THE NEW INTERPRETER'S® BIBLE
IN TWELVE VOLUMES

VOLUME SIX

THE NEW INTERPRETER'S® BIBLE

GENERAL ARTICLES
&
INTRODUCTION, COMMENTARY, & REFLECTIONS
FOR EACH BOOK OF THE BIBLE
INCLUDING
THE APOCRYPHAL/DEUTEROCANONICAL BOOKS
IN
TWELVE VOLUMES

VOLUME
VI

ABINGDON PRESS
Nashville

THE NEW INTERPRETER'S BIBLE
VOLUME VI

Copyright © 1994 by Abingdon Press

This book is printed on recycled, acid-free paper.

Library of Congress Cataloging-in-Publication Data

The New Interpreter's Bible: general articles & introduction,
   commentary, & reflections for each book of the Bible, including the
Apocryphal/Deuterocanonical books.
      p.   cm.
   Full texts and critical notes of the New International Version and
the New Revised Standard Version of the Bible in parallel columns.
   Includes bibliographical references.
      ISBN 0-687-27819-8 (v. 6: alk. paper)
      1. Bible—Commentaries.   2. Abingdon Press.   I. Bible.   English.
New International.   1994.   II. Bible.   English.   New Revised
Standard.   1994.
BS491.2.N484 1994
220.7'7—dc20   94-21092
                                                                                     CIP

ISBN 13: 978-0-687-27819-0

The HebraicaII® and GraecaII® fonts used to print this work are available from Linguist's Software, Inc., PO Box 580, Edmonds, WA 98020-0580. Tel (425) 775-1130. Web www.linguistsoftware.com

PUBLICATION STAFF
President and Publisher: Neil M. Alexander
Editorial Director: Harriett Jane Olson
Senior Editor of Reference Resources: Michael R. Russell
Production Editor: Linda S. Allen
Hebrew and Greek Editor/Assistant Editor: Lynn Allan Kauppi
Assistant Production Editor: Melanie Munnell
Production and Design Manager: Walter E. Wynne
Designer: J. S. Laughbaum
Copy Processing Manager: Sylvia S. Street
Composition Specialist: Kathy M. Harding
Publishing Systems Analyst: Glenn R. Hinton
Prepress Manager: Billy W. Murphy
Prepress Systems Technicians: J. Calvin Buckner
                                            Phillip D. Elliott
Director of Production Processes: James E. Leath
Scheduling: Laurene M. Martin
                  Tracey D. Craddock
Print Procurement Coordinator: Martha K. Taylor

10 11 12 13 14 15 16 — 15 14 13 12 11 10 9 8 7 6 5

MANUFACTURED IN THE UNITED STATES OF AMERICA

CONSULTANTS

NEIL M. ALEXANDER
President and Publisher
The United Methodist Publishing House
Nashville, Tennessee

OWEN F. CAMPION
Associate Publisher
Our Sunday Visitor
Huntington, Indiana

MINERVA G. CARCAÑO
Director
Mexican American Program
Perkins School of Theology
Southern Methodist University
Dallas, Texas

V. L. DAUGHTERY, JR.
Retired Pastor
South Georgia Conference
The United Methodist Church

SHARON NEUFER EMSWILER
Pastor
First United Methodist Church
Rock Island, Illinois

JUAN G. FELICIANO VALERA
Director
Development Office
Evangelical Seminary of Puerto Rico
San Juan, Puerto Rico

CELIA BREWER MARSHALL
Lecturer
University of North Carolina at Charlotte
Charlotte, North Carolina

NANCY C. MILLER-HERRON
Attorney and clergy member of
the Tennessee Conference
The United Methodist Church
Dresden, Tennessee

ROBERT C. SCHNASE
Pastor
First United Methodist Church
McAllen, Texas

BILL SHERMAN
Pastor Emeritus
Woodmont Baptist Church
Nashville, Tennessee

RODNEY T. SMOTHERS
Pastor
Ousley United Methodist Church
Lithonia, Georgia

WILLIAM D. WATLEY
Pastor
St. James African Methodist Episcopal Church
Newark, New Jersey

TALLULAH FISHER WILLIAMS[†]
Superintendent
Chicago Northwestern District
The United Methodist Church
Chicago, Illinois

SUK-CHONG YU
Superintendent
Nevada-Sierra District
The United Methodist Church
Reno, Nevada

[†] *deceased*

CONTRIBUTORS

ELIZABETH ACHTEMEIER[†]
  Adjunct Professor of Bible and Homiletics
  Union Theological Seminary in Virginia
  Richmond, Virginia
  (Presbyterian Church [U.S.A.])
  Joel

LESLIE C. ALLEN
  Professor of Old Testament
  Fuller Theological Seminary
  Pasadena, California
  (Baptist)
  1 & 2 Chronicles

GARY A. ANDERSON
  Associate Professor of Religious Studies
  University of Virginia
  Charlottesville, Virginia
  (The Roman Catholic Church)
  Introduction to Israelite Religion

DAVID L. BARTLETT
  Lantz Professor of Preaching and
      Communication
  The Divinity School
  Yale University
  New Haven, Connecticut
  (American Baptist Churches in the U.S.A.)
  1 Peter

ROBERT A. BENNETT, PH.D.
  Cambridge, Massachusetts
  (The Episcopal Church)
  Zephaniah

ADELE BERLIN
  Robert H. Smith Professor of Hebrew Bible
  Associate Provost for Faculty Affairs
  University of Maryland
  College Park, Maryland
  Introduction to Hebrew Poetry

[†] *deceased*

BRUCE C. BIRCH
  Dean and Woodrow W. and Mildred B. Miller
      Professor of Biblical Theology
  Wesley Theological Seminary
  Washington, DC
  (The United Methodist Church)
  1 & 2 Samuel

PHYLLIS A. BIRD
  Associate Professor of Old Testament
      Interpretation
  Garrett-Evangelical Theological Seminary
  Evanston, Illinois
  (The United Methodist Church)
  The Authority of the Bible

C. CLIFTON BLACK
  Otto A. Piper Professor of Biblical Theology
  Princeton Theological Seminary
  Princeton, New Jersey
  (The United Methodist Church)
  1, 2, & 3 John

JOSEPH BLENKINSOPP
  John A. O'Brien Professor of Biblical Studies
  Department of Theology
  University of Notre Dame
  Notre Dame, Indiana
  (The Roman Catholic Church)
  Introduction to the Pentateuch

M. EUGENE BORING
  I. Wylie and Elizabeth M. Briscoe Professor of
      New Testament, Emeritus
  Brite Divinity School
  Texas Christian University
  Fort Worth, Texas
  (Christian Church [Disciples of Christ])
  Matthew

ix

WALTER BRUEGGEMANN
William Marcellus McPheeters Professor of
Old Testament
Columbia Theological Seminary
Decatur, Georgia
(United Church of Christ)
Exodus

DAVID G. BUTTRICK
Professor of Homiletics and Liturgics
The Divinity School
Vanderbilt University
Nashville, Tennessee
(United Church of Christ)
The Use of the Bible in Preaching

RONALD E. CLEMENTS
Samuel Davidson Professor of Old Testament
King's College
University of London
London, England
(Baptist Union of Great Britain and Ireland)
Deuteronomy

RICHARD J. CLIFFORD, S.J.
Professor of Old Testament
Weston Jesuit School of Theology
Cambridge, Massachusetts
(The Roman Catholic Church)
Introduction to Wisdom Literature

JOHN J. COLLINS
Holmes Professor of Old Testament
Criticism and Interpretation
Yale University Divinity School
New Haven, Connecticut
(The Roman Catholic Church)
Introduction to Early Jewish Religion

ROBERT B. COOTE
Professor of Old Testament
San Francisco Theological Seminary
San Anselmo, California
(Presbyterian Church [U.S.A.])
Joshua

FRED B. CRADDOCK
Bandy Distinguished Professor of Preaching
and New Testament, Emeritus
Candler School of Theology
Emory University
Atlanta, Georgia
(Christian Church [Disciples of Christ])
Hebrews

† *deceased*

SIDNIE WHITE CRAWFORD
Professor and Chair of Classics and Religious
Studies
University of Nebraska—Lincoln
Lincoln, Nebraska
(The Episcopal Church)
Esther; Additions to Esther

JAMES L. CRENSHAW
Robert L. Flowers Professor of
Old Testament
The Divinity School
Duke University
Durham, North Carolina
(Baptist)
Sirach

KEITH R. CRIM†
Pastor
New Concord Presbyterian Church
Concord, Virginia
(Presbyterian Church [U.S.A.])
Modern English Versions of the Bible

R. ALAN CULPEPPER
Dean
The School of Theology
Mercer University
Atlanta, Georgia
(Southern Baptist Convention)
Luke

KATHERYN PFISTERER DARR
Associate Professor of Hebrew Bible
The School of Theology
Boston University
Boston, Massachusetts
(The United Methodist Church)
Ezekiel

ROBERT DORAN
Professor of Religion
Amherst College
Amherst, Massachusetts
1 & 2 Maccabees

THOMAS B. DOZEMAN
Professor of Old Testament
United Theological Seminary
Dayton, Ohio
(Presbyterian Church [U.S.A.])
Numbers

JAMES D. G. DUNN
Lightfoot Professor of Divinity
Department of Theology
University of Durham
Durham, England
(The Methodist Church [Great Britain])
1 & 2 Timothy; Titus

ELDON JAY EPP
Harkness Professor of Biblical Literature and
Chairman of the Department of Religion
Case Western Reserve University
Cleveland, Ohio
(The Episcopal Church)
*Ancient Texts and Versions of the New
Testament*

KATHLEEN A. ROBERTSON FARMER
Professor of Old Testament
United Theological Seminary
Dayton, Ohio
(The United Methodist Church)
Ruth

CAIN HOPE FELDER
Professor of New Testament Language and
Literature
The School of Divinity
Howard University
Washington, DC
(The United Methodist Church)
Philemon

TERENCE E. FRETHEIM
Professor of Old Testament
Luther Seminary
Saint Paul, Minnesota
(Evangelical Lutheran Church in America)
Genesis

FRANCISCO O. GARCÍA-TRETO
Professor of Religion and Chair of the
Department of Religion
Trinity University
San Antonio, Texas
(Presbyterian Church [U.S.A.])
Nahum

CATHERINE GUNSALUS GONZÁLEZ
Professor of Church History
Columbia Theological Seminary
Decatur, Georgia
(Presbyterian Church [U.S.A.])
*The Use of the Bible in Hymns, Liturgy,
and Education*

JUSTO L. GONZÁLEZ
Adjunct Professor of Church History
Columbia Theological Seminary
Decatur, Georgia
(The United Methodist Church)
*How the Bible Has Been Interpreted in
Christian Tradition*

DONALD E. GOWAN
Robert Cleveland Holland Professor of Old
Testament
Pittsburgh Theological Seminary
Pittsburgh, Pennsylvania
(Presbyterian Church [U.S.A.])
Amos

DANIEL J. HARRINGTON, S.J.
Professor of New Testament
Weston School of Theology
Cambridge, Massachusetts
(The Roman Catholic Church)
Introduction to the Canon

RICHARD B. HAYS
Professor of New Testament
The Divinity School
Duke University
Durham, North Carolina
(The United Methodist Church)
Galatians

THEODORE HIEBERT
Professor of Old Testament
McCormick Theological Seminary
Chicago, Illinois
(Mennonite Church)
Habakkuk

CARL R. HOLLADAY
Professor of New Testament
Candler School of Theology
Emory University
Atlanta, Georgia
*Contemporary Methods of Reading the
Bible*

MORNA D. HOOKER
Lady Margaret's Professor of Divinity, Emeritus
The Divinity School
University of Cambridge
Cambridge, England
(The Methodist Church [Great Britain])
Philippians

DAVID C. HOPKINS
Professor of Old Testament
Wesley Theological Seminary
Washington, DC
(United Church of Christ)
Life in Ancient Palestine

LUKE T. JOHNSON
Robert W. Woodruff Professor of New
Testament and Christian Origins
Candler School of Theology
Emory University
Atlanta, Georgia
(The Roman Catholic Church)
James

WALTER C. KAISER, JR.
President and Colman M. Mockler
Distinguished Professor of Old Testament
Gordon-Conwell Theological Seminary
South Hamilton, Massachusetts
(The Evangelical Free Church of America)
Leviticus

LEANDER E. KECK
Winkley Professor of Biblical Theology,
Emeritus
Yale University Divinity School
New Haven, Connecticut
(Christian Church [Disciples of Christ])
Introduction to The New Interpreter's Bible

CHAN-HIE KIM
Professor of New Testament and Director
of Korean Studies
The School of Theology at Claremont
Claremont, California
(The United Methodist Church)
Reading the Bible as Asian Americans

RALPH W. KLEIN
Dean and Christ Seminary-Seminex Professor
of Old Testament
Lutheran School of Theology at Chicago
Chicago, Illinois
(Evangelical Lutheran Church in America)
Ezra; Nehemiah

MICHAEL KOLARCIK, S.J.
Assistant Professor
Regis College
Toronto, Ontario
Canada
(The Roman Catholic Church)
Book of Wisdom

ANDREW T. LINCOLN
Professor of New Testament
Wycliffe College
University of Toronto
Toronto, Ontario
Canada
(The Church of England)
Colossians

J. CLINTON MCCANN, JR.
Evangelical Associate Professor of Biblical
Interpretation
Eden Theological Seminary
St. Louis, Missouri
(Presbyterian Church [U.S.A.])
Psalms

ABRAHAM J. MALHERBE
Buckingham Professor of New Testament
Criticism and Interpretation, Emeritus
Yale Divinity School
New Haven, Connecticut
(Church of Christ)
*The Cultural Context of the New
Testament: The Greco-Roman World*

W. EUGENE MARCH
Dean and Arnold Black Rhodes Professor of
Old Testament
Louisville Presbyterian Theological Seminary
Louisville, Kentucky
(Presbyterian Church [U.S.A.])
Haggai

JAMES EARL MASSEY
Dean Emeritus and
Distinguished Professor-at-Large
The School of Theology
Anderson University
(Church of God [Anderson, Ind.])
*Reading the Bible from Particular Social
Locations: An Introduction; Reading the
Bible as African Americans*

J. MAXWELL MILLER
Professor of Old Testament
Candler School of Theology
Emory University
Atlanta, Georgia
(The United Methodist Church)
*Introduction to the History of Ancient
Israel*

PATRICK D. MILLER
Charles T. Haley Professor of Old Testament
Theology
Princeton Theological Seminary
Princeton, New Jersey
(Presbyterian Church [U.S.A.])
Jeremiah

PETER D. MISCALL
Denver, Colorado
(The Episcopal Church)
Introduction to Narrative Literature

FREDERICK J. MURPHY
Professor Department of Religious Studies
College of the Holy Cross
Worcester, Massachusetts
(The Roman Catholic Church)
Introduction to Apocalyptic Literature

CAROL A. NEWSOM
Charles Howard Chandler
Professor of Old Testament
Candler School of Theology
Emory University
Atlanta, Georgia
(The Episcopal Church)
Job

GEORGE W. E. NICKELSBURG
Professor of Christian Origins and Early
Judaism, Emeritus
School of Religion
University of Iowa
Iowa City, Iowa
(Evangelical Lutheran Church in America)
*The Jewish Context of the New
Testament*

IRENE NOWELL, O.S.B.
Community Formation Director
Mount St. Scholasticas
Atchison, Kansas
(The Roman Catholic Church)
Tobit

KATHLEEN M. O'CONNOR
William Marcellis McPheeters Professor
of Old Testament
Columbia Theological Seminary
Decatur, Georgia
(The Roman Catholic Church)
Lamentations

GAIL R. O'DAY
Associate Dean of Faculty and Academic
Affairs and Almar H. Shatford Professor of
Preaching and New Testament
Candler School of Theology
Emory University
Atlanta, Georgia
(United Church of Christ)
John

BEN C. OLLENBURGER
Professor of Biblical Theology
Associated Mennonite Biblical Seminary
Elkhart, Indiana
(Mennonite Church)
Zechariah

DENNIS T. OLSON
Professor of Old Testament
Princeton Theological Seminary
Princeton, New Jersey
(Evangelical Lutheran Church in America)
Judges

CAROLYN OSIEK
Professor of New Testament
Department of Biblical Languages and
Literature
Catholic Theological Union
Chicago, Illinois
(The Roman Catholic Church)
Reading the Bible as Women

SAMUEL PAGÁN
President
Evangelical Seminary of Puerto Rico
San Juan, Puerto Rico
(Christian Church [Disciples of Christ])
Obadiah

SIMON B. PARKER
Professor of Hebrew Bible and Harrell F. Beck
Scholar in Hebrew Scripture
The School of Theology
Boston University
Boston, Massachusetts
(The United Methodist Church)
*The Ancient Near Eastern Literary
Background of the Old Testament*

PHEME PERKINS
Professor of New Testament
Boston College
Chestnut Hill, Massachusetts
(The Roman Catholic Church)
Mark; Ephesians

DAVID L. PETERSEN
Professor of Old Testament
Candler School of Theology
Emory University
Atlanta, Georgia
(Presbyterian Church [U.S.A.])
Introduction to Prophetic Literature

CHRISTOPHER C. ROWLAND
Dean Ireland's Professor of the Exegesis of
Holy Scripture
The Queen's College
Oxford, England
(The Church of England)
Revelation

ANTHONY J. SALDARINI[†]
Professor of Biblical Studies
Boston College
Chestnut Hill, Massachusetts
(The Roman Catholic Church)
Baruch; Letter of Jeremiah

J. PAUL SAMPLEY
Professor of New Testament and Christian
Origins
The School of Theology and The Graduate
Division
Boston University
Boston, Massachusetts
(The United Methodist Church)
1 Corinthians; 2 Corinthians

JUDITH E. SANDERSON
Assistant Professor of Hebrew Bible
Department of Theology and Religious Studies
Seattle University
Seattle, Washington
*Ancient Texts and Versions of the Old
Testament*

EILEEN M. SCHULLER, O.S.U.
Professor
Department of Religious Studies
McMaster University
Hamilton, Ontario
Canada
(The Roman Catholic Church)
Malachi

[†] *deceased*

FERNANDO F. SEGOVIA
Professor of New Testament and Early
Christianity
The Divinity School
Vanderbilt University
Nashville, Tennessee
(The Roman Catholic Church)
Reading the Bible as Hispanic Americans

CHRISTOPHER R. SEITZ
Professor of Old Testament and Theological
Studies
St Mary's College
University of St. Andrews
Fife, Scotland
(The Episcopal Church)
Isaiah 40–66

CHOON-LEONG SEOW
Henry Snyder Gehman Professor of Old
Testament Language and Literature
Princeton Theological Seminary
Princeton, New Jersey
(Presbyterian Church [U.S.A.])
1 & 2 Kings

MICHAEL A. SIGNER
Abrams Professor of Jewish Thought and
Culture
Department of Theology
University of Notre Dame
Notre Dame, Indiana
*How the Bible Has Been Interpreted in
Jewish Tradition*

MOISÉS SILVA
Professor of New Testament
Westminster Theological Seminary
Philadelphia, Pennsylvania
(The Orthodox Presbyterian Church)
*Contemporary Theories of Biblical
Interpretation*

DANIEL J. SIMUNDSON
Professor of Old Testament
Luther Seminary
Saint Paul, Minnesota
(Evangelical Lutheran Church in America)
Micah

ABRAHAM SMITH
Associate Professor of New Testament
Andover Newton Theological School
Newton Centre, Massachusetts
(The National Baptist Convention, USA, Inc.)
1 & 2 Thessalonians

DANIEL L. SMITH-CHRISTOPHER
Associate Professor of Theological Studies
Department of Theology
Loyola Marymount University
Los Angeles, California
(The Society of Friends [Quaker])
Daniel; Bel and the Dragon; Prayer of Azariah; Susannah

ROBERT C. TANNEHILL
Academic Dean and Harold B. Williams
Professor of Biblical Studies
Methodist Theological School in Ohio
Delaware, Ohio
(The United Methodist Church)
The Gospels and Narrative Literature

GEORGE E. TINKER
Professor of American Indian Cultures and
Religious Traditions
The Iliff School of Theology
Denver, Colorado
(Evangelical Lutheran Church in America)
Reading the Bible as Native Americans

W. SIBLEY TOWNER
The Reverend Archibald McFadyen Professor
of Biblical Interpretation
Union Theological Seminary in Virginia
Richmond, Virginia
(Presbyterian Church [U.S.A.])
Ecclesiastes

PHYLLIS TRIBLE
Professor of Biblical Studies
The Divinity School
Wake Forest University
Winston-Salem, North Carolina
Jonah

GENE M. TUCKER
Professor of Old Testament, Emeritus
Candler School of Theology
Emory University
Atlanta, Georgia
(The United Methodist Church)
Isaiah 1–39

CHRISTOPHER M. TUCKETT
Rylands Professor of Biblical Criticism and
Exegesis
Faculty of Theology
University of Manchester
Manchester, England
(The Church of England)
Jesus and the Gospels

RAYMOND C. VAN LEEUWEN
Professor of Religion and Theology
Eastern College
Saint Davids, Pennsylvania
(Christian Reformed Church in North America)
Proverbs

ROBERT W. WALL
Professor of Biblical Studies
Department of Religion
Seattle Pacific University
Seattle, Washington
(Free Methodist Church of North America)
Acts; Introduction to Epistolary Literature

DUANE F. WATSON
Associate Professor of New Testament Studies
Department of Religion and Philosophy
Malone College
Canton, Ohio
(The United Methodist Church)
2 Peter; Jude

RENITA J. WEEMS
Ordained Elder, African Methodist Episcopal
Church
Public Lecturer
(African Methodist Episcopal Church)
Song of Songs

LAWRENCE M. WILLS
Associate Professor of Biblical Studies
The Episcopal Divinity School
Cambridge, Massachusetts
(The Episcopal Church)
Judith

VINCENT L. WIMBUSH
Professor of New Testament and Christian
Origins
Union Theological Seminary
New York, New York
(Progressive National Baptist Convention, Inc.)
The Ecclesiastical Context of the New Testament

N. Thomas Wright
    Canon Theologian
    Westminster Abbey
    London, England
    (The Church of England)
        Romans

Gale A. Yee
    Professor of Hebrew and Director of Feminist
        Liberation Theologies
    Episcopal Divinity School
    Cambridge, Massachusetts
    (The Roman Catholic Church)
        Hosea

FEATURES OF
THE NEW INTERPRETER'S® BIBLE

The general aim of *The New Interpreter's Bible* is to bring the best in contemporary biblical scholarship into the service of the church to enhance preaching, teaching, and study of the Scriptures. To accomplish that general aim, the design of *The New Interpreter's Bible* has been shaped by two controlling principles: (1) form serves function, and (2) maximize ease of use.

General articles provide the reader with concise, up-to-date, balanced introductions and assessments of selected topics. In most cases, a brief bibliography points the way to further exploration of a topic. Many of the general articles are placed in volumes 1 and 8, at the beginning of the coverage of the Old and New Testaments, respectively. Others have been inserted in those volumes where the reader will encounter the corresponding type of literature (e.g., "Introduction to Prophetic Literature" appears in Volume 6 alongside several of the prophetic books).

Coverage of each biblical book begins with an "Introduction" that acquaints the reader with the essential historical, sociocultural, literary, and theological issues necessary to understand the biblical book. A short bibliography and an outline of the biblical book are found at the end of each Introduction. The introductory sections are the only material in *The New Interpreter's Bible* printed in a single wide-column format.

The biblical text is divided into coherent and manageable primary units, which are located within larger sections of Scripture. At the opening discussion of any large section of Scripture, readers will often find material identified as "Overview," which includes remarks applicable to the large section of text. The primary unit of text may be as short as a few verses or as long as a chapter or more. This is the point at which the biblical text itself is reprinted in *The New Interpreter's Bible*. Dealing with Scripture in terms of these primary units allows discussion of important issues that are overlooked in a verse-by-verse treatment. Each scriptural unit is identified by text citation and a short title.

The full texts and critical notes of the New International Version and the New Revised Standard Version of the Bible are presented in parallel columns for quick reference. (For the Apocryphal/Deuterocanonical works, the NIV is replaced by The New American Bible.) Since every translation is to some extent an interpretation as well, the inclusion of these widely known and influential modern translations provides an easy comparison that in many cases will lead to a better understanding of a passage. Biblical passages are set in a two-column format and placed in green tint-blocks to make it easy to recognize them at a glance. The NAB, NIV, and NRSV material is clearly identified on each page on which the text appears.

Immediately following each biblical text is a section marked "Commentary," which provides an exegetical analysis informed by linguistic, text-critical, historical-critical, literary, social-scientific, and theological methods. The Commentary serves as a reliable, judicious guide through the text, pointing out the critical problems as well as key interpretive issues.

The exegetical approach is "text-centered." That is, the commentators focus primarily on the text in its final form rather than on (a) a meticulous rehearsal of problems of scholarship associated with a text, (b) a thorough reconstruction of the pre-history of the text, or (c) an exhaustive rehearsal of the text's interpretive history. Of course, some attention to scholarly problems, to the pre-history of a text, and to historic interpretations that have shaped streams of tradition is important in particular cases precisely in order to illumine the several levels of meaning in the final form of the text. But the *primary* focus is on the canonical text itself. Moreover, the Commentary not only describes pertinent aspects of the text, but also teaches the reader what to look for in the text so as to develop the reader's own capacity to analyze and interpret the text.

Commentary material runs serially for a few paragraphs or a few pages, depending on what is required by the biblical passage under discussion.

Commentary material is set in a two-column format. Occasional subheads appear in a bold green font. The next level of subdivisions appears as bold black fonts and a third level as black italic fonts. Footnotes are placed at the bottom of the column in which the superscripts appear.

Key words in Hebrew, Aramaic, or Greek are printed in the original-language font, accompanied by a transliteration and a translation or explanation.

Immediately following the Commentary, in most cases, is the section called "Reflections." A detailed exposition growing directly out of the discussion and issues dealt with in the Commentary, the Reflections are geared specifically toward helping those who interpret Scripture in the life of the church by providing "handles" for grasping the significance of Scripture for faith and life today. Recognizing that the text has the capacity to shape the life of the Christian community, this section presents multiple possibilities for preaching and teaching in light of each biblical text. That is, instead of providing the preacher or teacher full illustrations, poems, outlines, and the like, the Reflections offer *several* trajectories of possible interpretation that connect with the situation of the contemporary listeners. Recognizing the power of Scripture to speak anew to diverse situations, not all of the suggested trajectories could be appropriated on any one occasion. Preachers and teachers want some specificity about the implications of the text, but not so much specificity that the work is done for them. The ideas in the Reflections are meant to stimulate the thought of preachers and teachers, not to replace it.

Three-quarter width columns distinguish Reflections materials from biblical text and Commentary.

Occasional excursuses have been inserted in some volumes to address topics of special importance that are best treated apart from the flow of Commentary and Reflections on specific passages. Set in three-quarter width columns, excursuses are identified graphically by a green color bar that runs down the outside margin of the page.

Occasional maps, charts, and illustrations appear throughout the volumes at points where they are most likely to be immediately useful to the reader.

CONTENTS

VOLUME VI

INTRODUCTION TO PROPHETIC LITERATURE

DAVID L. PETERSEN

OUTLINE

PROPHETIC LITERATURE: DEFINITIONS AND ORIGINS

What is prophetic literature? Prophetic literature involves far more than words that prophets spoke. That much is clear. But how much more? Study of biblical literature offers several possible answers: the canonical answer, the authorial answer, and the redactional answer.

One important definition of prophetic literature derives from the traditional divisions of the Hebrew Bible canon.[1] This is the "canonical" answer. Both early Jewish and Christian traditions attest a tripartite understanding of the Hebrew Bible: Torah (*torah*), Prophets (*nebi'im*), and

---

1. The term "Hebrew Bible" is a more ecumenical way of referring to that body of literature otherwise known as the Old Testament.

Writings (*ketubim*). The second of these divisions, "the Prophets," is made up of Joshua, Judges, 1 and 2 Samuel, 1 and 2 Kings, as well as the major (Isaiah, Jeremiah, Ezekiel) and the minor (Hosea–Malachi) prophets. This list might appear odd. One would expect to find the books attributed to prophets here, but why is narrative, historical literature—the "former prophets"—also classified as prophetic literature?

Scholars have offered several different answers to this question, but their answers remain suggestive rather than definitive. First, the Deuteronomistic History (Deuteronomy–2 Kings) attests that God spoke to Israel through prophets during the course of its existence. The first book of that history, Deuteronomy, views Moses as a prophet (Deut 18:15-18), and the last book, 2 Kings, affirms that God had "warned Israel and Judah by every prophet and every seer" (2 Kgs 17:13).[2] These various historical books may attest to an understanding of history in which the prophets as those who admonished, indicted, and judged was of critical importance. Although kings are important, hence the title "Kings," prophets are even more so, especially since they were present—as personified by Moses, Deborah, Samuel, to name just three—even before kingship commenced in Israel.

A second reason for classifying these historical books—or "former prophets"—as prophetic literature derives from a different understanding of prophets. The books of Chronicles provide a key. There prophets are presented as historians. For example, 1 Chr 29:29 states, "Now the acts of King David, from first to last, are written in the records of the seer Samuel, and in the records of the prophet Nathan, and in the records of the seer Gad." To be sure, the books of Kings refer to sources that were used by the historian: for example, "Now the rest of the acts of Manasseh, all that he did, and the sin that he committed, are they not written in the Book of the Annals of the Kings of Judah?" (2 Kgs 21:17). However, no author for these sources is ever identified in Kings. In contrast, Chronicles attributes such sources to prophets, whom the chronicler apparently understood as historians. Hence, historical works, such as "Kings" (though not apparently Chronicles),

may be understood as "the prophets," since prophets were viewed as Israel's early historians.

Both of these answers share an important underlying and often unstated assumption—namely, that Israel's prophets were of fundamental importance for understanding Israelite history. Their presence testifies to God's concern for the people Israel. Still, valuable as this understanding might be, it presents problems. Few readers today would want to count Joshua or 2 Samuel as prophetic literature.

One may identify a second kind of answer to the question about prophetic literature: the "authorial" response. Some would suggest that prophetic literature is that which prophets wrote or spoke. One could count the words of Micah, Amos, or Haggai as prophetic literature. Here prophets are not so much historians as authors, those who created literature—whether oral or written—that has been preserved in the Old Testament.

An important component of the authorial definition for prophetic literature is a high evaluation of that which prophets are understood to have said. That is, such speeches are often understood to be God's own speech. Many utterances in the books attributed to prophets commence with the phrase "Thus says the LORD" (e.g., Amos 1:3). To hear these words is, as it were, to hear God's words. Moreover, some interpreters view poetry as "inspired" language, and, in the case of the Old Testament, inspired not simply by one of the muses but by Israel's God. Finally, if wisdom literature is written or spoken by Israel's sages, then by analogy prophetic literature must have been written or spoken by Israel's prophets.

Regrettably, the matter is not so simple. There is considerable literature *about* prophets, but not all of it was written by them. The Bible presents two clear examples. The first involves the prophet Elisha and the literature associated with him. The book of 2 Kings includes a number of stories about this prophet. These stories are routinely included in assessments of Israel's prophets, even though someone other than Elijah must have been the author. As we shall see, these stories most probably originated in an oral, storytelling environment. In fact, the Bible attests to such a setting:

> Now the king was talking with Gehazi the servant of the man of God, saying, "Tell me all the

2. Unless otherwise noted, Scripture quotations are from the NRSV.

great things that Elisha has done." While he was telling the king how Elisha had restored a dead person to life.... (2 Kgs 8:4-5)

One can read the story about Elisha, the Shunamite woman, and her son (2 Kgs 4:8-37) and well imagine Gehazi, or another of Elisha's supporters, the so-called sons of the prophets, as its author. Someone like Gehazi, not Elisha, is the author of these stories.

The same could be said about Baruch, Jeremiah's scribe. The book of Jeremiah includes a number of stories told about the turbulent character whose name heads the book. These stories are clearly biographical, not autobiographical. Someone other than the prophet wrote about important episodes (e.g., Jeremiah 28) or major periods in his life (Jeremiah 37–44). A good candidate for the author is Baruch, the scribe who wrote down words that Jeremiah had spoken (see Jer 45:1). Unless we want to exclude such chapters from the corpus of prophetic literature, we will need to think about scribes like Baruch, and not just people like Jeremiah, as authors of prophetic literature.

In short, some of the literature attributed to a prophet was clearly written by someone other than the prophet. The previous cases involved literature in which the prophet was described. However, one may also refer to instances in which the prophet ostensibly speaks or writes, but the content of the text makes it difficult to think that the prophet in question actually wrote or spoke such words.

We enter here a range of biblical scholarship that some may find troubling—namely, the attempt to discern the difference between "authentic" and "secondary" prophetic literature. For example, for over a century scholars have pored over the book of Isaiah, in part attempting to determine what portions of that book might be attributed to Isaiah ben Amoz, who lived in the late eighth and early seventh centuries BCE. There is now a consensus that much in that book (particularly in chaps. 40–66) dates to the sixth and fifth centuries. Put another way, Isaiah ben Amoz could not have written major portions of the book attributed to him (see the Commentaries on Isaiah 1–39 and Isaiah 40–66 for discussion of these issues). If one wants to construe most of the book of Isaiah as prophetic literature, then one must accept someone other than Isaiah as the author of that

prophetic literature. This same situation also holds for sections of many other prophetic books (e.g., Zechariah 9–14). Unless one is willing to deny that such material in prophetic books is prophetic literature, the authorial answer will not suffice.

What, then, is prophetic literature? Prophetic literature is literature that attests to or grows out of (i.e., is generated by) the activity of Israel's prophets. This is the generative answer. One can count the words of a prophet as prophetic literature, but one can also deem a story about a prophet to be prophetic literature. Prophets can produce prophetic literature, but so can someone who is not known as a prophet. Moreover, as the examples suggest, prophetic literature can be composed not only as poetry, but also as prose.

These considerations lead us to ask about the origins of prophetic literature. Obviously, one essential element is the presence and activity of a prophet or an intermediary.[3] That individual could either write or speak prophetic literature—such was the case with Isaiah and Habakkuk, who are attested as both speakers and writers (Isaiah 7–8; Habakkuk 1–2). However, as we have already seen, other individuals contemporaneous with "prophets"—Gehazi and Baruch—could also speak or pen prophetic literature.

These two sorts of prophetic literature (prose accounts and poetic speeches), dating to roughly the period in which a prophet was active, possessed remarkable generative abilities. For example, the images of Zion present in the accounts and speeches of and about Isaiah ben Amoz offered later Israelites profound and productive ways for thinking about Zion—Jerusalem as God's chosen abode. In times long after that of the eighth-century prophet Isaiah, such as the Persian period (fifth cent.), authors composed literature that made its way into the book of Isaiah (material that can be found in chaps. 56–66). These anonymous individuals—whether or not we understand them to be prophets is an interesting question—produced a significant percentage of what appears in prophetic books. We need to look to these anonymous individuals and their times for the origins of prophetic literature as well as to the times of the originating prophets (e.g., an Amos or Isaiah).

---

3. On the use of the term "intermediary," see R. Wilson, *Prophecy and Society in Ancient Israel* (Philadelphia: Fortress, 1980).

In sum, prophetic literature can be understood from multiple perspectives. Moreover, a search for the origins of prophetic literature may end at various places—with the prophet, with a contemporary of the prophet, or with tradents, the anonymous authors and editors who preserved and added to the emerging corpus of prophetic literature. The words of a prophet or the prophet's contemporaries generated remarkable literary activity. The prophet's sayings and accounts, or those of the prophet's contemporaries, remained alive and elicited new words and accounts, a process that resulted in extensive books like Isaiah or Jeremiah. Israelite prophetic literature seems to have had an almost inherent capacity to elicit elucidation at a later time.

ISRAEL'S PROPHETS

Although prophetic literature is the primary focus of this volume, we also need to keep the prophet in the field of vision. The term "prophet" derives from the Greek noun προφήτης (*prophētēs*). The Greek root means, primarily, "to foresee." To understand prophets in the Old Testament as "prophets" in this sense is unfortunate and misleading for at least two reasons. First, the notion of seeing into the future, of predicting what will happen, is only one facet of what Israel's prophets were about. To be sure, Israel's prophets could and did speak about the future, but they also addressed the present and referred as well to the past. They were not essentially in the business of providing horoscopes for those in Judah and Israel.

Diverse Roles. Second, the use of one title, "prophet," belies the diversity among Israel's prophets. We possess various evidence of this diversity. Perhaps most indicative are the various titles or role labels used to describe those individuals whom we consider prophets. There are four such titles in the Hebrew Bible: חזה (*ḥōzeh,* "seer"), ראה (*rō'eh,* "diviner"), איש האלהים ('*îs hā'ělōhîm,* "man of God"), and נביא (*nābî',* "prophet"). As the typical English equivalents suggest, two of the four nouns derive from words meaning "to see." The first noun, *ḥōzeh,* apparently means quite simply an individual who receives and reports visions, (e.g., Amos 7:12), but it also appears to function interchangeably with the noun *nābî'* (so Isa 29:10; 30:10). The noun

rō'eh is associated primarily with the figure of Samuel. In the pivotal scene in which this noun appears (1 Samuel 9), Samuel functions rather like a diviner—that is, someone who is able to communicate with the world of the sacred in order to discover information that will be useful to those who consult him: "Perhaps he will tell us about the journey on which we have set out" (1 Sam 9:6). After Saul and his companion reach the town, they must go with Samuel to a shrine and then eat with him. Divinatory activity may have taken place in either context.

The third title, '*îs hā'ělōhîm,* "man of God," is especially prominent in the stories about Elijah and Elisha, particularly the latter. The literary character of these stories corroborates a judgment that the "man of God" can best be understood as a "holy man," a type of individual attested in numerous religious traditions. Such people possess the power of the holy and, hence, are dangerous, powerful, and due appropriate respect. Unlike visionaries, who occasionally engage in trance or possession behavior, the holy man personifies the deity in the midst of the profane world. A classic example is provided by 2 Kgs 6:1-7. Elisha, here characterized as "the man of God," makes an iron ax head float to the surface of the Jordan River, into which it had accidentally fallen. Such powers belong to the world of the sacred. Elisha does not need to pray; he can simply act, since he possesses those powers.

The most frequent term for "prophet" is *nābî'.* Scholars have not reached a consensus about its root meaning, but the term probably signifies someone called to a certain task. Hence it is no accident that call or commissioning narratives appear in several prophetic books (e.g., Isaiah 6; Jeremiah 1; Ezekiel 1–2). Over time, this term became the standard one by means of which prophets were known, as 1 Sam 9:9 reflects: "for the one who is now called a prophet [*nābî'*] was formerly called a seer."

One suspects that the use of these four role labels for a prophet reflected linguistic usage in different times and places. Moreover, they surely emphasized different things a prophet did; for example, report visions or utter oracles. However, as a roster of contemporary role labels, such as clergyperson, priest, pastor, or minister, suggests, there was probably considerable overlap in what various prophets were about. Israel's prophets were writers and/or speakers. They could receive communications from the deity in various ways (i.e., auditions and visions). Still, it is possible to identify one element common to all prophets. They functioned as *intermediaries* between the human and the divine worlds. They could represent humans to God (e.g., Amos 7:2) or God to humans (Amos 5:4). They could act with the power of God within the mundane world (so Elisha). They could envision the cosmic world (Amos 7:4; Zech 1:7-17); they could participate in the divine council (1 Kings 22; Isaiah 6); and they could analyze the machinations of humans (Micah 3). Prophets were truly boundary figures.

If prophets are to be understood as boundary figures, as intermediaries, then some comment is necessary about the relationship between the two major classes of what might be called religious professionals: priests and prophets. An absolute distinction between prophets and priests did not exist in ancient Israel. Some prophets were also priests. Jeremiah was born into a priestly lineage that resided in Anathoth, a small town not far from Jerusalem. This priestly house probably traced its roots to Abiathar, who was exiled to Anathoth, the ancestral dwelling, for having supported Adonijah rather than Solomon (1 Kgs 2:26-27). Ezekiel, too, is accorded priestly status (Ezek 1:3), again as a function of his birth. Unlike Jeremiah, Ezekiel was probably a member of the priestly line of the Zadokites, who had primary responsibility for the Temple in Jerusalem. Zechariah was another prophet born into a priestly family. His genealogy, "Zechariah son of Berechiah son of Iddo" (Zech 1:1), is also attested in the book of Nehemiah (Neh 12:16), where the genealogy is part of the listing for priestly ancestral houses. At least three prophets—Jeremiah, Ezekiel, and Zechariah—belonged to priestly families.

The priest-prophet connection is even stronger than matters of lineage. The book of Joel offers a remarkable scenario in which the prophet appears to function as a priest. In a time of national crisis, Joel calls the Israelites to engage in ritual lamentation at the Temple (Joel 1:13-14). He then utters the words that the priest would have spoken to the deity (Joel 1:19). In response to their calls for help, the deity then speaks through the prophet, affirming that the concerns of the people have been heard (Joel 2:18-20). The prophet Joel undertakes just such work as one might expect from an intercessory priest. Another prophetic book, Zephaniah, depicts the prophet's (Zeph 3:14-15) calling Israelites to the service of song. They are to praise the deity for having moved from a time of judgment to a time of restoration.

In sum, we do well to remember that prophets not only could exercise various roles but also could even be, even act as, priests. Such behavior should prevent us from thinking about prophets in a simple and/or monolithic fashion.

Historical and Social Settings. Prophets, as a class of religious specialists, are not present in all times or, for that matter, in all societies. Similarly, prophets were not present in all periods of Israel's existence. For reasons made clear in the article "Introduction to the History of Ancient Israel,"[4] it is difficult to speak about Israelite society in any strong historical sense much before the time of David (c. 1000 BCE). In literature that depicts Israel's understanding of itself prior to that time (the Pentateuch or the books of Joshua and Judges), references to prophets are rare or unusual. Moses is a significant exception, which will be examined below. Abraham (Gen 20:7), Miriam (Exod 15:20), and Deborah (Judg 4:4) are labeled as prophets; yet, they seem so strange when viewed as prophets that other labels for these individuals seem more appropriate; for example, Deborah is better understood as a judge and Abraham as a patriarch. Certain notions of the prophetic role (e.g., intercession) have affected the ways in which Israelite authors viewed these individuals. An ancient Israelite writer may view Abraham as a prophet when he prays on someone else's behalf, even though intercession may be characteristic neither of much prophetic activity nor of Abraham's own behavior.

Individuals who function as intermediaries and who are known as prophets begin to appear at the time when Israel adopted statehood as its form of government—in biblical terms, when Israel gained a king. Moreover, within seventy-five years from the time Judah was destroyed (as an independent state with a king), individually named prophets seem to have become a thing of the past.

4. J. Maxwell Miller, "Introduction to the Religion of Ancient Israel," in *The New Interpreter's Bible,* 12 vols. (Nashville: Abingdon, 1994) 1:244-71.

Thus there is a strong correlation between Israel's existence as a monarchic state and the presence of prophets in its midst.

This correlation may reflect several different features of prophetic behavior. As Overholt and others have demonstrated, prophecy requires certain conditions to exist.[5] Among them are an "audience" that will recognize someone as a prophet. Moreover, moving beyond Overholt, there may be a need for someone to protect a prophet from harm due to his proclaiming something unpopular; for example, the powerful individuals who helped Jeremiah (Ahikam son of Shaphan [Jer 26:24] or Ebed-melech the Cushite [Jer 38:7-13]). Finally, certain historical moments may produce greater needs for prophecy than do other times. Israel, from roughly 1000 to 500 BCE—though not uniformly during this half-millennium—met these conditions.

During these five hundred years, Israel lived through a number of major changes or crises: the inception of statehood, national schism, Neo-Assyrian threats and the destruction of the northern kingdom, the Neo-Babylonian threat and the destruction of Judah, life in exile, and attempts at restoration in the land. Prophets addressed each one of these pivotal moments.

For example, Nathan and Gad appeared during the lifetime of David, Israel's first true king. Both these prophets interacted directly with the king; they did not speak to a larger public.[6] Nathan confronted David after he had impregnated Bathsheba and had her husband killed (2 Samuel 11–12) and is able to trick David into indicting himself for this blatant misuse of royal power. Gad, too, critiqued the king after he had undertaken a census designed to assay the number of men available for battle (2 Samuel 24). In both cases, the prophet challenges the holder of a new political office, the king, by calling him to account based on Israel's ancient religious and ethical traditions. In the midst of this new political configuration, Israelites must have been asking the question, What does it mean for a king to function in an Israelite/Yahwistic setting? In some measure, then, these prophets are a voice from the past, attempting to relate Israel's defining norms to a new political situation.

David's grandson faced the next critical challenge. Could the diversity represented by the northern and southern tribes remain integrated in the united monarchy that David had forged? The Deuteronomistic History reports that even before Rehoboam had angered representatives from northern tribes, a prophet, Ahijah the Shilonite, had informed Jeroboam that he would be king of the new northern kingdom (1 Kings 11). These events (c. 922 BCE) spelled the end of the united monarchy and the creation of two nations, both of which claimed Yahweh as their state god. What is important to note for our purposes is that writers of Israelite history affirm that a prophet played a critical role in the creation of the divided monarchy.

The next major development on the political landscape was the threat posed by the reconsolidated Neo-Assyrian Empire in the eighth century. Although his predecessors should be credited with major initiatives, it was Tiglath-Pileser III (745–727 BCE) who began military campaigns in Syria-Palestine. These attacks in the decade between 740 and 730 BCE are attested both in biblical texts (2 Kings 15) and Assyrian annals. Moreover, they provide the context for two prophetic books: Amos and Hosea.

During this period, Amos, a Judahite who came to Israel, and Hosea, a native Israelite, addressed those in the northern kingdom, which was subject to greater pressure from the Neo-Assyrians than was its southern neighbor Judah. Both Amos and Hosea understood the dire straits facing Israel. One can comb the books and discover various images of military attack and destruction. Amos speaks of people being taken into exile (e.g., Amos 6:7), forcibly removed from their homes and resettled elsewhere, a practice used by the Neo-Assyrians when assuming control of a new area. Hosea, likewise, refers to the decimation of warfare:

> Therefore the tumult of war shall rise against
> your people,
> and all your fortresses shall be destroyed.
>
> (Hos 10:14)

However, Hosea and Amos do more than simply see the signs of the times and state them in a poetic

---

5. See T. Overholt, *Channels of Prophecy: The Social Dynamics of Prophetic Activity* (Minneapolis: Fortress, 1989).
6. Other prophets would function in powerful ways with kings; e.g., one of Elisha's band anointed Jehu as king (2 Kgs 9:1-13); Ahijah the Shilonite proclaimed to Jeroboam that he would become king of Israel (1 Kgs 11:29-39).

way. Instead, these individuals, as did those who came after them, interpreted these events from the perspective of Israelite religious and ethical traditions. These prophets understand Yahweh's hand to be at work behind whatever the Neo-Assyrians are doing. It is for this reason that Hosea continually describes the deity's work in the first person:

> I will cast my net over them;
> I will bring them down like birds of the air;
> I will discipline them. (Hos 7:12)

Although Neo-Assyrian chariotry may set out against Israelite troops, Hosea understands that it is really Yahweh who is disciplining the Israelites.

In addition, Amos and Hosea tried to explain to those in Israel why they were to suffer such a dire fate. Interestingly, the reasons they offer are diverse. Amos inveighs against social and economic practices in the northern kingdom, whereas Hosea focuses on religious and political misdeeds. Still, although they offer different kinds of critiques, the prophets share two basic assumptions: (1) that the destruction is a punishment and (2) that Israel had violated that which they had earlier agreed to do. The prophets do not indict Israel for violating some new norm. If anything is new, it is the freedom with which the prophets talk about the deity. One might say that their theologies are more creative than their ethics.

The next pivotal moment involved the same empire, but now confronting Judah. New prophets are involved: Micah and Isaiah. Although it would be a mistake to read all prophetic texts as direct reflections of historical circumstances, some texts do attest to particular moments in a stark way. Micah 1:10-16 is such a text. These verses contain a number of city names. Those that have been identified with actual sites all sit to the south and west of Jerusalem. The Neo-Assyrian annals report that Sennacherib destroyed a number of Judahite cities. One of these, Lachish (Mic 1:13), has been excavated. There is one layer attesting to destruction brought by military means and that almost certainly reflects Sennacherib's campaign in 701 BCE. Micah sets such Neo-Assyrian action within the context of a Judah, and especially a Jerusalem, that is filled with rampant violence. Micah 3:1-4 indicts those who rule from Jerusalem. They are responsible for both the suffering they inflict in the capital and the suffering the Neo-Assyrians are inflicting throughout the land.

Isaiah, too, knows of this same set of events c. 701 BCE, events that were of such significance that they were narrated in both Isaiah and Kings (Isaiah 36–37; cf. 2 Kings 18–19). Moreover, what transpires provides a key for understanding much in the book of Isaiah. These chapters address a question that must have vexed those who heard Micah's words: Whom does the Lord support? One could hear Micah (and Amos and Hosea) and think that Yahweh supported the efforts of those who were attacking Judah. The Assyrians were the means by which God was punishing the people. According to Isa 36:10, the Assyrians themselves were making this very point. Isaiah, through a divine oracle, responds that God will protect Jerusalem, "for my own sake and for the sake of my servant David" (Isa 37:35). Isaiah, finally, knows more about what God will do—and why—than do the Assyrians. Through him, and other prophets, Israelites can understand such moments as an attack by an imperial enemy.

Almost a century passed before prophets appear prominently again, which they do as the Neo-Assyrian Empire is ousted from the ancient Near Eastern stage by the Neo-Babylonians. The book of Nahum might be read as a treatise on the necessity for such destruction. However, this is a minor chapter when compared with the role the Neo-Babylonians will play within Syria-Palestine. The Babylonians defeated Nineveh, the Neo-Assyrian capital, in 612 BCE. Then, in 597 and again in 587, they attacked Judah, destroying Jerusalem in the second campaign. It is, therefore, no accident that two of the three so-called major prophets date to this time. If Judahites had been asking questions in 701, they must have been shouting them in 587. How could Yahweh let Judah and the Temple in Jerusalem be destroyed? Before 587, Jeremiah and Ezekiel affirm the necessity of such punishment. And both before and after that date, they explain why such radical action had become necessary. Ezekiel focuses on the ways in which Judah had insulted God's holiness, whereas Jeremiah continues a line of attack begun by Hosea, but now directed against Judah: They have acted in a promiscuous fashion, worshiping other gods. Moreover, their political policies stand at odds with what Yahweh desires them to do. Here again, times of radical change elicit the need for radical explanations.

Both Jeremiah and Ezekiel stand astride the decisive date of 587 BCE. After the time of destruction, they and other prophets (e.g., Haggai and Zechariah) wrestle with questions about what comes next. Will God be with this people? Will there still be a covenant? Will the new chapter be written with those in exile or those who return to the land? Prophets, and not priests or sages, were the ones providing responses to such questions. Ezekiel addresses these questions by using visionary language about a field of bones: Could they live again (Ezekiel 37)? Deutero-Isaiah (the prophet responsible for Isaiah 40–55) thought about a Jerusalem that would have its streets paved with gold (Isa 54:11-12). Jeremiah spoke in terms of a new covenant (Jer 31:31). Haggai anticipated a restoration of the prior monarchic order (Hag 2:20-23). Zechariah envisioned a new order, with both priest and king in leading roles (Zechariah 4). Different though these perspectives are, they share one essential affirmation: God will continue to be with the people.

With the rebuilding of the Temple and its rededication in 515 BCE, such individually named intermediaries begin to pass from the scene. Prophetic literature continues to be written, but it now occurs in the form of notes, additions, and supplements to earlier words. As a province in the Persian Empire, Judah may no longer have required prophets or possessed the prerequisites for prophetic activity. Moreover, the very character of Yahwism had changed, from the religion of a nation-state roughly coextensive with the boundaries of Judah and Israel to a religion that could be practiced not only in the land, but also elsewhere, such as in Egypt and Mesopotamia. This new form of religion, oriented around divine instruction, did not so much need new "words," new oracles from the deity, as it needed interpreters of words that already existed, particularly those of the Torah or the Pentateuch. Judaism, this new religion, did not need prophets, as had its forebear religion, Yahwism.

Historical circumstance provides only one way in which to contextualize Israel's prophets. Social setting offers another fruitful angle of vision. A number of popular understandings of Israelite prophecy picture prophets as something akin to desert mystics, walking into Israelite cities and ravaging at the residential population.[7] Earlier comments about prophets as priests suggested problems with such a view. However, the question of the social setting for prophecy deserves even more attention.

Wilson and Petersen, among others, have attempted to classify the social location of Israel's prophets and then to compare that location with intermediaries in other cultures.[8] Such anthropological research has resulted in understandings of prophets quite different from earlier models. For example, most prophets appear to undertake their activities within an urban setting. In fact, most appear to have lived in cities or, at a minimum, to be associated with specific towns (e.g., Amos of Tekoa; Jeremiah of Anathoth).

The anthropologist Ioan Lewis theorized that intermediaries could appear either in a central or a peripheral setting.[9] By that, he meant that prophets could function in different places within society. An intermediary might be located in or near the circles of power. Alternatively, a prophet might be part of a disenfranchised group. Many popular understandings of Israel's prophets have placed them in the latter setting. Rarely, however, was that the case either in Israel or throughout the ancient Near East. One of the first prophets, Nathan, is embedded in the structure of the royal court. He has the direct ear of the king; he can judge the king and name the son who will succeed David. Likewise, over four hundred years later, one of the last prophets, Haggai, in the oracle with which the book named for him concludes, speaks to an heir of the Davidic house. Such proximity to the king or prince symbolizes the prophet's close connection to political power during many periods of ancient Israelite history.

To be sure, Israel's prophets spoke on behalf of those without power and on behalf of those oppressed by the powerful. Amos challenges those "who oppress the poor, who crush the needy" (Amos 4:1). However, Amos himself was apparently a well-off farmer who engaged in both

---

7. Scholars differ in their judgments about the prominence of ecstatic behavior or trance possession among Israel's prophets. One might compare S. Parker, "Possession Trance and Prophecy in Pre-exilic Israel," *VT* 28 (1978) 271-85, to R. Wilson, "Prophecy and Ecstasy: A Reexamination," *JBL* 98 (1979) 321-37.

8. See R. Wilson, *Prophecy and Society in Ancient Israel* (Philadelphia: Fortress, 1980), and D. Petersen, *The Roles of Israel's Prophets,* JSOTSup 17 (Sheffield: JSOT, 1981).

9. I. Lewis, *Ecstatic Religion: An Anthropological Study of Spirit Possession and Shamanism* (Baltimore: Penguin, 1975).

animal husbandry and the production of crops. Micah indicts those who "covet fields, and seize them;/ houses, and take them away;/ they oppress householder and house,/ people and their inheritance" (Mic 2:2). Yet, Micah may well have belonged to the group of elders who were responsible for the governance of Moresheth, his village. In sum, there is considerable evidence for thinking that the prophets were not impoverished or members of a lower economic class. Instead, they articulate values that involve concern for those who might be oppressed by powerful groups or structures in Israelite and Judahite society.

A final comment needs to be made about prophecy as a form of intermediation in ancient Israel. Prophecy, as such, may have a fatal flaw. Prophecy can work well if there is one prophet speaking to somebody who will take that prophet seriously. The situation becomes problematic when two prophets appear and say things that are contradictory, especially if both prophets use the standard language of an Israelite prophet. This problem has often been termed the conflict between true and false prophecy.

Classic exemplars appear in 1 Kings 22 and Jeremiah 28. In the latter case, Jeremiah confronted another prophet, Hananiah, who presented a divine oracle (Jer 28:2-4) from Yahweh. However, Hananiah's words of hope stood in stark contrast to the words of judgment that Jeremiah had been proclaiming. Although Jeremiah responded with his own comments, Hananiah used a symbolic action, removing an ox yoke that Jeremiah had been wearing. Jeremiah, without any other prophetic alternative, left the scene. Later, after Jeremiah had received a divine oracle, he could challenge Hananiah in public.

One can imagine the difficulties encountered by those who had witnessed the initial confrontation. They had no easy way of knowing which prophet was telling the truth. In fact, the deuteronomic rules that govern such a case (Deut 18:15-22) stipulate that one should wait and see which individual's words would turn out to be true. But when prophets' words require action, such inactivity would not be possible. Moreover, prophets could disagree about assessments of the present and the past, not just about pronouncements concerning the future. This potential for conflict between prophets may have provoked such diffi-

culty that other forms of seeking information from the deity developed, forms such as priestly admonition or scribal intermediation, neither of which allowed for a direct public challenge.

Prophets, then, appeared primarily in times of crisis during the period when Israel and Judah existed as monarchic states and shortly thereafter. And they addressed both the nation's leaders and the overall population based on their understanding of Israel's religious traditions. They were embedded in, rather than distinct from, the structures of Israelite society.

PROPHETIC LITERATURE IN THE ANCIENT NEAR EAST

Since intermediation is a well-attested form of religious behavior in many societies, it should come as no surprise that prophets appeared in ancient Near Eastern societies other than Israel. In fact, the OT reports both explicitly and implicitly—often polemically—that prophets of other religions existed. Deuteronomy 13:1-2 alerts us to the existence of such prophets:

> If prophets or those who divine by dreams appear among you and promise you omens or portents, and the omens or the portents declared by them take place, and they say, "Let us follow other gods" (whom you have not known) "and let us serve them."

The authors of Deuteronomy not only knew about the existence of such prophets, but they also understood something about their power. A story like Elijah's confrontation with the prophets of Baal on Mt. Carmel (1 Kgs 18:20-40) makes sense only if Israelites had experience with these prophets and understood them to be effective intermediaries between Baal and those who venerated him.

For obvious reasons, most references to prophets for gods other than Yahweh are couched in a polemical tone, just as are references to the veneration of those gods. As a result, the case of Balaam son of Beor (Numbers 22–24) is particularly interesting. Balaam was a non-Israelite but also, according to Israelite tradition, was able to function as an intermediary between Israel's God and a Moabite and Midianite audience. He utters an "oracle of one who hears the words of God, who sees the vision of the Almighty" (Num 24:4).

Although not an Israelite prophet, Balaam does the same sorts of things that one would expect from an Israelite prophet.

Our knowledge about this OT, but non-Israelite, prophet has been significantly enhanced by an important archaeological discovery in 1967. Archaeological work at Tell Deir 'Alla, which would have been part of ancient Ammon, revealed a fragmentary plaster inscription dating to the eighth century BCE. That inscription attests to the activities of an individual named Balaam, son of Beor, almost certainly the same individual whose work is described in Numbers 22–24. There could be no more graphic confirmation of Israelite prophecy as a phenomenon typical of the larger ancient Near Eastern environ.

The inscription begins with the following introduction:

> The account of [Balaam, son of Beor], who was a seer of the gods. The gods came to him in the night, and he saw a vision like an oracle of El.[10]

Thereafter the text recounts the lamentation he undertakes after apprehending the vision, which he then recounts. The gods assembled in a council (cf. 1 Kings 22; Jer 23:18) in order to plan a devastating destruction. Darkness and the reversal of the social order will ensue (elements attested prominently in OT prophetic texts as well; see, e.g., Isa 3:4; Amos 8:9). Although much of the remainder of the text is so fractured that it is difficult to read, the text that is legible presents a picture of prophetic behavior essentially similar to that in other OT texts. Visions in the night (i.e., dreams; cf. the Greek notion of "sleeping vision") were a typical form of communication between the prophet and the world of the deity. The divine council, in which Yahweh is surrounded by minor deities (in the OT, "all the host of heaven" [1 Kgs 22:19]; "heavenly beings" [lit., "sons of God," Job 1:6]), is important in many prophetic texts. For example, Isaiah is commissioned to work as a herald on behalf of such a council (Isaiah 6). Balaam, like Israelite prophets, responded in a public way to the "private" communication at night. In so doing, that which he knew became public knowledge: "Sit Down! I will tell you what the Saddayin

have done. Now, come, see the works of the gods!"[11] Finally, inside and outside Israel, such behavior was memorialized in written form to testify to the powerful revelation of what the gods were doing.

Perhaps the most important trove of ancient literature that illumines Israelite prophetic activity dates to a far earlier epoch than do Balaam or any Israelite prophets. On the upper Euphrates River, at the city of Mari, archaeologists have discovered an archive that dates to the eighteenth century BCE—just before Hammurabi, of law code fame, ruled in Babylon. This library contained not only economic and political records but also a series of clay tablets recording the work of various prophets. These Mari prophets were known by various titles, as were the Israelite prophets.

The Mari texts are all relatively brief, incised on clay tablets. One such text (ARM X 7) is here quoted in its entirety. Zimri-Lim is the king, Sibtu is his wife, and Selebum is a prophet situated at the temple of the deity Annunitum.

> Speak to my lord: Thus Sibtu your maid-servant. The palace is safe and sound. In the temple of Annunitu, on the third day of the month, Selebum went into a trance. Thus spoke Annunitum: "O Zimri-Lim, with a revolt they would put you to the test. Guard yourself. Put at your side servants, your controllers whom you love. Station them so they can guard you. Do not go about by yourself. And as for the men who would put you to the text, I shall deliver these men into your hand." I have now hereby dispatched to my lord the hair and fringe of the cult-player.[12]

This is a highly formulaic text; the phrase "Thus spoke Annunitum" is parallel to numerous OT texts, "Thus says Yahweh" (Amos 2:1). The prophetic messages are routinely addressed to the king. Some individual offers a message, which is then reported to the king by a confidant, whereas in ancient Israel the prophet often conveys his or her own message directly to the king (the case of Baruch's presenting Jeremiah's message is a notable exception). The text quoted above is typical of many Mari texts that focus on the safety and security of the king. Such focus on the monarch is present in Israel as well, though not always in pre-

10. J. Hackett, *The Balaam Text from Deir 'Alla,* HSM 31 (Chico, Calif.: Scholars Press, 1980) 29.

11. Ibid.
12. W. Moran, "New Evidence from Mari on the History of Prophecy," *Biblica* 50 (1969) 29-30.

serving his safety (e.g., Isaiah 7; 38). Mari texts do on occasion challenge the king, especially if the prophet thinks that the monarch has not been providing properly for the maintenance of a temple.

This same Mari text (ARM X 7) includes two other elements that require mention. First, the text refers to the means by which the prophet received information: a trance. Anthropologists describe this as possession behavior, for which there is some evidence in the Hebrew Bible (e.g., 1 Sam 19:20). More to the point, prophetic literature often identifies the means by which a prophet receives information about the world of the divine—namely, through audition, vision, or possession. Second, the final sentence of the text refers to the hem of the garment and the hair from the head of Selebum. Such items were garnered in order to identify and verify the source of a particular prophetic message. Some scholars have suggested similar origins for superscriptions to or within prophetic collections (e.g., Isa 8:1, 16). The prophets' messages were powerful; they could influence military behavior and matters of state. Kings, especially, could not afford to put up with irresponsible prophetic speech. Hence, those who exercised the role of prophet were held accountable in this way.

The Mari texts, though stored in an archive, betray no attempt to create a collection associated with an individual. Also, there is no evidence of later additions or reflections, as one finds in Israelite prophetic literature.

A final set of texts must also be mentioned—namely, those that reflect prophetic activity in the Neo-Assyrian period (i.e., roughly eighth–seventh centuries BCE). Though less well known than the Mari texts, these tablets, which have been recently published by Simo Parpola, chronicle prophets contemporaneous with Isaiah and Micah. These texts apparently present the oracles of nine women and four men known as prophets, a striking divergence from the gender of Israelite prophets. One well preserved text reads:

Fear not, Esarhaddon!
I am Bel. (Even as) I speak to you,
    I watch over the beams of your heart.
When your mother gave birth to you,
    sixty great gods stood with me and protected
    you.

Sin was at your right side, Samas at your left;
    sixty great gods were standing around you
    and girded your loins.
Do not trust in man.
    Lift up your eyes, look to me!
I am Ishtar of Arbela; I reconciled Assur with
    you.
When you were small, I took you to me.
    Do not fear; praise me!
What enemy has attacked you while I remained
    silent?
The future shall be like the past.
I am Nabu, lord of the stylus. Praise me!
By the mouth of the woman Baya, "son" of
    Arbela[13]

One feature of the Neo-Assyrian texts is particularly striking: More than one oracle is present on a tablet. One tablet from Nineveh includes five oracles, all apparently attributed to the same prophet. Moreover, the middle oracle seems to have been placed there because of its central importance for the overall sequence—namely, the basis for a covenant between the god Assur and the royal house of Assyria.[14] The third collection commences with a prologue or introduction prior to the citation of the oracles, and the oracles themselves have been arranged in a temporal sequence. One might view this text as a primal form of a prophetic book. The other collections include the utterances of different prophets. Still, Parpola writes: "It appears that the oracles collected in these tablets were arranged chronologically and, it seems, thematically, as well."[15]

In sum, we know that prophets were active both inside Israel and throughout the larger ancient Near Eastern cultural context. These prophets engaged in similar forms of activity, including reporting visions and uttering oracles. As a result, prophetic literature appears both in Israelite and other cultures. What is distinctive about things prophetic in ancient Israel is the monumental literary creations that derive from the work of these prophets. There is simply no prophetic text from ancient Mesopotamia, Syria-Palestine, or Egypt that can compare with the books of Isaiah and Hosea, whether viewed from the perspectives of length, breadth of vision, or literary complexity.

13. Text 1.4 in S. Parpola, *Assyrian Prophecies,* SAA 9 (Helsinki: Helsinki University Press, 1997) 6.
14. So ibid., xix.
15. Ibid., lxviii.

LITERARY PERSPECTIVES

Prophetic literature from the ancient Near East occurs in the form of single clay tablets or plaster inscriptions, each typically attesting to one prophetic performance. In contrast, the biblical prophetic books are, for the most part, collections of numerous speeches or incidents from a prophet's life. Most of these biblical books are more than a piling up of oracles, as if a series of clay tablets were simply lined up on a shelf and then copied. Some books represent a meaningful ordering and carefully structured presentation of speeches and reports. Ezekiel moves from indictment and judgment on Israel (chaps. 1–24) to judgment on foreign nations (chaps. 25–32) to hope for Israel (chaps. 33–48). Other books (e.g., Hosea) appear minimally ordered and without the aforementioned formulae. Some books include pre-existing collections (e.g., the oracles against the nations in Amos 1–2 or the series of oracles about kings in Jer 21:11–23:8). Others appear simply as one collection, without readily discernible subunits (e.g., Micah). Hence, the astute reader may recognize different levels of prophetic literature: the individual saying or report, intermediate collections of such units, and the prophetic book itself.

The categories of prose and poetry might seem to offer a convenient way of categorizing prophetic literature, if one meant that poetry equals speech and prose equals story, as some scholars have suggested. Unfortunately, the matter is not so simple for at least three reasons. First, the boundary between prose and poetry is not always easy to discern. For example, in comparing the RSV and the NRSV translations of Ezek 17:2-10, one discovers that the earlier group of translators deemed those verses to be prose, whereas the later group of translators deemed them to be poetry. The distinction between formal prose and loosely structured poetry is often difficult to discern. Second, some speeches, whether of the deity or of a prophet, are conveyed in prose (e.g., Ezekiel 25). Third, not all prose texts (apart from speeches) constitute stories—that is, prose that includes narrative structure. These difficulties notwithstanding, I propose two basic categories with which to understand prophetic literature: prose accounts and poetic speech.

Prose Accounts. Most exemplars of prophetic literature that report the activity of prophets are conveyed in prose. But they are not all stories, if by that we mean a prose narrative that includes what literary critics have described as an arc of tension or plot—namely, a beginning point, followed by a complication, which is then resolved. Put simply, a story may report, but not all chronicles or reports are stories in this strict sense.

Careful reading of accounts, most of which are composed in prose, should attend in the first instance to their literary features. For example, the accounts about Elisha present a peculiar figure, on occasion a troublesome miracle worker, on occasion a benevolent intercessor. One does well to ask questions such as, What sort of character has the writer depicted in an account? At what point does an account of his activity become a story?

It is helpful to identify at least seven basic types of prose accounts in Israelite prophetic literature:

1. Symbolic Action Report. The symbolic action report describes prophetic behavior that is designed to convey a message. Isaiah 20:1-6 provides a classic example of the straightforward form. God commands Isaiah to walk naked for three years "as a sign and a portent against Egypt and Ethiopia" (Isa 20:3). We are not told that Isaiah was to proclaim anything. Action, rather than words, provides the key element. As we work through this report, we discover that the message was directed not to these foreign nations but to "the inhabitants of this coastland," Judah's near neighbors. The text does not exhibit interest in any qualms Isaiah might have had about undertaking this task. Nor do we hear how those in Judah responded to this naked man in their midst. One can readily conceive an imaginative or entertaining story about Isaiah's having comported himself in this way. But the author was interested in using the form of the symbolic action report, not in exploring the narrative potential of such prophetic behavior. The book of Ezekiel includes a number of comparable examples of symbolic action reports (e.g., Ezek 4:1-3; 5:1-4). Reporting human behavior and its significance for an audience constitutes the key elements in such accounts.

2. Commissioning Report. These accounts, sometimes termed call narratives, do not occur in all prophetic books. But they are so interesting, and regular in general form, that they have elicited much attention.[16] Jeremiah 1:4-10; Isaiah 6; and Ezekiel 1–3 are the telling examples. (On formal grounds, Isa 40:1-11 may belong here as well.) All three texts identify a "conversation" between the deity and the prophet, which appears to depict the prophet's initiation into that role. However, these texts are not biography but, instead, highly theologized accounts, each one influenced by imagery and ideas important to the prophetic book of which it is a part (e.g., the prominence of word in the Jeremiah 1 versus the imagery of holiness in Ezekiel 1–3).

Commissioning reports are typically made up of six elements (divine confrontation, introductory word, commission, objection, reassurance, sign), all of which are present in another non-prophetic commissioning report: the commissioning of Abraham's servant, which may be found in Genesis 24. Norman Habel has argued that the regularity of the commissioning report in prophetic books is due to the use of such discourse in the commissioning of messengers throughout ancient Israel.

Like the symbolic action report, the report of commissioning does not comprise a story. One could easily imagine Isaiah 6 being told as a story—for example, an interest in whether Isaiah's "uncleanness" (v. 5) will prevent him from becoming a prophet—but the basic elements of narrative are absent. Instead, the ancient authors attest to the fact of commissioning, not why (or how) it happened. Moreover, these accounts focus on an essential element of an individual prophet's message or role (i.e., Jeremiah as a prophet to the nations who announces both destroying/overthrowing and building/planting); they do not explore the prophet's personality or human capacities.

3. Vision Report. Two of the four role labels used to describe prophets may be translated "seer." Hence, it is not surprising that visionary behavior—"this is what the Lord GOD showed me" (Amos 7:1) or "I looked up and saw. . . ." (Zech 2:1)—figures prominently in prophetic books. Such behavior is also attested formulae that introduce prophetic books—e.g., "the book of the vision of Nahum" (Nah 1:1); "the vision of Obadiah" (Obad 1); or "the oracle that the prophet Habakkuk saw" (Hab 1:1).

Several prophetic books contain reports of that which a prophet "saw." Two of these visions occur in the commission reports (Isaiah 6; Ezekiel 1–3). However, elsewhere, prophets offer vision reports that attest not only to the inauguration of their roles as prophets but also to their ongoing work as prophets. Interestingly, these vision reports regularly occur in a series. Amos reports five visionary experiences (Amos 7:1-9; 8:1-3; 9:1-4). Ezekiel offers four vision reports; they begin in 1:1; 8:1; 37:1; and 40:1, respectively. And Zechariah 1–6 contains eight vision reports. (Jeremiah offers two very brief reports [Jer 1:11-13].) Each book presents its vision reports in a regular, one might even say stereotypical, manner. Whatever the prophet experienced has been conveyed in a regularized manner.

In this type of literature, one finds a prophet experiencing that which is happening or is about to happen. In the earliest vision reports, those of Amos, the seer understands immediately what he has experienced. For example, Amos perceives the deity "calling for a shower of fire, and it devoured the great [watery] deep and was eating up the land" (Amos 7:4). Immediately thereafter, the prophet intercedes on behalf of Israel, an act that implies that Amos understood all too well what he had seen. The same is true for the visions of Ezekiel, though this prophet is now accompanied on his visionary journey by the deity, who explains to Ezekiel the implications of what he sees (e.g., Ezek 8:17-18). By the time of Zechariah, the prophet is not so easily able to comprehend what he sees: "And I looked up and saw four horns. I asked the angel who talked with me, 'What are these?' " (Zech 1:18-19). By this time, there has been a major change in the vision reports. Earlier the prophet had a vision and understood what it meant; now the prophet sees and needs some other agent to explain the vision's significance. (This tradition of the vision as separate from the interpretation continues in the apocalyptic visions of the book of Daniel: "As for me, Daniel, my spirit was troubled within me, and the visions of my head terrified me. I approached one of the attendants to ask him the truth concerning all this" [Dan 7:15-16].)

4. Legend. The legend is another major exemplar of the prose account; it offers a report about something holy, whether an object (e.g., the ark of God; see 2 Sam 6:6-7) or a person. As we

---

16. The classic study is N. Habel, "The Form and Significance of the Call Narrative," *ZAW* 77 (1965) 297-323.

saw earlier, one of the role labels for a prophet was "man of God." From the perspective of the history of religions, such an individual can be understood as a holy person, someone who possesses supernatural powers. As with the previous two types of literature, a legend need not be a story (though there is a strong tendency in this direction). For example, 2 Kgs 2:23-24—just two verses—makes up one such account. Elisha encounters some boys who taunt him, whereupon he curses them, and they are killed. This is an account, not a story. There is no tension to be resolved, but simply a report that when someone bothers a holy man, that person is likely to end up dead. However, most biblical prophetic legends are written as narratives. A good example is found in 2 Kgs 4:1-7 (cf. 1 Kgs 17:8-16). Here the widow of one of Elisha's band of prophetic disciples lives in dire straits due to her poverty. Her children are about to be taken in debt slavery. Elisha saves the day by having olive oil appear in superabundant quantities behind the closed doors of her dwelling. The creditors are kept miraculously at bay. Moreover, there is a subtle subplot; the widow could have had even more oil than she did since the oil "stopped flowing" when she ran out of vessels that she had collected. Her notions of what might be possible limited the amount that she would receive. The legend has become a story, one with a didactic aside.

5. Prophetic Historiography.[17] Both the books of Isaiah and Jeremiah include chapters that overlap material found in Kings. Isaiah 36–39 is essentially the same as 2 Kgs 18:13–19:37, and Jeremiah 52 is coextensive with 2 Kgs 24:18–25:30. Isaiah the prophet appears in Isaiah 36–39, whereas Jeremiah is not mentioned in Jeremiah 52. However, what Jeremiah said and did help to set the context for this later overview of Jerusalem's defeat. What appears in the historical books can appear in a prophetic book as well. This fact has a bearing on how we think about prophetic literature—namely, as literature that can attest to the interplay between prophetic activity and the events that prophets address.

Isaiah 36–39 provides an account of Sennacherib's attack on Jerusalem during the reign

of Hezekiah. The first chapter focuses on an Assyrian official's (the Rabshakeh) challenge to all those in Jerusalem. After Hezekiah laments this situation at the Temple, Isaiah offers an oracle (Isa 37:6-7) in which God promised to save Israel from this military threat: "I myself will put a spirit in him [Sennacherib], so that he shall hear a rumor, and return to his own land" (Isa 37:7). Then after another plea from Hezekiah, Isaiah again offers an oracle (Isa 37:21-35). After this speech, the Neo-Assyrian threat is lifted. For this historian, to narrate the events of Sennacherib's campaign is also to recount the prophetic oracles that this challenge elicited.

These chapters attest to the role of the prophet in major national affairs, especially those involving the monarch and military challenges to the nation. Moreover, such prophetic historiography presupposes that the prophet has a critically important role in times of national crisis. Hezekiah prays to God, and God offers a response through the prophet, so that the king, and others, know what will be happening. Not all Israelite history writing presumed such a role for the prophets, but even apart from such so-called prophetic historiography, there is evidence that ancient Israelites understood the prophetic word to have a major place in the historical process (e.g., "as he had foretold through all his servants the prophets," 2 Kgs 17:23; cf. 24:2).

6. Biography. Biography in the ancient world was not the same enterprise as the volumes we might purchase today. Along with an interest in an individual's life—a feature common to all biographies—ancient biographies included attention to a primary thesis or theme that could be elucidated by attention to that life. Not all accounts about a prophet are typical of ancient biographies. Some, however, are; Jeremiah 37–44 is one major example. These chapters cover both the last decade of Judah's existence and the early years of life after the defeat in 587. However, unlike prophetic historiography, to which they might seem similar, they refer to this history by focusing on the vagaries of Jeremiah's existence. The "primary" story of Israel in the early sixth century BCE involves life in the Babylonian exile. Thus 2 Kings 24 narrates two deportations, the first (597 BCE) during which King Jehoiachin, along with other leaders, was taken to Babylon, and the second

---

17. See esp., A. Rofe, *The Prophetical Stories: The Narratives about the Prophets in the Hebrew Bible. Their Literary Types and History* (Jerusalem: Magnes, 1988) 75-105.

(587 BCE) when King Zedekiah and another group were taken into exile. Only brief mention is made of an exile in another direction, one to Egypt (2 Kgs 25:26). In contrast, the way in which Judahites ended up in Egypt receives considerable attention in Jeremiah. Chapters 41–44 provide this account, one that runs counter to Jeremiah's own words; he prophesied on behalf of continued residence in the land. However, against his will, he was taken into Egypt, where he continued to work as a prophet, presumably until he died.

The author of these chapters seems as much interested in Jeremiah and his fate as he does the larger historical issues. Such focus on the person, and not on the message, is a hallmark of ancient biography. Moreover, there is, as one should expect, a thesis or principle being addressed by the author—namely, that Jeremiah's words received a positive response neither before nor after the devastating defeat of Jerusalem. One might have expected that the Judahites would pay attention to him after his earlier words had been borne out, but such was not the case. Even now, though God "persistently" continued to send prophets (Jer 44:4), the people did not respond. Such is the theme of this prophetic biography.

7. Divinatory Chronicle. The Hebrew Bible contains several texts that indicate the prophet could function like a diviner, an individual who could provide information or help from the world beyond that of normal human knowledge. Samuel functions this way in 1 Samuel 9. Ezekiel does as well. Ezekiel 20 presents a scene in which the prophet, living in exile, received representatives from "the elders of Israel." They had come to "inquire from Yahweh." Yahweh then speaks through the prophet, thereby responding to the elders. Perhaps the most straightforward case of a prophet's receiving a request for a divine oracle and then providing the expected response occurs in Zechariah 7–8. The citizenry of Bethel empowered legates to ask: "Should I mourn and fast in the fifth month . . . ?" (Zech 7:3). The prophet then responds: "The fast of the fourth month, and the fast of the fifth, and the fast of the seventh, and the fast of the tenth, shall be to the house of Judah seasons of joy and gladness" (Zech 8:19 RSV).

In these and other cases (e.g., Jeremiah and Zedekiah, Jer 38:14), prophetic literature attests to interaction between the intermediary and those who want information from the deity. The deity's response, which is communicated by the prophet, is only one, though important, part of the literary form. The prophet as diviner is clearly attested in one type of prophetic literature, the divinatory chronicle.

In sum, accounts as a basic type of prophetic literature occur in a number of subgenres. Moreover, the impulses for the creation of these accounts are diverse. They do, however, tend to focus on action, people's behavior, rather than speech, which comprises the other basic type of prophetic literature.

Poetic Speech. Important though prose accounts are, structured speech is the predominant form of prophetic literature. Most, though not all, prophetic speech is set as poetry. Hence, readers need to attend to the rules of Hebrew poetry in general as well as to the special features of prophetic speech.[18] In addition to attending to matters of poetic technique, readers of prophetic structured speech should consider the formal characteristics of those speeches. Scholars have invested considerable energy in understanding the form (hence, the term "form criticism") of speeches in prophetic books. They have identified speeches that are traced to the deity—that is, when the deity speaks in the first person (e.g., "I, the LORD, am its keeper; every moment I water it" [Isa 27:3]). Although the prophet might mouth these words, he or she is clearly the rhetorical mouthpiece of the deity. Such speeches may be described as "divine oracles." And some form critics have distinguished these divine oracles from those speeches in which the prophet speaks about God in the third person, such as:

> My joy is gone, grief is upon me,
>   my heart is sick.
> Hark, the cry of my poor people
>   from far and wide in the land:
> "Is the LORD not in Zion?
>   Is her King not in her?" (Jer 8:18-19)

Here a different rhetoric is at work. The prophet speaks on behalf of the deity's perspective, but not with the voice of the deity. Hence these utterances are known as "prophetic speeches."

18. Adele Berlin's article "Introduction to Hebrew Poetry" provides an excellent guide for readers of ancient Hebrew poetry. See Adele Berlin, "Introduction to Hebrew Poetry," in *The New Interpreter's Bible,* 12 vols. (Nashville: Abingdon, 1996) 4:301-15.

Those interested in the form of prophetic speeches or divine oracles have been particularly impressed and puzzled by texts like Amos 1–2 and Isa 10:5-19. Amos 1–2 is made up of a series of oracles that have a remarkably regular structure: "Thus says the LORD," followed by an indictment that is then linked to a judgment. Many of the oracles conclude with a brief formula, "says the LORD." Moreover, this basic form, known as the judgment oracle—an indictment followed by a sentence of judgment—appears in many other prophetic books (e.g., Jer 5:10-17; Mic 1:5-7). How should one explain such remarkable regularity? It seems very unlikely that Amos created such discourse, which was then copied by other prophets.

Form critics have observed the sorts of regularities we have just identified. They have then sought places in the ancient society in which such regular forms might have been created and preserved. In the aforementioned case, some form critics have argued that the language of indictment and sentence is most likely to have been at home in the law court. That social institution would have preserved such a form with great regularity, just as wills and contracts are preserved by our legal institutions today. Form critics suggest that prophets like Amos "borrowed" forms of speaking from various sectors of ancient Israelite society in order to make their points. Elsewhere in Amos, we find him using hymnic language, poetry created and preserved at the Temple or other ritual contexts (so Amos 4:13; 5:8-9; 9:5-6). So some poems that we find in the prophetic books have been forged using structures known both to prophets and to their audiences.

The readers of such poetry will need to be alert to the various forms they might encounter. The following incomplete list is designed to be suggestive rather than exhaustive: judgment oracle (Jer 6:16-21), woe oracle (Isa 10:1-4), lawsuit (Mic 1:2-7); lament (Jer 8:18-9:3), hymn (Hab 3:2-15), song (Isa 5:1-2), allegory (Ezek 17:2-10), and acrostic (Nah 1:2-8). As already mentioned, the judgment oracle is a speech made up of two basic parts: an indictment and a sentence. The woe oracle includes these same elements, though it commences with the Hebrew word הוי (*hôy*), which has been translated in various ways (e.g., "Ah," Isa 5:8; "Alas," Amos 5:18; "Ha," Isa

29:15; "Oh," Isa 30:1; "Woe," Isa 45:9). The woe formula (woe plus some name) was probably used originally to refer to someone who had just died. Both the judgment and the woe oracles pass a sentence on some individual or group, with the woe oracle offering the connotation that the party is as good as dead. In a similar legal vein, the lawsuit attests to the legal process that would have resulted in the passing of such a sentence. Parties are summoned, "Hear, you peoples" (Mic 1:2); interrogations are made, "What is the transgression of Jacob?" (Mic 1:5); and judgments are offered, "Therefore, I will make Samaria a heap in the open country" (Mic 1:6). As the notion of passing sentence or reference to a legal process suggests, these three forms of speech derive from Israel's law courts. The prophets used such legal forms of speech more than any other type. In contrast, the lament and the hymn derive from the world of ritual. The lament would have been used in funerary rites, whereas the hymn was sung at the Temple. Jeremiah used laments not only to express his concern for the people (Jer 8:18–9:3) but also to reflect about his own situation (Jer 15:10, 18). In addition, a number of prophets used the language of hymns (hymns typically begin with a plural imperative verb, like "Sing" or "Praise"), which is then followed by a statement expounding the character of the deity (e.g., Amos 9:5-6). This hymnic language attests to the character of the deity, who, despite judging the people, remains worthy of veneration and worship. Finally, the prophets used forms that one associates with the scribes or intellectuals: elaborate allegories (Ezek 17:2-10) and acrostics (Nah 2:1-8). Such formal variety attests to the broad cultural knowledge the prophets possessed along with their rhetorical abilities, which enabled them to use such diverse forms of verbal expression.

Great value may be achieved by undertaking such a process of form-critical classification. It is terribly important to know what sort of literature one is reading. A lament, which derives from the language of ancient funerals, bears certain connotations. To utter a lament over someone who is still alive would have jarred ancient readers (so Amos 5:1-2).

THE GROWTH OF PROPHETIC LITERATURE

The dominant model for understanding the composition of prophetic books is one in which various discrete units of discourse—account or speech—were preserved, collected, and edited. Various speeches or accounts could be combined to create collections. We have already referred to one such collection outside the Bible—namely, in a Neo-Assyrian text. The legends collected about Elisha (e.g., 2 Kings 4–6) offer a good example of a prose collection, as does the assemblage of Zechariah's vision reports (Zechariah 1–6). The book of Jeremiah presents several compelling examples of collections that include both prose and poetry. Jeremiah 21:11–23:8 comprises an assemblage of sayings about Judahite kingship; the collection begins with the phrase "concerning the royal house of Judah." Jeremiah 23:9-40 offers a comparable collection of sayings, but now about prophets; this collection bears the title "concerning the prophets" (Jer 23:9). These labeled collections provide graphic evidence for the ways in which prophetic literature came to be formed. Either the prophet or an editor placed sayings addressing a similar topic together.

A quite different mode of collecting lies behind Hosea 12–14. Although the sayings are all composed in poetry, they are not similar in their content. Rather, their very dissimilarity—some very negative, others hopeful—permit the creation of a collection that moves the reader from sentiments of judgment to that of restoration. This and other sections of prophetic books represent the activity of an editor who confronted sayings of very different sorts. The result was an ordering that moved from punishment to promise. One can imagine oracles of admonition such as those in Hos 14:1-3 originally spoken prior to oracles of judgment. Now, however, within the prophetic book, they are meant to be read after Yahweh has spoken: "Compassion is hidden from my eyes" (Hos 13:14).

Other dynamics resulted in the growth of prophetic literature. Readers of earlier oracles often found them difficult to understand or otherwise problematic. As a result, scribes proceeded to interpret them and to include the interpretation as part of the biblical text. A comparison of the MT and LXX texts of Jeremiah presents a number of such examples. The reader of the LXX form of Jer 28:16 ("Therefore thus says the LORD: I am going to send you off the face of the earth. Within this year you shall be dead") might have asked, Why does Jeremiah offer such a harsh and abrupt sentence? The MT answers that question by adding the following clause to the end of the verse: "because you have spoken rebellion against the LORD." Such commentary or explication contributed to the growth of prophetic literature.

But much more than collection and exegetical interpretation were at work. The original prophetic sayings and accounts possessed a generative power that resulted in the creation of new literature, which is particularly evident in the books of Isaiah and Zechariah. This new literature, sometimes called "deutero-prophetic," represents an attempt by Israelites to understand their own times by reformulating earlier prophetic words and accounts. In some cases, the new literature arose in the form of rather short comments. Another prophet might update that which had been said earlier: "On that day the Lord will extend his hand yet *a second time* to recover the remnant that is left of his people" (Isa 11:11); "This was the word that the LORD spoke concerning Moab *in the past. But now* the Lord says . . ." (Isa 16:13-14). These texts represent brief notes from the hands of those who preserved and venerated the words of the earlier prophets as they contemporized those earlier texts. However, these later figures composed not only compact sayings but also major compositions in their own right. This ability of prophetic literature to elicit newer prophetic literature is one of its hallmarks. The book of Isaiah contains two major exemplars of this process. The chapters that have often been known as Second (chaps. 40–55) and Third (chaps. 56–66) Isaiah have been composed based on the sayings and accounts attributed to Isaiah ben Amoz and integrated into a composition that presents those earlier sayings and accounts as a response to Israelites living in the Persian period, long after Isaiah ben Amoz had died. In this process, major topics like the role of Jerusalem/Zion and Babylon are explored over a long period of time.

The orientation of much prophetic rhetoric toward the future helps to explain this kind of literary creativity. Deuteronomy 18 informed Israelites that they could rely on a prophet's oracles if they proved true. To be sure, not all sayings were subject to clear verification. Nonetheless, one can imagine that when Jeremiah spoke of a seventy-year captivity (Jer 25:11), some would have started counting to see if he was correct. Both later prophetic (Zech 1:12) and nonprophetic (2 Chr 36:21) biblical writers reflected upon the nature and accuracy of that prediction.

There is a final type of literary development in prophetic literature, one exemplified by Hos 14:9 and Mal 4:4. The former text emphasizes the connection between Hosea's words and those who are wise, whereas the latter concludes the Minor Prophets, perhaps even the entire prophetic canon, by calling for obedience to torah. In both cases, these components of prophetic books link that literature to another portion of the canon: wisdom literature (e.g., Proverbs) and the pentateuchal torah respectively.

All of these elements—collection, comment, updating, and linkage—belong to the process by means of which the prophetic canon grew. Of these, the copious updating or contemporizing of prophetic words and traditions for a new generation seems to be a distinguishing feature of prophetic literature.

Ultimately, this process by means of which prophetic literature grew eventuated in the creation of prophetic collections and books. For much of the twentieth century, those who have studied prophetic literature have tried to discern the elemental building blocks of prophetic literature. For example, those who have written about Amos have taken pains to identify the constituent oracles in chapter 1. More recently, they have understood these oracles as part of a collection of oracles against nations, which makes up chapters 1–2. Now, most recently, they have studied the ways in which an entire prophetic book works. Such analysis has even moved to considering categories larger than an individual prophetic book. For example, some scholars have begun to read the so-called Minor Prophets, Hosea–Malachi, as one book, The Book of the Twelve.

To this end, some scholars have identified a "normative" form for a prophetic book: oracles against Judah, oracles against the nations, hope for Judah. Whereas this pattern appears in Isaiah, LXX Jeremiah, and Ezekiel, it is absent from most other prophetic books. As a result, it is difficult, indeed, to talk about the typical format of a prophetic book. However, most prophetic books do possess one typical element, the superscription. This element often links the activity of a prophet to that of a period defined by the reign of a king (Isaiah, Jeremiah, Ezekiel, Hosea, Amos, Zephaniah, Haggai, Zechariah). In other cases, the superscription simply characterizes the book as "word" (Joel), "oracle" (Nahum, Habakkuk, Malachi), or "vision" (Obadiah). Although some superscriptions do refer to their books as "words" (e.g., Amos), the use of a singular noun predominates. This use of a singular noun to refer to books filled with diverse sayings and accounts may indicate that the editors who composed these superscriptions thought of them as literary entities, not simply as collections. These entities have, therefore, become the object of study, as scholars ask: How does Amos work as a book? How does Hosea work as a book? Are they similar to or different from each other?

The book of Habakkuk offers an interesting example for this kind of analysis. The reader sensitive to the diversity of rhetoric in prophetic literature will read Habakkuk and experience the sharp moves from dialogue (1:2–2:5) through woe oracles (2:6-20) to theophanic hymn (3:1-15) and prophetic response (3:16-19*a*). It would be possible to think about Habakkuk as simply a collection. However, the reader may move beyond the aforementioned variety to perceive an integrated booklet. The prophet's voice continues even after explicit dialogue with the deity has ceased. Instead of direct encounter, the prophet moves into the Temple (2:20), utters a prayer (3:2), sings a hymn (3:3-15), and then reflects or meditates upon what he has just sung (3:16-19*a*). The book of Habakkuk revolves around the prophetic voice, not a voice challenging the people but a voice speaking to or about the deity in various modes:

O LORD, how long shall I cry for help, and you will not listen? (1:2)

O LORD, I have heard of your renown, and I stand in awe, O LORD, of your work. (3:2)

God, the LORD, is my strength; he makes my feet like the feet of a deer. (3:19)

The book begins with complaint and concludes with the language of vow and thanksgiving.

Hence, one may speak of the movement within and the coherence of this book. Such is also the case with other exemplars of prophetic literature.

RELIGIOUS AND ETHICAL ISSUES

Covenant and Imperium. If prophets are best understood as intermediaries, those who act and speak on behalf of Israel's deity, then they should, in principle, reflect the religious affirmations and theological norms of ancient Israel. And such is the case. But the emphasis here must be on diversity—norms, not norm. As a result, it is difficult, indeed, to talk about a single prophetic theology or a sole prophetic ethical perspective. One of the great strengths of von Rad's treatment of prophetic literature was his ability to discern the remarkable variety of theological traditions within the various prophetic books.[19] For example, traditions about Zion are constitutive of Isaiah, whereas they are absent from Hosea; the exodus is important in Hosea and unimportant in the literature attributed to Isaiah ben Amoz.

Despite such diversity, scholars have devoted considerable energy in attempting to discern a common core or element to prophetic literature. For example, Blenkinsopp has argued that prophecy in a military context was an essential early feature that continued to influence prophetic discourse.[20] Even more prominent have been assessments of the covenantal background of much prophetic literature.[21] For example, it is difficult to read Hos 4:2 and not hear echoes of the Ten Commandments, which are in some ways similar to the stipulations of a covenant or treaty. So, too, curses, as found in covenant texts (e.g., Deuteronomy 28), also appear in prophetic literature (e.g., Isa 34:11-17). In a similar vein, the lawsuits brought by God through the prophets reflect the covenant relationship between God and Israel (so Mic 6:1-8). Such observations have led many scholars to think about the prophets as spokespersons on behalf of Israel's covenant, calling Israel to obey that to which they had agreed at Sinai. Such

a covenant background is difficult to deny, especially when some of the later prophets wrestle with a new way to understand Israel's relationship to its God and in so doing use the image of a new covenant (Jer 31:31; cf. Ezek 36:26). The image of Moses, the quintessential covenant spokesman, as prophet (Deuteronomy 18, on which see below) adds further weight to this idea.

However, equally important is what I would term the imperial perspective of Israel's prophets. In prophetic literature, the image of God present in a theophany on Mt. Sinai is complemented by that of God enthroned in the divine council. This, after all, is the scene portrayed in the call narratives of both Isaiah and Ezekiel. The case of Isaiah is telling. The prophet envisions the deity in the Temple, which is the visible, earthly symbol for the heavenly divine council. In that context, Yahweh is surrounded by minor deities, to whom God speaks: "Whom shall I send, and who will go for us?" (Isa 6:8)—the "us" are the members of that council. Isaiah speaks up in that royal chamber, "Here am I; send me!" When he is given his "message"—"Go and say to this people. . . ." (Isa 6:9)—Isaiah then becomes nothing less than a herald from the divine council, empowered with its words and its power. Jeremiah 23:18 offers the same conciliar perspective.

Such a way of thinking about prophets helps to explain the remarkable sweep of their vision—a sweep considerably broader than that of the language of covenant between Israel and its God. Jeremiah provides a case in point. In his commissioning narrative, God designates Jeremiah as "a prophet to the nations" and says, "I appoint you over nations and over kingdoms" (Jer 1:5, 10). The prophet as one with an international role fits better with the notion of God as an imperial and cosmic sovereign than it does with the God who is covenant partner with Israel.

The international aspect of the prophet's work cannot be underestimated. Although Jeremiah is the only prophet officially designated as "a prophet to the nations," each of the "major" prophetic books includes a sizable collection of sayings and oracles devoted to nations other than Israel (Isa 13:1–23:18; Jer 46:1–51:58; Ezek 25:1–32:32). These chapters provide more than just jingoistic rhetoric. They exemplify a "plan" that God has for all people:

19. G. von Rad, *The Message of the Prophets* (New York: Harper & Row, 1965).

20. J. Blenkinsopp, *A History of Prophecy in Israel* (Louisville: Westminster/John Knox, 1996).

21. D. McCarthy, *Old Testament Covenant: A Survey of Opinions* (Richmond: John Knox, 1972); R. Clements, *Prophecy and Covenant*, SBT 43 (Naperville: Allenson, 1965).

This is the plan that is planned
concerning the whole earth;
and this is the hand that is stretched out
over all the nations. (Isa 14:26)

Even among the Minor Prophets, this testimony to God's international imperium remains in place. The book of Amos begins with a short set of oracles concerning Israel's neighboring states. Joel is concerned with a northern army (2:20) and includes rhetoric proclaimed "among the nations" (3:9). Obadiah is concerned almost exclusively with Edom and its relation to Judah. Jonah's eyes are set toward Nineveh. Micah sees both woe and weal from an international perspective: "Peoples shall stream to it [Zion], and many nations shall come" (Mic 4:1-2). Nahum is titled "an oracle concerning [against] Nineveh" (Nah 1:1). Habakkuk's vision is palpably international: "Look at the nations, and see! . . . For I am rousing the Chaldeans" (Hab 1:5-6). Zephaniah, like Amos, includes a short section devoted to foreign nations (Zeph 2:4-15). Haggai, perhaps the most "domestic" prophetic book, understands Judah's weal and wealth to derive from God, acting on a cosmic scale: "I am about to shake the heavens and the earth, and to overthrow the throne of kingdoms" (Hag 2:21-22). Zechariah, too, is written from a grand scale. The very first vision reports that the divine patrol has moved throughout "the whole earth" (Zech 1:11). Finally, Malachi's theological perspective is international: "My name is great among the nations" (Mal 1:11).

The prophets lived in the world of politics, both international and domestic. They did not think that Israel, and more so Judah, could have an international policy (e.g., treaties, alliances) that did not take into account the divine king's imperial plans. In sum, Israel's prophets serve as heralds for a cosmic God. As such, they offer an international perspective for what happens to Israel even as they affirm the importance of God's covenant with Israel.

Ethical Norms. Ethical norms inform much of the critique offered by Israel's prophets. At the risk of oversimplification, one might suggest that there are two different levels of norms: those common to all humanity and those that Israel understands as specific to it. These two levels complement the aforementioned imperial and covenant perspectives. The former infuse those sayings and

oracles devoted to foreign nations. One may read the judgment oracles that occur in Amos 1–2 and discover that those nations are indicted for behavior that all humans would ordinarily find heinous: genocidal acts (1:6, 9), violence against noncombatants (1:13), acts of ritual degradation (2:1). Oracles against the nations also include indictments for prideful behavior that offended Israel's God. Isaiah 14 includes a dirge directed at an unnamed Neo-Assyrian emperor who, in the eyes of the poet, had attempted to "ascend to heaven." Finally, there is a strain of language according to which God had designated certain imperial powers—the Neo-Assyrians and the Neo-Babylonians—to act on God's behalf to punish Israel. However, in both cases, Israel experienced such devastation that some prophets maintained these two countries had overstepped the roles assigned to them by Yahweh (Assyria: Isa 10:12-15; Babylon: Jer 51:11-49). Hence, they are to be destroyed. But the norm is one common to all people: excessive violence in time of warfare.

When the prophets move to discourse about Israel, things change. There are more specific ethical categories at work. They are not unique to Israel, since they also appear on the stele that preserves Hammurabi's law code, but they pervade much of what the prophets say.[22] The categories are righteousness and justice. Quite simply, righteousness involves the principle of beneficence, doing the good thing (e.g., in Israelite language to aid the widow or orphan). Justice addresses the question of how. In concrete terms, should one offer ten pounds of wheat to one widow or one pound of wheat to ten widows? Considerations of justice are apt when one attempts to act out beneficence.

Some recent interpreters have noted that less overt and more troubling values underpin much rhetoric in the Hebrew Bible, particularly involving the place of violence. Although some have viewed language of slaughter as simply a concomitant of ancient warfare, on occasion there seems to be an interest in graphic descriptions of terror for its own sake (Isa 34:5-7; Jer 46:10). Also, violence against women—often bordering on the pornographic—cannot be gainsaid (e.g., Ezekiel 23).

---

22. *Studies in the Book of the Covenant in the Light of Cuneiform and Biblical Law,* VTSup 18 (Leiden: Brill, 1970).

As the reference to Hammurabi's law code suggests, the king was theoretically responsible for administering justice in the ancient Near East. Such was the case in Israel as well. To be sure, prophets did address kings, but they also challenged the entire population. One could say that they democratized the responsibility for justice and righteousness. To act in such a fashion was, ultimately, the responsibility of all, not simply the job of those elders, judges, who were most prominent in the legal system.

Israelite prophets during the Neo-Assyrian period seem concerned about a particular form of social and economic development in the eighth century BCE, a style of life that stood in tension with the realization of basic norms. It was increasingly difficult to provide for economic justice as larger estates were being created. People's land was being taken away, high interest rates made it difficult to retain financial independence, and debt slavery was rampant. When addressing these issues, the prophets were indicting societal structures as well as the behavior of individuals.

Along with these categories known both to moral philosophers and religious ethicists, there is another norm. Micah 6:8 speaks of walking humbly with one's God. Just as there can be prideful behavior on the international scene, so also too much arrogance can occur on the domestic front. As a result, some prophets argue on behalf of a proper relationship with Yahweh. What such a relationship involves is explored in various ways, but one important motif involves the absence of loyalty to any other deity. Hosea and Jeremiah, especially, attack the attraction of Baal, whereas Ezekiel 8 makes clear that the veneration of many other gods and goddesses was at stake. Only Obadiah, Jonah, and Haggai do not include overt polemics against the veneration of deities other than Yahweh. Of course, veneration of Yahweh alone is a characteristic feature of God's covenant with Israel (Exod 20:3), so the section "Covenant and Imperium."

Later prophets wrestled with the realities of human behavior. References to a new covenant (Jer 31:31) or a new heart (Ezek 36:26) could be read as utopian solutions to the intractable tendency of humans to do the errant thing. The ethical norms had not changed, but one recognizes a realization in Jeremiah, Ezekiel, and Zechariah that to enact them is terribly difficult, requiring a moral and religious capacity not hitherto realized.

Hope. Despite the propensity of prophetic literature to identify the many ways in which humans have fallen short of both universal and Israelite ethical norms—along with the ensuing results—that literature also often strikes a hopeful note. However, the vocabulary and images of hope in prophetic books have troubled many scholars. How, they ask, could someone like Amos, who speaks about an end for Israel, also talk about a future of plenty (Amos 9:11-15)? The same question could be posed about Micah (Mic 2:12-13).

Scholars have offered a number of answers to explain this hopeful strain. Most prominent has been the judgment that the language of weal arises only after the disasters actually occurred. Hence, books like Micah, which speak of both disaster and hope for Judah, need to be read as composite compositions. According to these scholars, the negative material predates the assaults by the Neo-Assyrian and Neo-Babylonian empires, whereas the positive language (e.g., Mic 4:6-8) was added after 587 BCE.

Now, to be sure, as we have already seen, various additions did make their way into prophetic literature. However, the language of hope is truly pervasive in prophetic literature and, hence, requires an explanation beyond that of scribal addition. Westermann has maintained that such hopeful discourse in prophetic oracles is far more prominent than many readers have thought to be the case. Moreover, M. Sweeney has written, "In general, prophetic books tend to focus on the punishment and restoration of Israel/Judah, *with the emphasis on the latter.*"[23]

The sources for hope in prophetic literature are multiple. The vocabulary of hope may stem from rudimentary knowledge of what happens when there is military destruction; inevitably some people survive. The language of a remnant surely reflects this brute reality (e.g., Isa 11:11; cf. 7:3). Despite the thorough destruction of Jerusalem and deportation of many Judahites, the land was not left uninhabited. This reality would have been apparent even prior to the various defeats Israel

---

23. M. Sweeney, *Isaiah 1–39*, FOTL 16 (Grand Rapids: Eerdmans, 1996) 17.

and Judah experienced. An "end" did not mean the cessation of all human life.

Judah's theological traditions would also have contributed to the notion that God could continue to act on behalf of the people. The language of the so-called Davidic covenant included the expectation that this polity would continue "forever" (2 Sam 7:13). Hence, even well after the defeat of Judah, we hear about what "David" might mean for Israel, even when a prophet might mean something quite different from the restoration of the Davidic monarchy, as is almost certainly the case in Isa 55:3.

Finally, as masters of poetic expression, the prophets attest to the power of new words, of language itself. It is striking that Isaiah, Jeremiah, Ezekiel, and the Book of the Twelve all acknowledge that the future will see a renaming of Jerusalem. The city that for many prophets personified all that was wrong with Israel (e.g., Isa 1:21; Mic 3:12) will undergo the same sort of transformation as did Jacob, who became Israel. A new name will signify a new fate. Jeremiah thinks Jerusalem will be called "the throne of the LORD" (Jer 3:17). The book of Ezekiel concludes with a new name for Jerusalem: "The LORD Is There" (Ezek 48:35). Isaiah 62:4 refers to a new name that Yahweh will give, "Hephzibah," or "My Delight Is in Her." Finally, Zech 8:3, as part of the Book of the Twelve, offers the final exemplar: "City of Faithfulness" (TNK). In these diverse ways, prophetic literature attests to a future beyond the "end" that many of Israel's prophets foresaw.

Traditions About Prophets. Over time Israel was confronted with the task of thinking about prophets. To be sure, they knew that individuals known as prophets had been in their midst. But what was a prophet? Was there a typical or ideal prophet? Moreover, as canonical literature—the Torah, or Pentateuch, and the book of Psalms—began to emerge, Yahwists were confronted with the question of the relationship between prophetic literature and that of torah and that of the writings.[24] Moreover, as torah was increasingly understood to be canon—that is, a body of literature that was now essentially closed—how should one conceive of the relationship of

prophetic literature to other parts of the canon? The phrase "the law and the prophets," which post-dates the formation of the Hebrew Bible, hints at a way of addressing the matter in a later time.

Those biblical writers who depicted Moses as a prophet offered one important way in which torah and prophets might be linked. If Moses were a paradigmatic prophet (Deut 18:15), and if Moses is responsible for torah, then prophecy becomes part of torah, though still subordinate to it. Prophetic literature may consequently be understood as an exposition or admonition based on torah, rather than an independent word of the deity. That is why Ezekiel appears to be such a dangerous text, since it purports to be a new torah, "the law of the temple" (Ezek 43:12), which might stand in competition with the pentateuchal torah.

However, Moses was only one of several possible paradigmatic prophets. Elijah is another; he had special credentials, since, according to biblical tradition, he had never died. As a result, writers both in the Persian and the Greco-Roman periods could look forward to the return of Elijah "before the great and terrible day of the LORD comes" (Mal 4:5; cf. Matt 17:10-13). Closed though the prophetic writings might finally become, there was still an expectation that a prophet or prophecy would appear in the future (see Joel 2:28-29; Acts 2).

Another important tradition about prophets as such involved the notion that they suffered a violent fate. Although this may have occasionally been the case in ancient Israel (see the brief chronicle about the death of Uriah son of Shemaiah in Jer 26:20-23), the Persian (2 Chr 24:20-22; Neh 9:26) and Greco-Roman periods saw the development of a notion that many prophets were treated in this way (e.g., Luke 13:34; Acts 7:52). Jeremiah's own rhetoric (e.g., Jer 11:19) may well have encouraged such an understanding. In contrast to this tradition, one may review the reports about prophets in ancient Israel and be surprised that they were not treated brutally more often.

Apart from traditions about prophets themselves, there were also canonical formulations that attempted to integrate prophetic literature with other portions of the canon. These texts are of several different types. On the one hand, considerable amounts of psalmic language are embedded within prophetic literature (e.g., the so-called

---

24. Torah typically refers to the Pentateuch, whereas the Writings refers to the third part of the Hebrew canon (Torah, Prophets, Writings). Psalms is part of the Writings.

Amos doxologies [4:13; 5:8-9; 9:5-6] and the catena of thanksgiving and hymn in Isaiah 12). On the other hand, there are texts at the end of prophetic books that call for the reader to reflect on that text from the perspective of another portion of the canon (Hos 14:9 points to wisdom texts, Mal 4:4 to torah). From this perspective, the law and the prophets were perceived by early readers as a far more coherent body than has been supposed.

SUMMARY

Prophetic literature derives from the activity of Israel's prophets. Just as there were different kinds of prophets, so also prophetic literature is itself diverse. Primary forms occur as account (symbolic action report, commissioning report, legend, prophetic historiography, biography) and structured speech (divine oracle and prophetic speech). Although prophetic literature is known elsewhere in the ancient Near East—most notably Old Babylonian and Neo-Assyrian textual corpora—there are no extrabiblical exemplars comparable in size and sophistication to the biblical prophetic books, in considerable measure because of the generative power of Israelite prophetic literature. Prophetic literature is the product of creative speakers and writers who were influenced not only by contemporary events but also by a view of Yahweh as an international sovereign and by a profound understanding of God's relationship to Israel. These traditions contributed to a powerful theological and ethical amalgam. Phrases such as:

> Let justice roll down like waters,
>   and righteousness like an ever-flowing
>   stream. (Amos 5:24)

> They shall beat their swords into plowshares,
>   and their spears into pruning hooks;
> nation shall not lift up sword against nation,
>   neither shall they learn war any more.
>   (Mic 4:3)
> I am the first and I am the last;
>   besides me there is no god. (Isa 44:6)

embody some of the most enduring perspectives in prophetic literature—indeed, in all biblical literature.

BIBLIOGRAPHY

Blenkinsopp, J. *A History of Prophecy in Israel.* Louisville: Westminster/John Knox, 1996.

Clements, R. *Old Testament Prophecy: From Oracles to Canon.* Louisville: Westminster/John Knox, 1996.

Gitay, Y., ed. *Prophets and Prophecy.* Semeia Studies. Atlanta: Scholars Press, 1997.

Gordon, R., ed. *The Place Is Too Small for Us: The Israelite Prophets in Recent Scholarship.* SBTS 5. Winona Lake, Ind.: Eisenbrauns, 1995.

Lewis, I. *Ecstatic Religion: An Anthropological Study of Shamanism and Spirit Possession.* Baltimore: Penguin, 1975.

Nissinen, M. *References to Prophecy in Neo-Assyrian Sources.* SAAS 7. Helsinki: Helsinki University Press, 1998.

Overholt, T. *Channels of Prophecy: The Social Dynamics of Prophetic Activity.* Minneapolis: Fortress, 1989.

Parpola, S. *Assyrian Prophecies.* SAA 9. Helsinki: Helsinki University Press, 1997.

Petersen, D., ed. *Prophecy in Israel: Search for an Identity.* IRT. Philadelphia: Fortress, 1987.

———. *The Prophetic Literature: An Introduction.* Louisville: Westminster/John Knox, 2002.

Rad, G. von. *The Message of the Prophets.* New York: Harper and Bros., 1965.

Rofé, A. *The Prophetical Stories: The Narratives About the Prophets in the Hebrew Bible, Their Literary Types and History.* Jerusalem: Magnes, 1988.

———. *Introduction to Prophetic Literature.* Sheffield: Sheffield Academic, 1997.

Westermann, C. *Prophetic Oracles of Salvation.* Louisville: Westminster/John Knox, 1991.

Wilson, R. *Prophecy and Society in Ancient Israel.* Philadelphia: Fortress, 1980.

THE BOOK OF ISAIAH 1–39

INTRODUCTION, COMMENTARY, AND REFLECTIONS

BY
GENE M. TUCKER

INTRODUCTION

T he first rule of biblical interpretation should be this: Do not reverse the miracle at Cana. That is, do not turn wine into water. No interpretation, exegesis, commentary, or reflection can replace the text it addresses, particularly the rich and complex landscape that lies before all who read Isaiah 1–39. But herein lies a dilemma, for interpretation is both necessary and inevitable. Anyone who reads creates meaning. If a significant text—such as one in these chapters of Isaiah—is to have meaning and life, it will be only in the minds and hearts of its readers, each of whom will encounter something different based on various factors, including experience, culture, and their goals in reading. Moreover, the meaning of this text from antiquity seldom is self-evident; nor can it be taken for granted.

The aim of the commentary ahead is not to provide a substitute for reading the text, for there is none. The goal is to open up the text, to encourage an encounter with it, to make it more accessible. Disciplined interpretation wants to engage the text and not a preconceived notion about its meaning. Any exegesis that draws the reader into the text has served its main purpose.

Explanation and interpretation are not the same. Many features of ancient and foreign texts require explanation: Who was Hezekiah or Sennacherib? When was "the year that King Uzziah died"? Interpretation strives for more, for engagement with the text at the level of both its meaning (commentary) and its potential implications (reflection). In short, interpretation strives for understanding.

ISAIAH 1–39 AS A BOOK WITHIN A BOOK

Until quite recently, no critical interpreter would have found it necessary to justify or even explain a commentary that addressed Isaiah 1–39 apart from Isaiah 40–66. Biblical scholarship since the nineteenth century had demonstrated persuasively that the book was to be attributed to not one but at least three "Isaiahs," responsible in turn for chaps. 1–39, 40–55, and 56–66. Thus concern with the book as a whole in its canonical form had been overshadowed by the evidence for diverse authorship and date. In the last two decades of the twentieth century, however, the attention of scholarship has turned to the interpretation of the book as a whole and from a variety of perspectives. Virtually all such approaches continue to acknowledge the validity of the evidence for different dates and circumstances, but question the relative significance of the history of the development of the book.[1]

The move to consider the book as a whole is a long overdue change, and for at least two reasons. First, any text deserves to be interpreted in its context. That will include words in sentences, sentences in paragraphs or lines in stanzas, paragraphs in larger units, units within books, and books within the Scripture as a whole. In this respect, context within a book often has been neglected, but it is fundamental to understanding texts. Second, texts within books are the most accessible as well as the most important horizon for the interpreter. Both before and after one reaches conclusions concerning historical background or the history of the book's development (e.g., that a particular section is a secondary addition), the interpreter ought to face the text in its final form.

This shift in emphasis has generated a great deal of energy, bringing a variety of approaches to bear on the question of what the parts of the book of Isaiah have in common rather than what separates them. One commentator has focused on the entire sixty-six chapters as the work of an editor or author active c. 435 BCE.[2] Although most interpreters recognize that this date is too early for the latest material in the book, concern with the final editor's work is acknowledged as important. More widely accepted is the analysis of the book's unity in terms of a series of editorial productions, a redaction in the eighth century, another in the seventh century in the time of Josiah, an exilic, and a (final) post-exilic edition.[3] This position builds upon a great deal of redaction-critical analysis of particular parts of Isaiah.[4] One scholar has argued that an independent book of Deutero-Isaiah never existed; rather, the same poet who wrote chapters 40–55 edited what is now Isaiah 1–39 as the basis for his own work.[5]

1. The exceptions are traditional approaches that focus on the book as a whole, considering all of it to be the work of the 8th-cent. BCE prophet. See John N. Oswalt, *The Book of Isaiah, Chapters 1–39,* NICOT (Grand Rapids: Eerdmans, 1986).

2. John D. W. Watts, *Isaiah 1–33,* WBC (Waco, Tex.: Word, 1985).

3. R. E. Clements, "The Unity of the Book of Isaiah," *Int.* 36 (1982) 117-29.

4. One of the most important of these is Hermann Barth, *Die Jesaja-Worte in der Josiazeit* (Neukirchen: Neukirchener Verlag, 1977). For such work on Isaiah 1–39, see esp. Marvin A. Sweeney, *Isaiah 1–39, With an Introduction to Prophetic Literature,* FOTL XVI (Grand Rapids: Eerdmans, 1996).

5. H. G. M. Williamson, *The Book Called Isaiah: Deutero-Isaiah's Role in Composition and Redaction* (Oxford: Oxford University Press, 1994).

Some have come to view the book as a whole from either a literary or a canonical perspective.[6] In many cases, they argue that concern with the history of the development of the literature or its historical context is beyond recovery, irrelevant, or distracts attention from the meaning of the text itself.[7]

Still others have recognized the coherence, if not necessarily the unity, of the book as a whole in terms of one or another theme.[8] One motif that doubtless contributes to the unity of Isaiah is that of kingship, including the importance of the Davidic dynasty, the expectation of an anointed ruler, and the servant of the Lord.[9] Others stress the theological centrality of Zion as a unifying theme.[10] The theme of the exodus, it has been argued, serves as one of the primary means of uniting the first and second halves of the book.[11] Another motif that persists throughout the book is "holy" (קָדוֹשׁ *qādôš*, 6:3), especially in "the Holy One of Israel" (1:4; 5:16, 19, 24; 10:20; 12:6; 17:7; 37:23; 41:14; 43:3, 14; 45:11; 48:17; 54:5; 60:9, 14) and in the identification of Zion as "the holy mountain" (11:9; 27:13; 56:7, 13; 65:11, 25; 66:20).

From the point of view of the history of the book's composition, these connections among the parts of the book disclose that the materials in Isaiah 40–66 were composed in the light of and in continuation of the tradition of Isaiah 1–39. From the point of view of reading and, therefore, interpreting the book, the links demonstrate the value of viewing any individual text from the perspective of the total book.

So is it legitimate any longer to present an introduction to and a commentary on Isaiah 1–39 as distinct from the canonical book? Is Isaiah 1–39 an artificial "book," especially since the division of Isaiah into three parts has been shaped by critical inquiry in the last century and more? Beyond the evidence for different authorship, there are sufficient reasons to address these chapters as a distinct part of the book. In the first place, it is hardly possible to comprehend the whole of such a book all at once. One needs to pay attention to the particular parts, including individual units of discourse as well as large sections. In the interpretation of biblical literature, those parts need to be understood both on their own and in their context.

6. See Brevard S. Childs, *Introduction to the Old Testament as Scripture* (Philadelphia: Fortress, 1979); Brevard S. Childs, *Isaiah: A Commentary* (Louisville: Westminster John Knox, 2001). Childs's central concern is to read and interpret biblical books finally as the scriptures of communities of faith. See also Christopher R. Seitz, "Isaiah 1–66: Making Sense of the Whole," in *Reading and Preaching the Book of Isaiah,* ed. Christopher R. Seitz (Philadelphia: Fortress, 1988) 105-26.

7. For an approach that emphasizes the role of the reader, see E. W. Conrad, *Reading Isaiah,* OBT 27 (Minneapolis: Fortress, 1979).

8. R. E. Clements, "A Light to the Nations: A Central Theme of the Book of Isaiah," in *Forming Prophetic Literature: Essays on Isaiah and the Twelve in Honor of John D. W. Watts,* ed. James W. Watts and Paul R. House, JSOTSup 235 (Sheffield: Sheffield Academic, 1996) 57-69. See also David M. Carr, "Reading for Unity in Isaiah," *JSOT* 57 (1993) 61-80.

9. H. G. M. Williamson, *Variations on a Theme: King, Messiah, and the Servant in the Book of Isaiah* (Carlisle: Paternoster, 1998).

10. Christopher R. Seitz, *Zion's Final Destiny: The Development of the Book of Isaiah* (Minneapolis: Fortress, 1991).

11. Marvin A. Sweeney, *Isaiah 1–4 and the Post-Exilic Understanding of the Isaianic Tradition,* BZAW 171 (Berlin: Walter de Gruyter, 1988) 17-21.

Second, in spite of major questions concerning the end of the book at various stages in the history of its composition (see below), there can be little doubt that the most distinct break falls between chaps. 39 and 40. Isaiah 1–39 is not an arbitrary unit. Although some parts of the first half are similar to chaps. 40–55 (chap. 35 in particular), the shift beginning with chap. 40 is dramatic in terms of style, historical horizon, and message. The superscription (Isa 1:1) appears to identify all that follows in the book with a particular prophet in a particular time, Isaiah the son of Amoz from (what we now know to be) the second half of the eighth century BCE. That verse has been the main basis, from the first century CE to the modern age, for attributing all sixty-six chapters to a single prophet. But closer scrutiny reveals problems and even contradictions within the literature. First, this is not the only superscription in the book, so we cannot take for granted that it was meant to cover the whole. One appears at Isa 2:1 and another at 14:1, the latter followed by a text concerning a much later period. Significantly, the last reference to the prophet Isaiah, son of Amoz, appears in chap. 39. Thus, for reasons that go beyond questions of authorship and date, Isaiah 1–39 presents itself as an appropriate unit of prophetic literature.

THE STRUCTURE AND COMPOSITION OF ISAIAH 1–39

Interpretation ought to begin with a description of the configuration or outline of the text in view, in this case Isaiah 1–39. Remarkably, there is widespread agreement among commentators on the major blocks of literature that comprise the book. That consensus points to the fact that these chapters have a great many clear markers that signal divisions, beginning with the superscriptions noted above. These markers include headings such as those ("Oracle concerning X") that both link the sections of chaps. 13–23 together in a series and separate them one from another, and the opening cries of "Woe" that function similarly in chaps. 28–32 (see also 5:8-24). Other indicators include genre, especially shifts from one to another. So Isaiah 36–39, consisting of a series of historical narratives, is readily recognized as a distinct section. Thus, although there will be some significant variations, most outlines of Isaiah 1–39 will resemble the one that appears at the end of this Introduction.

The meaning of those divisions, however, and particularly their relationship to one another, is far more disputed. One can hardly think of Isaiah 1–39 as a single composition, organized sequentially, either in terms of development of thought or chronologically. To be sure, there are elements of organization and development. First, some historical principles have guided the organization. Generally speaking, the prophetic speeches and narratives concerning the earlier events of the time of Isaiah come before the later ones. Thus the prophet's words and activities in relation to King Ahaz and the Syro-Ephramitic war (735–732 BCE) appear in chaps. 7–8, and those concerning King Hezekiah and the Assyrian crisis of 701 BCE come in chaps. 28–33 and in the historical narratives of chaps. 36–39. But this organization is far from rigid and is broken by material relating to events much later than the eighth century; and in any case, the historical references in many instances resist identification.

Second, some formal principles of organization reveal themselves. The initial chapter functions as a summary introduction to the whole and, some insist, to the entire book. In at least two instances (chap. 12 and chap. 33), liturgical materials conclude larger sections. A large section (chaps. 13–23) consists of a series of proclamations concerning foreign nations, each with the same heading, although there is no obvious principle for the organization of the individual proclamations within that section. The units of chaps. 24–27 have strong generic and thematic affinities, and those in chaps. 28–32 relate for the most part to the same historical events and theme.

Third, however, although certain themes recur throughout Isaiah 1–39, there is no obvious thematic development. There is not even a clear progression from words of judgment to those of salvation. In fact, the last word of the "book" is the announcement of the Babylonian exile (Isa 39:5-8). Organizational design and thematic development are more evident within some sections of the book, such as the interpretive summary in 1:2-31.

For the most part, the reader is faced with major blocks of material (such as 6:1–9:7; 13–23; 24–27; 28–33) that in turn consist of individual units of varying length. Since both the major building blocks and their individual components exhibit evidence of different historical horizons, it is more accurate to think of collections of traditions, subsequently more or less organized by scribes and editors over the years. Consequently, one must account for the shape of the book and its organization in terms of the history of its composition rather than, for instance, as the product of a self-conscious author or even a single editor.

How much one can know about the process of composition or why an editor placed material where it is rather than somewhere else is uncertain, and in that uncertainty lies the basis for disagreement about the meaning of the book's shape. Since all reconstructions of prior stages of development are hypothetical, some interpreters reject the effort out of hand. But the evidence, including the complexity of the book, reveals this much: Isaiah 1–39 developed over at least four centuries, and the actual process would have been more—not less—complicated than any theoretical model yet produced. This is by no means a call for ever more detailed division of the literature according to the stages of its development. It is to insist that the evidence does not allow recovery of all the steps through which the present text passed before reaching its final form. However, some steps along the way can be recognized.

The apportionment of Isaiah 1–66 among three distinct periods of activity remains fundamentally unshaken. But discernment of the relationship among those parts and the understanding of how Isaiah 1–39 itself developed have taken a turn. Until relatively recently, historians of the literature tended to view the major blocks of literature, such as chaps. 24–27 or 40–55, as arising independently before finally being incorporated into the book. These days the tendency is to attribute more thoughtfulness and craft to the tradents than did earlier generations of scholars. More and more scholars think of a process by which subsequent generations supplemented the tradition they had received. So even if it is acknowledged that Isaiah 24–27 had been composed independently of the present book, one asks why it was incorporated into the Isaiah tradition and why in its particular location. It has to be significant, and not arbitrary, that these eschatological prophecies concerning the whole world follow the proclamations against individual nations.[12] Moreover, Isaiah 1–39 could not have reached its final form before the addition of Isaiah 40–55, for some of its parts, including chaps. 24–27, originated later than Deutero-Isaiah. The development of the book was a complex process.

Nowhere is that complexity more obvious than with regard to the question of the end of the first book of Isaiah. So long as the source-critical divisions prevailed—into three sections according to authorship and date—the answer was clear: Chapters 1–39 were to be associated with Isaiah of Jerusalem. Now, however, and for various reasons, many commentators take the end of that book to be chap. 33.[13] This development means that chaps. 34–35 and chaps. 36–39 have become the keys to the organization of the book of Isaiah as a whole. The main impetus for taking chap. 33 to be the end has come from redaction criticism, the effort to write and understand the stages in the book's editorial development. Clearly both chaps. 34–35 and chaps. 36–39 are among the latest materials, and now widely regarded as transitional in some way between the First and Second Isaiahs. Isaiah 35 in particular is very similar to chaps. 40–55, but is sufficiently different to suggest that it was composed on the basis of those chapters. Moreover, there is persuasive evidence that an edition of the book in the seventh century in the time of Josiah closed the book with chap. 32 or 33.[14]

Against the position that chaps. 34–35 and 36–39 are to be associated more with what follows than with what precedes and, in favor of chap. 39 as the conclusion, is the subject matter of chaps. 36–39 in particular. Those narratives concern the prophet Isaiah, King Hezekiah, and the city of Jerusalem in the time of the Assyrian monarch Sennacherib. These chapters, as well as chaps. 34–35, almost certainly were added to the book even after chaps. 40–55, but they are about Isaiah.

ISAIAH THE PROPHET AND ISAIAH THE BOOK

None of this reflection on the questions concerning the shape of the book as a whole is to suggest that everything attributed to or concerning the prophet in the eighth

12. Ronald E. Clements, *Isaiah 1–39,* NCNB (Grand Rapids: Eerdmans, 1980) 198.

13. John D. W. Watts, *Isaiah 1–33,* WBC (Waco, Tex.: Word, 1985). For an excellent and detailed analysis of the structure and redactional history of Isaiah 1–39 in the context of the book as a whole, including an account of the critical scholarship on the question, see Marvin A. Sweeney, *Isaiah 1–39, With an Introduction to Prophetic Literature,* FOTL XVI (Grand Rapids: Eerdmans, 1996) 39-62.

14. The work of Hermann Barth, *Die Jesaja-Worte in der Josiazeit* (Neukirchen: Neukirchener Verlag, 1977), has been widely accepted. See, also Clements, *Isaiah 1–39,* 5-6; Sweeney, *Isaiah 1–39,* 58-59.

century was written in his time. The issue of the meaning of the received form of the book or of its editorial stages can be distinguished from the question of the authorship, origin, or date of the individual parts. The material used by editors may be old or new.

It should not be surprising, therefore, that for more than a century many texts in Isaiah 1–39 have been recognized to be as late or even later than those in Isaiah 40–66. It is not some modern historical curiosity that provokes exploration of such matters, but the information in the texts themselves. What are we to believe: Isa 1:1, which attributes what follows to Isaiah in the eighth century BCE, or the allusions and explicit references to later events in the body of the material? For example, the superscription in Isa 13:1 claims directly that Isaiah son of Amoz was the author of what follows in chaps. 13–14, but there are clear and specific allusions in those chapters to events two centuries after the prophet. Moreover, some texts—such as the superscriptions and narratives about Isaiah—by their very perspective assume authors other than the prophet.

What, then, is the relationship between the book—specifically chaps. 1–39—and the prophet? Given the fact that some of the literature originated long after the eighth century BCE, is it possible to retrieve the words of Isaiah of Jerusalem? This was not a problem before the rise of critical inquiry, when tradition—including the citation of texts from all parts of the book in the NT—attributed everything to Isaiah. But once a Second and then a Third Isaiah had been recognized, it was inevitable that the same principles of investigation would be applied to Isaiah 1–39. These principles were the same that led to the documentary hypothesis of the Pentateuch. Is there evidence (allusions, perspective) of different historical periods? Are there significant or measurable differences in style (poetry, vocabulary, syntax, etc.)? Are there different theological perspectives? This last question led to some clear excesses, particularly with respect to the prophets. It was not uncommon through much of the twentieth century for scholars to conclude that the early prophets announced judgment and that any announcements of salvation must have been later additions to tone down or qualify the bad news. Although there are many instances where such conclusions are justified on other grounds (e.g., Amos 9:11-15), that approach is especially misleading with regard to Isaiah 1–39.

There were two particularly troubling aspects of this source-critical investigation of the prophets. First, although many readers of the prophetic books were disturbed by conclusions that such and such a passage did not originate with the prophet in question, even more misleading was the implication that one could, through such analysis, arrive at the authentic words of the prophet. Second, decisions concerning authorship or origin often entailed judgments about the relative value or validity of particular texts. Just as tradition valued the entire books as words of an inspired prophet, so also critics considered the "authentic" words of the prophet more valuable than those of the later editors. But it is only on the basis of a particular understanding of inspiration that the speeches of Isaiah of Jerusalem can be regarded as more theologically authoritative than later additions to the tradition. One is entitled to value judgments, but they should not be confused with judgments of fact concerning origin (see the Reflections at Isa 4:2-6).

Early in the twentieth century, students of the Bible more and more acknowledged the importance of the oral tradition that had preceded the written texts. This concern was particularly significant with regard to the prophetic literature, which routinely reports the speeches of the prophets, often directly to individuals or to groups. Moreover, a great many of the genres present themselves as those of oral discourse.[15] The early prophets, such as Isaiah, were speakers whose words were written down and subsequently edited, expanded, and interpreted in new contexts. One effect of such form-critical analysis of prophetic literature was to extend earlier attempts to retrieve the original (oral) discourse of individual prophets. This view is appropriately chastened by the research and interpretation of recent decades, in which the recovery of the "original" speeches is recognized as difficult, if not impossible. Although one may remain convinced that the prophets were speakers, that does not at all mean that one can reconstruct individual speeches by the prophets whose names stand at the heading of the book, and even less the particular circumstances under which individual addresses were delivered.

Nevertheless, the questions posed by such analysis remain key interpretive steps in the study of prophetic texts. Introductory and concluding formulas enable the reader to recognize distinct units within the literature, structures common to particular genres show more clearly what is distinctive about a passage and how it relates to others, and the concern with social context (setting) helps one to understand how texts functioned in antiquity. Moreover, such questions have proved to be productive when applied to entire books as well as to small units of discourse.

The literary pursuit of authorship and the search for the original oral discourse of Isaiah are considered both more difficult and less significant than was the case only a few decades ago. If earlier generations of critical scholarship privileged the oldest, often at the expense of the actual written text, the current tendency is to privilege the latest, or canonical, form of the literature, sometimes at the expense of individual units and their precanonical history. This leads to what should be another rule for biblical interpretation: Throw nothing away. All texts in these chapters and all layers of their development are potentially significant. The serious reader who wants to understand and be confronted by the biblical text will not realize that potential by deciding in advance which is the more significant. There is life both in and behind the texts. Nor should one neglect the subsequent life of these texts as they came to echo in later biblical books, including the New Testament. So to read such rich and highly textured literature requires bifocals and more; its depths should not be sacrificed to a focus on one or another of its strata. Finally, if one level or one text is to be considered more valuable or

15. For a summary see Gene M. Tucker, "Prophetic Speech," *Int.* 32 (1978) 31-45; reprinted in *Interpreting the Prophets,* ed. James Luther Mays and Paul J. Achtemeier (Philadelphia: Fortress, 1987) 27-40.

more authoritative than another, that should not be determined on the basis of relative antiquity but on carefully considered theological grounds.

So is it possible to sort out the words of the prophet from the words of the book? The best one can do is to establish relative proximity to Isaiah's time and place, and that only when there is sufficient evidence. Such determination, when possible, is important, for it opens the door to deeper understanding. In any case, one needs to be occupied mainly with the text more than with its background, or even the text regardless of its background or origin. The book rather than the prophet Isaiah is what lies before us. Nevertheless, preoccupation with the unity of the entire book should not be allowed to obscure its individual parts or its pre-history.

HISTORICAL CONTEXT

As attention has shifted to the final form of the book, some have argued that the historical background is less important than the analysis of the literature as it stands. Although the main focus ought to be the text, consideration of its historical context is both all but unavoidable and essential to understanding. History is unavoidable because those who turn to this book from antiquity will take with them some image of that antiquity, and reading it will evoke further images. The issue for interpretation is whether that image of the past is a critical reconstruction—that is, whether or not the historical imagination is disciplined. (See the Reflections at 36:1–37:8.)

Attention to history is essential, for a great deal would be lost were it to be abandoned. Prophetic literature, and Isaiah 1–39 in particular, is filled with historical allusions, including references to events, kings, and circumstances. In many cases, the text would be mute if the reader did not comprehend the references. Who was Ahaz or Hezekiah or Sennacherib? At the most basic level of comprehending words and sentences, one cannot engage the details of the book without understanding what can be known about those individuals and circumstances. For the sake of making sense of the texts, the more one can know about its circumstances or those it refers to, the better. Unfortunately, many, if not most, of those allusions to circumstances are far more obscure than commonly assumed. Just as scholarship is less confident about reconstructing the history of the development of the book than only a few decades ago, so, too, there is greater caution about what can be known of the history of Israel. Nevertheless, the very contents of Isaiah 1–39 call attention to a historical horizon.

The history relevant to understanding Isaiah 1–39 could encompass most of the story of Israel and Judah, certainly at least from the time of David to well into the Persian period. The book—and the book of 2 Kings as well—locates Isaiah in the second half of the eighth century BCE. But these chapters include passages that originated as late as the fifth or possibly even the fourth century BCE, and they incorporate traditions stretching back to the time of David, around 1000 BCE. Moreover, the rise and fall of ancient Near Eastern empires come into play.

To begin with the center of attention, the prophet Isaiah son of Amoz was active in Jerusalem throughout most of the second half of the eighth century BCE. Little is known of his life, but some conclusions can be drawn from the book, mainly the narratives of his actions. That he had access to kings—although they did not always respect his messages—suggests he was inside rather than outside the central institutions of Judah. Although neither the prophet nor those who passed down the traditions show any interest in his biography, accounts of his symbolic actions indicate that he had children (Isa 7:3; 8:1-4). He probably had a group around him ("disciples," Isa 8:16) who would have been the first to collect and treasure his words.

The best evidence for the beginning of Isaiah's life as a prophet appears in the first-person account of his vocation in the Temple in Jerusalem (chap. 6). "The year that King Uzziah died" (6:1) probably was 742, but could have been as late as 736 BCE. Most important, that king's death signaled the end of an era of relative independence for Judah. Tiglath-pileser III came to power in Assyria in 745 BCE and soon began to expand his empire to include the small states of Syria and Palestine. His successors would continue his military and political policies. During most of Isaiah's lifetime, Judah lived under the threat of Assyrian domination. Most of the prophetic words and deeds that can be associated with historical events are related to the actions of a series of Assyrian monarchs or to events set into motion by their actions. More than once in Isaiah 1–39, Assyria appears as a tool of Yahweh's plan ("rod of my anger," 10:5).

One crisis not directly involving the Assyrians but caused by their advance toward Syria-Palestine was the so-called Syro-Ephraimitic war of c. 735–732 BCE. The initial response of the prophet and a summary of the events that prompted his intervention appear in Isa 7:1-9 (see also 2 Kgs 16:1-20; 2 Chr 28:5ff.). When Tiglath-pileser III of Assyria began to move against the small states of Syria and Palestine, the leaders of those states formed a coalition to oppose him. Apparently because Ahaz of Judah refused to join them, kings Rezin of Damascus and Pekah of Samaria, the capital of the northern kingdom, moved against Jerusalem (about 734 BCE) to topple Ahaz and replace him with someone more favorable to their policies. Their effort failed, but not because the Judean king heeded the prophet. In fact, both the books of Isaiah and 2 Kings present Ahaz as fearful and faithless. Much of Isaiah 7–8 concerns Ahaz and the time of the Syro-Ephraimitic war. Within a decade (722/21 BCE), the Assyrian army under Sargon II had destroyed the city of Samaria and settled the population of Israel around the empire, thus ending the history of the northern kingdom.

The next era of prophetic activity that can be identified with some confidence concerns another effort to mobilize opposition to the advance of Assyria. This time (c. 715 BCE), the rebellion was encouraged, if not instigated, by Egypt. Ashdod and other Philistine city-states revolted against Assyrian rule. According to Isa 20:1-6, when Sargon II attacked Ashdod, Isaiah walked naked in the streets of Jerusalem for three years as a sign. His action is interpreted as a warning against relying on Egypt in the face of Assyrian threats. Trust in Egyptian power proved to be vain, since Sargon managed to put down the rebellion. Isaiah 18 and 14:28-32 may also relate to the events of this time.

The final period of Isaiah's prophetic work was during the Assyrian crisis of 705–701 BCE. When Sargon II died c. 705 and Sennacherib came to the throne, there was widespread revolt across the empire, beginning when the Babylonian Merodach-baladan asserted his independence. In Jerusalem, Hezekiah declared Judah free from Assyrian control. The deuteronomistic historians (2 Kgs 18:1-8) credit him with a religious reformation. It did not take long, however, for Sennacherib to deal with Babylon and move toward Judah. Once again, the possibility of a Judean alliance with Egypt arises, and Isaiah is reported to have counseled against it (Isaiah 28–31). The Assyrian army decimated the cities and towns of Judah and laid siege to Jerusalem in 701 BCE (Isaiah 36–37). Complex sources, both biblical and Assyrian (see the Commentary on 36:1–37:8), render historical reconstruction difficult. However, whether because Hezekiah paid tribute or the Lord intervened directly as promised by Isaiah, the Assyrians withdrew without taking the city.

The last one hears of Isaiah (chap. 39) comes not from eighth-century traditions but from a later writer. Within a story about Babylonian exiles to Hezekiah, Isaiah is said to have prophesied the Babylonian exile. Thus the story goes on well beyond the end of the eighth century BCE, and a great deal of it is reflected in Isaiah 1–39. After Hezekiah would come other kings, including Josiah, who would centralize worship in Jerusalem yet die on a battlefield at the hands of Pharaoh Necho. After Sennacherib the Assyrian would come Nebuchadnezzar the Babylonian, who would first capture and then destroy Jerusalem with its Temple on Mt. Zion (597 and 587 BCE), carrying off the last Davidic king and much of the populace to Babylon. Then the exile would end (539 BCE) with the rise of the Persian Empire and Cyrus. The city of Jerusalem and the Temple would be rebuilt and worship renewed there. Also the institution and perspective of prophecy as reflected in the earlier traditions would gradually be transformed into apocalypticism. Some of the latest literature in Isaiah 1–39 (chaps. 24–27) reflects some of the steps in that direction.

TRADITIONS AND THEOLOGICAL THEMES

From what has been said thus far, it should be clear that one could hardly separate the message of Isaiah from the message of Isaiah 1–39. However, in many instances one can distinguish the earliest materials from the later ones. The heart of the eighth-century material—prophetic addresses and reports—lies in Isa 6:1–9:6 and 28–31, plus most of 1–5. Subsequent growth and development for the most part engaged that foundational tradition. Finally, the reader will need to come to terms with the book as it has finally been handed down. Throughout, there is some genuine continuity as well as significant differences. Some of that continuity continues throughout the entire book, although the differences become more pronounced after chap. 40.

Isaiah did not simply originate a theological message out of thin air. Rather, the prophet and the book are rooted in a number of foundational traditions.[16] The day is long past when one could think of a prophet like Isaiah as a solitary and creative individual who introduced a new way of thinking, radical ideas, or new legal or moral expectations.

First, there is the prophetic tradition itself. Although among the earliest of the prophets whose words have come down in a book with their name, both Isaiah the prophet and Isaiah 1–39 are part of a community that originated much earlier and stretches over centuries. This is confirmed not only by the accounts of earlier prophets, such as Nathan in the time of David, but also by the way Isaiah and most of his successors in these chapters speak and write. Patterns of speech and narrative are shaped by practices in communities over time. Consequently Isaiah's report of his call and the accounts of his symbolic actions closely parallel others in the Old Testament. The form and substance of the prophetic addresses reflect the essence of the prophetic self-understanding: They speak to others the word of the Lord, and that word concerns the future.

Second, neither Isaiah nor the other prophetic and poetic voices heard in these chapters introduced new laws. Rather, any indictment of people, groups, or kings is on the basis of ancient understandings of Israel's responsibilities to Yahweh. To be sure, specific concerns emerge in the indictments, and it is not always possible to identify particular laws behind accusations. Moreover, there seems to be little or no awareness of the covenant on Mt. Sinai when the laws were revealed. Still, Isa 5:24 can stand as a summary that links the legal with the prophetic tradition: "You have rejected the law [תורה *tôrâ*] of the LORD Almighty and spurned the word of the Holy One of Israel" (NIV; NRSV, "instruction"; see also Isa 2:3).

Two closely related theological traditions undergird the distinctive theology of Isaiah 1–39. These concern the chosen king and the chosen city. Again, these views did not originate with Isaiah in the eighth century BCE but were part of an ancient faith. To provide for the government of the people of God, the Lord had chosen the dynasty of David, promising that one of his sons would always sit on the throne (see 2 Samuel 7; Psalms 2; 89). Thus the dynasty was more than a symbol of the Lord's grace; it was the concrete means by which their security was established. When present kings prove faithless, as does Ahaz in Isaiah 7–8, this tradition turns to messianic expectations, as in Isa 9:1-7 and 11:1-9.

The Lord also chose Jerusalem as the sacred place and its center, Mt. Zion, as the place where the Lord would encounter the people in the Temple. And so Isaiah experienced the terrifying presence of the Lord there (Isaiah 6). Throughout these chapters there seems to be a struggle over the question of whether the Lord will allow an enemy to take the city or not, but the dominant expectation is that Yahweh will protect Jerusalem (Isa 1:8; 3:17; 4:5; 10:24; 24:23; 29:8; 33:5). This tradition as well is firmly rooted in the Yahwistic faith. In the Song of Moses (Exodus 15), the holy place is the goal of the exodus (Exod 15:17), and Zion is praised and celebrated in worship (Pss

16. See esp. Gerhard von Rad, *Old Testament Theology,* vol. 2 (New York: Harper & Row, 1965).

48:1-3; 52:2; 74:2; 132:13). So in the new age of peace among all peoples, Zion will be lifted up, and all nations will come to it (Isa 2:1-4).

It is not easy to summarize the message of Isaiah 1–39, or that of the earliest tradition. At the most basic level, was the message of Isaiah and of the book good news or bad? How can one reconcile the song of the vineyard (Isa 5:1-7), which proclaims judgment on the people of God, with that vision of Jerusalem as the center of world peace in Isa 2:1-4 or the promise of justice under a righteous king in Isa 9:1-7? Sorting out the layers of tradition or the specific historical circumstances of particular units helps to resolve some of the tensions and contradictions: The word of God could be different in diverse situations, and one generation's interpretation could supplement or revise that of its predecessors. But those efforts cannot resolve all the tensions into a consistent summary of the teachings of the prophet or of the book, and in any case the reader needs to come to terms with Isaiah 1–39 as it stands, with all its complexity.

Consequently, any statement of the book's themes must be cautious not to suggest more coherence than the work allows, not to replace a rich and textured landscape with a simple map. Although one might argue that one or another theme defines the others, that does not mean the others have been left behind. It would distort the book to ignore the harsh words against foreign nations or to rush past the announcements of judgment to those of salvation. After all, regardless of their own convictions, the final editors have handed down all this complexity. Nevertheless, it is important to identify some of the more pervasive and distinctive aspects of the book's message, even when they seem— or actually may be—in tension with one another.

One typically prophetic motif is the indictment of the Lord's people, as well as other nations, for their sins. The range of accusations is wide. Sin may be characterized broadly as rebellion against the Lord (Isa 1:2-3), as failure to know or acknowledge the Lord (Isa 1:4), or as rejection of the law of the Lord and the word of the Holy One of Israel (Isa 5:24). The people are accused of trusting in the trappings of worship when they should be seeking justice and caring for the oppressed (Isa 1:10-17). They are accused of specific unjust economic, judicial, and social activities (Isa 5:8-24; 10:1-4). Leaders and the powerful come in for particular attention (Isa 3:1-15), particularly for failing in their responsibilities (Isa 28:1-8) or scoffing at the word of the Lord (Isa 28:11-15). The accusations do not stop at Judah's boundary. Foreign powers are indicated as well, including the king of Assyria, the rod of the Lord's anger, who has become arrogant (Isa 10:5-19).

Second, Isaiah, as well as his successors in these chapters, announces that the Lord is coming in judgment. Often, but not always, that divine intervention is presented as punishment for offenses. The vineyard will be destroyed because it yielded bloodshed instead of justice, a cry instead of righteousness (Isa 5:1-7). People, nation, and city will be thrown into chaos (Isa 3:1-5). King and people will be carried into exile (Isa 39:6-8). Frequently, judgment is characterized as the coming of the day of the Lord (Isa 2:12, 20; 4:1; 7:20; 13:6). The wrath of the Lord is not limited to Israel and Judah but can include foreign nations (Isaiah 13–23; 34), the hosts of heaven (Isa 24:2), and even the world itself (Isa 24:1-23).

Third, in some of the most memorable passages of the Bible, the prophet and the book proclaim good news. The Lord will act to save, to redeem, and to transform. Here is where those two themes of the Davidic dynasty and the Lord's choice of Zion come into play most prominently. A new king will establish peace and justice (Isa 9:1-8), and the reign of the son of David will inaugurate a transformation in the relationship among all creatures (Isa 11:1-9). Jerusalem will be protected from the Assyrians (Isa 31:4-5; 37:6-7; 37:33-34). Exiles will return to Jerusalem (Isa 11:10-16; 35:1-10). Just as foreigners came in for punishment, so also they will participate in the new age of peace (Isa 2:1-4).

Finally, in the prophets generally, one encounters relatively few admonitions or instructions about what to believe or how to behave. For the most part, what they expect must be read as the reverse of what they criticize. One admonition in these chapters, however, is both distinctive and foundational. It is the summons to trust in the Lord, the Holy One of Israel. Kings in particular and the people as a whole are told to neither fear nor trust nations and armies, but the one who has authority over all things (Isa 31:1). Isaiah tells Ahaz, "If you do not stand firm in faith, you shall not stand at all" (Isa 7:9). With Jerusalem in trouble, the message from the Holy One of Israel is: "In returning and rest you shall be saved; in quietness and trust shall be your strength" (Isa 30:15). This summons has something to do with the content of belief, particularly that the Lord has chosen the dynasty of David and the city of Jerusalem. But fundamentally it is not faith as affirmation of doctrine or ideas that is encouraged. Rather, it is faith as trust in God, as commitment to the Holy One of Israel.

BIBLIOGRAPHY

Commentaries:

Barton, John. *Isaiah 1–39.* OTG. Sheffield: Sheffield Academic, 1995. An excellent and highly readable handbook both to Isaiah 1–39 and to the issues that face the interpreter.

Blenkinsopp, Joseph. *Isaiah 1–39.* AB 19. Garden City, N.Y.: Doubleday, 2000. This volume appeared too late to be considered in this commentary.

Brueggemann, Walter. *Isaiah 1–39.* Westminster Bible Companion. Louisville: Westminster John Knox, 1998. The first of two volumes on Isaiah designed fundamentally for Christian laity, this "canonical" interpretation applies the book's themes to modern issues.

Childs, Brevard S. *Isaiah.* OTL. Louisville: Westminster John Knox, 2001. This volume appeared too late to be considered in this commentary.

Clements, R. E. *Isaiah 1–39.* NCNB. Grand Rapids: Eerdmans, 1980. Highly recommended for solid redaction-critical treatment and reliable analysis of individual texts.

Kaiser, O. *Isaiah 1–12: A Commentary.* Translated by R. A. Wilson. Philadelphia: Westminster, 1972; and *Isaiah 13–39: A Commentary.* Translated by R. A. Wilson. Philadelphia: Westminster, 1974. Historically oriented commentary that dates a great deal of Isaiah 1–39 quite late.

Oswalt, John N. *The Book of Isaiah, Chapters 1–39.* NICOT. Grand Rapids: Eerdmans, 1986. A lucid, if often polemical, interpretation that treats all of Isaiah 1–66 as the work of Isaiah of Jerusalem.

Seitz, Christopher R. *Isaiah 1–39.* Interpretation. Louisville: John Knox, 1993. Concerned mainly with the coherence and theological themes of larger units.

Sweeney, Marvin A. *Isaiah 1–39, With an Introduction to Prophetic Literature.* FOTL XVI. Grand Rapids: Eerdmans, 1996. An excellent form- and redaction-critical analysis; extensive bibliographies on all individual texts and particular issues.

Watts, John D. W. *Isaiah 1–33.* WBC 24. Waco, Tex.: Word, 1985. Interprets the book in the context of its final composition; employs a distinctive and problematic literary analysis.

Wildberger, H. *Isaiah 1–12.* Translated by Thomas H. Trapp. Minneapolis: Fortress, 1991; and *Isaiah 13–27.* Minneapolis: Fortress, 1997. The most detailed modern commentary on most critical issues; the second volume, including a lengthy introduction, has not been translated from German.

Specialized Studies:

Childs, Brevard S. *Isaiah and the Assyrian Crisis.* SBT. London: SCM, 1967. A formative study of the historical and theological issues concerning important texts.

Clements, R. E. *Isaiah and the Deliverance of Jerusalem: A Study in the Interpretation of Prophecy in the Old Testament.* JSOTSup 13. Sheffield: JSOT, 1980.

———. "The Unity of the Book of Isaiah." *Int.* 36 (1982). Good statement of recent developments and of an understanding of the book as a whole.

Conrad, E. W. *Reading Isaiah.* OBT 27. Minneapolis: Fortress, 1979. A reader-response interpretation of the book.

Fohrer, G. "The Origin, Composition and Tradition of Isaiah i–xxxix." *The Annual of the Lees University Oriental Society* 3 (1962–63).

Jensen, Joseph. *The Use of tora by Isaiah.* CBQMS 3. Washington: Catholic Biblical Association, 1973. Solid treatment of an important theme.

Melugin, Roy F., and Marvin A. Sweeney, eds. *New Visions of Isaiah.* JSOTSup 214. Sheffield: JSOT, 1996. Fine collection of recent studies, particularly on the shape of the whole.

Seitz, Christopher R., ed. *Reading and Preaching the Book of Isaiah.* Philadelphia: Fortress, 1988. Useful collection of essays on the entire book and its three main parts.

———. *Zion's Final Destiny: The Development of the Book of Isaiah.* Minneapolis: Fortress, 1991. Presentation of the author's understanding of the book's unifying theme.

Sweeney, Marvin A. *Isaiah 1–4 and the Post-Exilic Understanding of the Isaianic Tradition.* BZAW 171. Berlin: Walter de Gruyter, 1988. Important study on the first four chapters and on the book's development.

Tate, Marvin E. "The Book of Isaiah in Recent Study." In *Forming Prophetic Literature: Essays on Isaiah and the Twelve in Honor of John D. W. Watts,* ed. James W. Watts and Paul R. House. JSOTSup 235. Sheffield: Sheffield Academic, 1996. Review of current research.

Tucker, Gene M. "The Role of the Prophets and the Role of the Church." *Quarterly Review* 5 (1981). Reprinted in *Prophecy in Israel,* ed. David L. Petersen. Philadelphia: Fortress, 1987. An interpretation of the role of the prophets and its contemporary implications.

Watts, James W., and Paul R. House. *Forming Prophetic Literature: Essays on Isaiah and the Twelve in Honor of John D. W. Watts.* JSOTSup 235. Sheffield: Sheffield Academic, 1996. Contains useful articles, particularly on the final form of the book.

Whedbee, J. W. *Isaiah and Wisdom.* Nashville: Abingdon, 1971. Considers the relationship of Isaiah to wisdom literature and institutions.

Williamson, H. G. M. *The Book Called Isaiah: Deutero-Isaiah's Role in Composition and Redaction.*

Oxford: Oxford University Press, 1994. Significant study of the relation between Isaiah 1–39 and Isaiah 40–55.

Williamson, H. G. M. *Variations on a Theme: King, Messiah, and the Servant in the Book of Isaiah.* Carlisle: Paternoster, 1998. An important argument concerning the coherence of the entire book of Isaiah.

OUTLINE OF ISAIAH 1–39

I. Isaiah 1:1–12:6, Prophecies of Judgment and Salvation Concerning Judah and Jerusalem

A. 1:1-31, An Introduction to the Book
1:1, Superscription
1:2-20, A Lawsuit Against Israel
1:21-26, Corrupt Jerusalem Redeemed
1:27-31, Redemption for Zion and Judgment for Sinners

B. 2:1–4:6, Prophecies of Salvation and Judgment
2:1-5, Swords into Plowshares
2:6-22, The Day of the Lord
3:1-15, Judgment Against Judah's Leaders
3:16–4:1, Judgment Against Jerusalem's Women
4:2-6, Jerusalem Purified and Protected

C. 5:1-30, Justice, Woes, and Judgment
5:1-7, The Song of the Vineyard
5:8-24, One Woe After Another
5:25-30, Judgment Without End

D. 6:1–9:7, The Prophet, Children, and Kings
6:1-13, Isaiah's Commission
7:1-9, A Remnant Shall Return, If . . .
7:10-25, The Sign of Immanuel
8:1-22, Signs and Portents
9:1-7, The Light of a New King

E. 9:8–10:4, A Series of Judgments

F. 10:5–12:6, Judgment Against Assyria and Announcements of Salvation
10:5-19, Judgment Against Arrogant Assyria
10:20-34, Jerusalem Threatened but Delivered
11:1-9, A New King and a New World
11:10-16, Return of the Exiles
12:1-6, Songs of Thanksgiving

II. Isaiah 13:1–23:18, Oracles Concerning Foreign Nations

    A. 13:1–14:27, Proclamations Against Babylon and Its King

    B. 14:28-32, Proclamation Concerning Philistia

    C. 15:1–16:14, Proclamation Concerning Moab

    D. 17:1–18:7, Proclamation Concerning Damascus

    E. 19:1–20:6, Proclamation Concerning Egypt

    F. 21:1-10, Proclamation Concerning the Wilderness of the Sea

    G. 21:11-12, Proclamation Concerning Dumah

    H. 21:13-17, Proclamation Concerning the Desert Plain

    I. 22:1-25, Proclamation Concerning the Valley of Vision

    J. 23:1-18, Proclamation Concerning Tyre

III. Isaiah 24:1–27:13, The Isaiah "Apocalypse"

    A. 24:1-23, The Lord's Judgment on the Earth

    B. 25:1-12, Celebrating Life and the Lord's Deliverance

    C. 26:1-21, Songs and Prayers for God's Intervention

    D. 27:1-13, Images of That Day

IV. Isaiah 28:1–33:24, Jerusalem in the Eye of the Assyrian Storm

    A. 28:1-29, Prophecies and Parables Concerning Israel and Judah

    B. 29:1-14, Jerusalem in Trouble

    C. 29:15-24, Plans Human and Divine

    D. 30:1-33, Foolish Alliances, Healing, and Judgment on Assyria

    E. 31:1-9, The Lord, not Egypt, Protects Jerusalem

    F. 32:1-20, Promises and Warnings

    G. 33:1-24, A Liturgy of Hope

V. Isaiah 34:1–35:10, Eschatological Prophecies Concerning Edom and the Exiles

    A. 34:1-17, Doom for Edom

    B. 35:1-10, Return of the Exiles to Zion

ISAIAH 1:1–12:6

PROPHECIES OF JUDGMENT AND SALVATION CONCERNING JUDAH AND JERUSALEM

OVERVIEW

I t is not easy to read a prophetic book. The subject, style, genre, and mood keep changing, often without warning. Readers attempting to follow the train of thought frequently find themselves derailed, or at least shifted to a different track. So it is with the book of Isaiah. Both the substance of individual prophetic speeches and the organization of the book challenge and disorient the reader.

Doubtless some of this challenge and disorientation are by design, especially in the individual prophetic accusations and announcements, and sometimes also in the way the book has been put together. But some of the difficulties in following the book arise from its complicated history of composition as well as our unfamiliarity with ancient conventions of speech and literature.

This book is identified as "*the* vision of Isaiah" (Isa 1:1), just as the book of Hosea is called "the word of the Lord that came to Hosea" (Hos 1:1 NRSV; cf. Isa 2:1). But as it turns out, the book of Isaiah contains many distinct "words" and "visions" as well as stories and even prayers—that is, words not from God but directed to God.

That observation provides the first hint for the reader: Observe the changes in form or genre, speaker or addressee, subject matter or mood as indications of distinct units. Larger patterns, such as plot or progress of thought, may be present, but if so they are not so obvious in Isaiah as in, for instance, Genesis–Kings or Job. One needs to be constantly attentive to indications of both coherence and disjunction, for markers of unity and disunity. What are the parts that make up the whole, and what is the shape of the whole?

The development and testing of outlines help us to find our way through a book such as Isaiah. An outline that shows the relation of the parts to the whole needs to be as faithful as possible to the organization of the book itself. Such outlines help us above all to understand the point of view of the material and that of its authors and editors. They may also lead to suggestions concerning the historical development of the literature. This, in turn, may help us to link particular speeches or stories to their horizons in history, thus understanding them more fully.

Most commentators have recognized chaps. 1–12 as the first major section of Isaiah. On the one hand, there is a certain coherence: These chapters consist primarily of prophetic addresses concerning Judah and Jerusalem. On the other hand, Isa 13:1 marks a major disjunction in both form and content; what follows in chaps. 13–23 is a series of prophecies against foreign nations. Many interpreters have rushed to the conclusion that these chapters consist mainly of the earliest words of Isaiah, but actually there are examples from all periods of the prophet's life, and later additions as well.

Although a kind of unity, Isaiah 1–12 is a very complicated piece of literature, including virtually all major genres known in the OT prophetic books. Almost side by side we see announcements of judgment and announcements of salvation. There are stories or reports of prophetic activities from the point of view of a third party as well as the prophet's own report of his vocation. Moreover, the section concludes with songs of praise and thanksgiving.

Progress of thought is difficult to discern. Chapter 1 is a clear introductory chapter, an epitome of the message of the book, and chap. 12, with its songs of praise, provides a fitting conclusion. Between those bookends one finds several relatively distinct collections of prophetic tradition.

The first of these, chaps. 2–4, has its own superscription, suggesting that 2:1 may have once been the beginning of the "book." Most of the individual units in this collection announce judgment against Judah and Jerusalem, but it begins (2:2-5) with the remarkable announcement of peace and justice with Jerusalem at the center. Isaiah 5 includes the song of the vineyard (5:1-7), a series of woes (5:8-24), and announcements of judgment (5:25-30). But since the distinctive refrain of these announcements is resumed in 9:8, it seems likely that the next unit (6:1–10:4) has been inserted into a previously established collection. Isaiah 6:1–10:4 consists mainly—but not entirely—of narratives in the first- or third-person style concerning Isaiah's activities, leading many to identify this section or part of it as a prophetic memoir. But this complex section includes the messianic prophecy in 9:1-7 as well as the announcements of judgment of 9:8–10:4, linked with those at the end of chap. 5. The last collection of speeches (10:5–11:16) includes announcements of judgment, but ends on the high note of messianic expectations and announcements of salvation. Thus the first twelve chapters of Isaiah consist mainly of a series of collections, and collections within collections.

ISAIAH 1:1-31, AN INTRODUCTION TO THE BOOK

OVERVIEW

The first chapter of the book is a distinct unit framed by the superscription in 1:1 and 2:1. Although consisting of diverse materials from different periods of the prophet Isaiah's work, and even additions composed long after his time, this chapter was composed as a fitting introduction to and even summary of the message of the entire book. By considering the end of the chapter to be secondary additions, commentators have treated 1:2-26 as a summary of the message of the prophet Isaiah as expressed in chaps. 1–39.[17] But in its present form the entire chapter introduces, reviews, and interprets the book of Isaiah as a whole.

More than one organizational or compositional rationale can be detected in the shape of the chapter.[18] First, it is clear that there are quite distinct units of discourse, recognized by changes in form and content. Some of these divisions are recognizable by their opening formulas, such as the calls to hear in vv. 2 and 10 and the cry "Ah" (or "Woe") in v. 4, or concluding formulas, such as "for the mouth of the LORD has spoken" in v. 20. Second, some of these distinct units have been linked by catchwords—that is, expressions from one section appear in the subsequent unit. The most obvious use of catchwords is the allusions to Sodom and Gomorrah in v. 9 that conclude a unit and again in v. 10 that initiate a new topic; but there are others. The expression "children" links vv. 2-3 with vv. 4-6, and "justice" connects vv. 10-17, 21-26, and 27-31.[19] It seems likely that catchwords originated in the oral tradition as mnemonic devices. Third, the materials in this chapter are not simply prophetic addresses that have been linked as beads on a string but discourses that have been organized thematically so as to display an interpretation of the Lord's ways with the Lord's people and with the holy city; indeed, the chapter is organized as a theological interpretation of history. The theological movement also mirrors the judicial process, reflecting the style of a lawsuit or trial instigated against the people by the prophet on behalf of God.

Following the superscription of 1:1, the first prophetic address (vv. 2-3) presents the Lord's

17. G. Fohrer, "Jes 1 als Zusammenfssung der Verkündigung Jesajas," *ZAW* 74 (1962) 251-68.
18. See J. J. M. Roberts, "Form, Syntax, and Redaction in Isaiah 1:2-20," *Princeton Seminary Bulletin* 3 (1982) 293, for a summary of recent interpretations of the organization and authorship of most of the chapter. Roberts considers 1:2-20 to be a single unit composed by Isaiah himself.

19. Fohrer, "Jes 1 als Zusammenfssung der Verkündigung Jesajas," 249.

accusation against the children of God in the style of a lawsuit: Their crime or sin is their failure to know or understand. Second (vv. 4-9), the accusation continues, spelling out the nation's sinfulness and rejection of their Lord and then presenting the results of that rebellion as disaster for the people, especially focused on the holy city. Third (vv. 10-17), the prophetic voice now turns to instruction, continuing to criticize behavior but also pointing out what to do, and concluding (vv. 16-17) with admonitions that hold out the possibility of transformation and the direction for deliverance. Fourth (vv. 18-20), the decision for judgment or deliverance is stated explicitly: Obedience brings salvation, but rebellion brings the sword. Fifth (vv. 21-26), the initial theme of corruption is resumed, but the passage concludes with the divine promise that punishment will purge and purify people and city so that once again Zion will be "the city of righteousness, the faithful city."[20] The final part of the chapter (vv. 27-31) extends the promise of the renewal of Zion in language that carries the reader to the book's concluding chapters. It announces redemption to the repentant and destruction to rebels and sinners. Thematically the chapter moves from sin to punishment to repentance to renewal.

20. The outline to this point summarizes the conclusions of Fohrer, "Jes 1 als Zusammenfssung der Verkündigung Jesajas."

Isaiah 1:1, Superscription

NIV	NRSV
1 The vision concerning Judah and Jerusalem that Isaiah son of Amoz saw during the reigns of Uzziah, Jotham, Ahaz and Hezekiah, kings of Judah.	1 The vision of Isaiah son of Amoz, which he saw concerning Judah and Jerusalem in the days of Uzziah, Jotham, Ahaz, and Hezekiah, kings of Judah.

COMMENTARY

Most of the prophetic books begin with superscriptions such as the one before us. Few, if any, of the superscriptions, including Isa 1:1, were written by the prophets themselves, since they refer to both the prophet and the book that follows in the third person. In fact, in terms of both its location and its contents this verse presumes the existence of a book or scroll, is distinct from the body of the work, and also assumes that the work of the prophet has ended and is in the past. Thus the superscription to Isaiah comes from scribes who copied and saved the book, and also supplemented the original prophetic words with later materials. So the superscriptions are important as interpretations of the prophetic messages.

It is by no means clear which "book" this superscription originally had in view, the present sixty-six chapters of the work now before us or some part of it. It seems likely that the similar superscription in 2:1 was earlier and that chapter 1, with its superscription, was placed at the beginning to provide the introduction discussed above. Some commentators have argued that the superscription was composed for the entire book, making it one of the latest elements in Isaiah.[21] Others have taken it to be the heading for Isaiah 1–12 or 1–39, depending on differing interpretations of the history of the composition of the book. But even if an earlier book (such as chaps. 1–39) with this superscription was subsequently expanded, that expansion claimed the superscription. Thus 1:1 now stands over the entire book of Isaiah and invites the reader to view all sixty-six chapters under that heading.

This initial verse of the book of Isaiah appears to be simple and straightforward both in its contents and in its matter-of-fact style, but it makes very significant claims about what follows. Like most of the others, the superscription to Isaiah begins with the title of the book, "The vision of Isaiah son of

21. O. Kaiser, *Isaiah 1–12: A Commentary,* trans. R. A. Wilson (Philadelphia: Westminster, 1972) 1.

Amoz." Titles become necessary when one has access to collections of books and, therefore, needs to distinguish them one from the other. Therefore, the superscription is part of the process by which a canon of sacred Scripture was developed.[22] This superscription, like most of the others to the prophetic books, makes an important theological claim concerning the words that follow: This is the "vision" (חזון *ḥāzôn*) that Isaiah "saw" (חזה *ḥāzâ*). "Saw" (*ḥāzâ*) in this context functions as a technical term for divine revelation. The TNK reflects this sense in its translation: "The prophecies of Isaiah son of Amoz, who prophesied." The original oral discourses, and additions to them, now written on a scroll, are presented as the word of God. This answers the question, "Why should anyone read this book?"

The other elements of the superscription elaborate the title and also make serious assertions, suggesting how one should read the book. By identifying the prophet as a particular individual ("the son of Amoz") and specifying his dates in terms of the kings of Judah, the editors express both a historical and a theological concern: They locate the prophet in a specific time in the past and insist on the historical particularity of the word of God. Moreover, the prophetic words concerned specific places ("Judah and Jerusalem").

Since v. 1 sets the prophet in the reigns of particular kings of Judah, it typically is the starting point for locating Isaiah in his historical horizon. The chronological information in the superscription could have been obtained from the book itself, which contains allusions to these four kings and to events during their reigns. According to 6:1, Isaiah was not active during the reign of Uzziah but began his work in "the year that King Uzziah died" (c. 742 BCE), a major turning point in ancient Near Eastern history. Nor is there evidence that Isaiah lived through the entire reign of the fourth king mentioned here, Hezekiah, who died c. 687 BCE. Still, Isaiah of Jerusalem, the prophet responsible for much of the material in Isaiah 1–39, would have been speaking the word of God to Jerusalem and Judah for some forty years, 742–701 BCE.

22. Gene M. Tucker, "Prophetic Superscriptions and the Growth of a Canon," in *Canon and Authority: Essays in Old Testament Religion and Theology,* ed. George W. Coats and Burke O. Long (Philadelphia: Fortress, 1977) 56-70.

REFLECTIONS

Even such a mundane verse as the superscription engages the reader in serious theological issues, urging both reflection and response. This note stresses that we as readers are faced with a book attributed to a particular prophet and presented to us as the Word of God—that is, as divine revelation. The content of the superscription shows that the issues of authority and revelation are ancient ones, and not questions raised only in the modern world. Why would the scribes point out that what follows is divinely inspired unless the question were in doubt? So we are induced to ask how such a claim can be validated. Why this book and not some others? The answer of the superscription follows from the traditional patterns of prophetic speech, which frequently introduce or conclude addresses with expressions such as "Thus says the LORD." That is, these words are true and dependable because of their source; they are the words of God. But how can we know if that is true? Within the pages of Scripture, and even within the book of Isaiah, apparently contradictory words claim to come from God. Are all those words equally valid? So the claim of divine authority itself calls for the reader or hearer to "test the spirits to see whether they are from God; for many false prophets have gone out into the world" (1 John 4:1 NRSV).

The superscription's concern with the voice of the prophet and the voice of the book suggests that these questions may be considered from two perspectives: the issue of true and false prophecy and the question of a book as the Word of God.

1. In the Hebrew scriptures, various means of distinguishing between true and false prophecy emerged. Some in antiquity presumed that the form of inspiration could be a test for the veracity of a prophet's words. The authentic prophet, according to this line of reasoning, is the one who dreams dreams and sees visions or hears the word of God while in a special state of con-

sciousness. But the canonical prophets themselves were suspicious of such claims. Jeremiah said: "Thus says the LORD of hosts: Do not listen to the words of the prophets who prophesy to you, they are deluding you. They speak visions of their own minds, not from the mouth of the LORD" (Jer 23:16 NRSV), and "I have heard what the prophets have said who prophesy lies in my name, saying, 'I have dreamed, I have dreamed!' " (Jer 23:25 NRSV). Psychological state or physical behavior seldom were considered reliable tests of validity.

Then there was a test of the contents of a message. Jeremiah, among others, argued that true prophets only announced disaster (Jer 28:8-9), and those who prophesied salvation were false prophets. Although Jeremiah was proved right in prophesying the Babylonian exile; this solution does not hold up. First ancient Israel, then Judaism, and later the Christian church acknowledged as true prophets—ones who spoke the authentic word of God—those who announced good news as well as those who prophesied disaster. In fact, virtually every early prophetic book, including Isaiah, now includes announcements of salvation alongside words of doom. Even the book that bears Jeremiah's name includes such prophecies.

But there are in the Old Testament two dominant and useful responses to the question of true and false prophets, both with implications for the contemporary reader. The first was a practical test. When the words announced by a prophet come to pass, then all will know that this prophet spoke the word of God (see Jer 28:9). Clearly this standard validated many of the early prophets; Amos and Hosea were seen to have announced the end of the northern kingdom of Israel, so when it fell their status was confirmed. The problem, of course, is that one would like to know in advance, not just after the fact, who is telling the truth. Nevertheless, there is something to be said for this as a realistic principle. Words that claim to be ultimately true have to be tested in real human life, in the course of actual events. Do these words stand the test of time and experience?

The other substantial response was a theological one, spelled out especially in Deuteronomy. Even the prophets whose words come to pass are false prophets *if they call for the people to follow other gods* (Deut 13:1-3). This is the canon within the Hebrew canon: All claims to express the truth are to be measured against the affirmation of faith in the one God. This principle has practical theological applications. Allegiance to the one God—or whatever one determines to be the heart of a community's faith—can be the benchmark for all words that claim to be true and authoritative. Thus those who take the Bible seriously are urged to consider their benchmark, their canon within the canon. Asking about the truth of biblical texts calls for the readers to consider the center and meaning of their faith.

2. Not only is Isaiah presented as an authentic prophet, but also the book that bears his name is alleged to be the Word of God. What does it mean to say that the book of Isaiah—or the Bible, for that matter—is the Word of God? After all, the book itself is a physical object, consisting of pages with black marks on them. The single, unexciting sentence of the superscription suggests some answers.

First, since the words are said to have come from a particular person, an individual from a specific time and place, the Word of God comes through human mediation that is historically conditioned and limited. Consequently, although inspired, they are not timeless words, always the same in every time and place. (Recognition of this point may help the reader come to terms with the fact that the book, even the first thirty-nine chapters, contains diverse and even contradictory messages, all presented as divinely inspired.) These words are for particular times and places in the now-distant past.

Second, by setting out the historical horizon of the book and commending it to later generations, the superscription calls attention to the readers themselves. These words from the past are to engage future hearers and readers. Thus the initial verse invites readers to consider both the historical particularity of the words and the lessons that can be learned from them in a very different age. The author of the superscription looks both backward and forward, linking the ancient book with each new generation of readers.

Third, in bridging the gap between generations, the superscription is itself an interpretation of the book that follows, a commentary on the Word of God. Such commentary arose long before the completion of the Hebrew scriptures and was, in fact, central to their development. The book of Deuteronomy, for example, consists largely of sermons interpreting older laws handed down—it was believed—from God. Sometimes these interpretations were radical. Similarly, the prose speeches in the book of Jeremiah reinterpret and apply the older prophetic words—from God—to new circumstances. Even the author of Chronicles, a devout and faithful scribe, reinterpreted the sacred traditions about Israel's history in the light of a different age and a distinctive theology. This history of interpretation invites each new generation to interpret the sacred texts in and for its own time.

So how is the book of Isaiah—or the Bible—the Word of God? The only concise response that fits both the Bible and human realities is this: The Word of God may come to expression when the book of Isaiah or the Bible is read and heard. That is to say, the Word of God, or the "truth," is not *in* the pages of the Bible, but in the interaction of readers and hearers with those words. That is the biblical way of understanding the power, authority, or truth of books. Only in reading and interpretation can such books function at all, except perhaps as objects to observe or worship, like icons, or as paperweights.

This verse encourages the modern interpreter to read seriously and to consider both the old and the new meanings of this book.

Isaiah 1:2-20, A Lawsuit Against Israel

NIV	NRSV

²Hear, O heavens! Listen, O earth!
    For the LORD has spoken:
"I reared children and brought them up,
    but they have rebelled against me.
³The ox knows his master,
    the donkey his owner's manger,
but Israel does not know,
    my people do not understand."
 	
⁴Ah, sinful nation,
    a people loaded with guilt,
a brood of evildoers,
    children given to corruption!
They have forsaken the LORD;
    they have spurned the Holy One of Israel
    and turned their backs on him.
 	
⁵Why should you be beaten anymore?
    Why do you persist in rebellion?
Your whole head is injured,
    your whole heart afflicted.
⁶From the sole of your foot to the top of
        your head
    there is no soundness—
only wounds and welts
    and open sores,
not cleansed or bandaged
	²Hear, O heavens, and listen, O earth;
	    for the LORD has spoken:
	I reared children and brought them up,
	    but they have rebelled against me.
	³The ox knows its owner,
	    and the donkey its master's crib;
	but Israel does not know,
	    my people do not understand.
	
	⁴Ah, sinful nation,
	    people laden with iniquity,
	offspring who do evil,
	    children who deal corruptly,
	who have forsaken the LORD,
	    who have despised the Holy One of Israel,
	    who are utterly estranged!
	
	⁵Why do you seek further beatings?
	    Why do you continue to rebel?
	The whole head is sick,
	    and the whole heart faint.
	⁶From the sole of the foot even to the head,
	    there is no soundness in it,
	but bruises and sores
	    and bleeding wounds;

NIV

or soothed with oil.

⁷Your country is desolate,
  your cities burned with fire;
your fields are being stripped by foreigners
  right before you,
  laid waste as when overthrown by
    strangers.
⁸The Daughter of Zion is left
  like a shelter in a vineyard,
like a hut in a field of melons,
  like a city under siege.
⁹Unless the LORD Almighty
  had left us some survivors,
we would have become like Sodom,
  we would have been like Gomorrah.

¹⁰Hear the word of the LORD,
  you rulers of Sodom;
listen to the law of our God,
  you people of Gomorrah!
¹¹"The multitude of your sacrifices—
  what are they to me?" says the LORD.
"I have more than enough of burnt offerings,
  of rams and the fat of fattened animals;
I have no pleasure
  in the blood of bulls and lambs and goats.
¹²When you come to appear before me,
  who has asked this of you,
  this trampling of my courts?
¹³Stop bringing meaningless offerings!
  Your incense is detestable to me.
New Moons, Sabbaths and convocations—
  I cannot bear your evil assemblies.
¹⁴Your New Moon festivals and your appointed
    feasts
  my soul hates.
They have become a burden to me;
  I am weary of bearing them.
¹⁵When you spread out your hands in prayer,
  I will hide my eyes from you;
even if you offer many prayers,
  I will not listen.
Your hands are full of blood;
¹⁶ wash and make yourselves clean.
Take your evil deeds
  out of my sight!
Stop doing wrong,
¹⁷ learn to do right!

NRSV

they have not been drained, or bound up,
  or softened with oil.

⁷ Your country lies desolate,
  your cities are burned with fire;
in your very presence
  aliens devour your land;
  it is desolate, as overthrown by foreigners.
⁸ And daughter Zion is left
  like a booth in a vineyard,
like a shelter in a cucumber field,
  like a besieged city.
⁹ If the LORD of hosts
  had not left us a few survivors,
we would have been like Sodom,
  and become like Gomorrah.

¹⁰ Hear the word of the LORD,
  you rulers of Sodom!
Listen to the teaching of our God,
  you people of Gomorrah!
¹¹ What to me is the multitude of your sacrifices?
  says the LORD;
I have had enough of burnt offerings of rams
  and the fat of fed beasts;
I do not delight in the blood of bulls,
  or of lambs, or of goats.

¹² When you come to appear before me,ᵃ
  who asked this from your hand?
  Trample my courts no more;
¹³ bringing offerings is futile;
  incense is an abomination to me.
New moon and sabbath and calling of
    convocation—
  I cannot endure solemn assemblies with
    iniquity.
¹⁴ Your new moons and your appointed festivals
  my soul hates;
they have become a burden to me,
  I am weary of bearing them.
¹⁵ When you stretch out your hands,
  I will hide my eyes from you;
even though you make many prayers,
  I will not listen;
  your hands are full of blood.
¹⁶ Wash yourselves; make yourselves clean;

ᵃOr *see my face*

NIV

Seek justice,
  encourage the oppressed.[a]
Defend the cause of the fatherless,
  plead the case of the widow.

[18]"Come now, let us reason together,"
  says the LORD.
"Though your sins are like scarlet,
  they shall be as white as snow;
though they are red as crimson,
  they shall be like wool.
[19]If you are willing and obedient,
  you will eat the best from the land;
[20]but if you resist and rebel,
  you will be devoured by the sword."
    For the mouth of the LORD has spoken.

[a]17 Or / rebuke the oppressor

NRSV

remove the evil of your doings
  from before my eyes;
cease to do evil,
[17] learn to do good;
seek justice,
  rescue the oppressed,
defend the orphan,
  plead for the widow.

[18] Come now, let us argue it out,
  says the LORD:
though your sins are like scarlet,
  they shall be like snow;
though they are red like crimson,
  they shall become like wool.
[19] If you are willing and obedient,
  you shall eat the good of the land;
[20] but if you refuse and rebel,
  you shall be devoured by the sword;
    for the mouth of the LORD has spoken.

COMMENTARY

In terms of both form and content, this first section of chap. 1 consists of no fewer than three, and likely as many as five, distinct units that have been organized thematically. The structure as a whole resembles the movement of a lawsuit, and the initial summons to heavens and earth (v. 2) indicates that this is a prophetic lawsuit in which the Lord brings a case against the people of Judah and Jerusalem. While keeping in view the broader picture, it is helpful to see its individual parts as well. Even if arguments for the original independence of these units are not always convincing, individual paragraphs or stanzas still make sense when read independently. Consequently, and especially when reading prophetic literature, one must be careful to see both the trees and the forest, the individual sections as well as their part in the larger whole.

1:2-3. Although it now stands as part of a larger discourse, this initial speech can be viewed as a unit, conveying a complete message. It leaves a great deal unstated, some of which becomes explicit in subsequent verses. But the ambiguity and imprecision of this poetry also evoke the imaginative response of the hearers. The peculiar form

of address already suggests something rather specific about the sort of discourse before us. Yahweh, speaking through the prophet, calls on "heavens" and "earth" to hear a charge against these wayward children. Such divine calls to heaven and earth mark the prophetic lawsuit.

What follows the summons is the presentation of the case, or accusation against these "children," which the hearers must recognize as themselves, the people of God. They are the ones "reared" and "brought up" by Yahweh. The accused are mentioned in the third person, as in a trial when the prosecution addresses the court with a complaint against an offender. In the background of this case is the prior relationship between Yahweh and Israel—that is, a covenant—although Isaiah reflects no awareness of the covenant and election traditions of the Pentateuch. Hence, some scholars have identified this and similar addresses as covenant lawsuits.[23] However, the language is

23. H. B. Huffmon, "The Covenant Lawsuit in the Prophets," *JBL* 78 (1959): 285-95; Kisten Nielsen, *Yahweh as Prosecutor and Judge: An Investigation of the Prophetic Lawsuit (Rîb-Pattern),* JSOTSup 9 (Sheffield: JSOT, 1978).

even more intimate than that of the covenant between God and people. The relationship between God and people is like that of a parent and children. The charge is symmetrical—that is, in the first two lines the Lord's faithfulness is contrasted with Israel's rebellion, and in the next four lines the faithfulness of the domestic animals (the ox and the donkey) is contrasted with Israel's lack of knowledge.

"To know" and "to understand" are complex expressions in the OT generally and in Isaiah in particular. In Isa 5:13 lack of knowledge leads the people into exile and suffering. In 7:15-16, "to know" refers to the stage of awareness that enables one to judge between right and wrong, and thus to be accountable for decisions, and in 8:4 it refers to a developed level of intellectual maturity. In other instances (12:4; 19:12; 28:9; 38:19), "to know" seems to refer fundamentally to cognition, while in some instances it means "to acknowledge" (19:21; 26:13; 33:13). In certain cases, such as the book of Hosea, "to know" is a covenantal expression, concerning the relationship between God and people. Certainly the expression in these verses concerns the relationship between God and people. But "understand" (בין *bîn*) in particular suggests the point of view of wisdom literature.

Other features of this unit likewise parallel wisdom literature. These features include the motif of sonship (Prov 4:1; 5:1; 6:20) and the parable with its analogy from experience and an application to the contrary.[24] What is it here that Israel "does not know" or "understand"? The children do not know or understand that it was the Lord who "reared" them and "brought them up," who made them who they are. It is implied, but not stated, that they do not know what to do or how to respond to the one who cared for them. But "knowledge" here also means "acknowledgment." The ox and the ass "know"—that is, acknowledge—their master as master, but Israel does not.

The fundamental purpose of these two verses is to accuse Israel of its transgressions, to indict the people for their failures. However, those failures are set out only in the most general terms: Israel has "rebelled," "does not know" or "understand."

24. J. William Whedbee, *Isaiah and Wisdom* (Nashville: Abingdon, 1971) 26-42.

Such accusations make no sense except in the context of a long and intimate relationship between God and people. The general and metaphorical—but not vague—presentation of the accusation leaves a great deal unstated. No specific transgressions are mentioned, but they will be specified in due course. The general character of the accusation allows these verses to serve very well as the introduction to the sequence of prophetic speeches that follow. Thus the book begins with the tone of encounter and incrimination.

1:4-9. This unit could stand alone, but it does not. We have seen how these verses function as part of the larger composition of 1:2-31. Nevertheless, there are indications that these verses are a distinct discourse that probably once circulated apart from its surroundings in Isaiah 1. The cry with which it begins (הוי *hôy*) is a typical opening formula in prophetic speeches; there is a shift of addressees from the heavens and earth in vv. 2-3 to the nation and the city in vv. 4-9 to the "rulers" in vv. 10-17, and both the tone and the specific purpose of these verses are distinct from what precedes and from what follows. Moreover, in spite of some inner tensions—v. 4 speaks of the people in the third person, vv. 5-8 address them in the second person, and v. 9 uses the first person—these verses comprise a coherent thematic unit.

The translation of *hôy* as "Ah" in the NRSV and the NIV reflects the judgment that the word is simply an exclamation, a means of getting the attention of the hearers or readers. The word may be translated "Woe," as in the RSV, signaling either condemnation or disaster. This cry appears frequently in the prophetic literature, and typically—as here—is followed by a description of the addressees in terms of their shameful behavior (see Isa 5:8-24). Here the cry "Ah" initiates an indictment of those addressed by describing their reprehensible activity in two ways. First, the prophet characterizes the nation with four terms for bad action: "sinful," "iniquity," "do evil," and "deal corruptly" (v. 4*a*). Second, three relative clauses display the people's rebellion against "the Holy One of Israel": "forsaken," "despised," and "estranged" (v. 4*b*). In the remainder of the section (vv. 5-9), the results of this sinfulness and rebellion are spelled out. This account of disaster is not a prophetic announcement of punishment that the Lord will bring upon the nation because of their sins, but a description of what they have already brought upon themselves. Beginning with a rhetorical question (v. 5*a*), the speaker moves to an analogy of the sick and wounded body (vv. 5*b*-6) and then to a specific description of a national catastrophe. The destruction plainly is the result of a military invasion that leaves the countryside desolate, cities burned, and the land eaten up and occupied by foreigners (v. 7). Graphic similes portray the effects of the invasion on Jerusalem ("daughter Zion"). The first two use agricultural images to show the isolation of the holy city: "like a booth in a vineyard" and "a shelter in a cucumber field." The third simile is both metaphorical and literal. Jerusalem is, in fact (or has been), "a besieged city." Characteristically, Jerusalem is called "daughter Zion" (v. 8; see also 10:32; 16:1; 37:22). This is an affectionate personification of the city as a young woman. The translation "Daughter of Zion" (NIV) is misleading. On the other hand, in 3:16 "daughters [plural] of Zion" refers to the women of Jerusalem.

The key to the meaning of this discourse is its conclusion in v. 9. The prophet applies a well-known metaphor for destruction to the situation of the nation, "like Sodom and Gomorrah," which ancient hearers, as well as modern readers, would connect with the tale of the destruction of the two corrupt cities (Gen 18:1–19:29, esp. 19:24-26). But the reference is in the subjunctive and the past tense: "*If* the LORD of hosts had not left us a few survivors, we *would have been* like Sodom and Gomorrah" (NRSV, italics added). The sinful nation has brought the disaster upon itself. But the Lord intervened to stop the effects of evil and disloyalty just short of total destruction, leaving a few survivors and, significantly, the city of Jerusalem. Therefore, both in itself and within the context of Isaiah 1, these verses function as indictment, accusation, or reasons for punishment. Following the general accusation in vv. 2-3, this indictment is more elaborate, if not always more specific. Only the account of the disaster (vv. 5-8) is more concrete: Look at the trouble your sins have caused! But the concluding verse turns accusation into warning. The "us" of v. 9 are among those "survivors" who are to hear the woe, the accusation, and the description of destruction as a cautionary

tale. The speaker implies, but does not state, that these hearers should change their ways. By contrasting Yahweh's mercy with Israel's iniquity, the prophet wants those survivors to learn their lesson. The next time the people rebel, the Lord of hosts might not stop the effects of sin and disloyalty, and Jerusalem might then become like Sodom and Gomorrah.

Because vv. 7-9 present such a graphic portrait of a military invasion of the country with an unsuccessful siege of Jerusalem, it has been common to see in those verses allusions to specific historical events. Typically, commentators conclude that the invasion and siege were those of the Assyrian king Sennacherib in 701 BCE.[25] This campaign is reported in Isaiah 36–37 (see also 2 Kings 18–20) and recorded in Assyrian inscriptions.[26] It is entirely possible that this particular campaign was the background for this discourse, and even that Isaiah delivered it shortly after the siege had been lifted. If that is the case, this would be one of the last of the prophet's speeches. But it is notoriously difficult to date ancient literature so precisely, especially when it is poetry. The land of Israel saw many invasions that decimated the countryside but left Jerusalem standing. However, the fact that one cannot correlate the text with a specific historical event should not lead to the conclusion that it does not relate to concrete historical events. This prophetic poetry is addressed to a populace that has experienced a horrible military campaign but who lived to tell about it and look to the future. The prophet is less concerned about telling the story than interpreting the events in the light of cause, effect, and the future. The cause of the disaster, he concluded, was sin and rebellion. That the destruction was not total was the effect of divine intervention. Now, he suggests to the people, consider your future actions in that light.

The God who has held back total destruction is identified by means of two distinct expressions. The first title, "Holy One of Israel" (v. 4), seldom appears outside the book of Isaiah. It seems likely that this expression is distinctly related to Jerusalem and the Temple (6:3). The holy is the radically other, which cannot be approached with-

25. H. Wildberger, *Isaiah 1–12*, trans. Thomas H. Trapp (Minneapolis: Fortress, 1991) 21.

26. James B. Pritchard, *Ancient Near Eastern Texts Related to the Old Testament,* 3rd ed. (Princeton: Princeton University Press, 1969) 287-88

out proper preparation (Exod 19:8-15) or viewed without danger (Isa 6:5). Thus it is even more remarkable that this God has intervened to avert total disaster. "LORD of hosts" (v. 9) is one of the most common designations for the deity in Isaiah 1–39. The title couples the name of Israel's God, Yahweh, with the word for "armies." The background of the designation must lie in the holy war traditions of Israel, in which Yahweh fights on behalf of the people (see Exod 15:1-3; Josh 5:13-15; 6). "Hosts" in this expression has come to refer to the heavenly armies. Thus the title evokes the image of God intervening against enemy troops.

The reference to "a few survivors" (v. 9) suggests the idea of a remnant left after judgment. Although this particular word for "survivor" (שָׂרִיד *śārîd*) occurs only here in Isaiah, the motif is both common and important in Isaiah 1–39. The roots of the expression clearly are militaristic, referring to those who escaped the sword (e.g., Josh 8:22).[27] In Amos 5:3, the announcement that the city that sent a hundred will have ten left serves to emphasize the bad news rather than the good. In Isaiah, good news is frequently announced to or for the "remnant" (שְׁאָר *šĕˀār*) beyond judgment (e.g., 10:19-21; 11:11, 16; 28:5). In the text before us, the fact that some were left is the good news, testimony to the grace of God.

1:10-20. This section has a clear beginning with a summons to hear, but its conclusion is not so obvious. It certainly continues through the ringing conclusion in v. 17, and v. 18 begins with a new call for attention. However, vv. 18-20 extend and interpret the fundamental point of vv. 10-17, making the instructions to the people explicit and the results of their actions unmistakably plain.

The basic pattern is a prophetic introductory call to hear (cf. Amos 3:1; 4:1; 5:1), followed by a speech of Yahweh. The introductory call (v. 10) consists of two parallel sentences, each with three parts: the call, the characterization of what is to be heard, and the identification of the addresses. The summons is addressed to the leaders and the people of Jerusalem, identified derisively as "rulers of Sodom . . . people of Gomorrah." In the preceding verse, the cities had represented destruction, and citation of these names will always evoke the threat of judgment; but in this verse they exemplify

the sinfulness of the leaders and citizens. Thus the very identification of the hearers in the address contains an indictment and sets the tone of accusation. The message to those hearers is identified as "the word of the LORD," a prophetic formula, and "the teaching (תורה *tôrâ*) of our God," an allusion to a priestly function. Already this opening sets up the tension to be developed in the body of the address. (The traditional translation of *tôrâ* as "law" in the NIV is not entirely incorrect, but given the burden that term carries for readers of the Bible, it is somewhat misleading. In view here is not a fixed and authoritative body of revealed legislation but the living process of instruction. That is what the subsequent verses contain.)

Beginning in v. 11, the words of Yahweh are quoted directly in a two-part speech, first the negative and then the positive, stating what Yahweh rejects and then what Yahweh requires. A ringing rejection of cultic practices is followed by a forceful plea for justice. The speech moves from the rejection of specific cultic practices in the form of rhetorical questions (vv. 11-13*a*) to a rejection of religious practices with reasons (vv. 13*b*-15) to a series of positive instructions (vv. 16-17). The divine speech continues in vv. 18-20, but with the inclusion of the prophetic formula "says the LORD" (v. 18*a*). In these verses the fate of the people is set out before them. The Lord is willing to purify them of their sins, but the future depends on their response. Obedience will bring blessing, but rebellion will bring the sword.

Something of the tone of the courtroom continues, with confrontation and accusation, but beginning with v. 10 the discourse shifts from indictment or accusation to another genre, specifically identified as "torah," instruction. This unit, which closely parallels Amos 5:21-27 and Mic 6:6-8 in both form and content, could be seen as a response to the question posed in Mic 6:6: "With what shall I come before the LORD?" (NRSV). It has long been recognized that these prophetic texts derive from the priestly torah, or instruction to the laity concerning ritual questions, such as the distinction between clean and unclean.[28] Thus the prophet has employed a

---

27. See Wildberger, *Isaiah 1–12*, 28-29.

28. Joachim Begrich, "Die priesterliche Tora," BZAW 66 (Berlin: A. Töpelmann, 1936) 63-88. See also E. Würthwein, "Kultpolemik oder Kultbescheid?" in *Tradition und Situation: Studien zur alttestamentlichen Prophetie,* ed. E. Würthwein and O. Kaiser (Göttingen: Vandenhoeck & Ruprecht, 1963) 115-33.

priestly procedure to address the question of ritual. But whereas the priest would have interpreted or explained the law, the prophet speaks forth in the voice of Yahweh. Some scholars have argued that the prophetic torah speeches are rooted in Israelite wisdom literature and practices.[29] Although there are some parallels to such teaching, with the call to pay attention and the concern for right behavior, the links with the priestly instruction are stronger.

The catalog of ritual practices rejected is extensive. The prophet first hears the Lord rejecting various kinds of sacrifices (vv. 11-12). The general word for "sacrifice" (זבח *zebaḥ*) includes all gifts burned on the altar. "Burnt offerings" (עלות *'ōlôt*) of animals are only one of several sacrifices. Such gifts are not required when one appears before God, and processions ("Trample my courts") are rejected (v. 12). The disapproval of "offerings" (מנחות *minḥôt*, the broader category, including sacrifices as well as other gifts to God) is then extended to encompass incense (v. 13*a*) as well as all forms of religious celebration and assembly (v. 13*b*), including regular and unscheduled services of worship. At this point the hearers are given the first hint of the Lord's problem with religious observances, expressed with deep irony: "I cannot endure solemn assemblies with iniquity." Verse 14 repeats and underscores the Lord's repudiation of religious festivals: "Your new moons and your appointed festivals my soul hates"—that is, "I hate." Perhaps the most radical announcement of all comes in v. 15 with the rejection of prayer itself ("stretch out your hands" refers to the posture of prayer), and the reason for the Lord's refusal to hear makes the ironic rejection in v. 13 plain: "I will not listen; your hands are full of blood." Thus the negative sequence concludes with the vivid image of bloody hands, a metaphor for unspecified acts of violence.

The language of vv. 16-17 continues the form of direct address with a series of instructions or admonitions. This positive section, in which the

Lord turns from what is rejected to what is required, implicitly continues the imagery of v. 15. "Wash yourselves" is a rich and complex expression. It refers at the same time to the literal cleaning of bloody hands, to ritual purification, and to the transformation of one's life: "cease to do evil." The instructions that follow move from the general to the specific, making it perfectly clear that learning to do "good" and seeking "justice" are not empty abstractions; nor do they refer simply to changing one's attitudes. To seek justice is to care for the powerless members of the society: the oppressed, the orphan, and the widow. The aura of the courtroom, of legal process, and of justice in society is explicit not only in the call for justice but also in the terms "defend" and "plead for." Thus the leaders, in particular, and the people, in general, are instructed to use the courts for their fundamental purpose, to protect those least able to protect themselves.

The tone shifts with v. 18, and the speech in vv. 18-20 resumes the metaphor of the trial or lawsuit begun in 1:2, with one side arguing with the other. In ancient Israel there was no formal difference between civil and criminal judicial process. Both were adversarial procedures in which one party accuses and the other responds. The parties presented their cases, called for the judgment they considered to be fair, issued pleas to agree or accept, and even set forth alternatives. In vv. 18-20, the Lord, as plaintiff, no longer accuses and argues that punishment is necessary. Now the plaintiff or prosecutor assumes that the case has been made: Their sins are "like scarlet . . . red like crimson." The Lord pleads the case with the people, arguing for an outcome other than judgment. Remarkably, this prosecutor now calls for the people to repent of their sins and change their ways. God holds out the possibility that the sins of the people can be washed away (v. 18) and spells out the blessings for them if they are obedient (v. 19). But the sword still hangs over their heads. If they refuse to repent and continue to rebel, judgment awaits. So the plea for change includes both a promise and a warning.

29. J. Fichtner, "Jesaja unter den Weisen," *TLZ* 74 (1949) 75-80; Joseph Jensen, *The Use of Tôrâ by Isaiah,* CBQMS 3 (Washington: Catholic Biblical Association, 1973) 68-83.

REFLECTIONS

Readers who take these verses seriously will find it difficult to avoid consideration of a number of crucial theological problems. These include the issue of God as judge, the question of worship and social justice, and the relationship between human sin and divine grace.

1. The image or theme of the Lord as judge appears throughout prophetic literature, and many readers may consider this to be the only God known to the prophets. After all, the prophets commonly announce the Lord's judgment against Israel or against particular groups or against foreign nations. The issue arises in Isaiah 1 because of both the form and the content of the verses before us.

There are both positive and negative dimensions to the metaphor of God as judge. On the one hand, the confidence in a just and fair, rather than arbitrary, God is the foundation for all understandings of human justice in the scriptures. Moreover, when the prophets hear Yahweh pronouncing judgment, it is always in the light of laws and other expectations long known to those who are being judged.[30] On the other hand, the image may suggest a distant and dispassionate deity more concerned with right defined juridically than with individuals or nations. That recognition evokes reflection on the relationship between justice and mercy, between God's justice and God's love. That may be why the understanding of God as judge is so frequently qualified and modified in the biblical tradition. Perhaps the best-known case is Hosea 11, where Yahweh's compassion is heard to struggle with the sense of justified punishment, and compassion wins. When God listens to the prayers of the Ninevites and decides not to execute the promised destruction, Jonah says, in the tone of accusation: "You are a gracious God and merciful, slow to anger, and abounding in steadfast love, and ready to relent from punishing" (Jonah 4:2 NRSV). That is very similar to the direction Isaiah 1 moves on this issue (see Reflection number 3).

Moreover, the sense of divine judgment is not the whole story of the prophetic understanding of the relationship between acts and consequences. The disastrous effects of sinful actions are not always seen as legal sanctions imposed by Yahweh. Another idea or preunderstanding is a dynamistic view of acts and consequences—that is, a point of view that sees actions, whether good or bad, as entailing or setting into motion their consequences. At the very least, actions or events themselves are viewed in some contexts as portentous. More than that, such an understanding of reality sees justice as built in. Hosea 8:7 expresses such a perspective:

> For they sow the wind,
> and they shall reap the whirlwind. (NRSV)

Isaiah 1:4-9 reflects that perspective as well. That rebellion itself produces estrangement (1:4) is obvious to the prophet. The disasters spelled out as the consequences of iniquity, evil, corruption, and rebellion (1:5-9) are not future punishments or judgments, but the present effects of such actions. Likewise, at the end of this chapter, those who participate in fertility cults are not punished by the divine judge but set themselves on fire with their own deeds and are consumed (1:31). This perspective parallels the common proverb, "Those who play with fire get burned." Consequently, the interpretation of modern disasters as God's punishment of sin is not the only alternative available to those who take the prophets seriously. Acts have consequences, and foolish or sinful acts can lead to disaster.

2. Isaiah 1:10-17 in particular raises important issues concerning the relationship between worship and social justice. In fact, it is tempting to take these verses as a total rejection of cultic activity and a call for ethical behavior in its place. Many interpreters, especially in the Protestant

30. Gene M. Tucker, "The Law in the Eighth Century Prophets," in *Canon, Theology, and Old Testament Interpretation: Essays in Honor of Brevard S. Childs,* ed. Gene M. Tucker, David L. Peterson, and Robert R. Wilson (Philadelphia: Fortress, 1988) 201-16.

tradition, have been unable to resist that temptation. The words are strong and tinged with contempt. The clear contrast between this range of ritual activities and the resounding call for purification, rejection of evil, and justice and righteousness elicits serious consideration of the legitimacy of religious ceremonies. The prophet clearly places limits upon the sufficiency of ritual.

However, it would be a mistake to use this text to drive a wedge between piety and social action, between the life of prayer and worship, on the one hand, and intervention on behalf of the oppressed, on the other hand. This text does not force a decision for one and against the other. It seems unlikely that Isaiah himself ever put aside ritual. He was in the Temple when he had the vision of the Lord of justice (chap. 6). Moreover, Israel's songs of worship constantly emphasize the link between piety and concern for equity in society. The liturgies for entrance into the Temple make this explicit: "O LORD, who may abide in your tent? . . . Those who walk blamelessly, and do what is right" (Ps 15:1-2 NRSV; see also Psalm 24). Fundamental to coming into the presence of the Lord is living a life of obedience to that Lord's will for justice. This affirmation by both prophets and the worship tradition (cf. Deut 26:12-15) emphasizes that worship is legitimate when accompanied by attendance to justice in one's daily life.

Nor is the interpretation of legitimate worship here concerned fundamentally with the attitudes or feelings of the worshiper; for example, it is not concerned with the sincerity of the worshiper.[31] The prophets, like most of the Old Testament tradition, focus on right actions rather than right thinking, on orthopraxis rather than orthodoxy. Thus to wash oneself in preparation for worship is to deal justly in very specific ways.

3. Throughout this section moves the poignant, almost heartbreaking, contrast between human sin and divine mercy. The contrast brings both human failure and divine concern into sharp focus. Just as human rebellion is demonstrated in acts of corruption and injustice, so also the vulnerability of God becomes visible in God's willingness to bargain, to hold back the deserved punishment.

The movement has a chronological dimension, from past, through the present, and into the future. Isaiah 1:2-3 contrasts God's past care—like that of a parent—with the people's rebellion and stupidity. In 1:4-9, the past is not forgotten, but the tension is brought into the present, particularly in the description of the effects of rebellion. Most of 1:10-14 concerns the present failure of worship without justice, and then in 1:15-20 the focus shifts to the future. Here Yahweh is heard to argue for change that may lead to renewal. The word "repent" does not appear, but the concept does. The people are urged to be willing and obedient—that is, to turn around. It may be implied, but it is not stated, that confession of sin is required. Significantly, when cleansing and pardon come in 1:19-20, they are conditional: "If you are willing and obedient . . . *but if* you refuse and rebel" (NRSV, italics added). God takes, and will continue to take, the initiative, but human response will determine the future.

This tension between sin, with its judgment, and the promise of salvation persists throughout Isaiah 1–39. Israel is guilty over and over, and what will God do? This differs from Amos, where the answer is clear and unambiguous: The end has come. In Isaiah one finds both good news and bad, leaving each reader to struggle with the possibility that the word of God is not always the same in all times and places. The book, and this section, also invites all readers to take responsibility for their own actions—indeed, for their own lives—in the context of that struggle.

---

31. As suggested by G. G. D. Kilpatrick, "The Book of Isaiah, Exposition," in *The Interpreter's Bible,* 12 vols. (Nashville: Abingdon, 1956) 5:171-74.

Isaiah 1:21-26, Corrupt Jerusalem Redeemed

NIV

21See how the faithful city
    has become a harlot!
She once was full of justice;
    righteousness used to dwell in her—
    but now murderers!
22Your silver has become dross,
    your choice wine is diluted with water.
23Your rulers are rebels,
    companions of thieves;
they all love bribes
    and chase after gifts.
They do not defend the cause of the fatherless;
    the widow's case does not come
        before them.
24Therefore the Lord, the LORD Almighty,
    the Mighty One of Israel, declares:
"Ah, I will get relief from my foes
    and avenge myself on my enemies.
25I will turn my hand against you;
    I will thoroughly purge away your dross
    and remove all your impurities.
26I will restore your judges as in days of old,
    your counselors as at the beginning.
Afterward you will be called
    the City of Righteousness,
    the Faithful City."

NRSV

21 How the faithful city
    has become a whore!
She that was full of justice,
    righteousness lodged in her—
    but now murderers!
22 Your silver has become dross,
    your wine is mixed with water.
23 Your princes are rebels
    and companions of thieves.
Everyone loves a bribe
    and runs after gifts.
They do not defend the orphan,
    and the widow's cause does not come
        before them.

24 Therefore says the Sovereign, the LORD of
        hosts, the Mighty One of Israel:
Ah, I will pour out my wrath on my enemies,
    and avenge myself on my foes!
25 I will turn my hand against you;
    I will smelt away your dross as with lye
    and remove all your alloy.
26 And I will restore your judges as at the first,
    and your counselors as at the beginning.
Afterward you shall be called the city of
        righteousness,
    the faithful city.

COMMENTARY

These verses continue the theme of the preceding unit and advance the question of sinful Jerusalem's fate, but it is equally clear that vv. 21-26 can stand alone as a self-contained unit, and very likely did before being incorporated into their present context. The initial "How" (איכה 'êkâ) typically functions in biblical literature to begin a new unit, especially a dirge or lament. Such laments over Jerusalem are not uncommon (see esp. Lam 1:1; 2:1; 4:1). Moreover, the same key expression, "faithful city," appears in vv. 21 and 26, forming an inclusio that adds poetic coherence to the thematic unity. That the subsequent verses (vv. 27-31) are a distinct unit is indicated by a shift from direct address to third-person description and by the fact that they interpret and extend the point of vv. 21-26.

In this address to Jerusalem, its leaders, and its people, form and content are in tension with each other. Remarkably, the form of the prophecy of judgment concludes with a proclamation of salvation. Speaking through the prophet, the Lord once again spells out the sins of the citizens of Jerusalem, this time in the mood of a lament (vv. 21-23), and then proceeds with the expected and justified announcement of punishment (v. 24). But the proclamation of judgment takes a surprising turn. Yahweh will indeed strike ("turn my hand against you") the city and people of Jerusalem, but God's wrath (v. 24) will purify and renew rather than destroy. Then where one would expect the announcement of judgment, instead the Lord proclaims salvation, promising to restore Jerusalem's judges and counselors so that Jerusalem's name will be "city of righteousness, the faithful city" (v. 26). The sequence of circumstances and events is of great importance in these verses. Jerusalem must be indicted, stand convicted before the Lord, deserve punishment, experience the divine wrath, be purified of its corruption, then be granted divinely ordained leadership. Then, and only then ("Afterward," v. 26), it will be entitled to recognition as the city of righteousness.

1:21-23. First come the scathing accusations, initially (v. 21) in the sad rhythm of the dirge, as if the accused is already dead. The accusations are presented both metaphorically and with concrete detail. All the metaphors represent corruption. Even the tone of the death song conjures up the image of decay. To call the city a "whore" personifies Jerusalem as a woman, but one who has corrupted herself by selling her affections. Silver that has become dross and wine diluted with water (v. 22) are vivid images of the corruption of something good to something worthless.

But again, as in v. 17, abstractions and metaphors will not suffice. So the prophet spells out the accusation of corruption in specific and concrete indictments (v. 23). First he says what they are: The "princes" (NRSV) or "rulers" (NIV) are rebels (against God) and friends of thieves. The princes are not necessarily members of the royal family but comprise the judicial and administrative leadership. Second, he states what they do: Everyone loves a bribe and seeks special favors. Third, he asserts what they do not do: They do not defend the orphan or listen to the case of the widow—that is, those in authority do not advocate in the courts on behalf of the powerless. So corruption is defined in terms of very specific corrupt activities.

1:24. The "therefore" that initiates this verse is the standard prophetic transition from reasons for judgment to the announcement of punishment. The forceful series of divine titles ("the Sovereign, the LORD of hosts, the Mighty One of Israel") identifies the speaker and the author of that judgment about to be spelled out, emphasizing the Lord's

power and authority. Beginning with the "Ah" (or "woe"), Yahweh announces the intention to pour out wrath upon enemies, to take revenge upon foes. This is just the kind of pronouncement one might expect against Israel's enemies in the holy war.

1:25. The next verse, however, contains two dramatic turns. In the first, the Lord makes it clear that the leaders and citizens of Jerusalem are those very enemies who face the Lord's wrath: "I will turn my hand against you." This turn is characteristic of Amos, Isaiah's contemporary, who uses the old traditions of the holy war, in which the Lord was believed to intervene on behalf of Israel against the nation's enemies, to announce destruction in the form of military disaster. Yahweh will, indeed, act against his enemies, but they are the people of Israel themselves, and not foreigners. As in Amos, expectations have been reversed (Amos 5:18-20). In Amos 2:13-16, where Yahweh intervenes in a holy war against the enemies, Israel becomes the Lord's enemy.

The second turn in this verse is just as unexpected. Yahweh's intervention to judge and punish will be painful, but it will be a purifying fire, removing the corruption of the city and its people. In this turn to the future, the prophet resumes one of the metaphors for corruption or contamination: silver that has become dross. The impending disaster will be like a blistering smelter or like scalding lye that removes all impurities.

1:26. Concretely, what do these metaphors envision for the future of the city, its leaders, and its people? What will happen to the princes, those who love bribes and who do not defend the orphan and the widow? Some commentators have argued that the point of this verse is that the Lord will remove the corrupt leaders and replace them with proper judges and counselors.[32] Kaiser concludes: "God's judgment is not simply a punishment. It is a division between the devout and the godless. God rejects the base metal in order to preserve the pure silver. The destruction of the godless is followed by the renewal of the congregation (v. 26)."[33] Such an interpretation, especially concerning the leadership, is not entirely unrealistic.

32. Marvin A. Sweeney, *Isaiah 1–39, With an Introduction to Prophetic Literature,* FOTL XVI (Grand Rapids: Eerdmans, 1996) 85.
33. O. Kaiser, *Isaiah 1–12: A Commentary,* trans. R. A. Wilson (Philadelphia: Westminster, 1972) 20.

The prophet has in view an invasion by an enemy, such as Assyria, and in such an event the leaders would be the first to go—and for good political and military reasons. Moreover, to modern ears such a view sounds fair: God will remove the evil and leave the good. Thus the "dross" or the "alloy" represents the sinners among the people, especially the powerful. But it is not said that the Lord will turn a hand specifically against the evil ones, and an alternative interpretation is more likely. The city and all its inhabitants will be passed through the fire, and all will suffer. A corporate, rather than a discriminating, judgment is typical of the eighth-century prophets, and the "you" against whom the Lord will turn a hand is singular, referring to the city of Jerusalem itself (v. 21). Thus those who are left will not have survived because they were the righteous, but they are made righteous, refined and purified, in the trial by fire.

The announcement of salvation (v. 26) contains two parts. In the first, Yahweh promises to restore sound leadership to Jerusalem. The language for this leadership differs from that in v. 23, but the function of the "judges" and the "counselors" parallels that of the "rulers." All would have been high officials responsible for the administration of justice—very important in the light of the particular accusations in v. 23—and for the management of the government under the royal house. The promise here ("restore") assumes that once upon a time, perhaps in the era of David, Jerusalem's leadership was just and right. In the second part of the announcement, the effects of Yahweh's intervention are spelled out. Jerusalem will be known by two names, "City of Righteousness" and "Faithful City," titles that express the quality of life in it. This new reputation for the former whore is not something Yahweh will do, but something God will make possible by the purging punishment and the restoration of just leadership. (See Reflections at 1:27-31.)

Isaiah 1:27-31, Redemption for Zion and Judgment for Sinners

NIV	NRSV

27Zion will be redeemed with justice,
    her penitent ones with righteousness.
28But rebels and sinners will both be broken,
    and those who forsake the LORD will perish.
 	
29"You will be ashamed because of the
      sacred oaks
    in which you have delighted;
you will be disgraced because of the gardens
    that you have chosen.
30You will be like an oak with fading leaves,
    like a garden without water.
31The mighty man will become tinder
    and his work a spark;
both will burn together,
    with no one to quench the fire."
	27 Zion shall be redeemed by justice,
	    and those in her who repent, by
	      righteousness.
	28 But rebels and sinners shall be destroyed
	      together,
	    and those who forsake the LORD shall be
	      consumed.
	29 For you shall be ashamed of the oaks
	    in which you delighted;
	  and you shall blush for the gardens
	    that you have chosen.
	30 For you shall be like an oak
	    whose leaf withers,
	    and like a garden without water.
	31 The strong shall become like tinder,
	    and their work[a] like a spark;
	  they and their work shall burn together,
	    with no one to quench them.
	
	[a]Or its makers

COMMENTARY

The concluding portion of the chapter consists of two distinct but closely related parts, vv. 27-28 and vv. 29-31. Both are announcements concerning the future, although neither is identified as the words of Yahweh, who is mentioned in the third person (v. 28). The first part (vv. 27-28) is a passive announcement ("shall be") of salvation for Zion and the repentant and an announcement of judgment on rebels and sinners, making explicit the distinction between sinners and the righteous, only implied in the preceding section. There is no summons to repent but an announcement concerning what will happen. The second part (vv. 29-31) presents an unambiguous announcement of judgment on those who participate in non-Yahwistic fertility cults. The form is direct address to the condemned ("you"), presumed in this context to be the "rebels" and "sinners" of v. 28.

1:27-28. These verses could just as well be taken as part of the preceding unit (vv. 21-26), and many commentators read them in this way. They do interpret and extend the conclusion of that section concerning purifying judgment. However, that reading can miss the integrity of vv. 21-26 and accept the point of vv. 27-28, a later addition, as the meaning of vv. 21-26. Furthermore, the verses in their present arrangement are an important anticipation of vv. 29-31. The expression "for" (כי *kî*), which begins v. 29, is a transition that presumes a preceding statement. Typically in prophetic speech the reasons for punishment would be given before the announcement of judgment. Here the redemption of Zion and the destruction of rebels and sinners (vv. 27-28) is the foundation for the specific announcement against those involved in non-Yahwistic worship. Consequently, vv. 27-28 function as a transition that both continues what precedes and introduces what follows.[34]

Evidence supports the conclusion of the majority of commentators that both parts of this section originated long after the eighth century BCE as interpretations of the prophetic message for new times and circumstances.[35] Verses 27-28 depend on and reinterpret vv. 25-26, and the identification of rebellion in terms of participation in fertility cults, characteristic of Hosea, is virtually unheard of in the words of Isaiah of Jerusalem. On the other hand, references to "oaks" and "gardens" as cultic objects or places are common in the final chapters of the book of Isaiah (57:5; 65:3; 66:17), as is "choose" used to refer to non-Yahwistic worship (65:12; 66:3-4).[36] The parallels between the first and the final chapters of Isaiah argue that these verses are secondary additions. Perhaps more significant, these parallels are links stemming from the final editorial stage, stressing the coherence of the entire book of Isaiah.

Concern with Zion (v. 27) as the Lord's chosen city echoes throughout both this chapter and the entire book. That the city and those in it will "be redeemed" (תפדה *tippādeh*) expresses a hope with deep biblical roots. If it can be said to have a non-religious meaning, it refers to a release or a ransom, as a slave from an owner (Lev 19:20). In the pentateuchal traditions, "redeem" frequently refers to the Lord's act of bringing Israel out of slavery in Egypt (Exod 9:25; Deut 15:15; 24:18), and in the sacrificial cult it refers to buying back the firstborn from God (Exod 13:13, 15; Lev 27:27). The use here is closer to that in the psalms, in which one prays to be or is delivered from some form of adversity.[37] In any case, one is redeemed from some kind of trouble. What Zion and its repentant citizens are redeemed from is not stated here, but it is probably the destruction set out for the rebels and sinners. In the OT, "redemption" concerns the concrete, historical, and physical situation of those redeemed.

One of the more important questions concerning v. 27 is also the most difficult to answer: By whose "justice" and "righteousness" will Zion and those who repent be redeemed, the Lord's or the people's? These terms, especially when paired,

---

34. Wildberger states: "The redactor who put these two sections together wanted vv. 29ff. to clarify and further expand v. 28." H. Wildberger, *Isaiah 1–12,* trans. Thomas H. Trapp (Minneapolis: Fortress, 1991) 75.

35. So, e.g., Kaiser, *Isaiah 1–12,* 19, 21; R. E. Clements, *Isaiah 1–39,* NCNB (Grand Rapids: Eerdmans, 1980) 37; R. B. Y. Scott, "The Book of Isaiah, Chapters 1–39," in *The Interpreter's Bible,* 12 vols. (Nashville: Abingdon, 1956) 5:179. Sweeney considers 1:27-28 to be a redactional addition from the mid- to late fifth century but 1:29-31 to be the work of Isaiah, "albeit modified by the editorial work evident in v. 29" (Sweeney, *Isaiah 1–39,* 87). On the other hand, Wildberger takes these verses to be from Isaiah (Wildberger, *Isaiah 1–12,* 75-76).

36. See Wildberger, *Isaiah 1–12,* 75.

37. Ibid., 71.

---

typically refer to human behavior (1:21; 5:7; 9:7; 28:17; 32:1; Amos 5:7, 24; 6:12). The context, in which the Lord executes purifying punishment, suggests that it is the Lord's justice and righteousness that redeem, and these seem to be divine attributes in Isa 5:16.

1:29-31. The announcement of judgment in v. 29 alludes to a very different offense from the crimes mentioned to this point in the chapter. "Oaks" and "gardens" are the sacred groves of the Canaanite fertility cult. Thus, although there is no specific accusation of idolatry, "those who forsake the LORD" (v. 28) are the ones who have participated in non-Yahwistic worship (cf. 17:7-8; 65:3; Jer 3:6, 9; Hos 4:13). To "be ashamed" and to "blush"

are not the same as being guilty; it is to have one's guilt exposed.

The judgment announced in vv. 30-31 is ironic and requires no particular divine intervention or punishment. That the rebels shall be like the oak that withers is a reversal of expectations. The symbol for life, and for the renewal of life in the fertility cult, becomes a symbol for death. The NIV translation ("oak with fading leaves") suggests the normal loss of leaves in autumn, but this is too tame, as v. 31 shows. In that verse the disaster becomes a consuming fire ignited by the very work of "the strong," probably a reference to the strongest sinners. Those who participate in the fertility cults bring themselves to ruin.

REFLECTIONS

1. The final part of this chapter (esp. vv. 21-23 as well as vv. 16-17) begins to bring into focus a concern central to Isaiah as well as to virtually all the prophetic books: the meaning of justice.[38] But direct access to the content of justice in the prophets is rare. In most texts, including Isaiah, the prophetic understanding of justice must be deduced from the negative—that is, from the sins and crimes the prophets condemn. We read justice as a mirror image, the reverse of what is wrong. Moreover, the prophets introduce remarkably few new laws or expectations to their addresses but instead depend on ancient tradition. They assume that the people standing before them have long known how they were supposed to act toward their God and toward one another.[39] In this chapter, we see both the negative, or condemnation of injustice (vv. 21-23), and the positive, or call for justice (vv. 16-17). Although addressed to ancient hearers, these words evoke both reflection and response in our age as well.

As in so many other prophetic texts, "justice" is paired with and qualified by "righteousness." The Hebrew for "justice" comes from a verb meaning "to judge," so the Tanakh often translates it as "judgment" instead of justice. But especially when linked with "righteousness," justice is a moral value understood theologically.[40] "Righteousness," a more specifically religious expression, concerns the quality of one's relationship to God, who is righteous.

In the context of the prophetic message, "social justice" is almost tautological, for human justice always has to do with relationships to others in society. Furthermore, it concerns not just individual acts but the structure of the society's institutions. In Isaiah 1, the failure of justice and righteousness is made concrete and specific. It concerns both individuals and the political and economic structure of the society. The absence of justice and righteousness is epitomized by murder (1:21), rebellion (1:22), association with thieves (1:22), bribery (1:23), failure to defend the orphan or hear the widow's cause (1:23)—that is, go to court on their behalf. The orphan and the widow were economically and politically vulnerable. To establish justice is to exercise one's responsibilities toward the weakest members of the society. The main form of justice in this context is procedural; injustice lies in using the courts and high office against the powerless.

Consequently the prophetic voice from the past serves as a summons in every age to establish

---

38. See esp. James L. Mays, "Justice: Perspectives from the Prophetic Tradition," *Int.* 37 (1983) 5-17; reprinted in *Prophecy in Israel,* ed. David L. Petersen (Philadelphia: Fortress, 1987) 144-58.

39. Gene M. Tucker, "The Law in the Eighth Century Prophets," in *Canon, Theology, and Old Testament Interpretation: Essays in Honor of Brevard S. Childs,* ed. Gene M. Tucker, David L. Petersen, and Robert R. Wilson (Philadelphia: Fotress, 1988) 201-16.

40. Mays, "Justice," 147.

fair courts accessible to all, regardless of economic or social status. That voice also serves to remind its hearers that the very purpose of legal institutions is to protect the weak from the strong. Moreover, the prophetic call insists that justice concerns not just how one person behaves toward another but how every society ought to establish fair and just institions.

2. Isaiah regularly calls attention to the importance of political leadership. Those who have brought disaster upon the people are singled out for special punishment. Through Yahweh's justice and righteousness, the right social, political, and economic structures will be restored (1:26-31). Bad leadership is a curse for which all suffer; sound government is a blessing. The special responsibilities of leadership for this prophet are related to the royal house, the particular Davidic theology of Isaiah. The political institution to which Isaiah speaks is a theocracy, in which the divinely elected king rules on behalf of Yahweh. Consequently, although many aspects of the prophetic concern for just government reach across the ages, it is not always simple to see how that message addresses other situations or contexts, such as a democracy, especially one founded on the principle of separation of church and state. Nevertheless, those who take the prophetic words seriously will examine their own political institutions and individual leaders to ask how they are a blessing and how they are a curse.

3. What are we to make of the fact that Isaiah 1 is a thematic unity that consists of diverse units, some of which were composed long after the death of the eighth-century BCE prophet? First, it is worth remembering that judgments of *fact*—that a particular unit or line came not from Isaiah but from a later hand—are not to be confused with judgments of *value*—therefore, that line or unit is less significant than the "original" words of the prophet. Such determinations of date and circumstances may be very important in understanding the words. But later is not necessarily inferior. After all, communities of faith affirm the book, rather than just what may be determined to be its earliest stage of development, as Scripture.

Second, this chapter, consisting of many originally independent speeches from different times and circumstances, is itself an interpretation of the message of the entire book of Isaiah. Guided largely by the pattern of the prophetic lawsuit, it moves thematically from accusation of sin to the possibility of transformation, to punishment, to repentance, to renewal, which includes the destruction of rebels and sinners. The authors and editors of the chapter commend this theology of history to the reader and hearer as a structure through which to read the words that follow. But this raises problems as well as solutions. It would be a mistake to rush to that outline whenever any difficult text is encountered. The thematic and theological outline must not become a substitute for engaging the hard individual points of the book's messages; for example, failing to hear the indictments of sin because the outcome is known or because they are interpreted as warnings and not as the basis for the announcement of judgment or failing to hear the announcements of judgment because one knows that the answer—announcement of salvation—is found at the end of the book. After all, even this theology of history has no room for cheap grace, doubtless because its authors and their first readers had been through the fires that destroyed Jerusalem and—at least for a while and for some—seemed to bring the history of God with these people to an end.

ISAIAH 2:1–4:6, PROPHECIES OF SALVATION AND JUDGMENT

OVERVIEW

The new superscription in 2:1 marks a clear beginning. It is quite possible that this was the beginning of an earlier form of the book of Isaiah. If so, it is by no means clear where that book ended. Its presence indicates that some part of the book of Isaiah that begins here—either through the end of chap. 4, through 9:7, or perhaps as far as the end of chap. 11—once circulated independently. In any case, the superscription with its title serves as the heading for a collection of prophetic speeches. Another relatively distinct beginning appears with the shift in genre in 5:1, and an even more definitive one with the date formula that begins the prophet's report of his vocation in 6:1.

Following the superscription is a cluster of prophetic addresses.[41] Although some thematic threads link these addresses, virtually the only

41. Sweeney takes Isaiah 2–4 to be a composite unit organized by editors who used various earlier texts to present an ideal picture of Zion's future role. This was accomplished by drawing the contrast between the ideal Zion (2:2-4) and the current state of its people. See Marvin A. Sweeney, *Isaiah 1–39, With an Introduction to Prophetic Literature,* FOTL XVI (Grand Rapids: Eerdmans, 1996) 87-91.

factor they have in common is that they are words of Yahweh concerning the future. The dimension of that historical horizon varies, from distant to immediate, and one does hear descriptions of the sins and crimes that will set disaster into motion. The section is framed by announcements of salvation at the beginning and at the end. Although both focus on Zion and Jerusalem, they are quite different in scope. Isaiah 2:1-5 announces the elevation of Zion and the establishment of peace with justice among all nations; 4:2-6 proclaims sanctification of those who survive in Jerusalem, which will be a divinely protected sanctuary. Between these announcements of salvation are three clusters of prophecies of judgment. The first, 2:6-22, proclaims the day of the Lord as a time of disaster for Judah, the "house of Jacob" (2:6). The second, 3:1-15, consists of several prophecies against Judah and Jerusalem. In the third, 3:16–4:1, Yahweh is heard to accuse and condemn the women of Jerusalem, "the daughters of Zion" (3:16-17 NRSV).

Isaiah 2:1-5, Swords into Plowshares

NIV	NRSV
2 This is what Isaiah son of Amoz saw concerning Judah and Jerusalem:	**2** The word that Isaiah son of Amoz saw concerning Judah and Jerusalem.
[2]In the last days	[2] In days to come
the mountain of the LORD's temple will be established	the mountain of the LORD's house shall be established as the highest of the mountains,
as chief among the mountains;	
it will be raised above the hills,	and shall be raised above the hills;
and all nations will stream to it.	all the nations shall stream to it.
[3]Many peoples will come and say,	[3] Many peoples shall come and say,
"Come, let us go up to the mountain of the LORD,	"Come, let us go up to the mountain of the LORD,
to the house of the God of Jacob.	to the house of the God of Jacob;
He will teach us his ways,	that he may teach us his ways
so that we may walk in his paths."	and that we may walk in his paths."
	For out of Zion shall go forth instruction,

NIV

The law will go out from Zion,
   the word of the LORD from Jerusalem.
⁴He will judge between the nations
   and will settle disputes for many peoples.
They will beat their swords into plowshares
   and their spears into pruning hooks.
Nation will not take up sword against nation,
   nor will they train for war anymore.

⁵Come, O house of Jacob,
   let us walk in the light of the LORD.

NRSV

   and the word of the LORD from Jerusalem.
⁴He shall judge between the nations,
   and shall arbitrate for many peoples;
they shall beat their swords into plowshares,
   and their spears into pruning hooks;
nation shall not lift up sword against nation,
   neither shall they learn war any more.

⁵O house of Jacob,
   come, let us walk
      in the light of the LORD!

COMMENTARY

2:1. Distinct headings over individual speeches appear throughout the prophetic books. In Jeremiah the third person dominates ("The word that came to Jeremiah from the LORD," Jer 7:1; also, e.g., Jer 11:1; 14:1; 18:1), but in Ezekiel these usually are first-person reports ("The word of the LORD came to me," Ezek 1:3 RSV; also, e.g., Ezek 12:1; 13:1; 15:1; 17:1). The announcements against the foreign nations in Isaiah have the heading "The oracle concerning Babylon" (Isa 13:1 NRSV; "Moab," 15:1 NRSV). But 2:1 is a superscription paralleling those that begin prophetic books. It contains some of the same information found in 1:1 (name and ancestor of the prophet, identification of what follows as revealed, and focus of the message upon Judah and Jerusalem). The same verb used in 1:1 (חזה ḥāzâ, "saw") reports Isaiah's reception of the revelation, but here it is called the "word" (דבר dābār) instead of the "vision" (חזון ḥāzôn). Both function as technical terms for divine revelation.

It seems most likely that this verse marked the beginning of an earlier collection of prophecies attributed to Isaiah and that chap. 1 was added later. But since vv. 2-4 are virtually identical to Mic 4:1-3, it is possible that an editor added this superscription to clarify the question of the announcement's origin, to insist that it first came from Isaiah.[42]

2:2-4. Few texts in the book of Isaiah are better known than this magnificent prophecy of peace—and rightly so. Form and content work in concert to express in the form of a promise the

longing for peace with justice among nations, and the rhetorical power of the poetry makes the promise graphic and compelling. Almost as well known is the fact that the same lines appear in virtually identical form, with minor textual variations, in Mic 4:1-4. So the question of the origin or authorship of this vision urges itself upon the interpreter. Some argue that Isaiah must have composed this piece in the eighth century, mainly on the grounds of his deep ties with the specific traditions of Jerusalem and Mt. Zion.[43] A few have argued that the promise originated with Micah.[44] There is no way of determining which prophet depends upon the other. Indeed, it is possible that both occurrences are citations from an older tradition, known at the Temple in Jerusalem.[45] Even more likely, both were added to the words of the two eighth-century prophets in the process of the formation of the books.[46] The liturgical dimensions of the passage support the view that the tradition is older than Isaiah and Micah, but the particular eschatology expressed in the poem is more consistent with perspectives of the exilic or early postexilic eras. Consequently, the evidence for the date of this passage is inconclusive.

Far more important than the authorship or date

---

42. Peter R. Ackroyd, "A Note on Isa 2:1," *ZAW* 75 (1963) 320-21.
43. H. Wildberger, *Isaiah 1–12*, trans. Thomas H. Trapp (Minneapolis: Fortress, 1991) 85-87.
44. E. Cannawurf, "The Authenticity of Micah IV 1–4," *VT* 13 (1963) 26-33.
45. J. J. M. Roberts, "The Davidic Origin of the Zion Tradition," *JBL* 92 (73) 329-44.
46. James Luther Mays, *Micah* (Philadelphia: Westminster, 1976) 95.

of these verses is understanding and coming to terms with their message. Formally, the poem is unusual, although not without parallels in the Hebrew scriptures. The speaker is not identified but must be deduced from the point of view. A prophetic voice announces what will happen and what Yahweh and others will do. There is no specific claim of prophetic authority (e.g., "thus says the LORD"), but this is what prophets do: proclaim what God will do in the future. Although there are liturgical allusions and even hymnic features—the implicit praise of Yahweh, the Temple, and Zion, the people's call to worship or pilgrimage in v. 3— the passage is not a hymn but a prophetic announcement or promise of salvation. The words are not addressed to God, as in a song of praise, but are indefinite. No particular addressee, such as the people of Israel or the nations of the world, is indicated. The editor who placed the superscription here interpreted the speech as one given to "Judah and Jerusalem" (v. 1), and Zion stands at the center of the promise. But this proclamation concerns all nations and addressees who will listen.

The sequence of future events is important. First, "the mountain of the LORD's house"—that is, Zion—will be elevated and exalted (v. 2*ab*). Second, there will be a pilgrimage of all peoples to the holy mountain (vv. 2*c*-3*a*). This is no simple sight-seeing trip or a military campaign but a purposeful journey to a holy place. Third, as they approach, the people will sing a call to pilgrimage that expresses their reasons for coming to Zion— namely, that the God of Jacob may teach them God's ways (v. 3*b*). Fourth, the motivation for the pilgrimage or the attraction of Zion is stated: "instruction" (or the "law," תורה *tôrâ*) and the word of Yahweh go forth from Jerusalem (v. 3*c*). Finally, in setting out the results of all that has transpired thus far, the speaker utters the name of the instigator of that future: Yahweh shall "judge between the nations," who will turn their instruments of war into farming tools, inaugurating a permanent reign of peace (v. 4).

Some of the events are characterized passively and others actively. The mountain "shall be established . . . and shall be raised" (v. 2), and instruction and the word of the Lord "shall go forth" (v. 3). The only actors in the drama of peace are Yahweh and "the nations," or "many peoples" (vv. 2-4). Yahweh takes on the role of teacher or instructor (v. 3), which traditionally was held by the priests in ancient Israel, and the duties of judge and administrator of justice (v. 4). The role of the nations is crucial. They come to Zion seeking instruction and revelation ("word of the LORD"), and they—not God—destroy the weapons of war. Consequently, their acknowledgment of Yahweh and trust in Yahweh's capacity to settle international disputes is the basis for peace.

The temporal phrase that initiates the anouncement opens an important question concerning the prophetic understanding of the future. Comparing the translations of the NRSV and the NIV accents the alternatives. The NRSV ("In days to come") is indefinite, while the NIV ("In the last days") advocates an eschatological, if not apocalyptic, understanding. Although the NIV follows the interpretation of the LXX and other ancient versions, it is misleading, suggesting an apocalyptic view, with a series of stages before the end. That is how the temporal expression is used in Dan 2:8 and 10:14, but not here. "In days to come" in this context is indefinite and distant, but not vague. It refers neither to the end of time nor beyond time, but within it. To be sure, the prophet expects a radical transformation of history, as the remainder of the prophecy demonstrates. Circumstances will change dramatically, and the Lord will reign, fundamentally as judge and peacemaker among nations.

"The mountain of the LORD's house" is Zion, the site of the Temple. Traditions concerning Zion as Yahweh's holy place and Jerusalem as the chosen city fuel the theology of Isaiah. But their roots are deep in ancient Near Eastern religion generally and the literature of Israel's worship in particular. Gods preferred mountains or high places. The Mesopotamian ziggurat, a mountain-shaped temple, was the house of the god, and the Canaanite deities lived on Mt. Zaphon as well as other peaks.[47] In praising God, Psalm 48 celebrates Mt. Zion as the city of the divine King, a citadel that can never be violated (see also Psalms 46; 76:2-3; 87; 122; 125; 132; Ezek 40:2). And never mind that Zion was not even the highest peak in the immediate neighborhood. Particular aspects of the Zion tradition appropriated in these verses include the pilgrimage of the nations to the holy mountain

47. R. J. Clifford, *The Cosmic Mountain in Canaan and the Old Testament* (Cambridge, Mass.: Harvard University Press, 1972) 31, 34-97, and (on Isa 2:2-4) 156-58.

(see also Isa 45:14-23; 60:1-18; 61:5-7) and the Lord's establishment of peace among nations, but generally through force:

> Come, behold the works of the LORD;
>   see what desolations he has brought on the
>   earth.
> He makes wars cease to the end of the earth;
>   he breaks the bow, and shatters the spear;
>   he burns the shields with fire.
>   (Ps 46:8-9 NRSV)

Thus the prophecy draws from Jerusalem's cultic traditions, but it is based as well on other institutions and ideas. The nations will come to Zion seeking "instruction, and the word of the LORD" (v. 3), the same language used in 1:10 for the priestly and the prophetic communication of the divine will. There is as well the concern for the administration of justice and the resolution of conflicts, applied to the arena of international politics. Yahweh will assume the role of judge and diplomat.

The Hebrew word for "peace" (שלום *šālôm*) does not appear in this vision of a world without war, but that is what the promise entails. Beyond the absence of military conflict, there will be justice, the resolution of conflicts on the basis of Yahweh's justice. Moreover, a major economic shift will occur. Swords and spears are relatively cheap today, but in antiquity their production diverted significant resources. The relatively simple mechanical transformation of swords into plowshares and spears into pruning hooks—any blacksmith could do it—represents the diversion of tools of destruction to tools that provide food.

2:5. This verse would not have been part of the original announcement of salvation. It does not appear in the parallel text in Mic 4:1-4, and the style shifts from proclamation of the future to second-person direct address. Formally, it is an admonition to the "house of Jacob"—that is, to the people of Judah. Because of the shift, some interpreters (so NRSV) see the verse as the beginning of the subsequent unit (2:5-22). Although there are connections with what follows, this verse is best seen as a call for response to the announcement of salvation (so NIV). "House of Jacob" picks up "house of the God of Jacob" from v. 3, and "walk" mirrors "walk in his paths" from v. 3.

The "nations" and "many peoples" of v. 4 would be everyone in the world, including the people of Judah and Jerusalem. But is there a particular role for the citizens of Yahweh's chosen territory? At some stage in the transmission and liturgical use of this text—if not when it was originally composed—that same question arose and was answered with the lines that stand in v. 5. The announcement is a vision of peace for all peoples, in which the foreign nations come to Jerusalem to learn the ways of justice. Having heard that proclamation, the congregation of the faithful in Jerusalem is called to "walk in the light of the LORD." The point seems clear: Those who already live in the presence of God are admonished to take the first steps on the path that all the nations will tread one day. "The light of the LORD" thus refers to the vision of God's reign, just announced. The appropriate response to this vision is to be guided by it, to actualize hope through obedience. The call to the congregation applies the good news of the announcement to the addressees.

REFLECTIONS

This text is rich in themes that call for theological reflection, including the future reign of God, international politics, war, and peace. But it also evokes deep emotional reactions: Who can read these verses and not long for world peace?

1. What are we to do with or about the announcement of the future reign of God? This is good news in the Old Testament prophetic sense. The poem is not a prediction but an affirmation that history will reach its goal. That goal, the reign of God, will involve a radical transformation of existing conditions, from nationalism and conflict to unity and peace. This is a proclamation that the future is God's, not a summons to people to bring in the new age. To be sure, human beings take part by responding to the Zion that has been elevated like a signal, by seeking instruction and following it, by transforming weapons into agricultural tools, and by turning away from war. The liturgical addition in 2:5 specifically invites the elect to participate in God's reign. That is what one does with the good news of God's reign in every age: respond and participate.

The time of this transformation of circumstances is not specified; indeed, the poem is vague on this point. But the announcement is concrete. That the vision of peace finds its setting within history and connected to specific places makes it all the more difficult to ignore. This is not some mythical vision of peace but one that invites all who hear it to see God's reign breaking forth in the concrete realities of human life. Any particular movement in the direction of peace with justice can be recognized as a sign of that reign.

2. This vision of the reign of God never mentions Yahweh as king or ruler but as teacher, judge, and arbitrator. To be sure, the center is Zion, where Yahweh is King; and the foundation for peace is instruction and the word of Yahweh. Particularly important in this new age is the understanding of God as judge (2:4a). This is not the typical prophetic image of the Lord as the judge who hands out punishment after establishing guilt or innocence. Like that image, the expectation here has deep roots in the understanding of Yahweh as just and in the prophetic calls for justice and righteousness. But the divine judge in Isa 2:2-4 is the one who settles disputes among the nations, resolving their differences so that peace can be established and maintained. Consequently, those who would respond to this vision of peace will seek to become peace makers, not accusing individuals or nations but acting as mediators and arbitrators among them.

3. This vision has international political dimensions. In fact, it is universal in the expectation that all nations will come to Jerusalem to know the one true God, and the result will be peace. Although the nations are not named, they are real nations. Consequently, the text, like so much of the book of Isaiah, challenges any claim that religion and theology have nothing to do with politics, including international relations. The variation in Mic 4:4 moves the promise from the realm of world politics to that of individuals. It brings the hope down to earth—literally—by envisioning the implications of world peace for country folks: "They shall all sit under their own vines and under their own fig tress, and no one shall make them afraid" (Mic 4:4 NRSV). Plowshares and pruning hooks make for economic security and the end of fear.

At least two problems arise in considering the promise of world peace. The first concerns its center. Is there an implicit nationalism in the expectation that all nations will come to Zion and will acknowledge Jerusalem's God? Does international peace require the recognition of a common and central authority? This is just what many people fear, and always have feared: that one's own individual or national self-interest would be subordinated to that of the common good of the world community. There is no easy or simple resolution of this issue, but reading this text may be enough to provoke reflection on the difference between patriotism and chauvinism. Isaiah 2:2-4 realistically expects conflicts, differences, and competing claims to continue. The difference in the new age is that they will be resolved peacefully. But that can happen only on the basis of some commonly accepted principles ("instruction," v. 3) that transcend individual or national self-interest. Yes, peace requires compromise, even in the reign of God.

A second problem arises when this text is seen in its wider biblical context. The question of the Bible's attitude toward war and peace is not settled by Isa 2:2-4, for alternatives to this vision abound. The sharpest contrast appears in Joel 3:10, variously understood as either an ancient proverb rewritten in Isa 2:4 (and Mic 4:3) or a transformation of the announcement of peace into a call for war: "Beat your plowshares into swords/ and your pruning hooks into spears/ let the weakling say, 'I am a warrior' " (Isa 2:4 NRSV).

Texts such as this, as well as the widespread biblical tradition of the holy war, seem to fuel the fires of international relationships more than do visions of peace. In any case, citing any single text—even one so powerful as Isa 2:2-4—provides no escape from difficult moral choices.

4. It is tempting for us, in an era of military conflict, nationalism, and international mistrust, simply to write off such an announcement as this one, either as unrealistic or as applying to an era only beyond history and not within it. It probably is unrealistic to expect peace among all nations in the immediate future. Should one, then, capitulate to such harsh realities? But this text, like so much of the Bible, confronts our resignation with the assurance that God will one day reign—and in peace. The passage brings home to all who hear it the power of expectation, and it kindles hope. International peace may not come, even as we visualize it and hope for it. Wishing, and even praying, will not necessarily make it happen. But it certainly will not come unless we imagine it, unless we believe and articulate the vision that God wills the end of war.

Since this text is such clear and evocative poetry and its content so significant, perhaps it should simply speak for itself. After all, the first rule of interpretation is to avoid reversing the miracle at Cana—that is, turning wine into water. So we could hardly do better than to read this text aloud in public, and often. There is no shortage of occasions in the cycle of the year, and in the life of nations, for which such a reading would be appropriate: Memorial Day, Veterans Day, the anniversary of the bombing of Hiroshima, the signing of peace treaties, or visits to the Vietnam War Memorial.

Isaiah 2:6-22, The Day of the Lord

NIV

[6]You have abandoned your people,
  the house of Jacob.
They are full of superstitions from the East;
  they practice divination like the Philistines
  and clasp hands with pagans.
[7]Their land is full of silver and gold;
  there is no end to their treasures.
Their land is full of horses;
  there is no end to their chariots.
[8]Their land is full of idols;
  they bow down to the work of their hands,
  to what their fingers have made.
[9]So man will be brought low
  and mankind humbled—
  do not forgive them.[a]

[10]Go into the rocks,
  hide in the ground
from dread of the LORD
  and the splendor of his majesty!
[11]The eyes of the arrogant man will be humbled
  and the pride of men brought low;
the LORD alone will be exalted in that day.

[12]The LORD Almighty has a day in store
  for all the proud and lofty,
  for all that is exalted

[a]9 Or *not raise them up*

NRSV

[6] For you have forsaken the ways of[a]
    your people,
    O house of Jacob.
Indeed they are full of diviners[b] from the east
    and of soothsayers like the Philistines,
    and they clasp hands with foreigners.
[7] Their land is filled with silver and gold,
    and there is no end to their treasures;
their land is filled with horses,
    and there is no end to their chariots.
[8] Their land is filled with idols;
    they bow down to the work of their hands,
    to what their own fingers have made.
[9] And so people are humbled,
    and everyone is brought low—
    do not forgive them!
[10] Enter into the rock,
    and hide in the dust
from the terror of the LORD,
    and from the glory of his majesty.
[11] The haughty eyes of people shall be
    brought low,
    and the pride of everyone shall be humbled;
and the LORD alone will be exalted in
    that day.
[12] For the LORD of hosts has a day

[a]Heb lacks *the ways of*   [b]Cn: Heb lacks *of diviners*

NIV

(and they will be humbled),
¹³for all the cedars of Lebanon, tall and lofty,
and all the oaks of Bashan,
¹⁴for all the towering mountains
and all the high hills,
¹⁵for every lofty tower
and every fortified wall,
¹⁶for every trading ship*ᵃ*
and every stately vessel.
¹⁷The arrogance of man will be brought low
and the pride of men humbled;
the LORD alone will be exalted in that day,
¹⁸ and the idols will totally disappear.
¹⁹Men will flee to caves in the rocks
and to holes in the ground
from dread of the LORD
and the splendor of his majesty,
when he rises to shake the earth.
²⁰In that day men will throw away
to the rodents and bats
their idols of silver and idols of gold,
which they made to worship.
²¹They will flee to caverns in the rocks
and to the overhanging crags
from dread of the LORD
and the splendor of his majesty,
when he rises to shake the earth.

²²Stop trusting in man,
who has but a breath in his nostrils.
Of what account is he?

ᵃ16 Hebrew every ship of Tarshish

NRSV

against all that is proud and lofty,
against all that is lifted up and high;*ᵃ*
¹³ against all the cedars of Lebanon,
lofty and lifted up;
and against all the oaks of Bashan;
¹⁴ against all the high mountains,
and against all the lofty hills;
¹⁵ against every high tower,
and against every fortified wall;
¹⁶ against all the ships of Tarshish,
and against all the beautiful craft.*ᵇ*
¹⁷ The haughtiness of people shall be humbled,
and the pride of everyone shall be
brought low;
and the LORD alone will be exalted on
that day.
¹⁸ The idols shall utterly pass away.
¹⁹ Enter the caves of the rocks
and the holes of the ground,
from the terror of the LORD,
and from the glory of his majesty,
when he rises to terrify the earth.
²⁰ On that day people will throw away
to the moles and to the bats
their idols of silver and their idols of gold,
which they made for themselves
to worship,
²¹ to enter the caverns of the rocks
and the clefts in the crags,
from the terror of the LORD,
and from the glory of his majesty,
when he rises to terrify the earth.
²² Turn away from mortals,
who have only breath in their nostrils,
for of what account are they?

ᵃC Compare Gk: Heb low   ᵇCompare Gk: Meaning of Heb uncertain

COMMENTARY

These verses, taken as a whole, are complicated and confusing. Most of the individual parts seem clear enough, but read together the section is one of the most chaotic in the book of Isaiah. There are signs of both coherence and dissonance. Some of the threads that tie the section together are the themes of judgment, the day of Yahweh, idolatry, and the exaltation of Yahweh. There is also the repetition of expressions that function somewhat like catchwords used to link distinct units or as refrains that lend coherence to the larger section ("And so people are humbled," vv. 9*a,* 11, 17; note similarity in vv. 11, 19, 21; "silver" and "gold" in both v. 7 and v. 20). Within the section, vv. 6-9 and vv. 12-17 are coherent, if not necessarily complete, units. If one read all these verses together, their theme could be called "apostasy brings judgment," although judgment upon whom is not set out consistently.

Attempting to sort out the most simple formal features of these verses shows that this is not a unified and coherent unit of speech but a collection of diverse materials from various periods assembled under the same general rubric: the fearsome day of the Lord. Point of view, speaker, addressee, and actor frequently shift. There is direct address to God—that is, prayer (vv. 6a, 9b)—direct address to the people (vv. 10, 19), and direct address to unidentified parties (v. 22). Verses 6b-9a present a third-person account of what people have done, what they are doing, and what is happening to them; and vv. 20-21 describe what the people will do on the terrible day. Verses 11-18 contain a prophetic announcement of the future, but it begins with a passive statement ("shall be brought low," v. 11), moves to active ("the LORD of hosts has a day," vv. 12-16), and concludes with a passive description of the future ("shall be humbled," vv. 17-18).

2:6a. By adding "the ways of," the NRSV construes the first half of this verse as an address to the "house of Jacob," whereas in the Hebrew (as in the NIV) it is an address to God—that is, a prayer. That the emendation allows the text to be read more smoothly is itself an argument against it. This language, traditionally at home in the complaint psalms, is placed here to provide an introduction to the accusations that follow.[48] The initial כִּי (*kî*) is asseverative, "Surely." Thus what would have functioned in a prayer complaining that God has forsaken the worshiper now introduces the reasons why God has, indeed, forsaken the people.

2:6b-9. The word *kî*, which begins the second half of the verse, introduces the reasons why Yahweh has forsaken the people and thus is translated "for." Verses 6b-8 amount to accusations of infidelity against the house of Jacob (i.e., Judah). The Hebrew of v. 6b does not make sense without the addition of "of diviners" (NRSV; NIV, "of superstitions"), an emendation justified on the basis of the ancient versions. Prohibition against such practices, considered to be foreign, is spelled out in Deut 18:9-14. To consult diviners or soothsayers was to mistrust Yahweh (cf. 1 Sam 28:9).

Likewise, the section closes (v. 8) with the strongest indictment of all, the violation of the second commandment (Exod 20:4-5; Deut 5:8-9) by filling the land with idols and worshiping them. Framed between these accusations concerning corrupt religious practices stands the description of a land full of great wealth and military resources ("silver and gold," "horses," and "chariots," v. 7). This sounds like a very solid economic, military, and, therefore, secure political situation. Ordinarily such descriptions could characterize blessings bestowed by God. In this context, however, it is an accusation. But what does it mean? Self-reliance instead of reliance on Yahweh? A false sense of security? We can only conclude that riches and corrupt practices are taken to go hand in hand.[49]

Following the indictments of vv. 6b-8, v. 9 contains, not an announcement of punishment by means of divine intervention, but a passive description of the effects of corruption. There is an element of irony: Those who "bow down to the work of their hands" (v. 8) are "brought low" (v. 9). Then the section concludes as it began, with a prayer, in this case not a complaint but a petition spoken by the prophet: "Do not forgive them" (v. 9).

2:10-11. These verses continue the theme of v. 9 with a general call to hide from the terrible appearance of the Lord, and then an announcement that the people shall be humbled and brought low, paralleling the description in v. 9. The Lord will be exalted in judgment.

2:12-18. This section, linked to the previous one by the catchword "day," presents an announcement of judgment in terms of the day of the Lord. This idea has a past and a future. The day of the Lord has roots in Israel's holy war traditions as the day of Yahweh's victory over enemies. The theme plays a prominent role in the book of Amos, where expectations are reversed. That Amos 5:18-20 ridicules those who eagerly look forward to the day of the Lord suggests that it was viewed by the prophet's audience as a time when the Lord would intervene to save Israel from its enemies. In announcing that it will be "a day of darkness and not light," Amos claims that it is, indeed, a day when the Lord will act against

---

48. H. Wildberger, *Isaiah 1–12*, trans. Thomas H. Trapp (Minneapolis: Fortress, 1991) 102.

49. But since cause and effect are not specified, this does not necessarily mean that prosperity leads to corruption, as Kaiser suggests. See O. Kaiser, *Isaiah 1–12: A Commentary*, trans. R. A. Wilson (Philadelphia: Westminster, 1972) 35.

enemies, but Israel has become the enemy. Later than the prophetic expectation of the day of the Lord is the apocalyptic understanding of a day of final judgment. Military motifs occur in this intertestamental and New Testament description of the day, for example, in the Qumran scroll *The War of the Sons of Light Against the Sons of Darkness*. An important aspect of this tradition is that, as in the ancient holy war, the people of God will triumph over their enemies.

The day of the Lord in vv. 12-16 has cosmic, almost apocalyptic, dimensions, but it does not signal the triumph of the people of God over their enemies. Jacob is the subject of the accusation that precedes the Lord's intervention on that day, but fundamentally the day of Yahweh is against all humankind. And not only that, the Lord will intervene against natural as well as cultural phenomena: cedars, oaks, mountains, hills, towers, fortified walls, ships of Tarshish, and "all the beautiful craft." What do all of these have in common? They are "proud and lofty" (v. 12). No reasons are given for this sweeping judgment against the world beyond the exaltation of Yahweh. There is an implicit accusation of v. 17: "haughtiness of people," "pride of everyone." The note about the disappearance of the idols in v. 18 seems to be an afterthought, but it ties this section to vv. 6-8.

2:19-22. The summons to flee from the Lord's terrible appearance (v. 19) is a close parallel to v. 10, and then the theme of the day of the Lord ("On that day") resumes. This time the people discard their idols "to the moles and to the bats" (v. 20) and obey that summons to hide in the caves from the terror of the Lord (v. 21). The meaning of the reference to moles and bats is elusive. All one can say with confidence is that it trivializes idols. It is very difficult to make any sense of v. 22, almost certainly a late addition. If the imperative translated "turn away" were singular, it might be a prayer of intercession that the Lord have pity on mere mortals (cf. Amos 7:5). But it is plural and thus could be taken as a plea to an unidentified group (Judeans?) to have no trust in humankind but instead—implicitly—to trust in God. Sweeney takes the verse to be a wisdom saying, a "plea to desist from human self-reliance."[50]

50. Marvin A. Sweeney, *Isaiah 1–39, With an Introduction to Prophetic Literature*, FOTL XVI (Grand Rapids: Eerdmans, 1996) 105-6.

REFLECTIONS

Among the issues raised by Isa 2:6-22 are the closely related problems of idolatry and magic. Here, as throughout the Old Testament, these are considered to be corrupt religion, bad religion, or the wrong religion.

1. As one considers the translation or application of the biblical concern with idolatry into the modern world, it is important to keep in mind that in ancient Israel this language is quite literal. Prophetic, legal, and narrative texts were concerned with concrete, everyday problems of the cultural context in ancient Israel. The veneration of idols in worship, even in everyday life, was a real alternative to the biblical faith and practice. All religions of the ancient Near East included images of the gods in their worship. Israel was the exception, both in insisting on the worship of only one God, Yahweh, and in prohibiting the making or worship of idols, "whether in the form of anything that is in heaven above, or that is on the earth beneath, or that is in the water under the earth" (Exod 20:4).

It is too easy—and unfair—to write off those who worshiped idols as simpleminded people who did not know the difference between what they had made with their own hands and the divine (cf. Isa 44:9-20). Idols were considered to be representations of deities or were ritually dedicated and sanctified as appropriate receptacles of the god's presence.

One way to approach the issue of idolatry is to put it in terms of faith and culture. On the one hand, the biblical faith seems uncompromising: Trust in the Lord alone, rejecting all symbols of the alternative religions in the surrounding culture. But purity was—and remains—impossible. Even that magnificent Temple on Mt. Zion, so central to the thought of Isaiah and his contemporaries, was modeled after Canaanite temples and was even designed by a foreign architect.

And it was not totally without images, although not images of God or the gods. When Solomon died and the northern kingdom established its own capital in Samaria, Jeroboam dedicated golden calves in the sanctuary (1 Kgs 12:28). These images are condemned throughout the Old Testament, but it remains unclear whether they, in fact, represented Canaanite gods or were understood to be symbols for Yahweh.

The references to silver, gold, horses, and chariots in the context of the condemnation of the creation and worship of images raise a tempting possibility for the modern interpreter. The worship of money, wealth, military power, and even means of transportation could be seen as contemporary forms of idolatry. Such an interpretation is not necessarily off the mark, but reflection on the meaning of idolatry could go even deeper.

Theologically, to identify any religious objects or symbols with God is idolatry. That is the heart of the biblical heritage about God: Confuse nothing in this world with God, who, although in it and active in it, is not the same as anything in the world. Thus the second commandment—the prohibition of images and idolatry—clearly follows from the first, that the people of God are to worship only the Lord.

It is commonplace to conclude that Christianity, Judaism, and Islam are religions of the word and not of images. That may solve one problem, at least in theory, but it opens the door for another form of idolatry: the identification of particular words with God. Individuals and groups have been known to give their full devotion to particular doctrines or understandings of God or of God's will. It is entirely possible that the most persistent form of idolatry among contemporary Christians is the worship of the Bible itself as an icon, a talisman, or a good luck charm.

2. There is an intimate relationship between the critique of idolatry and the rejection of magic: The first concerns worship, devotion, or commitment, and the second concerns the control of the power or powers of the universe. Magic and divination entail the manipulation of reality, either for the purposes of knowledge (What will happen in the future?) or for control (How can I exert my will through some secret key to the force or forces that control events?).

Various forms of divination were common and legitimate in antiquity. It was believed that the future left its tracks in advance, for example, in the liver of a sacrificial sheep or in the flights of birds, and could be known by experts. There were specialists who were believed to have some kind of power, to see the future or to communicate with the dead. Magic was dangerous, and thus some forms of it—the use of such powers for evil purposes—were forbidden in virtually all cultures. But what was forbidden was common, so in ancient Mesopotamia there developed long catalogs of procedures to remove curses. The third commandment, "You shall not make wrongful use of the name of the LORD your God" (Exod 20:7), prohibits cursing someone in the name of the Lord, thereby attempting to manipulate the deity.

Generally, the biblical tradition condemns all forms of magic and divination, insisting that God alone knows the future and cannot be controlled by words or actions (Deut 18:9-12). But there are numerous biblical texts in which magical or divinatory practices are mentioned without condemnation and various approved practices that could legitimately be called magical. These include the casting of lots, trial by ordeal, blessings and curses, and even the swearing of oaths that are conditional self-curses. The dominant means of knowing the future in the biblical tradition was the prophetic word. Consistently, the prophets insist that they have no special powers and that the revelation of the future comes from God. Still, even in the biblical tradition the line between magic and religion is difficult to draw. Is it possible that prayer, say for victory before a football game, could be an example of magic, of using the name of the Lord for a wrongful purpose?

Isaiah 3:1-15, Judgment Against Judah's Leaders

NIV

3 See now, the Lord,
the LORD Almighty,
is about to take from Jerusalem and Judah
both supply and support:
all supplies of food and all supplies of water,
2   the hero and warrior,
the judge and prophet,
the soothsayer and elder,
3the captain of fifty and man of rank,
the counselor, skilled craftsman and clever
enchanter.
4I will make boys their officials;
mere children will govern them.
5People will oppress each other—
man against man, neighbor against
neighbor.
The young will rise up against the old,
the base against the honorable.

6A man will seize one of his brothers
at his father's home, and say,
"You have a cloak, you be our leader;
take charge of this heap of ruins!"
7But in that day he will cry out,
"I have no remedy.
I have no food or clothing in my house;
do not make me the leader of the people."

8Jerusalem staggers,
Judah is falling;
their words and deeds are against the LORD,
defying his glorious presence.
9The look on their faces testifies against them;
they parade their sin like Sodom;
they do not hide it.
Woe to them!
They have brought disaster upon
themselves.

10Tell the righteous it will be well with them,
for they will enjoy the fruit of their deeds.
11Woe to the wicked! Disaster is upon them!
They will be paid back for what their hands
have done.

12Youths oppress my people,
women rule over them.

NRSV

3 For now the Sovereign, the LORD of hosts,
is taking away from Jerusalem and from
Judah
support and staff—
all support of bread,
and all support of water—
2warrior and soldier,
judge and prophet,
diviner and elder,
3captain of fifty
and dignitary,
counselor and skillful magician
and expert enchanter.
4And I will make boys their princes,
and babes shall rule over them.
5The people will be oppressed,
everyone by another
and everyone by a neighbor;
the youth will be insolent to the elder,
and the base to the honorable.

6Someone will even seize a relative,
a member of the clan, saying,
"You have a cloak;
you shall be our leader,
and this heap of ruins
shall be under your rule."
7But the other will cry out on that day, saying,
"I will not be a healer;
in my house there is neither bread nor
cloak;
you shall not make me
leader of the people."
8For Jerusalem has stumbled
and Judah has fallen,
because their speech and their deeds are
against the LORD,
defying his glorious presence.

9The look on their faces bears witness
against them;
they proclaim their sin like Sodom,
they do not hide it.
Woe to them!
For they have brought evil on themselves.

O my people, your guides lead you astray;
  they turn you from the path.

¹³The LORD takes his place in court;
  he rises to judge the people.
¹⁴The LORD enters into judgment
  against the elders and leaders of his people:
"It is you who have ruined my vineyard;
  the plunder from the poor is in your houses.
¹⁵What do you mean by crushing my people
  and grinding the faces of the poor?"
          declares the Lord, the LORD Almighty.

¹⁰ Tell the innocent how fortunate they are,
  for they shall eat the fruit of their labors.
¹¹ Woe to the guilty! How unfortunate they are,
  for what their hands have done shall be
          done to them.
¹² My people—children are their oppressors,
  and women rule over them.
O my people, your leaders mislead you,
  and confuse the course of your paths.

¹³ The LORD rises to argue his case;
  he stands to judge the peoples.
¹⁴ The LORD enters into judgment
  with the elders and princes of his people:
It is you who have devoured the vineyard;
  the spoil of the poor is in your houses.
¹⁵ What do you mean by crushing my people,
  by grinding the face of the poor? says the
          Lord GOD of hosts.

COMMENTARY

A new section begins in 3:1, and 3:16 initiates another clear unit in terms of both form and content. The section between these two beginnings, 3:1-15, concentrates on the leaders or the ruling class of Jerusalem and Judah, while 3:16 shifts attention to the women of Jerusalem. But in spite of the common subject matter, there are marks of discontinuity within these fifteen verses,[51] including changes in person, speaker, tense, mood, and genre. The section begins by referring to Yahweh in the third person, but shifts without warning in v. 4 to direct divine speech. Yahweh first announces the future directly (v. 9a), but then the future is described passively (vv. 9b-7). Verses 8-9 present the reasons for the troubles in Jerusalem and Judah, v. 10 gives instructions (Is the Lord speaking to the prophet?) to reassure the innocent, and v. 11 is a woe of judgment against the guilty. Verse 12 could be seen as a summary of the previous accusations against the ruling class, but expressed in the tone of a lament over the fate of the people. The clearest unit of this section is vv. 13-15, Yahweh's lawsuit, but it has two distinct

introductions. In v. 13 the Lord is said to judge "the peoples," but in v. 14 the Lord's case is against "the elders and princes of his people." Consequently, 3:1-15 is not an original unit of discourse; rather, it consists of several different prophecies against Judah and Jerusalem, only secondarily collected under the common theme of leadership.

3:1-8. The word כִּי (kî), which begins the section, often translated "For," is better understood as an asseveration, an emphatic declaration, and thus translated "Surely" (cf. the NIV's "See now"). As vv. 2-3 make clear, the "support" and "staff" of v. 1 are metaphors for leadership. Their interpretation to mean food and water (v. 1b) is almost certainly secondary, a note by some prosaic soul who could not leave the poetry alone. The interpretation basically misses the point. What will be lost is the leadership upon which the people can lean. So the announcement that leaders will be lost is not judgment only upon the ruling classes, but upon the population as a whole.

The list of offices and officeholders the Lord will take away (vv. 2-3) provides insight into the social structure of leadership in ancient Jerusalem and

51. See Wildberger, *Isaiah 1–12,* 126.

Judah. The roster includes official and unofficial positions, professionals and amateurs—that is, those who earn their living from their office and those who do not—as well as both legitimate and illegitimate functionaries. The catalog would seem at first glance to include all those upon whom the people might lean for "support." Curiously, however, it leaves out the king and the priest.[52] It is not difficult to account for the omission of the king, who, in Isaiah's theology, has a special divinely appointed role and, in any case, would represent a level of authority above those being enumerated. But why the priest is left out remains a mystery, especially since the prophet appears in the list and Isaiah certainly was capable of reprimanding the priesthood (28:7-10). There is no evidence to support the suggestion that a later—and presumably priestly—hand deleted an original reference to priests.[53]

The "skillful magician and expert enchanter" seem out of place in a list of otherwise legitimate offices. If these functions were not explicitly prohibited (cf. Deut 18:9-14 and 1 Sam 28:9), they certainly were held in suspicion by authorized leaders, and elsewhere Isaiah condemns similar practices (2:6). They must be included here to indicate that all to whom the people might turn for guidance will be swept away.

The Lord's declaration in v. 4 to "make boys their princes" and cause "babes" to rule over them certainly is bad news, an announcement of punishment. The experienced leaders will be replaced with children. Metaphorically, one might take this to mean that the leaders will act like children or will be replaced because they have acted childishly. Remarkably, a similar image stands at the heart of the announcement of peace in Isa 11:6: "and a little child shall lead them" (NRSV)—that is, will lead the animals. But in this text children do not personify innocence, but inexperience and perhaps even ignorance. As vv. 5-7 make clear, the rule by children signals chaos, the kind of social disorder that is the opposite of šālôm, or peace. Everyone will be oppressed by someone else; insolence will replace respect for the elder and the honorable citizen (v. 5). Anarchy will reach the point at which anyone thought to have a cloak will be asked by his relatives to be a leader, but he will refuse (vv. 6-7). Thus judgment against the leaders turns out to bring suffering upon the people as a whole.

Finally, the reasons (v. 8) for this disorder are set out, although in vague and general terms. That Jerusalem "has stumbled" and Judah "has fallen" has a double meaning. It refers both to the chaotic state of the society described in the previous verses and also to the cause of that turmoil, the people's stumbling out of its path, their falling away from loyalty to the Lord. The second half of the verse is somewhat more concrete, but still not very specific. The people's "speech" and "deeds" are against the Lord. What they have said or done is not stated, only that they have defied the Lord's "glorious presence." Clearly they have acted with disloyalty and disrespect, but we are not told how.

Attempting to connect this unit of discourse to a particular historical situation is futile. To be sure, specific events and occasions lie behind these words, but the allusions to those events and occasions are not sufficiently specific to allow us to reconstruct or even date them. The removal of Jerusalem's leadership may refer to deportation by a foreign power. It is not even clear, however, that a foreign power is in view, or if so which one and when.[54] Virtually all that is specified in this section could be the result of corrupt leadership leading to anarchy, and this could have occurred virtually any time during the monarchic period in Judah.

3:9-12. These verses, which do not comprise a clear and distinct unit of discourse, continue the theme of chaos in Jerusalem because of the failures of the people. The antecedents of "their" and "them" in v. 9 (i.e., the ones accused) are the people of Jerusalem and Judah (as in v. 8), and not the leading citizens listed in vv. 2-3. In this context, the loss of the leadership is a judgment on the people, who suffer from the resulting disorder and confusion. The first half of v. 9 alludes to the "sin" of the people but makes a further accusation: Their sin is obvious ("The look on their faces"), they seem even to be proud of it ("proclaim their sin"), and they have no shame ("do not hide it"). The second half of v. 9 contains the first of two "woe" sayings in the unit, emphasizing that the sinners will reap what they have sown. Disaster has been set into motion by their sinful actions (see 1:4-9; see also the Commentary on 1:4-9).

---

52. Ibid., 129.
53. Kaiser, *Isaiah 1–12*, 41.

54. Sweeney finds in 3:1-9 allusions to the aftermath of Hezekiah's revolt against Assyria in 701 BCE. See Sweeney, *Isaiah 1–39,* 109.

Verses 10-11 interpret the point of v. 9*b,* that actions bring their appropriate results. Verse 10 turns from curse to blessing as the speaker tells someone to address the righteous with a word of reassurance. Just as sinners bring evil upon themselves, so also the righteous will "eat the fruit of their labors." If one defines the sinners by their speech and deeds against the Lord (v. 8), then the righteous must be those who do not defy but honor the Lord's "glorious presence." Then in v. 11 the second "woe" saying repeats the point of the first one: What the "guilty" do will be done to them. The trouble that follows transgression thus is not necessarily the result of divine judgment and intervention to punish, but the consequence of the actions themselves.

The mood and tone shift in v. 12 to the somber notes of a lament in which the Lord grieves over the fate of the people of Jerusalem and Judah. The grounds for that grief return to the themes of vv. 1-8, the chaos and confusion because of the loss of good leadership. But the problem is characterized in two ways. In the first half of the verse, children oppress the people and women rule them, recalling v. 4, where "boys" and "babes" take the place of the established authorities. Here there can be no mistaking the implications concerning the place of women in the ancient society. That women rule over the people is taken as both a disaster and an insult. But in the second half of the verse the "leaders" who mislead and confuse very likely are those established authorities themselves. This puts a different twist on the theme of the section. Whereas the loss of leadership has been seen as the result of the people's sins, here the leaders themselves are held responsible for chaos in the society.

3:13-15. As in 1:2-20, the Lord presents accusations in the form of a lawsuit. This one has two distinct introductions. The first (v. 13) is strange in this context, for the prophet reports that the Lord is arguing a case in which God will "judge the peoples." The NIV smooths the tension between the two beginnings by translating the Hebrew plural in the singular, "people" (עם *'am*) (the LXX reads "his people" [ὁ λαός αὐτοῦ *ho laos autou*]). But the plural "peoples" (עמים *'ammîm*) is a common term in Isaiah, used to designate the nations of the world (e.g., 2:3-4; 8:9; 10:13-14; 11:10; 14:6). Both the context and the substance of the indictment (vv. 14*b*-15) support the conclusion that the introduction of v. 13 is secondary. In the second introduction (v. 14*a*), the prophet reports that the Lord is entering into "judgment"—or opening a suit—against "the elders and princes of his people." Then, in vv. 13*b*-14 the Lord speaks. Given what has been said in 3:1-12, a trial scene at this point is not surprising. One would anticipate an announcement of judgment following the accusations or reasons for punishment set out in vv. 1-12. But that is not what transpires. Yahweh does not announce judgment, but convenes the court and initiates a legal process against the accused, assuming the role of a plaintiff. The procedure begins—as the trial should—with accusations, a presentation of what the elders and princes have done that justifies a lawsuit. The accusations are in the form of direct address to the accused and begin with a metaphor: The elders and princes have "devoured the vineyard." This metaphor is used and explained in 5:1-7: "The vineyard of the LORD of hosts is the house of Israel, and the people of Judah are his pleasant planting" (5:7). Then follows a concrete and specific accusation: "The spoil of the poor is in your houses"—that is, the Lord accuses the elders and princes of robbing the poor. Finally, in a style appropriate for a legal argument, the accusation is stated in the form of rhetorical questions (v. 15). The leaders of the Lord's people are hauled into court to answer for "crushing" those very people, for oppressing the poor. The parallel lines of this accusation strongly suggest that "the poor" and the people of God ("my people") are the same.[55] These concluding lines are the clearest indication of the reasons for the Lord's removal of the leaders of Judah and Jerusalem, set out in vv. 1-13.

---

55. Wildberger, *Isaiah 1–12*, 144.

REFLECTIONS

Power is the concern that drives this discourse, political and economic power considered in terms of a society's leadership. It is difficult to read Isaiah, or any of the other prophetic books, and not be moved to reflect on the structures of power. What are the dangers of political and economic power? Are they inherently evil? Is it wrong for some to exert authority over others in a society?

Isaiah 3:1-15 addresses some of these questions directly, announcing that the Lord will remove all structures of authority because the leaders have abused their power. But indirectly and unintentionally the text reveals some important perspectives on politics.

There are few societies that have not experienced the chaos described here, the anarchy resulting from the loss of all traditional leadership. In fact, many societies seem to live on the edge of such disorder. That the Lord will remove Jerusalem's leading officers and offices is a disaster, not just for those leaders but for the society as a whole. By viewing the removal of leaders as judgment, the text affirms the importance of the exercise of power by those in leadership. Anarchy, including disrespect for the elderly and the honorable (3:5), becomes the alternative to order and peace.

But the prophets never hold political and religious leadership—up to and including the king—above the law or above criticism. And who has not railed against leadership, against those in power? Isaiah certainly raises his voice against politicians as well as religious leaders. What is the perspective from which these accusations against leaders come? Neither Isaiah nor the editors of this text are revolutionaries calling for the overthrow of the established order, or even for the removal of particular leaders. There is no critique of the social structure as such, calling for a new order—e.g., the powerless rising up to challenge those in authority. Quite the contrary. In Isaiah—if not in all the prophets—the criticism comes from within the structures of power, from a member of that very ruling class. It is not the structures of power or the political system, but the exercise of power, leaders who mislead (3:12), and especially the abuse of political power for economic oppression (3:15) that undermine the structures of the society. Moreover, those who have authority bear the burden of greater responsibility for the well-being of a society.

All reflections on law and order are limited by cultural circumstances. This text, like so much of the biblical tradition, presumes particular social, political, and economic frameworks as the norm. Inadvertently, this text reveals some of the problems inherent in a traditional patriarchal structure: Leaders who mislead are ridiculed as women (3:12), although there are many examples of women as strong and effective leaders in ancient Israel. Certainly some systems of power are better than others. Some provide more order, and others provide more justice. But how can one determine which is better? This text suggests two criteria, one moral and the other theological. The moral test is the protection of the politically weak and the economically poor (3:15). Theologically, this text—with the overwhelming weight of the biblical tradition on its side—affirms that all structures of power and all political and religious leaders must be evaluated in the light of God's justice.

Isaiah 3:16–4:1, Judgment Against Jerusalem's Women

NIV

[16]The LORD says,
"The women of Zion are haughty,
walking along with outstretched necks,
flirting with their eyes,
tripping along with mincing steps,
with ornaments jingling on their ankles.
[17]Therefore the Lord will bring sores on the
heads of the women of Zion;
the LORD will make their scalps bald."

[18]In that day the Lord will snatch away their
finery: the bangles and headbands and crescent
necklaces, [19]the earrings and bracelets and veils,
[20]the headdresses and ankle chains and sashes,
the perfume bottles and charms, [21]the signet rings
and nose rings, [22]the fine robes and the capes and
cloaks, the purses [23]and mirrors, and the linen
garments and tiaras and shawls.

[24]Instead of fragrance there will be a stench;
instead of a sash, a rope;
instead of well-dressed hair, baldness;
instead of fine clothing, sackcloth;
instead of beauty, branding.
[25]Your men will fall by the sword,
your warriors in battle.
[26]The gates of Zion will lament and mourn;
destitute, she will sit on the ground.

4 In that day seven women
will take hold of one man
and say, "We will eat our own food
and provide our own clothes;
only let us be called by your name.
Take away our disgrace!"

NRSV

[16] The LORD said:
Because the daughters of Zion are haughty
and walk with outstretched necks,
glancing wantonly with their eyes,
mincing along as they go,
tinkling with their feet;
[17] the Lord will afflict with scabs
the heads of the daughters of Zion,
and the LORD will lay bare their secret parts.

[18]In that day the Lord will take away the finery of the anklets, the headbands, and the cres-
cents; [19]the pendants, the bracelets, and the
scarfs; [20]the headdresses, the armlets, the sashes,
the perfume boxes, and the amulets; [21]the signet
rings and nose rings; [22]the festal robes, the man-
tles, the cloaks, and the handbags; [23]the garments
of gauze, the linen garments, the turbans, and the
veils.

[24] Instead of perfume there will be a stench;
and instead of a sash, a rope;
and instead of well-set hair, baldness;
and instead of a rich robe, a binding of
sackcloth;
instead of beauty, shame.[a]
[25] Your men shall fall by the sword
and your warriors in battle.
[26] And her gates shall lament and mourn;
ravaged, she shall sit upon the ground.

4 Seven women shall take hold of one man
in that day, saying,
"We will eat our own bread and wear our
own clothes;
just let us be called by your name;
take away our disgrace."

[a]Q Ms: MT lacks shame

COMMENTARY

This section clearly is distinct from the preceding one (vv. 1-15), mainly in its shift of theme from the leaders in Judah and Jerusalem to the women of the capital city. But the two are linked in that this unit picks up a motif that appeared in 3:12: the role of women. Moreover, both units press accusations against particular groups and not against the people as a whole. Most important, these verses continue the general topic of judgment against Jerusalem because of the sins and failures of its inhabitants, prophesying disaster in the form of military defeat.

As with 3:1-15, there are cracks in the surface of the text that suggest the section has been assembled from previously independent units of discourse. The introduction (3:16, "The LORD said") is inconsistent with the subsequent speech, which refers to the Lord in the third person (3:17-18). Consequently, it is unclear whom we are to understand to be the speaker. A coherent judgment speech against Jerusalem's leading women (3:16-17, 24) is disrupted by 3:18-23. This list of rich clothing and jewelry certainly is a secondary editorial expansion. It is prose in the middle of poetry, and it interrupts the clear flow of the address. Another shift occurs in 3:25-26, where the feminine pronouns refer not to the women of the city but to the city itself, personified as a woman.

3:16-24. Like so many prophecies of judgment in the prophetic literature, this one has two main parts. The first is the indictment or presentation of reasons for punishment (v. 16). Exceptional, however, is the introduction of those reasons with "because" (יַעַן כִּי *ya'an kî*) instead of making the logical connection after the reasons and before the announcement proper. (By omitting "because" in v. 16 and beginning v. 17 with "Therefore," the NIV translates to reflect the more common pattern.) Neither the charge nor the pronouncement of punishment is addressed directly to the accused, who are spoken of in the third person. The reasons for punishment are stated first in general terms ("Because the daughters of Zion are haughty") and then are elaborated by describing the posture and attire of the women of Jerusalem (the remainder of v. 16).

Likewise, the announcement of judgment,

which spells out the effects of a military defeat, moves from a more comprehensive or general statement (v. 17) to a series of comparisons between the present beauty and attire of the women to the horrors of their impending situation (vv. 18-23). The meaning of the last line of v. 17 is uncertain. That the Lord will "lay bare their secret parts" (NRSV) would refer to captives stripped naked. The more accurate reading is "make their scalps bald" (NIV), which forms a closer parallel to the first half of the verse and is a more likely meaning of the words in question. This interpretation is accepted by most modern translations and contemporary commentators.[56] Baldness, like nakedness, refers to the humiliation of captives shorn of their long hair.

Verse 24 continues to sketch the image of judgment with a series of graphic contrasts between the former beauty of Jerusalem's women and their future disgrace. That future goes beyond humiliation. All the images correspond to what is known to happen to women of cities defeated in warfare: the "stench" of death, the "rope" of captivity, the "baldness" already promised. The "sackcloth" that will replace the "rich robe" refers either to poverty or to mourning or to both. The list of rich clothing and jewelry in vv. 18-23, a commentary both on what precedes and what follows, adds little of substance. Still, it emphasizes the image of the women of Isaiah's Jerusalem as wealthy and pretentious, and soon to lose all reasons for conceit.

3:25–4:1. References to female figures continue, as does the description of future judgment in terms of military disaster, but the victim of the suffering has shifted. The pronouns "your" (fem. sing.), "her," and "she" in vv. 25-26 now refer to the city of Jerusalem, personified as a woman. What had begun as an announcement concerning the actual "daughters of Zion" (vv. 16-17) evokes the metaphor of "daughter Zion," although that actual expression does not appear here (cf. 1:8; 10:32; 16:1; 37:22). Verse 25 looks both backward and forward, connecting the indictment of the women to the city. Thus the prophecy against the

---

56. For example, O. Kaiser, *Isaiah 1–12: A Commentary,* trans. R. A. Wilson (Philadelphia: Westminster, 1972) 48; H. Wildberger, *Isaiah 1–12,* trans. Thomas H. Trapp (Minneapolis: Fortress, 1991) 149-50.

women of Jerusalem is expanded to include the city as a whole. But still the plight of the women is prominent (4:1), although it is no longer restricted to those who are "haughty." No specific indictment of the city is presented. In the present form of the text one could presume that the judgment is the continuation of vv. 16-24, and therefore the pride or haughtiness of the women will bring disaster upon the city.

The death of the men, and especially the warriors (v. 25), is presented from the perspective of their mothers, wives, and daughters and its effects on them. So Zion is personified as a woman ravaged, wailing a dirge, and sitting on the ground in the posture of mourning (v. 26). In the context of 3:16–4:1, although the scope is broadened from a particular group of women to the city as a whole,

the punishment fits the crime: Haughtiness and pretension lead to disgrace; pride is transformed into shame. If there had been any doubt about the dependent status of women in ancient Jerusalem, it is removed by the words of the widows and orphans cited in 4:1. The emphasis is not on their obvious economic dependence, for the women vow to provide their own food and clothing. The concern is their "disgrace," which will have included lack of protection. Thus seven women are heard to plead with one man to marry them. The expression "called by your name" comes from the marriage ceremony and in this case paints a picture of polygamy. All security is lost; the women are in danger and afraid, most of the men are dead, and drastic measures are called for.

REFLECTIONS

In many respects, Isa 3:16–4:1 is an embarrassing reminder of the perception of women and their roles in ancient Israel and in many biblical texts. The well-dressed and "haughty" women are an easy target for condemnation and blame, just as are the women of Samaria for Amos, who calls them "cows of Bashan" (4:1-3). In Hosea and Ezekiel women are the symbolic personification of unfaithfulness to Yahweh (Ezekiel 16; 23; Hosea 1–3). But unfaithfulness in the sense of selling oneself to other gods is not a central issue in Isaiah 1–39. Here it is the behavior and attitude of the women that come under attack. Even when the prophetic voice can muster a measure of compassion for the widowed women of Jerusalem (4:1), it reflects the patriarchal double standard. The polygamy behind this image is a specific type: Marriage of one man to more than one wife is allowed, but not the reverse. And the widows, even if they can provide for themselves, are humiliated and defenseless if they do not bear a man's name. So even when the women's voices are heard, they are quoted by and from the perspective of men.

The description of the women's behavior in 3:16 as "glancing wantonly with their eyes" (NRSV) or "flirting with their eyes" (NIV) indicates that the issue is not only gender but also sex and sexuality. Women in particular are blamed for sexual corruption. Does this characterization feed the image—or the male fantasy—of women as sexually hungry, and at the same time as sex objects?

The issues are far from simple. This is not the only thing Isaiah or the book of Isaiah says, and it is not only women who are singled out for blame. In the immediately preceding section it was the male political and economic leadership. But here women are shown to share responsibility. And more may be suggested by the juxtaposition of these units. The context, especially 3:1-15, is concerned with power, political and economic. It is not strange that the other major and persistent human concern, sex and sexuality, should follow. Moreover, the accusation against the women concerns not only gender but class as well. Wealth and elevated social status are suggested by the women's attire and attitude.

So reading this text evokes reflection on gender relationships and on the place of women in the structures of power. In modern times we have come to recognize how biblical texts such as this one undergird and shape demeaning and unfair images of women, and how the biblical tradition has been used to limit the role and power of women in society. When read in the context of Isaiah 1–39 and of the scriptures as a whole, this narrow and negative view of half the human race must be rejected and replaced with one that refuses to base worth or authority on gender but instead affirms that male and female are equally children of God.

Isaiah 4:2-6, Jerusalem Purified and Protected

NIV

²In that day the Branch of the LORD will be beautiful and glorious, and the fruit of the land will be the pride and glory of the survivors in Israel. ³Those who are left in Zion, who remain in Jerusalem, will be called holy, all who are recorded among the living in Jerusalem. ⁴The Lord will wash away the filth of the women of Zion; he will cleanse the bloodstains from Jerusalem by a spirit[a] of judgment and a spirit[a] of fire. ⁵Then the LORD will create over all of Mount Zion and over those who assemble there a cloud of smoke by day and a glow of flaming fire by night; over all the glory will be a canopy. ⁶It will be a shelter and shade from the heat of the day, and a refuge and hiding place from the storm and rain.

[a]4 Or the Spirit

NRSV

2On that day the branch of the LORD shall be beautiful and glorious, and the fruit of the land shall be the pride and glory of the survivors of Israel. ³Whoever is left in Zion and remains in Jerusalem will be called holy, everyone who has been recorded for life in Jerusalem, ⁴once the Lord has washed away the filth of the daughters of Zion and cleansed the bloodstains of Jerusalem from its midst by a spirit of judgment and by a spirit of burning. ⁵Then the LORD will create over the whole site of Mount Zion and over its places of assembly a cloud by day and smoke and the shining of a flaming fire by night. Indeed over all the glory there will be a canopy. ⁶It will serve as a pavilion, a shade by day from the heat, and a refuge and a shelter from the storm and rain.

COMMENTARY

Isaiah 2:1-5 and 4:2-6 are the bookends to the collection of materials in chaps. 2–4, surrounding a section full of words of disaster with the language of hope. Both units place Zion at the center of that hope. But there are significant differences between these two expressions of confidence in the future. The unit before us is more prosaic and more self-preoccupied than 2:1-5. There is no pilgrimage of the peoples to Zion and no concern with the establishment of justice and peace among nations, but there is concern with the sanctification of the survivors in the city. Jerusalem is not the center of justice but a sanctuary for the elect. In the organization of the book, 4:2-6 is a response to the immediately preceding announcement of judgment on Daughter Zion. The content of this unit moves a few steps from a prophetic to an apocalyptic understanding of the future, but formally it resembles prophecies of salvation. However, it is presented neither as a vision of the future nor as a message from God. It is, rather, a third-person description of the Lord's future saving acts.[57]

Most modern commentators have correctly taken this unit to be a relatively late addition to the book of Isaiah. Its prosaic style and content are quite different from other texts in the context, and its historical perspective is much later than the eighth century BCE, presuming that the destruction announced has taken place. The theological language and outlook, including the radical transformation of circumstances in history, correspond to those of the Persian period in Judah. It is less certain that the expansion took place in two stages, first v. 2 and then vv. 3-6,[58] although it is clear that v. 2 speaks of "Israel" and vv. 3-6 of Zion and Jerusalem.

This description of future salvation does not deny the validity of the old prophecies of judgment but sees beyond them. In effect, it affirms that the prophecies—as the creative word of God—have been effective and that their goal was the purification of the city of Jerusalem and its inhabitants. Thus this late text, like many others in the prophetic books, reinterprets the prophetic tradition and applies it to a new situation. The authors

57. Marvin A. Sweeney, *Isaiah 1–39, With an Introduction to Prophetic Literature,* FOTL XVI (Grand Rapids: Eerdmans, 1996) 109.

58. So H. Wildberger, *Isaiah 1–12,* trans. Thomas H. Trapp (Minneapolis: Fortress, 1991) 164-65, and others.

do not see themselves as living in this time of salvation, but they still look forward to it. Judgment has come, but even more lies ahead. The promises and expectations expressed here presume certain problems for the residents of Jerusalem, including the shortage of food and insecurity. And not so remarkably, those who have survived or will survive see themselves as the righteous remnant, purified and sanctified in the fires of judgment.

The section has a remarkable concentration of theologically significant expressions, many of which echo in later Hebrew scriptures, intertestamental literature, and the New Testament. It begins with a temporal phrase, "on that day," which many have taken to be eschatological. The formula has deep roots in ancient Israel's traditions, probably referring to the day of the Lord's victory in the holy war. Amos in particular turns that old hope around, seeing the day as one of judgment upon Israel (Amos 5:18-20). "That day" in 4:2 is not the end of time, as it will come to be in later apocalyptic literature. Reinforcing an eschatological reading of the text is the interpretation—as early as the Targum—of "the branch of the LORD" (v. 2) as the Messiah. The NIV has expressed a similar understanding by capitalizing "Branch." But the context, in which "branch" parallels "fruit of the land," strongly suggests a hope for the fertility and fruitfulness of the land. Such pictures are common in similar visions of the coming age of salvation (e.g., Amos 9:13-15).

References to "the survivors of Israel" (v. 2) and "whoever is left in Zion and remains in Jerusalem" (v. 3) pick up the idea of a remnant left over from judgment. The image, if not always the same language, appears frequently in Isaiah (1:9; 6:13; 10:19-22; 11:11, 16; 37:32; see also Amos 5:3). It is possible that these escapees were thought to have survived because they were more righteous than those who were destroyed. But it is more likely that they will be "called holy" (v. 3) because they were "recorded among the living in Jerusalem" (v. 3)—that is, they have been purified by the purging fire and not saved because they were already pure. Purification here is different from the ritual cleansing in 1:9. In this case it

appears to be once and for all, along with the transformation of the city. The expression "recorded for life" suggests, but does not refer to, the later "book of life" containing the names of those who will be saved in a final judgment (Phil 4:3; Rev 3:5; 13:8; 20:15), but more likely to a census of those who survived.

Although allusion to "the filth of the daughters of Zion" (v. 4) picks up the theme of 3:16-24, it is far more harsh than anything set out in chap. 3, seeming to blame divine judgment on the women of Jerusalem. The LXX spreads the responsibility to the people as a whole by inserting "sons" after "daughters." The "bloodstains" most likely refer to blood guilt, the culpability incurred through particular crimes and sins (cf. Exod 22:1; 1 Sam 25:26).

Themes from the Pentateuch fuel the images of v. 5. The main verb, "create" (ברא $b\bar{a}r\bar{a}'$), is the one used in Genesis 1, and in the Hebrew it never refers to human activity. The background of the "cloud by day and smoke and the shining of a flaming fire by night" can only be the smoke and fire leading Israel in the wilderness (Exod 13:21-22; 40:34-38). Here, however, it stays put over the holy city as a symbol of the protective presence of God. "All the glory" suggests the presence of God, as in the wilderness traditions and elsewhere in Isaiah (6:3; 10:16; 24:23). It is surprising that there would be a "canopy" over even the divine presence, but in Exod 40:34 "the cloud covered the tent of meeting, and the glory of the LORD filled the tabernacle." In Isa 2:10, 19-21 the glory of the Lord is terrifying; here it is a comforting presence.

The passage concludes (v. 6) with the image of Zion as a safe and secure place, where the holy remnant is afforded protection from the natural forces of the sun and the rain. Although the weather is not domesticated, it is not experienced as a problem. And what would even the sanctified people of God do without sun and rain? More directly, this final peaceful image introduces some tension into the unit: How can nature be fruitful (v. 2) without the sun and the rain?

REFLECTIONS

1. Along with most modern commentaries, this one has concluded that this text is a relatively late addition to the book of Isaiah. What bearing does such a conclusion have on the authority readers attribute to it? Especially in an earlier critical age, terms such as "secondary" and "inauthentic," particularly when applied to prophetic literature, reflected negative value judgments. Behind such evaluations lay the assumption that the authentic Word of God was communicated by the original prophet, who had presumably heard that word directly from God. But to disparage or even delete texts—as some critics have done—because they are determined to be later than the words of the original prophet is to confuse judgments of "fact" with judgments of "value." Why should one privilege the earliest stage of the tradition, or words that one attributes to the inspired individual whose name stands at the heading of the book (see Reflections at 1:1)? All the words in Isaiah are equally canonical. They are not all equally profound or valid in the context of the canon as a whole, but value judgments need to rest on theological or moral foundations rather than historical ones. With this text we have one model of how subsequent readers and writers engaged the sacred traditions in their own times. So if the authors of the biblical texts can interpret and reinterpret the scriptures handed down to them, so can modern readers. The authors of this particular text were guided in their understanding of the old tradition by theological principles, especially their confidence in God's will to save. Such a principle may likewise guide modern readers as they evaluate individual texts.

2. The community that developed this description of salvation knew the old prophetic announcements of judgment and the tragic history that included the destruction of Jerusalem. That knowledge left them with questions that trouble all communities of faith. Can any good come out of disaster? Has God abandoned them? After all, they believed that catastrophes were God's judgment on their sins and the sins of their ancestors.

Contemplation of human disaster and the ways of God can lead in many directions. One limit on that reflection seems always to have been accepted in the Old Testament: The unity of God will not be compromised. There is no demonic force to blame for trouble. History is seen to be the result of the interaction of God and human beings. The community behind this description of salvation has accepted culpability and then looks to the future. That is another way that tradition shapes this vision: Affirmation of faith is preceded by confession of sin. People who experience the world as unsatisfying or outright dangerous affirm that God's ultimate will is peace and security. No, God has not and will not abandon them or us. Remarkably, a spiritual vision of purification, sanctification, and the presence of God is framed by attention to ordinary physical concerns, envisioning a time when there will be no shortage of food and shelter. Suffering—at least the particular suffering of Jerusalem—has a purpose and direction: the sanctification of those who survive.

Doubtless it is easier for people in our time who have experienced disaster to identify with the hope for a day when all will be made right than it is to see a meaning in disasters, whether natural or caused by human agency. Often, however, one hears victims who have experienced natural disasters, yet who escaped with their lives, say they will never be the same. That may or may not be perceived as purification, but it certainly is transformation. Or one who has caused a disaster, such as a deadly automobile accident while intoxicated, will find it difficult if not impossible to face life without confessing and acknowledging responsibility.

ISAIAH 5:1-30, JUSTICE, WOES, AND JUDGMENT

OVERVIEW

If we view chap. 5 as a whole, its coherence and import are clear enough. There is a distinct beginning with the song of the vineyard (vv. 1-7), a series of accusations in the form of seven woe speeches (vv. 8-24), and an announcement of judgment (vv. 25-30), including the summons to a distant people. A certain progress of thought is recognizable, from a general accusation to more specific indictments to a comprehensive announcement of judgment. Moreover, chap. 6 marks the beginning of a new unit, with a shift from speeches to a first-person report of the prophet's vocation.

But viewed in the larger context, it seems that chap. 5 has reached an end, but not yet a conclusion. The problem arises when we observe that the woes and the refrain ("For all this his anger has not turned away, and his hand is stretched out still," v. 25) are resumed after 9:8. Furthermore, 6:1–9:8 is a relatively coherent section on its own. These features are best accounted for in terms of the history of the composition of the book. It

seems most likely that 6:1–9:8 was inserted into a previously completed collection. Many commentators have treated 9:8–10:4 with 5:1-30, thus attempting to restore a previous unity.[59] Although the disjunctions are more obvious than the connections between the sections, the present sequence probably made sense to someone at some stage of the book's development. However, attempts to discern its coherence or purpose have been unsuccessful.[60] Nevertheless, since the order is the only one we have, the texts are best examined in their biblical sequence.

59. Wildberger treats the woe speech in 10:1-4 with the others in 5:28-24 and deals with 5:25-30 when he takes up 9:8-20. See H. Wildberger, *Isaiah 1–12,* trans. Thomas H. Trapp (Minneapolis: Fortress, 1991) 188-245.

60. This includes efforts to explain the organization in terms of some historically arranged presentation. Seitz argues that the materials at the end of chap. 5 have been placed before 6:1–9:8 so as to set the material in chaps. 6–9 concerning the Syro-Ephraimite war in the Assyrian context. See Christopher R. Seitz, *Isaiah 1–39,* Interpretation (Louisville: John Knox, 1993) 26, 30. Not only are the historical allusions vague, but also it is unclear why such a presentation would be important for the author or editor and the readers.

Isaiah 5:1-7, The Song of the Vineyard

NIV	NRSV

5 I will sing for the one I love
    a song about his vineyard:
My loved one had a vineyard
    on a fertile hillside.
²He dug it up and cleared it of stones
    and planted it with the choicest vines.
He built a watchtower in it
    and cut out a winepress as well.
Then he looked for a crop of good grapes,
    but it yielded only bad fruit.
 	
³"Now you dwellers in Jerusalem and men
        of Judah,
    judge between me and my vineyard.
⁴What more could have been done for my
        vineyard
    than I have done for it?
	5 Let me sing for my beloved
	        my love-song concerning his vineyard:
	My beloved had a vineyard
	    on a very fertile hill.
	²He dug it and cleared it of stones,
	    and planted it with choice vines;
	he built a watchtower in the midst of it,
	    and hewed out a wine vat in it;
	he expected it to yield grapes,
	    but it yielded wild grapes.
	
	³And now, inhabitants of Jerusalem
	    and people of Judah,
	judge between me
	    and my vineyard.
	⁴What more was there to do for my vineyard
	    that I have not done in it?

NIV

When I looked for good grapes,
    why did it yield only bad?
⁵Now I will tell you
    what I am going to do to my vineyard:
I will take away its hedge,
    and it will be destroyed;
I will break down its wall,
    and it will be trampled.
⁶I will make it a wasteland,
    neither pruned nor cultivated,
    and briers and thorns will grow there.
I will command the clouds
    not to rain on it."

⁷The vineyard of the LORD Almighty
    is the house of Israel,
and the men of Judah
    are the garden of his delight.
And he looked for justice, but saw bloodshed;
    for righteousness, but heard cries of distress.

NRSV

When I expected it to yield grapes,
    why did it yield wild grapes?

⁵And now I will tell you
    what I will do to my vineyard.
I will remove its hedge,
    and it shall be devoured;
I will break down its wall,
    and it shall be trampled down.
⁶I will make it a waste;
    it shall not be pruned or hoed,
    and it shall be overgrown with briers
      and thorns;
I will also command the clouds
    that they rain no rain upon it.

⁷For the vineyard of the LORD of hosts
    is the house of Israel,
and the people of Judah
    are his pleasant planting;
he expected justice,
    but saw bloodshed;
righteousness,
    but heard a cry!

COMMENTARY

This passage, one of the most famous in Isaiah, is a self-contained unit, quite distinct from what precedes and what follows. It begins with a definitive introduction, moves to a clear conclusion, and is followed (vv. 8-24) by a series of indictments that generally carry forward the theme—criticism of the behavior of the people—but in a very different form. It comes to us as the account of a rhetorically compelling prophetic address to the people of Jerusalem and Judah.

The fundamental point of this unit is clear and relatively simple, but the route to that point is circuitous and sophisticated. Is this really a song? If so, what kind? Who is speaking, and on behalf of whom? In many cases in prophetic literature, identification of speaker or genre is difficult because of problems in the history of composition, but in this instance the mystery is part of the rhetorical design. Initially, the speaker announces that he will sing a song, but when one examines the unit

as a whole, it becomes clear that the song is limited to vv. 1*b*-2. If it is not a song, then what is it? In order to understand just what kind of literature this is, and how the speaker leads us to the conclusion in v. 7, we will need to chart the shifts of speaker or role and the outline of the poem.

Readers as well as hearers are to understand that the speaker who issues the call in v. 1 is the prophet Isaiah of Jerusalem, in the eighth century BCE. But what role does he assume? In vv. 1-2 the prophet speaks as the friend of the bridegroom. Decisive here is the translation of לידידי (*lîdîdî*, "my beloved," NRSV) as "my friend,"[61] and the realization that in the song he does not speak of his own "vineyard" but that of another. The prophet asks to sing a "love song," but on behalf of his friend, a bridegroom. Already in the first half-verse, three characters appear: (1) the prophet

---

61. See Ronald E. Clements, *Isaiah 1–39*, NCB (Grand Rapids: Eerdmans, 1980) 58; Wildberger, *Isaiah 1–12*, 175, 179-80.

as friend of (2) the bridegroom and (3) the vineyard as the bride. It is common in Hebrew love poetry for the vineyard to represent the beloved (Cant 1:6, 14; 2:15; 8:12). In vv. 3-6, the prophet assumes another role, that of the owner of the vineyard, who speaks now for himself. That owner brings charges against his vineyard, reporting as if in court, asking the audience to act as judge (v. 3). He argues that he had done everything necessary to promote growth, but the vineyard had failed him. So he announces the punishment. Roles shift again in v. 7 when the prophet speaks as prophet, indicting Israel on behalf of Yahweh. This application makes transparent what had only been hinted at in v. 6 ("I will command the clouds"): that the owner is Yahweh, and the vineyard is Israel. Thus it turns out that in the initial love song Isaiah had spoken as the friend of Yahweh.

Once he has the attention of the audience, the prophet begins a love song (v. 1*b*), perhaps even singing one already known in Israel. But already in v. 2 the tone and contents of the song have changed to suit his purpose, ending in an accusation against the "vineyard": "He expected it to yield grapes, but it yielded wild grapes" (v. 2). Then, in the role of the owner of the vineyard, the prophet addresses the audience directly. First (vv. 3-4), he asks that they "judge between me and my vineyard" (v. 3)—that is, determine which of the two is guilty of failure. Second (vv. 5-6), the owner, assuming that the verdict is against the vineyard, pronounces judgment on the vineyard. He will execute that judgment, returning the land to a waste and even prohibiting the clouds from raining on it.

It appears, then, that what began as a song, and a love song at that, has now become a trial in which Isaiah, on behalf of and even speaking for the owner of the "vineyard," argues a case before an Israelite audience. The closest parallel to this passage is the prophet Nathan's confrontation of David with the parable of the poor man's lamb (2 Sam 12:1-15). After David has taken Bathsheba and had her husband Uriah killed, Nathan comes to David with the tale of a rich man who stole a poor man's favorite lamb. David responds in anger against the criminal, and when he pronounces judgment on the rich man, Nathan says, "You are the man" (2 Sam 12:7 NRSV). Likewise in Isa 5:1-7, the accused hear a parable that leads them to pronounce judgment on an unproductive vineyard, thereby pronouncing judgment upon themselves. There are features of various genres, especially the love song and elements of juridical process. But taken as a whole, Isa 5:1-7, like 2 Sam 12:1-15, is a juridical parable.[62]

Isaiah 5:1-7 thus has three uneven parts, recognized by clear markers or shifts in speaker or addressee. Verse 1*a* is an introduction seeking the attention of an audience, vv. 1*b*-6 contain the parable of the vineyard, and v. 7 gives the concluding application. That conclusion reveals the identity of the partners: The vineyard is Israel, and the "owner" is the Lord of hosts. Then the indictment implied in the parable is made explicit: "He expected justice, but saw bloodshed; righteousness, but heard a cry!" These concluding lines continue the sophisticated rhetoric by means of plays on words, determined by the Hebrew words for "justice" (משפט *mišpāṭ*) and "righteousness" (צדקה *ṣĕdāqâ*). He expected *mišpāṭ* ("justice") but saw משפח (*mišpāḥ,* "bloodshed"), *ṣĕdāqâ* ("righteousness") and heard צעקה (*ṣĕ'āqâ,* "a cry"). As in most good poetry there is remarkable restraint—spaces between the lines that require the hearer or reader to supply what is missing. Specifically, the conclusion (v. 7) does not go as far as the parable did. In the parable, the owner moved on from indictment to the pronouncement of judgment, but the conclusion stops with the indictment. That leaves the final emphasis on the accusation, but the implications are not to be forgotten. The hearers are left, like David in 2 Samuel 12, to apply to themselves the judgment as well as the indictment.

In the middle of the parable, the prophet, speaking as the vineyard's "owner," directly addresses the "inhabitants of Jerusalem and people of Judah" (v. 3). Finally, however, the indictment is against the "house of Israel and the people of Judah" (v. 7). For many interpreters, the meaning of "Israel" here has been a key to dating the original address, presumed to have been delivered in Jerusalem. Eventually, "Israel" came to be a comprehensive term for the chosen people, and in Isaiah it

62. J. William Whedbee, *Isaiah and Wisdom* (Nashville: Abingdon, 1971) 47; G. T. Sheppard, "More on Isaiah 5:1-7 as a Juridicial Parable," *CBQ* 44 (1982) 45-47; G. A. Yee, "A Form Critical Study of Isaiah 5:1-7 as a Song and a Juridicial Parable," *CBQ* 43 (1981) 30-40. For a summary of the alternatives, see John T. Willis, "The Genre of Isaiah 5:1-7," *JBL* 96 3 (1977) 337-62.

commonly is used in more of a religious than a political or geographical sense.[63] If "Israel" refers here to the northern kingdom, then the parable of the vineyard probably would have originated before 722 BCE, when Samaria fell to the Assyrians. But the historical allusions in the context are not sufficiently specific to allow reliable conclusions.

The accusation is comprehensive, but it lacks details. First, within the parable, the vineyard, in spite of its owner's care for it, is charged with yielding "wild grapes" (NRSV) or "bad fruit" (NIV). Before hearing the concluding application, one could take this to mean that the vineyard has failed to be what it was created to be, that it has not fulfilled its purpose. The conclusion affirms that Judah and Israel were created by the Lord ("his pleasant planting") to embody justice and righteousness, but they have instead lived by violence. The failure of justice and righteousness is a

frequent theme in the early prophets in particular (Isa 1:10-17, 21-22; Amos 5:21-24; Mic 6:6-8). "Justice," particularly in Isaiah, refers to fair and equitable relationships within society grounded in the just will of the Lord and established through honest procedures. When such justice fails, it is because the economically and/or politically powerful have taken advantage of the weak. "Righteousness" refers to that relationship with the Lord from which springs loyalty to the Lord's expectations of justice.

If the punishment of the vineyard is applied to Judah and Israel—and that is what the parable expects—then the results of the failure of justice and righteousness are devastating. It is not difficult to translate the imagery of the vineyard, "devoured," "trampled down," its wall and hedge torn down (v. 5), into a scene of enemy military triumph over Jerusalem. And as if that were not enough, the "pleasant planting" will revert to a patch of overgrown briers and thorns, on which no rain falls (v. 6).

63. "Isaiah uses 'Israel' primarily in a religious sense for the heirs of the old Davidic-Solomonic empire." Clements, *Isaiah 1–39*, 58.

REFLECTIONS

1. Quite apart from its dramatic content, the song of the vineyard is a lesson in rhetoric for preachers and teachers or anyone else who needs to communicate an important message. Sometimes the prophets use the sledgehammer, confronting their hearers directly and bluntly. The sledgehammer comes out here, but it is concealed until the very end. The approach is subtle and inviting, not only catching the attention of the audience but also drawing them into a process that leads to a decision. Moreover, like the parables of the Gospels, the song of the vineyard asks the hearers—and now the readers—to draw the conclusion, in this case to pronounce judgment upon themselves. Like David in Nathan's story of the rich man's lamb, the hearers have become convinced of the logic of the argument before recognizing that it applies to them.

2. Once again, and not for the last time, a text in Isaiah invites its readers to reflect on justice, and on justice and righteousness. That is its central concern. But the prophetic accusation is broad to the point of being open. This text does not say what injustice is or what justice should be, except to contrast justice with violence and righteousness with a cry of pain. That openness, however, can become a challenge to reflect on the meaning of justice, to fill in the blanks from our own situation and time.

"Justice" is a potent word in any language, and it is an abstraction. Consequently, everyone knows what it means, and yet no one does. It is as difficult to define as are "right" and "wrong." Fortunately, Isaiah and the other prophets seldom stop with a simple cry for justice or a condemnation of injustice; rather, they say what they mean. The various uses of "justice" may be organized into several overlapping categories, most of them familiar in our own culture. First is *distributive justice,* concerned with the equitable distribution of resources, such as land (Isa 5:8). Then there is *retributive justice,* the sense that the scales must be balanced through punishment or retribution. This is the foundation for prophetic announcements of judgment, and in virtually all legal traditions it is the foundation for sanctions against violators. If many consider retribution to be unjust, it is because it may degenerate into revenge. Others see retributive justice as supporting a basic sense of fairness, and "an eye for an eye" means *only* an eye for an eye. Any society that ignores its victims' desire for retribution, or dismisses it too quickly, does so at its peril. Justice must be done, and known to be done, or confidence in fairness dissipates, and with it the stability of the society.

A third category is *procedural justice,* which attends to the administration of justice, the rules and procedures by which a society operates to maintain itself. Long before constitutional governments or the United States Bill of Rights, the biblical tradition knew that "due process" was essential to the good society (see Amos 5:10-12).

Finally, there is *substantive justice,* that by which all other forms are defined. In the biblical perspective, the foundation of all calls for human justice is the conviction that God is just. In Isa 5:1-7, the prophet contrasts the justice and generosity of the Lord with the unjust behavior of God's people, and justice is understood in relationship to righteousness.

The most certain way to perpetuate injustice is to allow "justice" to remain in abstraction. But it is not difficult to make the prophetic call for justice specific and concrete. The existence of poverty indicates that resources—including education and opportunities—are not distributed with equity. Law courts and other institutions administering justice must be established on laws and guided by procedures that ensure fairness and equity. Equally important, the officers of those institutions must also be dedicated to fair and due process. In democratic societies, responsibility for justice in all its forms rests in the hands of all citizens.

Isaiah 5:8-24, One Woe After Another

NIV

[8]Woe to you who add house to house
  and join field to field
till no space is left
  and you live alone in the land.

[9]The LORD Almighty has declared in my hearing:

"Surely the great houses will become desolate,
  the fine mansions left without occupants.
[10]A ten-acre[a] vineyard will produce only a bath[b]
  of wine,
  a homer[c] of seed only an ephah[d] of grain."

[11]Woe to those who rise early in the morning
  to run after their drinks,
who stay up late at night
  till they are inflamed with wine.
[12]They have harps and lyres at their banquets,
  tambourines and flutes and wine,
but they have no regard for the deeds of
  the LORD,
  no respect for the work of his hands.
[13]Therefore my people will go into exile

a10 Hebrew ten-yoke, that is, the land plowed by 10 yoke of oxen in one day   b10 That is, probably about 6 gallons (about 22 liters)   c10 That is, probably about 6 bushels (about 220 liters)   d10 That is, probably about 3/5 bushel (about 22 liters)

NRSV

[8]Ah, you who join house to house,
  who add field to field,
until there is room for no one but you,
  and you are left to live alone
    in the midst of the land!
[9]The LORD of hosts has sworn in my hearing:
Surely many houses shall be desolate,
  large and beautiful houses, without
    inhabitant.
[10]For ten acres of vineyard shall yield but
    one bath,
  and a homer of seed shall yield a
    mere ephah.[a]

[11]Ah, you who rise early in the morning
  in pursuit of strong drink,
who linger in the evening
  to be inflamed by wine,
[12]whose feasts consist of lyre and harp,
  tambourine and flute and wine,
but who do not regard the deeds of the LORD,
  or see the work of his hands!
[13]Therefore my people go into exile without
    knowledge;

aThe Heb bath, homer, and ephah are measures of quantity

NIV

for lack of understanding;
their men of rank will die of hunger
and their masses will be parched with thirst.
[14]Therefore the grave[a] enlarges its appetite
and opens its mouth without limit;
into it will descend their nobles and masses
with all their brawlers and revelers.
[15]So man will be brought low
and mankind humbled,
the eyes of the arrogant humbled.
[16]But the LORD Almighty will be exalted by
his justice,
and the holy God will show himself holy
by his righteousness.
[17]Then sheep will graze as in their own pasture;
lambs will feed[b] among the ruins of the rich.

[18]Woe to those who draw sin along with cords
of deceit,
and wickedness as with cart ropes,
[19]to those who say, "Let God hurry,
let him hasten his work
so we may see it.
Let it approach,
let the plan of the Holy One of Israel come,
so we may know it."

[20]Woe to those who call evil good
and good evil,
who put darkness for light
and light for darkness,
who put bitter for sweet
and sweet for bitter.

[21]Woe to those who are wise in their own eyes
and clever in their own sight.

[22]Woe to those who are heroes at drinking wine
and champions at mixing drinks,
[23]who acquit the guilty for a bribe,
but deny justice to the innocent.
[24]Therefore, as tongues of fire lick up straw
and as dry grass sinks down in the flames,
so their roots will decay
and their flowers blow away like dust;
for they have rejected the law of the
LORD Almighty
and spurned the word of the Holy One
of Israel.

[a]14 Hebrew Sheol   [b]17 Septuagint; Hebrew / strangers will eat

NRSV

their nobles are dying of hunger,
and their multitude is parched with thirst.

[14]Therefore Sheol has enlarged its appetite
and opened its mouth beyond measure;
the nobility of Jerusalem[a] and her multitude
go down,
her throng and all who exult in her.
[15]People are bowed down, everyone is
brought low,
and the eyes of the haughty are humbled.
[16]But the LORD of hosts is exalted by justice,
and the Holy God shows himself holy by
righteousness.
[17]Then the lambs shall graze as in their pasture,
fatlings and kids[b] shall feed among the ruins.

[18]Ah, you who drag iniquity along with cords of
falsehood,
who drag sin along as with cart ropes,
[19]who say, "Let him make haste,
let him speed his work
that we may see it;
let the plan of the Holy One of Israel hasten
to fulfillment,
that we may know it!"
[20]Ah, you who call evil good
and good evil,
who put darkness for light
and light for darkness,
who put bitter for sweet
and sweet for bitter!
[21]Ah, you who are wise in your own eyes,
and shrewd in your own sight!
[22]Ah, you who are heroes in drinking wine
and valiant at mixing drink,
[23]who acquit the guilty for a bribe,
and deprive the innocent of their rights!
[24]Therefore, as the tongue of fire devours
the stubble,
and as dry grass sinks down in the flame,
so their root will become rotten,
and their blossom go up like dust;
for they have rejected the instruction of the
LORD of hosts,
and have despised the word of the Holy
One of Israel.

[a]Heb her nobility   [b]Cn Compare Gk: Heb aliens

COMMENTARY

The song of the vineyard concluded with a "cry" instead of righteousness (5:7). Now the prophet voices his own cry, one of woe. This section is defined by a series of six prophetic woes (seven, if one includes 10:1-4; see below) that charge particular parties with unrighteous and injust behavior. It is not difficult to recognize the parts of this collection of speeches. The units, each initiated by the cry, "Woe," are vv. 8-10, 11-14, 18-19, 20, 21, and 22-24. In three cases the accusations or indictments are followed by announcements or descriptions of punishment, introduced by "therefore" (vv. 13, 24) or a formula indicating that the prophet has heard the Lord (v. 9). The announcement of punishment in vv. 14-17 appears to be a secondary expansion of the one in v. 13.

Because of its frequent and significant, but somewhat ambiguous, use in the prophetic literature, the little Hebrew word הוֹי (*hôy*) has evoked considerable research and disagreement concerning its translation and meaning. The recent history of interpretation has pursued two dominant explanations of the background of the prophetic usage of this term. Some have seen the roots of the expression in the funeral, as a cry of mourning.[64] That tends to interpret the force of the word as an expression of doom, or perhaps even an announcement of judgment: "Judged or dead are those doing XYZ." The other interpretation sees the background of the word in wisdom thinking or popular circles.[65] That is, the word is the antithesis of "blessed," expressing condemnation: "Bad or reprehensible are doing XYZ."[66] Since the exclamation invariably is followed by descriptions of immoral behavior, this view has more to recommend it.

Brushing aside considerations of the possible roots of the expression, many recent interpreters argue that *hôy* is simply an exclamation, and so it is read "Ah" by the NRSV and some other recent

translations.[67] It is, indeed, an exclamation, but one that carries negative, and possibly even ominous, connotations. Therefore, the ambiguous but negative English "Woe" (so NIV) represents the force of *hôy* better than does the neutral "Ah."

Regardless of the roots of the word, in the prophetic corpus it introduces a distinctive genre of speech that serves particular purposes. This much is clear: These woe speeches are not "oracles" in the formal sense of communications from God, nor do they announce the future. They are human (prophetic) utterances concerning past and present human conduct. These little speeches commonly appear in series and follow a typical pattern: The persons addressed are characterized—usually in the third person—in terms of their reprehensible behavior, which almost always is described with participles: "Woe, those who are joining house to house" (5:8). The woes themselves are not announcements of judgment, although such announcements may follow.[68] At most they are the indictments or reasons for the proclamations of disaster. In some cases, but not in most, the condemnation or accusation is followed by an announcement of judgment (see 5:9, 13-14, 24; 10:3-4*a*). But even when there is the turn to the announcement of judgment, only in 5:9 is there anything like a messenger formula, or attribution of the words concerning the future directly to Yahweh. The condemned behavior itself can be sufficient to set negative consequences into motion.

The common theme of the woes is social injustice. The allegations range from very specific, such as overindulgence in alcohol (vv. 11, 22), to broad, such as "iniquity" (v. 18) or reversing good and evil (v. 20). They include both particular actions, such as acquiring real estate (v. 8) or taking bribes (v. 23), and attitudes, such as arrogance (v. 21). Most of the accusations entail economic dimensions and assumptions about the class of the accused. They are the powerful, the "nobility of

---

64. W. Janzen, *Mourning Cry and Woe Oracle*, BZAW 125 (Berlin: Walter de Gruyter, 1972). See also H. J. Krause, "Hoj als prophetische Leichenklage über das eigene volk im 8. Jahrhundert," *ZAW* 85 (1973) 15-46.

65. E. Gerstenberger, "The Woe-Oracles of the Prophets," *JBL* 81 (1962) 249-63; Whedbee, *Isaiah and Wisdom*, 80-110.

66. The NEB apparently followed this line of thinking by translating *hôy* as "Shame on you!"

67. J. J. M. Roberts, "Form, Syntax, and Redaction in Isaiah 1:2-20," *Princeton Seminary Bulletin* 3 (1982) 296-300; J. J. M. Roberts, *Nahum, Habakkuk, and Zephaniah* (Westminster: John Knox, 1991) 118.

68. Contrary to C. Westermann's conclusions in *Basic Forms of Prophetic Speech,* trans. H. C. White (Philadelphia: Westminster, 1967) 189-94. Westermann suggested that "woe" was a weakened curse.

Jerusalem" (v. 14), the wealthy landowners, those with time to drink and with influence in the judicial system. Moreover, the prophet connects their reprehensible behavior directly to the failure of faith in Yahweh. They refuse to acknowledge Yahweh's authority and power (vv. 19, 24). One should not, however, assume that all of these woes are addressed to the same groups or individuals.

5:8-10. Viewed apart from the series of woe speeches, these verses closely parallel the typical three-part structure of prophecies of punishment. First, the woe itself (v. 8), spoken by the prophetic voice and directed against actions of wealthy landowners, provides the indictment or reasons for punishment and already suggests the consequences of those deeds. Second, the transition in v. 9a indicates that what follows is the word of Yahweh. Finally, punishment is announced against the accused (vv. 9b-10). Characteristically, the woe is not directed against individuals or groups as such, but against their conduct. The transitional attribution of the pronouncement of punishment to Yahweh is elliptical. The Hebrew reads, literally, "In my hearing the LORD of hosts," suggesting that the prophet has overheard the Lord in the heavenly council (cf. 6:8). The future devastation is described passively, following from the actions of the accused, and not as direct divine intervention to punish. The punishment does not just fit the crime; it is genuinely ironic. Those who take all the houses and land will be left alone in that land.

This prophetic speech concerning houses and fields—what we call real estate—presumes traditional Israelite understandings of land and justice, economics and power. Those who "join house to house, who add field to field" (v. 8), subvert the ancient order concerning land—the land promised to the patriarchs, divided among the tribes and their families, and never to be treated as real estate that can be sold (Lev 25:23). So the greedy development of large estates by the few at the expense of the many is social and economic injustice, creating or expanding a class of homeless people. But it is more than that. It is the violation of a divinely established order, taken to be the expression of election as well as justice. Land is not to be treated as property to be accumulated. It belongs to the Lord, whose equitable distribution of it among the tribes and clans as trustees is to be maintained in

perpetuity. In the eighth century BCE, economic shifts in the direction of capitalism were undermining the traditional ideas of stewardship of the land.

The punishment implied in v. 8b is the isolation of the greedy. Verses 9b-10 sketch a scene of judgment as an empty landscape, "desolate" and presumably ruined mansions whose owners and occupants have vanished. Such devastation may result from military invasion, but in this case the cause is crop failure. "Ten acres" (lit., "ten yoke," the land that can be worked by ten yoke of oxen in a day) of vineyard will produce only about five and a half gallons of wine, and "a homer of seed shall yield a mere ephah"—that is, the harvest will be one-tenth of the seed planted. Since this announcement is the word of Yahweh, it sets judgment into motion. Remarkably, as in Gen 3:17-19, the Lord punishes sinners by cursing the land.

5:11-13. The second woe indicts a particular group, those whose pursuit of pleasure obscures their perception of Yahweh's activity (vv. 11-12). With the appropriate logical connection ("Therefore"), there follows an announcement of judgment on the people as a whole (v. 13). The woe is not addressed directly to the drinkers, as the NRSV suggests, but speaks of them in the third person, as in the NIV.

The charges consist of two parts: what the accused are doing and what they are not doing. What they do is drink to the point of intoxication ("inflamed by wine") from early morning until late at night and spend their time at feasts with musical entertainment. The translation of שֵׁכָר (šēkār) as "strong drink" is misleading because it suggests distilled liquor, a relatively modern invention. It probably is "beer," common in the grain-producing areas of the ancient Near East.[69] The risks of overindulgence in alcohol are addressed elsewhere in Isaiah (5:22; 28:7; 29:9), but drinking is taken for granted. In the immediately preceding woe (v. 10), loss of the wine crop is a judgment of the landowners. The problems here are twofold: overindulgence and the pursuit of pleasure that obscures the vision of the Lord's work.

Thus the second part of the accusation concerns what the revelers fail to do: They "do not regard

---

69. Cf. O. Kaiser, *Isaiah 1–12: A Commentary,* trans. R. A. Wilson (Philadelphia: Westminster, 1972) 67.

the deeds of the LORD, or see work of his hands!" Certainly this juxtaposition contrasts excessive appetites with piety, but either could stand alone as sufficient grounds for condemnation. The precise meaning of disregarding the deeds and works of the Lord is unclear. Are the "deeds" the historical acts of the Lord on behalf of Israel, and the "work of his hands" the fruits of creation? Or are those deeds and acts what the Lord is about to do in the future, suggesting that the carousers are ignoring the consequences of their deeds?[70]

Although the indictments would seem to concern personal morality and piety, they embrace issues of social justice and economic inequities. The revelers are not specifically identified as members of the wealthy, leisure class; but who else can afford such feasts? The tragedy is that the corruption of a group leads to the suffering of the people as a whole, not just the "nobles" but the "multitude"—indeed, the exile of the Lord's ("my") people (v. 13).

5:14-17. Although these verses might be considered part of the preceding section, the new transition ("Therefore") indicates that they are better seen as an elaboration of the announcement of judgment in v. 13. Most likely, these verses are fragments of announcements concerning Jerusalem that have been included here, possibly on the basis of the appearance of "multitude" in vv. 13-14, and the similarity of the "brawlers and revelers" in v. 14 to the image of drunken feasts in vv. 11-12. In any case, this section presents announcements of judgment against Jerusalem and its inhabitants. That the underworld ("Sheol") is greedy (v. 14) is not unusual, for eventually the grave takes everyone (Prov 27:20; 30:16); but here the audience is confronted with the horrifying image of Sheol's swallowing up all the inhabitants of Jerusalem. All suffer for the sins of some; there is a solidarity of the people in judgment, if not in reasons for it. Verse 15 echoes the refrain in 2:9, 11, and 17 concerning human pride, and in v. 16 the concern for human "justice" and "righteousness" is shown to be founded on the divine character. The pastoral scene in v. 17 is hardly a positive note, for it pictures the sacred city in ruins.

5:18-19. The third woe is both broad and specific. The general accusation of wrongdoing (v. 18) draws a picture of people tied up in their sins and iniquities and pulling them along like a cart. The sins are specified and proved in v. 19 by quoting the words of the accused themselves, a common practice in prophetic indictments. The tone of the quotation is mocking and its substance both arrogant and cynical. The sinners' sin is challenging "the Holy One of Israel" to act according to God's "plan," certainly based on the assumption that God either cannot or will not do so. This amounts to a refusal to acknowledge Yahweh's authority and power. The specific acts of the accused are their words, which reveal their failure to trust Yahweh. It is not difficult to hear in this indictment the implied threat that the sinners will indeed be caught up in the fulfillment of the Lord's plan.

5:20. This woe also indicts a group of individuals for verbal actions, although the words are not quoted directly. The charge is comprehensive but not concrete, against those who use words ("call evil good and good evil") to reverse the moral order. That the meanings of "good" and "evil" are self-evident to the prophet is emphasized by his use of a series of contrasting metaphors: darkness and light, bitter and sweet. The poetic structure of reversal ("darkness for light and light for darkness") further underscores the reversal of morality.

5:21. In its condemnation of those who are "wise in their own eyes" (the NIV correctly reads the third person), this fifth woe parallels the third one (vv. 18-19) in charging the accused with arrogance and adds to it the allegation of conceit or pride.

5:22-24. The final woe in this immediate context contains two distinct accusations whose juxtaposition emphasizes the connection between private and public morality. The first is a close parallel to vv. 11-13, condemning those who drink too much and are proud of it. The epithets "heroes" and "valiant" are sarcastic terms that cast doubt not only on the actions but also on the character of those so identified. Whereas the drinkers in vv. 11-13 had disregarded "the deeds of the LORD . . . the work of his hands," these are guilty of corrupting the courts. The drunkards function—as could all full citizens—as judges,[71] and in that role

---

70. Clements takes it to mean the latter. See Ronald E. Clements, *Isaiah 1–39*, NCB (Grand Rapids: Eerdmans, 1980) 63-64.

71. There is no evidence for "professional royal judges in Jerusalem" in the time of Isaiah, as suggested by Kaiser, *Isaiah 1–12*, 69-70.

they accept bribes to absolve the guilty; thus they "deny justice to the innocent" (NIV). The NRSV ("deprive the innocent of their rights") is seriously misleading at this point. There is no word for or concept of the modern idea of individual rights in the Hebrew Bible. Both key words in v. 23*b* are forms of the root צדק (*ṣdq*), typically translated "righteous" or "righteousness," used here as technical legal terms. Thus the Tanakh reads "withhold vindication from him who is in the right." The charge focuses on the responsibilities of the officers of the court rather than the rights of the victims. Those with power to adjudicate cases side with the wealthy against the innocent.

The announcement of judgment in v. 24 certainly is based on the indictment of vv. 22-23, but it may also, in the context, function as a summary verdict justified by all the accusations in vv. 8-23. Following the transitional "Therefore," destruction is set out passively, and not as direct divine intervention, by means of two similes and two metaphors. The similes compare the fate of the accused with fire on stubble, grass in flame, artistically reversing subjects. Continuing the imagery of destroyed vegetation, the metaphors show roots that have become rotten and blossoms that have turned to dust. Because the antecedents of the pronouns "their" and "they" are not specified, it is not self-evident whose "root" and "blossom" will decay. Does this apply to the people as a whole or to a particular group? Certainly the condemned include the drunken citizens who corrupt the courts, and possibly all those indicted by the previous woes as well. Contained within the announcement is a more comprehensive and fundamental justification of ("for") the sentence of death that also identifies the condemned in terms of their activities. They are those who have refused to heed the Lord's will expressed in "instruction" (תורה *tôrâ*) or "word"—that is, through the prophets (cf. Isa 1:10 and the Commentary on 1:10).

REFLECTIONS

It is impossible to read Isaiah 1–39 and not be moved to reflect on morality, both generally and in terms of particular activities. What, in general, is right and wrong, and how is one to know? What specific activities or attitudes are right or wrong, and why? The accusations introduced by "Woe" bring these issues into the foreground.

The very clarity and decisiveness of the prophetic criticisms of wrongdoing are enough to make the hearers uneasy. This is especially the case for modern hearers in a pluralistic culture. Are there, as these cries against injustice and misbehavior suggest, absolute standards for behavior? In our culture, on life-and-death questions such as capital punishment and abortion, advocates on both sides of the issues are certain that they are right. Consequently, many have become cautious about certainty, especially moral certainty, and rightly so. Context is crucial. But this legitimate worry about absolutism can lead to rationalizing, to finding excuses for what we want to do. The prophetic tradition confronts this rationale with a sharp line between right and wrong.

What is the source of this prophetic morality and the basis for recognizing that line between right and wrong? First, it is important to keep in mind that the prophets do not present a set of laws or a code of behavior. We must read the prophetic understanding of right and wrong mainly from the negative, from their accusations and criticisms about bad behavior. Second, each prophet invents new laws or codes of conduct, but holds the people accountable to the legal and theological traditions that were revealed long before their time. Specifically, the substance of justice, of what is right and what is wrong, is founded on the understanding of God as just; and Isaiah is convinced that reprehensible behavior by groups or individuals stems directly from the failure of faith in Yahweh. At the very least, this suggests that those who take these texts seriously will set their moral and ethical deliberations within a theological framework. People act on the basis of their most deeply held beliefs, and their actions reveal their convictions, including convictions about God.

Two other general points concerning prophetic morality deserve consideration. First, as in the case of law, when morality is broad it may not be concrete or specific, as in generic or abstract accusations of sinfulness (5:18) or of calling evil good (5:20); but when morality is very specific (5:8, 11, 22-23), it is easy to apply to one context—say, in antiquity—but not necessarily to others. Second, the prophetic accusations make it difficult to sustain a significant line between private and public morality, for the actions of individuals or groups are shown to have serious implications for others, and for the people as a whole.

This leads to reflection on two specific concerns in these verses: drinking and land. In a culture such as ours, undergirded by a vigorous individualism, it is easy to argue that whether to drink alcohol or how much to drink is a private decision. And so it is. But private morality has implications for public responsibility. Drinking, especially drinking too much and under particular circumstances, can be dangerous. At certain levels that is widely recognized, or else states and nations would not have laws against driving while intoxicated. But even if private decisions about drinking do not physically endanger others, they can become public health problems that the society as a whole pays for. Moreover, as suggested by 5:22-23, drinking that affects the performance of public duties can lead to gross injustice.

With regard to land, 5:8-10 continues a central theme of the Hebrew scriptures by insisting that land and land ownership are not simply economic or political issues but are spiritual and theological matters as well. The problem set out here is driven by greed, by those who overthrow the ancient tradition that the tribes, clans, and families of Israel are trustees of the Lord's land in order to acquire more than they need. These verses evoke reflection on environmental, political, and economic issues. Treating land simply or primarily as property narrows the vision of the environment as a whole. Was the world created just to satisfy excessive human appetites? Political and military conflicts persist—and not just in modern Israel—because people disagree about God's selection of stewards of particular lands, or, whether with theological justification or not, they disagree about conflicting claims to particular lands. Few in our time can understand the spiritual attachment to land or the economic disaster of not having it better than those who have lost farms that had been held in their family for generations.

Isaiah 5:25-30, Judgment Without End

NIV	NRSV
²⁵Therefore the LORD's anger burns against his people; his hand is raised and he strikes them down. The mountains shake, and the dead bodies are like refuse in the streets. Yet for all this, his anger is not turned away, his hand is still upraised. ²⁶He lifts up a banner for the distant nations, he whistles for those at the ends of the earth. Here they come, swiftly and speedily! ²⁷Not one of them grows tired or stumbles, not one slumbers or sleeps; not a belt is loosened at the waist,	²⁵ Therefore the anger of the LORD was kindled against his people, and he stretched out his hand against them and struck them; the mountains quaked, and their corpses were like refuse in the streets. For all this his anger has not turned away, and his hand is stretched out still. ²⁶ He will raise a signal for a nation far away, and whistle for a people at the ends of the earth; Here they come, swiftly, speedily! ²⁷ None of them is weary, none stumbles, none slumbers or sleeps, not a loincloth is loose,

NIV

not a sandal thong is broken.
²⁸Their arrows are sharp,
    all their bows are strung;
their horses' hoofs seem like flint,
    their chariot wheels like a whirlwind.
²⁹Their roar is like that of the lion,
    they roar like young lions;
they growl as they seize their prey
    and carry it off with no one to rescue.
³⁰In that day they will roar over it
    like the roaring of the sea.
And if one looks at the land,
    he will see darkness and distress;
    even the light will be darkened by
        the clouds.

NRSV

not a sandal-thong broken;
²⁸ their arrows are sharp,
    all their bows bent,
their horses' hoofs seem like flint,
    and their wheels like the whirlwind.
²⁹ Their roaring is like a lion,
    like young lions they roar;
they growl and seize their prey,
    they carry it off, and no one can rescue.
³⁰ They will roar over it on that day,
    like the roaring of the sea.
And if one look to the land—
    only darkness and distress;
and the light grows dark with clouds.

COMMENTARY

This section consists of two parts, which rest uneasily both with each other and with their immediate context. Verse 25 describes punishment in the past, and vv. 26-30 are an announcement of punishment in the (apparently immediate) future. There is, to be sure, a certain progress of thought in Isaiah 5, from the general accusation in vv. 1-7 to the more specific indictments in vv. 8-24 to the words of judgment in this concluding part. Moreover, there is a distinct beginning in v. 25 with "therefore," although this transition typically presumes a presentation of accusations. There is no doubt that what follows v. 30, beginning with Isaiah's report of his call, is a distinct new section on the basis of both form and content. Consequently, since v. 25 in particular fits with 9:8–10:4, it seems most likely that 6:1–9:7 has been inserted by an editor into an earlier collection of the Isaiah tradition.

5:25. This verse describes how the Lord became angry in the past and punished "his people." But the concluding refrain reveals that both the anger and the judgment were continued, that this was not the last blow. The verse makes more sense as part of a series of accounts of punishment, and the concluding formula, "For all this his anger has not turned away, and his hand is stretched out still," is a refrain that concludes four other units: 9:8-12, 13-17, 18-21; and 10:1-4. The last of these also begins with "Woe."

What is the point? The devastation was like an earthquake ("the mountains quaked"), leaving death in its wake. The judgment—the Lord's exercise of his power ("hand")—was in response to some unspecified actions that angered the Lord. But what is the purpose of reporting past judgments? Was the purpose of punishment to evoke repentance? Is Yahweh's hand still stretched out because they have not yet learned their lesson? That is not clear. It could be that the punishment, either as penalty for offenses or as purging, simply is not finished.

The closest parallel to this pattern of reporting a series of past disasters and concluding with a refrain appears in Amos 4:6-12. In that refrain, Yahweh addresses the people, "Yet you did not return to me." So past disasters are interpreted as calls to repent. But the purpose of the recital of past judgments prepares for the concluding announcement of a meeting with Yahweh: "Prepare to meet your God" (Amos 4:12). Thus in Amos, and possibly also Isaiah, the account of the past becomes an indictment: Because you refused to accept or learn from the disasters, the end has come.

5:26-30. This proclamation of disaster is not a speech of Yahweh but describes events the Lord sets into motion. The third person dominates, with shifts in the English translations between singular and plural marking the parts of the presentation of future events. The third-person singular at the outset ("He") refers to Yahweh (v. 26a). The third-person plural ("they," "them," "their") refers to the enemy that Yahweh calls against the people (vv. 26c-30a), and the third-person singular for the observer of the devastation (v. 30b) is indefinite, meaning anyone who is left to see what has happened.

By sight ("signal") and by sound ("whistle") the Lord calls for a distant and foreign nation, like a master calls a dog. What approaches is not a nation but an enemy army. Although it is not stated directly, clearly Yahweh has summoned them (cf. 10:5) to act against God's own people. The wider context indicates that the enemy will approach Judah and Jerusalem.[72] The invader is not named,

but it can only be Assyria (cf. 7:18-20; 8:5-8; 10:5-11).

As with Yahweh's summons, the description of the enemy army appeals both to the eye and to the ear. The hearer is invited to see the troops and recognize their speed, stamina, discipline, preparedness, and weapons (vv. 26c-28). The description of "horses" and "wheels" refers to chariotry. When describing the sounds of the advancing army, the prophetic poet turns to metaphors: The noise is "like a lion, like young lions they roar" (v. 29; cf. Amos 3:4, 8). In v. 30, the roaring of the lion turns into the roaring of the sea.

This final verse echoes an important theological theme. "That day" is an allusion to the tradition concerning the day of the Lord, originally the day of the Lord's victory over enemies. But here, as in Amos 5:18-20, the Lord's own people have become the enemy, and the day is one of darkness.

72. Seitz argues that chapter 5 as a whole pertains to both Judah and Israel. See Christopher R. Seitz, *Isaiah 1–39*, Interpretation (Louisville: John Knox, 1993) 50-51.

REFLECTIONS

Prophetic announcements or descriptions of disaster as divine punishment evoke uneasiness in modern readers—and they should. They appear to treat devastation, whether natural (5:25) or military (5:26-30) as the will of God. The view that all disasters are God's will is a problem that calls for serious reflection.

To the extent that these prophetic words attempt to account for disaster, they do insist that there is purpose and direction in history, and God has a hand in that. What are the alternatives? One would be to conclude that there is no meaning or purpose in life or the events of the world, and that would be inconsistent with the biblical confidence in a God of history. Another alternative would be to attribute trouble to an evil power, such as a devil; and such a dualism would conflict with the biblical insistence that there is only one God worthy of the name.

In the Hebrew scriptures, it seems almost impossible to separate the course of events in human history from moral considerations. So it is not an arbitrary God who intervenes, but one who responds to human injustice or sins. Consequently, history, including catastrophes, is created by the interaction of the human and the divine wills.

Verse 25 entails a particular perspective, the view that suffering may be didactic, like a good parent disciplining a child to elicit change, to teach a lesson, or to make someone better. The prophet begins with the reality of suffering and works to find a way to honor that reality and the theological reality of the presence of God.

Coming to grips with the prophetic understanding of disaster does not provide easy solutions for our questions concerning evil and suffering. This is particularly the case when we recognize that the prophets believed that when bad things happen to bad people, good people suffer as well. In fact, the view that all suffering is "the will of God" may itself cause suffering. But these prophetic announcements of judgment call for us to consider the moral dimensions of historical events and may lead us to consider the relation between divine justice and mercy. Moreover, like all fundamental theological problems, this question needs to be considered in the context of the biblical tradition as a whole.

ISAIAH 6:1–9:7, THE PROPHET, CHILDREN, AND KINGS

OVERVIEW

This section has long been recognized as a distinct literary unit within the book of Isaiah. As noted already, it interrupts a sequence begun in 5:25-30 and resumed in 9:8, suggesting that 6:1–9:7 was an independent unit inserted into another collection. Beyond that, when one views these chapters broadly, a number of unifying factors can be recognized, including genre, chronology, and theological themes.

The dominant literary genres of this section are quite different from those in its context. Whereas everything before and most of what follows is prophetic address, the reader now encounters narratives. Some are autobiographical in style if not necessarily in purpose—that is, the prophet himself reports about events such as his vision of the Lord (chap. 6) or what he did and said at particular times, including symbolic actions and his encounters with the king (chap. 8). Others are third-person narratives, accounts about the prophet's activities (see chap. 7). These features have led many commentators to identify the section as Isaiah's "memoirs" (German *Denkschrift*), compiled by the prophet and comprising the earliest stage in the Isaiah tradition.[73] Although it is doubtful that Isaiah himself compiled this unit, it does relate to his own self-understanding, comes from a relatively early period in his work, and could very well be the earliest collection of traditions concerning Isaiah.

There is some chronological coherence to the section. Many of the events reported here share the same historical horizon, the one presumed in 7:1-9, the Syro-Ephraimitic war of 735–732 BCE. This certainly includes the accounts of the prophet's activities in 7:1–8:18. If "the year that king Uzziah died" (6:1) is as late as 736 BCE, then that would put the prophet's vision of the Lord and his commission not long before the other events,

and 6:1 becomes an appropriate heading for this large unit as well as the call itself. Both chronologically and in terms of genre, 9:1-7 has the least affinity with the other parts of the section. It is the announcement of the future on the basis of the birth of a crown prince. However, the introduction in 9:1 attempts to locate it historically, and—as in some of the prophetic narratives—a child is a sign from God.

Thematically, there is evidence of some progression of thought. The section begins with the prophet's summons to present an unqualified message of judgment, moves through indictments and warnings in which the central theme is faith and the situation is military danger, to conclude with an announcement of a time of peace and justice under a future Davidic king. Specifically, the harsh commission (6:9-10) corresponds to what happens to the prophet's words in the time of Ahaz, and 8:16 brings the theme to culmination. Ward sees the coherence of the section differently, in terms of the theme of kingship. Chapter 6 is a vision of Yahweh as King, chaps. 7 and 8 contain oracles and signs for the reigning king, and 9:1-7 announces the new king.[74]

So the parts of this section cohere in more than one way. But the more deeply one looks into this forest, the more distinct become the individual trees. Although most of the literature is narrative, the individual units belong to quite different narrative genres. There seem to be chronological affinities, but many dates are uncertain, and others are absent. "The year that king Uzziah died" is debated, and the identity (and thus the date) of the crown prince born or to be born in 9:1-8 is uncertain. Moreover, even when broad common themes are recognized, the individual issues are very different. Finally, some transitions between stories are rough and connections unclear. Consequently, it seems highly unlikely that these chapters were composed by a single author at one time. Rather,

---

73. Karl Budde, *Jesajas Erleben. Eine gemeinverständliche Auslegung der Denkschrift des Propheten Jesaja (Kap. 6, 1-9, 6)* (Gotha, 1928); O. Kaiser, *Isaiah 1–12: A Commentary,* trans. R. A. Wilson (Philadelphia: Westminster, 1972) 73. See also Ronald E. Clements, *Isaiah 1–39,* NCB (Grand Rapids: Eerdmans, 1980) 4.

74. James M. Ward, *Thus Says the Lord: The Message of the Prophets* (Nashville: Abingdon, 1991) 38, 48.

an editor, using originally independent traditions, has put the section together and organized it on the basis of some broad literary, historical, and theological principles.

The major sections are Isaiah's report of his call (6:1-13), two third-person symbolic action reports concerning children (7:1-9, 10-25), a series of third-person symbolic action reports (8:1-22), and the messianic poem promising a reign of peace (9:1-7).

Isaiah 6:1-13, Isaiah's Commission

NIV

6 In the year that King Uzziah died, I saw the Lord seated on a throne, high and exalted, and the train of his robe filled the temple. ²Above him were seraphs, each with six wings: With two wings they covered their faces, with two they covered their feet, and with two they were flying. ³And they were calling to one another:

"Holy, holy, holy is the LORD Almighty;
the whole earth is full of his glory."

⁴At the sound of their voices the doorposts and thresholds shook and the temple was filled with smoke.

⁵"Woe to me!" I cried. "I am ruined! For I am a man of unclean lips, and I live among a people of unclean lips, and my eyes have seen the King, the LORD Almighty."

⁶Then one of the seraphs flew to me with a live coal in his hand, which he had taken with tongs from the altar. ⁷With it he touched my mouth and said, "See, this has touched your lips; your guilt is taken away and your sin atoned for."

⁸Then I heard the voice of the Lord saying, "Whom shall I send? And who will go for us?"

And I said, "Here am I. Send me!"

⁹He said, "Go and tell this people:

" 'Be ever hearing, but never understanding;
be ever seeing, but never perceiving.'
¹⁰Make the heart of this people calloused;
make their ears dull
and close their eyes.ᵃ
Otherwise they might see with their eyes,
hear with their ears,
understand with their hearts,
and turn and be healed."

¹¹Then I said, "For how long, O Lord?"

ᵃ*9,10 Hebrew; Septuagint 'You will be ever hearing, but never understanding; / you will be ever seeing, but never perceiving.' / ¹⁰This people's heart has become calloused; / they hardly hear with their ears, / and they have closed their eyes*

NRSV

6 In the year that King Uzziah died, I saw the Lord sitting on a throne, high and lofty; and the hem of his robe filled the temple. ²Seraphs were in attendance above him; each had six wings: with two they covered their faces, and with two they covered their feet, and with two they flew. ³And one called to another and said:

"Holy, holy, holy is the LORD of hosts;
the whole earth is full of his glory."

⁴The pivotsᵃ on the thresholds shook at the voices of those who called, and the house filled with smoke. ⁵And I said: "Woe is me! I am lost, for I am a man of unclean lips, and I live among a people of unclean lips; yet my eyes have seen the King, the LORD of hosts!"

6Then one of the seraphs flew to me, holding a live coal that had been taken from the altar with a pair of tongs. ⁷The seraphᵇ touched my mouth with it and said: "Now that this has touched your lips, your guilt has departed and your sin is blotted out." ⁸Then I heard the voice of the Lord saying, "Whom shall I send, and who will go for us?" And I said, "Here am I; send me!" ⁹And he said, "Go and say to this people:

'Keep listening, but do not comprehend;
keep looking, but do not understand.'
¹⁰ Make the mind of this people dull,
and stop their ears,
and shut their eyes,
so that they may not look with their eyes,
and listen with their ears,
and comprehend with their minds,
and turn and be healed."

¹¹ Then I said, "How long, O Lord?" And he said:
"Until cities lie waste
without inhabitant,
and houses without people,

ᵃ*Meaning of Heb uncertain*   ᵇ*Heb He*

NIV

And he answered:

"Until the cities lie ruined
  and without inhabitant,
until the houses are left deserted
  and the fields ruined and ravaged,
[12] until the LORD has sent everyone far away
  and the land is utterly forsaken.
[13] And though a tenth remains in the land,
  it will again be laid waste.
But as the terebinth and oak
  leave stumps when they are cut down,
  so the holy seed will be the stump in the land."

NRSV

and the land is utterly desolate;
[12] until the LORD sends everyone far away,
  and vast is the emptiness in the midst of
  the land.
[13] Even if a tenth part remain in it,
  it will be burned again,
like a terebinth or an oak
  whose stump remains standing
  when it is felled."[a]
The holy seed is its stump.

[a] Meaning of Heb uncertain

COMMENTARY

The location of Isaiah's report of his call in the book of Isaiah is unusual, and not only because it interrupts a previously established collection of the prophet's speeches. Those of Jeremiah and Ezekiel are found more logically at the very beginning of the books. Given the relation of this account to the narratives that follow, it seems likely that the vocation report once stood at the beginning of an early collection of traditions concerning the prophet. Efforts to account for this location historically (e.g., that the words and events in chaps. 1–5 took place before those in chaps. 6–9), have been unsuccessful.[75]

The vocation and visionary experiences of prophets and other servants of God would have been very private and individual matters. It is all the more remarkable, therefore, to discover that Isaiah's report of his call has a great many features in common with other OT vocation reports.[76] These include those of Moses (Exod 3:1–4:17), Gideon (Judg 6:11-24), Jeremiah (Jer 1:4-10), and Ezekiel (Ezekiel 1–3). In all cases there is a report of an encounter with God, either directly or through a messenger; a commission to do the Lord's will or speak the Lord's word; and a ritual act or sign symbolizing the designated role. In all instances except Ezekiel, the one who is called objects to the vocation and then receives reassurance from God.

In its more specific features, Isaiah 6 closely parallels Ezekiel 1–3.[77] Both are reports of visions of the Lord's heavenly throne. Similar also is the scene described by Micaiah ben Imlah in 1 Kgs 22:19-22: "I saw the LORD sitting on his throne, with all the host of heaven standing beside him." Neither Isaiah nor Ezekiel sees God directly, but both have the sense of being on the outskirts of the heavenly throne room and hearing the deliberations going on there. This OT imagery is indebted to ancient Near Eastern traditions concerning the heavenly court. In those polytheistic traditions the court included the chief god and other deities; in the OT, God holds court with messengers (see also Job 1:6-12).

In part because of its location in the book and in part because this report has some distinctive features, some scholars have questioned whether Isaiah 6 is actually a vocation report.[78] Although it is possible that the experience reported here might not have been the inaugural vision that first set the prophet on his path, it shares both form and function with other vocation accounts. Like all the other reports, it has distinctive elements and a particular purpose. Frequently the authority of prophets to speak was challenged (see Jer 1:6-8; Amos 7:10-17), especially when they proclaimed

75. J. Milgrom, "Did Isaiah Prophesy During the Reign of Uzziah?" *VT* 14 (1964) 164-82.
76. N. Habel, "The Form and Significance of the Call Narratives," *ZAW* 77 (1965) 297-323.

77. W. Zimmerli, *Ezekiel,* Hermeneia (Philadelphia: Fortress, 1979) 1:97-100.
78. Seitz, *Isaiah 1–39,* 53-55.

judgment. Since prophets in Israel had no "official" standing comparable to that of, for example,
priests, their right to speak in the name of the Lord
was open to question. The vocation reports were
their responses to such challenges. They were not
only entitled but also compelled to speak because
God had called them to do so; they had not sought
the role, but it had been thrust upon them. In the
case of Isaiah 6, the prophet specifically justifies
his harsh message ("keep listening, but do not
comprehend," vv. 8-10) by reporting his vision of
the Lord on a throne.[79]

This chapter is a fully self-contained unit, presented as the first-person report by the prophet of
what happened to him, what he saw and heard,
and what he said. So it is a story, in form a personal account by the prophet of a momentous
event in his life, the defining vision. There is a
plot, and there are characters. The main ones are
the prophet and God; but there are others, including the seraphs, the heavenly court, and, of
course, offstage, "this people" (v. 9) to whom
Isaiah is sent. Some of the characters speak, both
moving the story along and bringing the listeners
up short. The account, consisting mainly of dialogue, is continuous and complete, and its main
parts are easily discernible on the basis of shifts of
genre, speaker, and content. Broadly, the elements
include the account of the vision and audition (vv.
1-4), the prophet's reaction (v. 5), the account of
the ritual of purification (vv. 6-7), Yahweh's question and Isaiah's response (v. 8), Yahweh's commission to the prophet (vv. 9-10), and Isaiah's
objections with the Lord's response (vv. 11-13).

6:1-4. The vocation report begins with a date
formula, which also sets the mood. "The year that
King Uzziah died" could have been as early as 742
or as late as 736 BCE, but that king's death signaled
the end of an era of relative independence for
Judah. Tiglath-pileser III came to power in Assyria
in 745 BCE, and, after consolidating his power in
Mesopotamia, began to expand his empire to
include the small states in Syria and Palestine. His
successors would continue his military and political policies. During most of Isaiah's lifetime, Judah
lived under the threat of Assyrian domination.

In addition to reminding the readers of the
international events that followed the death of

Uzziah, the date formula functions, as do those in
contracts, to verify and thus validate the report
that follows.[80] It also serves a theological function
similar to that of superscriptions to the prophetic
books—that is, to locate the revelation in a particular time (see the Commentary on 1:1). Finally,
the date refers to the time of the experience and
indicates that the report itself was written later.

The story begins with the description of an awe-
inspiring vision of Yahweh as King on a throne.
The fact that "the hem of his robe" (v. 1) filled the
Temple indicates that the prophet stands at the
entrance to the sacred precincts and that the ark
on the sanctuary's elevated most holy place was
understood to be the symbolic throne of Yahweh
(for a description, see 1 Kgs 8:6-8). Other aspects
of temple worship are the antiphonal hymn of
praise sung by the seraphim and the smoke—from
offerings or incense or both—that filled the
"house"—that is, the Temple. The seraphim who
attended the Lord must cover both their "feet" (a
euphemism for their nakedness) and their faces;
no one can appear naked before the Lord, and no
one can see God directly and live, not even the
supernatural beings that guard the throne.
Seraphim (lit., "fiery ones"; the English simply
transliterates the Hebrew) elsewhere are serpents
(Num 21:6; Isa 14:29; 30:6; cf. 1 Kgs 6:23-28; 2
Kgs 18:4), but here they have six wings.[81]
Whatever their form, their function is clear. Like
the cherubim in Ezekiel 1, they are attendants
around the divine throne, and they praise the
Lord.

The description of the appearance of the deity
has already prepared for the song of praise, which
emphasizes the Lord's power and sacredness. The
"LORD of hosts" is the leader of armies, both earthly
(1 Sam 17:45) and heavenly (Isa 40:26). "Holy" is
that which pertains only to God, emphasizing the
radical otherness of the Lord. Although the hem of
God's robe may fill the Temple, the "whole earth"
is filled with the "glory," the powerful presence of
the one who is radically other.

Other sights and sounds accompany the
singing, recalling the traditions of the appearances
of the Lord. The shaking of the "doorposts and
thresholds" and the smoke (v. 4) are like the

79. R. Knierim, "The Vocation of Isaiah," *VT* 18 (1968) 47-68.

80. Ibid., 49-50.
81. See Karen R. Jones, *Serpent Symbolism in the Old Testament* (Haddonfield, N.J.: Haddonfield House, 1974) 42-60.

appearance of the Lord on Mt. Sinai (Exod 19:9, 18; cf. Judg 5:4-5) and elsewhere (Hab 3:6).

6:5. Isaiah's response to the theophany is a cry of woe (v. 5). He literally fears for his life ("I am lost"). In the context of other vocation reports, this is not unlike expressions of resistance or inadequacy (Exod 3:13; 4:1, 10, 13; Jer 1:6). The content of Isaiah's declaration, however, is similar to a confession of sin and an expression of mourning both for himself and for his people. In the presence of the Lord, he knows that he is unclean, although by the priestly criteria he would have been judged ritually clean before he approached the Temple. The meaning of "unclean" in this context is unclear; no particular violation of ritual purity is stated.

6:6-7. In direct response to the prophet's confession, one of the seraphs performs a ritual of purification that combines word and action. Isaiah had confessed that he was "a man of unclean lips" (v. 5), so the seraph touches the prophet's mouth with a coal from the altar and pronounces that his guilt is removed and his sin forgiven. This ritual parallels those in the vocation reports of both Jeremiah (Jer 1:9) and Ezekiel (Ezek 2:8–3:3) in that all of them concern the mouth of the prophetic spokesman for God. The image of purifying fire appears elsewhere in Isaiah (1:25-26). The seraph solemnly pronounces the prophet free of "guilt" and "sin." The meanings of these two broad terms overlap. Moreover, "guilt" in ancient Israel was not so much a feeling as a state of being brought about by wrong behavior. For sin and guilt to have "departed" or to have been "blotted out" means that the effects of wrongful actions have been ended or removed.

Remarkably, the ritual has cleansed the prophet but not addressed the other aspect of his confession: that he lives "among a people of unclean lips" (v. 5). This suggests that Isaiah has now been set apart from the people.[82]

6:8. For the first time Yahweh speaks, and not directly to the prophet. The vision report reaches its climax when the prophet overhears the Lord asking the heavenly court who should be sent, and the prophet steps forward without hesitation. The closest biblical parallel to this scene and these speeches appears in 1 Kgs 22:19-23, where the Lord asks the heavenly council how best to bring judgment (see also Jer 23:18). Seen in that context, the harsh commission that follows is not surprising.[83]

6:9-10. Now the Lord speaks directly to Isaiah with his commission, setting forth how the prophet is to bring judgment upon "this people." There are two parts to Yahweh's address. In the first (vv. 9-10*a*) the Lord commands Isaiah what to say and do, and in the second (v. 10*b*), the Lord sets out the purpose of those words and actions. The prophet is to tell the people to listen but not comprehend, to look but not understand; he is to prevent the people from understanding, hearing, or seeing lest they see, listen, and comprehend and "turn and be healed." Isaiah's mission is clear: He is to prevent repentance and healing.

The force of the prophet's question is by no means self-evident. Viewed in the context of other biblical vocation reports, this could serve, along with v. 5, as an expression of resistance or reluctance. Although he does not explicitly object to the commission, he does raise a question about it. Behind these words stands a long tradition of prayer in ancient Israel. "How long?" is a common opening in the individual complaint psalms, the preface to a petition (Pss 13:2; 74:10; 75:5; 80:4; 89:46; 90:13). Thus "Isaiah begs for mercy."[84] Since the petition is on behalf of others ("this people"), it is a prayer of intercession (see also Amos 7:2, 5).

The Lord's initial responses offer no hope. The commission will not be fulfilled until the land is completely destroyed, not just cities and houses but those who live in them as well (v. 11). Verse 12, which speaks of Yahweh in the third person, shifts the focus slightly to an exile that leaves the land empty. Verse 13 uses the imagery of trees and fire to emphasize that what has been burned will be burned again, including the stumps of fallen trees. Only the last line of the chapter, "the holy seed is its stump," offers a glimmer of hope beyond destruction. The meaning and translation of v. 13, and especially its last line, are quite uncertain; it is very likely that the final line is a secondary

82. See Christopher R. Seitz, *Isaiah 1–39,* Interpretation (Louisville: John Knox, 1993) 54-55.

83. Knierim, "The Vocation of Isaiah," 54-55.
84. Kaiser, *Isaiah 1–12,* 54-55.

addition or a modification of an earlier form of the tradition.[85]

No reason is given for this announcement of disaster, only that the word of the Lord through the prophet is to make repentance impossible and thus to effect judgment. There is a hint of indictment in the prophet's initial reaction to the vision of the Lord: "and I live among the people of unclean lips" (v. 5). The prophet but not the people had

85. Many commentators have considered 6:12-13 to be secondary, probably reflecting the circumstances of the Babylonian exile, and the final clause of 6:13 to be later still. See Clements, *Isaiah 1–39*, 78.

been cleansed. It is possible that the judgment announced here is finally to purify the people. There is a kind of symmetry, if not a parallel, between the cleansing of the prophet by means of the coal from the altar and the "cleansing" of the people through the destruction. At the end, even the stump is burned, and then—in the final form if not in the original vision report—there is the seed, the possibility of renewal. The editors of the book, if not Isaiah or the earliest tradents, saw that the national disaster could be a cleansing punishment and that new life could grow out of it.

REFLECTIONS

1. The most obvious issues this chapter raises concern vocation in general and the call to a prophetic role in particular. Isaiah 6:8, with the Lord's invitation and the prophet's unhesitating response, has been the focus of attention, particularly in Protestant circles. For generations of readers, Isaiah has been lifted up as the heroic model of the servant of God. But this heroism—if it is that—did not appear out of thin air. For the prophetic voice that reports the call and commission, the sequence of events leading up to this point is important. There had been the encounter with the presence of God, confession, a ritual of purification, overhearing the Lord addressing the heavenly council, and then acceptance of the commission. It is also important that God does not address Isaiah directly, but the one purified by the divine messenger is able to hear the call and accept the commission to go as God's representative, to take the place of the angels. The prophet could proclaim the most difficult message because he had experienced the presence of the God whose glory fills the whole earth.

Although at that critical moment the prophet shows no hesitation, there are two points of resistance. Isaiah's first words confess his unworthiness (6:5), and he intercedes for the people when he learns the message he is to bring (6:11*a*). The persistence of reluctance or resistance in vocation reports indicates that resistance to the call is not linked so much to individual personalities as it is to the experience of standing in the presence of God. It is part of the office, even verifying that one is called by God, to feel unworthy in one way or another. Moreover, it does not go too far to conclude that one test of an authentic call to confront others is to identify with the accused. Isaiah questioned the harsh message and interceded for the people. In the Old Testament, one is allowed to resist, to disagree with, and to challenge even the God whose glory fills the whole earth. Questions are always allowed.

If standing in the presence of God were not enough, the biblical prophets believed that their words had genuine power. Because their words are the human expression of the words of God, what they say changes the course of events. What could be more intimidating to a messenger? The prophet is empowered with words that will prevent repentance and will bring judgment. Are there any modern words that have—or are understood to have—such power? Although we seldom believe that our words are the direct Word of God, we know that words have power. To be sure, some words have more power than others, but none are "off the record." Rituals and official language are particularly powerful. If one says, for example, "I now pronounce you husband and wife," then reality has been changed, even if the marriage does not last.

One other point concerning the prophetic call deserves consideration. The vision in the Temple, the hymn, the smoke of the offering, and the ritual of purification show that the prophet is in the sanctuary. Such texts as this make it difficult to drive a wedge between a prophetic and a priestly vocation. The contemporary call to respond prophetically to social problems such as racism, poverty, and other forms of injustice typically is experienced in the context of prayer and worship. Likewise, prophetic words and actions gain conviction and force when expressed out of genuine piety. Moreover, worship and prayer are shallow without awareness of and concern for the specific and concrete problems of human societies.

2. When Isaiah 6 appears in church lectionaries the reading usually ends with the prophet's exclamation in v. 8: "Here am I, send me!" That may be the climax, but it is not the end. The church tradition that selected the lectionary lost its nerve when it came to the contents of the prophet's commission, what he was told to say and do. Serious problems arise when one considers the message that Isaiah was commissioned to deliver. This command to prevent hearing, to "make the mind of this people dull," has long been a problem for readers. (The Greek text tried to tone it down by changing the imperatives of 6:10 to indicatives.)[86]

The meaning of the message is unmistakable. These lines confront their readers with the bad news. Many prefer to interpret even the prophetic announcements of disaster as warnings, to encourage repentance and thus avert the announced judgment. Here the prophet is to *prevent* repentance: "so that they may *not* look . . . listen . . . comprehend . . . and turn and be healed" (italics added).

To be sure, this message needs to be interpreted in its wider context in Isaiah 1–39, the entire book of Isaiah—indeed, the biblical tradition as a whole. This is neither the only nor the last word. But readers, and especially modern readers, tend to move over it too quickly. Is it ever possible that the Word of God, the truth for the present and future, is the proclamation of judgment? The Word of God is not a dogma, requiring the same proclamation in all times and places. Thus there is a time and an occasion not only for judgment, but also for salvation. We could miss the yes because we have not heard the no.

Do circumstances have to get worse before they can get better? Something like that is suggested in the final form of Isaiah 6. With that glimmer of hope in the final line, "the holy seed is its stump," the editors of the text did not deny the announcement of disaster—in fact, they may have experienced it—but they could see beyond judgment.

3. Undergirding this text, including the call of the prophet and his horrible commission, is a profound understanding of God. Virtually every line emphasizes that God is holy. The prophetic account of standing in the awesome presence of God describes what many have considered to be the heart of religious experience. The experience is both mysterious and awesome.[87] To encounter that presence is to acknowledge one's own imperfection. Does one need such a dramatic encounter to experience God, the Holy One?

If one reads only 6:3 and 8, then Isaiah becomes a text for Trinity Sunday in Christian lectionaries. The threefold "holy" and the Lord's self-reference in the plural ("who will go for *us*") were, for the early church, obvious references to the Trinity. The famous Christian hymn "Holy, Holy, Holy" derives in part from this text. But the text is not about the Trinity, a doctrine that arose in the early church long after the Bible had been written. This text does, however, reflect the experience of God that leads to such a doctrine. It includes all the essential elements: First, God is experienced as transcendent and all-powerful. The hem of the Lord's robe alone fills the Temple; thus a metaphor of size or dimension expresses the inexpressible. Second, God's presence fills the whole earth. Third, with the call and the active word, God intervenes in history through a human vessel.

---

86. See Seitz, *Isaiah 1–39*, 55.
87. R. Otto, *The Idea of the Holy* (New York: Oxford University Press, 1958; originally published 1923).

Isaiah 7:1-9, A Remnant Shall Return, If . . .

NIV

7 When Ahaz son of Jotham, the son of Uzziah, was king of Judah, King Rezin of Aram and Pekah son of Remaliah king of Israel marched up to fight against Jerusalem, but they could not overpower it.

²Now the house of David was told, "Aram has allied itself with*ᵃ* Ephraim"; so the hearts of Ahaz and his people were shaken, as the trees of the forest are shaken by the wind.

³Then the LORD said to Isaiah, "Go out, you and your son Shear-Jashub,*ᵇ* to meet Ahaz at the end of the aqueduct of the Upper Pool, on the road to the Washerman's Field. ⁴Say to him, 'Be careful, keep calm and don't be afraid. Do not lose heart because of these two smoldering stubs of firewood—because of the fierce anger of Rezin and Aram and of the son of Remaliah. ⁵Aram, Ephraim and Remaliah's son have plotted your ruin, saying, ⁶"Let us invade Judah; let us tear it apart and divide it among ourselves, and make the son of Tabeel king over it." ⁷Yet this is what the Sovereign LORD says:

" 'It will not take place,
    it will not happen,
⁸for the head of Aram is Damascus,
    and the head of Damascus is only Rezin.
Within sixty-five years
    Ephraim will be too shattered to be
        a people.
⁹The head of Ephraim is Samaria,
    and the head of Samaria is only
        Remaliah's son.
If you do not stand firm in your faith,
    you will not stand at all.' "

ᵃ2 Or has set up camp in   ᵇ3 Shear-Jashub means a remnant will return.

NRSV

7 In the days of Ahaz son of Jotham son of Uzziah, king of Judah, King Rezin of Aram and King Pekah son of Remaliah of Israel went up to attack Jerusalem, but could not mount an attack against it. ²When the house of David heard that Aram had allied itself with Ephraim, the heart of Ahaz*ᵃ* and the heart of his people shook as the trees of the forest shake before the wind.

3Then the LORD said to Isaiah, Go out to meet Ahaz, you and your son Shear-jashub,*ᵇ* at the end of the conduit of the upper pool on the highway to the Fuller's Field, ⁴and say to him, Take heed, be quiet, do not fear, and do not let your heart be faint because of these two smoldering stumps of firebrands, because of the fierce anger of Rezin and Aram and the son of Remaliah. ⁵Because Aram—with Ephraim and the son of Remaliah—has plotted evil against you, saying, ⁶Let us go up against Judah and cut off Jerusalem*ᶜ* and conquer it for ourselves and make the son of Tabeel king in it; ⁷therefore thus says the Lord GOD:
    It shall not stand,
        and it shall not come to pass.
⁸ For the head of Aram is Damascus,
        and the head of Damascus is Rezin.
    (Within sixty-five years Ephraim will be shattered, no longer a people.)
⁹ The head of Ephraim is Samaria,
        and the head of Samaria is the son of
            Remaliah.
    If you do not stand firm in faith,
        you shall not stand at all.

ᵃHeb his heart   ᵇThat is A remnant shall return   ᶜHeb cut it off

COMMENTARY

Chapter 7 consists of two distinct, but connected, units, vv. 1-9 and vv. 10-25. They are bound by their common historical situation, the fact that both are reports of symbolic actions involving sons of the prophet and that both involve encounters between Isaiah and Ahaz. The clear transition in v. 10 ("Again the LORD spoke to Ahaz") is a mark of conjunction as well as disjunction, indicating that two separate prophetic reports have been joined. Thus the narrative framework that continues through 8:22 both links and separates a series of episodes.

This particular unit is a self-contained report of a prophetic sign act or symbolic action, consisting of three parts. The first part (vv. 1-2) provides the essential background or historical setting for the episode. In the second part (vv. 3-6), the Lord gives instructions to the prophet concerning what to do and say: that he is to take his son Shear-jashub and confront King Ahaz. The third part (vv. 7-9) is a prophetic address, an announcement of salvation to be presented in a time of national danger. There is narrative, to be sure, but most of the space is given to speeches by Yahweh, first to the prophet and then to the king and, by implication, to the people.

Reports of symbolic actions appear throughout the prophetic books and elsewhere in the OT. One of the more dramatic is the story of the prophet Elijah on his deathbed (2 Kgs 13:14-19), who has the king actually perform the sign. The brief stories may be third-person accounts about actions performed by the prophets (Isaiah 20; Jeremiah 19; 32; Hos 1:2-8) or in first-person style (Hosea 3). Generally, such reports include or imply three movements: divine instructions for the action, fulfillment of the instructions, and interpretation of the action's meaning. What is missing in Isa 7:1-9, although clearly implied, is the account of Isaiah's execution of the instructions. The instructions themselves are so vivid that the reader needs no repetition. Even the reaction of the audience—the king—is anticipated. Symbolic actions were one thing: They were designed to communicate, and also to set into motion, the word of the Lord. But why, the reader will ask, do we have the report? The story of the action becomes a means of communicating that word in different contexts for those who did not witness the sign but can read about it.

At a time of international crisis, Isaiah intervenes in political decisions with a word from Yahweh. Although the encounter with the king does not make explicit use of the prophet's son, the message is embodied in his name, Shear-jashub, "A Remnant Shall Return." Through the prophet, Yahweh reassures Ahaz that he has nothing to fear from his present enemies and concludes with a warning that he should "stand firm in faith" (v. 9). Isaiah counseled nonresistance based on

faith in the ancient promise to David that one of his sons would always occupy the throne in Jerusalem. This message does not implement the commission reported in chap. 6. With the name "Shear-jashub," this unit picks up the concluding note of the chapter, which suggests that a remnant will be saved from destruction. But it does not give the harsh message of preventing repentance; the opposite is the case.

7:1-2. These verses first sketch the general situation (v. 1) and then, by means of a graphic metaphor, characterize the reaction of the king and "his people" to the threat. The historical information is presented not out of curiosity, but because this prophetic message concerns that particular time and situation, including both the international threat and the reaction of the king and the people to the threat. The historical events summarized here are spelled out in somewhat greater detail in 2 Kgs 16:1-20 (cf. 2 Chr 28:5ff.). When the Assyrian king Tiglath-pileser III began to move against the small states of Syria and Palestine, the leaders of those states responded by forming a coalition to oppose him. Apparently because Ahaz of Judah refused to join them, King Rezin of Damascus and King Pekah of Samaria, the capital of the northern kingdom, moved against Jerusalem (about 734 BCE) to topple Ahaz and replace him with someone more favorable to their policies.

Dynastic factors are essential to this passage. As will become more clear, identification of Pekah as "son of Remaliah" is meant to be demeaning. The reference to Ahaz as "the house of David" is no accident but is calculated to set the theme of what follows. The allusion to Ahaz as "son of Jotham son of Uzziah" both helps to tie this unit to Isaiah 6 and serves to reinforce the sense of the importance of the Davidic dynasty.

7:3-6. Following a standard introductory formula, Yahweh instructs Isaiah, concerning first what he is to do (v. 3) and then what he is to say (vv. 4-6). He is told to take his son Shear-jashub and meet King Ahaz "at the end of the conduit of the upper pool on the highway to the Fuller's Field." There must have been some special significance to the location of the encounter, and the original hearers and readers would have known precisely where it was. All we can know for sure is that it was in the environs of Jerusalem.

Something of the role and social location of the prophet is revealed here. Isaiah does have access to the king, but he does not go to the royal court. He waits for the king to come out and then addresses him without hesitation—or that is what we presume from the instructions.

Shear-jashub, "A Remnant Shall Return," plainly is a symbolic name and would have been given to the child long before this occasion, but it is mentioned only here. Its translation is open to question; moreover (as with the names of the other children in chaps. 7–8), it is enigmatic and, like the Oracle at Delphi, subject to various interpretations. It is not even self-evident whether the name itself conveys a promise or a threat or both. In Amos, allusions to a "remnant" emphasize that destruction will be virtually total (Amos 4:11; 5:3, 15; 3:12; 9:1-4). Does it refer here to the survival of some or to a religious turning, such as repentance?[88] If one reads the name according to the announcement in 10:20-23, then it emphasizes judgment: "*only* a remnant of them will return." In the context of chap. 6, one can hear hope for those who survive the coming disaster.[89] In the present literary setting, however, the message to Ahaz indicates that the name is a distinctly positive symbol. Thus it may very well indicate that only a remnant of the enemies who presently threaten Judah and Jerusalem will return.

The prophet's message to Ahaz (vv. 4-6) is a word of reassurance, an oracle of salvation. There are two pairs of admonitions at the beginning— "take heed, be quiet" and "fear not, do not let your heart be faint"—followed by what the king is not to fear: neither the anger of these enemies nor their actions. The context to some extent parallels the ancient tradition of the holy war, where the leader inquires of God through some means concerning the decision to go into battle. Typically such oracles begin with the third admonition in the address, "fear not," and emphasize that the Lord will be with the army (e.g., Josh 8:1). Here the king is encouraged to be calm in the face of the enemy coalition. (The NRSV's "Jerusalem" does not appear in the Hebrew text, which reads "let us

go up against Judah and cut it off.") The enemies are characterized scornfully. The king of Israel is designated not by name but only as "the son of Remaliah," and the pretender whom the coalition would set up in Judah is called only "the son of Tabeel."

7:7-9. This speech of Yahweh ("therefore thus says the LORD God") continues under the heading of the instructions given to Isaiah, but it is different from what precedes. First, it is in poetry, and second, it gives the explicit announcement concerning the future and the reasons for what will happen. Actually, the proclamation concerns what will not happen. It announces salvation by means of defeat to the enemies. The "it" that will not stand is the plot, including an attack on Jerusalem and the replacement of Ahaz with "the son of Tabeel."

Verses 8-9*a* present the reasons for the failure of the enemies. They will not succeed, because "the head of Aram is Damascus and the head of Damascus is Rezin." How are these facts—listing each country, its capital city, and its king—reasons for the announcement that the plot will fail? Evidently the statement is elliptical, presuming but not stating something that should be obvious to the hearers and readers. The attack will fail because the head of Judah is Jerusalem, and the head of Jerusalem is the son of David. The ridicule of the enemies presupposes Isaiah's confidence in the ancient promise to David and the election of Jerusalem as the Lord's holy place.

The note that Ephraim, the northern kingdom, will be destroyed and will no longer be a people "within sixty-five years" is a later addition, but one that is difficult to relate to particular historical events. The northern kingdom was, indeed, destroyed and its people scattered over the Assyrian Empire, but much earlier than suggested here. The Assyrians captured Samaria in 722/21 BCE, and the circumstances of this prophetic message are the Syro-Ephraimitic war, in about 734 BCE.

The final two lines of v. 9 return to admonitions directed to Ahaz. They make the proclamation of deliverance conditional and indicate how the king is to respond to the Lord's promise. Translations have attempted to capture the wordplay in these lines: "stand firm in faith [תאמינו *ta'ămînû*]" and "stand at all [תאמנו *tē'āmēnû*]" stem from the same

88. See H. Wildberger, *Isaiah 1–12,* trans. Thomas H. Trapp (Minneapolis: Fortress, 1991) 297.

89. Cf. O. Kaiser, *Isaiah 1–12: A Commentary,* trans. R. A. Wilson (Philadelphia: Westminster, 1972) 90-91, who sees the name as the epitome of the entire message of Isaiah.

Hebrew form, the root of "amen," that rare Hebrew word that has made it into the English language. "Faith" here certainly does not refer to believing in a particular doctrine, but to having confidence, trusting in the Lord's care for Jerusalem and the dynasty of David. Failure of such trust—as reflected in the king's trembling before his enemies (v. 2)—leads to failure. So these final words convey both warning and reassurance.

REFLECTIONS

Who could read the book of Isaiah and suggest that religion and politics do not mix? Here, as elsewhere (Isa 20:1-6, 18; 14:28-32), we encounter the prophet involved in political affairs. Isaiah confronts the king to give direct advice about international politics, but there is more. He tells the king how to behave based on what God has in store in the immediate future. He urges the king to remain calm and await the failure of a military invasion. The prophet's counsel is founded on specific theological traditions concerning the capital city and the monarchy. There are lessons here for the relationship between religion and politics, church and state, theology and public policy.

Those who look to the Hebrew scriptures for indications of how political and religious issues and institutions should be related must be cautious, however. A deep gulf separates ancient Israel from modern Western nations. Above all, Israel was a theocracy, a state presumed to be "under God" in very concrete and specific ways. It was a monarchy as well, but at least in Judah in the eighth century BCE, the king as the descendant of David was Yahweh's chosen ruler. Within that theocracy there were distinct institutions, but "church" and "state" were coterminous. There was only one legitimate faith; both political and religious institutions were accountable to Yahweh. However, that did not eliminate disagreements concerning the implications of that faith in specific national circumstances. In political matters, authority is the issue, even in a theocracy— perhaps especially in a theocracy, where the people as a whole and the leadership in particular are to be guided by the will of God. Conflicts among institutional representatives were common. The high priest as representative of the king accused Amos of sedition and prohibited the prophet from speaking in Israel (Amos 7:10-17). Jeremiah's conflicts with the king got him incarcerated (Jeremiah 38) and hauled into court by authorities who asked for the death penalty (Jeremiah 26). When he sent a scroll to the king, the king burned it (Jeremiah 36).

Thus we cannot easily take refuge in the fact that ours is a more complex society, that our religious institutions are distinct from the political ones, that no modern Western nation is a theocracy, and that diverse religions and faiths demand respect. Throughout most of its history in the West, Christianity has been an established religion. Religious freedom was the force that drove the so-called separation of church and state in the United States. But the prohibition of the establishment of (a particular) religion need not be interpreted to mean that religious voices should be silent in political affairs.

To the contrary, the prophetic tradition insists that all people of faith have responsibility for public policies. That would seem to be the case especially in a democracy. This need not mean that the prophetic voice will announce the future or declare whether God wishes the nation to enter a particular war or not—but it might. At the very least, the specifically religious role in public political discourse entails the theological interpretation of events. There is a voice that should be heard in the public discourse, a voice shaped by engagement with deep theological traditions.

Everyone knows the danger of religious voices in the establishment of political policy. It is the danger of absolute truth, including the conviction that God is on the side of a particular nation or group. This can conjure up visions of the French Revolution or of the Spanish Inquisition, when absolute truth became a matter of life and death. Viewed in its context in Isaiah, however, the word of God is not a dogma. Remarkably, the word of reassurance in Isa 7:1-9 comes immediately after the prophet's commission to prevent repentance and set judgment into motion. The prophetic tradition is aware that different circumstances require different messages. Whether this almost chaotic diversity of perspectives comes from Isaiah or from the editors of the book is irrelevant for this point. The complexity of this book, to say nothing of the scriptures as a whole, shows how the religious and theological interpretation addresses complex political events.

It is, indeed, a more complicated situation in the modern world. In a democracy, one cannot directly confront the head of state, and seldom even one's elected representatives. But there are some models in the prophetic texts. One can use words as well as actions—symbolic and otherwise—to criticize, propose, and influence policies. Voices shaped by religious convictions—even diverse religious convictions—are essential to the establishment of justice and righteousness. The tyranny of absolute truth can be realized only if there is just one voice in the public discourse.

Isaiah 7:10-25, The Sign of Immanuel

NIV

[10]Again the LORD spoke to Ahaz, [11]"Ask the LORD your God for a sign, whether in the deepest depths or in the highest heights."

[12]But Ahaz said, "I will not ask; I will not put the LORD to the test."

[13]Then Isaiah said, "Hear now, you house of David! Is it not enough to try the patience of men? Will you try the patience of my God also? [14]Therefore the Lord himself will give you[a] a sign: The virgin will be with child and will give birth to a son, and[b] will call him Immanuel.[c] [15]He will eat curds and honey when he knows enough to reject the wrong and choose the right. [16]But before the boy knows enough to reject the wrong and choose the right, the land of the two kings you dread will be laid waste. [17]The LORD will bring on you and on your people and on the house of your father a time unlike any since Ephraim broke away from Judah—he will bring the king of Assyria."

[18]In that day the LORD will whistle for flies from the distant streams of Egypt and for bees from the land of Assyria. [19]They will all come and settle in the steep ravines and in the crevices in the rocks, on all the thornbushes and at all the water holes. [20]In that day the Lord will use a razor hired from beyond the River[d]—the king of Assyria—to shave your head and the hair of your legs, and to take off your beards also. [21]In that day, a man will keep alive a young cow and

[a]14 The Hebrew is plural.   [b]14 Masoretic Text; Dead Sea Scrolls *and he* or *and they*   [c]14 Immanuel means *God with us.*
[d]20 That is, the Euphrates

NRSV

10Again the LORD spoke to Ahaz, saying, 11Ask a sign of the LORD your God; let it be deep as Sheol or high as heaven. 12But Ahaz said, I will not ask, and I will not put the LORD to the test. 13Then Isaiah[a] said: "Hear then, O house of David! Is it too little for you to weary mortals, that you weary my God also? 14Therefore the Lord himself will give you a sign. Look, the young woman[b] is with child and shall bear a son, and shall name him Immanuel.[c] 15He shall eat curds and honey by the time he knows how to refuse the evil and choose the good. 16For before the child knows how to refuse the evil and choose the good, the land before whose two kings you are in dread will be deserted. 17The LORD will bring on you and on your people and on your ancestral house such days as have not come since the day that Ephraim departed from Judah—the king of Assyria."

18On that day the LORD will whistle for the fly that is at the sources of the streams of Egypt, and for the bee that is in the land of Assyria. 19And they will all come and settle in the steep ravines, and in the clefts of the rocks, and on all the thornbushes, and on all the pastures.

20On that day the Lord will shave with a razor hired beyond the River—with the king of Assyria—the head and the hair of the feet, and it will take off the beard as well.

[a]Heb *he*   [b]Gk *the virgin*   [c]That is *God is with us*

NIV

two goats. ²²And because of the abundance of the milk they give, he will have curds to eat. All who remain in the land will eat curds and honey. ²³In that day, in every place where there were a thousand vines worth a thousand silver shekels,^a there will be only briers and thorns. ²⁴Men will go there with bow and arrow, for the land will be covered with briers and thorns. ²⁵As for all the hills once cultivated by the hoe, you will no longer go there for fear of the briers and thorns; they will become places where cattle are turned loose and where sheep run.

^e23 That is, about 25 pounds (about 11.5 kilograms)

NRSV

21On that day one will keep alive a young cow and two sheep, ²²and will eat curds because of the abundance of milk that they give; for everyone that is left in the land shall eat curds and honey.

23On that day every place where there used to be a thousand vines, worth a thousand shekels of silver, will become briers and thorns. ²⁴With bow and arrows one will go there, for all the land will be briers and thorns; ²⁵and as for all the hills that used to be hoed with a hoe, you will not go there for fear of briers and thorns; but they will become a place where cattle are let loose and where sheep tread.

COMMENTARY

In the context, the reader is to take this episode as either a second meeting between the prophet and the king or simply a continuation of the encounter reported in 7:1-9.[90] We are to understand this narrative under the heading in 7:1-2 and presume that the second symbolic action also took place during the Syro-Ephraimitic war (see the Commentary on 7:1-9). Yet the seams between the two reports are rough. The introductory "Again the LORD spoke to Ahaz, saying," marks both a break and a continuation, but one that does not continue the previous instructions to the prophet. The discourse shifts from a prophetic announcement to a dialogue between Yahweh and Ahaz. Throughout vv. 10-17 in particular, the distinction between the voice of Yahweh and the voice of Isaiah blurs. However, this unit clearly depends on and presumes at least 7:1-2, since the sign of Immanuel concerns the "two kings" mentioned there as well as the fear that gripped Ahaz (v. 16).

This section consists of two parts. The first (vv. 10-17) is a report of a symbolic action or sign act performed by the prophet before the king. The second (vv. 18-25) is a series of four prophetic announcements that continue and extend the concluding interpretation of the sign, each beginning with "On that day" (vv. 18, 20-21, 23).

7:10-17. Just as vv. 1-2 had set the context for

90. See Wildberger, *Isaiah 1–12,* 279-318, and other commentaries.

the symbolic action that follows, so also these verses set the scene for the sign of Immanuel. The circumstances are presented in the form of a dialogue between Yahweh and Ahaz. The king is invited to ask for a sign—any sign—but he declines, hiding behind a pious refusal to "put the LORD to the test" (v. 12; see Exod 17:2; Deut 6:16; Judg 6:17). Much is left unsaid. The Lord's offer of a sign must refer to a signal of reassurance. Given the context, the king's response is to be seen as a failure of faith, an unwillingness to be reassured. It was common, however, for kings or other leaders to inquire of the Lord, often through prophets, before deciding to go to battle (see 2 Kgs 13:14-19). Yahweh responds angrily through the prophet (the NRSV and the NIV have "Isaiah" in v. 13 where the Hebrew has only a pronoun, "he"), who is the speaker in vv. 13-17. The Lord will give a sign: "Look, the young woman is with child and shall bear a son, and shall name him Immanuel" (v. 14).

Then follows the interpretation of the sign (vv. 16-17), a promise that before the child knows how to "refuse the evil and choose the good"—that is, within a short time—the present military threat from "the two kings" (Rezin of Damascus and "the son of Remaliah" of Israel, vv. 1-2) will have ended. Although the means are not stated, the prophet promises that God will intervene to save king and people.

Seen in its historical and narrative framework, these verses are an announcement of salvation to the king and the people of Judah concerning the immediate future. The prophet gives no specific timetable but speaks in terms of the birth and development of the child. When the baby eats "curds and honey" probably refers to the first solid food after mother's milk; when the child can "refuse the evil and choose the good" (vv. 15-16) would refer to some degree of moral accountability, but no biblical traditions indicate a particular age.[91] This is not the only report in this section of Isaiah in which the birth of a baby is a symbol of hope (see 9:1-7). Here the good news is carried by the child's name, "Immanuel" (v. 14), "God is with us." Deliverance will come, not through alliances or military might, but through divine intervention, by a God who keeps promises.

Few textual and translation problems in the OT have generated more controversy than those of Isa 7:14. However, there can be little doubt about the meaning or translation of the crucial word. The Hebrew word עלמה ('almâ) is correctly rendered by the NRSV and almost all other modern translations as "young woman." The term is neutral with regard to her marital status or sexual experience. It was the Greek translation of Isaiah that introduced the rendering "virgin" (παρθένος parthenos), thus setting the stage for the particular messianic interpretation of the passage expressed in the NT. The bridge between the eighth century BCE and the early church is thus yet another historical and theological context, that of the translation of the Hebrew scriptures for Jews in a Hellenistic, pre-Christian culture. It is equally clear that the Hebrew text of Isaiah originally read here "young woman" and that the Evangelists inherited a translation of Isaiah that read "virgin."

Central to the interpretation of the text are the tenses of the verbs in v. 14b. The Hebrew clearly begins with the present tense and moves to the future: "the young woman is with child and shall bear a son" (so NRSV and most other modern translations). As in most other prophetic announcements or symbolic actions, Isaiah has the immediate future in view, and thus the woman and the child are his contemporaries. The prophet indicates to the king a woman who is already pregnant; the sign is not the pregnancy but the birth and name of the child. However, the identity of the woman is difficult, if not impossible, to establish. In view of a context that stresses the significance of the Davidic dynasty, many commentators have taken the child to be the crown prince and the woman as the wife of Ahaz. Others, seeing the passage in some ways parallel to Isa 8:1-4, have argued that the woman was the wife of the prophet and the child his son. It is quite likely, however, that the "young woman" was simply a pregnant woman whom Isaiah saw as he was addressing the king.

One of the keys to the meaning of this passage is the word "sign" (אות 'ôt, vv. 11, 14). It is the same word used in the tradition about the "signs and wonders" performed in Egypt before the exodus, and thus has come to be associated in modern minds with the so-called miraculous. However, such signs may be ordinary events as well as extraordinary ones. The decisive point in the OT view is that a "sign" is revelatory, that it communicates God's word or will or nature. Thus it is not remarkable that in Isaiah 7 something as common—and also as wonderful—as the birth of a baby boy is a message from God and a revelation of the future. The name embodies the promise of God's saving presence.

Verse 17 is a curious note in its context, and most commentators take it as secondary, although possibly even added by Isaiah after the king refused to accept the sign of good news.[92] Without the syntactically awkward "the king of Assyria," it could be taken as either positive or negative; good times or bad times are coming. The reference to the king of Assyria sounds like bad news—inconsistent with what has preceded—but it could mean that the king of Assyria will deal with Judah's enemies. In fact, he did.

7:18-25. Four announcements, each beginning with "On that day," seem to expand and extend the explanation of the symbolic action in vv. 10-17. The fact that the sign and its interpretation are enigmatic has invited such additions, most of which are connected with the sign of Immanuel by key words or concepts. Typically, when editors expand and modify they tend to soften the word of judgment or see beyond it to a time of salvation. But here, with the exception of vv. 21-22, the

---

91. See Wildberger, *Isaiah 1–12*, 315.

92. See Ronald E. Clements, *Isaiah 1–39*, NCB (Grand Rapids: Eerdmans, 1980) 89.

additions move in the direction of judgment. "On that day" refers to the day of the Lord's judgment, but it is not yet the eschatological concept it will become in apocalyptic literature.

The first and second prophecies present Assyria as a threat, presumably against Judah, but this is not stated. The "fly" and the "bee" (v. 18) function here as metaphors for Egypt—unexpected in this literary and historical context—and Assyria, who will fill the land (v. 19). In v. 20 the metaphor shifts from plagues of insects to Assyria the razor in the hand of Yahweh, similar to Assyria the rod of the Lord's anger (10:5). "The River" is the Euphrates; "feet," as in 6:2, is a euphemism for sexual organs.

Agricultural images dominate the last two units. The prophecy in vv. 21-22 seems to begin as an announcement of trouble, when one will struggle to keep alive a few domestic animals, but turns to a vision of plenty. "Curds" in v. 22 picks up the reference to the child's development in v. 15. The final announcement (vv. 23-25) sets out a scene in which rich vineyards have become a dangerous wilderness, where cultivated land has become fit only for grazing cattle and sheep.

REFLECTIONS

Texts such as this one, especially when read in the context of Christian worship, sharpen the tension between the historical meaning and the homiletical or theological interpretation of the Bible, and of the Old Testament in particular. What Isa 7:10-25 meant in its original contexts and what it means in the shadow of Matt 1:18-25 may be quite different. Matthew quotes Isa 7:14 as a prophecy of the conception and birth of Jesus, while Isaiah almost certainly had in view a particular woman and child in his own time. Because the church's commitment to the Bible includes the Old Testament, Christian readers should seek to allow the words from Isaiah to be heard in their own terms first and to consider not only how the New Testament interprets the Old, but also how the Old Testament enriches the New Testament.

Regardless of the extent and limits of our understanding of the passage in its own literary and historical context, it is hardly possible for a Christian congregation to hear the Immanuel prophecy without thinking of the birth of Jesus. What, then, are we to do with the tension between the ancient and the Christian meanings? It is difficult, but essential, to sustain the tension, to refuse to resolve it quickly by choosing the one while rejecting the other. Even a typological interpretation that sees the woman and her son as a model of Mary and Jesus should be attentive to what it is that has been reinterpreted, to what "Immanuel" meant in its ancient context.

Living with Isa 7:10-16 itself helps interpreters to keep their feet on the ground of history and human experience. The particular kind of good news proclaimed here by the ancient Israelite prophet should not be forgotten. It is a message that sees pregnancy and birth—even when not understood as miraculous—as signs of God's concern for God's people. That good news comes into a world with such concrete problems as international politics and threats of war. The fact that the prophet and his message are so directly involved in political events may move us to ask if such expectations as his, along with the message of the coming of Jesus, are legitimate hopes for the people of God. Is the coming of Jesus related to international politics or not? Those who take the full biblical context seriously, including Isa 7:10-16, will conclude that the answer to this question is yes.

Isaiah 8:1-22, Signs and Portents

NIV

8 The LORD said to me, "Take a large scroll and write on it with an ordinary pen: Maher-Shalal-Hash-Baz.[a] 2And I will call in Uriah the priest and Zechariah son of Jeberekiah as reliable witnesses for me."

3Then I went to the prophetess, and she conceived and gave birth to a son. And the LORD said to me, "Name him Maher-Shalal-Hash-Baz. 4Before the boy knows how to say 'My father' or 'My mother,' the wealth of Damascus and the plunder of Samaria will be carried off by the king of Assyria."

5The LORD spoke to me again:
6"Because this people has rejected
    the gently flowing waters of Shiloah
and rejoices over Rezin
    and the son of Remaliah,
7therefore the Lord is about to bring
        against them
    the mighty floodwaters of the River[b]—
    the king of Assyria with all his pomp.
It will overflow all its channels,
    run over all its banks
8and sweep on into Judah, swirling over it,
    passing through it and reaching up to
        the neck.
Its outspread wings will cover the breadth of
        your land,
    O Immanuel[c]!"

9Raise the war cry,[d] you nations, and
        be shattered!
    Listen, all you distant lands.
Prepare for battle, and be shattered!
Prepare for battle, and be shattered!
10Devise your strategy, but it will be thwarted;
    propose your plan, but it will not stand,
    for God is with us.[e]

11The LORD spoke to me with his strong hand upon me, warning me not to follow the way of this people. He said:

12"Do not call conspiracy

NRSV

8 Then the LORD said to me, Take a large tablet and write on it in common characters, "Belonging to Maher-shalal-hash-baz,"[a] 2and have it attested[b] for me by reliable witnesses, the priest Uriah and Zechariah son of Jeberechiah. 3And I went to the prophetess, and she conceived and bore a son. Then the LORD said to me, Name him Maher-shalal-hash-baz; 4for before the child knows how to call "My father" or "My mother," the wealth of Damascus and the spoil of Samaria will be carried away by the king of Assyria.

5The LORD spoke to me again: 6Because this people has refused the waters of Shiloah that flow gently, and melt in fear before[c] Rezin and the son of Remaliah; 7therefore, the Lord is bringing up against it the mighty flood waters of the River, the king of Assyria and all his glory; it will rise above all its channels and overflow all its banks; 8it will sweep on into Judah as a flood, and, pouring over, it will reach up to the neck; and its outspread wings will fill the breadth of your land, O Immanuel.

9 Band together, you peoples, and be dismayed;
    listen, all you far countries;
gird yourselves and be dismayed;
    gird yourselves and be dismayed!
10 Take counsel together, but it shall be brought
        to naught;
    speak a word, but it will not stand,
    for God is with us.[d]

11For the LORD spoke thus to me while his hand was strong upon me, and warned me not to walk in the way of this people, saying: 12Do not call conspiracy all that this people calls conspiracy, and do not fear what it fears, or be in dread. 13But the LORD of hosts, him you shall regard as holy; let him be your fear, and let him be your dread. 14He will become a sanctuary, a stone one strikes against; for both houses of Israel he will become a rock one stumbles over—a trap and a snare for the inhabitants of Jerusalem. 15And many among

NIV

everything that these people call
conspiracy[a];
do not fear what they fear,
and do not dread it.
[13]The LORD Almighty is the one you are to
regard as holy,
he is the one you are to fear,
he is the one you are to dread,
[14]and he will be a sanctuary;
but for both houses of Israel he will be
a stone that causes men to stumble
and a rock that makes them fall.
And for the people of Jerusalem he will be
a trap and a snare.
[15]Many of them will stumble;
they will fall and be broken,
they will be snared and captured."

[16]Bind up the testimony
and seal up the law among my disciples.
[17]I will wait for the LORD,
who is hiding his face from the house of Jacob.
I will put my trust in him.

[18]Here am I, and the children the LORD has given me. We are signs and symbols in Israel from the LORD Almighty, who dwells on Mount Zion.
[19]When men tell you to consult mediums and spiritists, who whisper and mutter, should not a people inquire of their God? Why consult the dead on behalf of the living? [20]To the law and to the testimony! If they do not speak according to this word, they have no light of dawn. [21]Distressed and hungry, they will roam through the land; when they are famished, they will become enraged and, looking upward, will curse their king and their God. [22]Then they will look toward the earth and see only distress and darkness and fearful gloom, and they will be thrust into utter darkness.

[a]12 Or Do not call for a treaty / every time these people call for a treaty

NRSV

them shall stumble; they shall fall and be broken;
they shall be snared and taken.

16Bind up the testimony, seal the teaching among my disciples. [17]I will wait for the LORD, who is hiding his face from the house of Jacob, and I will hope in him. [18]See, I and the children whom the LORD has given me are signs and portents in Israel from the LORD of hosts, who dwells on Mount Zion. [19]Now if people say to you, "Consult the ghosts and the familiar spirits that chirp and mutter; should not a people consult their gods, the dead on behalf of the living, [20]for teaching and for instruction?" Surely, those who speak like this will have no dawn! [21]They will pass through the land,[a] greatly distressed and hungry; when they are hungry, they will be enraged and will curse[b] their king and their gods. They will turn their faces upward, [22]or they will look to the earth, but will see only distress and darkness, the gloom of anguish; and they will be thrust into thick darkness.[c]

[a]Heb it [b]Or curse by [c]Meaning of Heb uncertain

COMMENTARY

This chapter consists of four distinct units (vv. 1-4, 5-10, 11-15, 16-22), but all are closely related to each other as well as to the prophetic narratives in the previous chapter. Whereas the symbolic action reports in chap. 7 were in the third person, these are first-person narratives or speeches set in an autobiographical framework. The first two narratives (vv. 1-4 and 5-10) clearly have to do with the same circumstances as Isaiah 7: the Syro-Ephramitic war, the fearlessness of King Ahaz, and a prophetic message of reassurance in the face of that fear. The actions in the previous chapter had been performed before and for the king, but no audience is indicated in this chapter. The first unit is another symbolic action report concerning the birth and name of a child, Maher-shalal-hash-baz. The second, a report of the reception and delivery of a word from the Lord, picks up and extends the symbolism of the sign of Immanuel from 7:14. The last two units focus more on the prophetic life and activity in relation to an audience that refuses to listen. The third unit (vv. 11-15) reports another message from the Lord, but this time containing instructions for the prophet and—in contrast to what has preceded it—pointing to punishment for both Israel and Judah. In the final unit (vv. 16-22), the prophet issues instructions for the "testimony" to be bound up and the "teaching" to be sealed among his disciples, pointing out that he and his children are "signs and portents" and issuing warnings about the future.

8:1-4. This brief narrative is a classic report of a prophetic symbolic action (see 1 Kgs 11:29-32; Ezek 37:15-28; see also the Commentary on 7:1-9).[93] Although autobiographical in style, its goal is not to present information about the prophet but to convey the message embodied in the sign. After the introductory speech formula ("Then the LORD said to me . . . ") come the instructions to the prophet to perform the sign, to take a tablet and write on it "belonging to Maher-shalal-hash-baz" (v. 1). The NRSV, following the ancient versions, has the instructions continuing into v. 2, but in the Hebrew text v. 2 begins the account of the prophet's performance of the sign. This included having the tablet attested to by "reliable witnesses," whose names are given (v. 2), and going in to the prophetess, who conceived a son (v. 3a). Again come instructions from the Lord to name the boy Maher-shalal-hash-baz (v. 3b). Finally, the speech of the Lord continues with the interpretation (introduced by "for") of the sign: Before the boy can say "my father" or "my mother," the king of Assyria will have laid ruin to Damascus and Samaria.

All three elements of symbolic action reports are here—instructions, performance, and interpretation—but not in a simple sequence. The initial report of instructions does not include everything that was done, and further instructions come after the birth of the child. This makes it appear that there is more than one sign, but all elements are related. The first action, writing the name and having it attested to by witnesses, seems mysterious. The sentence preceded by "to" or "belonging to" includes a proper name, "Maher-shalal-hash-baz." The purpose of the writing is to verify that the prophet knew in advance what was to happen because he had heard it from the Lord. In Israelite and other Near Eastern contracts, witnesses confirmed transactions and their dates. The witnessed document supports the validity of the sign of Maher-shalal-hash-baz itself, conveyed by the name. The message of this sign can be trusted because it was known even before the boy was conceived.

The name itself, which means "the spoil speeds, the prey hastens," is enigmatic but suggests disaster. However, the interpretation of the sign makes the point of the action unmistakable. Disaster is, indeed, coming, but for Judah's enemies in the Syro-Ephraimitic war (see the Commentary on 7:1-9). So the sign is an announcement of salvation for its hearers. The instrument of Israel's deliverance will be the king of Assyria.

The child clearly is the son of Isaiah,[94] as was Shear-jashub (7:3), but the role of his mother is less certain. Does the designation "the prophetess" refer simply to Isaiah's wife or to a prophetic function?

---

93. For other examples, see H. Wildberger, *Isaiah 1–12,* trans. Thomas H. Trapp (Minneapolis: Fortress, 1991) 334.

94. The proposal by H. M. Wolf, "A Solution to the Immanuel Prophecy in Is. 7:14–8:22 [8:1-2, 16]," *JBL* 91 (1972) 449-56, that Maher-shalal-hash-baz and Immanuel were the same child is unconvincing.

Since wives in the OT never are identified by the role or vocation of their husbands, it seems likely that she was a religious functionary of one kind or another.[95] Others identified as "prophetesses" in the OT are Miriam (Exod 15:20), Deborah (Judg 4:4), Hulda (2 Kgs 22:4; 2 Chr 34:22), and Noadiah (Neh 6:14).

Temporal considerations are important in the message and its validation. The writing of the name obviously would have been at least nine months before the name was given to the child. The sign and its interpretation reveal that the deliverance from the two enemies is to be soon, but not immediately. The stage at which a child is able to say "my father" or "my mother," of course, varies, but would have indicated approximately a year. In this respect as in others, the message of this symbolic action parallels that of the sign of Immanuel in 7:10-16. Although there is a degree of imprecision in the promise, this is a particular message in a particular time, and as such it is good news. It also includes confirmation that the prophet's words are the word of Yahweh.

In fact, the announcement did come true, beginning in 732 BCE when Tiglath-pileser III defeated Damascus, removed Pekah in Samaria, and set up Hoshea as king in Israel. But according to the deuteronomistic authors of Kings, Ahaz of Judah sold out to Assyria in the process (2 Kings 16; cf. 2 Kgs 15:29). This capitulation was only one of the reasons why Ahaz is considered a corrupt and evil king in the books of Kings and Chronicles (2 Chronicles 28).

8:5-10. These verses contain two distinct parts, vv. 5-8 and 9-10. Although the first-person narrative framework continues, the text has moved from the world of sign acts to that of prophetic announcements. This is a prophetic announcement, revealed to Isaiah, proclaiming that Assyria will sweep over Judah. The formula for the reception of the word (v. 5) parallels that in v. 1 but with the addition of "again," indicating that this speech is to be read as a continuation of vv. 1-4. This is particularly interesting, since the words in vv. 5-8 directly contradict the message of the sign act in vv. 1-4.

The reasons for punishment (v. 6), introduced

by "because," assume the information in 7:1-9, and especially the condition for survival set out in 7:9. The call to stand firm and trust, however, had been addressed to the king; now "this people" has failed by persisting in their fear of the enemy kings. Metaphors of water and waters characterize both the failure and the announcement of punishment. That the people have "refused the waters of Shiloah" refers to a little stream out of the Gihon Spring in Jerusalem, which provided clean drinking water. Here the stream represents the Davidic dynasty (see the Commentary on 7:1-9). The announcement of judgment (vv. 7-8), introduced with the typical transition "therefore," employs the image of the floodwaters of "the River"—that is, the Euphrates. The metaphor of the overflowing and flooding river is explained as representing "the king of Assyria and all his glory."

The first half of v. 8 continues the metaphor of the flood, with the water—that is, the Assyrians—filling the land of Judah "up to the neck." This suggests that it will come up to, say, Jerusalem, but will not drown it, that Judah will be devastated but not completely destroyed. More problematic is the second half of the verse, in which the metaphor shifts and the pronouns leave questions open. If the wings of the mighty bird represent Assyria, then the announcement of judgment continues, and the allusion to Immanuel would be ironic. On the other hand, if "its" wings are to be understood as "his" (i.e., Yahweh's) wings, then a common image for the Lord's protecting presence has been added by a later redactor who knew how events turned out[96] and has used the sign of Immanuel as the lens for interpreting this announcement.

Verses 9-10 shift to direct address in the plural, a summons to the "nations." A traditional summons to battle has been turned into a call to be defeated, and in the context the addressees are the Assyrians. Although it appears that the enemies are carrying out their own plans, they will be defeated, for "God is with us" ("Immanuel," v. 10).

8:11-15. This report in autobiographical style often has been called a "private" oracle, a message to the prophet concerning his role and behavior. The account has personal, almost confessional,

95. O. Kaiser, *Isaiah 1–12: A Commentary,* trans. R. A. Wilson (Philadelphia: Westminster, 1972) 111; cf. Wildberger, *Isaiah 1–12,* 337.

96. So Wildberger, *Isaiah 1–12,* 347.

aspects, is introduced as a powerful encounter with the Lord ("while his hand was strong upon me"), and is concerned with the prophet's integrity. Like the report of Jeremiah's vocation (Jer 1:4-10), it presumes that the prophet has encountered some opposition from the "people." At the very least, prophet and people disagree about what is conspiracy and what to fear, probably a reference to the coalition against Judah and the frightened reaction by the king and the people. So the message to Isaiah is to fear only the Lord (v. 13).

But why is Isaiah reporting this experience? A "private" oracle would not be expressed in public and preserved in the prophetic traditions unless it also conveyed a message to those people. So what begins personally turns into an announcement of disaster for Jerusalem and its inhabitants (vv. 14-15). The prophet addresses the people as third parties in the speech. In effect, Isaiah lets the people overhear what Yahweh has told him, thus accusing them of misunderstanding conspiracy and lacking faith. In this way the report parallels 7:1-9, as an address to the fears of the king and people. Moreover, the proclamation that Yahweh will become a "trap and a snare" is consistent with the hard commission given the prophet in 6:9-10. But the message is subtle, depending on who hears it and with whom they identify. If the hearers are those "disciples" mentioned in v. 16, and if they put themselves in the prophet's place, then they may hear not only a threat but also encouragement that there is no one to fear but the Lord.

8:16-22. This first-person report from the prophet, although lacking an introductory formula, has a clear beginning with the shift to direct address. It serves as a fitting conclusion to the collection that began in chap. 6, since both units concern the prophetic commission and activity and both are first-person reports. The addressee of the opening imperative (v. 16) is unclear, but the message as a whole is for Isaiah's disciples, the "you" in v. 19. The style is autobiographical, but not the intention. The text concerns the authenticity and validity of the prophetic word, not the personal life of the prophet. When his message is not heard—that is, accepted as the word of God—he writes it down and entrusts it to the disciples. This move from the spoken to the written word corresponds to that in Jeremiah 36.

It is not surprising for Isaiah to identify the

prophetic message as "instruction" (תורה *tôrâ,* 1:10). To call it "testimony" or evidence means that it will serve in the future as proof that Yahweh spoke to the prophet, spelling out in advance what would happen. Isaiah 30:8-11 is a close parallel and could very well be a duplicate account of the same events. It is possible that the words are to be sealed in a scroll, as in 29:11-12, so that they cannot be read. More likely, however, the sealing of the prophecy is like that of a contract or a deed, so that when the case comes up there will be proof of the transaction. This conclusion is confirmed by the note that the prophet and his children are "signs and portents" (v. 18; see also 30:8). Deutero-Isaiah uses just such earlier prophetic words as evidence that Yahweh is the one who has acted in history (48:3-5).

But for the time being, the prophet will withdraw ("wait for the Lord," v. 17). Since the Lord is hiding his face, there is no prophetic word to give. The silence of God is the result of a failure of the king and the people to trust in that God. No one knows who these "disciples" were,[97] but there is an old tradition of groups around a prophetic leader (1 Sam 10:5, 10-12; 19:20; 2 Kgs 4:1, 38; 6:1). How such associations functioned in the eighth century BCE is unclear, but Isaiah's words would not have been preserved at all unless some group considered his speeches to be valid and important, if not authoritative. "The children" (v. 18) would include those mentioned in 7:3 and 8:1-4.

In the process of entrusting the teaching to his disciples, Isaiah expresses his "hope in the Lord" (v. 17) and his faith in the word of God, as revealed to the prophet and made public as signs. The grounds for the prophet's confidence are that his message comes "from the Lord of hosts, who dwells on Mount Zion" (v. 18). In contrast, the prophet turns to a threat about resorting to other forms of revelation. The word of the Lord is not even to be compared with what one learns through consultation of mediums and wizards. If, because the Lord is silent, people consult "ghosts and the familiar spirits . . . their gods, the dead," then their words will not see the light of day (vv. 19-20). To be sure, these practices were illegal in

97. They are not the witnesses named in 8:2, as Clements proposes. See Ronald E. Clements, *Isaiah 1–39,* NCB (Grand Rapids: Eerdmans, 1980) 100.

ancient Israel (Lev 19:31; 20:6; Deut 18:10-14; 1 Sam 15:23), but that did not put an end to them (1 Sam 28:7-19).

Verse 21 is somewhat abrupt, beginning what most likely is a secondary expansion of the tradition. This final verse shifts to the description of a people wandering through the land, distressed and hungry. "They" would refer in the broad context to the people after a defeat by Assyria, explained here as those who turned to false sources of instruction. Eventually they will curse their king and their gods whom they had consulted. No answers and no hope will be found on earth or in heaven, but only "distress and darkness . . . anguish . . . thick darkness" (v. 22). This image sets the scene for the dramatic shift in 9:1-7.

REFLECTIONS

1. Few modern readers can see these reports about the names of the prophet's children without asking, "How could he do that to a child?" Those names, "A Remnant Shall Return" and "Speedy Spoil-Prompt Plunder," are not only strange to modern ears, but were unusual even in Isaiah's time. Both their form and their content are unlike typical Hebrew names. Hosea's children carried similar burdens, with the names "Jezreel" (after the location of a bloodbath), "Not Pitied," and "Not My People" (Hos 1:4-9). These names were designed to convey messages and to attract attention, but little, if any, thought seems to have been given to the effect on the children.

So these stories raise for us questions about the relationship between vocation and family responsibilities, between devotion to one's calling and devotion to one's children. One may wonder if the prophets and the prophetic tradition have set a bad example. These are not, to be sure, the questions of the text itself, which does not dwell at all on the life of the prophet, except in terms of his message. We cannot know how the symbolic names would have affected the children, nor do we have any details about the relationships in the family. There is a certain touching quality to the image of the prophet going out to meet the king with his son at his side, and his identification with them when he says that "I and the children whom the Lord has given me are signs and portents" (8:18). Certainly parents' vocations and careers have an important bearing on their children, for good and for ill.

2. Most modern readers, in an age of individualism, tend to think of the prophets as solitary individuals, independent thinkers working outside of and mainly against the established institutions. The allusions to Isaiah's disciples (8:16) is just one of many indications that this image misses the mark. The prophets were part and parcel of their communities, both small and large. The very way they spoke bears the marks of tradition, shaped and continued by communities over centuries, including groups of prophets. One could even call prophecy itself an institution. It is also clear that the prophets were engaged, in differing ways to be sure, in the central institutions of state and cult. From the time of David, prophets were mentioned alongside generals and priests as more or less officials of the king (cf. 1 Kgs 1:7-8). Moreover, Isaiah was a part of a community of faith that was both deep and broad. He knew its depth through the history of the people and its faith. In fact, when he calls the king and the people to trust the promise to the dynasty of David, he is appealing to ancient communal traditions. So if the prophets are models to be emulated, then it is a mistake to think of them as outside their communities and looking in.

Even such a creative and charismatic leader as Martin Luther King, Jr., did not arise out of thin air. Without diminishing the importance of his individual courage and imagination, one can recognize that he was also shaped by many forces and institutions. These included the church, especially the black church community, shaped by slavery and racial discrimination. And although he was a distinctly American leader, shaped by democratic ideals and the United States Constitution, he had learned as well from Gandhi and the independence movement in India.

3. If the warning about consulting ghosts and familiar spirits does not necessarily touch a modern nerve, it certainly points to a deep and persistent human concern: How can we know the future? Particularly in times of uncertainty, when God seems to be silent, people will turn to any form of revelation that seems to offer hope: magic, divination, consulting the dead, and so forth. Although illegal in ancient Israel, various forms of divination were practiced widely and officially in the ancient Near East. There are extensive records from Mesopotamia concerning the consultation of the liver of the sacrificial lamb, along with detailed models identifying the various parts of the liver. The priests kept records correlating the appearance of the liver with historical events so that they would know the meaning of the omens. It was believed that future events left their tracks in advance, if only one knew where to look.

In our modern culture, we are no less interested in knowing the future in advance. The legitimate forms of determining what will happen—the calculation of evidence on the basis of past experience—are rational, as in forecasting the weather or figuring the odds or deciding on investments or setting out trends for the future. The more one can know about the future, the more wise are one's decisions, from planning a picnic to anticipating retirement to going to war. Still there is no shortage of less rational approaches to such questions, such as fortune-tellers, horoscopes in the daily newspaper, or séances. Such approaches have religious—many say, false religious—dimensions. Moreover, the line between magic and discernment shaped by religious faith often is blurred and, in fact, they appear the same to many in modern culture.

The one certainty is that the future remains inherently uncertain. This and other prophetic texts are clear: There is only one legitimate way to know what will happen—through the word of God. But even that has its problems. Whom can we trust? Just because some people claim to have heard the word of God does not prove that they have. Isaiah's message in these texts goes far deeper than sorting out what will happen in the future. He counsels trust based on God's faithfulness and confidence in the face of uncertainty concerning the future.

Isaiah 9:1-7, The Light of a New King

NIV

9 Nevertheless, there will be no more gloom for those who were in distress. In the past he humbled the land of Zebulun and the land of Naphtali, but in the future he will honor Galilee of the Gentiles, by the way of the sea, along the Jordan—

[2]The people walking in darkness
    have seen a great light;
on those living in the land of the shadow
        of death[a]
    a light has dawned.
[3]You have enlarged the nation
    and increased their joy;
they rejoice before you
    as people rejoice at the harvest,
as men rejoice
    when dividing the plunder.
[4]For as in the day of Midian's defeat,

[a]2 Or *land of darkness*

NRSV

9 [a]But there will be no gloom for those who were in anguish. In the former time he brought into contempt the land of Zebulun and the land of Naphtali, but in the latter time he will make glorious the way of the sea, the land beyond the Jordan, Galilee of the nations.
[2b] The people who walked in darkness
    have seen a great light;
    those who lived in a land of deep darkness—
        on them light has shined.
[3] You have multiplied the nation,
    you have increased its joy;
    they rejoice before you
        as with joy at the harvest,
        as people exult when dividing plunder.
[4] For the yoke of their burden,
    and the bar across their shoulders,
        the rod of their oppressor,

[a]Ch 8.23 in Heb   [b]Ch 9.1 in Heb

NIV

you have shattered
the yoke that burdens them,
the bar across their shoulders,
the rod of their oppressor.
⁵Every warrior's boot used in battle
and every garment rolled in blood
will be destined for burning,
will be fuel for the fire.
⁶For to us a child is born,
to us a son is given,
and the government will be on his
shoulders.
And he will be called
Wonderful Counselor,ᵃ Mighty God,
Everlasting Father, Prince of Peace.
⁷Of the increase of his government and peace
there will be no end.
He will reign on David's throne
and over his kingdom,
establishing and upholding it
with justice and righteousness
from that time on and forever.
The zeal of the LORD Almighty
will accomplish this.

ᵃ6 Or *Wonderful, Counselor*

NIV

you have broken as on the day of Midian.
⁵ For all the boots of the tramping warriors
and all the garments rolled in blood
shall be burned as fuel for the fire.
⁶ For a child has been born for us,
a son given to us;
authority rests upon his shoulders;
and he is named
Wonderful Counselor, Mighty God,
Everlasting Father, Prince of Peace.
⁷ His authority shall grow continually,
and there shall be endless peace
for the throne of David and his kingdom.
He will establish and uphold it
with justice and with righteousness
from this time onward and forevermore.
The zeal of the LORD of hosts will do this.

COMMENTARY

This text, containing some of the best-known and most compelling lines in the Bible, is the final unit of the cluster of traditions that began in 6:1. The collection consists mainly of reports of prophetic activities in the first or third person. After the report of the prophetic vocation (6:1-13), the accounts deal with events taken to have happened during and immediately following the Syro-Ephraimitic war of c. 734 BCE (7:1-2; cf. 2 Kgs 16:5-9). The location of this unit in this particular context indicates the first discernible stage in its interpretation. By placing the poem at this point, the disciples of the prophet (cf. 8:16) or editors of the traditions saw it as a message during or, more likely, immediately following the Syro-Ephraimitic war. Moreover, its association with a series of reports of symbolic actions concerning children and their names is an important clue to its interpretation.

Although many commentators in the late nineteenth and early twentieth centuries took the present passage to be a post-exilic addition to the book of Isaiah, it is now widely accepted that it comes from Isaiah in the eighth century BCE. The precise date is difficult to establish; there doubtless are historical allusions within the poem, but they are obscure. Some scholars have seen the poem as part of the coronation ritual for a particular Judean king, most commonly identified as Hezekiah in 727 BCE. However, it is more likely that the prophetic hymn was composed to celebrate the birth of a new crown prince sometime after 732. The sign of God's deliverance is the birth of a new descendant of David.

The unit consists of two basic elements, the historical-geographical notation (v. 1) and the poem itself (vv. 2-7). The difference in versification between the Hebrew and the English (from the

LXX) is a clue to the relationship of 9:1 to the context. It is distinct from vv. 2-7 and provides a link with the end of chap. 8, which had drawn a picture of a time of darkness when God was silent. Verse 1 picks up on the time of darkness and trouble from 8:21-22. The first sentence of v. 1 ("But there will be no gloom for those who were in anguish") is a clumsy clause that could be read either with the previous unit or, more likely, as a transition from that unit to the one that follows. Consequently, it is the latest feature of the unit, probably added as the book was being compiled. The remainder of v. 1 interprets vv. 2-7 as a promise concerning a particular time and place. The territories mentioned correspond roughly to the sections of northern Israel annexed by Tiglath-pileser III beginning in 732 BCE (cf. 2 Kgs 15:29).[98]

In many ways the overall structure of the poem (vv. 2-7) resembles hymns of thanksgiving. The poem consists of two distinct parts. First, the song gives an account of trouble and salvation (vv. 2-3; cf. Pss 18:5-20; 32:3-5), and, second, it offers praise by enumerating reasons for celebration (vv. 4-7). There are three reasons for thanksgiving, each introduced by "for" (כִּי *kî*). The mood, tone, and style are hymnic, as in joyous celebration, and the "rejoicing" (v. 3) is cultic (cf. Pss 21:2; 19:15; 13:6; 31:8).[99] At least the first four verses are addressed directly to Yahweh: "You have made," "your presence." The first two reasons for celebration (vv. 4-5) concern release from military and political danger. The Lord is praised as the one who has broken "the rod of their oppressor" and is destroying all the battle gear of enemy warriors. Likely these lines have in view a particular deliverance, but the poetry is so comprehensive and compelling that it stirs up the vision of an end to all oppression and war. Verse 4 does speak of the destruction of "all the boots" and "all" the bloody garments. The third reason also is political, beginning with the announcement of a birth (v. 6) and looking to a reign of justice and righteousness (v. 7).

Particularly in the light of the history of the interpretation of this text, it is important to clarify the tenses in the poem. Verses 2-5 clearly speak of past events. The verbs in vv. 2-3 are participles ("the people are walking" or "the people walked"), perfects ("have seen" or "saw"), and infinitives ("when they divide spoil"). This pattern continues in vv. 4-5 ("you have shattered"), with the exception of the final clause, which has been translated "shall be burned." However, this is a result clause that can be read in the present tense. More decisive, the verbs in v. 6 are perfects and consecutive imperfects, the normal narrative tense in Hebrew. They must be read as reporting past action or, in view of the passives, possibly as present: "A child has been born to us . . . authority rests upon his shoulders." Only in v. 7 does the poem turn to the future tense, describing how the reign of the one who has been born will grow, concluding with the affirmation that "the zeal of the LORD of hosts will do this." The implications of this analysis are quite clear: The reasons for celebration—release from an oppressor, destruction of battle gear, and the birth of the "Prince of Peace"—are not in the future but in the past. These events form the basis for confidence in the future.

The poem certainly is not an ordinary prophetic speech, such as an announcement of salvation. There is no messenger formula or similar phrase to indicate that a prophet is conveying the word of Yahweh. Rather, words are addressed *to* Yahweh. The basic structure is that of a hymn of thanksgiving, but this observation alone does not adequately characterize the poem.

Other aspects of the unit have been made the basis for its interpretation. In vv. 6-7, royal motifs predominate. This fact has led a number of commentators to identify the unit with the ritual for the enthronement of a Davidic king. It has been called a dynastic oracle "uttered on the occasion of the anointing of a new king, or at the anniversary celebration of this event."[100] The prophet has been given the responsibility for writing "a cult oracle for a coronation ceremony."[101] In this view, the royal names (v. 6) are explained as parallels to the "great names" or throne names that the Egyptian pharaoh was given when he ascended to the throne.[102] Even more important for this view is

98. Albrecht Alt, "Jesaja 8:23–9:6. Befreiungsnact und Krönungstag," *Kleine Schriften* (München: C. H. Beck, 1959) 2:206-25.

99. H. Wildberger, *Isaiah 1–12*, trans. Thomas H. Trapp (Minneapolis: Fortress, 1991) 396, suggests that there are affinities with the thanksgiving psalm of the king.

100. M. B. Crook, "A Suggested Occasion for Isaiah 9:2-7 and 11:1-9," *JBL* 68 (1949) 213-24.

101. Scott, *IB*, 5:232.

102. Wildberger, *Isaiah 1–12*, 401.

the interpretation of v. 6a as the adoption formula in the enthronement ceremony. Such a ritual undoubtedly existed in Israel, and Yahweh's "adoption" of the king was a central element, as Psalms 2 and 89 testify. So the unit does employ a great many of the motifs of the enthronement ritual and clearly belongs to a tradition of dynastic theology. One commentator has assembled a list of parallels to the David-kingship motifs, especially in relation to the temple cult.[103] However, these motifs are borrowed for a specific purpose. The poem is not a coronation hymn.

The key to the genre, and thus to the setting is v. 5a: "for a child is born [better: "has been born"] to us, a son is given [better: "was given"] to us." In the coronation ceremony, the adoption formula was pronounced by Yahweh or, in affirmation of the adoption, by the king. Nowhere in the poem does Yahweh—or the king—speak. Rather, the words are addressed to Yahweh by the prophet on behalf of the people, by the people ("to us") or, possibly, by or on behalf of the royal household. These lines constitute a birth announcement, similar to others found in the OT: "cursed is the one who brought news to my father saying: 'A child was born to you, a boy!' " (Jer 20:15; see also Job 3:3). Such announcements are common to all cultures. In ours they ordinarily take the form first of an exclamation (e.g., "It's a boy!"), followed by a more formal written announcement that gives the child's name, date of birth, and other data.

The poem has features that are characteristic of other genres as well: the hymn of thanksgiving,

the ritual of enthronement, and birth announcements. However, in view of the apparent setting and intention, it is also a report of a sign. The literary context (6:1–9:7) contains other references to births and children (7:1-16; 8:1-4). All of these are either reports of or references to sign acts involving births or children's names. In 9:1-7, the proclamation of a birth has been made the focal point of a song of thanksgiving. This birth, and the accompanying celebration, function as a sign.

The royal titles, as well as the language of v. 7 ("and upon the throne of David"), indicate unambiguously that no ordinary birth is announced, not even an ordinary birth in the palace. The occasion for celebration is the birth of a crown prince.[104] Probably, as most commentators suggest, the honorific names here follow the pattern of Egyptian throne names given to the pharaoh.[105] Typically, the child is identified with Hezekiah, but there is not sufficient evidence to relate the song to the birth of a particular crown prince.

From Isaiah's perspective, the birth announced in v. 6 is a sign of hope. The ancient promise of a son of David on the throne is reaffirmed. Both the names of the child and the final lines of the poem promise perpetual peace with justice and righteousness. This continues the pattern of the other sign acts of the names, and especially 7:1-9, where the promise to the Davidic dynasty is the basis for hope in the face of military threat.

103. Scott, "The Book of Isaiah," 5:232.

104. Sigmund Mowinckel, *He That Cometh* (Nashville: Abingdon, 1954) 109.
105. See Ronald E. Clements, *Isaiah 1–39*, NCB (Grand Rapids: Eerdmans, 1980) 107-8.

REFLECTIONS

1. One important way to reflect on this poem is to consider the power of its graphic images, each with its accompanying mood and tone. First, there are the contrasting images of darkness and light (9:2). Darkness is a metaphor for depression and death. The NEB makes that explicit in the final line: "dwellers in a land as dark as death" (cf. Ps 23:4). Light symbolizes life and joy, and evokes them as well.

Second, in the language of prayer, the prophet sketches a scene of celebration. One can almost see and hear the festivities. People shout and sing to their God, as if it were the thanksgiving festival at the end of a good harvest or the spontaneous expression of joy when a war has ended and a time of peace begun.

Third, contrasting images again come to the fore, the harsh pictures of the instruments of war and oppression, on the one hand, and a gathering lighted by a fire in which those instruments are burned, on the other hand. The mood of joy and celebration from the previous images continues. What begins as the deliverance from a particular oppressor—doubtless the heel of Assyria—becomes a vision of perpetual peace: military boots and bloody uniforms are burned.

Fourth, we see a messenger emerging from the royal palace with the good news that a son—a crown prince—has been born. This birth announcement is the central scene of the poem. Like the symbolic action reports in the immediate context in the book of Isaiah (7:10-16; 8:1-4), the birth of a baby is a sign of God's saving activity on behalf of the people of God.

Finally, and with no dramatic transition, the scene shows us the future, moving to the throne room of the king and even beyond. The newborn baby is now shown to be the righteous and just king, sitting on the throne of David. This son of David will administer justice, establish righteousness, and inaugurate a reign of peace, all of which corresponds to the will of God and thus will extend forever.

Do images such as these have any power? We know they can change moods and feelings, and that alone is powerful. Good news is communicated not only by what is said but also by how it is said, by establishing a mood of celebration, and these images do just that. Can they change external realities as well? It would be naive, of course, to think that images alone, however compelling, could change the world, could lead to peace instead of war, to justice instead of oppression. Deliberation, planning, and hard work are required. But images, like ideas and commitments, fuel the imagination, which stimulates planning and action. Such a day of peace and justice as envisioned in this text may never come, but it certainly will not if there is no image drawing people toward it.

2. If there were any doubt that ancient texts could legitimately have diverse meanings, texts such as this should lay those doubts to rest. In the eighth century BCE, the words were uttered about the birth of a specific king in Judah, subsequently applied to other kings and even later to an expected messiah. The early church heard that promise and saw it fulfilled in Jesus, and Christians at worship will hear these words as proclamation of the birth of Jesus. All that is as it should be, for this ancient song helps faithful Christian hearers understand the meaning of Christmas. One of our struggles as interpreters faced with such texts is to proclaim the Christian meaning without thereby either ignoring or obscuring the ancient Israelite significance.

The central message of this text is that the birth and its celebration are signs of hope, grounds for confidence in God's future. But there are other important matters as well. Since this passage speaks above all of the nature of the king's reign as one of perpetual peace, founded on justice and righteousness—one that will bring an end to the dark, harsh, loud, and bloody martial alternative (vv. 2-5)—it concerns the messy world of politics. That makes it difficult to separate spiritual or religious matters from government. God's instrument for establishing justice in this case is a monarchy, to be sure, but one that exercises power in accordance with the Lord's will. Our familiarity with the text should not obscure its remarkable theme: In Isaiah's view, God's will for justice, righteousness, and peace is made flesh in the weakest of human creatures, a little baby.

ISAIAH 9:8–10:4, A SERIES OF JUDGMENTS

NIV

8The Lord has sent a message against Jacob;
   it will fall on Israel.
9All the people will know it—
   Ephraim and the inhabitants of Samaria—
who say with pride
   and arrogance of heart,
10"The bricks have fallen down,
   but we will rebuild with dressed stone;
the fig trees have been felled,
   but we will replace them with cedars."
11But the LORD has strengthened Rezin's foes
   against them
   and has spurred their enemies on.
12Arameans from the east and Philistines from
      the west
   have devoured Israel with open mouth.

Yet for all this, his anger is not turned away,
   his hand is still upraised.

13But the people have not returned to him who
      struck them,
   nor have they sought the LORD Almighty.
14So the LORD will cut off from Israel both head
      and tail,
   both palm branch and reed in a single day;
15the elders and prominent men are the head,
   the prophets who teach lies are the tail.
16Those who guide this people mislead them,
   and those who are guided are led astray.
17Therefore the Lord will take no pleasure in the
      young men,
   nor will he pity the fatherless and widows,
for everyone is ungodly and wicked,
   every mouth speaks vileness.

Yet for all this, his anger is not turned away,
   his hand is still upraised.

18Surely wickedness burns like a fire;
   it consumes briers and thorns,
it sets the forest thickets ablaze,
   so that it rolls upward in a column
      of smoke.
19By the wrath of the LORD Almighty
   the land will be scorched
and the people will be fuel for the fire;

NRSV

8 The Lord sent a word against Jacob,
   and it fell on Israel;
9 and all the people knew it—
   Ephraim and the inhabitants of Samaria—
but in pride and arrogance of heart
      they said:
10 "The bricks have fallen,
   but we will build with dressed stones;
the sycamores have been cut down,
   but we will put cedars in their place."
11 So the LORD raised adversaries[a] against them,
   and stirred up their enemies,
12 the Arameans on the east and the Philistines
      on the west,
   and they devoured Israel with open mouth.
For all this his anger has not turned away;
   his hand is stretched out still.

13 The people did not turn to him who
      struck them,
   or seek the LORD of hosts.
14 So the LORD cut off from Israel head and tail,
   palm branch and reed in one day—
15 elders and dignitaries are the head,
   and prophets who teach lies are the tail;
16 for those who led this people led them astray,
   and those who were led by them were left
      in confusion.
17 That is why the Lord did not have pity on[b]
      their young people,
   or compassion on their orphans
      and widows;
for everyone was godless and an evildoer,
   and every mouth spoke folly.
For all this his anger has not turned away;
   his hand is stretched out still.

18 For wickedness burned like a fire,
   consuming briers and thorns;
it kindled the thickets of the forest,
   and they swirled upward in a column
      of smoke.
19 Through the wrath of the LORD of hosts
   the land was burned,

aCn: Heb *the adversaries of Rezin*   bQ Ms: MT *rejoice over*

NIV

no one will spare his brother.
²⁰On the right they will devour,
  but still be hungry;
on the left they will eat,
  but not be satisfied.
Each will feed on the flesh of his own
      offspring*ᵃ:
²¹ Manasseh will feed on Ephraim, and
      Ephraim on Manasseh;
  together they will turn against Judah.

Yet for all this, his anger is not turned away,
  his hand is still upraised.

10 Woe to those who make unjust laws,
      to those who issue oppressive decrees,
²to deprive the poor of their rights
  and withhold justice from the oppressed of
      my people,
making widows their prey
  and robbing the fatherless.
³What will you do on the day of reckoning,
  when disaster comes from afar?
To whom will you run for help?
  Where will you leave your riches?
⁴Nothing will remain but to cringe among
      the captives
  or fall among the slain.

Yet for all this, his anger is not turned away,
  his hand is still upraised.

ᵃ20 Or *arm*

NRSV

and the people became like fuel for the fire;
  no one spared another.
²⁰ They gorged on the right, but still
      were hungry,
  and they devoured on the left, but were
      not satisfied;
they devoured the flesh of their own kindred;ᵃ
²¹ Manasseh devoured Ephraim, and Ephraim
      Manasseh,
  and together they were against Judah.
For all this his anger has not turned away;
  his hand is stretched out still.

10 Ah, you who make iniquitous decrees,
      who write oppressive statutes,
² to turn aside the needy from justice
  and to rob the poor of my people of
      their right,
  that widows may be your spoil,
  and that you may make the orphans
      your prey!
³ What will you do on the day of punishment,
  in the calamity that will come from
      far away?
To whom will you flee for help,
  and where will you leave your wealth,
⁴ so as not to crouch among the prisoners
  or fall among the slain?
For all this his anger has not turned away;
  his hand is stretched out still.

ᵃOr *arm*

COMMENTARY

As indicated already (see the Overview to 5:1-30), this section of the book probably once followed 5:8-30. The refrain ("For all this his anger has not turned away, and his hand is stretched out still," 5:25) resumes here and provides the structure for the entire section (9:12, 17, 21; 10:4). Moreover, the concluding unit (10:1-4) begins with the same cry of woe that organizes the parts of 5:8-24. Finally, the intervening material (6:1–9:8) is a relatively coherent section on its own, probably inserted into a previously completed collection of sayings.

As this section appears in the book it may be recognized as a single unit with four distinct parts, 9:8-12, 9:13-17, 9:18-21, and 10:1-4. The common concluding refrain marks it, along with at least 5:25-30, as a series of speeches. In the prophetic literature, such series may be explained in one of two ways. In some cases, they are the result of collecting and editorial activity in which originally independent speeches were combined on the basis of similarity of form and perhaps also of content. Such probably is the case with the series of woe addresses in Isa 5:8-24 and, for example, the series of vision reports in Amos 7:1–9:1 (even apart from the other material that surrounds those reports). In other instances, however, such series would have formed a composition, a single long and organized speech. Amos 1:3–2:16 is a clear instance of the former, although there have been some subsequent additions. Those chapters form a strong rhetorical whole, with two distinct parts: the announcements against the neighbors and the announcement against Israel. That almost certainly is the case with Isa 9:8–10:4. Each part depends on the other, and although each makes sense on its own, its force comes from the accumulation of the Lord's decisions to keep God's anger and God's "hand" against those who have not learned from repeated punishments.

The nearest parallel to Isa 9:8–10:4 and 5:25-30 is Amos 4:6-12[13] with its refrain, "yet you did not return to me, says the LORD." In both instances the refrain frames a history of divine intervention, the purpose of which is to promote repentance—explicitly in Amos and implicitly in Isaiah. (Note that Isa 9:13, "Nor seek the LORD of hosts," echoes the refrain in Amos 4.)

The transition from 9:1-7 to this series is abrupt and difficult to understand. The turn is from the future to the past, from an unqualified hope for a time when the Lord's "zeal" will establish a reign of peace and justice, to accounts of how the Lord's "anger" has persistently exercised judgment. Four distinct units are both set off from one another and linked together by the concluding refrain, indicating even through the last verse that the Lord has brought judgment after judgment and still is not finished. The first three units (9:8-12, 13-17, 18-21) speak of the accused in the third person, while the fourth (10:1-4) is in the form of direct address.

In part the shift of focus can be explained by the different addressees or objects of concern in 9:1-7 and 9:8–10:4. Whereas 9:1-7 had to do with Judah, at least the first three accounts of judgments that failed to evoke repentance are about the northern kingdom of Israel. Certainly in the redactional context, this entire sequence is taken to refer to the anger of Yahweh against the northern kingdom, from the time of the Syro-Ephraimitic war until after the fall of Samaria. Some scholars have seen the sequence as a warning to the leadership of the northern kingdom that its continued rebellion against Yahweh will lead to destruc-

tion.[106] Clearly the first three units have in view the Lord's judgments on the north ("Israel," vv. 8, 14; "Ephraim," v. 9; "Manasseh . . . Ephraim," v. 21), and the text stresses the responsibility of the leadership (vv. 14-16), but the historical allusions are not sufficiently specific to date the material. Such a recounting of punishments of Israel would have served as warnings to Judah after the northern kingdom fell to the Assyrians in 721 BCE, regardless of their purpose before that time.

9:8-12. Generally, each of these individual segments follows a similar pattern. First comes a report of reasons for punishment, then a description of the judgment, followed by the concluding refrain, "for all this his anger has not turned away; his hand is stretched out still." This unit begins with an introduction to the word of Yahweh (vv. 8-9), which already presents an indictment. Although the word had been sent and the people knew it, they exercised their "pride and arrogance of heart." Verse 10 cites their own words as evidence against them. That "the bricks have fallen . . . the sycamores have been cut down" refers to a disaster initiated by Yahweh. But the people brush it off as nothing, treating the disaster as the foundation for better things ("dressed stones," "cedars"). Because of the people's refusal to accept correction through disaster ("So," v. 11), the Lord raised up their enemies, the Aramaeans and the Philistines, against them (vv. 11-12).

9:13-17. This section has a twofold pattern of indictment and account of punishment. The initial indictment (v. 13) is an important clue to the meaning of the entire series, since it accuses the people of failing to "turn to him who struck them." The punishment for such failure is stated as a metaphor (v. 14) that is then explained (v. 15): In a single day the Lord cut off the elders and dignitaries, who are the head, and the prophets who teach lies, the tail. This is similar to Isa 3:1-5, which announces that the Lord is punishing Judah and Jerusalem by removing their leadership. The second accusation comes in v. 16, that those leaders led the people astray. The second account of punishment (v. 17) is harsh: The Lord did not have pity on young people, orphans, and widows. There is a summary accusation that everyone was

106. Marvin A. Sweeney, *Isaiah 1–39, With an Introduction to Prophetic Literature,* FOTL XVI (Grand Rapids: Eerdmans, 1996) 195.

godless and "spoke folly," followed by the concluding refrain.

9:18-21. This unit, clearly concerning the northern kingdom, sets out the evils of Israel and emphasizes their disastrous results. The initial "for" should be read as an asservation, "Surely." Verse 18 shows the complicated relationship between "wickedness" and disaster. Taken metaphorically, this verse underscores just how widespread the evil was. But viewed more literally it suggests that the "wickedness" actually ignited the fire that burned throughout the land. If that suggests a dynamistic understanding in which sin has its effects, then v. 19 moves in a juridical direction indicating that Yahweh's wrath burned in judgment because of the sins of the people.[107] The fire in vv. 18-19, with the people themselves as the fuel, suggests the aftermath of a military invasion and defeat. Taken literally, that "they devoured the flesh of their own kindred" (v. 20) could refer to starvation leading to cannibalism. However, the subsequent verse (v. 21) interprets this as a metaphor for political or military action of the tribes against one another, and specifically against Judah, as in the Syro-Ephraimitic war. Such political and military actions are reasons for the reported destruction.

10:1-4. In the book of Isaiah, these verses function as the conclusion to the unit that began in 5:25 and resumed in 9:8. The refrain, which appears here for the last time, makes the connection. Most likely, an editor of the work added the refrain to bring the series to an end.[108] However, although this unit concludes like the others in the context, it is quite distinct from them. In fact, in both form and content, these verses closely parallel the series of woe speeches in 5:8-24. The unit began with the cry "woe" ("Ah"; see the Commentary on 5:8-24), followed by a description of the addressees (in the third person) in terms of their reprehensible actions. When it turns to punishment, it concerns the future and not the past (as in the previous units in this sequence), using a rhetorical question (v. 3) to imply that judgment will come upon the accused.

Whereas the previous addresses (9:8-21) had concerned Yahweh's repeated punishments of the northern kingdom, these verses are concerned with law, justice, the poor, widows, and orphans. Those "who make iniquitous decrees, who write oppressive statutes" probably are judges or court officials; but given what little is known about juridical process in ancient Israel and Judah, they could be anyone with power to control the law. The "iniquitous decrees" would have been some kind of formal legal or political documents that deprive the poor and the needy of their day in court. The accusation is distressingly common in the eighth-century prophets (Isa 1:17, 23; 10:2; cf. Amos 2:7; 4:1; 5:11; 8:4, 6). The indictment is broader than the others and could be against any group, north or south, even reflecting the situation of the fall of Samaria. But, like the other woes in 5:8-24, this address likely had in view a Judean audience. The issues are not international politics but justice within the community.

One could call what follows the indictment an announcement of judgment (vv. 3-4a), but it is not set out directly as a statement of future events. Rather, the long ironic rhetorical question that asks the accused how they will respond "on the day of punishment" only alludes to the disaster, but takes it for granted as inevitable. The question is recognized as rhetorical because it makes a statement: You will have no one to call for help and nowhere to go to escape, but will be either a prisoner or a corpse.

107. Gene M. Tucker, "The Law in the Eighth Century Prophets," in *Canon, Theology, and Old Testament Interpretation: Essays in Honor of Brevard S. Childs,* ed. Gene M. Tucker, David L. Petersen, and Robert R. Wilson (Philadelphia: Fortress, 1988) 201-16. See also Christopher R. Seitz, *Isaiah 1–39,* Interpretation (Louisville: John Knox, 1993) 90.

108. See Gerald T. Sheppard, "Isaiah 1–39," in *Harper's Bible Commentary* (San Francisco: Harper & Row, 1988) 557.

REFLECTIONS

1. The series of addresses, each concluding with the refrain "For all this his anger has not turned away, and his hand is stretched out still," appears to interpret a history of disasters as the effects of divine intervention. One force that drives this viewpoint is the need to make sense of trouble and disaster, to rationalize it in the framework of an understanding of God and history. Here the continuing catastrophes—mostly military in nature—are taken either as the more or less direct results of the wickedness itself (9:18) or as God's response to human actions. It does not necessarily settle the problem of evil that punishment in this context is seen to be didactic (cf. 5:25); that is, its purpose is to evoke change in behavior. (For further discussion of these issues see the Reflections at 5:25-30.)

2. The history of the traditions and of their literary development raises both problems and possibilities. On the one hand, it might appear that a Judean editor or collector of the Isaiah traditions has made a point of emphasizing the failures of the northern kingdom. Thus in an early stage of the transmission of this history of disasters, possibly from Isaiah himself and put together during or soon after the Syro-Ephramitic war (c. 734 BCE; see the Commentary on 7:1-9), there is a chauvinistic edge to the interpretation of history. On the other hand, this material eventually was handed down and used in the south, in Judah. After 732 BCE, the northern kingdom no longer existed. After that time, the history of disasters and Israel's refusal to learn from them were seen as warnings before Samaria fell to the Assyrians and, therefore, as cautionary words for Judah and Jerusalem. What had been said concerning the north would have been read and heard as the words of God, now appropriate for the south. This editorial process can serve as a model for the reinterpretation and/or application of old "words of God" in and for new times and places. So we are not inventing the process when we struggle to determine if and how old Scripture speaks in our time and place. When we struggle with the modern meaning of ancient texts, as we prepare to teach, preach, or engage in personal study, we are treading a well-worn path.

ISAIAH 10:5–12:6, JUDGMENT AGAINST ASSYRIA AND ANNOUNCEMENTS OF SALVATION

OVERVIEW

Formally, this block of material consists of a number of diverse announcements of the future and the hymn (chap. 12) that concludes the first major section of the book of Isaiah (see the Overview to 1:1–12:6). The main units are 10:5-19; 10:20-34; 11:1-9; 11:10-16; and 12:1-6. Two major themes run through the announcements: judgment against Assyria and salvation to Judah, the latter developed primarily in terms of a remnant beyond judgment and a new royal figure (11:1-9). Chapter 12 is the more or less liturgical conclusion to the prophetic speeches and stories in the first eleven chapters. However, chap. 12 is tied specifically to these particular chapters through the expression "in that day" (12:1; cf. 10:20)—that is, a time of salvation in the future such as is announced in 10:20–11:16.

If there is any thematic unity in the announcements, it is very broad, a concern with the future of nations. One may recognize, at least in broad strokes, some progression of thought. The focus on the future moves from drawing the limits for Assyrian aggression, presuming that Israel has fallen but that Judah will not, to the remnant of destruction, to the announcement of a Davidic messiah with transformation of the world, and concluding with the eventual reconciliation of Judah and Israel. There is some movement from concern with the more immediate to the more distant future.

Various commentators have seen this block as a coherent unit,[109] but it is doubtful that these materials existed as an independent composition. The diversity of subjects, variations in style, and the catchword "remnant" in 10:19-20 suggest a collecting process. Moreover, not all sections are from

the same time (see the Commentary on 10:5-19). The final form, therefore, is late, probably exilic or post-exilic. The initial unit is loosely connected to what precedes by the initial cry of "Woe" ("Ah," NRSV) that appears in 10:1. It is likely that some of the earliest materials relate to the Assyrian threats against Judah under Sargon II (720 BCE) and others to Sennacherib's invasion of Judah and siege of Jerusalem (701 BCE). Mainly the late sections (10:12, 24-27; 11:10-11) are expansions and interpretations of earlier material.[110]

109. Sweeney sees a "structural unity" to 10:5–12:6. See Sweeney, *Isaiah 1–39,* 198. See also Gerald T. Sheppard, "Isaiah 1–39," *HBC* (San Francisco: Harper & Row, 1988) 557-58.

110. Sweeney's reconstruction of three major stages of development is possible but difficult to prove. See Sweeney, *Isaiah 1–39,* 210-11.

Isaiah 10:5-19, Judgment Against Arrogant Assyria

NIV	NRSV
[5]"Woe to the Assyrian, the rod of my anger, in whose hand is the club of my wrath! [6]I send him against a godless nation, I dispatch him against a people who anger me, to seize loot and snatch plunder, and to trample them down like mud in the streets. [7]But this is not what he intends, this is not what he has in mind; his purpose is to destroy, to put an end to many nations. [8]'Are not my commanders all kings?' he says. [9] 'Has not Calno fared like Carchemish? Is not Hamath like Arpad, and Samaria like Damascus? [10]As my hand seized the kingdoms of the idols, kingdoms whose images excelled those of Jerusalem and Samaria— [11]shall I not deal with Jerusalem and her images as I dealt with Samaria and her idols?' "	[5] Ah, Assyria, the rod of my anger— the club in their hands is my fury! [6] Against a godless nation I send him, and against the people of my wrath I command him, to take spoil and seize plunder, and to tread them down like the mire of the streets. [7] But this is not what he intends, nor does he have this in mind; but it is in his heart to destroy, and to cut off nations not a few. [8] For he says: "Are not my commanders all kings? [9] Is not Calno like Carchemish? Is not Hamath like Arpad? Is not Samaria like Damascus? [10] As my hand has reached to the kingdoms of the idols whose images were greater than those of Jerusalem and Samaria, [11] shall I not do to Jerusalem and her idols what I have done to Samaria and her images?"
[12]When the Lord has finished all his work against Mount Zion and Jerusalem, he will say, "I will punish the king of Assyria for the willful pride of his heart and the haughty look in his eyes. [13]For he says: " 'By the strength of my hand I have done this, and by my wisdom, because I have understanding.	[12]When the Lord has finished all his work on Mount Zion and on Jerusalem, he[a] will punish the

[a]Heb *I*

NIV

I removed the boundaries of nations,
   I plundered their treasures;
   like a mighty one I subdued[a] their kings.
[14]As one reaches into a nest,
   so my hand reached for the wealth of
      the nations;
as men gather abandoned eggs,
   so I gathered all the countries;
not one flapped a wing,
   or opened its mouth to chirp.' "

[15]Does the ax raise itself above him who
      swings it,
   or the saw boast against him who uses it?
As if a rod were to wield him who lifts it up,
   or a club brandish him who is not wood!
[16]Therefore, the Lord, the LORD Almighty,
   will send a wasting disease upon his sturdy
      warriors;
under his pomp a fire will be kindled
   like a blazing flame.
[17]The Light of Israel will become a fire,
   their Holy One a flame;
in a single day it will burn and consume
   his thorns and his briers.
[18]The splendor of his forests and fertile fields
   it will completely destroy,
   as when a sick man wastes away.
[19]And the remaining trees of his forests will be
      so few
   that a child could write them down.

[a]13 Or / I subdued the mighty,

NRSV

arrogant boasting of the king of Assyria and his
haughty pride. [13]For he says:
   "By the strength of my hand I have done it,
      and by my wisdom, for I have
         understanding;
   I have removed the boundaries of peoples,
      and have plundered their treasures;
      like a bull I have brought down those who
         sat on thrones.
[14] My hand has found, like a nest,
      the wealth of the peoples;
   and as one gathers eggs that have been
         forsaken,
      so I have gathered all the earth;
   and there was none that moved a wing,
      or opened its mouth, or chirped."

[15] Shall the ax vaunt itself over the one who
         wields it,
      or the saw magnify itself against the one
         who handles it?
   As if a rod should raise the one who lifts it up,
      or as if a staff should lift the one who is
         not wood!
[16] Therefore the Sovereign, the LORD of hosts,
      will send wasting sickness among his stout
         warriors,
   and under his glory a burning will be kindled,
      like the burning of fire.
[17] The light of Israel will become a fire,
      and his Holy One a flame;
   and it will burn and devour
      his thorns and briers in one day.
[18] The glory of his forest and his fruitful land
      the LORD will destroy, both soul and body,
      and it will be as when an invalid
         wastes away.
[19] The remnant of the trees of his forest will be
         so few
      that a child can write them down.

COMMENTARY

The announcement of judgment against Assyria, personified in the future of its king, consists of the two major elements typical of such prophetic speeches. First (vv. 5-15), the cry, "Woe," initiates an indictment or a presentation of the reasons for punishment. Second (vv. 16-19), the transitional "therefore" and the invocation of the name of the Lord signal the announcement of punishment. Shifts in the speaker mark important turning points in the address. Although there is no specific introduction to a divine speech, it is clear that Yahweh speaks in the beginning ("rod of my anger," v. 5; "I send him," v. 6). Then the Lord quotes the words of Assyria (or its king) in vv. 8-14, except for the third-person interruption in v. 12. Finally, in the announcement of the future (vv. 16-19), the prophetic voice speaks of Yahweh, Assyria, and Israel in the third person.

Since this passage includes concrete references to Assyrian aggression and other details about events that can be reconstructed historically, many scholars have presumed that the speech or speeches could be dated with some precision. But disagreements abound. Some interpreters have concluded that vv. 16-19, as well as v. 12, are later than the indictment of Assyria in vv. 5-15. Certainly an Assyrian invasion (or invasions) of Judah lies in the background. The main alternatives would be Sennacherib's invasion of Judah in 705–701 BCE (see Isaiah 36–38) or c. 717, after the fall of the north when the Philistine states led a revolt against Sargon.[111]

Although some of the details are problematic, the point of this unit can be stated succinctly. Assyria, the instrument of the will of the Lord against "a godless nation" (v. 6) has, quite literally, overreached itself, both going beyond what the Lord set into motion and arrogantly failing to recognize that it is but the "ax" and not "the one who wields it" (v. 15). Consequently, the Lord will bring disaster upon Assyria and its army in particular.

111. Clements summarizes the alternatives and argues for the earlier date. See Ronald E. Clements, *Isaiah 1–39*, NCB (Grand Rapids: Eerdmans, 1980) 109-11.

10:5-15. The indictment against Assyria begins with the cry "Woe," but both its form and its content are quite different from the other woe speeches in Isaiah (e.g., 5:8-24) and elsewhere. First, Yahweh as speaker is unusual for such addresses. Second, it does not describe the wrongful actions of the addressees; instead it speaks of the accused in the third person. Finally, when the address turns to accusation it is not concerned with unjust behavior within society but with international politics and military actions.

The description of the role of Assyria as the rod with which the Lord expresses anger (vv. 5-6) provides the context for the accusation. This reference to the Lord's "anger" may or may not be an allusion to the recurring refrain in the previous section (9:12, 17, 21; 10:4), but it does continue the theme of judgment executed by the enemies of Israel and Judah. It is taken for granted that when Assyria took spoil and plunder the Lord was punishing "a godless nation." In view of the address as a whole, as well as the use of this same term for Israel in 9:17, we are to conclude that this "nation" was the northern kingdom. Thus these verses may very well contain an allusion to the destruction of Samaria in 722/21 BCE.

Assyria's plunder and pillage in the north, however, is not the problem. So the voice of the Lord through the prophet presents the case against the world power (vv. 7-15). Verse 7 is a remarkable reflection upon the thoughts and motives of Assyria, and it begins to sound more and more like the king of Assyria. He intended to do more than the Lord planned, including the destruction of nations. As in other prophetic indictments, this one makes the case by citing the words of the accused (vv. 8-11, 13-14). He is heard to boast that his commanders are "like kings" (v. 8)—that is, each of them is superior to the kings they face, such as the kings of Israel and Judah. Moving roughly from north to south, the Assyrian king uses rhetorical questions to assert that to him the next city to conquer is just like the last one. The key to this recital, and to the invader's arrogance, is the declaration that Jerusalem "and her idols" (v. 11) are just as vulnerable as other cities that stood in his way. In moving against Jerusalem he has gone beyond his commission as Yahweh's instrument. Behind this accusation stands the tradition that Zion, as the Lord's chosen place, is inviolable (see 7:1-9 and the Commentary on 7:1-9). Moreover, in identifying Jerusalem with idols he has made the fundamental mistake of failing to acknowledge Yahweh as the one who set these events into motion. Of course, idols are not worshiped in Jerusalem, but the king of Assyria does not know that. When Sennacherib laid siege to Jerusalem, his chief officer (the Rabshakeh) challenged Hezekiah with a speech similar in tone and even in some of its content to these words attributed to the king of Assyria (36:4-10).

Both the form and the substance of v. 12 show it to be a later addition. It is prose in the middle of poetry, a report about the Lord's intentions for the king of Assyria. Moreover, it has the advantage of hindsight, knowing of Sennacherib's siege of Jerusalem under Hezekiah in 701 BCE (see Isaiah 36–37).

As the citation of the king of Assyria's words continues in vv. 13-14, his words convict him of arrogantly claiming all power for himself. It was his "hand" and not the hand of the Lord, his own "wisdom" and "understanding" and not the Lord's design that erased the boundaries of nations, plundered peoples, and deposed kings. All are powerless against him as he takes what he wants. In this respect, his pride becomes blasphemy.[112]

Verse 15 is a dramatic summation of the indictment, presented as a series of rhetorical questions that return to the initial image and expand it. No ax, saw, rod, or staff can assert itself against the one who uses it.

10:16-19. Now punishment will come upon the king of Assyria ("his," vv. 16-19). The indictment or reasons for punishment are linked to the announcement by "therefore" and the invocation of the name of the Lord. This is not, however, a typical announcement of punishment, for no longer is the speaker Yahweh, but the Lord's actions in the future are described from the perspective of the prophet as a third party.

The disaster that will befall the king of Assyria is set out in three connected movements. First, the Lord will send a "wasting sickness" among his soldiers (v. 16a). This seems to be an allusion to the relief of Sennacherib's siege of Jerusalem reported in 37:36-37. Second, disaster is presented as "a burning" under the "glory" of the Assyrian king, devouring "his thorns and briars in one day" (vv. 16b-17). The "light of Israel" and "Holy One" are names for the God who reigns in Jerusalem. Third, and extending the imagery of a destructive fire, the Lord will decimate the Assyrians' forest and "fruitful land" (vv. 18-19). Is this language literal or figurative? Does the announcement envision a fire sweeping over Assyria and burning all the vegetation, or do the "thorns," "briars," "forest," and "fruitful land" represent the soldiers and subjects of the Assyrian king? Most commentators understand these as metaphors[113] and that is possible but by no means self-evident. Note, finally, the reference to the "child" who will be able to count what "trees" remain after the fire (v. 19). Many children appear in Isaiah 7–11.

112. Cf. Clements, *Isaiah 1–39,* 110.

113. See, e.g., Oswalt, *The Book of Isaiah Chapters 1–39,* 267, and Christopher R. Seitz, *Isaiah 1–39,* Interpretation (Louisville: John Knox, 1993) 93-94.

REFLECTIONS

1. The persistent issue raised in prophetic announcements of the future such as this one concerns God's control of events. Here, however, the question arises with a distinctive and important twist: Who makes history, and how? God acts to set events into motion but is seen to accomplish that future through proximate or so-called secondary causes. In this case Assyria—or the Assyrian king—is the instrument of the divine will. For a while that agent seems to be out of control, but finally is not when the Lord acts to reign him in and punish him. The main problem of the "rod" of the Lord's anger is that the Assyrian king considers himself in charge of events and thus goes too far; that is, he attempts to cause what the Lord neither set into motion nor intended.

One form of the question of God's action in history is the virtually insoluble issue of free will, or determinism. Divine determinism, or even predestination—the doctrine that God knows and controls everything in advance—could very well be good theology. It seems consistent with an affirmation of God's omnipotence and omniscience. That view, however, is not the Bible's perspective. Fundamentally that is the case because the biblical texts are stories—or rely upon stories—and not doctrine. Stories entail drama, conflict, and uncertainty. History as the continuing sequence of events over time is seen to be created by the interaction of divine and human wills. This text presumes that the Lord intended to use Assyria to punish the kingdom of Israel. That happened, but then the arrogant will of the king of Assyria intervened. So the Lord intervenes again. Moreover, even the initial action to call Assyria was the divine response to the actions of human agents.

According to this text, plainly it is possible for individuals and groups of people to function as agents of the will of God without knowing it. Although the king of Assyria did not know he was the agent of the Lord's will, he is held accountable when he goes too far. We might be moved to ask if that is fair. How could he know that he had gone too far if he did not know he was exercising the will of the Lord in the first place? Still, he is shown to be capable of introspection. He reflects on motives and expresses his inner thoughts. His failure is, finally, a religious and theological one: He did not acknowledge the authority and justice of the God who reigned in Jerusalem.

2. Reading of the words and the fate of the king of Assyria might evoke reflection on the arrogance of the mighty and on the overweening ambitions of world powers generally. Lord Acton's famous saying fits this text: "Power tends to corrupt, and absolute power corrupts absolutely." Power does corrupt, and the name—or the source—of that corruption is arrogance. Power and pride tend to go hand in hand. The second part of Acton's saying is not as well-known: "Great men are almost always bad men." Does this follow? To take the lead from this text, we could say that power is good; it derives from God and can be exercised in accordance with God's will. But when pride takes control—that is, when one arrogates to oneself total authority (and so becomes "great")—then power is corrupt.

Ahab of Israel responded to the arrogance of the Aramaean king Ben-hadad with the saying, "One who puts on armor should not brag like one who takes it off" (1 Kgs 20:11). One lesson of Isa 10:5-19 is that it is not wise to boast even *after* one has won the battle and taken off one's armor.

One need not be a head of state, of course, to exercise power and be corrupted by it. Most readers of this text will recognize in themselves the temptation of the arrogance of power. Sooner or later, everyone wants to exercise his or her will over other people and things. On a personal and psychological level, these days that tendency often is called a "control" problem, the emotional need to be in control of others and circumstances. This common malady can lead to difficulties with interpersonal relationships and to internal conflicts.

But the desire for and the exercise of power are inescapable, both at the personal and at the political levels. Even if one wants to be able to empower others, that "be able to" is the power to exercise one's will—for good. One could even argue that the goal of military intervention is peace, and often it is. So the imposition of peace can be the exercise of power. That certainly was the case with ancient Assyria: They wanted peace but, of course, on their own terms. That power and the exercise of power are inevitable is taken for granted in this text. The problem addressed here is not power but the arrogance of power, which stems from the failure to acknowledge the limits and the source of all human power.

Isaiah 10:20-34, Jerusalem Threatened but Delivered

NIV

20In that day the remnant of Israel,
  the survivors of the house of Jacob,
will no longer rely on him
  who struck them down
but will truly rely on the LORD,
  the Holy One of Israel.
21A remnant will return,[a] a remnant of Jacob
  will return to the Mighty God.
22Though your people, O Israel, be like the sand
  by the sea,
  only a remnant will return.
Destruction has been decreed,
  overwhelming and righteous.
23The Lord, the LORD Almighty, will carry out
  the destruction decreed upon the
  whole land.

24Therefore, this is what the Lord, the LORD Almighty, says:
"O my people who live in Zion,
  do not be afraid of the Assyrians,
who beat you with a rod
  and lift up a club against you, as Egypt did.
25Very soon my anger against you will end
  and my wrath will be directed to their
  destruction."

26The LORD Almighty will lash them with a whip,
  as when he struck down Midian at the
  rock of Oreb;
and he will raise his staff over the waters,
  as he did in Egypt.
27In that day their burden will be lifted from
  your shoulders,
  their yoke from your neck;
the yoke will be broken
  because you have grown so fat.[b]

28They enter Aiath;
  they pass through Migron;
  they store supplies at Micmash.
29They go over the pass, and say,
  "We will camp overnight at Geba."
Ramah trembles;
  Gibeah of Saul flees.

NRSV

20On that day the remnant of Israel and the survivors of the house of Jacob will no more lean on the one who struck them, but will lean on the LORD, the Holy One of Israel, in truth. 21A remnant will return, the remnant of Jacob, to the mighty God. 22For though your people Israel were like the sand of the sea, only a remnant of them will return. Destruction is decreed, overflowing with righteousness. 23For the Lord GOD of hosts will make a full end, as decreed, in all the earth.[a]

24Therefore thus says the Lord GOD of hosts: O my people, who live in Zion, do not be afraid of the Assyrians when they beat you with a rod and lift up their staff against you as the Egyptians did. 25For in a very little while my indignation will come to an end, and my anger will be directed to their destruction. 26The LORD of hosts will wield a whip against them, as when he struck Midian at the rock of Oreb; his staff will be over the sea, and he will lift it as he did in Egypt. 27On that day his burden will be removed from your shoulder, and his yoke will be destroyed from your neck.

He has gone up from Rimmon,[b]
28   he has come to Aiath;
  he has passed through Migron,
    at Michmash he stores his baggage;
29 they have crossed over the pass,
    at Geba they lodge for the night;
  Ramah trembles,
    Gibeah of Saul has fled.
30 Cry aloud, O daughter Gallim!
    Listen, O Laishah!
    Answer her, O Anathoth!
31 Madmenah is in flight,
    the inhabitants of Gebim flee for safety.
32 This very day he will halt at Nob,
    he will shake his fist
  at the mount of daughter Zion,
    the hill of Jerusalem.

33 Look, the Sovereign, the LORD of hosts,
    will lop the boughs with terrifying power;

NIV

³⁰Cry out, O Daughter of Gallim!
  Listen, O Laishah!
  Poor Anathoth!
³¹Madmenah is in flight;
  the people of Gebim take cover.
³²This day they will halt at Nob;
  they will shake their fist
at the mount of the Daughter of Zion,
  at the hill of Jerusalem.

³³See, the Lord, the LORD Almighty,
  will lop off the boughs with great power.
The lofty trees will be felled,
  the tall ones will be brought low.
³⁴He will cut down the forest thickets with
      an ax;
  Lebanon will fall before the Mighty One.

NRSV

  the tallest trees will be cut down,
    and the lofty will be brought low.
³⁴ He will hack down the thickets of the forest
      with an ax,
    and Lebanon with its majestic trees[a]
      will fall.

[a]Cn: Compare Gk Vg: Heb *with a majestic one*

COMMENTARY

There is a distinct break between the previous section (10:5-19) and this series of speeches. The theme shifts from the punishment of Assyria for its arrogant exercise of power to the fate of a remnant of Israel and Judah. There are, however, distinct links between this body of prophetic texts and the previous section. First, the initial unit of this collection is linked to the preceding one by the appearance of the catchword "remnant" in vv. 19-20. This suggests an editorial process in which diverse traditions were collected rather than the composition of a long address at one time. Second, specific elements of the prophecy against Assyria are resumed in this section. These include the admonition not to fear Assyria (vv. 24-27), the approach of an enemy from the north (vv. 28-32), and the announcement that the Lord will destroy the forest of the enemy (vv. 33-34), as in 10:17-19.

This passage consists of four distinct prophecies or parts of prophecies that are only loosely connected. The breaks between them and the shifts of theme are more obvious than their continuity. The units are vv. 20-23, vv. 24-27a, vv. 27b-32, and vv. 33-34. They do have in common the announcement of the future in view of a military threat to Jerusalem. However, there is compelling evidence that most of these materials are not the words of

Isaiah of Jerusalem. Given the context following 10:5-19, those who edited and transmitted these prophecies related them to an Assyrian invasion of Judah.

10:20-23. Although not presented as the words of the Lord through a prophet, these lines contain an announcement of the Lord's acts in the future. It is clear enough that this future concerns a "remnant" and "survivors" of disaster, but is it good news or bad, announcement of judgment or salvation? In vv. 20-21 it seems to be good news, at least for the survivors, including the remnant of both Israel and Judah. Their faith will have been transformed by the tragedy that struck the people. That they will no longer "lean on the one who struck them" means that they will not rely on Assyria, but will "lean on the LORD" (v. 20). Finally, presumably after military defeat, Isaiah's admonition to Ahaz (7:9) will be followed, by the people if not by the king. Remarkably, even those left in the northern kingdom ("remnant of Jacob") will return to the God who reigns in Zion (v. 21). Thus the sign of Shear-jasub ("a remnant will return," 7:3) will be fulfilled.

Verses 22-23, however, are an announcement of judgment. These lines take the "remnant" to emphasize the severity of disaster: "only a remnant of them will return" (v. 22). This is comparable to Amos 5:3: "The city that marched out a thousand shall have a hundred left." The final line is stronger still, announcing a "full end" in all the "land" (v. 23; read with the NRSV footnote). Specifically, these verses comprise an announcement of punishment against Israel. This prophecy relates to the destruction of Samaria in 721 BCE and the exile of the population of Israel and most likely was composed after the fact, either in the time of Josiah[114] or even in the post-exilic period.[115] Given the tension between good news and bad, it appears that vv. 20-23 reflect at least two stages of development: one that envisioned the destruction of the north (vv. 22-23) and another that saw beyond that to the reconciliation of a remnant of Israel and Judah (vv. 20-21). In this way these verses are a commentary on Isa 10:5-19.

10:24-27a. These verses address the question of the limits of Assyria's advance as the "rod" (v. 24) of the Lord's "anger" (v. 25), as in vv. 5-19. The prose here is a mixture of speech from Yahweh (vv. 24-25) and announcement about Yahweh's actions (vv. 26-27a), but the section as a whole addresses the people of Jerusalem. The assumed setting is the Assyrian siege of the city as reported in chaps. 36–38. Clearly this unit is secondary and is probably from the post-exilic era. Favoring this conclusion are the prose style, the absence of specific details, and, above all, the use of the exodus and wilderness traditions (v. 26) in combination with the Zion tradition. Remarkably, there are no references to these pentateuchal traditions in the speeches of Isaiah of Jerusalem. Deutero-Isaiah (chaps. 40–55) brings together the exodus, Zion, and messianic traditions.

These verses announce salvation by means of an oracle of reassurance to the inhabitants of Zion. After an expanded messenger formula (v. 24a), the Lord tells the people not to fear (v. 24b). The formula "fear not" very likely has its roots in the ancient holy war traditions (Josh 8:1; 10:8) as the divine response to prayer before the battle, and it

would have been used as the priestly response to prayers of complaint and petition. The remaining lines (vv. 25-27a) give the reasons why the people should not fear, both negatively and positively. Negatively, the Lord will exercise wrath on the enemy just as God did against Midian and the Egyptians (vv. 25-26). Positively, the Lord will deal graciously with those who live in Jerusalem (v. 27a).

10:27b-32. With no introduction at all, these verses move from promise to threat. They first report and then predict the approach of an enemy who will threaten the sacred Mt. Zion in Jerusalem. The invader, variously identified in the singular ("he," vv. 27b, 28, 32) and the plural ("they," v. 29), is not named. By locating the passage in a context that concerns Assyria as the rod of the Lord's anger, the editors mean for the reader to understand this as a report of an Assyrian invasion, either that of Sargon II in 717 BCE or Sennacherib in 701 BCE (cf. Isaiah 36–38). But all the places that can be identified are north of Jerusalem, and the extra-biblical sources show that the Assyrians advanced on Jerusalem from the south.[116] It is entirely possible that this describes the itinerary of the coalition of Syria and Ephraim against Jerusalem, mentioned in 7:1-2 (see the Commentary on 7:1-9).

10:33-34. As it stands, this metaphorical announcement of judgment makes sense of the preceding report of the approach of an enemy army toward Jerusalem. Yahweh does not speak, but a prophetic voice proclaims that "the Sovereign, the LORD of hosts" will exercise awesome power to prune and then cut down the tall trees and the thickets. Even the legendary trees of Lebanon will fall. The announcement, which recalls vv. 18-19, clearly is a metaphor in which the trees stand for the arrogant invader ("the lofty will be brought low," v. 33), whom we are to understand as Assyria. In the context of the threat against Jerusalem, these verses function as words of reassurance in the light of the enemy advance. The Lord will protect Mt. Zion (v. 32).

---

114. Clements, *Isaiah 1–39*, 114-15.
115. H. Wildberger, *Isaiah 1–12*, trans. Thomas H. Trapp (Minneapolis: Fortress, 1991) 436.

116. Ronald E. Clements, *Isaiah 1–39*, NCB (Grand Rapids: Eerdmans, 1980) 117; Wildberger, *Isaiah 1–12*, 451.

REFLECTIONS

The "remnant" is a powerful and evocative religious and theological symbol. Its use in Isa 10:20-23 shows it to be not only a rich but also a complicated and even ambiguous expression. Here it expresses both good news and bad, the announcement that only a few will be left and the promise that those who are left will not only have survived but will also have learned from the tragedy that struck the community of faith.

Different terms for "a remnant" are used throughout the Old Testament, reflecting important perspectives on the understanding of the people of God in history. It is important to keep in mind that whichever word is used, the term refers to concrete, physical realities, that it concerns real life and death. It means, quite literally, the group or body of those who are left—the survivors of devastation. Use of the expression, either as a report or as a prophecy, presumes that some people—in fact, most—will be or have been destroyed or exiled and that a few survivors remain. Probably the image arose in prophetic usage as the announcement of the severity of the judgment to come: *Only* a remnant will be left or will return (Isa 10:22). Even when this term is used in an expression of hope for the future, it presumes that disaster has come, that most of the nation is gone.

"Remnant" became central to the self-understanding of the post-exilic community. The people knew that the nation had been devastated by military defeat and exile and that they were the ones who had survived, the remnant (2 Chr 34:9; Hag 1:12). Their survival proved that God had not completely abandoned God's people. Texts from that era in particular reveal what always had been assumed—namely, that "remnant" is a corporate and historical symbol. More important than the survival of individuals is the survival of the people, for without a remnant the history of God with the people ends (Ezra 9:8, 14-15; cf. Isa 1:9).

It is possible, of course, that thinking of oneself or one's group as a "remnant" can lead to self-righteousness. The ones who survived may come to believe that they are a righteous remnant, that God punishes those who deserve it. But that is by no means the theology that drives the prophetic use of this expression. Disaster, like the rain, can fall on the just as well as the unjust, and the innocent will suffer for the sins of others. In Isa 10:20-21, the remnant leans on the Lord. This suggests that they were not chosen to survive because they were righteous but that they were changed because they had survived as a remnant.

Individuals and groups are changed by becoming remnants, by surviving among the dead. Survivors of the Holocaust were dramatically affected by that experience and by the fact that they survived it. People who survive a disaster, such as an airline crash that took others' lives, know that they have been changed forever. Many believe that they quite literally have a new lease on life. Some may even vow to live out the rest of their lives as thanksgiving for survival.

Isaiah 11:1-9, A New King and a New World

NIV

11 A shoot will come up from the stump
of Jesse;
from his roots a Branch will bear fruit.
2 The Spirit of the LORD will rest on him—
the Spirit of wisdom and of understanding,
the Spirit of counsel and of power,

NRSV

11 A shoot shall come out from the stump
of Jesse,
and a branch shall grow out of his roots.
2 The spirit of the LORD shall rest on him,
the spirit of wisdom and understanding,
the spirit of counsel and might,

NIV

the Spirit of knowledge and of the fear of
the LORD—
[3]and he will delight in the fear of the LORD.

He will not judge by what he sees with his
eyes,
or decide by what he hears with his ears;
[4]but with righteousness he will judge the needy,
with justice he will give decisions for the
poor of the earth.
He will strike the earth with the rod of
his mouth;
with the breath of his lips he will slay
the wicked.
[5]Righteousness will be his belt
and faithfulness the sash around his waist.

[6]The wolf will live with the lamb,
the leopard will lie down with the goat,
the calf and the lion and the yearling[a]
together;
and a little child will lead them.
[7]The cow will feed with the bear,
their young will lie down together,
and the lion will eat straw like the ox.
[8]The infant will play near the hole of the cobra,
and the young child put his hand into the
viper's nest.
[9]They will neither harm nor destroy
on all my holy mountain,
for the earth will be full of the knowledge of
the LORD
as the waters cover the sea.

[a]6 Hebrew; Septuagint *lion will feed*

NRSV

the spirit of knowledge and the fear of
the LORD.
[3]His delight shall be in the fear of the LORD.

He shall not judge by what his eyes see,
or decide by what his ears hear;
[4]but with righteousness he shall judge the poor,
and decide with equity for the meek of
the earth;
he shall strike the earth with the rod of
his mouth,
and with the breath of his lips he shall kill
the wicked.
[5]Righteousness shall be the belt around
his waist,
and faithfulness the belt around his loins.

[6]The wolf shall live with the lamb,
the leopard shall lie down with the kid,
the calf and the lion and the fatling together,
and a little child shall lead them.
[7]The cow and the bear shall graze,
their young shall lie down together;
and the lion shall eat straw like the ox.
[8]The nursing child shall play over the hole of
the asp,
and the weaned child shall put its hand on
the adder's den.
[9]They will not hurt or destroy
on all my holy mountain;
for the earth will be full of the knowledge of
the LORD
as the waters cover the sea.

COMMENTARY

Few texts in all of biblical literature are better known or loved than this one—and for good reason. For all who read or hear them read aloud, these verses articulate the deep and persistent human hope for justice and peace, and within the Christian church, this text expresses the promise of a Messiah who will establish peace on earth. This is magnificent poetry, but it is not a poem. Nor is it a typical prophetic address, for the usual formulas attributing the words to the Lord are missing, and there is no direct address to an audi-ence. However, a prophetic voice speaks, referring to Yahweh in the third person, proclaiming what the Lord will accomplish in the future.

The unifying theme of this proclamation or announcement of salvation is the coming reign of God, understood and presented in two ways. The first part (vv. 1-5) concerns the reign of God in the sociopolitical order by means of the birth or ascension of a new and ideal king from the line of David. The second element (vv. 6-9) promises the reign of God in the order of creation with the establishment of peace and tranquility among all creatures, including predators and their prey. It should be emphasized that this vision of the peaceable kingdom has nothing to do with "nature" as such. Here, as throughout the Hebrew Bible, the world is understood as God's creation.

Some have argued that these two units arose independently or that vv. 6-9 were composed after the first section.[117] There are very few internal links between the two parts, although in the concluding lines (v. 9b) a major theme ("knowledge of the LORD") from the first part (v. 2) concludes the whole. In the context in which these two elements are juxtaposed, however, the cosmic peace of the second unit is viewed as the consequence of the rise of the king in the line of David. There is no good reason either to treat 11:6-9 as late or as separate from 11:1-5. They are two parts of the same proclamation concerning the future reign of peace. The vision of the peaceable kingdom in Isaiah is distinctly related to the promise of a Davidic king and with that to the celebration of kingship in the psalms (see especially Psalm 72), and quite likely also to wider ancient Near Eastern traditions.[118]

The question of the authorship and date of this passage has been the subject of considerable debate and disagreement. Does the passage, or any of its parts, come from Isaiah in the eighth century BCE or from a later hand? The answer, at least for vv. 1-5, turns primarily on the interpretation of "the stump" (or "stock," REB) of Jesse in v. 1. Those commentators who take the passage to be late see "the stump" as an allusion to a time when the Davidic dynasty had been cut down—that is, in the exilic or post-exilic era. Although that is how the term probably would have been heard in those later times, the language more likely refers simply to the lineage—the family tree—of David. Nothing in vv. 1-5 in particular is inconsistent with the thought or language of Isaiah of Jerusalem;[119] its closest parallel is Isa 9:1-7. While the first part of the promise (vv. 1-5) draws out the implications of the Davidic tradition, the second part (vv. 6-9)

depends on the Zion tradition and in important respects corresponds to 2:1-4. Both are central in the thought of Isaiah of Jerusalem.

Some commentators have argued that this text, like 9:1-7, is related either to the inauguration of an actual king in the time of Isaiah, such as Hezekiah, or belongs to the time of a later king, such as Josiah.[120] Such readings thus take at least vv. 1-5 as being connected to actual expectations for the king, even if they did not turn out to be realized. Others see the promise as stemming from the prophet Isaiah's disappointment with Hezekiah, and his vision for a king in some unspecified future who would embody the Davidic royal ideal.[121] Those commentators who take it to be exilic or post-exilic tend to see the promise as an unrealistic hope for the revival of the Davidic monarchy.

11:1-5. The proclamation in these verses consists of two parts. First comes the promise of a future king from the line of David (v. 1). The promise is expressed metaphorically in typical Hebrew parallelism, in terms of a "branch" from the "stock of Jesse," the father of David and a "shoot from his roots." Second, the prophet describes the future king in terms of his character and his activities as a ruler (vv. 2-5). In ancient Israel, confidence in the reign of a Davidic king in Jerusalem was based on the promise expressed in 2 Samuel 7 and was celebrated regularly in worship (see Psalms 2; 45; 72; 110). Isaiah saw the Davidic monarchy as Yahweh's means of implementing Yahweh's will, first for Judah and Jerusalem, and then for the world as a whole. In later centuries, the hope for such a messiah (lit., "anointed one," a term that does not appear in this passage) was linked more and more to the culmination or fulfillment of God's will for human history.

The character of the ruler (vv. 2-3a) will be shaped by the "spirit of the LORD." The first line of v. 2 is a general statement of the gift of the spirit, comparable to the ancient idea of the charismatic election of Israel's leaders. This "spirit" (רוח *rûaḥ*) represents the active and creative divine presence known at creation (Gen 1:2) and in the inspiration

117. Ronald E. Clements, *Isaiah 1–39,* NCB (Grand Rapids: Eerdmans, 1980) 122.

118. H. Wildberger, *Isaiah 1–12,* trans. Thomas H. Trapp (Minneapolis: Fortress, 1991) 463-64.

119. See ibid., 465-66, for a list of scholars who attribute the passage to Isaiah, those who take it to be late, and a summary of the arguments on both sides. Wildberger concludes that it is Isaianic.

120. Marvin A. Sweeney, *Isaiah 1–39, With an Introduction to Prophetic Literature,* FOTL 14 (Grand Rapids: Eerdmans, 1996) 196-217.

121. Wildberger, *Isaiah 1–12,* 469.

of prophets (2 Kgs 2:9; Mic 3:8). The coming of the spirit ordained and authorized kings (1 Sam 11:6; 16:13) and other leaders (Judg 6:34). In this case, the ancient charismatic ideal of leadership is applied to a dynastic royal figure. The spirit of the Lord endows the king with three pairs of gifts, each described as "the spirit of": "wisdom and understanding," "counsel and might," "knowledge and the fear of the LORD" (v. 2*b*). These are the credentials of the ideal ruler.

The terms in the first pair, "wisdom" (חכמה *ḥokmâ*) and "understanding" (בינה *bînâ*), frequently appear together, not only in the wisdom literature (e.g., Prov 3:13, 19; 8:1; 10:13) but throughout the OT (e.g., Isa 10:13; Jer 10:12; 51:15; Ezek 28:4). Consequently, it is difficult to determine with confidence the specific differences between the two.[122] Together in this context the terms refer to practical wisdom that enables a ruler to face reality and deal with it fairly, including in political and judicial matters.[123] Solomon prayed for and was granted understanding (1 Kgs 3:9, 11), and "a ruler who lacks understanding is a cruel oppressor" (Prov 28:16). The second pair, "counsel" (עצה *'ēṣâ*) and "might" (גבורה *gĕbûrâ*), refer to diplomatic and military judgment and authority. The third pair, "knowledge" (דעת *da'at*) and "the fear of the LORD" (יראת יהוה *yir'at YHWH*), refer to the ideal king's piety. The focus is not "knowledge" in general, but knowledge of the Lord, as stated explicitly in 11:9. Thus piety consists in acknowledgment of and reverence for the Lord. Remarkably, the fear of the Lord "is itself a gift of God."[124]

The description of this king's administration (vv. 3*b*-5) concentrates on his establishment of justice and righteousness. If he does not judge by what he sees and hears, then how? Will he judge by the motivation of those he faces? By preference for those in need? In the light of the gifts of the Spirit, he will act as one who sees and hears deeper than the surface and will ensure that the "poor" and the "meek"—that is, those least able to protect

themselves—have full protection under the law (Ps 72:4, 12-14). Such establishment of justice entails the enforcement of sanctions. Words have the power to transform, even to destroy (Jer 1:9-10; Hos 6:5; Amos 1:2), so the king is said to strike with "the rod of his mouth," to slay the wicked with "the breath of his lips." The language is, to be sure, metaphorical, but it could be taken as describing a judicial pronouncement of a death sentence or a military leader's commands to attack. The ideal king exercises power to protect the weak. The character and administration of the king here are those that the people hoped for—but never fully realized—as each new descendant of David took the throne in Jerusalem.

11:6-9. The move from v. 5 to v. 6 is abrupt, shifting from the promise of a new king wearing righteousness and faithfulness as the symbols of his office to a proclamation that predators and prey shall live together in peace. Although the word itself does not appear in this passage, the unity of vv. 1-5 and 6-9 is in שלום (*šālôm*), "peace." The rule of justice in human society is followed or paralleled by a transformation in the relationship among animals and between animals and human beings.

The vision of the new order is set forth in vv. 6-8, with v. 9 concluding the unit as a whole. Verse 6 first pairs predators with prey: wolf with lamb, leopard with kid, calf and "fatling" with the lion. That "a little child shall lead them" describes all these creatures in a pastoral scene, being led like a flock of sheep. The "little child" (v. 6), the "nursing child," and the "weaned child" (v. 8) represent children generally, human beings at their most vulnerable stages, and not any particular individual, just as no particular lion or calf is in view. If v. 6 had raised questions about the new diet of the carnivores, they are answered in v. 7. Not only the cow and the ox but also now the lion and the bear will eat grass and straw. The implications of these transformations for human beings become explicit in v. 8 with the scene of "the nursing child" and the "weaned child" playing safely where poisonous snakes live. The goal of nonviolent nature is to provide a world where human beings can live safely, without fear.[125]

122. Wildberger concludes that "wisdom" refers "to the type of wisdom which can handle problems of daily living" and "understanding" more to intellectual abilities "which are necessary for one to see beyond the details of a particular situation, make an appropriate assessment, and come to conclusions about necessary decisions." See ibid., 472.

123. See O. Kaiser, *Isaiah 1–12: A Commentary,* trans. R. A. Wilson (Philadelphia: Westminster, 1972) 158.

124. Wildberger, *Isaiah 1–12,* 473.

125. Gene M. Tucker, "Rain on a Land Where No One Lives: The Hebrew Bible on the Environment," *JBL* 116 (1997) 11-12.

The description of the peaceable kingdom shows it to be populated by little children and animals, but it mentions only those of the land, not those of the sea and the air. More significant is the distinction between wild and domestic animals. That domestic animals will be safe from wild creatures reflects a concern for human security and peace. This is genuinely a "pastoral" concern for the safety of flocks for the sake of humankind.[126] If this vision has a predecessor, it would be in the ancient myth of a nonviolent paradise at the beginning of time.[127] However, this picture of nonviolence among the animals goes far beyond any paradise as characterized in the creation stories of the Hebrew scriptures, although Gen 1:29-31 does suggest that no animals were carnivores since both human beings and animals are given "every green plant for food." Hosea 2:18 envisions a future time of peace that includes a covenant between human beings and animals.

Concerning the transformation of natural relationships in the animal world, Seitz talks of this as mythological and gives a fundamentally allegorical reading—that is, the animals are the military powers warring with one another, and the vision is one of international peace.[128] Such a reading is hardly justified. Isaiah 1–39 has no such allegory. When the prophetic voice speaks "symbolically," it is in terms of metaphors, and they are never so enigmatic as to identify particular animals with nations without explanation.[129]

Verse 9 brings together the two parts of the unit. The lines, which have a liturgical tone and cadence, are cited by Habakkuk (Hab 2:14) in the time of the Babylonian exile (see also Isa 65:25). The center of the peaceful cosmos is the same as that in Isa 2:1-5: Yahweh's "holy mountain," that is, Mount Zion in Jerusalem. As a consequence of the rule of justice and the transformation of nature, "the earth will be full of knowledge of the LORD" (v. 9). Or is it the reverse, that because the earth is filled with the knowledge of the Lord, justice and peace reign? In any case, the concluding metaphor is remarkably powerful: The earth will be as full of that knowledge as the sea is full of water. "Knowledge of the LORD" and "to know" appear frequently in Isaiah (e.g., 5:13; 26:13; 33:6, 13) and will have included cognition, intimate relationship, and acknowledgment. This promise for relationship with the Lord reverses the accusation set out in 1:2-3.

126. Gene M. Tucker, "The Peaceable Kingdom and a Covenant with the Wild Animals," in *God Who Creates: Essays in Honor of W. Sibley Towner,* ed. William Brown and Dean McBride (Grand Rapids: Eerdmans, 1999) 215-25.

127. H. Wildberger, *Isaiah 1–12,* trans. Thomas H. Trapp (Minneapolis: Fortress, 1991) 483. See also his list of ancient Near Eastern texts that describe nonviolence among animals at the beginning, ibid., 479.

128. Christopher R. Seitz, *Isaiah 1–39,* Interpretation (Louisville: John Knox, 1993) 106-7.

129. Tucker, "The Peaceable Kingdom," 218.

REFLECTIONS

1. The juxtaposition of 11:1-5 and 11:6-9 evokes reflection on the relationship among justice, mercy, and peace in human society, on the one hand, and harmony in the natural order on the other hand. This may be taken as a reminder that, as many have said, "If you want peace, work for justice." The text concerns peace in the sociopolitical/economic order as well as among all creatures. As a whole, this unit suggests that human justice leads to a transformed relationship between human beings and the rest of creation, just as Hos 4:1-3 shows that corruption within human society leads to destruction of the environment and all its creatures. However, it would distort the import of this text to turn it into instruction, admonition, or law. It does not set out what people ought to do within society or in relationship to the environment. To read it as such could distort both the content and the mood of these powerful lines. This passage is not a call for action or even a criticism of injustice. These lines simply present unqualified good news. Whether in this world and history or beyond, they cry joyfully that God wills—and one day will bring about—justice and peace for the world and all its living creatures. No interpretative comments should be allowed to obscure the tone of joyful hope.

2. The central message of this text is that God will establish justice and righteousness on earth and in history. The concluding verse in particular emphasizes that the more people know and acknowledge the Lord, the more justice will prevail. Characteristically for the prophets and the Old Testament generally, the peace that this rule of God brings is made concrete in human society and politics. Moreover, "the wicked" will be judged guilty, and "the poor" and "the meek" will be vindicated.[130] According to Isaiah, when God reigns it will be through a particular government, a monarchy in which the king is not only pious and faithful but also wise and perceptive. To be sure, in Israel as throughout the ancient Near East, religious and political institutions paralleled one another. So is there any way that Isaiah's vision of the reign of God makes sense in modern culture, particularly in a nation founded on the principle that church and state are separate? However the modern interpreter struggles with this question, the prophetic text insists that answers will address concrete social and political issues such as poverty and corruption and will be aware that particular institutions will work for or against justice and that acts of injustice ought to entail sanctions. Moreover, all behavior and all institutions will be evaluated in light of the conviction that God wills peace and justice.

3. As with Isa 9:1-7, what originated as the promise of a new king in ancient Jerusalem came to be understood as the prophecy of a messiah, fulfilled by the coming of Jesus. So the Christian reader must struggle to hear and understand both the ancient Israelite hope for a new descendant of King David who will be a just and faithful king, establishing justice and righteousness in governing a particular human society, and the faith of the church, which has seen that hope both fulfilled and transformed in Jesus of Nazareth.

For all its spirituality, this passage comes down to earth with the promised king's concrete and difficult judgments, leading to life and health for some ("the poor," "the meek") and death for others ("the wicked"). To capitalize "Branch" (11:1 NIV) and "Spirit" (11:2 NIV) tends to impose Christian theology upon the text.

4. The second part of this passage presents a vision of the world that has stimulated the human longing for the peaceable kingdom, as seen in the painting known by that name of the famous American Quaker artist Edward Hicks (1780-1845). This painting obviously portrays Isa 11:6-9, but off to the side of the beasts and little children playing together there is a scene of William Penn and other leaders making a treaty with the Native Americans, perhaps illustrating Isa 11:1-5 as well. Is this peaceable kingdom a realistic hope? It goes beyond the prophetic concern with history to hope for a new creation.

Within the context of the Bible's persistent affirmation of the goodness of creation, Isa 11:6-9, with its proclamation of a dramatic transformation of life among all creatures, could pose a serious problem. "Natural" enemies in the animal world will live together in peace, even changing their diets. On the one hand, as so frequently in the prophetic literature, the poem stresses the relationship among justice, mercy, peace, and harmony in the natural order (see Ezek 34:25; Hos 1:18). Who does not long for a world without fear and violence? But on the other hand, the lines seem to suggest that the world may have been created good, even very good, but not quite good enough. The text presumes a negative evaluation of the world as it is, filled with predators and prey, violence and death. One implication of the passage, to put it bluntly, is that there will come a time when the world will be made safe for domestic animals and for children.[131] This is the vision of that peaceable kingdom.

In view of the comprehensive statement that ends the unit, it is common to conclude that this vision of the change in nature is cosmic, reaching to all creation. But there are two ways in which the scope of the vision is limited. First, as noted in the Commentary, it does not encompass all the animals, but only those of the land (not those of sea and air), and it is based on the important distinction between wild and domestic animals. Its concern focuses on human

---

130. Wildberger states: "The gifts of the righteousness of God cannot become a reality unless they are given shape within the socio-economic sphere. The peace which this creates is not the 'peace of the soul' for the believer, characteristic of one who survives in the midst of a wicked world, but can be attained only when evil is overpowered, which alone can guarantee that insecurity and fear can be repelled. The anticipated condition of salvation is irrevocably grounded within a knowledge of Yahweh." See Wildberger, *Isaiah 1-12,* 484.

131. Tucker, "Rain on a Land Where No One Lives," 11-12.

security and peace. It is a genuinely "pastoral" concern for the safety of flocks for the sake of humankind. Second, although the "knowledge of God" will fill the earth, it is only on "my holy mountain" that "they will not hurt or destroy" (11:9). Certainly this mountain is Zion. Even if—as seems likely—the mountain stands for the whole of the land of Israel,[132] the envisioned peaceable kingdom is a particular sacred territory, and not the whole earth.

There is, to be sure, no explicit criticism of the world as it is, with some animals living by killing and eating others. The imagery is employed to characterize peace and security under the ideal ruler. In its context, the envisioned future is within history and falls short of an apocalyptic transformation of the world. However, the prophecy of the peaceable kingdom clearly is an expectation that could not be fulfilled within the framework of the creation.[133] Still, such an image of peace may fuel people's hope for a just and secure existence.

132. Ronald E. Clements, *Isaiah 1–39*, NCB (Grand Rapids: Eerdmans, 1980) 124.
133. Tucker, "The Peaceable Kingdom and a Covenant with the Wild Animals," XXX.

Isaiah 11:10-16, Return of the Exiles

NIV

[10]In that day the Root of Jesse will stand as a banner for the peoples; the nations will rally to him, and his place of rest will be glorious. [11]In that day the Lord will reach out his hand a second time to reclaim the remnant that is left of his people from Assyria, from Lower Egypt, from Upper Egypt,[a] from Cush,[b] from Elam, from Babylonia,[c] from Hamath and from the islands of the sea.

[12]He will raise a banner for the nations
    and gather the exiles of Israel;
he will assemble the scattered people of Judah
    from the four quarters of the earth.
[13]Ephraim's jealousy will vanish,
    and Judah's enemies[d] will be cut off;
Ephraim will not be jealous of Judah,
    nor Judah hostile toward Ephraim.
[14]They will swoop down on the slopes of
        Philistia to the west;
    together they will plunder the people to
        the east.
They will lay hands on Edom and Moab,
    and the Ammonites will be subject to them.
[15]The LORD will dry up
    the gulf of the Egyptian sea;
with a scorching wind he will sweep his hand
    over the Euphrates River.[e]
He will break it up into seven streams
    so that men can cross over in sandals.

[a]11 Hebrew *from Pathros*   [b]11 That is, the upper Nile region
[c]11 Hebrew *Shinar*   [d]13 Or *hostility*   [e]15 Hebrew *the River*

NRSV

10On that day the root of Jesse shall stand as a signal to the peoples; the nations shall inquire of him, and his dwelling shall be glorious.

11On that day the Lord will extend his hand yet a second time to recover the remnant that is left of his people, from Assyria, from Egypt, from Pathros, from Ethiopia,[a] from Elam, from Shinar, from Hamath, and from the coastlands of the sea.
[12]He will raise a signal for the nations,
        and will assemble the outcasts of Israel,
    and gather the dispersed of Judah
        from the four corners of the earth.
[13]The jealousy of Ephraim shall depart,
        the hostility of Judah shall be cut off;
    Ephraim shall not be jealous of Judah,
        and Judah shall not be hostile towards
            Ephraim.
[14]But they shall swoop down on the backs of
            the Philistines in the west,
        together they shall plunder the people of
            the east.
    They shall put forth their hand against Edom
            and Moab,
        and the Ammonites shall obey them.
[15]And the LORD will utterly destroy
        the tongue of the sea of Egypt;
    and will wave his hand over the River
        with his scorching wind;
    and will split it into seven channels,

[a]Or *Nubia*; Heb *Cush*

NIV

¹⁶There will be a highway for the remnant of his
people
    that is left from Assyria,
  as there was for Israel
    when they came up from Egypt.

NRSV

    and make a way to cross on foot;
¹⁶ so there shall be a highway from Assyria
    for the remnant that is left of his people,
  as there was for Israel
    when they came up from the land of Egypt.

COMMENTARY

Although composed of several relatively distinct elements, this section is a coherent unit on the theme of the return of a remnant of both Israel and Judah. Verses 10-11 are prose, and vv. 12-16 are poetry, but the passage as a whole is framed as a proclamation, in third-person style, of what the Lord will do in the future. Verse 10 is yet another announcement concerning the descendant of David, vv. 11-12 promise the return of the remnant of both Judah and Israel, vv. 13-14 announce the reconciliation of Judah and Israel and their triumph over the Philistines, and vv. 15-16 set forth how the return from exile will be like the exodus from Egypt.

The relationship of v. 10 to its context is problematic. Does it conclude vv. 1-9 or begin a new unit? Its initial formula ("On that day") typically begins a new unit of discourse. However, it does resume the messianic theme of 11:1-5, even picking up the language of v. 1 ("roots," "root"); so some commentators read it with the preceding section. Moreover, it does not advance the theme of the returning remnant that dominates vv. 11-16. But, on the other hand, v. 12 picks up the announcement concerning the descendant of the Davidic line as a "signal" for the nations and begins with the same formula as v. 12. In v. 10 all nations will unite as they come to "inquire" of God in Jerusalem (see 2:1-4). In v. 12, the "signal" calls for the return of the dispersed and outcasts of Judah and Israel. The fact that v. 10 is prose while the preceding lines are poetry supports the conclusion that it is secondary to the original unit or units.[134] Thus v. 10 functions as a bridge between the two parts of this chapter, linking vv. 1-9 to what follows in vv. 11-16. In the process, it adds an international dimension to the reign of the

Davidic ruler of vv. 1-5 and a messianic dimension to the return of the exiles in vv. 12-16.

Verses 11-16, like v. 10, are almost universally accepted as a secondary addition to earlier Isaianic traditions. One could envision an eighth-century BCE provenance for the promise of Israel's return from Assyria, but the words concerning Judah's return and the reconciliation of Judah and Israel presume the end of the Babylonian exile, and thus relate to the Persian period (after 538 BCE). Moreover, both the language and the ideas closely parallel those found in Isaiah 40–55, commonly dated to the beginning of the Persian period. These include reference to a "highway" for the returnees (v. 15; 40:3; 49:11), the "coastlands" (v. 11; 41:1, 5; 42:4, 10, 12; 49:1; 51:5), and the use of the exodus tradition in vv. 15-16. Rarely at all in Isaiah 1–39, and never in the speeches of Isaiah of Jerusalem, does one find references to this pentateuchal tradition (see 10:24-27a and Commentary there). Deutero-Isaiah (Isaiah 40–55) brings together the exodus, Zion, and messianic traditions. It is unlikely that these verses were composed by the author of Isaiah 40–55, but they do stress the connections among the various parts of the entire book. In adding these lines, a writer or writers have applied the announcements of salvation in 11:1-9 to their own time and extended them to fit those circumstances.

In this vision of the future, the Lord not only returns the remnant of Judah and Israel to their land but also gives them political independence and military power. This is achieved first through the reconciliation of the two kingdoms (v. 13) and then through victories over their enemies (v. 14). The means of the return from foreign lands is seen to be like the exodus from Egypt—that is, not by overthrowing the nations that hold the exiles but

---

134. So Wildberger, *Isaiah 1–12,* 463, and most other modern commentators.

by subduing the natural boundaries to travel. At the exodus the obstacle was "the sea" (v. 15), and in this return it is the desert between Assyria and the land of Israel (v. 16).

REFLECTIONS

The language and imagery of a remnant echoes throughout Isaiah 1–39 (7:1-9; 10:19-22; 14:22, 30; 15:9; 37:4, 31-32). The best-known usage is the name of Isaiah's child, Shear-jasub, "A Remnant Shall Return," in the prophet's symbolic action before King Ahaz (7:1-9). The text before us probably interprets that symbol in terms of later circumstances: Now that prophecy is seen as being fulfilled.

In its earliest prophetic expression, the image of a remnant—if not the exact language—expresses the announcement of judgment, stressing that destruction will be virtually total, with only a few left: "The city that marched out a thousand shall have a hundred left" (Amos 5:3; see also Amos 3:12; 4:11; 5:15; 9:1-4). Here, as in the symbolic action reported in Isa 7:1-9, survival of a remnant is good news. Still, these words stand out against a dark background. If there is only a remnant, what of all those others, those who have fallen? So this announcement of salvation marks the move from despair to hope, from death to life, even life for a new nation. But the new is seen to be in continuity with the old. The nation is not dead so long as a few survive to return to the sacred land and reestablish life there.

This passage would have been written by and for those who consider themselves the remnant. It fuels their hope, but such thinking can also be dangerous. The invidious side appears here in the promise of the subjugation of Israel's enemies. Is it necessary to believe that good news for some entails bad news for others? Two points in this text set the boundaries for any self-righteousness that might arise in the minds of those who consider themselves a remnant. First, the text gives no "moral" reasons for the survival of these specific ones, for example, that they survived because they were more just or righteous or pious than those who died. On this point the announcement is neutral. Second, it is explicit from beginning to end that the new future is created not by human hands but by the same Lord who brought Israel out of Egypt.

Isaiah 12:1-6, Songs of Thanksgiving

NIV

12 In that day you will say:

"I will praise you, O LORD.
    Although you were angry with me,
your anger has turned away
    and you have comforted me.
²Surely God is my salvation;
    I will trust and not be afraid.
The LORD, the LORD, is my strength and my song;
    he has become my salvation."
³With joy you will draw water
    from the wells of salvation.

⁴In that day you will say:
"Give thanks to the LORD, call on his name;

NRSV

12 You will say in that day:
    I will give thanks to you, O LORD,
    for though you were angry with me,
your anger turned away,
    and you comforted me.

² Surely God is my salvation;
    I will trust, and will not be afraid,
    for the LORD GOD[a] is my strength and
        my might;
    he has become my salvation.

3With joy you will draw water from the wells of salvation. ⁴And you will say in that day:

[a]Heb for Yah, the LORD

NIV

make known among the nations what he
has done,
and proclaim that his name is exalted.
⁵Sing to the LORD, for he has done
glorious things;
let this be known to all the world.
⁶Shout aloud and sing for joy, people of Zion,
for great is the Holy One of Israel
among you."

NRSV

Give thanks to the LORD,
call on his name;
make known his deeds among the nations;
proclaim that his name is exalted.

⁵ Sing praises to the LORD, for he has done
gloriously;
let this be known*ᵃ* in all the earth.
⁶ Shout aloud and sing for joy, O royal*ᵇ* Zion,
for great in your midst is the Holy One
of Israel.

*ᵃOr this is made known   *ᵇOr O inhabitant of

COMMENTARY

The location of Isaiah 12 within the book is by no means accidental. It provides a liturgical conclusion to the first major section of the work, chaps. 1–12. For the most part, the prophetic addresses and reports that preceded this unit are announcements concerning Judah and Jerusalem, and many probably stem from the early period of the prophet's activity. Isaiah 13:1 clearly signals a new block of material, mainly oracles against foreign nations, different in both form and content from the section concluded by chap. 12. More important for our understanding of this chapter is the fact that it directly follows a collection of prophecies concerning the Lord's saving acts for Jerusalem and Judah, acts that focus on the descendants of David. These materials include 9:1-7 and 11:1-9, as well as 11:10-16, all of which herald the new age of peace and justice under "the shoot from the stump of Jesse" (11:1).

Although it is not obvious whether this text contains a single song or two brief ones, along with liturgical instructions for their use, all of chap. 12 should be interpreted as a whole. In any case, the chapter contains two distinct parts, vv. 1-3 and vv. 4-6. (Verse 3 is to be taken with what precedes, not—as the NRSV divisions suggest—with what follows.) Each of the parts begins with the instructions, "You will say in that day." Although it is not clear in English translation, the lines are significantly different. In the Hebrew, v. 1*a* is second-person singular and v. 4*a* is second-person plural. Both are calls to give thanks, in v. 1

to an individual and in v. 4 to the community. The first section is a thanksgiving song of an individual, and the second a communal hymn of thanksgiving and praise. As v. 1 makes explicit, the background of songs of thanksgiving is deliverance from trouble and the celebration of that deliverance. Moreover, both the trouble and the deliverance are attributed to the same Lord.

The patterns and motifs of the chapter are familiar from the psalter. Expressions of thanksgiving, trust, or praise are followed by their reasons, introduced by "for" (vv. 1-2, 5-6). Confidence is expressed in the Lord as the individual's "strength," "song" (NIV), and "salvation" (v. 2, using the language of the Song of Moses, Exod 15:2). So the first two verses move from thanks for a specific divine act to generalizations about the nature of God as the one who saves. Songs of thanksgiving are prayers in which one calls to the Lord (v. 4). The second psalm (vv. 4-6) consists almost entirely of calls to give thanks and praise. God is praised especially for mighty deeds. Because God, the Holy One of Israel, is great, all the earth should know, and those who live in the shadow of the Temple in Zion should sing for joy. One sings for joy not only because the Holy One of Israel is great, but also because God is present with those who sing God's praises (v. 6).

"Psalms"—that is, hymns of praise, thanksgiving songs, and other lyrical cultic poetry—are not limited in the OT to the book of Psalms. One finds such songs frequently not only in the narrative books (e.g., Exod 15:1-8, 21) but in the prophetic books as well (e.g., Amos 4:13; 5:8-9; 9:5-6). This fact, which should not be surprising, is due mainly to two factors. First, the authors of the books or the prophets themselves would have been so steeped in the language of worship that they would have used such poetry where appropriate (see esp. Jeremiah's complaints; e.g., Jer 11:18-23; 12:1-6; 15:10-21). Second, as the books subsequently were read in the context of worship, psalms would have been added, similar to the publication of lectionary texts with all the readings for the particular days printed in the order of their use.

It is very unlikely that the prophet Isaiah wrote chap. 12. It was added as the sayings of the prophet were being collected, edited, and saved as a book. The chapter serves as a fitting response on the part of the community of faith to the reading of the promises of salvation. It is even possible that the juxtaposition of the hymn of thanksgiving with the word of God through the prophet reflects liturgical practice in the Second Temple, during the post-exilic period. The songs that conclude the first section of the book of Isaiah suggest that the prophetic book was used in worship even before an official canon of Scripture was established.

REFLECTIONS

These songs, rooted in ritual, serve as yet another reminder that it is difficult to drive a wedge between prophets and cult, between the prophetic concern for justice, righteousness, and God's act in human events, on the one hand, and ritual piety, on the other hand. Here the book quickly turns from the announcement of God's future to prayers of thanksgiving, sung by individuals and the community to that God. Moreover, the songs themselves emphasize the future and the hope for divine intervention in human events. The introductory phrases, "in that day" (11:1, 4), make the songs of thanksgiving into promises: There will come a time when the people of God will experience salvation and will sing. Because the coming of that day is assured, even the present can be a time of joy. The biblical integration of the prophetic and priestly words can serve as a model for contemporary prayer and worship, as songs of praise and thanksgiving respond to the word of God for the future.

Thematically as well this chapter picks up central themes in the previous chapters. Because of its reference to Zion, the city of David, and its location following the announcements in chapter 11, the hope expressed here concerns the messianic age. Finally, though it is "royal Zion" who sings for joy (11:6), the message of hope is by no means for a single city or a small circle. Giving thanks to the Lord means making "known his deeds among the nations" (11:4), proclaiming God's name "in all the earth" (11:5). Zion is the center, but when God is in its midst, the good news cannot be contained; it must reach out to all the world. In coming together to give thanks to God, the elect sing for the whole world. Consequently, any contemporary congregation of the elect will see itself in the context of God's concern for all peoples.

ISAIAH 13:1–23:18

ORACLES CONCERNING FOREIGN NATIONS

OVERVIEW

These chapters comprise a distinct collection of materials within the book of Isaiah, recognized first by the common heading "The oracle concerning X" and also by the dominant genre, the announcement of judgment against a foreign nation. Comparable collections of prophecies against foreign nations appear also in Jeremiah (chaps. 46–51) and Ezekiel (chaps. 25–32). The heading in this collection, with some variations, appears ten times. Although it is apparent that there are more than ten distinct units of discourse within these chapters, those headings and the sections of material they set off should be the point of departure for analysis of the collection. Presumably correcting an oversight by the early editors, both the NRSV and the NIV insert a heading before 14:24 that is not present in the Hebrew: "An Oracle Concerning Assyria," or "A Prophecy Against Assyria," paralleling those throughout the section. Only the first of the headings (13:1) specifically associates what follows with Isaiah, indicating that this particular formula is designed as the heading for the collection as a whole.

The ten major units, therefore, are 13:1–14:27, Babylon; 14:28-32, Philistia; 15:1–16:14, Moab; 17:1–18:7, Damascus; 19:1–20:6, Egypt; 21:1-10, the wilderness of the sea; 21:11-12, Dumah; 21:13-17, the desert plain; 22:1-25, the valley of vision; 23:1-18, Tyre. Because the formula that begins 14:28-32 differs significantly from the others, some see nine units, with 14:28-32 as "an appendix" to the Babylon oracle.[135] The date formula ("In the year that King Ahaz died") may be designed to relate it to the preceding section, but even if it functions as an appendix, it clearly is marked as a distinct unit.

This collection would have been the product of an editor whose guiding principle was the headings for the particular announcements concerning foreign nations. Did other considerations also shape the arrangement of these prophecies? Neither a geographical nor a thematic development in the sequence can be discerned.[136] Rather, the oracles jump around the map of the ancient Near East instead of moving systematically from one direction to another. Nor is there a progression in terms of world powers, seriousness of offenses, or severity of punishment. It is important, however, that the first nation treated is Babylon.

Although the headings and the dominant genre are the most obvious features of this section, neither fully accounts for all of the material. First, the length of the units under each of these headings varies considerably. The oracles concerning Philistia (14:28-32), Dumah (21:11-12), and the desert plain (21:13-17) are quite short, while some of the longer units marked by the opening formula consist of more than one oracle. These include 13:1–14:27 and 17:1–18:7 (18:1-7 concerns Ethiopia and not Damascus). Second, not everything in this section is an oracle concerning a foreign nation. At least the first part of the unit concerning the valley of vision (22:1-25) is about Jerusalem, and other addresses concern Judah or Israel as well. Most striking, perhaps, is the presence among the prophecies of two narratives. The narrative concerning Sargon's commander-in-chief and of Isaiah's walking naked in the street (20:1-6) is, perhaps, connected with the oracle concerning Egypt and Ethiopia because Isaiah's sign warns against calling on those powers in the face of

---

135. Marvin A. Sweeney, *Isaiah 1–39, With an Introduction to Prophetic Literature,* FOTL XVI (Grand Rapids: Eerdmans, 1996) 212.

136. Kaiser struggles to see a theological development in the collection. See O. Kaiser, *Isaiah 13–39: A Commentary* (Philadelphia: Westminster, 1974) 5.

Assyrian threats. The speech and narrative concerning Shebna, Hezekiah's official (22:15-25), appears to support the theme of a context concerned with Jerusalem's sins and punishment. These factors support the conclusion that this collection is the product of editorial work and that many of the units have been expanded, either before or after the collection itself was shaped.[137] The obviously complex editorial history of these chapters, as well as allusions to events as late as the sixth century, indicate that many hands have created this material. Doubtless some of the traditions stem from the time of Isaiah in the eighth century BCE, but sorting out the earlier from the later is always difficult and often impossible.

Debate has focused on the meaning of the key term in the headings to these units. "Oracle" (משא *māśśā'*) is used eleven times here and only one other time in Isaiah 1–39—in Isa 30:6, as the heading of an address concerning the animals of the Negeb. The two other times the word appears in the entire book of Isaiah (46:1-2), they are not headings for "oracles" but refer to "burdens," the etymological background of the term. The word means "burden" in Num 4:15, 19, 24; 17:21-27. In Jer 23:33-40 it is a double entendre, meaning both "burden" and "oracle"—that is, a message

from the Lord. The word appears as a superscription for prophetic addresses in Zech 9:1 and 12:1, and even as the superscription for prophetic books in Nah 1:1; Hab 1:1; and Mal 1:1. One should not make too much of the etymology meaning "burden." As the heading to prophetic addresses, it simply indicates a word from the Lord concerning the future.

Although the development of a theological argument is not discernible, the section as a whole has a theme, expressed in the language of 23:9 (concerning Tyre):

> The LORD of hosts has planned it—
> to defile the pride of all glory,
> to shame all the honored of the earth. (NRSV)

Seitz has expressed it well: The oracles against the nations "are concerned with establishing Israel's God as God of all peoples and as judge over all forms of human pride and idolatry."[138] He also correctly emphasizes that these judgments against the foreign nations are not primarily announcements of salvation for Israel.[139] Moreover, although most of the oracles are quite specifically against particular nations, some also advance the theme of total world destruction.

---

137. Cf. Christopher R. Seitz, *Isaiah 1–39,* Interpretation (Louisville: John Knox, 1993) 117.

138. Ibid., 126
139. Ibid., 122.

ISAIAH 13:1–14:27, PROCLAMATIONS AGAINST BABYLON AND ITS KING

NIV	NRSV
13 An oracle concerning Babylon that Isaiah son of Amoz saw:	**13** The oracle concerning Babylon that Isaiah son of Amoz saw.

²Raise a banner on a bare hilltop,
    shout to them;
beckon to them
    to enter the gates of the nobles.
³I have commanded my holy ones;
    I have summoned my warriors to carry out
        my wrath—
    those who rejoice in my triumph.
 	
⁴Listen, a noise on the mountains,
    like that of a great multitude!
	²On a bare hill raise a signal,
	    cry aloud to them;
	wave the hand for them to enter
	    the gates of the nobles.
	³I myself have commanded my
	        consecrated ones,
	    have summoned my warriors, my proudly
	        exulting ones,
	    to execute my anger.

NIV

Listen, an uproar among the kingdoms,
　like nations massing together!
The LORD Almighty is mustering
　an army for war.
[5]They come from faraway lands,
　from the ends of the heavens—
the LORD and the weapons of his wrath—
　to destroy the whole country.

[6]Wail, for the day of the LORD is near;
　it will come like destruction from
　　the Almighty.[a]
[7]Because of this, all hands will go limp,
　every man's heart will melt.
[8]Terror will seize them,
　pain and anguish will grip them;
　they will writhe like a woman in labor.
They will look aghast at each other,
　their faces aflame.

[9]See, the day of the LORD is coming
　—a cruel day, with wrath and
　　fierce anger—
to make the land desolate
　and destroy the sinners within it.
[10]The stars of heaven and their constellations
　will not show their light.
The rising sun will be darkened
　and the moon will not give its light.
[11]I will punish the world for its evil,
　the wicked for their sins.
I will put an end to the arrogance of
　　the haughty
　and will humble the pride of the ruthless.
[12]I will make man scarcer than pure gold,
　more rare than the gold of Ophir.
[13]Therefore I will make the heavens tremble;
　and the earth will shake from its place
at the wrath of the LORD Almighty,
　in the day of his burning anger.

[14]Like a hunted gazelle,
　like sheep without a shepherd,
each will return to his own people,
　each will flee to his native land.
[15]Whoever is captured will be thrust through;
　all who are caught will fall by the sword.

NRSV

[4]Listen, a tumult on the mountains
　as of a great multitude!
Listen, an uproar of kingdoms,
　of nations gathering together!
The LORD of hosts is mustering
　an army for battle.
[5]They come from a distant land,
　from the end of the heavens,
the LORD and the weapons of his indignation,
　to destroy the whole earth.

[6]Wail, for the day of the LORD is near;
　it will come like destruction from
　　the Almighty![a]
[7]Therefore all hands will be feeble,
　and every human heart will melt,
[8]　and they will be dismayed.
Pangs and agony will seize them;
　they will be in anguish like a woman
　　in labor.
They will look aghast at one another;
　their faces will be aflame.
[9]See, the day of the LORD comes,
　cruel, with wrath and fierce anger,
to make the earth a desolation,
　and to destroy its sinners from it.
[10]For the stars of the heavens and their
　　constellations
　will not give their light;
the sun will be dark at its rising,
　and the moon will not shed its light.
[11]I will punish the world for its evil,
　and the wicked for their iniquity;
I will put an end to the pride of the arrogant,
　and lay low the insolence of tyrants.
[12]I will make mortals more rare than fine gold,
　and humans than the gold of Ophir.
[13]Therefore I will make the heavens tremble,
　and the earth will be shaken out of
　　its place,
at the wrath of the LORD of hosts
　in the day of his fierce anger.
[14]Like a hunted gazelle,
　or like sheep with no one to gather them,
all will turn to their own people,
　and all will flee to their own lands.
[15]Whoever is found will be thrust through,

[a]6 Hebrew *Shaddai*

[a]Traditional rendering of Heb *Shaddai*

NIV

[16]Their infants will be dashed to pieces before
their eyes;
their houses will be looted and their
wives ravished.

[17]See, I will stir up against them the Medes,
who do not care for silver
and have no delight in gold.
[18]Their bows will strike down the young men;
they will have no mercy on infants
nor will they look with compassion
on children.
[19]Babylon, the jewel of kingdoms,
the glory of the Babylonians'[a] pride,
will be overthrown by God
like Sodom and Gomorrah.
[20]She will never be inhabited
or lived in through all generations;
no Arab will pitch his tent there,
no shepherd will rest his flocks there.
[21]But desert creatures will lie there,
jackals will fill her houses;
there the owls will dwell,
and there the wild goats will leap about.
[22]Hyenas will howl in her strongholds,
jackals in her luxurious palaces.
Her time is at hand,
and her days will not be prolonged.

14 The LORD will have compassion on Jacob;
once again he will choose Israel
and will settle them in their own land.
Aliens will join them
and unite with the house of Jacob.
[2]Nations will take them
and bring them to their own place.
And the house of Israel will possess the nations
as menservants and maidservants in the
LORD's land.
They will make captives of their captors
and rule over their oppressors.

[3]On the day the LORD gives you relief from suffering and turmoil and cruel bondage, [4]you will take up this taunt against the king of Babylon:

How the oppressor has come to an end!
How his fury[c] has ended!

---

[a]19 Or *Chaldeans'*   [b]4 Dead Sea Scrolls, Septuagint and Syriac; the
meaning of the word in the Masoretic Text is uncertain.

NRSV

and whoever is caught will fall by
the sword.
[16] Their infants will be dashed to pieces
before their eyes;
their houses will be plundered,
and their wives ravished.
[17] See, I am stirring up the Medes against them,
who have no regard for silver
and do not delight in gold.
[18] Their bows will slaughter the young men;
they will have no mercy on the fruit of
the womb;
their eyes will not pity children.
[19] And Babylon, the glory of kingdoms,
the splendor and pride of the Chaldeans,
will be like Sodom and Gomorrah
when God overthrew them.
[20] It will never be inhabited
or lived in for all generations;
Arabs will not pitch their tents there,
shepherds will not make their flocks lie
down there.
[21] But wild animals will lie down there,
and its houses will be full of
howling creatures;
there ostriches will live,
and there goat-demons will dance.
[22] Hyenas will cry in its towers,
and jackals in the pleasant palaces;
its time is close at hand,
and its days will not be prolonged.

14 But the LORD will have compassion on
Jacob and will again choose Israel, and will
set them in their own land; and aliens will join
them and attach themselves to the house of Jacob.
[2]And the nations will take them and bring them to
their place, and the house of Israel will possess the
nations[a] as male and female slaves in the LORD's
land; they will take captive those who were their
captors, and rule over those who oppressed them.

[3]When the LORD has given you rest from your
pain and turmoil and the hard service with which
you were made to serve, [4]you will take up this
taunt against the king of Babylon:

How the oppressor has ceased!
How his insolence[b] has ceased!

---

[a]Heb *them*   [b]Q Ms Compare Gk Syr Vg: Meaning of MT uncertain

NIV

⁵The LORD has broken the rod of the wicked,
  the scepter of the rulers,
⁶which in anger struck down peoples
  with unceasing blows,
 and in fury subdued nations
  with relentless aggression.
⁷All the lands are at rest and at peace;
  they break into singing.
⁸Even the pine trees and the cedars of Lebanon
  exult over you and say,
 "Now that you have been laid low,
  no woodsman comes to cut us down."

⁹The graveᵃ below is all astir
  to meet you at your coming;
 it rouses the spirits of the departed to
    greet you—
  all those who were leaders in the world;
 it makes them rise from their thrones—
  all those who were kings over the nations.
¹⁰They will all respond,
  they will say to you,
 "You also have become weak, as we are;
  you have become like us."
¹¹All your pomp has been brought down to
    the grave,
  along with the noise of your harps;
 maggots are spread out beneath you
  and worms cover you.

¹²How you have fallen from heaven,
  O morning star, son of the dawn!
 You have been cast down to the earth,
  you who once laid low the nations!
¹³You said in your heart,
  "I will ascend to heaven;
 I will raise my throne
  above the stars of God;
 I will sit enthroned on the mount of assembly,
  on the utmost heights of the sacred
    mountain.ᵇ
¹⁴I will ascend above the tops of the clouds;
  I will make myself like the Most High."
¹⁵But you are brought down to the grave,
  to the depths of the pit.

¹⁶Those who see you stare at you,

ᵃ9 Hebrew Sheol; also in verses 11 and 15   ᵇ13 Or the north;
Hebrew Zaphon

NIV

⁵The LORD has broken the staff of the wicked,
  the scepter of rulers,
⁶that struck down the peoples in wrath
  with unceasing blows,
 that ruled the nations in anger
  with unrelenting persecution.
⁷The whole earth is at rest and quiet;
  they break forth into singing.
⁸The cypresses exult over you,
  the cedars of Lebanon, saying,
 "Since you were laid low,
  no one comes to cut us down."
⁹Sheol beneath is stirred up
  to meet you when you come;
 it rouses the shades to greet you,
  all who were leaders of the earth;
 it raises from their thrones
  all who were kings of the nations.
¹⁰All of them will speak
  and say to you:
 "You too have become as weak as we!
  You have become like us!"
¹¹Your pomp is brought down to Sheol,
  and the sound of your harps;
 maggots are the bed beneath you,
  and worms are your covering.

¹²How you are fallen from heaven,
  O Day Star, son of Dawn!
 How you are cut down to the ground,
  you who laid the nations low!
¹³You said in your heart,
  "I will ascend to heaven;
 I will raise my throne
  above the stars of God;
 I will sit on the mount of assembly
  on the heights of Zaphon;ᵃ
¹⁴I will ascend to the tops of the clouds,
  I will make myself like the Most High."
¹⁵But you are brought down to Sheol,
  to the depths of the Pit.
¹⁶Those who see you will stare at you,
  and ponder over you:
 "Is this the man who made the earth tremble,
  who shook kingdoms,
¹⁷who made the world like a desert
  and overthrew its cities,

ᵃOr assembly in the far north

NIV

they ponder your fate:
"Is this the man who shook the earth
and made kingdoms tremble,
[17]the man who made the world a desert,
who overthrew its cities
and would not let his captives go home?"

[18]All the kings of the nations lie in state,
each in his own tomb.
[19]But you are cast out of your tomb
like a rejected branch;
you are covered with the slain,
with those pierced by the sword,
those who descend to the stones of the pit.
Like a corpse trampled underfoot,
[20] you will not join them in burial,
for you have destroyed your land
and killed your people.

The offspring of the wicked
will never be mentioned again.
[21]Prepare a place to slaughter his sons
for the sins of their forefathers;
they are not to rise to inherit the land
and cover the earth with their cities.

[22]"I will rise up against them,"
declares the LORD Almighty.
"I will cut off from Babylon her name
and survivors,
her offspring and descendants,"
declares the LORD.
[23]"I will turn her into a place for owls
and into swampland;
I will sweep her with the broom of
destruction,"
declares the LORD Almighty.

[24]The LORD Almighty has sworn,

"Surely, as I have planned, so it will be,
and as I have purposed, so it will stand.
[25]I will crush the Assyrian in my land;
on my mountains I will trample him down.
His yoke will be taken from my people,
and his burden removed from
their shoulders."

[26]This is the plan determined for the
whole world;

NRSV

who would not let his prisoners go home?"
[18]All the kings of the nations lie in glory,
each in his own tomb;
[19]but you are cast out, away from your grave,
like loathsome carrion,[a]
clothed with the dead, those pierced by
the sword,
who go down to the stones of the Pit,
like a corpse trampled underfoot.
[20]You will not be joined with them in burial,
because you have destroyed your land,
you have killed your people.

May the descendants of evildoers
nevermore be named!
[21]Prepare slaughter for his sons
because of the guilt of their father.[b]
Let them never rise to possess the earth
or cover the face of the world with cities.

[22]I will rise up against them, says the LORD of
hosts, and will cut off from Babylon name and
remnant, offspring and posterity, says the LORD.
[23]And I will make it a possession of the hedgehog,
and pools of water, and I will sweep it with the
broom of destruction, says the LORD of hosts.

[24]The LORD of hosts has sworn:
As I have designed,
so shall it be;
and as I have planned,
so shall it come to pass:
[25]I will break the Assyrian in my land,
and on my mountains trample him
under foot;
his yoke shall be removed from them,
and his burden from their shoulders.
[26]This is the plan that is planned
concerning the whole earth;
and this is the hand that is stretched out
over all the nations.
[27]For the LORD of hosts has planned,
and who will annul it?
His hand is stretched out,
and who will turn it back?

[a]Cn: Compare Gk: Heb *like a loathed branch*   [b]Syr Compare Gk:
Heb *fathers*

NIV

this is the hand stretched out over all
    nations.
[27]For the LORD Almighty has purposed, and
    who can thwart him?
His hand is stretched out, and who can
    turn it back?

COMMENTARY

Four distinct units comprise this section, identified as "the oracle concerning Babylon" (13:1). The units in this section are quite diverse in length, genre, and subject matter. Such diversity supports the view that this is not a unified composition but a collection of materials that originated independently. Only the first unit, the announcement of judgment in 13:2-22, actually concerns Babylon. The second unit (14:1-2) is a promise of salvation to "Jacob" and "Israel." Its prose stands out in the midst of poetic prophecies. Although the third section (14:3-23) parallels the first in many ways, it is not a proclamation against Babylon but a taunt song over the king of Babylon. Most commentators treat the fourth unit (14:24-27) as a distinct section, since it concerns not Babylon but Assyria. In fact, both the NRSV and the NIV supply a heading not found in the Hebrew, "An Oracle Concerning Assyria" or "A Prophecy Against Assyria." The absence of the heading as well as parallels to language and themes in 5:26-29 and 10:5-15 tend to support the conclusion that the unit has been moved into this context from elsewhere in the collection of Isaiah traditions.

The guiding theme of these chapters is twofold. On the one hand, the arrogance of Babylon and its king are held up to ridicule and condemnation. Babylon has become the "final symbol of national arrogance and blind disregard for the ways of Israel's God and his chosen people Israel."[140] On the other hand, underlying all these proclamations is the conviction that the Lord's authority extends over all the world, and especially over the great powers, even those who have worked God's will against Israel.

13:1. The initial verse, as a superscription, is separate from what follows in vv. 2-22. This heading is both parallel to and distinct from the others that mark the units in chaps. 13–23. The identification of Isaiah as "son of Amoz" corresponds to the superscriptions in 1:1 (see the Commentary on 1:1) and 2:1, as does the technical terminology for revelation, "saw." There is a tension between the attribution in v. 1 and the contents that follow. Although v. 1 specifically ascribes what follows to Isaiah, the prophecies in chaps. 13–14 contain allusions to events far later than the eighth century BCE. Although some recent commentators identify part or all of the material in this section with Isaiah of Jerusalem,[141] the evidence supports those others who conclude that most or all of these lines have been shaped by voices from the time of the Babylonian exile or later.[142] Although the enemy of his time was Assyria, it is certainly possible that Isaiah himself could have known of Babylon and spoken against it. However, both the oracle against Babylon (13:2-22) and the taunt song against the king of Babylon (14:5-23) presume events of the sixth century or later, when Babylon fell to the Persians (cf. 13:17).

13:2-22. Although it consists of a number of parts, this section is a coherent and relatively consistent prophecy.[143] Differences of perspective and even tensions become visible as the lines ebb and flow, but there is a fluid movement from beginning

---

140. Christopher R. Seitz, *Isaiah 1–39*, Interpretation (Louisville: John Knox, 1993) 119.

141. J. J. M. Roberts, "Isaiah," *HarperCollins Study Bible,* 1031-35; S. Erlandsson, *The Burden of Babylon: A Study of Isaiah 13:2–14:23,* ConBOT 4 (Lund: Gleerup, 1970).

142. H. Wildberger, *Isaiah 13–27: A Continental Commentary* (Minneapolis: Fortress, 1997) 16-17; Seitz, *Isaiah 1–39,* 120. Clements argues that while most of the material is late some of it may stem from the eighth century. See Ronald E. Clements, *Isaiah 1–39,* NCB (Grand Rapids: Eerdmans, 1980) 129-33.

143. Against Clements, *Isaiah 1–39,* 132-38, who sees here five distinct prophecies.

to end. If v. 1 had not informed us that the prophecy is against Babylon, we would not have known the object of the Lord's wrath until v. 19, where that name first appears in the oracle. This oracle is either a proclamation of punishment or an announcement of judgment on a particular foreign nation, but at points the Lord's intervention to judge is said to encompass "the whole earth" (v. 5), "the world" itself (v. 11), and to include "every human heart" (v. 7; cf. v. 12). So the prophecy is both local and universal.[144] The thread that connects the elements of this prophecy is "the day of the LORD" (vv. 6, 9), an ancient tradition related to the holy war in Israel. The "day of the LORD" was the day the Lord intervened on behalf of Israel against her enemies. A major turning point in this tradition is its use in Amos 5:18-20:

> Alas for you who desire the day of the LORD!
>
> . . . .
>
> It is darkness, not light. (NRSV)

Clearly the prophet reverses the expectation that the day of the Lord would bring victory for the Lord's people. Israel has become Yahweh's enemy and thus will be punished on that day. The future of the day of the Lord tradition lies in apocalyptic literature, where it is believed that the day of the Lord will be the last day, and the day of war.

Consistent with the day of the Lord theme, images of warfare dominate this oracle: The Lord "of hosts" (i.e., of armies) musters "an army for battle" (v. 4) and will use the "weapons of his indignation" (v. 5). Eventually the enemy will flee as from the battlefield (v. 14), those who are caught will "fall by the sword" (v. 15), infants will be killed, houses will be plundered (v. 16), and "young men" will be slaughtered by the bow (v. 18).

With a few exceptions, the speaker throughout the oracle is Yahweh. The Lord ("I myself") begins with a summons to prepare for war (vv. 2-3), calling for a "signal" to be raised. Less clear in this summons is the identity of the addressees. Certainly they are the Lord's "warriors," "consecrated" for the holy war. Would the ones who are to execute the wrath of the Lord be the "Medes" (v. 17), whom the Lord sends against Babylon (v. 17)? Given the present shape of the chapter, this is

the most likely reading. On the other hand, some take the summoned nation to be Babylon, arguing that the pronouncement of judgment or parts of it originally were directed either to Assyria[145] or to Israel itself.[145]

The next section (vv. 4-5) begins with another summons, a call to hear the sound of "a great multitude," "an uproar of kingdoms." The lines are spoken not by Yahweh but by a prophetic voice describing God's actions. The theme of preparation for war continues, but the scene has shifted. The army the Lord musters is not a single nation but "nations." Nor is the destination of that army's march a particular state. The goal is the destruction of "the whole earth" (v. 5). It may be that in the time of this poet Babylon had come to represent the known world, but the fact that armies come "from a distant land, from the end of the heavens" (v. 5) indicates that a genuinely cosmic destruction is in view.

Like the two previous parts of chap. 13, the next one (vv. 6-10) begins with a summons, in this case to mourn ("Wail," v. 6). The theme of universal destruction dominates these verses, set out in terms of the coming of the day of the Lord. Since the Lord is mentioned in the third person more than once, it is a prophetic voice that speaks. What this prophet sees on the horizon is the direct intervention of Yahweh. The image of people fleeing from the Lord's destruction is similar to that in Amos 2:14-16, but while Amos pictures soldiers in panicked retreat, this text shows all humanity under attack and in flight. The "wrath and cruel anger" come from the Lord, and will reach not only all human beings but even "the heavens and their constellations" (v. 10). It will be indeed a day of darkness (cf. Amos 5:18-20. In Josh 10:12-13 the Lord is said to have stopped the sun in the context of a holy war.)

In vv. 11-12 Yahweh speaks directly, promising to punish "the world for its evil" (v. 11). (The exception is v. 13*b*, which refers to the Lord in the third person.) First, the Lord promises to intervene to judge the world because of human wickedness (vv. 11-13). Then follows a passive description of the effects of divine intervention (vv. 14-16), stressing the flight and death of humanity. Among

---

144. Kaiser, *Isaiah 13–39*, 9.

145. Clements, *Isaiah 1–39*, 133; see also Seitz, *Isaiah 1–39*, 132-33.
146. Wildberger, *Isaiah 13–27*, 12.

the most horrible of lines in Scripture are those in v. 16 promising that "their infants will be dashed to pieces . . . and their wives ravished." As if those violent acts were not sufficient, one must notice that the perspective is not that of the children and women, but of the men. The picture stresses their pain at seeing such horrors. The loss of the children is a punishment for their fathers.

The Lord speaks directly again in v. 17, in this case announcing an intervention against Babylon through the instrumentality of the Medes. The remainder of the announcement (vv. 18-22) again articulates the effects of that divine intervention in passive form, noting what will happen as the Medes move against the mighty kingdom of Babylon. As in Isa 1:9, "like Sodom and Gomorrah" (v. 19) is the ultimate metaphor for divine judgment upon a sinful city. The details of that judgment go even beyond wiping out the great city and its inhabitants, spelling out Yahweh's promise in v. 11 to "punish the world." Babylon, the symbol of the highest civilization, and its very cradle, will return to chaos. It will never again be inhabited but will become such a wilderness as to be shunned by nomads and shepherds. It will be, in effect, a haunted place, approached only by "wild animals," "howling creatures," "ostriches," "goat-demons," "hyenas," and "jackals"; in short, the opposite of civilization.

Fundamentally, this chapter is an announcement of judgment. But where are the reasons for judgment that one ordinarily finds in such announcements against Israel? They appear only as allusions of the most general sort to the "evil" and "iniquity" (v. 11) of the condemned. Some other references to the wrongdoing of the guilty, such as the "pride of the arrogant" and the "insolence of tyrants" (v. 11), are somewhat more specifically addressed to the Babylonian Empire. But it is remarkable that the specific crimes or sins that would explain such horrible divine intervention are not enumerated. This leaves the emphasis upon the authority of the one who will judge the earth.

14:1-2. These verses contrast dramatically with the oracles in both the immediate and the wider context. Between the announcements of the judgment of the world and the overthrow of Babylon, on the one hand, and the taunt song over the king of Babylon, on the other hand, these lines

proclaim the good news of the restoration of Israel. Yahweh does not speak directly but Yahweh's future actions are described passively. Instead of expressing wrath, the Lord "will have compassion" and renew Israel's election ("again choose") and reestablish them in the promised land. This is that rare allusion to the exodus from Egypt within Isaiah 1–39. In v. 1 "aliens" will be welcome in the land (cf. Isa 2:2-5). But in v. 2 they have become slaves, and the conditions of oppressor and oppressed will be reversed.

There can be little doubt that this section is late.[147] It even seems likely that the two verses come from different periods, for they certainly express different attitudes toward the outsiders. In its promises of return and restoration, v. 1 presumes the exilic period, assuming that the people of God are dispersed from the land. Verse 2, however, does not so clearly presuppose the situation of exile for it can look back to such circumstances as past ("were their captors," "those who oppressed them"). Both verses presuppose a time of trouble and oppression for Israel at the hand of world powers. The perspective of v. 1 approaches that of Isaiah 40–55 (cf. 40:2; 49:22-23), while that of v. 2 reflects the attitude of Isaiah 56–66 toward non-Israelites (cf. 60:4-16; 61:5-7). Thus these verses support the perspective of the book of Isaiah as a whole: that Israel will suffer exile but later will be reestablished in the land promised to their ancestors.

The translation and interpretation of the little word that begins the chapter (כִּי, *kî*) is important in understanding both these two verses and the way they interpret the surrounding oracles. The NIV and REB leave it unexpressed, apparently reading it as a particle of emphasis ("indeed," or "surely") and not a conjunction. That is a legitimate possibility, but not likely. The word functions as a conjunction, e.g., "But" (NRSV, TNK), thus contrasting the fate of Israel with that of Babylon. Even stronger, the conjunction may be read as "for," giving the reasons for or the purpose of what has just been set out in chap. 13. The Lord will judge Babylon in order to restore

147. See virtually all modern commentaries. Exceptions are Oswalt, *Isaiah 1–39*, 312-13, and John H. Hayes and Stuart A. Irvine, *Isaiah the Eighth Century Prophet: His Times and His Preaching* (Nashville: Abingdon, 1987) 229-30.

Israel.[148] Neither the oracle against Babylon (13:2-22) nor the taunt song over the king of Babylon (14:4b-21) refers to Israel at all, but later editors have interpreted these announcements of judgment as good news for Israel.

14:3-23. Following a narrative introduction (vv. 3-4a) comes one of the most riveting and ominous poems in the Bible, the ironic dirge celebrating the death of the king of Babylon (vv. 4b-21). By means of a temporal clause ("When the LORD has given you rest"), the introduction links the taunt song to the preceding proclamation concerning the restoration of Israel. It leaves no doubt that the taunt concerns the Babylonian tyrant, whose death coincides with Israel's "rest" from servitude. This "rest" recalls Israel's relief from warfare and security in the land, as reported in the deuteronomistic history (Joshua–2 Kings; e.g., Josh 1:15; 11:23; 14:15; 22:4). The "king of Babylon" (v. 4) remains unnamed, and it is futile to search for his identity. By the end of the poem, this tyrant seems virtually to stand for the power of the Babylonian Empire, whose death is celebrated. The perspective is clear enough. Although the introductory instructions to "take up" the song are addressed in the second-person masculine singular ("you"), they actually seem to be addressed to Israelites who have suffered under the heel of the world power and have been set free.

The introduction also names the genre of the poem, a "taunt," from the Hebrew משל (māšāl). Elsewhere this term refers to proverbial sayings or similes (Prov 1:1; 10:1; 25:1), but there are other instances of the same sense as here, as a "mocking saying" (e.g., Deut 28:37; 1 Sam 10:12; Jer 24:9). The saying is also a song. Both its meter (3 + 2) and its contents show it to be patterned after the dirge or funeral song. Like the dirge, it uses the common cry "How" (vv. 4, 12) and describes the death of someone. But instead of mourning, this parody of the dirge provides the occasion for joyful celebration. Whereas the cry "how" would have expressed reluctance to accept the death of a friend or family member, now it serves to set a tone that is reversed. This is not the only instance of the use of funeral songs in prophetic literature to express something other

than grief. Amos sings a lament over "maiden Israel" (Amos 5:1-3) to announce that the nation is as good as dead. So the dirge here is ironic and even satirical.

With stunning poetry and vivid imagery the death song moves from one scene and one set of characters to another, finally encompassing the earth, the heavens, and the underworld. The first episode (vv. 4b-6) sets the scene for the whole by giving an account of the death of the oppressor. Like other biblical dirges, it gives an account of the death and contrasts the past with the present, the life of the one who has gone with his loss to death (2 Sam 1:19-27). Here the arrogance and power of the tyrant contrast with his broken staff and scepter. (This may be an allusion to the messianic expectation expressed in Isa 9:4.) The scene's setting is the political and military arena, and its characters are the king, the people whom he oppressed, and the Lord, who has crushed his power and taken his life.

The next scene (vv. 7-8) moves to the earth itself. Just as the taunt song will be sung when Israel is at "rest" (v. 3), so also all creation is shown to be "at rest and quiet." But this is just the pause before it breaks out into song. (Instead of reading "whole earth . . . they break forth" with the NRSV or "All the lands . . . they break forth" with the NIV, read "All the earth . . . loudly it cheers" with the TNK or "The whole world . . . it breaks into cries of joy" with the REB.) Even the great trees sing out in celebration, for they now are safe from the tyrant's ax.

In vv. 9-11, the scene moves to the underworld ("sheol," or "the grave"), and the dead king is addressed directly in mocking pictures of the realm of the dead. Sheol, the destination of all when they die, is personified. If we interpret the Hebrew term for the "inhabitants" (רפאים rĕpāʾîm) of Sheol in its OT and ancient Near Eastern context, then "shades" (NRSV) is a sound translation. They have no power, but lie there in the darkness (else why would they need to be roused?), eventually losing their identity (Ps 88:13; Eccl 9:5) and even fading away. They are "weak" (v. 10). To see them as the "spirits of the departed" (NIV) reads later ideas from Greek and Christian thought into these ancient texts and suggests more life than was believed to be present in this shadowy place. It is all the more remarkable, then, that Sheol

148. Kaiser, *Isaiah 13–29,* 23-25; H. Wildberger, *Isaiah 1–12,* trans. Thomas H. Trapp (Minneapolis: Fortress, 1991) 5, 33-35.

rouses from their thrones the shades of dead leaders and kings to greet the king of Babylon. Even tyrants, they remind him, come to the same end as all flesh. Power becomes weakness. Instead of harps to lull him to sleep, the king will lie on "maggots" and be covered with "worms" (v. 11).

The next scene (vv. 12-14), introduced, as was the first, with the cry, "How," takes place at the opposite extreme of the cosmos, in heaven. With more than a little irony, the tyrant is called "Day Star, Son of Dawn," divinities in the ancient Near East. In fact, this scene closely resembles the myths of the Canaanite gods as reported in the Ugaritic texts. Baal and the other gods gathered, and also fought with one another, on the "mount of assembly," on Mt. "Zaphon" (v. 13).[149] That the king seeks to "ascend to the tops of the clouds" recalls an epithet of Baal, "the cloud rider." The idea that the god would be "brought down to Sheol" (v. 15) lives on in the later tradition of Lucifer (Luke 10:18; 2 Pet 2:4). But all this talk of sacred mountains and gods serves to condemn the Babylonian king of hubris, of seeking to make himself "like the Most High" (v. 14).

As if to remind readers that the one who stormed the heavens is dead, the drama's setting shifts back to the underworld (vv. 15-20a). This section parallels the previous visit to Sheol (vv. 7-8), with the shades ridiculing the fallen despot. The comparison of his past glory and ruthless power with his present state makes a point of accusing the Babylonian king of refusing "to let his prisoners go home" (v. 17), an obvious allusion to the Babylonian exile. Moreover, here it is not the dead kings who scorn him but the inhabitants of the pit in general. That makes it possible for the sarcastic speech to compare the king of Babylon to other monarchs. Whereas they all have their glorious tombs, his carcass will be scattered and trampled as on a battlefield (vv. 18-19). He will be dishonored in death because he brought disaster upon his own land (v. 20).

The section concludes with a prayer or plea that goes even beyond the death of the king, asking that his sons be killed and that he have no descendants (vv. 20b-21). With the introduction (vv. 3-4a), these verses frame the taunt song itself. The hope expressed in these lines is first a further condemnation of the king of Babylon, for without

descendants he truly vanishes from the earth. Second, they express the positive hope that the power of the tyrant's empire will never again rule the earth. In this there is a blending of the specific and the general, the focus on the evil king and concern for all "evildoers."

Appended to the taunt song against the king of Babylon is a prophecy of judgment against Babylon (vv. 22-23). In prose instead of poetry, it uses ancient prophetic formulas ("says the LORD of hosts"), giving an account of Yahweh's promise to wipe Babylon from the earth. The proclamation is linked to v. 21 with the catchword "rise." It picks up and expands the hope that the king will have no one to carry on his name and echoes the motif of 13:20-22 that the center of civilization will revert to wilderness. The Lord will accomplish this with "the broom of destruction."

14:24-27. The heading before v. 24 in the NRSV and the NIV represents an interpretation and not a translation, for it does not appear in the Hebrew text. Certainly the interpretation is justified, for the words that follow concern Assyria. But, like the oracle against Babylon in 13:2-22, these lines are both specific and general; they concern "the whole earth" (v. 26) as well as Assyria. The introductory oath formula (v. 1a) informs the reader that what follows is a divine speech. Such divine oaths appear in Amos (4:2; 6:8; 8:7) and elsewhere in Isaiah (5:9; 22:14) and serve to emphasize the announcements they introduce. However, only the first part of the material that follows contains the words of Yahweh. Verse 26 describes the divine plan passively, and v. 27 speaks of the Lord in the third person.

The announcement's fundamental point is that Assyria will be broken, and on the Lord's own land. The passage echoes expressions found earlier in the book of Isaiah. The references to the "yoke" and the "burden" in v. 25 allude to 9:4. The fact that the language of the Lord's outstretched hand parallels the formula concluding a series in 5:25; 9:12, 17, 21; and 10:4 has led some scholars to conclude that the oracle originally belonged in that context and has been moved to its present location because it announces judgment on a foreign nation.[150]

---

149. See R. J. Clifford, *The Cosmic Mountain in Canaan and the Old Testament* (Cambridge, Mass.: Harvard University Press, 1972) 160-69.

150. Hermann Barth, *Die Jesaja-Worte in der Josiazeit* (Neukirchen: Neukirchener Verlag, 1977) 103-19. Seitz sees the theme of the Lord's outstretched hand as an organizing principle of the collection of oracles against foreign nations. See Christopher R. Seitz, *Isaiah 1–39*, Interpretation (Louisville: John Knox, 1993) 137.

REFLECTIONS

This text, like most of the oracles against the foreign nations, cannot be worked easily into a theological scheme or brought into line with conventional understandings of the world or of God. It is troubling and, therefore, provocative. Like so many prophetic texts, it cannot be domesticated or brought under our control. This provides all the more reason for us to listen, to allow ourselves to be challenged by what may seem to be alien perspectives. Serious readers will struggle to let the text speak before they rush in to reject it, to listen and look before speaking. If the reader is prepared for such effort, then these chapters raise several issues that call for serious reflection.

1. Contemporary readers recoil in horror to repudiate texts such as these that celebrate the suffering and death of enemies. Even if we can share some of the glee over the poetic account of the death of the king of Babylon, we are offended by lines such as those in 13:16-18 that envision the slaughter of children. Small wonder that verses like the last part of Psalm 137 found no home in Christian lectionaries:

Happy shall they be who take your little ones
 and dash them against the rock! (Ps 137:9 NRSV)

Psalm 137, like Isaiah 13–14, also concerns Babylon, and the line before it reads:

O daughter Babylon, you devastator!
 Happy shall they be who pay you back
 what you have done to us! (Ps 137:8 NRSV)

But such texts have at least two very important functions for readers separated by centuries from these voices. First, instead of rejecting such words from a superior and self-righteous perspective, we need to allow them to show us a different point of view. Context and perspective are everything here. This poetry, which comes from the time of the Babylonian exile and later, expresses the point of view of those oppressed by the superior power of Babylon. An important function of the text is to enable its readers to identify with the oppressed. Oppression is not just a modern idea, but the language used by the community to describe itself (14:2). Especially those who are comfortable and have lived their lives in powerful nations may come to learn something of the feeling of living under the thumb of aggressive forces over which they have no control.

Second, the Lord's judgment against Babylon sounds like a cry for revenge, especially insofar as it seems also to entail salvation for Israel. Although it is not self-evident that revenge lies at the foundation of these proclamations, they certainly can be and actually were used to express vengeance. Before we rush to condemn such feelings out of hand, it is valuable for us to acknowledge that such emotions are deeply embedded in the human experience and that they may be related to the cry for justice, at least justice in the form of retribution. Moreover, these texts enable us to recognize such vengeance within ourselves, to put us in touch with our own heart of darkness. To be sure, the desire for revenge is nothing to be proud of, but the reality must be acknowledged, else it cannot be exorcised. Feelings of hatred need to be confessed in order to be forgiven.

2. In the final form of this section, if not in all its individual parts, bad news for Babylon translates into good news for the people of God. Political and religious perspectives are intertwined, and God is seen to be the author of military destruction. Such understandings lead to consideration of issues of might and right and to ask whether God is on one side and not another.

We live in a violent world, particularly at the national level of struggles among nations.

Sources of war include conflicting national interests as well as different religious convictions and traditions. There is hardly a place where religious faith does not run deep that also does not have a violent history. Obvious examples include Northern Ireland and the state of Israel. It is no secret that the most violent of wars are holy wars, conflicts in which one side or both are convinced that they are executing the will of God. Have texts such as these contributed to holy wars?

3. Every nation and every community is entitled to its own identity. The announcements against the foreign nations emphasize the lines between Israel and the others. Thus one of the functions of these pronouncements is the establishment of community identity by distinguishing one's nation or group from the other. The negative side of this identity is a religious nationalism that seems at times to deny genuine identity to all others, but the positive side is the establishment and conservation of identity, especially when it is threatened by such disasters as exile.

4. What are we to think of the God who could be responsible for the devastation spelled out in Isaiah 13–14? We have seen that a central concern in this section is the assertion of God's jurisdiction over all the world, and particularly over Babylon, which earlier had executed God's judging will against Israel. Divine authority, power, and transcendence over the world and history come through as major themes of these chapters. But God, as seen here, is also both ambivalent and ambiguous. Divine ambivalence shows in the Lord's expression of feelings such as anger, wrath, and even concern for a special people. Such expressions also reveal the ambiguity of the God of the Bible, who is both affected and determined by human actions, if only in response. This God is by no means immutable.

Nor is it putting it too strongly to say that even God does not know what the future will bring. History, on all the pages of the Hebrew Bible, is worked out through the interaction of God and humanity. Assyria was the rod of God's anger, but then later was judged for arrogance. So it was with Babylon. It is typical of the prophetic understanding of God and history that circumstances change God's plans.

The reference to God's "plan that is planned" (14:26-27) seems to suggest a different direction; if not predetermination, then something like that. But the very emotion expressed in God's decision tends to confirm the view of ambiguity. Why would this have to be emphasized so strongly? Moreover, that very plan was set out in reaction to human behavior, and not before the beginning of time.

5. The various parts of the oracle against Babylon and the king of Babylon reflect something of the wide spectrum in the Bible's attitudes toward the relationship between civilization and the natural environment. On the one hand, the city of Babylon is the epitome of corruption, like Sodom and Gomorrah (13:19). Judgment against that civilization will entail a return to chaos, to a primitive and terrifying wilderness inhabited only by wild animals (13:20-22). In this vision, the uncultivated is frightening. On the other hand, the natural environment is embraced warmly as the trees celebrate the death of the tyrant who would cut them down (14:7-8). There is an implicit criticism of the expansion of civilization as it uses and possibly even exhausts natural resources. Trees are required to build such cultural artifacts as cities and weapons. Common to both these perspectives is a suspicion of civilization, at least in the form of great cities and empires. The splendor and glory of urbanization and empire lead to arrogance. Babylon is no sacred city.

ISAIAH 14:28-32, PROCLAMATION CONCERNING PHILISTIA

NIV

28This oracle came in the year King Ahaz died:

29Do not rejoice, all you Philistines,
    that the rod that struck you is broken;
from the root of that snake will spring up
        a viper,
    its fruit will be a darting, venomous
        serpent.
30The poorest of the poor will find pasture,
    and the needy will lie down in safety.
But your root I will destroy by famine;
    it will slay your survivors.

31Wail, O gate! Howl, O city!
    Melt away, all you Philistines!
A cloud of smoke comes from the north,
    and there is not a straggler in its ranks.
32What answer shall be given
    to the envoys of that nation?
"The LORD has established Zion,
    and in her his afflicted people will
        find refuge."

NRSV

28In the year that King Ahaz died this oracle came:

29 Do not rejoice, all you Philistines,
    that the rod that struck you is broken,
    for from the root of the snake will come forth
        an adder,
    and its fruit will be a flying fiery serpent.
30 The firstborn of the poor will graze,
    and the needy lie down in safety;
but I will make your root die of famine,
    and your remnant I[a] will kill.
31 Wail, O gate; cry, O city;
    melt in fear, O Philistia, all of you!
For smoke comes out of the north,
    and there is no straggler in its ranks.

32 What will one answer the messengers of
        the nation?
"The LORD has founded Zion,
    and the needy among his people
        will find refuge in her."

aQ Ms Vg: MT *he*

COMMENTARY

A new unit is marked off clearly by the heading in v. 28. Although this superscription differs from the others in chaps. 13–23, both form and substance identify the section as one of the oracles concerning foreign nations.[151] It lacks the name of the particular nation, but that appears in the subsequent verse. More significant, this is the only one of the proclamations with a date, "in the year that King Ahaz died."

Long ago, J. Begrich correctly argued that the date in the superscription is fundamental to under-

standing this proclamation.[152] Verse 28 indicates that the oracle that follows pertains to a particular time, "the year that King Ahaz died." Begrich concluded that the superscription was original, not added by an editor, and that the unit came, if not from Isaiah himself, at least from the basic level of the Isaiah tradition. The lines that follow, like most in the prophetic literature, arose in and addressed particular historical circumstances. However, it is by no means certain that the superscription was not added later to help make sense of an enigmatic

151. Mainly on the basis of the distinctive superscription, Sweeney considers this unit an appendix to the oracle against Babylon rather than a distinctive section. See Marvin A. Sweeney, *Isaiah 1–39, With an Introduction to Prophetic Literature,* FOTL XVI (Grand Rapids: Eerdmans, 1996) 221.

152. Joachim Begrich, "Jesaja 14, 28-32. Ein Beitrag zur Chronologie der israelitischejüdischen Königszeit," *ZDMG* 86 (1933) 66-79; reprinted in *Gesemmelte Studien zum Alten Testament,* ed. W. Zimmerli, TB 21 (München, 1964).

proclamation. Nor can we even be certain which year it was when Ahaz died. The most widely accepted date is 727 BCE, but some historians put it as late as 724 BCE. One should thus be reluctant to explain the oracle on the basis of a precarious interpretation of international events in the eighth century BCE.

The proclamation begins as an oracle—that is, a speech from the deity. Unlike the other oracles concerning the foreign nations, this one purports to be addressed directly to the nation in question. But, of course, the real audience is not Philistia but Judeans. The speech consists of two main parts: an address to Philistia (vv. 29-31) and instructions presumably to Jerusalem concerning a response to "the messengers of the nation" (v. 32). The address to Philistia in turn has two parts, first a negative admonition (vv. 29-30) and then a positive one (v. 31). Both, however, amount to the same cry: to refrain from rejoicing (v. 29) and instead to "Wail" or cry out in fear (cf. 13:6). The mood and tone of the dirge in the taunt song over the king of Babylon continues here.

The Philistines, occupants of five coastal cities, had been enemies of Israel since before the time of David. They are instructed not to celebrate the death of a king who had oppressed them ("the rod that struck you is broken," v. 29), for his successor will be even worse. In the context of the reference to the death of the Ahaz, it is possible this refers to the Judean king. More likely, however, it refers to some Assyrian king.[153] The chronological uncertainties render identification of that king highly speculative. But the point is clear enough: Rejoicing would be foolish because the king's successor will be even more dangerous than the one who has just died. The reasons for the admonition are set out in a series of dramatic, but mixed, metaphors. "Root," referring to the ancestry of the new oppressor, is plant imagery, and it is followed by figures from the animal kingdom ("snake," "adder") and even beyond ("flying fiery serpent"; cf. 6:2; Num 21:6-9). In the continuation of the threat, "root" (v. 30) is used again, but in a different sense, to represent the utter destruction of the Philistines.

The other part of the instructions to the Philistines conjures up the image of a city or nation in mourning and fear as an enemy army approaches "out of the north" (v. 31). The "smoke" comes from cities and villages that had been torched as the army moved through the land. That there is "no straggler in its ranks" epitomizes the rapid and disciplined army on the move. The "enemy from the north" is a persistent theme in prophetic literature, especially in Jeremiah (e.g., Jer 1:13-15; 4:6; 6:1). In the eighth century BCE, this certainly would have been the Assyrian invaders. Functionally, the admonitions to the Philistines amount to a prophecy of disaster.

In the second part of the unit (v. 32), a question introduces a speech. Neither the speaker nor the addressees are identified, but the quote shows the question to be addressed to the inhabitants of Jerusalem. The context suggests that "the messengers of the nation" are emissaries from Philistia who are asking Judah to join them against Assyria.[154] The response need not be the answer to any specific question. It is a credo or confession of faith in the Lord's election and protection of Zion. Faith in Yahweh's foundation of the city with its Temple has deep roots (see esp. Psalms 46; 48; 132:13-18) and is one of the distinctive elements in Isaiah's message. In fact, the confession here seems precisely the answer Isaiah wanted to hear from Ahaz during the Syro-Ephraimitic war (see 7:1-9).[155] If the instructions to Philistia (vv. 29-31) amount to an announcement of judgment, then this verse is the equivalent of an announcement of salvation to Jerusalem.

Some tensions are visible even in these five verses. Although the first part is attributed to Yahweh ("I will make your root die," v. 30), the Lord is referred to in the third person in the final section (v. 32). The ancient versions recognized and attempted to deal with this conflict by changing the first person to the third ("he" or "it") in v. 30.

The strong affirmation of the Zion tradition (v. 32) is only one of several clear links with other

153. See esp. Brevard S. Childs, *Isaiah and the Assyrian Crisis,* SBT (London: SCM, 1967) 60.

154. O. Kaiser, *Isaiah 13–39: A Commentary* (Philadelphia: Westminster, 1974) 59.

155. See H. Wildberger, *Isaiah 1–12,* trans. Thomas H. Trapp (Minneapolis: Fortress, 1991) 102.

texts in Isaiah 1–39. The reference to "the year that King Ahaz died" echoes 6:1, the "remnant" is a persistent motif (10:19-22; 11:11, 16; 14:22), and the "root" recalls the promise in 11:1, 10 (see also 5:24; 27:6; 37:31).

REFLECTIONS

One theme that underlies and connects the elements of this unit is hope and the relationship between hope and faith. What is hopeful? The text sets hope against false hope. The admonitions to the Philistines not to rejoice but to mourn presume they have become hopeful because of the death of a tyrant. Throughout all ages, such an event could well be the basis for celebration by those who had suffered under oppression or whose nation had been subject to such a leader. The proclamation in 14:28-32 conveys the message that such hope can be false hope, that joy will be turned to sorrow, that political change may bring something worse instead of something better.

On the other hand, according to this proclamation, genuine hope and help are found only in the Lord. The prophet calls for the people of God to confess their faith, a faith based on the belief that the Lord has chosen and will protect a particular people in a specified place, Zion. We know from history and experience that political hopes can be dashed. Is such religious hope as that expressed here also naive and unrealistic? Should the people of God trust in God instead of political and military leadership? These are tensions felt by all people of faith as they live in the world of politics.

Although we cannot be certain of the specific historical context of this message, it is wise to remember that the call for confidence in the Lord's protection of Zion had a particular historical horizon. In the time of Isaiah, in the eighth century BCE, confidence in that promise turned out to be justified. The Assyrians were unable to overthrow Jerusalem. But such hopes were dashed in the sixth century by the Babylonians. Still later, during the Persian period, the city and its Temple were rebuilt, only to be destroyed again c. 70 CE by the Romans.

Hope can be genuine only if it is based on what is ultimate, on fundamental convictions concerning history and the world. Thus Peter and the apostles are reported to have said, "We must obey God rather than any human authority" (Acts 5:29). Similarly, Shadrach, Meshach, and Abednego refused to worship the gods of Nebuchadnezzar and affirmed that their God would be able to save them from the fiery furnace (Dan 3:16-18). However, they seem to have accepted the possibility that their hope might be unrealistic. "Even if we are wrong" ("but if not"), they said, they refused to place their faith in what they knew not to be God. Trusting, even if naive, hope is preferable to false hope.

The risk involved in decisions concerning hope comes when and because faith and hope must face specific and concrete times and places. Will the next king be the salvation of the nation? Will our God protect our particular place? Those questions cannot be resolved in the abstract, but must be asked anew each day.

ISAIAH 15:1–16:14, PROCLAMATION CONCERNING MOAB

NIV	NRSV
15 An oracle concerning Moab:	**15** An oracle concerning Moab.
Ar in Moab is ruined,	Because Ar is laid waste in a night,

NIV

destroyed in a night!
Kir in Moab is ruined,
    destroyed in a night!
[2] Dibon goes up to its temple,
    to its high places to weep;
Moab wails over Nebo and Medeba.
Every head is shaved
    and every beard cut off.
[3] In the streets they wear sackcloth;
    on the roofs and in the public squares
they all wail,
    prostrate with weeping.
[4] Heshbon and Elealeh cry out,
    their voices are heard all the way to Jahaz.
Therefore the armed men of Moab cry out,
    and their hearts are faint.

[5] My heart cries out over Moab;
    her fugitives flee as far as Zoar,
    as far as Eglath Shelishiyah.
They go up the way to Luhith,
    weeping as they go;
on the road to Horonaim
    they lament their destruction.
[6] The waters of Nimrim are dried up
    and the grass is withered;
the vegetation is gone
    and nothing green is left.
[7] So the wealth they have acquired and stored up
    they carry away over the Ravine of
        the Poplars.
[8] Their outcry echoes along the border of Moab;
    their wailing reaches as far as Eglaim,
    their lamentation as far as Beer Elim.
[9] Dimon's[a] waters are full of blood,
    but I will bring still more upon Dimon[a]—
a lion upon the fugitives of Moab
    and upon those who remain in the land.

16 Send lambs as tribute
    to the ruler of the land,
from Sela, across the desert,
    to the mount of the Daughter of Zion.
[2] Like fluttering birds
    pushed from the nest,
so are the women of Moab
    at the fords of the Arnon.

[a] Masoretic Text; Dead Sea Scrolls, some Septuagint manuscripts and Vulgate *Dibon*

NRSV

    Moab is undone;
because Kir is laid waste in a night,
    Moab is undone.
[2] Dibon[a] has gone up to the temple,
    to the high places to weep;
over Nebo and over Medeba
    Moab wails.
On every head is baldness,
    every beard is shorn;
[3] in the streets they bind on sackcloth;
    on the housetops and in the squares
    everyone wails and melts in tears.
[4] Heshbon and Elealeh cry out,
    their voices are heard as far as Jahaz;
therefore the loins of Moab quiver;[b]
    his soul trembles.
[5] My heart cries out for Moab;
    his fugitives flee to Zoar,
    to Eglath-shelishiyah.
For at the ascent of Luhith
    they go up weeping;
on the road to Horonaim
    they raise a cry of destruction;
[6] the waters of Nimrim
    are a desolation;
the grass is withered, the new growth fails,
    the verdure is no more.
[7] Therefore the abundance they have gained
    and what they have laid up
they carry away
    over the Wadi of the Willows.
[8] For a cry has gone
    around the land of Moab;
the wailing reaches to Eglaim,
    the wailing reaches to Beer-elim.
[9] For the waters of Dibon[c] are full of blood;
    yet I will bring upon Dibon[c] even more—
a lion for those of Moab who escape,
    for the remnant of the land.

16 Send lambs
    to the ruler of the land,
from Sela, by way of the desert,
    to the mount of daughter Zion.
[2] Like fluttering birds,
    like scattered nestlings,

[a] Cn: Heb *the house and Dibon*   [b] Cn: Compare Gk Syr: Heb *the armed men of Moab cry aloud*   [c] Q Ms Vg Compare Syr: MT *Dimon*

165

NIV

3 "Give us counsel,
    render a decision.
Make your shadow like night—
    at high noon.
Hide the fugitives,
    do not betray the refugees.
4 Let the Moabite fugitives stay with you;
    be their shelter from the destroyer."

The oppressor will come to an end,
    and destruction will cease;
    the aggressor will vanish from the land.
5 In love a throne will be established;
    in faithfulness a man will sit on it—
    one from the house[a] of David—
one who in judging seeks justice
    and speeds the cause of righteousness.

6 We have heard of Moab's pride—
    her overweening pride and conceit,
    her pride and her insolence—
    but her boasts are empty.
7 Therefore the Moabites wail,
    they wail together for Moab.
Lament and grieve
    for the men[b] of Kir Hareseth.
8 The fields of Heshbon wither,
    the vines of Sibmah also.
The rulers of the nations
    have trampled down the choicest vines,
which once reached Jazer
    and spread toward the desert.
Their shoots spread out
    and went as far as the sea.
9 So I weep, as Jazer weeps,
    for the vines of Sibmah.
O Heshbon, O Elealeh,
    I drench you with tears!
The shouts of joy over your ripened fruit
    and over your harvests have been stilled.
10 Joy and gladness are taken away from
        the orchards;
    no one sings or shouts in the vineyards;
no one treads out wine at the presses,
    for I have put an end to the shouting.
11 My heart laments for Moab like a harp,
    my inmost being for Kir Hareseth.

[a]5 Hebrew tent   [b]7 Or "raisin cakes," a wordplay

NRSV

so are the daughters of Moab
    at the fords of the Arnon.
3 "Give counsel,
    grant justice;
make your shade like night
    at the height of noon;
hide the outcasts,
    do not betray the fugitive;
4 let the outcasts of Moab
    settle among you;
be a refuge to them
    from the destroyer."

When the oppressor is no more,
    and destruction has ceased,
and marauders have vanished from the land,
5 then a throne shall be established in
        steadfast love
    in the tent of David,
    and on it shall sit in faithfulness
a ruler who seeks justice
    and is swift to do what is right.

6 We have heard of the pride of Moab
    —how proud he is!—
of his arrogance, his pride, and his insolence;
    his boasts are false.
7 Therefore let Moab wail,
    let everyone wail for Moab.
Mourn, utterly stricken,
    for the raisin cakes of Kir-hareseth.

8 For the fields of Heshbon languish,
    and the vines of Sibmah,
whose clusters once made drunk
    the lords of the nations,
reached to Jazer
    and strayed to the desert;
their shoots once spread abroad
    and crossed over the sea.
9 Therefore I weep with the weeping of Jazer
    for the vines of Sibmah;
I drench you with my tears,
    O Heshbon and Elealeh;
for the shout over your fruit harvest
    and your grain harvest has ceased.
10 Joy and gladness are taken away
    from the fruitful field;

NIV

12When Moab appears at her high place,
  she only wears herself out;
when she goes to her shrine to pray,
  it is to no avail.

13This is the word the LORD has already spoken concerning Moab. 14But now the LORD says: "Within three years, as a servant bound by contract would count them, Moab's splendor and all her many people will be despised, and her survivors will be very few and feeble."

NRSV

and in the vineyards no songs are sung,
  no shouts are raised;
no treader treads out wine in the presses;
  the vintage-shout is hushed.[a]
11 Therefore my heart throbs like a harp
  for Moab,
  and my very soul for Kir-heres.
12When Moab presents himself, when he wearies himself upon the high place, when he comes to his sanctuary to pray, he will not prevail.
13This was the word that the LORD spoke concerning Moab in the past. 14But now the LORD says, In three years, like the years of a hired worker, the glory of Moab will be brought into contempt, in spite of all its great multitude; and those who survive will be very few and feeble.

[a]Gk: Heb *I have hushed*

COMMENTARY

The theme of death and destruction continues, as do the notes of lamentation and the tone of mourning heard in the previous proclamations of chaps. 13–14. In addition to these themes and moods, the material in chaps. 15–16 is unified mainly by its common attention to the country of Moab (the exception is 16:4b-5). There is another unifying feature, difficult to notice in English translations. The little Hebrew particle כִּי (*kî*), often translated "for" or "because," occurs a dozen times in these two chapters. The word is left untranslated in some modern versions (NIV, REB), and in others it is read as "Ah" or "O" (TNK). The NRSV renders most instances as "because" (15:1), "for" (15:5, 8-9; 16:8-9), or "when" (16:4, 12), but leaves some untranslated (15:6). Understanding the word as a deictic particle, such as "Ah" or "Look," is the most likely reading;[156] therefore, it is legitimate to leave it unexpressed. However, the word certainly ties together the parts of the pronouncement against Moab, if only in its repetitive sound in the original language.

Under the umbrella of these features is a collage of sometimes diverse materials and subjects. After the by now familiar heading "An Oracle Concerning," the first section (chap. 15) consists of two songs of lamentation over Moab, or one song with two parts (15:1-5, 6-9). There is no good reason to doubt that the chapter is a genuine dirge. It lacks the marks of a mocking or ironic poem seen in the taunt song over the king of Babylon (14:3-21).[157] Although neither the singer nor the one whose "heart cries out for Moab" (15:5) is identified, the voice must be one sympathetic to the plight of Moab. The second unit (16:1-4a) has the Moabites fleeing and seeking refuge and justice at Zion. The third piece (16:4b-5) has nothing to do with Moab at all but must be linked here because of the reference to Zion in 16:1. It is a messianic promise looking to the day when the dynasty ("tent") of David will be reestablished, presumably in Jerusalem. The next part (16:6-12) resumes the mood and content of lament over Moab's devastation. Finally, a very different voice looks back on the mourning for Moab as the Lord's word in the past, but now announces judgment on that country (16:13-14).

156. See H. Wildberger, *Isaiah 1–12,* trans. Thomas H. Trapp (Minneapolis: Fortress, 1991) 131.

157. With most commentators but against Van Zyl, *The Moabites* (Leiden: E. J. Brill, 1960) 20-21. Likewise to be rejected is Kaiser's conclusion that the dirge is "a stylistic device to re-emphasize the severity of the blow which has struck Moab, rather than an expression of genuine feeling." See O. Kaiser, *Isaiah 13–39: A Commentary* (Philadelphia: Westminster, 1974) 68.

Several different voices speak here; four come through quite distinctly. In most of the body of the proclamation, sympathetic singers mourn for Moab. A second voice responds in 16:4*b*-5 to the accounts of destruction and looks to a time of peace and justice under a Davidic ruler. The third and fourth voices come from readers of the laments over Moab who did not like what they read. One of them speaks for the Lord, announcing yet more destruction on Moab (15:9*b*). The final one (16:13-14) has interpreted the oracle, and in such a way as to point out that it is wrong. More accurately, sympathy for Moab might have been the word of God in the past, but it is not the word of God for the present and the future.

The text bristles with geographical references, many of which can be located today.[158] Moab occupied and controlled the region east of the Dead Sea and periodically came into conflict with Israelites to their north who claimed that part of Transjordan. Attempts to date either the proclamation itself or the events bemoaned here have proved futile.[159] An attack or attacks on Moab by a superior military force must have given rise to the songs, but there is insufficient evidence to determine which one.

15:1-9. The first part of this song (vv. 1-4) reports disaster and mourning in third-person descriptive language, concentrating on the mourning rituals. There is no attribution to a particular speaker or speakers, although it definitely is not a speech of the deity. At the beginning and end of the second section (vv. 5-9), we hear first-person speech. The major focus of this cry of sorrow is the plight of fugitives. Verse 5 is an actual expression of mourning ("My heart cries out"), but again the speaker is not identified. In the final verse, however, one can only conclude that the words are attributed to the Lord. Who else could "bring upon Dibon even more"? This shift in speaker and turn to the future strongly suggests that at least v. 9*b* is a secondary addition.

Descriptions of and allusions to the cause for mourning indicate a military disaster. The country and specific cities are "laid waste" and "undone" (v. 1), and "fugitives flee" (v. 5). But there are allusions as well to possible natural disasters, for "the grass is withered, the new growth fails" (v. 6). Indications of agricultural failures are even stronger in the next chapter (16:8-10).

What are these references to natural disasters doing in a lament over military defeat? The lament over Moab is shaped fundamentally by the community ritual of mourning. People would have joined together not only to mourn for losses in war, but on other occasions for other troubles as well, including crop failure and famine. So, although the event behind this song is a military defeat, it is not surprising that conventional expressions from standard ceremonials crop up.

Descriptions of specific activities show that a community ritual of mourning stands behind these lines. Weeping takes place in the "temple," "the high places," and "every" head is bald and "every" beard shorn (v. 2). Although places of worship were the center of activities, all people participate "on the housetops and in the squares" by putting on sackcloth, wailing, and crying (v. 3). Such community services of mourning would not have been part of the regular ritual calendar, but neither were they ad hoc events. Rather, they were familiar rituals of the community when disaster struck the people as a whole, just as funerals functioned when individuals died.

The dirge or lamentation is closely related to the complaint of the community or of the individual, as in the psalms. In fact, what many call laments in the book of Psalms are actually complaints, or prayers of petition for help in time of trouble (e.g., Psalms 5–7; 88). The tone of both is similar. The difference is the plea to God for help in the face of danger, especially danger that could lead to death for the individual or the community.

16:1-4a. Interpretation of v. 1 in particular is rendered uncertain by textual difficulties. The reading adopted by the NIV and the NRSV takes the verse to contain instructions to messengers from Moab to take tribute to the "ruler" in Jerusalem. The rest of the section shows that these emissaries come not to seek a political or military alliance but to beg for refuge for the "outcasts," the "fugitive" (v. 3) from Moab. Verses 3-4*a* quote those sent from Moab to Zion. In effect, the "justice" (v. 3) they seek is refuge—that is, to be

158. For a list of the places in these chapters that can be correlated with contemporary place-names, see J. Maxwell Miller, *Introducing the Holy Land* (Macon, Ga.: Mercer University Press, 1982) 68. See also J. Maxwell Miller, "Moab," *Anchor Bible Dictionary*, 6 vols. (New York: Doubleday, 1992) 4:882-93. On the geography as well as the rhetoric, see Brian Jones, *Howling Over Moab: Irony and Rhetoric in Isaiah 15–16*, SBLDS 157 (Atlanta: Scholars Press, 1996).

159. Most modern commentators agree on this point. See, e.g., Kaiser, *Isaiah 13–39*, 62, 65; H. Wildberger, *Isaiah 13–27*, (Minneapolis: Fortress, 1997) 122-26; Marvin A. Sweeney, *Isaiah 1–39, With an Introduction to Prophetic Literature*, FOTL XVI (Grand Rapids: Eerdmans, 1996) 247.

granted the status of resident aliens in Judah.[160] Although the mission of the ambassadors and their words are presented in a sympathetic light, the response by the "ruler" in Jerusalem is not reported.

16:4b-5. These verses look beyond the horizon of concrete geopolitical realities reflected in the previous verses (15:1–16:4*a*) to a time when "the oppressor is no more, and destruction has ceased" (v. 4). This little section is secondary to the poem concerning Moab and a commentary on the issues it raises. The visionary poet sees the answer to the problems of refugees from war to be in a ruler descended from David, on the throne in Jerusalem. The passage is messianic in this hope for an anointed one in the future. Its vision of a time of peace under a just ruler reiterates the themes of 11:1-5. Although it does not provide an answer to the specific request for justice in the form of refuge, requested in the previous section, it does give a general response to the call for justice.

16:6-12. A summons to mourn (v. 7) is preceded by the only lines in the section that could amount to reasons for the disaster (v. 6). The connection is made explicit by the "therefore" that begins the call to mourn in v. 7. Moab is indicted for its "arrogance" in such a way as to emphasize that pride goes before a fall. Functionally, the summons to corporate mourning is similar to calls to praise in the psalms (e.g., Pss 30:4; 33:1-3; 66:1-3; 96:1-3; 100:1-2). On the one hand, both reflect rituals in which leaders or choirs sing and ask for a response, but on the other hand, the calls already express what they call for: praise or mourning. The "we" who report on Moab's pride, although not identified, must be outsiders, likely Israelites. But the words could just as well be from the mouths of those in distress, quoting those who see and ridicule their suffering as well deserved.

Although it could be the result of a military inva-

160. Kaiser, *Isaiah 13–39,* 72.

sion, the disaster that calls for mourning in vv. 8-11 is basically agricultural. "Fields languish," vines do not produce wine, and the joy and gladness of harvest have disappeared, turned into sorrow. There is no mistaking the depth of the poet's despair for the land. The final verse of the unit (v. 12) is more accurately rendered in poetic lines, as in the NIV and others, instead of in the prose of the NRSV. Some commentators take the verse as an indictment of Moabite religion, but it can just as well further express the nation's despair by bemoaning the fact that even prayers bring no help.

16:13-14. This little section explicitly claims to be interpreting and reinterpreting the preceding proclamation concerning Moab. "This . . . word that the LORD spoke concerning Moab in the past" must refer to the substance of 15:1–16:12. The editor who added these lines presumes that the Lord is reversing an earlier message ("word"). But there are problems. In the first place, with the exception of the implied attribution of the words in 15:9 to the Lord, the proclamation concerning Moab is not a word of the Lord. Moreover, these verses presume a time when Moab is in its "glory," while the preceding sections were filled with mourning over Moab's destruction.

So what in the proclamation concerning Moab does this writer reject as an old word of the Lord, one that is no longer valid? It can only be the sympathy expressed for the old enemy nation that rings throughout the poetry (e.g., 15:1; 16:9ff.) and the implied positive response to the refugees who seek asylum in the shadow of Zion (16:1-4). However, although this writer hears a new word from the Lord, an announcement of judgment on Moab for its pride and glory, he does not go so far as to delete the older message.

REFLECTIONS

1. Given especially the diverse perspectives within these two chapters, and even tensions between different parts, serious readers will ask themselves what they are to believe. What is the center of the text, the part by which the rest is to be interpreted? Which text or part of the text interprets the others? What is the "canon" in this little canon? That is a question that faces every thoughtful reader of every biblical text. One could even take it further to ask which of all the biblical texts is one to read and believe or agree with or even to decide to be worth repeating.

In this case, one could take the center to be the dominant voice, the one sympathetic to the suffering of a foreign—and sometimes enemy—nation. Or one might interpret the rest in terms of the messianic vision of a descendant of David who will seek justice and do what is right. Again, the concluding announcement of disaster on Moab could be taken not only as the last but also the decisive word, leading to the interpretation of the earlier disaster as deserved.

More important, on what basis does one make such decisions? Is the rule that the last shall be first—that is, that the latest element interprets the younger? That is, in fact, what the last contributors to the text claimed. Or is it that the first shall be first—that is, the earliest tradition or one that might be attributed to the inspired prophet is the foundation for interpreting the rest, and thus the more valid perspective? Fundamentally one must use moral or theological criteria to evaluate various claims to truth. That is, in fact, what we do most commonly—to "know" what is right. Wildberger seems to argue both on the basis of what dominates the text as well as theological grounds, concluding that "the greatest weight must be given to the voice that expressed deep sympathy for Moab, and that must be taken seriously."[161] He takes the messianic expectations here to be part of that sympathy, seeking hope for Moab. Such efforts to find the center ought to be carried out, but thoughtfully. If one claims biblical authority, or even significance, then such an enterprise should be pursued in the light of decisions about the center of the canon as a whole.

One further lesson can be learned from that commentator who added the last verses. Although he disagreed with what he had before him, he did not discard it but engaged it. Engaging even what seems disagreeable and wrong helps us to put into perspective what we think we know. It is more difficult, but also more productive, to engage what one may find disagreeable.

2. These chapters are filled with cries of grief, descriptions of suffering, and images of mourning rituals. Since this is not the grief or suffering of an individual, the chapters call attention to the communal, corporate dimension of suffering and the response to it. Thus the proclamation over Moab evokes reflection on the role of funerals and funeral songs, on the importance of ritual even in the face of death.

First, people work through grief in part by expressing it, by acknowledging loss instead of denying it. Second, just because conventional and perhaps even clichéd language is used does not mean that the expression of grief is not genuine. Words and expressions persist and are even polished because they continue to say what people want and need to say. Moreover, in crisis circumstances in particular, it is reassuring not to be required to reinvent the wheel, to start from scratch or create what one wants to say. There is comfort in the familiar. Therein, even in the face of death, ritual functions to provide stability. Third, in addition to the support given by stable words and actions, one is enabled to work through grief with the support of the community, whether of the nation, the neighborhood, or the family. Those who have survived help themselves and one another by clinging together. The notion that there is such a thing as private grief is a price we pay for the modern understanding of individuality. As personal and as painful as it may be, grief is experienced in and with communities. If there is a lesson here it is a call to bear one another's burdens and to rely upon our communities when we grieve.

161. H. Wildberger, *Isaiah 13–27* (Minneapolis: Fortress, 1997) 153.

ISAIAH 17:1–18:7, PROCLAMATION CONCERNING DAMASCUS

NIV	NRSV
17 An oracle concerning Damascus:	**17** An oracle concerning Damascus.

NIV

"See, Damascus will no longer be a city
    but will become a heap of ruins.
²The cities of Aroer will be deserted
    and left to flocks, which will lie down,
    with no one to make them afraid.
³The fortified city will disappear from Ephraim,
    and royal power from Damascus;
    the remnant of Aram will be
    like the glory of the Israelites,"
                    declares the LORD Almighty.

⁴"In that day the glory of Jacob will fade;
    the fat of his body will waste away.
⁵It will be as when a reaper gathers the
        standing grain
    and harvests the grain with his arm—
    as when a man gleans heads of grain
    in the Valley of Rephaim.
⁶Yet some gleanings will remain,
    as when an olive tree is beaten,
    leaving two or three olives on the topmost
        branches,
    four or five on the fruitful boughs,"
                    declares the LORD, the God of Israel.

⁷In that day men will look to their Maker
    and turn their eyes to the Holy One of Israel.
⁸They will not look to the altars,
    the work of their hands,
    and they will have no regard for the
        Asherah poles[a]
    and the incense altars their fingers have made.

⁹In that day their strong cities, which they left
because of the Israelites, will be like places abandoned to thickets and undergrowth. And all will
be desolation.

¹⁰You have forgotten God your Savior;
    you have not remembered the Rock,
        your fortress.
    Therefore, though you set out the finest plants
        and plant imported vines,
¹¹though on the day you set them out, you make
        them grow,
    and on the morning when you plant them,
        you bring them to bud,
    yet the harvest will be as nothing

a8 That is, symbols of the goddess Asherah

NRSV

See, Damascus will cease to be a city,
    and will become a heap of ruins.
² Her towns will be deserted forever;[a]
    they will be places for flocks,
    which will lie down, and no one will make
        them afraid.
³ The fortress will disappear from Ephraim,
    and the kingdom from Damascus;
    and the remnant of Aram will be
    like the glory of the children of Israel,
                    says the LORD of hosts.

⁴ On that day
    the glory of Jacob will be brought low,
    and the fat of his flesh will grow lean.
⁵ And it shall be as when reapers gather
        standing grain
    and their arms harvest the ears,
    and as when one gleans the ears of grain
    in the Valley of Rephaim.
⁶ Gleanings will be left in it,
    as when an olive tree is beaten—
    two or three berries
    in the top of the highest bough,
    four or five
    on the branches of a fruit tree,
                    says the LORD God of Israel.

⁷On that day people will regard their Maker,
and their eyes will look to the Holy One of Israel;
⁸they will not have regard for the altars, the work
of their hands, and they will not look to what
their own fingers have made, either the sacred
poles[b] or the altars of incense.

⁹On that day their strong cities will be like the
deserted places of the Hivites and the Amorites,[c]
which they deserted because of the children of
Israel, and there will be desolation.

¹⁰ For you have forgotten the God of
        your salvation,
    and have not remembered the Rock of
        your refuge;
    therefore, though you plant pleasant plants
        and set out slips of an alien god,

ᵃCn: Compare Gk: Heb *the cities of Aroer are deserted*   ᵇHeb
Asherim   ᶜCn: Compare Gk: Heb *places of the wood and the
highest bough*

NIV

in the day of disease and incurable pain.

¹²Oh, the raging of many nations—
　they rage like the raging sea!
Oh, the uproar of the peoples—
　they roar like the roaring of great waters!
¹³Although the peoples roar like the roar of
　　surging waters,
　when he rebukes them they flee far away,
driven before the wind like chaff on the hills,
　like tumbleweed before a gale.
¹⁴In the evening, sudden terror!
　Before the morning, they are gone!
This is the portion of those who loot us,
　the lot of those who plunder us.

18 Woe to the land of whirring wings^a
　　along the rivers of Cush,^b
²which sends envoys by sea
　in papyrus boats over the water.

Go, swift messengers,
to a people tall and smooth-skinned,
　to a people feared far and wide,
an aggressive nation of strange speech,
　whose land is divided by rivers.

³All you people of the world,
　you who live on the earth,
when a banner is raised on the mountains,
　you will see it,
and when a trumpet sounds,
　you will hear it.
⁴This is what the LORD says to me:
　"I will remain quiet and will look on from
　　my dwelling place,
like shimmering heat in the sunshine,
　like a cloud of dew in the heat of harvest."
⁵For, before the harvest, when the blossom
　　is gone
　and the flower becomes a ripening grape,
he will cut off the shoots with pruning knives,
　and cut down and take away the spreading
　　branches.
⁶They will all be left to the mountain birds
　　of prey
　and to the wild animals;
the birds will feed on them all summer,
　the wild animals all winter.

NRSV

¹¹ though you make them grow on the day that
　　you plant them,
　and make them blossom in the morning
　　that you sow;
　yet the harvest will flee away
　in a day of grief and incurable pain.

¹² Ah, the thunder of many peoples,
　they thunder like the thundering of the sea!
Ah, the roar of nations,
　they roar like the roaring of mighty waters!
¹³ The nations roar like the roaring of
　　many waters,
　but he will rebuke them, and they will
　　flee far away,
chased like chaff on the mountains before
　　the wind
　and whirling dust before the storm.
¹⁴ At evening time, lo, terror!
　Before morning, they are no more.
This is the fate of those who despoil us,
　and the lot of those who plunder us.

18 Ah, land of whirring wings
　　beyond the rivers of Ethiopia,^a
² sending ambassadors by the Nile
　in vessels of papyrus on the waters!
Go, you swift messengers,
　to a nation tall and smooth,
to a people feared near and far,
　a nation mighty and conquering,
　whose land the rivers divide.

³ All you inhabitants of the world,
　you who live on the earth,
when a signal is raised on the mountains, look!
　When a trumpet is blown, listen!
⁴ For thus the LORD said to me:
　I will quietly look from my dwelling
　like clear heat in sunshine,
　like a cloud of dew in the heat of harvest.
⁵ For before the harvest, when the blossom
　　is over
　and the flower becomes a ripening grape,
he will cut off the shoots with pruning hooks,
　and the spreading branches he will
　　hew away.

^a1 Or of locusts　　^b1 That is, the upper Nile region

^aOr Nubia; Heb Cush

NIV

⁷At that time gifts will be brought to the LORD Almighty

from a people tall and smooth-skinned,
    from a people feared far and wide,
an aggressive nation of strange speech,
    whose land is divided by rivers—

the gifts will be brought to Mount Zion, the place of the Name of the LORD Almighty.

NRSV

⁶ They shall all be left
    to the birds of prey of the mountains
    and to the animals of the earth.
And the birds of prey will summer on them,
    and all the animals of the earth will
        winter on them.

⁷At that time gifts will be brought to the LORD of hosts from[a] a people tall and smooth, from a people feared near and far, a nation mighty and conquering, whose land the rivers divide, to Mount Zion, the place of the name of the LORD of hosts.

[a] Q Ms Gk Vg: MT *of*

COMMENTARY

Under the standard heading (17:1) for the main sections in Isaiah 13–23 appear four quite distinct units, recognized by shifts in subject matter as well as traditional formulas of introduction and conclusion. One could just as well call this section "proclamations concerning Damascus, Israel, idolatry, the enemies of Israel, and Ethiopia." To be sure, there are some unity and coherence, if only that established by the editor who organized Isaiah 13–23 and grouped material under these headings. So it is not surprising that some commentators emphasize the unity of these two chapters for various reasons, including what they take to be a common historical horizon as well as a central theological theme.[162] Whether scholarly determinations of the date are accurate or not, the passage has been shaped at least in part by traditions concerning a particular era in the eighth century, the Syro-Ephraimitic war (734–32 BCE) and subsequent events. The theological theme that runs through these chapters is a broad one: the affirmation of the Lord's authority over the nations. Somewhat more specifically, the dominant and unifying message is that Judah is to beware of entangling foreign alliances, whether with Damascus (Syria), Israel, or whatever power rules in Egypt. Instead,

they should trust in the Lord alone (cf. Isa 7:1-9). In terms of literary features, agricultural metaphors, especially of the harvest as a means of characterizing the Lord's judgment, recur throughout the section.

But viewing the two chapters as a whole, one sees that their unity is secondary, created by the combination of at least four distinct parts. First, as indicated by the heading, there is the proclamation concerning Damascus (17:1-6); but even this section is not limited to Damascus, since its second part (17:4-6) concerns "Jacob"—that is, the northern kingdom of Israel. Second are prophetic sayings (17:7-11) concerning the effects of idolatry and other non-Yahwistic religious practices. The third section (17:12-14) is an announcement of judgment against unidentified enemies of Jerusalem. Finally comes a proclamation (18:1-7) concerning Ethiopia, but the text does not include the expected heading, "Oracle concerning Ethiopia."

17:1-6. Two announcements of judgment form this section. The heading, "An oracle concerning Damascus," comes from the first of these (vv. 1-3). Each of the announcements has an introductory formula or cry, "See" (v. 1) and "On that day" (v. 4), and each concludes with the oracle formula "says the LORD," expanded in slightly different ways (vv. 3, 6). Thus both these parts are speeches in which a prophetic voice presents the Lord's

162. Sweeney, *Isaiah 1–39*, 254. Seitz considers the units of chap. 17 to be linked by a common historical horizon as well as theological theme, but he sees a new section beginning after chap. 17, since chaps. 18:1–20:16 concern Ethiopia and Egypt. See Christopher R. Seitz, *Isaiah 1–39,* Interpretation (Louisville: John Knox, 1993) 141-43.

word concerning future disaster. However, it is not that the first announcement concerns Damascus and the second concerns "Jacob"—that is, the northern kingdom. "Ephraim," another designation for the northern kingdom, already is linked to Damascus in v. 3. "Damascus" stands for the kingdom of which it is the capital: "Aram" (v. 3).

Verses 1-3 promise that the cities of Aram and the northern kingdom of Israel will disappear, be turned into ruins, and deserted. Verses 4-6 focus on the destruction of "the glory of Jacob" (v. 4), characterized by means of a series of metaphors. The first, that "the fat of his flesh will grow lean," announces a famine. The others are agricultural images, specifically concerning harvest. Israel is the crop that will be taken as by reapers harvesting the ears of standing grain (v. 5*a*), and as gleaners take what is left over (v. 5*b*). What is left will be like an olive tree after it is beaten to harvest the olives: two or three berries at the very top or "four or five" on a fruit tree (v. 6). The image of gleaning and the thorough harvesting of trees suggests that if there is to be a remnant it will be only the remnant of a remnant. No indictment or accusation justifies the punishment to be brought against these two nations. Some have argued that if the historical context is indeed the Syro-Ephraimitic war, the reasons for judgment against these nations that threatened Judah and Jerusalem would have been self-evident.[163] The clear message of this section is that both Damascus and the northern kingdom of Israel will suffer total destruction.

There is no good reason to doubt that the announcements against Damascus and Israel come from Isaiah. The linking of the two countries to the north as enemies of Judah and Jerusalem seems to presume the same historical background as Isa 7:1-9, the Syro-Ephraimitic war of 734 BCE.[164] The events of the crisis for Judah are summarized in Isa 7:1-2 and are spelled out in somewhat greater detail in 2 Kgs 16:1-20 (cf. 2 Chr 28:5ff.). When the Assyrian King Tiglath-pileser III began to move against the small states of Syria and Palestine, the leaders of those states responded by forming a coalition to oppose him. When Ahaz of Judah refused to join them, kings Rezin of Damascus and Pekah of Samaria, the capital of the northern kingdom, moved against Jerusalem (about 734 BCE) to topple Ahaz and replace him with someone more favorable to their policies.

17:7-11. The subject of this section is idolatrous and faithless worship. These verses, which very well could be taken as two or three separate units, include two pronouncements, each introduced by "On that day" (vv. 7-9) followed by a specification of reasons for the trouble ahead, introduced by "for" (vv. 10-11). The announcements in vv. 7-9 are in the third-person prose, while the remainder of the section is poetry in the second person, addressed directly to the accused.

The first announcement (vv. 7-8) is actually a prophecy of salvation, declaring that unidentified "people" will turn to their "Maker," the "Holy One of Israel," and away from altars, idols, "sacred poles," and "altars of incense." All these are allusions to the trappings and practices of fertility religions, which are associated here with northern Israel. The second announcement (v. 9) is a prophecy of judgment against "strong cities," which will become deserted. This verse alludes to the conquest of the promised land by Israel under Joshua, suggesting a reversal of what Yahweh had accomplished then. The cities are not identified, but the context strongly suggests they are in the northern kingdom, as mentioned in the previous parts of the chapter. Also supporting this identification is the statement of the reasons for judgment in vv. 10-11 that accuse people of forgetting "the God of your salvation," a clear reference to Yahweh. The indictment in vv. 10-11 again refers to non-Yahwistic religious practices. Forgetting "the God of your salvation . . . the Rock of your refuge" either leads to or is replaced by planting "pleasant plants" and "slips of an alien god" (v. 10). Clearly in view here is some kind of fertile garden, set out with fast-growing plants to ensure a good harvest. Confidence in such rituals is misplaced, for instead of a successful harvest there will be a "day of grief and incurable pain" (v. 11).

17:12-14. Although this section begins with the cry "Woe," or "Ah," it is not a typical prophetic woe oracle, such as those in 5:8-24. Instead follows a description of "many peoples"/"nations" approaching, sounds like "the thundering of the sea," the

163. H. Wildberger, *Isaiah 13–27* (Minneapolis: Fortress, 1997) 164.

164. So most modern commentaries, e.g., Ronald E. Clements, *Isaiah 1–39*, NCB (Grand Rapids: Eerdmans, 1980) 156-57; Wildberger, *Isaiah 13–27*, 164.

"roaring of mighty waters." This is imagery of the ear rather than the eye, but the threat is clear. But "he," presumably Yahweh, will "rebuke them" so that they flee. Now comes the visual imagery, for they are blown away like "chaff," like dust before a thunderstorm (v. 13). The final image is mysterious: terror in the evening, and in the morning the nations have disappeared (v. 14). Only in the concluding lines is there a hint of who was threatened by the many peoples and delivered by Yahweh: This is what happens to "those who despoil *us*" (v. 14, italics added). So it must have been Jerusalem that was threatened by its enemies.

But who are these enemies? The immediate context, related to the Syro-Ephraimitic war of 734 BCE, suggests they are the coalition of Damascus and northern Israel, moving to force Judah to join them against Assyria by capturing Jerusalem and replacing its king with a puppet. In the wider context of the book, however, the description of the approach of the enemy army and its flight corresponds more closely to the Assyrian siege under Sennacherib, reported in chaps. 36–37. The immediate problems with this identification are the plural references, to "many peoples" and to "nations." Given the vague and mysterious language, it is not surprising that these verses have been interpreted eschatologically as a prophecy of the end time when foreign nations will gather against the people of God.

18:1-7. There is a relatively clear break between the end of chap. 17 and the beginning of chap. 18, although 18:1 opens with the cry "Ah," or "Woe," as does 17:12. The initial subject matter is Cush, or Ethiopia, but other themes appear; and important questions about the meaning of the section are difficult to answer. Some of the problems of interpretation doubtless are because of a long history of composition. Most likely part of the unit goes back to Isaiah at a time when Egypt was under the control of the Ethiopians, who wanted to form alliances to oppose Assyria (724 BCE; see 2 Kgs 17:4). But the early tradition has been expanded in later centuries. Certainly v. 7 is a later addition, and quite likely also vv. 3 and 6.[165]

Verses 1-2 concern "ambassadors" sent from Ethiopia, presumably to the royal court in Jerusalem. However, although addressed to "swift messengers," the prophet's words are meant to be heard by the court and the citizens of the holy city. First the land and the travel by the ambassadors is reported (vv. 1-2*a*), with appropriate local color. Then (v. 2*b*) the prophet instructs "messengers" to go to that same land, the one "the rivers divide." Are these messengers the same as the ambassadors sent from Ethiopia? It is somewhat confusing that before messengers arrive they are sent. Consequently, some interpreters conclude that they are different, the ones sent being Judean emissaries to Egypt.[166] But more likely it is the Ethiopian ambassadors who are instructed to return home with a message.

In the present and final form of the book, that message would be the remainder of the chapter. Verse 3 functions here as a summons to all people of the earth to pay attention to what the prophet is about to say. Then the message proper begins with the prophetic formula for a word received from the Lord (vv. 4-6). It is not unusual for such messages to move from the first person ("I") to the third ("he," v. 5*b*), from direct quote to report of what the Lord plans to do. The message itself is elliptical, if not enigmatic. It certainly is a prophecy of disaster, but unlike the typical announcement, the focus of the Lord's wrath is not specified. Beginning with weather images (v. 4), the message moves to metaphors of the harvest (v. 5) and then to analogies of birds and animals. The point is that the Lord is going to "quietly look" and then intervene to judge, cutting off "shoots" and "spreading branches," leaving them to the "birds of prey." The concluding verse provides an interpretation in the context of the oracle concerning Ethiopia—that is, Egyptian power—that the powerful nation will bring tribute to Mt. Zion. The importance and centrality of Zion are that the name of the Lord is there (see Deuteronomy 12).

Again, as in Isa 7:1-9 and elsewhere, in the context of a question concerning foreign alliances, the prophet asserts the power and authority of Yahweh over nations and over the future. Thus, as most commentators have concluded, this chapter is another message from the prophet counseling against trust in entangling foreign alliances and encouraging trust in the Lord alone.[167]

---

165. Wildberger, *Isaiah 13–27*, 225-26.

166. Sweeney, *Isaiah 1–39*, 257.

167. Sweeney, ibid., 262, takes all of Isaiah 17–18 to function as counsel to the royal court against making an alliance with Egypt.

REFLECTIONS

A prominent issue raised in 17:7-11 concerns the worship of idols, forms of false religion equated with forgetting "the God of your salvation," "the Rock of your refuge." Remarkably, this issue rarely arises in Isaiah 1–39, whereas the worship of idols is a recurring theme in Isaiah 40–66. Likewise, Canaanite fertility religious practices are central concerns in Hosea as well as in Deuteronomy and the deuteronomistic history (Deuteronomy–2 Kings). Those texts, as well as many others, emphasize sole allegiance to Yahweh, with explicit prohibitions of non-Yahwistic religious practices. That is the heart of the biblical tradition as expressed in the first of the ten commandments: "You shall have no other gods before me" (Exod 20:3). Moreover, it could be said that the defining expression of Judaism is the Shema: "Hear, O Israel: The LORD is our God, the LORD alone" (Deut 6:4).

It is worth observing that the accusation in Isaiah 17 comes in the context of the condemnation of the northern kingdom; and Judean traditions, especially those, such as the book of Isaiah, that see Zion in Jerusalem as Yahweh's abode, frequently considered northern religion to be corrupt. In this passage, such practices are said to lead to disaster. So in antiquity, as in modern times, the definition of true religion has its political dimensions.

In this text, and especially in Deuteronomy, the line between true and false religion seems clear and distinct, like the difference between black and white. However, as one reflects on it, the line between legitimate and illegitimate religious behavior often is difficult to recognize, and purity is elusive. Israelite religion, even in its deuteronomistic form, was unable to avoid influence from "foreign" ideas and practices. The sacred calendar itself, set out in Deuteronomy and elsewhere, followed the agricultural year and was shaped by pre-Yahwistic practices celebrating the fertility of the earth. Even the Temple in Jerusalem, so sacred to Isaiah, was designed like Phoenician and Syrian temples, and major parts of it were fashioned by a Phoenician artisan, Hiram of Tyre (1 Kings 6–7). It is remarkable that the same context that condemns fertility practices (Isaiah 17–18) is filled with metaphors of the harvest. (To be sure, the active agent clearly is Yahweh and not fertility deities or the earth itself.) Moreover, many of the earliest Christian sanctuaries were built on the sacred sites where the mystery religions were practiced. One could interpret that as the destruction of the pre-Christian religions or as the absorption of some of their essence into the Christian faith. Purity in worship, as in all religious traditions, is difficult to find.

It is common for reflection on the biblical condemnation of idolatry to seek modern parallels and to find them in the worship of material goods. Such reflections are by no means misguided, especially in affluent societies preoccupied with the accumulation of possessions, with the acquisition of more than one needs. People who devote themselves to possessions can reach the point of being possessed by them.

However, this and similar biblical texts focus on the ritual dimensions of idolatry, religious practices considered to be corrupt. The practices in view here are the worship of idols and the planting of ritual gardens to promote fertility. The latter is considered to be a form of magic, and the biblical tradition draws a clear line between trust in the Lord and belief in magic, specifically in magical causation, the idea that one can change the future by performing certain "rituals" or saying certain words. Contemporary parallels to such practices are perhaps not as obvious as the worship of material goods, but they persist because superstitions die hard.

With regard to idolatry, the second commandment of the Decalogue ("You shall not make for yourself an idol," Exod 20:4) depends on the first one: "You shall have no other gods before me" (Exod 20:3). The Decalogue assumes the existence of other gods and commands worship of only one. That is, it presupposes, as does Isaiah 17–18, that people face real alternatives. The fundamental point is that unless the reality to which we commit or dedicate ourselves is ultimate, we worship idols. That could even be material things or even a revered religious object, such as the

Bible. It could also be the expression of an idea or a doctrine. All religious rites and ideas are symbolic; that is, they cannot replicate the reality they celebrate or express, but only point to it. The biblical faith is in and of the world. That is why it is so easy to mistake the symbol for what it symbolizes and why religious purity is impossible. One must choose one's rituals and symbols carefully and realize that they are themselves less than God.

This text sets against idolatry and magical practices a call for people to remember the God of their salvation. Thus it concerns habits of the heart and an understanding of faith as commitment by recalling the God who is their refuge. Faith certainly entails ritual practices and the expression of ideas, but fundamentally it is the decision about whom—or what—to trust.

ISAIAH 19:1–20:6, PROCLAMATION CONCERNING EGYPT

NIV

19 An oracle concerning Egypt:

See, the LORD rides on a swift cloud
  and is coming to Egypt.
The idols of Egypt tremble before him,
  and the hearts of the Egyptians melt
    within them.
2"I will stir up Egyptian against Egyptian—
  brother will fight against brother,
  neighbor against neighbor,
  city against city,
  kingdom against kingdom.
3The Egyptians will lose heart,
  and I will bring their plans to nothing;
they will consult the idols and the spirits of
    the dead,
  the mediums and the spiritists.
4I will hand the Egyptians over
  to the power of a cruel master,
and a fierce king will rule over them,"
  declares the Lord, the LORD Almighty.

5The waters of the river will dry up,
  and the riverbed will be parched and dry.
6The canals will stink;
  the streams of Egypt will dwindle and
    dry up.
The reeds and rushes will wither,
7   also the plants along the Nile,
  at the mouth of the river.
Every sown field along the Nile

NRSV

19 An oracle concerning Egypt.

See, the LORD is riding on a swift cloud
  and comes to Egypt;
the idols of Egypt will tremble at his presence,
  and the heart of the Egyptians will melt
    within them.
2 I will stir up Egyptians against Egyptians,
  and they will fight, one against the other,
  neighbor against neighbor,
  city against city, kingdom against kingdom;
3 the spirit of the Egyptians within them will be
    emptied out,
  and I will confound their plans;
they will consult the idols and the spirits of
    the dead
  and the ghosts and the familiar spirits;
4 I will deliver the Egyptians
  into the hand of a hard master;
a fierce king will rule over them,
  says the Sovereign, the LORD of hosts.

5 The waters of the Nile will be dried up,
  and the river will be parched and dry;
6 its canals will become foul,
  and the branches of Egypt's Nile will
    diminish and dry up,
  reeds and rushes will rot away.
7 There will be bare places by the Nile,
  on the brink of the Nile;
and all that is sown by the Nile will dry up,

will become parched, will blow away and
be no more.
[8]The fishermen will groan and lament,
all who cast hooks into the Nile;
those who throw nets on the water
will pine away.
[9]Those who work with combed flax will
despair,
the weavers of fine linen will lose hope.
[10]The workers in cloth will be dejected,
and all the wage earners will be sick
at heart.

[11]The officials of Zoan are nothing but fools;
the wise counselors of Pharaoh give
senseless advice.
How can you say to Pharaoh,
"I am one of the wise men,
a disciple of the ancient kings"?

[12]Where are your wise men now?
Let them show you and make known
what the LORD Almighty
has planned against Egypt.
[13]The officials of Zoan have become fools,
the leaders of Memphis[a] are deceived;
the cornerstones of her peoples
have led Egypt astray.
[14]The LORD has poured into them
a spirit of dizziness;
they make Egypt stagger in all that she does,
as a drunkard staggers around in
his vomit.
[15]There is nothing Egypt can do—
head or tail, palm branch or reed.

[16]In that day the Egyptians will be like women.
They will shudder with fear at the uplifted hand
that the LORD Almighty raises against them. [17]And
the land of Judah will bring terror to the
Egyptians; everyone to whom Judah is mentioned
will be terrified, because of what the LORD
Almighty is planning against them.

[18]In that day five cities in Egypt will speak the
language of Canaan and swear allegiance to the LORD
Almighty. One of them will be called the City of
Destruction.[b]

---

a13 Hebrew *Noph* *b18* Most manuscripts of the Masoretic Text;
some manuscripts of the Masoretic Text, Dead Sea Scrolls and Vulgate
City of the Sun (that is, Heliopolis)

be driven away, and be no more.
[8]Those who fish will mourn;
all who cast hooks in the Nile will lament,
and those who spread nets on the water
will languish.
[9]The workers in flax will be in despair,
and the carders and those at the loom will
grow pale.
[10]Its weavers will be dismayed,
and all who work for wages will be grieved.

[11]The princes of Zoan are utterly foolish;
the wise counselors of Pharaoh give
stupid counsel.
How can you say to Pharaoh,
"I am one of the sages,
a descendant of ancient kings"?
[12]Where now are your sages?
Let them tell you and make known
what the LORD of hosts has planned
against Egypt.
[13]The princes of Zoan have become fools,
and the princes of Memphis are deluded;
those who are the cornerstones of its tribes
have led Egypt astray.
[14]The LORD has poured into them[a]
a spirit of confusion;
and they have made Egypt stagger in all
its doings
as a drunkard staggers around in vomit.
[15]Neither head nor tail, palm branch or reed,
will be able to do anything for Egypt.

[16]On that day the Egyptians will be like
women, and tremble with fear before the hand
that the LORD of hosts raises against them. [17]And
the land of Judah will become a terror to the
Egyptians; everyone to whom it is mentioned will
fear because of the plan that the LORD of hosts is
planning against them.

[18]On that day there will be five cities in the
land of Egypt that speak the language of Canaan
and swear allegiance to the LORD of hosts. One of
these will be called the City of the Sun.

[19]On that day there will be an altar to the
LORD in the center of the land of Egypt, and a

---

*a*Gk Compare Tg: Heb *it*

NIV

¹⁹In that day there will be an altar to the LORD in the heart of Egypt, and a monument to the LORD at its border. ²⁰It will be a sign and witness to the LORD Almighty in the land of Egypt. When they cry out to the LORD because of their oppressors, he will send them a savior and defender, and he will rescue them. ²¹So the LORD will make himself known to the Egyptians, and in that day they will acknowledge the LORD. They will worship with sacrifices and grain offerings; they will make vows to the LORD and keep them. ²²The LORD will strike Egypt with a plague; he will strike them and heal them. They will turn to the LORD, and he will respond to their pleas and heal them.

²³In that day there will be a highway from Egypt to Assyria. The Assyrians will go to Egypt and the Egyptians to Assyria. The Egyptians and Assyrians will worship together. ²⁴In that day Israel will be the third, along with Egypt and Assyria, a blessing on the earth. ²⁵The LORD Almighty will bless them, saying, "Blessed be Egypt my people, Assyria my handiwork, and Israel my inheritance."

20 In the year that the supreme commander, sent by Sargon king of Assyria, came to Ashdod and attacked and captured it— ²at that time the LORD spoke through Isaiah son of Amoz. He said to him, "Take off the sackcloth from your body and the sandals from your feet." And he did so, going around stripped and barefoot.

³Then the LORD said, "Just as my servant Isaiah has gone stripped and barefoot for three years, as a sign and portent against Egypt and Cush,ᵃ ⁴so the king of Assyria will lead away stripped and barefoot the Egyptian captives and Cushite exiles, young and old, with buttocks bared—to Egypt's shame. ⁵Those who trusted in Cush and boasted in Egypt will be afraid and put to shame. ⁶In that day the people who live on this coast will say, 'See what has happened to those we relied on, those we fled to for help and deliverance from the king of Assyria! How then can we escape?' "

ᵃ3 That is, the upper Nile region; also in verse 5

NRSV

pillar to the LORD at its border. ²⁰It will be a sign and a witness to the LORD of hosts in the land of Egypt; when they cry to the LORD because of oppressors, he will send them a savior, and will defend and deliver them. ²¹The LORD will make himself known to the Egyptians; and the Egyptians will know the LORD on that day, and will worship with sacrifice and burnt offering, and they will make vows to the LORD and perform them. ²²The LORD will strike Egypt, striking and healing; they will return to the LORD, and he will listen to their supplications and heal them.

²³On that day there will be a highway from Egypt to Assyria, and the Assyrian will come into Egypt, and the Egyptian into Assyria, and the Egyptians will worship with the Assyrians.

²⁴On that day Israel will be the third with Egypt and Assyria, a blessing in the midst of the earth, ²⁵whom the LORD of hosts has blessed, saying, "Blessed be Egypt my people, and Assyria the work of my hands, and Israel my heritage."

20 In the year that the commander-in-chief, who was sent by King Sargon of Assyria, came to Ashdod and fought against it and took it— ²at that time the LORD had spoken to Isaiah son of Amoz, saying, "Go, and loose the sackcloth from your loins and take your sandals off your feet," and he had done so, walking naked and barefoot. ³Then the LORD said, "Just as my servant Isaiah has walked naked and barefoot for three years as a sign and a portent against Egypt and Ethiopia,ᵃ ⁴so shall the king of Assyria lead away the Egyptians as captives and the Ethiopiansᵇ as exiles, both the young and the old, naked and barefoot, with buttocks uncovered, to the shame of Egypt. ⁵And they shall be dismayed and confounded because of Ethiopiaᵃ their hope and of Egypt their boast. ⁶In that day the inhabitants of this coastland will say, 'See, this is what has happened to those in whom we hoped and to whom we fled for help and deliverance from the king of Assyria! And we, how shall we escape?' "

ᵃOr Nubia; Heb Cush   ᶜOr Nubians; Heb Cushitesᵈ

COMMENTARY

Under the heading "An oracle concerning Egypt" (19:1) are three distinct units: 19:1-15; 19:16-25; and 20:1-6. These units have in common a geographical focus shared with the final part of the previous section, the proclamation concerning Ethiopia (18:1-7). All relate in one way or another to Egypt. Although some of the material in this section comes from long after the time of Isaiah, the earlier traditions share the same historical horizon in the prophet's time, the period of Egyptian conflict with the Assyrian Empire, beginning about 715 BCE. Although the messages to and concerning Egypt in this unit vary dramatically, from bad news to good news, the common themes are the Lord's authority over nations and the prophet's counsel against foreign alliances. Although the style in which these themes are expressed varies considerably, they are woven through chap. 19 in particular by references to the "plan" of Yahweh (vv. 12, 17; cf. v. 3). The clear meaning is that the Lord will control future events for ill or for good, even over Egypt.

The first unit (19:1-15) presents an announcement of judgment against Egypt, with vv. 1-10 setting out the disaster and vv. 11-15 specifying the reasons for punishment. The second unit (19:16-25) is a series of five prose announcements concerning Egypt, including both judgment and salvation. The final section (20:1-6) is a prose narrative concerning a prophetic sign act performed by Isaiah, set in the time of Sargon's attack on the Philistine city of Ashdod.

19:1-15. After the heading that defines the units in chaps. 13–23, the body of this prophecy against Egypt begins with an introduction describing the Lord's appearance (v. 1). The Lord appears riding on a cloud, striking terror in the hearts of the Egyptians and their "idols" as well. The image of the deity on a cloud (see also Ps 104:3) is common in ancient Near Eastern traditions. In the Ugaritic texts, one epithet of the god Baal is "the cloud rider," probably an allusion to his function as the storm god. The translation "idols," which follows the tradition of the Greek versions, is somewhat misleading. The Hebrew אלילים ('ĕlîlîm) is a scornful expression for foreign or false gods.

Just as v. 1 introduces the substance of the announcement, its first section concludes with an oracle formula, "says the Sovereign, the LORD of Hosts" (v. 4). What lies between the introduction and this formula is a speech attributed to Yahweh, the "I" of vv. 2-4. The Lord intervenes indirectly, first by pitting Egyptians against Egyptians, allowing them to destroy themselves. Such internal conflict was not uncommon throughout the history of Egypt, particularly between upper and lower Egypt. Second, the Lord will work against the Egyptians by confusing their plans, rendering their ritual and magical practices ineffective. Then Yahweh will act directly, turning them over to a "hard master," a "fierce king" (v. 4). These words seem to have in view a particular historical situation, but which one is uncertain. Nor is it even clear whether this king is a foreigner or an Egyptian tyrant. The picture of civil strife in v. 2 suggests a domestic rather than a foreign power.

The announcement of judgment continues in vv. 5-10, but both style and content shift. Instead of divine speech, the coming judgment is described passively, and instead of political strife the disaster is a natural one with direct economic effects. The announcement reflects some knowledge of Egypt's dependence upon the regular and predictable floods of the Nile. For those floods to fail was a catastrophe of monumental proportions. The "canals" (v. 6) for irrigation would dry up, crops along the riverbank would die and blow away (v. 7), and those who fished with hooks or with nets would suffer (v. 8), as would all who depend on the food produced by the great river (v. 9).

Why will the Lord bring such troubles upon Egypt? Verses 11-15 answer that question, providing the reasons for punishment. The indictment cites the "princes of Zoan" for their arrogance, for their claims to wisdom (vv. 11-13), and especially for their reliance on "sages" who have no idea of the plans of the Lord of hosts against Egypt. Just as the previous verses reflected knowledge of the economy of Egypt, so also these display an awareness of the Egyptian court's trust in "wise counselors." The wisdom in view here is political competence rather than wisdom broadly understood.

The Lord intends to intervene against Egypt by confounding the counselors, pouring on them "a spirit of confusion" (v. 14). A close parallel to this form of divine intervention appears in 2 Sam 15:31–17:23. In the story of the later life of David (2 Samuel 9–1 Kings 2), God seldom is said to act directly in human affairs. But in the story of Absolom's rebellion, the Lord intervened indirectly to defeat David's son by leading him to follow the bad advice of a particular counselor: "For the LORD had ordained to defeat the good counsel of Ahithophel, so that the LORD might bring ruin on Absalom" (2 Sam 17:14 NRSV). Likewise in the announcement in Isaiah 19, the Lord will bring defeat and confusion upon Egypt through misguided political counsel.

19:16-25. This passage, generally considered to be much later than the time of Isaiah, consists of five discrete announcements concerning Egypt's future, written in prose rather than poetry. Each begins with the phrase "on that day," so the five parts are readily recognized as vv. 16-17, 18, 19-22, 23, and 24-25. It is not clear whether this is a collection of distinct pronouncements added to the prophecy concerning Egypt or a unified composition.[168] It is impossible to connect these pronouncements to particular historical circumstances. With the exception of the first of these announcements (vv. 16-17), the unit is a sharp contrast to the preceding material, bringing good news rather than bad to and concerning Egypt. Supporting the conclusion that this is an intentional composition is the progress of thought, with each announcement moving toward an ever more glorious and comprehensive image of the future role of Egypt.

Nonetheless, the initial unit (vv. 16-17) envisions trouble for Egypt, as its people "tremble" in the face of what Yahweh is doing to them. They will fear not only the Lord, but Judah as well. This is doubtless because Judah is seen to have a role in the Lord's "plan" against the Egyptians. The reference to this plan provides an explicit link to the previous section (cf. vv. 12-13). Moreover, this initial pronouncement functions to interpret and extend the message of 19:1-15, specifically by showing Judah to be, in effect, the rod of the Lord's anger.

That five cities in Egypt will speak "the language of Canaan" and "swear allegiance to the LORD of hosts" probably refers to the presence of Jews who had brought Egyptians into their faith. There is good evidence from papyri discovered at Elephantine near Asswan that this was in fact the case in the fifth century BCE, if not earlier (see Jeremiah 44).[169] Hebrew is one of the Canaanite dialects.

The third proclamation (vv. 19-22) carries the conversion of Egyptians to faith in Yahweh a step further, envisioning an "altar to the LORD" in the center of the land and signs of allegiance to the Lord at its boundaries. (There were, in fact, altars to the Lord in Egypt, at Elephantine and later at Leontopolis, but their existence did not mean that the Egyptians had turned to the Yahwistic faith.) Yahweh will defend Egypt from its enemies and will be revealed to the Egyptians, who will offer prayers and sacrifices to the Lord. When the Lord strikes Egypt, it will be to heal and evoke repentance (v. 22). In other words, the relationship between the Lord and Egypt will be parallel to that between the Lord and Israel. The reference to the Lord being made known to the Egyptians and striking them alludes to the story of Israel's exodus from Egypt (for "know," see Exod 6:7; 7:5; 9:14; 14:4; for "strike," see Exod 9:3; 12:3, 23).

The last two proclamations (vv. 23, 24-25) link worship to international relations and set out the place of Egypt in the Lord's plan. Instead of imperialistic warfare among nations, a highway will join Assyria and Egypt, whose people together will worship the Lord. Finally, we see a vision of world peace and order in which Israel is ranked with the two great political powers, Egypt and Assyria, all of which are a "blessing in the midst of the earth" and all of whom are blessed by the Lord. They are thus seen to be in covenant with one another and with the Lord.[170]

20:1-6. This chapter stands out as a narrative in the midst of prophetic proclamations concerning the future. It is located here under the heading "Oracle concerning Egypt" because of the point of the story. Isaiah's action in the narration is interpreted as a warning against relying on Egypt and Ethiopia in the face of Assyrian threats. Narratives

---

168. So H. Wildberger, *Isaiah 13–27* (Minneapolis: Fortress, 1997) 264.

169. Ronald E. Clements, *Isaiah 1–39,* NCB (Grand Rapids: Eerdmans, 1980) 171.

170. Wildberger, *Isaiah 13–27,* 264.

such as this are common to prophetic literature. This is a symbolic action report like those in Isa 7:10-14; 8:1-4; Jeremiah 19; 32; Hosea 1; 3; and Ezekiel 4–5.[171] The behavior is bizarre, but that is what prophets do. The heart of the story must stem from the time of Isaiah in the eighth century BCE, but it has grown over the centuries. It is important to distinguish between the event (the sign act as performed) and the report of it. The story, like most in the prophets, reports more spoken words than actions. More significant, the story itself is a word, a message, and as such is subject to repeated interpretation, reinterpretation, and application to ever-new situations.

The style of the chapter is remarkably matter-of-fact, given the shock and embarrassment expected from such behavior. And it is not that in antiquity people were more prone to walk around the city naked. The report is in the third person—that is, it is not the prophet, as in some accounts of sign acts, but a third party who tells the story. The chapter begins with an introduction (v. 1) that establishes the date in terms of a specific event. The year that Sargon's "commander-in-chief" put down a revolt in Philistia ("Ashdod") most likely was 711 BCE. The importance of this chronological information is both to set the stage and to indicate from the beginning the outcome of the events. Encouraged, if not instigated, by Egypt, Ashdod and other Philistine city-states revolted against Assyrian rule. The three years Isaiah is said to have walked around naked possibly correspond to the three years of the Philistine revolt.[172] Trust in Egyptian power proved to be vain as Sargon sent his troops to put down the rebellion. The awkward transition between v. 1 and v. 2 suggests that the historical reference could be secondary to the report itself, considered necessary for future readers to make sense of Isaiah's acts and words.

Following the historical introduction, the symbolic action report proceeds according to the three-part structure typical of such narratives. First come instructions to the prophet from Yahweh (v. 2*ab*). Without explanation, the Lord tells Isaiah to remove his clothes and sandals. Second is the report that the prophet carried out the assignment, walking "naked and barefoot" (v. 3*c*). Third, the

bulk of the account is given to the interpretation of the meaning of this odd behavior (vv. 3-6). The interpretation is given in another speech of Yahweh and, remarkably, is presented as if a third party is reporting the Lord's explanation of Isaiah's behavior. More typically, such interpretations are presented by the prophet or by a third party telling what the prophet said.

The point of the sign act seems simple, but there are at least three levels of meaning, corresponding in part to the history of the composition of the chapter. First, the prophetic act explicitly concerns Egypt and Ethiopia, whose people will be carried off as prisoners, "naked and barefoot," humiliated and exiled. The agent of this shameful defeat is "the king of Assyria" (v. 6). Second, as the introduction shows, the sign concerns the city of Ashdod and the Philistine revolt ("the inhabitants of this coastland," v. 6). The insurrection against Assyria will fail because of the rebels' reliance upon Egypt. The "they" of v. 5, who put their hope in Egypt, would have been the people of Ashdod. But, third, the real message is addressed to those who would have observed the symbolic action and heard its interpretation, the leaders and people of Judah and Jerusalem. The direct meaning is that the rebellion fomented by Egypt will lead to disaster. The indirect message to those listening in Jerusalem is to avoid this entangling foreign alliance. The sign serves as a warning against joining such coalitions, specifically against trusting in Egypt and Ethiopia.[173] Although there is no explicit call to trust Yahweh, this sense is consistent with the core of Isaiah's message (cf. Isa 7:1-9).

It is easy for modern readers to miss the power attributed to prophetic symbolic actions in antiquity. Isaiah's strange public nakedness does not simply dramatize something, although it does do that. It is more than a visual device to communicate a message; it is a "sign and a portent" (v. 3). In the prophets' understanding, as well as that of their contemporaries, such acts set events into motion. One finds a clear example of this belief in the prophetic actions of Elisha on his deathbed

---

171. G. Fohrer, *Die symbolischen Handlugen der Propheten*, ATANT 54 (Zurich: Zwingli Verlag, 1968).
172. So Clements, *Isaiah 1–39*, 173.

173. Wildberger, *Isaiah 13–27*, 288, is probably correct in concluding that the original text included only 20:2-5 and that the function of the symbolic action was to warn Judah against an alliance with Egypt. However, the subsequent additions in 20:1 and 6, in addition to applying the sign to the Philistines, provide the proper historical setting for Isaiah's concern for an Egyptian alliance.

(2 Kgs 13:14-19). When King Joash of Israel was faced with the question of whether to go to war against Aram, he came to the dying prophet to seek an oracle, a word from God. Would the Lord give victory? Since Elisha was too weak to get up, he directed the king to perform what was in effect two prophetic sign acts. First, the prophet told Joash to take his bow and shoot an arrow eastward. The interpretation of the sign was just what the king came for: This is "the LORD's arrow of victory, the arrow of victory over Aram!" (2 Kgs 13:17 NRSV). But the man of God then had the king perform another symbolic action, taking the arrows and striking the ground. When he struck only three times, Elisha was furious: "You should have struck five or six times; then you would have struck down Aram until you had made an end of it, but now you will strike down Aram only three times" (2 Kgs 13:19 NRSV).

By no means is this story to be taken as a comment on the limits of the king's resolve or courage. Both acts, the arrow of victory and the three strikes to the ground, not only reveal what will happen but also are believed to set the future into motion. Prophetic symbolic actions are like the prophetic word when it is the word of the Lord. Both words and actions are effective, like the word of God in Genesis 1. When the Lord roars from Zion, "the pastures of the shepherds wither, and the top of Carmel dries up" (Amos 1:2). Likewise, armed with the word of God, Jeremiah was appointed over nations,

> to pluck up and to pull down,
> to destroy and to overthrow,
> to build and to plant. (Jer 1:10 NRSV)

REFLECTIONS

It is difficult to ignore the story of Isaiah walking around naked and barefoot, but what are we to make of it? It is not surprising to hear of bizarre actions by many of the other prophets, given their place in society and what we know of their personalities. These would include Jeremiah, always on the outer fringes of power, or Ezekiel, who sees weird visions, or Amos, a man from the country in the capital city, or Hosea, who married a prostitute. But Isaiah? He was among the urban elite, with access to kings, often in and around both the court and the Temple.

The persistence of such reports about such diverse prophets calls attention to two points. First, the performance of symbolic actions was deeply rooted in the institution of prophecy and not in the individual prophets' personalities or social locations. Second, the acts were not about the prophets but about their messages and vocations. They were not preoccupied with themselves. None of these prophetic symbolic actions is self-serving.

We might look for contemporary parallels to prophetic symbolic actions in the sometimes outrageous behavior of religious leaders or other public personalities. It is not difficult to identify individuals who make careers out of being outrageous, in words or actions or both. But here some discernment is required and possibly even some insight from the prophetic tradition. Self-serving actions that call attention to the actor hardly qualify for the label "prophetic." The message, and not the messenger, will need to be the focus of attention. Moreover, symbolic actions in the biblical tradition will be more than attempts to get the attention of an audience, more than audio-visual devices. The act can embody and even set the future into motion. Examples can be found in the civil rights movement of the 1960s. By entering a schoolhouse and sitting in a formerly all-white classroom, a young woman in Arkansas performed a genuinely prophetic symbolic action. She changed the future, and the future was like her act. Through peaceful civil disobedience, Martin Luther King, Jr., and others embodied their dream for a new world and started it on its way.

Actions are messages that can speak louder than words, but they do become words. Isaiah 20 is a story, and the story is a word, a message. Like all stories, this one evokes a particular reality. It may take us for a while to another time and place. There is, however, more here than the basic power of narrative. This story is, as the Word of God, a creative word. At least some sense of the power of words and symbolic actions to change the future persists even in the modern world. It is obvious that taking vows, such as wedding vows, and participating in rituals not only express commitments but also set a new future into motion. Consider international diplomacy or labor negotiations. Even before the formal negotiations begin there have to be negotiations to determine where people sit at the table. The participants know that the symbolic act of taking a particular place at the table can determine the future realities. Moreover, taking their seats at the table commits the participants to that different future.

ISAIAH 21:1-10, PROCLAMATION CONCERNING THE WILDERNESS OF THE SEA

21 An oracle concerning the Desert by the Sea:

Like whirlwinds sweeping through the
    southland,
    an invader comes from the desert,
    from a land of terror.
²A dire vision has been shown to me:
    The traitor betrays, the looter takes loot.
Elam, attack! Media, lay siege!
    I will bring to an end all the groaning
        she caused.
³At this my body is racked with pain,
    pangs seize me, like those of a woman
        in labor;
I am staggered by what I hear,
    I am bewildered by what I see.
⁴My heart falters,
    fear makes me tremble;
the twilight I longed for
    has become a horror to me.
⁵They set the tables,
    they spread the rugs,
    they eat, they drink!
Get up, you officers,
    oil the shields!
⁶This is what the Lord says to me:
"Go, post a lookout
    and have him report what he sees.
⁷When he sees chariots
    with teams of horses,
riders on donkeys

21 The oracle concerning the wilderness of the sea.

As whirlwinds in the Negeb sweep on,
    it comes from the desert,
    from a terrible land.
²A stern vision is told to me;
    the betrayer betrays,
    and the destroyer destroys.
Go up, O Elam,
    lay siege, O Media;
all the sighing she has caused
    I bring to an end.
³Therefore my loins are filled with anguish;
    pangs have seized me,
    like the pangs of a woman in labor;
I am bowed down so that I cannot hear,
    I am dismayed so that I cannot see.
⁴My mind reels, horror has appalled me;
    the twilight I longed for
    has been turned for me into trembling.
⁵They prepare the table,
    they spread the rugs,
    they eat, they drink.
Rise up, commanders,
    oil the shield!
⁶For thus the Lord said to me:
"Go, post a lookout,
    let him announce what he sees.
⁷When he sees riders, horsemen in pairs,
    riders on donkeys, riders on camels,
let him listen diligently,
    very diligently."

NIV

or riders on camels,
let him be alert,
fully alert."
[8]And the lookout[a] shouted,
"Day after day, my lord, I stand on the
watchtower;
every night I stay at my post.
[9]Look, here comes a man in a chariot
with a team of horses.
And he gives back the answer:
'Babylon has fallen, has fallen!
All the images of its gods
lie shattered on the ground!' "
[10]O my people, crushed on the threshing floor,
I tell you what I have heard
from the LORD Almighty,
from the God of Israel.

[a]8 Dead Sea Scrolls and Syriac; Masoretic Text *A lion*

NRSV

[8]Then the watcher[a] called out:
"Upon a watchtower I stand, O Lord,
continually by day,
and at my post I am stationed
throughout the night.
[9]Look, there they come, riders,
horsemen in pairs!"
Then he responded,
"Fallen, fallen is Babylon;
and all the images of her gods
lie shattered on the ground."
[10]O my threshed and winnowed one,
what I have heard from the LORD of hosts,
the God of Israel, I announce to you.

[a]Q Ms: MT *a lion*

COMMENTARY

All of Isaiah 21 could be understood and treated as a single unit with three short sections, but the editor of the proclamations concerning the foreign nations (chaps. 13–23) set out three separate units by means of the headings that organize this large block of material. The headings in this chapter, which likely are secondary to the material that follows them, call attention to geographical distinctions: "the wilderness of the sea" (v. 1), "Dumah" (v. 11), and "the desert plain" (v. 13). Beyond their simple juxtaposition, it is difficult to recognize significant connections among the three proclamations.

Isaiah 21:1-10 is one of the more difficult passages to understand in the book, and thus it has produced quite diverse interpretations. Speakers, addressees, scenes, topics, and moods shift so quickly that the reader becomes dizzy. Who is the speaker reporting this vision, the "me" (v. 2) and the "I" (vv. 3-4, 10)? Who or what is the "betrayer" and "destroyer"? The heading itself raises questions. What is "the wilderness of the sea"? The obvious answer comes in v. 9: Babylon, which has fallen. This had been hinted at already in v. 2 with the calls to Elam and Media, powers to the east of Babylon, encouraged to "lay siege." But if

that is the case, why does the presumably Judean poet writhe in anguish (vv. 3-4) over the fall of the city and nation that had oppressed the Lord's people?

Most commentators have tried to explain the text by determining its historical context, and they have reached very different conclusions about its date, ranging from the time of Isaiah in the eighth century BCE to the post-exilic era.[174] The author's apparent agony over the fall of Babylon has led some to date the poem at a time when Babylon was allied with Judah against Assyria (c. 690 BCE), shortly before Sennacherib's army destroyed Babylon. However, why would it be so remarkable that a Judean seer would be appalled by a vision of the fall of a great empire, even an oppressive one? In the book of Revelation, on the other hand, the famous line of v. 19, "fallen is Babylon," is applied to Rome and is cited wihtout sympathy (Rev 18:2). In any case, the fall of Babylon evokes the image of a world in chaos, even for the oppressed. Others have attempted to make sense of the tensions and apparent conflicts within the

174. For a summary of the main alternatives, see Ronald E. Clements, *Isaiah 1–39*, NCB (Grand Rapids: Eerdmans, 1980) 176-77.

verses in terms of their history of composition.[175] However, it seems unlikely that more than one author contributed to the unit.

It is possible to make sense of the section. In fact, the problem is that it is possible to make sense of it in many different ways. That is true, of course, of any written or oral expression; but is especially the case with poetry, which is open-ended. It seems most likely, in fact, that the poetry is highly restrained and even enigmatic by design.[176] Problems are only multiplied when one tries to take the poetry as literal historical allusions. For example, the cry that Babylon has "fallen" could mean a literal destruction of the city, as by the Assyrians in 689 BCE, or the end of the empire, as in the more peaceful conquest of the capital by Cyrus in 539 BCE. The expression recalls the language of the dirge over the dead (2 Sam 1:19, 25, 27; Amos 5:2), but the death could be of Babylon or of its power.

Not all the questions posed in reading the text can be answered. However, many of them can be resolved if we begin with what is clear and then move to what is less certain. What we do know is that the passage concerns the fall of Babylon. Moreover, the structure of the unit is not difficult to outline. Following the superscription typical of this part of the book, an unidentified individual reports a visionary experience. There is a break at v. 5 with the messenger formula introducing a speech of Yahweh. However, vv. 1b-4 concentrate on the experience itself and the author's reactions to it, and vv. 5-9 on the substance of the vision. His anguish (vv. 3-4) emphasizes the terror of the experience rather than the message communicated in the vision. After all, he began by describing the vision as like a "whirlwind" from the desert (v. 1). In v. 5 he begins to describe what he saw, first a banquet scene and then a call to arms. Verse 6 is a turning point, for now the Lord speaks within the vision, commanding the visionary to "post a lookout" who will proclaim what he sees, in fact, describing what he is to watch for (v. 7). Prophets could understand themselves as watchmen (Ezekiel 33), but this visionary is instructed to "post a lookout," and then reports the sentry's

activities. In vv. 8-9, still from within the vision, the watchman is heard to cry out to Yahweh that he watched faithfully and tirelessly. When he saw the expected riders, he gave the announcement that forms the heart of the vision: "Fallen, fallen is Babylon, and all the images of her gods." Although stated in the past tense, this functions as an announcement of a future event, for it was seen in a vision. The unit concludes as the visionary turns to address the "threshed and winnowed one" to confirm that the vision is a message from the Lord.

Reports of visions are not uncommon in the prophetic books. One could even say that the dominant form of revelation in Ezekiel is the vision report. But such visions are rare in Isaiah and Jeremiah. In fact, both Jeremiah and Isaiah were suspicious of those who claimed to have visions from the Lord (Isa 29:10; 30:10; Jer 14:14; 23:16). The only other vision report in Isaiah 1–39 is the one in chap. 6, the account of Isaiah's vocation. The technical vocabulary of "to see" as in a vision appears as a designation for the book of Isaiah, and it is used in other superscriptions or headings in the book (2:1; 13:1). This use of such technical terminology, however, is a later interpretation by editors of the book (see the Commentary on 1:1). But Isaiah of Jerusalem does not report visions of this sort. Thus the form, the style, and the content of this section argue that it did not originate with Isaiah but with a later figure.[177] It is more accurate to call the author of these verses a seer rather than a prophet or poet.

The vision of the fall of Babylon most likely originated in the exilic or post-exilic age and served to further the leading theme of the oracles concerning foreign nations—that the Lord of hosts is God over all nations and peoples. The Lord not only knows in advance but also determines the fall of Babylon, the "betrayer" and "destroyer" (v. 2), asserting authority also in the destruction of the "images of her [Babylon's] gods" (v. 9). The vision also offers encouragement to God's people, the "threshed and winnowed one" (v. 10), likely an allusion to the destruction of Jerusalem and the exile of the people in Babylon. (See Reflections at 21:13-17.)

175. E.g., O. Kaiser, *Isaiah 1–12: A Commentary,* trans. R. A. Wilson (Philadelphia: Westminster, 1972) 122.

176. See H. Wildberger, *Isaiah 13–27* (Minneapolis: Fortress, 1997) 307.

177. See ibid., 311.

ISAIAH 21:11-12, PROCLAMATION CONCERNING DUMAH

NIV

¹¹An oracle concerning Dumah[a]:

Someone calls to me from Seir,
  "Watchman, what is left of the night?
  Watchman, what is left of the night?"
¹²The watchman replies,
  "Morning is coming, but also the night.
  If you would ask, then ask;
  and come back yet again."

[a]*11 Dumah* means *silence* or *stillness,* a wordplay on *Edom.*

NRSV

¹¹ The oracle concerning Dumah.

One is calling to me from Seir,
  "Sentinel, what of the night?
  Sentinel, what of the night?"
¹² The sentinel says:
  "Morning comes, and also the night.
  If you will inquire, inquire;
  come back again."

COMMENTARY

Even such a short unit as this one contains many voices. We hear first the voice of someone calling to a sentinel, asking about the night, then that of the sentinel who answers. There is also the voice of the one reporting the dialogue, the "me" who hears the call from Seir. It is possible, but unlikely, given the third-person form of the report in v. 12, that the voice of the sentinel and the reporter are the same. Finally, there is the one who frames the whole with the heading, identifying it as "The oracle concerning Dumah."

That heading functions to distinguish these two verses from those around them, but there are some connections among the units. The theme, if not the same vocabulary, of the "lookout" (vv. 7-8) is continued in the image of the sentinel in the night. These verses might be linked geographically to those that follow concerning Arabia, since Dumah was in the Arabian desert. Seir, on the other hand, was in Edom. So the relations among these units are complicated. At one point in the development of the book, these two verses must have been taken as a continuation of vv. 1-10, on the basis of the theme of the sentinel. But at a different stage—the one when the heading was put over the unit—they were regarded as concerning different places and circumstances.

Although there is some uncertainty about the geographical reference within the passage (Seir), clearly it directs the reader's eyes to a foreign land, presumably from the perspective of Judah. A little

scene is described in the first person ("calling to me," v. 11), defined by the dialogue between an inquirer and a sentinel. Both the question and the sentinel's answer are enigmatic.

Context is everything, especially if we are to make sense of enigmatic expressions. If we heard this dialogue on the street in the middle of the night or in a story about a city and its watchman, we might take it to be a simple response to a simple question. "What of the night?" probably is a question about the time. The NIV's "What is left of the night?" while possibly correct, is explanatory and is clearer than the Hebrew. The answer under any circumstances is vague. To read it in the future tense, with the NIV, as "morning is coming" or in the present tense, with the NRSV, as "morning comes" suggests that morning is near, that night is almost gone. But the Hebrew is a past tense, "Morning came, and so did the night" (TNK).[178] The watchman seems to be reminding the inquirer of the cycle of day and night. Morning came, and it will come again, and so will the night.

If that were not sufficiently ambiguous, the context of the report both complicates and deepens the possibilities for meaning. It is not the broad context of the Bible as a whole that is revealing, for not every expression is fraught with theological or moral import just because it is in the scriptures. But this ordinary event with enigmatic language is

178. Wildberger, *Isaiah 13–27,* 337.

given a heading like all others in Isaiah 13–23, forming the content of the oracle or proclamation concerning Dumah. Given the substance of the other proclamations concerning the foreign nations, one expects threatening words, or at least a warning. Certainly night and day, darkness and light, are persistent and powerful symbols. Those who expect the day of the Lord to be light will find it to be darkness (Amos 5:18). Thus the message could be this: Since morning came, and so did the night, be aware of the cycle of good times and bad and keep on asking which is which; keep inquiring.

It is possible that the message would have been clearer to those aware of the particular historical circumstances in which it was proclaimed. Some have argued for c. 690 BCE, when Dumah was allied with Babylon (see the Commentary on 21:1-10) and was attacked by the Assyrians.[179] Heard by Judeans in the time of the Babylonian exile, it could suggest that the present oppression would end, but another would come. (See the Reflections at Isa 21:13-17.)

179. Marvin A. Sweeney, *Isaiah 1–39, With an Introduction to Prophetic Literature,* FOTL XVI (Grand Rapids: Eerdmans, 1996) 285.

ISAIAH 21:13-17, PROCLAMATION CONCERNING THE DESERT PLAIN

NIV

¹³An oracle concerning Arabia:

You caravans of Dedanites,
    who camp in the thickets of Arabia,
¹⁴ bring water for the thirsty;
you who live in Tema,
    bring food for the fugitives.
¹⁵They flee from the sword,
    from the drawn sword,
from the bent bow
    and from the heat of battle.
¹⁶This is what the Lord says to me: "Within one year, as a servant bound by contract would count it, all the pomp of Kedar will come to an end. ¹⁷The survivors of the bowmen, the warriors of Kedar, will be few." The LORD, the God of Israel, has spoken.

NRSV

¹³ The oracle concerning the desert plain.

In the scrub of the desert plain you will lodge,
    O caravans of Dedanites.
¹⁴ Bring water to the thirsty,
    meet the fugitive with bread,
    O inhabitants of the land of Tema.
¹⁵ For they have fled from the swords,
    from the drawn sword,
from the bent bow,
    and from the stress of battle.

¹⁶For thus the Lord said to me: Within a year, according to the years of a hired worker, all the glory of Kedar will come to an end; ¹⁷and the remaining bows of Kedar's warriors will be few; for the LORD, the God of Israel, has spoken.

COMMENTARY

This section consists of two relatively distinct elements, vv. 13-15 and 16-17. These two units are connected on the basis of their common geography and their concern with trouble in the form of military disaster. All the places and peoples are Arabian, specifically related to the northern Arabian desert. Although they are associated geographically, the places and peoples are distinct. Moreover, the style, mood, attitude toward the people of the desert, and content of the two parts are quite different. The first piece expresses an almost poignant concern for an Arab group that has been the victim of a military attack. While the first unit is poetry, the second section is prose. Without regret or obvious sympathy, it announces judgment against yet another Arabian group, the people of Kedar.

Following the heading, the first segment (vv. 13-15) mentions two different peoples, the Dedanites and the "inhabitants of the land of Tema." It opens with a statement addressed to the Dedanites concerning the future—not unlike a prophetic announcement, but without attributing the words to Yahweh. For reasons to be made clear in v. 15, the unidentified speaker informs the Dedanites that they will live in the scrub of the desert (v. 13). This could be taken as a general statement about their destiny; that is, the desert plain is their homeland. However, it quickly becomes clear that they are homeless and in trouble, for the speaker instructs the people of Tema to meet them, the thirsty fugitives, with water and food. Now the reasons for their situation are presented, introduced by "for" (v. 15). They are fugitives who have escaped a military attack, running away from the sword and the bow.

Some commentators are confident that they can identify the aggressor and the historical circumstances, mainly on the basis of the context in chap. 21. Dates range from the time of Isaiah to well into the Persian period. A common date given by recent commentators is 689 BCE, when the Assyrians under Sennacherib attacked Babylon as well as its Arabian allies.[180] It is possible that the text comes from that period, but the evidence is too meager for any historical conclusions at all. In any case, it is unlikely that these lines come from Isaiah. Whatever its date of origin, these verses call for one desert group to come to the aid of another one that is fleeing a military attack. It is not necessary to conclude that the prophet's sympathy for the fugitive is motivated by politics—that is, that they were allies of Judah.[181]

If the attitude toward Arabian groups in vv. 13-15 is one of concern for their health and safety, then vv. 16-17 presume a posture of condemnation toward Kedar. Although in prose rather than poetry, these two verses follow the typical pattern of the announcement of judgment, introduced with the prophetic word of the Lord formula and concluded with another affirmation that the words come from Yahweh. However, both the usual pattern of such speeches and the "for" that begins it presume some reasons for the announcement. The preceding verses provide neither reasons for judgment nor indictment of Kedar. One could imagine the possibility that Kedar had been the aggressor who attacked the Dedanites (v. 13) and now is to suffer the wrath of God, but that conclusion is suggested by no more than the juxtaposition of the units.

Framed by the word of the Lord formulas, the substance of this little unit is a reported speech of Yahweh to a prophetic figure ("me," v. 16). The word of the Lord concerns the future military disaster that will bring an end to "the glory" of Kedar. As in most prophecies of disaster, this one concerns what is expected soon; but it is more specific than usual, promising that the trouble will come "within a year" (v. 16). The phrase "a year, according to the years of a hired worker" hints that the time before the glory of Kedar is brought to an end will be a hard time, that it will seem to move slowly. That would seem to be from the perspective of those who would be happy to see the disaster come, not the perspective of the condemned. The specific chronological reference reinforces the impression that the announcement has some specific historical situation in view, but there is not enough detail to know which one it might be.

The announcement of vv. 16-17 advances the leading theme of the oracles concerning the foreign nations in Isaiah 13–23, as expressed in 23:9 (concerning Tyre):

> The LORD of hosts has planned it—
>   to defile the pride of all glory,
>   to shame all the honored of the earth. (NRSV)

Yahweh is over all nations and peoples. Although reasons for the Lord's intervention against Kedar are not spelled out, they are implied in the judgment against its "glory."

---

180. Sweeney, *Isaiah 1–39*, 287. Kaiser, *Isaiah 13–39*, 135, disagrees.
181. So Clements argues, *Isaiah 1–39*, 181.

EXCURSUS: HEBREW POETRY

The complex and almost mysterious poetry of Isaiah 21 evokes reflection on poetry itself and on the relationship between poets and visionaries.

Most prophetic language is written in poetry of one kind or another. What is remarkable in prophetic books are prose passages in the middle of the poetry. Poetry is one of the factors that distinguishes prophetic from other discourse and links it with certain other types of literature, both within and beyond the Bible. There are bits and pieces of poetry, and even entire chapters, in the narrative books of the Old Testament. Beyond the prophetic literature, however, poetry dominates the third part of the Hebrew canon, the Writings, including wisdom literature and the book of Psalms. The poetic character of the wisdom books, such as Proverbs, Job, and Ecclesiastes, calls attention to the creative, artistic dimension of such expression.

The psalms as well are filled with artistic expression. Some are closely related to wisdom literature, but most were tied more or less directly to rituals of prayer, praise, petition, and thanksgiving. Why use poetry for such occasions? For the most part, the lines were to be sung or chanted, and thus they were cast into lyrical poetic style. Moreover, one can often detect in the psalms the relationship between poetic and ritual rhythms. Even more significant, one is aware that the special situation of coming before God requires a distinctive, elevated language.[182] The style and mood of poetry are inseparable from its content; each reinforces the tone and substance of the communication.

Nor does God speak in ordinary language, although there are reports of divine talk that is more typical of everyday speech in biblical narratives. But even there the attribution of a speech or address to God gives the words a certain tone. One can hardly hear the words of God from Mt. Sinai or at the creation of the world as normal talk. The main business of the prophets was to communicate the word of God. No wonder, then, that prophecies are in the exalted and memorable language of poetry.

Hebrew poetry has its distinctive features.[183] Translators of the Bible into English and other languages help the reader to recognize and understand Hebrew poetry by attempting to replicate its shape. That shape is defined by parallelism; in its simplest form, two virtually synonymous lines, as in 21:14:

> Bring water to the thirsty,
>> meet the fugitive with bread . . . .

Although these two lines clearly are parallel, they do not say the same thing. Each complements the other to draw attention to the needs of the escapees. Although variously understood, Hebrew poetry employs a kind of meter, patterns of accented syllables in lines. The dirge, for example, alternates lines of three and two accented syllables. Hebrew poetry also employs other features, such as wordplays and assonance—that is, the use of similar, if not rhyming, sounds. And like all enduring poetry, it often leaves a great deal to the imagination of the hearer or reader.

182. See E. Gerstenberger, *Psalms, Part 1, With an Introduction to Cultic Poetry,* FOTL XIV (Grand Rapids: Eerdmans, 1988) 5.
183. For a good introduction see David L. Peterson and Kent H. Richards, *Interpreting Hebrew Poetry* (Philadelphia: Fortress, 1992).

REFLECTIONS

1. People have been known to fear poetry, and well they should. Poetry puts a heavy burden on the reader or hearer, who must work to understand and to fill in blanks. Moreover, poetry entails risk, including the risk of misunderstanding. The poet is willing to give up a measure of control over what the reader or the hearer makes of the poetry, to allow for the possibility that it could be understood in various ways, or even misunderstood, and certainly misused. Would we prefer to have all the blanks filled in, everything explained in such a way that there was no room for our imagination? Many people do wish to have everything set out directly; hence, the expression, "More truth than poetry." Furthermore, poetry can be subversive, with its power and indirection. In that way it is like prophecy, which can call into question and even undermine conventional understandings.

It is, perhaps, not surprising that an author who has been identified as a visionary has produced enigmatic poetry like Isa 21:1-10. Both vision and poetry require imagination and openness. With regard to this and other biblical accounts of visions, readers have been known to ask whether the report is the description of an experience or a literary creation. This is an old question, but not a very productive one. The poetic imagination and the visionary experience are not so different. Poetic visionaries often see themselves as sentinels or, as with the author of 21:1-10, someone who is to call others to be on the lookout for trouble on the horizon. Poets, it may turn out, serve practical functions.

2. The summons to the people of Tema to bring water and food to the fleeing Dedanites (21:14-15) strikes a sensitive chord in this—or, sadly, any—age. The text is not a law or even an admonition to future readers to act in a particular way, but it does evoke reflection on the plight of fugitives, refugees, the homeless, and the hungry. It would be disrespectful of the text for us to simply lift a line out of context and apply it randomly to particular problems. Nonetheless, even in its context it calls attention to important concerns.

Here, in the framework of the proclamations concerning foreign nations, a Judean author is sympathetic to foreigners in need. Perhaps even more significant, this writer views other foreigners as both able and willing to provide help to those in need. One could say that the problem of suffering as a result of war is an international problem with international solutions. The parties involved here are Judeans, Arabs, and an unidentified aggressor.

To be sure, this concern for foreign refugees stands out all the more because of its context, of proclamations heralding divine judgment on various and sundry foreign nations and peoples. This fact emphasizes the need for serious reflection on the relationships between those who see themselves as the people of God (and most religious people do) and other peoples. The Bible seldom provides direct or simple answers to such problems.

ISAIAH 22:1-25, PROCLAMATION CONCERNING THE VALLEY OF VISION

NIV	NRSV
22 An oracle concerning the Valley of Vision: What troubles you now,	**22** The oracle concerning the valley of vision. What do you mean that you have gone up,

NIV

that you have all gone up on the roofs,
²O town full of commotion,
O city of tumult and revelry?
Your slain were not killed by the sword,
nor did they die in battle.
³All your leaders have fled together;
they have been captured without using
the bow.
All you who were caught were taken prisoner
together,
having fled while the enemy was still
far away.
⁴Therefore I said, "Turn away from me;
let me weep bitterly.
Do not try to console me
over the destruction of my people."

⁵The Lord, the LORD Almighty, has a day
of tumult and trampling and terror
in the Valley of Vision,
a day of battering down walls
and of crying out to the mountains.
⁶Elam takes up the quiver,
with her charioteers and horses;
Kir uncovers the shield.
⁷Your choicest valleys are full of chariots,
and horsemen are posted at the city gates;
⁸   the defenses of Judah are stripped away.

And you looked in that day
to the weapons in the Palace of the Forest;
⁹you saw that the City of David
had many breaches in its defenses;
you stored up water
in the Lower Pool.
¹⁰You counted the buildings in Jerusalem
and tore down houses to strengthen
the wall.
¹¹You built a reservoir between the two walls
for the water of the Old Pool,
but you did not look to the One who made it,
or have regard for the One who planned it
long ago.

¹²The Lord, the LORD Almighty,
called you on that day
to weep and to wail,
to tear out your hair and put on sackcloth.
¹³But see, there is joy and revelry,

NRSV

all of you, to the housetops,
²you that are full of shoutings,
tumultuous city, exultant town?
Your slain are not slain by the sword,
nor are they dead in battle.
³Your rulers have all fled together;
they were captured without the use of
a bow.ᵃ
All of you who were found were captured,
though they had fled far away.ᵇ
⁴Therefore I said:
Look away from me,
let me weep bitter tears;
do not try to comfort me
for the destruction of my beloved people.

⁵For the Lord GOD of hosts has a day
of tumult and trampling and confusion
in the valley of vision,
a battering down of walls
and a cry for help to the mountains.
⁶Elam bore the quiver
with chariots and cavalry,ᶜ
and Kir uncovered the shield.
⁷Your choicest valleys were full of chariots,
and the cavalry took their stand at the gates.
⁸He has taken away the covering of Judah.

On that day you looked to the weapons of the
House of the Forest, ⁹and you saw that there were
many breaches in the city of David, and you collected the waters of the lower pool. ¹⁰You counted
the houses of Jerusalem, and you broke down the
houses to fortify the wall. ¹¹You made a reservoir
between the two walls for the water of the old
pool. But you did not look to him who did it, or
have regard for him who planned it long ago.

¹²In that day the Lord GOD of hosts
called to weeping and mourning,
to baldness and putting on sackcloth;
¹³but instead there was joy and festivity,
killing oxen and slaughtering sheep,
eating meat and drinking wine.
"Let us eat and drink,
for tomorrow we die."

ᵃOr without their bows   ᵇGk Syr Vg: Heb fled from far away
ᶜMeaning of Heb uncertain

NIV

slaughtering of cattle and killing of sheep,
     eating of meat and drinking of wine!
"Let us eat and drink," you say,
     "for tomorrow we die!"

[14]The Lord Almighty has revealed this in my hearing: "Till your dying day this sin will not be atoned for," says the Lord, the Lord Almighty.

[15]This is what the Lord, the Lord Almighty, says:

"Go, say to this steward,
     to Shebna, who is in charge of the palace:
[16]What are you doing here and who gave you permission
     to cut out a grave for yourself here,
hewing your grave on the height
     and chiseling your resting place in the rock?

[17]"Beware, the Lord is about to take firm hold of you
     and hurl you away, O you mighty man.
[18]He will roll you up tightly like a ball
     and throw you into a large country.
There you will die
     and there your splendid chariots will remain—
     you disgrace to your master's house!
[19]I will depose you from your office,
     and you will be ousted from your position.
[20]"In that day I will summon my servant, Eliakim son of Hilkiah. [21]I will clothe him with your robe and fasten your sash around him and hand your authority over to him. He will be a father to those who live in Jerusalem and to the house of Judah. [22]I will place on his shoulder the key to the house of David; what he opens no one can shut, and what he shuts no one can open. [23]I will drive him like a peg into a firm place; he will be a seat[a] of honor for the house of his father. [24]All the glory of his family will hang on him: its offspring and offshoots—all its lesser vessels, from the bowls to all the jars.

[25]"In that day," declares the Lord Almighty, "the peg driven into the firm place will give way; it will be sheared off and will fall, and the load hanging on it will be cut down." The Lord has spoken.

[a]23 Or throne

NRSV

[14]The Lord of hosts has revealed himself in my ears:
     Surely this iniquity will not be forgiven you until you die,
     says the Lord God of hosts.

[15]Thus says the Lord God of hosts: Come, go to this steward, to Shebna, who is master of the household, and say to him: [16]What right do you have here? Who are your relatives here, that you have cut out a tomb here for yourself, cutting a tomb on the height, and carving a habitation for yourself in the rock? [17]The Lord is about to hurl you away violently, my fellow. He will seize firm hold on you, [18]whirl you round and round, and throw you like a ball into a wide land; there you shall die, and there your splendid chariots shall lie, O you disgrace to your master's house! [19]I will thrust you from your office, and you will be pulled down from your post.

[20]On that day I will call my servant Eliakim son of Hilkiah, [21]and will clothe him with your robe and bind your sash on him. I will commit your authority to his hand, and he shall be a father to the inhabitants of Jerusalem and to the house of Judah. [22]I will place on his shoulder the key of the house of David; he shall open, and no one shall shut; he shall shut, and no one shall open. [23]I will fasten him like a peg in a secure place, and he will become a throne of honor to his ancestral house. [24]And they will hang on him the whole weight of his ancestral house, the offspring and issue, every small vessel, from the cups to all the flagons. [25]On that day, says the Lord of hosts, the peg that was fastened in a secure place will give way; it will be cut down and fall, and the load that was on it will perish, for the Lord has spoken.

COMMENTARY

This chapter consists of two quite distinct parts, vv. 1-14 and vv. 15-25, but all of it deals with people and events in and around Jerusalem. In that respect, it stands out in the collection of proclamations concerning foreign nations in chaps. 13–23. It is not at all obvious why the material in chap. 22 was placed here. The fact that both chap. 21 and chap. 22 have unusual headings and that in both of them the Elamites attack hardly accounts for the inclusion of this chapter in its present context.[184] But for some reason, the editor of this collection has included the section here and affixed the heading "The oracle concerning the valley of vision," from the reference in 22:5.

The first part of the chapter (vv. 1-14) is, in the last analysis, an announcement of judgment against Jerusalem and its inhabitants; but the way to that announcement is by no means direct, nor is it typical of such prophecies. The second part (vv. 15-25) contains two related narratives concerning officials of the royal court. Although there are some later additions in both parts, most of the material in this chapter originated with the prophet Isaiah in the eighth century BCE.

22:1-14. The leading motif of this section is the day of the Lord. As in other prophetic allusions to the theme, this one concerns the day when the Lord will intervene in human affairs, ordinarily by means of a holy war against the Lord's enemies. As Amos made clear, however, those enemies could turn out to be the Lord's own people (Amos 5:18-20). Allusions to the day of the Lord are common in Isaiah (e.g., 2:11, 17, 20; 3:7, 18; 5:30) and are especially prominent in the collection of oracles against the nations (e.g., 13:6, 9, 15; 17:4, 7, 9; 19:16, 18, etc.). Usually the day of the Lord is seen in the future, but here it concerns the past. References to "that day" both sustain the movement in this passage and set off its parts from one another, introducing new sections in vv. 5, 8*b*, 12 and marking the transition to an addition in v. 25.

It is not at all clear who speaks in vv. 1-4—the prophet or the Lord through the prophet. Suggesting the latter is the warm and affectionate reference to "my beloved people" in v. 4; suggesting

184. So Christopher R. Seitz, *Isaiah 1–39*, Interpretation (Louisville: John Knox, 1993) 158.

the former is the mention of the Lord in the third person in the subsequent section (v. 5). In any case, in prophetic discourse the line between these two often is difficult to distinguish. These verses begin by criticizing the people of Jerusalem for celebrating in the midst of tragedy. Then the speaker describes the disaster: The dead were not slain in battle (v. 2*b*), and the leaders fled but still were captured (v. 3). Finally, the speaker affirms that he must weep over the destruction of "my beloved people," and he refuses to be comforted. This speech presumes that disaster has come and that both people and leaders behaved badly, the leaders by running away and the people by celebrating rather than mourning.

The next part (vv. 5-8) begins like a typical prophetic announcement of the future day of the Lord, but quickly turns to an account of events that have already happened. Walls are battered down, and a cry for help goes up to the mountains. An enemy army has invaded. Chariots and cavalry filled the valleys and "took their stand at the gates" (v. 7). These verses clearly describe an invasion of Judah and a siege, almost certainly of Jerusalem.

A prose section (vv. 9-11) begins with the key phrase "that day." In this case, however, it does not refer to the day of the Lord as such but simply to that time in the past when the enemy invaded. There follows a description of preparations for a siege, presented in the form of a second-person plural address. The prophet paints a picture of leaders and people scurrying about, looking for weapons in the royal armory ("the House of the Forest," v. 9; see 1 Kgs 7:2; 10:17), taking inventory of the "breaches" in the wall of the old city ("city of David," v. 9), caring for the water supply (see 7:3) , and even tearing down houses to repair the city walls. With all this frantic activity, they failed in the most important preparation: respecting and relying upon "him who planned it long ago" (v. 11). Thus the point is not to remind the leaders and the people of how well they had prepared for the attack but to accuse them of failing to trust in the God of history.

The final part of the unit (vv. 12-14) continues to characterize the day of the Lord in terms of past events. The Lord called for "weeping and mourning" and the accompanying rituals of wearing sackcloth and shaving of heads, but instead there was only celebration. The people cited what was doubtless an old saying, "Let us eat and drink,/ for tomorrow we die" (v. 13). One cannot know if that is what the people actually said, but for the prophet it epitomizes their attitudes in the face of danger. He certainly does not approve of the attitude expressed by the saying.

With the last verse the prophet moves to the future, introducing a one-sentence announcement with the affirmation that it comes from the Lord and concluding it with the oracle formula. The announcement is simple: The Lord will not forgive "this iniquity" until you die (v. 14). What was that iniquity? The previous thirteen verses have answered that question. In a time of trouble, the leaders and the people relied on their own preparations instead of the Lord, upon military strategy rather than Yahweh. Moreover, when circumstances called for mourning and lamentation, they celebrated and ate and drank. The language that frames the announcement indicates a very strong affirmation of Yahweh's decision to judge, but on the surface the content does not seem strong. Remarkably, the judgment announced does not mention the destruction of Jerusalem, but only that iniquity will not be forgiven. This judgment, however, is far stronger than it may appear to modern eyes. This means that the sinful acts will have their consequences, will work out their own punishment. Yahweh will not intervene to hold back the effects of sin.[185] The translation in the REB is not literally accurate but it captures the spirit of the announcement:

> Assuredly your wickedness will never be wiped out;
>> you will die for it.

Clearly this prophetic announcement of judgment presumes particular historical events known to the original speaker and hearers. Some of the activities are so stereotypical and common that they could refer to many circumstances. This applies to the description of the invading army and the siege of the city, all too common in the ancient Near East. Evidence for such assaults abound, both in words and in pictures from Assyrian sources.[186] But many of the allusions in Isaiah's address are detailed and precise, presented in the matter-of-fact tones typical of an eyewitness report. Some scholars argue that the unit does not provide sufficient information to relate it to a known and specific historical event, but could refer to any siege of Jerusalem by troops under Assyrian control.[187]

Although it is not possible to be certain of its date, the message and most of the details of this passage can be explained and understood in terms of Sennacherib's siege of Jerusalem and decimation of the Judean countryside in 701 BCE. That is the conclusion of most recent commentators.[188] Some of the details of that siege are well-documented, but some of the most important questions cannot be answered. The Assyrian king Sennacherib himself describes how he invaded Judah and laid siege to Jerusalem:

> As to Hezekiah, the Jew, he did not submit to my yoke, I laid siege to 46 of his strong cities, walled forts and to the countless small villages in their vicinity, and conquered [them] by means of well-stamped [earth-]ramps, and battering-rams brought [thus] near [to the walls] . . . I drove out [of them] 200,1500 people, young and old, male and female, horses, mules, donkeys, camels, big and small cattle beyond counting, and considered [them] booty. Himself I made a prisoner in Jerusalem, his royal residence, like a bird in a cage.[189]

The biblical texts also document the invasion in which Sennacherib destroyed much of Judah and laid siege to Jerusalem (2 Kings 18–19; Isaiah 36–37; see the Commentary on 36:1–37:38). The Assyrian army returned home without capturing Jerusalem, and the reasons for that failure have been debated by historians, ancient and modern, ever since.

---

185. See H. Wildberger, *Isaiah 13–27* (Minneapolis: Fortress, 1997) 275. For a discussion of the relationship between acts and consequences in the prophetic understanding of punishment, see Gene M. Tucker, "Sin and 'Judgment' in the Prophets," in *Problems in Biblical Theology: Essays in Honor of Rolf Knierim*, ed. Henry T. C. Sun et al. (Grand Rapids: Eerdmans, 1997) 373-88.

186. See, e.g., the Assyrian reliefs of Sennacherib's exploits in *ANEP,* 129-31.

187. Brevard S. Childs, *Isaiah and the Assyrian Crisis* (London: SCM, 1967) 26.

188. E.g., Clements, *Isaiah 1–39,* 183; Wildberger, *Isaiah 13–27,* 358, 361.

189. *ANET,* 288.

Most of the text before us presumes that the siege has been lifted. The prophet reports what had happened before the Assyrians arrived, during the siege, and after they departed. As the enemy approached, preparations were made to withstand the attack. When Sennacherib's army withdrew, the people congratulated themselves on their success and celebrated their survival against the most powerful army in the world. But Isaiah called for mourning. After all, the entire Judean countryside had been decimated ("the covering of Judah," v. 8), even if one allows for some exaggeration in Sennacherib's report. Moreover, the prophet, who had long ago said to trust in Yahweh instead of armies (7:1-9), had not changed his theology in his old age. If the substance of this speech comes from 701 BCE, it would have been one of his last appearances as a prophet. Some of this message makes good sense during the time of the siege, but now it is reported as part. Isaiah's confidence in the Lord's election of Jerusalem does not prevent him from proclaiming that the Lord will not forgive such iniquity, such failure of faith. They did not look to God during the siege, did not acknowledge that the Lord was the one who saved them, and did not grieve over the destruction of the cities and towns of Judah.

22:15-25. These verses present two different but related prophecies concerning officials in the royal household, Shebna (vv. 15-19) and Eliakim (vv. 20-25). The prophecies must have been placed in this particular context because the first part of the chapter concerns the sins and judgment of Jerusalem and its leadership, and probably also because tradition connected these two officials with the events taken to lie behind vv. 1-14: Sennacherib's invasion of Judah and siege of Jerusalem.

There is clear evidence of growth and editorial development in these two units. The foundation for that development lies in vv. 15-18, most likely an authentic tradition from Isaiah in the eighth century BCE. Introduced by the messenger formula, "Thus says the LORD God of hosts," the prophet reports his instructions to confront the steward Shebna with an accusation and a threat. The location of the confrontation is not given, but the allusion "here" (v. 16) indicates that it is at the place of Shebna's offense, where he is having an impressive grave prepared for himself. Isaiah accuses him

of having a tomb cut in the rock. What is wrong with that? It is not difficult to read between the lines. By means of a rhetorical question, the prophet reminds Shebna that he has no relatives here (v. 16) and thus has no right to such a place. He is an interloper. Moreover, both the expense of such a tomb and the allusion to Shebna's "splendid chariots" (v. 18) indicate excessive exploitation of economic resources. When the prophet calls him a "mighty man" (v. 17 NIV; NRSV, "my fellow"), his tone is ironic and contemptuous.[190] Shebna has taken advantage of his position and misused his office. Thus he is a "disgrace" to his "master's house"—that is, to the king. Consequently, the Lord is about to grab him, whirl him around in the air, and throw him into "a wide land." This can only be a prophecy of exile into Assyria.

But the final sentence of the prophecy against Shebna (v. 19) promises a different judgment: that the Lord will remove him from office. That would seem to be anticlimactic, and in any case expulsion from the country into exile certainly would remove him from office. Moreover, the prophecy shifts from a third-person report of what the Lord is about to do to the first person ("I will thrust you"). Since the next unit (vv. 20-25) announces that Eliakim will now be given Shebna's office, v. 19 must be a secondary editorial transition, noting how Shebna lost his office before it was given to Eliakim.

With the introductory "on that day" (v. 20) the text turns from an announcement of judgment against one royal official to an announcement of salvation for another, Eliakim son of Hilkiah. The first part of the section (vv. 20-24) is a coherent prophecy quoting the Lord, the "I" in vv. 20-23. Although the speech purports to be addressed to Shebna ("your robe," "your sash," "your authority," v. 21), it is unlikely to have originated with Isaiah. It seems that Shebna's office as steward and "master of the household" (v. 15) will be transferred to Eliakim, and this will effect stability and security for Jerusalem and Judah. Eliakim will exercise the authority of the royal house and will be like "a peg in a secure place" (v. 23).

All this changes dramatically with v. 25, for the peg will "give way," "be cut down and fall." Even worse, all that it had supported will perish. This

---

190. Clements, *Isaiah 1–39,* 189.

change to an announcement of the fall of Jerusalem must be a later reinterpretation of the prophecy, probably from the perspective of the Babylonian exile.

Both Shebna and Eliakim are known from the accounts of Hezekiah's reign, and particularly in the reports of Sennacherib's siege of Jerusalem. In Isa 36:3 and 1 Kgs 18:18, Eliakim is the higher official, the one "in charge of the palace," while Shebna is called "the secretary." Along with a third official, both went out to negotiate on behalf of the king. These accounts provide no explanation for Isaiah's condemnation of Shebna or why he is "master of the household" in Isa 22:15 and "secretary" in 36:3.

REFLECTIONS

1. The saying attributed by the prophet to the people in 22:13 certainly provides food for thought: "Let us eat and drink, for tomorrow we die." This famous line calls for reflection in two ways: as a specific response to an immediate threat and as a general observation about life.

First, as we encounter it here, the saying has a particular literary context that presumes a specific historical situation. When faced with a dangerous military threat, the Assyrian siege of the city, the accused decided to enjoy themselves. The prophet puts these words into the mouths of the people of Jerusalem as part of an accusation and an indictment. Faced with death, this is what they said. Certainly the prophet was using this citation to criticize the attitude of the inhabitants of Jerusalem. But what attitude did the saying represent? Was it denial of the seriousness of the threat or resignation to the inevitable? Is the emphasis on eating and drinking or on the possibility of dying tomorrow? More is suggested than eating and drinking, however, for both are essential to life. The saying in this context represents a flippant attitude in the face of a serious situation. At least implied is that additional line in the familiar saying from Ecclesiastes: "Eat, drink and be merry" (8:15 KJV; NRSV, "enjoy himself"). What is beyond a doubt, however, is that in this context the saying also functions as a warning. Isaiah says, in effect, "If you live for the day, whether in celebration or in resignation, that is all you get. But if you do something else—in this case, repent, appeal to, and trust Yahweh—you will not die—at least not right away." For readers in any age, the point is clear: Be serious in the face of trouble.

Second, this saying commonly is taken as a general observation about life. The perspective it expresses is virtually universal, for sayings similar to this one appear all over the world and throughout history.[191] There is an analogous Spanish saying: "Drink, brother, for life is short."

In this general usage, it is not at all obvious what attitude such sayings express. In fact, like all sayings or proverbs, there is both a transparency, a clear point, and an openness to diverse meanings. One reason why such sayings persist is that they can and do express more than one point of view. Although Isaiah cites this particular saying as part of a serious accusation, sayings such as this one can be playful as well as serious. Moreover, when one quotes a saying to make a point, someone else can always cite one supporting the opposite point; and, within limits, both may be valid. It is true that "haste makes waste," but it is also true that "the one who hesitates is lost." So timing is everything. One is genuinely wise who knows when to use which saying.

The saying in question here can and does make different points, just as there are various ways that people respond in the face of death or to the awareness that they are mortal. Above all, this saying acknowledges that life has limits: If we do not die tomorrow, we will die someday—and it is important to decide what we will do within those limits. We may respond with resignation, with denial, or with an affirmation of the life we have. This last seems to be the most typical use of this saying. But a flight to immediate pleasure, generally called hedonism, can represent an attempt to deny those limits. On the other hand, to eat and drink in the awareness of one's limits can express a call to live for the day, to focus on the present, to enjoy life to the full as a gift.

191. For a catalog of similar ancient Near Eastern sayings, see H. Wildberger, *Isaiah 13–27* (Minneapolis: Fortress, 1997) 373-75.

Moreover, to think about the saying in this way is to raise the question of deferred gratification, of finding the right balance between enjoyment of the fullness of life in the present and preparing for the future.

In at least one biblical book, Ecclesiastes or Koheleth, this saying is almost a theology, an approach to faith and life. Koheleth is resigned—almost stoic—in his attitude toward the world and human limits, but he has some recommendations for dealing with those boundaries: "Whoever is joined with all the living has hope, for the living dog is better than a dead lion" (Eccl 9:4). And over and over he repeats: "There is nothing better for mortals than to eat and drink, and find enjoyment in their toil" (Eccl 2:24), and "Enjoy life with the wife whom you love, all the days of your vain life that are given you under the sun, because that is your portion in life" (Eccl 9:9).

It may be small comfort, but it is some comfort to make the most of one's limited place in God's creation. Thus in view of the fact that all living things age and die, there is a tone of acceptance, if not resignation, in those most famous lines from Koheleth's book:

> For everything there is a season, and a time for every matter under heaven:
> a time to be born, and a time to die;
> a time to plant, and a time to pluck up what is planted. (Eccl 3:1-2 NRSV)[192]

The saying in Isa 21:13 is quoted in 1 Cor 15:32. Like Isaiah, Paul cites it unfavorably, as expressing a perspective he rejects. But he uses the saying to make a different point from Isaiah, to argue for faith in resurrection. He says, in effect, that if there is no resurrection, then we might as well eat and drink, for tomorrow we die. But is Paul's perspective so different from that of Isaiah after all? Both pose the saying as the alternative to trust in God's affirmation of life.

2. The two prophecies that end this chapter concern leadership and politics and provide the occasion for reflection on such matters. The text presents two sharply contrasting pictures, each almost amounting to a political caricature. The prophet describes Shebna as an arrogant and self-seeking official who is willing to use public resources to preserve his own memory. Isaiah confronts him at the place where he is having a magnificent tomb for himself cut into the rock. This activity hardly amounts to planning his funeral to save his descendants the trouble. The expenditure of resources for such a tomb can only have been to ensure the perpetuation of his name, to build a monument to himself. For this arrogant gesture, this use of his position for his own interests instead of for those of his city and state, he is condemned to exile in a foreign land, where his name surely will be forgotten.

Building a tomb or a monument to oneself with public funds is, of course, not the only way people misuse resources to make a lasting name for themselves. Nor is such arrogance limited to political figures.

According to Isaiah, such a tomb is more than Shebna deserves. It does not appear that the prophet disapproved of grand monuments in principle, but like so many considerations of political office and power, issues of class may have influenced his perspective. The language of the accusation suggests that Shebna is building a tomb in a place where he does not belong, where he has no family and thus was not among the aristocracy.[193] Isaiah, on the other hand, was among the elite of Jerusalem. Although it would go too far to suggest that the prophet sounds jealous, he does seem to reflect a certain class prejudice against a usurper. Class identity may quickly reveal itself in criticism of political figures.

The picture of Eliakim, on the other hand, is almost too good to be true. It does, however, set the mark for the role and behavior of a legitimate leader, ordained and blessed by God. Such a

---

192. Gene M. Tucker, "For Everything There Is a Season," in *Reflections on Aging and Spiritual Growth*, ed. Andrew J. Weaver, Harold G. Koenig, and Phyllis C. Roe (Nashville: Abingdon, 1998) 79-87.
193. See Wildberger, *Isaiah 13–27*, 387.

one will have full authority and will exercise it like a father for his family. He will not seek to preserve his own memory, but honor will be accorded to him. This ideal, which persists into democratic and egalitarian societies, is not without its problems. The image it endorses has paternalistic dimensions that have the power to impede the development of autonomous authority among those under such leadership.

But, as the final editors of this passage know, even leaders with the full authority of the throne, and even of God, are not necessarily capable of avoiding disaster for the nation.

ISAIAH 23:1-18, PROCLAMATION CONCERNING TYRE

NIV

23 An oracle concerning Tyre:

Wail, O ships of Tarshish!
  For Tyre is destroyed
  and left without house or harbor.
From the land of Cyprus[a]
  word has come to them.

[2]Be silent, you people of the island
  and you merchants of Sidon,
  whom the seafarers have enriched.
[3]On the great waters
  came the grain of the Shihor;
the harvest of the Nile[b] was the revenue
      of Tyre,
  and she became the marketplace of
      the nations.

[4]Be ashamed, O Sidon, and you, O fortress of
      the sea,
  for the sea has spoken:
"I have neither been in labor nor given birth;
  I have neither reared sons nor brought
      up daughters."
[5]When word comes to Egypt,
  they will be in anguish at the report
      from Tyre.

[6]Cross over to Tarshish;
  wail, you people of the island.
[7]Is this your city of revelry,
  the old, old city,

[a]1 Hebrew *Kittim*   [b]2,3 Masoretic Text; one Dead Sea Scroll
Sidon, / who cross over the sea; / your envoys [3]are on the great waters. / The grain of the Shihor, / the harvest of the Nile,

NRSV

23 The oracle concerning Tyre.

Wail, O ships of Tarshish,
  for your fortress is destroyed.[a]
When they came in from Cyprus
  they learned of it.
[2]Be still, O inhabitants of the coast,
  O merchants of Sidon,
  your messengers crossed over the sea[b]
[3] and were on the mighty waters;
your revenue was the grain of Shihor,
  the harvest of the Nile;
  you were the merchant of the nations.
[4]Be ashamed, O Sidon, for the sea has spoken,
  the fortress of the sea, saying:
"I have neither labored nor given birth,
  I have neither reared young men
  nor brought up young women."
[5]When the report comes to Egypt,
  they will be in anguish over the report
      about Tyre.
[6]Cross over to Tarshish—
  wail, O inhabitants of the coast!
[7]Is this your exultant city
  whose origin is from days of old,
whose feet carried her
  to settle far away?
[8]Who has planned this
  against Tyre, the bestower of crowns,
whose merchants were princes,
  whose traders were the honored of
      the earth?

[a]Cn: Compare verse 14: Heb *for it is destroyed, without houses*
[b]Q Ms: MT *crossing over the sea, they replenished you*

NIV

whose feet have taken her
  to settle in far-off lands?
[8]Who planned this against Tyre,
  the bestower of crowns,
whose merchants are princes,
  whose traders are renowned in the earth?

[9]The LORD Almighty planned it,
  to bring low the pride of all glory
  and to humble all who are renowned on
    the earth.

[10]Till[a] your land as along the Nile,
  O Daughter of Tarshish,
  for you no longer have a harbor.
[11]The LORD has stretched out his hand over the sea
  and made its kingdoms tremble.
He has given an order concerning Phoenicia[b]
  that her fortresses be destroyed.
[12]He said, "No more of your reveling,
  O Virgin Daughter of Sidon, now crushed!

"Up, cross over to Cyprus[c];
  even there you will find no rest."
[13]Look at the land of the Babylonians,[d]
  this people that is now of no account!
The Assyrians have made it
  a place for desert creatures;
they raised up their siege towers,
  they stripped its fortresses bare
  and turned it into a ruin.

[14]Wail, you ships of Tarshish;
  your fortress is destroyed!

[15]At that time Tyre will be forgotten for seventy years, the span of a king's life. But at the end of these seventy years, it will happen to Tyre as in the song of the prostitute:

[6]"Take up a harp, walk through the city,
  O prostitute forgotten;
play the harp well, sing many a song,
  so that you will be remembered."
[17]At the end of seventy years, the LORD will deal with Tyre. She will return to her hire as a prostitute and will ply her trade with all the kingdoms on the face of the earth. [18]Yet her profit and her earnings will be set apart for the LORD; they

a10 Dead Sea Scrolls and some Septuagint manuscripts; Masoretic Text Go through   b11 Hebrew Canaan   c12 Hebrew Kittim
d13 Or Chaldeans

NRSV

[9]The LORD of hosts has planned it—
  to defile the pride of all glory,
  to shame all the honored of the earth.
[10]Cross over to your own land,
  O ships of[a] Tarshish;
  this is a harbor[b] no more.
[11]He has stretched out his hand over the sea,
  he has shaken the kingdoms;
the LORD has given command concerning
    Canaan
  to destroy its fortresses.
[12]He said:
  You will exult no longer,
    O oppressed virgin daughter Sidon;
  rise, cross over to Cyprus—
    even there you will have no rest.

[13]Look at the land of the Chaldeans! This is the people; it was not Assyria. They destined Tyre for wild animals. They erected their siege towers, they tore down her palaces, they made her a ruin.[c]
[14]Wail, O ships of Tarshish,
  for your fortress is destroyed.
[15]From that day Tyre will be forgotten for seventy years, the lifetime of one king. At the end of seventy years, it will happen to Tyre as in the song about the prostitute:
[16]Take a harp,
  go about the city,
    you forgotten prostitute!
  Make sweet melody,
    sing many songs,
    that you may be remembered.
[17]At the end of seventy years, the LORD will visit Tyre, and she will return to her trade, and will prostitute herself with all the kingdoms of the world on the face of the earth. [18]Her merchandise and her wages will be dedicated to the LORD; her profits[d] will not be stored or hoarded, but her merchandise will supply abundant food and fine clothing for those who live in the presence of the LORD.

aCn: Compare Gk: Heb like the Nile, daughter   bCn: Heb restraint
cMeaning of Heb uncertain   dHeb it

NIV

will not be stored up or hoarded. Her profits will go to those who live before the LORD, for abundant food and fine clothes.

COMMENTARY

This final pronouncement in the collection of oracles concerning foreign nations (chaps. 13–23) is entitled "The oracle concerning Tyre." It is by no means obvious why this chapter forms the conclusion to this distinct section of the book. It certainly is not a climax either in the scope of what it says or in the relative significance of the nation in question. If there is any explanation, other than the chronology of the section's development by its editors, it could be because v. 9 includes the key to the theme of the section as a whole:

> The Lord of Hosts has planned it—
> to defile the pride of all glory,
> to shame all the honored of the earth.

The proclamations concerning the foreign nations persistently affirm that Yahweh is Lord over all the earth and is working to humble the proud and the powerful. From the perspective of Israel, from the time of Isaiah until the completion of the book of Isaiah no earlier than the Persian period, all other nations were perceived as honored, glorious, and proud of their power, which most were thought to exercise arrogantly.

The chapter contains two distinct parts, both related to the same general geographical location defined by the heading, but distinguished from each other in terms of temporal focus, style, and message. Verses 1-14 concern the past and the present; they are a call for mourning over Tyre and the other Phoenician centers. Verses 15-18 presume the substance of the first part of the chapter but turn to the future with announcements of judgment followed by announcements of salvation. Even with those two distinct parts and editorial additions, the chapter follows a plot of sorts, a story line. The point of departure is mourning over the metaphorical death of the Phoenician cities, to a period when they are forgotten, to their revival as trading centers, con-

cluding finally with their devotion of their gains to the service of the Lord.

It would assist our understanding of this chapter to know who wrote it and when, but unfortunately that is not possible. Virtually all interpreters agree that it did not originate in the eighth century BCE at the hands of Isaiah of Jerusalem. Moreover, the chapter would have developed over several centuries, with the first part (vv. 1-14) earlier than the second (vv. 15-18). Some interpreters conclude that most of the material was composed as early as the late seventh century, in the time of King Josiah, and that it is even based on traditions that go back to Isaiah's response to Phoenicia's capitulation to Sennacherib in 701.[194] But other events concerning Phoenicia are equally likely as occasions for the calls to mourn, including 681 and 678 BCE.[195] The final form, including the addition of v. 13 to the first section with its reference that looks to a new age, is no earlier than the time of the Babylonian exile, and perhaps even later.

Most important for interpretation of the text would be knowing the circumstances of those who wrote it, not the date of the events it refers to. Clearly the Phoenician cities experienced devastating attacks, if not total destruction. This text alone shows that the reaction among Israelites over the centuries was diverse, from mocking calls to mourn that in effect celebrated the fall of the powerful, to the hope that one day even the Phoenicians would use their seafaring and trading talents in service of the Lord (v. 18).

23:1-14. This proclamation is unusual among the oracles concerning the foreign nations in that it does not look to future judgment but in effect celebrates disaster that has already fallen upon a great power. The passage celebrates the disaster by

194. Marvin A. Sweeney, *Isaiah 1–39, with an Introduction to Prophetic Literature,* FOTL XVI (Grand Rapids: Eerdmans, 1996) 306-7.
195. See Ronald E. Clements, *Isaiah 1–39,* NCB (Grand Rapids: Eerdmans, 1980) 191.

calling for a communal lament or mourning over Tyre. But the disaster is even more widespread. In the final form of the unit, if not necessarily in its earliest stage, the lamentation includes not only Tyre but other cities as well. By mentioning Sidon (v. 4), the address means to encompass Phoenicia as a whole.[196]

Formally, this section is a general summons to communal mourning over the destruction of the Phoenician cities. It is organized as a series of six calls or commands (vv. 1*b*, 2, 4, 6, 10, and 14) that echo the sad note of grief throughout the poem, which is framed at the beginning and the end with the same summons to wail shouted to the "ships of Tarshish."[197] These imperatives to the cities and their people are addressed to Tyre, to Sidon, to the "inhabitants of the coast" (v. 6), and to the ships returning from Tarshish, but only formally. The intended audience would have been Judeans. The tone is not exactly what one expects in a genuine summons to mourn. There is irony, if not sarcasm, in the way that the powerful traders, masters of the Mediterranean coasts, are called to mourn the destruction of their cities.

Although there have been efforts to read these verses as an announcement or prophecy of future events, clearly they presume that Tyre and Sidon have been destroyed.[198] The point of the poem is to account for that disaster, to show how and why the mighty have fallen. The author leaves no doubt that the Lord ordained the devastation of Phoenicia and that the purpose of the Lord was to "defile the pride of all glory, to shame all the honored of the earth" (v. 9).

In the process of establishing that point, the poet gives Phoenicia its due. The cities on the coast north of Israel indeed ruled the waves, "crossed over the sea . . . on the mighty waters" (vv. 2-3), to the far reaches of the Mediterranean, even to Tarshish. Although the precise location of Tarshish is not settled, it was at the opposite end of the sea, probably on the southern coast of Spain, and thus had become a symbol for the end of the

earth (Jonah 1:3). Ships from the Phoenician seaport cities of Tyre and Sidon carried and traded goods among all the major seaports of the ancient Mediterranean world. Thus their rule of the seas was commercial rather than military ("merchant to the nations," v. 3), although they did establish trading colonies on the northern coast of Africa as early as the ninth century BCE. The most famous and powerful of these cities was Carthage, which became a military force in its own right in subsequent centuries.

This poem expresses a certain respect, if not awe, for the Phoenicians' mastery of the waves. Given Israel's proximity to the ocean, there is remarkably little orientation to the sea in the OT.

The motif of the summons to communal mourning that defines this section is shaped by ritual, if not by liturgical patterns. It is as if a leader or messenger is addressing people to call a service to order and to set its tone. The occasion for the lament is death, as in the death of Saul and Jonathan (2 Sam 1:17-27), or in this case the death of the Phoenician cities and their inhabitants. As in the lament over the death of an individual, the present state of wretchedness is contrasted with past glory. The wailing or weeping is not addressed in prayer to God, as in complaint songs asking for relief from trouble. The call to God, even over the destruction of Jerusalem in Lam 2:18-21, sad as it is, presumes the possibility of renewal in some form. Missing in this section is the authentic tone of mourning or any genuine regret that the Phoenician cities and their citizens have suffered.

Most of the calls to mourn follow the imperative with the reasons for mourning or wailing, as in v. 1. Those reasons express and reiterate the end of Tyre and Sidon. Verses 1-3 ask the "ships of Tarshish" to wail because their fortress has been destroyed. These would have been Phoenician ships returning home from a distant journey to the other end of the Mediterranean. Then the citizens of the coast are instructed to be quiet, recalling how in the past they had been "the merchant of the nations" (v. 3). In vv. 4-5, Sidon is to be ashamed. The reason for shame is enigmatic: "The sea . . . the fortress of the sea" has spoken mysteriously that it has not given birth. Verses 5-7 refer to the report of destruction arriving in Egypt, call again for wailing, and then pose a rhetorical and ironic question about the "exultant city," suggest-

196. Most recent commentators concur in this decision, but Kaiser argues that the passage originally concerned Sidon and was supplemented by material concerning Tyre.

197. Sweeney, *Isaiah 1–39,* 304. Sweeney identifies the section as a call to communal complaint, but that is somewhat misleading. The Phoenicians are not called to complain about their fate but to mourn it.

198. So most modern commentators, e.g., Wildberger, *Isaiah 13–27,* 413; Clements, *Isaiah 1–39,* 192.

ing a mocking contrast between its past and present states.

Having now set the stage, the poet turns to the central issue: the theological explanation for the downfall of the Phoenician cities (vv. 8-12). The poet poses a question (v. 8) in order to answer it (vv. 9-12). Yahweh "planned" the destruction of Tyre and Sidon in order to "defile the pride of all glory, to shame all the honored of the earth" (v. 9). This "plan" was not what theologians would call predestination. To the contrary, it is the divine response to human behavior and attitudes. This is not the only reference to the Lord's plan in Isaiah 1–39 (see 5:19; 14:24, 26-27; 19:12, 17; 25:1; 30:1; 37:27). The plan here extends far beyond the Phoenicians. The Lord plans to judge "all the honored of the earth." Finally, in the Lord's direct address to Sidon (v. 12), concern turns to the future. It is not, however, a prophetic announcement of a future judgment. Rather, looking beyond the devastation, it promises that Sidon will find no rest, even if its populace should migrate to Cyprus.

Verse 13, which seems to continue the citation of the Lord's address, is a secondary addition, a reinterpretation of the preceding lament over Tyre. It is as if an early interpreter added a note or gloss in the margin that subsequently was included in the text as such. The author of these lines presumed that the proclamation was taken to refer to an Assyrian destruction of Tyre and Sidon, and he means to correct that interpretation. He insists that the Phoenicians were destroyed by the Babylonians ("Chaldeans"). The author of the verse may have been attempting to bring this chapter into line with the proclamation concerning Tyre and Sidon in Ezekiel 27–28, which

relates to the Babylonian era. The section ends as it had begun, with the call for the ships of Tarshish to mourn over the destruction of their fortress (v. 14).

23:15-18. These verses are secondary to the previous part of the chapter, probably having been added in two stages (vv. 15-16 and vv. 17-18). These lines presume the circumstances of the pronouncement over Tyre and Sidon but now turn to a future beyond the destruction of those Phoenician cities. Verses 15-16 announce that Tyre will be forgotten for seventy sad years. In Jer 25:11-12, seventy years is given as the length of the Babylonian exile. The city is personified as a prostitute singing a poignant song so that she will be remembered.

The last two verses announce what will happen at the end of those seventy years. First, as a result of the Lord's intervention ("will visit"), Tyre will resume its trading practices, presumably throughout the Mediterranean coasts. The metaphor of the prostitute is taken up, but differently from vv. 15-16. Prostitution itself is a business, the sale of sexual services, but here it becomes a metaphor for business or trade itself. Precisely how Tyre will "prostitute herself" through trade is unclear, but the comparison is pejorative if not contemptuous. Remarkably, the final verse promises a reversal of both the character and the circumstances of Tyre. The wages of that prostitution, the profits of trade, will be devoted to the Lord, providing "abundant food and fine clothing for those who live in the presence of the LORD" (v. 18)—that is, providing for the priests and for the maintenance of the Temple.

REFLECTIONS

1. The central assertion of this chapter, that the Lord has planned the fall of powerful cities, calls for serious reflection. In fact, although the explicit language of God's plan does not appear on every page of Scripture or in every paragraph of theology, one could argue that this is the central concern of all theology and all Scripture. What does God intend for the world and its people? Few who believe in God doubt that God has a plan or plans concerning the world, history, nations, and individuals. To discern the plan or plans, however, is a different matter.

The author of Isaiah 23, looking back on particular events, is convinced that they had taken place because the Lord planned them. Although the interpretation of God's designs and ways with the world in history reflect more than one perspective in the Old Testament, two points seem consistent. First, for the most part, concern focuses on nations and peoples more than on particular individuals. When individuals are in view, most of them are kings or other leaders whose fate is tied directly to that of nations. Second, in no case should reference to the plan of God be taken to refer to what theologians call predestination. That is, in the biblical understanding, the events of history have not been set out from the beginning. Rather, history in the Old Testament is understood to be the result of the interaction of divine and human purposes and acts. The Lord wanted the people of Israel to live forever in the land promised to their ancestors, but because of their unfaithfulness the land was taken from them and they were sent into exile. Fundamentally because of the independence granted to human beings, even God does not know what the future may bring. To be sure, in reaction to human actions, the Lord plans a response. When the Lord sent Jonah to proclaim to Nineveh that the city would be destroyed, that was the divine plan. But when the king and all the people repented, the Lord also "repented" ("changed his mind," Jonah 3:10 NRSV) and withdrew the decision for destruction.

The various additions to the earlier text in this chapter show that readers continued to meditate on God's plan for the arrogant, the prideful. First, God was seen to have planned judgment "to defile the pride of all glory" (23:9). But the story does not end there. There is a period of seventy years when the Phoenician cities are forgotten (23:15-16). Finally, the divine plan includes more than destruction, more than shaming the proud. That goal is taken to be transformation from accumulation of wealth to the service of the Lord. To be sure, one could argue that this service is understood narrowly, from the point of view of priests in the Temple. But it is service of the Lord, nonetheless. So nations, whether they know it or not, have roles to play in God's design for the world. Moreover, the fact that generation after generation continued to reflect on God's plan for a proud people encourages us to continually engage such questions.

Confidence that God has plans enables us to make sense of the world and of history, and it can engender hope. In another context that also refers to seventy years, in this case the seventy years of the Babylonian exile, the word of the Lord from Jeremiah is explicit on this point: "For surely I know the plans I have for you, says the Lord, plans for your welfare and not for harm, to give you a future with hope" (Jer 29:11).

On the other hand, ideas about God's plan can be dangerous and harmful. Particularly when coupled with a biblical theology of retribution and applied to individual lives, such beliefs can lead to a great deal of suffering, especially to unwarranted guilt. It is not uncommon in contemporary life to hear those who are suffering ask what they have done to deserve it, or for one who has experienced loss to say that the particular death must be part of God's plan. It may be helpful to remember that in the Old Testament God's plans, and especially acts of judgment against sin, are corporate rather than individualistic. More important, reflection on God's plan is best viewed in a broad biblical context. While Deuteronomy tends to link blessings with obedience and curses with disloyalty to God, other traditions are not so clear. The book of Job is an explicit challenge to the idea that human suffering is directly linked to the depth of an individual's piety. Moreover, both the Old and the New Testaments affirm that God's plan ultimately is salvific.

2. What are the citizens of nations that are "the honored of the earth" (23:8-9) to make of this divine judgment against such peoples? Condemnation of pride and of proud peoples is a familiar theme both in the proclamations concerning foreign nations and in the biblical tradition as a whole. In this instance, there is no expression of divine preference for the poor, the weak, or the oppressed; nor is there even a suggestion that the Phoenician cities are suffering because they had been the oppressors.

Theologically, pride and power carry with them the risk that the power of God will go unrecognized or unacknowledged. That is the theme in Isaiah 14, where the king of Babylon is accused of placing himself among the gods: "I will raise my throne above the stars of God" (14:13). And it is the theme of Isa 10:15-19, where Assyria as the rod of the Lord's anger has magnified "itself against the one who handles it." It is not just that pride goes before a fall, but that power generates a false sense of self-sufficiency.

In the biblical texts, powerful peoples generally are viewed from the perspective of the politically vulnerable. Israel and Judah, through most of their history, had to live under the threat of powerful nations and empires. So one thing that citizens of mighty nations and empires could learn from such texts is how better to view themselves as the rest of the world sees them.

3. The descriptions of the Phoenicians as sailors and traders can evoke consideration of the attitudes toward various occupations and professions. On the one hand, the Phoenicians' mastery of the sea and their success as traders seems to be highly regarded. Their "merchants were princes" (23:8) who traveled where few others could. Even this praise, however, has an edge, for the honored have been shamed. On the other hand, the characterization of trade as prostitution (23:16-17) hardly conceals the author's contempt. The author would likely have been a scribe close to, if not part of, the priesthood, and he would have lived in an agricultural environment. His attitude can serve as a reminder that occupations and professions may be held in greater or lesser esteem by the public and that resentment and jealousy frequently rear their heads when members of one profession consider another. This story is as old as that of Cain and Abel, which reflects the tensions between the farmer and the herdsman.

Such contempt for occupations other than one's own may come from envy, prejudice, ignorance, or even familiarity. The final verse of the chapter acknowledges that even a "comtemptible" occupation could serve God, encouraging us to reflect on our attitudes toward other professions and to consider the definition of honorable work.

ISAIAH 24:1–27:13

THE ISAIAH "APOCALYPSE"

OVERVIEW

These four chapters constitute a discrete body of material within the book of Isaiah in terms of both form and content. It is clear that the proclamations concerning the foreign nations, with each marked by its heading, concluded with chap. 23. Equally clear is that a new body of prophetic speeches begins in chap. 28. So this section is framed by two other collections of prophetic literature. Early in the history of critical biblical scholarship, scholars recognized the distinctiveness of these chapters, calling the section "The Isaiah Apocalypse." This designation became common in the late nineteenth century, and, in spite of serious reservations, the heading has persisted.[199]

This characterization of the section is based on the observation that it contains certain features typical of apocalyptic literature and that it is quite different from the prophetic speeches of Isaiah. First, the judgment foreseen from the beginning is unlike that in the proclamations concerning the nations in chaps. 14–23. The announcements in chaps. 24–27 encompass the whole earth and all who live in it. Moreover, it appears to proclaim the final drama of history rather than a startling and significant turning point for particular peoples; that is, its ideas are eschatological, dealing with the last things. Furthermore, specific motifs or ideas appear that are generally found in apocalyptic literature, including the resurrection of the dead (26:19), divine judgment on the angels ("heavenly host," 24:21-22) and their imprisonment, the trumpet of the Lord calling for the elect (27:13), an eschatological banquet of the nations on Mt. Zion

(25:6-8), the Lord's defeat of Leviathan (27:1), the darkening of the sun and moon (24:23), and others.[200]

However, the presence of certain ideas and motifs does not justify identifying Isaiah 24–27 as an apocalypse. Reading this section of Isaiah provides the occasion to consider how prophetic and apocalyptic literature are similar and different. Many who continue to identify this block of literature as an apocalypse tend to use a loose definition of apocalypse, such as the following: "Isa. 24–27 contains a significant apocalypse, by which term is meant revelation, disclosure."[201] That is true enough, and it is based on the use of the term for a distinct apocalypse in the Bible, the Revelation (from the Greek for "apocalypse") of John. Prophecy and apocalypse both concern the future as revealed by God, but they are very different in the way this is understood and described. What is missing from this text are the fundamental marks of the genre of apocalypse, the detailed revelation of the future, usually set out in a series of eras, to a visionary through a dream or vision. Moreover, although there are dramatic and even mythological elements in these chapters, they lack the bizarre and otherworldly characteristics of the vision reports in Daniel and Revelation. The esoteric or secret character of the revelation in an apocalypse, that the future is a mystery revealed

199. For an extensive account of the various interpretations of the history of the composition of these chapters, see William R. Millar, *Isaiah 24–27 and the Origin of the Apocalyptic,* HSM 11 (Missoula: Scholars Press, 1976) 1-22; H. Wildberger, *Isaiah 13–27* (Minneapolis: Fortress, 1997) 447-51.

200. D. S. Russell, *The Method and Message of Jewish Apocalyptic* (Philadelphia: Westminster, 1964) 91. See also Marvin A. Sweeney, *Isaiah 1–39, With an Introduction to Prophetic Literature,* FOTL XVI (Grand Rapids: Eerdmans, 1996) 313 and the literature cited there. On the apocalyptic genre, see John J. Collins, *The Apocalyptic Imagination: An Introduction to Jewish Apocalyptic Literature* (Grand Rapids: Eerdmans, 1998) 1-42. Concerning the social location of apocalypticism and its relationship to prophecy, see Stephen L. Cook, *Prophecy and Apocalypticism: The Postexilic Social Setting* (Minneapolis: Fortress, 1995).

201. Elmer A. Leslie, *Isaiah, Chronologically arranged, translated and interpreted* (New York: Abingdon, 1963) 261.

only to the elect so they will know how to behave in the last days, is also missing.

It is useful to distinguish between an apocalypse, apocalyptic eschatology, and apocalyptic themes or ideas.[202] An apocalypse is a particular literary genre, found full-blown in the Bible only in the book of Revelation and in Daniel 7–12. It flourished from the second century BCE into the early Christian centuries. Apocalyptic eschatology, the defining religious perspective in an apocalypse but also found in many other genres, is the view that history, typically understood as a distinct series of eras from the beginning until the end, is quickly moving to its resolution, when God will judge the wicked and establish God's reign. Prophetic announcements, on the other hand, expect God to act within history but not bring it to a close. Apocalyptic motifs and ideas are those associated with apocalyptic eschatology, such as the ones noted above. Thus in some respects the material in Isaiah 24–27 has moved in the direction of apocalyptic, but neither in terms of theological content nor formal literary features is this section an apocalypse. Both its style and its ideas are closer to those of prophetic literature. The mode of revelation, with frequent references to what the Lord announces for the future, continues the prophetic tradition, and a form of the prophetic word formula appears in 24:3. The section is best identified as a collection of eschatological prophecies. To be sure, these announcements of the future judgment and the reign of the Lord provided grist for the mill of apocalyptic eschatology.

Some scholars have interpreted these chapters as a single, coherent composition, often as a prophetic liturgy.[203] But, as most commentators have recognized, these chapters are by no means a single or unified work. Rather, the section includes a great variety of material from different times and places. There are diverse genres, including announcements of judgment (24:1-13, 17-20; 25:10b-12; 27:1), announcements of salvation (24:21-23; 25:6-10a; 27:2-6, 12-13), hymns of praise (25:1-5; cf. 24:14-16), a victory song (26:1-6), and a complaint song or prayer (26:7-19). Sweeney argues that some of these materials have been constructed as disputation speeches (24:14-23; 27:7-13).[204]

But if the chapters are not a singular composition by one author, neither is the collection of materials entirely haphazard. The consistent eschatological and universal focus holds the individual units together. The dominant genres are announcements of the future and liturgical songs. Moreover, there is some thematic development, moving from the punishment of the earth (chap. 24) to the announcement of blessings for the earth and especially for Israel.[205] Within that broad structure, the individual chapters may be viewed as sections, each including several distinct parts and some thematic development. Isaiah 24 moves from announcement of judgment on the earth and all its inhabitants to the reign of the Lord on Mt. Zion, heralding the pattern of the section as a whole. In chapter 25, praise and celebration dominate, but it ends with pronouncement of judgment on Moab (25:10b-12). Chapter 26 begins with the promise that a song of victory will be sung in Judah, moves to prayer, and concludes with a call for the people of God to hide until the Lord finishes punishing the people of the earth. After a single verse announcing that the Lord will kill the dragon of chaos (27:1), chap. 27 announces salvation for Israel and promises that all nations will be gathered on the holy mountain in Jerusalem.

For more than a century, scholars have been all but unanimous in agreeing that these chapters did not originate with Isaiah of Jerusalem in the eighth century BCE. Most have concluded that they are among the latest parts of the book of Isaiah. Dates for the material range as late as the second century BCE. Unfortunately, there are no concrete historical allusions that would confirm a specific date.[206] The promise of restoration in 27:2-11 seems to presume the Babylonian exile, but if that is the case, it only means that the passage was composed after 587 BCE. The possible allusions to historical events are so clothed in eschatological poetry as to be unidentifiable. A case in point is the destruction of "the city of chaos" (24:10-12). This

202. Paul D. Hanson, *The Dawn of Apocalyptic* (Philadelphia: Fortress, 1975) 1-31; and Paul D. Hanson, *Old Testament Apocalyptic* (Nashville: Abingdon, 1987) 25-43.

203. G. Fohrer, "Der Aufbau der Apokalypse des Jesajabuches (Jes 24–27)," *CBQ* 25 (1963) 34-35. Also arguing for the unity of the section is P. L. Redditt, "Isaiah 24–27: A Form-Critical Analysis" (Ph.D. diss., Vanderbilt University, 1972). Likewise, Sweeney, *Isaiah 1–39*, 316-17, sees here "a high degree of coherence and unity of purpose" in this section.

204. Sweeney, *Isaiah 1–39*, 314.

205. Ibid., 311-13.

206. See ibid., 316.

could refer, as some have argued, to the destruction of Babylon by Alexander the Great in 311 BCE. However, it is by no means certain that this city is Babylon. It could just as well be any or every city, and a symbol for the powers of evil on the earth.

Given the diversity of the material in these chapters, it is highly unlikely that all the units come from the same time. The history of ideas and of the development of biblical literature, however, supports the general conclusion that this section is no earlier than the fifth century BCE. Moreover,

there is good evidence that the collection as a whole was inserted into its present location at a relatively late stage in the development of the book of Isaiah. These chapters provide an appropriate extension of the proclamations concerning the nations in Isaiah 14–23. Moreover, they contain numerous citations from earlier parts of the book of Isaiah.[207]

207. Marvin A. Sweeney, "Textual Citations in Isaiah 24–27," *JBL* 107 (1988) 39-52.

ISAIAH 24:1-23, THE LORD'S JUDGMENT ON THE EARTH

NIV

24 See, the LORD is going to lay waste the earth
and devastate it;
he will ruin its face
and scatter its inhabitants—
²it will be the same
for priest as for people,
for master as for servant,
for mistress as for maid,
for seller as for buyer,
for borrower as for lender,
for debtor as for creditor.
³The earth will be completely laid waste
and totally plundered.
The LORD has spoken this word.

⁴The earth dries up and withers,
the world languishes and withers,
the exalted of the earth languish.
⁵The earth is defiled by its people;
they have disobeyed the laws,
violated the statutes
and broken the everlasting covenant.
⁶Therefore a curse consumes the earth;
its people must bear their guilt.
Therefore earth's inhabitants are burned up,
and very few are left.
⁷The new wine dries up and the vine withers;
all the merrymakers groan.
⁸The gaiety of the tambourines is stilled,

NRSV

24 Now the LORD is about to lay waste the earth and make it desolate,
and he will twist its surface and scatter its inhabitants.
² And it shall be, as with the people, so with the priest;
as with the slave, so with his master;
as with the maid, so with her mistress;
as with the buyer, so with the seller;
as with the lender, so with the borrower;
as with the creditor, so with the debtor.
³ The earth shall be utterly laid waste and utterly despoiled;
for the LORD has spoken this word.

⁴ The earth dries up and withers,
the world languishes and withers;
the heavens languish together with the earth.
⁵ The earth lies polluted
under its inhabitants;
for they have transgressed laws,
violated the statutes,
broken the everlasting covenant.
⁶ Therefore a curse devours the earth,
and its inhabitants suffer for their guilt;
therefore the inhabitants of the earth dwindled,
and few people are left.
⁷ The wine dries up,

NIV

the noise of the revelers has stopped,
the joyful harp is silent.
⁹No longer do they drink wine with a song;
the beer is bitter to its drinkers.
¹⁰The ruined city lies desolate;
the entrance to every house is barred.
¹¹In the streets they cry out for wine;
all joy turns to gloom,
all gaiety is banished from the earth.
¹²The city is left in ruins,
its gate is battered to pieces.
¹³So will it be on the earth
and among the nations,
as when an olive tree is beaten,
or as when gleanings are left after the
grape harvest.

¹⁴They raise their voices, they shout for joy;
from the west they acclaim the LORD's
majesty.
¹⁵Therefore in the east give glory to the LORD;
exalt the name of the LORD, the God
of Israel,
in the islands of the sea.
¹⁶From the ends of the earth we hear singing:
"Glory to the Righteous One."

But I said, "I waste away, I waste away!
Woe to me!
The treacherous betray!
With treachery the treacherous betray!"
¹⁷Terror and pit and snare await you,
O people of the earth.
¹⁸Whoever flees at the sound of terror
will fall into a pit;
whoever climbs out of the pit
will be caught in a snare.

The floodgates of the heavens are opened,
the foundations of the earth shake.
¹⁹The earth is broken up,
the earth is split asunder,
the earth is thoroughly shaken.
²⁰The earth reels like a drunkard,
it sways like a hut in the wind;
so heavy upon it is the guilt of its rebellion
that it falls—never to rise again.

²¹In that day the LORD will punish
the powers in the heavens above

NRSV

the vine languishes,
all the merry-hearted sigh.
⁸ The mirth of the timbrels is stilled,
the noise of the jubilant has ceased,
the mirth of the lyre is stilled.
⁹ No longer do they drink wine with singing;
strong drink is bitter to those who drink it.
¹⁰ The city of chaos is broken down,
every house is shut up so that no one
can enter.
¹¹ There is an outcry in the streets for lack
of wine;
all joy has reached its eventide;
the gladness of the earth is banished.
¹² Desolation is left in the city,
the gates are battered into ruins.
¹³ For thus it shall be on the earth
and among the nations,
as when an olive tree is beaten,
as at the gleaning when the grape harvest
is ended.

¹⁴ They lift up their voices, they sing for joy;
they shout from the west over the majesty
of the LORD.
¹⁵ Therefore in the east give glory to the LORD;
in the coastlands of the sea glorify the
name of the LORD, the God of Israel.
¹⁶ From the ends of the earth we hear songs
of praise,
of glory to the Righteous One.
But I say, I pine away,
I pine away. Woe is me!
For the treacherous deal treacherously,
the treacherous deal very treacherously.

¹⁷ Terror, and the pit, and the snare
are upon you, O inhabitant of the earth!
¹⁸ Whoever flees at the sound of the terror
shall fall into the pit;
and whoever climbs out of the pit
shall be caught in the snare.
For the windows of heaven are opened,
and the foundations of the earth tremble.
¹⁹ The earth is utterly broken,
the earth is torn asunder,
the earth is violently shaken.
²⁰ The earth staggers like a drunkard,

NIV

and the kings on the earth below.
²²They will be herded together
    like prisoners bound in a dungeon;
they will be shut up in prison
    and be punished*a* after many days.
²³The moon will be abashed, the sun ashamed;
    for the LORD Almighty will reign
on Mount Zion and in Jerusalem,
    and before its elders, gloriously.

a22 Or *released*

NRSV

it sways like a hut;
its transgression lies heavy upon it,
    and it falls, and will not rise again.

²¹ On that day the LORD will punish
    the host of heaven in heaven,
    and on earth the kings of the earth.
²² They will be gathered together
    like prisoners in a pit;
they will be shut up in a prison,
    and after many days they will be punished.
²³ Then the moon will be abashed,
    and the sun ashamed;
for the LORD of hosts will reign
    on Mount Zion and in Jerusalem,
and before his elders he will manifest
    his glory.

COMMENTARY

The central theme of this chapter is the announcement of the day of the Lord, when God will lay waste to the earth and the Lord's reign will be established on Mt. Zion. The poetic imagery is vivid and compelling, difficult to reduce to prose. In spite of references to a particular but unnamed city (v. 10), the promised judgment is virtually universal, shaking the whole earth and leaving only Mt. Zion in Jerusalem. In fact, this day of judgment goes even beyond the earth, encompassing the heavenly host along with the kings of the earth (v. 21). No schedule for the cataclysm is given, but the eschatological prophet believes it to be imminent, just over the horizon.

In at least one section of the chapter, reasons for this judgment are presented, as is typical in earlier prophetic announcements. The Lord plans to judge the earth because its inhabitants have polluted it by violation of laws and statues, breaking "the everlasting covenant" (v. 5). There is also the contrast between the two cities, the city of chaos and Jerusalem, but this is not presented as a contrast between good and evil, so that evil must be wiped out. On the other hand, the chapter's conclusion indicates that the goal of the destruction of the earth is the reign of the Lord and the manifestation of the Lord's glory (v. 23). This glory will be

recognized and praised throughout the earth (vv. 14-16).

The organization and composition of this chapter may be understood in different ways. On the one hand, in terms of contents, the initial (vv. 1-6) and concluding (vv. 18*b*-23) sections form a coherent announcement of the Lord's impending intervention against all creation. The middle parts (vv. 7-18*a*), which may very well be secondary additions, elaborate on the central announcement. On the other hand, the shifts of tense and literary genre show the composition differently. Verses 1-3 announce the future and then vv. 4-13 describe chaos and destruction in the present tense, concluding with the announcement that this is the way it will be in the future (v. 13). Verses 14-16 begin by reporting songs of praise but conclude with a first-person song of woe. Verses 17-20 mix present and future, describing the staggering and stumbling of the earth iself. The concluding verses (21-23) return to the future tense, announcing cosmic punishment followed by the reign of the Lord on Mt. Zion.

24:1-3. The opening lines of the chapter sound the note for the Isaiah apocalypse as a whole, chaps. 24–27. The Lord is about to bring devastation upon the earth. It is possible but not certain that the twisting of the surface of the earth alludes to a massive earthquake, but even if that is the case, the reader should not confuse what the future holds with a natural phenomenon. The purpose of this divine intervention is to "scatter" all people, and v. 2 explains in painful detail that the disaster will affect all the earth's inhabitants. The list of classes or categories of people is a series of opposites, first contrasting the high with the low: "people" (that is, ordinary people, "layman" in TNK) and priest, slave and master, maid and mistress. The final contrasts are economic roles: buyer and seller, lender and borrower, creditor and debtors. The effect is to include everyone. Then the initial announcement of destruction is restated passively, "the earth shall be utterly laid waste," but a concluding prophetic formula makes it clear that the Lord is the one who will act.

24:4-13. Except for the concluding verse, this section gives a description of the present, what is happening to the earth and its people. One could argue that this is, in fact, a vision of the future in which the prophetic poet sees coming events as if they were present, but this seems unlikely. The present disaster described here is the beginning of the end. Again, the initial description focuses on the earth, this time with the imagery of drought that closely parallels the earlier announcement concerning the land in Hos 4:3.

Also as in Hos 4:1-3, the earth suffers because of human sin, as commonly understood in the Hebrew Bible. Thus what follows in vv. 5-6 is the most explicit explanation for the coming trouble in the entire section (chaps. 24–27). The earth withers because it has been "polluted" by its inhabitants. Three sources of the pollution are listed, but they are actually one. The first two, transgression of laws and violation of statutes, parallel one another, and amount to the third, breaking "the everlasting covenant" (v. 5). Which covenant does the author have in view? The obvious answer is the covenant with Noah (Gen 9:1-17), since it is called "an everlasting covenant," and extends to all people and creatures of the earth.[208] On the other hand, the reference to laws and statutes leaves open the possibility that this is the Sinai

covenant (Exod 19–Num 9). In this context, and somewhat in tension with vv. 1-3, the disaster comes not from divine intervention against the people and the earth, but from the "curse" that has its effects, polluting and devastating all creation. "Guilt" need not be punished because it sets terrible effects into motion. So NIV reads "its people must bear their guilt" (v. 6), that is, they have set the tragedy into motion.[209] The pollution of the earth (v. 5) through human disobedience is a fundamentally priestly or ritual understanding, related to the distinction between clean and unclean (cf. Deut 21:1-9). In Num 35:33 the people are commanded not to pollute the land with blood or by incurring blood guilt, and in Jer 3:2, 9 the land is polluted through adultery and false worship or unfaithfulness to the Lord. Whereas those texts refer to the pollution of the land of Israel, chap. 24 concerns the pollution of the whole earth.

When the earth dries up, so does the vine that produces wine (v. 7), and without wine, mirth and music will disappear (vv. 6-9). Joy evaporates as the earth dries up. It is worth noting that the prophetic poet obviously considers festivities with wine and music to be good things that are lost as the earth withers, but there may be as well the implication that those who were frivolous brought trouble upon themselves (cf. 5:11-13, 22-24).

Verses 10-12 continue the theme of joylessness in the description of the city of chaos. The "broken down" (v. 10) city whose gates are in "ruins" (v. 12) may be one that has suffered a military attack, but it could just as well be one that has decayed along with the earth, its gates fallen off their hinges. The dominant image is that of people shut up in their houses, and the banishment of gladness (v. 11). The city is identified only by the appellation "of chaos" (תהו, *tōhû*), which in Gen 1:2 refers to the state of the world before creation. Wildberger translates the phrase, "the nothing city."[210] But the more likely reference here is to the wilderness as in Deut 32:10, that is, to a city that has reverted to the uncivilized, uncultivated state. The fact that the city is unnamed has opened

208. So O. Kaiser, *Isaiah 13–39: A Commentary* (Philadelphia: Westminster, 1974) 183. But see also Donald C. Polaski, "Reflections on a Mosaic Covenant: The Eternal Covenant (Isaiah 24.5) and Intertextuality," *JSOT* 77 (1998) 55-73.

209. On this understanding of the relationship between sin and its effects, see the Reflections at 1:2-20. See also Gene M. Tucker, "Sin and 'Judgment' in the Prophets," in *Problems in Biblical Theology: Essays in Honor of Rolk Knierim,* ed. Henry T. C. Sun et al. (Grand Rapids: Eerdmans, 1997) 373-88.

210. H. Wildberger, *Isaiah 13–27* (Minneapolis: Fortress, 1997) 469.

the door for speculation about its identity. In another context, such as Isaiah 3, where a prophet is passing judgment on his own people, this could be Jerusalem. But since Jerusalem in Isaiah 24 is the center of the reign of Yahweh, some interpreters have taken the city of chaos to be Babylon.[211] More likely, however, this description applies to any and all cities when the end comes. That certainly is the point of v. 13, which announces the sad future for all nations.

24:14-16. Suddenly in v. 14 the mood shifts from despondency to joy with a third-person report of songs of praise. The reporter hears voice from the west praising the majesty of the Lord, and from the east and the coastlands of the sea, songs glorifying the name of the Lord. The chorus of hymns comes from the very ends of the earth, the same earth that is to be laid waste by the Lord (vv. 1-3). These songs of praise celebrate the reign of Yahweh, announced in v. 23, but they come from all the world, not just from the people of God. Thus these songs function as doxologies of judgment, sung even by the condemned as they acknowledge God's justice.[212] The story of Achan in Joshua 7 provides a clear example of this pattern in OT thought and practice. Achan had violated the ban by taking from Jericho booty that was devoted to the Lord, thus causing the Israelites to suffer a defeat in their next battle. When Joshua identified him as the guilty party, he said, "My son, give glory to the LORD God of Israel and make confession to him." The sinner is expected to confess his or her sin and to praise ("give glory to") God. For later readers of the book of Amos, who had experienced the exile as judgment, the prophet's announcements of judgment could function as confession, and a series of three doxologies in the book expressed praise.[213]

However, joyous praise is not the last word in this account of responses to the coming of the reign of God. In v. 16b singing continues, but both mood and voice shift, from corporate songs of praise to an individual's song of lament, similar to those in the psalter. A solitary voice utters cries of woe, in agony because "the treacherous deal treacherously." The triumph of the Lord has not yet come. The dark imagery and grim tones of the lament provide a transition to the announcement that follows. Thus some translations and commentators treat the lament as the introduction to the next section.

24:17-20. The chapter's initial and central theme of cosmic disaster resumes with the announcement of the destruction of the earth's inhabitants (vv. 17-18a) and the shattering of the earth itself (vv. 18b-20). In Hebrew, the threat is forcefully set out with assonance: Each of the words translated "terror," "pit," and "snare" begin with the same letter and sound very similar. Identical language appears in Jer 48:43-44, and the imagery of the impossibility of escaping the wrath of the Lord even in hell appears in Amos 9:1-4 (cf. Amos 5:18-19). "The pit" here is the same as sheol, the underworld where the shades of the dead go, eventually to fade away. There is no escape from the day of judgment, not even in hell.

The description of the catalysm visited upon the earth is rich in the language and imagery of the priestly account of creation and the flood, indicating that creation is about to be reversed. God had fashioned a dome over the earth to hold back the waters above (Gen 1:6-9), and in the time of Noah opened those "windows of the heavens" (Gen 7:11; 8:2) to destroy all life except what was in the ark. Throughout the OT, as well as in the ancient Near East generally, it was believed that the created world, the flat earth with the dome of the heavens, was surrounded by the primeval waters. So the text suggests but does not describe a universal flood, in stark contrast to the desolation of vv. 4-10, caused by drought. The prophetic poets responsible for this chapter draw upon every possible natural disaster to portray the coming catastrophe. Thus instead of mentioning along with the windows of the heavens the "fountains of the great deep" (Gen 7:11; 8:2), as one would expect, the visionary turns to the trembling of "the foundations of the earth" (v. 18). The breaking, tearing, shaking, and staggering of the earth (vv. 19-20) uses the imagery of the earthquake, but this is no ordinary earthquake. It will strike the whole earth with violence beyond measure.

24:21-23. The announcement of disaster "on that day" expands beyond the earth and its inhabitants to include "the host of heaven" and the

---

211. Marvin A. Sweeney, *Isaiah 1–39, With an Introduction to Prophetic Literature,* FOTL XVI (Grand Rapids: Eerdmans, 1996) 318-19, 331. For a discussion of the main alternatives, see Miller, *Isaiah 24–27 and the Origin of Apocalyptic,* 15-22.

212. Cf. Ronald E. Clements, *Isaiah 1–39,* NCB (Grand Rapids: Eerdmans, 1980) 203.

213. F. Horst, "Die Doxologien im Amobuch," reprinted in *Gottes Recht* (München: Kaiser, 1961) 155-66.

heavenly bodies (vv. 21-23a), and then states the goal of the judgment of the earth, namely, the reign of the Lord on Mt. Zion (v. 23b). So if there is an end there is also a new beginning. The Lord will establish a reign, and will put an end to all powers, both cosmic and earthly, that could stand in opposition to the Lord's authority. The "host of heaven" as well as the moon and sun, are, to be sure, the bodies one can see in the sky. Yet in the cultural and religious context of the Bible, they were viewed as divinities, which Israel was forbidden to worship (Zeph 1:5; Jer 8:12; Deut 4:19; Ps 82:1). The priestly author of Genesis 1 has almost systematically demythologized the heavenly bodies, explaining that they were created as clocks and calendars, to mark day and night, times and seasons (Gen 1:14-19). In subsequent apocalyptic texts, the heavenly host has become the army of angels (*Enoch* 18:11-18; Rev 9:1), with at least one faction in opposition to God, and the image of their imprisonment is elaborated.

The good news that concludes this chapter would not have been a new concept to the author. The enthronement of the Lord of hosts on Mt. Zion is celebrated in numerous psalms (e.g., 47; 93; 96), and also is a leading theme in Isaiah 1–39 (2:1-4; 10:24-27; 14:32; 31). The substance of Yahweh's reign is not described, but it presumes the punishment of evildoers and all powers that oppose the Lord.

REFLECTIONS

1. The claim of this text that human beings pollute the earth through their actions strikes a sensitive nerve in contemporary culture. "Pollution" in chapter 24 is a religious and moral concept, deeply rooted in biblical understandings of clean and unclean. Pollution has become a common expression in the vocabulary of modern societies. It is now a scientific as well as a moral category, but pollution nonetheless. Most types of pollution in the contemporary world can be measured against a theoretical criterion of purity. Thus it is not difficult to know the precise levels of air pollution in major cities or of water pollution in rivers or drinking water. One even hears of levels of noise pollution, to say nothing of debates concerning holes in the ozone layer of the atmosphere caused by certain pollutants.

The Bible has little to contribute directly to this contemporary definition or measurement of pollution. It does, however, suggest directions for reflection on the moral dimensions of the situation. One line of thought in Isaiah 24 sets out the impending disaster to the earth and all its inhabitants as God's judgment on human sin. After all, God is ultimately in charge of the future. If the earth withers and even dies, that is God's punishment of human beings for their sins. But running through this chapter, and also in other prophetic announcements of impending calamity, lies the perspective that immoral human activity itself has set the woeful future into motion. To sow the wind is to reap the whirlwind (Hos 8:7). Those who put their hands in a fire will be burned; no further "punishment" for foolish or wrong behavior is necessary.

This understanding of the relationship between human commitments, actions, and the effects on what we would call their natural environment is set out clearly in Hos 4:1-3, a classic statement of ecological disaster set into motion by human immorality. These verses describe a striking sequence of events, amounting to a series of causes and their effects. First there is the human failure of commitment and faithfulness to God at the deepest level ("There is no faithfulness or loyalty," Hos 4:1 NRSV). As a result, the earth and all of its inhabitants—human beings as well as creatures of field, air, and sea—languish and finally disappear ("Therefore the land mourns, and all who live in it languish" (Hos 4:3 NRSV). The whole cosmos suffers from the effects of human sinfulness.[214] This prophetic address clearly presumes that human beings have the power—but not the authority—to disrupt and even destroy the rest of creation.

The pollution of the earth is a moral issue. In the biblical tradition the environmental implications of particular human crimes or sins is not always obvious. We can understand how dump-

---

214. H. W. Wolff, *Hosea* (Philadelphia: Fortress, 1974) 68. See also Patrick D. Miller, *Sin and Judgment in the Prophets: A Stylistic and Theological Analysis*, SBLMS 27 (Chico, Calif.: Scholars Press, 1982) 9-11; and Tucker, "Sin and 'Judgment' in the Prophets."

ing industrial waste into a river pollutes it. But how does the violation of, e.g., some of the Ten Commandments "cause" the land to mourn and fish to die? On this issue, as on so many others, the biblical tradition calls for those who take it seriously to reflect more deeply upon human responsibilities to both the earth and all its inhabitants. Moreover, it should not be surprising that prophecies concerning the virtual destruction of the earth elicit reflection on the environment, for many contemporary writers on the subject claim that the environmental crisis has apocalyptic implications. Those who destroy or use up natural resources will lose those resources, or their descendants will.

2. Although critical interpreters debate the identity of the city of chaos (v. 10), subsequent tradition took it to be the evil city, Babylon, and contrasted it with Jerusalem. That opened the door for the even more dramatic contrast between the two cities in Revelation, Babylon (i.e., Rome), and the heavenly city of God. This text is not to that point, of course, but suggests the direction for later belief. Beyond the New Testament, some (mainly gnostic) Christian interpretation saw in this contrast the reasons for the day of judgment: Earth and what is earthly are evil in themselves. But there is no Old Testament parallel for the explanation. The earth and its inhabitants are not evil in themselves. The goal of the cataclysm is not the replacement of the earthly with the spiritual, but the establishment of God's righteous reign on earth. Even in Revelation, the heavenly city comes down to earth.

3. The announcement that the Lord will open "the windows of heaven" and bring a flood upon the earth presents a problem in the wider biblical context. As shown in the Commentary, the author of Isaiah 24 knows the priestly accounts of creation and the flood. But did he not know how the flood story ended, or knowing it, did he disagree? In the covenant with Noah and all his future descendants, God promised "that never again shall all flesh be cut off by the waters of a flood, and never again shall there be a flood to destroy the earth" (Gen 9:11). The rainbow, as a sign of the covenant, was to remind God of that promise: "When I bring clouds over the earth and the bow is seen in the clouds, I will remember my covenant that is between me and you and every living creature of all flesh; and the waters shall never again become a flood to destroy all flesh" (Gen 9:14-15). Remarkably, this promise is not restricted to human beings but explicitly extends to all life on the earth.

Is God's covenant not "everlasting," at least in the eyes of the author of Isaiah 24? Has the human condition become so corrupt that even the ancient promise no longer holds? No clear answer presents itself from the text. Certainly the eschatological prophet has employed earlier tradition to describe the impending devastation of the earth, but it is not even clear that he has deliberately reinterpreted that tradition. However, there is no way that both Genesis 9 and Isa 24:18 can be equally valid. So the interpreter is faced with the problems of responding to apparently contradictory messages. One way to respond is to rationalize these into some theological scheme, thus imposing the scheme on the Bible. Another is to decide that each message is or may be valid for a different time or place. Or one may choose between the competing claims on the basis of what is taken to be the center of the biblical tradition, the canon of or within the canon.

ISAIAH 25:1-12, CELEBRATING LIFE AND THE LORD'S DELIVERANCE

NIV	NRSV

25 O Lord, you are my God;
I will exalt you and praise your name,
   for in perfect faithfulness
     you have done marvelous things,
	25 O Lord, you are my God;
	I will exalt you, I will praise your name;
	   for you have done wonderful things,
	     plans formed of old, faithful and sure.

NIV

things planned long ago.
²You have made the city a heap of rubble,
  the fortified town a ruin,
  the foreigners' stronghold a city no more;
  it will never be rebuilt.
³Therefore strong peoples will honor you;
  cities of ruthless nations will revere you.
⁴You have been a refuge for the poor,
  a refuge for the needy in his distress,
  a shelter from the storm
    and a shade from the heat.
  For the breath of the ruthless
    is like a storm driving against a wall
5   and like the heat of the desert.
  You silence the uproar of foreigners;
    as heat is reduced by the shadow of a cloud,
    so the song of the ruthless is stilled.

⁶On this mountain the LORD Almighty
    will prepare
  a feast of rich food for all peoples,
  a banquet of aged wine—
    the best of meats and the finest of wines.
⁷On this mountain he will destroy
  the shroud that enfolds all peoples,
  the sheet that covers all nations;
8   he will swallow up death forever.
  The Sovereign LORD will wipe away the tears
    from all faces;
  he will remove the disgrace of his people
    from all the earth.
                    The LORD has spoken.
⁹In that day they will say,

"Surely this is our God;
  we trusted in him, and he saved us.
This is the LORD, we trusted in him;
  let us rejoice and be glad in his salvation."

¹⁰The hand of the LORD will rest on this
    mountain;
  but Moab will be trampled under him
    as straw is trampled down in the manure.
¹¹They will spread out their hands in it,
  as a swimmer spreads out his hands
    to swim.
  God will bring down their pride
    despite the cleverness*a* of their hands.

a11 The meaning of the Hebrew for this word is uncertain.

NRSV

²For you have made the city a heap,
  the fortified city a ruin;
  the palace of aliens is a city no more,
    it will never be rebuilt.
³Therefore strong peoples will glorify you;
  cities of ruthless nations will fear you.
⁴For you have been a refuge to the poor,
  a refuge to the needy in their distress,
  a shelter from the rainstorm and a shade
    from the heat.
When the blast of the ruthless was like a
    winter rainstorm,
5   the noise of aliens like heat in a dry place,
  you subdued the heat with the shade
    of clouds;
  the song of the ruthless was stilled.

⁶On this mountain the LORD of hosts will
    make for all peoples
  a feast of rich food, a feast of well-aged
    wines,
  of rich food filled with marrow, of well-
    aged wines strained clear.
⁷And he will destroy on this mountain
  the shroud that is cast over all peoples,
  the sheet that is spread over all nations;
⁸he will swallow up death forever.
Then the Lord GOD will wipe away the tears
    from all faces,
  and the disgrace of his people he will take
    away from all the earth,
  for the LORD has spoken.
⁹It will be said on that day,
  Lo, this is our God; we have waited for
    him, so that he might save us.
  This is the LORD for whom we have waited;
    let us be glad and rejoice in his salvation.
¹⁰For the hand of the LORD will rest on this
    mountain.

The Moabites shall be trodden down in
    their place
  as straw is trodden down in a dung-pit.
¹¹Though they spread out their hands in the
    midst of it,
  as swimmers spread out their hands
    to swim,

NIV

¹²He will bring down your high fortified walls
 and lay them low;
he will bring them down to the ground,
 to the very dust.

NRSV

 their pride will be laid low despite the
  struggle*a* of their hands.
¹² The high fortifications of his walls will be
  brought down,
 laid low, cast to the ground, even to
  the dust.

*a*Meaning of Heb uncertain

COMMENTARY

The first part of this chapter contrasts sharply with the preceding one. Whereas the dominant note of chap. 24 is the day of the Lord's judgment, concluding to be sure with the promise of the Lord's reign on Mt. Zion, 25:1-10a joyfully celebrates life and the deliverance that comes from the Lord. The language and rituals of celebration appropriately follow the proclamation of the Lord's victorious reign (24:33). The final section of the chapter (vv. 10*b*-12) returns to words of judgment. However, that declaration is not universal, as in chap. 24, but particular, proclaiming the destruction of a specific nation, Moab, as in the oracles concerning the foreign nations in Isaiah 14–23.

25:1-10a. These verses include two distinct parts and a concluding affirmation. The first piece (vv. 1-5) is a song of praise and thanksgiving addressed to God, similar to such hymns in the psalter (e.g., Psalm 145). Like other hymns, it begins by announcing the singer's intention to praise God (v. 1*a*) and then consists of praise itself and reasons for praise. The Lord is honored, on the one hand, for the destruction of cities and, on the other hand, for providing a refuge for the poor and needy. The second part of the unit (vv. 6-9) is an announcement of salvation with strong eschatological tones. The Lord's salvation includes the provision of a ritual meal on Mt. Zion ("the mountain," v. 6), and bringing an end to suffering (vv. 7-8). These acts will evoke praise and joy from the Lord's people (v. 9). The banquet on the mountain recalls the ritual meal on Mt. Sinai in the time of Moses (Exod 24:9-11). God shares this meal with "all peoples," signifying reconciliation and communion. In Isa 2:1-4, the nations will come to Zion for instruction and will participate in the peace established by the Lord. Here they come to

eat together in harmony. The concluding sentence (v. 10*a*) affirms that the Lord's power ("hand") will be present on Zion to accomplish what is promised.

That this passage is concerned with the world order and not solely with Judah and Jerusalem is repeatedly evident in the text: "strong peoples" (v. 3), "ruthless nations" (v. 3), "aliens" (vv. 2, 5), "all peoples" (vv. 6, 7), "all nations" (v. 7), "all faces" (v. 8), and "all the earth" (v. 8) are some of the terms that express the scope of God's activity. The passage gains its focus, however, by centering on two cities. One is an unnamed city, perhaps representative of the unbelieving world. This place is called "city of chaos" (24:10), "the fortified city" (25:2), "the palace of aliens" (25:2), and "the lofty city" (26:5); and it is the object of God's wrath (25:2). In contrast is the city on and around God's mountain, the place of God's splendid favor (25:6-10*a*). This most certainly is Jerusalem. The passage celebrates the punishment of the one and the blessing of the other.

It is important to hear the recital of punishment and restoration in the canticle of praise, which is set forth in unusual symmetry. Verses 1 and 9 frame the recital. Verse 1 praises the Lord for being faithful to the plan of God laid down ages ago. In other words, what will happen to the world, both punishment and salvation, is the unfolding of God's will. Ultimately it is not military prowess, political shrewdness, or any chance turn of events that provides history's final chapter, but God's "plans formed of old, faithful and sure." In v. 9, God is praised for keeping the promises, for carrying out the plans formed in the beginning. There was long waiting, to be sure; more than one generation asked the question, "How long, O Lord, will you tarry?" But on the day of deliverance, the faithful will say, "This is the LORD for whom we have waited; let us be glad and rejoice in his salvation" (v. 9). The verse parallels the words of Psalm 9. In the song the people affirm that God is theirs, that they have waited in the expectation that he would save them, and they rejoice in that salvation. Full homage and honor are accorded to God alone.

Between the framing words of praise in vv. 1 and 9 the passage does not fall simply into two divine acts, punishment of the wicked and redemption of the faithful. God does act on behalf of the poor, the needy, and the oppressed. The imagery used to portray God's benevolent intervention is touchingly beautiful: "a refuge," "a shelter in the storm," "shade from the heat," and welcomed quiet (vv. 4-5). God does refresh and nourish the holy city as with a banquet of unimagined plenty (v. 6). But remarkably, the effect of God's gracious activity is positive even among the ruthless and unbelieving. Faced with the demonstration of God's faithful love, "strong peoples will glorify you; cities of ruthless nations will fear you" (v. 3).

The best-known lines in this passage, and for good reason, are those in vv. 7-8. They express the deepest human hopes for an end to mourning ("the shroud that is cast over all peoples"), to death itself, and to all grief ("wipe away the tears from all faces"), and they do so in highly evocative images and poetic cadences. These lines also are familiar in part because they are paraphrased by Paul in 1 Cor 15:26, 54-55. Consequently, it is difficult to hear that the Lord "will swallow up death forever" in its ancient context, long before the rise of the ideas of an afterlife in Christianity and Judaism.[215] So it is helpful to look into the background of the expressions here. This imagery, along with the fertility motifs in the section, echo Cananite mythology, in which the chief god Baal defeats the gods Yam (Sea) and Mot (Death),[216] who was known to "swallow" all living creatures. But the construction of the language and theology are quite distinct here. Death is not another deity,

but a human reality, and its defeat does not recur each year in the spring. It is a single act of God when the new age begins. From the historical perspective, these lines appear in a context that sees the end of Israel's shameful exile. Thus some interpreters have taken them to refer to the end of military destruction and the mourning it produces.[217]

How are we to understand the promise that the Lord "will swallow up death forever"? Is it to be taken literally or metaphorically? Certainly the language is metaphorical, but the prophecy looks to a time when death will be no more. In this respect these lines are virtually without parallel in the OT. One may think of Isa 26:19 and Dan 12:1-4 as parallels, but both these texts anticipate a revival after death, and then only of some, not the end of death for everyone. The new age, which in this case can only mean beyond history, will entail a radical transformation, even of the human condition. In the meantime, for the author of this text and all its subsequent readers, mourning, death, and tears continue. Moreover, while readers may see the end of death as the focal point, the text emphasizes the end to mourning. That is, the stress is upon the pain that death creates for those still alive, the survivors who mourn their loss. Even in this respect the emphasis is upon life and the living.

However one interprets these lines, the prophetic voice declares that life, not death, is what God endorses. The line between life and death was not so clear in ancient Israel as it may seem in modern Western societies. The more one's capabilities for life diminish, the more one approaches death. Death is understood as any power that threatens life.[218] So the affirmation of life, and of God's affirmation of life, entails the end to grief and mourning. Such declarations come at the table, the banquet on Mt. Zion, thus defining the fullness of life as communion.

215. For discussion of ideas of resurrection and the afterlife, see George W. E. Nickelsburg, *Resurrection, Immortality, and Eternal Life in Intertestamental Judaism,* HTS XXVI (Cambridge, Mass.: Harvard University Press, 1972); John J. Collins, *Daniel,* Hermeneia (Minneapolis: Fortress, 1993) 394-98.

216. See Marvin A. Sweeney, *Isaiah 1–39, With an Introduction to Prophetic Literature,* FOTL XVI (Grand Rapids: Eerdmans, 1996) 337.

217. See O. Kaiser, *Isaiah 13–39: A Commentary* (Philadelphia: Westminster, 1974) 200-202.

218. H. Wildberger, *Isaiah 13–27* (Minneapolis: Fortress, 1997) 533. See also G. von Rad, "Statements of Faith in the Old Testament About Life and About Death," in *God at Work in Israel* (Nashville: Abingdon, 1980) 183-209, and esp. C. Barth, *Die Erretung vom Tode in den individuellen Klage-und Dankliedern des Alten Testaments* (Stuttgart: Kohlhammer, 1997; originally published 1947). The review of the most recent edition of this volume by H. P. Nasuti, *CBQ* 62 (2000) 312-13, includes an excellent summary of Barth's major conclusions.

25:10b-12. This brief announcement of judgment on Moab seems out of place. Both its form and content would appear more at home among the other proclamations concerning foreign nations (chaps. 13–23). Specifically, why it is here and not included with the sweeping oracle concerning Moab in 15:1–16:14 is a mystery. Most commentators since the late nineteenth century have concluded that these verses are an intrusive addition. But why here? Did an author or editor want to make it clear that Moab was not to be included among "all peoples" (vv. 6-8) invited to the Lord's banquet?[219] (For a discussion of the history and geography of Moab, see the Commentary on 15:1–16:14.)

The announcement of Moab's fate is not presented as a speech of Yahweh but, like many other prophecies, states in the passive voice what will happen to Moab. The prophecy is expressed by means of two vivid images. The second (v. 12) envisions the destruction of Moab's walls, presumably as a result of a foreign military invasion. That is a very common announcement of judgment, whether against foreign nations, Israel, or Judah. The first image (vv. 10b-11), while it describes no bloodshed, is a disgusting and vile scene of the Moabites trodden down in a cess pool. Even if they pray for deliverance ("spread out their hands"), "their pride will be laid low," and they will look like swimmers in a sewer. This image of the Moabites is a sharp contrast to the promise that the "disgrace" (v. 8) of God's people will come to an end.

This and the other judgments announced against Moab present the dominant OT attitude toward Judah's neighbors. It is not the only perspective, however. Ruth, the heroine of the book that bears her name and a traditional ancestress of King David, was a native of Moab.

---

219. Kaiser, *Isaiah 13–39*, 204; Ronald E. Clements, *Isaiah 1–39*, NCB (Grand Rapids: Eerdmans, 1980) 210.

REFLECTIONS

Like so much of the Bible, the main issue in this passage concerns life and death. The dominant tone of 1:10a is joy, and the central theme is the celebration of life. As the text sings of celebration it proclaims an end to mourning, and promises that death will be swallowed up. This does not amount to an affirmation of everlasting life, or resurrection. (On this subject, see the Reflections at 26:1-21.) It does, however, encourage readers to reflect on the power of death. Death not only ends life, but also cripples it. Death exercises power over life, both as individuals recognize their own mortality, and as they suffer the loss of those they love.

Because Isaiah 25:1-9 is eschatological in nature, it is not surprising that early Christian writers drew from it in portrayals of God's final victory. One hears v. 7 in Paul's triumphant shout, "Death has been swallowed up in victory" (1 Cor 15:54 NRSV). The prophet of the Apocalypse who, like Isaiah, envisions God's redemption of the holy city, draws on v. 8 in assuring the reader of God's tender presence: "he will wipe every tear from their eyes" (Rev 21:4 NRSV). As chap. 25 stresses, God affirms life. God does not desire that any should perish (2 Pet 3:9).

ISAIAH 26:1-21, SONGS AND PRAYERS FOR GOD'S INTERVENTION

NIV	NRSV
26 In that day this song will be sung in the land of Judah: We have a strong city;	**26** On that day this song will be sung in the land of Judah: We have a strong city;

NIV

God makes salvation
  its walls and ramparts.
²Open the gates
  that the righteous nation may enter,
  the nation that keeps faith.
³You will keep in perfect peace
  him whose mind is steadfast,
  because he trusts in you.
⁴Trust in the LORD forever,
  for the LORD, the LORD, is the Rock eternal.
⁵He humbles those who dwell on high,
  he lays the lofty city low;
he levels it to the ground
  and casts it down to the dust.
⁶Feet trample it down—
  the feet of the oppressed,
  the footsteps of the poor.

⁷The path of the righteous is level;
  O upright One, you make the way of the
    righteous smooth.
⁸Yes, LORD, walking in the way of your laws,ᵃ
  we wait for you;
your name and renown
  are the desire of our hearts.
⁹My soul yearns for you in the night;
  in the morning my spirit longs for you.
When your judgments come upon the earth,
  the people of the world learn righteousness.
¹⁰Though grace is shown to the wicked,
  they do not learn righteousness;
even in a land of uprightness they go on
    doing evil
  and regard not the majesty of the LORD.
¹¹O LORD, your hand is lifted high,
  but they do not see it.
Let them see your zeal for your people and be
    put to shame;
  let the fire reserved for your enemies
    consume them.

¹²LORD, you establish peace for us;
  all that we have accomplished you have
    done for us.
¹³O LORD, our God, other lords besides you have
    ruled over us,
  but your name alone do we honor.

ᵃ8 Or judgments

NRSV

he sets up victory
  like walls and bulwarks.
²Open the gates,
  so that the righteous nation that keeps faith
    may enter in.
³Those of steadfast mind you keep in peace—
  in peace because they trust in you.
⁴Trust in the LORD forever,
  for in the LORD GODᵃ
  you have an everlasting rock.
⁵For he has brought low
  the inhabitants of the height;
  the lofty city he lays low.
He lays it low to the ground,
  casts it to the dust.
⁶The foot tramples it,
  the feet of the poor,
  the steps of the needy.

⁷The way of the righteous is level;
  O Just One, you make smooth the path of
    the righteous.
⁸In the path of your judgments,
  O LORD, we wait for you;
your name and your renown
  are the soul's desire.
⁹My soul yearns for you in the night,
  my spirit within me earnestly seeks you.
For when your judgments are in the earth,
  the inhabitants of the world learn
    righteousness.
¹⁰If favor is shown to the wicked,
  they do not learn righteousness;
in the land of uprightness they deal perversely
  and do not see the majesty of the LORD.
¹¹O LORD, your hand is lifted up,
  but they do not see it.
Let them see your zeal for your people, and
    be ashamed.
  Let the fire for your adversaries
    consume them.

¹²O LORD, you will ordain peace for us,
  for indeed, all that we have done, you have
    done for us.
¹³O LORD our God,
  other lords besides you have ruled over us,
  but we acknowledge your name alone.

ᵃHeb in Yah, the LORD

NIV

¹⁴They are now dead, they live no more;
  those departed spirits do not rise.
You punished them and brought them to ruin;
  you wiped out all memory of them.
¹⁵You have enlarged the nation, O LORD;
  you have enlarged the nation.
You have gained glory for yourself;
  you have extended all the borders of
    the land.

¹⁶LORD, they came to you in their distress;
  when you disciplined them,
  they could barely whisper a prayer.ᵃ
¹⁷As a woman with child and about to give birth
  writhes and cries out in her pain,
  so were we in your presence, O LORD.
¹⁸We were with child, we writhed in pain,
  but we gave birth to wind.
We have not brought salvation to the earth;
  we have not given birth to people of
    the world.

¹⁹But your dead will live;
  their bodies will rise.
You who dwell in the dust,
  wake up and shout for joy.
Your dew is like the dew of the morning;
  the earth will give birth to her dead.

²⁰Go, my people, enter your rooms
  and shut the doors behind you;
hide yourselves for a little while
  until his wrath has passed by.
²¹See, the LORD is coming out of his dwelling
  to punish the people of the earth for
    their sins.
The earth will disclose the blood shed
    upon her;
  she will conceal her slain no longer.

ᵃ16 The meaning of the Hebrew for this clause is uncertain.

NRSV

¹⁴The dead do not live;
  shades do not rise—
because you have punished and destroyed
    them,
  and wiped out all memory of them.
¹⁵But you have increased the nation, O LORD,
  you have increased the nation; you are
    glorified;
  you have enlarged all the borders of
    the land.

¹⁶O LORD, in distress they sought you,
  they poured out a prayerᵃ
  when your chastening was on them.
¹⁷Like a woman with child,
  who writhes and cries out in her pangs
  when she is near her time,
so were we because of you, O LORD;
¹⁸ we were with child, we writhed,
  but we gave birth only to wind.
We have won no victories on earth,
  and no one is born to inhabit the world.
¹⁹Your dead shall live, their corpsesᵇ shall rise.
  O dwellers in the dust, awake and sing
    for joy!
For your dew is a radiant dew,
  and the earth will give birth to those
    long dead.ᶜ

²⁰Come, my people, enter your chambers,
  and shut your doors behind you;
hide yourselves for a little while
  until the wrath is past.
²¹For the LORD comes out from his place
  to punish the inhabitants of the earth for
    their iniquity;
the earth will disclose the blood shed on it,
  and will no longer cover its slain.

ᵃMeaning of Heb uncertain   ᵇCn: Compare Syr Tg: Heb *my corpse*
ᶜHeb *to the shades*

COMMENTARY

Three distinct but related units comprise this chapter. The parts are linked primarily by their common use of the language of cultic song, prayer, and by the theme of trust. First (vv. 1-6), an eschatologi-

cal prophetic voice announces that one day the inhabitants of Judah will sing a song thanking the Lord for victory. The second section (vv. 7-19) contains prayers for help, meditations on the travail of the Lord's righteous ones, and expressions of hope. Finally (vv. 20-21), an unidentified voice calls for people to seek cover, for the Lord is coming in wrath to exercise judgment on the earth. Only the last lines of this chapter contain strong apocalyptic images and motifs. The remainder blends the moods and language from the life of communal prayer with reflective meditation on the ways of God, the latter reminiscent of wisdom literature.

26:1-6. The initial line frames what follows as an announcement concerning the future. Out on the horizon looms a great day when the people of Judah will sing a song thanking the Lord for victory over their enemies. The cry to "open the gates" for the entry of the "righteous nation that keeps faith" reveals the hymn to be a pilgrim song, sung by the congregation as it moves first into the city and then to the temple precincts. As other such hymns show (see esp. Psalm 24), one does not approach the sacred place without appropriate questions and answers concerning one's heart and behavior. In Psalm 24 the question is asked directly, and not rhetorically: "Who shall ascend the hill of the LORD?" (Ps 24:3 NRSV). The response specifies the qualifications: "Those who have clean hands and pure hearts, who do not lift up their souls to what is false, and do not swear deceitfully" (Ps 24:4 NRSV). The question itself does not appear in chap. 26, but the answer to the implied challenge comes in vv. 2-3. Its substance is the same as that in Psalm 24. If they are to be deemed worthy to approach, the people will need to be righteous, keep faith, and trust in the Lord.

Verses 4-6 shift from direct hymnic address to the Lord to an admonition to the congregation, that they indeed trust in the Lord. But the reasons for that trust, signaled by "for" (v. 4*b*), in fact continue to express praise and thanksgiving for the Lord's actions. Fundamentally, the Lord is praiseworthy because he has "brought low the inhabitant of the height" and laid low "the lofty city" (v. 5). This city is probably the same one identified in the previous chapter as "the fortified city" (25:2), "the palace of aliens" (25:2). As in chap. 25, the text contrasts this city with Jerusalem, the "strong city" of 26:1. To conclude that the poet had in view the historical Babylon before its fall in 539 BCE[220] would entail dating the text earlier than the

literary evidence allows. It must be significant that the city is left unnamed. The celebration does not focus upon the downfall of a particular city or political power but on the expectation that the high and mighty will be brought down and trampled by the "poor" and the "needy" (v. 6).

26:7-19. Mood, tone, and tense shift throughout this section filled with the language of petition and praise addressed to God. In fact, with two exceptions (vv. 10, 18) the Lord is addressed directly in every verse of this unit, either by name or by means of the second-person singular pronoun "you." The tone, however, is meditative and reflective, so that the language of prayer at points sounds almost like a soliloquy.

The leading themes of these verses are the fate of the righteous and the justice of God, initiated in v. 7 where the Lord is invoked as "O Just One," and the poet affirms that "the way" of the righteous is level because God makes it so. But then speaking first in the singular and then in the plural on behalf of the people (vv. 8-9), the poet "yearns" for and seeks the Lord, assuming that the Lord has not yet acted to establish justice. "Soul" in these verses translates the Hebrew נפש (*nepeš*), a reference to the self or the life force, as in "the breath of life," נפש חיה (*nepeš ḥayyâ*), in Gen 2:7. This is not the soul as in Christian theology. In this instance, as in a great many other poetic texts, "soul" is not a metaphysical statement but a metaphor for the self. Then follows a meditation on righteousness. When God acts in judgment, the people of the world will learn righteousness (v. 9*b*). Divine judgment therefore is didactic, teaching right and wrong; "the wicked" will not become righteous if "favor is shown" to them (v. 10). The failings of the wicked are both in terms of behavior ("deal perversely") and their faith: They refuse to see, that is, to acknowledge, the "majesty" and power ("hand") of the Lord (vv. 10*b*-11*a*).

Now the prayer becomes a petition that the Lord's "zeal" for his people be demonstrated to the wicked, and that the Lord consume them (v. 11). Again, such a prayer presumes that justice has not yet been established on the earth. The song then praises the Lord for what God will do in the future, "ordain peace" for God's people. The singer's confidence is based on the affirmation that whatever God's people have done, God has done

---

220. Dan G. Johnson, *From Chaos to Restoration: An Integrative Reading of Isaiah 24–27.* JSOTSup 61 (Sheffield: JSOT, 1988) 59-61, 67-70.

for them (v. 12). The prayer for peace is reinforced by an affirmation of faith. The "other lords" that have ruled over God's people may refer to political figures, but may refer as well to other gods. If the existence of other gods that have ruled over the Lord's people is granted, this would only strengthen the affirmation, "we acknowledge your name alone" (v. 13). This presumes the same understanding of God among the gods expressed in the first commandment (Exod 20:1-3), and amounts to the claim that the community has been obedient to its most fundamental obligation.

Verse 14 calls the reader up short—its simple assertion that "the dead do not live; shades do not rise" appearing to have no connection with what precedes it. The lines have the ring of a familiar saying, a statement of what would have an indisputable fact to those who heard it in ancient Israel and most of the ancient Near East. Commentators have attempted to make sense of the lines in this context by arguing that "the dead" are the political lords who have ruled over Israel.[221] Certainly that makes sense in the light of the second half of v. 14, which affirms that God has "destroyed them," and v. 15, which contrasts the fate of God's "nation" with its oppressors. The initial lines of v. 14 are thus both a general observation—the dead do not rise—and a comment on the fate of Israel's enemies: They surely will die and be forgotten.

With v. 16 begins a prayer that reports past prayers of God's people. In their helplessness, suffering under the Lord's disciplining punishment, they prayed for help. The metaphor of a woman in labor characterizes both the passionate prayer and the suffering that provoked it ("cries out in her pangs when she is near her time," v. 17). Both the cries to God for help and the suffering itself were futile, bringing forth not a baby but "wind" (v. 18). The prayer goes on to translate the metaphor into literal terms, "no one is born to inhabit the world" (v. 18); that is, we have no progeny, no future.

Although the language of address to God continues at the beginning of v. 19, tone and content shift dramatically, from a painful petition for help

to an affirmation that the dead will live.[222] Particularly for Christian readers, this verse has been a crux, and not just for understanding this particular passage. Unfortunately, its sense is not at all obvious. The references of the pronouns are not certain, although both instances of "your" probably refer to the Lord. There is a textual variant in a key expression, with the Hebrew reading "my corpse" while most translations follow ancient versions that read "their corpses." Many have taken the singular of the Hebrew to be a change from an original plural, thus interpreting the text as supporting belief in the resurrection of the individual. But that is the central question for this verse. Does it refer metaphorically to the resurrection of the nation, as in Ezekiel's vision of the valley of dry bones (Ezekiel 37), or does it have in view the literal resurrection of individuals who have died, as seems to be the case in Dan 12:1-4? When the verse is seen in its context to function as an oracle of salvation responding to the prayer of petition that precedes it, the most plausible interpretation is to understand the lines as an affirmation that the Lord will give life to the community that considers itself as good as dead.[223]

26:20-21. If there is to be a revival of the people of God, it will come in the future. They must yet endure the great day of judgment that the Lord plans. This divine intervention goes beyond what the prophets had announced against particular nations or groups, including Israel. The Lord intends to "punish the inhabitants of the earth for their iniquity" (v. 21). This appears to be a virtually universal judgment, not one in which God acts against a nation or separates the righteous from the wicked. That is why the Lord summons the elect to hide themselves from the wrath to come, recalling the Passover night in Egypt when anyone found outside the house, or in a house not marked with the blood of the Passover lamb, would die (Exod 12:21-28).

221. E.g., Wildberger, *Isaiah 13–27*, 564; Clements, *Isaiah 1–39*, 215.

222. Because of the sharp contrast and the reference to raising the dead, some commentators have taken this to be a secondary and late addition, reacting to v. 14. So O. Kaiser, *Isaiah 13–39: A Commentary* (Philadelphia: Westminster, 1974) 215-20.

223. Wildberger, *Isaiah 13–27*, 567-70; Clements, *Isaiah 1–39*, 217.

REFLECTIONS

The promise in v. 19 that the dead will live, in its own context, most likely announces the rebirth of the nation that considers itself to be dead. However, in subsequent interpretation the verse has become a virtual proof-text for the resurrection of individual bodies. Because this issue is raised so sharply here, it provides an important point of departure for the consideration of death and resurrection, both in the context of the Old Testament and more broadly as well. Contemporary readers of this text may take it as an opportunity to reexamine their own ideas of life after death to better understand whether those views are consistent with the biblical perspective.

The initial lines of 26:14 state the consistent perspective of the Old Testament on life beyond death, a perspective shared with Mesopotamian and Canaanite religions. For every individual, death is the end. The "shades" of the living have no life, but are shadows that persist in the underworld, sheol, until they eventually fade away (see the Commentary on 25:7-8). The nation or the family may live on through history, but the individual dies. This might lead us to ponder the fact that the faithful in ancient Israel turned to God without looking for rewards or punishment beyond this life. It is possible that many religious people today hold the view that their faith is a way of earning their way into heaven. That view is challenged by the ancient biblical trust in God without any expectation of life beyond the grave.

Only two texts in the Hebrew Bible affirm any expectation of life after death comparable to that of the New Testament. They are Isa 26:19 and Dan 12:1-4 (cf. also Isa 25:7-8).

Both the text in Daniel and the traditional interpretation of the one before us set hope for resurrection in the context of apocalyptic eschatology. That is, the resurrection of the dead is seen to be a part of God's plan for the radical transformation of the world and of history. That is also the case for texts in the period between the testaments—such as the Dead Sea Scrolls; some books in the Greek Old Testament such as and some books in the so-called pseudepigrapha, such as *1 Enoch, Jubilees,* and the New Testament.

Within that apocalyptic understanding, it is important to distinguish between belief in the immortality of the soul and belief in the resurrection of the dead. If there are at most two texts in the Hebrew Bible expressing hope for the resurrection of the dead, there is no idea at all of an immortal soul, some essence of the individual that continues beyond death. That view comes from Greek religion and philosophy. The biblical, fundamentally New Testament, faith in resurrection presumes that all people die. The passion stories of the Gospels as well as the early Christian creeds make that very explicit concerning Jesus: "crucified, dead, and buried, and on the third day." Early New Testament faith on this point looks to a time when the world will be transformed, and all those who have died will be raised. Raised, to be sure, to eternal life. The central point is that what happens beyond death does not depend upon the nature of individuals—their immortal souls—but on God's intervention.

Finally, behind Isa 26:19 and Dan 12:1-4 is the issue of justice, particularly in the context of faith in the righteousness of God. The authors and early audience of this chapter saw evil times ahead. Indeed, they had already experienced such times. How could it be fair that the oppressors live and the faithful die, or that the powerful nation survives and the nation chosen by God disappears? Thus 26:11 is a prayer for the punishment of the wicked. The apocalyptic text in Daniel expects justice to be worked out at the end of the age. Likewise, Isaiah 26 reflects on the righteousness and justice of God and finally expresses confidence that the Lord will establish justice. Like Isa 25:7-8, this text is struggling toward the affirmation that nothing can separate the faithful from God, or from God's concern for them (cf. Rom 8:35-39).

Where does this consideration of the biblical views of life beyond death lead the contemporary reader? It may lead to the acknowledgment that many popular ideas rely less on the Bible than on other traditions. The heart of the biblical perspective on this as on all other points is the affirmation of a just and trustworthy God whose purposes are salvific and who finally will reign over all things, including death.

ISAIAH 27:1-13, IMAGES OF THAT DAY

27 In that day,

the LORD will punish with his sword,
his fierce, great and powerful sword,
Leviathan the gliding serpent,
Leviathan the coiling serpent;
he will slay the monster of the sea.

²In that day—

"Sing about a fruitful vineyard:
³ I, the LORD, watch over it;
I water it continually.
I guard it day and night
so that no one may harm it.
⁴ I am not angry.
If only there were briers and thorns
confronting me!
I would march against them in battle;
I would set them all on fire.
⁵Or else let them come to me for refuge;
let them make peace with me,
yes, let them make peace with me."

⁶In days to come Jacob will take root,
Israel will bud and blossom
and fill all the world with fruit.

⁷Has ₍the LORD₎ struck her
as he struck down those who struck her?
Has she been killed
as those were killed who killed her?
⁸By warfare[a] and exile you contend with her—
with his fierce blast he drives her out,
as on a day the east wind blows.
⁹By this, then, will Jacob's guilt be atoned for,
and this will be the full fruitage of the
removal of his sin:
When he makes all the altar stones
to be like chalk stones crushed to pieces,
no Asherah poles[b] or incense altars
will be left standing.
¹⁰The fortified city stands desolate,
an abandoned settlement, forsaken like
the desert;
there the calves graze,

27 On that day the LORD with his cruel and
great and strong sword will punish
Leviathan the fleeing serpent, Leviathan the twisting serpent, and he will kill the dragon that is in
the sea.

²On that day:
A pleasant vineyard, sing about it!
³ I, the LORD, am its keeper;
every moment I water it.
I guard it night and day
so that no one can harm it;
⁴ I have no wrath.
If it gives me thorns and briers,
I will march to battle against it.
I will burn it up.
⁵Or else let it cling to me for protection,
let it make peace with me,
let it make peace with me.

⁶In days to come[a] Jacob shall take root,
Israel shall blossom and put forth shoots,
and fill the whole world with fruit.

⁷Has he struck them down as he struck down
those who struck them?
Or have they been killed as their killers
were killed?
⁸By expulsion,[b] by exile you struggled
against them;
with his fierce blast he removed them in
the day of the east wind.
⁹Therefore by this the guilt of Jacob will be
expiated,
and this will be the full fruit of the removal
of his sin:
when he makes all the stones of the altars
like chalkstones crushed to pieces,
no sacred poles[c] or incense altars will
remain standing.
¹⁰For the fortified city is solitary,
a habitation deserted and forsaken, like
the wilderness;

---

[a]8 See Septuagint; the meaning of the Hebrew for this word is uncertain.   [b]9 That is, symbols of the goddess Asherah

[a]Heb *Those to come*   [b]Meaning of Heb uncertain   [c]Heb
Asherim

NIV

there they lie down;
they strip its branches bare.
¹¹When its twigs are dry, they are broken off
and women come and make fires
with them.
For this is a people without understanding;
so their Maker has no compassion on them,
and their Creator shows them no favor.

¹²In that day the LORD will thresh from the flowing Euphrates[a] to the Wadi of Egypt, and you, O Israelites, will be gathered up one by one. ¹³And in that day a great trumpet will sound. Those who were perishing in Assyria and those who were exiled in Egypt will come and worship the LORD on the holy mountain in Jerusalem.

[a]12 Hebrew River

NRSV

the calves graze there,
there they lie down, and strip its branches.
¹¹ When its boughs are dry, they are broken;
women come and make a fire of them.
For this is a people without understanding;
therefore he that made them will not have
compassion on them,
he that formed them will show them
no favor.

12On that day the LORD will thresh from the channel of the Euphrates to the Wadi of Egypt, and you will be gathered one by one, O people of Israel. ¹³And on that day a great trumpet will be blown, and those who were lost in the land of Assyria and those who were driven out to the land of Egypt will come and worship the LORD on the holy mountain at Jerusalem.

COMMENTARY

The final chapter of the distinct collection of eschatological prophecies generally called the Isaiah apocalypse contains four separate units, vv. 1, 2-6, 7-11, and 12-13. It is difficult to discern links between them, or progress of thought from one to the other. In fact, some commentators take v. 1 as the conclusion to 26:20-21,[224] but that ignores the clear markers that signal beginnings and endings. With the formula "On that day," v. 1 sets a definite boundary between the chapters, and vv. 12-13 provide a conclusion to the section as a whole (chaps. 24–27). The materials in the chapter have in common more-or-less eschatological expectations of the Lord's decisive intervention, both to judge and to save.[225] The initial verse stands quite alone as an announcement of the Lord's judgment on Leviathan. Verses 2-6 call for singing about the Lord's vineyard, announcing salvation for Judah. The third section, vv. 7-11, is the most difficult in the chapter, but it appears to proclaim that the guilt and sin of Jacob have been removed. Verses 12-13 express the promise that the Lord will bring the exiles home. That

announcement covers both the political and religious life of the people in a new age.

27:1. The phrase that initiates this section, "On that day," is a common biblical expression with a wide range of meanings. In this case, as with many others in prophetic literature, the expression refers to the future.[226] However, it is not the formula itself but the substance of the Lord's anticipated intervention that identifies the verse as eschatological. It will be no ordinary day in the future when the Lord "will punish Leviathan the fleeing serpent." "Leviathan the fleeing serpent," "the twisting serpent," and "the dragon that is in the sea" all refer to the same "creature."

To identify Leviathan as a creature is to raise important theological and religious issues. In the ancient Near Eastern religions of Mesopotamia and Syria-Palestine, the beast here identified as the dragon of the sea figured prominently in creation stories under various names. The dragon of chaos generally opposed the creator god, as did

224. Johnson, *From Chaos to Restoration,* 81-84.
225. Both Clements, *Isaiah 1–39,* 218, and Wildberger, *Isaiah 13–27,* 574, describe the parts of the chapter as "eschatological impressions."

226. Simon J. DeVries, *Yesterday, Today and Tomorrow: Time and History in the Old Testament* (Grand Rapids: Eerdmans, 1975) 314, 316. Against most of the evidence, DeVries argues that the formula introduces a conclusion to the first verses of chap. 26.

Tiamat, who was defeated by Marduk in the Babylonian account of creation. When Leviathan and other versions of the dragon of chaos appear in the Hebrew Bible, they may indeed stand in opposition to Yahweh, but their power is never to be compared with that of the Lord God. Psalm 74:14 praises the Lord as the one who worked acts of salvation and created the world, crushing Leviathan and turning him into food for wild creatures. In Job 41, Leviathan seems to have been reduced to a fearsome sea creature. Most delightful of all is the image in Ps 104:26. The poet praises God for creating the sea, "and Leviathan that you formed to sport in it." The old dragon of chaos has become God's playmate, consistent with Psalm 104's affirmation of all God's world, including its wild things.

In the present verse, the Lord will defeat Leviathan "on that day." If this is not the last day, it certainly is a time of decisive intervention in history. It has long been noticed that biblical reflection on the end sees a return to the conflicts of creation. God is seen here to defeat the last and oldest enemy, taken as a force, if not *the* force, of evil. Many interpreters have understood the dragon of the sea to stand for some political power, such as Egypt or Babylon.[227] But the evil represented here is religious and not political. Subsequent apocalyptic texts move reflection on the final struggle in different but related directions, some political and some metaphysical. The animals from the sea in Daniel 7 do represent political powers. After all, the forces of evil are known to be incarnate, to work in and through history. In the book of Revelation, the symbolism links the cosmic and the political dimensions. The dragon of chaos is explicitly identified with "the Devil and Satan" (12:9; 20:2),[228] and the beast from the sea is Rome (Revelation 13).

27:2-6. Although this section also begins with "On the day," anticipating a time in the future, it contains no explicit announcement of the Lord's intervention until its concluding verses. Rather, the passage paints an image of a time when the Lord will care for a "pleasant vineyard," while at the same time alluding to past relationships between the Lord and that vineyard. Doubtless the inspiration for these lines comes from 5:1-7.

The vineyard sung about here is the one in the song of the vineyard. So an author from the post-exilic period has reinterpreted the earlier prophetic text. The close parallels to the language indicate that the writer of 27:2-6 had Isaiah 5 before him.[229] Some of the images of chap. 5 have been used but transformed. Moreover, the present unit follows to some extent the pattern of 5:1-7, with the parable of the unidentified vineyard, identified only in the concluding line. Whereas the briers and thorns would have represented the fruit of the original vineyard, here they have become virtual allegories for foreign or impure elements among the people. In most respects this passage is a reversal of the earlier song of the vineyard. Instead of accusation and judgment there is good news, qualified to be sure by the conditions in v. 4. When this unit turns to the future, it becomes an announcement of salvation for Israel (v. 6). But the author has also reflected upon the earlier announcement of judgment, rationalizing what in fact had happened with the Babylonian Exile. The punishment, the author argues, was justified, so there is a summons to make peace with the Lord (v. 5), lest disaster strike again. Now, if only the people will "cling" to the Lord, the Lord will care for them so that no harm will come to them.

Remarkably, whereas the original song of the vineyard concerned Judah and Jerusalem (5:7), v. 6 anticipates in particular the return of Israel and the reestablishment of the northern kingdom. Consequently, some take v. 6 as the beginning of the next section, which also speaks of Jacob (v. 8).[230]

27:7-11. It is difficult to make sense of this complex unit because it seems to consist of bits and pieces, the antecedents of many pronouns are uncertain, and the allusions and images too often are baffling. One unifying feature is the use of agricultural metaphors, which also link this section with vv. 2-6. Generally, vv. 7-9 interpret the Lord's judgment ("he," "his fierce blast") upon the northern kingdom ("Jacob," v. 9) as purging punishment, and vv. 10-11 describe total judgment upon an unidentified "fortified city" (v. 10).

227. For a catalog of the possibilities, see H. H. Wildberger, *Isaiah 13–27* (Minneapolis: Fortress, 1997) 576-79.
228. Ibid., 580.

229. Nielson argues that this is the production of a new text based on Isa 5:1-7 rather than a reinterpretation of it. K. Nielsen, *There Is Hope for a Tree: The Tree as Metaphor in Isaiah,* JSOTSup 65 (Sheffield: JSOT, 1989) 116-23.
230. Wildberger, *Isaiah 13–27,* 590-91.

Initially (vv. 7-9*a*), the punishment that has purged Israel's sin seems to be in the past, fundamentally the "exile" of its population. The language of the NRSV and NIV characterizing the Lord's removal of guilt and sin ("expiation," "atone") is perhaps a bit too theological. The language of the TNK is more neutral: "purged away," "removing guilt." In any case, God is seen to have dealt with sin and guilt through punishment of the guilty. But then the Lord's intervention to judge seems to continue into the future. Verse 9*b* indicates that sin and guilt will be removed once the Lord has crushed the altars and torn down the "sacred poles." So the author views corrupt worship, including idolatry, as a continuing problem for the northern kingdom.

It would be easier to draw firm conclusions about the meaning of the unit if the "fortified city" (v. 10) had been identified. The common and most plausible solution is to take the city as Samaria since "Jacob" refers to the northern kingdom,[231] and to conclude that the passage reflects the Jewish-Samaritan conflict.[232] If that is the case, dates for the origin of the material could be any time from the early post-exilic period to well into the Hellenistic era. The conflict between Judeans and Samaritans stretched out over centuries. It is clear that the author has used old images from Isaiah ("people without understanding" recalls Isa 1:3 and 5:13) and Hosea ("will not have compassion" depends upon Hos 1:6).

27:12-13. This prose section also begins with the formula "On that day," initiating an announce-

ment of the Lord's future intervention to gather and save a scattered people. The image of divine action is virtually apocalyptic since the Lord will act in such a comprehensive way, threshing "from the channel of the Euphrates to the Wadi of Egypt" (v. 12), an expression that indicated the ideal boundaries of the land of Israel (cf. Gen 15:18; 1 Kgs 8:65; Ezek 47:15-20). In v. 13, however, the scope of the Lord's activity is broader, including Assyria and Egypt. The day of the Lord ("that day") will be a time of harvest when the exiles are brought home. The metaphor of threshing (or beating out) suggests the violent act of separating grain from the chaff (cf. Amos 9:9). If there is any sense of judgment if is only in the verb for threshing, signifying the act of sorting out the good from the waste. The concern focuses upon the grain, the fruits of the harvest that represent, of course, the people of Israel. That they will be gathered "one by one" (v. 12) suggests tender care for each grain, for each individual. The blowing of the "great trumpet" (v. 13) calling the exiles home is another apocalyptic image.

Although within the Hebrew Scriptures "Israel" may refer to the northern kingdom or to the nation as a whole, the exiles called home here would have been the northerners.[233] Verse 12 seems to have in view what the southerners, the Judeans, would have considered the mixed population of post-exilic Samaria, from which the Israelites will be separated. Verse 13, on the other hand refers to exiles taken by the Assyrians centuries earlier, beginning in 722 BCE. The return of Israel to worship at "the holy mountain at Jerusalem" represents a reestablishment of all Israel at the one legitimate sacred place.

---

231. Ibid., 595-96, and many others. Clements says this could be any of a number of fortified Israelite cities. See Ronald E. Clements, *Isaiah 1–39*, NCB (Grand Rapids: Eerdmans, 1980) 222.

232. R. J. Coggins, *Samaritans and Jews: The Origins of Samaritanism Reconsidered* (New York: Oxford University Press, 1975) 222.

233. Marvin A. Sweeney, *Isaiah 1–39, With an Introduction to Prophetic Literature,* FOTL XVI (Grand Rapids: Eerdmans, 1996) 351.

REFLECTIONS

The "Isaiah Apocalypse" (Isaiah 24–27) is not, as we have seen, an apocalypse in the technical sense. Instead it is a series of prophecies and other genres, many of which focus on a dramatic if not radical transformation of things as they are. Still, these texts, including some in chap. 27, contain motifs and ideas that are sufficiently eschatological and even apocalyptic to provoke reflection on expectations of the end and their implications for life and faith. These motifs include the announcement that the Lord will kill the dragon of chaos (27:1), the trumpet of the Lord calling for the elect (27:13), the summons to hide while the Lord judges the earth (26:20-21), divine judgment on the angels ("heavenly host," 24:21-22) and their imprisonment, an eschatological banquet on the nations on Mt. Zion (25:6-8), the darkening of the sun and moon (24:23), and other texts that seem to refer to a virtually universal judgment.

Reflection on the issues raised by these images and motifs ought to begin with the acknowledgment that apocalyptic literature and ideas have been troubled ground for many, if not the majority, throughout Jewish and Christian history. For comfortable folks, such discourse often seems both strange and threatening. Yet, there have always been those who put this literature and its ideas at the center of their faith and life. From the time of the Qumran community before the Christian era to the present day, apocalyptic groups have been outside the mainstream. However, it would be a serious mistake to relegate apocalyptic ideas to the margin or to leave them to those who believe that the end is coming soon, although they belong to them as well. Apocalyptic ideas are too close to the heart of the biblical faith—at least in the New Testament—to be left to sects that focus on the end, many of which have been spawned by this literature.

First, the defining conviction of apocalyptic literature is the expectation that God will one day reign with justice over all powers, whether of this or any possible world. In a general sense, this perspective undergirds prophetic literature as well, with its announcements that God will intervene to judge and to save. The distinctive features of apocalyptic faith are its scope—encompassing all powers—and the fact that it anticipates a radical transformation of history and of the world. Regardless of how dire circumstances may appear—or even actually be—for the world and for those who consider themselves the elect, God will be victorious and will finally establish a just order. Thus confidence in God's present and future dominion overcomes the experience of trouble and suffering. That is why the people of God are able to sing hymns of praise, even as they may be suffering judgment, for they anticipate God's eventual triumph.

Second, the apocalyptic vision of the future leads to an ever sharper distinction between good and evil, including moral, physical, and even metaphysical evil. Again, such distinctions are known throughout the biblical tradition, but in the apocalyptic vision have become more than human disobedience or rebellion against God. In the later apocalyptic literature, the last days will witness a struggle between the powers of good and the powers of evil, as in the Qumran text, "The war of the sons of light against the sons of darkness." That struggle is reflected in the Lord's killing Leviathan on the last day (27:1). The dragon of the sea, as the Lord's enemy, certainly represents evil, and eventually comes to symbolize metaphysical evil.[234] Later gnostic thought will suggest that the day of judgment is coming because earth and whatever is earthly are evil in themselves. But there is no support in the Hebrew Scriptures for this interpretation of the world itself as evil.

Third, under the shadow of the coming reign of the righteous God, what should human beings do? How should they live their lives? The elect are called to live out justice mainly in terms of faith and faithfulness to the God who reigns and will reign over all. But apocalyptic believers have responded in almost opposite ways to the conviction that God will intervene to change the world. In modern times, most apocalyptic groups have retreated from the world understood as ordinary society. For others, in particular the Jewish community in the second century BCE, apocalyptic faith as reflected in the book of Daniel supported engagement in the present world with all its political problems.

It may seem remarkable that something so focused on the world to come could be so deeply involved in political realities. That can happen because evil is believed to be incarnate, just as well as God's justice is incarnate, present in the world. Institutions themselves may be salvific as well as evil. So apocalyptic believers seek either to transform institutions, even through revolution, or establish their own societies distinct from those of the world. In this regard, it is important to recognize that within the eschatological vision of Isaiah 24–27, the faithful see God's reign established with its center in the true sanctuary, where they celebrate and sing praises to the God who reigns.

234. Wildberger, *Isaiah 13–27*, 580.

Both revolution and withdrawal, when guided by apocalyptic beliefs, have in common a deep sense of urgency concerning moral and religious decisions. What God will bring about seems clear, if not determined. Signs of the coming of God's reign are recognized in historical events. In a similar fashion, the prophets saw signs of God's reign where there were peace and justice, and when evil was judged. So it is up to human beings to decide whether or not to be a part of God's reign, and quickly. Along with that urgency comes a dedication to persevere, even in the face of impossible odds. Common themes in the parables of the kingdom are this urgency and perseverance.

Those who take the biblical tradition seriously will take apocalyptic literature, ideas, and convictions seriously and not consign them to the religious or social margins. First, over and over and in various ways, these themes insist upon the proclamation of the good news that God reigns over history and over the whole cosmos. That good news shines its light into the darkest of times and circumstances, comforting the powerless and challenging the powerful. Second, one does not wait quietly for God's reign to appear but responds to the good news with urgency and perserverance, expecting God's triumph any day, but acting each day as a citizen of a domain in which justice and righteousness are expected to prevail.

ISAIAH 28:1–33:24

JERUSALEM IN THE EYE OF THE ASSYRIAN STORM

OVERVIEW

In terms of both form and content, these chapters comprise the fourth major and distinctive block of literature in the book of Isaiah. After the long series of oracles concerning the nations in chaps. 13–23 and the collection of eschatological prophecies and related texts in chaps. 24–27, we return to the language and topics familiar from chaps. 1–12. Instead of prophecies concerning the last days and the world as a whole, prophetic addresses to and concerning Judah and Jerusalem dominate the section, although it begins with an announcement of judgment against the northern kingdom (28:1-6). The old familiar figure of Assyria rears its head again, as do the dominant themes of the centrality of Zion, the responsibilities of the nation's leaders, and trust in the Lord rather than political forces or alliances.

Most modern commentators have correctly concluded that much of the material in this section, especially in chaps. 28–31, stems from the eighth century, from the earliest Isaiah tradition, if not necessarily direcly from the prophet himself. There are, to be sure, literary contributions from the seventh and the fifth century BCE, but for the most part we have before us traditions concerning Isaiah's words in the last part of his life.[235] The circumstances of this period, the time of Hezekiah's revolt against Sennacherib in 705–701 BCE are reported and interpreted in Isaiah 36–39. That Judean insurrection against Assyria entailed a series of political and military maneuvers, including an alliance with Egypt. The texts presently before us do not report but only allude to these events, for their concern is the prophet's message in difficult times. The political and military

activities that prompted the prophetic addresses must be reconstructed from other biblical and extra-biblical sources. The speeches in this section provide insight into the prophetic political role and message concerning political policy, especially foreign, but also domestic.

Is Isaiah 28–33 a collection of diverse materials or a composition guided by some leading theme? As is the case with most prophetic literature, these chapters contain a great many relatively short units of discourse. The reader's first impression is that of discontinuity, of moving from one address to another. So the section reflects some characteristics of a collection of prophetic sayings. However, in its present form this body of literature is much more than a haphazard assortment of units. Rather, it is relatively coherent and organized. In fact, these discourses appear to be arranged according to several different but related principles of organization. These include formal, chronological, and thematic systems.

First, at the level of formal arrangement, major sections are set off by the introductory cry "Woe," visible in the NIV but commonly translated "Ah" in the NRSV, and the single use of "See" (הן *hēn*, 32:1). Although it is not possible to ascertain with confidence the stage in the section's development when it was organized this way, the use of these headings cannot be accidental, any more than the division or units in chaps. 13–23 under the common heading "Oracle concerning X" is accidental. Using this marker as a guide, the units therefore are 28:1-29; 29:1-14; 29:15-24; 30:1-33; 31:1-9; 32:1-20; and 33:1-24. The only anomaly in this pattern is the "Woe" in 29:15, which does not quite correspond to the other divisions or subdivisions. The shift from "Woe" to "see" at 32:1 is a small but telling change of expression to signal a

235. See Ronald E. Clements, *Isaiah 1–39*, NCB (Grand Rapids: Eerdmans, 1980) 223-24, for a list of texts generally considered to be secondary to this Isaiah tradition.

pause for the conclusion.[236] In addition to the indication of major sections by means of "Woe" or "See," another aspect of the formal structure is a series of collections of prophetic addresses (chaps. 28–32) with a liturgical conclusion (chap. 33). So the broadest outline would have two parts, chaps. 28–32 and chap. 33. This corresponds in some respects to chaps. 1–12, a series of prophetic addresses and reports with a hymnic conclusion (chap. 12). In fact, some have argued that chap. 33 formed the conclusion to the first half of the book of Isaiah as a whole.[237]

Second, at least within chaps. 28–31, a chronological organization appears to be at work.[238] The text does not contain an account of what happened, but rather includes Isaiah's prophetic speeches during the course of a particular series of events. Thus, in order to interpret his messages as well as recognize their chronological organization, it is necessary to summarize the political and military events that transpired in Judah toward the end of the prophet's lifetime. Unfortunately, this is a difficult task with regard to some of the most important details. By most standards for ancient history, the circumstances of the period are well-documented. There are at least two biblical accounts, one in 2 Kgs 18:17–19:37, and a slightly different version in Isaiah 36–39. In addition there is the virtually contemporary Assyrian record in the annals of Sennacherib. The biblical accounts are hardly objective reports, but rather, like Isaiah's words, theological interpretations of history. Moreover, the Assyrian king and his scribes also had an ax or two to grind.

Nevertheless, some of the key events can be reconstructed with confidence.[239] The political

protagonists of the drama of 705–701 BCE were King Hezekiah of Judah and King Sennacherib of Assyria. Since the fall of Samaria in 722/21, Assyria under Sargon II has asserted control over Syria-Palestine through a series of military campaigns in 720, 716, and 712 BCE. When Sargon II died, revolts against Assyrian authority began in Babylon and rippled throughout the empire. In 705, Hezekiah declared Judah's independence. According to the biblical tradition, this was both a political act and a religious reform, including returning the Temple to the worship of Yahweh alone. Sennacherib, son of Sargon II, promptly mounted a military campaign against the rebels, beginning with Babylon. By 701 his troops reached Judah, decimating the countryside and laying siege to Jerusalem. The final act in the drama shows Sennacherib's army withdrawing from the siege and returning to Assyria. The cause of this retreat is the most disputed question in ancient sources. In the meantime, the Judean royal house had carried on negotiations for an alliance with Egypt, which even a decade earlier had stirred up the states in the region against Assyria. (For more detail on these events, see the Overview to 36:1–39:8.)

Although only three direct references to Assyria appear in these chapters (27:13; 30:31; 31:8), many of the prophetic speeches address the events of Sennacherib's campaign, and in rough chronological order. A significant exception is 28:1-4, which concerns not Judah but condemns Israel and announces its destruction. It would thus be the oldest unit in this context, originating before the fall of Samaria in 722/21 BCE. Isaiah 28:7-13 is the earliest address of the prophet during the revolt, and 31:4-9 his last word, coming from the final phases of Sennacherib's siege of Jerusalem.[240] It is thus possible to see how Isaiah interpreted and responded to critical political and military actions.

Third, in the final form of this section, which includes both old traditions of Isaiah's words and later additions, it is possible to discern a thematic development. One motif that echoes throughout these chapters is concern for Zion.[241] Clearly the city of Jerusalem and the Temple Mount in

236. So Marvin A. Sweeney, *Isaiah 1–39, With an Introduction to Prophetic Literature,* FOTL XVI (Grand Rapids: Eerdmans, 1996) 353-54, who excludes 29:15 and 33:1 from the pattern. Although he recognizes the importance of these formal markers, he emphasizes the thematic development in the section. See also Christopher R. Seitz, *Isaiah 1–39,* Interpretation (Louisville: John Knox, 1993) 206, who suggests that the organization of the woes is designed to recall those in Isaiah 5.

237. Sweeney, *Isaiah 1–39,* 353.

238. See esp. Hans Wildberger, *Jesaja: Kapitel 28–39,* BKAT 10 (Neukirchen-Vluyn: Neukirchener Verlag, 1982) 1557. On the historical circumstances as well as the organization of the section, see Christopher R. Seitz, *Zion's Final Destiny: The Development of the Book of Isaiah* (Minneapolis: Fortress, 1991) 79-80.

239. For an excellent brief summary, see Clements, *Isaiah 1–39,* 223-24, and R. E. Clements, *Isaiah and the Deliverance of Jerusalem: A Study of the Interpretation of Prophecy in the Old Testament,* JSOT 13 (Sheffield: JSOT, 1980) 9-27.

240. See Wildberger, *Jesaja 28–39,* 1557.

241. Seitz, *Isaiah 1–39,* 205.

particular stand at the center of the concluding liturgy in chap. 33, and the prophecies also concern the threat to Zion and the Lord's response. This should not be surprising given Sennacherib's siege of the city where Isaiah lived. But the historical traditions concerning the city, the king, and Assyria have been shaped to express and even advocate particular theological affirmations. In general terms, the move is from accusation and announcement of judgment to salvation, interpreting the ways of God, past and future. Some commentators see a more specific development of thought, moving toward the emergence of a royal

savior and the downfall of Assyria as the ultimate purpose or result of Yahweh's bringing the Assyrians against Jerusalem.[242] To the extent that this is the case, it is the product of the last editors and redactors, probably during or after the Babylonian exile. The details of that editorial process are elusive. Doubtless they were even more complex than any reconstruction one might work out.

242. Sweeney, *Isaiah 1–39*, 354. Sweeney's identification of the genre of this body of literature as instruction is less persuasive. On the importance of this theme in the book as a whole, see Christopher R. Seitz, *Zion's Final Destiny: The Development of the Book of Isaiah* (Minneapolis: Fortress, 1991).

ISAIAH 28:1-29, PROPHECIES AND PARABLES CONCERNING ISRAEL AND JUDAH

NIV	NRSV
28 Woe to that wreath, the pride of Ephraim's drunkards,	**28** Ah, the proud garland of the drunkards of Ephraim,
to the fading flower, his glorious beauty, set on the head of a fertile valley— to that city, the pride of those laid low by wine!	and the fading flower of its glorious beauty, which is on the head of those bloated with rich food, of those overcome with wine!
²See, the Lord has one who is powerful and strong. Like a hailstorm and a destructive wind, like a driving rain and a flooding downpour, he will throw it forcefully to the ground.	² See, the Lord has one who is mighty and strong; like a storm of hail, a destroying tempest, like a storm of mighty, overflowing waters; with his hand he will hurl them down to the earth.
³That wreath, the pride of Ephraim's drunkards, will be trampled underfoot.	³ Trampled under foot will be the proud garland of the drunkards of Ephraim.
⁴That fading flower, his glorious beauty, set on the head of a fertile valley, will be like a fig ripe before harvest— as soon as someone sees it and takes it in his hand, he swallows it.	⁴ And the fading flower of its glorious beauty, which is on the head of those bloated with rich food, will be like a first-ripe fig before the summer; whoever sees it, eats it up as soon as it comes to hand.
⁵In that day the LORD Almighty will be a glorious crown, a beautiful wreath for the remnant of his people.	⁵ In that day the LORD of hosts will be a garland of glory, and a diadem of beauty, to the remnant of his people;
⁶He will be a spirit of justice to him who sits in judgment, a source of strength	

NIV

to those who turn back the battle at
the gate.

⁷And these also stagger from wine
and reel from beer:
Priests and prophets stagger from beer
and are befuddled with wine;
they reel from beer,
they stagger when seeing visions,
they stumble when rendering decisions.
⁸All the tables are covered with vomit
and there is not a spot without filth.

⁹"Who is it he is trying to teach?
To whom is he explaining his message?
To children weaned from their milk,
to those just taken from the breast?
¹⁰For it is:
Do and do, do and do,
rule on rule, rule on rule^a;
a little here, a little there."

¹¹Very well then, with foreign lips and
strange tongues
God will speak to this people,
¹²to whom he said,
"This is the resting place, let the
weary rest";
and, "This is the place of repose"—
but they would not listen.
¹³So then, the word of the LORD to them will
become:
Do and do, do and do,
rule on rule, rule on rule;
a little here, a little there—
so that they will go and fall backward,
be injured and snared and captured.

¹⁴Therefore hear the word of the LORD, you
scoffers
who rule this people in Jerusalem.
¹⁵You boast, "We have entered into a covenant
with death,
with the grave^b we have made an
agreement.
When an overwhelming scourge sweeps by,
it cannot touch us,

---

^a10 Hebrew / sav lasav sav lasav / kav lakav kav lakav (possibly
meaningless sounds; perhaps a mimicking of the prophet's words);
also in verse 13   ^b15 Hebrew Sheol; also in verse 18

NRSV

⁶and a spirit of justice to the one who sits in
judgment,
and strength to those who turn back the
battle at the gate.

⁷These also reel with wine
and stagger with strong drink;
the priest and the prophet reel with
strong drink,
they are confused with wine,
they stagger with strong drink;
they err in vision,
they stumble in giving judgment.
⁸All tables are covered with filthy vomit;
no place is clean.

⁹"Whom will he teach knowledge,
and to whom will he explain the message?
Those who are weaned from milk,
those taken from the breast?
¹⁰For it is precept upon precept, precept
upon precept,
line upon line, line upon line,
here a little, there a little."^a

¹¹Truly, with stammering lip
and with alien tongue
he will speak to this people,
¹²   to whom he has said,
"This is rest;
give rest to the weary;
and this is repose";
yet they would not hear.
¹³Therefore the word of the LORD will be
to them,
"Precept upon precept, precept upon
precept,
line upon line, line upon line,
here a little, there a little;"^a
in order that they may go, and fall backward,
and be broken, and snared, and taken.

¹⁴Therefore hear the word of the LORD,
you scoffers
who rule this people in Jerusalem.
¹⁵Because you have said, "We have made a
covenant with death,

---

^aMeaning of Heb of this verse uncertain

NIV

for we have made a lie our refuge
  and falsehood[a] our hiding place."

16So this is what the Sovereign LORD says:

"See, I lay a stone in Zion,
  a tested stone,
a precious cornerstone for a sure foundation;
  the one who trusts will never be dismayed.
17I will make justice the measuring line
  and righteousness the plumb line;
hail will sweep away your refuge, the lie,
  and water will overflow your hiding place.
18Your covenant with death will be annulled;
  your agreement with the grave will
    not stand.
When the overwhelming scourge sweeps by,
  you will be beaten down by it.
19As often as it comes it will carry you away;
  morning after morning, by day and by night,
  it will sweep through."

The understanding of this message
  will bring sheer terror.
20The bed is too short to stretch out on,
  the blanket too narrow to wrap around you.
21The LORD will rise up as he did at Mount
    Perazim,
  he will rouse himself as in the Valley
    of Gibeon—
to do his work, his strange work,
  and perform his task, his alien task.
22Now stop your mocking,
  or your chains will become heavier;
the Lord, the LORD Almighty, has told me
  of the destruction decreed against the
    whole land.

23Listen and hear my voice;
  pay attention and hear what I say.
24When a farmer plows for planting, does he
    plow continually?
  Does he keep on breaking up and
    harrowing the soil?
25When he has leveled the surface,
  does he not sow caraway and scatter
    cummin?
Does he not plant wheat in its place,[b]
  barley in its plot,[b]

NRSV

and with Sheol we have an agreement;
when the overwhelming scourge passes
    through
  it will not come to us;
for we have made lies our refuge,
  and in falsehood we have taken shelter";
16 therefore thus says the Lord GOD,
  See, I am laying in Zion a foundation stone,
    a tested stone,
  a precious cornerstone, a sure foundation:
    "One who trusts will not panic."
17 And I will make justice the line,
  and righteousness the plummet;
hail will sweep away the refuge of lies,
  and waters will overwhelm the shelter.
18 Then your covenant with death will be
    annulled,
  and your agreement with Sheol will
    not stand;
when the overwhelming scourge passes
    through
  you will be beaten down by it.
19 As often as it passes through, it will take you;
  for morning by morning it will pass through,
    by day and by night;
and it will be sheer terror to understand the
    message.
20 For the bed is too short to stretch oneself
    on it,
  and the covering too narrow to wrap
    oneself in it.
21 For the LORD will rise up as on Mount
    Perazim,
  he will rage as in the valley of Gibeon;
to do his deed—strange is his deed!—
  and to work his work—alien is his work!
22 Now therefore do not scoff,
  or your bonds will be made stronger;
for I have heard a decree of destruction
  from the Lord GOD of hosts upon the
    whole land.

23 Listen, and hear my voice;
  Pay attention, and hear my speech.
24 Do those who plow for sowing plow
    continually?
  Do they continually open and harrow
    their ground?

---

a15 Or false gods   b25 The meaning of the Hebrew for this word
is uncertain.

NIV

and spelt in its field?
²⁶His God instructs him
and teaches him the right way.

²⁷Caraway is not threshed with a sledge,
nor is a cartwheel rolled over cummin;
caraway is beaten out with a rod,
and cummin with a stick.
²⁸Grain must be ground to make bread;
so one does not go on threshing it forever.
Though he drives the wheels of his threshing
cart over it,
his horses do not grind it.
²⁹All this also comes from the LORD Almighty,
wonderful in counsel and magnificent in
wisdom.

NRSV

²⁵ When they have leveled its surface,
do they not scatter dill, sow cummin,
and plant wheat in rows
and barley in its proper place,
and spelt as the border?
²⁶ For they are well instructed;
their God teaches them.

²⁷ Dill is not threshed with a threshing sledge,
nor is a cart wheel rolled over cummin;
but dill is beaten out with a stick,
and cummin with a rod.
²⁸ Grain is crushed for bread,
but one does not thresh it forever;
one drives the cart wheel and horses over it,
but does not pulverize it.
²⁹ This also comes from the LORD of hosts;
he is wonderful in counsel,
and excellent in wisdom.

COMMENTARY

This chapter consists of three distinct elements, whose relationship to one another is by no means self-evident. First (vv. 1-6), introducing both the chapter and the larger section (chaps. 28–33) comes an announcement of judgment against Ephraim, the northern kingdom, specifically indicting its leaders. This unit in turn consists of two parts, the old announcement against Israel in vv. 1-4 and a later promise concerning "the remnant." The second segment (vv. 7-22), an announcement of judgment against Jerusalem because of the actions and attitudes of its prophets, priests, and other leaders, is typical of the focus of interest in the larger section to follow. This elaborate announcement was composed of several distinct traditions. Finally (vv. 23-29), the prophet tells the parable of the farmer showing the wisdom of knowing when to cultivate and plant particular crops, and how to prepare the harvested grain without destroying it. The general point of the parable is clear enough: The farmer's wisdom comes from and corresponds to that of the Lord. The particular message, however, must be discerned from the context. Certainly the parable has been included here to qualify and interpret Isaiah's announcements against Jerusalem.

How does the prophetic oracle against Ephraim function among announcements concerning Judah and Jerusalem? It does not serve quite the same purpose as the series of oracles against foreign nations in Amos 1–2, to frame a concluding announcement against Israel. Taken as a prophecy before the fall of Samaria (see the Overview to 28:1–33:24), this announcement will reinforce the authenticity of the prophetic words concerning the future of Judah and Jerusalem. The word of the Lord through Isaiah was true concerning Samaria, and therefore will be validated concerning Jerusalem. Thus the woe against Israel can serve as a warning to Judah. The most obvious link between vv. 1-6 and 7-22 is their common accusations against the leaders of the respective capital cities.

Like the other units in this larger section, this one begins with the cry "Woe." As with other prophetic woe speeches, these typically follow the cry with a description of the accused in terms of their wrongful activities (see the Commentary on 5:8-24 and 1:3). The woeful deeds evoke punishment that fits the crime.[243] The woe speeches in

243. See Miller, *Sin and Judgment,* 45-51.

this context are like others in that they are set out in a series. In fact, each major unit in the section begins with a woe speech consisting of a few verses, and then is followed by other discourses.

28:1-6. Although not presented as a direct speech of the Lord, this section contains two prophecies announcing the Lord's future acts. The first (vv. 1-4) has the typical features of a prophecy of punishment. The prophet addresses the accused directly with an indictment of their activities (v. 1) and then (vv. 2-4) describes their future punishment. The indictment or statement of reasons for punishment begins with the form of address, "drunkards of Ephraim," and then is spelled out in sarcastic language describing their excesses: "bloated with rich food . . . overcome with wine" (v. 1). Thus the prophet accuses the rich and powerful of attending to their appetites instead of their responsibilities, of self-deception and arrogant over-confidence in past glories. The "proud garland," a crown of flowers whose beauty is fading, serves as a metaphor referring generally to the pride and glory of Ephraim, and probably specifically to the walled city of Samaria.[244]

The announcement of judgment is rich in imagery and thin on specific details. It appears to declare that Samaria and its people are about to be swept away by an invading Assyrian army under its king, the "one who is mighty and strong" (v. 2). Most commentators correctly conclude that this address originated before the fall of Samaria to Sargon II in 722/21 BCE.[245] The first images (v. 2) characterize the invasion as a storm that brings hail, wind, and flood. This, however, is not a natural disaster but a military one. The "overflowing waters" recall the image of the Assyrian invasion in 8:7, flooding over Judah. The second picture (v. 3) shows the "proud garland" being trampled under foot, suggesting the destruction of the city. Finally (v. 4), metaphors are mixed, with the "fading flower" of the garland compared to a "first ripe fig" ready to be eaten by anyone who comes along. These analogies amount to a prophecy of destruction.

The announcement in vv. 5-6 is a subsequent addition to the old prophecy concerning the

northern kingdom. Picking up the images of "garland" and "glory," a voice from the time of the Babylonian exile or later provides a theological reinterpretation. Whatever the "garland" had represented in the old tradition, it now becomes a metaphor for the Lord. The Lord, not cities or walls, will be the pride and glory for "the remnant of his people" (v. 5). In the context following an announcement concerning Ephraim, the "remnant of his people" could have in view those left from the northern kingdom, but it could mean Judeans, or it could mean both. The "one who sits in judgment" most likely refers to the Lord's anointed king who will establish a spirit of justice, as in 11:1-5. "Those who turn back the battle at the gate" could be an allusion to the relief of the Assyrian army's siege of Jerusalem in 701 BCE, or to any who defend the sacred city.

28:7-22. This section begins without an introduction, the "also" of v. 7 joining this prophetic word to the one in vv. 1-4, connecting the drunken priests and prophets with the "drunkards of Ephraim" (v. 1), and at the same time indicating that a different set of drunkards comes into view. It will eventually become clear that these accused are in Jerusalem (vv. 14, 16), but this is not obvious at the outset. The culprits are not only priests and prophets (v. 7), but also those "who rule this people in Jerusalem" (v. 14). Thus this extended prophecy ridicules drunken leaders, both religious and political, and announces judgment because of their failure to understand the word of the Lord and because they have made "a covenant with death" (vv. 15, 18).

As with many prophecies of judgment, this section moves from accusation and indictment (vv. 7-12) to announcement of punishment (vv. 13-22), culminating with the prophet's affirmation that he has heard "a decree of destruction" from the Lord (v. 22). But the discourse is complicated, with several distinct declarations of the Lord's coming judgment, and additional accusations as well.

The initial charge is leveled against the priest and the prophet, that their drunkenness confuses their "vision" and their "judgment" (vv. 7-8). This drunkenness must be both literal and metaphorical, given the vivid description of a stinking banquet hall and the allusions to the basic functions of these offices. Prophets report visions and priests instruct or teach, in addition

---

244. See Clements, *Isaiah 1–39*, 225.
245. A major exception is O. Kaiser, *Isaiah 13–39: A Commentary* (Philadelphia: Westminster, 1974) 237-40, who argues that the unit is late.

to their ritual functions. Concerning the intoxicating beverages mentioned here, the NIV has it right. Wine and "beer" were standard fare in antiquity. "Strong drink" (NRSV, etc.) suggests distilled liquor, unknown in the ancient Near East. As the charge continues, it focuses on teaching and understanding. Rhetorical questions imply that the priest cannot "teach understanding" nor can the prophet "explain the message" (v. 11). Given what follows, this message must be that of Isaiah, which the drunks neither understand nor can they explain. In vv. 9-10 they mimic the language of the prophet, as if it were the unintelligible babbling of infants. The Hebrew of v. 10 (repeated in v. 13) makes less sense than most translations of it, although the NIV captures its tone. The lines are designed to ridicule the mutterings of the drunken priests and prophets as something like baby talk, making light of the word of the Lord.

Those responsible for the interpretation of the word of God only mutter and stammer, preventing the people from hearing the message of rest to the weary (v. 12), transmitted through Isaiah. Consequently, the Lord ("he," v. 11) will speak through the "foreign lips and strange tongues" (NIV) of the Assyrians, to whom they will fall (v. 13*b*). Thus the first punishment, introduced by "therefore" and identified as the word of the Lord, is that the people will indeed hear only mutterings instead of the divine word of peace, and be conquered.

A second announcement of punishment, also introduced by "therefore" and a summons to hear the word of the Lord, turns in direct address to "those who rule in Jerusalem" (v. 14), that is, the king and his trusted advisers. Thus a prophecy concerning the political leadership has been combined with one against the priests and prophets. As in other prophecies of punishment, the prophet ridicules and condemns his addressees by quoting their own words. But would they have actually said what Isaiah attributes to them? Surely they would not have claimed to have made "lies" their refuge, taken shelter in "falsehood" (v. 15). So it seems unlikely that they would have also claimed to have made "a covenant with death." Thus the quotation is a sarcastic caricature of what they have done; they have made a treaty, most likely the one with Egypt against Assyria. The leaders

believe this in fact amounts to life; the prophet asserts that it will lead to death.

Yet again (v. 16), "therefore" and the formula for the word of the Lord introduces an announcement, but it is not clear at the outset whether the message will be good news or bad. That the Lord is establishing a sure foundation in Zion should enable Jerusalem's people to rest secure, especially since the stone has a name or an inscription: "One who trusts will not panic" (v. 16).[246] The sense if not the precise language is comparable to Isaiah's message to Ahaz during the Syro-Ephraimitic war: "If you do not stand firm in faith, you will not stand at all" (Isa 7:9). That is, the Lord can establish Zion in security. The Lord expects the trust of the leaders and people, and the Lord expects them to do justice and righteousness rather than rely on treaties with foreign powers.

Subsequent verses explain that Jerusalem is being tested and will be found wanting. The metaphor of construction, initiated with the foundation stone, continues. Justice and righteousness will serve as the "measuring line" and the "plumb line" (v. 17; cf. Amos 7:7-9) to determine that trust in Yahweh has failed. The "covenant with death" will be annulled, and the Assyrian army ("overwhelming scourge") will sweep through, destroying anything that stands in its way. When this happens the leaders in Jerusalem will understand the message in terror. That message is summarized by means of a proverbial saying: The bed is too short and the covering too narrow (v. 20); that is, the treaty with Egypt will provide no protection.

The concluding lines of the passage (vv. 21-22) leave no doubt that the Lord is the author of the dreaded invasion. Yahweh will intervene as at Perazim, where David defeated the Philistines (2 Sam 5:17-21), and as at Gibeon, where the sun stood still (Josh 10:1-11). However, instead of defeating their enemies, the Lord will turn against "the whole land" with a "decree of destruction." No wonder that this divine deed is called "strange," the work of the Lord "alien" (v. 21). As in 10:5-6, Assyria will be the Lord's instrument of judgment, the "rod of his anger."

28:23-29. The parable of the farmer must be

---

246. The Hebrew of this verse is very difficult, and its translation is disputed. See J. J. M. Roberts, "Yahweh's Foundation in Zion (Isa 28:16)," *JBL* 106 (1987) 27-45.

here only to make sense of the prophet's message of judgment against Jerusalem. The parable itself is simple enough, and standing alone would seem quite innocent. But what is its point, particularly in this context, located between two prophecies that indictment and announce the Lord's judgment against Jerusalem?

The parable is framed neatly between the prophet's summons to hear what he is about to say (v. 23) and his affirmation that what he has said comes from the Lord, who is "wonderful in counsel," "excellent in wisdom" (v. 29), with another concluding observation about God's instructions dividing the two parts (v. 26). The language of these concluding affirmations indicates what the substance of the parable will make clear, namely, that proverbial wisdom is being employed in the service of the prophetic message.[247] Within the framework, the parable itself is a neatly constructed extended saying with two parts. The first (vv. 24-26) uses rhetorical questions to point out the wisdom of the farmer's sequence of plowing and planting, concluding that the wisdom to know what to do and when to do it comes from divine instruction. The second part (vv. 27-29) moves beyond plowing and planting and beyond the harvest to the preparation of the fruits of the field. The farmer has the good sense to thresh the small grains (dill and cumin) one way and the large

247. See esp. J. William Whedbee, *Isaiah and Wisdom* (Nashville: Abingdon, 1971) 51-67.

grains ("grain for bread," v. 28) another way, taking care in both cases not to destroy the edible parts of the plants.

On its own, quite apart from this or any context, the parable makes not just one but several general points. First, the framing verses affirm that the wisdom to be a good farmer—or to do anything for that matter—comes from God. The two elements of the parable itself could stand apart from this theological interpretation of wisdom. Second, the first part (vv. 24-26) establishes the importance of timing: There is a time to plow and a time to plant (cf. Eccl 3:1-8). Third, the second part (vv. 27-29) observes that the grains are prepared with violence, but violence appropriate to the harvest—violence that is not so harsh as to destroy the seeds.

In the context, between prophecies against Jerusalem, the parable responds, enigmatically to be sure, to the readers' questions concerning the Lord's ways. In effect, the parable becomes a commentary on the Lord's "strange" deed, "alien" work (28:21). In this literary setting, the wise farmer stands for Yahweh, and the crop for Judah and Jerusalem. The parable allows the reader to conclude that the Lord has a time for judgment and a time for salvation, that the violence of judgment is or will be limited to separating the grain from the chaff. Judah and Jerusalem may be crushed, but not destroyed.

REFLECTIONS

1. Drunken priests, prophets, and political leaders are easy targets, and for good reason. As Isaiah shows no mercy in blaming them for Jerusalem's troubles, so his words invite us to consider the place of the prophetic voice before corrupt leaders, both religious and political.

From antiquity to the modern day, the prophetic role has entailed confrontation and conflict. The language of the text before us reveals that the priests and prophets are arguing with Isaiah about his message, and even mocking him. The political leaders as well are called "scoffers" who rejected what he had to say. So to challenge institutions and leaders requires the courage to risk, at the very least, ridicule and isolation.

The old image of the prophet as a solitary individual outside of and standing against the central institutions distorts ancient Israelite prophecy and could be a hazardous model for any society, however. Here and elsewhere, Isaiah and other biblical prophets may see themselves against the majority, against the more powerful. Nonetheless, Isaiah lived his life as a part of the central religious institutions of Judah and Jerusalem. When he speaks against prophets he is addressing his peers, those who share his vocation. Nor do his accusations against the priests and temple rituals set him apart from the cult. After all, he reports that his call to be a prophet took place in the Temple (Isaiah 6). Moreover, he seems to have had regular access to kings. Thus he speaks from within, not from outside the institutions. To be sure, the relationship of Israel's prophets to the central institutions differed from time to time and place to place. Isaiah was hardly the same as Amos of Judah, speaking in Israel, and accused of sedition (Amos 7:10-17).

Isaiah, by his very criticism, stresses the importance of the roles of prophet, priest, and "rulers." They have failed in their responsibilities and thus are leading the nation to disaster. The failure of the prophets and priests is characterized sarcastically as drunkenness and their refusal or inability to accept the word of the Lord. Thus they are preoccupied with themselves instead of their responsibilities. This accusation evokes reflection on the relationship between personal morality and public responsibility. The prophet describes the failure of the political leadership strictly in terms of what he considers to be misguided public policy. This leads to the next issue raised by these lines—the place of the prophetic voice in political affairs.

2. Questions concerning the prophet's involvement in politics and concerning the relationship between faith and national policy persistently arise in the prophetic literature, and especially in this chapter. Here Isaiah specifically assaults the ruling group as "scoffers" (v. 14) because they have made a particular alliance, presumably a treaty with Egypt against Assyria. His grounds were in part practical, arguing that the treaty will not save them, but were fundamentally religious. Instead of putting their trust in military might or international alliances, the leaders and their people should trust in the Lord and the Lord's election of Zion as his holy place (v. 16). However, lest the call to trust be misunderstood, the prophet observes that justice and righteousness will be the measure of faith and action. No wonder people scoffed.

Some interpreters see Isaiah's call for trust in the Lord instead of military resistance as some form of pacifism. Grounds for this interpretation are weak. He seems to have responded to this and other particular crises on the basis of his understanding of the word of God for that moment. Whether he was a pacifist or not, the text raises for our thoughtful consideration the issue of when to fight and when to withdraw.

Isaiah lived in a different political system from ours, to be sure, so his perspective is not directly transferable to modern states. However, this text still opens for us the question of the role of faith, and of religious leaders, in political policies and decisions. Do some religious leaders in the United States, for example, use the separation of church and state as an excuse to withdraw? The apparent ineffectiveness of religious institutions in modern politics could be another excuse to remain aloof from politics. The Old Testament, and the prophetic tradition in particular, resists such withdrawal. How can one take the scriptures seriously and not insist that faith should guide public policy, domestic politics, and even international relationships? Decisions concerning national life cannot be based on pragmatic considerations alone. Even pragmatic factors will be driven by values of one kind or another, including self-interest or greed. So the prophetic tradition would suggest that calls for, e.g., justice and righteousness, should at the very least be part of the conversation in a pluralistic society, and perhaps even part of arguments concerning the values that drive political decisions. Even a call to trust in God rather than political treaties or weapons can serve to emphasize that no state or nation is ultimate; only God is.

3. The stone described in v. 16 and its inscription have captivated the imagination of readers and echoed through later traditions. Some NT texts turn it into a messianic promise. First Peter 2:6 cites the verse (from the LXX) in combination with references from Ps 118:22 and Isa 8:14-15, interpreting Jesus as the stone that will become the means of separation between believers and unbelievers (cf. Rom 9:33).[248] In Isaiah, the stone concerns not the Messiah, or the Davidic king,

---

248. John D. W. Watts, *Isaiah 1–33,* WBC 24 (Waco, Tex.: Word, 1985) 372.

but Zion as God's chosen and secure place. Nevertheless, the NT interpretations call attention to a theological issue central to Isaiah 28. The inscribed stone is a symbol of assurance, of the good news of God's presence. But at the same time the good news is a test. The leaders and people are called to respond in faith to this good news. This faith, however, is not the affirmation of particular beliefs, but trust in God and living according to justice and righteousness.

ISAIAH 29:1-14, JERUSALEM IN TROUBLE

NIV

29 Woe to you, Ariel, Ariel,
the city where David settled!
Add year to year
and let your cycle of festivals go on.
[2]Yet I will besiege Ariel;
she will mourn and lament,
she will be to me like an altar hearth.[a]
[3]I will encamp against you all around;
I will encircle you with towers
and set up my siege works against you.
[4]Brought low, you will speak from the ground;
your speech will mumble out of the dust.
Your voice will come ghostlike from the earth;
out of the dust your speech will whisper.

[5]But your many enemies will become like
fine dust,
the ruthless hordes like blown chaff.
Suddenly, in an instant,
[6]   the LORD Almighty will come
with thunder and earthquake and great noise,
with windstorm and tempest and flames of
a devouring fire.
[7]Then the hordes of all the nations that fight
against Ariel,
that attack her and her fortress and
besiege her,
will be as it is with a dream,
with a vision in the night—
[8]as when a hungry man dreams that he is eating,
but he awakens, and his hunger remains;
as when a thirsty man dreams that he is drinking,
but he awakens faint, with his thirst
unquenched.
So will it be with the hordes of all the nations
that fight against Mount Zion.

[a]2 The Hebrew for *altar hearth* sounds like the Hebrew for *Ariel.*

NRSV

29 Ah, Ariel, Ariel,
the city where David encamped!
Add year to year;
let the festivals run their round.
[2] Yet I will distress Ariel,
and there shall be moaning and
lamentation,
and Jerusalem[a] shall be to me like an Ariel.[b]
[3] And like David[c] I will encamp against you;
I will besiege you with towers
and raise siegeworks against you.
[4] Then deep from the earth you shall speak,
from low in the dust your words shall come;
your voice shall come from the ground like
the voice of a ghost,
and your speech shall whisper out of
the dust.

[5] But the multitude of your foes[d] shall be like
small dust,
and the multitude of tyrants like
flying chaff.
And in an instant, suddenly,
[6]   you will be visited by the LORD of hosts
with thunder and earthquake and great noise,
with whirlwind and tempest, and the flame
of a devouring fire.
[7] And the multitude of all the nations that fight
against Ariel,
all that fight against her and her
stronghold, and who distress her,
shall be like a dream, a vision of the night.
[8] Just as when a hungry person dreams of eating
and wakes up still hungry,
or a thirsty person dreams of drinking

[a]Heb *she*   [b]Probable meaning, *altar hearth*; compare Ezek 43.15
[c]Gk: Meaning of Heb uncertain   [d]Cn: Heb *strangers*

NIV

⁹Be stunned and amazed,
  blind yourselves and be sightless;
be drunk, but not from wine,
  stagger, but not from beer.
¹⁰The LORD has brought over you a deep sleep:
  He has sealed your eyes (the prophets);
  he has covered your heads (the seers).

¹¹For you this whole vision is nothing but words sealed in a scroll. And if you give the scroll to someone who can read, and say to him, "Read this, please," he will answer, "I can't; it is sealed." ¹²Or if you give the scroll to someone who cannot read, and say, "Read this, please," he will answer, "I don't know how to read."

¹³The Lord says:

"These people come near to me with
    their mouth
  and honor me with their lips,
  but their hearts are far from me.
Their worship of me
  is made up only of rules taught by men.ª
¹⁴Therefore once more I will astound
    these people
  with wonder upon wonder;
the wisdom of the wise will perish,
  the intelligence of the intelligent
    will vanish."

ª13 Hebrew; Septuagint *They worship me in vain; / their teachings are but rules taught by men*

NRSV

and wakes up faint, still thirsty,
so shall the multitude of all the nations be
  that fight against Mount Zion.

⁹Stupefy yourselves and be in a stupor,
  blind yourselves and be blind!
Be drunk, but not from wine;
  stagger, but not from strong drink!
¹⁰For the LORD has poured out upon you
  a spirit of deep sleep;
he has closed your eyes, you prophets,
  and covered your heads, you seers.

11The vision of all this has become for you like the words of a sealed document. If it is given to those who can read, with the command, "Read this," they say, "We cannot, for it is sealed." ¹²And if it is given to those who cannot read, saying, "Read this," they say, "We cannot read."

¹³The Lord said:
Because these people draw near with
    their mouths
  and honor me with their lips,
  while their hearts are far from me,
and their worship of me is a human
    commandment learned by rote;
¹⁴so I will again do
  amazing things with this people,
  shocking and amazing.
The wisdom of their wise shall perish,
  and the discernment of the discerning shall
    be hidden.

COMMENTARY

This unit is marked at the beginning by an opening "Woe" and at the end is signaled by another initial "Woe" in 29:15. However, the themes initiated in this section continue well into the next one.[249] Between these two cries of woe lie three distinct units, each addressing different listeners and concerned with different topics. The first (vv. 1-8) addresses "Ariel," that is, Jerusalem, and then

shifts, talking not to but about the city and what will happen to it. The theme is the siege of the city and its deliverance from its enemies. In the second part (vv. 9-11), both addressee and subject shift as the prophet speaks to the prophets and seers. In v. 13 both addressee and subject change yet again as the speaker turns directly to the people with accusations condemning their worship as superficial (vv. 13-14).

29:1-8. The woe cry introduces a prophecy of future events presented in two parts. The first (vv. 1-4) announces that the Lord will lay siege to

249. Sweeney treats chap. 29 as a single unit, but recognizes that the connections between vv. 1-14 and 15-24 are "tenuous in that they are thematic." See Marvin A. Sweeney, *Isaiah 1–39, With an Introduction to Prophetic Literature,* FOTL XVI (Grand Rapids: Eerdmans, 1996) 375, 381.

"Ariel." This unusual name certainly refers to Jerusalem or perhaps more specifically the Temple Mount, as the context clearly indicates. However, the meaning or origin of the name is uncertain and this is the only time it refers to the city. The name closely corresponds to the Hebrew term translated "altar hearth" in Ezek 43:15-16, and that would make sense. In fact, the final line of v. 2 seems based on that etymology, or at least a play on words, for Jerusalem is about to be turned into a burning altar. The "city where David encamped" (v. 1) alludes to the account of David's taking the city from its previous inhabitants, the Jebusites (2 Sam 5:6-10), but also conjures up the memory of the long association of Jerusalem with the Davidic dynasty.

Indictment of the addressees by describing their actions usually follows the prophetic "Woe." What follows here is the summons to the city to keep on doing what it has always done, "let the festivals run their round." As an accusation that could indicate preoccupation with things as they are, or overconfidence in the rituals and the sacred place. In vv. 2-4 the Lord promises—using human instrumentalities to be sure—to attack Jerusalem and besiege it, evoking cries from its inhabitants "like the voice of a ghost" (v. 4). This expresses one of the distinctive notes in Isaiah's understanding of the Lord's selection of Zion as his sacred place, namely, that any attack on the city is the Lord's doing, working out the divine plan in history.[250]

In the second part (vv. 5-8), the prophecy turns from judgment to salvation. Yahweh is no longer the enemy of Jerusalem, but the enemy of Jerusalem's enemies. Although the "foes" are almost beyond counting, the Lord will intervene unexpectedly against them (vv. 5b-6), and their anticipation of feasting on Jerusalem will be like a dream (vv. 7-8). So the nations that fight against Ariel will disappear. The description of the Lord's dramatic appearance in storm, earthquake, and fire (v. 6) draws upon the tradition of the theophany associated with those two holy mountains, Sinai and Zion (Exod 19:16-20; 1 Kings 19; Pss 18:15; 68:7-10).[251] The prophecy of the Lord's

actions here also draws on the tradition of the holy war, in which the Lord throws Israel's enemies into a panic and routs them (cf. Judg 4:11-16; 7:19-23).

The two parts of vv. 1-8 can be summarized into a coherent prophecy: The Lord will bring an enemy to besiege Jerusalem, but before the city falls to the enemy, the Lord will intervene to save. The final word is that Jerusalem will be delivered. However, tension between these two parts is unmistakable. Some commentators resolve the tension between threat and deliverance by taking vv. 5-8 as a secondary addition.[252] Others account for the deliverance following the threat by interpreting the voice from the ground (v. 4) as a cry of repentance that the Lord heeded, but that explanation seems unlikely. The key does lie in v. 4: The voice from the ground, the whisper out of the dust, represents the people of Jerusalem who are barely alive, but not yet dead. The siege is a threat, but one not carried to its conclusion. So room for hope remains, opening the door to what follows in vv. 5-8.

Although this text contains prophecies of the future, and the enemy that will surround the city and then flee in panic is unnamed, the context in the book of Isaiah definitely links the words to Sennacherib's invasion of Judah and siege of Jerusalem in 701 BCE. It is impossible to determine whether part or all of this unit was uttered before the Assyrian invasion, but its final editorial form had the advantage of hindsight. In fact, according to both the biblical and the Assyrian records, Sennacherib decimated the Judean countryside, laid siege to Jerusalem, but withdrew without taking the city (2 Kgs 18:13-15; Isa 37:21-36). Verse 3 gives a vivid description of a siege, with troops surrounding the city and building towers and "siegeworks." The account from Sennacherib's annals is no less graphic:

> As to Hezekiah, the Jew, he did not submit to my yoke, I laid siege to 46 of his strong cities, walled forts and to the countless small villages in their vicinity, and conquered [them] by means of well-stamped [earth] ramps, and battering-rams brought [thus] near [to the walls] [combined with]

---

250. J. H. Hayes, "The Tradition of Zion's Inviolability," *JBL* 82 (1963) 426.

251. See Jörg Jeremias, *Theophanie: Die Geschichte einer alttestamentlichen Gattung,* WMANT 10 (Neukirchen: Neukirchener Verlag, 1965).

252. R. E. Clements, *Isaiah and the Deliverance of Jerusalem: A Study in the Interpretation of Prophecy in the Old Testament,* JSOTSup 13 (Sheffield: JSOT, 1980) 47-48; and Ronald E. Clements, *Isaiah 1–39,* NCB (Grand Rapids: Eerdmans, 1980) 234-36.

the attack by foot soldiers, [using] mines, breeches as well as sapper work. . . . Himself I made a prisoner in Jerusalem, his royal residence, like a bird in a cage. I surrounded him with earthwork in order to molest those who were leaving his city's gate.[253]

29:9-12. Both form and content shift abruptly with v. 9, from an announcement of the future deliverance of Jerusalem to an imperative directly addressed to the prophets and seers. No transition or introduction accounts for the relationship of these verses to what precedes them, or for the circumstances that prompted the address.

Two distinct parts comprise the unit, vv. 9-10 and 11-12. In the first, the speaker orders the prophets and seers to "stupefy" themselves, to be "blind," but not from "strong drink" (better: NIV, "beer"; see the Commentary on 28:7). This resembles the accusation of drunkenness against the prophets and priests in 28:7-8, but indicates that drink alone cannot explain the failure of the accused to understand and to see. Although the instructions in v. 9 would presume that the prophets and seers have control over their failures, v. 10 explicitly states that they do not. They are unable to see or hear because the Lord "has poured out" on them "a spirit of deep sleep," closed their eyes and covered their heads. One cannot miss the similarity of this action to Isaiah's commission. A truly remarkable element of that commission was his call to "Make the mind of this people dull, and stop their ears, and shut their eyes" (6:10). In that case Isaiah was to prevent repentance so that the Lord's judgment could run its course. The purpose is unstated here, but certainly the stupidity of these visionaries is seen to be part of the Lord's purpose.

As most modern translations indicate, the second part of this unit (vv. 11-12) is not poetry but prose, already raising questions about its connections to the early prophetic tradition. These two verses continue the theme of the inability to perceive, but only in a general way. Now the focus has moved from the oral to the written revelation, and from a specific address to prophets and priests to a general audience. Ostensibly, the "sealed document" is presented as an example of the difficulty in understanding "the vision of all this," the meaning of which is not explained but likely refers to Isaiah's prophecy.[254] Some of the addressees cannot understand because they refuse to break the seal, but others cannot understand because they cannot read. These verses must have been included as a commentary on the preceding ones at a time when there was in fact a "document," when the focus was shifting from the oral tradition to the mysteries of the written text. The claim "we cannot read" would not be an empty assertion, for literacy in antiquity was the exception rather than the rule. Thus when Ezra presents the law to the people (Neh 8:1-12), he reads it aloud to them, and others interpret what is read. The motif of the inability to see or hear resumes in 29:18, and the concern with the written prophecy in 30:8.

29:13-14. This brief but compelling prophecy is connected to its context by the theme of its announcement of judgment—that "wisdom" shall perish and "discernment" be hidden—present both in vv. 9-12 and 15-16. In fact, the larger section, 29:9-24, could be called "human ignorance and the LORD's plans." But these two verses form a distinct unit, complete in itself.

Following the formula for the word of the Lord come the two most consistent features of a prophecy of punishment, an indictment or reasons for punishment (v. 13) and the announcement of punishment. The accused ("these people," v. 13) are not addressed directly but are described in the third person. The accusation concerns shallowness of worship, that is, going through the words and motions of ritual without sincerity, perhaps recalling the reference in 29:1 to the cycle of festivals. Their words and actions may be appropriate, but their hearts and motives are not. Famous as this passage is, its perspective is more common in modern times than in antiquity, where thoughts and feelings generally were not at the center of attention.

The Lord vows to get the attention of these people whose worship is simply "learned by rote" by doing "shocking" and "amazing" things. If the "again" has in view some tradition of divine intervention, the action is not mentioned. The punishment is neither military nor natural disaster, neither death nor exile. In one sense, the crime sets

---

253. *ANET,* 288.

254. Conrad takes this as a reference specifically to Isaiah 6–39. See Edgar W. Conrad, *Reading Isaiah* (Minneapolis: Fortress, 1979) 130-32.

its "punishment" into motion: The penalty for any religion without depth is a loss of wisdom. But in another sense, the Lord will impose the judgment in some dramatic fashion. As in vv. 9-10 and 6:10, the Lord will withdraw the capacity to see and understand. Remarkably, while the indictment concerned the cult, the realm of the priests, the punishment concerns the realm of "the wise." Given the context of this announcement and especially its proximity to the parable of the farmer in 28:23-29, however, the judgment is not against the institution of wisdom as such, but against the counsel of the wise in particular circumstances.[255]

255. Wedbee, *Isaiah and Wisdom,* 140.

REFLECTIONS

The most compelling lines of this section, particularly among Protestants, are those of v. 13. The Lord's indictment of "these people" consists of two parts. The first condemns those who approach the Lord with their mouths and honor God with their lips but not with their hearts, and the second denounces worship that is "a human commandment learned by rote." Thus this text evokes reflection on and self-examination concerning the meaning and practice of piety and religion.

The point of this verse seems clear and the implications appear to be self-evident, and in some sense they are. By its criticism of hypocrisy and religious routine, the verse calls for the reverse, sincerity of devotion and worship from the heart. Religion is thus identified as internal and individual, if not individualistic; its validity measured by motives and feelings.

However, it is familiar texts, such as this one, which call for the most reexamination. There have been and continue to be negative as well as positive uses of this indictment of shallow religion. Is it appropriate to employ these lines in support of the argument that ritual and rote are inferior to worship from the heart, or to suggest that any religion other than one's own is a mere "human commandment"? John Calvin saw the link between the two parts of the indictment, understanding the first as hypocrisy and the second as superstition: "Hypocrisy is never free from ungodliness or superstition; and, on the other hand, ungodliness or superstition is never free from hypocrisy." Then he used the verse as a proof-text against the Roman Catholic Church: "We may easily conclude from this what value ought to be set on that worship which Papists think that they render to God, when they worship God by useless ringing of bells, mumbling, wax candles, incense, splendid dresses, and a thousand trifles of the same sort; for we see that God not only rejects them, but even holds them in abhorrence."[256] Many have followed Calvin's example, using these powerful lines to attack others rather than to examine their own hearts.

This verse has long figured prominently in debates concerning authentic piety. It is cited in Matt 15:7-8 and Mark 7:6-7 as Jesus attacks the Pharisees and scribes, calling them hypocrites. In Matthew he accuses them of voiding the word of God, and in Mark of abandoning the commandment of God in favor of human tradition. Particularly in Matthew, the emphasis falls on the first half of the verse. In the context, Jesus cites the passage in response to the accusation that his disciples have not been observant, failing to wash their hands before eating. The conflict seems to be between internal and external religion, but it also lends support to criticism of tradition, setting against it the word of God, as communicated by the prophet Isaiah. Thus our text focuses attention on the tension between the law—which some identify with the "human commandment" here—and the spirit.

It would hardly be faithful to the spirit of this text, or its citation in the New Testament, to turn it against ritual or against concern with law and tradition. All religion, even the most

256. John Calvin, *Commentary on the Book of the Prophet Isaiah,* trans. William Pringle, vol. 2 (Edinburg: Calvin Translation Society, 1851) 323.

spontaneous and personal, is shaped by tradition and ritual. That applies to the most charismatic of worship services as well as the most formal of ceremonies. Consequently, a simple external examination of worship practices and procedures cannot determine the sincerity and devotion of the participants. Who can say that participation in a regular Mass is less hypocritical and more sincere than private meditation on the psalms? Therefore it would be inappropriate to use these lines to criticize the practices of others, but appropriate to use them to challenge one's own devotion.

To criticize worship or religion when it is "a human commandment" is to pose difficult and important questions. Calvin called this superstition, and Barth contrasted the Christian faith with religion, for him a negative category. But is not all "religion" the human response to the experience of the divine? Religion is the human attempt to understand and respond to God. Even if one contrasts religion as human with revelation, as in the Bible, even that revelation can only be heard and passed on from one human community to another. But it is not uncommon to think that all is human, except one's own religion, which is divinely revealed. That may be the case, but it has to be heard by human ears, seen by human eyes, and understood by human reason.

Remarkably, although v. 13 is frequently cited, the following verse (v. 14) seldom is remembered: "Yet I will again do amazing things with this people, shocking and amazing." Yet this announcement is linked directly to the famous sentences. It is God's promised intervention because of the indicted behavior. So these verses together criticize ritual without devotion from the heart and the wisdom of the wise. That God promises to do amazing things supports a sense of the spirit, of spontaneity, of the unexpected. So v. 14 could be taken to deconstruct, to even criticize, v. 13. Thus one who is "religious" will be prepared to be confounded, to experience the unexpected, what is beyond reason. Who knows what amazing, shocking work God will do?

ISAIAH 29:15-24, PLANS HUMAN AND DIVINE

NIV

15Woe to those who go to great depths
    to hide their plans from the LORD,
who do their work in darkness and think,
    "Who sees us? Who will know?"
16You turn things upside down,
    as if the potter were thought to be like
        the clay!
Shall what is formed say to him who formed it,
    "He did not make me"?
Can the pot say of the potter,
    "He knows nothing"?

17In a very short time, will not Lebanon be
        turned into a fertile field
    and the fertile field seem like a forest?
18In that day the deaf will hear the words of
        the scroll,
    and out of gloom and darkness
    the eyes of the blind will see.

NRSV

15 Ha! You who hide a plan too deep for
        the LORD,
    whose deeds are in the dark,
    and who say, "Who sees us? Who
        knows us?"
16 You turn things upside down!
    Shall the potter be regarded as the clay?
Shall the thing made say of its maker,
    "He did not make me";
or the thing formed say of the one who
        formed it,
    "He has no understanding"?

17 Shall not Lebanon in a very little while
        become a fruitful field,
    and the fruitful field be regarded as a forest?
18 On that day the deaf shall hear
        the words of a scroll,
    and out of their gloom and darkness

NIV

¹⁹Once more the humble will rejoice in
        the LORD;
    the needy will rejoice in the Holy One
        of Israel.
²⁰The ruthless will vanish,
    the mockers will disappear,
    and all who have an eye for evil will be
        cut down—
²¹those who with a word make a man out to
        be guilty,
    who ensnare the defender in court
    and with false testimony deprive the
        innocent of justice.

²²Therefore this is what the LORD, who
redeemed Abraham, says to the house of Jacob:

    "No longer will Jacob be ashamed;
    no longer will their faces grow pale.
²³When they see among them their children,
    the work of my hands,
    they will keep my name holy;
    they will acknowledge the holiness of the
        Holy One of Jacob,
    and will stand in awe of the God of Israel.
²⁴Those who are wayward in spirit will gain
        understanding;
    those who complain will accept instruction."

NRSV

    the eyes of the blind shall see.
¹⁹ The meek shall obtain fresh joy in the LORD,
    and the neediest people shall exult in the
        Holy One of Israel.
²⁰ For the tyrant shall be no more,
    and the scoffer shall cease to be;
    all those alert to do evil shall be cut off—
²¹ those who cause a person to lose a lawsuit,
    who set a trap for the arbiter in the gate,
    and without grounds deny justice to the
        one in the right.

²²Therefore thus says the LORD, who
redeemed Abraham, concerning the house of
Jacob:
    No longer shall Jacob be ashamed,
    no longer shall his face grow pale.
²³ For when he sees his children,
    the work of my hands, in his midst,
    they will sanctify my name;
    they will sanctify the Holy One of Jacob,
    and will stand in awe of the God of Israel.
²⁴ And those who err in spirit will come to
        understanding,
    and those who grumble will accept
        instruction.

COMMENTARY

As this text lies before us it consists of three sections, related in that the second two parts respond to and interpret the first. The section begins (vv. 15-16) with another prophetic woe speech indicting the addressees in terms of their actions. They are doing the unthinkable, believing they can hide their plans from God. The second part (vv. 17-21) contains an announcement of the Lord's own plan, to bring salvation through a transformation of nature and destruction of "the tyrant," the "scoffer," and evildoers. The final section (vv. 22-24), both linked to and set off from the preceding by an introductory "therefore," presents another announcement of salvation for the "house of Jacob."

The authorship and date of these verses are disputed. Some take the entire section as an address by Isaiah concerning the northern kingdom, composed after its fall and incorporation into the Assyrian Empire in 722 BCE.[257] Many others judge the entire unit to be late, stemming from the post-exilic era.[258] More likely, however, vv. 15-16 come from Isaiah in the time of the Assyrian crisis of 701 BCE, while vv. 17-24 bear strong marks of the exilic or post-exilic period.[259]

29:15-16. As with other prophetic woe speeches, the introductory cry is followed by an indictment of the addressees by describing what they are doing. The speech does not name the accused explicitly, but in the context they can only

257. Marvin A. Sweeney, *Isaiah 1–39, With an Introduction to Prophetic Literature,* FOTL XVI (Grand Rapids: Eerdmans, 1996) 382.
258. Ronald E. Clements, *Isaiah 1–39,* NCB (Grand Rapids: Eerdmans, 1980) 241.
259. See O. Kaiser, *Isaiah 13–39: A Commentary* (Philadelphia: Westminster, 1974) 275-76.

be the leaders in Jerusalem. The prophet accuses them of concealing their "plan" from the Lord, and then provides evidence for their culpability in the form of a quotation of their own words. They say, "Who sees us? Who knows us?" (v. 15). The allegation that their "plan [is] too deep for the LORD" drips with irony if not sarcasm. In fact, nothing is "too deep" for the Lord. The accusation could be a general theological one, applying to anyone who challenges God's wisdom or knowledge. Here, however, it would apply to the political plans of Hezekiah and his court, plans that go against the Lord's design for Jerusalem.

The accusation continues in an argumentative tone in v. 16. A series of rhetorical questions, each presuming the answer "no," claims that the addressees are thinking they can reverse reality, "turn things upside down." The leaders cannot claim to know better than God, nor does it make sense to think they can change those divine plans with designs of their own. It would be just as easy for a pot to say to its maker, "You did not make me." The metaphor of God as potter and human beings as clay suggests the account of the Lord's creation of the first human being from "the dust of the ground" (Gen 2:7). Specifically, Isaiah is attacking Jerusalem's reliance on Egypt for relief from Assyrian aggression. In effect, the leadership has refused to take the prophet's word seriously as the word of God. They have been both arrogant and faithless.

29:17-21. Instead of the expected announcement of judgment following an indictment, this passage announces salvation, and the establishment of justice. It brims with reversals of previous proclamations of judgment against God's people. In the context, these verses interpret the indictment in vv. 15-16 to mean: You have no idea how dramatically God can change circumstances, both in the external world and among human beings! Its substantive link with what precedes, then, is in terms of human wisdom contrasted with God's wisdom. In addition, the pattern of rhetorical questions continues in v. 17, suggesting a possible formal link to the preceding unit.

All the discourse in these verses, including the rhetorical questions, concerns the future. At least on the surface, v. 17 proclaims a transformation of nature, a reversal of present circumstances. The mountain of Lebanon will become "a fruitful field" and "the fruitful field" a forest. That would be dif-

ficult to understand in the context of an announcement of good news, so the language must be metaphorical, with Lebanon regarded as Judah or Israel and the "fruitful field" as their enemies. That makes sense in the light of the reference to the "tyrant" in v. 20. Even more important, the announcement fundamentally concerns power and the powerful, proclaiming the reversal of status. The deaf will hear, the blind see, the meek and needy will celebrate, the tyrant and scoffer will be no more, and those who corrupt the courts to deny justice to those who need it will be cut off.

The promise that the deaf will "hear the words of a scroll" and the blind shall see (v. 18) ties the oral to the written word. Moreover, this promise alludes back to and reverses the announcement in 29:11-12, and anticipates the affirmation in 30:8 that words written on a tablet, in a book, will stand in the future as a witness. The "meek" and "neediest people" who will "exult in the Holy One of Israel" (v. 19) could refer to the Lord's people as a whole, but could mean a particular class or group. The promise that "the tyrant," probably a foreign king, "shall be no more" (v. 20) suggests that the people as a whole are in view. On the other hand, the affirmation that justice will be established in the courts (v. 21) seems to presume that the powerless among the people are intended. This verse presumes the usual legal practice in ancient Israel, where parties to a civil or criminal proceeding would meet to argue their case (cf. Amos 5:12; 2:6-7). The good news is that no one will be allowed to interfere with the judicial process so as to "deny justice to the one in the right" (v. 21).

29:22-24. "Therefore" and the formula for the word of the Lord introduce the final unit in this section, another announcement of salvation concerning "the house of Jacob" (v. 22). The identification of the Lord as the one "who redeemed Abraham" is unusual. In fact, this is the only occurrence of the name of that patriarch in Isaiah 1–39, although it appears in the second part of the book (41:8; 51:2; 63:16). This fact alone lends credence to the conclusion—also supported by the language and ideas of the rest of the unit—that the announcement comes from the time of the Babylonian exile or later.

What is the meaning of the phrase "who redeemed Abraham"? Does this refer to some episode in the story of Abraham? Some interpreters have suggested that this alludes to the Lord's "redemption" of Abraham from the non-Yahwistic deities of Haran, and some late pseud-epigraphical texts interpret the expression that way.[260] In fact, however, 29:22 provides the only biblical instance of this particular phrase, so it is impossible to know what it may refer to. More important, the expression "who redeemed Abraham" is a theological rather than a biographical statement. It is less concerned with Abraham than with affirming the Lord as the one who redeems, thus emphasizing the continuity of divine care from the earliest ancestor to the present day.

Nor is the denotation of "Jacob" or the "house of Jacob" self-evident. The name may refer to Israel as a whole, the traditional descendants of that patriarch's twelve sons, or it may refer more narrowly to the northern kingdom. Both meanings appear in Isaiah 1–39, and in Isaiah 40–66 "Jacob" invariably refers to the nation or the people as a whole, with the old political divisions virtually forgotten. Although some have taken this instance as a reference to the northern kingdom, captured by the Assyrians in 722/21,[261] the context supports the other more inclusive meaning, as in Isaiah 40–66.

The language and expectations in this prophecy of salvation are thoroughly religious and spiritual, not political. The "house of Jacob" will "no longer be ashamed," because its descendants will "sanctify" the name of the Lord, the "Holy One of Jacob," standing in awe in the presence of the God of Israel. That the people will no longer be ashamed presumes that they are or have been ashamed. One could readily relate this to political subjugation or the Babylonian exile. Insofar as that is the case, the context suggests that the roots of this shame lie in the religious question: Do such disasters mean that the God of Israel has abandoned Jacob, or is subordinate to the gods of Babylon? This promise, set before Jacob's "children" (v. 23), presents a clear answer. Those "children," the actual addressees of these verses, will acknowledge the Holy One of Jacob as worthy of awe.

The concluding verse (24) returns to the theme of wisdom and stupidity, promising a reversal of what was expressed in v. 14 (cf. also 29:9-12 and 15-16). Its sentiments parallel those of Prov 1:17: "The fear of the LORD is the beginning of knowledge." That is, true piety leads to wisdom, and instruction leads to true piety.

260. See Kaiser, *Isaiah 13–39*, 280-81.
261. Such a reading is used in support of an eighth-century BCE date for the unit. See Sweeney, *Isaiah 1–39*, 382.

REFLECTIONS

1. In continuing the theme of the limitations of human wisdom from the first part of the chapter, vv. 15-16 evoke consideration of the relationship of human plans to divine knowledge. Addressed to the leaders in Jerusalem concerning their political plans, the prophetic voice accuses those leaders of the highest form of deception. They think they can plan in the dark and thus hide their schemes from the Lord. Obviously, one problem is that those plans run against what the Lord has designed for the city and its people. Even more fundamental, however, is the delusion that any human activities could be concealed from the creator of all life. The accusation makes sense to the faithful. That nothing can be hidden from God is self-evident, and to challenge divine wisdom is as if the pot denied that it was turned into a pot by the potter. Nevertheless, the existence of the accusation indicates that some within the prophet's hearing would not agree with the assertion that God knows all and created all.

In the contemporary world, thinking about God's knowledge may lead to consideration of a doctrine of omniscience and to attempts to sort out the relationship between divine knowledge and divine power. Or it may lead to more personal considerations, both comforting and troubling. God may be experienced as the one who knows our very hearts, who understands our thoughts and feelings even before we express them. Conversely, such all-encompassing knowledge may be experienced as threats to our own identity and integrity. If one is guided by the biblical images, the tension between divine knowledge and authority on the one hand and human autonomy on the other is never fully resolved.

2. Like so much of prophetic discourse, this passage bristles with reversals of circumstances. Even more, the metaphor of the potter and the clay (29:16) expresses the accusation that the hearers have reversed reality itself, thinking they (the clay) can become the potter (God). Mostly, however, reversals concern the future as announced by prophets. For example, the prophet Amos, in a time of relative peace and prosperity, proclaimed that God would reverse Israel's circumstances, that the nation would fall to an enemy and be carried into exile. The Lord would rise up as in the holy war against the enemies, but the Lord's own people would be the enemy.

The announcement of reversals in this passage addresses people in trouble: the deaf, the blind, the meek, the neediest people. The language is both literal and figurative as the promise comes that these will hear, see, be joyful, and exult in the Holy One of Israel. The transformation will be accomplished by reversing the circumstances of the powerful. The tyrant, the scoffer, those who plot evil, and those who corrupt the courts will cease to exist. Moreover, even natural circumstances will be transformed: Lebanon, representing the uncultivated wilderness, will become a fruitful field, and the fruitful field will become a forest. Thus those in trouble, whether physical, political, economic, or legal, are urged to take hope.

A more general implication would be: Anyone who listens for the word of God, whether through prophetic voices or in any possible way, should be prepared for surprises. Many of those surprises will turn out to be reversals of expectation (cf. Mark 10:31; Luke 13:30). We might do well to be guided by that line from one of the early Puritan covenants, "We pledge ourselves to the ways of God, known or to be made known to us."

ISAIAH 30:1-33, FOOLISH ALLIANCES, HEALING, AND JUDGMENT ON ASSYRIA

NIV

30 "Woe to the obstinate children,"
declares the LORD,
"to those who carry out plans that are not mine,
forming an alliance, but not by my Spirit,
heaping sin upon sin;
[2] who go down to Egypt
without consulting me;
who look for help to Pharaoh's protection,
to Egypt's shade for refuge.
[3] But Pharaoh's protection will be to your shame,
Egypt's shade will bring you disgrace.
[4] Though they have officials in Zoan
and their envoys have arrived in Hanes,
[5] everyone will be put to shame
because of a people useless to them,
who bring neither help nor advantage,
but only shame and disgrace."

[6] An oracle concerning the animals of the Negev:

NRSV

30 Oh, rebellious children, says the LORD,
who carry out a plan, but not mine;
who make an alliance, but against my will,
adding sin to sin;
[2] who set out to go down to Egypt
without asking for my counsel,
to take refuge in the protection of Pharaoh,
and to seek shelter in the shadow of Egypt;
[3] Therefore the protection of Pharaoh shall become your shame,
and the shelter in the shadow of Egypt your humiliation.
[4] For though his officials are at Zoan
and his envoys reach Hanes,
[5] everyone comes to shame
through a people that cannot profit them,
that brings neither help nor profit,
but shame and disgrace.

[6] An oracle concerning the animals of the Negeb.

NIV

Through a land of hardship and distress,
  of lions and lionesses,
  of adders and darting snakes,
the envoys carry their riches on donkeys' backs,
  their treasures on the humps of camels,
to that unprofitable nation,
[7] to Egypt, whose help is utterly useless.
Therefore I call her
  Rahab the Do-Nothing.

[8]Go now, write it on a tablet for them,
  inscribe it on a scroll,
that for the days to come
  it may be an everlasting witness.
[9]These are rebellious people, deceitful children,
  children unwilling to listen to the Lord's
    instruction.
[10]They say to the seers,
  "See no more visions!"
and to the prophets,
  "Give us no more visions of what is right!
Tell us pleasant things,
  prophesy illusions.
[11]Leave this way,
  get off this path,
and stop confronting us
  with the Holy One of Israel!"

[12]Therefore, this is what the Holy One of Israel
says:

"Because you have rejected this message,
  relied on oppression
  and depended on deceit,
[13]this sin will become for you
  like a high wall, cracked and bulging,
  that collapses suddenly, in an instant.
[14]It will break in pieces like pottery,
  shattered so mercilessly
that among its pieces not a fragment will
    be found
  for taking coals from a hearth
  or scooping water out of a cistern."

[15]This is what the Sovereign Lord, the Holy
One of Israel, says:

"In repentance and rest is your salvation,
  in quietness and trust is your strength,
  but you would have none of it.
[16]You said, 'No, we will flee on horses.'

NRSV

Through a land of trouble and distress,
  of lioness and roaring[a] lion,
  of viper and flying serpent,
they carry their riches on the backs
    of donkeys,
  and their treasures on the humps
    of camels,
to a people that cannot profit them.
[7] For Egypt's help is worthless and empty,
  therefore I have called her,
  "Rahab who sits still."[b]

[8] Go now, write it before them on a tablet,
  and inscribe it in a book,
so that it may be for the time to come
  as a witness forever.
[9] For they are a rebellious people,
  faithless children,
children who will not hear
  the instruction of the Lord;
[10] who say to the seers, "Do not see";
  and to the prophets, "Do not prophesy to
    us what is right;
speak to us smooth things,
  prophesy illusions,
[11] leave the way, turn aside from the path,
  let us hear no more about the Holy One
    of Israel."
[12] Therefore thus says the Holy One of Israel:
  Because you reject this word,
  and put your trust in oppression and deceit,
  and rely on them;
[13] therefore this iniquity shall become for you
  like a break in a high wall, bulging out, and
    about to collapse,
  whose crash comes suddenly, in an instant;
[14] its breaking is like that of a potter's vessel
  that is smashed so ruthlessly
that among its fragments not a sherd is found
  for taking fire from the hearth,
  or dipping water out of the cistern.

[15] For thus said the Lord God, the Holy One
    of Israel:
In returning and rest you shall be saved;
  in quietness and in trust shall be your
    strength.

[a]Cn: Heb *from them*   [b]Meaning of Heb uncertain

NIV

Therefore you will flee!
You said, 'We will ride off on swift horses.'
Therefore your pursuers will be swift!
¹⁷A thousand will flee
  at the threat of one;
at the threat of five
  you will all flee away,
till you are left
  like a flagstaff on a mountaintop,
  like a banner on a hill."

¹⁸Yet the LORD longs to be gracious to you;
  he rises to show you compassion.
For the LORD is a God of justice.
  Blessed are all who wait for him!

¹⁹O people of Zion, who live in Jerusalem, you will weep no more. How gracious he will be when you cry for help! As soon as he hears, he will answer you. ²⁰Although the Lord gives you the bread of adversity and the water of affliction, your teachers will be hidden no more; with your own eyes you will see them. ²¹Whether you turn to the right or to the left, your ears will hear a voice behind you, saying, "This is the way; walk in it." ²²Then you will defile your idols overlaid with silver and your images covered with gold; you will throw them away like a menstrual cloth and say to them, "Away with you!"

²³He will also send you rain for the seed you sow in the ground, and the food that comes from the land will be rich and plentiful. In that day your cattle will graze in broad meadows. ²⁴The oxen and donkeys that work the soil will eat fodder and mash, spread out with fork and shovel. ²⁵In the day of great slaughter, when the towers fall, streams of water will flow on every high mountain and every lofty hill. ²⁶The moon will shine like the sun, and the sunlight will be seven times brighter, like the light of seven full days, when the LORD binds up the bruises of his people and heals the wounds he inflicted.

²⁷See, the Name of the LORD comes from afar,
  with burning anger and dense clouds
    of smoke;
  his lips are full of wrath,
    and his tongue is a consuming fire.
²⁸His breath is like a rushing torrent,
  rising up to the neck.

NRSV

But you refused ¹⁶and said,
  "No! We will flee upon horses"—
    therefore you shall flee!
and, "We will ride upon swift steeds"—
    therefore your pursuers shall be swift!
¹⁷ A thousand shall flee at the threat of one,
  at the threat of five you shall flee,
until you are left
  like a flagstaff on the top of a mountain,
  like a signal on a hill.

¹⁸ Therefore the LORD waits to be gracious
      to you;
  therefore he will rise up to show mercy
      to you.
For the LORD is a God of justice;
  blessed are all those who wait for him.

19Truly, O people in Zion, inhabitants of Jerusalem, you shall weep no more. He will surely be gracious to you at the sound of your cry; when he hears it, he will answer you. ²⁰Though the Lord may give you the bread of adversity and the water of affliction, yet your Teacher will not hide himself any more, but your eyes shall see your Teacher. ²¹And when you turn to the right or when you turn to the left, your ears shall hear a word behind you, saying, "This is the way; walk in it." ²²Then you will defile your silver-covered idols and your gold-plated images. You will scatter them like filthy rags; you will say to them, "Away with you!"

23He will give rain for the seed with which you sow the ground, and grain, the produce of the ground, which will be rich and plenteous. On that day your cattle will graze in broad pastures; ²⁴and the oxen and donkeys that till the ground will eat silage, which has been winnowed with shovel and fork. ²⁵On every lofty mountain and every high hill there will be brooks running with water—on a day of the great slaughter, when the towers fall. ²⁶Moreover the light of the moon will be like the light of the sun, and the light of the sun will be sevenfold, like the light of seven days, on the day when the LORD binds up the injuries of his people, and heals the wounds inflicted by his blow.

²⁷ See, the name of the LORD comes from
      far away,

NIV

He shakes the nations in the sieve of
destruction;
he places in the jaws of the peoples
a bit that leads them astray.
29And you will sing
as on the night you celebrate a holy festival;
your hearts will rejoice
as when people go up with flutes
to the mountain of the LORD,
to the Rock of Israel.
30The LORD will cause men to hear his
majestic voice
and will make them see his arm
coming down
with raging anger and consuming fire,
with cloudburst, thunderstorm and hail.
31The voice of the LORD will shatter Assyria;
with his scepter he will strike them down.
32Every stroke the LORD lays on them
with his punishing rod
will be to the music of tambourines and harps,
as he fights them in battle with the blows of
his arm.
33Topheth has long been prepared;
it has been made ready for the king.
Its fire pit has been made deep and wide,
with an abundance of fire and wood;
the breath of the LORD,
like a stream of burning sulfur,
sets it ablaze.

NRSV

burning with his anger, and in thick rising
smoke;*a*
his lips are full of indignation,
and his tongue is like a devouring fire;
28 his breath is like an overflowing stream
that reaches up to the neck—
to sift the nations with the sieve of destruction,
and to place on the jaws of the peoples a bri-
dle that leads them astray.

29You shall have a song as in the night when a
holy festival is kept; and gladness of heart, as
when one sets out to the sound of the flute to go
to the mountain of the LORD, to the Rock of Israel.
30And the LORD will cause his majestic voice to be
heard and the descending blow of his arm to be
seen, in furious anger and a flame of devouring
fire, with a cloudburst and tempest and hailstones. 31The Assyrian will be terror-stricken at
the voice of the LORD, when he strikes with his
rod. 32And every stroke of the staff of punishment
that the LORD lays upon him will be to the sound
of timbrels and lyres; battling with brandished
arm he will fight with him. 33For his burning
place*b* has long been prepared; truly it is made
ready for the king,*c* its pyre made deep and wide,
with fire and wood in abundance; the breath of
the LORD, like a stream of sulfur, kindles it.

*a*Meaning of Heb uncertain   *b*Or *Topheth*   *c*Or *Molech*

COMMENTARY

Under the typical heading ("Woe") that organizes the larger sections of chaps. 28–33 appear
three discrete parts (vv. 1-17, 18-26, and 27-33),
each of which in turn consists of several units.[262]
Clearly the chapter contains materials that originated over a long period, from as early as the time
of Isaiah in the eighth century BCE, to the
Babylonian exile, and even as late as the return of
the exiles in the sixth century. Recognizing a
theme that unified the chapter is difficult if not

impossible. Viewed as it stands, however, there is
a development of thought that includes themes
from virtually the full spectrum of thought in
prophetic literature. The chapter opens with accusations and indictments followed by prophetic
announcement of disaster (vv. 1-17). Then comes
a prophecy of salvation to God's people (vv. 18-
26), but salvation proclaimed in the midst of disaster and announcing its end. Finally (vv. 27-33),
judgment is proclaimed on that ancient enemy of
Judah and Israel, Assyria, accompanied by joyful
celebration by the Lord's people.

In fact, concern with Assyria begins and ends
the chapter. Although that nation is not mentioned

262. Sweeney, ibid., 386-92, divides the chapter into two main units
under the general heading "Prophetic Instruction Speech," with vv. 1-
26 taken as the instruction proper and vv. 27-33 as an announcement
concerning Assyria.

in the first part, the Assyrian Empire and its expansionistic policies are presumed here, and cast a shadow over the scene. It was the threat from Assyria that motivated Judah's alliance with Egypt, which is condemned by the prophet.

30:1-17. United by the same historical circumstances and the common theme of the folly of an alliance with Egypt against Assyria are three sections, vv. 1-5, 6-7, and 8-17. In addition to the "woe" that marks the beginning, there is a new heading in v. 6, and a clear shift in speaker, addressee, and specific issues in v. 8. As almost all modern interpreters have recognized, these materials stem from Isaiah and concern the Assyrian crisis that Jerusalem faced in 705–701 BCE, including the events reported in Isaiah 36–37. These units concern the international intrigues generated by the advance of Assyria into the region, and in particular by Hezekiah's negotiations concerning an alliance with Egypt against Assyria (see 36:6).[263] From the point of view of international politics, one can readily see why Egypt would encourage alliances with the states in Syria-Palestine. It was to their advantage to set up buffer states that would at the very least slow the Assyrian advance toward Egypt, and force the Assyrian army to burn up resources and stretch out its supply lines. By the same token, one could understand why Judah would seek shelter under the wing of Egypt against the Assyrians, but small states often pay the price for struggles among the dominant powers.

Isaiah responded unambiguously to the negotiations with Egypt, condemning them out of hand and announcing that reliance on Egypt would lead to disaster (see also 31:1-3).[264] One may ask to what extent this judgment was based on political or religious foundations.[265] The traditions preserved in this and the subsequent chapter present faith in Yahweh as the alternative to trust in foreign alliances. Those who advocate an alliance with Egypt are "rebellious children" (v. 1), acting

against the will of the Lord, rejecting the word of the Lord through the prophets and seers (v. 10).

The cry "Woe" (v. 1; see the Commentary on 5:8-24) introduces more than a warning against the alliance with Egypt. Unlike most prophetic woe speeches, this one is attributed directly to the Lord. The woe cry initiates a classic prophecy of judgment (vv. 1-5), with the indictment of the addressees or the reasons for punishment following the woe (vv. 1-2). Then comes the announcement proper, introduced by "therefore" (vv. 3-5). As usual, the lines immediately following the woe describe the accused in terms of their actions. These activities are characterized first generally as rebellion against the Lord (v. 1), the address as "rebellious children" recalling the accusation in 1:2, 4. They have undertaken plans of their own, not considering the Lord's plan (see 29:15-16).[266] Then the actions are set out more specifically as going to Egypt to make an alliance or treaty and "seeking shelter in the shadow of Egypt" (v. 2). The Lord need not intervene to punish, for disaster will follow directly, and will fit the sinful actions. The results of rebellion, "shame and disgrace" (v. 5), appear somewhat vague, but probably entail the humiliation of military defeat.

To "carry out a plan" that is not the Lord's and to "make an alliance" against the Lord's will (v. 1) refer not to general avoidance of divine expectations but to specific procedures that, according to tradition, were to be carried out before involving the people in wars or treaties. How does one determine the will of the Lord? One is expected to ask for the Lord's counsel (v. 2). In the case of the holy war, various forms of consultation were possible (Judg 1:1; 6:36-40; 20:18; 1 Sam 13:41). Likewise, the leaders of Israel in the time of Joshua were condemned for failing to consult the Lord before making a treaty (Josh 9:14-21).

Although originally a distinct unit with its own heading, vv. 6-7 here amplify the theme of the previous verses: It is foolish to seek help from Egypt. The heading, "An oracle (משא *maśśá'*; see the Commentary on 13:1-22) concerning the animals of the Negeb," parallels the superscriptions of the oracles concerning the foreign nations in Isaiah

---

263. Seitz points out that Hezekiah is not mentioned by name here and doubts the particular concern with the king in this section. See Christopher R. Seitz, *Isaiah 1–39,* Interpretation (Louisville: John Knox, 1993) 215-17.

264. See also R. E. Clements, *Isaiah and the Deliverance of Jerusalem: A Study in the Interpretation of Prophecy in the Old Testament,* JSOTSup 13 (Sheffield: JSOT, 1980) 29-31.

265. Clements, ibid., 29-32, emphasizes the political dimensions, and Seitz, *Isaiah 1–39,* 219, stresses its religious basis.

266. Although clearly a prophetic address, many of the expressions and ideas are closely related to the wisdom traditions. See J. William Whedbee, *Isaiah and Wisdom* (Nashville: Abingdon, 1971) 132.

13–23. The "Negeb" was the semidesert between Judah and Egypt, and the "animals of the Negeb" listed are those that pose threats to any who venture into the region, including a camel caravan bearing "riches" and "treasures." The burdens of the donkeys and camels in this context suggest either trade with or the possibility of tribute carried to Egypt. Verse 7 emphasizes the folly of an alliance with Egypt by ridiculing Egypt's help as worthless. Although the Hebrew is uncertain and often emended, clearly Egypt is given a sarcastic title. "Rahab the Do-Nothing" (NIV) is based on one of the names of the chaos dragon slain by the deity (see 27:1). Rahab is known as a synonym for Egypt (cf. Ps 87:4).

A new section begins with v. 8 with a shift of addressee and continues through v. 11. Up to this point the prophet had presented the word of the Lord to the leadership in Jerusalem, and perhaps to the people as a whole. Now the Lord is heard to give instructions to the prophet, referring to the people in the third person (vv. 8, 9, 10). However, the people are expected to overhear those instructions, particularly as Isaiah reported what he had heard. The reference to "foolish children" (v. 9; cf. v. 1) links this section to vv. 1-5.

The instructions are similar to those in 8:1-4, 16-18 in that the prophet receives a message from the Lord telling him to write something down as evidence that the word of the Lord was known in advance. In the background is the sense, if not the actual practice, of legal contracts and juridical procedures in ancient Israel, which relied upon witnessed documents to prove past actions or agreements. Later, Second Isaiah will refer to past prophecies that prove Yahweh acted because the deeds were announced in advance. Here the written words will be "a witness forever" (v. 8) that the people rebelled against the Lord.

Verses 8-11 function as specifications of that rebellion. As in v. 1 (see also 1:2, 4), the rebellious people are called children. Here their rebellion is characterized generally as refusal to hear the "instruction" (תורה *tôrâ,* v. 9) of the Lord.[267] Specifically, they attempt to censor the voices that communicate divine instruction, the seers and the prophets, by telling them either to receive no

revelations ("do not see") or to prophesy only pleasant things, that is, "illusions." In fact, they want the mediators of revelation out of their way so that they will not have to listen to anything about the Holy One of Israel, or, if they must speak, to tell lies. This indictment, like so many others, is validated by citing the words of the accused.

The "therefore" and the messenger formula of v. 12 signal a move from indictment to announcement of punishment. Still, the accusation is repeated: "because you reject this word and put your trust in oppression and deceit" (v. 12*b*). "This word" must refer to a particular prophetic message, such as the one that follows in vv. 15-17. The second "therefore" (v. 13) begins the announcement of judgment itself. But it is not necessary for the Lord to intervene directly, for the "iniquity shall become" the disaster. This is another instance of a dynamistic rather than a juridical understanding of the relationship between acts and consequences (see the Reflections at 1:2-20 and the Commentary on 9:8–10:4). The coming catastrophe is set out by means of two similes: a breaking wall, and a smashed pot. The first simile actually describes the thing itself, a break in a wall about to collapse, and a sudden crash. This amounts to a successful siege of the city. The simile of the potter's vessel smashed ruthlessly recalls the metaphor of the potter and clay of 29:16. The pot is smashed—note the passive formulation—so completely that not even a sherd of usable size remains. Certainly Isaiah has in view the negotiations with Egypt, which he expects to produce disaster.[268]

A new and expansive introductory formula for the word of the Lord ("For thus says the Lord God, the Holy One of Israel," v. 15) begins a new section of this unit. However, the initial "For" (כי *kî*) links it to the preceding verses. Under such a heading one expects a prophetic announcement, and that is what appears. The indictment comes in the form of an account, a report of what the Lord had said and how the people had responded. The Lord had presented an alternative to foreign alliances that produce debacles, namely, salvation and strength—including political security—come from "returning and rest," "quietness and trust" (v. 15). The vocabulary setting out the alternative to

---

267. See Joseph Jensen, *The Use of tôrâ by Isaiah,* CBQMS 3 (Washington: Catholic Biblical Association, 1973) 112-20.

268. Clements, *Isaiah and the Deliverance of Jerusalem,* 29-31.

disaster is complex. The term translated "returning" in the NRSV (שׁובה *šûbâ*) appears only here, and the word for "rest" is uncommon. In spite of interpretations that move these terms in the direction of either a political understanding or a particular religious sense (e.g., "repentance" as in the NIV), the more vague sense of "returning" is to be preferred.[269] The sense of the second pair ("quietness and trust") is clear enough to support the conclusion that the words taken as a whole add up to a call for faith in the Lord and in the Lord's protection of Zion. Thus in important respects this invitation parallels 7:1-9. In both instances Isaiah urges faith in the Lord's promises instead of trust in foreign alliances.

The indictment (v. 16*a*) comes in the form of a quotation of how the leaders in Jerusalem reacted to the Lord's instructions. Instead of quiet faith, they vowed to flee on horseback; instead of calm, they panicked. "Therefore" introduces the announcement of judgment (vv. 16*b*-17), a punishment that matches the violation. Those who trusted in horses will indeed flee, but their pursuers will be even swifter (cf. Amos 2:14-16). The final image reveals nothing left but a "flagstaff on the top of a mountain" (cf. 5:1-7).

30:18-26. Again an announcement of the future begins with the transitional "Therefore," but unlike the others in this chapter, this one prophesies salvation. Moreover, nothing connects this proclamation to what precedes. The form is direct address, the "you" of v. 18 identified in v. 19 as "people in Zion." Only v. 18 is poetry; that vv. 19-26 are prose already suggests they are a later interpretation. Both the theological motifs and the assumptions about historical circumstances strongly indicate that this material comes from the time of the Babylonian exile or perhaps even later.[270] The theme of the passage is that the Lord will bring healing beyond a time of punishment. Those who suffer adversity (v. 20) are encouraged to remain faithful by the assurance that a punishment will purge them and by the promise of restored prosperity.

This announcement of salvation parallels virtually all others in the OT in that no human action justifies the salvific deeds. Rather, the reason lies in the Lord's decision to be merciful because the Lord is a God of justice (v. 18). This description of the glorious future presumes a great deal concerning the circumstances into which the Lord will intervene. That those will be blessed "who wait for him" (v. 18) and that the Lord will respond to the "cry" of the people (v. 19) assumes a period of prayerful suffering. The promise presupposes that the Lord who is coming to save is responsible for the suffering itself ("Though the LORD may give you the bread of adversity . . ." v. 20; "heals the wounds inflicted by his blow," v. 26). Moreover, the expectation that when the people are shown the right way they will "defile" and "scatter" their idols and images (v. 22) presumes they have given homage of some type to the symbols of non-Yahwistic religions. The passage as a whole expresses eschatological if not apocalyptic views, including the expectation of an unidentified "Teacher," a "day of great slaughter" (v. 25), and a dramatic change in the light from the moon and the sun (v. 26).[271]

The last paragraph of the promise of salvation turns to the fruitfulness of the land as a gift of God. The fertility of what we now call "nature" is a common theme in exilic and post-exilic announcement of salvation (e.g., Amos 9:13-15). The scene is one of domestic tranquility filled with the riches of agriculture and animal husbandry, all of which come as the result of a gift of God, the rain. The vision here corresponds closely to the understanding of the Yahwist's creation account, in which the Lord provides the rain and the human being the labor.[272] Thus the two in effect function as co-creators of the world, understood as the "cultivated ground" (אדמה *'ădāmâ*). But, remarkably, with the reference to "every lofty mountain and every high hill" (v. 25), the vision of fertility suggests imagery used elsewhere to condemn fertility religion (2 Kgs 14:23; 17:10; Jer 2:20; 3:6; 17:2). The vision closes with the violent image of "a day of great slaughter," when the lights in the heavens herald the Lord's intervention to heal.

30:27-33. The controlling theme of this passage is the proclamation of judgment, specifically against Assyria. It consists of two main parts. First

---

269. Hans Wildberger, *Jesaja: Kapitel 28–39* (Neukirchen-Vluyn: Neukirchener Verlag, 1982) 1180.

270. Ibid., 1193-95, and most modern commentators.

271. See O. Kaiser, *Isaiah 13–39: A Commentary* (Philadelphia: Westminster, 1974) 301.

272. See Theodore Hiebert, *The Yahwist's Landscape: Nature and Religion in Early Israel* (New York: Oxford University Press, 1996).

(vv. 27-28), the terrible approach of the Lord is announced. Then (vv. 29-33) as the purpose of the Lord's appearance is revealed to be the punishment of Assyria, rejoicing breaks out. The authorship and date of this section are difficult if not impossible to determine; the possibilities range from the time of Isaiah to the second century.[273] Indeed, it is unlikely that all these lines originated at the same time. While in their juxtaposition, the two parts amount to a proclamation of the Lord's judgment against Assyria, each could easily stand alone. Verses 27-28 make no mention of a particular object of the Lord's wrath but proclaim that Yahweh is coming in anger against the nations. Verses 29-33 see the Lord's wrath focused upon Assyria, but they are in the form of direct address to the Lord's own people, announcing that they will celebrate on Zion ("the mountain of the LORD," v. 29) the Lord's appearance to judge. In other respects the parts are different formally. The fact that vv. 29-33 may be construed as either prose or poetry is reflected in the different translations, with NRSV reading as prose and NIV (cf. also TNK and REB) taking the lines as poetic.

The mention of the "name of the LORD," particularly in a context that refers to the Temple Mount in Jerusalem, recalls the theology of Deuteronomy ("choose as a dwelling place for his name," Deut 12:11). Some of the language in these verses recalls the theophany tradition, in which the appearance of the Lord is accompanied by disturbing natural phenomena. However, here the Lord does not "come down" but marches forth. Metaphors are mixed. The Lord's advance is like a fire, but also like an "overflowing stream" (vv. 27-28). Indeed, v. 30 draws upon a wide range of traditions concerning the theophany: The Lord appears through God's "voice," the descending blow of his arm," a "flame of devouring fire," and the "cloudburst and tempest and hailstones." However, unlike many other theophany reports, Yahweh's appearance is not for the purpose of revelation but in anger to "sift the nations with the sieve of destruction," v. 28). Thus the "name" is like the standard carried at the head of an advancing army.

Verses 30-32 are filled with remarkable imagery, particularly combining a scene of celebration on the "mountain of the LORD" with one of destruction, the sound of musical instruments with that of the Lord's angry voice. The music is related to rituals in the Temple, but the fight to the music of timbrels and lyres is reminiscent of the noise of the holy war (Josh 6:1-20). "Tophet" (NIV) or "his burning place" (NRSV, see the footnote) was a place just outside of Jerusalem where human sacrifices had been offered to the god Molech (see Lev 18:21; 2 Kgs 23:10). It was not the hell of subsequent tradition but certainly provided some of the imagery for later ideas of that place.

273. For a summary of the main alternatives, see Ronald E. Clements, *Isaiah 1–39,* NCB (Grand Rapids: Eerdmans, 1980) 252.

REFLECTIONS

1. The accusations against the people in vv. 10-11 could sound familiar in any age. Leaders as well as people in general have been known to tell their seers and prophets to "speak to us smooth things, prophesy illusions," to tell them only what they want to hear. In politics, and in public discourse generally, bad news is not welcome. It may even be suggested that anyone who brings bad news in wartime is a traitor, giving aid and comfort to the enemy. Certainly that was true in the United States in the time of the Vietnam war. Often one hears that bad news is a self-fulfilling prophecy, and that military defeat or bad times can be avoided if only one would not talk about them. Frequently one hears that to talk about an economic recession, for example, is to increase the likelihood that it will happen.

This appears on the face of it to be a foolish idea, but why is it so persistent? To be sure, there can be some truth to it. Public attitudes, and therefore actions, can be shaped by expectations. Moreover, one just might make matters worse by obsessing on them. And there are such things as self-fulfilling prophecies. Another factor could be residual belief in magical causation. To say something is to cause it. And certainly the human capacity for denial is a significant factor.

However, confrontation with the facts of a situation, even when that consists of harsh news, is fundamental to facing reality and, when possible, doing something about it or coming to terms with it.

With regard for the process of facing the truth in questions of national policy or action, is there any place at all for prophetic voices in secular states? No doubt, confrontation with the possibility of disaster arising from particular decisions on both foreign and domestic policy is important in public debate in democratic societies. That debate continues, for example, concerning the Vietnam war, with many arguing that the protests against American action finally brought the conflict to an end, and others arguing it only prolonged the war and prevented victory by the United States forces. This text, however, claims divine authority for pronouncements concerning foreign alliances, accusing the leaders of refusing to hear the "instruction of the LORD" (v. 9). Where is the place, if any, for such claims in modern states? Is it a sufficiently prophetic act to make the moral and political dimensions clear? To be sure, whether religious authority is claimed or not, most moral assertions are informed by religious commitments.

Behind the prophetic accusations in this text lies the ancient Israelite practice of consultation before going to war, seeking to determine God's will through formal inquiry or ritual. Consultation in modern states takes the form of collecting information and seeking the judgment of experts. Many leaders are reported to pray over decisions, but that is hardly the same as consulting an oracle. On the one hand, all who take the biblical tradition seriously can appreciate leaders whose decisions are shaped by their faith in God. But on the other hand, there are risks. Even prayer might be a way to hear only "smooth things," "illusions." Some of those prayers even seem to be taking the name of the Lord in vain, as in praying for victory before a football game.

Not only with regard to national policy but also in relation to individuals, families, and small groups there can be a time and place for hard prophetic words. In fact, care, including pastoral care, must include telling the truth, even when it is not what a listener wants to hear. Even the prophetic announcements of judgment could function positively. In most instances, the indictments in such proclamations mean to make the disaster understandable, reasonable. In some cases such punishment is viewed as purging (Isa 1:18-20; Hos 2:1-15; 3:1-5). At least in some cases, while the prophetic purpose was to bring about punishment, the effect could be repentance and thus avoidance of the disaster. That is the situation with Jonah, whose message was the announcement of judgment upon Nineveh (Jonah 3:4), but first the people and then God repented (3:6-10). In the exilic and post-exilic periods, the earlier prophetic words of judgment were reinterpreted as warnings (see the prose speeches in Jeremiah). Ezekiel appears to have seen his role in such a light (Ezek 3:16-21; 33:7-16). In fact, echoing the concerns of Isa 30:9-11, some blamed the disaster of the exile on prophets who had not told the truth, and thus failed in their duty to "restore the fortunes" of the people:

Your prophets have seen for you;
    false and deceptive visions;
they have not exposed your iniquity
    to restore your fortunes,
but have seen for you oracles
    false and misleading. (Lam 2:14 NRSV)

Moreover, it was the pre-exilic interpretations of the national disaster as the result of sin that laid the basis for a hopeful future. The exile did not mean that history was meaningless or chaotic, but it was Yahweh's reaction to the failures of the covenant people. So the old prophetic indictments could serve later generations as confession of sin and thus the basis for a new covenant.

Whether before groups or individuals, the prophetic role involved, and continues to involve, confrontation. This was even the case in many of the announcements of salvation, such as those of Isaiah 40–55, which ran against the popular expectations. A classic but typical instance of prophetic confrontation is the response of Nathan to David's adultery with Bathsheba and his murder of her husband Uriah (2 Samuel 12). Uninvited, the prophet condemns the king's actions and announces the death penalty. When David confesses and repents, the sin still has its effects, but the punishment is modified.[274]

2. Some especially troubling expressions appear in 30:18-20, 26, expressions that assume the Lord is responsible for suffering. Clearly these lines were composed at a time when the people of the Lord were in trouble, suffering either during the Babylonian exile or later. It was not, however, just the expectation of better days ahead that enabled them to endure such distress, although such anticipation would have been comforting, empowering the people with hope. Even more important, grounds for confidence can be recognized in the very lines that may seem most troubling, the affirmations that the Lord was the author of the trouble. That would have enabled the faithful to affirm that their God was over events, and that their history, including times when they were punished for their sins, had meaning. Thus the faithful could see a direct connection between the justice and the mercy of God (v. 18).

274. Gene M. Tucker, "Old Testament Traditions and Theology of Care," *Dictionary of Pastoral Care and Counseling* (Nashville: Abingdon, 1990) 803-4.

ISAIAH 31:1-9, THE LORD, NOT EGYPT, PROTECTS JERUSALEM

31 Woe to those who go down to Egypt
  for help,
who rely on horses,
who trust in the multitude of their chariots
  and in the great strength of their horsemen,
but do not look to the Holy One of Israel,
  or seek help from the LORD.
[2]Yet he too is wise and can bring disaster;
  he does not take back his words.
He will rise up against the house of the wicked,
  against those who help evildoers.
[3]But the Egyptians are men and not God;
  their horses are flesh and not spirit.
When the LORD stretches out his hand,
  he who helps will stumble,
  he who is helped will fall;
  both will perish together.

[4]This is what the LORD says to me:

"As a lion growls,
  a great lion over his prey—
and though a whole band of shepherds

31 Alas for those who go down to Egypt
  for help
and who rely on horses,
who trust in chariots because they are many
  and in horsemen because they are
    very strong,
but do not look to the Holy One of Israel
  or consult the LORD!
[2]Yet he too is wise and brings disaster;
  he does not call back his words,
but will rise against the house of the evildoers,
  and against the helpers of those who work
    iniquity.
[3]The Egyptians are human, and not God;
  their horses are flesh, and not spirit.
When the LORD stretches out his hand,
  the helper will stumble, and the one
    helped will fall,
  and they will all perish together.

[4]For thus the LORD said to me,
  As a lion or a young lion growls over its prey,

NIV

is called together against him,
he is not frightened by their shouts
or disturbed by their clamor—
so the LORD Almighty will come down
to do battle on Mount Zion and on
its heights.
[5]Like birds hovering overhead,
the LORD Almighty will shield Jerusalem;
he will shield it and deliver it,
he will 'pass over' it and will rescue it."

[6]Return to him you have so greatly revolted against, O Israelites. [7]For in that day every one of you will reject the idols of silver and gold your sinful hands have made.

[8]"Assyria will fall by a sword that is not of man;
a sword, not of mortals, will devour them.
They will flee before the sword
and their young men will be put to
forced labor.
[9]Their stronghold will fall because of terror;
at sight of the battle standard their
commanders will panic,"
declares the LORD,
whose fire is in Zion,
whose furnace is in Jerusalem.

NRSV

and—when a band of shepherds is called
out against it—
is not terrified by their shouting
or daunted at their noise,
so the LORD of hosts will come down
to fight upon Mount Zion and upon its hill.
[5] Like birds hovering overhead, so the LORD
of hosts
will protect Jerusalem;
he will protect and deliver it,
he will spare and rescue it.

6Turn back to him whom you[a] have deeply betrayed, O people of Israel. [7]For on that day all of you shall throw away your idols of silver and idols of gold, which your hands have sinfully made for you.
[8] "Then the Assyrian shall fall by a sword, not
of mortals;
and a sword, not of humans, shall
devour him;
he shall flee from the sword,
and his young men shall be put to
forced labor.
[9] His rock shall pass away in terror,
and his officers desert the standard
in panic,"
says the LORD, whose fire is in Zion,
and whose furnace is in Jerusalem.

[a]Heb *they*

COMMENTARY

Four brief but distinct parts comprise this unit: vv. 1-3, 4-5, 6-7, and 8-9. Although considerably shorter than the preceding chapter, this unit parallels chap. 30 in both structure and content. Thus there are the same thematic development and coherence among the individual parts seen in the preceding chapter. The unit begins (vv. 1-3) with condemnation of the Egyptian alliance in the face of the threat from Assyria, moves to an affirmation of the Lord's care for Jerusalem (vv. 4-5), and concludes (vv. 8-9) with an announcement of judgment against Assyria. With the exception of vv. 6-7, the material in this chapter most likely stems from the prophet

Isaiah in the time of the Assyrian crisis of 705–701 BCE.

Verses 6-7 are a prose admonition that has no obvious connection with the context. This call for the people to reject their idols certainly is a later addition. Two factors likely prompted the addition of these lines here. First, the worship of idols instead of the Lord relates broadly to the theme of trust in Yahweh, and, second, the issue appears in the previous and parallel chapter. Isaiah 30:22 is an announcement that the people would indeed reject their idols.

Viewed as a whole, this unit may be taken as an argument against the alliance with Egypt, with the announcements of judgment presented as warnings and the affirmation of the Lord's care as encouragement.[275]

31:1-3. The cry "Woe" begins the chapter, as it does other units of chaps. 28–33. In this case, as in 30:1-5, the prophet indicts those leaders who seek to make a treaty with Egypt. Although his name is not mentioned, the king under whom these negotiations took place was Hezekiah.

These verses are structured as a typical prophetic announcement of judgment, but with one significant difference: At no point does the Lord speak directly to set out the future; rather, the entire address comes from the prophet, who refers to what Yahweh will do. First comes the indictment, or the reasons for judgment (v. 1). Where one would ordinarily see a transition from indictment with "therefore" and some form of the formula for the word of the Lord, there appears an affirmation of the Lord's wisdom and the certainty that what the Lord says will come to pass (v. 2*a*). Consequently, it is difficult to take these three verses as a warning. If the Lord, through the prophet, proclaims disaster, that is what will happen.[276] The announcement of that disaster (vv. 2*b*-3) begins with Yahweh's intervention (v. 2*b*) against "the house of the evildoers" and then what can only be construed as military disaster upon the Egyptians, who, after all, are mere mortals. Judgment will fall upon both "helper" (Egypt) and "the one helped" (Judah). Thus all will "perish together."

As in chap. 30, the issue is trust. Those who trust in chariots and horses instead of the Lord are condemned—that is, they are criticized and doomed to "perish." In this context, the evil and the iniquity can only be understood as misplaced trust. This misplaced trust, however, is by no means just an internal or a spiritual matter. Rather, the "evildoers . . . the helpers of those who work iniquity" are the ones who have made a particular international treaty. "Consult" (v. 1) is the technical term for the process of ascertaining the will of the Lord (see 30:9-11 and the Commentary on 30:1-33). The contrast between human and divine

wisdom underlies the indictment: The leaders in Jerusalem think they are wiser than the Lord. Likewise, the announcement contrasts human and divine power ("his hand," v. 3).

31:4-5. The prophet reports the revelation of the word of the Lord that came to him. The message articulates the promise that the Lord (mentioned in the third person) will protect Jerusalem.[277] The transitional "for" (כִּי *kî*, v. 4) presumes something has gone before. Although the themes of vv. 1-3 and 4-5 and are related, in terms of form and content the preceding unit does not connect to this one. Verse 3 had concluded with the pronouncement that "all," including those in Jerusalem, would "perish." Consequently, many see vv. 4-5 as an originally independent tradition.[278]

Assurance for Jerusalem is presented in the form of two similes. The first, that of a lion and its prey (v. 4), is curious. The lion is a common metaphor in the OT, but in almost all instances it represents disaster (Job 10:16; Pss 7:2; 17:12; Prov 28:15), particularly in the prophetic literature (Isa 5:29; 38:13; Hos 13:7-8; Amos 3:4-8). Here, however, the lion protecting its prey represents the Lord fighting for Jerusalem. Use of this wild animal in a similar fashion occurs in Hos 11:10-11, where the Lord roars like a lion calling its children home. Lion symbolism appeared on the temple furniture (1 Kgs 7:29, 36) and on Solomon's throne (1 Kgs 10:19-20; 2 Chr 9:18-19), and the Assyrians that occupied Samaria were said to have been attacked by lions (2 Kgs 17:25-26). The lion and eagle imagery of these verses is linked in the first of the four beasts in Daniel's vision: It was "like a lion and had eagles' wings" (Dan 7:4).

The second half of v. 4 sets out the meaning of the simile. Like a lion furiously defending its prey, so the Lord will fight on Mt. Zion.[279] In the back-

---

275. See Marvin A. Sweeney, *Isaiah 1–39, With an Introduction to Prophetic Literature,* FOTL XVI (Grand Rapids: Eerdmans, 1996) 401-8.

276. Gene M. Tucker, "Prophetic Speech," *Int.* 32 (1978) 31-45; reprinted in *Interpreting the Prophets,* ed. James L. Mays and Paul J. Achtemeier (Philadelphia: Fortress, 1987) 27-40.

277. Brevard S. Childs, *Isaiah and the Assyrian Crisis,* SBT, 2nd series 3 (London, 1967) 57-59.

278. Hans Wildberger, *Jesaja: Kapitel 28–39,* BKAT 10 (Neukirchen-Vluyn: Neukirchener Verlag, 1982) 1238-40.

279. The Hebrew preposition עַל (*'al*), translated by the NRSV and the NIV as "on," can also mean "against," and so it is read in the TNK. Given this possibility and the simile of the lion, some interpreters read this section as an announcement of judgment against Jerusalem. See R. E. Clements, *Isaiah and the Deliverance of Jerusalem: A Study in the Interpretation of Prophecy in the Old Testament,* JSOTSup 13 (Sheffield: JSOT, 1980) 32-33; Sweeney, *Isaiah 1–39,* 403-8. However, this interpretation relies on questionable arguments that 31:5 is secondary. The only way that 31:4 and 5 are consistent is to understand *al* as "upon."

ground would be Sennacherib's invasion and siege of Jerusalem in 701 BCE (see 29:1-8; 37:21-38). The expectation that the Lord would fight against the enemies of Israel has deep roots in the tradition of the holy war (Deut 20:1-4) and the understanding of the Lord as a warrior.[280] Isaiah did not invent the idea he expresses here, that the Lord will defend the sacred city. Nor is the belief one that developed only after Sennacherib's siege of the city was lifted. The confidence in the Lord's protection of Zion, expressed over and over by Isaiah and in the psalms, has its roots in ancient Jerusalem traditions, especially the story of the bringing of the ark to the city (2 Samuel 6).[281]

The second simile also employs the imagery of wildlife. The Lord will be "like birds hovering overhead," watching over Jerusalem, "to protect and deliver it," "to spare and rescue it." There is no close OT parallel to this metaphor.[282] The visual image is clear enough, however, and its point is stated directly. Like birds guarding their nests, Yahweh will protect and rescue Jerusalem.[283] This is not unlike the image of the Lord's care for the people in Deut 32:11-12: "As an eagle stirs up its nest/ and hovers over its young;/ as it spreads its wings, takes them up/ and bears them aloft on its pinions/ the LORD alone guided him" (NRSV).

31:6-7. These prose lines, almost universally recognized as late additions, continue the broad issue of trust in and faithfulness to the Lord. However, instead of political decisions that reflect lack of trust in the Lord's protection, they pose the matter of betrayal and sin in terms of the worship of idols. The readers are admonished to repent from their betrayal ("turn back to him") by discarding their idols made by human hands.

31:8-9. The expansive messenger formula that concludes these lines ("says the LORD," v. 9) shows them to be a prophetic announcement, in this case of disaster against Assyria. The place of this proclamation in its context connects the defeat of Assyria with the rescue of Jerusalem in the time of Hezekiah. That Assyria "shall fall by a sword, not of mortals, and a sword, not of humans" (v. 8) connects this announcement to that of 31:1-3, the reminder that the Egyptians are "human, not God." What is this sword? Certainly it is the hand of Yahweh, but the speaker leaves that for the hearers to conclude. The flight of the Assyrians (v. 8) and the desertion of the officers in "panic" (v. 9) characterize the effect of divine intervention as in the holy war. Compare the account of the departure of Sennacherib's army from Jerusalem in 37:36-38. "Forced labor" refers to the enslavement that comes from military defeat.

The concluding formula is unusual both in its length ("says the LORD" ordinarily is sufficient) and in the way it characterizes the Lord. Clearly the Lord's "fire in Zion" and "furnace in Jerusalem" stress the centrality of the city and the Temple. It is uncertain whether the fire and the furnace refer to the Lord's altar or more broadly to Yahweh's power.

---

280. Patrick D. Miller Jr., *The Divine Warrior in Early Israel* (Cambridge, Mass.: Harvard University Press, 1973).

281. John H. Hayes, "The Tradition of Zion's Inviolability," *JBL* 82 (1963) 419-26, esp. 425-26.

282. The argument advanced by Clements that the simile was designed to refute the boast put in the mouth of the king of Assyria in Isa 10:14 is not persuasive. See Ronald E. Clements, *Isaiah 1–39*, NCB (Grand Rapids: Eerdmans, 1980) 257-58.

283. Sweeney argues unsuccessfully that the birds are scavengers who come to the carcass killed by the lion and that together the similes announce judgment. See Sweeney, *Isaiah 1–39*, 407.

REFLECTIONS

One who reads this text, not just as an ancient artifact but also as if spoken to modern times, will face difficult questions. Should we trust in God or in powerful allies? That is the leading question of this chapter, one that has come up at several points in Isaiah 1–39 (see 28:1-29) and one that may arise any time people of faith reflect seriously upon political issues. This is not a theoretical question but one taken up in the awareness that decisions will come in real situations, for the issue becomes especially prominent in times of national and international crisis. At the level of practical, political decisions, it is not easy to decide where to place one's trust. Nor was the question simple in the time of the Assyrian crisis, to which Isaiah responded. It would be foolish to suggest that all political alliances are bad. The one Judah sought with Egypt was for the sake of self-protection, of survival, viewed from the side of both parties. That often seems to be the case with alliances. But alliances also have the potential to create and maintain solidarity among nations and peoples.

Perhaps a more practical way to pose the question would be: Which political decision is consistent with trust in God? Political decisions are inevitable, particularly for those in positions of leadership or power. Certainly the prophets, and especially Isaiah, insist that is the case. So for the person of faith it is not a matter of choosing between faith in God or making political decisions. Even to withdraw from political affairs is to make a political decision, to leave it to the snake. This is particularly true in democratic societies, where at least ideally all citizens participate in political decisions.

One could construe this as an issue of religion and politics. But "religion" is not a sufficiently strong or deep term for what is at stake here. "Religion" suggests the practices of the cult or other external behavior. Trust is a different matter, going to the heart of what must lie beneath religion. This is faith not as the affirmation of ideas or beliefs or as the practice of piety, but as trust in God, who is ultimately over history and the world.

But religious practices and traditions certainly shape one's faith, as they did Isaiah's understanding of trust in God. In Isa 7:1-9, the prophet's counsel of nonresistance was founded on specific theological traditions concerning the capital city and the monarchy. Then, in the time of the Syro-Ephraimitic war, the central foundation for confidence was the Lord's promise to David; here it is on the basis of the election of Jerusalem as the Lord's dwelling place. However, it would be a mistake to take this trust in the Lord's choice of Jerusalem as a form of religious nationalism. Even if one reads 31:4 as an expression of the Zion tradition, that the Lord will protect the holy city, the prophet proclaims judgment against Judah in 31:1-3 and elsewhere. Isaiah certainly expected trouble for Judah and Jerusalem in the time of Hezekiah, but not the end of the sacred city.

Clearly Isaiah does not hesitate to introduce theology into politics, both providing a theological interpretation of events and attempting to influence the direction of affairs. Is there a lesson in this for modern readers? Certainly at the very least, theologians, including clergy and thoughtful laypeople, are obliged to interpret events, including international politics, theologically. They are called to make sense of events both pragmatically and in the light of their understanding of God and God's will and deeds.

Is there any way that trust in God's promises should guide decisions concerning international relations? Two considerations suggest themselves from these prophetic texts for those who take the biblical tradition seriously. First, certainly the claim that God's reign is enduring and that human states are not can give grounds for confidence—even if that means particular states will be absorbed by others or even that they will die. No human state or empire, not even mighty Egypt or arrogant Assyria, endures forever. Second, for Isaiah, it is not simply that Yahweh lives in Zion, but that Yahweh is the judge of all the world, including nations and empires. So justice is the key to divine actions, expressed here in terms of judgment on evildoers. Likewise, justice is to be the guide for human actions.

ISAIAH 32:1-20, PROMISES AND WARNINGS

NIV

32 See, a king will reign in righteousness
and rulers will rule with justice.
²Each man will be like a shelter from the wind
   and a refuge from the storm,
like streams of water in the desert
   and the shadow of a great rock in a
      thirsty land.

³Then the eyes of those who see will no longer
      be closed,
   and the ears of those who hear will listen.
⁴The mind of the rash will know and
      understand,
   and the stammering tongue will be fluent
      and clear.
⁵No longer will the fool be called noble
   nor the scoundrel be highly respected.
⁶For the fool speaks folly,
   his mind is busy with evil:
He practices ungodliness
   and spreads error concerning the LORD;
the hungry he leaves empty
   and from the thirsty he withholds water.
⁷The scoundrel's methods are wicked,
   he makes up evil schemes
to destroy the poor with lies,
   even when the plea of the needy is just.
⁸But the noble man makes noble plans,
   and by noble deeds he stands.

⁹You women who are so complacent,
   rise up and listen to me;
you daughters who feel secure,
   hear what I have to say!
¹⁰In little more than a year
   you who feel secure will tremble;
the grape harvest will fail,
   and the harvest of fruit will not come.
¹¹Tremble, you complacent women;
   shudder, you daughters who feel secure!
Strip off your clothes,
   put sackcloth around your waists.
¹²Beat your breasts for the pleasant fields,
   for the fruitful vines
¹³and for the land of my people,

NRSV

32 See, a king will reign in righteousness,
and princes will rule with justice.
² Each will be like a hiding place from the wind,
   a covert from the tempest,
like streams of water in a dry place,
   like the shade of a great rock in a
      weary land.
³ Then the eyes of those who have sight will
      not be closed,
   and the ears of those who have hearing
      will listen.
⁴ The minds of the rash will have good
      judgment,
   and the tongues of stammerers will speak
      readily and distinctly.
⁵ A fool will no longer be called noble,
   nor a villain said to be honorable.
⁶ For fools speak folly,
   and their minds plot iniquity:
to practice ungodliness,
   to utter error concerning the LORD,
to leave the craving of the hungry unsatisfied,
   and to deprive the thirsty of drink.
⁷ The villainies of villains are evil;
   they devise wicked devices
to ruin the poor with lying words,
   even when the plea of the needy is right.
⁸ But those who are noble plan noble things,
   and by noble things they stand.

⁹ Rise up, you women who are at ease, hear
      my voice;
   you complacent daughters, listen to
      my speech.
¹⁰ In little more than a year
   you will shudder, you complacent ones;
for the vintage will fail,
   the fruit harvest will not come.
¹¹ Tremble, you women who are at ease,
   shudder, you complacent ones;
strip, and make yourselves bare,
   and put sackcloth on your loins.
¹² Beat your breasts for the pleasant fields,
   for the fruitful vine,
¹³ for the soil of my people

NIV

a land overgrown with thorns and briers—
yes, mourn for all houses of merriment
   and for this city of revelry.
[14]The fortress will be abandoned,
   the noisy city deserted;
citadel and watchtower will become a
      wasteland forever,
   the delight of donkeys, a pasture for flocks,
[15]till the Spirit is poured upon us from on high,
   and the desert becomes a fertile field,
   and the fertile field seems like a forest.
[16]Justice will dwell in the desert
   and righteousness live in the fertile field.
[17]The fruit of righteousness will be peace;
   the effect of righteousness will be quietness
      and confidence forever.
[18]My people will live in peaceful dwelling
      places,
   in secure homes,
   in undisturbed places of rest.
[19]Though hail flattens the forest
   and the city is leveled completely,
[20]how blessed you will be,
   sowing your seed by every stream,
   and letting your cattle and donkeys
      range free.

NRSV

growing up in thorns and briers;
yes, for all the joyous houses
   in the jubilant city.
[14] For the palace will be forsaken,
   the populous city deserted;
the hill and the watchtower
   will become dens forever,
   the joy of wild asses,
   a pasture for flocks;
[15] until a spirit from on high is poured out on us,
   and the wilderness becomes a fruitful field,
   and the fruitful field is deemed a forest.
[16] Then justice will dwell in the wilderness,
   and righteousness abide in the fruitful field.
[17] The effect of righteousness will be peace,
   and the result of righteousness, quietness
      and trust forever.
[18] My people will abide in a peaceful habitation,
   in secure dwellings, and in quiet resting
      places.
[19] The forest will disappear completely,[a]
   and the city will be utterly laid low.
[20] Happy will you be who sow beside every
      stream,
   who let the ox and the donkey range freely.

[a]Cn: Heb *And it will hail when the forest comes down*

COMMENTARY

Although this chapter is quite different from those that precede it, chaps. 28–33 are best viewed as a collection within the book, based on the opening woes and the concluding liturgical chapter (chap. 33). The shift from "Woe" (הוי *hôy*) at the beginning of the previous sections to "See" (הן *hēn*) in v. 1 is a small but telling change of expression, signaling both continuity and a shift, a pause for the conclusion. It either is a climax or prepares for one, reflecting the sense of the composition of the collection. Moreover, "Woe" would not begin an announcement of salvation, which we have here.

The chapter consists of three distinct sections, vv. 1-8, 9-14, and 15-20.[284] The first part expresses the promise of a king who will establish a righteous and just reign. The second is a warning against complacent women of Jerusalem. The concluding unit announces peace with justice for the Lord's people.

Primarily on the basis of literary style and theological perspective, there is every good reason to agree with the conclusions of most recent commentators that the various parts of this chapter did not originate with Isaiah in the eighth century BCE. However, no consensus has been reached concerning the date and circumstances that gave rise to these texts. Some date it as early as the time of Josiah in the seventh century,[285] while others locate some or all of the material to the exilic or post-exilic periods.[286]

284. Sweeney takes the chapter as a single unit with three parts: vv. 1-8, vv. 9-19, and v. 20 as a concluding beatitude. See Marvin A. Sweeney, *Isaiah 1–39, With an Introduction to Prophetic Literature,* FOTL XVI (Grand Rapids: Eerdmans, 1996) 409-10.

285. Clements, *Isaiah 1–39,* 259; Hermann Barth, *Die Jesaja-Worte in der Josiazeit,* WMANT 48 (Neukirchen-Vluyn: Neukirchener, 1977) 213-215.

286. Hans Wildberger, *Jesaja: Kapitel 28–39,* BKAT 10 (Neukirchen-Vluyn: Neukirchener Verlag, 1982) 1265-66; O. Kaiser, *Isaiah 13–39: A Commentary* (Philadelphia: Westminster, 1974).

32:1-8. These verses begin by looking to the future, and at first glance they have the appearance of a messianic promise.[287] Verse 1 recalls some of the language of the announcements in 9:1-7 and 11:1-5. Clearly the poet looks to a time when Israel's government will be based on righteousness and justice, when eyes wil be opened and all persons will be recognized for what they are. In terms of form, these verses do not constitute a prophecy—that is, a word of the Lord revealed through a mediator. There is no direct address or clear sense of an audience. The poetry is reflective and makes heavy use of wisdom vocabulary and ideas ("fool," "fools," vv. 5-6; see Prov 16:12-15). Although "a king," clearly a human being and not Yahweh, is expected, no vocabulary of the Davidic dynasty appears. This expectation of a king and princes who will look out for righteousness and justice is virtually proverbial, anticipating general circumstances rather than a particular individual (cf. Prov 8:15-16; 29:14).[288] It thus seems likely that the text arose in scribal circles. Certainly some Isaianic ideas are employed, such as justice and righteousness, although this is the only instance where the order is reversed.[289]

The future described in vv. 1-5 includes first a king and then princes whose rule is fair, establishing circumstances of security for their people. A series of metaphors describe this security: The righteous and just rulers will be a "hiding place" from the wind, a refuge from the storm, like water in a dry land, and "like the shade of a great rock in a weary land." This is a general, rather than a particular, hope. The second aspect of the future is even more broad. People will open their eyes and ears, and even the "rash" will have "good judgment" and "stammerers" will speak without hesitation (v. 4). Moreover, fools and villains will be recognized for what they are. This amounts to the establishment of the order taught by Israel's sages.

Verses 6-8 no longer describe the future but offer meditations on the foolishness of folly, including speaking "error" concerning the Lord and failing to care for the needy (v. 6). The unit concludes with outright instruction that contrasts "villains" (v. 7) with "those who plan noble things" (v. 8).

32:9-14. This unit reflects an unsual pattern for prophetic literature. It consists of a series of instructions to "complacent" women, with reasons given for each directive. The initial instructions in the form of direct address and a summons to hear (v. 9) strongly resemble those common to wisdom literature (Prov 1:8-9; 3:1-2, 11-12). At first the tone is that of reproof, criticizing "ease" and complacency (v. 9) because trouble lies ahead in the form of the failure of the vintage and the "fruit harvest" (v. 10). The Hebrew idiom translated "in little more than a year" is incertain. The translation "at the turn of the year" (REB) fits the reference to the agricultural calendar.

The tone soon turns to one of sorrow, and the women are called to perform the rituals of mourning (vv. 11-12). They are asked to grieve for the loss, not of the harvest itself, but of the "vine," the "soil," and even all the "joyous houses in the jubilant city" (vv. 12-13). The reference to "thorns and briers" (v. 12) recalls the song of the vineyard that functioned to proclaim judgment (5:1-7). To this point there seemed to be no reason to take the failure of the harvest as symbolic of any other disaster, but the final reason announces that the "palace" and the "populous city" will be forsaken and deserted and that the cultivated land will be taken over by "wild asses" and flocks (v. 14). This reiterates the frequent fear that it would be a tragedy for cities and arable land to revert to wilderness or even to land fit only for grazing. Although the unit contains no prophetic formula, this final verse strongly resembles a prophecy of disaster expressed passively.

It is not unheard of for warnings or announcements of punishment to be addressed to particular groups, including women (Isa 3:16–4:1; Amos 4:1-3). Here they represent complacency in the face of impending doom; but, more than that, they have a particular role in the rituals of mourning. There is no clear indictment or reasons for the trouble ahead. The expected disaster could very well be a natural one. Crops fail. In the context of these chapters concerning the Assyrian crisis, however, the agricultural failure with the desertion of the city more likely is viewed as the result of warfare. The text probably reflects the fall of the

287. See Sweeney, *Isaiah 1–39*, 411.
288. H. G. M. Wiliamson, *Variations on a Theme: King, Messiah, and the Servant in the Book of Isaiah* (Carlisle: Paternoster, 1998) 62-72.
289. Williamson, ibid., 69, argues that 32:3 is a reversal of 6:9-10 and suggests this should be ascribed to himself.

city of Jerusalem to the Babylonians in 598 and 587 BCE rather than to its siege by the Assyrians.[290]

32:15-20. The substance and tone of these verses (except v. 19) contrast sharply with the preceding section. Instead of warnings and descriptions of disaster, they offer a picture of a fruitful natural world, a reign of justice and righteousness, with happiness and security for people and domestic animals alike. Moreover, instead of a voice instructing the women, someone speaks on behalf of the people as a whole ("us," v. 15), another voice (the Lord?) refers to "my people" (v. 18), and finally the people are addressed directly ("you," (v. 20).

However, the temporal preposition "until" (עד 'ad) links this vision of a glorious future to what has gone before. These verses, which may very well be a secondary addition to the section, thus indicate that the desertion of the city and the return of the land to the wild asses (v. 14) will not be forever. It will last "until a spirit from on high is poured out on us." Although to capitalize "Spirit" (NIV) is to introduce an unjustified theological interpretation, the word certainly refers to the power of God that will establish what is proclaimed here.

The passage directly reverses the disaster of vv. 13-14 in that "the wilderness becomes a fruitful field" (v. 15). It also reiterates the promise in vv. 1-8 that justice and righteousness will be established. But there is more. These verses constitute a virtual catalog of the blessings for human beings in the world: prosperity from the fruitful land, "quietness and trust" (v. 17), peace, security, and happiness. The concluding image is both charming and profound, the farmer will "sow beside every stream" and allow the ox and the donkey to roam where they will, without fear that they will be stolen or killed.

Verse 19, which proclaims disaster for both forest and city, makes no sense in this context. It may have become displaced, or something may be missing, indicating that the forest and the city here are those of another nation.

290. Clements, *Isaiah 1–39,* 262-3.

REFLECTIONS

In many respects, this chapter is a summary of the message of Isaiah 1–39 as a whole, although not necessarily all of its individual parts. Although less specific and concrete than much of the rest of Isaiah 1–39, the chapter includes most of the important themes: the expectation of a just and righteous ruler, critical words against a particular group, expectation of disaster ahead, and then a future time when all will be well for the world and the people of God. In fact, some interpreters see chapter 32 as the appropriate conclusion for an edition of the book in the time of Josiah.[291]

But for all that, the reader of this chapter, as of so much of Isaiah 1–39, is not allowed to rest easy with simple conclusions or easy explanations of tensions and inconsistencies. There is both good news and bad here. How are they related to one another? Will Jerusalem be destroyed or will Yahweh protect the city, as Isa 31:4-5 had indicated? To be sure, the flow of the book and of its major sections points to a final resolution in salvation, to the reign of God, to the redemption of God's people. In fact, that is the pattern in most of the prophetic books. So should we then either ignore or pass over quickly the accusations and announcements of punishment? That is always a temptation for readers who know that good news is the last word.

In this chapter, one little preposition, "until," attempts to make sense of the course of history. Certainly the message of this chapter as a whole is that the power of God prevails for good. One fundamental rule of literature generally is that the last shall be first—that is, that the final word is the decisive one. Here a vision of peace, prosperity, justice, and righteousness leads people on. Nevertheless, the poets and editors responsible for this unit refused to delete the warnings and descriptions of serious, almost disastrous, trouble. They knew, probably on the basis of their own

291. Clements, *Isaiah 1–39,* 263.

experience, that neither the vision of peace nor its reality is won easily. Theologically, they could affirm that one has to face God's "No" before hearing God's "Yes." There will be mourning before celebration, trouble before peace and security.

Those of us eager to rush to the good news at the conclusion might, therefore, find it important to acknowledge the hard news as well.

ISAIAH 33:1-24, A LITURGY OF HOPE

NIV

33 Woe to you, O destroyer,
  you who have not been destroyed!
Woe to you, O traitor,
  you who have not been betrayed!
When you stop destroying,
  you will be destroyed;
when you stop betraying,
  you will be betrayed.

[2] O LORD, be gracious to us;
  we long for you.
Be our strength every morning,
  our salvation in time of distress.
[3] At the thunder of your voice, the peoples flee;
  when you rise up, the nations scatter.
[4] Your plunder, O nations, is harvested as by
      young locusts;
  like a swarm of locusts men pounce on it.

[5] The LORD is exalted, for he dwells on high;
  he will fill Zion with justice and
      righteousness.
[6] He will be the sure foundation for your times,
  a rich store of salvation and wisdom and
      knowledge;
  the fear of the LORD is the key to this
      treasure.[a]

[7] Look, their brave men cry aloud in the streets;
  the envoys of peace weep bitterly.
[8] The highways are deserted,
  no travelers are on the roads.
The treaty is broken,
  its witnesses[b] are despised,
  no one is respected.
[9] The land mourns[c] and wastes away,
  Lebanon is ashamed and withers;

[a]6 Or *is a treasure from him*   [b]8 Dead Sea Scrolls; Masoretic Text / *the cities*   [c]9 Or *dries up*

NRSV

33 Ah, you destroyer,
  who yourself have not been destroyed;
you treacherous one,
  with whom no one has dealt treacherously!
When you have ceased to destroy,
  you will be destroyed;
and when you have stopped dealing
      treacherously,
  you will be dealt with treacherously.

[2] O LORD, be gracious to us; we wait for you.
  Be our arm every morning,
  our salvation in the time of trouble.
[3] At the sound of tumult, peoples fled;
  before your majesty, nations scattered.
[4] Spoil was gathered as the caterpillar gathers;
  as locusts leap, they leaped[a] upon it.
[5] The LORD is exalted, he dwells on high;
  he filled Zion with justice and
      righteousness;
[6] he will be the stability of your times,
  abundance of salvation, wisdom, and
      knowledge;
  the fear of the LORD is Zion's treasure.[b]

[7] Listen! the valiant[a] cry in the streets;
  the envoys of peace weep bitterly.
[8] The highways are deserted,
  travelers have quit the road.
  The treaty is broken,
  its oaths[c] are despised,
  its obligation[d] is disregarded.
[9] The land mourns and languishes;
  Lebanon is confounded and withers away;
  Sharon is like a desert;

[a]Meaning of Heb uncertain   [b]Heb *his treasure*; meaning of Heb uncertain   [c]Q Ms: MT *cities*   [d]Or *everyone*

NIV

Sharon is like the Arabah,
and Bashan and Carmel drop their leaves.

10"Now will I arise," says the LORD.
"Now will I be exalted;
now will I be lifted up.
11You conceive chaff,
you give birth to straw;
your breath is a fire that consumes you.
12The peoples will be burned as if to lime;
like cut thornbushes they will be
set ablaze."

13You who are far away, hear what I have done;
you who are near, acknowledge my power!
14The sinners in Zion are terrified;
trembling grips the godless:
"Who of us can dwell with the
consuming fire?
Who of us can dwell with everlasting
burning?"
15He who walks righteously
and speaks what is right,
who rejects gain from extortion
and keeps his hand from accepting bribes,
who stops his ears against plots of murder
and shuts his eyes against contemplating
evil—
16this is the man who will dwell on the heights,
whose refuge will be the mountain fortress.
His bread will be supplied,
and water will not fail him.

17Your eyes will see the king in his beauty
and view a land that stretches afar.
18In your thoughts you will ponder the
former terror:
"Where is that chief officer?
Where is the one who took the revenue?
Where is the officer in charge of
the towers?"
19You will see those arrogant people no more,
those people of an obscure speech,
with their strange, incomprehensible
tongue.

20Look upon Zion, the city of our festivals;
your eyes will see Jerusalem,
a peaceful abode, a tent that will not
be moved;

NRSV

and Bashan and Carmel shake off
their leaves.

10 "Now I will arise," says the LORD,
"now I will lift myself up;
now I will be exalted.
11 You conceive chaff, you bring forth stubble;
your breath is a fire that will consume you.
12 And the peoples will be as if burned to lime,
like thorns cut down, that are burned in
the fire."

13 Hear, you who are far away, what I have done;
and you who are near, acknowledge
my might.
14 The sinners in Zion are afraid;
trembling has seized the godless:
"Who among us can live with the
devouring fire?
Who among us can live with everlasting
flames?"
15 Those who walk righteously and speak
uprightly,
who despise the gain of oppression,
who wave away a bribe instead of accepting it,
who stop their ears from hearing of
bloodshed
and shut their eyes from looking on evil,
16 they will live on the heights;
their refuge will be the fortresses of rocks;
their food will be supplied, their water
assured.

17 Your eyes will see the king in his beauty;
they will behold a land that stretches
far away.
18 Your mind will muse on the terror:
"Where is the one who counted?
Where is the one who weighed the tribute?
Where is the one who counted the
towers?"
19 No longer will you see the insolent people,
the people of an obscure speech that you
cannot comprehend,
stammering in a language that you cannot
understand.
20 Look on Zion, the city of our appointed
festivals!

its stakes will never be pulled up,
    nor any of its ropes broken.
²¹There the LORD will be our Mighty One.
    It will be like a place of broad rivers
        and streams.
No galley with oars will ride them,
    no mighty ship will sail them.
²²For the LORD is our judge,
    the LORD is our lawgiver,
the LORD is our king;
    it is he who will save us.

²³Your rigging hangs loose:
    The mast is not held secure,
    the sail is not spread.
Then an abundance of spoils will be divided
    and even the lame will carry off plunder.
²⁴No one living in Zion will say, "I am ill";
    and the sins of those who dwell there will
        be forgiven.

Your eyes will see Jerusalem,
    a quiet habitation, an immovable tent,
whose stakes will never be pulled up,
    and none of whose ropes will be broken.
²¹ But there the LORD in majesty will be for us
    a place of broad rivers and streams,
where no galley with oars can go,
    nor stately ship can pass.
²² For the LORD is our judge, the LORD is
        our ruler,
    the LORD is our king; he will save us.

²³ Your rigging hangs loose;
    it cannot hold the mast firm in its place,
    or keep the sail spread out.

Then prey and spoil in abundance will
        be divided;
    even the lame will fall to plundering.
²⁴ And no inhabitant will say, "I am sick";
    the people who live there will be forgiven
        their iniquity.

COMMENTARY

Because of its generic as well as its theological complexity, this chapter has evoked more questions than answers. Major differences of interpretation depend on whether one focuses primarily on the historical or the literary context and on whether one emphasizes the structural or the thematic features and order of the chapter. Although these approaches lead in different directions, there is no need to limit oneself to a single angle of vision. Certainly the reader needs to understand how the chapter functions in its literary context. But that does not mean that the passage and its individual parts had no life before being nestled after chap. 32 and before the remainder of the book of Isaiah. Different approaches may be complementary rather than mutually exclusive.

Because it is most accessible, although not always self-evident, the place and function of the unit in its context should come into view first. Just as the songs of thanksgiving in Isaiah 12 provide a liturgical conclusion to the first section of the book, so also chap. 33 brings closure to Isaiah 28–33. The external structure of a series of units, each beginning with "Woe," reflects at the very least an editorial ordering of the section (see the Overview to 28:1–33:24). In fact, some have argued that this chapter provides the conclusion to the first half of the book of Isaiah, taken to end with chap. 33 rather than chap. 39.²⁹² In any case, a series of prophetic addresses and related units concludes with liturgical material. It is possible, although unlikely, that the pattern of prophetic texts followed by liturgical material reflects the use of texts in corporate worship. More likely, the organization is literary, influenced by liturgical patterns.

Thematically, the chapter is complex, but there can be no doubt that vv. 17-24 set forth its main concern: the Lord's establishment of a just rule over a secure and peaceful Jerusalem. But is the

292. Marvin A. Sweeney, *Isaiah 1–39, With an Introduction to Prophetic Literature*, FOTL XVI (Grand Rapids: Eerdmans, 1996) 430.

"king" (v. 17) an earthly ruler[293] or the Lord?[294] Verse 22 affirms explicitly that "the LORD is our king." Certainly it is the Lord's majesty that prevails in Zion, whether a messianic figure is in view or not. But leading up to that theme are several others, including the destruction of the destroyer (v. 1), prayers of the people for help (vv. 2-4), expressions of confidence in the Lord (vv. 5-6), descriptions of trouble for the people even from the Lord (vv. 7-12), and words about the different futures for the sinners and the righteous (vv. 13-16). Thus one can recognize some thematic development leading to the concluding good news.

Formally, the most fruitful analysis recognizes the chapter as a liturgy consisting of five units: threats with prayer and reassurance, vv. 1-6; lament or complaint, vv. 7-9; divine oracle, vv. 10-13; entrance of torah liturgy, vv. 14-16; and promise of salvation, vv. 17-24.[295] In turn, each of these units is complex. Nevertheless, the language of prayer combined with words from God and patterns that mirror some in the psalter (see the Commentary on 33:14-16) support the conclusion that the passage reflects a kind of prophetic liturgy. It goes too far to conclude that these materials in their present form actually were used liturgically. This is a piece of literature that has been shaped following a liturgical model.[296] An alternative view sees the chapter as being organized differently and takes it as a royal liturgy that may actually have been used in a festival in Persian-period Judah.[297]

The question of the date of composition of this passage is highly disputed, and for good reason. In addition to the absence of concrete historical allusions, liturgical texts are notoriously difficult to date. Until recently, almost all commentators took chap. 33 to be later than the time of Isaiah, but there was wide disagreement concerning how much later.[298] Now, however, some argue that there is no reason not to attribute all or most of the

chapter to Isaiah.[299] To be sure, the passage presently functions to interpret the Asyrian crisis of 701 BCE, but its style, point of view, and the fact that it appears to assume the destruction of Jerusalem and to make use of and reverse some earlier Isaianic sayings argue for the development of this chapter in the post-exilic or Persian period.[300] It is an outstanding example of how a later prophetic tradition reflected upon important events of the past, in particular those of 701 BCE.[301]

33:1-6. The chapter begins with the by now familiar cry, "Woe" (see Isa 5:8-24 and the Commentary on 1:3), initiating an indictment in the form of a direct address to the accused. Unlike most others, this woe moves directly from accusation to promise of punishment. The address itself, "you destroyer," begins the indictment, and the speech continues with repeated plays on words, in which the punishment corresponds to the crime. For its poetic power, nothing specific is given about the destructive and treacherous deeds or identity of this "destroyer." In 21:1-10, the "destroyer" is Babylon. The larger literary context (Isaiah 28–33) concerning the Assyrian crisis of 705–701 BCE would suggest Assyria.[302] The fact that no name appears opens the text to applications in diverse times and circumstances.

Unexpectedly, v. 2 shifts to the language of communal prayer, a complaint or lament song in which the people ask for the Lord's help (v. 2) and affirm their confidence by reciting how in the past "peoples" fled and "nations" scattered before the Lord's "majesty" (vv. 3-4). The petition is further reinforced by a hymn of praise (vv. 5-6) focused on the Lord's care for Zion through "justice and righteousness" and the establishment of "stability." Although the appearance of hymnic language in the context of a petition is not unheard of, the shifts of reference are noteworthy, from direct address, "O LORD" (v. 5), to the third-person reference, "The LORD" (v. 5), to direct address to the

293. So Christopher R. Seitz, *Isaiah 1–39*, Interpretation (Louisville: John Knox, 1993) 235.

294. Sweeney, *Isaiah 1–39*, 422.

295. H. Gunkel, "Jesaia 33, eine prophetische Liturgie," *ZAW* 42 (1924) 177-208.

296. John Barton, *Isaiah 1–39* (Sheffield: Sheffield Academic, 1995) 99.

297. Sweeney, *Isaiah 1–39*, 426, 430.

298. For a list of the main alternatives, see Sweeney, *Isaiah 1–39*, 428-29.

299. Seitz, *Isaiah 1–39*, 233-35; J. J. M. Roberts, "The Divine King and the Human Community in Isaiah's Vision of the Future," in *The Quest for the Kingdom of God: Studies in Honor of George E. Mendenhall*, ed. H. B. Huffmon, F. A. Spina, and A. R. W. Green (Winona Lake: Eisenbrauns, 1983) 127-36.

300. Hans Wildberger, *Jesaja: Kapitel 28–39*, BKAT 10 (Neukirchen-Vluyn: Neukirchener Verlag, 1982) 1287-88.

301. Brevard S. Childs, *Isaiah and the Assyrian Crisis*, SBT (London: SCM, 1967) 114.

302. So Seitz, *Isaiah 1–39*, 235.

people who presumably uttered the prayer ("your times," v. 6).

33:7-9. The fundamental point of these verses is that in the absence of the fear of the Lord human order collapses and the land itself "mourns and languishes" (cf. Hos 4:3). In form and function, however, this is a complaint about circumstances, describing the distress faced by the community. That "the treaty is broken," oaths and obligations disregarded, could be taken as a reference to the international agreements in the time of the Assyrian crisis (see the Commentary on 30:1-7 and the Overview to 28:1–33:24). More likely, however, the complaint concerns broken and unreliable contracts, representative of social disorder.[303]

33:10-13. With another abrupt shift, the Lord now speaks directly, announcing that God will arise and be exalted. The Lord's words are addressed to an anonymous "you" (v. 11). In view of the reference to "the peoples" (v. 12) and the address to "you who are far away . . . and you who are near" (v. 13), the objects of the speech must be people in general, whose frailty and capacity to produce only "chaff" and "stubble" (v. 11) are set in contrast to the Lord's majesty and "might" (v. 13). No one can survive the searing fire of the Lord's appearance.

33:14-16. In the context following vv. 10-13, these verses address the question of who can survive the appearance of God. In themselves, they express the heart of the entrance or torah liturgy. That liturgy, reflected most clearly in Psalms 15 and 24, has a worshiper or the community approaching the temple precincts and inquiring of a priest concerning the qualifications for coming into the presence of the Lord. Here the question is stated explicitly: "Who among us can live with the devouring fire?" (v. 14*b*).

The response (v. 15) comes from a different voice, as if that of a priest, speaking in the third person, listing the qualifications to live in the presence of God. The list presents six characteristics, but they all amount to aspects of the first: "walk righteously." All are behaviors that define righteousness, including acts of the mouth, the heart, the will, the ears, and the eyes. Those who live such lives will not only endure the burning

presence of God but also will live safe and secure, provided with food and water (v. 16).

33:17-24. After words of judgment, prayers for help, and liturgies setting out the qualifications for living in the Lord's presence comes the good news. This section is not a prophecy of salvation, for there is no prophetic formula or attribution of the words to the Lord. Rather, what the Lord will do is mentioned more than once (vv. 21-22). This is a promise of salvation directly addressed to a people who presumably have not yet experienced the fullness of the Lord's rule. The substance of the promise is that in the age to come not an economy dependent on stately ships but one dependent on the Lord's majesty will prevail in Zion: No one will be sick in body or oppressed by want or sins (cf. Ezek 34:11-31; 47:1-12; Matt 11:5).

It cannot be determined whether this is a messianic vision in the sense that "the king" (v. 17) is the Lord's designated ruler.[304] Certainly there is no mention of the line of David, and v. 22 designates the Lord as "judge," "ruler," and "king." Terror in the form of enemies who took tribute and "counted the towers" (possibly of the city under siege) will only be memories (v. 18). The reference to foreign tongues that no longer will be heard (v. 19) likely depends on the story of Sennacherib's siege of Jerusalem (36:4-10; see also 28:11).

At the center of this promise stands Zion, where the "appointed festivals" are celebrated. It will be peaceful, secure, "an immovable tent" (v. 20). This image is consistent with and even goes beyond the assurance of the Lord's protection of the sacred place (29:5-8). The metaphor characterizing the Lord's majesty is curious, "a place of broad rivers and streams," but one where galleys and ships cannot go (v. 21). There are remarkably few references to ships and the sea in the OT. Some see here the use of Canaanite mythological motifs about the home of the gods, supplied with sufficient water but protected from attack by ships.[305] Others take this as a means of contrasting Jerusalem with Babylon and its river traffic.[306] Whatever the sense of those lines, because of the Lord's rule in Jerusalem there will be abundance for all (v. 23*b*), no one will be sick, and all will "be forgiven their iniquity" (v. 24).

---

303. Clements, *Isaiah 1–39*, 267.

304. Clements, *Isaiah 1–39*, 269, sees here a close parallel to the promise of a king in Isa 32:1-5.
305. Roberts, "Annotations, Isaiah," *HarperCollins Study Bible*, 1059.
306. Clements, *Isaiah 1–39*, 270.

REFLECTIONS

1. Even the prophetic books provide occasion to reflect upon liturgy and worship. As the Commentary indicates, many have identified this chapter as a prophetic liturgy. Whether or not one finds that identification convincing, it is clear that the literary genres identified with worship often appear in the middle of prophetic texts. This fact alone calls into question the common perception that prophets always stood against the priests and the institutions of worship. Even more, however, the substance of the liturgy for entrance into the Temple (33:15) shows that the prophetic call for justice is consistent with an Old Testament understanding of worship, that piety and social responsibility go hand in hand. Essential to coming into the presence of the Lord is living a life of obedience to the Lord's will for justice (see the Reflections at 1:10-17). Fundamental to both prophetic morality and piety is the conviction that human life is corporate. Neither justice nor worship is individualistic.

2. This chapter provides the liturgical conclusion to a series of texts concerned mainly with a particular crisis, Sennacherib's invasion of Judah and siege of Jerusalem. Without suggesting that this liturgy was actually used after that crisis had ended—for it is much later—its placement here indicates the importance of worship in times of crisis. Here is a model for our time as well. The experience of being in the house of the Lord and gathered with the Lord's people can be particularly powerful after or during events that threaten the existence of the people. What is there to do in times of trouble but ask for help? For the faithful, that means asking for God's help. What is there for them to do after the experience of being rescued but to give thanks to God?

Many of the different moods and modes of ancient Israel's worship are reflected in this chapter. Different voices are heard to speak, including questions and responses. There are cries for help as an expression of need and affirmations of confidence in God. Beneath all this language—petition, praise, and thanksgiving—lies the experience of dependence upon the God who created the world and participates with human beings in history. That sense of coming into the presence of God is what makes worship, both ancient and modern, different from all other public gatherings.

Moreover, corporate worship has the potential to constitute and maintain communities. Above all, such worship brings together those who participate, and at many levels. But even more than that, worship establishes solidarity over time as well among the present participants. The language and rituals of biblical worship in particular incorporate past events, communities, and individuals. They look to the future as well, including a future that the present worshipers will not live to see. This history is more than the line in which the people stand, accounting for where they have come from and where they are going. Since God's acts of salvation as well as judgment are fundamental, it is a sacred history—one in which we continue to share and shape.

3. A potential tension appears between 33:15, which states the qualifications for approaching the Lord, and 33:24, which promises forgiveness to the Lord's people. Although this is not a necessary contradiction, it has become an issue in the history of Christian theology, expressed as a choice between justification by faith or works. How does the promise of forgiveness relate to the qualifications for approaching the Lord? Does one need to be "righteous" to enter the Temple? In Isa 6:5 the prophet responded to the vision of the Lord's terrifying presence by confessing his sin. Then his sin was taken away, his lips were purified (6:5-7), and he could stand in the Lord's presence. This suggests that those who come before God in any time and place should confess both their sins and, if not their righteousness, at least their efforts to live among their neighbors with justice.

ISAIAH 34:1–35:10

ESCHATOLOGICAL PROPHECIES CONCERNING EDOM AND THE EXILES

OVERVIEW

A clear new summons to hear (34:1) initiates a new section. These two chapters may be considered as a separate segment in the book of Isaiah mainly because they are framed by two other quite distinct collections or compositions, Isaiah 28–33, on the one hand, and Isaiah 36–39, on the other. The kind of section they constitute, however, is not self-evident. Since there is no formal link between them, one could even argue that the chapters contain not one but two quite distinct units. In both style and substance they are very different. Two poems—one promising disaster and one promising salvation—are simply juxtaposed. To the extent that they comprise a unit their goal is to contrast the expected devastation of Edom (34:1-17) with the glorious future in store for the exiles (35:1-10). The most specific theological and literary link is in the interpretation of both disaster for Edom and salvation for the people of God as the Lord's "vengeance" (נקם *nāqām,* 34:8; 35:4).

In both style and substance, chap. 34 closely resembles the oracles concerning the nations of chaps. 13–23. Remarkably, that collection does not include an oracle concerning Edom as such.[307] A more aggressive editor of Isaiah 1–39 would have provided chap. 34 with the appropriate heading, "Oracle concerning Edom," and placed with the others in chaps. 13–23. Such speculation leads to the conclusion that for the tradents of the book of Isaiah, the chapter must have served an important function in its present location, including the juxtaposition with the following announcement of salvation for Judah.

The location and the character of these two chapters raise the question of the extent of the prophetic book associated with Isaiah of Jerusalem. Furthermore, the question of the place of these chapters in their context in the book is closely related to the issue of the date of the composition. Isaiah 34 stands out in sharp contrast to the immediately preceding chapter as a harsh prophecy of judgment with almost apocalyptic overtones, finally against Edom, Judah's neighbor. Chapter 35 returns to the theme of chap. 33, the future of the exiles, and closely parallels the language and ideas of Isaiah 40–66. The subsequent section, Isaiah 36–39 is an appendix to the prophetic collection containing narrative accounts concerning Isaiah of Jerusalem. Literary style, historical perspective, and theology indicate that neither of these chapters originated earlier than the end of the Babylonian exile. Both these chapters would have been composed quite late, most likely in the post-exilic period since they depend upon the work of Second Isaiah (Isaiah 40–55).[308] It thus seems likely that at one stage in the growth of the book, chap. 35 stood either as the conclusion to the book of Isaiah of Jerusalem or as the transition to the words of Second Isaiah in chapters 40–55.[309]

This section frequently has been called "the little Isaiah apocalypse," considered by some to be parallel in many respects to chaps. 24–27, called "the Isaiah apocalypse." But the appellation

---

307. The short proclamation concerning Dumah (Isa 21:11-12) refers to Seir, which may or may not have in view a city in Edom. The only explicit references to Edom in the book of Isaiah outside this chapter are in 11:14 (with Moab) and 63:1 (with Bozrah).

308. See Ronald E. Clements, *Isaiah 1–39,* NCB (Grand Rapids: Eerdmans, 1980) 271.

309. Seitz argues that the placement of these chapters, followed by the narratives of chaps. 36–39, serves to blur the distinction between "First" and "Second" Isaiah and that the technical midpoint of the book of Isaiah, according to the Masoretic verse count, is at 33:20. See Christopher R. Seitz, *Isaiah 1–39,* Interpretation (Louisville: John Knox, 1993) 241. See also Edgar W. Conrad, *Reading Isaiah* (Minneapolis: Fortress, 1991) 122-24.

"apocalypse" fits this section even more poorly than it does chaps. 24–27 (see the Overview to 24:1–27:13). There are, to be sure, some cosmic dimensions to the future set out before the readers, and some mythological motifs in 34:1-4, but the kind of transformation of history and the world envisioned by apocalyptic literature appears in neither of these chapters. It would be more accurate to identify them as eschatological prophecies, and of two very different sorts. Chapter 34 does bear some resemblance to parts of chaps. 24–27, but even more to the oracles concerning the nations in chaps. 14–23. Chapter 35, however, resembles neither of these sections in its most important respects and instead looks ahead to chaps. 40–55 for close parallels.

ISAIAH 34:1-17, DOOM FOR EDOM

NIV

34 Come near, you nations, and listen;
pay attention, you peoples!
Let the earth hear, and all that is in it,
the world, and all that comes out of it!
[2] The LORD is angry with all nations;
his wrath is upon all their armies.
He will totally destroy[a] them,
he will give them over to slaughter.
[3] Their slain will be thrown out,
their dead bodies will send up a stench;
the mountains will be soaked with
their blood.
[4] All the stars of the heavens will be dissolved
and the sky rolled up like a scroll;
all the starry host will fall
like withered leaves from the vine,
like shriveled figs from the fig tree.

[5] My sword has drunk its fill in the heavens;
see, it descends in judgment on Edom,
the people I have totally destroyed.
[6] The sword of the LORD is bathed in blood,
it is covered with fat—
the blood of lambs and goats,
fat from the kidneys of rams.
For the LORD has a sacrifice in Bozrah
and a great slaughter in Edom.
[7] And the wild oxen will fall with them,
the bull calves and the great bulls.
Their land will be drenched with blood,
and the dust will be soaked with fat.

[8] For the LORD has a day of vengeance,

---

[a]2 The Hebrew term refers to the irrevocable giving over of things or persons to the LORD, often by totally destroying them; also in verse 5.

NRSV

34 Draw near, O nations, to hear;
O peoples, give heed!
Let the earth hear, and all that fills it;
the world, and all that comes from it.
[2] For the LORD is enraged against all the nations,
and furious against all their hoards;
he has doomed them, has given them
over for slaughter.
[3] Their slain shall be cast out,
and the stench of their corpses shall rise;
the mountains shall flow with their blood.
[4] All the host of heaven shall rot away,
and the skies roll up like a scroll.
All their host shall wither
like a leaf withering on a vine,
or fruit withering on a fig tree.

[5] When my sword has drunk its fill in
the heavens,
lo, it will descend upon Edom,
upon the people I have doomed
to judgment.
[6] The LORD has a sword; it is sated with blood,
it is gorged with fat,
with the blood of lambs and goats,
with the fat of the kidneys of rams.
For the LORD has a sacrifice in Bozrah,
a great slaughter in the land of Edom.
[7] Wild oxen shall fall with them,
and young steers with the mighty bulls.
Their land shall be soaked with blood,
and their soil made rich with fat.

[8] For the LORD has a day of vengeance,

NIV

a year of retribution, to uphold Zion's cause.
⁹Edom's streams will be turned into pitch,
  her dust into burning sulfur;
  her land will become blazing pitch!
¹⁰It will not be quenched night and day;
  its smoke will rise forever.
From generation to generation it will
    lie desolate;
  no one will ever pass through it again.
¹¹The desert owl*a* and screech owl*a* will possess it;
  the great owl*a* and the raven will nest there.
God will stretch out over Edom
  the measuring line of chaos
  and the plumb line of desolation.
¹²Her nobles will have nothing there to be
    called a kingdom,
  all her princes will vanish away.
¹³Thorns will overrun her citadels,
  nettles and brambles her strongholds.
She will become a haunt for jackals,
  a home for owls.
¹⁴Desert creatures will meet with hyenas,
  and wild goats will bleat to each other;
there the night creatures will also repose
  and find for themselves places of rest.
¹⁵The owl will nest there and lay eggs,
  she will hatch them, and care for her young
    under the shadow of her wings;
there also the falcons will gather,
  each with its mate.

¹⁶Look in the scroll of the LORD and read:

None of these will be missing,
  not one will lack her mate.
For it is his mouth that has given the order,
  and his Spirit will gather them together.
¹⁷He allots their portions;
  his hand distributes them by measure.
They will possess it forever
  and dwell there from generation to
    generation.

a11 The precise identification of these birds is uncertain.

NRSV

a year of vindication by Zion's cause.*a*
⁹ And the streams of Edom*b* shall be turned
    into pitch,
  and her soil into sulfur;
  her land shall become burning pitch.
¹⁰ Night and day it shall not be quenched;
  its smoke shall go up forever.
From generation to generation it shall
    lie waste;
  no one shall pass through it forever
    and ever.
¹¹ But the hawk*c* and the hedgehog*c* shall
    possess it;
  the owl*c* and the raven shall live in it.
He shall stretch the line of confusion over it,
  and the plummet of chaos over*d* its nobles.
¹² They shall name it No Kingdom There,
  and all its princes shall be nothing.
¹³ Thorns shall grow over its strongholds,
  nettles and thistles in its fortresses.
It shall be the haunt of jackals,
  an abode for ostriches.
¹⁴ Wildcats shall meet with hyenas,
  goat-demons shall call to each other;
there too Lilith shall repose,
  and find a place to rest.
¹⁵ There shall the owl nest
  and lay and hatch and brood in its shadow;
there too the buzzards shall gather,
  each one with its mate.
¹⁶ Seek and read from the book of the LORD:
  Not one of these shall be missing;
  none shall be without its mate.
For the mouth of the LORD has commanded,
  and his spirit has gathered them.
¹⁷ He has cast the lot for them,
  his hand has portioned it out to them
    with the line;
they shall possess it forever,
  from generation to generation they shall
    live in it.

a Or of recompense by Zion's defender   b Heb her streams
c Identification uncertain   d Heb lacks over

COMMENTARY

This prophecy of judgment reads as a unified and coherent composition, not a collection of different materials, nor even an editorial combination of originally independent pieces. To be sure, however, the prophecy makes use of themes from various and diverse earlier traditions. One may call it an announcement of disaster against Edom, but with reservations, since it also proclaims doom on all nations, and even on the cosmos itself. Particularly in view of the beginning as a proclamation against the whole world, one may ask why Edom is singled out. Some seek the answer in particular historical events in which Edom was thought to have taken advantage of Judah, such as during the Babylonian exile. In the book as the whole, to be sure, Edom is not singled out, but enters a long list of foreign nations upon which judgment is to fall (chaps. 13–23, as well as 10:12-19, Assyria). But to the extent that Edom in particular is thought to have earned the Lord's vengeance (v. 8), one need look no further than the fact that Edom was a direct neighbor of Judah. Boundaries, like fences, do not necessarily make for friendly relations, but often the contrary. Proximity, like family intimacy, evokes strong emotional responses.

The order and composition of the prophecy will be viewed differently depending on whether one emphasizes its formal or thematic features. Viewed thematically, two distinct parts will be recognized. Verses 1-4 summon all nations—indeed, the entire world and everything in it—to witness and experience the wrath of the Lord. Verses 5-17 proclaim in painful detail the Lord's judgment on a single nation, Judah's neighbor Edom. Form and content to a great extent overlap, but noting the particular formal markers shows a different outline or division from the one indicated by theme and contents.[310] One important indicator of the poem's organization is the Hebrew particle כִּי (*kî*), "for," that appears in vv. 2, 5, 6*b*, and 8.[311] The

NIV leaves the first two instances untranslated, apparently taking the force to be emphatic, and the NRSV reads the instance in v. 5 as temporal, "When." But in each case "for" presents reasons for the peoples to heed the initial summons from the Lord (see TNK and REB). This catalog of reasons reaches across the announcement against the world and into the proclamation against Edom, thus reinforcing the unity of the chapter.

Whether one focuses attention on form or thematic content, the prophecy unfolds in a series of graphic and horrible scenes of destruction, addressed to all nations and peoples. Actually, however, the intended audience would have been Judeans in the post-exilic period living with the memory of the Exile.

34:1-4. In the opening verse a voice like a prophet issues a summons to all peoples, the earth itself, and "all that fills it" to give heed and hear. The call to attention, in the form of direct address to an audience, is common in prophetic speech (Isa 1:10; 7:13; 28:14, 23; 32:9; 33:13; Amos 3:1; 4:1; 5:1; 8:4). More typically, however, the summons includes some formula for the word of the Lord. For the most part, in this chapter the Lord does not speak directly, but what Yahweh intends to do in the future is reported by the unidentified prophetic voice. The exception comes in v. 5, where the Lord is heard to say "my sword." The opening imperative recalls the summons to heavens and earth as witnesses in 1:2.

Those called before the Lord here, however, are not witnesses but defendants, the objects of the Lord's wrath. "For" in v. 2 introduces the general reason for the summons: Yahweh is "enraged," "furious," and has "doomed" all the nations to slaughter. The judge who is also executioner presents no explanation for the harsh intervention. The butchery here is not a sacrifice (see also 65:12; Jer 48:15; Ezek 21:10, 22), although the motif of animal sacrifice will echo the theme of bloodshed in v. 6. The image suggests that of a vast army, fallen without anyone to bury their corpses, their blood covering the mountains.[312]

Only the universal scope of the slaughter

---

310. Sweeney divides the chapter into two main sections, vv. 1-15 and vv. 16-17, based on the two masculine plural imperatives to the nations at v. 1 and v. 16. See Marvin A. Sweeney, *Isaiah 1–39, With an Introduction to Prophetic Literature,* FOTL XVI (Grand Rapids: Eerdmans, 1996) 437-40. However, given the substance of what follows the second imperative, this organization is arbitrary.

311. James Muilenberg, "The Literary Character of Isaiah 34," *JBL* 70 (1947) 339-65.

312. Clements takes this prophecy to be "a further extension of that foretold in Hag 2:22." See Clements, *Isaiah 1–39,* 272.

suggests a parallel to apocalyptic eschatology, some final judgment, but the parallels are closer when judgment is pronounced on the "host of heaven" and even the skies themselves (v. 4). The "host of heaven" are the heavenly bodies taken as deities by non-Yahwistic peoples, so the proclamation includes polemic against the religions of foreign powers. The demise of the sun, moon, and stars is depicted with the metaphor of withering leaves and fruit, perhaps ridiculing the function of the astral deities to ensure fertility.

34:5-17. Now the prophetic voice turns to announce the destruction of one particular nation, Edom. The initial word (vv. 5-7) continues the theme of a world slaughter, with Yahweh's bloody sword (see Ezek 21:3-21; Jer 46:10) turning from the heavens to the Edomites. Now the people of Edom will fall, not as in battle, but like animals for sacrifice. The image is driven home vividly with a long catalog of sacrificial animals, their parts, and their blood (on sacrifices, see Leviticus 3–7).[313] The Lord will sacrifice in Bozrah, a major city in northern Edom, but the slaughter will include the whole land, with blood and fat soaking the soil (v. 7). With this note, the metaphor of animal sacrifice has become a description of the actual judgment.

The next scene (vv. 8-10) is introduced with a pronouncement concerning the meaning of Edom's disaster as a day of the Lord's "vengeance." This could be an answer to a prayer such as the one uttered in Ps 137:7: "Remember O LORD against the Edomites the day of Jerusalem's fall." The divine justice in view here is retribution, vindicating "Zion's cause" (v. 8), linking disaster for the neighbor with a positive result for Zion.[314] One purpose of biblical sacrifices was to atone for sins. Here the presumed sinner (Edom) becomes the sacrificial victim. The "day" is the day of the Lord's victory over Israel's enemies (on the day of the Lord, see 2:6-22 and the Commentary there; 7:18-25; 13:1-22 and the Commentary on 13:1–14:27). The scene itself reeks with the smell of sulfur and "burning pitch" (v. 9) as disaster is visited on the very land, rendering it not just

uninhabitable but a hell impossible to traverse, and forever (v. 10). Whether directly or indirectly, the burning land draws from the story of the destruction of Sodom and Gomorrah (Gen 19:24-29).

In the final scene (vv. 11-17) Edom has been turned over to the birds and animals of the wilderness. (Never mind that the land and water had become an uninhabitable furnace in vv. 8-10.) The extensive catalog of wild creatures and wilderness plants begins with four birds (11a, reading the difficult Hebrew as "screech owl" with NIV), only to be interrupted by the even more comprehensive announcement that Edom will return to the pre-creation chaos (תהו *tōhû*, v. 11b) mentioned in Gen 1:2 (see also Jer 4:23-28). Just as God had ordered chaos into creation, now instruments of order ("line," "plummet") will reverse the creation. The prophetic voice extends the concept of chaos to the political realm: Edom's leaders ("nobles," "princes," vv. 11-12) will become nothing, and the name of the place will be changed to "No Kingdom There."

Then the description of a return to wilderness resumes first with plants ("thorns," "nettles," and "thistles," v. 13) that are the enemies of the farmer and then a long list of wild creatures of land and sky. Whether this list also includes demons is open to question. Where NRSV reads "goat demons" and "Lilith" (known in ancient Near Eastern texts and the Talmud as a demonic threat), the REB reads "he-goats" and "nightjar."[315] Compounding the problem is the fact that the flora and fauna of the OT are notoriously difficult to identify and translate. Nevertheless, the vision of Edom following the day of the Lord is clear enough. It will revert to an uncultured wilderness uninhabited by human beings, who will even fear to go there. Although the reference to "chaos" (v. 11) presumes the priestly understanding of creation expressed in Genesis 1, the concept of the wilderness as the uncreated and the cultivated land as the created recalls the Yahwist's view of the world.[316]

The final verses (vv. 16-17) move outside the terrible vision for Edom to address the audience ("Seek and read"), emphasizing that the

---

313. For an excellent introduction to this topic with a bibliography, see Gary A. Anderson, "Sacrifice and Sacrificial Offerings (OT)," in *The Anchor Bible Dictionary,* ed. David Noel Freedman et al., 6 vols. (New York: Doubleday, 1992) 5:870-87.
314. But see the NRSV footnote for the alternative reading, "of recompense by Zion's defender."

315. Clements, *Isaiah 1–39,* 274, takes these to be animals rather than demons.
316. Theodore Hiebert, *The Yahwist's Landscape: Nature and Religion in Early Israel* (New York: Oxford University Press, 1996).

announcement can be trusted. Those who hear the announcement of doom can believe it, for it is written in the "book of the LORD." What is that book, and could modern readers consult it? Some suggest it is "that book in which are recorded the names of all his creatures."[317] One commentator, comparing the scene of vv. 14-16 to that of the animals before Noah entered the ark (Gen 6:19–7:3), has speculated that the book could be one in which the Noah story appears.[318] But the context presumes a written prophecy of a disaster such as this, and that even names these creatures.[319]

Further confirmation of the validity of the prophecy is the formula, "For the mouth of the LORD has commanded," and the affirmation that the Lord's "spirit has gathered them"—that is, prepared the wild creatures to occupy Edom. Moreover, just as the land was divided among the tribes of Israel by lot, so the Lord has "cast the lot" (v. 17, cf. Ps. 16:5-6; Mic 2:5) to assign Edom to the wild creatures, who will possess it in perpetuity.

317. A. S. Herbert, *The Book of the Prophet Isaiah 1–39,* CBCNE (Cambridge: Cambridge University Press, 1973) 194.
318. Seitz, *Isaiah 1–39,* 237.
319. Clements, *Isaiah 1–39,* 274, however, goes beyond the evidence to suggest particular texts.

REFLECTIONS

Those who have read through the book of Isaiah will wonder if there is no end to the pronouncements of disaster on foreign nations. But once again in this chapter the reader is brought face-to-face with the troubling issue of divinely sanctioned doom on a neighboring people. How could God do such things, and how could such texts be included in the Bible?

Although modern readers may react in disgust at such thoughts, it could be a serious mistake to write off texts such as this one too easily. First, modern readers may use such texts to understand the cries of those oppressed by more powerful forces, even if those cries take the form of the desire for revenge. Second, one has only to look around or look inside oneself to recognize just how deep and pervasive is the desire for vengeance. It is a fundamental and almost universal human response to injustice perpetrated by another, or even thought to be caused by others. (See the Reflections at 13:1–14:27.)

Vengeance as a feeling and a force asserts itself in various ways. It plays an important role in various matters of justice. Both opponents and proponents of the death penalty would do well to acknowledge that the desire for justice in the form of revenge is a significant but often ignored factor in the call for the ultimate sanction. Some people experience their own suffering as revenge by someone else or as divine retribution for real or imagined offenses. In fact, many nations have been driven by an ethos of revenge, often guided by religious faith. Wars have broken out, or been justified on such grounds.

This chapter offers a distinctive angle of vision on the question. On the one hand, Edom is said to suffer the wrath of the Lord as vengeance, as vindication for Zion (34:8). On the other hand, this chapter clearly is paired with chap. 35, which proclaims salvation for the people of God. While many of the other proclamations of disaster on the foreign nations do not explain that calamity as recompense for what they may have done to the Lord's people or link their bad news to good news for the elect, this one does both. The first of these is an expression of justice as retribution, related to the *lex talonis*—that is, an eye for an eye.

But the second opens the question of how much good there is to go around. Must good news for some be bad news for others? Is there only so much wealth, happiness, security, and peace to go around? After all, economics is the management of limited, finite resources. There is only so much land, and if one occupies it another cannot. So there may be some truth to the idea that some will suffer if others prosper. But in this instance, what does Judah gain from Edom's suffering?

Certainly not its land, for in this vision the land has become less than worthless. Only, it would appear, revenge, a certain sense of justice as retribution, the belief that they got what they deserved.

"Don't get mad, get even" is a common reaction to real or perceived hurt inflicted by others. Those too timid to get even themselves may be happy for God to do it for them, and may even pray for it. Are anger and revenge the only two alternatives? If so, which is better? Is there any way for individuals—or nations, for that matter—to get beyond anger and beyond retribution to other forms of justice? A first step would be acknowledging the power of the desire for revenge.

ISAIAH 35:1-10, RETURN OF THE EXILES TO ZION

NIV

35 The desert and the parched land will
　　be glad;
　the wilderness will rejoice and blossom.
Like the crocus, [2]it will burst into bloom;
　it will rejoice greatly and shout for joy.
The glory of Lebanon will be given to it,
　the splendor of Carmel and Sharon;
they will see the glory of the LORD,
　the splendor of our God.

[3]Strengthen the feeble hands,
　steady the knees that give way;
[4]say to those with fearful hearts,
　"Be strong, do not fear;
your God will come,
　he will come with vengeance;
with divine retribution
　he will come to save you."

[5]Then will the eyes of the blind be opened
　and the ears of the deaf unstopped.
[6]Then will the lame leap like a deer,
　and the mute tongue shout for joy.
Water will gush forth in the wilderness
　and streams in the desert.
[7]The burning sand will become a pool,
　the thirsty ground bubbling springs.
In the haunts where jackals once lay,
　grass and reeds and papyrus will grow.

[8]And a highway will be there;
　it will be called the Way of Holiness.
The unclean will not journey on it;
　it will be for those who walk in that Way;

NRSV

35 The wilderness and the dry land shall
　　be glad,
　the desert shall rejoice and blossom;
like the crocus [2]it shall blossom abundantly,
　and rejoice with joy and singing.
The glory of Lebanon shall be given to it,
　the majesty of Carmel and Sharon.
They shall see the glory of the LORD,
　the majesty of our God.

[3]Strengthen the weak hands,
　and make firm the feeble knees.
[4]Say to those who are of a fearful heart,
　"Be strong, do not fear!
Here is your God.
　He will come with vengeance,
with terrible recompense.
　He will come and save you."

[5]Then the eyes of the blind shall be opened,
　and the ears of the deaf unstopped;
[6]then the lame shall leap like a deer,
　and the tongue of the speechless sing for joy.
For waters shall break forth in the wilderness,
　and streams in the desert;
[7]the burning sand shall become a pool,
　and the thirsty ground springs of water;
the haunt of jackals shall become a swamp,[a]
　the grass shall become reeds and rushes.

[8]A highway shall be there,
　and it shall be called the Holy Way;
the unclean shall not travel on it,[b]

[a]Cn: Heb *in the haunt of jackals is her resting place*　　[b]Or *pass it by*

279

NIV

wicked fools will not go about on it.[a]
9 No lion will be there,
    nor will any ferocious beast get up on it;
    they will not be found there.
But only the redeemed will walk there,
10   and the ransomed of the LORD will return.
They will enter Zion with singing;
    everlasting joy will crown their heads.
Gladness and joy will overtake them,
    and sorrow and sighing will flee away.

[a]8 Or / the simple will not stray from it

NRSV

but it shall be for God's people;[a]
    no traveler, not even fools, shall go astray.
9 No lion shall be there,
    nor shall any ravenous beast come up on it;
    they shall not be found there,
but the redeemed shall walk there.
10 And the ransomed of the LORD shall return,
    and come to Zion with singing;
everlasting joy shall be upon their heads;
    they shall obtain joy and gladness,
    and sorrow and sighing shall flee away.

[a]Cn: Heb for them

COMMENTARY

This chapter is paired with the preceding one (see Isaiah 34–35, Overview), and together they are significant in the structure of the book of Isaiah as a whole. It is chap. 35, however, that plays the key role. In order to understand that role, it is important to recognize its relationship to what follows and what precedes in its wider context in the book of Isaiah.

Because of its similarities to the poetry in Isaiah 40–55, many commentators have attributed Isaiah 35 to the same prophet, Second Isaiah, who wrote those words in 539 BCE. On closer examination, however, it appears that the author of Isaiah 35 knew and depended upon Second Isaiah.[320] The poet frequently cites but often reinterprets expressions from that prophet of the end of the Babylonian exile: "highway" (v. 8) from 40:3, "streams in the desert" (v. 6) from 43:19, the appearance of the "glory of the LORD" (v. 2) from 40:3, 5, and more. However, where Second Isaiah had announced the return of the Judean exiles from Babylon along a highway in the desert, the poet of chap. 35 expects even more. The dispersed of Israel from throughout the world shall return to Zion, and the desert will become a fertile garden. The vision in our passage is even more cosmic and eschatological than that of Second Isaiah. Consequently, some interpreters have viewed this

chapter as an introduction to and summary of the message of Isaiah 40–55, later interrupted by the insertion of the material in Isaiah 36–39.

But Isaiah 35 also makes prominent use of themes from the first half of the book as well, particularly the theme of the highway that leads to Zion. So the chapter functions as an editorial bridge between the two major parts of the book.[321] It does indeed provide an introduction to the message that follows in chaps. 40–55, but it links them to Isaiah 1–34 as well. Its dependence on Second Isaiah alone shows that chap. 35 would have been composed in the post-exilic period.

The poem itself closely resembles a prophetic announcement of salvation, but is different in subtle ways. It does proclaim that God is coming to save, and there is a sense of an audience being addressed. But unlike traditional announcements, whether of judgment or salvation, the word from the Lord is not introduced by a messenger or other prophetic formula. Although it has its parts, its stanzas, this is a single, coherent poetic composition, using older traditions creatively. Moreover, it bears the marks of a written composition, not the recording of an oral tradition. Likely it was composed in writing, to be read by those who turned to the book of Isaiah, or to be read aloud. A poet

320. Ronald E. Clements, Isaiah 1–39, NCB (Grand Rapids: Eerdmans, 1980) 271-75; Marvin A. Sweeney, Isaiah 1–39, With an Introduction to Prophetic Literature, FOTL XVI (Grand Rapids: Eerdmans, 1996) 450; Hans Wildberger, Jesaja: Kapitel 28–39, BKAT 10 (Neukirchen-Vluyn: Neukirchener Verlag, 1982) 1357-59.

321. O. H. Steck, Jesaja 35 als redaktionelle Brücke zwischen dem Ersten und dem Zweiten Jesaja, Stuttgarter Bibelstudien 121 (Stuttgart: Katholisches Bibelwerk, 1985), summarized on 101-3. See also Sweeney, Isaiah 1–39, 451. Clements, Isaiah 1–39, 275, stresses the function of the chapter as a summary of Isaiah 1–34.

has assumed the role of one who speaks on behalf of the Lord. The themes and language also indicate that the author has moved beyond the traditional prophetic attention to specific historical events to more universal, eschatological expectations. Its central theme is the proclamation that the natural order will be dramatically transformed and that the "ransomed of the LORD" (v. 10) will come in joy to Zion.

No addressee is specified in the first stanza (vv. 1-2), which proclaims that the desert will be changed into a place flourishing with vegetation, so that even the land itself will "rejoice." It is not said but assumed that the Lord will bring about this transformation, since its purpose or result is the revelation of "the glory of the LORD, the majesty of our God." The antecedents of several pronouns in these verses are not self-evident. "It" appears twice in v. 2, in both instances referring to the dry land or the desert of v. 1. Thus the arid land will be as glorious with vegetation as Lebanon, Carmel, and Sharon. With the expression "our God," the poet identifies with the audience, and also hints that other people have other gods. Who are "they" who shall witness the glory of the Lord (v. 2)? In 40:5 it is all peoples who will see the glory of the Lord, and in 60:1 it is the Lord's own people. Here the reference is unclear. It could even refer to the desert and dry land of v. 1. Remarkably, for all the wonderful blossoming of the desert, there is no vision here of productive agriculture, of crops to feed the people (cf. Amos 9:13-15).

The next stanza (vv. 3-4) consists of an exhortation in which neither speaker nor addressee is identified. Since the imperatives ("Strengthen," "Say") are plurals, and God is mentioned in the third person, one must conclude that the prophetic voice is addressing the people as a whole or a group within them. They are urged to strengthen the weak and to declare to the fearful that their God is present (40:9), and coming with "vengeance," and "divine retribution" (read with NIV) to save them. Those who are afraid will gain courage from the announcement that help is coming.

There are echoes here of the old tradition about the theophany, the arrival of God and the dramatic and terrifying effect of the Lord's appearance on the world. Here, however, as the next stanza (vv.

5-7) sets out, the sick are healed and streams flow in the desert. The vision of water in the wilderness, streams in the desert (v. 6), recollects the tradition of the Lord's care for Israel in the wilderness, and echoes Deutero-Isaiah's image of the return of the Exiles from Babylon (41:18-19). Is one to understand the good news that the disabled ("blind," "deaf," "lame," "dumb," vv. 5-6a) will be healed literally or metaphorically, e.g., from spiritual inabilities? In 42:18-20, as well as many other biblical texts, "blind" and "deaf" clearly characterize the people's ignorance or inability to understand. Some interpreters, emphasizing the eschatological dimensions of the chapter as a whole, take the language to be literal, promising a radical transformation so that there will be no physical disabilities in the age to come.[322] That is the sense of the loose citation of these lines in the NT (Matt 11:15; Luke 7:22). The force of the language in the poem cannot be determined with certainty, and in any case this may pose the wrong question. In reflections on the future reign of God, physical and spiritual well-being are difficult if not impossible to separate.[323]

The leading theme of the final stanza (vv. 8-10) is the return of the redeemed, the dispersed people of Israel, to Zion. Here, too, nature is transformed, made into a well-watered land, and fitted with a highway called "the Holy Way" (v. 8). The familiar threats to travelers in the desert—dry land, wild beasts, and enemies—no longer exist. The final lines (v. 10) catch the tone of the entire poem: joy and gladness, for "sorrow and sighing shall flee away."

This "highway" plays an important role in Deutero-Isaiah's message proclaiming the return of the exiles from Babylon (40:3-5; cf. also 11:16), but the present context indicates a broader vision, possibly including all the people of Israel scattered from the holy place. The name of the road, "Holy Way" (v. 8) suggests a pilgrim's highway. This sacred road is restricted to those who are holy—that is, the ritually "unclean" (טמא ṭāmē) may not travel on it. Although "holy" (קדוש qōdeš) is widely used throughout the book of Isaiah (e.g., "the Holy One of Israel," 1:4; 5:24; 30:11, 12, 15; 41:14, 16; 43:3; 60:9, 14), the

---

322. Clements, *Isaiah 1–39*, 276; O. Kaiser, *Isaiah 13–39: A Commentary* (Philadelphia: Westminster, 1974) 362.
323. Wildberger, *Jesaja 28–39*, 1362-63.

concern with ritual purity parallels that in the final part of the book, Isaiah 56–66. The highway to Zion will be so plain that even fools (among God's people, to be sure) can find and travel this path (v. 8*b*). Moreover, passage will be safe, for no "lion" or any "ravenous beast" (v. 9*a*) will threaten travelers.

In the proclamation in vv. 9-10 the meaning of some key terms requires serious and subtle analysis. What does it mean that the "redeemed" and the "ransomed of the LORD" will return to Zion? It is tempting to read such powerful theological words in terms of religious status or spiritual transformation, but that would be misleading. "To redeem" (גאל *gā'al*) comes from the realm of family law and refers to buying back someone from slavery, a person or property from debt (Ruth 3:13; Lev 25:33), and an animal from a sacrificial obligation (Lev 27:13, 15, 19). The term is used commonly in the Exodus traditions referring to the Lord's reclaiming Israel from Egyptian bondage.[324] Deutero-Isaiah also employs the term for the Lord's reclaiming the exiles from Babylon (41:14; 43:1, 14; 44:6, 22-24). Likewise, "ransom" (פדה *pādâ*) is an economic and cultic term for buying back a person or an animal from an

obligation (Exod 13:13, 15; 34:20; Lev 27:27; Num 18:15), also employed with reference to the exodus from Egypt (Deut 7:8; 13:6; 9:26), including in Deutero-Isaiah (50:2; 51:11).[325] So this language is rooted in concrete realities, as in being set free from political captivity. To the extent that "the highway" (v. 8) is a metaphor for being on the right road, it is also an actual feature of the landscape. The "redeemed," the "ransomed of the LORD," are people who have been released by the Lord's intervention—from Babylon and elsewhere—and thus are free to return to Zion.

And return they shall, forming a festive procession with singing and joyful celebration (v. 10). The motif of joy and gladness returns to the initial verse of the chapter; then it was the wilderness that would rejoice, now it is God's people. The concluding note, that "sorrow and sighing shall flee away," presumes that those who hear this proclamation are experiencing trouble, although their particular difficulties are not mentioned. This good news to the suffering is the most dramatic eschatological line of the entire poem. How can sorrow and sighing flee away and joy be everlasting while there is pain and suffering?

324. Many commentators, including Sweeney, *Isaiah 1–39*, 453, have noted the use of exodus traditions in vv. 8-10 (cf. Num 20:17; 21:22; Deut 2:8).

325. On these two terms see Wildberger, *Jesaja 28–39*, 1365-66, and on "ransom" see H. Wildberger, *Isaiah 1–12*, trans. Thomas H. Trapp (Minneapolis: Fortress, 1991) 71-72.

REFLECTIONS

1. This prophetic poem echoes with the familiar religious symbols "redeemed" and "ransomed." It is all but inevitable that contemporary readers will hear more in these words than a reference to the return of exiles to a particular holy place, and so they should. For Christians, "redeemed" and "ransomed" tend to refer to transformations of their status, to their spiritual salvation. But, particularly because the language is so familiar, this text from the ancient world should provoke readers to ask what the words actually refer to. Those who use such terms regularly might reflect on the relation of those symbols to concrete realities, such as exile, slavery, and the joy of coming home.

What does it mean to be "redeemed," to be "the ransomed of the LORD"? Are these only spiritual conditions; do they refer only to political and economic realities? The analysis of the text indicates that they refer fundamentally, but not only, to release from actual captivity. But whether they are one or the other in the ancient text, their meaning is an important consideration as each generation of readers responds to and even applies the biblical text in contemporary circumstances.

For those inclined to hear such language as reference to a religious status, the biblical tradition provides a corrective. "Redeem" and "ransom" have political and economic meaning in the OT. In the story of the exodus tradition, these terms, as well as "salvation," meant actual release from physical slavery. (Whether the stories are historically accurate or not is beside the point.

They were believed to refer to real events.) For those, on the other hand, who emphasize the political or economic force of the language, release from captivity and reestablishment in one's own land certainly have spiritual and emotional dimensions as well. This text points to the joy of those set free. So "redemption" is both physical and spiritual. Moreover, about one point there can be no doubt: The people of God will not redeem or ransom themselves. In this text, redemption and ransom are effected by God, and God alone. Through divine action, the people of God become the redeemed of God, and that transforms their lives in every possible way.

2. Above all, both the tone and the substance of Isaiah 35 proclaim the good news of God's care for the people of God. Those who experience their lives as exile, those who pass through a wilderness, those who are weak or even disabled may shout for joy, for God will transform all things. Furthermore, it is even possible that the proclamation of such good news may have the power to transform ordinary lives and the realities of the world.

Behind this text, however, lie dark and troubling realities. Those to whom it was and is addressed have not yet seen sorrow and sighing flee away (35:10). There are "weak hands" that need to be strengthened, "feeble knees" that must be made firm, "fearful" hearts that need courage and encouragement (35:3-4). Even more dramatically, the message concerns the blind, deaf, lame, and the dumb (35:5-6). Every reader of every generation knows that all these, and more, are persistent human realities. That fact helps explain the longing, the need for hope, for the end to sighing and sorrow, if not in this world then in the world to come. The reader who is not willing to give up on God's concern to save will struggle to balance the announcement of God's good news with the acknowledgment that suffering persists.

ISAIAH 36:1–39:8

ISAIAH, HEZEKIAH, AND THE FATE OF JERUSALEM

OVERVIEW

The chronological heading and the shift from prophetic address in poetry to prose narration indicate that a distinct and quite different unit begins with 36:1. It is equally obvious that the section continues through the end of chap. 39, for chap. 40 resumes with announcements of salvation similar to that of chap. 35. Although more than one unit and various literary genre appear in chaps. 36–39, these chapters comprise a coherent section.

Narratives are, to be sure, found elsewhere in Isaiah 1–39, and some of the accounts here of Isaiah's words and actions in relationship to King Hezekiah are similar to the shorter accounts of the prophet's encounters with an earlier king, Ahaz (chap. 7).[326] But the narratives in Isaiah 36–39 are fundamentally different, closely resembling the particular type of historical narratives found in the book of Kings. In fact, with some variants, all this material except 38:9-20 is found in 2 Kgs 18:13–20:19. The meaning of this parallel requires explanation.

But when viewed in their context, these chapters form what is virtually a separate book.[327] At the center of these stories stands the question of the fate of Jerusalem and the reactions of Hezekiah, Isaiah, and—above all—the Lord, to the siege of the city by the Assyrian armies of Sennacherib. The story plays out in three parts, each in turn consisting of various elements. The longest and most complex of these is 36:1–37:38, the account of Sennacherib's invasion of Judah and siege of Jerusalem. This account contains two distinguishable versions of the events, but according to both of them, the Assyrian army decimated the towns of the Judean countryside, laid siege to Jerusalem, but left without capturing or destroying the holy city. The second part (38:1-22) appears unrelated to the first, containing the story of Hezekiah's life-threatening illness, his recovery, and prayer of thanksgiving. The third section (39:1-8) presents the story of how Hezekiah welcomed some other foreigners, a delegation from Babylon, and how Isaiah responded to the king's actions.

Interpreters have long recognized that these chapters parallel the account in 2 Kgs 18:13–20:19 very closely (see also 2 Chronicles 32, which is a shorter version that clearly depends on 2 Kings). The most significant difference is the addition of the psalm of Hezekiah in 38:9-20.[328] More important are the materials in 2 Kings that do not appear in Isaiah. First, the account in Kings is part of the deuteronomistic history (Deuteronomy–2 Kings). This means it has a large narrative context, the history of Israel and Judah beginning with the exodus from Egypt. The account of the events in and around Jerusalem in the time of Hezekiah comes late in the story, which will end in the disaster of the Babylonian Exile, with a little enigmatic note about the last Judean king as a prisoner at the court of the king of Babylon (2 Kgs 25:27-30). After David in a long line of rulers, only two kings, Hezekiah and Josiah, received unqualified approval by the authors and editors of this history. Obviously, none of the kings of the northern kingdom

---

326. Peter Ackroyd, "Isaiah 36–39: Structure and Function," in *Festschrift van der Ploeg*, AOAT 211 (1982) 3-21, has compared these chapters with Isa 6:1–9:7 and concluded that one purpose of Isaiah 36–39 is to contrast Hezekiah with Ahaz.

327. As Clements puts it, "The chapters should be considered as a whole, forming a trilogy of stories concerning Isaiah, Jerusalem and the Davidic kingship." See Ronald E. Clements, *Isaiah 1–39*, NCB (Grand Rapids: Eerdmans, 1980) 278.

328. Sweeney notes a number of points where the narrative from Kings has been changed in subtle ways to glorify Hezekiah. See Marvin A. Sweeney, *Isaiah 1–39, With an Introduction to Prophetic Literature*, FOTL XVI (Grand Rapids: Eerdmans, 1996) 481-83.

could qualify, since the central criterion applied by the historians was the purity of the worship of Yahweh at the sole legitimate sanctuary on Zion. The introduction to the reign of Hezekiah (2 Kgs 18:1-8) does not appear in Isaiah.

But the most significant difference between 2 Kings and Isaiah is that the latter does not include the other account of Sennacherib's siege of Jerusalem, the one in which Hezekiah capitulated to the Assyrian king (2 Kgs 18:13-16). This fact is a key to the relationship between the account in the deuteronomistic history and the one in Isaiah, but it is also important evidence for understanding how accounts function in the book of Isaiah.

Comparison of the books of 2 Kings and Isaiah confirms the judgment of virtually all interpreters that these narratives were originally composed for the historical books and only subsequently included in the scroll of Isaiah (e.g., 36:7 assumes but does not include the information concerning Hezekiah's reform in 2 Kgs 18:3-6). To be sure, that composition relied upon diverse earlier traditions, which were then interpreted over the decades if not centuries. This process is apparent from the complexity of the stories, even if it is not possible to reconstruct all the stages of their literary development. The narrative of Sennacherib's departure from his siege of Jerusalem appears in two versions in Isaiah, identified by scholars as the B[1] and B[2] accounts, and the report left out of Isaiah (2 Kgs 18:13-16, called the A account) tells a very different story.

It is not difficult to see why a history of Israel and Judah would contain accounts such as these, but why is the material repeated here in a prophetic book? One purpose could simply be to provide information on Isaiah, Hezekiah, and the events of the time. But stories, especially historical narratives, never have the sole purpose of presenting information. The reader always needs to ask the historian, "Why are you telling me this, and in this way?" This is important because a particular version of the past legitimizes some claim in the present. With this in view, it appears that one purpose of this set of narratives is to confirm the prophetic power of Isaiah. That helps explain why the version that reports the salvation of Jerusalem and not its capitulation (as in version A, 2 Kgs 18:13-16) is included, along with the announcement of the fall of the city to the Babylonians in the future (39:5-8).

Moreover, the narratives present a particular perspective on Yahweh's care for the city in the time of a faithful king, Hezekiah, and the Lord's subsequent judgment on the city and the people because of a history of apostasy.

An important and related question concerns the placement of the section in this particular context. Until relatively recently in the history of the interpretation of the book, the location of these chapters would not have been considered a serious problem. In the traditional view in church and synagogue, everything up to this point was taken to have come from or be directly about Isaiah, and now the reader is provided a trustworthy account of the events of the prophet's time. Moreover, the words about Babylon in chap. 39 introduce what were taken to be Isaiah's words concerning that time in the future (chaps. 40–66). In a form-critical interpretation of the book as a collection of various materials, the organization could be more or less random. The narrative traditions might as well be here as elsewhere. In the source-critical analysis of the book as the work of two or three major authors, Isaiah 36–39 makes sense as an appendix inserted at the end of one book (chaps. 1–39) and before the beginning of another (chaps. 40–55). A close parallel exists in the final chapter of Jeremiah (Jeremiah 52) that concludes with an historical "appendix" that corresponds to the substance of 2 Kgs 24:18–25:30.[329]

But as attention has shifted to the shape of the book as a whole and to the question of the meaning of that shape, either as the goal of an editor or as the final form of the canonical book, it has become more and more apparent that "appendix" is not an adequate designation of this material. Such a title implies that these chapters are not an integral part of the book of Isaiah. So why here? One reason for their location must be the proximity to the traditions in Isaiah 28–33 concerning the same Assyrian crisis. The problem, of course, is that chaps. 34–35 intervene. Given the similarity of chap. 35 to chaps. 40–55, it seems most likely that chaps. 36–39 were inserted into its context quite late in the history of the book's composition, after chap. 35 had been added (see the Commentary on 35:1-10). This means the narratives

---

329. See Hans Wildberger, *Jesaja: Kapitel 28–39,* BKAT 10 (Neukirchen-Vluyn: Neukirchener Verlag, 1982) 1370.

in this chapter were added after 539 BCE, the date of Second Isaiah, and probably also written after that as well, since the Deuteronomistic History was completed no earlier than the middle of the sixth century BCE.[330] The function of these historical narratives, then, was to provide a bridge between the prophecies for the Assyrian period and those for the time of the Babylonian exile.[331] This does not entirely resolve the question of why

chaps. 36–39 follow rather than precede chap. 35, which functions as an introductory summary for chaps. 40ff. It does seem clear, however, that a book of Isaiah had been completed before chaps. 34–35 and 36–39 were added. That does not mean everything in 1–33 was included in that book, but both these final sections presume the existence of the work of both Isaiah of Jerusalem and of Second Isaiah. So both 34–35 and 36–39 are transitional, with 35 providing the most obvious introduction to 40–55 and 36–39 linking the Assyrian to the Babylonian period.

---

330. Some argue that there was an earlier edition of this history from the time of Josiah. See Frank Moore Cross, *Canaanite Myth and Hebrew Epic* (Cambridge, Mass.: Harvard University Press, 1973) 287-89.

331. Clements, *Isaiah 1–39*, 277.

ISAIAH 36:1–37:38, SENNACHERIB'S THREAT AND THE LORD'S RESPONSE

NIV

36 In the fourteenth year of King Hezekiah's reign, Sennacherib king of Assyria attacked all the fortified cities of Judah and captured them. [2]Then the king of Assyria sent his field commander with a large army from Lachish to King Hezekiah at Jerusalem. When the commander stopped at the aqueduct of the Upper Pool, on the road to the Washerman's Field, [3]Eliakim son of Hilkiah the palace administrator, Shebna the secretary, and Joah son of Asaph the recorder went out to him.

[4]The field commander said to them, "Tell Hezekiah,

" 'This is what the great king, the king of Assyria, says: On what are you basing this confidence of yours? [5]You say you have strategy and military strength—but you speak only empty words. On whom are you depending, that you rebel against me? [6]Look now, you are depending on Egypt, that splintered reed of a staff, which pierces a man's hand and wounds him if he leans on it! Such is Pharaoh king of Egypt to all who depend on him. [7]And if you say to me, "We are depending on the LORD our God"—isn't he the one whose high places and altars Hezekiah removed, saying to Judah and Jerusalem, "You must worship before this altar"?

NRSV

36 In the fourteenth year of King Hezekiah, King Sennacherib of Assyria came up against all the fortified cities of Judah and captured them. [2]The king of Assyria sent the Rabshakeh from Lachish to King Hezekiah at Jerusalem, with a great army. He stood by the conduit of the upper pool on the highway to the Fuller's Field. [3]And there came out to him Eliakim son of Hilkiah, who was in charge of the palace, and Shebna the secretary, and Joah son of Asaph, the recorder.

4The Rabshakeh said to them, "Say to Hezekiah: Thus says the great king, the king of Assyria: On what do you base this confidence of yours? [5]Do you think that mere words are strategy and power for war? On whom do you now rely, that you have rebelled against me? [6]See, you are relying on Egypt, that broken reed of a staff, which will pierce the hand of anyone who leans on it. Such is Pharaoh king of Egypt to all who rely on him. [7]But if you say to me, 'We rely on the LORD our God,' is it not he whose high places and altars Hezekiah has removed, saying to Judah and to Jerusalem, 'You shall worship before this altar'? [8]Come now, make a wager with my master the king of Assyria: I will give you two thousand horses, if you are able on your part to set riders on them. [9]How then can you repulse a single captain

NRSV

8" 'Come now, make a bargain with my master, the king of Assyria: I will give you two thousand horses—if you can put riders on them! 9How then can you repulse one officer of the least of my master's officials, even though you are depending on Egypt for chariots and horsemen? 10Furthermore, have I come to attack and destroy this land without the LORD? The LORD himself told me to march against this country and destroy it.' "

11Then Eliakim, Shebna and Joah said to the field commander, "Please speak to your servants in Aramaic, since we understand it. Don't speak to us in Hebrew in the hearing of the people on the wall."

12But the commander replied, "Was it only to your master and you that my master sent me to say these things, and not to the men sitting on the wall—who, like you, will have to eat their own filth and drink their own urine?"

13Then the commander stood and called out in Hebrew, "Hear the words of the great king, the king of Assyria! 14This is what the king says: Do not let Hezekiah deceive you. He cannot deliver you! 15Do not let Hezekiah persuade you to trust in the LORD when he says, 'The LORD will surely deliver us; this city will not be given into the hand of the king of Assyria.'

16"Do not listen to Hezekiah. This is what the king of Assyria says: Make peace with me and come out to me. Then every one of you will eat from his own vine and fig tree and drink water from his own cistern, 17until I come and take you to a land like your own—a land of grain and new wine, a land of bread and vineyards.

18"Do not let Hezekiah mislead you when he says, 'The LORD will deliver us.' Has the god of any nation ever delivered his land from the hand of the king of Assyria? 19Where are the gods of Hamath and Arpad? Where are the gods of Sepharvaim? Have they rescued Samaria from my hand? 20Who of all the gods of these countries has been able to save his land from me? How then can the LORD deliver Jerusalem from my hand?"

21But the people remained silent and said nothing in reply, because the king had commanded, "Do not answer him."

NRSV

among the least of my master's servants, when you rely on Egypt for chariots and for horsemen? 10Moreover, is it without the LORD that I have come up against this land to destroy it? The LORD said to me, Go up against this land, and destroy it."

11Then Eliakim, Shebna, and Joah said to the Rabshakeh, "Please speak to your servants in Aramaic, for we understand it; do not speak to us in the language of Judah within the hearing of the people who are on the wall." 12But the Rabshakeh said, "Has my master sent me to speak these words to your master and to you, and not to the people sitting on the wall, who are doomed with you to eat their own dung and drink their own urine?"

13Then the Rabshakeh stood and called out in a loud voice in the language of Judah, "Hear the words of the great king, the king of Assyria! 14Thus says the king: 'Do not let Hezekiah deceive you, for he will not be able to deliver you. 15Do not let Hezekiah make you rely on the LORD by saying, The LORD will surely deliver us; this city will not be given into the hand of the king of Assyria.' 16Do not listen to Hezekiah; for thus says the king of Assyria: 'Make your peace with me and come out to me; then everyone of you will eat from your own vine and your own fig tree and drink water from your own cistern, 17until I come and take you away to a land like your own land, a land of grain and wine, a land of bread and vineyards. 18Do not let Hezekiah mislead you by saying, The LORD will save us. Has any of the gods of the nations saved their land out of the hand of the king of Assyria? 19Where are the gods of Hamath and Arpad? Where are the gods of Sepharvaim? Have they delivered Samaria out of my hand? 20Who among all the gods of these countries have saved their countries out of my hand, that the LORD should save Jerusalem out of my hand?' "

21But they were silent and answered him not a word, for the king's command was, "Do not answer him." 22Then Eliakim son of Hilkiah, who was in charge of the palace, and Shebna the secretary, and Joah son of Asaph, the recorder, came to Hezekiah with their clothes torn, and told him the words of the Rabshakeh.

NIV

²²Then Eliakim son of Hilkiah the palace administrator, Shebna the secretary, and Joah son of Asaph the recorder went to Hezekiah, with their clothes torn, and told him what the field commander had said.

37 When King Hezekiah heard this, he tore his clothes and put on sackcloth and went into the temple of the LORD. ²He sent Eliakim the palace administrator, Shebna the secretary, and the leading priests, all wearing sackcloth, to the prophet Isaiah son of Amoz. ³They told him, "This is what Hezekiah says: This day is a day of distress and rebuke and disgrace, as when children come to the point of birth and there is no strength to deliver them. ⁴It may be that the LORD your God will hear the words of the field commander, whom his master, the king of Assyria, has sent to ridicule the living God, and that he will rebuke him for the words the LORD your God has heard. Therefore pray for the remnant that still survives."

⁵When King Hezekiah's officials came to Isaiah, ⁶Isaiah said to them, "Tell your master, 'This is what the LORD says: Do not be afraid of what you have heard—those words with which the underlings of the king of Assyria have blasphemed me. ⁷Listen! I am going to put a spirit in him so that when he hears a certain report, he will return to his own country, and there I will have him cut down with the sword.' "

⁸When the field commander heard that the king of Assyria had left Lachish, he withdrew and found the king fighting against Libnah.

⁹Now Sennacherib received a report that Tirhakah, the Cushite[a] king ⸤of Egypt⸥, was marching out to fight against him. When he heard it, he sent messengers to Hezekiah with this word: ¹⁰"Say to Hezekiah king of Judah: Do not let the god you depend on deceive you when he says, 'Jerusalem will not be handed over to the king of Assyria.' ¹¹Surely you have heard what the kings of Assyria have done to all the countries, destroying them completely. And will you be delivered? ¹²Did the gods of the nations that were destroyed by my forefathers deliver them—the gods of Gozan, Haran, Rezeph and the people of Eden who were in Tel Assar? ¹³Where is the king of

[a]9 That is, from the upper Nile region

NRSV

37 When King Hezekiah heard it, he tore his clothes, covered himself with sackcloth, and went into the house of the LORD. ²And he sent Eliakim, who was in charge of the palace, and Shebna the secretary, and the senior priests, covered with sackcloth, to the prophet Isaiah son of Amoz. ³They said to him, "Thus says Hezekiah, This day is a day of distress, of rebuke, and of disgrace; children have come to the birth, and there is no strength to bring them forth. ⁴It may be that the LORD your God heard the words of the Rabshakeh, whom his master the king of Assyria has sent to mock the living God, and will rebuke the words that the LORD your God has heard; therefore lift up your prayer for the remnant that is left."

5When the servants of King Hezekiah came to Isaiah, ⁶Isaiah said to them, "Say to your master, 'Thus says the LORD: Do not be afraid because of the words that you have heard, with which the servants of the king of Assyria have reviled me. ⁷I myself will put a spirit in him, so that he shall hear a rumor, and return to his own land; I will cause him to fall by the sword in his own land.' "

8The Rabshakeh returned, and found the king of Assyria fighting against Libnah; for he had heard that the king had left Lachish. ⁹Now the king[a] heard concerning King Tirhakah of Ethiopia,[b] "He has set out to fight against you." When he heard it, he sent messengers to Hezekiah, saying, ¹⁰"Thus shall you speak to King Hezekiah of Judah: Do not let your God on whom you rely deceive you by promising that Jerusalem will not be given into the hand of the king of Assyria. ¹¹See, you have heard what the kings of Assyria have done to all lands, destroying them utterly. Shall you be delivered? ¹²Have the gods of the nations delivered them, the nations that my predecessors destroyed, Gozan, Haran, Rezeph, and the people of Eden who were in Telassar? ¹³Where is the king of Hamath, the king of Arpad, the king of the city of Sepharvaim, the king of Hena, or the king of Ivvah?"

14Hezekiah received the letter from the hand of the messengers and read it; then Hezekiah went up to the house of the LORD and spread it

[a]Heb he   [b]Or Nubia; Heb Cush

NIV

Hamath, the king of Arpad, the king of the city of Sepharvaim, or of Hena or Ivvah?"

¹⁴Hezekiah received the letter from the messengers and read it. Then he went up to the temple of the Lord and spread it out before the Lord. ¹⁵And Hezekiah prayed to the Lord: ¹⁶"O Lord Almighty, God of Israel, enthroned between the cherubim, you alone are God over all the kingdoms of the earth. You have made heaven and earth. ¹⁷Give ear, O Lord, and hear; open your eyes, O Lord, and see; listen to all the words Sennacherib has sent to insult the living God.

¹⁸"It is true, O Lord, that the Assyrian kings have laid waste all these peoples and their lands. ¹⁹They have thrown their gods into the fire and destroyed them, for they were not gods but only wood and stone, fashioned by human hands. ²⁰Now, O Lord our God, deliver us from his hand, so that all kingdoms on earth may know that you alone, O Lord, are God.ᵃ"

²¹Then Isaiah son of Amoz sent a message to Hezekiah: "This is what the Lord, the God of Israel, says: Because you have prayed to me concerning Sennacherib king of Assyria, ²²this is the word the Lord has spoken against him:

"The Virgin Daughter of Zion
    despises and mocks you.
The Daughter of Jerusalem
    tosses her head as you flee.
²³Who is it you have insulted and blasphemed?
    Against whom have you raised your voice
and lifted your eyes in pride?
    Against the Holy One of Israel!
²⁴By your messengers
    you have heaped insults on the Lord.
And you have said,
    'With my many chariots
I have ascended the heights of the mountains,
    the utmost heights of Lebanon.
I have cut down its tallest cedars,
    the choicest of its pines.
I have reached its remotest heights,
    the finest of its forests.
²⁵I have dug wells in foreign landsᵇ
    and drunk the water there.

ᵃ20 Dead Sea Scrolls (see also 2 Kings 19:19); Masoretic Text *alone are the* Lord   ᵇ25 Dead Sea Scrolls (see also 2 Kings 19:24); Masoretic Text does not have *in foreign lands*

NRSV

before the Lord. ¹⁵And Hezekiah prayed to the Lord, saying: ¹⁶"O Lord of hosts, God of Israel, who are enthroned above the cherubim, you are God, you alone, of all the kingdoms of the earth; you have made heaven and earth. ¹⁷Incline your ear, O Lord, and hear; open your eyes, O Lord, and see; hear all the words of Sennacherib, which he has sent to mock the living God. ¹⁸Truly, O Lord, the kings of Assyria have laid waste all the nations and their lands, ¹⁹and have hurled their gods into the fire, though they were no gods, but the work of human hands—wood and stone—and so they were destroyed. ²⁰So now, O Lord our God, save us from his hand, so that all the kingdoms of the earth may know that you alone are the Lord."

21Then Isaiah son of Amoz sent to Hezekiah, saying: "Thus says the Lord, the God of Israel: Because you have prayed to me concerning King Sennacherib of Assyria, ²²this is the word that the Lord has spoken concerning him:

She despises you, she scorns you—
    virgin daughter Zion;
she tosses her head—behind your back,
    daughter Jerusalem.

²³ "Whom have you mocked and reviled?
    Against whom have you raised your voice
and haughtily lifted your eyes?
    Against the Holy One of Israel!
²⁴ By your servants you have mocked the Lord,
    and you have said, 'With my many chariots
I have gone up the heights of the mountains,
    to the far recesses of Lebanon;
I felled its tallest cedars,
    its choicest cypresses;
I came to its remotest height,
    its densest forest.
²⁵ I dug wells
    and drank waters,
I dried up with the sole of my foot
    all the streams of Egypt.'

²⁶ Have you not heard
    that I determined it long ago?
I planned from days of old
    what now I bring to pass,
that you should make fortified cities

NIV

With the soles of my feet
  I have dried up all the streams of Egypt.'

26"Have you not heard?
  Long ago I ordained it.
In days of old I planned it;
  now I have brought it to pass,
that you have turned fortified cities
  into piles of stone.
27Their people, drained of power,
  are dismayed and put to shame.
They are like plants in the field,
  like tender green shoots,
like grass sprouting on the roof,
  scorched[a] before it grows up.
28"But I know where you stay
  and when you come and go
  and how you rage against me.
29Because you rage against me
  and because your insolence has reached
    my ears,
I will put my hook in your nose
  and my bit in your mouth,
and I will make you return
  by the way you came.

30"This will be the sign for you, O Hezekiah:

"This year you will eat what grows by itself,
  and the second year what springs from that.
But in the third year sow and reap,
  plant vineyards and eat their fruit.
31Once more a remnant of the house of Judah
  will take root below and bear fruit above.
32For out of Jerusalem will come a remnant,
  and out of Mount Zion a band of survivors.
The zeal of the Lord Almighty
  will accomplish this.

33"Therefore this is what the Lord says concerning the king of Assyria:

"He will not enter this city
  or shoot an arrow here.
He will not come before it with shield
  or build a siege ramp against it.
34By the way that he came he will return;
  he will not enter this city,"
                  declares the Lord.

a27 Some manuscripts of the Masoretic Text, Dead Sea Scrolls and some Septuagint manuscripts (see also 2 Kings 19:26); most manuscripts of the Masoretic Text *roof / and terraced fields*

NRSV

crash into heaps of ruins,
27 while their inhabitants, shorn of strength,
  are dismayed and confounded;
they have become like plants of the field
  and like tender grass,
like grass on the housetops,
  blighted[a] before it is grown.

28 I know your rising up[b] and your
    sitting down,
  your going out and coming in,
  and your raging against me.
29 Because you have raged against me
  and your arrogance has come to my ears,
I will put my hook in your nose
  and my bit in your mouth;
I will turn you back on the way
  by which you came.

30"And this shall be the sign for you: This year eat what grows of itself, and in the second year what springs from that; then in the third year sow, reap, plant vineyards, and eat their fruit. 31The surviving remnant of the house of Judah shall again take root downward, and bear fruit upward; 32for from Jerusalem a remnant shall go out, and from Mount Zion a band of survivors. The zeal of the Lord of hosts will do this.

33"Therefore thus says the Lord concerning the king of Assyria: He shall not come into this city, shoot an arrow there, come before it with a shield, or cast up a siege ramp against it. 34By the way that he came, by the same he shall return; he shall not come into this city, says the Lord. 35For I will defend this city to save it, for my own sake and for the sake of my servant David."

36Then the angel of the Lord set out and struck down one hundred eighty-five thousand in the camp of the Assyrians; when morning dawned, they were all dead bodies. 37Then King Sennacherib of Assyria left, went home, and lived at Nineveh. 38As he was worshiping in the house of his god Nisroch, his sons Adrammelech and Sharezer killed him with the sword, and they escaped into the land of Ararat. His son Esar-haddon succeeded him.

aWith 2 Kings 19.26: Heb *field*   bQ Ms Gk: MT lacks *your rising up*

NIV

35"I will defend this city and save it,
    for my sake and for the sake of David
        my servant!"
36Then the angel of the LORD went out and put to death a hundred and eighty-five thousand men in the Assyrian camp. When the people got up the next morning—there were all the dead bodies! 37So Sennacherib king of Assyria broke camp and withdrew. He returned to Nineveh and stayed there.

38One day, while he was worshiping in the temple of his god Nisroch, his sons Adrammelech and Sharezer cut him down with the sword, and they escaped to the land of Ararat. And Esarhaddon his son succeeded him as king.

COMMENTARY

These two chapters report the drama that transpired when the Assyrian army under Sennacherib invaded Judah and laid siege to Jerusalem. The central figures are Hezekiah, king of Judah; Sennacherib, king of Assyria; the Rabshakeh, emissary of Sennacherib; and the prophet Isaiah. Offstage, and communicating through the prophet as well as through actions, is Yahweh. The tension develops and is resolved around the question of what the Lord will do. Will the Lord intervene to save Jerusalem from the Assyrians or not?

As noted already (see the Overview to 36:1–39:8), the story is complex, including two related but distinct versions of the main events.[332] However, because the narrative transitions and introductions are clear, it is not difficult to discern the major divisions in the literature. Having set the stage by reporting the Assyrian invasion and siege, the first scene (36:1-22) finds the Rabshakeh, representing Sennacherib, addressing a long speech to Hezekiah, heard by his high officials and the people. In fact, this entire account contains more words than action. Once Hezekiah's representatives have reported the Rabshakeh's scandalous

speech to the king, the second scene (37:1-7) is played out by Hezekiah and Isaiah. The matter seems to have been resolved by the prophet's oracle of salvation in which Yahweh promises to inspire ("put a spirit in him," 37:7) Sennacherib to return home, where he will die by the sword.

But the Rabshakeh is not finished. In the next episode (37:8-20) he meets his king at the Judean city of Libna. Having heard of Judah's alliance with Egypt, Sennacherib gives the Rabshakeh another threatening message for Hezekiah, presumably in written form. Once the Judean king reads the message he prays to the Lord for deliverance. In the final scene (37:21-38), Isaiah presents the Lord's answer to the prayer. The response is twofold, an extended announcement of judgment on the Assyrian king and a promise to defend Jerusalem, both of which are said to have come to pass (37:36-38).

Two versions of the siege and deliverance of Jerusalem have been woven together into a narrative that moves from setting the scene, to complication and rising action, to resolution. The first account includes 36:1–37:9a plus 37:37-38. The second then consists of 37:9b-36.[333] In both instances the siege was lifted through divine inter-

332. For analysis of the texts and the issues, as well as the specific parallels to 2 Kings, see Brevard S. Childs, *Isaiah and the Assyrian Crisis,* SBT (London: SCM, 1967) esp. 69-103; R. E. Clements, *Isaiah and the Deliverance of Jerusalem: A Study in the Interpretation of Prophecy in the Old Testament,* JSOTSup 13 (Sheffield: JSOT, 1980).

333. See Clements, *Isaiah 1–39,* 278; Wildberger, *Jesaja 28–39,* 1378-1438; Childs, *Isaiah and the Assyrian Crisis,* 76-103.

vention, but there are duplicate versions both of the Rabshakeh's message and the fate of the invaders.

The message of this report as a whole is unmistakable. The Lord protects Zion. Or at least: The Lord protected Zion when it was ruled by a faithful king, under attack by an arrogant enemy, and when the Lord's word could be proclaimed by the prophet Isaiah.

Historical questions are inevitable when one reads accounts such as this that report important political and military events. What, we are bound to ask, happened? The question becomes difficult on the one hand because there is too much evidence. The texts themselves give more than one answer to our question. This story in Isaiah, itself made up of two strands of tradition, appears to conflict with the account in 2 Kgs 18:13-16, which reports Hezekiah's capitulation to Sennacherib. Moreover, yet a different account appears in the Assyrian records. On the other hand there is too little evidence. None of these sources are unbiased or objective, and all lack important details.

The tendency of historians has been to place more confidence in the Assyrian records than those from the OT, but they, like the biblical accounts, are far from neutral. Sennacherib boasts that it was the "terror-inspiring splendor of my lordship" that overwhelmed Hezekiah, who sent tribute to Nineveh, "my lordly city."[334] Is there any reason to suppose that the Assyrian account is more trustworthy than that of the OT?[335] There are no reasons except that the Assyrian texts actually stem from the time of the events or very shortly thereafter, while the biblical account comes from much later. To be sure, the OT accounts may derive from royal or temple records from the time of Hezekiah. But those records no longer exist and would have to be reconstructed from much later biblical accounts, and even later actual written texts. Moreover, the annals of Sennacherib, for all their bombast, contain a great many details of the siege of Jerusalem in 701 BCE.[336]

Some historians have attempted to resolve the problem of the sources by positing not one but two

Assyrian sieges of Jerusalem.[337] Although this theory seems to take account of the conflict between the report in 2 Kgs 18:14-16 of Hezekiah's submission and tribute to the Assyrians and the other reports that describe the invaders' dramatic retreat, it is both unsatisfactory and unnecessary. Different versions of the same event are common, particularly when they are found in traditions that have been passed down for decades if not centuries, as is the case with these biblical accounts. One alternative is to conclude that the historical questions cannot be answered.[338] The other is to acknowledge that, while certainty cannot be reached, the evidence tends to support certain conclusions. It is most likely that Sennacherib laid siege to Jerusalem once (in 701 BCE), but that he did not capture the city.[339] Both the Assyrian records and one biblical account (2 Kgs 18:14-16) agree that Hezekiah paid tribute, and that is what saved the city.[340] But all the biblical accounts, and especially those in chaps. 36–37, interpret the events theologically, as the Lord's salvation of Jerusalem.[341]

36:1-22. This section consists mainly of speeches but they are set within a narrative framework. What is about to happen took place in the "fourteenth year of king Hezekiah," generally believed to be 701 BCE. The circumstances are presented with a straightforward description, moving from general to specific events (vv. 1-3). The language is simple but the events dramatic: Sennacherib of Assyria invaded the land, capturing all the "fortified cities" of Judah. The writer takes it for granted that the reader will know Jerusalem was not included in that number. When that had happened, the Assyrian king sent the Rabshakeh—the word is a title for a high official and not a proper name—to speak on his behalf to Hezekiah. It is not said but assumed that Jerusalem is surrounded and under siege, with no hope for relief from other Judeans. The Rabshakeh took a position outside the city, where he was met by three of Hezekiah's officials. Thus the Assyrian and Judean kings communicated with one another through representatives.

334. *ANET,* 288.

335. Christopher R. Seitz, *Isaiah 1–39,* Interpretation (Louisville: John Knox, 1993) 252-53.

336. See *ANET,* 287-88, and the Commentary on Isa 29:1-14, where some of this text is cited.

337. This view was developed and popularized in John Bright, *A History of Israel,* 2nd ed. (Philadelphia: Westminster, 1972) 282-86, 296-308.

338. See Childs, *Isaiah and the Assyrian Crisis,* 118-20.

339. J. Maxwell Miller and John H. Hayes, *A History of Ancient Israel and Judah* (Philadelphia: Westminster, 1986) 358-63.

340. Clements, *Isaiah and the Deliverance of Jerusalem,* 90-91.

341. Ibid., 90-108.

When the Rabshakeh first speaks (vv. 4-10) it becomes clear that his overt goal is to persuade Hezekiah to surrender. He first ridicules Judah's reliance on its alliance with Egypt. "Mere words," that is, a treaty, are no substitute for military "strategy" and strength (v. 5). With a wonderful metaphor he belittles Judah's ally. Egypt, a land of reeds, is itself a reed, not a staff, that will pierce the hand that leans on it (v. 6). Then he ridicules Hezekiah's reliance on Yahweh, alluding to that king's efforts to centralize worship in Jerusalem by destroying Yahweh's worship centers elsewhere (2 Kgs 18:3-6; cf. Deuteronomy 12). In his next move he scorns the king's military resources, promising to give Hezekiah two thousand horses if he could provide them with riders (v. 8), and vowing that the troops under the command of a single "captain" could take the city (v. 9). Finally, the Rabshakeh becomes a theologian, affirming that Assyrian victory is assured because they have come at the Lord's instruction (v. 10). The idea corresponds to Isaiah's earlier affirmation that Assyria is the rod of the Lord's anger (10:5). By now the speech has become propaganda, designed to demoralize the people of Jerusalem.

Now the three Judean officials speak and the Rabshakeh responds (vv. 11-12). They plead with him to speak in Aramaic, the diplomatic language of the Assyrian Empire, rather than "the language of Judah" because the people sitting on the wall can understand everything. Scornfully, the Assyrian representative admits that his speech is not just for the king but for all the people of Jerusalem. He means to incite, if not rebellion, at least desertion by reminding them of the hardships of a long siege. Without food and water they are doomed "to eat their own dung and drink their own urine" (v. 12).

The Rabshakeh speaks again (vv. 13-20), this time addressing the people directly, telling them not to follow Hezekiah's call to trust in the Lord and the promise that the city cannot be taken (vv. 14-15). Speaking as a messenger for Sennacherib, he explicitly calls for peace, that is, surrender, in which case "everyone of you will eat from your own vine and your own fig tree and drink water from your own cistern" (v. 16) instead, he implies, of the starvation and thirst brought on by the siege. But in the next breath (v. 17) the Assyrian threatens the populace with exile. Again, the argumenta-

tion and propaganda turn to theology as the Rabshakeh warns against reliance on Yahweh. None of the gods of the other and more powerful nations saved them, so why should anyone believe that the Lord will save Jerusalem? (vv. 18-20). That last line poses the central question that drives the entire story: Can and will the Lord save Jerusalem?

The narrative framework (vv. 21-22) reports that, in obedience to Hezekiah's command, no one responded to the Assyrian messenger's speech, and that the three Judean officials came in mourning ("with their clothes torn") before the king and reported what they had heard.

37:1-7. The king responds to the threat in two ways. First he assumes the posture of mourning and lament by tearing his clothes and putting on sackcloth and going to the Temple (v. 1), presumably to pray. Second, he sends his high officials to consult the prophet Isaiah. Two of these, Eliakim the major domo and Shebna the secretary, had been Hezekiah's delegates when the Rabshakeh presented Sennacherib's case. However, the third, Asaph the recorder, is replaced by "the senior priests" (v. 2). Afraid and in mourning, this delegation meets Isaiah with a message from the king. The deferential tone shows respect for the prophet, and their speech takes nothing for granted. They lament the situation, punctuating their report with a proverbial saying, "children have come to birth and there is no strength to bring them forth" (v. 3; cf. Hos 13:13).[342] Then they present a selective précis of the message from the Rabshakeh, emphasizing that his king had sent him "to mock the living God" (v. 4). This summary is designed to support their request, that Isaiah intercede on behalf of those left in Jerusalem (v. 5).

Prophets most commonly are known to hear the word of the Lord and speak it to the people, but here Isaiah is asked to do the reverse, to intercede with the Lord on behalf of the people. There are instances of prophets in Israel, as mediators between God and human beings, interceding with the Lord. One could take the lines in 6:11 as such a prayer, "How long, O LORD?" The response of Amos to the first two visions of destruction clearly is to intercede on behalf of the people (Amos 7:2, 5). Here Isaiah responds to the request with a

342. Brevard S. Childs, *Isaiah and the Assyrian Crisis*, SBT (London: SCM, 1967) 90.

prophetic announcement, a message not to but from Yahweh. His opening words, "Fear not," are familiar from the consultation at the beginning of the holy war (Josh 11:6) and from the priestly oracle of salvation. This injunction is followed by the statement of the reasons not to fear, that the Lord will intervene; indeed, has already acted to put "a spirit" in the Assyrian king, who will hear a rumor and return to his own land. Moreover, the Lord, "will cause him to fall by the sword" there (v. 7). This amounts to a promise that Jerusalem will not fall to the Assyrians.

37:8-20. Verse 8 marks a clear narrative shift with the report that the Rabshakeh left to meet his king at Libnah, having finished with the Judean stronghold of Lachish. (Although not spelled out in this account, Sennacherib's defeat of Lachish is illustrated in gruesome detail in a series of reliefs from his palace walls.)[343] The narrative becomes a bit awkward, reflecting the introduction of the second account of the Assyrian siege of Jerusalem (beginning in v. 9*b*). Having heard of the plans of the Egyptians ("King Tirhkah of Ethiopia," v. 9), Sennacherib sends his messengers to warn Hezekiah not to rely on his God's promise that Jerusalem will not fall to the Assyrians (v. 10). They are also to remind the Judean king that the gods of the other nations have not protected them (vv. 11-13). Although anonymous messengers have replaced the Rabshakeh, the account of the threats parallels the one in 36:4-20.

Remarkably, beginning in 37:14, Hezekiah is said to have received not an oral communication but a "letter." In this account, no Judean officials are mentioned, and the king does not call for Isaiah to intercede. Instead, he takes the letter directly to the Lord, spreading it out in the Temple (v. 14) and offering a prayer for help (vv. 15-20). The prayer follows cultic traditions but its style is similar to that of the deuteronomistic historian, and the king's piety fits that writer's interpretation of history.[344] Hezekiah's invocation begins with words of praise, indicating that he prays before the ark as the throne of the Lord (v. 15; cf. 6:1). The Lord is praised as the only God over all kingdoms, the creator of heaven and earth. Then Hezekiah presents his petition, first calling for the Lord to listen

(v. 17*a*), then reminding the Lord what Sennacherib has said (v. 17*b*) and what the Assyrians have done to other nations and their "gods" (vv. 18-19), and finally asking the Lord to "save us" from Sennacherib (v. 20*a*). The petition is reinforced by reminding the Lord of the positive effect of such divine intervention: "so that all the kingdoms of the earth may know that you alone are the Lord" (v. 20*b*).

37:21-38. This long section continues the second account of the rescue of Jerusalem from the Assyrian army, focusing upon Isaiah's intervention. (See 2 Kgs 19:20-34.) The final verses (37-38), however, come originally from the first account (36:1–37:9*a*), giving its conclusion. Isaiah serves in this account as Yahweh's messenger to deliver the answer to the prayer.

The answer is not initially addressed to the petitioner, Hezekiah, but begins in the form of an announcement of judgment against Sennacherib and addressed to him (vv. 22-29). Most of the prophecy consists of the traditional elements, accusations or reasons for punishment (vv. 23-28, 29*a*) and announcement of judgment (v. 29*b*), but it also includes a reminder of the Lord's authority (vv. 26-28). "She" (v. 22) is Jerusalem ("virgin daughter Zion," "daughter Zion") and the "you" whom she scorns is Sennacherib. By means of rhetorical questions, the prophet (referring to the Lord in the third person) indicts the Assyrian king of blasphemy (v. 23), continuing the accusation directly by citing the words of Sennacherib (vv. 24-25). The boastful tone and the contents of the citation amount to a charge of arrogance. In language reminiscent of 10:5-6, the brash monarch is reminded that everything he has done was "determined . . . long ago" (v. 26) by the Lord. Finally, the arrogance implied in the citation of the words of the accused is made explicit and linked to blasphemy (v. 29*a*) as the foundation for the announcement of judgment. Just as the Lord determined how Sennacherib would advance, so will the Lord turn him back the same way, with a "hook" in his nose and a "bit" in his mouth. These tools for control may refer to those used for animals, wild and domestic, or to those used to lead prisoners away (cf. Ezek 19:4, 9; 38:4; Ps 32:9; Prov 26:3).

Beginning in v. 30 the prophet turns from announcement of judgment against Sennacherib

---

343. See *ANEP,* plates 371-74.
344. Childs, *Isaiah and the Assyrian Crisis,* 99-100.

to a direct address to Hezekiah, giving him a sign that will confirm a positive answer to his prayer. In the context, the message appears to be that in the third year agricultural conditions will have returned to normal. But proverbial sayings such as this one seldom have a single meaning. The description of better benefits from the fields in each of three years suggests that the change from adversity to prosperity is gradual. This sign with its agricultural images then is turned first into a promise that "the remnant of the house of Judah" (v. 31) will take root and flourish, and then (v. 32) that a remnant shall "go out" from Mt. Zion. This complex address in prose appears to be more than one elaboration on the announcement against Sennacherib.[345] The promise of a sign depends on 7:14-16; 8:4, and the concern with a "remnant" recalls 10:20-22 as well as the name of Isaiah's son, Shear-jashub ("A Remnant Shall Return," 7:3). These parallels serve to contrast faithless Ahaz with faithful Sennacherib.

The prophet's role concludes (vv. 33-35) with the explicit announcement that the king of Assyria shall not enter the city. Nor will he succeed in

345. Ronald E. Clements, *Isaiah 1–39*, NCB (Grand Rapids: Eerdmans, 1980) 286-87.

shooting an arrow in it, come close with a shield, or even build a siege ramp against it. Instead he shall go back the way he came. The Lord promises to defend and save the city, in order to demonstrate that the Lord is God and to confirm the Davidic dynasty. Thus the historian brings together two themes central to Isaiah 1–39, the Lord's election of David and choice of Jerusalem.

Although the concluding narrative (vv. 36-38) reads coherently, it includes the resolution of the crisis from both narrative strands in chaps. 36–37. According to the one (v. 36), "the angel of the Lord" decimated the Assyrian army, killing one hundred eighty-five thousand. An angel of the Lord appears in the Bible either as the presence of the Lord (Exod 3:2-6) or, as here, the agent of God's will in some event. Some interpreters take this report as a theological interpretation of a plague that struck Sennacherib's army, and link it to the story told by Herodotus of a plague of mice that gnawed the Assyrian's bowstrings. In the conclusion to the other account (B[1], vv. 37-38), Sennacherib is said to have returned home, where two of his sons killed him and another, Esar-haddon, succeeded him. In either case, Jerusalem was saved through divine intervention.

REFLECTIONS

Historical texts such as this provoke reflection on the meaning of history, beginning with the definition and use of that common term and reaching to the substance and significance of history itself. First, one may reflect on the problem and importance of history in general. Second, questions concerning the sense and significance of history within the biblical context and for theology need to be addressed.

Although the word "history" is casually—and not inappropriately—used to refer to the past in general, or to particular events in the past, that usage masks the problem of history. Originally and essentially, the word refers to a narrative, a story that claims to be a true account of events. In modern times, that claim to truth—or at least to accuracy—became increasingly important, so that by the late nineteenth century the goal of the historian came to be the determination of what actually happened. Historians weigh available evidence to reconstruct the story of the past. But since the early twentieth century, it has become increasingly clear that one cannot write "the" story of the past but *a* story of it.

The difficulty of reducing the past to a single true account arises for many reasons. Not the last of these is the difference in perspective among historians or storytellers, especially from generation to generation. No one can be entirely neutral, nor is it reasonable to expect complete objectivity. Not only are there interests to be served, but there are different concerns or purposes, for example, with different aspects of the past. Moreover, the evidence or sources upon which one bases an account of the past are always ambiguous. Commonly, anyone who wants to know what happened will be faced with conflicting evidence, as with the biblical and Assyrian texts concerning Sennacherib's invasion of Judah and siege of Jerusalem.

All accounts, whether from the past or the present, are limited; but all accounts are valuable. No single perspective can capture any event with precision, but every report is correct and valuable in some respect. At the very least it is a source for the point of view it expresses, a witness to the time it was recorded. That is, of course, assuming one can determine what time that was. It remains a valid premise of historical inquiry that any text gives us more information about the time of its own composition than it does about any prior periods, including the one it describes. Furthermore, the most interesting part of history is the hardest part: What caused these events? And specifically, what were the actors thinking when they did or said something? The authors of these old histories—both biblical and Assyrian—were interested in these questions as well, but that does not necessarily mean they got it right. Thus anyone who wants to know what happened must weigh all available evidence carefully.

History, therefore, is not "what happened," but a story written and told by human beings, at its best a critical reconstruction of past human events, but one that will also require the writer to use the historical imagination.[346] The object of the historian's quest is not what happened, but what is the most likely reconstruction of what happened, based on the available evidence. The historian must at every point assume the burden of proof. The evidence for any reconstruction must be presented and analyzed critically. The texts will need to be cross-examined and their testimony confirmed. Historians must always limit themselves to establishing the balance of probability, and seldom can that be done beyond a reasonable doubt. To be sure, there are a great many instances in which there simply is insufficient evidence for a critical reconstruction.[347]

Whether a critical reconstruction of past events is possible in any given instance or not, historical thinking is—in the modern world—inevitable, possible, and essential. Everyone engages in historical thinking every day, and often it is even a matter of life and death. One of the best models for this enterprise is the law court, in which the goal, day in and day out, is determining what happened in the past. This determination will go far deeper than establishing the "facts," which are the evidence on which the alternative reconstructions are based. The facts will be used to determine "what happened," and even motives—what was going on in human minds and hearts in the past. Then the meaning of the events so reconstructed within this particular interpretive community (the legal system) will be determined in the light of the law. In the American court system that will be spelled out by a judge for a jury. If the jury should determine that thus and so is what happened, it is a crime and, if so, what kind. Trials proceed according to due process, especially focusing upon the rules of evidence. The kinds of evidence include eyewitness testimony, physical evidence, and "circumstantial evidence," all of which is subject to cross-examination—that is, its meaning is never taken for granted. All that one can expect to reach is a judgment "beyond a reasonable doubt." Reason is the fundamental criterion and method. One will then arrive at a reconstruction of events and even of motives, or at least one that is persuasive to a jury.

Another model for historical reconstruction, without the explicit adversarial dimensions of the American law court, is the fact-finding work of such agencies as the National Transportation Safety Board. (And most nations have similar agencies.) When an airplane crashes, teams of "detectives"—analysts of various kinds—rush in to collect and interpret all the available evidence—physical, eyewitness, etc.—and to reconstruct what happened. They operate under the strict rules of reason and logic, and usually are able to draw persuasive conclusions. Persuasive, that is, except to some parties with particular interests in the results: Pilots generally do not like to hear the conclusion "pilot error," and parties to lawsuits over the crash certainly have their vested interests. At their best, the NTSB and similar agencies have only one interest: to establish the facts of the past in order to reduce the possibility of future disasters.

---

346. R. G. Collingwood, *The Idea of History* (New York: Oxford University Press, 1956) 231-48.

347. On this point and what follows, see Gene M. Tucker, "The Futile Quest for the Historical Prophet," in *A Biblical Itinerary: In Search of Method, Form, and Content. Essays in Honor of George W. Coats,* ed. Eugene E. Carpenter, JSOTSup 240 (Sheffield: Sheffield Academic, 1997) 144-52.

While history as the reconstruction or construction of the past may not be a matter of life and death every day, it is essential to human self-understanding, including the way people appropriate the biblical traditions. The stories people tell define who they are. The stories of the ancestors and of the exodus from Egypt enabled ancient Israelites to understand the meaning of their lives as the Lord's people. The Deuteronomistic History (Deuteronomy–Kings) was an interpretation of history from the exodus to the Babylonian exile, emphasizing the sins of the people and a series of kings. In its final form it could function for the exiles in Babylon and those who later returned to Judah as an explanation of the catastrophe: The exile was the Lord's punishment for a history of sin.

That belief is but one instance of what is common to virtually all biblical history: The biblical accounts of past events are founded on the conviction that those events are significant because the God who created all that is engages human beings in time and space. In short, history has ultimate significance because the story goes on through the interaction of divine and human forces. This history of the Assyrian siege of Jerusalem, like virtually all in the OT, is theological history; that is, God is seen to act in the ongoing drama.

This perspective poses a problem for the critical reconstruction of history. One may weigh and judge evidence concerning human actions and even motives, but the acts and plans of God will not fit on the same scale. Is God active, intervening in human events? And if so, how? These are theological problems that require serious reflection by all who take the biblical tradition seriously. Moral judgments both past and future imply such theological reflection: Was slavery the will of God? Were the bloody wars to reclaim the Holy Land from the Moslems a correct or incorrect interpretation of the will of God? Which course for the future is consistent with the will of God?

The critical historical task is important because posing the historical questions is all but inevitable and because understanding the past is essential to self-understanding. Recognizing that "objective" history is not possible may encourage readers of the Bible to focus more on the text than upon some reconstructed account of the past. After all, it is the text—not history—that is canonical. But at the same time, everyone who reads a prophetic book will do so in the light of some image of the past to which the book refers and from which it originated. Reading and understanding will be enhanced by the informed image of those historical horizons.

ISAIAH 38:1-22, HEZEKIAH'S ILLNESS

NIV

38 In those days Hezekiah became ill and was at the point of death. The prophet Isaiah son of Amoz went to him and said, "This is what the LORD says: Put your house in order, because you are going to die; you will not recover."

²Hezekiah turned his face to the wall and prayed to the LORD, ³"Remember, O LORD, how I have walked before you faithfully and with wholehearted devotion and have done what is good in your eyes." And Hezekiah wept bitterly.

⁴Then the word of the LORD came to Isaiah: ⁵"Go and tell Hezekiah, 'This is what the LORD, the God of your father David, says: I have heard

NRSV

38 In those days Hezekiah became sick and was at the point of death. The prophet Isaiah son of Amoz came to him, and said to him, "Thus says the LORD: Set your house in order, for you shall die; you shall not recover." ²Then Hezekiah turned his face to the wall, and prayed to the LORD: ³"Remember now, O LORD, I implore you, how I have walked before you in faithfulness with a whole heart, and have done what is good in your sight." And Hezekiah wept bitterly.

4Then the word of the LORD came to Isaiah: 5"Go and say to Hezekiah, Thus says the LORD, the God of your ancestor David: I have heard your

NIV

your prayer and seen your tears; I will add fifteen years to your life. [6]And I will deliver you and this city from the hand of the king of Assyria. I will defend this city.

[7]" 'This is the LORD's sign to you that the LORD will do what he has promised: [8]I will make the shadow cast by the sun go back the ten steps it has gone down on the stairway of Ahaz.' " So the sunlight went back the ten steps it had gone down.

[9]A writing of Hezekiah king of Judah after his illness and recovery:

[10]I said, "In the prime of my life
    must I go through the gates of death[a]
    and be robbed of the rest of my years?"
[11]I said, "I will not again see the LORD,
    the LORD, in the land of the living;
no longer will I look on mankind,
    or be with those who now dwell in
      this world.[b]
[12]Like a shepherd's tent my house
    has been pulled down and taken from me.
Like a weaver I have rolled up my life,
    and he has cut me off from the loom;
    day and night you made an end of me.
[13]I waited patiently till dawn,
    but like a lion he broke all my bones;
    day and night you made an end of me.
[14]I cried like a swift or thrush,
    I moaned like a mourning dove.
My eyes grew weak as I looked to the heavens.
    I am troubled; O Lord, come to my aid!"

[15]But what can I say?
    He has spoken to me, and he himself has
      done this.
I will walk humbly all my years
    because of this anguish of my soul.
[16]Lord, by such things men live;
    and my spirit finds life in them too.
You restored me to health
    and let me live.
[17]Surely it was for my benefit
    that I suffered such anguish.
In your love you kept me
    from the pit of destruction;

[a]10 Hebrew *Sheol*   [b]11 A few Hebrew manuscripts; most Hebrew manuscripts *in the place of cessation*

NRSV

prayer, I have seen your tears; I will add fifteen years to your life. [6]I will deliver you and this city out of the hand of the king of Assyria, and defend this city.

[7]"This is the sign to you from the LORD, that the LORD will do this thing that he has promised: [8]See, I will make the shadow cast by the declining sun on the dial of Ahaz turn back ten steps." So the sun turned back on the dial the ten steps by which it had declined.[a]

[9]A writing of King Hezekiah of Judah, after he had been sick and had recovered from his sickness:
[10] I said: In the noontide of my days
    I must depart;
    I am consigned to the gates of Sheol
    for the rest of my years.
[11] I said, I shall not see the LORD
    in the land of the living;
    I shall look upon mortals no more
    among the inhabitants of the world.
[12] My dwelling is plucked up and removed
      from me
    like a shepherd's tent;
like a weaver I have rolled up my life;
    he cuts me off from the loom;
    from day to night you bring me to an end;[a]
[13] I cry for help[b] until morning;
    like a lion he breaks all my bones;
    from day to night you bring me to an end.[a]

[14] Like a swallow or a crane[a] I clamor,
    I moan like a dove.
My eyes are weary with looking upward.
    O Lord, I am oppressed; be my security!
[15] But what can I say? For he has spoken to me,
    and he himself has done it.
All my sleep has fled[c]
    because of the bitterness of my soul.

[16] O Lord, by these things people live,
    and in all these is the life of my spirit.[a]
    Oh, restore me to health and make me live!
[17] Surely it was for my welfare
    that I had great bitterness;

[a]Meaning of Heb uncertain   [b]Cn: Meaning of Heb uncertain
[c]Cn: Compare Syr: Heb *I will walk slowly all my years*

NIV

you have put all my sins
    behind your back.
[18]For the grave[a] cannot praise you,
    death cannot sing your praise;
those who go down to the pit
    cannot hope for your faithfulness.
[19]The living, the living—they praise you,
    as I am doing today;
fathers tell their children
    about your faithfulness.

[20]The LORD will save me,
    and we will sing with stringed instruments
all the days of our lives
    in the temple of the LORD.

[21]Isaiah had said, "Prepare a poultice of figs and apply it to the boil, and he will recover."
[22]Hezekiah had asked, "What will be the sign that I will go up to the temple of the LORD?"

[a]18 Hebrew *Sheol*

NRSV

but you have held back[a] my life
    from the pit of destruction,
for you have cast all my sins
    behind your back.
[18] For Sheol cannot thank you,
    death cannot praise you;
those who go down to the Pit cannot hope
    for your faithfulness.
[19] The living, the living, they thank you,
    as I do this day;
fathers make known to children
    your faithfulness.

[20] The LORD will save me,
    and we will sing to stringed instruments[b]
all the days of our lives,
    at the house of the LORD.

[21]Now Isaiah had said, "Let them take a lump of figs, and apply it to the boil, so that he may recover." [22]Hezekiah also had said, "What is the sign that I shall go up to the house of the LORD?"

[a]Cn: Compare Gk Vg: Heb *loved*   [b]Heb *my stringed instruments*

COMMENTARY

This chapter forms a distinct unit within the narratives concerning Isaiah, Hezekiah, and the fate of Jerusalem (chaps. 36–39), as the introductory phrase ("In those days," v. 1) and the new subject matter indicate. Another discrete unit begins with its own chronological heading in 39:1. Chapter 38 presents the story of Hezekiah's life-threatening illness and divinely decreed recovery. The substance of this narrative, except for the prayer of thanksgiving (vv. 9-20), appears, with some variations, in 2 Kgs 20:1-11. This is another story that contains more speech than action. The speakers are the prophet, the king, and the Lord. Isaiah speaks on behalf of the Lord, Hezekiah speaks to the Lord, praying for help, the Lord speaks a word for Hezekiah to Isaiah, and the king offers a prayer of thanksgiving.

One can readily discern the major units of the chapter on the basis of the narrative transitions. Verses 1-8 contain the story of the king's illness and the divine promise of recovery. Hezekiah's

thanksgiving song, introduced as "a writing," then follows (vv. 9-20). The final unit (vv. 21-22) appears to be out of sequence, for it reports the procedure for the healing already celebrated by the song and the question of v. 22 ("What is the sign?") had been answered in vv. 7-8. These verses appear in the more logical location in 2 Kgs 20:1-11, and thus the REB has placed vv. 21-22 between vv. 6-7. Since the placement of the verses at the end of the story appears to serve no particular purpose, it seems reasonable to conclude that they were not an original part of the text and were added from 2 Kings 20 by a later editor.[348]

38:1-8. "In those days" is an indeterminate reference to the time of Hezekiah, appropriate in the original location of this chapter in 2 Kings. The juxtaposition of this chapter with the preceding ones connects the king's illness with the Assyrian threat to Jerusalem. The only specific reference to

348. Clements, *Isaiah 1–39*, 288.

the siege comes in v. 6, in which the Lord, in addition to answering the king's prayer for recovery, unexpectedly promises to deliver Hezekiah and Jerusalem from the king of Assyria. This promise likely is an editorial effort to date the illness to the time of the Assyrian invasion.

Although everything that transpires is seen to be the result of divine intervention, the effect of the story is to emphasize the piety of Hezekiah and to show the prophetic power of Isaiah. Moreover, the theme of the power of Hezekiah's prayers runs through chaps. 36–38.

All narratives create and maintain the interest of the reader or hearer by developing tension and finally resolving it. The tension in this story focuses upon the king's illness. The problem is set out immediately and then resolved quickly. Hezekiah is deathly ill. Will he die or not? It is significant that the story begins by reporting simply and directly that the king became ill and was about to die. The reader is not told that Yahweh caused the illness, or that it was punishment for some sin. Immediately, however, and uninvited, Isaiah appeared to present the word of the Lord (v. 1). Formally, the prophetic address contains an instruction and the reasons for it, but the speech amounts to a death sentence: Prepare to die. Hezekiah's reaction is depression ("turned his face to the wall") but not hopelessness, for he prays for relief (vv. 2-3). The tone and contents of the brief prayer parallel the individual complaint songs of the psalter. The heart of the petition, such as "help me," is unstated but implied by the reasons presented in support of a request. Prayers of complaint may be supported by confessions of sin and promises to change, but more commonly in the psalter one finds confessions of faithfulness and righteousness such as expressed here (Psalms 17; 26).

The Lord answers Hezekiah's prayer by instructing Isaiah to go to the king and pronounce an oracle of salvation with two elements. The first (v. 5) is that, having heard Hezekiah's prayer and seen his tears, the Lord has determined to add fifteen years to his life. The divine appellation, "the God of your ancestor David," cannot be accidental, but is a reminder of the Lord's election of David's sons—including Hezekiah—to rule in Jerusalem. The second element (v. 6) proclaims the Lord's resolve to deliver and defend Jerusalem (cf. 37:33-35).

It is not unheard of for the Lord's death sentence to be withdrawn in response to prayers by the condemned. The story of the prophet Nathan's pronouncement of judgment on King David for taking Bathsheba and killing her husband Uriah is but one example. When the king confesses, punishment continues, but the death sentence is lifted (2 Sam 12:13). When, in response to Jonah's announcement of judgment, the people of Nineveh repent, they and their city are saved (Jonah 3).

Up to this point in the story elements of the royal novella have dominated.[349] As the Lord's instructions continue in vv. 7-8, however, the story resembles prophetic legends that demonstrate how the power of God was manifest through a holy figure (2 Kgs 1:3-16; 2:8; 2:19-22; 4). The Lord promises to confirm the promise with a "sign" (cf. Isa 7:11), that the shadow of the "declining" sun will go back ten steps (cf. Josh 10:12-13). It is not important to the sense of the story whether one translates the Hebrew literally as "steps" (NIV) or takes it to mean (sun) "dial" (NRSV). Like many accounts of prophetic signs, this one is elliptical. It does report that the sign came to pass, but fails to mention that Isaiah did as the Lord instructed, that is, communicated the oracle to the king. The reader has no difficulty filling in the gap. Now the tension has been resolved. The sign validates the Lord's promise through Isaiah that Hezekiah will not die but will live fifteen more years.

38:9-20. A brief introduction (v. 9) identifies the prayer that follows as a "writing" of King Hezekiah and dates it to the time of his recovery from the illness. It cannot be accidental that this verse is a close formal parallel to the historical superscriptions to many psalms, especially those that attribute specific psalms to David at some particular time in his life. The superscription to Psalm 18 is but one example: "A Psalm of David the servant of the Lord, who addressed the words of this song to the Lord on the day when the Lord delivered him from the hand of all his enemies, and from the hand of Saul" (see also the superscriptions to Psalms 3; 30; 34; 51; 52; 54; 56; 57; 59;

---

349. Sweeney considers the royal novella to be the genre of the chapter as a whole. See Marvin A. Sweeney, *Isaiah 1–39, With an Introduction to Prophetic Literature,* FOTL XVI (Grand Rapids: Eerdmans, 1996) 493-94.

60; 63). So this single verse serves several important functions. It places the prayer in a particular historical context, attributes it to Hezekiah, and subtly associates Hezekiah with the piety and the poetry of the founder of the dynasty, King David.

Although commentators have identified the prayer variously on the basis of some of its elements,[350] what follows is a typical individual thanksgiving psalm, such as those used in the temple service of thanksgiving for deliverance from suffering (see Psalms 32; 116).[351] In times of trouble or danger, such as sickness, an individual in ancient Israel would pray for help, setting out the case before God and giving reasons (as in 38:3) for God to intervene. There is sufficient evidence to show that the individual complaint or lament psalms were part of a prayer service in which various parties participated, including the family and friends of the sufferer and cultic officials.[352] Often the sufferers promised offerings or services in the Temple once they were healed (Ps 116:17-18). That the song is identified here as a "writing" shows it was to be such an offering.

The song of thanksgiving was the individual's response to answered prayer. Hezekiah's words begin with lamentation and complaint (vv. 10-15), but that is not unusual. Thanksgiving songs frequently include a recital of the pain and suffering, as well as the prayers, that lead up to the thanksgiving. The king reports in detail what he "said" (v. 10). While still young ("in the noontime of my days") he faces death, no longer to see either the Lord or human beings (vv. 10-11). Compelling metaphors characterize the end of life: a house taken away, a tent plucked up, an unfinished cloth cut off the loom and rolled up (v. 12). Unlike the narrative of vv. 1-8, the singer attributes his impending death to God: "he cuts me off from the loom" (v. 12), "like a lion he breaks all my bones" (v. 13). Then the prayer becomes first a complaint directly addressed to the Lord ("you bring me to an end," v. 13) and then a plea: "O LORD, I am oppressed; be my security!" (v. 14). The prayer during suffering then acknowledges the futility of praying for help to the very one responsible for

that suffering ("he himself has done it," v. 15). Still, the petition for help becomes explicit, and directly addressed to the Lord: "restore me to health and make me live!" (v. 16). Such pleas are the heart of complaint psalms. All the other elements, including description of the suffering and the reasons for God to hear, support the petition.

Although continuing to allude to the past suffering and to reasons why God should intervene, vv. 17-19 express thanks to God for deliverance. The singer acknowledges that the suffering was for his own good (v. 17a); still, the Lord rescued him from the brink of death (v. 17b). Again, unlike the narrative account, the psalm identifies suffering with sin and restitution to life with release from sin (v. 17c). Lines such as those in v. 18 often appear in complaint psalms as reasons for the Lord to help. Death is the end, and if the sufferer is allowed to die then the Lord will lose a voice in the earthly choir that praises God (Pss 6:4-5; 30:9). The living are the ones capable of thanking God, and so the singer does, calling upon each generation to pass on to the next the reminder that God is faithful (v. 19). The psalm concludes, as other songs of thanksgiving, with praise, and the promise to continue that praise in the Temple (v. 20).

38:21-22. These lines are, quite literally, anticlimactic. The threat to Hezekiah's life has not only been resolved but also celebrated in song. Now the reader is informed about how it has been resolved. As noted already, these verses appear in their more logical location in 2 Kgs 20:1-11, prior to the words and actions reported in 38:7. It is easier to understand why a scribe who noticed the omission from 2 Kings would bring these details into chap. 38 than to understand why that scribe would tack these verses to the end of the story. The desire to see that nothing was lost must have been stronger than the need for logical order.

Isaiah's instructions for the application of a healing "lump of figs" belongs, with the story of the sign (vv. 7-8), to the legendary tradition that shows him to be a vehicle for the power of God. At the outset the king's illness has not been identified, but here the figs are to heal a "boil" (v. 21). Hezekiah's request for a sign anticipates its performance, but his intention ("go up to the house of the Lord," v. 22) anticipates the presentation of his song of thanksgiving.

350. For a summary of different designations of the genre, see ibid., 494-96.

351. Hans Wildberger, *Jesaja: Kapitel 28–39*, BKAT 10 (Neukirchen-Vluyn: Neukirchener Verlag, 1982) 1455-56.

352. Ernard Gersternberger, *Psalms I, with an Introduction to Cultic Poetry*, FOTL 14 (Grand Rapids: Eerdmans, 1988) 9-14.

REFLECTIONS

One could say that this story of answered prayer reports a miracle, the healing of the king through divine intervention mediated by a prophet. Moreover, the sun's shadow, if not explicitly the sun itself, is said to have moved backward. Miracle stories and miracles present problems for modern readers of the Bible. Does God suspend the laws of the universe on special occasions?

This story opens questions concerning "nature" similar to those the previous chapters (chaps. 36–37) raised concerning history. Does God intervene in human lives, particularly in response to prayer? And if so, how? One may be confident in the view that God acts to heal through medical science and competent physicians, but have doubts about divine intervention through a prophet's words.

Everyone knows that what happens in history and nature is not entirely caused by human actions. Weather is a good example of forces beyond human control. Is that why insurance companies call hurricanes and tornadoes acts of God? Is everything that happens in the universe fully rational, and human beings just do not know enough yet? Advances in science may lead some to believe that human beings can know the causes of everything and have control over all forces. Or one could believe that what happens is just a series of random acts. Among the alternatives is some form of deism: God was here once, set the universe into motion, and let it go on its own.

Biblical stories such as this one confront the reader with the mystery that God engages human beings in response to their words and actions. Contemporary readers will need to discern the activity, and perhaps even the intervention, of God in their world. Perhaps the little note of 38:21 about the use of a poultice suggests a direction for our reflection. Even the prophet used "medicine." Healing is no less a miracle when the work of medical science and competent professionals than when it comes as a word directly from heaven.

Stories of divine healing present special problems for modern readers. Although they mean to demonstrate God's love of life and of individual human lives, they make many contemporary readers uneasy. Not everyone who prays for a healing miracle has one. Is it because some are not sufficiently pious or faithful while others are? The biblical stories seem to suggest that if only one really believed he or she could be healed. It is a small step from this belief to the view that God causes each case of illness. So it is not surprising that the psalm of Hezekiah attributes suffering to God. Certainly such beliefs, often deeply held, create harm, not least in the guilt they generate. Thus, while they can generate hope, they also have the capacity to add to suffering.

ISAIAH 39:1-8, HEZEKIAH, ISAIAH, AND THE AMBASSADORS FROM BABYLON

NIV

39 At that time Merodach-Baladan son of Baladan king of Babylon sent Hezekiah letters and a gift, because he had heard of his illness and recovery. [2]Hezekiah received the envoys gladly and showed them what was in his storehouses—the silver, the gold, the spices, the fine oil, his entire armory and everything found among his treasures. There was nothing in his palace or in all his kingdom that Hezekiah did not show them.

NRSV

39 At that time King Merodach-baladan son of Baladan of Babylon sent envoys with letters and a present to Hezekiah, for he heard that he had been sick and had recovered. [2]Hezekiah welcomed them; he showed them his treasure house, the silver, the gold, the spices, the precious oil, his whole armory, all that was found in his storehouses. There was nothing in his house or in all his realm that Hezekiah did not show them. [3]Then the prophet Isaiah came to King Hezekiah

NIV

³Then Isaiah the prophet went to King Hezekiah and asked, "What did those men say, and where did they come from?"

"From a distant land," Hezekiah replied. "They came to me from Babylon."

⁴The prophet asked, "What did they see in your palace?"

"They saw everything in my palace," Hezekiah said. "There is nothing among my treasures that I did not show them."

⁵Then Isaiah said to Hezekiah, "Hear the word of the LORD Almighty: ⁶The time will surely come when everything in your palace, and all that your fathers have stored up until this day, will be carried off to Babylon. Nothing will be left, says the LORD. ⁷And some of your descendants, your own flesh and blood who will be born to you, will be taken away, and they will become eunuchs in the palace of the king of Babylon."

⁸"The word of the LORD you have spoken is good," Hezekiah replied. For he thought, "There will be peace and security in my lifetime."

NRSV

and said to him, "What did these men say? From where did they come to you?" Hezekiah answered, "They have come to me from a far country, from Babylon." ⁴He said, "What have they seen in your house?" Hezekiah answered, "They have seen all that is in my house; there is nothing in my storehouses that I did not show them."

5Then Isaiah said to Hezekiah, "Hear the word of the LORD of hosts: ⁶Days are coming when all that is in your house, and that which your ancestors have stored up until this day, shall be carried to Babylon; nothing shall be left, says the LORD. ⁷Some of your own sons who are born to you shall be taken away; they shall be eunuchs in the palace of the king of Babylon." ⁸Then Hezekiah said to Isaiah, "The word of the LORD that you have spoken is good." For he thought, "There will be peace and security in my days."

COMMENTARY

The clear beginning with a temporal formula ("At that time") both sets this chapter out as a distinct unit and links it to the preceding story of the king's illness. The connection is made explicit in v. 1*b,* for Hezekiah's illness and recovery are the occasion if not the excuse for the visit by the Babylonian envoys. Although the chapter begins as a story about international relations, most of it concerns a series of dialogues between Isaiah and Hezekiah. Formally, vv. 1-2 report the visit of the Babylonian ambassadors to Jerusalem and vv. 3-8 report a series of three interchanges between prophet and king.[353] Like the other narratives in chaps. 36–39, this one contains more talk than action.

The doubtless historically reliable account of the diplomat visit provides the occasion for interpretation of the history of Judah, Jerusalem, and the Davidic dynasty. When the Babylonians arrive, Hezekiah welcomes them and shows them all the treasures of the kingdom. Hearing of this, Isaiah confronts the king, questions him, and announces the Lord's judgment that all those treasures will be "carried to Babylon" (v. 6), as will some of the king's descendants. Hezekiah accepts the prophecy as valid.

The story addresses a serious theological problem. Why was Jerusalem saved from the Assyrians in 701 BCE but not from the Babylonians in 597 and 587 BCE? Isaiah's prophecy provides an answer if not an explanation. No reason for the judgment appears in this chapter. It is tempting to see the king's opening the treasure houses to the visitors as the reason, but that connection is not drawn. The historians do not hold Hezekiah responsible for the exile. But there is a sense of irony here. In the time of Hezekiah it was safe to show the treasures to the Babylonian officials, and little more than a century later Babylonians would carry those treasures off.

The fuller explanation for the exile comes in the deuteronomistic history, from which this

353. Sweeney, *Isaiah 1–39,* 505-7.

story is drawn (2 Kgs 20:12-19). Moreover, Isaiah's prophecy of the Babylonian exile is consistent with a pattern in that history, that of prophecy and fulfillment (e.g., 1 Kgs 13:2-3; 20:13ff.; 21:19). The account of the fulfillment of Isaiah's prophecy comes in 2 Kings, but not in Isaiah. However, with chap. 40 the book of Isaiah moves into the Babylonian era. In its context in the book of Isaiah, this chapter facilitates the transition to the next section. It also provides a significant qualification of the theology concerning both Jerusalem and the Davidic dynasty. Theology has to take account of the historical evidence. Jerusalem and Hezekiah were indeed saved from the Assyrians, but even at that time the Lord had determined that the city would fall and the last of the sons of David would be carried off to exile.[354]

That the literary and historical sequence of events in Isaiah 36–39 do not coincide stresses the significance of the placement of the story of the Babylonian ambassadors at the end. Sennacherib's invasion would have been in 701 BCE, but most interpreters agree that the delegates from Merodach-baladan would have come earlier, when both Babylon and Judah rebelled against Assyria, about 705–703 BCE.[355] The story would have been composed much later, but before it was incorporated first into 2 Kings and then into the book of Isaiah. The fact that the prophecy anticipates the looting of the Temple and palace by the Babylonians but not their destruction provides persuasive evidence that the account was composed after the capture of Jerusalem in 597 BCE but before the city and the Temple were destroyed in 587 BCE.[356]

Up to this point in the narratives concerning Isaiah, Hezekiah, and the fate of Jerusalem, the king has been the model of piety and good judgment. That changes subtly here, not to the point that he is identified as a sinner according to the standards of the deuteronomistic historians, but

problems arise.[357] Isaiah, however, comes out unscathed.

39:1-2. Although no Mesopotamian documents record the diplomatic delegation mentioned, Merodach-baladan is known as a Babylonian monarch who opposed the Assyrian Empire. The envoys were sent to Hezekiah, ostensibly to inquire about his health, but probably to encourage his rebellion against Assyria. The "letters" (v. 1) would have contained more than the best wishes of one king to another. In contrast to the brevity of the note about the sending of the delegation, the account of Hezekiah's welcome is expansive, detailed, and repetitive. The effect of this catalog of assets is to suggest an image of Hezekiah as boastful and lacking in discretion if not good judgment.

39:3-8. Without mentioning that the ambassadors left, the narrator reports that Isaiah confronted Hezekiah. Three dialogues between king and prophet follow. In the first (v. 3), Isaiah asks the monarch who those visitors were and where they came from. When Hezekiah answers, the prophet wants to know what they have seen, and the king tells him what the reader already knows from v. 2. He showed them everything (v. 4). Isaiah's abrupt questions suggest but do not express disapproval. The prophet's attitude is the same as always. Foreign alliances should be avoided, for they compromise trust in Yahweh (cf. 7:3-9; 30:3-5).

In the third dialogue (vv. 5-8) Isaiah proclaims the word of the Lord directly to the king, and it is an announcement of disaster. The word of the Lord begins with the proclamation that "all that is in your house," every last thing, shall be carried off to Babylon (v. 6). Moreover, some of the king's descendants will be exiles, "eunuchs in the palace of the king of Babylon" (v. 7). Although the announcement follows the implicit criticism of Hezekiah's display of the treasures, his actions are not given as reasons for judgment against him, or against the nation in the future. The treasures shown to the Babylonians seem to serve as a sign for those taken in the future.

One should not take Hezekiah's response ("The word of the LORD that you have spoken is good," (v. 8a) as a moral judgment but only as affirmation

---

354. On the function of this chapter to qualify the theology of divine protection, see R. E. Clements, *Isaiah and the Deliverance of Jerusalem: A Study in the Interpretation of Prophecy in the Old Testament,* JSOTSup 13 (Sheffield: JSOT, 1980) 65-66; and Ronald E. Clements, *Isaiah 1–39,* NCB (Grand Rapids: Eerdmans, 1980) 279.

355. Sweeney, *Isaiah 1–39,* 508; Clements, *Isaiah and the Deliverance of Jerusalem,* 66-67.

356. Clements, *Isaiah and the Deliverance of Jerusalem,* 67-68; Clements, *Isaiah 1–39,* 294.

357. Sweeney, on the other hand, considers this story to be another one that emphasizes the piety of Hezekiah. See Sweeney, *Isaiah 1–39,* 510-11.

of the validity of the announcement. These words are consistent with his piety. But the final sentence has the king musing about the good news for him implicit in the bad news for the future: "For he thought, 'There will be peace and security in my days' " (v. 8b). One may even detect a note of bit-terness in the final line as the author of the story reads the mind of Hezekiah. A writer who had seen the treasures of the palace and the Temple carried off knew that Hezekiah, facing the threat of the Assyrians, had been spared. Why should he care about the future?

REFLECTIONS

That thought attributed to Hezekiah in the final line of the chapter is contrary to most bibli-cal reflection on one's responsibility toward future generations. To be sure, no one could know what the king actually would have thought when he heard a prophecy to be fulfilled a century later. So the line reveals more about its author than it does about Hezekiah. That author does not blame Hezekiah for the disaster that has come in his generation, when Babylon looted Jerusalem and later destroyed it. But through the lens of deuteronomic theology, that author saw the national catastrophe of the Babylonian period as set into motion by previous generations, specifically by a line of corrupt rulers. The author of these lines also knew that Hezekiah and his generation suffered far less than did his.

One does not accept all the tenets of the theology of Deuteronomy to know that decisions in the present have powerful consequences for future generations, both for good and for ill. Each present generation can look back to its predecessors either with gratitude or resentment, or a measure of both. It is widely accepted, for example, among historians of the twentieth century that the treatment of Germany at the end of World War I was a major factor in the rise of National Socialism and therefore of World War II.

Do leaders of nations, or the public in general, tend to care more about "peace and security" in their own days than about the possibility of disaster in the distant future? One need not look for to identify issues where nations and individuals seem forced to choose between "security" in the present and "security" for those who will come later. One of these concerns fiscal policy and national debts. It is not uncommon to buy security for the present and leave the debts to be paid by the children and grandchildren. That security may be literal, when a nation goes into debt to fund its military forces. Few would doubt that some circumstances require such hard decisions, for example, when there is strong evidence that without such expenditures and debt there might be nothing for future generations to inherit. But it is a different matter when security in the pres-ent is understood as lower taxes.

One finds the question of future generations at the heart of arguments concerning environ-mental policies and practices. If a generation or two depletes the earth's fossil fuels, how will those in the future have heat, light, and transportation? Of course, that is an issue only if one acknowledges that natural resources are finite. The process of global warming—if one believes it is happening at all—is so slow that should the polar ice caps melt, a century or more will pass before the level of the oceans is raised enough to flood major cities along every coast line on the planet. So if one has any regard for future, including distant future, generations, then the ques-tion is how much of its "security" is the present generation willing to sacrifice for their sake. The obvious alternative is to let future generations pay the price for the excesses of the present. The preponderance of the biblical message, including that of Isaiah 1–39, argues against that alter-native and in favor of concern for future generations. Individuals, groups, and generations are called to transcend themselves in their concern for those who will follow.

THE BOOK OF ISAIAH 40–66

INTRODUCTION, COMMENTARY, AND REFLECTIONS

BY

CHRISTOPHER R. SEITZ

THE BOOK OF
ISAIAH 40–66

INTRODUCTION

The reader who comes to the section of the book of Isaiah now popularly called "Second Isaiah" will expect some introductory material dealing with setting, author, religious context, major themes, and the like. A discussion of these matters can be found later in this Introduction. The first two sections to follow, however, discuss the suitability of providing an introduction midway through a book of prophecy that, until the modern period, was treated as a single work. The discussion in these opening two sections takes its point of departure from more recent treatments of Isaiah 40–66, which view proper commentary on these twenty-seven chapters to demand at least a serious inquiry into the book's larger unity. Only then, it could be argued, should the interpretation of chapters 40–66 proceed.

To be sure, some readers may find the discussion more comprehensible if the traditional sections (dealing with setting, historical period, author, and literary form and composition) are studied first. However, what is at issue is the justification of such introductory material following Isaiah 39, in spite of the fact that presentation of this material has been the standard operating procedure for roughly a century and a half.

I hope that a fresh approach to these twenty-seven chapters can be set forth in the commentary proper and that suitable introductory matter might also be found that does justice both to their independence and to their coordinated integration (so it will be argued) with "Former Isaiah" (chaps. 1–39). Also requiring clarification is some explanation for the use of the term "Third Isaiah" alongside "Second Isaiah." That matter, too, is taken up in the introductory sections to follow. It might also be appropriate to say here that much of what has counted for introduction to "Second Isaiah" has been incorporated within the Overview sections of the commentary, and this is particularly true of chapter 40. The larger concern is with limiting and modifying a view of chapters 40–66 as independent of the book of Isaiah as a whole.

THE LOGIC OF ISAIAH 40–66: FRONT MATTER, MIDDLE MATTER, OR NO MATTER?

In *The Interpreter's Bible,* the decision was made to assign the major section of chapters 40–66 to its own author for introduction and commentary, independent of Isaiah 1–39. In doing this, the *IB* was following the well-nigh universal practice of the day of seeing in the book of Isaiah at least two, if not more, individual collections, worthy of their own special treatment.

We might pause to consider that this practice, while widespread, was in some sense unique in the context of the Old Testament (or New Testament) canon. Whatever one may make of similar divisions within books, prophetic or otherwise, none called for such a special and specialized examination as Isaiah 40–66. "Deutero" or "Trito" Zechariah, for example, or the prose narratives of Jeremiah or the Temple Vision of Ezekiel (chaps. 40–48) did not rise to the level of such individualized treatment as was reckoned justified for Isaiah 40–66. And yet in some sense, each of these acts of subdivision belonged to the same climate of assured or semiassured results of critical methodology, by then already utilized for over a century.

In an almost breathtaking sense, the liberation of these twenty-seven chapters from the larger book of Isaiah also set free characters who would become household words within that narrow context better known as historical-critical education. Indeed, "Second" and "Third Isaiah" have now become so familiar in the vocabulary of the late modern West (whether one is ignorant of historical-critical labor or a devoted practioner of it) that one could imagine a major American newspaper referring to "Second Isaiah" without further ado. "Thus saith Second Isaiah" could easily ring out after a church reading from chapters 40–55.

In the *IB* Isaiah volume, James Muilenberg produced a lengthy (disproportionately so) introductory front matter that summarized the findings of the day and also set forth his own characteristic approach to these twenty-seven chapters. Muilenberg took the opportunity to say things about his "rhetorical method" that had been said by him in lapidary or only more general terms before, thus making his front matter treatment a classic example of that approach. Indeed, his interest in rhetorical analysis, it could be said, was tailor-made to these chapters of prophecy from the book of Isaiah. Whether this tailor-made character meant we were talking about a method to be employed more widely in the literature of the Old Testament or only about a set of pertinent observations of what made Isaiah 40–66 distinctive as such is not a topic for the front matter of this commentary in *The New Interpreters Bible.*

It is worth noting, just the same, that Muilenberg's heavy investment in defending a rhetorical approach in Isaiah 40–66, integrated with and by no means at odds with previous critical (mostly form-critical) analyses, saw to it that the division of the book of Isaiah into two sections was maintained with the same high seriousness as had been true for over a century. It would be ironic if his rhetorical method succeeded both in capturing the distinctive character of these twenty-seven chapters and in assuring that they remained virtually unique in the history of critical interpretation, in terms of their special, independent treatment in the various commentary series. If a method claims to account for so much distinctiveness, it can literally displace the material, dissociating it from its own literary relations within the selfsame corpus of texts (the larger book of Isaiah).

So, in the last century and a half, the more one could say about the special character of these chapters of Isaiah, the more their rootedness in the larger book was rejected, ignored, or simply assumed as unworthy of, even passing, productive comment. Second Isaiah (and Third Isaiah) were here to stay. To produce commentary, with front matter the equivalent of, or more robust than, what was true for other prophetic books (including now a "First Isaiah") could pass without comment.

But for several reasons this is no longer true. On the one hand, these twenty-seven chapters have proved on the whole resistant to Muilenberg's rhetorical conclusions. This can be said here with deep appreciation for his learning and his sensitivity as an exegete; the reader will find that the commentary to follow is indebted at many points to findings adduced in the *IB.* The problem is that continued division of the book of Isaiah into distinctive sections, as was for Muilenberg a truism, has succeeded in generating rival and contradictory accounts of the origins of, arrangement of, editing of, and independence and integrity of these same twenty-seven chapters. An older form-critical/rhetorical consensus, if such it was, has given way to literary analysis somewhat reminiscent of nineteenth-century approaches, with the focus on individual texts and editorial touches and highly complex reconstructions of redactional history. That these recent redactional approaches are now undertaken with an eye toward the larger book of Isaiah and its literary history is itself an ironic commentary on the history of critical reading of Second Isaiah. For these recent approaches, front matter, or "middle matter," would now not matter much. Yet it is difficult to see how such approaches are not the logical heirs of a method that divided the book firmly into two or more sections and gave such prominence to a "Second Isaiah," the great prophet of the exile.

On the other hand, renewed interest in the place of these twenty-seven chapters within the larger book of Isaiah has not found it necessary to reject the sort of integrative literary analysis deployed by Muilenberg, in favor of a complex redaction-historical conception. And yet precisely at this juncture, because of the interest in relating these chapters—as an integrated and rhetorically persuasive composition in something of the manner meant by Muilenberg—with the material found in chapters 1–39, it becomes far less clear how much of what belonged to the genre of "introduction" should properly be pursued. Matters of who, what, when, where, how—insofar as these are subsumed under attention to author, setting, historical period, literary analysis, and provenance, as in the standard introduction—are suitable within a historical-critical climate concerned with Second Isaiah, his life and times and message. But once one sees these questions as relevant only to the degree that they are correlated with an interpretation of the book of Isaiah as a whole, then the very genre of "introduction" in the middle of a major prophetic work like the book of Isaiah becomes problematic.

It is from such a vantage point, therefore, that we pause before commenting on Isaiah 40–66 to examine matters peculiar to the intepretation of these twenty-seven chapters. In doing so, we will be saying nothing about the appropriateness of the practice of writing front matter in the middle of a book, except as I have called attention to that here and now. Is there a way forward that appreciates the literary advances manifest in Muilenberg's commentary, that integrates these with attention to the logic and coherence of Isaiah as a single (sixty-six chapters) work and that refuses so to honor the "life and times" of a "Second Isaiah" that the path back to reading these twenty-seven chapters as Isaiah's powerful conclusion is not blocked off or made unduly complex?

JUST WHAT IS AN "INTRODUCTION" TO ISAIAH 40–66?

In the middle of the twentieth century, form-critical readings of Isaiah 40–66 predominated. Yet, this predomination came with a caveat: The prophets Deutero- and Trito-Isaiah utilized older forms and then, often radically, adapted them to new ends. This would require of the form-critic the skill to identify the scope and form of a unit of text and the creative adaptation of it, both in some measure the mark of the prophet's genius as inspired author. Interpreters spoke of the inspired freedom of Deutero-Isaiah, who "bent" older forms so as to fit them within a discourse suited for proclamation to Israelites languishing in Babylonian exile. Often it was said that this bending of forms was tied up with a new manner of proclamation. Rather than brief oral utterances, spontaneously delivered, the prophet had crafted longer rhetorical compositions (there was some disagreement about how long; this was a topic pursued with energy by Muilenburg in the *IB*), which were read or heard in a new "fuller-form" presentation. Perhaps this had to do with the social conditions under which the prophet labored; perhaps one should speak of an evolution in prophecy, undergoing modifications because of the awareness of prophecy as a written legacy, available and demanding correlation of some sort, in these special times of crisis and disruption. Perhaps one should simply say that the prophet is his own man, and what we see in these forms of speech has to do with Deutero-Isaiah and with his Trito-Isaiah disciple as inspired individuals. But whatever conclusion was reached, most recognized that in Isaiah 40–66 we stood on a borderline between older presuppositions about prophecy and later, new ones. Even the plain sense of the material in chapters 40–66 spoke this way when it used the language of "former things" and "latter" or "new things" to describe God's dealings with the people Israel.

It has taken several decades to recognize the full significance of the liminal state of these chapters as Israelite prophetic literature. The practice of simply treating the authors of Isaiah 40–66 as individuals, giving them names like Deutero- or Second Isaiah, and bestowing on them authorship of separate volumes of prophecy has held on, however, and is manifest in the majority of treatments available today (whether in commentary series or in general discussion). The usual practice of binding into separate volumes commentary on Isaiah 1–39, Isaiah 40–55, and Isaiah 56–66 will be, inadvertently, set aside here (as it was in the *IB*) because the entire Isaiah corpus is being treated with other major prophets associated with it in the canon, in one single volume.

Now this practical reality takes a further turn of significance in the case of Isaiah, because in recent decades the notion of independent prophets, following in some manner in the train of Isaiah and other pre-exilic voices, and therefore deserving of separate commentary treatment, is giving way to a different picture in the case of Isaiah 40–66. But this raises an important question, and it lies over the heart of the commentary to follow and the practice of writing introductions to prepare the reader for meeting "Deutero-" and "Trito-Isaiah." The terms refer here not to literary sections of Isaiah, but to authors in fixed social settings that can be described, with this or that distinctive theological message, over against other Isaiahs and other prophets, working out of this or that historical setting, as was true of Jeremiah, Nahum, Hosea, or the Isaiah of the Syro-Ephraimite crisis of the eighth century BCE.

In a word, if we are prepared to accept a distinctly new form of prophecy in Isaiah 40–66, however one understands that, should we also break ranks and bend the form of typical commentary front matter in the case of these chapters? Why, in other words, is introduction necessary here, following chapter 39 and preceding chapter 40, and what form should such introduction take? If our alleged "Deutero-Isaiah" has creatively adapted forms that he inherited, how might he be taken as an appropriate example for the genre of commentary writing as well?

The older practice insisted upon, first, a reconstruction of the historical and social setting of the prophecy. This was to drive home the fact that the setting (i.e., social-historical setting) of chapters 40–66 was decidely not to be confused with the setting of Isaiah 1–39 (which presented its own problems). Second, the literature was classified as to form (units and larger organization) and situated within a developmental picture of Israelite prophecy attentive to the social and historical circumstances referred to at points in the literal sense. References to Babylon, Cyrus, fleeing from diaspora, and lack of mention of David, Temple, Assyria (though see the Commentary for problems of occasional reference) conspired to produce a reasonable picture of prophetic speech, in new forms of presentation, delivered to those in exile and, later, to those in the land, following some sort of return of exiles to Jerusalem. Then the limits for the contributions were set, with most assigning chapters 40–55 to a Second Isaiah author, while chapters 56–66 were the work of a Trito-Isaiah. A related task was, of course, determining additions to these major collections and rearrangements and dislocations. Recent work on chapters 40–66 indebted to this general manner of approach has focused in particular on matters of arrangement and on certain long-standing difficulties.[1] So some divide all of chapters 40–55 into various redactional levels and seek to coordinate these with similar features in chapters 56–66, or a major division is sought at chapter 49, or, more ambitiously, redactional levels are coordinated with portions of text in chapters 1–39. All of this has complicated any simple talk about who, what, when, where, or how as this pertains to Isaiah 40–66.

While there is at present interest in the larger unity and coherence of Isaiah as a whole book, it would not be fair to say that this interest is what presents the major challenge to any simple deployment of the genre of "introduction" for chapters 40–55 or 40–66. Recent redactional-critical studies, because they analyze the manifestly anonymous, often minute additions and rearrangements of this material, assigning to these theological significance within a study of the whole book's theological evolution, also cannot give easy answers to the old questions of author, social setting, audience, and historical location. Indeed, these recede in importance as the redactional decisions, made within the literature, carry the chief theological weight the material seeks to convey. To speak of a "Deutero-" or "Trito-Isaiah" has become more difficult than talking of a "Zion tradition" or a "pro-nations level" or an "anti-temple redaction." Setting stops being geographical location, historical moment, or individual "poetic" contribution ("The Great Prophet of the Exile") and becomes instead this or that literary evidence of this or that theological shift, within a much broader reconstruction of the later years of Israelite religion (exilic and post-exilic).

On all accounts, then, return to a simple "author, setting, audience" form-critical approach, with its usual introductory roll call of topics to be treated before reading chapter 40, must now face the challenge of a host of newer approaches. It is not just the existence of these chapters within a larger book that raises questions about the appropriateness of discussing author and setting; it is also the sheer complexification of form-critical methodology into redaction and *tendenz*-oriented literary criticism in recent years. The provenance of these chapters has become increasingly literary and scribal and anonymous, making use of the terms "Deutero-" and "Trito-Isaiah"—except as literary designations—nostalgic simplification.

1. See esp. R. F. Melugin, *The Formation of Isaiah 40–55,* BZAW 141 (Berlin: Walter de Gruyter, 1976).

SETTING

The term "setting" is used in its social-historical sense here, mindful that efforts to describe the setting of these chapters must rely quite heavily, if not exclusively, on the literary evidence of the chapters in question.

In an early reassessment, Childs raised the possibility that clearer signs of the book's historical and social location had been muted when the chapters were shaped to function in the larger book.[2] Another way to take Childs's suggestion is as a simple recognition that chapters 40–66 do not choose to highlight their historical and social setting in ways historical-critics might wish and in ways that do in fact exist in other parts of the canon (e.g., Jeremiah or Ezra-Nehemiah). To say such a thing is not a reflection of simple laziness or lack of resolve about historical questions (a century of work on these questions in Isaiah 40–66 shows otherwise). But it is significant to note, and often is not sufficiently noted, how content these chapters are to work with a low degree of historical referentiality. Whether the reason for that has to do with the existence of chapters 1–39 as its own "setting" for chapters 40–66 is a separate question, to be taken up below. The "authorizing voice(s)" at work in our literature may have felt no need to stipulate a setting that, for the first audience, was everywhere pre-supposed and self-evident. This would be true whether such authorizing voices were aware of the voice of Isaiah or not (more on this below). What is noteworthy is that the material of chapters 40–66 was not supplied with editorial comment locating it in time and space, as is true of other prophetic books, and here the transmission of these oracles together with Isaiah 1–39 is surely relevant.

Reference to Cyrus in this discourse (Isa 45:1) does not appear to be an interpolation, but belongs intimately to the argument of the context. Cyrus was, of course, the Persian monarch who, history and parts of Scripture record (2 Chr 36:22-23; Ezra), brought about the end of Neo-Babylonian rule in the region and, indeed, saw to it that those in diaspora could return. It is not possible, given the form of the proclamation about him, more precisely to date the message of chapters 40–66. He is clearly modeled on typological grounds, in relationship to the depiction of Assyria earlier in Isaiah (10:5), and consistent with the new exodus language of much of these chapters, as a "second pharaoh" witnessing God's mighty acts. There is no reason to assume that the language about Cyrus is not roughly contemporaneous with his historical existence. But here again, it would probably be saying too much to argue that knowledge of Cyrus, in the terms expressed in these texts, requires the author and the audience to have been in Babylonian exile or to have been concerned about something so imminent as to fix this proclamation at one moment in time only.

2. B. S. Childs, *Isaiah*, OTL (Louisville: Westminster John Knox, 2000). Trobisch discusses the concrete form such editorial efforts to "de-historicize" (Childs's term) literature might take in his treatment of the Pauline letters. See D. Trobisch, *Paul's Letter Collection: Tracing the Origin* (Minneapolis: Fortress, 1994).

At several points in chapters 40–55 reference is made to Israel in dispersion. The dispersion is global (e.g., Isa 43:5-7) and is not described with any constraint on our participating from only one point of view—say, with a "prophet of the exile." Indeed, from the standpoint of the literature's own presentation, as Duhm long ago noted,[3] the perspective is, if anything, Jerusalemite in orientation. This did not, however, prevent Duhm from locating the actual author in Phoenicia in an odd bit of exegesis, showing that Duhm knew the difference between the setting of the author (a matter for close literary and historical analysis) and the setting the literature itself appears to work with. Hence, the words directed to those in dispersion in Babylon are to go forth *from there* (Isa 48:20), not, as it were, from here, and at other places, the Zion-orientation of the literature is unmistakeable (Isa 49:14–55:13). A handful of scholars has always registered objections to an exilic provenance.[4]

Once one respects Duhm's distinction between the literature's perspective and the author's actual historical location, a conclusion not unlike Childs's comes back into play. One need not conclude that these chapters once had a more concrete setting that was removed when the chapters began to form the conclusion of Isaiah 1–39. Rather, one need only respect the literature's Zion orientation and note the general concern for Israel in every compass point of dispersion (and the nations' similar location as anticipated recipients of God's name and glory). Then the constraining of the literature into some exilic context seems both unnecessary and less plausible, both on literary and on historical grounds.

Consequently, another major scholarly consensus will also need to be reviewed: the division of the book into two sections based upon the geographical reality of exile for one section (chaps. 40–55) and return for the other (chaps. 56–66), a distinction manifestly awkward when one notes the interest in Zion and its children running from chapter 49 to the final depiction of the book (66:10-16).

HISTORICAL PERIOD

If setting is an effort to get at the question of where, then in this section the question of when is addressed. When, at which historical period, is it proper to situate these twenty-seven chapters, or portions thereof? As we shall see, a question like this is fraught with the same sort of problems as setting raised, precisely because "where" and "when" are in fact allied inquiries.

As stated already, chapters 40–66 presuppose the collapse of the Neo-Babylonian Empire. Stated in the terms of Isaiah's own temporal bearings, the "former things" have passed away when we come to chapter 40. The period of judgment spoken of in Isaiah

3. Bernhard Duhm, *Das buch Jesaia,* HKAT (Göttingen: Vandenhoeck & Ruprecht, 1892).

4. J. D. Smart, *History and Theology in Second Isaiah* (Philadelphia: Westminster, 1965); C. C. Torrey, *The Second Isaiah* (New York: Scribner's, 1928); Recently questions have been raised afresh. See R. Clements, "Beyond Tradition-History: Deutero-Isaianic Development of First Isaiah's Themes," *JSOT* 31 (1985); J. van Oortschot, *Von Babel zum Zion,* BZAW 206 (Berlin: Walter de Gruyter, 1993).

6 has reached its conclusion, and only now are we in a position to hear about forgiveness and new things, on the other side of that judgment. Historically speaking, chapters 40–66 are self-consciously later speech than that of Isaiah of Jerusalem, from the period following Babylonian collapse.

This establishes a general *terminus ab quo* (earliest date) for the proclamation of Isaiah 40–66, but what of the *terminus ad quem* (latest possible date)? In some measure, this is both a historical and a literary question, for there is a time frame operating within the presentation of these twenty-seven chapters that allows us to note movement and change and development in the literature's argument, just as there is a narrower question about when such and such text was written, over against other texts, within and outside these twenty-seven chapters.

Beuken, more than any modern commentator, has taught us to pay attention to certain key words and themes in this discourse, and here he inadvertently raises a question of temporal location.[5] For all the centrality of the word "servant" in chapters 40–52, there is also some difficulty in knowing how to identify and interpret the servant's role and mission. Is the servant one and the same person, regardless of context? Is there a cycle of "servant songs" in which the servant is always the same person, or is to speak of a cycle already to prejudge the matter?

What is beyond controversy, however, is that the plural form, "servants," appears only at chapter 54 and nowhere before that and that these "servants" (cf. also "seed/offspring") play a decidedly central role in the presentation of especially chapters 56–66. Beuken has established this beyond doubt in a series of important essays.

In the Commentary to follow, these servants are taken to be the followers of the servant, in the same manner as Isaiah raises up around himself disciples (8:16). That is, the servants function on analogy with the generation that were to carry out the will of God as manifested to the prophet Isaiah. In Isaiah's day, there had to be a period of waiting, for the prophet's speech was not to be heeded but ignored—indeed, it made hearers deaf and blind (6:10). So it was the task of the disciples to bind up the testimony that it might be preserved and opened for a later day (see also 29:11-12, 19). As at other places where prophets are described in the Old Testament, the prophet's followers can be understood as his children or offspring (e.g., in the Elijah/Elisha stories).

The time frame envisioned by this scenario of rejection and punishment is not over-specified in Isaiah; we know only that a period of judgment, devastating in scope, is to be visited upon God's people and that a remnant will survive (6:11-13). We know also that Hezekiah will be spared seeing this period of judgment (39:5-8). When we read into chapter 40 and following, it is clear that the day of judgment is past (40:2, "she has served her term—her penalty is paid"). The former things contained the record of this coming judgment and of God's commissioning of its agent of release (41:21-29). It is in

5. W. A. M. Beuken, "The Main Theme of Trito-Isaiah: The Servants of Isaiah," *JSOT* 47 (1990).

the light of possession of this "former" record that Israel is a unique witness, able to produce what the nations cannot, and the possession of this knowledge is likewise testimony to the unique and sole lordship of Israel's God.

If the temporal relationship, in precise terms, between Isaiah and the testimony of the disciples released for a latter day is imprecise, we are able to infer that it involved movement from the period of Assyrian judgment and blasphemous threat (Isaiah 36–37), to a time centuries later (39:5-7), with Cyrus as the agent of release from judgment (cf. Isa 13:17 and 41:25).

The relationship, temporally, between the servant and the servants would appear more compressed. While the nomenclature "servants" is somewhat vague, there is no reason to assume that the "servants" of chapters 56–66 represent several successive generations; indeed, there is good evidence to believe that we are talking about the generation immediately after the servant, who is the author and subject of the core proclamation of Isaiah 40–66. At the close of chapter 59, we hear of a covenant made with several generations. God's spirit will be given to those ("offspring," "seed") who follow in the train of the servants, and the perspective is a future, not a past, one. At most, the book appears to describe a generation or two of servant disciples, and the steady attention of chapters 56–66, as Beuken has clearly shown, remains on them. They are the promised "seed" of the servant (53:10).

It remains to be established whether the temporal distinction represented by the movement in the literature from "servant" (singular) to "servants" (plural) also correlates with what was an alleged geographical distinction (exilic chapters, 40–55, and Jerusalemite-return chapters, 56–66). It is notable that the plural use of "servants" comes first in chapter 54, not in chapter 56. I have already registered my skepticism about whether the literature makes an important distinction between "Deutero" and "Trito" sections as traditionally held; in the Commentary the only distinction followed is between the discourse of the servant and the discourse of the servants. For this, the dividing line is the tribute to the servant, found in 52:13–53:12 (the so-called suffering servant song).

In the final chapters of Isaiah, controversy over the Temple is clearly in evidence. Most of the language of restoration in Isaiah focuses on Zion's discovery of her many children, some birthed without any labor (66:7; cf. 54:1-2; 60:4). When reference is made to concrete restoration, it tends still to focus on Zion's resplendent dress (Isaiah 54; 60–61), and not on the sort of concrete scenario (foundation stone, altar, walls, city) envisioned in Ezra–Nehemiah. If it were necessary to set a *terminus ad quem* for the discourse of the servants in chapters 54–66, the most that could be safely said would be the period of the first generations concerned with the restoration of Zion. Chapter 66 is more about rival building proposals and false religion than about precise moments in the restoration of the cult as Ezra sets this forth.

In sum, the perspective of the literature is of several generations, during the time of return and restoration, depicted from the standpoint of Zion-Jerusalem, where the full return of all the dispersed is a lively hope and with that, the inclusion of the nations as worshipers of God and witnesses to the glory of YHWH (66:18-23).

AUTHOR

It is important that we understand what the term "author" means when we look at Isaiah 40–66. We can start by attending to "the author" on the literature's own terms:

(1) The author of the material in chapters 40:1–52:12 is not identified by name.

(2) The author of this material does not speak in the first person, as prophets do in reference to themselves (when not speaking for God); this changes at 48:16d ("and now the LORD God has sent me and his spirit").

(3) Thereafter, the author speaks of himself in the first person and as God's servant (49:1-7; 50:4-9), all the while maintaining his primary role as "divine voice" in the manner familiar in chapters 40–48, though now with special attention to discharging the responsibility to comfort Zion (in fulfillment of the charge of 40:1-11).

(4) This author does not use, nor do others ever use, the familiar term "prophet" (נביא *nābî'*) to describe himself.

(5) The closest thing to what might be termed a "call narrative" (describing the setting apart of the individual for God's service) is to be found in 49:1-7, but it is more retrospective than prospective, and it entails a commissioning of the individual servant to be "Israel" (49:3), which gives rise to complaint about a past vocation.

Because the author is not called a prophet and because for much of the discourse he does not step forward (indeed, when he does so, it is due to divine compulsion and spirit possession; 48:16d), the term "author" must be understood along the lines of "authorizing" voice. This begs the question as to what sort of form-critical discourse the material of chapters 40–52:11 and 53:12–66:24 is (on this, see the section following).

In the opening chapters (chaps. 40–48) it is not necessary for the material to supply us with some account authorizing the speech. How is that possible? We are used to that in other prophetic material, even if it is only brief notices supplied clearly by an editor.

Several explanations lie close at hand. The first involves the relationship between the discourse of chapters 40–66 and what precedes in the book of Isaiah. In the commentary to follow, it will be shown that the "former things" perspective assumed in chapters 40–48 operates with knowledge of a prior prophetic record, involving most crucially oracles from Isaiah of Jerusalem. The opening pericope (40:1-11) is not, as many have noted, a call narrative, however much we may feel entitled to one at the point of entry into this material and however much it may resemble such a narrative (e.g., Isaiah 6). The voices that speak are those from the heavenly council. We are meant to know that the voices who addressed Isaiah in former times with a word of judgment for God's people (see 6:3-5, 9-10) are here, as in chap. 6, deferential to the word the Lord has spoken: formerly for judgment (6:8-10), latterly for forgiveness (40:5), with the announcement of God's holy presence before all flesh (40:5, 10). What is missing in our account is a prophet on analogy with Isaiah. Instead we have voices speaking to one another, as before, but no named prophet. Consistent with this, in what follows we have divine speech without any presentation of the authorized voice. For that we must wait until 48:16d and 49:1-7, and even then what we find is indebted to former prophetic records (49:1-7 resembles Jer 1:4-10) and is not a full reproduction of them for a new prophet.

It is not clear that the speaker or his audience believes prophecy can exist at this period without further ado as a simple extension of what had pertained in the days of Isaiah, Jeremiah, or even Ezekiel (who is nearly contemporaneous). It is likely no accident that Isaiah 40–66 never circulated as a separate prophetic collection (in spite of Duhm's clever hypothesis to the contrary) in any reception-history capable of verification, and indeed that the only form we have of it is as it exists now: as the final chapters of a vision of Isaiah. As we shall see, the notion that there was to be a series of prophets, and a specific prophet "like Moses" (Deut 18:15), may have carried with it a further assumption—namely, that at some point prophecy would come to a close in eschatological fulfillment of God's plans for it. It is necessary here only to register that the peculiar depiction of the literature, focused on a servant and servants but not on a prophet, belongs to the specific presentation of the book of Isaiah as a whole and this particular moment in God's revelation of the word to Israel.

What stands out in Isaiah 40–66 is the notion of God's independent word accomplishing what God wills (55:11). This notion is rooted in the presentation of Isaiah 1–39, where we learn that Isaiah's word to one generation would go unheeded, but would remain God's word nonetheless for a later generation. The author lives under this perspective and does not seek to encroach upon it. Indeed, when in chapter 49 he speaks for himself, it is clear that he regards his vocation as heretofore fruitless, however, and in whatever form it took in chapters 40–48. His own hope is in God's accomplishing potential (49:4).

It remains for the commentary proper to sort out the details of this understanding of the author, based upon a close reading. It will be argued that the servant is given in 49:3 the role announced as Israel's in 42:1-8, is persecuted and afflicted (50:4-9), and dies (52:13–53:12). He accomplishes what God had promised in comforting Zion, in removing sin, and in becoming thereby a light to the nations, if in an eschatological realm only (52:13-15). The moving tribute to the servant is provided by the servants, who glimpsed into the mystery of his death and saw there not an end but a fulfillment and an inauguration. The remainder of the book is their own written legacy.

Is it possible to assign this new mode of inspired speech to some social or religious setting? Yes, most certainly. What is less clear is whether this would add to or detract from our appreciation of the discourse as it lies before us in the book of Isaiah. I remain fairly certain that we are reading this material on something of the terms those who preserved it meant for us to—that is, as an extension of the vision of Isaiah. Reading these chapters, or hearing them read aloud, in other words, may not be far from how they first functioned. At points the intertextuality of the material (i.e., its reutilization of other parts of Scripture) is so strong that one must imagine a highly trained author and audience; trained, that is, in the knowledge of the specific literary content of Israel's legacy of divine speech. This, in turn, points to the strong possibility that the composition of these twenty-seven chapters never originated as public, spontaneous, brief utterances, in the manner understood by nineteenth- and twentieth-century German scholars, only secondarily to be committed to writing, arranged and rearranged, until we have what sits before us now.

The sheer invisibility of the prophetic voice within the discourse itself may mean that the author was faced by oppression and challenge from within his circle. If this is true, it would provide an explanation for why such radically hopeful and forgiving speech exists together with descriptions of persecution and affliction, even unto death. In the final chapters, this conflict emerges into the full light of day, forms the center of the discourse, until the servants are separated from their wicked persecutors (65:13). Here as well, the descriptions of affliction and persecution sit right alongside language bursting with hope and promise.

We know that the office of prophet nearly tore Jeremiah in two. The servant-author and the servant followers move the discourse about Israel and the nations into truly unprecedented territory (cf. Jeremiah's appointment as prophet over nations and kingdoms in Jer 1:10) and therein may lie the source of the conflict. The servant and the servants insist that Israel be a light to the nations and that God may well use affliction and even death to accomplish this. It is hard to imagine a more difficult word to be given to deliver. The form of the presentation, with its hidden author who steps forward in the role of servant Israel, light to the nations, dies and gives birth to a new generation of servants, allows us to glimpse but partially the social world in which the message was first delivered. But that may not be an accident of history. The text from its beginning was felt to have an ongoing, eschatological import, beyond the circumstances of its first delivery, and that understanding goes back to Isaiah himself. To read the literature on its own terms is to respect this eschatological message and its capacity to transcend historical reconstructions.

In sum, I would argue for a single author, joined by a generation of servant followers, later termed those who tremble at God's word (66:2, 5). These latter form the core of a group who heard and transmitted the servant's oracles to a yet wider audience. In that transmission came friction and dissent. In the tribute to the servant and in the life of the servants we learn that this friction and dissent also belonged to God's plans for the people and inaugurated God's final purposes for all creation and all flesh.

LITERARY FORM AND COMPOSITION

Second Isaiah was a form-critical proving ground in the middle of the twentieth century. In the first phase, the focus was on exact delimitation of units and classification of them in terms of genre. These chapters seemed to lend themselves to this sort of task, because of the sharpness of transition and the general tidiness of expression. Still, sharp disagreements existed over both the number and the genre of the units discovered.

In the second phase, more attention was paid—in spite of these disagreements—to the life-setting of the speech units, now separated from their present literary arrangement ("situation-in-text"). Again, very little agreement was forthcoming about the social setting of the proclamation and the proper description of the office of the prophet Deutero-Isaiah. Some of this was the frustration of conjecturing about a setting for which we have very little collateral testimony (allegedly, life in Babylonian exile). Was the prophet operating in a cultic context, a preaching context, or some other context? Or was he, say, writing down his proclamation and sending it out piecemeal? Then an additional complicating factor extruded itself: What if the prophet was using genre familiar to him and his audience, but only in terms of literary imitation—that is, already at one stage removed from whatever situation-in-life they had first functioned in and had in turn affected their form? If this turned out to be the case, then form criticism could only point to its own built-in limitations, in the case of Isaiah 40–66.

In a third phase, then, attention returned to the text itself and to theories about the present structure and arrangement of the material. Here it seemed commentators felt themselves to be on firmer ground. Westermann and Melugin are classic examples of those who worked with the literary and formal aspects of the previous critical phase, but who sat easier to the search for setting-in-life, preferring instead an effort to account for the organization of the chapters in Isaiah 40–55.[6] Westermann extended his own analysis into chapters 56–66, and in large measure one could conclude that he was representative of a general trend, of seeing in "Third Isaiah" a much more heterogeneous and haphazardly arranged collection of formal units. The Commentary follows these two approaches (Westermann's and Melugin's) closely throughout.

This interest in editorial shaping has continued, but it has taken two different directions. Mention has been made already about the newer redactional studies, and these represent one direction. A second direction can be seen in the work of Muilenberg and various other literary approaches.[7] These seek to see in the final form of Isaiah 40–55 a rhetorically effective, highly organized, only lightly redacted presentation. Redactional studies are more interested in identifying divergence and literary tension, and then delineating wide-scale levels of redaction and alteration, which run across

6. C. Westermann, *Isaiah 40–66*, trans. David Stalker, OTL (Philadelphia: Westminster, 1969); R. F. Melugin, *The Formation of Isaiah 40–55*, BZAW 141 (Berlin: Walter de Gruyter, 1976).

7. J. Muilenburg, "The Book of Isaiah: Chapters 40–66," in *The Interpreter's Bible* (Nashville: Abingdon, 1956) vol. 5.

tidy structural divisions—not only within chapters 40–55 or 56–66, but also across these sections (indeed, into the oracles of First Isaiah).

In the Commentary to follow, a third approach is taken. It will be shown that the structure of Isaiah 40–66 is highly thought out, is the product of the servant's own efforts, and reaches beyond chapters 40–55, especially in relationship to the former things of Isaiah (chaps. 1–39). The major literary divisions are adjusted, however, away from a Second and Third Isaiah orientation, in favor of (I) chapters 40–48; (II) chapters 49:1–52:12; (III) chapters 52:13–53:12; and (IV) chapters 54–66, with the third section transitional and not sharply independent.

It is the view of the Commentary to follow that the servant has taken older forms and has adapted these with great freedom to produce a literary work. Here the rhetorical direction of Muilenberg and others is followed up and taken a step further. The servant poems are not to be understood as either part of a distinctive cycle, on the one hand, or a more random appearance (in chaps. 40–48), on the other hand. Rather, it will be shown that both types of servant proclamation have been coordinated in the final form of the literature and that they function differently based on their appearance before or after the central poem at 49:1-9.

More will not be said here because in the Commentary to follow the practice is adopted of providing major Overview sections that discuss literary matters relevant to the section under discussion, arguing in each case for the intentionality of the structural division and the cogency of the argument of the literature contained within it. It is not my intention at this point to allow the "front matter" to mislead one into conceiving commentary on Isaiah 40–66 as an independent matter. Interpretation of Isaiah 40–66, we shall see, is interpretation of the book of Isaiah.

BIBLIOGRAPHY

Commentaries:

Baltzer, K. *Deutero-Isaiah: A Commentary on Isaiah 40–55.* Hermeneia. Minneapolis: Fortress, 2001. Shortly to appear in English translation, this commentary presents a novel dramatic interpretation of Isaiah 40–55, which the author locates in a Jerusalem-Judean context, in the period of Nehemiah.

Childs, B. S. *Isaiah.* OTL. Louisville: Westminster John Knox, 2001. A fresh effort to read Isaiah 40–66 within the context of the canonical book of Isaiah. Knowledgeable and impeccably researched, with attention to newer redactional and canonical readings.

Hanson, P. D. *Isaiah 40–66.* Interpretation. Louisville: Westminster John Knox, 1995. An accessible introduction to the "prophet Second Isaiah," with an emphasis on his personality, inspiration, and unique features of his thought. The author tries to find a middle way between form criticism and rhetorical-literary criticism, with modern homilectical remarks extrapolated from the socioreligious world of the prophet.

Muilenburg, J. "The Book of Isaiah: Chapters 40–66." In *The Interpreter's Bible.* 12 vols. (Nashville: Abingdon, 1956). Vol. 5. Presents the argument for a "rhetorical reading" of Second Isaiah chapters. Frequently full of insight, Muilenburg is sensitive to poetic details.

Westermann, C. *Isaiah 40–66.* Translated by David Stalker. OTL. Philadelphia: Westminster, 1969. The classic form-critical treatment, with scattered attention to the final structure of the literature. The author works very closely with the prophet's forms of speech and is committed to locating these forms in Israel's religious life.

Specialized Studies:

Bellinger, W. H., and W. R. Farmer, eds. *Jesus and the Suffering Servant: Isaiah 53 and Christian Origins.* Harrisburg, Pa.: Trinity Press International, 1998. English translations of many of the essays from *Der leidende Gottesknecht* (see below), along with fresh individual treatments.

Beuken, W. A. M. "The Main Theme of Trito-Isaiah: 'The Servants of Yahweh.' " *JSOT 47* (1990). An important study of how "Third Isaiah" is related to "Second Isaiah" and the book of Isaiah, by a brilliant critical interpreter of Isaiah.

Clements, R. "Beyond Tradition-History: Deutero-Isaianic Development of First Isaiah's Themes." *JSOT* 31 (1985). A representative essay by one of the recent new interpreters of Isaiah, focusing on internal Isaianic development.

Janowski, B., and P. Stuhlmacher, eds. *Der leidende Gottesknecht.* FAT 14. Tubingen: Mohr-Siebeck, 1996. Essential reading on the role of the servant poems in Isaiah 40–66, with attention to their subsequent history of interpretation.

Meade, D. G. "Authorship, Revelation and Canon in the Prophetic Tradition." In *Pseudonymity and Canon.* WUNT 39. Tubingen: Mohr-Siebeck, 1986. A balanced analysis of the way "authorship" emerged in antiquity, with special attention to the Isaiah traditions.

Melugin, R. F. *The Formation of Isaiah 40–55.* BZAW 141. Berlin: Walter de Gruyter, 1976. The classic investigation of forms and their arrangement in the literature of Isaiah 40–55, presenting the strengths and weaknesses of the older form-critical method. Essential reading.

Melugin, R., and M. Sweeney, eds. *New Visions of Isaiah.* JSOTSup 214. Sheffield: JSOT, 1996. An up-to-date assessment of recent trends in Isaiah interpretation.

Seitz, C. R. "How Is the Prophet Isaiah Present in the Latter Half of the Book? The Logic of Chapters 40–66 Within the Book of Isaiah." *JBL* 115 (1996). A consideration of the way Isaiah 40–66 relates to preceding chapters on the matter of "authorial" (human) voice, with special attention to the role of chaps. 48–49.

Smith, P. A. *Rhetoric and Redaction in Trito-Isaiah.* VTSup 62. Leiden: Brill, 1995. An up-to-date, useful analysis of the poems of Isaiah 56–66 and their critical interpretation.

Wilcox, P., and D. Paton-Williams. "The Servant Songs in Deutero-Isaiah." *JSOT* 42 (1988). A pivotal essay on the role of Isaiah 49 in the theological movement of Deutero-Isaiah chapters.

OUTLINE OF ISAIAH 40–66

I. Isaiah 40:1-31, A Word at Once New and Old

    A. 40:1-11, A Highway for God

    B. 40:12-31, Pre-trial Statement

II. Isaiah 41:1–48:22, Draw Near for Judgment

    A. 41:1-29, Two Called, One Caller

    B. 42:1-13, The Servant Presented, Addressed, Hymned

    C. 42:14-25, Blind Leading the Blind?

    D. 43:1-28, An Isaian Exodus

    E. 44:1-23, I Formed You

    F. 44:24–48:22, Cyrus and the Nations

        44:24–45:8, Cyrus, Unwitting Agent
        45:9-25, Every Knee Shall Bow
        46:1-13, Heavy Laden
        47:1-15, Zion's Foiled Foil
        48:1-22, Former Things, New Things

III. Isaiah 49:1–53:12, Servant, Light to the Nations

    A. 49:1-26, Servant and Zion

    B. 50:1-11, The Taught One

    C. 51:1–52:12, The Last Speech of the Servant Like Moses

        51:1-23, The Taught One Teaches
        52:1-12, Final Testimony

    D. 52:13–53:12, The Servant's Abiding Legacy

IV. Isaiah 54:1–66:24, Vindication of the Servant by God

    A. 54:1-17, The Heritage of the Servants

    B. 55:1-13, The Reversal Continues

    C. 56:1-8, Gathered to the Holy Mountain

    D. 56:9–57:21, God's Peace—and Its Cruel Opposite

    E. 58:1–59:21, God's Righteous Sentinel Speaks

ISAIAH 40:1-31

A WORD AT ONCE NEW AND OLD

OVERVIEW

Chapter 40 has a special position in the book of Isaiah as a whole and also as an introduction to the new discourse represented by chapters 40–66. Analysis of the chapter begins with a discussion of its relation to the immediately preceding narratives of Zion's deliverance (chaps. 36–39) and the poetic section before that (chaps. 34–35). Because Isaiah 40–66 is unique as prophetic literature, due to its relationship to the "former things" testimony of Isaiah, the character of commentary writing is affected. It will be necessary to dwell on this chapter of Isaiah at greater length than will be the practice for subsequent chapters.

Also, as was argued in the Introduction, chapter 40 is the first chapter of the first main division of Isaiah 40–66—i.e., chaps. 40–48. It sets us firmly in the context of a trial from the heavenly council, in which Israel and the nations are litigants. This setting is maintained until chap. 48, at which point the servant, who had been presented before the heavenly council and commissioned for a task to the nations (so, crucially, in 42:1-9), is identified with the author of the discourse; otherwise, in this opening section (chaps. 40–48) the author remains anonymous, and, it will be argued, intentionally so. The trial leads to a judgment of the nations in chap. 46, on the other side of which the servant will take up his task to be "light for the nations" in chaps. 49–66. This task involves suffering and death; confession and insight from the servants in Israel; and, in an eschatological sense, the acknowledgment of the nations (52:13-15).

CHAPTER 40 IN THE BOOK OF ISAIAH

Commentators ancient and modern agree that at chap. 40 we cross a significant boundary in the book of Isaiah. Suddenly the Babylonian victory over Judah and Jerusalem, if earlier intimated (chaps. 13–14; 21), is now fully presupposed. Jerusalem has, not in prediction but in fact, "received from the LORD's hand double for all her sins" (40:2). Where once she had been spared the fate of the cities of Judah at the hands of mighty Assyria (36:1), through the prayer of King Hezekiah (37:16-20) and the word of the prophet Isaiah (37:33-35), now she has shared in defeat and been forced to "serve her term" (40:2) as God's final judgment at last extended to her. Assyria had reached up to the neck (8:8) and then been halted (37:36-38), in fulfillment of the prophet's promise. Yet in the chapters that follow this remarkable account of Zion's deliverance, another prophetic word has sought fulfillment and found it:

> Days are coming when all that is in your house, and that which your ancestors have stored up until this day, shall be carried to Babylon; nothing shall be left, says the LORD. (39:6 NRSV)

It is against this backdrop that chap. 40 sounds its stunning word of hope and encouragement, "Comfort, O comfort my people, says your God."

It is important not to lose sight of this earlier Isaiah backdrop as one crosses into chap. 40. Isolating "Second Isaiah" and "Third Isaiah" from the perspective established in earlier chapters can lead to a one-sided approach to reading the final twenty-seven chapters of the book. So conceived, the most important context for interpretation becomes the circumstances out of which the literature was generated, as these can be reconstructed using form-critical (setting-in-life; social circumstances governing speech) and historical tools (including authorial and audience redescription). This is good so far as it goes, since chaps. 40–66 reflect a dispensation in which one can talk about "former things" in distinction to "latter" or "new things" (41:22; 42:9; 43:9, 18; 46:9). That is, a new and distinctive historical situation is indeed what grounds the literary presentation of "new things" to be contrasted with "former things."[8] The former/latter theme appears frequently enough in chaps. 40–48 to be regarded as an organizing refrain. It sets in place an obvious temporal framework in which the events of preceding chapters have already taken place and now stand at a considerable remove. At the same time, this framework calls attention to important literary and theological perspectives the literature itself has chosen to emphasize. That is, the material in chapters 40–66 self-consciously functions in relationship to earlier Isaiah chapters and other "former things."[9] This warns against artificially isolating the proclamation in the context of Babylonian exile as the proper way to appreciate the temporal distance of chaps. 40–66. The literature is more complex than that, reflecting as it does new historical circumstances, yet all the while retaining its integral connection with the literary perspective set by the larger book itself.

This is nowhere clearer than in the very first verses of chap. 40. The solemn declaration of served term, paid penalty, and double receipt is directed *to Jerusalem* (40:2). It was her destiny around which the narratives of chaps. 36–39 swirled, even as they spoke of the king and the royal house as well (e.g., 38:6). The book of Isaiah opens with an address to Jerusalem (1:21-23). God is about to do a new thing, and this involves God's own personal return to Zion (40:3, 9-11), to be witnessed by the same cities of Judah (40:9) that had been overrun in the days of King Sennacherib (36:1). Chapter 39 had spoken of the hauling away of royal house and treasuries, and we are to assume in the chapter that follows that this prophecy has been fulfilled. But where, then, are we when we enter the world of chap. 40? In Babylonian exile? With a new prophet? In a social

and historical context, the laying bare of which is a prerequisite for our being able to read these powerful chapters? No, we enter chap. 40 from the selfsame perspective established in the larger book of Isaiah, within which a response to the word of judgment sounded at 39:6-8 is capacitated—that is, God's perspective, coordinated with the wide variety of concerns articulated in preceding Isaiah chapters. That we move so abruptly to this powerful new proclamation is not a sign of the independence of "Second" and "Third Isaiah." Rather, the abruptness serves to emphasize that a word is being spoken from the void, against all hope and all expectation, by God, from the council of God's own sovereign will, about the faithless but elect and forgiven city Zion/Jerusalem.

Here also are given clues why we do not get a clear profile of the prophetic voice responsible for these chapters as we enter the world of their discourse, as often happens in prophetic literature (e.g., Jer 1:1-13). Two explanations account for this. On the one side, there is the word of God as it had already sounded forth in chaps. 1–39 (in whatever form and scope these chapters existed), which constitutes a profound "anxiety of influence" over the unknown author.[10] And, as we shall see, "former things" are chiefly, but not exclusively, prophecies of Isaiah; there is a considerable prophetic legacy upon which this proclamation is based (see the Commentary on 49:1-6).[11] The reference to the word of God and what "the mouth of the LORD has spoken" in the first section of chap. 40 (vv. 5, 8) is consistent with this observation regarding literary influence, as well as the language of what many consider the final chapter of "Second Isaiah" (chap. 55):

> So shall the word be that goes out from my mouth; it shall not return to me empty, But it shall accomplish that which I purpose. (55:11)

8. See Christopher R. Seitz, "How Is the Prophet Isaiah Present in the Latter Half of the Book? The Logic of Chapters 40–66 Within the Book of Isaiah," *JBL* 115 (1996) 219-40.

9. Compare the discussion of C. R. North, "The 'Former Things' and the 'New Things' in Deutero-Isaiah," in *Studies in Old Testament Prophecy* (Edinburgh: T. & T. Clark, 1950) 111-26, and the assessment of it by B. S. Childs, *Introduction to the Old Testament as Scripture* (Philadelphia: Fortress, 1979).

10. The phrase is taken from Harold Bloom, *The Anxiety of Influence: A Theory of Poetry* (London: Oxford University Press, 1997). Childs speaks of "a coercion exerted by the biblical text itself, as authoritative scripture." See B. S. Childs, *Isaiah*, OTL (Louisville: Westminster John Knox, 2001) 422-23. He is speaking of how the NT writers used Isaiah and OT Scripture "in its struggle to understand the suffering and death of Jesus Christ." This coercion exists within the development of the Isaiah tradition itself, moreover, and the model for the early church's handling of the Old Testament has its roots in the Old Testament. The relationship between "former" and "latter" Isaiah is one of the best examples of this.

11. See also B. Sommer, "Allusions and Illusions: The Unity of the Book of Isaiah in Light of Deutero-Isaiah's Use of Prophetic Literature," in *New Visions of Isaiah*, ed. R. Melugin and M. Sweeney, JSOTSUP 214 (Sheffield: JSOT, 1996).

There is an independence to the word of God addressing the prophet that requires the prophet's own self-presentation to recede.[12] In chap. 40, the word of God comes to him as a "voice" (קוֹל *qôl*; see vv. 3, 6), and a measure of the independence of that voice is never fully lost, just as the prophet's own persona never takes up much space within the literature, especially at the beginning and in the opening section (chaps. 40–48). Accommodation is made for the word that addresses the prophet as well as the earlier literary context out of which the proclamation now sounds forth—namely, the "former things" of Isaiah. Further literary testimony held in trust by Israel has likewise influenced the presentation (see the Commentary on 41:1-29).

On the other side, in terms of religious history, Israel appears to be grappling at this moment with just what the prophetic office is, whether it is being extended or transformed or whether it has died out altogether.[13] Many have seen evidence of a "divine council scene" in 40:1-9—that is, a heavenly throne room, with divine attendants, where verdicts are rendered (cf. 1 Kings 22; Psalm 82).[14] To speak of a divine council in the opening chapter—where God speaks to voices, who respond in kind, with the prophetic voice only vaguely, if at all, accounted for (v. 6)—is to reckon with a new form for authorizing divine speech. Both the inner subjectivity and the public character of the prophet, as described by the literature itself, have receded to the point of invisibility. The reader is confronted with a form of discourse not unlike that which opens the book of Job, whose author is not relevant to the discourse related. The book of Zechariah likewise opens with the prophet discovering himself in the midst of a midair colloquy ("I saw in the night"), with exchanges between God and angelic voices bearing tidings for Zion and Jerusalem (Zech 1:7-17). Through the medium of this depiction, God speaks to the reader directly, without any subsequent prophetic activity

undertaken by the prophet (Zechariah) himself. He is instructed to go proclaim things by the divine emissary (Zech 1:14-17) that are, in fact, only "proclaimed" by our reading them, in the context of an exchange between God, divine agents, and the prophet. What the "author" of the Isaiah discourse has to "say," as a prophetic individual, is fully subsumed by the message he hears and passes on, in as direct and immediate a manner as possible, in unbroken continuity with the former "vision of Isaiah." This is a new form of prophetic mediation, and it assumes a different sort of audience. Moreover, this form of mediation makes the prophetic word available to us on terms very close to that of the "original" audience.

The remainder of chap. 40 (vv. 12-31), following the opening colloquy (vv. 1-11), demonstrates a remarkable convergence of historical, literary, and theological contexts. The discourse addresses matters of God's sovereignty (v. 12), the absurdity of idol manufacture (vv. 18-20), the non-existence of other "gods" (vv. 24-25), prior testimony from God to which Israel holds title (vv. 27-28*a*), and God's strengthening of those who wait on God (vv. 29-31). The remarkable nature of the assembly of themes is not just that they are relevant to the circumstances of Babylonian exile, historically reconstructed. True as this may be, it fails to push to the heart of the matter. Rather, what is striking is that virtually all of these issues are taken up in the narratives immediately preceding chap. 40—that is, narratives within the literary context of Isaiah and not the historical context of exile in Babylon. The Assyrian emissary sent from Lachish to Jerusalem said that Israel's God is one among many (36:18-20), that his "great king" is the one sovereign over all nations (37:10-13), that the strong are nothing before him (36:4-10). During all this, Hezekiah has waited on God (37:14-20), disputed the efficacy of idols (37:19), and called upon the Lord as his only source of strength, "that all the kingdoms of the earth may know that thou alone art the LORD" (37:20). When God comes through and vindicates this faithful servant and delivers Jerusalem, this constitutes solid proof, to which Israel might subsequently refer (40:21-23), when times grow yet darker and judgment by Babylon is a reality. Even the motif of prior reference, such as we find it in this discourse of a later Isaiah, has its counterpart within the narratives that precede chap.

12. For a good assessment, see D. G. Meade, "Authorship, Revelation and Canon in the Prophetic Tradition," in *Pseudonymity and Canon,* WUNT 39 (Tubingen: Mohr-Siebeck, 1986).

13. See Seitz, "How Is the Prophet Isaiah Present in the Latter Half of the Book?" See also the helpful remarks of G. Sheppard, "The 'Scope' of Isaiah as a Book of Jewish and Christian Scripture," in Melugin and Sweeney, *New Visions of Isaiah*. C. R. Seitz, "The Prophet Moses and the Canonical Shape of Jeremiah," *ZAW* (1989) 1-21.

14. F. M. Cross, "The Council of Yahweh in Second Isaiah," *JNES* 12 (1953) 274-77.

40, at Isa 37:26-27: "Have you not heard that I determined it long ago?" This makes the reiteration in 40:21-23 ("Have you not heard?") all the more forceful. God brings princes to nought (40:23); the proof of this was established for all the world to see outside the gates of Jerusalem, and in an especially personal way for mighty King Sennacherib, who was killed by his own sons, "as he was worshiping in the house of his god Nisroch" (37:38).

It should be clear that the connections between the "opening" chapter of this new discourse and what precedes in chaps. 36–39 are not merely literary and allusive, intended to satisfy close readers in search of correspondence. The "author" of this new discourse addresses his "audience" insofar as he has been addressed by a prior word and because he believes that word to be pressing for further and further fulfillment. The fit that exists between past testimony (from Isaiah's vision and from other sources of Israel's knowledge of God) and the present historical reality is what the "author" knows to be the word of God addressing him and others. The example of Zion's deliverance provided in chapters immediately preceding this discourse showed Israel that the claims now being made by Babylonian "victory" had an analogy in the past, and there, too, they were groundless—even as they required enormous faith and fortitude from God's servants. The Assyrian Rabshakeh ("chief steward") had boasted that the citizens of Jerusalem "would be taken away to a land like your own" (36:17), and even his word would ultimately prove true, though by the hand of another agent. Yet God's establishment of sovereignty over mighty Assyria served notice of sovereignty over Babylon and all other nations as well. When the Rabshakeh boasted, "Is it without the LORD that I have come up against this land?" (36:10), he had no idea just what he was saying and what fate awaited him.[15]

Finally, too, we should note the correspondences between chap. 40 and chaps. 34–35. These correspondences have been frequently pointed out, to the extent of arguing for common authorship. That sort of diachronic judgment (based on precise historical, authorial, and/or editorial reconstruction) will not be pressed too hard in the present treatment.[16] There remains no final way to adjudicate such matters, and it remains a fact that the book has acquired a particular shape and organization. I regard this as a datum worthy of consideration. The effect of hearing the opening voice respond to God (vv. 2-5) with words drawn virtually verbatim from these chapters (e.g., "they shall see the glory of the LORD"; "a highway shall be there") should not be lost on the reader (see Isa 35:1-4, 8-10). In this way it is demonstrated in the divine council that God has made good on what was earlier promised, even before the assault on Jerusalem is narrated in chaps. 36–39.[17] There would be an international judgment on a massive scale (34:1-4), from which would ensue a day of vengeance for Zion (34:8), with the glory of the Lord viewed by the nations, and the weak and feeble saved by God. To hear these themes sounded again from the divine council is to know God's word is good and that it can be trusted, even when mortals grow weary and forget. This is what it means to be addressed by a word not of our making, and in that experience is constituted "the prophetic." In the case of the discourse here, the experience is so pure as to leave "the author" fully hidden from view, overshadowed by God's word and by voices duty bound to bring it back to mind when it is forgotten.

STRUCTURE AND FUNCTION

The opening chapter of this Isaiah discourse is typically divided into two units: vv. 1-11 and vv. 12-31. Under the influence of a conception of chap. 40 as inaugurating a section of independent prophecy, called "Second Isaiah" of "Deutero Isaiah," most commentators regard the first unit as portraying the prophet's call, since this is what one might expect in a new and independent prophetic collection. This conclusion is not materially affected by the recognition that the form of a call narrative has here been adapted, either to serve the purposes of offering an introduction or prologue to the entire Second Isaiah corpus or under

15. See C. R. Seitz, *Zion's Final Destiny: The Development of the Book of Isaiah* (Minneapolis: Fortress, 1993).

16. For a full treatment, see C. R. Mathews, *Defending Zion: Edom's Desolation and Jacob's Restoration (Isaiah 34-35) in Context,* BZAW 236 (Berlin: Walter de Gruyter, 1995).

17. See C. R. Seitz, "On the Question of Divisions Internal to the Book of Isaiah," *SBLSP* (Atlanta: Scholars Press, 1993) 260-66.

the influence of a closely related form, involving the scenery of the heavenly council (speech from an entourage of attendants; plural address, i.e., "comfort ye," to these same attendants; divine verdict announced), within which the prophet is commissioned.[18] That a heavenly council scene is clearly presented, or presupposed on the basis of a known form, would seem logical if the unit is intended to work in coordination with the earlier commissioning of Isaiah (chap. 6). There the voices other than God's are supplied with specific identities: They are seraphim. This could also explain why the voices in this unit speak without any further ado or any need to rehearse the scenario of chap. 6.[19] But this must remain conjecture.

The theory of a "prologue" is sometimes bolstered if one can identify a clear structure in the composition of "Deutero-Isaiah," matched by an epilogue, which would mark the closing lines of the arrangement for which the prologue was constructed. Chapter 55 has traditionally served this purpose, but even if that judgment is accepted, it begins to ask a lot of this unit—that it do the duty of literary prologue, prophetic call narrative, and heavenly council commissioning, not to mention making a clear connection backward to chap. 6 and the prophet Isaiah's commissioning. Moreover, the clearest candidate for a text in coordination with 40:1-11 within the discourse under discussion is not chap. 55, but 52:1-12.[20] The good-tidings bearer of 40:9 appears there (52:7); the promised return of the Lord (40:10) is there referenced (52:8); the people are comforted (40:1; 52:9); the glory all flesh were to see at 40:5 becomes the salvation all the ends of the earth see at 52:10. The language parallels are clear and beyond dispute. The significance of this for the structure of this discourse will be taken up below.

To talk about a call narrative in the case of 40:1-11 may require a commitment to the independent character of this material, for which some such authorizing narrative, familiar from other prophetic books, would be expected. This approach, however, may misunderstand the peculiar circumstances under which this new unit must operate—namely, beginning a new discourse, but in an old setting, which has its own authorizing narrative for the prophet Isaiah in chap. 6. What is striking and uncontroversial about this unit is its paucity of autobiographical detail. Westermann comments on vv. 6-7: "No intimation of a call could be briefer."[21] If one were to read the MT of v. 6 quite literally, even an intimation would be eliminated. The ואמר (we'āmar, "and he said," "and one said"; KJV, "and it said") would then have as its subject a voice in the heavenly entourage who is not sure whether the lead of the proclaiming voice of v. 3 can be followed, because all flesh is like grass that withers when God's breath blows on it (v. 7).[22] The text form here employed to depict the issuance of new proclamation is so fresh and innovative—precisely in its indebtedness to a variety of older forms—that the text-critical tradition bears witness to a degree of puzzlement regarding the text's plain sense. To say that the text as rendered by a first-person "I" is clearer and that the form is thereby revealed to be a call narrative of the prophet Second Isaiah would be overstatement. The text is not operating in this climate of prophetic commissioning—familiar from independent prophetic books like Jeremiah, Ezekiel, or Hosea—precisely because it is not an independent book, but a new and later thing connected to an old and former thing.

To raise a question about the character of the opening unit as relating the prophet's call should also raise a question as to how the entire opening chapter should be properly divided or, better, what "divisions" mean as literary features within prophecy like this. At the heart of this characteristic of the discourse lie the seeds of the debate between strict form-critical versus rhetorical analysis.[23] That debate centered on two questions: (1) How independent were the individual units in Isaiah 40–55? (2) How related were they to one another, in the order we presently find them?

---

18. See the helpful discussion of R. F. Melugin, *The Formation of Isaiah 40–55,* BZAW 141 (Berlin: Walter de Gruyter, 1976) 82-86.

19. See C. R. Seitz, "The Divine Council: Temporal Transition and New Prophecy in the Book of Isaiah," *JBL* 109 (1990) 229-47.

20. See J. van Oorschot, *Von Babel zum Zion,* BZAW 206 (Berlin: Walter de Gruyter, 1993).

21. C. Westermann, *Isaiah 40–66,* trans. David Stalker, OTL (Philadelphia: Westminster, 1969) 7.

22. The fact that there is a text-critical problem here (DSS and LXX reading first-person "I"; so RSV, NRSV) should not push one toward simple this-or-that resolution. See D. Carr, "Reaching for Unity in Isaiah," *JSOT* 57 (1993). Rather, the text-critical problem inheres with the text's own intrinsic, complex presentation; text-critical divergences simply bear witness to this.

23. The flavor of that debate can be seen in irenic form in James Muilenburg's commentary in the *IB.*

There can be little doubt that the opening unit rounds itself off at the close of v. 11 and that at v. 12 a longer unit, with a loose structure provided by a series of rhetorical questions (note vv. 12-13, 18, 21, 25-28), begins.

Yet one feature is fully consistent with the unit that begins this discourse. The voice that speaks in 40:12-31 is not God's—who is referred to in the third person (with the single exception, perhaps rhetorically motivated, of v. 25)—but an unknown narrator. To say, instead, "this is the prophet speaking," would be to ignore the very problem, or characteristic feature, introduced in the opening unit, where the transition from God to voice to prophet seems particularly underdetermined. Who, for example, is speaking of God in the third person in v. 10? The prophet? The voice? These transitions are slippery and fully understated (see esp. the movement from v. 7 to v. 8). It is here that the opening unit of the discourse displays one striking divergence from other so-called heavenly commissioning scenes in the OT; in these the reader visits the divine realm and witnesses a transaction there between God and attendants, with a judgment or a charge delivered and received in anticipation of action in the mundane realm. In such scenes we can generally follow who is speaking to whom, even when the exchange is strange or obscure (e.g., "And the LORD answered gracious and comforting words to the angel who talked with me," Zech 1:13; cf. 1 Kgs 22:19-23; Job 1–2; Isa 6:1-13). At any event, when chap. 41 opens, God is speaking quite clearly and directly in the first person, and the characteristic feature of chap. 40 has given way to a different form of expression.

In sum, one feature holding the entire chapter together is the recession of the prophetic voice, as distinctly and independently depicted, and the emergence of voices—not God's—who nevertheless speak for God. These voices defend God and speak with an authority consistent with the divine realm. The spirit at work in the author of the proclamation to follow is one dispatched from the heavenly council, with an authority no earthly council can bestow or inspire. It is an authority based on the Word of God, which stands forever (40:8). God's Word, sovereign over flesh, grass, and the flower of the field (40:6-7), manifests now a sovereignty on the other side of withering and fading for God's people Israel. As for the rulers of the earth, "scarcely has their stem taken root in the earth, when he blows on them and they wither" (v. 24). The theme of God's sovereign, promised, and fulfilled purpose for the people and for the nations of the earth spans the two "units" of chap. 40 (vv. 1-11, 12-31). This theme serves as a fitting opening for the discourse to follow. The sovereign purposes of God are newly revealed; yet by their very nature they are eternally established in the will and character of God. Their import is differently conceived, however, for those who hear God's word (v. 8) and for the princes and rulers of the earth (vv. 23-24).

ISAIAH 40:1-11, A HIGHWAY FOR GOD

NIV	NRSV
40 Comfort, comfort my people, says your God.	**40** Comfort, O comfort my people, says your God.
² Speak tenderly to Jerusalem, and proclaim to her that her hard service has been completed, that her sin has been paid for, that she has received from the LORD's hand double for all her sins.	² Speak tenderly to Jerusalem, and cry to her that she has served her term, that her penalty is paid, that she has received from the LORD's hand double for all her sins.
³ A voice of one calling:	³ A voice cries out:

NIV

"In the desert prepare
  the way for the LORD[a];
make straight in the wilderness
  a highway for our God.[b]
[4]Every valley shall be raised up,
  every mountain and hill made low;
the rough ground shall become level,
  the rugged places a plain.
[5]And the glory of the LORD will be revealed,
  and all mankind together will see it.
    For the mouth of the LORD has spoken."

[6]A voice says, "Cry out."
  And I said, "What shall I cry?"

"All men are like grass,
  and all their glory is like the flowers of
    the field.
[7]The grass withers and the flowers fall,
  because the breath of the LORD blows
    on them.
Surely the people are grass.
[8]The grass withers and the flowers fall,
  but the word of our God stands forever."

[9]You who bring good tidings to Zion,
  go up on a high mountain.
You who bring good tidings to Jerusalem,[c]
  lift up your voice with a shout,
lift it up, do not be afraid;
  say to the towns of Judah,
  "Here is your God!"
[10]See, the Sovereign LORD comes with power,
  and his arm rules for him.
See, his reward is with him,
  and his recompense accompanies him.
[11]He tends his flock like a shepherd:
  He gathers the lambs in his arms
and carries them close to his heart;
  he gently leads those that have young.

[a]3 Or *A voice of one calling in the desert: / "Prepare the way for the
LORD*   [b]3 Hebrew; Septuagint *make straight the paths of our God*
[c]9 Or *O Zion, bringer of good tidings, / go up on a high mountain. /
O Jerusalem, bringer of good tidings*

NRSV

"In the wilderness prepare the way of
  the LORD,
make straight in the desert a highway for
  our God.
[4]Every valley shall be lifted up,
  and every mountain and hill be made low;
the uneven ground shall become level,
  and the rough places a plain.
[5]Then the glory of the LORD shall be revealed,
  and all people shall see it together,
for the mouth of the LORD has spoken."

[6]A voice says, "Cry out!"
  And I said, "What shall I cry?"
All people are grass,
  their constancy is like the flower of
    the field.
[7]The grass withers, the flower fades,
  when the breath of the LORD blows upon it;
  surely the people are grass.
[8]The grass withers, the flower fades;
  but the word of our God will stand forever.
[9]Get you up to a high mountain,
  O Zion, herald of good tidings;[a]
lift up your voice with strength,
  O Jerusalem, herald of good tidings,[b]
lift it up, do not fear;
say to the cities of Judah,
  "Here is your God!"
[10]See, the Lord GOD comes with might,
  and his arm rules for him;
his reward is with him,
  and his recompense before him.
[11]He will feed his flock like a shepherd;
  he will gather the lambs in his arms,
and carry them in his bosom,
  and gently lead the mother sheep.

[a]Or *O herald of good tidings to Zion*   [b]Or *O herald of good tidings to Jerusalem*

COMMENTARY

God here announces in terse fashion the intention for the people and for the city, Jerusalem (vv. 1-2). This statement, issued within God's own council, stands over the entire discourse that follows and stipulates the terms with which God is now prepared to treat a people once deaf and blind (6:10) and a city once a whore (1:21). There follows a series of reactions from the divine council (vv. 3-8), culminating in the announcement of a theophany (vv. 9-10), which holds the promise of gathering and protection for God's people (v. 11).

40:1-2. Plural imperatives are quite frequent in Isaiah 40–66 (see, e.g., 41:1; 42:10; 43:9; 44:23; 45:8, 20). Here it is not stipulated clearly who is being addressed (cf. 41:1). This gives the opening charge a certain lofty character, appropriate to its form and content. Those charged are told to comfort, speak, and cry. The voice in v. 3 does, in fact, "cry," and the voice of v. 6 reflects on a similar vocation, so it seems clear that these voices are the ones being charged. Moreover, as v. 1 speaks of "your [pl.] God," the first voice responds appropriately with first-person plural "our God" at v. 3. To say that these voices are the ones charged is, however, to remain in obscure terrain, since all that is stipulated about them is that they are voices. My position is that in vv. 1-2 God is charging those in the council. The notion of a divine entourage is familiar from the psalms (Psalm 82) as well as from other OT contexts.

In 1 Kings 22, when God addresses "all the host of heaven standing beside him on his right hand and on his left" (1 Kgs 22:19), the text reports a similar colloquy of voices in response: "Then one said one thing, and another said another" (1 Kgs 22:20). Isaiah 6 records that the seraphim who attend God both call to one another and speak out (6:3) in such a way that the prophet Isaiah is a witness to the effects of the voice that crys out (קול הקורא *qôl haqqôrē*)—namely, the shaking of the pivots of the threshhold of the Temple (6:4). The language employed in Isaiah 6 is quite similar to what we have here, while the scene of 1 Kings 22, with God dispatching the host in attendance for a specific task, matches fairly closely the opening charge of 40:1-2. This would not rule out some

critical reconfiguration of the actual terminology deployed in 1 Kings 22 (e.g., "all the host of heaven," 1 Kgs 22:22). As this chapter unfolds, when God speaks in the first person (vv. 25-26), it is to assert that the host are under God's control and that God calls them each by name.

What is intriguing in this connection is that something of the mechanics of how God's word gets spoken are revealed when one studies these heavenly council scenes. There is a sort of deployment phase, as God speaks and then that will is communicated subsequently, through voices, spirits, or seraphic attendants. It is important to keep this in mind as we reflect on the charge given concerning "my people" and Jerusalem. Comfort is not instantaneously experienced, and while the term has been served, the penalty has been paid, and the sins have been completely punished, it belongs to the mediation of the discourse of Isaiah 40–66 to drive that fact home.

There is division of opinion regarding the plain sense of "double" payment in v. 2. Some believe this refers to a payment in surplus ("she has paid overmuch"). Others consider the Hebrew word כפלים (*kiplayim*) to be more in the direction of "complete" or "full," and so without surplus. If we consider the larger context of the proclamation as a whole, it is clear in the later depiction of Zion as regarding her suffering as enormous (see, e.g., 49:14). There is, however, no explicit statement from Zion that her punishment was intended by God as a form of *unjust* humiliation—an overdoing of it, a gratuitous affliction, as it were. It is probably safest to conclude that we are hearing from God's own council a verdict that ought to quell all doubt: Zion is fully forgiven. She has paid all that God required her to pay, and the term of service is over. The judgment, first visited upon the cities of Judah by Assyria, then upon Zion by Babylon, constitutes all that was necessary, and a new day is now dawning.

40:3-5. The divine attendants act independently, though the text does not reflect on this reality for its own sake. The voice responds appropriately to the charge of God to "cry"; yet the content of what is proclaimed is fresh and beyond what the opening verses had asked for. Moreover, what the narrator hears from this voice is not relevant for Jerusalem or God's own people only. Creation itself is affected. God's glory will be revealed, and "all people shall see it together" (v. 5).

Westermann is typical in considering the reference to the wilderness in v. 3 as that "which, of course, separates the people of Israel from their homeland."[24] Likewise, for the image of the "highway" (מסלה *mĕsillâ*) is frequently sought a Babylonian parallel, the great processional highways of gods and kings, prepared for triumphal entry into the city of Babylon. Very quickly this highway becomes the way for exiles to travel on their way back from Babylon to Jerusalem, as the two distinct concepts are merged, and wilderness becomes the specific territory separating the exiles from Jerusalem as once the wilderness lay between the promised land and Egyptian bondage.

Before moving too quickly to this popular "Second Exodus" interpretation, reinforced by a conception of the prophet Second Isaiah among exiles in Babylon, it is important to let the text have its say. There is as yet no reference to exiles in Babylon. The word pair "wilderness"/"desert" is familiar from 35:1, and there and elsewhere its primary referent is a "place of destruction's aftermath." The association of "haunt of jackals" in chap. 34 with the Lord's "day of judgment" is clear, and in chap. 35 this same "haunt" appears in connection with the blooming wilderness:

> For waters shall break forth in the wilderness
>   and streams in the desert;
> the burning sand shall become a pool,
>   and the thirsty ground springs of water.
>   (35:6-7 NRSV)

In this place of judgment's aftermath and God's reversal of that, there will be a highway leading to Zion (35:8-10). The desolation of the earth and its reduction to desert as a consequence of massive divine judgment is the chief theme of chaps. 24–27, and one can spot it more specifically tied to Jerusalem in chap. 1, where Jerusalem has become almost as desolate as Sodom and Gomorrah (1:7-9).

What these verses mean to relate is a massive upheaval and reversal in nature, signaling the end of Zion's desolation and the appearance of God's glory, like the rainbow after the flood, for all

people to see. The way of the Lord and the highway of God are as yet only related to this theophanic context, and we have yet to move, as happens eventually in chap. 35, from a description of theophany and the reversal of judgment marked in creation, to God's way becoming the way for the ransomed to come to Zion. Instead, following the charge to address Zion/Jerusalem in v. 2, a divine attendant calls for preparation for God's way in the wilderness. The coming of God will mean upheavals in the created realm, but especially in the place where once God had come in judgment. This "wilderness" lies not between Zion and Babylon, but constitutes the graphic location of God's wrath in judgment. So Zion has her own "waste and desolate places" (49:19), and the Lord "will comfort Zion; he will comfort all her waste places, and will make her wilderness like Eden, her desert like the garden of the LORD" (51:3). The way that leads to Zion does not stretch from Babylon; it is, rather, the way that erupts in the desert Zion had become but is no longer, that gives right-of-way to all Israel wherever she had been cast forth in judgment.

There has been a creative adaptation of two related notions in the OT. On the one hand, God's choice of Zion and ongoing support of her is likened, especially in the psalms, to the signal act of creation, such that if this were canceled or annulled in judgment, the world would, in fact, fall back into chaos. It would be a desert. At the same time, the judgment wrought upon God's people has had as its specific consequence the dispersion of God's people among the nations round about, to the "four corners of the earth" (11:12). Unlike the first exodus, God's people did not migrate peaceably into a region beyond, later to encounter a pharaoh who knew not Joseph; they were sent forth in judgment. In the language of God's word to Isaiah, where the timetable for judgment is set forth:

> "Until cities lie waste without inhabitant,
> and houses without people,
>   and the land is utterly desolate;
> until the LORD sends everyone far away."
>   (6:11-12*a* NRSV)

The act that initiates their return, that signals the time has come, is God's decision, announced by an attendant, to set in the desert *God's* way. This way is the way of restoration, and it belongs to God.

24. Westermann, *Isaiah 40–66*, 37.

It was remarked that the voice speaking in these verses does not simply respond to the opening charge, but speaks of matters over and above what was said by God there. The final line of v. 5 makes it clear, however, that what is being said is what God had already said, "for the mouth of the LORD has spoken." This may well mean that the divine attendant is actually quoting a word that we can track down, that already exists in the record. If so, the significance of chaps. 34–35 and their location within the "former things" of Isaiah is underscored, for there we learn not only that the judgment God will exact will reduce the world and Zion within it to a wilderness, but also that the "desert shall rejoice and blossom" (35:1), the glory of the Lord will be seen beyond Israel (35:2), and "a highway shall be there," where once there had been desert.

40:6-8. That the heavenly assembly is not marked by unrefracted obedience and praise is evident in the majority of the OT accounts in which such scenes are described in detail. There is the enticing spirit who goes out and becomes a lying spirit in the mouth of the prophets (1 Kgs 22:22); in Psalm 82, children of the Most High are summarily demoted from their high place in the divine council for failing to judge with impartiality. Both Zechariah and Job know of a single figure in the heavenly court who is an accuser and spotter of human infraction, according to his own standard (Job 1:6-12; Zech 3:1-2). In Job, the שׂטן (śāṭān) walks the earth and is given a distinct measure of evil independence.

It is not clear whether the voice of v. 6 that reflects on the inconstancy of human nature rises to this level or not. Problematic is the translation of the second line of the verse, where the MT has (instead of "And I said") "and one said" or "and he said" (third-person singular masculine). Even this leaves it unclear whether the objection is lodged by the same voice who says, "Cry out!" or another voice in the heavenly assembly. The verb אמר ('mr, "say") is used at 39:8 to indicate interior reflection ("for he thought," consecutive form), so we might translate: "A voice says, 'Cry out!' but then considered, 'what shall I cry?' " Reference was made above to the significance of the text-critical confusion, and it would seem prudent to respect that. I have argued elsewhere that one can explain a shift toward a first-person "and I said" as accommodating

a prophetic "I" much easier than a movement toward the present reading of the MT.[25] For the purposes of this discussion, that reading will be pursued here.

The image of grass applied to human endeavor can be found at Isa 37:27, where God describes fortified cities crashing into ruins, becoming like tender grass vulnerable to blight. Also at 28:1 the "fading flower" is used as a description of the garland on the head of the "drunkards of Ephraim." So the voice is not telling a lie, even as he dwells on the negative (so also the *satan* in Job). The NRSV renders the difficult Hebrew חסדו (ḥasdô) of v. 6b as "constancy," and this is a good solution for an unusual usage of the common חסד (ḥesed, "steadfast love"), here given a third-person masculine suffix. The connections that have been argued to exist between this "prologue" and an "epilogue" found at chap. 55 were mentioned earlier. Whatever the merits of such a theory, it is striking that while here reference is made to the inconstancy of human nature, there (55:3) the steadfast love God has for David is enlarged to include the people, with whom an everlasting covenant is made. What the voice remarks is lacking in mortals, God will supply, as if the entire nation were David. Yet within the context of this scene, no effort is made to counter the observation that grass withers and flowers fade, and such is humanity. God's spirit can wreak an awesome judgment on humanity, and in fact that has happened. Yet the word spoken in judgment has also spoken in promise, and that word endures forever (v. 7) and is now on the horizon of fulfillment.

40:9-11. The opening scene reaches its culmination in these verses. The argument against the appositional rendering of מבשרת ציון (mĕbaśśeret ṣiyyôn) as "O Zion, herald of good tidings" (NRSV) is cumulative in character; the NIV translation, then, is preferred here: "you who bring good tidings to Zion." Zion is nowhere depicted in the active role of a tidings bringer anywhere else in chaps. 40–66; nowhere else are the "cities of Judah" the special recipients of tidings from Zion; and elsewhere when mention is made of a tidings-bearer, the recipient is Zion/Jerusalem ("I give to Jerusalem a מבשר [mĕbaśśēr]," 41:27; "how beautiful upon the mountains are the feet of the

---

25. See Carr, "Reaching for Unity in Isaiah."

"messenger" *mĕbaśśēr*... who says to Zion, 'Your God reigns,' " 52:7). The similarity of the last reference to vv. 9-11 is unmistakable and, indeed, argues for an intentional association.

What has probably given rise to the appositional reading is the fact that a feminine participial form appears here, in distinction to the other passages. But forms such as these are familiar elsewhere in the OT (קהלת *qôhelet*, "the Preacher"), and the exact gender of the messenger cannot necessitate an appositional reading. Zion's *mĕbaśśeret*, who is instructed to speak to the cities of Judah, is so closely identified with Zion that a feminine form and feminine imperatives are used. The "bearer of good tidings" is Zion's own special emissary and emblem who gets up on a high mountain in order best to see God's approach on the horizon. It was the job of the tidings-bearer to announce the results of warfare, and they were usually dispatched from the front (see 2 Sam 18:19-30). Here the scenario is altered for dramatic effect, since God has won the victory without Israel's help. What is announced to the cities of Judah is God's triumphal arrival, which these outlying cities will witness first before God's return and entrance into Zion, as the heavenly emissary had announced (vv. 3-5) with a word based on the promises of chaps. 34–35. Just as the cities of Judah had been the first to bear the brunt of Sennacherib's assaults, so also they are first to witness God's victory and triumph. The ultimate "comforting" of Zion is God's own final reclaiming of her, and the depiction of that is dramatically portrayed in later chapters.

In sum, the herald of good tidings is not Zion, but is Zion's representative. This emissary speaks first to the cities of Judah, announcing God's victorious entrance, before tidings are delivered to Zion herself (so 41:27; 52:7).

It is striking how a conventional scene of battle victory and triumphal entry has here been subtly altered, with God as lone victor, Zion as comforted bride, heralds sent forth for news of a triumph in a battle they were not aware was taking place. Most striking is the portrayal of the final verse. The victor typically comes home with spoils of war, with booty, with "reward and recompense" (v. 10). In the days of holy war, this booty, "man and woman, child and infant, ox and sheep, camel and donkey," was to be given over to God, whose victory it was (see 1 Sam 15:1-35). But here the booty is of a different order, appropriate to this unconventional victory and victor. Driven like a flock before a careful shepherd, and even carried on the arm of battle, are the spoils of war, God's own children, returned to Mother Zion, under the images of lambs and nursing mothers. Here we have but an adumbration of a scene of reunion that is spelled out in greater detail in the second major section of this powerful discourse (49:14 and following chapters). So while this opening unit is not a prologue in the strict sense, it does depict from the standpoint of the heavenly council events that will transpire in the course of the chapters to follow.

REFLECTIONS

In the reflections here and throughout the remainder of Isaiah 40–66, I will seek to illustrate key theological issues that the relevant portion of text raises, especially problems or theological challenges a close reading of Isaiah may evoke. As a general rule, the reflections begin with close exegetical questions that the text engenders, often as a consequence of the way the text has been traditionally heard or reinterpreted in the New Testament. Where multiple reflections are included, they should move in the general direction of more topicality. The reflections are not intended, however, to displace the work of the preacher or teacher, nor are they to generate set answers to problems in such a timebound way that they are out of date for a next generation. The main concern of the reflections is simple: Allow the edge of the text to assert itself.

With the earliest readers of Scripture, the church fathers, what we wish to know is the text's plain sense. Then what we desire is obedience. With these two in place—an exegetical and an ascetical discipline—our duty before God's Word should be clear.

1. In the reading presented here, the prophet "Second Isaiah" never appears at all. The

literature shows no interest in grounding the bold proclamation in flesh and blood in a new prophet, but is content to let God and the heavenly assembly speak. What is spoken is both new and old, promised and unexpected. What has been forgotten is brought to mind by God and the heavenly servants. There is emerging within Israel a legacy of faithful speech and testimony, to which appeal can be made. As Zechariah understands it, while individual prophets do not live forever, the word God has spoken to them and through them has the power to outlive them, to survive and speak a word on another day, overtaking and ambushing generation after generation (Zech 1:5-6). Indeed, that is exactly what prophecy—true prophecy—is: an accomplishing word, landing again and again to speak a new word to a new generation from the vortex of lived experience with the Holy One of Israel, by God's servants the prophets. Prophecy is not dying out; it is being transformed in ways that make it forever reliable and forever alive. Even the heavenly voice speaks a word that had already been delivered in Israel.

Herein lies the mystery of these Isaiah chapters, now found within a larger prophetic word, that no reconstruction of a new prophet should seek to undo. God can take out of the treasure house things old and new and in so doing remind us that God's word always comes out of the void, however much we can contextualize it and understand its origins. And that is what also makes it possible for it to speak yet again.

Were it otherwise, domestication or magical repetition would set in, and God's voice would be stilled and controlled. But God refuses to speak on terms other than God's own. "My thoughts are not your thoughts," God will later say.

The reason for such care in handling God's word, in attending to the form of God's mode of speaking, is that it inheres with God's identity. Exegesis is always a combination of prayer, care, and obedience to what lies before us in the text. No generation exhausts this. Each generation learns afresh. But God's Word will abide forever.

2. In the New Testament, John the Baptist does not say he is "the prophet," understood as the forerunner for the Christ, or the Christ himself, when questioned by priests and Levites from Jerusalem (John 1:19-23). The heavenly voice directing speech to the wilderness becomes the voice of John in the wilderness: "I am the voice of one crying out in the wilderness . . . as the prophet Isaiah said" (John 1:23 NRSV). Just as in the opening scene of Isaiah 40, the word of God has generated something new and something old, whose truthfulness will be measured by God's ensuing work and word. What is old is the command to "make straight the way of the LORD." In every age only faithfulness to this command can make room for God's dramatic victory and entrance into the desert of our lives, where judgment and defeat are signs of God's clearing away the brush and dry rot that have kept God safely at distance.

John has not misread Isa 40:3. The voice that cries there from heaven is his own voice in his own day. Their message, this hidden Isaiah's and John's, is the same one, and John has no doubt whatsoever that he has been dispatched for the task he is undertaking by God and that it will entail a special revelation to Israel of God's own son (John 1:31-34). There is a congruence between the old word from Isaiah and the new circumstances in which he has stepped out in faith that can only be described as the accomplishing power of God's Word in history. John says "to the cities of Judah, 'Here is your God!' " (Isa 40:9*b* NRSV) with the words, "Here is the Lamb of God who takes away the sin of the world!" (John 1:29 NRSV). The lamb being carried on God's victorious arm (Isa 40:11) is carried forth here as well, for a different task in a different day, as old word and new word converge for a final dramatic purpose.

3. At the convergence of new word and old word in this Isaiah discourse, there is a discouraging word as well: "All people are grass, their constancy like the flower of the field" (40:6 NRSV). When God decides to do a new thing in a dramatic way, there is resistance at the very highest level. Its force can be felt throughout all creation, and we can feel it at times as a force within the marrow of our bones; we know it is larger than us, that it demands our cooperation, and that it can only be halted at the highest level. No sooner does the Spirit come upon Jesus than he is driven by that same Spirit into the wilderness from which the voice heralding him from Isaiah first spoke (Mark 1:1-13). A battle must be fought, and the evil one must be acknowledged as a word to be faced. There can be no repression of this difficult truth, accompanying God's promises for good and intended victories on our behalf. Isaiah 40 does not hide from this reality. The voice is heard along with the others.

In Isaiah, the victory of God is dramatically that of God's flock and the people Israel, a triumph for the defeated Jerusalem and the cities of Judah. But the despondent voice does not single out God's people only: "all people are grass"—Israel and the nations alike. It will require a yet greater act of victory, foreshadowed by the one here as a combination of sheer triumphant might and tender compassion (40:10-11), for that voice to be stilled as a rival to God's intentions for Israel and for all people. The victory is not one we can effect by an act of will, from the side of our flesh. It must come with the fullest initiative of God, to whom our wills must be conformed and conjoined, through acts of daily preparation for the way of the Lord.

4. Our Advent and Christmas hymns rejoice with the words of Isaiah, "Comfort, comfort my people." Just as at Isaiah 40, a new day dawns with the birth of Jesus Christ. But Jesus does not come as a bolt from the blue or from a history leading into a void.[26] He comes prepared by former things. So our rejoicing stands in continuity with the praises of Israel. Luke captures this well by showing the faithful within the bosom of Israel, filled with the Holy Spirit, as those who first bear witness to the coming of John and Jesus Christ. Their joy comes both at what is totally new, even beyond their wildest imagination, and at how what is new fulfills dreams long cherished: "Blessed be the Lord God of Israel, for he has visited his people and redeemed them" (Luke 1:68). Comfort comes to those who are prepared, who have waited, whose sins God has forgiven in Christ.

Our received testimony from Isaiah comes in two main parts, a former and a latter part, and it mirrors the canon of Christian Scripture.[27] Our joy at Christmas is being brought within the fellowship of Jesus Christ, the hope of Israel and the "light for revelation to the Gentiles" (Luke 2:32 NRSV). When Simeon looks for the consolation of Israel (Luke 2:25), he is looking for what Isaiah announced in his day. At both times the former thing of Isaiah—from Isaiah the Former for our discourse and from Isaiah the Latter for Simeon—gave words to guide his joy. In both cases, the new thing that evokes such joy is the "knowledge of salvation . . . by the forgiveness of their sins" (Luke 1:77 NRSV).

It is difficult, therefore, to pull apart forgiveness of sins and the announcement of comfort before God's new and dramatic act in Jesus Christ. They come both at the same time, and for this reason our joy is overflowing. The former word of promise and the new word of fulfillment double what we might ever have imagined true joy to be.

26. R. Bultmann, "The Significance of Jewish Old Testament Tradition for the Christian West," in *Rudolf Bultmann: Essays Philosophical and Theological* (New York: Macmillan, 1955) 262-72.
27. C. R. Seitz, " 'Of Mortal Appearance': Earthly Jesus and Isaiah as a Type of Christian Scripture," *Ex Auditu* 14 (1998) 31-41.

ISAIAH 40:12-31, PRE-TRIAL STATEMENT

NIV

¹²Who has measured the waters in the hollow
  of his hand,
  or with the breadth of his hand marked off
    the heavens?
Who has held the dust of the earth in a basket,
  or weighed the mountains on the scales
  and the hills in a balance?
¹³Who has understood the mind[a] of the LORD,
  or instructed him as his counselor?
¹⁴Whom did the LORD consult to enlighten him,
  and who taught him the right way?
Who was it that taught him knowledge
  or showed him the path of understanding?

¹⁵Surely the nations are like a drop in a bucket;
  they are regarded as dust on the scales;
  he weighs the islands as though they were
    fine dust.
¹⁶Lebanon is not sufficient for altar fires,
  nor its animals enough for burnt offerings.
¹⁷Before him all the nations are as nothing;
  they are regarded by him as worthless
  and less than nothing.

¹⁸To whom, then, will you compare God?
  What image will you compare him to?
¹⁹As for an idol, a craftsman casts it,
  and a goldsmith overlays it with gold
  and fashions silver chains for it.
²⁰A man too poor to present such an offering
  selects wood that will not rot.
He looks for a skilled craftsman
  to set up an idol that will not topple.

²¹Do you not know?
  Have you not heard?
Has it not been told you from the beginning?
Have you not understood since the earth
  was founded?
²²He sits enthroned above the circle of the earth,
  and its people are like grasshoppers.
He stretches out the heavens like a canopy,
  and spreads them out like a tent to live in.
²³He brings princes to naught
  and reduces the rulers of this world to nothing.

ᵃ13 Or *Spirit* ; or *spirit*

NRSV

¹²Who has measured the waters in the hollow
  of his hand
  and marked off the heavens with a span,
enclosed the dust of the earth in a measure,
  and weighed the mountains in scales
  and the hills in a balance?
¹³Who has directed the spirit of the LORD,
  or as his counselor has instructed him?
¹⁴Whom did he consult for his enlightenment,
  and who taught him the path of justice?
Who taught him knowledge,
  and showed him the way of understanding?
¹⁵Even the nations are like a drop from a bucket,
  and are accounted as dust on the scales;
  see, he takes up the isles like fine dust.
¹⁶Lebanon would not provide fuel enough,
  nor are its animals enough for a burnt
    offering.
¹⁷All the nations are as nothing before him;
  they are accounted by him as less than
    nothing and emptiness.

¹⁸To whom then will you liken God,
  or what likeness compare with him?
¹⁹An idol? —A workman casts it,
  and a goldsmith overlays it with gold,
  and casts for it silver chains.
²⁰As a gift one chooses mulberry wood[a]
  —wood that will not rot—
then seeks out a skilled artisan
  to set up an image that will not topple.

²¹Have you not known? Have you not heard?
  Has it not been told you from the
    beginning?
Have you not understood from the
  foundations of the earth?
²²It is he who sits above the circle of the earth,
  and its inhabitants are like grasshoppers;
who stretches out the heavens like a curtain,
  and spreads them like a tent to live in;
²³who brings princes to naught,
  and makes the rulers of the earth as
    nothing.

ᵃMeaning of Heb uncertain

NIV

²⁴No sooner are they planted,
    no sooner are they sown,
    no sooner do they take root in the ground,
than he blows on them and they wither,
    and a whirlwind sweeps them away
        like chaff.

²⁵"To whom will you compare me?
    Or who is my equal?" says the Holy One.
²⁶Lift your eyes and look to the heavens:
    Who created all these?
He who brings out the starry host one by one,
    and calls them each by name.
Because of his great power and mighty
        strength,
    not one of them is missing.

²⁷Why do you say, O Jacob,
    and complain, O Israel,
"My way is hidden from the LORD;
    my cause is disregarded by my God"?
²⁸Do you not know?
    Have you not heard?
The LORD is the everlasting God,
    the Creator of the ends of the earth.
He will not grow tired or weary,
    and his understanding no one can fathom.
²⁹He gives strength to the weary
    and increases the power of the weak.
³⁰Even youths grow tired and weary,
    and young men stumble and fall;
³¹but those who hope in the LORD
    will renew their strength.
They will soar on wings like eagles;
    they will run and not grow weary,
    they will walk and not be faint.

NRSV

²⁴ Scarcely are they planted, scarcely sown,
    scarcely has their stem taken root in
        the earth,
when he blows upon them, and they wither,
    and the tempest carries them off like
        stubble.

²⁵ To whom then will you compare me,
    or who is my equal? says the Holy One.
²⁶ Lift up your eyes on high and see:
    Who created these?
He who brings out their host and
        numbers them,
    calling them all by name;
because he is great in strength,
    mighty in power,
    not one is missing.

²⁷ Why do you say, O Jacob,
    and speak, O Israel,
"My way is hidden from the LORD,
    and my right is disregarded by my God"?
²⁸ Have you not known? Have you not heard?
The LORD is the everlasting God,
    the Creator of the ends of the earth.
He does not faint or grow weary;
    his understanding is unsearchable.
²⁹ He gives power to the faint,
    and strengthens the powerless.
³⁰ Even youths will faint and be weary,
    and the young will fall exhausted;
³¹ but those who wait for the LORD shall renew
        their strength,
    they shall mount up with wings like eagles,
they shall run and not be weary,
    they shall walk and not faint.

COMMENTARY

Chapter 41 introduces a trial scene that continues for a further eight chapters. This backdrop is implicit, but it extends through chap. 48 and forms a loose organizing structure for the various units of speech found there.

Preceding this, a long speech is made on behalf of God (40:12-31). It is directly attached to the opening statement from the heavenly council (40:1-11) and forms its appropriate continuation.

There is no reason to speak of another voice at work here than the voice that last spoke in v. 11. Thundering forth from the divine council is a statement reminding Israel who the Lord is. The statement defines God's relationship to the nations, to other gods, to idolatry, to the divine testimony already delivered, and to those who would speak on God's behalf from the divine assembly. This is a pre-trial statement, made to Israel, before the lens widens and others find themselves summoned to the divine courtroom to be witnesses, litigants, defendants, and, on occasion, accused. The judge in all of this is the Holy One of Israel, the Lord of all creation.

Characteristic of this extended section is the posing of questions, the answers to which are not so much given as inferred or left hanging over the listener. Most commentators note the resemblance between the form deployed here and in the book of Job, in the divine speech from the whirlwind (Job 38:1–41:34), where God poses a series of questions that put Job off guard. It is not clear, however, that such is the purpose of this speech, which falls short of pure disputation. Also, the speeches of Job are defenses of God by God, with an intentional piling-up of the first person. This serves to underscore that Job is meeting God, and not another, eye to eye (Job 42:5).

The point of this long speech, moreover, is at a considerable distance from rebuff. Those addressed here are not being shown something new or something on the far horizon of what they might have thought about God (cf. Job 42:5). The speech intends to drive home matters about God that Israel already knows but has forgotten, and its final purpose is to lift up, to increase strength, to bolster and rejuvenate (40:28-31). The appeal here is not to something unknown or insufficiently grasped, but precisely to something Israel has known and heard and been shown from eternity, from the very foundation of the heavens and the earth (vv. 21, 28).

40:12-17. The units in this speech are not to be divided sharply, and the divisions followed here are for convenience of treatment only. The first one insists that the creative order and design, everywhere visible, has its source in only one place: Israel's Lord. God does not take counsel and instruction, but gives it. As was argued in the Overview, the basis for these assertions about God is not general philosophical observation and deduction, though that is fine so far as it goes. Rather, appeal is made to a testimony in the record bequeathed to Israel; that is, when the nations are most elaborately prepared for mighty demonstrations of power, precisely then they are brought low. This is the testimony of Isa 36:1–37:38, in the contest between Yahweh and the king of Assyria. In other words, what the voice here

asserts is that God's power in creation is not a one-time demonstration from which God now stands back. Rather, creation consists of the will of God manifesting itself on a daily basis in the destinies of all nations. That which appears to us to be the most obvious, present mobilization of daily authority—that of earthly national power—is before God's will mere vapor (v. 17).

Note that the particular collocation of creative and national authority introduced here (in the transition from v. 14 to v. 15) is characteristic of the entire chapter. In this way, the created order and God's superintendence of the nations are decisively connected (vv. 12-14 and 15-17; vv. 21-22 and 23-24; vv. 25-27 and 28-31). The reverse direction—from national might to powerful use/misuse of the created order—is familiar at other points in Isaiah. Sennacherib boasts of felling Lebanon's tallest trees and boring to the earth's recesses for water, and even drying up the streams of Egypt (37:24-25). Similar language is used of Babylon (14:8), within a span or realm almost broader than creation's limits, from Sheol to the stars of heaven and beyond (14:9-14). Similar expressions of national power exhibited through manipulation of nature are found throughout the oracles against the nations (chaps. 13–23). Yet before God, the nations are less than תהו (*tōhû*; NRSV, "emptiness," v. 17). This is the same word used in Gen 1:1 to designate the primal void existing before God's purposeful, good creative act. Less than this primal void are the nations, at their most powerful reach.

40:18-20. Many regard this unit as intrusive, belonging to a secondary layer concerned with applying the prophet's teaching to the specific problem of idolatry (see esp. 44:9-20). Westermann excises vv. 19-20 in order to keep the focus on the incomparability of Yahweh, rather than the fashioning of idols.[28] It is possible that the reference to Lebanon's, famous for its great forests (37:24), not having sufficient wood for a suitable offering for God (40:16) has triggered a reference to the sort of fine wood necessary for good idol manufacture. Instead of offering to God the fruit of God's own created bounty and largesse, one takes

---

28. C. Westermann, *Isaiah 40–66*, trans. David Stalker, OTL (Philadelphia: Westminster, 1969). Westermann, *Isaiah 40–66*, 54, here follows Bernhard Duhm. Compare the treatment of J. Barr, *Biblical Faith and Natural Theology* (Oxford: Clarendon, 1993).

the best of creation and fashions an idol out of it, using special human skill and ingenuity. The wrongful manipulation of nature by powerful nations has its religious counterpart. (The same connection is likewise made clear at 37:19.)

40:21-24. Here and at v. 28 an appeal is made to what Israel already knows and has heard and has been told. Again, it belongs to the way God has created the world (which Israel should remember) that the destinies of nations and rulers are under God's authority. The assertion of this fact, from the divine council, is clearly being made in the face of a rival view of the matter. We can get glimpses of this view by examining relevant ancient Near Eastern literature, with its rival cosmogonies. Alternatively, one can glean a partial picture by looking at the OT's own indigenous understanding of the claims with which foreign powers validate and undergird their activity.

In Isaiah 14, Babylon is addressed as an astral deity, which ascends back to heaven, having won mighty victories (14:12-13). Reaching the very height of the clouds, all the military victories find their deepest motivation revealed at last: "I will make myself like the Most High" (14:14). Yet the Lord does not live in the heavens, like a star, but creates them, and "sits above the circle of the earth" (40:22). You cannot reach the Lord, even when that is your deepest motivation, but will at greatest reach appear a mere grasshopper. Identification with an astral deity does not mean you return from where you first came, when victory establishes that some cherished "god" has blessed your endeavors. No one was with God when the world was established. Israel's creation account makes that clear.

In Psalm 82, we have a depiction that also lies close at hand. Nations have their "gods." Yet if justice and protection of the weak are not exhibited, these gods are no better than mortals, and they will "fall like any prince" (Ps 82:7). In v. 21, the MT reads, literally, "Have you not understood the foundations of the earth?" Yet under the influence of the temporal perspective introduced in the second line, the text is frequently emended (as in the NRSV), "Have you not understood *from* the foundations of the earth?" Psalm 82 also mentions the earth's foundations as being shaken and threatened (Ps 82:5) because of the unjust rule of national "gods." The founding of the earth

excludes rival deities, or even divine consultants, according to vv. 12-14. To understand the way God has created the world—and this Israel has known, has heard, has been told—is to know that no ruler can claim identity with God or gods, and no divine endorsement or undergirding is responsible for victories that are in turn rewarded by a return to the heavenly place. To go that high is to make the very foundations of the earth shake, and the result is a fall into the depths of Sheol, to visit the graves of other such claimants (14:15-20).

The final verse of this passage (v. 24) also reports a fact to which Israel can make clear reference in the literary record. The fate of Assyria is depicted with much of this same language (chap. 10). No sooner does Assyria "take root" in the earth for a task of administering God's justice against Israel, than its boughs are lopped off with terrifying power (10:33). Finally, Isa 37:27 uses the image of tender field grass, "scorched before it grows up" (NIV), and this is the same image the despondent voice of 40:6 uses of "all people." Yet here the application is specifically to "princes and rulers," the lofty in distinction to those who wait on God (so the next unit).

40:25-31. The final unit offers the closest formal parallel to actual disputation, with its reference to Israel's complaint against God.[29] Up to this point we have been left in the dark as to Israel's specific state of mind. This offers among other things a brilliant transition from the speech of the heavenly council, made on behalf of God, to the trial proper, which opens in chap. 41. That transitional character is further underscored with the appearance of first-person speech at v. 25, the only such speech of its kind in this pre-trial statement from the heavenly council. The effect here is to relativize even the speech made on behalf of God, in preparation for God's own address, beginning with the divine summoning of the farthest nations to a trial in 41:1.

In this opening chapter, we have closely observed the depictions of heavenly council scenes as these appear in the OT and alongside them descriptions of national triumph and power in relationship to the divine realm. In 1 Kings 22, it would appear that the voices that speak up and the

29. See R. F. Melugin, *The Formation of Isaiah 40–55,* BZAW 141 (Berlin: Walter de Gruyter, 1976) 35-36.

spirit that comes forward to entice the prophets belong to "the host of heaven" ranged to the right and left of God (1 Kgs 22:19). So, too, Babylon (Isa 14:12) is identified as the Day Star, son of Dawn (בן־שחר *ben-šāḥar*), a familiar Canaanite astral deity. However these several descriptions are to be fitted together, in this final unit it is made clear that the host of heaven is fully under the control of the One God, the Holy One, the Creator of heaven and earth. God calls them, having been the one who first gave them a name. This emphasis on God's total grasp of every star in the sky—not one missing—is meant to anticipate the concern of Jacob/Israel that somehow God has disregarded or forgotten about the way of the people. The one who calls each of the host of heaven by name and who can tell if just one is missing has an understanding that is unsearchable. The issue is not God's grasp, but Israel's weariness and exhaustion. The final verses allow God to get the true issue on the table, by ignoring the content of the disputation in the name of addressing the real underlying problem: Israel's exhaustion and weariness, which have been wrongly translated into disregard by God. But all this is still preliminary to God's fullest design, which will be to address Israel's concern in the context of a massive trial, before all the nations. This is neither a sentimental nor an intramural problem. It has to do with how Israel understands itself within the larger created order and how it properly understands God's superintendence of that order, which it has up to now misinterpreted.

REFLECTIONS

1. Two different views of prophecy have emerged in recent times. One regarded prophets as unique conduits for a divine word with no prior reference whatsoever, thus insisting on a detachment of the traditional linkage of "law and prophet." The prophet was Israel's religious genius. Nothing lay before him; the law was a later ossifying and conservative reaction. A second view was a modification of this extreme position, though it did not reject the basic notion of prophecy as a lively phenomenon pre-dating the finished Pentateuch, as a public, literary document. In this view, the prophet relied on traditions (rather than the law), and the prophetic genius consisted of proper reactualization and adaptation of a former theme or concept (e.g., exodus, David, Zion, wilderness) rooted in Israel's collective memory and kept alive within some religious setting.

The appeal made in Isaiah 40 is to something more formal than traditions. The piling up of exhortations ("have you not known, have you not heard, have you not been told") consists of an appeal to a public record, whose difference from the public records of other peoples and cultures is beginning to be felt—and felt strongly. What Israel knows is not general religious musing, more or less on target, but a quite specific account of how the world was made, how God chose a people, how God was and is God. There is nothing casual or serendipitous about what Israel knows of God, and precisely the possession and good stewardship of this knowledge is what it means for Israel to be God's elect people in the first place. Paul makes the same point: "They were entrusted with the oracles of God" (Rom 3:2).

It is striking that precisely at this moment of despair and darkness, the thing that is brought back to mind is just how precious and irreplaceable and life-giving is the word entrusted to Israel. It enlivens even the heavenly voices themselves. Indeed, here in Isaiah we see that what makes Israel different and capable of hope is possession of the special record, given to this people in trust. The question for the church today is whether it has retained this sense of the privilege of being in possession of God's word at all, even before the special character of that word and the special responsibility of attending to it is appreciated.

2. We know from earlier passages in Isaiah that an entire generation in Isaiah's lifetime had their ears shut and their eyes closed and that the word of God itself had this effect (Isa 6:9-10). Yet in chapter 40 a new generation is appealed to in the strongest possible terms: to listen and see and know again, for God's word does not require assent to remain true and abiding. Of its own nature, it is that. It stands forever (40:8). It was not that an entire generation did not have God's word present and alive around them; they did, and Isaiah continued to bear witness even as the word went unheeded. It was that the word was not heard, received, heeded in the manner God intended. Possession of God's word turned from joy to judgment.

What a strange, but accurate, perception it is that our ears must be opened to hear aright; hearing is more than sound waves bouncing off our inner ear, seeing more than light refracting off print. Each generation must be taught to hear and see by God. This reality stands at the absolute center of the book of Isaiah, as it moves from one epoch to another. It gives one pause to realize that it is more than possession of the right text or mere proximity to the word of God. A switch must be flipped, and no human hand can touch it. Isaiah lived with that reality day and night. It is no accident that as a new epoch begins, it begins with sustained speech by God, the only one capable of flipping that switch, together with obedient servants in the heavenly council.

3. We no longer live in a time when rival deities, national gods, or rival cosmogonies make clear, and divergent, claims on us, for which we are publicly accountable—at least not in the same way as Nisroch (Isa 37:38), Bel, and Nebo (Isa 46:1-2) jealously guard their identities and demand the loyalty of their worshipers. Yet we know that rival "theories" (e.g., the physical origin of the universe) and "mythologies" (Jung's "personality types") and "national epics" (the Romantic frontier; the global village) do, indeed, exist in our day, dealing with all aspects of human life and desire. Moreover, these are frequently coordinated with beliefs in God. Rarely, however, are these "theories" and "epics" given the personality and identity of what in Isaiah's day were called "gods." We are much more subtle, though ironically naive, in our polytheism and idolatry. Speaking about the privilege of Gentile inclusion, Robert Jenson states it this way:

> Precisely being able to turn from their gods to the true God occasioned "the joy" with which the apostles' gentile converts "received the word." In the act of faith, gentile believers recognize themselves as those who have worshiped or might have worshiped Moloch the baby-killer or Astarte the universal whore or *Deutsches Blut* or the Free Market or the Dialectic of History or the Metaphor of our gender or ethnic ressentiment, and on through an endless list of tyrants. Only a naivete impossible for the apostolic church, which fully inhabited the religious maelstrom of late antiquity, can think that religion as such is a good thing or that gods are necessarily beneficent.[30]

In the place of "gods" to worship, we have substituted the abstraction, "We all worship the same God." But the effect is largely the same. No particular claims for God's identity and action in time and space can be lodged, so God ends up a pluriform abstraction, exercising power in local, mysterious, and attenuated ways.

Animating this abstraction is a commitment to tolerance and civility, on the one hand, coupled with a universalistic instinct borne of an overwhelming awareness of the size and complexity and diversity of our world. Does such an abstraction, however, contain within it the power to actually stand in the way of comprehending how God might be actively, and distinctively, at work in the world today? As P. T. Forsyth insisted, the One God is Holy because holiness is an active will to create and impart God's own character to creatures.[31] God's jealousy is central to Old Testament convictions and insists above all else that God lays claim, for God's own sake and purposes.[32]

How are we to make sense of the Word of God from the Old Testament when it so clearly understands itself as a distinctive word? It requires enormous sensitivity and insight to translate

30. Robert Jenson, *The Triune God,* vol. 1 of *Systematic Theology* (New York: Oxford University Press, 1997) 50-51.

31. Lee Keck, *Who Is Jesus? History in Perfect Tense* (Columbia: University of South Carolina Press, 2000) 134-37. Quoting Forsyth, Keck summarizes his treatment of God's holiness, "Holiness is the eternal moral power which must do, and do, till it sees itself everywhere." See P. T. Forsyth, *Positive Preaching and the Modern Mind* (London: Independent Press, 1907) 240.

32. See Jenson's treatment of Yahweh's jealousy, *The Triune God,* 47.

the understanding of God and gods everywhere at work in the Old Testament—and the New—into a modern framework, and to do so with responsibility and accountability. Yet without this, the Word of God that sounds forth from the Bible will be patronized or consigned to a period we now reckon as quaint and old-fashioned—which view may effectively be closing ears for God's providential judgment in our day. The challenge is to let the Old Testament have its say about gods, jealousy, and the danger of polytheism and to follow where it leads.[33]

4. It is a difficult but essential discipline to learn how rightly to assess our degree of weariness and exhaustion in the walk of faith. Sometimes these twins are directly responsible for our inability to hear God, and for misunderstanding how God is actively at work. The final appeal of Isaiah 40 (vv. 27-31) acknowledges that Israel is convicted by a sense that God has abandoned her and no longer understands her way. God addresses this charge not by insisting Israel is wrong, that God has not disregarded her rights, but by strengthening and encouraging Israel and by insisting that weakness and powerlessness are never roadblocks to God's grace, while their opposites almost surely are. As for Israel's "right" (40:27), her sense of justice is forfeit; God will address that most pivotal concern at the proper moment and in the proper way (42:1-4). First, there must be a grounding and stabilizing of Israel at the most basic level, and for that only God's direct address concerning the deity and the record of God's past faithfulness will suffice (41:1-29).

The Old Testament records the cry of God's people, honest and anguished and bold. It records that God's people set their outrage and complaint before God as the one who is the source both of anguish and of hope. It records that God answers on those terms, yet with divine freedom and wisdom. It is on these same terms that we deal with the Holy One of Israel, whose faithfulness has been displayed before all the world in the raising of Jesus. There can be no place of discouragement, for all has been seen and lived and redeemed in the Son of God, to the glory of the Father. This means we know where our hope lies, eternally and surely.[34]

33. See J. C. O'Neill, *The Bible's Authority: A Portrait Gallery from Lessing to Bultmann* (Edinburgh: T. & T. Clark, 1991).

34. In his treatment of Job, Barth clearly sees that our protagonist never flees, seriously or sustainedly, to "another god" to deliver him from the One Lord Yahweh. See K. Barth, "The True Witness," in *Church Dogmatics,* vol. 4: *The Doctrine of Reconciliation* (Edinburgh: T. & T. Clark, 1961) IV.3.1. Quoting de Pury (against Luther), "The remarkable thing about this Book is that Job makes not a single step of flight to a better God, but stays resolutely on the field of battle under the fire of the divine wrath. He flees to the God whom he accuses" (424).

ISAIAH 41:1–48:22

Draw Near for Judgment

Overview

LITERARY STRUCTURE

Virtually all modern interpreters—including those, like Westermann, who are committed to traditional form-critical separation of individual units—argue for a major structural division of "Second Isaiah" into two halves.[35] This division seems appropriate for the following reasons: (1) The fixed pair, Jacob/Israel (introduced at 40:27), is addressed throughout chaps. 40–48, while from 49:14 onward, Zion/Jerusalem takes center stage. (2) A prominent theme introduced in chaps. 40–48 involves reference to "former things" over against "new things" and "latter things" (41:22-23; 42:9; 43:9, 18-19; 46:9-10; 48:3, 6), alongside a more general appeal to matters declared earlier to Israel (41:27; 45:21; 48:5). This theme is missing in the address to Zion in the second section. Indeed, the final reference makes it clear it is the last one, for now new things "created now, not long ago" (48:6) will be the subject of the discourse. (3) It is frequently pointed out that reference to Israel as servant is repeated throughout the first section (41:8-9; 42:19; 43:10; 44:1-2, 21, 26; 45:4), culminating in the redemption of "servant Jacob" at 48:20, while in the second section the term only appears in the so-called servant songs (49:6; 52:13). The single exception is to be found in 54:17, and there, strikingly, the term appears for the first time in the plural ("this is the heritage of the servants of the Lord"). This permits a transition to chaps. 56–66, where the term is always in the plural.[36]

Another way to put this is that Zion is not "servant," whoever the servant is, both inside and outside the traditional cycle of "servant poems." This explains why in the second section the term is less prominent.

Several other literary features can be added to bolster the argument for a division at chap. 49:

(1) There is a randomly placed (some disagree) series of brief hymnic portions, which are more prominent in the first section (42:10-13; 44:23; 45:8). The one that appears in the second section (49:13) may have to do with the significance of the transitional character of the first block of material (49:1-12), after which Zion is first introduced (49:14). When in chap. 54 Zion is directed to sing (54:1), we are no longer talking about a hymnic fragment, but something far more substantial.

(2) There is an interesting parallel between the opening appeal of chap. 41 ("Listen to me in silence, O coastlands") and that of chap. 49 ("Listen to me, O coastlands"), introducing the second major section. Such appeals appear only at these two points, introducing the two main sections of the discourse. Yet in the second section, the coastlands are not called by God, but by the servant, and what they are asked to attend to is a new thing regarding the destiny of the nations (49:6).

(3) I have argued elsewhere for a connection between the declaration of 48:7—that no longer will former things be appealed to, but rather "things created now"—and the emergence of the first true first-person voice that is not God's at 48:16.[37] This voice speaks again in 49:1-7 in a

35. See P. Wilcox and D. Paton-Williams, "The Servant Songs in Deutero-Isaiah," *JSOT* 42 (1988) 79-102. Their discussion of the "servant songs" involves a close analysis of the structure of chaps. 40–55. Westermann's structural argument can be found in the monograph. See C. Westermann, *Sprache und Struktur der Prophetie Deuterojesajas* (Stuttgart: Calwer, 1981). See also the fine discussion of R. F. Melugin, *The Formation of Isaiah 40–55*, BZAW 141 (Berlin: Walter de Gruyter, 1976).

36. W. A. M. Beuken, "The Main Theme of Trito-Isaiah, 'The Servants of YHWH,' " *JSOT* 47 (1990) 67-87.

37. See C. R. Seitz, "The Divine Council: Temporal Transition and New Prophecy in the Book of Isaiah," *JBL* 109 (1990) 245-47; C. R. Seitz, "How Is the Prophet Isaiah Present in the Latter Half of the Book? The Logic of Chapters 40–66 Within the Book of Isaiah," *JBL* 115 (1996) 233-36.

modified call narrative, showing us for the first time the actual "author" of the material before us. The "new things" are what we hear from chap. 49 onward, involving nations no longer on trial, but now serving as witnesses to a new work involving the servant (49:6-7).

(4) I am also less persuaded that the theory of a cycle of four servant songs, now broken up and distributed across the two main sections of the present collection, is persuasive.[38] The middle two are closely related; both are first-person reports (49:1-6; 50:4-9) followed by brief third-person commentary (49:7; 50:10-11). The final poem is quite distinctive (52:13–53:11). This leaves only one poem in the first section, and here one is struck by the fact that all the numerous surrounding references to "servant" clearly identify the servant as Israel—e.g., the first one at 41:8. This raises a question about whether a "cycle" extends across two very distinctive sections of discourse.

Two additional details should be briefly mentioned. The mission of Cyrus is a theme that extends no further than chap. 48. This is probably related to Babylon's downfall, depicted in chap. 47, and the charge for exiles to leave the city, which closes off the first section (48:20-22). Furthermore, older commentators noted the division of chaps. 40–66 into three sections of nine chapters each, closed by similar refrains regarding the fate of the wicked (49:22; 57:20-21; 66:24). The implications of this for our understanding of just how and where "Second Isaiah" chapters conclude will have to be taken up below. But this observation is consistent with the judgment that a major break is to be identified at the close of chap. 48.

A TRIAL SETTING?

The argument in favor of a distinctive section comprising chaps. 41–48 is at potential odds with the conclusion of form criticism that the basic building block of "Second Isaiah" is the individual genre unit. How can there be distinctive individual forms that at the same time are amenable to arrangement and coordination within a recognizable section? This is not the place to pursue this discussion in detail.[39]

One brief example can serve to illustrate the problem. Is it possible to talk about fifteen distinctive units of speech,[40] running through the first three chapters of this section (chaps. 41–43), which have nevertheless been meaningfully and purposefully ordered? Oracles of salvation, trial speeches, hymnic fragments, disputation, and "fear not" oracles stand side by side without obvious interpretive guidelines for integration. It seems obvious that the discourse represented by these chapters offers a bold and innovative adaptation of older prophetic works, by virtue of being found within a larger prophetic collection to begin with. In addition, it has been forcefully argued that the "author" has made use of traditional forms, but has done so in a distinctly literary way, which allows the freedom to shape and mold forms of speech that no longer have a point of origin—and therefore a certain fixity—in public, oral, spontaneous address. It is for this reason that one can talk about the possibility that diverse forms have been coordinated under a larger conceptual design that extends over a major literary section, in this case running from chap. 41 through chap. 48.

One specific formal marker can be identified throughout the first section. That is the appeal to draw near, present evidence, and produce witnesses, all pertinent to the setting of a trial.

> Let us together draw near for judgment. (41:1)
> Set forth your case . . . bring your proofs. (41:21)
> Who among you will give heed to this? (42:23)
> Let the peoples assemble. . . . Let them bring their witnesses. (43:9)
> Accuse me, let us go to trial; set forth your case. (43:26)
> Let them declare and set it forth before me. (44:7)
> Assemble yourselves and come together. (45:20)
> Declare and present your case. (45:21)
> Assemble, all of you, and hear! (48:14)

When one considers further that a trial consists of more than calling for litigants or rebuttal, even this listing is too restricted to one sort of formal marker of legal proceedings. The appeal to "former things," for example, which runs throughout this section, belongs to the evidentiary portion of the trial. The lamentation over Babylon, which com-

---

38. See T. N. D. Mettinger, *A Farewell to the Servant Songs,* Scriptora Minora 13 (Lund: Gleerup, 1983).

39. Melugin, *The Formation of Isaiah 40–55,* 93, has done a good job assessing the debate and offering his own proposal.

40. So C. Westermann, *Isaiah 40–66,* trans. David Stalker, OTL (Philadelphia: Westminster, 1969).

prises the entirety of chap. 47, is a brilliantly modified form of sentencing, appropriate to the literary character of this proceeding. The hymns serve to break up the movement (42:10-13; 44:23; 45:8) and offer a sort of modified "chorus," reminding us that it is, after all, the Lord of all the universe who here deigns to be put on trial, on behalf of the people Israel, before all the nations. Central to the Lord's defense, as we shall see, is the assertion that Cyrus is in fact doing not his own, but God's and Israel's bidding. That bit of evidence is introduced early on (41:25-29), is central to the section (45:1-7, 13), and keeps the discourse tied to historical realities that are presently unfolding (48:14-15).

The setting of a trial, with the coastlands as witnesses and creation as chorus, is furthermore compatible with the divine council setting with which the discourse opens. God announces the intention for Zion (40:1-2). The divine entourage lift their voices (40:3-31). God is introduced to Israel as the twin Lord of creation and national destinies, within which Israel has and continues to have special purpose. Then God initiates a solemn procedure, summoning to God's divine presence the widest possible audience for courtroom drama of the highest significance (41:1). The composition that follows reintroduces familiar prophetic speech forms, but now in service to one overarching drama, involving testimony from the past, fresh evidence, challenge and rebuttal, encouragement, hymnody, sarcasm, sentencing, and presentation of God's special servant before all there arrayed (42:1-4).

LITERARY UNITS

If the argument for a larger design, toward which individual formal units have been conformed, is convincing, this alters the way one thinks about dividing the text into smaller pericopes for discussion. The impression must be avoided that the most important context for interpretation is the historical setting out of which a given form was generated, since this is now fully subservient to the dramatic structure of the literary composition itself. These settings have become fossilized through the process of constructing a complex literary presentation, overshadowed by the creative activity of the "author" who has not slavishly reproduced older forms or worked within the constraints of an original situation-in-life. This is what it means to have "literary license."

For the purposes of this commentary treatment, the decision has been made to simply discuss one chapter at a time, examining the units that comprise that one block of material. No claim is being made for the importance of chapter divisions; in fact, the opposite conclusion is to be reached. The chapters represent arbitrary divisions within a larger structure and, therefore, neither detract from nor enhance that larger design. Instead, they present us with a reasonably sized collection of discourse, which will be further broken down in the course of the discussion.

ISAIAH 41:1-29, TWO CALLED, ONE CALLER

NIV

41 "Be silent before me, you islands!
Let the nations renew their strength!
Let them come forward and speak;
    let us meet together at the place of judgment.

2 "Who has stirred up one from the east,
    calling him in righteousness to his service[a]?
He hands nations over to him
    and subdues kings before him.

[a] 2 Or / whom victory meets at every step

NRSV

41 Listen to me in silence, O coastlands;
let the peoples renew their strength;
let them approach, then let them speak;
    let us together draw near for judgment.

2 Who has roused a victor from the east,
    summoned him to his service?
He delivers up nations to him,
    and tramples kings under foot;
he makes them like dust with his sword,

NIV

He turns them to dust with his sword,
  to windblown chaff with his bow.
³He pursues them and moves on unscathed,
  by a path his feet have not traveled before.
⁴Who has done this and carried it through,
  calling forth the generations from the
    beginning?
I, the LORD—with the first of them
  and with the last—I am he."

⁵The islands have seen it and fear;
  the ends of the earth tremble.
They approach and come forward;
⁶ each helps the other
  and says to his brother, "Be strong!"
⁷The craftsman encourages the goldsmith,
  and he who smooths with the hammer
  spurs on him who strikes the anvil.
He says of the welding, "It is good."
  He nails down the idol so it will not topple.

⁸"But you, O Israel, my servant,
  Jacob, whom I have chosen,
  you descendants of Abraham my friend,
⁹I took you from the ends of the earth,
  from its farthest corners I called you.
I said, 'You are my servant';
  I have chosen you and have not rejected you.
¹⁰So do not fear, for I am with you;
  do not be dismayed, for I am your God.
I will strengthen you and help you;
  I will uphold you with my righteous
    right hand.

¹¹"All who rage against you
  will surely be ashamed and disgraced;
those who oppose you
  will be as nothing and perish.
¹²Though you search for your enemies,
  you will not find them.
Those who wage war against you
  will be as nothing at all.
¹³For I am the LORD, your God,
  who takes hold of your right hand
and says to you, Do not fear;
  I will help you.
¹⁴Do not be afraid, O worm Jacob,
  O little Israel,
for I myself will help you," declares the LORD,

NRSV

  like driven stubble with his bow.
³He pursues them and passes on safely,
  scarcely touching the path with his feet.
⁴Who has performed and done this,
  calling the generations from the beginning?
I, the LORD, am first,
  and will be with the last.
⁵The coastlands have seen and are afraid,
  the ends of the earth tremble;
  they have drawn near and come.
⁶Each one helps the other,
  saying to one another, "Take courage!"
⁷The artisan encourages the goldsmith,
  and the one who smooths with the
    hammer encourages the one who
    strikes the anvil,
  saying of the soldering, "It is good";
  and they fasten it with nails so that it
    cannot be moved.
⁸But you, Israel, my servant,
  Jacob, whom I have chosen,
  the offspring of Abraham, my friend;
⁹you whom I took from the ends of the earth,
  and called from its farthest corners,
saying to you, "You are my servant,
  I have chosen you and not cast you off";
¹⁰do not fear, for I am with you,
  do not be afraid, for I am your God;
I will strengthen you, I will help you,
  I will uphold you with my victorious
    right hand.

¹¹Yes, all who are incensed against you
  shall be ashamed and disgraced;
those who strive against you
  shall be as nothing and shall perish.
¹²You shall seek those who contend with you,
  but you shall not find them;
those who war against you
  shall be as nothing at all.
¹³For I, the LORD your God,
  hold your right hand;
it is I who say to you, "Do not fear,
  I will help you."

¹⁴Do not fear, you worm Jacob,
  you insectᵃ Israel!

ᵃSyr: Heb *men of*

your Redeemer, the Holy One of Israel.
[15]"See, I will make you into a threshing sledge,
new and sharp, with many teeth.
You will thresh the mountains and
crush them,
and reduce the hills to chaff.
[16]You will winnow them, the wind will pick
them up,
and a gale will blow them away.
But you will rejoice in the LORD
and glory in the Holy One of Israel.

[17]"The poor and needy search for water,
but there is none;
their tongues are parched with thirst.
But I the LORD will answer them;
I, the God of Israel, will not forsake them.
[18]I will make rivers flow on barren heights,
and springs within the valleys.
I will turn the desert into pools of water,
and the parched ground into springs.
[19]I will put in the desert
the cedar and the acacia, the myrtle and
the olive.
I will set pines in the wasteland,
the fir and the cypress together,
[20]so that people may see and know,
may consider and understand,
that the hand of the LORD has done this,
that the Holy One of Israel has created it.

[21]"Present your case," says the LORD.
"Set forth your arguments," says
Jacob's King.
[22]"Bring in ⌐your idols⌐ to tell us
what is going to happen.
Tell us what the former things were,
so that we may consider them
and know their final outcome.
Or declare to us the things to come,
[23]   tell us what the future holds,
so we may know that you are gods.
Do something, whether good or bad,
so that we will be dismayed and filled
with fear.
[24]But you are less than nothing
and your works are utterly worthless;
he who chooses you is detestable.

I will help you, says the LORD;
your Redeemer is the Holy One of Israel.
[15] Now, I will make of you a threshing sledge,
sharp, new, and having teeth;
you shall thresh the mountains and
crush them,
and you shall make the hills like chaff.
[16] You shall winnow them and the wind shall
carry them away,
and the tempest shall scatter them.
Then you shall rejoice in the LORD;
in the Holy One of Israel you shall glory.

[17] When the poor and needy seek water,
and there is none,
and their tongue is parched with thirst,
I the LORD will answer them,
I the God of Israel will not forsake them.
[18] I will open rivers on the bare heights,[b]
and fountains in the midst of the valleys;
I will make the wilderness a pool of water,
and the dry land springs of water.
[19] I will put in the wilderness the cedar,
the acacia, the myrtle, and the olive;
I will set in the desert the cypress,
the plane and the pine together,
[20] so that all may see and know,
all may consider and understand,
that the hand of the LORD has done this,
the Holy One of Israel has created it.

[21] Set forth your case, says the LORD;
bring your proofs, says the King of Jacob.
[22] Let them bring them, and tell us
what is to happen.
Tell us the former things, what they are,
so that we may consider them,
and that we may know their outcome;
or declare to us the things to come.
[23] Tell us what is to come hereafter,
that we may know that you are gods;
do good, or do harm,
that we may be afraid and terrified.
[24] You, indeed, are nothing
and your work is nothing at all;
whoever chooses you is an abomination.

[b]Or trails

NIV

25"I have stirred up one from the north, and
        he comes—
    one from the rising sun who calls on
        my name.
He treads on rulers as if they were mortar,
    as if he were a potter treading the clay.
26Who told of this from the beginning, so we
        could know,
    or beforehand, so we could say, 'He
        was right'?
No one told of this,
    no one foretold it,
    no one heard any words from you.
27I was the first to tell Zion, 'Look, here
        they are!'
    I gave to Jerusalem a messenger of
        good tidings.
28I look but there is no one—
    no one among them to give counsel,
    no one to give answer when I ask them.
29See, they are all false!
    Their deeds amount to nothing;
    their images are but wind and confusion.

NRSV

25 I stirred up one from the north, and he
        has come,
    from the rising of the sun he was
        summoned by name.ᵃ
He shall trampleᵇ on rulers as on mortar,
    as the potter treads clay.
26 Who declared it from the beginning, so that
        we might know,
    and beforehand, so that we might say, "He
        is right"?
There was no one who declared it, none
        who proclaimed,
    none who heard your words.
27 I first have declared it to Zion,ᶜ
    and I give to Jerusalem a herald of
        good tidings.
28 But when I look there is no one;
    among these there is no counselor
    who, when I ask, gives an answer.
29 No, they are all a delusion;
    their works are nothing;
    their images are empty wind.

ᵃCn Compare Q Ms Gk: MT *and he shall call on my name*   ᵇCn:
Heb *come*   ᶜCn: Heb *First to Zion—Behold, behold them*

COMMENTARY

A trial, announced by God from the divine council, is the general setting into which all of chaps. 41–48 have been fitted. At 49:1, the coastlands are again summoned, but for a different purpose, by a different agent. That a divine council setting is compatible with a trial proceeding is made clear by Psalm 82. There the "gods" are summoned to the divine council and are sentenced. That possibility is ruled out in this discourse by the pre-trial speech, where members of the divine council make it clear that the Holy One is God alone. Gods and nations are on trial here in a more subtle sense than could be communicated by calling them in and demoting them, then and there. For here a chief aspect of the trial involves persuading an Israel whose right, it has been asserted, is disregarded by God (40:27).

A typical subdivision of the chapter finds six discrete units comprising vv. 1-5, vv. 6-7, vv. 8-13, vv. 14-16, vv. 17-20, and vv. 21-29 (with some dis-

agreement about the independence of vv. 6-7).[41] The genres represented are trial speech (vv. 1-5[7], 21-29), salvation-oracle (vv. 8-13, 14-16), and proclamation of salvation (vv. 17-20). Even with this traditional form-critical analysis, one can see the difficulty in insisting on too sharp a line between individual units—to the point of reaching the opposite conclusion, clear rhetorical unity.[42] The middle three units are closely related by form, and the first and last are identical (trial speech). The same verb עור (*'wr*, "rouse") is used in both units to describe God's rousing of the agent of victorious purpose, the first called from the east (41:2), the second from the north and the east (41:25). Virtually all modern commentators regard this agent as one and the same, Cyrus of Persia. God's first line of defense is the divine rousing of

41. Compare the treatments of Westermann, *Isaiah 40–66*, and Melugin, *The Formation of Isaiah 40–55*.
42. See Muilenberg's introduction in "The Book of Isaiah: Chapters 40–66," in *IB*, 12 vols. (Nashville: Abingdon, 1956) vol. 5:381-419.

Cyrus on Israel's behalf. Interestingly, Cyrus is not as yet named; for that we must wait until 44:28. In both texts, the agent is left undesignated.

The argument in favor of reading the agent as Cyrus has not gone unchallenged, in either the modern or the pre-critical periods. Torrey and others took the reference to be to none other than the patriarch Abraham, in part by appeal to consistency of content.[43] In the unit 41:8-13, it is Abraham who has been taken from the ends of the earth, "called from its farthest corners" (v. 9). Here the question of method immediately raises its head. If form-critical units are so discrete, one need not expect anything like consistency in content from one unit to the next. The calling of Cyrus in the first unit is an example of defending the offspring of Abraham in the ensuing unit. That connection is sufficient to associate two discrete units, without the agent in the first being Abraham.

A more serious objection to the identification of the agent roused in 41:2 as Abraham involves the seemingly peripheral character of such an appeal. How could the nations be in any way impressed, or interested, in the internal affairs of Israel? That is, how in any way would this constitute proof of a compelling character of God's actions for anyone beyond Israel's own immediate circle? And yet precisely a wider circle is addressed by the question, "Who roused a victor from the east?"

One further issue needs to be considered. Why is the agent unnamed? Is this meant to add a certain drama to the movement, resolved when Cyrus is directly addressed in 45:1-7? Childs and others have noted the correspondence between the verb used here and the earlier reference to the punisher of evil Babylon, dispatched by God in 13:17 and identified there as "the Medes" (see also 20:2).[44] Such an identification could presumably be extended to include the Persian Cyrus, now bringing to completion God's "former thing" as promised concerning Babylon. The first line of association, in other words, relevant to the larger shape of the book of Isaiah, is God's promise to "stir up" an agent of judgment against mighty Babylon. Moreover, this dispatching of a foreign nation for a divinely appointed task belongs to the

general proclamation of Isaiah, especially concerning Assyria: "rod of my anger . . . against a godless nation I send him" (10:5-6). Against this specific backdrop, God again argues for a special commissioning now of "a victor from the east" (41:2) and "one from the north" (41:25). This last association is also familiar from earlier prophetic discourse, especially Jeremiah: "Out of the north disaster shall break out on all the inhabitants of the lands" (Jer 1:14; cf. Jer 4:6). Destruction from the north (Jer 4:6) is here directed not against Judah, but on its behalf (so 41:10).

In terms, then, both of the direction ("north") and of the action ("roused"), traditional language and concepts are used to describe God's intention with the people in such a way as to compel witnesses to recognize God's authority and supremacy. The final unit at 41:21-29 associates the "traditional" character of this intention with God's reliability through time. That is, more than a present assertion, made intramurally, is at work. The God of Israel *is* God, because what is happening now God alone said would happen, and the truly wondrous thing is that this prior word even had to do with events beyond Israel's own history. The God of Israel can announce beforehand and bring to completion the activity in history of a foreign agent, when even the gods of the country whose agent God is fail to produce such evidence of prior calling (41:21-24).

The view held here is that the force of the larger argument of the chapter requires that Cyrus be the agent God "stirred up from the north," in fulfillment of an announcement made earlier (41:22). He is unnamed (until 44:28) so that the emphasis might remain on the traditional character of the appeal, as constituted by the God of Israel's more general use of foreign nations and rulers to work the divine will, within the book of Isaiah. The identity of the agent called from the north (and the east) in 41:25 as Cyrus does not, however, necessarily oblige one to accept that identification at 41:2. What would the point of such a repetition be, within the context of this single chapter, when the following chapters are content to remain silent on such a specific commissioning of Cyrus until 44:8? Why is the traditional agent of judgment from the north combined with a calling from the east in 41:25—thus appropriate for Cyrus—not

43. See C. C. Torrey, *The Second Isaiah* (New York: Scribner's, 1928) 310-21.

44. B. S. Childs, *Introduction to the Old Testament as Scripture* (Philadelphia: Fortress, 1979) 330.

introduced in this way at 41:2? The answer will be provided through a close reading of the individual units of the chapter, which are by no means casually arranged or mechanically linked through catchword or rhetorical device alone. Correct interpretation of individual units flows from and does not precede some larger understanding of the way the chapter as a whole means to make its point. It is significant that at the beginning and the end an agent of God's rousing is sent on a mission, that the final one is plausibly related to the mission of Cyrus the Persian, as this takes explicit form in chap. 45, and that the vagueness of the first reference is intentional and is only cleared up as one reads on to see how the logic of the individual units unfolds.

41:1-7. The coastlands and peoples summoned in v. 1 are the witnesses beyond Israel, lying at the farthest reaches of the inhabited world. The trial setting is made explicit right away ("let us draw near for judgment"). The term מִשְׁפָּט (mišpāṭ) was introduced as that which was disregarded by God in the preceding chapter (40:27). In the chapter to follow, mišpāṭ is repeated three times in the course of four verses, forming the central item to be established by the servant (42:1-4). It should be understood in the general sense of "a grasp of the divine order of things, as this manifests the will of YHWH." It has a larger context than Israel, though that is where it is manifested for the nations' beholding.

Earlier commentators who preferred Abraham as the one here called from the east frequently rendered the צֶדֶק (ṣedeq) of v. 2 as a divine name, as this sometimes happens in the Genesis narratives (e.g., Gen 31:53): "The Righteous One called him to his service." The specific context to which the passage referred was Abram's routing and further pursuing of a powerful alliance of four eastern kings beyond the borders of Israel, all the way north of Damascus (Gen 14:1-16). It was a stunning victory, involving hot pursuit, battle, further pursuit, and rescue. Perhaps even more significant for the purposes of this commentary, the victory was in turn followed by homage from the king of Salem, Melchizedek (Gen 14:17-20).

How would this Isaiah passage (vv. 1-5) have been heard? As related to Cyrus or as exposition of Genesis 14 (or an appeal to the tradition behind it)? God as first and last, as calling every genera-

tion from the beginning (41:4)—would this apply to the early calling of Abraham or the much later calling of Cyrus? Are the coastlands and ends of the earth those beyond the offspring of Abraham, offering proper tribute, like Melchizedek? Or are they simple idolaters, like the king of Sodom or the idolaters of a later age, wrongly reacting to God's dispatching of Abraham or Cyrus? The text is capable of both interpretations; indeed, there might be good reason to say that is exactly its point, as a typological association has been made at the most basic level of the text. The final two verses (vv. 6-7) are frequently taken as an addition, but the verbs employed (עזר 'zr "help"; חזק ḥzq "be strong") would seem integrally to anticipate God's strengthening and encouraging of Abraham-Jacob-Israel in the following unit (vv. 8-10), in sarcastic contrast to the encouraged manufacture and undergirding of idols.

How the passage is heard should take seriously its twin audience: an Israel whose "right has been disregarded" (40:27), and also the foreign coastlands. There is a lesson from Israel's indigenous history, concerning God's calling of Abraham and support of him, and a lesson concerning God's calling of another agent from the east, to be developed in further detail at the close of the chapter (vv. 25-28). The initial reference to the "east" only (v. 2; cf. v. 25) allows the text to remain open to interpretation, within the context of Israel's past testimony and, outside it, to Cyrus and a generation presently called.

41:8-13. Westermann calls this unit an "oracle of salvation" whose "birthplace was Israel's worship."[45] Just how abrupt a shift we have from the trial setting of the first unit (and a diatribe against idolatry) entails one's larger understanding of the form-critical task in this Isaiah discourse. The references to choosing, calling, taking from earth's ends, and even the "victorious right hand" (v. 10) are all anticipated nicely by the preceding unit. The final assurance of triumph over "those who contend" and "those who war" (v. 12) fits both the context of present trial and past record of battle victory from the days of Abraham.

Here for the very first time we are introduced to the term עֶבֶד ('ebed, "servant"), which plays so

45. C. Westermann, *Isaiah 40–66,* trans. David Stalker, OTL (Philadelphia: Westminster, 1969) 67-68.

signal a role in this discourse. Whatever obscurity might surround the use of the term in certain poems, the first reference makes it clear who the servant is in this context: the offspring of Abraham, Jacob/Israel (v. 8). The dual use of the name is typical in this discourse and should probably conjure up the larger context of ancestor narratives, concerning the wily patriarch (Genesis 25–50). Here again we are working with the assumption that a public, fixed record is being appealed to by the author of the discourse, constituting a word that stands forever, and not just memories or traditions. The final predication, "whom I took from the ends of the earth, and called from its farthest corners" (v. 9), attaches more easily to the immediately aforementioned Abraham than to Jacob, so the larger ancestral election, calling forth, and strengthening are what forms the context central to the appeal. Language familiar from the calling of individual prophets ("I have chosen you . . . do not fear, for I am with you") is here associated with God's most foundational calling of the people. It is fitting that the opening appeal to God's specific act of creation (40:12-31) is followed immediately by God's own bringing into evidence the choosing and strengthening of the ancestors. The piece of evidence best suited to the present circumstances is the victory of Abraham over the eastern kings and, alongside it, the narratives that speak of God's covenant with Abraham's seed (Genesis 17; 28). The "Israel" addressed in Isa 40:27 takes its very identity and name from a set of specific circumstances whose governing center is calling, strengthening, and presence. This is what sets Israel apart and forms the ground and logic of its *mišpāṭ* with God.

The typological association between Abraham's past victory and Israel's present victory begins with a slight contrast: The enemies will not even be found, for they are "as nothing at all" (v. 12) due to God's presence. It is difficult to know how best to judge this contrast, but its point may unfold as we move to the next unit.

41:14-16. It is by no means unusual to find in this discourse one formal unit followed by another of the same basic type, here an "oracle of salvation." The designation of Jacob as "worm" is unusual, and the term is unfamiliar from the ancestral narratives. Begrich's tracing of the term to laments ("I am a worm and not human," Ps

22:6 NRSV) and the association with Babylonian lament psalms is learned, but it strays from the image central to the unit—namely, that of threshing and winnowing.[46] The worm is known from Jonah (Jonah 4:7) and the curses of Deuteronomy (Deut 28:39) as an agent of destruction, slow but quite effective (and not even slow in Jonah's case!). Now the worm becomes a sledge with razor-sharp teeth (v. 15).

The curiosity that Israel's enemies have virtually or really evaporated ("you shall not find them," v. 12) has already been mentioned. This could just be rhetorical overplay, not to be taken literally. At the same time, here there is an object of Israel's threshing, crushing, and winnowing of mountains and hills. The concluding image introduced in v. 16 harks back to 40:24, where, as a result of God's action against rulers and princes, "the tempest carries them off." Now because of God's presence with Israel, that is the consequence of the threshing: "The wind shall carry them away and the tempest shall scatter them" (41:16). In the very first speech from the heavenly council, itself harking back to chaps. 34–35, mountains and hills were to be leveled to prepare God's way (40:4). The text insists that Israel will accomplish this in a manner overshadowing Jacob's or Abraham's efforts against the nations, but only as the consequence of renewed divine presence (underscored by the repeated assurances of vv. 10, and 13-14), to a degree never before experienced. The consequence of all this is the praise and glory of the "Holy One" (קדוש‎ *qādôš*), Isaiah's special name for God (1:4).

41:17-20. This unit effects the transition to the chapter's conclusion at vv. 21-29. It offers an assurance, grounded in past testimony, of God's wondrous, unanticipated provision. If the narratives of Genesis directly or indirectly influence this author's forms of expression, several episodes from that testimony come to mind. Hagar finds herself in the wilderness on two different occasions (Gen 16:7-14; 21:14-19). There God miraculously supplies water to her when all hope was lost (Gen 21:19). Similar stories are found in the basic stock of wilderness narratives in Exodus and Numbers. Yet now the provision by Israel's Holy One will

---

46. J. Begrich, "Das priesterliche Heilsorakle," *ZAW* 52 (1934) 87; C. Westermann, "Struktur und Geschichte der Klage im Alten Testament," *ZAW* 66 (1954) 284.

have an even wider circle of witnesses (so Isa 40:20), and here is where the transition to the final unit is made clear. God's rearrangement of creation will take place, not just to supply Israel's need (vv. 17-18), but to testify to God's Lordship over creation, "that all may see and know, all may consider and understand." As Clements has pointed out, this piling up of verbs is important for another reason: Here we have a point-by-point reversal of the charge of Isaiah 6, now accomplished for Israel *and all flesh.*[47] In 6:10, they were not "to see" (ראה *r'â*), "to hear" (שמע *šm'*), "to comprehend" (בין *byn*), or "to turn back" (שוב *šwb*), while here they "see" (*r'â*), "know" (ידע *yd'*), "take to heart" (שים *śym*), and, indeed, fully "understand" (שכל *śkl*). "Together" (יחדו *yaḥdāw*) recollects the promise of 40:5, enlarging the new comprehension to include those beyond Israel's circle.

41:21-29. What was true and decisive as evidence for Israel is here set forth for a wider purpose, consistent with v. 20, but also in challenge. Here the original summons is recalled from v. 1. God addresses those outside the elect relationship so that those inside might know just how special has been God's peculiar relationship with Israel, from creation, through the calling of Abraham, through various wildernesses, to the present moment. The "us" is presumably *qādōš,* "the Holy One," and the divine entourage; but the people Israel could also be implied.

Verse 24 establishes the truthfulness of what had been announced to Israel in promise at v. 12, and here the promise is grounded in empirical fact. The nations are not able to link promises made in the past by their gods to any present or anticipated fulfillment. The Holy One can do that on behalf of God's own people. That is, God can point to concrete testimony of having made good on the divine word. God promised to make of Abraham and Sarah a people, and dod so. God promised to guard and keep them through hostile times, and did so. God promised to provide for them when they were thirsty and in need, and did so. Yet now a special challenge is being presented, and God is

poised to give evidence of an act the gods of the nations should be able to boast about, since it involves them; but they have nothing to say (v. 24).

The unit moves through two phases, represented by conclusions at vv. 24 and 28.[48] It is important to note this twofold structure because of the confusing wording in v. 27. The first section presents a challenge to the gods, and their silence is taken as proof that they cannot respond with testimony, as can God. The specific content of the proof is revealed in the second phase: God stirred up one from the north. In this instance (cf. v. 2), given the present appeal based upon past prediction (v. 26), the most likely candidate is Cyrus the Persian. Just as God called Abraham in the past and faithfully supported him in the cause of his people, so also now God has called a foreign ruler to do the divine bidding on behalf of Israel. One would expect foreign "gods" to be better informed about one of their own, and their inability to produce testimony to this effect proves that they are "empty wind" (v. 29).

Janzen has defended the MT's peculiar הנה הנם (*hinnēh hinnām,* "Behold, behold them") at v. 27 against efforts at emendation by associating the referent with "the previously mentioned flock of exiles returning to Zion under the aegis of Yahweh and through the instrumentality of Cyrus" (connected to the *hinnēh* of 40:9-11).[49] Laudable is his appeal to context, as against emendation. What is clear is that Zion has received testimony (v. 27) that is lacking for those challenged (vv. 28-29) and that this testimony is perceived as having been given מראש (*mērō'š*) and מלפנים (*millēpānîm*), "beforehand" (v. 26). I take this to refer to the "stirring up" of the Medes against Babylon, as spoken beforehand by Isaiah—as this is interpreted by the author of this material from his own later perspective in the exilic period. That is, I am not arguing for "Isaianic authorship" of 13:17—which is probably an anachronistic notion—but that the author of this material regarded the calling of Cyrus as having been predicted long "beforehand" within Israel.

The nearer contextual referent for *hinnām* ("behold them") is to be found within the second

---

47. R. E. Clements, "Beyond Tradition-History: Deutero-Isaianic Development of First Isaiah's Themes," *JSOT* 31 (1985) 95-113. Interestingly, while Clements studies closely the theme of deafness and blindness, he does not treat this particular passage (cf. 35:5; 42:18-19; 43:8; 44:18).

48. See Westermann, *Isaiah 40–66,* 82-83.

49. J. Janzen, "Isaiah 41:27: Reading הנה הנומה in 1QIsa and הנה הנם in the Masoretic Text," *JBL* 113 (1994) 602.

verse-half. The verse should be thus paraphrased, "First to Zion/Jerusalem God has given a messenger of good tidings; behold them." The problem is how to render the sentence properly in terms of temporal perspective. The herald of good tidings was referred to as having been dispatched at 40:9, and here what is being said to the gods is that the message delivered is based on past testimony once delivered by God through Isaiah of Jerusalem to Zion and beyond, concerning the commissioning of Cyrus. The messengers within Israel are able to say a word concerning external affairs that the gods, whose business one might argue Cyrus is, cannot: "But when I look there is no one; among these there is no counselor who, when I ask, gives an answer" (41:28). There is no counselor who instructs the deity (40:13), but there are counselors and messengers instructed by God who obediently give testimony concerning Cyrus, both then and now.

It has been pointed out that the gods of foreign nations do, in fact, defend themselves as faithful predictors of events.[50] This text is in some ways more complex than that. It depicts a trial in which

50. See Westermann, *Isaiah 40–66,* 83.

foreign gods are unable to give testimony about a matter that should concern them and that, therefore, establishes that they are not gods at all. All activity, wherever it takes place, is under the control of only one God, the Holy One of Israel. There is no such thing as local dispatching for local purposes. Israel's God is not better than the others; the others are not. The nearest text for comparison here is to be found in the exchange between the Rabshakeh, Isaiah, and Hezekiah (Isaiah 36–37). The worldview of the Rabshakeh concerning "gods" is accepted long enough to demonstrate its complete inadequacy. The nub of the matter is exposed at 37:18-20:

> "Truly, O LORD, the kings of Assyria have laid waste all the nations and their lands, and have hurled their gods into the fire, though they were no gods, but the work of human hands—wood and stone—and so they were destroyed. So now, O LORD our God, save us from his hand, so that all the kingdoms of the earth may know that you alone are the LORD." (NRSV)

The prayer answered by God's victory (37:36-38) is here answered by an extended demonstration, by God, of God's authority over gods, which are not.

REFLECTIONS

1. To the charge that God has disregarded the right of Israel there is at first encouragement and strengthening of the most basic sort (40:29-31). But very soon, God takes the charge seriously and mounts a defense Israel can take seriously. God does not tell Israel how great it is, how the right that constitutes its special relationship with God is intact and special. God does not begin with Israel in its present situation at all. Rather, God emphasizes who God has been *for Israel,* in the context of those who think otherwise.

There is a great lesson for us in this. God does not permit Israel to adopt a governing perspective that the Holy One then feels obliged to conform to. God widens the lens, bringing in what is relevant. Israel is not in despair because its right has been disregarded, but because it has failed to understand just how that right is, in fact, constituted. It does not involve a personal, private line of credit upon which the people can draw when the going gets tough, allowing them to endure the blandishments of enemies with fortitude or equanimity. Why? Because any assault on Israel's worth is, in fact, an assault on God. Apart from God, Israel has no identity, so any question of Israel's right that truly merits response will have to be taken up in the wider context of the coastlands, the peoples, and the "gods" that are no gods. And just as for Israel, so, too, for the church.

When the first Christians were under the sort of assault that might have been construed as the disregarding by God of their right, the prayer they lifted to God did not begin with a petition to stop any further assaults (Acts 4:24-31). Their prayer began with an extended address reminding God and themselves who God is: "Sovereign Lord, who made the heaven and the earth, the seas and everything in them" (Acts 4:24). Only later did the subject of their particular dilemma come up (Acts 4:29). The tide that makes all things turn is not when God pays attention to us and our special cicrumstances, but when we are put in mind of the divine power and the long-standing character of God's faithfulness, which allows us to see just who we are and where we stand. Job learned this (Job 38:1–42:6). The saints in every day experience this truth. Our prayer should be to be counted among them, in suffering obedience if need be, if that is the way God is calling us to be God's body in the world.

When the first disciples recall who God is, the prayer they lift up concerning themselves is that they might be able to persist in bold speech on God's behalf—that is, that they might persist in the very behavior that got them in hot water to begin with (Acts 4:29). We know that God is addressing us when we are given boldness to speak of matters pertaining to God, beyond our own circle of concern.

2. Election is a two-edged sword. To be specially called is to live a life of victory or defeat, trembling or courage, servant or antagonist of the Holy One. The call to be servant is immediately a call to "fear not, for I am with you," in the face of contention, shame, disgrace, and warfare (Isa 41:9-13). It is not to look back on a period of sweet companionship or blessed comfort. Only when we take the charge seriously, "fear not," and then press ahead can the discovery be made that there is a presence who does not remove adversity, but who can make the greatest of real challenges as if they were nothing at all.

The alternative to this sort of life is never morally neutral: If we do not follow the Holy One of Israel, we will and must make other gods for ourselves. We will and must be God's antagonist, the virulent counterpart to Abraham, "my friend." Isaiah 41 never contemplates some spot in creation where excuses serve to ward off full and faithful service or accountability before the Holy One of the most serious sort. Even the gods are taken seriously enough to have it revealed that they are nothing. This was a risky move, but the alternative would be for God to arrogantly assert sovereign "Godness" but fail to come to terms with real and dedicated challenges to divine sovereignty. Here the Holy One takes these challenges seriously without compromising God's holiness, God's special way with Israel, or God's designs for the whole world. Counting equality with God a thing to be grasped would protect both God and the Son, but it would also fail to address creation's most painful and distorting realities. God goes the harder way on behalf of creation and all the nations of the earth.

3. There must be more to the final challenge to the "gods" than a mechanical "I said it; you didn't" in respect of Cyrus. How are we to assess the fact that neither at 13:17 nor at 41:25 is the actual name of Cyrus mentioned? The "foe from the north," traditionally an agent of God's judgment, is here conflated with the one from the east. It is argued in the commentary that this latter fact has triggered an association with Abraham of old, also called by God for a task of victory (41:2-10).

The author will have more to say about Cyrus in due course (44:28; 45:1-7; 48:14), and what we will learn is the special character of the ruler's mission as instrumental and beneficial to God's people, Israel, and God's place, Zion. The traditional foe from the north (Jer 1:14; 4:6), famous for colossal show of strength (Isa 13:1-16; Jer 4:23-31), has become one called from the east, with a positive, upbuilding role in God's economy, as Jeremiah had promised, on the far side of plucking up and pulling down (Jer 1:10). This promise of an end to God's judgment and the sending forth of a new agent for a new time of violence halted is what is recalled as central to the testimony of God to Israel. It is not just that Cyrus was promised of old to Zion, but that he was promised within a larger plan (e.g., 14:24; 37:26), around which the message of the prophet Isaiah swirled, guarding God's sovereignty, freedom to one day open stopped ears, and ability to send alongside agents of judgment agents of grace and favor. The word of the prophet Isaiah conveying that plan would one day be opened and read, and a new generation would see there words meant for them, plans laid down of old (29:11-12; 30:8). For the author of Isaiah, that plan and that word of old were true not just for a new generation within Israel, but for that generation within the context of nations and gods and the wider created *mišpāṭ* itself. Isaiah's plan of old has become the trigger for the association of former and latter things, spanning the ages (41:22; 43:9; 44:7-8; 45:21; 46:9; 48:3-5), now on the horizon of fulfillment and giving way to new things (42:8; 43:18; 48:6).

We do well to consider this when we find ourselves in places of darkness or doubt. Like the proverbial hunting dog that must return to where the scent was lost, God will return us to the place where the divine plan was revealed and will show us how God means to make good on promises. God may be about to do a new and strange thing in commissioning something we simply could not have imagined when we first were shown the way. But if this is the strange way God means now to act, we should expect confirmation in no uncertain terms, as consistent with divine plans from of old.

4. What the Holy One promises to do is to bring coherence to our times. God means to reassert, especially at this time when God's providence seems hardest to trust, that all times are in God's hands. This constitutes the Holy One's distinctiveness against the "gods," whose silence in this regard is deafening.

It is not that this coherence knows no assault or is immune from our modern skepticisms (these the Bible shows us are always threatening God's rule). No, God's sovereignty takes up within it our times and promises without exception to draw lines of connection that span darkness, disregard, and doubt. God does this, not just in response to our complaints that it appears otherwise, but so that "all may see and know, all may consider and understand, that the hand of the LORD has done this, the Holy One of Israel has created it" (Isa 41:20).

We are not to welcome times of hardship and judgment, nor are we to seek them out. But God will, indeed, use them to make us a people who cling to God as our only source of life, strength, and hope. It is up to us, therefore, to press our case before God, to insist that our right has been disregarded, if indeed that is the way it seems. But when God responds, and how God responds, will remain secrets only God's heavenly council is privileged, if at all, to glimpse. And the final upshot will not be the reestablishment of some old familiar equilibrium, but a whole new vista onto the past and the future within God's providence and a breaking forth of what we know in the service of the world God has made. Suffering and disregard are never simply relieved, but they are redeemed and pressed into service, to the glory of God.

The Bible does many things. It stirs the imagination. It tells us our duty. It displays a God who is rhetorically overwhelming and incapable of domestication. It shows us a pattern into which God and Jesus Christ and the end make sense. But it also locates us temporally within the holy and good judgment of the sovereign God. That was true for Israel in Isaiah's day, it was true even amid ecclesial confusion, and it remains true today. The Bible seeks to display the "strange new world" that bids us find our place in God's history, not in the historicisms of modernity.[51] The Holy One demands that we find our place under God's judgment in time. This is what it means to believe in history at all.

---

51. See Neil MacDonald, *Karl Barth and the Strange New World Within the Bible* (Carlisle: Paternoster, 2000). On providence and the silence of Scripture in the West, see E. Radner, *The End of the Church: A Pneumatology of Christian Division in the West* (Grand Rapids: Eerdmans, 1998); and W. Abraham, *Canon and Criterion in Christian Theology: From the Fathers to Feminism* (Oxford: Clarendon, 1998).

ISAIAH 42:1-13, THE SERVANT PRESENTED, ADDRESSED, HYMNED

NIV

42 "Here is my servant, whom I uphold, my chosen one in whom I delight;
I will put my Spirit on him
  and he will bring justice to the nations.
²He will not shout or cry out,
  or raise his voice in the streets.
³A bruised reed he will not break,
  and a smoldering wick he will not snuff out.
In faithfulness he will bring forth justice;
⁴   he will not falter or be discouraged
till he establishes justice on earth.
  In his law the islands will put their hope."

⁵This is what God the LORD says—
he who created the heavens and stretched
    them out,
  who spread out the earth and all that comes
    out of it,
who gives breath to its people,
  and life to those who walk on it:
⁶"I, the LORD, have called you in righteousness;
  I will take hold of your hand.
I will keep you and will make you
  to be a covenant for the people
  and a light for the Gentiles,
⁷to open eyes that are blind,
  to free captives from prison
  and to release from the dungeon those who
    sit in darkness.

⁸"I am the LORD; that is my name!
  I will not give my glory to another
  or my praise to idols.
⁹See, the former things have taken place,
  and new things I declare;
before they spring into being
  I announce them to you."

¹⁰Sing to the LORD a new song,
  his praise from the ends of the earth,
you who go down to the sea, and all that is
    in it,
  you islands, and all who live in them.
¹¹Let the desert and its towns raise their voices;

NRSV

42 Here is my servant, whom I uphold,
  my chosen, in whom my soul delights;
I have put my spirit upon him;
  he will bring forth justice to the nations.
² He will not cry or lift up his voice,
  or make it heard in the street;
³ a bruised reed he will not break,
  and a dimly burning wick he will
    not quench;
  he will faithfully bring forth justice.
⁴ He will not grow faint or be crushed
  until he has established justice in the earth;
  and the coastlands wait for his teaching.

⁵ Thus says God, the LORD,
  who created the heavens and stretched
    them out,
  who spread out the earth and what comes
    from it,
who gives breath to the people upon it
  and spirit to those who walk in it:
⁶ I am the LORD, I have called you in
    righteousness,
  I have taken you by the hand and kept you;
I have given you as a covenant to the
    people,ᵃ
  a light to the nations,
⁷   to open the eyes that are blind,
  to bring out the prisoners from the dungeon,
  from the prison those who sit in darkness.
⁸ I am the LORD, that is my name;
  my glory I give to no other,
  nor my praise to idols.
⁹ See, the former things have come to pass,
  and new things I now declare;
before they spring forth,
  I tell you of them.

¹⁰ Sing to the LORD a new song,
  his praise from the end of the earth!
Let the sea roarᵇ and all that fills it,

ᵃMeaning of Heb uncertain   ᵇCn Compare Ps 96.11; 98.7: Heb
Those who go down to the sea

    let the settlements where Kedar lives
      rejoice.
Let the people of Sela sing for joy;
    let them shout from the mountaintops.
[12]Let them give glory to the LORD
    and proclaim his praise in the islands.
[13]The LORD will march out like a mighty man,
    like a warrior he will stir up his zeal;
with a shout he will raise the battle cry
    and will triumph over his enemies.

    the coastlands and their inhabitants.
[11] Let the desert and its towns lift up their voice,
    the villages that Kedar inhabits;
let the inhabitants of Sela sing for joy,
    let them shout from the tops of the
      mountains.
[12] Let them give glory to the LORD,
    and declare his praise in the coastlands.
[13] The LORD goes forth like a soldier,
    like a warrior he stirs up his fury;
he cries out, he shouts aloud,
    he shows himself mighty against his foes.

COMMENTARY

We now enter a distinctive section of the discourse. It remains in the context of trial and divine council, but now Israel forms the focus of attention, while the nations and their no-gods fall silent before the Holy One's testimony and speech to Israel.

Yet first a presentation is made of God's servant before those assembled (vv. 1-4). This is followed by a word to the servant (vv. 5-9) concerning his task and a hymn to God, enjoined of all creation (vv. 10-13).

It is structurally significant that on a later occasion when such a hymnic fragment appears (45:8), it follows God's explicit commissioning of Cyrus (45:1-7). A presentation of Cyrus to the divine council is not made on exact analogy with God's servant (42:1-4). For that we are to rest content with what appears in the chapter just discussed (41:25-29), where the stirring up of Cyrus is connected to God's prior speech in testimony to the Holy One's exclusive divine status before the nations and their "gods." Moreover, as we shall see, the presentation of the servant constitutes a pledge of his future success in carrying out a mission to the nations. Cyrus is *already* at work. What happens in his case is different; he must have it clarified just how and why and for whom he is about his business. In any event, there is a structural similarity in that the commission of Cyrus likewise constitutes a bold step forward, and it is followed by a brief hymnic fragment (45:8) on analogy with 42:10-13. The next such hymn

appears in the second major section of discourse (49:1–52:12), following the acceptance by an individual of the role of servant in 49:1-12 as anticipated and promised in 42:1-9. The hymn, or call to sing, appears at 49:13.

It is also significant, then, that major new sections of discourse are introduced and then followed by brief hymnic refrains. The first of these sections introduces God's servant (vv. 1-13). It is followed by an extensive section dealing with Israel's past blindness and deafness, its potential for persistence, and its removal (42:14–44:22). Consistent with the structural overview, this section also concludes with a hymn (44:23) before a transition to the Cyrus proclamation (44:24-28).[52]

42:1-4. It is Jacob-Israel-Abraham who is first and, clearly, called "servant" in 41:8-9. This designation was derived from the covenant relationship that God established with the ancestors (Gen 17:1-22). What is striking in that Genesis text is the repeated association of Abraham and Sarah in the context of God's ברית (*běrît,* "covenant") with *the nations* (Gen 17:4-6, 16). Within the covenant relationship, Yahweh is Lord, and Abraham is servant. The term עבד (*'ebed,* "servant") does not appear in the Genesis narratives, though it is

---

52. On the role of hymns as structural devices, see R. F. Melugin, *The Formation of Isaiah 40–55,* BZAW 141 (Berlin: Walter de Gruyter, 1976) 77-82. Eva Hessler, in particular, pursued this line of approach in her dissertation ("Gott der Schöpfer: Ein Beitrag zur Komposition und Theologie Deuterojesajas" [Ph.D. diss., Greifswald, 1961]), with adaptations by C. Westermann, *Sprache und Struktur der Prophetie Deuterojesajas* (Stuttgart: Calwer, 1981) 161.

clearly consistent with the covenant frame of reference. In other words, in the case of God's covenant with Abraham, the covenant partners ("servants") not only are the ancestor and his immediate offspring, but also the nations as the anticipated progeny of this "father of a multitude" (Gen 17:4):

> I will make you exceedingly fruitful; and I will make nations of you, and kings shall come from you. I will establish my covenant between me and you, and your offspring after you throughout their generations, for an everlasting covenant ברית עולם [bĕrît 'ôlām], to be God to you and to your offspring after you. (Gen 17:6-7)

Note that reference to the generations, "called from the beginning" (Isa 41:4), immediately preceded the declaration to "Israel, my servant, Jacob, whom I have chosen, the offspring of Abraham, my friend" (Isa 41:8; the unusual collocation "nations and kings" is also found in Isa 41:2).

It is not the purpose of the discourse in chap. 41 to stress the connection between the covenant with Abraham and the nations after him, because the chapter is more concerned with the challenge presented to Israel by the claims of the "gods." As we saw, God addressed that challenge by drawing attention, for Israel and the nations, to the close association between the calling and the triumph of both Abraham and Cyrus, both from the east, separated in time but not in divine purpose. But as chap. 42 opens, it is precisely the relationship between God's servant, equipped with משפט (mišpāṭ, "justice"), and the nations that comes to the fore (vv. 1, 4). Once the "gods" of the nations are shown to be nothing and a delusion, the nations, the coastlands, and the wider earth are placed in a position where they might see and receive the mišpāṭ that the One God means to be theirs, as offspring of servant Abraham.

Form criticism has been most helpful—and in general agreement—regarding the genre and background of this text. Where there remains some question is the actual scope of the first unit. What is the form of vv. 5-9, and how are these verses related to vv. 1-4? In this connection, it is significant to note that the next two "servant songs" are also followed by extensions or elaborations (49:1-6 and 49:7-12; 50:4-9 and 50:10-11), whose precise form-critical designation and rela-

tionship to the main unit are matters for discussion. However, in the case of 42:1-4 and 42:5-9, it is not possible to talk about a main text and a brief elaboration; the units are of equal length.

Most scholars agree that the opening phrase, "Behold my servant," is taken from a royal setting, where the king or the king's successor is formally presented before an audience (e.g., 1 Sam 9:15-16). So, too, the role of bringing forth justice, spoken of in v. 1b and repeated two more times in the course of three verses, is clearly the decisive theme of the unit and has been argued to be a royal function. At the same time, the spirit endowment is by no means restricted to a royal setting (1 Samuel 16), but frequently is associated with prophetic commissioning. Westermann speaks of "two lines of mediation," by word (prophetic) and by action (royal; judges), "reunited in the servant" consistent with the frequent use of the term "servant" for the figure of Moses, "in whose person the lines were still one."[53]

Kaiser had earlier argued for a distinctive royal setting for both vv. 1-4 and vv. 5-9.[54] The first unit is an imitation of the liturgical drama in which the deity presents a king before the heavenly court, while the second unit relates the commissioning made directly to the king himself. This is a preferable reading, and it solves the problem of how the units are to be related. They are, in fact, episodes, the first involving the presentation of the servant, the second the commissioning of him. Another way to put this would be that the first scene involves God's statement of the servant's purpose, made to those assembled, as in the preceding chapter, involving the specific mission of the servant to the nations. The second scene involves God's own word to the servant and to Israel (there is a relationship here, as we shall see), explaining to the servant directly what his task entails. This explains not only the different emphases in each unit, but also their relationship. While it is correct to talk about a creative adaptation of forms by the author ("Second Isaiah") in this instance, the creativity extends across both units (vv. 1-4 and vv. 5-9) and involves their actual episodic association.

53. C. Westermann, *Isaiah 40–66*, trans. David Stalker, OTL (Philadelphia: Westminster, 1969) 97. This is a succinct and accurate summary.
54. O. Kaiser, *Der konigliche Knecht*, FRLANT 70 (Gottingen: Vandenhoeck und Ruprecht, 1962) 16-18.

Beuken has stressed the continuation of a theme introduced in the previous chapters involving *mišpāṭ,* and that, too, is fully on target.[55] When one takes the previous context into account, the interpretation of the first servant poem is more easily gained. It is clear above all that the servant has a task to the nations. The verbs all stress "bringing forth" (יוֹצִיא *yôṣî',* v. 1; *yôṣî',* v. 3) and establishing *mišpāṭ*—not within Israel—but in the earth and among the coastlands (ישים בארץ *yāśîm bāʾāreṣ).* There is, furthermore, no evidence of hostile demeanor from the nations, expected or depicted. The coastlands wait for the servant's תורה *tôrâ,* or instruction, in something of the irenic manner of Isa 2:1-4, where peoples and nations go up to Zion to learn God's ways and to be taught from God's *tôrâ.* This is due to the fact that the "gods" who pretend to represent them have been silenced and thrown down (for an explicit depiction of this, cf. Psalm 82).

Yet there is another important consideration here, based on the introduction of the "offspring of Abraham my friend," servant Israel, in chap. 41. If the interpretation given above is correct, the emphasis falls there on the covenant promises to Abraham, Sarah, and their offspring, most immediately Isaac and Jacob/Israel, but more extensively as well, involving the nations, for whom Abraham and Sarah are founding father and mother. The author of the Isaiah discourse knows these promises, made to servant Abram by the Lord and, more important, knows them to remain on the horizon of fulfillment. Now the servant commissioned for this task is presented by God to the heavenly council and all those assembled, who are instructed as to the servant's task. Within the context of a trial setting, still loosely maintained, this amounts to a pledge of future success made on the part of the Holy One. It belongs to the "I intend to show X" portion of a trial, where the jury and the witnesses are put on notice as to what will transpire in the course of the proceedings. As Westermann puts it, the words of 42:1 "represent the public designation of the one chosen by God to perform the task he wishes carried out."[56] This task is in fact one with very old roots, traceable to the promises made to Abraham and Sarah,

conjoined here with the concrete manifestations of the promise: *mišpāṭ* and *tôrâ. Mispat* here refers to the established will of the One God, now made known in and through all creation in fulfillment of the promise to Abraham (Gen 12:1-3).

The declaration made here by God emphasizes the servant's ultimate success, apparently in the face of expectations to the contrary. Note the adverbial לאמת (*leʾĕmet,* "faithfully") in v. 3*b* and the verbal repetition in v. 4, "he will not grow faint, he will not be crushed until he has established justice." Alongside this assurance comes a description of the servant's demeanor that likewise serves to ward off doubt, since it is unusual behavior for king or for prophet. One might naturally expect spirit endowment to lead to speech and royal commissioning to lead to action of a decisive, if not also triumphant, sort. The images used here to describe the servant's activity apparently wish to emphasize just the opposite (vv. 2-3), and in that consists their special character, for success will ensue just as surely as if the traditional endowments gave rise to traditional behaviors.

It has been argued that these descriptions of the servant's demeanor are actually keyed to later manifestations of his activity within the cycle of "servant poems." That is, depictions in this first song "anticipate(s) the sufferings the servant is to endure during his mission, sufferings that are elaborated fully in the other Songs (xlix 4; l 6; liii)."[57] Even if one is not wedded to the theory of a "servant-song cycle," what is striking here would be the notion of literary anticipation. That is, the author has so planned his work that he anticipates resolutions or clarifications and is free to forestall them at an earlier juncture. An alternative to be pursued here is that a description of the servant's vocation and ultimate success constitutes God's word to the author, made before the divine council, and like the words to which appeal has been made earlier, we must wait for fulfillment, just as surely as do the coastlands. More than a literary technique is at work here in the declaration before the heavenly court of the servant's final success. A promise has been made, and God will have to make good on it.

Westermann had spoken of two lines of mediation that, in Moses, had yet to come apart. His

55. W. A. M. Beuken, *"Mispat:* The First Servant Song and Its Context," *VT* 22 (1972) 1-30.
56. Westermann, *Isaiah 40–66,* 94.
57. Beuken, *"Mispat,"* 26.

temporal scheme is fine, but he should have pressed back even further in Israel's history, to the period of the ancestors and the promises made to the covenanted Abraham, in order to set the proper context for this servant poem. There it is that concern for the nations within God's created design surfaces. The nations—"all the families of the earth"—are part of a promise of blessing through Abraham that is not yet realized (Gen 12:1-3). The covenant made with Abraham promises not only that nations (and kings) will issue forth from him, but also, and more important, that Yahweh "will be their God" (Gen 17:8). The servant is dispatched to bring those promises to completion, armed now with a *mišpāṭ* and a *tôrâ* that Israel has come to associate with God's servant Moses, as well as the prophet Isaiah (Isa 1:10; 2:3; 8:16).

42:5-9. The first messenger formula here introduces God's speech to Israel. The lengthy predication of v. 5 ("he who created the heavens"; "who gives breath . . . and life to those who walk on [earth]") is consistent with the preceding unit in stressing the universality of God's claim, here announced to God's particular people, Israel. The breath all humanity draws has one source (Gen 2:7). In v. 6, Israel is addressed, and the role God has given the people in vv. 1-4 is described to them, again with emphasis on their relationship to the nations. For this the terse phrase, the word ברית עם (*běrît 'ām*), "covenant to the nations," is used, in parallel to אור גוים (*'ôr gôyim*), "light of the nations." Israel was formed, like the first human being, with this particular role in mind. The whole force of the unit is to define Israel's role within the context of all peoples to whom God has given breath and life.

The centrality of the concept of covenant for understanding the discourse of these chapters has been emphasized throughout, and here the term "covenant" (*běrît*) appears. The Hebrew of v. 6b is quite dense. It is unclear whether Israel is a "covenant people"—and in this very role (based on understanding of the proximity of Genesis 17 to this discourse) has a defined relationship to the nations—or whether the final two phrases are in stricter parallelism, with *'ām* and *gôyim* paired. This would produce the (perhaps intentionally) novel reading: "I made you a covenant vis-à-vis the people, a light vis-à-vis the nations." In either case,

the emphasis remains on Israel's defined role in relationship to the nations. Therefore, the opening of blind eyes and freeing from prisons of darkness (v. 7) applies not to Israel, but to humanity in the most general sense. There is an implicit irony here, which will be addressed in short order: How can a blind and deaf and imprisoned Israel be of any help to those outside its number? This topic is discussed in detail in the section to follow (42:14–44:22), especially because blindness and deafness are well-known problems in the book of Isaiah (see 6:9-10); but this unit simply foreshadows that discussion with the concluding words, "the former things have come to pass" (v. 9). The new thing remains on the horizon, and it involves the relationship of the servant Israel to the nations. God is announcing it ahead of time in the spirit of the former things, which have now come to pass and give way to a new cycle of announcement and anticipated fulfillment.

The servant designated for a task vis-à-vis the nations is Israel, according to an old design and purpose. In Isaiah 40–48, the identification of the servant with Israel is frequent and in most instances unequivocal (41:8-9; 42:19; 43:10; 44:1-2, 21; 44:26; 45:4; 48:20). To say this is not, however, to resolve a very complex presentation of Israel's servant status; this is pressed home almost immediately over the next three chapters (42:14–44:22). Moreover, it leaves untouched the question of the identity of the servant in the second section and beyond (chaps. 49–66). At this juncture what is clear is that Israel, according to an old identity, is presented as servant to the divine council and those assembled for trial, including most especially the nations. There they are told that through the agency of servant Israel the nations will receive God's *mišpāṭ* and *tôrâ* and that they can be sure of this, despite the unusual character of the agent and the agency. It is, moreover, not enough that the nations hear of the unusual agent and agency; Israel must be told that it has this task, since, however rooted in former things such an understanding is, what is truly new is the announcement that this task is about to be undertaken—and undertaken with success.

42:10-13. Befitting a new thing is a new song. Again, consistent with the wide lens of the previous units, those enjoined to sing are not Israel specifically but the wider creation generally. The images of vv. 10-11 are meant to emphasize expanse and reach. At the most distant and most unlikely places—desert, sea, mountains, coastlands, end of the earth—let song arise to the God of all creation.

This song may well take as a point of reference, and departure, the concluding hymn of Isa 12:1-6, often regarded as a sort of signature piece, or incipit, in which the prophet's name (ישעיהו *yěša'yāhû*) is alluded to with the repeated reference to "salvation" (ישועתי *yěšû'ātî*, v. 2*a*; לישועה *lîšû'â*, v. 2*b*; הישועה *hayšû'â* v. 3*a*). That song tells of a future day (ביום ההוא *bayyôm hahû'*) when an individual will give praise and thanksgiving for God's comfort and forgiveness. This spills over to a plural reference in vv. 3-6, and we learn that the nations, too, are to know of God's ways (v. 3). What God has done "is known in all the earth." Yet this vision clearly remains on the distant horizon, and the hymn concludes with Zion singing God's praises (v. 6).

What that hymn sees in the distance, this hymn has begun to participate in. Some commentators speak of the eschatological character of the hymn in order to blur the precise temporal framework. That is, we know that God's activity through servant Israel, on behalf of the wider creation, still awaits fulfillment. At the same time, what God has announced deserves response of the only sort appropriate, and so all creation is enjoined to break forth in song. What Isaiah had announced of old is now coming into being. What an unknown audience was to say "in that day" has now been said, as God's deeds are to be made known by servant Israel "among the peoples" (Isa 12:4). The final verse (v. 13) clearly intends to ease the transition to the passage that follows (42:14-17). It also insists that the God active in the past as divine warrior, in exodus and in occupation and in prophetic judgment, remains active now toward a new end: the vanquishing of foes who would prevent God's being known in all the earth.

REFLECTIONS

1. The similarity of Mark 1:11 to Isa 42:1 has been frequently noted (with additional influence from Ps 2:7). It is a "voice from heaven" that pronounces the words, "You are my Son, the Beloved; with you I am well pleased." In Mark as in Isaiah, what is clarified is the *character* of the relationship between the one sent and the sender. In Isaiah, we know that the servant is fully supported by God, is fully pleasing to God, is fully endowed by God. The character of that relationship alone begs for mission, implies a vocation with God's own stamp on it. In the case of John's baptism of Jesus, the image the evangelist uses to convey the sense of urgency implied by the relationship is that "the heavens were torn apart" (Mark 1:10). Heaven cannot hold speech like this any more than it could in the days of Isaiah. The Spirit given to the servant in Isa 42:1 likewise must take form in Mark, and the form the eye sees is the dove, descending on Jesus.

Taken literally, the image is an unusual one. It cannot be easily explained as being pressed on the evangelist from some strange Old Testament setting. At the same time, the unusual character of the Spirit's descent may well find its home in the mission of the servant in Isaiah, in which the Spirit's endowment gives rise to behaviors not generally associated with kings or prophets: no shouting, no sounding off in a public show, "a bruised reed he will not break, and a dimly burning wick he will not quench" (42:2). The descent of the Spirit like a dove may be an effort after all to capture something of the strange mixture of assured success—he will not break or crush, but neither will he be broken or crushed—and peaceful inner resolve that is not the innate human bearing. When we see this in the ordinary human being, we speculate it has a source from heaven. In the case of Jesus of Nazareth, the evangelist leaves no doubt: The heavens are torn apart; what issues forth is a dove.

Then the Spirit drives him immediately into the wilderness (Mark 1:12). Neither the Son nor the servant—pleasing as each is to God—hangs around very long, basking in that status. God unabashedly describes a mission; it will be difficult, but it is meant to set in right order a plan and a design long overdue for completion: "And the coastlands wait for his teaching" (Isa 42:4). Mark describes that teaching in terse form: "The time is fulfilled, and the kingdom of God has come near; repent and believe in the good news" (Mark 1:14). The promise embedded in God's word to Abraham and embodied in Isaiah's servant Israel is here manifested in the man Jesus.

2. It is now clear that one of the places historical-critical method overreached itself was in trying to establish a hermeneutical lens through which consistency and authorial intention were valued, in the face of a biblical record that operated internally with very different constraints and expectations. This is true not just of the way the New Testament hears the Old, but in the way both Testaments reflect on earlier traditions within their own compass. Suddenly there was no way to appreciate, short of rationalistic explanation, what is arguably the most decisive element at work in the New Testament witness to Jesus Christ: pressure from Israel's scriptures.

In the reading of the servant adopted here, much has been made of the covenant with Abraham and especially the references to nations that appear in Genesis 17, alongside the more constrained "offspring." Did the author of Genesis 17—now reckoned to be the priestly writer—mean that the God of Israel (the son of Abraham) would in time be recognized as the one God of all the nations? Suprisingly, for all the value placed on single authorial intention in the tradition of historical criticism, a survey of modern commentaries will show a true variety of interpretations, some stressing the universal capacity of the text's plain sense, others a restriction to Israel as nation.

The point is not to resolve the issue once and for all, but to recognize that no diachronic or historic approach can ever constrain the way a text (or even a tradition) might have been heard within Scripture itself. To seek the meaning the priestly writer intended offers a good starting point and helps us to calibrate a range of interpretations, but it may still fail to understand how that same text might have been heard within the biblical tradition.

What good biblical interpretation seeks is close reading of the plain sense and an eye toward seeing how a range of interpretations can open up as God's Word presses forward—not without limit, but also not without power to accomplish a new thing under God's providence. What is striking about Genesis 17 is that it seeks such an ambitious horizon. It talks of offspring and nations and even kings, and then without nailing down the referent it concludes, "and I will be their God" (Gen 17:8). The text could refer to Abraham and his immediate progeny only or to those who take possession of the land in time to come. Yet at the same time the text has ambitiously called Abram "Abraham," father of a multitude and has gone on to call him "the ancestor of a multitude of nations," the one from whom nations and kings will arise. Ishmael—not Isaac—is circumcised in the same chapter.

The author of Isaiah is aware of these promises and of Israel's strained relationship to the nations as falling short of what God intends for the larger created order. And so a servant is dispatched with a new task, meant to complete an old promise, just as in a latter day another servant will take up that same task, inaugurated by a voice from heaven, speaking words new and old. Did this author hear the message of Genesis 17 rightly? God alone knows.

"God alone knows" is not a counsel of despair but a claim that, in the freedom of the Holy Spirit, God takes the Word and drives it home to us as God wills. This was true for the author of Isaiah, and it remains true of the way God uses the divine Word with us and for us today. Just as the search for single authorial intention missed the patterns of Scripture itself, so, too, it diminished the freedom of God to speak in more than one way, through the testimony of a single tradition. In the history of interpretation it was meaningful to speak of a "double literal sense" and multiple spiritual and moral senses.[58] That is true not because the history of interpretation was blind to authorial intention, but because it reckoned with God as author and the Word as being under God's pedagogical control. What we must pray for is a rejuvenated sense of God's providence, the superintendence through time of God's Word to the church.

58. B. S. Childs, *"Sensus Literalis*: An Ancient and Modern Problem," in *Beitrage zur alttestamentlichen Theologie* (Gottingen: Vandenhoeck & Ruprecht, 1976); K. Greene-McCreight, *Ad Litteram: How Augustine, Calvin, and Barth Read the "Plain Sense" of Genesis 1–3* (New York: Peter Lang, 1999).

3. There are times when the only possible response to news of great moment is to break forth in song. To label this a genre ("hymn") fails to do justice to all that a song conveys. The commands (e.g., "let the sea roar"; "let the desert and towns lift up their voice"), of course, suggest that we do not yet have singing, but only the anticipation of faithful joining in from all corners of creation.

The contrast with the servant is striking. His silent, faithful bearing leads to worldwide justice, which in turn sparks an explosion heard throughout the universe: roaring, shouting, praising. He does not lift up his voice in the streets (Isa 42:2), and as a consequence, the deserts, the towns, and the villages lift up theirs (Isa 42:11).

Perhaps the hardest trial of faith is to persevere, to "bear under" (cf. Job and the commendation of him in Jas 5:11), in silence or with cries, through time, unsure of the outcome, guided only by a sure, small voice insisting that you are God's servant and you will be upheld. We need reminders such as these that silence is often the most productive bearing of all, because it can permit another sort of conception and gestation to take place, sometimes "three days" in its deafening character. Yet into this seeming vacuum, this dark and silent tomb, comes a rush from heaven unlike that of a dove or even torn skies as all the powers of death and darkness and despair are robbed of their inner nerve. So it is fitting that the stones themselves are enjoined to sing (Isa 41:11), that the commands are turned into indicative, as God goes forth in triumph against foes unnamed, greater and older than any mere national power. Room has been created by the servant's faithful, entombed silence, and into this room the Holy One comes victorious, finishing and perfecting the work of the servant in establishing true justice in all the earth. In fulfillment of Isaiah, even the stones sing the praises of the Holy One, the servant, the Son.

ISAIAH 42:14-25, BLIND LEADING THE BLIND?

NIV

[14]"For a long time I have kept silent,
  I have been quiet and held myself back.
But now, like a woman in childbirth,
  I cry out, I gasp and pant.
[15]I will lay waste the mountains and hills
  and dry up all their vegetation;
I will turn rivers into islands
  and dry up the pools.
[16]I will lead the blind by ways they have
    not known,
  along unfamiliar paths I will guide them;
I will turn the darkness into light before them
  and make the rough places smooth.
These are the things I will do;
  I will not forsake them.
[17]But those who trust in idols,
  who say to images, 'You are our gods,'
  will be turned back in utter shame.

[18]"Hear, you deaf;

NRSV

[14] For a long time I have held my peace,
  I have kept still and restrained myself;
now I will cry out like a woman in labor,
  I will gasp and pant.
[15] I will lay waste mountains and hills,
  and dry up all their herbage;
I will turn the rivers into islands,
  and dry up the pools.
[16] I will lead the blind
  by a road they do not know,
by paths they have not known
  I will guide them.
I will turn the darkness before them into light,
  the rough places into level ground.
These are the things I will do,
  and I will not forsake them.
[17] They shall be turned back and utterly put
    to shame—
  those who trust in carved images,

NIV

look, you blind, and see!
¹⁹Who is blind but my servant,
and deaf like the messenger I send?
Who is blind like the one committed to me,
blind like the servant of the LORD?
²⁰You have seen many things, but have paid
no attention;
your ears are open, but you hear nothing."
²¹It pleased the LORD
for the sake of his righteousness
to make his law great and glorious.
²²But this is a people plundered and looted,
all of them trapped in pits
or hidden away in prisons.
They have become plunder,
with no one to rescue them;
they have been made loot,
with no one to say, "Send them back."

²³Which of you will listen to this
or pay close attention in time to come?
²⁴Who handed Jacob over to become loot,
and Israel to the plunderers?
Was it not the LORD,
against whom we have sinned?
For they would not follow his ways;
they did not obey his law.
²⁵So he poured out on them his burning anger,
the violence of war.
It enveloped them in flames, yet they did not
understand;
it consumed them, but they did not take it
to heart.

NRSV

who say to cast images,
"You are our gods."

¹⁸ Listen, you that are deaf;
and you that are blind, look up and see!
¹⁹ Who is blind but my servant,
or deaf like my messenger whom I send?
Who is blind like my dedicated one,
or blind like the servant of the LORD?
²⁰ He sees many things, but doesᵃ not
observe them;
his ears are open, but he does not hear.
²¹ The LORD was pleased, for the sake of his
righteousness,
to magnify his teaching and make it
glorious.
²² But this is a people robbed and plundered,
all of them are trapped in holes
and hidden in prisons;
they have become a prey with no one
to rescue,
a spoil with no one to say, "Restore!"
²³ Who among you will give heed to this,
who will attend and listen for the time
to come?
²⁴ Who gave up Jacob to the spoiler,
and Israel to the robbers?
Was it not the LORD, against whom we
have sinned,
in whose ways they would not walk,
and whose law they would not obey?
²⁵ So he poured upon him the heat of his anger
and the fury of war;
it set him on fire all around, but he did not
understand;
it burned him, but he did not take it
to heart.

ᵃHeb *You see many things but do*

COMMENTARY

We now enter a new section of discourse (42:14–44:22), with a hymn at its conclusion (44:23). A problem has been introduced in the commissioning of servant Israel as light to the nations—namely, Israel's own track record as being blind and deaf and its own present impris-

onment and subjugation. These issues are addressed by God in this section. As the past is taken up and set before Israel, calling for acknowledgment and repentence, God also sets before the servant a new thing, in the present time. The ועתה (*wĕ'attâ,* "but now") of 43:1 and 44:1 introduces this new frame of reference and allows God to describe what is now to be done (43:1-7; 44:1-8). Interspersed are also challenges to the nations (43:8-15) and to Israel (43:22-28) to go ahead and accuse or bring witnesses. These passages remind us that the trial proceedings have not been set aside, even as a variety of forms of speech (oracle of salvation, disputation, "fear-not" assurance, trial speech) has been creatively adapted to that setting.

42:14-17. Verse 16 suggests that its form is an oracle of salvation. Yet the larger context in which the passage now functions has influenced that form considerably.[59] The picture of long-standing constraint with which the unit opens is connected with the preceding "divine warrior" depiction. The marching forth of God against foes has been delayed, because God has so planned it. Perhaps an objection to the contrary lies behind this depiction (e.g., God is weak; God is slow; cf. chaps. 63–64), but this must remain conjecture.

The literal rendering of מעולם (*mēʿôlām*, v. 14) would be "from eternity." This may be rhetorical flourish, meant to highlight the energy about to be released—not unlike an overlong pregnancy (v. 14). It may also be related to the period spanned by the book of Isaiah's own internal time frame. The reference to blindness and darkness, closely tied to the preceding charge to the servant (see v. 7), and there linked to humanity's more universal condition, will become in the unit that follows more specifically Israel's blindness and deafness. There it is reasonably clear that this condition is traceable to the times and mission of Isaiah of Jerusalem (6:9-10) quite specifically. The period of judgment—and magnification of תורה *tôrâ* (v. 21)—is also closely related to the book of Isaiah's own internal temporal framework and logic.

Still, this first unit holds back that context in order to speak about more general human darkness, within which Israel's more specific condition presents problems as well as possibilities. The mission servant Israel is to be about—opening blind eyes, removing prison's darkness (vv. 6-7)—is God's own personal mission as well, and it involves the world God has made in the broadest

sense. This shuttling back and forth from God's activity to Israel's activity is a hallmark of the discourse, and we are prepared for it in chap. 41, where Israel threshes mountains with God's help, so that all might know "the hand of the LORD has done this" (41:20). The servant's activity has the warrant and backing of the one who upholds (42:1).

Seen in this context, the opening reference, "from forever," may be more than rhetorical flourish or an appeal to Isaiah's own internal judgment clock (see esp. 6:11). The darkness and blindness that have persisted throughout creation, "from forever," God will tolerate no longer. The rough places were to be turned to plain, 40:4 insisted and 42:16 reiterates, so that God's glory might be revealed, and "all people shall see it together" (40:5). The universal mission of the servant is here the subject of the Holy One's own work. If this temporal perspective is correct, then it takes its bearings from the division of the nations in the primeval period (see Genesis 1–11), scattered in judgment. Isaiah's "people who walk in darkness" (9:2) are but one segment of a much larger problem. God intends now to address this through the agency of the servant.

42:18-25. The call to hear and to see in Isaiah tragically led to no understanding, to no knowledge, to dulled hearts, to clogged ears, and to veiled eyes (6:9-10). Yet the prophet was to continue his mission, seemingly that this condition might grow worse still—that is, until full judgment had fallen (6:11-12). But even then God had promised that there would be a holy seed, refined by fire, a charred reminder of God's cleansing *mišpāṭ,* (6:13).

That condition so poignantly depicted in the days of Isaiah is here brought back to mind. God's servant, presented before the heavenly assembly and earth's widest reaches, is no ideal figure whose past has been sanitized or obliterated or even forgotten. God's dedicated servant bears fully the marks of that obdurate generation that preceded him, both in election and in merited judgment. Verse 20 has every indication of meaning to invoke Isaiah's earlier commissioning scene, where, though seeing, a former generation did not see, and, though having ears, they failed to hear. The servant commissioned by God for a special task is no stranger to the biblical landscape. Nor

59. Melugin apparently feels this influence was felt even earlier, in the history of the form itself, as an oracle of salvation was explicitly shaped to address a communal lament. See R. F. Melugin, *The Formation of Isaiah 40–55*, BZAW 141 (Berlin: Walter de Gruyter, 1976) 102.

will this complex admixture of beloved and blind lend itself to resolution by speaking of one "ideal" servant here and another less winsome there.[60] This is the servant Israel whom God is presently commissioning, a servant with open ears and eyes that frequently fail to take in what God displays. But that has never drawn down the balance of God's own righteousness, as the people fail to live up to God's public statements about them. In the same section of the book of Isaiah where we hear about the divine word, about teaching's shutting ears, and about even darker days to come (8:17-22), תורה (tôrâ) and testimony will survive, sealed among God's disciples. It is that which bears witness to God's righteousness, foresaken in one day, but resplendent in another for those who wait on God (8:16-17). Here lie the roots of the somewhat unique expression that for the sake of righteousness, God "magnified tôrâ and made it glorious" (see v. 42).

The syntax of v. 22 intends to lay emphasis on sharp contrast: Nevertheless, at the same time, "this is a people robbed and plundered." The poet here underscores that whatever deficiencies Israel exhibited in a prior day, it has now fully borne a difficult judgment.[61] With this description of grim imprisonment, the mission of the servant to alleviate the general human condition is recalled and rounded out as we learn that alongside deafness and blindness (v. 6), dungeons and prisons of dark-

ness (v. 7) are fates Israel has come to know first-hand (v. 22). The servant does not step into regions unfamiliar, but ones where blindness, deafness, and imprisonment have become the means of God's grace.

The final section of the unit (vv. 23-25) is unique in several respects. A question is posed to a plural audience concerning who will take in the truth of what is being communicated. "Is comprehension at last possible?" the text seems to be asking. The testimony from an earlier day—the refusal to hear and understand—still seems to haunt the servant. The question is then posed, "Who brought about this situation of distress?" "Was it accident? Arbitrary divine wrath? Faulty comprehension apparatus?" For the first time in the discourse we get a glimpse at the audience, as first-person plural response—thus far unique—is given: The Lord was the agent of judgment, for we sinned against God (v. 24). I have argued elsewhere that this unique form of speech is similar to confessional refrains in the book of Jeremiah (e.g., Jer 3:24-25), where a present generation accepts responsibility and asks for forgiveness for the sins of a previous generation and for their own sins.[62] This confession allows a new beginning for God's people, signaled by the "but now" ועתה (wĕ'attâ) of 43:1. The final verse of the chapter merely describes the sentence of judgment against God's people that we should know well from the former things of Isaiah (1:7, 31; 6:13). But that sentence now describes a past reality, already experienced. It was not understood or taken to heart—but God is about to change all that, so that the servant might be about a new thing in God's service.

---

60. Herein lie the roots of a conception of "servant songs" over against the other servant passages, like this one, where the servant is not "ideal." This conception was given a sort of canonical status after Duhm's 1892 treatment. Duhm spoke of the "hero" of the songs, "innocent, disciple of the LORD, daily illumined by him, quiet in service, with a mission to the nations" to be contrasted with Israel as servant, "blind and deaf, imprisoned and plundered, a worm, full of sin." See B. Duhm, *Das Buch Jesaia,* HKAT (Göttingen: Vandenhoeck & Ruprecht, 1892) 284.

61. Duhm felt that this specific description did not comport with what we know of life in exile and "proved that Deutero-Isaiah did not live in Babylon." Ibid., 294.

62. See C. R. Seitz, "How Is the Prophet Isaiah Present in the Latter Half of the Book? The Logic of Chapters 40–66 Within the Book of Isaiah," *JBL* 115 (1996) 232.

REFLECTIONS

1. The central, if not greatest, evangelical truth is that God takes what is weakness and sin in us and uses precisely these to reconstruct us in service. There are not two servants: one ideal, one deaf and blind. The messenger God sends (42:19) not only is unequipped for the task, in terms of creaturely endowment, but also has a history of disobedience and failure to heed, the burden of which frustrates God's capacity to begin anew. It is as though there are two potential hindrances facing us in God's service: our resistance to God in the most basic sense and our knowledge that this resistance has a history and a legacy in us.

The first deficiency, God is prepared to work with. We must come to accept this reality about ourselves, however, as the ground of our identity and our life in God and not believe that God uses only our "talents" or our "best" innate skills and traits. How attractive a view it is that the Christian life consists in matching our natural endowments and proclivities with tasks worthy of and compatible with them. Israel also was tempted to think this way about God's choice and use of it, as if *by nature* Israel possessed the endowments requisite for God's service and could reflect on these as justifying God's decision to "set his heart" on this nation, "out of all the peoples on earth to be his people" (Deut 7:6-7). Yet God's love of Israel is a mystery, and the freedom with which God chose Israel is the only ground of its affection and obedience in return (Deut 7:8). Doubtless this passage from Deuteronomy, like Isaiah 42, was written, not from the standpoint of anticipated obedience from a godly people, but with full knowledge of Israel's weakness and failure, in the wilderness that lay before them and in the wilderness of exile that lay further ahead (Deut 30:1-10). Paul's having been chosen in Christ does not dislodge this mystery, even as it brings it into poignant focus (Rom 9:1-5) and asks for a similar awareness of utter unworthiness at having been loved by God, in Christ, and set free for service.

The second matter—sin's burden and the weight of the knowledge of disobedience—must be confronted in a different sense. If we must *accept* our innate human blindness as a reality unable to block God's love and commissioning of us in service, we must *confess* the history of failure and the fruit of that blindness as offensive to God and not just as an unfortunate failure to match our best skills with what God would have us be and do, leading to our present depression or unhappy state. There had to be a connection between sin and accountability to God before any new thing could start. And the new status quo was not a new Israel, with new ears and new eyes that this time promised unfailing recognition, but an Israel *redeemed* (43:1) and recommissioned on the same grounds as before: "because you are precious in my sight, and honored, and I love you" (43:4). Nothing more, but also nothing less.

2. What is striking, if not also difficult and offensive to the modern mind, is the seriousness of both sides of this dialectic of "judging love." God truly poured on Israel "the heat of his anger and the fury of war" (42:25). The failure to hear and see what God says and manifests carries with it the maximum penalty possible, short of complete annihilation. Even the tenth burned again (6:13), and the right testimony of Joshua and Caleb (Numbers 13–14) sadly only underscore the maximal seriousness with which God demands our obedience and affection. We lose God at our peril, in the most absolute sense.

Yet with that same seriousness God reaches out to resuscitate and commission the deaf and blind servant. There are no half-measures, no splitting of the difference, no saying that the first half of the equation was too highly calibrated. Only that seriousness can effect a confession of sin whose consequence is forgiveness and new life. There is full condemnation (2 Cor 3:9) precisely that "he might have mercy upon all" (Rom 11:32). Isaiah 42 bears as eloquent a testimony to this reality, in the choosing of blind servant Israel, as can be found anywhere else in Scripture.

3. "Your prophets . . . have not exposed your iniquity to restore your fortunes." So the author of Lam 2:14 reflects on the punishment of God and the failure of the prophets to properly expose iniquity. Within this same frame of reference lies the perspective of the psalmist, who reckons that God's judgments are matters to long for, "Let the daughters of Judah rejoice because of thy judgments" (Ps 48:11). Without the judgment of God, we are left with our blindness and deafness in a world where only vague shapes appear: "They look like trees walking" (Mark 8:24).

Yet with God's judgment an avenue is opened up, into which confession and acknowledgment of guilt are channeled. This road requires painful self-reflection and may at times seem so exceedingly narrow that we simply cannot start down it. This is why one properly longs for *God's* judgment, for the choice is not whether there must be judgment, but whose. Israel's confession here is brief but unmistakable (42:23-25). It comes within the context of extended divine assurances, exhortation, challenge, and recommissioning—in short, it comes within the common prophetic legacy, here taken up by God, of exposing guilt so as to restore fortune.

Efforts to lift the spirits by therapeutic encouragement and avoidance of "judgmentalism" must carefully assess whether God's judgments are, in fact, at work. This does not mean conjuring them up but asking the harder question: where and how and whether they are already being experienced in some way that God positively intends. Removing the language of judgment from our worship and discourse may only allow us to persist in blindness and never know the widest range of what God intends for us, as we find places of blindness, deafness, and imprisonment transformed under divine judgments.

ISAIAH 43:1-28, AN ISAIAN EXODUS

NIV

43 But now, this is what the LORD says—
he who created you, O Jacob,
he who formed you, O Israel:
"Fear not, for I have redeemed you;
I have summoned you by name; you are mine.
[2] When you pass through the waters,
I will be with you;
and when you pass through the rivers,
they will not sweep over you.
When you walk through the fire,
you will not be burned;
the flames will not set you ablaze.
[3] For I am the LORD, your God,
the Holy One of Israel, your Savior;
I give Egypt for your ransom,
Cush[a] and Seba in your stead.
[4] Since you are precious and honored in
my sight,
and because I love you,
I will give men in exchange for you,
and people in exchange for your life.
[5] Do not be afraid, for I am with you;
I will bring your children from the east
and gather you from the west.
[6] I will say to the north, 'Give them up!'
and to the south, 'Do not hold them back.'
Bring my sons from afar
and my daughters from the ends of
the earth—
[7] everyone who is called by my name,
whom I created for my glory,
whom I formed and made."

[a] 3 That is, the upper Nile region

NRSV

43 But now thus says the LORD,
he who created you, O Jacob,
he who formed you, O Israel:
Do not fear, for I have redeemed you;
I have called you by name, you are mine.
[2] When you pass through the waters, I will be
with you;
and through the rivers, they shall not
overwhelm you;
when you walk through fire you shall not
be burned,
and the flame shall not consume you.
[3] For I am the LORD your God,
the Holy One of Israel, your Savior.
I give Egypt as your ransom,
Ethiopia[a] and Seba in exchange for you.
[4] Because you are precious in my sight,
and honored, and I love you,
I give people in return for you,
nations in exchange for your life.
[5] Do not fear, for I am with you;
I will bring your offspring from the east,
and from the west I will gather you;
[6] I will say to the north, "Give them up,"
and to the south, "Do not withhold;
bring my sons from far away
and my daughters from the end of
the earth—
[7] everyone who is called by my name,
whom I created for my glory,
whom I formed and made."

[a] Or Nubia; Heb Cush

NIV

⁸Lead out those who have eyes but are blind,
    who have ears but are deaf.
⁹All the nations gather together
    and the peoples assemble.
Which of them foretold this
    and proclaimed to us the former things?
Let them bring in their witnesses to prove
        they were right,
    so that others may hear and say, "It is true."
¹⁰"You are my witnesses," declares the LORD,
    "and my servant whom I have chosen,
so that you may know and believe me
    and understand that I am he.
Before me no god was formed,
    nor will there be one after me.
¹¹I, even I, am the LORD,
    and apart from me there is no savior.
¹²I have revealed and saved and proclaimed—
    I, and not some foreign god among you.
You are my witnesses," declares the LORD,
    "that I am God.
¹³   Yes, and from ancient days I am he.
No one can deliver out of my hand.
    When I act, who can reverse it?"

¹⁴This is what the LORD says—
    your Redeemer, the Holy One of Israel:
"For your sake I will send to Babylon
    and bring down as fugitives all the
        Babylonians,ᵃ
    in the ships in which they took pride.
¹⁵I am the LORD, your Holy One,
    Israel's Creator, your King."

¹⁶This is what the LORD says—
    he who made a way through the sea,
    a path through the mighty waters,
¹⁷who drew out the chariots and horses,
    the army and reinforcements together,
and they lay there, never to rise again,
    extinguished, snuffed out like a wick:
¹⁸"Forget the former things;
    do not dwell on the past.
¹⁹See, I am doing a new thing!
    Now it springs up; do you not perceive it?
I am making a way in the desert
    and streams in the wasteland.
²⁰The wild animals honor me,

ᵇ14 Or Chaldeans

NRSV

⁸ Bring forth the people who are blind, yet
        have eyes,
    who are deaf, yet have ears!
⁹ Let all the nations gather together,
    and let the peoples assemble.
Who among them declared this,
    and foretold to us the former things?
Let them bring their witnesses to justify them,
    and let them hear and say, "It is true."
¹⁰ You are my witnesses, says the LORD,
    and my servant whom I have chosen,
so that you may know and believe me
    and understand that I am he.
Before me no god was formed,
    nor shall there be any after me.
¹¹ I, I am the LORD,
    and besides me there is no savior.
¹² I declared and saved and proclaimed,
    when there was no strange god among you;
    and you are my witnesses, says the LORD.
¹³ I am God, and also henceforth I am He;
    there is no one who can deliver from
        my hand;
    I work and who can hinder it?

¹⁴ Thus says the LORD,
    your Redeemer, the Holy One of Israel:
For your sake I will send to Babylon
    and break down all the bars,
    and the shouting of the Chaldeans will be
        turned to lamentation.ᵃ
¹⁵ I am the LORD, your Holy One,
    the Creator of Israel, your King.
¹⁶ Thus says the LORD,
    who makes a way in the sea,
    a path in the mighty waters,
¹⁷ who brings out chariot and horse,
    army and warrior;
they lie down, they cannot rise,
    they are extinguished, quenched like
        a wick:
¹⁸ Do not remember the former things,
    or consider the things of old.
¹⁹ I am about to do a new thing;
    now it springs forth, do you not perceive it?
I will make a way in the wilderness
    and rivers in the desert.

ᵃMeaning of Heb uncertain

NIV

the jackals and the owls,
because I provide water in the desert
and streams in the wasteland,
to give drink to my people, my chosen,
21 the people I formed for myself
that they may proclaim my praise.

22"Yet you have not called upon me, O Jacob,
you have not wearied yourselves for me,
O Israel.
23You have not brought me sheep for burnt
offerings,
nor honored me with your sacrifices.
I have not burdened you with grain offerings
nor wearied you with demands for incense.
24You have not bought any fragrant calamus
for me,
or lavished on me the fat of your sacrifices.
But you have burdened me with your sins
and wearied me with your offenses.

25"I, even I, am he who blots out
your transgressions, for my own sake,
and remembers your sins no more.
26Review the past for me,
let us argue the matter together;
state the case for your innocence.
27Your first father sinned;
your spokesmen rebelled against me.
28So I will disgrace the dignitaries of
your temple,
and I will consign Jacob to destruction[a]
and Israel to scorn.

[a]28 The Hebrew term refers to the irrevocable giving over of things or
persons to the LORD, often by totally destroying them.

NRSV

20 The wild animals will honor me,
the jackals and the ostriches;
for I give water in the wilderness,
rivers in the desert,
to give drink to my chosen people,
21 the people whom I formed for myself
so that they might declare my praise.

22 Yet you did not call upon me, O Jacob;
but you have been weary of me, O Israel!
23 You have not brought me your sheep for
burnt offerings,
or honored me with your sacrifices.
I have not burdened you with offerings,
or wearied you with frankincense.
24 You have not bought me sweet cane
with money,
or satisfied me with the fat of your
sacrifices.
But you have burdened me with your sins;
you have wearied me with your iniquities.

25 I, I am He
who blots out your transgressions for my
own sake,
and I will not remember your sins.
26 Accuse me, let us go to trial;
set forth your case, so that you may be
proved right.
27 Your first ancestor sinned,
and your interpreters transgressed
against me.
28 Therefore I profaned the princes of
the sanctuary,
I delivered Jacob to utter destruction,
and Israel to reviling.

[a]Meaning of Heb uncertain

COMMENTARY

Chapter 43 consists of four coordinated units: vv. 1-7, vv. 8-15, vv. 16-21, and vv. 22-28. An oracle of salvation, introduced by "but now" (v. 1), shifts the focus from Israel's prior blindness and judgment (42:18-25) to God's present word of assurance. The second unit (vv. 8-15) is likewise familiar in a formal sense;[63] individual trial speeches appear here and elsewhere in this long

63. So Westermann and others. Melugin further subdivides the second unit into vv. 8-13 and vv. 14-15, and he labels vv. 8-13 a "trial speech" and vv. 14-15 a salvation speech. See R. F. Melugin, *The Formation of Isaiah 40–55*, BZAW 141 (Berlin: Walter de Gruyter, 1976) 110. Here one sees the difficulty of adopting a too strict form-critical approach, since many of the types are mixed in such a way as to invite subdivision when a change of content can be detected.

section (chaps. 41–48) to remind us of the ongoing character of the trial proceedings from the divine council and Israel's role as special witness to God, now as the reassured and recommissioned servant. This is followed by a second salvation speech (vv. 16-21) and another trial or disputation speech (vv. 22-28). A theme that further holds the various units together is the appeal to exodus motifs (passing through water, v. 2; ransom, v. 3; chariots and horses, v. 16; water in the desert, v. 20). Some scholars regard these motifs as being referenced by the phrase "former things" (vv. 9, 18). Both of these views will be examined in detail. The final unit (vv. 22-28) introduces a concern that, on the face of it, is unrelated to either exilic life or the exodus: failure to offer sacrifice.

43:1-7. The notion that God created and formed Jacob/Israel puts before us the two verbs ברא (*br'*, "created") and יצר (*ysr*, "formed"), sometimes thought to represent rival or distinctive understandings, associated with God's creation of humankind and the entire cosmos (Gen 1:1; 2:7). The ancestors are "called" by God, beginning with Abraham (Gen 12:1-3), but the notion that the ancestor Jacob/Israel was "created" and "formed" like the first man, Adam (1:27; 2:7), is unusual enough to call for comment and reflection.

Noting the provocative collocation, Westermann relates God's creative activity with Jacob/Israel to that "saving act by which (God) brought Israel into being"; for Westermann, that saving act is the exodus.[64] It is difficult to know the degree to which he has pre-judged the matter, either anticipating what appear to be references to exodus events in the larger unit (vv. 2-3) or as a result of the generally heavy emphasis placed on the exodus as Israel's birth-event by neo-orthodox interpreters (e.g., von Rad; B. Anderson). As we have seen thus far, Jacob/Israel can mean precisely what it says: the people Israel in the context of ancestral election. This theme is arguably also present—and significant—in the larger chapter. The important thing is not to adopt too restrictive an interpretation too quickly, but to work toward a comprehensive reading.

How critical is the exodus context for the proper interpretation of the unit? We want to hold out for the likelihood that the first verse is speaking

of that signal act by which Israel came into being—namely, God's electing of the offspring of Abraham and covenanting with servant Jacob. The "fear not" directed to Abraham (Gen 15:1) is heard again here. And just as Jacob was once given a new name, "Israel," which clarified his destiny with God (Gen 32:28), so also now that calling and that special relationship are here evoked (v. 1).

Verse 2 opens with what appears to be a reference to the exodus event, and yet the description is rather bloated: waters are joined by rivers, and fire is joined by flame. The latter is foreign to the exodus context, but it is well known as an image of judgment in Isaiah (v. 25; 1:7, 25, 31; 6:13). Within the book of Isaiah, moreover, water as an image of judgment appears in connection with Assyria:

> The Lord is bringing up against it the mighty flood waters of the River, the king of Assyria and all his glory . . . it will sweep on into Judah as a flood, and, pouring over, it will reach up to the neck. (8:7-8 NRSV)

The promise was made in this latter context that Immanuel would not be swamped by the river, consistent with the promise here that "the rivers, they shall not overwhelm you" (v. 2). It would probably be saying too much that what was true of Immanuel is now true of God's servant people as a royal people, replacing David.[65] In sum, the relationship to the exodus narratives is not to be denied, but the association is secondary and allusive and has been generated by the language of judgment (fire, water) already familiar from the larger book of Isaiah.

This is equally true of the next two verses, where the exodus context seems much clearer. Egypt was a ransom for Israel in the events of the first exodus (Exodus 12–13). Yet here Egypt is joined by Ethiopia and Seba, who play no real role in the exodus events. It is a common move, therefore, to begin to relate the ransoming defeat of Egypt in the first exodus with the activity of Cyrus, who will defeat this threesome, in the view of "Deutero-Isaiah," in place of and to the benefit of Israel. That is, the exodus backdrop of the first verses is here revealed as contemporaneously

---

64. C. Westermann, *Isaiah 40–66,* trans. David Stalker, OTL (Philadelphia: Westminster, 1969) 117.

65. This is frequently argued for other texts in Isaiah 40–55. See Edgar Conrad, *Reading Isaiah,* OBT (Minneapolis: Fortress, 1991) 143-52.

significant, for just as God did in the days of Egyptian bondage, so also now in the days of Cyrus, God does on behalf of Israel. For this reading to work, it is necessary that the prophet Deutero-Isaiah be sufficiently ill informed about Cyrus's actual military activity, since there are problems with this contemporaneous interpretation of Persian triumphs over Egypt, Ethiopia, and Seba.[66] Why Ethiopia and Seba would be singled out—relative bit players in the world power game played by Persia and its predecessors—is also unclear.

Within the biblical record, the table of nations (Genesis 10) explains that Seba is related to Cush (Ethiopia). For the specific pairing of Ethiopia and Egypt, the most obvious literary context is again the book of Isaiah. An oracle concerning judgment over Ethiopia precedes one over Egypt in the nation oracles section of Isaiah (chaps. 18–19). Then, in chap. 20, Isaiah walks naked for three years to enact the stripping and exiling that await Egypt and Ethiopia at the hands of the Assyrians. In other words, reading the former things of Isaiah could well generate an interpretation that, while the river Assyria failed to reach beyond Israel's neck, Egypt and Ethiopia were not so fortunate. In this former action there is relevance for the present: Nations have been given in exchange for Israel, and this "ransom" pays for the returning of exiles, wherever they are found and not just in a Babylonian bondage on analogy with the earlier Egyptian one. Just as once the righteous judgment on Egypt spared the firstborn of Israel, so also it will be in the days of the prophet Isaiah. This "former thing" grounds new prophetic speech in a Persian, not Assyrian, context. Yet both are types of God's selfsame action on behalf of Israel.

We remain fully in the Isaiah context when reference is made to offspring from east, west, north, and south (43:5-6), for such was the perspective of Isa 11:12, where a signal for the nations is set up and the "outcasts of Israel" are gathered from "the four corners of the earth." The fire that does not burn servant Israel now (43:2) once did (6:13), just as God's "scorching wind" once waved its hand over the river, Assyria (11:15), stilling its "vaunted ax" (10:15) so that Israel might return

home (11:15-16). Here we find a clear reference to God's making the river into a footpath for crossing, as a highway extends from Assyria as it once did from Egypt (11:16). When this image is collated with the return of the dispersed from all compass points, we discover the working ingredients of the Isaiah proclamation.

In sum, the author of this proclamation is confronted by the word of God rooted in earlier divine speech concerning Israel's destiny among the nations. That earlier proclamation, to be sure, involves Israel's ransoming from Egyptian bondage. But the primary context for such proclamation is now found in the book of Isaiah. On the basis of Isaiah's former things, associations are made with God's present and former actions, in the events of the exodus and in the calling of the ancestors out of foreign regions and foreign hostilities. With its references to calling, creating, forming, and making, the final verse (v. 7) recalls the opening address to Jacob/Israel, applied now to God's people at the very ends of the earth (43:6), among the nations as once Abram and Sarah had been (Gen 11:10-32).

43:8-15. Some scholars make a division at v. 14 because of the messenger formula, "Thus says the LORD"; vv. 14-15 are then taken as a separate unit. It can also be read as the culmination of the preceding trial speech (vv. 8-13), as God renders judgment on behalf of Israel in the presence of the assembled nations. This reading is adopted here.

The summons to gather is addressed to two audiences: (1) the blind and deaf servant people and (2) the nations and peoples. With its unusual word order, v. 8 signals that God has reversed the circumstances of Isa 6:9-10, a situation prepared for by the confession at the close of the previous chapter (42:23-24). Isaiah's blind people do yet have eyes; the deaf do yet have ears. The nations, on the face of it, suffer no such ailments and have undergone no such transformation, positive or negative. They should be able to offer testimony. The challenge is almost identical to the one offered in 41:21-29. The witnesses should come forward, present testimony, let it be heard and discussed as to rightness, and let the verdict fall in their favor. As before, the silence signals more than pre-emption: God knows there are no such witnesses.

Israel, however, is a witness in two different

66. See B. Duhm, *Das Buch Jesaia,* HKAT (Göttingen: Vandenhoeck & Ruprecht, 1892) 285.

senses. First, there is testimony available for it to bring that is not contaminated by its former blindness and deafness. Israel has recourse to the former things, which the nations are unable to declare. Here we are within a specifically Isaian frame of reference. Blindness and deafness were hallmarks of the generation addressed by the prophet. The prophet's former speech ricocheted off those he addressed like so much foreign gibberish (28:13); God's work became alien and strange (28:21); "the vision of all this" was sealed for those who could read, and it was open only in paradox for those who could not read in the first place (29:11-12). But in several places we learn quite clearly that God's word remains true, even if unheeded, because it is divinely sent and because it will be heard and received as testimony in a different day, for a different generation.

> Go now, write it before them on a tablet,
>   and inscribe it in a book,
> so that it may be for the time to come
>   [אחרון *'aḥărôn*]
>   as a witness [עד *'ad*] forever. (30:8 NRSV)

Similar language is used of the "testimony and teaching" sealed among the prophet's disciples in 8:16. What God said through Isaiah truly ricocheted off a generation, but only to become testimony for a new day, providing evidence of God's dealings with Israel among the nations, the producing of which shuts eyes and ears in a new sense. Now it is the nations who are without testimony. "Blind" and "deaf" to the testimony available to a people once similarly endowed, they are, in addition, mute.

Israel is a witness in another sense as well. Usually witnesses are called in to give testimony on behalf of another, in this case God. That is, they are in possession of information or evidence necessary to establish a positive verdict for someone else. Ironically, Israel must be told that it possesses this information to begin with (Israel is deaf but has ears!). And the possession of this testimony benefits not so much God as it does Israel itself. God never takes the challenge of the nations all that seriously, but what God does take seriously is that Israel's testimony has the capacity to reconnect it to God in the most basic sense—a sense that was undone in the days of Isaiah, leading to Israel's death and destruction. "You are my wit-

nesses," God says to Israel, "so that you may know and believe me and understand that I am he" (v. 10). Knowing and believing and understanding were what failed, leaving a previous generation blind to God's ways (6:8-10). The reestablishment of these faculties constitutes the most fundamental connection possible, a bringing back from the dead. No wonder the poet makes persistent reference to the calling of Abraham and the ancestral election; for all intents and purposes, this generation is meeting God as if for the first time. "I, I am the LORD" (v. 11) sounds like the solemn declaration made to Abraham at Gen 15:7. There, as here, God is about to bring forth a people from "Ur of the Chaldees," from the Babylonian region of the diaspora.

The final verses of the unit (vv. 14-15) pronounce the solemn verdict of God on behalf of Israel. God is the Lord, the Holy One, Creator, King—a constellation evoking the call of Abraham, of Isaiah's Holy One, of the creation of all nations, and of God's particular rule over this particular people. God as King is reminiscent of Book IV of the psalter (Psalms 90–106), following upon the lament of David in Psalm 89. It is not a rejection of or dismissal of Davidic promises, but a reassertion of their underlying rationale, set forth in the psalter in Psalm 2.[67] There and here, at this juncture in Israel's history, the reassertion of God's kingship must precede any discussion of the role of the Davidic house. We are at a far more rudimentary level, not unlike that of the first ancestors.

Central to our discourse is the promise of the return of exiled and judged Israel, which has been scattered to the four winds (vv. 5-6), to be reunited with the witnesses assembled and addressed and re-created here. The voice of the discourse is not *in exile,* as is so frequently insisted. It never highlights its geographical bearings in this way. Its point of orientation is Zion, and so the Holy One of Israel announces the intention to *send* to Babylon to break down bars. Babylonian imprisonment is surely central to the discourse, as perhaps the most stunning and most

---

67. See C. R. Seitz, "Royal Promises in the Canonical Books of Isaiah and the Psalms," in *Word Without End* (Grand Rapids: Eerdmans, 1998) 150-67. Childs's formulation is cautious: "It is important to see in this relation that the promise to David has not been repudiated by Second Isaiah, but extended and transferred to the mission of the servants of the Lord." See B. S. Childs, *Isaiah,* OTL (Louisville: Westminster John Knox, 2001) 437.

recent example of God's judgment by means of the nations. And the release of those cast off to Babylon is critical because it presages a wider return of all God's people. With this will come about the completion of God's promise to open blind eyes and deaf ears and to "bring out the prisoners from the dungeon" (42:7). As with blindess and deafness, the mission of the servant begins with Israel's own restoration.

43:16-21. Unmistakable here is the exodus predication: Israel's Lord is the one who defeated Egypt's hosts and delivered the people at the sea. This language previously found its way into the book of Isaiah, to be further transformed there (e.g., 11:15-16), while here we come cleanly into contact with the old exodus tradition. It doubtless appears here to bolster the announcement of Babylon's defeat and Israel's anticipated release (vv. 14-15). The exodus tradition likewise constitutes a "former thing" to which appeal can be made, outside the book of Isaiah.[68] Here we are reminded that as the author uses it, "former things" are a wide-ranging complex of traditions, not restricted to the book of Isaiah.

These former things, however, are not to be dwelt on because God is proposing to do a new thing. In this sense, the "former things" referred to here play a different role in the discourse (cf. 41:21). They are not introduced to supply testimony; nor are they intended to expose the impotence of the nations. Rather, they set up an *a fortiori* appropriate to the circumstances of Israel's diaspora (cf. 42:9). Strictly speaking, we are familiar with the notion of God's making a way through the sea from the exodus narratives. But now God proposes to make a way in the wilderness, which sounds like an elaboration or extension of the old exodus language into a new framework. The image of a wilderness way is familiar from 40:3, but there the way is God's own, and only later do we learn that God intends to travel on this way like a shepherd, conducting flocks (40:10-11). It is not clear from the old wilderness traditions that God actually makes a way through the wilderness,

like a way through the sea. God guides Israel and directs its travel. But here greater intentionality is involved in the passage *from* bondage *back to* Zion. The older wilderness tradition also included a highly complex, far from uniform depiction of complaint, scarce resources, divine absence, and the judgment of death over an entire generation. This may partly explain why the "former things," in this instance, are not to be remembered but are in contrast to a new thing, springing forth now (v. 19). We are no longer talking about the wondrous production of water at Marah but about full-fledged rivers in the desert (vv. 19-20). Instead of a tradition of murmuring, now we have a tradition of praise (v. 21).

It has been noted in connection with 40:1-11 that the wilderness tradition in the book of Isaiah was closely associated with God's judgment and was distinctive over against the old exodus-wilderness tradition. Within that complex of images, the jackal and ostrich appear (13:21-22; 34:13; 35:7), marking the return to briers and thistles—another key image of judgment in Isaiah (e.g., 5:6; 7:24-25; 9:18; 10:17; 27:4). To be destined for wild animals (13:21; 14:23; 23:13) is to become a wilderness of God's judgment, shorn of grand and majestic trees (10:33-34). Now that wilderness of judgment, collated loosely with the old wilderness separating Egypt and the promised land, is about to be transformed, leaving the wild animals, jackals, and ostriches—unknown in the first wilderness—free to honor God. With this, even the depiction of chaps. 34–35 has been advanced.

43:22-28. This concluding unit presents a puzzle that has long challenged interpreters. How could an Israel in exile be upbraided for not offering sacrifices to God?[69] The most common solution to this problem is to regard the polemic—if that is, in fact, what it is—as dealing with the age-old problem of false worship, appropriate to any period.[70] Still, why would such a harsh verdict be included at this particular juncture?

An explanation for the past temporal perspective is to be found by comparison with the

68. B. W. Anderson, "Exodus Typology in Second Isaiah," in *Israel's Prophetic Heritage: Festschrift in Honor of James Muilenburg*, ed. B. W. Anderson and W. Harrelson (New York: Harper and Bros., 1962) 177-95. Cf. B. S. Childs, *Introduction to the Old Testament as Scripture* (Philadelphia: Fortress, 1979); and C. R. Seitz, "How Is the Prophet Isaiah Present in the Latter Half of the Book? The Logic of Chapters 40–66 Within the Book of Isaiah," *JBL* 115 (1996).

69. Torrey comments summarily, "Viewed in any light, it would be altogether out of place in an 'exilic' composition." See C. C. Torrey, *The Second Isaiah* (New York: Scribner's, 1928) 342.

70. Westermann states, "This verdict here, a retrospect, is passed upon pre-exilic Israel's worship *in toto.*" See C. Westermann, *Isaiah 40–66*, trans. David Stalker, OTL (Philadelphia: Westminster, 1969) 132.

preceding chapter. There, too, at the conclusion (42:23-25), Israel's past circumstances are recalled, and confession is given in order to set up the oracle of assurance, introduced by "but now," which immediately follows (43:1-7). A similar movement, now lacking confession but including reference to God's forgiveness (v. 25), is present in the transition to the following chapter and its introductory oracle of assurance (44:1-5) for the present generation ("but now," 44:1). The past-tense perspective of the NRSV is to be preferred at v. 28 over the NIV's future rendering.[71]

Correct interpretation of the passage demands attention to where the denouement is located and how the logic of the rebuke works. It is not a question of other gods—instead of Yahweh—having been the actual recipients of otherwise proper offerings (i.e., "not to *me* were brought X"). Nor is this a polemic against sacrifice and offerings per se, though this is frequently asserted. In this connection, it is important to note what appears to be a close verbal association with the Isaianic polemic at 1:11-15, and in that context improper, overloaded offerings are in fact being condemned. Moreover, the "come now, let us argue it out" of 1:18 seems to find a rough counterpart here: "accuse me, let us go to trial, set forth your case, so that you may be proved right" (43:26). In other words, the earlier Isaiah passage, with its sharp attack on improper offerings (as well as kindred OT texts), may well form the backdrop of this unit, and readers/hearers may well have been expected to know and be familiar with that backdrop. But the unit assumes that backdrop in order to go a new way. In fact, something of the reverse logic of that earlier Isaiah text appears to come into play.

The first verse (v. 22) sets up the logic: A play is made on proper and improper "burdening" of God, which is elaborated in the lines that follow (vv. 23-24a). The resolution is forestalled until v. 24b. There is a familiar context of improperly burdening God with sacrifices, known from Isaiah 1. There the point is that when one is internally burdened with sin and guilt, an internal change is necessary before any external offerings will be

acceptable: "cease to do evil, learn to do good" (1:17; cf. Ps 51:16-19). That all sacrificial offerings are wrong as such would be going beyond even the sharpest of the prophetic denunciations.

Here the logic runs in a different direction. God has been burdened with Israel's sins and iniquities (v. 24) but has experienced nothing of the sort of improper burdening of sinful offerings known of old. One cannot just stop making offerings altogether and have it follow that sin and iniquity will disappear. This would be a perversion of the logic of Isaiah 1 and Psalm 51. To forgo sacrifice and offering is not necessarily an abstemious bulwark against wrong sacrifice; it, too, may just cover up the underlying problem: "you have burdened me with your sins; you have wearied me with your iniquities" (43:24). And deeper still, "you have been weary of me, O Israel!" At the root of Israel's abstention are baseline weariness and neglect, which are no better or no worse than zealous sacrificing and offering.

The final verses only serve to reinforce this bold new adaptation of older prophetic denunciation. God remains the one capable of blotting out transgression, though, as before, it will take a direct encounter with God of the most personal kind (v. 26). Lots of sacrifices, or none at all in counter-reaction, cannot stand in the way of this encounter: "I, I am He who blots out your transgressions for my own sake" (v. 25). The forgiveness of sins has as much to do with God's own character as it does with Israel's desire for health and restitution. The final two verses, like the final verse of chap. 42, simply remind the present generation of a past judgment. Because the former generation sinned and transgressed (see Isaiah 1), God finally brought sacrificial worship to an end. Here we come to learn why no burnt offerings, sacrifices, offerings, frankincense, sweet cane, or fat—overmuch or just right—have come before God. The previous generation's sins brought an end to the sanctuary. But that did not bring an end to sin and transgression, in some perverse misreading of Isaiah 1. Rather, it means only that a new generation is about to be confronted by God's grace in a new, yet every bit as direct, sense (44:1-5).

Some prefer to take "first ancestor" (אביך הראשון *'ăbîkā hāri'šôn*) in the specific sense of the patriarch Jacob (NRSV annotation). Hosea 12:2-5 presents a picture of Jacob as deserving

---

71. The MT points the verbs as though implying otherwise, but the context—especially 44:1—argues in favor of the consecutive reading of the Hebrew verbs by the LXX (so NRSV) and a consistently past perspective for the entire unit (43:22-28).

punishment for having striven with God and prevailed, which in turn required weeping and intercession and ultimate forgiveness. "Interpreters" is likewise an obscure expression, occurring only here. It may refer to Israel's intercessors, the prophets. This combination would mean that all Israel, right back to the ancestral period, had sinned and deserved the punishment that eventually fell. What we do know is that the term *hāri'šôn* ("former," "first") makes frequent appearance in this discourse, where it is contrasted with the present generation or the present proclamation. However far back Israel's sin is considered to have stretched, it culminated in God's judgment over the sanctuary. Now a new thing is about to take place.

REFLECTIONS

1. Sins of commission are more easily numbered and identified than sins of omission, whose potential range is infinite. But before God both are sin and an offense to God's righteousness, plain and simple.

Isaiah of Jerusalem knew he was confronting a deceitful generation that lacked even the sort of basic, instinctive sense of God's presence that an animal has of its master (1:2-3). With that sort of rudimentary understanding and obedience missing, it no doubt struck him as the height of religious perversion to witness people's apparent zeal in worship and their multitudinous sacrifices. This sort of extreme disconnection had to be exposed and rebuked. But even then the route of cynicism and abject condemnation was disallowed. Appeals for a new start continued to go forth (1:18-20), and even an anticipated judgment had as its final purpose not annihilation, but cleansing and restoration (1:24-26) for those who repented.

Interestingly, Isaiah 43 does not assume that an apparent alternative—that is, abstaining from offerings and sacrifice—is any more pleasing to God. These are the fruit of a heart, once broken and contrite, that is now tuned to God's will and pleasure (Ps 51:17). In Isaiah 43 the initiative for this remains God, who forgives sin "for my own sake" (43:25); in Psalm 51, God is the one who builds up Zion and Jerusalem anew, and that divine act in turn gives rise to righteous sacrifices and delightful whole burnt offerings (Ps 51:18-19). It would be so much easier if we could just keep all proper religious bearing *counterfactual:* If hypocritical sacrifices are wrong, get rid of them altogether, and all will be right. If the heart is too lifted up, break it just to get it down and contrite, as an end to itself. But God wants neither the obvious wrong nor its obvious counterfactual, but forgiveness and new life "for my own sake," because it is consistent with God's own character as God.

2. The creation account speaks of God's forming the universe out of chaotic nothingness. Here the calling of Jacob/Israel is said to be an act of creation, on analogy with that signal first divine act. And yet right away reference is made to extreme trial, of the sort one might regard as creation's potential undoing: a passing through waters of chaos (43:2). Creation, it turns out, is not an event long ago, but a continuous activity of God in the face of extreme challenge to divine rule.

And yet right away the larger Isaiah context reminds us that fire and flame were God's own measures taken against a disobedient people. They were not forces hostile to God's rule, but dispatchers of it. And these are placed next to rivers and waters, symbolizing not only Assyria's cleansing judgment, but also evoking the waters parted by God on behalf of Israel, destroying the Egyptian host. This admixture presents a challenge of major theological significance. How are we to know when adversity is sent in judgment or on our behalf? The fire sent by God to punish before is not now present for that purpose. How does Israel know that? By hearing it from God.

The previous generation could not hear. God's word became gibberish, incomprehensible, alien. But here God speaks of creating a people, evoking the calling of Jacob/Israel. Ears hear, and eyes see that fire and water remain forces to contend with. This new people, hearing God as though for the first time, are not treated to a new creation in which fire and flood have been removed, never to bother them again. What they now know is that God has not sent them in judgment.

What calls for further reflection is whether this fact can itself constitute freedom from anxiety. We have come to believe that adversity—natural and personal—is so much random grunting and groaning of impersonal forces, even while we suffer as much under the sheer impersonality of this portrayal as our forebears did under one more personal and providential. Within the older system, however, there apparently is a further dimension: assurance that adversity, when it does come, cannot destroy, even to the extent of miraculous deliverance ("when you walk through fire you shall not be burned"). To know that fire and flood are not acts of judgment entails a revelation, from God, to that effect; and with that comes the assurance of deliverance and protection.

3. A yet more difficult dimension opens up in this same passage. Israel's new life, its capacity to move through real fire and real tempest unharmed, *costs* something. God does not manipulate the created order and introduce entirely new categories: fireless existence. Rather, God *redeems* what God has made, and redemption involves an exchange within the created realm. A price is paid in order to set things back the way they were. Sons and daughters are bought back, as once the ancestors were called out of Ur of the Chaldees, but now at the cost of the nations.

This same context of exchange and payment figures prominently in the suffering servant text later in Isaiah (52:13–53:12), and there a distinctive picture emerges, though still within this framework. What is striking is that ransom frees Israel from past sin and guilt—deafness, blindness, imprisonment—and with the same stroke opens up a completely new existence within the old created order. Is not Israel getting the slate wiped clean, returning to where it was before, but with an added bonus: divine protection through fire and tempest? Yes, though the connection with the ancestral promise suggests this was always Israel's destiny with God. Why this happens is to be traced to God's sheer, unmerited love: "because you are precious in my sight, and honored, and I love you" (43:4).

To speak of a personal God, personally and intimately involved with people, is to speak of God's love in sacrifice. A cost is paid; there is a movement, an exchange, that ultimately traces back to God. "For God so loved the world that he gave his only son" is the culmination of this understanding shared with Israel on behalf of the world God made. It is inseparable from the self-understanding of the one sent by God who said, "The Son of Man came to give his life as a ransom." Our offenses make a dividing wall of separation between us and God—an exile—from which we must not only be brought back but also must be bought back, by God, in sacrifice. The Christian gospel begins as an act of costly redemption: the love of God overcoming our willed alienation from the deity.

As we will see, Israel shares in both the bounty of God's special love and in the cost of that love as it begins to spill over and be made manifest beyond Israel's sphere of comprehension. In both contexts, it is a love that costs God something so precious that the only way to describe it is through the figure of father/son, parent/child. God made a choice, and within the constraints of that choice God redeemed Israel, and through them, in God's Son, the church that confesses his name. With that choice come benefits and responsibilities—and the assurance that when we pass through fire, we shall not be burned, and when death takes us, it will not have the final word.

4. Within the book of Isaiah there are times when the former things are to be recollected for a positive purpose (41:27; 46:9), but other times when they are to defer to new things God is about to do (42:8; 43:18-19). The former things constitute testimony Israel can use in the face of challenge, establishing a special relationship, over time, with the God of all creation. But the present relationship consists of more than memory of past faithfulness, decisive though that be in certain contexts. "I am about to do a new thing" (43:19) signals the freshness of God's ways and the continual possibility of a sudden, unexpected turn of fortune.

This dialectic appears frequently enough that we ought to be sure we understand it. It is a dialectic that is fundamental to our understanding of how God works over time, as much now as in Isaiah's day. Being told not to remember the former things does not entail a criticism of them, with an emphasis on discontinuity between the new thing God will do and the memory of the former things God has sought to underscore on other occasions. The emphasis falls, rather, on the radical newness of what God is up to. Each element is critical within its own appropriate context, and one belongs inextricably to the other as part of the dynamic, selfsame activity of God. The freshness of this announcement that wild animals will honor God in the wilderness is grasped within the framework of a former wilderness the people recall, but will never think of in the same way again.[72] The challenge for the church is to remain open to the radical freedom of God "to do a new thing," yet fully within the context of prior divine activity.

At the heart of this dialectic also stands an insight about how the two Testaments of Christian Scripture are related for those brought near in Christ. Nations arrive at last and receive instruction along with Israel, as in another context Isaiah also promised (2:1-4). But they come to grasp the centrality of the former things from the standpoint of the new thing itself, and not the other way around (Luke 24:27), coming as they do as aliens and strangers to the former "covenants of promise" (Eph 2:12). Yet, ironically, part of the radical newness in this case involves an introduction to "former things," on the basis of which their eventual inclusion is identified both as radically new and as fully consistent with God's former testimony to Israel. When Egypt and Ethiopia appear again, it is armed with the confession, "God is with you alone, and there is no other" (45:14) and "truly thou art a God who hides himself, O God of Israel, the Savior" (45:15). The confession of those outside made in Isaiah is a "former thing," integrally related to and then dramatically trumped by God's "new thing" in Christ Jesus. The God who has hidden is more than disclosed. God is revealed, is fully poured out in the suffering sacrifice of the Son, that all creation might know God, a new thing wrought before the foundations of the earth.

72. See J. Louis Martyn, "Listening to John and Paul on the Subject of God and Scripture," *Word and World* 12 (1992) 68-81.

ISAIAH 44:1-23, I FORMED YOU

NIV

44 "But now listen, O Jacob, my servant,
Israel, whom I have chosen.
²This is what the LORD says—
he who made you, who formed you in
the womb,
and who will help you:
Do not be afraid, O Jacob, my servant,
Jeshurun, whom I have chosen.
³For I will pour water on the thirsty land,
and streams on the dry ground;
I will pour out my Spirit on your offspring,

NRSV

44 But now hear, O Jacob my servant,
Israel whom I have chosen!
² Thus says the LORD who made you,
who formed you in the womb and will
help you:
Do not fear, O Jacob my servant,
Jeshurun whom I have chosen.
³ For I will pour water on the thirsty land,
and streams on the dry ground;
I will pour my spirit upon your descendants,
and my blessing on your offspring.

NIV

and my blessing on your descendants.
⁴They will spring up like grass in a meadow,
    like poplar trees by flowing streams.
⁵One will say, 'I belong to the LORD';
    another will call himself by the name
        of Jacob;
  still another will write on his hand,
    'The LORD's,'
  and will take the name Israel.

⁶"This is what the LORD says—
  Israel's King and Redeemer, the
    LORD Almighty:
I am the first and I am the last;
    apart from me there is no God.
⁷Who then is like me? Let him proclaim it.
  Let him declare and lay out before me
what has happened since I established my
    ancient people,
  and what is yet to come—
  yes, let him foretell what will come.
⁸Do not tremble, do not be afraid.
  Did I not proclaim this and foretell it
    long ago?
You are my witnesses. Is there any God
    besides me?
  No, there is no other Rock; I know
    not one."

⁹All who make idols are nothing,
  and the things they treasure are worthless.
Those who would speak up for them are blind;
  they are ignorant, to their own shame.
¹⁰Who shapes a god and casts an idol,
  which can profit him nothing?
¹¹He and his kind will be put to shame;
  the craftsmen are nothing but men.
Let them all come together and take
    their stand;
  they will be brought down to terror
    and infamy.

¹²The blacksmith takes a tool
  and works with it in the coals;
he shapes an idol with hammers,
  he forges it with the might of his arm.
He gets hungry and loses his strength;
  he drinks no water and grows faint.

NRSV

⁴They shall spring up like a green tamarisk,
  like willows by flowing streams.
⁵This one will say, "I am the LORD's,"
  another will be called by the name
    of Jacob,
yet another will write on the hand,
    "The LORD's,"
  and adopt the name of Israel.

⁶Thus says the LORD, the King of Israel,
  and his Redeemer, the LORD of hosts:
I am the first and I am the last;
  besides me there is no god.
⁷Who is like me? Let them proclaim it,
  let them declare and set it forth before me.
Who has announced from of old the things
    to come?ᵃ
  Let them tell usᵇ what is yet to be.
⁸Do not fear, or be afraid;
  have I not told you from of old and
    declared it?
  You are my witnesses!
Is there any god besides me?
  There is no other rock; I know not one.

⁹All who make idols are nothing, and the things
they delight in do not profit; their witnesses neither
see nor know. And so they will be put to shame.
¹⁰Who would fashion a god or cast an image that
can do no good? ¹¹Look, all its devotees shall be put
to shame; the artisans too are merely human. Let
them all assemble, let them stand up; they shall be
terrified, they shall all be put to shame.

¹²The ironsmith fashions itᶜ and works it over
the coals, shaping it with hammers, and forging it
with his strong arm; he becomes hungry and his
strength fails, he drinks no water and is faint.
¹³The carpenter stretches a line, marks it out with
a stylus, fashions it with planes, and marks it
with a compass; he makes it in human form, with
human beauty, to be set up in a shrine. ¹⁴He cuts
down cedars or chooses a holm tree or an oak and
lets it grow strong among the trees of the forest.
He plants a cedar and the rain nourishes it. ¹⁵Then
it can be used as fuel. Part of it he takes and
warms himself; he kindles a fire and bakes bread.

ᵃCn: Heb *from my placing an eternal people and things to come*
ᵇTg: Heb *them*   ᶜCn: Heb *an ax*

NIV

¹³The carpenter measures with a line
   and makes an outline with a marker;
he roughs it out with chisels
   and marks it with compasses.
He shapes it in the form of man,
   of man in all his glory,
   that it may dwell in a shrine.
¹⁴He cut down cedars,
   or perhaps took a cypress or oak.
He let it grow among the trees of the forest,
   or planted a pine, and the rain made
      it grow.
¹⁵It is man's fuel for burning;
   some of it he takes and warms himself,
   he kindles a fire and bakes bread.
But he also fashions a god and worships it;
   he makes an idol and bows down to it.
¹⁶Half of the wood he burns in the fire;
   over it he prepares his meal,
   he roasts his meat and eats his fill.
He also warms himself and says,
   "Ah! I am warm; I see the fire."
¹⁷From the rest he makes a god, his idol;
   he bows down to it and worships.
He prays to it and says,
   "Save me; you are my god."
¹⁸They know nothing, they understand nothing;
   their eyes are plastered over so they
      cannot see,
   and their minds closed so they cannot
      understand.
¹⁹No one stops to think,
   no one has the knowledge or understanding
      to say,
"Half of it I used for fuel;
   I even baked bread over its coals,
   I roasted meat and I ate.
Shall I make a detestable thing from what
      is left?
   Shall I bow down to a block of wood?"
²⁰He feeds on ashes, a deluded heart
      misleads him;
   he cannot save himself, or say,
   "Is not this thing in my right hand a lie?"

²¹"Remember these things, O Jacob,
   for you are my servant, O Israel.
I have made you, you are my servant;

NRSV

Then he makes a god and worships it, makes it a carved image and bows down before it. ¹⁶Half of it he burns in the fire; over this half he roasts meat, eats it and is satisfied. He also warms himself and says, "Ah, I am warm, I can feel the fire!" ¹⁷The rest of it he makes into a god, his idol, bows down to it and worships it; he prays to it and says, "Save me, for you are my god!"

18They do not know, nor do they comprehend; for their eyes are shut, so that they cannot see, and their minds as well, so that they cannot understand. ¹⁹No one considers, nor is there knowledge or discernment to say, "Half of it I burned in the fire; I also baked bread on its coals, I roasted meat and have eaten. Now shall I make the rest of it an abomination? Shall I fall down before a block of wood?" ²⁰He feeds on ashes; a deluded mind has led him astray, and he cannot save himself or say, "Is not this thing in my right hand a fraud?"

²¹ Remember these things, O Jacob,
   and Israel, for you are my servant;
I formed you, you are my servant;
   O Israel, you will not be forgotten by me.
²² I have swept away your transgressions like
      a cloud,
   and your sins like mist;
return to me, for I have redeemed you.

²³ Sing, O heavens, for the LORD has done it;
   shout, O depths of the earth;
break forth into singing, O mountains,
   O forest, and every tree in it!
For the LORD has redeemed Jacob,
   and will be glorified in Israel.

NIV

O Israel, I will not forget you.
²²I have swept away your offenses like a cloud,
        your sins like the morning mist.
Return to me,
        for I have redeemed you."

²³Sing for joy, O heavens, for the LORD has
            done this;
        shout aloud, O earth beneath.
Burst into song, you mountains,
        you forests and all your trees,
for the LORD has redeemed Jacob,
        he displays his glory in Israel.

COMMENTARY

We remain in trial proceedings. The hymn at 44:23 establishes a structural seam concluding the foregoing section (42:14–43:22), as was the case following the presentation of the servant (42:10-13). The next, shorter section consists of the presentation of Cyrus (44:24-28; 45:1-7). As with the servant, the introduction of Cyrus is concluded with an appeal to creation to respond to God's bold action (45:8). The trial character is revealed explicitly in vv. 7-8 and in v. 11, in the idol polemic (44:9-20). Form critics also designate 44:6-8 (and for some, vv. 21-22 as a continuation of the unit) a "trial speech."

There are several important features in 44:1-23 that present a challenge to form-critical purists. The opening unit (vv. 1-5) looks like a typical oracle of salvation, and yet this form usually has a substantiating clause after the "fear not" assurance, "which consists of nominal sentences and verbs in the perfect tense."[73] Instead we have imperfects (vv. 3-5), suitable to the content of what is being announced, which here involves future descendants. For this reason, some view the past-tense declaration as assumed from the preceding unit, where God says transgression has been blotted out (v. 25). This judgment seems sound, even as it calls into question the basic notion of originally discrete units. The close connection between 43:22-28 and 44:1-5 has already

been noted, patterned on the transition from 42:23-25 to 43:1-7, where a past situation of transgression is contrasted with God's new action in the present. Other connections will be noted in the Commentary.

Another challenge is the long idol polemic found in vv. 9-20. A similar challenge presented itself earlier (40:18-20; 41:6-7), where idol manufacture is condemned in what many regard as interpolated pieces; here, however, the satire is much more elaborate. Since Duhm, many have argued it is a secondary addition and have sought to connect (reconnect) the small fragment following it (vv. 21-22) with the brief trial speech preceding it (vv. 6-8). Yet here, too, problems arise. The "fear not" declaration is somewhat out of place in a trial speech (v. 8), and so to link this "assurance of salvation" with "substantiations" in v. 21 (so Westermann), begins to encroach on the original form-critical logic. Again, these connections are rooted in the discourse at a most basic level. At a whole host of levels—verbal, thematic, ironic—the idol polemic is inextricably related to its present literary context. In sum, the logic of the literary arrangement is a first-order concern of the author, who has creatively adapted older forms fully to his purposes.

In this regard, it is striking that this section closes in much the same way as do chaps. 42 and 43. That is, there is reference to Israel's transgressions (44:22) as in 42:24 and 43:25, and the same

---

73. See R. F. Melugin, *The Formation of Isaiah 40–55,* BZAW 141 (Berlin: Walter de Gruyter, 1976) 115; C. Westermann, *Isaiah 40–66,* trans. David Stalker, OTL (Philadelphia: Westminster, 1969) 134.

verb (מחה *mḥh*, "blot out," "sweep away") is used in the two final contexts. Here, however, there is no need for further confession (as in chap. 42) or rehearsal of past sins (as in chap. 43). What Israel is to remember is not past transgression, but the transparent foolishness of idol manufacture in and of itself, but more important, in the light of God's own special fashioning of Israel. Verse 21 forms an inclusio with v. 1, and hard on the announcement of forgiveness the section concludes with a call to sing out (v. 23), similiar in form and function to 42:10-13.

In the collection of units running from v. 1 to v. 23, we confront some of the most intricate, subtle shaping and arrangement in all of the discourse. The idol satire, in particular, introduces us for the first time to actual witnesses, before summoned but never appearing. In so doing, it forms an integral extension of the trial setting of vv. 6-8 and is no mere interpolation or disconnected apostrophe. The announcement of forgiveness in the final unit (vv. 21-22), appearing in the context of acknowledged transgression, is the third such unit of its kind (42:23-25 and 43:25-28). It represents a final denouement in respect of this theme. We are now prepared for creation's wider praise and the presentation from God's wider realm of a new agent dispatched for a new purpose, different in character from a former "rod of my anger" (10:5).

44:1-5. The ועתה (*wĕ'attâ*, "but now") of v. 1 serves the same purpose as in 43:1: to contrast the preceding context of past judgment with the present context of assurance. The predications likewise recall those of 43:1, but here "election" (בחר *bḥr*) stands where "creation" (ברא *br'*) appeared before. The references to choosing and spirit endowment are particularly evocative of the original presentation of the servant (42:1-8), while the calling from the womb nicely anticipates the next major servant poem (49:1-7). These linkages establish that the same general framework is being maintained across distinct sections, though the author sticks fairly loosely to strict chronological distinctions. As we have seen, Israel is addressed in the present situation; yet within the specific context of ancestral traditions from the past, with a new vocation entailing justice and the nations still on the horizon. These three perspectives can be identified, even as they are merged and rearranged and creatively combined.

The blessing spoken of in v. 3 provides a good illustration of this. Spirit is given in 42:1 in conjunction with the servant's task of bringing משפט (*mišpāṭ*) to the nations, but here it is set in parallel with blessing and is specifically directed to the future descendants of Jacob/Israel (v. 3). The singular use of the term "blessing" here can be explained as being rooted in the ancestral traditions. The barrenness of Rebekah was removed by the prayer of Isaac (Gen 25:21), and Jacob was formed in the womb, along with his brother, Esau, in a surprise divine reversal (Gen 25:23). Through memorable ingenuity, and with Rebekah's help, Jacob won a blessing (Genesis 27). The forming, choosing, and blessing of Jacob are here clearly evoked, but now applied to the descendants of reviled and destroyed Jacob (Isa 43:28; 44:3). The unexpected choosing and blessing of Jacob, and not Esau, has its more dramatic counterpart here: a fresh start for a generation thought dead and cursed and their offspring after them. The original promise to Abraham is here maintained, following a season of transgression and profanation and elaborated according to the present circumstances.

Water is used in this unit in a way very different from in 43:1-7. It produces growth. Conjoined with spirit and ancestral blessing, it rejuvenates fresh generations and permits continued growth and sustenance. The image of trees may be more than general wisdom reflection (e.g., Ps 1:3). Total deforestation of Assyria is contrasted sharply with the promise of a Davidic shoot in Isa 10:28–11:9. The influence here is probably indirect, yet it serves nicely as a contrast to a different sort of deforestation, spelled out in the idol polemic. There, too, great trees, nourished by rain, are cut down (44:14): not only to serve as fuel, for warmth and for cooking, but also to make an idol for worship (14:15-17). Sitting over all the units of this section is the ironic contrast between God's forming of a people (vv. 2, 21), sustained by God's water, "like willows by streams" (v. 4); and human creating of gods, from great cedars, nourished by waters, even given human form (v. 13). Inscribing "The LORD's" (v. 5) is contrasted with styling a god according to a blueprint (v. 13). Depletion is taken seriously by God in Israel's case, while workers tired out by their idol manufacture cook food with the same fuel they use to make gods, in a crazy cycle of ongoing depletion.

A textual and translation problem is hidden by the NIV and NRSV renderings of v. 4. Hebrew בין (bên) and חָצִיר (ḥāṣîr) are taken as types of trees in the NRSV; the NIV retains ḥāṣîr as "grass" and takes the other term to mean "meadow." Torrey renders v. 4, "they shall spring up like grass amid waters."[74] The MT, while difficult, can be rendered, "they shall spring up in the midst of grass." The Hebrew ḥāṣîr ("grass") is not unusual, and it appears earlier in 40:6: "all flesh is grass, and all its constancy like the flower of the field." In other words, in the midst of human frailty, surrounded by inconstancy, Jacob/Israel will take root and grow like willows. This new creation amid the old will be named by God, as was the first Israel, and will be named of God, with "the LORD's" inscribed on the hand (v. 5).

In this same connection, an explanation may be found for the curious wording of v. 14 in the idol satire. The shrewd idolmaker also recognizes differentiation among the various types of trees (cedar, holm, oak) and chooses wisely from these for his various projects. He, too, knows how to plant a tree and understands the necessity of water for growth. The same rain that brings about good creation from God's hand is used by the craftsman to an end for which it was not suited: idol manufacture. Idolaters are not alchemists; they are abusers of created good. They are that grass whose root will fail (40:8) because it is ungrounded in God's Word. In the midst of that grass, Israel will spring up like willows planted by good water.

44:6-20. A new unit would seem to be suggested by the opening messenger formula ("Thus says the LORD") and by a distinct change in form and content. Here a challenge is presented in the context of an assertion by God to be God, and God alone (vv. 6-8). The call to come forward and produce evidence (v. 7) and the reference to witnesses (v. 8) are familiar from the Isaiah discourse (41:21-29; 43:8-13) and mark the unit as a trial speech. In addition to reminding us of the larger setting into which the various forms of speech have been placed (trial proceedings from the divine council), the unit accommodates a smooth transition to the long idol satire (vv. 9-20). Three times it is repeated that Israel's God is Lord alone.

74. C. C. Torrey, *The Second Isaiah* (New York: Scribner's, 1928) 235.

The first of these assertions recalls 41:4b, where God's exclusivity involves a temporal category. God as "Alpha and Omega" is inextricably related to the reliability of God's word through time. The same terms are used in connection with the "former" (רִאשׁוֹן ri'šôn) and "latter" (אַחֲרוֹן 'aḥărôn) things, testifying to God's having beforehand announced to Israel matters now transpiring. God is not just "first and last" in some isolated sense, but in connection with the people Israel and God's word to them. Earlier this logic was used to demonstrate that "gods" are "indeed nothing" (41:24); here it appears with that context presupposed. The second assertion, in the form of a question ("Who is like me?"), sets up the idol polemic to follow. The second half of the verse presents a translation problem. The MT contrasts God's having established an "eternal people" in the past with things to come that those summoned are challenged to reveal. The final assertion, that God is the rock and that no one stands beside God, may simply present a play on the predication "rock" (צוּר ṣûr) and the immediately following "make," "form" (יצר yṣr).

As in the past, witnesses have been summoned, but none ever appear and offer testimony, presumably because they have nothing to say or bring forward. It could be consistent with the genre employed that the possibility of rival witnesses for rival gods is entertained only to the point of rejecting such a conception altogether. The nonappearing witnesses are evidenced by their absence.

That being said, here the genre begins to go a different way. The opening verses of the satire clearly pick up the theme introduced in this unit, involving testimony and witnesses. Idols are said to have "their witnesses" in v. 9, and in v. 11b the verbs employed are consistent with the usual trial summons, "let them all assemble, let them stand up" (NRSV). In other words, it is as if the author asked, "What would such witnesses look like if they were to step forward? What sort of evidence might they reasonably bring in defense of their rival gods?" In what follows, however, we do not get an objective description of the logic of idolmaking. The flow of the unit and the logic of its unfolding are dictated, as pointed out earlier, by a host of concerns completely indigenous to the discourse. This explains why there is such peculiar emphasis on water, fire, food, hunger, exhaustion, various woods, and other matters peripheral to a discussion of idolmaking, strictly speaking. It should also be pointed out that the witnesses who appear here are for the most part third-person, though the form is punctuated by occasional first-person speech (vv. 16-17, 19-20). In other words, the witnesses who come forward do so as the author has styled them. This protects the form from the interpretation that such rival views should be taken seriously and accounts for the high degree of satire present. It is not that Israel failed to understand the subtlety of idol manufacture and its religious logic; it is never taken that seriously. Subtlety belongs to the satire, not to the thing being satirized.

One further sign of craftsmanship in the form needs to be pointed out. The collocation at vv. 18-19 is unmistakably associated with the theme of deafness and blindess that is so central to the logic of the larger Isaiah presentation. All that was once said about an Israel who had become like the nations is now true in a special way of those who fashion idols. Verses 18-19 present a point-by-point reassertion of the logic of 6:9-10. Those witnesses called forward are too deluded by the thrall of their own religious system to be able to set forth the logic of what they are doing.

This constitutes, in essence, nothing but a variation on the motif of non-appearing witnesses. They appear, but they fail to understand what they themselves are up to. Verse 19 drives this point home. Israel once heard God's word as alien gibberish. This delusion of mind makes the words out of one's own mouth incomprehensible and deluded.

The themes present in the satire are familiar from other places in the discourse. Israel as witness is to fear not (43:8); these witnesses are in dread (44:11). The ironsmith toils over his fire (44:12); Israel passes safely through fire (43:2). The Lord's "victorious right hand" upholds Israel (41:10); the smith forges with his strong arm (44:12). The poor and needy seek water, and God gives it (41:17); God gives power to the faint (40:29). Here the strong smith is faint and hungry, and yet the carpenter appears to be the one who finally eats. Yet the very project that provides the fuel to cook is what produces the hunger to begin with. What a brilliant narrative depiction of the

weariness and exhaustion of the strong with which the discourse began (40:30). And the larger point remains the play on fashioning: God fashions Israel, and not the other way around.

44:21-23. Given the intricate relationship between the various units of this section, how are we to take the opening appeal to Jacob to "remember these things"? To what does the author refer? The answer is consistent with the craftsmanship of the arrangement. Israel is to remember that God formed it, on the one hand, and yet within the context of another sort of possible forming: that of deluded idol manufacture. There may well be a specific connection as well with the odd phrase in v. 7b in which God establishes an "eternal people." Despite transgression, God has not forgotten this eternal people whom God formed (v. 21); instead, God has forgiven them and made their transgressions like mist. Israel is to remember that God does not forget.

The focus of the previous hymn (42:10-13) was on the comprehensiveness of praise and song to God in the light of the presentation of the servant. Servant Jacob/Israel was, however, deaf and blind (42:18), imprisoned (42:22), laden with sin (42:24). These matters have been addressed, one by one, in the section now concluding. Now Israel is a *forgiven* and *redeemed* servant (44:22). The hymn here simply references the former comprehensiveness with the pairing of "heavens" and "depths." The second pairing, "mountains" and "forest," is less obvious. A further elaboration, "and every tree in it," may well serve as commentary on the preceding idol satire. The trees in the forest are the one God's, and they exist to praise God and reflect God's glory. To fashion these trees into gods is to abuse the created design and to blaspheme, not honor, the maker of heaven and earth.

We might also recollect that the destruction of the sanctuary was clearly referred to in the context of failure to bring offerings (43:22-28). In the next section, the announcement is made that Jerusalem will be rebuilt and the Temple reestablished (44:28). This constitutes a proper use of the trees of the forest and the establishment of God's earthly mount as well. The hymn does a superb job of closing off one section and preparing us for the presentation of Cyrus in the next.

REFLECTIONS

1. One of the easiest tendencies imaginable for the modern mind is the dismissal of idolatry as simply belonging to another day; irrelevant, if elaborate, foolishness. The logic of it seems too crass. We may not be helped in this instance by the high level of satire resident in the description of idolatry (44:9-20). Not many of us know people who spend time fashioning real idols, to be set up and worshiped as gods in elaborately prepared shrines or household sanctuaries.

When, however, we read the passage closely, it is possible to catch some of the flavor of this enterprise that does not seem outmoded or patently objectionable. There is an underlying situation of dread or anxiety (44:11). Then great effort is expended to the point of exhaustion (44:12). Close attention and care and precision and beauty each takes its rightful place (44:13). Then follow discrimination and adaptability and comfort (44:15-17). Not one of these matters could fail to be taken as a virtue. Even anxiety and dread are part of the human condition; they need not be the fruit of exposed lies and false worship. But at some point a line is crossed and "god" appears, beckoning and asking for worship, which all this effort sees as consistent and the logical culmination of things.

At a minimum this requires some serious reflection about where our most careful and concerted efforts come from. What motivates them? To what end are we laboring and selecting and styling and creatively adapting? There can be no doubt that even the most exhausting and demanding projects have their nourishing moments. So while we may not have a shrine in the backyard where we fashion something we call "god," how different is it to find that our deepest and most sustained efforts have begun to ask for worshipful attention to the exclusion of the one we know to be God? "Fool, today your life is required of you" sounds quite close to the delusion depicted at the close of chapter 44, and yet nowhere was the suggestion made that the man with full barns was out praying to them: "Save me, for you are my god." But was not the effect the same?

The one point the satire fails to develop is the one with which it opens. Fear and shame and dread and terror are to be the consequences of the exposure of false worship, when "all who make idols" assemble and learn of God's judgment (44:9-11). All these anti-virtues, of course, were present at the start of the construction; indeed, we could conclude that they were driving the enterprise to begin with, at every point along the way. What does all the attention to detail and effort and exertion—potentially but not actually virtuous—say about the undertaking in the first place?

What we learn is that the New Testament parable of the talents has its opposite—that is, lots of overdiligent effort covering up deeper anxiety and dread. Here in Isaiah what we see is not a hoarding away of talents but an expenditure of them in bouts of activity aimed more at busyness and self-will than in godly creation. The result is not just a return to dread and fear, but delusion and self-reproach, "Is not this thing in my right hand a fraud?" Such is God's only judgment over activity undertaken without God's blessing and care.

2. The appeal to ancestral promise, forming, and blessing to bolster God's servant Israel in the present is not without its potential problem. Ancestor worship, condemned for the covenant community, is nothing but the final culmination of a scheme for orientation in the present based on past lineage and the fixed significance of "family tree." In the oracle concerning Egypt (Isa 19:1-25), idolatry is associated without further ado with consulting the spirits of the dead (19:14). This is how Egypt determines its plans for the present and for the future: by a backward glance at "the ghosts and the familiar spirits" (19:4). But God has a plan, and it confounds theirs.

In the case of Isaiah 44, however, two things make the appeal to ancestral promise, election, and formation distinctive. First, appeal is made to an Israel who believes those promises are null and void because of the accumulated weight of sin, blindness, and deafness. The curses of

Deuteronomy have fallen upon Israel, and blessing—ancestral and otherwise—has disappeared. Against that backdrop, the eternal promises to the ancestors—blessing, progeny, guidance, and divine presence—enable Israel to move beyond curse. The cleansing judgment of Isaiah was accomplished. "How long?" (6:11) had found its answer in the present, reconnected remnant: servant Jacob/Israel (6:11). Appeal to ancestor promises in this case grounds Israel's movement from curse back to blessing.

Second, a double name is inscribed on the new generation: not only the name of the ancestor Israel, but also the Lord's name. There is an identity in association with the ancestor, but deeper than that, and in addition to that, there is the identifying name of God. The "first and the last" has intimate fellowship with an "eternal people" (44:7 MT) who understand their relationship to the past ancestors and the past promises dynamically, as forever opening onto a new thing ("now it springs forth, do you not see it?"). All this stands in steady contrast to the consulting of idols and ancestors in order to discover a secret "plan." God's plan is not secret; rather, it is public, on display before all who choose to assemble. It involves promises made of old, durable through transgression and blindness for no reason but one: "for my own sake" (43:25).

ISAIAH 44:24–48:22, CYRUS AND THE NATIONS

OVERVIEW

This section is introduced with a formal unit (44:24–45:7) that is responded to by a hymn (45:8), which is analogous to the presentation of the servant at the opening of 42:1–44:23. At 42:1-13 and here, the unit serves to set forth God's bold design, the content of which is then elaborated, disputed, and otherwise parsed in what follows. How can a blind, transgressor servant do what God has said? This was the concern of 42:14–44:23. Here, Cyrus is commissioned, which in turn leads to disputation (45:9-25), anticipation of Babylonian defeat (46:1-13), depiction of that defeat (47:1-15), and a transition to new things and release (48:1-22). Cyrus is mentioned by name or by allusion at 45:13; 46:11; and 48:14-15. We are to understand the defeat of Babylon as having been accomplished by him as God's agent (chaps. 46–47). In sum, God's work through Cyrus is the governing concern of this main section, and in 44:24–45:8 that activity is introduced.

There is one important shift in this section that should be noted. The trial setting has not disappeared. Calls to assemble and present evidence continue to punctuate the discourse concerning Cyrus (45:20; 48:6, 14), less frequent, perhaps, but sufficient to keep the larger disputational backdrop in place. The same emphasis on unmediated first-person divine speech is also maintained throughout (with a significant transition at 48:16b), as God continues direct address from the divine council. What is new is that the disputation has taken a different turn with the commissioning of Cyrus. In the preceding section, Israel is reestablished as God's servant, for Israel's sake, but within the context of the challenge of the nations. The nations are to provide witnesses and testimony; their failure to do so entails God's claim, before the people and the nations, that Yahweh is God alone, maker of heaven and earth. Ironically, the servant will ultimately have a mission to these same nations, manifesting God's mišpāṭ.

This section, however, opens on a different note. One from among the nations, Cyrus, is the focus of God's plans. Before Israel can be servant, as God intends, Israel must—though blind and deaf—see and hear and repent and be forgiven (44:21-22). But Israel also must be set free in order to "bring out the prisoners from the dungeons" (42:7). Here Cyrus will find his role. But the very way the introductory unit (44:24-28) inches up on this fact, beginning with what is known and moving toward its chief, but astounding, conclusion, signals that the commissioning of

Cyrus from the nations is controversial. Consequently, in this section the challenge to assemble is joined by the more general call to listen and attend (46:8, 12; 48:1, 12). Israel—not the nations—stands at the center of these calls to listen and assemble. Now it is Israel—"recall it to mind, you transgressors" (46:8)—and not the nations, who must attend to the former things in order to grasp the logic of what God is up to (46:9-11). Now the possibility of idolatry lies within Israel's range of options—even if sarcastically entertained (48:5)—alongside its former role as an absurdity to be appropriately satirized or condemned (44:25; 45:16, 20; 46:1-2, 6-7). By shifting the focus to Cyrus, it follows that a new set of concerns confronts servant Israel.

Though subtle, with this shift we can begin to see something of the intermingling of Israel and the nations anticipated in the initial presentation of the servant (42:1, 4, 6). Some aspects of this are more lavish than others and have already received adequate comment—e.g., the predication for Cyrus at 45:1, "my anointed" (משיחו *mĕšîḥô*; cf. Ps 2:2), alongside "shepherd" (44:28) and "man for my purpose" (46:11; cf. 48:14), not to mention the generally novel suggestion that a Persian ruler will deliver, not punish, God's own people. Other aspects are more obliquely registered. God created humankind (45:12), and not just Israel (43:1). Egypt and Ethiopia, the former objects of ransom (43:3), here approach, do homage, and make confession (45:14-15). It is likely that "survivors of the nations" (45:21) means the ransomed of Israel, but in the same context "all the ends of the earth" are to "turn to me and be saved" (45:22; cf. 45:23). With the dramatic punishment of Babylon, Zion's counterpart, there may be something of a new beginning for the nations, on indirect analogy with the announcement that Israel has been forgiven and is, though a transgressor (46:8), God's servant, freed and commissioned for a special task (48:20).

Isaiah 44:24–45:8, Cyrus, Unwitting Agent

NIV	NRSV

²⁴"This is what the LORD says—
    your Redeemer, who formed you in
        the womb:
 	
I am the LORD,
who has made all things,
who alone stretched out the heavens,
who spread out the earth by myself,
 	
²⁵who foils the signs of false prophets
    and makes fools of diviners,
who overthrows the learning of the wise
    and turns it into nonsense,
²⁶who carries out the words of his servants
    and fulfills the predictions of his messengers,
 	
who says of Jerusalem, 'It shall be inhabited,'
    of the towns of Judah, 'They shall be built,'
    and of their ruins, 'I will restore them,'
²⁷who says to the watery deep, 'Be dry,
    and I will dry up your streams,'
²⁸who says of Cyrus, 'He is my shepherd
	²⁴ Thus says the LORD, your Redeemer,
	    who formed you in the womb:
	I am the LORD, who made all things,
	    who alone stretched out the heavens,
	    who by myself spread out the earth;
	²⁵ who frustrates the omens of liars,
	    and makes fools of diviners;
	who turns back the wise,
	    and makes their knowledge foolish;
	²⁶ who confirms the word of his servant,
	    and fulfills the prediction of his
	        messengers;
	who says of Jerusalem, "It shall be inhabited,"
	    and of the cities of Judah, "They shall
	        be rebuilt,
	    and I will raise up their ruins";
	²⁷ who says to the deep, "Be dry—
	    I will dry up your rivers";
	²⁸ who says of Cyrus, "He is my shepherd,
	    and he shall carry out all my purpose";

NIV

and will accomplish all that I please;
  he will say of Jerusalem, "Let it be rebuilt,"
  and of the temple, "Let its foundations be
      laid." '

45 "This is what the Lord says to his
     anointed,
  to Cyrus, whose right hand I take hold of
to subdue nations before him
  and to strip kings of their armor,
to open doors before him
  so that gates will not be shut:
²I will go before you
  and will level the mountains[a];
 I will break down gates of bronze
  and cut through bars of iron.
³I will give you the treasures of darkness,
  riches stored in secret places,
so that you may know that I am the Lord,
  the God of Israel, who summons you
      by name.
⁴For the sake of Jacob my servant,
  of Israel my chosen,
 I summon you by name
  and bestow on you a title of honor,
  though you do not acknowledge me.
⁵I am the Lord, and there is no other;
  apart from me there is no God.
I will strengthen you,
  though you have not acknowledged me,
⁶so that from the rising of the sun
  to the place of its setting
men may know there is none besides me.
  I am the Lord, and there is no other.
⁷I form the light and create darkness,
  I bring prosperity and create disaster;
  I, the Lord, do all these things.

⁸"You heavens above, rain down righteousness;
  let the clouds shower it down.
Let the earth open wide,
  let salvation spring up,
let righteousness grow with it;
  I, the Lord, have created it.

a2 Dead Sea Scrolls and Septuagint; the meaning of the word in the Masoretic Text is uncertain.

NRSV

and who says of Jerusalem, "It shall be
    rebuilt,"
  and of the temple, "Your foundation shall
    be laid."

45 Thus says the Lord to his anointed, to
     Cyrus,
  whose right hand I have grasped
to subdue nations before him
  and strip kings of their robes,
to open doors before him—
  and the gates shall not be closed:
²I will go before you
  and level the mountains,[a]
I will break in pieces the doors of bronze
  and cut through the bars of iron,
³I will give you the treasures of darkness
  and riches hidden in secret places,
so that you may know that it is I, the Lord,
  the God of Israel, who call you by
     your name.
⁴For the sake of my servant Jacob,
  and Israel my chosen,
I call you by your name,
  I surname you, though you do not
    know me.
⁵I am the Lord, and there is no other;
  besides me there is no god.
  I arm you, though you do not know me,
⁶so that they may know, from the rising of
    the sun
  and from the west, that there is no one
    besides me;
  I am the Lord, and there is no other.
⁷I form light and create darkness,
  I make weal and create woe;
  I the Lord do all these things.

⁸Shower, O heavens, from above,
  and let the skies rain down righteousness;
let the earth open, that salvation may
    spring up,[b]
  and let it cause righteousness to sprout
    up also;
  I the Lord have created it.

aQ Ms Gk: MT the swellings   bQ Ms: MT that they may bring forth salvation

COMMENTARY

44:24-28. Form critics have debated both the genre and the scope of this unit. The repeated participial introductions are striking, and they have urged some scholars to speak of a hymnlike composition. Yet there is a distinctly disputational tone to the piece as well, which has led others to adopt that classification. The striking repetition of participles (eleven in all), three of which are identical and conclude the unit ("who says"), distinguishes the unit from anything we have seen thus far. I agree with Westermann that this serves the purpose of introducing, in a somewhat deliberative way, the royal oracle concerning Cyrus in the following unit (45:1-7) and, therefore, is not, strictly speaking, a separate unit at all. Rather, it is a hymnlike introduction. This is, of course, more of a literary category than a form-critical category, consistent with the creative freedom of the unknown author.

The unit opens with phraseology in distinct continuity with the preceding section, and, indeed, that is its purpose. God is Israel's redeemer and creator from the womb (so 44:1 and 22). The import of the next line ("maker of all") could be seen as congenial with previous predications (42:5), but the close juxtaposition with the preceding is unusual. We are quite used to the bundling of predications, but the focus has up to now remained on who God is for Israel/Jacob (cf. 43:1 or 44:1). Moreover, it remains unclear how we are to take the generic "all" (by rendering "all things," the NIV and the NRSV have made an interpretation of sorts, likely on the basis of the following line). Yet the repetitive element of the speech-unit tends to frustrate associations of two lines only, as we are driven forward to see where the participial descriptions are taking us. Repetitions like this urge some final resolution where the point of the series is made clear.

The craftsmanship and logic of the unit are quite effective. Verse 25 presents us with just the sort of information we have come to expect: God's rejection of various forms of divination or "wisdom," especially when set over against v. 26. It is the servant's word, not omens, that will be established by God. We also know about "messengers" (here the term is מלאך [*mal'āk*]) with tidings for

Jerusalem (40:9; 41:27), though God's word to Zion/Jerusalem is here given more concrete specificity (v. 26*b*). The fact that yet further is said of a familiar character in the next line (v. 27), only then to double back to Zion/Jerusalem's reestablishment, interrupts the sense of piling up and moving forward characteristic of the unit until its end. By this means the chief point is underscored: It is Cyrus through whom God's purpose will be carried out. The effect of this is to catch the audience off guard, as God's plans announced from the divine council back in 40:1-11 here come to center on the Persian ruler Cyrus. The mysterious new foe from the northeast, summoned by name by God (40:25), is now identified and named for Israel as well.

45:1-7. Already mentioned is the formal analogy between the presentation and commissioning of the servant, followed by a hymn (42:1-13), and the commissioning of Cyrus, with hymn (45:1-8). There is one slight difference. The servant poem fell into two sections, and the first was the presentation of the servant to the divine council, while the second consisted of the commissioning of the servant by God in a more direct sense, with clarification of God's role. Here the presentation aspect is covered by the preceding unit (44:24-28), which presumably includes Israel as witness as well. The address to the servant (42:5-8) has its counterpart here, but an important difference can be detected. Cyrus remains an unwitting agent of God's will on behalf of Israel, while that activity is being carried out. Twice it is said (vv. 4-5), "you do not know me." Others will come to know (v. 6), and perhaps in time Cyrus, too, will know (v. 3). But the sense remains that here an important difference exists between the activity of the servant and the activity of Cyrus: At his commissioning by God, Cyrus, ironically, remains unaware of who is naming him for this task.

This is further clarified when we consider the explicit way God must contend with and overcome Israel's blindness and deafness in the previous section. In the previous section there is no emphasis on what Israel remains unaware of, but just the opposite. What Israel knows and is capacitated through forgiveness to remember as God's servant is the chief concern. When all is said and done, Israel not only knows God again, but inscribes God's name on the hand (44:5), while of Cyrus it is said, "I surname you, though you do not know me" (45:4). Idolators "do not know, nor do they comprehend" (44:18), and their blindess and delusion are the consequences of false worship. In sum, this section is not concerned to alleviate or remove the condition that keeps Cyrus without knowledge, while exactly that removal is arguably the concern in the case of Israel. God is fully able to work with Cyrus as is. The problem will be in getting Israel to understand and accept what God is doing on its behalf through Cyrus. Another way to put this is that no scene, such as we witness for Egypt and Ethiopia (vv. 14-15), involves Cyrus in a comparable way. His activity is to lead to the knowledge of God for others beyond Israel (v. 6), but that same activity transpires without Cyrus's own knowledge of Yahweh, the God of Israel. Whatever knowledge God indicates Cyrus will have (v. 3) is not present at his commissioning.

It is important to maintain these several distinctions in order to best understand how Cyrus is both distinctive and typical as an agent dispatched by Israel's God. Assyria, too, was sent by God as "the rod of my anger" (10:5). But its own mind is elsewhere (10:7), because it does not know God. Assyria is an ax that vaunts itself over the one who wields it (10:15). The Rabshakeh insists that God actually spoke to Sennacherib, granting the ruler knowledge of divine plans to the extent of boasting:

> Is it without the LORD that I have come up against this land to destroy it? The LORD said to me, Go up against this land, and destroy it. (36:10 NRSV)

This is blasphemy of such high order that God avenges it. Not content with destroying the host threatening Jerusalem, Sennacherib, the narrative concludes, is slain by his own sons "as he was worshiping in the house of his god Nisroch" (37:38). God's capacity to commission Cyrus does not require Cyrus's knowledge of God, and the text makes that clear: "I arm you, though you do not know me" (45:5). In this sense, Cyrus is typical, even while bearing the title "anointed one."

On the other hand, Cyrus has a different task

from that which Assyria had in a former day. While he does not know the God of Israel, Cyrus as commissioned and active will ensure that the God of Israel is finally known "from the rising of the sun, and from the west" (v. 6, anticipating vv. 14-15). Hezekiah's plea to God, that with the deliverance of Jerusalem, "all the kingdoms of the earth may know that you alone are the LORD" (36:20) is, through another unknowing agent, Cyrus, on the horizon of fulfillment. Seen through the lens of that "former thing," the author can even conclude that when treasures of darkness (אוצרות חשך 'ōṣĕrôt ḥōšek) become Cyrus's, he will "know that it is I, the LORD, the God of Israel, who call you by name" (v. 3). It was "everything found in his treasures [באצרתה bĕ'ōṣĕrōt]" that Hezekiah showed Babylonian emissaries in a scene foreshadowing the exile (39:1-8). Perhaps with their return and with the rebuilding of Zion/Jerusalem, the author could anticipate Cyrus's gaining knowledge of God. That particular scenario is depicted at vv. 14-15 when treasures ("wealth," "merchandise") are at last presented; confession then follows by the nations in fulfillment of Hezekiah's former prayer, "God is with you alone, and there is no other . . . O God of Israel, the Savior" (vv. 14b-15; cf. 36:20). When treasures are returned and Zion is adorned again, confession by the nations, including even Cyrus, will follow.

The Cyrus Cylinder, a historical record of the Persian ruler's reign, describes Cyrus's own claim to have been sent by Marduk, "lord of the gods," to destroy "his city" Babylon, much like an Assyria sent by God against "a godless nation," the people Israel.[75] Additionally, here Cyrus could be said to occupy the same role as Sennacherib in another day, when the Rabshakeh quotes him as saying, "Is it without the LORD that I have come up against this land to destroy it?" The text guards carefully against any such arrogation, even as it sets this caution next to one of the boldest promises in the discourse: that through this "anointed one," all nations will come to know that the God of Israel, the Lord, is God alone.

The form "royal commissioning" has been adapted for a special purpose in vv. 1-7. This is

75. J. Begrich, *Studien zu Deuterojesaja, ThB* 20, ed. W. Zimmerli (Munich: Kaiser, 1963). See text and discussion in C. Westermann, *Isaiah 40–66,* trans. David Stalker, OTL (Philadelphia: Westminster, 1969) 158.

connected with the concern to depict Cyrus as one who does not know God. How do you commission someone directly and say that he or she does not know you? For this reason, Begrich early on classified the unit a "salvation oracle" addressed to Israel.[76] It would be Israel who would need clarification as to how a foreign ruler, unaware of their God, could in fact be God's "anointed one," a role clearly, though not exclusively, associated with David (2 Sam 5:3; Ps 2:3), who in another place is called "head of the nations" (Ps 18:43). As such, vv. 1-7 are only an imitation of an actual royal commissioning, functioning here as an oracle of salvation, clarifying to Israel how Cyrus will execute his office in such a way as to finally carry out God's purposes for Zion/Jerusalem (44:28).

The final three verses of the unit further strain even a modified commissioning-salvation oracle, as the lens widens beyond the concerns of Israel and Zion/Jerusalem. Cyrus's lack of knowledge sets up an ironic contrast with the knowledge others will gain because of him (vv. 5*b*-6*a*)—even from the same "rising of the sun" where he was dispatched (41:25). God's intention in calling a foreign ruler who will bring about knowledge of God in every corner of creation could be taken as rhetorically powerful, a tribute to God's overwhelming generosity and kindness. But it could also be taken as some sort of ill-timed pre-emption of Israel's own role and place, a generosity that ignores its condition and blurs the particularity of the moment in which Israel, servant, finds itself: among the nations, within and without, at home and dispersed.

The final verse seems to catch some of the chiaroscuro of this difficult "announcement of salvation." It should not, however, be abstracted beyond this context, as so often happens when individual verses are too quickly universalized. Does the verse mean to describe the origins of evil as being lodged in God ("I make weal and create woe")? Given the context of the discussion, the text would not appear to be working at that level of theological abstraction. We are talking about the

76. Begrich, *Studien zu Deuterojesaja,* 14.

commissioning of an unwitting Cyrus, as military adjutant appropriate for the task at hand. "Evil" here is set in contrast with שלום (*šālôm*), a word absent from the creation account or affiliated texts. The destructive force about to be unleashed in Cyrus is not to be sentimentalized; he will subdue nations and ungird the loins of kings (v. 1; the text closest to this one is the opening chapter of Habakkuk). How can God dispatch the terrible, violent Chaldeans as any sort of agent of judgment? The answer to that question is not won through theological discussion or sublime reflections on the origins of evil as an independent force, either in Habakkuk or here. At some point it is bound up with the sovereign mystery, "I am the LORD, and there is no other," in the face of powerful, and transitory, national might.

45:8. The placement of the hymn is also significant in this discussion. Unlike the others (42:10-13; 44:23), it includes God's own speech. The terse conclusion, "I have created it" (בראתיו *běrā'tîw*), picks up the verb of the preceding line, "I create woe." "It" has no clear referent. Does it refer to the righteousness (צדקה *ṣĕdāqâ*) of the preceding stich? Or, more generally, does it refer to God's present activity as such? What we do know is that creation is to bear witness to emerging righteousness and to participate in its springing forth. Whether experienced as *šālôm* or as violence, God's activity with Israel, with Cyrus, and with the nations is consistent with and a manifestation of divine righteousness. This is a hymnic response similiar to the one given the prophet Habakkuk (Hab 3:2-19).

In the reference to salvation's (ישע *yeša'*) springing up, a word rare in this discourse, it is tempting to see an allusion to the name of the prophet of the former things, "Isaiah" (ישעיהו *yĕša'yāhû*). Salvation as associated with him included the knowledge of God by Israel and by the nations (2:1-4; 37:20). When his eye looked to the "latter time" (9:1), it could see a just reign (9:2-7) and a day "when the earth will be full of the knowledge of God as the waters cover the sea" (11:9). Paradoxically, Cyrus is to initiate the securing of that day.

REFLECTIONS

1. God has guarded the divine freedom to do a new thing and here does it. God places it within the context of something Israel knows already (44:24-28) or has been trained to know. Moreover, the notion that God was stirring up someone from the north and from the rising of the sun (41:25) was a former testimony, the possession of which was intended to expose the claims of the nations and their gods. God's defense of the prior word in this matter constituted the ground on which God stood, enabling God to reconstitute, form, bless, and empower a servant people all but dead. Here that agent is named.

It is difficult to know what the reaction was to God's word here. We have a somewhat glamorized view of Cyrus, which is partly deserved when measured against most of his marauding ancient Near Eastern counterparts. The sticking point was surely not Cyrus's personality or policy, but the fact that God was using him in a role once belonging to David, God's anointed, founder, with Solomon, of nation and sanctuary. The same David is even conceived of in the psalter and in Isaiah 11 as having a specific role to the nations.

Would it have helped much to know that Cyrus did not know what he was doing and who was sending him, or would that have made the oracle even more arch in tone? The text does not tell us these things, though in short order we will be able to construct a partial picture (45:9-25). To insist that Israel/Jacob remains God's servant doubtless had the rejuvenating effect intended. But the discourse now associates that proclamation with matters related to it in the first place, and so not altogether new: "in you all the families of the earth shall be blessed" (Gen 12:3 NRSV). The knowledge of God is to come to all peoples, and Isaiah reiterates that (45:6). But the terms of the brokering of that knowledge are unanticipated, centering now on a godless or god-filled ruler who does not know really what he is doing. In this sense he is not even like Abimelech, to whom God came in a dream and warned just who he was dealing with (Gen 20:3-7).

How often the richest promises made good on by God entail combinations of things neither bargained for nor anticipated. There was David; the nations; present imprisonment; God's word of old to Isaiah and older still to the ancestors; even an Assyrian ax or roused Chaldean host—each familiar enough in its own way and in its own field of association. But God's freedom to do a new thing does not mean that it is *ex nihilo,* with stuff never before seen under the sun. It is the particular constellation of the familiar and the trustworthy, rearranged and recast for a new purpose, that reveals God as fully faithful, sovereign, and free to be God on behalf of the people and the world God has made. The logic of that old bromide, "Be careful what you pray for, because you might get it," is here partly revealed.

2. God will demonstrate the ability to work with the strong reaction of the people to the word as well in the unit to follow (45:9-25). As in a later day, with a yet more profound combination of the old and the new, there will be limits (Matt 2:1-23). God's freedom to bring forth "my anointed" from Bethlehem never overrides Herod's freedom to reject the man of God's purpose and to seek his death. Nor does it interfere with the freedom, stirring the spirits of those from the rising of the sun (Matt 2:1), to unexpectedly come and do homage and bring offerings for the building up of an unexpected temple, lying in the crude house at Bethlehem (Matt 2:11) or hanging on a cross (Matt 27:51). The God who keeps hidden (Isa 45:15) makes Divinity fully known, in birth and in death. The how and why of who comes to adore are lodged within the same mysterious counsel that dispatched Cyrus. Toward that mystery inclines the force of the final two verses, involving God's freedom and God's righteousness (45:7-8). At a similiar juncture, Paul knew the same truth:

> O, the depth of the riches and wisdom and knowledge of God! How unsearchable are his judgments, and how inscrutable his ways! . . . For from him and through him and to him are all things. To him be the glory forever. Amen. (Rom 11:33, 36 NRSV)

Isaiah 45:9-25, Every Knee Shall Bow

NIV

[9]"Woe to him who quarrels with his Maker,
    to him who is but a potsherd among the
        potsherds on the ground.
Does the clay say to the potter,
    'What are you making?'
Does your work say,
    'He has no hands'?
[10]Woe to him who says to his father,
    'What have you begotten?'
or to his mother,
    'What have you brought to birth?'

[11]"This is what the LORD says—
    the Holy One of Israel, and its Maker:
Concerning things to come,
    do you question me about my children,
    or give me orders about the work of
        my hands?
[12]It is I who made the earth
    and created mankind upon it.
My own hands stretched out the heavens;
    I marshaled their starry hosts.
[13]I will raise up Cyrus[a] in my righteousness:
    I will make all his ways straight.
He will rebuild my city
    and set my exiles free,
but not for a price or reward,
    says the LORD Almighty."
[14]This is what the LORD says:

"The products of Egypt and the merchandise
        of Cush,[b]
    and those tall Sabeans—
they will come over to you
    and will be yours;
they will trudge behind you,
    coming over to you in chains.
They will bow down before you
    and plead with you, saying,
    'Surely God is with you, and there is no other;
        there is no other god.' "

[15]Truly you are a God who hides himself,
    O God and Savior of Israel.
[16]All the makers of idols will be put to shame
        and disgraced;

[a]13 Hebrew him   [b]14 That is, the upper Nile region

NRSV

[9] Woe to you who strive with your Maker,
    earthen vessels with the potter![a]
Does the clay say to the one who fashions it,
    "What are you making"?
    or "Your work has no handles"?
[10] Woe to anyone who says to a father, "What
        are you begetting?"
    or to a woman, "With what are you
        in labor?"
[11] Thus says the LORD,
    the Holy One of Israel, and its Maker:
Will you question me[b] about my children,
    or command me concerning the work of
        my hands?
[12] I made the earth,
    and created humankind upon it;
it was my hands that stretched out
        the heavens,
    and I commanded all their host.
[13] I have aroused Cyrus[c] in righteousness,
    and I will make all his paths straight;
he shall build my city
    and set my exiles free,
not for price or reward,
    says the LORD of hosts.
[14] Thus says the LORD:
The wealth of Egypt and the merchandise
        of Ethiopia,[d]
    and the Sabeans, tall of stature,
shall come over to you and be yours,
    they shall follow you;
    they shall come over in chains and bow
        down to you.
They will make supplication to you, saying,
    "God is with you alone, and there is
        no other;
    there is no god besides him."
[15] Truly, you are a God who hides himself,
    O God of Israel, the Savior.
[16] All of them are put to shame and confounded,
    the makers of idols go in confusion together.
[17] But Israel is saved by the LORD
    with everlasting salvation;

[a]Cn: Heb *with the potsherds*, or *with the potters*   [b]Cn: Heb *Ask
me of things to come*   [c]Heb *him*   [d]Or *Nubia*; Heb *Cush*

NIV

they will go off into disgrace together.
¹⁷But Israel will be saved by the LORD
  with an everlasting salvation;
you will never be put to shame or disgraced,
  to ages everlasting.

¹⁸For this is what the LORD says—
  he who created the heavens,
    he is God;
  he who fashioned and made the earth,
    he founded it;
  he did not create it to be empty,
    but formed it to be inhabited—
  he says:
"I am the LORD,
  and there is no other.
¹⁹I have not spoken in secret,
  from somewhere in a land of darkness;
I have not said to Jacob's descendants,
  'Seek me in vain.'
I, the LORD, speak the truth;
  I declare what is right.

²⁰"Gather together and come;
  assemble, you fugitives from the nations.
Ignorant are those who carry about idols
    of wood,
  who pray to gods that cannot save.
²¹Declare what is to be, present it—
  let them take counsel together.
Who foretold this long ago,
  who declared it from the distant past?
Was it not I, the LORD?
  And there is no God apart from me,
a righteous God and a Savior;
  there is none but me.

²²"Turn to me and be saved,
  all you ends of the earth;
  for I am God, and there is no other.
²³By myself I have sworn,
  my mouth has uttered in all integrity
  a word that will not be revoked:
Before me every knee will bow;
  by me every tongue will swear.
²⁴They will say of me, 'In the LORD alone
  are righteousness and strength.' "
All who have raged against him
  will come to him and be put to shame.

NRSV

you shall not be put to shame or confounded
  to all eternity.

¹⁸ For thus says the LORD,
  who created the heavens
    (he is God!),
  who formed the earth and made it
    (he established it;
  he did not create it a chaos,
    he formed it to be inhabited!):
I am the LORD, and there is no other.
¹⁹ I did not speak in secret,
    in a land of darkness;
  I did not say to the offspring of Jacob,
    "Seek me in chaos."
  I the LORD speak the truth,
    I declare what is right.

²⁰ Assemble yourselves and come together,
    draw near, you survivors of the nations!
  They have no knowledge—
    those who carry about their wooden idols,
  and keep on praying to a god
    that cannot save.
²¹ Declare and present your case;
    let them take counsel together!
  Who told this long ago?
    Who declared it of old?
  Was it not I, the LORD?
    There is no other god besides me,
  a righteous God and a Savior;
    there is no one besides me.

²² Turn to me and be saved,
    all the ends of the earth!
  For I am God, and there is no other.
²³ By myself I have sworn,
    from my mouth has gone forth in
      righteousness
    a word that shall not return:
  "To me every knee shall bow,
    every tongue shall swear."

²⁴ Only in the LORD, it shall be said of me,
    are righteousness and strength;
  all who were incensed against him
    shall come to him and be ashamed.

25But in the LORD all the descendants of Israel
will be found righteous and will exult.

25 In the LORD all the offspring of Israel
shall triumph and glory.

COMMENTARY

We enter one of those stretches of discourse where the scope of text discussed is determined as much by external as by internal factors. A hymn concludes the commissioning of Cyrus and marks an obvious transition to the present section (v. 8), while in chap. 46 the anticipation of Babylon's defeat is depicted through another polemic against idolatry. Cyrus (vv. 9-13) and idolatry (vv. 16-17, 20-21) are also topics in the present section, so it would be wrong to draw lines too sharply. The portion of text treated here is in some sense a matter of convenience.

More difficult in some ways is determining how to break up and analyze individual units according to form. This is a place where smaller units seem to be the rule. Verses 9-13 are an obvious disputation speech. Verses 14-17 are not always regarded as a single unit, though for our purposes it will be treated as such. Its form is unclear, but it participates with other Isaiah texts (49:22-23; 60:1-22) in themes of homecoming, homage of the nations, and procession to Zion with treasures. Here the latter two themes predominate. Verses 18-19 and 20-21 could be taken together, the first part consisting of divine self-declaration, which introduces a summons to trial in the second part. Others regard vv. 20-25 as comprising an individual unit, taken to be a trial speech, and leave vv. 18-19 to a different classification. The difficulty here is illustrative of a more general problem of division and genre assignment in the chapter. However, after chap. 45 the opposite tendency will be the rule— that is, longer compositions with fairly clear lines of demarcation.

45:9-13. This is obviously a disputation speech, and the background for it is equally clear; it need not be inferred, as is sometimes the case. God's commissioning of Cyrus has met with objection. The oracle does not move immediately to this, but allows a more general indictment to set up the specific complaint. In v. 13, however, the stirring up of "him" can be no other than Cyrus

(the same verb is employed at 41:13; it is used also at 13:17 for the Medes). The righteous character of this decision was also a theme anticipated in the hymn of v. 8. The more specific task of building Jerusalem, "my city" (v. 13), mentioned in 44:28, is here joined by that for which Cyrus is more generally renowned: the freeing of "exiles" (גלות *gālût*). This is the first time in the discourse where that specific term is employed.

These different tasks—city building and exile returning—are also closely related by the chronicler. The edict circulated by Cyrus throughout all his kingdom (2 Chr 36:22-23) stipulates that Yahweh, the God of heaven, "has charged me to build him a house at Jerusalem" (36:23), before mention is made of liberation from exile. The same edict serves to introduce Ezra–Nehemiah, though it adds that the returning exiles will "rebuild the house of the LORD, the God of Israel" (Ezra 1:3). This potential confusion could well be intentional, for it sets up the following narrative sequence (out of order in strict chronological terms) brilliantly. Only when search is made in the archives in Ecbatana, in Media, is it discovered that the hindered work of the exiles was not only permitted by Cyrus, but underwritten as well: "let the cost be paid from the royal treasury" (Ezra 6:4). The accounts of the chronicler and of Ezra–Nehemiah are presumably later than this Isaiah discourse, and they may represent an effort at coordination with it. In any event, the notion that Cyrus would rebuild the Temple and the city is not taken as rhetorical overplay and may well be rooted, and realistically so, in discourse such as this. It clearly augments the popular picture of Cyrus (and Deutero-Isaiah) as chiefly having to do with exiles and their return. In equal proportion to this is a concern with Cyrus as a second David: the anointed one, (re-)establisher of Jerusalem and its cultic center (44:26, 28; 45:13). This depiction is also coordinated with a text taken as curious or peripheral in the discourse (see the Commentary on 43:22-28). The sanctuary's princes were profaned by God, and Jacob/Israel was destroyed in a former day. Cyrus, however, will rebuild Jerusalem, raise up the ruins of Judah (44:26), and see to it that the temple foundations are laid (through financial support, as Ezra 5 has it).

Here, too, we may find an explanation for the final verse of the unit, "not for price or reward" (v. 13). Liberation and rebuilding will not cost anything (cf. 55:1). Both were costly in the first exodus; one recalls the motif of Egyptian despoiling, if not also the death of the firstborn. The sanctuary was also provided for by freewill offerings. Neither is going to be required this time (a fact Ezra takes quite literally). With this final statement, the transition to the following unit is nicely accomplished.

The disputation opens on a more general note (v. 9), with the image of the potter and his work. Israel would already be familiar with the language of forming and fashioning from the preceding chapters (43:1; 44:2, 9, 21). God has formed, created, made, sustained, chosen *Israel*. The divergence between the NRSV and the NIV readings in v. 9 reflects a somewhat awkward Hebrew, though the NIV has tried to read the MT as it has been vocalized. The sense of the second half of the first line is, "woe to the potsherd who contends with (other) potsherds"—and not just with the potter himself. This reading finds support at v. 12: God created the earth and "humankind" (אדם *'ādām*) in the most general sense (Gen 1:27). We are in a larger context than Israel and its maker, appropriate to God's calling of Cyrus.

God's freedom to form Israel from the womb, and to encourage it on that ground (44:2), gives rise to a further ramification Israel had apparently not expected. The questions posed in v. 9*b* would traditionally apply to Israel: Formed by God in a certain way, for a certain purpose, Israel ought not to question how that way and purpose are working themselves out (see esp. Isa 29:16). Yet v. 10 makes it clear that Israel is not asking about its own curious purpose and form, but the form and purpose of something else God has conceived. The work of God's hands whom Israel is not to question is Cyrus.[77] God's freedom to form, and reform

Israel, has its counterpart—unexpected or unwelcome though it be—in God's conception of Cyrus and rousing of him to action on Israel's behalf.

45:14-17. This passage is referred to in detail earlier because of its importance in revealing the final purpose of God's call of Cyrus, "that they may know, from the rising of the sun, and from the west, that there is no one besides me" (45:6). The references to wealth and merchandise in the opening verse (v. 14) may pick up and extend the preceding reference to priceless rebuilding and freeing by Cyrus (v. 13). The first release from slavery in Egypt was likewise to accomplish the widespread acknowledgment of Israel's Lord as God alone. This is a persistent theme through Exodus 6–14 (e.g., 6:7; 7:5, 17; 9:16, 29; 10:2; 14:18), culminating in the victory at the sea and the confession of the Egyptian host (Exod 14:25). Pharaoh's frequent acknowledgments of God's power and existence were grudging, fleeting, and made only under duress (Exod 8:8, 28; 9:20, 27; 10:7-11, 17; 12:31). Some of that backdrop remains here, but in addition there is actual supplication and acknowledgment (vv. 14-15). Whatever wealth and merchandise accrue from Cyrus's subjugation of nations (45:1) accrues not for Cyrus, but for Israel and the acknowledgment of "the God of Israel, the Savior" (v. 15).

Westermann (and in their own way the NRSV and the NIV) regards v. 15 as independent of the preceding confession made by the nations. He goes one step further in reckoning the verse an astonished, but favorable, response to God's work in Cyrus, thus expressing "an insight of the highest importance" otherwise missing in 45:9-13.[78] The reasoning he gives is full of religious insight, but unfortunately it is impossible to establish. What is hidden is the activity of a God who had formerly fought openly on behalf of the people, and occasionally against them, but who now no longer would do so: "Henceforth God's action in history is a hidden one."[79] This is the response of a writer interpolating his favorable reception of God's action in Cyrus. This interpretation asks us to see unwarranted discontinuity between God's action in Assyria and God's action in Cyrus, of a sort that occasioned an independent one-verse response, unmarked but there nonetheless.

---

77. The first half of the second line of v. 11 MT is rendered as, "inquire of me about the things to come, about my children." The things to come are apparently God's accomplishment of God's purpose through Cyrus, whom God has formed.

78. *C. Westermann, Isaiah 40–66,* trans. David Stalker, OTL (Philadelphia: Westminster, 1969) 170.

79. Ibid.

The alternative is to simply take the verse as an extension of the quoted acknowledgment of the nations doing homage. The God of Israel is not made known in some universal way, independently of the people and the actions toward them. The "Savior" of Israel is none other than the one who delivers from defeat and imprisonment, here through the agency of Cyrus. God's actions are not hidden to Israel in some new way, hitherto unexperienced. They have been and remain hidden to the nations, who come to know God and God's ways only as they witness God's actions with the people Israel, here ironically and mysteriously accomplished through a foreign ruler. The contrast with the exodus is striking. Here we have a foreign liberator who does not know God, whose liberation of Israel leads to the acknowledgment of God by foreign nations, but who is greeted with resistance by God's own people, Israel.

The final two verses serve to conclude the unit by offering a contrast between shamed worshipers of idols and an Israel saved by God, unashamed to all eternity. The "Savior," referred to by the nations in acknowledgment, here speaks on behalf of his people. If vv. 14-17 constitute a traditional form-critical unit, these final verses would mark it as an oracle of salvation. The oracle is delivered in the specific context of acknowledgment by the nations (v. 14-15), which is itself closely tied to the oracle commissioning Cyrus (v. 6). The other way to describe this is not that smaller, independent units are here juxtaposed by an editor, but that a longer, single composition (vv. 9-25) attempts to comprehend the range of concerns sparked by the decision to commission a foreign ruler to save Israel (vv. 1-7). The author proceeds by simply examining various facets of this decision and reactions to it. This gives "units" in the chapter the appearance of having been loosely strung together on the basis of catchword. But, in fact, here we are simply observing the mind of the author at work as he moves from one aspect to the next, one association giving rise to another.

45:18-25. For reasons just given, the final verses of this chapter are treated as a complex unity. The confession by the nations that the God of Israel, from their perspective, keeps hidden (v. 15), has triggered a reflection on just how this is so. The key words appear in the first two verses: "secret" and "chaos" and "land of darkness" (vv.

18-19). These verses reflect a self-predication from God that intends to clarify the confession of the nations for Israel and introduce the trial speech of vv. 20-24.

The opening verses make their point by means of counterfactuals. To say that God is the transcendent "maker of heaven and earth" does not mean that creation is a random, disorderly, arbitrary habitation in which God's will is known by accident or through penetration into realms of darkness and confusion. The God who has nevertheless chosen to be revealed and has spoken truthfully and clearly to the offspring of Jacob. By this means the divine will can be made known throughout all nations, for creation has been designed by God for this purpose. God did not ask Israel to seek God in chaos, and neither is this God's intention for the nations. With this wider, clarifying lens in place, the nations are summoned.

The striking thing about this trial speech is that it does not result in defeated silence or rebuff, as has been the rule thus far. Even the opening address, "survivors of the nations," is new, and it signals the possibility of a fresh handling of the destiny of those beyond Israel. The term could be interpreted with reference to Israel, as those who have survived the nations' onslaught over against a more appositional reading of the construct פְּלִיטֵי הַגּוֹיִם (pĕlîṭê haggôyim, e.g. "the nations' survivors"). The context serves to clarify matters (again pointing out how a traditional form-critical approach could be impaired). The succeeding reference to idolatry (cf. v. 16) anticipates nicely the introduction of the chapter to follow (46:1-7), where Babylonian "survivors," burdened with idols, go into exile. The challenge to present testimony further establishes the appeal to assemble as directed to the nations, as this motif is a persistent feature in all the previous trial speeches (41:21-24; 43:8-13; 44:7). The nearest one (44:6-20) is the most elaborate, as we saw, and there the explicit context of idols as potential conveyors of testimony was exposed, polemicized, and condemned.

It is not clear whether we are to understand the testimony from long ago as pointing to a single, specific content (Cyrus) or whether at this juncture the appeal is somewhat stereotypical. Attractive is the possibility that what the nations cannot bear testimony to, uttered long ago by God, is their own salvation and inclusion in God's designs (v. 22). This testimony exists within Israel's discourse with God (2:2-4). It may also be rooted in a particular interpretation made by our unknown author of the promises to the ancestors, as these spill over and engage "all the families of the earth" (12:1-3; 17:1-8). These promises made long ago are testimony to God's present decision to address the nations, by means of Cyrus and Israel, and exhort them, "turn to me and be saved, all the ends of the earth" (v. 22).

Proper interpretation of v. 23 would also serve to clarify the character of the testimony. Instead, the issue becomes more complicated. Both the NRSV and the NIV render the verbs in the past tense, suggesting that God's oath involving the nations' eventual worship was delivered in time past.[80] This would be consistent with the perspective of v. 21 and could constitute testimony from long ago. Others treat the oath as being presently delivered, anticipating the ensuing oath of the nations (vv. 24-25), to the effect that "only in the LORD . . . are righteousness and strength."[81] The exact rendering of לי אמר (lî 'āmar, "it shall be said") is somewhat unclear in the context of v. 24. If there is an anticipated oath, extending to the end of the chapter, it might be rendered: "Surely in the LORD [one will say of me] are righteousness and strength, while all who raged against him will come and be ashamed." Verse 25 either is spoken by the divine voice or is a continuation of the confession: "But in the LORD all the descendants of Israel will be found righteous and exult" (v. 25). If this latter interpretation is adopted, then the similarity with vv. 14-15 is what comes to the fore. The nations will confess the Lordship of Israel's God, and also the righteousness obtained by God's people, Israel.

---

80. In poetry (even with a more prosaic character, as in this discourse), strict tense or aspect differentiation is often missing.

81. So Westermann, *Isaiah 40–66,* 174-76. The NIV treats 45:24*b* only as the oath sworn by the nations. The NRSV reports God's oath only (45:23*b*) and presumably leaves the final two verses divine speech.

REFLECTIONS

1. The difficulty in rendering the Hebrew in the final verses of chapter 45 is more than a matter of missing quotation marks or the terseness of poetic expression. It has also to do with the difficult subject matter being handled. By commissioning unwitting Cyrus in a David-like role and arming him in such a way that knowledge of God will be grasped to the very ends of the earth, the author strains at the limits imposed by particular election, here conjoined with universal knowledge. The nations' confession acknowledges both the Holy One and Israel's particular election: God is *with you* alone (45:14); in the Lord the offspring of Israel shall triumph and glory (45:25). The widest possible knowledge of God includes with it a recognition that the place of God's privileged speech and life is with a particular people and is experienced by others in relationship to that speech and life.

It is little wonder that Isaiah so permeates the latter chapters of Romans. Paul refuses to cut the work of God in Christ loose from its moorings in God's Word and life of old with Israel. This would amount to a questioning of what God had promised and done long ago. Even if Israel were to become an enemy of God, those outside can know that only through the lens of "for your sake" (Rom 11:28). All clay is imprisoned in disobedience, so that God might have mercy on all (Rom 11:32). Any effort to correct the balance of these dispensations or to step outside the merciful freedom of God to make things right upsets either the particular election or the universal generosity of God through Israel and through the greater anointed one, Israel's king and the one at God's right hand through whom heaven and earth were made.

Isaiah 45 is brilliant in portraying the complex welter of emotions ignited by the theological difficulty of protecting the particular, while at the same time using it to manifest God's grander purposes. God may have planned long ago to dispatch Cyrus to free the people, but here we are talking about a service, unwitting though it be, that begins at Zion and reaches to the ends of the earth. Israel is being asked at the moment of forgiveness and reformation to find its place in a new dispensation as old as Abraham. What if it were to turn out that those who once held Israel captive were the ones who could say, in the same breath that confesses Israel's Lord as God, "in the LORD all the descendants of Israel will be found righteous" (Isa 45:25)? Paul is wrestling with just this sort of dialectic when he argues, "They have now been disobedient, in order that by the mercy shown to you, they too may now receive mercy" (Rom 11:31). But finally he knows that he stands before a mystery locked in the counsel of God, who hides and is revealed according to Divinity's own unsearchable wisdom (Rom 11:33-36).

2. What a challenge images of subjugation and obeisance present for modern men and women in the West. This is the subservient posture not only of the nations before God, but before Israel as well, "they shall come over in chains and bow down to you" (45:14). This is because we assume such posture to be about humiliation and aggrandizement, traceable to the misuse of power.

How would this text have been heard within its own frame of reference? Ethiopia is a "nation mighty and conquering" (Isa 18:2). Yet the day will come, Isaiah says, when this "people feared near and far" will bring gifts to the Lord of hosts (18:7). Mighty Egypt, it is said, will be "delivered into the hand of a hard master" (Isa 19:4) on account of idolatry and consulting the dead. Yet the prophet speaks as well of a day when blessing will come upon Egypt. Together with Israel, it will be called "my people" (Isa 19:25).

Perhaps the harder question is spotting subjugation in its less obvious, but nevertheless virulent, forms or coming to the false apprehension that God is more about "let my people go" than "that they might serve me."[82] It gives one pause that the central image of the discourse is "servant"—not "slave"—but far closer to that than "master" or "colleague." "Servant" is not replaced by "friend"; the two stand side by side (Isa 41:8). It is only from the perspective of God's Lordship that the term "friend" is appreciated and accepted as the merciful bestowal it is (the NT version of this, with Jesus as Lord, is found in John 15:15). Egypt had once to bow to a "hard master" (Isa 19:4), but in bowing to this Lord and this people, Egypt finds itself fulfilling the promise of Isaiah: "Blessed be Egypt my people, and Assyria the work of my hands, and Israel my heritage" (Isa 19:25).

3. In Phil 2:10-11, as several commentators have noted, there is a clear reference to Isa 45:23.[83] But the point is not to do with good use of a concordance. The Isaiah text speaks of God's swearing "by myself" that "to me every knee shall bow, every tongue swear." It goes on to speak of all peoples declaring that of the Lord, alone, come righteousness and strength. That is, the named God of Israel, Yahweh, is to be confessed as God alone throughout all creation.

Often the point is made, for a variety of reasons, that early Christian creeds and Christian Scripture are two quite different matters. Indeed, they can and should be seen as in some considerable tension. Nontheless, what some interpreters have shown is that the judgments rendered by the creedal language "of one substance" or "of one being" are fully consistent with the judgments of Christian Scripture, when the force of Phil 2:6-11 is heard properly in relation to Isaiah 45's promise. That is, God has given to Jesus God's own sacred name (YHWH), so that at this name, "the name of Jesus," the promises of Isaiah 45 might be fulfilled "to the glory of God the father."

Simply trying to match the conceptual frameworks of Scripture and creeds, or Scripture and our world, will often fail to see the logic of the judgments rendered by the texts, especially when one is, like the pre-modern history of interpretation (in its manifold expressions), seeking to hear

82. See the insightful criticism of problematic "liberation" applications of Israel's exodus traditions in Jon Levenson, "Exodus and Liberation," in *The Hebrew Bible, The Old Testament, and Historical Criticism* (Louisville: Westminster John Knox, 1993) 127-59.

83. David Yeago, "The New Testament and Nicene Dogma: A Contribution to the Recovery of Theological Exegesis," *Pro Ecclesia* 3 (1994) 152-64; Richard Bauckham, *God Crucified* (Carlisle: Paternoster, 1998). See also C. R. Seitz, "Handing Over the Name: Christian Reflection on the Divine Name YHWH," in *Trinity, Time, and the Church: A Response to the Theology of Robert W. Jenson,* ed. C. E. Gunton (Grand Rapids: Eerdmans, 2000) 23-41.

the whole counsel of Christian Scripture.[84] The church will suffer from ill-diagnosed forms of amnesia unless it can grasp something of how earlier interpreters (and that includes a fourth-century Athanasius CE in conflict with Arianism) read Scripture. Fortunately, we can go to school again within the book of Isaiah itself, which, as we have repeatedly seen, works with very subtle intratextual combinations, seeking to hear the word of God as it arcs from former to latter dispensations of God's selfsame working.

84. See Frances Young, *Biblical Exegesis and the Emergence of Christian Culture* (Cambridge: Cambridge University Press, 1998). Compare R. Greer, *Theodore of Mopsuestia: Exegete and Theologian* (Westminster: Faith Press, 1961).

Isaiah 46:1-13, Heavy Laden

NIV

46 Bel bows down, Nebo stoops low;
their idols are borne by beasts of
burden.[a]
The images that are carried about are
burdensome,
a burden for the weary.
[2] They stoop and bow down together;
unable to rescue the burden,
they themselves go off into captivity.

[3] "Listen to me, O house of Jacob,
all you who remain of the house of Israel,
you whom I have upheld since you were
conceived,
and have carried since your birth.
[4] Even to your old age and gray hairs
I am he, I am he who will sustain you.
I have made you and I will carry you;
I will sustain you and I will rescue you.

[5] "To whom will you compare me or count
me equal?
To whom will you liken me that we may
be compared?
[6] Some pour out gold from their bags
and weigh out silver on the scales;
they hire a goldsmith to make it into a god,
and they bow down and worship it.
[7] They lift it to their shoulders and carry it;
they set it up in its place, and there it stands.
From that spot it cannot move.
Though one cries out to it, it does not answer;
it cannot save him from his troubles.

[8] "Remember this, fix it in mind,

---
[a] 1 Or *are but beasts and cattle*

NRSV

46 Bel bows down, Nebo stoops,
their idols are on beasts and cattle;
these things you carry are loaded
as burdens on weary animals.
[2] They stoop, they bow down together;
they cannot save the burden,
but themselves go into captivity.

[3] Listen to me, O house of Jacob,
all the remnant of the house of Israel,
who have been borne by me from your birth,
carried from the womb;
[4] even to your old age I am he,
even when you turn gray I will carry you.
I have made, and I will bear;
I will carry and will save.

[5] To whom will you liken me and make
me equal,
and compare me, as though we were alike?
[6] Those who lavish gold from the purse,
and weigh out silver in the scales—
they hire a goldsmith, who makes it into
a god;
then they fall down and worship!
[7] They lift it to their shoulders, they carry it,
they set it in its place, and it stands there;
it cannot move from its place.
If one cries out to it, it does not answer
or save anyone from trouble.

[8] Remember this and consider,[a]
recall it to mind, you transgressors,
[9] remember the former things of old;

---
[a] Meaning of Heb uncertain

NIV

take it to heart, you rebels.
⁹Remember the former things, those of
    long ago;
    I am God, and there is no other;
    I am God, and there is none like me.
¹⁰I make known the end from the beginning,
    from ancient times, what is still to come.
    I say: My purpose will stand,
    and I will do all that I please.
¹¹From the east I summon a bird of prey;
    from a far-off land, a man to fulfill
        my purpose.
    What I have said, that will I bring about;
    what I have planned, that will I do.
¹²Listen to me, you stubborn-hearted,
    you who are far from righteousness.
¹³I am bringing my righteousness near,
    it is not far away;
    and my salvation will not be delayed.
    I will grant salvation to Zion,
    my splendor to Israel.

NRSV

for I am God, and there is no other;
    I am God, and there is no one like me,
¹⁰ declaring the end from the beginning
    and from ancient times things not yet done,
    saying, "My purpose shall stand,
    and I will fulfill my intention,"
¹¹ calling a bird of prey from the east,
    the man for my purpose from a far country.
    I have spoken, and I will bring it to pass;
    I have planned, and I will do it.

¹² Listen to me, you stubborn of heart,
    you who are far from deliverance:
¹³ I bring near my deliverance, it is not far off,
    and my salvation will not tarry;
    I will put salvation in Zion,
    for Israel my glory.

COMMENTARY

This chapter is brilliantly crafted. It is possible to detect shifts that are for the most part rhetorical in character; that is, they are not evidence of once independent form-critical units. Imperatives at v. 3, v. 8, and v. 12 mark these. The motifs of "bearing" (עמס *'ms*), "carrying" (נשׂא *nś'*), and "delivering" (מלט *mlṭ*), associated with God's life with Israel (vv. 3-4), are introduced in the opening verses in connection with the Babylonian deities Bel and Nebo (vv. 1-2). Unfortunately, these verses present considerable translation difficulty, persuading many commentators to adopt some sort of emendation scheme or simply rearrange the word order. Part of the complication is traceable to the craftsmanship of the author, who wishes to make an ironic contrast between God's carrying Israel into "old age" (שׂיבה *śêbâ*) and "the going into exile" (שׁבי *śěbî*) of gods or idols or the beasts carrying them (v. 2).[85] It is a brilliant play on who carries

whom and what in fact is burdensome, but the exact sense of the opening lines is unclear.[86]

In addition, the term משׂא (*maśśā'*, "burden") has a further association—namely, a prophetic utterance (used, e.g., within the nations oracle section of Isaiah, at 13:1; 14:28; 15:1; 17:1; 19:1; 21:1; 21:13; 22:1; 23:1). The author may wish to associate the great effort expended, resulting in no delivery of a *maśśā'* (v. 2), with the failure of Bel or Nebo to deliver a word. This same motif is present in v. 7, applied to the idol ("it does not answer"), and in vv. 8-11, where God can point to speech of old, now coming to pass (v. 11), in a manner with which we are now familiar. Israel is to listen (vv. 3, 12) and remember (vv. 8-9) because God speaks and has spoken. The gods do not speak or deliver a "burden" (*maśśā'*) but are

---

85. Torrey notes: "The difficulty which exegetes have found in this verse is due in part to text-corruption (though this is only slight), but still more to the unexpected vigor of the poet's language." See C. C. Torrey, *The Second Isaiah* (New York: Scribner's, 1928) 364.

86. Torrey translates the MT without emendation: "Bel sinks, Nebo breaks down! They [their idols] have proved like the beasts and the cattle." This maintains the usual sense of חיה (*ḥyh*) with the preposition ל (*lě*). Compare C. Westermann, *Isaiah 40–66*, trans. David Stalker, OTL (Philadelphia: Westminster, 1969) 177, who follows the emendation suggestion of C. F. Whitley, "Textual Notes on Deutero-Isaiah (46:1)," *VT* 11 (1961) 459.

themselves compelled to go into exile, weighted down to the point of collapse.

The goal of the chapter is revealed in the final verse. God will put salvation in Zion. Here we come into contact with what will be the major theme of the second major section, beginning at chap. 49. The Zion introduced here has a counterpart, the city under special protection of Bel-Marduk: Babylon. In chap. 47, "daughter Babylon" is introduced and her ignominious defeat portrayed. The personified Zion does not speak until 49:14, but with the humiliation of Babylon, Zion's exultation is signaled as now possible. God promised to return to Zion (40:10) that God's glory might be revealed (40:5). As God's agent, Cyrus would be Babylon's vanquisher (45:1). With Babylon's defeat, the glory promised in 40:5 would again be possible. The various strands of the discourse (sanctuary, Cyrus, idolatry, former things, the gods) are beginning to coalesce. Yet to find full expression, however, is the plight of Zion. This strand of the discourse is taken up following Babylon's fall and the stepping forward of God's special servant in 49:1-12.

46:1-2. The chapter opens with this brief two-verse depiction of idols, anticipating themes employed to describe God's way with Israel (vv. 3-4). I agree with Torrey that the textual problems are slight compared with the "unexpected vigor of the poet's language." I will follow his lead here in attempting an interpretation.

Bel and Nebo are Babylonian deities, the former (with Marduk) associated with the city Babylon, the latter with dynastic legitimation (the names "Nebuchadnezzar" and "Nabopolassar" reflect this). We know of accounts of Babylonian kings gathering together the gods (idols) from their shrines and hustling them off to safety. In this way, the idols were protected from theft and could presumably continue to offer protection. Such is the trope the author of Isaiah exploits.

The first line is the difficult one. In a case like this it is helpful to work with what is known, and that is only revealed subsequently. Israel has been a "burden" carried by God "from womb to tomb" (vv. 3-4). Animals are likewise able to bear burdens, even very heavy and wearying ones (v. 1b). Now we have the ingredients necessary to read the text. Bel and Nebo are sinking under an undesignated load. In this they are like beasts and cattle. If we think of the resolution involving Israel and God's carrying of them, then the gods should be weighted down from carrying their national burden. Instead, the idols are themselves the weight that makes animals groan and stoop and are thus carried into exile (šĕbî), while Israel is carried to old age (śêbâ). Here is another instance in which idol manufacture is stunningly polemicized in conjunction with a word of assurance to Israel.

46:3-4. The remnant of Jacob referred to here has a counterpart introduced in the previous chapter, the "survivors of the nations" (45:20). Babylon's anticipated fall, heralded by the faltering of Bel and Nebo, has ramifications, as we saw, beyond Israel's borders. But here God returns to speak directly to the people, whom God formed in the womb (44:1) for a special task within the clay of humankind (45:12), a potsherd among other potsherds (45:9). Israel has been borne, carried, and conducted from the womb. Finally, Israel will also be "delivered" (ואמלט *wa'ămallēṭ*), in the very same way a prophet delivers a burden under divine compulsion. The result in this case is the reverse of Babylon's destiny. Babylon goes into exile as Israel comes forth. The motif of lifting up, employed in the last line (v. 4), anticipates the following depiction of idols being lifted on the shoulder (v. 7). It also sets the stage for the stunning portrayal of Zion's children being carried back home on the shoulder of nations in the role of foster parents (49:22). All this will serve to complete God's original promise to Zion (made at 40:11) that God will gather and carry the people back home. God can be relied on to carry them not just from the womb, but through the hardship of exile and into old age.

46:5-11. The polemic against idol manufacture found here is familiar enough; one thinks of the extensive satire found at 44:9-20 or the briefer treatments at 40:18-20 and 41:7. The first of these (40:18-20) is particularly close to this passage, and it also can be found in connection with appeal to former testimony (40:21-23; 46:8-11). The connection here serves to remind the reader/listener that Cyrus stood at the center of God's former purpose of old and that the collapse of Babylon is not due to Cyrus's strength or even to his claim that Marduk sent him to punish his own people (so the Cyrus Cylinder). Idols, by contrast, cannot speak, no matter how much attention one lavishes on their manufacture and care.

Even the double call to remember is set in sharp contrast to the silence of the idol and those who would take guidance from it; instead they hear nothing and can recall nothing. God not only speaks, but has spoken. The famous "plan" (יצר *yēṣer*) of Isaiah (see 14:26; 22:11; 30:1; 37:26) finds its own special expression in this discourse, where it is viewed in retrospect and is seen as now coming to pass and even giving way to new things. The plan of old, as it found earlier expression in Isaiah, was clearly connected to God's sovereignty over the nations. The outstretched hand of God was "over all the nations," based upon God's plan "that is planned concerned the whole earth" (14:26). Even at 37:26, the plan concerning Sennacherib's downfall is regarded as having been established "long ago," in God's counsel from eternity. The dispatching of Cyrus belongs to that same plan of old, and the glimpse that is given us of Babylon's fall in chaps. 13–14 is chilling. Striking there as well is the reference to God's stirring (the verb used of Cyrus at 41:25 and 45:13) of the Medes to crush mighty Babylon, "who have no regard for silver and do not delight in gold"

(13:18). This reference may have influenced the author of 45:13 ("not for price or reward"); it presents as well a nice contrast to the pouring forth of gold and silver here, as idols that cannot save are made even heavier and more burdensome.

The forward influence of this passage can be seen as well. Chapter 55 speaks of a nourishment that costs nothing and that is contrasted with costly expenditure that provides nothing (55:1-2). God's word accomplishes for free what God intends for it (55:11). Here we have costly silence, preparatory to heavy-laden captivity.

46:12-13. Cyrus is called from afar (v. 11). The same term is used to describe the distance of the stubborn of heart from God's righteousness and deliverance. Then the verb employed in the final verse depicts the inexorable approach of God's righteousness. God will overcome the distance by divine effort. God will put salvation *in Zion*. The stubborn of heart consist of more than an Israel in exile, despondent on that basis. Those far from God's righteousness are to be found all over, including within the exiled Zion, in the wasteland and desert it has become, forfeit of God's presence (49:19).

REFLECTIONS

1. "Come unto me all ye that are heavy laden and I will refresh you" is one of the best-known lines in the Gospels (Matt 11:28). These are "comfortable words," as *The Book of Common Prayer* puts it. There is an honesty about the description that underscores its compelling character. To be "heavy laden" is not an accident of fate, occasioned by an unfortunate mishap or a sudden loss or bad news. It belongs to our existence at some basic level that we cannot shed by our own effort.

Striking in the depiction here is the even heavier burden borne by those things in which hope is wrongly placed in times of hardship. Not only do they fail to sustain us, but also they are themselves the source of great captive weight, and they bow down to the point of exhaustion and collapse.

This is the last time Isaiah speaks of the futility of idolatry, for the proof of that is now to be established beyond any doubt as the once mighty Babylon is humiliated and cast down, even further than the fallen gods and idols in which Babylon had placed its hope (chap. 47). To be sure, there is an occasional backdraft (48:5), but the discourse is shifting away from present events spoken of long ago to Israel toward new things. Even the threat of idolatry must give way to new challenges, and central among these is the despondency of Zion itself. This is occasioned not by the heavy-laden fruit of idol reliance, but by the core conviction that God had forgotten Israel's plight altogether (49:14). Which form of heavy-ladenness is heavier is hard to gauge, but God deals with each one in a manner appropriate to its own character and to God's sovereign design. False religion is exposed first, and then God is free to address the heaviness of Zion's heart as a matter of utmost importance.

2. It is unclear how and why God suddenly decides to close the gap between divine righteousness and those far from deliverance. There is little calculating in the discourse about just why Zion could now be regarded as having paid its penalty, reckoned as having received "from the LORD's hand double for all her sins" (40:2). There is no recourse to a time-scheme (Jeremiah's 70 years), no death of one generation, giving rise to a new one (the book of Numbers). Isaiah's former "How long?" received a reply so ghastly as to defy numbering and adding up altogether (6:11), and even it appeared to entail yet further cleansing and smelting (6:13). The promise of an end to Babylonian "justice" was uttered long enough ago, and in sufficiently vague terms for those wanting to calculate, that it could not serve as the cause of God's forgiveness, but only the manifestation of it, for the "tenth part remaining, burned again" (Isa 6:13).

Once the decision was made, however, the discourse hastens to its denouement, displayed in a series of interlocking episodes: Israel forgiven, Cyrus commissioned, Babylon defeated, Zion restored, God's glory revealed, the nations drawing near in obeisance and confession. God's salvation is "nearer to us now than when we became believers," to use the New Testament equivalent for this perspective. Still, it remains an eschatological event when all is said and done, for all the haste that is being evidenced. To know that the gap is being closed, at God's own initiative, within the logic of God's own eternal plan, is good news enough to amount to salvation and glory for those with ears to hear (46:13). Faith, then and now, is the substance of things hoped for, built upon the sure rock of God's word.

Isaiah 47:1-15, Zion's Foiled Foil

NIV

47 "Go down, sit in the dust,
    Virgin Daughter of Babylon;
sit on the ground without a throne,
    Daughter of the Babylonians.[a]
No more will you be called
    tender or delicate.
²Take millstones and grind flour;
    take off your veil.
Lift up your skirts, bare your legs,
    and wade through the streams.
³Your nakedness will be exposed
    and your shame uncovered.
I will take vengeance;
    I will spare no one."

⁴Our Redeemer—the LORD Almighty is
        his name—
    is the Holy One of Israel.

⁵"Sit in silence, go into darkness,
    Daughter of the Babylonians;
no more will you be called
    queen of kingdoms.
⁶I was angry with my people

NRSV

47 Come down and sit in the dust,
    virgin daughter Babylon!
Sit on the ground without a throne,
    daughter Chaldea!
For you shall no more be called
    tender and delicate.
² Take the millstones and grind meal,
    remove your veil,
strip off your robe, uncover your legs,
    pass through the rivers.
³ Your nakedness shall be uncovered,
    and your shame shall be seen.
I will take vengeance,
    and I will spare no one.

⁴ Our Redeemer—the LORD of hosts is
        his name—
    is the Holy One of Israel.

⁵ Sit in silence, and go into darkness,
    daughter Chaldea!
For you shall no more be called
    the mistress of kingdoms.
⁶ I was angry with my people,
    I profaned my heritage;

ᵃ1 Or *Chaldeans*; also in verse 5

NIV

and desecrated my inheritance;
I gave them into your hand,
    and you showed them no mercy.
Even on the aged
    you laid a very heavy yoke.
[7]You said, 'I will continue forever—
    the eternal queen!'
But you did not consider these things
    or reflect on what might happen.

[8]"Now then, listen, you wanton creature,
    lounging in your security
and saying to yourself,
    'I am, and there is none besides me.
I will never be a widow
    or suffer the loss of children.'
[9]Both of these will overtake you
    in a moment, on a single day:
    loss of children and widowhood.
They will come upon you in full measure,
    in spite of your many sorceries
    and all your potent spells.
[10]You have trusted in your wickedness
    and have said, 'No one sees me.'
Your wisdom and knowledge mislead you
    when you say to yourself,
    'I am, and there is none besides me.'
[11]Disaster will come upon you,
    and you will not know how to conjure
        it away.
A calamity will fall upon you
    that you cannot ward off with a ransom;
a catastrophe you cannot foresee
    will suddenly come upon you.

[12]"Keep on, then, with your magic spells
    and with your many sorceries,
    which you have labored at since childhood.
Perhaps you will succeed,
    perhaps you will cause terror.
[13]All the counsel you have received has only
        worn you out!
Let your astrologers come forward,
those stargazers who make predictions month
        by month,
    let them save you from what is coming
        upon you.
[14]Surely they are like stubble;
    the fire will burn them up.

NRSV

I gave them into your hand,
    you showed them no mercy;
on the aged you made your yoke
    exceedingly heavy.
[7]You said, "I shall be mistress forever,"
    so that you did not lay these things to heart
    or remember their end.

[8]Now therefore hear this, you lover of
        pleasures,
    who sit securely,
who say in your heart,
    "I am, and there is no one besides me;
I shall not sit as a widow
    or know the loss of children"—
[9]both these things shall come upon you
    in a moment, in one day:
the loss of children and widowhood
    shall come upon you in full measure,
in spite of your many sorceries
    and the great power of your enchantments.

[10]You felt secure in your wickedness;
    you said, "No one sees me."
Your wisdom and your knowledge
    led you astray,
and you said in your heart,
    "I am, and there is no one besides me."
[11]But evil shall come upon you,
    which you cannot charm away;
disaster shall fall upon you,
    which you will not be able to ward off;
and ruin shall come on you suddenly,
    of which you know nothing.

[12]Stand fast in your enchantments
    and your many sorceries,
    with which you have labored from
        your youth;
perhaps you may be able to succeed,
    perhaps you may inspire terror.
[13]You are wearied with your many
        consultations;
    let those who study[a] the heavens
stand up and save you,
    those who gaze at the stars,
and at each new moon predict

[a]Meaning of Heb uncertain

NIV

They cannot even save themselves
    from the power of the flame.
Here are no coals to warm anyone;
    here is no fire to sit by.
[15]That is all they can do for you—
    these you have labored with
    and trafficked with since childhood.
Each of them goes on in his error;
    there is not one that can save you.

NRSV

            what[a] shall befall you.

[14]See, they are like stubble,
    the fire consumes them;
they cannot deliver themselves
    from the power of the flame.
No coal for warming oneself is this,
    no fire to sit before!
[15]Such to you are those with whom you
            have labored,
    who have trafficked with you from
            your youth;
they all wander about in their own paths;
    there is no one to save you.

[a]Gk Syr Compare Vg: Heb *from what*

COMMENTARY

Commentators generally agree that in chap. 47 we find a unified composition. Traditional form-critical analysis usually gives way to a discussion of "strophes," with attention to the unique literary form and language of the poem.[87] For some earlier commentators, this may have led to the conclusion that the poem was not authored by Deutero-Isaiah; its tone, moreover, was reckoned too vindictive for our unknown poet.[88] The mood has shifted, however, in the light of the work of Muilenberg and others. Now attention is paid not only to the rhetorical craft of the poem, but also to its affiliations with other parts of the discourse. These will be noted in the Commentary. It is clear that the depiction of Daughter Babylon is intended to serve as a foil, introducing the address to Daughter Zion in chaps. 49–55. "What happens to Jerusalem is the opposite of all that happened to Babylon."[89]

Discussion of the form of the poem has centered on questions about the exact timing of Babylon's downfall. "Triumph song" or "mocking song" are viewed as unsuitable designations by those who wish to locate the delivery of the poem before Babylon's actual historical collapse. This controversy may introduce an index somewhat peripheral to the poem and its function within the discourse. A reasonable conclusion is that the poem is in the form of a taunt, influenced by the style of the prophetic oracle.[90] Seen within the perspective of the book of Isaiah, it is reminiscent of the oracles against the nations (chaps. 13–23). What is foreseen regarding Babylon in chaps. 13–14 is here on the horizon of fulfillment, and the prophet's proclamation serves to assure Israel that it is, indeed, to be so.

At the same time, the poem here has not been composed in one-to-one correspondence with the depiction of chaps. 13–14. It is content to go its own distinctive way, appropriate to the context and the movement from deaf and blind Israel, restored and forgiven (chaps. 41–46), to despondent Daughter Zion, widowed and bereft of children (chaps. 49–55). Cyrus is not named as the victor over Babylon in the poem, but reference to him in the preceding chapters clarifies that Babylon will, indeed, meet the concrete judgment promised at 13:17-22 and will be removed forever from its place as "Babylon, the glory of the kingdoms" (13:19). With this accomplished, the poet

---

87. Westermann states: "The chapter contains about forty words not found elsewhere in Deutero-Isaiah." C. Westermann, *Isaiah 40–66,* trans. David Stalker, OTL (Philadelphia: Westminster, 1969) 188.

88. See, e.g., R. N. Whybray, *Isaiah 40–66* (London: Oliphants, 1975) 126.

89. Chris A. Franke, "The Function of the Satiric Lament over Babylon in Second Isaiah (XLVII)," *VT* 41 (1991) 416.

90. R. F. Melugin, *The Formation of Isaiah 40–55,* BZAW 141 (Berlin: Walter de Gruyter, 1976) 135.

turns for the last time to the "former things" in chap. 48, only to announce that they have given way to new things and are no longer to be remembered (48:3-6). Central within that appeal was the promise that Cyrus was roused by God of old to crush mighty Babylon. Isaiah 48:3 reports that has, in fact, happened, and the proclamation of chap. 47 prepares us for that announcement.

The poem is generally divided into five strophes: vv. 1-4, vv. 5-7, vv. 8-9, vv. 10-12, and vv. 13-15, though the last two are not always drawn the same way. This is not critical for the text's interpretation. Verse 13 introduces those experts who have assisted Daughter Babylon "from her youth" (v. 14); they, too, will be consumed along with her. This is a further elaboration of Babylon's own studied use of magic and sorcery, described in the fourth strophe. To speak of strophes is already to reckon with a more integrated composition whose further division is not pivotal.

47:1-4. Chapter 14 speaks about a fall from the stars all the way to the depths of Sheol for once mighty Babylon. There the gallery of slain rulers, each in his tomb, greets the nation; but even its corpse finds no resting place but is cast away like "loathsome carrion" (14:19).

The discourse speaks of a fall appropriate to the context: Queen Babylon becomes a common slave girl, forced to grind and mill, stripped and humiliated. The command "sit" (שׁבִי šĕbî, 2nd fem. sing.) is repeated twice here and again at v. 5. It is a homonym with שׁבִי (šĕbî, "captivity"), such as we find it in the previous chapter (46:2); the effect is obvious. The second command to "sit" locates the place for that as "the earth" (הארץ hāʾāreṣ), which is a common allusion to the netherworld.[91] If that is intended here, the central image of chap. 14 is evoked; there (14:12), too, Babylon is cut to the ground (lāʾāreṣ), and the netherworld association is explicit. The throne that was raised above the stars (14:13) does not accompany it to the netherworld, there or here. In short, the opening verses signal that the taunt to be taken up against the king of Babylon, "when the LORD has given you rest from the pain and turmoil and hard service with which you were made to serve" (14:3), is now being delivered. The taunt against the king of

91. Franke, "The Function of the Satiric Lament over Babylon in Second Isaiah (XLVII)," 414.

Babylon is here joined by one against Daughter Babylon, "mistress of the kingdoms," Queen Mother (גברת gĕberet) and progenitor of all things Babylonian.

The common term for "exile" (גלות gālût) comes from the verb "to strip bare" (גלה gillâ), and here it is used twice in association with unveiling and the baring of legs. Most scholars agree that the image of passing through rivers seems out of place, strictly speaking, in this scenario. The only explanation for its appearance is the association with rivers elsewhere in the discourse, tracing back to previous Isaiah chapters. Rivers are a symbol of God's destructive potential ("the River, the king of Assyria and all his glory," 8:7) through which Israel will now pass unharmed (43:2; 44:27); they also stand in contrast to a different sort of sustaining water ("the waters of Shiloah that flow gently," 8:5) that God is prepared to produce to support the people (43:20; 44:3; 55:1). Slave Babylon is about to endure the first, as naked and vulnerable as it can be.

Striking is the final confession, presumably made by Israel (v. 4), in the light of the strong preceding statement that no one is to be spared. The plural "our" points to those who have been redeemed through similar trial and not obliterated. The appellation "Holy One of Israel" is reminiscent of Isaiah of Jerusalem, who was told not only of the sternest possible punishment, but also of a remnant purged by fire (6:13). Those who have passed through rivers ahead of Babylon know that they were redeemed by the Holy One, and here their confession drives home the still greater severity of Babylon's punishment.

47:5-7. The reasons for the extreme judgment over Babylon emerge slowly and are different in kind. Daughter Babylon is again charged to sit in silence and darkness, fitting images for the underworld or for the silence appropriate to those who cannot bring testimony. The charge leveled here begins with an acknowledgment that God directed the punishment of Israel, against whom God was angry. Reference to profaning the sanctuary (or its officials) was made at 43:28 and is joined here by a different object, broader in scope ("my heritage"). It was God who gave Israel into the hands of Babylon. But in a manner familiar from the earlier Isaiah chapters, where Assyria overstepped its role, Babylon also was ruthless and went beyond what was a reasonable execution of the role of conqueror. The author may have in mind the sort of treatment recorded in 2 Kgs 25:6-7 (the blinding of King Zedekiah following the execution of his sons), but this is impossible to determine. The text reports excessive treatment of the elderly and does not stipulate any further cruelties alongside this. The final verse introduces us to what may be the more salient charge. Daughter Babylon ironically claimed to be the eternal "mistress forever," when she did not know there would be an end consequence superintended by the one who is *mišpāṭ* and whose word is not just first but last. The term "end" (אחרית *'aḥărît*) is the same one used of God's claim to be first and last, alone capable of knowing and establishing the link between former things with their outcome (44:6-8).

47:8-9. The command to "sit" is here replaced by "listen." Babylon as addressed is sitting (יושבת *yôšebet*) securely already. The quote given here reveals what Babylon had said in her heart; it is repeated again in the next strophe (v. 10). It is almost identical to God's own self-predication at 45:21 and elsewhere. Babylon is, of course, not entirely alone; she has children and a consort. Yet the force of the nation's claim is that it will *always* have these; it will never suffer the loss of children. The opposite of perpetuity is instantaneousness, and God's justice coordinates them both. In an instant Babylon is both of the things it claimed it would never be: a widow, and one without children. The final verse eases the transition to the next strophe; magic and enchantment cannot prevent what God is about to do.

47:10-12. The security Babylon experienced was based in evil and in the claim to being seen by no one. The claim to perpetuity is joined by one to moral invisibility. The knowledge and wisdom that are her possessions lead her astray. She was,

according to Jeremiah, to mete out a threefold judgment on Judah and Jerusalem: pestilence, captivity, sword (Jer 43:11), and pestilence, sword, famine (Jer 16:1-4; 21:7). Now Babylon experiences "evil" (רעה *rā'â*), "disaster" (הוה *hôwâ*), and "ruin" (שואה *šô'â*), for which her magic is no prophylactic. She can give it her best shot, but to no avail (v. 12).

47:13-15. "Counsel" (NIV) and "consultation" (NRSV) are renderings of the Hebrew עצה (*'ēṣâ*), the same term referred to by God as the "plan" or "purpose" (so, e.g., 46:10*b*). God has one consistent plan; Babylon has many stratagems and strategizers. We have heard of Babylon's sorcery and enchantment and charms; now we learn of astrology and astrologers. This is exactly the same art/science with which we are familiar today. To divide the heavens (v. 13) is above all to learn the constellations and study their movements, from which predictions can then be made. "When Mars approaches the moon and stands, the moon will cause evil to inhabit the land"—so runs a typical astrological prediction, in this case unfavorable.[92]

The end visited upon these experts is reminiscent of Isaiah's opening chapter (1:31). Babylon was to undergo the fate of Sodom and Gomorrah (13:19), also mentioned in the opening chapter (1:9). There a few survivors testify to the awesome judgment visited upon Jerusalem, without which "we would have been like Sodom, and become like Gomorrah" (1:9). For Babylon, in distinction to Zion (46:13), there is no salvation whatsoever (47:15). In contrast to the preceding chapter, this bitter taunt is unrelieved in its portrayal of a final judgment—swift, sure, without exception—visited upon Daughter Babylon and her associates.

92. Westermann, *Isaiah 40–66*, 193.

REFLECTIONS

1. In the major section we have been working with thus far, the Holy One of Israel establishes before Israel and before those summoned to trial that "I am the first and I am the last; besides me there is no god" (44:6). Rival national deities are exposed as "nothing and your work nothing at all." The "work" of a deity involves a people, a sanctuary, and a word, which establishes itself as true through time and the working out of events in strict accordance with God's prior word and plan. God's people live by the reliability of this word, and that reliability is established by God before the nations in Isaiah 40–46. Jacob/Israel is given new life on the basis of former things: promises to the ancestors; promises made good on in another wilderness and house of bondage; and promises of an agent of judgment who would bring an end to Babylon's reign of excess and terror, without even knowing he was sent by Israel's God, the one and only God.

Infrequent but clear have also been references to God's sanctuary. Jerusalem is to be comforted (40:1-2); heralds are to announce God's return to Zion (40:9). The sanctuary and its officials had been profaned by God on account of long-standing sin and transgression (43:26-28); that sin is now blotted out (43:25). Cyrus does not just win military victory over one more, perhaps final, foe and thereby pave the way for the knowledge of the true God. God's plan with Cyrus involves a mighty apostrophe to the sanctuary, "Who says of the temple, 'Your foundation shall be laid' " (44:28). Where tribute is brought, where God is "with you alone" (45:14-16), is God's sanctuary in Zion. The salvation not slow to come is salvation "I will put in Zion" (46:13).

The depiction of the end of Daughter Babylon can also serve as a grand apostrophe to the sanctuary, and to the figure of Daughter Zion, who is addressed directly in 49:14 through chapter 52 and beyond. The book of Jeremiah sits more exclusively on this particular period in the history of Israel; it begins with reference to Babylon's destructive agency and ends with lengthy accounts of its fall, far more elaborate than what we find in Isaiah 47. That prophetic record finds its center and pivot in Jeremiah 25, where the nations assemble to drink God's cup of wrath, passed at last to Babylon. In the final chapters (Jeremiah 50–52), God's punishment of Babylon is to be reported in Zion as "vengeance for his temple" (Jer 50:28). The spirit of the "kings of the Medes" is stirred up by God to destroy Babylon, "for that is vengeance of the LORD, vengeance for his temple" (Jer 51:11). Babylon and the inhabitants of Chaldea are repaid "for all the wrong they have done in Zion" (Jer 51:24). The final chapter (Jeremiah 52) gives something of the flavor of that, even as it understands the judgment over Judah and the house of David to have been merited: "Indeed, Judah and Jerusalem so angered the LORD that he expelled them from his presence" (Jer 52:3).

God's presence is manifested in different ways, but certainly in a special way in Zion. Daughter Babylon finds her place next to the king of Babylon (14:4-21) in the book of Isaiah on account of Zion and God's plan for her: "The LORD has founded Zion, and the needy among his people will find refuge in her" (14:32). Chapter 47 is not about the vindictiveness of an author's portrayal or an odd moment of poetic excess. Babylon's Bel and Nebo are not empty threats, devoid of any power to enthrall; rather, they are the trustees of an elaborate religious system, complete with appeals to the stars, sorcery, enchantment, and various charms. Daughter Babylon thrives on these, stands or falls in relationship to these, in the same way Daughter Zion lives by God's presence and Word. Just as there is no god besides the Holy One, so also there is no sanctuary but Zion. Cyrus will build up its foundations, but first its counterpart must step aside, and then Zion must be addressed and comforted, as the heavenly voice first announced at the very highest levels of eternal government (40:1-2).

2. Probably one of the worst features of our late modern culture (in the West) is naïveté about monotheism. It is assumed to exist by all rational people who think of themselves as "religious," while polytheism or the notion of rival gods is presumed to be "irrational." Yet pierce not very deeply below this veneer of rationalism, and one can see all sorts of spiritual forces laying claim to us: consumerist spirits, fitness spirits, rights and entitlement spirits, and even spirits of religious rightness and zeal.

The Old Testament exists in a context where this battleground cannot help being a conscious reality, and in that sense, it has some distinct advantages over our supposedly "enlightened" rationalism, with its immature but very real and very widespread spiritualities vying for our devotion. We may not build shrines for the god of shiny new automobiles or Sunday football, but we know without a doubt just how much of a financial investment our culture has in these things. Isaiah has a word to say to each one of us on this score.

3. The New Testament does not move away from the realm of sanctuaries and rival deities. Athens is full of shrines, and its people are very religious (Acts 17:22). The Jerusalem of Jesus' day presented a sanctuary, literally, from the claims of the naturally religious instincts, in the Temple, where the One Holy Lord was worshiped and the holy name praised. We long for this place of purity and holiness to cleanse us from our daily compromises with the spirits of our age. We long not only to be clean, but also to live in holy fellowship with our holy and eternal Lord. That instinct is there naturally, too, but it must find its target in the one and only true Lord, the maker of heaven and earth.

When the light that was to rise and shine over Zion for all nations and kings to see (Isa 60:1-3) rises and settles over the little child in Bethlehem (Matt 2:9), we learn that our true and lasting sanctuary is forever open, its altar light ever burning brightly, its high priest forever about his service for us. We need never worry that the spirits of our age or the depth of our sins is any genuine rival to the cleansing and forgiving power of Jesus Christ. We must make our own pilgrimage to see this Lord, and the way is costly because we must give up our selfish dreams of control, commerce, and a righteousness sought out of pride, not received as a child. But the light is shining as brightly as ever it did that night long ago. There is no season, no hour, no minute when it cannot be visited. That is what it means for the prophet Isaiah to tell of a mighty God, a God without rival: giving us a holy sanctuary for cleansing, forgiveness, and new life with God. "Our redeemer—the LORD of hosts is his name—is the Holy One of Israel" (47:4).

Isaiah calls us to another sanctuary and another God, the one in whom surrender is freedom and death to self, the one who is life eternal. May we depart from our anxiety borne of idolatry and the worship of spirits unable to save into God's peace, and there watch as God makes good on earth as it is in heaven, through the mediation and intercession of the great high priest.

Isaiah 48:1-22, Former Things, New Things

NIV

48 "Listen to this, O house of Jacob,
you who are called by the name of Israel
and come from the line of Judah,
you who take oaths in the name of the LORD
and invoke the God of Israel—
but not in truth or righteousness—
[2]you who call yourselves citizens of the
holy city
and rely on the God of Israel—
the LORD Almighty is his name:
[3]I foretold the former things long ago,
my mouth announced them and I made
them known;

NRSV

48 Hear this, O house of Jacob,
who are called by the name of Israel,
and who came forth from the loins[a]
of Judah;
who swear by the name of the LORD,
and invoke the God of Israel,
but not in truth or right.
[2] For they call themselves after the holy city,
and lean on the God of Israel;
the LORD of hosts is his name.

[3] The former things I declared long ago,

[a]Cn: Heb *waters*

NIV

then suddenly I acted, and they came
  to pass.
⁴For I knew how stubborn you were;
  the sinews of your neck were iron,
  your forehead was bronze.
⁵Therefore I told you these things long ago;
  before they happened I announced them
    to you
so that you could not say,
  'My idols did them;
  my wooden image and metal god ordained
    them.'
⁶You have heard these things; look at them all.
  Will you not admit them?

"From now on I will tell you of new things,
  of hidden things unknown to you.
⁷They are created now, and not long ago;
  you have not heard of them before today.
So you cannot say,
  'Yes, I knew of them.'
⁸You have neither heard nor understood;
  from of old your ear has not been open.
Well do I know how treacherous you are;
  you were called a rebel from birth.
⁹For my own name's sake I delay my wrath;
  for the sake of my praise I hold it back
    from you,
  so as not to cut you off.
¹⁰See, I have refined you, though not as silver;
  I have tested you in the furnace of affliction.
¹¹For my own sake, for my own sake, I do this.
  How can I let myself be defamed?
  I will not yield my glory to another.

¹²"Listen to me, O Jacob,
  Israel, whom I have called:
I am he;
  I am the first and I am the last.
¹³My own hand laid the foundations of
    the earth,
  and my right hand spread out the heavens;
when I summon them,
  they all stand up together.

¹⁴"Come together, all of you, and listen:
  Which of ⌊the idols⌋ has foretold
    these things?

The LORD's chosen ally

NRSV

they went out from my mouth and I made
  them known;
  then suddenly I did them and they came
    to pass.
⁴ Because I know that you are obstinate,
  and your neck is an iron sinew
  and your forehead brass,
⁵ I declared them to you from long ago,
  before they came to pass I announced them
    to you,
so that you would not say, "My idol did them,
  my carved image and my cast image
    commanded them."

⁶ You have heard; now see all this;
  and will you not declare it?
From this time forward I make you hear
    new things,
  hidden things that you have not known.
⁷ They are created now, not long ago;
  before today you have never heard of them,
  so that you could not say, "I already
    knew them."
⁸ You have never heard, you have
    never known,
  from of old your ear has not been opened.
For I knew that you would deal very
    treacherously,
  and that from birth you were called a rebel.

⁹ For my name's sake I defer my anger,
  for the sake of my praise I restrain it for you,
  so that I may not cut you off.
¹⁰ See, I have refined you, but not like ᵃ silver;
  I have tested you in the furnace of adversity.
¹¹ For my own sake, for my own sake, I do it,
  for why should my name ᵇ be profaned?
  My glory I will not give to another.

¹² Listen to me, O Jacob,
  and Israel, whom I called:
I am He; I am the first,
  and I am the last.
¹³ My hand laid the foundation of the earth,
  and my right hand spread out the heavens;
when I summon them,
  they stand at attention.

ᵃCn: Heb *with*   ᵇGk Old Latin: Heb *for why should it*

NIV

will carry out his purpose against Babylon;
  his arm will be against the Babylonians.*

¹⁵I, even I, have spoken;
  yes, I have called him.
I will bring him,
  and he will succeed in his mission.

¹⁶"Come near me and listen to this:

"From the first announcement I have not
    spoken in secret;
  at the time it happens, I am there."

And now the Sovereign Lord has sent me,
  with his Spirit.

¹⁷This is what the Lord says—
  your Redeemer, the Holy One of Israel:
"I am the Lord your God,
  who teaches you what is best for you,
  who directs you in the way you should go.
¹⁸If only you had paid attention to
    my commands,
  your peace would have been like a river,
  your righteousness like the waves of the sea.
¹⁹Your descendants would have been like
    the sand,
  your children like its numberless grains;
their name would never be cut off
  nor destroyed from before me."

²⁰Leave Babylon,
  flee from the Babylonians!
Announce this with shouts of joy
  and proclaim it.
Send it out to the ends of the earth;
  say, "The Lord has redeemed his
    servant Jacob."
²¹They did not thirst when he led them
    through the deserts;
  he made water flow for them from the rock;
he split the rock
  and water gushed out.

²²"There is no peace," says the Lord, "for
    the wicked."

*14 Or Chaldeans; also in verse 20

NRSV

¹⁴Assemble, all of you, and hear!
  Who among them has declared
    these things?
  The Lord loves him;
    he shall perform his purpose on Babylon,
    and his arm shall be against the Chaldeans.
¹⁵I, even I, have spoken and called him,
  I have brought him, and he will prosper
    in his way.
¹⁶Draw near to me, hear this!
  From the beginning I have not spoken
    in secret,
  from the time it came to be I have
    been there.
And now the Lord God has sent me and
    his spirit.

¹⁷Thus says the Lord,
  your Redeemer, the Holy One of Israel:
I am the Lord your God,
  who teaches you for your own good,
  who leads you in the way you should go.
¹⁸O that you had paid attention to my
    commandments!
  Then your prosperity would have been like
    a river,
  and your success like the waves of the sea;
¹⁹your offspring would have been like the sand,
  and your descendants like its grains;
their name would never be cut off
  or destroyed from before me.

²⁰Go out from Babylon, flee from Chaldea,
  declare this with a shout of joy, proclaim it,
send it forth to the end of the earth;
  say, "The Lord has redeemed his
    servant Jacob!"
²¹They did not thirst when he led them
    through the deserts;
  he made water flow for them from
    the rock;
  he split open the rock and the water
    gushed out.

²²"There is no peace," says the Lord, "for
    the wicked."

COMMENTARY

Commentators agree that numerous special problems exist in this chapter; they disagree over how they are to be resolved. In the opening unit (vv. 1-11) there is a shift between plural and singular addressee, and yet dividing the chapter along these lines makes no sense. Others take the combination of rebuke (vv. 1*d*, 4, 5*b*, 7*b*, 8*b*-10) with more typical trial defense as the sign of a later hand glossing the trial speech with negative predications.[93] The text can be divided along these lines to produce a fairly typical trial speech, but that is not the text that lies before us.[94] It would be a mistake to undo the creative activity of the author in order to retrieve a form he modified for another purpose. Why a glossator would proceed as he has done is also unclear. The passage as presently before us can be situated within the logic and flow of the chapter as a whole, making appeals to secondary disturbance unnecessary.

The opening unit rehearses rather familiar language about the former things, but now in order to inaugurate quite distinctive new things. The second unit (the term is being used quite loosely) is taken by Westermann to run through v. 17, but only through v. 15 by Melugin, who calls it a trial speech. Reference to the calling of Cyrus (v. 14) would connect with the theme of the former things reviewed in the opening unit. The passage begging for proper interpretation is found at v. 16; with the close of the verse, we have a very clear first-person reference without any true analogy thus far in the discourse. It sounds like a reference to commissioning. How the two preceding "I" references in the verse work with this last one will require further analysis.

The messenger formula at v. 17 introduces a conditioned divine word, positive in its promise (vv. 17-19). The work of Cyrus, referred to in the second unit (v. 14), finds its conclusion in the hymn of 48:20-21. The final refrain at v. 22 has counterparts at the close of chap. 57 and chap. 66, and it appears to be editorially supplied, perhaps so

that the last twenty-seven chapters of the book of Isaiah will be read together.

Chapter 48 speaks of the former things for the last time. Something new is about to happen, though the content of that is either missing or to be inferred or supplied at a later point. Since we know the former things to have been most especially about the rousing of Cyrus, it is fitting that his work comes to fruition here, in terms of God's purpose against Babylon (here made explicit following the portrayals of chaps. 46 and 47). The servant Jacob has received sight, hearing, and forgiveness. Now he will be set free. This is the last we hear of Cyrus.

48:1-11. It has been a while since Jacob was addressed directly in this manner. We must go back before the commissioning of Cyrus in chap. 45, to 44:1 and 21. The call to assemble issued in 45:20 was addressed to the survivors of the nations; though they are unnamed, we assume the transgressors (46:8) and the stubborn of heart (46:12) refer to Israel. The sharp tone that rises in this passage is not so strange, then, when one considers the larger context of address.

"Hear this" has a counterpart at v. 16. There, however, the main content of what is to be heard is supplied immediately, while here we listen first to a series of predications for the "house of Jacob." The NRSV judges the content as provided in part within the predications themselves (vv. 1-2), while the NIV understands "this" as God's word beginning in v. 3, concerning the former things (vv. 3-6*a*) and new things (vv. 6*b*-11). The problem is an old one and involves (1) the proper interpretation of כִּי (*kî*) at the beginning of v. 2 and (2) how the lines within the first two verses are to be divided. The NIV rightly sees a series of predications interrupted by the parenthetical "but not in truth or in righteousness." The *kî* in this instance follows the negative לֹא (*lōʾ*), "no," in a concessive sense—that is, "though they call themselves by the holy city and rely on the God of Jacob." In this way, the positive sense of all predications—even when misused by Israel, as with false invoking—is maintained throughout. In other words, no causal connection is implied by the *kî* and the preceding "not in truth," as the NRSV reads. This translation

93. C. Westermann, *Isaiah 40–66,* trans. David Stalker, OTL (Philadelphia: Westminster, 1969) 194-96.

94. Melugin comments: "Whatever the history of the text may have been, we can interpret it now only in its present form." R. F. Melugin, *The Formation of Isaiah 40–55,* BZAW 141 (Berlin: Walter de Gruyter, 1976) 40.

would seem to imply that calling oneself by the holy city and leaning on the God of Israel are negative, examples of "not in truth or right." The NIV better captures the sense here, as all predications remain on the same positive level.

The reference to former things that follows is the last one of its kind, and it nicely prepares us for the final mention of Cyrus as God's agent against Babylon (v. 14) and the final hymn (vv. 20-21). Why the rebuking tone? One likely explanation is that a contrast is being set up with the new things, which have no history of prior delivery. It is as though the fact of Israel's having forgotten the former things—think of the repeated charge to remember, consider, bring to mind, and so forth within chaps. 40–46—impinges itself at the moment of God's deciding to do a new thing. Though announced long ago (and then forgotten), God's ability to bring the former things quickly and effectively to pass means that Israel cannot simply cover up their forgetfulness with a yet worse claim: "My idol did it." This is an astute rhetorical move, and it sets up nicely the chief content the author wishes to convey, the "this" the house of Jacob is to listen to. As God begins to deliver a new word to a new Israel, they are reminded of their past forgetfulness and tendency toward idolatry. The rebuking tone has a distinct purpose: to put Israel on notice that God is about to do something new, and they are not to forget it.

The predications of v. 8 are reminiscent of Isaiah's generation (6:9-11). Now they serve a different purpose—namely, to emphasize the newness of what is being said (vv. 6-7), which *could not* have been heard or known. The final verses (vv. 9-11) also provide a backward glance at language familiar from Isaiah of Jerusalem and a former generation, from which a purged remnant has emerged, as God promised (1:24-26; 6:13; 31:6-9), to hear a new word. All this comes only because God so willed it, for God's own sake and for God's own glory; Israel is no less prone to rebellion now than then (v. 8). The discussion also calls to mind the death of an old generation and the birth of the new in Num 14:10b-35, where concern for God's glory and name stays an immediate punishment.[95] The new generation existed

by the grace of God. The only advantage they had, if one should call it that, was the memory of past failure and God's punishment, to serve as a warning (Deut 9:1-29). That same tone permeates Isa 48:1-11.

48:12-16. There is no agreement about proper division at this juncture, as was noted above. The problem is not a form-critical one only, but goes hand-in-glove with the difficulty of knowing just what is being said, at the most basic level, in vv. 14-16. What is clear is that the messenger formula at v. 17 introduces direct divine speech in preparation for the final hymn (vv. 20-21). The chief question for interpretation, then, focuses on vv. 14-16 and a determination of just who is being spoken of there.

The unit opens with a traditional appeal. Jacob and Israel (treated in the singular) are to listen (v. 12a). God is first and last, the creator (vv. 12b-13). All this is familiar from the discourse up to this point; 44:6-8 uses the same language within a similar context of proof from former prophecy. But perhaps the text nearest to this one is found at 41:26. There the contrast between what Israel knows and what the nations fail to produce is set in sharp contrast, in respect of God's rousing of Cyrus (41:25). No one can respond and give testimony; Zion/Jerusalem has such recourse (41:27).

This passage is different in that the role of the nations has changed. In the larger chapter, Israel is the one being rebuked. The nations play no obvious role. Chapter 47 had one particular nation in its sights: Babylon. Yet within the larger plans of God for Cyrus, as was noted above, the generally negative portrayal of the nations has undergone a modification (see esp. 45:6, 22-25). Babylon's judgment through Cyrus (46:11) clears the way for that. In chap. 48, the provision of new things has been set within the context of failure to attend to former things. That is, the former things serve a different role from positive testimony, the lack of which on the nations' part reveals the impotence of their gods. It serves to rebuke an Israel on the verge of learning a new thing.

This makes it difficult to interpret the "you" (pl.) and "them" (pl.) contrast at v. 14.[96] In 41:26 the contrast between Israel and the nations was

---

95. D. Olson, *The Death of the Old and the Birth of the New* (Chico: Calif.: Scholar's Press, 1985).

96. Qumran texts have consistent 3rd plural readings; versional manuscripts have consistent 2nd plural.

already vague enough, though the larger context made clear who was intended. Here things are much more compressed. In 43:9, a similar question is posed: "Who among them declared this?" The nations are the subject of this query. We could imagine, then, that Israel is called to assemble and listen and note for one last time that the nations ("who among them") failed to give evidence of the calling of Cyrus. The one whom God loves would be Cyrus, through whom God executes the desired plan.

The reason for staying with the problem of reference further involves the final line of v. 16, whose translation is comparatively simple to come by: "and now the Lord GOD has sent me and his spirit." Here we have the clear commissioning of an individual who is not Cyrus. Spirit endowment was a feature of God's servant (42:1). The reference to sending is too general to admit of only one interpretation, but it would be consistent with the dispatching of a prophetic figure. The suggestion has been made that the verse is somehow associated with 49:1-6 and was subsequently "inserted into the text at a wrong place."[97] The "and now" (ועתה *wĕʿattâ*) means to contrast the present with the past and is consistent with the issuance of new things, referred to earlier in the chapter, "from this time forward" (מעתה *mēʿattâ*). The inference that the phrase is associated with 49:1-6 is a strong one; rather than arguing for a misplacement, however, the reference may be an intentional introduction to the servant's first-person speech, strongly prophetic in character, now found at 49:1-6. But we are still left with the problem of integrating the final line at v. 16c within its present context. What is striking is that, if the question posed at 48:14 is not merely rhetorical in character, then the final line gives an answer to it. Who declared these things? God did, and now God has sent "me and his spirit."

In other words, the difficulty of determining the proper referent for the pronouns in the unit involves the force of the final line and the argument of the larger chapter itself, where the nations play little role and where Israel is reminded of its poor track record in recalling God's former word. "The LORD loves him," strictly speaking, is not an answer to the question, "Who among them has

declared this?" If the question is not rhetorical only, an alternative reading would be: "The LORD loves the one who declared this." This one is not from among the nations—that is impossible—but from within God's own people, all of whom, save this one, merit the rebuke for having failed to recall God's former things. God's action against Babylon is in part confirmation of the one who faithfully declared these things—that is, the heretofore unknown author of the discourse. In v. 16, then, the veil falls from the one who has been speaking, and he steps forward and announces his spirit endowment and his having been dispatched by God. With the accomplishment of God's former word concerning Cyrus, faithfully spoken and witnessed to ("from the time it came to be I have been there"), the speaker now tells of a prophetic-like commissioning, about which we will hear more in the next chapter, when the servant speaks of his earlier calling and frustration (49:1-4).

The reason why it is difficult to know whether God is the one who did not speak in secret "from the beginning," or the voice at v. 16c, is that they up to now have been one and the same. Only here do we see a distinction between the divine voice and the prophetic voice, and it is one that will obtain throughout chaps. 49–53. This cannot be coincidental. Nor is the emergence of this voice in conjunction with the announcement of new things surprising. The one who declared these things faithfully in respect of Cyrus now steps forward to declare new things as well. No longer is his word the recapitulation of God's word of old, but a fresh word uttered in the light of prior frustration, concerning Zion's comforting and the charge given to the servant Israel to be a light to the nations.

In sum, the difficulty of determining the referents of the pronouns in 48:14-16 involves this very significant transition in the discourse. The mission of Cyrus is clearly the subject of vv. 14b-15. However, we are hearing of that for the last time, as the former things give way to new things. The voice that had proclaimed faithfully what God had announced of old also witnesses this key fulfillment, "from the time it came to be I have been there" (v. 16). With Cyrus having accomplished his task (vv. 20-21 announce this clearly), the voice of God and the voice of the prophet are set in clearer relationship to each other, "and now the

---

97. Westermann, *Isaiah 40-66*, 203.

Lord GOD has sent me and his spirit."[98] The question that remains to be considered is whether the voice here speaking understands himself as the servant God commissioned back in 42:1-4, who would bring justice to the nations. Is this the same voice who speaks, summoning the coastlands and peoples as once God did (41:1), in the servant poem of 49:1-6? Is the reference there to laboring in vain (49:4) connected with his career, as we have observed it in chaps. 40–48, or is something more intended, involving the entire history of prophecy?[99] These questions and others will be addressed in the treatment of that key text below.

48:17-19. This divine speech, uttered by the voice introduced at v. 16c, is unusual in that it expresses a wish (vv. 18-19). Both the NIV and the NRSV are correct in adopting a past-tense perspective: "O that you had paid attention. . . ." In other words, the past punishment could have been avoided. This voice, singular within its generation, is capable of seeing things from the divine perspective. As in the opening unit (vv. 1-11), the past is recalled right on the verge of the delivery of new things. Here the tone is not rebuke, however, but the longing expression from God that it need not have gone as it did, if Israel had attended to God's commandments (v. 18).

The torah, or instruction, for which the coastlands wait (42:4), was to have been a guide for God's own people. In the opening verse (v. 17), God's role as teacher introduces this exhortation. The verb למד (*lmd*), "to teach," also has clear associations with Isaiah and his "disciples" (8:16)—that is, those "taught" (למדי *limmudāy*) who bear witness to the testimony and teaching for a later generation (8:16-22). The servant at 50:4 understands himself as one taught למודים (*limmûdîm*), which is the necessary precondition for teaching. This recognition is further evidence that the voice that in 48:17-19 speaks for God understands himself as bearing proper testimony to God's word of old.

48:20-22. The announcement is sent forth: Jacob is redeemed; it is time to come back home from Babylon. The entire earth witnesses this, moreover, and is given notice of God's redemption of Jacob. The first exodus and wilderness are recalled in v. 21—not the trials and the testing of God, but God's gracious provision.

The final verse of the chapter and of this major section, however, introduces a more somber note. Similiar notices are found at the close of chaps. 57 and 66, each heightening the sense of foreboding and judgment associated with God's mercy and release. The placement of these divides the entire discourse into three sections and is intended to keep them related. Within the context of recalling the first wilderness and God's gracious provision, the death of an entire generation who failed to trust God is not forgotten. The editor has added the notice in that spirit, mindful of the argument of the entire discourse represented by Isaiah 40–66.

---

98. In the context of this discussion of the voice here and in the ensuing servant poems, note the singular expression for "God" at 48:16c, אדני יהוה (*'ădōnāy* YHWH; "the Lord GOD," NRSV; "the Sovereign LORD," NIV), and its repeated appearance in the third "servant poem" (50:4-5, 7, 9) and within "Third Isaiah" in a similar form of discourse (61:1).

99. See C. R. Seitz, "How Is the Prophet Isaiah Present in the Latter Half of the Book? The Logic of Chapters 40–66 Within the Book of Isaiah," *JBL* 115 (1996); and cf. P. Wilcox and D. Paton-Williams, "The Servant Songs in Deutero-Isaiah," *JSOT* 42 (1988) 79-102.

REFLECTIONS

1. It is a misconception that we possess one standard "call narrative" in the Old Testament, whose business it is to record the inaugurating episode by which a prophet becomes a prophet, before which he or she was just a common Israelite. It is arguable that Isaiah 6 never means to record such a first-time reception of God's word; its very location renders such a view problematic.[100] Many prophetic books lack any such account altogether. Amos 7:14-15 is a retrospective report, given to Amaziah, of what happened when God's word confronted Amos. Its purpose is largely to clarify that Amos was not a prophet by profession or by genes, but a herdsman addressed by God's word. The prophetic oracles associated with his name do not contain a call narrative, strictly speaking. Examples such as these could be compounded; they ask us to be sensitive to the unique way in which various prophetic and non-prophetic books go about reflecting on the vocation and mission of the individual by whose name they are now known.

---

100. See C. R. Seitz, *Isaiah 1–39,* Interpretation (Louisville: Westminster John Knox, 1993) 52-59.

Isaiah 48 has an added feature: It exists within a collection already associated with the prophet Isaiah. That collection had within it, however, the seeds from which later conception was not only possible or desirable, but necessary (8:16-22; 30:8-9). One generation would not hear what another would be privileged to discover, even in the face of their own forgetfulness, their own selfsame rebellious character, and their own painful knowledge that the sins of their forebears had been visited in an especially focused way on them.

Just as Isaiah stood virtually alone in his day, amid his generation, so also does the voice that speaks up in chapter 48. This voice had until now relayed God's word without interference of his own person or even the slightest concern to report how it was that he said what he said, as this particular man sent to this particular people. The reason was not personal reticence, but an awareness that what he was reporting was not, in fact, a new word at all, but an old one, with roots in Israel's former time, that all the people had forgotten or chosen to ignore. We shift here to rebuke for a reason. The former things have served their purpose in rejuvenating Israel, in reminding them of old promises now coming to fruition, in exposing the fraudulence of the claims of nations, gods, and idols, silent before a testimony only one people can bring and, within them, just one anonymous voice who up to now has remained hidden from view. On the verge of God's announcement of new things and the introduction of the one who will speak these as faithfully as he had transparently done so up to this time, Israel must be reminded that they are prone to forget. If that was true of a former generation, it remains true now and has an even stronger relevance because of the radical newness of what God intends to say through and in this servant. The speech they will hear could not even be attributed to an idol (48:5), because it is concerned to address, through the servant and through Israel, those who up to this time were their devotees and worshipers, but who are about to be stripped of every excuse for false religion.

Isaiah stood virtually alone amid his generation: "Seal the teaching among my disciples" (8:16). While not literally one of Isaiah's children, "teaching and instruction" (8:20) are provided through the one we have come to call "Second Isaiah." He might as easily be called *Shear-jasub,* "Remant Shall Return," for through this "seconder" of Isaiah's former word and testimony a remnant, even rebels from their birth (48:8), are brought before what the former Isaiah called "a witness forever," intended for "the time to come" (30:8). The Holy One of Israel is the Sovereign God for this seconder of Isaiah. What he now has to say, inspired by the spirit of the Sovereign God who sent him (48:16), involves "hidden things . . . created now" (48:6), not reliant on the word spoken to the former Isaiah. What we begin to hear of this will find its extension and summation in the next section of discourse, chapters 49–53.

2. It is striking that God's most extreme acts of grace and mercy frequently lead straight into a wilderness. The author speaks here of a wilderness where rocks were split in a manner every bit as dramatic as the signal event at the sea during the exodus. Waters gushed forth where once they rushed back, so Israel could go through on dry ground while Pharaoh's host was engulfed. But the wicked are themselves like the tossing sea, as the next concluding refrain puts it (57:20). They are not moved about by God's spirit and will, but toss up mud and mire.

The final, somber verse (48:22) no longer is content to distinguish between the hosts of Pharaoh and Israel; it reflects on wickedness in and of itself. What some viewed as gracious provision in the wilderness, as a sign of good things to come, others resented and saw as a sign to return to Egypt, where all had been well! Both witnessed the same things, but peace was found only within the breasts of those who believed that what God had promised and inaugurated God would carry through despite whatever present challenges stood in the way. They had the capacity to take what they knew and had experienced of God's graciousness and wear it through the darkest moments. This led to the remarkable discovery that darkness could itself yield great treasures, like rocks from which water flowed.

It takes leaders with vision to see and bear witness to these dark moments yielding fruit, persons who are leaders precisely in proportion to that endowment and that insight. One has just stepped forward in this discourse, and others will follow in his wake. It has ever been so, for the source of this witness is God's spirit, God's dispatching, God's own sovereign self.

ISAIAH 49:1–53:12

SERVANT, LIGHT TO THE NATIONS

OVERVIEW

The larger working conception has at its center the conviction that this discourse is above all an *interrelated* one. Not unlike the Epistle to the Romans, attention must be given to following the argument carefully from chapter to chapter, and not isolating a section or playing one off against another. To do so would be to miss the flow—"dramatic" is not a bad term—that characterizes the composition of the chapters in their present arrangement.

As we have seen, the first section was concerned to introduce, in turn, God (within the divine council), the servant Israel, the necessary confession and restoration, Cyrus, the new eyes necessary for a new thing, the repudiation of idolotry, and the defeat of Daughter Zion, in preparation for the address to the disconsolate and uncomforted Zion. With chap. 49, the next major section begins.

Unlike chap. 48, however, this section contains a much more complex presentation than single, direct divine speech from a trial setting before Israel and the nations (and their gods). There the prophetic personality is totally and completely hidden behind the discourse itself, allowing for a sustained and provocative assertion by God of matters spoken of long ago ("the former things") through Isaiah and others. The servant, Cyrus, Jacob/Israel, Daughter Babylon—each remains a plastic image, fully under the power of expression that belongs to the divine voice. Only once does the direct speech of Israel rise to the surface, and then only briefly and for the purpose of confession (42:24). But toward the close, with the introduction of new things "created now, not long ago" (48:7), we witness the brief but striking emergence of a new voice, alongside the divine, speaking for that voice, as that voice: "and now the Lord YHWH has sent me and his spirit" (48:16c, author's trans.).

This index is decisive for interpreting the present section, which concludes with the suffering servant poem of 52:13–53:12. Instead of sustained presentation from the divine council, however, we confront a very different form of discourse. There are three reasons for this. First, the voice that was introduced at 48:16, alongside the divine voice theretofore at work, is that of the second two "servant songs" (49:1-6; 50:4-9), as well as that of God, in the traditional manner of the prophets (e.g., 49:22-26; 51:1-23). Second, the indirect speech of Zion is presented, along with the reaction to it, provided by this same voice (e.g., 49:14-21; 50:1-3; 52:1-10). Daughter Zion functions here in a way not unlike Jacob/Israel in the first section, never speaking directly in any sustained way, her views and attitudes revealed through the servant's direct response to them. The third aspect that is different in this presentation involves the dramatic conclusion: the report of the suffering and death of the servant (52:13-15; 53:7-9) and the related confession by a plural audience of the significance of that death for them (53:1-6) and for others (53:10-12). In my view, the one whose death is reported is the same first-person servant of the middle two poems, who is also the voice who speaks for God and Zion and himself, introduced at 48:16c. The details and circumstances of his death remain obscure; all we know of these we learn in the suffering servant poem, which will be discussed further below.

This dramatic account at the close of the section helps explain the presence of another level of tradition within the presentation of chaps. 49–53: the responses and elaborations that can be found at the close of the two servant poems (49:7;

50:10-11). These serve to comment upon and respond to the servant's original first-person speech in the light of the significance of his death, which they anticipate, as this is reported by the same hand(s) in 52:13–53:12. Attributed to this same hand(s) are the second, longer elaboration at 49:8-12 and the hymnic fragment at 49:13, composed in the light of the servant's own word at 52:1-10, with which his own contribution concluded. Here we find the fulfillment of the charge to comfort Zion, as originally set forth in 40:1-9.

The authors of this level of the discourse are the servant followers of the servant. They saw deeper significance in his death than others saw in his death and the fulfillment of God's earlier promises—promises both within this discourse in respect of the nations and outside it in respect of the provision of a prophet like Moses (Deut 18:15). They take the "likeness" in this instance to be complete, if not surpassing. These servants are responsible for the chapters that follow (chaps. 54–66), the first one of which (chap. 54) concludes with reference to "the heritage of the servants of the LORD, and their vindication from me" (54:17). The servant's task, as they saw it, was among other things to "apportion the desolate heritages" (49:8), as Moses did in days of old. Chapter 54 is a paean to the servant's accomplishment of that task through his word of comfort to Zion. The servants are to the servant as Joshua and Caleb were to Moses, though now the apportionment and the generation to be apportioned are new, befitting God's new work. The focus is on Zion—in place of the wider promised land of old—and on a people of God no longer simply identified as "Israel" or defined over against the nations. There are the righteous servants, who suffer as did the servant, and the nations "who join themselves to the LORD" (56:6). This radical and bracing proclamation the servants judge to be the continuation of the work of the servant, whose death did not bring defeat but the possibility of a new beginning.

Many have noted the close correspondences between chap. 55 and chap. 56. Attention to this correspondence has lessened the influence on commentators to follow Duhm and see a sharp break between "Deutero-" and "Trito-Isaiah," whose individual prophetic contributions comprise chaps. 40–55 and 56–66 respectively. The boundary between the work of the servant and that of the servants is not sharply fixed, precisely because the close relationship between the two has its literary and editorial counterpart. If one were to seek a "conclusion" to the work of this unknown servant-poet, it would be located at 52:1-1012, the passage that most merits the title "epilogue" in relation to the "prologue" of 40:1-9. Here we have the intended fulfillment of the charge that is set forth there, to comfort Zion and bear witness to God's return to her.

It is not my intention here to present yet another complex diachronic theory to explain how the discourse takes the form it does, without which we could not read and interpret the material as it lies before us. I trust this proposal is both simple enough to account for new features in this section of the discourse, while at the same time not getting in the way of what remains the most important interpretive task: reading the material before us true to the manner of its own literary unfolding and presentation. If one needs complexity for success in interpretation, many diachronic proposals presently available far surpass the one set forth here.

ISAIAH 49:1-26, SERVANT AND ZION

NIV	NRSV

49 Listen to me, you islands;
    hear this, you distant nations:
 Before I was born the LORD called me;
    from my birth he has made mention of
       my name.
	49 Listen to me, O coastlands,
	    pay attention, you peoples from far away!
	 The LORD called me before I was born,
	    while I was in my mother's womb he
	       named me.

NIV

[2]He made my mouth like a sharpened sword,
   in the shadow of his hand he hid me;
he made me into a polished arrow
   and concealed me in his quiver.
[3]He said to me, "You are my servant,
   Israel, in whom I will display my splendor."
[4]But I said, "I have labored to no purpose;
   I have spent my strength in vain and
      for nothing.
Yet what is due me is in the LORD's hand,
   and my reward is with my God."

[5]And now the LORD says—
   he who formed me in the womb to be
      his servant
to bring Jacob back to him
   and gather Israel to himself,
for I am honored in the eyes of the LORD
   and my God has been my strength—
[6]he says:
"It is too small a thing for you to be my servant
   to restore the tribes of Jacob
   and bring back those of Israel I have kept.
I will also make you a light for the Gentiles,
   that you may bring my salvation to the
      ends of the earth."

[7]This is what the LORD says—
   the Redeemer and Holy One of Israel—
to him who was despised and abhorred by
      the nation,
   to the servant of rulers:
"Kings will see you and rise up,
   princes will see and bow down,
because of the LORD, who is faithful,
   the Holy One of Israel, who has
      chosen you."
[8]This is what the LORD says:

"In the time of my favor I will answer you,
   and in the day of salvation I will help you;
I will keep you and will make you
   to be a covenant for the people,
to restore the land
   and to reassign its desolate inheritances,
[9]to say to the captives, 'Come out,'
   and to those in darkness, 'Be free!'

"They will feed beside the roads
   and find pasture on every barren hill.

NRSV

[2] He made my mouth like a sharp sword,
   in the shadow of his hand he hid me;
he made me a polished arrow,
   in his quiver he hid me away.
[3] And he said to me, "You are my servant,
   Israel, in whom I will be glorified."
[4] But I said, "I have labored in vain,
   I have spent my strength for nothing
      and vanity;
yet surely my cause is with the LORD,
   and my reward with my God."

[5] And now the LORD says,
   who formed me in the womb to be
      his servant,
to bring Jacob back to him,
   and that Israel might be gathered to him,
for I am honored in the sight of the LORD,
   and my God has become my strength—
[6] he says,
"It is too light a thing that you should be
      my servant
   to raise up the tribes of Jacob
   and to restore the survivors of Israel;
I will give you as a light to the nations,
   that my salvation may reach to the end of
      the earth."

[7] Thus says the LORD,
   the Redeemer of Israel and his Holy One,
to one deeply despised, abhorred by
      the nations,
   the slave of rulers,
"Kings shall see and stand up,
   princes, and they shall prostrate
      themselves,
because of the LORD, who is faithful,
   the Holy One of Israel, who has
      chosen you."

[8] Thus says the LORD:
In a time of favor I have answered you,
   on a day of salvation I have helped you;
I have kept you and given you
   as a covenant to the people,[a]
to establish the land,
   to apportion the desolate heritages;

[a]Meaning of Heb uncertain

NIV

[10]They will neither hunger nor thirst,
  nor will the desert heat or the sun beat
    upon them.
He who has compassion on them will
    guide them
  and lead them beside springs of water.
[11]I will turn all my mountains into roads,
  and my highways will be raised up.
[12]See, they will come from afar—
  some from the north, some from the west,
  some from the region of Aswan.[a]"

[13]Shout for joy, O heavens;
  rejoice, O earth;
  burst into song, O mountains!
For the LORD comforts his people
  and will have compassion on his
    afflicted ones.

[14]But Zion said, "The LORD has forsaken me,
  the Lord has forgotten me."

[15]"Can a mother forget the baby at her breast
  and have no compassion on the child she
    has borne?
Though she may forget,
  I will not forget you!
[16]See, I have engraved you on the palms of
    my hands;
  your walls are ever before me.
[17]Your sons hasten back,
  and those who laid you waste depart
    from you.
[18]Lift up your eyes and look around;
  all your sons gather and come to you.
As surely as I live," declares the LORD,
  "you will wear them all as ornaments;
  you will put them on, like a bride.

[19]"Though you were ruined and made desolate
  and your land laid waste,
now you will be too small for your people,
  and those who devoured you will be
    far away.
[20]The children born during your bereavement
  will yet say in your hearing,
  'This place is too small for us;
    give us more space to live in.'

[a]12 Dead Sea Scrolls; Masoretic Text *Sinim*

NRSV

[9]saying to the prisoners, "Come out,"
  to those who are in darkness, "Show
    yourselves."
They shall feed along the ways,
  on all the bare heights[a] shall be
    their pasture;
[10]they shall not hunger or thirst,
  neither scorching wind nor sun shall
    strike them down,
for he who has pity on them will lead them,
  and by springs of water will guide them.
[11]And I will turn all my mountains into a road,
  and my highways shall be raised up.
[12]Lo, these shall come from far away,
  and lo, these from the north and from
    the west,
  and these from the land of Syene.[b]

[13]Sing for joy, O heavens, and exult, O earth;
  break forth, O mountains, into singing!
For the LORD has comforted his people,
  and will have compassion on his
    suffering ones.

[14]But Zion said, "The LORD has forsaken me,
  my Lord has forgotten me."
[15]Can a woman forget her nursing child,
  or show no compassion for the child of
    her womb?
Even these may forget,
  yet I will not forget you.
[16]See, I have inscribed you on the palms of
    my hands;
  your walls are continually before me.
[17]Your builders outdo your destroyers,[c]
  and those who laid you waste go away
    from you.
[18]Lift up your eyes all around and see;
  they all gather, they come to you.
As I live, says the LORD,
  you shall put all of them on like
    an ornament,
  and like a bride you shall bind them on.

[19]Surely your waste and your desolate places
  and your devastated land—

[a]Or *the trails*   [b]Q Ms: MT *Sinim*   [c]Or *Your children come
swiftly; your destroyers*

NIV

²¹Then you will say in your heart,
  'Who bore me these?
I was bereaved and barren;
  I was exiled and rejected.
Who brought these up?
I was left all alone,
  but these—where have they come from?' "

²²This is what the Sovereign LORD says:

"See, I will beckon to the Gentiles,
  I will lift up my banner to the peoples;
they will bring your sons in their arms
  and carry your daughters on their shoulders.
²³Kings will be your foster fathers,
  and their queens your nursing mothers.
They will bow down before you with their
    faces to the ground;
  they will lick the dust at your feet.
Then you will know that I am the LORD;
  those who hope in me will not be
    disappointed."

²⁴Can plunder be taken from warriors,
  or captives rescued from the fierce*ᵃ* ?

²⁵But this is what the LORD says:

"Yes, captives will be taken from warriors,
  and plunder retrieved from the fierce;
I will contend with those who contend
    with you,
  and your children I will save.
²⁶I will make your oppressors eat their
    own flesh;
  they will be drunk on their own blood, as
    with wine.
Then all mankind will know
  that I, the LORD, am your Savior,
  your Redeemer, the Mighty One of Jacob."

ᵃ24 Dead Sea Scrolls, Vulgate and Syriac (see also Septuagint and
verse 25); Masoretic Text *righteous*

NRSV

surely now you will be too crowded for your
    inhabitants,
  and those who swallowed you up will be
    far away.
²⁰ The children born in the time of your
    bereavement
  will yet say in your hearing:
"The place is too crowded for me;
  make room for me to settle."
²¹ Then you will say in your heart,
  "Who has borne me these?
I was bereaved and barren,
  exiled and put away—
  so who has reared these?
I was left all alone—
  where then have these come from?"

²² Thus says the Lord GOD:
I will soon lift up my hand to the nations,
  and raise my signal to the peoples;
and they shall bring your sons in their bosom,
  and your daughters shall be carried on
    their shoulders.
²³ Kings shall be your foster fathers,
  and their queens your nursing mothers.
With their faces to the ground they shall bow
    down to you,
  and lick the dust of your feet.
Then you will know that I am the LORD;
  those who wait for me shall not be put
    to shame.

²⁴ Can the prey be taken from the mighty,
  or the captives of a tyrant*ᵃ* be rescued?
²⁵ But thus says the LORD:
Even the captives of the mighty shall be taken,
  and the prey of the tyrant be rescued;
for I will contend with those who contend
    with you,
  and I will save your children.
²⁶ I will make your oppressors eat their own flesh,
  and they shall be drunk with their own
    blood as with wine.
Then all flesh shall know
  that I am the LORD your Savior,
  and your Redeemer, the Mighty One
    of Jacob.

ᵃQ Ms Syr Vg: MT *of a righteous person*

COMMENTARY

The division of chap. 49 into units is comparatively easy. Commentators are in general agreement about the assignment of these, and the form-critical task of describing genres is also relatively uncontroversial. This is true even as one encounters a fair degree of creative freedom on the part of the author in modifying and adapting older forms to his specific purpose. So, for example, there is general agreement that 49:1-6 constitutes a "servant song" and that, as with 42:1-4 and 42:5-9, we find an elaboration appended to the main unit at 49:7-12. This is then followed by a hymn (49:13), in the same manner observed at 42:10-13. The remainder of the chapter is taken up with the response to Zion, as one specific case of uncomforted existence, over against the people at large (49:13b). This rather lengthy unit is composed of smaller rhetorical strophes (vv. 14-18, 19-21, 22-23, 24-26) instead of discrete form-critical units.[101]

The genre assignment of the opening "servant song" is the most difficult of all. There are several distinctive features here. Early form critics (e.g., Begrich) spoke of a hymn of thanksgiving from an individual. This was an effort to account for the note of despondency around which the poem centers (v. 4), which is effectively responded to in the final verses, introduced by "and now" (vv. 5-6). At the same time, the commissioning language that introduces the poem (vv. 1-3) is undeniable; it has prompted others to speak of a royal (Kaiser) or royal-prophetic (Westermann, Melugin) commissioning report.

Striking is the retrospective character of the report, which runs through v. 4 and includes a note of dejection: The servant has *already* labored in vain. If we speak of a commissioning, it is made against a backdrop of prior activity. Language familiar from the call of the prophet Jeremiah (Jer 1:1-9), for example, is not associated with the present-tense word to the servant from God; rather, it forms his own reflection on a vocation that already lies behind him. These distinctive features must be borne carefully in mind. "Hymn of Thanksgiving" is a correct designation insofar as it keeps this aspect to the fore. The one taking up the hymn is the servant, and his answered complaint entails his vocation as one "called from the womb," like Jeremiah. "Commissioning" or "Recommissioning Report" is correct insofar as the word of response given to the servant in the final verse entails his specific vocation as servant (v. 6). The cause for thanksgiving is the restatement, made personally to the servant, of the role and function first established for him by God.

The question to be taken up involves the function of the elaboration at 49:7-12. Westermann has combined two units, each introduced by a messenger formula, into one and has labeled it "Deutero-Isaiah's original utterance," a "proclamation of salvation" in formal terms.[102] What this solution entails is an elimination of the very problem constituted by the existence of two discrete oracles to begin with. As more recent interpreters have seen,[103] v. 7 appears more prospectively related to the final servant poem at 52:13–53:12 than retrospectively affiliated with 42:5-9. The reverse is true of 49:8-12, which shares with 42:5-9 the singular expression "covenant to the people," positively anticipating the servant's success in liberating God's people everywhere, rather than pointing to the destiny of suffering and affliction at the hands of the nations (cf. 49:7 and 52:13-15). It is difficult to know whether both, or just the first, have been editorially supplied in an effort to affiliate the servant's work with the charge given the servant Israel at 42:1-9 (so the second) and the final destiny of the servant, whose suffering and death are recorded at 52:13–53:12 (so the first). Alternatively, only the first has been editorially supplied, under the influence of the final "suffering servant poem"; the second would then be God's further word of response to the servant, elaborating in a distinctive manner the word given at 49:6. The

---

101. Melugin opts for three units (vv. 14-21, vv. 22-23, and vv. 24-26), "each [unit] complete in terms of form; each is capable of being understood without the other." Whether "capable" moves in the direction of "obliged" or "necessary" is the question. Methodological consistency could be at odds with the intention of the material. See R. F. Melugin, *The Formation of Isaiah 40–55,* BZAW 141 (Berlin: Walter de Gruyter, 1976) 148-51.

102. C. Westermann, *Isaiah 40–66,* trans. David Stalker, OTL (Philadelphia: Westminster, 1969) 214.

103. R. G. Kratz, *Kyros im Deuterojesaja-Buch,* FAT 1 (Tübingen: Mohr-Siebeck, 1991); O.H. Steck, "Aspecte des Gottesknechts in Deuterjesaja 'Ebed-Jahwe Liedern," *ZAW* 96 (1984) 372-90; B. S. Childs, *Isaiah,* OTL (Louisville: Westminster John Knox, 2001) 386.

placement of the hymn at v. 13 is by now familiar (cf. 42:10-13; 45:8), and it points to a high degree of intentionality in the final shaping of the material.

49:1-7. The opening address to the coastlands and the people has its precise counterpart at 41:1. Now not God, from within the divine council, but the servant himself addresses the known world. The servant was before presented to the council and those assembled; now he steps forward and speaks as once God did. He reports the call that has already taken place (vv. 1-3). Language used to describe God's relationship to Israel (44:1) is here applied to the individual servant (49:1b), who stepped forward at 48:16c. It is augmented with a more typically individual, "prophetic" predication, "from the belly of my mother he named me" (cf. Jer 1:5). This reference fits an individual better than Israel as a nation.[104] The references to hiddenness, together with effective speech, match perfectly the role the servant has had up to this point (v. 2).

"Israel" in v. 3 cannot be an interpolation, but belongs inextricably to the text in its present and previous life (if such there be).[105] Williamson's argument that "Israel" is not to be taken as vocative, indicating the addressee ("you are my servant, O Israel"), but as predicative, making a statement ("you are my servant, [you are] Israel") is also convincing.[106] This frees the unit (and a syntactically problematic v. 4) for a fresh interpretation, which has as an additional benefit the possibility of coordinating this poem with preceding and ensuing discussions of the role of the servant. The servant presented by God before the divine council in 42:1-4 was the same Jacob/Israel servant consistently addressed that way in chaps. 40–48. Now the speaker—who nowhere explicitly adopts the title "prophet" (נביא *nābîʾ*), nor is it applied to him—accepts as an individual the role set forth by God for the nation Israel. The servant knows himself to have been called by God and empowered for a hidden and, in its own mysterious way, speech-filled vocation (vv. 1-2). It is then clarified to him, "You are my servant—you

are Israel, in whom I will be glorified." It would be wrong to term this a call narrative because of the singularity of the office of prophet, witnessed to in the discourse, within the context of the larger book of Isaiah and its own complex presentation (see the Reflections at 48:1-22). Rather, it is a recommissioning in the light of developing circumstances at this particular juncture in the discourse, involving the role of Israel, the servant-author, and the nations.

To this the servant responds in objection. He has already labored mightily, but in vain. To what is this a reference? Wilcox and Paton-Williams answer: "These verses describe the recommissioning of the prophet, to do what Israel was called to do."[107] In other words, the prophet Deutero-Isaiah was frustrated in effecting Israel's assumption of the role of servant, as sketched forth in 42:1-9 and in the following chapters in the opening section (chaps. 40–48).

I have argued elsewhere for a modification of this interpretation. The servant who has stepped forward in chap. 48 reflects on his frustration in accomplishing what was said of the servant in 42:1-9, and behind this failure lies the entire history of prophecy as that was directed through Israel to the nations (e.g., Jer 1:5, "I appointed you a prophet to the nations"; Jer 1:10, "See, today I set you over nations and kingdoms"). "That is, it is a mission based upon all prior prophecy at its own potential end point and dissolution.... This servant carries Israel's history with prophecy in him, and in so doing, is 'Israel' in a very specific sense."[108] I would add here only that this profound insight, borne witness to by the servant, is seen by him through the specific lens of his having brokered the proclamation of chaps. 40–48, where God's mission to the nations, through servant Jacob/Israel and through Cyrus, stands at the center of the discourse.

Language once applied to Israel is now applied to the servant, whose task (though once hidden) has been and remains to Jacob/Israel (v. 5). Here is the one place where the genre designation "thanksgiving" truly applies: "I am honored in the sight of the LORD, and my God has become my

---

104. P. Wilcox and D. Paton-Williams, "The Servant Songs in Deutero-Isaiah," *JSOT* 42 (1988) 90.

105. See Wilcox and Paton-Williams, "The Servant Songs in Deutero-Isaiah," 79-102; T. N. D. Mettinger, *A Farewell to the Servant Songs,* Scriptora Minora 13 (Lund: Gleerup, 1983) 32.

106. Noted by Wilcox and Paton-Williams, "The Servant Songs in Deutero-Isaiah," 102n. 36.

107. Ibid., 92.

108. C. R. Seitz, "How Is the Prophet Isaiah Present in the Latter Half of the Book? The Logic of Chapters 40–66 Within the Book of Isaiah," *JBL* 115 (1996) 236.

strength" (v. 5b). The servant recalls the task he has had with Jacob and Israel, and he knows it to be bound up with God's honoring and strengthening of him. The final verse (v. 6b) reminds the servant of Israel's task to the nations (so 42:6); this task is now to be his own, who had formerly been Israel's faithful servant of address, in chaps. 40–48. The mission to the nations is not the "new thing" (48:6), but the individual servant's bearing of it. His hidden mission to Israel is here augmented to include a public mission to the nations, as this was once Israel's more broadly. These are the nations the servant addresses in v. 1. The "servant song" in its entirety (49:1-6) clarifies to them how it is that he has come to be empowered by God to this particular service. The one who spoke for God in similar, though hidden, terms at 41:1 now speaks publicly of God's special word to him, the one who is "Israel" according to a prophetic calling, "light to the nations" (49:6).

Reference to the nations at v. 6 has triggered a gloss (v. 7), which serves to anticipate the servant's final destiny (52:13–53:12). The one "deeply despised, abhorred by the nations" is the servant. Nevertheless, the unit insists, the nations will come to proper acknowledgment and worship, as had been promised earlier (45:14) in connection with the mission of Cyrus. What Cyrus was meant to effect through military victory, the servant will accomplish through suffering and death. This note is supplied by the servant followers of the servant, who have composed the final poem in tribute to the paradoxical accomplishment of the servant, who becomes a light to the nations through affliction, death, and blood expiation.

49:8-13. Whether this unit belongs to the same level of tradition is unclear. The central question in part is, Who is being answered (v. 8): Israel or the servant of vv. 1-6? It would not simplify matters to say they were one and the same; the identical problem of vv. 1-6 would surface. How does Israel have a mission to Israel?[109] And in this unit (vv. 8-12), how does servant Israel establish the land for Israel? Even an exilic servant (over against Israel as such) does not work well, for it sounds as though the servant speaks to prisoners (v. 9) who are themselves being escorted by God

from the broadest diaspora (v. 12). The task of apportioning heritages was an individual one, either assigned to Moses (Num 26:52-56; 34:1-15) or delegated by him to Joshua and Eleazar (Num 32:28-32; 34:16-29).

It is to be inferred that 49:8-12 is an elaboration akin to 42:5-8, further stipulating the role of the servant. The task that belonged to Israel as servant in 42:5-8 now belongs to the individual servant of 49:1-6. Since 49:1-6 is not divine speech commissioning the servant, but the servant's own hymn of thanksgiving in reflection upon his past and future vocation, the elaboration of 49:8-12 cannot be his own word to himself or his own word to an Israel who will apportion the land and free the prisoners. Rather, it is an elaboration made by the servants, promising that God's intention with the servant will finally prevail. They understand the servant as a prophet, like Moses, who is responsible for a new exodus like the first (vv. 9b-11), but far more expansive in its points of origin (v. 12) and far less fraught with wilderness privation. The individual servant is a "covenant to the people" (ברית עם bĕrît 'ām). He is the concrete means by which God's relationship with Israel is embodied and manifested. Moses cut a covenant; the servant is a covenant. Moses apportioned inheritances in a new land; the servant apportions desolated ones in a new wilderness. The servants' editorial elaboration here points forward to chap. 54. At that juncture, fully comforted Zion herself sings out, as she and her children are reunited. The long poem concludes: "This is the heritage of the servants of the LORD, and their vindication from me, says the LORD" (54:17). In other words, apportioning the land in the case of the new exodus has its focal point at Zion, whose righteous children are God's servants.

The hymn that follows (49:13) comes at the same juncture as 42:10-13, indicating the studied character of this planned composition. Heavens and earth and mountains are to witness God's comforting of Israel. In view of the preceding reference to the turning back home of scattered Israel (49:12), the reference is closely tied to the comforted diaspora of all compass points. Comfort begins with their return. The final reference, however, will trigger a response from Zion. Has God had compassion on the afflicted ones? One particular suffering case is crying out for attention and redress.

---

109. See, e.g., the typical discussion of Melugin, *The Formation of Isaiah 40–55,* 146.

49:14-26. The book of Lamentations showcases the extreme situation of Daughter Zion. Within the first chapter alone, five times the refrain is repeated, "she has no one to comfort her" (Lam 1:2, 9, 16, 17, 21). Zion's fate is viewed, first, by means of personification, as the city takes the role of a lamenting widow (Lam 1:1) whose children are dead or dying (Lam 1:16, 18; 2:22; 4:2), while she herself has been invaded by enemies (Lam 1:3, 10; 2:4, 7, 16; 4:12; 5:18). Second, her fate is viewed by means of sympathetic narration, which sometimes spills over into plural confession and lament (Lam 3:40-47; 5:1-22), and which frequently acknowledges the rightness—though extreme—of God's sentence (Lam 1:8-9; 2:8, 17; 4:11, 16, 22). The phrase quoted here, "The LORD has forsaken me," has its unrelenting counterpart in Lamentations, alongside other charges and statements of anguish.

In some respects, the larger Isaiah discourse is an address to the situation described in Lamentations, and specifically the plaintive, "there is no one to comfort her" (Lam 1:17). Comfort is more than emotional understanding; it entails restitution and explanation—from God. Lamentations contains a far greater proportion of acknowledged guilt and wrongdoing on Zion's part than we find in Isaiah. That is because that discourse and those circumstances are presupposed here, as the argument of Isaiah 40–66 attempts to move to the next stage in Zion's destiny: comfort and restitution. Lamentations also contains the statement: "Your prophets . . . have not exposed your iniquity to restore your fortunes" (Lam 2:14). The "prophet" of the Isaiah discourse is about both of these tasks, in the manner God now deems appropriate to the time and circumstance of Jacob/Israel and Daughter Zion.

As numerous commentators have noted, "Jacob" and "Israel" no longer appear after 48:14; they have been replaced by the personified Zion, who takes center stage. Alongside this, however, one needs to take seriously the transition reflected in 49:1-13, whereby the servant takes up the role of "Israel," later to be accompanied by "servants" (54:17). The specific task of comforting Zion/Jerusalem, set forth in 40:1-9, is here taken up by the author in his address of Zion's charge, "the LORD has forgotten me" (49:14), with which this section opens.

The argument begins on Zion's own territory. Mothers are not given to forgetting their children (see Lamentations); and even if they were, God would not forget them. By means of this address we come to see immediately how inextricably Zion's own personal destiny is tied up with the destiny of her children. The servant understands Zion's ruined physical condition, not for its own sake, but in connection with the return of children. The translation difficulty at v. 17 (cf. the NRSV and the NIV) stems from the similiarity in Hebrew between the words for "children," "sons" (בניך *bānàyik*), and "builders" (בניך *bōnayik,* so several versions). Perhaps builders or sons are arriving to replace the former destroyers. There can be little doubt, however, that v. 18 describes the arrival of Zion's children, whom she wears as a bride proudly wears ornaments.

Two unexpected facts are then related to Zion (vv. 19-21). She has children who were born during the time of her bereavement that, understandably, she did not know she had; and they are so numerous that her concern should shift toward coming to terms with anticipated complaints about crowded conditions. What a shock this news would be for the bereft Zion whom we encounter in Lamentations. The langauge of v. 21 could not make it clearer. Zion's condition makes even Sarah's look hopeful. A barren widow, cast off, exiled, alone (cf. Lam 1:1) has a right to ask where all these children are coming from.

The signal raised in v. 22 was promised by God in Isa 11:12, for the "outcasts of Israel . . . and the dispersed of Judah from the four corners of the earth." Reference is made there as well to God's hand (11:11; cf. 49:21), which had been outstretched in judgment (5:25; 9:12, 17, 21; 10:4), but now extends to gather the remnant from numerous localities, all the way to the "coastlands of the sea" (11:11). The same geographical perspective and scope are in force here. The children returning to Zion come from all compass points, even if principally from Babylon, because of God's word of promise from the days of Isaiah. With one hand God raises a signal; with the other, raised formerly in judgment, God gathers Israel, and in so doing judges the nations.

In a brilliant stroke, the question of who has reared the mysterious children is answered: Kings and queens were foster parents. In the first exodus, Moses was reared in the foster care of Pharaoh's daughter and her retinue, though suckled by a woman brought from his own people (Exod 2:5-9). Even that special treatment is trumped here (v. 23). Moreover, God had promised in the first exodus that by God's act of deliverance Pharaoh and the Egyptians would know "that I am the LORD, when I stretch out my hand against Egypt and bring the Israelites [the children of Israel] out from among them" (Exod 7:5; cf. Exod 14:18) in order to "make my name resound through all the earth" (Exod 9:16). The promise remained centered, however, on Israel's own knowledge of God through this deliverance (Exod 6:7; 7:17; 10:2). The servant picks up that promise again here, as the "foster nations" come to Zion with her children: "then you [Zion] will know that I am the LORD" (Isa 49:23). The nations not only let Zion's children go free, but also rear them and then escort them back home, eventually to do homage and acknowledge God's name themselves (so 45:14). Isaiah (and his children) waited for the Lord (8:17); those who wait in the latter time, we learn, are not to be disappointed. Zion's children testify to God's faithfulness.

The final verses of this address to Zion (vv. 24-26) reassure her that, no matter how harsh the oppressors of her children are, they shall be rescued. The final line reminds us both of the promise to Moses of old and of the divine voice of 40:5 and the seraphim of 6:3. God's rescue of this people, even in harsh judgment, is meant for one purpose only: to convey the knowledge of God to all flesh, as Israel's savior, redeemer, mighty one.

REFLECTIONS

1. It is one thing for God to answer Zion's question, "Who reared these?" In a master stroke, appropriate to a new exodus with new parameters, God responds in such a way that the listeners should recall Moses, Pharaoh's daughter, another people in bondage, and another experience of coming to the knowledge of God in deliverance and in judgment. Here Zion comes to the knowledge of God in an especially profound sense. What was true of God's people in bondage in Egypt is yet more true of God's people scattered to the four winds, the care of whom has been handed over to kings and queens.

What Zion knows of God at this dramatic moment extends as well to the question, "Who has borne me these?" Zion was alone, barren, exiled. The answer to that question is constituted by the return of children, on the one hand, and by the discourse represented by chapters 40–48, on the other hand. God has brought a people into being, out of exile, out of death, out of the "stuff of nothingness": "But now thus says the LORD, he who created you, O Jacob, he who formed you, O Israel . . . I have called you by name, you are mine." Pharaoh's daughter does not give the name, nor in this case can we track down Jacob/Israel's "parents." For all of the reliance on a powerful human metaphor—of conceiving, naming, mothering, suckling, rearing—the limits of that metaphor are then exploded. God has created a people, children of Zion, in the same way water is brought forth out of rock or springs appear in a desert: simply by God's will and word. In the way the first human being was created (Gen 2:7) or Abraham was made a great nation (Gen 12:2), out of the ashes of God's cleansing judgment, a new people is formed. As the barrenness of Sarah is no hindrance to God, neither is the barrenness of Zion. Jacob is not just chosen by God, but is "formed in the womb" (Isa 44:2), formerly and latterly.

The New Testament depiction of Jesus is at so many points indebted to this discourse that it is difficult to know where to begin and end. The virginal birth related by the evangelists Matthew and Luke belongs within a much wider nexus than Isaiah 7:14 alone (see Matt 1:23). It belongs within the context of the raising of Lazarus, healings, feedings, and raising up from stones children of Abraham, each traceable to the sovereign freedom of God witnessed to in discourse such as that of Isaiah, which reaches its climax in the rolling back of the stone and the harrowing of the underworld, that final exile and wilderness.

There and here the text is not talking about magic or alchemy, the changing of categories of creation to thrill or astound, but the sovereign God's ability to form out of the "stuff of nothingness"—the desert, the barren womb, the grave of exile, the depths of despair—new life and abundance. In each and every case there is some form of remnant and reminiscence, some "former thing" conjoined with the word of promise and God's enlivening presence and spirit. What is created and fashioned and resurrected bears witness to the fidelity of God through time. It belongs to the warp and woof of both Testaments that God will neither abrogate material promises nor be limited by human imagination or religion. Former things and new things are two sides of one coin. Zion knows her children when she sees them, even as she cannot account for who bore them in her time of bereavement. Will her imagination and religion tolerate this bold freedom of God? That is one question. Will this freedom conform to a justice she has come to live by and trust, rooted in God's character? That is the other. Only God can answer questions like these, which is why Zion began where she did, "The LORD has forsaken me, my LORD has forgotten me" (49:14). No other court of appeal will suffice when the problem must be taken to the highest court.

2. The chapter begins and ends with reference to the nations. What God is doing with Zion and her children is to be witnessed to by "peoples from far away" (49:1) and by "all flesh" (49:26). It is too light a thing, God tells the servant, for Jacob/Israel to be reunited with Zion, brought back from all compass points, or displayed before her for the very first time. The servant is to be a "light to the nations."

What this phrase means has been variously interpreted. What seems clear is that the nations are to be illuminated through the servant's activity and existence. A light is not a focus of attention itself, but serves to open eyes to something previously not perceived. This pledge has been set over against a sharply contrasting alternative—that is, that the servant will accomplish nothing and that the nations will ignore, wrongly perceive, or in fact prevent the servant from accomplishing what God desires. In other words, the alternative to the nations' seeing something and acknowledging its divine origin, through the servant, is not to continue to go their own way, outside the range of God's activity and purpose with the servant. It is to come into contact with the servant's work in an unavoidable way and to persist in their oppression and their ignorance of the Holy One of Israel. God assures the servant that the first will happen, but the second will issue into final recognition: "Kings shall see and stand up, princes, and they shall prostrate themselves" (49:7). The path the servant will take, however, entails obvious affliction. The nations will come to the knowledge God seeks to convey by overcoming through acknowledgment of their wrongful stance and demeanor (see 49:7, 24-26).

To be a "light to the nations" does not, therefore, mean going out and converting "peoples from far away" by word and thereafter associating with them on equal terms. Instead it means bearing affliction and hardship—brought about on account of obedience to God—and precisely thereby conveying the knowledge of God. To witness to the God of Israel is not to share information with others but to be faithful to God in such a way that confrontation will occur but will not be an end in itself. The witness leaves the final accomplishment to God, assured that affliction and hardship will be the means through which "my salvation shall reach to the ends of the earth" (49:6).

The other side of this assurance is revealed at 49:26, by the servant, to Zion. God will "contend with those who contend with you" (49:25). By virtue of the work of the servant, God will judge the nations and take up the cause of Zion. The servant will not both grant knowledge and mete out justice, but God will do that on account of him. That is the servant's word to Zion and her children, coming on the heels of God's own word to him (49:6). Distinctions are not undone by God—all flesh knows the Lord is Israel's savior—even as they are redeemed and reconstituted by a common confession, with neither the servant nor Zion nor the nations ever the same again thereafter. It is little wonder that Isaiah has the reputation in the history of Christian interpretation of being more evangelist than prophet.[110]

110. See J. Sawyer, *The Fifth Gospel: Isaiah in the History of Christianity* (Cambridge: Cambridge University Press, 1996). Cf. C. R. Seitz, " 'Of Mortal Appearance': Earthly Jesus and Isaiah as a Type of Christian Scripture," *Ex Auditu* 14 (1998).

ISAIAH 50:1-11, THE TAUGHT ONE

NIV

50 This is what the LORD says:

"Where is your mother's certificate of divorce
  with which I sent her away?
Or to which of my creditors
  did I sell you?
Because of your sins you were sold;
  because of your transgressions your mother
    was sent away.
[2]When I came, why was there no one?
  When I called, why was there no one
    to answer?
Was my arm too short to ransom you?
  Do I lack the strength to rescue you?
By a mere rebuke I dry up the sea,
  I turn rivers into a desert;
their fish rot for lack of water
  and die of thirst.
[3]I clothe the sky with darkness
  and make sackcloth its covering."

[4]The Sovereign LORD has given me an
      instructed tongue,
  to know the word that sustains the weary.
He wakens me morning by morning,
  wakens my ear to listen like one
    being taught.
[5]The Sovereign LORD has opened my ears,
  and I have not been rebellious;
  I have not drawn back.
[6]I offered my back to those who beat me,
  my cheeks to those who pulled out
    my beard;
I did not hide my face
  from mocking and spitting.
[7]Because the Sovereign LORD helps me,
  I will not be disgraced.

NRSV

50 Thus says the LORD:
Where is your mother's bill of divorce
  with which I put her away?
Or which of my creditors is it
  to whom I have sold you?
No, because of your sins you were sold,
  and for your transgressions your mother
    was put away.
[2]Why was no one there when I came?
  Why did no one answer when I called?
Is my hand shortened, that it cannot redeem?
  Or have I no power to deliver?
By my rebuke I dry up the sea,
  I make the rivers a desert;
their fish stink for lack of water,
  and die of thirst.[a]
[3]I clothe the heavens with blackness,
  and make sackcloth their covering.

[4]The Lord GOD has given me
  the tongue of a teacher,[b]
that I may know how to sustain
  the weary with a word.
Morning by morning he wakens—
  wakens my ear
to listen as those who are taught.
[5]The Lord GOD has opened my ear,
  and I was not rebellious,
  I did not turn backward.
[6]I gave my back to those who struck me,
  and my cheeks to those who pulled out
    the beard;
I did not hide my face
  from insult and spitting.

[7]The Lord GOD helps me;

[a]Or *die on the thirsty ground* [b]Cn: Heb *of those who are taught*

NIV

Therefore have I set my face like flint,
   and I know I will not be put to shame.
[8]He who vindicates me is near.
   Who then will bring charges against me?
   Let us face each other!
Who is my accuser?
   Let him confront me!
[9]It is the Sovereign LORD who helps me.
   Who is he that will condemn me?
They will all wear out like a garment;
   the moths will eat them up.

[10]Who among you fears the LORD
   and obeys the word of his servant?
Let him who walks in the dark,
   who has no light,
trust in the name of the LORD
   and rely on his God.
[11]But now, all you who light fires
   and provide yourselves with flaming
      torches,
go, walk in the light of your fires
   and of the torches you have set ablaze.
This is what you shall receive from my hand:
   You will lie down in torment.

NRSV

   therefore I have not been disgraced;
therefore I have set my face like flint,
   and I know that I shall not be put to
      shame;
[8]   he who vindicates me is near.
Who will contend with me?
   Let us stand up together.
Who are my adversaries?
   Let them confront me.
[9] It is the Lord GOD who helps me;
   who will declare me guilty?
All of them will wear out like a garment;
   the moth will eat them up.

[10] Who among you fears the LORD
   and obeys the voice of his servant,
who walks in darkness
   and has no light,
yet trusts in the name of the LORD
   and relies upon his God?
[11] But all of you are kindlers of fire,
   lighters of firebrands.[a]
Walk in the flame of your fire,
   and among the brands that you
      have kindled!
This is what you shall have from my hand:
   you shall lie down in torment.

[a]Syr: Heb *you gird yourselves with firebrands*

COMMENTARY

Chapter 50 breaks into three basic units. In the middle of the chapter is the poignant third "servant song" (vv. 4-9); the form of this "song" will be discussed below. This central unit has given rise to a response at vv. 10-11. I argued above for taking this elaboration on the same terms as 49:7, which followed the second "servant song." That is, in the light of the servant's death and the confession made by the servants in the dramatic fourth "suffering servant song" (52:13–53:12), the middle two servant poems have occasioned responses. These responses seek to anticipate the final song in literary terms and to clarify theologically just how the servant's suffering, even unto death, was to be interpreted by the wider community. The elaborations clarify that the servant's

suffering was not in vain, nor did it stand outside God's purposes. Rather, it belonged to the central aim of God in commissioning the servant to be "light to the nations." The elaboration here, however, does not so much clarify as exhort. Its target is the community that has witnessed the servant's activity and yet persists in lighting its own fires, rather than walking in the light of the servant.

The opening unit (vv. 1-3) shares much in common with the address to Zion of the previous chapter. However, a new unit is called for because the addressants have changed. Not Zion, but her children, are those who are confronted by the servant. The question posed at v. 2 is answered by the "servant song" of vv. 3-9. In other words, vv. 1-3 have not been composed as an independent form-critical unit, but, mindful of the legacy of prophetic address within Israel, are here adapted to serve the purpose of introducing the obedient servant, who answered when God called.

50:1-3. The question posed in v. 2 has a familiar ring to it. We encountered a similar rhetorical question at 41:26-28; whenever there is an appeal to the former things, it is generally prefaced with a question, "Who declared this?" (43:9; 44:7; 45:21). In those contexts, however, the question is put to the nations, and the disputation involves God's challengers, who fail to produce testimony. The question posed here also assumes the failure of anyone to respond, but it is clear that in this case the failure exists within God's own people.

To what exactly does this accusation pertain, if not to former things, or to the inability of the nations to present witnesses? Following the flow of the argument as closely as possible, one suggestion lies in chap. 48, where the former things were recalled by God one last time as a way of introducing new things and a new servant. Israel failed to hear and respond appropriately before, in the light of God's prior word: "From of old your ear has not been opened" (48:8). The question in this unit comes out of the same context of past failure, but its rhetorical force is in anticipating a positive response—namely, that of the servant of 50:4-9. In other words, both in chap. 48 and here, the mission of God's obedient servant is set in contrast to Israel at large, specifically in respect of his having been there when God came and his having answered when God called (50:2).

It is important to pay close attention to the pronouns and suffixes of v. 1. Addressed are Zion's children. The subject is Zion, their mother: Can they produce the bill of divorce God wrote in her case? Only then is their own specific situation referred to: Was God indebted to anyone such that he was forced to pawn his own people? The answer to both questions, however, involves them and only them. They were sold because of their sins, not because God was in debt. Their mother, on the other hand, was not put away because of her sins, but because of their sins. This depiction, if followed through to its conclusion, could imply Zion's innocent, perhaps vicarious, suffering. Yet Isa 40:2 does not go this far, and neither does the book of Lamentations. At most we might conclude from 40:2 that Zion paid her debt for sin *overmuch,* "double" (כפלים *kiplayim*).

She was not innocent (consistent with the depiction in Lamentations) even as her suffering was extreme—if not also borne on behalf of her children.

In the light of these circumstances, the rhetorical question of v. 2 gains its force: One of Zion's children should have stepped forward when God called. God did not issue a punishment of annihilation; God remains ready to redeem and deliver. One might well expect an oracle of salvation to follow at this juncture, but instead we get a lengthy predication, involving images of death and desert. The sea and rivers rebuked here are evocations of Babylon and Assyria (Isa 8:7; 21:1), approaching even more apocalyptic descriptions (Isa 24:4; 27:1), whose destinies are set in contrast with that of Zion. These images of destructive force, wrought by God's judgment, must be understood over against the blandishments the servant endures, faithfully and not disobediently.

50:4-9. Striking in this poem, which describes for the first time the servant's suffering and affliction, is the repetition of the divine name introduced at 48:16c: אדני יהוה (*'ǎdōnāy YHWH*), "Sovereign LORD" (NIV). Fully four of the six verses comprising the poem open with this special divine name, giving the poem a particularly personal feel as the servant reports that God has taught him, prepared him, and helped him. I agree with Westermann, on this account and on others, that the poem is not in the form of an individual lament, but rather is an individual psalm of confidence. Missing completely is any complaint to God, on any score, either as giver of the painful situation (so, e.g., Jer 15:18; 20:7) or as one slow to respond to it (Lam 5:20). There is even no declaration that the affliction the servant bears is the cause of any serious anguish or doubt whatsoever; in fact, the opposite is true (vv. 7-9). "Individual psalm of confidence" is precisely a correct interpretation of the poem before us.

Descriptions of suffering and affliction can be found in the psalter (Psalms 22; 69; 88), in Jeremiah, and in Lamentations. Those that appear here serve to illustrate God's sustaining attention and strengthening presence. That is, they are not, as is so often the case in psalms of lament, issues demanding address and redress from God. They remain subsidiary to the chief burden the poem wishes to communicate—namely, that God has faithfully responded to the servant *within* his situation of distress. In fact, it is in the context of God's attending to the servant that affliction arises and yet is borne without either complaint or resistance to bearing additional afflictions.

Unlike Israel of a previous generation (6:10-11), and unlike the generation that has failed to recall the former things, whose "ear has not been opened" (48:8), the servant has ears opened by God. God "stirred up" (העירותי *ha'îrôtî*) Cyrus (41:25); God has "stirred up" (יעיר *ya'îr*) morning by morning the ear of the servant, enabling him to hear as one taught. The significance of the term employed by the servant to describe God's relationship to him has already been mentioned. He has the tongue of one taught (למודים *limmûdîm*); the NRSV adopts a plausible translation of the term: "teacher." However, the term's usage here is a conscious evocation of 8:16, where the testimony vouchsafed to Isaiah is sealed among his "disciples" (בלמדי *bělimmudāy*). No mention was made of the tongue of the previous generation, since it was the tongue of the prophet that ricocheted off their closed ears and dulled understanding; presumably their speech would have been as much gibberish as was the prophet's to them (28:13). The prophet heard the word faithfully and transmitted what he heard to a generation whose only other faithful receivers were to be found among his disciples—and even that must be inferred.

What the servant hears gives him the capacity to know how to sustain the weary. Now this represents a narrowing or specifying of the prophet's audience, different in kind from what was represented in the former things of Isaiah's day. The word he has to speak involves the weary. The term was used at 40:30 to stipulate who God was prepared to strengthen: not the strong or the virile, but the faint, the powerless, the weary, and the exhausted (40:29-31). Here the weary are those addressed effectively by the servant.

Verse 5 again sets the servant off against those in chap. 48, whose ears from of old have not been opened (48:8). The insults borne by the servant are similar to those borne by the "one who has seen affliction" in Lamentations 3 (see Lam 3:30). The identity of this "afflicted one" is obscure; some opt for Zion, others for a sort of "everyman"

figure. The descriptions could be stereotypical ones, but what is striking is how they are related to the open-ear language of vv. 4-5. The servant is not rebellious *precisely* in his willingness to endure such suffering. In Lamentations a similar note is sounded: "It is good for one to bear the yoke . . . to give one's cheek to the smiter and be filled with insults" (Lam 3:27, 30). The "goodness" there entails the sense that the punishment is merited and is being borne with this due sense, "For the LORD will not reject forever" (Lam 3:31).

Here the poem seems to go another way, suggesting a different context of affliction—and theological reflection about it—than that of Zion depicted in Lamentations. Verse 7 clarifies that the servant is helped by God precisely in his ability to bear assaults. God is the source more of strength than of merited justice, and God will in time vindicate the servant. No one is able to declare the servant guilty, v. 9 concludes. Just as in the trial speeches of the first section, rhetorical questions that have no answer imply no answer is there to be given. "All of them will wear out like a garment" the servant says (v. 9), just as before God had said, "You, indeed, are nothing, and your work is nothing at all" (41:24). God and the servant are one.

Here the contrast with the books of Jeremiah and Lamentations is striking. It is hard to imagine a more solid confession of confidence than what we find here. What we do not know for sure is just where the affliction is coming from and why. In Jeremiah, the prophet is buffeted by his own people (Jer 11:21-23), "even your kinsfolk and your own family" (Jer 12:6). In Lamentations, the affliction would appear to be generated by those who have invaded Zion (e.g., Lam 1:5), whom God had dispatched for this purpose (Lam 2:5), whereupon God withdrew "his right hand from them in the face of the enemy" (Lam 2:3). It is one thing to contrast the open ear and ready tongue of the servant with generations past and present within Israel; it is another thing to see within his own generation, within Israel, the source of his affliction. A clue is provided by the final verses of the chapter (vv. 10-11), but before we can turn to this clue we should discuss the unit and its position following the servant poem proper, which is structurally analogous to the elaborations found after the two previous servant poems (42:5-9; 49:7-12).

50:10-11. Westermann sees great difficulties with this unit in its present location, even as he acknowledges expansions of the servant songs previously. The failure of a hymn to appear (so 42:10-13; 49:13) is partly the problem, but other difficulties appear to surface in his reading. His solution is to relocate the unit within the next chapter, following 51:1*a* and preceding 51:4.[111] Melugin goes in something of the opposite direction. The purpose of the psalm of confidence of vv. 4-9 is not to express trust but "to lay the foundation for the condemnation of the unfaithful," as this is proclaimed in vv. 10-11. Why? Because a standard psalm of confidence ought not to conclude in this manner.[112] The approach taken in this commentary will be to retain the central poem as a formal unit (against Melugin), commented upon by the elaboration now found in a discrete unit in 50:10-11. No relocation is desirable or necessary (against Westermann).

There is a translation problem in v. 10, unresolved by the NRSV, but resolved by the NIV and by Westermann. Each of the latter, somewhat differently, reads the second half of the verse as introducing a command—e.g., "Let him who walks in the dark, who has no light, trust in the name of the LORD" (NIV). What we do know is that a contrast is set up between walking in darkness and trusting in God nonetheless, as against lighting fires of one's own making. Those who fear God listen to the voice of the servant—that is, they are those whose ears, like that of the servant (vv. 4-5), are open. The Hebrew word אֲשֶׁר (*'ăšer*) is translated "who" and is followed by a singular form of the verb "to walk," with its near antecedent "the servant." The servant is the one who must walk in darkness, without any light, and trust in God. This construal would be a reading of the servant in the central poem fully consistent with his depiction there. Those who fear God are to listen to the voice of the servant; that voice, we learned at v. 4, was poised to speak to the weary.

The final verse addresses another possible audience: those who seek to provide their own light for their endeavors. The images of fire judgment are familiar from Isa 1:13 and 6:13, and they

anticipate the final verses of the book of Isaiah (66:24). They have been adapted here to set up a contrast with the servant, who walks without a torch through darkness, but is nevertheless a light to the nations (49:6). This is a stunning picture of the work of the servant.

This exhortation, based on a reflection on the work of the servant in the preceding unit (vv. 4-9), has been provided by the servants, who have composed the final suffering servant poem in tribute to the servant. If this is true, or if it captures at least something of the intention of the content of vv. 10-11, it follows that the affliction the servant reports in vv. 4-9 cannot be laid at the feet of the nations (so Lamentations) or narrowly traced to one group of harassers (as, on occasion, in Jeremiah). The affliction the servant endures emerges from some internal oppression. The "kindlers of fire" (v. 10) have not heeded the voice of the servant. It is reasonable to assume that they represent forces hostile to the servant, against whom the servant knows he will find strength and vindication in God (vv. 8-9). What the servant says in defense of himself, the servants reiterate, in a climate of ongoing oppression, in the final verses of chap. 50.

The oppressors who contend with the servant need not be one narrowly defined group, because the discourse has begun to radically reconsider Israel's relationship to the nations. For the time being it is prudent to conclude that the servant's opponents are not just to be found among the nations. The servant's challenge to his adversaries at v. 8 is intentionally reminiscent of God's challenge to the nations, issued repeatedly in chaps. 40–48. Yet what is clear about their identity earlier, set over against Israel and its possession of the testimony of the former things, is by no means clear here. When one adds to that the rebuke of chap. 48 and the commissioning of one servant who is Israel, light to the nations, the safest conclusion to reach is that, from chap. 48 onward, adversaries can no longer be neatly divided along Israel/the nations' lines.

Chapter 51 contains several appeals to those who pursue righteousness or know it (51:1, 7) or who are afflicted (51:21-23). Chapter 50 concludes with a contrast between those who emulate the servant, as God-fearers, and those who light their own lights. Already in the discourse

111. C. Westermann, *Isaiah 40–66,* trans. David Stalker, OTL (Philadelphia: Westminster, 1969) 233-34.

112. R. F. Melugin, *The Formation of Isaiah 40–55,* BZAW 141 (Berlin: Walter de Gruyter, 1976) 152-53.

usually associated with "Deutero-Isaiah" we are beginning to witness themes that take a much more obvious form in "Trito-Isaiah" chapters, where the servants, followers of the one servant, are set over against the unrighteous *within Israel.* Here the text indicates that the servants responsible for the final chapters of the book of Isaiah fol- lowed the servant in representing a particular way of life that not all would choose to follow or to interpret as consistent with God's design for Israel and for the larger created order. The usual repre- sentation of a sharp division at chap. 56 onward must be reconsidered. More will be said about this at the appropriate junctures.

REFLECTIONS

1. We are all aware of the uneven character of punishment. The Old Testament wrestles mightily with the depiction of God deploying nations as instruments of judgment who turn out to be far more wicked and deserving of judgment than those God first set out to correct. Isaiah testifies strongly, if at times indirectly, through the presentation of an Assyria replaced by Babylon. It is never clear whether a rightly commissioned Babylon simply overstepped itself, as did Assyria in its day (Isa 10:1-19), or whether from the beginning Babylon's claims to dominion fully contaminated any possible sense that God could have justly dispatched it (Isa 13:1–14:21). The transition is noted, whereby Assyria is replaced by Babylon (23:13), but with barely a theo- logical assessment. Hezekiah reckons God's word about the coming Babylonian exile as "good" (39:8), but only as an obedient response to the prophet Isaiah's word, combined with a sense of gratitude at his own sparing. The transition from Assyrian to Babylonian sections of the book of Isaiah effected by chapter 39 leaves us largely in the dark as to how we might theologically inter- pret the role of Babylon within God's stated designs for Israel and for all creation.

Judgments meted out by such violent agents are frequently messy. Isaiah 24–27 spells this out; it is as though creation itself threatens to come undone. In the spillover of massive force unleashed, some get burned more than others. Zion's children sinned, and their mother was the one put away because of their actions, over and above whatever uncleanness was found in her own skirts (Lam 1:9). She was not innocent, but neither was her punishment fully proportion- ate to her crime.

The text does not attempt to resolve this dilemma and the seeming injustice it represents. It poses other questions altogether: Why does the punishment for sin, divinely sent if dispropor- tionately felt, have such a paralyzing effect? And why does it entail an assumption that the God who has judged cannot also be the God who wills to save? The fury of divine rebuke testifies to the energy God is prepared to expend to save: "Is my hand shortened that it cannot redeem?" (Isa 50:2). Can the disproportionate character—traceable to Babylon, and not to the one who sent her—itself create this paralyzing stance?

It is worth pondering the sequence of thought represented by Isa 50:1-3. How is it that pun- ishment we know issues forth from God leads to the conclusion that God means to obliterate, and not redeem? And why is it that we, like the "friends" of Job, are averse to suffering that has spilled over and cost someone or some group more than others? Each of these questions is sig- nificant in its own right. But here they come as a one-two punch.

2. The servant is God's response, not ideas or a tidy theological resolution to the very difficult problem of the origins and injustice of raw evil. God does not announce that the punishment was wrongheaded or that Jacob/Israel's sins were unjustly handled. The servant finds his voca- tion precisely in the trenches where Zion was afflicted. It is difficult to judge whether these verses represent an honest advance over any previous reflection on affliction, or whether they are a singular response to a singular circumstance, no less profound for being so, but also diffi- cult to compare. This is not "the LORD gave, and the LORD has taken away; blessed be the name of the LORD" (Job 1:21 NRSV); but neither is it, "cursed be the day on which I was born" (Jer

20:14 NRSV) or even "heal me, O LORD, and I shall be healed" (Jer 17:14 NRSV). The servant appears to understand his capacity to withstand assault as the embodiment of obedience, "I was not rebellious, I did not turn backward" (Isa 50:5 NRSV).

At the same time, the servant does not escape to some place beyond pain. He issues a challenge to those who would contend with him. God will judge him innocent and vindicate him against them. What is perhaps striking here is the servant's refusal to understand his grim situation as sent by God for just punishment. He can endure the sort of affliction usually associated with Zion and yet never draw the conclusion others apparently wish to draw that he is being put to shame or being found guilty in God's eyes.

There is a flavor of the wisdom of the maturing Job here, though the circumstances are quite different. The servant's affliction is interpreted, finally, as an expiation for others (53:4-6). In the book of Job, this insight appears only in the final epilogue (Job 42:7-9), and there it comes as divinely given insight, as God instructs the "friends" to ask Job to pray for them, which Job does. The servant goes into this situation of affliction—some of it merited, some of it a spillover, all of it difficult and preferably avoided—fully conscious of the significant place of his affliction. His is a response of obedience that he has been prepared to accept because God has instructed him as to its purpose and has helped him. Nowhere does the servant imply that he is taking a risk in respect of knowing what God is up to. God has opened his ears and taught him, and he has responded obediantly to God and defiantly to those who would interpret it otherwise.

It is crucial to remember that, as tragedies go, the crucifixion of Jesus was neither the worst nor was it even remotely a singular event in its time; many were such executions in his day. What set it apart was that God had opened Jesus' ears as to its larger significance, allowing him the measure of confidence that did not remove the anguish but made it bearable. It was the knowledge of the righteousness of his obedience, and his love for those imperiled by evil, with a name and a spillover capacity and a potential to obliterate, that kept him moving down that particular road and up a cross. But behind it all was the voice of the one who sent him, who opened his ears and taught him and helped him, even against forces of death with millennia of momentum, foreshadowed by Babylon, overshadowing all but the Son of God himself. That voice kept Good Friday "good" and not another tragedy. It enabled that particular servant to empower and inspire other servants, who would follow his lead and take up the cross God set aside for them as well.[113]

---

113. See C. R. Seitz, *Seven Lasting Words: Meditations on the Death of Jesus* (Louisville: Westminster John Knox, 2001).

ISAIAH 51:1–52:12, THE LAST SPEECH OF THE SERVANT LIKE MOSES

OVERVIEW

It is necessary to treat the content and form of the servant's discourse preceding the climactic suffering servant poem in a special fashion. The material in chaps. 51–52 is not amenable to traditional or even modified, form-critical treatment, even of the sort employed throughout the commentary thus far, which has attempted to take seriously the author's creative freedom and sheer rhetorical brilliance. Most commentators recognize that something unusual is going on at this juncture in the discourse, and they generally allow for the possibility of longer compositional units. Westermann, for example, conceives of two fairly sizable units (51:1-2, 4-8; 50:10-11; and 51:9–52:3), the first of which includes portions of the preceding chapter, the second of which is a "single consciously designed unit," some eighteen verses in length.[114] The unit at 52:7-10 represents the finale of the discourse as this has been anticipated by the original heavenly council scene in 40:1-11. The last two verses (52:11-12) can be read together with it; they simply give the charge to exiles in diaspora to return home, as all has been prepared through God's word to the servant. The unit at 52:4-6 is unusual and will require special comment.

There is evidence of structural linkages woven into the composition as a whole that should be noted. Repetitions at 51:9, 12, 17; and 52:1 ("awake, awake"; "I, I"; "rouse yourself, rouse yourself"; "awake, awake") help to set off rhetorical units. Arguably, these repetitions are intended to evoke the double imperative with which the discourse began ("comfort, comfort," 40:1). The single comforter of 51:12 uses the emphatic "I, I" in a striking modification of the initial double charge. Especially telling in this section of the larger unit (51:9–52:12) are the frequent and evenly dispersed allusions to the initial heavenly council scene (40:1-11). The arm of God has been abstracted from the opening scene (40:10-11) in order to be addressed directly at 51:9-10, anticipated in the nearer context by the reference at 50:2 to God's redeeming capacity, "Is my hand shortened, that it cannot redeem?" Comforted are both the people (51:12) and Zion (51:17-23) in fulfillment of 40:1-2. The herald of good tidings announces God's return (40:9; 52:8); plural sentinals are even accounted for (52:8), as at 40:9, who see here eye to eye what God had promised all flesh would eventually witness (40:5), a promise reiterated here as well (52:10). Finally, God's faithful accompanying of those returning to Zion (52:12) was promised at 40:11.

The first section of the discourse (51:1-8) has a more immediate contextual relationship with the preceding chapters. It serves to introduce the recapitulation and finale represented by 51:9–52:12. Especially prevalent in this section is the repetition of forms of the word "righteousness" together with "salvation" (vv. 1, 5-8). Addressed are first "pursuers of righteousness" (vv. 1-3), then God's own people (vv. 4-6), and then finally "knowers of righteousness" and those in whose hearts God's law is found (vv. 7-8). The backdrop for this escalating appeal is to be found in the preceding chapter, where the servant's special role is held up to others for emulation and contrasted with the fate of those who walk in the flame of their own fire. The degree to which themes from "former Isaiah" are here pressing for fulfillment, especially in vv. 4-8, will be examined in greater detail; it may be possible that the threefold reference to "salvation" (ישע *yēša'*; ישועה *yēšû'â*; וישועתי *wîšû'ātî*) constitutes a deliberate evocation of the prophet Isaiah's own name and legacy. That name is recalled here as the one servant addresses his servants, just as once Isaiah surrounded himself with disciples or "taught ones" (8:16) in the midst of an obdurate and unheeding generation.

There appear to be at least three specific literary or tradition complexes lying very close to the servant's proclamation here. The first is composed of the narrative traditions concerning Abraham, Sarah, and their descendants. Blessing and multiplication are obvious references to the ancestor narratives (51:2). The overcoming of Sarah's barrenness has been creatively combined with Zion's own unexpected regeneration, itself traced back to the Genesis stories of Eden (Gen 2:8-9).

In the second complex (51:4-6), "former Isaiah" stands close at hand, with the references to "my nation" (1:4),[115] "teaching" (2:3), and "heavens" and "earth" (1:2). Those original witnesses to God's indictment of the people become a "nation" like Sodom. Here they are dismissed in the face of God's enduring salvation (*wîšû'ātî*)—itself an evocation of ישעיהו (*yēša'yāhû*), "Isaiah."

The third narrative complex impinging on the discourse is arguably the most important one. Its role here, however, must be inferred on the basis of much larger themes and a general conviction about the character of the prophecy represented by the discourse, especially at this juncture. The transition from servant to servants, made explicit at 54:17 but suggested as well by the force of the

---

114. C. Westermann, *Isaiah 40–66*, trans. David Stalker, OTL (Philadelphia: Westminster, 1969) 232-48. The problems with the first compositional unit were discussed above, preferring to read 50:10-11 in its present location as a commentary from the servants on the preceding poem of 50:4-9.

115. Instead of גוי חטא (*gôy ḥōṭē'*, "sinful nation"), 51:4 uses the more neutral לאומי (*lĕ'ummî*), which generally applies to non-Israelites (so 55:4), but could not exclude them. In other words, to apply the term *gôy* to Israel at 1:4 is to seek a clear rhetorical effect; to use לאום (*lĕ'ōm*) with עמי (*'ammî*, "my nation") at 51:4 is to set that earlier motivation to the side in the name of a new thing that is about to happen, for God's people and for the nations.

servant's own speech in chap. 50, is similar in kind to the transition from Moses, the servant of the Lord (Deut 34:5), to Joshua and his faithful followers. We have a new generation with a new possibility: Isaiah's unheeding "nation" has become again "my people" (51:4); whore Zion (1:21) again has righteousness (51:1, 7) lodged in her (1:26); and again these are people in whose heart is God's law (51:7; recalling Deut 30:1-6; Isa 2:3; Jer 31:33-34). Zion has become an Eden; out of her will go instruction. The new generation has the opportunity of Abraham and Sarah again. The promised land will be apportioned (49:8), but with direct movement to Zion as the focus of desolation removed and with a different understanding of inheritance (54:17). This generation is no better equipped than that of Joshua, nor is it any less prone to disobedience. But it is being given a completely fresh start.

Deuteronomy contains two important texts pertaining to prophecy (Deut 18:15-22; 34:10-12). Most commentators understand the promise of God's raising up "a prophet like Moses" (Deut 18:15) in a generally linear sense. That is, Deuteronomy teaches that after Moses' death, a lineage or succession of prophets "like Moses" will emerge, beginning with Joshua. Critical interpreters also take this text to reflect full knowledge of prophecy's lengthy history in Israel. The text represents an effort to coordinate prophecy as a large-scale phenomenon with law or to describe how the dynamic character of Mosaic speech, such as we find it in Deuteronomy, continued subsequently in God's "servants the prophets" (2 Kgs 24:2). Thus what was manifested in figures like Samuel and Isaiah and Jeremiah had its beginnings in Moses. Whether this is an effort to tamp down independent prophetic charism or to elevate law to a form of dynamic prophetic speech continues to be debated.[116]

Of course, the OT nowhere describes or seeks to put forward a notion of unbroken prophetic succession, beginning with Moses, whose gaps or final dissolution would then present a serious critical problem.[117] Things are not that tidy. Instead, it appears as though Israel's prophets and the messages they delivered—at this moment and at that, as God saw fit—were evaluated and edited and cherished according to a basic evaluative *discrimens:* How and to what degree was the prophet one like Moses? (This is especially true of the deuteronomistically oriented traditions; see Deut 18:15-22; Jer 15:1-4.) A double concern may have been at work here. Moses and his life with Israel may have represented a sort of benchmark against which the succeeding prophets were measured and coordinated through editorial shaping.[118] Late in Israel's experience with prophecy, another sort of concern may have emerged alongside this one, not replacing it but seeking to comprehend the underlying rationale of Deuteronomy's conception of a "prophet like Moses." Coordination and evaluation of prophecy according to a Mosaic standard were not undertaken for the purposes of ranking former prophetic worthies; these processes evolved over time into a more eschatological concern. The more prophets God sent, the more the original notion of prophecy as such, beginning with Moses, underwent thoughtful consideration. From the notion of "successors" of Moses developed a search not for prophets of Mosaic bearing, but for, literally, "a prophet like Moses"—that is, one single prophetic figure whose proximity to Moses would bring prophecy to its wonted fulfillment regarding God's plans for Israel and the world at large.

The "servant" at work in this discourse operates consciously or unconsciously within this climate of theological reflection. He is fully aware of the history of prophecy as it lies before him, running all the way back in time to God's servant Moses, and especially of its frustrated moments (49:4). These frustrated moments were there from the beginning. They involved an unfaithful generation who died in the wilderness after having been given life; Moses' own suffering and persecution; his death outside the promised land; and perhaps also his expiation for the sins of his own deaf generation (Deut 4:21), so that a new generation under the leadership of the faithful servants Joshua and Caleb might have life. Such moments also persisted throughout prophecy's long history, and the

116. See S. B. Chapman, *The Law and the Prophets,* FAT 27 (Tubingen: Mohr Siebeck, 1999).

117. On the "end" of prophecy, see T. W. Overholt, "The End of Prophecy: No Players Without a Program," *JSOT* 42 (1988) 103-15. He has cited all the relevant secondary literature on this question. See also E. Conrad, "The End of Prophecy and the Appearance of Angels/Messengers in the Book of the Twelve," *JSOT* 73 (1997) 65-79.

118. C. R. Seitz, "The Prophet Moses and the Canonical Shape of Jeremiah," *ZAW* 101 (1989) 1-21.

servant was doubtless aware of these episodes of seeming unfulfillment, of God's words falling unheeded on a generation doomed. What did it mean, for example, that God had chosen Jeremiah to be a "prophet to the nations" (Jer 1:5), appointed "over nations and over kingdoms" (Jer 1:10)? These nations had certainly proven good agents of judgment, but by no means enjoyed both tearing down and subsequent building up (Jer 1:10). The servant's role as "light to the nations" is the assumption, divinely mandated, of God's stated prophetic intention with the nations, especially as this is manifested in the proclamation of "former Isaiah" (Isa 2:1-4; 19:23-25; 37:20).

There is some tension between the notion of prophets or a prophet like Moses (Deut 18:15-22) and the final claim of the book of Deuteronomy, that "never since has there arisen a prophet in Israel like Moses, who knew the LORD face to face" (Deut 34:10). The singular character of Moses is carefully guarded and acknoweldged even as the radical potential exists that one like Moses will arise, into whose mouth God will put God's very own words. The servant lives within this tension, and even more so do those who reflect on his life, mission, and death—i.e., the servant successors of the servant.

Within the servant's last speech here, and earlier, we see movement toward identification with Moses and his generations—an old one dying and a new one on the banks of the Jordan, with God's law in their midst—that is unmistakable. This identification is further influenced by the wider knowledge of God's ways with the former prophet Isaiah, all the way back to the generations of Sarah and Abraham (who is himself called a prophet at Gen 20:7). The servant addresses for the last time those who would pursue righteousness, including Zion, consistent with Isaiah's former word (1:1-31). He recalls God's mighty arm of deliverance (51:10), in creation and in exodus redemption. Quoting Deut 18:15-22 almost verbatim, he speaks of God's having put "my words in your mouth," together with God's having hidden him in the shadow of God's hand (Isa 49:2). After he faithfully discharges his vocation to comfort Zion, he witnesses the fulfillment of God's promises to her (52:7-10). Heralds observe what is on the horizon, and approaching.

As his final act, the servant dispatches the priests as did Moses in his day (Deut 31:9), not to carry the law—which goes forth now from Zion or is found in the heart of "knowers of righteousness" (51:7)—but the vessels once hauled off to Babylonian exile (2 Kgs 25:13-17; 2 Chr 36:18). The actual arrival of scattered Israel at Zion he will not, however, witness. Like Moses, he can only see them from afar, as they approach, together with the nations, to see "the salvation of our God" (52:10). If we can only infer his death just this side of the return of God and the scattered to the new "promised land," Zion, on the basis of the Moses analogy, then the servants who report his death in the climactic suffering servant poem following (52:13–53:12) make it explicit. Whatever movement the servant might have made toward an identification with "the prophet like Moses," they complete from their own side.

One particular silence at this point begs for comment, though it is difficult to judge its significance. The voice of the discourse never uses for himself the actual title "prophet" (נביא *nābî*), and neither do those who record his expiatory death, which they judge to be like that of Moses. Perhaps the servant's prophetic status is simply assumed. "Servant" is, of course, the term applied to the prophet Moses by Deuteronomy, and it has its counterpart in the history associated with the editorial efforts of the deuteronomists: "according to the word of the LORD that he spoke by his servants the prophets" (2 Kgs 24:2 NRSV).

Could it be the case that the servant's identification with Moses has as a prior working assumption that prophecy has in fact been extinguished? Had the rough succession of prophetic figures in Israel's history been terminated with the state itself? We know, for example, that Israel's kings were measured over against the prototype David in the Deuteronomistic History (e.g., "He did not do what was right in the sight of the LORD his God, as his ancestor David had done," 2 Kgs 16:2 NRSV), in a similar manner to what is described in terms of Moses and the prophets who came after him. Yet kingship came to an end in the figure of Zedekiah, whose sons were executed before he himself was blinded and rendered unfit for rule. If the word of Isaiah to Hezekiah were to be taken literally, then the royal descendants would one day be "eunuchs in the palace of the king of Babylon" (Isa 39:7). Hopes attached to Jehoiachin and his offspring (2 Kgs 25:27-30) still constitute more of a resuscitation of a thing judged and terminated than the continuation of a succession temporarily knocked off course. Ezra–Nehemiah's use of the term "king" to refer to foreign rulers (Nebuchadnezzar, Cyrus, Darius, Artaxerxes) or even to David (Ezra 3:10), but not to Zerubbabel, in some sense matches the perspective of the prophet Ezekiel. Ezekiel, too, speaks of the "king of Babylon" (Ezek 21:21); yet when he describes the restoration of Davidic kings, he seems to prefer other language to speak of them (prince, servant, shepherd).

Seen against this backdrop, the servant—and the servants—may judge his activity to constitute such an identification with Moses that to use the term "prophet" would imply an adjusted continuation of a former thing, rather than a completely fresh beginning. With Jeremiah's return to Egypt, the curses of Deuteronomy were called down upon an evil generation, who would die in exile as once a generation had died in Egypt. (In Deut 17:16 the king is not to "return the people to Egypt . . . since the LORD has said to you, 'You must never return that way again,' " NRSV) Did prophecy as an extension of the Mosaic office also

die there? If so, then this might have freed texts like Deut 18:15-18 or Deut 34:10-12 for a fresh appraisal. There never would be another prophet like Moses who knew God face-to-face at Sinai and in Egypt (Deut 34:10), but there would be another one raised up into whose mouth God would place words. The one like Moses was not a prophet; he was a servant with a particular mission, passed on to others within Israel as "the heritage of the servants of the LORD, and their vindication from me" (54:17). In this way continuity with old promises and hopes is maintained, even as a new thing is introduced. Here is the logic of "former things" and "new things" in its characteristic, dialectical expression, manifested in the identity and mission of the servant and comprehended as such by the servants who pick up where he left off. Where this one is most like Moses, he is also most himself and most in accordance with God's new thing for Israel and the nations: "You are my servant, Israel, in whom I will be glorified" (49:3). The servant is not Moses *redivivus,* but Israel after God's own heart. In that role he will re-create God's people, and in doing that task he will become a "light to the nations."

Isaiah 51:1-23, The Taught One Teaches

NIV

51 "Listen to me, you who pursue
righteousness
and who seek the LORD:
Look to the rock from which you were cut
and to the quarry from which you
were hewn;
[2]look to Abraham, your father,
and to Sarah, who gave you birth.
When I called him he was but one,
and I blessed him and made him many.
[3]The LORD will surely comfort Zion
and will look with compassion on all
her ruins;
he will make her deserts like Eden,
her wastelands like the garden of the LORD.
Joy and gladness will be found in her,
thanksgiving and the sound of singing.

[4]"Listen to me, my people;

NRSV

51 Listen to me, you that pursue
righteousness,
you that seek the LORD.
Look to the rock from which you were hewn,
and to the quarry from which you
were dug.
[2] Look to Abraham your father
and to Sarah who bore you;
for he was but one when I called him,
but I blessed him and made him many.
[3] For the LORD will comfort Zion;
he will comfort all her waste places,
and will make her wilderness like Eden,
her desert like the garden of the LORD;
joy and gladness will be found in her,
thanksgiving and the voice of song.

[4] Listen to me, my people,

NIV

hear me, my nation:
The law will go out from me;
   my justice will become a light to
         the nations.
⁵My righteousness draws near speedily,
   my salvation is on the way,
   and my arm will bring justice to the nations.
The islands will look to me
   and wait in hope for my arm.
⁶Lift up your eyes to the heavens,
   look at the earth beneath;
the heavens will vanish like smoke,
   the earth will wear out like a garment
   and its inhabitants die like flies.
But my salvation will last forever,
   my righteousness will never fail.

⁷"Hear me, you who know what is right,
   you people who have my law in your hearts:
Do not fear the reproach of men
   or be terrified by their insults.
⁸For the moth will eat them up like a garment;
   the worm will devour them like wool.
But my righteousness will last forever,
   my salvation through all generations."

⁹Awake, awake! Clothe yourself with strength,
   O arm of the LORD;
awake, as in days gone by,
   as in generations of old.
Was it not you who cut Rahab to pieces,
   who pierced that monster through?
¹⁰Was it not you who dried up the sea,
   the waters of the great deep,
who made a road in the depths of the sea
   so that the redeemed might cross over?
¹¹The ransomed of the LORD will return.
   They will enter Zion with singing;
   everlasting joy will crown their heads.
Gladness and joy will overtake them,
   and sorrow and sighing will flee away.

¹²"I, even I, am he who comforts you.
   Who are you that you fear mortal men,
   the sons of men, who are but grass,
¹³that you forget the LORD your Maker,
   who stretched out the heavens
   and laid the foundations of the earth,
that you live in constant terror every day

NRSV

and give heed to me, my nation;
for a teaching will go out from me,
   and my justice for a light to the peoples.
⁵I will bring near my deliverance swiftly,
   my salvation has gone out
   and my arms will rule the peoples;
the coastlands wait for me,
   and for my arm they hope.
⁶Lift up your eyes to the heavens,
   and look at the earth beneath;
for the heavens will vanish like smoke,
   the earth will wear out like a garment,
   and those who live on it will die
         like gnats;ᵃ
but my salvation will be forever,
   and my deliverance will never be ended.

⁷Listen to me, you who know righteousness,
   you people who have my teaching in your
         hearts;
do not fear the reproach of others,
   and do not be dismayed when they
         revile you.
⁸For the moth will eat them up like a garment,
   and the worm will eat them like wool;
but my deliverance will be forever,
   and my salvation to all generations.

⁹Awake, awake, put on strength,
   O arm of the LORD!
Awake, as in days of old,
   the generations of long ago!
Was it not you who cut Rahab in pieces,
   who pierced the dragon?
¹⁰Was it not you who dried up the sea,
   the waters of the great deep;
who made the depths of the sea a way
   for the redeemed to cross over?
¹¹So the ransomed of the LORD shall return,
   and come to Zion with singing;
everlasting joy shall be upon their heads;
   they shall obtain joy and gladness,
   and sorrow and sighing shall flee away.

¹²I, I am he who comforts you;
   why then are you afraid of a mere mortal
         who must die,

ᵃOr in like manner

NIV

because of the wrath of the oppressor,
who is bent on destruction?
For where is the wrath of the oppressor?
¹⁴ The cowering prisoners will soon be set
free;
they will not die in their dungeon,
nor will they lack bread.
¹⁵For I am the LORD your God,
who churns up the sea so that its
waves roar—
the LORD Almighty is his name.
¹⁶I have put my words in your mouth
and covered you with the shadow of
my hand—
I who set the heavens in place,
who laid the foundations of the earth,
and who say to Zion, 'You are my people.' "

¹⁷Awake, awake!
Rise up, O Jerusalem,
you who have drunk from the hand of
the LORD
the cup of his wrath,
you who have drained to its dregs
the goblet that makes men stagger.
¹⁸Of all the sons she bore
there was none to guide her;
of all the sons she reared
there was none to take her by the hand.
¹⁹These double calamities have come
upon you—
who can comfort you?—
ruin and destruction, famine and sword—
who can^a console you?
²⁰Your sons have fainted;
they lie at the head of every street,
like antelope caught in a net.
They are filled with the wrath of the LORD
and the rebuke of your God.

²¹Therefore hear this, you afflicted one,
made drunk, but not with wine.
²²This is what your Sovereign LORD says,
your God, who defends his people:
"See, I have taken out of your hand
the cup that made you stagger;
from that cup, the goblet of my wrath,

^a19 Dead Sea Scrolls, Septuagint, Vulgate and Syriac; Masoretic Text /
how can I

NRSV

a human being who fades like grass?
¹³ You have forgotten the LORD, your Maker,
who stretched out the heavens
and laid the foundations of the earth.
You fear continually all day long
because of the fury of the oppressor,
who is bent on destruction.
But where is the fury of the oppressor?
¹⁴ The oppressed shall speedily be released;
they shall not die and go down to the Pit,
nor shall they lack bread.
¹⁵ For I am the LORD your God,
who stirs up the sea so that its waves roar—
the LORD of hosts is his name.
¹⁶ I have put my words in your mouth,
and hidden you in the shadow of my hand,
stretching out^a the heavens
and laying the foundations of the earth,
and saying to Zion, "You are my people."

¹⁷ Rouse yourself, rouse yourself!
Stand up, O Jerusalem,
you who have drunk at the hand of the LORD
the cup of his wrath,
who have drunk to the dregs
the bowl of staggering.
¹⁸ There is no one to guide her
among all the children she has borne;
there is no one to take her by the hand
among all the children she has brought up.
¹⁹ These two things have befallen you
—who will grieve with you?—
devastation and destruction, famine
and sword—
who will comfort you?^b
²⁰ Your children have fainted,
they lie at the head of every street
like an antelope in a net;
they are full of the wrath of the LORD,
the rebuke of your God.

²¹ Therefore hear this, you who are wounded,^c
who are drunk, but not with wine:
²² Thus says your Sovereign, the LORD,
your God who pleads the cause of
his people:

^aSyr: Heb *planting*   ^bQ Ms Gk Syr Vg: MT *how may I comfort
you?*   ^cOr *humbled*

NIV

you will never drink again.
[23]I will put it into the hands of your tormentors,
who said to you,
'Fall prostrate that we may walk over you.'
And you made your back like the ground,
like a street to be walked over."

NRSV

See, I have taken from your hand the cup
of staggering;
you shall drink no more
from the bowl of my wrath.
[23] And I will put it into the hand of your
tormentors,
who have said to you,
"Bow down, that we may walk on you";
and you have made your back like the ground
and like the street for them to walk on.

COMMENTARY

The previous section made clear that chap. 51 is but a portion of a longer section running up to the suffering servant poem at 52:13–53:12. For the sake of convenience, the traditional chapter division will be followed, with the contents of chap. 51 treated first, before moving to 52:1-12.

As indicated, the chapter breaks into several rhetorical units whose ligatures are indicated by the presence of the imperative "listen": vv. 1-3, vv. 4-6, vv. 7-8. These give way to repeated imperatives and a double "I": "awake, awake" (vv. 9-11); "I, I" (vv. 12-16); "rouse yourself, rouse yourself" (vv. 17-23). In point of fact, however, the chapter is even more replete with commands than even this division would imply; there are eight plural imperatives in vv. 1-8 alone. This gives the chapter a decidedly urgent character.

51:1-3. It has been commented that to "do righteousness" is a characteristic of chapters associated with "Third Isaiah" (56:1) over against "Second Isaiah" chapters, where the emphasis is on God's own righteousness bestowed on the community (e.g., 51:5-6, 8).[119] The implication is that "Third Isaiah" is more concerned with practical behavior and proper conduct within the community. There will be opportunity to test this notion below, but it is to be noted here that the servant has no trouble speaking of the pursuit of righteousness, which is paired with seeking the Lord. These construct (genitive) forms recall 50:10 and the appeal to those who fear the Lord made

there.[120] The servant addresses here those who would distinguish themselves by their pursuit of righteousness.

The collocation of appeal to the ancestors, together with comfort to Zion, is unusual, since these belong to different sections of the larger discourse. Westermann notes what he regards as the unusual depiction of Zion as a wilderness, as against the territory separating exiles from their homeland on analogy with the exodus event; for this and other reasons he treats v. 3 by itself as the fragment of a lost hymn.[121] Right along I have argued against this restricted understanding of desert and wilderness in this discourse (see the Commentary on 40:1-11). What is striking about the present collocation is that the appeal to the ancestors Abraham and Jacob/Israel, familiar from the first half of the discourse (41:1, 8, 14; 43:1; 44:1), is here augmented by the reference to the matriarch Sarah. Sarah was once barren, as Abraham was once old and but one. Zion's comforting will lead to joy and gladness in her, as her children return to a new Eden. She who was as barren as Sarah—as well as bereaved, exiled, put away (49:21)—not only anticipates the songs of her unexpected children, but her complete transformation to an Eden-like unspoiledness as well. We see further elaboration of Eden's original state, applied to Jerusalem, in 65:17-25.

51:4-6. The general appeal of vv. 1-3 is here

119. R. Rendtorff, "Isaiah 56:1 as a Key to the Formation of the Book of Isaiah," in *Canon and Theology,* OBT (Minneapolis: Fortress, 1993) 181-90.

120. Partly for this reason, Westermann rearranges the material so that 51:1 is directly followed by 50:10-11. See C. Westermann, *Isaiah 40–66,* trans. David Stalker, OTL (Philadelphia: Westminster, 1969) 232, 34.
121. Ibid., 237.

followed by a narrower one. The argument was made earlier for an especially close association between this unit and the opening material of "former Isaiah" (1:1–2:4). There Israel was addressed as one of the "nations" (1:4), as corrupt offspring in an unfaithful city, with rulers of Sodom, righteousness forfeited, and heaven and earth called in to witness God's indictment. And yet the promise of God's instruction going forth from a cleansed city, for Israel and for all the nations who streamed there, followed the indictment (2:1-4). Afterward, God said of Zion, "You shall be called the city of righteousness, the faithful city" (1:26).

Here Zion's unexpected children are addressed, once again as God's people and not as children who "have rebelled against me" (1:3), "offspring who do evil, children who deal corruptly" (1:4). Ears can hear now (cf. 6:9-10). God's instruction goes forth (2:3). Divine justice illuminates the nations, who await God's judgment (2:4). In a previous day, the people ignored Isaiah's instruction and instead turned their faces upward or looked to the earth, but saw nothing but gloom and anguish (8:21-22). Now they look up and down, only to see the former witnesses to their iniquity (1:2) dismissed, with simply God's righteousness remaining. This is not incipient apocalypticism, but the intertextual signal that a new day, looked for of old, is dawning for the rescued children of Zion. The tongue of God's taught one speaks God's word and God's instruction to a new generation, capable of being taught. For those in whose hearts is God's law, instruction of a former character is no longer even necessary (vv. 7-8).

51:7-8. In this third in a series of appeals, the servant addresses those who would be servants and follow his example. These are not pursuers of righteousness (v. 1), but those who know it. When the prophet Jeremiah speaks of a new generation, it is a forgiven generation, in which people will not need to teach one another or say to one another " 'Know the LORD,' for they shall all know me" (Jer 31:34). God's instruction is written on their hearts (31:33). The servant here appeals to this new generation with language identical to Jeremiah's: "Listen to me, you who know righteousness, you people who have my teaching in your hearts" (Isa 51:7), even as the phrase "new covenant" does not appear.

The servant's "teaching" does not involve

imparting new information; it consists, rather, of encouragement through oppression and hardship. Note that the same language used by the servant to describe his own conviction of God's vindication (50:9) is here applied to the circumstances of those addressed. The servant is commissioning servants to a similar vocation through affliction. The final line of v. 8 repeats practically verbatim the concluding line of v. 6. In the suffering servant poem to follow, the servants will reach the conclusion that "the righteous one, my servant, shall make many righteous" (53:11). Without his yet knowing it, it will be through the servant that God's righteousness is manifested and shared, from one generation to the next.[122]

51:9-11. Here begins a series of rhetorical units that leads us into chap. 52 (51:9-11; 51:12-16; 51:17-23; 52:1-2). At the same time, there is continuity with preceding units as well. Verse 11 tells of the singing of the redeemed who are returning to Zion, just as the comforted Zion was informed of the voice of song that would again be found in her, who once was like Sarah (51:3). There was reference to the Lord's redeeming hand preceding the servant poem at 50:2 and to God's drying up of the sea; the same language is found in 51:9-10, as the arm of God is directly addressed. The servant has taken this image from the opening heavenly council scene (40:10-11).

The future generations (דור דורים *dôr dôrîm*) that will witness God's righteousness and salvation (51:8) have their counterpart in the past, "generations of long ago" (דרות עולמים *dôrôt 'ôlāmîm*). These latter witnessed God's act of creation, here described with reference to the chaos monster Rahab (cf. Job 26:12; Pss 74:14; 89:10; Isa 27:1). This prototypical event has its echo at the Red Sea (Exod 15:1-18), an event that foreshadows God's founding of Zion (Pss 46:1-7; 93:1-5). Here it is collated, not with Zion's firm founding, but with the deliverance of the ransomed diaspora, as though passing again through the Red Sea, en route directly to Zion. Creation, exodus, and Zion all testify to the selfsame arm of God, at work long ago in previous generations, at work now in redemption, providing salvation and righteousness throughout all future time (v. 8).

---

122. On the significance of צדק (*ṣdq*) in the transition from servant to servants, see W. A. M. Beuken, "The Main Theme of Trito-Isaiah: 'The Servants of YHWH,' " *JSOT* 47 (1990) 67-87.

51:12-16. The circumstances of oppression are again recalled (cf. v. 7; 50:4-9), though particularly at v. 14 the more detailed description is obscure. The NIV thinks concretely of "prisoners . . . in their dungeons"; the NRSV speaks of "the oppressed . . . down to the Pit." At 63:1 the same rare Hebrew term (צעה *ṣ'h*) appears to refer to the great weight borne by one with bloodstained battle garments—that is, one "stooped." "Release" (NRSV) is a possible interpretation of the Hebrew הפתח (*hippātēaḥ*); variant terms (פקח *pqḥ,* "open"; הוציא *hôṣî',* "bring out") are used in the charge to the servant Israel at 42:7; there quite clearly the reference is to the liberation of prisoners from the dungeon. If that same context is to be inferred here, then the servant, through whom God speaks, here follows through on the charge given earlier to servant Israel. This would make the personal address to the servant in v. 16 by no means out of place. God reminds the servant at v. 16 of his prior commissioning language, "in the shadow of his hand he hid me away" (49:2), which may be another way to express the somewhat passive, but nevertheless effective, mode of servant "proclamation" first introduced at 42:2-3.

Noted above are the direct correlation between the expression "I have put my words in your mouth" (v. 16) and the promise of a prophet like Moses whom God intends to raise up: "I will put the words in the mouth of my prophet, who shall speak to them everything that I command" (Deut 18:18). The expression is sufficiently general to prohibit a case being made on the basis of this verse alone, but the cumulative evidence would suggest that an effort is being made—by the servant and the servants—to comprehend his vocation in relationship to that of Moses long ago. In any event, the expression does not appear in this form in the earlier servant poems, so its usage here cannot simply be the reproduction of some previous stock phrase (cf. "hidden you in the shadow of my hand," Isa 51:16). God's designation and equipping of the servant is of the same order as the most basic acts of creation, which now entail the creation of children for barren, bereaved, cast-off Zion (v. 16).

The situation of distress revealed in the opening verses (vv. 13-14) suggests that the servant and the wider community are under fairly constant assault, "You fear continually all day long because of the fury of the oppressor" (v. 13). We know very little about life in Babylonian exile, and what we learn of it from Daniel, Ezekiel, or Esther is not entirely consistent with such a picture. Duhm long ago argued that an earlier description of grim prison life in this discourse ("all of them trapped in holes and hidden in prisons," 42:22) was "proof positive that Deutero-Isaiah did not live in Babylon."[123] What such descriptions do match are the presentations of life in a ruined and overrun Judah and Jerusalem, now found in the book of Lamentations and especially in the latter chapters of Jeremiah (e.g., Jeremiah 37–43). There we have internal strife, murder, fear of foreign reprisals, oppression, imprisonment, and a destroyed Zion. The Isaiah discourse operates from within this perspective, even as it keeps its eye on far horizons from which other prisoners will one day come (e.g., 52:11-12). To be "among the nations" is not just to be literally in exile (cf. Lam 1:1, 3, 10, 17 with Lam 4:15, 20), just as Zion can be described as having her own specific wilderness and exile (Isa 49:21; 51:3; Lam 4:22).

51:17-23. This passage looks like a page taken out of the book of Lamentations. The judgment Jerusalem has endured was sent by God (v. 17; cf. Lam 2:1-8). Her children cannot come to her aid (v. 18; cf. Lam 1:16-17). Instead, the streets are lined with their corpses (v. 20), "as their life is poured out on their mother's bosom" (Lam 2:12). The children themselves acknowledge God's rebuke (v. 20; cf. Lam 3:40-47).

Zion is not charged to rise from the dust because of her oppression, anguish, and affliction only. She has fallen into a torpor induced by drinking God's cup of wrath. Associated images appear earlier in Isaiah (19:14; 28:1-8), but the central image is unfolded in more detail in Jer 25:15-29. There all the nations, beginning with "Jerusalem and the towns of Judah" (Jer 25:18) and ending with Babylon (Jer 25:26), take turns drinking from God's cup of wrath. Now "your Sovereign, the LORD" (cf. Isa 50:4-5, 7, 9) announces that the cup is to pass to others.

The "two things" that have befallen Jerusalem refer to two destructive pairs, combined for

123. B. Duhm, *Das Buch Jesaia,* HKAT (Göttingen: Vandenhoeck & Ruprecht, 1892) 294.

alliteration in Hebrew (השד והשבר והרעב והחרב *haššōd wĕhaššeber wĕhārāʿāb wĕhaḥereb*). This foursome trumps Jeremiah's typical use of triads (e.g., sword, famine, and pestilence; 21:7; 27:8; 28:8; 38:2). "Two things" (שתים *šĕttayim*) here may correspond to "double" (כפלים *kiplayim*) at 40:2, where the initial statement of Zion's receipt of judgment is made. This "double full" notion is also roughly consistent with the statement at 50:1, where Zion's just judgment also entails the payment for her children's sins. The introduction of a notion of gratuitous judgment is quite possibly being flirted with here, but never with the suggestion that God's justice is under scrutiny. Lamentations strains even harder at stretching this dialectic. This collection of statements about Zion's punishment serves to lay the groundwork for a conception of unbalanced, though fully just, punishment, the surplus of which could accrue to the benefit of others. In the servant's comforting speech to Zion lie the seeds of the servants' own portrayal of their leader's affliction and death and their profound appraisal of innocent, expiatory suffering, different in character but similar in kind to that of Zion.

REFLECTIONS

1. Here and elsewhere the servant displays profound insight into Zion's situation. He is able to take seriously her anguish and distress, and yet at the same time interpret these theologically. He does not take sides—here with God, there with Zion. Neither does his comforting take the form of sentimental participation in her pain. Nowhere is the effort made by the servant to say that he knows what her situation is like. True comfort, as the text means it, does not amount to collapsing the distance that separates the one who addresses and the one who is being addressed, so that a common territory opens up between them and mutually interprets their common anguish. The servant, too, knows anguish and affliction (50:4-9). He never, however, uses these to build an explicit bridge to Zion. She knows nothing of what he says to God and to us. If there is a commonality, we are the ones who must identify it.

Seen against this backdrop, what is striking is the servant's willingness to risk comprehending Zion's punishment as fully just, and yet also as massive in proportion and degree. Nowhere does he indulge that sort of risky comprehension in his own case. We know nothing of the servant's guilt or innocence at anything like the same level of concern. We know only that in the face of those who interpret his present affliction as a sign of God's disfavor, his response is to throw up the challenge, "Who will declare me guilty?" (50:9). The servant has the fortitude to declare Zion's anguish as coming to an end, even as his own persists, without making any comparisons or efforts at a uniform perspective. Zion remains Zion, the servant the servant. His ability to speak comfort to her does not derive from the firm foundation of his own innocence or from a firmer grasp of the contours of or reasons for the oppression that besets him, but from God's inspiration alone, "That I may know how to sustain the weary with a word" (50:4).

His ability in chapter 51 and elsewhere to admit that "overfull" punishment can and does occur, without questioning or compromising God's justice, constitutes the servant's inspiration at a point of maximum penetration. It breaks open, as well, the possibility that in the word he speaks to the weary, one is able to identify a word that will apply to him as well. In laying bare Zion's predicament theologically, the path is exposed by which others will come to understand his sacrifice, not as a tragic finale, but as the bestowal of God's righteousness in life through the means of atoning death (53:11). It belongs to the sacrifice of the servant in its most mature expression that as he comforts Zion and attempts to comprehend surplus aspects of her suffering, he does so without any reference to himself. When the servants confess, "Surely he has borne our infirmities and carried our diseases" (53:4), they do so partly in reflection on the servant's comforting witness to Zion, as that takes form in chapter 51 and earlier.

2. The anguish and distress of those who are oppressed (51:13-14) and bear reproach (51:7) presents a slightly different face and challenge for the servant, over against that of Zion. Zion has finished drinking the cup of merited wrath and is about to confront unexpected children; however, for precisely those "who have my teaching in your hearts" (51:7), reviling, reproach, and oppression will constitute a different cup of wrath. This cup, one might assume, could well be thought of as being handed over by the same just God who once set out to judge Israel and every nation on earth (Jer 25:15-27). How could the reproach borne formerly in judgment now turn a corner and become no longer God's rebuke, but reviling traceable to "a mere mortal who must die, a human being who fades like the grass" (Isa 51:12), not to be taken as divinely sent?

What is required in a situation such as this is one who knows that no confrontation mounted at the human level can convict him of rightful shame and guilt (50:8-9). Without ever protesting his moral superiority or claiming some special virtuous discipline or prophetic immunity from discouragement, the servant knows the line tracing his affliction stops with wrongful adversaries, and he goes no further. Behind their insults stands not God, but only their own clothing of iniquity, about to be consumed by moth and worm (50:9; 51:8). We cannot know how the servant could interpret anguish in one instance as "overfull" but divinely sent, and in another as stemming from the "mortal who must die," to be borne not as Zion must bear a cup of God's wrath, but as simply that through which God promises to work in vindication and release. The only answer the text gives is that the servant's ear has been opened (50:4), and with his tongue he faithfully discharges his reponsibility to "sustain the weary with a word," in one way to Zion, and in another to those "who know righteousness," in whose heart is God's law (51:7). Jeremiah's new covenant people are not exempt from affliction; they have been forgiven, and, therefore, they know the difference between just punishment and the sort of affliction that paradoxically accompanies the gift of having been set free. God has as distinctive a word for them as that for Zion.

3. Is it necessary to add that all the ingredients of the gospel can be found here? There is the righteous servant, whose atoning death bestows righteousness on those whose eyes and ears are opened to see God's will at work in him. There is Zion, justly bearing the weight of her sins, and, in addition, a surplus thrown up by justice gone awry in the hands of agents of evil purpose. There are those pursuing righteousness and fearing God who stand on the outskirts of fuller fellowship. There are those in whose hearts is God's law, who should be ready to bear affliction in imitation of the servant. There are kings who shut their mouths or are otherwise brought into submission, and there are those who remain potent brokers of power, outside God's purposes. There is the possibility that the nations—those without God in the world (Eph 2:12)—might by the work of the servant find a light that illuminates God's purposes with them and Israel and the world God has made. All is coming to a boil at this juncture in the book of Isaiah. This is why the prophet Isaiah has been regarded as an evangelist, not a prophet, in the history of interpretation, and why the book associated with him has been termed, "the fifth Gospel."[124]

When Augustine inquired of Ambrose what book of the Bible should be his starting point in coming to understand the gospel now invading his soul, "Isaiah" was the answer the bishop gave. Yet Augustine was frustrated in his efforts to read the prophet's message. He went instead to the New Testament. Justin Martyr, by contrast, insists it is the scriptures of Israel that validate the truth of the gospel for him. Here we see the indissolubility of the two-Testament witness to Jesus Christ. The gospel lies latent in the Old and becomes patent in the New, as the traditional expression puts it, and neither witness exists without the other.

In the righteous servant we have a prophecy of Jesus Christ in one very specific sense. The book of Isaiah is not here predicting Jesus of Nazareth; language like "the latter days" or "in that

---

124. See C. R. Seitz, "The Book of Isaiah (First Isaiah)," in *The Anchor Bible Dictionary*, 6 vols., ed. D. N. Freedman (Garden City, N.Y.: Doubleday, 1992) 3:490-501.; J. A. Sawyer, *The Fifth Gospel* (Cambridge: Cambridge University Press, 1996).

---

day" is completely missing from the discourse at this point. Rather, the book of Isaiah is sketching the lineaments of God's righteous servant in the very same sense as it spoke of the former thing proclaimed by God in days ago, now coming to fruition. Here God, by means of a former thing, establishes a fixed mark. From this mark bearings will be taken by which to measure the work of God in Jesus Christ, such that God might be shown to be faithful in bringing to fullness a word that had gone forth from God's mouth long ago and would not return empty, but would accomplish a new thing. The gospel is that new thing, consistent with, but then overflowing, the former word, revealing itself to be *the* fixed mark from which new bearings will be taken, according to a plan of God set from all eternity.

Isaiah 52:1-12, Final Testimony

NIV

52 Awake, awake, O Zion,
clothe yourself with strength.
Put on your garments of splendor,
    O Jerusalem, the holy city.
The uncircumcised and defiled
    will not enter you again.
²Shake off your dust;
    rise up, sit enthroned, O Jerusalem.
Free yourself from the chains on your neck,
    O captive Daughter of Zion.

³For this is what the LORD says:

"You were sold for nothing,
    and without money you will be redeemed."
⁴For this is what the Sovereign LORD says:

"At first my people went down to Egypt to live;
    lately, Assyria has oppressed them.

⁵"And now what do I have here?" declares the LORD.

"For my people have been taken away
        for nothing,
and those who rule them mock,ᵃ"
                   declares the LORD.
"And all day long
    my name is constantly blasphemed.
⁶Therefore my people will know my name;
    therefore in that day they will know
that it is I who foretold it.
    Yes, it is I."

⁷How beautiful on the mountains
    are the feet of those who bring good news,
who proclaim peace,
    who bring good tidings,

ᵃ5 Dead Sea Scrolls and Vulgate; Masoretic Text *wail*

NRSV

52 Awake, awake,
put on your strength, O Zion!
Put on your beautiful garments,
    O Jerusalem, the holy city;
for the uncircumcised and the unclean
    shall enter you no more.
² Shake yourself from the dust, rise up,
    O captiveᵃ Jerusalem;
loose the bonds from your neck,
    O captive daughter Zion!

3For thus says the LORD: You were sold for nothing, and you shall be redeemed without money. ⁴For thus says the Lord GOD: Long ago, my people went down into Egypt to reside there as aliens; the Assyrian, too, has oppressed them without cause. ⁵Now therefore what am I doing here, says the LORD, seeing that my people are taken away without cause? Their rulers howl, says the LORD, and continually, all day long, my name is despised. ⁶Therefore my people shall know my name; therefore in that day they shall know that it is I who speak; here am I.

⁷ How beautiful upon the mountains
    are the feet of the messenger who
        announces peace,
who brings good news,
    who announces salvation,
    who says to Zion, "Your God reigns."
⁸ Listen! Your sentinels lift up their voices,
    together they sing for joy;
for in plain sight they see

ᵃCn: Heb *rise up, sit*

452

NIV

who proclaim salvation,
who say to Zion,
   "Your God reigns!"
[8]Listen! Your watchmen lift up their voices;
   together they shout for joy.
When the L<small>ORD</small> returns to Zion,
   they will see it with their own eyes.
[9]Burst into songs of joy together,
   you ruins of Jerusalem,
for the L<small>ORD</small> has comforted his people,
   he has redeemed Jerusalem.
[10]The L<small>ORD</small> will lay bare his holy arm
   in the sight of all the nations,
and all the ends of the earth will see
   the salvation of our God.
[11]Depart, depart, go out from there!
   Touch no unclean thing!
Come out from it and be pure,
   you who carry the vessels of the L<small>ORD</small>.
[12]But you will not leave in haste
   or go in flight;
for the L<small>ORD</small> will go before you,
   the God of Israel will be your rear guard.

NRSV

   the return of the L<small>ORD</small> to Zion.
[9]Break forth together into singing,
   you ruins of Jerusalem;
for the L<small>ORD</small> has comforted his people,
   he has redeemed Jerusalem.
[10]The L<small>ORD</small> has bared his holy arm
   before the eyes of all the nations;
and all the ends of the earth shall see
   the salvation of our God.

[11]Depart, depart, go out from there!
   Touch no unclean thing;
go out from the midst of it, purify
   yourselves,
you who carry the vessels of the L<small>ORD</small>.
[12]For you shall not go out in haste,
   and you shall not go in flight;
for the L<small>ORD</small> will go before you,
   and the God of Israel will be your
   rear guard.

COMMENTARY

This chapter is composed of four separate units. The first (52:1-3) forms a continuation of the series begun in 51:9, each unit marked with a double imperative (51:9, 17) or similar rhetorical features (51:12). Zion has risen from her stupor, induced by God's cup of wrath (51:17-23), and now she will be newly clothed in garments befitting her holy status. The garments of the iniquitous adversaries (50:9; 51:8) have their counterpart in Zion's resplendent vesture.

The final two units are closely related (vv. 7-10 and vv. 11-12). Together they constitute the finale toward which the opening heavenly council scene (40:1-11) has been inexorably moving, as the servant here faithfully concludes his comforting of Zion with a portrayal of God's promised return (40:9-11). As mentioned above, the charge to those who bear the vessels taken into exile (52:11-12) is analogous to Moses' dispatching of the priests "who carried the ark of the covenant of the L<small>ORD</small>" (Deut 31:9), just before the entrance into the promised land. The discourse does not anticipate a new law as such being delivered, but a law written on the heart (51:7; Jer 31:34), which in itself constitutes a "new" character. What is brought back from exile are not instructions from Sinai, but vessels once hauled off from a destroyed Temple, now to be restored to their former place in a comforted and resplendent Zion.

Virtually all commentators regard the unit at 52:3-6 as intrusive. Westermann is prepared to read the first half of v. 3 with the preceding unit (52:1-2), and then take vv. 4-6 as "a marginal gloss in prose linking on to the word 'for nothing' in v. 3."[125] There is a clear problem here that will be discussed further.

52:1-3. Here the judged and cleansed Zion (cf. 1:26) is charged to rise and put on glorious apparel. The contrast with the garments of adversaries consumed by moth and worm is unmistakable (50:9; 51:8). Former Isaiah's faithful city

---

125. C. Westermann, *Isaiah 40–66,* trans. David Stalker, OTL (Philadelphia: Westminster, 1969) 248.

(1:26) is here called the holy city, as at 48:2, for the servant wishes to emphasize here that with the return of God and the scattered people to Zion, the unclean and uncircumcised "shall enter you no more" (v. 1) or "again." The context for this promise is retrospective as well as prospective; Lamentations makes abundantly clear that the defilement of Zion was brought about by those enemies who "stretched out their hands over all her precious things" (Lam 1:10). This, and the blood of the righteous shed in the midst of her (Lam 4:13), rendered her unfit for God's presence. Both here and at the close of this section (Isa 52:11) there is concern to portray the rejuvenated Zion as one worthy of God's lavish attention and presence. She is a holy city again.

This language is not at odds with the promises made in chap. 56, which envisions all manner of proselytes—those who "join themselves to the LORD" (56:6)—being brought to God's holy mountain (56:7). It is a bold extension of the description found here, which wishes to insist that former uncleanness and defilement are now being done away with. How that happens involves the work of the servant, described in the unit that follows this section (52:13–53:12), hard upon the charge to "touch no unclean thing" and "purify yourselves" (52:11).

The description of Zion's captivity and yoke in v. 2 again underscores that to think of this discourse through the primary lens of "prophet among exiles in Babylon" would be to restrict the scope of the servant's message and concern.[126] Until God returns to a cleansed Zion, the entire cosmos is in bondage and captivity and exile. Verse 3 could be read as the conclusion of this brief exhortation to Zion, but only from the perspective just mentioned; the addressant is no longer Zion, but a people with a legacy of exilings. The thrust of v. 3 is consistent with earlier formulations (50:1; 45:13).

52:4-6. The first two verses here appear to offer an interpretation of the phrase "for nothing" (חנם *ḥinnām*) of v. 3. An ironic twist has been put on it. "For nothing" is taken as meaning

"gratuitously"—that is, "without cause" (באפס *běʾepes,* v. 4). Here God acknowledges the gratuitous character of the judgment Israel has endured, first (and most obviously) in Egypt, where they were only sojourners, not punished exiles, and, second, at the hands of the Assyrians. One reading "former Isaiah" could easily draw this latter conclusion on the basis of texts like 10:7 or the narrative complex in chaps. 36–37. In the oracle concerning Assyria at 14:24-27, the promise is made that "his yoke shall be removed from them, and his burden from their shoulders" (14:25; cf. 9:4). This may have provided the trigger for the reflection found here, as the bonds from captive Daughter Zion fall away in 52:2, explaining the interesting collocation of Egypt and Assyria (cf. Lam 5:6).

The interpretation of v. 5 is much more difficult. The NIV seeks a literal translation, whose thrust is captured by the more paraphrastic NRSV: The past treatment by Egypt and Assyria is trumped by the present experience of gratuitous punishment, presumably at the hands of Babylonians and others. Qumran and Aquila understand the verb in v. 5*b* as "mock" (יהללו *yěhallēlû*) rather than "wail" or "howl" (יהילילו *yěhêlîlû*), the former being "a verb used to describe the insolent folly of godless men."[127] The rulers are not Israel's, in anguish, but captors, who mock.

The final verse of the unit is extraordinarily difficult. The despised name (v. 5) will be known by God's people (v. 6*b*). Then there follows yet a second "therefore." Qumran lacks this second לכן (*lākēn*), which allows a different line division than the Masoretic one: "therefore my people will know my name on that day." This reading makes good sense. It frees the final phrase, "for I am he who is speaking; here am I," to be simply a strong conclusion from the speaker's own voice. The last word, הנני (*hinnēnî,* "here am I") could only with some difficulty apply to God, while it is a stock prophetic response (Isa 6:8; Exod 3:4). What we have here is the signature of the servant, similar in content and function to 48:16*c,* "and now the LORD God has sent me and his spirit." The servant here promises, and gives himself as surety, that the people of God will acknowledge God's vindicated name on the other side of their present affliction. The signature here, "prophetic" in character,

---

126. Duhm saw the problem here, as Torrey enthusiastically notes. His own solution—to make the language entirely figurative—creates a Hobson's choice. Zion is literally captive; and the proclamation makes complete sense when viewed from a Jerusalem perspective, not unlike, and indeed in conversation with, the book of Lamentations. See C. C. Torrey, *The Second Isaiah* (New York: Scribner's, 1928) 406.

127. Ibid., 407.

functions as an inclusio to the first one at 48:16*c*, which introduced him. Now, however, we stand at the end of the servant's discourse.

52:7-12. These six verses represent the culmination of the discourse, as this has taken its bearings from the opening charge in the heavenly council. The servant sees the heralds of good tidings appearing on the mountains, announcing to Zion that God has returned to reign. The conception of God as enthroned as king in Zion is a familiar one from the psalms (e.g., Psalms 97; 99). The recession of God's kingship would lead to chaos, the assaults of the nations, the defilement of the sanctuary, and the loss of God's own anointed one. It was against precisely this backdrop—not unlike the backdrop Psalm 89 serves for Psalms 90–106 (Book IV)—that God made the opening pronouncement in the heavenly council. The servant has stepped forward to comfort both "my people" (40:1) and "Jerusalem" (40:2), and now in his final speech he proclaims as now having arrived what God had promised.

Where once anonymous voices in the heavenly court responded to the divine announcement (40:3-8), here we have the voices of sentinels (52:8), together breaking into song. Their "eye to eye" recalls Moses; "face to face" (Deut 34:10) from a former time. "All people" were to see God's glory at Isa 40:5; the arm of 40:10-11 is what all the nations here observe (52:10), bringing with it God's victory. The depiction of v. 9, where Jerusalem's own desolated places ("ruins," חרבות *ḥārĕbôt*) sing out, is consistent with the other references that have been noted, which insist that Zion/Jerusalem is itself a wilderness, an exile, and a desert (49:19; 51:3; 52:2). The way of the Lord (40:3) has been prepared in the wilderness of Zion, with the consequence that her desolated places sing out again.

The final two verses pick up the motif with which the chapter began—namely, the insistence that the unclean and uncircumcised would not again enter God's sanctuary. That motif is partially backward-looking, for it involves the shameful violation of Zion by enemies bent on defilement. Lamentations provides one witness to this. The other is found in the Deuteronomistic History (2 Kgs 25:8-17), with the chronicler's related account (2 Chr 36:5-7). The first relates—in some detail—the inventory of vessels carried off by

Nebuchadnezzar's forces, following the burning of the Temple;[128] the latter gives brief notice only, so as to prepare for the account of Ezra 1:7-11. There it is related that Cyrus personally brought out the vessels from Nebuchadnezzar's possession, where they had been installed in "the house of his gods" (Ezra 1:7). An inventory accompanies their transfer over to proper hands for the return trip to Judah and Jerusalem (vv. 9-11).

This tradition is expressed in its own distinctive form here, where it has been collated with the original departure traditions from Egyptian, not Babylonian, bondage. The turning aside from uncleanness (סורו סורו . . . טמא אל־תגעו *sûrû sûrû . . . ṭāmēʾ ʾal-tiggāʿû*) is consistent with the concern of 52:1—"the unclean [*ṭāmēʾ*] shall enter you no more"—as is the reference to purification. The charge is not, as is sometimes assumed, made from the perspective of exile itself. The priests are commanded to "go forth from there" (צאו משם *ṣĕʾû miššām*), not "go up from here." The servant delivers a charge to those into whose care the temple vessels have been placed. They represent, as has been noted, the tokens of continuity between the former and the new times.[129] The dispatching of priests, ritually purified, bringing holy vessels into the holy city, matches the scene found on the banks of the Jordan, as this is reported in Deuteronomy 31. Neither Moses nor the servant will witness their arrival.

The reference to uncleanness is not dependent upon historical realities alone—that is, upon what it meant that the temple vessels, or those who bore them, were in a specifically unclean place (e.g., Nebuchadnezzar's "house of his gods," Ezra 1:7; cf. Dan 5:1-4). The reference is at least partly dependent on the old exodus traditions. This is made particularly evident in v. 12. "Haste" recalls the deportment necessary for the first departure, specifically in reference to the passover meal, eaten with staff in hand (Exod 12:11, "you shall eat it hurriedly. It is the passover of the LORD"). Another tradition speaks of the failure to leaven

128. Probably the Temple's interior was destroyed and rendered unfit for worship. By and large, temples were not torn down in antiquity, but were invaded and defiled by conquering armies. Restoration, then, was partly a ritual matter, partly a physical matter. See B. Halpern, "The Ritual Background of Zechariah's Temple Song," *CBQ* 40 (1978) 167-90.

129. P. R. Ackroyd, "The Temple Vessels: A Continuity Theme," in *Studies in the Religion of Ancient Israel*, VTSup 23 (Leiden: Brill, 1972) 166-81.

the bread as also involving haste (Exod 12:34, "So the people took their dough before it was leavened," NRSV); here the concern is that of the Egyptians themselves, who urged the Israelites to go, "for they said, 'We shall all be dead' " (Exod 12:33). This also provided an explanation for why the Egyptians handed over their costly jewelry, in fulfillment of God's word to Moses (Exod 3:21-22; 11:2-3).

It would be a reasonable conjecture that the concern for not touching anything unclean has been generated in part as a reflection on these older traditions. The nations are not to be plundered to build or otherwise ornament the sanctuary this time; they will themselves approach with offerings, as once did Israel in the wilderness, on the other side of the judgment in the golden calf affair (Exod 36:1-7). The theme of offering nations appears earlier at 45:14; it finds mature expression at 60:5-6, 11-13. In sum, there is no need for the returning diaspora to bother itself about anything this time, except the faithful return of holy vessels for a holy city, about to be resplendent again. God will keep watch and guard as in the wilderness, when an unruly generation was headed by God's faithful servant Moses.

REFLECTIONS

1. Does the servant make identification in this last speech, the faithful execution of the charge of 40:1-11, with God's servant Moses on the banks of the Jordan? The final verses are so clearly formed in reference to the first exodus that it is difficult to avoid the conclusion that, just as Moses dispatched the priests and his servants Joshua and Eleazar at the head of a new generation with a new possibility for life in the promised land, so also the servant found his vocation reaching its appointed end, in the context of his faithful carrying out of the mission to comfort Zion and God's people.

On one interpretive model, the prophets were isolated figures, vouchsafed powerful but also singular visions of God's will. On another model, the prophets were vigorous interpreters of traditions handed down to Israel, creatively adapted to the situation at hand. Here in the book of Isaiah we are talking about a different sort of inspiration. The servant finds himself in a "path prepared for him to walk in," as *The Book of Common Prayer* puts it. Moses' treasured experience as God's man at Israel's foundational moment echoes again here as the servant faces his own generation on the banks of the Jordan and his own premonitions as to the final point of God's hand hard on him. The servant does not step out into a void, even as he knows the episode for which he has been called to take his part has no rehearsal or opportunity at a dry run. However much we may take guidance from those who walk the path of faith before us, the time must come when we understand our own distinctive path as that which constitutes our identity and purpose, and walk by faith and not by sight.

The servant is not scanning Israel's past in the hopes of finding an appropriate role model or compass heading. He is simply obediant in the place God has called him to be, and through the lens of that obediance vistas open up that seem at once new and old. It is not that no other prophetic figure had an experience of affliction and testing; it is that this servant comprehends his experience, through his willingness to move forward into areas God will not call foresaken, in communion with these previous servants, in relationship to a whole legacy of hard-fought prophetic obedience. In that decision and in that willingness, the face of Moses rises up as the one who began it all, whose walk with God, though unequaled, was a benchmark by which other walks would be measured and, in this case, emulated to the point of overflow and transformation.

2. When identification is made of the servant with prior servants, of the Christian with the one whose name he or she bears, whose full stature represents starting point and goal, the possibility of a most unlikely stance in the midst of affliction looms large. The servant can rejoice, as did Moses before him, in the promise for a new generation he will not himself share: "How beautiful upon the mountains are the feet of the messenger who announces peace, who brings good news" (52:7 NRSV). The servant can rejoice in Zion's coming joy, can speak of sentinels who sing for joy, in the same way Moses laid hands on Joshua, filling him with the spirit of wisdom to guide a generation into a land Moses could only see from afar (Deut 34:9).

It has been held that one possible interpretation of the first line of the suffering servant poem (52:13) could yield a translation, "Behold, my servant will make wise," and that precisely this understanding has influenced the text of Dan 12:3, where those who are wise in turn "lead many to righteousness" (cf. Isa 53:11).[130] The roots of this, however, may well be traceable to Moses' transfer of the spirit of wisdom to Joshua. The servants responsible for the final suffering servant tribute understand the servant as imparting both wisdom and righteousness through his atoning sacrifice. This is their tribute in return to him, a profound response to his words of comfort and joy.

Moses is able to hear as his final words from God, "You shall not cross over there" (Deut 34:4) without resentment or anguish because of his solidarity with God's purposes (Deut 34:10). This frees him, like the servant who follows in his steps, to bestow wisdom and righteousness and joy on a new generation with equanimity and grace. The only source for that sort of empowerment is the presence of God.

This divine presence is the source of the servant's massive and memorable accomplishment, which overshadows his own identification for posterity. The text never provides such identification. The most we have, if the reading adopted in the Commentary is correct, is the old prophetic "here am I," running from Moses to Isaiah, found without fanfare at Isa 52:6. It is enough that the servant says these words at the end of his career—not at the beginning—for otherwise we would have virtually no personal signature whatsoever. About Moses' own final signature, the tradition has its own special counterpart, "No one knows his burial place to this day" (Deut 34:6 NRSV). The shrine left behind for pilgrimage is not a head marker, but the legacy of righteous, wise, faithful, privileged speech and a new generation who carried that speech forward. Such is the legacy of the servant as well, to whom can also be added an atonement that spills over and constitutes in some profound way the fulfillment of the promise, "I will give you as a light to the nations" (49:6 NRSV).

130. H. L. Ginsberg, "The Oldest Interpretation of the Suffering Servant," *VT* 3 (1963) 400-404.

ISAIAH 52:13–53:12, THE SERVANT'S ABIDING LEGACY

NIV	NRSV
[13]See, my servant will act wisely[a];	[13] See, my servant shall prosper;
he will be raised and lifted up and highly exalted.	he shall be exalted and lifted up, and shall be very high.
[14]Just as there were many who were appalled at him[b]—	[14] Just as there were many who were astonished at him[a]
his appearance was so disfigured beyond that of any man	—so marred was his appearance, beyond human semblance,
and his form marred beyond human likeness—	and his form beyond that of mortals—
	[15] so he shall startle[b] many nations;
[a]13 Or *will prosper* [b]14 Hebrew *you*	[a]Syr Tg: Heb *you* [b]Meaning of Heb uncertain

NIV

[15]so will he sprinkle many nations,[a]
   and kings will shut their mouths because
      of him.
For what they were not told, they will see,
   and what they have not heard, they will
      understand.

53 Who has believed our message
   and to whom has the arm of the LORD
      been revealed?
[2]He grew up before him like a tender shoot,
   and like a root out of dry ground.
He had no beauty or majesty to attract us
      to him,
   nothing in his appearance that we should
      desire him.
[3]He was despised and rejected by men,
   a man of sorrows, and familiar with
      suffering.
Like one from whom men hide their faces
   he was despised, and we esteemed him not.

[4]Surely he took up our infirmities
   and carried our sorrows,
yet we considered him stricken by God,
   smitten by him, and afflicted.
[5]But he was pierced for our transgressions,
   he was crushed for our iniquities;
the punishment that brought us peace was
      upon him,
   and by his wounds we are healed.
[6]We all, like sheep, have gone astray,
   each of us has turned to his own way;
and the LORD has laid on him
   the iniquity of us all.

[7]He was oppressed and afflicted,
   yet he did not open his mouth;
he was led like a lamb to the slaughter,
   and as a sheep before her shearers is silent,
so he did not open his mouth.
[8]By oppression[b] and judgment he was taken away.
   And who can speak of his descendants?
For he was cut off from the land of the living;
   for the transgression of my people he was
      stricken.[c]

[a]15 Hebrew; Septuagint *so will many nations marvel at him*   [b]8
Or *From arrest*   [c]8 Or *away. / Yet who of his generation considered / that he was cut off from the land of the living / for the transgression of my people, / to whom the blow was due?*

NRSV

kings shall shut their mouths because
      of him;
for that which had not been told them they
      shall see,
   and that which they had not heard they
      shall contemplate.

53 Who has believed what we have heard?
   And to whom has the arm of the LORD
      been revealed?
[2] For he grew up before him like a young plant,
   and like a root out of dry ground;
he had no form or majesty that we should
      look at him,
   nothing in his appearance that we should
      desire him.
[3] He was despised and rejected by others;
   a man of suffering[a] and acquainted with
      infirmity;
and as one from whom others hide
      their faces[b]
   he was despised, and we held him of no
      account.

[4] Surely he has borne our infirmities
   and carried our diseases;
yet we accounted him stricken,
   struck down by God, and afflicted.
[5] But he was wounded for our transgressions,
   crushed for our iniquities;
upon him was the punishment that made us
      whole,
   and by his bruises we are healed.
[6] All we like sheep have gone astray;
   we have all turned to our own way,
and the LORD has laid on him
   the iniquity of us all.

[7] He was oppressed, and he was afflicted,
   yet he did not open his mouth;
like a lamb that is led to the slaughter,
   and like a sheep that before its shearers
      is silent,
so he did not open his mouth.
[8] By a perversion of justice he was taken away.
   Who could have imagined his future?
For he was cut off from the land of the living,

[a]Or *a man of sorrows*   [b]Or *as one who hides his face from us*

NIV

⁹He was assigned a grave with the wicked,
　　and with the rich in his death,
though he had done no violence,
　　nor was any deceit in his mouth.

¹⁰Yet it was the LORD's will to crush him and
　　cause him to suffer,
　　and though the LORD makes*ᵃ* his life a guilt
　　　　offering,
he will see his offspring and prolong his days,
　　and the will of the LORD will prosper in
　　　　his hand.
¹¹After the suffering of his soul,
　　he will see the light ⸢of life⸣,*ᵇ* and be
　　　　satisfied*ᶜ*;
by his knowledge*ᵈ* my righteous servant will
　　　　justify many,
　　and he will bear their iniquities.
¹²Therefore I will give him a portion among
　　the great,*ᵉ*
　　and he will divide the spoils with
　　　　the strong,*ᶠ*
because he poured out his life unto death,
　　and was numbered with the transgressors.
For he bore the sin of many,
　　and made intercession for the transgressors.

ᵃ10 Hebrew *though you make*　　*ᵇ11* Dead Sea Scrolls (see also
Septuagint); Masoretic Text does not have *the light ⸢of life⸣,*.
ᶜ11 Or (with Masoretic Text) *¹¹He will see the result of the suffering
of his soul / and be satisfied*　　*ᵈ11* Or *by knowledge of him*
ᵉ12 Or *many*　　*ᶠ12* Or *numerous*

NRSV

　　stricken for the transgression of my
　　　　people.
⁹They made his grave with the wicked
　　and his tomb*ᵃ* with the rich,*ᵇ*
although he had done no violence,
　　and there was no deceit in his mouth.

¹⁰Yet it was the will of the LORD to crush him
　　with pain.*ᶜ*
When you make his life an offering for sin,*ᵈ*
　　he shall see his offspring, and shall
　　　　prolong his days;
through him the will of the LORD
　　shall prosper.
¹¹　　Out of his anguish he shall see light;*ᵉ*
he shall find satisfaction through his
　　knowledge.
　　The righteous one,*ᶠ* my servant, shall
　　　　make many righteous,
and he shall bear their iniquities.
¹²Therefore I will allot him a portion with
　　the great,
　　and he shall divide the spoil with
　　　　the strong;
because he poured out himself to death,
　　and was numbered with the transgressors;
yet he bore the sin of many,
　　and made intercession for the
　　　　transgressors.

*ᵃ*Q Ms: MT *and in his death*　　*ᵇ*Cn: Heb *with a rich person*
*ᶜ*Or *by disease*; meaning of Heb uncertain　　*ᵈ*Meaning of Heb
uncertain　　*ᵉ*Q Mss: MT lacks *light*　　*ᶠ*Or *and he shall find satisfaction. Through his knowledge, the righteous one*

COMMENTARY

It is the thesis of the present study that the chief reason for confusion in interpreting the final suffering servant poem is the failure properly to appreciate how many distinct concerns and prior contexts have been creatively merged here, to the point of overflow and seeming paradox.[131] These include, chiefly (a) the *servant* as one like Moses in suffering and expiatory death on behalf of a new generation of the people Israel; (b) the *servants* as acknowledgers of the work of the servant for Israel's collective redemption, as this has found specific expression earlier in the discourse; and (c) the portrayal by the servants of the acknowledgment of the *nations,* also as this has been anticipated within the discourse. Because this acknowledgment occurs alongside the confession of the servants as part of their own portrayal of God's fulfillment of the work of the servant, it must be assessed in conjunction with their own. In and of itself, the acknowledgment has profound theological significance, as the

131. A litany of traditional concerns can be found in summary form in H. G. Reventlow, "Basic Issues in the Interpretation of Isaiah 53," in *Jesus and the Suffering Servant: Isaiah 53 and Christian Origins,* ed. W. H. Bellinger and W. R. Farmer (Trinity Press International, 1998) 23-38.

present confession of Israel is expressed within the framework of an anticipated—one could say "eschatologically inaugurated"—confession of the nations. Thus through Israel the nations find a "voice," as Israel makes confession and acknowledges the sacrifice of the servant.

We stand at a critical juncture in the movement of the discourse. Before considering the content and structure of the poem, it is necessary to set the proper framework for hearing this extraordinary composition. Thus three aspects of this unit will be discussed: (1) its placement within the larger Isaiah text, (2) the intermingling referred to above, and (3) the role of Moses and the nations within the unit.

Placement. This poem represents the culmination of all that precedes and constitutes the decisive boundary line in the larger discourse (chaps. 40–66), as the text moves from the achievement of the servant (40:1–52:11) to the work of the servants (54:1–66:24), which is an elaboration and ramification of that prior legacy. This boundary (52:13–53:12) is every bit as significant as the final chapters of Deuteronomy, which separate the received torah and a dying generation from an ongoing and productive instruction within a new generation of Israel under new leadership. What is truly bold and without precedent, however, is the effort to think about that transition within a new set of parameters determined by God's word to the servant involving the role of the nations. For this theme there is no obvious precedent in the earlier transition from Moses to Joshua. This transition has here been creatively reconfigured, appropriate for a new dispensation, as a movement from the servant to servants, who now find themselves "among the nations," yet with both of them on the other side of a decisive boundary constituted by this tribute to the servant.

The Servant, the Servants, and the Nations. The greatest challenge of this profound tribute to the suffering servant—decisive for exegesis—involves a correct appraisal of who is speaking. Many commentators regard it as self-evident that the nations, not Israel, make the acknowledgment that lies at the heart of 53:1-12, for which 52:13-15 serves as an introduction.[132] The prob-

lem is complicated by two additional factors, beyond the simple difficulties of correctly perceiving the content and the form and the exchange of voices that characterize this complicated composition. First, we must distinguish between who has conceived and crafted the text, on the one hand, and the first-person voices that announce that they see and comprehend something they had misunderstood, on the other hand. This comprehension in turn leads to extended, direct-speech response: "He has borne our infirmities and carried our diseases" (53:4). In other words, the voices that speak up in the poem—giving it a character quite singular within the discourse thus far—are not necessarily the same voices responsible for the tribute's form and existence in the first place.

The "voices" responsible for this poem are the servant followers of the servant, who see in his death the bringing to fruition of God's design for him, that he be a "light to the nations" (42:6; 49:6). The salvation that was to reach to the ends of the earth (49:6), the preceding unit claims is on the near horizon of fulfillment (52:10b), as God bares "his holy arm before the eyes of all the nations" (52:10a). That arm has now been bared for those to whom it has been revealed (53:1). The "voices" who have constructed this dramatic text have done so in such a way that we do not have a straightforward "martyr account," with an emphasis on omniscient description and bold final speech or witness before meeting death (see, e.g., Acts 7). Instead, the authors introduce third-party witnesses (52:14) whose acknowledgment is to be occasioned by the report of the servants (chap. 53). Through this report we learn the fate of the servant, the significance of his life and death, and especially his anguish and affliction (53:1-9).

The second problem surfaces at this point, in connection with the problem of "voice" in the poem. It is a distinctive feature of the discourse thus far that while a distinction is maintained between "Israel" or "Zion," on the one side, as against "the nations," "the peoples," and "the coastlands," that distinction is being brought before a new set of divine constraints and expectations. The Commentary has carefully plotted this distinction throughout the discourse: from the summoning of hostile national challengers or their no-gods (chaps. 41–44); to the calling of Cyrus the Persian (chap. 45); to the challenge of Israel in the

132. See R. F. Melugin, *The Formation of Isaiah 40–55,* BZAW 141 (Berlin: Walter de Gruyter, 1976) 167; C. C. Torrey, *The Second Isaiah* (New York: Scribner's, 1928) 409, 411. See also M. Weippert, "Die 'Konfessionen' Deuterojesajas," in *Schopfung und Befrieung. FS C. Westermann,* ed. R. Albertz et al. (Stuttgart: Calwer, 1989) 110.

light of the potter's new pots (chaps. 45–48); to the reiteration of claims made in chaps. 40–48, e.g., "to me every knee shall bow" (45:23), now seen through the lens of the succinct word to the servant that he will be a "light to the nations, that my salvation may reach to the ends of the earth" (49:6). Although the discourse has been focused of late on the specific comforting of Zion (49:14–52:12), the servant's affliction and expected vindication have likewise been in the forefront (chaps. 50–51). We should not, therefore, be caught entirely off guard by the lengthy descriptions of anguish and ignominy found in this poem, even as they may move us in new ways.

What is fresh here, and worthy of reflection, is the coalescing of several distinctive concerns, chief among them the servant as light to the nations. This theme is treated in conjunction with an interpretation of his suffering and vindication, through the confession of servant followers, whose "voices" are the means by which we hear the anticipated voice of the nations, in recognition and acknowledgment. For all these reasons, it is important to keep the various issues at hand before us as we read this text—the nations, atoning death, the servant and the servants—for only in this way can we appreciate how they are being merged and resolved, through the form of the suffering servant composition. In other words, the "we" that speaks at 53:1 must be kept distinct from the voice from the nations. It is through Israel's voice that the nations come to find voice. The catalyst for all of this is the death of the servant who was himself "Israel, in whom I will be glorified" (49:3). In other words, there had already been a distinctive transfer at work, whereby "Israel" was embodied in the servant and his specific vocation, but without at the same time losing a mission to a Jacob/Israel whose identity and vocation remained intact. The introduction of this sort of inner-Israel distinction opened up the possibility for a fresh understanding of Israel and the nations. That possibility is exploited to its maximal potential in the suffering servant tribute.

This particular-eschatalogical dialectic, if that is the way to describe it, also accounts for why the text has remained eschatologically open in its history of interpretation. That is, the work of the servant does not end with the once-upon-a-time acknowledgment by specific Israel or generic nations. The very generality of the "we" and the very specificity of the servant's suffering and death combine to produce a text that cannot but draw into the circle of recognition and acknowledgment readers who have closely followed the discourse up to this point. We are likewise those at the "ends of the earth" (52:10) before whom the arm of the Lord is bared in the work of the servant; and the question of 53:1, "to whom has the arm of the LORD been revealed?" is directed at any and all, within Israel and without, because of the prior promises associated with his vocation, "I will give you as a light to the nations" (49:7). Here is the fitting, final tribute to the servant—one that is *not* final, but has the capacity to draw within the circle of recognition generations to come, including those who see the work of the servant once again at Calvary, when the former and new things combine so powerfully that "kings shut their mouths" (52:15; John 18:37-38).

Moses, Israel, the Nations. Attention needs to be called to one further aspect of the poem: earlier the identification of the servant with Moses, who is likewise regarded as one who bore the sins of a generation with whom he died in the wilderness (Deut 4:21-24) and whose intercession stayed an immediate judgment (Deut 9:25-29). Those same themes are clearly expressed here, for example, in the poem's final line: "yet he bore the sin of many, and made intercession for the transgressors" (53:12). Yet the servant is nowhere explicitly identified with Moses, here or earlier, but with Israel (49:3). What has happened here is that the servant's vocation as "light to the nations" has caused a modification of the older Mosaic traditions, even as much as they are evoked here. In Deuteronomy, the concern with the nations involves what they would say if an entire generation were to die in the wilderness—namely, "The LORD was not able to bring them into the land that he promised them, and because he hated them, he brought them out to let them die in the wilderness" (Deut 9:28).

Here, in contrast, the identification of the servant with Israel sets up a different, though affiliated, conception. The servant's death is reckoned as representative of Israel's death and suffering *at the hands of the nations.* Whatever justice was required in God's judgment of the people, it is also true that, as with Zion (40:1-2), they bore a punishment at the hands of the nations that was over-full, on the one hand, and misunderstood and mis-interpreted by the nations themselves, on the other hand (so the entire force of chaps. 40–48). But with the death of this individual servant, the servants depict the nations coming to an under-standing of Israel's destiny, while Israel, in its own way, also understands that this individual expres-sion of "Israel," in the servant (49:3), has effected the removal of sin, in the same way as Moses' death and intercession brought new life, for Israel. The dual mission of the servant—restoration of the survivors of Israel and as "Israel," a light to the nations (49:6)—is here confessed by the servants as fully accomplished. The accomplishment war-rants the servant's exultation and effects righ-teousness and wisdom for generations to come, including even the nations among these "many" (the term is repeated five times in the frame units; see below).

To summarize the remarks up to this point, in this poem the servants come to acknowledge the life and death of the servant, as an individual, as expiatory for themselves. But because the servant, as an individual, has understood himself as the embodiment of "Israel, in whom I will be glori-fied" (49:6), especially with a vocation to the nations, the poem functions at yet another level. The individual servant's suffering and death are Israel's on behalf of the nations. The servants let rise, in their tribute to the servant, an anticipated, astonished acknowledgment from the nations that sees as divinely purposed the servant's role both as a "light to the nations" and as the embodiment of Israel. "For that which had not been told them they shall see, and that which they had not heard they shall contemplate" (52:15).

The servant's suffering and death are his own, on behalf of the servants. At the same time, the servant's suffering and death are Israel's, on behalf of the nations. These two distinctive themes are here woven together so tightly as to refuse disen-tanglement; and in this joining consists the ser-vant's tribute of the servant as "Israel" glorified before the nations.

52:13-15. As redactionally oriented studies have noted, the first three verses resemble the form of presentation of the servant poem at 42:1-4. That is, they consist of divine speech announc-ing in formal, public terms the ultimate destiny of

the servant.[133] As such, they move temporally beyond the main body of the poem (53:1-9) to tell of the servant's ultimate exaltation. It is not likely that they were added simply to calibrate the poem with what was found at 42:1-4, since they func-tion as well in conjunction with 53:10-12. Indeed, the three-part structure of the entire unit (52:13–53:12) could be described as a main sec-tion, consisting of confession by Israel of the work of the servant, as this has taken place already (53:1-9); this in turn is placed within a frame con-sisting of divine speech, which tells of the servant's destiny (52:13-15; 53:10-12).

It is important to take note of this structure. To hear of the servant's vindication *after* the confes-sion of the servants (53:10-12) means that misun-derstanding and a cruel sentence of death are not the final word. As such, the confession of the ser-vants moves the poem in a positive direction: The confession is met by promise.

A different effect is registered in the opening unit (52:13-15). God speaks personally of the ser-vant ("behold, my servant will prosper"). We have no formal confession in respect of the servant's past action. Rather, there is an intimation of his physical treatment (v. 14), within which a promise is made about a future reaction. In other words, the exaltation promised in the opening unit is not simply fulfilled in the final unit. Rather, the open-ing unit tells of an exaltation made before the eyes of nations and kings. As stated above, moreover, the nations and kings are not the speakers in the main body of the poem. These speakers acknowledge their own share in the servant's suffering, whether that means they caused it or more simply that they were not prepared to understand or accept its providential meaning, and hence their confession and acknowledgment.

On the other hand, it would be wrong to con-clude that a distinction between the nations and the confessors in 53:1-9 is not to be found in the text at all. Verse 15 speaks explicitly about the nations coming to an understanding that hereto-fore they did not possess. The language of reversal, familiar in the preceding chapters for Israel (6:10;

---

133. See B. S. Childs, *Isaiah*, OTL (Louisville: Westminster John Knox, 2001) 412. Childs's reading is very close to that of this commen-tary. See C. R. Seitz, "How Is the Prophet Isaiah Present in the Latter Half of the Book? The Logic of Chapters 40–66 Within the Book of Isaiah," *JBL* 115 (1996) 219-40.

35:5; 43:8), is here applied to the nations as well. In this we are meant surely to see the completion of the work of the servant in his action, not toward Israel, but toward the nations, for whom he is to be a light (49:6). If we are in any doubt about this, the redactional anticipation at 49:7 makes it crystal clear: "Kings shall see and arise . . . because of the LORD, who is faithful." Here in 52:13-15, the faithfulness of God toward the servant is confirmed.[134]

At the same time, it is appropriate to keep the temporal horizons of the two framing pieces flexible, yet coordinated. The first piece speaks of an ultimate recognition by the nations, and it is a recognition that nowhere takes place within the main body of the poem. The promise of vindication after death with which the poem closes is intimately bound up with the overlap of its statements with those of the confessors in the main unit (cf. the bearing of iniquities in vv. 6 and 11 or the reference to death in vv. 9 and 12; intercession for transgressors in v. 12 and a similar notion in v. 5). The servant will be exalted in the final unit because of his work of intercession and his affliction unto death, as this has been acknowledged by the servants. Indeed, his work unto death has a future horizon, as v. 11 understands it, beyond the first circle of recognition.

What we see in the opening unit is an exaltation of the servant that entails the recognition of the nations; in that sense, it is either eschatological in character, or it is promissory and nowhere is depicted within the poem proper as having been fulfilled. It possibly resides in the existence of the confession of the servants, which is its inaugural starting point.

The language of extreme exaltation goes beyond what was said of Zion in 2:2, but the association may not be accidental. The exalting of Zion was to serve the purpose of divine action vis-à-vis the nations, and so it is here as well. What the former Isaiah spoke of on the other side of Zion's just sentence (1:25), latter Isaiah tells of in respect of God's servant. The sentence here, however, is directed toward the innocent servant, and its justice is transformed into a mystery of confession and the bearing away of sin. By this action, the nations will come to an understanding that had not been theirs before.

The language of blood sprinkling seems to appear in v. 15, but recent diachronic (historical-developmental) studies have contested any mature blood atonement theology alluded to with the (admittedly unusual) use of the verb נזה (*nzh;* NRSV, "startle"; NIV, "sprinkle").[135] For different reasons, it should be questioned whether such cultic associations can be read from a single verb within what is arguably a wisdom context (esp. the verbs "prosper" or "make wise" and "to see" and "to understand"). The nations come to the knowledge of a thing, and they gain insight because of the work God intends to do through this servant. It is a valid question to inquire, as will be done, about the cultic association found in the body of the poem, but these have to do with intra-Israelite confessions and their own distinctive theological rationale.

Before moving too quickly forward, note should be made of the immediate context of 52:7-10 and 52:11-12. The comforting of Zion happens before all the nations, as promised in 40:6. The going up high of messengers is announced in 40:9 and is alluded to again in 52:7. The going forth "from her" has in the modern period been taken to refer to Babylonian exile, a place of uncleanness (v. 11), even though the previous feminine reference is to Jerusalem (v. 10).

Could one possibility, then, be that the servant's exaltation is the higher and more final going up, which brings about what God had promised before Zion in chap. 40—brought to initial form in the commissioning of servant Israel in chap. 42, transferred to the profound mystery of the individual servant's vocation in chap. 49, and here brought to its final elevated purpose? By this purpose Zion and the servants are comforted and cleansed of all iniquity and uncleanness, and the nations bear witness to this action in fulfillment of the promises uttered thus far in the discourse.

In the context of this reference to uncleanness, we need to reconsider the proper conceptuality to bring to the main portion of the text (53:1-9). Three factors will need to be borne in mind. First, as Reventlow rightly stresses, we do not find in this text an elaborately prepared theological

---

134. Childs's view diverges here. See Childs, *Isaiah,* 413.

135. K. Elliger, *Leviticus,* HAT I, 4 (Tubingen: Mohr Siebeck, 1966) 76; B. Janowski, "Er trug unsere Sunden: Jes 53 und die Dramatik der Stellvertretung," in *Der leidende Gottesknecht,* ed. B. Janowski and P. Stuhlmacher, FAT 14 (Tubingen: Mohr-Siebeck, 1996) 27-48.

treatise on atonement or righteous suffering.[136] The text is poetic in the very basic sense of the word. That is, the confession of the servants is in the nature of the thing a discovery of something that they themselves are struggling to describe. Hence, for example, the tendency of the text to back over terrain more than once or to pile up descriptions as if searching for the proper words.

Second, and related to this, we need to consider the degree to which what is being described is a genuine *novum,* or new thing, however much the paints and brushes used to depict what is happening have a legitimate history of prior use. That is, the suffering and affliction and death of the servant, and the inner meaning of them all, gain their compelling character precisely as known categories are being combined, expanded, and, as a result, transformed. To say that the text is concerned with ritual cleanness or with juridical absolution or with the language of cultic sacrifice or with prophetic intercession (with models available in Moses, Jeremiah, Ezekiel, and others) or even with coloration from royal and priestly spheres— all these things may, indeed, be partly true. However, the death of the servant, and particularly the comprehensiveness of what is being claimed that it accomplishes, at this moment in the history of Israel and the nations expresses God's decision to deal with sin and estrangement at their most global expression. Israel sees this. The nations, when they see it, will be astounded and will shut their mouths. We must take seriously the text's own claim that it is telling us an unbelievable report, something not heard or comprehended before now (53:1).

Third, modern and ancient commentators have been right to stress the "second Moses" character of the servant's vocation. When one brackets out just what this might mean in a "second" Moses sense, what would a "first" Moses context bring with it to the text? We take our cues in part from Psalm 90, written at a time arguably close to that of the Isaiah discourse.[137] Psalm 89, which precedes, sees the death of familiar markers, the covenant with David supreme among these. We find ourselves at a time when few, if any, covenantal protections seem to provide assurance.

So, if evocations of Moses are found in the poem, then what is evoked in part is a time when kingship, prophecy, priesthood, and wisdom are yet to be differentiated in the ways we later see and have learned to distinguish from one another. If Moses is being evoked, so, too, are the later (differentiated) traditions that Israel saw united in the person of Moses. So we ought not to be surprised that it is difficult to disentangle in a "second Moses" figure traditions associated with the Jerusalem cult and the levitical blood theology; traditions associated with prophets, like Moses, who are intercessors and bear the judgment (even innocently) of the people at large; and traditions associated with wisdom and kingly rule, for prior to the monarchy and David/Solomon, even the roots of these traditions were sought in the man Moses.

So to conclude: What does this opening framing piece tell us? (1) The servant's death and expiation for the servants will finally cause the nations to see what they need to see. (2) The confession of the servants to follow (53:1-9) has its own special character inside God's plans for Israel. (3) And the horizon of the servant's work not only encloses most immediately the acknowledgment that follows (53:1-9), but also anticipates, as the nations see what the report of Israel entails, the inaugurating of all nations' coming to knowledge of the one light of Yahweh.

53:1-9. Efforts to assign these verses to the core or earliest level of tradition have foundered, for reasons provided by Reventlow and others.[138] It is not wrong, however, to see them as comprising a distinctive section. The first-person plural voice ("we") extends in measured fashion over vv. 1-6. The third-person description of the servant's affliction, such as we have it in vv. 2-3, is matched formally by vv. 7-9.

Some break down the unit into three sections, the outer two dealing with the servant's rejection (vv. 1-3 and vv. 7-9) and a middle section (vv. 4-6),

---

136. Reventlow comments: "All these uncertainties are typical of poetry. Poetry thrives on allusions, on impressions which touch the feeling, never using explicit definitions, but rather referring to a knowledge carefully hidden in the subconscious of the hearers." See H. G. Reventlow, "Basic Issues in the Interpretation of Isaiah 53," in *Jesus and the Suffering Servant: Isaiah 53 and Christian Origins,* ed. W. H Bellinger and W. R. Farmer (Harrisburg, Pa.: Trinity Press International, 1998) 30.

137. See C. R. Seitz, "Royal Promises in the Canonical Books of Isaiah and the Psalms," in *Word Without End* (Grand Rapids: Eerdmans, 1998).

138. Reventlow, "Basic Issues in the Interpretation of Isaiah 53," 30.

"which stresses the significance of the servant's suffering."[139] The more compelling structural argument, however, is for the resemblance of the framing units (52:13-15 and 53:10-12), especially with the fivefold repetition of "many" (רבּים *rabbîm*) found within them.[140] So 53:1-9 can be treated as a subsection by process of subtraction, and further internal divisions are not that consequential. Especially in the light of the fact of word repetition in general terms, the unit is clearly passing over matters in a poetic fashion and is not subject to strict rules of literary logic.[141]

Childs argues for a close connection between 53:1 and the final verse of the preceding unit, in accordance with his view that in both places one and the same group within Israel is referred to.[142] He is right to see the connection, verbally or conceptually, between the language in both verses having to do with seeing and revealing and (not) "hearing" and "report" (from the same Hebrew root [שׁמע *śm'*]). A contrast is in place here—that is, the servants who are making confession regarding the work of the servant (in 53:1-9) begin by stating that what they have come to know was not and is not in any way obvious. Their report, that which they would pass on for hearing—who, they wonder, will comprehend it? Comprehension will require the arm of the Lord revealing it, and, they ask, to whom will God reveal what they are about to report?

Verse 1 states ahead of time that the nations will—how, it is not said—hear and understand matters heretofore outside their ken. This statement exists in the realm of promise, not in the realm of blunt indicative fact. God is promising that what the servants have come to understand, which they are about to share as "our report" in the following verses, will also come to astound kings and nations. And tied up with that promise is the fulfillment of the destiny of the servant, to be the nation's light (see 49:6-7). The servants confess their massive misunderstanding of the servant's suffering and affliction in the lines that

follow. This same servant-Israel can also be described, however, as "one deeply despised, abhorred of the nations" (49:7); the servant suffers at the hands of those within Israel, but also more generally. The servants' confession can be interpreted as a template for that of the nations, though this future acknowledgment is to occur within God's providential design, and it is not worked out beyond the promise of 52:15.

The report proper begins, then, at v. 2. The language is unusual and not easily located, although many of the psalms of the suffering righteous individual can be pointed to as well as descriptions of the afflicted Zion in Lamentations. His natural growth is described as if, quite apart from any ill treatment, he was always physically unprepossessing. Very similar language is used of Jerusalem's infancy in Ezek 16:1-7, the point there being that Jerusalem was made resplendent and fetching only under the conditions of God's merciful action toward her: "Live, and grow up like a plant of the field" (Ezek 16:6-7), thus reversing her natural condition ("cast out on the open field, for you were abhorred," Ezek 16:5). The servant, in form, features, appearance, and general bearing, is undesirable.

The description intensifies in v. 3, as the phrases are heaped up in unusual fashion; four are provided in the first verse-half alone. On the one hand, the phrases emphasize how isolated he was ("cut off from humanity"; "before him faces were hidden"). They also indicate that he was sickly. On the face of it, none of this points directly to actions taken against the servant, such as we hear in 50:6-7, but to more of a matter of communal neglect and possible derision. "He was despised and we esteemed him not" captures the passive character of his afflicted condition, without stipulating further the reasons or the agents. The possessive pronouns are not attached to descriptions of his affliction, but only to the consequences of them for the "we." There are despising, rejection, sorrow, sickness, smiting (by God), wounding, bruising, chastisement, stripes, oppression, and judgment; but they are uniformly unstipulated in respect of agency (cf. 49:7). What *is* stipulated are the beneficiaries of all this.

In v. 4, the prior estimation of v. 3 is confessed as being wrong—and seriously so. And since we should not consider the repetition of phrases used

---

139. G. P. Hugenberger, "The Servant of the Lord in the 'Servant Songs' of Isaiah: A Second Moses Figure," in *The Lord's Anointed: Interpretation of Old Testament Messianic Texts,* ed. P. E. Satterthwaite, R. S. Hess, and G. J. Wenham (Carlisle: Paternoster, 1995) 114.

140. Reventlow, "Basic Issues in the Interpretation of Isaiah 53," 29.

141. P. R. Raabe, "The Effect of Repetition in the Suffering Servant Song," *JBL* 103 (1984) 77-81.

142. Childs, *Isaiah,* 413.

of the servant ("sickness" and "wounds") applied also to the "we" voices as accidental, a new effect is achieved. The servant is confessed actively to be bearing conditions that belong to the confessors, as they see it. "Surely he has borne our griefs and carried our sorrows"—that is, his natural and/or afflicted condition was made to serve the purpose of bearing something not naturally his alone, but rightly accruing to others.

Without describing the agents of his affliction, v. 5 nevertheless suggests more directly that the servant was actively (and not simply due to his natural fate), physically assaulted, hence drawing us closer to the portrayal he himself gave in chap. 50. Here, too, language drawn not simply from the physical but rather from the moral or cultic realm is directly employed. Sins and iniquities the servant is bearing are not divinely sent as warranted in his case (as v. 4 had implied), but for the sake of others. The confession of sin and iniquity is clear as it rises from the lips of the servants. Whether they were the agents of his distress or not, they are most assuredly the beneficiaries of his suffering, and this even while they had failed to comprehend it and, indeed, had regarded him as afflicted to another end altogether. No, "the LORD has laid upon him the iniquity of us all."

The final verses of this main section (vv. 7-9) move more straightforwardly in their narrative depiction. The "we" confession of sin and accompanying insight into its transference are here replaced by a blunt account of the servant's final days (in the third person). The minority position of Whybray and others regarding these verses is faulty, for reasons already rehearsed.[143] The servant dies. We are not just hearing standard phrases from the psalms about the approach to death. Such a view urges itself forward only when one judges the final description of resititution as incongruent with death. The language of this text is clear enough: There is a grave and death. There is also the momentum and acceleration of the wrongdoing, pushing beyong the compressed and intensive portrayal of vv. 1-6, whose logic moves inexorably to the final insult and ignominy: false judgment and a sentence of death. To try to remove this final episode into the realm of metaphor or figure is inconsistent with the graphic character of the description up to this point.

The variety of textual emendations on offer, especially in vv. 7-9, is wide. Nevertheless, the main force of the text, in spite of various options, is reasonably clear.[144] What comes to the fore in these verses is the violent and aggressive character of his mistreatment. Over against this is the depiction of his innocence and silence. In retrospect, it is hard now not to see the language of 42:2, "he will not cry or lift up his voice, or make it heard in the street," as being of particular moment, given the ultimate fate of the servant-Israel in this mysterious transaction of bringing instruction to the nations. He was to establish justice (42:4), and he does so by forgoing justice in his own death (53:8; NRSV, "by a perversion of justice").

The second phrase of v. 8a is rendered by the NRSV in such a way as to make the term דורו (dôrô, "his generation") the object of the verb (it would appear to have an object marker, את 'et) and so, "who could have imagined his future?" The reading preferred here takes the 'et in the sense of the RSV, "as for his generation," and continues with the question, "Who gave any regard [to him]?" The circle of his own generation did not perceive what the servants now perceive, as those "to whom the arm of the LORD has been revealed." The important point is that the death of the servant required illumination by God. Just being among the circle of the witnesses did not enhance one's powers of reception; indeed, the obverse was the case, as v. 4 makes clear: "We esteemed him smitten by God." This underscores the hope of the servants when they imagine as well the final astonishment of kings and nations, who also learn something they did not experience firsthand.

Verse 8b is elliptical in its final clause. "Cut off from the land of the living," though it can have a figural or spiritual meaning in the psalms, need not be taken as figural in Isaiah in the light of the reference to death and burial in v. 9a. What follows in the final clause in BHS is "from, by the sin of my people; blow for him." A Qumran reading has "his people," thus permitting, "there was a wound for him by the transgression of his people." But again, the general sense of unmerited death is clear in either case.

143. R. N. Whybray, *Thanksgiving for a Liberated Prophet: An Interpretation of Isaiah Chapter 53*, JSOTSup 4 (Sheffield: JSOT, 1978).

144. B. S. Childs, *Isaiah*, OTL (Louisville: Westminster John Knox, 2001) 416-17.

Verse 9 is problematical not in the sense of syntax but in its vocabulary. His grave is with the wicked. This seems consistent with the injustice thus far portrayed. Verse 9*b* reads, "with a rich person in his death," and the parallel with v. 9*a* is not so obvious (rich, but improperly gained wealth?), thus calling forth emendations to "with evil doers" or "with demons." Some take the reference as a Mosaic allusion. Israel, and a Moses who failed to maintain holiness (Deut 32:51), died in an unclean land (Amos 7:17). Just as Moses' grave was hidden in the wilderness, so also the servant's grave was with wilderness "goat-demons."[145]

The allusions to Moses can be permitted to inform our understanding of the work of the servant, as the servants seek to portray him without requiring such minute correlations, which are difficult to corroborate. The servant's death was like that of Moses, who bore the sins of a wicked generation (Num 14:26-35; Deut 4:21-22). It is also like that of Ezekiel, who, we are told, symbolically bore the punishment of the house of Israel (Ezek 4:4).[146] And yet, the servant is depicted as innocent in a way that outstrips the portrayal of Moses or Ezekiel, and in that sense it would be wrong to seek too fine a correlation beyond what is helpful for understanding the context that may function for the authors of Isaiah. Was the death of the servant viewed as the culmination of promises thought to be associated with the coming of a prophet like Moses (Deut 18:15)? That is quite likely. But more important is the more general figural link between the generation of the servants of old and these servant followers, whose task in the wake of the servant's offering will involve God's dramatic activity among the nations, with Zion as the center of God's plans for a new creation (see chaps. 54–66).

53:10-12. Verse 10 picks up the theme of the work of the servant in the future, beyond his death. The phrase "to prolong days" (v. 10*b*) may suggest a future in contrast with that of Moses,[147] though in

a poetic sense: The servant's "afterlife" in the promised land of God's new generation is assured. This afterlife has a continuity that outstrips that between even Moses and Joshua. The "seed" is clearly understood in chaps. 54–66 as the "servants." From the agony of his travail, the servants proclaim (v. 11), this innocent servant will see and know what he has accomplished and will be satisfed. How this happens, in practical terms, is not spelled out, and we must respect the text's poetic and reticent character at this juncture and not seek to fill out too much detail. What the Lord seeks to accomplish through the servant, God's delight in the power set loose by the servant to bring to proper completion (v. 10*b*), is what the text seeks to highlight.

It is from this perspective (theological-eschatological) that the reference to "offering" (אשם *'āšām*) in v. 10*a* is to be understood. To move directly from a single word into the full-orbed universe of Leviticus (esp. Leviticus 5; see also Ezekiel 40–48) is pushing things too far (leaving aside arguments for this or that dating of Israel's cultic theology).

A sharp separation between the juridical and the cultic realms, on the other hand, can also push things too far in an effort to rule out the latter.[148] This text is *sui generis* as well as indebted to a previous religious history. The servant is not obliterating sin, in the conceptual world of Leviticus; he is carrying something off, lifting it, bearing it unto himself. But there "is nothing automatic or intrinsic in the servant's act that would result in forgiveness."[149] Everywhere the text speaks of God's granting insight into the work of the servant, which points to God's authority over the "prospering" of the "power" or "capacity" of what the servant has done, both for Israel and finally for the nations. "Through him the will of the LORD shall prosper" (v. 10*b*). This prospering is to do with the accounting as right of many by virtue of the work of the one righteous servant. In this is his "*asam*" service for God.

The reference to "booty" (שלל *šālāl*) has been explained by one interpreter as a reference to the success of the "whole salvation plan of

145. E. Sellin, *Introduction to the Old Testament,* Eng. trans. of 3rd German ed. (London: Hodder and Stoughton, 1923) 143; Hugenberger, "The Servant of the Lord in the 'Servant Songs' of Isaiah," 121, 136.

146. See H. G. Reventlow, "Basic Issues in the Interpretation of Isaiah 53," in *Jesus and the Suffering Servant: Isaiah 53 and Christian Origins,* ed. W. H Bellinger and W. R. Farmer (Harrisburg, Pa.: Trinity Press International, 1998) 36-37.

147. See Hugenberger, "The Servant of the Lord in the 'Servant Songs' of Isaiah," 138.

148. Childs, *Isaiah,* 418.

149. Clements, 1993, 50; J. Kaminsky, *Corporate Responsibility in the Hebrew Bible,* JSOTSup 196 (Sheffield: Sheffield Academic, 1995).

Yahweh."[150] This is, in turn, disputed by Reventlow, who speaks of "a metaphor indicating that the servant will be integrated again into the community from which he was separated by illness and suffering" (though in a non-literal sense).[151] In the realm of second-Moses allusions, it bears notice that the term is used in Jeremiah in a similar context. The two exceptions to the judgment in Jeremiah's generation (Baruch and Ebed-Melech; cf Joshua and Caleb), we are told, will survive and retain their life as "a prize of war [*šālāl*]" (Jer 39:18; 45:5).[152] Isaiah's servant is contrasted both with Jeremiah and with Moses, even as the particular details of his sharing booty with the strong is not spelled out. He is numbered "among the saints," as it were.

The three references to "the many" (*rabbîm*; rendered "great" by the NRSV in v. 12*a*) in vv. 11*b*-12 have their counterpart in the opening frame (52:13-15).[153] Many will be made righteous (v. 11*b*). He bore the sins of many (v. 12*b*). He will have his portion among these same "many" (v. 12*a*). Many were astonished (52:14), and many nations will likewise be startled by what they come to learn (52:15). The servant is bringing to completion the "salvation plan of the LORD" and in that is his "reward."[154] It is a "booty" greater than that of generations following the great Moses or the great Jeremiah, though it is built upon the foundation of all God's servants, the prophets. The servant has, by God's grace, stood in the place of transgressors.[155] That is what it means to say that he has made intercession. This intercession outstrips what Moses or Jeremiah was called to do, within their own exalted place in the whole salvation plan of the Lord. For this reason, it is right to that the servant, shall prosper, he shall be exalted and lifted up, and shall be very high" (52:13).

---

150. H.-J. Hermission, "Das vierte Gottesknechtslied im deuterojesa-janischen Kontext," in *Der leidende Gottesknecht,* FAT 14 (Tubingen: Mohr-Siebeck, 1996) 18.

151. Reventlow, "Basic Issues in the Interpretation of Isaiah 53," 26.

152. See C. R. Seitz, "The Prophet Moses and the Canonical Shape of Jeremiah," *ZAW* 101 (1989) 1-21.

153. See Reventlow, "Basic Issues in the Interpretation of Isaiah 53," 29.

154. H.-J. Hermission, "Der Lohn des Knechts," in *Die Botschaft und die Boten, FS. H. W. Wolff,* ed. J. Jeremias and L. Perlitt (Neukirchen-Vluyn: Neukirchener, 1981) 269-87.

155. For this translation of the root פגע (*pgʿ*) at 53:12, see C. R. North, *The Second Isaiah* (Oxford: Clarenden, 1964) 203.

REFLECTIONS

1. Interpreters of the New and the Old Testament alike have called this text an "erratic block."[156] That is, it is a text that breaks through conventions and sits alone, both in what it says of itself and in its history of interpretation. Not until the New Testament does the text gain the sort of sustained hearing it has come to have in association with Christian articulation of the gospel, the death of Jesus Christ, and the meaning of this death for Israel and the whole world.

This interpretation seems right. The text even says about itself that it consists of a report that is astounding: "Who has believed what we have heard?" (53:1). The work of the servant required God's illumination to lift it out of the realm of brute facts and into the realm of saving providence. Otherwise, it was just another death among deaths, another case of picking on the weak and undesirable, another instance of some good man going wrongly to the grave, done in by a corrupt justice system.

In a memorable statement, Leander Keck once said of the crucifixion of Jesus, "All three men were equally dead by sundown."[157] One of those men claimed nothing for himself and threw himself on Jesus' mercy. The other chided Jesus. But all three were dead by sundown.

---

156. The term is that of Klaus Koch, "Suhne und Sundenvergebung um die Wende von der exilischen zur nachexilischen Zeit," in *Spuren des hebraischen Denkens: Beitrage zur alttestamentlichen Theologie* (Neukirchen-Vluyn: Neukirchener, 1991) 203. It appears in the English translation of H. G. Reventlow, "Basic Issues in the Interpretation of Isaiah 53," in *Jesus and the Suffering Servant: Isaiah 53 and Christian Origins,* ed. W. H Bellinger and W. R. Farmer (Harrisburg, Pa.: Trinity Press International, 1998) 31, who says it continues, "an erratic block [which] remained behind without being understood until the days of the New Testament." For a discussion of this issue, see W. H. Bellinger and W. R. Farmer, eds., *Jesus and the Suffering Servant: Isaiah 53 and Christian Origins* (Harrisburg, Pa.: Trinity Press International, 1998), in which Reventlow's essay appears. See also B. S. Childs, *Isaiah,* OTL (Louisville: Westminster John Knox, 2001) 420-23.

157. L. Keck, *A Future for the Historical Jesus: The Place of Jesus in Preaching and Theology* (Nashville: Abingdon, 1971).

It was not the first crucifixion, nor by any means was it the last. In a line that stretches from Abel to Auschwitz, and from there until God is all in all, innocent women and men will be put to death. They will suffer and die in mundane and forgotten circumstances, and they will suffer and die with the heat of religious lights and moral certainty pouring down on them (surely he was "struck down by God").

There are occasions when, due to the plan of God, things come to a certain boil and a situation of outrageous injustice becomes a lens onto eternity itself. In Isaiah 53, we have a poignant and powerful scene of injustice. But we also have promises put into the air by God concerning a "light to nations," concerning prophets like Moses, concerning the gathering back of Israel (cf. 49:5), and concerning the forgiveness of sin. What we could not have known was how God would bring out of all this suffering some sort of issue deserving the claim of divine purpose and stewardship.

But that is what lifts this scene of injustice out of the line stretching from Abel to Calvary and beyond. God provided ahead of time all the ingredients necessary, so that when this event occurred, the capacity to see something in it, precisely in its status as an "erratic block," would be there. The report got written, even though a generation had got it wrong at first. The report got written, and it was not tragic because God had the final word, and that final word included even the promise that, not just us, but the servant himself saw something of God's purpose within his agony and was satisfied.

2. It is important to keep this in view when we consider the New Testament portrayal of Jesus' death. John seems to reach a crescendo where we may not suspect it. When does the dramatic moment occur? When Jesus cries out, "It is finished"? When the God who was silent spoke and raised Jesus from the dead? When Thomas came to faith or when those who were not there were blessed and came to faith through what they received in testimony, beyond the circle of the Twelve? Each of these episodes belongs, of course, to one connected "climax"; it would be artificial to pose the question too sharply in the manner I have done.

But surely one can hear the drum roll especially loudly and deeply when John reports the handling of Jesus' corpse. The soldiers do not break his legs; he was dead already. They pierce his side, and out comes blood and water. John gathers himself and says, "He who saw it has borne witness—his testimony is true, and he knows that he tells the truth—that you also may believe. For these things took place that the scriptures might be fulfilled" (John 19:35-36 RSV). And then he quotes from the book of Psalms and from Zechariah.

The death of Jesus was provided an interpretation—by Jesus himself—ahead of time. This is especially true in John, but it is also true of the Synoptics. Jesus said plainly that he would die. He also spoke of giving his life as a ransom (Mark 10:45).

But when it comes to the dramatic moment itself, those who offer their astonishment see this death as having been calibrated from before the foundations of the world. And the way they make that clear is by the insight given them out of the depth of Israel's scriptures. No exegetical technique reveals this. No special reading glasses provided by earned knowledge or piety bring it to light. The use of Old Testament texts to "prove" that Jesus died to such and such a purpose, for rational debate does not get to the heart of the matter.

As with the servant, God provides illumination by bringing what God has said and promised into a specific congruence in time and space, under temporal judgment, catalyzed by the obedience of the servants, including finally God's own Son and our Savior. We can see into the mystery of Jesus' death and resurrection, as did those first witnesses, because God has provided a testimony ahead of time, which will be used to interpret and illuminate and, indeed, guarantee the exaltation of God's servant.

And a deeper truth is exposed in this "former/latter" congruence: The grasping of what is going on in Jesus' death, or in the servant's death before him, does not require us to be first witnesses, to be there on the spot. Indeed, had we been there, we likely would have gotten it wrong. The scriptures, because they are God's word, are commandeered by God to further the divine purpose. They can communicate what God intends, because about God's word it can be said that it accomplishes what God purposes (Isa 55:11). Isaiah sets forth this truth and shows it coming to pass in the report concerning the servant. The report, in turn, promises an ultimate recognition by the nations. All these things have their purpose in their own day, but they also serve a larger purpose in setting the stage for the dramatic finale of all time: Jesus' death before Israel and kings and nations. Any Gentile who saw into the mystery of Jesus' death was foreseen by the record of Israel's witness. Such Gentiles were our forerunners from outside the covenants. We all come now, from Israel or from the nations, to see the truth of this death for us as a fulfillment, a filling to the full, of God's accomplishing word from Isaiah.

3. The form of Isaiah 53 is striking. It is a connected narrative. It has movement and drama. It is much longer than the other so-called servant songs. It repeats and doubles back. It contains a variety of voices.

In the report about the servant's death, the witnesses state certain truths that they are absolutely convicted of. The propositions, if such they are (e.g., "the LORD laid on him the iniquity of us all"), arise out of a passionate rehearsal of a truth that has grasped them, not one that they are grasping. God has acted in such a way as to convict them of the fragility of any assumptions they, once upon a time, held so boldly and unswervingly; and God has raided their sensibility and intellect in the work of the servant, transforming and baptizing them toward the deepest perception of divine truth and intention. So now, within the report they give, the witnesses speak of the truth that has come upon them and loosed their tongues for a different sort of report than they had ever before given.

This is surely the way the gospel, in the Old Testament and in the New Testament, communicates its truth. It takes hold of us and changes us. It defeats old notions and first impressions. It gets inside our very bones. It shakes us and shows us ourselves in a new light—not so that we can turn back on ourselves and rejoice at the space we have moved, but so that we might be free to look on God anew, know God as our Savior, and trust God's continual working in our lives because of what was done for us in the servant.

There are times when we must simply surrender because we can find no way forward without God's grace and truth. There are times when we must surrender because the ways we have chosen to go bear only God's judgment, and we know that. But there are also times when we must surrender because God has laid hold of us so dramatically that we can scarcely do else. When this happens, the speech we get is directly from God. It comes upon us and shows us a truth we never before could have entertained. And then our tongue is free for confession and release; our sins do not overwhelm us because we can see them clearly and report them freely, because they have been clearly and freely taken away from us and laid upon another.

How we go about providing additional witness is another question. God surely has a hand in that task as well, as our individual testimony is fitted within with the testimony of saints and martyrs, living and dead, our community of fellowship. But such witness is never a substitute for the passionate rehearsal, and it always flows from it in one direction. We may not be able to say what it means for sin to be taken up and removed and placed upon another, but we can say that it has happened and that we are free. And perhaps the surest testimony to this being grasped by God is the awareness that what has happened for us in Christ or for Israel in the servant is not about us only, but means to spill out into every corner of time and space and lay hold of every creature God has made. When we can see everyone, all people from highest to lowest estate, as potential speakers forth of God's praise, as they are grasped by what God has done so surely in us, then we can be sure that the work of God is abroad. Our God seeks to do mighty things, and in the single acts of divine forgiving mercy is every such act in every time and in every place, until God is all in all.

VINDICATION OF THE SERVANT BY GOD

OVERVIEW

The remaining chapters of the book of Isaiah are concerned with demonstrating God's vindication of the servant, as promised in 52:13–53:12. Yet this vindication does not happen in any straightforward way. The composers of this material have understood the resolution of the servant's life and death in a transformed and specific way. At the center of this transformation stands the figure of Zion.

It is to be noted, therefore, that following hard upon the final report and confession concerning the servant, the topic shifts to Zion. She, too, is afflicted and "storm-tossed" (54:11), as was the servant. Where the suffering servant poem spoke of the servant's "seeing offspring" (53:10), it is Zion who actually gives birth to this righteous progeny (54:3), "taught by the LORD" (54:13) as was the servant (50:4), as was Isaiah's own righteous remnant (8:16). The servant was to be "exalted, lifted up, very high" (52:13)—signs of his exaltation, intended, among other things, to convict the nations (52:15). In the presentation of chaps. 54–66, the servant has become a figure of the past, as he now lives on in the righteous deportment of the servants. But the actual destiny God had described as his is in some measure envisioned through the destiny of Zion, the afflicted one who is comforted and vindicated (chap. 54), the one to whom the nations stream (chap. 60), high and lifted up for the ends of the earth to see (62:10-12).

The pressure for this transformation, if we are entitled to so describe it, may be due in part to the testimony of Isaiah 1–39. The promise that the nations would stream to the Lord's house, "established as the highest of the mountains" (2:2), for the "instruction" (תורה *tôrâ*) of Zion (2:3) is a foundational theme in early Isaiah chapters (see esp. chap. 33). The servant was to "see offspring" according to the promise of 53:10 and "make many righteous" (53:11). It is Zion who becomes the means of that procreation, as chap. 54 depicts it. The fate of the servants, followers of the servant, is intimately bound up with the fate of Zion (54:13-17). Even foreigners who join themselves to the Lord and keep covenant can earn the right to be called servants of God (56:6). The various promises associated with the servant in chaps. 40–53, and especially in the final tribute (52:13–53:12), concerning the nations, the making righteous of a community (רבים *rabbîm*, "many"), and the vindication of an offspring are tied up in chaps. 54–66 with the destiny and exaltation of Zion, in fulfillment of promises associated with Isaiah of Jerusalem.

Yet almost right away, we are brought up against a characteristic feature of these final Isaiah chapters: the presence of intra-community conflict. Even chap. 54, which is part of a programmatic introduction (54:1–56:8), with all its enjoyment of Zion's beautification, understands this finally against a backdrop of hostility and challenge—for the city and for the servants (54:14-17). Chapter 55 likewise issues a warning to the wicked and the unrighteous (55:6-9). The exhortatory tone of 56:1-2 has long been noted, as the controversial notion of foreigners gaining access to God's house of prayer is introduced. In sum, even this first opening section, connected by reference to the term ברית (*běrît*, "covenant"; 54:10; 55:3; 56:6), for Zion, for her children, and for foreigners keeps before our eyes the presence of conflict within the community.

The next section runs from 56:9 to 59:21. Characteristic of it is the opposition of two distinct progenies.[158] Over against the proper banquet at

---

158. See W. A. M. Beuken, "The Main Theme of Trito-Isaiah: 'The Servants of Yahweh,' " *JSOT* 47 (1990) 69-70.

Zion, described in chap. 55, we find a drunken, adulterous, idolatrous orgy (56:7–57:21). Alongside this, however, are appeals to proper conduct and promises of God's sure vindication for those who are faithful (57:14–58:14). The section ends with a call for repentance and a description of God's own personal intervention (59:1-20). The final notice reminds us of the presence of a righteous cadre within Israel's midst, as the covenant language returns with a vengeance (59:21).

Virtually all commentators read chaps. 60–62 as a collection, some treating it as the very core proclamation of the prophet and its originating germ. What we have here is a reiteration of the promises associated with Zion, now reasserted against the backdrop of obvious intra-community strife. In glorious language, virtually unsurpassed in expressions of hope and vindication, as the nations lavish treasures on God's married spouse, we are told again of Zion's triumph. Chapter 61 stands as a representative speech for any and all who possess God's spirit among the righteous servants. It is a speech replete with language familiar from other sections of Isaiah 40–53, and one gets the sense of an ideal figure here, the true culmination of what God had in mind in the servant. The theme of Zion's vindication is taken up again in chap. 62, with the added dimension of the nearness of that action. Sentinals have been posted on the walls (62:6); the reward and recompense of God for Zion, recalling 40:11, is again on the moment of fruition (62:11).

In the next section (63:1–64:12), God does,

indeed, put in an appearance, as the watchmen detect the presense of the divine warrior, returned from battle and announcing vindication (63:1-6). The defeat of Edom, as described in Isaiah 34, was to be emblematic of his victory over all national forces hostile to Zion. Yet at this point in the presentation, a deeply ironic turn seems to be taken. The victory over Edom appears to give rise to thanksgiving (63:7-9), as God's gracious deeds of old are recalled when Israel's enemies were defeated. Yet this line of reflection leads, for the author, to a recognition that God also treated Israel as an enemy, having grieved God's holy spirit (63:10); this reads like exegesis of Isa 1:24. God's faithfulness to Israel in the past only serves to shame Israel in the present, and the people lament their sorry condition (63:10-19). This communal lament, as it has been termed, continues up to the close of chap. 64.

God's response to this lament forms the content of the following chapter (chap. 65). The vindication of Zion and the servants that God has in mind is a far more dramatic, apocaplyptic deliverance than what has as yet been described. The curses of Gen 3:14-19 are revoked (Isa 65:23-24), and the fulsome promises of Isa 11:6-9 are recalled and interspersed with this new creation hope. The final chapter maintains this vision within the context of God's righteous judgment. One can also note the resurfacing of older Isaianic prophecies from the earlier sections of the book as the chapter accomplishes a sort of inclusio finale.

❖   ❖   ❖   ❖

EXCURSUS: "THIRD ISAIAH"

A "Third Isaiah" was necessitated, for various reasons, once a "Second Isaiah" took his place beside Isaiah of Jerusalem. It is worth examining those reasons briefly, as we will be working with a different model in this commentary. It is not clear which of the various reasons ought to be given greater priority; in some sense, they are interrelated.

I have questioned the notion of an exilic (Babylonian) provenance for the material treated thus far, and it should not be necessary to cover that ground again here. Yet insofar as the material of chaps. 40–55 was located by critics in Babylon, the references to life in Judah found in chaps. 56–66 required some explanation—if only that "the prophet of the exile" had at last found his way home. In fact, this particular way of understanding the geographical change never caught on.[159] Rather, a new and different prophetic voice at work in Judah was argued for.

---

159. See a modern version of this older theory in Jurgen van Oorschot, *Von Babel zum Zion* (Berlin: Walter de Gruyter, 1993), for whom movement from Babylon to Judah takes place already in chaps. 40–55.

That prophetic voice was far more concerned with cult and matters priestly, according to Duhm.[160] The prophet was a writer, not a speaker; concerned with heresy, not promises; dogmatic, not realistic, and so forth. In sum, for Duhm and others, no sharper contrast could exist between the content and the proclamation of "Second Isaiah" and "Third Isaiah."[161]

The final matter to be determined was where this distinctive prophetic legacy began. As we have seen, various literary arguments conspired to see that boundary at chapter 56. Chapter 55 was regarded as an epilogue to the prologue of 40:1-11. Melugin summarizes the argument this way: "The collection ends, then, as it begins. It is fitting that the collection ends with assertions about the reliability of Yahweh's word (55:10-11) and a promise of the exodus (v. 12-13)."[162]

It should be noted that within chaps. 56–66 there is a good deal of material—esp. chaps. 60–62—that has rightly been viewed as quite close in content and message to what we find in chaps. 40–55. This similarity should be mentioned, as it makes it all the more necessary to establish the notion of a distinct boundary. Otherwise, what lies at the middle section could be too easily conformed with the thrust of what proceeds in chaps. 40–55.

But what problems arise with the theory? Some have noted that, strictly speaking, a far more suitable epilogue can be argued for at 52:7-12.[163] Some recent commentators have seen the close association that exists between chaps. 55 and 56.[164] Both chapters speak of a covenant (55:3; 56:4). In both, the nations come to Israel (55:5; 56:6). Beuken has especially drawn attention to the fact that the proper banquet introduced in chap. 55 has its clear counterpart in the corrupt banquet of 56:9–57:21.[165] Furthermore, the final verses of chap. 54 (54:14-17) are far from being free of a sense of tension within the community. Like chaps. 55 and 56, chap. 54 makes reference to a covenant (54:10). Even more important, what unites chaps. 54–66 is the preference for the plural form "servants," the first reference appearing in 54:17.[166] Finally, only in chap. 54 is Zion "married"—an image that is fully consistent with the perspective to follow (62:4).[167] Perhaps forgotten in the present climate is Karl Elliger's learned, detailed argument in favor of taking both chap. 54 and chap. 55, on linguisitic and stylistic grounds, as part of the contribution of his own version of "Third Isaiah."[168] From a different methodological climate, I concur with Elliger's judgment.

The notion that "Third Isaiah" alone is concerned with intra-community disputes is one mentioned as faulty above. Especially noteworthy in this regard is 50:10-11. The very fact that suffering occurs in connection with the work of the servant—whether at the hands of Israel or others—implies that we are in a situation of conflict that would not leave the community untouched in some way, already within the compass of chaps. 40–53. What accounts for the sharp expression of conflict within these final chapters is a distinction between the servants— followers of the servant of Isaiah 40–53—and their unrighteous opponents. Only with the death of the servant and the (contested?) claims made about that death does the possibility open up for yet sharper disagreement within the community. This disagreement is most clearly manifested at 65:13-15 as consisting of a dispute between "the servants" and others; yet it is also clearly anticipated, as Beuken has shown, in 56:9–57:21.

160. Duhm termed him "a theocrat of purest ilk." See B. Duhm, *Das Buch Jesaia,* HKAT (Göttingen: Vandenhoeck & Ruprecht, 1892) 390.

161. See C. R. Seitz, in *The Anchor Bible Dictionary,* 6 vols., ed. D. N. Freedman (Garden City, N.Y.: Doubleday, 1992) 3:490-501.

162. R. F. Melugin, *The Formation of Isaiah 40–55,* BZAW 141 (Berlin: Walter de Gruyter, 1976) 174.

163. See M. A. Sweeney, *Isaiah 1–4 and the Post-Exilic Understanding of the Isaianic Tradition,* BZAW 171 (Berlin: Walter de Gruyter, 1988); Beuken, "The Main Theme of Trito-Isaiah."

164. J. van Oortschot, *Von Babel zum Zion,* BZAW 206 (Berlin: Walter de Gruyter, 1993); C. Westermann, *Isaiah 40–66,* OTL (Philadelphia: Westminster, 1977).

165. W. A. M. Beuken, "Isa. 56:9-57:13—An Example of the Isaianic Legacy of Trito-Isaiah," in *Tradition and Re-interpretation in Jewish and Early Christian Literature,* ed. J. W. Van Henten et al. (Leiden, 1986) 48-64.

166. See Beuken, "The Main Theme of Trito-Isaiah," 67-87.

167. I am grateful for the paper of Kathryn Schifferdecker, "Zion and Servant: Context and Function of Isaiah 54" (unpublished).

168. Karl Elliger, *Deuterojesaja in seinem Verhaltnis zu Tritojesaja* (Stuttgart: Kohlhammer, 1933) 135-67.

Since this commentary regards the report and confession of 52:13–53:12 as the work of the servant followers of the servant, then their contribution can properly be regarded as beginning there. But as this report brings to a close the preceding chapters, it is best regarded as the centerpiece of chaps. 40–66; therefore, chap. 54 is the opening chapter, as it were, of the final section of the book.

It should be mentioned, as well, that various theories have been put forward as to the time gap separating "Second" and "Third" Isaiah—at a minimum, sufficient time for the people of Israel to have made their way home from exile. In the model proposed here, there is no time gap whatsoever. With the death of the servant, the servants' work begins. As for the status of the Temple, what we learn in these chapters is not clear. Very little mention is actually made of the Temple, which is odd under the circumstances attending the usual dating scenarios. Most of the language involves Zion's beautification, and most of it is hyperbolic, poetic, and eschatological, not concrete (cf. Ezra–Nehemiah). Where concrete reference is made, the sanctuary is described as "trampled down," on one occasion (63:18); apparently not to be built, on another (66:1); and (presumbly) intact on yet another (56:5). These passages need to be looked at in their context. Suffice it to say here that the final chapters speak in great and lavish detail about Zion's marriage and beautification, but this provides us with practically no information at all about the actual temple structure itself.

❖   ❖   ❖   ❖

ISAIAH 54:1-17, THE HERITAGE OF THE SERVANTS

NIV

54 "Sing, O barren woman,
     you who never bore a child;
burst into song, shout for joy,
     you who were never in labor;
because more are the children of the
          desolate woman
than of her who has a husband,"
                         says the LORD.
2"Enlarge the place of your tent,
     stretch your tent curtains wide,
     do not hold back;
lengthen your cords,
     strengthen your stakes.
3For you will spread out to the right and to
          the left;
     your descendants will dispossess nations
     and settle in their desolate cities.

4"Do not be afraid; you will not suffer shame.

NRSV

54 Sing, O barren one who did not bear;
     burst into song and shout,
          you who have not been in labor!
For the children of the desolate woman will
          be more
     than the children of her that is married,
          says the LORD.
2 Enlarge the site of your tent,
     and let the curtains of your habitations be
          stretched out;
     do not hold back; lengthen your cords
     and strengthen your stakes.
3 For you will spread out to the right and to
          the left,
     and your descendants will possess
          the nations
     and will settle the desolate towns.

4 Do not fear, for you will not be ashamed;

NIV

Do not fear disgrace; you will not be
    humiliated.
You will forget the shame of your youth
    and remember no more the reproach of
        your widowhood.
⁵For your Maker is your husband—
    the LORD Almighty is his name—
the Holy One of Israel is your Redeemer;
    he is called the God of all the earth.
⁶The LORD will call you back
    as if you were a wife deserted and distressed
        in spirit—
a wife who married young,
    only to be rejected," says your God.
⁷"For a brief moment I abandoned you,
    but with deep compassion I will bring
        you back.
⁸In a surge of anger
    I hid my face from you for a moment,
but with everlasting kindness
    I will have compassion on you,"
    says the LORD your Redeemer.

⁹"To me this is like the days of Noah,
    when I swore that the waters of Noah
        would never again cover the earth.
So now I have sworn not to be angry with you,
    never to rebuke you again.
¹⁰Though the mountains be shaken
    and the hills be removed,
yet my unfailing love for you will not
    be shaken
    nor my covenant of peace be removed,"
    says the LORD, who has compassion on you.

¹¹"O afflicted city, lashed by storms and
        not comforted,
    I will build you with stones of turquoise,ᵃ
    your foundations with sapphires.ᵇ
¹²I will make your battlements of rubies,
    your gates of sparkling jewels,
    and all your walls of precious stones.
¹³All your sons will be taught by the LORD,
    and great will be your children's peace.
¹⁴In righteousness you will be established:
    Tyranny will be far from you;
        you will have nothing to fear.

ᵃ11 The meaning of the Hebrew for this word is uncertain.   ᵇ11
Or lapis lazuli

NRSV

do not be discouraged, for you will not
        suffer disgrace;
for you will forget the shame of your youth,
    and the disgrace of your widowhood you
        will remember no more.
⁵For your Maker is your husband,
    the LORD of hosts is his name;
the Holy One of Israel is your Redeemer,
    the God of the whole earth he is called.
⁶For the LORD has called you
    like a wife forsaken and grieved in spirit,
like the wife of a man's youth when she is
        cast off,
    says your God.
⁷For a brief moment I abandoned you,
    but with great compassion I will
        gather you.
⁸In overflowing wrath for a moment
    I hid my face from you,
but with everlasting love I will have
        compassion on you,
    says the LORD, your Redeemer.

⁹This is like the days of Noah to me:
    Just as I swore that the waters of Noah
        would never again go over the earth,
so I have sworn that I will not be angry
        with you
    and will not rebuke you.
¹⁰For the mountains may depart
    and the hills be removed,
but my steadfast love shall not depart
        from you,
    and my covenant of peace shall not
        be removed,
    says the LORD, who has compassion
        on you.

¹¹O afflicted one, storm-tossed, and not
        comforted,
    I am about to set your stones in antimony,
    and lay your foundations with
        sapphires.ᵃ
¹²I will make your pinnacles of rubies,
    your gates of jewels,
    and all your wall of precious stones.
¹³All your children shall be taught by the LORD,

ᵃOr lapis lazuli

NIV

Terror will be far removed;
    it will not come near you.
[15]If anyone does attack you, it will not be
        my doing;
    whoever attacks you will surrender to you.

[16]"See, it is I who created the blacksmith
    who fans the coals into flame
    and forges a weapon fit for its work.
    And it is I who have created the destroyer to
        work havoc;
[17]   no weapon forged against you will prevail,
    and you will refute every tongue that
        accuses you.
This is the heritage of the servants of the LORD,
    and this is their vindication from me,"
                        declares the LORD.

NRSV

and great shall be the prosperity of your
    children.
[14]In righteousness you shall be established;
    you shall be far from oppression, for you
        shall not fear;
    and from terror, for it shall not come
        near you.
[15]If anyone stirs up strife,
    it is not from me;
    whoever stirs up strife with you
        shall fall because of you.
[16]See it is I who have created the smith
    who blows the fire of coals,
    and produces a weapon fit for its purpose;
    I have also created the ravager to destroy.
[17]   No weapon that is fashioned against you
        shall prosper,
    and you shall confute every tongue that
        rises against you in judgment.
This is the heritage of the servants of
    the LORD
    and their vindication from me, says
    the LORD.

COMMENTARY

In the opening heavenly council scene, the charge went forth to "speak tenderly to Jerusalem" (40:2). Zion has been promised comfort (51:3). Sons and daughters were to be returned to her (49:22). The servant's final words to Zion, as these are recorded in the epilogue of 52:7-12, are words of comfort and restitution as God returns to Zion. Now here, on the other side of the servant's death, the servants take up where the servant left off. God not only returns to Zion but also takes Zion as wife (54:5) and promises many, many offspring (54:1-3). The new generation, set free by the servant's death, here take possession of their promised land, Zion. "This is the heritage of the servants of the LORD, and their vindication from me, says the LORD" (54:17).

There is general agreement that the chapter is composed of several subunits, though whether these are traceable to originally independent speech forms is a matter of scholarly assessment. A fairly distinctive break would appear to fall at the end of v. 10 with the words "says the LORD, your comforter." Less-pronounced breaks may appear at the end of v. 3 and v. 8, the former closing off the opening appeal (vv. 1-3), the latter setting up the comparison with the Noachic judgment that follows (vv. 9-10). But by and large the movement of the poem is clear and without disjunction.

The final unit (vv. 11-17) is somewhat more complicated. Zion is addressed. Promises are made to her. Yet there is the clear anticipation of strife and challenge, not unlike what she had formerly endured. Only now, God promises, such assault will come to nought. Form-critically, the oracle is an assurance of salvation.

54:1-3. The notion of large-scale, unexpected progeny can be traced to 50:20-21, though there we hear only of their number, not the actual place of their abode. Here the image of the tent, spread out broadly and staked down, comes into play. The author may be aware of the tradition associated with descriptions of Zion in chap. 33:

Look on Zion . . . an immovable tent,
whose stakes will never be pulled up,
    and none of whose ropes will be broken.
(33:20 NRSV)

Promises associated with Zion in chap. 33, are now coming to fruition. The reference to many descendants (רבים *rabbîm,* v. 1) may pick up the promise made to the servant in 53:11 that he would make many (לרבים *lārabbîm*) righteous. Surely a connection is implied between 53:10 and 54:3, where the key word זרע (*zera',* "seed," "offspring," "descendants") is repeated. The legacy of the servant in respect of the many who have been vindicated and the promise of an ongoing generation are here realized in Zion's children.

54:4-8. Here the painful past is mentioned and acknowledged for what it was: a time of shame, disgrace, and derision. The double reference to shame and the mention of youth evoke the memory of the faithful city gone awry in chap. 1: "you shall be ashamed of the oaks in which you delight" (1:29), the city of Isaiah's time. If this is the case, it is not just the state of childlessness that causes Zion anguish and shame or the (seeming) loss of her husband—but the derision and shame that accompanied actual apostasy and unfaithfulness, precisely of the sort referred to in chap. 1. There God's eyes are hidden and God's ears are closed (1:15); here reference is made to God's having hidden God's face (54:8). "Overflowing wrath" (54:8) has its counterpart in 1:24-25. Yet all this simply forms a strong contrast with God's present decision: to gather, to love, to comfort, to declare the deity as husband.

54:9-10. Then God reaches even further back in the dealings with an unjust and corrupt creation, to the time of Noah and the flood. Reference to Zion's husband as "the God of the whole earth" at v. 5 finds its correlate in God's general relationship with creation before the call of Abraham. We know from the psalms that God's founding of Zion can be regarded as a primordial event not unlike any other signal act of creation (Ps 93:2; cf. Ps 50:1-2). The floodwaters of chaos that threatened creation—and became the means of judgment in the time of Noah—also lift up their voice against God's habitation in Zion (Ps 93:3-4; cf. Ps 46:1-5). Yet here God insists that no threat can harm special Zion; the former anger and rebuke (again see

chap. 1) are gone for good now. The final verse of the unit (v. 10) is reminiscent of Psalm 46: the "habitation of the Most High" will not be moved, "though the earth should change, though the mountains shake" (Ps 46:2, 4). This special relationship with Zion is called "my covenant of peace" (54:10). In sum, the sort of permanent defense and protection by God of Zion that is assumed in the book of Psalms, if undone by Zion's apostasy, is here again asserted.

Use of the term ברית (*běrît,* "covenant") here, specifically directed to God's relationship with Zion, has its counterpart in 55:3 and 56:4 concerning the people who hearken and those who keep sabbath, respectively. Its appearance can also be explained in the context of the foregoing remarks about Zion's status. In chaps. 24–27, the depiction of destruction in the earth, caused by God's judgment, is likened to a breaking of "the everlasting covenant" (24:5)—that is, a return to the chaos against which the Noachic covenant was to have been an earnest. Here God reasserts the promise that waters of chaos may remove mountains and hills, but not Zion. The "covenant of peace" will not be removed. In this is constituted God's marriage vows to Zion.

54:11-17. In this final unit the horizon of the proclamation to Zion is enlarged a bit so that the effect of God's protection of her might be spelled out for her children as well. What begins as a lavish description of Zion's adornment, appropriate more for a bride than for a city built with human hands, shifts quickly to take into account her children.

We might recall that in 50:1, Zion is sold into bondage on account of her children's trangressions. The relationship between the people of God and Zion is a fractured and unhappy one. Here that relationship is explored in exactly the opposite terms. Now it is the case that Zion's divine protection will serve to resist any assault. Verse 14 asserts that Zion has become the righteous city promised in 1:26: "afterward you shall be called the city of righteousness." Chapter 1 had envisioned assaults from God meant to cleanse and remove all alloy (1:25). The agents of that judgment were the nations. God reasserts divine control over all national force (vv. 16-17), but now to the effect that Zion's status is enhanced, not threatened. Strife will exist as before. But now it will be fully under God's control, with positive consequences for Zion. Zion's dross was removed in its former judgment; it is time for her to enjoy new status as God's chosen bride.

Chapter 1 had also spoken, in the context of Zion's cleansing, about her citizens and their future beyond judgment (1:26). Here those citizens are described as Zion's children, "taught by the LORD" (54:13). The phrase "taught by the LORD" (למודי יהוה *limmûdê YHWH*") has enormous significance, not least when considered against the descriptions of Zion's citizens in chap. 1—citizens who neither know nor understand, who are children brought up by God only to rebel (1:2-3). Alone among the faithful of Isaiah's day were his "disciples" (למודים *limmûdîm*), into whose possession was committed God's teaching and instruction (8:16-20). Isaiah and his children were signs and portents—not so much on behalf of as against Israel. Now Zion and her children must face adversity of a different kind, but God's gracious healing and protection for them means that we have entered a new day. No longer are the prophet and the remnant alone within a rebellious people. Zion's righteous children—all of them—are to be taught by God. They will endure adversity because of God's lavish care for Zion, their habitation. No floodwaters—of the mighty river Assyria or even the floodwaters of Noah—can touch those who put their trust in that Zion whom God has taken back, cleansed, forgiven, and remarried. The wretched scenario of Isaiah 7–8 will not be replayed, as the promises associated with Isaiah's "taught ones" are here lavished on Zion's children.

In many ways, chap. 54, sitting as it does as the preface to Isaiah's concluding chapters, offers a conscious counterpoise to Isaiah's opening chapter. Zion begins again, as do her righteous children. But that is not all. The vision of a redeemed and forgiven Zion in chap. 1 ("city of righteousness," 1:26) concludes with a sharp warning. "Justice" (משפט *mišpāṭ*) and "righteousness" (צדקה *sĕdāqâ*) are the means by which the repentant regain favor (see 56:1). But destruction awaits those who persist in rebellion and sin (1:27). Here we find a foreshadowing of the theme of strife found at 54:15, and of false judgment at 54:17. Chapter 54 introduces these themes, even for the redeemed Zion, as consistent with the original vision of Isaiah. The truth of this will be borne out in the chapters to follow, where the false worship described in 1:29 emerges as a reality (see 56:9–57:21) and a counterpoise to the lavish banquet of chap. 55.

REFLECTIONS

1. What are we to make of the persistence of strife and false judgment in the face of so lavish a scene of restoration? Why is it that pure, undefiled, and undeserved acts of forgiveness and restitution fail to eliminate human pride and antagonism? The experience of Zion's remarraige could not be more lavishly drawn. All that she has lost is returned. The Lord has turned the fortunes of Zion, as the psalmist petitioned (Psalm 126). Whatever judgment was endured is now over—for good. God has set a seal on this with a covenant of peace (Isa 54:10).

Not all are prepared to accept God's previous sentence of judgment and to see it as an act of cleansing, necessary for full life in God's future plans. It is those who repent, we are told in 1:27, who will see God's justice and righteousness anew and will move gladly in this direction. All has been stripped away. New vision is thereby granted. But to rebel against God's judgment is to miss its redemptive purpose. It is a holding on to the status quo as bearable, even justifiable, instead of accepting the darkness of God's justice as the only path leading to God's light and truth.

So the rebellion is not quashed by God. There can be judgment, but there cannot be forced repentance. God will allow the evil and strife to persist, once God has rendered the verdict designed for new life and hope.

Yet notice that this reality in no way diminishes God's gracious action toward Zion and her taught children. The persistence of sin and rebellion does not need to be intellectually squared with God's free gift of redemption and new life. God takes another tack on this matter. God promises that such persistent rebellion will not gain the victory over these lavishly restored people. There is no diminishment of God's mighty power to redeem by the existence of forces to the contrary. Even the ravager is under God's control, to his or her own peril.

2. God had promised that the servant would "see his offspring" (53:10). There are times when the outcome of God promises is truly beyond comprehension. In fact, one suspects that the true nature of God's power and sovereignty are most on display when we have run out of cause to hope, when the way ahead is only dark. And yet those promises keep pressing their way into our consciousness. Then when the skies clear, as they do in this magnificent chapter, what God shows us catches us offguard, so stunning is the display of divine richness.

We must press on in times of hopelessness, not because we can summon up strength, but because we cannot. In those times, all we have left to trust is God's word alone and the assurance that it is in the darkness when God is doing something unexpected, for which our eyes will have to adjust. Zion had been told that things would be put back together for her. Yet clearly she could not believe it. Finally, however, the day arrived when God not only took her back and restored her past fortunes, but promised as well that any future assault would not be from God—and that God would guard her as never before. That was a promise fulfilled worth waiting for through the darkest times.

Were we to expect that the offspring the servant would see would turn out to be these children of Zion, taught by the Lord? Is this the way God intended to make good on the promise in 53:10? And in what sense does the servant himself actually see them, as promised? That we cannot know for sure. But many servants are made righteous by the servant, as promised. Their dwelling is the righteous city itself, Zion, made new again. Zion is their heritage, and it is a heritage that will weather any new assaults. No ravager or weapon will prosper (54:17); rather, the will of God will prosper (53:10) by means of the servant's sacrifice. Chapter 54 testifies to the accomplishment of the servant on behalf of Zion and her offspring. It is not too much to hope that the servant also has found "satisfaction through his knowledge" (53:11).

ISAIAH 55:1-13, THE REVERSAL CONTINUES

NIV

55 "Come, all you who are thirsty,
come to the waters;
and you who have no money,
come, buy and eat!
Come, buy wine and milk
without money and without cost.
²Why spend money on what is not bread,
and your labor on what does not satisfy?
Listen, listen to me, and eat what is good,
and your soul will delight in the richest
of fare.
³Give ear and come to me;
hear me, that your soul may live.
I will make an everlasting covenant with you,
my faithful love promised to David.

NRSV

55 Ho, everyone who thirsts,
come to the waters;
and you that have no money,
come, buy and eat!
Come, buy wine and milk
without money and without price.
² Why do you spend your money for that
which is not bread,
and your labor for that which does not satisfy?
Listen carefully to me, and eat what is good,
and delight yourselves in rich food.
³ Incline your ear, and come to me;
listen, so that you may live.
I will make with you an everlasting covenant,
my steadfast, sure love for David.
⁴ See, I made him a witness to the peoples,

NIV

⁴See, I have made him a witness to the peoples,
  a leader and commander of the peoples.
⁵Surely you will summon nations you
      know not,
    and nations that do not know you will
      hasten to you,
  because of the Lord your God,
    the Holy One of Israel,
    for he has endowed you with splendor."

⁶Seek the Lord while he may be found;
  call on him while he is near.
⁷Let the wicked forsake his way
  and the evil man his thoughts.
  Let him turn to the Lord, and he will have
    mercy on him,
    and to our God, for he will freely pardon.

⁸"For my thoughts are not your thoughts,
  neither are your ways my ways,"
                declares the Lord.
⁹"As the heavens are higher than the earth,
  so are my ways higher than your ways
    and my thoughts than your thoughts.
¹⁰As the rain and the snow
  come down from heaven,
    and do not return to it
    without watering the earth
  and making it bud and flourish,
    so that it yields seed for the sower and bread
      for the eater,
¹¹so is my word that goes out from my mouth:
  It will not return to me empty,
    but will accomplish what I desire
    and achieve the purpose for which I sent it.
¹²You will go out in joy
  and be led forth in peace;
    the mountains and hills
    will burst into song before you,
  and all the trees of the field
    will clap their hands.
¹³Instead of the thornbush will grow the
      pine tree,
    and instead of briers the myrtle will grow.
  This will be for the Lord's renown,
    for an everlasting sign,
    which will not be destroyed."

NRSV

  a leader and commander for the peoples.
⁵ See, you shall call nations that you do
      not know,
    and nations that do not know you shall
      run to you,
  because of the Lord your God, the Holy One
    of Israel,
    for he has glorified you.

⁶ Seek the Lord while he may be found,
    call upon him while he is near;
⁷ let the wicked forsake their way,
    and the unrighteous their thoughts;
  let them return to the Lord, that he may
      have mercy on them,
    and to our God, for he will abundantly
      pardon.
⁸ For my thoughts are not your thoughts,
    nor are your ways my ways, says the Lord.
⁹ For as the heavens are higher than the earth,
    so are my ways higher than your ways
    and my thoughts than your thoughts.

¹⁰ For as the rain and the snow come down
      from heaven,
    and do not return there until they have
      watered the earth,
  making it bring forth and sprout,
    giving seed to the sower and bread to
      the eater,
¹¹ so shall my word be that goes out from
      my mouth;
    it shall not return to me empty,
  but it shall accomplish that which I purpose,
    and succeed in the thing for which I sent it.

¹² For you shall go out in joy,
    and be led back in peace;
  the mountains and the hills before you
    shall burst into song,
    and all the trees of the field shall clap
      their hands.
¹³ Instead of the thorn shall come up
      the cypress;
    instead of the brier shall come up the myrtle;
  and it shall be to the Lord for a memorial,
    for an everlasting sign that shall not be
      cut off.

COMMENTARY

It is noted above that 54:1-17; 55:1-13; and 56:1-8 have in common the key word ברית (*běrît*, "covenant"); for this and other reasons, the chapters form a roughly continuous section of discourse. Zion was the subject of chap. 54; yet, the discussion of her children at the close offers a nice transition to chap. 55. The covenant established in this chapter is not with Zion, but with those who have come to drink her waters.

Elliger was right in seeing a close connection between chaps. 54 and 55, as have others following him.[169] The language in both is unique, over against the language of chaps. 40–53, and that is particularly true of the images chosen in chap. 55. We have confronted as yet very little of the vocabulary in the chapters preceding, though, as we will see, several of the images have a distinct rootage in Isaiah 1–39. This pattern is fully consistent with the intertextual character of the compositions in these final Isaiah chapters. We have already seen the degree to which chap. 54 was indebted to the portrayal and time frame of Isaiah 1.

Commentary that is form-critically oriented seeks to discover the life setting of the opening unit (vv. 1-5) in particular. A popular choice has been "an invitation on the part of Wisdom to be guests at her table."[170] Comparisons are made with Proverbs 9. A more concrete life setting is urged by Westermann, "In the cries of the water-sellers and others who shouted their wares in the market."[171] Yet even Westermann acknowledges that the summons to buy and eat is an odd and unexpected one over against the typical exhortations of "Deutero-Isaiah."

55:1-5. The approach adopted here is prepared to see the value in form-critical searches for life settings and genre comparisons with other OT forms. However, this sort of analysis may not go far

enough and, therefore, might miss the exegetical character of the compositions. The opening exhortation, "come to the waters," does not, in fact, sound like an invitation to seek wisdom, nor does it sound like a summons literally to buy water. We had reference to floodwaters in chap. 54—that is, to waters of Noah that would not assault the earth. In the judgment address of Isaiah to Ahaz, the king of Assyria is likened to mighty floodwaters (8:7) that will "sweep on into Judah as a flood" (8:8). So, in fact, the reference in chap. 54 is quite fitting.

What is striking in that same passage (chap. 8) is the prophet's admonishment that "this people" have refused other, sustaining waters, "the waters of Shiloah that flow gently" (8:6), that offered strength and support because they were associated with God's promises to the house of David (7:13). Is it against this intertextual backdrop that the appeal to come to the waters finds its proper force? The possibility is strengthened by the references in chap. 54 to waters of destruction, now no longer a threat.

Further support for this interpretation can be found by attending to the other images deployed in chap. 55. The force of the opening two verses is on (1) abundance and no cost, as against profitless striving, and (2) the concrete gifts of wine, milk, and bread. In later verses of the chapter, the provision of bread by God's creative power is likened to the power of God's word to accomplish what God desires (vv. 10-11). And in the final verses, the familiar Isaianic image of "briers and thorns" appears, set in contrast to the myrtle and cypress of God's goodness and restorative power.

When we return to the context of chaps. 7–8 and the challenge put to "this people" and King Ahaz, it is apparent that all these various images find their home there. Many have noted that in the catalog of "on that day" oracles closing off the word to Ahaz (7:18-25), there is a curious admixture of positive and negative images. Those left in the land will have milk in abundance (7:22), even though there is not much livestock. Very expensive vines will become briers and thorns (7:23).

Chapter 55 capitalizes on the word of God from Isaiah's day and sees it accomplishing what God

---

169. Karl Elliger, *Deuterojesaja in seinem Verhältnis zu Tritojesaja* (Stuttgart: Kohlhammer, 1933) 135-167. Melugin also treats the chapters together in his analysis of unit delineation. This may only be due, however, to the fact that the chapters are hedged in on either side by the constraints of the traditional model—on the front by the dramatic suffering servant poem (52:13–53:12), and on the back by the beginning of "Trito-Isaiah." See R. F. Melugin, *The Formation of Isaiah 40–55*, BZAW 141 (Berlin: Walter de Gruyter, 1976) 169-75.

170. The quote is from J. Begrich as cited in C. Westermann, *Isaiah 40–66*, trans. David Stalker, OTL (Philadelphia: Westminster, 1969) 281.

171. Ibid., 282.

intends in the present day. The waters that were once rejected—those connected with Zion's secure status (Psalm 46)—are once again a source of strength (55:1). Wine and milk can be bought without money, for the expensive vines that became briers and thorns (7:23) are again there to be had (free wine) because they have been changed into mytle and cypress (55:13). Abundant milk had been promised in Isaiah's day for "everyone left in the land"; that word has now come to fruition. (This reading also squares with the view that these chapters concern life for a remnant in the land.)

Striking as well is the appeal to "listen carefully" (שִׁמְעוּ *šim'û šāmôa'*) and to "incline the ear"—reversals of Isaiah 6 made possible by the proclamation of the servant in chaps. 40–52. The period of desolation is now over (6:11-12). But we must also be prepared for further refining (1:28-31; 6:13).

Much has been written about the so-called transfer of the Davidic covenant to the people, said to occur at 55:3.[172] Some speak of democratizing the royal promises, say, over against the laments of Psalm 89. These laments about the fall of the Davidic line, it is argued, are addressed by a prophecy like this that transfers the promises to others, the people at large.[173] Views such as this are quite popular among commentators.[174]

The problem with such an interpretation is that it tries to claim too much against an alleged backdrop of frustration and disappointment. Surely there is no criticism of the royal house to be found here, as is sometimes maintained. Otherwise, why would the prophecy continue with a description of David in a positive light, as "witness to the peoples, a leader and commander for the peoples" (v. 4)? This description can be traced to Ps 18:43, where David thanks God, for "you made me head of the nations;/ people whom I had not known served me" (NRSV).

What the prophecy states, and boldly, is that that aspect of the Davidic covenant pertaining to

David's role vis-à-vis the nations has been enlarged to encompass God's people at large. The sure love for David, expressed in God's promises to him with respect to the nations, is now the purview of the people who incline their ears and listen, as a former generation had not. One might add here another aspect related to the work of the servant in chaps. 40–52. There it appeared that the role given to the people, as light to the nations (42:1-7), was taken up by the servant himself (49:6), a task that is mentioned clearly in the final servant tribute (52:15). Both the city Zion and the servant followers of the servant take up the role once located in the servant, who himself embodied God's promises to Israel in chaps. 49–53. What would be saying too much is that the promises associated with David have now ceased, having been handed over to the people. The text does not state this, as the extended predication of vv. 4-5 makes clear.

55:6-11. That such a promise was bold in its expectations may be underscored by the thrust of this unit. Especially vv. 8-11 emphasize the mysterious character of God's plans over against human pretensions and expectations. God's word also seeks out an accomplishing end that God alone determines, an end that may seem to be as incomprehensible to human plotting as the transition from rain to bread.

The opening two verses (vv. 6-7) stress the need for repentance and pardon, as in 1:27. Wicked and unrighteous thoughts will be in no position to comprehend, even out of awe, the higher thoughts of God. Only repentance and pardon can open eyes and minds to the ways of God and the mysterious accomplishment of God's word.

55:12-13. The final two verses are generally related to a "second exodus" motif, whereby exiles are depicted as returning home from Babylon. Yet the removal of thorns and briers is a promise rooted in Isaiah's former word concerning the remnant in the land, the rejuvenated "pleasant vineyard" (see 27:2-4). Briers and thorns are what the land is reduced to under God's judgment (5:6; 7:24-25), to be removed by God's gracious action. In the lavish promises of God, the people will come and go from Zion in joy and peace, as all nature salutes God's dramatic turning of fortunes.

---

172. See, O. Eissfeldt, "The Promises to David in Isaiah 55.1-5," in *Israel's Prophetic Heritage,* ed. B. Anderson and W. Harrelson (New York: Harper and Bros., 1962) 196-207.

173. So Westermann, *Isaiah 40–66,* 284.

174. See C. R. Seitz, "Isaiah and the Search for a New Paradigm: Authorship and Inspiration," in *Word Without End* (Grand Rapids: Eerdmans, 1998) 150-67.

This will constitute an everlasting memorial on precisely those terms—that God has wiped out the days of judgment and given those who repent a fully new lease on life.

REFLECTIONS

It is striking what sort of flexibility God is prepared to show with the word once delivered. Clear reversals of judgment, promised beforehand, are executed. Waters once rejected are offered again. Promises of an everlasting covenant with David are enlarged to include God's people. The former word has gone forth and has not returned empty. In other cases, it has gone forth and undergone surprising adaptations, which no one could have imagined. Our thoughts are not God's thoughts, the prophet reminds us; and yet God's word, once delivered, maintains a sure continuity through time, accomplishing what God had planned originally. So there is a limit to what we can entertain as truly discontinuous and still of God, even as strange and unexpected developments occur.

Even here, however, note that such parameters are relevant in a situation when God has drawn near: "Seek the LORD while he may be found" (55:6). In times of darkness and uncertainty about God's will, discussions of discontinuity and radical change may be misplaced. The proper stance at such times may be waiting and repentance, as eyes and ears strain to hear an old word sound forth with conviction again. Even now, as God proposes enlarging the promises to David, this remains in a context in which the wicked and the unrighteous must forsake their ways, if they are to come anywhere near comprehending God's thoughts—radical though they may be—for their day.

ISAIAH 56:1-8, GATHERED TO THE HOLY MOUNTAIN

NIV

56 This is what the LORD says:

"Maintain justice
    and do what is right,
for my salvation is close at hand
    and my righteousness will soon be revealed.
[2]Blessed is the man who does this,
    the man who holds it fast,
who keeps the Sabbath without desecrating it,
    and keeps his hand from doing any evil."

[3]Let no foreigner who has bound himself to
        the LORD say,
    "The LORD will surely exclude me from
        his people."
And let not any eunuch complain,
    "I am only a dry tree."

[4]For this is what the LORD says:

NRSV

56 Thus says the LORD:
    Maintain justice, and do what is right,
for soon my salvation will come,
    and my deliverance be revealed.

[2] Happy is the mortal who does this,
    the one who holds it fast,
who keeps the sabbath, not profaning it,
    and refrains from doing any evil.

[3] Do not let the foreigner joined to the LORD say,
    "The LORD will surely separate me from
        his people";
and do not let the eunuch say,
    "I am just a dry tree."
[4] For thus says the LORD:
To the eunuchs who keep my sabbaths,
    who choose the things that please me

NIV

"To the eunuchs who keep my Sabbaths,
    who choose what pleases me
    and hold fast to my covenant—
⁵to them I will give within my temple and
        its walls
    a memorial and a name
    better than sons and daughters;
I will give them an everlasting name
    that will not be cut off.
⁶And foreigners who bind themselves to
        the LORD
    to serve him,
    to love the name of the LORD,
    and to worship him,
    all who keep the Sabbath without
        desecrating it
    and who hold fast to my covenant—
⁷these I will bring to my holy mountain
    and give them joy in my house of prayer.
Their burnt offerings and sacrifices
    will be accepted on my altar;
for my house will be called
    a house of prayer for all nations."
⁸The Sovereign LORD declares—
    he who gathers the exiles of Israel:
"I will gather still others to them
    besides those already gathered."

NRSV

    and hold fast my covenant,
⁵I will give, in my house and within my walls,
    a monument and a name
    better than sons and daughters;
I will give them an everlasting name
    that shall not be cut off.

⁶And the foreigners who join themselves to
        the LORD,
    to minister to him, to love the name of
        the LORD,
    and to be his servants,
    all who keep the sabbath, and do not
        profane it,
    and hold fast my covenant—
⁷these I will bring to my holy mountain,
    and make them joyful in my house
        of prayer;
    their burnt offerings and their sacrifices
        will be accepted on my altar;
for my house shall be called a house of prayer
    for all peoples.
⁸Thus says the Lord GOD,
    who gathers the outcasts of Israel,
I will gather others to them
    besides those already gathered.ᵃ

ᵃHeb *besides his gathered ones*

COMMENTARY

The secret to proper interpretation of this unit lies in the degree of caution one exercises in using other biblical texts to reconstruct the sociohistorical context in which it allegedly fits. There is, to be sure, an element of newness here—hence the force of the prophetic word—but again we must be careful to understand the specific character of what is being said. Reviewing the various texts over against which commentators have been prone to plot the force of the passage, P. A. Smith concludes that foreigners were not *de facto* excluded from the post-exilic cult, even as depicted in Ezra–Nehemiah.[175] That there were distinct stipulations is everywhere assumed by the text here. The problems of reconstructing post-exilic

life are fraught with terminological and sociological complexities, some of which admit of no obvious solution. In addition, we are already prepared to accept the reality of conflict within the community of Israel itself, as this has been mentioned throughout the preceding chapters. When one adds to that tensions between remnant communities in the land and those returning from Babylonian exile, then the difficulty of gaining a clear picture is compounded.[176]

It has been held that the interest in eunuchs displayed in this text is not so specialized as it might sound. Whybray has argued that it was not unusual for such a physical condition to have been accepted in order for one to advance into official

175. P. A. Smith, *Rhetoric and Redaction in Trito-Isaiah* (Leiden: Brill, 1995) 50-66.

176. C. R. Seitz, *Theology in Conflict: Reactions to the Exile in the Book of Jeremiah* (Berlin: de Gruyter, 1989).

circles in the Persian or Babylonian courts or for other reasons related to court life (see 39:7).[177] Moreover, what is at stake here is not simple admission to the Temple and a setting aside of deuteronomic law regarding crushed testicles (23:1)—arguably a different matter anyway—but the possibility of gaining some sort of monument in the temple precincts in lieu of children (cf. 2 Sam 18:18). What this section seems to want to communicate, culminating in v. 8, is that God is gathering outcasts, over and above the gathering of Israel. Isaiah 40:11 introduced the image of gathering, and here it is enlarged yet further.[178]

Use of the verb שׁמר (*šmr*, "maintain," "keep") in vv. 1-2, 4, and 6 creates a coherent movement and unity. Terms that have appeared in the immediately preceding passages ("justice," "right," "covenant," "name") reappear here, reinforcing the sense that the author is working with some larger conception at this juncture of the work. We have seen treatments of covenant in respect of Zion and her children; now those who hold fast to God's covenant are unsure of their status. The word delivered to them is that *all* who do justice and righteousness and hold fast to the divine covenant are God's servants.

The passage opens with a psalm-like exhortation (vv. 1-2). The appeal to "justice" (משׁפט *mišpāṭ*) and "righteousness" (צדקה *ṣĕdāqâ*) is frequently interpreted as Trito-Isaiah's paraenetic leveling of earlier theological proclamation—that is, as an exhortation to act in a righteous way— regarding *God's* impending justice and righteousness.[179] An alternative is to see in the opening appeal of Isaiah 1 the source of this prophetic word: "Zion shall be redeemed by justice, and those in her who repent, by righteousness" (1:27). God's *full and complete* redemption of Israel is contingent upon the display of justice and righ-

teousness within Zion, however bracing may have been the earlier proclamation of God's will to save and deliver. The wisdom-like refrain insists that this sort of conduct has its own reward (Ps 1:1-2).

Verse 3 is quite clear about what sort of foreigner is being addressed here: one "joined to the LORD." Calvin comments, "This consolation belongs to those only who have followed God when he called them; for there are many 'eunuchs' on whom God does not bestow his favour, and many 'foreigners' who do not join themselves of the people of God."[180] One who has already joined oneself to the Lord and is a foreigner is concerned that he or she will now be separated (v. 3). The eunuch's concern is lack of progeny—not admission to the Temple per se. What shall not be cut off is the "name" (שׁם *šēm*) of the eunuch. Here the motif of 55:13 is consciously developed; the brier become myrtle gives God a name that will not be cut off, and in the same way what was lost to the eunuch ("monument" is Hebrew יד [*yād*], a euphemism for "penis") is transformed and restored by God's grace, "better than sons and daughters" (56:5).

Attention returns to the foreigner (vv. 7-8). Here we get a pretty clear sense of what "joining" entails, as the stipulations are set forth in a catalog of three infinitive and two participial phrases. What we learn is that the holy mountain of Zion, backdrop of chaps. 54–55, is to include foreign worshipers who have fully joined themselves to Israel's Lord. Isaiah 55:5 had said the same thing in more general terms. This passage is once again the fulfillment of former Isaianic proclamation, concerning "days to come" (this time Isa 2:2-4). Many peoples were to stream to Zion to learn torah and be taught God's ways (2:3). Now joining Zion's children taught by God (54:13) are those from the peoples. God has gathered them twice (56:8). The original vision of Isaiah is seen as coming to fruition in this fresh prophetic instruction.

177. R. N. Whybray, *Isaiah 40–66,* NCB (Grand Rapids: Eerdmans, 1975) 198.

178. Efforts to subdivide the unit have been numerous; see Smith, *Rhetoric and Redaction in Trito-Isaiah,* 51-54.

179. See Westermann, *Isaiah 40-66,* 309-10.

180. John Calvin, *Calvin's Commentaries: Isaiah,* vol. 3 (Grand Rapids: Associated Publishers and Authors, n.d.) 746.

REFLECTIONS

There is clearly an air of newness and urgency in this proclamation. The role of foreigners in Israel's worship prior to the exile was to some degree not a pressing concern. The threat, rather, was to the consolidation of Israel's identity and worship in the face of rival gods and rival understandings that threatened to erode covenant fidelity.

We are in a new day. The prophet does not retrieve inflexible teachings from the past and apply them in a situation calling for something new. Neither does he pass judgment on past understandings of God's will. One looks in vain here for debate and counterproposal; an objection is being lodged from within, which is met with a word of promise and consolation. Still, in this new circumstance, the emphasis remains on religious fidelity: keeping the sabbath, guarding against profanation, holding fast to the covenant stipulations. The prophet has not drifted off into abstraction and sentimentality, change for change's sake. The opening appeal is sober and direct: Maintain justice and do what is right. The content for these matters comes from the teaching God had promised long ago to share with the nations (Isa 2:3). Justice and righteousness are not virtues to be summoned up from our natural sense of equality and fair play. They are linked with attention to what God requires of us and obedience to God's instruction.

What we fail to find in this passage is any abstracting or universalizing logic under which is subsumed outreach and care for the outcast. Through and through the passage is concerned with pure and undefiled worship of God in ways that can be seen and known and acted upon.

ISAIAH 56:9–57:21, GOD'S PEACE—AND ITS CRUEL OPPOSITE

NIV

⁹Come, all you beasts of the field,
   come and devour, all you beasts of the forest!
¹⁰Israel's watchmen are blind,
   they all lack knowledge;
they are all mute dogs,
   they cannot bark;
they lie around and dream,
   they love to sleep.
¹¹They are dogs with mighty appetites;
   they never have enough.
They are shepherds who lack understanding;
   they all turn to their own way,
   each seeks his own gain.
¹²"Come," each one cries, "let me get wine!
   Let us drink our fill of beer!
And tomorrow will be like today,
   or even far better."

57 The righteous perish,
   and no one ponders it in his heart;

NRSV

⁹ All you wild animals,
   all you wild animals in the forest, come
      to devour!
¹⁰ Israel's[a] sentinels are blind,
   they are all without knowledge;
they are all silent dogs
   that cannot bark;
dreaming, lying down,
   loving to slumber.
¹¹ The dogs have a mighty appetite;
   they never have enough.
The shepherds also have no understanding;
   they have all turned to their own way,
   to their own gain, one and all.
¹² "Come," they say, "let us[b] get wine;
   let us fill ourselves with strong drink.
And tomorrow will be like today,
   great beyond measure."

a Heb *His*   *b* Q Ms Syr Vg Tg: MT *me*

NIV

devout men are taken away,
  and no one understands
that the righteous are taken away
  to be spared from evil.
²Those who walk uprightly
  enter into peace;
  they find rest as they lie in death.

³"But you—come here, you sons of a sorceress,
  you offspring of adulterers and prostitutes!
⁴Whom are you mocking?
  At whom do you sneer
  and stick out your tongue?
Are you not a brood of rebels,
  the offspring of liars?
⁵You burn with lust among the oaks
  and under every spreading tree;
you sacrifice your children in the ravines
  and under the overhanging crags.
⁶The idols₁ among the smooth stones of the
      ravines are your portion;
  they, they are your lot.
Yes, to them you have poured out
      drink offerings
  and offered grain offerings.
  In the light of these things, should I relent?
⁷You have made your bed on a high and
      lofty hill;
  there you went up to offer your sacrifices.
⁸Behind your doors and your doorposts
  you have put your pagan symbols.
Forsaking me, you uncovered your bed,
  you climbed into it and opened it wide;
you made a pact with those whose beds
      you love,
  and you looked on their nakedness.
⁹You went to Molechᵃ with olive oil
  and increased your perfumes.
You sent your ambassadorsᵇ far away;
  you descended to the graveᶜ itself!
¹⁰You were wearied by all your ways,
  but you would not say, 'It is hopeless.'
You found renewal of your strength,
  and so you did not faint.

¹¹"Whom have you so dreaded and feared
  that you have been false to me,

ᵃ9 Or to the king   ᵇ9 Or idols   ᶜ9 Hebrew Sheol

NRSV

57 The righteous perish,
  and no one takes it to heart;
the devout are taken away,
  while no one understands.
For the righteous are taken away
      from calamity,
²   and they enter into peace;
those who walk uprightly
  will rest on their couches.
³ But as for you, come here,
  you children of a sorceress,
  you offspring of an adulterer and a whore.ᵃ
⁴ Whom are you mocking?
  Against whom do you open your
      mouth wide
  and stick out your tongue?
Are you not children of transgression,
  the offspring of deceit—
⁵ you that burn with lust among the oaks,
  under every green tree;
you that slaughter your children in the valleys,
  under the clefts of the rocks?
⁶ Among the smooth stones of the valley is
      your portion;
  they, they, are your lot;
to them you have poured out a drink offering,
  you have brought a grain offering.
  Shall I be appeased for these things?
⁷ Upon a high and lofty mountain
  you have set your bed,
  and there you went up to offer sacrifice.
⁸ Behind the door and the doorpost
  you have set up your symbol;
for, in deserting me,ᵇ you have uncovered
      your bed,
  you have gone up to it,
  you have made it wide;
and you have made a bargain for yourself
      with them,
  you have loved their bed,
  you have gazed on their nakedness.ᶜ
⁹ You journeyed to Molechᵈ with oil,
  and multiplied your perfumes;
you sent your envoys far away,
  and sent down even to Sheol.
¹⁰ You grew weary from your many wanderings,

ᵃHeb an adulterer and she plays the whore   ᵇMeaning of Heb
uncertain   ᶜOr their phallus; Heb the hand   ᵈOr the king

NIV

and have neither remembered me
　　nor pondered this in your hearts?
Is it not because I have long been silent
　　that you do not fear me?
¹²I will expose your righteousness and
　　　　your works,
　　and they will not benefit you.
¹³When you cry out for help,
　　let your collection ˷of idols˷ save you!
The wind will carry all of them off,
　　a mere breath will blow them away.
But the man who makes me his refuge
　　will inherit the land
　　and possess my holy mountain."

　¹⁴And it will be said:
"Build up, build up, prepare the road!
　　Remove the obstacles out of the way of
　　　　my people."
¹⁵For this is what the high and lofty One says—
　　he who lives forever, whose name is holy:
"I live in a high and holy place,
　　but also with him who is contrite and
　　　　lowly in spirit,
　to revive the spirit of the lowly
　　and to revive the heart of the contrite.
¹⁶I will not accuse forever,
　　nor will I always be angry,
　for then the spirit of man would grow faint
　　　　before me—
　　the breath of man that I have created.
¹⁷I was enraged by his sinful greed;
　　I punished him, and hid my face in anger,
　　yet he kept on in his willful ways.
¹⁸I have seen his ways, but I will heal him;
　　I will guide him and restore comfort to him,
¹⁹　creating praise on the lips of the mourners
　　　　in Israel.
　Peace, peace, to those far and near,"
　　says the LORD. "And I will heal them."
²⁰But the wicked are like the tossing sea,
　　which cannot rest,
　　whose waves cast up mire and mud.
²¹"There is no peace," says my God, "for
　　the wicked."

NRSV

but you did not say, "It is useless."
You found your desire rekindled,
　　and so you did not weaken.

¹¹ Whom did you dread and fear
　　so that you lied,
and did not remember me
　　or give me a thought?
Have I not kept silent and closed my eyes,[a]
　　and so you do not fear me?
¹² I will concede your righteousness and
　　　　your works,
　　but they will not help you.
¹³ When you cry out, let your collection of
　　　　idols deliver you!
　The wind will carry them off,
　　a breath will take them away.
But whoever takes refuge in me shall possess
　　　　the land
　　and inherit my holy mountain.

¹⁴ It shall be said,
"Build up, build up, prepare the way,
　　remove every obstruction from my
　　　　people's way."
¹⁵ For thus says the high and lofty one
　　who inhabits eternity, whose name is Holy:
I dwell in the high and holy place.
　　and also with those who are contrite and
　　　　humble in spirit.
to revive the spirit of the humble.
　　and to revive the heart of the contrite.
¹⁶ For I will not continually accuse,
　　nor will I always be angry;
for then the spirits would grow faint
　　　　before me,
　　even the souls that I have made.
¹⁷ Because of their wicked covetousness I was
　　　　angry;
　　I struck them, I hid and was angry;
　but they kept turning back to their
　　　　own ways.
¹⁸ I have seen their ways, but I will heal them;
　　I will lead them and repay them
　　　　with comfort,
　creating for their mourners the fruit of
　　　　the lips.[b]

[a]Gk Vg: Heb *silent even for a long time*　[b]Meaning of Heb uncertain

NRSV

19 Peace, peace, to the far and the near, says the
      Lord;
    and I will heal them.
20 But the wicked are like the tossing sea
    that cannot keep still;
    its waters toss up mire and mud.
21 There is no peace, says my God, for
      the wicked.

COMMENTARY

Recent commentary has rightly stressed two aspects of this passage. The first is its rhetorical unity.[181] The second is its extraordinary intertextuality, reaching into both the legacy of the servant (Isaiah 40–52) and the proclamation from the former things of Isaiah.[182] Neither aspect was particularly highlighted in an earlier form-critical climate. Instead, smaller units of speech were isolated, and the intertextual character was frequently interpreted as a sign that portions of this long passage were legitimately pre-exilic in provenance (e.g., 57:7-13).[183] How and why they found their way into "Trito-Isaiah" were questions fully at home in a diachronic inquiry content to set to the side the present shape and organization of the literature as secondary and derivative concerns.

The craftmanship of the passage is quite apparent and suggests a hand at work (1) fully aware of the legacy of prophetic speech in Isaiah and (2) shaping and directing that legacy in a fresh literary way toward sharp and effective address in a new day. The passage is held together by vocabulary, repetition, and counterpoint.

The fates of the wicked and the righteous are set in contrast (56:9-12; 57:1-2; 57:3-13; 57:14-19;

57:20-21). Peace awaits the righteous, even in suffering and martyrdom, imitating the servant (57:2; 57:18-19), while there can be no peace for the wicked oppressors who persist in their apostasy (57:21). The verb "to sleep" or "to rest" (שכב *škb*) and its noun form (משכב *miškāb*) appears in several rhetorical units (56:10; 57:2, 7-8); the expression translated "no one takes it to heart" at 57:1 is repeated at 57:11 ("did not . . . give me a thought").

Some controversy over the purpose of the second-person feminine address in 57:6-13, shifting from the preceding second-person plural masculine (57:3-5), as well as the identity of this "female" addressant, persists among interpreters. Biddle argues that here we have Zion's "alter ego": "Zion, herself, in a troubling manifestation."[184] Lady Babylon has fallen, and we expect Zion's exaltation, following the movement from 47:1-15 to 49:14-26; 51:17–52:10; and 54:1-17. But first the "Old Jerusalem" must fall as well; "Jerusalem will not be restored, but replaced."[185] Beuken, too, sees the close connection between language used here and language used to depict Babylon in chap. 47 and concludes that here Trito-Isaiah is depicting the "adulterous Zion" in antithesis of "my holy mountain" of chap. 54 (see 57:13).[186]

The position adopted here is that the observations about associating 57:6-13 with previous oracles regarding Zion and Babylon are correct. The children of an adulterous woman are contrasted with the righteous progeny promised the servant (53:10). Yet as these righteous offspring have

181. G. Polan, *In the Ways of Justice Toward Salvation: A Rhetorical Analysis of Isaiah 56–59* (New York: Peter Lang, 1986).

182. W. A. M. Beuken, "Isa. 56:9–57:13—An Example of the Isaianic Legacy of Trito-Isaiah," in *Tradition and Re-interpretation in Jewish and Early Christian Literature: Festschrift for J. C. A. Lebram,* ed. J. van Henton et al. (Leiden: Brill, 1986) 48-64; Mark E. Biddle, "Lady Zion's Alter Ego: Isaiah 47:1-15 and 57:6-13 as Structural Counterparts," in *New Visions of Isaiah,* ed. Roy F. Melugin and Marvin A. Sweeney (Sheffield: Sheffield Academic, 1996); P. A. Smith, *Rhetoric and Redaction in Trito-Isaiah,* VTSup 62 (Leiden: Brill, 1995) 67-96.

183. Westermann comments: "56:9-57:13 represent a short, self-contained collection of prophetic oracles of doom dating from the pre-exilic period" See C. Westermann, *Isaiah 40–66,* trans. David Stalker, OTL (Philadelphia: Westminster, 1969) 325.

184. Biddle, "Lady Zion's Alter Ego," 137.
185. Ibid., 139.
186. Beuken, "Isa. 56:9–57:13," 53.

already been promised Zion (54:3), and the righteous and cleansed Zion has been claimed and married by God, there is no reason to regard such a scenario as set aside here.[187] What the author wants to emphasize is the contrast between the righteous progeny who "inherit my holy mountain" (57:13) and those who by their adulterous actions hinder God's intention. In their behavior, they are reminiscent of Babylon (chap. 47) for the author. Their mother is not Zion, but Zion's "Babylonian" counterpart. There is likely an actual backdrop of self-conscious apostasy in place here, in which Israel's religious leaders have oppressed the righteous followers of the servant and sought their own portion elsewhere (note the contrast between 57:6 and 53:12). This sort of affliction, first visited on the servant (50:4-9; 53:13–53:12), has now come upon the servants. We were prepared for this already in 50:10.

56:9-12. The opening subunit sets the scene, which will be pursued in the larger movement of the passage as a whole. As Beuken suggests, what we have here is a perversion of the feast depicted in chap. 55.[188] All were to come to the waters and eat and drink without cost (55:1-2). The wicked were called to forsake their ways (55:7); here we see the cost of their refusal to do so.

The image of the watchman is familiar from other OT sources, especially the book of Ezekiel (3:17; 33:7), where it applies positively to the prophetic vocation of Ezekiel and negatively to false prophets and leaders. In Ezekiel 39, wild animals are called to a great sacrificial feast (Ezek 39:17). Here, too, their role is that of consumer as opposed to the consumed. The reason why they are able to come with this destructive role is that the watchmen have not done their duty.

The watchman is also familiar in the nearer context of Isaiah. In both prologue and epilogue of the servant's legacy (40:1-11; 52:7-12), the watchman has a key role: to bear witness to God's return to Zion (40:9, "herald of good tidings"; in 52:7-8, the roles are set next to each other). This return was set in contrast to the oppression of God's people ("for nothing," 52:5) while the rulers howled. The

blindness of the sentinals is precisely what God had come to reverse in the preceding chapters (chaps. 40–52), as against the former days of Isaiah (6:10). The knowledge granted by the servant's sacrifice (52:11) is not a knowledge these sleeping leaders share (56:10). The same point is repeated at 56:11, under the image of "shepherd"—again, the image deployed at 40:11 to describe God's faithful superintendence of the people.

The servants confessed in 53:6 that they wrongly turned each to his own way, leaving the servant to bear their punishment. Here the shepherds knowingly persist in wrongdoing (56:11), turning to their own ways, ignoring the wisdom imparted at God's feast on Zion (55:8), in order to overconsume and misconsume the new wine offered there (55:1; 56:12). In so doing, they imitate the drunkards of Isa 5:11, 22 who let God's vineyard fall into ruin in the former days of Isaiah.

The controlling image of this opening unit is surfeit. The appetite has been so overly indulged that all perception is fatally dulled, and sleep results. One day follows another as a search for more to eat and drink. The beds of these leaders will become the beds of the adulterous woman of 57:7; both are contrasted in the next subunit with the bed of the righteous (57:2).

57:1-13. This subunit can be delimited with attention to its beginning and end, where the contrast is set up between the righteous (vv. 1-2, 13) and the apostate (vv. 3-12). It has been noted already that there is repetition of phrases in v. 1 and v. 11 regarding failure to attend—first, to the death of the righteous and, second, to the consequences of apostasy—and the contrast between the bed of the righteous and the bed of adultery (vv. 2, 7-8). The true righteousness of vv. 1-2 is contrasted with the false righteousness of v. 12, which does not profit.

Verse 2 is difficult to translate. The NRSV would interpret the resting on beds as the peace of those who walk uprightly. The NIV allows the starker image of death and suffering, introduced in v. 1, to extend into v. 2; the peace found comes from death and, therefore, removal from further abuse. What is clear is that righteous suffering and affliction can lead to death, in ignominy and without concern. This is consistent with the fate of the servant as confessed by the servants (53:3). The servant was to make many righteous (v. 11); the fate

---

187. Biddle says, "Isaiah 57 problematizes this almost automatic, mechanical sequence of events" in order to place a New Jerusalem before our eyes. But such a Jerusalem has already been introduced in chap. 54. The problematizing has already been an episode in Zion's destiny, but it is now past. See Biddle, "Lady Zion's Alter Ego," 139.

188. Beuken, "Isa. 56:9–57:13," 50-53.

that was his is shared by those who follow in his way.

A sharp contrast is introduced in v. 3, captured well in the NRSV's "But as for you." These are the progeny, not of Zion or the servant, but of sorcery and adultery. Here is recalled the indictment of Babylon in chap. 47. At the close of that chapter, the author spoke of those who had trafficked with Babylon and of the fate in store for them (47:14-15), reminiscent of the judgment oracle of 1:29-31. The profitless character of her enchantments there (47:12) is here likened to the false righteousness displayed by the adultress (57:12).

The indictment of the false seed (vv. 3-5) is quite sharp and suggests the sort of mistreatment endured by the servant. These are children of transgression (פשע *pešaʿ*); the servant was stricken for the transgression (*pešaʿ*) of the people. Now these iniquities are not confessed, but gloated over (v. 4).

As has been noted, there is a change of addressant in v. 6, from the children to the mother. Many commentators have accounted for this change by simply arguing that Israel is addressed in the second-person feminine singular.[189] But why would such a change occur suddenly here? Others interpret the feminine address more literally, as involving Zion or Zion's "alter ego." It should be noted that the change occurs at the juncture in the indictment where the children, referred to in vv. 3-5, are condemned for sacrificing *their* children. At this point, the children are simply identified with the false source of their adulterous worship, and "she" is addressed directly. Just as Zion's children were to find identity and refuge in her, so also these children were to find succor with the source of their strength and devotion. This is not Zion's alter ego but her infamous counterpart, condemned earlier under the figure of Lady Babylon (chap. 47). Her "portion" (חלק *ḥeleq*) stands in contrast to the portion of the servant (53:12), even as he has poured out his soul to death, while she apparently thrives, pouring out libations and making wide her bed. The indictments are largely sexual in character and are reminiscent of the pre-exilic statements of Hosea. There is no reason to seek their provenance there, however. It is the false worship of the exilic and post-exilic period that is condemned, a cult of death that has spilled over to assaults on the righteous servants of the servant.

Beuken has called attention to the connection that exists between this passage and the two preceding passages (55:1-13; 56:1-8), in that they are all concerned with God's holy mountain (56:7).[190] Chapter 54 should be included in this connection as well, as the final line of the subunit makes clear. Isaiah 54:17 referred to Zion and her protection against rebuke for the servants as constituting their inheritance; the same note is sounded in 57:13*b*. Death is not the final word for the servants who take refuge in Zion, but it is the final destiny of false worshipers and those who trust in idols, in spite of their seeming triumph or pretensions at righteousness.

57:14-21. The final passage is frequently taken as an isolated form-critical unit, though the strictness of the method has given way in many instances to a different set of concerns.[191] It is treated here in conjunction with 56:9-12 and 57:1-13 because of the continuing contrast between the fate of the righteous servants ("peace") and the fate of the wicked persons who assault them (57:20-21). The final note appears to be modeled on 48:22. Alternatively, 48:22 has found its way into the legacy of the servant (chaps. 40–52) so that the final section in its entirety (chaps. 40–66) might fall into thirds (chaps. 40–48; 49–57; 58–66), thereby stressing continuity across these chapters instead of a sharp break at chap. 55 or chap. 56.

Zimmerli is representative of the view that with "Trito-Isaiah" we move from a certain historical realism, typical of "Deutero-Isaiah," to a more figurative or spiritualized sense. The call to prepare the way, found at 40:3, was intended literally, while what we have here has "become part of general devout parenesis."[192] The problem is with determining what is meant by *literal* sense at 40:3. Zimmerli and others typically mean by this historical sense—that is, referring to the way through the wilderness from exile for the prophet's audience. It is not clear, however, that "the way of the LORD" referred to in 40:1-11 means anything like that. The way of Lord is stipulated at 40:10, in its literal sense, as involving a theophany: "See, the

---

189. For a full discussion, see Biddle, "Lady Zion's Alter Ego."

190. Beuken, "Isa. 56:9—57:13," 50.
191. A good survey of the shift in method—and ongoing challenges to it—can be found in Smith *Rhetoric and Redaction in Trito-Isaiah,* 67-96.
192. Quoted in English translation in C. Westermann, *Isaiah 40–66,* trans. David Stalker, OTL (Philadelphia: Westminster, 1969) 327.

Sovereign LORD comes with power" (NIV). The Lord's way entails God's sovereign approach to this people.

Seen in this light, there is very little to differentiate what we have here from the preceding usage, even when one notes that in this case "the way" can be referred to in shorthand fashion. The way of the people, mentioned at the close of v. 14, is to be cleared of obstructions. But this is precisely so that God can "revive" (v. 15), "heal," "comfort," and sustain mourners (v. 18). This is precisely the same intention as at chap. 40, though now in very different circumstances in the light of the work of the servant. Now the past punishment of God's people is truly past and can be referred to retrospectively in a way that moves out beyond Isaiah 40–52. But the chief difference lies in the references to God's special attention to those who are contrite and humble in spirit (v. 15). "My people" meant at 40:1 exactly what one expected: God's people Israel. Here, however, God's special dwelling entails God's "way" to a specific entity within Israel whose ways God has seen, but who are now the objects of God's reviving. Read in the

context of what immediately precedes, and anticipating the final notice at 57:20-21, salvation is addressed to the righteous servants who follow in the footsteps of the servant as over against the apostate wicked (57:3-13).

The double imperative (v. 14) is reminiscent of exhortations in the work of the servant. ("It shall be said"/"And it will be said" is an addition in both the NIV and the NRSV renderings, respectively, presumably meant to ease the transition from v. 13.) We are familiar with the use of the predication "Holy One" standing alone for God, as this is typical of usage throughout Isaiah. Here (v. 15) we have a different usage, with "high and lofty" serving this purpose. These adjectives were applied to the servant's promised exaltation (52:13). Here they describe God's permanent dwelling and help to set up the contrast with God's descent in comfort and reviving. Use of the term "contrite" (דכא *dakāʾ*; נדכאים *nidkāʾîm*) reminds one here of the servant's mission: He "was smitten" (מדכא *mĕdukāʾ*) for the iniquities of the servants (53:5).

REFLECTIONS

1. Two things are immediately striking about this passage. The first is that the righteous will suffer and die. Second, the foundational sin is not failing to do our best in and with God's world but is, rather, deserting God. It is leaving God for some other god and some other form of devotion. The pragmatic among us identify the religious good with some sort of quantifiable, demonstrable outcome *in this world.* On this measurement, the righteous have failed in that they have borne suffering and have perished. They have changed nothing in the world at all. Their only legacy is fidelity to God. At this point, we see the connection between the death of the righteous and the demand for fidelity to God as the highest calling.

When one considers the pragmatic concerns of this author, his insistence on doing justice and righteousness (56:1)—which could well serve as a motto over his entire word to us—it is all the more striking that this is the turn he here makes. The chief sin is not pre-exilic or post-exilic, but infects every age. The dramatic version we have before us plays out in sexual terms. To cause suffering and to extend the sin against God's servants, begun with the servant, is to engage, religiously, in a confused and misplaced devotion. It is to seek a sort of religious pleasure, springing from the sources of our own sexual desires, which ebb and flow but can be revived through effort of will and proper manipulation (57:10). The point at which false devotion slips into absorption in the realm of the sensory is nearly invisible. No logical argument is produced here that tracks the movement from oppression to apostasy to religiously endowed sensation. The prophet merely reports what has transpired. The only sure fact is that the righteous suffer and die in the face of such apostasy. There is no such thing as harmless apostasy, hurting only those who are engaged in the behavior.

The word of God here calls us to repent and be sure of our devotion. Ezekiel never tired of insisting that Israel had truly forgotten who God is. It was that simple. The only solution to the darkness in which the people lived was a fresh encounter with the living God. Only then "will they know that I am the LORD"—to quote the word that most punctuates his teaching.

The word of the prophet also implies that such knowledge and pure devotion will entail suffering and death. There is refuge in Zion that leads to peace and removal from the onslaughts of the wicked. But this is no stronghold against suffering and death. The legacy of the servant, if followed boldly, creates peace and healing. It cannot remove one from the ultimate scourge of the evil of this world.

2. The final unit is directed to the righteous (57:14-21). It is not the case that God's righteous ones have no record of sin. Quite to the contrary. God has seen their ways, and they are backsliding and self-centered ways, betraying God and bringing forth God's righteous anger (57:17). In the past of the righteous stands the memory of God's judgment and wrath. No one who seeks to model holiness of life and righteousness gets there on a road of self-confident striving. God breaks down and humbles those who strive toward a righteousness of their own making. Such efforts are too clogged with sin and human folly to enjoy God's blessing. They constitute an obstruction in the way of God's people (57:14) that must give way to another sort of approach from God.

There is, at the same time, a propensity to despair that associates itself with righteous judgment and anger from God's cleansing hand. Will the spirit of humanity not be crushed and obliterated under God's direct and unmediated address? There can come a period of darkness and despair as one seeks to allow the grace of God to stand in and replace old patterns of apostasy and self-centeredness. The familiar has been burned away, but what will now serve as our guide and bulwark? How will God's peace come near when we sense our distance and our contrition?

The word that is needed at such times is a distinctly *healing* word, and it can come from no lips but God's alone. Only God's special sort of speech has the power to heal and "revive the spirit of the humble" (57:15). The reason for this is that we are not talking about a despair generated for human reasons or a weakness of spirit that has come upon us due to circumstance or accident. The despair has been generated by God as a consequence of divine anger toward sin in us. And because it has God's signature on it, we know that it means to lead to our restoration. The words that most testify to this spiritual truth are found in 57:16: "for then the spirits would grow faint before me." God's just cleansing reduces us before the Lord in order to prepare us for restoration. It is not despair that can kill, but a sense that God is neither just nor healing. In one fell swoop, the righteous learn that God is both in equal measure: as high and lofty as divine holiness demands, and as low and accessible as human sinful nature requires (57:15). That balance constitutes God's very identity; it can never be relaxed if we are to know God as God is: "Peace, peace, to the far and the near, say the LORD; and I will heal them" (57:19). To forfeit this knowledge is to become like the tossing sea, which cannot be still.

ISAIAH 58:1–59:21, GOD'S RIGHTEOUS SENTINEL SPEAKS

NIV

58 "Shout it aloud, do not hold back.
Raise your voice like a trumpet.
Declare to my people their rebellion
and to the house of Jacob their sins.
²For day after day they seek me out;
they seem eager to know my ways,
as if they were a nation that does what is right
and has not forsaken the commands of
its God.
They ask me for just decisions
and seem eager for God to come near them.
³'Why have we fasted,' they say,
'and you have not seen it?
Why have we humbled ourselves,
and you have not noticed?'

"Yet on the day of your fasting, you do as
you please
and exploit all your workers.
⁴Your fasting ends in quarreling and strife,
and in striking each other with wicked fists.
You cannot fast as you do today
and expect your voice to be heard on high.
⁵Is this the kind of fast I have chosen,
only a day for a man to humble himself?
Is it only for bowing one's head like a reed
and for lying on sackcloth and ashes?
Is that what you call a fast,
a day acceptable to the LORD?

⁶"Is not this the kind of fasting I have chosen:
to loose the chains of injustice
and untie the cords of the yoke,
to set the oppressed free
and break every yoke?
⁷Is it not to share your food with the hungry
and to provide the poor wanderer
with shelter—
when you see the naked, to clothe him,
and not to turn away from your own flesh
and blood?
⁸Then your light will break forth like the dawn,
and your healing will quickly appear;
then your righteousness*ᵃ* will go before you,

ᵃ*8 Or your righteous One*

NRSV

58 Shout out, do not hold back!
Lift up your voice like a trumpet!
Announce to my people their rebellion,
to the house of Jacob their sins.
²Yet day after day they seek me
and delight to know my ways,
as if they were a nation that practiced
righteousness
and did not forsake the ordinance of
their God;
they ask of me righteous judgments,
they delight to draw near to God.
³"Why do we fast, but you do not see?
Why humble ourselves, but you do
not notice?"
Look, you serve your own interest on your
fast day,
and oppress all your workers.
⁴Look, you fast only to quarrel and to fight
and to strike with a wicked fist.
Such fasting as you do today
will not make your voice heard on high.
⁵Is such the fast that I choose,
a day to humble oneself?
Is it to bow down the head like a bulrush,
and to lie in sackcloth and ashes?
Will you call this a fast,
a day acceptable to the LORD?

⁶Is not this the fast that I choose:
to loose the bonds of injustice,
to undo the thongs of the yoke,
to let the oppressed go free,
and to break every yoke?
⁷Is it not to share your bread with the hungry,
and bring the homeless poor into
your house;
when you see the naked, to cover them,
and not to hide yourself from your
own kin?
⁸Then your light shall break forth like
the dawn,
and your healing shall spring up quickly;

NIV

and the glory of the LORD will be your
  rear guard.
⁹Then you will call, and the LORD will answer;
  you will cry for help, and he will say: Here
    am I.

"If you do away with the yoke of oppression,
  with the pointing finger and malicious talk,
¹⁰and if you spend yourselves in behalf of
    the hungry
  and satisfy the needs of the oppressed,
then your light will rise in the darkness,
  and your night will become like the
    noonday.
¹¹The LORD will guide you always;
  he will satisfy your needs in a sun-
    scorched land
  and will strengthen your frame.
You will be like a well-watered garden,
  like a spring whose waters never fail.
¹²Your people will rebuild the ancient ruins
  and will raise up the age-old foundations;
you will be called Repairer of Broken Walls,
  Restorer of Streets with Dwellings.

¹³"If you keep your feet from breaking
    the Sabbath
  and from doing as you please on my
    holy day,
if you call the Sabbath a delight
  and the LORD's holy day honorable,
and if you honor it by not going your
    own way
  and not doing as you please or speaking
    idle words,
¹⁴then you will find your joy in the LORD,
  and I will cause you to ride on the heights
    of the land
  and to feast on the inheritance of your
    father Jacob."
        The mouth of the LORD has spoken.

59 Surely the arm of the LORD is not too
      short to save,
  nor his ear too dull to hear.
²But your iniquities have separated
    you from your God;
your sins have hidden his face from you,
  so that he will not hear.

NRSV

your vindicator[a] shall go before you,
  the glory of the LORD shall be your
    rear guard.
⁹ Then you shall call, and the LORD will answer;
  you shall cry for help, and he will say, Here
    I am.

If you remove the yoke from among you,
  the pointing of the finger, the speaking
    of evil,
¹⁰ if you offer your food to the hungry
  and satisfy the needs of the afflicted,
then your light shall rise in the darkness
  and your gloom be like the noonday.
¹¹ The LORD will guide you continually,
  and satisfy your needs in parched places,
  and make your bones strong;
and you shall be like a watered garden,
  like a spring of water,
  whose waters never fail.
¹² Your ancient ruins shall be rebuilt;
  you shall raise up the foundations of many
    generations;
you shall be called the repairer of the breach,
  the restorer of streets to live in.

¹³ If you refrain from trampling the sabbath,
  from pursuing your own interests on my
    holy day;
if you call the sabbath a delight
  and the holy day of the LORD honorable;
if you honor it, not going your own ways,
  serving your own interests, or pursuing
    your own affairs;[b]
¹⁴ then you shall take delight in the LORD,
  and I will make you ride upon the heights
    of the earth;
I will feed you with the heritage of your
    ancestor Jacob,
  for the mouth of the LORD has spoken.

59 See, the LORD's hand is not too short
      to save,
  nor his ear too dull to hear.
² Rather, your iniquities have been barriers
    between you and your God,

[a]Or vindication   [b]Heb or speaking words

NIV

³For your hands are stained with blood,
   your fingers with guilt.
Your lips have spoken lies,
   and your tongue mutters wicked things.
⁴No one calls for justice;
   no one pleads his case with integrity.
They rely on empty arguments and speak lies;
   they conceive trouble and give birth to evil.
⁵They hatch the eggs of vipers
   and spin a spider's web.
Whoever eats their eggs will die,
   and when one is broken, an adder
      is hatched.
⁶Their cobwebs are useless for clothing;
   they cannot cover themselves with what
      they make.
Their deeds are evil deeds,
   and acts of violence are in their hands.
⁷Their feet rush into sin;
   they are swift to shed innocent blood.
Their thoughts are evil thoughts;
   ruin and destruction mark their ways.
⁸The way of peace they do not know;
   there is no justice in their paths.
They have turned them into crooked roads;
   no one who walks in them will know peace.

⁹So justice is far from us,
   and righteousness does not reach us.
We look for light, but all is darkness;
   for brightness, but we walk in deep shadows.
¹⁰Like the blind we grope along the wall,
   feeling our way like men without eyes.
At midday we stumble as if it were twilight;
   among the strong, we are like the dead.
¹¹We all growl like bears;
   we moan mournfully like doves.
We look for justice, but find none;
   for deliverance, but it is far away.

¹²For our offenses are many in your sight,
   and our sins testify against us.
Our offenses are ever with us,
   and we acknowledge our iniquities:
¹³rebellion and treachery against the LORD,
   turning our backs on our God,
fomenting oppression and revolt,
   uttering lies our hearts have conceived.
¹⁴So justice is driven back,

NRSV

and your sins have hidden his face from you
   so that he does not hear.
³ For your hands are defiled with blood,
   and your fingers with iniquity;
your lips have spoken lies,
   your tongue mutters wickedness.
⁴ No one brings suit justly,
   no one goes to law honestly;
they rely on empty pleas, they speak lies,
   conceiving mischief and begetting iniquity.
⁵ They hatch adders' eggs,
   and weave the spider's web;
whoever eats their eggs dies,
   and the crushed egg hatches out a viper.
⁶ Their webs cannot serve as clothing;
   they cannot cover themselves with what
      they make.
Their works are works of iniquity,
   and deeds of violence are in their hands.
⁷ Their feet run to evil,
   and they rush to shed innocent blood;
their thoughts are thoughts of iniquity,
   desolation and destruction are in
      their highways.
⁸ The way of peace they do not know,
   and there is no justice in their paths.
Their roads they have made crooked;
   no one who walks in them knows peace.

⁹ Therefore justice is far from us,
   and righteousness does not reach us;
we wait for light, and lo! there is darkness;
   and for brightness, but we walk in gloom.
¹⁰ We grope like the blind along a wall,
   groping like those who have no eyes;
we stumble at noon as in the twilight,
   among the vigorous*ᵃ* as though we
      were dead.
¹¹ We all growl like bears;
   like doves we moan mournfully.
We wait for justice, but there is none;
   for salvation, but it is far from us.
¹² For our transgressions before you are many,
   and our sins testify against us.
Our transgressions indeed are with us,
   and we know our iniquities:
¹³ transgressing, and denying the LORD,

ᵃMeaning of Heb uncertain

NIV

and righteousness stands at a distance;
truth has stumbled in the streets,
honesty cannot enter.
¹⁵Truth is nowhere to be found,
and whoever shuns evil becomes a prey.

The LORD looked and was displeased
that there was no justice.
¹⁶He saw that there was no one,
he was appalled that there was no one
to intervene;
so his own arm worked salvation for him,
and his own righteousness sustained him.
¹⁷He put on righteousness as his breastplate,
and the helmet of salvation on his head;
he put on the garments of vengeance
and wrapped himself in zeal as in a cloak.
¹⁸According to what they have done,
so will he repay
wrath to his enemies
and retribution to his foes;
he will repay the islands their due.
¹⁹From the west, men will fear the name of
the LORD,
and from the rising of the sun, they will
revere his glory.
For he will come like a pent-up flood
that the breath of the LORD drives along.ᵃ

²⁰"The Redeemer will come to Zion,
to those in Jacob who repent of their sins,"
declares the LORD.

²¹"As for me, this is my covenant with them,"
says the LORD. "My Spirit, who is on you, and my
words that I have put in your mouth will not
depart from your mouth, or from the mouths of
your children, or from the mouths of their descendants from this time on and forever," says the
LORD.

ᵃ19 Or *When the enemy comes in like a flood, / the Spirit of the
LORD will put him to flight*

NRSV

and turning away from following our God,
talking oppression and revolt,
conceiving lying words and uttering them
from the heart.
¹⁴Justice is turned back,
and righteousness stands at a distance;
for truth stumbles in the public square,
and uprightness cannot enter.
¹⁵Truth is lacking,
and whoever turns from evil is despoiled.

The LORD saw it, and it displeased him
that there was no justice.
¹⁶He saw that there was no one,
and was appalled that there was no one
to intervene;
so his own arm brought him victory,
and his righteousness upheld him.
¹⁷He put on righteousness like a breastplate,
and a helmet of salvation on his head;
he put on garments of vengeance for clothing,
and wrapped himself in fury as in a mantle.
¹⁸According to their deeds, so will he repay;
wrath to his adversaries, requital
to his enemies;
to the coastlands he will render requital.
¹⁹So those in the west shall fear the name of
the LORD,
and those in the east, his glory;
for he will come like a pent-up stream
that the wind of the LORD drives on.

²⁰And he will come to Zion as Redeemer,
to those in Jacob who turn from
transgression, says the LORD.
²¹And as for me, this is my covenant with them,
says the LORD: my spirit that is upon you, and my
words that I have put in your mouth, shall not
depart out of your mouth, or out of the mouths of
your children, or out of the mouths of your children's children, says the LORD, from now on and
forever.

COMMENTARY

In the previous unit Israel's shepherds and sentinels were condemned for allowing God's banquet, so lavishly displayed in chap. 55, to be invaded by wild animals (56:9-12). The consequence was affliction for the righteous (57:1-2) and the emergence of a substitute for Lady Zion and her children (57:3-13), modeled on Lady Babylon and her traffickers (47:1-15). The passage ended with a healing speech, directed to the righteous progeny of Zion (57:14-21). What we see in the present text is the emergence of the proper sentinel, warning and exhorting as God would have it. Not blind or silent (56:10), this sentinel is called to "shout out . . . lift up your voice like a trumpet" (58:1).

The passage can be divided into several smaller rhetorical units. There is a slight transitional break at 58:6, as the sentinel moves to address the people's complaint. This address closes in 58:14 with the words "for the mouth of the LORD has spoken" (cf. 40:5). Chapter 59 continues the address of the sentinel, but the subject of his discourse and the forms employed change; 59:1-8 constitutes an indictment that serves to set up a communal lament in 59:9-15*a*. The response that is given is found in the closing unit (59:15*b*-20). Here we find an inclusio that justifies treating these two chapters as a single extended unit: The transgressions of Jacob ("their rebellion" [פשעם *piš°ām*] and "their sins" [חטאתם *ḥaṭṭō'tām*]) were to be announced by God's sentinel in the opening verse (58:1); God will come to Zion as redeemer for those who turn from transgression (לשבי פשע *lĕšobê peša'*) in Jacob (59:20).

The first address (chap. 58) chiefly concerns proper fasting, with an emphasis on clarifying what constitutes true righteousness (58:2). The second address deploys a strong indictment of the people in order to bring to the surface their underlying complaint (59:9-15*a*). As in the preceding passage (56:9–57:21), one gets the sense that the people are suffering from despair and anger over their sins and God's apparent abandonment of them to a deserved evil (57:12-13). As in chap. 58, the key words that reappear are those introduced in 56:1: "justice" (משפט *mišpāṭ*) and "righteousness" (צדקה *ṣĕdāqâ*; 58:2, 8; 59:4, 8-9, 11, 14, 17). The final verse retrieves the emphasis on

covenant found back in chaps. 54–56 and attaches it to God's special prophetic vocation for the sentinel and his "children." In that sense it closes off this first major section (chaps. 54–59) and prepares us for the sentinel's powerful address in chaps. 60–62.

Steck has argued for the unity of these two chapters within a larger section comprising 56:9–59:21. In the first part (56:9–57:21) the leaders of the people are singled out for address, while in the second part (58:1–59:21) it is the people themselves whom the prophet addresses.[193] The close connection between chap. 58 and the injunction of 56:1 has been explored in detail by Polan.[194] It is as though chap. 58 serves to stipulate just what the poet had in mind by the exhortatio, "maintain justice, and do what is right." In both 56:1-8 and chap. 58 the concern with proper sabbath observance comes to the fore (58:13-14). The observations concerning justice (*mišpāṭ*) and righteousness (*ṣĕdāqâ*) apply in derivative measure to chap. 59 as well, where the terms appear frequently (see above). The broad designation of Steck does capture something of the transition from 56:9–57:21 to 58:1–59:21.

58:1-5. Efforts have been made to further subdivide the unit because of the roughness of the transition from v. 2 to v. 3. Steck classified all of chap. 58 as a prophetic commissioning directed only to the prophet.[195] This element can be most clearly identified in vv. 1-2. At v. 3, a transition is marked by the shift to second-person plural speech, "you serve your own interest on your fast day," which sounds like direct address to the people themselves. It is clear that the author has adapted speech forms in a literary composition with diverse elements that cannot now be isolated and assigned discrete form-critical status. Therefore, it is better to seek markers of rhetorical shift and redirection, rather than to separate units according to strict form-critical logic.

This opening unit initiates an indictment of inappropriate fasting by citing the complaint of the

193. O. Steck, *Studien zu Tritojesaja* (Berlin: de Gruyter, 1991) 182-86.

194. G. Polan, *In the Ways of Justice Toward Salvation: A Rhetorical Analysis of Isaiah 56–59* (New York: Peter Lang, 1986) 315.

195. Steck, *Studien zu Tritojesaja,* 182-86.

people (v. 3). We are used to this sort of move in the discourse, whereby the situation into which prophetic speech is directed is obliquely revealed. This comes to full flower in chap. 59, where the communal lament of the people is given in larger scope and detail (59:9-15*a*). The opening verses represent an effort in literary terms to introduce the speaker and assign him appropriate status as God's sentinel. It seems to "re-echo two earlier prophetic utterances, Hos. 8:1 . . . and Micah 3:8."[196] Here, however, we move immediately away from prophet to prophetic address. The references to seeking and knowing God's ways (v. 2) are reminiscent of 55:6-7; the references to doing righteousness and justice, of 56:1. It sounds as though the prophet's auditors are not unmovable ojects of God's wrath, even as they fast falsely, but are those whom the prophet sincerely seeks to bring to repentance and change of life. This will require that the content of justice and righteousness be spelled out clearly.

We know about fasting rituals during the exilic period from Zechariah 7–8. The same tone is adopted here. Fasting cannot be mechanized, for it will devolve into mere ceremony without proper consequence. Fasting is not being rejected as such, in spite of the harsh force of 58:5. Verse 4 shows the behavior associated with improper fasting, and this sets up a contrast with 58:6-7 (cf. Zech 7:5-11). The fasting the prophet condemns contains the proper ritual content and self-denial (v. 3), but its fruit serves to condemn it as improperly motivated.

58:6-12. The first four verses (vv. 6-9) designate the proper fruit of fasting. Verse 9 establishes the link back to the complaint of v. 3, that God took no notice of the people. God will answer and be available—but only when proper righteousness is manifested, and not hypocrisy. While using different terminology, the reference to healing in v. 8 establishes a connection with the final unit of the preceding chapter (57:14-21). Healing will come, the prophet promises, when the fruit of proper devotion is in evidence.

Most commentators agree that the catalog regarding proper justice found in vv. 6-7 focuses on the specific need for release from bondage (cf.

61:1).[197] These are not generic problems, but belong to the circumstances presupposed throughout this discourse: of hardship, bondage, oppression, and unmerited suffering, during the exilic period. God's righteous servant bore suffering and affliction, and it has been clear that the same treatment has been meted out to God's servants (57:1-2). Fasting that does not alleviate these conditions, but worsens them, stands under prophetic condemnation. Fasting is meant to be a response of penitence and contrition, seeking God's favor. Such attitudes are inconsistent with oppression and disregard for those in need. Verse 8*b* picks up imagery from the discourse of the servant (52:12) and attaches it specifically to the righteous deportment of God's people.

Verses 9*b*-12 elaborate the prophet's appeal. The "if" clauses signify God's final intention to bring forth salvation, not condemnation. Both here and in chap. 59, the situation of the people addressed by the prophet sounds unusually grim. Darkness, gloom, parched places, ruins, breaches—the spiritual state of the people is mirrored in the material conditions of hardship. In other words, there is oppression and selfishness from those who are themselves in dire straits. It is not indictment of wicked leadership and wrongly wielded power such as we found in the preceding passage (56:9–57:21). The prophet is condemning false righteousness (58:2) among a people for whom there is the hope and the possibility of true righteousness. The connection here with 56:1-8 is clear. Polan puts it this way, "56:1 is the skeletal message of the relationship between right and just actions and salvation, while 59 is the flesh and blood which enlivens the impact of that kernal message with literary development."[198] The beginning of the process of filling out the content of 56:1 can be found in chap. 58.

58:13-14. A clear connection with 56:1-8 can be seen in these verses. Westermann emphasizes their detachable character from what precedes and argues that they have been redactionally placed here to form a section running from 56:1–58:14.[199] This is to misunderstand the way in which chap. 58 in its entirety serves to flesh out the content of 56:1-8. The transition to concern

196. C. Westermann, *Isaiah 40–66,* trans. David Stalker, OTL (Philadelphia: Westminster, 1969) 334.

197. Ibid., 337.
198. Polan, *In the Ways of Justice Toward Salvation,* 315.
199. Westermann, *Isaiah 40–66,* 340-41.

with the sabbath is completely natural, following the movement at 56:2, 4, 6. Reference was made at 56:7 to the actual house of God, and this same context is spoken of in 58:12. Here, however, the restoration imagery spills over into the broader "heritage of your ancestor Jacob" (58:14). The connection between Zion, the land, righteousness, and inheritance was established in chap. 54 (vv. 3, 14, 17). Here the spiritual and material conditions are linked, as in vv. 9*b*-12. The sabbath is not a day to go one's own way (compare v. 13 and v. 3), but a day "holy" and "honorable" and a "delight." Similarly, 56:7 speaks of the joy shared by those who keep the sabbath, who come to God's holy mountain.

The history of sabbath observance in Israel demands a complex reconstruction. What we learn of the sabbath here is that it is a day set apart ("the holy day of the LORD"). This is described through a series of contrasts, all of which center on pursuing one's own ordinary, day-to-day interests. The sabbath is to be a day for God, set apart, honored. Not to be preoccupied with one's own things is the height of worship, and gives access to the material joy that God wants to give (v. 14). As the chapter closes, it is clear that issues of social justice, religious observance, daily relations, and sabbath obedience are woven together, and together they constitute what the poet understands as practicing true righteousness (58:2).

59:1-21. There is a general consensus that chap. 59 subdivides into three sections: vv. 1-8, vv. 9-15*a*, and vv. 15*b*-21). Less clear is the form-critical classification of the subunits and their relationship to one another. A special problem exists in vv. 9-15*a*. Is this a communal lament? How does one explain the presence of confessional elements (vv. 12-13)? Who is speaking: prophet, people, both? What seems reasonably clear is that v. 20 works on the basis of a distinction now set forth in chaps. 58–59—namely, between those who heed the prophet's admonitions and turn from sin and those who do not, thus meriting God's wrath (v. 18).

The final notice in v. 21 has been the subject of much commentary. We have had reference to covenant at 54:10; 55:3; and 56:4, 6. A further reference can be found at 61:8 in connection with "descendants" (זרעם *zarʿām,* 61:9). "Children" (lit., "seed" [זרע *zeraʿ*]) is a key word in these chap-

ters; it may be closely related to the promise given the servant that he would "see his offspring" (53:10), a theme picked up in the preceding chapters (54:3;) and maintained further (61:9; 65:23).[200] The promise of spirit and speech sounds prophetic in character, and the extent of the endowment has been enlarged to include all the "offspring" of the servant, which is not likely to be meant literally. More on this below.

59:1-8. The unit opens in a fashion with which we are familiar, where the complaint of the people is obliquely related in the context of a larger treatment. It corresponds roughly with 58:3, in that God's *not hearing* and *not saving* are in the foreground of the complaint, just as before his failure to take notice was registered by the people. The prophet then goes on to clarify, as in 58:3*b*-5, why the complaint is misdirected. Here, the indictment is very strong. God has been blockaded by the sins of the people and is unable to hear. The catalog of sins is wide ranging, general, and lengthy. What begins in direct address ("you and your God") shifts at v. 4 to third-person ("they speak lies"). The effect of this is to put greater distance between the indicter and the crimes themselves.

We see here the familiar emphasis on failure to produce justice (*mišpāṭ;* vv. 4, 8). Other vocabulary has appeared earlier as well ("deeds," "thoughts," "iniquity," "highway," "way of peace," "crooked"), some of it familiar from chaps. 40–52. The way of peace was referred to in 57:14-21 and belonged to the promises of the righteous in 57:1-2. This has been forfeited in the current context. There is no clear movement in the catalog of indictment, and the effect is simply one of accumulation. What the prophet wishes to emphasize is not only God's immunity from criticism, but the opposite: the people's massive accumulation of sin, taking the form of a barrier that separates them from God. The shift from second to third person only underscores this objectification of sin. In the final verse we have a summary that provides a fitting contrast to the way of the righteous (57:1-2).

59:9-15a. The difficult thing to determine here is the relationship of this unit to the preceding one. The first-person plural voice is maintained throughout. The form seems to be composite, with

---

200. See W. A. M. Beuken, "The Main Theme of Trito-Isaiah: 'The Servants of YHWH,'" *JSOT* 47 (1990) 67-87.

elements of a communal lament, but also with clear notes of confession (vv. 12-13). The question for exegesis is: Are we to take the confession of wrongdoing as directly related to the catalog of crimes in the opening unit (vv. 1-8)? Does the prophet deliver a strong indictment that is appropriately responded to by those speaking in vv. 9-15*a*? If so, why do elements of complaint still persist (vv. 9-11)? Has the prophet not clarified why justice and righteousness are lacking?

The position adopted here understands the first-person plural voice as that of the prophet, speaking on behalf of the righteous among the people.[201] Justice and righteousness (v. 9) are lacking for two reasons, one of which is clearly articulated in the following confession, the other having to do with the circumstances related in vv. 1-8. Justice and salvation (v. 11) are missing in part because of the people's transgressions, which the prophet relates in vv. 12-13. That is, he speaks on behalf of those penitent ones who concur with the indictment preceding (both in 59:1-8 and in chap. 58). But truth is also lacking in the public square (59:14-15). There is a dimension of the perversion of God's will that is so overwhelming, as related in 59:1-8, that the entire community suffers, over and above what their own transgressions have brought upon them. This reading explains the combination of confession and complaint that characterize the speech.

59:15b-20. In point of fact, v. 15 is to be divided merely for reasons of commentary. The first half of the verse summarizes the previous predicament, and is a natural extension of v. 14. At the same time, God's failure to see any justice is fully consistent with the cry that those who *do* turn aside from evil are despoiled (v. 15*a*). Now the complexity of the preceding unit finds its resolution. The complaint about lack of justice (v. 11) is not entirely a matter of the people's sins (v. 12). Even those who turn away from evil are vulnerable to abuse. This calls for a response, which God provides, whose culmination is the promise oracle at the close (v. 20). For those who turn aside from transgression, God *will* come as redeemer.

It is important to note the way in which this final unit responds to the complaint-confession that precedes. The final note sounded in that unit was not confession (vv. 12-13), but rather a return to complaint (vv. 14-15*a*), along something of the same lines as at the opening (vv. 9-11). Justice and righteousness stand at a distance; this is the same note sounded in vv. 9 and 14. Dimensions of this are traceable to the confession of wrongdoing, but that is not all. There is a public dimension to evil that has not been confessed and whose persistence plagues the community, especially those who seek God's righteousness and justice, if first through the avenue of their own confession.

There is considerable similarity between this unit (59:15*b*-20) and the one that follows the core proclamation (60:1–62:12), appearing in 63:1-6 (cf. esp. 59:16 and 63:5). In both the emphasis is on God's singular intervention. God's epiphany in judgment is described, using language familiar from pre-exilic prophecy, where the enemies to be judged are clearly extramural. Language like this can be found at 1:24; 42:13; and 52:10. Commentators frequently note the problem of its appearance here.[202] Yet at 1:24-26 we find a similar use of divine warrior motifs: Judgment on God's enemies includes the expression of divine wrath on Israel. This is the force of the unit under discussion, with a slight variation.

The preceding unit has clarified that injustice is an intramural concern. Verse 15*b* follows just as we would expect from vv. 14-15*a*. The "enemies" and "adversaries" under judgment in v. 18 correspond to those who have persisted in injustice, overwhelming the confession that precedes and frustrating divine response. The traditional language of divine warrior, on behalf of Israel, is retained, and remnants of the older form are most in evidence in v. 18*c:* "to the coastlands he will render requital." But even here, the extramural reference merely serves to set up the range intended by the poet for acknowledgment of God's epiphany (v. 19). The final verse resolves the dilemma and complaint, running back to 58:1. God's redemption is to take place for those in Jacob who turn from evil. The judgment has this final intention.

What remains to be clarified are the expressions

201. See P. A. Smith, *Rhetoric and Redaction in Trito-Isaiah,* VTSup 62 (Leiden: Brill, 1995) 122.

202. Westermann notes: "The section can only be taken as using language that is not appropriate." Westermann, *Isaiah 40–66,* 350.

employed in v. 16. Verse 16 speaks clearly about the lack of a human intervener. There is "no man" (אֵין אִישׁ *'ên 'îš*) and no one to intervene (אֵין מַפְגִּיעַ *'ên mapgîa'*). In some ways this corresponds to the prior work of the servant, whose intercessory work was for transgressors (53:12). Transgression was removed through the death of the servant. The servant made others righteous. But here we have an evil afflicting those who have themselves turned aside from wickedness (v. 15*ba*). Seeing no one to intervene in this instance, God relies on his own arm (cf. 53:1). Seeing no justice and righteousness, he girds these on himself for battle. The work undertaken by the servant here becomes God's own direct intervention, in the changed circumstances confronting the servants.

59:21. This final verse demands special comment. Many see a clear connection with 61:8-9. Some argue that the covenant referred to here has been drawn up on the basis of language found in chaps. 40–55, and in this location it serves to reinterpret the covenant of 61:8.[203] That is, the person now referred to in 61:1, and his descendants, become the covenant itself referred to at 61:8, on the basis of the editorial rereading supplied at this juncture in 59:21.

Yet the verse is too closely related to what precedes to serve that primary function. The covenant "with them" refers to those who have turned aside from transgression in Jacob. The content of the covenant does appear unusual, in that it is the promise of persistent spirit and speech from one generation to the next, for "them." The reference to spirit endowment recalls 42:1 (where "justice" is also a key word), there applied to Israel, and 44:3; it also recalls especially 48:16*c*, which, as argued above, involved a distinct transference of Israel's role to God's individual servant, confirmed in 49:1-6. Striking in 49:1-6 is the emphasis on speech ("he made my mouth like a sharp sword," 49:3) typical of prophetic commissioning (cf. Jer 1:9; see also Isa 51:16, "I have put my words in your mouth"). Both of these elements appear here in conjunction with an emphasis on the generations ("seed," "descendants" [*zera'*]).[204] This

key word was introduced in 53:10 and can be tracked further at 54:3 and 57:3 (see also 61:9). The covenantal promise is of eternal prophetic speech and spirit, for those who turn aside from evil.

How does this affect our reading of what follows? Here we need to avoid diachronic (developmental) theories about which texts were composed first and prefer to judge the final movement of the material as itself worthy of reflection. We can assume that an editor (or the author himself) intended us to read, not just his hypothetical erasures, but also the final organized shaping of the material.

In some sense, the emergence of clear language of commissioning, following previous prophetic speech, is similar to what occurs in the discourse of the servant (chaps. 40–52). Only at 48:16*c* do we have reference to individual commissioning. The fuller account at 49:1-6 clarifies this. Do we not have the same sort of movement here? The notice at 59:21 clarifies the commissioning—not just of the servant, but also of the servants who are his "offspring." (This notion is familiar from 8:16.) Their presence in the community constitutes God's eternal covenant with the contrite.

It should not be surprising, therefore, that we have a clear speech (long noted to be analogous to the servant speeches of chaps. 40–55) in 61:1-4, in which the prophetic "I" steps forward. When reference to the "everlasting covenant" appears at 61:8, it comes in a context of a prior statement, confirming God's love of justice and hatred of injustice (v. 8*a*). This intends to clarify what we learn at 59:21, that the covenant "with them" refers to a covenant with "those in Jacob who turn from transgression." Even if it were to be argued that chaps. 60–62 represent the core proclamation of a pristine "Trito-Isaiah," whose message is "salvation and nothing but salvation,"[205] that message has not formed the final word of the present Isaiah discourse. The emphasis on salvation remains in all its force, but it has been directed toward those within Jacob who are obedient to the prophetic word delivered from the servant and his "offspring." In chaps. 60–62, that servant steps forward with greatest clarity. Here we see and hear core proclamation to be sure. But the conclusion to be drawn from this is not that a secondary

203. B. Gosse, "L'alliance d'Isaïe 59,21," *ZAW* 101 (1989) 116-18.
204. Beuken draws special attention to 44:3 and 51:16 in connection with 59:21. See W. A. M. Beuken, "Servant and Herald of Good Tidings: Isaiah 61 as an Interpretation of Isaiah 40-55," in *The Book of Isaiah*, ed. J. Vermeylen (Leuven: Brill, 1989) 416.

205. Westermann, *Isaiah 40-66*, 296.

misreading or transformation has occurred, but rather that the proclamation of God's cleansing judgment and its specific attachment to captives, prisoners, the brokenhearted, and those who mourn (61:1-2) has been sharpened, not loosened, in the final presentation of the material. This is particularly evident in 56:1–59:21. A similar move is even more clearly evidenced in 63:1–66:24, on the other side of this core proclamation.

REFLECTIONS

1. This section is interesting for what it reveals about the state of mind of those who seek God's righteousness. One of the real hallmarks of this discourse (chaps. 54–66) is its propensity to share with us the various objections and complaints that surface in the community. This is in particular evidence at three points here: 58:3 and 59:1, 9-15*a*. Because the prophet identifies with the community he addresses and seeks to range himself with other righteous servants (see 65:13-15), we are able to glimpse something of the mood of the community he addresses. We lack a similar perspective in much pre-exilic prophecy.

This is not a community for which the prophet has no sympathy. In distinction, the rebuke that falls on the wicked leaders in 56:9–57:21 offers very little in the way of hope for a restored future for them. The righteous suffer at their hands (57:1-2).

Here, however, we see a people who seek righteousness (58:2). They are involved in fasting. But they feel that God has let them down. Their fasting is not acknowledged (58:3). Their prayers are not heard (59:1).

The prophet does not sympathize with them, but instead calls forth God's righteous judgment as the means by which their reinstatement will be accomplished. The prophet identifies a disjunction between their religious practices and their actual, manifest injustice. This has to be cleared up first. Fasting and prayer are always appropriate, when they are appropriately motivated.

What is striking is that the prophet's rebuke, in fact, leads to proper confession (59:9-15*a*), in which complaint still persists. God honors the circumstantial character of their sinful condition, and promises to come in vindication, precisely when the sins are confessed and the transgressions that the prophet has laid bare are acknowledged. It is all too easy to get a mechanical view of the way God means to deal with our conditions of hardship. Here, what came first was painful honesty about wrongly motivated religion. Then an even sharper portrait was painted explaining why God was not listening. Only then did confession emerge, allowing the true complexity of the situation to emerge in the light of day, and be honored and addressed by God. Often there is more to our anguish than the selfish assaults of others on us. There is a deeper reality that God seeks to get at first, involving our own dishonesty and transgressions. Here we may even get more than we bargained for out of a sense that what needed remedy was God or the evil around us.

2. If the reading of the communal lament in 59:9-15*a* is correct, it is the prophet himself who takes the lead. The remedy of confession in the midst of complaint requires leadership. It is easy to begin where the pain and misdirection are most obvious and testify to the need for God's intervention (59:9-10). All of us are forced to "grope like the blind along a wall" at moments in our walk toward obedient righteousness. The pain of waiting for deliverance can be overwhelming (59:11). But to see yet deeper into the abyss of our own transgressions takes prophetic courage. It is easier to blame God and neighbor than to seek a deeper, more painful look at our own shortcomings as the avenue on which justice will be found and confirmed around us.

The prophet and the people go down this road. Then the longed-for justice and righteousness are provided in ways we could not achieve—for ourselves in our own circumstance of transgression or to redress the truthless evil in the world around us. God comes with garments of righteousness, which simultaneously expose and cleanse our filthy garments and fully contend with the evil around us we were convinced could not be eradicated. This proximity and leadership, from prophet to people, is then seen for what it is in the final verse: as constituting an eternal covenant whose purpose is always to redeem those who turn away from transgression, "from now on and forever" (59:21).

ISAIAH 60:1–62:12, ZION'S EXALTATION

OVERVIEW

Special attention is generally given to these three chapters as a unit. The reasons for this involve a theory about the growth and development of tradition in chapters 55–66 in relation to Deutero-Isaiah material. First, "Trito-Isaiah" is understood as that individual who works most closely in association with Deutero-Isaiah. Material in these three chapters is thought to involve "salvation and nothing but salvation";[206] thus, if that is one's notion of Deutero-Isaiah's proclamation, it would follow that here we see the greatest proximity in tone and substance. Second, it is frequently held that these chapters betray the greatest demonstrable influence from chaps. 40–55. Third, the "I" voice of chap. 61 (and usually of chap. 62) is thought to be a clear manifestation of the prophet "Trito-Isaiah." Fourth, the community addressed in these chapters is "all Israel" or "all Jerusalem's inhabitants" without internal differentiation. This would, in theory, be consistent with Deutero-Isaiah, and inconsistent with chaps. 56–59. Finally, while distinctions are thought to exist between the appeal to historical realities, so prevalent in Deutero-Isaiah, and the appeal to more mythological or theological motifs in these core chapters,[207] the greatest proximity along this axis is found between the proclamation of chaps. 40–55 and that of chaps. 60–62. These chapters deal with the earthly Jerusalem and her inhabitants, and with real, not mythical, nations.

Considerable problems exist with this otherwise simple and straightforward reconstruction, based upon unilateral development and change. First, it is wrong to characterize the proclamation of 40–52(55) as "salvation and nothing but salvation." The servant's suffering and the anticipation of similar suffering for those who follow him (50:10-11; 51:12-16) suggest that the message of salvation from the servant's discourse is nuanced through and through. It is another question altogether whether and why such themes might appear in these three chapters, at this juncture in the discourse of chaps. 54–66. Second, there are clear signs of influence from other sections of Isaiah (not just "Deutero-Isaiah") in chaps. 54–59 that suggest a development of themes at work in the "suffering servant poem"—among them an interest in righteousness, the servants, and the progeny of the servant. There is no singular Deutero-Isaiah influence to be noted in 60–62 that would set these chapters apart, even when a density of intertextuality can be detected. The explanation for this density may have more to do with the subject matter itself than with a theory of chaps. 60–62 forming the core proclamation of "Trito-Isaiah."

The question as to whether chaps. 60–62 envision a uniform Israel, without internal differentiation (as over against 54–59), is an important one and will be taken up in the commentary below. The issue must be seen from the perspective of the entire movement of chaps. 54–66, and not isolated for the purpose of pursuing a theory of tradition-development alone. It has been argued, for example, that the author of 61:1-2 has in mind a specific group within Israel, not unlike the "righteous" of chaps. 54–59.[208] Again, the issue may be

206. C. Westermann, *Isaiah 40–66,* trans. David Stalker, OTL (Philadelphia: Westminster, 1969) 296.

207. Westermann, ibid., 353, states: "Here [salvation] . . . is not expected, as in Deutero-Isaiah, to be inaugurated by a definite historical event, but by the divine, miraculous transformation of a condition, the nation's oppression and its impoverishment, into its opposite."

208. W. A. M. Beuken, "Servant and Herald of Good Tidings: Isaiah 61 as an Interpretation of Isaiah 40–55," in *The Book of Isaiah,* ed. J. Vermeylen (Leuven: Brill, 1989) 411-42.

over-finessed—in either direction—if the larger context is ignored completely. It appears that 59:21 seeks to establish an important transition linking chaps. 58–59 to what follows in 60–62. If this is a correct appraisal, such a linking need not be artificial, but may well seek to highlight features latent in both collections, sharpening and clarifying what is at stake in the mature development of the material. What is decisive here is not so much making an either/or commitment to plotting theoretical change from an original or emphasizing mature development; what is decisive is becoming sensitive through a close reading of the contours and movements of the literature.

Indeed, precisely for this reason I regard it as probable that the voice that speaks up in chaps. 60–61 is indeed the voice of the prophet at work in the literature thus far. We view him here, as in chaps. 54–59, as a servant follower of the martyred servant of 52:13–53:12. This explains the transition to the plural form at 54:17 and the distinctive development of aspects of the suffering servant poem in chaps. 54–59. Here the affiliation with so-called Deutero-Isaiah material is to be expected. What comes as a surprise is the adaptation and development of aspects of the older servant's discourse.

The case can also be made positively for the placement of these chapters within a larger movement begun prior to chap. 54. Darkness and gloom and looking for light are spoken of in 59:9-10. The light's arrival and the gloom's transference to the peoples are described in 60:1-3. The arrival of children and adornment of Zion described in 60:4-7 was foreshadowed in chap. 54, as well as in 56:7-8. The subservience of the nations is a fulfillment of aspects of the servant's proclamation in chaps. 40–52; it represents a theme to be isolated from that of the inclusion of foreigners in 56:1-8. The righteousness missing in chaps. 56–59 is in full evidence at 60:21. The promise that ruins would be rebuilt, remarkable at 58:12, is reiterated at 61:4. The covenant and descendants (61:8) were spoken of at 59:21. Proper sentinels appear in 62:6, replacing false and overindulged ones at 56:10. The call to prepare the "way of the people" repeats almost verbatim a similar appeal at 57:14. The "redeemed of the LORD" at 62:12 recalls the promise of 59:20: "He will come to Zion as Redeemer." Finally, 59:15b-19 closely resembles 63:1-6, suggesting that chaps. 60–62 form an important transition before the former declaration can be pursued in detail at 63:1-6, now with a different nuance.

A great many interpreters are prepared to accept chaps. 60–62 in their present literary integrity as a unit. This coheres in some measure with the notion of a core "Trito-Isaiah" message. Efforts to detect complex redactional levels and rearrangements in the final form have not met with widespread acceptance.[209] Some wish to extend the primary unit to include 63:1-6 as well, believing these verses exemplify the vengeance on Edom called for in chaps. 61–62, on Edom.[210] As we regard the material in its entirety as meaningfully arranged and interrelated, distinctions such as these are less crucial. It is not enough to consider chaps. 60–62 before discussing 63:1-6.

The three chapters do treat distinct, though related, topics. Chapter 60 keeps at the center of its focus the city Zion. It is not concerned as much with Zion's present inhabitants as with the nations and with Zion's children who have yet to be gathered. In contrast, chap. 61 concerns itself with "those who mourn in Zion" (v. 3). Chapter 62 emphasizes the theme of Zion's vindication. The city and its present inhabitants are brought together only at the close (vv. 10-12).

209. J. Vermeylen's work utilizes this sort of approach. See J. Vermeylen, *Du Prophete Isaie a l'apocalyptique* (Paris: J. Gabalda, 1977).
210. P. A. Smith, *Rhetoric and Redaction in Trito-Isaiah,* VTSup 62 (Leiden: Brill, 1995) 38-44.

Isaiah 60:1-22, Zion, the Divine Light of the World

NIV

60 "Arise, shine, for your light has come,
and the glory of the LORD rises upon you.
²See, darkness covers the earth
and thick darkness is over the peoples,
but the LORD rises upon you
and his glory appears over you.
³Nations will come to your light,
and kings to the brightness of your dawn.

⁴"Lift up your eyes and look about you:
All assemble and come to you;
your sons come from afar,
and your daughters are carried on the arm.
⁵Then you will look and be radiant,
your heart will throb and swell with joy;
the wealth on the seas will be brought to you,
to you the riches of the nations will come.
⁶Herds of camels will cover your land,
young camels of Midian and Ephah.
And all from Sheba will come,
bearing gold and incense
and proclaiming the praise of the LORD.
⁷All Kedar's flocks will be gathered to you,
the rams of Nebaioth will serve you;
they will be accepted as offerings on my altar,
and I will adorn my glorious temple.

⁸"Who are these that fly along like clouds,
like doves to their nests?
⁹Surely the islands look to me;
in the lead are the ships of Tarshish,ᵃ
bringing your sons from afar,
with their silver and gold,
to the honor of the LORD your God,
the Holy One of Israel,
for he has endowed you with splendor.

¹⁰"Foreigners will rebuild your walls,
and their kings will serve you.
Though in anger I struck you,
in favor I will show you compassion.
¹¹Your gates will always stand open,
they will never be shut, day or night,
so that men may bring you the wealth of
the nations—

ᵃ9 Or *the trading ships*

NRSV

60 Arise, shine; for your light has come,
and the glory of the LORD has risen
upon you.
² For darkness shall cover the earth,
and thick darkness the peoples;
but the LORD will arise upon you,
and his glory will appear over you.
³ Nations shall come to your light,
and kings to the brightness of your dawn.

⁴ Lift up your eyes and look around;
they all gather together, they come to you;
your sons shall come from far away,
and your daughters shall be carried on
their nurses' arms.
⁵ Then you shall see and be radiant;
your heart shall thrill and rejoice,ᵃ
because the abundance of the sea shall be
brought to you,
the wealth of the nations shall come to you.
⁶ A multitude of camels shall cover you,
the young camels of Midian and Ephah;
all those from Sheba shall come.
They shall bring gold and frankincense,
and shall proclaim the praise of the LORD.
⁷ All the flocks of Kedar shall be gathered
to you,
the rams of Nebaioth shall minister to you;
they shall be acceptable on my altar,
and I will glorify my glorious house.

⁸ Who are these that fly like a cloud,
and like doves to their windows?
⁹ For the coastlands shall wait for me,
the ships of Tarshish first,
to bring your children from far away,
their silver and gold with them,
for the name of the LORD your God,
and for the Holy One of Israel,
because he has glorified you.
¹⁰ Foreigners shall build up your walls,
and their kings shall minister to you;
for in my wrath I struck you down,
but in my favor I have had mercy on you.

ᵃHeb *be enlarged*

NIV

their kings led in triumphal procession.
¹²For the nation or kingdom that will not serve
you will perish;
it will be utterly ruined.

¹³"The glory of Lebanon will come to you,
the pine, the fir and the cypress together,
to adorn the place of my sanctuary;
and I will glorify the place of my feet.
¹⁴The sons of your oppressors will come bowing
before you;
all who despise you will bow down at
your feet
and will call you the City of the LORD,
Zion of the Holy One of Israel.

¹⁵"Although you have been forsaken and hated,
with no one traveling through,
I will make you the everlasting pride
and the joy of all generations.
¹⁶You will drink the milk of nations
and be nursed at royal breasts.
Then you will know that I, the LORD, am
your Savior,
your Redeemer, the Mighty One of Jacob.
¹⁷Instead of bronze I will bring you gold,
and silver in place of iron.
Instead of wood I will bring you bronze,
and iron in place of stones.
I will make peace your governor
and righteousness your ruler.
¹⁸No longer will violence be heard in your land,
nor ruin or destruction within your borders,
but you will call your walls Salvation
and your gates Praise.
¹⁹The sun will no more be your light by day,
nor will the brightness of the moon shine
on you,
for the LORD will be your everlasting light,
and your God will be your glory.
²⁰Your sun will never set again,
and your moon will wane no more;
the LORD will be your everlasting light,
and your days of sorrow will end.
²¹Then will all your people be righteous
and they will possess the land forever.
They are the shoot I have planted,
the work of my hands,

NRSV

¹¹ Your gates shall always be open;
day and night they shall not be shut,
so that nations shall bring you their wealth,
with their kings led in procession.
¹² For the nation and kingdom
that will not serve you shall perish;
those nations shall be utterly laid waste.
¹³ The glory of Lebanon shall come to you,
the cypress, the plane, and the pine,
to beautify the place of my sanctuary;
and I will glorify where my feet rest.
¹⁴ The descendants of those who oppressed you
shall come bending low to you,
and all who despised you
shall bow down at your feet;
they shall call you the City of the LORD,
the Zion of the Holy One of Israel.
¹⁵ Whereas you have been forsaken and hated,
with no one passing through,
I will make you majestic forever,
a joy from age to age.
¹⁶ You shall suck the milk of nations,
you shall suck the breasts of kings;
and you shall know that I, the LORD, am
your Savior
and your Redeemer, the Mighty One
of Jacob.

¹⁷ Instead of bronze I will bring gold,
instead of iron I will bring silver;
instead of wood, bronze,
instead of stones, iron.
I will appoint Peace as your overseer
and Righteousness as your taskmaster.
¹⁸ Violence shall no more be heard in your land,
devastation or destruction within
your borders;
you shall call your walls Salvation,
and your gates Praise.
¹⁹ The sun shall no longer be
your light by day,
nor for brightness shall the moon
give light to you by night;^a
but the LORD will be your everlasting light,
and your God will be your glory.
²⁰ Your sun shall no more go down,

^aQ Ms Gk Old Latin Tg: MT lacks *by night*

NIV

for the display of my splendor.
²²The least of you will become a thousand,
    the smallest a mighty nation.
I am the LORD;
    in its time I will do this swiftly."

NRSV

or your moon withdraw itself;
    for the LORD will be your everlasting light,
    and your days of mourning shall be ended.
²¹ Your people shall all be righteous;
    they shall possess the land forever.
They are the shoot that I planted, the work of
    my hands,
    so that I might be glorified.
²² The least of them shall become a clan,
    and the smallest one a mighty nation;
I am the LORD;
    in its time I will accomplish it quickly.

COMMENTARY

It could be helpful to talk about strophes or smaller rhetorical units in this text—elements that move the material along. Yet most agree that it is a long, unified composition. The precise determination of units is therefore less decisive for interpretation.

In both the opening and the closing sections (vv. 1-3 and vv. 19-22) the motif of light predominates. The pairing "nations/kings" is introduced in 60:3, and pursued further at vv. 10-12. The poem speaks of the return of Zion's children in the context of the nations' approach, obeisance, and offering. Zion's fortification and salvation are on the verge of fulfillment (v. 22*b*). In many respects, the poem reiterates and elaborates themes introduced in chap. 54 (return of Zion's children, Zion's protection, and Zion's adornment). In that chapter greater emphasis is laid on the moment of marriage and renewed comfort (54:4-10). Here the emphasis shifts to Zion's dramatic exaltation, the place to which her children and all the nations stream.

60:1-3. Light is, of course, the opposite of darkness. Thus far in the discourse (e.g., chaps. 56–59) there has been more emphasis on darkness than on light (59:9-10). Earlier in the discourse of the servant, light was a prominent theme. Most notably, it was used in connection with the nations. The servant is to be "light to the nations" (42:6; 49:6). It is the servant whom nations and kings will acknowledge (52:15). The servant will also be high and lifted up (52:13). In short, all that

was said of the servant—first, of Israel as servant, then of the individual "servant Israel"—is here associated with Zion. She is to rise up; nations and kings are to stream to her light. This light is identified clearly with God's epiphany: "the LORD will arise upon you, and his glory will appear over you." The connection here is established with the promise of 59:20 that God would come to Zion as redeemer.

What occurs is the coalescing of various themes introduced in the discourse of the servant. Zion was promised in 40:1-11 that God would come to her and that all people would witness God's glory as a result. The association of Zion with the streaming of the nations was established in 49:22. To a degree the promises associated with the servant and his exaltation come to fruition in this paean to Zion. The promise that all her people will be righteous, which comes in the final verse (v. 21), is likewise related to the mission of the individual servant (53:11), a theme that has been traced throughout chaps. 54–59 as well.

It should not pass notice that another key text may well have influenced the poet in these verses. In the "former things" of Isaiah, a time of darkness and distress is foretold, when people will turn their faces upward, only to see the "gloom of anguish" (8:22). This former time is then set in contrast to the latter time—a contrast that may well figure prominently in the logic of the discourse of the servant (chaps. 40–48). At this latter time, a "great light" is seen by those who had walked in darkness: "on them light has shined" (9:2). The oracle goes on to relate this to the birth of a Davidic scion. The author, however, has connected the great light to Zion and her time of resplendence, now that the former time has passed. The darkness now covers the people, thereby increasing Zion's visibility.

60:4-7. The first half of v. 4 presents word-by-word the text of 49:18*a*, where the original promise was made to Zion that she would put on her children like adornments. That was a context of despair into which a word of hope was delivered to a forsaken Zion. The actual fulfillment of the promise is closer here as the poet strains to depict a grand and joyous homecoming. Verse 5 may represent an effort to contrast the terrifying and dread river that once threatened Zion's existence in the former times (see 8:7) with the swollen and enlarged heart of Zion as the abundance of the sea comes now in the form of the nations' wealth (cf. 45:14). These various offerings, the finest from the representative nations, are acceptable for God's altar—the same phrase used at 56:7. The point of the gifts now is not Zion's adornment, which has occurred in earlier chapters (52:1; 54:11-12), but the glorifying of God's house, and specifically the sanctuary and altar (see also v. 13).

60:8-13. The litany of gifts continues. The swiftness of the return is likened to clouds and doves. The ships of Tarshish are in the lead, bringing back the dispersed. In the former things of Isaiah, the wealth of Tyre is to be dedicated to the Lord, in the time to come (23:17-18). If that text lies close at hand here, then "their silver and gold" would be the wealth of the ships of Tarshish, not of Zion's children.

In this scenario, which deals with the influx of the nations' carrying Zion's children home, kings and nations are depicted as doing service (cf. Rev 21:24-27). Upon arrival, they deposit Zion's children and the offerings for the sanctuary. The offerings motif finds an irenic narration in Ezra 6:8-12. Here, in the light of Israel's former oppression by the nations, the roles are reversed. This occurs, not for its own sake, but so that God's sanctuary might be glorified and beautified.

60:14-16. The feet the descendants of oppressors bow down to belong to Zion. In a context that focuses on Zion's debasement, sharper images are deployed (see 45:14; 49:23; 51:23). Here the point is not simple debasement, but acknowledgment that Zion is God's special, holy place of dwelling. Interpreters who seek to isolate layers in chaps. 40–66 based on the depiction of the nations often fail to give due emphasis to the specific place in which a given depiction occurs.[211] Kings and queens are foster fathers and nursing mothers in 49:23, before they do extreme obeisance: "They shall bow down to you, and lick the dust of your feet." Here the image is essentially maintained, but the point is Zion's recognition of the Lord's redemption—promised at 59:20. Moreover, the text speaks of *children* ("descendants") of former oppressors, thus introducing a distinction that may well coordinate with the depiction of their role vis-à-vis Zion (over against what we saw of the previous generation of oppressors in chaps. 40–52). Incidentally, here we see the only real temporal distinction operative in the literature itself that differentiates the discourse of the servant (chaps. 40–52) from that of the servants (52:13–53:12; 54–66)—namely, the movement from one generation to the next.

60:17-22. The final verses are often taken as distinctive within the chapter, if not also separated for that reason and viewed as independent. The first two of these verses simply emphasize that Zion will now be greater than any former display of magnificence. The reference to overseers and taskmasters in v. 17*b* goes together closely with what follows in v. 18. Instead of violence and senseless oppression, as before, now Zion's "overseers" are the epitome of peace and righteousness. Violence is over—this is fully consistent with the preceding images of obeisance, whose purpose is proper acknowledgement of Zion as God's holy city.

More difficult to square with what precedes are the final verses (vv. 19-22). The mood seems more pronouncedly apocalyptic. The motif of Zion's divine light, introduced in 60:1-3, is picked up again in these verses. Now the light is so prominent and everlasting, the cycles of sun and moon are shut down (v. 20). Zion's exaltation has cosmic, transnational consequences. Here the depiction begins to approach the form found later in the discourse (65:17-25). The end of all mourning

---

211. O. Steck, *Studien zu Tritojesaja* (Berlin/New York: de Gruyter, 1991) 182-86.

(v. 20) is a theme at 65:19 as well, and it is developed at the start of the next chapter (61:2-3). Even the notion that *all* of Zion's children will be righteous seems to outstrip the mundane reality described thus far.

One solution has been to isolate the discourse of these chapters in their entirety (60–62) and describe them as the core proclamation of Trito-Isaiah. Yet even here interpreters note a movement in vv. 17-22 that is taken to be distinctive over against the preceding verses (vv. 1-16), to be labeled "apocalyptic."[212]

It is important not to introduce distinctions too quickly, or when they are inconsistent with the discourse itself. Verse 2 speaks of "deep darkness" enshrouding the nations, a theme likely developed on the basis of prior Isaianic texts, and hardly one amenable to "the confines of this world and of history."[213] The wealth of nations being continuously

hauled through gates never shut also borders on apocalyptic depiction. Many other images in the poem could be pointed out as well in this regard.

We must not let the dramatic and enthusiastic poetic force of the material be translated too quickly into social and mundane realities. The text speaks of a marvelous transformation of Zion and the nations. It does so because this is the intention of God as it has pressed itself on the mind of the author. It is inspired speech. Some of its inspiration is "borrowed"—drawn from the promises of God long ago, according to the principle introduced at 55:11. The final verse reminds us that the vision of Zion's glorification is fully under God's sovereign time and intention. It is not content, in the manner of its own expression, to set forth a program, whose point-by-point completion can be monitored. It is God's statement from the prophet about divine final intentions for Israel, Zion, and the nations. Its accomplishment will be swift, according to a time only God knows. (See Reflections at 61:1–62:12.)

---

212. Westermann, *Isaiah 40–66,* 364, comments: "In all the rest of ch. 60 the salvation proclaimed never transcends the confines of this world and of history."

213. See ibid., 364, who remarks: "When 60.1ff. speak of God's being a light, they way they do so is completely different."

Isaiah 61:1–62:12, The Holy People, the City Not Forsaken

61 The Spirit of the Sovereign LORD is on me,
   because the LORD has anointed me
   to preach good news to the poor.
He has sent me to bind up the brokenhearted,
   to proclaim freedom for the captives
   and release from darkness for the prisoners,[a]
[2] to proclaim the year of the LORD's favor
   and the day of vengeance of our God,
to comfort all who mourn,
[3] and provide for those who grieve in Zion—
to bestow on them a crown of beauty
   instead of ashes,
the oil of gladness
   instead of mourning,
and a garment of praise
   instead of a spirit of despair.
They will be called oaks of righteousness,
   a planting of the LORD
   for the display of his splendor.

a1 Hebrew; Septuagint the blind

61 The spirit of the Lord GOD is upon me,
   because the LORD has anointed me;
he has sent me to bring good news to the
      oppressed,
   to bind up the brokenhearted,
to proclaim liberty to the captives,
   and release to the prisoners;
[2] to proclaim the year of the LORD's favor,
   and the day of vengeance of our God;
   to comfort all who mourn;
[3] to provide for those who mourn in Zion—
   to give them a garland instead of ashes,
the oil of gladness instead of mourning,
   the mantle of praise instead of a faint spirit.
They will be called oaks of righteousness,
   the planting of the LORD, to display his glory.
[4] They shall build up the ancient ruins,
   they shall raise up the former devastations;
they shall repair the ruined cities,
   the devastations of many generations.

NIV

⁴They will rebuild the ancient ruins
  and restore the places long devastated;
they will renew the ruined cities
  that have been devastated for generations.
⁵Aliens will shepherd your flocks;
  foreigners will work your fields and
    vineyards.
⁶And you will be called priests of the LORD,
  you will be named ministers of our God.
You will feed on the wealth of nations,
  and in their riches you will boast.

⁷Instead of their shame
  my people will receive a double portion,
and instead of disgrace
  they will rejoice in their inheritance;
and so they will inherit a double portion in
    their land,
  and everlasting joy will be theirs.

⁸"For I, the LORD, love justice;
  I hate robbery and iniquity.
In my faithfulness I will reward them
  and make an everlasting covenant
    with them.
⁹Their descendants will be known among
    the nations
  and their offspring among the peoples.
All who see them will acknowledge
  that they are a people the LORD has blessed."

¹⁰I delight greatly in the LORD;
  my soul rejoices in my God.
For he has clothed me with garments
    of salvation
  and arrayed me in a robe of righteousness,
as a bridegroom adorns his head like a priest,
  and as a bride adorns herself with her jewels.
¹¹For as the soil makes the sprout come up
  and a garden causes seeds to grow,
so the Sovereign LORD will make righteousness
    and praise
  spring up before all nations.

62 For Zion's sake I will not keep silent,
  for Jerusalem's sake I will not
    remain quiet,
till her righteousness shines out like the dawn,
  her salvation like a blazing torch.
²The nations will see your righteousness,

NRSV

⁵Strangers shall stand and feed your flocks,
  foreigners shall till your land and dress
    your vines;
⁶but you shall be called priests of the LORD,
  you shall be named ministers of our God;
you shall enjoy the wealth of the nations,
  and in their riches you shall glory.
⁷Because their*a* shame was double,
  and dishonor was proclaimed as their lot,
therefore they shall possess a double portion;
  everlasting joy shall be theirs.

⁸For I the LORD love justice,
  I hate robbery and wrongdoing;*b*
I will faithfully give them their recompense,
  and I will make an everlasting covenant
    with them.
⁹Their descendants shall be known among
    the nations,
  and their offspring among the peoples;
all who see them shall acknowledge
  that they are a people whom the LORD
    has blessed.
¹⁰I will greatly rejoice in the LORD,
  my whole being shall exult in my God;
for he has clothed me with the garments
    of salvation,
  he has covered me with the robe of
    righteousness,
as a bridegroom decks himself with a garland,
  and as a bride adorns herself with
    her jewels.
¹¹For as the earth brings forth its shoots,
  and as a garden causes what is sown in it
    to spring up,
so the Lord GOD will cause righteousness
    and praise
  to spring up before all the nations.

62 For Zion's sake I will not keep silent,
  and for Jerusalem's sake I will not rest,
until her vindication shines out like the dawn,
  and her salvation like a burning torch.
²The nations shall see your vindication,
  and all the kings your glory;
and you shall be called by a new name
  that the mouth of the LORD will give.

*a*Heb *your*   *b*Or *robbery with a burnt offering*

NIV

and all kings your glory;
you will be called by a new name
    that the mouth of the LORD will bestow.
³You will be a crown of splendor in the
    LORD's hand,
    a royal diadem in the hand of your God.
⁴No longer will they call you Deserted,
    or name your land Desolate.
But you will be called Hephzibah,ᵃ
    and your land Beulahᵇ;
for the LORD will take delight in you,
    and your land will be married.
⁵As a young man marries a maiden,
    so will your sonsᶜ marry you;
as a bridegroom rejoices over his bride,
    so will your God rejoice over you.

⁶I have posted watchmen on your walls,
        O Jerusalem;
    they will never be silent day or night.
You who call on the LORD,
    give yourselves no rest,
⁷and give him no rest till he establishes
        Jerusalem
    and makes her the praise of the earth.

⁸The LORD has sworn by his right hand
    and by his mighty arm:
"Never again will I give your grain
    as food for your enemies,
and never again will foreigners drink the
        new wine
    for which you have toiled;
⁹but those who harvest it will eat it
    and praise the LORD,
and those who gather the grapes will drink it
    in the courts of my sanctuary."

¹⁰Pass through, pass through the gates!
    Prepare the way for the people.
Build up, build up the highway!
    Remove the stones.
Raise a banner for the nations.

¹¹The LORD has made proclamation
    to the ends of the earth:
"Say to the Daughter of Zion,
    'See, your Savior comes!

ᵃ4 Hephzibah means my delight is in her.   ᵇ4 Beulah means married.   ᶜ5 Or Builder

NRSV

³You shall be a crown of beauty in the hand of
        the LORD,
    and a royal diadem in the hand of your God.
⁴You shall no more be termed Forsaken,ᵃ
    and your land shall no more be termed
        Desolate;ᵇ
but you shall be called My Delight Is in Herᶜ
    and your land Married;ᵈ
for the LORD delights in you,
    and your land shall be married.
⁵For as a young man marries a young woman,
    so shall your builderᵉ marry you,
and as the bridegroom rejoices over the bride,
    so shall your God rejoice over you.
⁶Upon your walls, O Jerusalem,
    I have posted sentinels;
all day and all night
    they shall never be silent.
You who remind the LORD,
    take no rest,
⁷and give him no rest
    until he establishes Jerusalem
    and makes it renowned throughout the earth.
⁸The LORD has sworn by his right hand
    and by his mighty arm:
I will not again give your grain
    to be food for your enemies,
and foreigners shall not drink the wine
    for which you have labored;
⁹but those who garner it shall eat it
    and praise the LORD,
and those who gather it shall drink it
    in my holy courts.

¹⁰Go through, go through the gates,
    prepare the way for the people;
build up, build up the highway,
    clear it of stones,
    lift up an ensign over the peoples.
¹¹The LORD has proclaimed
    to the end of the earth:
Say to daughter Zion,
    "See, your salvation comes;
his reward is with him,
    and his recompense before him."
¹²They shall be called, "The Holy People,

ᵃHeb Azubah   ᵇHeb Shemamah   ᶜHeb Hephzibah   ᵈHeb Beulah   ᵉCn: Heb your sons

NIV	NRSV

See, his reward is with him,
    and his recompense accompanies him.' "
[12]They will be called the Holy People,
    the Redeemed of the LORD;
and you will be called Sought After,
    the City No Longer Deserted.
	The Redeemed of the LORD";
	    and you shall be called, "Sought Out,
	    A City Not Forsaken."

COMMENTARY

Many commentators have noted the degree to which especially 61:1-4 is indebted to language, motifs, and expressions found earlier in the discourse of "Second Isaiah."[214] Spirit endowment is spoken of in connection with the servant (42:1; 48:16) and more generally with Jacob/Israel's offspring at 44:3. Anointing appears in connection with Cyrus (45:1). "Bringing good news" (לבשׂר *lĕbaśśēr*) is an expression that appears frequently in Deutero-Isaiah chapters, connected with the heralds who announce tidings to Jerusalem (40:9; 41:27; 52:7).

Just as important are the connections within our present discourse. At 59:21 we have the announcement of spirit endowment for the prophet at work in our material. As mentioned above, two concepts seem to have been combined there: the prophetic commissioning associated with God's servant (42:1; 48:16), and the generational extension of that spirit, based on 44:3. This fact, God announces, itself constitutes a covenant "with them"—a reference to those who have turned from transgression in Jacob in the preceding verse (59:20), prefaced by God's promised return to Zion. That epiphany was the subject of chap. 60. In chap. 61, the prophet acts in the spirit of the covenant announced in 59:21. To repeat: the content of the covenant is *his actual prophetic (speech and spirit) relationship to the repentant.* This (on the face of it) unusual content of the covenant may be anticipated at 42:6, where reference is made to a ברית עם (*bĕrît 'ām,* "a people-covenant" or "a covenant of/for the people"). If the connection is real and not mistaken, 59:21

sees this covenant enacted in the particular relationship between the prophet and a specific group in Israel: those who turn from evil.[215]

If this view of the matter is accurate, it runs counter to the prevailing opinion that chaps. 60–62 contain the core proclamation of nothing but salvation, addressed to all Israel. The position adopted in this commentary is based on a close reading of the material *in its present form,* taking seriously the notice at 59:21 and the preceding movement of the material, where a distinction is clearly introduced between the righteous servants and their oppressors. These righteous ones are not without transgression, but they are addressed by the prophet and told to turn away in repentance.

This position can be further strengthened by attention to chaps. 63–66. I will only note the most salient matters at this point. The everlasting covenant is spoken of again in 61:8, coordinating with 59:21. The seed (זרעם *zar'ām,* "their descendants") of those within the covenant are mentioned in 61:9, picking up the generational motif of 44:3, here affiliated with the promise associated with the prophet and his "seed" in 59:21. We have tracked the use of the term זרע (*zera'*) from the final servant poem (53:10) and have seen it to be significant in the movement of the material. The true vindication of the servants culminates in chap. 65. In 65:9, the righteous remnant is identified. Out from Jacob, the text says, God brings forth a seed (NRSV, "descendants") on behalf of the servants (65:8). These inherit the holy mountain, as God's servants, and settle there. A distinction is being clearly drawn in this chapter between an unrighteous, apostate group—such as

214. See W. A. M. Beuken, "Servant and Herald of Good Tidings: Isaiah 61 as an Interpretation of Isaiah 40-55," in *The Book of Isaiah,* ed. J. Vermeylen (Leuven: Brill, 1989); Smith, *Rhetoric and Redaction in Trito-Isaiah,* 24-25.

215. Cf. the (popular) interpretation of Smith, ibid., 26 and others, who view Isaiah 60–62 as earlier and more universal than other material in chaps. 56–66.

we saw in chaps. 56–59—and God's righteous seed. At the close of chap. 62, the righteous are called God's "Holy People" and their sure residence in an exalted Zion is also stipulated. These "redeemed of the LORD" correspond to the ones God promises to redeem (59:20). What is less clear, but worthy of consideration, is whether the notion of a righteous and holy seed is based in part on 6:13: "the holy seed is its stump"—a reference to a remnant after protracted judgment.

Taken together, these various texts reveal that the address to "those who mourn in Zion" (61:3) in chaps. 61–62 is not a generic address, but is issued within the parameters already drawn in chaps. 56–59. There we learn that the covenant God establishes is grounded in a relationship between the prophet and his seed and those who turn from sin in Jacob. Whatever its pre-history may have been, chap. 61 is open to scholarly speculation, of course. But the presentation of the material as we now have it suggests a clear picture, in which the prophet steps forward to address the audience set apart in chap. 59, which will be further so designated in chaps. 63–66.

61:1-3. Here the mission of the servant is made manifest. The form resembles 49:1-6. This section is not a "call narrative" as such; rather, like 49:1-6, it consists of a modification of that older form. In some sense it offers a clarification of a call already under way. That is not so unusual in the book of Isaiah.[216] What is unusual is the causal clause (יַעַן *ya'an,* "because"), which begins in v. 1*a* and extends to the various infinitive clauses that follow. Strictly speaking, there are seven of these clauses in all. The prophet's spirit possession entails his specific function with the community, which is spelled out in the infinitive clauses. This is fully consistent with the force of 59:21; the prophet's mission is comprehended through the lens of his relationship to that segment of the community God seeks to redeem (59:20).

We find aspects of the prophet's mission coordinated with that of the servant earlier. He is anointed and sent, and so represents a coalescing

of roles once belonging to Cyrus (as liberator) and servant (within Israel; see esp. 42:1-7). The oppressed (lit., "afflicted" [עֲנָוִים *'ănāwîm*]) and brokenhearted resemble not only the contrite persons of 57:15 and the suffering servant himself, but also the afflicted Zion (51:21; 54:11)—a sense now no longer apposite. Verse 1*b* seems to have been influenced by 42:7, although the exchange is not exact. The depiction of a day of vengeance and year of favor appears to be a coalescing of 34:8 and 59:17, on the one hand, with a positive outcome ("favor") for those whom the prophet here addresses, on the other hand. "Comfort" is a virtual motif-word in Deutero-Isaiah, and here it is expressly tied to those who mourn in Zion. The "faint spirit" of v. 3*b* recalls both 57:16 and 42:1, thus again bringing together aspects of the present and earlier discourse. The thrust is that continuity has been maintained from servant to the generation of the servants, even in new and changed circumstances. Our prophet knows who he is with reference to what God has said and what the servant has done. The intertextuality is not just a technique to be traced out, but has important implications for the prophet's own self-understanding.

The final line (v. 3*b*) picks up certain aspects of 60:21, thus justifying the notion that all three of these chapters are closely related. The righteous people are to be "God's own planting" (מַטַּע יהוה *matta' YHWH*), so that God might get glory. This promise is reiterated here and joined up with the image of righteous oaks.

61:4-7. The transition at this point is not all that sharp; some would read v. 4 with the preceding unit. It is not decisive for exegesis. Yet again we get a clear reiteration of earlier material. Verse 4 expands and elaborates the promise of 58:12. That promise was made within the context of conditionality—*if* those addressed did righteousness and justice. Here the promise is delivered full-stop, appropriate to the genre of the chapter itself, an oracle of salvation for the righteous remnant. Verse 5 follows loosely the logic of 60:7, but here serves primarily to set up a contrast. The nations' gifts referred to in chap. 60 were to serve as offerings (60:7); for such offerings priests and ministers are required. A double portion is deemed appropriate to a double bearing of shame. Though the terms used are different, the "double" payment for

<hr/>

216. See C. R. Seitz, *Isaiah 1–39,* OTL (Louisville: Westminster, 1993) for the treatment of the placement of Isaiah 6. Also in the discourse of chaps. 40–52, a similar move can be detected; see the commentary above. The prophet never steps fully into view until well into the discourse. So too here.

sin referred to in 40:2 may lie close at hand. The shift from second-person plural to third-person plural (somewhat rough in v. 7*a,* text-critically) eases the transition to the following unit, and anticipates a focus on descendants there, appropriately spoken of in the third-person plural (v. 9).

61:8-11. The significance of vv. 8-9 has been treated in some detail already for the proper interpretation of chaps. 60–62. The key words "covenant" and "descendants/offspring" are coordinated with 59:21, and here refer to the objects of prophetic speech, within the covenant God has established between prophet and those who turn from sin (59:20-21). In the future, this offspring will be acknowledged by the nations. Here is a fulfillment of the promise to the servant (52:13) that the nations would come to understand, now brought to fruition through the persistence and destiny of the righteous "seed"—again, in clear relationship to the promise of 53:10.

The final two verses (vv. 10-11) return us to the prophet's own first-person praise. "Righteousness" is clearly the main concern in these verses. The clothes God puts on in order to establish justice—within and without (59:17)—are here garments of the righteous servant. The recognition of the nations is again the final theme of the chapter. The work of the servant is being accomplished in the next generation, and in generations to come. Promises of Deutero-Isaiah retain their force in new and changed circumstances (44:3; 52:13; 53:10), combined with the concerns of a new day (59:20-21; 60:21).

62:1-5. The extremely close association between Zion and her "taught children" demands at this point a return to concern with her vindication. Chapter 60 described an exalted Zion in terms also reminiscent of the servant. Nations and kings were to acknowledge her, in the same way that the righteousness manifested by the servants will "spring up before all nations" (61:11). The NRSV renders "vindication" for צדקה (*ṣĕdāqâ*), the term otherwise translated "righteousness." The term is repeated in v. 2. The general image of light deployed at the opening of chap. 60 is joined here by others: dawn's first light and a burning torch. The righteousness the servant was to establish (53:11) is manifested in the servants and the restored Zion. God's creation of these two sure realities is what testifies to divine

power, and gives sure witness before the nations of the continuity of God's promises from generation to generation.

The abandonment motif appears frequently in respect to Zion in earlier chapters; indeed, it is the first word out of Zion's mouth (49:14; see also 54:6). Zion has a new name here, given by God (v. 2) as if in a betrothal naming. Most modern interpreters regard the Hebrew בניך (*bānāyik,* "your sons") at v. 5*a* as inappropriate[217] and opt for בניך (*bōnêk,* "your builder") instead (cf. 49:17). The NIV has retained the older tradition here. This is consistent with the close relationship the prophet asserts between Zion's righteous children and their mother (see 54:13). What it might mean for Zion's "builder" to marry her remains unclear in any event, and in some sense offers no obvious resolution. The union of God and Zion is analogous, in the poetic expression of v. 5, with Zion and her children.

62:6-9. As Westermann notes, there is a close parallel between v. 6 and v. 1.[218] Sentinels (NRSV) were mentioned in 52:8, though a different Hebrew term is used there. In 52:7-10 there is a corresponding epilogue to 40:1-11; now the messengers and sentinels announce what God had earlier promised from the heavenly council. Here a different term is used, toward a somewhat different end. These "watchmen" (NIV) are dispatched by the prophet to ceaselessly keep God on notice about Zion's establishment in the sight of the nations. At the forefront here is not Zion's marriage or exaltation, but rather her protection and vindication before the entire earth (vv. 8-9; 11). It is important to note these themes as we approach 63:1-6. The situation the prophet calls for here—alert sentinels on Jerusalem's walls—is acted out in 63:1-6, and the emphasis there is on military victory.

62:10-12. These verses contain a virtual collage of images drawn from previous chapters. The "way of the people" was referred to at 57:14. The "highway" of God's theophany was introduced at 40:3. The "ensign" (נס *nēs*) was an image frequently employed in former Isaiah for dispatching God's instruments of judgment (5:26; 13:1) or for

217. Torrey calls it nonsense. See C. C. Torrey, *The Second Isaiah* (New York: Scribner's, 1928) 455.

218. C. Westermann, *Isaiah 40–66,* trans. David Stalker, OTL (Philadelphia: Westminster, 1969) 377.

signaling a time of ingathering (11:12). In v. 11*c*, 40:10*b* is quoted verbatim. Here God is referred to somewhat differently from at 40:10. God is "Saviour" (יֹשֵׁעֵךְ *yiš'ēk*), a possible play on the word "Isaiah." The "Holy People" correspond to the promised seed of 6:13, the sole hopeful image in

the scene of Isaiah's call, seen from afar, with vast judgment still to come. Zion also is the city of faithfulness and righteousness emerging after judgment at 1:26. Now she is on the verge of laying claim to new names in addition to those already granted (60:4; 62:4; 62:12).

REFLECTIONS

1. The horizon this text introduces is a broad one. Nations come from afar. All the earth witnesses Zion's establishment. Kings and foreigners bring gifts and do service. Before all the nations, righteousness springs up.

It is striking that the means by which God brings about universal and broad-reaching knowledge of God's righteousness remains specified and particular. There is one place and one people to which the nations come. The promise made to Abraham long ago (Gen 12:3) has been transformed, but the same content remains, now focused on Zion and her children—"a people whom the Lord has blessed" (61:9).

The apostle Paul considers God's election of Israel in the Letter to the Romans. On the face of it, the transition from chapter 8 to chapter 9 in Romans might appear abrupt, given the movement that precedes. These chapters begin with the universal condition, move to the work of Christ for both Jews and Gentiles, shift from justification to sanctification, and end with glorification and the inseparable character of God's claim on the elect in Christ. Why, then, a return to God's word to Israel?

The answer is given in Romans 11. There is one tree, not two or more. God does not work with those outside the commonwealth of Israel apart from the work begun in them. To speak of "natural branches" is to recognize what Isaiah 60–62 strains to put before our eyes. It is "out of Zion" (Rom 11:26) that a deliverer (Isa 62:11) comes. To talk about the treatment of the nations apart from this theological reality, carried over bodily in the gospel, is to shift attention away from God's original promises and future plans, centered on Zion and her righteous children. When those plans are honored, the widest possible reach of God's knowledge becomes operative. Judgment—of Israel and the nations—ironically becomes the means by which God is fully and most widely acknowledged. Only through this judgment can one begin true and lasting fellowship with the one God, revealed to Israel, shared with the world in Jesus Christ.

2. Exclusion is also a theme here. God is winnowing his own people, in the context of Zion's universal acknowledgment. The demands of election are such that those within the relationship who turn their back on God and on proper worship of God bring oppression and suffering upon God's obedient righteous ones and find themselves outside the covenant that binds God's word, through the prophet, to the people (59:21). Then the word of salvation—so bold and so maximal in these three chapters—becomes an address that initiates deeper seeking for one group, even in a penitential form (63:7–64:12), but increased apostasy and closed ears for another (65:1-7). The original exhortation, "seek the Lord while he may be found," contained the admonishment, "let the wicked forsake their way" (55:6-7). Without attention to this demand, the words of salvation will become a reality for one group only, "for the people that sought me" (so 65:10), but will fail to make inroads with another.

The same reality prevailed in the days of former Isaiah (6:9-10; 28:16). The same reality persists into the New Testament, there as here, not neatly coordinated between Israel and the Gentiles, but now placing an equal demand on both, in the light of the gospel message of salvation (Matt 21:44; Rom 11:21). The truth of God's word of salvation, in Old Testament and New, is always like Isaiah's foundation stone in Zion: it makes some fall, while others find their sure rest and hope there (Isa 28:16; Matt 21:42; Rom 9:33). It creates in one penitent seeking and longing to be heard, and in another confidence in self and vain worship only.

3. The placement of these chapters calls for theological comment. Why does a word of glorious redemption stand in the middle of the proclamation of these chapters, and not at the close? At the close we find exclusion and judgment, alongside new visions of restoration, some of them extending the horizon found here. Should God's word of salvation lead to rejoicing, or to lengthy penitential response? What is it like to hear such words of hope and promise, when they stand in apparent disjunction with present reality (63:18)? Many want to have chaps. 60–62 be a *response* to the laments that follow. But in the presentation we have before us, they *occasion* or *elicit* this response of penitence and complaint; they are not themselves an effort to comprehend or answer such prior speech.

For the righteous who seek God's will, this disjunction is frequently present. God seeks to bolster the righteous through prophetic address. Yet at times of real hardship, salvation can be more difficult to comprehend than judgment, and the response to both can be resistance. God is prepared, however, to work through the resistance that comes from hearing the divine word of promise and has in fact bypassed it. Israel, and all those who find themselves in places forlorn, can only recall better days in the past (63:7) upon hearing of a future bright but incomprehensible.

The movement at this point in the discourse is a critical one, expressesing a deep spiritual truth. The disciples, even after several encounters with the risen Lord, could still "disbelieve for joy" (Luke 24:41). We have the same sort of complex reaction here, in the face of such grand promises to Zion and her righteous children. Here, however, the righteous are driven to deeper and more penetrating reflection on God's sovereign purposes, linking past, present, and future. It is not out of their own wisdom that they sense final purpose and the truth of God's lavish promises, stated in these chapters. Through that experience—not bypassing it or uttering false platitudes of confidence—God will speak a fresh word that confirms what God has said here (65:13). Then an even greater picture of God's promised future emerges, greater than they could have asked for or imagined (65:17-25). The righteous move from promise to promise, through dark valleys of anguish and despair. For God demands to be God in all these places, and especially asks that we seek the Divine and turn away from wickedness in times of despair. God will be found.

4. The prophet here takes measures to put God on notice (62:6). He may himself sense the lavish character of what God has promised, and the need to "remind the LORD . . . and give him no rest." This, too, marks a critical moment in our struggles for faith. The character of persistence and the concrete strategies to press God and demand an enactment of what has been promised belong to the walk of faith. God can correct the overzealous appeal, especially when it issues into self-righteousness (see Job). But the obverse is never true. God cannot work with those who reject words of promise and turn to their own ways. The middle course we see here: persistent reminding of God, carrying—in penitence and in boldness—our concern that the divine word accomplish every good thing God has promised and intends. This too belongs to the way of the righteous.

ISAIAH 63:1-6, GOD'S PROMISED VINDICATION

NIV

63 Who is this coming from Edom,
from Bozrah, with his garments stained
crimson?
Who is this, robed in splendor,
striding forward in the greatness of his
strength?

"It is I, speaking in righteousness,
mighty to save."

²Why are your garments red,
like those of one treading the winepress?

³"I have trodden the winepress alone;
from the nations no one was with me.
I trampled them in my anger
and trod them down in my wrath;
their blood spattered my garments,
and I stained all my clothing.
⁴For the day of vengeance was in my heart,
and the year of my redemption has come.
⁵I looked, but there was no one to help,
I was appalled that no one gave support;
so my own arm worked salvation for me,
and my own wrath sustained me.
⁶I trampled the nations in my anger;
in my wrath I made them drunk
and poured their blood on the ground."

NRSV

63 "Who is this that comes from Edom,
from Bozrah in garments stained crimson?
Who is this so splendidly robed,
marching in his great might?"

"It is I, announcing vindication,
mighty to save."

² "Why are your robes red,
and your garments like theirs who tread
the winepress?"

³ "I have trodden the winepress alone,
and from the peoples no one was with me;
I trod them in my anger
and trampled them in my wrath;
their juice spattered on my garments,
and stained all my robes.
⁴ For the day of vengeance was in my heart,
and the year for my redeeming work
had come.
⁵ I looked, but there was no helper;
I stared, but there was no one to sustain me;
so my own arm brought me victory,
and my wrath sustained me.
⁶ I trampled down peoples in my anger,
I crushed them in my wrath,
and I poured out their lifeblood on
the earth."

COMMENTARY

This is a fascinating text, in terms of its placement in the discourse, in terms of the larger book of Isaiah and its presentation, and in terms of its own content. The connections between 63:1-6 and the oracle concerning Edom in Isaiah 34 stand out. Both passages place the judgment over Edom within the larger context of God's dealing with the nations (63:6; 34:2). Similar phrases are used, especially "day of vengeance" (34:8). Both presuppose that such "vengeance" (requital) involves Zion's vindication; it is not an act of isolated judgment, for its own sake.

Connections within the present discourse are also clear. In 62:6, the prophet dispatched sentinels. Although the parties are unnamed, it is apparent that the scene drawn in 63:1-6 involves the exchange between a sentinel and God. It includes a divine speech, initiated by a query from a sentinel—a sort of "who goes there?" in v. 1*a*. The theme of vindication (63:1*b*) and the day/year motif (63:4) appeared in the previous section (61:2; 62:1-2).

It is one thing to detect these connections and another to explain just what the passage is about at this juncture in the discourse. Why a sudden and specific interest in Edom? This question has occupied scholars, regarding this passage and others, where Edom plays a singular, if not also somewhat representative role (Genesis 27; Num 20:14-21; Ps 137:7-9; Isaiah 34; Ezekiel 35).[219] Historical theories, based upon these texts and other references in ancient literary finds, suggest that Edom played a particularly dastardly role in the fall of Jerusalem (Ps 137:7-9), exacerbated by the fact of the close, though not unconflicted (Genesis 27), relationship between these two "brothers." Whether specific historical realities, contemporaneous with the discourse, have given rise to this text is an ongoing matter of speculation.[220] An alternative would be to seek an explanation in more strictly literary terms, involving specifically the previous Isaiah text in chap. 34.[221] The judgment of God over Edom, promised in Isaiah 34, has here transpired. Such a judgment was to vindicate Zion (34:8) and initiate a period of joy and redemption in Zion (35:1-10).

Those historically concerned ask whether such a military victory over Edom fits with the time frame and setting of the discourse of Trito-Isaiah. The text's referential connection to events in history is a primary consideration for exegesis, as having given rise to the oracle itself. Was Edom not destroyed by Nabonidus in the mid-sixth century? If so, can the prophet speak about a present destruction as meaningful (assuming that he is of a later period historically)? Did Edom experience a resurgence that necessitated or encouraged the delivery of this oracle? Was it the case, for example, that "Edom remained to be fully punished and to be removed from Jewish territory," according to the best reconstruction?[222]

219. See Claire Mathews, *Defending Zion* (Berlin: Walter de Gruyter, 1994); B. Dicou, *Edom, Israel's Brother and Antagonist: The Role of Edom in Biblical Prophecy and Story* (Sheffield: Sheffield Academic, 1994); J. Bartlett, *Edom and the Edomites* (Sheffield: Sheffield Academic, 1989).
220. See the discussion in Smith, who works this angle. P. A. Smith, *Rhetoric and Redaction in Trito-Isaiah,* VTSup 62 (Leiden: Brill, 1995) 40-41.
221. See O. Steck, "Der Rachetag in Jesaja 61,2: Ein Kapital redaktionsgeschichtliche Kleinarbeit," *VT* 36 (1986) 323-38. Matthews (*Defending Zion*) pursues aspects of Steck's redactional explanation, especially in his *Bereitete Heimkehr* (Stuttgart: Katholisches Bibelwerk, 1985).
222. Smith, *Rhetoric and Redaction in Trito-Isaiah,* 41.

Proper interpretation of the passage, like others, turns on allowing the right proportion of historical and literary concerns to come into play. The intertextual dimension is one force that has been at fairly constant work in the composition of this particular material. But such work does not go on in a complete vacuum. Certainly a level of historical referentiality exerts pressure on the proclamation that is delivered. The problem in the past has been that this dimension was judged the only factor about which the exegete should be concerned, and in the end it generated a rival industry of reconstructions in competion with each other—this labor all justified in the name of sharpening our exegetical eye. Particularly in the later period, we must contend with the existence of a literary legacy, known to the community and to those who address it. This legacy has helped the "prophet" or tradent (the one handing on the legacy) to see how God's word of old might be coming to fruition in circumstances out beyond its own historical horizon. Almost all agree that at this point in Israel's history, such a legacy is in place. The problem has been calibrating the legitimate concerns of form-critical and other historical inquiries with the intertextual dimension.

It is clear that Isaiah 34 stands close at hand to the text. Efforts to coordinate redactional levels across the larger book of Isaiah, and to determine which texts are earlier than others, need not be a preoccupation for us here. One needs to work under the assumption that the final editors left the material in the shape they did, mindful that they were bridging the last stages of growth and the first stages of reading and interpreting the material. Isaiah 34 had seen the defeat of Edom as a signal that Zion's vindication was at hand, and also that God's larger work of judgment against the nations was under way. Our text operates from a similar perspective.

We assume that, as a historical fact, the nation of Edom had been severely affected by Babylonian assaults on the region, and had suffered as had Judah and other neighboring states, though the degree to which some felt these incursions more sharply than others is a matter for ongoing research. Jeremiah 40:11-12 gives one a sense of commonality binding those under Babylonian hegemony, even as chaps. 39–42 report tensions among these various neighbor-states. It is not our purpose here to clarify why Edom is frequently singled out at this time for separate discussion. What we do know is that this perspective is at work in the larger book of Isaiah.

An oracle that is not usually discussed in this connection is Isa 21:11-12. The larger context of the chapter (21:1-10) involves the fall of Babylon at the hands of the Persians. This "stern vision" is vouchsafed by the prophet Isaiah (21:2); it makes him ill (21:3-4), in the same way Daniel is distraught by terrifying events outside his frame of reference (Dan 10:8). In that oracle in chap. 21, a watchman is also appointed for continual duty (as in 62:6), day and night. The watchman sees the fall of Babylon and reports this.

Now what is striking in this connection is the brief oracle that follows in 21:11-12, concerning Dumah. The town is considered to be located in Arabia, but it may be some sort of symbolic name for Edom. What is uncontroversial is the reference to Seir, an Edomite city (Gen 32:3), in v. 11. One is calling from Seir to a sentinel—the same term as is used here (62:6). The sentinel has no word to give, *as yet*. He says, "If you will inquire, inquire; come back again" (21:12). It appears that the voice calling from Seir wants to know from the sentinel what he has seen or will see—the appeal "what of the night?" is obscure.

One explanation for the content and position of the passage under discussion is the double influence of Isaiah 34 and 21:1-12. The sentinel reappears, as before (61:1). Now he poses a question, asking both "Who goes there?" and "Why?": "Why do you look as you do?" The sentinel does know the answer, however, from where the figure has come: He comes from "Edom," a word with associations in Hebrew to "red" (see Gen 25:25).

So it is reasonable to surmise that along with the pressure from Isaiah 34, with its depiction of the judgment over Edom initiating a much larger vindiction on behalf of Zion (34:2), the prophet was aware of the sentinel text regarding Seir and the Babylonian defeat from former Isaiah (21:1-12). What the posted sentinel learns is that God is *already* at work vindicating Zion; the day of vindication has arrived, and this means a year of redeeming work on behalf of Zion (63:4)—a clear modification of 34:8. The sentinel of 21:11-12 has no answer to give because there must be a later return for inquiry. Now that later time has arrived; now the sentinel himself witnesses a new judgment, over Seir/Edom. God has executed a plan of judgment that was deferred at 21:11-12, was spelled out in Isaiah 34, and is testified to here by God.

The salvation referred to at the end of v. 1 picks up on the same root (ישׁע *ys'*) used at the close of the preceding chapter (62:11). "Vindication" in v. 1 is from the root for righteousness (צדק *ṣdq*). The promised depiction of God's defeat of adversaries within Zion (59:18) has its counterpart here in God's vindication and victory over the nations, exemplified in Edom's defeat.

The motif of lone vengeance (63:5) is likewise familiar from 59:16. Westermann is probably right when he conjectures that this motif goes back to mythic origins, and has nothing to do with the Cyrus theme of Deutero-Isaiah; it is an agentless victory in this case.[223] The motif is most closely related to another Deutero-Isaiah conception: God's sovereign incomparability (40:12-21), here extended into the martial sphere. The thrust of the passage is that God has already begun the process of vindication on behalf of Zion. The action is under way, proven by God's own testimony to the prophet, via the sentinel.

223. Westermann, *Isaiah 40–66*, 382.

REFLECTIONS

1. Twice in this Isaiah discourse we hear of God's word's accomplishing something, not according to what the prophet himself thinks, or what an author might be reconstructed as having thought, but according to what God has in mind: God's word will not return empty, we are told (45:23; 55:11). The subjectivity of the authorial mind, and its intentions, is used by God, of course, but in ways that remain under divine disposition. One might rightly say that the vocation of Isaiah is to speak as God tells him, and to remain in service to a word he, Isaiah, must watch unfold in its claim on hearers or its lack thereof, or to attend to its preservation for another day.

So many successful projects—as God means that adjective—demand a period of sheer obscurity and rejection for their proper incubation. God remains sovereign over visions the deity grants. If Isaiah's words shut ears or become so much gibberish in his day, the challenge for the prophet is not to alter the words, or to try harder, or to seek a receptive audience somewhere else. That would be to kill off the "accomplishing potential" and would be the greatest act of disobedience, greater even than flight or silence. The challenge is to "bind up the teaching" and to remain obedient when no one listens, and this can be the hardest challenge of all. Who can be sure that rejection or failure to be heard is not a sign of poor preaching or false vocation? Why could one comfort oneself with the belief that, in a later day, one's words would at last be listened to? Why would such a hope not be a sign of vanity or self-delusion?

What is required is what God supplies, in the former and latter dispensations covered by Isaiah. What is required is a word from God, as sure as the preached word God demands be spoken, even though the word is not for us or our generation, and we must rightly receive rebuke and endure our own season of confusion, because God has something else in mind. Is it not enough to rest on the assurance that the word is of divine origin, and that its non-reception makes the word no less divine and us no less God's servants? If we stumble on this truth, is it because God has not set us apart for this sort of task? No one from the former day of Isaiah could know exactly what use God would make of the word that went forth but was not received. God was strong to make assurance, and less clear about satisfying the need to know what the accomplishment would look like when it happened. The thing that kept Isaiah strong in resolve was not cleverness or adaptability, but God's word assuring him that his question "How long?" was meaningful and capable of an answer—even an answer that portended anguish for him and his people. God was sovereign over divine promises and over divine words, and the reward for the prophet was resolution and resolve about that.

Now, then, when we see the word opened up afresh, in a latter day, and see it bearing fruit—in judgment, in promise, in rebuke, in direction, in demand even for further patience—are we not to rejoice in the sheer providence of God, who makes sure that the words given to us to speak remain open for fulfillment even long after their delivery by us? This makes us marvel at the obedience of servants God chooses and at God's wisdom in choosing them according to the needs God knows must be met, for them and for the recepients of what they have to say. That includes us in the latter days of Isaiah's vision, who are privileged to oversee the ages joined, even after generations have passed and much darkness has remained, by nothing but God's word in its going forth and its accomplishing.

2. God speaks here of vindication of the Divine. Whatever else may be true of scenes of vindication in Scripture (see esp. the book of Revelation), they are chiefly to do with God's justice and righteousness, as worthy unto themselves, and only secondarily related to our *quid pro quo* needs or hopes.

This must be one of the hardest lessons Scripture teaches, because it defies our sense of compassion and mercy in the name of confounding our limited and always unjust systems of justice. We would rank mercy above justice, because we cannot understand holy righteousness, never having seen it in ourselves or in others. Should we not be honest and say that mercy cannot be greater than justice, except to the degree that we have yet to experience true and lasting and unrequited and bone-jarring injustice of the sort that still exists in this world? And even then, should we ever know such injustice, we would long for justice as a distillate of a mercy we also strain to comprehend.

We count on God alone to show us mercy and justice and to teach us how both are gifts consistent with God's character as God, but unavailable on any other terms than that—that is, as glimpses for a second into God's character as God: holy, just, and loving all at once. God is the God of pure and holy vengeance, who is accompanied by no other (63:5), so that we might believe that justice and mercy are in God one and the same thing, and cannot exist as separate attributes except in our world of sin. Without the grace of a transcendent God come down in Jesus Christ, mercy is sentimentalism and vengeance lacks any connection to God's holiness.

ISAIAH 63:7–64:12, RETROSPECT, PROSPECT: SUPPLICATION, CONFESSION

NIV

⁷I will tell of the kindnesses of the LORD,
    the deeds for which he is to be praised,
    according to all the LORD has done for us—
yes, the many good things he has done
    for the house of Israel,
    according to his compassion and many
        kindnesses.
⁸He said, "Surely they are my people,
    sons who will not be false to me";
    and so he became their Savior.
⁹In all their distress he too was distressed,
    and the angel of his presence saved them.
In his love and mercy he redeemed them;
    he lifted them up and carried them
    all the days of old.
¹⁰Yet they rebelled
    and grieved his Holy Spirit.
So he turned and became their enemy
    and he himself fought against them.

¹¹Then his people recalled[a] the days of old,
    the days of Moses and his people—
where is he who brought them through the sea,
    with the shepherd of his flock?
Where is he who set
    his Holy Spirit among them,
¹²who sent his glorious arm of power
    to be at Moses' right hand,
who divided the waters before them,
    to gain for himself everlasting renown,
¹³who led them through the depths?
Like a horse in open country,
    they did not stumble;
¹⁴like cattle that go down to the plain,
    they were given rest by the Spirit of the LORD.
This is how you guided your people
    to make for yourself a glorious name.

[a]11 Or But may he recall

NRSV

⁷I will recount the gracious deeds of the LORD,
    the praiseworthy acts of the LORD,
because of all that the LORD has done for us,
    and the great favor to the house of Israel
that he has shown them according to
      his mercy,
    according to the abundance of his
      steadfast love.
⁸For he said, "Surely they are my people,
    children who will not deal falsely";
and he became their savior
⁹   in all their distress.
It was no messenger[a] or angel
    but his presence that saved them;[b]
in his love and in his pity he redeemed them;
    he lifted them up and carried them all the
      days of old.

¹⁰But they rebelled
    and grieved his holy spirit;
therefore he became their enemy;
    he himself fought against them.
¹¹Then they[c] remembered the days of old,
    of Moses his servant.[d]
Where is the one who brought them up out
    of the sea
    with the shepherds of his flock?
Where is the one who put within them
    his holy spirit,
¹²who caused his glorious arm
    to march at the right hand of Moses,
who divided the waters before them
    to make for himself an everlasting name,
¹³   who led them through the depths?
Like a horse in the desert,
    they did not stumble.

[a]Gk: Heb anguish   [b]Or savior. 9In all their distress he was distressed; the angel of his presence saved them;   [c]Heb he
[d]Cn: Heb his people

NIV

¹⁵Look down from heaven and see
> from your lofty throne, holy and glorious.
> Where are your zeal and your might?
>> Your tenderness and compassion are with-
>> held from us.
¹⁶But you are our Father,
> though Abraham does not know us
> or Israel acknowledge us;
> you, O Lord, are our Father,
> our Redeemer from of old is your name.
¹⁷Why, O Lord, do you make us wander from
>> your ways
> and harden our hearts so we do not
>> revere you?
> Return for the sake of your servants,
> the tribes that are your inheritance.
¹⁸For a little while your people possessed your
>> holy place,
> but now our enemies have trampled down
>> your sanctuary.
¹⁹We are yours from of old;
> but you have not ruled over them,
> they have not been called by your name.^a

64 Oh, that you would rend the heavens
> and come down,
> that the mountains would tremble
>> before you!
²As when fire sets twigs ablaze
> and causes water to boil,
> come down to make your name known to
>> your enemies
> and cause the nations to quake before you!
³For when you did awesome things that we did
>> not expect,
> you came down, and the mountains
>> trembled before you.
⁴Since ancient times no one has heard,
> no ear has perceived,
> no eye has seen any God besides you,
> who acts on behalf of those who wait
>> for him.
⁵You come to the help of those who gladly
>> do right,
> who remember your ways.
> But when we continued to sin against them,

^a19 Or *We are like those you have never ruled, / like those never
called by your name*

NRSV

¹⁴ Like cattle that go down into the valley,
> the spirit of the Lord gave them rest.
> Thus you led your people,
> to make for yourself a glorious name.
¹⁵ Look down from heaven and see,
> from your holy and glorious habitation.
> Where are your zeal and your might?
>> The yearning of your heart and your
>> compassion?
> They are withheld from me.
¹⁶ For you are our father,
> though Abraham does not know us
> and Israel does not acknowledge us;
> you, O Lord, are our father;
> our Redeemer from of old is your name.
¹⁷ Why, O Lord, do you make us stray from
>> your ways
> and harden our heart, so that we do not
>> fear you?
> Turn back for the sake of your servants,
> for the sake of the tribes that are
>> your heritage.
¹⁸ Your holy people took possession for a
>> little while;
> but now our adversaries have trampled
>> down your sanctuary.
¹⁹ We have long been like those whom you do
>> not rule,
> like those not called by your name.

64 O that you would tear open the heavens
> and come down,
> so that the mountains would quake at
>> your presence—
^{2a}as when fire kindles brushwood
> and the fire causes water to boil—
> to make your name known to your
>> adversaries,
> so that the nations might tremble at your
>> presence!
³ When you did awesome deeds that we did
>> not expect,
> you came down, the mountains quaked at
>> your presence.
⁴ From ages past no one has heard,
> no ear has perceived,
> no eye has seen any God besides you,

^aCh 64.1 in Heb

NIV

you were angry.
How then can we be saved?
⁶All of us have become like one who is unclean,
and all our righteous acts are like filthy rags;
we all shrivel up like a leaf,
and like the wind our sins sweep us away.
⁷No one calls on your name
or strives to lay hold of you;
for you have hidden your face from us
and made us waste away because of our sins.

⁸Yet, O LORD, you are our Father.
We are the clay, you are the potter;
we are all the work of your hand.
⁹Do not be angry beyond measure, O LORD;
do not remember our sins forever.
Oh, look upon us, we pray,
for we are all your people.
¹⁰Your sacred cities have become a desert;
even Zion is a desert, Jerusalem a desolation.
¹¹Our holy and glorious temple, where our
fathers praised you,
has been burned with fire,
and all that we treasured lies in ruins.
¹²After all this, O LORD, will you hold
yourself back?
Will you keep silent and punish us
beyond measure?

NRSV

who works for those who wait for him.
⁵ You meet those who gladly do right,
those who remember you in your ways.
But you were angry, and we sinned;
because you hid yourself we
transgressed.ᵃ
⁶ We have all become like one who is unclean,
and all our righteous deeds are like a
filthy cloth.
We all fade like a leaf,
and our iniquities, like the wind, take us
away.
⁷ There is no one who calls on your name,
or attempts to take hold of you;
for you have hidden your face from us,
and have deliveredᵇ us into the hand of
our iniquity.
⁸ Yet, O LORD, you are our Father;
we are the clay, and you are our potter;
we are all the work of your hand.
⁹ Do not be exceedingly angry, O LORD,
and do not remember iniquity forever.
Now consider, we are all your people.
¹⁰ Your holy cities have become a wilderness,
Zion has become a wilderness,
Jerusalem a desolation.
¹¹ Our holy and beautiful house,
where our ancestors praised you,
has been burned by fire,
and all our pleasant places have
become ruins.
¹² After all this, will you restrain yourself,
O LORD?
Will you keep silent, and punish us
so severely?

ᵃMeaning of Heb uncertain   ᵇGk Syr Old Latin Tg: Heb *melted*

COMMENTARY

The passage breaks without difficulty into brief rhetorical units (63:7-9, 10-4, 15-19; 64:1-5*a*, 5*b*-7, 8-12). We are not dealing in this instance with once-discrete units, but rather with a long poem, carefully crafted and designed to be read as such. Its form appears to be a community lament. It resembles other such texts in the psalms and in the book of Lamentations. Like Psalm 89, it begins with a positive retrospect (63:7-14; Ps 89:1-37), before setting this off against the present situation of despair and seeming rejection.

There are numerous connections between the lament and the foregoing sections (60:1–63:6).[224]

224. For a summary, see P. A. Smith, *Rhetoric and Redaction in Trito-Isaiah,* VTSup 62 (Leiden: Brill, 1995) 44-46.

Both 64:11 and 60:7 speak of the "glorious house" בית תפארתי (*bêt tip'artî*)—the only two such occurrences in the OT. The root for "glorify" (פאר *p'r*) appears frequently in these two sections (60:7, 9, 13, 21; 61:3; 62:3; 63:12; 64:9). "Sanctuary" (in reference to the Jerusalem Temple) also occurs only at 60:13 and 63:18 in the Isaiah tradition (cf. 8:14; 16:12). Striking in the lament is reference to God's spirit (63:10-11 ,14). I have had occasion to note the special reference to Spirit at 59:21 and its significance for interpreting chaps. 60–62. The lament gives utterance to questions about the persistence of God's Spirit, in contrast to the Mosaic period. God's silence is referred to, with different rhetorical effect, at 62:1, 6 and 64:12.

The conclusion Smith draws, following Westermann, is that the core proclamation of chaps. 60–62 is meant to correspond to and answer the lament of 63:7–64:11.[225] Services of lamentation during the exile are mentioned by Zechariah (7:5). Trito-Isaiah responds to these laments with the salvation proclamation of chaps. 60–62. In other words, in the present arrangement of the material, the movement depicted is in reverse order: first, 63:7–64:11, then, in response, 60:1–62:12. In Westermann's model, a consideration of the final presentation is irrelevant; the response is the same no matter whether chaps. 60–62 precede or follow. (He also regards, for that matter, 59:1-15*a* as lament as well.) Furthermore, laments are not the work of Trito-Isaiah, as their "genuine" home is in worship.[226] Here we see the form-critical method at work with very little modification (e.g., Westermann's inquiry into the way units may once have responded to one another, prior to their final rearrangement or misarrangement).

Two factors speak in favor of a consideration of the present arrangement of the material as purposefully constructed. First, it is clear that the actual response to the lament is not found in the preceding chaps. (60–62), but in chap. 65. The connections between 60:1–63:6 and 63:7–64:11 remain important, but do not serve as evidence of a movement in reverse of the present arrangment. Second, the opening retrospective is intended to work in conjunction with 63:1-6. God's victory over Edom brings to mind God's praiseworthy acts of old (63:7-14). God's unaided victory, underscored at 59:16 and 63:5, has its counterpart in the days of Moses (63:9, 12). Then, as now, God was their savior (62:11; 63:8).

As for the form of the rhetorical composition represented by 63:7–64:11, it would be too simple to accept a single designation (e.g., lament), in light of the composite and carefully crafted literary achievment that lies before us. For comparison, one is put in mind of the psalms of recital (Psalms 44; 66; 78; 105; 106; 107).[227] But even this is an uneven and imprecise form-critical category; other scholars have proposed other psalms for comparison as a consequence of their different understanding of genre within the psalter itself (so, Psalms 77; 135; 136).[228] In some places, such recital leads to praise of God as its governing formal component (Psalms 66; 68; 105; 107; 135; 136). At other places, lament and protestation control the focus of the recital, as if to "blackmail" or persuade or merely reproach God on the basis of past faithfulness, presently absent (Psalms 44; 89; Lamentations).

It should also be noted that formal observations regarding 63:7–64:11 can be significantly influenced by narrower preoccupation with social and political reconstruction as the key to exegesis. The best popular example of this can be seen in the work of Paul Hanson.[229] Older form-critical attention to genre gives way to what he calls a "typological contextual" approach, which attempts to date precisely Hebrew poetry and morphological shifts according to a very specific chronological grid (this is what he means by "typology"). Then one moves rather straightforwardly to social-historical analysis, entirely controlled by a preliminary judgment about protest and conflict among various parties in the exilic and post-exilic period. In Hanson's hands, our text's meaning becomes fully a function of his dating and sociological scheme. For example, the meaning of 63:16, "Abraham does not know us, Israel does not acknowledge us," becomes for Hanson a protest of ousted Levitical priests who had not been in exile against Abraham/Israel, "the group returning

225. Ibid., 44-46; C. Westermann, *Isaiah 40–66*, trans. David Stalker, OTL (Philadelphia: Westminster, 1969) 300.
226. Ibid., 300-301.
227. See the valuable discussion of Hugh Williamson, "Isaiah 63,7–64,11. Exilic Lament or Post-Exilic Protest?" *ZAW* 102 (1990) 48-58.
228. See ibid., 55.
229. Paul Hanson, *The Dawn of Apocalyptic* (Philadelphia: Fortress, 1975).

from exile under the leadership of the Zadokite priests."[230] Williamson's careful analysis and critique of Hanson is difficult to improve upon. I shall refer to this as is warranted below.

Williamson has helpfully shown that one needs to deploy the form-critical analysis very carefully. What is distinctive about this lament/complaint (setting it off, e.g., from Pss 44; 89) is the clear statement of confession (64:5b-7). This makes the closest parallel Psalm 106 or Nehemiah 9, where recital leads to confession. Lamentations also contains this element, quite centrally, as it moves to plaintive petition.

One further element will have to be brought into play, completely repudiated by Hanson's approach, and not of particular concern to Williamson, working with the constraints imposed by the topic of his essay. This element is the larger literary context, and most particularly the following response of 65:1-25, but also the preceding unit as well (63:1-6). Isaiah 63:1-6 shows the mighty warrior, Israel's Lord, in full battle attire, emerging from a lone victory over Edom (63:5). The text then moves to a recollection of YHWH as victor from days of old (63:7-9). There, too, no one was with the Lord in the Lord's saving acts (63:9)—there was no angel of presence (Exod 33:2). Yet Moses was God's faithful servant, and a portion of his spirit was distributed to others for faithful fellowship (Num 11:17).

Moses was God's servant, but Moses was also the one on Israel's side, precisely because he was on the Lord's side when the people were not (see the dramatic presentation of Exod 32:30–34:10). Now, however, there is no Moses among the people. There is the memory of Moses (63:11). There is a memory of God's saving acts and God's saving servant, from whose spirit God enlarged the divine presence among them (63:10-14). The lament with recital does not ignore sin and the need for confession, but indeed gives full utterance to these (64:5b-7). Yet it longs for intercession and restored presence (64:7). No longer is Moses present; no longer do Abraham and Israel recognize the sinful generation here speaking (63:16). Will God attend to the servants, without the servant Moses (63:17b)? Previously there were mourning, guilt, and acts of contrition (Exod 33:16). The servant

Moses offered his life and stayed the full judgment (Exod 32:33-34; 34:6-10), assuring God's presence and not that of a surrogate, on the strength of the Mosaic intercession reminding God of the promises to the ancestors. Can God act thus again for a new generation, on the basis of a new petition, now with a confession of iniquity, not from Moses, but from the servant followers of the servant? The answer God gives is found, not in chaps. 60–61 (pace Westermann), but in the following chap. (65:1-25), with its resounding separation of the servants (65:13-15) in a cleansing vis-à-vis.

63:7-9. Here the element of recital familiar from the psalter appears. The exodus events are not highlighted exclusively at the beginning. God's past faithfulness is more generous and more generic, "because of all that the LORD has done for us" (63:7). Though the reference to divine assistance appears to evoke Exod 33:1-3, following a situation of disobedience (as an alternative form of presence, a sort of "Yahweh stand-in," due to the obligations of God's holiness), our text is content to recall the positive side of all this. God went with the faithful people; God's attributes of holiness, love, and mercy were fully intermingled and fully present. The announcement of the holy name recapitulates and intensifies the revelation to Moses as we see it in Exodus 3 (see 33:19 and 34:6-9). God's announcement of the divine name is an announcement of God's own presence and not that of a surrogate.

The textual problem at 63:9 cannot be easily resolved, though the versions and the Massoretes themselves have tried. In spite of all that, I would argue that any translation provided must hold on to the fundamental idea of a contrast between God's presence and a potential go-between, however that contrast is rendered into English. The NRSV has done this. The contrast is critical to the sense in Isaiah as well as the larger exodus environment against which the text makes its point.

63:10-14. When the tone shifts at v. 10, it is not surprising, in spite of its sharpness. This transition to rebellion is familiar from psalms of recital (e.g., Psalm 78). Yet v. 11 contrasts the depicted rebellion with a time past, the days of old, of Moses. For this reason, the rebellion cited in v. 10 is not an ancient one, but a present one, figurally congruent with but also distinct from the rebellion in the wilderness. The language used here is very

230. Ibid.

close to what appears in Isaiah 1, where the Holy One is rebelled against, and where, as a consequence, God becomes an enemy (1:24-26). As I describe below, at the close of Isaiah the opening vision of the book is intratextually close at hand. The typological-figural orientation of the authors of Isaiah is unsurpassed. We move from wilderness rebellion, to rebellion of former Isaiah days, to present rebellion—which takes the concrete form in all three epochs of idolatry and false worship (Exodus 32; Isaiah 1–4; 65–66).

Verse 11 is not easily rendered from the Hebrew, because of the apparent pronomial unclarity. Even this is likely not accidental, in the text as original or in its history of use, given the point that God and Moses collaborate as Lord and servant. As mentioned above, the reference to "Holy Spirit" is likely tied to the description of Numbers 11. In Nehemiah 9 (a tradition from the same historical vantage point as Isaiah 63–64), there is also a recital in which rebellion figures prominently, and where the theme of God's Spirit is highlighted within the usual wilderness litany. In Neh 9:20, the juxtaposition of Spirit and manna points to a close reading of Numbers 11 in the form that we now have it, where the two themes are likewise sitting astride. Ezra speaks of God giving "your good spirit to instruct them" (9:20); Isaiah 63:11 speaks of "his holy spirit." Yet who is speaking here? The poet, God himself, or both? And about what? Moses' spirit, or God's, or both?

The answer is likely to be found at v. 14, where it is clearly the Lord's own spirit that gave Israel necessary leadership. God gave the divine spirit to Moses and to "the shepherds of his flock" (63:11), consistent with Number 11. Moses was in the prominent place, of course, and God's own right hand accompanied Moses at the sea (leading to the aggrandizing correlation of Exod 14:31, "the people believed in the LORD and in his servant Moses"). Here the plural reference (shepherds) means not to encroach on Moses, but serves as a fitting plural reference, given the context of the discourse of servant-followers of the servant as we now have it.

63:15-19. The plural-servants motif is made explicit in 63:17, "turn back for the sake of your servants." The notion that heaven is God's true and lasting abode, the place of sovereign and eternal judgment, is consistent with the depiction of

Isa 66:1-2, and also with other similar contexts of judgment (e.g., 1 Kgs 8:30, "O hear in heaven your dwelling place; heed and forgive"). Even as Solomon builds God's earthly dwelling, at the moment where the presence of God in concrete structure is most stressed, we are nevertheless to know that demolition of the house would not mean defeat of God or serious encroachment on divine sovereign justice and providential rule. God's abode is in heaven. The question to be considered seriously within the present situation would not be God's sovereignty, but the twin foundations of election (eternal promises to Abraham and Israel) and forgiveness by intercession (Moses in Exodus; Moses in Psalm 90 in response to Psalm 89 and the "broken" Davidic covenant).[231] These twin foundations appear under assault.

When the promises to David or the Mosaic covenant seemed in question, appeal was made to the promises to the ancestors, as underriding and permanent—the "firewall," as it were, against final curse (Deuteronomy) or desperate, intercessorless existence. In some measure, the appeal to the "former things" as promises to Abraham and Jacob/Israel serve this function in Isaiah 40–49, in a context of judgment and dejection.

Yet here the situation is worse still. Even Abraham ("father of many") and Israel (that is, the patriarch) cannot offer assurance. They do not recognize the present generation and those mortally endangered within it. Though the appellation "Father" is rare in the OT, its usage here is stunning and fully explicable, against the backdrop of Abraham and promises associated with him, as well as in the light of early Genesis chapters.

The father of many nations (Abraham) may not know this Israel, nor Israel (Jacob) the present generation. Promises to David, intercession from Moses, election in Abraham—under them all stands God's own eternal and cosmic lordship, in heaven when not in house (demolished and trampled down, in spite of the holy people of old, so 63:18). So the servant-followers beg, "You, O LORD, are our Father" and boldly adopt this form of address. The treatment given Pharaoh and his recalcitrant hosts has here become the punishment

231. See my discussion of the transition from Psalm 89 to Psalm 90 in C. R. Seitz, "The Royal Promises in the Canonical Books of Isaiah and the Psalms," in *Word Without End* (Grand Rapids: Eerdmans, 1998) 158-67.

for God's own people (63:17), in view of their rebellion against God. But can the present intercession fail to bring about a turn of fortune, in this case not based upon the plea of the servant Moses, nor that of the servant (53:12), but of the servant-followers themselves, for their own sakes and for the sake of a generation hardened as was Pharaoh? The plea to God "our Father" turns on the ancestral promises, a petition here uttered not by Moses but by the servants.

More should be said here about the appellation "Father," as it appears in an identical phraseology at 64:8 ("Yet, O LORD, thou art our Father"). The double reference is striking and should be accounted for. This brings us to the context of the early Genesis chapters and their significance for adjudicating the problem of the broken covenant.

Again we face the question: Why does the term "Father" appear at this juncture of the book when we see it so infrequently elsewhere in the OT? It is obviously not a context where "maleness" as against "femaleness" would urge the deployment of a term for God based upon the appropriateness of a human projection—this is a context of sin, guilt, despair, and confession of hardness of heart and lack of fear of God (63:17). The situation is not one of successful patriarchy, thus urging a usage of a human metaphor for God heretofore avoided.

What we can see in the final chapters of Isaiah (65–66) is an obvious allusion to the early chapters of Genesis, that is, *before* the promises to Abraham and the ancestors have been made by God. New heavens and new earth, no labor agony, long age, peace between animal and human creatures—these themes bespeak a mitigation of conditions, if not a reversal of conditions, present in the early chapters of Genesis. And in the text presently under discussion, there are references to these same chapters at 64:8*b*, in the verse where the reference to God as Father appears ("we are the clay, and you are our potter; we are all the work of your hand"). The answer to the question, Why does this term for God ("our Father") appear here?, lies close at hand when one considers the context of the early Genesis accounts. When the covenantal promises as a series (Noah, Abraham, Moses, David, and Zion) are abrogated, and yet still retain their character as covenants made by the Holy One of Israel,

recourse must be made to some underlying sovereign protection guarding God's character as the covenanting and electing One who cannot finally cast off Israel because of the character of the named God of Israel. Just as Moses puts God in mind of promises to the ancestors when all seems lost at the foot of the mountain, so, too, appeal here is to a covenantal ground floor, below which there is nothing but the checked forces of chaos and void. Why, then, is the appeal to God as Father constitutive of this ground floor?

The answer would seem to lie in how the early chapters of Genesis were being "closely read" at this period, when Isaiah was reaching its final form. We are talking here, not about Genesis traditions, or "P" or "J" or some such scholarly reconstruction, but about a narrative tradition in something like the form we now see it in the received text of Genesis. To speak of "close reading" is to reckon with a pressure from literature and narrative form, different from traditions or the memory of oral recitation. Genesis 5:1-5 is obviously a redactional unit. That is, it seeks to coordinate the presentations of creation (Gen. 1:1–2:3) and the garden (Gen. 2:4–3:24) by showing Adam to be in relationship to his son, Seth, made in his image (5:3), in the same way that "humanity" (אדם ʾādām, male and female) is made in the image and likeness of Elohim (5:1). Adam is the first male individual, and the father of progeny "made in his image." Adam is also humanity in general, male and female, in some way to be understood as the progeny of God, as Seth is the progeny of Adam. תולדת Tôlēdōt (NRSV, "descendants") is physical generation in the most obvious sense in the majority of the genealogies of Genesis (5:1; 10:1; 11:10; 25:12). Tôlēdōt can also mean "aftermath," or something akin to this, as in Genesis 2:4*b;* the heavens and earth are to the created realm more generally, as is God to humanity, as is Adam to Seth. This generating is not comprehensible by reference to God "as a human mother," and hence the lack of reference to Eve or an Eve/life, Adam/image parallel.

The reference to "Our Father" in the context of broken covenant and supplication indicates how central the creation account has become in times of distress and estrangement. God "Our Father" is an appeal to the basic creation goodness and compassion of God, who has made male and female in

God's own image. Even the murder of Abel will not and cannot break God's covenant with humanity; the image God bestows is an unbreakable fact of creation itself that perdures beyond all assault, from the side of creation. Seth captures the image and likeness of God by virtue of being the son of Adam, and no murder or interruption can affect this ground of imaging. The cry to "Our Father" in the midst of this petition is based upon theological bearings set by the creation story and its aftermath in early Genesis chapters.

The final three verses of this subunit constitute the heart of the present dilemma, and ground the poignant appeal with which it opens, "Why, O LORD?" The hardening of heart referred to (v. 17) coalesces the exodus theme, as involving Pharaoh, but also the Isaiah call "to make dull" mind, ear, and eye (6:10). Possession by a "holy people" (v. 18) would appear to refer to the initial possession of the sanctuary, upon occupation of Zion and the promised land, but this reference clearly reaches up to and includes the time of recent dispossession and the defiling of the sanctuary. The servants are living at a time when the sanctuary is trampled by adversaries, and God is called upon to reassert God's rule, on behalf of the servants.

64:1-5a. The direct, second-person appeal is elaborated. God is reminded of powerful theophanies. Knowing, hearing, perceiving, seeing—in the most elevated and true sense, these modes of apprehension pertained to how God had once made known, not only the divine word through the prophets, but God's own self, without remainder. "O that you would tear open the heavens and come down" refers to God's self-manifestation at Sinai, when the divine name was made known. Israel did not expect that awesome display, for what it said of God could not have fit on the register of comprehension as we mean that in reference to eyes, ears, sensation, knowledge, and perception. The servants cry out for this again. In this way redress for the situation described in the foregoing unit—assault from adversaries, trampled sanctuary—can be had. The testimony before adversaries and nations may evoke the opening refrain of 52:13-15, where the servants had spoken of recognition by the nations of the work of the servant, thus fulfilling the Servant's vocation to be light to the nations. But here the cry is more urgent, given the delay and the manifest, ongoing hostility of the nations and non-recognition by the adversaries. It is hard to know where the hope for vindication against the nations and vindication for the servants begins and ends, as they are two sides of one coin.

64:5b-7. Now we see a distinct formal change, as the first-person plural "we" emerges to join the "Thou" address. With this change comes a change in tone and form. This is confession of iniquity replacing petition and cry. The communal confession can appear and does appear in similar contexts in the psalms and Lamentations. Even its abrupt appearance, as here, is familiar.

At points the confession of sin and iniquity is reminiscent of the prologue of our Isaiah discourse (40:1-11). Fading away, like dying vegetation, is descriptive of the condition of iniquity at both 40:7-8 and 64:6. The repetition of the phrase "all of us" (כֻּלָּנוּ *kullānû*) at 64:6 likewise is suggestive of links to the confession of the servants in the final servant tribute (53:6). What demands further reflection is the phrase "there is no one who calls" (אֵין־קוֹרֵא *'ên-qôrē'*) because of its possible association with the voices of the Isaiah heavenly counsel (קוֹל קוֹרֵא *qôl qôrē;* see 40:3, 6). In that scene, a voice despaired of calling (40:6) and said "What shall I cry, all flesh is grass?" But the voice was quickened, as it were, and divine speech came forth in reply (40:8).

Here, by contrast, there is "no one who calls" (*'ên-qôrē'*). The servant was properly to have fulfilled, in life and speech, the role of bearing tidings to Zion (compare 40:9 and 52:7); further, in his dying he was to have borne the iniquity of the servants. What we have here is allusion to those texts and those circumstances, but now with an obvious dilemma (a painful reversal of the prior resolution) crying out for divine redress and compassion. The servants suffer under their iniquity—indeed they have become like unclean menstrual cloths, cleansed not by the sprinkling of the servant (52:15) who gave up his life for expiation (53:10) for "all of us." In addition, there is no one to call on their behalf, as was the situation of 40:1-11, which was resolved through the life-work of the servant. The servant followers have been handed over to an iniquity that once was double (40:2) and yet was borne away (53:4-6). God has hidden altogether, as if undoing the circumstances of disclosure ("God is with you alone . . . there is no god besides him"); this also occurs at 45:14-15, which in turn occasioned the confession based upon that recognition, "you are a God who hides himself, O God of Israel, the Savior." Now God is hidden again, fully, and there is no one to call upon the divine name, such that the nations might learn of God (see 45:14-16; 45:22-25). God is now no "Savior" but the hidden and absent One.

Mention should be made, if briefly, of the translation problems in this unit; they are several and they are difficult. The NRSV has sought to give a causal reading at v 5: "because you hid yourself we transgressed." This cannot be pressed too hard for theological meaning, however, as though God is being held responsible for the condition now in place for the servants. The force of other statements in the unit make it clear that the servants know they are responsible for the condition they must endure, which includes as a consequence the withdrawal of God.

64:8-12. The "Father language" used here has been discussed above (see 63:15-19). What needs to be stressed at this point is the persistence of the plural-communal terms, as these were operative in the previous confession. "Our" Father means God as established in the creative act of making humanity (*'ādām*) in the divine image, and the "all of us" (*kûllānû*) of the preceding unit is repeated here in the context of creation ("we are all the work of your hand"). The phrase is repeated yet a fourth time at 64:9, "we are all your people." As discussed above, reference to God as "Our Father" is based upon a close reading of the

Genesis accounts of creation, as they now exist in the first five chapters, in order to ground God's fundamental relationship with Israel, below all subsequent covenanting actions with Noah, Abraham, Moses, David, and Zion. On this ground of creation, the appeal is made.

What is paradoxical, however, is that the plural emphasis clearly falls on the servants and the people of Israel, as such. This is made obvious in the final three verses of the chapter, where reference is made to the destruction of Zion/Jerusalem, and all the pleasant places of God's people; it is Israel, "all of them" as God's people, and not just a select portion within Israel, who is to be the object of God's renewed favor and forgiveness. That is, an appeal to the creation of humanity as the ground of God's maintenance of relationship with humanity in general ("adam," male and female) and an appeal on behalf of "all of us" (servants/Israel) are not seen as rival or alternative appeals. The "us" seeking God's presence and release from punishment is not humanity at large (who calls God "Father" based upon the logic of Genesis 1–5) but all Israel, and not a portion thereof. However we are to understand the paradox here; it does not appear to beg for comment, as constructed in this petition. The emphasis is obviously on a comprehensive favor from God, for all Israel, and not for a select portion within Israel. It is critical that this emphasis be grasped, if God's response in the following chapter is properly to be understood and interpreted.

REFLECTIONS

1. It is striking how the most poignant and emotional pleas to God for forgiveness and renewed presence do not begin with the state of isolation and estrangement as the chief starting point, but somewhere else. Whatever disorientation, guilt, and sin cloud the petitioner's state of mind, this must be measured against an awareness of God's awesome grace and former good-pleasure. It is the memory of God's sure mercies that orients the plea and gives it its divine bearings (see 63:7-9).

But how are we properly to understand this starting point? Several possibilities suggest themselves. First, God is put in mind of the divine character and activity of old chiefly to extort divine favor now. This would serve a certain emotional purpose, by placing the anger and hurt at some place where it *rightly* belongs: in God's own self and will. Alternatively, the petitioner is indulging, understandably, in an act of spiritual nostalgia. Whatever is true about the distress presently experienced, it has not always been so: "Let's remember the God of our past clarity and his past beneficence." "It has not always been this bad."

Yet the opening lines would require less content for these explanations to find plausibility, however appealing they may be. What is the logic of this introduction?

The petitioner recalls that God has in fact been faithful, not just to him, but to Israel, all Israel. Allusion is made to a past episode where God could have divided the people into the Moses-group and the evil group, or could have sent a substitute. Instead, God refers to the logic that is operative later in the petition: the people of Israel are God's own children, and they will not deal falsely to the point of severing the Father bond. God is Father in fullest presence—in love, pity, and compassion. Israel knows this to be true of God, and the people's memory, even at this moment of distress, has not faded or failed.

How hard it is to genuinely recall God's pure love and goodness when these are absent, and when distress is the governing condition. How much easier it is to assume that we were led astray by descriptions of God's character, or that the good God has done for us in the past was not really divine goodness at all, but a stroke of fate. Yet Israel's hope is genuinely grounded in God's character as God. Even if the deity is absent, petition is not an effort to get God to show up. Petition is an effort to get God to be true to a character we know to be divine when we are assaulted by our enemies or our sins. Yet how hard it is to speak about our distress in theological terms and not anthropological terms. We are taught here, as elsewhere in Israel's prayers overheard, that reversal of human fortune is *not* a matter of discovering we were wrong about God's goodness and love, or that these characteristics were in shorter supply than we had reckoned, or that our experience of divine judgment meant a diminishment of how we might talk about God. Whatever confusion or distress we may feel under the hand of God, God remains truly God and truly good. We must interpret God's absence as a request, a demand, that we come to terms with God as God is.

2. It is striking that the memory of the wilderness, in terms of God's presence, has here taken the more specific form of talk about the spirit. We had been told that God was truly with Israel in the wilderness, and not an angel or some other surrogate (63:9). Grieving God's Holy Spirit (63:10), and grieving God, without remainder, are clearly the same thing as we read on. The reason for Israel's protection and guidance in the wilderness entailed the spirit of the Lord giving them rest (63:14). The spirit given to Moses was given through him to others.

Yet the reference in v. 10 is not to God's becoming an enemy in the past only, in the wilderness period, but right now as well. This language of God becoming a warrior against Israel appears elsewhere in Isaiah (e.g., 1:25). To grieve God's Holy Spirit is not to drive God out, but to cause God to come in judgment against those whom God loves. God hardens hearts and even leads astray (63:17), and the petitioner does not state that such a condition is God's untrustworthiness manifesting itself. This is what happens when the people God loves grieve God's active, holy presence.

The appeal to a change in fortune, in other words, entails an awareness that God can be grieved, has been grieved, but in such conditions comes in judgment as a sign of the presence of God's Holy Spirit. Even the condition of straying and dulled hearts is God's own work. How difficult it is to understand judgment as God's presence in holiness, and not God's withdrawal into a vagary that somehow is as true of God as we know it to be of ourselves. To be like those God no longer rules would be the very worst thing that could be said of any person or group; it would entail, virtually, a confession that God had stopped being the Father of children, in the way we know that to be a biological impossibility in the human realm of fathers and mothers.

Yet the dilemma here, apparently, is that God threatens to withdraw in such a way as to differentiate divine rule within those who are children of God. That is, God insists that the individual cry of 63:7, which moved immediately to the "all of us" of past and present Israel, cannot be assumed any longer. The individual and the righteous children of the Father who are here pleading or pleaded for, note well, never operate with the assumption that God could act this way. God refused to divide and differentiate the manner of being God in the wilderness, one way with some and one way with another, and so the petitioner never goes down this road. Neither does the petitioner assume it is a way to understand their common dilemma. When he speaks of holy people, and "all of us"—the plural forms so emphasized throughout this text—we are not to assume he means it any other way than the obvious way. All God's people are holy, and when God is grieved, the Holy Spirit will bring judgment upon a holy people altogether and without exception. To withdraw from one would be to withdraw from all, and that would be the most unthinkable fate of all.

In other words, God will be the one who insists on separation, if that is necessary. The form of our discourse must be respected at this juncture. The first-person plural emphasis is real. The petition is not for some but for all. Our prayer cannot be, in the first instance, "separate our righteous selves from our unrighteous fellows, for that is why God is angry and has struck out against us." Our prayer is our common memory of God as Father—loving, forgiving, and guiding us all—and of God as grieved judge, working among us to bring us to common repentance and common recognition. It will always take another form of speech, to follow, not precede, this way of prayerful approach and appeal. That form comes in the final chapters, and its location after this petition and not before it demands attention and respect.

3. Notice how God can hide and still be active in holy judgment (64:7). So, too, God can be silent and be active in severe punishment (64:12).

At times I wonder if we need a late-modern Christian spirituality that can speak this language with meaningfulness. How much the Old Testament resonates with paradox and carnality when it speaks of God and creatures, so much so that to bring any abstraction or systematizing into play threatens to undo the raw transparency of this language for God and for us, God's children! And yet, to hear talk about spirituality and exercises of this or that sort would seem to be the very last thing the Old Testament has in view. It suggests a self-consciousness about prayer and even God that is, not surprisingly, as foreign to the Old Testament as it is to any serious relationship in which people are vulnerable and yet capable of identity, holiness, and jealousy.

In this section of Isaiah we are confronted by the Old Testament's ever-vigilant guard against sentimentality, spiritualism, or false exceptions to the rule. God takes us seriously. At the moment the most tender images are used (and we need to recall that the use of Father—so rare in the Old Testament alongside King, Judge, and Holy One—belongs here), God is also grieved to the heart. To ratchet-up the personal and intimate language for God is to make God more, not less, holy and jealous, and less, far less, abstract, banal, universal, or benign. To speak of God's people and God's self is to hear this sort of language from Isaiah, "Yet"—the adverb is critical, "You, O LORD, are our Father . . . will you keep silent, and punish us so severely?"

ISAIAH 65:1–66:24, FINAL JUDGMENT, FINAL VISION

65 "I revealed myself to those who did not
ask for me;
I was found by those who did not seek me.
To a nation that did not call on my name,
I said, 'Here am I, here am I.'

65 I was ready to be sought out by those
who did not ask,
to be found by those who did not seek me.
I said, "Here I am, here I am,"
to a nation that did not call on my name.

NIV

2All day long I have held out my hands
    to an obstinate people,
who walk in ways not good,
    pursuing their own imaginations—
3a people who continually provoke me
    to my very face,
offering sacrifices in gardens
    and burning incense on altars of brick;
4who sit among the graves
    and spend their nights keeping secret vigil;
who eat the flesh of pigs,
    and whose pots hold broth of unclean meat;
5who say, 'Keep away; don't come near me,
    for I am too sacred for you!'
Such people are smoke in my nostrils,
    a fire that keeps burning all day.

6"See, it stands written before me:
    I will not keep silent but will pay back in full;
    I will pay it back into their laps—
7both your sins and the sins of your fathers,"
    says the LORD.
"Because they burned sacrifices on the
        mountains
    and defied me on the hills,
I will measure into their laps
    the full payment for their former deeds."

8This is what the LORD says:

"As when juice is still found in a cluster
        of grapes
    and men say, 'Don't destroy it,
    there is yet some good in it,'
so will I do in behalf of my servants;
    I will not destroy them all.
9I will bring forth descendants from Jacob,
    and from Judah those who will possess my
        mountains;
my chosen people will inherit them,
    and there will my servants live.
10Sharon will become a pasture for flocks,
    and the Valley of Achor a resting place
        for herds,
    for my people who seek me.

11"But as for you who forsake the LORD
    and forget my holy mountain,
who spread a table for Fortune
    and fill bowls of mixed wine for Destiny,

NRSV

2I held out my hands all day long
    to a rebellious people,
who walk in a way that is not good,
    following their own devices;
3a people who provoke me
    to my face continually,
sacrificing in gardens
    and offering incense on bricks;
4who sit inside tombs,
    and spend the night in secret places;
who eat swine's flesh,
    with broth of abominable things in
        their vessels;
5who say, "Keep to yourself,
    do not come near me, for I am too holy
        for you."
These are a smoke in my nostrils,
    a fire that burns all day long.
6See, it is written before me:
    I will not keep silent, but I will repay;
I will indeed repay into their laps
7   their*a* iniquities and their*a* ancestors'
        iniquities together,   says the LORD;
because they offered incense on the mountains
    and reviled me on the hills,
I will measure into their laps
    full payment for their actions.
8Thus says the LORD:
As the wine is found in the cluster,
    and they say, "Do not destroy it,
    for there is a blessing in it,"
so I will do for my servants' sake,
    and not destroy them all.
9I will bring forth descendants*b* from Jacob,
    and from Judah inheritors*c* of my
        mountains;
my chosen shall inherit it,
    and my servants shall settle there.
10Sharon shall become a pasture for flocks,
    and the Valley of Achor a place for herds to
        lie down,
    for my people who have sought me.
11But you who forsake the LORD,
    who forget my holy mountain,
who set a table for Fortune
    and fill cups of mixed wine for Destiny;
12I will destine you to the sword,

*a*Gk Syr: Heb *your*   *b*Or *a descendant*   *c*Or *an inheritor*

NIV

¹²I will destine you for the sword,
  and you will all bend down for
    the slaughter;
for I called but you did not answer,
  I spoke but you did not listen.
You did evil in my sight
  and chose what displeases me."

¹³Therefore this is what the Sovereign LORD says:

"My servants will eat,
  but you will go hungry;
my servants will drink,
  but you will go thirsty;
my servants will rejoice,
  but you will be put to shame.
¹⁴My servants will sing
  out of the joy of their hearts,
but you will cry out
  from anguish of heart
  and wail in brokenness of spirit.
¹⁵You will leave your name
  to my chosen ones as a curse;
the Sovereign LORD will put you to death,
  but to his servants he will give another
    name.
¹⁶Whoever invokes a blessing in the land
  will do so by the God of truth;
he who takes an oath in the land
  will swear by the God of truth.
For the past troubles will be forgotten
  and hidden from my eyes.

¹⁷"Behold, I will create
  new heavens and a new earth.
The former things will not be remembered,
  nor will they come to mind.
¹⁸But be glad and rejoice forever
  in what I will create,
for I will create Jerusalem to be a delight
  and its people a joy.
¹⁹I will rejoice over Jerusalem
  and take delight in my people;
the sound of weeping and of crying
  will be heard in it no more.

²⁰"Never again will there be in it
  an infant who lives but a few days,
  or an old man who does not live out
    his years;

NRSV

and all of you shall bow down to
    the slaughter;
because, when I called, you did not answer,
  when I spoke, you did not listen,
but you did what was evil in my sight,
  and chose what I did not delight in.
¹³ Therefore thus says the Lord GOD:
My servants shall eat,
  but you shall be hungry;
my servants shall drink,
  but you shall be thirsty;
my servants shall rejoice,
  but you shall be put to shame;
¹⁴ my servants shall sing for gladness of heart,
  but you shall cry out for pain of heart,
  and shall wail for anguish of spirit.
¹⁵ You shall leave your name to my chosen to
    use as a curse,
  and the Lord GOD will put you to death;
but to his servants he will give a
    different name.
¹⁶ Then whoever invokes a blessing in the land
  shall bless by the God of faithfulness,
and whoever takes an oath in the land
  shall swear by the God of faithfulness;
because the former troubles are forgotten
  and are hidden from my sight.

¹⁷ For I am about to create new heavens
  and a new earth;
the former things shall not be remembered
  or come to mind.
¹⁸ But be glad and rejoice forever
  in what I am creating;
for I am about to create Jerusalem as a joy,
  and its people as a delight.
¹⁹ I will rejoice in Jerusalem,
  and delight in my people;
no more shall the sound of weeping be heard
    in it,
  or the cry of distress.
²⁰ No more shall there be in it
  an infant that lives but a few days,
  or an old person who does not live out
    a lifetime;
for one who dies at a hundred years will be
  considered a youth,

NIV

he who dies at a hundred
    will be thought a mere youth;
he who fails to reach[a] a hundred
    will be considered accursed.
²¹They will build houses and dwell in them;
    they will plant vineyards and eat their fruit.
²²No longer will they build houses and others
        live in them,
    or plant and others eat.
For as the days of a tree,
    so will be the days of my people;
my chosen ones will long enjoy
    the works of their hands.
²³They will not toil in vain
    or bear children doomed to misfortune;
for they will be a people blessed by the LORD,
    they and their descendants with them.
²⁴Before they call I will answer;
    while they are still speaking I will hear.
²⁵The wolf and the lamb will feed together,
    and the lion will eat straw like the ox,
    but dust will be the serpent's food.
They will neither harm nor destroy
    on all my holy mountain,"
                            says the LORD.

66 This is what the LORD says:

"Heaven is my throne,
    and the earth is my footstool.
Where is the house you will build for me?
    Where will my resting place be?
²Has not my hand made all these things,
    and so they came into being?"
                        declares the LORD.

"This is the one I esteem:
    he who is humble and contrite in spirit,
    and trembles at my word.
³But whoever sacrifices a bull
    is like one who kills a man,
and whoever offers a lamb,
    like one who breaks a dog's neck;
whoever makes a grain offering
    is like one who presents pig's blood,
and whoever burns memorial incense,
    like one who worships an idol.
They have chosen their own ways,

ᵃ20 Or / the sinner who reaches

NRSV

and one who falls short of a hundred will
        be considered accursed.
²¹ They shall build houses and inhabit them;
    they shall plant vineyards and eat
        their fruit.
²² They shall not build and another inhabit;
    they shall not plant and another eat;
for like the days of a tree shall the days of my
        people be,
    and my chosen shall long enjoy the work of
        their hands.
²³ They shall not labor in vain,
    or bear children for calamity;[a]
for they shall be offspring blessed by
        the LORD—
    and their descendants as well.
²⁴ Before they call I will answer,
    while they are yet speaking I will hear.
²⁵ The wolf and the lamb shall feed together,
    the lion shall eat straw like the ox;
    but the serpent—its food shall be dust!
They shall not hurt or destroy
    on all my holy mountain,   says the LORD.

66 Thus says the LORD:
Heaven is my throne
    and the earth is my footstool;
what is the house that you would build for me,
    and what is my resting place?
² All these things my hand has made,
    and so all these things are mine,[b]
                            says the LORD.
But this is the one to whom I will look,
    to the humble and contrite in spirit,
    who trembles at my word.

³ Whoever slaughters an ox is like one who
        kills a human being;
    whoever sacrifices a lamb, like one who
        breaks a dog's neck;
    whoever presents a grain offering, like one
        who offers swine's blood;[c]
    whoever makes a memorial offering of
        frankincense, like one who blesses
        an idol.
These have chosen their own ways,

ᵃOr sudden terror   ᵇGk Syr: Heb these things came to be
ᶜMeaning of Heb uncertain

NIV

and their souls delight in their abominations;
⁴so I also will choose harsh treatment for them
    and will bring upon them what they dread.
For when I called, no one answered,
    when I spoke, no one listened.
They did evil in my sight
    and chose what displeases me."

⁵Hear the word of the LORD,
    you who tremble at his word:
"Your brothers who hate you,
    and exclude you because of my name,
        have said,
'Let the LORD be glorified,
    that we may see your joy!'
Yet they will be put to shame.
⁶Hear that uproar from the city,
    hear that noise from the temple!
It is the sound of the LORD
    repaying his enemies all they deserve.

⁷"Before she goes into labor,
    she gives birth;
before the pains come upon her,
    she delivers a son.
⁸Who has ever heard of such a thing?
    Who has ever seen such things?
Can a country be born in a day
    or a nation be brought forth in a moment?
Yet no sooner is Zion in labor
    than she gives birth to her children.
⁹Do I bring to the moment of birth
    and not give delivery?" says the LORD.
"Do I close up the womb
    when I bring to delivery?" says your God.
¹⁰"Rejoice with Jerusalem and be glad for her,
    all you who love her;
rejoice greatly with her,
    all you who mourn over her.
¹¹For you will nurse and be satisfied
    at her comforting breasts;
you will drink deeply
    and delight in her overflowing abundance."

¹²For this is what the LORD says:

"I will extend peace to her like a river,
    and the wealth of nations like a
        flooding stream;
you will nurse and be carried on her arm

NRSV

and in their abominations they
    take delight;
⁴I also will choose to mockᵃ them,
    and bring upon them what they fear;
because, when I called, no one answered,
    when I spoke, they did not listen;
but they did what was evil in my sight,
    and chose what did not please me.
⁵Hear the word of the LORD,
    you who tremble at his word:
Your own people who hate you
    and reject you for my name's sake
have said, "Let the LORD be glorified,
    so that we may see your joy";
    but it is they who shall be put to shame.

⁶Listen, an uproar from the city!
    A voice from the temple!
The voice of the LORD,
    dealing retribution to his enemies!

⁷Before she was in labor
    she gave birth;
before her pain came upon her
    she delivered a son.
⁸Who has heard of such a thing?
    Who has seen such things?
Shall a land be born in one day?
    Shall a nation be delivered in one moment?
Yet as soon as Zion was in labor
    she delivered her children.
⁹Shall I open the womb and not deliver?
    says the LORD;
shall I, the one who delivers, shut the womb?
    says your God.

¹⁰Rejoice with Jerusalem, and be glad for her,
    all you who love her;
rejoice with her in joy,
    all you who mourn over her—
¹¹that you may nurse and be satisfied
    from her consoling breast;
that you may drink deeply with delight
    from her glorious bosom.

¹²For thus says the LORD:
    I will extend prosperity to her like a river,

ᵃOr to punish

NIV

and dandled on her knees.
¹³As a mother comforts her child,
    so will I comfort you;
    and you will be comforted over Jerusalem."

¹⁴When you see this, your heart will rejoice
    and you will flourish like grass;
    the hand of the LORD will be made known to
        his servants,
    but his fury will be shown to his foes.
¹⁵See, the LORD is coming with fire,
    and his chariots are like a whirlwind;
    he will bring down his anger with fury,
    and his rebuke with flames of fire.
¹⁶For with fire and with his sword
    the LORD will execute judgment upon
        all men,
    and many will be those slain by the LORD.

¹⁷"Those who consecrate and purify themselves to go into the gardens, following the one in the midst of*ᵃ* those who eat the flesh of pigs and rats and other abominable things—they will meet their end together," declares the LORD.

¹⁸"And I, because of their actions and their imaginations, am about to come*ᵇ* and gather all nations and tongues, and they will come and see my glory.

¹⁹"I will set a sign among them, and I will send some of those who survive to the nations—to Tarshish, to the Libyans*ᶜ* and Lydians (famous as archers), to Tubal and Greece, and to the distant islands that have not heard of my fame or seen my glory. They will proclaim my glory among the nations. ²⁰And they will bring all your brothers, from all the nations, to my holy mountain in Jerusalem as an offering to the LORD—on horses, in chariots and wagons, and on mules and camels," says the LORD. "They will bring them, as the Israelites bring their grain offerings, to the temple of the LORD in ceremonially clean vessels. ²¹And I will select some of them also to be priests and Levites," says the LORD.

²²"As the new heavens and the new earth that I make will endure before me," declares the LORD, "so will your name and descendants endure.

ᵃ17 Or *gardens behind one of your temples, and*   *ᵇ18* The meaning of the Hebrew for this clause is uncertain.   *ᶜ19* Some Septuagint manuscripts *Put* (Libyans); Hebrew *Pul*

NRSV

    and the wealth of the nations like an
        overflowing stream;
    and you shall nurse and be carried on
        her arm,
    and dandled on her knees.
¹³ As a mother comforts her child,
    so I will comfort you;
    you shall be comforted in Jerusalem.
¹⁴ You shall see, and your heart shall rejoice;
    your bodies*ᵃ* shall flourish like the grass;
    and it shall be known that the hand of the
        LORD is with his servants,
    and his indignation is against his enemies.
¹⁵ For the LORD will come in fire,
    and his chariots like the whirlwind,
    to pay back his anger in fury,
    and his rebuke in flames of fire.
¹⁶ For by fire will the LORD execute judgment,
    and by his sword, on all flesh;
    and those slain by the LORD shall be many.

¹⁷Those who sanctify and purify themselves to go into the gardens, following the one in the center, eating the flesh of pigs, vermin, and rodents, shall come to an end together, says the LORD.

¹⁸For I know*ᵇ* their works and their thoughts, and I am*ᶜ* coming to gather all nations and tongues; and they shall come and shall see my glory, ¹⁹and I will set a sign among them. From them I will send survivors to the nations, to Tarshish, Put,*ᵈ* and Lud—which draw the bow—to Tubal and Javan, to the coastlands far away that have not heard of my fame or seen my glory; and they shall declare my glory among the nations. ²⁰They shall bring all your kindred from all the nations as an offering to the LORD, on horses, and in chariots, and in litters, and on mules, and on dromedaries, to my holy mountain Jerusalem, says the LORD, just as the Israelites bring a grain offering in a clean vessel to the house of the LORD. ²¹And I will also take some of them as priests and as Levites, says the LORD.

²² For as the new heavens and the new earth,
    which I will make,

---

*ᵃ*Heb *bones*   *ᵇ*Gk Syr: Heb lacks *know*   *ᶜ*Gk Syr Vg Tg: Heb *it is*   *ᵈ*Gk: Heb *Pul*

NIV

23From one New Moon to another and from one Sabbath to another, all mankind will come and bow down before me," says the LORD. 24"And they will go out and look upon the dead bodies of those who rebelled against me; their worm will not die, nor will their fire be quenched, and they will be loathsome to all mankind."

NRSV

shall remain before me, says the LORD;
  so shall your descendants and your
    name remain.
23 From new moon to new moon,
  and from sabbath to sabbath,
all flesh shall come to worship before me,
  says the LORD.
24And they shall go out and look at the dead bodies of the people who have rebelled against me; for their worm shall not die, their fire shall not be quenched, and they shall be an abhorrence to all flesh.

COMMENTARY

Much hard work has gone into the interpretation of these two chapters. The reasons for this are varied, but certainly interest in the larger shape of Isaiah as a whole corpus has contributed to the fresh investment of labor.[232]

The standard form-critical treatment is best represented by Westermann.[233] He divides the chapters into six smaller units (65:1-7; 65:8-16a; 65:16b-25; 66:1-4; 66:5; 66:6-16) and even suggests verse rearrangement from as far away as 59:21 in the final four subsections (66:17; 66:18-9, 21; 66:20, 22-24); he types the units according to form; and finally he assigns the units to points in time and to settings, largely in relationship to chaps. 60–62, which constitute for him the authentic Trito-Isaiah proclamation.[234] His approach continues to find a following among redaction-oriented studies, which seek to build upon older form-critical labors in the name of assessing the final editorially arranged product.[235]

Alongside this as a minority voice was the work of Liebreich in the late 1950s.[236] Liebreich sought an altogether different angle of vision, beginning with chap. 65 and extending to chap. 66. In essence, he concluded that these final chapters formed an inclusio with Isaiah 1 and were composed in order to unite the overall Isaiah tradition—hence the title of his essay, "The Compilation of the Book of Isaiah." These conclusions were based upon a straightforward concordance logic, which revealed a high degree of lexical and thematic correspondence between the last two chapters and the first chapter of the Isaiah tradition. To break ranks with form-critical preoccupation with discrete units was no mere gesture; it pointed to terrain that had not been sufficiently plowed by the reigning methods. Cultic abuse is a major theme in both locations (1:29-31; 66:17); so, too, the motifs of shame and fire-judgment for the unrepentant (1:29; 1:31; 66:5; 66:24); in addition, the new name given Jerusalem in 1:31 finds its counterpart in the righteous of 65:15. Lack picked up the concordance observations of Liebreich, and moving beyond the form-critical acceptance of three Isaiahs comprised of discrete units sought to find signs of structural organization in the Isaiah corpus as a whole.[237] He also noted

232. See New Visions of Isaiah, ed. R. F. Melugin and M. A. Sweeney, JSOTSup 214 (Sheffield: Sheffield Academic, 1996). D. M. Carr's essay, "Reading Isaiah from Beginning (Isaiah 1) to End (Isaiah 65–66): Multiple Modern Possibilities," ibid., 188-218, offers a good overview of work on Isaiah 65–66 and Isaiah 1, with astute exegesis of these three chapters.

233. C. Westermann, Isaiah 40–66, trans. David Stalker, OTL (Philadelphia: Westminster, 1969) 398-429.

234. He wonders if 59:21 should be inserted in the gap he created between 66:20 and 66:22. Ibid., 427.

235. See, e.g., S. Sekine, Die tritojesajanische Sammlung (Jes 56–66) redaktionsgeschichtlich untersucht, BZAW 175 (Berlin: de Gruyter, 1989). For an overview, see C. R. Seitz, "Isaiah (Third), the Book of," ABD 3:490-501.

236. L. J. Liebreich, "The Compilation of the Book of Isaiah," JQR 46 (1955–56) 276-77; and JQR 47 (1956-57) 126-27.

237. R. Lack, La symbolique du livre d'Isaie: Essai sur l'image littéraire comme l'element de structuration, AnBib 59 (Rome: Pontifical Biblical Institute, 1973) 139-41.

differences between the opening and closing chapters, but these were evidence of a conscious intertexual relationship, not accidental or form-critically discrete themes. Sweeney is the most recent exegete to accept and build on these two studies through his own work on Isaiah 1–4.[238]

A related work should be mentioned in this same context. Beuken has defended the novel view that chaps. 65–66 comprise studied, intentional closures, editorially supplied, to Trito-Isaiah chapters (56–64), Deutero-Isaiah chapters combined with them (40–64), and finally, the book of Isaiah as a coordinated whole (1–66).[239] So, for example, the unit 65:1–66:14 is the fitting conclusion to the dramatic movement begun in chap. 56: the righteous are rewarded as the suffering seed, promised in chap. 53 as progeny for the servant. The unit 66:15-20*a* brings a combined Deutero-and Trito-Isaiah to conclusion; there is the promised theophany, the acknowledgment of the nations, and language reminiscent of Deutero-Isaiah, according to Beuken ("all flesh," "tongues," "sign"). The entire, coordinated Isaiah corpus then finds its own special conclusion at 66:22-23. Judgment by fire (1:31; 6:13), new moon and sabbath (1:13), and even the witness of the dead bodies (37:38) are recycled here by Beuken's final "epilogist," based upon their appearance in Former- or Proto-Isaiah.

One should acknowledge the enormous difficulty of establishing such a complex thesis, and in this respect Beuken is to be congratulated for his extraordinarily close reading of these chapters, the consequence of his effort to demonstrate such subtle, intratextual connections. He is forced, however, to establish so many things at once. First, the final two chapters make sense as a "coherent text complex"[240] unto themselves. Second, one portion of text forms an epilogue to one developing section of Isaiah tradition, then another to two combined, and finally a third to three combined. And yet Beuken himself acknowledges that the influence

of Proto-Isaiah was felt by his second epilogist,[241] and this should not be suprising, since there is a certain artificiality in retaining a strict 1-2-3 Isaiah framework, when sections 2 and 3 are themselves *already indebted* to Isaiah traditions that lay before them. This is particularly true in the case of so-called Trito-Isaiah. Indeed, more than any other expositor, it has been Beuken who pointed the way in assessing the proclamation of Trito-Isaiah through a set of theological assumptions he inherited from the Deutero-Isaiah traditions, chief among them: servants, seed, righteousness, suffering, and vindication. This being the case, it requires a deft surgical touch to speak of an epilogue to Trito-Isaiah that can be distinguished from one for Deutero-Isaiah and Trito-Isaiah combined.

Mention should also be made of Steck's recent foray into Trito- and Deutero-Isaiah work. His work is a painstaking effort to combine formal and redactional analysis that is unlikely to find a rival in sheer complexity of reconstruction.[242] It is with a certain irony, then, that Steck has emerged as a defender of chaps. 65–66 as one textual unit in two parts (65:1–66:4 and 66:5-24). Steck argues that the conclusion of the corpus of Trito-Isaiah (and thus Isaiah) provides a unified response in chaps. 65–66 to the preceding lament (63:7–64:11). This amounts to a full rejection of the approach of Westermann and his students, and finds curious analogy at this point with *The Interpreter's Bible* 1956 contribution of James Muilenberg.[243] Muilenberg had argued both for reading chaps. 65 and 66 together and for seeing a clear connection between the preceding lament and this response from God, at once caustic and comforting. Steck likewise sees his first text unit (65:1–66:4) as God's response to the apostates in Israel, while the final unit of the book (66:5-24) is addressed to the righteous. In so doing, the assumptions of a unified and comprehensive Israelite lament, such as is found in 63:17–64:11, are questioned and repudiated. A lament that sought divine redress and response for an afflicted people serves to introduce a rebuke and a final divine division,

238. M. Sweeney, *Isaiah 1–4 and the Post-Exilic Understanding of the Isaiah Tradition,* BZAW 171 (Berlin: de Gruyter, 1988).

239. W. A. M. Beuken, "Isaiah Chapters LXV-LXVI: Trito-Isaiah and the Closure of the Book of Isaiah," in *The Congress Volume: Leuven 1989,* ed. J. A. Emerton, VTSup 43 (Leiden: Brill, 1991) 204-21. Also relevant, W. A. M. Beuken, "Does Trito-Isaiah Reject the Temple? An Intertextual Inquiry into Isa. 66:1-6," in *Intertextuality in Biblical Writings. Essays in Honor of Bas van Iersel,* ed. Sipke Draisma (Kampen: Uitgeversmaatschappij J. H. Kok, 1989) 53-66.

240. Beuken, "Isaiah Chapters LXV-LXVI," 221.

241. Ibid., 208.

242. O. H. Steck, *Studien zu Tritojesaja,* BZAW 203 (Berlin: de Gruyter, 1991).

243. J. Muilenberg, "The Book of Isaiah, Chapters 40–66," in *The Interpreter's Bible,* 12 vols. (Nashville: Abingdon, 1956) vol. 5.

cleaving Israel and raising in such a context the theological destiny of the nations under one Lord. Finally, mention should be made of the creative work of Conrad, which regarding these final chapters finds an unexpected ally in the conclusions of Steck. Conrad's larger concern is to spot evidence of an intended audience for the book of Isaiah as a whole, revealed within the text and not merely inferred as a historical or new-critical reality. Not suprisingly, perhaps, evidence is produced in the opening and closing chapters of just such an audience. A confession at 1:9, followed by an appeal to hear the word of the Lord (1:10), finds its counterpart in the final chapters of Isaiah, with a lament (63:7–64:11) and the cry, "Hear the word of the LORD, you who tremble at his word" (66:5). Conrad identifies both groups as consisting of the remnant survivors, either specifically referenced or promised, at numerous points in the Isaiah presentation (1:9; 6:13) and especially contrasted with the impious abusers of cult and divine presence in these final chapters.

One can spot yet further thematic linkages between these two important textual blocks, so that the notion of intratexuality affecting the composition of chaps. 65–66 appears on solid footing. (For example, the reference to spreading out hands in chapter one, and its ironic reversal in 65:1-3, 24.) The theme of God's calling and speaking, before being called upon or spoken to, is a motive now uniting the final two chapters; (c.f. 65:12 and 66:4).

What can we conclude, then, about the formation and purpose of these critical closing chapters of the book of Isaiah? First, Beuken is correct to spot a high degree of intratextuality in these last two chapters, even as his efforts to sort this out along the lines of specific correspondence within sections of the preceding corpus appear unnecessarily ambitious. What would such a finding in fact imply? In the view of this commentary and in agreement with much of Beuken's other work, this finding puts too great an emphasis on the discrete character of chaps. 56–66, which are provided with an epilogue before ensuing epilogists go to work on larger combinations. The very fact that Proto-Isaiah and Deutero-Isaiah seem to intrude in epilogue number one ought to be no surprise, as it is clear that these final chapters are calibrated to the presentation of, and indeed are an

explicit continuation of, the work of the servant by the servants (chaps. 40–53 with 54–64). Perhaps one should conclude that Beuken's first epilogue is an effort to bring to a close a continuous project undertaken by the servants, which extends back to include the presentation of chaps. 40–53. In that sense, the vindication of the righteous appears as a particularly dense theme here (65:1–25) and serves as the crowning resolution of the conflict between the righteous afflicted servants and their opponents within the community of Israel. In chap. 65, this resolution appears as a divine verdict on behalf of the servants (65:13-16), where in chap. 66, the righteous are addressed directly (66:5ff.) and their vindication is the means by which the nations come to knowledge of the one God's holy reign over all the earth. Israel's judgment becomes the occasion for the nations' worship.

This brings us to the second major finding. It seems clear that when one seeks to establish the basis for intratextual commentary in these final chapters, chap. 1 in particular comes into play. But even this finding can be wrongly stretched. The final chapters work with an obvious remnant theology. Such a theology is adumbrated in chap. 1 (1:9, 27), and also at other points in First and Second Isaiah chapters (6:13; 50:10-11) and in the separation of the righteous within chaps. 54–64. The burning and cleansing judgment is a key motif in chap. 1 (1:24-31); however, the ironic fire judgment that sweeps over Zion and also over the nations, seemingly dividing one from the other, finds expression at other key points in First Isaiah (e.g., 29:5-8). Still, it is important to note that opening and closing chapters of Isaiah's vision seem calibrated for readers of the entire corpus. Differences between them are not proof that they are independent, but that they have been coordinated to make different points at different junctures in the book.

Not suprisingly, the opening chapter allows the main focus to fall on Israel—the possibility of repentance, the cleansing of Zion, and the final warning judgment exhortation. The last chapter would make no sense as mere repetition of these themes, given all that has transpired in the larger Isaiah corpus, and especially in chaps. 40–64. So, the language and orientation of this prominent opening chapter is evoked in order to signal continuity with former things, but also a new thing—here, the deployment of a familiar conceit or poetic image from Second Isaiah that outstrips what we found in those chapters (compare 48:6 and 65:17ff.). Zion has been cleansed and made new; children are birthed aright, in wonderous and righteous conception; the judgment has begun on Israel, as promised in chap. 1, and will soon involve "all flesh" (66:16)—for which the Assyrian defeat is but a type (37:36). False worship, then by an Israel become Sodom (1:10-17) and by the nations as such (chaps. 13-23; 37:37-38), now by Israel and by all flesh (65:1-6; 66:3-4; 66:17), will give way to right worship and reverence of Israel's Lord by the whole earth (66:18-23). What is clear in comparing the opening and closing chapters is not just evidence of wordplays, reversals, and intratextuality, but also a manifest desire to produce a coherent presentation at the close of Isaiah that is at once in continuity with former things, but also presents the outer, bold fringes of the vision given to God's servant Isaiah and those servants who speak and act in his stead.

And finally, there is a third finding to consider: the connection between these final two chapters and the preceding lament. Recent scholarship has rejected the notion that these final chapters are unrelated to what precedes, a view made popular in older form-critical treatments and the legacy they represent.[244] One sees clearly that the division within Israel, so prominent a theme in chaps. 65–66, is missing or is at least too subtly expressed in 63:7–64:11. Moreover, since, strictly speaking, older form-critical labors never expected the final organization of units to mean anything of significance for interpretation, one chief task was moving units to new locations and devising ways to understand theological shifts from the angle of these relocations. It is important to mention this here because of the recent redactional work of Steck. Steck feels that the position of chaps. 65–66 is intentional and that these two chapters are meant to respond to the lament of 63:7–64:11.

244. See, e.g., D. Carr, "Reading Isaiah from Beginning (Isaiah 1) to End (Isaiah 65–66): Multiple Modern Possibilities," in *New Visions of Isaiah,* ed. R. F. Melugin and M. A. Sweeney, JSOTSup 214 (Sheffield: JSOT, 1996) 204, who cites Whybray's view that "there is no connexion between the two passages" (R. N. Whybray, *Isaiah 40–66,* NCB [London: Oliphants, 1975] 266) as typical of a position he is seeking to set aside. Also in line with Whybray are Westermann and Paul Hanson, *The Dawn of Apocalyptic* (Philadelphia: Fortress, 1975) 80-81.

This is a *redactional* judgment, however, in the sense that the content and present placement of chaps. 65–66 serve to *correct* an understanding at work in the preceding lament, namely, that Israel as a whole is entitled to God's response. Stated differently, another hand has sought to modify and recast a theological view at work in the lament with which it took issue. The manifestly tendentious relationship between levels of tradition and texts in Isaiah 56–66 is typical of Steck's reconstruction. Chapters 65–66 are meant to follow and respond to what precedes, but only through the lens of redactional intentionality, not in the plain-sense presentation of the canonical text as such.

Conrad, by contrast, seeks to read the relationship between the lament and the final chapters at a different level of intentionality. The final chapters respond to the preceding lament at the level of its own argument. Those responsible for Isaiah's final word do not seek to correct or recast a theological view they regarded as faulty and yet as intended by the author in the terms expressed. The response of chaps. 65–66 is a divine response to the supplication made on behalf of all Israel, as Conrad sees it, properly lodged by the prophetic voice therein. The view adopted here is that Conrad's efforts are in the right direction, as against the (redactionally tendentious) reconstruction of Steck. That is, the supplication is indeed heard by God on its own terms. Within this frame of reference, God effects a distinction the supplication was not urging, as it gave expression to true confession and heartfelt appeal. God reveals in the final chapters that the supplication *cannot* hold true: for those who do not wish it, who do not seek him, and who do not reckon God's glorification to involve the ones who, ironically, are making supplication on their behalf (66:5). The irony the text underscores in its present arrangement is poignant and tragic. The Holy One cannot and will not hear the cries of those who have repudiated God and who have as well rejected the righteous ones who cry out on behalf of all Israel, including their opponents.

In sum, the final chapters respond forthrightly to the preceding supplication, though in a way that reveals God's judgment over those who have not sided with God's servants. The "where is the one?" of 63:11 finds its proper response at 65:1, "Here I am, here I am." The "there is no one who calls on your name" (64:7) is followed in 65:1 by "a nation that did not call on my name." The rebellious people of 65:2 are foreshadowed in 63:10. The phraseology "walk in a way that is not good" (65:2) likewise recalls 63:17 and 64:5; "keep silence" in 65:6 and 64:12; "iniquities" in 65:7 and 64:6-7, 9; "all of you" in 65:12 and 64:6, 9.[245] God's judgment over rebels in Israel becomes the occasion for the journey of the nations to Zion, as promised in Isa 2:1-4. The peaceful scene of the nations and Israel on the holy mountain is reissued in 65:25, with an obvious evocation of Isa 11:9. But the final picture is one of fire judgment, as a preparation for proper worship by all flesh (66:17-24).

The interpretation both of individual units within the logic of Isaiah's conclusion and of how such units work in close connection with previous sections of Isaiah must be attended to. The author of this final section knows about the "former things" of Isaiah, and he seeks to let God speak God's final word in this "vision of Isaiah" in response to, coordinated with, and obedient to a word that did not go forth in vain, but kept on accomplishing in accordance with God's purposes, which are found within Israel's legacy of divine speech. Central in this regard is the opening vision of Isaiah (1:1–4:6) and the speech to Zion and the servants at the transition after the servant's death (54:1–55:13). Allusions to early chapters found now in Genesis, especially in 65:17-25, suggest that for this author the "former things" are not restricted to the legacy of divine speech found in Isaiah only. To speak of new heavens and new earth is of necessity to refer to the context of divine speech about creation and first disobedience such as we find in Genesis 1–3. That, too, is a "former thing."

65:1-7. Here is the divine response to the preceding lament and petition. For the purpose of commentary, I restrict the response to these seven verses, though it is obvious that the divine speech of 65:8-16 and 65:17-25 is elaboration based upon this initial word. In all three units it is to be assumed that a division is being made by God between the righteous servants and the wicked, and that the latter are engaged, proudly and self-consciously, in religious acts unworthy of the Holy

One of Israel. Ironically, it would appear that the wicked have charged the servants with being insufficiently religious or holy (65:5); apparently, therefore, they would accept the various descriptions of their worship given here (65:3-4; 65:11), but would defend them, and have defended them before the servants, as appropriate to the worship of the God of Israel.

Less clear, perhaps, is the relationship between this indictment of false religion parading as true, and the concerns of chap. 66, as these touch upon the Temple (66:1-6). True worship, as God intends this, is not worship without form or substance of any kind. At the same time, the detailing of false worship, such as we see it in chap. 65, persists in like manner in chap. 66, as is made clear in 66:3 and 66:17. It cannot be concluded without further ado that God is arguing for some sort of purely spiritual worship, of a sort discontinuous with worship as it is known in Israel. The retribution visited by God against false worship is retribution from the Temple. The final description of the worship of Israel and the nations speaks the familiar language of Israel's cult as God has revealed it (66:20-23). I will take up below the nature of the divine rebuke concerning God's house (66:1-2). Not suprisingly, the tension between indictment of false worship, on the one hand, and the maintenance of true religion, on the other, is reflected in chap. 1 as well as in the final chapters of Isaiah.

On another front, it would not be proper to merely sociologize these indictments from God, that is, reduce the characterizations found in 65:3-4 and elsewhere to what one makes up about one's opponents so as to discredit them. There is an authentic disagreement here over the nature of true worship, and it runs in both directions. God is adjudicating that disagreement in favor of the servants, who have been charged by the wicked and have been afflicted and persecuted. The servants are described later as those "who tremble" at God's word (66:2, 5) and are hated by their own people (66:5). If the persecution and affliction are true—and there is no good reason to question this—then the false worship, down to the details, must also be reasonably reflected in these verses. To not "tremble" at God's word is to walk in one's own way, and that begins in false worship.

Having said that, it is not easy to know the con-

245. See Muilenburg, "The Book of Isaiah, Chapters 40–66," 745.

tent of the worship practices enumerated here (and elsewhere in chaps. 65–66). The text is, in the nature of the thing, not giving us a dispassionate sociological analysis. Worship of the dead, or manipulation of the realm of the dead spirits on behalf of the living, is a practice well known in antiquity, and it appears on occasion in the Old Testament (1 Samuel 28). Garden-sacrificing would appear to involve nature rites of some kind, but again we get half-glimpses only in places like Hosea 1–3, and these suggest some effort to conflate human sexuality and nature and the divine realm. There is as well here mention of dietary practices at odds with the Torah of Moses. It is only conjecture, but the servants seem to be under assault from a group claiming special knowledge, which exempts them from the law as related to death, sex, and food; and that this is done on the basis of claims to holiness.

The divine response to the petition of the servants in the preceding chapter is unequivocal. There can be no meaningful use of the term כלנו (*kūllānû,* "all of us") as the petitioner sought (64:6, 8). The petition of the servant for the "all of us" who went astray made sense as the servants eulogized the servant in their tribute at 52:11–53:12. But God draws the line here, in this response. The servants' appeal for "all of us" is responded to by God's indictment of false worship. God makes a distinction between those who tremble at the divine word and those who dispense with it in pursuit of special knowledge and holiness.

The reference to fire and smoke in 65:5, in the context of false worship, and the iniquity of ancestors (65:7), could well be calibrated with Isaiah 1. False worship (1:10-15), the punishment of iniquity within Israel for those who forsake the Lord (1:28), and the fire consuming them and their work (1:31), that is, the gardens of 1:29, would appear to be a similar set of concerns as here. The NRSV places a colon after "See, it is written before me" (v. 6) to signal that what follows is what has been written down. Another possibility is that the indictment of Isaiah 1, against the iniquities of the ancestors, and God's word of coming judgment found there, is what God refers to as written before God. The iniquities of the present generation, together with those of the former times, are together here judged. It is as if the forgiven

iniquities—double in intensity and doubly forgiven—that are spoken of in Isaiah 40 have here given way to fresh iniquities of a sort reminiscent of the false worship of Isaiah's day. Translations struggle at v. 7, though there can be little doubt that a former time and a latter time of iniquity are being conflated and punished in full measure (cf. 40:2).

65:8-16. Beuken has rightly taught us to pay attention to the key word "seed" through chaps. 54–66. English translations often render the Hebrew word in terms of "ancestors, descendants" and so forth. Beuken wants us to understand the promise to the servant that he would "see seed" (53:10; compare 6:13 and 54:3) as being carefully followed up in these chapters. The seed of the servant are the disciples (servants) who bear the same relationship to him as he did to the former Isaiah: they are taught by him (see 50:4 and 8:16). As the disciples of Isaiah in his day guarded the testimony vouchsafed by God to Isaiah, so, too, the disciples of the servant in this generation. The collocation of "my chosen" and "my servant" is familiar from 42:1. Here it is pluralized, appropriate to our context (65:9). The seed of the servant are the servant children, borne to Zion (cf. chap. 54 and 65:17-25), "offspring [זרע *zeraʿ*] blessed of the LORD" (65:23). The promises made at 59:21, of spirit endowment from one generation of the seed of the servant to the next, are here reiterated, now in the context of the separation of the righteous servants from their persecutors. Beuken is right to emphasize both the careful planning of these chapters around this theme, and its resounding climax in our unit here (65:13-14).

The language of seeking out appears in 65:1 and again here (65:10), and it appears to work in conjunction with the rousing hymn in chap. 55: "Seek the LORD while he may be found, call upon him while he is near" (55:6). The wicked, as stated then, were to forsake their ways (55:7) in order to trigger God's lavish pardon. Instead of the banquet of joy, feasting, eating, drinking and delight, promised by God in chap. 55 for God's servants, however, the wicked are set apart for punishment. They have not forsaken their ways, are not richly pardoned, and seek their own delight, not God's. The eating, drinking, and joy are not taken back, but remain the possession of those who heeded the admonition of chap. 55.

Vineyard imagery occurs elsewhere in Isaiah (5:1-7; 27:1-6) as does the dialectic of threshing in judgment and cleansing for purification. On the one hand, God watches God's vineyard like a hawk, guarding it fiercely, but looking for good grapes as well. Yet, we know from 27:4, "if it gives me thorns and briers . . . I will burn it up." Here the dialectic is resolved by means of a division within Israel. Destined for the sword are those whose false worship amounts to a forsaking of the Lord (65:11-12), while the servants are vindicated and given a new name (65:15). This naming mirrors the promises given to Zion in 62:2; as for Zion, so, too, for her servant-children.

Language appears in this unit that is reused at 66:4. God calls, but there is no answer; God speaks, and there is no listening. It has been established that Isaiah was to prophesy and that the consequence would be no listening and no comprehension (6:9-10). It has also been established that the "How long?" conditions were fulfilled in the circumstances of exile and forgiveness, and that the servant Israel, though deaf and blind, yet has eyes to see again and ears to hear God's new word (43:8). The logic of the discourse of Isaiah 40–48 turns on this release from deafness and blindness, as former things give way to new things. It may be, then, that the logic of the language's usage here (65:12) is that the opponents of God and the servants, living on the other side of Isaiah's "how long?" have returned themselves to the era of judgment that constituted the former things. The indictments of false worship from Isaiah's day are as true for these opponents as they were before, but with the added dark reality that standing as they do on the other side of an era of forgiveness and release from blindness, they constitute more serious offense. To turn away from the lavish forgiveness proffered by God and brought about by the sacrifice of the servant is a worse offense than to stand under Isaiah's "former thing" judgment. And so, too, the punishment is more severe. God called and spoke anew, but some refused to listen and answer, choosing instead a way of death (65:15).

65:17-25. This unit is introduced through a transitional figure, as God announces the death of the persecutors of the servants and the new naming of the servants. The former things are over and gone and forgotten. The servants' vindication is full and complete.

Here again we can feel the presence of chap. 1, with its call to heavens and earth to serve as witnesses against rebellious children. But so far gone are those days, enclosing the wicked opponents of the servants as well, that God announces an imminent plan: the creation of a new heavens and a new earth. The final vindication of the servant and the servants was to involve the reconstitution of Zion and her repopulation with children she did not know she had even conceived. So, naturally, those themes appear here (v. 18).

But the descriptions accompanying this new heaven and new earth are more than the natural fulfillment of promises God has made, even as they are that, to be sure. The most graphic example of this is seen in the final verse (65:25). Here a word-for-word recycling of verses from Isa 11:6-9 appears. That is, God is making good on the word of promise to Isaiah's generation, when God spoke of a day to come when enemies in the realm of nature would peacefully coexist. Yet, appended to this is reference to the serpent and the curse upon him, based upon Gen 3:14. To speak of a new heaven and a new earth is to return to creation and the curses that followed upon the very first act of disobedience. It is to go back beyond the rebellions of Isaiah's generation, or of the present generation; back to the very point of rupture. In order for the former things to be put away for good, God must begin all over again.

Mention of the curse over evil as embodied in the serpent—that creature that cannot coexist with other creatures except as a parasite—makes clear that Genesis language and context are pivotal in the construction of this unit. When this is clear, then one can see the force of other allusions as well. Advanced years, like the ages of the great ancestors from Genesis, will be like youth, and there will be no premature dying (65:20). Human labor will not be marked by the "thorns and thistles" of Genesis (3:18) nor by Isaiah's briers and thorns (5:6; 7:24, 25; 27:4; 55:13). Children will be born without labor pains, in line with the promises to Zion (54:1; 66:7), and with obvious resonance to Gen 3:16. Blessing stands (65:23) where curse—over ground, creation, procreation, and human labor—ruled before. The "seed" the servant was to see becomes, in this new heaven and earth, a new creation altogether. In the enjoyment of one's work in long life (65:22), humankind is likened to a tree in its longevity, and one can hear in this verse no reference to a tree of life to be contrasted with a tree of knowledge of good and evil. Something truly new is being set forth, against the backdrop of these former things.

The critical wording of v. 24 requires comment, given the remarks above on 65:12 (and 66:4). Here appear the calling and speaking, answering and hearing collocation again. In the new creation the blessed seed is heard and answered before any calling or speaking takes place. This does not move in the same direction as with 65:12 (or 66:4). This is human calling and human speaking, and God promises to hear and answer before such even takes place. It is hard not to see in this an evocation of the tragedy of not calling and not speaking in the garden, at the moment when the serpent posed its terrible question (3:1). In the ruptured existence after disobedience, God must call to humankind, who is hiding. And, mortals must now call on God, in a different dispensation of communication, fraught with sin and anguish and avoidance and rebellion. But in the age described in 65:17-25, all that is confused and wreaked in divine-human exchange is gone. This is not unlike the language associated with new covenant in the Deuteronomy–Jeremiah traditions: "I will put my law within them, and I will write it on their hearts . . . they shall all know me, from the least of them to the greatest" (Jer 31:33-34 NRSV; Deut 30:14). That aspect of human-divine communication, disrupted by the corrupt human will and heart, will be addressed by God, and the consequence will be a new creation, in which hearing and attending are indistinguishable.

66:1-24. Four things need to be noted about this chapter. First, chap. 66 and chap. 65 should be read together. The language links are obvious—heaven and earth; verbs for slaughtering, sacrifice, and offering; the centrality of joy and rejoicing for the servants; calling and speaking (not responded to); Zion's new birthing; and fire judgment. The indictment against false worship and the separation of the servants is heightened here, yet the terms of the dispute are set in chap. 65. Chapter 66 is a logical, direct, sustained continuation of the argument of chap. 65.

Second, Beuken's view regarding chap. 66's relationship to the book of Isaiah is *generally* sus-

tained by a close reading. That is, the first part of the chapter (vv. 1-9) tends to relate more to chap. 65 than the larger book as such, while the second section (vv. 10-16) relates to Deutero-Isaiah material as well. The final section (vv. 17-24) brings in the entire book's shape and direction. But this is only a general observation, since obvious exceptions can be noted. For example, the stunning vindication of the servants (a Trito-Isaiah theme notable in chap. 65) is found in the final section of chap. 66, where the "seed" is declared part of God's permanent worship community (66:22). On the other hand, the condemnation of false worship, found in the first section (66:1-6) has much in common with chap. 1 of Isaiah. So there is an admixture at work in chap. 66 that resists simple alignment with critically determined sections of Isaiah. Striking is what a sustained role is played by previous prophecy from Isaiah (chaps. 1; 11; 19; 40; 49; 62).

Third, the only way to make sense of chap. 66's indictment of false worship is to seek to follow a consistent reading that can integrate the whole chapter. If such can be found, the burden will remain on those who follow the more common procedure of dividing the chapter into units that present divergent and disagreeing positions on worship and the nations. I believe a consistent reading can be adduced without flattening the descriptions found across verses of chap. 66.

Finally, certain themes run throughout the chapter, chief among these the concern with joy and rejoicing (66:5, 10, 14) and the revelation of God's glory (66:5, 11, 19). The worship by all flesh (66:23) is a rebuke to those within Israel who have chosen another worship, according to "their own ways" (66:3), and who are closed out. They taunted the servants with the production of God's glory, so as to bring joy (66:5), and God obliges by bringing joy to Zion and the servants through God's glorification, inclusive of the witness of the nations. In the final verses (vv. 17-24), problems of determining the proper pronominal referent are alleviated by context, that is, the fact of intratextuality at work in the composition of the text.

66:1-6. The only serious question about delimiting the unit comes in v. 6. Either the verse stands alone (what follows in vv. 7–11 relates to Zion), or it closes the indictment of 66:1-5 with an oracle of accomplished judgment. I choose the latter reading here.

The problem of the unit is obvious: Do we have a condemnation, without further ado, of a theology of presence in God's house? This would amount, in some sense, to a rejection of previous theologies of presence, as these took root in Israel, and would be arguably consistent with the sharp condemnation of false worship in, e.g., Isaiah 1 and 65. The force of the unit would be, then, God dwells not in "houses made with human hands" (Acts 7:48). Solomon's temple-building was either wrong or misguided, and now is being rejected altogether (cf. Acts 7:44-46). Using some form of historical analysis, it is frequently held that a party within Israel, represented here, is rejecting the post-exilic efforts to build the Temple again (for this, see, e.g., Ezra and Nehemiah).

What is striking, however, is how the Solomonic building project uses the exact same language. That is, the report of 1 Kgs 8:1-53 states throughout that God dwells in heaven, called specifically "your dwelling place" (8:30) not on earth, but "in heaven" (8:32, 34, 36, 39, 43, 45, 49). The repetition is obvious and belongs to the central rhetorical force of the prayer at the Temple's dedication. Indeed, the account is crafted with obvious knowledge of the eventual destruction of the Temple in judgment (see 1 Kgs 9:8-9). When one adds to this the references to the Temple at Isa 66:6 and 66:20, then it becomes far less clear that what is at issue here is simple renunciation of a former temple ideology, or of one repeating it in the post-exilic situation of rebuilding. The Temple is the location of God's voice of judgment at 66:6, just as in former Isaiah (6:8-13). When proper offerings are brought at the close of chap. 66, again alongside the typical "holy mountain" language appears a reference to the "house of the LORD" (NIV, "temple of the LORD") and indeed to priests and Levites (see vv. 20-21). What is contested (and this is true in Acts as well) is a notion that God dwells in some restricted or merely carnal sense in the place built for God, and this set of potential misperceptions constrains the cautious descriptions in 1 Kings 8–9.

In this unit, the emphasis is slightly different, however. God repeats the theology of 1 Kings 8, and the focus seems then to shift to *who* is doing the building on behalf of *whom* and whether it is

appropriate to even use this language. In v. 2, God refers to the divine act of creation (there is a text-critical alternative to consider in v.2*a*). The contrast is picked up later in the unit, where the false worshipers are said to have followed "their own ways" (v. 3). This in turn contrasts with the servants, "who tremble at his [God's] word" (v. 5) and presumably follow ways not their own, but those that God has set these forth.

In view of this I must consider the literal rendering into English of the Hebrew אי־זה (*'ê-zeh*), that is, "where is this house?" The force of the condemnation is not that God is rejecting a previous temple theology of presence; indeed, God repeats the one already given at 1 Kings 8. Rather, God rejects a house-building project that stands over against what God has already accomplished: "All these things my hand has made and so all these things are mine" (or, "came to be"). There can be no new building grounded in any other logic.

It stands to reason that one possibility that exists for those represented as religious innovators (in 65:2-4 and 66:3) is building a different house (so, "where is this house?"; is this a reference to the temple at Elephantine?) or rebuilding the present one ("what is this house?") along the lines of their own ideology. So God thwarts this by reminding them of past theological grounding and past commitments ("all these my hand has made") to the Temple built by Solomon. If this is true, then it helps in interpreting the difficult v. 3. Proper worship practice is improper and worse when carried out independently of God's will. The same lesson is explicit in the rejection of Saul on the occasion of his defeat of the Philistines (1 Samuel 13) and again in the sacrifices at Gilgal (1 Samuel 15). As I shall discuss, it is of the same character as improper worship *tout court* (Isa 66:17). Proper worship wrongly undertaken, and improper worship conducted with rigor and enthusiasm—neither have God's blessing, while both have God's most severe and final judgment.

Verse 4 extends the image of new creation at 65:24, but in an ironic contrast. The new creation of righteous servants is to be marked by dramatically new communication, between themselves and God. That this is not happening in 66:4 is just more evidence of a cleavage. "Those who tremble at God's word" are those prepared with new ears and new voices by God. Their respect for God's word means that their offerings will prove acceptable, by contrast with what is described in v. 3. This contrast is played out in the final verses of the chapter (66:17-21).

As noted above, the final thrust of this section involves the caustic challenge of the wicked, in respect of God's glory, and God's promised self-glorification on behalf of the persecuted servants. This glorification, moreover, amounts to a fulfillment of the promise from the divine council, viz., "and all flesh shall see it together" (40:5). That is, it involves the gathering of "all nations and tongues, and they will come and see my glory" (66:18), while those within Israel conducting false or wrongly ordered worship will be forfeit. In the words of the opening Isaiah vision, they will have become God's enemies (1:24; 66:6).

66:7-16. It is best to describe this section, not as an independent unit, but as an elaboration of the preceding speech, in two main parts (vv. 7-11; vv. 12-16). The abrupt transition at v. 7 is to be explained by reference to the contents of Isaiah 1 and to the themes of the immediately preceding chapters. To speak of the Temple and the city (66:6) triggers recollection of the language of explicit promise associated with a righteous Zion, after cleansing judgment and purification ("afterward you will be called the city of righteousness," 1:26), such as appears in Isa 49:14–54, 55, and 60–62.

It is difficult to avoid the conclusion that two contexts are operating in the expression of vv. 7-8: creation and new creation (no labor pains) consistent with chap. 65; and the discovery of children delivered but as yet unknown to bride Zion (49:21: "who bore me these?"). Painless childbirth is joined with wondrous and prodigous delivery. The address is not directed to Zion, however, as was true in Isaiah 49–56. Rather, it is to the children of Zion, formerly in mourning, now birthed and ready to be nourished in delight and overflowing abundance. New creation is also new national identity and a new beginning inside of a history with God set in motion long ago. Election, Zion, creation: all were threatened, and all are being renewed in a dramatic configuration, as dramatic as birth without gestation or labor pain.

The second brief section (vv. 12-16) is also a compendium of previous promise and judgment language, familiar from our Isaiah discourse. The comforting of Zion, promised from the heavenly council, has been accomplished, and in this is comfort for Zion's new children. Her children see her peace. The promise of 40:11, that God would personally and gently lead "those that have young" finds its dramatic focus in daughter Zion, and the spill-over of this is comfort for the righteous servants.

The sharp transition to judgment, on the hinge of servant vindication (v. 14), is familiar in these closing chapters of Isaiah (63–66). Again, the pressure from former prophecies is likely in evidence here: from Isaiah 1's larger vision (with fury, fire, anger, and rebuke) and from Isaiah 36–38 the dramatic rescue of Zion, king and people/children, is the consequence of God's word to Isaiah and Hezekiah.

Yet the ambiguity of chap. 1 is also important to recall. There as here we have reversal: Zion becomes not bride but harlot (1:21); Israel, the children, becomes forfeit and sinful גוי (gôy, 1:4), like the people of Gomorrah, with rulers like those of Sodom (1:10). The same reversals are coming into play here, but toward a different end. Zion and her children are restored—but with the severe separation from her ranks of wicked children. The generic foe of 1:24 remains the object of God's wrath, but counted among their number are portions of God's own inheritance, on the tragic far side of forgiveness and promise squandered. To use the language of 1:28, they are exposed in the servants' vindication as "rebels and sinners" meriting God's full judgment, as in the days of Assyria's humiliation before the gates of Jerusalem (37:36).

66:17-24. Superficially, a similarity exists between the conclusion of the book of Isaiah and the book of Daniel. Both have an apocalyptic tenor. Both appear to heap up elaborations, though in the case of Daniel these are frequently regarded as adjustments and corrections made in the light of failed prophecy. The alternative position is that later editors returned to the original Daniel visions and pressed further for their details, armed with the conviction that prophecy cannot fail, except from the standpoint of the interpreter's confusion.

The final verses of Isaiah do display a heaping up of elaborations, made on the basis of previous Isaianic contexts. This is the virtual hallmark of

Isaiah, especially as the book draws to a close: the density of intratextual reference (e.g., 65:25; 66:4; 66:7-8; 66:12, to which compare 23:18; 66:13; 66:15). So it is not surprising to find elaborations in extremely dense form at the final verses, before which lie the vast field of Isaianic prophecy.

Verse 17 elaborates the character of false worship described in 66:3, without the ironic contrast necessary in this earlier context. Here we have straightforward description and straightforward condemnation. Leader and follower in these spurious rituals will meet their end together. It is likely that the reference to consecration and purification further attaches to the charge of 65:5, made by the opponents of the servants, "I am too sacred for you." Verse 17 gives further evidence of the nature of the opposition, though still in sufficiently lapidary form in respect to their practices. We should be in no doubt, however, that the practices are rigorously religious in character, and not absent of piety, ritual, polity, and regimen. This brief judgment oracle triggers its own elaboration in v. 18: God's coming in punishment against the religiously wicked will serve as the occasion of the revelation of God's glory.

The language of v. 18 requires close scrutiny, given the possibility for intratextual reference. Unfortunately, as annotation and translation reveal, the first half of the verse is quite difficult. The effort seems to be in the direction of connecting the judgment of v. 17 with some attendant divine action. The divine action is itself clear: the gathering of nations and tongues to see God's glory. This action finds yet further, detailed stipulation in the adjoining unit (vv. 19-21).

The promise of all flesh seeing God's glory is inherent in the Isaiah discourse (40:5). The streaming of the nations to Zion is also attested (2:1-5). Isaiah is a book that has much to do with the fate and final destiny of foreign peoples (chaps. 13–21). The concept of a remnant of survivors found at all compass points closes off the discourse of Isaiah 1–12 (11:10-16), and there appears the banner or sign set up as a rallying point for God's ingathering of Israel (11:10, 12; cf. 66:19). It would appear that within the context of God's judgment of Israel, that is, of the "religious" opponents of the servants, has been added the gathering of nations outside Israel to witness God's glory, in fulfillment of one portion of former Isaiah and another of latter Isaiah.

One further context needs to be considered, given the predilection of these closing chapters for referring to key Genesis themes. The Table of Nations, with its list of nations and tongues (Gen 10:1-32), is juxtaposed, positively, to the story of the flood and God's judgment on all creation in the Noah episodes (Gen. 6:1–9:29). The national identities emerge not in the context of judgment, as in the ensuing Babel Tower debacle (11:1-9), but in the context of divinely intended dispersion, the being fruitful and multiplying and filling the earth fulfillment of the original creation charge (1:28). God notes the imagination of humankind's heart, that it is "evil from childhood" (8:21) and forswears any future global judgment as the remedy.

In the unit following (vv. 19-21), the nations listed are not special in any strictly Isaianic sense, even as one can identify associations elsewhere in the book of Isaiah (for Tarshish, see esp. Isaiah 23; for distant isles, see 11:11 and 42:4; etc.). They do, however (and perhaps not surprisingly), correspond to the non-Semitic sons of Noah, in their nations and in their languages (so the terms of Genesis 10). What sort of adaptation of that Genesis-creation-judgment tableau do we find before us?

As the consequence, not of global flood judgment (which God forswore), but of judgment over a sinful people within Israel, there is a positive outcome, as there was in Genesis 10. There the positive outcome was the emergence of national identity in fulfillment of Gen 1:28. Isaiah has modified this picture for his own situation, but under constraint of its first expression; namely, the emergence of the nations, now gathered to witness God's glory in Zion, God's new creation.

The sign set up in the ensuing unit (vv. 19-21) is not the bow in the clouds, strictly speaking, but the sign we heard of in 11:12, to be set up for the survivors of Israel among the nations, here doing a sort of double-duty for the bow of Gen 9:12-16, "the sign of the covenant that I make between me and you and every living creature." That sign of covenantal kindness toward all nations is here the sign promised for the exiles among the nations. This means that God reveals divine glory and covenantal goodness in two ways: by gathering "all nations and tongues" to Zion, and by setting up a sign akin to the rainbow, visible outside of

Israel and Zion, so that those who have not heard of God (cf. 45:14-15) might see God's glory, where they are in their national distinctiveness and particularity.

One major difficulty in interpretation must be faced at this point: the obscurity of reference in the pronoun "they," running right across vv. 18-21. "They" in the second half of v. 18 clearly means the nations. The problem, however, begins in v. 19. Because the promise is that God's glory will be proclaimed among the nations by those who survive (presumably, the judgment implied by God's theophany in vv. 17-18), the question is: Who are the survivors, and of what?

One possibility for a referent is the group of those among the gathered nations who survive and who report the glory of God as they were promised they would see it in v. 18. They report this glory and witness to it among their fellow nations.

Another possibility for a referent is the group of those who survive within Israel, who are then sent out to the nations. If this were the preferred interpretation, then the radicality of the next verses would be dampened. Israel is making an offering of her own people, and in so doing, before the nations, from her number are selected priests and Levites.

It is for the reason of forfeiting the radicality that we prefer the first interpretation, without which the rhetorical force of the verses is lost. Offerings are brought by the nations, in fulfillment of 56:1-8, wherein we are told that foreigners will come to God's holy mountain (56:7), and "their burnt offerings and sacrifices will be accepted on my altar." The false religion of the servants' opponents is replaced by right worship by the nations. This comes in fulfillment of that previous oracle's conclusion, "I will gather still others to them besides those already gathered" (56:8). The consistency this reading achieves, in the context of the last verses of Isaiah and in the light of previous prophecy, commends it as preferable to an Israelite-only reading. It finds futher warrant in the oracle concerning Egypt in Isa 19:16-25. Instead of an altar in Egypt (19:19), however, the nations unambiguously come to Zion to worship, with sacrifices and grain offerings according to the final chapter. The sign is not an altar in Egypt (19:19) but a sign among the nations to gather themselves

and Israel, with the latter constituting the proper offering to the Lord in Zion.

It should be noted in passing how extraordinarily close this particular interpretation of Isaiah's last scene is to the plain sense of Zech 8:20-23 and 14:16-21. In the latter passage, the survivors are unambiguously those from the nations, and they are strictly enjoined to journey to Zion to worship in accordance with Israel's torah. Here, too, we can detect the logic of Isa 66:20, wherein holiness and purity, associated with ceremonially clean vessels, is extended to bells on horses and all common cooking pots (Zech 14:20). In this mood of expansion, coupled with attention to the torah revealed to Israel, it is no far leap to proclaim, "I will select some of them also to be priests and Levites" (Isa 66:21 NIV). In Isaiah, as in Zechariah, radicality and novelty are joined with strict concern for obedience to God's ordinances.

So it is that vv. 22-23, which precede the solemn concluding coda (v. 24), continue to refer to New Moon and Sabbath, just as Zechariah refers to strict observance by all peoples of the Feast of Tabernacles. The reference to "all mankind bowing down before me" (v. 23) may pick up the solemn oath of 45:23, "By myself I have sworn . . . a word that will not be revoked: before me every knee will bow." As many have recently noted, a further reference to this key text can be seen in Phil 2:10.

The final coda takes the form of a solemn warning, by utilizing a description of judgment against all who rebel against God. This motif is obvious from Isa 1:28 ("rebels and sinners will be broken"). Also, the language is arguably influenced by Isaiah 36–37 and the description of Assyrian defeat, which has here become a type of all national and internal rebellion. For there we read, "When the people got up the next morning— there were all the dead bodies!" (37:36 NIV). The eternally restless character of their judgment recalls the two previous organizing refrains, at 49:22 and 57:20-21. The scene of judgment on rebels matches what we find in Zech 14:12-15, only the order is different. It is the survivors of national rebellions and warfare against Zion who make up the contingent headed for proper worship in Jerusalem. In Isaiah, the same motif appears, but the final verse sets a solemn warning, attributing an eternal and unceasing punishment against all rebellion. This is the final, not the penultimate verse of the book of Isaiah. It sits astride the preceding language of radical promise, as its twin. There is worship of God by all flesh, or there is rebellion meriting punishment of a haunting and unrelieved sort.

REFLECTIONS

1. The end of Isaiah is very similar to its beginning. In both, there is a dramatic and extended scene of judgment. Israel's false worship comes under indictment (1:11-17; 66:3ff.). There is a call to hear the word of the Lord (1:10; 66:8). Still, God's approaching judgment is overwhelming and sure (1:24-25; 66:15-16).

This final chapter has distinctive notes, however. In the first chapter, the prophet addresses an Israel that has become, as it were, one of the nations (1:4). Her rulers are from Sodom and her people from Gomorrah (1:10). There is no such sarcastic portrayal in Isaiah 66. Israel is riven in two. Those who tremble at God's word are those who receive hatred and rejection in God's own name from God's own people (66:5). And the nations remain who they are in this final tableau. They are not the sinful Israel or the agents of God's cleansing judgment as in former Isaiah, but neither are they neutral observers. In fulfillment of Isaiah 2, they stream to Zion (2:2; 66:18-21). They come with God's people to the house of the Lord (66:20).

Divine judgments have a purpose only God can bring about. All pride and arrogance are flattened. Self-confident religious speech is exposed for hypocrisy (66:5). False worship is not merely empty and vain; it is wicked and viral (66:3). Under such conditions, zealous religious programs are demonic and must be exposed as such by God (66:1).

In a lecture and response to a prominent atheist of his day, Karl Barth spoke in a manner not unlike our prophet, facing the religious hypocrisy of his day:

> The atheism that is the real enemy is the "Christianity" that professes faith in God very much as a matter of course, perhaps with great emphasis, and perhaps with righteous indignation at atheism wild or mild, while in its practical thinking and behaviour it carries on exactly as if there were no God.[246]

In such a climate, God can only respond as God does in Isa 66:1, "What is the house that you would build for me?"

However, there remain the humble who tremble at God's word (66:2, 5). God speaks clearly to these humble souls, attends to them and cares for them; God sets them apart and makes lavish promises to them. God provides what has become in latter Isaiah the greatest sign of God's love: comfort (66:13). This comfort is not mere words or occasional affection or remote but well-meaning sympathy. The humble are fed, are carried, are protected, are made to know joy and peace (66:12-15). The humble do not seek retribution and it is not their job to expose religious fraud. By virtue of their constancy and humility before God's word, they have their reward. Here in Isaiah's final chapter we see the lesson of the beatitudes (Matt 5:3-12).

No one in the Christian church lives without persecution, from within and from without. To walk the way of the cross obliges us to suffer and to refuse to return evil for evil. This disposition is not a stoic virtue, achieved by techniques or habit of mind. It is a gift of the Holy Spirit, given to those who know themselves to be forgiven and comforted.

Like Daniel in exile, thriving on God's word, the comforted of God become vehicles of transformation for the nations and the outsiders to God's word and ways. "Now I, Nebuchadnezzar, praise and extol and honor the King of heaven,/ for all his works are truth,/ and his ways are justice;/ and he is able to bring low/ those who walk in pride" (Dan 4:37 NRSV). In the book

---

246. Karl Barth, *Fragments Grave and Gay*, ed., M. Rumscheidt (London: Collins, 1971) 46-47.

of Isaiah, the nations stream to Zion bringing their own lavish gifts (66:12, 18-21). And in the book of Ezra, the house of the Lord is restored by foreign endowment (Ezra 7:21-26).

So the final scene of Isaiah becomes the final scene of the gospel story as well. God uses the innocent, obedient judgment of Jesus Christ as the vehicle by which all creation is transformed. This is the final destiny of God's Son, God's people, God's creation. We can be guided by this word if we tremble before it and receive it with constancy and humility.

We may for the time being suffer and experience rejection and hatred, even from within the household of faith. But that is not God's final word. Rather, God's final word is comfort and peace that pass all understanding. Isaiah's final vision is a vision into which we must lean, drawing comfort and assurance from it as if we were little children again, nursing from the riches of God's own glorious provision (66:11).

2. The final chapters of Isaiah also take us back to the very beginning, back before Isaiah 1 to the creation itself (Isa 65:17-25). What God is up to is nothing less than making a new heaven and a new earth. Irenaeus spoke of "recapitulation" as that act of God in Christ whereby the entire story of God's dealings with the chosen people is reclaimed, chapter by chapter, from the very beginning right through to the end. It is never enough that God comforts the individual soul, apart from the transformation of all created things.

The vision of 65:17-25 may strike us as wishful thinking or as the prophet's rhetorical excess. Yet when we consider the work of God in Christ, we see that this vision of Isaiah entails the actual project God has undertaken through the obedience of his Son. This is not high-flying rhetoric, but a genuine description of what God accomplished in Jesus Christ.

God reclaimed creation. Jesus harrowed Hades and recovered all that had been lost before his new creation, starting with Adam and moving right through the line of prophets and holy women and men to his own time.

In the second century, Justin regarded the truth of the gospel as revealed from before all time, through the witness of Israel's scriptures; and he was followed by Irenaeus later in the century. In the third century, Origen spoke of the dual authority of these ancient archives of God and the witness of Jesus Christ. In the fourth century, Ambrose sent Augustine to Isaiah to hear the gospel. Today, we cannot regard the final vision of Isaiah as anything less than true and inspired, because the gospel recapitulates its word and establishes beyond doubt the work of God, which is God being satisfied with nothing less than total reclamation of the world. Isaiah saw dimly and in shadows, not because his vision was unclear or his speech ambiguous, which it is not, but because the grandeur of what God accomplished in the Son put this vision in a new light. We are able to see into the gospel of Jesus with the aid of this vision, and in return, we see this vision as that final report of God's ultimate purposes for the world.

It has been said recently that the content of the Christian hope is not imaginary but "irreducibly imaginative" because it draws us "out of our present world in the direction of another, which makes us aware in the process that it points beyond itself to something which is, strictly speaking, unimaginable."[247] This is the nature of prophecy, one might say, as God's unimaginable word bears forward on the goal of God's purposes for the world.

The book of Revelation naturally draws from the well of God's word to Isaiah so as to give us hope and direction in our faith. The Christian knows where she or he is headed, guided by the lamp of Isaiah and the confirming witness of God's word in Jesus. It is this dual testimony that lies at the heart of the promising and fulfilling God, the Elohim of promise and the Yahweh of fulfillment, as Rashi understood it.[248] And it is this dynamic and faithful character Christians confess to be God's own inner life as the Father, and the Son, and the Holy Spirit.

247. R. Bauckham and T. Hart, *Hope Against Hope: Christian Eschatology at the Turn of the Millenium* (Grand Rapids: Eerdmans, 1999).

248. M. Rosenbaum and A. M. Silbermann, eds., *Pentateuch with Rashi's Commentary: Exodus* (New York: Hebrew Publishing Company, n.d.) 24-25.

In Isaiah's last chapters, we get yet again a glimpse into the mystery that is Isaiah's greatest gift to the Israel of God. The gift is made explicit at an earlier juncture: "So shall my word be that goes forth from my mouth; it shall not return to me empty, but it shall accomplish that which I purpose, and succeed in the thing for which I sent it" (55:11). God's word spoken through the witness of his servant Isaiah cannot come to an end, until of course God is all in all.

This final vision belongs to the one who inspired it, the Holy One of Israel. We see it with eyes of faith, lean into it with the Holy Spirit's aid, and find it ratified by Christ and continually accomplishing its purpose, to the glory of God the Father. Until that day when wolf and lamb feed together, and hurt or destruction finds no place on all God's holy mountain—until then, we feed on this word and see in it sure promises of God.

"So shall my word be that goes forth from my mouth." Amen.

THE BOOK OF JEREMIAH

INTRODUCTION, COMMENTARY, AND REFLECTIONS

BY

PATRICK D. MILLER

THE BOOK OF
JEREMIAH

INTRODUCTION

T he book of Jeremiah is one of the longest books in the Bible, surpassed in number of pages of text only by the book of Psalms. While not all of the book is necessarily from the prophet Jeremiah himself, the vast extent of his prophetic career and its setting in one of the most critical times in the history of Israel—from the reform of Josiah through the downfall of Judah and into the time of exile—suggest why this book looms so large in Scripture. The great crisis of Israel's history in the Old Testament period involved the destruction of the Temple, the dwelling place of the Lord of Israel, and the exile of God's people. Much of the biblical literature either deals with those matters or comes from that time in Israel's history. No other biblical book so enables readers to comprehend theologically what was going on at that time—to hear both what happened and why it happened—as does the book of Jeremiah.

HISTORICAL CONTEXT

The two great events of Judah's history during the years of Jeremiah's prophecy were the religious reform of Josiah (622 BCE) and the destruction of Jerusalem and Judah (587 BCE) and the exile of many of its leaders and citizens (597 and 587 BCE). These events, however, took place in the context of major geopolitical upheavals in the ancient Near East, affairs of nations in conflict with one another that are constantly reflected in the book of Jeremiah and were often the focus of attention in his oracles. Jeremiah began to proclaim the divine word during the time of Assyrian decline and the ensuing conflict between Egypt and Babylon for domination of the Fertile Crescent. The demise of Assyria was under way during the first part of Josiah's reign (640–609 BCE). The last great king of Assyria, Asshurbanipal, died in the year given as the date of Jeremiah's call, 627 BCE (Jer 1:2). Thereafter, Assyria was unable to resist the rise of Babylon, even with help from Egypt. Nabopolassar took Babylon from Assyrian control in 626 BCE and made himself its king. Having broken Egypt free from Assyrian control under Psammetichus, his successor, Necho, sought to help Assyria, probably to exercise some power in Syria-Palestine, but also to resist the greater threat of Babylonian dominance. Meanwhile, the Medes supported the Babylonians. Over the years there were various battles and engagements involving these nations against each other, which resulted in the loss of important Assyrian cities: Asshur, Nineveh, and Harran.

The loss of Assyrian control in Syria-Palestine permitted a more independent stance on the part of Judah, especially during the reign of Josiah. It was manifest especially in his religious reform, which included the removal of all Assyrian religious practices that had become a part of the religious life of Jerusalem and elsewhere and also in political reform, his taking control of the Assyrian provinces that had once constituted the northern kingdom, Israel.

The reform, which is dated to Josiah's eighteenth year (622 BCE) by 2 Kgs 22:3 and 23:3, may, in fact, have begun earlier (2 Chr 34:3-7). In any event, it seems to have been quite comprehensive, according to the account in 2 Kings 23, and even seems to have extended into the former northern kingdom (2 Kgs 23:15-20; 2 Chr 34:6). The reform was the most extensive and far-reaching in Israel's history, though its effects were not very lasting, if the prophecy of Jeremiah is any indication. It seems to have had its impetus in nationalistic stirrings during the decline of Assyrian domination. Josiah's ability to take control of northern territory inevitably meant conflict with the northern shrines, which were regarded as idolatrous by those in Jerusalem. The reform, however, was not only a political endeavor. The discovery of a law book while the Temple was being renovated, itself a part of Josiah's reforming activity, gave significant impetus to the impulse for reform. There is no reason to doubt the judgment of Kings that Josiah was a committed Yahwist as well as an assertive nationalist.

During his reform, Josiah eliminated all non-Yahwistic cults and practices, both those manifest in the Temple and its paraphernalia and those in the high places or shrines. The reform was massive and involved the destruction of all the shrines outside Jerusalem, whether Yahwistic or not, and the complete centralization of worship in the capital city and its Temple. This reform meant the destruction especially of the shrines in the northern kingdom and their personnel, which would have been regarded as idolatrous almost by definition. The priests of the outlying shrines of Judah were invited to come to Jerusalem.

However successful Josiah's reform may have been, resistance to the reform is evident

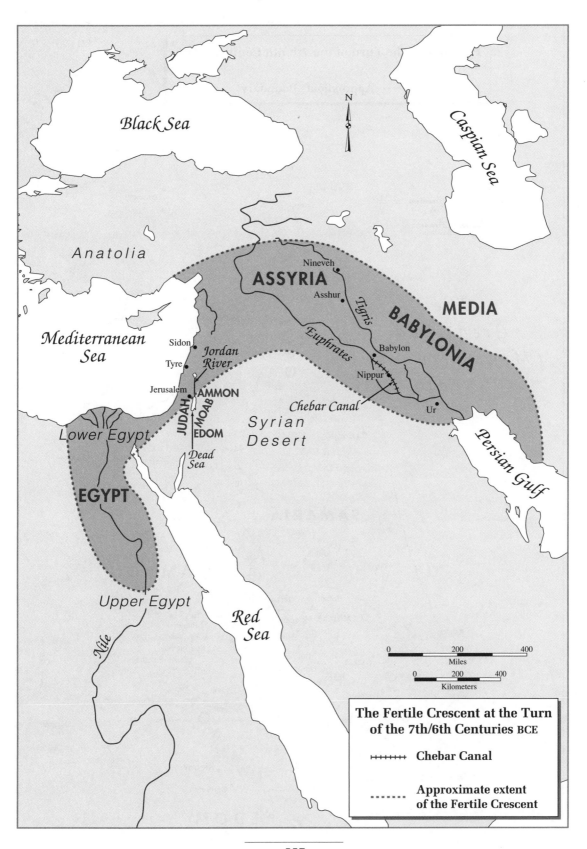

Black Sea

Caspian Sea

Anatolia

N

ASSYRIA

Nineveh

Asshur

Tigris

BABYLONIA

MEDIA

Mediterranean
Sea

Sidon

Euphrates

Babylon

Tyre

*Jordan
River*

Nippur

Jerusalem

AMMON

Chebar Canal

Ur

JUDAH

MOAB

EDOM

*Syrian
Desert*

Dead
Sea

Lower Egypt

Persian Gulf

EGYPT

Upper Egypt

Red
Sea

Nile

0	200	400

Miles

0	200	400

Kilometers

**The Fertile Crescent at the Turn
of the 7th/6th Centuries BCE**

+++++++ Chebar Canal

.... Approximate extent
of the Fertile Crescent

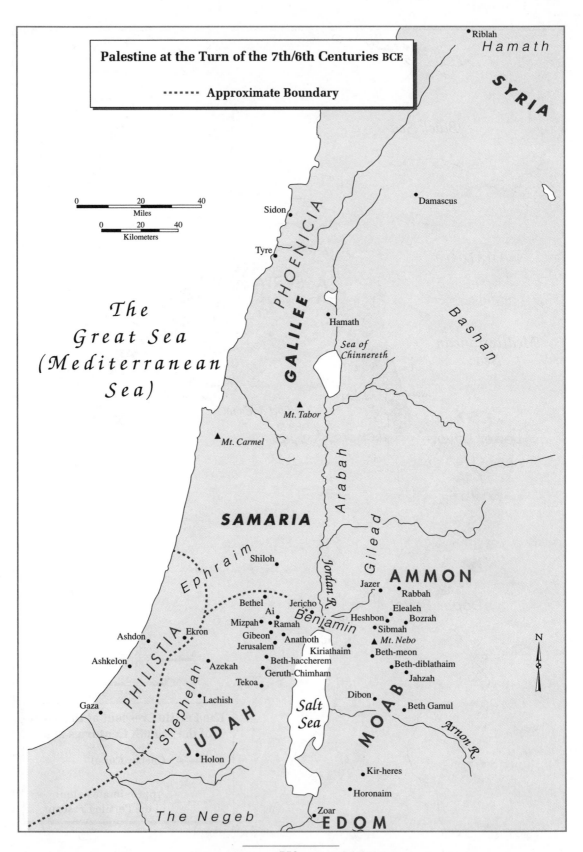

Palestine at the Turn of the 7th/6th Centuries BCE

- - - - - - - Approximate Boundary

0   20   40
Miles

0   20   40
Kilometers

The
Great Sea
(Mediterranean
Sea)

Riblah
Hamath

SYRIA

Sidon

PHOENICIA

GALILEE

Damascus

Tyre

Hamath

*Sea of
Chinnereth*

Bashan

▲ *Mt. Tabor*

▲ *Mt. Carmel*

Arabah

SAMARIA

Gilead

Ephraim Shiloh

Benjamin

Jazer

AMMON

Rabbah

Jordan R.

Bethel
Ai   Jericho
Mizpah   Ramah
Gibeon   Anathoth
Jerusalem

Elealeh
Heshbon   Bozrah
Sibmah

▲ *Mt. Nebo*

Kiriathaim

N

Ashdon
Ashkelon

Ekron

PHILISTIA

Beth-haccherem

Beth-meon

Azekah

Beth-diblathaim

Geruth-Chimham

Jahzah

Tekoa

Shephelah

Lachish

Gaza

Dibon

MOAB

Beth Gamul

Arnon R.

*Salt
Sea*

JUDAH

Holon

Kir-heres

Horonaim

The Negeb

Zoar

EDOM

558

from the book of Jeremiah. Both the testimony of narrative texts in Jeremiah to the worship of other gods because of their apparent productivity (Jer 44:15-19) and his countereffort to insist that the other gods did not "profit" suggest that there was fairly widespread continuing devotion to other cults than the worship of Yahweh or that the single devotion to Yahweh in the one sanctuary was fairly short-lived.

Josiah was killed at Megiddo in 609 BCE when he met and sought to stop Necho, the king of Egypt, and his army from going to the assistance of Assyria when it tried to retake Harran. The Egyptian-Assyrian coalition failed to counter Babylon's strength, and by 605 BCE, with Nebuchadnezzar's defeat of the Egyptians at Carchemish (Jeremiah 46), Assyrian power was at an end. Meanwhile, Necho had sought, successfully, to regain Egyptian control of Palestine. The people of Judah had anointed Josiah's son Jehoahaz as king after Josiah's death, but Necho deposed him after only three months and deported him to Egypt, imposing tribute on Judah. He placed another son of Josiah on the throne and changed his name from "Eliakim" to "Jehoiakim." Jehoiakim paid the tribute by heavily taxing the citizenry.

Jehoiakim reigned until 598 BCE, when he died or possibly was assassinated. If Jeremiah's response to Jehoiakim (Jer 22:13-19) and the latter's disdain of Jeremiah's prophetic word (Jer 36:20-26) are any indication, Jehoiakim's rule served well the interests of those opposed to Josiah's reform, he showed no interest in the covenantal norms. Meanwhile, the defeat of the Egyptians at Carchemish in 605 BCE allowed the Babylonians to move westward and begin to establish control of Syria-Palestine. In the period after the battle at Carchemish, Jehoiakim transferred his allegiance to Babylon (2 Kgs 24:1). That submission to Babylonian rule was, however, fairly short-lived. Within three years, Jehoiakim, probably in response to pro-Egyptian elements and nationalistic zeal, rebelled against the Babylonian king Nebuchadnezzar (2 Kgs 24:1). That was a big mistake. By 598 BCE, the Babylonian army was in Judah. Jehoiakim died that year, and his young son was made king. Within about three months, Jerusalem surrendered to the Babylonian army, and the young king, together with the queen mother and many officials and citizens, was deported to Babylon.

Jehoiachin's uncle Zedekiah was placed on the throne by the Babylonians, whereupon the nation went through a decade of unrest. Zedekiah was a relatively weak king. Jeremiah's encounters with him indicate that he had some good intentions but was unable to stand up to those who opposed him. The record of Zedekiah's reign, preserved primarily in the book of Jeremiah, shows a vacillating rule that ended in terrible defeat at the hands of those who had set him up as king. That some considered his predecessor, Jehoiachin, still to be the rightful king of Judah, even though in exile (see chap. 28), did not help him rule with the support of his subjects.

A rebellion in Babylon in 595 BCE seems to have stirred hopes of Judah's breaking free of Babylonian domination. In 594 (Jer 28:1), envoys from Edom, Moab, Ammon, Tyre, and Sidon met with Zedekiah in Jerusalem to plan a revolt against Babylon, a move that

Jeremiah thought was a disaster, even contrary to God's will. The plans did not go anywhere, and Zedekiah sent to Babylon (Jer 29:3), or went to Babylon (Jer 51:59), to settle things with the Babylonians and assure them of his loyalty. Within five years, however, Judean leadership with pro-Egyptian and anti-Babylonian sympathies had pushed Zedekiah into open rebellion. The Babylonians reacted quickly. The account of their siege of Jerusalem and the end of Judah is preserved in the final chapters of the books of Kings and Jeremiah. Jerusalem and its Temple were destroyed after the Temple was looted. Many of the leaders were executed, and many people were taken into exile in Babylon. Zedekiah was forced to watch his sons being executed before the Babylonians put out his eyes and dragged him off to Babylon.

A number of Judeans were left behind, including Jeremiah. The Babylonians appointed Gedaliah, a member of an important Judean family whose father and grandfather had been officials in the court, as governor of Judah. He counseled the people to remain in the land and accept Babylonian control, the same message Jeremiah had offered. Unfortunately, Gedaliah was assassinated by Ishmael, a member of the royal family, who failed to gain any support for his action and fled to the Ammonites. Fearful of Babylonian retaliation because of the murder of Gedaliah, some of the remaining leaders ignored Jeremiah's counsel to stay put and insisted on fleeing to Egypt, taking Jeremiah and his scribe Baruch with them (Jeremiah 43). We last hear him preaching a sermon against the Judean refugees in Egypt, accusing them of idolatry and abandoning their allegiance to the Lord of Israel (Jeremiah 44).

THE PROPHET JEREMIAH

While the book of Jeremiah is not intended to tell the story of the prophet, the figure of Jeremiah is often the focus of attention in the book. In the commentary that follows, the treatment of particular texts seeks to show the ways in which the prophet's life—what happens to him, what he thinks, and how he acts—is a part of the message of the text. There are, however, two issues that need to be identified and discussed as a part of introducing the book.

One is the whole question of how much, if any, access to the "historical" Jeremiah is provided by the book of Jeremiah. Opinion on that question ranges from the conviction of William Holladay,[1] who proposes a detailed chronology of the prophet and believes that most of the oracles in the book of Jeremiah can be dated to some time in his prophetic career, to Robert Carroll's[2] equally vigorous argument that the book provides little access to the prophet and his words and thoughts because so much of the book is an editorial product from a later time. These two extremes, not surprisingly, do reflect features of the book. The prophet is so prominent in the book, proclaiming many oracles that were highly appropriate to specific circumstances, that one can hardly believe

1. W. L. Holladay, *Jeremiah 1: A Commentary on the Book of the Prophet Jeremiah, Chapters 1–25*, Hermeneia (Philadelphia: Fortress, 1986) 1-10 .
2. R. P. Carroll, *Jeremiah*, OTL (Philadelphia: Westminster, 1986) 33-37.

his prophetic activity is not attested in the book. Furthermore, the references to his dictating oracles and the identification of a scribe who wrote them down and who was himself involved in the story of the last days of Judah tend to move in the same direction. There is little doubt, however, that the process of formation of a prophetic book was long and complex with considerable creative editing activity as oracles were added and interpreted, sometimes moved from one place to another, expanded by words and phrases and the like. The existence of two different forms of the book in the Hebrew (or Masoretic) text and the Greek (or Septuagintal) text further confirms the complex growth of the book, which can hardly be confined to Jeremiah's prophetic activity. Nor can one refer even to the laments of Jeremiah as a presumably authentic view into the life and mind of the prophet. Their language is typical of the psalmic laments and are not peculiar to Jeremiah or to his experience.[3]

Out of the whole—remnants of Jeremiah's prophecy and editorial additions, expansions, and the like—there comes a picture of the prophet that cannot be labeled as either historical or unhistorical, fact or fiction. Some have spoken of this image as the *persona* of the prophet, a coherent depiction of the prophet as presented by the book. One may presume that much of what is recorded there accurately conveys the experiences and happenings of Jeremiah as well as his prophetic message. But that depiction is also the result of the growth of the book and so may involve embellishment from a later time. The reference to Baruch's recording of many of Jeremiah's oracles suggests that the book has a nucleus of Jeremiah's actual oracles. One may assume a high degree of consistency between the portrait of the prophet in the book and the actual events and experiences of Jeremiah's prophetic career. With regard to particular details and the ascription of particular oracles to the prophetic activity of Jeremiah, one may not always be able to say with certainty how close the connection is between the presentation of the prophet and the life of the prophet. In this commentary, oracles and narratives are interpreted as they relate to the picture of the prophet they present without trying to differentiate between the historical prophet and the presented prophet.

A second question addresses the beginning of Jeremiah's ministry. When did he receive his call and what oracles can be associated with his early career? The superscription at the beginning of the book places Jeremiah's call in the thirteenth year of Josiah's reign, which would be 627 BCE. That date is accepted by many scholars as accurate. Others observe that the book shows little indication of Jeremiah's connection with the reform of Josiah and no oracles can be assuredly dated to the time prior to Josiah's reform in 622 BCE. Only one passage, 3:6-11, is actually dated to "the days of Josiah," while the other references to him allude to his sons and assume Josiah's death (chap. 22). The oracle in 3:6-11 illustrates the problem. William Holladay, who tends to assign as many oracles as possible to Jeremiah, nevertheless says that these verses "are

---

3. On the relation of Jeremiah's laments to their narrative context and their use of typical lament language and expressions found in the book of Psalms, see Patrick D. Miller, *Interpreting the Psalms* (Philadelphia: Fortress, 1986).

generally agreed to be late and unauthentic to Jrm."[4] John Bright associates them with prophetic preaching in Josiah's time, and Jack Lundbom sees that as a real possibility also. Bright, however, puts these verses prior to the reform of Josiah, while Lundbom says they would have to be late enough for the reform to have been judged a failure.[5] The association of Jeremiah's preaching with Josiah's time is further complicated by the problem of the identity of the "foe from the north," a topic prominent in the early chapters of the book. In Josiah's time, this could hardly have been Assyria, which was no longer attacking Syria-Palestine, or Babylon, which had not yet started to move west. The most likely candidate for the foe from the north is still Babylon, but, such an identification would involve dating those texts to a later time.

The absence of explicit date formulas in chaps. 2–20, where one would expect to find Jeremianic oracles from Josiah's time, creates an ambiguous situation. Some scholars have connected various oracles in chaps. 1–6 to that period.[6] Others have sought to explain in different ways the apparent silence about Josiah's time and his reform. Some have accepted the date in 1:2 but assumed long periods of inactivity on Jeremiah's part. Others see the superscription as conventional and stereotypical and thus unreliable for deriving biographical information.[7] The identification of Jeremiah as a boy when he was called and as having been called before he was even born (1:5-7) has led others to see in these references clues for distinguishing between his "call" and the time he actually began to act as a prophet. One solution is that of Holladay, who sees the dating of Jeremiah's call to the thirteenth year of Josiah as a reference to the prophet's birth—a plausible proposal in the light of the fact that Jeremiah was consecrated and appointed a prophet before he was born.[8] His actual public ministry as a prophet began sometime later. Lundbom distinguishes between Jeremiah's call (1:4-12) and the word of the Lord coming to Jeremiah "a second time" in 1:12-19. He would see in this "second time" a commissioning of Jeremiah to begin his public ministry, an act that would have taken place at a later time than his call, which came when he was quite young.[9] Both Holladay and Lundbom put great weight on 15:16, where Jeremiah says: "Your words were found, and I ate them." They see here a reference to the "finding" of the book of the law in the Temple (2 Kgs 22:8, 13; 23:2) and Jeremiah's ingesting of these words as his acceptance of the call. For Lundbom, this means that the beginning of the prophetic ministry was in 622 BCE; for Holladay, it means simply that the public ministry began sometime after 622.

4. W. L. Holladay, *Jeremiah 1*, 77.

5. John Bright, *Jeremiah*, AB 21 (Garden City, N.Y.: Doubleday, 1965) 26; Jack R. Lundbom, *Jeremiah 1–20*, AB 21A (Garden City, N.Y.: Doubleday, 1999) 308.

6. E.g., Bright, ibid.

7. E.g., Carroll, *Jeremiah*.

8. Holladay, *Jeremiah 1*, 1. See also Holladay, *Jeremiah: A Fresh Reading* (New York: Pilgrim, 1990) 13-15.

9. Lundbom, *Jeremiah 1–20*, 107-9.

These difficulties cannot be resolved now. In the commentary that follows, there is no attempt to date precisely the individual oracles. The book does present most of Jeremiah's prophetic activity as stemming from the time of Jehoiakim and Zedekiah. If there are earlier oracles (and there probably are), they seem to be consistent with his proclamation from 609 BCE onward—in their condemnation of the religious and social practices of the Judeans. It is possible that some of that condemnation could have come before Josiah's reform. It is more likely, however, that such rhetoric followed the deterioration after the reform.

Jeremiah as a prophet is so prominent in the book that any interpretation is forced to pay attention to him and to see in his story and in his struggles something of the book's own proclamation. The anguish of the prophet over the heedlessness of the people overlaps with the anguish of God. Jeremiah's laments provide a glimpse into the inner struggle of those figures who were called by God to an often demanding and, indeed, terrible task. Jeremiah was not alone in resisting and fighting God over the burden laid upon him; witness Elijah and Jonah, for instance. But no other book so vividly portrays that inner anguish created by a burden imposed that cannot be laid down. The biographical material in the book tells the reader something of the cost of obedience to the prophetic calling, a testimony echoed in the lives of other prophets as well. As much as anything, therefore, the overall presentation of the prophet, which centers in his frequent conflicts with false prophets, with kings, with the religious and political leaders of the community, and finally with his God, provides important material for understanding and interpreting the prophetic role in the Old Testament.

COMPOSITION

The beginning of the formation of the book of Jeremiah is evident within the book itself. The first indication is the reference to Jeremiah's dictation of a large collection of his oracles to Baruch, who wrote them down on a scroll (36:2; 45:1). This probably contained significant portions of what is now found in chaps. 1–25, though it could not have been too long if it was read three times in a single day (Jeremiah 36). The summary of Jeremiah's preaching in 25:1-13 is dated to the same year as Jeremiah's dictation to Baruch. Hence that year, 605 BCE, may be the starting point for the preservation and written transmission of Jeremiah's oracles.

That this initial writing down of Jeremiah's oracles did not constitute the final form of the book is indicated not only by the continuation of Jeremiah's prophetic activity for another twenty years but also by the information that after King Jehoiakim burned the scroll Baruch had written, Jeremiah redictated the oracles, Baruch wrote them down again, "and many similar words were added" (36:32). And these are not the only references to oracles being written down. The "Book of Consolation" (chaps. 30–31) receives its customary title from a statement at the beginning in which the Lord tells

Jeremiah to "write in a *book*/scroll all that I have spoken to you" (30:2). It is another document that makes up part of the book of Jeremiah, though it, like the other collections, was probably edited and expanded in the process of transmission. Finally, at the end of the book, there is a reference to Jeremiah's writing down oracles against Babylon on a scroll (51:60), presumably what is now chaps. 50–51.

It is clear, therefore, that the process of recording a prophet's oracles does not happen all at once. Nor is it a matter of someone following him around and copying as he speaks, though that may have happened on occasion. That the text makes a point of indicating that the oracles of the first scroll covered a period of "twenty-three years" (25:3) suggests that there was a long process of oral communication. The oracles were first preserved in the memory of the prophet or of the prophet's disciples and then were written down. If the book of Isaiah is any indication, the purpose of writing them down was to provide a way of validating the truth of the prophet's message because, at a later time, one could read the record and see that the prophet had announced ahead of time what was going to happen (Isa 8:16-22). Like Baruch's scroll of Jeremiah's oracles, the process of writing down and adding continued.

It is not possible to say now what the two Baruch scrolls consisted of, though many hypotheses have been proposed. In the light of the Lord's desire to bring the people to repentance (36:2-3), expressed in the first scroll, one may assume that those oracles in the first part of the book that urge repentance in order that the Lord might forgive the people would have been prominent in the first scroll. Inasmuch as the Lord's instruction to write the words down a second time includes an announcement of punishment of the king and the people (36:28-31), the second scroll would probably have included the announcements of judgment that are so prominent in Jeremiah's prophecy. One may presume, further, that not only were the two scrolls brought together but additions were made to both over a considerable period of time.

There is considerable evidence of a long period of composition. The most obvious is the presence of two different textual witnesses to the Hebrew of Jeremiah: one in the Masoretic Text and the other in the Septuagint (see below). It is difficult to derive either one of these from the other. The Jeremianic tradition was dynamic and not fixed. A second indicator of a complex history of the formation of the book is the number of duplications and repetitions within it (e.g., 6:12-15 and 8:10-12 or 10:12-16 and 51:15-19). It is possible that some of the repetitions are the prophet's own reuse of stock material, but in some instances it appears as if they are the result of an editing process. Furthermore, there are also places where the words of the prophet are duplications of verses or passages from other prophetic books. Yet another signal to the reader that the book went through a process of growth that extended beyond Jeremiah's own words is the appendix at the end, Jeremiah 52, which is preceded by the sentence, "Thus far are the words of Jeremiah" (51:64). One might take that sentence as a testimony that everything in the first 51 chapters comes from Jeremiah, but when one notices how much of the book is *about* the prophet and not simply his words, it becomes clear that the book is built on Jeremiah's oracles but has grown both due to his long prophetic career and due to the editorial process that started with the narratives about Jeremiah.

Three kinds of material have been brought together in the composition of the book: (1) prophetic oracles in poetic style (esp. in chaps. 2–25); (2) biographical material (esp. chaps. 26–29 and 34–45); and (3) prose sayings by the prophet, often showing deuteronomic affinities. This last type occurs as long prose discourses (e.g., 7:1–8:3; 11:1-17; 25:1-11), as shorter prose oracles and sayings scattered throughout the poetry (e.g., 3:6-11), and as prose sayings transmitted in connection with the biographical material (e.g., 21:1-10). Considerable debate has arisen over the degree to which these different types of material, specifically the poetic oracles and the prose sayings, come from the prophet himself or represent later additions to the Jeremianic collection. It is generally assumed that the poetic oracles were proclaimed by the prophet. Certainly most of the pre-exilic prophetic writings are poetic in form. One must be careful, however, about assuming that the poetic form certifies authenticity. In other poetic books, such as Amos 9, there are clearly poetic additions to the original core of the book, and the same is probably the case with Jeremiah.

The prose prophetic sayings have provoked the most discussion. The clear presence of deuteronomic language in many has led some scholars to see them as essentially deuteronomic or deuteronomistic constructions from a later time. Others have argued that while the form may be prose, the language is as much Jeremianic as it is deuteronomic and not infrequently is anticipated in the poetic oracles. This would mean that either these prose sayings should be attributed to Jeremiah or that they at least originate with Jeremiah and preserve, as Bright puts it, the "gist" of Jeremiah's proclamation, now edited and cloaked in language that reflects verbal expansion or adaptation of the prophet's word by deuteronomic or other editors.[10] This process of preserving, transmitting, and reformulating Jeremiah's oracles sometimes may have produced prose versions that were close to the prophet's perspective and at other times may have led to more self-conscious theological reworking in the light of a new situation confronting those who preserved and transmitted Jeremiah's prophetic legacy.

Linguistic arguments have been used in various ways in this debate. The fact that language usage in these prose sermons can be interpreted in different ways suggests that the process of composition whereby Jeremianic oracles were expanded and added to was multiform. That would include simple expansions and more thorough theological reworking with a particular *Tendenz*. But it also may have involved exegesis or comment on earlier texts in such a fashion that was quite particular and ad hoc, not part of a coherent theological or systematic reworking of the entire book.[11]

10. Bright, *Jeremiah*, 59.
11. W. McKane, "Relations Between Poetry and Prose in the Book of Jeremiah with Special Reference to Jeremiah III 6–11 and XII 14–17," *Congress Volume Vienna 1980*, ed. J. A. Emerton, VTSup (Leiden: E. J. Brill, 1981) 220-37.

Brevard Childs has suggested that chap. 25 points to an oral communication of the oracles from Josiah's time to Jehoiakim's time (the poetic oracles) and then to a recording of them in "a written condensation of prophetic threat" (prose sermons), which interpreted the prophet's proclamation and ministry in relation to Scripture—namely Deuteronomy.

> From the perspective of the tradition a new understanding of Jeremiah emerged from the events of history, which, far from being a distortion, confirmed the prior word of scripture. The canonical shaping of the Jeremianic tradition accepted the Deuteronomic framework as an authentic interpretation of Jeremiah's ministry which it used to frame the earlier poetic material.[12]

Such an understanding may be too simple a handling of a complex problem and suggests more coherence than many see in the final outcome. To the extent, however, that one finds in the prose material a later editing that shows some significant affinities with deuteronomic language and theology, Childs's approach resists the tendency to dismiss this level of the text in favor of the authentic Jeremiah material, as many are wont to do. His interpretation refocuses the reader's attention on the final outcome, but without ignoring earlier levels of the text.

Variations of this effort to see a coherent and theological development arising out of the prose sayings and sermons can be found elsewhere. For example, Walter Brueggemann has proposed a two-stage development of the book, a move from judgment to hope that reflects the two literatures of the book, Jeremianic and deuteronomic.[13] This two-stage development has been argued in a more detailed way by Louis Stuhlman, who sees a move from dismantling the old world in chaps. 1–25 to new beginnings from that shattered world being worked out in chaps. 26–52. Stuhlman suggests that the prose discourses have been carefully placed to provide a framework for chaps. 1–25, one that helps to provide equilibrium, echoing and enunciating notes that are present in the poetry and ultimately creating "structural unity and cohesion." The result is a "narratorial construction" that makes three major claims: (1) Judah has rejected the prophetic word of Jeremiah, (2) the result of that rejection is an impending and just punishment, and (3) the end of the old system prepares the groundwork for a newly emergent community.[14] These salutary efforts to see some coherence in the various "sources" or tradition complexes and to affirm the significance of the later editorial stages of the book's composition should not cause the interpreter to ignore or smooth over inconcinnities in the text, signs of a less tidy growth that surely was a part of the creation of the book, as is clearly indicated in the different textual forms of Jeremiah.

12. Brevard Childs, *Introduction to the Old Testament as Scripture* (Philadelphia: Fortress, 1979) 345-47.
13. Walter Brueggemann, "A Second Reading of Jeremiah After the Dismantling," *Ex Auditu* 1 (1985) 156-68.
14. Louis Stuhlman, *Order Amid Chaos: Jeremiah as Symbolic Tapestry,* The Biblical Seminar 57 (Sheffield: Sheffield Academic, 1998) chap. 1.

TEXT

The significant variation between the two main ancient versions of the book of Jeremiah, the Hebrew (or Masoretic Text, MT) and the Greek (or Septuagint, LXX), presents the interpreter with major problems. The Greek text is about one-seventh to one-eighth shorter than the MT, which means that either a considerable amount of text has been lost by scribal error or intention in the Greek or text has been added to the Hebrew. Sometimes the differences are just a word or a phrase, but often they are several verses (e.g., 8:10-12; 33:14-26; 39:4-13 are not present in the Greek). Furthermore, the order of chapters in the LXX differs from that of the MT after 25:13a. The oracles against the foreign nations in chaps. 46–51 appear in the LXX after 25:13a and in a different order from that of the MT of chaps. 46–51. The discovery of some fragments of Jeremiah among the Hebrew texts from Qumran has put the discussion of this difference on a new footing, especially since the texts include Hebrew fragments reflecting the Hebrew behind both the Septuagint and the Masoretic Text.[15]

It is now the general consensus that we have, in effect, two texts of Jeremiah that reach back to earlier Hebrew forms of the book, one apparently coming from Egypt and preserved in the Septuagint and one apparently coming from Babylon or Palestine and preserved now in the Masoretic Text. It also seems that the Greek text is not generally an abbreviated text, while the MT tends to be expansionistic. This tendency of the MT is especially evident with regard to the addition of formulas, epithets, and the like. In this regard, the LXX testifies to a superior text, if one means by that an earlier form in which expansions evident in the Hebrew of the MT had not yet occurred.[16] But the divergences are significant enough that we must ask whether they do not reflect a development of the text in two different contexts such that the end result is not simply a superior text testifying to an earlier form of the Hebrew (that is, the LXX); rather, it may be a combination of two Hebrew texts that had a separate history over a long enough time to represent, in part at least, different developments of the book and not merely scribal mistakes and corrections in transmission. The MT and the LXX represent not simply two different stages but also two different streams in the literary history of the book—one given more to expansion, the other less so. Literary growth and textual transmission, therefore, have blurred considerably. The result, as one interpreter has put it, is "a fluid tradition, our written remains serving as 'snapshots' capturing the situation of a moment."[17] To what extent the differences in the growth of the text are systematic and wide-ranging or more ad hoc and particular remains debatable.

15. These fragments have been published in *Qumran Cave 4. X: The Prophets,* Discoveries in the Judean Desert 15, ed. Eugene Ulrich et al. (Oxford: Clarendon, 1997) 145-207. For a brief discussion of what is contained in the fragments, see Jack R. Lundbom, *Jeremiah 1–20,* AB 21A (Garden City, N.Y.: Doubleday, 1999) 62-63. For the earliest and still primary discussion of the text-critical significance of the Qumran material, see J. Gerald Janzen, *Studies in the Text of Jeremiah,* HSM 6 (Cambridge, Mass.: Harvard University Press, 1973) 173-84.

16. Lundbom, *Jeremiah 1–20,* 57-62, has argued on behalf of the superiority of the Masoretic Text, claiming a much larger number of haplographies in the Hebrew lying behind the Greek than most text critics have been prepared to do.

17. David J. Reimer, *The Oracles Against Babylon in Jeremiah 50–51: A Horror Among the Nations* (San Francisco: Mellen, 1993) 155.

The position and order of the oracles against the nations (chaps. 46–51) are two elements within the larger differences. Janzen has argued plausibly that the oracles against the nations circulated separately as one of the component parts of the book of Jeremiah (like the Book of Consolation in chaps. 30–31, for instance).[18] They were inserted into the middle of the book (so the LXX), reflecting a tendency also evident in Isaiah and Ezekiel to put the oracles concerning other nations in the middle of a prophetic book. Chapter 25 already provided a connection with its oracular material having to do with foreign nations. Janzen further supposes that this new form of the Jeremianic corpus would have made other manuscripts obsolete in their existing form and that, rather than simply destroying them, scribes would have attached the corpus of oracles against the nations to the end of the book as an appendix. Because the order of the oracles in the Hebrew corresponds roughly to the order of the nations listed in 25:19-26, Janzen assumes that this is a secondary development designed to make these oracles conform to their context; there is no clear reason for a secondary development producing the Greek order of the oracles.[19]

If such an analysis is correct, and if there are other data to support it, then the reader is still confronted with two different traditions. One may grow out of the other, but the results are different traditions and texts. There is a sense in which once the egg is broken and scrambled this much, it is not possible to put it back together again. That is, the community of faith that carries forward the MT as its Scripture reads this material in a different way than is reflected in the LXX. The book comes to an end now in its Hebrew form with the oracles against the nations and especially with the oracle against Babylon. That ending gives a particular direction or shape to the book (see the Commentary).

The interpreter, faced with this complex textual situation, may be able to use one version to help establish a "better" text or to make corrections of obvious mistakes in the transmission of the Jeremianic corpus. But in the end, it is still necessary to choose which of these two ancient textual traditions of the book of Jeremiah will function as the base text, the subject of interpretation for the interpreter and the community to which he or she belongs. Both texts have functioned as Scripture for parts of the Jewish and Christian communities. In this instance, the basis for comment and interpretation is the text that has been my own Scripture and that of most of the readers of this commentary series, the Hebrew Old Testament. This commentary, therefore, is based on the Masoretic Text and does not seek to reconstruct an earlier form of the text of Jeremiah, except in cases where obvious and unintentional errors have occurred.

18. Janzen, *Studies in the Text of Jeremiah.*
19. Ibid.

BIBLIOGRAPHY

Commentaries:

Bright, John. *Jeremiah*. AB 21. Garden City: Doubleday, 1965. A fresh translation with critical notes and brief comment. The passages dealing with the life of the prophet have been brought together in one place and arranged chronologically.

Brueggemann, Walter. *A Commentary on Jeremiah: Exile and Homecoming*. Grand Rapids: Eerdmans, 1998. A superb theological and expository commentary; awareness of critical issues is placed in the service of excellent interpretation. The best commentary for the preaching task.

Calvin, John. *Commentaries on the Book of the Prophet Jeremiah and the Lamentations*. 5 vols. Grand Rapids: Eerdmans, 1950. These classic commentaries are still rich in exegetical and theological comment.

Carroll, Robert P. *Jeremiah*. OTL. Philadelphia: Westminster, 1986. A useful commentary that tends to read much of the text as the result of much later editing and interpretive activity and less the actual product of Jeremiah's prophetic ministry.

Clements, Ronald. *Jeremiah*. Interpretation. Atlanta: John Knox, 1988. Valuable insights for preaching and teaching.

Craigie, Peter, Page H. Kelley, and Joel F. Drinkard Jr. *Jeremiah 1–25*. WBC 26. Dallas: Word, 1991.

Keown, Gerald L., Pamela J. Scalise, and Thomas J. Smothers. *Jeremiah 26–52*. WBC 27. Dallas: Word, 1995. This two-volume series is a comprehensive and very useful resource, covering all aspects of the exegetical process. Extensive bibliography on every passage.

Holladay, William L. *Jeremiah 1: A Commentary on the Book of the Prophet Jeremiah Chapters 1–25*. Hermeneia. Philadelphia: Fortress, 1986.

———. *Jeremiah 2*. Hermeneia. Philadelphia: Fortress, 1989. A massive commentary that is especially strong in philological, historical, and exegetical matters. Seeks to work out a chronology of the prophet's preaching. Especially useful for showing where and how Jeremiah's language is used in other contexts. Extensive bibliography on every passage.

Lundbom, Jack R. *Jeremiah 1–20*. AB 21A. New York: Doubleday, 1999. The first volume of a comprehensive treatment of all facets of the book with special emphasis on rhetorical criticism.

McKane, William. *A Critical and Exegetical Commentary on Jeremiah*. 2 vols. ICC. Edinburgh: T. & T. Clark, 1986, 1996. Especially strong on textual, philological, compositional, and literary dimensions of the text.

O'Connor, Kathleen. "Jeremiah." In *The Women's Bible Commentary*. Edited by Carol A. Newsom and Sharon H. Ringe. Louisville: Westminster/John Knox, 1992. Keen attention to social issues, especially in regard to gender.

Thompson, J. A. *The Book of Jeremiah*. NICOT. Grand Rapids: Eerdmans, 1980. A comprehensive commentary written from an evangelical stance.

Specialized Studies:

Baumgartner, Walter. *Jeremiah's Poems of Lament*. Sheffield: Sheffield Academic Press, 1987. A translation of the major German form-critical study of Jeremiah's laments in the twentieth century.

Berridge, John MacLennan. *Prophet, People, and the Word of Yahweh: An Examination of Form and Content in the Proclamation of the Prophet Jeremiah*. Basel Studies of Theology 4. Zürich: EVZ-Verlag, 1970. A form-critical study of the book to address the individuality of the prophet and his proclamation.

Holladay, William L. *The Architecture of Jeremiah 1–20*. Lewisburg: Bucknell University Press, 1976. The application of rhetorical criticism to the first twenty chapters to work out structural patterns.

Holladay, William L. *Jeremiah: A Fresh Reading.* New York: Pilgrim, 1990. A helpful short presentation of the results of his large two-volume commentary study of the prophet. Reconstructs the life and work of the prophet, drawing upon many texts. Very readable.

Janzen, J. Gerald. *Studies in the Text of Jeremiah.* HSM 6. Cambridge, Mass.: Harvard University Press, 1973. An important study of the text of Jeremiah, taking account of the Qumran fragments of Jeremiah and confirming the general textual superiority of the Septuagint (Greek) over the Masoretic Text (Hebrew).

King, Philip J. *Jeremiah: An Archaeological Companion.* Louisville: Westminster/John Knox, 1993. Sheds light on various aspects of the book from the world of material culture.

Lundbom, Jack R. *Jeremiah: A Study in Ancient Hebrew Rhetoric.* SBLDS 18. Missoula: Scholars Press, 1975; 2nd ed., Winona Lake: Eisenbrauns, 1997. A rhetorical-critical study of Jeremiah.

Nicholson, Ernest. *Preaching to the Exiles: A Study of the Prose Tradition in the Book of Jeremiah.* Oxford: Blackwell, 1970. The subtitle properly describes this work. The author argues that the biographical narratives and prose sermons were the product of the deuteronomists and represent a theological tradition out of the period of the exile.

O'Connor, Kathleen M. *The Confessions of Jeremiah: Their Interpretation and Role in Chapters 1–25.* SBLDS 94. Atlanta: Scholars Press, 1988. The best treatment of Jeremiah's laments, with particular attention to their context.

Overholt, Thomas W. *The Threat of Falsehood: A Study in the Theology of the Book of Jeremiah.* SBTSS 16. Naperville: Allenson, 1970. Treats a major theme in the book of Jeremiah with particular attention to texts that have to do with true and false prophecy.

Perdue, Leo G., and Brian W. Kovacs, eds. *A Prophet to the Nations: Essays in Jeremiah Studies.* Winona Lake: Eisenbrauns, 1984. A wide-ranging collection of studies on various aspects of the book of Jeremiah giving an idea of the state of scholarly discussion of the book at the time it was published.

Stuhlman, Louis. *Order Amid Chaos: Jeremiah as Symbolic Tapestry.* The Biblical Seminar 57. Sheffield: Sheffield Academic, 1998. A fine study that seeks to show how the book reflects an intentional organization of two main parts and a final theological message communicated by the shape of the whole.

OUTLINE OF JEREMIAH

I. Jeremiah 1:1–10:25, The Prophet's Call and Words of Judgment

    A. 1:1-19, The Prologue

        1:1-3, The Superscription
        1:4-19, The Call of Jeremiah

    B. 2:1–4:4, Indictment for Apostasy and Call to Repentance

    C. 4:5–6:30, Sin and Judgment

        4:5-31, Disaster Overtakes Disaster
        5:1-31, Deeds of Wickedness
        6:1-30, The Wages of Sin

    D. 7:1–8:3, A Sermon in the Temple

JEREMIAH 1:1–10:25

THE PROPHET'S CALL AND WORDS OF JUDGMENT

OVERVIEW

The book of Jeremiah begins with a proper prophetic introduction. It identifies the central figure of the book by recounting his call. In doing so, the call narrative identifies various dimensions of the book that are evident especially in the first ten chapters. The call is accompanied by a vision report that seems to refer to a hostile threat coming from the north. In the chapters that follow, that enemy is evident, although never named. The prophet is also given a mission that includes plucking up and pulling down, destroying and overthrowing (1:10). The bulk of the prophecies that follow involve announcing judgment upon the nation and giving the reasons why that judgment comes. A number of the prophecies in chaps. 1–10 may have to do with Jeremiah's early career. It is not possible, however, to determine precise dates for many of them, though some oracles clearly seem close to the time of the Babylonian invasion and exile. Even the few passages that are given some historical reference may come from a later period. In somewhat reverse fashion, passages that seem to identify an enemy already at hand may be earlier than the Babylonian destruction, even though they anticipate it.

The oracles of the first ten chapters are directed largely toward Judah and Jerusalem and their inhabitants, with specific denunciations directed toward religious and other leaders. At the same time, some of the oracles speak also of and to the northern kingdom, even though by Jeremiah's time it no longer existed as an independent political entity but was part of an Assyrian province. Even though allusion to the northern kingdom, Israel, shows the depth of Judah's sin, Jeremiah also addresses the remnants of that sister kingdom, calling them to repentance.

Among the themes and features that dominate these chapters are the judgment of God for Judah's and Israel's apostasy, the depiction of the people using the image of an unfaithful lover and bride, the unwillingness of the people to be corrected, the endemic presence of lying in every aspect of the people's lives, and the terrible devastation of military defeat that lies ahead. The prophet calls the people to repent and to amend their ways, a dimension of his preaching that falls away in the next sections. Before this section is over, the reader also comes to understand that the sin of the people exists not only in their worship but also in their social life and their relationships with one another. So as the oracles continue, one hears increasing sounds of lament—on the part of the people, the prophet, and the Lord.

JEREMIAH 1:1-19, THE PROLOGUE

OVERVIEW

The opening chapter of Jeremiah does two things of an introductory sort, both of them appropriate to a prophetic book. First of all, it provides some historical context for the book—to let the reader know the answers to such basic questions as who, when, and where: Who is this book about? When and where did the things talked about in the book take place? Such information is characteristic of prophetic books and occurs typically, in longer or shorter fashion, at the beginning of the book in a format customarily called a *superscription* (e.g., Isa 1:1; Hos 1:1; Amos 1:1). Such superscriptions serve in a sense as a title for the book, but they do more than that. Their primary function seems to be to identify the prophet with whom the words or oracles that follow are to be associated. They sometimes do little more than that (e.g., Joel 1:1; Obad 1). They may take the reader directly into the narrative (e.g., Ezek 1:1; Jonah 1:1). Most often, as in the case of Jeremiah, they give some basic information that sets the prophet and his words in a historical setting. That information tends to be of two sorts: time and place. For those prophets who prophesied before the fall of Jerusalem and the end of kingship in the northern (Israel) and the southern (Judah) kingdoms, the time or date is typically indicated by reference to the rule of a king or kings over one or both of the kingdoms. The geographical setting identifies the community to whom the words of the prophet were addressed. Most often we are told that the prophet spoke words or the word of the Lord "concerning" the community then being identified as "Israel" (Amos 1:1), "Judah and Jerusalem" (Isa 1:1), "Samaria and Jerusalem" (Mic 1:1), or the like. Such superscriptions are not confined to the beginning of prophetic books. Not infrequently, there will be later superscriptions in the body of the book that identify a particular chapter or set of chapters as words or oracles concerning some group (e.g., Jer 47:1; 48:1; 49:1, 7).

Second, the prologue to the book of Jeremiah narrates his call, how Jeremiah came to be a prophet. Again, such call reports occur elsewhere in the prophetic books (e.g., Isaiah 6; Ezekiel 1–3; Amos 7:14-15) as well as in narratives about other prophetic figures, such as Moses (Exodus 3–4) and Samuel (1 Samuel 3). While none of these call stories is exactly alike, they do share certain formal commonalities (see Commentary). One may conclude, therefore, that such reports of included certain features essential for identifying the prophet as authentically under the direction and command of the Lord. The presence of such reports of the call of the prophet indicates that the authenticity and authority of the prophet was a real issue, as indeed it was. Jeremiah is sufficient proof of that, for he was in constant conflict with other prophets who claimed to speak the Word of the Lord but one quite different from what Jeremiah himself proclaimed (e.g., 14:13-16; 23:9-22; 28). The report of the call thus serves to tell the reader that what follows is legitimately God's Word, that Jeremiah was truly the bearer of the divine message to ancient Judah. His credentials as a prophet are set out at the very beginning. So we may continue on through the book with confidence. The issue for the reader is not whether the word of Jeremiah can be trusted as the word of the Lord. The call report settles that matter. The issue now becomes whether it will be obeyed. That is the force of the call reports—then and now.

Jeremiah 1:1-3, The Superscription

NIV

1 The words of Jeremiah son of Hilkiah, one of the priests at Anathoth in the territory of Benjamin. [2]The word of the LORD came to him in the thirteenth year of the reign of Josiah son of Amon king of Judah, [3]and through the reign of Jehoiakim son of Josiah king of Judah, down to the fifth month of the eleventh year of Zedekiah son of Josiah king of Judah, when the people of Jerusalem went into exile.

NRSV

1 The words of Jeremiah son of Hilkiah, of the priests who were in Anathoth in the land of Benjamin, [2]to whom the word of the LORD came in the days of King Josiah son of Amon of Judah, in the thirteenth year of his reign. [3]It came also in the days of King Jehoiakim son of Josiah of Judah, and until the end of the eleventh year of King Zedekiah son of Josiah of Judah, until the captivity of Jerusalem in the fifth month.

COMMENTARY

1:1. The first piece of information provided in this introductory note is about the "author" of the book: Jeremiah. The superscription adds only two other pieces of data about this person. One is about his father, a fairly common mark of personal identification in prophetic superscriptions (e.g., Isa 1:1; Hos 1:1; Joel 1:1; Zeph 1:1; Zech 1:1). The paternal relationship serves as a sort of last name. But the reference to the father of the prophet is not always given in the prophetic superscriptions (e.g., Amos 1:1; Mic 1:1; Nah 1:1).

The significance of this information may be found in the rest of the sentence, for Jeremiah and his father are identified further as belonging to a priestly line that resided in Anathoth, a town in the territory of Benjamin. Even as the reference to the prophet Amos's being a "shepherd" (Amos 1:1) serves to let the reader know that he was not a typical prophet (see Amos 7:14-15), so also it is important in Jeremiah's superscription for those who read and hear his words to know that he was of a priestly lineage. Anathoth, just north of Jerusalem, was one of the cities assigned to the levitical priests (Josh 21:18). It was the place to which Solomon banished one of David's two chief priests, Abiathar, because of his support of Solomon's rival, Adonijah, in the struggle for the throne after David's death. Abiathar apparently belonged to the house of Eli, the priest under whom the young Samuel ministered at the shrine of Shiloh, where the ark of the covenant resided in the period of the Judges (1 Kgs 2:27). By this simple reference, we are made aware of two things about Jeremiah: He was a member of the religious establishment by birth and family association, and that association would have meant that he was familiar with the ancient traditions of Israel, the Mosaic exodus and covenantal foundations of Israel's life and faith. Both of these facts are reflected in different ways in the rest of the book. However, his priestly lineage was no protection for him. The kinsfolk at Anathoth make a disturbing appearance in 11:21-23 as plotters against Jeremiah's life. Thus his priestly heritage seems only to have increased his isolation and enhanced the danger to him. Further, Jeremiah's association with Anathoth and its history makes it unsurprising that he is the one prophet who mentions Shiloh (7:12, 14; 26:6, 9)

and Samuel (15:1). His ancestry gave him direct connection with that early and formative period in Israel's history.

1:2-3. In the rest of the superscriptions, two things happen. Most of the text is a typical dating formula, including reference to the rule of the kings during the time of Jeremiah's prophecy. But before that, there is an even more important element, the identification of the words of Jeremiah as being "the word of the LORD." Literally, vv. 1-2*a* read: "The words of Jeremiah . . . which was the word of the LORD to him." These may be the words of Jeremiah, but their "authorship" is not that simple. The very character of prophetic speech is to be a word that is passed on. Later in the book, we encounter an elaboration of the view of the prophet as a herald or messenger of the Word of the Lord decreed in the heavenly council, the political authority that rules heaven and earth (23:18-22). Here we are simply told that all that follows, which are indeed words of Jeremiah— though some of them seem to have been later words associated with him and thus belonging to the Jeremianic tradition—came to him from the Lord. The opening rubric, "the words of Jeremiah," does not occur again until the book's conclusion, where we read: "Thus far are the words of Jeremiah" (51:64; chap. 52 is an appendix from the end of the books of Kings). But we hear over and over again the clause at the beginning of v. 2 or its equivalent:

> "The word of the LORD that came to Jeremiah . . ."
> (14:1)
> "The word that came to Jeremiah from the LORD"
> (e.g., 7:1; 11:1; 18:1; 21:1; 25:1; 34:1; 35:1)
> "The word of the LORD came to me" (e.g., 1:4,
> 11, 13; 2:1; 13:3, 8; 16:1; 18:5; 24:4)
> "Thus says the LORD" (e.g., 6:22; 7:3; 9:23;
> 25:32)

The rest of the superscription places this word of the Lord through Jeremiah at a particular time, albeit a fairly extended period. By the reckoning of the regnal formulae in these verses, Jeremiah prophesied from 627 BCE, the thirteenth year of Josiah's rule over Judah, to 587 BCE, the eleventh year of Zedekiah and the year of the fall of Jerusalem to the Babylonians. By this reckoning, therefore, Jeremiah's prophetic activity covered a long time and took place over a tumultuous period of Judah's history, from one of its greatest moments, the reign of King Josiah, who sought to reform the religious life of the nation, to its lowest moment, the fall of Jerusalem and Judah, the exile of many in Judah to Babylon, and even Jeremiah's own exile to Egypt. These were among the most important events in the history of ancient Israel.

Historically, therefore, the prophecy of Jeremiah begins in a time of glory and ends in a time of judgment and disaster. In the lifetime, or more specifically, the "career" of one prophet, Judah goes from faithfulness and obedience (from the reform of Josiah) to its downfall, which is proclaimed by this prophet as the judgment of God. The speed of that downhill run has something to do with why Jeremiah is known as a prophet of doom and gives us one of the more colorful English terms for denunciatory and pessimistic speech, a "jeremiad." The superscription lets the reader know where the book is headed—to the captivity and exile of Jerusalem. It prepares us for the heavy focus on that city and the hortatory and condemning words that are directed toward its leaders and citizens.

The accuracy of the dating of Jeremiah's prophetic work in the superscription is a matter of debate, at least with regard to the front end of that dating. Jeremiah's disappearance from the scene shortly after the fall of Jerusalem is confirmed by the rest of the book. But there is some uncertainty whether he in fact began to prophesy as early as 627 BCE. The book seems to locate most of Jeremiah's prophetic activity in the reign of Jehoiakim and afterward. There is little indication of his connection with or reaction to Josiah's reform, an enterprise that would have been very consistent with themes of his prophecy. Thus some would see his prophetic work as beginning a good bit later, but there is no agreement on the part of such counterproposals about when that would have been.[20]

Jeremiah 25:3 confirms the date of the superscription, so that there is little doubt about when the editors of the book believed Jeremiah's call to prophesy came. But the reader must be mindful of the uncertainty about these matters and their implications for the difficulty of precise dating of many of Jeremiah's oracles—no easy matter in some cases, even if one could be sure of the date of Jeremiah's call.

---

20. For an extended proposal for the chronology of Jeremiah's life and oracles that assumes the date of 627 BCE as the date of the prophet's birth rather than his call, see William L. Holladay, *Jeremiah 1,* Hermeneia (Philadelphia: Fortress, 1986) 1-10, and *Jeremiah 2,* Hermeneia (Minneapolis: Fortress, 1989) 24-35. An extended interpretation of the chronology of Jeremiah's career that assumes he was called in 627 BCE and only later commissioned to begin his public ministry is to be found in Jack Lundbom, *Jeremiah 1–20,* AB 21A (Garden City, N.Y.: Doubleday, 1999).

REFLECTIONS

1. The frequency with which data having to do with historical circumstances are set at the beginning of the prophetic books is a clue to the importance of the historical context for understanding what is to follow. While the growth and formation of a prophetic book may have been quite complex, occurring over a long period of time and often incorporating later oracles that did not come from the prophet named in the superscription, the superscription serves to place these words in the warp and woof of history, concretely in the life of a community and its affairs, its ups and downs, its obedience and its sinfulness. Whatever enduring truth may be evident in the prophetic words, that cannot finally be abstracted from history. The historical-critical task is in part thrust upon the interpreter by the very nature of the biblical material. These words were addressed to a community and had to do with its affairs. They often deal with matters of life and death. Our rehearing and understanding of them is in relation to their place in history, as best we can discern that. That is generally true of the prophets, and it is especially true of Jeremiah. No other prophet, save Ezekiel, is presented so thoroughly and explicitly in the context of the events and experiences of his time. His own life became a significant part of the prophetic word. Thus the history of the community and the biography of the prophet were joined as the vehicle of the prophetic word.

Such a reminder of the historicity of these words also serves to warn us that they may not always be easy to hear or comprehend. The historical character of the material carries with it a strangeness that the reader needs to feel because it is there. The prophet's world is strange to us in many ways. We cannot simply re-create in our minds what life was like two and a half millennia ago in that small Mediterranean land of tribal units blended into small states, of religious systems that involved features such as sacrifice and divination. The task of interpretation must take such strangeness into account.

At the same time, these prophetic words have a continuity in the midst of a community that also has a continuity. They have not been excavated from some archaeological site. The community in which they were set has endured, ever-changing but in constant touch with these words. Their very character as Scripture serves to indicate that they can connect with later times and places, that the particularity of their first location does not exclude their continuing force in different historical circumstances. Indeed, that original particularity may provide important clues for the way the prophetic word of the Lord speaks afresh in the later community or communities that still identify themselves with the Israel addressed by Jeremiah and other prophets.

2. The identification of Jeremiah with a place (Anathoth) and with a group (the priests) that were significant in the religious history of Israel and the locus and guardians of the Mosaic or covenantal traditions gave him a grounding in those traditions, and they were formative in his proclamation. The superscription thus implicitly identifies the way in which the prophet's familial association with and attention to the religious tradition prepared him and gave him a direction that was crucial to his prophetic message. The faith in which he was presumably steeped from earliest days shaped his understanding of Judah's responsibility and its failure. Such early grounding in the faith of the family and the community was a touchstone for all that followed in his words and deeds.

This grounding did not automatically guarantee a commitment to the fundamental traditions, to the story of redemption and the instruction for life that grew out of it and was reflected in the various legal codes and traditions of Israel. His kinsfolk were among those who most resisted his message and went to extreme lengths to stop it. We cannot, therefore, generalize or universalize too much about the significance of Jeremiah's heritage. It gave him a place to stand but did not guarantee that he would do so. What separated Jeremiah from his kin in this regard? We cannot know altogether.

The superscription, however, does give one clue to the difference. While he shared with his kin a rooting in the Mosaic traditions and the responsibilities of covenantal life under the Lord of Israel, the crucial factor for Jeremiah was that his words were not his own. They came from that same Lord. The rest of chapter 1 tells how that came to be the case.

But already in the rather bland introductory tones of the superscription, the word of the prophet is identified with the word of the Lord. The prophetic authority rests on that ground alone. These are the words of Jeremiah. But their significance, their power, and their authority are only comprehended by the further indication that they came from the Lord. Throughout the book, the particular words of Jeremiah to individuals or to the people are regularly prefaced by some indication of this transcendent origin. The hearers then and now cannot escape the true source of these often difficult and even terrifying words. They are the word of the Lord, set in a particular time and place, as is always true of the divine word.

The particularity of that moment, indicated in the specifying of the years of Jeremiah's prophecy by the kings who ruled then, makes the reader aware that the timelessness of the prophet's message is precisely in its timeliness to particular circumstances. It was under these kings—Josiah, Johiakim, and Zedekiah—that the word of the Lord through Jeremiah made its claim. By preserving these words and discerning their scriptural character, the community of faith presses all later times to find the timeliness of these words, to sense their resonance with other equally particular situations where issues of faith and faithlessness, of sin and judgment, of idolatry, immorality, unfaithful religious and political leadership, and social injustice may signal afresh the liveliness of the word of the Lord that came to Jeremiah.

Jeremiah 1:4-19, The Call of Jeremiah

NIV

⁴The word of the LORD came to me, saying,
⁵"Before I formed you in the womb I knew*ᵃ* you,
   before you were born I set you apart;
   I appointed you as a prophet to the nations."
⁶"Ah, Sovereign LORD," I said, "I do not know how to speak; I am only a child."

⁷But the LORD said to me, "Do not say, 'I am only a child.' You must go to everyone I send you to and say whatever I command you. ⁸Do not be afraid of them, for I am with you and will rescue you," declares the LORD.

⁹Then the LORD reached out his hand and touched my mouth and said to me, "Now, I have put my words in your mouth. ¹⁰See, today I appoint you over nations and kingdoms to uproot and tear down, to destroy and overthrow, to build and to plant."

¹¹The word of the LORD came to me: "What do you see, Jeremiah?"

"I see the branch of an almond tree," I replied.

¹²The LORD said to me, "You have seen correctly, for I am watching*ᵇ* to see that my word is fulfilled."

¹³The word of the LORD came to me again: "What do you see?"

"I see a boiling pot, tilting away from the north," I answered.

¹⁴The LORD said to me, "From the north disaster will be poured out on all who live in the land. ¹⁵I am about to summon all the peoples of the northern kingdoms," declares the LORD.

"Their kings will come and set up their thrones
   in the entrance of the gates of Jerusalem;
they will come against all her surrounding walls
   and against all the towns of Judah.
¹⁶I will pronounce my judgments on my people
   because of their wickedness in forsaking me,
in burning incense to other gods
   and in worshiping what their hands have made.
¹⁷"Get yourself ready! Stand up and say to them whatever I command you. Do not be terrified by them, or I will terrify you before them.

ᵃ5 Or *chose*   *ᵇ12* The Hebrew for *watching* sounds like the Hebrew for *almond tree.*

NRSV

4Now the word of the LORD came to me saying,
⁵ "Before I formed you in the womb I knew you,
   and before you were born I consecrated you;
   I appointed you a prophet to the nations."
⁶Then I said, "Ah, Lord GOD! Truly I do not know how to speak, for I am only a boy." ⁷But the LORD said to me,
   "Do not say, 'I am only a boy';
   for you shall go to all to whom I send you,
   and you shall speak whatever I command you.
⁸ Do not be afraid of them,
   for I am with you to deliver you,
                              says the LORD."
⁹Then the LORD put out his hand and touched my mouth; and the LORD said to me,
   "Now I have put my words in your mouth.
¹⁰ See, today I appoint you over nations and over kingdoms,
   to pluck up and to pull down,
   to destroy and to overthrow,
   to build and to plant."

11The word of the LORD came to me, saying, "Jeremiah, what do you see?" And I said, "I see a branch of an almond tree."*ᵃ* ¹²Then the LORD said to me, "You have seen well, for I am watching*ᵇ* over my word to perform it." ¹³The word of the LORD came to me a second time, saying, "What do you see?" And I said, "I see a boiling pot, tilted away from the north."

14Then the LORD said to me: Out of the north disaster shall break out on all the inhabitants of the land. ¹⁵For now I am calling all the tribes of the kingdoms of the north, says the LORD; and they shall come and all of them shall set their thrones at the entrance of the gates of Jerusalem, against all its surrounding walls and against all the cities of Judah. ¹⁶And I will utter my judgments against them, for all their wickedness in forsaking me; they have made offerings to other gods, and worshiped the works of their own hands. ¹⁷But you, gird up your loins; stand up and tell them everything that I command you. Do not break

*ᵃ*Heb *shaqed*   *ᵇ*Heb *shoqed*

NIV	NRSV
¹⁸Today I have made you a fortified city, an iron pillar and a bronze wall to stand against the whole land—against the kings of Judah, its officials, its priests and the people of the land. ¹⁹They will fight against you but will not overcome you, for I am with you and will rescue you," declares the LORD.	down before them, or I will break you before them. ¹⁸And I for my part have made you today a fortified city, an iron pillar, and a bronze wall, against the whole land—against the kings of Judah, its princes, its priests, and the people of the land. ¹⁹They will fight against you; but they shall not prevail against you, for I am with you, says the LORD, to deliver you.

COMMENTARY

Unlike most accounts of prophetic calls, this one occurs at the beginning of the prophetic book. Its form is similar to other prophetic call stories, but in some of its particulars, especially in the commissioning language (v. 10), notes are sounded that are peculiar to the work and message of Jeremiah, notes that resound throughout the rest of the book.[21]

The chapter has three parts, all of which are dimensions of the call narrative. The call proper is found in vv. 4-10. Two reports of visions that Jeremiah receives from the Lord follow the call, one of an almond rod (vv. 11-12) and one of a boiling pot (vv. 13-16). These visions confirm the call and anticipate various dimensions of Jeremiah's prophetic preaching. Finally, the call is reiterated in vv. 17-19, but with special emphasis on the assurance of divine presence and support in Jeremiah's prophetic ministry, an assurance already given in briefer form in the call itself (v. 8).

The relation of the literary report to the actual call is a matter of considerable debate. The formal and somewhat stereotypical character of the call report as a genre lends support to the view of some interpreters that the call report testifies to the authority of the prophet but should not itself be read as a biographical datum about this particular prophet. We cannot be certain how much of the formulation of his oracles and the reports of his experiences were constructed significantly by the later community (see the Introduction). Whether or not the call reported here reflects historical fact, it does conform with what follows in the rest of

the book, in terms of both what it says about his task and message and what it intimates about his experiences. One need not resolve the questions of biographical authenticity and editorial reconstruction to appreciate the consonance between the call and the rest of the book. Indeed, that consonance is so obvious that however the call narrative came to be, it is what later readers are expected to hear and appropriate.

1:4-10. The call begins with the *revelation,* or *reception of the divine word.* This revelation, of course, is not peculiar to Jeremiah. Indeed, such divine initiative is a regular feature of call reports, in some cases far more prominently set forth than in Jeremiah's case. Moses, for example, encounters the bush that burns without being consumed and is told that he is on holy ground as the Lord speaks to him, calling him to leadership of the people (Exod 3:1-6). The angel of the Lord comes to Gideon while he is in the field beating wheat (Judg 6:11-12). Isaiah has an overwhelming vision of the Lord enthroned on high in the midst of the heavenly assembly (Isa 6:1-5). The appearance of the Lord to Ezekiel, calling him to bear the prophetic word, is so powerful and complex that it takes a whole chapter. For Jeremiah, the visionary dimension of the call comes at the end and does not involve a revelation of the deity's presence. The muted form of this first part of the typical call narrative, however, places the weight on Jeremiah and his prophetic word.

The revelatory formula, "the word of the LORD came to me," which repeats and thus echoes the superscription in v. 2, initiates each section in this chapter except the final reassurance (vv. 4, 11, 13). Indeed, it carries over and introduces the first

21. For the form and character of call narratives, see Norman Habel, "The Form and Significance of the Call Narratives," *ZAW* 77 (1965) 297-323; and Holladay, *Jeremiah 1,* 27.

set of prophetic oracles in the book in 2:1. The superscription and the call confirm each other and emphasize a critical point of the book: that Jeremiah's prophetic ministry began and remained under the impetus of the divine word. While that may seem obvious to later readers, it clearly was a matter of contest in his own time as others claimed to be the true bearers of the word of the Lord, even though their message opposed Jeremiah's. The question of whether or not those other voices had indeed received the Word of the Lord comes up explicitly in the book (e.g., 23:16-22). It is important, therefore, from the beginning to identify the words of Jeremiah with the words of the Lord, to emphasize again and again their divine source, for many in Judah did not want to listen to these words and chose to see them as the words of an unduly pessimistic prophet. There were plenty of other prophetic voices around to sound a more pleasant note.

The *divine commission* to Jeremiah is set forth in v. 5. The reiterated "before" clauses establish Jeremiah's calling from the beginning as not his own choosing. That seems regularly to have been the case with the prophets who bore the word of the Lord; they did so under the divine commission. But in Jeremiah's case, the prophet's vocation was given to him before he was even born—before he was formed in embryonic state (v. 5*a*), before he came forth from his mother's womb (v. 5*b*). The call of Jeremiah is one of the clearest and most explicit biblical formulations of the experience of election. Indeed, it is a genuine example of predestination, but not in the sense of a predestination to salvation or damnation. The destiny that matters in Jeremiah's case is his calling, his vocation. Jeremiah was predestined to be the bearer of God's word. He came into being under the divine commission. There was certainly no escaping this calling. He could not even go back to some other vocation, as Amos did. Jeremiah was brought into the world to be a prophet of the Lord.

The other aspect of Jeremiah's commission is found in the sequence of first-person verbs that describe the manner and intention of the Lord's election of him: "I knew you"; "I consecrated you"; "I set you as a prophet to the nations." Each of these actions expresses a dimension of Jeremiah's election and calling. When God says, "I

knew you," two things are implied: knowing in the sense of choosing and knowing in the sense of watching over and caring for. When Amos speaks the Word of the Lord, "You only have I known of all the families of the earth" (Amos 3:2), it is God's choosing of Israel to be a people special to the Lord that is in view. When the psalmist declares, "The LORD knows the way of the righteous" (Ps 1:6), it is God's watching over and keeping safe the lives of the righteous ones. In Jeremiah's case, we may assume that the divine declaration involves both things. Surely the former is meant. Even as God "knew" Abraham that he might "charge his children and his household after him to keep the way of the LORD by doing righteousness and justice" (Gen 18:19), so also God "knew" Jeremiah before he was born so that he might proclaim the word of the Lord to the people. But the experience of the prophet, who constantly came under attack and suffered threats to his life, who declared the agony of his prophetic task and received a special word of assurance at his call, surely testifies to the other sense of God's knowing Jeremiah. Even before he was born, God was watching over and protecting him. Implicit in that idea is an assurance that such divine protection perdures long after birth, when the prophet was set to the task for which God "knew" him.

The declaration that God "consecrated" Jeremiah—that is, set him apart to the prophetic task—is unusual. This is the only place where it is said of a prophet. It is commonly spoken of priestly designation, however, and it may be that the word is used for Jeremiah's commission because of his priestly lineage. Of a priestly family, he is set apart to a different role in the government of God. He is not the priestly mediator of God's holiness in the sanctuary. He is the proclaimer of that holiness and its demands in the streets of Jerusalem.

Finally, God has set Jeremiah as "a prophet to the nations." The assignment is rather unusual, and not what one customarily expects of a Hebrew prophet. Their messages were usually aimed at specific internal situations—the religious, political, and social ills and sins of the people. Certainly that was the case with Jeremiah. Nor is there any indication of his going to a foreign nation to prophesy, in the way, for example, of Jonah, though Jeremiah does send a scroll to Babylon with prophecies against that nation (51:59-64).

The assignment, however, is not altogether anomalous or inconsistent with this prophet or with other prophets. Several prophetic books include oracles concerning other nations (e.g., Isaiah, Ezekiel, Amos), and two brief books, those of Obadiah and Nahum, are entirely concerned with or directed to other nations (Edom and Assyria respectively). In like manner, the last part of the book of Jeremiah is composed of a series of oracles concerning "the nations" (46:1). While his primary people of address were the Judeans, Jeremiah's words from the Lord did address other nations, beginning with the former northern kingdom, Israel, and extending to other smaller and then larger nations of the ancient Near East. There is a sense in which the commission of Jeremiah takes the typical commissioning of a prophet and writes it larger than usual. Thus his calling cannot be set at some moment of life; he was called before he was born. His audience is not simply Israel or Judah, as is customarily the case. He addresses a much larger audience. Thus already in the commission, something of the grandeur of this prophetic voice is signaled. That his name is probably more widely associated with biblical prophecy than any other is not surprising. His calling identifies him as the prophet par excellence, the prophet writ large.

That such a calling is a burden is immediately perceived by the prophet when he responds in v. 6 with his objection that he is only a lad. Three things are important here:

First, his *objection* to the call is not simply a matter of personal recalcitrance—or if it is, such reluctance is endemic to the calling, for it was often a part of the call reports or of the response of persons whom the Lord called to an office or a task. So we find Moses objecting several times (Exodus 3–4), as does Gideon (Judg 6:15). Furthermore, the person called often objected out of some sense of incapacity or inadequacy before the task (Exod 4:10; Judg 6:15; 1 Sam 9:21; cf. 2 Sam 7:18; Amos 7:14-15). The objection to the prophetic calling makes sense both from the standpoint of the one being called and in the eyes of the audience to whom the call report was addressed as an authenticating and authorizing word. The task was, indeed, a large one, and any sensible person might well resist, both for fear of being unable to fulfill the calling and for fear of the consequences

if one did. The careers of the prophets or the prophetic figures, like Moses, certainly do not suggest that it was an easy life. Such an objection, however, also indicated to the people to whom the prophet was sent that the task was not sought or desired. On the contrary, it was resisted. Thus the listeners are given a sense of the divine compulsion as the initiative of prophecy rather than a personal desire for whatever reason.

Second, the initial response of the prophet, "Ah, LORD God," is language that customarily belongs to prayer and complaint to God (Jer 4:10; 32:17; Ezek 9:8; 11:13).[22] The prophet Ezekiel uses this expression in specific complaints against God's assignment (Ezek 4:14; 20:49). Jeremiah's initial response, therefore, has the tone of lament and complaint to God, thus anticipating the later and more extensive complaints against the prophetic assignment and its effects on his life. In this way, the call report introduces an issue that will appear throughout the book.

Third, Jeremiah's particular resistance is the claim to be only a youth without the gifts for speaking that one might expect of a proclaimer of the divine word. Such an objection was not new to the call experience. It was voiced by Moses when the Lord called him and evoked God's anger, who then promised to give him a mouthpiece in his brother, Aaron. In Jeremiah's case, the objection may be a clue that the call of God came rather early to him. It is also a clear indication of the significance of the act of speaking and proclamation as a part of the prophetic task. Jeremiah's objection, however, prompts the important divine rejoinder that the capacities and abilities of the prophet as a person were not an issue (v. 7). There is little indication that the divine call ever came out of some recognition of special talent or particular piety or readiness for prophetic vocation. On the contrary, the prophet is a vessel of the divine word, and the next verses answer the objection of the prophet in a final way—though in the chapters that follow we hear Jeremiah's continuing objections to the prophetic task more than we do for any other prophet.

22. On this expression, see John M. Berridge, *Prophet, People, and the Word of Yahweh: An Examination of Form and Content in the Proclamation of the Prophet Jeremiah,* Basel Studies of Theology 4 (Zürich: EVZ-Verlag, 1970) 410-11.

The *divine response* to Jeremiah's objection possesses several features. One is an explicit rejection of the objection. While not with the anger that finally explodes from the Lord against Moses to his objection about his inability to speak (Exod 4:10-17), the Lord flatly refuses to accept the appeal to inexperience and youthfulness. There is, however, a clear reason for discounting Jeremiah's objection. In giving that reason, the Lord in effect renews the commission. Jeremiah's worries are deemed irrelevant because the issue is not what he can or cannot do but that his activity is totally under the initiative of God. As a prophet, he is sent to speak. That is what prophets in ancient Israel were—messengers and mouthpieces for the word of the Lord. Indeed, later in the book, the distinction between false and true prophets lies in the fact that the former were not "sent" from the divine council, from the heavenly government, and did not proclaim "my words" (Jer 23:21-22). One might seek to make a case based on the eloquence of the prophets; they did speak powerfully with their poetry. But such a case is not made in Scripture. In fact, it seems to be the opposite. The character of the prophet as a vessel is accentuated; the role of the prophet is not so much as preacher but as the messenger of someone else's word. This does not mean that the prophet's own person and thought do not enter into the formulation of the word, but it is clearly understood, as fully as possible, as a word that comes from outside. The attacks on the prophets were classic examples of attacks on the messenger, the bearers of bad news, not the originators of that news.

This point is made even more explicit in v. 9*b* when the Lord touches the mouth of the prophet and says, "I have put my words in your mouth." Again, two different matters are addressed simultaneously in these verses: the objection of the prophet to the call and the questions of the audience who hear or read the report of the call. Jeremiah cannot resist God because of his inability and inexperience, and the hearers of these words cannot resist on the grounds that the words do not matter or are not truly those of the Lord, whose rule they acknowledge.

The authority of the prophet is accentuated further by the similarity between what the Lord says to Jeremiah and the promise in Deuteronomy that the Lord will, in the future, raise up a prophet like Moses. Verses 7*b* and 9*b* of Jeremiah's call report are virtually identical to the promise given in Deut 18:18: "I will put my words in his mouth, and he will speak to them all that I command him."

The similarity suggests deuteronomistic influence on the call report. More important, however, is the indication that in the person of Jeremiah the community is to see the fulfillment of the Lord's intention as set forth in Deuteronomy. Jeremiah is indeed a prophet like Moses who bears the Lord's word and speaks on behalf of the Lord's work.

In v. 8 the prophet answers an objection that is not spoken by Jeremiah but is apparently implicit in what he says: He is afraid of the task to which he is being called and of what may happen to him. At this stage in the book, we do not know why that fearfulness is there, but it does not take much looking ahead to find out. We are not told at this point who the "them" are that Jeremiah is not to fear, but the book will go a long way toward identifying "them." Jeremiah, however, does not need to be prescient at the time of his call in order to be afraid. The fate of the prophets was well known by this time in Judah. Indeed, the book includes a conversation about the fate of an earlier prophet, Micah, who survived (26:18-19) and the report of the fate of a contemporary prophet who did not (26:20-23). The oracle of salvation that is given to Jeremiah at this point is elaborated and developed at the end of the chapter (see below).

The *commission,* given in v. 5, is now reiterated and developed in significant ways (vv. 9-10). The mission of the prophets to the nations is restated and emphasized in language that points to the prophet's role in the politics or government of God. Jeremiah is an "appointee," an official of the divine government, appointed to a task. The language is similar to the way the report in 2 Kings 25 tells of the king of Babylon's appointing Gedaliah as governor over the people who remained in the land of Judah after the Babylonian exile (2 Kgs 25:22-23). The assignment is spelled out in detail in a series of responsibilities given to Jeremiah:

First, they have to do with the Lord's activity— that is, these are responsibilities given to Jeremiah in his call. But when we see these actions carried out in the course of the book, it is in fact the Lord who acts in these ways. There is a significant consonance between the divine and human activities, between the work of the prophetic servant and that of the Lord who calls him. Jeremiah's representative role is once more firmly identified. His words are the words of the Lord. His power to speak is given by the Lord. His assignment is to do what, in fact, the Lord will do through him.

Second, the series of verbs in this commission is formative for the message of Jeremiah. Again and again, the hearer or reader will find the Lord speaking of doing just what is assigned to Jeremiah in his call. It is often the case that the call report gives important clues to the actual message of the prophet that follow in the rest of the book. That is clearly the case, since the Lord later speaks of plucking up and pulling down, of destroying and overthrowing, of building and planting (12:17; 18:7, 9; 24:6; 31:28, 40; 42:10; 45:4). The words that are paired here are often paired elsewhere and in some instances are heaped up in a way similar to their usage in the call report. The fundamental message and task of the prophet is set forth in these verbs.

Third, both negative and positive actions are assigned, but there is some variation in the negative group. That is, the Lord appoints Jeremiah to represent the divine government not only in negative ways but also in positive ones. The verbs for the positive or "constructive" work of the Lord—"build" and "plant"—do not vary. But one notes that there is a larger vocabulary for the "destructive" work of the Lord and more variation in the way it appears. While the positive pair remains constant ("build" and "plant"), the negative pair or group is variable ("pluck up" and "pull down," "pluck up" and "destroy," "overthrow" and "pluck up," etc.). Indeed, other words are added to this list in the various oracles from the Lord in the rest of the book. This difference in the constructive and destructive vocabulary seems to be "a device for 'ringing the changes' on what was the main burden of Jeremiah's message."[23] The work of the Lord in Jeremiah is usually remembered as negative. He is recalled as a prophet of doom and judgment. The call report indicates that was indeed the largest part of his responsibility. It also reminds us that even as the judgmental word is never the last one in the story of Israel's way with the Lord, this prophet was also called to proclaim the intention of God to build and plant new

nations and kingdoms, to reseed and start over in the kingdom of God. Such proclamation is not a large part of the book of Jeremiah. The call report does not lead us to expect that. But it is there, and the report invites the reader to expect and look for the words of hope and renewal as well as the words of judgment and doom.

1:11-16. Two reports of visions that, like the preceding verse, serve a double function follow. They reflect Jeremiah's call, but they also point forward into the rest of the book. The vision reports are here as *signs confirming the call,* often to part of the call reports. They also open up further aspects of the prophetic proclamation.

The first of the vision reports involves a play on words (cf. Amos 8:1-3). It is terse; there is no report of a vision, simply the question of the Lord: "What do you see?" It is almost as if there is a kind of test here about Jeremiah's receptivity and perception, for when Jeremiah says that he sees an almond rod, the Lord compliments him, as if to say that Jeremiah is perceptive and has given the right answer. Is this a check on the Lord's own decision? The text seems to provide a sign confirming this call to Jeremiah. But the response of the Lord suggests that the vision also confirms to God the choice of Jeremiah to be the prophetic messenger of "my words."

Here, however, as in most of the vision reports of the OT prophets, the meaning or significance of what is seen is not clear until the Lord interprets it. The interpretation does not have anything to do with almond rods. The connection between the interpretive comment in v. 12*b* and the almond rod is in the wordplay between the Hebrew for "almond rod" (שָׁקֵד *šāqēd*) and for "watch" (שֹׁקֵד *šōqēd*). Such visions are thus both enigmatic and revelatory. The visual experience is always accompanied by the interpretive word, and it is only with that word that the point of the strange vision becomes clear.

It is characteristic of call stories that the one being called receives some kind of sign to confirm the call (Exod 3:12; Judg 6:17; 1 Sam 10:7). The vision of the almond rod probably serves that function here. The rod is a sign that the Lord has called and commissioned Jeremiah that "overcomes objection and reassures by confirming the authenticity of the commission."[24] But if so, it is like the

23. J. Gerald Janzen, *Studies in the Text of Jeremiah,* HSM 6 (Cambridge, Mass.: Harvard University Press, 1973) 35.

24. Burke Long, "Reports of Visions Among the Prophets," *JBL* 94 (1976) 358.

sign that is given to Moses in Exod 3:12. The confirmation comes only at the end. The almond rod is a sign that "my word(s)" (vv. 9, 12), which Jeremiah is to proclaim, will in fact be fulfilled—that is, that the Lord will surely do what Jeremiah declares as the word of the Lord. Frequent reference is made to "my word(s)" in the course of the book (e.g., 6:19; 11:10; 13:10; 18:2; 23:22, 28). The word of the Lord, specifically "my word," proclaimed, put in the mouth of the prophet (cf. 5:14), heard, not heard, and so on, is very important in this book. So this vision serves to confirm the call and to focus attention on the word of the Lord, assuring the prophet that what he prophesies really will happen; it will be accomplished. The vision report is thus closely tied both to the call and to the rest of the book.

The latter linkage is clear, since the verb *šāqad*, not used frequently in the OT, appears nearly half the time in the sense of "watching" or "watching over" in the book of Jeremiah. Two instances are worth noting: (1) In 31:28, the Lord speaks of having "watched over" (*šāqad*) the house of Israel and the house of Judah, the northern and southern kingdoms, "to pluck up and break down, to overthrow, destroy, and bring evil"—that is, to make sure that what Jeremiah is to do in his prophecy comes to pass. Thus the vision report is once more linked to the confirmation of Jeremiah's call. (2) Then in 44:27-29, the Lord speaks of the Judean migrants to Egypt after the Babylonian destruction who have turned to the worship of the Queen of Heaven and speaks in a way that is once again reminiscent of the conversation with Jeremiah that is reported in the call narrative:

> I am going to watch over them for harm and not for good . . . and all the remnant of Judah, who have come to the land of Egypt to settle, shall know *whose words will stand, mine* or theirs! This shall be the *sign* to you, says the LORD, that I am going to punish you in this place, in order that you may know that *my words* against you will surely be carried out.

Both texts make clear that the vision report identifies one of the major themes of the book as a whole: the vindication of the Lord's word of judgment and salvation as spoken by the prophet Jeremiah.[25]

A second vision is reported in vv. 13-16. Its form is the same except that the positive judgment of the Lord on Jeremiah's seeing is not repeated. Further, the vision report in this instance is symbolic, in distinction from the wordplay vision report of the preceding verses. The vision in this instance is of a pot with some unidentified liquid boiling in it. It is tilted from a northerly direction. The interpretation of the vision is given in simple form in v. 14: Some kind of disaster will befall Judah, and it will come from the north. Then this interpretation is elaborated in some detail in the next two verses, first with a description of the Lord's calling kings from the north against Jerusalem (v. 15) and then with an indication that all of this is the Lord's judgment against Judah for its apostasy and idolatry (v. 16). In both respects, the vision points to significant dimensions of the message of the book and the circumstances and events of those times.

The enemy from the north is a theme of Jeremiah's oracles, from chap. 4 onward. There has been much debate about the identity of the enemy from the north, and that debate has revolved in part around how one dates the texts. Verse 15 makes it seem as if there are multiple kingdoms from the north. In the present form of the book, however, the foe from the north clearly is to be identified with the Babylonian Empire (cf. Ezek 26:7). It is the kingdom that destroys Judah, and its coming is understood as the judgment of the Lord.

The picture of the kings setting up thrones at the gates of Jerusalem and around the walls of Jerusalem and the cities of Judah is a siege motif. Indeed, there are Assyrian reliefs of the siege of Lachish that show Judean captives bowing before an enthroned King Sennacherib.[26] The judgment motif that follows in v. 16 may already be anticipated in the picture of the thrones set up for the kings. In the account of the building of Solomon's palace, it is reported that: "He made the Hall of the Throne where he was to pronounce judgment, the Hall of Justice, covered with cedar from floor to floor" (1 Kgs 7:7). The thrones before Jerusalem may be a symbol of judgment as well as one of conquest.

25. Ernest Nicholson, *Preaching to the Exiles* (Oxford: Basil Blackwell, 1970) 114-15.

26. See James B. Pritchard, ed., *The Ancient Near East in Pictures Relating to the Old Testament* (Princeton: Princeton University Press) 129.

In any event, the invasion of the foe from the north is explicitly identified in the next verse as an act of divine judgment. The "judgments" the Lord will utter against Judah and Jerusalem refer to the judgment speeches Jeremiah is to announce against them. This is one of the most common forms of prophetic speech in pre-exilic prophecy, where much of the prophetic proclamation, in the north as well as in the south, was denunciation of political, religious, and social sins. The judgment speech uses the discourse of the law court—that is, it is a legal genre. Indeed, the expression of v. 16, "utter judgment(s) against" someone, occurs in Jeremiah in a narrative account of the king of Babylon pronouncing sentence against the king of Judah (39:5 = 52:9). The judgment speech can have considerable variation, but its primary elements are an accusation or indictment and a verdict or pronouncement of sentence. That is, the judgment speech identifies the sin or crime of the people or their leaders and then announces as a sentence of judgment the punishment the Lord will bring because of the crime. A variant legal form is that of the lawsuit. Jeremiah's oracles contain numerous judgment speeches (e.g., 5:10-17; 7:8-15; 23:10-15) and lawsuits (e.g., 2:4-9; cf. 12:1; 25:31).

The primary accusation against the people is anticipated in the interpretation of the second vision. It is their abandonment of the Lord of Israel in the worship of other gods and of idols. In the course of the book, many specific charges are laid against the people and their leaders. Some of them are for the sin of social oppression, for false prophecy, and for poor leadership. But underlying all of this is the fundamental failure at the most critical point in the covenantal relationship between Israel and its God—the full and total allegiance in faith and life to the God who redeemed them and blesses their lives. That this is the critical point, the life-and-death issue (see 8:1-3; see also Deut 30:15-20) is made very clear when the chapter immediately after the call story begins the indictments against the people with an extended account of their faithlessness and their pursuit of other gods.

1:17-19. The account of Jeremiah's call concludes with a reiteration of that call and an extended assurance of the Lord's protective care over Jeremiah in the face of the dangers his prophetic work will entail.

The reiteration begins with an emphatic address

to the prophet: "As for you," here is what all this means. The commission is repeated: "Tell them everything that I command you" (cf. v. 7b). But a new dimension is added now: "Gird up your loins; stand up." This new element points us to something suggested already (v. 8) that is now becoming dominant in the reiteration of the call: The task that is being placed upon Jeremiah may be difficult and painful, from the point of view of both the resistance of the people and the demand placed upon him by God. The former is signaled clearly in the remaining verses of this chapter as well as in the several biblical references to girding oneself with strength or for battle (Ps 18:32, 39; 93:1; Isa 8:9); but so is the latter. A dire threat is set out in the Lord's command to Jeremiah not to break down before the people or else the Lord will break him down (v. 17b)! It is worth noting, therefore, that the expression "gird up your loins" appears only two other places, both times in God's response to Job's questioning complaint:

> "Gird up your loins like a man,
>   I will question you, and you shall declare to me.
> "Where were you when I laid the foundation of
>   the earth?
>
> . . . .
>
> "Will you even put me in the wrong?
>   Will you condemn me that you may be justified?"
>   (Job 38:3-4; 40:7-8 NRSV)

While, therefore, the call to Jeremiah to gird up his loins may be a command to prepare to do battle prophetically with the people, it may be as much or even more a command to prepare to confront the Lord. Certainly in the rest of the book, Jeremiah complains to the Lord and receives not only rebukes from the Lord for having done so but also intimations that complaints will evoke heavier burdens (e.g., 12:1-6).

The final verses of the chapter (vv. 18-19) continue the reassurance given in v. 8. Together, they make up a prime example of the *oracle of salvation,* the fundamental OT word of assurance and help that God speaks to those who cry out to the Lord in distress, suffering, and oppression.[27] The basic elements of the salvation oracle are present:

---

27. For extended discussion of this form of speech in the OT and in extra-biblical texts, see Patrick D. Miller, *They Cried to the Lord: The Form and Theology of Biblical Prayer* (Minneapolis: Fortress, 1994) 135-77.

a personal address ("but you," v. 17); the basic word of assurance that one does not have to be afraid (v. 8*a*); the reason or basis for the assurance, which is a promise of God's presence and of God's help ("I am with you to deliver you," vv. 8*b*, 19*b*); and an elaboration of what the Lord will do in this instance to help (vv. 18-19).[28]

Why is this elaborate oracle of salvation here? Words of assurance were fairly standard in the call stories—assurance that the one called could do the task. But these words are not directed toward feelings of inadequacy. The Lord addresses that in v. 7. The oracle of salvation is that fundamental gospel word of assurance that rings throughout the scriptures to people in situations of terrible distress. That is why it occurs in this context, for Jeremiah more than any other prophet will come up against threats and dangers, will experience imprisonment and near death, will be terribly frightened and tempted to run. In these words of assurance, the Lord addresses Jeremiah like any person in deep distress, anticipating what the book

reveals again and again. Thus the call report once more looks forward into the book where "kings, princes, priests, and the people of the land" threaten Jeremiah in various ways.

The word of the Lord is thus a powerful message of support at the beginning of Jeremiah's prophetic career. The words of v. 18, "I have made you a fortified city," echo the Hebrew words of v. 9, "I have set my words in your mouth." In other words, the one who places the prophetic burden and assignment on the prophet also sets him like a mighty rock, like an impregnable fortress in the face of powerful foes. The imagery is heaped up—fortified city, iron pillar, bronze wall—all images conveying the protection that the Lord will provide Jeremiah, the resistance to attacks that is as strong as iron and bronze, as secure against threats as the great wall of a fortified city against a siege.

So in the final section of this chapter, as in all the previous sections, there is anticipation of a major theme or component of the book to follow—in this case, the attacks and threats the prophet whose call opens the book will have to endure. The oracle of salvation is anticipatory, but it is appropriate, for Jeremiah will cry out often to the Lord. But he will also endure, because of the protective presence of God.

---

28. In v. 8*a*, "do not break down" (אל־תירא *'al-tîrā'*) appropriately translates a Hebrew expression that regularly parallels "do not be afraid" in the oracles of salvation and is customarily translated in other contexts as "do not be dismayed." In a single phrase, therefore, Jeremiah receives both threat and assurance. The ambiguity of the expression is almost unbearable, as Jeremiah's experience demonstrates.

REFLECTIONS

1. The call of Jeremiah, and indeed his whole career as a prophet, makes it clear that prophetic proclamation is neither a simple matter nor a desirable "occupation." There is a lot we do not know about how professional prophets may have been.

There are indications that some prophets, at least, occupied a position as a professional or as full-time as that of a priest. But while both priest and prophet occupied significant positions in the divine government of Israel, and so continue to be recognized roles in the ongoing communities of faith that look to Israel's story for direction, they are vastly different in character. While the role of the priest was a hereditary position, the prophet was often more ad hoc. The priest's responsibilities continued for a lifetime. The prophet's task could be long or short; there was no telling. Those in the priesthood knew their place, and their place and responsibilities were recognized by others. It is surely no accident that the term *priest* continues as a designation for those who are in full-time, continuing ministry, persons recognizable by others as having an ongoing religious function. The same could be true of the prophet, but there are significant differences. One of them is found in this first. The prophets whose oracles are remembered and preserved in Scripture assumed their roles and responsibilities under the call of God. There seems to have been a lot of ambiguity about that role and about the authority of the prophet to speak and say what he or she said. There were rival priesthoods and conflicts among them, but such rivalries were more like political parties vying for power, moving in and out of control. For the prophet, the conflict seems always to have been about whether or not the oracle being uttered was really the word of the Lord. And often the decision about which prophet spoke the truth—that is, which spoke truly from the divine government and represented it—was a life-or-death matter. Their oracles were about the large issues of moral conduct, political policy, religious leadership. Different prophets sometimes gave diametrically opposite messages.

The question of authenticity and authority was thus no small matter. The claim to stand under the call of God was absolutely crucial. There are all sorts of indications, many here in the book of Jeremiah, that more than one person could make that claim, and the prophetic audience did not have an easy task deciding in the face of conflicting claims. But the call was a kind of credential, an indication that the one who speaks does so under the aegis of God, under commission, not on his or her own, not even voluntarily. While there may have been persons who signed up or enlisted as prophets, those whose names and oracles are remembered as truly the word of the Lord were not volunteers for the task. The prophetic rose was instrumental, and not originary. It was compulsory, and not voluntary.

For all these reasons, the identification of prophetic ministry in our time continues to be a knotty issue, whether for those who listen for a prophetic word or for those who wonder whether they have a prophetic ministry.[29] The call story here and elsewhere gives us at least a couple of clues that need to be taken into account even if they never completely settle the matter. The most obvious is the sense of being called, of being under divine commission. Thus the "call" is for many Christian communities a very important part of the identification of persons for the ministry, the call experienced and the call recognized. The proclaimer of the divine word, whether heard in some difficult to describe personal experience—visionary, revelatory, etc.—as in the cases of the biblical prophets or found in the pages of Scripture and interpreted, stands under some divine compulsion. Without some indication of the divine authority lying behind the words of the prophet, the audience will treat the declarations and claims that are made no more seriously than the mouthings of politicians or the ravings of end-of-the-world apocalypticists. When, in contemporary gatherings of the church, whether official meetings of church courts, occasions of worship, or more personal and ad hoc occasions of Christian fellowship, the minister is called upon or volunteers to give some accounting of God's calling into the ministry of the church, there is a direct line to the prophet Jeremiah and others like him who laid their cards on the table—or others did so for them—and said, "Here are my credentials."

2. If the identification of authentic prophecy, the truthful word from the Lord, was and is not a simple matter, then prophecy also was and is not a particularly desirable "occupation." It is worth paying attention to the fact that prophets resisted and objected to the calling. It was not sought. It was pushed away. There are two things very apparent in that resistance. One is that while Jonah is regularly condemned for running away from his prophetic calling, in a paradoxical way, one of the primary measures of authentic prophecy is that it is an enterprise taken up only reluctantly. There is little sign that the prophets of Israel enjoyed the task. If there is not some hesitation at being the spokesperson for the divine word, at directing the light of God's word in all its brightness—and sometimes that light is harsh—on the human scene, on the affairs of God's people, then maybe the spokesperson is not truly the messenger of God's word. (Again, Jonah's failure as a prophet was not so much his running from the difficult task as it was his running because he did not really believe that God would follow through on the judgment. His resistance was not to the difficult task but to the divine mercy.) Confidence in one's ability to proclaim God's Word to the people does not seem to have been a part of the prophetic credentials. On the contrary, a sense of ineptness, of inability to do such an awesome task seems to have been a part of the claim that was set forth to persuade hearers and readers that what they confront is truly the word of God.

The other side of this resistance, of course, is the clear indication that prophetic ministry is a difficult and demanding task, not a way of endearing one to the people, often a risk to life and

---

29. See W. Sibley Towner, "On Calling People 'Prophets' in 1970," *Interpretation* 24 (1970) 492-509.

---

limb. The extent to which the prophetic task is conceived of as a part of the ministry of Christ is a measure of the extent to which those who take up that ministry are open to the threats and dangers, to the mental, emotional, and sometimes physical suffering that seems to go with the prophetic task. If the work of the ministry is fairly comfortable and nonthreatening, it is very likely that one will find a prophetic dimension there only with difficulty, for such threats to one's well-being and happiness were a part of the case that the prophets made to document their claim to be the authentic messengers of the word God wanted the people to hear.

3. The particular formulation of Jeremiah's commission in 1:5 suggests that an identity and a task are being given to Jeremiah in the same terms as the ancient and traditional way in which Israel understood its identity and its task in the world. The language, "I have *known* you," has its primary resonance with Gen 18:19 and Amos 3:2, both of which are statements about the Lord's knowing Israel and doing so to give them a task in the world, "to keep the way of the LORD by doing righteousness and justice" (Gen 18:19). Both form and substance suggest that Jeremiah now takes up that task, as one known or chosen and one for whom the Lord's way of righteousness and justice will be uppermost in his preaching. So it is with the Lord's declaration to Jeremiah: "I have consecrated you," "I have made you holy," echoes the designation of Israel as a "holy nation" (Exod 19:6), an understanding of Israel as set apart to the Lord that is repeated in the opening words of the first oracle after the call (Jer 2:3) with reference to the time in the wilderness. What Israel was meant to be at the beginning but has failed to be in the end is what Jeremiah is appointed to be—holy, consecrated to the Lord. Finally, the call of Jeremiah to be a prophet to the nations is reminiscent of the way in which the call of Abraham was for the sake of "all the families of the earth" (Gen 12:3).

Thus a note is sounded here at the very beginning of the book that will reverberate throughout and much beyond the book of Jeremiah: The one acts in place of as well as on behalf of the many. The calling given to the people of Israel has been vitiated by the sinfulness of the nation, north and south. So the Lord moves to call one in the language and mode that the many were called and set apart to the work and the way of the Lord. The failure of God's people means now that the prophet embodies and continues the task, the identity, the purpose of Israel. He is now the chosen and elect one, the holy one, mediating God's way with the nations. The stream of those individuals who are called of God to act in the place of, on behalf of, and over against those who have rejected the divine calling does not begin or end with Jeremiah. But it goes through him, and he becomes one of the biblical figures who embody that calling of the one out of the many when the many do not get the job done, when the many reject their identity and their task.

4. The call of the prophet sets before us a dimension of the divine government, of the politics of God. The prophet's role was clearly set in the "machinery" by which the Lord ruled the affairs of nations and peoples. Divine decisions made in heaven were communicated through the prophet to the community on earth. The imagery behind this notion is that of the heavenly assembly, the divine council in the midst of which the Lord rules (see 23:18-22). In this context, the important thing to note is that the prophetic proclamation is not simply a religious phenomenon in the way most preaching is regarded. It is seen as the means by which the Lord announces and works out the divine policy. The political character of the prophetic proclamation is further indicated by the way in which its address is precisely to the political communities, "nations and kingdoms." From the start, we hear that the work of this prophet is not a private or in-house matter. It has to do with the rule of God over the world and over the cosmos. It is not even confined to the particular community of which this "preacher" was a part. Through the prophet, the divine word about what is going on in the world, about what God is doing to direct the affairs of peoples and nations toward a righteous and just humanity is set forth.

5. Jeremiah's call makes us aware of the synergism of divine and human activity that is so common in the biblical story, whether in the wars of Israel or the words and deeds of the prophets. The latter were highly individual and powerful personalities. At the same time, they were simply messengers and agents for the divine activity. When viewed more closely, their actions, strange as they often were, seem to have been less the result of strong and unusual personality than the burden placed upon them by a transcendent source, the Lord of Israel. There is a strange paradox that we cannot fully work out. But it is certainly the case that those who dare to speak as the messengers of God, the bearers of the divine spirit, the proclaimers of the divine word—whether rightly or not—often seem strange to the rest of us. It may be that there really is something outside ourselves that breaks in upon us in a different way than the routines and styles to which we are accustomed when the divine word and work are under way in particular individuals.

6. The dangers to the prophet's life and well-being are manifest often in the chapters that follow. But we must not miss the danger that is suggested in the mix of divine promise and warning. The one who stands under the call of God is given a powerful word of assurance, but that assurance does not allow the call to be taken lightly—ever. There will be times when Jeremiah will want to let go, when the forces aligned against him will beat him down sufficiently that he cries out to and against God. The assurance of God's protection is clear and sufficient, but the one who is under the divine commission is not to flinch from the demands placed upon him or her. The larger danger to the prophet is the judgment of God, not the hostilities of the human community. There is protection against the latter. Against the former, there is no preventive save obedience to the commission God has imposed and has promised to support.

JEREMIAH 2:1–4:4, INDICTMENT FOR APOSTASY AND CALL TO REPENTANCE

NIV

2 The word of the LORD came to me: ²"Go and proclaim in the hearing of Jerusalem:
" 'I remember the devotion of your youth,
how as a bride you loved me
and followed me through the desert,
through a land not sown.
³Israel was holy to the LORD,
the firstfruits of his harvest;
all who devoured her were held guilty,
and disaster overtook them,' "
                    declares the LORD.

⁴Hear the word of the LORD, O house of Jacob,
all you clans of the house of Israel.
⁵This is what the LORD says:

"What fault did your fathers find in me,
that they strayed so far from me?
They followed worthless idols
and became worthless themselves.
⁶They did not ask, 'Where is the LORD,

NRSV

2 The word of the LORD came to me, saying:
²Go and proclaim in the hearing of Jerusalem, Thus says the LORD:
I remember the devotion of your youth,
your love as a bride,
how you followed me in the wilderness,
in a land not sown.
³ Israel was holy to the LORD,
the first fruits of his harvest.
All who ate of it were held guilty;
disaster came upon them,
                    says the LORD.

4Hear the word of the LORD, O house of Jacob, and all the families of the house of Israel. ⁵Thus says the LORD:
What wrong did your ancestors find in me
that they went far from me,
and went after worthless things, and became
worthless themselves?

NIV

who brought us up out of Egypt
and led us through the barren wilderness,
through a land of deserts and rifts,
a land of drought and darkness,[a]
a land where no one travels and no one
lives?'
⁷I brought you into a fertile land
to eat its fruit and rich produce.
But you came and defiled my land
and made my inheritance detestable.
⁸The priests did not ask,
'Where is the LORD?'
Those who deal with the law did not know
me;
the leaders rebelled against me.
The prophets prophesied by Baal,
following worthless idols.

⁹"Therefore I bring charges against you again,"
declares the LORD.
"And I will bring charges against your children's children.
¹⁰Cross over to the coasts of Kittim[b] and look,
send to Kedar[c] and observe closely;
see if there has ever been anything like this:
¹¹Has a nation ever changed its gods?
(Yet they are not gods at all.)
But my people have exchanged their[d] Glory
for worthless idols.
¹²Be appalled at this, O heavens,
and shudder with great horror,"
declares the LORD.
¹³"My people have committed two sins:
They have forsaken me,
the spring of living water,
and have dug their own cisterns,
broken cisterns that cannot hold water.
¹⁴Is Israel a servant, a slave by birth?
Why then has he become plunder?
¹⁵Lions have roared;
they have growled at him.
They have laid waste his land;
his towns are burned and deserted.
¹⁶Also, the men of Memphis[e] and Tahpanhes
have shaved the crown of your head.[f]

NRSV

⁶They did not say, "Where is the LORD
who brought us up from the land of Egypt,
who led us in the wilderness,
in a land of deserts and pits,
in a land of drought and deep darkness,
in a land that no one passes through,
where no one lives?"
⁷I brought you into a plentiful land
to eat its fruits and its good things.
But when you entered you defiled my land,
and made my heritage an abomination.
⁸The priests did not say, "Where is the LORD?"
Those who handle the law did not know
me;
the rulers[a] transgressed against me;
the prophets prophesied by Baal,
and went after things that do not profit.

⁹Therefore once more I accuse you,
says the LORD,
and I accuse your children's children.
¹⁰Cross to the coasts of Cyprus and look,
send to Kedar and examine with care;
see if there has ever been such a thing.
¹¹Has a nation changed its gods,
even though they are no gods?
But my people have changed their glory
for something that does not profit.
¹²Be appalled, O heavens, at this,
be shocked, be utterly desolate,
says the LORD,
¹³for my people have committed two evils:
they have forsaken me,
the fountain of living water,
and dug out cisterns for themselves,
cracked cisterns
that can hold no water.

¹⁴Is Israel a slave? Is he a homeborn servant?
Why then has he become plunder?
¹⁵The lions have roared against him,
they have roared loudly.
They have made his land a waste;
his cities are in ruins, without inhabitant.
¹⁶Moreover, the people of Memphis and
Tahpanhes
have broken the crown of your head.

NIV

¹⁷Have you not brought this on yourselves
    by forsaking the L ORD your God
    when he led you in the way?
¹⁸Now why go to Egypt
    to drink water from the Shihor^a?
And why go to Assyria
    to drink water from the River^b?
¹⁹Your wickedness will punish you;
    your backsliding will rebuke you.
Consider then and realize
    how evil and bitter it is for you
when you forsake the L ORD your God
    and have no awe of me,"
          declares the Lord, the L ORD Almighty.

²⁰"Long ago you broke off your yoke
    and tore off your bonds;
    you said, 'I will not serve you!'
Indeed, on every high hill
    and under every spreading tree
    you lay down as a prostitute.
²¹I had planted you like a choice vine
    of sound and reliable stock.
How then did you turn against me
    into a corrupt, wild vine?
²²Although you wash yourself with soda
    and use an abundance of soap,
    the stain of your guilt is still before me,"
          declares the Sovereign L ORD.
²³"How can you say, 'I am not defiled;
    I have not run after the Baals'?
See how you behaved in the valley;
    consider what you have done.
You are a swift she-camel
    running here and there,
²⁴a wild donkey accustomed to the desert,
    sniffing the wind in her craving—
    in her heat who can restrain her?
Any males that pursue her need not tire
        themselves;
    at mating time they will find her.
²⁵Do not run until your feet are bare
    and your throat is dry.
But you said, 'It's no use!
    I love foreign gods,
    and I must go after them.'

²⁶"As a thief is disgraced when he is caught,

^a*18* That is, a branch of the Nile   ^b*18* That is, the Euphrates

NRSV

¹⁷ Have you not brought this upon yourself
    by forsaking the L ORD your God,
    while he led you in the way?
¹⁸ What then do you gain by going to Egypt,
    to drink the waters of the Nile?
Or what do you gain by going to Assyria,
    to drink the waters of the Euphrates?
¹⁹ Your wickedness will punish you,
    and your apostasies will convict you.
Know and see that it is evil and bitter
    for you to forsake the L ORD your God;
    the fear of me is not in you,
          says the Lord G OD of hosts.

²⁰ For long ago you broke your yoke
    and burst your bonds,
    and you said, "I will not serve!"
On every high hill
    and under every green tree
    you sprawled and played the whore.
²¹ Yet I planted you as a choice vine,
    from the purest stock.
How then did you turn degenerate
    and become a wild vine?
²² Though you wash yourself with lye
    and use much soap,
    the stain of your guilt is still before me,
          says the Lord G OD.
²³ How can you say, "I am not defiled,
    I have not gone after the Baals"?
Look at your way in the valley;
    know what you have done—
a restive young camel interlacing her tracks,
²⁴   a wild ass at home in the wilderness,
in her heat sniffing the wind!
    Who can restrain her lust?
None who seek her need weary themselves;
    in her month they will find her.
²⁵ Keep your feet from going unshod
    and your throat from thirst.
But you said, "It is hopeless,
    for I have loved strangers,
    and after them I will go."

²⁶ As a thief is shamed when caught,
    so the house of Israel shall be shamed—
they, their kings, their officials,
    their priests, and their prophets,

NIV

so the house of Israel is disgraced—
they, their kings and their officials,
their priests and their prophets.
27They say to wood, 'You are my father,'
and to stone, 'You gave me birth.'
They have turned their backs to me
and not their faces;
yet when they are in trouble, they say,
'Come and save us!'
28Where then are the gods you made for yourselves?
Let them come if they can save you
when you are in trouble!
For you have as many gods
as you have towns, O Judah.

29"Why do you bring charges against me?
You have all rebelled against me,"
declares the LORD.
30"In vain I punished your people;
they did not respond to correction.
Your sword has devoured your prophets
like a ravening lion.
31"You of this generation, consider the word of
the LORD:

"Have I been a desert to Israel
or a land of great darkness?
Why do my people say, 'We are free to roam;
we will come to you no more'?
32Does a maiden forget her jewelry,
a bride her wedding ornaments?
Yet my people have forgotten me,
days without number.
33How skilled you are at pursuing love!
Even the worst of women can learn from
your ways.
34On your clothes men find
the lifeblood of the innocent poor,
though you did not catch them breaking in.
Yet in spite of all this
35 you say, 'I am innocent;
he is not angry with me.'
But I will pass judgment on you
because you say, 'I have not sinned.'
36Why do you go about so much,
changing your ways?
You will be disappointed by Egypt
as you were by Assyria.

NRSV

27who say to a tree, "You are my father,"
and to a stone, "You gave me birth."
For they have turned their backs to me,
and not their faces.
But in the time of their trouble they say,
"Come and save us!"
28 But where are your gods
that you made for yourself?
Let them come, if they can save you,
in your time of trouble;
for you have as many gods
as you have towns, O Judah.

29 Why do you complain against me?
You have all rebelled against me,
says the LORD.
30 In vain I have struck down your children;
they accepted no correction.
Your own sword devoured your prophets
like a ravening lion.
31 And you, O generation, behold the word of
the LORD![a]
Have I been a wilderness to Israel,
or a land of thick darkness?
Why then do my people say, "We are free,
we will come to you no more"?
32 Can a girl forget her ornaments,
or a bride her attire?
Yet my people have forgotten me,
days without number.

33 How well you direct your course
to seek lovers!
So that even to wicked women
you have taught your ways.
34 Also on your skirts is found
the lifeblood of the innocent poor,
though you did not catch them breaking in.
Yet in spite of all these things[a]
35 you say, "I am innocent;
surely his anger has turned from me."
Now I am bringing you to judgment
for saying, "I have not sinned."
36 How lightly you gad about,
changing your ways!
You shall be put to shame by Egypt
as you were put to shame by Assyria.

[a]Meaning of Heb uncertain

NIV

7You will also leave that place
    with your hands on your head,
for the LORD has rejected those you trust;
    you will not be helped by them.

3 "If a man divorces his wife
    and she leaves him and marries another
        man,
should he return to her again?
    Would not the land be completely defiled?
But you have lived as a prostitute with many
        lovers—
    would you now return to me?"
                        declares the LORD.
2"Look up to the barren heights and see.
    Is there any place where you have not been
        ravished?
By the roadside you sat waiting for lovers,
    sat like a nomad*a* in the desert.
You have defiled the land
    with your prostitution and wickedness.
3Therefore the showers have been withheld,
    and no spring rains have fallen.
Yet you have the brazen look of a prostitute;
    you refuse to blush with shame.
4Have you not just called to me:
    'My Father, my friend from my youth,
5will you always be angry?
    Will your wrath continue forever?'
This is how you talk,
    but you do all the evil you can."

6During the reign of King Josiah, the LORD said to me, "Have you seen what faithless Israel has done? She has gone up on every high hill and under every spreading tree and has committed adultery there. 7I thought that after she had done all this she would return to me but she did not, and her unfaithful sister Judah saw it. 8I gave faithless Israel her certificate of divorce and sent her away because of all her adulteries. Yet I saw that her unfaithful sister Judah had no fear; she also went out and committed adultery. 9Because Israel's immorality mattered so little to her, she defiled the land and committed adultery with stone and wood. 10In spite of all this, her unfaithful sister Judah did not return to me with all her heart, but only in pretense," declares the LORD.

*a*2 Or *an Arab*

NRSV

37 From there also you will come away
    with your hands on your head;
for the LORD has rejected those in whom
        you trust,
    and you will not prosper through them.

3 If*a* a man divorces his wife
    and she goes from him
and becomes another man's wife,
    will he return to her?
Would not such a land be greatly polluted?
You have played the whore with many lovers;
    and would you return to me?
                        says the LORD.
2 Look up to the bare heights,*b* and see!
    Where have you not been lain with?
By the waysides you have sat waiting for
        lovers,
    like a nomad in the wilderness.
You have polluted the land
    with your whoring and wickedness.
3 Therefore the showers have been withheld,
    and the spring rain has not come;
yet you have the forehead of a whore,
    you refuse to be ashamed.
4 Have you not just now called to me,
    "My Father, you are the friend of my
        youth—
5 will he be angry forever,
    will he be indignant to the end?"
This is how you have spoken,
    but you have done all the evil that you
        could.

6The LORD said to me in the days of King Josiah: Have you seen what she did, that faithless one, Israel, how she went up on every high hill and under every green tree, and played the whore there? 7And I thought, "After she has done all this she will return to me"; but she did not return, and her false sister Judah saw it. 8She*c* saw that for all the adulteries of that faithless one, Israel, I had sent her away with a decree of divorce; yet her false sister Judah did not fear, but she too went and played the whore. 9Because she took her whoredom so lightly, she polluted the land, com-

*a*Ms Gk Syr: MT *Saying, If*   *b*Or the trails   *c*Q Ms Gk Mss Syr: MT *I*

NIV

¹¹The LORD said to me, "Faithless Israel is more righteous than unfaithful Judah. ¹²Go, proclaim this message toward the north:

" 'Return, faithless Israel,' declares the LORD,
  'I will frown on you no longer,
for I am merciful,' declares the LORD,
  'I will not be angry forever.
¹³Only acknowledge your guilt—
    you have rebelled against the LORD your God,
  you have scattered your favors to foreign gods
    under every spreading tree,
    and have not obeyed me,' "
                    declares the LORD.

¹⁴"Return, faithless people," declares the LORD, "for I am your husband. I will choose you—one from a town and two from a clan—and bring you to Zion. ¹⁵Then I will give you shepherds after my own heart, who will lead you with knowledge and understanding. ¹⁶In those days, when your numbers have increased greatly in the land," declares the LORD, "men will no longer say, 'The ark of the covenant of the LORD.' It will never enter their minds or be remembered; it will not be missed, nor will another one be made. ¹⁷At that time they will call Jerusalem The Throne of the LORD, and all nations will gather in Jerusalem to honor the name of the LORD. No longer will they follow the stubbornness of their evil hearts. ¹⁸In those days the house of Judah will join the house of Israel, and together they will come from a northern land to the land I gave your forefathers as an inheritance.

¹⁹"I myself said,
" 'How gladly would I treat you like sons
    and give you a desirable land,
    the most beautiful inheritance of any nation.'
I thought you would call me 'Father'
    and not turn away from following me.
²⁰But like a woman unfaithful to her husband,
    so you have been unfaithful to me, O house
      of Israel,"
                    declares the LORD.
²¹A cry is heard on the barren heights,
    the weeping and pleading of the people of
      Israel,
because they have perverted their ways
    and have forgotten the LORD their God.

NRSV

mitting adultery with stone and tree. ¹⁰Yet for all this her false sister Judah did not return to me with her whole heart, but only in pretense, says the LORD.

11Then the LORD said to me: Faithless Israel has shown herself less guilty than false Judah. ¹²Go, and proclaim these words toward the north, and say:

Return, faithless Israel,   says the LORD.
  I will not look on you in anger,
    for I am merciful,   says the LORD;
  I will not be angry forever.
¹³ Only acknowledge your guilt,
    that you have rebelled against the LORD
      your God,
  and scattered your favors among strangers
      under every green tree,
    and have not obeyed my voice,
                    says the LORD.
¹⁴ Return, O faithless children,   says the LORD,
    for I am your master;
  I will take you, one from a city and two from
    a family,
    and I will bring you to Zion.

15I will give you shepherds after my own heart, who will feed you with knowledge and understanding. ¹⁶And when you have multiplied and increased in the land, in those days, says the LORD, they shall no longer say, "The ark of the covenant of the LORD." It shall not come to mind, or be remembered, or missed; nor shall another one be made. ¹⁷At that time Jerusalem shall be called the throne of the LORD, and all nations shall gather to it, to the presence of the LORD in Jerusalem, and they shall no longer stubbornly follow their own evil will. ¹⁸In those days the house of Judah shall join the house of Israel, and together they shall come from the land of the north to the land that I gave your ancestors for a heritage.

¹⁹ I thought
    how I would set you among my children,
  and give you a pleasant land,
    the most beautiful heritage of all the
      nations.
  And I thought you would call me, My Father,
    and would not turn from following me.

NIV

22"Return, faithless people;
    I will cure you of backsliding."

"Yes, we will come to you,
    for you are the LORD our God.
23Surely the ‚idolatrous‚ commotion on the hills
    and mountains is a deception;
surely in the LORD our God
    is the salvation of Israel.
24From our youth shameful gods have consumed
    the fruits of our fathers' labor—
their flocks and herds,
    their sons and daughters.
25Let us lie down in our shame,
    and let our disgrace cover us.
We have sinned against the LORD our God,
    both we and our fathers;
from our youth till this day
    we have not obeyed the LORD our God."

4 "If you will return, O Israel,
    return to me,"
                    declares the LORD.
"If you put your detestable idols out of my
        sight
    and no longer go astray,
2and if in a truthful, just and righteous way
    you swear, 'As surely as the LORD lives,'
then the nations will be blessed by him
    and in him they will glory."

3This is what the LORD says to the men of Judah
and to Jerusalem:

"Break up your unplowed ground
    and do not sow among thorns.
4Circumcise yourselves to the LORD,
    circumcise your hearts,
    you men of Judah and people of Jerusalem,
or my wrath will break out and burn like fire
    because of the evil you have done—
    burn with no one to quench it.

NRSV

20 Instead, as a faithless wife leaves her hus-
        band,
    so you have been faithless to me, O house
        of Israel,   says the LORD.

21 A voice on the bare heights[a] is heard,
    the plaintive weeping of Israel's children,
because they have perverted their way,
    they have forgotten the LORD their God:
22 Return, O faithless children,
    I will heal your faithlessness.

"Here we come to you;
    for you are the LORD our God.
23 Truly the hills are[b] a delusion,
    the orgies on the mountains.
Truly in the LORD our God
    is the salvation of Israel.
24 "But from our youth the shameful thing has
devoured all for which our ancestors had labored,
their flocks and their herds, their sons and their
daughters. 25Let us lie down in our shame, and let
our dishonor cover us; for we have sinned against
the LORD our God, we and our ancestors, from
our youth even to this day; and we have not
obeyed the voice of the LORD our God."

4 If you return, O Israel,   says the LORD,
    if you return to me,
if you remove your abominations from my
        presence,
    and do not waver,
2 and if you swear, "As the LORD lives!"
    in truth, in justice, and in uprightness,
then nations shall be blessed[c] by him,
    and by him they shall boast.
3For thus says the LORD to the people of Judah
and to the inhabitants of Jerusalem:
Break up your fallow ground,
    and do not sow among thorns.
4 Circumcise yourselves to the LORD,
    remove the foreskin of your hearts,
    O people of Judah and inhabitants of
        Jerusalem,
or else my wrath will go forth like fire,
    and burn with no one to quench it,
    because of the evil of your doings.

[a]Or the trails   [b]Gk Syr Vg: Heb *Truly from the hills is*   [c]Or *shall
bless themselves*

COMMENTARY

The heading identifies two primary concerns in these chapters. The oracles of Jeremiah begin with some of the harshest condemnations in the whole book. The focus of the accusation in chap. 2 is the fundamental issue for Israel's life: its covenantal loyalty to the Lord of Israel. The sins of Israel (both northern and southern kingdoms) are spelled out in detail and with richly developed imagery. There follows an equally powerful series of oracles that call the people to turn from their ways, to repent and live in obedience to the Lord and under God's blessing.

Specific features mark off chaps. 2 and 3 from each other, while other features bind them together in a single whole. The distinction between the two chapters may be discerned particularly in the prominent use of the thematic verb "return"/"repent" (שׁוּב *šûb*), which occurs sixteen times in chap. 3 and only a couple of times in chap. 2, but not in the same sense of calling the people to repentance. Yet main images, such as "the way" (2:17-18, 23, 33, 36; 3:2, 21) and "going after" (2:2, 5, 8, 23, 25; 3:17, 19), the imagery of "bride" (2:1-3, 32) and "wife" (3:1-5, 20), joined with the language and imagery of harlotry (e.g., 2:20-25, 33-37; 3:1-10, 12-13, 20), the language of shame (2:26, 36; 3:24-25), and the divine epithet "my father" (2:27; 3:4, 19), run through both chapters, indicating much shared content. Attention to both kingdoms, Israel and Judah, further holds these chapters together. Thus we will read these two chapters individually and together to get their full impact.

At the heart of chap. 2 is the covenant lawsuit that the Lord brings against Israel for its faithlessness (2:4-13). The two dimensions of faithlessness, both religious and political—that is, both alliances with other gods and alliances with other nations—are the subject of further oracles. The relation of husband and wife is the chief vehicle for speaking about the various forms of faithlessness and provides the major bridge to chap. 3 where, as in the case of Jeremiah's predecessor Hosea, the family imagery is extended from the sphere of spousal relationship to that of filial relationship as Israel and Judah are portrayed not only as faithless wives or lovers—and sisters—but also as rebellious children (3:4-5, 19, 21-22*a*). The judgment speeches

of the Lord through the prophet continue in chap. 3, but the judgment speeches now are mixed with hope for and a summons to repentance. The initial verses of chap. 4 round off the call to repentance, whereupon 4:5 opens up a new section of oracles having to do with the foe from the north.

2:1-3. The initial half-verse offers a triple introductory formula. The first of these, "The word of the LORD was to me," directly ties this word and all the words to follow with the call, for that formula is repeated three times in the call narrative (1:4, 11, 13). In this fashion, the opening indictment flows directly out of the preceding chapter and continues the transmission of the divine word to the prophet. One cannot view these harsh words of Jeremiah any differently from those that laid upon him, against his wishes, the prophetic burden. From beginning to end, he is simply passing on the word of the Lord.

The second introductory formula, "Go and proclaim in the hearing of Jerusalem," also ties this word and what follows to the call of Jeremiah (cf. 1:7), but it also identifies the audience to whom these words are directed. That audience seems obvious in the light of Jeremiah's Judean location, but the matter is more complex, for in vv. 4-13, the prophet addresses ("O house of Jacob and all the families of Israel") the northern kingdom, or what was left of it, whether still in the north, in Assyrian exile, or in Judah. Later texts in this section also seem to address the people of the northern kingdom (e.g., 3:19-20).[30] But once these oracles are placed under the divine command at the beginning to "go and proclaim in the hearing of Jerusalem," then the words to the Israelites also become words for Jerusalem and the Judeans.

The final piece of introductory word is the typical prophetic formula "Thus says the LORD," so common in prophetic books. In fact, it is the messenger formula per se and reminds the hearer that the one who speaks does so as herald and messenger from the divine government, sent with a word, a message to transmit. This messenger formula always conveys its transcendent source and

---

30. For a possible early recension to the north underlying the present form of these chapters, see William L. Holladay, *Jeremiah 1: A Commentary on the Book of the Prophet Jeremiah Chapters 1–25*, Hermeneia (Philadelphia: Fortress, 1986) 62-81.

authority. In this case, the instinct to kill the messenger of bad news will take over.

The first word of the Lord through Jeremiah, then, is a powerful and poignant recollection of Israel's youthful love and devotion (vv. 2*b*-3). The wilderness experience after the exodus and the covenantal moment at Sinai are often depicted with the imagery of youth—that is, as the early stages of the growth and development of God's people. The point of the divine memory is not to identify an ideal time but to point to a relationship as it was and is still meant to be. The emphasis, therefore, is not so much on an ideal early period as it is on loyalty and devotion to the Lord of Israel and what that involves.

The specifics of that loyalty are set forth in two modes. One is with the abstract, but theologically weighty, terms *devotion* and *love.* The former is the very common term חסד (*ḥesed*), most often translated in the NRSV as "steadfast love" but here as "devotion" to avoid the double use of the word "love" (אהבה *'ahăbâ*) and to set the abstract language in the context of the bridal imagery. Both terms signify the appropriate response of Israel to its creator and covenanting God. These words have to do with a kind of unqualified and persistent loyalty to the Lord that helps all of life express a kind of devotion that can only be described with the human notion of love. The bridal imagery, even though participating in the patriarchal character of much biblical imagery, is appropriate in this context because of the way that marriage is the most visibly covenantal of all human institutions. Elements of love, loyalty, full devotion, jealousy, and forgiveness all belong to the marriage relationship, where two persons bind themselves in covenantal obligation and promise to live together and to turn to no other one to express or receive such full devotion.

These characteristics that the Lord remembers as belonging to the people's early history, their "youth," were indeed expectations of ancient Israel from the beginning. Thus the embodiment of the whole law, of all of Israel's covenantal obedience in the Shema identifies that obedience with the "love" of the Lord (Deut 6:4). The prophets knew that the "steadfast love" (i.e., devotion) of Israel for its Lord was the prime good, the *sine qua non* for its existence. So we find in some of the most familiar and definitive prophetic words about

what was expected of Israel the call to love the Lord, to set the steadfast love of the Lord above all other religious activities (Hos 6:6; Mic 6:8). So also Israel was "holy" to the Lord (Exod 19:6; Deut 7:6) and lived under a Torah that taught the meaning and reality of such holiness. The holiness code, coming from a later period but understood as identifying the way for Israel from its beginning, set the imitation of the Lord's holiness as one of the fundamental ways of defining Israel's moral life: "You shall be holy, for I the LORD your God am holy" (Lev 19:2 NRSV).

The second way of defining the specifics of Israel's loyalty to the Lord occurs in the language of "going after" or "following" (v. 2*b*). Here, in the beginning of Jeremiah's oracles, we encounter one of the critical and thematic expressions of these chapters. It occurs a number of times in the oracles to follow, but this is the only time that it is used positively. This verse defines the standard, the expected, the remembered way against which the people are measured and from which they fall short when they "go after the baals." The expression occurs most often in the negative, "going after other gods," in Jeremiah (see below) as well as in Deuteronomy (Deut 6:14). The imagery of "following after" is one of several ways of expressing the demand that is present in the first commandment, to have no other Gods before or besides the Lord.

In v. 3, the prophetic speech moves to the other side of the relation. Having remembered the covenantal loyalty and devotion of Israel at an earlier time, God now speaks about the divine election and protection of Israel, the steadfast love of the Lord for Israel as well as Israel's devotion to the Lord. What is in view is the setting apart of Israel as the Lord's special possession (Exod 19:4-6) that involved not only Israel's devotion but also the Lord's protection and favor. The language here is not that of personal relationships (as in v. 2) but comes from the cultic and sacral sphere—"holy," "become guilty." God elects Israel. But that choice is couched in ways that point to the protection and providence of God over the people, already indicated in the reference to "a land not sown" where God provided for the people, but a choice indicated further by reference to the guilt and disaster that came upon those who sought to devour the people whom the Lord had elected (v. 3*b*).

There is another kind of language present as well. Along with the personal and the relational, the sacral and the cultic, there is also the language of property and produce in v. 3. The power and beauty of the poetry of this oracle may be observed in the way the reference to the land not sown— that is, to the wilderness experience that is the context for the bridal imagery—is a bridge for a wholly different kind of imagery to speak about the same thing, the beginning of the relation of the Lord and Israel. The new imagery is agricultural and proprietary. The primary thing the Lord is doing in the world is first reflected in God's way with Israel. Those who stand in the way of that by "devouring" or "eating" the Lord's firstfruits, Israel, incur guilt before the Lord and consequent disaster.

The divine memory, however, is an aching one, and the words are a setup. They clearly presuppose more to follow. The memory of Israel's devotion is precisely that, a memory, a recollection from the past. The present is another story. That story is what we encounter in the many oracles that follow. It is a story; it is still recollection—but not a pleasant one. Only from the oracles that follow can one comprehend the poignancy of the first memory in vv. 2b-3.

2:4-13. The heart of chaps. 2–3 is the covenant lawsuit.[31] The plaintiff, God, brings a case or a claim against the defendant, Israel. The lawsuit indicts more than it announces judgment. The declaration of God's judgment is central to the form of the judgment speech, which we will encounter often in the oracles of Jeremiah. The lawsuit genre (ריב *rîb*, "accuse")is rooted in the covenant and sets an indictment against the people for breach of covenant. Prophetic speech here borrows a form or genre from the courtroom because the intention is to argue a case against someone who has violated the contractual relationship.

The covenant lawsuit begins with a summons to those who are being called into court (v. 4). The critical thing in this instance is the identity of those being summoned, called here "house of Jacob" and "house of Israel." In all likelihood, this is a reference to the northern kingdom, Israel (see Isa 9:8), which suggests that the oracles—or at least a

good portion of them—between 2:4 and 4:2, where the address switches to Judah and Jerusalem, comprise a collection addressed to the north (see above), possibly in connection with King Josiah's efforts to carry his cultic reform to the northern kingdom. That could well have been a long process, continuing right up to Josiah's death in 609 BCE.

The lawsuit continues in vv. 5-8 with the indictment in the form of historical recital. The question in v. 5 identifies the issue and sets the theme: the Lord's righteousness and Israel's faithlessness. There follows a succinct summary of Israel's history— but with a particular slant. The story of Israel from God's perspective is a long history of Israel's forsaking the Lord. The question of v. 5, "What wrong did your ancestors find in me?" is rhetorical in that it expects the clear answer that nothing "wrong" was found in the Lord's part of the covenantal story. The question opens up a biblical formulation of the *via negativa,* the negative attributes of God. The righteous God is one who does not do "wrong," a term that seems rooted in the judicial process in what is not to be done in the law court—showing partiality, accepting bribes, and the like.

The point of the question is that the action of the ancestors in turning far away from the Lord (v. 5a) was inappropriate and stupid, inappropriate because they left a God who was just and righteous (v. 5a). But the people's leaving the Lord was also stupid because it was useless and utterly ineffective (v. 5b). Not only did they abandon the God who had done no wrong to them, but also they went after "worthless things" and thus became themselves "worthless." The play on words of the NRSV is reflected in the Hebrew. There is no question what the "worthless things" are. They are the idols. That is evident in the language of "going after," which is the same expression used in v. 2 with reference to Israel's "following after" the Lord in the wilderness and is regularly used to indicate allegiance to a deity. Elsewhere in Jeremiah, the expression "worthless things" refers to idols and other gods worshiped by the ancestors, by previous generations of Israelites:

Our ancestors have inherited nothing but lies,
   worthless things in which there is no profit.
Can mortals make for themselves gods?
   Such are no gods!
(16:19-20 NRSV; cf. 8:19; 10:15; 44:22; 51:18)

---

31. On this form, see Herbert Huffmon, "The Covenant Lawsuit in the Prophets," *JBL* 78 (1959) 285-95.

The divine accusation is that the previous generations left the Lord to find gods that would be productive and useful to them, but to no avail. In vv. 8 and 11, the point is made in another way, centering around the word "profit." In v. 5, the people go after emptiness and worthlessness. In v. 8, the prophets go after what does not profit. Verse 11 identifies the sin of the people as exchanging one God for what does not profit—that is, for a non-productive, non-effective deity. The theme that binds all these verses together is the abandonment of the Lord for what does not work, failing to recognize that in the God they worship is to be found the source of life, fertility, and good or well-being. Seeking this elsewhere is an utterly fruitless task. The search for God becomes a search for whatever enhances my (or our) well-being, makes my land more productive, increases my wealth and my place and my status. The decision of translators to use "profit" for the Hebrew verb יעל (*yāʿal*) is a good one. It suggests, correctly, that the effort to find a deity who will benefit and profit oneself is the primary concern. The wordplay in the English translation of v. 8*b* ("prophet"/"profit") does not occur in the Hebrew. However, the prophetic rhetoric creates a Hebrew wordplay between "Baal" (בעל *bāʿal*) and "profit" (*yāʿal*); two of the three Hebrew consonants are the same and stand in the same order. This wordplay makes the point indirectly but forcefully: "Baal" = "no profit."

The term "profit" is used almost entirely negatively in prophetic polemic; the word occurs in polemic against false gods. Isaiah 30:5 calls Egypt a people that cannot profit. So why go to them in political alliance? It will not benefit. Increasingly in the prophets the expression "What does not profit . . . ?" describes idols and the worship of other gods. In Jeremiah and elsewhere, what does not profit will also be called false and a lie (e.g., 16:19). There is one positive use of the word (*yāʿal*) in the prophetic literature, and it provides the counterpoint to the many negative uses, the discernment of what truly profits:

> I am the LORD your God,
>   who teaches you for your own good,
>   who leads you in the way you should go.
> O that you had paid attention to my
>   commandments!
>   Then your prosperity [שלום *šālôm*] would have

> been like a river
> and your success [צדקה *ṣĕdāqâ*] like the waves
>   of the sea. (Isa 48:17-18 NRSV)

Prosperity, success, and profit have only one source: the way of the Lord.

The Deuteronomistic History includes a long explanatory speech accounting for the fall of the northern kingdom because of its apostasy (2 Kgs 17:7-23). The prophet recalls the stubbornness of the people's ancestors (v. 14). Among the list of sins for which Israel was punished is their going after what is worthless and becoming themselves worthless (v. 15), exactly the sin for which these early oracles of Jeremiah condemn the people. The condemnation of the northern kingdom in 2 Kings 17 thus echoes the Jeremianic lawsuit against that same kingdom.

The rest of this historical recital makes different points. The recital seeks first of all to make the case *for* the Lord (vv. 6-7*a*) and then the case *against* the people (vv. 7*b*-8). The case for the Lord is a kind of brief history of salvation or credo statement that focuses on the three critical moments in Israel's early history: exodus ("who brought us up from the land of Egypt"), wilderness journey ("who led us in the wilderness"), and settlement of the land ("I brought you into a plentiful land")—all of which were manifestations of the Lord's faithfulness. The recitation describes all that the Lord had done that has clearly profited Israel. It offers a picture of the Lord leading them through all sorts of disasters and impossible situations and also of God providing them with a productive and rich land.

But such massive evidence for the Lord's strength and blessing on Israel's behalf was insufficient to hold the allegiance of the people. The prophet makes the case against the people in two parts, both of which revolve around the accusation, "They/the priests did not say, 'Where is the LORD?' " (vv. 6*a*, 8*a*). This question, which the Lord expected to hear but does not, expresses the longing of those who cry out in complaint or lament. Thus Gideon says: "If the LORD is with us, why then has all this happened to us? And where are all his wonderful deeds?" (Judg 6:13 NRSV). In Isa 63:11, 15, such a question is part of a communal prayer for help, what the people say when they have rebelled and the Lord has punished them:

"Where is the one who brought them up out of the sea? . . . Where are your zeal and might?" Elihu says to Job that those who are oppressed cry out for help, but no one says, "Where is God my Maker, who gives strength in the night?" (Job 35:10). The Lord's accusation, therefore, is that in the failure to ask, "Where is the LORD?" the people either assume a self-sufficiency in not crying out to the Lord in time of trouble or they cry out to other gods. Certainly v. 7*b* carries forward the indictment of the people specifically in terms of their having polluted the land God gave them by worshiping other gods.

God's indictment of the leaders of Israel and Judah is a prominent issue in the book of Jeremiah. It begins in these verses when the same accusation is made against them, or at least against the priests—namely, that they do not call upon the Lord. The sin of the people involves, at least in part, the result of a failure of leadership. Neither party is absolved of responsibility, for priests and people have known from the early days in the wilderness who it is that guides their life (vv. 2-3).

But the priests are only one part of the failure of the political and religious leadership. Those responsible for the instruction and teaching of the Lord's Torah—possibly the priests but certainly the wise men, the scribes (cf. 10:8)—do not know the Lord. Jeremiah may be indicting them for not saying, "Where is the LORD?" The charge may have in mind the same idea one finds in 22:16, where the knowledge of God is directly related to the maintenance of justice in the community. That is, the teachers do not, in fact, teach the law and ensure that its calls for justice and compassion and the right worship of God are carried out in the community. The absence of justice in Israel is always a religious, and not just a social, matter.

The indictment of the kings for their transgressions is broad. One would have to look at the history of both kingdoms to discern the specific charges. Jeremiah 22:16 is illustrative here. It presents an indictment of the king for being concerned about royal perquisites and luxuries but not about the cause of the poor and the needy. The accusation against the prophets that they turned to Baal takes us back into the history of the northern kingdom and the coalition of royal and prophetic enthusiasm for the worship of Baal, which involved looking for rain and fertility from another

power than the one that brought Israel out of the wilderness and sustained them on their way.

This recital of good and bad history turns into a lawsuit in v. 9 as the Lord brings suit against Israel for breach of covenant, for failure to worship and serve no other God but the Lord, the fundamental principle of the covenant relationship. The indictment is restated in vv. 10-11 in address to an unknown group. The court? The heavens? Verse 12 would suggest the latter in their function as the court or as witnesses. God asks if there is any precedent for such behavior anywhere (Cyprus and Kedar probably represent western and eastern geographical extremes). In the repetition of the indictment in v. 11 (cf. v. 13), the defendants are spoken of as "my people," the covenantal designation of this community.

The shocking character of the people's action in abandoning the Lord for gods that do not accomplish anything may not be hyperbole. Israel's behavior in letting go of its national deity in favor of other gods may have been genuinely unusual. Addition of foreign gods to a nation's pantheon was not unusual in the ancient Near East. However, Jeremiah claims that the abandonment of the god of the tribe, people, or nation in favor of other gods is unprecedented and utterly appalling.

This exchange of one deity for another may be reflected in the puzzling "two evils" or two crimes of v. 13. It would be possible to read the forsaking of the Lord (v. 13*a*) and the digging of cisterns in this way, the latter a way of speaking about the people's going after what does not profit, what does not work. Jeremiah's use of water imagery offers another way of speaking about the exchange of one God for other gods, one ultimate claim of faith that has sustained and cared for them throughout their whole history—living water—for cisterns full of stagnant water that does not refresh and nourish and, in fact, simply does not last because the water trickles away through cracks in the cistern. The issue is the difference between the continuous, fresh, vital water, symbolizing the Lord, and the stagnant and gradually disappearing water of the broken cisterns, symbolizing the other gods (cf. 17:13).

2:14-19. The indictment of Israel now moves more specifically to the political plane. Apostasy, the central sin of Israel according to the lawsuit brought in vv. 4-13, is still the issue. Twice we hear of Israel's "forsaking the LORD your God" (vv. 17, 19; cf. v. 13). The expression "the LORD your God" echoes the Shema, with its confession that "the LORD our God" is God alone and its call to "love the LORD your God" completely and without reserve. But the manifestation of apostasy, the path of abandonment identified here, is political. It is found in Israel's pursuit of alliances with other nations, specifically Egypt and Assyria. The divine and prophetic claim that alliances with other nations are demonstrations of bad faith and unwillingness to trust in the Lord is a theme already known from Isaiah's oracles in the eighth century BCE (Isa 28:14-15; 30:1-5; 31:1-3). Such political activity is another example of not saying, "Where is the LORD?" Instead, the people have turned to other powers, other sources of might and help.

The theme of apostasy is found not only in the equation of political alliances with "forsaking" the Lord but also in the depiction of that action as going to drink from the waters of the chief rivers of the two countries, the Nile in Egypt and the Euphrates in Assyria. Implicit in that imagery is the repeated judgment that such water will not sustain life. It is bad and bitter (v. 19); to drink it is to drink to their death. The people have brought their downfall upon themselves, a case of poetic justice. The prophet argues that going to other nations in effect brings them back upon you— Memphis and Tahpanes were major cities of Egypt and quite possibly places where negotiations with Egyptian representatives would have taken place.[32] The outcome of such negotiations, however, is not deliverance. Israel, a free people by the redemptive grace of God, has become both slave and plunder—literally, as the people are taken into exile and their land is plundered. The people who were created in liberation from slavery by the Lord and guided along the way of the wilderness have taken another way, which culminates in a return to slavery.

2:20-28. In coarse and disturbing language, the prophetic voice describes the ways in which Israel has forsaken the Lord. Images, particularly animal metaphors, are heaped upon one another to describe the people's apostasy. The first is that of an ox, or some domesticated animal, that breaks the yoke or the reins and refuses to submit to the owner or do the necessary work. The expression "I will not serve" is not only ironic, in the light of the previous passage's identification of the people's servitude to the political powers, but it also carries a double meaning. The verb עבד ('ābad) can mean to do work in the sense of manual labor or tilling the ground. It is also the word for serving a master and, more specifically, for serving God or other gods, as, for example, in the commandment prohibiting bowing down to or serving—that is, worshiping—other gods (Exod 20:5). The rebellious ox is an image, then, for breach of covenant. As Holladay puts it, "On the level of the animal metaphor Israel says, 'I will not work!' and on the level of covenant Israel says, 'I will not submit!' "[33]

Sexual imagery figures prominently in the unit, first as the nation is depicted as a prostitute by virtue of its participation in the fertility cult worship "on every high hill and under every green tree," a standard cliché for the sites of such worship (v. 20b).[34] It is possible that the whore/prostitute imagery is chosen as an image for the people's infidelity not only because of its appropriateness as a metaphor for breach of covenant but also because the worship of the baals may have involved sexual activity, although the evidence for that is uncertain. In any event, the sexual imagery becomes even stronger in vv. 23-25 where images of a camel and a wild ass are brought into the picture. The former is not so much an animal in heat as it is an image for the unreliable, uncontrollable people who wander off for other gods as easily as a young camel goes off the track and wanders around without direction. The more extended image involves the wild ass. Israel is depicted as a wild ass that will "lie" with anyone who comes along, a sexually insatiable animal that will pick up any stranger. Here gross sexual appetite is the analogy for Israel's unrestrained lust for the baals and other objects of religious devotion.

> If the young camel cannot walk straight, then the female wild ass in heat walks only too straight, so impetuously that one cannot deal with her. Both animals in their diffferent ways are perfect symbols for Israel's tracks to Baal.[35]

---

32. On poetic justice in the prophets, see Patrick D. Miller, *Sin and Judgment in the Prophets: A Stylistic and Theological Analysis,* SBLMS 27 (Chico, Calif.: Scholars Press, 1982).

33. William L. Holladay, *Jeremiah 1: A Commentary on the Book of the Prophet Jeremiah Chapters 1–25,* Hermeneia (Philadelphia: Fortress, 1986) 97-98.

34. See S. Ackerman, *Under Every Green Tree: Popular Religion in Sixth-Century Judah,* HSM 46 (Atlanta: Scholars Press, 1992) 152-53.

35. Holladay, *Jeremiah 1,* 97-98.

What the wild ass says (v. 25) functions as a kind of imposed confession of guilt. The statement uses the language of sexual imagery but also picks up the thematic language of this chapter, "going after." Verse 25 is directly related to the final verse of the passage. Just as a whore/prostitute will stop any stranger on the street, so also Israel "goes after" or offers its loving attention to every god that comes around. The reference to gods as numerous as the towns of Judah may be a reference to worship of local gods of the towns of Judah. Such reference may also be a hyperbolic statement to make the point that Israel has "gone after" Baal and other profitless objects of religious devotion.

The "confession" of guilt in v. 25 expresses defiance. The language of "love" clearly alludes to the sexual appetite of the "wild ass"/"whore." However, it is hardly appropriate to speak of such purely sexual activity that has no real love involved in it. But the term "love" is covenantal and here echoes its use in v. 2, referring to the people's abandonment of their devotion to the Lord. Those who had "gone after" the Lord and "loved" the Lord in the past now "go after" and "love" strangers—that is, the gods of the land and probably also the foreign powers referred to in vv. 14-19.

Other images fill out this passage. Isaiah's song of the vineyard (Isa 5:1-7) echoes in the background of v. 22, where Israel's disloyalty is compared to a choice vine that is planted (by the Lord) as a reliable stock (lit., "seed of faithfulness") but ends up bearing strange or foreign fruit (v. 21). Verse 22 reminds us of Lady Macbeth's "damned spot" that will not come out, a permanent, unremovable testimony to guilt. Finally, a comparison to the shame of a thief who has been caught concludes the indictment against the people and their leaders (v. 26). The useless and profitless outcome of their pursuit of other gods and other powers is accented in the closing verses (vv. 27-28). They can do nothing. The powerlessness of the gods other than Yahweh is a major prophetic theme. Here is Jeremiah's voice in that loud chorus of prophetic ridicule and mockery.

2:29-37. The charges go forward as the Lord wistfully and angrily argues the case against the people using terms already encountered in preceding verses. The judicial/legal setting is signaled at the beginning as the Lord expresses astonishment that the people would claim any case against their God in the light of the degree of their own rebellion (v. 29). The evidence is clearly loaded one way, and the following verses reiterate that point with the rhetoric of interrogation, sarcasm, and exclamation. The self-indicting words of the people are quoted frequently in these verses, their claims to "religious freedom" from the covenant, the right to choose whatever deity they wish (v. 31), and the even more amazing claims of innocence and righteousness (v. 35), claims that by their very audacity in the face of all the evidence before the court will ensure a verdict of guilt. Those who claim innocence are in fact the ones who have harmed the innocent and the poor (v. 34), the first indication in the book of Jeremiah of the social injustices of the community as a part of their indictment; that theme will resound loudly in later chapters. As already indicated in vv. 14-19, judgment will work itself out in the failure of Israel's alliances with Egypt and Assyria and the consequent shame and humiliation the people will endure (vv. 36-37a), an outcome that, while couched in political terms, is entirely the work of the Lord of Israel (v. 37b).

Images and themes from earlier verses continue to be prominent. Thus Israel's sin of forgetting the Lord is compared unfavorably to the inconceivability of a bride discarding and forgetting her wedding dress (see vv. 1-3). And the language of "wilderness" and "land," which, in those same verses, reflects God's care, now appears as a part of God's incredulous querying of the people's casual turning away and forgetting the Lord (v. 31). Here also the prophet sets forth a notion of God's judgment as a form of correction and discipline, a kind of judgment (cf. v. 19) where the punishment of wickedness is in fact a disciplining through judgment that the people's wickedness has evoked.[36] A particular rhetorical form that Jeremiah uses a number of times occurs in v. 31 (cf., e.g., v. 14; 3:5). The Lord asks two rhetorical questions: "Have I been a wilderness?" "Or a land of thick darkness?" The Lord then asks, "Why . . . ?" The first two questions state a traditional, generally acceptable presupposition, with which the hearers

---

36. The word for "punish" (יסר *yāsar*) in 2:19 is the same as the word for "correction" in 2:30. The allusion to the killing of the prophets in 2:30 is unclear. See Neh 9:26.

should agree. Then the third question, "Why?" suddenly and sharply turns the argument against the hearers by drawing the implications of the consensus just established.[37] Jeremiah's rhetoric thus joins the many instances in the prophetic oracles in which the prophet disputes and counteracts the assumptions of the people by discerning the way in which the assumptions have in them the seeds of judgment.

3:1-5. The mode of speech of the opening verse is the request for a priestly ruling about a matter of law or ritual in which a situation is posed and a question is asked about how the matter should be understood or dealt with (see Hag 2:12-13).[38] The situation posed is drawn from the law of divorce in Deut 24:1-4, whose subject matter is less divorce than it is the question of remarriage to a first husband by a wife who has been twice divorced (or widowed). In this manner, the prophet returns to the harlotry imagery, the metaphor of Israel as a bride in an adulterous relationship. In chap. 2, Jeremiah focuses on the manifestation of this adultery, particularly in the people's religious life, though with an allusion to the doing in of the "lifeblood of the innocent poor" (v. 34). In chap. 3, the issue is the possibility of "return," and from two directions: the Lord's wishing to return to the spouse who has gone off to other lovers and the spouse who wishes to return again to the first spouse. The passage incorporates into the denunciations the question of repentance—that is, of return. This topic becomes the focus of attention in the oracles that follow, even though indictment for the sins of both the northern kingdom and the southern kingdom is still very much in view.

The opening verse (v. 1) sets the relationship between the Lord and the people in analogy to the husband who has divorced a wife. The first half of v. 1 ends with two questions: Will he (the Lord) return to her, and would the defilement of the wife not defile the whole land? An obvious response by the audience would be to reject any idea of the husband's return to the wife who had gone off to another husband, much less with many lovers, as v. 1*b* and the preceding chapter make clear. The

oracle, with its rhetorical questions based on well-known and accepted law, thus serves as a kind of self-indictment on the part of the people who would respond so vigorously and thus implicate themselves as they are represented in the figure of the wife.

There are two critical turns in the argument of v. 1. One is a significant variation on the law of Deuteronomy, which is about the wife's returning to the husband, while Jeremiah's oracle speaks of the husband's returning to the wife. The initiative shifts from the wife to the husband. The hearer learns at the start that this text is as much about the move the Lord makes toward the people as it is about what they should do in order to restore their relationship with the Lord.

The other critical turn in the argument may be found in the ambiguity of the final line of the sentence, which both the NRSV and the NIV translate as a question: "Would you return to me?" Such a rhetorical question assumes a negative answer on the analogy of the divorce and remarriage law of Deuteronomy. But the sentence is equally capable of being translated as an imperative, "[Nevertheless] return to me!" The translation of this phrase as an imperative suggests that the Lord will break the Lord's own law and take Israel back if the people will repent. The word "return" thus carries both the notion of repentance, for this is the standard Hebrew word for repentance (שׁוּב *šûb*), and the restoration of relationship as the wife is reunited with her husband, or as Israel is brought back into relationship with its Lord. "It is this tension between the legal impossibility of return and the religious possibility of repentance and divine remission that is captured in the ambiguous phrase 'thus shall you return to me.' "[39] The essential point of this whole section is thus set forth in the opening verse. The affection of the Lord for this people is so great that God is willing to violate God's own law, willing to risk pollution and defilement, if the people will turn in loyalty once more to the Lord of Israel.

In vv. 2-5, the case concerning the "adultery" of the people is made once more, in language that, in Hebrew, is very coarse. The scene is reminiscent of the story of Tamar, who wore the paraphernalia of a prostitute and waited by the road to attract the

37. See W. Brueggemann, "Jeremiah's Use of Rhetorical Questions," *JBL* 92 (1973) 358-74.

38. Michael Fishbane, *Biblical Interpretation in Ancient Israel* (Oxford: Clarendon, 1985) 307.

39. Ibid., 310.

attention of her father-in-law, Judah. It also recalls the alluring prostitute in Prov 7:10-27, who lies in wait at every corner. Israel's whoring and promiscuity are rampant and unabashed (cf. 6:15–8:12), and the outcome has been devastating for the land. Defilement and drought follow such violation of the relation between the people and the Lord (cf. 12:4; 14:1-6). There is irony here in that the turning of the people to the fertility cults of the land would have been intended to ensure the fertility of the land, but the reverse has been the case.[40]

Perhaps in response to the devastating drought, the people appeal to the mercy of God that their theological tradition has always claimed and their history has constantly illustrated. The address to the Lord as Father and friend in v. 4 may reflect covenantal categories. Verses 4-5a show the people drawing upon the tradition, articulated so powerfully in Psalm 103, that knows the compassion of God like that of a father and the unwillingness of God to remain forever angry at the people because of their sins (Ps 30:5).

The passage ends, however, with things quite up in the air about either party's returning because of the many sins of the people (v. 5b). In other words, there is no contrition or penitence, only an utter incongruity between the words of the people and their actions. They have spoken in this way while all the time continuing to do as much wickedness as they could.

3:6-11. In this prose text, probably from a later time than the verses surrounding it, the "turn" or "return" (šûb) language strikes again an important theme, but it is used now in a quite different fashion from the first five verses. Its use in vv. 1-5 is entirely in terms of the possibility of reconciliation and repentance. Will the husband return to the wife who has gone off? Will she and can she return to him?

Now, however, the term šûb in its various formations takes on another use and refers to "turning" away from the Lord. A term has been coined for these verses: "faithless/apostate [משבה méšubâ] Israel," appropriately translated by W. Holladay as "Turncoat Israel."[41] The passage builds upon and works with themes and language of the preceding text and clearly depends on it. This relationship is evident not only in the "return to me" phraseology but also in the frequent reference to harlotry, the spelling out of the religious apostasies with the picture of things happening "on the high hill" (cf. v. 2), which seem to be a part of the fertility cults of the Canaanites, and especially the "decree of divorce" (v. 8), a term that appears only one other place besides its use here and in Deut 24:1-4, the text that lies behind the opening verse of this chapter.

The "decree of divorce" in this section seems to have in mind the exile of the northern kingdom. The text looks back at vv. 1-5, which probably was addressed to Judah, as an account of the sin of the northern kingdom, Israel, but only to make the point that Judah's sins were worse than those of Israel, a culpability made more acute by Judah's failure to pay any attention to or learn from the Lord's judgment on the northern kingdom.

The reference to Josiah may indicate that the sin of Judah involves the failure of the people to carry out the reforms instituted by that king. The critical verse of the indictment of Judah is v. 10, where one hears the thematic language of the prophet and an echo of the deuteronomic measuring rod of reform, the Shema. The prophet says that Judah did not "return" to the Lord "with all her heart," a clear reference to the call to love the Lord "with all your heart" in Deut 6:4 and frequently in Deuteronomy. But the "return" has been turned into a "lie," a term that Jeremiah regularly uses to describe all that is false in the community.[42] One may assume that the assertions made by the people in the preceding chapters (e.g., "I am innocent . . . I have not sinned" [2:35]), are examples of this "false" return.

3:12-13. The ambiguity of the "return" language in v. 1 is now broken open completely as the Lord issues a passionate call for faithless Israel to "return." As a message addressed to the north (v. 12), the imperative "Return!" may have geographical connotations. It may reflect the return from exile of citizens of the northern kingdom, or it may be a call to the north to be reunited with the southern kingdom, Judah, consistent with Josiah's efforts to achieve a political reunion of north and south. But in this context, the return language becomes a call for repentance. In the

40. Robert P. Carroll, *Jeremiah,* OTL (Philadelphia: Westminster, 1986) 143.
41. Holladay, *Jeremiah 1,* 58.

42. Robert P. Carroll, *Jeremiah,* OTL (Philadelphia: Westminster, 1986) 146.

context of Jeremiah, the words to the north are ultimately to be heard as a call to Judah as well. (In the next section, the same imperative opens the text, but this time it is not "Return, faithless Israel," but "Return, faithless *children*.") Words to the north are always addressed to the south as well. The whole people of Israel, in whatever form they may exist, stand under judgment and receive the call to repentance.

The connections of these verses to v. 5 and to Psalm 103 are obvious. The passage is about the will of God to forgive and to be compassionate. At the end of v. 5, it seems as if the claims of Psalm 103 may not be valid. Now in v. 12, it is clear that they are. The Lord is indeed merciful and does not remain angry forever. But the tension is real—between the grace of the God who will not follow the law but risks breaking it in compassion and the urgent call to repentance upon which the divine forgiveness rests. That theological tension is one that Scripture never seems to let go of. Nowhere is it played out more elaborately than in this chapter.

3:14-18. The will of the Lord to bring the people back is set forth in uncompromising terms. The tension just described is present again as the text opens with the call to "Return!" and immediately moves to an extended divine announcement of God's intention to bring the people back. These verses belong with that great visionary and eschatological text of Isa 2:2-4 (= Mic 4:1-5), for here is a forward look to "that time" (v. 17), to "those days" (vv. 16, 18) when Judah and Israel will be reunited as one faithful people, experiencing the promise of divine blessing (v. 16 echoes the blessing of Gen 1:28) and be given true and faithful "shepherds" (leaders). Jerusalem will be the center, to which will come not only the inhabitants of the northern and the southern kingdoms, but all the nations of the earth as well. And, in the language so prominent in chap. 2, "they," which here incorporates the nations as well as Israel and Judah, will no longer "go after" the stubbornness of their own hearts.

The political dream of Josiah to reunite Israel and Judah lies in the background, but it takes shape in this instance in an even larger vision of the community of nations united before the Lord in obedience to the Lord's way rather than in stubborn insistence upon their own way. The text is rooted in the politics of late pre-exilic and exilic

Judah, but it points the community forward to a hope it never relinquishes of a truly ecumenical and obedient community whose center is the Lord.[43]

3:19-20. The pathos of God continues to break out in these verses, the passionate desire of God to restore the people of Israel/Judah to the intimate relationship that is suggested by both the familial images (parent/child, v. 19; husband/wife, v. 20). Both images recall vv. 1-5. It is clear that the parent/spouse, the Lord, wishes to be called "My Father," as the people are reported doing in v. 5; but that has no meaning on the lips of a faithless people. The prophetic word continues to play on the *šûb* ("turn"/"return") language that so dominates chaps. 2 and 3. Here the verb is used negatively to depict what a faithful Israel would do—that is, "not turn" from following the Lord. Returning (repentance) to the Lord and not turning (obedience) from following the Lord are notes sounded again and again in chap. 3. The prophetic and divine insistence on such returning/not turning stands in continuing tension with the powerful impetus to grace and mercy that is so obviously in the heart of Israel's God.

3:21-25. We now begin to hear the weeping or crying of the people who have sinned (v. 25), followed by the words of confession and shame that have to this point been thoroughly missing (vv. 22*b*-25). The confession arises out of a further summons to "Return, faithless children" (v. 22*a*). This is the third such summons; each one has held out a promise from God if confession and repentance take place:

> I will not be angry for I am merciful. (v. 12)
> I am your master [i.e., your *ba'al*]. I will return you to Zion. (v. 14)
> I will heal your faithlessness. (v. 22*a*)

Some have seen this confession as ironic. It may be authentic, however. It is at least a way of saying quite specifically what is called for, putting words in the mouths of the exilic or post-exilic community what is called for:

---

43. The note that the ark of the covenant is no longer remembered in this context is a part of the move to see *all* Jerusalem as the throne of the Lord. But it may be a reflex of the eclipse of the ark in the late period and its ultimate loss. See William L. Holladay, *Jeremiah: A Fresh Reading* (New York: Pilgrim, 1990) 120-21.

Return to the Lord: "Behold we are going to come to you" (v. 22*b*).

Declaration of allegiance "for you are the Lord our God" (v. 22*b*).[44]

Confession of sin joined with confession of faith: "Truly the hills are a delusion" (v. 23*a*) and "Truly in the LORD our God is the salvation of Israel" (v. 23*b*).

Confession of sin continues as the one who had no shame now has it (vv. 24-25*a*).

The traditional and explicit confessional formula: "We have sinned against the Lord our God" (v. 25*b*).[45]

There is an important tie back to the beginning of this section in Jer 2:2, where the Lord remembers the "devotion of your youth." Now we hear the confession of the people that "from our youth" they have sinned against the Lord. This long recollection (two chapters) of disobedience and faithlessness, punctuated again and again with calls for repentance and return and promises of mercy, now comes to an end with a full confession of what the people were accused of from the beginning. The reader cannot know when these words were spoken, whether before the exile or long after exile and punishment. They are, however, what the Lord longs to hear. They define for the rest of the book the response that God wishes so passionately from this people. In their present context, the words of confession are only temporary. Prophetic denunciation and judgment will continue throughout much of the rest of Jeremiah. But the reader knows from these chapters what the Lord is after and the way the Lord works.

4:1-4. The literary unit comprising chaps. 2–3 is not quite over, however. While 4:3-4 begins to make the transition into the next section of the book as it pairs Judah and Jerusalem in a way that anticipates their pairing in 4:5, there is a final call to repentance at the beginning of chap. 4, which clearly continues the line of thought already set forth in chap. 3. (The NIV translation of v. 1*a* is probably correct.) The thematic verb *šûb* ("turn"/"return") is used in its double sense as the Lord tells the people of Judah that their "turning" should be a "returning" to the Lord. This section, which continues the line of thought that God is

open in mercy to a repentant people, also makes clear what such repentance involves. It involves a turning away from certain modes of conduct, identified in the vile abominations and the wandering aimlessly of their lives to this point (v. 1*b*).[46] It also includes turning toward a style of life that is marked by righteousness, justice, and truth-telling. Verse 2*a* alludes to the oath in the court, calling for what the commandment against taking the Lord's name in vain insists upon: the serious use of the Lord's name, especially in the courts. The integrity of the oath by the Lord's name is a final guard against the manipulation of the courts on behalf of unrighteousness and injustice. The way of repentance, therefore, is marked not only by faithfulness and steadfastness in devotion to the Lord but also by righteousness and justice in dealings with the neighbor. The consequence of such a reversal of this people's way would be enormous (v. 2*b*). It would mean the enactment of the ancient promise to Abraham: the blessing of the nations through the obedience of Abraham and his "seed." Verse 2 echoes the theology expressed in Gen 18:19, where the choosing of Abraham and his descendants manifests the way of justice and righteousness on earth. No less than the whole earth may benefit!

The call to repentance that has dominated in the preceding chapter has its final sounding in vv. 3-4, but in fresh imagery as the poetry of the prophet seeks once more to engender renewal and change. The familiar practices of farming are the first imaginative vehicle as the prophet tells the people it is time to turn the soil over and start afresh and not to involve themselves in the counterproductive, useless, and indeed dangerous soil of the other gods. Then the prophet invokes another familiar practice: circumcision. He speaks of it metaphorically in much the same way that one finds in Deuteronomy. The dedication and purification that may have been at the heart of the physical act of circumcision need to be manifest in the heart and will of this people. The physical and symbolic act means little without its reflection in the dedication of heart, mind, and soul to the

44. We hear in this declaration the confessional language of the Shema in Deut 6:4: "Hear, O Israel, the LORD is our God, the LORD alone."

45. See Patrick D. Miller, *They Cried to the Lord: The Form and Theology of Biblical Prayer* (Minneapolis: Fortress, 1994) 250-52.

46. The closest parallel to this usage of the verb נוד (*nûd,* "to wander") is Cain's wandering the earth in Gen 4:14, leading Holladay to suggest, in the light of the reference to the Abrahamic blessing in 4:2*b*, that "the implication here seems to be, 'If you stop being like Cain, you can begin to be like Abraham.' " See Holladay, *Jeremiah 1,* 127.

Lord.[47] Without this conversion, this turning of mind and will to the Lord, there is no averting the judgment that the evil deeds of God's people invites.

47. On this imagery and its use in the NT, see Patrick D. Miller, *Deuteronomy*, Interpretation (Louisville: John Knox, 1990) 125-27.

REFLECTIONS

1. The beginning of this section uncovers an important hermeneutical dimension at work in the composition of the book of Jeremiah. The second introduction, "Go and proclaim in the hearing of Jerusalem," serves to bring all the words that follow into an address to Jerusalem. Since some of those words seem to have been addressed to the northern kingdom or to inhabitants of that territory, the proclamation serves to do what all good interpretation does: take words addressed to one audience and reapply them to a new and different one. The interpretive enterprise that is assumed in the proclamation of Scripture is not peculiar to a later age. It is already going on within Scripture itself. Thus the contemporary interpreter takes some cues, at least methodologically, from the signals already in the text. A trajectory of interpretation is already under way, and the later proclamation joins with that trajectory, even as it recognizes the canonical character of its beginning part.

2. The language of "following after" or "going after," in its negative formulation with reference to going after Baal and the things that do not profit (e.g., 2:5, 8) and especially in its positive form at the beginning of Jeremiah's proclamation in 2:2, where it is set in divine speech as a definition of Israel's way, the original and root relationship between the people and their Lord, is the Old Testament vocabulary for what in New Testament terms is known as *discipleship*. When Jesus says, "If any want to become my followers [lit., "come after me"], let them deny themselves and take up their cross and follow me" (Mark 8:34), he draws directly on the Old Testament way of defining an exclusive relationship of allegiance and loyalty. Jesus' use of this language is a powerful movement of identity with the Lord of Israel, who, as the book of Jeremiah so roundly insists, is the only one after whom this people may go. Thus the way of discipleship is set in the many Old Testament texts that, like this one, seek to define a way of obedience and counteract tendencies to go after other things that seem to invite our loyalty.

3. Defining what "following after" means pervades these chapters, but it has its weightiest manifestation in the opening verses of chap. 2 and the covenant lawsuit that follows in 2:4-13. The presupposition of this prophetic word is the reality of a community that has lived long and fully under the care of the Lord. The particularities of God's protecting (2:6) and providential care (2:2*d*, 7) are spelled out in detail. The record is written in history that this people was delivered from oppression and suffering and led through dangers to new life *by this God*. That history also knows an acknowledgment of the obligations of the relationship: a community faithful to the Lord, disciples of this God who redeemed them.

The point of the prophetic word is that (1) the one who watched over, cared for, and protected the people has been forsaken for other allegiances and (2) the shift of allegiance has been an utterly fruitless enterprise. God's people are faulted, therefore, on two accounts: for their infidelity and faithlessness, and for their absurd and stupid actions that bring no good result. Theologically and practically, Israel has blown it.

There is both tacit and explicit indication that allegiance to a deity is related to the deity's provision and care, that the relationship involves getting something out of it. So in this text, the Lord spells out in detail what Israel has gotten out of the covenantal relationship. That, however, is apparently no longer sufficient, so the people have turned to other sources for the goods of life, for the provision of well-being. But there is a large difference. The original relationship was not a matter of the people's searching for the god or the power that could benefit them most. It was a people captured and kept by a loving and providing grace that drew them into relationship. What has happened now is that Israel has stepped outside that relationship of grace to look for the best bargain, the most productive power, the richest benefactor. They have assumed that the question of who ultimately directs our lives, shapes our destiny, and claims our allegiance is negotiable and exchangeable. It does not work that way. Those who have been led in the right way and sustained by the true Lord cannot shift and get someone else to do that.

The issue is not a dead one. Theological arguments continue in our own time about whether Christian faith needs a more polytheistic framework, as if we could in fact exchange the God who has made us for some other. The argument has been made that things would make more sense and work better with a multiplicity of centers of value, of gods who would give variety to our life and provide for us in different ways. What this Jeremiah text says is that discipleship is not whimsical. We cannot casually follow after one Lord and then decide to go after another.

The other dimension here is the *fruitlessness* of thinking that there is some other power at work that can make things better for us. There is no other power. What we may assume can sustain us is in fact a poof of air, nothing, and can profit us not at all. That language, of course, indicates that the kinds of actions described here, in effect, turn the matter of allegiance to the Lord of life and of the universe into a kind of game, searching for the most productive power to fatten our wallets, increase our crops and other investments, provide us better houses, and the like. So this text addresses a kingdom that has gone after other lords, and it also addresses a later people who do the same thing. What we have is all we need and is better than any other possibility. Common sense tells us that to turn elsewhere is to grasp at thin air or to gasp thin air. It is nothing but air, and we will suffocate in the process. If common sense does not make that clear, the prophetic word spells it out in detail.

4. The reference to "living water" and "cracked cisterns" (2:13) takes us into a sphere of rich biblical imagery that belongs always to the proclamation of this text. That is so not least of all because the imagery is taken up directly by Jesus in his conversation with the woman at the well (John 4:7-15) in which he revealed that the source of living water is himself. Here again there is an explicit identification of Jesus with the God who delivered Israel. The metaphor is quite direct. The Lord is called a "fountain of living water," and in John 4:13-14, Jesus is identified as the source of living water, the access to the fresh and vital water that is the Lord's sustaining presence. The Johannine text is even more explicit, however. The water that Jesus gives is "a spring of water gushing up to eternal life" (John 4:14). The living water gives life.

5. The picture of Israel's early history set forth by the Lord at the beginning of chap. 2 is an example of the Lord's "selective memory" and how it seems to work in favor of the people. It is selective in the direction of grace, of setting the people in a better light than the tradition in fact sets them. The wilderness narratives of the Pentateuch are full of stories of the faithlessness of the people and of the Lord's anger toward them. But, like a parent, God has a predisposition to remember the good.

In this case, the imagery is not parental but marital. Whether such selective memory is typical of marriage relationships, however, is beside the point. The text is describing a relationship, not modeling one. We cannot simply do a one-to-one correlation between the imagery and all of our experiences of marriage, while we do, in fact, hear and receive the imagery in the light of familiarity with that institution.

6. Reference to the prominent marital imagery of this text raises the issue of the depiction of Israel as the whoring wife threatened with punishment by her husband, the Lord. Such imagery is not peculiar to Jeremiah. We encounter it in Hosea, Ezekiel, and elsewhere. Many sit very uncomfortably before such couching of the divine/human relationship in gender terms reflecting a cultural ethos in which women were in a significantly subordinate relationship to their husbands, subject in various ways to their control and dominance. The cultural disgust with illicit female promiscuity was a powerful vehicle for the word of Jeremiah. The marital imagery allows for the depth of emotion and passion that belongs to the Lord's relationship with this people. It also provides an image that fully uncovers the ruling, if loving, power of the Lord over this people.

It is difficult, however, for a contemporary audience to encounter such imagery without some discomfort, at the least, and for many real anger and rejection. It is a reflection of a cultural situation in which women experienced various kinds of oppression precisely because of the relationship implied in Jeremiah's use of marital imagery. The text comes from a male perspective and tends to undergird abusive punishment of wives by their husbands while easily depicting women/wives as prone to betrayal and promiscuity. Thus any interpretation of these texts has to listen and subvert at the same time, has to learn from them something of what is expected in the covenantal relationship between the Lord and those who would be the Lord's people while recognizing that the covenant of marriage that Christian theology articulates resists such subordination and power domination. Issues of loyalty, devotion, passionate love, and anger at betrayal properly sound as the imagery of marriage and infidelity comes into play. But there can be no transference from this depiction to human relationships. It is difficult to continue to play with the biblical imagery. The proper assumptions we make about the equality of husband and wife, the resistance we have to abusive relationships as well as to claims of dominance and rule by husbands, makes it virtually impossible for us to carry forward the biblical imagery into contemporary theological construction. It is genuinely dangerous. The transcendent relationship between God and humanity is not explicable in such detailed way via the man-woman relationship, whether in or out of marriage. So our proclamation must seek to comprehend the biblical text critically, in every sense of that word.

JEREMIAH 4:5–6:30, SIN AND JUDGMENT

OVERVIEW

These chapters represent as well as any the gist of Jeremiah's prophecy. They mix indictment and denunciation of the people's sins—including the particular sins of the leadership—with announcement of judgment that at many points seems to be right at their doorstep. The particular historical locus of the oracles in these chapters is not easy to discern. The vivid description of siege elements and the laying waste of the land (4:19-26) suggests that the devastation prophesied has in fact been experienced. But the oracles as a whole are anticipatory in form and character. Whatever the particular moment of Jeremiah's proclamation—or of editorial addition—the oracles point to the future and announce a judgment that is imminent. The prophet warns of a foe from the north who is close at hand and will soon bring destruction (cf. 1:15). The identity of that foe has been the subject of

much discussion. While the reference to a "foe from the north" may have some mythological background and, indeed, some intentional vagueness reflecting the north as the typical source of attack, in the present context of the book, that foe has clearly come to be understood as the Babylonians, who twice besieged Jerusalem, conquering Judah and exiling leaders and citizens.[48]

The first set of oracles (4:5-31) announces the imminent disaster and destruction. Chapter 5 then turns the prophetic lens upon the people to lay out in some detail what has been going on that merits such devastating attack by a foreign power. Whatever may have been the political reasons con-

48. For discussion of the foe from the north and the various views about this term, see William L. Holladay, *Jeremiah 1: A Commentary on the Book of the Prophet Jeremiah Chapters 1–25,* Hermeneia (Philadelphia: Fortress, 1986) 42-43; Ronald Clements, *Jeremiah,* Interpretation (Atlanta: John Knox, 1988) 20-21.

tributing to the Babylonian move against Judah, this chapter makes clear that the attack is an act of divine judgment for sins that are both social and spiritual, enumerated at length. Whereas the focus of 2:1–4:4 was on the apostasy and idolatry of the people, in this section the sins that are lifted up as the basis for judgment are primarily social injus-

tices and the failure and corruption of the religious and political leaders of the community. In chap. 6, the prophet returns to the themes of chap. 4, warning the people of the disaster at hand, while here and there continuing to remind them of the justice of the judgment they are about to endure.

Jeremiah 4:5-31, Disaster Overtakes Disaster

NIV

5"Announce in Judah and proclaim in Jerusalem
    and say:
    'Sound the trumpet throughout the land!'
Cry aloud and say:
    'Gather together!
    Let us flee to the fortified cities!'
6Raise the signal to go to Zion!
    Flee for safety without delay!
For I am bringing disaster from the north,
    even terrible destruction."

7A lion has come out of his lair;
    a destroyer of nations has set out.
He has left his place
    to lay waste your land.
Your towns will lie in ruins
    without inhabitant.
8So put on sackcloth,
    lament and wail,
for the fierce anger of the LORD
    has not turned away from us.

9"In that day," declares the LORD,
    "the king and the officials will lose heart,
the priests will be horrified,
    and the prophets will be appalled."
10Then I said, "Ah, Sovereign LORD, how completely you have deceived this people and Jerusalem by saying, 'You will have peace,' when the sword is at our throats."

11At that time this people and Jerusalem will be told, "A scorching wind from the barren heights in the desert blows toward my people, but not to winnow or cleanse; 12a wind too strong for that comes from me.a Now I pronounce my judgments against them."

13Look! He advances like the clouds,

a12 Or comes at my command

NRSV

5Declare in Judah, and proclaim in Jerusalem,
and say:
    Blow the trumpet through the land;
        shout alouda and say,
    "Gather together, and let us go
        into the fortified cities!"
6 Raise a standard toward Zion,
    flee for safety, do not delay,
for I am bringing evil from the north,
    and a great destruction.
7 A lion has gone up from its thicket,
    a destroyer of nations has set out;
    he has gone out from his place
to make your land a waste;
    your cities will be ruins
    without inhabitant.
8 Because of this put on sackcloth,
    lament and wail:
    "The fierce anger of the LORD
        has not turned away from us."

9On that day, says the LORD, courage shall fail the king and the officials; the priests shall be appalled and the prophets astounded. 10Then I said, "Ah, Lord GOD, how utterly you have deceived this people and Jerusalem, saying, 'It shall be well with you,' even while the sword is at the throat!"

11At that time it will be said to this people and to Jerusalem: A hot wind comes from me out of the bare heightsb in the desert toward my poor people, not to winnow or cleanse— 12a wind too strong for that. Now it is I who speak in judgment against them.
13 Look! He comes up like clouds,

aOr shout, take your weapons. Heb shout, fill (your hand)   bOr the trails

NIV

his chariots come like a whirlwind,
his horses are swifter than eagles.
  Woe to us! We are ruined!
¹⁴O Jerusalem, wash the evil from your heart
    and be saved.
  How long will you harbor wicked thoughts?
¹⁵A voice is announcing from Dan,
  proclaiming disaster from the hills of
    Ephraim.
¹⁶"Tell this to the nations,
  proclaim it to Jerusalem:
'A besieging army is coming from a distant
    land,
  raising a war cry against the cities of Judah.
¹⁷They surround her like men guarding a field,
  because she has rebelled against me,' "
                        declares the LORD.
¹⁸"Your own conduct and actions
  have brought this upon you.
This is your punishment.
  How bitter it is!
  How it pierces to the heart!"

¹⁹Oh, my anguish, my anguish!
  I writhe in pain.
Oh, the agony of my heart!
  My heart pounds within me,
  I cannot keep silent.
For I have heard the sound of the trumpet;
  I have heard the battle cry.
²⁰Disaster follows disaster;
  the whole land lies in ruins.
In an instant my tents are destroyed,
  my shelter in a moment.
²¹How long must I see the battle standard
  and hear the sound of the trumpet?

²²"My people are fools;
  they do not know me.
They are senseless children;
  they have no understanding.
They are skilled in doing evil;
  they know not how to do good."

²³I looked at the earth,
  and it was formless and empty;
and at the heavens,
  and their light was gone.
²⁴I looked at the mountains,

NRSV

his chariots like the whirlwind;
his horses are swifter than eagles—
  woe to us, for we are ruined!
¹⁴ O Jerusalem, wash your heart clean of
    wickedness
  so that you may be saved.
How long shall your evil schemes
  lodge within you?
¹⁵ For a voice declares from Dan
  and proclaims disaster from Mount
    Ephraim.
¹⁶ Tell the nations, "Here they are!"
  Proclaim against Jerusalem,
"Besiegers come from a distant land;
  they shout against the cities of Judah.
¹⁷ They have closed in around her like watchers
    of a field,
  because she has rebelled against me,
                        says the LORD.
¹⁸ Your ways and your doings
  have brought this upon you.
This is your doom; how bitter it is!
  It has reached your very heart."

¹⁹ My anguish, my anguish! I writhe in pain!
  Oh, the walls of my heart!
My heart is beating wildly;
  I cannot keep silent;
for I[a] hear the sound of the trumpet,
  the alarm of war.
²⁰ Disaster overtakes disaster,
  the whole land is laid waste.
Suddenly my tents are destroyed,
  my curtains in a moment.
²¹ How long must I see the standard,
  and hear the sound of the trumpet?
²² "For my people are foolish,
  they do not know me;
they are stupid children,
  they have no understanding.
They are skilled in doing evil,
  but do not know how to do good."

²³ I looked on the earth, and lo, it was waste
    and void;
  and to the heavens, and they had no light.
²⁴ I looked on the mountains, and lo, they were
    quaking,

[a]Another reading is *for you, O my soul,*

NIV

and they were quaking;
all the hills were swaying.
[25] I looked, and there were no people;
every bird in the sky had flown away.
[26] I looked, and the fruitful land was a desert;
all its towns lay in ruins
before the LORD, before his fierce anger.

[27] This is what the LORD says:

"The whole land will be ruined,
though I will not destroy it completely.
[28] Therefore the earth will mourn
and the heavens above grow dark,
because I have spoken and will not relent,
I have decided and will not turn back."

[29] At the sound of horsemen and archers
every town takes to flight.
Some go into the thickets;
some climb up among the rocks.
All the towns are deserted;
no one lives in them.

[30] What are you doing, O devastated one?
Why dress yourself in scarlet
and put on jewels of gold?
Why shade your eyes with paint?
You adorn yourself in vain.
Your lovers despise you;
they seek your life.

[31] I hear a cry as of a woman in labor,
a groan as of one bearing her first child—
the cry of the Daughter of Zion gasping for
breath,
stretching out her hands and saying,
"Alas! I am fainting;
my life is given over to murderers."

NRSV

and all the hills moved to and fro.
[25] I looked, and lo, there was no one at all,
and all the birds of the air had fled.
[26] I looked, and lo, the fruitful land was a desert,
and all its cities were laid in ruins
before the LORD, before his fierce anger.

[27] For thus says the LORD: The whole land shall
be a desolation; yet I will not make a full end.
[28] Because of this the earth shall mourn,
and the heavens above grow black;
for I have spoken, I have purposed;
I have not relented nor will I turn back.

[29] At the noise of horseman and archer
every town takes to flight;
they enter thickets; they climb among rocks;
all the towns are forsaken,
and no one lives in them.
[30] And you, O desolate one,
what do you mean that you dress in crimson,
that you deck yourself with ornaments of
gold,
that you enlarge your eyes with paint?
In vain you beautify yourself.
Your lovers despise you;
they seek your life.
[31] For I heard a cry as of a woman in labor,
anguish as of one bringing forth her first
child,
the cry of daughter Zion gasping for breath,
stretching out her hands,
"Woe is me! I am fainting before killers!"

COMMENTARY

4:5-8. These verses create a sharp and abrupt shift from the preceding text. Whereas the possibility of repentance is set forth and called for in chap. 3 and 4:1-4, now the prophetic voice shouts out calls to flee for safety from the enemy that is at hand. The final line of 4:4 forms the bridge into these verses. The reader assumes that the change of heart and way has not happened and so the wrath of God goes forth because of the evil doings of the people. The prophet uses the summons to flee, a typical form of prophetic speech that occurs especially in the oracles against the nations (e.g., 48:6-8, 28; 49:2; 50:8-10; 51:6, 45); but here it is directed to Judah and Jerusalem (cf. 6:1). The prophet's "trumpet call" to the people is intended to stir them up, to shock them into awareness of the terrible danger into which their conduct is leading them. Complacent in Zion, they assume it is always secure, a false security the prophet attacks directly in chap. 7. Here the prophet says it is a time for hiding and lamentation. There is no security in this situation.

4:9-10. The Lord anticipates the reaction of the leaders. They display both a loss of courage—"the heart perishes," according to the Hebrew—and an incredulous astonishment. The fainthearted-ness of the political leaders is understandable in the face of such a devastating military force. The astonishment of the religious leaders is understandable in the light of the prayer of Jeremiah that follows (v. 10). He offers a complaint prayer, in which we hear the first of several complaints of Jeremiah that he and the people have been deceived by the Lord. Jeremiah contends that the Lord has allowed the false prophets to say that everything is all right, to say repeatedly, "Peace, peace," when war is at hand (6:14). Jeremiah's words, "It shall be well with you," are actually a quotation of these prophets (23:17). The consistent problem with "the prophets" in the book of Jeremiah is this assurance of security to the people in the face of terrible danger. In this situation, Jeremiah begins the dialogue of complaint against God that will erupt again and again; indeed, this same complaint appears in 14:13. That the complaint has some sting is suggested by the repeated insistence on the part of the deity that these prophets do speak falsely (6:14; 14:14-16) and are not the Lord's representatives (23:16-22). This argument between Jeremiah and the Lord is reminiscent of the scene in 1 Kings 22, where the Lord sends a lying spirit to put a message of false hope in the mouths of the prophets in order to bring about the downfall of King Ahab. However, there is a major difference between 1 Kings 22 and Jeremiah. The false words of the prophets in Jeremiah's time are their own and are simply a reflex of the people's assumption that all will be well in the Lord's city and the Lord's place. It is that fundamental misreading of history and Israel's own theology that Jeremiah attacks in his great temple sermon (chap. 7).

4:11-18. The terrible and furious onset of an enemy invasion is expressed again in powerful poetic images centering around the force of a mighty wind that sweeps everything before it. Different voices are heard in these verses, conveying something of the confusion evoked by this terrible event—the people's lament (v. 13*b*), the

prophet's call for repentance (vv. 14-15), and the shouts of the sentries in the north, bracketed on either side by the Lord's announcement of judgment (vv. 11-12, 16-18). The panicked lament of the people seems to open up once more the possibility of repentance. But that is deceptive. As the prophecy of Jeremiah goes on, the possibility of turning back on the part of the people seems so remote that this call for repentance, very much like the imperatives of Amos 5, is a call for a conduct that is now too late. Still it identifies a primary need: repentance in order to be saved. The sound of the coming judgment, heard on either side of the call for repentance, suggests that "v. 14 occupies a position of sad isolation in a passage which is laden with doom."[49] This is not the last time we will hear the call for repentance in the book of Jeremiah. But in the chapters that follow, words about repentance will be primarily about the refusal of the people to "turn" or repent (5:3; 8:5-6; 9:6 LXX).

The undefined character of the threat invites the hearer to focus less on historical and political identities and facts than on the real danger and the reasons for it. The oracles of Jeremiah are more interested in the specifics of the reasons than the specifics of the danger. Here we are simply given the fundamental theological interpretation of the events in Judah's history. They are the Lord's doing, whatever may be the complexity of the affairs of people and nations. The disastrous turn of affairs that is announced here is not finally due to any kind of foreign policy or internal Judean politics. Throughout these verses, we hear that the deeper reality in all these events is the outcome of wicked schemes and rebellion against the Lord. There is an ambiguity in the words of the Lord in v. 18 that is worth noting. When the Lord says, "Your own conduct and actions have brought this upon you," the text may announce a retribution that the Lord will bring upon the people because of their conduct. But the statement can also indicate a kind of direct connection between the conduct and its consequences, that the way of living this people have engaged in brings about events that ultimately do them in. Even in this reading, however, there is no doubt that the connection between the conduct and its consequence is under

---

49. W. McKane, *A Critical and Exegetical Commentary on Jeremiah*, ICC (Edinburgh: T. & T. Clark, 1986) 99.

the direction of the Lord. Jeremiah makes it clear again and again that what is happening is not simply consequence. It is also punishment. As both consequence and punishment, the fate of this people testifies to a moral order at the core of the Lord's rule.

4:19-22. The anguish of the prophet is intense as he sees the impending doom. The sounds of war are almost in his tent. It is as if somebody were in a house with bombs falling all around. That prophetic anguish shades into divine frustration at the people's wickedness (v. 22). The implications of this language of angry frustration are important. It reflects the way in which the perspective of wisdom as we encounter it in the OT identifies wickedness with foolishness. The way this people are acting is wrong. It is also stupid (v. 22; cf. 5:21). The wise person pays attention to consequences and determines conduct in relation to that. Wisdom is fundamentally the skill of making life work. The only skill evident in this community is a perverse one. Jeremiah's language is ironic, even sarcastic. The people and their leaders are "wise" or "skilled" only in wickedness, which by definition is the very opposite of wisdom. In a further wordplay, the reader hears a resonance between the opening words of the divine speech—"they do not know me"—and the closing words—"they do not know how to do good." The connection is critical for Jeremiah. One defines the other. The proper knowledge of God is where good is carried out, where justice is maintained and the welfare of the community is sought even for the weakest and lowest members. This equation between knowing God, both in the sense of true acknowledgment of the Lord and living in relation to God, and doing the right and the good is a powerful prophetic theme. It is enunciated by Hosea (Hos 4:1-9; 6:6) and Amos (Amos 5:4-5, 14-15) and made a criterion for true kingship in the oracles of Jeremiah (22:15-16). The next chapter takes up this language and spells out the stupidity and "perverse" skill that does not know God or good.

4:23-28. The frantic picture of an army invading and devastating the land moves to another plane. The prophet has a vision of the destruction that is cosmic in scope. In language that echoes Genesis 1–2 (waste and void, Gen 1:2; light, Gen 1:3; no one [האדם *hā'ādām*], Genesis 2), the prophet reports a vision of desolation that is a virtual dismantling of

creation, a return to chaos. The mythic images of creation time and end time become a vehicle for picturing the judgment of the Lord. The nothingness that remains will be like the pre-creation state. The references to desert and fruitful land (v. 26), however, place this vision within the context of Israel's history, for the language of desert and fruitful land echoes the story of the Lord's care of Israel in its youth in chap. 2, when the Lord guided the people through the desert or wilderness (2:2, 6) and brought them into a plentiful or fruitful land (2:7). The devastation of the enemy from the north that seems to transform creation back into chaos is no generalized, abstract picture. It offers a clue to the intensity of the Lord's moral outrage at the behavior of this people, who will find their cities in ruins and their fruitful land turned back into wilderness. So creation and divine providence are intertwined with obedience. Covenant and creation are so connected that the dissolution of the one threatens the other (cf. 5:22).

The seriousness and finality of this judgment are indicated not only in its being couched as the undoing of creation but also in the seriousness of the Lord's will, an intention that cannot be changed (v. 28*b*). In the early story of Israel, when the people were faced with the divine wrath and imminent destruction, the intercession of a figure such as Moses (Exod 32:11-14) or Amos (Amos 7:1-6) brought about a divine relenting, a change of mind on God's part. In the book of Jeremiah, despite the calls to repentance, the breach of covenant is so serious, that God will not even allow intercession (7:16; 11:14; 14:11-12; 15:1).

The divine statement in v. 27 is an enigma. What does it mean that the Lord will not make a full end? One should not put too much weight on this word. Some would emend it to make it an emphatic statement of full destruction. Others would see here a later gloss in the light of what actually happened. Some would understand it to say that the devastation was not fully completed. The simplest reading is what we find in the NIV and the NRSV, an indication that the destruction is not total. Since this claim stands in such tension with what precedes and follows, we may need to acknowledge the possibility that the sentence is a later addition, drawn from its presence elsewhere (e.g., 5:10, 18). (The tendency of Jeremiah's oracles to repeat themes and language could be an argument for its originality.) However the text arose, we cannot simply pass by what is there.

The phrase "not a full end" is a signal, whether from Jeremiah's time or later, that despite the devastating, cataclysmic, and unavoidable judgment, it will not be the final end. Judah cannot escape the destruction, but there is a kind of promissory note about the future, a self-imposed caveat by the Lord. Perhaps, this is a more oblique indication of what is spelled out in more detail in chap. 32 when the prophet is ordered to buy a field in the land that is about to be destroyed and to do so because houses and fields will be bought again in the land.

4:29-31. This powerful picture of overwhelming destruction and desolation at the hands of an invading foe comes to an end when Zion is addressed. Jerusalem is personified here to represent the people. The passage begins in astonishment at the conduct of Jerusalem and its citizens. In the face of such a terrible prophecy as Jeremiah has brought forth, one would expect the people to flee for safety, as they have been urged to do in the preceding oracles. Instead "she" has carried on as before, primping and dolling up for her lovers, decking herself out for another fling (note that the imagery of the prostitute appears once more). In this case, as previously, the lovers seem to be foreign powers. Yet they arrive not to help but to rape and to kill. In the final verse, the imminent fate of the people is given a terrible poignancy as the anguish expressed by the prophet (v. 19) is now voiced by "daughter Zion" as a pregnant mother, her pleading hands stretched out to her rapist killers. The picture is a terrible one, reflective of the practices of war then and now.[50] The prophet seeks once again to shock the people out of their present ways as he employs imagery that is full of violent contrast and sarcasm but ends in wrenching pathos and anguish. (See Reflections at 6:1-30.)

---

50. Brueggemann says about Jeremiah here that "the prophet presses to find a metaphor raw enough to carry the truth." See W. Brueggemann, *A Commentary on Jeremiah: Exile and Homecoming* (Grand Rapids: Eerdmans, 1998) 62.

Jeremiah 5:1-31, Deeds of Wickedness

5 "Go up and down the streets of Jerusalem,
     look around and consider,
search through her squares.
If you can find but one person
     who deals honestly and seeks the truth,
     I will forgive this city.
[2]Although they say, 'As surely as the LORD
          lives,'
     still they are swearing falsely."

[3]O LORD, do not your eyes look for truth?
     You struck them, but they felt no pain;
     you crushed them, but they refused correction.
They made their faces harder than stone
     and refused to repent.
[4]I thought, "These are only the poor;
     they are foolish,
for they do not know the way of the LORD,
     the requirements of their God.
[5]So I will go to the leaders
     and speak to them;

5 Run to and fro through the streets of
          Jerusalem,
     look around and take note!
Search its squares and see
     if you can find one person
who acts justly
     and seeks truth—
so that I may pardon Jerusalem.[a]
[2] Although they say, "As the LORD lives,"
     yet they swear falsely.
[3] O LORD, do your eyes not look for truth?
You have struck them,
     but they felt no anguish;
you have consumed them,
     but they refused to take correction.
They have made their faces harder than rock;
     they have refused to turn back.

[4] Then I said, "These are only the poor,
     they have no sense;

[a]Heb *it*

NIV

surely they know the way of the LORD,
    the requirements of their God."
But with one accord they too had broken off
        the yoke
    and torn off the bonds.
⁶Therefore a lion from the forest will attack them,
    a wolf from the desert will ravage them,
    a leopard will lie in wait near their towns
    to tear to pieces any who venture out,
for their rebellion is great
    and their backslidings many.

⁷"Why should I forgive you?
    Your children have forsaken me
    and sworn by gods that are not gods.
I supplied all their needs,
    yet they committed adultery
    and thronged to the houses of prostitutes.
⁸They are well-fed, lusty stallions,
    each neighing for another man's wife.
⁹Should I not punish them for this?"
    declares the LORD.
    "Should I not avenge myself
    on such a nation as this?

¹⁰"Go through her vineyards and ravage them,
    but do not destroy them completely.
Strip off her branches,
    for these people do not belong to the LORD.
¹¹The house of Israel and the house of Judah
    have been utterly unfaithful to me,"
        declares the LORD.

¹²They have lied about the LORD;
    they said, "He will do nothing!
No harm will come to us;
    we will never see sword or famine.
¹³The prophets are but wind
    and the word is not in them;
    so let what they say be done to them."

¹⁴Therefore this is what the LORD God
Almighty says:

    "Because the people have spoken these words,
    I will make my words in your mouth a fire
    and these people the wood it consumes.
¹⁵O house of Israel," declares the LORD,
    "I am bringing a distant nation against you—
an ancient and enduring nation,

NRSV

for they do not know the way of the LORD,
    the law of their God.
⁵ Let me go to the rich[a]
    and speak to them;
surely they know the way of the LORD,
    the law of their God."
But they all alike had broken the yoke,
    they had burst the bonds.

⁶ Therefore a lion from the forest shall kill
        them,
    a wolf from the desert shall destroy them.
A leopard is watching against their cities;
    everyone who goes out of them shall be
        torn in pieces—
because their transgressions are many,
    their apostasies are great.

⁷ How can I pardon you?
    Your children have forsaken me,
    and have sworn by those who are no gods.
When I fed them to the full,
    they committed adultery
    and trooped to the houses of prostitutes.
⁸ They were well-fed lusty stallions,
    each neighing for his neighbor's wife.
⁹ Shall I not punish them for these things?
        says the LORD;
    and shall I not bring retribution
    on a nation such as this?

¹⁰ Go up through her vine-rows and destroy,
    but do not make a full end;
strip away her branches,
    for they are not the LORD's.
¹¹ For the house of Israel and the house of Judah
    have been utterly faithless to me,
        says the LORD.
¹² They have spoken falsely of the LORD,
    and have said, "He will do nothing.
No evil will come upon us,
    and we shall not see sword or famine."
¹³ The prophets are nothing but wind,
    for the word is not in them.
Thus shall it be done to them!

¹⁴ Therefore thus says the LORD, the God of
        hosts:

[a]Or the great

NIV

a people whose language you do not know,
    whose speech you do not understand.
¹⁶ Their quivers are like an open grave;
    all of them are mighty warriors.
¹⁷ They will devour your harvests and food,
    devour your sons and daughters;
  they will devour your flocks and herds,
    devour your vines and fig trees.
  With the sword they will destroy
    the fortified cities in which you trust.

¹⁸"Yet even in those days," declares the LORD, "I will not destroy you completely. ¹⁹And when the people ask, 'Why has the LORD our God done all this to us?' you will tell them, 'As you have forsaken me and served foreign gods in your own land, so now you will serve foreigners in a land not your own.'

²⁰ "Announce this to the house of Jacob
    and proclaim it in Judah:
²¹ Hear this, you foolish and senseless people,
    who have eyes but do not see,
    who have ears but do not hear:
²² Should you not fear me?" declares the LORD.
    "Should you not tremble in my presence?
  I made the sand a boundary for the sea,
    an everlasting barrier it cannot cross.
  The waves may roll, but they cannot prevail;
    they may roar, but they cannot cross it.
²³ But these people have stubborn and rebellious
        hearts;
    they have turned aside and gone away.
²⁴ They do not say to themselves,
    'Let us fear the LORD our God,
  who gives autumn and spring rains in season,
    who assures us of the regular weeks of
        harvest.'
²⁵ Your wrongdoings have kept these away;
    your sins have deprived you of good.

²⁶ "Among my people are wicked men
    who lie in wait like men who snare birds
    and like those who set traps to catch men.
²⁷ Like cages full of birds,
    their houses are full of deceit;
  they have become rich and powerful
²⁸   and have grown fat and sleek.
  Their evil deeds have no limit;

NRSV

Because they[a] have spoken this word,
  I am now making my words in your mouth a
        fire,
    and this people wood, and the fire shall
        devour them.
¹⁵ I am going to bring upon you
    a nation from far away, O house of Israel,
                says the LORD.
  It is an enduring nation,
    it is an ancient nation,
  a nation whose language you do not know,
    nor can you understand what they say.
¹⁶ Their quiver is like an open tomb;
    all of them are mighty warriors.
¹⁷ They shall eat up your harvest and your food;
    they shall eat up your sons and your
        daughters;
  they shall eat up your flocks and your herds;
    they shall eat up your vines and your fig
        trees;
  they shall destroy with the sword
    your fortified cities in which you trust.

¹⁸But even in those days, says the LORD, I will not make a full end of you. ¹⁹And when your people say, "Why has the LORD our God done all these things to us?" you shall say to them, "As you have forsaken me and served foreign gods in your land, so you shall serve strangers in a land that is not yours."

²⁰ Declare this in the house of Jacob,
    proclaim it in Judah:
²¹ Hear this, O foolish and senseless people,
    who have eyes, but do not see,
    who have ears, but do not hear.
²² Do you not fear me? says the LORD;
    Do you not tremble before me?
  I placed the sand as a boundary for the sea,
    a perpetual barrier that it cannot pass;
  though the waves toss, they cannot prevail,
    though they roar, they cannot pass over it.
²³ But this people has a stubborn and rebellious
        heart;
    they have turned aside and gone away.
²⁴ They do not say in their hearts,
    "Let us fear the LORD our God,

^aHeb you

NIV

they do not plead the case of the fatherless
to win it,
they do not defend the rights of the poor.
²⁹ Should I not punish them for this?"
declares the LORD.
"Should I not avenge myself
on such a nation as this?

³⁰ "A horrible and shocking thing
has happened in the land:
³¹ The prophets prophesy lies,
the priests rule by their own authority,
and my people love it this way.
But what will you do in the end?

NRSV

who gives the rain in its season,
the autumn rain and the spring rain,
and keeps for us
the weeks appointed for the harvest."
²⁵ Your iniquities have turned these away,
and your sins have deprived you of good.
²⁶ For scoundrels are found among my people;
they take over the goods of others.
Like fowlers they set a trap;ᵃ
they catch human beings.
²⁷ Like a cage full of birds,
their houses are full of treachery;
therefore they have become great and rich,
²⁸   they have grown fat and sleek.
They know no limits in deeds of wickedness;
they do not judge with justice
the cause of the orphan, to make it prosper,
and they do not defend the rights of the
needy.
²⁹ Shall I not punish them for these things?
says the LORD,
and shall I not bring retribution
on a nation such as this?

³⁰ An appalling and horrible thing
has happened in the land:
³¹ the prophets prophesy falsely,
and the priests rule as the prophets direct;ᵇ
my people love to have it so,
but what will you do when the end comes?

ᵃMeaning of Heb uncertain   ᵇOr *rule by their own authority*

COMMENTARY

5:1-9. Like Diogenes with his lantern searching for a single honest man, the Lord calls for an extensive investigation throughout Jerusalem to see if there is anybody in that great city, and by inference in the whole land, who demonstrates the justice and faithfulness that both reflect the God who rules this people and lie at the heart of the covenant relationship between God and Israel (see Deut 32:4, where the same terms, "justice" [משפט *mišpāṭ*] and "faithfulness" [אמונה *'ĕmûnâ*] are used to describe the character of the Lord). It is like the call in 2:10 to send to the far lands to see if any people have changed their gods as have this people. This same mode of speech, a command to initiate a careful search and investigation, identifies two dimensions of the people's sin: apostasy and the absence of justice and integrity in human relations. Nothing is more characteristic of Jeremiah's prophecy than the insistence on these two spheres of Judah's sin. While all sorts of theological interpretations of this sin are given, such as rebellion against God (e.g., 4:17), the actuality of that rebellion and disobedience is in the turning to other sources of ultimate loyalty and the failure to maintain justice, in the larger sense of that term—that is, fairness toward the neighbor and oppression of none. This chapter focuses particularly on this latter failing. Verse 2 puts particular weight on the issue of integrity, offering the concrete example of false oaths. The prophet indicts disobedience of the commandment against misuse or empty use of the Lord's name. Taking oaths by the Lord's name and then telling lies is both a sin against the one whose name has been invoked as the grounding of the oath and an ultimate breakdown of the system of justice. If, inside the courtroom and out, one may not depend on truthfulness, there is no way to ensure justice and integrity in any human interactions. If the court is full of lies, a society faces chaos. It is no wonder that Jeremiah again and again sounds like the character Big Daddy, striding across the stage in Tennessee Williams's play *Cat On a Hot Tin Roof,* shouting, "Mendacity, mendacity, mendacity." The lie is a way of life, and when the lies are told in God's name, the sin is doubly wrong.

In this opening verse, we hear something akin to the dialogue between the Lord and Abraham over the fate of Sodom and Gomorrah (Genesis 18) in the notion of the innocent few who secure forgiveness and mercy for the sinful many. The point is not simply to call attention in exaggerated fashion to the extent of the people's wickedness but to find an openness, if at all possible, for God to forgive and pardon. In Genesis 18, Abraham keeps pushing the Lord to leave the door open even if there are only ten innocent people in Sodom and Gomorrah. In Jeremiah, we see where the Genesis conversation is really headed. If there is one doer of good, even a single person manifesting integrity and fidelity in human relationships, that is enough to evoke the Lord's pardon and mercy. The judgment about which Jeremiah speaks is not really an equitable justice. It is always open to the divine inclination to deliver and to redeem. With all the clear and inescapable words of judgment in the first part of Jeremiah, it is hedged all about with the possibility of stopping the judgment and offering forgiveness. But the picture here is bleak (cf. Ps 14:1-3*d*).[51]

There are some further clues about what is going on in God's punishment and judgment in v. 3. The Lord's wrath has two aims:

(1) Divine judgment is intended to elicit anguish and remorse. Verse 22 reinforces this as fear before the Lord, paralleled by anguish or trembling before the Lord. To see what is desired, we may turn back to 4:19-21, where the prophet experiences anguish in the face of the enemy's destructive appearance. The problem is that the prophet is the only one who responds in anguish before the enemy.

(2) Divine judgment can result in a sinful people's learning to act differently. It has a disciplining function; it is the Lord's act to teach the people. This is terminology from the realm of wisdom. But the wisdom and skill of this people are only in doing wrong (4:22). They have not learned from any experiences of the Lord's hand upon them. In a favorite expression of Jeremiah's, the people have "refused to take correction" (2:30; 7:28; 17:23; 32:33; 35:13). They have learned nothing. Even when punished—in what way we are not told—the people stubbornly refuse to repent and change their ways.

The search for someone who follows the Lord's way and manifests the kind of justice the Lord promotes goes on in vv. 4-5, but to no avail. The poor are not excused ("they *all alike* had broken the yoke," v. 5*b,* italics added), but their ignorance might make their casual way with oaths more tolerable. The powerful and the leaders are expected to know better, but they do not do any better. Here, therefore, is part of the grounding for the severe indictment of Judah's leaders, so characteristic of Jeremiah's prophecy.

So judgment is announced once more (v. 6), this time in language that echoes the call of Jeremiah with its picture of a leopard "watching" (שֹׁקֵד *šāqad;* cf. 1:12) over the cities to destroy them. The imagery of wild beasts can refer to conquering armies converging on Jerusalem, or it may be a way of imaging the Lord as a destroying warrior.

Verses 7-9 may be viewed as a separate unit from the preceding one, but they clearly look back to v. 1 and God's intent to pardon Jerusalem. As one interpreter has put it, "The movement of the dialogue is thus from the dangled possibility of divine forgiveness (v. 1) to its final removal (v.

---

51. It is possible that the hyperbolic and utterly pessimistic view of the character of the people represents a later justification of the divine judgment, "an attempt at theodicy from a period when the subject was a matter of urgent discussion" (Robert P. Carroll, *Jeremiah,* OTL [Philadelphia: Westminster, 1986] 177). But the theological explanation that these verses then give to the destruction of Jerusalem still reflects an understanding of the divine will for mercy that is consistent with Genesis 18 and other passages of Scripture.

9)."[52] In this divine soliloquy, we are once more let into the mind and heart of God. The rhetorical questions that bracket this section receive their answer in the indictment they surround. Again, we encounter images of prostitution, adultery, and sexual license, though in this case it is applied to the men of the land. Verse 7 suggests that it is not necessarily actual adultery that is meant but adultery again as an image for apostasy. The "adultery" happens after the Lord has fully provided for the people. They have gone after other gods (their neighbor's wife) even though their own God has fully provided for them.

The language is ambiguous, however, and we cannot rule out the possibility that sexual sins and religious sins are both in view. The next time there is explicit reference to adultery (7:9), it alludes to the Decalogue and clearly refers to the act of adultery.[53]

5:10-17. A summons to battle addressed to an unknown host (The armies of the Lord? The armies of Babylon?) is sounded because of the people's treachery. In this context, both the northern and the southern kingdoms are included in the general indictment of faithlessness (cf. 3:7, 10, 20, where both Israel and Judah are described as faithless or false). The specifics of that faithlessness are spelled out in vv. 12-17. The particular sin is lying about the Lord. It is not in this case apostasy or injustice, but rather a word about the Lord, specifically the arrogant assurance that the Lord will not do anything to them, no matter what they do. Presumably, the people are so confident in the Lord's protection of Zion and the Temple (see chap. 7) that they do not feel any need to worry about danger. No prophet so constantly accuses the people of lying and deceit as does Jeremiah. In this chapter and these verses we get to the root of that accusation and why it is so intense. There is lying in the courts when oaths sworn in the Lord's name are not kept (v. 2), and there is lying in the streets and in the places of worship when the prophets declare, falsely, that everything is fine and no one need worry (vv. 13, 31a). Moreover,

the people buy into these deceitful and disastrously misleading words (vv. 11-12, 31b, "My people love it so!").

Two announcements of judgment then complete this prophetic judgment speech, the first in v. 14 and the second in vv. 15-17. Both are superb instances of poetic justice, a common feature of prophetic style and theology.[54] The punishment of those who spoke a false word about the Lord will be a judging word from the Lord (v. 14). It will be a devouring fire spoken through the mouth of Jeremiah, an explicit reference back to the call of Jeremiah in 1:9b and an early indication of why the prophet would encounter the marked hostility anticipated in his call and manifest in his prophetic career. Judgment will also come upon those who thought no evil "will come upon us" (v. 12b). They will hear that God is "going to bring upon you" (v. 15) a foreign nation. Finally, those who thought no ill would come upon them (v. 12b) will endure both sword (v. 17c) and famine (v. 17ab).

5:18-19. A particular form of prophetic speech is introduced in v. 19, one that appears several more times in the book (e.g., 9:12-16[11-15]; 13:12-14; 15:1-4; 16:10-13; 22:8-9; and 23:33).[55] It is a question-and-answer schema that addresses the issue of theodicy device, a justification of the divine judgment, as a shaken and devastated people look back and ask why such terrible things have happened to them. This form may have arisen out of the prophetic preaching of the exile, or it may be a literary convention that comes out of the circles of the deuteronomistic historian (Joshua through 2 Kings), since it is found twice in that work (Deut 29:22-25[21-24]; 1 Kgs 9:8-9), both times probably in exilic texts. The question-and-answer form found in Assyrian texts "states succinctly that a catastrophe be understood as the result of a broken treaty, and hence as the work of the gods who sanctioned the arrangement."[56] The use of this schema in the book of Jeremiah, therefore, may have direct connections to the covenant or treaty form. This form of prophetic preaching justifies the severity of the punishment with reference to the breach of covenant and the enactment

---

52. P. C. Craigie et al., *Jeremiah 1–25*, WBC (Dallas: Word, 1991) 88.

53. Holladay notes that Jeremiah "forces the hearer to think about human adultery, and past it to theological adultery—all irresponsible." See William L. Holladay, *Jeremiah 1: A Commentary on the Book of the Prophet Jeremiah Chapters 1–25*, Hermeneia (Philadelphia: Fortress, 1986) 180-81.

54. P. D. Miller, *Sin and Judgment in the Prophets*, SBLMS, 27 (Chico, Calif.: Scholars Press, 1982).

55. On this prophetic form, see B. O. Long, "Two Question and Answer Schemata in the Prophets," *JBL* 90 (1971) 129-39.

56. Ibid., 133.

of the covenant curses. In every text in Jeremiah and the Deuteronomistic History where the question being asked is, "Why has this happened?" or "Why has our God done this to us?" the answer is always, "Because Israel/Judah has forsaken the Lord or the law or the covenant" (5:19; 9:11-15; 16:10-13; 22:8-9; Deut 29:22-25[21-24]; 1 Kgs 9:8-9). Thus the whole experience of destruction and exile is rooted in the covenant faith and theology of Israel. The special relationship embodied in the covenant always included requirements and consequences. The book of Jeremiah testifies to a time when both seem to have been ignored.

Standing alongside this explanation is again the caveat, heard first in 4:27 and then again earlier in 5:10, that the Lord will not make a full end to this people. Here is a crucial qualifier to the divine judgment. God is not finished with this people. Anticipating a salvation oracle that appears later in the book (30:11), in the midst of all these harsh words of judgment, the Lord insists with equal intensity that it is not all over.

5:20-31. The prophet now offers a long series of indictments culminating in the rhetorical question of v. 29. The text is ultimately an announcement of judgment, but like all such announcements it comes—as one would expect from the juridical background of the judgment speech—only after the evidence has been made and the case laid out. The sins of the people are listed in powerful and imaginative ways. These are not primarily sins of religious apostasy in the strict sense, though that is suggested in the language of v. 23. These are the sins of social injustice and oppression, the rich and powerful oppressing the poor and the weak, particularly through the legal processes that were supposed to provide protection for just such people (vv. 27-28). Instead the rich trap the poor, filling their fine houses with the substance or possessions of the poor gained by fraudulent economic practices. The "deceit" or "treachery" (v. 27a) may refer to lying and deceit in court oaths, contracts, and the like (cf. v. 2). Although v. 28 seems to suggest unlimited wickedness, the text more likely says that they "pass over deeds/words of evil" in the sense of winking at or turning a blind eye to lawless and deceitful activities.[57] This is a strong indictment of

a community in which the politically powerful and the well-to-do amass possessions and wealth at the expense of the marginal and those in society who do not have protection and power, in which flagrant manipulation of the socioeconomic system to the advantage of the advantaged is simply ignored. The picture is as familiar at the beginning of the third millennium CE as it was in the first millennium BCE.

Throughout the first part of the passage there is repetition and play on words that poetically presses the case. The text sets the paradox of a call to hear (vv. 20b, 21a) for those who cannot hear. (Note the echoes of Isa 6:9-10.) There is a hearing problem in Judah, a large one. Central to the problem is the play within the meaning of the word שׁמע (šāmaʿ) between "hearing" and "obeying." What seems to be simply hearing of the ear is in fact more than that, as is further suggested by the wordplay between "seeing" (ראה rāʾâ) and "fearing" (ירא yārēʾ). Those who do not "see" (לא יראו lōʾ yirʾû) do not "fear" (לא תיראו lōʾ tîrāʾû). Also in these verses, repeated references to another part of the body, the heart or mind, carry the indictment forward: a senseless people (lit., "without heart," v. 21), a people of stubborn and rebellious hearts (v. 23), a people who do not say in their hearts, "Let us fear the LORD" (v. 24).

Notable in this text is the connection between creation and covenant (cf. 4:23-28).[58] The strong doxological language speaks of the power of God at work in the creation—the natural world, the seasons, and the fertility of nature. This creation language initially offers the grounds for challenging the people who do not fear and tremble before the creator of the universe. Then it becomes the context of judgment for breach of covenant. That is, the potential praise to the Lord who provides the natural order is not possible because the people's refusal to make that doxology has itself affected the natural order (vv. 24-25).

At the close of this chapter, Jeremiah focuses on the priests and prophets again (vv. 30-31). But the betrayal of leadership of God's people is just what the people want. They want to hear the good

57. John Bright, *Jeremiah*, AB 21 (Garden City: Doubleday, 1965) 40.

58. On the relation between creation and covenant generally, see Patrick D. Miller, "Creation and Covenant," in S. J. Kraftchick, C. D. Myers Jr., and B. C. Ollenburger, *Biblical Theology: Problems and Perspectives in Honor of J. Christiaan Beker* (Nashville: Abingdon, 1995) 155-68.

(false) words and have their situations supported and confirmed by the priests and prophets. Then comes the poignant, terrible question at the end of the chapter. It is a perduring, inescapable question: What will you do when the end comes? Its answer is terrifying because the question assumes a point of no return, human impotence before the terrible judgment of God. (See Reflections at 6:1-30.)

Jeremiah 6:1-30, The Wages of Sin

NIV	NRSV
6 "Flee for safety, people of Benjamin! Flee from Jerusalem! Sound the trumpet in Tekoa! Raise the signal over Beth Hakkerem! For disaster looms out of the north, even terrible destruction.	**6** Flee for safety, O children of Benjamin, from the midst of Jerusalem! Blow the trumpet in Tekoa, and raise a signal on Beth-haccherem; for evil looms out of the north, and great destruction.

NIV

6 "Flee for safety, people of Benjamin!
  Flee from Jerusalem!
Sound the trumpet in Tekoa!
  Raise the signal over Beth Hakkerem!
For disaster looms out of the north,
  even terrible destruction.
²I will destroy the Daughter of Zion,
  so beautiful and delicate.
³Shepherds with their flocks will come against
    her;
  they will pitch their tents around her,
  each tending his own portion."

⁴"Prepare for battle against her!
  Arise, let us attack at noon!
But, alas, the daylight is fading,
  and the shadows of evening grow long.
⁵So arise, let us attack at night
  and destroy her fortresses!"

⁶This is what the LORD Almighty says:

"Cut down the trees
  and build siege ramps against Jerusalem.
This city must be punished;
  it is filled with oppression.
⁷As a well pours out its water,
  so she pours out her wickedness.
Violence and destruction resound in her;
  her sickness and wounds are ever before me.
⁸Take warning, O Jerusalem,
  or I will turn away from you
and make your land desolate
  so no one can live in it."

⁹This is what the LORD Almighty says:

"Let them glean the remnant of Israel
  as thoroughly as a vine;
pass your hand over the branches again,
  like one gathering grapes."

¹⁰To whom can I speak and give warning?
  Who will listen to me?

NRSV

6 Flee for safety, O children of Benjamin,
    from the midst of Jerusalem!
Blow the trumpet in Tekoa,
  and raise a signal on Beth-haccherem;
for evil looms out of the north,
  and great destruction.
² I have likened daughter Zion
  to the loveliest pasture.ᵃ
³ Shepherds with their flocks shall come
      against her.
  They shall pitch their tents around her;
  they shall pasture, all in their places.
⁴ "Prepare war against her;
  up, and let us attack at noon!"
"Woe to us, for the day declines,
  the shadows of evening lengthen!"
⁵ "Up, and let us attack by night,
  and destroy her palaces!"
⁶ For thus says the LORD of hosts:
Cut down her trees;
  cast up a siege ramp against Jerusalem.
This is the city that must be punished;ᵇ
  there is nothing but oppression
      within her.
⁷ As a well keeps its water fresh,
  so she keeps fresh her wickedness;
violence and destruction are heard within
      her;
  sickness and wounds are ever before me.
⁸ Take warning, O Jerusalem,
  or I shall turn from you in disgust,
and make you a desolation,
  an uninhabited land.

⁹ Thus says the LORD of hosts:
Gleanᶜ thoroughly as a vine
  the remnant of Israel;

ᵃOr *I will destroy daughter Zion, the loveliest pasture*   ᵇOr *the city of license*   ᶜCn: Heb *They shall glean*

NIV

Their ears are closed[a]
  so they cannot hear.
The word of the LORD is offensive to them;
  they find no pleasure in it.
[11] But I am full of the wrath of the LORD,
  and I cannot hold it in.

"Pour it out on the children in the street
  and on the young men gathered together;
both husband and wife will be caught in it,
  and the old, those weighed down with years.
[12] Their houses will be turned over to others,
  together with their fields and their wives,
when I stretch out my hand
  against those who live in the land,"
                              declares the LORD.
[13] "From the least to the greatest,
  all are greedy for gain;
prophets and priests alike,
  all practice deceit.
[14] They dress the wound of my people
  as though it were not serious.
'Peace, peace,' they say,
  when there is no peace.
[15] Are they ashamed of their loathsome conduct?
  No, they have no shame at all;
  they do not even know how to blush.
So they will fall among the fallen;
  they will be brought down when I punish
    them,"
                              says the LORD.

[16] This is what the LORD says:

"Stand at the crossroads and look;
  ask for the ancient paths,
ask where the good way is, and walk in it,
  and you will find rest for your souls.
  But you said, 'We will not walk in it.'
[17] I appointed watchmen over you and said,
  'Listen to the sound of the trumpet!'
  But you said, 'We will not listen.'
[18] Therefore hear, O nations;
  observe, O witnesses,
  what will happen to them.
[19] Hear, O earth:
I am bringing disaster on this people,
  the fruit of their schemes,
because they have not listened to my words

a 10 Hebrew uncircumcised

NRSV

like a grape-gatherer, pass your hand again
  over its branches.

[10] To whom shall I speak and give warning,
  that they may hear?
See, their ears are closed,[a]
  they cannot listen.
The word of the LORD is to them an object
    of scorn;
  they take no pleasure in it.
[11] But I am full of the wrath of the LORD;
  I am weary of holding it in.

Pour it out on the children in the street,
  and on the gatherings of young men as well;
both husband and wife shall be taken,
  the old folk and the very aged.
[12] Their houses shall be turned over to others,
  their fields and wives together;
for I will stretch out my hand
  against the inhabitants of the land,
                              says the LORD.

[13] For from the least to the greatest of them,
  everyone is greedy for unjust gain;
and from prophet to priest,
  everyone deals falsely.
[14] They have treated the wound of my people
    carelessly,
  saying, "Peace, peace,"
  when there is no peace.
[15] They acted shamefully, they committed
    abomination;
  yet they were not ashamed,
  they did not know how to blush.
Therefore they shall fall among those who
    fall;
  at the time that I punish them, they shall be
    overthrown,
                              says the LORD.

[16] Thus says the LORD:
Stand at the crossroads, and look,
  and ask for the ancient paths,
where the good way lies; and walk in it,
  and find rest for your souls.
  But they said, "We will not walk in it."
[17] Also I raised up sentinels for you:

a Heb are uncircumcised

NIV

and have rejected my law.
²⁰ What do I care about incense from Sheba
or sweet calamus from a distant land?
Your burnt offerings are not acceptable;
your sacrifices do not please me."

²¹Therefore this is what the LORD says:

"I will put obstacles before this people.
Fathers and sons alike will stumble over
them;
neighbors and friends will perish."

²²This is what the LORD says:

"Look, an army is coming
from the land of the north;
a great nation is being stirred up
from the ends of the earth.
²³ They are armed with bow and spear;
they are cruel and show no mercy.
They sound like the roaring sea
as they ride on their horses;
they come like men in battle formation
to attack you, O Daughter of Zion."

²⁴ We have heard reports about them,
and our hands hang limp.
Anguish has gripped us,
pain like that of a woman in labor.
²⁵ Do not go out to the fields
or walk on the roads,
for the enemy has a sword,
and there is terror on every side.
²⁶ O my people, put on sackcloth
and roll in ashes;
mourn with bitter wailing
as for an only son,
for suddenly the destroyer
will come upon us.

²⁷ "I have made you a tester of metals
and my people the ore,
that you may observe
and test their ways.
²⁸ They are all hardened rebels,
going about to slander.
They are bronze and iron;
they all act corruptly.
²⁹ The bellows blow fiercely
to burn away the lead with fire,

NRSV

"Give heed to the sound of the trumpet!"
But they said, "We will not give heed."
¹⁸ Therefore hear, O nations,
and know, O congregation, what will happen to them.
¹⁹ Hear, O earth; I am going to bring disaster on
this people,
the fruit of their schemes,
because they have not given heed to my
words;
and as for my teaching, they have rejected
it.
²⁰ Of what use to me is frankincense that comes
from Sheba,
or sweet cane from a distant land?
Your burnt offerings are not acceptable,
nor are your sacrifices pleasing to me.
²¹ Therefore thus says the LORD:
See, I am laying before this people
stumbling blocks against which they shall
stumble;
parents and children together,
neighbor and friend shall perish.

²² Thus says the LORD:
See, a people is coming from the land of the
north,
a great nation is stirring from the farthest
parts of the earth.
²³ They grasp the bow and the javelin,
they are cruel and have no mercy,
their sound is like the roaring sea;
they ride on horses,
equipped like a warrior for battle,
against you, O daughter Zion!

²⁴ "We have heard news of them,
our hands fall helpless;
anguish has taken hold of us,
pain as of a woman in labor.
²⁵ Do not go out into the field,
or walk on the road;
for the enemy has a sword,
terror is on every side."

²⁶ O my poor people, put on sackcloth,
and roll in ashes;
make mourning as for an only child,

NIV

but the refining goes on in vain;
    the wicked are not purged out.
30They are called rejected silver,
    because the LORD has rejected them."

NRSV

most bitter lamentation:
    for suddenly the destroyer
    will come upon us.

27 I have made you a tester and a refiner[a]
        among my people
    so that you may know and test their ways.
28 They are all stubbornly rebellious,
    going about with slanders;
they are bronze and iron,
    all of them act corruptly.
29 The bellows blow fiercely,
    the lead is consumed by the fire;
in vain the refining goes on,
    for the wicked are not removed.
30 They are called "rejected silver,"
    for the LORD has rejected them.

[a]Or a fortress

COMMENTARY

6:1-8. Once more there is the call to flee (vv. 1-2) and the call to fight (vv. 4-6), one trumpet sounding the battle cry, another the cry of alarm. The terrible enemy from the north is on the march. The chapter begins with the Lord warning Jerusalem's inhabitants to get out while they can because disaster is on its way from the north. Verse 2 is difficult to translate and may refer either to the Lord's destroying a beautiful and pampered Jerusalem (so NIV) or to the Lord's making the city into a beautiful pasture (so NRSV). The striking thing about the imagery here is the very negative use of the shepherding metaphor. The shepherds in view here are described in apparently neutral language as coming into the meadow, pitching their tents, and pasturing. But the context shapes the usually appealing and trust-effecting imagery of the shepherds, the flock, and the pasture into an ominous, threatening picture (cf. 4:16-17). A powerful inversion of the shepherding imagery takes place. As Carroll states, "The beautiful meadow infested with shepherds grazing their sheep is in reality a city under siege from a formidable enemy. Sheep may not graze safely here."[59]

The call to battle (v. 4) is a call to holy war, literally, "sanctify war against her." A further inversion thus takes place since the people who took the land in sacral warfare now hear that a holy war is being called against them.[60] The ideology of holy war that undergirded the claims of Israel to the land of Canaan is subverted as its language and ritual become a part of the prophetic call for judgment that will remove the people from the land. The dissolution of the gift and blessing of land from the covenant demands that went with it now means the revocation of the blessing.

The calls to attack at noon or night may reflect the confidence of the enemy that it can take the city whenever it wills. The woe cry (v. 5) may be the voice of the enemy regretting the rapid passage of daylight before they can take the city. More likely, in the light of the use of "woe to us" in Jeremiah and elsewhere (e.g., 4:13, 31; see also 10:19; 15:10; 1 Sam 4:7-8; Lam 5:16), it is a cry of anguish and panic as the people sense that their time is running out.

59. Robert P. Carroll, *Jeremiah,* OTL (Philadelphia: Westminster, 1986) 191.

60. See G. von Rad, *Holy War in Ancient Israel* (Grand Rapids: Eerdmans, 1991); Patrick D. Miller, "The Divine Council and the Prophetic Call to War," *VT* 18 (1968) 100-107; and the literature cited in both works.

The Lord speaks in the last three verses (vv. 6-8), both to reiterate the call to fight against Jerusalem and to lay out the rationale for such a terrible fate invoked against the Lord's own earthly dwelling place. The rationale draws upon the stock of prophetic vocabulary that regularly identifies the social crimes of both kingdoms: "oppression in its midst," "wickedness," and "violence and destruction" (22:3, 17; see also Isa 59:6-7; 60:18; Ezek 45:9; Amos 3:9-10; Hab 1:2). In and around the use of these terms, one hears of evictions—by legal, but oppressive, and by illegal means—from land belonging to the family inheritance or allotment (see Ezek 45:9; see also Isa 5:8; Mic 2:2), of robbery (22:3), of shedding innocent blood (22:3, 17), of improper financial gains (see the Commentary on 6:13), and of illegal holding of personal property taken in pledge or collateral for loans (see Hab 2:6).[61] The language betrays rampant social and economic oppression whose primary, but not only, victims are the poor and the unprotected. As the next section indicates (v. 13), almost everyone is seeking to get a cut of the action at somebody else's expense.

Two features of v. 7 are worth noting. One is the use again of water imagery (cf. 2:13; 17:13). This time the simile is disorienting, since the positive picture of water kept pure and fresh in a well is used to depict the people's wickedness. They store it up and keep it fresh, ready to pour it out at the first opportunity. The incongruity of well-fresh water ready and available to drink and pent-up wickedness ready to be vented on someone is one of many jarring poetic features in the rhetoric of this prophet.

The ambiguity in the final line is further evidence of the poetic force in this speech. In the Hebrew of the Masoretic Text, the sickness and wounds are connected to the preceding lines and thus are a part of the portrayal of the moral sickness of the people or of the consequences of their social violence. In the Greek and Syriac translations, however, "sickness" and "wounds" are connected to v. 8 and refer to the attacks of the invading army, which ought to serve as a corrective, evoking a more moral and covenantal behavior on the part of the people. This latter alternative is what is suggested by other uses of these terms in Jeremiah (e.g., 10:19; 30:12-15), but neither possibility can be clearly ruled out. The imagery of illness and battle wounds bespeaks as powerfully the condition of a morally corrupt society as it does a besieged and devastated city. One senses that the ambiguity was intended by the poet.

God's will not only to punish but also to correct and discipline in order to effect a change of behavior is intimated again in v. 8. The disciplinary character of divine judgment is emphasized by Jeremiah. If the people can be instructed by what they go through, the Lord may hold back a full destruction, the total desolation of land and people. The great problem is that the "medicine" of correcting judgment seems never to have taken effect (2:30; 5:3; 7:28; 17:23; 32:33; 35:13).

6:9-15. Reminiscent of 5:10-17, this section seems initially addressed to Jeremiah (see 5:10), whose words are meant to be an instrument of gleaning (see 5:14). The particular force of the imagery is ambiguous, and interpreters read it differently. The gleaning and the reference to a remnant may suggest that Jeremiah is trying to save a few folk,[62] a process that the prophet then says is hopeless (v. 10). Or one may see in the gleaning of the remnant a kind of mopping-up operation for a people who have been previously punished that is going to clean out the very last element that is left.[63] Neither of these contradictory interpretations can be ruled out.[64] The imagery of harvesting in 5:10 and elsewhere (see Isa 17:4-6) is thoroughly a negative image, suggesting extensive and full judgment, and the parallel passage in 5:10-17 tends to confirm that interpretation. But the character of Jeremiah's question in v. 10 suggests that the command of God invites the search for a responsive audience that will attend to the word of the Lord and subsequently be saved. So the reader is left in a quandary, hearing both possibilities in the text.

What is quite clear in the text is the outcome of Jeremiah's prophetic activity. Just as their hearts are "uncircumcised," or stubborn, so also their

61. For an actual seventh-century BCE Hebrew petition seeking return of a farm laborer's coat confiscated by a superior and not returned, see K. A. D. Smelik, *Writings from Ancient Israel: A Handbook of Historical and Religious Documents* (Louisville: Westminster/John Knox, 1991) 93-100.

62. See, e.g., McKane, *A Critical and Exegetical Commentary on Jeremiah,* 1:143-48.
63. See Holladay, *Jeremiah 1,* 213-14. See also Carroll, *Jeremiah,* 195, for the way the imagery suggests final and total destruction.
64. Carroll, *Jeremiah,* 196, claims that "the text is too allusive to allow one definitive meaning."

ears are "uncircumcised," or closed. The particular formulation of the people's response to the prophetic word resonates with the language of Psalm 1, a psalm that echoes elsewhere in the prophecy of Jeremiah (e.g., 17:5-8). The word of the Lord, whether in prophetic oracle or torah instruction, is the subject of scorn and mockery. With that response, the people in effect take a seat with the scorners about whom Ps 1:1 warns. Unlike the righteous way described in Ps 1:2, there is no "delight" in God's word (v. 10c). Thus, by reversing the way set forth in Psalm 1, the people have *de facto* followed the way of the wicked rather than the way of the righteous. The inevitable outcome of such a way as described in Ps 1:6 is the judgment Jeremiah is called to announce: The way of the wicked shall perish.

As chap. 5 has already indicated (5:1, 4-5), the whole community seems to be implicated, both in the sins that are rampant in the land and in the judgment that is to come (vv. 11-13). The picture of Judahite society in the book of Jeremiah is one of widespread corruption that draws in "everyone," even the lesser members of the community (v. 13). The rich and the leadership receive the brunt of the prophetic critique, but everyone wants a share and will say and do whatever is necessary to get in on the action. The "unjust gain" (v. 13) is literally "a cut" (בצע *beṣaʿ*). As Holladay has suggested, the action described here is what is typified in the slang phrase, "taking a cut": "This is the world of baksheesh and worse, palms greased, expenses padded. The context is made clear by 22:17: there we must not understand the king to be 'taking a profit'; no, he is 'in on the take' and so, by the evidence of the present passage is everybody else."[65]

The parallel expression in v. 13 is dealing falsely and is a part of taking a cut. Such practices include bribery, fudging, juggling of figures, the use of false weights and balances, and the like. They are a part of systemic corruption where people achieve economic gain by varied—often ingenious—questionable practices.

The prophet then lays particular responsibility again on the leaders of the community. Although v. 13 suggests their participation in the economic corruption of the people, v. 14 points to another

kind of perversion of the truth: lying for God, falsifying the divine word. Drawing again on the imagery of sickness and healing, through the prophet the Lord accuses the religious leaders of the community of placing a bandage over a gushing artery and saying, "Don't worry, you will be all right." One may refer to the chief priest Amaziah, who confronts Amos and would suppress the disturbing prophetic message to keep the peace, while the rotten underbelly of life in Israel is a sign that the end is near (Amos 7:10-17). Such perversion of the priestly and prophetic responsibilities has reached such a point that there is no longer embarrassment at official malfeasance. As they participate in the pervasive sin of the community, they will go down with it (v. 15). There is no lightning from on high, no fire from the Lord (cf. Lev. 10:1-7). The forces of the Lord are the forces of history. The foe that comes from the north (vv. 22-23) will carry the leaders into exile first of all.

6:16-21. In an elaborate judgment speech with alternating indictment for sin (vv. 16-17, 19b-20) and announcement of the judgment evoked by the sins (vv. 18-19a, 21), the Lord through the prophet not only spells out what is going to happen and why but also attests once more to the divine frustration at the stubbornness of a people who are reminded again and again of their covenantal responsibilities but refuse to pay attention to or do anything about them. Readers of Jeremiah are accustomed to the pathos of the prophet's frustration and anger in the face of the attempts on his life and freedom and the resistance of the community to his word. But because Jeremiah's frustration and anger are often directed to the Lord, it is easy to miss the fact that such frustration and anger are shared by the one who commissions him. Again and again, we see the Lord trying to shake the people loose, sending signals to them that are ignored (v. 17), suggesting where they can look to find the way to life rather than death (v. 16). Although the prophecy of Jeremiah is full of announcements of judgment, they often are interspersed with various calls to repentance, warning signs, and indications of what is needed. The Lord does not simply point out the sin and announce the judgment. At times, there is an almost painful kind of explanation. The bond between the people and their God is so strong that the divine will does not easily bring

65. William L. Holladay, *Jeremiah 1*, 216.

forth the judgment that seems inevitable in the face of such stubborn refusal to live by the covenant that made them the people of the Lord.

The great text in this passage occurs in the opening verse (v. 16), the call to the congregation to look to its past history, to check its memory, to find the ways that have been forgotten, to remember the God who has delivered and directed. What is meant here is the ancient story and the implications of that story found in the Decalogue, the laws of Exodus and Leviticus 19–26 and Deuteronomy, the latter explicitly laying out the "good way." The call is similar to that covenantal drawing of the line that Moses sets before the people in Deuteronomy: "See, I have set before today you life and prosperity. . . . Choose life . . . loving the LORD your God, obeying [him]" (Deut 30:15-20 NRSV). The words and Torah to which the people do not attend (v. 20) are both instruction and story. Torah involves more than the commands and teachings of the Lord (5:4-5), but it is also the whole story of God's way with this people from the beginning to now (cf. 2:17-18). The story of torah has been marked by the people's experience of good; it was intended to show them the good way in which they should walk. A similar note is sounded by Isaiah:

> Look to the rock from which you were hewn,
> and to the quarry from which you were dug.
> Look to Abraham your father
> and to Sarah who bore you;
> for he was but one when I called him,
> but I blessed him and made him many.
> (Isa 51:1-2 NRSV)

The people have forgotten the story and its implications. Their forgetting is seen here as a conscious act: "We will not walk in it." In such a manner, Jeremiah portrays the hardness of heart and the uncircumcised ears and heart that manifest themselves in the daily conduct of the people.

Jeremiah 34 provides a good example of the return to the ancient way and what that would mean as well as the failure of the people to do that. The king calls for the reinstitution of the ancient sabbatical release of bonded servants so that they are not forever in economic slavery. The people release their slaves, but afterward make them slaves again. Personal greed and the pain of economic loss impel the people once again to abandon the ancient ways, the good way of torah.

This call also involves the possibility of looking for and finding the ancient and good ways, which has a kind of therapeutic dimension: rest for weary and undone souls. Over against the false claims of the prophets that there is well-being and prosperity in their present ways, the Lord summons this people to walk down a path that truly leads to rest.

But that possibility is rejected. The Judahites fail to pay attention (vv. 17, 19) to the torah and to the word, presumably the prophetic words (cf. 6:10). The fate of the people is the effect of their deeds (v. 19a). Their acts have consequences, and in these consequences, "the fruit of their schemes," judgment is effected. The text here holds together a conviction of an unbroken connection between the way the people act and what happens to them, but it makes clear that it is the Lord who effects the connection and so the judgment. And, consistent with the prophetic word generally, when Torah is not operative, when the guidelines for righteous living in the community are not in place, there is no religious act, no sacrifice, no generous offering that can evoke the Lord's positive response, even if it is an especially precious and valuable offering (v. 20).

6:22-26. A battle scene opens up again, but not this time a call to flee or fight. It depicts the now inevitable conquest of Jerusalem. Whenever this text was delivered or written down, the Babylonian army was in mind. The terror of this merciless horde evokes an anguished lament from the people in which we hear for the first time a catchword of Jeremiah's prophecy: "Terror is on every side" (see also 20:3, 10; 46:5; 49:29; Ps 32:14; Lam 2:22). With its frequent depictions of the enemy threat, its calls to flee for safety, and its constant stress on the terrible judgment that is to come, no prophetic book so vividly depicts the terror that is all around a people who have so thoroughly given themselves over to greed, the values of royal consumption, and self-interest at the expense of others whose protection is their first responsibility. The imagery of a woman in the pain of labor rises again as a vehicle for conveying the terrible anguish of this people (4:31) as once again the experience of women becomes a prophetic vehicle for speaking to the people. Woman as whore and woman as mother—these are the constant rhetorical weapons of the prophets, Jeremiah especially. The reader may not pass by them casually as if they do not reflect and elicit the pain of a woman's life, whether by her nature as a mother or by her existence in a male-dominated and often woman-abusing society.

6:27-30. Finally, at the end of this part of the book, there is a word about Jeremiah's vocation that contains in it a play on one of the powerful prophetic images of judgment: testing and refining by smelting.[66] In some contexts, the smelter's fire is simply and powerfully an image of judgment (Ezek 22:18-22). Elsewhere testing and refining are acts of judgment, but as a part of the correcting and disciplining that God seeks to effect in judgment (Isa 1:24-26). Here it refers to an activity of the prophet, laid upon him in language reminiscent of his call in chap. 1: "I have made you a tester and refiner among my people" (cf. 1:5). But its outcome is more in line with the word of the Lord to Ezekiel, Jeremiah's contemporary, rather than with Isaiah's refining and purifying fire. The technical analysis of the process here described is complicated. It probably involves the refining of

impure silver by introducing lead into the process—not enough lead, and the whole process ends up as a mess.[67] Whatever the details of the process, however, the outcome is clear: The result of the prophet's testing of this people is that they now wear the label "Reject Silver." There is no purity and no value in this people. They are a metallic mess, corrupted by corruption, rebellion, and malicious gossip (v. 28); so they are to be tossed away. The reader should not miss the repeated "all" in v. 28. The corruption is as pervasive as the impurity in the rejected silver. This metallurgical imagery joins with the vision of the plumb line in Amos 7:7-9, showing how out of plumb is the "house" of Israel and with Jeremiah's later use of the potting image with the spoiled clay in the potter's hand (18:4). The imagery of testing recurs several times in the course of this book (e.g., 9:6; 11:20; 12:3; 17:10; 20:12) precisely because it aptly identifies what the Lord is doing—and the negative results.

66. Patrick D. Miller, *Sin and Judgment in the Prophets: A Stylistic and Theological Analysis,* SBLMS 27 (Chico, Calif.: Scholars Press, 1982) 137.

67. For details of the metallurgical processes indicated here see William L. Holladay, *Jeremiah 1: A Commentary on the Book of the Prophet Jeremiah Chapters 1–25,* Hermeneia (Philadelphia: Fortress, 1986) 230-32; and William McKane, *A Critical and Exegetical Commentary on Jeremiah,* ICC (Edinburgh: T. & T. Clark, 1986) 1:154-57.

REFLECTIONS

1. The word of judgment is so strong in chapters 4–6 that one may miss the degree to which the Lord who brings the judgment resists doing so and experiences frustration and despair at the continued disobedience and wrongdoing of the people. The frequent references to refused correction (e.g., 5:3), the call to look for the good way, the various queries to the people, "Do you not fear me" (5:22), the divine search for at least *one* just person so that the Lord may pardon Jerusalem (5:1), and the inner dialogue within the mind and heart of God that is made public in these chapters ("Shall I not punish them for these things?" 5:9; note the third-person address, indicating the deity is talking to self or to the prophet) all suggest that judgment comes hard for the Lord, who has loved this people so. A prophecy that speaks so clearly of the wrath of God becomes also a prism through which to view that wrath in less simple and reductionistic tones. There is great resistance by God to what seems to be required. One of the experiences of a steady reading through Jeremiah, at least in the first half of the book, is a kind of monotony in the face of the litany of sins and wrongs and announcements of judgment. But that is a part of the literary uncovering of the divine ambivalence, if not the divine anguish at having to move against a people whom the Lord has designated as a "treasured possession," as God's people (Deut 7:6). It is not a simple and quick decision. All these judgment speeches are a part of the divine pathos and agony at how this has all turned out. This is no hard-nosed CEO, making brutal decisions and cutting jobs without blinking an eye.

There is a subtle blending of the anguish of the prophet and the anguish of God in 4:19-22 as the hearer or reader has to try to figure out where the prophet's voice ends and God's voice begins. The "my people" of 4:22 is clearly the voice of God, but that verse flows so clearly out of the preceding ones that the reader is led to identify the one who speaks about "my anguish" in 4:19 with the one who speaks about "my people" in 4:22. Most interpreters would see the speaker of 4:19 as the prophet, but the text raises another possibility, one that other prophets, such as Hosea, reinforce: Anguish and complaint in the prophet are reflections of anguish and complaint in God. There is nothing in the character of God that makes judgment any less disturbing for God than it is for those who experience it or view it. In various ways, the prophet shows us the divine pathos in the midst of divine anger.[68]

2. The search for the one person whose just and faithful actions will elicit God's pardon of Jerusalem (5:1) is part of a major thread that runs through the Scriptures: the one for the many, the innocent one who saves the guilty. There are various ways in which this theme is played out. I have already pointed to God's openness to holding back judgment on Sodom and Gomorrah if even a few righteous or innocent ones could be found. Even earlier, the righteous and blameless Noah does not save the rest of corrupt humanity, but God's protection of him becomes the start of a new humanity. The clearest manifestation of this theme in the Old Testament is, of course, the servant of the Lord who suffers, despite his innocence, for the sins of the many and whose life and death are a successful intercession for the guilty. Finally, the pardon of the many through the one righteous person is central to the meaning of the death of Jesus in the New Testament. As Jeremiah and other Old Testament witnesses testify, that move on God's part should not surprise us. It is one example of the many ways in which the Lord of Israel is "bent" toward that community of creatures whom God brought into being and has loved throughout the ages. The story of judgment is always capable of being blown open, of being nullified by the faithfulness and innocence and justice of a single person. The Diogenes-like search of Jer 5:1 might seem hyperbolic if we did not read it in the context of the whole story and know that the Lord really is like that.

3. The several times that this section specifically identifies the social sins of the people make us aware that the gap between then and now, which often seems large, is hardly there at all, at least when it comes to speaking about the personal and corporate injustices of a community. Never is the text more clearly a mirror of our own time than here as we encounter an uncomfortably familiar picture of economic greed and that allows some to stuff their pockets at the expense of others by all sorts of legal and illegal manipulations of the system. Thus contracts are manipulated or voided and facts are falsely reported; insider information enables a few to create wealth from which others are closed off; advertising gives us "a market-place in which ubiquitous deception is accepted";[69] and executives accumulate more and more wealth and possessions out of their obscenely exaggerated compensation while workers lower down on the economic ladder struggle to make ends meet. The ease with which most of us wink at morally questionable practices in our own businesses, professions, and institutions is remarkably reflective of what Jeremiah was talking about. And the "cut" is pervasive. It is perhaps symbolized best by a legal system that allows some lawyers to function as predators, skimming off as much as possible of every case through exaggerated expenses and excessively high hourly billing prices. They are, however, only the most obvious example of many ways that persons in power, even modestly so, get in on the take. The blatant way in which the political system encourages our leaders to find ways of building up personal and campaign resources by manipulating the system astonishes nearly all of us, even as we seem willing to put up with it and at times to participate fully in it. And nothing may be more indicative of the corruption of a society in the manner of ancient Judah than the ease with which wealthy politicians cut the opportunities of those at the lowest scale of the social order—widow, poor, and orphan (in today's culture, the child of a single mother)—to exist at even a minimal subsistence level.

68. See J. J. M. Roberts, "The Motif of the Weeping God in Jeremiah and Its Background in the Lament Tradition of the Ancient Near East," *Old Testament Essays* 5 (1992) 361-74.
69. J. A. Barnes, *A Pack of Lies: Towards A Sociology of Lying* (Cambridge: Cambridge University Press, 1994) 46.

4. A passage such as 6:1-8 is, like others in this section, set in the heat of battle, reminding us that Israel's and Judah's lives were often like that. Just as the problems were social and corporate, so also the experience of interaction with the divine, of chastisement and judgment, was social and corporate, the agents of God's judgment being the opposing nations whose imperial and aggressive actions become the vehicle of the divine judgment. Through such texts, we are sharply reminded of what it meant to be Israel and what it means to have Israel's story as our Scripture. The work of God is wrought in the affairs of a people and their involvements with other people. The "land" is often in view. One cannot spiritualize the reality of Israel, the expectations of God for the way that Israel/Judah should go or the way in which God's judgment comes into human life. It is very much the stuff of this world, the things that we encounter all the time in our existence as persons who belong to communities that seek to live harmoniously—often failing to do so—yet who find themselves in tension with other communities and peoples.

Jeremiah 6:1-8 creates a kind of tension. The battle is at hand. Jerusalem is told to flee. We hear the warriors of the enemy army shouting to go up and besiege the city. But this is not a judgment speech in its typical form of indictment and sentence of judgment. Here the prophet announces judgment, on the one hand, and issues a warning, on the other hand. The word of the prophet places Judah between chastisement and destruction and so in its very character speaks to the readers about the tight spot in which a community with oppression in its midst and rampant with violence and destruction exists. The chastising and correcting judgment of God seems already at work. But it is possible for such an encounter with the enemy to be a warning, a discipline that can teach. If that does not happen, the sick patient will die, to use the imagery of the text. Once again, the question is, How do you hear (5:21; 6:10)? Or to those of us who come on the scene at a later time, How do you read?

5. The call to look to the ancient paths in order to find the good way suggests the importance of a community's living by its story and the implications drawn from it. This is another way of speaking of the lessons of history, in this instance the experience of the people in the past and the instruction God has given them. The present way to go is marked by the way they have gone in the past. In no small measure, here is the impetus for the creation of Scripture. The ways of old, the story of God's deliverance and guidance, the commandments long ago given are remembered, retold, corrected, and written down so that the later community will have some guidelines, some road signs to know which way to go. That becomes especially crucial if the community has lost its way and is unsure or if it has, in fact, chosen to go down paths that lead to destruction. How does one know? Read and tell the story. Recall the things that worked and did not in the past. Go back and read the "handbook" that Grandmother and Grandfather carried on their journey. The good way is not difficult to identify if we pay attention to the story that has brought us to this point.

6. In the midst of all the accusations of injustice, deceit, and other kinds of economic and social sins, there is a persistent focus on the stubbornness and refusal to receive correction. The prophecy thus not only marks the explicit wrongdoings of the people but also indicts them just as thoroughly because of their hardheaded refusal to learn any lessons, even the lessons of history. Here is a community whose preachers and prophets have reminded them again and again about the requirements of their life and have repeatedly pointed out the failings, but to no avail. Even when bad things happen, there is no anguish or penitence, no learning from what has happened. Refusal to pay any attention to the word of the Lord that comes to them is as much the problem as anything. The persistence of sin is dramatically illustrated in the experience of Judah. Modes of conduct into which people slip, especially when they are self-serving, become impossible to break. It is like the biblical theme of the hardening of the heart. Continuous hardening and unwillingness to be instructed by chastening events seem finally to turn the people's hearts to stone. The only anguish is God's. Such stubbornness arises in no small part from people's greater attentiveness to those who give them good and comfortable words (5:31; 6:14) than to those who identify serious problems and call for major change.

JEREMIAH 7:1–8:3, A SERMON IN THE TEMPLE

NIV

7 This is the word that came to Jeremiah from the LORD: ²"Stand at the gate of the LORD's house and there proclaim this message:

" 'Hear the word of the LORD, all you people of Judah who come through these gates to worship the LORD. ³This is what the LORD Almighty, the God of Israel, says: Reform your ways and your actions, and I will let you live in this place. ⁴Do not trust in deceptive words and say, "This is the temple of the LORD, the temple of the LORD, the temple of the LORD!" ⁵If you really change your ways and your actions and deal with each other justly, ⁶if you do not oppress the alien, the fatherless or the widow and do not shed innocent blood in this place, and if you do not follow other gods to your own harm, ⁷then I will let you live in this place, in the land I gave your forefathers for ever and ever. ⁸But look, you are trusting in deceptive words that are worthless.

⁹" 'Will you steal and murder, commit adultery and perjury,ᵃ burn incense to Baal and follow other gods you have not known, ¹⁰and then come and stand before me in this house, which bears my Name, and say, "We are safe"—safe to do all these detestable things? ¹¹Has this house, which bears my Name, become a den of robbers to you? But I have been watching! declares the LORD.

¹²" 'Go now to the place in Shiloh where I first made a dwelling for my Name, and see what I did to it because of the wickedness of my people Israel. ¹³While you were doing all these things, declares the LORD, I spoke to you again and again, but you did not listen; I called you, but you did not answer. ¹⁴Therefore, what I did to Shiloh I will now do to the house that bears my Name, the temple you trust in, the place I gave to you and your fathers. ¹⁵I will thrust you from my presence, just as I did all your brothers, the people of Ephraim.'

NRSV

7 The word that came to Jeremiah from the LORD: ²Stand in the gate of the LORD's house, and proclaim there this word, and say, Hear the word of the LORD, all you people of Judah, you that enter these gates to worship the LORD. ³Thus says the LORD of hosts, the God of Israel: Amend your ways and your doings, and let me dwell with youᵃ in this place. ⁴Do not trust in these deceptive words: "This isᵇ the temple of the LORD, the temple of the LORD, the temple of the LORD."

5For if you truly amend your ways and your doings, if you truly act justly one with another, ⁶if you do not oppress the alien, the orphan, and the widow, or shed innocent blood in this place, and if you do not go after other gods to your own hurt, ⁷then I will dwell with you in this place, in the land that I gave of old to your ancestors forever and ever.

8Here you are, trusting in deceptive words to no avail. ⁹Will you steal, murder, commit adultery, swear falsely, make offerings to Baal, and go after other gods that you have not known, ¹⁰and then come and stand before me in this house, which is called by my name, and say, "We are safe!"—only to go on doing all these abominations? ¹¹Has this house, which is called by my name, become a den of robbers in your sight? You know, I too am watching, says the LORD. ¹²Go now to my place that was in Shiloh, where I made my name dwell at first, and see what I did to it for the wickedness of my people Israel. ¹³And now, because you have done all these things, says the LORD, and when I spoke to you persistently, you did not listen, and when I called you, you did not answer, ¹⁴therefore I will do to the house that is called by my name, in which you trust, and to the place that I gave to you and to your ancestors, just what I did to Shiloh. ¹⁵And I will cast you out of my sight, just

ᵃ9 Or *and swear by false gods*

ᵃOr *and I will let you dwell*   ᵇHeb *They are*

NIV

[16]"So do not pray for this people nor offer any plea or petition for them; do not plead with me, for I will not listen to you. [17]Do you not see what they are doing in the towns of Judah and in the streets of Jerusalem? [18]The children gather wood, the fathers light the fire, and the women knead the dough and make cakes of bread for the Queen of Heaven. They pour out drink offerings to other gods to provoke me to anger. [19]But am I the one they are provoking? declares the LORD. Are they not rather harming themselves, to their own shame?

[20]" 'Therefore this is what the Sovereign LORD says: My anger and my wrath will be poured out on this place, on man and beast, on the trees of the field and on the fruit of the ground, and it will burn and not be quenched.

[21]" 'This is what the LORD Almighty, the God of Israel, says: Go ahead, add your burnt offerings to your other sacrifices and eat the meat yourselves! [22]For when I brought your forefathers out of Egypt and spoke to them, I did not just give them commands about burnt offerings and sacrifices, [23]but I gave them this command: Obey me, and I will be your God and you will be my people. Walk in all the ways I command you, that it may go well with you. [24]But they did not listen or pay attention; instead, they followed the stubborn inclinations of their evil hearts. They went backward and not forward. [25]From the time your forefathers left Egypt until now, day after day, again and again I sent you my servants the prophets. [26]But they did not listen to me or pay attention. They were stiff-necked and did more evil than their forefathers.'

[27]"When you tell them all this, they will not listen to you; when you call to them, they will not answer. [28]Therefore say to them, 'This is the nation that has not obeyed the LORD its God or responded to correction. Truth has perished; it has vanished from their lips. [29]Cut off your hair and throw it away; take up a lament on the barren heights, for the LORD has rejected and abandoned this generation that is under his wrath.

[30]" 'The people of Judah have done evil in my eyes, declares the LORD. They have set up their detestable idols in the house that bears my Name and have defiled it. [31]They have built the high places of Topheth in the Valley of Ben Hinnom to

NRSV

as I cast out all your kinsfolk, all the offspring of Ephraim.

[16]As for you, do not pray for this people, do not raise a cry or prayer on their behalf, and do not intercede with me, for I will not hear you. [17]Do you not see what they are doing in the towns of Judah and in the streets of Jerusalem? [18]The children gather wood, the fathers kindle fire, and the women knead dough, to make cakes for the queen of heaven; and they pour out drink offerings to other gods, to provoke me to anger. [19]Is it I whom they provoke? says the LORD. Is it not themselves, to their own hurt? [20]Therefore thus says the Lord GOD: My anger and my wrath shall be poured out on this place, on human beings and animals, on the trees of the field and the fruit of the ground; it will burn and not be quenched.

[21]Thus says the LORD of hosts, the God of Israel: Add your burnt offerings to your sacrifices, and eat the flesh. [22]For in the day that I brought your ancestors out of the land of Egypt, I did not speak to them or command them concerning burnt offerings and sacrifices. [23]But this command I gave them, "Obey my voice, and I will be your God, and you shall be my people; and walk only in the way that I command you, so that it may be well with you." [24]Yet they did not obey or incline their ear, but, in the stubbornness of their evil will, they walked in their own counsels, and looked backward rather than forward. [25]From the day that your ancestors came out of the land of Egypt until this day, I have persistently sent all my servants the prophets to them, day after day; [26]yet they did not listen to me, or pay attention, but they stiffened their necks. They did worse than their ancestors did.

[27]So you shall speak all these words to them, but they will not listen to you. You shall call to them, but they will not answer you. [28]You shall say to them: This is the nation that did not obey the voice of the LORD their God, and did not accept discipline; truth has perished; it is cut off from their lips.

[29] Cut off your hair and throw it away;
  raise a lamentation on the bare heights,[a]
for the LORD has rejected and forsaken
  the generation that provoked his wrath.

[a]Or the trails

NIV

burn their sons and daughters in the fire—something I did not command, nor did it enter my mind. [32]So beware, the days are coming, declares the LORD, when people will no longer call it Topheth or the Valley of Ben Hinnom, but the Valley of Slaughter, for they will bury the dead in Topheth until there is no more room. [33]Then the carcasses of this people will become food for the birds of the air and the beasts of the earth, and there will be no one to frighten them away. [34]I will bring an end to the sounds of joy and gladness and to the voices of bride and bridegroom in the towns of Judah and the streets of Jerusalem, for the land will become desolate.

8 " 'At that time, declares the LORD, the bones of the kings and officials of Judah, the bones of the priests and prophets, and the bones of the people of Jerusalem will be removed from their graves. [2]They will be exposed to the sun and the moon and all the stars of the heavens, which they have loved and served and which they have followed and consulted and worshiped. They will not be gathered up or buried, but will be like refuse lying on the ground. [3]Wherever I banish them, all the survivors of this evil nation will prefer death to life, declares the LORD Almighty.'

NRSV

[30]For the people of Judah have done evil in my sight, says the LORD; they have set their abominations in the house that is called by my name, defiling it. [31]And they go on building the high place[a] of Topheth, which is in the valley of the son of Hinnom, to burn their sons and their daughters in the fire—which I did not command, nor did it come into my mind. [32]Therefore, the days are surely coming, says the LORD, when it will no more be called Topheth, or the valley of the son of Hinnom, but the valley of Slaughter: for they will bury in Topheth until there is no more room. [33]The corpses of this people will be food for the birds of the air, and for the animals of the earth; and no one will frighten them away. [34]And I will bring to an end the sound of mirth and gladness, the voice of the bride and bridegroom in the cities of Judah and in the streets of Jerusalem; for the land shall become a waste.

At that time, says the LORD, the bones of the kings

8 of Judah, the bones of its officials, the bones of the priests, the bones of the prophets, and the bones of the inhabitants of Jerusalem shall be brought out of their tombs; [2]and they shall be spread before the sun and the moon and all the host of heaven, which they have loved and served, which they have followed, and which they have inquired of and worshiped; and they shall not be gathered or buried; they shall be like dung on the surface of the ground. [3]Death shall be preferred to life by all the remnant that remains of this evil family in all the places where I have driven them, says the LORD of hosts.

[a]Gk Tg: Heb *high places*

COMMENTARY

The chapter is presented as a prophetic address by Jeremiah to the people of Judah as they come to the Temple for worship. While much of the chapter is a collection of oracles that do not necessarily come from such a setting, chap. 26 tells of an occasion when Jeremiah preached in the court of the Temple, dating it to the beginning of the reign of Jehoiakim, Josiah's son, in 609 BCE (26:1). As a result of that preaching Jeremiah was put on trial

for his life. The content of the sermon, abbreviated at the beginning of chap. 26, is similar enough to the contents of 7:1-15 to lead most interpreters to connect the two events and to see in 7:1-15 the heart of Jeremiah's proclamation, albeit possibly expanded by later editors who also would have appended the oracles that follow in the rest of the chapter. The matter is somewhat complicated by the fact that most of the first two verses of the

Hebrew text of chap. 7, which place Jeremiah at the Temple proclaiming these words to the entrants, are missing from the Greek translation and are judged by most scholars to be an expansion in the Hebrew. If so, they attest both to the fact that the text is the result of a complex process of editing and revision and to the intention of the ones responsible for the process of equating these words with the event described in chap. 26.

The text does not identify the actual occasion of the sermon. One assumes that it would have been when many people were at the Temple. Some have suggested that the occasion was Jehoiakim's inauguration, others that it was one of the major pilgrimage festivals, presumably the autumn festival. Whatever the moment, the trial outcome of the sermon indicates the significant impact of the sermon on the hearers and suggests that the occasion was not a casual one.

The temple sermon proper is the primary focus of attention in this section of the book. It addresses two perennial and interrelated issues in the Judean community: (1) the incongruity between the worship of the people and their way of life and (2) the inviolability of the Temple. The underlying question was whether the continued existence of the Temple as God's dwelling place—even in the face of dangerous threats in the past, especially in Isaiah's time—constituted a security blanket over the land, especially Jerusalem, ensuring God's protection from harm for Zion, no matter what the people did or how they behaved. The point of the sermon is a clear and emphatic no to the widespread assumption that Zion was secure, that God would never let anything happen to the Temple.

This focus on the center of worship carries over into the rest of the oracles in this chapter as they deal largely with other aspects of the worship of the people: popular devotion to the queen of heaven (vv. 16-20), proper sacrifices (vv. 21-29), child sacrifice (vv. 30-34), and the worship of the astral hosts (8:1-3). These oracles are quite different in character, but underlying all of them is the issue of true and false worship of God, the same concern that, in another way, is at the center of vv. 1-15.

7:1-15. The opening verses establish the context. Jeremiah addresses "all you people of Judah, you that enter these gates to worship the LORD." This characterization of the audience does two

things. By means of the first phrase, "all you people of Judah," the reader gains information about the major occasion that is the setting of the sermon—that is, an occasion in which "all" Judah might be expected to be present. In the second, they are identified as those entering to worship the Lord. The words that follow have to do precisely with that worship, what legitimates it and what nullifies it, indeed, what defines that worship. The words also turn Jeremiah's proclamation into a kind of prophetic "entrance liturgy," a term that has been used to describe Psalms 15 and 24, which seem to have been liturgies for those entering the Temple, liturgies that would identify moral qualifications, the manifestations of a holy life that were appropriate for anyone coming before the holy God. In the psalms, this check on the proper qualifications for worship comes in the form of questions. For the prophet, questions are unnecessary. The absence of the qualifications is transparent, and the prophet's words effectively forbid entrance until those qualifications are met. He is unable to prevent the people from entering, however; indeed, chap. 26 will show his absence of power as he is placed on trial for having made this speech. But his words identify the danger to "all Judah" coming in to worship the Lord if those qualifications are not met.

What are those qualifications? They are set forth in a rhetorical sequence that occurs twice between vv. 3 and 8:

> exhortation to change = amending   one's ways (vv. 3*b*, 5);
> result of the change = God will let them dwell there (vv. 3*c*, 7);
> prohibition = do not trust in lying words (vv. 4, 8).

Initially, the exhortation is a general call to the people to change their behavior so that the Lord may let them dwell there.[70] There is a serious textual problem in v. 3, demonstrated in the differences between the translation of the verb "dwell" (שכן *šākan*) in the NRSV, which reflects versional

---

70. The "and let me dwell" of the NRSV is better translated as "so that I may dwell," and the note's "and I will let you dwell" as "so that I may let you dwell." In like manner, the NIV may be understood as "so that I may let you live."

evidence, and in the NIV (reflected in the NRSV note), which reflects the Masoretic, or Hebrew, Text. The difference has to do with how the consonants of the Hebrew are to be vocalized. The matter is complicated by the same verb's appearing in v. 7 in the same form as in the Hebrew text of v. 3. The NRSV defines the consequence of changed conduct as the Lord's continued abiding with the people in the Temple ("I will dwell with you"). The NIV, or Hebrew, reading sets the consequence as the Lord's continuing to let the people abide or dwell in the land ("I will let you dwell"), a point that is made clearly in v. 7. If we follow the NRSV translation, it is likely that the reference in v. 3 is to the Lord's continued residence in the Temple, a quite plausible reading. This view would be directly related to the people's assumption that "the temple of the LORD" will always be there. Either reading is fully plausible, and the difference between the NRSV and the NIV reflects the fact that interpreters from earliest times have been unable to reach agreement on this matter. The parallel structures in vv. 3-4 and 5-8 tend to weight the argument toward reading the text the same way in both v. 3 and v. 7, whichever alternative is chosen.

The general exhortation for the people to change their ways so that the Lord may dwell there or let them dwell there is followed by a warning against a pernicious kind of false security, the assumption that God will never let the Temple, the Lord's dwelling place, be harmed, that the Lord will always be present in the Temple and thus keep it and the people worshiping there from any kind of ultimate threat or danger. Threats to the Temple and to Jerusalem had taken place in earlier times (e.g., in the days of Hezekiah; see Isaiah 36–37), but the Temple endured. The promise of the Lord to defend the city (Isa 37:35) was probably remembered well by later generations, who saw in that promise and in the Temple, as the earthly abode of the almighty God, a kind of protecting shield over Jerusalem that could not be penetrated. What this did not account for was the Lord's own decision to remove the shield.

The repetition of the words "the temple of the LORD" in v. 4 probably reflects what the people had been saying—constantly repeating these words, perhaps throwing them in Jeremiah's face when he spoke of dangers to Jerusalem. They had become a kind of religio-political cliché that everybody simply

assumed was not debatable. But rather than reflecting the substantive reality of a nation whose life is ordered to conform to the holiness and righteousness of the Lord of the Temple, these words are a patina over a societal structure that is rotten to the core. Or to use the language of the text, they are, in fact, a lie. The only way the assumption implicit in the people's automatic chant, "the temple of the LORD," can be turned from lie to truth is by a radical alteration of the moral life.

The rhetorical movement of Jeremiah's sermon in vv. 3-4 is then taken up again in vv. 5-8, but it is expanded and intensified as the sermon builds. The imperative formulation of v. 3 for the people to amend their ways now shifts to a conditional "If you amend . . . ," but the effect is the same. In both v. 3 and v. 5, the result of being allowed to dwell in the land depends on the change of behavior. The intensification from the first movement (vv. 3-4) to the second (vv. 5-8) is evident in the emphatic Hebrew verbal constructions of v. 5, reflected in the NRSV's "truly" (NIV, "really"). Jeremiah is raising the rhetorical level a notch or two. Even more important is his development of the general call for a change of behavior to spell out what is required if they have any hope of dwelling securely in this land:

dealing justly in all human relations (v. 5*b*);
not taking advantage of weaker or powerless members of the society (v. 6*a*);
not committing violence against others (v. 6*b*);
not worshiping other gods (v. 6*c*).

One might be inclined to press the sermonic character of Jeremiah's words to see in these verses illustrations of what was needed. The preceding chapters have made clear that these are more than illustrations. They are it. The specifics are many and varied, and Jeremiah spells out a number of them in preceding and following chapters. But the bottom line is clear in these verses: Fair and just dealings; protection and care of the innocent and weak members of society;[71] and unqualified devotion and loyalty to the Lord are required.

71. One may assume various kinds of extortions here, such as excessive rents, high prices that keep the poor indebted, and other forms of manipulating the system to extract the money of the poor, who lack the capabilities of defending themselves against such oppressive practices.

What we encounter in these verses is a series of fundamental principles governing Israel's covenant life as a people of the Lord. They had some set character to them, for we find them much the same in 22:3, 15-17. Jeremiah thus provides an encapsulation of fundamental covenantal principles, such as we know from other prophets (e.g., Isa 1:16-17; Ezek 45:9; Mic 6:8; Zech 7:8-10). This is prophetic exhortation in imperative and prohibitive forms, setting forth fundamental principles of Israel's life, which are spelled out in greater detail in case laws and prophetic indictments.

The result of Judah's revival of these basic guidelines in their corporate life is reiterated: their continuing existence in the land the Lord gave them (v. 7). There follows the rejection of the "lying words," presumably the repeated and hollow words "the temple of the LORD." The intensity of the prophet's rhetoric increases as he turns the prohibition (v. 4) into an accusation (v. 8) and adds a further word. Like their pursuit of other gods, the people's false attachment to the Temple as a safety device "does not profit" (2:9, 11). This is another part of the exposure of the lie. Over against the presumption of the exclamation in v. 10 ("We are saved!"), the people will, in fact, be done in. There is nothing to be gained by trusting in the Temple to keep them safe. (Cf. the identification in v. 6 of the pursuit of other gods as bringing harm rather than prosperity.)

The case against Judah is then developed in vv. 9-12. As in Amos and other prophets, Jeremiah's rhetorical questions here serve as indictments that spell out the sins and highlight the outrageous incongruity between the extensive violation of covenantal requirements in the society and the worship of God in the Temple. The indictment makes specific reference to the prohibitions that we know from the Decalogue, including the worship of other gods and four of the sins against the neighbor. What is astonishing in the Lord's eyes is that the people can violate the most fundamental of the covenantal stipulations and yet go into worship in the Temple, claiming liturgically its security ("We are safe") and go right back out to commit the same crimes and sins. The people have no shame (cf. 3:3)! The Temple is no longer a place of worship under these circumstances. It is, literally, what the Lord calls it (v. 11)—a gathering place for thieves, adulterers, extortioners, and the like.

The "congregation of the LORD," the "house which if called by my name," has been turned into a lair for criminals. That being the case, there is no alternative but to get rid of it, and so in vv. 13-15, the corollary is drawn. The sentence follows from the indictment and the self-evident guilt of the accused: destruction of the Temple.

As that sentence is pronounced, several things are to be noted. First, the Lord tries to shake the Judahites from their unshakable confidence by identifying an earlier instance where the people's sins elicited a judgment that included the destruction of the Lord's own house, the central sanctuary at Shiloh. It is as if the Lord is still trying to break the unreasoned self-confidence of this people by laying out some hard data before them that cannot be ignored and surely should serve as a dash of cold water to sober up this recalcitrant and unashamed people: "Take a quick tour up to Shiloh and check out the ruins there. That should knock some sense into your heads."

Second, such extreme measures as the destruction of the Temple come only after persistent reminders and warnings, matched only by even more persistent ignoring of all such blatant signals of the danger ahead. In that sense, the people are correct to assume that the Lord will protect as fully as possible the place of the Lord's dwelling. Their mistake is to assume that such protection is unlimited and to ignore the fact that they have converted the Lord's dwelling place into something else quite altogether—a den of thieves that needs to be destroyed.

Finally, all the characteristics that would seem to guarantee the protection of the Temple are spelled out to underscore the enormity of the situation. It is the house "called by my name," the place in which the people trusted, and the place given by the Lord to the ancestors of this people and to them (v. 14). None of those aspects of the Temple and its history are sufficient to save it now. The Lord, who has been watching (v. 11), will cast this people out of this house and out of sight.

7:16-20. This text first introduces us to a prophetic function of great importance, but one that is highly ambiguous in Jeremiah's case: intercession. One of the responsibilities that seems to have accompanied the prophetic enterprise was to stand before God on behalf of a sinful people, even a people who have time and again disobeyed the Lord, even a people who over and over threaten the life and well-being of the prophet himself, as in the case of Jeremiah.[72] The intercessory activity may be observed in prophets from Abraham to Ezekiel. However, for Jeremiah, more than once intercession by him is either prohibited by the Lord (as here) or deemed fruitless (15:1; cf. 14:11). There is a reason for this divine resistance to the prophet's engaging in intercession. Although Jer 26:3 indicates the Lord's openness to a change of mind about the judgment if the people will only listen, virtually all the instances where the Bible speaks of a divine change of mind are occasions of a positive response by the Lord to the intercession of a prophet for mercy toward the people (e.g., Exod 32:14; Amos 7). Indeed, Ezek 13:5 and 22:30-31 indicate a clear expectation on God's part that prophets will pray for the people, and the Lord will take that prayer into account. Here the intercession does have an effect. The intercessory prayer of a prophet does move God. One should note, for example, in Exodus 32 how even when God wants to be left alone to carry out the judgment, the prophet Moses, in going ahead, accomplishes his goal of changing the Lord's mind. That is the point. The prophet's prayer for the people can influence the divine will and activity. There seems to be a responsiveness to such intercessory prayers that resides in the very nature of God. That is why God puts off Jeremiah's intercession in this instance. This is not a time for intercession (cf. Amos 7:7-9; 8:1-3). Things have gone too far; things are so out of hand that only judgment is possible, and God does not want to be vulnerable at this point to the cries for mercy of God's servant, the prophet.

In v. 16, it is important that the negative of the prohibition is the particle אל (*'al*) rather than the negative particle לא (*lō'*), which would mean permanent prohibition. Jeremiah is not prohibited forever from making intercession. But in this moment, when the Lord has come up against the divided loyalties of the people in their worship of other Gods—the violation of the fundamental stipulation of the covenant—the Lord will move against this people and wants no intercession to stop the intended correction. In 11:14, where this

prohibition of intercession is given again, it is for a similar reason. So at this moment, Jeremiah is not to intercede, though he may do so in the future—and, indeed, does (e.g., Jeremiah 42).

The reason for this unmovable judgment is a particular activity—the worship of the queen of heaven—though other activities of worship described in the rest of the chapter contribute to the immutability of this divine judgment. The queen of heaven was one of the goddesses of the West Semitic pantheon, probably Astarte. The worship of the queen of heaven seems to have been a feature of popular religion, or more specifically family religion, in the seventh–sixth centuries BCE. It involved domestic activities that were given a cultic function, such as feeding the deity, a practice not common in Israel's worship of the Lord but fairly standard in Mesopotamian religion, which is the ultimate source of the worship of the queen of heaven.[73] A somewhat later Phoenician inscription from Cyprus gives information about a festival meal for Astarte that included some of the same ritual elements described in Jeremiah: a procession through the streets of the city (see Jer 7:17), singing and lighting a fire for the queen of heaven, sacrifice, and baking bread for Astarte and cakes for the participants in the festival.[74] The one other reference to these practices occurs in Jer 44:15-20 and indicates the prominent role of the women or wives of Judah in the worship of the queen of heaven. This is one of several instances in the OT where women were as much on the margins of the proper worship of the Lord as they generally were on the margins of the power and participatory structures of society. There may have been some corollary between those two margins in the experience of women, for we encounter the women of Judah in other references to unorthodox or heterodox practices (e.g., 2 Kgs 23:7; Ezek 8:14).[75] The later reference in Jeremiah 44

72. On prophetic intercession, see Samuel E. Balentine, "The Prophet as Intercessor: A Reassessment," *JBL* 103 (1984) 161-73; and Patrick D. Miller, *They Cried to the Lord: The Form and Theology of Biblical Prayer* (Minneapolis: Fortress, 1994) chap. 8.

73. On the cakes for the queen of heaven, see Walter E. Rast, "Cakes for the Queen of Heaven," in *Scripture in History and Theology: Essays in Honor of J. Coert Rylaarsdam*, ed. A. L. Merrill and T. W. Overholt (Pittsburgh: Pickwick, 1977) 167-80; Philip J. King, *Jeremiah: An Archaeological Companion* (Louisville: Westminster/John Knox, 1993) 102-9. On Astarte as the queen of heaven, see John Day, *Yahweh and the Gods and Goddesses of Canaan*, JSOTSup 265 (Sheffield: Sheffield Academic, 2000) 148-50.

74. Brian Peckham, "Phoenicia and the Religion of Israel: The Epigraphic Evidence," in *Ancient Israelite Religion: Essays in Honor of Frank Moore Cross*, ed. P. D. Miller Jr., P. D. Hanson, and S. D. McBride (Philadelphia: Fortress, 1987) 84-85.

75. See Phyllis Bird, "The Place of Women in the Israelite Cultus," in ibid., 397-419.

indicates the reason for the cult of the queen of heaven: It is because the people believe that as long as they bake the cakes, pour out the libations, and whatever other activities may have been necessary for the queen of heaven, they will prosper and suffer no misfortune, but when they stopped doing these things, the situation would turn bad (44:17-18). This is one of the clearest texts in Scripture for identifying a fundamental reason for turning to other gods. It is precisely what Jeremiah labels it: a search for what profits. There are, however, two problems that he keeps identifying: The people are not free to worship the queen of heaven or any other deity, and to do so does not finally profit.

7:21-29. The critique of Israel's worship in the face of its disobedience continues in these verses with what at first glance seems to be a strange and contradictory word. The people are told to add one offering to another and eat the sacrificial meat. Then they are told that the Lord never commanded sacrifices at the beginning of Israel's story. What is going on here? The biblical accounts of the people coming out of Egypt to Sinai are filled with regulations and instruction from God about proper sacrifice! Several things are involved in this indictment:

(1) The indictment here is not so much of the whole sacrificial cult as it is of the individual offerings that people bring voluntarily. Such offerings are an affront to the Lord in the face of the moral turpitude of the ones who bring them.[76]

(2) The burnt offering and the sacrifice were quite separate offerings, the former to be burned entirely, the latter being partly consumed by the worshiper. What the Lord says, in effect, is, "You might as well throw it all together and eat the whole mess for what little good or meaning it has to me." In other words, the normal rules of sacrificial offering to the Lord are moot when the worshiper's sacrifice is tainted with the blood of the innocent and the disobedience of a covenanted people.

76. Jacob Milgrom, "Concerning Jeremiah's Repudiation of Sacrifice," *ZAW* 89 (1977) 273-75. Others see here reflection of a more deuteronomic mode of thinking that regarded the sacrificial cultus as secondary to the demand for obedience to the Decalogue. In Deuteronomy, the sacrificial instruction is taught by Moses, whereas the Decalogue is commanded directly by the Lord. Yet even in Deuteronomy, the instruction of Moses is understood to originate from the Lord. See Moshe Weinfeld, "Jeremiah and the Spiritual Metamorphosis of Israel," *ZAW* 88 (1976) 17-56.

(3) The Lord's words about not commanding sacrifice at the beginning suggest that one needs to distinguish between what the Lord commands or requires—obedience—and what the Lord provides—a sacrificial cultus. The psalmist says that the Lord does not ask or require sacrifice (Ps 40:6[7]). Similarly, one of the classic legal-ethical summaries of the OT, Mic 6:8 asks what the Lord requires and answers with no word about sacrifice of any sort, only about justice and kindness—those things that are absent in Jeremiah's time. The influence of Deuteronomy may be felt at this point, for that same question about the Lord's requirements is answered there with words about fearing and serving the Lord and walking in the Lord's ways (Deut 10:12), just the point Jeremiah's prophecy makes. Indeed, none of the legal-ethical summaries of the prophets (e.g., Isa 1:12-17; Zech 8:16) call for sacrifice, and a number of them set the demand for justice and righteousness over against the human preference for sacrifice. The latter may be understood better as a part of the provision of the Lord, but not on the same level as these other matters—indeed, thoroughly problematic when carried out in the absence of doing good, justice, and protecting the weak and the powerless.

(4) The fundamental claim of the passage, therefore, is once again an insistence that the covenantal relationship is about obedience. The priority of obedience to sacrifice has always been clear in Israel's religion (1 Sam 15:22). That has been the bottom line from the beginning of the story, and it has always been the trouble spot—only now the spot is a large and growing stain.

(5) The Lord, who has provided sacrifice as a procedure for relating to the deity, for seeking help and forgiveness, for expressing thanks, and the like, has also provided another procedure for helping the people keep on the right track: the prophets. But that apparatus is working no better than did the sacrificial one. Again and again, the prophet says, "They did not listen/obey" (six times!). They did not accept correction, and lying is the only mode of speech in town (v. 28). The stubbornness of the people thus renders both divine provisions moot. The only process left is judgment.

7:29-34. It is not clear whether v. 29 belongs to this part of chap. 7 or to the preceding unit. As a call for lament, it is equally applicable to both parts. But it seems to prepare the way for the announcement of judgment that comes at the end of the chapter.

These verses identify two other worship practices that are perversions of the true worship of Yahweh and are unacceptable: idolatry (v. 30) and child sacrifice (v. 31). They then pronounce once more the harsh judgment of God upon the sins of the people (vv. 32-34). The abominations in the Temple, referred to in v. 30, refer to idols in the Temple, either in the time of an earlier king, such as Ahaz or Manasseh, or at a later time in a regressive falling away from the reforms of Josiah. The term "abomination" (שקוצים *šiqqûṣîm*) denotes something that is particularly reprehensible, repugnant, and impure or unclean. The presence of idols in the Temple pollutes the holy place, making it unclean and unfit for habitation by the Holy One of Israel.

Equally repugnant to the deity is the practice of child sacrifice, the dedication of babies to the deity by burning them in a place called "the fireplace" (תפה *tōpet,* vocalized with the vowels for Hebrew "shame"). Josiah's destruction of the Tophet is reported in 2 Kgs 23:10. If that record is true, then Jeremiah may be speaking in relation to the renewal of child sacrifice after Josiah's death. The purpose of such sacrifices was sometimes dedicatory, as in a foundation sacrifice for a city (1 Kgs 16:34); more likely, and more often, babies or children were sacrificed in times of crisis and calamity to secure the favor of the gods (see 2 Kgs 3:27). In the light of the report that the worship of the queen of heaven was to secure prosperity that had gone away (see above), the latter rationale most likely accounts for the renewal of child sacrifice in Judah at the beginning of the sixth century BCE.

Similar references to this practice as it is described in 7:31 appear in 19:5 and 32:35. In those cases, the deity to whom the sacrifices were dedicated is Baal. Yet, the strange statement that also occurs in each of these three verses, "which I did not command nor did it come into my mind," suggests that the people also considered these sacrifices to be permissible within their worship of Yahweh, an assumption that the Lord's statement is designed to refute. In Lev 20:3 and Ezek 23:38-39, there is mention of the sacrifice of children and on the same day the people's coming into the Lord's sanctuary, suggesting that this was done alongside other, more traditional Yahwistic prac-

tices (see Ezek 20:25-26). While such practices seem to have had little precedent in Israel's normative worship practices, the command of the Lord in Exod 22:29-30, calling for the consecration of the firstborn sons as well as oxen and sheep, may have been interpreted by some as permission, if not instruction, to sacrifice sons as they would oxen and sheep. When this practice became a regular part of the ritual, there was a procedure for redemption of the firstborn.[77]

The Lord indicates that such an interpretation of the law is a gross misreading. The outcome will once again be a matter of poetic justice because the place where babies were killed will become a slaughtering place of judgment, so extensive that there will not be sufficient room to bury all the bodies. Joy and laughter will turn into utter silence before the awful, annihilating judgment. It is a harsh picture, impossible to ameliorate.

8:1-3. The imagery of heaped-up corpses as a kind of poetic judgment continues in the final verses of this section. It speaks of a future desecration of the graves of the people—the leaders, against whom so many of Jeremiah's oracles are set, are listed first—in an act of ironic judgment, as the bones are exposed to the astral bodies they had served for life only to find death, a dramatic demonstration of the way to destruction that such worship leads. Verse 2 includes a heaping up of all the words that were supposed to express devotion to the Lord—"loving," "serving," "following," "inquiring," and "worshiping"—but they were instead a manifestation of the people's devotion to the heavenly bodies, things the Lord had made, not deities to be worshiped.

The final sentence in v. 3 is a play on the crucial and decisive message of Deut 30:15-20: "See, I have set before you life and . . . death. . . . Choose life so that you and your descendants may live, loving the LORD your God, obeying him, and holding fast to him." The choice has been made. It is for death, a choice vividly displayed in the bones of the kings, officials, and people laid out before the sun and the moon and, ironically, then chosen also by those who have been sent away into exile. When the choice of life was rejected in the manner of life, it meant that the people would finally reject it in the manner of destiny.

---

77. For further biblical references that might connect the practice of human sacrifice to the worship of the Lord, see Robert P. Carroll, *Jeremiah,* OTL (Philadelphia: Westminster, 1986) 223.

REFLECTIONS

1. Jeremiah's joining of a fundamental set of moral and religious principles (7:6-7) with several of the commandments of the Decalogue (7:9) provides a fairly unique ethic of command in the Old Testament. There are other places of prophetic exhortation that set forth similar injunctions as those in 7:6-7, and there are a few references to the Decalogue. But these references do not come together as they do here. The reader is thus given one of those summaries of the law, of what matters in the relationship with God, that is already indicated by the Shema (Deut 6:4-5) and that we find later in the Great Commandment. Here is the heart of the matter in defining the moral life in ancient Israel. While, on the one hand, the covenantal stipulations are spelled out in great detail and encompass many chapters of books, it is also possible to point, in brief scope, to the basics. That is what Jeremiah does in his temple sermon. Such encapsulation of the divine will enables readers to cut through the morass of legislation that is often obscure, at least to modern readers, and seemingly irrelevant to daily life in the contemporary world in order to discern the shape of the life God intends to elicit through such detailed instruction.

The fundamental guidelines provided by the Ten Commandments join with basic concerns for justice and protecting the life and security of those on the margins of society or without the means to sustain or protect themselves. That joining suggests that an ethic based on the Old Testament will not depend exclusively on the commandments; nor will it be reduced to prophetic calls for justice. The moral life in covenant with God involves rejecting those ways in which we can harm a neighbor's life, property, marriage, and name. It also calls for a continuing attitude of fairness and a special concern for the weaker members of the community. Neither should it be missed that in this significant summary of the moral life, both parts—prophetic principles and Ten Commandments—set devotion and proper allegiance to the Lord as an essential ingredient. There is no separation of ethics from religion and devotion to God.

2. The refusal to separate the attitude toward God and the attitude toward the neighbor is at the heart of this sermon and places before us the intimate relation between worship and ethics that seems to be fundamental to the prophetic message. Surely there are few themes so repeatedly enunciated in the prophets than the insistence on a strict correlation between what goes on inside the sanctuary and what takes place outside it. In this case, the focus is on the meaninglessness of the sanctuary and what it suggests about divine presence and protection when the life-style of the community runs counter to the will of the God who dwells within. The Temple of old, like the temple or church sanctuary of the present, is a powerful symbol of divine presence and security. Such symbols are rendered meaningless when their adherents have violated the divine instruction and have used their economic and other powers for personal gain at the expense of others. This text is a critique of religious sloganeering—"the temple of the LORD," "I have been baptized," or "justification by faith"—and of an easiness in Zion that assumes living *the* good life is not finally dependent upon living *a* good life.

3. The text raises this question, "Where does your ultimate trust lie?" The community Jeremiah addressed placed its trust in a secondary point of reference, the Temple, and not in the ultimate One. The language used by Jeremiah, "Do not *trust in* these deceptive words," customarily has the Lord as its object (cf. Pss 4:5[6]; 31:6[7]; 56:3[4]). Misplaced trust is an issue that continues as the community of faith is tempted, individually and communally, to count on other means of safeguarding its life than the Lord it worships.

4. In like manner, the later conversation between Jeremiah and the people uncovers the degree to which we human beings give religious devotion to that which profits us, to what benefits us, and also the way in which we may totally misread the situation. The people really thought that worship of the queen of heaven profited them. The activity of God is dependent upon faith and a faithful reading of what happens. People may see that differently. The Judeans who spoke with Jeremiah really thought that another worship benefited them.

The narrative reflects the way in which human beings tie the worship of God to notions of benefit. In contemporary society, one often hears people speaking about how worshiping God and going to church have given them a good life and kept them healthy. This is not inherently wrong. Indeed, part of the divine argument in the book of Jeremiah is against a faulty realization of where the "profit" lies. The problem is the ease with which people relinquish their loyalty to the source of good, who has guided and sustained their lives and their destiny, in order to find some quick fix for immediate problems.

5. In the New Testament, a connection is made between the attitude of the people toward the Temple in Jeremiah's time and the same attitude in Jesus' time (Matt 21:13// Mark 11:17// Luke 19:46; see also John 2:13-16). The circumstances are not the same, but the mercenary activities that Jesus encountered in the Temple, the "use" of the Temple by the people to support their financial enterprises, echoes the situation in Jeremiah's time and in so doing alerts us to the perennial danger of covering our sins with our religious practices. As Douglas Hare states in his commentary on the Gospel of Matthew, "The allusion to Jeremiah . . . suggests that the market represents to Jesus the secularization of the temple by worshipers (buyers and sellers) whose lives do not conform with their religious profession but who claim nonetheless to find security in their religiosity ('We are delivered!')."[78]

6. There is ambiguity in the text of 7:3, 7, leading to the different readings in the NRSV and the NIV. If the translation of the NRSV is correct, "that I may dwell with you in this place," then the text reminds its readers of the freedom of God, even relative to the Lord's own choices, God's own "life." The Temple chosen, as the earthly dwelling place of God, did not inhibit the freedom of God to take it all back, to "live" elsewhere. Those things that have to do with God's own self are responsive to the human situation. God is both free and responsive. The way God is present to the human community is not immutably set, nor is it unrelated to the way the community is present to God.

78. Douglas R. A. Hare, *Matthew,* Interpretation (Louisville: Westminster/John Knox, 1993) 241.

JEREMIAH 8:4–10:25, JUDGMENT AND LAMENT

OVERVIEW

The temple sermon and related oracles in Jer 7:1–8:3 interrupt the many judgment speeches and the sounds of lament anticipating the coming of the foe from the north who will bring the judgment of God upon a sinful Judah and Jerusalem. Those words of judgment and cries of lament pick up again in these chapters, with the sounds of lament growing louder. The smaller units in this block are not tightly integrated, but their concerns and themes are consistent. They are like a running conversation, a polyphony of voices: God, prophet, people, mourners, praisers, and even a strange Aramaic voice (10:11; Aramaic is a Semitic language). But within that conversation, there is a persistent movement from sin to judgment to lament. The movement is not always straightforward. The text keeps turning from one to the other. But the logic is that in this movement a sinful people evoke God's judgment and end up in grievous lamentation, a lament that is shared by the prophet and by God. Thus the sins of the people are laid out in 8:4-8, 10b-12a, in the midst of which judgment is announced (8:9-10*a*), and there follows an extended lament in 8:14–9:1. In the next section, this movement occurs twice:

Sin 9:2-6, 8	Sin 9:12-14
Judgment 9:7, 9, 11	Judgment 9:15-16
Lament 9:10	Lament 9:17-22

Other distinctive features in these chapters are the elaborated description of the idols and the sharp contrast between the idols and the Lord of Israel (chap. 10).

Continuities with the chapters before the temple sermon are evident in the references to the foe from the north, the concern for turning or repentance, the uncircumcised heart, the failure of the leaders, and the prophets who speak falsely about peace. Also, the divine activity to test and to correct, already identified in chaps. 2–6, is reiterated in chaps. 8–10. There is a sameness to Jeremiah's message for it was set out over a long period of time as covenantal violations persisted. Even where later hands have elaborated his message, they do not significantly alter the main threads of his proclamation. But that sameness is freshly and differently articulated in every oracle, in every prophetic proclamation. So the reader gets a different slant, another image, a new vehicle for hearing more clearly the persistent word as each new text is taken up.

One cannot easily assign these texts to particular moments in Jeremiah's years. They are probably from the last years of the seventh century and the first decade of the sixth. The persistence of Judah's abandonment of the earlier reforms and of covenantal obedience is so clear and the sounds of the enemy forces in the background is so loud that we cannot be too far from Judah's last days.

Jeremiah 8:4–9:1, No Balm in Gilead

NIV

⁴"Say to them, 'This is what the LORD says:

" 'When men fall down, do they not get up?
    When a man turns away, does he not
        return?
⁵Why then have these people turned away?
    Why does Jerusalem always turn away?
They cling to deceit;
    they refuse to return.
⁶I have listened attentively,
    but they do not say what is right.
No one repents of his wickedness,
    saying, "What have I done?"
Each pursues his own course
    like a horse charging into battle.
⁷Even the stork in the sky
    knows her appointed seasons,
and the dove, the swift and the thrush
    observe the time of their migration.
But my people do not know
    the requirements of the LORD.

⁸" 'How can you say, "We are wise,
    for we have the law of the LORD,"
when actually the lying pen of the scribes
    has handled it falsely?

NRSV

⁴You shall say to them, Thus says the LORD:
    When people fall, do they not get up again?
        If they go astray, do they not turn back?
⁵Why then has this people[a] turned away
    in perpetual backsliding?
They have held fast to deceit,
    they have refused to return.
⁶I have given heed and listened,
    but they do not speak honestly;
no one repents of wickedness,
    saying, "What have I done!"
All of them turn to their own course,
    like a horse plunging headlong into battle.
⁷Even the stork in the heavens
    knows its times;
and the turtledove, swallow, and crane[b]
    observe the time of their coming;
but my people do not know
    the ordinance of the LORD.

⁸How can you say, "We are wise,
    and the law of the LORD is with us,"
when, in fact, the false pen of the scribes

[a]One Ms Gk: MT *this people, Jerusalem*,   [b]Meaning of Heb uncertain

NIV

⁹The wise will be put to shame;
  they will be dismayed and trapped.
Since they have rejected the word of the LORD,
  what kind of wisdom do they have?
¹⁰Therefore I will give their wives to other men
  and their fields to new owners.
From the least to the greatest,
  all are greedy for gain;
prophets and priests alike,
  all practice deceit.
¹¹They dress the wound of my people
  as though it were not serious.
"Peace, peace," they say,
  when there is no peace.
¹²Are they ashamed of their loathsome conduct?
  No, they have no shame at all;
  they do not even know how to blush.
So they will fall among the fallen;
  they will be brought down when they are
    punished,
                              says the LORD.

¹³" 'I will take away their harvest,
                    declares the LORD.
There will be no grapes on the vine.
There will be no figs on the tree,
  and their leaves will wither.
What I have given them
  will be taken from them.ᵃ' "

¹⁴"Why are we sitting here?
  Gather together!
Let us flee to the fortified cities
  and perish there!
For the LORD our God has doomed us to perish
  and given us poisoned water to drink,
  because we have sinned against him.
¹⁵We hoped for peace
  but no good has come,
for a time of healing
  but there was only terror.
¹⁶The snorting of the enemy's horses
  is heard from Dan;
at the neighing of their stallions
  the whole land trembles.
They have come to devour
  the land and everything in it,
  the city and all who live there."

ᵃ13 The meaning of the Hebrew for this sentence is uncertain.

NRSV

has made it into a lie?
⁹ The wise shall be put to shame,
  they shall be dismayed and taken;
since they have rejected the word of the LORD,
  what wisdom is in them?
¹⁰ Therefore I will give their wives to others
  and their fields to conquerors,
because from the least to the greatest
  everyone is greedy for unjust gain;
from prophet to priest
  everyone deals falsely.
¹¹ They have treated the wound of my people
    carelessly,
  saying, "Peace, peace,"
  when there is no peace.
¹² They acted shamefully, they committed
    abomination;
  yet they were not at all ashamed,
  they did not know how to blush.
Therefore they shall fall among those who fall;
  at the time when I punish them, they shall
    be overthrown,   says the LORD.
¹³ When I wanted to gather them, says the
    LORD,
  there areᵃ no grapes on the vine,
  nor figs on the fig tree;
even the leaves are withered,
  and what I gave them has passed away
    from them.ᵇ

¹⁴ Why do we sit still?
  Gather together, let us go into the fortified
    cities
  and perish there;
for the LORD our God has doomed us to perish,
  and has given us poisoned water to drink,
  because we have sinned against the LORD.
¹⁵ We look for peace, but find no good,
  for a time of healing, but there is terror
    instead.

¹⁶ The snorting of their horses is heard from
    Dan;
  at the sound of the neighing of their stal-
    lions
  the whole land quakes.

ᵃOr I will make an end of them, says the LORD. There are
ᵇMeaning of Heb uncertain

NIV

17"See, I will send venomous snakes among you,
  vipers that cannot be charmed,
  and they will bite you," declares the LORD.

18O my Comforter*a* in sorrow,
  my heart is faint within me.
19Listen to the cry of my people
  from a land far away:
"Is the LORD not in Zion?
  Is her King no longer there?"

"Why have they provoked me to anger with
    their images,
  with their worthless foreign idols?"

20"The harvest is past,
  the summer has ended,
  and we are not saved."

21Since my people are crushed, I am crushed;
  I mourn, and horror grips me.
22Is there no balm in Gilead?
  Is there no physician there?
Why then is there no healing
  for the wound of my people?

9 1Oh, that my head were a spring of water
    and my eyes a fountain of tears!
I would weep day and night
  for the slain of my people.

a18 The meaning of the Hebrew for this word is uncertain.

NRSV

They come and devour the land and all that
    fills it,
  the city and those who live in it.
17 See, I am letting snakes loose among you,
  adders that cannot be charmed,
  and they shall bite you,   says the LORD.

18 My joy is gone, grief is upon me,
  my heart is sick.
19 Hark, the cry of my poor people
  from far and wide in the land:
"Is the LORD not in Zion?
  Is her King not in her?"
("Why have they provoked me to anger with
    their images,
  with their foreign idols?")
20 "The harvest is past, the summer is ended,
  and we are not saved."
21 For the hurt of my poor people I am hurt,
  I mourn, and dismay has taken hold of me.

22 Is there no balm in Gilead?
  Is there no physician there?
Why then has the health of my poor people
  not been restored?

9 *a*O that my head were a spring of water,
    and my eyes a fountain of tears,
  so that I might weep day and night
    for the slain of my poor people!

aCh 8.23 in Heb

COMMENTARY

8:4-7. The text begins with one of the central Jeremianic themes: turn and return (שוב *šûb*). As in chaps. 3 and 4, the prophet plays with the language, using some form of this verb twice in v. 4*b* and three times in v. 5. In each verse, the verb is used both to speak about the "turning" away and about the "returning." In vv. 4-7 another instance of the rhetorical device noted earlier occurs (see the Commentary on 2:29-37) in which the prophet asks a series of rhetorical questions, the first two of which "establish the presupposition of his speech and a consensus with his hearers," and the final "why," together with the sentences that follow in the next three verses, "abruptly turns the

argument against the hearers by drawing the implications of the consensus just established."[79] The rhetorical questions in v. 4 are pieces of practical wisdom used as an analogy: Does not the person who falls down, who has an accident and stumbles, always want to get up and return to the proper and normal situation? And will not the one who wanders off the path in the wrong direction want to get back on the path headed in the right direction? Then surely, those who turn away, who get off the right path, will want to turn back and

79. Walter Brueggemann, "Jeremiah's Use of Rhetorical Questions," *JBL* 92 (1973) 374.

not stay forever on the wrong track. By analogy from the obvious answers to the first two questions, that should surely be the case. But it turns out not to be. And that is just the point. There is nothing wrong with the practical wisdom applied in all the questions. What is wrong is that "Israel's acting out of character and inconsistently with conventional wisdom has brought trouble. Nothing in nature or history has betrayed Israel. Israel has rather been tested by the way things naturally and normally are and has been found out of kilter."[80]

In the midst of the indictment, the prophet adds another term to the theological vocabulary of deceit that plays such a large role in his proclamation: תַּרְמִית (tarmît), which appears also in 14:14 and 23:26. The latter text may give a clue to the deception to which the people hold fast. In those texts, the "deceit" of the heart is the lie of the prophet, the promise that everything will be all right. Chapter 7 suggests another form of self-deception, one of equal tenacity: It is the trust in the Temple as a false source of security.

Verse 6 sets forth one of the many biblical pictures of the ears of God being attuned to human voices. It is like God's looking for a prophet to stand in the breach and intercede so that divine judgment will not have to happen (Ezek 13:5; 22:30-31). Here, however, the Lord is looking for the people to turn and repent, to cry out in remorse, "What have I done?" But there is only silence. We have to assume that, should the cry come, God would be open to the human word; the malleable God would respond as much to the confession and remorse of repentant hearts as to the prophetic prayers of intercession.

It becomes clear, however, that there is only one kind of "turning" in this community: turning away to their own course, doing what is right in their own eyes. Here again the prophet-poet uses an analogy to describe the turning of the people. Theirs is not a passive, slow degeneration or decline in morality, but an aggressive and full-force turning away, like the excited, headlong plunge of a warhorse into the midst of battle—and just as stupid. Their apostasy is driven by zeal.

An argument from the order of creation follows in v. 7. Even the birds know their place and their

appointed times and seasons. They keep to those places and times, thus following the way the Lord has set for them. Surely the people with whom the Lord lives in perpetual relationship, who know in their minds and hearts the providential care of the Lord, will outdo the birds. But the facts show that not to be the case. In another play on words, the prophet says, "They do not know the ordinance [מִשְׁפַּט mišpāṭ] of the LORD." They do not know the order (mišpāṭ) of the Lord for their lives, an order that is centered in justice (mišpāṭ). They also do not know the judgment (mišpāṭ) that is to come into their lives.

8:8-13. The argument of vv. 4-7 continues now in a specific way, moving back and forth between indictment or accusation (vv. 8, 9b, 10b-12) and announcement of judgment (vv. 9a, 10a, 12b). Verse 8 suggests that by this time there was some kind of written torah, with persons having specific responsibility for writing it down. We cannot be specific about what that written torah was, though some have suggested that it might have been some form of Deuteronomy. The "false pen of the scribes" is even more enigmatic. Is the falsity in their writing down the torah or in their interpretation or commentary on it? We cannot be sure. At best we can say that there are some leaders, perhaps the priests, perhaps the wise (v. 9), who have some responsibility for the keeping of the torah and presumably for its recitation and instruction. But their behavior vis-à-vis the torah makes them stupid and deceiving. It is much like their attitude toward the Temple. As long as the Temple is around, everything will be all right, no matter what the people do. Likewise, as long as they have the torah at hand, they can do whatever they want.

Verse 9a gives the lie to that assumption, and the second half of the verse restates the sin of this "we" group of leaders or wise types. They claim wisdom because of the torah, but if they reject the word of the Lord, what does that mean for their wisdom? Here the issue is not so much the written word versus the oral word or the wise person versus the prophet but the possession of a visible form of the word versus keeping and doing it.

In the back-and-forth movement of this text, the prophet then announces once more the judgment that is to come. It is, indeed, a harsh one: They will lose their wives and fields to others. In this

80. Ibid., 361.

case, the audience is probably males, for the leaders, the wise people, and the scribes for the most part would have been males. But the suffering that is inflicted upon them in judgment also extends to the women who are their spouses. The corporate experience of judgment is thus sharply underscored, and the women of the community are caught up in a punishment that, in this instance, is for the sins of their husbands (see also 7:18; 44:14-19).

The accusation against some of the leaders now moves out to incorporate the entire community (vv. 10b-12). This sudden shift is jarring and may be accounted for in part by recognizing that these words, which do not occur in the Greek translation, were probably not original to the text but have been inserted here from 6:12-13, possibly because a copyist wrote 6:12-13 in the margins of the text. In any event, those verses have now become a part of this passage, and it behooves us to ask what the text now means. One may suggest several things:

(1) The enigmas of the preceding verses are broken open. Readers are reminded again of the greediness of the community, of the economic character of this people's sin. At this point, the indictment picks up on Jeremiah's words in the temple sermon (chap. 7) about not oppressing the widow and the orphan. They are among the first and chief victims of this corporate greediness.

(2) An implicit correlation is suggested between the judgment that gives fields to the conquerors (v. 10a) and the greediness that has amassed unjustly derived wealth in order to "add field to field" (see Isa 5:8). The reader is reminded of Amos's announcement that those who had built fancy houses and planted pleasant vineyards would not live in the houses or drink the wine from the vineyards (Amos 5:11).

(3) The relation of the fasle prophets to deceit (v. 5) receives confirmation here, since the indictment is placed upon the prophets of (false) peace.

(4) Being ashamed and not knowing how to blush echoes the picture of the people/leaders who do not know the ordinance of the Lord as well as do the birds. These people are impervious to what they are doing, a gross and culpable ignorance or amorality.

(5) The word about falling in v. 12b echoes the beginning of vv. 4-7. What was a proverb-like say-

ing now becomes a word of judgment. Just as the second illustrative question about turning in v. 4 becomes concretized in v. 5 in the "turning" of the people, so also now the first illustrative question about falling becomes concretized in v. 12 in the "falling" of the people. The accusation of "turning away" leads to the judgment of falling.

8:14-17. As the military references and the allusion to the sounds of armies from the north (Dan) suggest, these verses are still a part of that complex of materials, beginning at 4:5, that deals with the coming of the enemy from the north. In words steeped in irony, the prophet envisions the people assessing their situation. The call to flee, "Gather together, let us go into the fortified cities," echoes 4:5. But what follows comes as a shock when compared to the earlier statement. The move to the fortified cities should be in preparation for and protection from the enemy. Instead, it is a move to judgment. That this understanding of the cities is both a move to protection and resistance and a move to judgment is confirmed by the similarity of v. 14a to the words of the lepers in 2 Kgs 7:3, who sat outside the gate of a besieged and desperate Samaria, surrounded by an Aramaean army. They ask themselves, "Why should we sit here waiting to die?" and decide to enter the Aramaean camp so that they can escape death. Hence v. 14 begins as a message to flee in order to escape judgment and ends up saying that flight is to judgment; moreover, v. 15 suggests the same thing. Hoping to get away to the safety of fortified cities, to find שלום (šālôm), safety and security, the people find only catastrophe, terror instead of healing or rest. The text is similar to Amos 5:18-19 as well and the escape to judgment described in that sentence parable.

It is not clear whether the "poisoned waters" of v. 14 are to be understood metaphorically or literally—that is, whether God will poison the water of the city and so destroy the people because of their sin. The matter is further complicated by the ambiguity of the phrase, as noted by the NIV translation. The Hebrew phrase could also be read as "tears," producing a different image but still one of judgment.

The imagery of judgment that began with poisoned waters moves now to the mighty horses of the invading army and then on to the snakes. The picture of the horses alludes to a scorched-earth policy, the utter devastation of the whole land and everything in it; this policy was to a large degree carried out by the Babylonian army, which had destroyed the cities of Judah on the way to doing the same to Jerusalem. The snakes are a different kind of menace. While we might understand them metaphorically, the references to poisoned water and the army of horses suggest that we give them a more literal reading. In the ancient Near East, the attack of wild animals was one of the curses set forth for disobedience of treaty stipulations. The reference to snakes here also evokes again the sentence parable of Amos 5:19 with its story of a retreat to safety from the threatening menace, only to find in the place of safety (home in Amos; fortified cities in Jeremiah) the final, inescapable menace, in both texts conveyed by the lethal bite of the snake.

8:18–9:1. The prophet now moves from the description of sin and announcements of judgment to a lament over the resulting distress of the people. The textual unit is clearly related with what precedes and with what follows. The presence of the divine voice in 8:17 opens up the possibility—indeed, the likelihood—that the first-person speaker of 8:18–9:1[8:18-23] is the Lord.[81] While it is customary to understand the speaker of these words as the prophet lamenting over the people, over "my people" (NRSV, "my poor people"), it is equally possible, as the context suggests, that we have here the voice of God. There is no real separation between the anguish and pathos of the prophet over what is happening to the people and the anguish and pathos of God. The divine word of v. 19c, which should not necessarily be read parenthetically as in the NRSV, helps to confirm this reading. Furthermore, elsewhere we encounter the Lord lamenting over the people (12:7-13), sometimes through the voice of the prophet (see Reflections on 4:19-22). In 14:17, it appears that the prophet is being told to lament for the Lord. There, too, the laments of prophet and God are followed by a lament addressed to the Lord, as is the case here (vv. 19-20). The reader would do well, therefore, to make no sharp distinction between prophetic and divine voices in these verses. There is no inherent reason why the anguish of the prophet should be greater than that of God over what has happened to "my people."

81. For full discussion of the case for seeing God as the one lamenting in these verses, see J. J. M. Roberts, "The Motif of the Weeping God in Jeremiah and Its Background in the Lament Tradition of the Ancient Near East," *Old Testament Essays* 5 (1992) 361-74.

At the end of the unit, there are clear links with the following text. The unit 9:2-9[9:1-8] is connected to this unit by its beginning, "O that . . . ," which echoes the same expression in 9:1. The joining of the two units also reinforces a reading of the first-person speaker as the Lord (see 9:3b).

At the beginning and end of the passage, we hear the anguish of the prophet/God, so sick at heart (8:18) that there are not enough tears to convey the sorrow (9:1). Within the passage, one hears the people cry for help, uttering the words that have done them in. In the rhetorical sequence that Jeremiah uses again and again (see the Commentary on 2:29-37 and 8:4-7), the first two questions ("Is the Lord not in Zion? Is her King not in her?") give a traditional, generally accepted presupposition, and the final question ("Why have they provoked me to anger . . . ?") becomes accusatory, challenging the assumption or logic of the first two in the light of the conduct of the people. The people assume that God will save them, since God is in Zion, or that if they will just wait, the Lord will come rushing in and miraculously deliver them, as God rescued them when Sennacherib threatened Jerusalem (Isaiah 36–37). The voice of God in the middle undercuts that assumption. God is offended by these claims, and the sense of offense is matched only by the divine distress over what that means for the people.

Another series of three rhetorical questions occurs in 8:22, the first two of which reflect traditional notions. The area of Gilead, east of the Jordan, was noted for trading in balm, a kind of aromatic resin that was regarded as having properties that either eased pain or covered the smell of festering wounds. Yes, there should be healing in Gilead, so why not healing for the people? The third question, as in the earlier instances (see above), uncovers the real situation. The reason why there is no hope for the people, no healing in Gilead or anywhere else, is given in 9:2-6. The reference to "balm in Gilead," a phrase well known to readers of Scripture, is especially poignant because it is said in the midst of weeping for the people. But they are tears for a people who have been slain (9:1). The prophet laments uncontrollably for a sick and dying people for whom there is no healing, no closing of the wound. There are not enough tears to equal the disaster that lies ahead as the prophet/God, knowing what terrible things lie ahead, "feels his way to the end of the process."

REFLECTIONS

1. The imagery of the way or the path is prominent in Scripture. It comes to play once more in the opening verses of this section. The richness of that image is hinted at by this text and is suggested in even greater fashion when it is brought into relation with other texts. Here it sets before the interpreter a picture, even a kind of action story, of persons going for a walk and losing their way, who are then faced with the alternatives of retracing their steps, "asking for the ancient paths" (6:16), to get back on track or proceeding recklessly down the wrong path that leads to a very uncertain end. Interpretation of the text might well take up the image of the way and bring it into juxtaposition with, for example, Psalm 1 with its depiction of two ways, the way of the righteous and the way of the wicked, one that is productive, fruitful, and durable like a tree planted by waters, and one that is transient, nonproductive, useless like chaff. Elsewhere Jeremiah connects with Psalm 1 (Jer 17:8), but 8:4-7 works the same soil from a different angle. In both Jer 8:4-7 and Psalm 1, the listener/reader is faced with sharp alternatives and is invited to make a decision. The text becomes a lesson from the past that poses afresh the issue of the way of obedience and the way of personal interest.

2. What is clear in this text is that self-interest and common sense indicate clearly which path to take. Indeed, this is one of many texts in Jeremiah where the rhetoric and appeal to the people are sensible, where the people are urged to do what any thinking person would do. We do not always think of the prophets as making strong rational arguments, but they do that all the time, appealing to what is in the best interests of the people, using logic, illustrating their points with stories and examples. The various three-part rhetorical questions identified several times in 8:4–9:1 as well as earlier are good examples of the prophet's persuasive rhetoric, of a proclamation that uses the logic of the hearers to cut the ground out from under them. The mode of speech in such a text as this and others like it suggests something of the way the contemporary proclaimer of the text might communicate.

3. The anthropomorphic imagery of Scripture comes into play here in indirect fashion as we are given a picture of a listening God, of the ears of God, or the divine antenna, attuned to hear human voices. Such a picture can be seen in Scripture as early as the Cain and Abel story, where the blood of Abel cries out and is heard by God. Such imagery suggests several points:

The first idea this imagery suggests is the openness of God to human need and to human appeals. This is something for which God actively listens. It is the particular "wavelength" to which God is attuned. So the picture of God listening intimates the responsiveness of God, the awareness that human life is not on its own and without resort in the world. God is listening all the time.

Second, this text suggests that at least one of the things for which God listens is the confession of those who have done wrong, the repentant cry, "We have sinned." The confession of sin is a fairly routine matter in contemporary liturgy, given little sense of urgency, of the fact that God is intently listening for such confession and repentance. Yet urgency is what we associate with cries for help. Jeremiah makes us aware that God's urgency may be about repentance and the prayers that say to God, "What have I done?!" with as much fervor as "What have you done?!"

Third, the responsiveness of God is such that the divine intention can be affected and even altered by words of confession and repentance. Indeed, most of the examples of God's change of mind in Scripture have to do with the Lord's decision not to bring judgment when the community has sinned greatly. That may be because of prophetic intercession (see the Commentary on chaps. 7 and 15), as in the account of Moses' prayer on behalf of the people when they made the golden calf, or as in the story of the repentant Ninevites in the book of Jonah. In either case, there is a willingness, if not a strong desire, on God's part to avert judgment. But divine action is not apart from what is happening on the human scene.

4. There seems often to be a point of no return in human conduct that elsewhere in Scripture is called hardening of the heart. Self-interest and personal gain may control one's actions for so long that it is not possible for that person to see or act differently, even when circumstances indicate that a change of heart and a different mode of conduct are, in fact, in one's own self-interest. A society that focuses on the acquisitive instinct, on personal fulfillment, on ambition, and on accumulation bids fair to create an ethos of just such "hardening," where patterns or paths of conduct are so set that they cannot be given up, even when they are wrongheaded and disastrous. Prophetic preaching is often set in just such circumstances—now as well as then. It may be no more successful now than it was then.

5. While we cannot be sure what is meant by "the false pen of the scribes," enough is indicated to make the contemporary scribe, the contemporary keeper of the word—whether theologian, teacher, priest, or preacher—nervous about ways in which by our preaching, our interpretation, our mode of living we turn the divine word into a lie, using it to support the way we wish to see things or to have them be. We may turn the hard words of Scripture into easy ones, not because of the gospel but because of our desire to maintain the status quo, not to offend friends and parishioners. And so we have "made it into a lie." We have offered a "balm" that we did not have. We may turn the gracious words of Scripture into hard ones and so cut off persons from the experience of healing that is offered by those words, thus making them into "a lie." There *is* a balm in Gilead to make the wounded whole. One of the critical tasks for contemporary proclamation is to know whether such balm is available and how and when the offer of such balm is to treat "the wounds of my people carelessly" (6:14).

6. Jeremiah 8:10*b*-12 seems to be an intrusion from chap. 6 (see the Commentary on 8:4-13). That perception makes it easy to ignore these verses by saying that they do not fit or that they are a later gloss on the text. But that may be just the point, that in the midst of everything that is said there constantly intrudes the reality that these people who claim to live by God's command are completely focused on their own gain and are perfectly willing to get their "cut" of the action out of the hides of those less well off than they. That is wrong. That is a violation of God's commands. That is a breach of the covenantal relationship. There is no way to equivocate or justify such actions. Its obvious contemporary instantiation is in the vigorous, sometimes fanatical, efforts of those with large financial holdings to make sure that capital gains taxes on those investments are cut to pad their wallets, thereby taking that gain out of monies cut from the support of dependent children and single parents.

Jeremiah 9:2-26, What Can I Do with My Sinful People?

NIV

²Oh, that I had in the desert
    a lodging place for travelers,
so that I might leave my people
    and go away from them;
for they are all adulterers,
    a crowd of unfaithful people.

³"They make ready their tongue
    like a bow, to shoot lies;
it is not by truth

NRSV

²ᵃ O that I had in the desert
    a traveler's lodging place,
    that I might leave my people
    and go away from them!
For they are all adulterers,
    a band of traitors.
³ They bend their tongues like bows;
    they have grown strong in the land for
        falsehood, and not for truth;

ᵃ Ch. 9.1 in Heb

NIV

that they triumph[a] in the land.
They go from one sin to another;
    they do not acknowledge me,"
                    declares the LORD.
4"Beware of your friends;
    do not trust your brothers.
For every brother is a deceiver,[b]
    and every friend a slanderer.
5Friend deceives friend,
    and no one speaks the truth.
They have taught their tongues to lie;
    they weary themselves with sinning.
6You[c] live in the midst of deception;
    in their deceit they refuse to acknowledge
    me,"
                    declares the LORD.
7Therefore this is what the LORD Almighty says:

"See, I will refine and test them,
    for what else can I do
    because of the sin of my people?
8Their tongue is a deadly arrow;
    it speaks with deceit.
With his mouth each speaks cordially to his
    neighbor,
    but in his heart he sets a trap for him.
9Should I not punish them for this?"
    declares the LORD.
"Should I not avenge myself
    on such a nation as this?"

10I will weep and wail for the mountains
    and take up a lament concerning the desert
    pastures.
They are desolate and untraveled,
    and the lowing of cattle is not heard.
The birds of the air have fled
    and the animals are gone.

11"I will make Jerusalem a heap of ruins,
    a haunt of jackals;
and I will lay waste the towns of Judah
    so no one can live there."

12What man is wise enough to understand this? Who has been instructed by the LORD and can explain it? Why has the land been ruined and laid waste like a desert that no one can cross?

---

a3 Or lies; / they are not valiant for truth   b4 Or a deceiving Jacob   c6 That is, Jeremiah (the Hebrew is singular)

NRSV

for they proceed from evil to evil,
    and they do not know me, says the LORD.

4 Beware of your neighbors,
    and put no trust in any of your kin;[a]
for all your kin[b] are supplanters,
    and every neighbor goes around like a
    slanderer.
5 They all deceive their neighbors,
    and no one speaks the truth;
they have taught their tongues to speak lies;
    they commit iniquity and are too weary to
    repent.[c]
6 Oppression upon oppression, deceit[d] upon
    deceit!
    They refuse to know me, says the LORD.

7 Therefore thus says the LORD of hosts:
I   will now refine and test them,
    for what else can I do with my sinful
    people?[e]
8 Their tongue is a deadly arrow;
    it speaks deceit through the mouth.
They all speak friendly words to their
    neighbors,
    but inwardly are planning to lay an ambush.
9 Shall I not punish them for these things? says
    the LORD;
    and shall I not bring retribution
    on a nation such as this?

10 Take up[f] weeping and wailing for the
    mountains,
    and a lamentation for the pastures of the
    wilderness,
because they are laid waste so that no one
    passes through,
    and the lowing of cattle is not heard;
both the birds of the air and the animals
    have fled and are gone.
11 I will make Jerusalem a heap of ruins,
    a lair of jackals;
and I will make the towns of Judah a
    desolation,
    without inhabitant.

---

aHeb in a brother   bHeb for every brother   cCn.: Compare Gk: Heb they weary themselves with iniquity. b Your dwelling   dCn: Heb Your dwelling in the midst of deceit   eOr my poor people   fGk Syr: Heb I will take up

NIV

[13]The LORD said, "It is because they have forsaken my law, which I set before them; they have not obeyed me or followed my law. [14]Instead, they have followed the stubbornness of their hearts; they have followed the Baals, as their fathers taught them." [15]Therefore, this is what the LORD Almighty, the God of Israel, says: "See, I will make this people eat bitter food and drink poisoned water. [16]I will scatter them among nations that neither they nor their fathers have known, and I will pursue them with the sword until I have destroyed them."

[17]This is what the LORD Almighty says:

"Consider now! Call for the wailing women to
    come;
  send for the most skillful of them.
[18]Let them come quickly
    and wail over us
till our eyes overflow with tears
    and water streams from our eyelids.
[19]The sound of wailing is heard from Zion:
    'How ruined we are!
    How great is our shame!
We must leave our land
    because our houses are in ruins.' "

[20]Now, O women, hear the word of the LORD;
    open your ears to the words of his mouth.
Teach your daughters how to wail;
    teach one another a lament.
[21]Death has climbed in through our windows
    and has entered our fortresses;
it has cut off the children from the streets
    and the young men from the public squares.

[22]Say, "This is what the LORD declares:

" 'The dead bodies of men will lie
    like refuse on the open field,
like cut grain behind the reaper,
    with no one to gather them.' "

[23]This is what the LORD says:

"Let not the wise man boast of his wisdom
    or the strong man boast of his strength
    or the rich man boast of his riches,
[24]but let him who boasts boast about this:
    that he understands and knows me,
    that I am the LORD, who exercises kindness,

NRSV

[12]Who is wise enough to understand this? To whom has the mouth of the LORD spoken, so that they may declare it? Why is the land ruined and laid waste like a wilderness, so that no one passes through? [13]And the LORD says: Because they have forsaken my law that I set before them, and have not obeyed my voice, or walked in accordance with it, [14]but have stubbornly followed their own hearts and have gone after the Baals, as their ancestors taught them. [15]Therefore thus says the LORD of hosts, the God of Israel: I am feeding this people with wormwood, and giving them poisonous water to drink. [16]I will scatter them among nations that neither they nor their ancestors have known; and I will send the sword after them, until I have consumed them.

[17] Thus says the LORD of hosts:
  Consider, and call for the mourning women to
    come;
    send for the skilled women to come;
[18] let them quickly raise a dirge over us,
    so that our eyes may run down with tears,
    and our eyelids flow with water.
[19] For a sound of wailing is heard from Zion:
    "How we are ruined!
    We are utterly shamed,
  because we have left the land,
    because they have cast down our
      dwellings."

[20] Hear, O women, the word of the LORD,
    and let your ears receive the word of his
      mouth;
  teach to your daughters a dirge,
    and each to her neighbor a lament.
[21] "Death has come up into our windows,
    it has entered our palaces,
  to cut off the children from the streets
    and the young men from the squares."
[22] Speak! Thus says the LORD:
  "Human corpses shall fall
    like dung upon the open field,
  like sheaves behind the reaper,
    and no one shall gather them."

[23]Thus says the LORD: Do not let the wise boast in their wisdom, do not let the mighty boast in their might, do not let the wealthy boast in their

NIV

justice and righteousness on earth,
for in these I delight,"
                    declares the LORD.

²⁵"The days are coming," declares the LORD, "when I will punish all who are circumcised only in the flesh— ²⁶Egypt, Judah, Edom, Ammon, Moab and all who live in the desert in distant places.^a For all these nations are really uncircumcised, and even the whole house of Israel is uncircumcised in heart."

^a26 Or *desert and who clip the hair by their foreheads*

NRSV

wealth; ²⁴but let those who boast boast in this, that they understand and know me, that I am the LORD; I act with steadfast love, justice, and righteousness in the earth, for in these things I delight, says the LORD.

²⁵The days are surely coming, says the LORD, when I will attend to all those who are circumcised only in the foreskin: ²⁶Egypt, Judah, Edom, the Ammonites, Moab, and all those with shaven temples who live in the desert. For all these nations are uncircumcised, and all the house of Israel is uncircumcised in heart.

COMMENTARY

9:2-11[1-10]. The connecting point between this unit and the end of chap. 8 is the catchword expression "O that . . ." in 9:1-2. This repeated exclamation, together with the ongoing first-person speech, suggests that one should continue to hear in these words the voice of the Lord, speaking through the prophet.[82] These verses now spell out why there can be no healing for this people, the question raised in 8:22: their immoral conduct. Verses 2-3, however, clearly belong to the verses that follow, since they spell out the sins of the people and the repeated reference to not "knowing" the Lord. The movement from sin to judgment to lament is evident again in these verses, though it does not happen in a simple, linear process. The sins of the people are spelled out in vv. 2-6 and 8, the judgment of God against them in vv. 7, 9, and 11, and the lament in v. 10. There is an intensifying movement in the elaboration of the crimes of the people, or at least in the way this is turned into a theological sin. The sins cataloged in v. 3 are climaxed by the conclusion: "They do not know me." As the catalog grows larger and the sins are heaped one upon another (v. 6), the Lord characterizes these actions as a demonstration of not just that "they do not know me" but that "they *refuse* to know me." This characterization of the people is consistent with the many indications in Jeremiah that the people persisted in their disobedience and sin even when they were

reproved, that they refused to accept discipline and correction when it came, that they continued down the wrong path, ignoring opportunities to turn back and renew their way. In other words, the conduct does not simply demonstrate or result in a lack of acknowledgment and a lack of relationship with the Lord. It is, rather, a willful refusal to make any attempt to do so.

The opening verse sounds as if it may be the prophet saying he wishes to get completely away from this sinful people. But we may not simply assume that such anthropomorphic language could not apply to God. Elsewhere, there is a similar picture of the Lord "like a traveler turning aside for the night" (14:8). Once again, the verse may give us the blended voices of prophet and God, similarly and together disgusted enough with the conduct of "my people" to want to get out of town and have nothing to do with them.

The sin of the people as described in this text is that of the tongue, the many ways in which language and speed betray, hurt, deceive, and destroy others. The initial description of this sin in v. 3 may be a more generalized reference to the way in which the sins of the people betray their relationship with the Lord. That is, the reference to adultery may have in mind that particular sin as being rampant in the community (Jer 5:7), but earlier in the book (chap. 2) as well as in the prophet Hosea, adultery has been an image for the people's violation of their relationship with the Lord, and that may well be the point here. The Hebrew for

82. See Roberts, "The Motif of the Weeping God in Jeremiah and Its Background in the Lament Tradition of the Ancient Near East."

"band" (עצרת '*ăṣeret*) often refers to a cultic assembly. If that is the case in this instance, then the Lord is addressing again the way in which the cultic activities in worship of God are betrayed by the people's conduct outside the sanctuary. If this reading of v. 3 is on target, then the text moves from the general identification of the sins of the people as a kind of fundamental treachery against their covenantal obligations to the Lord to the specific ways in which what they say in their everyday life renders harm.

The absence of truthful speech is identified again as a major problem in Judean society (cf. 5:1-3, 12, 30; 6:13-14; 7:4, 8; 8:5, 8). The lying speech and the sin of the tongue take the form of slander, malicious speech directed against other members of the community, what one interpreter has described as a kind of "internecine warfare."[83] With striking imagery reminiscent of Ps 64:3-4, the prophet speaks of words that shoot out of the mouth like arrows and wound just as painfully (vv. 3, 8). The picture that unfolds is of a society in which truth has disappeared and terrible things are said to one another about others such that no one can be trusted and nothing spoken can be believed.

The repeated reference to "neighbor" and "kin" or "brother" sharpens the sense of how bad the situation has gotten. The Hebrew expression lying behind the translation "all your kin are *supplanters*" (NRSV) or "every brother is a *deceiver*" (NIV) plays on the name "Jacob" (עקוב יעקב '*āqôb ya*'*qôb*). Additionally, the different words for "deceit" in v. 5 (תלל *tālal*) and v. 6 (מרמה *mirmâ*) come to play in the Jacob story when he tells his wives that their father, Laban, cheated (*tālal*) him (Gen 31:7) and Jacob is said to have taken his brother's blessing deceitfully (*mirmâ*, Gen 27:35; note also a later act of deceit by Jacob in Gen 34:13). Thus the present situation seems to hark back to the beginnings when Israel's ancestor both deceived his kin and was deceived by his kin, implicitly suggesting that there is something in the very heritage of this people that seems to predispose them to deceit and cheating.[84]

No one in the community can be trusted. They pretend to care about each other and are superficially nice, but behind people's backs, they spread all sorts of gossip and slanderous talk (cf. 6:28). These people have taught their tongues how to inflict wounds and tell lies (cf. 4:22). It has become a practiced art for them. And they show no inclination to change (v. 5*b*).

So, in a kind of divine soliloquy, the Lord asks what to do about this sinful people (v. 7) and answers the question with the obvious and inescapable answer: Judgment must be made against them (v. 9). (On the image of the Lord as the refiner and tester, see the Commentary on 6:27-30.)

The NIV translation of v. 10 is probably correct. (The more difficult reading of the Hebrew text has the first-person "I will take up [weeping]," as distinguished from the Greek version, which has an imperative, "Take up [weeping]," that conforms to the character of the related speech in v. 18, where it is the community that laments.) That understanding leaves open, however, the question of who the speaker is, whether Jeremiah or God. Some interpreters would see here two separate fragments, the first a lament by the prophet and the second a word of judgment by the Lord. It is possible that the text represents the joining of several shorter pieces, but there are problems with that understanding of the speakers. The content of the two verses is sufficiently similar in their depiction of a land laid waste, and the back-and-forth movement from deity (vv. 7-9), to prophet (v. 10), to deity (v. 11) sufficiently jarring that some interpreters have preferred the Greek reading because it enables one to keep the divine voice speaking consistently through these verses. But there is no reason not to see the Lord as the subject of the verb "I will take up [weeping]" that the Hebrew text represents.

Verse 9 should be understood as the lament of God set in sharp juxtaposition with the announcement of judgment in v. 10. The picture of God weeping and lamenting over a disobedient and doomed people is not unique to this chapter. In 12:7-13, God laments and judges the people at the same time. Moreover, the concluding unit of chap. 8 also depicts God lamenting over the plight of the people in the midst of declarations of judgment (see the Commentary on 8:18–9:1). The devastated land is at one and the same time the consequence

83. William McKane, *A Critical and Exegetical Commentary on Jeremiah,* 2 vols., ICC (Edinburgh: T. & T. Clark, 1986, 1996) 1:199.

84. William L. Holladay, *Jeremiah 1: A Commentary on the Book of the Prophet Jeremiah Chapters 1–25,* Hermeneia (Philadelphia: Fortress, 1986) 301.

of the Lord's intentional decision and the source of great anguish in God's heart. It is not difficult to imagine such anguish in viewing the devastation of the place where the Lord of Israel has dwelt with this covenanted people.

9:12-16[11-15]. Using a question-and-answer scheme (vv. 12-14) that occurs several times elsewhere in Jeremiah (see the Commentary on 5:19), one that always explains or justifies the divine judgment, the writer places the next question not in the mouths of the people but as one that the Lord has raised. The question and its answer, in effect, create an inverted judgment speech. Instead of announcing a coming judgment on the basis of an accusation or indictment, as the judgment speech typically does, the question looks back from the judgment to ask why and so to discover the grounds for that judgment.

The opening line suggests that with careful discernment one can figure out what has happened and that its meaning has been revealed by God. The relation between the discernment and the revelation is vague in this context, but the wise person will seek to determine the meaning of the events and will do so in relation to the word of the Lord that announced them. The query assumes an experience of devastation. So even if the question is posed by the Lord, it anticipates what the people will try to understand after the Babylonian army has devastated the land. The answer, in retrospect, is the same one that has regularly been given: breach of covenant, evident in the failure of the people to live by the instruction and teaching (torah) of the Lord, a failure most clearly represented in the avid pursuit of other gods. The text plays with the familiar language of "going after" (see the Commentary on 2:1-3), giving that expression two objects: their own stubborn hearts and the "baals." These are not really separate items, but the first of the two picks up the persistent problem that is identified again and again: the people's resistance to correction, to change, to turning around, and hence to repentance. Their own desires and self-interests, reflected in the attention they give to the fertility gods, is their all-consuming passion. The Lord and the Lord's way have been displaced from first place in their hearts. The devastated land is a manifestation of the continuing power of the Lord.

This indictment leads, then, into another announcement of judgment, revolving around the imagery of eating and drinking poison. The "wormwood" may represent the bitterness of life in a devastated land or in exile, or it may be understood, with the poisonous water, to imply that the judgment is, in effect, a poisoned drink, a fatal cup. The poison signifies both exile and death.

9:17-22[16-21]. The words of indictment and judgment culminate once again in lament, this time not prophetic or divine lament but a call for mourning women to come forward and lift up the sounds and wails of a dirge, the kinds of sounds that are heard when death is at hand. That these women are trained mourners is indicated both by the reference to "skilled women" in v. 17 and by the call for the women to teach their daughters a dirge (v. 20). The picture that evolves is powerfully clear: Death stalks the land, and the only appropriate response is to evoke the dirges that are regularly sung over the dead. When repentance does not take place, then there is nothing to do but weep for the shame of defeat and conquest.

The middle verses underscore how bad things are with the command to teach dirges and laments to their daughters and neighbors. There are not enough professional mourners to wail over the devastation, for death is everywhere. It is an active force, coming into houses, attacking children in the streets. The scene suggests plague and pestilence striking down everyone. There are so many corpses and so few people left alive that the bodies lie where they fell and rot on the ground. It is a horrific image. No wonder the wailing women are summoned.

The picture of death at the window (v. 21) has been traced to a story in Syro-Palestinian mythology that depicts the Canaanite god Baal building a palace for himself and resisting the proposal by the architect, another deity, to place windows in the palace. It has been suggested that Baal resists because he fears that the god of death, Mot, might enter the palace through the windows. Other ancient Near Eastern texts depict death or a demon coming in through the window to prey on people.

9:23-24[22-23]. In the midst of these words of sin and judgment, of weeping and wailing over destruction, the prophet sets a kind of plumb line, a statement that succinctly identifies the wrong way and the right way, what is needed and what is missing. These brief verses join wisdom style with prophetic norms. The reference to wisdom and the expression "Let not someone boast in . . ." (see 1 Kgs 20:11; Prov 23:17-18*a*) associate this way of speaking with the modes and concerns of the sages and the circles of the wise. The first part of this section is thus a traditional saying about what counts and what does not, about assuming one is in good shape only to find out that is not the case. The categories of wisdom, strength, and riches represent fundamental grounds of security: intellectual skill and the ability to make things work in life, power and might in oneself or in one's armies, and wealth that enables one to acquire whatever one needs. There may be an implicit critique of the royal establishment in the rejection of these grounds for boasting, but they are ultimately more universal than that. These are the things that represent the primary avenues for personal self-enhancement and security. One may hear in the triad a kind of ironic play on the three dimensions of love of the Lord in the Shema (Deut 6:5): the "heart" or "mind" (לבב *lēbāb*); the "soul" (נפש *nepeš*), which here seems to mean one's life or physical strength; and the "muchness" (מאד *mĕ'ōd*) that is not so much physical strength as it is all that one has or owns.

Such comparison is invited further by what is set over against these false grounds for boasting: comprehension of who the Lord is and what the Lord is like and an acknowledgment of that Lord. The wisdom that matters is not the intellectual skill of the sage or the technical skill of the administrator. It is the good sense to know that the Lord, whose way is characterized by steadfast love, justice, and righteousness, is the only one who can provide solid security. Such discernment and acknowledgment mean that one is pledged to another way than that which involves pursuit of wisdom, might, and riches. It is a way that manifests a lasting care and love, equity and fairness in all human dealings and affairs, and a conformity to God's will for right conduct and right relationship. This triad is meant to effect a kind of *imitatio dei,* defining the chief expectations of the Lord for human conduct by identifying the chief characteristics of the Lord's own way. Over against wisdom, might, and riches—typical grounds for boasting— the prophet suggests that there is only one ground of security: the Lord's way. Here, therefore, the

prophet joins other prophets, such as Isaiah (Isa 1:16-17), Hosea (Hos 6:6), Amos (Amos 5:14-15, 24), and Micah (Mic 6:8), who set forth in succinct fashion the Lord's requirements for the people.

Paul takes up this text more than once, but particularly to radicalize it, to identify God's way with foolishness, weakness, and lowliness, precisely the opposite of the presumably more desirable ways of wisdom, might, and riches (1 Cor 1:31). In so doing, all these other grounds for boasting of one's place are reduced to nothing. There is no alternative but to boast in the Lord (see 2 Cor 10:17).

9:25-26[24-25]. These verses sit loosely in their context but are a part of a continuing critique reaching back to other texts that speak about the circumcision of the heart (4:4; 6:10) as well as to chap. 7, which rejects any assumption that ritual propriety can help one withstand the judgment for moral turpitude. It has been suggested that this group of nations represents a political coalition of circumcised nations against the uncircumcised Babylonians.[85] No record, however, has been preserved to confirm that suggestion. No formal religious act or symbol—whether circumcision or temple—can offset the judgment of God when it is not backed up with proper quality of life. The gist of v. 26 is best indicated in the NIV: These nations, even though circumcised, will face divine judgment, some because, though circumcised, they have no relation to the Lord and "the house of Israel." Their pervasive apostasy, injustice, and selfishness betray hearts that are not bent toward the Lord and the Lord's way. They are circumcised, but it means nothing. A formal physical act is not matched by the "cutting" of the will. They are "uncircumcised in heart." Paul puts the matter this way in his letter to the Romans:

> For a person is not a Jew who is one outwardly, nor is true circumcision something external and physical. Rather, a person is a Jew who is one inwardly, and real circumcision is a matter of the heart—it is spiritual and not literal. (Rom 2:28-29*a* NRSV)

---

85. "Those with shaven temples who live in the desert" is probably a reference to Arab tribes who are distinguished by their particular type of haircut.

REFLECTIONS

1. The identification of deceit, lies, and treachery as some of the major problems in Judean society sets before us the reality of lying and the use of hurtful words as major social issues. There is a tendency to see lying as a kind of individual or personal sin, but it nearly always has negative effects on others. Jeremiah challenges the contemporary community to examine the way we speak and the integrity of our dealings with others. When business contracts are drawn up that hide information from one of the parties, lying is a tool of economic deceit. When a spouse pretends to be faithful while showering attention and affection on another person, lying is part of the rot that undoes the marriage relationship. When a son or a daughter does not tell a parent the truth about what he or she has been doing, the family becomes more vulnerable to breakdown. When a politician fails to disclose her or his ties to private interests that lead to favoritism in making decisions and legislation, the democratic process is skewed. When a person lies to the court in any capacity, society's last resort for integrity and fair dealing no longer functions and there can be no guarantee of justice anymore. Perjury receives a severe sentence precisely because the failure of the courts means that there is no protection for the community, no redress in the face of the oppression of power, wealth, and lies. The picture Jeremiah paints is of a community that is totally broken down because nothing can be counted upon. There is no trustworthy social intercourse. There is only deceit and the suspicion that it breeds. Charles Swezey has aptly described the social breakdown that accompanies persistent and pervasive mendacity:

> Freedom of choice depends upon a knowledge of the case at hand, which lies take away. Integrity depends upon speaking from one's own perspective, which lies remove. When lies are habitual and the words of everyday discourse unreliable, we plunge into doubt and suspicion. Life together is not possible without a minimal trust in the veracity of words. An unwritten law exists: Unless checks are placed on the proclivity to evade truthfulness, corporate existence flounders and is altogether nasty and brutish.[86]

It is not only overt lying that does in the community. The tongue can afflict and wound and hurt in many ways that are not technically lying, and that is what Jeremiah has in mind in this chapter. The New Testament Letter to James speaks of the tongue as a fire and says, "How great a forest is set ablaze by a small fire!" (Jas 3:5-6). So in gossip and slander, as well as in lies, injury is inflicted upon others in the community. The image of the tongue as an arrow (9:8) is powerful. An arrow even fits the shape of the tongue, and it readily suggests how a word shoots out of the mouth toward someone or about someone and pierces in a way a real arrow can, perhaps causing even greater harm. It is easy for us to repeat what we have heard, to say exaggerated things about others that turn a fault into a sin and so destroy a reputation. To modify the old saying, "Sticks and stones may break my bones, but words can *really* hurt me!"

2. In the interpretive literature on Jeremiah 8–9, there is some resistance to seeing God as the subject of the first-person lamenting speech. In part this is due to the apparent contradiction between God's threatening judgment in one verse (e.g., 9:9), lamenting in the next verse (9:10), and promising devastating judgment in the next one (9:11). But such contradiction is better perceived as a tension within the heart and character of God. Two things are at odds: the steadfast and faithful love of God for this people and the intention of God to have an obedient and faithful people in the world. The Scriptures are full of testimony to both dimensions of God's relationship with Israel. That such equally strong dimensions of the divine reality can be at odds with each other, creating painful tension within God's own mind, is indicated in various texts, such as in the conversation between Moses and God when the Lord threatens to destroy the people after the making of the golden calf (Exod 32:7-14) or in the divine soliloquy in Hosea 11. The

---

86. Charles M. Swezey, "Exodus 20:16—'Thou shalt not bear false witness against thy neighbor,'" *Int.* 34 (1980) 407.

church's theology has focused heavily on the judgment of God and on the sovereign power of God, particularly in its reading of the Old Testament. It has often passed by all those moments when God weeps and laments, when the heart of God is saddened and grieves over what has gone on in the world, especially over the failure of God's beloved people—those with whom the Lord has entered into perduring covenantal relationship—who toss aside binding commitments in ways that anger and sadden at the same time. There are sufficient analogies on the human scene to create no surprise that God's wrath and tears may flow forth simultaneously. One need only think of the marital setting when a spouse discovers the unfaithfulness of her or his partner. Grief and anger may erupt at the same time. So it is with the Lord of Israel discovering the unfaithfulness of God's covenant partner.

3. The ground for boasting is a theme that merits continuing attention, as Paul's several references to the topic suggest. There is a sense that the move to glory in God rather than in the typical human values—wisdom, power, wealth—effects a radical change in the shape of life. The juxtaposition of these human values with the three divine virtues surely suggests the primacy of the latter over the former. There is no denigration of wisdom, power, and wealth per se, but there is a devaluing of the more evident and typical grounds for self-acclaim and the acclaim of others. The intellectual, the politician, and the entrepreneur are legitimate roles in society—then and now—but the inclination of such individuals to exalt themselves or of others to exalt them is to be resisted. When it is God who is glorified, another set of values is lifted up: justice, righteousness, and steadfast love. The exaltation of God shifts in a radical way the categories of human valuation. Thus the Red Cross worker, the civil rights worker, the legal aid lawyer, the nurse, and the parent, and the friend become modes of human existence that reflect some ways that God is at work in the world. They are not grounds for boasting. Rather, they are ways of knowing and acknowledging God.

Jeremiah 10:1-16, God Versus the Idols

NIV

10 Hear what the LORD says to you, O house of Israel. ²This is what the LORD says:
"Do not learn the ways of the nations
   or be terrified by signs in the sky,
   though the nations are terrified by them.
³For the customs of the peoples are worthless;
   they cut a tree out of the forest,
   and a craftsman shapes it with his chisel.
⁴They adorn it with silver and gold;
   they fasten it with hammer and nails
   so it will not totter.
⁵Like a scarecrow in a melon patch,
   their idols cannot speak;
they must be carried
   because they cannot walk.
Do not fear them;
   they can do no harm
   nor can they do any good."

NRSV

10 Hear the word that the LORD speaks to you,
       O house of Israel. ²Thus says the LORD:
Do not learn the way of the nations,
   or be dismayed at the signs of the heavens;
   for the nations are dismayed at them.
³ For the customs of the peoples are false:
a tree from the forest is cut down,
   and worked with an ax by the hands of an
      artisan;
⁴ people deck it with silver and gold;
   they fasten it with hammer and nails
   so that it cannot move.
⁵ Their idols*a* are like scarecrows in a cucumber
      field,
   and they cannot speak;
   they have to be carried,
   for they cannot walk.

*a*Heb *They*

NIV

⁶No one is like you, O Lord;
    you are great,
    and your name is mighty in power.
⁷Who should not revere you,
    O King of the nations?
    This is your due.
  Among all the wise men of the nations
    and in all their kingdoms,
    there is no one like you.
⁸They are all senseless and foolish;
    they are taught by worthless wooden idols.
⁹Hammered silver is brought from Tarshish
    and gold from Uphaz.
  What the craftsman and goldsmith have made
    is then dressed in blue and purple—
    all made by skilled workers.
¹⁰But the Lord is the true God;
    he is the living God, the eternal King.
  When he is angry, the earth trembles;
    the nations cannot endure his wrath.

¹¹"Tell them this: 'These gods, who did not make the heavens and the earth, will perish from the earth and from under the heavens.' "[a]
¹²But God made the earth by his power;

    he founded the world by his wisdom
    and stretched out the heavens by his
      understanding.
¹³When he thunders, the waters in the heavens
      roar;
    he makes clouds rise from the ends of the
      earth.
  He sends lightning with the rain
    and brings out the wind from his storehouses.

¹⁴Everyone is senseless and without knowledge;
    every goldsmith is shamed by his idols.
  His images are a fraud;
    they have no breath in them.
¹⁵They are worthless, the objects of mockery;
    when their judgment comes, they will
      perish.
¹⁶He who is the Portion of Jacob is not like
      these,
    for he is the Maker of all things,
  including Israel, the tribe of his inheritance—
    the Lord Almighty is his name.

*11 The text of this verse is in Aramaic.

NRSV

  Do not be afraid of them,
    for they cannot do evil,
    nor is it in them to do good.

⁶ There is none like you, O Lord;
    you are great, and your name is great in
      might.
⁷ Who would not fear you, O King of the
      nations?
    For that is your due;
  among all the wise ones of the nations
    and in all their kingdoms
    there is no one like you.
⁸ They are both stupid and foolish;
    the instruction given by idols
    is no better than wood![a]
⁹ Beaten silver is brought from Tarshish,
    and gold from Uphaz.
  They are the work of the artisan and of the
      hands of the goldsmith;
    their clothing is blue and purple;
    they are all the product of skilled workers.
¹⁰ But the Lord is the true God;
    he is the living God and the everlasting
      King.
  At his wrath the earth quakes,
    and the nations cannot endure his
      indignation.

11 Thus shall you say to them: The gods who did not make the heavens and the earth shall perish from the earth and from under the heavens.[b]

¹² It is he who made the earth by his power,
    who established the world by his wisdom,
    and by his understanding stretched out the
      heavens.
¹³ When he utters his voice, there is a tumult of
      waters in the heavens,
    and he makes the mist rise from the ends
      of the earth.
  He makes lightnings for the rain,
    and he brings out the wind from his store-
      houses.
¹⁴ Everyone is stupid and without knowledge;
    goldsmiths are all put to shame by their
      idols;

*Meaning of Heb uncertain   *This verse is in Aramaic

NRSV

for their images are false,
and there is no breath in them.
[15] They are worthless, a work of delusion;
at the time of their punishment they shall
perish.
[16] Not like these is the Lord,[a] the portion of
Jacob,
for he is the one who formed all things,
and Israel is the tribe of his inheritance;
the Lord of hosts is his name.

[a]Heb lacks the Lord

COMMENTARY

These verses show evidence of a complex history of transmission and so raise questions about their unity. Among the pieces of such evidence are the incongruity of the superscription (v. 1), which identifies these as words of the Lord, and the rest of the text, which includes extensive words both about and to the Lord; a significant difference between the Hebrew text and the Greek text of these verses with both forms of text having been preserved in Hebrew MSS at Qumran; the location of v. 9 of the Greek text next to vv. 4-5, where it seems to fit better; the presence of a single verse of Aramaic in an otherwise Hebrew text; various shifts back and forth between singular and plural forms; the repetition of vv. 12-16 in 51:15-19; and various real or apparent incongruities in the text, such as that between the fear of the heavenly signs in v. 2 and the making of the idols in v. 3. The extent to which any of the verses can be traced directly to Jeremiah is a matter of considerable debate. The different tone of this chapter from much of Jeremiah's denunciatory words suggests to some a different author,[87] while others reach the same conclusion on the basis of the similarity of the polemic against idols to passages in Isaiah (Isa 40:18-20; 41:7; 44:9-20; 46:5-7).[88]

Determination of the date and authorship of these verses or of the original text is no less difficult here than in many other parts of the book of Jeremiah. The main issues could have been appropriately addressed to remnants of either the northern kingdom (e.g., v. 2) or to Judeans anytime from the last years of Judah, particularly after the first deportation, down into the exile and the centuries that followed. The question of authorship must simply remain open.[89] However, even though recovery of an original text is virtually impossible, the present form of the text does not lack signs of unity and a clear point, whatever the history of its formation. It is that point and its development toward which interpretation should be directed.

The essential intention of the text is set forth in its opening verses: a warning against Israel's following "the way of the nations" and "the customs of the peoples." That way is then identified with a fondness for making idols of their deities, though in the opening verse it is specifically understood to be the omens and portents that come forth from astronomical phenomena, a major dimension of Babylonian religion as attested by the many astrological and astronomical texts from Mesopotamia. The association of the astral deities with the signs and omens of the heavens makes a natural association of that "way of the nations" with their love of idols, which were seen as manifestations of the presence and power of their deities. All of this is understood to be, in typical Jeremianic terms, "worthless" (v. 4; cf. the NIV of v. 8; see also v. 15;

87. E.g., Carroll, *Jeremiah,* 254.
88. E.g., Bright, *Jeremiah,* 79.

89. For a cautious argument for the Jeremianic authorship of this passage on the basis of style and linguistic affinities, see William L. Holladay, *Jeremiah 1: A Commentary on the Book of the Prophet Jeremiah Chapters 1–25,* Hermeneia (Philadelphia: Fortress, 1986) 329-30.

2:5; 8:19; 14:22; 16:19). The rest of this passage argues the case for the worthless and useless character of the idols and does so by alternating mockery of the idols (vv. 2-5, 8-9, 11, 14-15) with hymnic praise of the Lord (vv. 6-7, 10, 12-13, 16), thus effecting a powerful contrast between the Lord and idols.

Part of the mockery takes place in an elaborated description of the making of the idols, how they are carved and then covered with precious metals and painted with bright-colored dyes.[90] The author acknowledged that such work was a craft, requiring skill and training (v. 9); but also that there is an inherent contradiction in the use of such skill in such a stupid enterprise, exerting so much effort and artistry for something that represents nothing at all. The stupidity and ineffectiveness of all this labor and cost are spelled out in various ways, all of which in some fashion uncovers the utter powerlessness of the idols—and of the gods they represent.

Their origin in human artistry is the first indication of the ineffectiveness of these idols. The character of the idols as "made" or "work" (עשׂה, 'āśâ) of human hands is asserted several times (vv. 3, 9 [2 times], 15) and is contrasted with the Lord, who not only is not "made" but also "made" all that is, the whole creation (vv. 12-13). Verses 11-12 make the contrast even more explicit, sharply contrasting the gods, who did not make heaven and earth, with the God who did, indeed, make heaven and earth. The motif of heaven and earth provides a further vehicle for the contrast when the praise of the Lord as the one who stretches out the heavens and brings water from the heavens (vv. 12-13) is set against the words about the nations fearing the signs of the heavens (v. 2). These verses also underscore this same point: gods who did not make heaven and earth; gods perishing from the earth and from under heaven; the Lord making the earth and stretching out the heavens.

The do-nothing character of the idols provides another point for mockery and taunt. They have to be secured in place so they will not wobble or totter off their pedestals (v. 4b). They cannot walk or speak; they have to be carried (v. 5a). They can do nothing at all (v. 5b). This stands in contrast to the Lord of Israel, who is great and whose name is great in might (v. 6), whose power is so great that it could create a world (v. 12), who not only can speak but whose speech can bring forth rain to water the earth and make it fruitful (v. 13).[91] Over against the deluding and false gods of the idols (vv. 14-15) is the Lord, who is real and is truly God (v. 10). Unlike the idols and false gods, who may flourish for a time but eventually perish (vv. 11, 15), the Lord is "the living God" and the "everlasting King." The hymnic portions of the text offer typical statements about the Lord of Israel, including assertions of incomparability (vv. 6-7; cf. Exod 15:11) that gain a special force because of the way they respond to the polemic against the idols. The Lord is, indeed, the only reality that is true, living, effective, and lasting.

While all these words are relevant to the life and faith of the people, there are three places where the text specifically addresses the Judahite community. One is at the beginning, with the words to "the house of Israel"—a richly open expression that may refer to the northern kingdom, the whole of ancient Israel, or any community that defines itself in any way as the Israel of God. Israel should not learn the ways of other peoples. A second instance occurs in v. 6, where the speaker (either the Lord or the prophet) gives a word of assurance that complements the exhortation of v. 2. The Lord not only warns against the people's paying attention to idols and the gods they represent but also reassures a community that is confronted with evidence of the power of these other gods. The word of the Lord, therefore, is not only instructional and prohibitive (v. 2) but also a word of salvation and assurance that the people are not under the power of these deities, for they can neither hurt nor help, neither bless nor curse. Then at the end the author underscores the point of the whole passage: *Not like these* is the portion of Jacob. There is no way in which the Lord of Israel, the creator and fashioner of all that exists, is like these manufactured, powerless, stupid, inanimate, dead, and useless idols. The reference to Israel as "the portion of Jacob" and "the tribe of his inheritance" echoes the opening verses by reminding the people once more of their special place in the world by virtue of the Lord's choice of them as covenant partner.

---

90. On the details of the construction of idols as described here, see Philip J. King, "Jeremiah's Polemic Against Idols: What Archaeology Can Teach Us," *The Bible Review* 10 (December 1994) 22-29.

91. For this particular contrast, see Isaiah 40–55, where the power of the Lord to affect nature and history by the divine word is set over against the silent ineffectiveness of the idols.

REFLECTIONS

1. The "ways of the nations" and the "customs of the people" receive a particular interpretation in the history of the formation of this text. Those expressions probably had a more open-ended reference at an earlier stage, of which idolatry was one example. They do serve as a pointer to the peculiarity of Israel and lift up the significance of distinctiveness, the possibility of a counterculture in a community that is not the same as every other group. The point is not simply difference for the sake of difference but difference in a particular direction, and this text aims to identify that direction in particular ways. Many other texts in the Old Testament suggest that being chosen by the Lord meant and means charting a different way in the world, a way of holiness that sets one apart precisely because it is not the way that others go. It is more demanding, more just, more oriented toward others. Such peculiarity is not a mark for boasting, as chapter 9 has made very clear. Nor is it seen as simply one alternative to be chosen out of a smorgasbord of life-styles. It is a covenantal way that is the only option for the people of the Lord. Accommodation to the general culture and the ways of other communities, whether religious or not, is unacceptable for the community of this book. To determine what such accommodation might involve and so to shy away from it is one of the reasons why we read and attend to the book of Jeremiah, for it stands as an enduring critique of the tendency to let the customs and ways of other groups determine what the people of "the Way" (Acts 9:2) will do.

2. One of the strongest barriers to the appropriation of the full force of the Old Testament in the contemporary world is the seemingly innocuous and unreal character of the words about other gods and idols. That problem is acutely present in a text, such as this one, that focuses on the making of idols. For a society in which plastic images of various forms are not really conceived of as loci of ultimate power, these texts seem archaic and irrelevant. At the same time, the issue of idolatry persists and has been the focus of theological and moral concern throughout the history of Judaism and Christianity. If, as has been suggested, idolatry is "any nonabsolute value that is made absolute and demands to be the center of dedicated life," then the issue is a continuing one and happens all the time.[92] While it may seem to be a cliché to speak of money, for example, as an idol, Karl Marx minced no words in building a philosophical and political system on just such an assumption: "Money is the Jealous God of Israel before whom no other god may exist. Money degrades all the gods of mankind and converts them into commodities. Money is the general, self-sufficient value of everything."[93]

The failure of the Marxist proposal in our time does not belie his point. It may simply demonstrate it all the more, for it is a capitalist system that so regards money that has won the battle—for the time being. But even the Marxist revolution is an example of crossing the line between value and absolute value, between devotion and total devotion, that represents the idolatrous turn. In noting this, Halbertal and Margalit have called attention to the documentation of some experiences of the failure of the Communist revolution in a book with the unsurprising title *The God That Failed.*[94] The power of a political philosophy or of a political system to claim ultimacy is demonstrated all the time in our world. The idols that are attractive by their economic value or power—made of silver and gold (10:9)—or their promise to enhance our lives—to do good (10:5*b*)—do not disappear with the move away from wood and metal images. They take shape in equally seductive and alluring form, even in the guise of theological systems to which we commit ourselves in an ultimate sense without even noticing.

92. See Moshe Halbertal and Avishai Margalit, *Idolatry* (Cambridge, Mass.: Harvard University Press, 1992) 246.
93. See ibid., 243.
94. Arthur Koestler et al., *The God That Failed,* ed. R. Crossman (New York: Harper, 1963).

Jeremiah 10:17-25, A Severe Wound

NIV

17Gather up your belongings to leave the land,
you who live under siege.
18For this is what the LORD says:
"At this time I will hurl out
those who live in this land;
I will bring distress on them
so that they may be captured."

19Woe to me because of my injury!
My wound is incurable!
Yet I said to myself,
"This is my sickness, and I must endure it."
20My tent is destroyed;
all its ropes are snapped.
My sons are gone from me and are no more;
no one is left now to pitch my tent
or to set up my shelter.
21The shepherds are senseless
and do not inquire of the LORD;
so they do not prosper
and all their flock is scattered.
22Listen! The report is coming—
a great commotion from the land of the
north!
It will make the towns of Judah desolate,
a haunt of jackals.

23I know, O LORD, that a man's life is not his
own;
it is not for man to direct his steps.
24Correct me, LORD, but only with justice—
not in your anger,
lest you reduce me to nothing.
25Pour out your wrath on the nations
that do not acknowledge you,
on the peoples who do not call on your
name.
For they have devoured Jacob;
they have devoured him completely
and destroyed his homeland.

NRSV

17 Gather up your bundle from the ground,
O you who live under siege!
18 For thus says the LORD:
I am going to sling out the inhabitants of the
land
at this time,
and I will bring distress on them,
so that they shall feel it.

19 Woe is me because of my hurt!
My wound is severe.
But I said, "Truly this is my punishment,
and I must bear it."
20 My tent is destroyed,
and all my cords are broken;
my children have gone from me,
and they are no more;
there is no one to spread my tent again,
and to set up my curtains.
21 For the shepherds are stupid,
and do not inquire of the LORD;
therefore they have not prospered,
and all their flock is scattered.

22 Hear, a noise! Listen, it is coming—
a great commotion from the land of the
north
to make the cities of Judah a desolation,
a lair of jackals.

23 I know, O LORD, that the way of human
beings is not in their control,
that mortals as they walk cannot direct
their steps.
24 Correct me, O LORD, but in just measure;
not in your anger, or you will bring me to
nothing.

25 Pour out your wrath on the nations that do
not know you,
and on the peoples that do not call on your
name;
for they have devoured Jacob;
they have devoured him and consumed him,
and have laid waste his habitation.

COMMENTARY

This passage opens with the Lord's announcement of judgment to Jerusalem (vv. 17-18), manifest in a siege (v. 17) by the foe from the north (v. 22; see the Commentary on 1:11-16 and the Overview of 4:5–6:30). This army, which is on its way, will carry out widespread destruction in the land (v. 22 b) and send the people into exile (v. 18). The exile is anticipated by the call to the people to gather their bundles preparatory to being ejected from the land. The imagery, as the NIV and the NRSV indicate, is that of a rock being hurled from a sling. Such imagery symbolizes the swift and violent dispatch of the people.

This fate evokes terrible lament on the part of Mother Zion (vv. 19-20), identified as the recipient of this judgment speech by the second-person feminine suffixes throughout the first two verses and the reference to "my children" in v. 20. Personified Zion laments over the condition of the city and the community, the place and the people. Several images come together in the description of their plight. First there is the metaphor of sickness, which is typical of laments, ancient and modern, for depicting trouble and disaster of all sorts. Then there is a picture of a family's tent dwelling being destroyed, which may well carry in it an allusion to the destruction of the Temple inasmuch as tent language is applicable to the tabernacle. Finally, there is the image of a mother bereft of all her children, who have been killed or kidnapped, evoking a sorrow that knows no bounds (cf. Rachel weeping for her children in 31:15). There is no complaint to God at this point, not even the plea for help that often appears in a lament. Quite the contrary, the appropriateness of punishment is acknowledged.

In v. 21, the shepherd image lets the reader discern the immediate basis for the punishment. Regularly depicted as shepherds, the civil leadership has done two things that have resulted in the dispersal of the flock, the citizens of the city and the land. First, they have acted stupidly, conduct that may involve everything from their moral direction to their political strategy. Second, they have not inquired of the Lord, an expression that regularly refers to seeking a word from the Lord. Implicit in this indictment is the assumption that the people have not listened to the direction Jeremiah has given them, regularly described by him as the word of the Lord. These two indictments come together in the realization that failure to discern what the Lord is doing and what the Lord desires is an act of the greatest stupidity.

At the close of the chapter (v. 25), the lament of vv. 19-20 is picked up again, only now the lament is truly a prayer, drawing upon typical lament expressions in the OT. Interpretation of v. 23 is helped by reference to a similar passage in Prov 16:9: "The human mind plans the way,/ but the LORD directs the steps." While v. 23 can be read as a rejection of responsibility, it may also be an acknowledgment that the Lord is in control and that the destiny of the people is shaped by the divine hand. Read in that light, the one praying, Mother Zion, who laments earlier about having to bear the punishment (v. 19), uses language reminiscent of Pss 6:1 and 38:1 to urge God to keep the inevitable punishment just—that is, bearable and not so severe as to reduce the people to nothing. The irony that the people now ask to be corrected in the light of their regular resistance to correction (see 2:30; 5:3; 7:28; 17:23) should not be missed. While the plea is legitimate, it comes in the face of a judgment that is so overwhelming that correction now looks good.

From 8:4 onward, this section, which focuses on sin and judgment evoking lament, comes to a conclusion with a traditional prayer against the enemies (cf. Ps 79:6-7). The form of the lament or of the plea for help invites the prayer for God's judgment against the enemies, even if they are the instruments of God's judgment. Though not acting apart from the Lord's control of history, their ignoring the Lord and their brutality toward Israel and Judah legitimize the prayer for their destruction. Here, at least, one may comprehend some of the rationale and force of those imprecations against the enemies in the psalms (e.g., Psalms 10; 109; 137; 139:19-22). The words of Isaiah about the Assyrian king Tiglath-pileser III (Isa 10:5-19) reflect this ambiguity about the enemy not only as the agent of divine destruction but also, ultimately, as the recipient of that same destructive power.

REFLECTIONS

1. The specific problem that evokes divine judgment and subsequent lament in this text is the failure of leadership, and specifically effort to go it alone without reference to God. The text reminds us that independence and self-direction are not really biblical virtues. On the contrary, they are more likely to be problems. Such a perspective runs counter to the modern mentality, whether it is Ralph W. Emerson's "trust thyself" or David Riesman's exaltation of the inner-directed person.[95] Autonomy is the great virtue of the Enlightenment and post-Enlightenment world, but not of Scripture. The text from Jeremiah, however, is not talking about a herd mentality. The issue is not a matter of heteronomy or following the crowd. Precisely the contrary. Going with the crowd is the big problem, whether it is learning the way of the nations (10:2ff.) or not bothering to check with the Lord on what one should do (10:21) and how Israel/Judah might bring themselves into conformity with what God is doing in the world. The issue is whether a community that goes by the name of the Lord will choose theonomous existence. It is not enough to go by that name if one does not call upon it. Nor is the issue purely a theoretical one or simply a matter of what happens in church. If the God of Jeremiah is in control of history as the prophet declared, then failure to inquire of the Lord in all matters is truly stupid. Moreover, it is very dangerous.

2. The mix that is found in the lament-prayer elements of this text is worth noting, for it says something about the conglomeration of things that is often a part of troubled prayer. Here is the weeping of a mother who faces great loss, particularly of her children, the deepest anguish of all. But here also is a kind of confession and acknowledgment of God's justice operative in the human situation. At the same time, there is always a hope that such justice will be just that, a feeling that if the response to sin is shaped by anger, then fairness and justice go out the window. The anger of God is an anthropomorphic way of speaking about the intention of God to judge— that is, to deal justly with the wicked and the unrighteousness. But the one who feels that judgment senses that if the compassion of God can show mercy overflowing, then the anger of God can also make punishment overflowing. It is appropriate for those who stand under judgment to ask for a staunching of that flow, for a punishment appropriate to the sin. The word of Scripture is that God is inclined to such appeals and tends to place the punishment significantly under the control of the divine compassion (Ps 30:5; Isa 54:7-8).

The mix of prayer in this text also includes a powerful rage against the violence of those who, though instruments of divine judgment, mete out a terror that itself demands a just response. So tears, rage, confession, submission, and plea pile one upon another as the voice of a community is articulated in the form of a mother's prayer. We expect mothers' prayers to be more sentimental because we are sentimental about mothers. But this is Mother Zion, and sometimes the mother's loss can be an outcome of the mother's sin. That is not, of course, axiomatic in the universe. Most often the mother's loss is simply that. And after all, Zion is not a real mother. Let us not assume, however, that confession, rage, and submission may not follow lest we deprive mothers of the right and the responsibility to be human. Nor should we assume that mothers are through with crying in this book. There is more to come, and there will be a different outcome (31:15). But if Rachel's weeping in chapter 31 is heard as authentically the voice of a mother who has lost all, then we cannot rule that out for Mother Zion also, even if the prayer is more discordant and less palatable.

---

95. David Riesman with Reuel Denney and Nathan Glazer, *The Lonely Crowd: A Study of the Changing American Character* (New Haven: Yale University Press, 1969).

JEREMIAH 11:1–20:18

LAMENTS AND PROPHECIES CONCERNING JUDGMENT

OVERVIEW

These chapters are among the most debated texts of the entire book of Jeremiah. The focus of that discussion is a series of passages containing prophetic prayers to God and the Lord's responses, which form the core of the book (11:18–12:6; 15:10-21; 17:14-18; 18:18-23; 20:7-18). These prayers, often called Jeremiah's confessions, are more accurately understood as laments or prayers for help and are to be compared with the laments of the psalter and the dialogues in Job. The debate centers around how they are to be understood. Are they actual prayers Jeremiah prayed while he was attacked for his work as a prophet? Or are they typical laments that have been placed on the prophet's lips by later editors? Do they represent Jeremiah as a mediator for the people, lifting up their plight? Is the "I" of these prayers really the prophet representing the concerns of the people?

Definitive answers have not been given to these questions. The commentary that follows reflects some judgments about the relationship of the laments of chaps. 11–20 to the prophet, to the community, and to the book. With regard to the first issue, one can readily discern evidence of traditional prayers. These prayers, including specific words and phrases, are paralleled by laments in the psalter. This fact, however, tells nothing about whether such traditional language was spoken by Jeremiah. When someone prayed asking God for help in desperate circumstances, that individual used traditional language and forms of speech.

It is difficult, however, to separate these prayers from the persona of the prophet. They no doubt reflect the prophet's experiences. There are many ways in which the prayers are related to the prophet's circumstances. In some instances, the

connection is made where the prayer occurs (e.g., 11:21-23; 18:18).

These prayers or laments belong with this prophet. At the same time, we cannot be too sure of how autobiographical they are. They are appropriate to the persona or the presentation of the prophet in the book, which may stem from literary as much as biographical processes.

Kathleen O'Connor has demonstrated that the lament prayers give clues to what is happening in this section of the book.[96] The close connections of these prayers to the call of Jeremiah (chap. 1) indicate that they are related to the public presentation of his vocation and the responses to his prophetic activity. The placing of the lament prayers of Jeremiah entirely within the complex of chaps. 11–20 involves the way this section moves beyond the presentation of Jeremiah's message and the frequent calls for repentance and amendment, as present in chaps. 2–10, to identify both the negative response to that message and its ultimate vindication.

Interspersed among these prophetic laments are other prophetic speeches or divine oracles. Their thrust is largely judgment. Particularly noticeable are the signs of lament on the part of God over the judgment that must and will come (e.g., 12:7-13) and a series of passages that involve various kinds of symbols and symbolic actions (13:1-14; 16:1-13; 17:19-27; 18:1-12; 19:1–20:6). In this section as a whole, therefore, several things happen. The focus on repentance and amendment diminishes. The word of judgment is underscored and heightened with a clear focus on its vindication, a focus that receives particular emphasis in the dialogue

96. Kathleen M. O'Connor, *The Confessions of Jeremiah: Their Interpretation and Role in Chapters 1–25*, SBLDS 94 (Atlanta: Scholars Press, 1988).

between the prophet and the Lord. The lament prayers, which by their associations with the call confirm the authenticity of the call and the authority of the prophetic word, join with the reports of symbolic actions by the prophet to focus attention on the prophet's proclamation. The prophet now not only speaks but also acts out the word in a very public and dramatic fashion. The response to this spoken and enacted prophetic word by the people, as reflected particularly in the prayers of the prophet and the Lord's responses, becomes a major feature of these chapters.

This part of the book of Jeremiah ends in chap. 20 with the last of Jeremiah's laments, in some ways the nadir of his despair. We do not hear the lamenting and complaining voice of the prophet in the remaining chapters of the book. There is a shift, already evident in the final chapter of this section, toward a narrative demonstration of the

grounds for the prophet's complaint, the real suffering and pain he experienced in carrying out his calling, which is spelled out in the second half of the book. By placing the laments early on, the composers of the book of Jeremiah have given to the reader not only third-person narrative reports of the trials and tribulations of the prophet but also an interior view of the prophet's reaction to what he was encountering and the ways it challenged his vocation and his relationship to the Lord who called him. The struggle so depicted vindicates both his calling and his message.

Finally, one may recognize that some of this anguished prayer may have functioned also as an expression of the despair of the exiles. The sound of their laments is not much different from that of Jeremiah, and they probably found in his voice an anticipation of their own, as indeed later members of the community of faith have done.

JEREMIAH 11:1-17, THE BROKEN COVENANT

NIV

11 This is the word that came to Jeremiah from the LORD: ²"Listen to the terms of this covenant and tell them to the people of Judah and to those who live in Jerusalem. ³Tell them that this is what the LORD, the God of Israel, says: 'Cursed is the man who does not obey the terms of this covenant— ⁴the terms I commanded your forefathers when I brought them out of Egypt, out of the iron-smelting furnace.' I said, 'Obey me and do everything I command you, and you will be my people, and I will be your God. ⁵Then I will fulfill the oath I swore to your forefathers, to give them a land flowing with milk and honey'—the land you possess today."

I answered, "Amen, LORD."

⁶The LORD said to me, "Proclaim all these words in the towns of Judah and in the streets of Jerusalem: 'Listen to the terms of this covenant and follow them. ⁷From the time I brought your forefathers up from Egypt until today, I warned them again and again, saying, "Obey me." ⁸But they did not listen or pay attention; instead, they followed the stubbornness of their evil hearts. So

NRSV

11 The word that came to Jeremiah from the LORD: ²Hear the words of this covenant, and speak to the people of Judah and the inhabitants of Jerusalem. ³You shall say to them, Thus says the LORD, the God of Israel: Cursed be anyone who does not heed the words of this covenant, ⁴which I commanded your ancestors when I brought them out of the land of Egypt, from the iron-smelter, saying, Listen to my voice, and do all that I command you. So shall you be my people, and I will be your God, ⁵that I may perform the oath that I swore to your ancestors, to give them a land flowing with milk and honey, as at this day. Then I answered, "So be it, LORD."

6And the LORD said to me: Proclaim all these words in the cities of Judah, and in the streets of Jerusalem: Hear the words of this covenant and do them. ⁷For I solemnly warned your ancestors when I brought them up out of the land of Egypt, warning them persistently, even to this day, saying, Obey my voice. ⁸Yet they did not obey or incline their ear, but everyone walked in the stubbornness of an evil will. So I brought upon them

NIV

I brought on them all the curses of the covenant I had commanded them to follow but that they did not keep.' "

⁹Then the LORD said to me, "There is a conspiracy among the people of Judah and those who live in Jerusalem. ¹⁰They have returned to the sins of their forefathers, who refused to listen to my words. They have followed other gods to serve them. Both the house of Israel and the house of Judah have broken the covenant I made with their forefathers. ¹¹Therefore this is what the LORD says: 'I will bring on them a disaster they cannot escape. Although they cry out to me, I will not listen to them. ¹²The towns of Judah and the people of Jerusalem will go and cry out to the gods to whom they burn incense, but they will not help them at all when disaster strikes. ¹³You have as many gods as you have towns, O Judah; and the altars you have set up to burn incense to that shameful god Baal are as many as the streets of Jerusalem.'

¹⁴"Do not pray for this people nor offer any plea or petition for them, because I will not listen when they call to me in the time of their distress.

¹⁵"What is my beloved doing in my temple
　　as she works out her evil schemes with
　　　　many?
　Can consecrated meat avert ₗyour
　　　　punishment₎?
　When you engage in your wickedness,
　　then you rejoice.ᵃ"

¹⁶The LORD called you a thriving olive tree
　　with fruit beautiful in form.
　But with the roar of a mighty storm
　　he will set it on fire,
　　and its branches will be broken.

¹⁷The LORD Almighty, who planted you, has decreed disaster for you, because the house of Israel and the house of Judah have done evil and provoked me to anger by burning incense to Baal.

ᵃ15 Or *Could consecrated meat avert your punishment? / Then you would rejoice*

NRSV

all the words of this covenant, which I commanded them to do, but they did not.

9And the LORD said to me: Conspiracy exists among the people of Judah and the inhabitants of Jerusalem. ¹⁰They have turned back to the iniquities of their ancestors of old, who refused to heed my words; they have gone after other gods to serve them; the house of Israel and the house of Judah have broken the covenant that I made with their ancestors. ¹¹Therefore, thus says the LORD, assuredly I am going to bring disaster upon them that they cannot escape; though they cry out to me, I will not listen to them. ¹²Then the cities of Judah and the inhabitants of Jerusalem will go and cry out to the gods to whom they make offerings, but they will never save them in the time of their trouble. ¹³For your gods have become as many as your towns, O Judah; and as many as the streets of Jerusalem are the altars you have set up to shame, altars to make offerings to Baal.

14As for you, do not pray for this people, or lift up a cry or prayer on their behalf, for I will not listen when they call to me in the time of their trouble. ¹⁵What right has my beloved in my house, when she has done vile deeds? Can vowsᵃ and sacrificial flesh avert your doom? Can you then exult? ¹⁶The LORD once called you, "A green olive tree, fair with goodly fruit"; but with the roar of a great tempest he will set fire to it, and its branches will be consumed. ¹⁷The LORD of hosts, who planted you, has pronounced evil against you, because of the evil that the house of Israel and the house of Judah have done, provoking me to anger by making offerings to Baal.

ᵃGk: Heb *Can many*

COMMENTARY

The most obvious features of this text belong together. They are its focus on the subject of covenant and its articulation in highly deuteronomic or deuteronomistic language and phraseology. This is in some respects the central covenantal text of the book, articulating the relationship of Israel to God in terms that are deeply rooted in the formative identity of Israel as covenant partner with the Lord, bound in obligation to the one who redeemed them from slavery and brought them into a land of abundance and plenty. The most extended formulation of that covenant understanding is to be found in the book of Deuteronomy. The question of whether or not the words of this literary unit come from Jeremiah or are the results of deuteronomistic editing and redaction cannot be answered readily. Nor can one easily determine if these words were directly connected to the failure of the reform of Josiah or represent a later address to the community that explains what has happened to them. The focus is clear and obviously was understood to be illuminating for comprehending what happened to Judah in the late pre-exilic days.

11:1-5. The initial section of the passage sets forth in concise terms an understanding of the covenant, its fundamental character, sanctions, and benefits. "This covenant" is the subject of the divine speech and the prophet's proclamation (v. 2). The demonstrative pronoun joins with the several specific references in 11:1-17 to the people of Judah and Jerusalem—and even to the "house of Israel" (v. 17)—to make the reference very specific. One is not to understand here a vague general relationship to God but a very specific involvement on God's part with a particular community, one that has large implications for their existence. The full force of those implications is indicated by the rubric under which the proclamation is set: cursed by anyone who does not heed the words of this covenant. The people are to understand that the situation is now one where the question of sanctions for disobedience is legitimately to be raised (see Deuteronomy 28). The reference in these verses is back to the initial enactment of the covenant at Sinai, to the words of the Lord to "your ancestors," the generation that was delivered from Egyptian slavery (the iron smelter in which Israel was tested and refined)—in an act of divine liberation that established the grounds for the Lord's claim on the people. The claim is expressed in several words: "the words of this covenant," "my voice," "all that I command you" (see Exod 19:1-6). The concrete specificity lying behind these general terms can only be determined by: (a) going back to the Sinai pericope in Exodus 19–24 and its recollection in Deuteronomy 5 and listening again to the specific stipulations or (b) by inference from examining the oracles of Jeremiah that identify the different ways in which the people have disobeyed the covenant. The oath referred to in v. 5 is a significant part of the covenantal procedure and reminds the people that even the deliverance from Egypt grew out of a commitment on the part of God to the ancestors Abraham, Isaac, and Jacob to provide for them a good place to live. All this "command" or demand that seems to fall so heavily on the people only arises because of the way in which they have been bound to the Lord by God's care and provision. What that means is stated here in the simplest form in which the covenantal relationship appears in the OT: You will be my people and I will be your God (see Exod 6:7). It is as simple as that. But the inhabitants of Judah, Jerusalem, and the house of Israel have not kept their part of the obligation, for their identity and character as the Lord's people are expressed precisely in their obedience to the stipulations of the covenant.

11:6-8. The seriousness of this covenantal relation is carried further as the Lord moves from a basic characterization of the covenant to a historical retrospect that recollects the disobedience of an earlier generation that chose an autonomous mode of existence in direct contradiction to the theonomous one that was realized in the enactment of the covenant. The point of the retrospect is in the last line: "So I brought upon them all the words of this covenant." The "words" referred to here are the curses or sanctions invoked upon the disobedient covenant partner. Covenant is a serious matter, and willful disregard of it has had—and will have—serious and terrible consequences.

11:9-14. The point is a familiar one: The lessons were not learned. Deuteronomic language joins with the language of other Jeremianic oracles to identify why the sanction of curse is at hand. Thus in v. 10 one finds again the negative use of the word "turn" (שוב *šûb*) in reference to the people's "turning back" to the sins of their ancestors (see 3:19; 8:5-6) and the "refusal" of this people to heed the words of the covenant. Elsewhere it is a refusal to be ashamed (3:3), to take correction (5:3), to "return" to the Lord (5:3; 8:5), and to know the Lord (9:6), this last being covenant language for acknowledging the Lord who enters into covenant. And, of course, the cardinal sin is this people's "going after other gods to serve [worship] them" (v. 10), the language of both Jeremiah (2:4, 8*b*, 23, 25; 7:7, 9) and Deuteronomy (e.g., 5:7, 9*a*; 6:14; 7:4, 15) for speaking of the violation of the first and basic principle of the covenant: complete and uncompromising allegiance to the Lord of Israel. The reforms of Josiah achieved no more enduring commitment to the covenant than had earlier reforms of Hezekiah and others.

The use of the term "conspiracy" to describe the totality of the sins of Judah and Jerusalem is an appropriation of a word from the political sphere into the religious. Because the covenant structure of the relationship is drawn from political treaty models that involve modes of regulation of political loyalty, the conspiracy metaphor is highly suggestive for speaking about the way in which the people have colluded in various ways to develop a "rebellion" against the Lord, by turning to other deities and ignoring the stipulations of the political treaty (i.e., covenant).

The outcome of such conspiracy is God's invoking the sanctions of covenant, the curse of judgment. The extremity of the situation has no better indicator than what is said in v. 11. The very framework of Israelite faith and the divine/human relationship assumed the responsiveness of the deity to the cries and prayers of the people. The earlier history of apostasy is nevertheless also a story of the cries of the people and of their mediators for the Lord's mercy, many of which were answered. There comes a time, however, when the resistance is such that it is no longer possible to hold back the judgment. In the vision reports of Amos 7–8, twice the prophet intercedes and the Lord relents. But the last two visions of judgment do not elicit a plea from the prophet. When things have gotten so bad in the human community, when the structure of the relationship embodied

in the metaphor of covenant is broken, it may no longer be capable of repair. So the prayers are not heard by God.

As at other points in the book (e.g., 7:16-20; 14:11-12; 16:5-9), the prophet is forbidden to intercede for the people. The difference here is striking. While the cries of the people are unheard by God, the prophet is forbidden from even uttering the cry. Why is that? The reason is clear when one looks at the history of prophecy and the history of intercession. One of the primary functions of the prophet was to stand before the Lord and speak on behalf of the people. Such prophetic intercession evoked a change in the heart of God again and again, even when the wrath of God burned hot against the people (e.g., Exod 32:11-14). God so builds into the divine action an openness to the prophetic intercession that it is necessary to prevent such intercession if the judgment is going to take place (see the Commentary on 7:16-20).

The words about the other gods (vv. 12-13) serve primarily to imply the impotence of these other deities that have seemed so attractive to the people. The sarcastic comment that "your gods are as many as your towns" occurs earlier in Jer 2:28, where there is a similar and equally sarcastic dismissal of these gods as completely powerless to save the people when circumstances deteriorate.

11:15-17. Two poems and images conclude the discussion of the broken covenant. They are joined editorially to the preceding discussion by v. 17, which ends exactly as did v. 13, with reference to "making offerings to Baal." The first of the poems invokes the image of the beloved bride or lover who has betrayed her spouse. The gender is mixed in this case with both feminine and masculine forms referring to the lover (this may be the result of textual corruption, which is evident in these verses). The beloved has betrayed the relationship and so can no longer claim a place in the house (i.e., Temple). It would be pointless anyway, for the usual religious acts would be to no avail. Here the prophet echoes other prophetic words that reject the assumption that ritual and worship can offset disobedience, sin, and social injustice (e.g., Hos 6:6; Amos 5:21-24; Mic 6:1-8).

A second image portrays the faithless people as a ripe and fruitful olive tree, a positive image like that of the bride. But the tree has turned sour. The positive regard for the people is replaced by a fiery judgment that will bring them down. The final word (v. 17) involves poetic justice: The "evil" (רעה *rā'â*) of the people will bring "disaster" (רעה *rā'â*) from the Lord. *Rā'â* evokes *rā'â*. The final words reiterate the heart of the matter in this broken covenant: the violation of the basic stipulation of the covenant—absolute loyalty to the Lord, the covenantal partner.

REFLECTIONS

Jeremiah is one of those biblical books in which the covenant and covenant theology are highly visible. Most of the attention to covenant has been focused on Jeremiah 31 and the words about a new covenant inscribed on the heart. But we cannot talk about a new covenant without talking first about the old covenant, about what has happened and why it is even necessary to speak about *new* covenant. Conversation jumps too quickly to the new without coming to terms with its antecedents.

Few texts of Scripture so forthrightly uncover what the biblical covenant was all about as does this one. So it becomes a rich source for thinking abou that relationship. The priority of divine mercy and even divine obligation is the starting point. While the focus of covenantal thinking is usually on the demands placed on the human community, and perhaps rightly so, for there is where our part of the covenantal relationship is defined, the whole business makes no sense if one does not reach back to the ground of the covenant, to the very rationale for entering into such a relationship.

This text reminds us that the covenant is not simply an abstract metaphor for speaking about relationship with God. It is the effecting of a relationship out of particular historical events: the Lord's deliverance of Israelite slaves from Egypt and the promise of a place for living that God made to their ancestors. These two dimensions of God's beneficent and redemptive care of a community are what evoke the covenant relationship. Covenant is thus the community's experience of having been redeemed and the possibilities for life that God promises. But it is not finally a covenantal relationship until the community takes on its responsibility to the redeeming and promising God. The formation of the text in the first five verses is revealing. It begins with the deliverance from Egypt and ends with the land flowing with milk and honey. Bracketed between those two divine gifts is the call to "listen to my voice" and the covenant formulary: You shall be my people, and I will be your God. The movement from redemption to life is through the covenant. The small word *that* at the beginning of v. 5 is explicit in the Hebrew and indicates that the abundant life springs out of living in covenantal relationship with God, committing oneself to a life that is shaped and directed by God's instruction, by God's ways. The life in the land, which is the Old Testament understanding of the gift of abundant life, is tied to that commitment, that obedience, in complex ways. Obedience to the divine instruction is an obligation. That is the point of the covenant. It is the community's part of the covenantal obligation, as the oath to provide life in the land is God's part. But such obedience to God's instruction, commonly understood as the law, is also the *way* to life, the *means* to life. The book of Deuteronomy, which rings through the language of this chapter, makes that point again and again. How then shall we live? This is how we do it—by living according to this teaching. At the conclusion of the book, the point is made in a sharp way as Moses tells the people that in the teaching he has given them, the divine instruction called torah, he has set before them life and prosperity, death and adversity (Deut 30:15). It is up to them to choose which it will be (Deut 30:19). One way leads to the good life; that is the way of obedience. The other way leads to death. That is the way of disobedience. So the divine instruction embodied in the law becomes also a gift that offers the possibility of rich outcomes. And when the gift is not accepted, when God's instruction is not followed, the outcome is death. That is what the book of Jeremiah is about.

JEREMIAH 11:18–12:6, THE PROPHET UNDER ATTACK

NIV

¹⁸Because the LORD revealed their plot to me, I knew it, for at that time he showed me what they were doing. ¹⁹I had been like a gentle lamb led to the slaughter; I did not realize that they had plotted against me, saying,

"Let us destroy the tree and its fruit;
  let us cut him off from the land of the living,
    that his name be remembered no more."
²⁰But, O LORD Almighty, you who judge
    righteously
  and test the heart and mind,
let me see your vengeance upon them,
  for to you I have committed my cause.

²¹"Therefore this is what the LORD says about the men of Anathoth who are seeking your life and saying, 'Do not prophesy in the name of the LORD or you will die by our hands'— ²²therefore this is what the LORD Almighty says: 'I will punish them. Their young men will die by the sword, their sons and daughters by famine. ²³Not even a remnant will be left to them, because I will bring disaster on the men of Anathoth in the year of their punishment.' "

12 You are always righteous, O LORD,
    when I bring a case before you.
  Yet I would speak with you about your justice:
    Why does the way of the wicked prosper?
    Why do all the faithless live at ease?
²You have planted them, and they have taken root;
    they grow and bear fruit.
  You are always on their lips
    but far from their hearts.
³Yet you know me, O LORD;
    you see me and test my thoughts about you.
  Drag them off like sheep to be butchered!
    Set them apart for the day of slaughter!
⁴How long will the land lie parched*ᵃ*
    and the grass in every field be withered?
  Because those who live in it are wicked,
    the animals and birds have perished.
  Moreover, the people are saying,
    "He will not see what happens to us."

ᵃ4 Or *land mourn*

NRSV

¹⁸ It was the LORD who made it known to me,
    and I knew;
  then you showed me their evil deeds.
¹⁹ But I was like a gentle lamb
    led to the slaughter.
  And I did not know it was against me
    that they devised schemes, saying,
  "Let us destroy the tree with its fruit,
    let us cut him off from the land of the living,
      so that his name will no longer be
      remembered!"
²⁰ But you, O LORD of hosts, who judge
    righteously,
  who try the heart and the mind,
  let me see your retribution upon them,
    for to you I have committed my cause.
²¹Therefore thus says the LORD concerning the people of Anathoth, who seek your life, and say, "You shall not prophesy in the name of the LORD, or you will die by our hand"— ²²therefore thus says the LORD of hosts: I am going to punish them; the young men shall die by the sword; their sons and their daughters shall die by famine; ²³and not even a remnant shall be left of them. For I will bring disaster upon the people of Anathoth, the year of their punishment.

12 You will be in the right,
      O LORD,
    when I lay charges against you;
    but let me put my case to you.
  Why does the way of the guilty prosper?
    Why do all who are treacherous thrive?
² You plant them, and they take root;
    they grow and bring forth fruit;
  you are near in their mouths
    yet far from their hearts.
³ But you, O LORD, know me;
    You see me and test me—my heart is
      with you.
  Pull them out like sheep for the slaughter,
    and set them apart for the day of slaughter.
⁴ How long will the land mourn,
    and the grass of every field wither?

NIV

5"If you have raced with men on foot
    and they have worn you out,
    how can you compete with horses?
If you stumble in safe country,^{a}
    how will you manage in the thickets by^b the
        Jordan?
6Your brothers, your own family—
    even they have betrayed you;
    they have raised a loud cry against you.
Do not trust them,
    though they speak well of you.

^{a}5 Or *If you put your trust in a land of safety* ^{b}5 Or *the flooding of*

NRSV

For the wickedness of those who live in it
    the animals and the birds are swept away,
    and because people said, "He is blind to
        our ways."^{a}

5 If you have raced with foot-runners and they
        have wearied you,
    how will you compete with horses?
And if in a safe land you fall down,
    how will you fare in the thickets of the
        Jordan?
6 For even your kinsfolk and your own family,
    even they have dealt treacherously with
        you;
    they are in full cry after you;
do not believe them,
    though they speak friendly words to you.

^{a}Gk: Heb *to our future*

COMMENTARY

11:18-20. This section is ordered around a sequence of prophetic laments (11:18-20; 12:1-4), followed in each case by a divine response (11:21-23; 12:5-6). The text begins quite abruptly out of the extended prose treatment of the covenant. Calvin and others have argued that it was the evil deeds of the people generally that Jeremiah had in mind.[97] But it is more likely that the "evil deeds" (NIV, "plot") refer to the "schemes" devised against Jeremiah. Now the reader is brought abruptly from the fate of the community, and the extended theological analysis of it, into the inner mind and heart of the prophet, into the personal and painful suffering of the one whom God has called to announce and interpret the judgment.

The sense of some kind of plot against Jeremiah, which is confirmed immediately in the verses that follow, is suggested in v. 18 as the prophet indicates that he came to know something was going on when he was previously unaware of threats against him. How the Lord made this known to Jeremiah, we are not told, but there is no sense that it was in any other fashion than by prophetic revelation. The opening verse indicates that this long sequence of laments and prayers of Jeremiah begins in an innocence that is only broken by the Lord's revelation of the plot. That revelation triggers the prayers and the complaints.[98]

The first complaint occurs in v. 19, a typical lament about the enemies, mixed with language and images characteristic of prayers for help. The prophet's lack of awareness of the plots against him is here underscored as he depicts himself as an innocent lamb led to slaughter, going about his business quite unaware that the butchers are ready to cut his throat. The image has at least three dimensions: (1) It is perfect for expressing the prophet's sense about his situation, his blissful ignorance of the dangers before him. (2) It is also a characteristic image of lament prayers (Ps 44:12). And when one hears the image from the background of Psalm 44, where the one who leads the people to the slaughter like sheep is the Lord, one cannot help asking whether that is inferred in Jeremiah's use of that image here. Certainly, the

97. John Calvin, *Commentaries on the Book of the Prophet Jeremiah and the Lamentations* (Grand Rapids: Eerdmans, 1950) 2:106-9.

98. Because 12:6 is a divine word revealing the threats against Jeremiah, some have suggested that it originally belonged after 11:18 or that 12:1-6 as a whole would have preceded 11:18-20. It is best, however, to deal with the text as received, with all its tensions and spasms.

prophet increasingly lays the blame for his condition on God, as the lament in 12:1-6 indicates. (3) Further, by its resonance with the picture of the suffering servant in Isaiah 53 as a lamb led to the slaughter, it draws Jeremiah's experience into that line of God's suffering servants who, in doing the will of the Lord, find themselves under attack and oppression. That resonance is sharpened by the reference to being cut off from the land of the living (v. 19; cf. Isa 53:8). Jeremiah's response, however, is quite different from that of the servant in Isaiah 53, where the image of the lamb conveys the silence of the victim. Jeremiah is anything but silent before the threats to his life.

The depiction of the threat as a matter of the enemy's devising evil schemes is also characteristic of the lament psalms, where such schemes and plots were a common feature of the dangers faced by those who prayed (e.g., Pss 7:14; 10:2; 35:4; 36:4; 41:7; 140:2). Indeed, Jeremiah demonstrates for the reader of the psalms the concreteness of such threats. Here the general language of the lament prayer is given specificity immediately in the words that follow in vv. 21-23 and later in 18:18, as well as in some of the narrative biographical sections of the book. Evil schemes really were being devised against the one who prayed.

The second half of v. 19 presents the prophet as quoting or projecting what his opponents are saying and threatening to do. Such quotations of the enemy's intent are a common feature of lament prayers (e.g., Pss 2:3; 12:4; 35:25; 71:11). Here the quotation unequivocally identifies the plan against the prophet: his death. Once again, there are echoes of the lament psalms, in this case Ps 83:4, where lamenting Israel quotes the nations as plotting against them to wipe them out so that "the name of Israel will be remembered no more."

The imagery of the fruitful tree is ironic since this image often conveys the notion of rich fruitfulness, of one who is blessed and successful (e.g., 17:8; Pss 1:3; 92:12-14). In this case, the point is the destruction of the still fruitful—that is, active and vital—tree, here the prophet.

There is irony in the threat to eliminate Jeremiah's name from memory by killing him. Later in these chapters, Jeremiah is instructed by the Lord not to marry and not to have any children, the primary vehicle by which a name would have been created. There is a particular purpose in that command (see the Commentary on 16:1-9), but its implications for Jeremiah's life are no less than what is intended in the threat to kill him. It is no surprise that the lament of the prophet is a profound complaint against God. That is often the case with laments, but Jeremiah's personal experience suggested more directly than most that his chief source of pain and suffering was the Lord.

The petition that is always at the heart of lament prayers unfolds in v. 20, again in language typical of such prayers or the psalms generally: "judge righteously" (Pss 7:11; 9:4); "test the heart and mind" (cf. Pss 7:9; 26:2); "to you I have committed my cause" (Ps 22:8); "your vengeance" (cf. Pss 18:47; 94:1; 149:7). The appellation "you who judge righteously" is a significant part of the appeal of Jeremiah. The possibility of his surviving this predicament depends on his being able to count on the Lord to uphold righteousness, to decide equitably between the innocent and the wicked, which in this case means acting on behalf of an innocent Jeremiah and against his destructive and wicked enemies. Prayer involves the laying out of a case before God on the assumption that God will assess and act appropriately. So the prophet, counting on such fair assessment and righteous intervention, presents as part of his case his own innocence and righteousness. Implicit in such language is the assumption that the heart and mind of the person praying can stand the test, a point made explicit in Psalm 7, which provides so much of the language of this verse:

> The LORD judges the peoples;
> judge me, O LORD, according
> to my righteousness
> and according to the integrity
> that is in me.
> O let the evil of the wicked come to an end,
> but establish the righteous,
> you who test the minds and hearts,
> O righteous God. (Ps 7:8-9 NRSV)

In all of the expressions in v. 20, the prophet is making the case, making the appeal, and also motivating the deity. Nearly every part of the prayer for help that makes up the lament gives reasons to God that invite divine intervention. The appeal to the character of God as righteous judge and the indication of an innocent person that his or her cause is in the hands of such a judge are designed to arouse God, in this case to bring "your vengeance" against the prophet's enemies. The possessive pronoun is important here. Vengeance is the action of God to acquit and save the righteous or innocent and to thwart and put down the wicked. It is an act of divine sovereignty and righteousness. It is not a matter of Jeremiah's revenge. Those who oppress the wicked are by definition set against God, and the vindication—perhaps a better term than "vengeance" or "retribution" in this instance—of God is accomplished as the enemies are defeated.

11:21-23. The divine response to Jeremiah's prayer uncovers the details of the threat and answers the prayer with a promise that his enemies will be overcome. The threat is more terrifying than expected: His own people, his own family, conspire against him and seek to do him in. That is made explicit in 12:6, but the first reference to Jeremiah in the whole book has identified him as coming from "the priests who were in Anathoth." The "people of Anathoth" are kinsfolk. The threat of Jeremiah's message becomes all the clearer when even his family cannot accept his message. It is so dangerous that his own people are at work to stop him, even to kill him to stop the word of the Lord.

The passage has its closest analogy to Amos 7:10-17, another instance where a prophet is told to stop prophesying, in that case by the chief priest of the land. The opposition of priest and prophet is thus underscored by these two texts, which show the religious establishment vigorously resisting the prophetic word.

The similarity to Amos's encounter with the priest Amaziah is further indicated by the parallel forms of punishment. It is not simply those who oppose the prophetic word who will be punished. Even their sons and daughters will die in battle and famine. In fact, the punishment seems to be against the next generation, in contrast to the words later on in the book of Jeremiah about a time when it shall no longer be that children are punished for their parents' sins (31:29-30). What seems to be involved here, however, as well as in the case of Amos, is not so much a shifting of the punishment from the sinning generation to an innocent generation but the effects of the sins of the parents upon the children. The sword and famine are those that come with war. The judgment against Judah and Jerusalem that will take effect in the coming of the conquering army will inevitably destroy the children as they are killed in battle or die of the famine that results from widespread devastation of the land. The punishment of Jeremiah's enemies is part of the larger punishment of the people, inasmuch as their sin against Jeremiah is part of the larger resistance to the divine word of reproval and correction.

12:1-4. The complex interrelationship of Jeremiah's laments with one another is evident when one compares these verses with the first lament in 11:18-20. They share a number of features: the address to God as the one "who judges righteously" (11:18) and as the one who "will be in the right" (12:1); the juridical word "case" or "cause"(ריב *rîb*) in 11:20 ("my cause") and 12:1 ("lay charges," a verbal form); the imagery of the sheep for slaughter (11:19; 12:3); the imagery of the tree with its fruit (11:19; 12:2); the sequence of "know" and "see" (11:18; 12:3); and the testing of the heart (11:20; 12:2) and the mind (11:20; 12:3). Yet, there are significant differences in the way these phrases and themes come to expression in the two laments.

The case that is presented *to* the Lord in 11:20 in the context of a plea for help becomes a case *against* the Lord in 12:1. The lament of 11:18-20, therefore, now becomes unequivocally a complaint. As such, it is again typical of the psalmic complaints against God, with the characteristic "Why?" questions addressed to the deity.[99] The first question lies at the heart of virtually all the complaints against God: Why do the wicked prosper? It is a direct challenge to the assumptions of Psalm 1—namely, that the righteous prosper and the wicked perish. The question becomes even more an issue of theodicy with the assertion that God plants the "treacherous and they take root, grow, and flourish while being far from God in their hearts."

The sheep to be led to slaughter are now the enemies of Jeremiah. What he experienced now becomes his hope for them. There is a kind of poetic justice in such a plea for retribution just as there is in the picture of the enemies, rather than Jeremiah, as the cut-down tree.

---

99. On the complaint against God, see Craig C. Broyles, *The Conflict of Faith and Experience in the Psalms: A Form Critical and Theological Study,* JSOTSup 52 (Sheffield: Sheffield Academic, 1989); Patrick D. Miller, *They Cried to the Lord: The Form and Theology of Biblical Prayer* (Minneapolis: Fortress, 1994).

A further complaint is added in the typical lament question "How long?" At this point, Judah's plight is brought into the prophet's lament, indicating once again how much Jeremiah identifies with his people and does not simply stand over against them, even though the "rightness" of the judgment against them is acknowledged (v. 4*b*).

The lament of the previous chapter, therefore, has become a complaint, and Jeremiah, like Job, lays out a case (lit., "judgments," v. 1*a*) against the deity. But it is still the Lord to whom Jeremiah appeals, and his presupposition in v. 1 is that "you will be in the right." Is this a way to motivate the deity, or is it Jeremiah's awareness that he cannot win this argument? If the latter, there is a painful tension in the text, for the claim of v. 3*a* is really a protestation of innocence, the confidence of the prophet that, when tested, he will be found innocent. It is no accident that this claim is followed by the single petition of the prayer: that God will pull the wicked out like sheep for the slaughter. The praying prophet is sure that the test will lead God to vindicate him and overthrow the wicked.

12:5-6. Again comes the divine response. But it is quite different from the first one in 11:21-23. Here we encounter the kind of response that the Lord made to Elijah at Mt. Sinai when he complained or to Job when he questioned God. The dialogue has brought a word of assurance to Jeremiah in the form of a judgment oracle against his enemies (11:21-23), but it has also brought the disturbing announcement in v. 5: "You think it is bad now? You haven't seen anything yet!" The prophetic burden has never been more sharply etched than in this statement of the Lord. It is not a message of reassurance but a question of how much Jeremiah can withstand, because his troubles have only just begun. An emphatic clue to that effect is provided by the use of "even" (גַּם *gam*) three times in v. 6 (though shown only twice in translation): "*even* your kinsfolk . . . *even* your family . . . *even* they are in full cry after you." Jeremiah is not safe anywhere. What was intimated with reference to the people of Anathoth (11:21) is now made very explicit: The plots against Jeremiah are coming from his own family.

REFLECTIONS

1. While it may seem a little strange to our notions of prayer to think of it as an act of urging and persuading God, the laments of Jeremiah, like those of the book of Psalms, show that to be the case. In various ways, the prophet seeks to lay his situation out before the Lord in a manner that will appeal to one who seeks justice and righteousness in the world. Indeed, the very appellation of the deity as "righteous judge" is a reminder of that which is the ground of Jeremiah's appeal. The one who is the righteous judge can hardly ignore the cause of this innocent and besieged prophet.

Such efforts to push God to act in certain ways may seem to be a kind of human manipulation of the deity. But that is a superficial judgment. The case presented and the appeals set forth are such that they, in effect, call upon and urge God to be and to act in ways that are already understood to be consistent with God's nature and character. The prayer offers the situation of the praying one as an opportunity for the God who has been revealed as a righteous judge, as one who cares about the oppressed, and as one who works in the world for good and life and against evil and death. The openness of the Lord to the prophet's prayers for the people, an openness that is so strong that God actually has to forbid such intercession when judgment is called for (see 11:14), is a signal of the power of prayer to persuade the Lord to respond. Something very important is thus indicated about what goes on in the act of prayer. Jeremiah's prayer assumes the receptivity of God to the argument he makes in prayer. That assumption means, however, that not just anything goes in prayer. The plea and the case are consistent with what is true and fundamental about God and what God is doing in the world. Trivialities are not what is going on in such praying, certainly not in Jeremiah's prayers.[100]

---

100. On prayer as an act of persuasion, see P. D. Miller, "Prayer as Persuasion: The Rhetoric and Intention of Prayer," *Word and World* 13 (1993) 356-62.

2. The passage makes the reader aware that the fundamental concerns of contemporary theodicies—that is, the desire to comprehend and justify the ways of God in the face of human realities that seem to call God's way into question—are not a modern discovery. The questions of "Why?" and "How?" which we are compelled to ask in the face of evil and tragedy, are very much at the heart of the biblical story. Alongside Psalm 1, we read Jeremiah's complaints and know that God's people have always struggled to comprehend the absence of apparent justice in the world, the prosperity of the bad and the wicked. The text does not give an answer to the question, but it assumes that it is going to be present on the lips of even God's chosen and called ones. It is not so much that the text gives permission to the contemporary person of faith as that it recognizes the inevitability of such questions and complaints as a part of human existence, more acutely present in the context of a deep relationship with God. Not only does the experience of that relationship not protect us from such questions, but it may also force us to ask them all the more sharply.

3. A feature worth noting in this text is the claim of the prophet, in this instance more implicit than direct, that he is not guilty of sin and that the oppression he experiences is undeserved. The assumption of a deep, pervasive, and unavoidable sinfulness as a part of the human condition is not to be found here. There is instead a claim on the part of the prophet that he has been a faithful and obedient servant and so can claim God's help rather than God's punishment. There is something quite important and healthy here that often gets lost in the picture of humanity and of persons of faith as being so contaminated with sin that they, by definition, are undeserving and can only claim God's mercy against their just deserts. The lamenting ones of the psalms and of Jeremiah as petitioners for help are willing to set their lives under examination. It *is* possible to live a just and obedient life. Human life is not perverted insofar that there is no possibility of righteous living. Jeremiah is even willing to be tested at that point.

4. Both of Jeremiah's pleas receive responses from God. That is usually the case in Scripture. What is interesting in this case is the character of the response. Most often, the word received is an oracle of salvation assuring the petitioner that he or she need not be afraid, that God is present to help and deliver (see the Commentary on 1:17-19). But the responses here suggest something of the diversity of God's reactions to the prayers of the faithful. There is a positive answer to Jeremiah's prayer in 11:18-20. God will bring deliverance, but it is a deliverance that is to be wrought in the fires of judgment (11:22-23). It is not a happily ever after promise. One has only to read Jeremiah's story to know that while he does survive, he also endures some of the devastation of the judgment, ending up finally in exile in Egypt (see chaps. 43–44).

There is also a response to Jeremiah's second prayer, and it is most assuredly not a promise of deliverance. Instead, we hear what happens on some other occasions when profound queries go up to heaven from those who are being done in, when the "Why?" and the "How long?" sound their most poignant. In 12:5-6, the response of God is not an oracle of salvation. God's reaction to the questions of Jeremiah is, in turn, to ask some questions back to the prophet. There is no assurance of deliverance. Instead, there is a querying of the prophet's own questions. It is particularly with those markedly faithful ones—Elijah, Jeremiah, and Job—that the Lord seems to push the demand to its ultimate. Elijah, who wished to cut loose from all the dangers and ardors of being God's prophet; Job, who knew he was innocent and would not stop until he was given an accounting; and Jeremiah, whose life and liberty are under constant threat because he does what the Lord tells him—all cry out to God, only to be queried back or told to get back into the hot kitchen where it is only going to get hotter. Likewise, when the exiles at a later time complain to God, their complaints are met not only with oracles of salvation but also with challenges to their assumptions about what God is doing or not doing in the world (Isa 40:27-31). The Scriptures suggest again and again that our prayers are heard and that the reassuring promise of God's presence and power, a promise underscored in the life and death of Jesus Christ, is given to us. But sometimes our questions may only be thrown back at us or thrust aside in the renewed call for us to take up the tasks that have brought us into weariness, danger, and defeat. At the beginning of the book, Jeremiah is given the assurance of God's presence to deliver (1:19). One may assume that this promise was sure and could be counted upon. But it surely did not mean an easy life and a final rest—not for this faithful servant of the Lord. And it has not been for a lot of others.

JEREMIAH 12:7-17, MY HERITAGE A DESOLATION

NIV

⁷"I will forsake my house,
    abandon my inheritance;
I will give the one I love
    into the hands of her enemies.
⁸My inheritance has become to me
    like a lion in the forest.
She roars at me;
    therefore I hate her.
⁹Has not my inheritance become to me
    like a speckled bird of prey
    that other birds of prey surround and attack?
Go and gather all the wild beasts;
    bring them to devour.
¹⁰Many shepherds will ruin my vineyard
    and trample down my field;
they will turn my pleasant field
    into a desolate wasteland.
¹¹It will be made a wasteland,
    parched and desolate before me;
the whole land will be laid waste
    because there is no one who cares.
¹²Over all the barren heights in the desert
    destroyers will swarm,
for the sword of the LORD will devour
    from one end of the land to the other;
    no one will be safe.
¹³They will sow wheat but reap thorns;
    they will wear themselves out but gain nothing.
So bear the shame of your harvest
    because of the LORD's fierce anger."
¹⁴This is what the LORD says: "As for all my wicked neighbors who seize the inheritance I gave my people Israel, I will uproot them from their lands and I will uproot the house of Judah

NRSV

⁷I have forsaken my house,
    I have abandoned my heritage;
I have given the beloved of my heart
    into the hands of her enemies.
⁸My heritage has become to me
    like a lion in the forest;
she has lifted up her voice against me—
    therefore I hate her.
⁹Is the hyena greedy*ᵃ* for my heritage at my
    command?
Are the birds of prey all around her?
Go, assemble all the wild animals;
    bring them to devour her.
¹⁰Many shepherds have destroyed my vineyard,
    they have trampled down my portion,
they have made my pleasant portion
    a desolate wilderness.
¹¹They have made it a desolation;
    desolate, it mourns to me.
The whole land is made desolate,
    but no one lays it to heart.
¹²Upon all the bare heights*ᵇ* in the desert
    spoilers have come;
for the sword of the LORD devours
    from one end of the land to the other;
    no one shall be safe.
¹³They have sown wheat and have reaped
    thorns,
they have tired themselves out but profit
    nothing.
They shall be ashamed of their*ᶜ* harvests
    because of the fierce anger of the LORD.

ᵃCn: Heb *Is the hyena, the bird of prey*   ᵇOr *the trails*   ᶜHeb *your*

NIV

from among them. [15]But after I uproot them, I will again have compassion and will bring each of them back to his own inheritance and his own country. [16]And if they learn well the ways of my people and swear by my name, saying, 'As surely as the LORD lives'—even as they once taught my people to swear by Baal—then they will be established among my people. [17]But if any nation does not listen, I will completely uproot and destroy it," declares the LORD.

NRSV

14Thus says the LORD concerning all my evil neighbors who touch the heritage that I have given my people Israel to inherit: I am about to pluck them up from their land, and I will pluck up the house of Judah from among them. [15]And after I have plucked them up, I will again have compassion on them, and I will bring them again to their heritage and to their land, everyone of them. [16]And then, if they will diligently learn the ways of my people, to swear by my name, "As the LORD lives," as they taught my people to swear by Baal, then they shall be built up in the midst of my people. [17]But if any nation will not listen, then I will completely uproot it and destroy it, says the LORD.

COMMENTARY

12:7-13. As in chaps. 8–10, compassion and judgment, lament and anger are intertwined in this divine speech. Two types of repetition reveal the passionate mix of anger and lament. One type is the repeated "my" with reference to the people, who are consistently called "my heritage" (NIV, "my inheritance") or "my portion" (NIV, "my field") or similar expressions of relationship. The terms "heritage" and "portion" mean essentially the same thing and identify the people of Judah as the particular and beloved possession of the Lord. In the background is the notion, found in Deut 32:8-9 and elsewhere, that in God's division of the peoples of the earth, the Lord chose Israel as an "allotted share" (Deut 32:9; cf. Deut 7:6). These verses thus heap up terms to describe the Lord's sense of special relationship to this people. The other repeated word is "desolation" (4 times in vv. 10-11). Its use reflects language elsewhere that depicts the people as ravaged and the land as destroyed. The point of the text is, perhaps, best conveyed by v. 7b: "I have given the beloved of my heart into the hands of her enemies." The pathos of the whole section is caught up in that one sentence, with its identification of the one whom the Lord has given over to her enemies as "the beloved of my heart." It is captured in another way when the Lord says of "my heritage," "I hate her" (v. 8).

Two other features of the text need to be noted.

One is the use of images of the hyena, birds of prey, and wild animals as being poised over the people to devour them and of shepherds who have made the land into a desolation. These rather negative images about the Lord's instruments of destruction prepare the way for the next passage, in which the Lord turns against these destructive forces. Then in the final verse of the unit, the reader hears again (cf. chap. 2) that whatever the people have done, they have gotten no profit from it, an echo of the earlier condemnation of the people as betraying the Lord to follow Baal but finding no profit in doing so. All of the earlier indictments lie in the background of this text. The anger of the Lord is as sharp and real as is the Lord's passionate affection.

12:14-17. A second speech of the Lord carries forward the claims of the preceding verses but incorporates them into strong language about the nations who are the Lord's instruments of anger and destruction. Here, they, too, suffer the fate of Judah, being plucked up or uprooted. The expression "my evil neighbors who touch the heritage that I have given my people Israel to inherit" is an unusual one. It not only ties these verses to the preceding ones through the use of the "heritage" language, but it also speaks of the other peoples not just as Judah's neighbors but as "my neighbors." The involvement of the Lord in the fate of Israel is again underscored. Furthermore, the move of the other nations, whoever they may be, to "touch" God's people and their land cannot be without consequence. These nations are not without culpability.

The last two verses not only announce the restoration of Judah but also make the same promise to other nations. The text then outruns anything we have yet heard from Jeremiah: the call to the nations to convert to Yahwism. "To swear by my name" is to give allegiance to the Lord. The oracle invites the other nations to turn around, and does so with real irony. Just as these nations taught Israel/Judah to walk in other ways and give allegiance to other gods, so also they are now invited to learn Israel's—that is, God's—ways and to swear by Israel's God. The text betrays a powerful universalistic impulse. The Lord invites and welcomes all the "neighbors" into the community of faith that is constituted by Israel. The invitation is real. It also has a catch to it: There is no other alternative (v. 17).

Finally, one should note how thoroughly this text is cast in the words of the Lord's commission to Jeremiah in his call (1:5*b*, 10). Jeremiah was appointed a prophet to and over the nations, "to pluck up" and "to build." The former verb appears three times in the Lord's statement about what is going to happen to Judah and "my evil neighbors." The latter verb is the promise to those same neighbors that if they will learn the ways of Israel and swear by the name of the Lord, "they shall be built up."

REFLECTIONS

1. Again we encounter the pathos of God in Scripture. That is nowhere more sharply indicated than in the reality of the cross and its mix of God's judgment and God's suffering. But these and other words of the prophet also portray the power of that reality. We see, even if in the very earthen vessel of prophetic proclamation, a true glimpse into the way in which divine judgment against those whom the Lord has loved so dearly is always mixed with great sadness and loss. The anthropomorphic portrayal of the "heart" of God is crucial for comprehending the depth of what has happened. The judgment can never be understood lightly or as some inherent dimension of a God who is prone to anger and wrath. It is there only because the human community that the Lord has called and loved into being has refused to live as a called and loved and obedient people. Precisely because of the depth of God's care and sense of identification with this people, the anger is so fierce. But that fierceness cannot be easily dismissed. This is a God who called a people into being and not only loved them but set them as a people to show the Lord's way in the world. When that did not work out, the Lord put that process on hold and would not tolerate the continued betrayal of "my heritage." That "hold" is not the last word, but it cannot be skipped over, historically or theologically.

2. The historical context of 12:14-17 is debated, with some arguing for this text as coming from Jeremiah and his time and others seeing it as a projection backward from the time of exile or later. It ultimately does not matter where it can be located historically. Its connection to the preceding words reiterates what we hear again and again in the Old Testament: The anger and judgment of God are not the last word. The critical words are, "I will again have compassion on them." We cannot ameliorate the fierce anger we discover in 12:13, but neither can we end the story there or draw a definitive picture of God's way with this frail, disobedient, wandering people. There is no temporizing about obedience. The Lord promises to start over with Judah and invites others to become a part of the story. But there is only one way to do that, and there is no pussyfooting around about whether the Lord will put up with resistance to the way of justice and righteousness, faithfulness and loyalty, which God has intended for this planet from the beginning. "No way," says the prophet (12:17).

3. Judgment against all those "evil neighbors" who "touch" the heritage of "my people" Israel is announced in 12:14. This passage in its context is similar in meaning and force to Zech

2:8: "For thus said the LORD of hosts . . . regarding the nations that plundered you: Truly, one who touches you touches the apple of my eye." This was one of the passages that so impressed itself upon Dietrich Bonhoeffer after the Krystalnacht pogrom against the Jews. His friend Eberhard Bethge believed that it was in reading this and other texts in the light of that event that Bonhoeffer made his commitment to stand with the Jews and against the tyranny of National Socialism.[101] Such texts make it clear that Israel was and remains so dear to the Lord that those who "touch" Israel do harm to that which is the very apple of God's eye. Christian theology and practice can never forget that.

4. The narrow provincialism that many read into the Old Testament is broken through here. The purpose of God incorporates the full community of nations as those who live and walk by the law of the Lord. Thus 12:15-17 joins with Isa 2:2-5; 19:16-25; and Mic 4:1-5 to envision a time when all the peoples of the earth will swear by the Lord and live by the Lord's teaching, a time when justice and righteousness will prevail among all and the former enemies become the Lord's people and the Lord's heritage along with Israel. No vision of God's future, whether soon or late, can afford to let go of that hope, of that expectation. These are the pictures of the future that can shape the present and create an imagination that is not content with the present hostilities, oppressions, and enmities.[102]

101. Eberhard Bethge, *Friendship and Resistance* (Grand Rapids: Eerdmans, 1995) 58-71.
102. See Walter Brueggemann, *The Prophetic Imagination* (Philadelphia: Fortress, 1978).

JEREMIAH 13:1-27, PROPHETIC SYMBOLS

NIV

13 This is what the LORD said to me: "Go and buy a linen belt and put it around your waist, but do not let it touch water." [2]So I bought a belt, as the LORD directed, and put it around my waist.

[3]Then the word of the LORD came to me a second time: [4]"Take the belt you bought and are wearing around your waist, and go now to Perath[a] and hide it there in a crevice in the rocks." [5]So I went and hid it at Perath, as the LORD told me.

[6]Many days later the LORD said to me, "Go now to Perath and get the belt I told you to hide there." [7]So I went to Perath and dug up the belt and took it from the place where I had hidden it, but now it was ruined and completely useless.

[8]Then the word of the LORD came to me: [9]"This is what the LORD says: 'In the same way I will ruin the pride of Judah and the great pride of Jerusalem. [10]These wicked people, who refuse to listen to my words, who follow the stubbornness of their hearts and go after other gods to serve and

[a]4 Or possibly *the Euphrates*; also in verses 5-7

NRSV

13 Thus said the LORD to me, "Go and buy yourself a linen loincloth, and put it on your loins, but do not dip it in water." [2]So I bought a loincloth according to the word of the LORD, and put it on my loins. [3]And the word of the LORD came to me a second time, saying, [4]"Take the loincloth that you bought and are wearing, and go now to the Euphrates,[a] and hide it there in a cleft of the rock." [5]So I went, and hid it by the Euphrates,[a] as the LORD commanded me. [6]And after many days the LORD said to me, "Go now to the Euphrates,[a] and take from there the loincloth that I commanded you to hide there." [7]Then I went to the Euphrates,[a] and dug, and I took the loincloth from the place where I had hidden it. But now the loincloth was ruined; it was good for nothing.

8Then the word of the LORD came to me: [9]Thus says the LORD: Just so I will ruin the pride of Judah and the great pride of Jerusalem. [10]This evil people, who refuse to hear my words, who stubbornly follow their own will and have gone after other

[a]Or *to Parah*; Heb *perath*

NIV

worship them, will be like this belt—completely useless! ¹¹For as a belt is bound around a man's waist, so I bound the whole house of Israel and the whole house of Judah to me,' declares the LORD, 'to be my people for my renown and praise and honor. But they have not listened.'

¹²"Say to them: 'This is what the LORD, the God of Israel, says: Every wineskin should be filled with wine.' And if they say to you, 'Don't we know that every wineskin should be filled with wine?' ¹³then tell them, 'This is what the LORD says: I am going to fill with drunkenness all who live in this land, including the kings who sit on David's throne, the priests, the prophets and all those living in Jerusalem. ¹⁴I will smash them one against the other, fathers and sons alike, declares the LORD. I will allow no pity or mercy or compassion to keep me from destroying them.' "

¹⁵Hear and pay attention,
    do not be arrogant,
    for the LORD has spoken.
¹⁶Give glory to the LORD your God
    before he brings the darkness,
    before your feet stumble
    on the darkening hills.
You hope for light,
    but he will turn it to thick darkness
    and change it to deep gloom.
¹⁷But if you do not listen,
    I will weep in secret
    because of your pride;
my eyes will weep bitterly,
    overflowing with tears,
    because the LORD's flock will be taken captive.

¹⁸Say to the king and to the queen mother,
    "Come down from your thrones,
for your glorious crowns
    will fall from your heads."
¹⁹The cities in the Negev will be shut up,
    and there will be no one to open them.
All Judah will be carried into exile,
    carried completely away.

²⁰Lift up your eyes and see
    those who are coming from the north.
Where is the flock that was entrusted to you,
    the sheep of which you boasted?

NRSV

gods to serve them and worship them, shall be like this loincloth, which is good for nothing. ¹¹For as the loincloth clings to one's loins, so I made the whole house of Israel and the whole house of Judah cling to me, says the LORD, in order that they might be for me a people, a name, a praise, and a glory. But they would not listen.

12You shall speak to them this word: Thus says the LORD, the God of Israel: Every wine-jar should be filled with wine. And they will say to you, "Do you think we do not know that every wine-jar should be filled with wine?" ¹³Then you shall say to them: Thus says the LORD: I am about to fill all the inhabitants of this land—the kings who sit on David's throne, the priests, the prophets, and all the inhabitants of Jerusalem—with drunkenness. ¹⁴And I will dash them one against another, parents and children together, says the LORD. I will not pity or spare or have compassion when I destroy them.

¹⁵Hear and give ear; do not be haughty,
    for the LORD has spoken.
¹⁶Give glory to the LORD your God
    before he brings darkness,
    and before your feet stumble
    on the mountains at twilight;
while you look for light,
    he turns it into gloom
    and makes it deep darkness.
¹⁷But if you will not listen,
    my soul will weep in secret for your pride;
my eyes will weep bitterly and run down
        with tears,
    because the LORD's flock has been taken
        captive.

¹⁸Say to the king and the queen mother:
    "Take a lowly seat,
for your beautiful crown
    has come down from your head."ᵃ
¹⁹The towns of the Negeb are shut up
    with no one to open them;
all Judah is taken into exile,
    wholly taken into exile.

²⁰Lift up your eyes and see
    those who come from the north.

ᵃGk Syr Vg: Meaning of Heb uncertain

NIV

21What will you say when ₍the LORD₎ sets over
      you
   those you cultivated as your special allies?
Will not pain grip you
   like that of a woman in labor?
22And if you ask yourself,
   "Why has this happened to me?"—
it is because of your many sins
   that your skirts have been torn off
   and your body mistreated.
23Can the Ethiopian*a* change his skin
   or the leopard its spots?
Neither can you do good
   who are accustomed to doing evil.

24"I will scatter you like chaff
   driven by the desert wind.
25This is your lot,
   the portion I have decreed for you,"
                        declares the LORD,
   "because you have forgotten me
   and trusted in false gods.
26I will pull up your skirts over your face
   that your shame may be seen—
27your adulteries and lustful neighings,
   your shameless prostitution!
I have seen your detestable acts
   on the hills and in the fields.
Woe to you, O Jerusalem!
   How long will you be unclean?"

a23 Hebrew Cushite (probably a person from the upper Nile region)

NRSV

Where is the flock that was given you,
   your beautiful flock?
21 What will you say when they set as head
         over you
   those whom you have trained
   to be your allies?
Will not pangs take hold of you,
   like those of a woman in labor?
22 And if you say in your heart,
   "Why have these things come upon me?"
it is for the greatness of your iniquity
   that your skirts are lifted up,
   and you are violated.
23 Can Ethiopians*a* change their skin
   or leopards their spots?
Then also you can do good
   who are accustomed to do evil.
24 I will scatter you*b* like chaff
   driven by the wind from the desert.
25 This is your lot,
   the portion I have measured out to you,
         says the LORD,
   because you have forgotten me
   and trusted in lies.
26 I myself will lift up your skirts over your face,
   and your shame will be seen.
27 I have seen your abominations,
   your adulteries and neighings, your
         shameless prostitutions
   on the hills of the countryside.
Woe to you, O Jerusalem!
   How long will it be
   before you are made clean?

aOr Nubians; Heb Cushites   bHeb them

COMMENTARY

13:1-11. This is the first of several symbolic actions in the book of Jeremiah.[103] A regular part of prophetic proclamation, symbolic actions were the means by which the word of the Lord was dramatically illustrated. The basic form of the symbolic act is simple. The prophet receives a command from the Lord to carry out some deed.

The narrative gives a report of the action taken. Then there is an interpretive explanation of the symbolic act. In this case, the action takes place out of a series of commands (vv. 1-7), followed by an extended explanation (vv. 8-11).

There are two interpretive problems reflected in the NIV and NRSV translations and in the literature on this text. The Hebrew word פרת (*pĕrāt*) was understood by the earliest versions to refer to the Euphrates River in Mesopotamia (NRSV). The diffi-

103. For a list of Jeremiah's symbolic actions, see William L. Holladay, *Jeremiah 1: A Commentary on the Book of the Prophet Jeremiah Chapters 1–25,* Hermeneia (Philadelphia: Fortress, 1986) 394-95.

culty of conceiving of the prophet's making several journeys from Judah to the Euphrates has led some scholars to understand *pĕrāt* as referring to a Benjaminite place named Parah (NIV?), near Jeremiah's family town of Anathoth. The other problem is related to the meaning of *pĕrāt*. If the word refers to the Euphrates, then perhaps this is not an account of a symbolic action. Some would understand this text to be a report[104] or a parable, spoken or acted,[105] not as an actual sequence of journeys. Matters are complicated by the way the translation of *pĕrāt* affects whether this passage speaks about exile. If the word refers to the Euphrates, then an allusion to the exile is likely. If it refers to a Judaean town, however, then exile is not the point of the parable. Since these problems of interpretation cannot be satisfactorily resolved, the story should be read as it is given to us.

The loincloth that the prophet is told to take from its hiding place at the Euphrates may symbolize the people of Judah (and Israel, v. 11) and represent the exile of the people, who were once intimately and permanently bound to the Lord but are now separated and undone. It may, however, that the loincloth represents the corruption of the people through Assyrian or Babylonian influences. They have, in effect, gone to Assyria by adopting Assyrian practices (cf. 7:16-20; 44:15-19).

Both interpretations are possible in the light of the explanatory words in vv. 8-11. While exile is not explicitly referred to in those verses, v. 9 gives as the initial general explanation of the symbolic action the Lord's destruction of Judah and Jerusalem. Moreover, it makes direct connection to v. 7, with its "just so" and the use of the verb "ruin" (שחת *šāḥat*): Just as the loincloth was ruined, so also the Lord will ruin the pride of Judah and Jerusalem. Verses 10-11 suggest that the symbolic action has to do with the corruption of the people, whether under Assyrian influence or by some other means. The unwashed and now ruined loincloth is the Lord's people whom the Lord has kept as close as clothes on one's body. That is the way Israel is meant to be to the Lord. "The constant wearing of the loincloth is an indication of Yahweh's continuous care for his people and the indissolubility of their relationship."[106]

The corruption of the people, which means that they, like the loincloth, are now good for nothing, is described in the familiar terms of refusal to obey the Lord, stubbornness, and the worship of other gods.

Verse 11 poignantly reveals the mind and heart of God. The Lord had great hopes for this people. In the people's unceasing devotion to the Lord's way, the Lord would have a people "for me," and by their actions the Lord's name would be lifted up and praised. But that is now all gone because they would not listen.

13:12-14. The oracle of the prophet takes up another symbol, a wine jar. But this is not a symbolic action. Instead, an interpretation is given to a saying, one that is either proverbial in some sense—everything has its proper use—or that is simply banal. The latter is more likely due to the response of the citizens, who treat the remark as obvious. The statement then becomes a judgment speech as the Lord declares the divine intent to fill all these "wine-jars" with drunkenness. The list of people in v. 13 expresses both a judgment on the leaders, as Jeremiah often does, and the totality of judgment. The drunkenness imagery may connote loss of control and self-destruction as drunks lose control, make fools of themselves, and endanger themselves and others.[107] The motif of drinking from the cup of wine, however, is used elsewhere in Jeremiah (25:15-29; 48:26; 49:12) and in other prophetic oracles (e.g., Ezek 23:31-34; Hab 2:15-16) to express the notion of drinking from the cup of the Lord's wrath. The image is similar to the depictions of the Lord's giving the people poison to drink (Jer 8:14; 9:15; 23:15).

It is uncertain whether the drunkenness imagery continues in v. 14, but there is no question that the judgment at the hands of the Lord continues in these verses. The language of smashing "each against his brother, parents and children together" may suggest indirectly internecine strife taking place in the community that brings about self-destruction. The relentlessness of God's judgment is underscored in the final sentence. All instinct for God to deal mercifully (the book of Jeremiah and the OT in general attest regularly to that instinct; see, e.g., Exod 34:6-7; Ps 103:8-13) is suppressed in the face of the outrageous conduct

104. So Calvin, *Commentaries on the Book of the Prophet Jeremiah and the Lamentations,* 2:160-65.
105. R. Carroll, *Jeremiah* (Philadelphia: Westminster, 1986) 297.
106. William McKane, *A Critical and Exegetical Commentary on Jeremiah,* 2 vols., ICC (Edinburgh: T. & T. Clark, 1986, 1996) 1:290.
107. Walter Brueggemann, *A Commentary on Jeremiah: Exile and Homecoming* (Grand Rapids: Eerdmans, 1998).

of this people, conduct that is identified again and again in the judgment oracles of the first half of the book.

13:15-17. With great pathos, the prophet calls for the people to let go of their pride. What that means is suggested by the call in v. 16 to "give glory to the LORD your God." The prophet addresses once again the self-sufficiency and stubbornness of the people, who go their own way, following their own desires and wants, their own predilections, rather than the law of the Lord. The Lord's disappointment at the way the people's actions fail to redound to the praise and glory of God (v. 11) is shared here by the prophet, who sees the gathering darkness. He weeps at the stubbornness of the people who will not let go of their pride. The words suggest that there is still time; perhaps there is, but the mood of these verses is gloomy, the sadness of a prophet who already sees the outcome (v. 17).

13:18-19. The pathos of the preceding verses continues in this address to the king and the queen mother, probably Jehoiachin and his mother, Nehusta. His reign was short, and both of them were taken in the first and partial exile of 597 BCE (2 Kgs 24:8-17). Yahweh admonishes Jehoiachin to accept his fate: the impending loss of his throne and deportation. It is only the beginning of the larger fate of Judah (v. 19). The heavy hyperbole of v. 19 is probably a matter of poetic license, though some have suggested that Jeremiah anticipated an exile of larger dimensions than in fact took place.

13:20-27. The familiar verse of this passage is also its fundamental point: It is as likely that a person or an animal can change the color of its skin as it is that the people of Judah can change their propensity for evil and start doing good. The fate of Judah, described here in graphic terms as an outcome of their sins, their alliances, and the Lord's exposing their iniquity, is not the consequence of a harsh deity or of circumstances beyond their control. It grows directly out of the direction they have set for their lives. The problem is not unlike that of the pharaoh whose heart became so hardened that it was not possible for it ever to be softened again. The prophet invokes feminine imagery again because the feminine-personified Jerusalem is being addressed (see v. 27 and the sequence of feminine verbs) and because

the experience of war and devastation is meted out horrendously on women. So the judgment speech moves through images of a pregnant woman in labor (v. 21), of a woman being sexually violated (v. 22), and of an adulterous woman being exposed (vv. 26-27). Such imagery conveys indictment (vv. 22-23, 25*b*, 27*a*) and judgment (vv. 20-21, 24-25*a*, 26, 27*b*), which recalls earlier sections of the book, particularly 2:1–4:4.

Just as the previous oracle addressed the royal leaders and their downfall, so also now the Lord's message is addressed to the royal city, accusing it of not having tended to its flock. The prophet refers to the foe from the north (see the Commentary on 1:15), which has moved against Judah; the disappearing flock may refer to those who have gone into exile. In v. 21*a*, the prophet uses the pain of a woman in labor as a way of speaking about the travail of the city (see 4:3; 6:24; 22:23). The question in v. 22 is a lament, the "Why?" that belongs to the experience of terrible suffering. The prophet's response turns the whole passage into a theodicy, a justification of the suffering of Jerusalem, an explanation that seeks in this instance to answer the "Why?" directly. The extent of suffering matches the "greatness" of the city's sin. In the verses that follow, it is difficult to tell how literally or metaphorically one should read the text. The mention of forgetting the Lord and trusting in falsehood (v. 25) clearly refers to the people's apostasy, their turning to what does not profit and is not the truth—the other gods they have chosen to adore and serve. The imagery of vv. 26-27 may have the same thing in mind, invoking again the picture of the adulterous bride who turns to other "lovers" and worships other gods on the hills and under the trees (see 2:1–4:4). But the language may also reflect actual adultery and prostitution among the citizens of the community (see 5:7-8). The shocking and disturbing language of the violated woman (vv. 22, 26) serves all too well as a vehicle for conveying the experience of shame, humiliation, and physical attack. The destruction of Jerusalem, which surely involved the rape and assault of women, is itself understood by that same imagery. In that process, the shame of an iniquitous people will be exposed as a husband might expose the sexual sin of a wife.

REFLECTIONS

1. We often feel our hopes dashed when others do not live up to our expectations of them. When friends and family fail us, we are saddened, and possibilities that seemed large and grand are lost. We are less likely to think of dashed hopes as a part of God's experience, but the Bible is one long narrative of God's dashed hopes. That is not the whole story. But honesty about the failures of human beings as depicted in Scripture should give us pause. We may not have paid sufficient attention to the disappointment this causes the Lord. Chapter 13 momentarily sets before us just such sadness in the heart of God. The failure of God's people to live by the way the Lord has set is not just a matter for judgment. It is a source of genuine disappointment as well.

2. It is not difficult for us to think of our fate as being tied to what God does. This text reminds us, however, as do the prayers of Moses (Exod 32:11-14; Num 14:13-19) and the community laments (Psalm 44), that God's reputation is tied to what human beings do. That is, the one who has chosen to make the loincloth cling so closely is genuinely affected by what happens to it. God's glory depends in some fashion on what the community of faith does. How the Lord is perceived and responded to by the world is determined in no small measure by how the Lord's way is revealed through the life and work of those people who bear the Lord's name.

3. Use of imagery of the sexual activity and sexual violation of a woman to describe the sin of the people and the judgment of God places the reader in a serious tension. The imagery is powerful and communicates effectively. But it is itself a form of assault as it makes the vulnerability of a woman to sexual assault and shame the vehicle for speaking about human sin and divine judgment. The *yes* that the image raises by its communication is immediately negated by the *no* of the reader who sees in the image the ease with which literary and religious expression can victimize women. Poetic rape is not the same thing as actual rape, but it is no more palatable.

What is to be noticed in this instance—and perhaps elsewhere—is the way the development of the image in the passage serves to subvert the aim of the text. The denunciation and exposure of the faithless city become the shame and violation of a woman, and the sympathies of the reader are aroused along with the sense of justice. This subversion starts in the complaint of the victimized woman in 13:22. That her victimization turns out to be punishment does not diminish the reader's sense of her suffering. When that is heightened by the Lord's own involvement in the exposure of the sexual shame, the subversion continues. It receives its final turn when one moves from the oracles of judgment in Jeremiah to the plaintive laments of this same suffering woman, Jerusalem, in Lamentations and hears the cries for help of the one who has been violated and shamed and abandoned.

JEREMIAH 14:1–15:9, PRAYER THAT DOES NOT WORK

NIV	NRSV

14 This is the word of the LORD to Jeremiah concerning the drought:
 ²"Judah mourns,
  her cities languish;
	14 The word of the LORD that came to Jeremiah concerning the drought:
	 ² Judah mourns
	  and her gates languish;

they wail for the land,
  and a cry goes up from Jerusalem.
³The nobles send their servants for water;
  they go to the cisterns
  but find no water.
They return with their jars unfilled;
  dismayed and despairing,
  they cover their heads.
⁴The ground is cracked
  because there is no rain in the land;
the farmers are dismayed
  and cover their heads.
⁵Even the doe in the field
  deserts her newborn fawn
  because there is no grass.
⁶Wild donkeys stand on the barren heights
  and pant like jackals;
their eyesight fails
  for lack of pasture."

⁷Although our sins testify against us,
  O LORD, do something for the sake of your
    name.
For our backsliding is great;
  we have sinned against you.
⁸O Hope of Israel,
  its Savior in times of distress,
why are you like a stranger in the land,
  like a traveler who stays only a night?
⁹Why are you like a man taken by surprise,
  like a warrior powerless to save?
You are among us, O LORD,
  and we bear your name;
  do not forsake us!

¹⁰This is what the LORD says about this people:

"They greatly love to wander;
  they do not restrain their feet.
So the LORD does not accept them;
  he will now remember their wickedness
  and punish them for their sins."

¹¹Then the LORD said to me, "Do not pray for the well-being of this people. ¹²Although they fast, I will not listen to their cry; though they offer burnt offerings and grain offerings, I will not accept them. Instead, I will destroy them with the sword, famine and plague."
¹³But I said, "Ah, Sovereign LORD, the prophets

they lie in gloom on the ground,
  and the cry of Jerusalem goes up.
³ Her nobles send their servants for water;
  they come to the cisterns,
they find no water,
  they return with their vessels empty.
They are ashamed and dismayed
  and cover their heads,
⁴ because the ground is cracked.
  Because there has been no rain on the land
the farmers are dismayed;
  they cover their heads.
⁵ Even the doe in the field forsakes her
    newborn fawn
  because there is no grass.
⁶ The wild asses stand on the bare heights,ᵃ
  they pant for air like jackals;
their eyes fail
  because there is no herbage.

⁷ Although our iniquities testify against us,
  act, O LORD, for your name's sake;
our apostasies indeed are many,
  and we have sinned against you.
⁸ O hope of Israel,
  its savior in time of trouble,
why should you be like a stranger in the land,
  like a traveler turning aside for the night?
⁹ Why should you be like someone confused,
  like a mighty warrior who cannot give help?
Yet you, O LORD, are in the midst of us,
  and we are called by your name;
  do not forsake us!

¹⁰ Thus says the LORD concerning this people:
  Truly they have loved to wander,
  they have not restrained their feet;
therefore the LORD does not accept them,
  now he will remember their iniquity
  and punish their sins.

11 The LORD said to me: Do not pray for the welfare of this people. ¹²Although they fast, I do not hear their cry, and although they offer burnt offering and grain offering, I do not accept them; but by the sword, by famine, and by pestilence I consume them.

ᵃ Or *the trails*

NIV

keep telling them, 'You will not see the sword or suffer famine. Indeed, I will give you lasting peace in this place.' "

¹⁴Then the LORD said to me, "The prophets are prophesying lies in my name. I have not sent them or appointed them or spoken to them. They are prophesying to you false visions, divinations, idolatries[a] and the delusions of their own minds. ¹⁵Therefore, this is what the LORD says about the prophets who are prophesying in my name: I did not send them, yet they are saying, 'No sword or famine will touch this land.' Those same prophets will perish by sword and famine. ¹⁶And the people they are prophesying to will be thrown out into the streets of Jerusalem because of the famine and sword. There will be no one to bury them or their wives, their sons or their daughters. I will pour out on them the calamity they deserve.

¹⁷"Speak this word to them:

" 'Let my eyes overflow with tears
   night and day without ceasing;
for my virgin daughter—my people—
   has suffered a grievous wound,
   a crushing blow.
¹⁸If I go into the country,
   I see those slain by the sword;
if I go into the city,
   I see the ravages of famine.
Both prophet and priest
   have gone to a land they know not.' "

¹⁹Have you rejected Judah completely?
   Do you despise Zion?
Why have you afflicted us
   so that we cannot be healed?
We hoped for peace
   but no good has come,
for a time of healing
   but there is only terror.
²⁰O LORD, we acknowledge our wickedness
   and the guilt of our fathers;
   we have indeed sinned against you.
²¹For the sake of your name do not despise us;
   do not dishonor your glorious throne.
Remember your covenant with us
   and do not break it.

NRSV

13Then I said: "Ah, Lord GOD! Here are the prophets saying to them, 'You shall not see the sword, nor shall you have famine, but I will give you true peace in this place.' " ¹⁴And the LORD said to me: The prophets are prophesying lies in my name; I did not send them, nor did I command them or speak to them. They are prophesying to you a lying vision, worthless divination, and the deceit of their own minds. ¹⁵Therefore thus says the LORD concerning the prophets who prophesy in my name though I did not send them, and who say, "Sword and famine shall not come on this land": By sword and famine those prophets shall be consumed. ¹⁶And the people to whom they prophesy shall be thrown out into the streets of Jerusalem, victims of famine and sword. There shall be no one to bury them—themselves, their wives, their sons, and their daughters. For I will pour out their wickedness upon them.

¹⁷You shall say to them this word:
   Let my eyes run down with tears night and
      day,
      and let them not cease,
   for the virgin daughter—my people—is
         struck down with a crushing blow,
      with a very grievous wound.
¹⁸If I go out into the field,
      look—those killed by the sword!
   And if I enter the city,
      look—those sick with[a] famine!
   For both prophet and priest ply their trade
         throughout the land,
      and have no knowledge.

¹⁹Have you completely rejected Judah?
      Does your heart loathe Zion?
   Why have you struck us down
      so that there is no healing for us?
   We look for peace, but find no good;
      for a time of healing, but there is terror
         instead.
²⁰We acknowledge our wickedness, O LORD,
      the iniquity of our ancestors,
      for we have sinned against you.
²¹Do not spurn us, for your name's sake;
      do not dishonor your glorious throne;

NIV

²²Do any of the worthless idols of the nations
    bring rain?
    Do the skies themselves send down showers?
No, it is you, O LORD our God.
    Therefore our hope is in you,
    for you are the one who does all this.

15 Then the LORD said to me: "Even if Moses and Samuel were to stand before me, my heart would not go out to this people. Send them away from my presence! Let them go! ²And if they ask you, 'Where shall we go?' tell them, 'This is what the LORD says:

" 'Those destined for death, to death;
those for the sword, to the sword;
those for starvation, to starvation;
those for captivity, to captivity.'

³"I will send four kinds of destroyers against them," declares the LORD, "the sword to kill and the dogs to drag away and the birds of the air and the beasts of the earth to devour and destroy. ⁴I will make them abhorrent to all the kingdoms of the earth because of what Manasseh son of Hezekiah king of Judah did in Jerusalem.

⁵"Who will have pity on you, O Jerusalem?
    Who will mourn for you?
    Who will stop to ask how you are?
⁶You have rejected me," declares the LORD.
    "You keep on backsliding.
So I will lay hands on you and destroy you;
    I can no longer show compassion.
⁷I will winnow them with a winnowing fork
    at the city gates of the land.
I will bring bereavement and destruction on
        my people,
    for they have not changed their ways.
⁸I will make their widows more numerous
    than the sand of the sea.
At midday I will bring a destroyer
    against the mothers of their young men;
suddenly I will bring down on them
    anguish and terror.
⁹The mother of seven will grow faint
    and breathe her last.
Her sun will set while it is still day;
    she will be disgraced and humiliated.

NRSV

    remember and do not break your
        covenant with us.
²² Can any idols of the nations bring rain?
    Or can the heavens give showers?
Is it not you, O LORD our God?
    We set our hope on you,
    for it is you who do all this.

15 Then the LORD said to me: Though Moses and Samuel stood before me, yet my heart would not turn toward this people. Send them out of my sight, and let them go! ²And when they say to you, "Where shall we go?" you shall say to them: Thus says the LORD:
    Those destined for pestilence, to pestilence,
        and those destined for the sword, to the
            sword;
    those destined for famine, to famine,
        and those destined for captivity, to captivity.
³And I will appoint over them four kinds of destroyers, says the LORD: the sword to kill, the dogs to drag away, and the birds of the air and the wild animals of the earth to devour and destroy. ⁴I will make them a horror to all the kingdoms of the earth because of what King Manasseh son of Hezekiah of Judah did in Jerusalem.

⁵ Who will have pity on you, O Jerusalem,
    or who will bemoan you?
Who will turn aside
    to ask about your welfare?
⁶ You have rejected me, says the LORD,
    you are going backward;
so I have stretched out my hand against you
        and destroyed you—
    I am weary of relenting.
⁷ I have winnowed them with a winnowing
        fork
    in the gates of the land;
I have bereaved them, I have destroyed my
        people;
    they did not turn from their ways.
⁸ Their widows became more numerous
    than the sand of the seas;
I have brought against the mothers of youths
    a destroyer at noonday;
I have made anguish and terror
    fall upon her suddenly.
⁹ She who bore seven has languished;

NIV	NRSV
I will put the survivors to the sword before their enemies," declares the LORD.	she has swooned away; her sun went down while it was yet day; she has been shamed and disgraced. And the rest of them I will give to the sword before their enemies, says the LORD.

COMMENTARY

The opening superscription signals a new block of material (cf. 2:4; 7:1; 11:1; 46:1; 47:1). Its structure involves the repeated movement from a description of Judah's plight—first drought (14:1-6), later battle and siege (14:17-18)—to the lament of the people (14:7-9, 19-22) and to the response of the Lord (14:10-16; 15:1-9). Particularly prominent are the repeated references to drought or famine, the sequence "sword" and "famine" (14:12-13, 15-16, 18; 15:2; see also 15:3, 9) with "pestilence" included twice in the sequence (14:12; 15:2). In addition, in each sequence the Lord resists intercession (14:11-12; 15:1). The lament of Jeremiah that begins in 15:10 returns to the dialogue between the prophet and the deity that began in 11:18–12:6.

William Holladay has made the interesting suggestion that this section is a "counter-liturgy, Jrm's imitation of the official liturgy of the people in time of need."[108] He proposes that such liturgical activity would have gone on during the fast day proclaimed by King Jehoiakim (Jer 36:6). Jeremiah's "counter-liturgy" was not, in Holladay's judgment, a public activity but a private revelation of the Lord to Jeremiah. Such a hypothesis is difficult to substantiate, but it would help to account for the way in which this section both resembles an actual communal liturgy in time of distress and departs from it in various ways.

14:1-6. The speaker of these verses is not identified. The poetry depicts a sustained and vivid depiction of drought, the things people and animals do in that situation, and the effects of the drought. Thus the oracle begins with Judah and its towns ("gates") withering and languishing under the effects of a terrible drought (v. 2a). The ground is so dry it is cracked. There is no grass. Farmers can grow nothing. Wild animals cannot find any

food; they stand gasping for air and going blind for lack of adequate nutrition. Even the mother of the fawn abandons its young to find grass.

Such a terrible plight evokes two responses. One is shame and humiliation on the part of the uppermost (the nobles) and the lowest (the hired farmers) in the face of their incapacity and distress. The other response is signaled at the beginning of the passage. It is the crying out of the people, the lament or prayer for help that arises from a community in suffering. We hear that cry in the following verses.

14:7-9. The communal lament of the people involves both a confession of sin (v. 7) and a petition for help (vv. 7a, 9c). Between confession and plea is an extended complaint. In that complaint, one finds a basic feature of the communal lament: an appeal that seeks to tie the fate of the people to the Lord's own reputation and fate. Twice the people note that the very name of God is at stake in what happens to them. That the plea for God to act "for your name's sake" is an appeal to God's reputation is emphasized in v. 9, when the people point out that they bear the Lord's name. Whatever happens to them is going to be seen as a reflection on the power and greatness of the Lord. Verses 8-9 then underscore this point with queries that suggest that if nothing is done to deliver them, then the Lord will be seen as a God who is helpless and not even at home in the territory in which the deity has chosen to dwell. In such a manner, the people claim that whatever befalls them will reflect badly on the deity. Hence, they seek to motivate the Lord to intervene to deliver them now as in the past (v. 8a). The affirmation that God is in their midst is probably an indirect reference to the Temple, perpetuating the theology, Jeremiah attacks in chap. 7.

14:10-16. The expected response to the plea

108. Holladay, *Jeremiah I*, 425.

for help is an oracle of salvation, a word of deliverance.[109] But the opposite happens here. A word of judgment is given in v. 10. Rather than follow after the Lord, the people have wandered away; indeed, they have "loved to wander" after other loyalties and other interests; the previous chapters have spelled out this behavior in detail. The sins of the people will be punished rather than forgiven. The term "accept" (רצה rāṣâ, v. 10) is a technical word taken from the vocabulary of sacrifice. It refers to sacrifices acceptable to the deity (Lev 1:4; 7:18; 19:7; Amos 5:22; Mic 6:7) or the person making the sacrifice (2 Sam 24:23; Ezek 20:40-41). When the time of punishment in exile is over, it is this word of acceptance that the Lord speaks in Isa 40:2: "Her penalty is paid" (NRSV).

The situation is serious and the divine decision firm (vv. 11-12). While the Lord's response is not technically a response to the lament of vv. 7-9, it does continue to make the point that forgiveness is out of the question. The point implicit in the first ten verses now becomes explicit: God will not listen to the prayer of the people. Confession is insufficient at this point, and the attempt to persuade the Lord by appealing to the divine reputation is resistible. The Lord takes up each of the modes of appealing to God and effecting a positive response from the deity: prayer, sacrifice, and intercession. The OT is full of indications that these ways of seeking God's help or forgiveness are effective. But not now. One should note the prohibition of intercession on Jeremiah's part (v. 11). It echoes 7:16: the power of prophetic intercession to change the mind and heart of God (see the Commentary on 7:16-20). That power is so real and God is so open that the Lord will not risk entertaining such intercession.

Like the preceding two verses, vv. 13-16 are not a part of the response of judgment to the lament and petition of vv. 7-9. But the conversation that began in vv. 11-12 continues as Jeremiah points out that other prophets are giving a different message to the people (v. 13). They are announcing salvation, "true peace" in the land, while he is announcing death and destruction. The future of famine (14:1-6) and sword (14:17-18) announced by Jeremiah is rejected by other prophets. But God's response to that news is unequivocal. These prophets are a part of the endemic problem in Judah: mendacity. Their words are not the word of the Lord. They did not receive them from the Lord, as v. 14b (cf. 23:21-23) makes clear. Because of their lies, the prophets of "good" will come under the same judgment as will befall the people. It is poetic justice that the sword and famine they denied will come to them and to the ones who welcomed their prophetic good news, for both groups are full of wickedness.

14:17-18. The movement that runs through 14:1-16—plight/lament/divine response—occurs again in 14:17–15:9. The development of ideas is similar, but this unit has its own specific modes of expression. This section is similar to the preceding passage; both convey the picture of a land, city and countryside, devastated by sword and famine (v. 18). It is difficult to tell whether the oracle represents the situation at the time of its utterance or is meant to be understood as anticipating devastation yet to come. The depiction of the terrible disaster coming upon the people is formulated as both announcement of judgment and lament. As judgment, it depicts battlefields full of the dead and a city full of people starved to death by siege. The word of judgment, however, is uttered through tears (v. 17a), tears that are usually said to be those of the prophet, but in their context are just as likely—if not more so—to be the tears of God. The expression "my people" occurs in Jeremiah nearly forty times. The vast majority of the instances are spoken by God; no instance is unambiguously the expression of the prophet alone. Again, it is not always possible to draw sharp distinctions between the pathos of the prophet before the plight of the people and the pathos of God (see the Commentary on 8:18–9:1). In any case, the picture of judgment is clearly set forth by a voice that looks with horror and pain on what is happening, someone who speaks of those who lie dead with the intimate language of "my people" and "virgin daughter."

The meaning of the final sentence in v. 18 is unclear, as the varying translations of the NRSV and the NIV indicate. The NRSV suggests that the religious leaders go about their business without comprehending or acknowledging God; "do not know" could be understood either way. The NIV suggests that the land to which the prophet and the priest have gone is Sheol, the grave (23:11-12).[110]

109. Patrick D. Miller, *They Cried to the Lord: The Form and Theology of Biblical Prayer* (Minneapolis: Fortress, 1994) chap. 4.

110. Holladay, *Jeremiah 1,* 437-38.

14:19-22. The picture of disaster evokes another communal lament (see 14:7-9). Its opening words are couched in a sequence of rhetorical questions (v. 19*a*), a form found a number of times in Jeremiah, each sequence having a different content or point (see the Commentary on 2:29-37). Here, as elsewhere, the rhetorical questions express a traditional belief and seek "to establish a basis of consensus between covenant partners on the basis of which appeal can be made."[111]

In this instance, the prophet appeals to the complaint of the people on the grounds of the Lord's covenantal commitment to the people ("Have you completely rejected . . . ?") and on the assumption of God's continuing mercy and compassion ("Why have you struck us down?"). The assumption is that the Lord cannot and surely will not break the covenant and let Zion fall. A second set of rhetorical questions (v. 22) assumes the unique power of the Lord against the impotence of the idols. Only the Lord is able to bring rain from the heavens. This claim is related to the depiction of drought at the beginning of the chapter.

There is, of course, a powerful irony in these words. They assume the Lord's commitment to the covenant while the people themselves have broken the covenant time and again. They assume the power of the Lord in contrast to the other gods, even though the people sought other gods. The word for "idols" is הבל (*hebel*), which the prophet often uses to refer to the "worthless," "unprofitable" gods of the other peoples (2:5; 8:19; 10:3, 8, 15; 16:19). As Brueggemann has noted, the call to the Lord to "remember" the covenant is a dangerous request. The Lord might just do that—remember the covenant with its terrible sanctions for disobedience by the people (see v. 10).[112]

The lament shares with its predecessor in 14:7-9 the confession of sin, which, as was the case in the former passage, may be ironic rather than reflecting authentic contrition. And, like vv. 7-9, this lament pleads for God not to forsake or reject the people (v. 21*a*), grounding that petition in motivation clauses that once again appeal to the Lord's reputation: "for your name's sake" and "do not dishonor your glorious throne." The final irony of the passage occurs in the third motivation clause in v. 21, where the people plead for the Lord not to break the covenant even as they have been breaking it right and left. The text does not indicate which covenant is in mind, Mosaic or Davidic. It is quite likely the latter that the people have in mind, appealing to what was understood to be an enduring and unconditional assurance of Davidic rule and divine presence in the Temple on Zion (cf. 33:21; Ps 89:34). If that is the case, then in their prayer the people make the same mistake they make when they say over and over again "the temple of the LORD," "the temple of the LORD." They assume that God's covenant with the Davidic house will perdure. they are wrong, as the next verses make abundantly clear (on the absence of healing, see 8:22 and the Commentary on 8:18–9:1).

15:1-4. A response to the people's lament may be discerned in these verses, though they do not comprise a straightforward prophetic oracle. Rather, a familiar question-and-answer form, which probably has its roots in the request to prophets for an oracle from the Lord, conveys the divine word. Again, as in 14:10, the saying offers a word of judgment rather than the sought-for deliverance. The degree to which the community has violated the covenant and teaching of the Lord is clear because the Lord does not respond positively to the cries for help that are uttered by the people, not even with their confession of sin and guilt. The best indication of how bad the situation is may be the resistance once more to prophetic intercession on behalf of the people (7:16; 11:14; 14:11). This is exactly the kind of setting in which such intercession has often occurred. In the biblical tradition generally, Moses and Samuel are the great exemplars of prophetic intercession, an intercession that accomplishes a change of the Lord's mind and a withholding of judgment (e.g., Exod 32:11-14; Num 14:13-25; 1 Sam 7:8-9; 12:19). Not this time. The situation is so terrible—lying, apostasy, adultery, malfeasance of office, oppression of the poor—that not even the most successful intercessors could succeed. The Lord's heart has hardened in the face of continuing, unrelenting wickedness. The people's refusal to "turn," repent, and their refusal to receive correction is so persistent (e.g., 2:30; 3:10; 5:3; 8:5-6; 15:7) that "turning" is no longer possible.

---

111. W. Brueggemann, "Jeremiah's Use of Rhetorical Questions," *JBL* 92 (1973) 363n. 17.

112. Walter Brueggemann, *A Commentary on Jeremiah: Exile and Homecoming* (Grand Rapids: Eerdmans, 1998) 140.

The expression "Send them out [שלח šālaḥ] of my sight and let them go [יצא yāṣā']" (v. 1b) reverses what came to be technical terminology for the exodus, the former occurring frequently in the commands to Pharaoh to "let my people go" (e.g., Exod 4:21, 23; 5:1-2; 7:2, 14), and the latter, in its causative form, as a part of the ancient Israelite credo that rehearsed the mighty deeds of the Lord to "bring out" the people (e.g., Deut 6:21; 26:8; Josh 24:5-8). Now the Lord "sends" the people out to judgment and "lets them go" into exile.

The question of the people, "Where shall we go?" elicits a judgment speech in v. 2b. It is a fate that reflects rather accurately the outcome of the conflict with the Babylonians: disease, death in battle, famine, and exile. Attribution of judgment due to the sin of Manasseh may be traced to the hand of the deuteronomist. The Deuteronomistic History (Joshua–Kings) regards Manasseh's apostasy as the primary reason for the divine judgment on Judah (2 Kgs 21:1-18; 23:26; 24:3). The oracles of Jeremiah tend to place blame more on the people and the leaders generally, though one notes that an identification of Manasseh's sins as a primary cause of the judgment against Judah may be reflected in the people's claim about "the iniquity of our ancestors" (14:20).

15:5-9. This section seems to be an addition to the sequence that begins in 14:1. The element of lament in v. 5 and the elaboration of the Lord's judgment may be the reason why these verses have been joined to the larger literary unit. In any event, they continue to spell out the character of the judgment that is going to take place, though the past-tense verbs create ambiguity about whether they refer to a judgment already wrought (e.g., the first exile of 597 BCE) or are to be read as a kind of "prophetic perfect"—that is, a prophetic anticipation of the imminent judgment.[113]

113. See William McKane, *A Critical and Exegetical Commentary on Jeremiah,* 2 vols., ICC (Edinburgh: T. & T. Clark, 1986, 1996) 342-43.

Jerusalem as a figure for the community as a whole is the addressee here, and the feminine gender of the city name contributes to the feminine coloring of the passage.

The fundamental point is that enough is enough and the Lord has tired of relenting, of holding back the judgment (v. 6). The reason why is stated three ways: The people have rejected the Lord (v. 6); they have gone backward (v. 6), a play on "going after" other gods (cf. 2:2-4); and they have not turned from their ways (v. 7; cf. 5:3; 6:16; 7:5). The consequence of this backward move is articulated two ways. One is the repeated first-person verbs spoken by the Lord: "I have stretched out my hand"; "I have winnowed them"; "I have bereaved them"; "I have destroyed my people"; "I have brought a destroyer against the mother of their youths"; "I have made anguish and terror fall"; and "I will give the rest of them to the sword." Nowhere in Jeremiah is the divine intent to judge and the sense of divine agency more emphatically stated. The second consequence of the people's backward move is the lamenting queries of mother Jerusalem (v. 5). They are carried forward in the depiction of the different kinds of women whose fate in this judgment is particularly devastating and cannot be overlooked or whitewashed. The death of the men leaves widows without support, protection, or power. The judgment is so total the land will be full of widows. The mother of seven is a traditional image for fertility and blessing. But that blessing only underscores her terrible fate. Her "swooning" probably results from the news of the deaths of all her sons. The absence of husbands and sons is a shaming reality that means those women who survive are no better off than the sons and husbands who died. The picture of Jerusalem crying with no one to pity or bemoan her fate is confirmed in Lamentations, where Jerusalem the fallen sits mourning, with no one to comfort her (e.g., Lam 1:9, 17).

REFLECTIONS

1. For the way in which prayer functions as an act of persuasion, see the Reflections at 11:18–12:6. What is especially daring in the communal laments is the very open way in which the people challenge God by suggesting rather directly that the Lord is not quite up to the task, that the suffering of the people is an intimation of the failure of the deity in some respects and that the only way to demonstrate that God is really God, the only way to restore the reputation of the Lord before the world, is in acting to deliver the people in their present plight. One cannot miss the resonance with the experience of the Jewish people and the way in which post-Holocaust theological discussion has raised exactly the question of the presence and power of God in the light of such devastating destruction.

2. Jeremiah does not comment on the "good news" of the false prophets. But one can begin to see why this section comes between two poignant laments on Jeremiah's part. Good news is always preferable to bad. The harsh and irrevocable word of judgment that comes from Jeremiah would have been no more desirable and acceptable to the people of Israel than are gloomy words about our future from modern-day prophets. It is always tempting to read the "signs" positively, both then and now. It is difficult enough to "speak truth to power" in any time; it is hard enough to suggest that human conduct is going to have its reward, that faithlessness and oppression will bring the judgment of God. That difficulty becomes even more acute when, as in Jeremiah's time, there are many preaching a comforting and comfortable word: "Everything is all right; God will give us peace in our time."

3. This passage announces a particular word of judgment upon religious leaders, priests, prophets, and preachers, who use their office to smooth things over, who betray their ministry by speaking soft words and denying the hard reality of how bad things really are. Like Amaziah, the chief priest/preacher at the national church of the northern kingdom (Amos 7:10-17), false prophets, who give the people what they want to hear and do it from the pulpit so that it has all the aura of faithful and true preaching, will find themselves under judgment as they are caught up in the larger judgment of the people.

4. The words of judgment in 14:10-16 have an echo in a later part of the book of Jeremiah, one that is quite different in tenor from this section. In a sequence of chapters that speak of restoration and healing after the punishment and judgment, the Lord announces, "I will forgive their iniquity, and remember their sin no more" (31:34; see 14:10). And the false prophecy of "true peace" (14:13) becomes the Lord's own hopeful word in 33:6, but only after the judgment is over. The punishment is not forever. The compassion of the Lord means that judgment is not the final word for this people whom the Lord has called "my people." But the story of Israel teaches us that grace is not cheap, that sin is not lightly passed over. The mercy of God finally controls our lives, but that does not mean that judgment is not real and sure. It is a long way from the first half of Jeremiah and his prophecies of judgment to the words of restoration later in the book. Because we know the story, we can anticipate them, but the God of Jeremiah, the same God we know in Jesus Christ, is not easily tampered with, not easily ignored by those who live in covenant with that God.

JEREMIAH 15:10-21, WOE IS ME!

[10]Alas, my mother, that you gave me birth,
    a man with whom the whole land strives
        and contends!
I have neither lent nor borrowed,
    yet everyone curses me.

10Woe is me, my mother, that you ever bore me, a man of strife and contention to the whole land! I have not lent, nor have I borrowed, yet all of them curse me. [11]The LORD said: Surely I have

NIV

11The Lord said,

"Surely I will deliver you for a good purpose;
  surely I will make your enemies plead
      with you
  in times of disaster and times of distress.

12"Can a man break iron—
  iron from the north—or bronze?
13Your wealth and your treasures
  I will give as plunder, without charge,
because of all your sins
  throughout your country.
14I will enslave you to your enemies
  in*a* a land you do not know,
for my anger will kindle a fire
  that will burn against you."

15You understand, O Lord;
  remember me and care for me.
  Avenge me on my persecutors.
You are long-suffering—do not take me away;
  think of how I suffer reproach for your sake.
16When your words came, I ate them;
  they were my joy and my heart's delight,
for I bear your name,
  O Lord God Almighty.
17I never sat in the company of revelers,
  never made merry with them;
I sat alone because your hand was on me
  and you had filled me with indignation.
18Why is my pain unending
  and my wound grievous and incurable?
Will you be to me like a deceptive brook,
  like a spring that fails?

19Therefore this is what the Lord says:
  "If you repent, I will restore you
    that you may serve me;
  if you utter worthy, not worthless, words,
    you will be my spokesman.
Let this people turn to you,
  but you must not turn to them.
20I will make you a wall to this people,
  a fortified wall of bronze;
they will fight against you
  but will not overcome you,
for I am with you

a14 Some Hebrew manuscripts, Septuagint and Syriac (see also Jer. 17:4); most Hebrew manuscripts *I will cause your enemies to bring you / into*

NRSV

intervened in your life*a* for good, surely I have imposed enemies on you in a time of trouble and in a time of distress.*b* 12Can iron and bronze break iron from the north?

13Your wealth and your treasures I will give as plunder, without price, for all your sins, throughout all your territory. 14I will make you serve your enemies in a land that you do not know, for in my anger a fire is kindled that shall burn forever.

15O Lord, you know;
  remember me and visit me,
  and bring down retribution for me on my
      persecutors.
In your forbearance do not take me away;
  know that on your account I suffer insult.
16Your words were found, and I ate them,
  and your words became to me a joy
  and the delight of my heart;
for I am called by your name,
  O Lord, God of hosts.
17I did not sit in the company of merrymakers,
  nor did I rejoice;
under the weight of your hand I sat alone,
  for you had filled me with indignation.
18Why is my pain unceasing,
  my wound incurable,
  refusing to be healed?
Truly, you are to me like a deceitful brook,
  like waters that fail.

19Therefore thus says the Lord:
  If you turn back, I will take you back,
    and you shall stand before me.
  If you utter what is precious, and not what is
      worthless,
    you shall serve as my mouth.
  It is they who will turn to you,
    not you who will turn to them.
10And I will make you to this people
    a fortified wall of bronze;
  they will fight against you,
    but they shall not prevail over you,
  for I am with you
    to save you and deliver you,
                    says the Lord.
21I will deliver you out of the hand of the
      wicked,

*a*Heb *intervened with you*   *b*Meaning of Heb uncertain

NIV

to rescue and save you,"

declares the LORD.
[21]"I will save you from the hands of the wicked and redeem you from the grasp of the cruel."

NRSV

and redeem you from the grasp of the ruthless.

COMMENTARY

The second of Jeremiah's laments over his prophetic task occurs in this section. As in 11:18–12:6, the sequence of thought moves from prophetic lament to divine response twice: (1) lament in v. 10 and response in vv. 13-14; (2) lament in vv. 15-18 and response in vv. 19-21. The second movement (vv. 15-21) is clear. The first movement (vv. 10-14), however, is problematic, presenting textual difficulties and posing compositional and redactional questions.

15:10-14. There are several interpretive problems in this passage. First, should v. 11 be understood as part of the Lord's response, as the Hebrew version clearly makes it, or as part of the prophet's complaint, as the Greek version presents the text (see RSV)? The NRSV and the NIV give some indication of the possible translations of the Hebrew text. No certainty about the reading and interpretation of this verse is possible, particularly in the light of the puzzling first verb (שריתך *šērîtikā*). Carroll gives a plausible reading of the Hebrew, understanding it as an oracle of salvation from the Lord to the prophet:

[The Lord said,] "Surely I have strengthened you
for good;
surely, I have intervened on your behalf in
time of evil and distress."[114]

O'Connor also has presented a plausible translation, but one that draws upon the Greek and understands v. 11 as a continuation of the complaint of the prophet in v. 10:

So be it, Lord, if I have not served you [שרת *šārat*]
for good,
If I have not entreated you for the enemy in
time of trouble
and in time of distress.[115]

No certainty on this matter is likely. Either interpretation is possible, but in the light of the difficulties, the weight of interpretative attention should be given to the other verses.

A second interpretive problem of this passage is the meaning of v. 12. The interpretation depends on what meaning is given to the obviously symbolic uses of iron and bronze in the verse. Again, O'Connor pays attention to the use of these terms elsewhere in Jeremiah. Noting that "iron from the north" probably refers to the enemy from the north, an interpretation followed by most scholars, and that "bronze" elsewhere in Jeremiah, including this passage, is a symbol for the prophet (1:18; 15:20), she would translate the verse in its most literal sense: "Can iron break iron from the north and bronze?" She understands this verse as a rhetorical question indicating that "iron," which must refer to the people of Judah, is not breakable—that is, it is not vulnerable to defeat by either the enemy from the north or Jeremiah. The question is thus a word of encouragement to the prophet, in effect saying, "Can Jeremiah's enemies, who appear as strong as iron, break God's instruments, the enemy from the north and the prophet?" The answer is clearly no.[116]

Another interpretive problem in this text is that vv. 13-14 seem to be a variant of 17:3-4; some would see them as being displaced from chap. 17 to chap. 15. Such a conclusion is difficult to prove or disprove.

Finally, the phrase at the beginning of v. 14 can be translated as either "I will cause your enemies to pass over" (so the Hebrew) or "I will cause you to serve your enemies" (so the Greek). If the former translation is chosen, then the passage may be interpreted as a word to the prophet; if the latter, then it is a word to the people (see below).

114. Robert P. Carroll, *Jeremiah,* OTL (Philadelphia: Westminster, 1986) 327. He regards the term "the enemy" as a marginal gloss identifying the meaning of "a time of evil and distress."
115. Kathleen O'Connor, *The Confessions of Jeremiah: Their Interpretation and Role in Chapters 1–25,* SBLDS 94 (Atlanta: Scholars Press, 1988) 27.

116. Ibid., 34-36.

The first lament of the prophet in this section is both a lament about his life and a protestation of his innocence (v. 10). The cursing of the day of birth is a motif of despairing lament (20:14; Job 3), but here it may also allude to his call inasmuch as he was appointed prophet before he was even born (1:5). The reference to "strife" (ריב *rîb*) and "contention" is double-edged. The context suggests the sort of contentions he has with his family and others, who have isolated him, belittled him, and treated him contemptibly, which is what is meant in the expression "curses me." But one must also reckon with the notion of the prophet as the bearer of the Lord's covenant lawsuit (see the Commentary on 2:4-13). Either kind of *rîb,* the personal or the theological, arouses the hostility and contempt of Jeremiah's fellow citizens and family members. What he expresses in the second sentence of v. 10 (and in v. 11, if it is to be read as the words of Jeremiah) is a typical protestation of innocence, a claim that he has not done those things that might have aroused contempt, such as borrowing and not paying back or lending and pressing others to pay him back (see Job 6:22). Verse 11, understood as the word of the prophet, presents Jeremiah's further claim to have done the intercessory task that the prophet is supposed to do.

The prayer of the prophet, which in this instance is confined to the lament, is answered by the Lord, possibly in v. 11, if read as a divine word of assurance, but at least in v. 12. The divine word continues in vv. 13-14. Possibly a later addition to the text, v. 13 is a word of judgment addressed to Jeremiah's enemies and thus, implicitly, a vindication of Jeremiah's prophetic vocation that has gotten him into such trouble. Verse 14 either continues that word of judgment, moving from their being defeated and plundered to their being taken into captivity (so the Hebrew), or is addressed to the prophet assuring him that those enemies who have threatened him and attacked him will eventually go into exile.

15:15-18. The second sequence of prophetic lament and divine response is much clearer than the first. While it is full of the typical language of lament and sounds like many of the psalms, it also resonates with the experience of Jeremiah as that is described in the rest of the book. The plea or petition that was absent from the previous lament

(though it may have been implicit) is now expressed with great vehemence in v. 15: "know," "remember," "visit" (NIV, "care for"), "avenge" (NRSV, "bring retribution"), "do not take away," "think of how" (NRSV, "know"). We hear the anguish of the prophet in the piling up of the petitions, partly for himself, partly against his enemies. He yearns for the Lord's attention. The plea to "remember" is common in the laments of the psalter (e.g., Pss 74:2, 18, 22; 89:47, 50). The appeal to the memory of God is an appeal to the faithfulness of God. The deliverance from Egypt in the exodus happened because the Lord heard the people's cry, the lament of the Hebrews, and remembered the covenant with their ancestors. In this case, Jeremiah pleads that God remember that God has called Jeremiah and promised to deliver him. The petition to "bring down retribution" or to "avenge" Jeremiah against his enemies is really a plea for God to vindicate him. When the prophet says "vindicate me" (הנקם *hinnāqem*), he pleads, in effect, "Confirm the rightness of my words and deeds and so vindicate me before my persecutors," an act that would be both a judgment against his enemies and a vindication of the Lord who called him. The expression "in your forbearance [NIV, "you are long-suffering"] do not take me away" is an appeal to the very character of God as Israel has known and confessed the deity from earliest times. This expression is also found in the ancient confessional liturgy, "The LORD, the LORD, a God merciful and gracious, slow to anger" (Exod 34:6 NRSV; cf. Ps 103:8). Here, the prophet wants the Lord not to delay in holding back the judgment. In the final sentence of v. 15, the prophet has in mind such taunts as the one he quotes in 17:15: "Where is the word of the LORD? Let it come!" But he also knows that his suffering lies at the hands of his enemies and that their downfall is his only way out.

Jeremiah continues to make the case for God's intervention on his behalf as he protests his innocence and his devotion to his prophetic calling (vv. 16-17). The claim to have found, eaten, and enjoyed "your words" in this context surely refers to the putting of the Lord's words in Jeremiah's mouth at his call and connotes Jeremiah's appropriation of the words of the Lord—that is, of the oracles of the Lord that he proclaims (1:9; cf. Ezek 3:1-3). The reference to the name of the Lord being called over Jeremiah (v. 16*b*) is a legal statement. Just as God claims ownership of the Temple, for which this same formulation is used (7:10), so also, Jeremiah says, God has claimed him as a special possession.

Jeremiah advances his case for fidelity to his calling (v. 17). It has meant his isolation from those who were enjoying life, whether the false prophets of peace or the people. His harsh words of judgment, intended by the term "indignation," have made him unwelcome at the party! God has put him into this terrible spot. The "weight of your hand," or, more simply, "your hand," alludes to the prophetic call or burden. He is under the claim, the authority of the Lord, and because of that is thrust into this position of isolation and loneliness.

So he cries out in pain and anger, drawing on two kinds of imagery: sickness and water. He is like a person whose sickness never ends, a pain that just goes on and on without ever healing. And "the fountain of living water" (2:31) has become, for Jeremiah, "a deceitful brook." God has become for Jeremiah like a wadi in the wilderness that promises water for the thirsty traveler, only to be dry when water is most needed. What seemed to be an unceasing source of strength and life and support has failed him. There could hardly be a sharper accusation against the deity. God has done what the people have done: The Lord has deceived Jeremiah. The expressions here are emphatic. Jeremiah claims that God is like waters that are "untrustworthy," "unreliable." God cannot be counted upon. What the Lord's deception of Jeremiah entails is not indicated, but it is surely God's assurance in Jeremiah's call that, though many would fight against him, they would not prevail. In fact, however, they seem to have done just that.

15:19-21. The divine response comes once more as an oracle of salvation. It echoes directly the oracle of salvation accompanying Jeremiah's call in chap. 1 (v. 20 is virtually a quotation from 1:17-19). What God says is reminiscent of both that assuring oracle and the divine response in 12:5-6 in that all three texts place a kind of caveat on the promise of deliverance. That caveat states that the road ahead is still going to be very rough (1:17; 12:5-6) but that Jeremiah needs to stay at the task, come what may (1:17; 15:19). Verse 19,

therefore, is something of a rebuke. It is a call for repentance, something unusual in the relationship between prophet and God. God understands the protest of Jeremiah's lament as resistance to the prophetic task. Hence the Lord calls Jeremiah to return to the faithful exercise of his prophetic duties. If he "returns," then he may continue to represent the Lord's word ("you shall stand before me . . . you shall serve as my mouth"). The prophet is as free as anyone to cry out for help in time of trouble; but he is liable to rebuke from the Lord who calls him. The "worthless word" may be the complaints and the accusations against God in the lament of the previous verses. The "precious words" are the truthful oracles the Lord gives him to proclaim.

This is no typical word of assurance to a person in trouble. The Lord's response is both a rebuke and, like 12:5-6, a call to stand firm in his prophetic calling. His repentance means that he may continue to bear the terrible burden! Verses 20-21 add to these words the more typical oracle of salvation. They do not take away the conditionality of v. 19, but they do undergird the call to "return" with an assurance that in the heat of the fray, Jeremiah will not be alone and will not finally be done in (see the Commentary on 1:17-19).

The relationship between the prophet and his God, which seems frayed already in 11:18–12:6, undergoes a deepening tension. The prophet's "Why?" (already present in 12:1) is reiterated here (v. 18) but ends up now in an accusation of unfaithfulness. The warning of the Lord that the situation is only going to get worse (12:5-6) now moves to a rebuke of the prophet for his own unfaithfulness to his calling. To be the Lord's prophet involves a special relationship, but it is not an easy one. The relationship between these two is a rocky road. It only becomes more so as the book goes along.

This passage includes a further dimension, involving the word word שוב (*sûb*), "turn" or "return." This word occurs four times in v. 19. But that word is most often used in reference to the return or repentance of the people (cf. 3:1–4:4). It is likely, therefore, that the conversation between the Lord and Jeremiah came to be heard by later Israelites as a message to them, as a combination of rebuke and assurance to a people who had turned away and ended up in the suffering of exile, crying out to the Lord, as did Jeremiah. Walter Brueggemann has described this text as follows:

> What Jeremiah knows in his prophetic vocation, Israel comes to know in its exile, where it also senses abandonment. As Jeremiah can address God abrasively, so can Israel in exile. As Jeremiah is pressed to more serious obedience by Yahweh, so is Israel in exile. As Jeremiah receives a promise of God's solidarity in trouble, so does Israel in exile. In exile, Israel found Jeremiah's prayer and experience of God to be paradigmatic for its own destiny with God as a people of troubled faith.[117]

117. Walter Brueggemann, *A Commentary on Jeremiah: Exile and Homecoming* (Grand Rapids: Eerdmans, 1998) 150.

REFLECTIONS

1. The initial complaint of Jeremiah in 15:10 is stereotypically a part of human laments and cries to God, and rightly so. He gives voice to elemental feelings of one who is beset and done in by others, especially when the one who cries out in fear and pain has suffered despite living an upright life, despite seriously attempting to live faithfully. One of those feelings, which probably comes at the very lowest point, is a wish to avoid the terrible pain of the present by never having been born. The corollary of that is, "I wish I could die," the kind of lament often heard from those in dire sickness or pain. The other feeling that is often voiced by those in trouble is what we have called the protestation of innocence. "Why me, Lord?" or "What have I done to deserve this?" Implicit in such questions is a conviction that the lamenter has done what he or she ought to have done and has done nothing to merit such punishment. The prophet's lament is clearly tied to his particular circumstance. But it is also universal language, so that the lament of the prophet articulates the deepest feelings of those with similar troubles. The form of prayer permits and almost seems to require, if the frequency of these themes is any clue, such expression of these deep feelings. Here, therefore, the particulars of the story of Jeremiah become a vehicle for the articulation of common human laments.[118]

2. The laments of the prayers for help regularly identify the suffering as three-dimensional in its causality. There is something going on internally in the petitioner; but there is a problem with God; and there is also usually some outside source of trouble and suffering. Jeremiah's lament reflects this threefold causality: He experiences pain and isolation; God's hand weighs upon him, and God has been a "deceitful brook" to him; and there are persons who persecute him. These three sources of distress are not always present, but they are common enough to remind those who listen and learn from these prayers that suffering is personal, spiritual, and social, that one cannot deal with human plight on one of these levels alone. Sickness, loneliness, guilt, and the weight of sin can almost do us in. But along with these we may also have the sense of being done in by the weight of God's hand upon us. Cries of "Why me?" express implicitly and often explicitly a sense that God is part of the problem as well as the solution. And there is nearly always somebody else or some others in the picture, whether as oppressing forces or those from whom one is cut off and before whom one is shamed. The human condition as reflected in prayers for help, laments such as those Jeremiah utters, cannot be examined and understood, much less dealt with, except in awareness of all three dimensions of pain and suffering.[119]

3. The fluidity of the text at 15:19-21 in addressing the particular and somewhat unique situation of the prophet and the larger situation of the people in exile is both a reminder of the rich possibilities of the biblical word and a warning about fixing its meaning and applicability at any one point. A stream of reception is opened up in this text that continues to operate as the text resonates with personal experience, particularly the experience of those who stand under some

118. See Patrick D. Miller, *Interpreting the Psalms* (Philadelphia: Fortress, 1986) 57-63.
119. Ibid., 56-57.

dimension of divine demand and calling, and with communal conditions of exile, isolated and cut off, hearing again in the biblical text a call to repentance and a word of assurance. In the incarnation of God in Jesus Christ, the Christian community finds that same powerful call to repentance (Mark 1:14-15) and that enduring word of assurance (Luke 2:10-11).

JEREMIAH 16:1-21, JEREMIAH'S CELIBACY AS A WORD OF JUDGMENT

NIV

16 Then the word of the LORD came to me: 2"You must not marry and have sons or daughters in this place." 3For this is what the LORD says about the sons and daughters born in this land and about the women who are their mothers and the men who are their fathers: 4"They will die of deadly diseases. They will not be mourned or buried but will be like refuse lying on the ground. They will perish by sword and famine, and their dead bodies will become food for the birds of the air and the beasts of the earth."

5For this is what the LORD says: "Do not enter a house where there is a funeral meal; do not go to mourn or show sympathy, because I have withdrawn my blessing, my love and my pity from this people," declares the LORD. 6"Both high and low will die in this land. They will not be buried or mourned, and no one will cut himself or shave his head for them. 7No one will offer food to comfort those who mourn for the dead—not even for a father or a mother—nor will anyone give them a drink to console them.

8"And do not enter a house where there is feasting and sit down to eat and drink. 9For this is what the LORD Almighty, the God of Israel, says: Before your eyes and in your days I will bring an end to the sounds of joy and gladness and to the voices of bride and bridegroom in this place.

10"When you tell these people all this and they ask you, 'Why has the LORD decreed such a great disaster against us? What wrong have we done? What sin have we committed against the LORD our God?' 11then say to them, 'It is because your fathers forsook me,' declares the LORD, 'and followed other gods and served and worshiped them. They forsook me and did not keep my law. 12But you have behaved more wickedly than your

NRSV

16 The word of the LORD came to me: 2You shall not take a wife, nor shall you have sons or daughters in this place. 3For thus says the LORD concerning the sons and daughters who are born in this place, and concerning the mothers who bear them and the fathers who beget them in this land: 4They shall die of deadly diseases. They shall not be lamented, nor shall they be buried; they shall become like dung on the surface of the ground. They shall perish by the sword and by famine, and their dead bodies shall become food for the birds of the air and for the wild animals of the earth.

5For thus says the LORD: Do not enter the house of mourning, or go to lament, or bemoan them; for I have taken away my peace from this people, says the LORD, my steadfast love and mercy. 6Both great and small shall die in this land; they shall not be buried, and no one shall lament for them; there shall be no gashing, no shaving of the head for them. 7No one shall break bread[a] for the mourner, to offer comfort for the dead; nor shall anyone give them the cup of consolation to drink for their fathers or their mothers. 8You shall not go into the house of feasting to sit with them, to eat and drink. 9For thus says the LORD of hosts, the God of Israel: I am going to banish from this place, in your days and before your eyes, the voice of mirth and the voice of gladness, the voice of the bridegroom and the voice of the bride.

10And when you tell this people all these words, and they say to you, "Why has the LORD pronounced all this great evil against us? What is our iniquity? What is the sin that we have committed against the LORD our God?" 11then you shall say to them: It is because your ancestors

Two Mss Gk: MT break for them

NIV

fathers. See how each of you is following the stubbornness of his evil heart instead of obeying me. [13]So I will throw you out of this land into a land neither you nor your fathers have known, and there you will serve other gods day and night, for I will show you no favor.'

[14]"However, the days are coming," declares the LORD, "when men will no longer say, 'As surely as the LORD lives, who brought the Israelites up out of Egypt,' [15]but they will say, 'As surely as the LORD lives, who brought the Israelites up out of the land of the north and out of all the countries where he had banished them.' For I will restore them to the land I gave their forefathers.

[16]"But now I will send for many fishermen," declares the LORD, "and they will catch them. After that I will send for many hunters, and they will hunt them down on every mountain and hill and from the crevices of the rocks. [17]My eyes are on all their ways; they are not hidden from me, nor is their sin concealed from my eyes. [18]I will repay them double for their wickedness and their sin, because they have defiled my land with the lifeless forms of their vile images and have filled my inheritance with their detestable idols."

[19]O LORD, my strength and my fortress,
my refuge in time of distress,
to you the nations will come
from the ends of the earth and say,
"Our fathers possessed nothing but false gods,
worthless idols that did them no good.
[20]Do men make their own gods?
Yes, but they are not gods!"

[21]"Therefore I will teach them—
this time I will teach them
my power and might.
Then they will know
that my name is the LORD.

NRSV

have forsaken me, says the LORD, and have gone after other gods and have served and worshiped them, and have forsaken me and have not kept my law; [12]and because you have behaved worse than your ancestors, for here you are, every one of you, following your stubborn evil will, refusing to listen to me. [13]Therefore I will hurl you out of this land into a land that neither you nor your ancestors have known, and there you shall serve other gods day and night, for I will show you no favor.

14Therefore, the days are surely coming, says the LORD, when it shall no longer be said, "As the LORD lives who brought the people of Israel up out of the land of Egypt," [15]but "As the LORD lives who brought the people of Israel up out of the land of the north and out of all the lands where he had driven them." For I will bring them back to their own land that I gave to their ancestors.

16I am now sending for many fishermen, says the LORD, and they shall catch them; and afterward I will send for many hunters, and they shall hunt them from every mountain and every hill, and out of the clefts of the rocks. [17]For my eyes are on all their ways; they are not hidden from my presence, nor is their iniquity concealed from my sight. [18]And[a] I will doubly repay their iniquity and their sin, because they have polluted my land with the carcasses of their detestable idols, and have filled my inheritance with their abominations.

[19]O LORD, my strength and my stronghold,
my refuge in the day of trouble,
to you shall the nations come
from the ends of the earth and say:
Our ancestors have inherited nothing but lies,
worthless things in which there is no
profit.
[20]Can mortals make for themselves gods?
Such are no gods!

21"Therefore I am surely going to teach them, this time I am going to teach them my power and my might, and they shall know that my name is the LORD."

[a]Gk: Heb *And first*

COMMENTARY

16:1-9. The prophetic burden, which weighs so heavily upon Jeremiah in the preceding passage, takes a different form in this chapter. The isolation and loneliness of the prophet, his lack of involvement in social and festive activities, are given another etiology. Jeremiah is prohibited by the Lord from marrying and having children (v. 2), a personal destiny that was out of accord with the accepted patterns of Israelite life. Little information is recorded about the marriages and families of the prophets. Whenever such information is found, it usually has to do with the prophetic message, as, for example, the reporting of the presence and names of Isaiah's children.[120] On three occasions, we hear about prophetic marriages, and in each case the prophet's life becomes a symbol of what elsewhere is proclaimed by prophetic oracle. Hosea is commanded to go and marry a harlot and dramatically embody the breakdown of the relationship between the Lord and Israel (Hosea 1–3). Ezekiel is told that his wife, the delight of his eyes, will die and that he must not mourn in order to symbolize the way the Lord will destroy the Temple, "my sanctuary" (Ezek 24:15-27). In chap. 16, Jeremiah is cut off from the joys of marriage and of having children so that his personal existence will dramatically emphasize and remind the people of the fate that is in store for them: the deaths of the sons and daughters and of the husbands and wives who bore them. Marriages and families will disappear from the land under the judgment of God. Just as Isaiah's children were walking reminders of the imminent fate of the people in the eighth century BCE, so also now Jeremiah is a reminder of the fate of the families of Judah, a fate that is spelled out in gory detail (v. 4).

The demand that Jeremiah embody the message goes a step further in vv. 5-9, where he is forbidden to mourn the dead at funerals. Again, this is in order to anticipate and demonstrate the absence of mourning that shall sweep the land when it is decimated by its enemies. The "house of mourning" (בית מרזח *bêt marzēaḥ*; cf. Amos 6:7) refers to an ancient custom, known from various parts of the ancient Near East, in which mourners gathered in a kind of club or association for a funerary banquet. The reference to revelry in Amos 6:7 and a mythological account of the Canaanite god El getting drunk at a *marzēaḥ* suggest that such places may have served as the locus for boisterous wakes.[121] Jeremiah's absence from funerals and their concomitant rituals is to be a continuing reminder of what lies ahead for the people: death without the normal rituals of mourning. Not only will the dead go unmourned (vv. 6-7), but they will remain unburied as well, food for the birds (v. 4). There will be nothing decent and civilized in the fires of judgment, no resting in decent graves with the ancestors who have gone before.

A third prohibition is then placed on Jeremiah (v. 8). While some would associate the "house of feasting" with the *marzēaḥ,* where feasting certainly went on, the reference here is more probably to marriage feasts, to celebratory, happy occasions. Jeremiah's absence is to be a sign that such celebration and joy will disappear from the land. The social isolation of which the prophet has spoken in the previous chapter is now declared as the Lord's intent and a mode of prophetic proclamation, not the effect of his unpopularity or negative preaching.

The reason for all this is given in v. 5. The Lord has taken away my "peace" (שלום *šālôm*), which is then explained as "my steadfast love and mercy." The claim seems to carry a double meaning. The peace that the people have sought (8:15; 14:19) and that the false prophets have promised (6:14; 8:11) is gone, and the God they have known and worshiped as "the LORD merciful and compassionate, slow to anger and abounding in steadfast love" (Exod 34:6 NRSV) now will be that way with them no more.

16:10-13. Using a familiar question-and-answer schema in which the people ask a question and the prophet gives an answer, these verses identify the cause of this horrendous judgment that has just been so graphically and brutally described. The indictment is a familiar one: the apostasy of this generation and of their ancestors, couched in the language of the Decalogue (v. 11;

---

120. The identification of Huldah's husband in 1 Kgs 22:14 is more a reflection of the social structure that tended to locate a woman's identity in relation to her husband.

121. See Philip King, *Jeremiah: An Archaeological Companion* (Louisville: Westminster/John Knox, 1993) 140-41.

cf. 3:25; 7:9; 14:20); their sin is worse than that of the previous generation (v. 12; cf. 3:6-11); they have not kept the law (v. 11; cf. 6:19; 9:13); they have stubbornly followed their own will (v. 12; cf. 3:17; 7:24; 9:14; 11:8); and they do not listen (v. 12; cf. 6:10; 11:8; 13:10). It is a wearying list, but then this people have wearied their God with their repeated sins.

16:14-15. In the midst of this fierce rhetoric comes a word that looks beyond all this to a future that is almost nonsensical in its context, a future beyond exile when a lost and destroyed people will be redeemed and reborn. The verses duplicate 23:7-8, where they fit better in a context of restoration prophecy. They may have been inserted here in the exilic or post-exilic periods. Still, the reader should not skip over them. Two things must be said. First, these words of promise cannot be excised from the context of judgment, no matter how much our logic or even our literary analysis might impel us to do so. Second, the text reminds us that God's way with Israel was defined in the exodus. The Lord who brought Israel out of bondage will bring Israel back from exile. The prophecy of Isaiah 40–55 attests to the way the Lord, who heard the cries of a distressed people and delivered them from slavery, hears again the cries of a judged people and delivers them from exile. The name, the being, the reality, the character, the actions of this God—all of that is embodied in such "bringing out."

16:16-18. The divine word now moves back to judgment. The picture of fishermen and hunters after their prey, the Judeans, is clear. The "ways" of the people, about which Jeremiah has spoken (e.g., 2:23; 4:18; 6:27; 7:3, 5), have brought about these calamities. The land is polluted with idols (cf. Deut 21:22-23), which will be heaped up like the corpses of the people, spoken about earlier in the chapter. There is considerable debate about the particular reference of "the fishermen" and "the hunters" who are sent by God successively to "catch" and to "hunt" the Judeans. Some think that these terms refer to the two Babylonian deportations (597 and 586 BCE). That idea is rein-

forced by the "double" in v. 18, although that term may mean "equivalent to." Others have seen in these two images a reference to Egyptians (cf. Isa 19:8) and to Babylonians; those two nations are paired twice in 2:18, 36. If that understanding is correct, then the oracle anticipates the successive arrivals of Egyptian and Babylonian forces to "catch" and "hunt" the Judeans. But the fishing metaphor is also applied elsewhere to the Babylonians (Hab 1:14-17). In either case, this imagery depicts these invaders as working hard to catch and hunt the iniquitous Judeans, so that no one will get away.

16:19-21. Verses 14-15 have let the reader know that this chapter bears surprises. The surprises continue as we hear a single voice begin with typical language of lament and thanksgiving, words of trust in the help of the Lord. In context, these can only be heard as the words of Jeremiah and so must be added to the sounds of complaint that have been heard in preceding chapters. Complaint is not the only kind of address to God that this prophet makes.

The connection of the first part of v. 19 to the second part is rough, and many would see here a composite text. The prophet reports a confession of the nations. While such a move sounds more like the prophecy of Isaiah 40–55, the language of the nations' confession is consistent with much in the book of Jeremiah—the reference to the sins of the ancestors, the characterization of the sins of the nations as lies and as "worthless things in which there is no profit" (cf. 2:4, 8), and the condemnation of idolatry. The sins of Judah are now confessed by the nations as their own sins.

The chapter concludes with a word from the Lord carried by the fourfold use of "know" (ידע yāda‘) that impressively demonstrates the divine purpose. The "them" is the nations of the preceding verse, who will see the Lord's power and might at work, probably in the return of the exiles from captivity. Like Judah, the nations will see the power and might of the Lord over against the lifeless, unprofitable idols demonstrated in the events of history.

REFLECTIONS

1. The text is not sentimental about the Lord's refusal to allow Jeremiah to marry and have children, the common experience of his peers. This is a divine command embodied in the life of the prophet. But it is an implicit reminder of the way in which the agent of that word, the bearer of the divine message, often experiences personal pain and anguish in the very act of proclamation. If one were to ask what features seemed to belong commonly to the prophetic office in order to try to identify prophetic figures in a later time, it would not be inappropriate to expect that the prophetic task would involve some kind of deprivation and suffering. That is not something that is recorded of every prophet, but it happens so often that it seems as if one should anticipate and recognize the agency of God in such situations. That such deprivations or unhappy experiences were often formal symbolic actions does not lessen their identity with the function of prophetic proclamation. It is a form of preaching "in word and deed," even if the deed is under divine command rather than human inclination. Jeremiah is a vivid example of the absence of an easy life and of popular acceptance on the part of the Lord's prophet. But he exemplifies what goes with the job—or calling—in any age.

2. The strange juxtaposition of the promising and hopeful words of 16:14-15 with the terrible denunciatory and judging words all around them merits some reflection. The God who leaves the bodies unburied for the birds is the same God who brings the captives home. The God who delivered an oppressed people from the tyranny of Egyptian slavery is the same God who brings famine, sword, and disease in judgment upon the descendants of those same people. Surely nowhere is the tension between the judging and redeeming activity of God more strongly felt than in this counterpoint. It is important to hear this and yet not to misread it. This is not a Janus-faced deity, angry one moment and in the next compassionate. These words are a reminder in the face of impending and terrible death that such a fate is not the last word with this God and with the Lord's way with Israel. One may not ameliorate the force of the judgment. But one may not simply stop there as if that were all God had to say. The compassion and peace that go away because of the disobedience of the people and their refusal to listen come back in full force. The ancient confession of Exod 34:6-7 is the controlling reality, but it includes judgment. So also does the cross.

3. The surprising outburst of the nations in 16:19-20 is a clue to the larger picture. The scope of the Lord's work is much larger than the focus on Judah and its sins would suggest. The gathering of the nations before the Lord is a biblical theme that is most familiar from such texts as Isaiah 2; Micah 4; and Matt 25:31-46. In a context such as Jeremiah 16, that theme injects an eschatological anticipation in the midst of the disasters, troubles, and breakdown of the contemporary world. But the two are related. The problems of the community of faith in its failure to live as God's people are not sharply different from the problems of other groups. There is a standard for Israel and the church, but it is not necessarily a double standard. If the hope for the nations is the same as the hope for Israel (Isa 2:2-5 would suggest that), then the confession of the nations is appropriately an echo of Israel's own confession of sin. So in the midst of our reading of the trials and tribulations of Judah, Jeremiah, and the Lord, we are reminded that this important piece of God's purpose is part of a larger whole: the gathering of all the peoples in confession, praise, and the desire to learn a different way of existence.

JEREMIAH 17:1-27, THE PROBLEM OF THE HEART AND OTHER MATTERS

NIV

17 "Judah's sin is engraved with an iron tool,
   inscribed with a flint point,
on the tablets of their hearts
   and on the horns of their altars.
²Even their children remember
   their altars and Asherah poles[a]
beside the spreading trees
   and on the high hills.
³My mountain in the land
   and your[b] wealth and all your treasures
I will give away as plunder,
   together with your high places,
   because of sin throughout your country.
⁴Through your own fault you will lose
   the inheritance I gave you.
I will enslave you to your enemies
   in a land you do not know,
for you have kindled my anger,
   and it will burn forever."

⁵This is what the LORD says:

"Cursed is the one who trusts in man,
   who depends on flesh for his strength
   and whose heart turns away from the LORD.
⁶He will be like a bush in the wastelands;
   he will not see prosperity when it comes.
He will dwell in the parched places of the
      desert,
   in a salt land where no one lives.

⁷"But blessed is the man who trusts in the
      LORD,
   whose confidence is in him.
⁸He will be like a tree planted by the water
   that sends out its roots by the stream.
It does not fear when heat comes;
   its leaves are always green.
It has no worries in a year of drought
   and never fails to bear fruit."

⁹The heart is deceitful above all things
   and beyond cure.
   Who can understand it?

---

a2 That is, symbols of the goddess Asherah   b2,3 Or hills / ³and
the mountains of the land. / Your

NRSV

17 The sin of Judah is written with an iron pen;
   with a diamond point it is engraved on the
tablet of their hearts, and on the horns of their
altars, ²while their children remember their altars
and their sacred poles,[a] beside every green tree,
and on the high hills, ³on the mountains in the
open country. Your wealth and all your treasures I
will give for spoil as the price of your sin[b] throughout all your territory. ⁴By your own act you shall
lose the heritage that I gave you, and I will make
you serve your enemies in a land that you do not
know, for in my anger a fire is kindled[c] that shall
burn forever.

⁵ Thus says the LORD:
   Cursed are those who trust in mere mortals
      and make mere flesh their strength,
      whose hearts turn away from the LORD.
⁶ They shall be like a shrub in the desert,
      and shall not see when relief comes.
   They shall live in the parched places of the
         wilderness,
      in an uninhabited salt land.

⁷ Blessed are those who trust in the LORD,
      whose trust is the LORD.
⁸ They shall be like a tree planted by water,
      sending out its roots by the stream.
   It shall not fear when heat comes,
      and its leaves shall stay green;
   in the year of drought it is not anxious,
      and it does not cease to bear fruit.

⁹ The heart is devious above all else;
      it is perverse—
      who can understand it?
¹⁰ I the LORD test the mind
      and search the heart,
   to give to all according to their ways,
      according to the fruit of their doings.

¹¹ Like the partridge hatching what it did not lay,

---

aHeb Asherim   bCn: Heb spoil your high places for sin   cTwo
Mss Theodotion: you kindled

NIV

¹⁰"I the LORD search the heart
  and examine the mind,
to reward a man according to his conduct,
  according to what his deeds deserve."

¹¹Like a partridge that hatches eggs it did not lay
  is the man who gains riches by unjust
    means.
When his life is half gone, they will desert
    him,
  and in the end he will prove to be a fool.

¹²A glorious throne, exalted from the beginning,
  is the place of our sanctuary.
¹³O LORD, the hope of Israel,
  all who forsake you will be put to shame.
Those who turn away from you will be
    written in the dust
  because they have forsaken the LORD,
    the spring of living water.

¹⁴Heal me, O LORD, and I will be healed;
  save me and I will be saved,
  for you are the one I praise.
¹⁵They keep saying to me,
  "Where is the word of the LORD?
    Let it now be fulfilled!"
¹⁶I have not run away from being your
    shepherd;
  you know I have not desired the day of
    despair.
What passes my lips is open before you.
¹⁷Do not be a terror to me;
  you are my refuge in the day of disaster.
¹⁸Let my persecutors be put to shame,
  but keep me from shame;
let them be terrified,
  but keep me from terror.
Bring on them the day of disaster;
  destroy them with double destruction.

¹⁹This is what the LORD said to me: "Go and stand at the gate of the people, through which the kings of Judah go in and out; stand also at all the other gates of Jerusalem. ²⁰Say to them, 'Hear the word of the LORD, O kings of Judah and all people of Judah and everyone living in Jerusalem who come through these gates. ²¹This is what the LORD says: Be careful not to carry a load on the Sabbath day or bring it through the gates of Jerusalem.

NRSV

so are all who amass wealth unjustly;
  in mid-life it will leave them,
  and at their end they will prove to be fools.

¹²O glorious throne, exalted from the
    beginning,
  shrine of our sanctuary!
¹³O hope of Israel! O LORD!
  All who forsake you shall be put to shame;
those who turn away from you^a shall be
    recorded in the underworld,^b
  for they have forsaken the fountain of liv-
    ing water, the LORD.

¹⁴Heal me, O LORD, and I shall be healed;
  save me, and I shall be saved;
  for you are my praise.
¹⁵See how they say to me,
  "Where is the word of the LORD?
    Let it come!"
¹⁶But I have not run away from being a
    shepherd^c in your service,
  nor have I desired the fatal day.
You know what came from my lips;
  it was before your face.
¹⁷Do not become a terror to me;
  you are my refuge in the day of disaster;
¹⁸Let my persecutors be shamed,
  but do not let me be shamed;
let them be dismayed,
  but do not let me be dismayed;
bring on them the day of disaster;
  destroy them with double destruction!

¹⁹Thus said the LORD to me: Go and stand in the People's Gate, by which the kings of Judah enter and by which they go out, and in all the gates of Jerusalem, ²⁰and say to them: Hear the word of the LORD, you kings of Judah, and all Judah, and all the inhabitants of Jerusalem, who enter by these gates. ²¹Thus says the LORD: For the sake of your lives, take care that you do not bear a burden on the sabbath day or bring it in by the gates of Jerusalem. ²²And do not carry a burden out of your houses on the sabbath or do any work, but keep the sabbath day holy, as I commanded your ancestors. ²³Yet they did not listen or incline

^aHeb *me*   ^bOr *in the earth*   ^cMeaning of Heb uncertain

NIV

²²Do not bring a load out of your houses or do any work on the Sabbath, but keep the Sabbath day holy, as I commanded your forefathers. ²³Yet they did not listen or pay attention; they were stiff-necked and would not listen or respond to discipline. ²⁴But if you are careful to obey me, declares the LORD, and bring no load through the gates of this city on the Sabbath, but keep the Sabbath day holy by not doing any work on it, ²⁵then kings who sit on David's throne will come through the gates of this city with their officials. They and their officials will come riding in chariots and on horses, accompanied by the men of Judah and those living in Jerusalem, and this city will be inhabited forever. ²⁶People will come from the towns of Judah and the villages around Jerusalem, from the territory of Benjamin and the western foothills, from the hill country and the Negev, bringing burnt offerings and sacrifices, grain offerings, incense and thank offerings to the house of the LORD. ²⁷But if you do not obey me to keep the Sabbath day holy by not carrying any load as you come through the gates of Jerusalem on the Sabbath day, then I will kindle an unquenchable fire in the gates of Jerusalem that will consume her fortresses.' "

NRSV

their ear; they stiffened their necks and would not hear or receive instruction.

24But if you listen to me, says the LORD, and bring in no burden by the gates of this city on the sabbath day, but keep the sabbath day holy and do no work on it, ²⁵then there shall enter by the gates of this city kingsᵃ who sit on the throne of David, riding in chariots and on horses, they and their officials, the people of Judah and the inhabitants of Jerusalem; and this city shall be inhabited forever. ²⁶And people shall come from the towns of Judah and the places around Jerusalem, from the land of Benjamin, from the Shephelah, from the hill country, and from the Negeb, bringing burnt offerings and sacrifices, grain offerings and frankincense, and bringing thank offerings to the house of the LORD. ²⁷But if you do not listen to me, to keep the sabbath day holy, and to carry in no burden through the gates of Jerusalem on the sabbath day, then I will kindle a fire in its gates; it shall devour the palaces of Jerusalem and shall not be quenched.

ᵃCn: Heb *kings and officials*

COMMENTARY

This chapter contains a collection of small pieces, including judgment speeches, wisdom sayings, hymnic exaltations, and prophetic lament. It ends with an extended sermon by Jeremiah on the sabbath. The individual pieces are for the most part independent literary units, but shared words and motifs, particularly the repeated reference to the heart in the first three units and the water motif in vv. 5-8 and 12-13, help to join all but the final sermon together into a whole.

17:1-4. The opening section is clearly a judgment speech. The first two-and-a-half verses indict Judah for apostasy, here described in typical language with reference to altars, sacred poles, and the places of apostasy (cf. 2:20; 3:6, 13). These elements were associated with the worship of Baal. The sacred poles, or asherim, were elements of the Baal cult that could have been legitimately

associated with the worship of the Lord but became separated and identified with a female goddess. The mention of the "children" remembering may refer to cultic paraphernalia and rituals that were destroyed in King Josiah's reform (2 Kings 23), or it may simply mean that the next generation continues to "remember" in the sense of observe (cf. Exod 20:8), the rituals associated with the worship of the Canaanite gods and goddesses.

Such sins have become such a deep part of the people's lives that they are indelibly engraved on their hearts. The image of the pen made of iron with a "diamond" (probably hard stone) point is meant to convey how permanently and deeply sin has become ingrained in this people. The statement that the people's sins are engraved on the horns of the altar is probably a way of saying that the very signs of cultic obedience, the altar and its horns, where the blood of sacrifices were smeared and persons could come for protection, have become symbols of cultic disobedience and no longer protective.

The last two verses conclude the judgment speech by announcing the Lord's judgment against the people. They will lose their material assets, they will lose their land, and they will be sent into exile. The final sentence reveals the depth of the divine rage at the conduct of the people, since the Lord's anger is as enduring as the sin that is permanently engraved on the heart.

17:5-8. What follows sounds like something out of the wisdom literature or, even more, like one of the psalms (e.g., Ps 92:13-14). The imagery is closely associated with Psalm 1, where tree imagery is also used to contrast the way of those who put their trust in the Lord with the way of those who trust in human resources. What is the difference between these ways? The images of the two trees spell that out: One is like a piece of dry scrub in the desert; it bears no fruit, has no permanent source of nourishment, no companionship. The other is altogether different. Using the same sentence that begins the image of the tree in Psalm 1, Jeremiah speaks of what it is like to move that tree (the verb is "transplanted" [שׁתל *šātal*], not "planted") from the desert and place it beside a stream. It sinks its roots deeply, becoming richly fertile and productive, unafraid of the assaults of the elements, particularly the heat. It is always fresh, even in dry, hot times. The absence of fear and anxiety is a significant part of this description. It is the choice between life and death.

17:9-10. The heart comes back into the picture for a third time. Earlier, Jeremiah spoke of the sin written on the heart (v. 1) and of the the heart that turns away from the Lord (v. 5); now it is the devious and perverse heart (v. 9). The text is not dissimilar from the first four verses of the chapter. There it was a specific message to Judah about the deeply rooted sins of the people. In both instances, the message comes from the Lord. But this time, it is more general, about the human condition as a whole (cf. Gen. 6:5). Verse 9 may be an utterance of the prophet, whose personal experience has convinced him that the mind and will of human

beings is deceitful and perverse (the word for "devious" [עקב *'āqôb*] derives from the same root as in the name "Jacob," an occasionally devious character) beyond comprehension. Just as vv. 1-4 suggest that the Lord knows the condition of the heart and will do something about it, so also these verses confirm that in different language. The prophet may not comprehend the human heart, but the Lord is testing it all the time (cf. 6:27-30; 9:7)—and acting accordingly. There is an order in the world, and one dimension of that order resides in the correspondence of deeds and consequences. The one who brought about the order of the world in creation sustains it in the lives of its creatures (v. 10*b*). That order is called justice and righteousness.

17:11. The point of the preceding verses is carried forward in the form of a proverb comparing the person who accumulates wealth in unjust ways to a bird that hatches eggs it did not lay. Just as the young birds eventually leave the nest, so also the ill-gotten gains will eventually abandon the rich person, to whom they really do not belong. The proverb shows how the point of v. 10 works itself out in human life. The equation of the fool with the wicked is also implicit in the final line of the proverb. It has been suggested that, in the light of 22:13, 17, the allusion here may be to King Jehoiakim, who is condemned by the prophet for having amassed wealth unjustly. The connection cannot be confirmed precisely because a proverb speaks universally and generally. But the openness of the proverbial speech makes application of it to Jehoiakim fully appropriate.

17:12-13. Some ambiguities exist in these verses, particularly in v. 12, but the thrust of the text can be determined without doubt. Verse 12 may be read as either a declarative statement (NIV) or a vocative address (NRSV). The throne may be the throne in heaven or the throne of the ark. In any event, the verse joins with v. 13*a* to offer a hymnic exaltation of the Lord. The equation of God enthroned in heaven with God enthroned in the Temple is a commonplace in the OT. This God, who dwells "on high" (i.e., "exalted"), is Israel's only hope. The doxology of vv. 12-13*a* becomes a word of judgment in the rest of the saying. The prophet indicts those who forsake or turn away from this God who is their only hope and their only possibility for life (cf.

2:13). Rejecting the living waters, they will find themselves in the land of death. The ambiguities in the passage grow with the realization that the expression translated properly as "hope of Israel" can also be translated as "pool of Israel." This is the water that sustains those who trust in the Lord. To forsake that pool of water is to die of thirst.

These two verses do much to bind together the disparate parts of chap. 17. Some have seen in them an introduction to the lament that follows. While vv. 14-18 are probably a separate literary unit, they pick up the theme of shame in vv. 12-13. These verses also look backward as they create implicit echoes and contrasts: the sin "written" (כתב *kātab*) on the heart (v. 1), and those who turn away "written" (*kātab*) in the earth (v. 13); the wealth that "leaves" (עזב *'āzab*) those who acquire it unjustly (v. 11) and those who "forsake" (*'āzab*) the Lord (v. 13); and especially the nourishing water that sustains those who trust in the Lord (v. 8) and the fountain of living water that is the Lord (v. 13).

17:14-18. The lamenting voice of the prophet is heard once more in these verses (cf. 11:18–12:6; 15:10-21). The lament, as always, is a prayer for help. In tone, it is somewhat different from the earlier ones and those that follow. Its complaint against God is more muted. The one who complained about an "incurable wound, refusing to be healed" in 15:18 now cries out for healing in the confidence that God can heal, that God can save (cf. 15:20). The imagery of sickness and healing may be understood figuratively. The next line interprets its meaning: Jeremiah is in trouble and needs help. The expression "for you are my praise" typically provides a rationale for God to respond, this time in the prophet's devotion to the Lord. How can God not respond to one whose life is lived in praise of God?

The force of the passage is carried by a sequence of emphatic pronouns in vv. 15-16 (see the Reflections on 5:10-21). The key to the passage lies in v. 15: words from an unidentified group who may be understood as the people, the false prophets, or the leaders.[122] Whoever "they" are,

they are Jeremiah's enemies, the "persecutors" of v. 18. They have taunted him, saying that the word he proclaimed has not come to pass. They do not believe it, and there is no evidence that they should. Thus the taunt is a challenge both to Jeremiah's authority as a prophet and to the credibility of Yahweh's word.

By its emphatic opening "I," v. 16 sets the prophet's innocence, good conduct, and proper obedience over against the taunts of the "they." What the prophet claims for himself, however, is difficult to determine. The NRSV and the NIV suggest that he is claiming faithfulness to his "shepherding" task. That may be correct, but "shepherding" in Jeremiah, as elsewhere, is generally associated with the political and religious leaders of the community (e.g., 2:8; 3:15; 10:21; 23:1-4; 25:34-38). Jeremiah may be declaring his own faithfulness in following the Lord's leading as a shepherd. Many interpreters have suggested that the NRSV's "from being a shepherd" (מרעה *mērō'eh*) should be repointed to read מרעה (*mērā'â*), "from evil," or corrected to "for evil" (לרעה *lērā'â*), with "evil" (רעה *rā'â*) and "shepherd" (רעה *rō'eh*) having the same consonants and only different vowels. Thus the prophet's words would be something like: "I have not pressed for evil; I have not longed for the calamitous day."[123] There is some textual evidence for this reading, and it meshes with the rest of the verse by understanding Jeremiah's words to say that he has not pressed for the day of calamity, that he has not "desired" (אוה *'āwâ*) or longed for the Lord's day of judgment, as the people of Amos's time mistakenly "desired" the day of the Lord (Amos 5:18). The emphatic "you," addressed to the deity (v. 16b), is a reminder to God that Jeremiah's faithfulness and the character of his preaching are known well to the Lord.

The prophet thus claims that the word of judgment is not his own, but the Lord has jeopardized his life, thus creating terror or dismay (the word "terror" [מחתה *mĕḥittâ*] is a nominal form of the verb translated "dismay" in v. 18) in him (v. 17). In vv. 17-18, the prophet asks God to remove the terror, dismay, and shame that Jeremiah experiences by confirming and vindicating the prophetic word. As in v. 14, the prophet

122. Kathleen M. O'Connor, *The Confessions of Jeremiah: Their Interpretation and Role in Chapters 1–25*, SBLDS 94 (Atlanta: Scholars Press, 1988) 49.

123. Ibid., 45.

seeks to persuade God so to act by claiming confidence in God as his protection and refuge (v. 17). Jeremiah's plea for deliverance is a plea for God to overcome those who are oppressing him. Thus he prays that his shame before the taunts of his persecutors may be turned into their shame before the powerful judgment of God, that his dismay at the failure of the word may be turned into their dismay. While he did not press for this day of disaster, since it is the Lord's word and the Lord's doing, the prophet does not hesitate to pray that his enemies—and the Lord's—may be overcome.

17:19-27. The lament of the prophet is not now followed by a divine response, as in 11:18–12:6 and 15:10-21, but by a sermon ascribed to the prophet and preached at one of the entrances to Jerusalem. In setting and form, as well as in its focus on an element of the Decalogue, this sermon reminds us of Jeremiah's sermon at the temple gate in chap. 7. But it is not at all certain that this text comes from Jeremiah or his time. Because of its style and subject matter, the sermon is often ascribed to an exilic or post-exilic setting in which the sabbath had greater prominence. Some would see the decline of sabbath observance after the destruction of the Temple as the context of these words. Others have noted the affinities to Neh 13:15-22 and the trend toward commercialization of the sabbath in the post-exilic era and have suggested that the sermon may come from that time.

Whatever the circumstances, the force of the text is clear. It reflects a situation when the practice of sabbath rest was being eroded and persons were working or selling the fruits of their labors on the sabbath in Jerusalem. The use of the word "burden" (משא *maśśāʾ*) in Neh 13:15, 19 to refer to commercial loads suggests that its use in this text (vv. 21-22, 24) has the same meaning. The sanctification of the sabbath for the life of the community has become a life-and-death matter. The sermon in chap. 7 made no mention of the sabbath in its call for observance of the Decalogue stipulations. However, that issue is now laid before the people. What the community does about the sabbath is made a criterion for its future existence. Careful observance of the sabbath's sacred character opens up the possibility for the city's restoration. The community will choose life or death, depending on whether it sets apart a time for rest from all human pursuits and economic endeavors to refresh themselves and attend to the things of the Lord.

REFLECTIONS

1. There are only two places in the book of Jeremiah where we hear of writing on the heart. The first is this chapter, and the second is 31:33. The latter is the more famous text, for it speaks of the new covenant the Lord will establish with the people. The Lord says, "I will put my law within them, and I will write it on their hearts." While we cannot argue for an intentional association of these two texts, the resonance between them is striking. As Brueggemann has put it, "Something will be written on the heart, either sin or torah."[124] The movement here is a fundamentally theological one, and even more fundamentally the movement of faith. The movement from repentance to sanctification is a movement from the sin written indelibly on the heart by human beings to the law written indelibly on the heart by God. That movement is embodied in the sacraments of baptism and the Lord's Supper, but it is carried by other images, such as washing and eating. The whole Letter to the Romans is Paul's way of describing the connection between the sin we write on our hearts and the law God writes there. The former is so deeply engraved that we cannot get away from it. Only by the grace and redemption of God can it be overcome. The possibilities of new life come only by that same grace, writing as deeply on our hearts the Lord's instruction for our lives. In both cases, what is written on the heart is who we are; thus both testaments know the possibility of a transformation of that heart, of different kinds of "writing."

---

124. Walter Brueggemann, *A Commentary on Jeremiah: Exile and Homecoming* (Grand Rapids: Eerdmans, 1998) 157.

2. Some texts do not tell the truth. Or perhaps they exaggerate. Or perhaps they do not tell the whole truth. Jeremiah 17:4*b* is such a text. It has to be heard full force or one will never sense how deeply the Lord feels about this people, how wounded the Lord is over their sin and disobedience. It is so deep that the rage threatens never to die. Such a text must be heard on its own with all its force. This God will not be toyed with or betrayed with impunity. The covenant is not simply an image for a relationship. It is a reality between God and the people who know themselves to have been created, redeemed, and led by the Lord. This covenant has expectations and sanctions to undergird them.

But such a text cannot be heard simply on its own. The same testament in which the book of Jeremiah rests bears witness again and again to the momentary and impermanent character of the Lord's anger. It is there in the ancient confession of Exod 34:6 and is repeated again and again in the psalms and other texts: God is "slow to anger . . . yet by no means clearing the guilty." But it is seen even more sharply in the actual experience of persons who come to know that God's "anger is but for a moment; his favor is for a lifetime" (Ps 30:5[6]). And precisely in the context of the exile and the experience of the enduring and burning wrath of the Lord, there is sounded a similar word:

> For a brief moment I abandoned you,
>> but with great compassion I will gather you.
> In overflowing wrath for a moment
>> I hid my face from you,
> but with everlasting love I will have compassion on you,
>> says the LORD, your Redeemer. (Isa 54:7-8 NRSV)

That text has to be placed alongside Jer 17:4—but not too quickly. Exile came. It was long and difficult. Sometimes the moment can seem like an eon. But it is only a moment in the divine reckoning.

3. The images of the shrub in the desert and the tree transplanted to a well-watered site are richly open to proclamation. They vividly illustrate the point that is being made and draw the hearer toward making a decision. One image repels, and the other attracts. The simile of the tree planted beside water has such appeal that if we can convey that trust in the Lord has those kinds of effects and benefits—durability, the ability to stand against the pressures of life and the changes of the seasons of life, freshness and productivity, and the loss of incapacitating anxiety—people will hear it and respond. It is important to keep the image in its context, however. It has to do with trusting the Lord and the effects of doing so. There may be all sorts of ways in which life is not productive and our way comes under assault. But there is a way to survive and continue, to live without being done in and weighed under. Even in the dry periods, there is a source of life that carries us through. It is like that tree.

The water imagery returns again in 17:13. Its continuity with the image of the transplanted tree is powerful, for the point is the same: the identification of a source of life, of water that is always flowing and always fresh. It can be counted on to be there. All of this water imagery is a way of saying, "The Lord is like that." Jesus picks up this theme directly in the conversation with the woman of Samaria in John 4, identifying himself with the water that will keep one from ever being thirsty, more specifically "a spring of water gushing up to eternal life" (John 4:14). Jeremiah suggests that the way to speak about trusting in the Lord is to speak about water. That is how to tell what such trust really means. It is not so much an obligation as it is a gift—or even better, a provision, the source of life, as desirable and necessary as water is to the thirsty.

4. Two ways, two modes of existence, as spoken of in 17:5-8. Contemporary culture also knows of two ways to live. One is the way of the self, which knows with confidence what it wants to do; it will not be controlled by corporate mentality or the mores of the community. The other is the way of the person, who goes along to get along or who does not know how to direct his or her own life and lets external forces set the direction and the pace. We tend to exalt and applaud those who are inner-directed and put down or disparage those who are other-directed.

The images of the two trees in 17:5-8 lump both these ways together and indicate that there is a still better way. It is not the way of autonomy, the direction of the self and the ego; nor is it the way of heteronomy, in which we allow others to control our lives. It is the way of theonomy, the way of "God's law" or, in the language of Jeremiah, trust in the Lord. Neither of the other ways can produce the kinds of results that the theonomous life can. The issue is not success. It is durability, freshness, and the possibility of living in the world without fear and anxiety. Hanging on to the Lord is a way of hanging in there, so the prophet says.

5. The heart is a theme in three successive texts in this chapter. It is an image that combines will, intention, disposition, and feeling. It may express the deepest devotion, and so each Valentine's Day the heart becomes the primary symbol for expressing the devotion and affection of lovers. But the heart can be twisted and devious. Imagery of the heart is a way of speaking about ourselves at our deepest, our inmost level. We speak of "the secrets of the heart," those thoughts and feelings we keep hidden. The heart gives us an image to express who we really are. So the turning away of the heart is a real abandonment. And God's searching our hearts (v. 10) is a probe of our innermost self, the exposure of what we are like down deep inside.

6. The sabbath is here given a place of significance. Its careful observation is something on which the fate of the nation hangs. That may seem to be a lot of weight to place on sabbath observance. At least it makes us aware that something is at stake in the keeping of the sabbath. Several things may be noted in that regard. The sabbath as breaks the feeling of economic dependency, underscoring that the community is finally dependent upon its Lord. The sabbath is a way of showing that our labor is not our final aim and that its products are not the consuming aim of our lives. Both labor and consumption are regularly to be set aside in favor of rest and non-consumption. And the commitment to productivity is to be set aside in favor of our loyalty to the Lord, who made us and gave us the sabbath. The commandment to honor the sabbath safeguards the first commandment, which reminds us wherein is our ultimate trust. In that respect, the sabbath sermon at the end of chapter 17 reinforces the point that is made in vv. 5-8: The source of our life is trust in the Lord.

JEREMIAH 18:1-23, THE POTTER AND THE CLAY

NIV

18 This is the word that came to Jeremiah from the LORD: 2"Go down to the potter's house, and there I will give you my message." 3So I went down to the potter's house, and I saw him working at the wheel. 4But the pot he was shaping from the clay was marred in his hands; so the potter formed it into another pot, shaping it as seemed best to him.

NRSV

18 The word that came to Jeremiah from the LORD: 2"Come, go down to the potter's house, and there I will let you hear my words." 3So I went down to the potter's house, and there he was working at his wheel. 4The vessel he was making of clay was spoiled in the potter's hand, and he reworked it into another vessel, as seemed good to him.

NIV

⁵Then the word of the LORD came to me: ⁶"O house of Israel, can I not do with you as this potter does?" declares the LORD. "Like clay in the hand of the potter, so are you in my hand, O house of Israel. ⁷If at any time I announce that a nation or kingdom is to be uprooted, torn down and destroyed, ⁸and if that nation I warned repents of its evil, then I will relent and not inflict on it the disaster I had planned. ⁹And if at another time I announce that a nation or kingdom is to be built up and planted, ¹⁰and if it does evil in my sight and does not obey me, then I will reconsider the good I had intended to do for it.

¹¹"Now therefore say to the people of Judah and those living in Jerusalem, 'This is what the LORD says: Look! I am preparing a disaster for you and devising a plan against you. So turn from your evil ways, each one of you, and reform your ways and your actions.' ¹²But they will reply, 'It's no use. We will continue with our own plans; each of us will follow the stubbornness of his evil heart.' "

¹³Therefore this is what the LORD says:

"Inquire among the nations:
   Who has ever heard anything like this?
A most horrible thing has been done
   by Virgin Israel.
¹⁴Does the snow of Lebanon
   ever vanish from its rocky slopes?
Do its cool waters from distant sources
   ever cease to flow?ᵃ
¹⁵Yet my people have forgotten me;
   they burn incense to worthless idols,
which made them stumble in their ways
   and in the ancient paths.
They made them walk in bypaths
   and on roads not built up.
¹⁶Their land will be laid waste,
   an object of lasting scorn;
all who pass by will be appalled
   and will shake their heads.
¹⁷Like a wind from the east,
   I will scatter them before their
      enemies;
I will show them my back and not my face
   in the day of their disaster."

ᵃ14 The meaning of the Hebrew for this sentence is uncertain.

NRSV

⁵Then the word of the LORD came to me: ⁶Can I not do with you, O house of Israel, just as this potter has done? says the LORD. Just like the clay in the potter's hand, so are you in my hand, O house of Israel. ⁷At one moment I may declare concerning a nation or a kingdom, that I will pluck up and break down and destroy it, ⁸but if that nation, concerning which I have spoken, turns from its evil, I will change my mind about the disaster that I intended to bring on it. ⁹And at another moment I may declare concerning a nation or a kingdom that I will build and plant it, ¹⁰but if it does evil in my sight, not listening to my voice, then I will change my mind about the good that I had intended to do to it. ¹¹Now, therefore, say to the people of Judah and the inhabitants of Jerusalem: Thus says the LORD: Look, I am a potter shaping evil against you and devising a plan against you. Turn now, all of you from your evil way, and amend your ways and your doings.

12But they say, "It is no use! We will follow our own plans, and each of us will act according to the stubbornness of our evil will."

¹³ Therefore thus says the LORD:
   Ask among the nations:
      Who has heard the like of this?
   The virgin Israel has done
      a most horrible thing.
¹⁴ Does the snow of Lebanon leave
      the crags of Sirion?ᵃ
   Do the mountainᵇ waters run dry,ᶜ
      the cold flowing streams?
¹⁵ But my people have forgotten me,
      they burn offerings to a delusion;
   they have stumbledᵈ in their ways,
      in the ancient roads,
   and have gone into bypaths,
      not the highway,
¹⁶ making their land a horror,
      a thing to be hissed at forever.
   All who pass by it are horrified
      and shake their heads.
¹⁷ Like the wind from the east,
      I will scatter them before the enemy.
   I will show them my back, not my face,
      in the day of their calamity.

ᵃCn: Heb *of the field*   ᵇCn: Heb *foreign*   ᶜCn: Heb *Are . . . plucked up?*   ᵈGk Syr Vg: Heb *they made them stumble*

NIV

¹⁸They said, "Come, let's make plans against Jeremiah; for the teaching of the law by the priest will not be lost, nor will counsel from the wise, nor the word from the prophets. So come, let's attack him with our tongues and pay no attention to anything he says."

¹⁹Listen to me, O LORD;
    hear what my accusers are saying!
²⁰Should good be repaid with evil?
    Yet they have dug a pit for me.
Remember that I stood before you
    and spoke in their behalf
    to turn your wrath away from them.
²¹So give their children over to famine;
    hand them over to the power of the sword.
Let their wives be made childless and
        widows;
    let their men be put to death,
    their young men slain by the sword in
        battle.
²²Let a cry be heard from their houses
    when you suddenly bring invaders against
        them,
    for they have dug a pit to capture me
    and have hidden snares for my feet.
²³But you know, O LORD,
    all their plots to kill me.
Do not forgive their crimes
    or blot out their sins from your sight.
Let them be overthrown before you;
    deal with them in the time of your anger.

NRSV

18Then they said, "Come, let us make plots against Jeremiah—for instruction shall not perish from the priest, nor counsel from the wise, nor the word from the prophet. Come, let us bring charges against him,ᵃ and let us not heed any of his words."

¹⁹ Give heed to me, O LORD,
    and listen to what my adversaries say!
²⁰ Is evil a recompense for good?
    Yet they have dug a pit for my life.
Remember how I stood before you
    to speak good for them,
    to turn away your wrath from them.
²¹ Therefore give their children over to famine;
    hurl them out to the power of the sword,
    let their wives become childless and
        widowed.
May their men meet death by pestilence,
    their youths be slain by the sword in battle.
²² May a cry be heard from their houses,
    when you bring the marauder suddenly
        upon them!
For they have dug a pit to catch me,
    and laid snares for my feet.
²³ Yet you, O LORD, know
    all their plotting to kill me.
Do not forgive their iniquity,
    do not blot out their sin from your sight.
Let them be tripped up before you;
    deal with them while you are angry.

ᵃHeb *strike him with the tongue*

COMMENTARY

Three separate units are brought together in this chapter. The first is a symbolic act involving the work of a potter in making a clay vessel (vv. 1-12; cf. 19:1-15); the second is a judgment speech against Israel/Judah for its idolatry (vv. 13-17); and the final section (vv. 18-23) presents another of the prophet's laments.

18:1-12. The symbolic action that takes place here is not performed by Jeremiah but something that he observes: the work of a potter in making a clay utensil (vv. 1-4). The prophet observes that a potter can take a molded pot and, before it is

glazed and fired, reshape and redo it if it is spoiled or blemished. The point of this parabolic action is given in the next two verses (vv. 5-6): The Lord's relation to the house of Israel is like that of the potter with the clay. The Lord can do the same thing with a blemished, not-quite-right people. The power and sovereignty of God over this people are asserted in a dynamic way, identifying an aspect of that sovereignty that is sometimes missed or ignored: the possibility of not simply destroying the people but remolding them.

With vv. 7-11 there is a transitioning as the Lord

moves from speaking of divine action on analogy with the work of a potter to speak about a correlation between the behavior of a nation and God's treatment of that nation. Here the text speaks less about malleability, as in the potter's work with the clay, and more about a dynamic of deed and consequence. But inasmuch as these verses follow on the interpretation of the potter's work, the force of that parable continues. The Lord is still speaking about the clay/Israel and the potter/God. The point is straightforward: God's mind can change in regard to dealing out catastrophe or good, depending on the way a nation acts. The rhetoric in which this point is couched is important. When v. 7 speaks of the Lord's declaring (through the prophet) an intention to "pluck up and break down and destroy," the language of Jeremiah's call is invoked (1:10), as it is when the Lord speaks of the intention to "build and plant it" (v. 9). Thus the general statement about the Lord's sovereign freedom to act differently, to respond to what is happening in the human community works itself out specifically in the work of Jeremiah and the people to whom Jeremiah "declares" the word of the Lord. That is further intimated by the correlation between the Lord's "change of mind" and the people's "turning" (שוב šûb) from evil, a constant theme in the book of Jeremiah (e.g., chap. 3).

Verse 11 applies this principle to the citizens of Judah and the capital city, Jerusalem. The formulation makes them an example of the first option the Lord mentions: moving away from disaster because the nation turns from its evil (v. 7). The image of the potter returns, although now it is more distant. The Lord announces an imminent event: "I am in the process of shaping disaster against you and devising a plan against you." Judgment is in the works; the Lord has a plan and is putting it into play. But that imminence also involves an openness, and, as v. 7 has made clear, it is possible to change the plan if the people will do as Jeremiah has told them to do in the temple sermon in chap. 7: turn from their bad ways and change so that God can change the plan (cf. 7:3, 5).

The tragedy of Judah's story is nowhere more poignantly set out than in the people's response to these words. It is not altogether clear whether v. 12 is an act of defiance, the stubbornness that has been attested again and again (e.g., 3:17; 7:24; 13:10; 16:12), or whether it is a response of despair, the confession of a people that they have gone too far to turn back. The verse may be an explanation for the disaster they have incurred. If so, it is a cogent theological explanation. The people who insisted on following their own "plans" came up against the "plan" of God.

18:13-17. These verses, while probably originally unconnected to the preceding ones, now carry forward the parable of the potter and its interpretation. The "plans" in which the stubborn people persist are spelled out. With a play on words, the editor shows that the "horrible thing" (שערורת ša'ărûrit, v. 13) the virgin Israel has done is the "stubbornness [שררות šĕrîrût] of our evil will" that has just been confessed in v. 12.[125] The particulars of that stubborn evil will are now spelled out.

In a text similar to the form of the covenant lawsuit in 2:4-13, the Lord opens a case against "my people" (v. 15) by summoning the nations and asking them a rhetorical question, suggesting that nothing as bad as what is going on among the Lord's people has been seen before (cf. 2:10-11). Verse 14 is nearly impossible to understand, but it is clearly meant to establish a contrast with v. 15. A similar contrast in 2:32 suggests that the Lord is suggesting something impossible only to emphasize the unbelievability of what Judah has done. It is as unexpected and strange as if nature were to stop acting with its expected consistency. The reliability of nature's ways is set in sharp contrast to the unreliability of the Lord's people. The core of the accusation is v. 15: As impossible as it may seem, the people have forgotten their Lord. What does that mean? The next lines make it clear: They have sacrificed to idols. The word "delusion" (NIV, "worthless") is equivalent to the things that do not profit in 2:8 and 11. Literally, the word means "empty," "nothing." They have turned away from the Lord in order to give their devotion to what is actually nothing and can do nothing. Throughout Jeremiah, there is a kind of divine incredulity that the Lord's people would go after gods that can do nothing, that offer them nothing, that are in fact nothing, no more substantial than thin air. Obviously, the people saw it differently. And that was their great mistake, for the pursuit of

125. Brueggemann, *A Commentary on Jeremiah,* 170.

this "delusion" was their undoing, sending them down strange paths, pulling them away from "the ancient roads" (see 6:16) to go down strange and unfamiliar ways. "This is imagery which conveys Israel's apostasy, her 'lostness' on paths which are dangerous and in traveling along which she is not rightly guided."[126]

And so the accusation moves inexorably to the announcement of judgment, which begins to happen in v. 16. Does the land become a desolation and a thing that horrifies all who see it because of what the people are doing in it or because of the devastation of the Lord's judgment? The text is properly ambiguous at that point. Surely both things are true. But by v. 17, the word of judgment is plain: The forgotten Lord will disperse the people before their enemies, a declaration that can involve both defeat by their enemies and being carried into exile. The final piece of that judgment is the powerful image of the turning of God's back on the people. This is equivalent to the hiding of the face, which the prophets use regularly as an image for God's judgment. What many laments identify as an experience of abandonment—God's hidden face— is here declared to be a very intentional act. We may assume that the image conveys God's turning away from the cries for help in the time of disaster. That is almost as unbelievable as if the cold flowing streams ran dry. Still, the text has already revealed that something as impossible as that has already happened: "My people have forgotten me."

18:18-23. The "plans" the people of Judah carry out according to the stubbornness of their evil will (v. 12) are exemplified in the "planning" or plotting against Jeremiah's life, reported in v. 18. And while an original connection of the lament in vv. 19-23 is uncertain, the appropriateness of this lament after such a report is reinforced by the verbal association between the plotters' "not heeding" (v. 18c) Jeremiah's words and Jeremiah's pleading with the Lord to "heed" (v. 19a).

Such plotting against Jeremiah has already been reported in the first of his laments (11:21-23). It again represents the effort to stop the prophetic word (cf. Amos 7:10-17). The "they" of v. 18 are not identified—they may be the false prophets, as

126. William McKane, *A Critical and Exegetical Commentary on Jeremiah,* 2 vols., ICC (Edinburgh: T. & T. Clark, 1986, 1996) 1:433.

some have suggested, or they may be the people of Anathoth who plot against Jeremiah in 11:21. The text may refer to all those elements in Judahite society who resisted the hard word of the prophet. The stubbornness of the people is once more evident in their common decision not to pay attention to anything Jeremiah says. But their intention goes further than that. "They" say, "Let us attack him with our tongues." The tongue as a weapon of destruction is well known in the laments (e.g., Psalm 64). In some instances, it may be used to slander, but here the NRSV is surely correct in discerning a reference to bringing charges in a court. Jeremiah 26 tells of an occasion when charges were formally lodged against the prophet in an effort to have him executed. It is worth noting that those bringing charges on that occasion are two of the groups mentioned in 18:18: the priests and the prophets. The references to instruction (torah) from the priest, counsel from the wise, and the word from the prophet identify the authority figures in the community and the sources of their authority (see Ezek. 7:26). Whoever the "they" of v. 18 are, they are the supporters of the establishment, the maintainers of the status quo who are unwilling to let anything be heard that subverts their claims to the truth. In contrast, not only are Jeremiah's words less acceptable but they also threaten the control and power of these leaders in the community. There are clear issues of self-interest and power at work in this resistance to Jeremiah.

So the prophet cries out in a lament that once more combines stereotypical lament language with the situation of the prophet (vv. 19-23). No one else will heed Jeremiah's words, and so his life is at stake. In this situation, however, it only matters that one subject will give heed: the Lord (v. 19). What the adversaries say is to be understood as their plot against Jeremiah; and before his prayer is over the prophet makes specific reference to their plans (v. 23). The question at the beginning of v. 20 is a protestation of innocence, a feature common to lament prayers. In the rest of the verse, Jeremiah spells out the "good" he has done. He has interceded for the people, has spoken out on their behalf, seeking to turn away the divine wrath. Such intercession, as we have seen, belongs to the prophetic office, part of Jeremiah's task. But it is also a good deed on behalf of the people, one that is now being rewarded with evil, the plot against his life.

The earlier words about planning and plotting are picked up in the lament, albeit with different language and with different imagery. Jeremiah's enemies have dug a pit and set snares to trap him (vv. 20, 22). His prayer now assumes the kind of ambush envisioned in v. 18. So the prophet, in some of his strongest language, calls for the Lord to step in and stop his enemies. The curse against the enemies in vv. 21-22 is strong and comprehensive. It is a call for their complete destruction—men, women, and children. In v. 22, the prophet urges God to bring about just the kind of prayer that he is now praying—but it will do no good, for the one who listens is now the one who judges. Finally, he pleads with the Lord not to make the kind of move that Jeremiah in his intercessory role always seeks and that Jeremiah knows is what one expects from the Lord, who is "a God merciful and gracious, slow to anger, and abounding in steadfast love . . . forgiving iniquity and transgression and sin" (Exod 34:6-7). Here Jeremiah sounds very much like Jonah, except that Jeremiah at least prays against persons who are trying to kill him! But he knows the propensity of his God to act mercifully, even in the midst of all the words of judgment that have been uttered. The sound of God's weeping is there also, and Jeremiah knows that the Lord is highly vulnerable if "a cry be heard" (v. 22). The final line is revealing: Jeremiah asks the Lord to deal with his enemies "in the time of your anger." That anger does not last long. The Lord's "overflowing wrath" gives way again and again to mercy and "everlasting love" (Isa 54:6-8; see the Reflections at 17:1-27). If Jeremiah does not get the Lord's attention in the time of wrath and judgment, the moment may pass.

REFLECTIONS

1. The story of the potter and its elaborated interpretation is a medium for reflection upon divine sovereignty and freedom. The passage means to assert both realities. The Lord's control over the history of nations and peoples is not willy-nilly, not a determinism that is set from the beginning, not an inflexible plan. There is language that clearly means to claim that sovereignty. When the Lord says, "I declare," we hear the decree of the Lord, uttered from the divine assembly where the fate of the cosmos is regularly under review and enacted (cf. Jer 23:18-23). The reference to the Lord's "plan" takes us also into the sphere of divine intentionality, planning, and rule. But the sovereign plan and intention are open, and so the text asserts immediately the freedom of God to "change my mind" (18:8-10). The context in which these words are uttered indicates at the same time the freedom of the human creature and the responsiveness of God to the human situation. The sovereignty of God takes account of the human way. That is indicated both in the image of the potter remolding the clay and in the Lord's speaking about a change of mind dependent upon what is happening on earth. This text gives us a means for trying to speak about divine sovereignty and freedom, about human freedom and destiny.

2. God's repeated openness to "change my mind" raises the question about the context for such a change, for such flexibility on the part of God. Of course, we cannot say in any definitive way. But it is worth noting that in virtually all the instances of the Lord's change of mind, the change is not from the intention to do good to an intention to destroy but the reverse. God's change of mind seems regularly to work for the people and the human community. The change that is regularly reported is a decision *not* to bring judgment. So in the wilderness, God's change of mind stops a planned and merited punishment of the people who have disobeyed (Exod 32:12, 14). The prayer of a prophet brings about a change of mind on the part of the Lord and the stopping of an intended judgment (Amos 7:3, 6). The repentance of a foreign nation evokes a merciful change of mind on God's part and the decision not to destroy Nineveh (Jonah 3:10). Exodus 34:6 is right: "The LORD, the LORD, a God merciful and gracious, slow to anger, and abounding in steadfast love and faithfulness."

3. The image of the potter remolding the clay, when appropriated to speak about God's way with the house of Israel, is an important image for understanding the place of judgment in the divine plan. While the context would seem to confine the remolding to the time before judgment, other images of refining fire (Isa 1:21-26; cf. Jer 6:27-30), a plumb line (2 Kgs 21:13; cf. Isa 28:17), and a wiped dish (2 Kgs 21:13) suggest that the process of judgment may itself be the remolding of the spoiled clay. The pot will not work in its present shape, so the potter molds it back into a lump of clay and begins to work afresh with it. Just as the dirty dish will not work until it is clean, the out-of-plumb wall will not hold up the building until it is taken down and rebuilt, and the metal will not be of value until it is melted down and refined of its impurities, so also the pot will not be what it is meant to be or do what it is meant to do in the eyes of the potter until it has been returned to a lump of clay and molded afresh. This is at least one significant dimension of the judging work of God as we encounter it in Israel's story. God is reshaping a blemished clay vessel so that it is right in God's eyes.

4. Jeremiah's lament in this chapter is his strongest prayer against his enemies. It is a classic imprecatory prayer, uttering curses against his enemies and thereby calling for their total destruction. Such prayers are not easily appropriated—and ought not to be. That is not the way the Lord taught us to deal with our enemies. Jesus' words were about praying *for* our enemies, not *against* them (Matt 5:44). Negative reaction to Jeremiah's prayer is to be expected. Not everything in the Bible is true, good, and beautiful!

At the same time, the reader needs to be in Jeremiah's shoes, if for no other reason than that Jeremiah here prays not just his particular prayer. His prayer is a standard lament, a typical prayer for help such as one finds in the psalms. There is something universal and generally applicable in this prayer. Others have prayed this way and will pray this way again. The value of Jeremiah's prayer is, at least in part, that it provides a glimpse of what evokes such terrible curses. It is the experience of outrageous oppression, of persons literally plotting to kill him, of constant plotting to destroy him, of loneliness and isolation and the oppression of the powers that be and the family that supposedly cares. That kind of predicament evokes rage. It can hardly be suppressed.

The crucial thing is that the prayer is lifted up to God. The predicament is placed in God's hands. The prayer is serious at the point of wanting to stop—in the most complete way possible—the trouble that is happening. It goes further than that in its desire for revenge. But such revenge is given over to God. That does not make it easier for us to stomach. But it means that it is up to God to take this prayer and do what needs to be done. Such taking of the prayer will be an act of vindication, not only for Jeremiah but also for God. One of the realities of Scripture that often is lost is that God really does have enemies. In this case, the effort to stop the prophet's word is a fierce opposition to the Lord and what the Lord is doing. So the prayer against Jeremiah's enemies is also a prayer for the Lord to stop what God's own enemies are doing. That is not an easy job, but it is what the wrath of God is all about. The New Testament tells us that it may take God's own suffering to bring it about. The cross is a strange kind of wrath.

JEREMIAH 19:1–20:6, A MESSAGE IN A JUG

NIV

19 This is what the LORD says: "Go and buy a clay jar from a potter. Take along some of the elders of the people and of the priests ²and go out to the Valley of Ben Hinnom, near the entrance of the Potsherd Gate. There proclaim the words I tell you, ³and say, 'Hear the word of the LORD, O kings of Judah and people of Jerusalem. This is what the LORD Almighty, the God of Israel, says: Listen! I am going to bring a disaster on this place that will make the ears of everyone who hears of it tingle. ⁴For they have forsaken me and made this a place of foreign gods; they have burned sacrifices in it to gods that neither they nor their fathers nor the kings of Judah ever knew, and they have filled this place with the blood of the innocent. ⁵They have built the high places of Baal to burn their sons in the fire as offerings to Baal—something I did not command or mention, nor did it enter my mind. ⁶So beware, the days are coming, declares the LORD, when people will no longer call this place Topheth or the Valley of Ben Hinnom, but the Valley of Slaughter.

⁷" 'In this place I will ruin*a* the plans of Judah and Jerusalem. I will make them fall by the sword before their enemies, at the hands of those who seek their lives, and I will give their carcasses as food to the birds of the air and the beasts of the earth. ⁸I will devastate this city and make it an object of scorn; all who pass by will be appalled and will scoff because of all its wounds. ⁹I will make them eat the flesh of their sons and daughters, and they will eat one another's flesh during the stress of the siege imposed on them by the enemies who seek their lives.'

¹⁰"Then break the jar while those who go with you are watching, ¹¹and say to them, 'This is what the LORD Almighty says: I will smash this nation and this city just as this potter's jar is smashed and cannot be repaired. They will bury the dead in Topheth until there is no more room. ¹²This is what I will do to this place and to those who live here, declares the LORD. I will make this city like Topheth. ¹³The houses in Jerusalem and those of

---

*a7 The Hebrew for *ruin* sounds like the Hebrew for *jar* (see verses 1 and 10).*

NRSV

19 Thus said the LORD: Go and buy a potter's earthenware jug. Take with you*a* some of the elders of the people and some of the senior priests, ²and go out to the valley of the son of Hinnom at the entry of the Potsherd Gate, and proclaim there the words that I tell you. ³You shall say: Hear the word of the LORD, O kings of Judah and inhabitants of Jerusalem. Thus says the LORD of hosts, the God of Israel: I am going to bring such disaster upon this place that the ears of everyone who hears of it will tingle. ⁴Because the people have forsaken me, and have profaned this place by making offerings in it to other gods whom neither they nor their ancestors nor the kings of Judah have known, and because they have filled this place with the blood of the innocent, ⁵and gone on building the high places of Baal to burn their children in the fire as burnt offerings to Baal, which I did not command or decree, nor did it enter my mind. ⁶Therefore the days are surely coming, says the LORD, when this place shall no more be called Topheth, or the valley of the son of Hinnom, but the valley of Slaughter. ⁷And in this place I will make void the plans of Judah and Jerusalem, and will make them fall by the sword before their enemies, and by the hand of those who seek their life. I will give their dead bodies for food to the birds of the air and to the wild animals of the earth. ⁸And I will make this city a horror, a thing to be hissed at; everyone who passes by it will be horrified and will hiss because of all its disasters. ⁹And I will make them eat the flesh of their sons and the flesh of their daughters, and all shall eat the flesh of their neighbors in the siege, and in the distress with which their enemies and those who seek their life afflict them.

10Then you shall break the jug in the sight of those who go with you, ¹¹and shall say to them: Thus says the LORD of hosts: So will I break this people and this city, as one breaks a potter's vessel, so that it can never be mended. In Topheth they shall bury until there is no more room to

---

*aSyr Tg Compare Gk: Heb lacks *take with you**

NIV

the kings of Judah will be defiled like this place, Topheth—all the houses where they burned incense on the roofs to all the starry hosts and poured out drink offerings to other gods.' "

¹⁴Jeremiah then returned from Topheth, where the LORD had sent him to prophesy, and stood in the court of the LORD's temple and said to all the people, ¹⁵"This is what the LORD Almighty, the God of Israel, says: 'Listen! I am going to bring on this city and the villages around it every disaster I pronounced against them, because they were stiff-necked and would not listen to my words.' "

20 When the priest Pashhur son of Immer, the chief officer in the temple of the LORD, heard Jeremiah prophesying these things, ²he had Jeremiah the prophet beaten and put in the stocks at the Upper Gate of Benjamin at the LORD's temple. ³The next day, when Pashhur released him from the stocks, Jeremiah said to him, "The LORD's name for you is not Pashhur, but Magor-Missabib.ᵃ ⁴For this is what the LORD says: 'I will make you a terror to yourself and to all your friends; with your own eyes you will see them fall by the sword of their enemies. I will hand all Judah over to the king of Babylon, who will carry them away to Babylon or put them to the sword. ⁵I will hand over to their enemies all the wealth of this city—all its products, all its valuables and all the treasures of the kings of Judah. They will take it away as plunder and carry it off to Babylon. ⁶And you, Pashhur, and all who live in your house will go into exile to Babylon. There you will die and be buried, you and all your friends to whom you have prophesied lies.' "

ᵃ3 *Magor-Missabib* means *terror on every side.*

NRSV

bury. ¹²Thus will I do to this place, says the LORD, and to its inhabitants, making this city like Topheth. ¹³And the houses of Jerusalem and the houses of the kings of Judah shall be defiled like the place of Topheth—all the houses upon whose roofs offerings have been made to the whole host of heaven, and libations have been poured out to other gods.

14When Jeremiah came from Topheth, where the LORD had sent him to prophesy, he stood in the court of the LORD's house and said to all the people: ¹⁵Thus says the LORD of hosts, the God of Israel: I am now bringing upon this city and upon all its towns all the disaster that I have pronounced against it, because they have stiffened their necks, refusing to hear my words.

20 Now the priest Pashhur son of Immer, who was chief officer in the house of the LORD, heard Jeremiah prophesying these things. ²Then Pashhur struck the prophet Jeremiah, and put him in the stocks that were in the upper Benjamin Gate of the house of the LORD. ³The next morning when Pashhur released Jeremiah from the stocks, Jeremiah said to him, The LORD has named you not Pashhur but "Terror-all-around." ⁴For thus says the LORD: I am making you a terror to yourself and to all your friends; and they shall fall by the sword of their enemies while you look on. And I will give all Judah into the hand of the king of Babylon; he shall carry them captive to Babylon, and shall kill them with the sword. ⁵I will give all the wealth of this city, all its gains, all its prized belongings, and all the treasures of the kings of Judah into the hand of their enemies, who shall plunder them, and seize them, and carry them to Babylon. ⁶And you, Pashhur, and all who live in your house, shall go into captivity, and to Babylon you shall go; there you shall die, and there you shall be buried, you and all your friends, to whom you have prophesied falsely.

COMMENTARY

Like the preceding chapter, chap. 19 opens with a parable centering around the work of a potter as the vehicle for symbolic action. The prophet is commanded to act out a judgment speech against the people of Judah and Jerusalem. The indictment is directed toward the idolatrous practices of the people, more specifically the child sacrifices at the Topheth. The similarity of subject matter and, even more, of specific linguistic expressions to 7:30-34, has evoked the plausible suggestion that just as chap. 26 is the narrative version of the sermon in 7:1-15, so also 18:1-13 is the narrative version of 7:30-34.[127]

Joined to the symbolic action and its interpretation in 19:1-13 is a brief report of a prophetic declaration by the prophet "when Jeremiah came from Topheth" (19:14-15). That brief sermon took place at the Temple, "where the LORD had sent him to prophesy." The temporal clause ties these two verses to the preceding account of the symbolic action, which took place at the Topheth. Setting them at the place where the Lord had sent Jeremiah "to prophesy" ties these verses to 20:1-6, which is an account of the imprisonment of Jeremiah because of his "prophesying" these things. In the present context, therefore, the imprisonment of Jeremiah is evoked by the prophetic proclamation of chap. 18. If the comparison with chap. 26 is valid, then one notes that the preaching of 7:1-15 also led to Jeremiah's arrest. In both cases there is a prophetic proclamation by Jeremiah, then his arrest, and then another statement after his arrest.[128]

19:1-13. The work of a potter, which was the focus of the parable in 18:1-12, is the vehicle again for the Lord's Word through a symbolic action on the part of Jeremiah. This time, however, Jeremiah is not an observer but the actor. The action builds in two stages, each followed by an announcement of judgment by the Lord.

The first stage is the Lord's command for Jeremiah to take a clay jug or flask and go, along with some of the elders and priests, out to the Potsherd Gate at the valley of Ben-Hinnom (vv. 1-2).

This valley may be the Tyropean Valley, which runs south of the Temple Mount, but the gate is unknown. Presumably it was a place where broken pots were discarded, a kind of city dump. Once there, Jeremiah proclaims a long judgment speech before his conscripted audience. The indictment (vv. 4-5) is comprehensive and familiar. It lists both the sin of apostasy, manifested particularly in child sacrifice, and the violent oppression of the poor ("the blood of the innocent," v. 4; cf. 2:34). With regard to the former sin, the Lord's expression, "which I did not command or decree, nor did it enter my mind" (v. 5), suggests that such sacrifices were genuinely syncretistic in that they were being made not only to Baal but also to the Lord. There is no way that such practices could be associated legitimately with the Lord of Israel. Verse 5 heaps up expressions to make that point. The Lord says, in effect, "I did not command or say this in any way; I did not even think such an idea. There is no way you can associate such activities with my worship."

And so the announcement of judgment comes (vv. 6-10). Among the noticeable features of this announcement are the many first-person verbs and the horror of the destruction. The first-person verbs underscore the divine agency in what is to happen. Anyone who comes upon the scene of destruction may think that all he or she is seeing is a terrible military defeat and its violent consequences. The horrific picture emphasizes the terrible fate that awaits a disobedient people. The rhetoric typical of treaty curses and other forms of malediction creates an effect of horror. The picture is one of siege that is so terrible that bodies cannot even be buried. Those who remain are forced to eat the flesh of their own children and their neighbors. One should not miss the irony inherent in the fate of the children. Those not consumed as offerings will be consumed by their parents. The picture is horrifying—intentionally so (vv. 3b, 8).

A particular linguistic connection is made between the symbol of the clay jug and the announcement of judgment. The divine announcement that "I will make void" (v. 7; NIV, "I will ruin") uses the verb בקק (*bāqaq*) and thus plays on the word for "clay flask," בקבק (*baqbuq*), a noun

127. William L. Holladay, *Jeremiah 1: A Commentary on the Book of the Prophet Jeremiah Chapters 1–25,* Hermeneia (Philadelphia: Fortress, 1986) 536-37.
128. Ibid., 537.

from the same verbal root. Prophetic speech is rich in its communicative power, often using wordplay with other forms of communication to vivify and impress. The audience sees and hears at the same time. Before the final stage of this symbolic action, the point of the clay jug has been scored.

The second stage comes in vv. 10-13 when the symbolic action is completed and an interpretation of it is given, again in the form of an announcement of judgment. The prophet is told to break the jug he is carrying. The symbolism is obvious but is spelled out anyway. The action reflects a divine decree that the people shall also be broken. There is something quite final about this act, in contrast to the potter in chap. 18. There, the point rests very much on the possibility of remolding unfired clay. Here the vessel is "finished," in more ways than one. The point is made explicit: It cannot be mended. This pot has had it. There may be other vessels for the Lord's use in the future, but not this one. The judgment speech then goes on to reiterate the reasons for such drastic and final actions: They are the same as the ones in the first part of this chapter, though in this stage of the sermon only apostasy, manifest in the terrible rites of the Topheth and in the worship of foreign gods and astral deities, is mentioned (v. 13). There is also a note of poetic justice in the judgment. The ones who sinned at the Topheth will find their city becoming a Topheth—defiled and a place of slaughter.

19:14-15. A brief sermon provides the transition from the symbolic action with the jug to the jailing of Jeremiah (20:1-6). The text reports that Jeremiah went from the Topheth and gave a brief judgment speech at the court of the Temple, saying that what the Lord has just laid out in much detail the Lord will do. The rationale for judgment this time is not the specifics of apostasy but the stubbornness of the people (cf. 18:12), their adamant refusal to pay attention to the words of warning, to receive any correction, to turn from their walk down the path to destruction.

20:1-6. A priest, Pashhur, who apparently had major administrative responsibilities at the Temple (but not the Pashhur of 21:1), heard "Jeremiah prophesying these things." Such rocking of the political-religious boat, as Jeremiah's words "in the court of the Lord's house" (19:14) manifest, must not be allowed to go on. And so the priest strikes the prophet and puts him in some kind of restraining device, apparently like the form of punishment known as the stocks. The passage then announces judgment on Pashhur and his associates in the context of the death and exile of all Judah. The subtext of the passage is the encounter between prophet and priest, between proclaimer of the divine word of judgment and one resisting that authority.

The physical abuse of the prophet, manifested in beating and restraint, does not accomplish its goal. Rather than silencing the prophet, it brings down judgment upon the priest who ordered it. The reversal of the situation is marked. We would expect that when Pashhur brought Jeremiah from detention to appear before him, the priest would give him some threat, an ultimatum. In fact, the voice of Pashhur is never heard again. Rather, Jeremiah speaks and is in obvious command of the situation even though he is under restraint.

Whereas the prophet was commanded to perform a symbolic action as a message of judgment in chap. 19, in these verses a name change conveys judgment. The message is explicit in the name the Lord gives to Pashhur: "Terror on every side." The operative word, as v. 4 indicates, is "terror." The "on every side," which does not alter the meaning of the name but only intensifies it, may be a later addition from 20:10. Missing from the Greek translation, the phrase appears a number of times in the book (6:25; 20:10; 46:5; 49:29; cf. Ps 31:14; Lam 2:22). The resistance of the priest to Jeremiah's proclamation of the word means that he and those associated with him will find themselves beset by terror. It is not Jeremiah or other opponents of Pashhur who will find him a terror but those who are his friends (vv. 4, 6) and his family (v. 6); his resistance to the prophetic word will bring judgment upon them all. Reference to family and friends may imply their complicity, or it may simply mean that the judgment Pashhur brings will include those about whom he cares. The final words of this section suggest that the friends are "victims" of his lying prophecy, but they may have been very happy to receive it. The extension of judgment to incorporate all Judah places the punishment of the priest within the context of the devastation, exile, and looting by the Babylonian army. That point is made explicit in v. 5 when the judgment pronounced on Pashhur includes joining the exiles in captivity, death, and burial in a foreign and unclean land (cf. Amos 7:17).

There is no question about who the foe is in this text. It is written in full awareness and anticipation of the attack by the Babylonians. This is the first time that Babylon is mentioned in the book of Jeremiah. From now on, the reader will encounter that name constantly. The shadowy "foe from the north" has been coming into clearer profile throughout the book. Hardly anything that happens henceforth in the book occurs without reference to Babylon.

REFLECTIONS

1. The terrible picture of massive destruction in this passage raises two theological issues. One is the depiction of God as wreaking punishment upon the Lord's people. There is no easy way around that depiction. It is not a sideline in the story. It dominates the prophecy of Jeremiah. While it is very important that the decision of the Lord to punish the people in strong fashion be set in the context of the loving and merciful character of God and that the announcements of judgment be set alongside the evidence of God's weeping over the fate of the people (see Reflections at 9:2-26), the reader cannot whitewash it. The God who speaks and is spoken about is not an easygoing, undemanding God. The "fire and brimstone" preachers of the past at least did not belittle God or minimize the seriousness of human choices and God's response. A proper caution in contemporary preaching about the nature of God's judgment upon us for our sins and a viewing of all judgment in the light of the reality of the cross is appropriate. But the God of Jesus Christ will not be mocked, and judgment is a central dimension of what takes place in the death of Christ. While it is mistaken to see in the biblical portrait the Janus-faced God who is always looking in two directions at the same time, always wrathful and always loving, it is equally mistaken to assume that this irascible, demanding, awesome, holy God whom we worship never looks in anger upon our actions or that any community of God's people might not be subject to terrible experiences of judgment.

2. The second theological problem is the way in which the judgment seems to carry all with it, innocent as well as guilty. With regard to that corporate and wholesale judgment, several things need to be said. First, the innocent oppressed may not see their fate as being so terrible as the outsider sees it. If one is being done in by the system, the reaction is often, "Let the system be done in!" When James Baldwin spoke about "the fire next time," he did not presume that oppressed African Americans could avoid the fire.[129] They already knew about it. He saw white America facing the fire also. If the fires are already in the inner cities, those consumed by them may not be as worried about a collective punishment that consumes everyone. Further, the notion of collective punishment, which runs against the grain of our notion of each person's suffering for his or her own sins (itself a biblical notion; see Ezekiel 18) incorporates an understanding of the community as a whole being responsible for the many and various sins of its peoples. No one really stands outside the system when systemic crimes and oppressions are operative. There are few, if any, citizens of the United States who do not participate in the "crimes" of this country against other nations in despoiling them of their resources and in acquiring goods made by their poorly rewarded laborers. There are few, if any, persons in this country who do not participate in the destructive racism that is woven into our history. Some of us are more resistant. Most of us acquiesce or are complicit in the national sins that cannot be denied. Our will to have and to acquire, a propensity that seems to be universal, is carried out in ways that inevitably leave "innocent blood in the streets." Some are more blatant than others in manifesting a commitment to what does not profit in pursuit of profit. Some are more responsible than others for the terrible oppression of the disadvantaged. But few of us can except ourselves from the fear of "the fire next time."

129. James Baldwin, *The Fire Next Time* (New York: Dial, 1963).

3. The encounter between the prophet Jeremiah and the priest Pashhur has been compared to that between the prophet Amos and the priest Amaziah, recorded in Amos 7:10-17. Each meeting has enough features in common that, whether or not we would argue for a specific genre of prophetic/priestly conflict, the reader recognizes a common pattern. When prophetic, critical, and challenging figures confront the community of faith with strong denunciations of its behavior, authority figures react. The establishment cannot allow the rocking of the boat, so it seeks to stop or thwart the critique. Pashhur, priest at the Lord's house, like Amaziah, chief priest of the northern sanctuary of Bethel, was not a bad guy. He was responsible for the proper carrying out of religious activities in the worship of the Lord of Israel. But by the time this passage is over, he, again like Amaziah, is under condemnation and judgment of that same Lord he ostensibly served. In both passages, the divine representative, the minister of the national church, has failed properly to serve the one whose service is his vocation. He is so tied to the maintenance, security, and proper care of the religious operation that he cannot hear the Lord's declaration that it is a whitewashed sepulchre. Presumably committed to utter loyalty to the Lord, both priests are committed to the maintenance of the status quo in the religious establishment. And that is their damnation.

The passage thus impels reflection on the continuing resistance of the church to the prophetic critique and the possibility that its ministers may be the perservers of the status quo, but not attenders to the prophetic word. That word calls us to a commitment to the Lord, who made us, and to a kind of life in community that cannot ignore the blood on the skirts, the lies that suggest those in power can maintain their political, economic, and religious dominance when the innocent, the poor, and the weak are downtrodden by oppressive acts and systemic neglect. Martin Luther King, Jr., remains an enduring example of the prophet who comes with the proclamation of the Lord and turns things upside down, reversing the power structures so that the ones who would humiliate and put him in the stocks become those who eventually are caught up in his truthful word. The religious establishment is no longer in charge when God's powerful word sweeps in and sets truth against falsehood.

4. But when truth is set against falsehood, someone has to discern the truth. The book of Jeremiah is a vivid indication of the difficulty of doing that, of deciding which prophetic word is the truthful one. This passage suggests that the decision is fraught with great consequence, life and death no less. But the problem may not be as difficult as we sometimes make it. The difficulty may be in our reluctance to hear a critical word from Scripture, to give up the comfortable circumstances of our life. Stopping the ears and eyes to the evident sounds and sights of a situation that we know well is not God's will and God's way. The problem of deciding between one prophetic voice and another is often the problem of an inclination to go with what we wish to hear because it is not offensive or disturbing. The comforting and comfortable word, uttered in comfortable circumstances, is not the biblical tendency. When that is what is being defended, then we may know that it is a lie, but we prefer to be "friends" with that sort of "prophesying" rather than with one that challenges all we are doing to the very core.

JEREMIAH 20:7-18, A PROPHET DECEIVED AND DESPAIRING

<table>
<tr><td>

NIV

⁷O LORD, you deceived[a] me, and I was
  deceived[a];
  you overpowered me and prevailed.
I am ridiculed all day long;
  everyone mocks me.
⁸Whenever I speak, I cry out
  proclaiming violence and destruction.
So the word of the LORD has brought me
  insult and reproach all day long.
⁹But if I say, "I will not mention him
  or speak any more in his name,"
his word is in my heart like a fire,
  a fire shut up in my bones.
I am weary of holding it in;
  indeed, I cannot.
¹⁰I hear many whispering,
  "Terror on every side!
  Report him! Let's report him!"
All my friends
  are waiting for me to slip, saying,
"Perhaps he will be deceived;
  then we will prevail over him
  and take our revenge on him."

¹¹But the LORD is with me like a mighty warrior;
  so my persecutors will stumble and not
    prevail.
They will fail and be thoroughly disgraced;
  their dishonor will never be forgotten.
¹²O LORD Almighty, you who examine the
    righteous
  and probe the heart and mind,
let me see your vengeance upon them,
  for to you I have committed my cause.

¹³Sing to the LORD!
  Give praise to the LORD!
He rescues the life of the needy
  from the hands of the wicked.

¹⁴Cursed be the day I was born!
  May the day my mother bore me not be
    blessed!

[a]7 Or persuaded

</td><td>

NRSV

⁷O LORD, you have enticed me,
  and I was enticed;
you have overpowered me,
  and you have prevailed.
I have become a laughingstock all day long;
  everyone mocks me.
⁸For whenever I speak, I must cry out,
  I must shout, "Violence and destruction!"
For the word of the LORD has become for me
  a reproach and derision all day long.
⁹If I say, "I will not mention him,
  or speak any more in his name,"
then within me there is something like a
    burning fire
  shut up in my bones;
I am weary with holding it in,
  and I cannot.
¹⁰For I hear many whispering:
  "Terror is all around!
  Denounce him! Let us denounce him!"
All my close friends
  are watching for me to stumble.
"Perhaps he can be enticed,
  and we can prevail against him,
  and take our revenge on him."
¹¹But the LORD is with me like a dread warrior;
  therefore my persecutors will stumble,
  and they will not prevail.
They will be greatly shamed,
  for they will not succeed.
Their eternal dishonor
  will never be forgotten.
¹²O LORD of hosts, you test the righteous,
  you see the heart and the mind;
let me see your retribution upon them,
  for to you I have committed my cause.

¹³Sing to the LORD;
  praise the LORD!
For he has delivered the life of the needy
  from the hands of evildoers.

¹⁴Cursed be the day

</td></tr>
</table>

NIV

¹⁵Cursed be the man who brought my father
    the news,
  who made him very glad, saying,
    "A child is born to you—a son!"
¹⁶May that man be like the towns
  the Lord overthrew without pity.
  May he hear wailing in the morning,
    a battle cry at noon.
¹⁷For he did not kill me in the womb,
  with my mother as my grave,
  her womb enlarged forever.
¹⁸Why did I ever come out of the womb
  to see trouble and sorrow
  and to end my days in shame?

NRSV

  on which I was born!
  The day when my mother bore me,
    let it not be blessed!
¹⁵Cursed be the man
  who brought the news to my father, saying,
  "A child is born to you, a son,"
    making him very glad.
¹⁶Let that man be like the cities
  that the Lord overthrew without pity;
  let him hear a cry in the morning
    and an alarm at noon,
¹⁷because he did not kill me in the womb;
  so my mother would have been my grave,
    and her womb forever great.
¹⁸Why did I come forth from the womb
  to see toil and sorrow,
  and spend my days in shame?

COMMENTARY

The last of Jeremiah's laments brings the section 11:1–20:18 to a close. It is the climax of the long walk of despair that is reflected in the prophet's laments.

20:7-13. The text occurs in the classic lament form: the prayer for help that begins in address to God (v. 7) and moves to convey the lament of the one praying, articulating that lament in the three-fold form of complaint against God (v. 7*a*), the pain and dissolution of the self (vv. 7*b*-9), and the lament against the "other," the enemy (v. 10). The expression of confidence (v. 11) then leads into the petition, the cry for help (v. 12). However, at the end there is something different: a song of praise.

The longest single part of this prayer is the lament proper (vv. 7-10), in which the prophet registers his predicament and what it is doing to him. It opens (v. 7) and closes (v. 10*b*) with two words that form an envelope or inclusio around the whole: "entice" or "deceit" (פתה *pātâ*) and "prevail" (יכל *yākōl*). The latter word is then repeated twice more within the lament proper (vv. 9, 11). This repetition identifies the two fundamental issues of the lament: the experience of deceit and the question of who will prevail. The first of these words, *pātâ*, has provoked consider-able discussion. Its range of meaning and nuance is well conveyed by the two translations: "entice" (NRSV) and "deceive" (NIV). The former meaning is clearly indicated for some uses of the verb, as, for example, in Delilah's enticement of Samson (Judg 14:15) or Prov 1:10, which refers to the danger of sinners "enticing" the young person to do wrong. Elsewhere, the verb clearly involves lying and deception (e.g., Prov 24:28). In two other instances, this verb is used in relation to the Lord's deceiving a prophet (1 Kgs 22:20-22; Ezek 14:9). The notion of deception is clearly at the heart of the complaint in these verses. At the same time, the choice of this particular word suggests also the nuance of being enticed into something; in this case the prophet is enticed by God into the prophetic vocation (v. 7) and by his enemies into some act that will get Jeremiah into trouble (v. 10).

Yet, if the primary force of the verb is "deceit," then what is the deception? We are not told explicitly, but a couple of possibilities may be inferred from the context. One is to be found in the other thematic word, "prevail" (*yākōl*). The final word of the Lord to Jeremiah at his call was the assurance that although the leaders and people would fight against him, they would not prevail.

However, Jeremiah has not experienced life that way. His lament in these verses closes with the report that his enemies are plotting to entice or deceive him so that they may prevail over him. This accusation of divine deceit may also address "Yahweh's slowness in executing the threatened judgment that exposed the prophet to peril and made him feel that God had deliberately deceived him."[130]

The complaint becomes even sharper as the prophet indicates that he has suffered not only the plots of his enemies but also the Lord's own power over him. He has been sucked in (or suckered in!) to this prophetic enterprise, and it is ultimately undoing him. Whether he can withstand the efforts of his enemies to prevail over him is uncertain, but the Lord has *already* done him in. That is evident in the reactions of those around him. His preaching has made him an object of ridicule, a laughingstock that nobody takes seriously (vv. 7*b*, 8*b*), even though we know that some thought he was dangerous (v. 10). But the reader must assume that he was taunted, particularly because some thought nothing of his judgment prophecy was happening. The language of vv. 7*b* and 8*b* is also found in a community lament in Ps 79:4, and the taunt (NRSV, "reproach"; NIV, "insult") is essentially the same as the one directed toward the community in Ps 79:10: "Where is your God?" This is regularly the character of the taunt of enemies (cf. Ps 42:3, 10[4, 11]; Joel 2:17). In Jeremiah's case, such taunting and derision could mean either that he is not sustained or that the word he proclaims is not sustained.

The cause of all this derision and mockery is identified in v. 8, though the verse is filled with ambiguity. Does it refer to the cry of Jeremiah as a victim in pain, which is often, if not regularly, the context in which the verb זעק (*zāʿaq*), "cry out," occurs? If so, then the outcry of "violence and destruction" may reflect his experience of violence and oppression, and the taunt is about his God's inability to sustain him. Another possibility is that the speaking out to which Jeremiah refers is his proclamation of the divine word. Certainly the other verbs, דבר (*dibber*, "speak") and קרא (*qārāʾ*, "shout" or "proclaim"), are both terms for

prophetic proclamation. Furthermore, the expression "violence and destruction" is part of the prophet's cry about the condition in Judah (6:7; cf. Hab 1:2). Both of these interpretations of v. 8 are possible. The fact that v. 9 is a response or reaction to what is described in v. 8 suggests that the prophet wants to stop his prophetic preaching, thus pointing us toward the second option.

The prophet decides to take things into his own hands and do the only practical thing: stop doing what brings the derision—that is, speaking in the name of the Lord (v. 9*a*). But there is a problem; he cannot stop being a prophet (v. 9*b*). To speak the prophetic word makes him the laughingstock of others, but to stop speaking the prophetic word is an impossibility, since the prophetic word is a burning fire that he cannot quench. The verse emphasizes the strong sense of the prophetic burden, an inner compulsion that will not allow him to give up the enterprise. When the prophet says, "I am weary of holding it in," he is speaking of the word burning within him. That word (6:11) involves "the wrath of the LORD," the word of judgment against this people that he is trying to hold in but cannot. The Lord prevails against him again through the word working in him. The word Jeremiah uses when he says "I cannot" is the thematic verb יכל (*yākōl*). Everybody here "prevails," "is able," except Jeremiah. This word first occurs in Jeremiah's call with the assurance that those against him would *not* prevail. But now they do. Even the Lord is overpowering Jeremiah, and he is unable to stand up against anybody.

The lament about enemies is uttered in v. 10, which reflects Jeremiah's overhearing of what they are saying about him. The language is in many ways typical of laments elsewhere, but at the same time the rhetoric is fully meaningful in Jeremiah's own story. Here one finds the specific link between this prayer and the preceding story of Jeremiah's persecution at the hands of Pashhur. "Terror" is the name that the Lord gives to Pashhur, and now it is what Jeremiah's foes are whispering. Verse 3 indicates that these words are to be understood as an oracle about the coming siege. But the verb in that sentence is regularly related to declaring, telling, and proclaiming. It may be, therefore, that the enemies are saying, "Let us proclaim for him, 'Terror all around.' " That is, they are mocking his prophetic message.

130. J. J. M. Roberts, "Does God Lie? Divine Deceit as a Theological Problem in Israelite Prophetic Literature," *Jerusalem Congress Volume*, SVT 40 (Leiden: E. J. Brill, 1988) 211-20.

So their hope that he will be deceived or enticed would have in mind the Lord's deception to which the prophet has already referred. The enemies may be saying, "Perhaps his message will prove false or the Lord will not protect him, and then we will have him." The "close friend" (אנוש שלומי *'ĕnôš šĕlômî*; lit., "one of my peace") occurs in a similar fashion in the lament of Ps 41:9[10] referring to a close friend who spreads malicious words.

It may seem strange to hear Jeremiah utter the words of v. 11 after the opening of this prayer, but his words here are a typical part of the prayer for help: an expression of confidence. No matter how strong the complaint against God, these are prayers of a person whose life is rooted in commitment to that God. Confidence in God is the ground on which complaint is possible. The expression of confidence anticipates the word of deliverance, the salvation oracle that the prayer for help seeks. Central to the divine word of promise is the assurance of God's presence with the one in trouble (cf. Isa 41:10). Here Jeremiah's prayer harks back to the oracle of salvation that was given at the time of his call: "They will fight against you; but they shall not prevail against you, for I am with you, says the Lord, to deliver you" (1:19; cf. 15:20). In this expression of confidence we hear the final occurrence of the word "prevail." Its movement through the prayer reflects the movement of the prayer. From the complaint against the Lord who prevails over him (v. 7), Jeremiah expresses his own frustration at not being able to prevail over the word that burns in him (v. 9*b*) and his fear that his enemies will prevail over him (v.

10), now to assert, finally, his confidence that the Lord will prevail over Jeremiah's enemies and deliver him (v. 11).

That confidence is undergirded with an implicit declaration of his innocence and righteousness, sufficient grounds for a righteous God to step into the situation and support the one who trusts in the Lord, to vindicate the righteous one who has faithfully performed his duties. The final word of the prayer is a petition for such justice to be worked out in overthrowing Jeremiah's enemies (v. 12).

Verse 13 may seem out of place, but it is appropriate to the formal structure of a lament. The prayer for help, uttered in deep despair about the human situation, but in powerful confidence in God, turns from lament to praise. Both the expression of confidence in v. 11 and the song of praise in v. 13 assume that Jeremiah receives a divine word of assurance, a saving word. The typical hymnic form—a call to praise and a reason for the praise—is once again the vehicle for the petitioner's joy at God's response.

20:14-18. The hymn of praise does not mean the end, however. Jeremiah's lowest point may lie in these verses, the last of his recorded laments. If the hymn of v. 13 comes as a surprise, the verses that follow are even more so. In the silence between the verses, the prophet is plunged into the lowest depths. A curse against himself (vv. 14-17), framed in the form of an imprecation against the day he was born and the one who brought the "good news" of his birth, is joined with a lament that ends this journey of despair in the question, "Why was I even born?"

REFLECTIONS

1. The mix of stereotypical lament language and particular Jeremianic experience is evident throughout the laments and certainly in this particular case. It is a clue to the way the laments of the Old Testament are universal prayers for help that are available in varying situations. The interpretation of the laments of Jeremiah in relation to the larger narrative and story of his life should not overlook the fact that these prayers have the capacity to become the prayers of other persons and later generations. While no prayer in Scripture is simply laid as a grid over contemporary experience, all the psalmic prayers (and this is one of them) have served as a vehicle for expressing the rage and despair and sense of need of persons throughout the ages. This particular one is offered as a prayer for those many prophetic figures in the history of the church who have been persecuted for their pursuit of God's word and their faithfulness to their calling. The sense of being overwhelmed by God's demand and done in by the slander and attacks of others is an experience that is widely a part of faithful attendance to one's vocation of ministry in difficult times.

Something even more basic comes to the surface in the second part of this lament section (20:14-18). There Jeremiah becomes a truly Joban figure, one beset by such terribly oppressive events and trials that existence itself is an unbearable burden. Here are words for those who have plunged to such depths that they would rather not go on. Suicide is never an option in Scripture. But persons then as much as now could be in circumstances that led them to such despair. The lament that we have here is the path that is offered for such persons as an alternative to suicide. Relentlessly expressive of the terror that makes non-existence and non-living a better alternative and presenting no easy response, such praying is from the pit without any confidence that one will ever get out. One of the reasons for learning the Scriptures is to have available such prayers when the pain is so great and a voice is needed to express it. It is difficult to recommend such a prayer. It is important that it be available for the grasping when there is nothing else to hold on to.

The rhetoric of the second prayer is an important indicator of the hyperbole of the imprecatory prayers. It is as much a curse prayer as any of the harshest imprecations of the psalms (e.g., Pss 137:7-9; 139:19-22). The hyperbole and rhetoric that such terrible despair evokes are a venting of rage beyond rational discourse. One needs to be careful about overweighting or literalizing the rhetoric. In this case, it is directed toward an individual who is not an enemy, whose identity is essentially unknown, whose act is one of utter innocence. Yet the situation of the petitioner is so terrible that he can utter terrible curses against the person who, probably in great joy, spread the news of his birth. Rage and despair move to a level of unutterable passions and misdirected anger. In this instance, the prayer cannot be taken seriously in a literal sense but only in regard to the authenticity of its despair, which lashes out in rage, even against the innocent. That being the case, we do well not to treat other curse prayers any more literally than this one. The petitions are really felt, but they may not always be acted upon. The language of curse is identified, in this prayer especially, as the expression of despair and rage more than the language of petition.

A further implication, growing out of the first, is that rational analysis is insufficient for interpreting such imprecations. Simply to read and analyze and judge such language with the dispassion of critical analysis is like saying, "Don't cry," to someone whose spouse and child have been killed in a car wreck. Such a response does not match the situation. There is a sense in which only someone in a similar situation can judge the appropriateness of such vented rage. This is self-denigration in the face of overwhelming circumstances. Judgment of how appropriate such a prayer is, theologically and spiritually, is not a simple matter of dispassionate analysis.

Even in the prayer against the "real" enemies, as in 20:12, the force of the prayer needs to be kept in mind. This is a prayer for "your retribution"—that is, for *God's* vindication of Jeremiah against his enemies. The particular situation of the praying person is placed in the larger context of the vindication of God's purposes and God's way. Not only are the personal experience and the personal rage given over to God in prayer, but also the deliverance is placed in the context of the accomplishment of God's will, the working out of God's purpose in this situation. "Retribution" is what the petitioner seeks personally; so that is an appropriate interpretation. But the word refers to *God's* vindication in the event. Something very important happens in that regard: The desire for the opponents to be undone is really there in the petition, but it is subsumed under God's purpose in the confidence that this is not simply a matter of personal vengeance but of the accomplishment of what God is about in the world. That is why the response to the hostility of one's enemies needs to stay at the level of prayer for God's justice and not move to action that seeks personal justice in anger and rage.

2. Two aspects of Jeremiah's prayers in this chapter seem rather jarring in their context. One is the bold expression of confidence in God of 20:11 that seems so startling in the face of the complaint of 20:7 and the general tenor of Jeremiah's laments. That jarring juxtaposition, however, is significant for the character and context of prayer. It reflects a fundamental tension that may run against our tendency to seek logical connections but is a part of the dialogue of faith that prayer becomes. It is the one who trusts in God who complains to God. The complaints and accusations, no matter how extreme, arise out of a fundamental relationship that is asserted as the grounds for the petition and thus a part of the urging of God that goes on in prayer. It is only the person who truly believes that God can and will help who dares to challenge the Lord so forthrightly.

The other somewhat jarring dimension of these verses is the move to singing and joy in 20:13. But, as has been suggested, that hymn is an important indicator that Jeremiah received a response from God, that he heard a word of assurance of God's powerful presence and support. This is not totally surprising in the light of similar words in 1:18-19 and 15:20. What is to be noted at this point is the characteristic movement of prayer that Scripture gives us. We remember well the laments of Jeremiah, and properly so. They are dominant, and they do not end with the song of joy in 20:13. But we need to keep in mind that the form and theology of prayer given to us in Scripture always anticipate the help of God and the movement from the depths to the heights, from despair to joy. Whatever we teach about the nature of prayer and its relation to human experience, this is central to the biblical understanding.[131] The prayer of the faithful moves from lament to praise, from fear to joy—even for Jeremiah.

There may be a certain amount of realism, however, in the movement from 20:13 to 20:14-18. The word of praise is not always the last word. The prophet, like many people, falls back from praise to lament. Deliverance is not necessarily final or even realized. The logic of faith—and that is the dominant word—is from lament to praise. But life often takes us from the heights back to the depths, as it did for Jeremiah.

131. On the movement from lament to divine response to hymnic exultation, see Patrick D. Miller, *They Cried to the Lord: The Form and Theology of Biblical Prayer* (Minneapolis: Fortress, 1994) chaps. 3–5.

JEREMIAH 21:1–25:38

AGAINST KINGS AND PROPHETS

OVERVIEW

These chapters are often regarded as an appendix to chaps. 1–20, which make up the first main part of the book and the primary collection of Jeremiah's oracles. The book itself, however, indicates no significant break or shift between chaps. 20 and 21. The prophetic activity goes on even after the despairing cry of the prophet at the end of chap. 20. The content of chaps. 21–25 echoes many of the themes that have been heard before: judgment at the hands of Babylon, the call to repentance, the possibility of hope beyond judgment, and the indictment of false prophets. Particularly noticeable in this section are the focus on the leadership of Judah, specifically kings and prophets, and the proximity of the judgment. Kingship is the particular subject of the oracles in chaps. 21 through the first part of chap. 23. In the rest of chap. 23, we encounter one of the most extensive collections of oracles concerning false prophets in the whole book. The fact that judgment is at hand is indicated at a number of points, specifically in the various references to the capture of King Jehoiachin and the taking of the first group of exiles to Babylon (22:24-30; 24) and the word to Judah's last king, Zedekiah, at the time of the Babylonian siege (21:1-7).

The final chapter in this section represents a kind of conclusion or break in the book. That happens in two ways: (1) 25:1-14 is a prose sermon presenting a summary of Jeremiah's preaching up to the fourth year of King Jehoiakim (605 BCE). At the end there is a reference to a "book" or scroll that contains "all the words that I have uttered against" the land. This is probably a reference to the first or second scroll that Jeremiah dictated to his scribe Baruch in the fourth year of King Jehoiakim, containing "all the words of the LORD that he had spoken to him" (36:4). The first part of chap. 25, therefore, represents a kind of closure, a late summary that serves to conclude the first part of the book and, in a sense, to wrap it up. (2) The further indication of a significant shift in chap. 25 is the fact that in the Greek edition of the book of Jeremiah the large section of oracles against the nations in chaps. 46–52 in the Hebrew text is placed after 25:13*a*, a placement that may have been earlier than the present Hebrew arrangement. In any event, the second part of chap. 25 has to do with the nations and belongs, in terms of content, with chaps. 46–51, with which it is in fact associated in the Greek form of the book.

JEREMIAH 21:1-10, THE BESIEGING CHALDEANS

21 The word came to Jeremiah from the LORD when King Zedekiah sent to him Pashhur son of Malkijah and the priest Zephaniah son of Maaseiah. They said: [2]"Inquire now of the LORD

21 This is the word that came to Jeremiah from the LORD, when King Zedekiah sent to him Pashhur son of Malchiah and the priest Zephaniah son of Maaseiah, saying, [2]"Please

NIV

for us because Nebuchadnezzar[a] king of Babylon is attacking us. Perhaps the LORD will perform wonders for us as in times past so that he will withdraw from us."

[3]But Jeremiah answered them, "Tell Zedekiah, [4]'This is what the LORD, the God of Israel, says: I am about to turn against you the weapons of war that are in your hands, which you are using to fight the king of Babylon and the Babylonians[b] who are outside the wall besieging you. And I will gather them inside this city. [5]I myself will fight against you with an outstretched hand and a mighty arm in anger and fury and great wrath. [6]I will strike down those who live in this city—both men and animals—and they will die of a terrible plague. [7]After that, declares the LORD, I will hand over Zedekiah king of Judah, his officials and the people in this city who survive the plague, sword and famine, to Nebuchadnezzar king of Babylon and to their enemies who seek their lives. He will put them to the sword; he will show them no mercy or pity or compassion.'

[8]"Furthermore, tell the people, 'This is what the LORD says: See, I am setting before you the way of life and the way of death. [9]Whoever stays in this city will die by the sword, famine or plague. But whoever goes out and surrenders to the Babylonians who are besieging you will live; he will escape with his life. [10]I have determined to do this city harm and not good, declares the LORD. It will be given into the hands of the king of Babylon, and he will destroy it with fire.'

[a]2 Hebrew *Nebuchadrezzar*, of which *Nebuchadnezzar* is a variant; here and often in Jeremiah and Ezekiel   [b]4 Or *Chaldeans*; also in verse 9

NRSV

inquire of the LORD on our behalf, for King Nebuchadrezzar of Babylon is making war against us; perhaps the LORD will perform a wonderful deed for us, as he has often done, and will make him withdraw from us."

3Then Jeremiah said to them: [4]Thus you shall say to Zedekiah: Thus says the LORD, the God of Israel: I am going to turn back the weapons of war that are in your hands and with which you are fighting against the king of Babylon and against the Chaldeans who are besieging you outside the walls; and I will bring them together into the center of this city. [5]I myself will fight against you with outstretched hand and mighty arm, in anger, in fury, and in great wrath. [6]And I will strike down the inhabitants of this city, both human beings and animals; they shall die of a great pestilence. [7]Afterward, says the LORD, I will give King Zedekiah of Judah, and his servants, and the people in this city—those who survive the pestilence, sword, and famine—into the hands of King Nebuchadrezzar of Babylon, into the hands of their enemies, into the hands of those who seek their lives. He shall strike them down with the edge of the sword; he shall not pity them, or spare them, or have compassion.

8And to this people you shall say: Thus says the LORD: See, I am setting before you the way of life and the way of death. [9]Those who stay in this city shall die by the sword, by famine, and by pestilence; but those who go out and surrender to the Chaldeans who are besieging you shall live and shall have their lives as a prize of war. [10]For I have set my face against this city for evil and not for good, says the LORD: it shall be given into the hands of the king of Babylon, and he shall burn it with fire.

COMMENTARY

21:1-7. Beginning with this passage, many of the oracles and narratives that follow are given some sort of dating or historical setting in the text. In this case, that is near the fall of the kingdom of Judah, during the time of its last king, Zedekiah (597–587 BCE), when Zedekiah has rebelled against the Babylonians (called here and elsewhere

"Chaldeans") and they are besieging the city. It is to be associated with two other accounts of oracles to Zedekiah, one also involving emissaries sent to Jeremiah to ask for his intercession (37:3-10) and the other an oracle announcing Zedekiah's personal fate (34:1-7). The placement of this particular oracle after chap. 20 may have to do with the common name "Pashhur" that occurs in 20:1-6 and 21:1, although the first Pashhur was a priest and the second one a prince (cf. 38:1-6). Pashhur is sent by Zedekiah, along with the priest Zephaniah, who is one of the emissaries in 37:3-10 and appears in one other episode (29:24-32) before his death at the hands of the king of Babylon is reported at the end of the book (52:24-27).

The particular assignment of the emissaries is ambiguous. The language "inquire of the LORD" (v. 2) is a typical expression for seeking an oracle from a prophet, in effect a word about what will happen to the king and the people. At the same time, the emissaries are sent to "inquire of the Lord *on our behalf,*" language that sounds more like a request for intercession. This interpretation is reinforced by the expressed hope "perhaps the LORD will perform a wonderful deed for us" (v. 2), more literally, "act with us according to all his wonderful deeds." That the request for an oracle is really the desire for intercession is confirmed by the parallel passage in 37:3-10, where the assignment to the emissaries is to ask Jeremiah explicitly to "pray for us to the LORD our God," but the Lord's reply interprets this act as an inquiry. The intercessory role of Jeremiah is well identified in the book (7:16; 11:14; 14:11; 15:1; 42:2, 4, 20), so it is no surprise that the king's request for the prophet to seek a word from the Lord is really a request to intercede on their behalf with the Lord. The "wonderful deeds" are the mighty acts of God manifested in the exodus and the journey into the land and in the whole history of this people whom the Lord has delivered from the hands of their enemy. Knowing that history, Zedekiah hopes—and prays—for such a magnificent deliverance now (cf. Isaiah 37).

The prayer is in vain. Exodus language occurs in the response of the Lord ("with outstretched hand and mighty arm"; see Deut 7:19; 11:2; 26:8), but it is an anti-exodus. It is the mighty deed of the Lord to punish the people. The weapons of war that are turned back are not those of the enemy but those of the Lord's people. The God who fought for Israel against Egypt in the exodus (Exod 14:14; Deut 1:30) now fights against Judah (v. 5). The God who delivered the Canaanites into the hands of the Israelites (Deut 2:24; 3:2) now delivers the Judeans into the hands of the Babylonians (v. 7). The divine warrior who fought on Israel's behalf out of compassion and concern (Exod 2:24-25) now fights against them "in anger, in fury, and in great wrath" (v. 5). The holy city of Jerusalem, whose security seemed so certain because it was the site of the Temple, the dwelling place of the Lord (chap. 7), will be a bloody site of destruction, and the royal son of David will be given over, together with all his entourage and his people, into the hands of the enemy.

21:8-10. This prophetic word may have been joined with the preceding one by virtue of the repetition of the expression "the Chaldeans who are besieging you." That shared subject matter makes them appropriately coordinate, and the present placement effects a coherent movement in the text. Having addressed the king about his fate, the prophet addresses the people with the word of the Lord about their fate. There is a potential difference in outcome. The people are now offered a chance for survival—but only in surrendering. The passage draws on language and themes from the great covenantal and climactic text of Deut 30:15-19. As in that decisive moment, the people are given the alternative of life or death. In Deuteronomy the choice was a matter of obedience to the Lord's instruction. Now that option is no longer open. Or rather, the people have chosen the way of death by failing to obey the Lord's commands. Yet, there is still a way out. It is in accepting the Lord's punishment administered by the new "rod of my anger" (Isa 10:5), "the Chaldeans who are besieging you." The prophetic word thus joins with other words in Jeremiah to identify a new kind of obedience to the Lord. It is to be found in an acceptance of the Lord's judgment for the people's sins (27:6-8; 38:2-3; 39:18; 45:5). Deuteronomy 30:15 indicates that the life-and-death choice is also a choice between good and evil, between blessing and curse. The word of the Lord is that the people have made that choice, and thus God's face is set against the city for evil rather than good. Those who acknowledge the Lord's hand at work through the Babylonian army and thus surrender can save their lives.

REFLECTIONS

1. The response of the Lord to the king is instructive in several ways. For one thing, it is a demonstration in the pages of Scripture of an answer to prayer that is most assuredly not the deliverance and help that was sought. The tradition is massively weighted with testimonies to the Lord's positive response to the prayers of those in trouble who cry out to God. This is not such a situation. The word of the Lord in this book is that the trouble is the Lord's doing. In the face of divine judgment, the prayer for deliverance is ineffective. That is said only in the context of the awareness of the extended history of disobedience. There are many indications of the Lord's willingness to withhold judgment. But as in the days of Amos (Amos 7:1-9), there can come a time when disobedience is so persistent that intercession is either forbidden or ineffective, and the cries of the people go unheeded. This is the hard part of the Bible's teaching about prayer (see Deut 1:45).

2. The text is also a classic case of the community of faith finding its own powerful ideology turned upon itself. The ideology that guided the community and in which it found its security, centering in the mighty acts of the Lord to deliver Israel, the covenant with the house of David, and the dwelling of the Lord on Zion, is turned upside down. The mighty act is *against* God's people. The royal theology is crushed as the scion of David is delivered over to his enemy. The once-secure Zion is turned into a place of death and destruction. Thus does the prophetic word and the experience of Israel undercut every ideological security, whether it is confidence in an exodus deliverance or in a cross and resurrection. The ideology always assumes a way of human existence and not simply a divine act. The choice that lies at the center of the deuteronomic instruction, whether to choose the way of life or the way of death, is placed before the people once more. The common tendency is to assume that the *magnalia dei* that ground our faith are also our security. But exodus is always followed by Sinai, deliverance by calling, the gospel by "therefore." A people who live only by the awareness of God's grace and not by the awareness of God's command risk the possibility that the coming of the Lord will be in anger and not in compassion.

3. The choice that is laid before the people opens up an odd kind of finding life in losing it, of saving one's life by surrendering it. Here that possibility rests in the realization that the possibilities of new life are found only in accepting the death of the old life. There is no way past the fires of judgment, but there is a way through them. Surrender and exile were not pleasant prospects. But the community under judgment may find in its exiled state, in its loss of control and dominance, in its forced submission to alien powers, whether political or cultural, a way out with all the ambiguity that is present in the text's own reference to "going out" (21:9). The possibility for life is found in exile. The church does not live under the threat of Babylonian armies. But it may find itself forced into a state of exile as its only way to survive. We are inclined to view such a condition with all the weeping and wailing of the Judeans. It may also be the hand of the Lord at work in judgment upon a people who have lost the way.[132]

132. For a development of the exilic image as a model for the church, see W. Brueggemann, "Rethinking Church Models through Scripture," *TToday* 48 (1991) 128-38. This essay is reprinted in W. Brueggemann, *A Social Reading of the Old Testament: Prophetic Approaches to Israel's Communal Life,* ed. Patrick D. Miller (Minneapolis: Fortress, 1994) 263-75.

JEREMIAH 21:11–23:8, ORACLES AGAINST AND FOR THE KING

NIV

[11]"Moreover, say to the royal house of Judah, 'Hear the word of the LORD; [12]O house of David, this is what the LORD says:

" 'Administer justice every morning;
 rescue from the hand of his oppressor
 the one who has been robbed,
or my wrath will break out and burn like fire
 because of the evil you have done—
 burn with no one to quench it.
[13]I am against you, ⌊Jerusalem,⌋
 you who live above this valley
 on the rocky plateau,
 declares the LORD—
you who say, "Who can come against us?
 Who can enter our refuge?"
[14]I will punish you as your deeds deserve,
 declares the LORD.
I will kindle a fire in your forests
 that will consume everything around you.' "

22 This is what the LORD says: "Go down to the palace of the king of Judah and proclaim this message there: [2]'Hear the word of the LORD, O king of Judah, you who sit on David's throne—you, your officials and your people who come through these gates. [3]This is what the LORD says: Do what is just and right. Rescue from the hand of his oppressor the one who has been robbed. Do no wrong or violence to the alien, the fatherless or the widow, and do not shed innocent blood in this place. [4]For if you are careful to carry out these commands, then kings who sit on David's throne will come through the gates of this palace, riding in chariots and on horses, accompanied by their officials and their people. [5]But if you do not obey these commands, declares the LORD, I swear by myself that this palace will become a ruin.' "

[6]For this is what the LORD says about the palace of the king of Judah:

"Though you are like Gilead to me,
 like the summit of Lebanon,
I will surely make you like a desert,
 like towns not inhabited.

NRSV

[11]To the house of the king of Judah say: Hear the word of the LORD, [12]O house of David! Thus says the LORD:

Execute justice in the morning,
 and deliver from the hand of the oppressor
 anyone who has been robbed,
or else my wrath will go forth like fire,
 and burn, with no one to quench it,
 because of your evil doings.

[13]See, I am against you, O inhabitant of the valley,
 O rock of the plain, says the LORD;
you who say, "Who can come down against us,
 or who can enter our places of refuge?"
[14]I will punish you according to the fruit of your doings, says the LORD;
 I will kindle a fire in its forest,
 and it shall devour all that is around it.

22 Thus says the LORD: Go down to the house of the king of Judah, and speak there this word, [2]and say: Hear the word of the LORD, O King of Judah sitting on the throne of David—you, and your servants, and your people who enter these gates. [3]Thus says the LORD: Act with justice and righteousness, and deliver from the hand of the oppressor anyone who has been robbed. And do no wrong or violence to the alien, the orphan, and the widow, or shed innocent blood in this place. [4]For if you will indeed obey this word, then through the gates of this house shall enter kings who sit on the throne of David, riding in chariots and on horses, they, and their servants, and their people. [5]But if you will not heed these words, I swear by myself, says the LORD, that this house shall become a desolation. [6]For thus says the LORD concerning the house of the king of Judah:

You are like Gilead to me,
 like the summit of Lebanon;
but I swear that I will make you a desert,

NIV

⁷I will send destroyers against you,
each man with his weapons,
and they will cut up your fine cedar beams
and throw them into the fire.

⁸"People from many nations will pass by this city and will ask one another, 'Why has the LORD done such a thing to this great city?' ⁹And the answer will be: 'Because they have forsaken the covenant of the LORD their God and have worshiped and served other gods.' "

¹⁰Do not weep for the dead ⌊king⌋ or mourn his loss;
rather, weep bitterly for him who is exiled,
because he will never return
nor see his native land again.

¹¹For this is what the LORD says about Shallum^a son of Josiah, who succeeded his father as king of Judah but has gone from this place: "He will never return. ¹²He will die in the place where they have led him captive; he will not see this land again."

¹³"Woe to him who builds his palace by unrighteousness,
his upper rooms by injustice,
making his countrymen work for nothing,
not paying them for their labor.
¹⁴He says, 'I will build myself a great palace
with spacious upper rooms.'
So he makes large windows in it,
panels it with cedar
and decorates it in red.

¹⁵"Does it make you a king
to have more and more cedar?
Did not your father have food and drink?
He did what was right and just,
so all went well with him.
¹⁶He defended the cause of the poor and needy,
and so all went well.
Is that not what it means to know me?"
declares the LORD.
¹⁷"But your eyes and your heart
are set only on dishonest gain,
on shedding innocent blood
and on oppression and extortion."

¹⁸Therefore this is what the LORD says about Jehoiakim son of Josiah king of Judah:

^a11 Also called *Jehoahaz*

NRSV

an uninhabited city.^a
⁷ I will prepare destroyers against you,
all with their weapons;
they shall cut down your choicest cedars
and cast them into the fire.
⁸And many nations will pass by this city, and all of them will say one to another, "Why has the LORD dealt in this way with that great city?" ⁹And they will answer, "Because they abandoned the covenant of the LORD their God, and worshiped other gods and served them."

¹⁰ Do not weep for him who is dead,
nor bemoan him;
weep rather for him who goes away,
for he shall return no more
to see his native land.
¹¹For thus says the LORD concerning Shallum son of King Josiah of Judah, who succeeded his father Josiah, and who went away from this place: He shall return here no more, ¹²but in the place where they have carried him captive he shall die, and he shall never see this land again.

¹³ Woe to him who builds his house by unrighteousness,
and his upper rooms by injustice;
who makes his neighbors work for nothing,
and does not give them their wages;
¹⁴ who says, "I will build myself a spacious house
with large upper rooms,"
and who cuts out windows for it,
paneling it with cedar,
and painting it with vermilion.
¹⁵ Are you a king
because you compete in cedar?
Did not your father eat and drink
and do justice and righteousness?
Then it was well with him.
¹⁶ He judged the cause of the poor and needy;
then it was well.
Is not this to know me?
says the LORD.
¹⁷ But your eyes and heart
are only on your dishonest gain,
for shedding innocent blood,

^aCn: Heb *uninhabited cities*

NIV

"They will not mourn for him:
'Alas, my brother! Alas, my sister!'
They will not mourn for him:
'Alas, my master! Alas, his splendor!'
¹⁹He will have the burial of a donkey—
dragged away and thrown
outside the gates of Jerusalem."

²⁰"Go up to Lebanon and cry out,
let your voice be heard in Bashan,
cry out from Abarim,
for all your allies are crushed.
²¹I warned you when you felt secure,
but you said, 'I will not listen!'
This has been your way from your youth;
you have not obeyed me.
²²The wind will drive all your shepherds away,
and your allies will go into exile.
Then you will be ashamed and disgraced
because of all your wickedness.
²³You who live in 'Lebanon,'ᵃ
who are nestled in cedar buildings,
how you will groan when pangs come upon
you,
pain like that of a woman in labor!

²⁴"As surely as I live," declares the LORD, "even if you, Jehoiachinᵇ son of Jehoiakim king of Judah, were a signet ring on my right hand, I would still pull you off. ²⁵I will hand you over to those who seek your life, those you fear—to Nebuchadnezzar king of Babylon and to the Babylonians.ᶜ ²⁶I will hurl you and the mother who gave you birth into another country, where neither of you was born, and there you both will die. ²⁷You will never come back to the land you long to return to."

²⁸Is this man Jehoiachin a despised, broken pot,
an object no one wants?
Why will he and his children be hurled out,
cast into a land they do not know?
²⁹O land, land, land,
hear the word of the LORD!
³⁰This is what the LORD says:
"Record this man as if childless,
a man who will not prosper in his lifetime,
for none of his offspring will prosper,

ᵃ23 That is, the palace in Jerusalem (see 1 Kings 7:2)   ᵇ24 Hebrew *Coniah*, a variant of *Jehoiachin*; also in verse 28   ᶜ25 Or *Chaldeans*

NRSV

and for practicing oppression and violence.
18Therefore thus says the LORD concerning King Jehoiakim son of Josiah of Judah:
They shall not lament for him, saying,
"Alas, my brother!" or "Alas, sister!"
They shall not lament for him, saying,
"Alas, lord!" or "Alas, his majesty!"
¹⁹With the burial of a donkey he shall be
buried—
dragged off and thrown out beyond the
gates of Jerusalem.

²⁰Go up to Lebanon, and cry out,
and lift up your voice in Bashan;
cry out from Abarim,
for all your lovers are crushed.
²¹I spoke to you in your prosperity,
but you said, "I will not listen."
This has been your way from your youth,
for you have not obeyed my voice.
²²The wind shall shepherd all your shepherds,
and your lovers shall go into captivity;
then you will be ashamed and dismayed
because of all your wickedness.
²³O inhabitant of Lebanon,
nested among the cedars,
how you will groanᵃ when pangs come upon
you,
pain as of a woman in labor!

24As I live, says the LORD, even if King Coniah son of Jehoiakim of Judah were the signet ring on my right hand, even from there I would tear you off ²⁵and give you into the hands of those who seek your life, into the hands of those of whom you are afraid, even into the hands of King Nebuchadrezzar of Babylon and into the hands of the Chaldeans. ²⁶I will hurl you and the mother who bore you into another country, where you were not born, and there you shall die. ²⁷But they shall not return to the land to which they long to return.
²⁸Is this man Coniah a despised broken pot,
a vessel no one wants?
Why are he and his offspring hurled out
and cast away in a land that they do not
know?

ᵃGk Vg Syr: Heb *will be pitied*

NIV

none will sit on the throne of David
or rule anymore in Judah."

23 "Woe to the shepherds who are destroying and scattering the sheep of my pasture!" declares the LORD. [2]Therefore this is what the LORD, the God of Israel, says to the shepherds who tend my people: "Because you have scattered my flock and driven them away and have not bestowed care on them, I will bestow punishment on you for the evil you have done," declares the LORD. [3]"I myself will gather the remnant of my flock out of all the countries where I have driven them and will bring them back to their pasture, where they will be fruitful and increase in number. [4]I will place shepherds over them who will tend them, and they will no longer be afraid or terrified, nor will any be missing," declares the LORD.

[5]"The days are coming," declares the LORD,
   "when I will raise up to David[a] a righteous
      Branch,
   a King who will reign wisely
      and do what is just and right in the land.
[6]In his days Judah will be saved
      and Israel will live in safety.
   This is the name by which he will be called:
      The LORD Our Righteousness.

[7]"So then, the days are coming," declares the LORD, "when people will no longer say, 'As surely as the LORD lives, who brought the Israelites up out of Egypt,' [8]but they will say, 'As surely as the LORD lives, who brought the descendants of Israel up out of the land of the north and out of all the countries where he had banished them.' Then they will live in their own land."

[a]5 Or *up from David's line*

NRSV

[29]O land, land, land,
      hear the word of the LORD!
[30]Thus says the LORD:
   Record this man as childless,
      a man who shall not succeed in his days;
   for none of his offspring shall succeed
      in sitting on the throne of David,
      and ruling again in Judah.

23 Woe to the shepherds who destroy and scatter the sheep of my pasture! says the LORD. [2]Therefore thus says the LORD, the God of Israel, concerning the shepherds who shepherd my people: It is you who have scattered my flock, and have driven them away, and you have not attended to them. So I will attend to you for your evil doings, says the LORD. [3]Then I myself will gather the remnant of my flock out of all the lands where I have driven them, and I will bring them back to their fold, and they shall be fruitful and multiply. [4]I will raise up shepherds over them who will shepherd them, and they shall not fear any longer, or be dismayed, nor shall any be missing, says the LORD.

[5]The days are surely coming, says the LORD, when I will raise up for David a righteous Branch, and he shall reign as king and deal wisely, and shall execute justice and righteousness in the land. [6]In his days Judah will be saved and Israel will live in safety. And this is the name by which he will be called: "The LORD is our righteousness."

[7]Therefore, the days are surely coming, says the LORD, when it shall no longer be said, "As the LORD lives who brought the people of Israel up out of the land of Egypt," [8]but "As the LORD lives who brought out and led the offspring of the house of Israel out of the land of the north and out of all the lands where he[a] had driven them." Then they shall live in their own land.

[a]Gk: Heb *I*

COMMENTARY

This part of the book is composed of a group of oracles, in poetry and prose, that have to do with the king or the royal city Jerusalem. The expression "concerning/to the king of Judah" (21:11a) is an introduction to the whole section comparable to the expression "concerning the prophets," which begins the next section (23:9). This heading joins with the content of these passages to indicate that we have an intentional grouping of this block of material dealing with the kings or kingship. Various kings are specifically addressed: Josiah's son Jehoahaz, called here Shallum (22:10-12); his successor and brother, Jehoiakim (22:13-19); and then Jehoiakim's successor, Jehoiachin, the next to the last king of Judah (22:24-30). Josiah is alluded to (22:15-16), so that Zedekiah, the last king of Judah, is the only king not addressed or referred to; he has already been addressed in the preceding chapter. The view of kingship here, is rooted in the covenant with David. It assumes and builds upon the responsibility of the king for the maintenance of justice and order in the community, a responsibility that often seemed to get lost in the shuffle of military endeavors, political maneuverings, and economic aggrandizement. While these oracles have to do with particular kings at a number of points, at the beginning (21:12) and the end (23:5) of this section the particular is set in the context of the larger view, the intention of God to effect a righteous rule through the house of David. The opening oracle sets the norm (21:11-12); the various oracles that follow (22:1–23:4), addressed to particular kings, identify the failure of kingship and do so quite specifically; the final oracle announces a future when the Lord will raise up a king for David who will rule wisely and justly (23:5-6).

It is difficult to speak to and about the king without also addressing the royal city, which is as central to the misrule as it is to the righteous rule of the house of David. So it is that, interspersed throughout the numerous oracles concerning the kings, there are also several that speak about Jerusalem and its fate (21:13-14; 22:8-9, 20-23).

21:11-12. This text joins with 22:13-19 to set the responsibility for justice as a matter of first order for the royal ruler. The passage has two introductions. While the first one, in v. 11, is an introduction to the whole section, 21:11–23:8, the second one, addressed to "the house of David," serves as a kind of comprehensive rubric. Specific kings are in view in these texts, but the requirement for the proper administration of justice is laid on all of them. It is an address to every king, the whole house of David, whoever might be on the throne at any given time.

The exhortation to judge justly echoes many prophetic injunctions to righteousness and justice (Isa 1:17; 56:1a; Amos 5:14-15; Mic 6:8). This passage, however, identifies the maintenance of justice as a particular responsibility of the ruler, a notion that belonged to royal ideology throughout the ancient Near East. In the Bible, that is indicated in a programmatic way in Ps 72:2-4, 12-14 but also in a number of narratives such as 2 Samuel 12; 14; and 15:1-6. The king was the primary guardian of justice in the kingdom, the one to whom those who had been unfairly dealt with or robbed in some fashion could appeal for help and justice.[133] That responsibility is a theme of this section (22:3, 15; 23:5). It assumes that the king is both the guarantor of the right and of the social order that justice and righteousness effect as well as the court of last resort in specific instances of injustice and oppression. The concern for the execution of this royal responsibility is such a large one in these passages that it serves to identify for the reader both the primary task of the king (see Psalm 72) and the basis for the Lord's judgment against kings. The two things that stand out in this passage are the insistence on the execution of justice as a regular, constant enterprise on the part of the king, to be carried out each morning (v. 12a), and the clear indication that the fate of the king and the kingdom depend on such continuing attention to the cause of justice and of the oppressed.

At the beginning of this literary block, therefore, this passage sets before the kings of Judah the fundamental requirement for their rule of the people and the norm by which they will be judged. At the end of this block, that norm is set out again as the primary characteristic of the reign of that future

---

133. On the king as the one to whom the oppressed and the marginal could appeal for justice see Richard Boyce, *The Cry to God in the Old Testament*, SBLDS 103 (Atlanta: Scholars Press, 1988).

king from the house of David whom the Lord will raise up to rule the people (23:5-6). In between, the norm is reiterated (22:1-5) and its breakdown identified (22:13-19).

21:13-14. In the midst of these words to the kings is set a judgment speech against a city, surely Jerusalem. No specific reason is given for the judgment except the general reference to punishing "according to the fruit of your doings." One has to read the earlier chapters to find out what those "doings" are. The text, however, does characterize the city as a place of arrogance and complacency, assuming it is invulnerable to attack and secure from any threat. It is not dissimilar to the attitude Jeremiah condemns in chap. 7, when the people assume that the presence of the Temple of the Lord makes them impervious to any danger. In the face of such misplaced arrogance, the Lord says, "The fire next time!" The forest in which the Lord's fire will be kindled is the royal palace and the Temple, both built of cedars from the forests of Lebanon. The palace was in fact called "the house of the forest [of Lebanon]" (1 Kgs 7:2; 10:17, 21; Isa 22:8). The Lord's judgment will start at the heart of the city at those places that embodied royal and religious misconduct but were assumed to be citadels of the city's security. The punishment by fire, which echoes the judgment in v. 12, may be the reason why this small oracle has been attached to 21:11-12 (cf. 22:7*b*). The reference to the cedar forest connects the text with the passages that follow (22:7*b*, 14-15, 20, 23).

22:1-7. These verses repeat the exhortation to the king to execute justice that is the subject of 21:11-12, and the reader is referred to the interpretive comments there (see also the Commentary on 7:1-15). Like 21:11-12, the threat of judgment hangs over the king who does not do justice. The demand for royal justice, however, is elaborated even more in these verses. Not only is there the positive call for justice and righteousness and the deliverance of those oppressed but also a negative formulation is set as a counterpart, a word of warning to the kings not to be the agents of oppression against the marginal, the powerless, the poor of the land. While one might read this as a way of rephrasing negatively what has been said positively in order to reinforce the basic demand, later in this chapter the reader will hear of a king who has, in fact, shed innocent blood. The prob-

lem is not simply inactivity, lassitude before rampant injustice, but the complicity of the king in deeds of injustice and violence (cf. 2:34). That complicity may be in the various ways the king seeks to enhance and extend power and territory. It also may happen as the king permits a royal entourage to do what is necessary to protect and build up the wealth of the royal establishment and the elite and upper class who have a mutual and interlocking economic dependency with the court. It is important to note that while the king is the primary addressee, the whole court is explicitly included. McKane has rightly translated the Hebrew of v. 2*b* as "you, your officials and those in your service."[134] The gates are the gates of the royal palace, and it is those people who regularly move in and out of the palace who are addressed by these words. No details are given, only the elaboration of the demand, the norm by which the kings—and their courts—will be judged.

The text sets forth this demand as a choice, a life-or-death choice (see 8:3; 21:8-10). Like many prophetic exhortations, it suggests a way of amending the situation and effecting life. The point of the passage as a whole is to set, in the either/or of the covenantal relationship, the criterion by which the kings of Judah are being and have been measured. The context, however, as in the case of the exhortations in Amos 5, suggests that the decision has already been made. By their placement, vv. 6-7, a separate oracle, serve to indicate that the "house of the king of Judah" (see 21:11; 22:1) has been found wanting by these criteria and now stands under imminent judgment. The judgment is against the "house," that is, the palace of the king; but that judgment obviously entails all who come and go through its doors. The reference to Gilead and Lebanon probably is an allusion to the fact that the palace was built of fine cedars (v. 15; cf. 2 Sam 7:2, 7; 1 Kgs 7:2-5). It was also built with a "hall of justice," where the king was "to pronounce judgment" (1 Kgs 7:7). This text suggests that the "hall of justice" has been vacated, so to speak, and has decayed. So the magnificent cedar timbers of the royal palace will fall before the unnamed destroyers who are prepared (lit., "consecrated" [קדשׁ *qdš*]) to that task by the Lord (v. 7*a*).

---

134. William McKane, *A Critical and Exegetical Commentary on Jeremiah*, 2 vols., ICC (Edinburgh: T. & T. Clark, 1986, 1996) 1:514.

22:8-9. Once again, the movement of the text turns our attention from the king and his court to the city of Jerusalem. In the form of the question-and-answer schema found elsewhere in Jeremiah (see the Commentary on 5:18-19), an explanation of the destruction of Jerusalem is given as an answer to the hypothetical question of the surrounding nations: Why has the Lord dealt in this way with that great city? The question implies a puzzlement on the part of the nations. Why in the world would the Lord want to destroy or allow to be destroyed such a magnificent city as Jerusalem—indeed, the place of the Lord's own dwelling? It is like the hypothetical claim that Moses made in his intercessions for the people in the wilderness when he questioned the Lord's decision to punish the disobedient people, saying that the nations would think that the Lord had it in for Israel in the first place (Exod 32:12) or that the Lord could not accomplish the conquest and settlement of the land (Num 14:15-16). The question in Jeremiah is after the fact, a looking back. But there is an apologetic agenda implicit in it, as is usually the case with the question-and-answer form. Jerusalem's fate is not the result of a divine evil intent (as in Exod 32:12) or the Lord's frustrated efforts (as in Num 14:15-16). There is one reason alone, and it has been indicated again and again in the book: The people have forsaken the covenant. The city and its ruling class—indeed, its citizens more generally—have failed to live by the commandments and the requirements of justice and righteousness that were set forth in the covenant stipulations recorded in the books of the Torah. There seems to be a discrepancy between the norms set forth for judging the kings in 21:11–22:7 (the maintenance of justice and righteousness) and the basis for judgment reported in 22:9 (the worship of other gods). That discrepancy is more apparent than real, however. In the comparable temple sermon of chap. 7, which is addressed to the whole community, the covenantal requirements that were lifted up for obedience included both the maintenance of justice and total allegiance to the Lord. Abandonment of the covenant referred to in v. 9 includes both justice for the oppressed and loyalty to the Lord.

22:10-12. Verse 11 is a prose commentary on the brief oracle in v. 10. As such it indicates that the two persons referred to in v. 10 are Josiah, who was killed in battle, and Jehoahaz, his son, who was placed on the throne by "the people of the land" (possibly the landed gentry of Judah), but after only three months was taken into exile in Egypt by Pharaoh Necho, who had killed Josiah at the Battle of Megiddo (2 Kgs 23:30-34). "Shallum" was the personal name of this son (1 Chr 3:15) and "Jehoahaz" the royal name that was given to him when he became king. The point of the oracle in v. 10 is that the people who had pinned their hopes so thoroughly on Josiah as the king who would restore the Davidic kingdom and overthrow all foreign domination should not keep on lamenting and pining over those lost hopes. It is already time to mourn over the next king, who is about to go into exile and will never come back. The story of the last kings of Judah is not one of triumph. It evokes only weeping and sadness.

22:13-19. The heavy focus of this text on the responsibility of the ruler of God's people to maintain justice and protect the weak becomes very pointed in these verses. As v. 18 indicates, the text is directed toward Jehoahaz's successor, Jehoiakim, and is a judgment speech against him for his failure to carry out the royal responsibility to ensure justice and righteousness in the land. The association of the whole text with Jehoiakim is confirmed by the comparison in vv. 13-17 between a just king (Josiah) and his unjust son (Jehoiakim).

The force of the opening "Woe" (הוי *hôy*) is indicated by the use of the same word in v. 18, there translated as "alas." As v. 18 shows, this is what people cry out at a funeral, the lament over the dead. In Jehoiakim's case, the king will not even receive the usual burial and funeral rites. His death will be so ignominious that mourning will not be possible. Rather than being given a magnificent state funeral, Jehoiakim's body will be dragged off and left in the open to rot as would be a dead donkey (cf. 36:30). The people who were told to stop their weeping for a dead Josiah and turn it to an about-to-be-exiled Jehoahaz now hear that there will be no weeping for the next king, Jehoiakim, when the judgment of God comes upon him. Why? While the surface answer is that it is because of the manner of his death, about which the historical record is unclear, the real answer is given in the indictment that precedes the announcement of judgment in vv. 18-19. That indictment, set forth in vv. 13-17, is pointed and telling.

Two intimately related issues dominate the indictment of Jehoiakim: royal aggrandizement and injustice. In this instance, they are one and the same thing. Royal power is exercised unjustly. The chief manifestations of the injustice and unrighteousness present in the land are at the hands of the king, whose building projects are accomplished on the backs of the people and without appropriate remuneration (v. 13). The opening line, therefore, summarizes the indictment (v. 13a): building a magnificent house or palace in a manner that is unjust. The rest of the passage elaborates the specifics of that indictment. The injustice is economic, as it often was in Israel and Judah (see Isa 5:7-8; Amos 2:6; 4:1; 5:11; Mic 2:1-2; 3:1-3). In this case, it is royal conscription, or forced labor, something well known in the history of the house of David; Solomon had used forced labor specifically to provide cedar from Lebanon to build the Temple (1 Kgs 5:13-14) and presumably his own magnificent palace (1 Kgs 7:1-12), a policy continued by his son Rehoboam (1 Kgs 12:1-11). One may presume such practices continued in both the northern and the southern kingdoms. In any event, history repeats itself in this regard when Jehoiakim builds a magnificent house with fancy rooms and big windows, all built of the finest cedar, such as Solomon used to build his house (1 Kgs 7:7), but without compensation for those who built it.

The issue as the prophet defines it is set forth starkly in vv. 15-17 in the comparison of Jehoiakim with his father, Josiah. It is the question of what makes a king (v. 15a). Is kingship represented by the possession of a magnificent palace, symbolized by the use of cedar? Or is it manifest in the securing of justice for the poor and the oppressed? The first question, however, discloses a second and deeper issue: What defines the true relationship between the king and the Lord (v. 16b)? The two questions are one and the same. True kingship is to be found in the ruler who "knows"—that is, acknowledges and lives in faithful relationship with—God. The content of that knowledge, that relationship, is specifically obedience to the requirements of justice and righteousness, the care of the poor and the needy that was central to the instruction of the Lord and the job description of the king (see Psalm 72; Isa 9:7; 11:5).

The comparison with Josiah makes the point. He was a just and righteousness ruler. To judge the cause of the poor and the needy under Josiah's reign (v. 16a) was to see that they did not suffer abuse, that their labor did not go uncompensated, that their property was not extorted from them, that the legal system was not manipulated by bribery and other devices to rob those who did not have much in the first place. Jehoiakim failed the test of kingship in every way. If the first part of this passage bids comparison with the forced labor of Solomon, the final indictment of Jehoiakim (v. 17) brings to mind the kangaroo court established by Ahab to expropriate the property of Naboth by setting up false witnesses to accuse him of blasphemy, allowing the king to execute him and appropriate his property for a vegetable garden (1 Kings 21). The aggrandizement of the king is accomplished by the abusive exercise of royal power. The result is the shedding of innocent blood and the practice of oppression and violence (v. 17b). Just as Ahab was judged and punished for that abuse of power, so also now the Lord announces a word of judgment against a later king who does the same thing.

There is one more thing to be noted in the comparison with Josiah (v. 15). It is in the words about Josiah's eating and drinking and doing justice and righteousness with the consequent judgment that "all went well." The point seems to be that the king was able to carry on his daily life-style in satisfactory fashion; he was able to live happily, while being sure to maintain the social order by regularly hearing the cases and the causes of the weak and the poor. Furthermore, such attention to the needs of the poor, to justice for the oppressed, is judged as having had good effects for him and apparently for the whole community. There is a clear sense that maintaining a just order leads to a good order, to the good life for all.

22:20-23. Once again, the word to the kings is correlated with a word to the royal city, Jerusalem. Placing these verses in this context may have to do with the reference to Lebanon, which also is mentioned in v. 6, and the references here and in vv. 7 and 14-15 to cedars, which come from Lebanon. The mountains referred to in v. 20 are high mountain ranges to the north (Lebanon), the northeast (Bashan), and the south (Abarim) of Jerusalem. As in 4:30 and elsewhere in the prophets (e.g., Ezek

23:5, 9), the "lovers" of Jerusalem are probably foreign powers that Judah has wooed for help or to which the country has allied itself. While many interpret the imperatives of v. 20 as a call to lament, the verb that is used there (צעק *ṣāʿaq*) commonly refers to crying out for help. As some interpreters have long recognized, there is a touch of satire or sarcasm in the call to Jerusalem in v. 20. McKane puts it this way:

> The satire consists in the suggestion that Jerusalem should shout for help from the most effective vantage points, directing her cries to her foreign allies. Let her ascend the highest mountains in order to broadcast her appeal, but it will all be in vain, for her allies are broken (or, will be broken), and they have power neither to help themselves nor to help her.[135]

Jerusalem has received plenty of warning from the prophets and has plenty of opportunity to change its ways but has refused to pay attention—a stubborn recalcitrance that is one of the themes of the book of Jeremiah (e.g., 6:10; 7:24-28; 11:8; 13:10-11). In many ways, it is too late to cry out now because the foreign allies and their gods are in the same boat as Jerusalem.

The sarcasm carries through to the end of the passage with the reference to the "inhabitant of [perhaps better, "enthroned in"] Lebanon, nested among the cedars." The allusion, of course, is to the cedars of the royal palace, by which Jehoiakim has sought to demonstrate his kingship, his royal prestige, and his power (vv. 14-15).

22:24-30. These verses announce judgment on the next to last king of Judah, Jehoiachin, who succeeded his father, Jehoiakim, in 597 BCE but ruled only three months before Jerusalem fell to the Babylonians. Jehoiachin was then taken with other leaders into exile in Babylon. In various ways, the passage is analogous to vv. 10-12. The similarities in the two texts are several: (a) judgment is announced on a king who ruled only three months before being deposed by a foreign power; (b) the judgment is exile, Jehoahaz to Egypt and Jehoiachin to Babylon; (c) no reason is given for the punishment because these kings ruled too briefly to accumulate any record, good or bad; and (d) the kings are referred to by names different

135. Ibid., 537.

from their throne names (Shallum and Coniah, possibly a variation on the regnal name Jehoiachin).

The thrust of the passage is the unqualified certainty of exile for Jehoiachin, no matter who he is or what he has done—or not done. The "signet ring" is the key to that thrust. It was the ring used to seal a document or letter of the king, representing his authority. In Hag 2:23, the Lord's announcement that Zerubbabel will be God's chosen ruler after exile is stated in the words "I will make you like a signet ring." Even if Jehoiachin were like that to the Lord, it would not save him. The finality of the announcement is reinforced with the terms "tear off" and "hurl." Further reinforcement occurs as the announcement of judgment heaps up the words about death and not returning. Jehoiachin's mother was a prominent figure on the scene, particularly in the light of the youthfulness of her son (see 13:18; 2 Kgs 24:8), and she, too, will go into exile; the writer of 2 Kgs 24:15 reports that both mother and son were, indeed, carried away into exile.

Finally, the word of judgment is scored again in vv. 28-30, and it becomes ever more clear that the intention of this passage is not only to announce judgment but also to cut off any hope on the part of persons in either Babylon or Jerusalem that Jehoiachin, the legitimate ruler, will return to his throne. There were clearly such expectations in Judah, as witnessed to by the false prophecy of Hananiah that the Lord would bring Jehoiachin and the exiles back to Judah (28:4). Such hopes have no basis in reality. This king is for all intents and purposes like a dead man. Nor should any Judeans pin their hopes on one of Jehoiachin's sons; though he did have offspring (see 1 Chr 3:17-18), the possibility that one of them will succeed to the throne is so out of the question that he can be regarded as childless.

The devastating force of these words and their poignancy are seen in the repeated "land, land, land" and the absoluteness of the word that seems to cut off forever the line of David, with whom the Lord had covenanted and whose eternal rule had been promised. But that covenant was premised on a rule of obedience, a rule of justice and righteousness (Psalms 72; 132), which is reiterated in this literary block of Jeremiah. The history of Judah and its kings in these last days was a record of the failure of obedience to the covenant, a failure so great that even an innocent Jehoiachin cannot endure.

23:1-8. The words about and against the kings come to a conclusion in these verses, reinforcing the basic point of the preceding oracles and announcing possibilities for the future beyond the present end. Three prose sermons are joined together to announce the end and to open up the future.

In the first of the prose sermons (vv. 1-4), a summary judgment against all the kings is made. The shepherd language draws on one of the most common images for kingship in the ancient Near East. While the experience of monarchy could be harsh, its ideology assumed the role of a shepherd, who watched over his flock, protected them, kept them together and in order, and made sure that any who were hurt were taken care of. But that is what these kings have failed to do, the cardinal example in Jeremiah's time being Jehoiakim (22:13-17) and the manner of failure being the perpetration of injustice and economic oppression. This brief prose sermon serves not only as a kind of summary of the preceding text, but also as an interpretation of what has happened. The emphatic construction "It is you who have scattered my flock" (v. 2*b*) makes it clear that while the judgment is the activity of the Lord, it is really the kings who, by their misrule, have scattered the flock and caused their exile. One of the primary clues, in the midst of this announcement of judgment, to the words of hope that are about to come—and quite unexpectedly—is the heavy relational language that the Lord uses: "my pasture," "my people," "my flock." The covenantal relationship is never relinquished by the Lord. A further emphatic construction at the beginning of v. 3 turns the whole thing around and opens up a door of hope and expectation beyond exile. The Lord says, "While it is *you* [the kings] who have scattered my flock, I, for my part, am going to gather my flock and bring them back into the fold." The shepherd imagery continues both in the depiction of the Lord's shepherding and in the announcement that the Lord will raise up new shepherds who will truly be that for the people.

Within the language of these verses are significant allusions to types of speech and style common to judgment and salvation oracles. The former is reflected in a kind of wordplay that creates a cor-

respondence between the sin of the kings and the judgment that is wrought against them, thus effecting a sense of poetic and appropriate justice: The "shepherds who shepherd" (רעה *rāʿâ*) will be punished for their "evil" (רעה *rāʿâ*) deeds, and those who do not "attend" (פקד *pāqad*) to the flock will be "attended" (פקד *pāqad*) to.[136] There is also an allusion to the basic assurance of the oracle of salvation in the Book of Consolation about the future restoration of the people in Jeremiah 30–31. That basic assurance is in the words "Do not fear; do not be dismayed" (cf. 30:10), here alluded to in the promise that in the future when the Lord has saved the people, they will not fear or be dismayed (v. 4).

The words of hope about new shepherds is made more specific in the second of the prose sermons of this section, vv. 5-6 (cf. 33:15-16). Having announced that no son of Jehoiachin will sit on the throne of David (22:30), the Lord now declares the divine intention to place a different descendant of David on the throne. It is not all over. An end has come, a real end. But there is more. This announcement sets forth one of the primary definitions of the rule God intends to accomplish through the human ruler: That ruler will come from the line of David, and the primary characteristic of his reign will be righteousness, a righteousness that manifests the Lord's way with this people (v. 6*b*). Righteousness is that all-encompassing notion of the proper relationship among God and people and king. Its specificity in the agency of the future king of God's rule is manifest in two ways: doing justice and righteousness (v. 5*b*) and the provision of safety for the people (v. 6*a*). The first of these is the thread that links this whole section together. "Doing justice and righteousness" is the injunction laid on the kings at Israel's beginning (22:3; cf. 21:12); it was the central sin of Jehoiakim that led to his downfall and that of the Davidic line (22:13, 15); and now it is once again the norm for the rule of God's righteous king. The safety and security of the people are directly tied to the rule of justice (see Psalm 72).

The name that is given to the future king, "the LORD is our righteousness," probably contains a play on the name of the last pre-exilic king of the

---

136. See Patrick D. Miller, *Sin and Judgment in the Prophets: A Stylistic and Theological Analysis*, SBLMS 27 (Chico, Calif.: Scholars Press, 1982).

Davidic line, "Zedekiah," which means "the LORD is my righteousness." This raises the possibility that this future oracle was uttered during Zedekiah's rule, but the wordplay could have come into use any time after Zedekiah ascended the throne. It creates a continuity and a discontinuity between the failed past and the announced future.

Finally, this word of hope declares that the future beyond judgment is so fraught with redemptive possibility that the God who brings it about will be known primarily by that saving work. The Lord of Israel has been defined as the God of the exodus.

The revelation of the name and character of God in the first part of the book of Exodus is of one "who brought you out of the land of Egypt, out of the house of slavery" (Exod 20:1). So definitive of the Lord's way and so powerful an act of redemption will be the Lord's deliverance of this destroyed and punished people that it will replace the exodus as the modifying clause whenever the Lord's name is taken in oath (e.g., "As the LORD lives . . ."). There is no homecoming without exile, and exile is the first and primary theme in Jeremiah. But it is not the last word God has for this people.

REFLECTIONS

1. This whole literary complex is dominated by the relationship between kingship and justice. That the two are mutually interdependent so that one cannot survive without the other is a central claim of these oracles. It is set forth so insistently that one must take the whole matter very seriously. Visions of the kingdom of God can function on a very spiritual plane, remote from the realities of human community. The Old Testament, however, persistently insists on that vision's centering in justice and regularly sets the criterion for determining whether justice is present in the way one treats the weakest members of the community, the powerless and the marginalized, the economically depressed, and the vulnerable. The judicial structures, including the appeal to the king, are the locus of justice, but the content of it rests in the treatment of the weak.

These texts reinforce that point with particular reference to the relationship between human rule and human justice. There is a claim here that the leader(s) of the people (one should remember that the whole of the king's court is in view, all of those who have anything to do with the seat of government) are responsible for the care of the stranger, the widow, and the orphan; their role in this matter is so fundamental that their own survival depends on how well they have carried it out. The normal structural procedures and guarantees for determining who rules and governs go out the door when the ruler(s) do not do justice, do not ensure the well-being of the people by attending to the needs of the poor and the weak. The whole system falls when the ruling power is self-aggrandizing and inattentive to the needs of the weak (see Psalm 82).

The spacious house, which is the focus of the indictment of Jehoiakim, is a continuing symbol of economic aggrandizement and the greedy consumerism of those who have access to the wealth of the land. These texts are an indictment of any leader or ruler or of any ruling system that allows the rich and the powerful to exploit the labor and energy of the poor and the weak in order to enhance their own life-styles in a conspicuously luxurious way. Even if the issue is built into the system (e.g., into the capitalistic system), the indictment still stands. The passage equates justice with the way one treats the weak and the poor; it also equates justice with economic dealings. The classic biblical case of injustice for economic enhancement is Ahab's judicial murder of Naboth in order to seize his property so that Ahab might have a better vegetable garden. Any society that allows the manipulation of political power to enhance the wealth of the powerful and the rulers/leaders at the expense of the poor and the weak stands under the indictment carried through these verses. In the 1990s, American society and American politics were a classic example of such manipulation of political power, as the "members of the court," the president and the administration together with the political rulers in Congress, cut the taxes of the rich, raised them for the poor, and sought to balance the national budget on the backs of children, dependent mothers, and immigrants, the contemporary equivalents of the widow, the poor, the orphan, and the stranger.

There is no indication in these texts that the fundamental matters in ruling the human community under God's direction and by God's instruction have anything to do with more or less government intervention. They have to do with whether or not that government attends to the security of the country by tending to the cause of the poor and the needy. This was the plumb line that Amos set in the middle of the northern kingdom that found it wanting. It is always the plumb line by which the Lord measures a people and the degree to which they embody the righteous rule that is the Lord's will and way for human life.

2. Consistent with this understanding is the way these texts equate the relationship to God, here characterized as "knowing" God (22:16), with the maintenance of justice in the human community. There is no separation of the social and the spiritual. What does the Lord expect of those who worship and acknowledge the Lord's claim on their lives? How do we live in good relation to the Lord who has saved us? The answer given here is echoed again and again in the prophets: by doing justice, by hating evil, and by loving the good, the specifics of which, once again, is the careful administration of justice (Amos 5:14-15). When Isaiah tells the people that Israel does not know (Isa 1:3), he goes on to spell out what that missing knowledge is: cease doing evil, learn to do good, seek justice, rescue the oppressed, defend the orphan, plead for the widow (Isa 1:17; cf. Mic 6:8). The willingness to ignore matters of justice while continuing to praise the Lord and worship is precisely the state of affairs that existed in late pre-exilic Judah. It brought about an end of that people and their government. It may do the same for any other, certainly for any people who seek to claim the covenantal relationship. There is no possibility of substituting "Praise the Lord!" for doing justice.

3. We need to pay attention to the implicit claim in the comparison of Josiah and his son Jehoiakim to the apparent indication that there is a relation between keeping justice and righteousness and how well society operates (22:15-16). This is not a matter of some kind of rational calculus that rewards according to good deeds. It is a recognition that there is some coherent relationship between a careful leader's attention to the needs of the people and the way things go in society. The community works better, and the social order enhances tranquillity and well-being when "the least of these" is tended to, protected, given an economic base. We tend to turn the matter on its head and assume that the good society is one that allows those with economic means to hold on to them and not worry too much about those who have nothing. There are significant moments in American history that give the lie to that notion. The trouble spots that exist in American cities confirm the sense that without attending to the economic oppression implicit in the system and experienced concretely by the poor of this country, it will not "go well" with us. Yet the "king" and those who go in and out the palace gates tend to seek the good in the good of the better off, and the rest of us are complicit in accepting that standard. It is not the Lord's way for things to work well. It is more likely to be the road to judgment.

JEREMIAH 23:9-40, CONCERNING THE PROPHETS

NIV

⁹Concerning the prophets:

My heart is broken within me;
  all my bones tremble.
I am like a drunken man,
  like a man overcome by wine,
because of the LORD
  and his holy words.
¹⁰The land is full of adulterers;
  because of the curse*ᵃ* the land lies parched*ᵇ*
  and the pastures in the desert are withered.
The ⌊prophets⌋ follow an evil course
  and use their power unjustly.

¹¹"Both prophet and priest are godless;
  even in my temple I find their wickedness,"
                    declares the LORD.
¹²"Therefore their path will become slippery;
  they will be banished to darkness
  and there they will fall.
I will bring disaster on them
  in the year they are punished,"
                    declares the LORD.

¹³"Among the prophets of Samaria
  I saw this repulsive thing:
They prophesied by Baal
  and led my people Israel astray.
¹⁴And among the prophets of Jerusalem
  I have seen something horrible:
  They commit adultery and live a lie.
They strengthen the hands of evildoers,
  so that no one turns from his wickedness.
They are all like Sodom to me;
  the people of Jerusalem are like Gomorrah."

¹⁵Therefore, this is what the LORD Almighty says
concerning the prophets:

"I will make them eat bitter food
  and drink poisoned water,
because from the prophets of Jerusalem
  ungodliness has spread throughout the land."

¹⁶This is what the LORD Almighty says:

ᵃ10 Or *because of these things*   *ᵇ10* Or *land mourns*

NRSV

9Concerning the prophets:
My heart is crushed within me,
  all my bones shake;
I have become like a drunkard,
  like one overcome by wine,
because of the LORD
  and because of his holy words.
¹⁰ For the land is full of adulterers;
  because of the curse the land mourns,
  and the pastures of the wilderness are dried
    up.
Their course has been evil,
  and their might is not right.
¹¹ Both prophet and priest are ungodly;
  even in my house I have found their
    wickedness,   says the LORD.
¹² Therefore their way shall be to them
  like slippery paths in the darkness,
  into which they shall be driven and fall;
for I will bring disaster upon them
  in the year of their punishment,
                    says the LORD.
¹³ In the prophets of Samaria
  I saw a disgusting thing:
they prophesied by Baal
  and led my people Israel astray.
¹⁴ But in the prophets of Jerusalem
  I have seen a more shocking thing:
they commit adultery and walk in lies;
  they strengthen the hands of evildoers,
  so that no one turns from wickedness;
all of them have become like Sodom to me,
  and its inhabitants like Gomorrah.
¹⁵ Therefore thus says the LORD of hosts
  concerning the prophets:
"I am going to make them eat wormwood,
  and give them poisoned water to drink;
for from the prophets of Jerusalem
  ungodliness has spread throughout the land."

16Thus says the LORD of hosts: Do not listen to
the words of the prophets who prophesy to you;
they are deluding you. They speak visions of their

NIV

"Do not listen to what the prophets are
    prophesying to you;
  they fill you with false hopes.
They speak visions from their own minds,
    not from the mouth of the LORD.
[17]They keep saying to those who despise me,
    'The LORD says: You will have peace.'
And to all who follow the stubbornness of
    their hearts
  they say, 'No harm will come to you.'
[18]But which of them has stood in the council of
    the LORD
  to see or to hear his word?
  Who has listened and heard his word?
[19]See, the storm of the LORD
    will burst out in wrath,
  a whirlwind swirling down
    on the heads of the wicked.
[20]The anger of the LORD will not turn back
    until he fully accomplishes
    the purposes of his heart.
In days to come
  you will understand it clearly.
[21]I did not send these prophets,
    yet they have run with their message;
I did not speak to them,
    yet they have prophesied.
[22]But if they had stood in my council,
    they would have proclaimed my words to
    my people
  and would have turned them from their evil
    ways
  and from their evil deeds.

[23]"Am I only a God nearby,"
            declares the LORD,
    "and not a God far away?
[24]Can anyone hide in secret places
    so that I cannot see him?"
            declares the LORD.
  "Do not I fill heaven and earth?"
            declares the LORD.

[25]"I have heard what the prophets say who
prophesy lies in my name. They say, 'I had a
dream! I had a dream!' [26]How long will this continue in the hearts of these lying prophets, who
prophesy the delusions of their own minds?
[27]They think the dreams they tell one another will

NRSV

own minds, not from the mouth of the LORD.
[17]They keep saying to those who despise the word
of the LORD, "It shall be well with you"; and to all
who stubbornly follow their own stubborn hearts,
they say, "No calamity shall come upon you."

[18] For who has stood in the council of the LORD
    so as to see and to hear his word?
  Who has given heed to his word so as to
    proclaim it?
[19] Look, the storm of the LORD!
    Wrath has gone forth,
  a whirling tempest;
    it will burst upon the head of the wicked.
[20] The anger of the LORD will not turn back
    until he has executed and accomplished
    the intents of his mind.
In the latter days you will understand it
    clearly.

[21] I did not send the prophets,
    yet they ran;
  I did not speak to them,
    yet they prophesied.
[22] But if they had stood in my council,
    then they would have proclaimed my
        words to my people,
  and they would have turned them from their
        evil way,
    and from the evil of their doings.

[23]Am I a God near by, says the LORD, and not
a God far off? [24]Who can hide in secret places so
that I cannot see them? says the LORD. Do I not fill
heaven and earth? says the LORD. [25]I have heard
what the prophets have said who prophesy lies in
my name, saying, "I have dreamed, I have
dreamed!" [26]How long? Will the hearts of the
prophets ever turn back—those who prophesy
lies, and who prophesy the deceit of their own
heart? [27]They plan to make my people forget my
name by their dreams that they tell one another,
just as their ancestors forgot my name for Baal.
[28]Let the prophet who has a dream tell the dream,
but let the one who has my word speak my word
faithfully. What has straw in common with
wheat? says the LORD. [29]Is not my word like fire,
says the LORD, and like a hammer that breaks a

NIV

make my people forget my name, just as their fathers forgot my name through Baal worship. [28]Let the prophet who has a dream tell his dream, but let the one who has my word speak it faithfully. For what has straw to do with grain?" declares the LORD. [29]"Is not my word like fire," declares the LORD, "and like a hammer that breaks a rock in pieces?

[30]"Therefore," declares the LORD, "I am against the prophets who steal from one another words supposedly from me. [31]Yes," declares the LORD, "I am against the prophets who wag their own tongues and yet declare, 'The LORD declares.' [32]Indeed, I am against those who prophesy false dreams," declares the LORD. "They tell them and lead my people astray with their reckless lies, yet I did not send or appoint them. They do not benefit these people in the least," declares the LORD.

[33]"When these people, or a prophet or a priest, ask you, 'What is the oracle[a] of the LORD?' say to them, 'What oracle?[b] I will forsake you, declares the LORD.' [34]If a prophet or a priest or anyone else claims, 'This is the oracle of the LORD,' I will punish that man and his household. [35]This is what each of you keeps on saying to his friend or relative: 'What is the LORD's answer?' or 'What has the LORD spoken?' [36]But you must not mention 'the oracle of the LORD' again, because every man's own word becomes his oracle and so you distort the words of the living God, the LORD Almighty, our God. [37]This is what you keep saying to a prophet: 'What is the LORD's answer to you?' or 'What has the LORD spoken?' [38]Although you claim, 'This is the oracle of the LORD,' this is what the LORD says: You used the words, 'This is the oracle of the LORD,' even though I told you that you must not claim, 'This is the oracle of the LORD.' [39]Therefore, I will surely forget you and cast you out of my presence along with the city I gave to you and your fathers. [40]I will bring upon you everlasting disgrace—everlasting shame that will not be forgotten."

[a]33 Or burden (see Septuagint and Vulgate)   [b]33 Hebrew; Septuagint and Vulgate 'You are the burden. (The Hebrew for oracle and burden is the same.')

NRSV

rock in pieces? [30]See, therefore, I am against the prophets, says the LORD, who steal my words from one another. [31]See, I am against the prophets, says the LORD, who use their own tongues and say, "Says the LORD." [32]See, I am against those who prophesy lying dreams, says the LORD, and who tell them, and who lead my people astray by their lies and their recklessness, when I did not send them or appoint them; so they do not profit this people at all, says the LORD.

[33]When this people, or a prophet, or a priest asks you, "What is the burden of the LORD?" you shall say to them, "You are the burden,[a] and I will cast you off, says the LORD." [34]And as for the prophet, priest, or the people who say, "The burden of the LORD," I will punish them and their households. [35]Thus shall you say to one another, among yourselves, "What has the LORD answered?" or "What has the LORD spoken?" [36]But "the burden of the LORD" you shall mention no more, for the burden is everyone's own word, and so you pervert the words of the living God, the LORD of hosts, our God. [37]Thus you shall ask the prophet, "What has the LORD answered you?" or "What has the LORD spoken?" [38]But if you say, "the burden of the LORD," thus says the LORD: Because you have said these words, "the burden of the LORD," when I sent to you, saying, You shall not say, "the burden of the LORD," [39]therefore, I will surely lift you up[b] and cast you away from my presence, you and the city that I gave to you and your ancestors. [40]And I will bring upon you everlasting disgrace and perpetual shame, which shall not be forgotten.

[a]Gk Vg: Heb What burden   [b]Heb Mss Gk Vg: MT forget you

COMMENTARY

No prophetic book talks more about prophets and prophecy than does the book of Jeremiah. On the one hand, there is the constant presence of the prophet himself, the account of his call and the constant references or allusions to it as well as the dialogues with the Lord about his vocation and where it has led him. On the other hand, there are the so-called false prophets, or in Jeremiah's terms, the prophets of peace and well-being, who seemed to be fairly numerous in his day and a chief problem for the effective communication of the word of the Lord, which was not peace and well-being but doom and disaster. This chapter presents us with a collection of oracles indicting and announcing judgment upon the prophets, and at the same time polemically seeking to counter their influence.

23:9-12. The indictment of the prophets begins with a more general statement describing the extent of the wickedness in the land, with which the religious leaders, both priest and prophet, collude. The opening words, reminiscent of the earlier laments of Jeremiah in chaps. 11–20, are written in the lament style. While v. 9 is sometimes read as an experience of ecstasy and sometimes as an indication of how shocked the prophet was, it is clearly an expression of distress. The NIV translation of the first half of the verse, with reference to the broken heart, is preferable to the NRSV. The brokenhearted are a category of sufferers about whom we hear elsewhere (e.g., Ps 34:18[19]; Isa 61:1), and the shaking bones remind the reader of the plight of the lamenter in Ps 22:14. The terrible words of the Lord have undone the prophet. It is not clear whether these are the words of indictment or of judgment. If they are what follows—(see the "for" at the beginning of v. 10) then it is both indictment and judgment that has elicited the distress.

The indictment has two parts: a nation full of adulterers (v. 10a), and religious leadership whose perversion of responsibility takes place even in the very sanctuary of the Lord (v. 11). We are not told what the specifics of that "ungodly" behavior are, though the accusation is repeated in v. 15. The "adultery" referred to may be the real thing, the breakdown of marital relationships and a casual involvement in affairs and sexual activity with other than the marriage partner (see 5:7), or it may be a metaphor for the faithlessness of the people to the service of the Lord. In the next passage, adultery is identified again, this time on the part of the prophets. There, too, it may be actual adultery, but the reference to the prophets' prophesying by Baal suggests the possibility that there, as well as here, the turning to other "lovers," to other gods and their enticements, may be in view. The imagery of Israel/Judah as a faithless spouse hotly pursuing other lovers instead of being devoted fully to the service of the Lord of Israel permeates chaps. 2–4.

The allusion to a "curse" seems to have in mind a drought as punishment for the sins of the people, and this may be part of what has distressed the prophet (v. 9). In any event, consistent with the form of the prophetic judgment speech, the indictment of vv. 10-11 is followed in v. 12 by the announcement of judgment. The punishment joins the outcome of going down the road the "adulterers," priests, and prophets have chosen to travel with a clear announcement that the darkness that lies ahead is the specific work of the Lord. Those who have done what is bad, what is evil (רעה *rā'â*, v. 10c), will receive the bad, disaster (*rā'â*, v. 12b).

23:13-15. The point that has just been made moves even more specifically into an announcement of judgment against the prophets. The indictment shares similarities with vv. 9-12 (see above), but the catalog of sins grows longer and ever more specific. Adultery, whether real or symbolic of apostasy, joins with prophesying in the name of another god (v. 13b), lying, not telling the truth about the divine intent and the future that is to come, and supporting the schemes and manipulations of other people (v. 14b). Rather than serving as a corrective in a corrupt society, the prophets contribute to a greater corruption, supporting the wealthy and powerful to do in the weak. A powerful metaphor leads into the punishment. The allusion to Sodom and Gomorrah (Genesis 18–19) evokes a symbol of absolute and total corruption and wickedness. It is difficult to believe that Judah at any time could be compared to Sodom and Gomorrah, but, even allowing for prophetic hyperbole, the comparison is a damning indictment and indicates the pervasiveness of human wickedness in Judah. As in an earlier piece of Jeremianic prophecy, the depth of Judah's sin, or in this case the sin of its prophets, is underscored by a comparison with that of the northern kingdom, Israel (3:6-14). In the Deuteronomistic History of 1 and 2 Kings, the sins of Jeroboam and the northern kingdom are the height of wickedness and disobedience to the Lord. But now it is no better in the south. There is a terrible contagion of godlessness in the land. But it will not last long.

23:16-22. There are three parts to this passage: vv. 16-17, vv. 18-20, and vv. 21-22. Whether or not these three parts were originally a whole, they are properly joined now. The opening section (vv. 16-17) is an indictment of the false prophets. The second section takes the reader more deeply into the matter to see where the source of the problem of the prophets lies and in doing so counters the word of the prophets. Finally, the third section answers the question posed in the second to clarify once and for all why the words of these prophets cannot be trusted. In this context, we are presented with one of the most pervasive and important symbols or images of the OT: that of the divine council or the heavenly assembly.

The accusation that is made in vv. 16-17 is essentially the same that is found in 14:13-16. The heart of the matter is that the prophets are telling the people that everything is all right (שָׁלוֹם šālôm), and that is a lie. It is not a correct assessment of the situation, and it is not a word that comes from the Lord. We do not know who the "prophets" are except in a particular case (see chap. 28), but they seem to be an extensive group whose message is fairly unanimous. Elsewhere, we encounter groups of prophets, sometimes called the "company of prophets" (e.g., 2 Kgs 2:3, 15). While it is customary to think about prophets as lone and named individuals, there were also prophetic bands or guilds whose particular identities are not known to us but who are recorded in the text as numbering 100 (1 Kings 18) or 400 (1 Kings 22; see 1 Kgs 18:19). Such groups could be authentic prophets of the Lord, as in 1 Kings 18. But they also could be those who did not speak the word of the Lord but fed the sentiments of the people and claimed it was the word of the Lord. That seems to have been the case here. These prophets, like Jeremiah, began their message to the people with "Thus says

the LORD" (cf. 29:2, 11). In this instance, it is a lie that serves to lull the people into complacency, feeding their own inclinations to keep on doing exactly what they want without being disturbed. Two of the most persistent problems of Judean society in Jeremiah's time are joined here: the falsehood of the prophets and the stubbornness of the people. The reader of the book to this point will have heard these points scored so often that their very repetition serves to make the point of stubbornness (3:17; 7:24; 9:14; 11:8; 13:10; 16:12; 18:12). There is a major prophetic conflict between those who repeatedly say, "All will be well and no harm will come to you" (cf. 4:12-13; 14:13), and Jeremiah, who speaks the opposite word constantly (e.g., 1:14; 4:6; 6:1; 11:11, 17, 23; 14:16). But how does one know which prophecy is correct?

It is to that question that the rest of this passage, specifically vv. 18, 21-22, is directed. We learn that the true word of the Lord comes only to the prophet who has stood in the council of the Lord, the heavenly assembly gathered around the throne of the Lord, and who has received the decree of the Lord that the prophet is to proclaim. The "council of the Lord," a prominent image in Israel's faith, was a way of conceptualizing the divine government of the cosmos. The image conveyed a sense of the rule of the Lord from above, a transcendent ground of divine action. The council or assembly is that group of generally nameless semi-divine beings, represented in various ways by such terms as "cherubim," "seraphim," "angels," or simply "divine ones." They worship the Lord and do the Lord's bidding. Among the biblical passages that have their setting in the heavenly council are 1 Kgs 22; Job 1–2; Psalm 82; Isaiah 6; and possibly Isa 40:1-11 (see also Amos 3:7; Zech 3:1-5). Many other texts make implicit allusion to the council. The divine council served as a kind of court, an entourage of the One seated on the heavenly throne, but a court that could serve a governmental function, decreeing and deciding what would happen on earth or marching into battle behind the Lord as the divine warrior. The decisions, however, were those of the Lord. None of the council had any autonomous or independent status, not even the "adversary" whose title "satan" (שָׂטָן śāṭān) came to be a proper name in the tradition.

This passage shows that prophecy had its conceptuality directly tied to this image. The prophet was understood to be the messenger of the Lord, the herald of the divine decree from the council of the Lord. That is explicitly the claim of vv. 18, 21-22, and it is confirmed in 1 Kings 22 where the prophet Micaiah is identified as the true prophet because he is able to reveal the actions of the Lord in the heavenly assembly (1 Kgs 22:19-23). The prophets who are saying all is well and that nothing bad will happen have not stood before the Lord and heard the Lord's decree in the heavenly council. If they had, they would not be saying that all is well. They are false prophets not only because their words are not true but also because they claim to speak the word of the Lord that comes only from the divine council, where these prophets have not been. If they had, indeed, stood before the Lord, their words would be quite different. The fact that the Lord assumes the people would have turned from their evil ways effects a kind of tension in the reader, for any close attention to Scripture reveals how often the people did not attend to the prophets. Yet there is a thread running through the prophetic books, insisting that the words of the prophets really were meant to induce the listeners to repent and change their ways (e.g., 1 Samuel 12; Jonah).

It is difficult for the interpreter to determine how it was that the prophet gained access to the council of the Lord. Isaiah 6 and 1 Kings 22 suggest the likelihood of some kind of visionary experience that may have belonged to the ecstatic dimension of prophecy. Contemporary language for this would be an "out-of-body experience." From a number of texts, we know that the prophets had visions; the superscriptions of the prophetic books often speak of the "vision" or words the prophet "saw" (e.g., Isa 1:1; Ezek 1:1; Amos 1:1; Obad 1; Nah 1:1). Such a revelatory medium is not accessible to rational analysis or objectification, but the authority of such a vision was profound and clearly part of the credentials of the true prophet. The only problem, of course, was that any prophet could claim to have a vision of the council of the Lord.

In the middle of this oracular discussion of true and false prophecy, vv. 19-20 place a separate oracle envisioning the judgment that is to come in the form of a mighty storm or tempest. While some interpreters would see these words as originating from another context, it is best to view them in the present context and thus as a confirming word that the prophets of an untrue peace, of a false word of calm, are dead wrong. They do not know the "intentions" (מזמות *mĕzimmôt*), the plans, or the decrees of the Lord, which are judgment and calamity (v. 20). When it is all over, the Lord says, you will see who was correct.

23:23-24. These verses assert the sovereignty of God, transcendent and immanent, with the accent on the transcendence. It is true that God is near, at hand, able to deliver; but what is sometimes forgotten is that God is also transcendent, filling heaven and earth, able to discern all that happens, and "from whom no secret is hid." These rhetorical questions intimate some kind of dispute, some challenge to which the Lord responds through the prophet.

While these verses fit rather loosely in their context, that context suggests that they have been brought into the argument about the false prophets. Apparently, the claim of God to be near, a claim that in Deuteronomy is asserted as one of the distinctive realities of Israelite faith, is used by the prophets of peace in a manipulative way; yet their claim to know the word of God is as false as the belief that the presence of the Temple was an automatic protection against any harm to the nation. In the face of both distortions, the assertion of the greatness and transcendence of God challenges such easy claims about God.

23:25-32. The continuing attack on the false prophets who say that all is well continues in these verses with a challenge to their prophetic dreams. Such dreams were a common way of discerning the intention and plan of God for the future and as such were acceptable modes of revelation in ancient Israel (e.g., the dreams in the Joseph story). Here, however, the dreams of the prophets come under attack, apparently because the prophets have told their dreams as the word of the Lord, when they are just their own imaginings; they are "lying dreams" (v. 32). The issue, however, is not the vehicle of revelation but the source. These prophecies are not the word of the Lord spoken faithfully; rather, they are deceitful words, originating not from the heavenly throne and the divine council but from "the deceit of their own heart" (v. 26), "their own tongues" (v. 31). The point is reinforced with the comparison of straw to wheat. One can no more claim these recounted prophetic dreams as the word of the Lord than one can regard straw as wheat. Rather than being testimony to the Lord and what the Lord is doing, these dreams turn the people away so that they forget the Lord's name.

The reference to forgetting the Lord's name, occurring twice in v. 27, is a way of saying that the prophets portray a god other than the one who has created and led this people. The name of God is an indicator of the Lord's character. They have presented a god who is easily accessible and manipulatible, undemanding, and no threat. But this God is not that way. The point is made in dramatic fashion with the comparison of the word of the Lord to fire and to a sledgehammer shattering a rock. This is a far cry from the easy assurance of the prophets of peace that the Lord of Israel will do no harm to the people.

In vv. 30-32, the Lord makes an emphatic statement of opposition, and thus judgment, against the false prophets. Three times comes the divine word: "See, I am against the prophets, who. . . ." The relative clauses serve to lay out the specifics of the indictment against these prophets. The fundamental and reiterated word is that their prophecies are lies ("lying dreams," "who use their own tongues and say, 'Says the LORD'"). The effect of their false message is to lead the people astray and to have them once again trusting in what does not profit (see the Commentary on 2:4-13). The reference to stealing "my words" from one another (v. 30) is somewhat enigmatic. It could have to do with the false prophets stealing oracles from true prophets, like Jeremiah. More likely, it has to do with their resorting to appropriating oracles from

one another, "repeating at second hand what they had heard others say, while pretending that this had come to them as a revelation from Yahweh."[137]

23:33-40. This long section against the prophets concludes with an oracular wordplay that is elaborated so that it becomes a part of the prophetic conflict presupposed in this chapter. The wordplay is in v. 33 with the word "burden" (משׂא *maśśā'*), which is a technical term for "oracle" and can also mean "burden." The point of the wordplay, therefore, is simple and clear: Whoever asks for an "oracle" will receive a "burden." The *maśśā'* is a *maśśā'*. Thus the people have become a burden that the Lord will cast off.

This wordplay is then developed into a prohibition against saying "the burden [oracle] of the LORD." Presumably, this is to stop the false prophets, who would have begun their lying oracles, in some instances at least, with an introductory or concluding "the oracle [burden] of the LORD." The prophetic oracle is so misused that the Lord will no longer permit the word *maśśā'* to be used in reference to the Word of the Lord. It can only refer to human words. The situation is so dire, the perversion of the prophetic office so great, that the Lord prohibits the use of *maśśā'* on the pain of being "cast off" (vv. 33, 39) just for having uttered the word. This is a way of reinforcing the already forceful, "I have set myself against the prophets." So corrupt and false have become all the claims to speak "the oracle/word of the LORD" that the very utterance of the phrase brings judgment.

137. John Bright, *Jeremiah*, AB 21 (Garden City: Doubleday, 1965) 155.

REFLECTIONS

1. The several occasions in Jeremiah where Judah is compared to Israel's wickedness and found wanting gnaw at the tendency to assume a kind of moral superiority by one part of the community of faith over against another. Israel's and Judah's experiences were particular and not repeatable. The tendency to moral arrogance is a specter that rises before any later community that reads these oracles. And thus it is a warning. It is a little like Jesus' words about observing the mote in your neighbor's eye, unaware of the beam in your own. The specifics in this case have to do with the prophets, but they are a microcosm of the whole community ("all of them," v. 14). The tendency to assume that the ills of other groups are surely not ours becomes a false security. How could anything be worse than what "they" have done? Jeremiah's prophecy cautions rather fiercely against such a reading of the present positively against a negative view of the past. There is little evidence of moral progress in the story of the human race. Precisely where that assumption is implicitly operative may be the point where the word of judgment strikes home.

2. This passage suggests two possible criteria for distinguishing the true prophet of the Lord. One of them, the access of the prophet to the council of the Lord, is difficult for the modern reader to grasp where that imagery has little concrete meaning and reality. The other criterion is less clearly a mark of the false prophet, but it so regularly appears in Jeremiah that one is thereby duly warned that it may often be the case. If the message of the prophetic bearers and interpreters of the Lord's Word and the Lord's way have nothing but good news to say in good times, then the listeners should be on their guard. Prophets did bring authentically good news. One hears such words even from the prophet Jeremiah (e.g., chaps. 30–31). But that good news comes to people who are down and think all is lost. The ones who have nothing to say but peace in a time when many in the community are enjoying all the good things of the good life may be doing nothing but feeding the desire for the status quo, undergirding confidence on the part of the well-to-do and powerful so that they can keep on doing as they are ("stubbornly following the stubbornness of their own hearts"), complacent in the face of obvious ills and sickness in the larger society. That was the case in Jeremiah's time. The community that has held on to this story and these words does not do so simply to understand the past. Readers who take up the text again do so to be challenged to hear the word of the Lord in their time.

The one Hebrew word that many people know, in and out of the community of faith, is the word *shalom,* "Peace." It is a good word, properly pointing to the intention of God for well-being and the enjoyment of God's good gifts. This chapter reminds us, however, that the word *shalom* can be uttered in the wrong time. It flows so easily from our lips that we may hear and utter it ignorant of or ignoring all the indicators that the situation in which we find ourselves is not a time of peace, that the future is not "good-time Charlie" but a dangerous and deadly prospect. The prophets of old said "Peace" now and "Peace" on the horizon, and they were dead wrong about both things. The minority voice, the tiny minority voice that calls the people to account against the norms and criteria of community conduct that pervade the scriptures, and particularly the prophetic books—do justice and righteousness; do no wrong or violence to the stranger, the orphan, and the widow—is often an unwelcome voice and not as mellifluous to our ears, much less to our hearts and minds, as the term "Shalom!" There are times when *shalom* is not the right word for the community to listen to or to speak, when it is the wrong word at the wrong time.

3. The image of the council of the Lord is so mythological in its character, with its setting in the divine world, a vision of heaven that has no concrete reality for human beings who know heaven only in poetic terms. But that may, indeed, be the point, that the poetic presentation points to a reality that cannot be made literal and can be apprehended only by a transcendent medium, like poetry or music, comprehensible to us in our depths but not subject to or reducible to rational explanation. The council of the Lord is a pointer to the rule of God, to the activity of God that takes place in our earthly world but has a transcendent origin. It is in this instance a way of identifying legitimate authority for the divine spokesperson. All sorts of words are said and authoritative claims are made. The Bible constantly reminds us that the word of the Lord comes to us from outside ourselves and is not to be handled as other things are. The prophetic word is part of the divine government, the means by which the Lord speaks in a situation that seems to be controlled by other forces and closed to divine intervention and rule. The prophet was part of a kind of heavenly checks and balances on the powers that be on earth. Thus through whatever avenues we may search for a contemporary prophetic word, it will probably play a similar kind of role—a word of the Lord that calls us to account on the basis of an authority that transcends all human authorities. For the community that lives by Scripture, that authority will probably be discerned most accurately in those words that reflect the instruction given to us in Scripture. If the church does not have prophets with visions of the heavenly council, it does have the stories of the prophets who did stand in the council of the Lord, and, as their visions and words have become canonical, they have become the authority by which we are called to faithful discernment of "the word of the LORD" in our own time.

4. Yet there is no infallible way of saying that this prophet truly speaks the word of the Lord and that one does not. It was terribly difficult for the people of Judah to discern between them, and it is surely no easier for us. That they had to struggle to determine the authentic word of the Lord surely means that we cannot avoid the same. Like ancient Judah, we may not know who has properly discerned what the Lord is doing in the world until after the fact. In the meantime, what do we do? Jeremiah is instructive in this regard, and this text is one of the most instructive. If we cannot be certain who has stood before the Lord, we might at least determine who is saying a word that we like to hear because it confirms us in our self-advantaged positions, supports us in what we want to hear, promises us no disturbance of our patterns of life, especially when they clearly work to our advantage, even when they work to the disadvantage of others in the community, specifically the lesser members, the poor and the disadvantaged. One of the problems in Jeremiah's time was that the people did not struggle enough over the question of which of the contradictory words they were receiving might be the word of the Lord. A sign to watch for with regard to false prophecy is whether the words feel good, whether the word of the Lord that is being proclaimed to us makes us comfortable. In Israel's time, that was almost always a sure sign that the proclamation was not the word of the Lord. The true word of the Lord came from those voices who spoke uncomfortable and disturbing words, who challenged the ways and conduct of the community, who called for radical change in no uncertain terms. It probably still does.

5. In the midst of the indictment of the false prophets of peace, there is a richly suggestive comparison of the word of the Lord to fire and a hammer. Fire illuminates, as does the divine word, but it also consumes. It cannot be touched. It is not easily contained. The one who claims to have hold of the word of God may find himself or herself terribly burned as well. Like fire, the word of the Lord can consume and destroy. It can shatter what it addresses like a sledgehammer shattering hard rock. There is thus both a negative and a positive message in this imagery, a warning about the dangers for those who claim to speak the word of the Lord and may find themselves burned or shattered by it, but there is a glimpse of the power of that word as it operates in human life and human history, raising up and putting down, holding things together and undoing them.

There is a powerful directive in this text to those who find themselves in any way entrusted with the word of the Lord: "Let the one who has my word speak my word faithfully" (v. 28). That is finally the fundamental issue for all who declare, teach, interpret, preach, or handle the word of the Lord in any fashion. Has the interpreter faithfully let the Lord's way come to light? Has Jesus been truthfully presented to those who would see him (John 12:21)? Job confronted his friends with the question: "Will you tell lies in God's behalf?" It is the same question to the prophets of Jeremiah's time and to any who handle the word of God. One thing is required: a faithful and true listening and declaring of the word that has been handed on.

6. Particularly in the formulations of 23:17 and 32, we encounter the way in which sinfulness is uncovered in the stubbornness of a people who hear what they want to hear, but a stubbornness that is also the outcome of the failure and sin of leaders who do not do what they are supposed to do. The stubbornness of the wider group is without doubt, but it is reinforced by a religious leadership that caters to and feeds the corruption of the people rather than challenging it. If one asks about what elicits the judgment of God—that is, about who is responsible—one finds that it is regularly a shared responsibility. On the one hand are stubborn hearts that seek their own self-aggrandizement, economic luxury, and personal security, all the while resistant to any words that would threaten those aims and force a wider concern for others in the community; on the other hand is a religious leadership that has lost its integrity and takes its bearings from the sentiments of the people as a weather vane gets its movements from the blowing of the wind. This is so regularly the case not only in Jeremiah but also in the prophets generally that one knows it is characteristic of the human situation. The sheep want to go their own way and will not follow the right way of the shepherd; yet the shepherd will not show them the right way but lets them go where they wish. The failure of the community of faith is persistently such a joint responsibility: people whose self-interest controls their conduct rather than the way of the Lord and leaders who lead the people down ways that "do not profit." When that was the situation in ancient Israel, God's judgment was on the horizon. One cannot help wondering if that is not always the case.

JEREMIAH 24:1-10, GOOD AND BAD FIGS

NIV

24 After Jehoiachin[a] son of Jehoiakim king of Judah and the officials, the craftsmen and the artisans of Judah were carried into exile from Jerusalem to Babylon by Nebuchadnezzar king of Babylon, the LORD showed me two baskets of figs placed in front of the temple of the LORD. ²One basket had very good figs, like those that ripen early; the other basket had very poor figs, so bad they could not be eaten.

³Then the LORD asked me, "What do you see, Jeremiah?"

"Figs," I answered. "The good ones are very good, but the poor ones are so bad they cannot be eaten."

⁴Then the word of the LORD came to me: ⁵"This is what the LORD, the God of Israel, says: 'Like these good figs, I regard as good the exiles from Judah, whom I sent away from this place to the land of the Babylonians.[b] ⁶My eyes will watch over them for their good, and I will bring them back to this land. I will build them up and not tear them down; I will plant them and not uproot them. ⁷I will give them a heart to know me, that I am the LORD. They will be my people, and I will be their God, for they will return to me with all their heart.

⁸"'But like the poor figs, which are so bad they cannot be eaten,' says the LORD, 'so will I deal

^a1 Hebrew *Jeconiah,* a variant of *Jehoiachin*   ^b5 Or *Chaldeans*

NRSV

24 The LORD showed me two baskets of figs placed before the temple of the LORD. This was after King Nebuchadrezzar of Babylon had taken into exile from Jerusalem King Jeconiah son of Jehoiakim of Judah, together with the officials of Judah, the artisans, and the smiths, and had brought them to Babylon. ²One basket had very good figs, like first-ripe figs, but the other basket had very bad figs, so bad that they could not be eaten. ³And the LORD said to me, "What do you see, Jeremiah?" I said, "Figs, the good figs very good, and the bad figs very bad, so bad that they cannot be eaten."

⁴Then the word of the LORD came to me: ⁵Thus says the LORD, the God of Israel: Like these good figs, so I will regard as good the exiles from Judah, whom I have sent away from this place to the land of the Chaldeans. ⁶I will set my eyes upon them for good, and I will bring them back to this land. I will build them up, and not tear them down; I will plant them, and not pluck them up. ⁷I will give them a heart to know that I am the LORD; and they shall be my people and I will be their God, for they shall return to me with their whole heart.

⁸But thus says the LORD: Like the bad figs that are so bad they cannot be eaten, so will I treat King Zedekiah of Judah, his officials, the remnant of Jerusalem who remain in this land, and those

NIV

with Zedekiah king of Judah, his officials and the survivors from Jerusalem, whether they remain in this land or live in Egypt. [9]I will make them abhorrent and an offense to all the kingdoms of the earth, a reproach and a byword, an object of ridicule and cursing, wherever I banish them. [10]I will send the sword, famine and plague against them until they are destroyed from the land I gave to them and their fathers.' "

NRSV

who live in the land of Egypt. [9]I will make them a horror, an evil thing, to all the kingdoms of the earth—a disgrace, a byword, a taunt, and a curse in all the places where I shall drive them. [10]And I will send sword, famine, and pestilence upon them, until they are utterly destroyed from the land that I gave to them and their ancestors.

COMMENTARY

The form of this narrative is that of a vision report, and as such it has similarities with 1:11-19 and to some extent with 18:1-12, though the latter focuses on an interpreted action rather than a symbol (cf. Amos 7:1–8:3). It begins with an introductory word that identifies the symbol as something that the Lord has shown to the prophet (vv. 1 *a,* 2). There follows a dialogue in which the Lord asks the prophet what he sees (v. 3*a*), and the prophet's answer (v. 3*b*) then evokes an interpretive oracular speech by the Lord that explains the meaning of the symbol (vv. 4-10). The date formula in v. 1*b* was probably added secondarily but anticipates the interpretation of the vision of the figs by locating this event after the first exile to Babylon and before the second.

It is that period and the division of the Judean community into two quite different geographical locales and circumstances that is the presupposition of the oracle. The passage reflects a tension between these two groups and clearly represents a judgment for one group and against the other.[138] The passage has been regarded as a piece of religious propaganda in behalf of the exiles in Babylon, and there is no denying that it serves their cause. It also represents a kind of canonical decision, in the process of the formation and redaction of the book of Jeremiah that the future of Judah centered in the community in exile rather than those who had escaped that fate and may

have presumed, for a time, that they were the true continuity of God's people.

The symbol and its interpretation are quite clear: The good fruit symbolizes the exiles in Babylon, and the rotten fruit the survivors at home. While one can recognize the propagandizing possibility in such an oracle, it is important to recognize how thoroughly it goes against the grain of what one might have expected and also how consistent it is with the message of Jeremiah as a whole—that is, with the word of the Lord from beginning to end. The danger and delusion of those who survived the first exile is to think of themselves as saved, as having no worries. The obvious disaster to the others and the fact of their survival would have tended to lull the inhabitants of Jerusalem into thinking that the judgment of God did not and would not affect them, that life—and the ills and sins of that communal life—could go on as before. Against that natural reading comes a contrary word: Only the community that has gone under judgment will come out the other end. Against all the evidence that would suggest the future belongs to the ones who escaped the Babylonian threat, the Lord announces that there is no escaping the judgment. This is not simply a matter of military conflict, with some going under and some surviving. The Babylonian force is, like the Assyrian army a century before, the rod of the Lord's anger (Isa 10:5). To all appearances, the Babylonian put-down of the first revolt under Jehoiakim was a simple matter of a powerful empire bringing a small rebellious nation into line and punishing its leadership with exile, which would also serve to deplete the locals who might

---

138. For a comprehensive study of the conflict among these groups as it is reflected in the book of Jeremiah and elsewhere, see Christopher Seitz, *Theology in Conflict: Reactions to the Exile in the Book of Jeremiah,* BZAW 176 (Berlin: Walter de Gruyter, 1989).

continue to be rebellious. Against that "normal" interpretation comes the claim that the exiles in Babylon are those "whom I have sent away from this place to the land of the Chaldeans" (v. 5). The larger act here is one of judgment not military conflict, but it is a judgment that cannot be escaped.

Thus there are two messages in the vision of the good and the bad figs. One is a word of continuing judgment against those who presumptuously think they are all right, convinced by their survival of their virtue. They shall become like rotten figs and shall undergo the same kind of judgment—destruction and exile. The remnant is not a saving remnant in this instance. The other word is a surprising announcement of new things, of hope beyond exile, of the intention of the Lord to keep working with this people, to continue the promise of land and life on it. Verses 5-7 embody as succinctly as anywhere in the book the future that God envisions beyond judgment. The repeated "I" is not to be missed—eleven first-person verbs in three verses! Here is the work of God in the midst of a history that seems totally controlled by the forces of human power. Each one of the first-person verbs makes an assertion that affects history and unfolds afresh the character and way of the Lord of Israel:

(1) "I will regard as good the exiles" and "I will set my eyes upon them for good" are different ways of saying the same thing. The situation of the exiles will turn around, but not by any human actions, not even by a belated repentance on the part of the people. In the sovereign, free, and gracious intent of the Lord—and only that way—will this people find their life turned from evil and disaster to good and well-being. The story of the creation has identified that good as the Lord's intention for the human community (Genesis 1). The covenantal relationship has always set the possibility of good before the people (Deut 30:15-20). Judgment is not the last word. God's "good" will continue to operate, and a people whom the Lord has placed under judgment will be re-created as a new community. This is an astonishing message set in the midst of a story of destroying Babylonian armies and a community torn apart by exile and foreign domination. But then, this is an astonishing God.

(2) "I will bring them back to this land" overturns the assumption that Israel/Judah's tie to the land is forever broken by exile, and the ancient promise of a place to live under God's rule is torn asunder. Israel is tied to the land, not by right or conquest but by the Lord's promise of a place for a redeemed slave people to live in freedom and goodness. Exile is temporary. Homelessness is not a state of being but an act of punishment. The Lord will start again with this people—on their land.

(3) "I will build them up, and not tear them down; I will plant them, and not pluck them up" draws together the key verbs of Jeremiah's call (1:10). Much of the proclamation of the prophet has been in conformity with his commission "to pluck up . . . and to overthrow." Now his prophecy is the vehicle of the Lord's announcement of a new time of "building" and "planting." The call of Jeremiah lets the reader know from the beginning that there is a positive tone to this prophetic message, and now it is heard loud and clear. The punishment is never purely retribution. The Lord intends to start over with this people.

(4) That point is made especially clear in v. 7. The one who called again and again for repentance now announces that things will be different. But it is not alone by human will. The Lord will give the ones of stubborn heart (23:17) a new heart (cf. Ezek 36:26), a heart that will be responsive to divine instruction. With that new heart, those who formerly did not listen and would not turn and repent will do so.

(5) The further indication of the Lord's intent to reestablish Israel not only on its land but also as the Lord's people is found in the covenantal formula in v. 7b: "they shall be my people and I will be their God." No single formulation more fully captures the divine imagination for the future than these words (cf. 7:23; 11:4; 30:22; 31:1, 33; 32:38). Israel was founded as a people this way, in covenant with the Lord, at Sinai (Exod 6:7). The breakdown of that relationship has happened as the people have constantly disobeyed the covenant stipulations. But the covenant is not at an end. Again, it is the freedom and grace of God that perdure and hold fast to the relationship.

REFLECTIONS

1. Much of what is to be absorbed from this text is around the "I" who speaks in the text, around the witness to the nature of the God of Israel who is known to us also in Jesus Christ. A text of uncertain date, wrought out of conflict among different elements of the Judean community, reveals a God who surprises us by reversing our very basic assumptions about where the action is and who is on top (cf. 1 Sam 2:1-10; Luke 1:46-55). This is a God who refuses to give up on a recalcitrant and disobedient people—the text regularly calls them "wicked"—even in judgment, who will finally do what the people seem unwilling or unable to do, a God who does not work with a precise calculus of reward and punishment but hangs in there to build a new community out of the fires of judgment. Synagogue and church have preserved this story so that later generations can know what sort of God it is that guides their lives. Whatever may be the particular circumstances of this or any of the other texts, the "I" who speaks through them and acts through them is attested in ways that are relevant for all future circumstances. Surprising, demanding, gracious, persistent, and free—such a God is the one who rules our lives. That is where we are, as much as ancient Judah. It is not easy being there, but it is enough to be in the hands of this God. It is an existence that is never without hope in a grace that can make us what we seem unable and unwilling to be.

2. The promise of a new heart is one of the gracious words of Scripture to those who know—and to those who do not know—that their will leads them to sin and disobedience. In the context of 24:7, that promise identifies a fundamental structure of existence before God that is as familiar from the New Testament as from the Old. The new heart is a divine gift, pure grace. But with that new heart, the people will "return," repent, "with their whole heart." The Letter to the Ephesians puts it this way: "For by grace are you saved through faith, and this is not your own doing; it is the gift of God" (Eph 2:8). There is that strange mixture of action and passivity, of gift and movement that defines the true life before God. There is no possibility without the work of God's grace in the hearts of stubborn and sinful people. But the changed heart is so that those now transformed by grace will turn to the Lord with their whole hearts and live lives in complete and full loyalty to the one whose unmerited and saving grace is real. The structure has two parts to it: the gift and the expectation. The Christian life is built on that structure. Neither part can be missing. Those who have known the power of that grace find themselves wanting to turn and give themselves in devotion and service to the Lord, whose eyes are set for good upon them.

3. The concreteness of life in this world is always the realm of God's activity in the Old Testament. Its particular representation here, as so often, is life on the land. The materiality of the promise never disappears in the Old Testament. It is important for Christian faith—which has spiritualized that concreteness and turned homelessness into a symbol of pilgrimage to a city without foundations, whose builder and maker is God—to hold firmly to this materiality, to know that the provision for life, the support of the helpless, the blessing of place and means for life are central to the promises of God. Neither Old Testament nor New ever assumes that the promises to Israel are passé. The Christian community needs both to comprehend the significance of land and place for the Jewish community that continued out of these fires of judgment and still hangs on in this world—by the grace of God—and to realize that the materiality of God's blessing and the salvific promises of the Old Testament are ours also. God did not create us for any world other than the one in which we live.

JEREMIAH 25:1-14, A SUMMARY JUDGMENT

NIV

25 The word came to Jeremiah concerning all the people of Judah in the fourth year of Jehoiakim son of Josiah king of Judah, which was the first year of Nebuchadnezzar king of Babylon. ²So Jeremiah the prophet said to all the people of Judah and to all those living in Jerusalem: ³For twenty-three years—from the thirteenth year of Josiah son of Amon king of Judah until this very day—the word of the LORD has come to me and I have spoken to you again and again, but you have not listened.

⁴And though the LORD has sent all his servants the prophets to you again and again, you have not listened or paid any attention. ⁵They said, "Turn now, each of you, from your evil ways and your evil practices, and you can stay in the land the LORD gave to you and your fathers for ever and ever. ⁶Do not follow other gods to serve and worship them; do not provoke me to anger with what your hands have made. Then I will not harm you."

⁷"But you did not listen to me," declares the LORD, "and you have provoked me with what your hands have made, and you have brought harm to yourselves."

⁸Therefore the LORD Almighty says this: "Because you have not listened to my words, ⁹I will summon all the peoples of the north and my servant Nebuchadnezzar king of Babylon," declares the LORD, "and I will bring them against this land and its inhabitants and against all the surrounding nations. I will completely destroy*ᵃ* them and make them an object of horror and scorn, and an everlasting ruin. ¹⁰I will banish from them the sounds of joy and gladness, the voices of bride and bridegroom, the sound of millstones and the light of the lamp. ¹¹This whole country will become a desolate wasteland, and these nations will serve the king of Babylon seventy years.

¹²"But when the seventy years are fulfilled, I will punish the king of Babylon and his nation, the land of the Babylonians,*ᵇ* for their guilt," declares the LORD, "and will make it desolate forever. ¹³I

ᵃ9 The Hebrew term refers to the irrevocable giving over of things or persons to the LORD, often by totally destroying them.   *ᵇ12* Or *Chaldeans*

NRSV

25 The word that came to Jeremiah concerning all the people of Judah, in the fourth year of King Jehoiakim son of Josiah of Judah (that was the first year of King Nebuchadrezzar of Babylon), ²which the prophet Jeremiah spoke to all the people of Judah and all the inhabitants of Jerusalem: ³For twenty-three years, from the thirteenth year of King Josiah son of Amon of Judah, to this day, the word of the LORD has come to me, and I have spoken persistently to you, but you have not listened. ⁴And though the LORD persistently sent you all his servants the prophets, you have neither listened nor inclined your ears to hear ⁵when they said, "Turn now, everyone of you, from your evil way and wicked doings, and you will remain upon the land that the LORD has given to you and your ancestors from of old and forever; ⁶do not go after other gods to serve and worship them, and do not provoke me to anger with the work of your hands. Then I will do you no harm." ⁷Yet you did not listen to me, says the LORD, and so you have provoked me to anger with the work of your hands to your own harm.

⁸Therefore thus says the LORD of hosts: Because you have not obeyed my words, ⁹I am going to send for all the tribes of the north, says the LORD, even for King Nebuchadrezzar of Babylon, my servant, and I will bring them against this land and its inhabitants, and against all these nations around; I will utterly destroy them, and make them an object of horror and of hissing, and an everlasting disgrace.*ᵃ* ¹⁰And I will banish from them the sound of mirth and the sound of gladness, the voice of the bridegroom and the voice of the bride, the sound of the millstones and the light of the lamp. ¹¹This whole land shall become a ruin and a waste, and these nations shall serve the king of Babylon seventy years. ¹²Then after seventy years are completed, I will punish the king of Babylon and that nation, the land of the Chaldeans, for their iniquity, says the LORD, making the land an everlasting waste. ¹³I will bring upon that land all the words that I have uttered against it, everything written in this book, which

*ᵃ*Gk Compare Syr: Heb *and everlasting desolations*

NIV

will bring upon that land all the things I have spoken against it, all that are written in this book and prophesied by Jeremiah against all the nations. ¹⁴They themselves will be enslaved by many nations and great kings; I will repay them according to their deeds and the work of their hands."

NRSV

Jeremiah prophesied against all the nations. ¹⁴For many nations and great kings shall make slaves of them also; and I will repay them according to their deeds and the work of their hands.

COMMENTARY

These verses serve in various ways to conclude the first part of the book, summarizing various themes, repeating some of the exhortations and warnings of the preceding chapters, and setting all of this within the context of a Jeremianic speech that looks back over twenty-three years of his prophetic ministry. The reference to "this book" in v. 13, which may have referred originally to the first or second scroll that Jeremiah dictated to his scribe Baruch, suggests a collection of material, further reinforcing the summary and concluding character of this text. The difficulties in syntax of the Hebrew and the numerous differences between the Hebrew and the usually shorter Greek text not only make translation somewhat difficult but also attest to the complicated process of growth and transmission of these verses. There is little doubt that in its present form this prose sermon is from the exile or later and thus is retrospective. To what extent Jeremiah's own words are present one cannot say. The fact that the oracles against the nations, which in the Hebrew text appear in chaps. 46–51, are placed after 25:13a in the Greek text of Jeremiah further underscores the break that is indicated by 25:1-14, particularly if the Greek text represents the original Hebrew order, as seems likely.

25:1-7. This section sets the text in a specific time, dating it to the fourth year of King Jehoiakim (i.e., 605 BCE), but referring back to the twenty-three years of Jeremiah's prophetic activity to that point. That date connects chap. 25 to chap. 36 and the report of Jeremiah's dictating all his prophetic oracles uttered to that point to his scribe Baruch and presenting the completed scroll to the king, who proceeded to tear it up and burn it, in response to which Jeremiah dictated it a second time. The two chapters together suggest, there-

fore, that chap. 25 provides the conclusion to a collection, which now may be understood as the preceding chapters, even though they include oracles from before and after 605, or possibly chaps. 1–20.

The content of the text reiterates fundamental themes from the preceding books. The heart of the matter is the call for repentance, upon which continued life in the land is dependent, a point that has been made persistently in the preceding chapters (e.g., 3:1–4:4; cf. chap. 7) and indeed has been a theme of other prophets before Jeremiah. The "evil way and wicked doings" (v. 5) centers in the people's apostasy and the ease with which they have turned to other gods to find their needs met and their loyalties directed. The history of Judah is thus reduced to a history of idolatry and continuous unattended prophetic denunciation of it. The critical histories of the southern kingdom naturally included a much more detailed and complex report than this reductionistic one. From Yahweh's perspective, this is all that matters in the end. It is a biased view of that nation's history.

25:8-14. The second part of this summary is, therefore, an announcement of judgment against Judah, though in the process of transmission allusions to the nations round about as objects of God's judgment have entered the text (v. 9; cf. v. 13b). Jeremiah's prophecy included not only calls for "turning" or repentance but also announcements of judgment in the face of continuing disobedience. The agent of that judgment has been identified in earlier chapters: "the tribes of the north" and, more specifically, the Babylonian king Nebuchadrezzar. The fact that these verses are dated to 605 BCE, the date of the Battle of Carchemish and the defeat of the Egyptians by the Babylonians, may have something to do with the inclusion of Nebuchadrezzar's name in the text inasmuch as the Greek text suggests an original Hebrew text that did not include specific reference to the Babylonian king. That is, the process of transmission has focused upon this critical moment and the transition of imperial dominance from Assyria and Egypt to Babylon, the eventual conqueror of Judah. The identification of Nebuchadrezzar as the servant of the Lord (v. 9) is notable. This designation appears two other times in the Hebrew text (27:6; 43:10) but not at all in the Greek text. All three occurrences may represent a corruption of the text in 27:6, where the Greek has "to serve him" instead of "my servant." However the text may have grown, it now ascribes to Nebuchadrezzar a direct connection to the work of the Lord, the term "servant" here referring to one who is consciously in relation to and acting obediently as agent of the Lord (see the Commentary on 27:5).

The sin of Judah is identified in v. 8 as disobedience. The judgment is conquest by a foreign nation and ruler. In language that echoes 7:34 and 16:9, the divine announcement of judgment spells out the plight of the people when the time comes. To the earlier descriptions of the absence of special moments of joy and celebration, such as a wedding, is added the absence of millstones grinding and lamps being lit, presumably referring to the beginning and end of an ordinary day's activities, the beginning of the day's work and the end of the day in the night's rest. Neither the ordinary affairs of life nor the special moments of joy will occur anymore. The ruin will be complete. And once more, the judgment is spoken of in terms of its effects upon the land (v. 11). For Israel, it always seems that life and death are tied up with the land. Its good deeds and its evil ones have effects upon the land.

The passage concludes by announcing that eventually—the force of the "seventy years" (v. 12) is unclear, but it may simply mean a genera-

tion—the conqueror shall also be conquered, the Babylonians suffering their own defeat and judgment (cf. Isaiah 10).[139] Such a word served a double function. One was to answer the kind of question reflected in the first chapter of Habakkuk in reaction to the announcement of the Lord's rousing up the Babylonians to wreak judgment on Judah (Hab 1:5-11):

> Your eyes are too pure to behold evil,
>   and you cannot look on wrongdoing;
> why do you look on the treacherous,
>   and are silent when the wicked swallow
> those more righteous than they?
>
> . . . .
>
> Is he then to keep on emptying his net,
>   and destroying nations without mercy?
>   (Hab 1:13, 17 NRSV)

A righteous God cannot and will not ignore the wickedness, even of the Lord's chosen agent. The announcement of judgment finally against Babylon is a vindication of the justice of God before the Lord's own (judged) people.

It is also a muted word of hope. The book of Jeremiah places Judah—and those who read about its fate—in a kind of tension. We have heard words about an anger that is kindled forever (15:14; 17:4). Now we hear about a limitation of seventy years. That is a long time, but it is not forever (cf. 3:5). The judgment is real and earnest, but it does come to an end. There is no joyous oracle of salvation here. That is quite premature for a people who stand before the fires of judgment. But the exile, the service of the Babylonian Empire, is not the final word. It is not all over with this people. The domination of the terrible Babylonian Empire reaches a limit—by the Lord's decision—and then it will fall.

---

139. For discussion of the meaning of "seventy years" and further bibliography, see Gerald L. Keown, Pamela J. Scalise, and Thomas G. Smothers, *Jeremiah 26–52*, WBC (Dallas: Word, 1995) 73-75.

REFLECTIONS

1. The Bible is notoriously slanted in its presentation of the events of the past. This text is a clear example. The history of Judah is told as a history of disobedience and ignored prophetic warning. The great moments of Hezekiah's and Josiah's reigns and the details of other kings' accomplishments are of no significance. This is a way of indicating to the reader what matters in history, particularly the history of those who live in covenant with the Lord of Israel. There is a bottom line that controls the whole. Some things matter more in that history than do others. The issue of fundamental loyalty to the Lord, to the one who creates and guides, who redeems and judges, is the touchstone for reading the history of the people of God. The text raises for the contemporary community the question of whether there is a similar way of viewing our history that transcends or relativizes the other matters that are part of any secular historical rendition. Does the community live in obedience to the Lord alone and by the instruction of the Lord? Does it listen? Does it heed the warnings that come from those prophetic voices, reminding us of our responsibilities as a people? They challenge the raising of lesser allegiances to ultimate status. In the United States, such misplaced status happens when patriotism brooks no voice of conscience, no criticisms, informed by Scripture or not, that suggest that the nation, the state, our country, is wrong and its actions must be resisted. Prophetic voices still challenge the dominance of economic self-interest that is as prominent now as it was then, national policy that fills the pockets of the rich and takes away the little that the poor have. Persistent warnings against such practices, when ignored, brought horrendous judgment in Jeremiah's time. We read them now to see if the warnings once ignored will now be heard. Jeremiah says this is finally what history is all about.

2. One of the most daring claims of this book arose in its formation and probably was not a part of its earliest inscription. It is the claim that the violent and destructive King Nebuchadrezzar of Babylon was a servant of the Lord—like Jacob, Moses, David, and the suffering one of Isaiah 40–55. That is a hard thought to swallow. But it is a testimony to the sovereign activity of God in the world, an insistence that in the affairs of history, the Lord is at work, often with strange and unusual instruments. One must see neither too little nor too much in the phrase "my servant." It is a reminder that the redeeming and judging work of God is often worked out through alien forces, through those whose morality can hardly be commended but whose, at best ambiguous, acts are the stuff with which the Lord rules and directs history. In Isaiah's time, it was Tiglath-pileser (Isaiah 10), no moral exemplar he. In the time of exile, it was a more enlightened king, Cyrus of Persia (cf. Isa 45:1-7). It is, indeed, a radical idea that the villains of history can be the agents of the Lord. We assume too easily that they can only be villains, so we may be surprised when our own time of accounting comes.

No instrument of the Lord, however, escapes being held to a moral accountability. That is one of the important points of the last part of this text and one that is earlier asserted with equal vigor in Isa 10:12-19. In the face of the modern blindness to the morality of divine sovereignty, the Scripture asserts the justice and righteousness of God that works itself out, sometimes over very long periods of time—in this instance, a generation or more. It may be only by the word of Scripture that any modern person can dare to hope for a vindication, an end to oppression, even the oppression that is the judgment of God. There is a strange ambiguity in the agent whose dirty work in behalf of the Lord can be the cause of the agent's own destruction, but that is what Jer 25:12-14 dares to assert. It may look to us as if the Lord's hands are also dirty. So be it. But the Lord will not let evil, even that which accomplishes the Lord's purposes, stand indefinitely. The text leaves us perplexed once more over how this good God can appropriate the dirtiness of historical oppression and destruction for divine purposes. It at least insists that the justice of God will finally triumph, even over that which the Lord has called up.

JEREMIAH 25:15-38, THE CUP OF WRATH

NIV

¹⁵This is what the LORD, the God of Israel, said to me: "Take from my hand this cup filled with the wine of my wrath and make all the nations to whom I send you drink it. ¹⁶When they drink it, they will stagger and go mad because of the sword I will send among them."

¹⁷So I took the cup from the LORD's hand and made all the nations to whom he sent me drink it: ¹⁸Jerusalem and the towns of Judah, its kings and officials, to make them a ruin and an object of horror and scorn and cursing, as they are today; ¹⁹Pharaoh king of Egypt, his attendants, his officials and all his people, ²⁰and all the foreign people there; all the kings of Uz; all the kings of the Philistines (those of Ashkelon, Gaza, Ekron, and the people left at Ashdod); ²¹Edom, Moab and Ammon; ²²all the kings of Tyre and Sidon; the kings of the coastlands across the sea; ²³Dedan, Tema, Buz and all who are in distant places^a; ²⁴all the kings of Arabia and all the kings of the foreign people who live in the desert; ²⁵all the kings of Zimri, Elam and Media; ²⁶and all the kings of the north, near and far, one after the other—all the kingdoms on the face of the earth. And after all of them, the king of Sheshach^b will drink it too.

²⁷"Then tell them, 'This is what the LORD Almighty, the God of Israel, says: Drink, get drunk and vomit, and fall to rise no more because of the sword I will send among you.' ²⁸But if they refuse to take the cup from your hand and drink, tell them, 'This is what the LORD Almighty says: You must drink it! ²⁹See, I am beginning to bring disaster on the city that bears my Name, and will you indeed go unpunished? You will not go unpunished, for I am calling down a sword upon all who live on the earth, declares the LORD Almighty.'

³⁰"Now prophesy all these words against them and say to them:

" 'The LORD will roar from on high;
  he will thunder from his holy dwelling
  and roar mightily against his land.
He will shout like those who tread the grapes,

^a23 Or *who clip the hair by their foreheads*   ^b26 *Sheshach* is a cryptogram for Babylon.

NRSV

15For thus the LORD, the God of Israel, said to me: Take from my hand this cup of the wine of wrath, and make all the nations to whom I send you drink it. ¹⁶They shall drink and stagger and go out of their minds because of the sword that I am sending among them.

17So I took the cup from the LORD's hand, and made all the nations to whom the LORD sent me drink it: ¹⁸Jerusalem and the towns of Judah, its kings and officials, to make them a desolation and a waste, an object of hissing and of cursing, as they are today; ¹⁹Pharaoh king of Egypt, his servants, his officials, and all his people; ²⁰all the mixed people;^a all the kings of the land of Uz; all the kings of the land of the Philistines—Ashkelon, Gaza, Ekron, and the remnant of Ashdod; ²¹Edom, Moab, and the Ammonites; ²²all the kings of Tyre, all the kings of Sidon, and the kings of the coastland across the sea; ²³Dedan, Tema, Buz, and all who have shaven temples; ²⁴all the kings of Arabia and all the kings of the mixed peoples^a that live in the desert; ²⁵all the kings of Zimri, all the kings of Elam, and all the kings of Media; ²⁶all the kings of the north, far and near, one after another, and all the kingdoms of the world that are on the face of the earth. And after them the king of Sheshach^b shall drink.

27Then you shall say to them, Thus says the LORD of hosts, the God of Israel: Drink, get drunk and vomit, fall and rise no more, because of the sword that I am sending among you.

28And if they refuse to accept the cup from your hand to drink, then you shall say to them: Thus says the LORD of hosts: You must drink! ²⁹See, I am beginning to bring disaster on the city that is called by my name, and how can you possibly avoid punishment? You shall not go unpunished, for I am summoning a sword against all the inhabitants of the earth, says the LORD of hosts.

30You, therefore, shall prophesy against them all these words, and say to them:

The LORD will roar from on high,
  and from his holy habitation utter his voice;

^aMeaning of Heb uncertain   ^b*Sheshach* is a cryptogram for *Babel*, Babylon

NIV

shout against all who live on the earth.
31The tumult will resound to the ends of the
earth,
for the LORD will bring charges against the
nations;
he will bring judgment on all mankind
and put the wicked to the sword,' "
declares the LORD.

32This is what the LORD Almighty says:

"Look! Disaster is spreading
from nation to nation;
a mighty storm is rising
from the ends of the earth."

33At that time those slain by the LORD will be
everywhere—from one end of the earth to the
other. They will not be mourned or gathered up or
buried, but will be like refuse lying on the ground.

34Weep and wail, you shepherds;
roll in the dust, you leaders of the flock.
For your time to be slaughtered has come;
you will fall and be shattered like fine
pottery.
35The shepherds will have nowhere to flee,
the leaders of the flock no place to escape.
36Hear the cry of the shepherds,
the wailing of the leaders of the flock,
for the LORD is destroying their pasture.
37The peaceful meadows will be laid waste
because of the fierce anger of the LORD.
38Like a lion he will leave his lair,
and their land will become desolate
because of the sword*a* of the oppressor
and because of the LORD's fierce anger.

*a38 Some Hebrew manuscripts and Septuagint (see also Jer. 46:16 and
50:16); most Hebrew manuscripts anger*

NRSV

he will roar mightily against his fold,
and shout, like those who tread grapes,
against all the inhabitants of the earth.
31 The clamor will resound to the ends of the
earth,
for the LORD has an indictment against the
nations;
he is entering into judgment with all flesh,
and the guilty he will put to the sword,
says the LORD.

32 Thus says the LORD of hosts:
See, disaster is spreading
from nation to nation,
and a great tempest is stirring
from the farthest parts of the earth!
33Those slain by the LORD on that day shall
extend from one end of the earth to the other.
They shall not be lamented, or gathered, or
buried; they shall become dung on the surface of
the ground.
34 Wail, you shepherds, and cry out;
roll in ashes, you lords of the flock,
for the days of your slaughter have come—
and your dispersions,*a*
and you shall fall like a choice vessel.
35 Flight shall fail the shepherds,
and there shall be no escape for the lords of
the flock.
36 Hark! the cry of the shepherds,
and the wail of the lords of the flock!
For the LORD is despoiling their pasture,
37   and the peaceful folds are devastated,
because of the fierce anger of the LORD.
38 Like a lion he has left his covert;
for their land has become a waste
because of the cruel sword,
and because of his fierce anger.

aMeaning of Heb uncertain

COMMENTARY

25:15-29. A fairly common OT image for judgment is the vehicle for an announcement of judgment against virtually all the nations of the region
(see 49:12; 51:7; Ps 75:8[9]; Isa 19:14-15; Ezek
23:31-34; Hab 2:15-16; cf. Jer 48:26). The cup of

the wine of wrath is a powerful symbol to convey
the effects of the Lord's judgment on the nations.
The imagery of drunkenness, staggering, vomiting,
and falling-down incapacitated vividly conveys the
chaos, the loss of control, the disintegration and

powerlessness that come from the Lord's judgment.[140] Very little specific information is given about the actuality of this destructive experience other than the two references to the sword that the Lord is sending among the nations (vv. 16, 27), suggesting military disasters. But the specifics are not the point. The issue is the Lord's control of history. It is not simply Israel's or Judah's destiny that is in the hands of the Lord of Israel. All the kingdoms of the earth are finally subject to the sovereign Lord. Their destiny, for good or for ill, is under the cosmic rule of Yahweh of Israel. No nation, not even Israel's greatest enemy, is outside the potential blessing of the Lord (Gen 12:1-3; Isa 19:24-25), and no nation is unaccountable to the Lord for its actions vis-à-vis the other nations.

We are not told what specifically these nations have done to merit punishment (v. 29). The long list of so many nations suggests the summary character of this part of chap. 25 also. Inasmuch as the Greek translation places the oracles against the nations of chaps. 46–51 just before these verses—that is, right after 25:13*a*—this section may have served as a kind of rounding-off summary of a broad sequence of oracles against the various nations that spelled out in more detail the grounds for the sentence being imposed, a sequence that is preserved in the Hebrew text in chaps. 46–51 (see the Overview of Jeremiah 46–51). One must turn to those chapters for some elaboration of the grounds for the punishment, though not all the nations mentioned in 25:15-29 are the focus of oracles in chaps. 46–51. Indeed, some of the places listed are unknown. The inclusion of Jerusalem at the beginning of the list of nations may be a later addition, but it now serves to identify the starting point of divine judgment with the Lord's own people. Placing Babylon (i.e., Sheshach) last is certainly done intentionally. Even

the mighty Babylonian Empire will eventually drink from the cup of the Lord's wrath (cf. 25:11-12). While there is little likelihood that Jeremiah actually preached to these nations, placing the cup of the wine of wrath in his hand to give to the nations to drink is consistent with the calling of Jeremiah to be a prophet to the nations "to pluck up and to pull down, to destroy and to overthrow" (1:10; cf. 1:5). The presentation of the prophet in the book of Jeremiah is where that part of the vocation of Jeremiah has its beginning.

25:30-38. Language from earlier prophets echoes afresh in these verses. The roaring of the Lord from the holy dwelling place is first heard in Amos 1:2, and the indictment of the Lord against the people announced in Hos 4:1 is extended now to become an indictment, or more accurately a legal suit against all the nations. The nations, and more specifically the rulers and leaders of the nations, alluded to here with the extended imagery of the shepherds and lords of the flock (vv. 34-38), will feel the judging hand of the Lord moving over them like a powerful gale, a tornado or hurricane that destroys everything in its path as it moves across sea and land (v. 32).

Mention of the roar of the Lord "from his holy habitation" is a way of speaking about the rule of the Lord that proceeds from the divine abode, from the throne of power and judgment. Imagery of king and lion (vv. 30, 38) asserts the sovereignty of this God over "all the inhabitants of the earth." The extended reference to the shepherds is a way of staking the claim of the Ruler of heaven and earth over all other rulers on heaven and earth. Those shepherds who think that their power over their flock, their nation and people, is absolute find that is not the case. The "anger of the LORD," which bespeaks the will of God for righteousness and justice, intimated by the reference to the lawsuit and the judging activity of God in v. 31, works itself out in the Lord's shaping of history toward the punishment of the guilty. Familiar though that claim may be, its radical character should not be missed.

---

140. On the possible background of the cup imagery in notions of ordeal and banqueting, see Robert P. Carroll, *Jeremiah,* OTL (Philadelphia: Westminster, 1986) 500-504; William McKane, *A Critical and Exegetical Commentary on Jeremiah,* 2 vols., ICC (Edinburgh: T. & T. Clark, 1986, 1996) 634-36; and Gerald L. Keown, Pamela J. Scalise, and Thomas J. Smothers, *Jeremiah 26–52,* WBC 27 (Dallas: Word, 1995) 277-79.

REFLECTIONS

While Jerusalem and Judah are mentioned in these verses, they are clearly not the focus that they have been for all the preceding chapters. Here the scope of the Lord's concern has moved far beyond the confines of those who worship the God of Israel. Interpretation seeks without success to find the bill of particulars against these many nations. While such particulars may be uncovered from chaps. 46–51, they are not really the issue here. The text is a kind of Old Testament depiction of the universal judgment day, when the Lord will judge "all flesh." Precisely because so many of the nations mentioned here seem remote from the biblical story or remote from the interests of the God of Israel, the text makes its particular claim about the lordship of Yahweh. The rule of the Lord of Israel is set within the affairs of nations and peoples, and there is no community outside of the sovereign activity of that God. We encounter here no narrow stream of holy history but a view of universal history that insists that the workings of divine justice are not confined to those who are called out and elected to God's service. All human communities are called to account, and even the mightiest have no final autonomy. The political leaders who seem to be in charge of the affairs of the world stand under a higher power, whether they are aware of it or not. The Bible, here and elsewhere, dares to claim that in the interactions of nations, in the conflicts and upheavals, a transcendent governance is manifest. Sometimes Scripture will be specific about that. At other times, such as in this chapter, the assertion is made without the specifics.

The prophecy of Jeremiah, like much of the Old Testament, ringss the changes on the sins of the chosen people. That does not mean that the Lord turns a blind eye to the sins of their enemies or even other nations with whom they have little contact. The text recognizes within the divine politics an insistence on a moral accountability that is not confined to those who worship the Lord. It is placed upon all nations. If what the Lord is about in the human story is the blessing of "all the families of the earth" along with Israel, then it is also the case that, along with Israel, the nations of the earth stand under the demands of the Lord of Israel for justice and fairness in their interactions with one another, for compassion and mercy in their internal rule, for care and support of the weak and the poor in their dispersion of the nation's wealth. None of this is alluded to in this text. But all of it can be inferred from the trial scene. The canons of judgment that were laid on Israel and Judah are the measuring sticks by which other human communities, other political systems, and other ruling powers are judged. History does not punish the guilty, but this text dares to assert that in what human beings see as the workings of history the Lord will punish the guilty. If the contemporary interpreter is bashful about identifying that in any particular way, he or she must at least hold fast to the fundamental assertion.

JEREMIAH 26:1–36:32

CONFLICT AND COMFORT

OVERVIEW

These chapters incorporate several blocks of material that are only loosely connected to each other. They are set at different times in the career of Jeremiah and the history of Judah, and they range from announcements of judgment to oracles of salvation. Chapter 26 opens this block by looking back to chap. 7 as it gives a narrative context for the temple sermon recorded there. It reiterates the call to repentance of the temple sermon and records a mixed reaction to that urging. Set at the beginning of the reign of Jehoiakim, this chapter forms a kind of frame with chap. 36 around the literary units of this collection.

Chapters 27–29 form a literary unit that has internal linguistic and thematic connections. They contain spellings of the names of Jeremiah, Zedekiah, and Nebuchadrezzar that are different from the usual spellings in the rest of the book. They are set in the same period, around 594 BCE, and have to do with increasing hopes that Judah and the surrounding nations would be able to rebel successfully against Babylonian domination, hopes that Jeremiah's word from the Lord vigorously opposes. That conflict between the desire to resist and rebel and the prophet's insistence that the Lord is working through Babylon to punish Judah and that that punishment must be accepted is a continuing and important dimension of the politics and theology of chaps. 26–45. Chapters 27–29 appropriately follow chap. 26 in that they report further conflict between Jeremiah and the priests and prophets of Judah. One of the things that begins to develop in these chapters is a focus upon the prophet and his experiences. That will continue in chaps. 37–45. The concern is not to produce a biography of the prophet but to set his prophetic word in relation to the events that are happening and to see in the interaction of

Jeremiah with those around him something of the impact and consequences of his prophetic preaching and the resistance to the word of the Lord as he set it forth. The laments of Jeremiah in chaps. 11–20 have let the reader know that the experience of the prophet in carrying out his vocation is a part of the story this book seeks to tell. In those chapters, we were exposed to the internal suffering of the prophet. In chaps. 26–29 and 37–45, the narrative lets us in on the external events that may have precipitated the laments or, at least, are to be seen as the kind of experiences that could have evoked them. The word of the prophet thus converges with the story of the prophet, and we are led to ask about how each illuminates what God was doing in the last days of Judah and what continues to matter about those events and the word that was spoken in the midst of them.

Chapters 30–33 are a word of hope about healing and redemption beyond the judgment. They are set in the midst of the story of Judah's downfall and look beyond it in ways that let the reader know that this downfall is not the end of the story. The judgment cannot be avoided, which the chapters that follow spell out in painful detail. The sting of the Lord's wrath is real, and Judah cannot hope to escape it by political machinations. But the Lord's wrath is for a moment and is not everlasting (cf. Ps 30:5[6]; Isa 54:7-8). Just as chap. 32 sets a hope for the future right in the middle of the judgment that is happening, so also chaps. 30–33 set that hope in the midst of the narrative of God's judgment's being accomplished.

Chapters 34 and 35 present two opposite pictures of elements in Judah in its last years. One is of broken covenant when a proclamation of sabbatical release of slaves is declared, only to be violated when the slaves are shortly reenslaved (chap.

768

34). The other is of rigorous faithfulness on the part of the Rechabites, whose strict adherence to the commands of their ancestor Jonadab is contrasted with the disobedience of the people of Judah to the commands of the Lord (chap. 35).

Chapter 36 serves as a kind of transition, a swing chapter, so to speak. Some interpreters see it as a part of the literary unit of the chapters that precede it; others associate it with chaps. 37–45. There are reasons for the disagreement, for the chapter clearly has connections to the material preceding it and to that which follows. In this commentary, it is being read in connection with the preceding and is understood as a kind of framing chapter, reaching back in particular ways to chap. 26 and bringing the material in chaps. 26–35 to a close in a way not dissimilar to the function of 25:1-14 in regard to the chapters preceding it. Chapter 26 is dated to the beginning of Jehoiakim's reign, while chap. 36 is set four years later. In chap. 26, the prophet calls for repentance on the part of the people. While his life is threatened by this action, there are people who stand up for him and accept his word as an authentic message from the Lord. Chapter 36 reiterates the call to repentance in language very reminiscent of chap. 26 (cf. 26:3 and 36:3), but it reports an unambiguous rejection of Jeremiah's message by King Jehoiakim. In both chap. 26 and chap. 36, Jehoiakim is depicted as a threat to any prophet with a word like that of Jeremiah (26:20-24; 36:26), and Jeremiah's freedom and safety are endangered.

The fact that chaps. 37–44 deal entirely with the last days of the southern kingdom while chap. 36 belongs to an earlier period—that is, the reign of Jehoiakim rather than that of Zedekiah—is one of the reasons for associating chap. 36 primarily with the preceding chapters. But it should be noted that while, along with chap. 26, it forms a kind of frame around chaps. 27–35, it also does something of the same with chap. 45 around 37–44. That is, chap. 36 tells of Jeremiah's dictation of a scroll of his oracles to Baruch in 605 BCE and of the subsequent burning of that scroll by Jehoiakim. Chapter 45 belongs to the same occasion as chap. 36 and refers to Baruch and the dictated scroll. Literarily, therefore, chap. 36 looks forward to chap. 45 as well as backward to chap. 25 and the chapters that follow. In this discussion, however, it will be taken up in relation to chaps.

26–35 inasmuch as the strongest connections seem to be with that block of material.[141]

The first half of the book of Jeremiah presents the oracles of the prophet *in extenso.* The second half now moves to lay out the responses of the people and the leaders to the prophet's words. While intimations of reaction to those words from the Lord are found in chaps. 1–25—both in Jeremiah's references to the people's stubborn unwillingness to listen and accept correction and in his laments, where indications of active hostility to the prophet appear (e.g., 11:21; 12:6)—the response to his prophetic activity only now becomes the focus of attention. The narratives of chap. 26 and following serve both to validate the prophetic activity of Jeremiah and to account for the fate of Jerusalem and its people. Clearly, the preservation and recording of much of this material comes from a later time. How much of it is recollection of actual events is difficult to tell, though surely many of the basic facts reported here are accurate—for example, Jeremiah in conflict with other prophets, tried, imprisoned, and taken into exile; the fate of the last kings of Judah; resistance to Babylonian domination on the part of various elements of the population and leadership; and the like. That recollection is part of an interpretive presentation of happenings from about 609 BCE onward, much of which is set forth in the light of the outcome of Jeremiah's prophetic activity. These chapters tell of the last days of Judah and even of events that followed afterward. The record is fully cognizant of what happened and remembers and interprets events in the light of the fall of Jerusalem and the two exiles in 597 and 587 BCE. Thus, just as the events of history served to authenticate the truthfulness of Jeremiah's prophecy, the presentation of his story in the light of that history is made in a way that underscores that authentication. There continues to be much debate and discussion about how this material is brought together, what elements represent historical recollection, and what dimensions of it are

141. On the question of the larger literary blocks and particularly the association of chap. 36 with the preceding or the following chapters, see William L. Holladay, *Jeremiah 2,* Hermeneia (Minneapolis: Fortress, 1989) 22-23; Robert P. Carroll, *Jeremiah,* OTL (Philadelphia: Westminster, 1986) 509-10, 513-14; and the interesting theologically and ideologically developed proposal for seeing chap. 36 in relation to chaps. 37–45 in Walter Brueggemann, *A Commentary on Jeremiah: Exile and Homecoming* (Grand Rapids: Eerdmans, 1998) 338-44.

reflective interpretation only loosely connected to the actual events. The interpretation that follows will not try to sift out layers of literary composition or arbitrate the discussion about the composition of these chapters. Too much of it is not susceptible to any final and conclusive judgment. We will try to comprehend the presentation of the prophet and the story of the end of Judah as they are set before us to hear what lessons they are meant to tell—and they are surely there to give lessons to the later generations that read this book.

JEREMIAH 26:1-24, PROPHETS UNDER THREAT

NIV

26 Early in the reign of Jehoiakim son of Josiah king of Judah, this word came from the LORD: ²"This is what the LORD says: Stand in the courtyard of the LORD's house and speak to all the people of the towns of Judah who come to worship in the house of the LORD. Tell them everything I command you; do not omit a word. ³Perhaps they will listen and each will turn from his evil way. Then I will relent and not bring on them the disaster I was planning because of the evil they have done. ⁴Say to them, 'This is what the LORD says: If you do not listen to me and follow my law, which I have set before you, ⁵and if you do not listen to the words of my servants the prophets, whom I have sent to you again and again (though you have not listened), ⁶then I will make this house like Shiloh and this city an object of cursing among all the nations of the earth.' "

⁷The priests, the prophets and all the people heard Jeremiah speak these words in the house of the LORD. ⁸But as soon as Jeremiah finished telling all the people everything the LORD had commanded him to say, the priests, the prophets and all the people seized him and said, "You must die! ⁹Why do you prophesy in the LORD's name that this house will be like Shiloh and this city will be desolate and deserted?" And all the people crowded around Jeremiah in the house of the LORD.

¹⁰When the officials of Judah heard about these things, they went up from the royal palace to the house of the LORD and took their places at the entrance of the New Gate of the LORD's house. ¹¹Then the priests and the prophets said to the officials and all the people, "This man should be sentenced to death because he has prophesied against this city. You have heard it with your own ears!"

NRSV

26 At the beginning of the reign of King Jehoiakim son of Josiah of Judah, this word came from the LORD: ²Thus says the LORD: Stand in the court of the LORD's house, and speak to all the cities of Judah that come to worship in the house of the LORD; speak to them all the words that I command you; do not hold back a word. ³It may be that they will listen, all of them, and will turn from their evil way, that I may change my mind about the disaster that I intend to bring on them because of their evil doings. ⁴You shall say to them: Thus says the LORD: If you will not listen to me, to walk in my law that I have set before you, ⁵and to heed the words of my servants the prophets whom I send to you urgently—though you have not heeded— ⁶then I will make this house like Shiloh, and I will make this city a curse for all the nations of the earth.

7The priests and the prophets and all the people heard Jeremiah speaking these words in the house of the LORD. ⁸And when Jeremiah had finished speaking all that the LORD had commanded him to speak to all the people, then the priests and the prophets and all the people laid hold of him, saying, "You shall die! ⁹Why have you prophesied in the name of the LORD, saying, 'This house shall be like Shiloh, and this city shall be desolate, without inhabitant'?" And all the people gathered around Jeremiah in the house of the LORD.

10When the officials of Judah heard these things, they came up from the king's house to the house of the LORD and took their seat in the entry of the New Gate of the house of the LORD. ¹¹Then the priests and the prophets said to the officials and to all the people, "This man deserves the sen-

NIV

[12]Then Jeremiah said to all the officials and all the people: "The LORD sent me to prophesy against this house and this city all the things you have heard. [13]Now reform your ways and your actions and obey the LORD your God. Then the LORD will relent and not bring the disaster he has pronounced against you. [14]As for me, I am in your hands; do with me whatever you think is good and right. [15]Be assured, however, that if you put me to death, you will bring the guilt of innocent blood on yourselves and on this city and on those who live in it, for in truth the LORD has sent me to you to speak all these words in your hearing."

[16]Then the officials and all the people said to the priests and the prophets, "This man should not be sentenced to death! He has spoken to us in the name of the LORD our God."

[17]Some of the elders of the land stepped forward and said to the entire assembly of people, [18]"Micah of Moresheth prophesied in the days of Hezekiah king of Judah. He told all the people of Judah, 'This is what the LORD Almighty says:

" 'Zion will be plowed like a field,
Jerusalem will become a heap of rubble,
    the temple hill a mound overgrown with
        thickets.'[a]

[19]"Did Hezekiah king of Judah or anyone else in Judah put him to death? Did not Hezekiah fear the LORD and seek his favor? And did not the LORD relent, so that he did not bring the disaster he pronounced against them? We are about to bring a terrible disaster on ourselves!"

[20](Now Uriah son of Shemaiah from Kiriath Jearim was another man who prophesied in the name of the LORD; he prophesied the same things against this city and this land as Jeremiah did. [21]When King Jehoiakim and all his officers and officials heard his words, the king sought to put him to death. But Uriah heard of it and fled in fear to Egypt. [22]King Jehoiakim, however, sent Elnathan son of Acbor to Egypt, along with some other men. [23]They brought Uriah out of Egypt and took him to King Jehoiakim, who had him struck down with a sword and his body thrown into the burial place of the common people.)

[a]18 Micah 3:12

NRSV

tence of death because he has prophesied against this city, as you have heard with your own ears."

[12]Then Jeremiah spoke to all the officials and all the people, saying, "It is the LORD who sent me to prophesy against this house and this city all the words you have heard. [13]Now therefore amend your ways and your doings, and obey the voice of the LORD your God, and the LORD will change his mind about the disaster that he has pronounced against you. [14]But as for me, here I am in your hands. Do with me as seems good and right to you. [15]Only know for certain that if you put me to death, you will be bringing innocent blood upon yourselves and upon this city and its inhabitants, for in truth the LORD sent me to you to speak all these words in your ears."

[16]Then the officials and all the people said to the priests and the prophets, "This man does not deserve the sentence of death, for he has spoken to us in the name of the LORD our God." [17]And some of the elders of the land arose and said to all the assembled people, [18]"Micah of Moresheth, who prophesied during the days of King Hezekiah of Judah, said to all the people of Judah: 'Thus says the LORD of hosts,

Zion shall be plowed as a field;
    Jerusalem shall become a heap of ruins,
    and the mountain of the house a wooded
        height.'

[19]Did King Hezekiah of Judah and all Judah actually put him to death? Did he not fear the LORD and entreat the favor of the LORD, and did not the LORD change his mind about the disaster that he had pronounced against them? But we are about to bring great disaster on ourselves!"

[20]There was another man prophesying in the name of the LORD, Uriah son of Shemaiah from Kiriath-jearim. He prophesied against this city and against this land in words exactly like those of Jeremiah. [21]And when King Jehoiakim, with all his warriors and all the officials, heard his words, the king sought to put him to death; but when Uriah heard of it, he was afraid and fled and escaped to Egypt. [22]Then King Jehoiakim sent[a] Elnathan son of Achbor and men with him to Egypt, [23]and they took Uriah from Egypt and brought him to King Jehoiakim, who struck him

[a]Heb adds men to Egypt

NIV	NRSV
24Furthermore, Ahikam son of Shaphan supported Jeremiah, and so he was not handed over to the people to be put to death.	down with the sword and threw his dead body into the burial place of the common people. 24But the hand of Ahikam son of Shaphan was with Jeremiah so that he was not given over into the hands of the people to be put to death.

COMMENTARY

The sequence of chapters that tell of actual conflict and resistance to the prophecies of Jeremiah begins with a report of the response of the leadership and the people to the sermon he preached in the Temple, which is reported in Jer 7:1-15. The earlier chapter focuses on the content of Jeremiah's word, while chap. 26 focuses on the reaction to it.

26:1-6. The earlier sermon is briefly summarized in these verses. The critical aspects of that summary are the openness of the Lord to a responsive repentance on the part of the people, a feature of chap. 7 also, and the comparison of the possible fate of Jerusalem to the earlier fate of Shiloh, the earlier central sanctuary and dwelling place of the ark, the divine throne (see the Commentary on 7:1-15).[142] The elements added to the story in this chapter are worth noting.

(1) One is the dating of the incident to the beginning of Jehoiakim's reign. Whatever judgment is made about the accuracy of the date formula, it sets this account of prophetic preaching and community response in the context of the reign of Jehoiakim. He makes no direct appearance in the story, but we have already been told of the character of his reign; and when this section comes to an end in chap. 36, his complicity in the resistance to, even disdain of, the prophetic word is evident and, indeed, exemplary. It is already intimated in the final part of this chapter, which reports the king's execution of another prophet who, like Jeremiah in chap. 7, "prophesied against this city and against this land." Just as his father, Josiah, was the model of faithfulness to the Lord and the covenantal law, so also Jehoiakim was the model of faithlessness and disobedience.

Appropriately, the resistance to the word of the Lord to Jeremiah is reported as beginning when Jehoiakim began to reign.

(2) Jeremiah is told not to "hold back a word." This is probably a way of insisting on the full force of the divine word being set forth. Jeremiah's call also included the command to proclaim "all" that the Lord commanded, no matter the consequences. The trial that follows here suggests why it might be appropriate for the Lord to insist that Jeremiah not mince words or fudge on the word of the Lord.[143]

(3) While chap. 7 couches the divine word entirely as a call for repentance so that the Lord may continue to let the people dwell in the land and/or continue to dwell with them in the land, here the note of judgment is already sounded in the reference to "the disaster that I intend to bring on them because of their evil doings" (v. 4). Just as the oracles of Jeremiah have conjoined calls to repentances with announcements of judgment that is going to happen, so also that tension is summarized in these verses with an announcement of judgment that is going to happen and a conditionality that leaves things open, a divine "perhaps" (v. 3) fraught with possibilities but also fragile and tenuous. The tension is "managed" in this passage through the word נחמתי (*nihamtî*), "that I may change my mind" (v. 4; cf. vv. 13, 19). The one thing that can stop the judgment is for God to *niham.* That divine openness to a change of mind when the decision for judgment has been made is one of the profound themes of Scripture, effected by prophetic intercession at other times (e.g., Exod 32:14; Amos 7:3, 6; cf. Num 14:20) and

---

142. On the biblical and archaeological data for Shiloh, see Gerald L. Keown, Pamela J. Scalise, and Thomas J. Smothers, *Jeremiah 26–52,* WBC 27 (Dallas: Word, 1995) 16-19.

143. For possible reasons a prophet might hold back a word of the Lord, see Waldemar Janzen, "Withholding the Word," in *Traditions in Transformation: Turning Points in Biblical Faith,* ed. Baruch Halpern and Jon D. Levenson (Winona Lake, Ind.: Eisenbrauns, 1981) 97-114.

offered once more in this prophetic proclamation. It is a way of indicating that the judgment of 587 BCE happened only after the door had been left open a long time. The "perhaps" (NRSV, "it may be"; cf. Amos 5:14) suggests, whether in anticipation of the destruction of Jerusalem or in retrospect, that divine expectations were not very high—and with good reason.

26:7-19. The response to Jeremiah's preaching moves through several stages. A crisis is triggered by the judgment of "the priests and the prophets and all the people" that Jeremiah should be executed for what he has prophesied (vv. 9-10). The words of Jeremiah's accusers suggest their reaction is due to the content of his preaching rather than to a question about whether he is a true prophet. But that alternative may be a false one. Their words suggest they do not believe that such a threat to the Temple and the city can come from the Lord. That is somewhat understandable because they know well the tradition of Temple and city as the chosen and permanent dwelling place of the Lord. Jeremiah's words, therefore, are doubly false or presumptuous inasmuch as they utter a claim that simply cannot be countenanced—to wit, that the Lord would announce an intention to destroy the divine dwelling place and the holy city, which the Lord had long ago chosen and preserved. Such an event could not happen; so such a word cannot come from the Lord. It is theologically and politically unacceptable.

The summary of Jeremiah's preaching given by the priests, the prophets, and the people (vv. 9, 11) leaves out some important features, creating a distortion of his words and underscoring a major dimension of this text: The people and their leaders do not listen. Two things happen: The conditionality of the judgment's depending upon whether the people keep the law and heed the words of the prophets simply drops out, and the divine first-person verbs of v. 6 identifying the destruction of the Temple and the city as acts of the Lord are changed into third-person announcements of future events. The word of the prophet is thus thoroughly detheologized (cf. Amos 7:9b, 11a), and its covenantal call to obedience is omitted. The religious leaders and the people hear only what they wish to hear. Their response, therefore, is a cardinal example of the failure to listen that is at the heart of what is happening in the book of

Jeremiah. The "it may be" of v. 3, the divine "perhaps," thus becomes more tenuous than ever.

A significant shift happens in v. 10. The royal officials of Judah, hearing the uproar around Jeremiah's preaching, or hearing about it, move onto the scene in a somewhat official way, taking their place in the gate. There is debate about whether this part of chap. 26 preserves a record of a trial. That cannot be determined with precision, but there is at least some sort of official investigation. The gate was where members of the community met to carry out legal and other matters, and the officials, who are regularly identified in relation to the king (1:18; 2:26; 4:9; 25:18) and who come under judgment along with the king, gather here to hear the charges against Jeremiah and make some determination. The charge that is brought in v. 11 is consistent with the reaction in vv. 8b-9: Prophecy against Jerusalem is a capital crime. Whether this was understood as blasphemy, treason, or false prophecy is difficult to determine. It may and could have been seen as all of these and from any of those angles would have been justifiably a capital charge.

What happens indicates, however, that the officials will not allow the mock justice of a kangaroo court. Jeremiah is given a chance to speak in his defense. That defense contains three elements. The first and last element of his defense, and perhaps the most important, is his insistence that what he speaks is truly (באמת be'ĕmet, v. 15) the word of the Lord. At the beginning (v. 12) and the end (v. 15) of his speech to the officials, he claims to have met the chief criterion of authentic Yahwistic prophecy: "the LORD sent me" (cf. chap. 1 and 23:18-23). Second, Jeremiah's defense becomes a platform for reiteration of the fundamental message that got him into trouble in the first place (v. 13). In this case, his words are not couched as the word of the Lord but as his own admonition to the community. In language that recapitulates the exhortation of chap. 7, Jeremiah calls the people to listen to the word of the Lord and make good (v. 13) their sinful ways. Finally ("as for me," v. 14), he recognizes the danger to his life in such proclamation, but that is a separate and secondary matter in the order of things. His death will only continue their sinful practices (cf. 2:34) and exacerbate the plight of the people he has described. Jeremiah's fate is clearly of a second order compared to his responsibility to call them to account and to a change of heart.

The response on the part of the officials and the people is an exoneration of Jeremiah, against the call of priests and prophets for his execution. While the accusation they brought against him had to do primarily with its substance—prophecy against Temple and capital—the exoneration is in terms of Jeremiah's authority—prophesying in the name of the Lord. There is a certain tension in the story at this point, because the priests and the prophets do not contest his prophesying in Yahweh's name. It is the content of such prophecy. The officials do not comment on the content. They are satisfied that the prophecy is authentically Yahwistic and thus deem Jeremiah not a false prophet, whatever the substance. How they determine that is not indicated by the passage and is not clear. But there may be a clue in what follows when some of the "elders of the land," leading citizens who may have had some responsibility for proper administration of justice, cite a precedent for Jeremiah's words and the decision not to charge or execute him in the words and experience of an earlier Judean prophet, Micah. Here the substance of Jeremiah's prophecy, which is what disturbs the priests and prophets, is taken up.

Prophecy of the destruction of the Temple and the capital city has some precedent in the oracles of the eighth-century prophet Micah. The elders give a quotation of Mic 3:12, suggesting that collections of prophetic oracles are already being made. It is not implausible that in Jeremiah's time, more than a hundred years after Micah's time, such collections had been preserved (cf. Jeremiah 36; 45:1; Isa 8:16-17). One may infer that contemporary prophecy in Jeremiah's time is being attended to by at least some of the community in the light of the past experience with prophets. Earlier prophecy becomes here a basis for making judgment about the authenticity of the prophetic word in the present.

The response of the eighth-century king Hezekiah and his people to the prophetic word is offered by the elders as a helpful analogy for the present. Words against the Temple and the city have been heard before in Judah from the mouth of a prophet. If attentive response to them then saved the city and the people, then the same may happen once more. There is no conditionality in

Micah's words, and the biblical records do not make connections between his words and the fate of Jerusalem in the eighth century. But the later community is interpreting history to make sense out of the present. The elders' words are thus a small window of light into the book of Jeremiah. Against the near unanimous resistance to the prophet's call for a change of heart and a renewed obedience to the covenantal law of the Lord, these words of the elders suggest that they comprehend the message of Jeremiah and see in Hezekiah a model of proper response: fear of the Lord.

26:20-24. This account of the fate of another prophet, a brief narrative that seems to interrupt the story of the charges against Jeremiah and their outcome, in fact is a crucial piece for understanding why, ultimately, the positive response of the elders to Jeremiah's message was ineffective or insufficient to stave off the judgment of God. The story of Uriah's execution is tied to the "trial" of Jeremiah by the contrast that is made at the end of the chapter between the fate of the two prophets, one being taken by force from Egypt and executed, the other being hidden and protected from execution.

But the critical contrast in these verses is not the one between Jeremiah and Uriah. It is the contrast between the way the kings Hezekiah and Jehoiakim respond to the prophetic word. While Jehoiakim plays no part in the charges against Jeremiah and his royal officials actually save Jeremiah's life, the force of the opening superscription becomes clearer now and gets its final unfolding in chap. 36. Jehoiakim, one of the specific objects of Jeremiah's prophecy (chap. 22), responds to the prophetic words against city and land in a manner totally different from the faithful and God-fearing king Hezekiah. He does not take the prophet's words seriously, repenting and entreating the Lord's favor as Hezekiah did, thereby effecting a change of mind on the part of the Lord so that Zion and Jerusalem were saved. Rather, Jehoiakim makes a massive political move to extricate, by kidnapping or extradition, the prophet who had announced judgment and executes him. The situation in the late seventh and early sixth centuries is radically different at this critical point. With Josiah dead, there is no God-fearing king who might listen to the word of the Lord and repent. Instead, the royal power is arrogantly and presumptuously dismissive of the prophetic word. Even when the prophet has fled the country and is no longer a specific threat, the king hunts him down and has him killed. The order of the day now is royal and political resistance to the word of the Lord calling for massive turning from social oppression and idolatry. When the leadership at the top is resolutely representative of those practices and arrogantly unwilling to countenance a word of criticism, the situation is hopeless. All that is left is the blowing of the hot anger of the Lord in judgment against a faithless nation and its leaders.

Reference to the king and the leaders presses us to take note of the various groups that appear in this chapter and the varying, even inconsistent, roles they play. The "elders of the land," those least associated with the Jerusalem establishment, represent an element within the Judean population that seems inclined to take seriously the prophetic word and the prophetic tradition. Following H.-W. Wolff, Walter Brueggemann has suggested that it is the elders "who are rooted in the old covenantal traditions and who maintain a vision of social reality and a historical perspective that was not preempted by royal definitions of reality."[144] This chapter, and particularly the words of the elders, lets the reader know that even with the judgment to come there is an element in the population that is attentive to the covenantal tradition and the words of the prophets (see v. 5). It is not surprising, perhaps, that these folk may have come from outside the capital city, where the powerful elite with their acquisitive instincts and concentrations of wealth were at home.

The primary opposition to Jeremiah and the Micah-Uriah-Jeremiah tradition of judgment prophecy are "the priests and the prophets" (vv. 7-8, 11, 16). Their attitude and their position are unambiguous. They are the ones who twice seek to bring the death penalty against Jeremiah (vv. 8, 11), and their rationale is clearly stated: He threatens the Temple and the capital city. The priests and prophets, therefore, are not those whose primary role is to instruct in the torah of the Lord and listen for the word of the Lord. That may be their "professional" assignment, but these two groups are the religious establishment that func-

tions as an establishment always does, working to protect its walls (literally) and to resist any rocking of the boat that would threaten the religious ("house") and political ("city") structures. They are guardians of the status quo and protectors of the political and religious institutions. The two primary groups that should be leading the people in a faithful obedience to the Lord of Israel, calling them to attend to the word of the Lord, are the primary opponents of the word and neglectors of the law.

Two other groups whose roles are more ambiguous are mentioned in this chapter. One is the cadre of officials who come down to examine the charge against Jeremiah and then pronounce him undeserving of the death sentence that was sought. These are persons with connections to the court of the king, and so one would expect their actions to reflect those of the king and vice versa. But that is not the case. What is clear from this story and from chap. 36 is that the royal officials often take their cue from the king, but not always. In chap. 36, they hear Baruch read from the dictated scroll of Jeremiah's oracles and are alarmed enough to report the words immediately to the king. But two things happen then that suggest there is a political savvy also operating with at least some of these officials and, as chap. 26 suggests, a response to prophetic activity that is not entirely hostile or unwilling to listen to the words of the prophets that threaten their situation. First, the officials tell Jeremiah and Baruch to hide themselves from the king, thus protecting Jeremiah once more. Then two of the officials, Elnathan and Delaiah, try to persuade the king not to burn the scroll in his anger. So the officials, in many ways complicit in and benefiting from the repressive and oppressive policies of the royal administration—at least as far as one may infer from the book—at times show themselves not totally devoid of sensitivity to what is going on. They are a mixed bag, and these two chapters indicate that in a way most of the rest of the book does not.

In a similar fashion, "the people," the general populace present and listening to Jeremiah's words, act in contradictory fashion, first aligning themselves with the priests and the prophets and calling for Jeremiah's death, then joining with the officials against the priests and prophets to protect Jeremiah, and, finally, in the last verse seeking his

144. Walter Brueggemann, *A Commentary on Jeremiah,* 236.

death. What is going on here? Many would argue that these contradictory stances reflect a multilayered text in which the compositional process has introduced inconsistencies. Such may have been the case, but the interpreter has some responsibility for asking about the present depiction, inasmuch as the inconsistencies would have been apparent at the beginning. The best reading of the text is to see in the populace something of the mixed reactions that are apparent in the presentation of the royal officials. The people are changeable, obviously subject to influence from different directions. The priests have significant control over the thinking of the people, but they would not be inattentive to the attitudes and conclusions of the royal officials, particularly when seeming to operate in some official capacity, as seems to be the case in vv. 10-11. The people move back and forth, sometimes acting in ways appropriate to the situation, and at other times reflecting the widespread sickness of Judean society. In the end, they are found to be in profound opposition to the word of the prophet and seek to kill him (v. 24). However mixed their reactions may be, the end of the story finds the people aligned against the prophet and the word of the Lord he declares.

REFLECTIONS

1. There is within Jeremiah's summary presentation a succinct definition of the source of direction for life that is lived in obedience to God. It is found in walking or living by the Torah, the law of the Lord, and paying attention to the warnings and directions of the prophets. The problem of human sin is not in our not knowing what to do or our inability to do it, but in not paying attention to what we are told by the prophets and in neglecting to follow the directions we are given in the law. The "law" has a particular function. "Torah" is often and properly translated as "instruction," and that is its function: to teach us the way to live. For Christians, that instruction incorporates the law of the Old Testament and the further instruction of Jesus and the apostles. How that instruction is applicable to the contemporary situation is not always easily discernible, and Christians have debated through the centuries about the relevance of the Old Testament law for the Christian life. But such debates can miss the force of Jeremiah's words and their contemporary resonance. The issue is over being willing to and making sure that one acts according to the instruction incumbent upon the community of faith. That instruction is reinforced by the words of the prophets, who continue to point to the divine instruction, who call us to faithfulness, and who warn us about the implications of not attending to that instruction. This text repeatedly speaks about people "listening" or not "listening," not "heeding" or "obeying." One of the tests of whether the community is acting faithfully is whether it pays attention to the prophetic words inscribed in Scripture and to their echoes in contemporary life. The community comes together for worship, to hear the scriptures read and preached in order to make sure that it regularly "listens" to the Word of the Lord and seeks direction from God's instruction. Part of paying attention to the prophets, however, is to hear their warnings about a Sunday listening that is not a Monday obedience.

2. The reaction to Jeremiah's sermon typifies, unfortunately, the way in which the prophetic word is often received. Two things happen just as in this text. One is that we hear what we want to hear and sift out the rest. The other is that we resist whatever in the word threatens our own security and set ways of living and acting. In the second half of the twentieth century, American culture was beset by two major upheavals: race relations and the Vietnam war. Both crises produced prophetic words and acts deeply rooted in the Lord's requirements of justice and peace so insistently set forth in the pages of Scripture. In the former instance, resistance to integration was rooted in the unwillingness to heed—as in Jeremiah's time—the law of Scripture, the teaching of God, and the admonitions of the prophets. This was in no small measure because of the way all these challenged the set ways and patterns of the culture and created upheaval of our comfortable modes of existence—housing patterns, school populations, work opportunities, and the like. In the latter instance—the resistance to the Vietnam war—the virulent reaction of many Americans reflected complete inability to hear how the denunciation of the war was rooted in faith and a vision of the ways of nations that was shaped by Scripture. The voices of conscience, which were also the voice of the Lord in the hearts of many persons, were seen only as human cowardice and lack of patriotism. The Christian community, therefore, has to watch constantly its unwillingness to listen to or heed the challenges to its comfortable ways and its tendency to transform such challenges into unacceptable human words rather than listening for the word of the Lord in the midst of them.

3. The citation of Micah's prophecy is an important clue for the way in which the community assesses contemporary prophecy. The Old Testament talks about the question of true and false prophecy at a number of points and raises the issue of distinguishing between them. How does one know whether the word that is being spoken in a prophetic way is truly a word from the Lord? That is a crucial question in the book of Jeremiah, as the next two chapters demonstrate in vivid fashion. Elsewhere in the book, criteria for distinguishing true and false prophecy are given (Jer 23:18-23). In this chapter, we find the community interpreting prophecy in the present by noting its consistency with prophecy in the past. That may be the best way for the contemporary community to try to discern the truth in the words of persons today who speak about what God is doing in the world or who call the community of faith to particular modes of conduct. How do their words and deeds compare with those of the prophets of old? Are the norms similar? Are the sources of authority like those of the prophets of Scripture? Do they speak out of a compulsion and against their own self-interest? In such a way the accounts of the lives and the words of the prophets of Scripture can serve as a guide for assessing possible prophetic words in the present. At the least the story of Jeremiah suggests that paying attention to the earlier prophets can be helpful in deciding about the authenticity of the word that is offered to us today.

4. The ambiguous picture of the royal officials and the people bids us think about the way in which the community of faith often reflects ambivalent attitudes about the hard issues of conduct and life. It is not always a simple matter of disobedience and inattention to the divine instruction and the words of the prophets. Sometimes we are just as much a mixed bag as were the people of Judah—self-sufficient and greed-directed; pursuing those gods that seem to ensure our well-being and enhance our wealth, status, and security; inattentive and indifferent to the needs of the poor and those without standing and power to secure their own well-being. At other times, we pay attention to the words of the prophets and seek to turn in a different direction. The biblical picture is often sharply etched, either good or evil and little sense of the way a community may move back and forth between faithfulness and sin. In this chapter, we see the people and even some of the political leadership being more attentive to the word of the Lord and are cautioned against oversimplifying our analysis of the contemporary scene.

JEREMIAH 27:1–29:32, COMING TO TERMS WITH BABYLON

OVERVIEW

The literary unity of these chapters—marked by linguistic peculiarities, a common date, and a focus on submission to Babylonian rule, including acceptance of the exile—has been noted in the Overview of chaps. 26–36. They demonstrate the political and theological conflict that arose in Jerusalem and Judah—indeed, among the surrounding peoples, who also chafed under the Babylonian yoke—about whether or not it was possible to break free from Babylonian domination. The natural assumption, then and now, would be that if such rebellion could be accomplished successfully, it should certainly take place. The harshness of the Babylonians needs no underscoring. In 597 BCE they had besieged Jerusalem and deported much of the leadership of the population as well as the treasures of the Temple. Clearly, any possibility of overthrowing Babylonian rule would be highly desirable. Not only is that view maintained among a large segment of the population, but there were also voices who deemed it possible, if not probable.

The large thrust of this section is to say as loudly as possible that rebellion against Babylonian rule by the remaining elements in Judah or by its neighbors is not only impossible but also wrong. Babylonian domination and deportation of Judeans to Babylon is the work of the Lord, an act of judgment that cannot be set aside. There is only one thing to do: Accept the punishment and learn to live with it, because the Lord is still at work and there is a hopeful future out there. Meanwhile, do not try to thwart the judging activity of God or fall prey to false hopes raised by false prophets. The yoke of Babylon has been placed on Judah by the Lord. For a period of time, it must be worn.[145]

It is possible that this stance represents a development in the prophecy of Jeremiah in the light of the events of 597. The call to submit to the yoke of Babylon in order to live is not reflected in the oracles of Jeremiah 1–20, where the word about Babylon is totally a word of destruction and exile.

> In 597 B.C., this language took on concrete form. It is only after the fulfillment of the prophetic word that a unique shift occurred in the prophet's perspective on the present and future. The concrete circumstances of 597 gave the prophet Jeremiah and his message a startling and forceful validation; at the same time, these circumstances gave rise to a distinct transformation of that message for the post–597 community in Judah who had experienced and survived the catastrophe. This transformation included a new focus directed toward the necessity of Judah's submission to Babylon, away from the often hyperbolic vision of military punishment as a judgment upon Judah's sins (Jer 9:10, 18, 21; 12:11; 14:8ff.).[146]

145. For detailed analysis of the particularities of language and thematic dimensions that support the reading of chaps. 25–29 as a literary whole, see Gerald L. Keown, Pamela J. Scalise, and Thomas J. Smothers, *Jeremiah 26–52*, WBC 27 (Dallas: Word, 1995) 35-38.

146. Christopher Seitz, *Theology in Conflict: Reactions to the Exile in the Book of Jeremiah*, BZAW 176 (Berlin: Walter de Gruyter, 1989) 207.

Jeremiah 27:1–28:17, The Yoke of Submission

NIV	NRSV
27 Early in the reign of Zedekiah*ᵃ* son of Josiah king of Judah, this word came to	**27** In the beginning of the reign of King Zedekiah*ᵃ* son of Josiah of Judah, this word came to Jeremiah from the LORD. ²Thus the LORD said to me: Make yourself a yoke of straps
ᵃ1 A few Hebrew manuscripts and Syriac (see also Jer. 27:3, 12 and 28:1); most Hebrew manuscripts Jehoiakim (Most Septuagint manuscripts do not have this verse.)	*ᵃAnother reading is Jehoiakim*

NIV

Jeremiah from the LORD: ²This is what the LORD said to me: "Make a yoke out of straps and crossbars and put it on your neck. ³Then send word to the kings of Edom, Moab, Ammon, Tyre and Sidon through the envoys who have come to Jerusalem to Zedekiah king of Judah. ⁴Give them a message for their masters and say, 'This is what the LORD Almighty, the God of Israel, says: "Tell this to your masters: ⁵With my great power and outstretched arm I made the earth and its people and the animals that are on it, and I give it to anyone I please. ⁶Now I will hand all your countries over to my servant Nebuchadnezzar king of Babylon; I will make even the wild animals subject to him. ⁷All nations will serve him and his son and his grandson until the time for his land comes; then many nations and great kings will subjugate him.

⁸" ' "If, however, any nation or kingdom will not serve Nebuchadnezzar king of Babylon or bow its neck under his yoke, I will punish that nation with the sword, famine and plague, declares the LORD, until I destroy it by his hand. ⁹So do not listen to your prophets, your diviners, your interpreters of dreams, your mediums or your sorcerers who tell you, 'You will not serve the king of Babylon.' ¹⁰They prophesy lies to you that will only serve to remove you far from your lands; I will banish you and you will perish. ¹¹But if any nation will bow its neck under the yoke of the king of Babylon and serve him, I will let that nation remain in its own land to till it and to live there, declares the LORD." ' "

¹²I gave the same message to Zedekiah king of Judah. I said, "Bow your neck under the yoke of the king of Babylon; serve him and his people, and you will live. ¹³Why will you and your people die by the sword, famine and plague with which the LORD has threatened any nation that will not serve the king of Babylon? ¹⁴Do not listen to the words of the prophets who say to you, 'You will not serve the king of Babylon,' for they are prophesying lies to you. ¹⁵'I have not sent them,' declares the LORD. 'They are prophesying lies in my name. Therefore, I will banish you and you will perish, both you and the prophets who prophesy to you.' "

¹⁶Then I said to the priests and all these people, "This is what the LORD says: Do not listen to the

NRSV

and bars, and put them on your neck. ³Send word[a] to the king of Edom, the king of Moab, the king of the Ammonites, the king of Tyre, and the king of Sidon by the hand of the envoys who have come to Jerusalem to King Zedekiah of Judah. ⁴Give them this charge for their masters: Thus says the LORD of hosts, the God of Israel: This is what you shall say to your masters: ⁵It is I who by my great power and my outstretched arm have made the earth, with the people and animals that are on the earth, and I give it to whomever I please. ⁶Now I have given all these lands into the hand of King Nebuchadnezzar of Babylon, my servant, and I have given him even the wild animals of the field to serve him. ⁷All the nations shall serve him and his son and his grandson, until the time of his own land comes; then many nations and great kings shall make him their slave.

8But if any nation or kingdom will not serve this king, Nebuchadnezzar of Babylon, and put its neck under the yoke of the king of Babylon, then I will punish that nation with the sword, with famine, and with pestilence, says the LORD, until I have completed its[b] destruction by his hand. ⁹You, therefore, must not listen to your prophets, your diviners, your dreamers,[c] your soothsayers, or your sorcerers, who are saying to you, 'You shall not serve the king of Babylon.' ¹⁰For they are prophesying a lie to you, with the result that you will be removed far from your land; I will drive you out, and you will perish. ¹¹But any nation that will bring its neck under the yoke of the king of Babylon and serve him, I will leave on its own land, says the LORD, to till it and live there.

12I spoke to King Zedekiah of Judah in the same way: Bring your necks under the yoke of the king of Babylon, and serve him and his people, and live. ¹³Why should you and your people die by the sword, by famine, and by pestilence, as the LORD has spoken concerning any nation that will not serve the king of Babylon? ¹⁴Do not listen to the words of the prophets who are telling you not to serve the king of Babylon, for they are prophesying a lie to you. ¹⁵I have not sent them, says the LORD, but they are prophesying falsely in my name, with the result that I will drive you out and

[a]Cn: Heb *send them* [b]Heb *their* [c]Gk Syr Vg: Heb *dreams*

prophets who say, 'Very soon now the articles from the LORD's house will be brought back from Babylon.' They are prophesying lies to you. [17]Do not listen to them. Serve the king of Babylon, and you will live. Why should this city become a ruin? [18]If they are prophets and have the word of the LORD, let them plead with the LORD Almighty that the furnishings remaining in the house of the LORD and in the palace of the king of Judah and in Jerusalem not be taken to Babylon. [19]For this is what the LORD Almighty says about the pillars, the Sea, the movable stands and the other furnishings that are left in this city, [20]which Nebuchadnezzar king of Babylon did not take away when he carried Jehoiachin[a] son of Jehoiakim king of Judah into exile from Jerusalem to Babylon, along with all the nobles of Judah and Jerusalem— [21]yes, this is what the LORD Almighty, the God of Israel, says about the things that are left in the house of the LORD and in the palace of the king of Judah and in Jerusalem: [22]'They will be taken to Babylon and there they will remain until the day I come for them,' declares the LORD. 'Then I will bring them back and restore them to this place.' "

28 In the fifth month of that same year, the fourth year, early in the reign of Zedekiah king of Judah, the prophet Hananiah son of Azzur, who was from Gibeon, said to me in the house of the LORD in the presence of the priests and all the people: [2]"This is what the LORD Almighty, the God of Israel, says: 'I will break the yoke of the king of Babylon. [3]Within two years I will bring back to this place all the articles of the LORD's house that Nebuchadnezzar king of Babylon removed from here and took to Babylon. [4]I will also bring back to this place Jehoiachin[a] son of Jehoiakim king of Judah and all the other exiles from Judah who went to Babylon,' declares the LORD, 'for I will break the yoke of the king of Babylon.' "

[5]Then the prophet Jeremiah replied to the prophet Hananiah before the priests and all the people who were standing in the house of the LORD. [6]He said, "Amen! May the LORD do so! May the LORD fulfill the words you have prophesied by bringing the articles of the LORD's house and all the exiles

[a]20, 4 Hebrew *Jeconiah,* a variant of *Jehoiachin*

you will perish, you and the prophets who are prophesying to you.

[16]Then I spoke to the priests and to all this people, saying, Thus says the LORD: Do not listen to the words of your prophets who are prophesying to you, saying, "The vessels of the LORD's house will soon be brought back from Babylon," for they are prophesying a lie to you. [17]Do not listen to them; serve the king of Babylon and live. Why should this city become a desolation? [18]If indeed they are prophets, and if the word of the LORD is with them, then let them intercede with the LORD of hosts, that the vessels left in the house of the LORD, in the house of the king of Judah, and in Jerusalem may not go to Babylon. [19]For thus says the LORD of hosts concerning the pillars, the sea, the stands, and the rest of the vessels that are left in this city, [20]which King Nebuchadnezzar of Babylon did not take away when he took into exile from Jerusalem to Babylon King Jeconiah son of Jehoiakim of Judah, and all the nobles of Judah and Jerusalem— [21]thus says the LORD of hosts, the God of Israel, concerning the vessels left in the house of the LORD, in the house of the king of Judah, and in Jerusalem: [22]They shall be carried to Babylon, and there they shall stay, until the day when I give attention to them, says the LORD. Then I will bring them up and restore them to this place.

28 In that same year, at the beginning of the reign of King Zedekiah of Judah, in the fifth month of the fourth year, the prophet Hananiah son of Azzur, from Gibeon, spoke to me in the house of the LORD, in the presence of the priests and all the people, saying, [2]"Thus says the LORD of hosts, the God of Israel: I have broken the yoke of the king of Babylon. [3]Within two years I will bring back to this place all the vessels of the LORD's house, which King Nebuchadnezzar of Babylon took away from this place and carried to Babylon. [4]I will also bring back to this place King Jeconiah son of Jehoiakim of Judah, and all the exiles from Judah who went to Babylon, says the LORD, for I will break the yoke of the king of Babylon."

[5]Then the prophet Jeremiah spoke to the prophet Hananiah in the presence of the priests and all the people who were standing in the

NIV

back to this place from Babylon. [7]Nevertheless, listen to what I have to say in your hearing and in the hearing of all the people: [8]From early times the prophets who preceded you and me have prophesied war, disaster and plague against many countries and great kingdoms. [9]But the prophet who prophesies peace will be recognized as one truly sent by the LORD only if his prediction comes true."

[10]Then the prophet Hananiah took the yoke off the neck of the prophet Jeremiah and broke it, [11]and he said before all the people, "This is what the LORD says: 'In the same way will I break the yoke of Nebuchadnezzar king of Babylon off the neck of all the nations within two years.' " At this, the prophet Jeremiah went on his way.

[12]Shortly after the prophet Hananiah had broken the yoke off the neck of the prophet Jeremiah, the word of the LORD came to Jeremiah: [13]"Go and tell Hananiah, 'This is what the LORD says: You have broken a wooden yoke, but in its place you will get a yoke of iron. [14]This is what the LORD Almighty, the God of Israel, says: I will put an iron yoke on the necks of all these nations to make them serve Nebuchadnezzar king of Babylon, and they will serve him. I will even give him control over the wild animals.' "

[15]Then the prophet Jeremiah said to Hananiah the prophet, "Listen, Hananiah! The LORD has not sent you, yet you have persuaded this nation to trust in lies. [16]Therefore, this is what the LORD says: 'I am about to remove you from the face of the earth. This very year you are going to die, because you have preached rebellion against the LORD.' "

[17]In the seventh month of that same year, Hananiah the prophet died.

NRSV

house of the LORD; [6]and the prophet Jeremiah said, "Amen! May the LORD do so; may the LORD fulfill the words that you have prophesied, and bring back to this place from Babylon the vessels of the house of the LORD, and all the exiles. [7]But listen now to this word that I speak in your hearing and in the hearing of all the people. [8]The prophets who preceded you and me from ancient times prophesied war, famine, and pestilence against many countries and great kingdoms. [9]As for the prophet who prophesies peace, when the word of that prophet comes true, then it will be known that the LORD has truly sent the prophet."

[10]Then the prophet Hananiah took the yoke from the neck of the prophet Jeremiah, and broke it. [11]And Hananiah spoke in the presence of all the people, saying, "Thus says the LORD: This is how I will break the yoke of King Nebuchadnezzar of Babylon from the neck of all the nations within two years." At this, the prophet Jeremiah went his way.

[12]Sometime after the prophet Hananiah had broken the yoke from the neck of the prophet Jeremiah, the word of the LORD came to Jeremiah: [13]Go, tell Hananiah, Thus says the LORD: You have broken wooden bars only to forge iron bars in place of them! [14]For thus says the LORD of hosts, the God of Israel: I have put an iron yoke on the neck of all these nations so that they may serve King Nebuchadnezzar of Babylon, and they shall indeed serve him; I have even given him the wild animals. [15]And the prophet Jeremiah said to the prophet Hananiah, "Listen, Hananiah, the LORD has not sent you, and you made this people trust in a lie. [16]Therefore thus says the LORD: I am going to send you off the face of the earth. Within this year you will be dead, because you have spoken rebellion against the LORD."

[17]In that same year, in the seventh month, the prophet Hananiah died.

COMMENTARY

Within the larger whole of chaps. 27–29, these two chapters are a subunit recounting a symbolic prophetic action that Jeremiah undertakes and interprets at length (chap. 27) and the counter-move of another prophet, Hananiah, whose symbolic action seeks to reverse the force of Jeremiah's (chap. 28). Herein lies one of the classic OT accounts of the conflict of true and false prophecy. What Jeremiah's oracles have spoken about in much detail—false prophets who oppose his message with words of peace—is vividly demonstrated in this narrative. The focus of the conflict is the matter of whether or not the word of the Lord is judgment (Jeremiah) or salvation (Hananiah). The specifics have to do with what is going to happen with regard to Babylonian control of Judah and, more specifically, with the temple vessels and treasures.

27:1-11. While the initial verse, missing from the Greek text of Jeremiah, seems to set this incident in the time of Jehoiakim, vv. 3 and 12 explicitly refer to Zedekiah, and vv. 16-22 presuppose that later time when the temple vessels have already been taken to Babylon. Thus the narrative, as v. 28 indicates, belongs in the reign of the last king of Judah, Zedekiah, sometime between 597 and 586 BCE. There is a conflict in the datings of 27:1 and 28:1 as to whether these events were understood as happening in the first year or the fourth year of Zedekiah's reign, and it is difficult to say which is correct.

Jeremiah is commanded to perform a simple but dramatic act, one that would be highly visible to the larger community. He is told to put on a yoke, customarily worn by oxen, and strap it to his neck (v. 2). This act is to symbolize the submission of Judah and other nations to the Babylonian "yoke," an interpretation given in an extended divine speech addressed to emissaries of the kings of Edom and Moab, the Ammonites, and to Tyre and Sidon. The speech is a theologically reflective interpretation that underscores four points:

(1) The Lord of Israel is in control of history, as indicated by Yahweh's power-manifesting creation of the earth and all that inhabits it. This is an assertion of the claim of the Lord over the other nations and what happens to them. After all, they are part of the "people and animals" the Lord made (v. 5).

The conclusion of this divine claim—"I give it to whomever I please" (lit., "I give it to whomever it seems right in my eyes to do")—provides the premise for the other themes.

(2) At this point in time and history, the Lord has given "it"—that is, "all these lands"—to the Babylonian king Nebuchadrezzar ("Nebuchadnezzar" in chaps. 27–29). The assertion here is that Babylonian domination is by the direct intent of the Lord, and the various nations of the area of Syria-Palestine will have to acknowledge this. Babylonian domination is neither an accident nor contrary to the intention of the creator God of Israel. The claim "I give/have given" is reiterated three times in vv. 5-6. This Babylonian hegemony will come to an end but not for a long time (v. 7), a point that is regularly made about the Lord's "use" of the Babylonian Empire, but not the main point of this symbolic act and its interpretation. The glimmer of light in the tunnel is to be noticed but not dwelt upon; it is far down the road. The mistaken assumption being addressed in these words is that Judah and the other nations think they can see light just around the corner.

(3) The only point that is made with more emphasis than the Lord's giving the lands and everything in them over to Nebuchadrezzar is the necessity for all their inhabitants to "serve" the king of Babylon. Seven times in these verses the verb "serve" is repeated. The point of the yoke around Jeremiah's neck is made abundantly clear: Neither rebellion nor false hopes of miraculous rescue is the order of the day. Failure of any of these nations to accept the necessity to subjugate themselves to Babylonian rule will mean an even worse fate (v. 8*b*).

To be noted in this connection is the second time Nebuchadrezzar is called "my servant" by the Lord (cf. 25:9; 43:10). The designation probably arose out of a textual corruption in v. 6, where the text probably read originally, "I have given . . . into the hand of Nebuchadnezzar, king of Babylon, *to serve him,*" reflecting a minor difference in the consonantal text of the Hebrew. The resulting phrase "my servant" was then brought over into 25:9 and 43:10, effecting a theological understanding of Nebuchadnezzar as not merely the instrument of the Lord's judgment but, as the term "my servant" implies, one who is in "a conscious and mutual relationship which is characterized by humble submission, obedience, and dedication to Yahweh on the part of the servant."[147] Such an understanding probably comes from a later period when Nebuchadrezzar was described in the tradition as having come to a direct acknowledgment of the sovereignty of the Lord of Israel (Dan 2:47; 3:28-29; 4:34-35, 37).[148]

(4) Do not listen to the prophets and others who think this submission to Babylon can be avoided. Jeremiah's reaction to the other prophets is consistent. The word of the Lord is once more that prophecies of a future without judgment are lies. They will be undone by the facts of the future. Furthermore, a decision relative to whose word will be confirmed is fraught with significance for the people. Submission to the yoke of Babylon will mean that those still in Judah can live on their land and survive. They can work their land and get a living off of it as they have done in the past (v. 11). The fulfillment of the words of doom in the first siege and in the exile of 597 leaves open the possibility of a future for those who survived that deportation and remain in Judah. Resistance to the Babylonian yoke will bring a certain end.

27:12-15. These verses reiterate the message of the preceding passage but now are addressed to Zedekiah and to the Judeans. It is worth noting that while the message is the same, it was first uttered to non-Israelite/Judean peoples and only then to the covenant community itself. This is one of those many places in the OT where the line between Israel and the other nations is not sharply drawn, where their stories coincide in the larger purpose of God.

27:16-22. Jeremiah's rejection of the word of the prophets who are announcing an immediate restoration and return from exile is made more insistent by its reiteration a third time. In this instance, the particular focus is the claim of the prophets of imminent salvation that the vessels or implements that were taken to Babylon in the conquest and exile of 597 will be returned shortly. We know from 2 Kings 24 that some of the vessels and treasures were taken by Nebuchadrezzar at that time, but the Kings report indicates that all of

them were taken and that the gold vessels were cut up. It is not possible to resolve this contradiction. The best that can be indicated is that some were taken in 597 and that a tradition in Jeremiah assumes some were still present in the Temple, for Jeremiah's retort to the prophets' prediction of the return of the vessels is that not only will they not be returned but the rest of them will be taken away as well (see 52:17-23). A tension is thus created in the chapter between the call to submit and live and the announcement that the rest of the temple implements will be carried into exile. This tension probably reflects different attitudes in the community over an extended time, one point of view seeing a possible future in the remaining Judean community if it submitted, with another, and possibly later perspective, represented in vv. 18-22 seeing Judah's future resting in the restoration of the exilic community, not in the folks who remained after 597. The latter point of view probably came to dominate after the destruction of the Temple and the second deportation of Judeans to Babylon in 586.[149]

As a part of his taunt of the false prophets, Jeremiah gives a fragmentary but important picture of what authentic prophecy is all about. In v. 18, those who would be prophets are those in whom the word of the Lord is to be found and who engage in intercession for the community. The book of Jeremiah regularly identifies intercession in time of trouble as a prophetic act (e.g., 7:16; 11:14; 14:11-12; 15:1). The prophets of salvation reveal their lack of credentials by prophesying salvation in a time when, like Jeremiah and earlier prophets, they should be praying for the people. The prophet was the intercessor *par excellence* in ancient Israel. The absence of intercession marks these prophets as truly not knowing what is going on, not knowing what time it really is.

28:1-11. Jeremiah's warning the people against listening to prophets who prophesied the immediate return of the temple vessels from Babylon forms a bridge from chap. 27 to chap. 28, for now we hear of such a prophet whose oracle not only promises the recovery of the implements and vessels of the Temple but also the return of the exiled Judean king Jehoiachin, together with all the Judeans deported to Babylon in 597. The

147. Werner Lemke, "Nebuchadrezzar, My Servant," *CBQ* 28 (1966) 46.
148. Ibid., 49-50.
149. On this tension in Jeremiah see Seitz, *Theology in Conflict*.

proclamation of that oracle becomes the context for one of the most direct encounters between opposing prophets in the OT.

The present form of v. 1 sets this confrontation in the same year as the symbolic action and interpretation of chap. 27, although such a temporal drawing together of the two accounts may be a redactional move because the phrase "in the same year" is missing from the better text of the Greek translation. In vv. 2-4, an oracle is given by a prophet named Hananiah, who is otherwise unattested in biblical and extra-biblical texts but who must have been known to the community at the time because he is identified as "the prophet from Gibeon." It is likely, therefore, that his appearance on the scene and his proclamation of an oracle would have been no more unusual than Jeremiah's doing so. The similarity to Jeremiah is further indicated by the form and content of the oracle Hananiah utters (vv. 2-4). It is fully comparable to those of Isaiah, Jeremiah, and other prophets, beginning with the words, "Thus says the LORD of hosts . . ." and presenting a divine speech announcing a future act of the deity, in this case, as often in the prophets, a word of deliverance: "I have broken the yoke of the king of Babylon." This salvation prophecy is spelled out in more detail with the announcement of the imminent return of the temple vessels, Jehoiachin, and the deported Judeans. The oracle is concluded with a typical "says the LORD." Then, following Jeremiah's response to this oracle (vv. 5-9), Hananiah performs a symbolic action, again comparable to what Jeremiah does on several occasions (cf. 13:1-12 and esp. 19:10-11). He breaks the yoke Jeremiah is wearing and says: "Thus says the LORD, 'This is how I will break . . .' " (cf. 13:9; 19:11). In this case, however, both the proclamation and the symbolic action are set as direct counters to the proclamation and symbolic action of Jeremiah. That should not be surprising, inasmuch as he has regularly set his word against the word of the other prophets, more specifically the prophets of peace, which is what Hananiah is in this story. Three things are thus prominent in the story:

(1) In formal ways—that is, in his manner of speech and action—Hananaiah is fully comparable to Jeremiah and other prophets of the Lord. Nowhere more dramatically than this is the reader placed before the conflict of prophecy that

seems to have been fairly common in Israel and Judah, a conflict of alternative, indeed contradictory visions of what God was doing in their time. The prophets whom Jeremiah opposed looked, talked, and acted as he did, proclaiming their words as the word of the Lord. Hananiah's words are "in the presence of the priests and all the people" (vv. 1, 5), before the religious leadership and the larger community, the same kind of setting in which Jeremiah regularly spoke the word of the Lord.

(2) The content of the prophetic speech and action of Hananiah is one of imminent salvation or deliverance. That was often the word of the Lord, but not now. Where does it come from? We do not know what sort of prophetic experience Hananiah may have had, but his prophecy here is understood to be ideological. At its time, it may have been perceived as a competing ideology with that of Jeremiah, one calling for political submission and the other for political resistance, one saying that Babylonian domination was something to be accepted, the other saying that independence was on the horizon. Each claimed his word to be the word of the Lord. In the context of the book of Jeremiah, the words of the other prophets, and the lessons of history, Hananiah's word is seen not to be the word of the Lord but the maintenance of a mistaken assumption that the Lord will preserve Zion and the people from any serious harm, that the unpleasant events of the present were a reprimand but not a serious reality of punishment and judgment. Whether drawing upon past words of assurance about Jerusalem, such as those of Isaiah, or simply reflecting the same kind of popular manifestation of the royal theology that was so confident that nothing would happen to king and Temple, the announcement of salvation was dead wrong, a popular word that couched a kind of nationalistic and establishment confidence in the garment of divine speech. That was—and is—ideology.

(3) Both the words and the actions of Hananiah are set in direct and visible opposition to the words and actions of Jeremiah. Hananiah's speech exemplifies what Jeremiah warns against in chap. 27, and Jeremiah's act of wearing the yoke, an action performed under divine command, is countered when Hananiah takes the yoke off Jeremiah and, with an accompanying divine explanatory speech,

breaks it. Here prophets do not simply differ, but prophecy is set against prophecy. The alternative visions are not compatible. Hananiah's symbolic act is a prophetic and political move to defeat the vision of Jeremiah, to claim the following and thus the appropriate actions of his audience, "the priests and all the people." Much is riding on this conflict, for the audience will act quite differently depending upon which prophet it believes is "truly sent."

Between Hananiah's oracle and his symbolic act, Jeremiah responds (vv. 5-9). His restraint is notable, and some would see in the depiction of Jeremiah a different authorial hand with a different characterization of the prophet, while others would draw their basic picture of the prophet from the presentation in these chapters. It is not finally that helpful to try to develop either a consistent picture of the prophet or to uncover varying depictions and assign them to different authorial or redactional sources. The book gives a complex presentation, and that is the one offered to our attention.

Here, a more measured response in the context of a narrative and a direct encounter with another prophet is the vehicle for Jeremiah's indirect challenge to the oracle of this prophet of peace. Contrary to his usual unqualified denunciation of the oracles of the prophets of peace, Jeremiah now seems open to the positive oracle of deliverance. What accounts for that is difficult to say. It may be that Jeremiah is being somewhat cautious in responding to so obviously popular and desirable a word as Hananiah's prophecy. After all, Jeremiah's response is also very public (v. 5). More likely, in confirming Hananiah's salvation prophecy with an "Amen" and the wish for God to make it happen, Jeremiah expresses his own wishes and hopes for a positive outcome to the present trials. There is little indication that Jeremiah enjoyed uttering his words of judgment and much indication of the pain that such prophecies caused him (see chaps. 11–20 and the account of the last days of Judah in chaps. 37–44). As Calvin has suggested with regard to the prophets of judgment, "They did not wholly put off every humane feeling, but condoled with the miseries of the people; and though they denounced on them destruction, yet they could not but receive sorrow from their own prophecies."[150]

A sharp "nevertheless" follows this instinctively "humane feeling," however, and Jeremiah challenges the hopeful words of Hananiah on two grounds, both of which belong to the criteria for assessing prophetic words. One is prophetic tradition, the experience of the community in the past with the words of the prophets. Here, Jeremiah does, in effect, what the elders did in chap. 26: He cites the record. While words of deliverance were prophesied in the past—by Isaiah, for example, whose prophecies may have inspired Hananiah—the large picture for the pre-exilic period is one of announcements of judgment. As the elders recognize when they vindicate Jeremiah, his terrible words of doom are consistent with the way prophets have addressed the people in the past. In the light of that history, one should be very suspicious of easy words of deliverance.

The second ground on which Jeremiah responds to Hananiah is the test of prophecy, the issue of what happens. Deuteronomy 18 sets that as the fundamental criterion for distinguishing between true and false prophecy. The word of the prophet truly sent by the Lord is the word that will come to pass. The catch, of course, is that one can only apply that criterion after the fact. History will have to tell which prophet was sent by the Lord. And there, of course, is the point of the story. It is preserved in the record precisely as a vindication of Jeremiah's prophecy, for the later readers know how things worked out. The decision between Jeremiah and Hananiah is easy for the readers of the story, not because of fine distinctions between form or content but because the word of Jeremiah came to pass and Hananiah's did not.

28:12-17. False prophecy, however, is not simply a matter of saying, "Oh, I made a mistake!" The one who misrepresents the word and work of the Lord stands in opposition to that word and that work and so is in some sense an "enemy" of the Lord, an exemplar of the bad faith that is endemic to the religious leadership of Judah in its last days. Hananiah's response to Jeremiah's warning on the basis of prophetic tradition and the test of prophecy is a defiant symbolic act to break the yoke Jeremiah wore. Such defiance in opposition to the divine word brings judgment on this false prophet of peace.

Two oracles are given by Jeremiah to Hananiah. The first one is in response to Hananiah's own ora-

---

150. John Calvin, *Commentaries on the Book of the Prophet Jeremiah and the Lamentations,* vol. 3 (Edinburgh: Calvin Translation Society, 1852) 392-93.

cle and symbolic act. They are both negated by the divine word that the broken wooden yoke or bar (singular) will only lead to the placement of iron bars (plural) upon Judah and the other nations. The oracle in v. 14 reiterates the original prophecy of Jeremiah in 27:6. The move from wood to iron and from singular to plural is a way of indicating how far off Hananiah is, how much he has gotten it wrong. Hananiah has utterly misread the situation, and with this word from the Lord, Hananiah's word is now clearly revealed as a lie.

So the second oracle of Jeremiah responds to what Hananiah has done, to the larger meaning of his act. The positive words of imminent deliverance would have been music to the ears of the people, causing them to assume all would be okay, and they would not have to do anything but await the Lord's deliverance. That response is just the opposite of what needs to happen, and so Hananiah's words of false security have caused the people to trust in a lie, to place their hopes in what is an impossibility. Rather than repenting and turning from their ways of idolatry, social injustice, and arrogant self-sufficiency, the people are lulled by

Hananiah's words into carrying on as usual. The indictment of Hananiah is a double one, but the two parts are really a single whole. Causing the people to trust in a lie (v. 15) is a form of rebellion against the Lord (v. 16). The latter indictment corresponds to the language of Deut 13:5[6], which calls for the sentence of death on prophets who turn the people from the way of the Lord. And so that sentence is pronounced upon Hananiah in a way that effects a kind of poetic justice common in the prophetic judgment speeches. His crime is to prophesy when the Lord did not "send" him (v. 15 b); his punishment is to be "sent" off the face of the earth (v. 16 a). The encounter between Jeremiah and Hananiah, which is really a conflict over truth and falsehood whose aim is to make clear at the center of the book who is in control of history and who is God's real spokesman, concludes with the perfunctory note about the fulfillment of the prophecy of Jeremiah: Hananiah died that very same year. The brief note is a further confirmation of the authenticity of Jeremiah as the true prophet of the Lord. His announcement of judgment against Hananiah came true.

REFLECTIONS

1. The ground of the Lord's claim to be at work in the domination of Babylon over the states of Palestine is based on a succinct but powerful joining of creation and history into a single sphere over which the Lord's sovereignty is manifest. Nowhere, perhaps, is creation more explicitly a ground for history than here. Nowhere is history more directly an outcome of creation. The easy tendency to separate these two spheres—creation and history, nature and culture—is negated in this text as the activity of God in history, seen in the effecting of judgment through the agency of Babylon and its king is a manifestation of the creative power of God. The text is thus resistant to theologies of salvation history and God's mighty deeds as well as to those that see creation as the horizon of theology, at least in the Old Testament.[151] The two are melded into one, creation and universal history, the particular activity of God in and through Israel and also the judgment of nations unrelated to Israel, the domination of a despotic ruler as the outcome of the power of God at work in creation. The divine speech in 27:4-11 begins in God's creative work and leads into the events of the early sixth century BCE as a manifestation of that creative power. Lest one forget that it is the work of the Creator that sets Babylon loose on these nations, the end of the divine speech in 27:11 returns to explicit creation language as the promise is made that any nation that properly submits to the yoke and "serves" (עבד 'ābad) the Babylonian king will be able to live on its "ground" (אדמה 'ădāmâ; cf. Genesis 1–2) and "till" ('ābad) it, which is the human vocation, according to the story of God's creation (Gen 2:15; 4:2 b). Submission to the Lord's rule of history, which is rooted in the creative power of God, leads to human life lived according to God's intent in the creation.

---

151. On the tendency to develop a theology of the OT from one of these directions or the other, see Walter Brueggemann, "The Loss and Recovery of Creation in Old Testament Theology," *TToday* 53 (1996) 177-90; and, more extensively, "A Shifting Paradigm: From 'Mighty Deeds' to 'Horizon,' " *The Papers of the Henry Luce III Fellows in Theology* I, ed. Gary Gilbert (Atlanta: Scholars Press, 1996) 7-47.

2. The maker of heaven and earth is the one who does with it whatever is the divine pleasure. That "pleasure," as the NRSV translates the end of 27:5, is really a manifestation of the Lord's righteous control of history. Against human expectations and even human hopes, against prophetic claims and political machinations, the Lord defines what is "right" for the world. The rule of a tyrannical king is in this case a manifestation of the action of God in history and a conformity with the norm that is the Lord's own. This is a difficult message for the contemporary hearer, who knows that the Lord who speaks in Scripture is compassionate and loving, wills the good of humankind, and attends to the oppressed. It does suggest that the "right" as the Lord defines it is not always manifested in what human beings see in a particular moment as "right." There is a larger view, which is one of the main things the book of Jeremiah contributes. And there is an understanding that human definitions, expectations, and desires do not always perceive or conform to the Lord's creative power at work in history. So readers of the signs of the times and those who would speak in God's behalf or even against God in behalf of the human, need to beware a misreading of what God is doing in the world, from the beginning until the end.

3. Theology and politics are once again joined in the prophecy of Jeremiah. There are such large claims here that one risks reading them as "religious" stuff or merely ideological rhetoric for pressing through a particular "party" line. The stuff of this text is, indeed, religious and ideological. Within both, there is an awareness that the realm of God's work in the world is the affairs of people and nations, the politics of alliances and the rise and fall of empires. "It is I," says the Lord, and the construction is explicitly emphatic (27:5). The destiny of the nations of the Fertile Crescent—not merely Israel—are at the direction of Yahweh, and—in the growing vision of the text—the Babylonian king is seen to be the one who does the will of the Lord. Yet even the "servant" of the Lord stands under divine control and judgment. What is going on in history is fraught with human decisions, inclinations, evil, and good. It is all the context in which the Lord is working out the divine purposes, a context that itself is provided by the Creator. The politics of human communities are found to be in some fashion coterminus with the politics of God. That is not something we can always discern or make sense of, and there may be times when we have to call human evil simply that and make no more of it. But Jeremiah suggests that we think about what is going on in the world as God's work, even with alien and strange instruments.

4. The line between faith and ideology is a very slim one. Indeed, any large perspective that speaks about the fate of a political community and seeks to spur particular kinds of responses and actions on the basis of an analysis or perception of present reality and future possibilities has an ideological bent to it, an underlying—somewhat explicit, somewhat implicit—conviction about the community's whence and whither and a program for bringing about the proper goal or outcome. That was no less true of Jeremiah than of Hananiah. What must never be missed is the Bible's conviction that ideologies are not all the same, that some bring us closer to what God is doing in the world and thus may be spoken of as faithful as well as ideological. Those programs for the future that build upon the biblical story and, like the prophets of old, use the language of Zion and claim divine guidance but are not consonant with that story and its direction, that do not really listen to the prophets of old, their instruction and warnings, are engaged in an ideology that is finally bad faith.[152]

5. Political expediency at times may be also an act of obedience. It is customary to see acts of resistance and rebellion as the proper manifestation of a religious or, even more specifically, Christian conscience, as, for example, in the lives of the martyrs, of a Dietrich Bonhoeffer.

---

152. On the difficult question of the relationship of faith and ideology, see Patrick D. Miller, Jr., "Faith and Ideology in the Old Testament," in *Magnalia Dei: The Mighty Acts of God: Essays on the Bible and Archaeology in Memory of G. Ernest Wright,* ed. Frank Moore Cross, Werner E. Lemke, and Patrick D. Miller, Jr. (Garden City, N.Y.: Doubleday, 1976) 464-79.

In Jeremiah's time, the proper submission to the will of God involved a submission to the political authorities, not because of some theory of church and state relations but because at that moment in time submission and acceptance of domination was the intention of God in history. One cannot extrapolate a general principle—one way or the other—about the correlation between prudence/resistance and obedience. But the story before us identifies a moment in history when the right political move was an acceptance of the bad situation because it was God's work, and not simply fate.

6. The encounter between Hananiah and Jeremiah makes us aware of the difficulty of discerning the times or of knowing whose wisdom, whose discernment, whose interpretation is "truly" (28:11) from the Lord. Formal characteristics will not finally tell us who speaks truly. Both Hananiah and Jeremiah spoke and acted "properly" as prophets of the Lord. We are not finally given some rules of the game that let us know whose word we can trust. The listeners must themselves discern who is "truly sent" and who is not. Once again, as in chap. 26, one way to get at that is set out in the text. It is the need to pay attention to what the prophets of the past have said. That is not an infallible criterion. Prophets of the past spoke "truly" oracles of salvation or peace as well as authentic words of the Lord's "war." In one sense, we learn from these chapters only about what happened in the early sixth century BCE in the Judean kingdom and the different ways prophets responded to that crisis and declared the word of the Lord. But Jeremiah's citation of the prophets of the past suggests that if we keep reading and listening to the prophetic voices of Scripture, who are for us the authentic word of the Lord, we may have the resources at hand for discerning the voices of those who are "truly sent" in our own time. There are no guarantees, no criteria of credibility that one can slip in to claim truth over falsehood. The only resource one has is attentive listening to the prophets of old to attune oneself for listening for the truth. (On Nebuchadrezzar as a servant of the Lord, see the Reflections at 25:1-14.)

Jeremiah 29:1-32, Accepting Exile

NIV

29 This is the text of the letter that the prophet Jeremiah sent from Jerusalem to the surviving elders among the exiles and to the priests, the prophets and all the other people Nebuchadnezzar had carried into exile from Jerusalem to Babylon. [2](This was after King Jehoiachin[a] and the queen mother, the court officials and the leaders of Judah and Jerusalem, the craftsmen and the artisans had gone into exile from Jerusalem.) [3]He entrusted the letter to Elasah son of Shaphan and to Gemariah son of Hilkiah, whom Zedekiah king of Judah sent to King Nebuchadnezzar in Babylon. It said:

[4]This is what the LORD Almighty, the God of Israel, says to all those I carried into exile from Jerusalem to Babylon: [5]"Build houses

[a]2 Hebrew *Jeconiah*, a variant of *Jehoiachin*

NRSV

29 These are the words of the letter that the prophet Jeremiah sent from Jerusalem to the remaining elders among the exiles, and to the priests, the prophets, and all the people, whom Nebuchadnezzar had taken into exile from Jerusalem to Babylon. [2]This was after King Jeconiah, and the queen mother, the court officials, the leaders of Judah and Jerusalem, the artisans, and the smiths had departed from Jerusalem. [3]The letter was sent by the hand of Elasah son of Shaphan and Gemariah son of Hilkiah, whom King Zedekiah of Judah sent to Babylon to King Nebuchadnezzar of Babylon. It said: [4]Thus says the LORD of hosts, the God of Israel, to all the exiles whom I have sent into exile from Jerusalem to Babylon: [5]Build houses and live in them; plant gardens and eat what they produce. [6]Take wives and have sons and daughters;

NIV

and settle down; plant gardens and eat what they produce. [6]Marry and have sons and daughters; find wives for your sons and give your daughters in marriage, so that they too may have sons and daughters. Increase in number there; do not decrease. [7]Also, seek the peace and prosperity of the city to which I have carried you into exile. Pray to the LORD for it, because if it prospers, you too will prosper." [8]Yes, this is what the LORD Almighty, the God of Israel, says: "Do not let the prophets and diviners among you deceive you. Do not listen to the dreams you encourage them to have. [9]They are prophesying lies to you in my name. I have not sent them," declares the LORD.

[10]This is what the LORD says: "When seventy years are completed for Babylon, I will come to you and fulfill my gracious promise to bring you back to this place. [11]For I know the plans I have for you," declares the LORD, "plans to prosper you and not to harm you, plans to give you hope and a future. [12]Then you will call upon me and come and pray to me, and I will listen to you. [13]You will seek me and find me when you seek me with all your heart. [14]I will be found by you," declares the LORD, "and will bring you back from captivity.[a] I will gather you from all the nations and places where I have banished you," declares the LORD, "and will bring you back to the place from which I carried you into exile."

[15]You may say, "The LORD has raised up prophets for us in Babylon," [16]but this is what the LORD says about the king who sits on David's throne and all the people who remain in this city, your countrymen who did not go with you into exile [17]yes, this is what the LORD Almighty says: "I will send the sword, famine and plague against them and I will make them like poor figs that are so bad they cannot be eaten. [18]I will pursue them with the sword, famine and plague and will make them abhorrent to all the kingdoms of the earth and an object of curs-

[a]14 Or *will restore your fortunes*

NRSV

take wives for your sons, and give your daughters in marriage, that they may bear sons and daughters; multiply there, and do not decrease. [7]But seek the welfare of the city where I have sent you into exile, and pray to the LORD on its behalf, for in its welfare you will find your welfare. [8]For thus says the LORD of hosts, the God of Israel: Do not let the prophets and the diviners who are among you deceive you, and do not listen to the dreams that they dream,[a] [9]for it is a lie that they are prophesying to you in my name; I did not send them, says the LORD.

10For thus says the LORD: Only when Babylon's seventy years are completed will I visit you, and I will fulfill to you my promise and bring you back to this place. [11]For surely I know the plans I have for you, says the LORD, plans for your welfare and not for harm, to give you a future with hope. [12]Then when you call upon me and come and pray to me, I will hear you. [13]When you search for me, you will find me; if you seek me with all your heart, [14]I will let you find me, says the LORD, and I will restore your fortunes and gather you from all the nations and all the places where I have driven you, says the LORD, and I will bring you back to the place from which I sent you into exile.

15Because you have said, "The LORD has raised up prophets for us in Babylon,"— [16]Thus says the LORD concerning the king who sits on the throne of David, and concerning all the people who live in this city, your kinsfolk who did not go out with you into exile: [17]Thus says the LORD of hosts, I am going to let loose on them sword, famine, and pestilence, and I will make them like rotten figs that are so bad they cannot be eaten. [18]I will pursue them with the sword, with famine, and with pestilence, and will make them a horror to all the kingdoms of the earth, to be an object of cursing, and horror, and hissing, and a derision among all the nations where I have driven them, [19]because they did not heed my words, says the LORD, when I persistently sent to you my servants the prophets, but they[b] would not listen, says the LORD. [20]But now, all you exiles whom I sent away from Jerusalem to Babylon, hear the word of the LORD: [21]Thus says the LORD of hosts, the God of Israel, concerning Ahab son of Kolaiah and

[a]Cn: Heb *your dreams that you cause to dream* [b]Syr: Heb *you*

NIV

ing and horror, of scorn and reproach, among all the nations where I drive them. ¹⁹For they have not listened to my words," declares the LORD, "words that I sent to them again and again by my servants the prophets. And you exiles have not listened either," declares the LORD.

²⁰Therefore, hear the word of the LORD, all you exiles whom I have sent away from Jerusalem to Babylon. ²¹This is what the LORD Almighty, the God of Israel, says about Ahab son of Kolaiah and Zedekiah son of Maaseiah, who are prophesying lies to you in my name: "I will hand them over to Nebuchadnezzar king of Babylon, and he will put them to death before your very eyes. ²²Because of them, all the exiles from Judah who are in Babylon will use this curse: 'The LORD treat you like Zedekiah and Ahab, whom the king of Babylon burned in the fire.' ²³For they have done outrageous things in Israel; they have committed adultery with their neighbors' wives and in my name have spoken lies, which I did not tell them to do. I know it and am a witness to it," declares the LORD.

²⁴Tell Shemaiah the Nehelamite, ²⁵"This is what the LORD Almighty, the God of Israel, says: You sent letters in your own name to all the people in Jerusalem, to Zephaniah son of Maaseiah the priest, and to all the other priests. You said to Zephaniah, ²⁶'The LORD has appointed you priest in place of Jehoiada to be in charge of the house of the LORD; you should put any madman who acts like a prophet into the stocks and neck-irons. ²⁷So why have you not reprimanded Jeremiah from Anathoth, who poses as a prophet among you? ²⁸He has sent this message to us in Babylon: It will be a long time. Therefore build houses and settle down; plant gardens and eat what they produce.' "

²⁹Zephaniah the priest, however, read the letter to Jeremiah the prophet. ³⁰Then the word of the LORD came to Jeremiah: ³¹"Send this message to all the exiles: 'This is what the LORD says about Shemaiah the Nehelamite: Because Shemaiah has prophesied to you, even though I did not send

NRSV

Zedekiah son of Maaseiah, who are prophesying a lie to you in my name: I am going to deliver them into the hand of King Nebuchadrezzar of Babylon, and he shall kill them before your eyes. ²²And on account of them this curse shall be used by all the exiles from Judah in Babylon: "The LORD make you like Zedekiah and Ahab, whom the king of Babylon roasted in the fire," ²³because they have perpetrated outrage in Israel and have committed adultery with their neighbors' wives, and have spoken in my name lying words that I did not command them; I am the one who knows and bears witness, says the LORD.

24To Shemaiah of Nehelam you shall say: ²⁵Thus says the LORD of hosts, the God of Israel: In your own name you sent a letter to all the people who are in Jerusalem, and to the priest Zephaniah son of Maaseiah, and to all the priests, saying, ²⁶The LORD himself has made you priest instead of the priest Jehoiada, so that there may be officers in the house of the LORD to control any madman who plays the prophet, to put him in the stocks and the collar. ²⁷So now why have you not rebuked Jeremiah of Anathoth who plays the prophet for you? ²⁸For he has actually sent to us in Babylon, saying, "It will be a long time; build houses and live in them, and plant gardens and eat what they produce."

29The priest Zephaniah read this letter in the hearing of the prophet Jeremiah. ³⁰Then the word of the LORD came to Jeremiah: ³¹Send to all the exiles, saying, Thus says the LORD concerning Shemaiah of Nehelam: Because Shemaiah has prophesied to you, though I did not send him, and has led you to trust in a lie, ³²therefore thus says the LORD: I am going to punish Shemaiah of Nehelam and his descendants; he shall not have anyone living among this people to see[a] the good that I am going to do to my people, says the LORD, for he has spoken rebellion against the LORD.

[a]Gk: Heb *and he shall not see*

NIV

him, and has led you to believe a lie, ³²this is what the Lord says: I will surely punish Shemaiah the Nehelamite and his descendants. He will have no one left among this people, nor will he see the good things I will do for my people, declares the Lord, because he has preached rebellion against me.'"

COMMENTARY

While the themes of this chapter continue from the preceding chapters, the form is rather unusual. Prophetic oracles are couched in a series of letters, by Jeremiah and others, back and forth between Jerusalem and Babylon. The heart of the chapter is a long letter from Jeremiah to the exiles who were deported to Babylon in 597 BCE (vv. 1-23), followed by the report of an exchange of letters reflecting conflict between Jeremiah and another prophet, Shemiah. The form of the chapter bears little resemblance to typical Hebrew letters, but the reference to the letter bearers (v. 3) and the Lord's self-identification as a witness (v. 23), which functions as a kind of countersignature to the letter inasmuch as its content is a message from the Lord, reinforce the claim of the opening verse that we have here a kind of prophetic-pastoral letter to the exiles.

The thematic foci of the chapter are two: the need for exiles to accept their fate and know that the God who has brought it upon them is at work for their ultimate good, and the danger (once more) of listening to false prophets who create a false hope of immediate deliverance. Just as chap. 27 addressed the Judean survivors of the 597 deportation, calling upon them to accept Babylonian domination of Judah and the surrounding countries, so also now chap. 29 calls upon the deportees to accept servitude in Babylon. For those at home and those away, this is a time of punishment, and the first order of business is to acknowledge that and live with it. But the muted indications of an end to the punishment in chap. 27 are here extended to become a larger part of the message. That word of hope for a future restoration has its full development in the chapters that immediately follow (chaps. 30–33).

There is one problem in the arrangement of the chapter that needs to be observed. There is an obvious disjunction (reflected in the NRSV's use of a dash) between v. 15, which returns to the matter of prophets, and the immediately following verses, which are words of judgment against the Judeans who remained in the land after the first deportation in 597. Some would argue that vv. 16-19 "cohere poorly with the concerns of chap. 29," and see in them a later expansion of the text to incorporate a word against the remaining Judeans into a passage that otherwise is directed only to Babylonian exiles.[153] But the pairing of the two communities in the form of positive words for the exiles and negative for the survivors is a feature of other Jeremianic texts, specifically chap. 24, with which this passage has its largest affinities.[154] However the text may have come to its present stage, the concerns of these chapters are fully consistent not only with Jeremiah in general but more specifically with the preceding chapters of this literary unit (chaps. 27–28). The disjunction between v. 15 and v. 16 may best be accounted for by assuming a process of error in the transmission of the Hebrew text that once may have had the sequence of vv. 1-14, 16-20, 15, 21-23. The disturbance of that order to produce what is presently before us would have happened by readily discernible processes of textual error and correc-

---

153. William McKane, *A Critical and Exegetical Commentary on Jeremiah*, 2 vols., ICC (Edinburgh: T. & T. Clark, 1986, 1996) 2:739.
154. For the way in which the present text of Jeremiah may have arisen out of redactional activity reflecting major theological conflicts around contrasting evaluations of the events of 597 BCE and attitudes toward the remnant community in Judah between 597 and the second and final deportation in 587, see Christopher Seitz, *Theology in Conflict: Reactions to the Exile in the Book of Jeremiah*, BZAW 176 (Berlin: Walter de Gruyter, 1989).

tion.[155] Because vv. 15 and 21-23 deal with the issue of false prophecy in Babylon, we will look at those verses in connection with vv. 8-9, where that matter first comes up in the chapter.

29:1-7. In what is a rather unusual piece of prophecy—a letter carried by royal emissaries from Judah to Babylon—Jeremiah now addresses not his usual audience of local Judeans and Jerusalemites but those who have already experienced divine judgment and have been deported to Babylon. It is, however, essentially the same message that he has delivered to the Judeans at home (chap. 27): "Do not resist; carry on your lives; learn to come to terms with your situation." If the words of this letter are a counterpart to the oracles addressing the Judeans in the land, they are also a counterpart to the "peace" prophecy of Hananiah in chap. 28 (see 28:9), for now we hear Jeremiah speaking of "peace" for the people. Three times the divine oracle speaks of peace in v. 7 and then once again in v. 11. But the peace and well-being the Lord promises to the exiles through Jeremiah are radically different from that promised by Hananiah and prophets like him. Such peace is not to be found in resistance and rebellion—and this letter may have been sent when there were signs of such in the Babylonian Empire—but in submission. It is not to be found in returning to home, land, and family but in settling into exile and building homes and farms and families there. The exiles are not to "pray for the peace of Jerusalem," as the psalmist commends (Ps 122:6 NRSV), but for the peace of Babylon! Psalm 122 gives us some idea of what sort of praying is envisioned:

> "May they prosper who love you.
> Peace be within your walls,
>   and security within your towers." (NRSV)

But such prayers of intercession would have included prayers for Babylon's deliverance from threats and dangers as well.

Within these commands to the exiles is an assurance that the divine blessing of fertility, well-being, productivity, and the regular provision of the possibilities of life continues even in exile. The punishment characteristic of what has happened is clear, and it is not quickly over. So for that very

reason, the exiles are enjoined to find their life now in this new and difficult place, assured by the command of God that life is possible, that home and family, food and shelter, the things that support and keep human beings human, are possible—and over the long haul. The creation blessing of Gen 1:28-30 continues, even in exile.

Jeremiah's letter is a rather astonishing manifestation of his commission "to build and to plant" (v. 5; cf. 1:10). It is worth noting that the divine commission in Jeremiah's call to "build and plant" comes after the other commands "to pluck up and to pull down, to destroy and to overthrow." Jeremiah's earlier words have been in fulfillment of the first part of that commission; now he is carrying out the second part, albeit quite strangely or unpredictably. The positive possibilities for life—home, productivity, and family—are to be found in exile. Strangest of all is the prayer for the enemy capital that brought about Judah's downfall.

There is a pragmatic dimension to the direction the Lord gives to the people through Jeremiah. Those who live in Babylon can find their possibilities for life only as Babylon is a viable place to live, secure and at peace. So seeking the peace and welfare of Babylon is not simply altruistic; it is a safeguard on the possibility of the deportees' finding their own well-being in a difficult situation. If Babylon is besieged and attacked, if it is subject to plague or famine, then the exiles will suffer also.

29:10-14. The divine counsel in the preceding verses is about how to live today in exile. But the letter to the exiles is not just about today. It also speaks about the future and does so in a way that underscores the moment of judgment that has to be endured even as it offers "a future with hope." Both judgment and hope are held together in the figure of the seventy years (v. 10). In 25:11, where we first hear of a Babylonian domination of seventy years, the announcement is clearly one of judgment, the terrible message of a long period of subjugation to a foreign power. In this context, however, that same word becomes a door to the future, for the stress now is on the period that is coming to an end.

The tension is nicely felt in comparing the translations of the NRSV ("Only when Babylon's seventy years are completed") and the NIV ("When seventy years are completed for Babylon"). The former stresses the weight of the judgment. Seventy years

---

155. See J. Gerald Janzen, *Studies in the Text of Jeremiah*, HSM 6 (Cambridge, Mass.: Harvard University Press, 1973) 118; and William L. Holladay, *Jeremiah 2*, Hermeneia (Philadelphia: Fortress, 1989) 135.

are a long time. It is not clear where the number "seventy" comes from.[156] Some would see it as a figure derived after the fact—that is, created by someone who knew how long the exile was. More likely, the number is a conventional one for a period of divine punishment, for it is known from Assyrian sources in that usage also, or that it simply represents the period of a lifetime (Ps 90:10). The exiles who received the letter could not expect to see home ever again.

Here, however, the Lord balances the counsel to settle in with the further word that such settlement is not final. It is for the duration, and not forever. Language that from one angle is the rhetoric of judgment from another perspective is turned into the speech of hope. That is true not only of the figure of seventy years but also of the language of "visiting," which often has to do with punishment (Exod 20:5b; Amos 3:2b, 14a) but here is a visit to fulfill a "gracious promise," a promise for "good" (טוב ṭôb). Likewise the language of "planning" or "devising" welfare and not "harm" (רעה rā'â) in v. 11 is a positive move in contrast to earlier words about the Lord's devising or planning disaster or evil (rā'â) against this same people (18:8, 11; 26:3; 36:3; cf. Lam 2:8). The people in exile are not to despair. They are to settle in and live their lives under the blessing of God (vv. 5-6); they are to find their peace and well-being as they seek and pray for that for their oppressors (v. 7); and they are to know that beyond exile and judgment, the Lord will bring them home and give to them peace and well-being in the future.

These chapters are about שלום šālôm "peace" and how the Judean community can find it. They cannot find it in a quick overthrow of Babylonian rule that seeks to bypass the judgment for their sins, which is the Lord's purpose. That is the message of the false prophets.[157] They can find it in accepting their punishment and living in exile. As they settle in and live their lives in captivity, as they seek and work for the well-being of their captors and the Babylonian community, they will find šālôm. And God will also give them šālôm in the future, once again in the place they call home.

This last promise is made quite specific in the rest of this section: The Lord will gather the exiles from all the places they have been in exile (notice the explicit divine agency in "where I have driven you") and will bring them home. Verses 12-13 make this homecoming an answer to prayer—that is, the exiles are to pray not only for the welfare of Babylon but also for the Lord's deliverance, with the clear promise that the Lord will listen and pay attention when the people cry out. The Lord thus expects to hear the prayers for help of the people in exile and will be responsive. (On the expression "restore your fortunes" see the Commentary on 30:1–31:40.)

29:16-19. It was noted earlier that this part of the letter is the most problematic and may come from a later hand. It is missing altogether in the Greek translation, but that bit of evidence is ambiguous, for some would argue that it has been dropped by textual error from the Greek rather than being a much later expansion of the Hebrew. At whatever stage it came into being, the oracle compares with chap. 24, not only in the way it presents a negative word of judgment against the Judeans remaining on the land after the 597 BCE deportation alongside the positive word about the exiles in Babylon, but also in its use of language that echoes chap. 24. This is most noticeable in the reference to bad/rotten "figs that may not be eaten" (24:2//29:17b), but it is also seen in the comparison of 29:18 with 24:9-10.

The prophecy, which is a typical judgment speech with indictment (v. 19) as the basis for an announcement of judgment (vv. 17-18), stands in some tension with the words of Jeremiah to the Judean survivors in chap. 27, where he counseled them to submit and live. The message to the Judeans is thus ambivalent. That may be because this text represents a later corrective by those who saw the 587 BCE destruction as a necessary part of God's judgment, while chap. 27 is more nearly Jeremiah's own understanding of the word of the Lord to the post-597 deportation. But the situation was probably quite ambiguous. The possibility of submitting and living ran up against both the political realities of Babylon's continued dominance and the urge to throw it off. It also was nullified, according to the picture we get from Jeremiah, by the failure of the people to heed the word of the Lord and turn from their evil ways. Whenever the

---

156. See Gerald L. Keown, Pamela J. Scalise, and Thomas J. Smothers, *Jeremiah 26–52*, WBC 27 (Dallas: Word, 1995) 73-75.

157. The difference between the Babylonian rule's ending after two years (so Hananiah) and after seventy years (so Jeremiah) is substantive and massive, as Shemaiah recognized (29:28).

text may have originated, the book as a whole judges the community for refusing to listen to the word of the Lord all the way along. Thus destruction and exile were magnified to incorporate the rest of the community in Judah.

29:8-9, 15, 20-23, 24-32. The second large topic in this letter to the exiles is the reiterated warning about trusting in lying prophets. There were prophets among the exiles in Babylon also, though they are not mentioned in the categories of deportees in v. 2. The names of three are given in this chapter (Ahab, Zedekiah, and Shemaiah), and Ezekiel seems to have been among them, indeed a prophet who was regularly consulted by the people. So the problem of the false prophets persists, even among the exiles. We are not told in vv. 8-9 what the lie of the prophets to the exiles is. It is simply a general warning against paying attention to prophets and diviners of the future. The generalized warning, however, suggests that the lies are the same as those that have been identified in the book earlier. The immediate context—that is, the conflict between Jeremiah and the other prophets, particularly Hananiah, over whether or not Babylonian domination would come to an end shortly and Judah and Jerusalem would be quickly restored to normalcy (chaps. 27–28)—suggests that was probably the same issue for prophecy in exile. Specific confirmation of that comes in the conflict between Shemaiah and Jeremiah in vv. 24-32. Shemaiah sends a letter back to Jerusalem calling for a rebuke to Jeremiah because of the contents of his letter to the exiles. He quotes the instruction in v. 5 to build houses and live in them and to plant gardens and eat the produce (v. 28). But he prefaces that quotation with the words, "It will be a long time," in effect a summary of v. 10. The focus of Shemaiah's protest is precisely Jeremiah's announcement of a long exile and the need to settle down. Jeremiah's response to Shemaiah is another letter to the exiles that is now specific relative to the earlier words of vv. 8-9. The Lord did not send Shemaiah, and his words are a lie. Even in exile, where such prophecies would be quite incendiary in terms of stirring up false hopes and possible politically dangerous moves, there are prophets who are lying about the future and are doing so in the name of the Lord, an assumption that one can

draw from the Lord's insistence that "I did not send him" (v. 31).[158]

Like Hananiah, this false prophet of a quick return to normality comes under divine condemnation, not for the content of the prophecy per se but because of its mendacity and its betrayal of the prophetic responsibility to the people: to speak truly the word of the Lord to them that they could act appropriately. If they trust in a lie, they will make all the wrong moves. There is a powerful testimony to the influence of the prophetic word, but there is also an indication of how open the community is to a word that promises quick and easy alleviation of its troubles without suffering the consequences of its sins or the change of heart necessary to effect a different future on God's part. The prophet who, presumably, announced a short duration for the exile, will not have—in good poetic justice—anyone around among his family and descendants to see when it is over, when God effects "good" once more for a chastised and punished people. Like Hananiah (28:16), Shemaiah is also dubbed a false prophet by one of the fundamental deuteronomic criteria: He preached rebellion or treason against Yahweh, the ruler of Israel (v. 32; cf. Deut 13:5).

Two other prophets, Ahab and Zedekiah, who, like Shemaiah, are unknown outside of this text, are also accused of prophesying lies in the name of the Lord to the exiles (vv. 20-23). They are further accused of immorality, specifically violation of the commandment against adultery. It is not altogether clear whether the "outrage in Israel" they have committed refers to the adultery and the lying words or to something more, but the former is probably the case. Either charge merited the sentence of death in ancient Israel. The assignment of the execution of these two prophets to Nebuchadrezzar might be a way of identifying his rule over the exilic community, but it may be an indication that the lies of these prophets were political in character. That is, they are likely to have been among the prophets announcing an end to exile and the overthrow of Babylonian rule, sufficient grounds for the political authorities to have them

158. Holladay has plausibly suggested that at 29:24-25 there was originally an oracle of salvation announced by Shemaiah to the exiles that has been lost in the transmission of the text. William L. Holladay, *Jeremiah 2*, Hermeneia (Philadelphia: Fortress, 1989) 136-37, 145-47.

executed. Thus all of the named prophets in this literary unit meet an untimely end: Hananiah (28:17), Ahab and Zedekiah (v. 21), and Shemaiah (v. 32).

REFLECTIONS

1. We need to become accustomed to the way the Bible skews or modifies our common understandings of the way things are or should be. That is surely nowhere more evident than in some of the things we learn about its notions and visions of peace. There are many ways in which they correspond to what we would expect and to our human instincts for peace and well-being. That is certainly the case in this chapter, in which home and family, place to live and productive lands, are the *šālôm* the Lord offers to the exiles. But to find one's peace in enemy territory is not expected. The *šālôm* for this very nationalistic community is to be found in submission and acceptance of foreign domination. If the components sound right, the place sounds wrong. But that is the point about the Lord's peace. There are often ways in which it will not fit what we expect or want. And there are lines of connection to the peace Christ gives that is not as the world gives (John 14:27). It is real, but it may come by way of a cross. William Alexander Percy captured this often paradoxical and surprising *šālôm* in his hymn about Jesus' disciples, "They Cast Their Nets in Galilee":

> The peace of God it is no peace,
> But strife closed in the sod.
> Yet, brothers, pray for but one thing—
> The marvelous peace of God.

2. Yet the vision is still one of peace; the blessing the Lord offers is the possibility of good and well-being in the midst of judgment and punishment. That seems a strange combination. We expect either/or. But the biblical story is often more complex and realistic than our own imaginations. The punishment is real; seventy years is a full lifetime, and those who went into exile will not return home. But in many ways that punishment is ameliorated. That should not be surprising to those who read of clothes the Lord made for a disobedient Adam and Eve or of a mark to protect a murderous Cain or a planter of vineyards to give relief from the cursed ground (Gen 5:28). Exile is no easy matter. The Bible does not view it positively and, even in this text, anticipates an end and the return home. But in the midst of exile, there is the possibility of life, even as Jeremiah claimed that in the midst of foreign domination there was the possibility of survival. Nor should we miss the way in which the words of Jeremiah called for the people to "multiply and not decrease" in exile (29:6), a reiteration of the blessing of creation in Gen 1:22. The blessing of God is—as it was once before—away from the place where we expect it. It may be down in Egypt and lead to slavery; it may come in Babylon in the midst of foreign exile. Blessing and peace and life are possible outside the customary parameters. Here, they are offered as gifts in the midst of judgment and punishment.

Patriotism and nationalism are so much the order of the day in contemporary society, and particularly on American soil, that it is hard to contemplate the call to accept domination, to make one's peace with being deported, to settle in and live normal lives on enemy territory. We are not Judean exiles, but there may be an underlying challenge to some of our absolutes in hearing about their story, if in no other way than making us think about the possible modes of judgment and survival for either church or nation in our own time. Exile might turn out to be our lot. If it does, at least we know there was a time when God's people were sent into exile and called to live there, to find their well-being by carrying on their lives in a hostile, foreign territory.

3. We must not overlook the Old Testament antecedent to the prayer for the enemies of which Jesus speaks more directly. One of the tasks of settling in to exile is to seek the good of the enemy—more specifically, to pray for the welfare of those who have deported you, to ask God's blessing on those who have destroyed your homeland. This outruns toleration of unfortunate circumstances. It is a call to find one's well-being in seeking the well-being of the enemy oppressor. Jeremiah's words were probably more pragmatic than we might expect. How does one live in captivity? Apparently, part of that is in tying oneself to the well-being of the captors. There is some good sense in that, but it is not just good sense. It is a different mode of existence from the permanent hatred of the enemy that is our instinct and even sometimes the word we hear from the Bible (e.g., Exod 17:16). Jesus suggested that praying for those who persecute us is a part of the way the kingdom of God is established on earth. For Israel, such praying began in Babylon.

4. In 29:10-14 we encounter one of many instances of the paradox of divine activity in Scripture. The saving work of God is what God has "planned" and purposed. That is the whole point of these verses. What is happening is fully the Lord's doing and is quite intentional, purposed ahead of time. That is true of the judgment—the destruction of Jerusalem and Judah and the deportation and exile of its citizens—and it is true of the deliverance—the return from exile after seventy years. The text is explicit about the length of time and the Lord's shaping of this history: "I know the plans I have for you" (the "I" is emphatic in the Hebrew).

At the same time, it is equally true that what happens is very much shaped and affected by human acts, human decision, human words. Such is the case with regard to the divine plan for judgment, for the Lord has spoken often through the prophet to call the people to turn from their sinful ways so that judgment might be averted, that the plan and intention of God might be changed (e.g., 18:8: "I will change my mind"). But the future deliverance is also shaped and affected by human words and actions as the prayers of the people go up to God and are heard (29:12-13). There are all sorts of indicators in Scripture that the prayers of the leaders or of the people influence the divine decision and the divine activity. What God intends to do is significantly affected by what human beings do. So the Lord who intends to bring the people home calls upon them to pray for just that thing to happen so that God may listen and respond. None of that may be quite logical, but it is that peculiar biblical claim about human freedom and divine will, or, if you will, divine freedom and human will. They are conjoined. One end of that polarity is not subordinated to the other. God's will and freedom do not run rampant over human words and deeds—good or bad—nor does human intentionality so control what happens that God is unable to effect the divine purposes. What "happens" occurs within that tension. So we count on God to be God and pray to God in order to bring that about.

JEREMIAH 30:1–33:26, WORDS OF COMFORT AND HOPE

OVERVIEW

These four chapters in the middle of the book of Jeremiah pick up the various words of hope scattered throughout the prior words of judgment and offer a sustained development of the theme of hope. Like the rest of Jeremiah, the composition of these chapters probably derives from a complex process. It is difficult to determine the authorship of a particular oracle. Chapter 32, an account of Jeremiah's life during the last days of the Judean kingdom, joins with chap. 29 and other passages to point to a future beyond exile and a restoration of the people's fortunes. There is no serious reason not to assume that such a message was a part of Jeremiah's prophecy, but it is equally the case that that message, like other parts of the book, may have been elaborated in the course of the creation and transmission of the book. As one interpreter has put it:

What we have here is the literary deposit outlining the message of hope that derived from Jeremiah's central conviction given in the hour of Judah's deepest crisis. It has been elaborated and filled out to offer a more complete picture of how renewal would come about, what it meant in theological and political terms, and also the range and nature of its authority. It would amount to a rebirth of the nation of Israel, drawing in not only the exile from Babylon but also those far earlier exiles of Israel who had been thrown out from

their homeland in the Northern Kingdom by Assyria (30:4-24).[159]

These words of hope and comfort take shape in three parts. The first comprises chaps. 30–31 and is commonly called "The Book of Comfort" or "The Book of Consolation." It is followed by a narrative of the last days of Judah (chap. 32), with the Babylonian army at the gates, recounting Jeremiah's purchase—at the command of the Lord—a plot of land as a sign that fields will be bought again in the land of Judah. Then in chap. 33, oracles, perhaps from a later time but now set in the very moment of the destruction of Jerusalem and tied chronologically to the preceding chapter, provide an extended message of hope for the future and the restoration of Judah. All four chapters are linked by the repeated thematic phrase "restore the fortunes" (שוב שבות šûb šĕbût), which has its most extensive use in chaps. 29–33, occurring eight times in these chapters (29:14; 30:3, 18; 31:23; 32:44; 33:7, 11, 26). In 30:3 and 33:26, the phrase serves as a kind of inclusio, or envelope, around these chapters, identifying their theme at the very beginning and at the end.[160]

159. R. E. Clements, *Jeremiah,* Interpretation (Atlanta: John Knox, 1988) 176.
160. John Bracke, "*sûb sebût:* A Reappraisal," *ZAW* 97 (1985) 233-44.

Jeremiah 30:1–31:40, The Book of Consolation

30 This is the word that came to Jeremiah from the LORD: [2]"This is what the LORD, the God of Israel, says: 'Write in a book all the words I have spoken to you. [3]The days are coming,' declares the LORD, 'when I will bring my people Israel and Judah back from captivity[a] and restore them to the land I gave their forefathers to possess,' says the LORD."

[a]3 Or *will restore the fortunes of my people Israel and Judah*

30 The word that came to Jeremiah from the LORD: [2]Thus says the LORD, the God of Israel: Write in a book all the words that I have spoken to you. [3]For the days are surely coming, says the LORD, when I will restore the fortunes of my people, Israel and Judah, says the LORD, and I will bring them back to the land that I gave to their ancestors and they shall take possession of it.

NIV

⁴These are the words the LORD spoke concerning Israel and Judah: ⁵"This is what the LORD says:

" 'Cries of fear are heard—
  terror, not peace.
⁶Ask and see:
  Can a man bear children?
Then why do I see every strong man
  with his hands on his stomach like a
    woman in labor,
  every face turned deathly pale?
⁷How awful that day will be!
  None will be like it.
It will be a time of trouble for Jacob,
  but he will be saved out of it.

⁸" ' In that day,' declares the LORD Almighty,
  'I will break the yoke off their necks
and will tear off their bonds;
  no longer will foreigners enslave them.
⁹Instead, they will serve the LORD their God
  and David their king,
  whom I will raise up for them.

¹⁰" 'So do not fear, O Jacob my servant;
  do not be dismayed, O Israel,'
                    declares the LORD.
'I will surely save you out of a distant place,
  your descendants from the land of their exile.
Jacob will again have peace and security,
  and no one will make him afraid.
¹¹I am with you and will save you,'
  declares the LORD.
'Though I completely destroy all the nations
  among which I scatter you,
  I will not completely destroy you.
I will discipline you but only with justice;
  I will not let you go entirely unpunished.'

¹²"This is what the LORD says:

" 'Your wound is incurable,
  your injury beyond healing.
¹³There is no one to plead your cause,
  no remedy for your sore,
  no healing for you.
¹⁴All your allies have forgotten you;
  they care nothing for you.
I have struck you as an enemy would
  and punished you as would the cruel,
because your guilt is so great

NRSV

⁴These are the words that the LORD spoke concerning Israel and Judah:
⁵Thus says the LORD:
We have heard a cry of panic,
  of terror, and no peace.
⁶Ask now, and see,
  can a man bear a child?
Why then do I see every man
  with his hands on his loins like a woman in
    labor?
  Why has every face turned pale?
⁷Alas! that day is so great
  there is none like it;
it is a time of distress for Jacob;
  yet he shall be rescued from it.

⁸On that day, says the LORD of hosts, I will break the yoke from off hisᵃ neck, and I will burst hisᵃ bonds, and strangers shall no more make a servant of him. ⁹But they shall serve the LORD their God and David their king, whom I will raise up for them.

¹⁰But as for you, have no fear, my servant
  Jacob, says the LORD,
  and do not be dismayed, O Israel;
for I am going to save you from far away,
  and your offspring from the land of their
    captivity.
Jacob shall return and have quiet and ease,
  and no one shall make him afraid.
¹¹For I am with you, says the LORD, to save you;
I will make an end of all the nations
  among which I scattered you,
  but of you I will not make an end.
I will chastise you in just measure,
  and I will by no means leave you
    unpunished.

¹²For thus says the LORD:
Your hurt is incurable,
  your wound is grievous.
¹³There is no one to uphold your cause,
  no medicine for your wound,
  no healing for you.
¹⁴All your lovers have forgotten you;
  they care nothing for you;
for I have dealt you the blow of an enemy,

ᵃCn: Heb *your*

NIV

and your sins so many.
¹⁵Why do you cry out over your wound,
    your pain that has no cure?
Because of your great guilt and many sins
    I have done these things to you.

¹⁶" 'But all who devour you will be devoured;
    all your enemies will go into exile.
Those who plunder you will be plundered;
    all who make spoil of you I will despoil.
¹⁷But I will restore you to health
    and heal your wounds,'
                        declares the LORD,
'because you are called an outcast,
    Zion for whom no one cares.'

¹⁸"This is what the LORD says:

" 'I will restore the fortunes of Jacob's tents
    and have compassion on his dwellings;
the city will be rebuilt on her ruins,
    and the palace will stand in its proper place.
¹⁹From them will come songs of thanksgiving
    and the sound of rejoicing.
I will add to their numbers,
    and they will not be decreased;
I will bring them honor,
    and they will not be disdained.
²⁰Their children will be as in days of old,
    and their community will be established
        before me;
    I will punish all who oppress them.
²¹Their leader will be one of their own;
    their ruler will arise from among them.
I will bring him near and he will come close
        to me,
    for who is he who will devote himself
    to be close to me?'
                        declares the LORD.
²²" 'So you will be my people,
    and I will be your God.' "

²³See, the storm of the LORD
    will burst out in wrath,
a driving wind swirling down
    on the heads of the wicked.
²⁴The fierce anger of the LORD will not turn back
    until he fully accomplishes
    the purposes of his heart.
In days to come
    you will understand this.

NRSV

the punishment of a merciless foe,
    because your guilt is great,
    because your sins are so numerous.
¹⁵ Why do you cry out over your hurt?
    Your pain is incurable.
Because your guilt is great,
    because your sins are so numerous,
    I have done these things to you.
¹⁶ Therefore all who devour you shall be
        devoured,
    and all your foes, everyone of them, shall
        go into captivity;
those who plunder you shall be plundered,
    and all who prey on you I will make a prey.
¹⁷ For I will restore health to you,
    and your wounds I will heal,
                        says the LORD,
because they have called you an outcast:
    "It is Zion; no one cares for her!"

¹⁸ Thus says the LORD:
I am going to restore the fortunes of the tents
        of Jacob,
    and have compassion on his dwellings;
the city shall be rebuilt upon its mound,
    and the citadel set on its rightful site.
¹⁹ Out of them shall come thanksgiving,
    and the sound of merrymakers.
I will make them many, and they shall not be
        few;
    I will make them honored, and they shall
        not be disdained.
²⁰ Their children shall be as of old,
    their congregation shall be established
        before me;
    and I will punish all who oppress them.
²¹ Their prince shall be one of their own,
    their ruler shall come from their midst;
I will bring him near, and he shall approach
        me,
    for who would otherwise dare to approach
        me?   says the LORD.
²² And you shall be my people,
    and I will be your God.

²³ Look, the storm of the LORD!
    Wrath has gone forth,

NIV

31 "At that time," declares the LORD, "I will be the God of all the clans of Israel, and they will be my people."

²This is what the LORD says:

"The people who survive the sword
    will find favor in the desert;
    I will come to give rest to Israel."

³The LORD appeared to us in the past,[a] saying:

"I have loved you with an everlasting love;
    I have drawn you with loving-kindness.
⁴I will build you up again
    and you will be rebuilt, O Virgin Israel.
Again you will take up your tambourines
    and go out to dance with the joyful.
⁵Again you will plant vineyards
    on the hills of Samaria;
the farmers will plant them
    and enjoy their fruit.
⁶There will be a day when watchmen cry out
    on the hills of Ephraim,
'Come, let us go up to Zion,
    to the LORD our God.' "

⁷This is what the LORD says:

"Sing with joy for Jacob;
    shout for the foremost of the nations.
Make your praises heard, and say,
    'O LORD, save your people,
    the remnant of Israel.'
⁸See, I will bring them from the land of the north
    and gather them from the ends of the earth.
Among them will be the blind and the lame,
    expectant mothers and women in labor;
    a great throng will return.
⁹They will come with weeping;
    they will pray as I bring them back.
I will lead them beside streams of water
    on a level path where they will not stumble,
because I am Israel's father,
    and Ephraim is my firstborn son.

¹⁰"Hear the word of the LORD, O nations;
    proclaim it in distant coastlands:
'He who scattered Israel will gather them
    and will watch over his flock like a shepherd.'
¹¹For the LORD will ransom Jacob

[a]3 Or LORD has appeared to us from afar

NRSV

a whirling[a] tempest;
    it will burst upon the head of the wicked.
²⁴ The fierce anger of the LORD will not turn back
    until he has executed and accomplished
    the intents of his mind.
In the latter days you will understand this.

31 At that time, says the LORD, I will be the God of all the families of Israel, and they shall be my people.

² Thus says the LORD:
The people who survived the sword
    found grace in the wilderness;
when Israel sought for rest,
³   the LORD appeared to him[b] from far away.[c]
I have loved you with an everlasting love;
    therefore I have continued my faithfulness
    to you.
⁴ Again I will build you, and you shall be built,
    O virgin Israel!
Again you shall take[d] your tambourines,
    and go forth in the dance of the
    merrymakers.
⁵ Again you shall plant vineyards
    on the mountains of Samaria;
the planters shall plant,
    and shall enjoy the fruit.
⁶ For there shall be a day when sentinels will
    call
    in the hill country of Ephraim:
"Come, let us go up to Zion,
    to the LORD our God."

⁷ For thus says the LORD:
Sing aloud with gladness for Jacob,
    and raise shouts for the chief of the
    nations;
proclaim, give praise, and say,
    "Save, O LORD, your people,
    the remnant of Israel."
⁸ See, I am going to bring them from the land of
    the north,
    and gather them from the farthest parts of
    the earth,
among them the blind and the lame,
    those with child and those in labor,
    together;

[a]One Ms: Meaning of MT uncertain   [b]Gk: Heb me   [c]Or to him
long ago   [d]Or adorn yourself with

NIV

and redeem them from the hand of those stronger than they.
[12]They will come and shout for joy on the heights of Zion;
they will rejoice in the bounty of the LORD—
the grain, the new wine and the oil,
the young of the flocks and herds.
They will be like a well-watered garden,
and they will sorrow no more.
[13]Then maidens will dance and be glad,
young men and old as well.
I will turn their mourning into gladness;
I will give them comfort and joy instead of sorrow.
[14]I will satisfy the priests with abundance,
and my people will be filled with my bounty,"
declares the LORD.

[15]This is what the LORD says:

"A voice is heard in Ramah,
mourning and great weeping,
Rachel weeping for her children
and refusing to be comforted,
because her children are no more."

[16]This is what the LORD says:

"Restrain your voice from weeping
and your eyes from tears,
for your work will be rewarded,"
declares the LORD.
"They will return from the land of the enemy.
[17]So there is hope for your future,"
declares the LORD.
"Your children will return to their own land.

[18]"I have surely heard Ephraim's moaning:
'You disciplined me like an unruly calf,
and I have been disciplined.
Restore me, and I will return,
because you are the LORD my God.
[19]After I strayed,
I repented;
after I came to understand,
I beat my breast.
I was ashamed and humiliated
because I bore the disgrace of my youth.'
[20]Is not Ephraim my dear son,
the child in whom I delight?
Though I often speak against him,

NRSV

a great company, they shall return here.
[9]With weeping they shall come,
and with consolations[a] I will lead them back,
I will let them walk by brooks of water,
in a straight path in which they shall not stumble;
for I have become a father to Israel,
and Ephraim is my firstborn.

[10]Hear the word of the LORD, O nations,
and declare it in the coastlands far away;
say, "He who scattered Israel will gather him,
and will keep him as a shepherd a flock."
[11]For the LORD has ransomed Jacob,
and has redeemed him from hands too strong for him.
[12]They shall come and sing aloud on the height of Zion,
and they shall be radiant over the goodness of the LORD,
over the grain, the wine, and the oil,
and over the young of the flock and the herd;
their life shall become like a watered garden,
and they shall never languish again.
[13]Then shall the young women rejoice in the dance,
and the young men and the old shall be merry.
I will turn their mourning into joy,
I will comfort them, and give them gladness for sorrow.
[14]I will give the priests their fill of fatness,
and my people shall be satisfied with my bounty,   says the LORD.

[15]Thus says the LORD:
A voice is heard in Ramah,
lamentation and bitter weeping.
Rachel is weeping for her children;
she refuses to be comforted for her children,
because they are no more.
[16]Thus says the LORD:
Keep your voice from weeping,
and your eyes from tears;

[a]Gk Compare Vg Tg: Heb *supplications*

NIV

I still remember him.
Therefore my heart yearns for him;
I have great compassion for him,"
declares the LORD.

21"Set up road signs;
put up guideposts.
Take note of the highway,
the road that you take.
Return, O Virgin Israel,
return to your towns.
22How long will you wander,
O unfaithful daughter?
The LORD will create a new thing on earth—
a woman will surround[a] a man."

23This is what the LORD Almighty, the God of Israel, says: "When I bring them back from captivity,[b] the people in the land of Judah and in its towns will once again use these words: 'The LORD bless you, O righteous dwelling, O sacred mountain.' 24People will live together in Judah and all its towns—farmers and those who move about with their flocks. 25I will refresh the weary and satisfy the faint."

26At this I awoke and looked around. My sleep had been pleasant to me.

27"The days are coming," declares the LORD, "when I will plant the house of Israel and the house of Judah with the offspring of men and of animals. 28Just as I watched over them to uproot and tear down, and to overthrow, destroy and bring disaster, so I will watch over them to build and to plant," declares the LORD. 29"In those days people will no longer say,

'The fathers have eaten sour grapes,
and the children's teeth are set on edge.'

30Instead, everyone will die for his own sin; whoever eats sour grapes—his own teeth will be set on edge.

31"The time is coming," declares the LORD,
"when I will make a new covenant
with the house of Israel
and with the house of Judah.
32It will not be like the covenant
I made with their forefathers
when I took them by the hand
to lead them out of Egypt,

NRSV

for there is a reward for your work,
says the LORD:
they shall come back from the land of the
enemy;
17 there is hope for your future,
says the LORD:
your children shall come back to their own
country.

18 Indeed I heard Ephraim pleading:
"You disciplined me, and I took the discipline;
I was like a calf untrained.
Bring me back, let me come back,
for you are the LORD my God.
19 For after I had turned away I repented;
and after I was discovered, I struck my
thigh;
I was ashamed, and I was dismayed
because I bore the disgrace of my youth."
20 Is Ephraim my dear son?
Is he the child I delight in?
As often as I speak against him,
I still remember him.
Therefore I am deeply moved for him;
I will surely have mercy on him,
says the LORD.

21 Set up road markers for yourself,
make yourself guideposts;
consider well the highway,
the road by which you went.
Return, O virgin Israel,
return to these your cities.
22 How long will you waver,
O faithless daughter?
For the LORD has created a new thing on the
earth:
a woman encompasses[a] a man.

23Thus says the LORD of hosts, the God of Israel: Once more they shall use these words in the land of Judah and in its towns when I restore their fortunes:
"The LORD bless you, O abode of
righteousness,
O holy hill!"

---

[a]22 Or will go about seeking,; or will protect their fortunes   [b]23 Or I restore their fortunes

[a]Meaning of Heb uncertain

NIV

because they broke my covenant,
    though I was a husband to^a them,^b"
                        declares the LORD.
³³"This is the covenant I will make with the
        house of Israel
    after that time," declares the LORD.
"I will put my law in their minds
    and write it on their hearts.
I will be their God,
    and they will be my people.
³⁴No longer will a man teach his neighbor,
    or a man his brother, saying, 'Know the LORD,'
because they will all know me,
    from the least of them to the greatest,"
                        declares the LORD.
"For I will forgive their wickedness
    and will remember their sins no more."

³⁵This is what the LORD says,

he who appoints the sun
    to shine by day,
who decrees the moon and stars
    to shine by night,
who stirs up the sea
    so that its waves roar—
    the LORD Almighty is his name:
³⁶"Only if these decrees vanish from my sight,"
    declares the LORD,
"will the descendants of Israel ever cease
    to be a nation before me."

³⁷This is what the LORD says:

"Only if the heavens above can be measured
    and the foundations of the earth below be
        searched out
will I reject all the descendants of Israel
    because of all they have done,"
                        declares the LORD.

³⁸"The days are coming," declares the LORD, "when this city will be rebuilt for me from the Tower of Hananel to the Corner Gate. ³⁹The measuring line will stretch from there straight to the hill of Gareb and then turn to Goah. ⁴⁰The whole valley where dead bodies and ashes are thrown, and all the terraces out to the Kidron Valley on the east as far as the corner of the Horse

^a32 Hebrew; Septuagint and Syriac / and I turned away from   ^b32 Or was their master

NRSV

²⁴And Judah and all its towns shall live there together, and the farmers and those who wander^a with their flocks.
²⁵ I will satisfy the weary,
    and all who are faint I will replenish.
²⁶Thereupon I awoke and looked, and my sleep was pleasant to me.

²⁷The days are surely coming, says the LORD, when I will sow the house of Israel and the house of Judah with the seed of humans and the seed of animals. ²⁸And just as I have watched over them to pluck up and break down, to overthrow, destroy, and bring evil, so I will watch over them to build and to plant, says the LORD. ²⁹In those days they shall no longer say:
"The parents have eaten sour grapes,
    and the children's teeth are set on edge."
³⁰But all shall die for their own sins; the teeth of everyone who eats sour grapes shall be set on edge.

³¹The days are surely coming, says the LORD, when I will make a new covenant with the house of Israel and the house of Judah. ³²It will not be like the covenant that I made with their ancestors when I took them by the hand to bring them out of the land of Egypt—a covenant that they broke, though I was their husband,^b says the LORD. ³³But this is the covenant that I will make with the house of Israel after those days, says the LORD: I will put my law within them, and I will write it on their hearts; and I will be their God, and they shall be my people. ³⁴No longer shall they teach one another, or say to each other, "Know the LORD," for they shall all know me, from the least of them to the greatest, says the LORD; for I will forgive their iniquity, and remember their sin no more.

³⁵ Thus says the LORD,
    who gives the sun for light by day
        and the fixed order of the moon and the
            stars for light by night,
    who stirs up the sea so that its waves roar—
        the LORD of hosts is his name:
³⁶ If this fixed order were ever to cease
        from my presence, says the LORD,

^aCompare Syr Vg Tg: Heb and they shall wander   ^bOr master

NIV

Gate, will be holy to the LORD. The city will never again be uprooted or demolished."

NRSV

then also the offspring of Israel would cease
   to be a nation before me forever.

37 Thus says the LORD:
   If the heavens above can be measured,
      and the foundations of the earth below can
         be explored,
   then I will reject all the offspring of Israel
      because of all they have done,
                              says the LORD.

38The days are surely coming, says the LORD, when the city shall be rebuilt for the LORD from the tower of Hananel to the Corner Gate. 39And the measuring line shall go out farther, straight to the hill Gareb, and shall then turn to Goah. 40The whole valley of the dead bodies and the ashes, and all the fields as far as the Wadi Kidron, to the corner of the Horse Gate toward the east, shall be sacred to the LORD. It shall never again be uprooted or overthrown.

COMMENTARY

These two chapters have long been recognized as a literary unit in the book of Jeremiah. They are marked off from their surroundings by their generally poetic character. They take the intimations of restoration in the preceding chapters and present a collection of oracles that spell out the restoration in much detail. They assume the experience of trouble found in a time of foreign domination, oppression, and exile. But, as is the case with earlier Jeremianic oracles, the community that is the subject of these oracles is not simply the southern kingdom of Judah. The northern kingdom, Israel, is also addressed, and some have seen in the collection and composition of these oracles an early form of the book focused on the north that was then reinterpreted and extended by the incorporation of further oracles to address the southern kingdom, Judah. Some of the oracles concerning the north may have occurred fairly early in Jeremiah's career, but the assignment of particular oracles to Jeremiah, much less to specific times in his prophetic career, is a difficult task. In any event, one may observe within these chapters the process by which earlier words were interpreted and addressed to a new situation.

These chapters look back to earlier parts of the book, using language and imagery—incurable pain, lovers who have forgotten—that occurs elsewhere and responding to issues and questions, to laments and woes expressed by Jeremiah or the people elsewhere.[161] The judgment that has been announced so thoroughly in the first half of the book is clearly kept in mind, alluded to, and interpreted further. But judgment becomes the stepping-stone for speaking about restoration.

30:1-4. The description of these chapters as "the book of comfort/consolation" is drawn in part from the opening verses, which tell of a divine word commanding Jeremiah to write a *book* or document. What follows, therefore, is understood as part of Jeremiah's message that is to be preserved for the future. This process may reflect the well-known criterion for true prophecy: In distinc-

161. For a brief summary of some of the specific connections to other parts of the book, see Gerald L. Keown, Pamela J. Scalise, and Thomas J. Smothers, *Jeremiah 26–52*, WBC 27 (Dallas: Word, 1995) 86.

tion from false prophecy that is not fulfilled, a true prophetic word comes to pass (Deut 18:22). Jeremiah is to make a written record of the Lord's intent. Indeed, one might describe this as "a letter of intent."[162] These opening verses say, quite succinctly, what that intent is: the restoration of the fortunes of both Israel and Judah and the return of the people to the land promised to them long ago through the Lord's oath to the ancestors. The oracles that follow will develop that intention in some detail, with eloquence, hope, and sensitivity to the pain that the people have experienced.

The promise is sweeping in that it is directed to "my people Israel and Judah" (v. 3). The expression "my people" is the ancient covenantal designation, which is still applicable. The judgment is a punishment of "my people," not a disowning of them, not an abandonment, though in the face of the Babylonian army and in the experience of exile, that has been the fear of the people (cf. Lam 5:22). So in this very simple identification, words of assurance are implicit. Further, the "people" here incorporates the *whole* of Israel. While the political split of the kingdom lies long in the past (922 BCE) and the Northern Kingdom's downfall and deportation a century past (721 BCE), the words of restoration are directed to the *whole people* on the *whole land*. The promise is twofold: restoration of fortune and return to the land. The prophet refers to restoration with a technical phrase that is used a number of times in the OT: שוב שבות (*šûb šĕbût*). The etymology of this phrase, translated as "restore fortune," is uncertain, but here it regularly refers to the Lord's reversal of judgment.[163] Thus while the initial word to the exiles is about the length of the exile (29:4-9), a point that Shemaiah accentuates in his summary reference to the letter ("It will be a long time," 29:28), the announcement in 29:14 that "I will restore your fortunes" reverses this message about settling down in Babylon and becomes an announcement of God's intention to bring the people back. In 30:18ff. as well, the restoration of fortune is reflected in the rebuilding of the cities (cf. 31:21, 24, 38-40) upon which judgment had been announced earlier (e.g., Jer. 2:15; 4:7, 26, 29; 5:17). Restoration also means an increase of popu-

lation, whereas the judgment had meant loss of children (e.g., 2:30; 3:24; 5:17; 10:20). Verse 4 then tells us that the following oracles are the "words that I have spoken to you" (v. 2), which depict this restoration of fortunes and return to the land.

30:5-7. It is startling, then, to hear in the very first words of the first oracle after the introductory oracular formula "thus says the LORD," cries of despair and terror rather than words of hope and assurance.[164] They show the situation into which the Lord's words of hope and promise are thrust, identifying the reality of the exile and the suffering of the people. The cry of despair in these verses is the presupposition of the words of assurance that follow. Just as the words of judgment did not close the door to the Lord's future action on behalf of the people, so also the announcement of that further work does not ignore the woe the Lord has inflicted upon the people (cf. v. 11*b*).

The imagery of the men standing with their hands on their loins as if in labor is ambiguous. Men do beget children, but they do not give birth to them. The image is thus one of absurdity, pain, shame, and anguish before the enemy. The absurdity points to the desperation of the situation. The pain of childbirth is once again an image for the terror of the destruction (see 4:31). But the warriors in pain like that of childbirth also express their terror, their anguish in the face of a superior conquering force, their helplessness before a destructive army they cannot withstand. We encounter this same image elsewhere in the book of Jeremiah. The pale face of v. 6*c* conveys the same idea. "The metaphor portrays faces drained of color, drained of life. The presence of death is pervasive."[165]

This image of the warriors acting like women in childbirth erupts into a cry of "Woe," the lament of the funeral dirge, that cry of grief when death is the focus of attention (cf. 22:13, 18). As it does in Amos 5:18, the "woe" announces the terrible day of the Lord. And, like Amos 5:18, the terror of the day of the Lord's coming is to be felt not only by Israel's enemies but also by Israel itself.

---

162. Ibid., 87.
163. Bracke, "*šûb šebût,*" 237.

164. Some interpreters would hold together all of 30:5-11 as a single literary unit, and that is quite possible. Within that complex, however, vv. 5-7, 8-9, and 10-11 represent three different foci and may be discussed separately without losing a sense of their context. For careful and helpful analysis of the literary form of Jeremiah 30–31, see Barbara A. Bozak, C.S.J., *Life "Anew": A Literary-Theological Study of Jer. 30–31,* AnBib (Rome: Pontifical Biblical Institute, 1991).
165. Ibid., 38.

The prophet paints a picture of terror and panic, of pain and death, of a time of destruction that is the day of the Lord's judgment. The heaped-up description, the sharpness of the picture in vv. 5-7*a,* only heightens the sudden and unexpected word of v. 7*b:* "yet he shall be rescued from it." In that movement is encapsulated the whole development of these chapters. The reality of pain and death this people have experienced and are now experiencing is real. But that is not the end. They will be delivered out of it. As other prophecies in the book indicate, this is not a magical act to make the pain and terror disappear. No, the pain is as real as the images convey. Further, to whatever "day" these verses may point, the judgment does not exclude Jacob. In the context of this book, the judgment on Jacob/Israel (and the terminology may have had the Northern Kingdom in mind but includes Judah) is the primary focus. But the Lord will move into that scene and deliver the people of Israel from their pain and terror.

30:8-9. These oracles of hope are tied directly to the preceding chapters by the imagery of the yoke. The prophet Hananiah had falsely declared the word of the Lord: "I will break the yoke of king Nebuchadnezzar of Babylon . . . within two years." Now the Lord does make such an announcement. It is not a promise of a short and meaningless period of exile, as Hananiah had claimed, but it is a promise that exile and Babylonian domination shall not go on forever. There is a world of difference between Hananiah's claim that judgment will not happen and the Lord's announcement that judgment will not go on forever. The same divine word, "I will break the yoke," thus means something quite different in chap. 28 and in chap. 30.

The image of the yoke has appeared before in Jeremiah. In 2:20 and 5:5, the prophet speaks of the people breaking the yoke of service to the Lord and keeping the Lord's covenant. So the reappearance of this image in vv. 8-9 joins the promise of redemption with the Lord's expectation of a people who, with their oppressive bonds broken, will bear with joy the bonds of covenant obedience and serve the Lord and the Lord's anointed. The new era will be not only a time of redemption but also a time of obedience.

30:10-11. The language of service joins these verses to the immediately preceding ones. The lan-

guage about both submission and absolute loyalty to a master and a position of status and honor is consistent with vv. 9-10. The community "yoked" to the Lord in obedient and loyal service is the community that stands before the Lord as the Lord's servant, as one who is beloved and lifted up (cf. Isa 41:8-9).

These two verses comprise an oracle of salvation, the type of speech that brings the good news of God's deliverance to those who have cried out and prayed to God for help. These words, therefore, may be understood as the response of God to the cries of the exiles.[166] The very personal mode of address characterizes the announcement of God's deliverance, calling the lamenter by name, "Israel," and addressing the community with the emphatic personal pronoun, "but you." The use of the terms "Israel" and "Jacob" allows the oracle to address the northern kingdom of Israel specifically, but those names also refer to the whole community descended from the ancient patriarch. Both kingdoms that have suffered foreign oppression and deportation hear a word addressed to them.

The fundamental word of the oracle of salvation, its basic assurance, is always, "Do not fear." This type of speech is designed to take away the fear of those who have cried out in trouble (cf. 46:27; 46:28; Ps 23:4; 34:4; Isa 41:14; 43:1, 5; 44:2; 54:4; Lam 3:57). The claim that one does not have to be afraid anymore is then grounded in specific reasons. (Note the "for" in v. 10*b* and at the beginning of v. 11 in the NRSV, unfortunately missing from the NIV translation in both places.) Those reasons are of two sorts. One involves the claim that the relationship between the Lord and the lamenter, in this case the community in exile, still perdures, addressing the fear of the exiles that the Lord has abandoned them (Isa 40:27; 41:9*b;* Lam 5:22). That claim is most often expressed in the words "I am with you," as in v. 11. The other reason why fear is no longer appropriate is the announcement that God will step into this situation to deliver those who cry out. This announcement, elaborated in vv. 10*b*-11*a,* includes three elements: deliverance from exile; defeat of the enemies who brought about the exile but whose own time will come, even though they functioned

166. On this type of speech as God's response to prayer, see Patrick D. Miller, *They Cried to the Lord: The Form and Theology of Biblical Prayer* (Minneapolis: Fortress, 1994) chap. 4.

as the Lord's agents of judgment; and the promise of rest and security (v. 10c). This latter promise is another form of the promise of *salôm* and is related to one of the most vivid and influential depictions of God's peaceable kingdom. When Micah repeats Isaiah's vision of the nations coming to the mountain of the Lord (Isa 2:2-4), he adds the words:

> But they shall all sit under their own vines
>   and under their own fig trees,
>   and no one shall make them afraid.
>   (Mic 4:4 NRSV)

That vision of a community secure and no longer under threat, no longer living in constant fear, is the end result of this oracle of salvation. But it is not a cheap peace that takes no account of the sins of the people. It is a peace and security that only God can provide, since God has been the one who has brought about the punishment (v. 11b).

30:12-17. The twofold activity of God as the redeemer from the punishment God has wrought is articulated in these verses again but in a reverse movement. The rhetorical power of this oracle, which now addresses the community with feminine pronouns,[167] is carried through the imagery of sickness, caring, and healing.[168] It is imagery that recurs in the book of Jeremiah, especially the language of grievous wounds and incurable sickness, to describe the condition of the people and the land (e.g., 6:7; 8:21-22; 10:19; 14:17, 19). In these verses, the language of incurable sickness is joined with two other types of expression: (1) legal language of v. 13a, citing the absence of anyone to uphold the people's cause, to plead their case in court, and (2) sexual imagery of the harlot whose many lovers have all abandoned her, here probably referring to the abandonment of Israel or Judah by its foreign allies.

No healing, no legal support, no support of friends and lovers—all of this language is heaped up in the Lord's description of the plight of the people. The form of this section would seem at first glance to be a judgment speech, but it is quite different at some key points. The indictment of the people for their sins is clear, repeated and thus emphasized in vv. 14-15. However, we cannot talk about meaningless suffering in this instance. It has great meaning, and that is what the Lord is setting forth. But the description of judgment and punishment is not an announcement of future punishment, as is customary in prophetic judgment speeches. The Lord describes what is happening right now! That fact is emphasized in the strange question, "Why do you cry out over your hurt?" (v. 15). That is, why do you offer lament prayers seeking God's help? Inasmuch as such crying out is usually appropriate and, indeed, one of the primary ways of speaking of the prayer of the sufferer and the oppressed, the Lord's challenge to such crying out now is surprising. Elsewhere in the book of Jeremiah, God either forbids Jeremiah to pray and intercede for the people or refuses to listen to their outcry because it is the Lord's intent to punish, and not to save (e.g., 7:16; 11:11; 14:11-12; 15:1). This is a time of judgment—no therapy or physician for the sick and wounded, no judge for the cause of the sufferer, no friend or loved one to care. The punishment is real, the reason is clear, and the agent is specified. As the incurable wounds are described again (vv. 12-13, 15a) and the guilt reiterated (vv. 14b, 15b), the text twice identifies all of this as the act of the Lord of Israel (vv. 14b, 15b). The last line of v. 15 underlines the whole point: "I have done these things to you."

That emphatic declaration makes the following verse all the more surprising. The "therefore" that typically identifies the announcement of judgment after a listing of sins and crimes leads into a word of judgment. Since the word of judgment is against the nations who have oppressed Israel, it becomes a word of restoration and healing for Israel. The nations who have inflicted such pain, whether Assyria against the Northern Kingdom or Babylon against the Southern Kingdom, have acted willfully and harshly. Poetic justice and irony are joined in the Lord's announcement (v. 15) that the devourer shall be devoured, the plunderer plundered, the preying one become prey. Their turn will come, and their judgment will lead to Israel's healing and redemption.

The turn at v. 16 is a remarkable one.

---

167. Bozak has called attention to the repeated alternation of masculine and feminine forms of address in chaps. 30–31 and has suggested various forms of literary, historical, and psychological significance that might be ascribed to the feminine forms of address. See Bozak, *Life "Anew,"* 154-72.

168. For an extended analysis of this passage, lifting up its imagery and rhetoric, see Walter Brueggemann, "The 'Uncared For' Now Cared For (Jer 30:12-17): A Methodological Consideration," *JBL* 104 (1985) 419-29 (reprinted in W. Brueggemann, *Old Testament Theology: Essays on Structure, Theme, and Text,* ed. Patrick D. Miller [Minneapolis: Fortress, 1992] 296-307).

Brueggemann has called attention to the shift in the Lord's attitude: "Nothing has changed about the propensity of Israel. Israel is still guilty, still sick, still under threat. Everything, however, has changed about God. Between v. 15 and v.16 there is a radical alteration in God's attitude, perspective, and inclination. The indignant One has become the compassionate One."[169]

Such sudden turning on God's part is not peculiar to this passage, as Brueggemann has noted. One might argue that such unexpected reversal by the Lord is, paradoxically, one of the most consistent things about this deity. The reason for the reversal seems often to result from one of two things—or both: the Lord's willingness to hear the cry of the sufferer and the Lord's compassion (e.g., Exod 22:27). The first of these is specifically rejected, and so the possibility of healing and support seems cut off by the end of v. 15. But the compassion of God so controls the divine will, so shapes the Lord's intent, that it overcomes the will to punish.

The last sentence of the passage is critical: There is no one to care about you, no one to take care of you, literally, "No one asks about you." In v. 14, this is the Lord's description of the plight of the people, a plight to which the whole world, including former friends and allies, is indifferent. At the end, a similar expression occurs on the lips of an unidentified "they." Here the situation of Zion/Israel has now elicited a taunt, a mocking of this people for whom no one on earth cares. That taunt becomes the ground for God's turning from the words of judgment to the words of healing and restoration ("because they have called you . . ."). In the psalms of lament, such taunts are part of the grounds for the lamenter's cry for help. Here it is God's own recognition of the taunts and the claim that Israel is utterly abandoned. The character of God is so bent toward compassion, toward caring for those for whom nobody else cares, toward protecting those who are "my people," that the will to judge is overcome by the will to care.

30:18-22. The turn that is taken in vv. 16-17 continues now with the reiteration of the phrase "restore the fortunes." The parallelism of v. 18 powerfully equates restoration of fortunes with compassion. The outcome (restoration) is rooted

in the deep feeling of God, the parental compassion that is moved to care and tenderness in the presence of the pain of the child (cf. 31:20). Towns and villages, royal cities and fortresses will all be restored. Jerusalem will be restored on its proper place, literally on its *tell.* Like the phoenix rising from the ashes, the Lord will raise from the destroyed city a new city, a new Jerusalem.

The "thanksgiving" sounds refer to the thanksgiving offering that the rescued one(s) presents to the Lord in gratitude for answered prayer and deliverance (v. 19). But along with the sound of laughter and mirth, the gratitude is lifted up into an ongoing sound of praise and celebration, of thanksgiving and joy, an enduring festival in the restored city and among the people now cared for. The formerly decimated band of people will become many. The mocked, taunted, and unsought will take places of honor. The Lord's command to the people about their life in exile ("multiply there, and do not decrease," 29:6) becomes the Lord's personal agenda in the restoration. God will multiply their number and lift the despised to seats of honor. All of this reflects divine caring, compassion, and restoration.

The political dimension of this vision of restoration is underscored with the announcement that the people shall once more live under the rule of one of their own (cf. Deut 17:15) and not under the tyranny of foreign kings and rulers. This leader will stand before the Lord as servant and worshiper, a ruler who knows his leadership is subordinate to the rule of God.

The essential feature in this vision of restoration is the renewal of the covenant relationship (v. 22; cf. Exod 6:7). What has broken down in the history of this people shall be renewed. The restoration of the intimate relation between the Lord and the people, between "my people" and "our God," is the ultimate goal of the divine activity of judgment and redemption. It is the final word in this vision of the future beyond judgment just as it is the final word in the biblical story (see Rev 21:3).

30:23–31:1. In a poetic version of 23:19-20, the prophet describes the theophany of the divine warrior in judgment against the wicked. In this context, these words are heard as a part of the restorative activity of the Lord. Reference to the punishment of the oppressors of Jacob (v. 10) suggests that the appearance of God like a wrathful

169. Walter Brueggemann, *A Commentary on Jeremiah: Exile and Homecoming* (Grand Rapids: Eerdmans, 1998) 277.

storm is directed toward that particular body of "the wicked." These verses conclude with the covenant formulary, suggesting that in this later time the covenant broken by Israel/Judah but never abandoned by the Lord will be renewed (31:1; cf. v. 22).

31:2-6. The covenant formula of 31:1 provides a transition into a series of oracles that announce the restoration of Israel and Judah. The first of these oracles locates the restoration hope of Israel in the Lord's declared love for this people. Drawing upon Exodus language, God speaks personally and directly to the exiled people (both Israel and Judah) to offer them a future that is grounded in the "grace," "love," and "faithfulness" of the Lord. In the present "wilderness," where the people experience the judgment of God and the apparent cessation of the covenant, they now learn that the covenant will be renewed (31:1). The choice of words is significant: "love" (אהבה 'āhăbâ) and "faithfulness" or "steadfast love" (חסד ḥesed). They refer to fundamental covenantal attributes of God—a gracious love that endures. The marriage metaphor rises naturally in such a situation (note the address to Israel in the feminine in v. 4). The Lord stresses a continuity between the present and prior experiences of the people with the Lord.

God effects a renewal of the people (vv. 4-6), underscoring it with the repeated "again." The "building" and "planting" language of Jeremiah's call (1:10) comes into play again. This rebuilding and replanting involve the building of their homes and the planting of their fields and vineyards (cf. 32:15, 41, 43-44). The joy of the redeemed is manifest in dancing and singing as they go up to celebrate the Lord's goodness and faithfulness in the house of the Lord. The language of Deuteronomy echoes in these verses, not only in "the LORD our God" and the reference to the love of the Lord for Israel (Deut 7:7-8), but also in the way the future deliverance reverses the curses of Deuteronomy (Deut 28:30). The futility curses that arose for breach of covenant will be nullified. What was before shall be again. The final verse of this proclamation of future salvation echoes the great vision of Isa 2:2-5: all the nations going up to the mountain of the Lord. The image of the kingdom of peace stands in the background in these verses.

31:7-14. The notes of restoration and joy from the preceding verses continue here. Psalmic language resounds through the images of the Lord as shepherd and keeper and the people being led by waters and on straight paths (see Psalms 23; 100; 121). The first section (vv. 7-9) seems to be addressed to Israel, the second section to the nations (vv. 10-14). The tone is one of sheer joy. The imperative "save!" (v. 7) seems peculiar because the shouts of joy usually come after the salvation has occurred. It should probably be seen as a reference back to the petition of the people, which is then answered by the words of the Lord, "I am going to bring them . . ." (v. 8). The Greek translation offers an alternative, "The Lord has saved his people." The matter remains uncertain.

The point of the divine announcement in vv. 7-9 is clear: The Lord will gather "the remnant of Israel," which probably encompasses the members of the northern kingdom along with the Judeans. The announcement describes the returning company primarily as a community of the weak, not an army of the strong—those blind and lame, women pregnant and with children. The Lord is again concerned about the weaker members of the community, not just the stronger ones. The picture of vv. 8-9 reverses that of 6:21-22, where a people "from the land of the north" and "from the farthest parts of the earth" are the instrument of judgment and where the Lord impedes the way of all, even the children. Those who "stumbled" in judgment (6:21) shall not "stumble" when the Lord leads them back (v. 9). These chapters announce an end to the judgment and a reversal of the people's fortunes.

With the image of the shepherd leading the people on the way and that of the father caring for the firstborn, the people are reminded about the special place they have in the heart of God. The notion of Israel as the firstborn of the Lord is rooted in the earliest moments of this people's history. It echoes the claim of God against Pharaoh's unyielding slavery of the Hebrews (Exod 4:22). Reference to Ephraim as firstborn not only includes the exiles from the northern kingdom in these words of deliverance and hope, but also alludes to the way in which Ephraim was chosen by Jacob as Joseph's firstborn. As Bozak has noted, the use of the name "Ephraim" highlights both the choice of the people, who are now made "the head of the nations" (v. 7), and the gratuitousness of God's gifts for them.[170]

---

170. Bozak, *Life "Anew,"* 87.

In vv. 10-14, we hear how fully God cares for these people. The nations among whom the exiles are scattered are recruited as the messengers of the good news. And that news is extravagantly good. God announces redemption and deliverance (v. 11), providing for all the physical needs of the people. The text depicts the return of the people to the land as participation in an unending banquet where all the good things of life are provided (v. 12). Sheer joy shall turn the tears and sorrow of the past into music and song, stumbling feet of judgment into dancing feet of celebration. In the concluding verses, God's reversal of Israel's fortunes echoes the exuberant claim of the psalmist after having been delivered: "You have turned my mourning into dancing" (Ps 30:11). Indeed, the banquet depicted in these verses may be understood as a great thanksgiving feast to celebrate the people's deliverance by the Lord—only this thanksgiving feast goes on forever. The promise of the Lord to satisfy the people with "my bounty" or "my good" (טובי *tôbî*) echoes the poetic depiction of Ps 104:28: "When you open your hands, they are satisfied with good things [טוב *tôb*]." The Lord's redemption of Israel will constitute a new creation, a renewal of God's provision for life.

31:15-22. The picture of Israel's restoration shifts dramatically from the sounds of music, dancing, and joy to those of weeping and lamentation and moaning. If the preceding verses are a vision of the future that nearly outruns believability for its picture of blessing and good, these verses insert a harsh realism, though without relinquishing the positive view of the future.

The passage presents a series of rich and poignant images of familial relationships. They begin with the inconsolable weeping of Mother Rachel for her children. Rachel, the wife of Jacob, was the mother of Joseph and Benjamin. The extremity of Israel's condition is sharply depicted in this picture of the ancestral mother, disconsolate because of the destruction of her children. The setting of Rachel's weeping in Ramah is probably to be connected to that town as the place from which the Judeans were taken into exile (40:1). The reason for such bitter and uncontrollable maternal weeping is clear: "They are not" (v. 15). Here that punishment is seen through the eyes of the mother whose children are being punished.

To this uncomforted mother come the only pos-

sible words of comfort. Echoes of Isa 40:1 may be heard in this passage: "Comfort, comfort, my people." Here as there, the comforting act is not a pat on the back but a move to restore the community to its place and land. The weeping of the mother becomes a prayer that is now answered, and the "there is not" receives a response in the twofold "there is" (vv. 16*b*, 17*a*). The Lord's answer to Mother Rachel's prayer is a kind of resurrection. Her "work," the work of weeping and praying, is rewarded by the only thing that can be termed reward; her hopelessness ("refusing to be comforted") will be turned to hope. The text emphasizes this point twice: "They shall come back" becomes "*Your children* shall come back."

Then the Lord turns from a mother weeping for her children to "my dear son," Ephraim, who also happens to be one of Rachel's "children" (vv. 18-20). If Rachel's lament receives a response from the Lord, then Ephraim also hears the word of deliverance at "his" confession of sin and repentance. The heart of God is moved by the prayer of the mother and by the repentant confession of the "gone" child. The pathos of divine investment in this "family" turns the destruction and exile of God's wrath and judgment into a marvelous restoration (see vv. 7-14), due to God's memory and mercy. Two infinitives absolute, placed before the words for "remember" and "have mercy," reinforce the depth of that memory and that compassion (v. 20). The Lord is profoundly moved by the tears of the mother and the repentance of the child. Divine vulnerability to the human situation is nowhere more explicit than here, where God's intent to punish cannot resist God's own compassionate attention to the prayers of the people. The tension and the way it is finally broken open are best identified in the line "As often as I speak against him, I still remember him [or better: I remember him so much]." This dialogue within the mind or heart of God recalls a similar one in Hos 11:1-9 that also involves the compassion of the Lord for Ephraim/Israel, "my son."

The final strophe of this section (vv. 21-22) seems quite different in subject and tone, but the repeated use of the thematic verb שוב (*šûb*, "return"), which occurs here twice in v. 21*b* and in the epithet "faithless" applied to Israel (v. 22*a*) as well as in both the preceding strophes in reference to the "return" from exile (vv. 16*b*, 17*b*, 18*b*

[2x]) and the "turning away" of Ephraim (v. 19*a*), clearly connects it with vv. 15-20. Furthermore, although the address to Virgin Israel as daughter is a shift from the address to Ephraim as son, the use of familial relationships as the vehicle of meaning is consistent with what has just gone before.[171] The commands to prepare the way and to return are ambiguous, capable of being read geographically as referring to the return from exile or spiritually as referring to the turning of the heart back to the Lord. As such, these verses sound like earlier exhortations to faithless Israel to turn around in conduct and like other words of promise of deliverance and new life. That ambiguity lets the hearer attend to both the powerful new thing the Lord is doing for Israel, intimated with equal ambiguity in v. 22, and the enduring covenantal requirements of faithfulness to the Lord and the Lord's way that are not obviated by the experience of judgment and the consequent compassionate intention of God to restore Israel to its original state of blessing (vv. 7-14).

The final line of this passage has baffled interpreters and produced many different interpretations. Bozak summarizes the main ones:

The woman will turn into a man; the woman will protect the man since there will be such peace that women will be able to protect the city (metaphor for complete peace); the woman will court the man, the wife will take the initiative with her husband (metaphor for Israel taking the initiative in her relationship with Yhwh); the woman will surround or embrace the man in the sense that there will once again be procreation in the land.[172]

I am inclined to accept the last interpretation, the new thing created in the land as Virgin Israel's becoming fruitful again and Rachel's having her lost children back.[173] The sentence points toward God's new creation, toward things that will happen for Israel in their new life in the new land.

31:23-26. The oracles of deliverance in these chapters carry forward in these verses with the Lord's promise of "a restoration of urban and rural

life in the land that will be focused on worship in Jerusalem."[174] There will be harmony and unity among all its inhabitants (cf. Ps 133:1), even between farmers and shepherds, often in conflict with one another. And there will be divine rest for the weary, a motif that echoes the picture of God's provision for life in Zion in 31:12 ("languish") and 31:14 ("satisfy").

Verse 26 is enigmatic. Who is the "I," and why do we encounter such a sudden reference to sleeping and waking? We cannot be sure, but it is best to understand the speaker as a prophet, whether Jeremiah or a later voice. The waking suggests that what has been seen in these chapters is visions of the future, "sweet dreams" anticipatory of God's future. Sleep and dreaming are modes of God's revelation (cf. Ps 126:1), and not just fantasy. As Brueggemann puts it cogently: "Hope is clearly understood as a dreamlike alternative imagination which accepts God's intent as more powerful than the present, seemingly intransigent circumstance."[175]

31:27-30. The promise of the future ("days are coming"; cf. vv. 31, 38) is couched in the promise of fertility and in the language of Jeremiah's call. The land will be full of people, and the animals that provide sustenance and support will also multiply. The close connection between the prophet's call and the message of the prophet is underscored again as the Lord speaks of a turn from deeds of judgment (1:10, 14) to acts of renewal. In this Book of Consolation the prophet carries out the commission "to build and to plant."

The coming days will negate the attitude, conveyed in the proverb of v. 29, that the children must pay for the sins of their mothers and fathers. Ezekiel 18 makes clear that this attitude was common among Judeans after the fall of their country. Instead, the Lord will build and plant a community different from the one of the past. In this future, when sin occurs it will be dealt with, but it will be a community that is not shaped by a long history of disobedience. The proverb thus does three things: (1) removes a despairing attitude from the mind of the community; (2) contributes to the picture of a renewal of community life by God's power; and (3) incorporates into this vision

---

171. Note also the repeated use, but with quite different meanings, of the word תמרורים (*tamrûrîm*) in v. 15 ("bitter") and v. 21 ("markers".
172. Bozak, *Life "Anew,"* 103.
173. See Bernhard Anderson, "The Lord Has Created Something New: A Stylistic Study of Jeremiah 31:15-22," in *A Prophet to the Nations,* ed. Leo Perdue and Brian Kovacs (Winona Lake, Ind.: Eisenbrauns, 1984) 367-80.
174. Gerald L. Keown, Pamela J. Scalise, and Thomas J. Smothers, *Jeremiah 26–52,* WBC 27 (Dallas: Word, 1995) 127.
175. Walter Brueggemann, *A Commentary on Jeremiah: Exile and Homecoming* (Grand Rapids: Eerdmans, 1998) 289.

of newness a realistic note that knows the reality of sin in the human condition but believes it will be checked and controlled, not pervasive and determinative in the new community.

31:31-34. In one of the most famous passages of Jeremiah, we hear about a "new covenant." This is the only reference to a new covenant in the OT, but the language and images of such newness are important in the restoration promises of other prophets, including a new heart and a new spirit (Ezek 11:19-20; 18:31; 36:26) and new things (Isa 42:9; 43:19; 48:6). The similarities of this text to Ezekiel's prophecy are especially important because they indicate that one of the key features of this new covenant—that it is written on the heart (v. 33) and does not have to be taught (v. 34)—was a part of the exilic and post-exilic vision for the future. Ezekiel also has in mind a future when God will effect a new kind of obedience. For Ezekiel, obedience will derive from a new spirit and a new heart; for Jeremiah, it will stem from God's writing the law on the heart. Ezekiel's joining of a new heart and a new spirit unites these motifs. In the next chapter of Jeremiah, the Lord reiterates the covenant formula that is declared in v. 33*b* ("I will be their God and they shall be my people") in the context of promising to give the people "one heart . . . that they may fear me for all time. . . . and I will put the fear of me in their hearts" (32:38-40). This idea is not unlike the shift in Deuteronomy from the command to "circumcise, then, the foreskin of your heart; and do not be stubborn any longer" (Deut 10:16 NRSV) to the promise, from the exilic period or later, "Moreover, the LORD your God will circumcise your heart and the heart of your descendants, so that you will love the LORD your God with all your heart and with all your soul, in order that you may live" (Deut 30:6 NRSV).[176] In all of these texts, God promises a new kind of obedience to the covenant stipulations. God will affect the human heart so that people can keep the covenant requirements.[177]

In Jeremiah and other prophets (e.g., Ezekiel 11; 36), this promise of the future will represent sharp discontinuity with the past. This history of constant disobedience has led to judgment, a history that the Lord speaks of (v. 32) as reaching back to the very beginning of the history of this people. This passage announces that the breaking of the covenant does not mean an end to that history. On the contrary, in the future the Lord will make a new covenant and will effect in the minds and hearts of the people the will to obey, to live as God's people, to acknowledge the Lord as their master, the one who secures their lives and provides for them.

All of this happens by a divine reversal, a change in the heart of God toward the people (v. 34*b*). This change is not all that surprising because it has happened again and again. The clear intent of God "to remember their iniquity and to punish their sins" (14:20) will be turned around in the future. God will forgive the people and no longer remember their sins. The anger of the Lord will not last forever (Ps 103:9). Divine forgiveness is not new, but there is a sense in which the promise here represents a radical disjunction, "not like" (v. 32) and "no longer" (v. 34), even as it is consistent with the way of God with this people from of old.

31:35-37. God's promise is related to the story of the cosmos in a doxology. Israel will perdure, just as the cosmos continues to exist. Just as the prophet Amos underscored the word of judgment with a sequence of doxologies exalting "the LORD, the God of hosts" (Amos 4:13; 5:8-9; 9:5-6), so also the prophecy of Jeremiah now underscores hope for the future in a similar way. Echoing the Noachian covenantal promise that the rhythms and order of creation would never cease, the Lord says that it is no more likely or possible that Israel could cease to exist. Analogously, the Lord's rejection of Israel—a likely inference from the explicit declarations that the destructive force of the Babylonians is a manifestation of the wrath of God—is no more plausible or possible than the ability of human beings to measure the heavens or plumb the earth. It may seem that Israel is rejected. In the mystery of God's gracious commitment to Israel, however—ultimately as impenetrable as the mysteries of the universe—the nation of Israel is held secure through judgment and suffering.

31:38-40. Still, the judgment and the suffering are real. These verses confirm hope as it grows out

---

176. The connection of Deut 30:6 to the promise in Jeremiah is further underscored by the reference in Deut 30:3 to the Lord's restoration of the fortunes of the people, the central theme of the Book of Consolation in Jeremiah.

177. The divine gift of "another heart" has precedents in Israel's story, for example, with reference to Saul at the beginning of his kingship, "God gave him another heart" (1 Sam 10:9), literally, "God turned another heart to him." Cf. Zeph 3:9: "At that time I will change the speech of the peoples to a pure speech, that all of them may call on the name of the Lord and serve him with one accord."

of realistic judgment. They announce, with the detail of an architect or contractor, the plan of the Lord to rebuild Jerusalem. Some of the references in these verses are to places in ancient Jerusalem. Others, such as Gareb and Goah, are not. The most startling announcement is that the valley of dead bodies and ashes, the Hinnom Valley, will be included in the Lord's holy city. This was where the Tophet was located, a place where people burned their sons and daughters, a place that the Lord renamed "valley of Slaughter" because of Judean bodies piled up in judgment. These sacred bones and ashes of the people were at least in part a result of the Babylonian destruction of Jerusalem. Beyond that judgment, but not apart from it, the Lord who called the prophet Jeremiah to "pluck up" and to "overthrow" (1:10; cf. 31:28) pronounces an end to that word in the final sentence of this chapter. The destroyer of Jerusalem pledges an eternal protection for the holy city.

REFLECTIONS

1. The promise of return to the promised land is one of the many instances in which God's deliverance is seen to belong to the very real and material world of human existence in time and space and not only to a spiritual realm. Salvation here has to do with place and the possibilities of life there. Chapter 29 makes it clear that life can go on outside the land. But home is not simply the place where the heart is; it is the gift of God. Scripture has much to say about finding a home and about God's providing home, welcoming home, bringing home. The image of returning home as a salvific act is so powerful that it comes to have a spiritual dimension as well, through the images of pilgrimage, of looking for a city without foundations, whose builder and maker is God. The language of "going home" is used not infrequently as a way of speaking about death. But these spiritual understandings are rooted in the this-worldly experience of the people of God. Their place in this world is God-given. They have a home because God has provided them a place and an opportunity. The return to the land long ago promised is a return home, and it is a return to the place of security, the place where the means to life can be found. That is a reality in Scripture, and it is one that people in our own time have known in hope or in frustration of hopes, from Jews deported and murdered who sought and found a home, praising God for it, to Palestinians who have lost a home as Jews have found one, to any number of peoples around the globe who have been forced out of their homes. Jeremiah reminds us of the centrality of the need for place and the longing for home in human experience and, even more, of the intention of God to fulfill the need and the yearning.

2. One of the most noticeable things in these oracles is the way in which the gospel, the announcement of good news to sinners and the oppressed, is addressed to those persons in ways that are fully cognizant of their condition, their suffering and their pain. It meets them where they are and starts from the assumption that things are really bad, that judgment has happened and pain has been inflicted. In this context, it is not "I'm okay. You're okay." Pain and hurt are the present reality. And the one who provides a way out is also the one who brought the people into this condition. In weal and woe, for evil and for good, the community of faith deals with the Lord. The gospel comes to this community, as it so regularly does, on two assumptions: that things are bad and good news is desperately needed, and that the Lord is involved in the bad as well as in the good. While not all suffering is laid at the hands of the Lord, the church should not forget that the biblical story tells us often of experiences of disaster that are the judgment of God. We cannot assume that chastisement does not come to us. The argument of Job against his friends is part of the story of human suffering, but so is the real event of exile as well as the story of a suffering servant whose bruises were for our iniquities.

3. The alternation of feminine and masculine forms of address in chaps. 30–31 bids us reflect on this surely significant literary device. The masculine address is fairly understandable with the references to Jacob and Israel in personal terms that contain allusions to the patriarch Jacob, to the northern kingdom, and to the whole people of God. But the text persists in coming back to feminine address, a feature used earlier in the book (e.g., 5:7). That may reflect an implicit address to the capital city Jerusalem, regularly spoken to and about in feminine language in the Bible. But when that Jerusalem is not explicitly indicated, the address to a feminine figure serves to connote the feminine in the relation of the people to the Lord. As Bozak has pointed out, attention to the place of women in ancient Israel suggests that the feminine here can convey notions of dependence, intimacy, and exclusive relationship—all of which are aspects of the relationship between God and Israel conveyed in these chapters. The feminine address, therefore, opens up our thinking about the utter dependence of the community of faith on its Lord and the intimate and personal character of that relationship, suggested also by the oracle of salvation, which addresses the people as an individual and speaks in direct and personal terms. Several times in these chapters there is emphasis on the Lord as Israel's God and the people as "my people" (e.g., 30:3, 22; 31:1, 33). The image of the marriage relationship is highly covenantal and is suggested in this use of the feminine. These are heuristic features of the style of the text and cannot be literalized any more than explicit metaphor can be. But their presence has possibilities for stimulating our thinking about the way in which the people and their Lord live together.

4. The reversal of God's way that takes place in these chapters is vividly articulated in 30:12-17. Once again the reader learns afresh a familiar word about the God we worship and why the community lives in praise and adoration of this God. The text reminds us again that the Lord of Israel is not a Janus-faced God, a God of wrath and a God of love. The wrath of God is always subordinated to the love of God. The purpose of God in and through Israel is identified at the very beginning as blessing for the covenant people but through them for all the earth (Gen 12:1-3). And curse is what is to be overcome. It is not a part of the purpose of God. Curse and judgment are always in reaction to the sins of the community. But the Lord is constantly switching directions from judgment to grace and healing and redemption. Something in the very heart of God is moved by suffering and hurt and pain, by the plight of the mocked and the ridiculed, the lonely and the desolate, the besieged and the afflicted. The Lord will not let the uncared for remain that way, will not let the taunts of the mockers go untended. This is what we know to be at the very center of the revelation of the love of God—in both the story of Israel and in the story of Jesus Christ. The grace of God triumphs over the judgment of God. That is very good news.

5. The imagery of the new Jerusalem, of the holy city that the Lord will build in the future in the midst of humanity, has one of its earliest formulations in Jer 30:18-22. That theme, which first occurs in a negative way in the Tower of Babel story (Genesis 11), continues through the rest of Scripture and is the vision with which the whole ends in Rev 21:1-4, a vision directly reflective of these verses of Jeremiah. In Revelation as well as in Jeremiah the city is not simply a political symbol, not just a concrete, material representation of human community under divine and human leadership. Rather, it is a manifestation of the compassion of God. It is the place where *shalom* finally resides, where the sounds are only of joy, where no one is ever put down again, where God and humanity live in commitment to each other and in the peaceable kingdom God envisioned from the creation. This utopian vision belongs to the most radical of political movements and has shaped countless revolutionary urges. But the vision also belongs to the deepest and most personal of hopes for a life with God beyond death.

6. The conclusion of chapter 30, with its indication that the vindication of God's purposes in the defeat of the wicked and the restoration of Israel is something "you will understand" in the latter days, is a reminder that God's purposes are not always discernible in the present moment. The church knows of a larger perspective and lives in the present by the promises of God for the future. It may not fully comprehend the meaning of its present experience, especially if that is one of pain and suffering. It lives in hope and an expectation that God will effect in us the understanding we need when we need it.

7. Surely there is no more powerful or extravagant depiction of the Lord's future provision of the good of the people than that of 31:10-14. It is an invitation to a party the likes of which this people have never known. It is a homecoming party, with all the good things parties are meant to have: the best food and wine, music and singing and dancing. It is intergenerational and full of fun and merriment. And it goes on forever. The picture of a marvelous party, where all are gathered before the Lord to enjoy all the benefits of God's goodness and celebrate in joy and singing and dancing, is a way of connecting the vision of the future with the reality of the present. There is no literal way of telling us about what God plans out there beyond our ken. But the language by which Israel spoke of and entrusted its future is the kind of appropriate imaginative construal of the way it will be. It's going to be party time!

8. The image of Rachel weeping for her children has been developed in powerful ways by Walter Brueggemann, who notes that this text has placed in the language and thought of both Judaism and Christianity a powerful image of the effects of brutality against Israel and the Jews. Thus Matthew returns to this image in Matt 2:18 to place Herod's terror against the Jewish babies alongside Babylon's destruction and exile of the Judeans. The text does not stop on the problem of the one destruction being a part of the judgment of God. Rachel's weeping is over the lost children regardless of who is ultimately responsible. But it may be that the ambiguity around the question of responsibility for the terror—tyrannical king or wrathful deity—is what has held the image of Rachel's weeping so powerfully in the tradition, enabling it to be recalled in the face of the terror and destruction of the Holocaust and in the depiction of the plight of the homeless. Brueggemann writes:

> Mother Rachel in Ramah, moreover, is not grudging with her tears. She will weep for all her children. The warehoused ones in New York City are present, then, with the baby at Bethlehem, and with the exiles in Babylon, and with the lost boy in Genesis. On the horizon of mother Rachel, all are the same, all her abused, destroyed children who must be grieved in perpetuity. And Kozol, in an act of courageous imagination, shows us that our policy on homelessness is indeed a "final solution," a betrayal of the beloved city, a city completely dissolved in tears.[178]

9. The new covenant announced in 31:31-34 poses several issues for the church's reflection. They revolve around the question of what comprises the new covenant and what that means for the old covenant. Who makes up the new covenant? And what happens to the community of the old covenant? The very expression "New Testament" serves to identify the new covenant with the Christ-event. The further identification of the blood of Christ and the cup of communion with the "new covenant" (Luke 22:20; 1 Cor 11:25) serves to underscore the New Testament claim to perceive the establishment of the new covenant relationship in the advent of Christ and the creation of a community that defines its relationship to God through Jesus Christ. The reference to the blood of Christ is a way of pointing to the divine act of salvation that, like the exodus, redeems a people by God's own power and grace. Christians know that particularly in the cross and celebrate it. Just as the exodus event is a pointer to the Christ event, so also the latter is a confirmation of the other.

Some of the New Testament texts go further in seeing the new covenant in Christ as a negation of the old covenant with Israel (e.g., 2 Cor 3:5-14; Heb 8:8-12; 10:16-17). Christians, in their legitimate desire not to be supersessionist, probably need to hear these texts both critically and appreciatively. That is, we need to remember that in this as in all matters Christians are grafted onto the Jewish tree (Romans 11) and "come derivatively and belatedly to share the promised newness."[179] This is the way we are drawn into the covenant, as members of a community of the new covenant. However God's covenant is renewed with Israel—and the word of Jeremiah

---

178. Walter Brueggemann, "Texts That Linger, Words That Explode," *Theology Today* 54 (1997) 186. The reference to the "lost boy in Genesis" is to Joseph for whom Jacob "refuses to be comforted" (Gen 37:35), a motif that is transferred to Rachel in Jer 31:15.
179. Brueggemann, *Jeremiah,* 295.

is that it is or will be—the Christian community enters anew to that new covenant through Christ. We may need to be very modest about what we say about God's covenant with the Israel that exists as God's people alongside the church, possibly more modest than Paul and the author of the Letter to the Hebrews, but not modest in our experienced conviction of what the sacrament regularly tells us, that in the death of Christ, God has acted graciously to create the relationship that makes us God's people and the Lord as our God. In both cases, the new covenant points us to a reality both experienced and anticipated—the work of God in our lives to make us obedient and responsive to God's love. The largest question about the new covenant is not about who belongs to it but about whether any of us, Jew or Christian, show forth the new heart and new spirit that God has promised to effect within us.

Jeremiah 32:1-44, A Field of Hope

NIV

32 This is the word that came to Jeremiah from the LORD in the tenth year of Zedekiah king of Judah, which was the eighteenth year of Nebuchadnezzar. [2]The army of the king of Babylon was then besieging Jerusalem, and Jeremiah the prophet was confined in the courtyard of the guard in the royal palace of Judah.

[3]Now Zedekiah king of Judah had imprisoned him there, saying, "Why do you prophesy as you do? You say, 'This is what the LORD says: I am about to hand this city over to the king of Babylon, and he will capture it. [4]Zedekiah king of Judah will not escape out of the hands of the Babylonians[a] but will certainly be handed over to the king of Babylon, and will speak with him face to face and see him with his own eyes. [5]He will take Zedekiah to Babylon, where he will remain until I deal with him, declares the LORD. If you fight against the Babylonians, you will not succeed.' "

[6]Jeremiah said, "The word of the LORD came to me: [7]Hanamel son of Shallum your uncle is going to come to you and say, 'Buy my field at Anathoth, because as nearest relative it is your right and duty to buy it.'

[8]"Then, just as the LORD had said, my cousin Hanamel came to me in the courtyard of the guard and said, 'Buy my field at Anathoth in the territory of Benjamin. Since it is your right to redeem it and possess it, buy it for yourself.'

"I knew that this was the word of the LORD; [9]so I bought the field at Anathoth from my cousin Hanamel and weighed out for him seventeen

[a]4 Or *Chaldeans*; also in verses 5, 24, 25, 28, 29 and 43

NRSV

32 The word that came to Jeremiah from the LORD in the tenth year of King Zedekiah of Judah, which was the eighteenth year of Nebuchadrezzar. [2]At that time the army of the king of Babylon was besieging Jerusalem, and the prophet Jeremiah was confined in the court of the guard that was in the palace of the king of Judah, [3]where King Zedekiah of Judah had confined him. Zedekiah had said, "Why do you prophesy and say: Thus says the LORD: I am going to give this city into the hand of the king of Babylon, and he shall take it; [4]King Zedekiah of Judah shall not escape out of the hands of the Chaldeans, but shall surely be given into the hands of the king of Babylon, and shall speak with him face to face and see him eye to eye; [5]and he shall take Zedekiah to Babylon, and there he shall remain until I attend to him, says the LORD; though you fight against the Chaldeans, you shall not succeed?"

6Jeremiah said, The word of the LORD came to me: [7]Hanamel son of your uncle Shallum is going to come to you and say, "Buy my field that is at Anathoth, for the right of redemption by purchase is yours." [8]Then my cousin Hanamel came to me in the court of the guard, in accordance with the word of the LORD, and said to me, "Buy my field that is at Anathoth in the land of Benjamin, for the right of possession and redemption is yours; buy it for yourself." Then I knew that this was the word of the LORD.

9And I bought the field at Anathoth from my cousin Hanamel, and weighed out the money to him, seventeen shekels of silver. [10]I signed the deed, sealed it, got witnesses, and weighed the

NIV

shekels[a] of silver. [10]I signed and sealed the deed, had it witnessed, and weighed out the silver on the scales. [11]I took the deed of purchase—the sealed copy containing the terms and conditions, as well as the unsealed copy— [12]and I gave this deed to Baruch son of Neriah, the son of Mahseiah, in the presence of my cousin Hanamel and of the witnesses who had signed the deed and of all the Jews sitting in the courtyard of the guard.

[13]"In their presence I gave Baruch these instructions: [14]'This is what the LORD Almighty, the God of Israel, says: Take these documents, both the sealed and unsealed copies of the deed of purchase, and put them in a clay jar so they will last a long time. [15]For this is what the LORD Almighty, the God of Israel, says: Houses, fields and vineyards will again be bought in this land.'

[16]"After I had given the deed of purchase to Baruch son of Neriah, I prayed to the LORD:

[17]"Ah, Sovereign LORD, you have made the heavens and the earth by your great power and outstretched arm. Nothing is too hard for you. [18]You show love to thousands but bring the punishment for the fathers' sins into the laps of their children after them. O great and powerful God, whose name is the LORD Almighty, [19]great are your purposes and mighty are your deeds. Your eyes are open to all the ways of men; you reward everyone according to his conduct and as his deeds deserve. [20]You performed miraculous signs and wonders in Egypt and have continued them to this day, both in Israel and among all mankind, and have gained the renown that is still yours. [21]You brought your people Israel out of Egypt with signs and wonders, by a mighty hand and an outstretched arm and with great terror. [22]You gave them this land you had sworn to give their forefathers, a land flowing with milk and honey. [23]They came in and took possession of it, but they did not obey you or follow your law; they did not do what you commanded them to do. So you brought all this disaster upon them.

[a]9 That is, about 7 ounces (about 200 grams)

NRSV

money on scales. [11]Then I took the sealed deed of purchase, containing the terms and conditions, and the open copy; [12]and I gave the deed of purchase to Baruch son of Neriah son of Mahseiah, in the presence of my cousin Hanamel, in the presence of the witnesses who signed the deed of purchase, and in the presence of all the Judeans who were sitting in the court of the guard. [13]In their presence I charged Baruch, saying, [14]Thus says the LORD of hosts, the God of Israel: Take these deeds, both this sealed deed of purchase and this open deed, and put them in an earthenware jar, in order that they may last for a long time. [15]For thus says the LORD of hosts, the God of Israel: Houses and fields and vineyards shall again be bought in this land.

16After I had given the deed of purchase to Baruch son of Neriah, I prayed to the LORD, saying: [17]Ah Lord GOD! It is you who made the heavens and the earth by your great power and by your outstretched arm! Nothing is too hard for you. [18]You show steadfast love to the thousandth generation,[a] but repay the guilt of parents into the laps of their children after them, O great and mighty God whose name is the LORD of hosts, [19]great in counsel and mighty in deed; whose eyes are open to all the ways of mortals, rewarding all according to their ways and according to the fruit of their doings. [20]You showed signs and wonders in the land of Egypt, and to this day in Israel and among all humankind, and have made yourself a name that continues to this very day. [21]You brought your people Israel out of the land of Egypt with signs and wonders, with a strong hand and outstretched arm, and with great terror; [22]and you gave them this land, which you swore to their ancestors to give them, a land flowing with milk and honey; [23]and they entered and took possession of it. But they did not obey your voice or follow your law; of all you commanded them to do, they did nothing. Therefore you have made all these disasters come upon them. [24]See, the siege-ramps have been cast up against the city to take it, and the city, faced with sword, famine, and pestilence, has been given into the hands of the Chaldeans who are fighting against it. What you spoke has happened, as you yourself can see. [25]Yet

[a]Or to thousands

NIV

²⁴"See how the siege ramps are built up to take the city. Because of the sword, famine and plague, the city will be handed over to the Babylonians who are attacking it. What you said has happened, as you now see. ²⁵And though the city will be handed over to the Babylonians, you, O Sovereign LORD, say to me, 'Buy the field with silver and have the transaction witnessed.' "

²⁶Then the word of the LORD came to Jeremiah: ²⁷"I am the LORD, the God of all mankind. Is anything too hard for me? ²⁸Therefore, this is what the LORD says: I am about to hand this city over to the Babylonians and to Nebuchadnezzar king of Babylon, who will capture it. ²⁹The Babylonians who are attacking this city will come in and set it on fire; they will burn it down, along with the houses where the people provoked me to anger by burning incense on the roofs to Baal and by pouring out drink offerings to other gods.

³⁰"The people of Israel and Judah have done nothing but evil in my sight from their youth; indeed, the people of Israel have done nothing but provoke me with what their hands have made, declares the LORD. ³¹From the day it was built until now, this city has so aroused my anger and wrath that I must remove it from my sight. ³²The people of Israel and Judah have provoked me by all the evil they have done—they, their kings and officials, their priests and prophets, the men of Judah and the people of Jerusalem. ³³They turned their backs to me and not their faces; though I taught them again and again, they would not listen or respond to discipline. ³⁴They set up their abominable idols in the house that bears my Name and defiled it. ³⁵They built high places for Baal in the Valley of Ben Hinnom to sacrifice their sons and daughtersᵃ to Molech, though I never commanded, nor did it enter my mind, that they should do such a detestable thing and so make Judah sin.

³⁶"You are saying about this city, 'By the sword, famine and plague it will be handed over to the king of Babylon'; but this is what the LORD, the God of Israel, says: ³⁷I will surely gather them from all the lands where I banish them in my

ᵃ35 Or *to make their sons and daughters pass through ₗthe fireⱼ*

NRSV

you, O Lord GOD, have said to me, "Buy the field for money and get witnesses"—though the city has been given into the hands of the Chaldeans.

26The word of the LORD came to Jeremiah: ²⁷See, I am the LORD, the God of all flesh; is anything too hard for me? ²⁸Therefore, thus says the LORD: I am going to give this city into the hands of the Chaldeans and into the hand of King Nebuchadrezzar of Babylon, and he shall take it. ²⁹The Chaldeans who are fighting against this city shall come, set it on fire, and burn it, with the houses on whose roofs offerings have been made to Baal and libations have been poured out to other gods, to provoke me to anger. ³⁰For the people of Israel and the people of Judah have done nothing but evil in my sight from their youth; the people of Israel have done nothing but provoke me to anger by the work of their hands, says the LORD. ³¹This city has aroused my anger and wrath, from the day it was built until this day, so that I will remove it from my sight ³²because of all the evil of the people of Israel and the people of Judah that they did to provoke me to anger—they, their kings and their officials, their priests and their prophets, the citizens of Judah and the inhabitants of Jerusalem. ³³They have turned their backs to me, not their faces; though I have taught them persistently, they would not listen and accept correction. ³⁴They set up their abominations in the house that bears my name, and defiled it. ³⁵They built the high places of Baal in the valley of the son of Hinnom, to offer up their sons and daughters to Molech, though I did not command them, nor did it enter my mind that they should do this abomination, causing Judah to sin.

36Now therefore thus says the LORD, the God of Israel, concerning this city of which you say, "It is being given into the hand of the king of Babylon by the sword, by famine, and by pestilence": ³⁷See, I am going to gather them from all the lands to which I drove them in my anger and my wrath and in great indignation; I will bring them back to this place, and I will settle them in safety. ³⁸They shall be my people, and I will be their God. ³⁹I will give them one heart and one way, that they may fear me for all time, for their own good and the good of their children after them. ⁴⁰I will make an everlasting covenant with them, never to

NIV

furious anger and great wrath; I will bring them back to this place and let them live in safety. [38]They will be my people, and I will be their God. [39]I will give them singleness of heart and action, so that they will always fear me for their own good and the good of their children after them. [40]I will make an everlasting covenant with them: I will never stop doing good to them, and I will inspire them to fear me, so that they will never turn away from me. [41]I will rejoice in doing them good and will assuredly plant them in this land with all my heart and soul.

[42]"This is what the LORD says: As I have brought all this great calamity on this people, so I will give them all the prosperity I have promised them. [43]Once more fields will be bought in this land of which you say, 'It is a desolate waste, without men or animals, for it has been handed over to the Babylonians.' [44]Fields will be bought for silver, and deeds will be signed, sealed and witnessed in the territory of Benjamin, in the villages around Jerusalem, in the towns of Judah and in the towns of the hill country, of the western foothills and of the Negev, because I will restore their fortunes,[a] declares the LORD."

[a]44 Or *will bring them back from captivity*

NRSV

draw back from doing good to them; and I will put the fear of me in their hearts, so that they may not turn from me. [41]I will rejoice in doing good to them, and I will plant them in this land in faithfulness, with all my heart and all my soul.

[42]For thus says the LORD: Just as I have brought all this great disaster upon this people, so I will bring upon them all the good fortune that I now promise them. [43]Fields shall be bought in this land of which you are saying, It is a desolation, without human beings or animals; it has been given into the hands of the Chaldeans. [44]Fields shall be bought for money, and deeds shall be signed and sealed and witnessed, in the land of Benjamin, in the places around Jerusalem, and in the cities of Judah, of the hill country, of the Shephelah, and of the Negeb; for I will restore their fortunes, says the LORD.

COMMENTARY

The purpose of the Book of Consolation is extended and confirmed in this narrative. Like the previous two chapters, this one affirms the harsh reality of judgment, judgment that would seem to end things forever for Judah. However, the prophet offers a powerful word about the future and the renewal of life in the land, not in a series of oracles but in the story of Jeremiah's purchase of a field in his home territory.

32:1-5. Although the first verse provides a precise date, v. 2 presents the truly salient facts for understanding what follows: The Babylonian army is besieging the city, and Jeremiah is in prison. Those facts underscore the apparent irrationality of what is to happen: Jeremiah's purchase of a piece of land in his hometown, Anathoth. Neither the general circumstances of the Judeans— besieged by a powerful army—nor the particular circumstances of Jeremiah—imprisoned in Jerusalem—provide a sound basis for the act of purchasing land for future use.

The detailed account of why Jeremiah was imprisoned by Zedekiah contains one of several prophecies given to Zedekiah by the prophet (e.g., 21:1-7; 32:1-5; 34:1-7; 37:1-10, 17; 38:14-28). The word of judgment to Zedekiah adds to the picture of improbability the note that Jeremiah would be purchasing a piece of property at this time. He has previously announced the defeat of the Judean king and his exile to Babylon, making clear, apparently, that this king and this people have no future in Judah.

The introductory words of the chapter, therefore, lay the groundwork for what follows. Jeremiah's improbable act seems to conflict with the circumstances and his own words. Only the power of God to redeem the future will make it a meaningful act. As Clements has put it, "The hope was in no way derivative from the events themselves."[180] There is nothing in the present situation that would precipitate investing in the future of Judah. Siege, defeat, and exile are the present realities.

32:6-15. The transaction by which Jeremiah purchases a field of land from his relative Hanamel is recounted in these verses. Two things are important about the whole account. First, everything that happens flows out of the word of the Lord to Jeremiah. Five times the prophet refers to the word of the Lord or says, "Thus says the LORD." None of this strange business deal is any of Jeremiah's doing. It is as implausible to him as to anyone else; one has the feeling that Jeremiah frequently refers to "the word of the LORD" to make clear why he is doing such strange things. The second thing about the transaction is that while it is carried out in utterly realistic fashion, as the details of vv. 9-12 make clear, the incident is still a prophetic symbolic action. It reminds us of the Lord's commands to Jeremiah to buy a loincloth and hide it (13:1-11) and to buy an earthenware jug and break it (chap. 19). One wonders if Jeremiah expects the land to be lost just as the loincloth was ruined and the earthenware jug broken, a symbol of coming judgment. In each case, Jeremiah is told to "buy" something (13:1; 19:1; 32:7-8, 25). These are all symbolic actions announcing judgment—until we get to 32:15. Then the meaning of the purchase changes radically. This time the act symbolizes God's intent to provide a future beyond the present judgment.

It has been suggested that Hanamel's visit to Jeremiah may have taken place during a brief period when the siege of the Babylonian army was lifted (cf. 37:5), permitting Hanamel to travel from Anathoth to Jerusalem. The text, however, does not tell us that and seems uninterested in how Hanamel could get to Jeremiah. No hint is given that some relief from the Babylonian threat is in view. However it happened, Hanamel appears and tells Jeremiah to purchase his land, "for the right of possession and redemption is yours." Hanamel refers here to the legal provision that protects the family inheritance or allotment of land from

permanent loss and thus the family from being deprived of its means of production and economic support. That provision is found in the jubilee law, where there is specific allowance for the selling of property to the next of kin, so that the inheritance does not permanently disappear from the family (Lev 25:23-28). It is not clear what has prompted Hanamel to sell the property; the account of its sale is aimed at the significance of the purchase, not the reasons for the sale. One may assume that Hanamel would have rejoiced at receiving money for property that seemed potentially worthless, whatever were his reasons for selling it.

The transaction is reported in great detail. Every step is recorded, including the price, the witnesses, the public setting, and the recording and preserving of the deeds. This detail underscores the nature of this symbolic action. Jeremiah paid out real money in front of witnesses and in public, and he preserved the deed. If it is a symbolic act, it is also a real event, real money paid for worthless land in front of an audience. Only in v. 15 is the meaning of this strange activity made clear. The rationale for the prophetic action is no less incredible, however, once it is understood by the prophet's report of the word of the Lord. The transaction is real because it rests in God's promise of a real future for this land: "Houses and fields and vineyards shall again be bought in this land." Jeremiah's purchase of property is a down payment on the future, a foretaste of the promise, but one that takes place in the midst of the reality of judgment. The detail of the symbolic action highlights the contrast between the act and present reality and the resonance between the act and the promised future. (For the role of Baruch in the book, see the Commentary on 36:1-32; 42:1–43:13; and 45:1-5.)

32:16-25. Jeremiah's symbolic action is followed by a prayer of "trustful incredulity"[181] whose fundamental theme is articulated in v. 17: "Nothing is too hard for you." The prayer arises from the incongruity between the action of buying the field (understood now in v. 25 as a divine command) and the present state of affairs: "See the siege ramps have been cast up against the city . . . and the city has been given into the hands of the

180. Ronald Clements, *Jeremiah,* Interpretation (Atlanta: John Knox, 1988) 195.

181. Walter Brueggemann, "A 'Characteristic' Reflection on What Comes Next (Jeremiah 32:16-44)," in *Prophets and Paradigms: Essays in Honor of Gene M. Tucker,* ed. Stephen B. Reid (Sheffield: Sheffield Academic, 1996) 19.

Chaldeans" (v. 24). It is essentially a doxological prayer, praising the power and might of God manifest in the acts of creation, redemption, and judgment. Its opening ("Ah, Lord God!") identifies the implicit theodicy issue in the prayer. Such address characteristically occurs in the face of trouble, representing despair and anguish, often with an implicit or explicit "Why?" (e.g., 4:10; 14:13; Josh 7:7; Ezek 9:8; 11:13). In traditional language drawn from the credo recitals of the Pentateuch and elsewhere, the prophet declares both the power and the graciousness of God and the consequent disobedience of the people, which now results in a word of judgment. All this is familiar and understandable. But in v. 25, there is an explicit linguistic and theological turn. "Yet *you...*" shatters the traditional order of things while still reflecting dependence upon God. The "trustful incredulity" is there between "Nothing is too hard for you" and "Yet *you* have said to me, 'Buy the field' . . . though the city has been given into the hands of the Chaldeans." The term "hard" (פלא *pālā'*) is the key here; it refers to doing the impossible.[182]

32:26-44. Transforming impossibilities into possibilities is the Lord's way: "See, I am the Lord, the God of all flesh; is anything too hard [פלא *pālā'*, "wonderful," "impossible"] for me?" (v. 27). This sentence serves as a counterpart to v. 17 and suggests that these words of the Lord respond to the implicit question of the prophet at the end of his prayer. The interpretation of the symbolic action follows in an extended recital of the judgment and the reason for it (vv. 28-35). God does not mince any words in elaborating in painful detail both the Babylonian destruction (v. 29), which is explicitly the work of the Lord of Israel (v. 28), and the sinful activities of the people (vv. 30-35). The latter draws together all the indictments of the book and

piles them up into a catalog of covenantal disobedience so unrelenting that one waits with certainty for the "Now therefore" that is surely to come as indictment leads into sentence of judgment.

Indeed, "Now therefore" follows in v. 36. Once more, however, expectations are overturned and the Lord of Israel breaks out of expected consistencies, leaping beyond the real and terrible judgment to speak of a future as unbelievable as buying land in front of a burning, destroying army. The reversal is signaled where the word about Jerusalem's being given into the hands of the Chaldeans, which twice has been explicitly the word of the Lord (vv. 3, 28), is now said to be what "you [the people] are saying" (cf. v. 43). The declaration that the Lord has given Jerusalem into the hands of the Chaldeans—an indubitable and important fact—seems to be, for Judah, the last word. But it is not the last word. Over against what "you are saying," the Lord now sets another word to "this city" (v. 36), echoing chaps. 30–31: There will be a gathering and a restoration. Once more, there is no tiptoeing over present harsh reality. This future gathering is necessary because of the Lord's wrathful scattering. The present terror cannot be bypassed; it can be overcome by the same power that effected it. Preceding chapters have shown that both the socioeconomic recovery of land and place and the theopolitical renewal of the covenant are constitutive for this restoration. Whereas chap. 31 characterized this covenant as "new," chap. 32 calls it an "eternal" covenant. The Lord is committed to doing good forever to "my people." This commitment is described as the Lord's "joy," and, in an unusual construction, the Lord commits to doing good in language that customarily describes what is expected of the people: "I will plant them in this land in faithfulness, *with all my heart and all my soul*" (cf. Deut 6:5). But the Lord also promises to effect one heart and one way in the people (cf. 31:33-34). Even the responsiveness of the Lord's initiative will create a response from the community.

182. On this word and its use, see Walter Brueggemann, " 'Impossibility' and Epistemology in the Faith Traditions of Abraham and Sarah (Genesis 18:1-15)," in W. Brueggemann, *The Psalms and the Life of Faith,* ed. Patrick D. Miller (Minneapolis: Fortress, 1995) 167-88.

REFLECTIONS

1. The text is about betting on the future, which belongs to the expectations, the habitus, the discipline of the community of faith. The story of Israel and of the church is constantly one of persons being called to bet on the future. But that is never guesswork, not even intelligent guesswork—like investing in the stock market after careful analysis. The stock market analogy is not inappropriate in this context, for the bet on the future in this text is couched in very concrete, economic terms; note the repeated use of the word "buy." The promise offered here is no generalized hope for better times. It is a call for putting one's money down now, for risking hard cash in the most speculative stock on the market at that time—a bankrupt company going under.

Betting on the future is thus an act of *trust* and *hope,* a risky act. But it is that element of trust that means the hope is not merely keeping one's fingers crossed. Christian hope is always tied to *promise,* as it is in this text. Christian hope has often been against good sense, against the tides in human affairs, but it is always in relation to the promise of the one who shapes the future in specific ways. So it is that the habit this text cultivates in its readers is one of trust. Trust is, presumably, a constant in the Christian life, but there are occasions when such trust is set in the midst of adversity and present misfortune and so is lifted to another level. The promise may not be as clear in the contemporary situation, but it is well grounded in the story of faith, both as recorded in Scripture and as experienced by our mothers and fathers of long ago and of more recent times. We may need to turn to such a text as this to get some clue about the future when the Babylonians are at the gate. (They have often been there and will be there again.) Misfortune, whether it is the judgment of God or disaster of other sorts—biblical "evil" can be either God's catastrophe laid upon us or disasters of any sort, including those from which we pray God's deliverance and help—is most often encompassed by promise. The biblical words let us know that there are occasions when that does not seem to be the case, and may indeed not be the case. But the tendency of the Lord of Israel and the creator of the universe is toward promising and keeping promises. If Scripture is reliable, then that tendency can be trusted; and faith bets against the future, but only because it knows that God controls that future and has let us know it is one of hope, of rebuilding, of fruitfulness, and of recovery.

2. This chapter is thus also about the marvelous power of God to effect a surprising future, a mix of power and grace at work to effect a radical reversal of present reality. The critical conversation of the text is between the repeated words about nothing being too difficult for the Lord and about buying fields in this land. The God who covenants with Israel can break out of all conventions and overcome all seeming constraints, including those of the Lord's own purposive actions, to effect a new reality, to turn punishment into redemption, devastation into good, danger and oppression into safety and security. The text here does not use the term "grace," but the promise of God is precisely what the New Testament and later theology understands by grace: the unmerited, free act of God to effect in our hearts a new spirit, a new life, a new way, to draw us to the fear of the Lord when we have been unwilling to go that way ourselves. The power that means nothing is too difficult for this God is not simply the power through and over Babylonian, and other, armies but the power through and over hard hearts and dead souls. And it is a power for good. That part is not new. It is just always being rediscovered.

3. The query, "Is anything too difficult, too wonderful for the Lord?" is voiced elsewhere in Scripture and so functions as a kind of theme, particularly when one pays attention to the contexts in which it appears. The first occurrence is when Sarah laughs at the suggestion that a woman as old as she will bear a child, to which the Lord responds similarly to Jeremiah's implicit question about the insanity of buying fields in a devastated land: "Is anything too hard/wonderful for the Lord?" (Gen 18:14). The impossibility not only becomes possible but also opens up the whole story of God's blessing for all humankind, even as the same rhetorical question in Jeremiah 32 opens up a whole new future for a people who were crying out, "Our bones are dried up, and our hope is lost; we are cut off completely" (Ezek 37:11 NRSV). This question is heard yet again, this time as an affirmation on the lips of the angelic messenger to Mary, the handmaid of the Lord: "For nothing will be impossible with God." At just those critical points when the future seems utterly restricted and without new possibilities, the God of wonders breaks out of the assumed constraints to create a future of blessing and hope, of restoration and good, of Immanuel and Jeshua.[183]

4. The chapter ends with the theme sounded at the beginning of this section of the book of Jeremiah: the restoration of fortunes for the people of God. By now it is evident that such restoration is rich and full-bodied, complex in every way, comprising economic and moral renewals, new hearts, and different modes of life. What is not too hard for this God is also not simple. It is a restoration that knows renewal and transformation cannot be confined to one sphere of life. Thus hope is kept from being simplistic, and participation in God's renewal and restoration knows that it encompasses all the complexities of life. Here again, the Old Testament reminds us of what it takes and all that is involved in God's new order.[184]

183. On "Israel's trust in impossibilities from God that shatter and recharacterize life" and the theological, economic, and epistemological significance of the trajectory of meaning identified here, see Brueggemann, " 'Impossibility' and Epistemology in the Faith Traditions of Abraham and Sarah (Genesis 18:1-15)."

184. On the nonreductionistic character of biblical thought and the necessity of nonreductionistic theological and ethical thought, see William Schweiker and Michael Welker, "A New Paradigm of Theological and Biblical Inquiry," in *Power, Powerlessness and the Divine: New Inquiries in Bible and Theology* (Atlanta: Scholars Press, 1997) 3-20.

Jeremiah 33:1-26, Restoration of Jerusalem and Its Leaders

NIV

33 While Jeremiah was still confined in the courtyard of the guard, the word of the LORD came to him a second time: [2]"This is what the LORD says, he who made the earth, the LORD who formed it and established it—the LORD is his name: [3]'Call to me and I will answer you and tell you great and unsearchable things you do not know.' [4]For this is what the LORD, the God of Israel, says about the houses in this city and the royal palaces of Judah that have been torn down to be used against the siege ramps and the sword [5]in the fight with the Babylonians[a]: 'They will be filled with the dead bodies of the men I will slay in my anger and wrath. I will hide my face from this city because of all its wickedness.

[6]" 'Nevertheless, I will bring health and healing to it; I will heal my people and will let them enjoy abundant peace and security. [7]I will bring Judah and Israel back from captivity[b] and will rebuild them as they were before. [8]I will cleanse them from all the sin they have committed against me and will forgive all their sins of rebellion against me. [9]Then this city will bring me renown, joy, praise and honor before all nations on earth that hear of all the good things I do for it; and they will be in awe and will tremble at the abundant prosperity and peace I provide for it.'

a5 Or Chaldeans   b7 Or will restore the fortunes of Judah and Israel

NRSV

33 The word of the LORD came to Jeremiah a second time, while he was still confined in the court of the guard: [2]Thus says the LORD who made the earth,[a] the LORD who formed it to establish it—the LORD is his name: [3]Call to me and I will answer you, and will tell you great and hidden things that you have not known. [4]For thus says the LORD, the God of Israel, concerning the houses of this city and the houses of the kings of Judah that were torn down to make a defense against the siege-ramps and before the sword:[b] [5]The Chaldeans are coming in to fight[c] and to fill them with the dead bodies of those whom I shall strike down in my anger and my wrath, for I have hidden my face from this city because of all their wickedness. [6]I am going to bring it recovery and healing; I will heal them and reveal to them abundance[b] of prosperity and security. [7]I will restore the fortunes of Judah and the fortunes of Israel, and rebuild them as they were at first. [8]I will cleanse them from all the guilt of their sin against me, and I will forgive all the guilt of their sin and rebellion against me. [9]And this city[d] shall be to me a name of joy, a praise and a glory before all the nations of the earth who shall hear of all the good that I do for them; they shall fear and tremble

aGk: Heb it   bMeaning of Heb uncertain   cCn: Heb They are coming in to fight against the Chaldeans   dHeb And it

NIV

[10]"This is what the LORD says: 'You say about this place, "It is a desolate waste, without men or animals." Yet in the towns of Judah and the streets of Jerusalem that are deserted, inhabited by neither men nor animals, there will be heard once more [11]the sounds of joy and gladness, the voices of bride and bridegroom, and the voices of those who bring thank offerings to the house of the LORD, saying,

"Give thanks to the LORD Almighty,
    for the LORD is good;
    his love endures forever."

For I will restore the fortunes of the land as they were before,' says the LORD.

[12]"This is what the LORD Almighty says: 'In this place, desolate and without men or animals—in all its towns there will again be pastures for shepherds to rest their flocks. [13]In the towns of the hill country, of the western foothills and of the Negev, in the territory of Benjamin, in the villages around Jerusalem and in the towns of Judah, flocks will again pass under the hand of the one who counts them,' says the LORD.

[14]" 'The days are coming,' declares the LORD, 'when I will fulfill the gracious promise I made to the house of Israel and to the house of Judah.

[15]" 'In those days and at that time
    I will make a righteous Branch sprout from
        David's line;
    he will do what is just and right in the land.
[16]In those days Judah will be saved
    and Jerusalem will live in safety.
This is the name by which it[a] will be called:
    The LORD Our Righteousness.'

[17]For this is what the LORD says: 'David will never fail to have a man to sit on the throne of the house of Israel, [18]nor will the priests, who are Levites, ever fail to have a man to stand before me continually to offer burnt offerings, to burn grain offerings and to present sacrifices.' "

[19]The word of the LORD came to Jeremiah: [20]"This is what the LORD says: 'If you can break my covenant with the day and my covenant with the night, so that day and night no longer come at their appointed time, [21]then my covenant with David my servant—and my covenant with the

[a]16 Or he

NRSV

because of all the good and all the prosperity I provide for it.

[10]Thus says the LORD: In this place of which you say, "It is a waste without human beings or animals," in the towns of Judah and the streets of Jerusalem that are desolate, without inhabitants, human or animal, there shall once more be heard [11]the voice of mirth and the voice of gladness, the voice of the bridegroom and the voice of the bride, the voices of those who sing, as they bring thank offerings to the house of the LORD:

"Give thanks to the LORD of hosts,
    for the LORD is good,
    for his steadfast love endures forever!"
For I will restore the fortunes of the land as at first, says the LORD.

[12]Thus says the LORD of hosts: In this place that is waste, without human beings or animals, and in all its towns there shall again be pasture for shepherds resting their flocks. [13]In the towns of the hill country, of the Shephelah, and of the Negeb, in the land of Benjamin, the places around Jerusalem, and in the towns of Judah, flocks shall again pass under the hands of the one who counts them, says the LORD.

[14]The days are surely coming, says the LORD, when I will fulfill the promise I made to the house of Israel and the house of Judah. [15]In those days and at that time I will cause a righteous Branch to spring up for David; and he shall execute justice and righteousness in the land. [16]In those days Judah will be saved and Jerusalem will live in safety. And this is the name by which it will be called: "The LORD is our righteousness."

[17]For thus says the LORD: David shall never lack a man to sit on the throne of the house of Israel, [18]and the levitical priests shall never lack a man in my presence to offer burnt offerings, to make grain offerings, and to make sacrifices for all time.

[19]The word of the LORD came to Jeremiah: [20]Thus says the LORD: If any of you could break my covenant with the day and my covenant with the night, so that day and night would not come at their appointed time, [21]only then could my covenant with my servant David be broken, so that he would not have a son to reign on his throne, and my covenant with my ministers the

NIV

Levites who are priests ministering before me—can be broken and David will no longer have a descendant to reign on his throne. ²²I will make the descendants of David my servant and the Levites who minister before me as countless as the stars of the sky and as measureless as the sand on the seashore.' "

²³The word of the LORD came to Jeremiah: ²⁴"Have you not noticed that these people are saying, 'The LORD has rejected the two kingdoms[a] he chose'? So they despise my people and no longer regard them as a nation. ²⁵This is what the LORD says: 'If I have not established my covenant with day and night and the fixed laws of heaven and earth, ²⁶then I will reject the descendants of Jacob and David my servant and will not choose one of his sons to rule over the descendants of Abraham, Isaac and Jacob. For I will restore their fortunes[b] and have compassion on them.' "

[a]24 Or *families*   [b]26 Or *will bring them back from captivity*

NRSV

Levites. ²²Just as the host of heaven cannot be numbered and the sands of the sea cannot be measured, so I will increase the offspring of my servant David, and the Levites who minister to me.

²³The word of the LORD came to Jeremiah: ²⁴Have you not observed how these people say, "The two families that the LORD chose have been rejected by him," and how they hold my people in such contempt that they no longer regard them as a nation? ²⁵Thus says the LORD: Only if I had not established my covenant with day and night and the ordinances of heaven and earth, ²⁶would I reject the offspring of Jacob and of my servant David and not choose any of his descendants as rulers over the offspring of Abraham, Isaac, and Jacob. For I will restore their fortunes, and will have mercy upon them.

COMMENTARY

33:1-13. The opening verse directly ties this chapter to the preceding one as well as to its time and circumstances, referring to a "second" divine word sent to Jeremiah while he was in prison (see 32:1-2). The chapter anticipates a future announced in the midst of terrifying judgment. The latter is depicted in a scene of carnage and devastation (vv. 4-5), verses that are textually corrupt and difficult to translate. But there is enough clarity to see again a picture of Babylonian destruction, represented in this case especially in the piling up of the dead bodies in the destroyed houses ("Torn down" translates נתץ [*nātaṣ*], one of the verbs in Jeremiah's commission in 1:10). The hymnic element in the divine word grounds the present judgment and the future healing in the power of the God who made the world and unfolds the future (cf. Amos 4:13; 5:8-9; 9:5-6). The "hidden things" represent all of what is declared here, the divine "I" at work in the midst of Babylonian havoc as well as the surprising future of healing and life.

The theme of restoration of fortunes continues the note first sounded in chap. 30 (see introductory comments on chaps. 30–33). Here that notion is made concrete: a vision of the future that holds quite specific ingredients—healing, security, prosperity, and joy—beyond the present death and terror, deprivation and sorrow. The scope of that future is comprehensive, incorporating both kingdoms, Israel and Judah (v. 7). But to that picture of health and security is added a further word of divine forgiveness. The reality of sin on the part of the people is no more masked here than it was in previous chapters. The overcoming of that sin is as clearly a divine activity of forgiveness and cleansing as the new heart and the new obedience are the work of God (31:31-34).

There are several ways in which the depiction of the future echoes or counters previous claims: (1) Within the passage, there is a sharp contrast between what "you say" about the present desolate waste—that is, the present laments of the people—and what God says about a future when people will dance in the streets for joy and celebrate the renewal and continuity of life in weddings and thanksgiving offerings, the last improbable in the present since there is nothing for which to be thankful.

825

(2) The false prophets had claimed that nothing would happen and that the people would enjoy ongoing "prosperity and security" (14:13). The deceit in that prophecy lay in its assumption that there would be no calling to account of a people who refused to live by the instruction of the Lord. The present announcement, in the midst of the judgment and the loss of prosperity and security, indicates that God intends to effect both "prosperity and security" (v. 6b); but the blessing of God given generously is not without demand. In the midst of the Babylonian siege, only God could make such a radical claim about the future.

(3) The Lord's announcement of a future "healing" now becomes a response to the earlier question: "Is there no balm in Gilead? . . . Why then has the health of my poor people not been restored?" (8:22). Restoration of health comes not from Gilead's balm but from the Lord's restorative powers.

(4) The promised end to joy and mirth, the sound of the bride and the bridegroom in a land made waste by God's judgment, an announcement of punishment reiterated again and again in the earlier prophecies of Jeremiah (7:34; 16:9; 25:10), is replaced now—in the very moment of judgment—by a promise of the restoration of those sounds in a renewed land.

33:14-26. In these oracles (missing from the Greek version and probably a later supplement to the first half of chap. 33), the prophet focuses on the leadership of the future, specifically the royal and priestly leadership of David and the Levites. The passage echoes chaps. 22 and 23 (see esp. 23:5-6) in recalling the failure of political leadership to render justice and righteousness in the community and announcing God's intention to provide leaders who will do that. The restoration of fortunes is not, therefore, simply a matter of abundance, productivity, and partying. It also includes the reestablishment of systems of governance and cult, creating leaders who will rightly render the affairs of the people and will lead them in their worship of the Lord.

The initial verses focus on the ruler and relate the rule of righteousness and justice with the well-being and security of the city. The prophetic vision of God's future seems always to place these characteristics of human rule to the fore. Jeremiah 23:6 says that "the LORD is our righteousness" is the name of the king who will come and rule

righteously. This chapter says that this is the name of the city. The repetition is not casual. The city is the place of God's rule, and the human ruler is the agent of that rule. The character of that rule is consistent and clear. It is exercised in the maintenance of the right as embodied in all the instruction of Moses and the prophets, in keeping faithful to relationships, in upholding the right of the wronged. A human community that goes by the name "the LORD is our righteousness" understands itself to be delivered, redeemed, and cared for by the Lord. That community understands itself to be committed to all those ways God has defined as right living in relationship with God and neighbor.

The identification of the leadership of the community as royal and priestly, as political and religious, goes back to the earliest period of the monarchy when priests were key figures alongside, but under, the king. These verses probably reflect the character of post-exilic community life. From other contexts, particularly the prophets Haggai, Zechariah, and Malachi, we can see indications of a kind of diarchy, or "twofold government by a secular governor and a religious leader" (e.g., Hag 1:1; 2:2; Zech 4:11-14).[185] Reference to the levitical priests may reflect a time when the legitimacy of the levitical line of priests was being asserted against the dominant Zadokite priestly line. The reference to "my covenant with my ministers the Levites" (v. 21) undergirds their claim to be the priestly leaders of the community. Such conflict is subdued in this text, which announces the renewal of the royal and priestly rule that had disappeared during the Babylonian oppression and exile. But it may be a clue to the reason for the rhetoric in vv. 19-26.

The rhetoric of these oracles is argumentative in the sense that it lays out a case to convince the prophet's hearers and readers. That rhetoric is covenantal and argues from the greater to the lesser, from God's covenant with the cosmos (vv. 20, 25) to the covenant with a single family. It is similar to the form of argument at the end of 31:35-37. It is a claim about divine fidelity, and it is repeated three times. The surety of the promise to the line of David and to the Levites can be counted upon as surely as day follows night. In v. 26 the argu-

185. See Richard D. Nelson, *Raising Up a Faithful Priest* (Louisville: Westminster/John Knox, 1993) 122-25.

ment is expanded to include the promise to the seed of Jacob, the covenant with Israel. It is an apologetic against the fears of many folk within the community. We are not sure who "these people" are in v. 24a, but they are probably a skeptical element within the community who think all the covenantal fidelities of the past are defunct (though it is possible that they are some of the surrounding peoples). The rhetoric in these verses proposes such skepticism, cynicism, and doubt. The Lord's covenantal fidelity never disappears. "Historical structures rooted in God's promises are as sure as cosmic sequences authored by God who creates and presides. God's love to Israel is as sure as God's ordering of creation."[186]

186. Walter Brueggemann, *A Commentary on Jeremiah: Exile and Homecoming* (Grand Rapids: Eerdmans, 1998) 320.

A final "Amen" to all of these promises and fidelities is given in the last verse, which sums up the theme of chaps. 30–33 and reiterates the catchphrase "restore the fortunes." These chapters have focused on two things: divine mercy and restoration. Verse 26, along with 30:3, creates a literary envelope that summarizes three issues. In the midst of a book whose primary subject matter involves God's judgment against a people who have abandoned the covenant, we find a counter-word of unbelievable proportions, so unbelievable that in this final section the promise has had to take the form of an argument. It is a word about restoration set in the midst of the experience of ongoing devastation, and it is a word from God, who does weal and woe (Isa 45:7) and will not let this people go—in their infidelity or in their suffering.

REFLECTIONS

1. The hymnic introduction to the prophecy of healing and restoration (33:2-3) is one of many clues in the book of Jeremiah to the character of prophecy and its significance for understanding the Lord of Israel and the interaction of divine word and deed. Here prophecy is explicitly depicted as revelatory, uncovering what is hidden. Prophecy is not presented as a form of magic and manipulation but as the divine decision to make known the future. For Israel the difference, if sometimes blurred, was significant, for here as elsewhere it is clear that revelation is from God, not a matter of human discernment. Various processes may have been involved (e.g., calling upon the Lord [33:3], which may have in mind prayer and petition), but these are not to be interpreted as devices for figuring out the future. They are the means by which one seeks the divine revelation, which may come at the desire of human beings (33:3a) or which may come unbidden, as on this occasion, and sometimes against other claims about the future, as in the case of false prophets. Biblical stories suggesting the possibility of human devices, rituals, and manipulations to discern God's future for us are deceptive. One of the most apparent is the case of Saul consulting the witch of Endor against his own instructions to expel mediums and wizards from the land. But the rising of Samuel from the dead is depicted as a final word from the Lord through God's prophet about Saul's fate. It is once again divine revelation, not human discernment. We are alerted, therefore, to maintain a healthy skepticism about claims on the part of human beings to discern the future, to read in the stars or any other medium what the future holds. The community of faith is given its scriptures, a story about the past that gives us directions, not predictions, about the future. As Moses suggested to the community about to enter the land, the revealed torah of the Lord is all the instruction the community needs. The prophets of Israel were God's messengers to Israel and Judah at a later time, revealing the Lord's will and purpose and calling the people to live by the instruction they had received. "The law and the prophets" give the community of faith the wholeness of its revelation. Neither as a corporate group nor as individuals do we expect or need human maneuvers to predict the future. We comprehend it through the careful study of God's Word and in God's response to our prayers, or we will simply not understand. There are no other avenues.

2. The social vision of restoration presented in chaps. 32 and 33 is not to be missed. Forgiveness of iniquity is clearly a dimension of God's future for the people (33:8), but both chapters set forth a detailed picture of renewal that takes place in economic and social ways. Business transactions will resume. Real estate deals will be possible. People will engage in the most human, intimate, and celebratory rituals of life—both personal (weddings) and cultic (thanksgiving offerings). Central modes of economic production and livelihood, such as shepherding, will be carried out in pastures now desolate. We are thus reminded once again that the vision of the future and of God's blessing that permeates the Scriptures is not simply spiritual, interior, and personal. It is richly material, life-enhancing, socially sustaining, and enjoyable. The general picture one has of the exilic promises is of deliverance from exile, salvation from Babylonian oppression. That picture is correct but partial, for the God who saves is also the God who blesses. That blessing is found in the provision and maintenance of life, in the continuities of birth and growth and marriage, in the sustaining of lives by work and economic gain, in the rich joy that human intercourse brings to individuals and the community. The holistic vision of the future put forth in chap. 33 addresses itself also to questions of leadership, indicating that politics and religion, the governance of the city and the service of God in worship, are part of the restoration that God effects.

The divine promises of Jeremiah keep us from translating the vision of hope into a purely otherworldly linguistic system that has no concrete connections with lived experience. They join with other Old Testament voices (e.g., Isa 2:1-4; 11:1-9) to announce a future that centers around the restoration of this world to its proper character as God's creation.

JEREMIAH 34:1–35:19, OBEDIENCE: TWO TEST CASES

OVERVIEW

With these chapters, the book returns to the present situation and the primary word of judgment. Two contrasting examples are set before the audience. One is a demonstration of the covenantal disobedience of the community as a whole, exemplified in this instance in their violation of the sabbatical principle inscribed in the deuteronomic code (chap. 15) and set forth by Zedekiah in a proclamation of release. The other is the continuing faithfulness of the Rechabites to the commands of their ancestor Jonadab about the lifestyle of their clan. The example of the Rechabites' obedience makes, by contrast, the same point as is made in the story of the violation of the sabbatical release: "You [this people] have not obeyed me" (34:17; 35:16).

Jeremiah 34:1-22, The Sabbath Release Undone

NIV

34 While Nebuchadnezzar king of Babylon and all his army and all the kingdoms and peoples in the empire he ruled were fighting against Jerusalem and all its surrounding towns, this word came to Jeremiah from the LORD: ²"This is what the LORD, the God of Israel, says: Go to Zedekiah king of Judah and tell him, 'This is what the LORD says: I am about to hand this city over to

NRSV

34 The word that came to Jeremiah from the LORD, when King Nebuchadrezzar of Babylon and all his army and all the kingdoms of the earth and all the peoples under his dominion were fighting against Jerusalem and all its cities: ²"Thus says the LORD, the God of Israel: Go and speak to King Zedekiah of Judah and say to him: Thus says the LORD: I am going to give this city

NIV

the king of Babylon, and he will burn it down. ³You will not escape from his grasp but will surely be captured and handed over to him. You will see the king of Babylon with your own eyes, and he will speak with you face to face. And you will go to Babylon.

⁴" 'Yet hear the promise of the LORD, O Zedekiah king of Judah. This is what the LORD says concerning you: You will not die by the sword; ⁵you will die peacefully. As people made a funeral fire in honor of your fathers, the former kings who preceded you, so they will make a fire in your honor and lament, "Alas, O master!" I myself make this promise, declares the LORD.' "

⁶Then Jeremiah the prophet told all this to Zedekiah king of Judah, in Jerusalem, ⁷while the army of the king of Babylon was fighting against Jerusalem and the other cities of Judah that were still holding out—Lachish and Azekah. These were the only fortified cities left in Judah.

⁸The word came to Jeremiah from the LORD after King Zedekiah had made a covenant with all the people in Jerusalem to proclaim freedom for the slaves. ⁹Everyone was to free his Hebrew slaves, both male and female; no one was to hold a fellow Jew in bondage. ¹⁰So all the officials and people who entered into this covenant agreed that they would free their male and female slaves and no longer hold them in bondage. They agreed, and set them free. ¹¹But afterward they changed their minds and took back the slaves they had freed and enslaved them again.

¹²Then the word of the LORD came to Jeremiah: ¹³"This is what the LORD, the God of Israel, says: I made a covenant with your forefathers when I brought them out of Egypt, out of the land of slavery. I said, ¹⁴'Every seventh year each of you must free any fellow Hebrew who has sold himself to you. After he has served you six years, you must let him go free.'ᵃ Your fathers, however, did not listen to me or pay attention to me. ¹⁵Recently you repented and did what is right in my sight: Each of you proclaimed freedom to his countrymen. You even made a covenant before me in the house that bears my Name. ¹⁶But now you have turned around and profaned my name; each of

ᵃ14 Deut. 15:12

NRSV

into the hand of the king of Babylon, and he shall burn it with fire. ³And you yourself shall not escape from his hand, but shall surely be captured and handed over to him; you shall see the king of Babylon eye to eye and speak with him face to face; and you shall go to Babylon. ⁴Yet hear the word of the LORD, O King Zedekiah of Judah! Thus says the LORD concerning you: You shall not die by the sword; ⁵you shall die in peace. And as spices were burnedᵃ for your ancestors, the earlier kings who preceded you, so they shall burn spicesᵇ for you and lament for you, saying, "Alas, lord!" For I have spoken the word, says the LORD.

6Then the prophet Jeremiah spoke all these words to Zedekiah king of Judah, in Jerusalem, ⁷when the army of the king of Babylon was fighting against Jerusalem and against all the cities of Judah that were left, Lachish and Azekah; for these were the only fortified cities of Judah that remained.

8The word that came to Jeremiah from the LORD, after King Zedekiah had made a covenant with all the people in Jerusalem to make a proclamation of liberty to them, ⁹that all should set free their Hebrew slaves, male and female, so that no one should hold another Judean in slavery. ¹⁰And they obeyed, all the officials and all the people who had entered into the covenant that all would set free their slaves, male or female, so that they would not be enslaved again; they obeyed and set them free. ¹¹But afterward they turned around and took back the male and female slaves they had set free, and brought them again into subjection as slaves. ¹²The word of the LORD came to Jeremiah from the LORD: ¹³Thus says the LORD, the God of Israel: I myself made a covenant with your ancestors when I brought them out of the land of Egypt, out of the house of slavery, saying, ¹⁴"Every seventh year each of you must set free any Hebrews who have been sold to you and have served you six years; you must set them free from your service." But your ancestors did not listen to me or incline their ears to me. ¹⁵You yourselves recently repented and did what was right in my sight by proclaiming liberty to one another, and you made a covenant before me in the house that

ᵃHeb as there was burning ᵇHeb shall burn

NIV

you has taken back the male and female slaves you had set free to go where they wished. You have forced them to become your slaves again.

¹⁷"Therefore, this is what the LORD says: You have not obeyed me; you have not proclaimed freedom for your fellow countrymen. So I now proclaim 'freedom' for you, declares the LORD— 'freedom' to fall by the sword, plague and famine. I will make you abhorrent to all the kingdoms of the earth. ¹⁸The men who have violated my covenant and have not fulfilled the terms of the covenant they made before me, I will treat like the calf they cut in two and then walked between its pieces. ¹⁹The leaders of Judah and Jerusalem, the court officials, the priests and all the people of the land who walked between the pieces of the calf, ²⁰I will hand over to their enemies who seek their lives. Their dead bodies will become food for the birds of the air and the beasts of the earth.

²¹"I will hand Zedekiah king of Judah and his officials over to their enemies who seek their lives, to the army of the king of Babylon, which has withdrawn from you. ²²I am going to give the order, declares the LORD, and I will bring them back to this city. They will fight against it, take it and burn it down. And I will lay waste the towns of Judah so no one can live there."

NRSV

is called by my name; ¹⁶but then you turned around and profaned my name when each of you took back your male and female slaves, whom you had set free according to their desire, and you brought them again into subjection to be your slaves. ¹⁷Therefore, thus says the LORD: You have not obeyed me by granting a release to your neighbors and friends; I am going to grant a release to you, says the LORD—a release to the sword, to pestilence, and to famine. I will make you a horror to all the kingdoms of the earth. ¹⁸And those who transgressed my covenant and did not keep the terms of the covenant that they made before me, I will make like*a* the calf when they cut it in two and passed between its parts: ¹⁹the officials of Judah, the officials of Jerusalem, the eunuchs, the priests, and all the people of the land who passed between the parts of the calf ²⁰shall be handed over to their enemies and to those who seek their lives. Their corpses shall become food for the birds of the air and the wild animals of the earth. ²¹And as for King Zedekiah of Judah and his officials, I will hand them over to their enemies and to those who seek their lives, to the army of the king of Babylon, which has withdrawn from you. ²²I am going to command, says the LORD, and will bring them back to this city; and they will fight against it, and take it, and burn it with fire. The towns of Judah I will make a desolation without inhabitant.

*a*Cn: Heb lacks *like*

COMMENTARY

34:1-7. Preceding the main component of the chapter is an oracle to and about Zedekiah. The oracle's context is the fierce fighting of the Babylonian army against Jerusalem (vv. 1, 6-7). Two oracles have been combined. The first is an announcement of judgment against the city, Jerusalem, and its king, Zedekiah (vv. 2-3). The second oracle, promising a peaceful end for Zedekiah and full royal burial (v. 5; cf. 2 Chr 16:14), seems to challenge this and other oracles that describe a negative fate for Zedekiah (e.g., 21:1-7) and stands in marked contrast to Zedekiah's actual fate—forced to watch his sons

killed, blinded, and taken into exile. These two oracles may derive from originally distinct settings, but their present juxtaposition suggests that the second oracle implied a peaceful end only on condition of Zedekiah's submission to the word of the Lord (v. 4)—that is, to the Lord's call for submission to the Babylonian Empire. The rest of the book and the rest of the story let us know that Zedekiah did not submit and, in an ironic play on v. 3*b*, saw not the king of Babylon "eye to eye" but the death of his own two sons (39:6).

34:8-22. The prophet announces a judgment speech. It is a case of double jeopardy arising out of the momentary and short-lived attention by the people to the legal requirement that Hebrew bonded servants be released from their servitude every seventh year. The deuteronomic law on this practice (Deut 15:12-13) is loosely quoted in v. 14. The release was to have been a regular part of Israelite life, but the text indicates that it had been neglected until the king gave an official decree proclaiming a release. The expression "proclaim liberty" (vv. 8, 15), comes from the law of the jubilee in Lev 25:10 (cf. Isa 61:1; Ezek 46:17), which called for the release of land and bonded servants (vv. 39-43) in the fiftieth year. The relation of this event to antecedent Israelite legal tradition is further complicated by the fact that the release is not done according to a set and regular time, as prescribed by the Torah, but by a royal proclamation, which was the way in which such release of debts and slaves occurred elsewhere in the ancient Near East, but not in Israel. Scholars have debated the relation of this event to the laws of release and to the historical context in which it is reported to have occurred. Various motives have been suggested: getting rid of the burden of caring for slaves in a time of siege, seeking to gain the mercy of God by an act of goodwill, ensuring the loyalty of the slaves, and the like. The reenslavement has been related to the break in the action when the Babylonians had to lift the siege of Jerusalem temporarily in order to deal with the approaching Egyptian army (vv. 21-22; cf. 37:5-11).

None of these matters can be settled with any certainty. What does seem clear is that the release reflects laws now present in Leviticus and Deuteronomy, thus placing the activity of the Judeans within the torah tradition, though with various points of conformity to the specific covenant requirements.[187] Covenant obedience is manifest in the act of release, which is linguistically associated with the Leviticus jubilee law, even though royal proclamation is nowhere envisioned in the pentateuchal traditions. Covenant disobedience is seen in the failure to provide for *regular* release of bonded servants from the chains of economic enslavement compounded by the people's rapid *reenslavement* of those released when the threat of danger seemed to have passed. The emphasis on covenant is explicit in the text, both in Zedekiah's reference to making (lit., "cutting") a covenant with the people in the proclamation of release (cf. v. 15) and in the Lord's reference to making or cutting a covenant with the ancestors at Sinai (v. 13) as well as to transgression and not keeping the covenant (v. 18).

Such double disobedience has simply compounded the violation of covenant. The Lord responds in an act of judgment framed in terms of a very precise correspondence of the punishment to the crime.[188] Those who have not obeyed "by granting a release" will find that the Lord "is going to grant them a release"—to sword, pestilence, and famine (v. 17). Those who have given a freedom that offers no freedom will be dealt with in the same way. Further, those who "cut" (v. 18; NRSV, "made") a covenant, by passing between the two parts of a calf, will be cut like the calf. One of the treaty curses in the Aramaic treaties of Sefire shows the covenantal character of this judgment word: "[Just as] this calf is cut to pieces, so may Mati'el be cut to pieces and his nobles be cut to pieces."[189] The conduct of the people as an act of covenantal disobedience is underscored by this invocation of a covenantal curse.

---

187. On the intertextual connections of the passage, see Simeon Chavel, " 'Let My People Go!' Emancipation, Revelation, and Scribal Activity in Jeremiah 34:8-14," *JSOT* 76 (December 1997) 71-95.

188. See Patrick D. Miller, "Sin and Judgment in Jeremiah 34:17-22," *JBL* 103 (1984) 611-13.

189. J. B. Prichard, ed., *Ancient Near Eastern Texts Relating to the Old Testament* (Princeton: Princeton University Press, 1955) 503-4.

REFLECTIONS

1. The word of the Lord through the prophet to the king shows that even within an oracle of judgment, the listener has the possibility of shaping the outcome, of determining the future. The message to Zedekiah is ambiguous by any reading, but that may be because the word of the prophet is often ambiguous in that one cannot know how it will turn out without knowing how the recipient of the message will respond to it. We need to note, therefore, the fluidity of prophecy against the usual assumption that the declaration of the word of the Lord means an immalleable future and a rigid control of history. Even when judgment is the appropriate outcome for what is happening, God is free, and the community is free to modify and alter that outcome through an appropriate response. This chapter, like so many others, demonstrates the missed opportunity and thus the inevitable (but only now inevitable) outcome of judgment.

2. The particular sin of the people in this instance has to do with violation of the sabbatical principle, one of the foundation stones of the Israelite understanding of justice and compassion for the disadvantaged. All of Israel's law codes had built into them as essential features provisions ensuring that economic bondage could not endure forever and that persons who had fallen onto hard times and had been forced into some kind of servitude could start over, free of obligations and with sufficient provisions to make a new start. Embodied especially in the sabbatical laws of the deuteronomic code (chap. 15), such provisions challenge the assumption current in our own time that one cannot break the chain of cause and effect that binds people to financial and economic straits and insist that a community living in relation to the Lord is to safeguard all its members from being permanently crushed economically. Such laws are often said to be utopian and surely are not to be taken seriously. Whether or not they worked well, this text most assuredly conveys they are to be taken seriously.

The narrative may be more "realistic" in describing reality as we regularly encounter it—people doing whatever it takes to hold on to their wealth and economic power, commodifying persons for profit, and refusing to give up anything to let someone else have a share. But that reality is not acceptable in the kingdom of God. There is, indeed, another way of dealing with those who are economically oppressed. Israel, in its governing polity, and Israel's God, in divine rule and judgment, insisted that the welfare of the community depended upon providing a means of release for those in economic bondage. No community that fails to provide such measures can seriously understand itself as being in accordance with the divine will or reflective of the society God intends.

3. An important linguistic shift takes place at 34:17. Those who have been described as "slaves" are now characterized by the Lord as "brother "/"sister" and "neighbor"/"friend." The law of Deuteronomy 15 uses this same language to speak of the male or female slave as "your brother/sister" (Deut 15:7, 12, "member of your community"). We are made aware in this shift of the moral significance of the way we perceive and describe the people with whom we interact. The terms "brother"/"sister" and "neighbor" carry heavy moral weight. These are persons with whom we live and have intimate contact. As long as we confine those who have debt to categories that identify them in terms of that condition, then it is easier to treat them as commodities. If we understand them as "brother"/"sister" and "neighbor"/"friend," then we are led—indeed, required—to deal with them. The question of the lawyer to Jesus, "Who is my neighbor?" remains one of the definitive moral and ethical questions because it has large implications for the way we deal with those around us.

Jeremiah 35:1-19, A Study in Contrasts

NIV

35 This is the word that came to Jeremiah from the LORD during the reign of Jehoiakim son of Josiah king of Judah: ²"Go to the Recabite family and invite them to come to one of the side rooms of the house of the LORD and give them wine to drink."

³So I went to get Jaazaniah son of Jeremiah, the son of Habazziniah, and his brothers and all his sons—the whole family of the Recabites. ⁴I brought them into the house of the LORD, into the room of the sons of Hanan son of Igdaliah the man of God. It was next to the room of the officials, which was over that of Maaseiah son of Shallum the doorkeeper. ⁵Then I set bowls full of wine and some cups before the men of the Recabite family and said to them, "Drink some wine."

⁶But they replied, "We do not drink wine, because our forefather Jonadab son of Recab gave us this command: 'Neither you nor your descendants must ever drink wine. ⁷Also you must never build houses, sow seed or plant vineyards; you must never have any of these things, but must always live in tents. Then you will live a long time in the land where you are nomads.' ⁸We have obeyed everything our forefather Jonadab son of Recab commanded us. Neither we nor our wives nor our sons and daughters have ever drunk wine ⁹or built houses to live in or had vineyards, fields or crops. ¹⁰We have lived in tents and have fully obeyed everything our forefather Jonadab commanded us. ¹¹But when Nebuchadnezzar king of Babylon invaded this land, we said, 'Come, we must go to Jerusalem to escape the Babylonianᵃ and Aramean armies.' So we have remained in Jerusalem."

¹²Then the word of the LORD came to Jeremiah, saying: ¹³"This is what the LORD Almighty, the God of Israel, says: Go and tell the men of Judah and the people of Jerusalem, 'Will you not learn a lesson and obey my words?' declares the LORD. ¹⁴'Jonadab son of Recab ordered his sons not to drink wine and this command has been kept. To this day they do not drink wine, because they obey their forefather's command. But I have

ᵃ11 Or Chaldean

NRSV

35 The word that came to Jeremiah from the LORD in the days of King Jehoiakim son of Josiah of Judah: ²Go to the house of the Rechabites, and speak with them, and bring them to the house of the LORD, into one of the chambers; then offer them wine to drink. ³So I took Jaazaniah son of Jeremiah son of Habazziniah, and his brothers, and all his sons, and the whole house of the Rechabites. ⁴I brought them to the house of the LORD into the chamber of the sons of Hanan son of Igdaliah, the man of God, which was near the chamber of the officials, above the chamber of Maaseiah son of Shallum, keeper of the threshold. ⁵Then I set before the Rechabites pitchers full of wine, and cups; and I said to them, "Have some wine." ⁶But they answered, "We will drink no wine, for our ancestor Jonadab son of Rechab commanded us, 'You shall never drink wine, neither you nor your children; ⁷nor shall you ever build a house, or sow seed; nor shall you plant a vineyard, or even own one; but you shall live in tents all your days, that you may live many days in the land where you reside.' ⁸We have obeyed the charge of our ancestor Jonadab son of Rechab in all that he commanded us, to drink no wine all our days, ourselves, our wives, our sons, or our daughters, ⁹and not to build houses to live in. We have no vineyard or field or seed; ¹⁰but we have lived in tents, and have obeyed and done all that our ancestor Jonadab commanded us. ¹¹But when King Nebuchadrezzar of Babylon came up against the land, we said, 'Come, and let us go to Jerusalem for fear of the army of the Chaldeans and the army of the Arameans.' That is why we are living in Jerusalem."

¹²Then the word of the LORD came to Jeremiah: ¹³Thus says the LORD of hosts, the God of Israel: Go and say to the people of Judah and the inhabitants of Jerusalem, Can you not learn a lesson and obey my words? says the LORD. ¹⁴The command has been carried out that Jonadab son of Rechab gave to his descendants to drink no wine; and they drink none to this day, for they have obeyed their ancestor's command. But I myself have spoken to you persistently, and you

NIV

spoken to you again and again, yet you have not obeyed me. ¹⁵Again and again I sent all my servants the prophets to you. They said, "Each of you must turn from your wicked ways and reform your actions; do not follow other gods to serve them. Then you will live in the land I have given to you and your fathers." But you have not paid attention or listened to me. ¹⁶The descendants of Jonadab son of Recab have carried out the command their forefather gave them, but these people have not obeyed me.'

¹⁷"Therefore, this is what the LORD God Almighty, the God of Israel, says: 'Listen! I am going to bring on Judah and on everyone living in Jerusalem every disaster I pronounced against them. I spoke to them, but they did not listen; I called to them, but they did not answer.' "

¹⁸Then Jeremiah said to the family of the Recabites, "This is what the LORD Almighty, the God of Israel, says: 'You have obeyed the command of your forefather Jonadab and have followed all his instructions and have done everything he ordered.' ¹⁹Therefore, this is what the LORD Almighty, the God of Israel, says: 'Jonadab son of Recab will never fail to have a man to serve me.' "

NRSV

have not obeyed me. ¹⁵I have sent to you all my servants the prophets, sending them persistently, saying, 'Turn now everyone of you from your evil way, and amend your doings, and do not go after other gods to serve them, and then you shall live in the land that I gave to you and your ancestors.' But you did not incline your ear or obey me. ¹⁶The descendants of Jonadab son of Rechab have carried out the command that their ancestor gave them, but this people has not obeyed me. ¹⁷Therefore, thus says the LORD, the God of hosts, the God of Israel: I am going to bring on Judah and on all the inhabitants of Jerusalem every disaster that I have pronounced against them; because I have spoken to them and they have not listened, I have called to them and they have not answered.

18But to the house of the Rechabites Jeremiah said: Thus says the LORD of hosts, the God of Israel: Because you have obeyed the command of your ancestor Jonadab, and kept all his precepts, and done all that he commanded you, ¹⁹therefore thus says the LORD of hosts, the God of Israel: Jonadab son of Rechab shall not lack a descendant to stand before me for all time.

COMMENTARY

In a different kind of symbolic action, the Lord lets a family be a lesson in obedience that vividly exposes the disobedience of the people. Jeremiah is commanded to bring the whole family of the Rechabites to a room in the Temple and offer them some wine to drink. The Rechabites refuse to drink the wine and give an extended explanation of their reason for doing so. Their ancestor Jonadab (cf. 2 Kgs 10:15-23) gave the family several instructions, including prohibitions against drinking wine, building houses, planting fields, and planting or owning vineyards. They were to live in tents; their means of subsistence is not reported here or elsewhere. The Rechabites claim that they have done "all that our ancestor Jonadab commanded" and explain their unexpected appearance in the capital city as being due to the threat of the Babylonian army. Several

things may be observed about this initial conversation.

(1) While our curiosity about this rather strange group is hard to suppress, it must be admitted that we know virtually nothing about the Rechabites and can only speculate about who these people were. They have been identified as nomadic herders, an ascetic protest movement, a clan of smiths (the root רכב [rākab], from which the name of the clan derives, means "ride"; the word "chariot" comes from the same root), and a group of former household servants. Whatever the case, their practices here have a single point: the commitment of an Israelite family to live by the commands of their ancestor.

(2) This is, of course, a kind of test, but not one that the Lord expects the Rechabite family to fail. On the contrary, their unflinching obedience to

the directions of their ancestor must have been widely known. So the offer of wine is an intentional sham to elicit from them a refusal and an explanation.

(3) The text makes the point of saying that the *whole family*—leader, brothers, children, "and the whole house of the Rechabites"—came to the Temple. The demonstration of obedience, therefore, is heightened as it presents not just an individual case but shows a whole people following the instructions given to them long ago, which

everyone in the family continues to keep. The analogy between all the Rechabites and all the Judeans is drawn in the following verses.

The function of the Rechabite episode as a lesson is made explicit in the second part of the text (v. 13). The family of Jonadab obeyed the commands of their ancestor. The "family" of Israel did not obey the commands of their Lord conveyed through the prophets. In the former case, obedience opens up a hopeful future (v. 19); in the latter case, disobedience means disaster.

REFLECTIONS

1. The text is didactic, unsubtle, making a single point that cannot be missed or avoided. The Rechabites provide an explicit object lesson in obedience. The contemporary community of faith, the church, cannot miss the lesson any more than could the ancient community. The lesson conveys the fact that obedience is possible, that we can find instances of faithfulness in large measure, instructing and, indeed, shaming us, demonstrating the real possibilities of full and total commitment. In this case, it is not insignificant that the obedience is total. If the Rechabites are any indication, it is not unrealistic to assume that a group *can* live by an ethic of obedience and obligation, that they *can* continue to follow the paths set out long ago for them. The passage of time has not made the ancient ways irrelevant, ambiguous, or unrealistic. No "acids of modernity" are allowed to erode the faithfulness of this family. Many may have looked at the Rechabites as an odd group with a peculiar discipline. The Lord says that such folk show the rest of us how to go. Their unflinching and unrelenting obedience to the commands of their leader provides a living, walking, talking illustration of what it means to be a people under a command.

2. As in so many texts that focus primarily on what is needed for the human community, this chapter reveals something about the God who rules that community. Persistence is characteristic of God's call to the people to live by their covenantal obligations as fully as did the Rechabites. That persistence is signaled prominently in 35:14-15 with the repeated "again and again" (NIV) or "persistently" (NRSV). But it is reiterated in the poignant conclusion of 35:17 with the words that the judgment to come is because "I have spoken to them and they have not listened, I have called to them and they have not answered." We rarely hear the word of judgment without catching something of this tone that wishes it were not so and that God has done all that is divinely possible to hold it off.

JEREMIAH 36:1-32, A KING'S ARROGANT DEFIANCE

NIV

36 In the fourth year of Jehoiakim son of Josiah king of Judah, this word came to Jeremiah from the LORD: ² "Take a scroll and write on it all the words I have spoken to you concerning

NRSV

36 In the fourth year of King Jehoiakim son of Josiah of Judah, this word came to Jeremiah from the LORD: ²Take a scroll and write on it all the words that I have spoken to you

NIV

Israel, Judah and all the other nations from the time I began speaking to you in the reign of Josiah till now. ³Perhaps when the people of Judah hear about every disaster I plan to inflict on them, each of them will turn from his wicked way; then I will forgive their wickedness and their sin."

⁴So Jeremiah called Baruch son of Neriah, and while Jeremiah dictated all the words the LORD had spoken to him, Baruch wrote them on the scroll. ⁵Then Jeremiah told Baruch, "I am restricted; I cannot go to the LORD's temple. ⁶So you go to the house of the LORD on a day of fasting and read to the people from the scroll the words of the LORD that you wrote as I dictated. Read them to all the people of Judah who come in from their towns. ⁷Perhaps they will bring their petition before the LORD, and each will turn from his wicked ways, for the anger and wrath pronounced against this people by the LORD are great."

⁸Baruch son of Neriah did everything Jeremiah the prophet told him to do; at the LORD's temple he read the words of the LORD from the scroll. ⁹In the ninth month of the fifth year of Jehoiakim son of Josiah king of Judah, a time of fasting before the LORD was proclaimed for all the people in Jerusalem and those who had come from the towns of Judah. ¹⁰From the room of Gemariah son of Shaphan the secretary, which was in the upper courtyard at the entrance of the New Gate of the temple, Baruch read to all the people at the LORD's temple the words of Jeremiah from the scroll.

¹¹When Micaiah son of Gemariah, the son of Shaphan, heard all the words of the LORD from the scroll, ¹²he went down to the secretary's room in the royal palace, where all the officials were sitting: Elishama the secretary, Delaiah son of Shemaiah, Elnathan son of Acbor, Gemariah son of Shaphan, Zedekiah son of Hananiah, and all the other officials. ¹³After Micaiah told them everything he had heard Baruch read to the people from the scroll, ¹⁴all the officials sent Jehudi son of Nethaniah, the son of Shelemiah, the son of Cushi, to say to Baruch, "Bring the scroll from which you have read to the people and come." So Baruch son of Neriah went to them with the scroll in his hand. ¹⁵They said to him, "Sit down, please, and read it to us."

NRSV

against Israel and Judah and all the nations, from the day I spoke to you, from the days of Josiah until today. ³It may be that when the house of Judah hears of all the disasters that I intend to do to them, all of them may turn from their evil ways, so that I may forgive their iniquity and their sin.

4Then Jeremiah called Baruch son of Neriah, and Baruch wrote on a scroll at Jeremiah's dictation all the words of the LORD that he had spoken to him. ⁵And Jeremiah ordered Baruch, saying, "I am prevented from entering the house of the LORD; ⁶so you go yourself, and on a fast day in the hearing of the people in the LORD's house you shall read the words of the LORD from the scroll that you have written at my dictation. You shall read them also in the hearing of all the people of Judah who come up from their towns. ⁷It may be that their plea will come before the LORD, and that all of them will turn from their evil ways, for great is the anger and wrath that the LORD has pronounced against this people." ⁸And Baruch son of Neriah did all that the prophet Jeremiah ordered him about reading from the scroll the words of the LORD in the LORD's house.

9In the fifth year of King Jehoiakim son of Josiah of Judah, in the ninth month, all the people in Jerusalem and all the people who came from the towns of Judah to Jerusalem proclaimed a fast before the LORD. ¹⁰Then, in the hearing of all the people, Baruch read the words of Jeremiah from the scroll, in the house of the LORD, in the chamber of Gemariah son of Shaphan the secretary, which was in the upper court, at the entry of the New Gate of the LORD's house.

11When Micaiah son of Gemariah son of Shaphan heard all the words of the LORD from the scroll, ¹²he went down to the king's house, into the secretary's chamber; and all the officials were sitting there: Elishama the secretary, Delaiah son of Shemaiah, Elnathan son of Achbor, Gemariah son of Shaphan, Zedekiah son of Hananiah, and all the officials. ¹³And Micaiah told them all the words that he had heard, when Baruch read the scroll in the hearing of the people. ¹⁴Then all the officials sent Jehudi son of Nethaniah son of Shelemiah son of Cushi to say to Baruch, "Bring the scroll that you read in the hearing of the

NIV

So Baruch read it to them. ¹⁶When they heard all these words, they looked at each other in fear and said to Baruch, "We must report all these words to the king." ¹⁷Then they asked Baruch, "Tell us, how did you come to write all this? Did Jeremiah dictate it?"

¹⁸"Yes," Baruch replied, "he dictated all these words to me, and I wrote them in ink on the scroll."

¹⁹Then the officials said to Baruch, "You and Jeremiah, go and hide. Don't let anyone know where you are."

²⁰After they put the scroll in the room of Elishama the secretary, they went to the king in the courtyard and reported everything to him. ²¹The king sent Jehudi to get the scroll, and Jehudi brought it from the room of Elishama the secretary and read it to the king and all the officials standing beside him. ²²It was the ninth month and the king was sitting in the winter apartment, with a fire burning in the firepot in front of him. ²³Whenever Jehudi had read three or four columns of the scroll, the king cut them off with a scribe's knife and threw them into the firepot, until the entire scroll was burned in the fire. ²⁴The king and all his attendants who heard all these words showed no fear, nor did they tear their clothes. ²⁵Even though Elnathan, Delaiah and Gemariah urged the king not to burn the scroll, he would not listen to them. ²⁶Instead, the king commanded Jerahmeel, a son of the king, Seraiah son of Azriel and Shelemiah son of Abdeel to arrest Baruch the scribe and Jeremiah the prophet. But the LORD had hidden them.

²⁷After the king burned the scroll containing the words that Baruch had written at Jeremiah's dictation, the word of the LORD came to Jeremiah: ²⁸"Take another scroll and write on it all the words that were on the first scroll, which Jehoiakim king of Judah burned up. ²⁹Also tell Jehoiakim king of Judah, 'This is what the LORD says: You burned that scroll and said, "Why did you write on it that the king of Babylon would certainly come and destroy this land and cut off both men and animals from it?" ³⁰Therefore, this is what the LORD says about Jehoiakim king of Judah: He will have no one to sit on the throne of David; his body will be thrown out and exposed

NRSV

people, and come." So Baruch son of Neriah took the scroll in his hand and came to them. ¹⁵And they said to him, "Sit down and read it to us." So Baruch read it to them. ¹⁶When they heard all the words, they turned to one another in alarm, and said to Baruch, "We certainly must report all these words to the king." ¹⁷Then they questioned Baruch, "Tell us now, how did you write all these words? Was it at his dictation?" ¹⁸Baruch answered them, "He dictated all these words to me, and I wrote them with ink on the scroll." ¹⁹Then the officials said to Baruch, "Go and hide, you and Jeremiah, and let no one know where you are."

²⁰Leaving the scroll in the chamber of Elishama the secretary, they went to the court of the king; and they reported all the words to the king. ²¹Then the king sent Jehudi to get the scroll, and he took it from the chamber of Elishama the secretary; and Jehudi read it to the king and all the officials who stood beside the king. ²²Now the king was sitting in his winter apartment (it was the ninth month), and there was a fire burning in the brazier before him. ²³As Jehudi read three or four columns, the king*a* would cut them off with a penknife and throw them into the fire in the brazier, until the entire scroll was consumed in the fire that was in the brazier. ²⁴Yet neither the king, nor any of his servants who heard all these words, was alarmed, nor did they tear their garments. ²⁵Even when Elnathan and Delaiah and Gemariah urged the king not to burn the scroll, he would not listen to them. ²⁶And the king commanded Jerahmeel the king's son and Seraiah son of Azriel and Shelemiah son of Abdeel to arrest the secretary Baruch and the prophet Jeremiah. But the LORD hid them.

²⁷Now, after the king had burned the scroll with the words that Baruch wrote at Jeremiah's dictation, the word of the LORD came to Jeremiah: ²⁸Take another scroll and write on it all the former words that were in the first scroll, which King Jehoiakim of Judah has burned. ²⁹And concerning King Jehoiakim of Judah you shall say: Thus says the LORD, You have dared to burn this scroll, saying, Why have you written in it that the king of

*a*Heb *he*

NIV

to the heat by day and the frost by night. ³¹I will punish him and his children and his attendants for their wickedness; I will bring on them and those living in Jerusalem and the people of Judah every disaster I pronounced against them, because they have not listened.' "

³²So Jeremiah took another scroll and gave it to the scribe Baruch son of Neriah, and as Jeremiah dictated, Baruch wrote on it all the words of the scroll that Jehoiakim king of Judah had burned in the fire. And many similar words were added to them.

NRSV

Babylon will certainly come and destroy this land, and will cut off from it human beings and animals? ³⁰Therefore thus says the LORD concerning King Jehoiakim of Judah: He shall have no one to sit upon the throne of David, and his dead body shall be cast out to the heat by day and the frost by night. ³¹And I will punish him and his offspring and his servants for their iniquity; I will bring on them, and on the inhabitants of Jerusalem, and on the people of Judah, all the disasters with which I have threatened them—but they would not listen.

32Then Jeremiah took another scroll and gave it to the secretary Baruch son of Neriah, who wrote on it at Jeremiah's dictation all the words of the scroll that King Jehoiakim of Judah had burned in the fire; and many similar words were added to them.

COMMENTARY

The function of this chapter as a transitional conclusion to the sequence of chaps. 26–35 and the opening of chaps. 37–45 is described in the Overview to chaps. 26–36. While this chapter looks forward and forms with chap. 45 a bracket around chaps. 37–44 (note, e.g., the reference in chap. 45 to the event that is described in detail in chap. 36), it also looks back to chap. 25, with its reference to the fourth year of Jehoiakim, in a sense nailing the coffin shut on the kingdom of Judah with its report of Jehoiakim's calm and deliberate dismissal of the prophet's words of accusation. While the Book of Comfort tells of a future beyond the judgment, the chapters that follow this one assume that the end is near. Why that end is unalterable is nowhere more clearly delineated than in Jehoiakim's reaction to the reading of Jeremiah's judgment speeches, which had been recorded by his scribe Baruch.

If Jeremiah 27–28 is a classic instance of the conflict between true and false prophet, this chapter, without ever bringing the prophet and the king into direct contact, provides a classic case of the confrontation between the prophetic word and royal power, confirming that royal power cannot overcome the prophetic word. We should read

these verses, therefore, with an ear to their political as well as theological overtones. While the chapter seems to couch everything theologically in terms of human sin and divine judgment, we may assume that Jehoiakim's reaction to the reading of the prophetic scroll and his attempt to arrest the prophet and his scribe is tied to the pro-Babylonian policy with which they have been associated (see esp. chaps. 27; 29; and 43:1-7).

36:1-8. The reference to the "fourth year of Jehoiakim" (v. 1) three times at pivotal points in the book of Jeremiah underscores the significance of that moment. It is a time when Jeremiah's oracles over many years (chap. 25 indicates it is twenty-three years) have been summarized (chap. 26) and written down (chaps. 36 and 45). According to chaps. 25 and following, it was possible that repentance and submission to Babylon might bring change from the future announced in the judgment oracles. In the opening verses of chap. 36, that possibility is still there. The inscription of Jeremiah's oracles offers an opportunity for the kingdom of Judah to read, hear, listen to, and reflect upon the extensive record of their disobedience. According to chap. 36, Jehoiakim's response signals the end of that possibility.

This scroll constituted a full collection of Jeremiah's oracles, since it incorporated oracles addressed to the northern kingdom, Israel, to the southern kingdom, Judah, and to other nations. (The oracles concerning the other nations occur later in the Hebrew form of the book of Jeremiah but are located after 25:13*a* in the Greek version.) The purpose of this collection is explicit: to evoke repentance on the part of the Judeans, a repentance that will lead to divine forgiveness and an avoidance of the judgment that is sure to come. We may assume that the inscription of these oracles is intended to preserve them as a faithful record against which the future can be checked (cf. Isa 8:16-22), especially in the light of the significant conflict between Jeremiah and the other prophets about that future.

We know little of Baruch except that he was Jeremiah's secretary, a kind of administrative assistant who helped him in various ways, including acting on Jeremiah's behalf (v. 5; cf. 32:9-16; 45:1-5). Jeremiah 43:3 suggests that Baruch may have played a prominent role, since he was accused of being the real source of Jeremiah's pro-Babylonian policy.[190] A seal impression bearing Baruch's insignia has been discovered on a collection of documents from the seventh century; seal impressions of two other figures mentioned in this chapter, Gemariah (vv. 10-11) and Jerahmeel (v. 26), have been found as well.[191]

36:9-26. Baruch's reading from the scroll of Jeremiah's oracles takes place in public at a religious occasion: in the Temple on a fast day before citizens of Jerusalem and those coming from the outlying towns. The fullness of the prophetic word that is read is matched by the totality of the community that is forced to listen: all the people of Jerusalem and all the people of Judah. This large contingent does not include the chief officials of the court, who are off by themselves in one of the administrative offices of the palaces. When word is reported to them of the contents of the scroll, they insist on a personal presentation by Baruch.

The text attests to the increasingly intense affect of the scroll. Each reading of the scroll effects a greater reaction. In the first instance, we hear nothing of the reaction of the people (this text is about royal reaction to prophetic proclamation; cf. chap. 26), but we are told of the quick movement of a palace official to to report to other officials and scribes. Their reaction is great alarm or fear, and they decide that they must report this to the king (v. 16). The king responds arrogantly and defiantly destroys the scroll (v. 23). At this point, the response no longer incorporates any fear or alarm on the part of the king and his servants, as the text notes explicitly (v. 24).

The effect of reading the words of the Lord/Jeremiah (cf. "the words of Jeremiah" in vv. 8, 10 with "the words of the Lord" in v. 11) is both complex and intense. The text makes a distinction between the "secretary" or "scribe" and the "officials" in the secretary's chamber, on the one hand (vv. 11-14), and the king's "servants," on the other hand (v. 24). Both groups are in the palace and thus are involved in the royal court. But the former group has respect for the scribe Baruch and for the words on the scroll. They react in horror at the king's burning of the scroll, pleading with him not to do so. Finally, they protect Jeremiah and Baruch—and thus the words of the Lord—by telling them to hide. The latter group are totally identified with the king's disdain of the divine words on the scroll. The scribes and officials are fully involved in the royal establishment, but they are more ambivalent in their reaction than were the king's servants. There is a sense that the scroll is serious business, to be respected and heeded.[192]

Finally, one must take special note of v. 24 for the way in which it evokes a recollection of the discovery of another scroll, "the book of the law" found in the Temple during the reign of Jehoiakim's father, Josiah (2 Kings 22).[193] The accounts of the reading of Jeremiah's scroll and of the finding of the book of the law, though different, share similarities. In both cases, the scroll is

190. On the significance of Baruch, see Walter Brueggemann, *A Commentary on Jeremiah: Exile and Homecoming* (Grand Rapids: Eerdmans, 1998) 338-44; and James Muilenburg, "Baruch the Scribe," in *Proclamation and Presence: Old Testament Essays in Honour of Gwynne Henton Davies,* ed. John I. Durham and J. Roy Porter (Richmond: John Knox, 1970) 215-38.

191. For references, see William L. Holladay, *Jeremiah 2,* Hermeneia (Philadelphia: Fortress, 1989) 215, 257, and 260.

192. J. Andrew Dearman has sought to show how this chapter, along with others, reflects a scribal "support group" around Jeremiah that was critical in the preservation of the prophet's words. See Dearman, "My Servants the Scribes: Composition and Context in Jeremiah 36," *JBL* 109 (1990) 403-21.

193. Charles D. Isbell, "II Kings 22:3–23:24 and Jeremiah 36: A Stylistic Comparison," *JSOT* 8 (1978) 33-45.

understood by a scribal official or secretary to be of great importance and something that the king would need to know about. In both cases the document is read to the king. At that point, the narratives point to a sharp contrast. When Josiah heard the words of the book of the law read, he immediately "tore" his garments (2 Kgs 22:11), was penitent, and humbled himself before the Lord (2 Kgs 22:19), initiating a major reform of the religious practices of Judah. Jehoiakim and his servants, therefore, are contrasted not only with the officials and scribes who were alarmed at Jeremiah's words but also with his own father. This time there is no royal penitence manifest in the tearing (v. 24) of the garments and royal reform of the nation's life—only utter dismissal and disdain for the divine word in the "tearing" (v. 23) of the scroll into pieces.

36:27-32. The final verses of this chapter signal the futility of the king's action and the finality of the divine judgment. Henceforth we will hear no more of repentance and forgiveness, which still remain a possibility at the beginning of the chapter (v. 3). Jehoiakim's actions have sealed the death warrant of the nation. A judgment speech is pronounced upon him and his servants because "they would not listen" (v. 31; cf. vv. 24-25) and burned

the scroll (v. 29). As is often the case, the judgment is a kind of poetic justice so that "the king's body will be 'cast out' [מֻשְׁלֶכֶת *muš leket*] to the heat by day [לַחֹרֶב בַּיּוֹם *laḥōreb bayyôm*] and the frost by night, he who could now sit comfortably in his winter house [בֵּית הַחֹרֶף *bêt haḥōrep,* v. 22], and who 'threw' [הִשְׁלִיךְ *hašlēk*] the cut scroll into the fire!" (v. 23).[194] The text focuses on the king and his servants, for their reaction to the scroll is what this incident is all about. But the text was first heard by the people—and like king, like people. The threatened judgments will come upon the people of Judah and Jerusalem, not just the royal power and his courtiers.

But the Word of the Lord endures. The burning of the scroll has not silenced it. Along with the command to speak an oracle against the king, the Lord calls for a new inscription of Jeremiah's prophetic oracles. Not only has the king failed to destroy the scroll, and thus the force of the oracles written on it, but the second scroll becomes the basis for a much larger collection and may be seen as the beginning of the book of Jeremiah as we know it, the permanent record of the word of the Lord through the words of this prophet.

194. Martin Kessler, "Form-Critical Suggestions on Jer 36," *CBQ* 28 (1966) 398.

REFLECTIONS

1. The writing down of Jeremiah's oracles in a complete collection on a single scroll is clearly a major step in the process of transforming his words into Scripture for the guidance of a later community. We are let in on the process by which a prophetic book comes into being and also on its function as a book. Not only are we told of the inscription of "all the words" (36:2) of the prophet up to a certain point and covering probably some twenty years of prophecy, but we are also informed that this scroll continued to grow as many more oracles were added to it (36:32).

These words of old become Scripture only as they are recorded to be held and read and reflected upon. Recorded prophetic oracles can continue to have effect beyond their time of deliverance. Some of the oracles in Baruch's scroll would have been uttered many years earlier. But they are still capable of touching the minds and hearts of the people; they are still functioning as the word of the Lord to the people. That is what Scripture is all about—the preservation of the words and deeds, of the oracles and stories by which the community was first instructed, for the sake of a later audience who will need them to know rightly what the Lord is doing and what the Lord desires of the community that lives under the divine rule. It is ironic that the act of the king to nullify, destroy, and dismiss the words of the prophet accomplishes instead their permanent inscription as a guide to later rulers and "all the people."

2. In this chapter, we learn that the Bible was a dangerous and threatening document right from the start. There is a political movement in the text that needs to be noted. The reading of the scroll to the people in a religious context triggers an immediate movement of an official to the palace (36:12), which in turn triggers a further and more alarmed movement of an official to the king himself. The prophetic words are understood to have potent political implications ("We must tell the king"). What it was specifically about the words of the prophet that alarmed the officials is not clear, but the political potency of the divine word is evident at every turn. These are not religious thoughts confined to some spiritual dimension of life. Like Amos's words in the time of Jeroboam II, Jeremiah's oracles have implications for the larger life of the community and for the fate of the leadership. When the representative of the Lord's way speaks truth to power and calls for the community to enact justice, to turn from its ways of idolatry, acquisitiveness, and indifference to the teaching of the Lord, there is going to be resistance. These things cannot happen without affecting the status quo both socially and politically. One may expect that when such potent words are read in a religious context, they will not be contained there. They will explode into the larger political climate, creating anxiety and resistance. No better indication of that is needed than the immediate counsel of the governmental officials to Baruch: You and Jeremiah had better hide.

When the word of judgment comes, it is meant to sound an alarm in the populace and among the rulers of the land. Being frightened upon hearing the divine words is an appropriate and healthy response. The problem the text reports is not the fright of the officials and scribes but the lack of a right response and defiance from the political leader and those around him. Political authority is rarely willing to listen to uncomfortable words, especially those that threaten its continued control and power, as Jeremiah's words did. The king did, indeed, hear the words of the scroll—but only certain ones, only the ones about Babylonian destruction and exile. The divine words calling for reform, repentance, obedience, and justice are ignored, and all that breaks through the selective hearing and resistance of political power are those words that threaten the present order.

The pleas of the officials and scribes are insufficient to deter royal arrogance, but their modest resistance to the king is an instance of human response affecting the future, even if it seems very slight and ineffective at the time. Their response, limited by the bureaucratic context of their positions, does nothing to change the political or religious situation, nothing to deter the king from his corrupt ways and nothing to fend off the inevitable judgment. But it does protect the prophet and his scribe, who live another day to rewrite the scroll and so preserve for posterity the divine word. The narrative is an example of the way prophetic proclamation can find some support within the societal structures even when the primary forces of power are set against any hearing of the call to repentance and reform.

JEREMIAH 37:1–45:5

THE LAST DAYS OF A KINGDOM AND A PROPHET

OVERVIEW

As chap. 36 came to a close, the divine decision to bring judgment upon the Lord's disobedient people became irrevocable (though it is still possible for individuals to save their lives by surrendering to the Babylonians). But its accomplishment remains to be spelled out. The chapters that complete the story of Jeremiah and the fall of Judah focus on the last days, on the destruction of Judah and Jerusalem and the exile of its leaders and people. They recount incidents from the final moments of the kingdom as well as from the last recorded events of Jeremiah's prophecy. The prophet has never been far out of the picture, even if his words have been the primary focus of attention. If the preceding sections of the book have put the weight on his prophetic proclamation in word and deed, this section brings the prophet and the things that happen to him and around him more into view while demonstrating that, to the end, his proclamation of the divine word to the people remains central.

Chapters 37–39 focus particularly on King Zedekiah and his relation to Jeremiah, ending with a detailed report of the king's unhappy fate and a word from the Lord about fulfilling "my words against this city." A salvation oracle for Ebed-melech the Ethiopian, who saves Jeremiah's life and thus demonstrates that he "trusted in me" (38:7-13; 39:15-18), anticipates that Jeremiah's scribe, like Ebed-melech, will be given his life as "a prize of war" (39:18; 45:5). Only such individual deliverance is possible (38:2).

Chapters 40–41 move the reader into events that follow closely after the Babylonian conquest of Jerusalem. They narrate the appointment of Gedaliah, son of Ahikam, as governor of the land of Judah, his subsequent murder by Ishmael, an officer of the king and member of the royal family,

and the avenging of his murder by Johanon son of Kareah, who had suspected Ishmael's conspiratorial intent.

The next two chapters (42–43) move the scene from Judah to Egypt as they recount Johanon's going to Egypt, despite God's explicit word that to do so would mean death. This section ends with the people going to Egypt and a symbolic action by the prophet that seals the fate of the—again—disobedient people. Chapter 44 recounts a single episode from the Egyptian period before this section about the last days of the nation and the prophet concludes in chap. 45 with a salvation oracle promising Baruch that he will survive the conflict with the Babylonians. This chapter, set in the same year as chap. 36 and referring to the scroll that Jeremiah dictated to Baruch, concludes the narrative about the end of Judah and highlights another major dimension of this literary block: the existence of a remnant that survives the Babylonian conquest of Judah. Here the story of Jeremiah as God's servant comes to an end, except for a brief reference at the conclusion of chap. 51, which, like chap. 45, focuses on the writing down of Jeremiah's oracles.

The reader of these chapters will note the prominence of realistic detail in the narratives, especially in chaps. 37–38. Some have thought this feature reflects an eyewitness report and have suggested that Jeremiah's scribe, Baruch, may be the source for some or much of this material. That is a plausible suggestion, but only that. We can tell no more about the authorship of this material than for most of the book. It does appear, however, that someone close to the scene, which could include the prophet himself, is responsible for at least the beginning stages of transmission of these chapters.

JEREMIAH 37:1–39:18, A KING AND A PROPHET

NIV

37 Zedekiah son of Josiah was made king of Judah by Nebuchadnezzar king of Babylon; he reigned in place of Jehoiachin[a] son of Jehoiakim. [2]Neither he nor his attendants nor the people of the land paid any attention to the words the LORD had spoken through Jeremiah the prophet.

[3]King Zedekiah, however, sent Jehucal son of Shelemiah with the priest Zephaniah son of Maaseiah to Jeremiah the prophet with this message: "Please pray to the LORD our God for us."

[4]Now Jeremiah was free to come and go among the people, for he had not yet been put in prison. [5]Pharaoh's army had marched out of Egypt, and when the Babylonians[b] who were besieging Jerusalem heard the report about them, they withdrew from Jerusalem.

[6]Then the word of the LORD came to Jeremiah the prophet: [7]"This is what the LORD, the God of Israel, says: Tell the king of Judah, who sent you to inquire of me, 'Pharaoh's army, which has marched out to support you, will go back to its own land, to Egypt. [8]Then the Babylonians will return and attack this city; they will capture it and burn it down.'

[9]"This is what the LORD says: Do not deceive yourselves, thinking, 'The Babylonians will surely leave us.' They will not! [10]Even if you were to defeat the entire Babylonian[c] army that is attacking you and only wounded men were left in their tents, they would come out and burn this city down."

[11]After the Babylonian army had withdrawn from Jerusalem because of Pharaoh's army, [12]Jeremiah started to leave the city to go to the territory of Benjamin to get his share of the property among the people there. [13]But when he reached the Benjamin Gate, the captain of the guard, whose name was Irijah son of Shelemiah, the son of Hananiah, arrested him and said, "You are deserting to the Babylonians!"

[14]"That's not true!" Jeremiah said. "I am not deserting to the Babylonians." But Irijah would

NRSV

37 Zedekiah son of Josiah, whom King Nebuchadrezzar of Babylon made king in the land of Judah, succeeded Coniah son of Jehoiakim. [2]But neither he nor his servants nor the people of the land listened to the words of the LORD that he spoke through the prophet Jeremiah.

3King Zedekiah sent Jehucal son of Shelemiah and the priest Zephaniah son of Maaseiah to the prophet Jeremiah saying, "Please pray for us to the LORD our God." [4]Now Jeremiah was still going in and out among the people, for he had not yet been put in prison. [5]Meanwhile, the army of Pharaoh had come out of Egypt; and when the Chaldeans who were besieging Jerusalem heard news of them, they withdrew from Jerusalem.

6Then the word of the LORD came to the prophet Jeremiah: [7]Thus says the LORD, God of Israel: This is what the two of you shall say to the king of Judah, who sent you to me to inquire of me: Pharaoh's army, which set out to help you, is going to return to its own land, to Egypt. [8]And the Chaldeans shall return and fight against this city; they shall take it and burn it with fire. [9]Thus says the LORD: Do not deceive yourselves, saying, "The Chaldeans will surely go away from us," for they will not go away. [10]Even if you defeated the whole army of Chaldeans who are fighting against you, and there remained of them only wounded men in their tents, they would rise up and burn this city with fire.

11Now when the Chaldean army had withdrawn from Jerusalem at the approach of Pharaoh's army, [12]Jeremiah set out from Jerusalem to go to the land of Benjamin to receive his share of property[a] among the people there. [13]When he reached the Benjamin Gate, a sentinel there named Irijah son of Shelemiah son of Hananiah arrested the prophet Jeremiah saying, "You are deserting to the Chaldeans." [14]And Jeremiah said, "That is a lie; I am not deserting to the Chaldeans." But Irijah would not listen to him, and arrested Jeremiah and brought him to the officials. [15]The officials were enraged at Jeremiah, and they beat him and imprisoned him in the

---

a1 Hebrew *Coniah,* a variant of *Jehoiachin*   *b5* Or *Chaldeans;* also in verses 8, 9, 13 and 14   *c10* Or *Chaldean;* also in verse 11

*a*Meaning of Heb uncertain

not listen to him; instead, he arrested Jeremiah and brought him to the officials. ¹⁵They were angry with Jeremiah and had him beaten and imprisoned in the house of Jonathan the secretary, which they had made into a prison.

¹⁶Jeremiah was put into a vaulted cell in a dungeon, where he remained a long time. ¹⁷Then King Zedekiah sent for him and had him brought to the palace, where he asked him privately, "Is there any word from the Lord?"

"Yes," Jeremiah replied, "you will be handed over to the king of Babylon."

¹⁸Then Jeremiah said to King Zedekiah, "What crime have I committed against you or your officials or this people, that you have put me in prison? ¹⁹Where are your prophets who prophesied to you, 'The king of Babylon will not attack you or this land'? ²⁰But now, my lord the king, please listen. Let me bring my petition before you: Do not send me back to the house of Jonathan the secretary, or I will die there."

²¹King Zedekiah then gave orders for Jeremiah to be placed in the courtyard of the guard and given bread from the street of the bakers each day until all the bread in the city was gone. So Jeremiah remained in the courtyard of the guard.

38 Shephatiah son of Mattan, Gedaliah son of Pashhur, Jehucal[a] son of Shelemiah, and Pashhur son of Malkijah heard what Jeremiah was telling all the people when he said, ²"This is what the Lord says: 'Whoever stays in this city will die by the sword, famine or plague, but whoever goes over to the Babylonians[b] will live. He will escape with his life; he will live.' ³And this is what the Lord says: 'This city will certainly be handed over to the army of the king of Babylon, who will capture it.' "

⁴Then the officials said to the king, "This man should be put to death. He is discouraging the soldiers who are left in this city, as well as all the people, by the things he is saying to them. This man is not seeking the good of these people but their ruin."

⁵"He is in your hands," King Zedekiah answered. "The king can do nothing to oppose you."

ᵃ1 Hebrew *Jucal,* a variant of *Jehucal*   ᵇ2 Or *Chaldeans;* also in verses 18, 19 and 23

house of the secretary Jonathan, for it had been made a prison. ¹⁶Thus Jeremiah was put in the cistern house, in the cells, and remained there many days.

¹⁷Then King Zedekiah sent for him, and received him. The king questioned him secretly in his house, and said, "Is there any word from the Lord?" Jeremiah said, "There is!" Then he said, "You shall be handed over to the king of Babylon." ¹⁸Jeremiah also said to King Zedekiah, "What wrong have I done to you or your servants or this people, that you have put me in prison? ¹⁹Where are your prophets who prophesied to you, saying, 'The king of Babylon will not come against you and against this land'? ²⁰Now please hear me, my lord king: be good enough to listen to my plea, and do not send me back to the house of the secretary Jonathan to die there." ²¹So King Zedekiah gave orders, and they committed Jeremiah to the court of the guard; and a loaf of bread was given him daily from the bakers' street, until all the bread of the city was gone. So Jeremiah remained in the court of the guard.

38 Now Shephatiah son of Mattan, Gedaliah son of Pashhur, Jucal son of Shelemiah, and Pashhur son of Malchiah heard the words that Jeremiah was saying to all the people, ²Thus says the Lord, Those who stay in this city shall die by the sword, by famine, and by pestilence; but those who go out to the Chaldeans shall live; they shall have their lives as a prize of war, and live. ³Thus says the Lord, This city shall surely be handed over to the army of the king of Babylon and be taken. ⁴Then the officials said to the king, "This man ought to be put to death, because he is discouraging the soldiers who are left in this city, and all the people, by speaking such words to them. For this man is not seeking the welfare of this people, but their harm." ⁵King Zedekiah said, "Here he is; he is in your hands; for the king is powerless against you." ⁶So they took Jeremiah and threw him into the cistern of Malchiah, the king's son, which was in the court of the guard, letting Jeremiah down by ropes. Now there was no water in the cistern, but only mud, and Jeremiah sank in the mud.

⁷Ebed-melech the Ethiopian,[a] a eunuch in the

ᵃOr *Nubian;* Heb *Cushite*

NIV

⁶So they took Jeremiah and put him into the cistern of Malkijah, the king's son, which was in the courtyard of the guard. They lowered Jeremiah by ropes into the cistern; it had no water in it, only mud, and Jeremiah sank down into the mud.

⁷But Ebed-Melech, a Cushite,ᵃ an officialᵇ in the royal palace, heard that they had put Jeremiah into the cistern. While the king was sitting in the Benjamin Gate, ⁸Ebed-Melech went out of the palace and said to him, ⁹"My lord the king, these men have acted wickedly in all they have done to Jeremiah the prophet. They have thrown him into a cistern, where he will starve to death when there is no longer any bread in the city."

¹⁰Then the king commanded Ebed-Melech the Cushite, "Take thirty men from here with you and lift Jeremiah the prophet out of the cistern before he dies."

¹¹So Ebed-Melech took the men with him and went to a room under the treasury in the palace. He took some old rags and worn-out clothes from there and let them down with ropes to Jeremiah in the cistern. ¹²Ebed-Melech the Cushite said to Jeremiah, "Put these old rags and worn-out clothes under your arms to pad the ropes." Jeremiah did so, ¹³and they pulled him up with the ropes and lifted him out of the cistern. And Jeremiah remained in the courtyard of the guard.

¹⁴Then King Zedekiah sent for Jeremiah the prophet and had him brought to the third entrance to the temple of the LORD. "I am going to ask you something," the king said to Jeremiah. "Do not hide anything from me."

¹⁵Jeremiah said to Zedekiah, "If I give you an answer, will you not kill me? Even if I did give you counsel, you would not listen to me."

¹⁶But King Zedekiah swore this oath secretly to Jeremiah: "As surely as the LORD lives, who has given us breath, I will neither kill you nor hand you over to those who are seeking your life."

¹⁷Then Jeremiah said to Zedekiah, "This is what the LORD God Almighty, the God of Israel, says: 'If you surrender to the officers of the king of Babylon, your life will be spared and this city will not be burned down; you and your family will live. ¹⁸But if you will not surrender to the officers

ᵃ7 Probably from the upper Nile region   ᵇ7 Or *a eunuch*

NRSV

king's house, heard that they had put Jeremiah into the cistern. The king happened to be sitting at the Benjamin Gate, ⁸So Ebed-melech left the king's house and spoke to the king, ⁹"My lord king, these men have acted wickedly in all they did to the prophet Jeremiah by throwing him into the cistern to die there of hunger, for there is no bread left in the city." ¹⁰Then the king commanded Ebed-melech the Ethiopian,ᵃ "Take three men with you from here, and pull the prophet Jeremiah up from the cistern before he dies." ¹¹So Ebed-melech took the men with him and went to the house of the king, to a wardrobe ofᵇ the storehouse, and took from there old rags and worn-out clothes, which he let down to Jeremiah in the cistern by ropes. ¹²Then Ebed-melech the Ethiopianᵃ said to Jeremiah, "Just put the rags and clothes between your armpits and the ropes." Jeremiah did so. ¹³Then they drew Jeremiah up by the ropes and pulled him out of the cistern. And Jeremiah remained in the court of the guard.

14King Zedekiah sent for the prophet Jeremiah and received him at the third entrance of the temple of the LORD. The king said to Jeremiah, "I have something to ask you; do not hide anything from me." ¹⁵Jeremiah said to Zedekiah, "If I tell you, you will put me to death, will you not? And if I give you advice, you will not listen to me." ¹⁶So King Zedekiah swore an oath in secret to Jeremiah, "As the LORD lives, who gave us our lives, I will not put you to death or hand you over to these men who seek your life."

17Then Jeremiah said to Zedekiah, "Thus says the LORD, the God of hosts, the God of Israel, If you will only surrender to the officials of the king of Babylon, then your life shall be spared, and this city shall not be burned with fire, and you and your house shall live. ¹⁸But if you do not surrender to the officials of the king of Babylon, then this city shall be handed over to the Chaldeans, and they shall burn it with fire, and you yourself shall not escape from their hand." ¹⁹King Zedekiah said to Jeremiah, "I am afraid of the Judeans who have deserted to the Chaldeans, for I might be handed over to them and they would abuse me." ²⁰Jeremiah said, "That will not happen. Just obey the voice of the LORD in what I say to you, and it

ᵃOr *Nubian;* Heb *Cushite*   ᵇCn: Heb *to under*

NIV

of the king of Babylon, this city will be handed over to the Babylonians and they will burn it down; you yourself will not escape from their hands.' "

¹⁹King Zedekiah said to Jeremiah, "I am afraid of the Jews who have gone over to the Babylonians, for the Babylonians may hand me over to them and they will mistreat me."

²⁰"They will not hand you over," Jeremiah replied. "Obey the Lord by doing what I tell you. Then it will go well with you, and your life will be spared. ²¹But if you refuse to surrender, this is what the Lord has revealed to me: ²²All the women left in the palace of the king of Judah will be brought out to the officials of the king of Babylon. Those women will say to you:

" 'They misled you and overcame you—
    those trusted friends of yours.
Your feet are sunk in the mud;
    your friends have deserted you.'

²³"All your wives and children will be brought out to the Babylonians. You yourself will not escape from their hands but will be captured by the king of Babylon; and this city will* be burned down."

²⁴Then Zedekiah said to Jeremiah, "Do not let anyone know about this conversation, or you may die. ²⁵If the officials hear that I talked with you, and they come to you and say, 'Tell us what you said to the king and what the king said to you; do not hide it from us or we will kill you,' ²⁶then tell them, 'I was pleading with the king not to send me back to Jonathan's house to die there.' "

²⁷All the officials did come to Jeremiah and question him, and he told them everything the king had ordered him to say. So they said no more to him, for no one had heard his conversation with the king.

²⁸And Jeremiah remained in the courtyard of the guard until the day Jerusalem was captured.

39 This is how Jerusalem was taken: ¹In the ninth year of Zedekiah king of Judah, in the tenth month, Nebuchadnezzar king of Babylon marched against Jerusalem with his whole army and laid siege to it. ²And on the ninth day of the fourth month of Zedekiah's eleventh year, the city

*23 Or *and you will cause this city to*

NRSV

shall go well with you, and your life shall be spared. ²¹But if you are determined not to surrender, this is what the Lord has shown me— ²²a vision of all the women remaining in the house of the king of Judah being led out to the officials of the king of Babylon and saying,

'Your trusted friends have seduced you
    and have overcome you;
Now that your feet are stuck in the mud,
    they desert you.'

²³All your wives and your children shall be led out to the Chaldeans, and you yourself shall not escape from their hand, but shall be seized by the king of Babylon; and this city shall be burned with fire."

24Then Zedekiah said to Jeremiah, "Do not let anyone else know of this conversation, or you will die. ²⁵If the officials should hear that I have spoken with you, and they should come and say to you, 'Just tell us what you said to the king; do not conceal it from us, or we will put you to death. What did the king say to you?' ²⁶then you shall say to them, 'I was presenting my plea to the king not to send me back to the house of Jonathan to die there.' " ²⁷All the officials did come to Jeremiah and questioned him; and he answered them in the very words the king had commanded. So they stopped questioning him, for the conversation had not been overheard. ²⁸And Jeremiah remained in the court of the guard until the day that Jerusalem was taken.

39 In the ninth year of King Zedekiah of Judah, in the tenth month, King Nebuchadrezzar of Babylon and all his army came against Jerusalem and besieged it; ²in the eleventh year of Zedekiah, in the fourth month, on the ninth day of the month, a breach was made in the city. ³When Jerusalem was taken,* all the officials of the king of Babylon came and sat in the middle gate: Nergal-sharezer, Samgar-nebo, Sarsechim the Rabsaris, Nergal-sharezer the Rabmag, with all the rest of the officials of the king of Babylon. ⁴When King Zedekiah of Judah and all the soldiers saw them, they fled, going out of the city at night by way of the king's garden through the gate between the two walls; and they went toward the Arabah. ⁵But the army of the Chaldeans pursued

*This clause has been transposed from 38.28

NIV

wall was broken through. ³Then all the officials of the king of Babylon came and took seats in the Middle Gate: Nergal-Sharezer of Samgar, Nebo-Sarsekim[a] a chief officer, Nergal-Sharezer a high official and all the other officials of the king of Babylon. ⁴When Zedekiah king of Judah and all the soldiers saw them, they fled; they left the city at night by way of the king's garden, through the gate between the two walls, and headed toward the Arabah.[b]

⁵But the Babylonian[d] army pursued them and overtook Zedekiah in the plains of Jericho. They captured him and took him to Nebuchadnezzar king of Babylon at Riblah in the land of Hamath, where he pronounced sentence on him. ⁶There at Riblah the king of Babylon slaughtered the sons of Zedekiah before his eyes and also killed all the nobles of Judah. ⁷Then he put out Zedekiah's eyes and bound him with bronze shackles to take him to Babylon.

⁸The Babylonians[c] set fire to the royal palace and the houses of the people and broke down the walls of Jerusalem. ⁹Nebuzaradan commander of the imperial guard carried into exile to Babylon the people who remained in the city, along with those who had gone over to him, and the rest of the people. ¹⁰But Nebuzaradan the commander of the guard left behind in the land of Judah some of the poor people, who owned nothing; and at that time he gave them vineyards and fields.

¹¹Now Nebuchadnezzar king of Babylon had given these orders about Jeremiah through Nebuzaradan commander of the imperial guard: ¹²"Take him and look after him; don't harm him but do for him whatever he asks." ¹³So Nebuzaradan the commander of the guard, Nebushazban a chief officer, Nergal-Sharezer a high official and all the other officers of the king of Babylon ¹⁴sent and had Jeremiah taken out of the courtyard of the guard. They turned him over to Gedaliah son of Ahikam, the son of Shaphan, to take him back to his home. So he remained among his own people.

¹⁵While Jeremiah had been confined in the courtyard of the guard, the word of the LORD came to him: ¹⁶"Go and tell Ebed-Melech the

*3 Or *Nergal-Sharezer, Samgar-Nebo, Sarsekim*   *4 Or *the Jordan Valley*   *5, 18 Or *Chaldean*   *8 Or *Chaldeans*

NRSV

them, and overtook Zedekiah in the plains of Jericho; and when they had taken him, they brought him up to King Nebuchadrezzar of Babylon, at Riblah, in the land of Hamath; and he passed sentence on him. ⁶The king of Babylon slaughtered the sons of Zedekiah at Riblah before his eyes; also the king of Babylon slaughtered all the nobles of Judah. ⁷He put out the eyes of Zedekiah, and bound him in fetters to take him to Babylon. ⁸The Chaldeans burned the king's house and the houses of the people, and broke down the walls of Jerusalem. ⁹Then Nebuzaradan the captain of the guard exiled to Babylon the rest of the people who were left in the city, those who had deserted to him, and the people who remained. ¹⁰Nebuzaradan the captain of the guard left in the land of Judah some of the poor people who owned nothing, and gave them vineyards and fields at the same time.

11King Nebuchadrezzar of Babylon gave command concerning Jeremiah through Nebuzaradan, the captain of the guard, saying, ¹²"Take him, look after him well and do him no harm, but deal with him as he may ask you." ¹³So Nebuzaradan the captain of the guard, Nebushazban the Rabsaris, Nergal-sharezer the Rabmag, and all the chief officers of the king of Babylon sent ¹⁴and took Jeremiah from the court of the guard. They entrusted him to Gedaliah son of Ahikam son of Shaphan to be brought home. So he stayed with his own people.

15The word of the LORD came to Jeremiah while he was confined in the court of the guard: ¹⁶Go and say to Ebed-melech the Ethiopian:[a] Thus says the LORD of hosts, the God of Israel: I am going to fulfill my words against this city for evil and not for good, and they shall be accomplished in your presence on that day. ¹⁷But I will save you on that day, says the LORD, and you shall not be handed over to those whom you dread. ¹⁸For I will surely save you, and you shall not fall by the sword; but you shall have your life as a prize of war, because you have trusted in me, says the LORD.

*Or *Nubian*; Heb *Cushite*

NIV

Cushite, 'This is what the LORD Almighty, the God of Israel, says: I am about to fulfill my words against this city through disaster, not prosperity. At that time they will be fulfilled before your eyes. [17]But I will rescue you on that day, declares the LORD; you will not be handed over to those you fear. [18]I will save you; you will not fall by the sword but will escape with your life, because you trust in me, declares the LORD.' "

COMMENTARY

37:1-2. These verses serve a transitional function in two ways. They move the historical stage abruptly from Jehoiakim through Jehoiachin to the last king of Judah, Zedekiah—placed on the throne by the Babylonians when Jehoiachin was taken into exile but now in rebellion against Babylon—and to the last days of the kingdom (see 2 Kings 24–25; cf. Jeremiah 52). More important, they make it clear that even in the final moments of the southern kingdom the problem that is at the heart of the preceding chapter persists: The king and his court ("his servants") do not listen to the word of the Lord spoken through Jeremiah, and, not surprising, neither do the people (see the Commentary on 36:1-32). The beginning of the final stages of the Judahite story and of the Jeremiah story thus lets the reader know that the outcome of the preceding section (chaps. 26–36), that a nation and a royal dynasty have reached a point of no return, is the presupposition of this last section of narrative about the final days of Judah.

37:3-10. In a report that can only be read ironically after the preceding verses, the king asks Jeremiah to intercede with the Lord. The irony is heightened to the level of hypocrisy by the appeal to "the LORD our God" (v. 3), the language of the Shema (Deut 6:4), whose call for uncompromising loyalty and obedience to the one Lord of Israel has been so utterly ignored by those who now seek the Lord's help. This plea opens up a series of conversations between the king and the prophet that forms a substantial part of chaps. 37–38 (see also chap. 21) and suggests a quite different relation between Jeremiah and Zedekiah than had been the case between the prophet and Jehoiakim.

The narrative then moves quickly to quell any assumption that the relief afforded against the siege of Jerusalem by the fact that the Babylonian army has to turn its attention to the army of Egypt, which has come to the aid of Judah (probably in the summer of 588 BCE), is anything but temporary.[195] The word of the Lord denies any possible connection between Egyptian presence and the appeal of the king for Jeremiah's intercession. Indeed, we do not know whether Jeremiah interceded for the king and the people. Moreover, we know of more than one occasion when the Lord prohibited any such intercession on Jeremiah's part (7:16; 14:11) or refused to pay any attention to it (15:1). The die is cast, and there is no avoiding the fate their own acts have evoked from the hand of the Lord (see v. 2). The point is underscored with the Lord's claim that Judah's doom is so certain that, even if conflict with the Egyptians left the Babylonian army so decimated that all that remained were soldiers lying wounded in their tents, the Babylonians would still succeed in utterly destroying Jerusalem. The hopelessness of the Judean cause against the Babylonians is thus made a further presupposition of the narrative of events that follows in chaps. 37–45.

37:11-16. The extent to which Jeremiah's own story, and more specifically his suffering and oppression at the hands of various officials and leaders of Jerusalem, is a central part of this narrative of Judah's end is now suggested by the report of Jeremiah's beating and imprisonment when he left the city. The prophet is recognized and

195. For the historical background of chaps. 37–45, see John Bright, *Jeremiah,* AB 21 (Garden City, N.Y.: Doubleday, 1965) xlix-liv.

accused of desertion, an accusation that, while false—as Jeremiah insists vehemently—might not be incredible in the light of his frequent call for submission to the Babylonians. The essential point of this brief account is to report the brutal beating and subsequent prolonged imprisonment he received from enraged "officials," presumably seeing him as the source of their troubles. Both his frequent words of doom and his insistence on submission to the Babylonian yoke could well have provoked the wrath of panicked and frustrated officials (cf. 38:4), in this case different from those "officials" named in chap. 36, who were also alarmed by Jeremiah's words but were moved to protect him from royal rage. The story portrays some of the further (personal) ramifications of Jeremiah's ministry, forecast long before in his call (1:19) and reiterated in his dialogue with the Lord (15:20).

37:17-21. Just as the chapter begins with Zedekiah's plea to Jeremiah for intercession, so also it concludes with his appeal to the prophet (this time secretly) for some word from the Lord. And he gets it—bluntly and succinctly. Surely the curt announcement, "You shall be handed over to the king of Babylon," is not what the king wanted to hear. But, unlike the officials in the preceding verses or Jehoiakim in the preceding chapter, he reacts with neither rage nor arrogant dismissal. Indeed, this may have been exactly what he expected to hear, confirmation of his worst fears. We hear nothing of Zedekiah's personal reaction to this unpleasant, but not unlikely, word. Instead, the text goes on to tell of Jeremiah's impassioned plea for relief from his imprisonment, words spoken with fervor and the genuine fear that he might die in the makeshift jail to which he has been confined (v. 15*b*). His appeal is grounded in two realities that he sets before the king: (1) He has done no wrong to anyone and quite specifically not to the king or any of his servants who have imprisoned him, and (2) his unpleasant words of prophecy have proven true in contrast to the assuring words of "*your* prophets," who said that nothing would happen. Jeremiah is thus doubly innocent and righteous. He has prophesied according to the criterion of true prophecy; his words have been confirmed by the events of history (Deut 18:22).

Zedekiah appears to take Jeremiah seriously. Whatever the character of his rule generally, as we shall see in the rest of his story, he does not sub-

ject Jeremiah to the violent fate that so often prophets suffer at the hands of kings. Jeremiah is not released, but Zedekiah orders him moved to a different and more comfortable venue in the court of the guard. The text makes clear that he is given food as long as it is available in Jerusalem. As Brueggemann has observed, such actions indicate an implicit acceptance of the prophet and the validity of his claims.[196] In these last days, the king quietly (the next chapter will show how quietly) acknowledges the prophet and the truthfulness of his claims.

38:1-13. Jeremiah's plight continues to be the focus of attention. The incident reported here does not seem to flow directly from the preceding chapter because it tells of another strong reaction to Jeremiah on the part of officials unhappy with his message and the putting of Jeremiah in the court of the guard. This is the same place he was at the end of chap. 37, thus leading some interpreters to regard this chapter as a duplicate version of chap. 37. Still, there are enough differences to suggest that the narrative is to be read as a separate incident. The incident is similar to that in the preceding chapter because in both harsher treatment is meted out to the prophet on the part of the officials than by the king. But dropping Jeremiah into a waterless, but miry, cistern heightens the harshness of the officials. Ebed-melech thought it would end in a slow and terrible death by starvation. Furthermore, Ebed-melech's report that there is no bread left in the city picks up directly on the final words of chap. 37, which report the king's order that Jeremiah should have bread as long as there was any left in the city. The story thus carries us farther down Jeremiah's rough road and further into the odd relationship between Zedekiah and the prophet.

At the same time, the story of the officials' attack on Jeremiah in this chapter may be read in tandem with the preceding report of their enraged beating of the prophet. Here the reader is given a rationale for such actions. Jeremiah's proclamation of the Lord's insistence that Judah capitulate to the Babylonians is viewed as treasonous. It would have discouraged the troops in battle. How can morale be kept up when a leading religious figure

---

196. Walter Brueggemann, *A Commentary on Jeremiah: Exile and Homecoming* (Grand Rapids: Eerdmans, 1998) 359.

is constantly urging the community to surrender? We may find some sympathy for the antagonism of an establishment committed to resisting Babylonian domination when it is being continuously undercut by such a prophetic voice. It is difficult to see how surrendering to the Babylonians could lead to anything but death or exile.

The problem, however, is the continuing misreading of the situation by these leaders and their refusal to allow any agenda or plan for national survival other than their own. They assume that Jeremiah's path—always, of course, presented as that of the Lord of Israel—will bring harm to the people and not preserve their well-being (שלום *šālôm,* v. 4). Indeed, Jeremiah proclaims "harm" against the people. This is the same word consistently used to speak of the "evil" or "disaster" that the Lord is bringing in judgment against the nation (e.g., 4:6; 11:17; 16:10; 18:8, 11; 21:10; 26:3; 39:16). The only way the people can find their well-being, their *šālôm,* their *survival,* is to accept the judgment of Babylonian domination. That is a message the political leadership is unwilling and unable to hear.

The plan of this group of officials is foiled by Ebed-melech. In one of those paradoxes that seems so common in Scripture, rescue and help come from an outsider, a Cyrene (Matt 27:32), a Samaritan (Luke 10:29-37), in this case one who is in some sense doubly an outsider, both Ethiopian and a eunuch. But Ebed-melech sees the "harm" (רעה *rā'â*) not in Jeremiah's words but in the conduct of the officials ("they have done wickedly [הרעו *hērē'û*]") and informs the king of what has happened to Jeremiah (v. 9). Once again, the response to the prophet and to his words is more complicated than one might sometimes imagine, as is exemplified here in the compassionate assistance of one belonging to the royal court yet not a part of the Israelite community. That complicated reaction to Jeremiah is carried further by Zedekiah's response to Ebed-melech. The king, who was helpless to withstand the officials' insistence on harsh treatment of the prophet, now sends Ebed-melech to counter the actions of these officials by rescuing Jeremiah. Ebed-melech's rescue effort is told in the same kind of rich detail as one finds in the account of the purchase of the field in chap. 32. The preservation of the prophet's life may be the divine intention, but it is carried

out by the humane and risky pleading of a royal official in a carefully worked-out plan. The depths of the pit are indicated by the fact that ropes were needed to lower Jeremiah into it and that padded ropes (to avoid rope burn) were needed to extricate him. Both the suffering of the prophet and the humanity of the servant are implicit in the way the story is told.

Then there is Zedekiah. Each episode in the account of his ongoing encounter with Jeremiah further testifies to the ambiguity of this king's actions. It is possible simply to judge him a weak king; he admits as much in the text (v. 5). Yet, his conduct is enigmatic; his response to Ebed-melech leads him to allow for Jeremiah's rescue. Perhaps, he is moved by the most immediate petitioner. Perhaps, he did not know what the officials had done. Perhaps, he believes the rescue of Jeremiah will not be discovered, though that is rather difficult to imagine. In any event, the king who allowed the officials to bury Jeremiah alive now permits Ebed-melech to rescue him from that fate.

38:14-28. As in 37:17-21, the king sends for Jeremiah to give him some oracle, some word from the Lord about his fate, and again Jeremiah fears that doing so will just get him into more trouble—as it always seems to do. In this instance, the prophetic oracle is longer and different in character from the one given in 37:17. Whereas the divine word in the prophet/king encounter of chap. 37 was a blunt announcement that Zedekiah would be handed over to the Babylonian king, here an alternative is offered, one that Jeremiah has been presenting often (e.g., 27:12-14; 38:2). Capitulation to the Babylonians can save Zedekiah and his household; it may even prevent the burning of the city (vv. 17, 20). While the judgment is sure and there is to be no miraculous escape from it, as in Hezekiah's time, options are still present. To the very end, the king and the people are being given the opportunity to listen to the divine word and, by responding, change their situation.

Jeremiah makes clear that if he does not act properly, the king will be handed over to a terrible fate at the hands of the Babylonians and the city will be destroyed by fire (vv. 18, 23*b*), a fate further described in vv. 22-23*a*. The prophet underscores the violent fate of the women of the court and their children: rape and enslavement for the women and likely execution or, at best, enslavement for the royal sons. The choice before the king is not simply a matter of his own fate. It has ramifications for everyone in his court. That connection is underscored by the lament Jeremiah places on the lips of the women being led to their violent fate. The lament of the women takes the form of a taunt song, accusing the king of being enticed by his trusted friends into a mode of conduct that brings about his own downfall. The lament of the women who suffer by the king's decision uncovers the underlying schema: the weakness of the king before other powerful officials (see v. 5) or his inability to see the foolishness of their counsel.

That the king's reaction is due in large part to his fear of his own officials is evident at the end of this chapter. He swears Jeremiah to secrecy and to a ruse to hide from the officials the fact that the king has turned to him for counsel or a word from the Lord. This concluding episode is once again marked by considerable realistic detail. As at the end of chap. 38, the king does not oppose the prophet's message. Again there is a kind of implicit acceptance of it but not a willingness to abide by it. This puppet king is afraid of everybody and seems powerless to act. He is obviously afraid of the Babylonian army—as well he should be. The prophet has told him to expect a bad end if he does not capitulate, but to do so is to put himself in the hands of the power that put him on the throne and against which he has now rebelled! Further, his own officials have power over him, and he is afraid of what they might do to him if he decided to surrender. Thus none of the possible scenarios look very good to the king. The outcome is a do-nothing approach that here, as always, becomes a do-something approach, in this case an implicit refusal to act according to the word whose validity he seems to acknowledge. By the next chapter the consequences of his choice are clear and consistent with the prophet's proclamation to him.

39:1-10. We were told at the beginning of this section that the king would not listen (37:2). Nothing has changed at the end, and so the judgment of God through the Babylonian army is played out in these verses. There is no reference in these verses to the Lord or to divine involvement in the affairs they recount. The preceding chapters have made it clear that failure to listen to the prophetic proclamation to submit to the Baby-

lonians would bring about Judah's destruction. This detailed account of the end of Zedekiah and of Judah is at one and the same time a report of the fulfillment of the word of the prophet, proclaimed over and over but rarely heeded.

The details of this chapter echo what we hear in 2 Kings 25 and Jeremiah 52 about the end of Judah. The Babylonian army breaks through and takes the city. The king and his warriors flee but are eventually captured, whereupon he is taken before the king of Babylon, who is in Syria (Hamath), forced to watch his sons and his nobles executed (see 38:23), blinded, and taken in chains into exile. We hear no more of him. The city is burned (see 37:8, 23), and the people have been exiled to Babylon (cf. 40:1)—all of this in accordance with the word of the Lord spoken by the prophet Jeremiah.

There is a brief note at the end of this report to the effect that the Babylonian commander Nebuzaradan left some of the poor people "who owned nothing" in Judah and gave them some vineyards and fields (cf. 2 Kings 25:12; Jer 52:16). This action can be regarded "both as an economic necessity and as a measure of pacification."[197] It may have been the way that Babylon converted Judah into a kind of province. Such provision by the Babylonians cannot be seen as fulfillment of the Jeremianic prophecy that "houses and vineyards and fields shall again be bought in this land" (32:15). No financial transactions are envisaged here. These are people "without anything." This verse is one of several indications that there was a community in Judah and that it was supported by the Babylonian government. Indeed, the rest of the "action" of the book involves that Judean community, not the people who were taken into exile.

39:11-14. Just as this section deals with the final fate of the king, the city, and the people, so also it tells about the fate of the prophet, whose personal trials and tribulations have been so important in these chapters. These verses are to be read with 40:1-6, which may be a variant report or a different episode. The pro-Babylonian stance of Jeremiah may have had much to do with the favorable treatment he receives from the Babylonians. As Brueggemann has noted, such treatment could

197. William L. Holladay, *Jeremiah 2*, Hermeneia (Philadelphia: Fortress, 1989) 293.

have confirmed in the minds of his opponents their judgment that he was a traitor to his country. More important, as both 39:12 and 40:4 indicate:

> The prophet is to have the decisive voice in determining his own future. Jeremiah's person now acts out the positive option Jeremiah had anounced for the community. He has urged "submit and live." As one who has *submitted,* he is permitted to *live.* His personal destiny is presented as what might have been available for Zedekiah and for all his cohorts, had they not believed their own war propaganda—their silly, false notion of well-being (*shalom*).[198]

198. Brueggemann, *A Commentary on Jeremiah*, 372.

The final word (39:14; 40:1-6) is that Jeremiah "stayed with his own people." He is not a deserter to the Babylonians. His words have been the word of the Lord, and not the words of an appeaser and quisling. Jeremiah's place and fate have always been with his people, so he does not choose to go to Babylon. He chooses to remain with the "remnant" of the people left in the land (40:6).

39:15-18. See the Commentary on 38:1-13 and the Reflections at 45:1-5.

REFLECTIONS

1. The degree to which these chapters focus on the prophet and his suffering at the hands of the officials reminds us of that strain within the scriptures telling of God's faithful ones who endure a degree of suffering that becomes a fundamental theme of the Lord's way, evident most fully in the suffering and death of Jesus of Nazareth. His fate is in various ways anticipated in the fate of others, especially Moses, who was not allowed to enter the promised land because the Lord was angry with him on account of the sins of the people (Deut 1:37; 3:26; 4:21), and the suffering servant of Isaiah 53, who was "wounded for our transgressions, crushed for our iniquities" (Isa 53:5). Jeremiah's suffering is not described as vicarious, but it is clearly a suffering that is borne out of his commitment to the Lord's way and the Lord's calling. It is in some ways also his destiny, as the call of Jeremiah and the Lord's response to his frequent laments make clear. Isolation and loneliness have been his plight all along. Now in the final days we find the suffering of the prophet more acute and physical with severe beatings, frequent imprisonment, and an entombment that would surely have meant his slow and terrible death apart from the intervention of Ebed-melech. He thus becomes a representative of the faithful way as well as indicative of what is often the fate of God's faithful servants in a world that does not like to hear its assumed autonomy challenged. The proclamation of God's call for repentance and a more just and obedient way is constantly resisted, and those who utter it, whether by visions from the divine council or by careful listening to Scripture, always risk the Jeremianic fate of resistance breaking over into physical danger and true suffering.

2. The reaction of the leadership to Jeremiah as articulated in 38:4 is an appropriate text for thinking about the resistance of political leaders to any kind of moral or religious direction, any kind of counsel of conscience that involves a threat to national honor. It is the danger of patriotism, but patriotism is too simple a cliché at this point. Our instincts are so set for resistance to any form of domination, for victory over our enemies, for pulling together in any sort of foreign conflict, that we cannot countenance another mode of conduct and cannot allow a moral claim that suggests we might not seek victory and must accept defeat. This is a kind of secularized form of the "God is on our side" claim that surreptitiously always guides national conduct. Any other conduct and any other proposal or counsel is automatically and inherently treasonous and to be suppressed.

The Vietnam war offers a particularly vivid example of this phenomenon. The "officials," and indeed many of the people, could not countenance the moral and religious claim that this was not a war to be fought, that national honor was better maintained by extrication and admission of defeat than by persevering. Even the religious assemblies of the nation were the scenes of accusations of treason and claims that those who opposed the war really sought the harm of the nation and were not working for its good.

Jeremiah's story is a reminder that sometimes the purposes of God are not identifiable with national well-being. One must ask further if there are not occasions when the community of faith must still recognize the judging purposes of God in the "harm" that threatens a nation. Certitude on such matters is hardly likely, but the lessons of Scripture are that the Lord of Israel and of the church, who is the Lord of the universe, works this way in the affairs of nations. Acceptance of such judgment may be an act of obedience and not an act of treason.

3. The words of Jeremiah to Zedekiah in chapter 38 are a reminder of one of the most horrendous outcomes of the inclination of royal and other (generally male) political leaders to take up the weapons of war. The brutality of war takes its largest toll on the women and children who have nothing to do with the decision or its execution. They are by definition its victims. At this point, we are confronted again with the harsh political reality of all that is going on in these times. This is not merely a spiritual conflict; the struggle for the heart and soul of Judah is carved out in the sociopolitical realities of early sixth-century BCE Judah. And its consequences are devastating for all. But this text focuses explicitly on the way the choices of male rulers to go to war automatically bring rape, enslavement, and death to innocent parties who are totally outside the decision-making process. The taunt of the women is one of the primary moral words of the book of Jeremiah. In its concrete particularity, it is a continuing condemnation of the tendency of rulers to invoke the horror of war over the shame of capitulation and surrender of arms. This text, in fact, turns the whole thing on its head. The shame is that of the king, and the women name it. Resort to arms is the way of death; surrender of arms is the way to life. Why do we always seem to choose the former and let our wives and sisters, our mothers and children, pay for it? Listen carefully, and you will still hear the women taunting and Rachel weeping (31:15).[199]

4. These chapters create an important tension in their presentation of the divine intent and the human options that intention opens up. The divine decision to bring judgment upon Judah is clear. Resistance to the prophetic call for repentance and a change of life has been manifest all the way through. The actions of Jehoiakim in chapter 36 and the opening words about Zedekiah's refusal to listen also have sealed Judah's fate. That has been a long process as the Lord again and again has sent the prophet with a word that is explicit about the outcome of disobedience but always opens up the possibility of a change in the divine intent if the leaders and the people are open to change. Now we seem to be at a point of no return. The word has not been heeded; indeed, it has been destroyed in its written form. The fulfillment of the divine announcement of judgment is the primary content of these chapters.

Even so, there is an openness; a possibility of survival for those who obey is offered right to the very end. It is there in the last words of Jeremiah to King Zedekiah just before the report of the Babylonian breach of the city. The Lord's mercy is available; more specifically, the offer of life rather than death is set before the people. It requires a painful obedience to what would have been seen as a shameful surrender. But obedience carries with it the possibility of life. The Lord of Israel seems always willing to keep the door open a crack, no matter how far down the road of disloyalty and disobedience the people have gone. The divine compassion and will to life is larger than the divine decision for judgment. Death is not an arbitrary imposition. It is a path taken, and there is always another option available in the kingdom ruled by this God.[200]

5. The somewhat curious note about Nabuzaradan's giving some vineyards and fields to the poor, to the people who have nothing, is a kind of indirect response to the constant question

199. See Brueggemann, "Texts That Linger."
200. See Ronald Clements, *Jeremiah,* Interpretation (Atlanta: John Knox, 1988) 219-23.

about the fairness of corporate judgment. Why should the victims of oppression suffer the punishment for that oppression? This particular text suggests that such may not be the outcome at all. For one thing, the poor may not be at all unhappy at disaster whose primary outcome is the overthrow of the rich establishment, the landowners, and the affluent citizenry. They have nothing to lose when they are those "who owned nothing" (39:10). And in this case, possibilities for the poor open up that were not there before. Those "who owned nothing" are now given property that provides a means of subsistence. The defeat of Judah effects a topsy-turvy turn of events, bringing about a redistribution of property in the midst of the judgment. The corporate punishment of the rich and the powerful has not created further harshness for their victims. In this instance, it opens up possibilities for them that were not present in the "peace" that the false prophets claimed to have existed in Judah.

JEREMIAH 40:1–41:18, CONSPIRACY AND MURDER AMONG THE JUDEAN REMNANT

NIV

40The word came to Jeremiah from the LORD after Nebuzaradan commander of the imperial guard had released him at Ramah. He had found Jeremiah bound in chains among all the captives from Jerusalem and Judah who were being carried into exile to Babylon. ²When the commander of the guard found Jeremiah, he said to him, "The LORD your God decreed this disaster for this place. ³And now the LORD has brought it about; he has done just as he said he would. All this happened because you people sinned against the LORD and did not obey him. ⁴But today I am freeing you from the chains on your wrists. Come with me to Babylon, if you like, and I will look after you; but if you do not want to, then don't come. Look, the whole country lies before you; go wherever you please.' ⁵However, before Jeremiah turned to go,ᵃ Nebuzaradan added, "Go back to Gedaliah son of Ahikam, the son of Shaphan, whom the king of Babylon has appointed over the towns of Judah, and live with him among the people, or go anywhere else you please."

Then the commander gave him provisions and a present and let him go. ⁶So Jeremiah went to Gedaliah son of Ahikam at Mizpah and stayed with him among the people who were left behind in the land.

⁷When all the army officers and their men who were still in the open country heard that the king

ᵃ5 Or *Jeremiah answered*

NRSV

40The word that came to Jeremiah from the LORD after Nebuzaradan the captain of the guard had let him go from Ramah, when he took him bound in fetters along with all the captives of Jerusalem and Judah who were being exiled to Babylon. ²The captain of the guard took Jeremiah and said to him, "The LORD your God threatened this place with this disaster; ³and now the LORD has brought it about, and has done as he said, because all of you sinned against the LORD and did not obey his voice. Therefore this thing has come upon you. ⁴Now look, I have just released you today from the fetters on your hands. If you wish to come with me to Babylon, come, and I will take good care of you; but if you do not wish to come with me to Babylon, you need not come. See, the whole land is before you; go wherever you think it good and right to go. ⁵If you remain,ᵃ then return to Gedaliah son of Ahikam son of Shaphan, whom the king of Babylon appointed governor of the towns of Judah, and stay with him among the people; or go wherever you think it right to go." So the captain of the guard gave him an allowance of food and a present, and let him go. ⁶Then Jeremiah went to Gedaliah son of Ahikam at Mizpah, and stayed with him among the people who were left in the land.

⁷When all the leaders of the forces in the open

ᵃSyr: Meaning of Heb uncertain

NIV

of Babylon had appointed Gedaliah son of Ahikam as governor over the land and had put him in charge of the men, women and children who were the poorest in the land and who had not been carried into exile to Babylon, [8]they came to Gedaliah at Mizpah—Ishmael son of Nethaniah, Johanan and Jonathan the sons of Kareah, Seraiah son of Tanhumeth, the sons of Ephai the Netophathite, and Jaazaniah[a] the son of the Maacathite, and their men. [9]Gedaliah son of Ahikam, the son of Shaphan, took an oath to reassure them and their men. "Do not be afraid to serve the Babylonians,[b]" he said. "Settle down in the land and serve the king of Babylon, and it will go well with you. [10]I myself will stay at Mizpah to represent you before the Babylonians who come to us, but you are to harvest the wine, summer fruit and oil, and put them in your storage jars, and live in the towns you have taken over."

[11]When all the Jews in Moab, Ammon, Edom and all the other countries heard that the king of Babylon had left a remnant in Judah and had appointed Gedaliah son of Ahikam, the son of Shaphan, as governor over them, [12]they all came back to the land of Judah, to Gedaliah at Mizpah, from all the countries where they had been scattered. And they harvested an abundance of wine and summer fruit.

[13]Johanan son of Kareah and all the army officers still in the open country came to Gedaliah at Mizpah [14]and said to him, "Don't you know that Baalis king of the Ammonites has sent Ishmael son of Nethaniah to take your life?" But Gedaliah son of Ahikam did not believe them.

[15]Then Johanan son of Kareah said privately to Gedaliah in Mizpah, "Let me go and kill Ishmael son of Nethaniah, and no one will know it. Why should he take your life and cause all the Jews who are gathered around you to be scattered and the remnant of Judah to perish?"

[16]But Gedaliah son of Ahikam said to Johanan son of Kareah, "Don't do such a thing! What you are saying about Ishmael is not true."

41 In the seventh month Ishmael son of Nethaniah, the son of Elishama, who was of royal blood and had been one of the king's officers,

[a]8 Hebrew *Jezaniah*, a variant of *Jaazaniah*   [b]9 Or *Chaldeans*; also in verse 10

NRSV

country and their troops heard that the king of Babylon had appointed Gedaliah son of Ahikam governor in the land, and had committed to him men, women, and children, those of the poorest of the land who had not been taken into exile to Babylon, [8]they went to Gedaliah at Mizpah—Ishmael son of Nethaniah, Johanan son of Kareah, Seraiah son of Tanhumeth, the sons of Ephai the Netophathite, Jezaniah son of the Maacathite, they and their troops. [9]Gedaliah son of Ahikam son of Shaphan swore to them and their troops, saying, "Do not be afraid to serve the Chaldeans. Stay in the land and serve the king of Babylon, and it shall go well with you. [10]As for me, I am staying at Mizpah to represent you before the Chaldeans who come to us; but as for you, gather wine and summer fruits and oil, and store them in your vessels, and live in the towns that you have taken over." [11]Likewise, when all the Judeans who were in Moab and among the Ammonites and in Edom and in other lands heard that the king of Babylon had left a remnant in Judah and had appointed Gedaliah son of Ahikam son of Shaphan as governor over them, [12]then all the Judeans returned from all the places to which they had been scattered and came to the land of Judah, to Gedaliah at Mizpah; and they gathered wine and summer fruits in great abundance.

13Now Johanan son of Kareah and all the leaders of the forces in the open country came to Gedaliah at Mizpah [14]and said to him, "Are you at all aware that Baalis king of the Ammonites has sent Ishmael son of Nethaniah to take your life?" But Gedaliah son of Ahikam would not believe them. [15]Then Johanan son of Kareah spoke secretly to Gedaliah at Mizpah, "Please let me go and kill Ishmael son of Nethaniah, and no one else will know. Why should he take your life, so that all the Judeans who are gathered around you would be scattered, and the remnant of Judah would perish?" [16]But Gedaliah son of Ahikam said to Johanan son of Kareah, "Do not do such a thing, for you are telling a lie about Ishmael."

41 In the seventh month, Ishmael son of Nethaniah son of Elishama, of the royal family, one of the chief officers of the king, came with ten men to Gedaliah son of Ahikam, at Mizpah. As they ate bread together there at

came with ten men to Gedaliah son of Ahikam at Mizpah. While they were eating together there, [2]Ishmael son of Nethaniah and the ten men who were with him got up and struck down Gedaliah son of Ahikam, the son of Shaphan, with the sword, killing the one whom the king of Babylon had appointed as governor over the land. [3]Ishmael also killed all the Jews who were with Gedaliah at Mizpah, as well as the Babylonian[a] soldiers who were there.

[4]The day after Gedaliah's assassination, before anyone knew about it, [5]eighty men who had shaved off their beards, torn their clothes and cut themselves came from Shechem, Shiloh and Samaria, bringing grain offerings and incense with them to the house of the LORD. [6]Ishmael son of Nethaniah went out from Mizpah to meet them, weeping as he went. When he met them, he said, "Come to Gedaliah son of Ahikam." [7]When they went into the city, Ishmael son of Nethaniah and the men who were with him slaughtered them and threw them into a cistern. [8]But ten of them said to Ishmael, "Don't kill us! We have wheat and barley, oil and honey, hidden in a field." So he let them alone and did not kill them with the others. [9]Now the cistern where he threw all the bodies of the men he had killed along with Gedaliah was the one King Asa had made as part of his defense against Baasha king of Israel. Ishmael son of Nethaniah filled it with the dead.

[10]Ishmael made captives of all the rest of the people who were in Mizpah—the king's daughters along with all the others who were left there, over whom Nebuzaradan commander of the imperial guard had appointed Gedaliah son of Ahikam. Ishmael son of Nethaniah took them captive and set out to cross over to the Ammonites.

[11]When Johanan son of Kareah and all the army officers who were with him heard about all the crimes Ishmael son of Nethaniah had committed, [12]they took all their men and went to fight Ishmael son of Nethaniah. They caught up with him near the great pool in Gibeon. [13]When all the people Ishmael had with him saw Johanan son of Kareah and the army officers who were with him,

Mizpah, [2]Ishmael son of Nethaniah and the ten men with him got up and struck down Gedaliah son of Ahikam son of Shaphan with the sword and killed him, because the king of Babylon had appointed him governor in the land. [3]Ishmael also killed all the Judeans who were with Gedaliah at Mizpah, and the Chaldean soldiers who happened to be there.

4On the day after the murder of Gedaliah, before anyone knew of it, [5]eighty men arrived from Shechem and Shiloh and Samaria, with their beards shaved and their clothes torn, and their bodies gashed, bringing grain offerings and incense to present at the temple of the LORD. [6]And Ishmael son of Nethaniah came out from Mizpah to meet them, weeping as he came. As he met them, he said to them, "Come to Gedaliah son of Ahikam." [7]When they reached the middle of the city, Ishmael son of Nethaniah and the men with him slaughtered them, and threw them[a] into a cistern. [8]But there were ten men among them who said to Ishmael, "Do not kill us, for we have stores of wheat, barley, oil, and honey hidden in the fields." So he refrained, and did not kill them along with their companions.

9Now the cistern into which Ishmael had thrown all the bodies of the men whom he had struck down was the large cistern[b] that King Asa had made for defense against King Baasha of Israel; Ishmael son of Nethaniah filled that cistern with those whom he had killed. [10]Then Ishmael took captive all the rest of the people who were in Mizpah, the king's daughters and all the people who were left at Mizpah, whom Nebuzaradan, the captain of the guard, had committed to Gedaliah son of Ahikam. Ishmael son of Nethaniah took them captive and set out to cross over to the Ammonites.

11But when Johanan son of Kareah and all the leaders of the forces with him heard of all the crimes that Ishmael son of Nethaniah had done, [12]they took all their men and went to fight against Ishmael son of Nethaniah. They came upon him at the great pool that is in Gibeon. [13]And when all the people who were with Ishmael saw Johanan son of Kareah and all the leaders of the forces with

[a]3 Or *Chaldean*

[a]Syr: Heb lacks *and threw them*; compare verse 9   [b]Gk: Heb *whom he had killed by the hand of Gedaliah*

NIV

they were glad. [14]All the people Ishmael had taken captive at Mizpah turned and went over to Johanan son of Kareah. [15]But Ishmael son of Nethaniah and eight of his men escaped from Johanan and fled to the Ammonites.

[16]Then Johanan son of Kareah and all the army officers who were with him led away all the survivors from Mizpah whom he had recovered from Ishmael son of Nethaniah after he had assassinated Gedaliah son of Ahikam: the soldiers, women, children and court officials he had brought from Gibeon. [17]And they went on, stopping at Geruth Kimham near Bethlehem on their way to Egypt [18]to escape the Babylonians.[a] They were afraid of them because Ishmael son of Nethaniah had killed Gedaliah son of Ahikam, whom the king of Babylon had appointed as governor over the land.

[a]18 Or *Chaldeans*

NRSV

him, they were glad. [14]So all the people whom Ishmael had carried away captive from Mizpah turned around and came back, and went to Johanan son of Kareah. [15]But Ishmael son of Nethaniah escaped from Johanan with eight men, and went to the Ammonites. [16]Then Johanan son of Kareah and all the leaders of the forces with him took all the rest of the people whom Ishmael son of Nethaniah had carried away captive[a] from Mizpah after he had slain Gedaliah son of Ahikam—soldiers, women, children, and eunuchs, whom Johanan brought back from Gibeon.[b] [17]And they set out, and stopped at Geruth Chimham near Bethlehem, intending to go to Egypt [18]because of the Chaldeans; for they were afraid of them, because Ishmael son of Nethaniah had killed Gedaliah son of Ahikam, whom the king of Babylon had made governor over the land.

[a]Cn: Heb *whom he recovered from Ishmael son of Nethaniah*
[b]Meaning of Heb uncertain

COMMENTARY

40:1-6. These verses have been largely treated in the Commentary on 39:11-14. Two further matters need to be noted, however. First, *a Babylonian* (vv. 2-3) confesses that what has happened to Jerusalem and Judah is, indeed, a fulfillment of the announcement of the Lord's intention to punish the people because of their sin. What the Judeans themselves could or would never accept in prospect and do not affirm in retrospect is given as a straightforward claim by a member of the conquering army. The one acknowledgment of the truthfulness of Jeremiah's prophecy in the whole book comes from the lips of the enemy.

Second, in this text we learn about a Babylonian plan to set up a governor over Judah, further evidence for the existence of a Judean community in the land. The person appointed is Gedaliah, son of Ahikam, whose leadership seems appropriate but whose naïveté about the dangers before him leads to his murder (41:2).

40:7-12. The appointment of Gedaliah as governor (lit., "appointed over the land," v. 7) has salutary effects on the populace remaining in Judah. Those placed formally under his charge by

the Babylonians now include two other significant components: various elements from the army who were scattered in the countryside and had not been captured by the Babylonians (v. 7; see 52:8*b*) and Judeans who had either migrated or fled to neighboring countries, such as Moab, Edom, and Ammon and now were returning.

The first part of this section (vv. 7-9) is virtually identical to the account in 2 Kgs 25:22-24, while the remainder, not found in Kings, elaborates the appointment of Gedaliah. These texts create a picture of Gedaliah that is very positive, setting forth genuine possibilities for new life in the devastated land. Gedaliah comes from an established family. His grandfather (Shaphan) and father (Ahikam) had both been involved in the discovery and handling of the scroll of the Torah found in the Temple during Josiah's reign. Moreover, his father had protected Jeremiah from execution by the people after his trial in chap. 26. There is thus some affinity between this family and the prophet.

Gedaliah's leadership offers promise for the future. Still, he is clearly in a ticklish position, needing to behave in a way that will not arouse the ire of the Babylonians who appointed him, but also needing not to seem a Babylonian puppet to the remaining Judeans, who would obviously hold great antipathy for their conquerors. He seems to have elicited trust on both sides and, in his words to the leaders of the remaining army forces, indicates his intention to represent the people to the Babylonians while also giving leadership to the people.

The latter is evident in his command for the Judeans to gather provisions from the land and to settle again in the towns of Judah. One cannot be sure how accurate this picture of the post-Babylonian destruction is. It may represent an idealized view—men, women, and children, the poor, the remnants of the military, and returning Judeans—and a "great abundance" of produce from the land.[201] Exaggerated as this picture may be, the main impression is that the devastation is not so great that people cannot find food and some kind of habitation. The words of Gedaliah are remarkably like those of Jeremiah to the exiles in 29:5 and are consistent with the message that Jeremiah has been giving all along: Find your life here by submitting to the Babylonians. While the submission is now forced by conquest rather than by surrender, and thus there has been a heavy toll on the people and their leadership who refused to obey the word of the Lord and capitulate, the community is now experiencing new possibilities for their life under Babylonian domination. Gedaliah's leadership effects a community life that embodies and realizes that for which the prophet had called.

40:13-16. There is a fatal flaw in that leadership, however: Gedaliah's apparent naïveté or his unwillingness to take strong preemptive action to preserve his position. One of the military leaders, Johanon, has discovered that his comrade in arms Ishmael is plotting a conspiracy against Gedaliah at the instigation of the king of Ammon, who is earlier implicitly identified with the Judean resistance to Babylonian domination (27:3) and so may not have cared for Gedaliah's cooperation with the Babylonian power. Political struggle is still the context in which the story of Jeremiah and Judah is worked out. Johanon, however, has cast his lot

with Gedaliah and believes in his leadership. He realizes the danger to their leader and thus to the stability of the surviving community (v. 15) and offers to strike first and kill Ishmael before he can do anything. Gedaliah's refusal to believe Johanon and set him free to carry out his own conspiracy against Ishmael—as, for example, David would surely have done with Joab—sounds his own death knell.

41:1-3. Ishmael's conspiracy is carried out as he and a number of his men treacherously kill Gedaliah in the middle of a meal they are having with him. They also wipe out everyone else who is at the meal, Judean and Babylonian alike. The political character of this murder of the governor, already indicated in the preceding chapter with reference to the alliance with the king of Ammon, is further suggested in the way that Ishmael is identified with the Judean royal power ("of the royal family, one of the chief officers of the king") and the explicit reference to Gedaliah's appointment by the Babylonian king.[202]

41:4-10. But it is not sufficient to characterize Ishmael's treachery simply as an act of political opposition representing a loyalist element that regards Gedaliah as a puppet of the Babylonians. His mass slaughter of all who are with Gedaliah is followed by a further act of brutality when he kills eighty men who have come from the north to sacrifice at the Temple. This murder of Gedaliah and his men in the middle of a meal where he is a guest is matched by his weeping before the mourning pilgrims,[203] apparently identifying with them in order to lull them into thinking he is to be trusted. Such is his lying invitation to "come to Gedaliah" (v. 6). The treachery of Ishmael in both instances indicates the way in which forces within the community dismantle the promising efforts of Gedaliah to bring about a viable and ordered community out of the remnant in Judah. Henceforth, the possibilities for new life will be oriented around the exiles in Babylon. That may reflect the victory of a particular ideology in the struggle

201. On the possible propaganda character of this picture of abundance and the return of many Judeans, see Gerald L. Keown, Pamela J. Scalise, and Thomas J. Smothers, *Jeremiah 26–52,* WBC 27 (Dallas: Word, 1995) 235-38.

202. The expression "one of the chief officers of the king" does not appear in the Greek text or in the parallel account in 2 Kgs 25:25, though Janzen has suggested that this phrase may be an old variant of "the royal family" or "ten men." See J. Gerald Janzen, *Studies in the Text of Jeremiah,* HSM 6 (Cambridge, Mass.: Harvard University Press, 1973) 199n. 59.

203. "Crocodile tears," as McKane properly recognizes. See William McKane, *A Critical and Exegetical Commentary on Jeremiah,* 2 vols., ICC (Edinburgh: T. & T. Clark, 1986, 1996).

among various post-destruction Judahites, one that sees the exilic community as the locus of the true Israel.[204] These chapters, at least, help to show how and why the remnant community in Palestine failed to become the center of the story of Israel after the divine judgment.

The text characterizes the eighty men who are murdered as pilgrims in mourning, preparing for religious rites at the Temple. Their journey from the north attests to the significance of Jerusalem as a center of worship for all Israel. That may be a testimony to the attraction of the Temple from its earliest days, or it may reflect the impact of Josiah's reform, which centralized all worship in Jerusalem. Inasmuch as the events of this chapter are placed in the seventh month, the men may have been on the way to the Feast of Tabernacles, which was held in that month. It is likely that their mourning symbols represent a reaction to the destruction of the Temple, about which they surely would have known. So this pilgrimage may have been a special penitential act that would have climaxed at the site of the now-destroyed Temple (see chap. 52).

The story of Ishmael's barbarity is fleshed out with the report that he literally filled a large (so NRSV, following the better Greek text) cistern that had been built many years before by King Asa (see 1 Kgs 15:22*b*) with the corpses of his murdered victims and then took everybody else who had been left in the care of Gedaliah as his captives to Ammon.

41:11-15. Ishmael's control of the situation is short-lived. Johanon, who had known of Ishmael's intentions and was a loyal supporter of Gedaliah, but obviously was not on the scene when the governor was murdered, moves to stop Ishmael and manages to do so before he can reach Ammon. Ishmael apparently has never had anything but a small cadre of soldiers (ten men in v. 1; eight in v. 15); so his captives, upon spotting Johanon and his forces, simply stop going with Ishmael and return back in joy to join up with Johanon while Ishmael manages to escape to Ammon. We hear no more about him.

41:16-18. Now in the safe hands of Johanon, the people who remain in Judah realize that they are in serious trouble. The murder of Gedaliah, when made known to the Babylonian authorities who appointed him, will surely bring down the wrath of the Babylonians upon the remnant in Judah. They have legitimate reason to fear harsh treatment even if they are innocent of murder. The better part of wisdom seems to be for them to leave the country. They decide to head to Egypt, which is not only in the opposite direction from Babylon but also is a country that has already indicated some willingness to help (37:5). On the surface, flight to Egypt is a sensible plan; but it is not God's plan for this people, as the next chapter will show.

---

204. On the conflict of theologies and ideologies in late Judah as reflected in Jeremiah and Ezekiel especially, see Christopher Seitz, *Theology in Conflict: Reactions to the Exile in the Book of Jeremiah,* BZAW 176 (Berlin: Walter de Gruyter, 1989).

REFLECTIONS

1. The words of the Babylonian captain Nebuzaradan to Jeremiah in 40:2-3 are an astonishing statement of Jeremianic theology, confirming that the destruction of Jerusalem and Judah was, indeed, the work of the Lord of Israel because of the sins of the people. Many interpreters assume this to be absurd and indicative of a corruption of the text that has transferred the oracle from Jeremiah's lips to the Babylonian's. That analysis cannot be ruled out, but the textual evidence indicates that this confession is made by Nebuzaradan. And the assumption of corruption seems to be largely guided by the prior assumption that it makes no sense to expect a biblical text to have a foreigner—indeed, an enemy—make such a confesssion of faith and be the primary interpreter of the meaning of such an epochal event.

But that is to ignore the several instances where just such a confession of faith by an outsider, by the nations or by a representative of the nations, is central to the biblical story. In the book of Jeremiah itself we are told that what happens in chapter 40 would indeed happen—that is, the nations will look upon destroyed Judah and conclude that the Lord of Israel had done this because of their breach of covenant (22:8). Furthermore, at other strategic moments, the primary confession of faith that testifies to the handiwork of the Lord in the events of the moment is made by a foreigner, a member of another nation (e.g., Rahab's confession in Joshua 2). In some places, the confession of the nations is the first word, the first acknowledgment of the Lord's work, as it is here. So in Ps 126:2 the nations, in the face of the Lord's restoration of the fortunes of Zion, proclaim that "the LORD has done great things for them." And it is only after that and in echo of this confession that the people themselves then say, "The LORD has done great things for us" (Ps 126:3). Even more significant, the first confession of the importance of the death of Jesus is uttered by the conquering nations in the form of a Roman centurion, who, in one account, praises God and confesses, "This one was righteous" (Luke 23:47), and in another account says that this one was God's Son (Matt 27:54), a claim that is mocked by the chief priests and the scribes and elders only a few verses earlier (Matt 27:43).

There is thus an important strain in Scripture that testifies to the capacity of those outside the community of faith sometimes to see more clearly what is going on in God's work in the world than those who seem to have the word. In some of these cases, and particularly in Jeremiah's time, it is the blindness of the community of faith that accentuates the significance of the confession of the outsider. Nebuzaradan is an example of one of the righteous Gentiles, who, even though a powerful representative of the conquering and destroying Babylonians, deals humanely with Jeremiah, instigates a plan for the recovery of the people in their own land, and sees through to the heart of the matter in a way that none around him seem capable of. If the nations ever do finally stream to the mountain of the Lord's house (Isa 2:2), they may beat the church and the synagogue there. It is often God's own elect people who are the most obtuse and resistant to the word of the Lord, blocked by blinders of self-interest from seeing what God is doing in the world. The assumption that "outsiders" will only be able to proclaim the Lord's power and might after the "insiders" have told them about it comes under radical challenge in this and other texts.

2. This text bids us think about the quiet and providential working out of God's way that is suggested by the possibilities of renewal and new life that were present in the appointment of Gedaliah over the land and his careful and sensible initiation of a plan for economic recovery and stabilization. The picture is so consistent with what Jeremiah had proclaimed earlier about the people's finding a way to survive and finding new life in the land under Babylonian rule, that we cannot help reading chapter 40 as a manifestation of the providence of God at work among the people. Through the words of the Babylonian captain of the guard, this chapter confesses God's hand in the Babylonian defeat. It then immediately begins to talk about renewal and restoration for the remnant. It even contains the theme of the gathering of the Jews from among the nations, in this case, from the immediately surrounding countries. The punishment is real, as Nebuzaradan states, but there follows not only exile for many of the Judeans but also the reestablishment of life in the land. Nothing is said about divine activity at this point, but this was what the Lord had called for. Thus in the activity of Gedaliah we may see not only some amelioration of the divine punishment but also the work of the Lord to begin afresh, in the ruins of destruction and in the surely bewildered and devastated remnant, to build a new community and to provide for its sustenance. Thus the blessing of God begins to operate again before the fires of destruction are fully out.

3. As the biblical story has confirmed about our human way from the beginning, the blessing of God to provide life and its possibilities in abundance is often undone by the evil machinations and willful self-interest of human creatures. One man's evil ways can do in a people. There are those who cooperate with him, but this is not a large wrecking crew. As is often the case, one person bent on treachery and taking advantage of the trust and goodwill of others creates such havoc that everything is undone. If Adolf Hitler is an extreme case of such one-man havoc, there are many other lesser ones along the way.

In these chapters of Jeremiah, we are beginning to see the seeds sown that sprout into different communities of Judeans—in the land of Judah, in Babylon, and in Egypt. The weakest of those communities was the one that started off with the greatest possibilities. Human sin at work in acts of treachery, brutality, and murder effectively blocks the will of God through human servants to rebuild this land.

JEREMIAH 42:1–43:13, EGYPT OR BUST

NIV

42 Then all the army officers, including Johanan son of Kareah and Jezaniah[a] son of Hoshaiah, and all the people from the least to the greatest approached ²Jeremiah the prophet and said to him, "Please hear our petition and pray to the LORD your God for this entire remnant. For as you now see, though we were once many, now only a few are left. ³Pray that the LORD your God will tell us where we should go and what we should do."

⁴"I have heard you," replied Jeremiah the prophet. "I will certainly pray to the LORD your God as you have requested; I will tell you everything the LORD says and will keep nothing back from you."

⁵Then they said to Jeremiah, "May the LORD be a true and faithful witness against us if we do not act in accordance with everything the LORD your God sends you to tell us. ⁶Whether it is favorable or unfavorable, we will obey the LORD our God, to whom we are sending you, so that it will go well with us, for we will obey the LORD our God."

⁷Ten days later the word of the LORD came to Jeremiah. ⁸So he called together Johanan son of Kareah and all the army officers who were with him and all the people from the least to the greatest. ⁹He said to them, "This is what the LORD, the God of Israel, to whom you sent me to present your petition, says: ¹⁰'If you stay in this land, I will build you up and not tear you down; I will plant you and not uproot you, for I am grieved over the disaster I have inflicted on you. ¹¹Do not be afraid of the king of Babylon, whom you now fear. Do not be afraid of him, declares the LORD, for I am with you and will save you and deliver you from his hands. ¹²I will show you compassion so that

ᵃ1 Hebrew; Septuagint (see also 43:2) Azariah

NRSV

42 Then all the commanders of the forces, and Johanan son of Kareah and Azariah[a] son of Hoshaiah, and all the people from the least to the greatest, approached ²the prophet Jeremiah and said, "Be good enough to listen to our plea, and pray to the LORD your God for us—for all this remnant. For there are only a few of us left out of many, as your eyes can see. ³Let the LORD your God show us where we should go and what we should do." ⁴The prophet Jeremiah said to them, "Very well: I am going to pray to the LORD your God as you request, and whatever the LORD answers you I will tell you; I will keep nothing back from you." ⁵They in their turn said to Jeremiah, "May the LORD be a true and faithful witness against us if we do not act according to everything that the LORD your God sends us through you. ⁶Whether it is good or bad, we will obey the voice of the LORD our God to whom we are sending you, in order that it may go well with us when we obey the voice of the LORD our God."

7At the end of ten days the word of the LORD came to Jeremiah. ⁸Then he summoned Johanan son of Kareah and all the commanders of the forces who were with him, and all the people from the least to the greatest, ⁹and said to them, "Thus says the LORD, the God of Israel, to whom you sent me to present your plea before him: ¹⁰If you will only remain in this land, then I will build you up and not pull you down; I will plant you, and not pluck you up; for I am sorry for the disaster that I have brought upon you. ¹¹Do not be afraid of the king of Babylon, as you have been; do not be afraid of him, says the LORD, for I am with you, to save you and to rescue you from his hand. ¹²I will grant you mercy, and he will have mercy

ᵃGk: Heb Jezaniah

NIV

he will have compassion on you and restore you to your land.'

¹³"However, if you say, 'We will not stay in this land,' and so disobey the LORD your God, ¹⁴and if you say, 'No, we will go and live in Egypt, where we will not see war or hear the trumpet or be hungry for bread,' ¹⁵then hear the word of the LORD, O remnant of Judah. This is what the LORD Almighty, the God of Israel, says: 'If you are determined to go to Egypt and you do go to settle there, ¹⁶then the sword you fear will overtake you there, and the famine you dread will follow you into Egypt, and there you will die. ¹⁷Indeed, all who are determined to go to Egypt to settle there will die by the sword, famine and plague; not one of them will survive or escape the disaster I will bring on them.' ¹⁸This is what the LORD Almighty, the God of Israel, says: 'As my anger and wrath have been poured out on those who lived in Jerusalem, so will my wrath be poured out on you when you go to Egypt. You will be an object of cursing and horror, of condemnation and reproach; you will never see this place again.'

¹⁹"O remnant of Judah, the LORD has told you, 'Do not go to Egypt.' Be sure of this: I warn you today ²⁰that you made a fatal mistake*ᵃ* when you sent me to the LORD your God and said, 'Pray to the LORD our God for us; tell us everything he says and we will do it.' ²¹I have told you today, but you still have not obeyed the LORD your God in all he sent me to tell you. ²²So now, be sure of this: You will die by the sword, famine and plague in the place where you want to go to settle."

43When Jeremiah finished telling the people all the words of the LORD their God—everything the LORD had sent him to tell them—²Azariah son of Hoshaiah and Johanan son of Kareah and all the arrogant men said to Jeremiah, "You are lying! The LORD our God has not sent you to say, 'You must not go to Egypt to settle there.' ³But Baruch son of Neriah is inciting you against us to hand us over to the Babylonians,*ᵇ* so they may kill us or carry us into exile to Babylon."

⁴So Johanan son of Kareah and all the army officers and all the people disobeyed the LORD's command to stay in the land of Judah. ⁵Instead, Johanan son of Kareah and all the army officers

ᵃ20 Or you erred in your hearts   ᵇ3 Or Chaldeans

NRSV

on you and restore you to your native soil. ¹³But if you continue to say, 'We will not stay in this land,' thus disobeying the voice of the LORD your God ¹⁴and saying, 'No, we will go to the land of Egypt, where we shall not see war, or hear the sound of the trumpet, or be hungry for bread, and there we will stay,' ¹⁵then hear the word of the LORD, O remnant of Judah. Thus says the LORD of hosts, the God of Israel: If you are determined to enter Egypt and go to settle there, ¹⁶then the sword that you fear shall overtake you there, in the land of Egypt; and the famine that you dread shall follow close after you into Egypt; and there you shall die. ¹⁷All the people who have determined to go to Egypt to settle there shall die by the sword, by famine, and by pestilence; they shall have no remnant or survivor from the disaster that I am bringing upon them.

18"For thus says the LORD of hosts, the God of Israel: Just as my anger and my wrath were poured out on the inhabitants of Jerusalem, so my wrath will be poured out on you when you go to Egypt. You shall become an object of execration and horror, of cursing and ridicule. You shall see this place no more. ¹⁹The LORD has said to you, O remnant of Judah, Do not go to Egypt. Be well aware that I have warned you today ²⁰that you have made a fatal mistake. For you yourselves sent me to the LORD your God, saying, 'Pray for us to the LORD our God, and whatever the LORD our God says, tell us and we will do it.' ²¹So I have told you today, but you have not obeyed the voice of the LORD your God in anything that he sent me to tell you. ²²Be well aware, then, that you shall die by the sword, by famine, and by pestilence in the place where you desire to go and settle."

43When Jeremiah finished speaking to all the people all these words of the LORD their God, with which the LORD their God had sent him to them, ²Azariah son of Hoshaiah and Johanan son of Kareah and all the other insolent men said to Jeremiah, "You are telling a lie. The LORD our God did not send you to say, 'Do not go to Egypt to settle there'; ³but Baruch son of Neriah is inciting you against us, to hand us over to the Chaldeans, in order that they may kill us or take us into exile in Babylon." ⁴So Johanan son of Kareah and all the commanders of the forces and

NIV

led away all the remnant of Judah who had come back to live in the land of Judah from all the nations where they had been scattered. ⁶They also led away all the men, women and children and the king's daughters whom Nebuzaradan commander of the imperial guard had left with Gedaliah son of Ahikam, the son of Shaphan, and Jeremiah the prophet and Baruch son of Neriah. ⁷So they entered Egypt in disobedience to the LORD and went as far as Tahpanhes.

⁸In Tahpanhes the word of the LORD came to Jeremiah: ⁹"While the Jews are watching, take some large stones with you and bury them in clay in the brick pavement at the entrance to Pharaoh's palace in Tahpanhes. ¹⁰Then say to them, 'This is what the LORD Almighty, the God of Israel, says: I will send for my servant Nebuchadnezzar king of Babylon, and I will set his throne over these stones I have buried here; he will spread his royal canopy above them. ¹¹He will come and attack Egypt, bringing death to those destined for death, captivity to those destined for captivity, and the sword to those destined for the sword. ¹²He*ᵃ* will set fire to the temples of the gods of Egypt; he will burn their temples and take their gods captive. As a shepherd wraps his garment around him, so will he wrap Egypt around himself and depart from there unscathed. ¹³There in the temple of the sun*ᵇ* in Egypt he will demolish the sacred pillars and will burn down the temples of the gods of Egypt.' "

ᵃ12 Or I   ᵇ13 Or in Heliopolis

NRSV

all the people did not obey the voice of the LORD, to stay in the land of Judah. ⁵But Johanan son of Kareah and all the commanders of the forces took all the remnant of Judah who had returned to settle in the land of Judah from all the nations to which they had been driven— ⁶the men, the women, the children, the princesses, and everyone whom Nebuzaradan the captain of the guard had left with Gedaliah son of Ahikam son of Shaphan; also the prophet Jeremiah and Baruch son of Neriah. ⁷And they came into the land of Egypt, for they did not obey the voice of the LORD. And they arrived at Tahpanhes.

8Then the word of the LORD came to Jeremiah in Tahpanhes: ⁹Take some large stones in your hands, and bury them in the clay pavement*ᵃ* that is at the entrance to Pharaoh's palace in Tahpanhes. Let the Judeans see you do it, ¹⁰and say to them, Thus says the LORD of hosts, the God of Israel: I am going to send and take my servant King Nebuchadrezzar of Babylon, and he*ᵇ* will set his throne above these stones that I have buried, and he will spread his royal canopy over them. ¹¹He shall come and ravage the land of Egypt, giving

those who are destined for pestilence, to pestilence,
and those who are destined for captivity, to captivity,
and those who are destined for the sword, to the sword.

¹²He*ᶜ* shall kindle a fire in the temples of the gods of Egypt; and he shall burn them and carry them away captive; and he shall pick clean the land of Egypt, as a shepherd picks his cloak clean of vermin; and he shall depart from there safely. ¹³He shall break the obelisks of Heliopolis, which is in the land of Egypt; and the temples of the gods of Egypt he shall burn with fire.

ᵃMeaning of Heb uncertain   ᵇGk Syr: Heb I   ᶜGk Syr Vg: Heb I

COMMENTARY

The issue of these chapters is a familiar one: listening or obeying (שמע *šāmaʿ*). From the opening of this portion of the book (37:2), which is echoed at the beginning of this section (cf. 37:3; 42:2), it has been clear that the fundamental problem of this people is their refusal to listen to the word of the Lord. Chapter 42 begins promisingly in that regard, but chap. 43 reveals that promise to be false. This section also brings Jeremiah back onto the scene. The small remnant (42:2) of Judah under the de facto leadership of Johanon after Gedaliah's murder and the escape of Ishmael is in chaos, uncertain of what to do, though the preceding chapter has reported their intention to go to Egypt to escape the expected retribution of the Babylonians because of Gedaliah's murder.

Narrative tension may be found between the end of chap. 41 and the beginning of chap. 42. In chap. 42, it appears that Johanon and the people do not know what to do and so seek God's direction, whereas chap. 41 revealed a definite intention. This tension is eventually resolved when the appeal for prophetic mediation becomes a charade (chap. 43) and we learn that the plan set out at the end of chap. 41 (to go to Egypt) has always been the intention of the group, and nothing will stop them—not even the prophetic word of the Lord.

A further tension in the forward movement of the story occurs between the end of chap. 42 and the beginning of chap. 43. The former includes a divine denunciation of the people's refusal to obey, even though the reader does not hear their negative response to the divine word until the beginning of chap. 43. This has led some to propose a transposition of 42:19-22 and 43:1-3. However, this rearrangement is unnecessary because, as these two examples cited here indicate, such anticipatory elements are not unusual in this narrative.

42:1-6. The remnant turn to the prophet and ask him to inquire of the Lord about what they should do. It is characteristic of the prophetic vocation to inquire of the Lord for individuals or groups and to pray to the Lord on their behalf.[205] The language of the latter activity is what we have

in v. 2—that is, a plea by this small dispirited group of folk that the prophet pray to the Lord for them. The rest of the narrative makes clear that they do not seek a prayer of intercession on their behalf but instead desire a typical inquiry of the Lord about what they are to do (e.g., 1 Kgs 22:5-6).

The conversation between Jeremiah and the group under Johanon sets the stage for what follows in two ways. Jeremiah indicates that he will do what they ask and give them a response, stressing that he will hold nothing back. This note, together with his promise to tell them everything the Lord says, suggests that the message may not be entirely welcome. The response of the remnant to this declaration offers a clue to the problem of this event. The people promise, rather vehemently and without reservation, to do whatever they are told. That vigorous commitment is signaled several ways: by the promise to "act according to everything that the Lord your God sends us through you," by the willingness to swear an oath to that end by the Lord's name ("May the Lord be a true and faithful witness against us"), by the indication that it does not matter whether the word is good or bad, and finally by the repeated promise to "*obey* the voice of the Lord our God" (v. 6). While some of this language belongs to the formal language used to inquire of the Lord, its cumulative effect underscores dramatically the people's ensuing disobedience (chap. 43).

42:7-17. The text tells us nothing of Jeremiah's prayer or inquiry, but the response that comes after a deliberate time ("ten days") indicates that he has, indeed, prayed on behalf of the people and has sought direction from the Lord. The divine response is both an oracle of salvation assuring the people of God's help and a judgment oracle announcing the Lord's intention for this people. The critical factor in determining whether this word will mean deliverance or judgment does not depend on what the Lord does. It is up to the people to determine whether the word of the Lord is a redemptive one or a punishing one. All hinges on the small word "if," which occurs three times: at the beginning of the oracle of salvation (v. 10), at the beginning of the accusatory part of the judgment speech (v. 13), and at the beginning of the

---

205. On the prophet as intercessor, see Patrick D. Miller, *They Cried to the Lord: The Form and Theology of Biblical Prayer* (Minneapolis: Fortress, 1994) chap. 8.

sentence of punishment, the second part of the judgment speech (v. 15). The reiteration of this conditional particle underscores the role of the people's response in determining what will happen.

This oracle of salvation is the most customary form of a divine response to human prayer.[206] Its heart is the reassurance, usually repeated as it is here, that you do not have to be afraid in what is clearly a fearful situation (v. 11*a*). But such a word, which always seems to stand against the facts of the case, is undergirded and grounded in fundamental claims of two sorts: (1) the promise of God's presence, "I am with you" (v. 11*b*), and (2) the further promise to intervene in the situation to help and to save (v. 11*c*). The fundamental assurance is then often elaborated and made specific, as it is here with the promise to build and plant rather than to pull down and pluck up (v. 10), language that echoes Jeremiah's commission (1:10), as well as the explicit promise that their particular and very real fear—the vengeance of the Babylonian ruler—will be laid to rest (v. 12). In this case, the good news, the rich possibilities for new life sounded in this oracle of salvation, is further underscored by the Lord's word, "I am sorry for the disaster" (v. 10). This word is to be read in the light of 18:7-10 as an assertion of the freedom of the Lord to exercise a change of mind. In this case, change of heart does not mean a reversal of history but a divine decision that the Lord will not carry the disaster forward.

With the people not yet even having a chance to react to the prophetic word, the prophet poses a sharp alternative in a conditional judgment speech (vv. 13-15). Such possibilities of judgment are so strong as to seem premature, even though the narrative has already anticipated the potentially negative response to the salvation oracle by telling us that the people are already on their way to Egypt. Those who ask the Lord to tell them which way to go are already on the way, following their own inclination.

In this new situation, living in post-Babylonian destruction and fearing Babylonian retribution, the fundamental issue for God's people has not

changed. In its more general and largest form it is still the refusal to listen and obey (v. 13). Moreover, the specific arena for obedience has not changed either. God insists that the people remain in or return to (the text is unclear which verb is intended in vv. 10*a* and 12*b*, where the NRSV has "remain" in the first instance and "restore" in the second) the land and live under Babylonian rule. That such an alternative has real possibilities has been demonstrated by preceding events. But it is a risky way, and the people (v. 14) choose the more pleasant prospects of Egypt: no war and sufficient food.

This judgment speech (vv. 13-17) is framed in the typical correspondence of punishment to the crime. Those who want to go to Egypt to escape war and to have plenty of food will be overtaken there, not by the Babylonian army but by the sword and famine they have sought to escape. What they fear in Judah, they will find in Egypt. No remnant of this group will be left. The judgment speech is couched in terms of the political realities of the time. The subtext to that reading is the perduring association of this people with the land of Canaan, now Judah and Samaria. The land of their previous slavery does not offer a better choice.

42:18-22. Anticipating the choice of the people as if it has already been made, the prophet underscores the word of judgment that has been uttered in several ways: (1) The people are commanded specifically not to go to Egypt (v. 19); (2) they are reminded that this word from the Lord comes *at their initiative* and of their firm and unreserved commitment to obey whatever direction they are given; and (3) the "if" of the preceding section disappears in the flat statement that the community will disobey and go its own way. The issue at the beginning of the chapter is still there at the end: "obeying the voice of the Lord your God" (v. 21). And the outcome of disobedience is what it has always been: the sanction of the covenant curses.

43:1-3. Although the text has offered numerous clues that make the reader expect a negative reaction to the prophetic word from the Lord, the ease with which it is rejected is still shocking. A largely responsible and faithful leadership to this point now becomes, by their actions, "insolent" as they accuse the prophet of lying to them. This may

---

206. Patrick D. Miller, "Prayer and Divine Action," in *God in the Fray,* ed. Timothy Beal and Tod Linafelt (Minneapolis: Fortress, 1998) 211-32. For a more extensive analysis of the oracle of salvation in the Bible generally, see Miller, *They Cried to the Lord,* chap. 4.

be a way of avoiding the force of the divine word because they argue that the Lord did not send Jeremiah to them with this word. But the accusation of lying is, in effect, a forthright refusal to do what the Lord has told them to do. If there is any playing fast and loose with the truth, it is in the claim of Johanon and others that the Lord did not say, "Do not go to Egypt." They are literally correct because they have changed the negative of the sentence from אַל ('al; as it appears in 42:19), which is not a permanent prohibition but a particular command for a particular moment, to לֹא (lō', 43:2), which makes the prohibition permanent and enduring. The word of the Lord at this moment in history is that they are to live their lives in the land of Judah under the Babylonians, even though that may be threatening. The people distort the prophetic word to their own ends, so that it is their words that become a lie.

The accusation against Baruch suggests that he may have been more than a scribe. The pro-Babylonian dimension of Jeremiah's preaching is here identified with his associate. While there is no way of being sure of whether the accusation of those who have set themselves against Jeremiah's prophetic word is true, there is reason to expect conformity between the perspective of the prophet and that of his chief aide, whichever of the two may have been the primary impetus for believing submission to Babylon was the stance for Judah.

43:4-7. But "they did not obey the voice of the Lord." This refrain, with which these verses (v. 4) begin and end (v. 7), has become monotonous in the narrative. It is the whole point, the theme of chaps. 37–45. The fall of Jerusalem, the destruction of Judah, and the exile of many to Babylon have not fundamentally altered the underlying sin of this community. Those realities have changed the context and its manifestation. What the narrative has anticipated in so many ways now happens. The people go to Egypt, arriving at Tahpanes, an Egyptian town in the northeastern part of the Nile Delta, near the border. Jeremiah and Baruch go with them.

43:8-13. The announcement of judgment upon the community if it goes to Egypt is reiterated in a different form once they have arrived there. Jeremiah uses another symbolic action, like the hiding of a loincloth at the Euphrates (13:1-11), the breaking of the clay pot (19:1-13), the wearing

of a yoke on his neck (27:1-15), and Hananiah's breaking of Jeremiah's yoke (28:10-11). The stones Jeremiah is to hide are to be the foundation of Nebuchadrezzar's throne when he conquers Egypt, which is the essence of this prophetic announcement. Calvin may understand the significance of the hiding properly when he says that "the time, indeed, for building the throne had not yet come; but God's purpose was to lay the foundations, so that they might be hid until the time arrived."[207] The reference to the throne and the king's canopy underscores Nebuchadrezzar's sovereignty over Egypt as surely as his sovereignty over the land of Judah. His conquest of Egypt will be as devastating as his conquest of Judah—burning the Temple, killing many inhabitants, and taking others into exile. But it is consistent with the Egyptian setting in the reference to breaking the obelisks (v. 13) and carrying the statues of the Egyptian gods into captivity, a common practice to demonstrate the power of the god(s) of the conqueror over the god(s) of the conquered.

The symbolic action, and its interpretation, is aimed at Egypt and is not couched as a word of judgment against the migrating Judeans. Still, in this context, it becomes a word to them as well, as is clear from the divine command, "Let the Judeans see you do it." Even more important in this respect is the focus upon Nebuchadrezzar as the conquering power and eventual ruler of Egypt (cf. 46:1-28). The escape to Egypt, perceived as an escape from the Babylonian ruler and the certain death or exile that the Judean remnant feared would be their fate, turns out to be a kind of "appointment in Samara." They have fled from the perceived, but unreal, danger of Babylon, only to encounter real danger in the place they thought would be safe. The incident reminds one of Amos's parable of the person who flees from a lion only to encounter a bear, gets away from the bear, and arrives safe at last in his house, only then to be bitten by a lethal snake as he leans against the wall in tired relief (Amos 5:19). Those who had thought they had finally escaped danger discover that this place they had assumed would be secure will become the place of their death.

---

207. John Calvin, *Commentaries on the Book of the Prophet Jeremiah and the Lamentations* (Edinburgh: Calvin Translation Society, 1854) IV:513. See also William L. Holladay, *Jeremiah 2*, Hermeneia (Philadelphia: Fortress, 1989) 302.

REFLECTIONS

1. One of the important theological features of this whole narrative is the convergence of the political events of the nations with the activity of the Lord of Israel. At several points, the prophetic word identifies the hand of the Lord in all that is going on. The promise that the king of Babylon would have mercy on the people is preceded by the assertion, "I will grant you mercy" (42:12), so that the mercy of the king is a kind of secondary causality to the mercy of God. Likewise, the sword, famine, and pestilence that are the promised fate of those who refuse to listen to God's word and stay put in Judah are described as "the disaster that I am bringing upon them" (42:17). Finally, this prophecy not only describes Nebuchadrezzar's actions in Egypt as the result of the Lord's sending him to Egypt, dubbing the Babylonian king "my servant" (43:10), but also reflects the sense of interaction between the king's actions and the Lord's actions in the way that the Hebrew and the Greek vary the personal pronoun in 43:10*b* and 12*a*.[208] The Hebrew has "I will set his throne" and "I shall kindle a fire," while the Greek has "he will set" and "he shall kindle." While the difference may be resolved in one direction or another in the textual history of the passage, the alternatives have arisen, in part, because of the convergence of human and divine agency that is at the heart of this story. The politics of the nations is the politics of God; the divine sovereignty is manifest over and through human sovereigns.

2. The double-edged character of the divine word through Jeremiah to the people in chapter 42 is a familiar feature of prophetic proclamation. It occurs in various ways, for example, in the prophet Isaiah, whose son's name, Shear-yashub, is an ambiguous oracle capable of meaning "(Only) a Remnant Shall Return" or "A Remnant Shall (Indeed) Return" (Isa 7:3; 10:20-23). Moreover, Isaiah's word to Ahaz, "If you do not stand firm in faith, you shall not stand at all" (Isa 7:9) contains the "if" that we see in Jeremiah 42, indicating that the outcome is very much up to Ahaz. He has a choice, and the choice he makes will determine whether he stands or falls.

The "flexibility" of the divine word at this point is a significant indicator of the openness of divine activity, fully responsive to the human response to it. That is, there is no deterministic notion of God's activity, no indication that things have been set according to some irrevocable plan. The malleability of the Lord's way with this people is constantly indicated, but no more clearly than here. Human decision is significantly a part of what shapes the future. The community is free to respond in freedom. But that choice is a weighty one. The Lord's intention for the future is here a complex mix of human petition, prophetic intercession, divine response, and human reaction to that. All of these things are what comprise the action of God in this situation. The "if" builds into the situation the power of human choice to affect what God does. The "now therefore" (a more accurate translation of the NRSV's weak "then" at the beginning of v. 15) announces consequences dependent upon the choice made. We are accustomed to the notion that our deeds have consequences. We may not have thought as deeply about the fact that God's control of history is significantly affected by both our prayers and our decisions. In this case, the choice that was made had significant historical results as it shifted the primary locus of the divine involvement with Israel and the possibilities of new life for that people from the surviving remnant of Judah to the exiles in Babylon. The people had promised to obey the divine word, whether it was "good or bad." What they failed to realize is that they would themselves determine whether it was good news or bad news, whether it was a word of salvation or a word of judgment.

3. The oracle of salvation, the divine word of assurance and promise to help, requires a large degree of trust. In most cases, when such oracles are uttered by priest or prophet, the circum-

---

208. On the textual and theological issues involved in the expression "my servant Nebuchadnezzar," see J. Gerald Janzen, *Studies in the Text of Jeremiah,* HSM 6 (Cambridge, Mass.: Harvard University Press, 1973) 54-57; and Werner E. Lemke, "Nebuchadnezzar, my Servant," *CBQ* 28 (1966) 45-50.

stances at the time do not look hopeful. The transformation of spirit and attitude that comes with the oracle of salvation arises from a confident trust in the faithfulness and power of God in the face of the continuing situation of trouble. Thus exiles were called to sing hymns of praise while they were still in exile because they had been told the good news that God had not abandoned them, that the Lord was with them and would uphold them and deliver them. Without a conviction that God is really present to help, nothing is changed. That trust is the missing component in this text, and without it there is no alleviation of the fear and the word of deliverance is turned into a word of judgment (43:13-17).

The announcement that God is at work to redeem the times is not always embraced as good news. The community of faith is called to act in the confidence that God's announcement really is true. Whether one really believes the good news from on high makes all the difference in the world. What is required may be a mode of life and action totally counter to the facts of the case from most perspectives, as is indicated in this text where the judgment speech anticipates the people's analysis of how things seem to be and gives a "rational" response to the situation (42:14). Our natural tendency is to do the sensible thing; the call of God is to live and walk by faith in the promises that have been declared and confirmed in the good news of God's redeeming love in Jesus Christ.

4. The degree to which these chapters are a reflection of the ideological interests of the Judeans in exile against the claims to legitimacy of what became a significant Judean community in Egypt is well articulated by Brueggemann, who writes: "The interplay of *vested interest* and *theological affirmation* is both evident and unavoidable. The text is not disinterested, but it operates on the conviction that the intent of God and the interest of this community of Babylonian exiles do indeed converge."[209] Here, as in so much of this book, sociopolitical interests are pervasive and cannot be removed from the story. Both Brueggemann and Seitz[210] have shown how much theological and ideological conflict permeates Jeremiah. The community of faith perceives the not-disinterested character of the text. After all, when are important texts ever disinterested? The Declaration of Independence is a thoroughly ideological and self-serving document, but its claims on those who live by it transcend the ideological conflict that produced it.

So it is with Scripture, whether it is the ideology that undermines the occupation of the land by its prior inhabitants or the ideology that combats the claims to legitimacy of particular groups within the community of Israel and the early church. One reads with critical, not innocent, eyes to perceive what is going on and with faithful, not skeptical, eyes to uncover the meaning of the memory Scripture preserves. In this case, the story of God's activity focuses on Babylon. The claim of the Judean homeland to be the center of the continuing story, which is the divine intent, is undone by human disobedience, while the claim of the Egyptian community is negated by the judgment of God on those who go that way. In fact, the working out of the divine word happened in a more complex way as all three of these communities became loci for the renewal of Judean/Jewish life in the centuries that lay ahead. Indeed, all three became preservers of the Word of the Lord as they nurtured and protected the scriptures of Israel.

As Brueggemann suggests: "The pro-Babylonian cast of the material is not simply political ideology or pastoral sensitivity toward exiles, but it is finally a daring judgment of faith about God's will and work in the world."[211] The present community of faith is no more able to free itself from ideological strains than was the ancient community. It hopes and prays that its ideologies can be transformed and absorbed into the divine activity, that "vested interest" and "theological affirmation" can still converge on behalf of truthful obedience and the purposes of God.[212]

209. Walter Brueggemann, *A Commentary on Jeremiah: Exile and Homecoming* (Grand Rapids: Eerdmans, 1998) 395.
210. Christopher Seitz, *Theology in Conflict: Reactions to the Exile in the Book of Jeremiah*, BZAW 176 (Berlin: Walter de Gruyter, 1989).
211. Brueggemann, *A Commentary on Jeremiah*, 344.
212. On the relation of faith and ideology, see Patrick D. Miller, "Faith and Ideology in the Old Testament."

JEREMIAH 44:1-30, DIFFERENT SETTING, SAME SIN

NIV

44 This word came to Jeremiah concerning all the Jews living in Lower Egypt—in Migdol, Tahpanhes and Memphis*ᵃ*—and in Upper Egypt*ᵇ*: 2"This is what the LORD Almighty, the God of Israel, says: You saw the great disaster I brought on Jerusalem and on all the towns of Judah. Today they lie deserted and in ruins 3because of the evil they have done. They provoked me to anger by burning incense and by worshiping other gods that neither they nor you nor your fathers ever knew. 4Again and again I sent my servants the prophets, who said, 'Do not do this detestable thing that I hate!' 5But they did not listen or pay attention; they did not turn from their wickedness or stop burning incense to other gods. 6Therefore, my fierce anger was poured out; it raged against the towns of Judah and the streets of Jerusalem and made them the desolate ruins they are today.

7"Now this is what the LORD God Almighty, the God of Israel, says: Why bring such great disaster on yourselves by cutting off from Judah the men and women, the children and infants, and so leave yourselves without a remnant? 8Why provoke me to anger with what your hands have made, burning incense to other gods in Egypt, where you have come to live? You will destroy yourselves and make yourselves an object of cursing and reproach among all the nations on earth. 9Have you forgotten the wickedness committed by your fathers and by the kings and queens of Judah and the wickedness committed by you and your wives in the land of Judah and the streets of Jerusalem? 10To this day they have not humbled themselves or shown reverence, nor have they followed my law and the decrees I set before you and your fathers.

11"Therefore, this is what the LORD Almighty, the God of Israel, says: I am determined to bring disaster on you and to destroy all Judah. 12I will take away the remnant of Judah who were determined to go to Egypt to settle there. They will all perish in Egypt; they will fall by the sword or die

ᵃ1 Hebrew Noph   ᵇ1 Hebrew in Pathros

NRSV

44 The word that came to Jeremiah for all the Judeans living in the land of Egypt, at Migdol, at Tahpanhes, at Memphis, and in the land of Pathros, 2Thus says the LORD of hosts, the God of Israel: You yourselves have seen all the disaster that I have brought on Jerusalem and on all the towns of Judah. Look at them; today they are a desolation, without an inhabitant in them, 3because of the wickedness that they committed, provoking me to anger, in that they went to make offerings and serve other gods that they had not known, neither they, nor you, nor your ancestors. 4Yet I persistently sent to you all my servants the prophets, saying, "I beg you not to do this abominable thing that I hate!" 5But they did not listen or incline their ear, to turn from their wickedness and make no offerings to other gods. 6So my wrath and my anger were poured out and kindled in the towns of Judah and in the streets of Jerusalem; and they became a waste and a desolation, as they still are today. 7And now thus says the LORD God of hosts, the God of Israel: Why are you doing such great harm to yourselves, to cut off man and woman, child and infant, from the midst of Judah, leaving yourselves without a remnant? 8Why do you provoke me to anger with the works of your hands, making offerings to other gods in the land of Egypt where you have come to settle? Will you be cut off and become an object of cursing and ridicule among all the nations of the earth? 9Have you forgotten the crimes of your ancestors, of the kings of Judah, of their*ᵃ* wives, your own crimes and those of your wives, which they committed in the land of Judah and in the streets of Jerusalem? 10They have shown no contrition or fear to this day, nor have they walked in my law and my statutes that I set before you and before your ancestors.

11Therefore thus says the LORD of hosts, the God of Israel: I am determined to bring disaster on you, to bring all Judah to an end. 12I will take the remnant of Judah who are determined to come to

ᵃHeb his

NIV

from famine. From the least to the greatest, they will die by sword or famine. They will become an object of cursing and horror, of condemnation and reproach. ¹³I will punish those who live in Egypt with the sword, famine and plague, as I punished Jerusalem. ¹⁴None of the remnant of Judah who have gone to live in Egypt will escape or survive to return to the land of Judah, to which they long to return and live; none will return except a few fugitives."

¹⁵Then all the men who knew that their wives were burning incense to other gods, along with all the women who were present—a large assembly—and all the people living in Lower and Upper Egypt,ᵃ said to Jeremiah, ¹⁶"We will not listen to the message you have spoken to us in the name of the LORD! ¹⁷We will certainly do everything we said we would: We will burn incense to the Queen of Heaven and will pour out drink offerings to her just as we and our fathers, our kings and our officials did in the towns of Judah and in the streets of Jerusalem. At that time we had plenty of food and were well off and suffered no harm. ¹⁸But ever since we stopped burning incense to the Queen of Heaven and pouring out drink offerings to her, we have had nothing and have been perishing by sword and famine."

¹⁹The women added, "When we burned incense to the Queen of Heaven and poured out drink offerings to her, did not our husbands know that we were making cakes like her image and pouring out drink offerings to her?"

²⁰Then Jeremiah said to all the people, both men and women, who were answering him, ²¹"Did not the LORD remember and think about the incense burned in the towns of Judah and the streets of Jerusalem by you and your fathers, your kings and your officials and the people of the land? ²²When the LORD could no longer endure your wicked actions and the detestable things you did, your land became an object of cursing and a desolate waste without inhabitants, as it is today. ²³Because you have burned incense and have sinned against the LORD and have not obeyed him or followed his law or his decrees or his stipulations, this disaster has come upon you, as you now see."

ᵃ15 Hebrew *in Egypt and Pathros*

NRSV

the land of Egypt to settle, and they shall perish, everyone; in the land of Egypt they shall fall; by the sword and by famine they shall perish; from the least to the greatest, they shall die by the sword and by famine; and they shall become an object of execration and horror, of cursing and ridicule. ¹³I will punish those who live in the land of Egypt, as I have punished Jerusalem, with the sword, with famine, and with pestilence, ¹⁴so that none of the remnant of Judah who have come to settle in the land of Egypt shall escape or survive or return to the land of Judah. Although they long to go back to live there, they shall not go back, except some fugitives.

15Then all the men who were aware that their wives had been making offerings to other gods, and all the women who stood by, a great assembly, all the people who lived in Pathros in the land of Egypt, answered Jeremiah: ¹⁶"As for the word that you have spoken to us in the name of the LORD, we are not going to listen to you. ¹⁷Instead, we will do everything that we have vowed, make offerings to the queen of heaven and pour out libations to her, just as we and our ancestors, our kings and our officials, used to do in the towns of Judah and in the streets of Jerusalem. We used to have plenty of food, and prospered, and saw no misfortune. ¹⁸But from the time we stopped making offerings to the queen of heaven and pouring out libations to her, we have lacked everything and have perished by the sword and by famine." ¹⁹And the women said,ᵃ "Indeed we will go on making offerings to the queen of heaven and pouring out libations to her; do you think that we made cakes for her, marked with her image, and poured out libations to her without our husbands' being involved?"

20Then Jeremiah said to all the people, men and women, all the people who were giving him this answer: ²¹"As for the offerings that you made in the towns of Judah and in the streets of Jerusalem, you and your ancestors, your kings and your officials, and the people of the land, did not the LORD remember them? Did it not come into his mind? ²²The LORD could no longer bear the sight of your evil doings, the abominations that you committed; therefore your land became a

ᵃCompare Syr: Heb lacks *And the women said*

NIV

²⁴Then Jeremiah said to all the people, including the women, "Hear the word of the LORD, all you people of Judah in Egypt. ²⁵This is what the LORD Almighty, the God of Israel, says: You and your wives have shown by your actions what you promised when you said, 'We will certainly carry out the vows we made to burn incense and pour out drink offerings to the Queen of Heaven.'

"Go ahead then, do what you promised! Keep your vows! ²⁶But hear the word of the LORD, all Jews living in Egypt: 'I swear by my great name,' says the LORD, 'that no one from Judah living anywhere in Egypt will ever again invoke my name or swear, "As surely as the Sovereign LORD lives."' ²⁷For I am watching over them for harm, not for good; the Jews in Egypt will perish by sword and famine until they are all destroyed. ²⁸Those who escape the sword and return to the land of Judah from Egypt will be very few. Then the whole remnant of Judah who came to live in Egypt will know whose word will stand—mine or theirs.

²⁹"'This will be the sign to you that I will punish you in this place,' declares the LORD, 'so that you will know that my threats of harm against you will surely stand.' ³⁰This is what the LORD says: 'I am going to hand Pharaoh Hophra king of Egypt over to his enemies who seek his life, just as I handed Zedekiah king of Judah over to Nebuchadnezzar king of Babylon, the enemy who was seeking his life.'"

NRSV

desolation and a waste and a curse, without inhabitant, as it is to this day. ²³It is because you burned offerings, and because you sinned against the LORD and did not obey the voice of the LORD or walk in his law and in his statutes and in his decrees, that this disaster has befallen you, as is still evident today."

²⁴Jeremiah said to all the people and all the women, "Hear the word of the LORD, all you Judeans who are in the land of Egypt, ²⁵Thus says the LORD of hosts, the God of Israel: You and your wives have accomplished in deeds what you declared in words, saying, 'We are determined to perform the vows that we have made, to make offerings to the queen of heaven and to pour out libations to her.' By all means, keep your vows and make your libations! ²⁶Therefore hear the word of the LORD, all you Judeans who live in the land of Egypt: Lo, I swear by my great name, says the LORD, that my name shall no longer be pronounced on the lips of any of the people of Judah in all the land of Egypt, saying, 'As the Lord GOD lives.' ²⁷I am going to watch over them for harm and not for good; all the people of Judah who are in the land of Egypt shall perish by the sword and by famine, until not one is left. ²⁸And those who escape the sword shall return from the land of Egypt to the land of Judah, few in number; and all the remnant of Judah, who have come to the land of Egypt to settle, shall know whose words will stand, mine or theirs! ²⁹This shall be the sign to you, says the LORD, that I am going to punish you in this place, in order that you may know that my words against you will surely be carried out: ³⁰Thus says the LORD, I am going to give Pharaoh Hophra, king of Egypt, into the hands of his enemies, those who seek his life, just as I gave King Zedekiah of Judah into the hand of King Nebuchadrezzar of Babylon, his enemy who sought his life."

COMMENTARY

The opening words of this chapter come as something of a surprise. What was an apparently small band of Judeans residing at Tahpanes on the border of Egypt is now a widespread immigration, resulting in Judean communities at three other towns besides Tahpanes. The inevitable inference from the text is that some time has passed and that people have entered Egypt and settled down there. This assumption, however, conflicts with the announced, but not yet accomplished, defeat of Pharaoh Hophra, whose rule ended within twenty years of the destruction of Jerusalem. We also are presented with a somewhat unreal picture of Jeremiah preaching to an assembly of all the Judeans from four different areas of Egypt and engaging them in conversation. Such features suggest that the chapter in its present form is not concerned primarily with reporting history as such. Its purpose, like much of this book, is of a different sort.

The character of Jeremiah's words and the response of the people would make this oracle appropriate for any earlier time in the history of his prophecy in Judah. In language and content often reminiscent of Deuteronomy as well as of the prophet's own earlier prophecies, Jeremiah proclaims a word from the Lord to the effect that the long history of disobedience that centers in the worship of other gods has not yet come to an end. As a result, the wrath and anger of the Lord are not yet at an end either. Indeed, the chapter underscores the degree to which the religious practices of the Judean community in Egypt are continuous with the practices of the people in Judah. They have even returned more vigorously to their apostate ways. This chapter focuses on worship of the queen of heaven, an activity already placed under prophetic condemnation in 7:16-20. (See the Commentary on 7:16-20 for an extended discussion of the worship of the queen of heaven as it is presented in both chaps. 7 and 44.)

44:1-14. The movement of Jeremiah's speech has three primary components: (1) He begins with a rehearsal of the past judgment against Judah and Jerusalem, which is meant to function as a kind of object lesson (vv. 1-6). The opening words of the speech, "You yourselves have seen" (v. 2), often are used to emphasize that the people have wit-

nessed to the mighty deeds of the Lord in the history of their salvation (see Exod 19:4; Deut 29:2-3; Josh 23:3). Now that same expression points to the witness of the people to the history of judgment. Just as in the past the eyewitness was meant to nurture faith and trust in the Lord, so also it is here. And as it often did not in the past, it does not here.

(2) In the second part of the speech (vv. 7-10), the prophet draws a large inference from the first part ("and now," or better, "now therefore," v. 7). He builds upon the story of the past to indict the present community in Egypt. That indictment is set out in a series of rhetorical questions, which are often used in a formal disputation. These questions are intended, therefore, to make the people question their actions and thus to persuade them to change their ways. The final verse of this section, however, indicates that the questions function instead to effect a kind of self-indictment of a people who show no inclination to change their ways "to this day" (v. 10). Verse 10 thus provides both a summary or general indictment of the people (for not following the Lord's law and statutes), the specifics of which are spelled out elsewhere in the text. Verse 10 also serves as a link to the final part of the speech, indicating that the sins of the past have continued to the present moment.

(3) This prophetic speech, a series of logical inferences that cannot be missed or escaped, is developed further with the "therefore" at the beginning of the final part (vv. 11-14). The prophet announces punishment upon those who have continued in the ways of the past and hence now hear about their fate—same song, second (or fifteenth!) verse. While the punishment announced in 43:8-13 is directed more to Egypt and by inference to those Judeans who refused to listen to the voice of the Lord and went on to Egypt anyway, this punishment is quite specifically directed at the Judeans. Their behavior as a covenant people is no better in Egypt than it was in Judah.

There is much repetition in these verses, and, as is often the case, the repeated language carries the thematic freight. The most repeated word is רעה (rā'â), variously translated as "disaster" (vv. 2, 11), "wickedness" (vv. 3, 5), "harm" (v. 7), and "crimes" (5 times in the Hebrew of v. 9). All these uses of *rā'â* are related. The logic is simple but devastating. The *rā'â* of the people, their "wickedness" and "crimes," which comprises a long history, as the several references to the "ancestors" (vv. 3, 9-10) indicate, brings about great "harm" because it "provokes" (vv. 3, 8) the Lord to bring "disaster" on the people.

The source of the provocation is indicated in another repeated phrase: "making offerings to other gods" (vv. 3, 8). The book of Jeremiah has identified the allure of the other gods as the fatal temptation of this people. In this summary account, we hear that what had been announced beforehand has now come to pass. The worship of other gods they did not "know," carried out in the face of repeated prophetic warnings (v. 4), has resulted in the "disaster" of the Babylonian destruction. Those who committed their "crimes" in "the land of Judah and the streets of Jerusalem" (v. 9) experienced the terrible disaster that the Lord brought upon "the towns of Judah and the streets of Jerusalem" (vv. 3, 6).

The effect of this destruction is characterized in several ways. It involves the traditional, but no less terrible, fate of death by "sword and famine" (vv. 12-13), already anticipated when the people claimed their flight to Egypt was to escape war and hunger (42:13-17). Moreover, the story about the fate of the people will be told with horror; they will be made the object of ridicule by other nations (vv. 8, 12, 22; cf. 24:9; 25:18; 29:18; 42:18). Finally, there will not be enough left to flee back to Judah when they finally realize that their best and only hopes are there (v. 14). They are being punished not only because of their apostasy, but also because of their decision to flee to Egypt against the express command of the Lord. The third part of the speech (vv. 11-14) reiterates the word of the Lord in 43:8-13, a strong word of judgment against the Judeans in Egypt that receives further emphasis by its repetition at the end of this chapter (44:27-28).

44:15-19. Once again, the people respond, "We are not going to listen" (v. 16). This time, however, rather than accusing the prophet of lying as an excuse to disobey, the people simply and arrogantly refuse to pay any attention. But we hear a new element; a rationale is given for their persistent behavior. The speakers are the women, the wives in the group (v. 19), which may be why the crimes or wickedness of "your wives" is specifically

cited in v. 9. Their argument offers a serious counter to Jeremiah's word and, in a sense, uses Jeremiah's argument against him. He proclaims sword, famine, death, and destruction if they continue in their present wickedness of making offerings to other gods. "But the women arrange and interpret the raw material of Jeremiah's argument differently. Disaster did not follow on disobedience to the prophetic word or on idolatry. It followed on the institution of exclusive centralized Yahwism and the suppression of syncretism."[213] The people argue that the disasters they have suffered would not have happened if they had not stopped making cakes and libations to the queen of heaven. It is not clear when worship of the queen of heaven ceased, but most scholars assume it would have been in Josiah's time. Hence the women are probably referring to the sequence of disasters following his reform, from Jeremiah's death to the destruction of Jerusalem and the various calamities afterward.[214] In any event, the women have no intention of stopping again, and they call attention to the fact that they do not do this without the implicit assent of their husbands, whose role in the worship of the queen of heaven is attested in 7:18. (For more extensive discussion of the worship of the queen of heaven, see the Commentary on 7:16-20.)

44:20-23. The conflict here is unresolvable. There are two very different views on what is happening and the way the gods are involved in the affairs of the people. Jeremiah challenges the claims of the women and vigorously asserts the opposite perspective. The disasters that have ensued down to the present are precisely the judgment of the Lord for just this kind of disobedience of the Lord's voice and the Lord's law.

44:24-30. This standoff between the worshipers of the queen of heaven and the prophet of the Lord is then set forth by the prophet as a test case whose resolution will occur in the course of history. Jeremiah tells the people—with some vehemence, according to the emphatic constructions in v. 25c—to go ahead and do what they are insisting on doing. But there will be a way of telling whose power is really at work and whose word endures, "mine or theirs" (v. 28). The language of "watching" (שׁקד *šāqad,* v. 27) echoes the

213. William McKane, *A Critical and Exegetical Commentary on Jeremiah,* 2 vols., ICC (Edinburgh: T. & T. Clark, 1986, 1996) 2:1089.
214. Ibid., 1087.

call of Jeremiah and the sign of the almond branch (1:11-12), testifying to the power of the Lord's word to effect history.

The connection between the sin of idolatry and the sin of disobeying the voice of the Lord and going to Egypt is made clear. The divine word refers several times to the people of Judah in the land of Egypt and once explicitly to those "who have come to the land of Egypt to settle" (v. 28). The punishment will come about "in this place" (v. 29). The people thought that going to Egypt and worshiping the queen of heaven would ensure their well-being and safety. Both acts, however, will accomplish just the opposite. The Lord's "harm" will reduce the remnant in Egypt to nothing but a few fugitives who escape back to Judah (vv. 14, 28). Thus both Judah and Egypt will no longer be places where a remnant of the Lord's people can begin again to new life. That will happen in and among the exiles in Babylon. The one who promised "good and not harm" (29:11) for the community in exile in Babylon now promises "harm and not good" (44:27) for the remnant community who fled Judah for Egypt. Here the text makes a judgment that is less historical, for communities of Judeans continued to exist in both the land of Judah and Egypt, than it is theological and ideological. The locus of the Lord's "building and planting" (1:10; 31:28) will be the community of the return, in Babylon (29:5, 28) and eventually again in Judah (24:6; 32:15).

The word of the Lord concludes with the promise of a sign. This is not a sign of what is to come in order to instill faith and confidence but an element of what is to come, which, when it happens, will confirm the Lord's word of judgment.[215] It is analogous to the sign given to Moses at the burning bush in the wilderness of Horeb: When the people were delivered, they would find themselves at that same mountain worshiping the Lord who had delivered them. Second Isaiah makes this announcement of what is to come beforehand the primary test of a true deity (Isaiah 41). It is not a test here, but the word is implicitly put forth as an assertion that it is the Lord, not the queen of heaven or any other deity, who determines what happens to the people of Israel.

The prophecy of the death of Pharaoh Hophra of Egypt, who reigned over Egypt from 588 to 569 BCE and was killed in a rebellion, may be a prophecy after the event. The Jeremianic tradition saw in that event the fulfillment of the word of the Lord to Jeremiah and a sign of the Lord's judgment on the Judean remnant in Egypt, though there is no indication of a special fate for them. The invasion of Nebuchadrezzar in 568/67 BCE provided a further confirmation of the inability of the fleeing Judeans to escape Babylonian control. The reference to Zedekiah may have a double significance. Hophra may have been involved in Zedekiah's revolt against Babylon. But the one who would destroy the royal scion of David would certainly be no less hesitant to destroy a king of an alien nation.

215. On the two types of signs, see John Calvin, *Commentaries on the Book of the Prophet Jeremiah and the Lamentations* (Edinburgh: Calvin Translation Society, 1854) 4:561-62.

REFLECTIONS

1. The double use of the word "provoke" (44:3, 8) and the reference to "wrath and anger" (44:6) invoke anthropomorphic language to convey the degree to which this correspondence of crime and punishment cannot be understood as a kind of deterministic view of history. This is not some fate-effecting deed that works automatically, the consequence flowing inevitably out of the deed. No, the God of Israel responds vigorously to the way the people act ("This abominable thing that I hate!"). The covenant is a relational framework, and in that relationship the deity is understood to be personally involved as much as the people. What happens "moves" God to act, even as the people are "moved" to act in certain ways. The "provocation" is the critical link between the "wickedness" and the "disaster."

The use of anthropomorphic language of Scripture in reference to deity, language that cannot be literalized but is nevertheless truthful, is a way of identifying the personal dimension of God's relation to the world. It is possible to read the anthropomorphic portrayal of God as a human projection of what is human because human beings (1) have no other conceptual tools or language to speak of God or (2) are inclined to take human features and push them to the limits and call that God. In the Christian faith, however, conceiving of God as personal is given "from above" rather than being a projection "from below." The incarnation of God in Jesus Christ is a confirmation of the deeply personal involvement of God in human life and of the fact that human, personal categories are appropriate, indeed *necessary,* for Christian faith to speak truthfully about God and to speak faithfully to God.

2. The conflict between the prophet of the word of the Lord and the women and others in the community is a dramatic example of reading the data differently. That reading is seen by both sides to be a life-and-death matter. The pursuit of other gods is not here an academic pastime. It happens out of a firm conviction that only by such devotion can one survive. That may always be the case, at least to the degree that ultimate loyalties that infringe upon our devotion to God often represent choices of those things that we believe will bring us life and blessing.

In this case, there is no final arbiter of the matter in the moment. The text proclaims, however, that there is a way of determining who it is that brings life and not death. The coming of the future, the effecting of history, will indicate who is in charge, and the signs of the times will show that. But such signs will always be ambiguous. After all, the Egyptian pharaoh Hophra died as a result of an internal Egyptian revolt, not by military defeat at the hands of the Babylonians. It is for just such ambiguities of history and life that the church receives and holds its scriptures. The story of Israel and the story of Christ become a genuine measuring stick (i.e., a canon), an instrument of apperception that enables those who still find their lives led by the Lord of Israel to look for the signs, to discern what is going on, to know how to respond, and to find the way. The queen of heaven does not have a continuing story, and so the test of history provides some vindication of Jeremiah's claim.[216] It is not a proof. But out of just such "reading" of history, the community, in faith, claims to know the way to truth, the God who is real, and the rule that benefits. (See also paragraph 4 in the Reflections at 7:1–8:3, which pertains to this chapter as well, and the discussion of idolatry and the worship of other gods in paragraph 3 in the Reflections at 2:1–4:4.)

216. See, in this regard, the perceptive remarks of Walter Brueggemann, *A Commentary on Jeremiah: Exile and Homecoming* (Grand Rapids: Eerdmans, 1998) 410-13, on the difference between the Lord and the queen of heaven in terms of long-term history and theological density, canonical literature, and interpretive commentary.

JEREMIAH 45:1-5, A PROMISE TO BARUCH

NIV

45 This is what Jeremiah the prophet told Baruch son of Neriah in the fourth year of Jehoiakim son of Josiah king of Judah, after Baruch had written on a scroll the words Jeremiah was then dictating: [2]"This is what the LORD, the God of Israel, says to you, Baruch: [3]You said, 'Woe to me! The LORD has added sorrow to my pain; I am worn out with groaning and find no rest.' "

[4]The LORD said, "Say this to him: 'This is what the LORD says: I will overthrow what I have built and uproot what I have planted, throughout the

NRSV

45 The word that the prophet Jeremiah spoke to Baruch son of Neriah, when he wrote these words in a scroll at the dictation of Jeremiah, in the fourth year of King Jehoiakim son of Josiah of Judah: [2]Thus says the LORD, the God of Israel, to you, O Baruch: [3]You said, "Woe is me! The LORD has added sorrow to my pain; I am weary with my groaning, and I find no rest." [4]Thus you shall say to him, "Thus says the LORD: I am going to break down what I have built, and pluck up what I have planted—that is, the whole land. [5]And you, do you seek great things for your-

NIV	NRSV
land. ⁵Should you then seek great things for yourself? Seek them not. For I will bring disaster on all people, declares the LORD, but wherever you go I will let you escape with your life.' "	self? Do not seek them; for I am going to bring disaster upon all flesh, says the LORD; but I will give you your life as a prize of war in every place to which you may go."

COMMENTARY

With these brief verses, this portion of the book, narrating the last days of Judah and the events that followed the Babylonian conquest, comes to an end. It is particularly concerned with Baruch. The chapter takes the reader back in time to the events recorded in chap. 36 and thus serves as a kind of echo of that chapter. It also concludes this section in a manner very similar to the way the first part ends (chaps. 37–39)—that is, with an oracle of salvation to one who has stayed faithful (see 39:15-18).

The disjunction between the date given in the first verse (fourth year of Jehoiakim), which places this chapter in 605 BCE, and the present literary setting, after the series of events and oracles involving the flight to Egypt after 586 BCE, has caused interpreters problems. Some have moved these verses so that they are connected with chap. 36 and the writing of the scroll on that occasion. Others regard the date formula in v. 1 as inaccurate and see the chapter as fitting in the period to which the preceding chapters belong—that is, the time of the Judean flight to Egypt.[217] There may be no way to resolve the tension between the date given by the text and the date suggested by the present literary location of these verses.

The date formula is important, for it underscores the significance of this year and relates events. The book refers to the fourth year of Jehoiakim at several key points: at the conclusion to the collection of oracles in chaps. 1–25 (25:1); at the conclusion to the next collection, chaps. 26–36, which ends with the writing of the scroll and Jehoiakim's arrogant destruction of the scroll, putting an end to the possibility of Judah's avoiding divine judgment (36:1); at the beginning of chap. 45, which concludes the next section of Jeremiah (chaps. 37–45); and at 46:2, which begins the oracles concerning the foreign nations.

Taylor rightly sees this date as signaling the judgment of God.[218] That judgment is further suggested by Baruch's complaint and by the Lord's announced intention to break down what has been built and pluck up what has been planted, a clear allusion to Jeremiah's call, but the only such allusion—and there are several—that places the planting and building as past events that are now being undone. These verses thus underscore the impression that chap. 36 and other references to the fourth year of Jehoiakim have made: The year 605 BCE was a decisive moment in Judah's history, the point of no return from the pending judgment.

But in its present literary context, the words to Baruch function also as a way out, a chance for life that is given in the face of death. It is the same word given to Ebed-melech at the conclusion of chap. 39 as a reward for his faithfulness. Baruch's "life as a prize of war" signals not only that war is imminent but also that he will endure and will find his life and not lose it. Like Ebed-melech, Baruch is rewarded because of his faithfulness to the Lord by his service to the prophet Jeremiah and presumably also because of his support of God's insistence on submission to the Babylonians.

No reason is given for Baruch's complaint, nor is there any explanation of the enigmatic "great things" Baruch seeks for himself (v. 5). The scribe is much like the prophet both in his complaint and in having the complaint summarily dismissed by the Lord. The dismissal, however, occurs in the context of a promise, as is the case with Jeremiah (e.g., 11:23; 15:20).

Three other elements of this text are important: (1) The reference to the scroll Jeremiah dictated to Baruch reminds the reader of the importance of this document as a continuing record of what happened and what was said (cf. chap. 36).

---

217. Marion Ann Taylor, "Jeremiah 45: The Problem of Placement," *JSOT* 37 (1987) 79-98.

218. Ibid., 89.

(2) The protection of Baruch's life points to the remnant that perdures, even though preceding chapters have suggested that there can be no survivors outside of exile. There are at least Ebed-melech and Baruch! The story of Jeremiah and Judah does not end without a modest hope for the future in the midst of a large act of judgment.

(3) The brief oracle of the Lord (vv. 4-5) suggests a broader framework for God's judgment than the book has hitherto set forth. Whereas most of the words about the Lord's judgment have been directed toward Judah and Israel, now we hear that the Lord is "going to bring disaster upon *all flesh*" (v. 5). The same thing may be indicated by כל־הארץ (*kol-hā'āreṣ*) in v. 4, which is translated in the NRSV as "the whole land" but could mean "the whole earth."[219] This broader reference foreshadows what is to follow: announcements of God's judgment upon the other nations.

219. The absence of this phrase in the Septuagint has led many to regard it as a much later explanatory gloss. If that is the case, then the issue remains what the interpretive gloss means to suggest—the land or the earth.

REFLECTIONS

"Your life as a prize of war" is a highly ambiguous promise, but it is not uncharacteristic of the promises of this God who speaks through Jeremiah. It ties together trust, promise, and a difficult life. This combination frequently marks the way of those whose loyalty is to God. The book of Jeremiah serves to underscore that ambiguous way and the combination of these elements in a life devoted to God as it presents the characters of Ebed-melech (chaps. 38–39) and Baruch in a similar fashion. Their faithfulness is marked not so much in pious acts as in holding fast in the face of the exigencies and situations that confront them. In Ebed-melech's case, there is no indication of any special religious qualities. He is simply willing to risk in compassion and concern for the Lord's prophet. Of Baruch, we know only of his loyalty to Jeremiah and his faithful performance of his duties as Jeremiah's scribe. In one case, a particular act of compassion; in the other, a lifetime of doing his job. The reward is not some great and magnificent blessing, not some large promise such as came to Abraham and to David. It is simply survival in a terrifying time.

Those who read of these two men match them with other persons who have done their job in a way that demonstrates in unheralded ways a trust in the Lord and so see a continuing line of nonheroic types whose faithfulness is deemed good by the Lord. The rewards for such faithfulness are sometimes no better than survival, but in time of trouble the promise of survival is a large one. "Your life as a prize of war" for services rendered may be the best possibility available—even for the church—in the midst of God's judging purposes.

JEREMIAH 46:1–51:64

ORACLES AGAINST THE NATIONS

OVERVIEW

This long section of oracles concerning various other nations of the ancient Near East at the end of the book of Jeremiah brings together both a common feature of prophecy and a particular feature of the book of Jeremiah. Several of the prophetic books include a body of oracles that address the affairs of other nations (e.g., Isaiah 13–23; Ezekiel 24–32; Amos 1:3–2:16). In that respect, Jeremiah is similar to other prophetic books. The rationale for including a number of oracles concerning other peoples in this book, however, derives from Jeremiah's original commission: "I appointed you a prophet to the nations" (1:5). Most of the prophetic call stories are typical in form but distinctive in content. Each one highlights a particular feature of the prophetic message or book. Jeremiah is no exception. Most of his prophecies are addressed to the Judeans, but early in the book one finds speeches addressed to the northern kingdom, Israel. Now at the end we encounter an extensive collection of both brief and lengthy prophetic speeches about other nations. They are grouped together under the prophetic rubric: "The word of the LORD that came to the prophet Jeremiah against the nations" (46:1).

This collection of prophecies against or about (the Hebrew preposition עַל ['al] can mean either "concerning" or "against") the nations also represents one of the major differences between the Hebrew, or Masoretic, text of Jeremiah and the Greek, or Septuagintal, text. While they appear at the end of the book in the Hebrew, in the Greek translation, which may represent an earlier stage in the formation of the text, they make up chaps. 25:14–31:44, having been attached to the words in 25:13 about "all the words that I have uttered against it"—that is, against Babylon—though the Greek makes no explicit reference to Babylon. The oracles also appear in a different order in the Greek than they do in the Hebrew.

These oracles speak about and to several different countries: Egypt, Philistia, Moab, Ammon, Edom, Damascus (Aram), Arabian tribes, Elam in Mesopotamia, and finally and most extensively Babylon. They share neither form nor tone. Some announce future destruction with some pathos, others with more fierce intent. Some anticipate restoration after the judgment of the nation; others do not. The explicit rationale for the judgment of a particular nation is occasionally apparent, in some instances hardly visible at all, and in the case of Babylon much more articulated. The oracles in chaps. 47–49 may reflect the impact of international treaties, with most of these nations seen as violating the suzerain power of the Lord of Israel exercised through the Babylonian ruler as the Lord's servant.[220] Various clues, such as the presence of treaty curses, may point in that direction. In any event, the oracles do indicate that the interaction of many nations in the events of the late seventh and early sixth centuries did not stand outside the purview of the Lord of Israel. The sovereign rule of that God over the whole earth is nowhere more clearly asserted than in the address of oracles to other nations without respect to their relationship to Israel/Judah.

> If these close neighbors of Judah were caught up in the same events, was not the same divine purpose that related to Judah also operational for them? Inevitable questions relating to the interpretation of the divine purpose for all nations arose out of the conviction that historical events manifested in some way a divine purpose.[221]

220. Gerald L. Keown, Pamela J. Scalise, and Thomas J. Smothers, *Jeremiah 26–52*, WBC 27 (Dallas: Word, 1995) 275-77.
221. Ronald Clements, *Jeremiah*, Interpretation (Atlanta: John Knox, 1988) 246.

The actual connection of Jeremiah to this collection is complex. It is likely that some of the oracles (e.g., the first one in 46:3-12) come from the prophet himself, while others were added to the collection as the book developed, a process already hinted at within the book (36:32). The oracles concerning Moab, Edom, Ammon, and the Philistines may be related to the events of 594 BCE, reported in chaps. 27–28, when those nations sent envoys to plan rebellion with Judah against Nebuchadrezzar.[222] Chapters 50–51, or large parts of the oracle against Babylon, have often been ascribed to later hands, though some interpreters have argued that much of this material is also Jeremianic. The final verses of chap. 51 even give a date for the words against Babylon.

222. Beat Huwyler, *Jeremia und die Völker: Untersuchungen zu den Völkersprüchen in Jeremia 46–49*, FAT 20 (Tübingen: Mohr Siebeck, 1997) 307-15.

JEREMIAH 46:1-28, AGAINST EGYPT

NIV	NRSV
46 This is the word of the LORD that came to Jeremiah the prophet concerning the nations:	**46** The word of the LORD that came to the prophet Jeremiah concerning the nations.
2Concerning Egypt:	2Concerning Egypt, about the army of Pharaoh Neco, king of Egypt, which was by the river Euphrates at Carchemish and which King Nebuchadrezzar of Babylon defeated in the fourth year of King Jehoiakim son of Josiah of Judah:
This is the message against the army of Pharaoh Neco king of Egypt, which was defeated at Carchemish on the Euphrates River by Nebuchadnezzar king of Babylon in the fourth year of Jehoiakim son of Josiah king of Judah:	

NIV

3"Prepare your shields, both large and small,
    and march out for battle!
4Harness the horses,
    mount the steeds!
Take your positions
    with helmets on!
Polish your spears,
    put on your armor!
5What do I see?
    They are terrified,
they are retreating,
    their warriors are defeated.
They flee in haste
    without looking back,
    and there is terror on every side,"
                declares the LORD.
6"The swift cannot flee
    nor the strong escape.
In the north by the River Euphrates
    they stumble and fall.

7"Who is this that rises like the Nile,

NRSV

3 Prepare buckler and shield,
    and advance for battle!
4 Harness the horses;
    mount the steeds!
Take your stations with your helmets,
    whet your lances,
    put on your coats of mail!
5 Why do I see them terrified?
    They have fallen back;
their warriors are beaten down,
    and have fled in haste.
They do not look back—
    terror is all around!   says the LORD.
6 The swift cannot flee away,
    nor can the warrior escape;
in the north by the river Euphrates
    they have stumbled and fallen.

7 Who is this, rising like the Nile,
    like rivers whose waters surge?
8 Egypt rises like the Nile,
    like rivers whose waters surge.
It said, Let me rise, let me cover the earth,
    let me destroy cities and their inhabitants.
9 Advance, O horses,

NIV

like rivers of surging waters?
⁸Egypt rises like the Nile,
  like rivers of surging waters.
She says, 'I will rise and cover the earth;
  I will destroy cities and their people.'
⁹Charge, O horses!
  Drive furiously, O charioteers!
March on, O warriors—
  men of Cush[a] and Put who carry shields,
  men of Lydia who draw the bow.
¹⁰But that day belongs to the Lord, the LORD
      Almighty—
  a day of vengeance, for vengeance on his foes.
The sword will devour till it is satisfied,
  till it has quenched its thirst with blood.
For the Lord, the LORD Almighty, will offer
      sacrifice
  in the land of the north by the River
      Euphrates.

¹¹"Go up to Gilead and get balm,
  O Virgin Daughter of Egypt.
But you multiply remedies in vain;
  there is no healing for you.
¹²The nations will hear of your shame;
  your cries will fill the earth.
One warrior will stumble over another;
  both will fall down together."

¹³This is the message the LORD spoke to
Jeremiah the prophet about the coming of
Nebuchadnezzar king of Babylon to attack Egypt:

¹⁴"Announce this in Egypt, and proclaim it in
      Migdol;
  proclaim it also in Memphis[b] and
      Tahpanhes:
  'Take your positions and get ready,
    for the sword devours those around you.'
¹⁵Why will your warriors be laid low?
  They cannot stand, for the LORD will push
      them down.
¹⁶They will stumble repeatedly;
  they will fall over each other.
They will say, 'Get up, let us go back
  to our own people and our native lands,
  away from the sword of the oppressor.'

ᵃ9 That is, the upper Nile region   ᵇ14 Hebrew Noph; also in verse 19

NRSV

and dash madly, O chariots!
Let the warriors go forth:
  Ethiopia[a] and Put who carry the shield,
  the Ludim, who draw[b] the bow.
¹⁰ That day is the day of the Lord GOD of hosts,
  a day of retribution,
    to gain vindication from his foes.
The sword shall devour and be sated,
  and drink its fill of their blood.
For the Lord GOD of hosts holds a sacrifice
  in the land of the north by the river
      Euphrates.

¹¹ Go up to Gilead, and take balm,
  O virgin daughter Egypt!
In vain you have used many medicines;
  there is no healing for you.
¹² The nations have heard of your shame,
  and the earth is full of your cry;
for warrior has stumbled against warrior;
  both have fallen together.

13The word that the LORD spoke to the prophet
Jeremiah about the coming of King Nebuchadrezzar of Babylon to attack the land of Egypt:
¹⁴ Declare in Egypt, and proclaim in Migdol;
  proclaim in Memphis and Tahpanhes;
Say, "Take your stations and be ready,
  for the sword shall devour those around
      you."
¹⁵ Why has Apis fled?[c]
  Why did your bull not stand?
    —because the LORD thrust him down.
¹⁶ Your multitude stumbled[d] and fell,
  and one said to another,[e]
"Come, let us go back to our own people
  and to the land of our birth,
  because of the destroying sword."
¹⁷ Give Pharaoh, king of Egypt, the name
  "Braggart who missed his chance."

¹⁸ As I live, says the King,
  whose name is the LORD of hosts,
one is coming
  like Tabor among the mountains,
  and like Carmel by the sea.

ᵃOr Nubia; Heb Cush   ᵇCn: Heb who grasp, who draw   ᶜGk: Heb Why was it swept away   ᵈGk: Meaning of Heb uncertain   ᵉGk: Heb and fell one to another and they said

NIV

¹⁷There they will exclaim,
'Pharaoh king of Egypt is only a loud noise;
he has missed his opportunity.'

¹⁸"As surely as I live," declares the King,
whose name is the LORD Almighty,
"one will come who is like Tabor among the
mountains,
like Carmel by the sea.
¹⁹Pack your belongings for exile,
you who live in Egypt,
for Memphis will be laid waste
and lie in ruins without inhabitant.

²⁰"Egypt is a beautiful heifer,
but a gadfly is coming
against her from the north.
²¹The mercenaries in her ranks
are like fattened calves.
They too will turn and flee together,
they will not stand their ground,
for the day of disaster is coming upon them,
the time for them to be punished.
²²Egypt will hiss like a fleeing serpent
as the enemy advances in force;
they will come against her with axes,
like men who cut down trees.
²³They will chop down her forest,"
declares the LORD,
"dense though it be.
They are more numerous than locusts,
they cannot be counted.
²⁴The Daughter of Egypt will be put to shame,
handed over to the people of the north."

²⁵The LORD Almighty, the God of Israel, says: "I
am about to bring punishment on Amon god of
Thebes,^a on Pharaoh, on Egypt and her gods and
her kings, and on those who rely on Pharaoh. ²⁶I
will hand them over to those who seek their lives,
to Nebuchadnezzar king of Babylon and his officers. Later, however, Egypt will be inhabited as in
times past," declares the LORD.

²⁷"Do not fear, O Jacob my servant;
do not be dismayed, O Israel.
I will surely save you out of a distant place,
your descendants from the land of their exile.

^a25 Hebrew No

NRSV

¹⁹ Pack your bags for exile,
sheltered daughter Egypt!
For Memphis shall become a waste,
a ruin, without inhabitant.

²⁰ A beautiful heifer is Egypt—
a gadfly from the north lights upon her.
²¹ Even her mercenaries in her midst
are like fatted calves;
they too have turned and fled together,
they did not stand;
for the day of their calamity has come upon
them,
the time of their punishment.

²² She makes a sound like a snake gliding away;
for her enemies march in force,
and come against her with axes,
like those who fell trees.
²³ They shall cut down her forest,
says the LORD,
though it is impenetrable,
because they are more numerous
than locusts;
they are without number.
²⁴ Daughter Egypt shall be put to shame;
she shall be handed over to a people from
the north.

²⁵The LORD of hosts, the God of Israel, said:
See, I am bringing punishment upon Amon of
Thebes, and Pharaoh, and Egypt and her gods and
her kings, upon Pharaoh and those who trust in
him. ²⁶I will hand them over to those who seek
their life, to King Nebuchadrezzar of Babylon and
his officers. Afterward Egypt shall be inhabited as
in the days of old, says the LORD.

²⁷ But as for you, have no fear, my servant Jacob,
and do not be dismayed, O Israel;
for I am going to save you from far away,
and your offspring from the land of their
captivity.
Jacob shall return and have quiet and ease,
and no one shall make him afraid.
²⁸ As for you, have no fear, my servant Jacob,
says the LORD,

NIV

Jacob will again have peace and security,
and no one will make him afraid.
[28]Do not fear, O Jacob my servant,
for I am with you," declares the LORD.
"Though I completely destroy all the nations
among which I scatter you,
I will not completely destroy you.
I will discipline you but only with justice;
I will not let you go entirely unpunished."

NRSV

for I am with you.
I will make an end of all the nations
among which I have banished you,
but I will not make an end of you!
I will chastise you in just measure,
and I will by no means leave you
unpunished.

COMMENTARY

46:1. The opening verse is an introductory superscription governing the whole collection of oracles against the nations. It links the final chapters to the rest of the book, a collection of prophecies by the prophet, who, in his commission, is twice identified as a prophet to the nations (1:5, 10). This part of his commission now comes to full bloom. The horizons of Jeremiah's prophetic activity, and of the reign of the Lord who called him, are now opened onto the international plane. It has already been clear that Judah and Israel interact constantly with other peoples and national entities, especially Babylon. But this rubric indicates that what follows is not primarily about Judah and Israel, though their fate is not forgotten. Now the decrees of the Lord reach out to encompass other nations.

46:2. A second superscription then is set over the chapter that follows, identifying this particular collection of oracles as addressing Egypt and connecting the first one with the defeat of the Egyptian army by the Babylonian army at the Battle of Carchemish in 605 BCE. The superscription ties the words of divine judgment that are to follow with a specific historical event. The work of the Lord of Israel does not take place in some vague and indefinite realm. Nebuchadrezzar's defeat of Pharaoh Necho is as much the work of the Lord as was the defeat of an earlier Egyptian pharaoh in the exodus. In this case, however, the occasion is not redemptive for Israel. Implicit in these oracles is the warning to Judah against seeking help from Egypt to resist Babylonian power. The outcome of the Battle of Carchemish joins with the words of the prophet to show what a vain hope Egypt would be.

46:3-12. Although Egypt was one of Israel's traditional oppressors, that nation is not depicted here as enemy or oppressor. These verses do not comprise a typical judgment speech, indicting the people for crimes or sins and then announcing a judgment. Rather, they are the summons to battle and/or the summons to flee, which is first met in 4:5-6 and 6:1-6 but is seen most often in the oracles against the nations (48:6-8, 28; 49:2; 50:8-10; 51:6, 45).[223] In this first instance, there is much irony and mockery. The call to battle (vv. 3-4) becomes a call to defeat (vv. 5-6). The warriors are immediately put to rout and are defeated at the river Euphrates, a reference to the battle at Carchemish, which was situated on the Euphrates. That reversal is then repeated in vv. 9-12, where the Egyptian warriors, including mercenaries from Cush, Put, and Ludim, who are called to go forth madly into battle (v. 9), are then depicted as falling all over one another in shameful defeat.[224]

This call to battle that ends in massive defeat includes several important features. One is the prophet's double taunting of the Egyptians. The first offers a picture of Egypt rising like the Nile to cover the earth (vv. 7-8). But this personification of Egypt's hubris is made a mockery by the defeat at Carchemish. The other taunt carries an implicit link with Jeremiah's earlier prophecies. Just as he

223. The relation of this form of speech to the early holy wars, or wars of Yahweh, and with war ideology and practice generally in the ancient Near East is a matter of much debate, but there is little doubt that the call to fight and the call to flee are rooted in the war practices of Israel and others. For the most recent extended discussion of the issue, see Huwyler, *Jeremia und die Völker*, 285-300.

224. Cush is probably Ethopia and Nubia; the locations of Put and Ludim are debated and less certain.

had earlier lamented the absence of any balm in Gilead to heal the people, so also now the prophet mocks Egypt by calling it to go up to Gilead and find a healing balm, knowing that no balm can heal the present sickness of Egypt (vv. 11-12). The stereotyped exclamation, "Terror is all around!" (v. 5; cf. 6:25; 20:3, 10; 49:29; Ps 31:14[13]), creates a further link with earlier prophecies, one with an implicit comparison between Judah's fate and Egypt's. The shorthand cliché for the threat to Judah is equally appropriate for the danger to Egypt and other nations.

At the center of the oracle lies the claim that this well-known and well-recorded battle between Egyptian and Babylonian armies was something more than a day of Babylonian victory and Egyptian defeat. It was a day of vindication for "the LORD God of hosts." The repetition of this name in v. 10 asserts the sovereignty of the Lord of Israel over all the armies of heaven and earth. The image of the day of the Lord points to the work of God in this great battle. That "day," which can be past, present, or future, is a time when the rule of the Lord is vindicated over all who would oppose it.[225] The depiction of the day as a mighty battle by the divine warrior and a sacrificial feast is similar to Isaiah 34. The Babylonian army becomes the agent of the Lord's judgment over the Egyptians, whose sin in this oracle is an arrogant claim to rule the earth. Significant dimensions of the book are reinforced as the reader both hears of the power of God at work through an enemy from the north (cf. 1:13-14) and learns that Egypt is not a power to rely upon—as many Judeans did—in hopes of avoiding divine judgment. Egypt, too, comes under that judgment.

46:13-26. A second superscription in v. 13 suggests that this oracle is related to a different time from the battle at Carchemish (v. 2). The superscription indicates that the oracle involves an invasion of Egypt by Nebuchadrezzar, but it is difficult to determine when that was or to know—as is also the case with the preceding oracle—whether the oracle was given before or after the event. Nebuchadrezzar moved against Egypt on several occasions after the Battle of Carchemish in 605 BCE, including one time when the Egyptian Pharaoh Hophra was coming to the aid of a

besieged Jerusalem (588 BCE; see 37:6-7). The range of possibilities extends from 604 to 568 BCE.[226] It should be noted, however, that some have seen in the explanation of the name of the king of Egypt in v. 17 ("he missed his chance"), a Hebrew play on the Egyptian name of Pharaoh Hophra as well as an accurate description of him, since he had a reputation for impetuous behavior.

This passage echoes the preceding one in several ways: (1) The oracle begins with a call to battle, only to announce the defeat of the warriors who are summoned to stand. Most of the oracle describes the defeat and flight of the Egyptian warriors and their mercenaries. Note the further use of the terms "stumble" and "fall" in v. 16 (cf. vv. 6, 12).

(2) The defeat is by an enemy from the north, clearly Babylon, though not specifically identified as such (v. 20). The text envisages the flight of the Egyptians back home or of mercenaries to their homelands (v. 16), but this conflict eventuates in both the destruction of Egyptian cities (Memphis) and exile (vv. 19, 24*b*). The reader is familiar with such a picture. But this time it is not Judah facing destruction and exile. Human devastation and divine judgment reach out to encompass other communities as well. The depiction of Egypt's defeat is rich in imagery: Egypt is represented as a handsome cow stung by a fly and a snake gliding away at the sounds of people coming toward it; the enemy is portrayed as a horde of tree cutters and compared to a locust plague (a common biblical image for an invading army; cf. Joel 1).

(3) In all this, Egypt is shamed (v. 24; see v. 12). Indeed, Egypt experiences the same fate that it inflicted upon Judah (2:36; cf. v. 26), though it is important to recognize that their treatment of Judah is not the motivation for Egypt's shaming.

(4) The day of vengeance or retribution of v. 10 is echoed here in the "day of calamity" (v. 21).

(5) The Lord of hosts remains central in this oracle (v. 18; cf. v. 10). The reiteration of that name and the addition of the term "king" (cf. 48:15; 51:57) emphasize the sovereign power of the Lord of Israel over the nations and the power behind the throne, so to speak, of Babylon, the

---

225. For discussion of the day of the Lord, see Joseph A. Everson, "The Days of Yahweh," *JBL* 93 (1974) 329-37.

226. For succinct presentation of the alternative datings, see Keown, Scalise, and Smothers, *Jeremiah 26–52;* Beat Huwyler, *Jeremia und die Völker: Untersuchungen zu den Völkersprüchen in Jeremia 46–49,* FAT 20 (Tübingen: Mohr Siebeck, 1997) 125-26.

"gadfly from the north." According to vv. 25-26, probably an addition to the text, the defeat of Egypt is entirely an act of the Lord of hosts. If Babylon and its king are victorious over Egypt and its kings and gods, that is only because the Lord of the hosts of heaven and earth has handed Egypt over to the Babylonian host.[227] (On v. 26*b* see the Commentary on 48:47 and the Reflections).

46:27-28. This oracle of salvation is virtually identical to 30:10-11, and the reader is referred to the Commentary on those verses for discussion of the details of this passage. Why is this oracle placed here, at the end of the oracles against Egypt? (There is an unresoved debate as to whether the oracle is original in chap. 30 or in chap. 46.) We should note first that this salvation word for Judah/Israel follows immediately upon the statement that after the judgment against it, Egypt will again be inhabited.

---

227. The Greek of 46:15 divides the Hebrew word נִסְחַף (*nishap,* "swept away") into two words, נָס (*nās,* "fled") and חַף (*ḥāp,* "Apis"), seeing in the second word a reference to the Egyptian god of fertility, Apis. The two readings are reflected in the NRSV, following the Greek, and the NIV, following the Hebrew.

The even more marvelous restoration of Israel offers an analogy. In the midst of this extended announcement of judgment on the nations, where does God's beloved, but judged and destroyed, Israel fit? The prophet makes this connection to the judgment of the nations in v. 28. Over against that word of a final end to all the nations—a word that is already compromised by grace in v. 26 with respect to Egypt (cf. 48:47; 49:6, 39)—comes an assurance that Israel will be disciplined but not finally abandoned. The Lord cannot begin this extended declamation against the nations without saying something more about this people with whom the Lord has struggled for so many generations. Nothing can separate them finally from God's redeeming grace. Over against the terror that faces the Egyptians, Israel need not fear. Even in the fires of exile, Judah does not have to be dismayed. There is a future of peace and security that comes from the very hand of the one who has brought judgment against Israel and will bring it against all the other nations as well. (See Reflections at 51:59-64.)

JEREMIAH 47:1-7, AGAINST PHILISTIA

NIV	NRSV
47 This is the word of the LORD that came to Jeremiah the prophet concerning the Philistines before Pharaoh attacked Gaza:	**47** The word of the LORD that came to the prophet Jeremiah concerning the Philistines, before Pharaoh attacked Gaza:
²This is what the LORD says:	² Thus says the LORD:
"See how the waters are rising in the north; they will become an overflowing torrent. They will overflow the land and everything in it, the towns and those who live in them. The people will cry out; all who dwell in the land will wail	See, waters are rising out of the north and shall become an overflowing torrent; they shall overflow the land and all that fills it, the city and those who live in it. People shall cry out, and all the inhabitants of the land shall wail.
³at the sound of the hoofs of galloping steeds, at the noise of enemy chariots and the rumble of their wheels. Fathers will not turn to help their children; their hands will hang limp.	³ At the noise of the stamping of the hoofs of his stallions, at the clatter of his chariots, at the rumbling of their wheels, parents do not turn back for children, so feeble are their hands,
⁴For the day has come to destroy all the Philistines	⁴ because of the day that is coming to destroy all the Philistines,

NIV

and to cut off all survivors
   who could help Tyre and Sidon.
The LORD is about to destroy the Philistines,
   the remnant from the coasts of Caphtor.[a]
⁵Gaza will shave her head in mourning;
   Ashkelon will be silenced.
O remnant on the plain,
   how long will you cut yourselves?

⁶" 'Ah, sword of the LORD,' ⌐you cry,⌐
   'how long till you rest?
Return to your scabbard;
   cease and be still.'
⁷But how can it rest
   when the LORD has commanded it,
when he has ordered it
   to attack Ashkelon and the coast?"

ᵃ4 That is, Crete

NRSV

to cut off from Tyre and Sidon
   every helper that remains.
For the LORD is destroying the Philistines,
   the remnant of the coastland of Caphtor.
⁵Baldness has come upon Gaza,
   Ashkelon is silenced.
O remnant of their power![a]
   How long will you gash yourselves?
⁶Ah, sword of the LORD!
   How long until you are quiet?
Put yourself into your scabbard,
   rest and be still!
⁷How can it[b] be quiet,
   when the LORD has given it an order?
Against Ashkelon and against the seashore—
   there he has appointed it.

ᵃGk: Heb *their valley*   ᵇGk Vg: Heb *you*

COMMENTARY

This announcement of judgment is directed toward Israel's and Judah's oldest enemies, the Philistines. But as is the case in other Jeremianic oracles against the nations, the judgment is not grounded in some act against the Judeans. In fact, the reason for the judgment is not given at all. The oracle simply depicts destruction of the five cities of the Philistine pentapolis. Gaza and Ashkelon are mentioned explicitly and Ashdod implicitly. The other two cities, Gath and Ekron, are not mentioned at all.

Much about this chapter remains unclear. We know about no move of a pharaoh against Gaza, though it was certainly possible because of the close proximity of Philistia to Egypt and the involvement of Egypt in this region. Further, it is likely that the reference to an attack against Gaza in v. 1 is secondary; it does not seem to be consistent with the oracle itself, which refers to "waters rising out of the north" as the destructive power. Throughout Jeremiah, the north regularly means the Babylonians. Inasmuch as Nebuchadrezzar sacked Ashkelon in 604 BCE, since Ashkelon is twice mentioned in this text as being attacked and silenced (vv. 5, 7), this event may lie behind the text.

The reader quickly sees, however, that the depiction of battle and defeat is couched in familiar and stereotypical tones that betray no specific occasion and could have been spoken at any time, before or after any battle. Numerous images and phrases found in other oracles against the nations, or even in more general announcements of judgment, occur here. The imagery of feeble or limping hands (v. 3*b*) appears not only in 50:43 but also in other scenes of judgment (Isa 13:7; Jer 6:24; Ezek 7:17; 21:7[12]; Zeph 3:16). The imagery of rising waters occurs in 46:7-8 and in an oracle against Philistia in Isa 14:31, where it is accompanied by a depiction of the Philistines wailing and crying out and of smoke coming "from the north" (see Jer 47:2). The specificity of the "day," which suggests a particular battle, is thoroughly rooted in the imagery of the Day of the Lord, already manifest in the oracle against Egypt in the preceding chapter (46:10, 21). The text may not intend for the reader to think about a specific day.

There is no call to battle or to flight in these verses, no indication of the reason for this devastation of the Philistine cities. The picture of a powerful and devastating flood that sweeps over everything (v. 2) is transformed into a thundering army of horses' hooves and chariot wheels (v. 3; cf. Isa 5:28)—weaponry familiar to the Babylonians. The text is just as unflinching as most biblical depictions of judgment in describing human fear and terror, so great that parents are too traumatized and paralyzed even to help their children flee. Baldness, gashing or cutting oneself, and silence are mourning rites (vv. 4-5; cf. 7:29; 16:6; 48:37). The text is emphatically clear that this destruction is the work of the Lord (vv. 4, 6). Hence, it is appropriate for this calamity to be viewed as the day of the Lord (see the Commentary on 46:3-12).

The imagery of the divine warrior coming against another one of the nations is reinforced in the final verses with the address to the personified "sword of the LORD" (vv. 6-7; cf. Isa 34). Someone (the poet/prophet? a Philistine?) calls for the sword to stop its deadly activity and sheath itself. But it cannot do so when the Lord has appointed it for destruction of the Philistines. A kind of inevitability hangs over the moment. There is no stopping this force, because the Lord is behind it. Like "Assyria, the rod of my anger" (Isa 10:5) at an earlier time, the Babylonian sword is under divine orders and will do its terrible work. (See Reflections at 51:59-64.)

JEREMIAH 48:1-47, AGAINST MOAB

NIV

48 Concerning Moab:

This is what the LORD Almighty, the God of Israel, says:

"Woe to Nebo, for it will be ruined.
　Kiriathaim will be disgraced and captured;
　the stronghold[a] will be disgraced and
　　shattered.
²Moab will be praised no more;
　in Heshbon[b] men will plot her downfall:
　'Come, let us put an end to that nation.'
You too, O Madmen,[c] will be silenced;
　the sword will pursue you.
³Listen to the cries from Horonaim,
　cries of great havoc and destruction.
⁴Moab will be broken;
　her little ones will cry out.[d]
⁵They go up the way to Luhith,
　weeping bitterly as they go;
on the road down to Horonaim
　anguished cries over the destruction are
　　heard.
⁶Flee! Run for your lives;
　become like a bush[e] in the desert.
⁷Since you trust in your deeds and riches,

NRSV

48 Concerning Moab.

Thus says the LORD of hosts, the God of Israel:
　Alas for Nebo, it is laid waste!
　　Kiriathaim is put to shame, it is taken;
　the fortress is put to shame and broken down;
²　　the renown of Moab is no more.
　In Heshbon they planned evil against her:
　　"Come, let us cut her off from being a
　　　nation!"
　You also, O Madmen, shall be brought to
　　silence;[a]
　　the sword shall pursue you.

³ Hark! a cry from Horonaim,
　　"Desolation and great destruction!"
⁴ "Moab is destroyed!"
　　her little ones cry out.
⁵ For at the ascent of Luhith
　　they go[b] up weeping bitterly;
　for at the descent of Horonaim
　　they have heard the distressing cry of
　　　anguish.
⁶ Flee! Save yourselves!
　　Be like a wild ass[c] in the desert!

a1 Or / *Misgab*　*b2* The Hebrew for *Heshbon* sounds like the Hebrew for *plot*.　*c2* The name of the Moabite town Madmen sounds like the Hebrew for *be silenced*.　*d4* Hebrew; Septuagint / *proclaim it to Zoar*　*e6* Or *like Aroer*

*a*The place-name *Madmen* sounds like the Hebrew verb *to be silent*　*b*Cn: Heb *he goes*　*c*Gk Aquila: Heb *like Aroer*

NIV

you too will be taken captive,
and Chemosh will go into exile,
together with his priests and officials.
⁸The destroyer will come against every town,
and not a town will escape.
The valley will be ruined
and the plateau destroyed,
because the LORD has spoken.
⁹Put salt on Moab,
for she will be laid waste*a*;
her towns will become desolate,
with no one to live in them.

¹⁰"A curse on him who is lax in doing the
LORD's work!
A curse on him who keeps his sword from
bloodshed!

¹¹"Moab has been at rest from youth,
like wine left on its dregs,
not poured from one jar to another—
she has not gone into exile.
So she tastes as she did,
and her aroma is unchanged.
¹²But days are coming,"
declares the LORD,
"when I will send men who pour from jars,
and they will pour her out;
they will empty her jars
and smash her jugs.
¹³Then Moab will be ashamed of Chemosh,
as the house of Israel was ashamed
when they trusted in Bethel.

¹⁴"How can you say, 'We are warriors,
men valiant in battle'?
¹⁵Moab will be destroyed and her towns
invaded;
her finest young men will go down in the
slaughter,"
declares the King, whose name is the LORD
Almighty.
¹⁶"The fall of Moab is at hand;
her calamity will come quickly.
¹⁷Mourn for her, all who live around her,
all who know her fame;
say, 'How broken is the mighty scepter,
how broken the glorious staff!'

a9 Or Give wings to Moab, / for she will fly away

NRSV

⁷Surely, because you trusted in your strongholds*a* and your treasures,
you also shall be taken;
Chemosh shall go out into exile,
with his priests and his attendants.
⁸The destroyer shall come upon every town,
and no town shall escape;
the valley shall perish,
and the plain shall be destroyed,
as the LORD has spoken.

⁹Set aside salt for Moab,
for she will surely fall;
her towns shall become a desolation,
with no inhabitant in them.

10Accursed is the one who is slack in doing the
work of the LORD; and accursed is the one who
keeps back the sword from bloodshed.

¹¹Moab has been at ease from his youth,
settled like wine*b* on its dregs;
he has not been emptied from vessel to vessel,
nor has he gone into exile;
therefore his flavor has remained
and his aroma is unspoiled.
12Therefore, the time is surely coming, says
the LORD, when I shall send to him decanters to
decant him, and empty his vessels, and break his*c*
jars in pieces. ¹³Then Moab shall be ashamed of
Chemosh, as the house of Israel was ashamed of
Bethel, their confidence.

¹⁴How can you say, "We are heroes
and mighty warriors"?
¹⁵The destroyer of Moab and his towns has
come up,
and the choicest of his young men have
gone down to slaughter,
says the King, whose name is the LORD of
hosts.
¹⁶The calamity of Moab is near at hand
and his doom approaches swiftly.
¹⁷Mourn over him, all you his neighbors,
and all who know his name;
say, "How the mighty scepter is broken,
the glorious staff!"

aGk: Heb works   bHeb lacks like wine   cGk Aquila: Heb their

NIV

¹⁸"Come down from your glory
    and sit on the parched ground,
    O inhabitants of the Daughter of Dibon,
for he who destroys Moab
    will come up against you
    and ruin your fortified cities.
¹⁹Stand by the road and watch,
    you who live in Aroer.
Ask the man fleeing and the woman escaping,
    ask them, 'What has happened?'
²⁰Moab is disgraced, for she is shattered.
    Wail and cry out!
Announce by the Arnon
    that Moab is destroyed.
²¹Judgment has come to the plateau—
    to Holon, Jahzah and Mephaath,
²²   to Dibon, Nebo and Beth Diblathaim,
²³   to Kiriathaim, Beth Gamul and Beth Meon,
²⁴   to Kerioth and Bozrah—
    to all the towns of Moab, far and near.
²⁵Moab's horn^a is cut off;
    her arm is broken,"

                        declares the LORD.

²⁶"Make her drunk,
    for she has defied the LORD.
Let Moab wallow in her vomit;
    let her be an object of ridicule.
²⁷Was not Israel the object of your ridicule?
    Was she caught among thieves,
that you shake your head in scorn
    whenever you speak of her?
²⁸Abandon your towns and dwell among the
        rocks,
    you who live in Moab.
Be like a dove that makes its nest
    at the mouth of a cave.

²⁹"We have heard of Moab's pride—
    her overweening pride and conceit,
her pride and arrogance
    and the haughtiness of her heart.
³⁰I know her insolence but it is futile,"
                    declares the LORD,
    "and her boasts accomplish nothing.
³¹Therefore I wail over Moab,
    for all Moab I cry out,
    I moan for the men of Kir Hareseth.

^a25 Horn here symbolizes strength.

NRSV

¹⁸ Come down from glory,
    and sit on the parched ground,
    enthroned daughter Dibon!
For the destroyer of Moab has come up
        against you;
    he has destroyed your strongholds.
¹⁹ Stand by the road and watch,
    you inhabitant of Aroer!
Ask the man fleeing and the woman escaping;
    say, "What has happened?"
²⁰ Moab is put to shame, for it is broken down;
    wail and cry!
Tell it by the Arnon,
    that Moab is laid waste.

    21Judgment has come upon the tableland, upon
Holon, and Jahzah, and Mephaath, ²²and Dibon,
and Nebo, and Beth-diblathaim, ²³and Kiriathaim,
and Beth-gamul, and Beth-meon, ²⁴and Kerioth,
and Bozrah, and all the towns of the land of Moab,
far and near. ²⁵The horn of Moab is cut off, and his
arm is broken, says the LORD.
    26Make him drunk, because he magnified him-
self against the LORD; let Moab wallow in his
vomit; he too shall become a laughingstock.
²⁷Israel was a laughingstock for you, though he
was not caught among thieves; but whenever you
spoke of him you shook your head!

²⁸ Leave the towns, and live on the rock,
    O inhabitants of Moab!
Be like the dove that nests
    on the sides of the mouth of a gorge.
²⁹ We have heard of the pride of Moab—
    he is very proud—
of his loftiness, his pride, and his arrogance,
    and the haughtiness of his heart.
³⁰ I myself know his insolence, says the LORD;
    his boasts are false,
    his deeds are false.
³¹ Therefore I wail for Moab;
    I cry out for all Moab;
    for the people of Kir-heres I mourn.
³² More than for Jazer I weep for you,
    O vine of Sibmah!
Your branches crossed over the sea,
    reached as far as Jazer;^a

^aTwo Mss and Isa 16.8: MT the sea of Jazer

NIV

³²I weep for you, as Jazer weeps,
  O vines of Sibmah.
Your branches spread as far as the sea;
  they reached as far as the sea of Jazer.
The destroyer has fallen
  on your ripened fruit and grapes.
³³Joy and gladness are gone
  from the orchards and fields of Moab.
I have stopped the flow of wine from the presses;
  no one treads them with shouts of joy.
Although there are shouts,
  they are not shouts of joy.

³⁴"The sound of their cry rises
  from Heshbon to Elealeh and Jahaz,
from Zoar as far as Horonaim and Eglath
    Shelishiyah,
  for even the waters of Nimrim are dried up.
³⁵In Moab I will put an end
  to those who make offerings on the high
    places
  and burn incense to their gods,"
                              declares the LORD.
³⁶"So my heart laments for Moab like a flute;
  it laments like a flute for the men of Kir
    Hareseth.
The wealth they acquired is gone.
³⁷Every head is shaved
  and every beard cut off;
every hand is slashed
  and every waist is covered with sackcloth.
³⁸On all the roofs in Moab
  and in the public squares
there is nothing but mourning,
  for I have broken Moab
like a jar that no one wants,"
                              declares the LORD.
³⁹"How shattered she is! How they wail!
  How Moab turns her back in shame!
Moab has become an object of ridicule,
  an object of horror to all those around her."

⁴⁰This is what the LORD says:

"Look! An eagle is swooping down,
  spreading its wings over Moab.
⁴¹Keriothᵃ will be captured
  and the strongholds taken.

ᵃ41 Or The cities

NRSV

upon your summer fruits and your vintage
  the destroyer has fallen.
³³ Gladness and joy have been taken away
  from the fruitful land of Moab;
I have stopped the wine from the wine
    presses;
  no one treads them with shouts of joy;
  the shouting is not the shout of joy.

³⁴Heshbon and Elealeh cry out;ᵃ as far as Jahaz they utter their voice, from Zoar to Horonaim and Eglath-shelishiyah. For even the waters of Nimrim have become desolate. ³⁵And I will bring to an end in Moab, says the LORD, those who offer sacrifice at a high place and make offerings to their gods. ³⁶Therefore my heart moans for Moab like a flute, and my heart moans like a flute for the people of Kir-heres; for the riches they gained have perished.

³⁷For every head is shaved and every beard cut off; on all the hands there are gashes, and on the loins sackcloth. ³⁸On all the housetops of Moab and in the squares there is nothing but lamentation; for I have broken Moab like a vessel that no one wants, says the LORD. ³⁹How it is broken! How they wail! How Moab has turned his back in shame! So Moab has become a derision and a horror to all his neighbors.

⁴⁰ For thus says the LORD:
  Look, he shall swoop down like an eagle,
    and spread his wings against Moab;
⁴¹ the townsᵇ shall be taken
    and the strongholds seized.
  The hearts of the warriors of Moab, on that
      day,
    shall be like the heart of a woman in labor.
⁴² Moab shall be destroyed as a people,
    because he magnified himself against the
      LORD.
⁴³ Terror, pit, and trap
    are before you, O inhabitants of Moab!
                              says the LORD.
⁴⁴ Everyone who flees from the terror
    shall fall into the pit,
  and everyone who climbs out of the pit
    shall be caught in the trap.

ᵃCn: Heb From the cry of Heshbon to Elealeh   ᵇOr Kerioth

NIV

In that day the hearts of Moab's warriors
will be like the heart of a woman in labor.
⁴²Moab will be destroyed as a nation
because she defied the LORD.
⁴³Terror and pit and snare await you,
O people of Moab,"
declares the LORD.
⁴⁴ "Whoever flees from the terror
will fall into a pit,
whoever climbs out of the pit
will be caught in a snare;
for I will bring upon Moab
the year of her punishment,"
declares the LORD.

⁴⁵"In the shadow of Heshbon
the fugitives stand helpless,
for a fire has gone out from Heshbon,
a blaze from the midst of Sihon;
it burns the foreheads of Moab,
the skulls of the noisy boasters.
⁴⁶Woe to you, O Moab!
The people of Chemosh are destroyed;
your sons are taken into exile
and your daughters into captivity.
⁴⁷"Yet I will restore the fortunes of Moab
in days to come,"
declares the LORD.
Here ends the judgment on Moab.

NRSV

For I will bring these things*ᵃ* upon Moab
in the year of their punishment,
says the LORD.

⁴⁵ In the shadow of Heshbon
fugitives stop exhausted;
for a fire has gone out from Heshbon,
a flame from the house of Sihon;
it has destroyed the forehead of Moab,
the scalp of the people of tumult.*ᵇ*
⁴⁶ Woe to you, O Moab!
The people of Chemosh have perished,
for your sons have been taken captive,
and your daughters into captivity.
⁴⁷ Yet I will restore the fortunes of Moab
in the latter days, says the LORD.
Thus far is the judgment on Moab.

ᵃGk Syr: Heb *bring upon it*   ᵇOr *of Shaon*

COMMENTARY

This long, often repetitive poem announces judgment against Moab, Judah's neighbor to the east across the Dead Sea. While there may be connections to Moab's fate at the hands of the Babylonians, the text refers to no specific event. Not only are they to be compared with oracles against Moab in other books (e.g., Isaiah 15–16; Ezek 25:8-11), but also some of the verses here are identical with those in other prophecies concerning Moab. They go further than the oracles against Egypt and Philistia in providing grounds for judgment. The sin of Moab is to be found in the arrogance and insolence of the nation. The allusions to Chemosh, the national god of the Moabites (vv. 7, 13, 46; cf. v. 35), and the report

that they have been arrogant toward the Lord of Israel (vv. 26, 42) and Israel's fate (v. 27) suggest religious and nationalistic rivalry behind these words against Moab. Through references to landscape, viticulture, and the many towns of Moab, the oracles reveal an intimate knowledge of that country and its character.

48:1-13. The first verse sounds the primary notes of this section and of the chapter as a whole:

(1) The cry of "woe" or "alas" at the beginning signals a lament or dirge over Moab, and the sounds and wails and acts of mourning reverberate in this chapter (vv. 17, 20, 31, 34-39).

(2) In the verb for "laid waste" or "ruined" (שדד *šādad*), often translated elsewhere in the chapter

as "destroy," one may hear the fundamental and repeated theme of the chapter: Moab is destroyed (vv. 3, 8, 15, 18, 20), a theme richly spelled out with other words and images for "destruction," notably the salting of Moab, which probably reflects placing the land under a curse or making it infertile (cf. Judg 9:45), and the imagery of the bloody sword (vv. 2, 10).

(3) The effect of the destruction is characterized as it is in v. 1: a terrible shame coming upon the nation, its towns, and its inhabitants. But there are other effects also: flight, anguished cries—including those of little children—and exile.

(4) The particularity of the punishment is underscored by reference to specific cities, Nebo and Kiriathaim in v. 1 as well as in the verses that follow.

Although there is no explicit conflict between the Lord and the god of Moab, there is an implicit claim that the Lord is sovereign over the gods of Moab. The text combines the reference to Chemosh's going into exile (v. 7) with the identification of the destruction of Moab as "the work of the LORD" (v. 10), a theme that echoes throughout the rest of the chapter. The carrying of images of deities into exile by conquering armies as an indication of the abandonment of the people by their gods or of the power of the gods of the conquering nation was a common occurrence in the ancient Near East and is reflected in the story of the capture of the ark of the covenant in 1 Samuel 4–6. The ark narrative in that text even more explicitly reflects the conflict between gods that lies beneath the surface of Jeremiah 48—its several references to Chemosh's fate and the power of the Lord of Israel to destroy the Moabites.[228]

This section concludes with the image of Moab as a rich wine in a bottle, decanter, or cask. In this case, the wine has remained on its lees, unopened, undisturbed, and thus still rich in bouquet. The cask has not been opened to let the wine begin to lose its flavor. The destruction that is to come is described via this image as an opening of the undecanted wine, pouring it from bottle to bottle, and finally simply breaking the vessels containing the wine. The wine is no longer preserved in its rich original state. It has been disturbed and ultimately disappears—wine and containers together.

228. See Patrick D. Miller and J. J. M. Roberts, *The Hand of the Lord* (Baltimore: Johns Hopkins University Press, 1977).

The significance of the image depends in part on what is meant by viewing Moab at ease and settled throughout its history. This may be neutral terminology rather than prophetic criticism. It is likely, however, that some critique is implied. The root for "being at ease" (שָׁאֵן *šĕʾn*) is used positively in several contexts (Isa 32:18; 33:20; Jer 30:10 = 46:27). But it also occurs in reference to a false, arrogant self-sufficiency that is overthrown by the events of history at the Lord's hand (e.g., Isa 32:9, 11; Amos 6:1). Two prophetic texts with similar imagery suggest that the security and ease of Moab are not intended as a neutral comment. In Zeph 1:12, the Lord announces punishment for the people of Jerusalem who "rest complacently [lit., "thicken"] on their dregs," believing that nothing will happen to them, that God will do nothing. Even more directly related to this text, Zech 1:14-15 attests to a divine announcement that the Lord is jealous for Jerusalem and Zion and very angry with the nations "that are at ease." They made the disaster of the Lord's anger against Jerusalem even worse. Jeremiah's oracle, set in the midst of the Lord's anger against the nations and words on behalf of Jerusalem/Zion, may reflect a similar perception of the "ease" of Moab. They have thought themselves secure under the protection of Chemosh, their god. But that will avail Moab no more than did confidence in the security of Bethel enabled Israel to survive.

48:14-28. The themes of the preceding verses continue here as Moab is depicted as powerless before its destroyer, put to shame by the devastation that is to occur within it. The secure nation is cast down from its mighty and glorious state. The list of towns (vv. 21-24) makes concrete the force of the pending destruction (cf. v. 34). The mourning of Moab's neighbors (v. 17) is really a taunt, exultation at the nation's fate (cf. Isa 14:3-4). The nation that laughed at a destroyed Israel will itself become a laughingstock. To the picture of shame and devastation, a nation reduced, is added a nation humiliated, depicted here as drunk (on its own wine?) and wallowing in its own vomit.

Again we hear about a theological dimension in these events that is manifest in several ways. For one, the breaking of the scepter and the staff of Moabite rule stands implicitly in contrast to the destroying power of "the King," "the LORD of hosts" (vv. 15-17). Further, the destruction of Moab is "judgment" or "justice" (מִשְׁפָּט *mišpāṭ*); the Hebrew word allows for either translation (v. 21). It is not fate or happenstance, but the outworking of God's purpose. The judgment is explained as the Lord's reaction to Moab's vaunting itself against the Lord (cf. v. 42). How this magnifying or defying of the Lord happens, we are not told. The allusion may be to a political event, perhaps the coalition of Moab and other nations— including Judah—against Nebuchadrezzar, mentioned in Jeremiah 27.[229] The context suggests something else, however. The taunting laughter of Moab at the fate of Israel may be understood as a mockery of its God (v. 27). This is a different reading of the judgment of Israel than what the rest of the book presents. But it is not inconsistent with Zech 1:14-15. The exultation of the nations over the fate of God's people, even if deserved, "made the disaster worse" and was an implicit denigration of the Lord, who brought the judgment. The fate of Israel was no laughing matter to the rest of the nations. Making it such turns their laughter on its head so that Moab will now become an object of derision (v. 39). Sin and punishment correspond as they do elsewhere in the prophets.[230] In similar fashion, Zeph 2:8-11 sets the taunts of Moab against "my people" as the basis for the Lord's judgment.

Several images help to carry the freight of the message. The arm and the horn that are broken (v. 25) are symbols of strength. The shaking of the head (v. 27) depicts a reaction of horror to the destruction, elsewhere seen as a natural and almost instinctive reaction (18:16). On the imagery of drinking from the cup of the Lord's wrath to become drunk and its association with the judgment of the nations, see the Commentary on 25:15-38 and the references given there.

48:29-39. In language similar to the oracles against Moab in Isaiah 15–16, the depiction of Moab's downfall continues. If the "being at ease" in earlier verses is ambiguous, the arrogance of Moab is now made explicit, a carryover of the

indictment of the nation for magnifying itself against the Lord. Judgment on such pride is manifest in the wailing and crying, here on the part of the Lord (vv. 31-32, 36), echoing the wailing and crying of the Moabite people (vv. 5, 20, 34, 38-39), and the disappearance of joy from the land (v. 33). Viticulture in Moab is reflected once more in the reference to the treading of the grapes and the winepresses as well as in the image of the broken vessel (כְּלִי *kĕlî*) of v. 38 (cf. *kĕlî* in vv. 11-12). The intensity of Moab's loss is emphasized by using the imagery of winemaking, a source of wealth and happiness, to depict it.

Twice in these verses, the reader is told that the destruction of Moab is the Lord's doing (vv. 35, 38). Here, however, the implicit conflict with Chemosh, the god of the Moabites, is expanded so that the judgment becomes a way of stopping sacrifices and offerings to other gods, presumably Chemosh and others who may have been worshiped by the Moabites. The divine resistance to the worship of other gods is carried forward to a community whose ostensible national god is somebody other than the Lord of hosts. But here is where the polytheistic world of those times stands in abrasive tension with the prophetic voice. Even the other nations find themselves under the rule of the Lord of Israel. While it is possible to read this announcement of the end of sacrifice and offering as simply an end to cultic activity along with viticulture and other kinds of commerce, the references to Chemosh elsewhere in the chapter (vv. 7, 13, 46) suggest that the end to cultic activity is an end to the cult of Chemosh, itself an indication of the rule of "the King, whose name is the LORD of hosts" (v. 15).

48:40-47. The eagle, elsewhere a powerful image of divine care (Exod 19:4; Deut 32:11), provides a simile for the coming of the destroyer against its Moabite prey (cf. 49:22). The motive for the judgment against Moab remains the same: "He magnified himself against the LORD" (v. 42; cf. v. 26), but this time the text offers no specific acts. The clues must be taken from the earlier context. The inevitability of the judgment is carried by the depiction of those in flight, escaping from one thing (terror) only to be caught in another (pit).

As in the case of Egypt (46:26), there is a final word of restoration. It is couched in language found in the Book of Comfort: restoration of fortunes. There is no elaboration of what this means,

229. See Gerald L. Keown, Pamela J. Scalise, and Thomas J. Smothers, *Jeremiah 26–52,* WBC 27 (Dallas: Word, 1995) 316-17; Beat Huwyler, *Jeremia und die Völker: Untersuchungen zu den Völkerspüchen in Jeremia 46–49,* FAT 20 (Tübingen: Mohr Siebeck, 1997) 307-15.

230. See Patrick D. Miller, *Sin and Judgment in the Prophets: A Stylistic and Theological Analysis,* SBLMS 27 (Chico, Calif.: Scholars Press, 1982).

as there is for Judah. Still, just as the judgment on Judah is not the last word and a future of restoration beyond judgment is announced, so also will it be with the Lord's judgment against the nations. (See Reflections at 51:59-64.)

JEREMIAH 49:1-6, AGAINST AMMON

NIV

49 Concerning the Ammonites:

This is what the LORD says:

"Has Israel no sons?
    Has she no heirs?
Why then has Molech[a] taken possession of
    Gad?
    Why do his people live in its towns?
[2]But the days are coming,"
    declares the LORD,
"when I will sound the battle cry
    against Rabbah of the Ammonites;
it will become a mound of ruins,
    and its surrounding villages will be set on
        fire.
Then Israel will drive out
    those who drove her out,"
                        says the LORD.
[3]"Wail, O Heshbon, for Ai is destroyed!
    Cry out, O inhabitants of Rabbah!
Put on sackcloth and mourn;
    rush here and there inside the walls,
for Molech will go into exile,
    together with his priests and officials.
[4]Why do you boast of your valleys,
    boast of your valleys so fruitful?
O unfaithful daughter,
    you trust in your riches and say,
    'Who will attack me?'
[5]I will bring terror on you
    from all those around you,"
            declares the Lord, the LORD Almighty.
"Every one of you will be driven away,
    and no one will gather the fugitives.

[6]"Yet afterward, I will restore the fortunes of
        the Ammonites,"
                        declares the LORD.

[a]1 Or *their king*; Hebrew *malcam*; also in verse 3

NRSV

49 Concerning the Ammonites.

Thus says the LORD:
    Has Israel no sons?
        Has he no heir?
    Why then has Milcom dispossessed Gad,
        and his people settled in its towns?
[2] Therefore, the time is surely coming,
        says the LORD,
    when I will sound the battle alarm
        against Rabbah of the Ammonites;
    it shall become a desolate mound,
        and its villages shall be burned with fire;
    then Israel shall dispossess those who dispos-
            sessed him,
        says the LORD.

[3] Wail, O Heshbon, for Ai is laid waste!
        Cry out, O daughters[a] of Rabbah!
    Put on sackcloth,
        lament, and slash yourselves with whips![b]
    For Milcom shall go into exile,
        with his priests and his attendants.
[4] Why do you boast in your strength?
        Your strength is ebbing,
    O faithless daughter.
        You trusted in your treasures, saying,
        "Who will attack me?"
[5] I am going to bring terror upon you,
        says the Lord GOD of hosts,
        from all your neighbors,
    and you will be scattered, each headlong,
        with no one to gather the fugitives.
    6But afterward I will restore the fortunes of the
Ammonites, says the LORD.

[a]Or *villages*   [b]Cn: Meaning of Heb uncertain

COMMENTARY

The oracle against Ammon consists of two judgment speeches (vv. 1-2, 4-5) with a call for mourning placed between them that is itself an announcement of judgment. Judgment speeches typically indict the recipient of the speech for a crime and then announce the sentence of punishment. In the first case, the announcement is characterized in a typical Jeremianic form with two rhetorical questions ("Has Israel no sons? Has Israel no heir [lit., "possessor"]?") whose answers are transparent and set up the entrapping final "why" question: "Why then has Milcom dispossessed Gad?"[231] The sin/crime of Ammon is the dispossession of Israelite territory—more specifically, the territorial allotment of the tribe of Gad, which bordered on Ammon. There was constant territorial conflict between the northern kingdom and Ammon, its Transjordanian neighbor, but it is not clear what Ammonite encroachment on Israelite territory is intended by this reference. The point is clear, however: Israel remains alive (sons, heirs), and Ammon cannot take its territory. In another example of the correspondence between crime and punishment, of poetic justice, the dispossessor (Ammon) will be dispossessed—and by the one who was dispossessed (Israel). The chief city of Ammon, Rabbah, and its outlying villages will all be destroyed by fire.

This announcement functions as a call for mourning because the chief god of the Ammonites, Milcom, will go into exile. At this point, the similarity to the oracle against Moab is apparent in the repetition of 48:7b, only with Milcom rather than Chemosh as the god taken into exile. The text is also similar to the Moab oracle because the reason for the second judgment speech, the confidence and the security of the Ammonites (vv. 4-5), is not unlike the "confidence" of Moab in Chemosh and the pride and arrogance of that same people (48:13, 29-30). What this confidence did not take into account was the intrusion of the Lord of hosts. The text creates a wordplay: "Who will come against me?" asks disdainful Ammon (v. 4b). "I am going to cause someone to come against you," says the Lord (v. 5a), and that will be the end.

A note of hope about the future is added at the end of the oracle against Ammon, reminiscent of the word about Moab at the end of chap. 48 (see the Commentary on 48:47). (See Reflections at 51:59-64.)

231. For other examples of this rhetorical device, see Jer 2:14, 31; 8:4-5, 19, 22; 14:19; cf. Mal 2:10. See also W. Brueggemann, "Jeremiah's Use of Rhetorical Questions," *JBL* 92 (1973).

JEREMIAH 49:7-22, AGAINST EDOM

NIV	NRSV
[7]Concerning Edom:	7Concerning Edom.
This is what the LORD Almighty says:	Thus says the LORD of hosts:

"Is there no longer wisdom in Teman?
    Has counsel perished from the prudent?
    Has their wisdom decayed?
[8]Turn and flee, hide in deep caves,
    you who live in Dedan,
for I will bring disaster on Esau
    at the time I punish him.
[9]If grape pickers came to you,
    would they not leave a few grapes?
	Is there no longer wisdom in Teman?
	    Has counsel perished from the prudent?
	    Has their wisdom vanished?
	[8] Flee, turn back, get down low,
	    inhabitants of Dedan!
	For I will bring the calamity of Esau upon him,
	    the time when I punish him.
	[9] If grape-gatherers came to you,
	    would they not leave gleanings?

NIV

If thieves came during the night,
    would they not steal only as much as they
        wanted?
[10]But I will strip Esau bare;
    I will uncover his hiding places,
        so that he cannot conceal himself.
His children, relatives and neighbors will
        perish,
    and he will be no more.
[11]Leave your orphans; I will protect their lives.
    Your widows too can trust in me."

[12]This is what the LORD says: "If those who do
not deserve to drink the cup must drink it, why
should you go unpunished? You will not go unpunished, but must drink it. [13]I swear by myself,"
declares the LORD, "that Bozrah will become a ruin
and an object of horror, of reproach and of cursing;
and all its towns will be in ruins forever."

[14]I have heard a message from the LORD:
    An envoy was sent to the nations to say,
    "Assemble yourselves to attack it!
    Rise up for battle!"

[15]"Now I will make you small among the
        nations,
    despised among men.
[16]The terror you inspire
    and the pride of your heart have deceived
        you,
    you who live in the clefts of the rocks,
        who occupy the heights of the hill.
Though you build your nest as high as the
        eagle's,
    from there I will bring you down,"
                                    declares the LORD.
[17]"Edom will become an object of horror;
    all who pass by will be appalled and will
        scoff
    because of all its wounds.
[18]As Sodom and Gomorrah were overthrown,
    along with their neighboring towns,"
                                    says the LORD,
    "so no one will live there;
        no man will dwell in it.

[19]"Like a lion coming up from Jordan's thickets
    to a rich pastureland,
    I will chase Edom from its land in an instant.

NRSV

If thieves came by night,
    even they would pillage only what they
        wanted.
[10] But as for me, I have stripped Esau bare,
    I have uncovered his hiding places,
        and he is not able to conceal himself.
His offspring are destroyed, his kinsfolk
    and his neighbors; and he is no more.
[11] Leave your orphans, I will keep them alive;
    and let your widows trust in me.

[12]For thus says the LORD: If those who do not
deserve to drink the cup still have to drink it, shall
you be the one to go unpunished? You shall not go
unpunished; you must drink it. [13]For by myself I
have sworn, says the LORD, that Bozrah shall
become an object of horror and ridicule, a waste,
and an object of cursing; and all her towns shall
be perpetual wastes.
[14] I have heard tidings from the LORD,
    and a messenger has been sent among the
        nations:
    "Gather yourselves together and come against
        her,
    and rise up for battle!"
[15] For I will make you least among the nations,
    despised by humankind.
[16] The terror you inspire
    and the pride of your heart have deceived
        you,
    you who live in the clefts of the rock,[a]
        who hold the height of the hill.
Although you make your nest as high as the
        eagle's,
    from there I will bring you down,
                                    says the LORD.
[17]Edom shall become an object of horror;
everyone who passes by it will be horrified and
will hiss because of all its disasters. [18]As when
Sodom and Gomorrah and their neighbors were
overthrown, says the LORD, no one shall live
there, nor shall anyone settle in it. [19]Like a lion
coming up from the thickets of the Jordan against
a perennial pasture, I will suddenly chase Edom[b]
away from it; and I will appoint over it whomever
I choose.[c] For who is like me? Who can summon
me? Who is the shepherd who can stand

[a]Or *of Sela*   [b]Heb *him*   [c]Or *and I will single out the choicest
of his rams.* Meaning of Heb uncertain

NIV

Who is the chosen one I will appoint for
    this?
Who is like me and who can challenge me?
    And what shepherd can stand against me?"
20Therefore, hear what the LORD has planned
    against Edom,
    what he has purposed against those who
        live in Teman:
The young of the flock will be dragged away;
    he will completely destroy their pasture
        because of them.
21At the sound of their fall the earth will
    tremble;
    their cry will resound to the Red Sea.a
22Look! An eagle will soar and swoop down,
    spreading its wings over Bozrah.
In that day the hearts of Edom's warriors
    will be like the heart of a woman in labor.

a21 Hebrew Yam Suph; that is, Sea of Reeds

NRSV

before me? 20Therefore hear the plan that the
LORD has made against Edom and the purposes
that he has formed against the inhabitants of
Teman: Surely the little ones of the flock shall be
dragged away; surely their fold shall be appalled at
their fate. 21At the sound of their fall the earth
shall tremble; the sound of their cry shall be heard
at the Red Sea.a 22Look, he shall mount up and
swoop down like an eagle, and spread his wings
against Bozrah, and the heart of the warriors of
Edom in that day shall be like the heart of a
woman in labor.

aOr Sea of Reeds

COMMENTARY

The prophet turns now to the southern neighbor of Moab, Edom, a nation-state whose customary wisdom, noted elsewhere in the OT (e.g.,
Obad 8), seems to have disappeared (v. 7) and
whose pride has made the nation assume it is
impervious to the dire threat (v. 16). The image of
the eagle reappears in these oracles, this time in a
double function: as a comparison to the height of
Edom's arrogance and as an image of the danger
that is going to swoop down upon this people (cf.
48:40). The divine "I," more muted in other oracles against the nations, dominates these verses:

"I will bring the calamity."
"I will punish him."
"I have stripped bare."
"I have uncovered. . . ."
"I will keep alive. . . ."
"I will make you least."
"I will bring you down."
"I will chase. . . ."
"I will appoint. . . ."

As elsewhere, the "I" acts through invading armies,
militant neighbors, and the like. But the outcome
is so complete that the disaster leaves less than a
thief would do in robbing a house or an efficient
gleaner would do when harvesting the fields (v. 9).

The force of the first-person statements about
the Lord's intention to destroy Edom completely
reaches a climax in v. 19 with powerful statements
about the incomparability of the Lord of Israel:
"Who is like me? Who can summon me? Who is
the shepherd who can stand before me?" Such
questions articulate the power of the Lord over all
the other gods and the nations who worship them
(see Exod 15:11). The shepherd who cannot stand
is presumably a human ruler, and the animal
imagery that recurs in this passage takes the form
of the flock that is devastated by the lion that
pounces upon its prey (cf. 4:7; 5:6), the "sheep"
(vv 19-20; cf. 50:44-46). The comparison of Edom
to Sodom and Gomorrah evokes the image of an
utterly lifeless and devastated land, incapable any
longer of supporting life (v. 18; cf. vv. 13, 33;
50:40; 51:43).

The apparent offer of divine protection in v. 10
is understood by some as the quotation of Edom's
neighbors, who offer to help but are unable to do
so. The meaning of the text is unclear, but v. 20
does not offer much hope for "the little ones." On
the cup of wrath in v. 12, see the Commentary on
25:15-29. (See Reflections at 51:59-64.)

JEREMIAH 49:23-27, AGAINST DAMASCUS

NIV

23Concerning Damascus:

"Hamath and Arpad are dismayed,
　for they have heard bad news.
They are disheartened,
　troubled like[a] the restless sea.
24Damascus has become feeble,
　she has turned to flee
　and panic has gripped her;
anguish and pain have seized her,
　pain like that of a woman in labor.
25Why has the city of renown not been
　　abandoned,
　the town in which I delight?
26Surely, her young men will fall in the streets;
　all her soldiers will be silenced in that day,"
　　　　　　　　declares the LORD Almighty.
27"I will set fire to the walls of Damascus;
　it will consume the fortresses of Ben-
　　Hadad."

[a]23 Hebrew on or by

NRSV

23Concerning Damascus.

Hamath and Arpad are confounded,
　for they have heard bad news;
they melt in fear, they are troubled like the sea[a]
　that cannot be quiet.
24 Damascus has become feeble, she turned to
　　flee,
　and panic seized her;
anguish and sorrows have taken hold of her,
　as of a woman in labor.
25 How the famous city is forsaken,[b]
　the joyful town![c]
26 Therefore her young men shall fall in her
　　squares,
　and all her soldiers shall be destroyed in that
　　day, 　　　　　says the LORD of hosts.
27 And I will kindle a fire at the wall of
　　Damascus,
　and it shall devour the strongholds of
　　Ben-hadad.

[a]Cn: Heb there is trouble in the sea　　[b]Vg: Heb is not forsaken
[c]Syr Vg Tg: Heb the town of my joy

COMMENTARY

This brief oracle is directed against the capital of Aram, or Syria, to the north of Israel and Judah. No particular historical moment is identifiable in these verses; no references to the life or culture or religion of Syria are made; and nothing is told of the reason for judgment. The passage describes what is going to happen to Damascus, a description that shares with other oracles against the nations in comparing the plight of the people to the suffering of a woman in labor (v. 24; cf. v. 22; 50:43). The expressions "the famous city" or "city of renown" and "the joyful city" (v. 25) may have been honorific labels reflecting the character of Damascus as a fruitful oasis on the edges of the Syrian wilderness, similar to modern appellations, such as "the pearl of the Orient" and "the eye of the East."[232]

232. W. Rudolph, *Jeremia*, Handbuch zum Alten Testament 12 (Tübingen: Mohr, 1958) 271; and Huwyler, *Jeremia und die Völker*, 307-15.

The announcement of judgment is a little milder in tone than some of the other oracles against the nations. The destruction of Damascus will be an event that causes fear and anxiety on the part of other Syrian cities, specifically Hamath and Arpad to the north.

The divine agency in the destruction is signaled only at the end in a verse whose style and language echo Amos 1:4, 14. Everywhere one turns in the oracles against the nations, echoes of other such oracles are heard either in general form (e.g., the calls to flee and the images of sword and cup) or in strong linguistic similarity (as in v. 27). This language represents a community store of ways of speaking about God's judgment on the nations—idioms and images appropriate to the depiction of such devastation. The prophets and those who added to their oracles or revised them drew upon this common store. (See Reflections at 51:59-64.)

JEREMIAH 49:28-33, AGAINST KEDAR AND THE KINGDOMS OF HAZOR

NIV

28Concerning Kedar and the kingdoms of Hazor, which Nebuchadnezzar king of Babylon attacked:

This is what the LORD says:

"Arise, and attack Kedar
   and destroy the people of the East.
29Their tents and their flocks will be taken;
   their shelters will be carried off
   with all their goods and camels.
Men will shout to them,
   'Terror on every side!'

30"Flee quickly away!
   Stay in deep caves, you who live in Hazor,"
                              declares the LORD.
"Nebuchadnezzar king of Babylon has plotted
   against you;
he has devised a plan against you.

31"Arise and attack a nation at ease,
   which lives in confidence."
                              declares the LORD,
"a nation that has neither gates nor bars;
   its people live alone.
32Their camels will become plunder,
   and their large herds will be booty.
I will scatter to the winds those who are in
   distant places[a]
and will bring disaster on them from every side,"
                              declares the LORD.
33"Hazor will become a haunt of jackals,
   a desolate place forever.
No one will live there;
   no man will dwell in it."

[a]32 Or *who clip the hair by their foreheads*

NRSV

28Concerning Kedar and the kingdoms of Hazor that King Nebuchadrezzar of Babylon defeated.

Thus says the LORD:
Rise up, advance against Kedar!
   Destroy the people of the east!
29 Take their tents and their flocks,
   their curtains and all their goods;
carry off their camels for yourselves,
   and a cry shall go up: "Terror is all
      around!"
30 Flee, wander far away, hide in deep places,
   O inhabitants of Hazor!   says the LORD.
For King Nebuchadrezzar of Babylon
   has made a plan against you
   and formed a purpose against you.

31 Rise up, advance against a nation at ease,
   that lives secure,   says the LORD,
that has no gates or bars,
   that lives alone.
32 Their camels shall become booty,
   their herds of cattle a spoil.
I will scatter to every wind
   those who have shaven temples,
and I will bring calamity
   against them from every side,
                              says the LORD.
33 Hazor shall become a lair of jackals,
   an everlasting waste;
no one shall live there,
   nor shall anyone settle in it.

COMMENTARY

Kedar refers to the Arabian tribes known as Kedarites, who roamed the Syrian-Arabian desert and are referred to several times in the OT (e.g., Gen 25:13; Ps 120:5; Isa 21:16-17; 42:11). While Hazor may have been a place in the Arabian desert (not the famous city in the north of Israel) or may be a now-disguised reference to חצר (ḥāṣēr), "court" (so the Greek) or "settlement," and thus a reference to unwalled Arab villages of a settled or semi-settled character, possibly inhabited also by Kedarites. A number of interpreters have identified two oracles joined together, the first against the nomadic tribes of Kedar (vv. 28*b*-29) and the second against the more sedentary Arabs in the unwalled (v. 31) villages (vv. 30-33)—that is, against the kingdoms (villages? chieftains?) of Hazor.[233] Hazor is mentioned in both parts of the text.

These two oracles, though not identical in form, share some common features. Each begins with the cry "Rise up, advance against . . . " (vv. 28*b*, 31*a*), and then characterizes the people under attack (vv. 29*a*, 31*b*), identifying their camels as a source of booty (vv. 29*b*, 32*a*). The flight of the people is described in each case: (1) as the imperative call to flight and the reason for flight (v. 30), a form of speech heard often in Jeremiah (e.g., 4:6; 6:1; 48:6; 49:8; cf. 48:28), and (2) as the Lord's intention to scatter the people (cf. v. 36*b*); shaven heads or temples refer to some kind of religious practice of haircutting among Arab tribes (cf. 9:26; 25:23). The unprotected character of the Arab settlements, indicated in the second oracle with reference to their false security in living by themselves and not bothering to build protected cities with walls and gates (v. 31), makes them particularly vulnerable to attack and loss of all their goods.

The result, in both oracles, is disaster (vv. 30*b*, 32*b*-33).

The two oracles make the same point, though in complex ways. They belong together, especially in the way they join human (v. 30*b*) and divine (v. 32*b*) agency only. In the first oracle, the destruction of the Kedarites is a result of the plan and purpose of Nebuchadrezzar. That is language one might have expected of the deity, but this oracle sets the whole matter on the human-political plane. Kedarite defeat is a part of Babylonian military strategy. Only with the reiterated word of judgment in the second oracle do we hear the expected word that the plan of the Babylonians is the act of God. The text says nothing about how the plan and purpose of the Babylonian king are to be understood as the action of the Lord of Israel.[234] But by juxtaposing these two oracles the prophet makes that claim explicit. One may speak about the event either as a military victory of Babylonians over Arabian tribes (we know from the Babylonian Chronicle that there was such an event in 599–598 BCE) or as a divine act, the Lord's scattering and bringing calamity. In either way, the outcome is the same: The Arab territory is decimated, an uninhabitable waste (v. 33). (See Reflections at 51:59-64.)

233. See William L. Holladay, *Jeremiah 1: A Commentary on the Book of the Prophet Jeremiah Chapters 1–25,* Hermeneia (Philadelphia: Fortress, 1986) 382-86; Gerald L. Keown, Pamela J. Scalise, and Thomas J. Smothers, *Jeremiah 26–52,* WBC 27 (Dallas: Word, 1995) 336-40; and Huwyler, *Jeremiah und die Völker,* 236.

234. The word "Nebuchadrezzar," is missing from the Greek and may have been absent from the original text, but the verse still refers to a king of Babylon.

JEREMIAH 49:34-39, AGAINST ELAM

34This is the word of the LORD that came to Jeremiah the prophet concerning Elam, early in the reign of Zedekiah king of Judah:

35This is what the LORD Almighty says:

"See, I will break the bow of Elam,
　the mainstay of their might.
36I will bring against Elam the four winds
　from the four quarters of the heavens;
I will scatter them to the four winds,
　and there will not be a nation
　where Elam's exiles do not go.
37I will shatter Elam before their foes,

34The word of the LORD that came to the prophet Jeremiah concerning Elam, at the beginning of the reign of King Zedekiah of Judah.

35Thus says the LORD of hosts: I am going to break the bow of Elam, the mainstay of their might; 36and I will bring upon Elam the four winds from the four quarters of heaven; and I will scatter them to all these winds, and there shall be no nation to which the exiles from Elam shall not come. 37I will terrify Elam before their enemies, and before those who seek their life; I will bring disaster upon them, my fierce anger, says the

NIV

before those who seek their lives;
I will bring disaster upon them,
even my fierce anger,"
declares the LORD.
"I will pursue them with the sword
until I have made an end of them.
38I will set my throne in Elam
and destroy her king and officials,"
declares the LORD.

39"Yet I will restore the fortunes of Elam
in days to come,"
declares the LORD.

NRSV

LORD. I will send the sword after them, until I
have consumed them; 38and I will set my throne
in Elam, and destroy their king and officials, says
the LORD.

39But in the latter days I will restore the fortunes of Elam, says the LORD.

COMMENTARY

If the oracles against the Arabian tribes of Kedar only uncover the divine activity near its end, the oracle against the Mesopotamian kingdom of Elam, east of the Tigris River, does the reverse. Here there is no vivid description of the people, their land and their culture, though the breaking of the bow of Elam (v. 36) may allude to the excellence of Elamite archers (cf. Isa 22:6). Nor does the text describe people's reaction to destruction, as is regularly the case in other oracles. Here there is only the divine "I" at work—from beginning to end (cf. vv. 7-22). The text shows no interest in the human agency of Elam's destruction. It is entirely the work of the Lord, who brings the winds from the corners of the earth to scatter the Elamites to the winds, whose fierce anger and

mighty sword (cf. 47:6; 48:2) destroy Elam and its rulers. The only throne left in Elam will be the one representing the rule of the Lord of hosts (vv. 35-38). This oracle concludes the series that makes up chap. 49. The wrath of the divine warrior against the nations of the earth represents the victory of the kingdom of God over the claims to sovereignty of human princes, even those far removed from the territory of the chosen people, Israel. The oracles thereby are seen to have an eschatological claim as they anticipate the Lord's rule over the far-flung peoples of the earth.

The last word in these oracles, however, is not a word of destructive power. Rather, it is a promise of restoration (v. 39; see the Commentary on 48:47). (See Reflections at 51:59-64.)

JEREMIAH 50:1–51:58, AGAINST BABYLON

NIV

50This is the word the LORD spoke through Jeremiah the prophet concerning Babylon and the land of the Babylonians^a:
2 "Announce and proclaim among the nations,
lift up a banner and proclaim it;
keep nothing back, but say,

^a1 Or Chaldeans; also in verses 8, 25, 35 and 45

NRSV

50The word that the LORD spoke concerning Babylon, concerning the land of the Chaldeans, by the prophet Jeremiah:
2 Declare among the nations and proclaim,
set up a banner and proclaim,
do not conceal it, say:
Babylon is taken,

NIV

'Babylon will be captured;
Bel will be put to shame,
Marduk filled with terror.
Her images will be put to shame
and her idols filled with terror.'
³ A nation from the north will attack her
and lay waste her land.
No one will live in it;
both men and animals will flee away.

⁴ "In those days, at that time,"
declares the LORD,
"the people of Israel and the people of Judah
together
will go in tears to seek the LORD their God.
⁵ They will ask the way to Zion
and turn their faces toward it.
They will come and bind themselves to the
LORD
in an everlasting covenant
that will not be forgotten.

⁶ "My people have been lost sheep;
their shepherds have led them astray
and caused them to roam on the
mountains.
They wandered over mountain and hill
and forgot their own resting place.
⁷ Whoever found them devoured them;
their enemies said, 'We are not guilty,
for they sinned against the LORD, their true
pasture,
the LORD, the hope of their fathers.'

⁸ "Flee out of Babylon;
leave the land of the Babylonians,
and be like the goats that lead the flock.
⁹ For I will stir up and bring against Babylon
an alliance of great nations from the land
of the north.
They will take up their positions against her,
and from the north she will be captured.
Their arrows will be like skilled warriors
who do not return empty-handed.
¹⁰So Babyloniaᵃ will be plundered;
all who plunder her will have their fill,"
declares the LORD.

ᵃ10 Or Chaldea

NRSV

Bel is put to shame,
Merodach is dismayed.
Her images are put to shame,
her idols are dismayed.
3For out of the north a nation has come up
against her; it shall make her land a desolation,
and no one shall live in it; both human beings and
animals shall flee away.

4In those days and in that time, says the LORD,
the people of Israel shall come, they and the people of Judah together; they shall come weeping as
they seek the LORD their God. ⁵They shall ask the
way to Zion, with faces turned toward it, and they
shall come and joinᵃ themselves to the LORD by an
everlasting covenant that will never be forgotten.

6My people have been lost sheep; their shepherds have led them astray, turning them away on
the mountains; from mountain to hill they have
gone, they have forgotten their fold. ⁷All who
found them have devoured them, and their enemies have said, "We are not guilty, because they
have sinned against the LORD, the true pasture,
the LORD, the hope of their ancestors."

8Flee from Babylon, and go out of the land of
the Chaldeans, and be like male goats leading the
flock. ⁹For I am going to stir up and bring against
Babylon a company of great nations from the land
of the north; and they shall array themselves
against her; from there she shall be taken. Their
arrows are like the arrows of a skilled warrior who
does not return empty-handed. ¹⁰Chaldea shall be
plundered; all who plunder her shall be sated,
says the LORD.

¹¹ Though you rejoice, though you exult,
O plunderers of my heritage,
though you frisk about like a heifer on the
grass,
and neigh like stallions,
¹² your mother shall be utterly shamed,
and she who bore you shall be disgraced.
Lo, she shall be the last of the nations,
a wilderness, dry land, and a desert.

ᵃGk: Heb toward it. Come! They shall join

NIV

¹¹"Because you rejoice and are glad,
  you who pillage my inheritance,
because you frolic like a heifer threshing grain
  and neigh like stallions,
¹²your mother will be greatly ashamed;
  she who gave you birth will be disgraced.
She will be the least of the nations—
  a wilderness, a dry land, a desert.
¹³Because of the LORD's anger she will not be
  inhabited
  but will be completely desolate.
All who pass Babylon will be horrified and scoff
  because of all her wounds.

¹⁴"Take up your positions around Babylon,
  all you who draw the bow.
Shoot at her! Spare no arrows,
  for she has sinned against the LORD.
¹⁵Shout against her on every side!
  She surrenders, her towers fall,
  her walls are torn down.
Since this is the vengeance of the LORD,
  take vengeance on her;
  do to her as she has done to others.
¹⁶Cut off from Babylon the sower,
  and the reaper with his sickle at harvest.
Because of the sword of the oppressor
  let everyone return to his own people,
  let everyone flee to his own land.

¹⁷"Israel is a scattered flock
  that lions have chased away.
The first to devour him
  was the king of Assyria;
the last to crush his bones
  was Nebuchadnezzar king of Babylon."

¹⁸Therefore this is what the LORD Almighty, the
God of Israel, says:

"I will punish the king of Babylon and his land
  as I punished the king of Assyria.
¹⁹But I will bring Israel back to his own pasture
  and he will graze on Carmel and Bashan;
his appetite will be satisfied
  on the hills of Ephraim and Gilead.
²⁰In those days, at that time,"
  declares the LORD,
"search will be made for Israel's guilt,
  but there will be none,
and for the sins of Judah,

NRSV

¹³Because of the wrath of the LORD she shall not
    be inhabited,
  but shall be an utter desolation;
everyone who passes by Babylon shall be
    appalled
  and hiss because of all her wounds.
¹⁴Take up your positions around Babylon,
  all you that bend the bow;
shoot at her, spare no arrows,
  for she has sinned against the LORD.
¹⁵Raise a shout against her from all sides,
  "She has surrendered;
her bulwarks have fallen,
  her walls are thrown down."
For this is the vengeance of the LORD:
  take vengeance on her,
  do to her as she has done.
¹⁶Cut off from Babylon the sower,
  and the wielder of the sickle in time of
    harvest;
because of the destroying sword
  all of them shall return to their own
    people,
  and all of them shall flee to their own land.

17Israel is a hunted sheep driven away by
lions. First the king of Assyria devoured it, and
now at the end King Nebuchadrezzar of Babylon
has gnawed its bones. ¹⁸Therefore, thus says the
LORD of hosts, the God of Israel: I am going to
punish the king of Babylon and his land, as I punished the king of Assyria. ¹⁹I will restore Israel to
its pasture, and it shall feed on Carmel and in
Bashan, and on the hills of Ephraim and in Gilead
its hunger shall be satisfied. ²⁰In those days and at
that time, says the LORD, the iniquity of Israel shall
be sought, and there shall be none; and the sins of
Judah, and none shall be found; for I will pardon
the remnant that I have spared.

²¹Go up to the land of Merathaim;[a]
  go up against her,
and attack the inhabitants of Pekod[b]
  and utterly destroy the last of them,[c]
                    says the LORD;
  do all that I have commanded you.

[a]Or of Double Rebellion [b]Or of Punishment [c]Tg: Heb destroy
after them

NIV

but none will be found,
for I will forgive the remnant I spare.

21"Attack the land of Merathaim
and those who live in Pekod.
Pursue, kill and completely destroy[a] them,"
declares the LORD.
"Do everything I have commanded you.
22The noise of battle is in the land,
the noise of great destruction!
23How broken and shattered
is the hammer of the whole earth!
How desolate is Babylon
among the nations!
24I set a trap for you, O Babylon,
and you were caught before you knew it;
you were found and captured
because you opposed the LORD.
25The LORD has opened his arsenal
and brought out the weapons of his wrath,
for the Sovereign LORD Almighty has work to
do
in the land of the Babylonians.
26Come against her from afar.
Break open her granaries;
pile her up like heaps of grain.
Completely destroy her
and leave her no remnant.
27Kill all her young bulls;
let them go down to the slaughter!
Woe to them! For their day has come,
the time for them to be punished.
28Listen to the fugitives and refugees from
Babylon
declaring in Zion
how the LORD our God has taken vengeance,
vengeance for his temple.

29"Summon archers against Babylon,
all those who draw the bow.
Encamp all around her;
let no one escape.
Repay her for her deeds;
do to her as she has done.
For she has defied the LORD,
the Holy One of Israel.

---

*a*21 The Hebrew term refers to the irrevocable giving over of things or persons to the LORD, often by totally destroying them; also in verse 26.

NRSV

22 The noise of battle is in the land, and great
destruction!
23 How the hammer of the whole earth
is cut down and broken!
How Babylon has become
a horror among the nations!
24 You set a snare for yourself and you were
caught, O Babylon,
but you did not know it;
you were discovered and seized,
because you challenged the LORD.
25 The LORD has opened his armory,
and brought out the weapons of his wrath,
for the Lord GOD of hosts has a task to do
in the land of the Chaldeans.
26 Come against her from every quarter;
open her granaries;
pile her up like heaps of grain, and destroy her
utterly;
let nothing be left of her.
27 Kill all her bulls,
let them go down to the slaughter.
Alas for them, their day has come,
the time of their punishment!

28Listen! Fugitives and refugees from the land
of Babylon are coming to declare in Zion the
vengeance of the LORD our God, vengeance for his
temple.

29Summon archers against Babylon, all who
bend the bow. Encamp all around her; let no one
escape. Repay her according to her deeds; just as
she has done, do to her—for she has arrogantly
defied the LORD, the Holy One of Israel.
30Therefore her young men shall fall in her
squares, and all her soldiers shall be destroyed on
that day, says the LORD.

31 I am against you, O arrogant one,
says the Lord GOD of hosts;
for your day has come,
the time when I will punish you.
32 The arrogant one shall stumble and fall,
with no one to raise him up,
and I will kindle a fire in his cities,
and it will devour everything around him.

NIV

³⁰Therefore, her young men will fall in the streets;
  all her soldiers will be silenced in that day,"
              declares the LORD.
³¹"See, I am against you, O arrogant one,"
  declares the Lord, the LORD Almighty,
  "for your day has come,
    the time for you to be punished.
³²The arrogant one will stumble and fall
    and no one will help her up;
  I will kindle a fire in her towns
    that will consume all who are around her."

³³This is what the LORD Almighty says:

"The people of Israel are oppressed,
    and the people of Judah as well.
All their captors hold them fast,
    refusing to let them go.
³⁴Yet their Redeemer is strong;
    the LORD Almighty is his name.
He will vigorously defend their cause
    so that he may bring rest to their land,
    but unrest to those who live in Babylon.

³⁵"A sword against the Babylonians!"
    declares the LORD—
"against those who live in Babylon
    and against her officials and wise men!
³⁶A sword against her false prophets!
    They will become fools.
A sword against her warriors!
    They will be filled with terror.
³⁷A sword against her horses and chariots
    and all the foreigners in her ranks!
    They will become women.
A sword against her treasures!
    They will be plundered.
³⁸A drought on^a her waters!
    They will dry up.
For it is a land of idols,
    idols that will go mad with terror.

³⁹"So desert creatures and hyenas will live there,
    and there the owl will dwell.
It will never again be inhabited
    or lived in from generation to generation.
⁴⁰As God overthrew Sodom and Gomorrah
    along with their neighboring towns,"

^a 38 Or A sword against

NRSV

³³Thus says the LORD of hosts: The people of
Israel are oppressed, and so too are the people of
Judah; all their captors have held them fast and
refuse to let them go. ³⁴Their Redeemer is strong;
the LORD of hosts is his name. He will surely plead
their cause, that he may give rest to the earth, but
unrest to the inhabitants of Babylon.

³⁵ A sword against the Chaldeans, says the
      LORD,
    and against the inhabitants of Babylon,
    and against her officials and her sages!
³⁶ A sword against the diviners,
    so that they may become fools!
A sword against her warriors,
    so that they may be destroyed!
³⁷ A sword against her^a horses and against her^a
      chariots,
    and against all the foreign troops in her
      midst,
    so that they may become women!
A sword against all her treasures,
    that they may be plundered!
³⁸ A drought^b against her waters,
    that they may be dried up!
For it is a land of images,
    and they go mad over idols.

³⁹Therefore wild animals shall live with hyenas in Babylon,^c and ostriches shall inhabit her;
she shall never again be peopled, or inhabited for
all generations. ⁴⁰As when God overthrew Sodom
and Gomorrah and their neighbors, says the LORD,
so no one shall live there, nor shall anyone settle
in her.

⁴¹ Look, a people is coming from the north;
    a mighty nation and many kings
    are stirring from the farthest parts of the
      earth.
⁴² They wield bow and spear,
    they are cruel and have no mercy.
The sound of them is like the roaring sea;
    they ride upon horses,
set in array as a warrior for battle,
    against you, O daughter Babylon!

^aCn: Heb his   ^bAnother reading is A sword   ^cHeb lacks in
Babylon

NIV

declares the LORD,
"so no one will live there;
    no man will dwell in it."

41"Look! An army is coming from the north;
    a great nation and many kings
    are being stirred up from the ends of the
        earth.
42They are armed with bows and spears;
    they are cruel and without mercy.
They sound like the roaring sea
    as they ride on their horses;
they come like men in battle formation
    to attack you, O Daughter of Babylon.
43The king of Babylon has heard reports about
        them,
    and his hands hang limp.
Anguish has gripped him,
    pain like that of a woman in labor.
44Like a lion coming up from Jordan's thickets
    to a rich pastureland,
I will chase Babylon from its land in an instant.
    Who is the chosen one I will appoint for
        this?
Who is like me and who can challenge me?
    And what shepherd can stand against me?"
45Therefore, hear what the LORD has planned
        against Babylon,
    what he has purposed against the land of
        the Babylonians:
The young of the flock will be dragged away;
    he will completely destroy their pasture
        because of them.
46At the sound of Babylon's capture the earth
    will tremble;
    its cry will resound among the nations.

51 This is what the LORD says:

"See, I will stir up the spirit of a destroyer
    against Babylon and the people of Leb
        Kamai.a
2 I will send foreigners to Babylon
    to winnow her and to devastate her land;
they will oppose her on every side
    in the day of her disaster.
3 Let not the archer string his bow,

a1 Leb Kamai is a cryptogram for Chaldea, that is, Babylonia.

NRSV

43 The king of Babylon heard news of them,
    and his hands fell helpless;
anguish seized him,
    pain like that of a woman in labor.

44Like a lion coming up from the thickets of
the Jordan against a perennial pasture, I will suddenly chase them away from her; and I will
appoint over her whomever I choose.a For who is
like me? Who can summon me? Who is the shepherd who can stand before me? 45Therefore hear
the plan that the LORD has made against Babylon,
and the purposes that he has formed against the
land of the Chaldeans: Surely the little ones of the
flock shall be dragged away; surely theirb fold shall
be appalled at their fate. 46At the sound of the capture of Babylon the earth shall tremble, and her
cry shall be heard among the nations.

51 Thus says the LORD:
I am going to stir up a destructive windc
    against Babylon
    and against the inhabitants of Leb-qamai;d
2 and I will send winnowers to Babylon,
    and they shall winnow her.
They shall empty her land
    when they come against her from every
        side
    on the day of trouble.
3 Let not the archer bend his bow,
    and let him not array himself in his coat of
        mail.
Do not spare her young men;
    utterly destroy her entire army.
4 They shall fall down slain in the land of the
        Chaldeans,
    and wounded in her streets.
5 Israel and Judah have not been forsaken
    by their God, the LORD of hosts,
though their land is full of guilt
    before the Holy One of Israel.

6 Flee from the midst of Babylon,
    save your lives, each of you!
Do not perish because of her guilt,

aOr and I will single out the choicest of her rams. Meaning of Heb
uncertain   bSyr Gk Tg Compare 49.20: Heb lacks their   cOr
stir up the spirit of a destroyer   dLeb-qamai is a cryptogram for
Kasdim, Chaldea

NIV

nor let him put on his armor.
Do not spare her young men;
    completely destroy[a] her army.
[4] They will fall down slain in Babylon,[b]
    fatally wounded in her streets.
[5] For Israel and Judah have not been forsaken
    by their God, the Lord Almighty,
though their land[c] is full of guilt
    before the Holy One of Israel.

[6] "Flee from Babylon!
    Run for your lives!
    Do not be destroyed because of her sins.
It is time for the Lord's vengeance;
    he will pay her what she deserves.
[7] Babylon was a gold cup in the Lord's hand;
    she made the whole earth drunk.
The nations drank her wine;
    therefore they have now gone mad.
[8] Babylon will suddenly fall and be broken.
    Wail over her!
Get balm for her pain;
    perhaps she can be healed.

[9] " 'We would have healed Babylon,
    but she cannot be healed;
let us leave her and each go to his own land,
    for her judgment reaches to the skies,
    it rises as high as the clouds.'

[10] " 'The Lord has vindicated us;
    come, let us tell in Zion
    what the Lord our God has done.'

[11] "Sharpen the arrows,
    take up the shields!
The Lord has stirred up the kings of the
        Medes,
    because his purpose is to destroy Babylon.
The Lord will take vengeance,
    vengeance for his temple.
[12] Lift up a banner against the walls of Babylon!
    Reinforce the guard,
station the watchmen,
    prepare an ambush!
The Lord will carry out his purpose,
    his decree against the people of Babylon.

[a]3 The Hebrew term refers to the irrevocable giving over of things or persons to the Lord, often by totally destroying them.   [b]4 Or Chaldea   [c]5 Or / and the land ₍of the Babylonians₎

NRSV

for this is the time of the Lord's vengeance;
    he is repaying her what is due.
[7] Babylon was a golden cup in the Lord's hand,
    making all the earth drunken;
the nations drank of her wine,
    and so the nations went mad.
[8] Suddenly Babylon has fallen and is shattered;
    wail for her!
Bring balm for her wound;
    perhaps she may be healed.
[9] We tried to heal Babylon,
    but she could not be healed.
Forsake her, and let each of us go
    to our own country;
for her judgment has reached up to heaven
    and has been lifted up even to the skies.
[10] The Lord has brought forth our vindication;
    come, let us declare in Zion
    the work of the Lord our God.

[11] Sharpen the arrows!
    Fill the quivers!
The Lord has stirred up the spirit of the kings of
the Medes, because his purpose concerning
Babylon is to destroy it, for that is the vengeance
of the Lord, vengeance for his temple.
[12] Raise a standard against the walls of Babylon;
    make the watch strong;
post sentinels;
    prepare the ambushes;
for the Lord has both planned and done
    what he spoke concerning the inhabitants
        of Babylon.
[13] You who live by mighty waters,
    rich in treasures,
your end has come,
    the thread of your life is cut.
[14] The Lord of hosts has sworn by himself:
Surely I will fill you with troops like a swarm
        of locusts,
    and they shall raise a shout of victory over
        you.

[15] It is he who made the earth by his power,
    who established the world by his wisdom,
and by his understanding stretched out the
    heavens.

NIV

¹³You who live by many waters
   and are rich in treasures,
your end has come,
   the time for you to be cut off.
¹⁴The Lord Almighty has sworn by himself:
   I will surely fill you with men, as with a
      swarm of locusts,
   and they will shout in triumph over you.

¹⁵"He made the earth by his power;
   he founded the world by his wisdom
   and stretched out the heavens by his
      understanding.
¹⁶When he thunders, the waters in the heavens
      roar;
   he makes clouds rise from the ends of the
      earth.
He sends lightning with the rain
   and brings out the wind from his storehouses.

¹⁷"Every man is senseless and without
      knowledge;
   every goldsmith is shamed by his idols.
His images are a fraud;
   they have no breath in them.
¹⁸They are worthless, the objects of mockery;
   when their judgment comes, they will perish.
¹⁹He who is the Portion of Jacob is not like
      these,
   for he is the Maker of all things,
including the tribe of his inheritance—
   the Lord Almighty is his name.

²⁰"You are my war club,
   my weapon for battle—
with you I shatter nations,
   with you I destroy kingdoms,
²¹with you I shatter horse and rider,
   with you I shatter chariot and driver,
²²with you I shatter man and woman,
   with you I shatter old man and youth,
   with you I shatter young man and maiden,
²³with you I shatter shepherd and flock,
   with you I shatter farmer and oxen,
   with you I shatter governors and officials.

²⁴"Before your eyes I will repay Babylon and all
who live in Babyloniaᵃ for all the wrong they have
done in Zion," declares the Lord.

ᵃ24 Or Chaldea; also in verse 35

NRSV

¹⁶When he utters his voice there is a tumult of
      waters in the heavens,
   and he makes the mist rise from the ends
      of the earth.
He makes lightnings for the rain,
   and he brings out the wind from his
      storehouses.
¹⁷Everyone is stupid and without knowledge;
   goldsmiths are all put to shame by their
      idols;
for their images are false,
   and there is no breath in them.
¹⁸They are worthless, a work of delusion;
   at the time of their punishment they shall
      perish.
¹⁹Not like these is the Lord,ᵃ the portion of
      Jacob,
   for he is the one who formed all things,
and Israel is the tribe of his inheritance;
   the Lord of hosts is his name.

²⁰You are my war club, my weapon of battle:
   with you I smash nations;
      with you I destroy kingdoms;
²¹with you I smash the horse and its rider;
   with you I smash the chariot and the
      charioteer;
²²with you I smash man and woman;
   with you I smash the old man and the boy;
   with you I smash the young man and the girl;
²³   with you I smash shepherds and their
      flocks;
   with you I smash farmers and their teams;
   with you I smash governors and deputies.

²⁴I will repay Babylon and all the inhabitants
of Chaldea before your very eyes for all the wrong
that they have done in Zion, says the Lord.

²⁵I am against you, O destroying mountain,
                              says the Lord,
   that destroys the whole earth;
I will stretch out my hand against you,
   and roll you down from the crags,
   and make you a burned-out mountain.
²⁶No stone shall be taken from you for a corner
   and no stone for a foundation,

ᵃHeb lacks the Lord

NIV

²⁵"I am against you, O destroying mountain,
  you who destroy the whole earth,"
                    declares the LORD.
"I will stretch out my hand against you,
  roll you off the cliffs,
  and make you a burned-out mountain.
²⁶No rock will be taken from you for a
    cornerstone,
  nor any stone for a foundation,
  for you will be desolate forever,"
                    declares the LORD.

²⁷"Lift up a banner in the land!
  Blow the trumpet among the nations!
Prepare the nations for battle against her;
  summon against her these kingdoms:
  Ararat, Minni and Ashkenaz.
Appoint a commander against her;
  send up horses like a swarm of locusts.
²⁸Prepare the nations for battle against her—
  the kings of the Medes,
  governors and all their officials,
  and all the countries they rule.
²⁹The land trembles and writhes,
  for the LORD's purposes against Babylon
    stand—
to lay waste the land of Babylon
  so that no one will live there.
³⁰Babylon's warriors have stopped fighting;
  they remain in their strongholds.
Their strength is exhausted;
  they have become like women.
Her dwellings are set on fire;
  the bars of her gates are broken.
³¹One courier follows another
  and messenger follows messenger
to announce to the king of Babylon
  that his entire city is captured,
³²the river crossings seized,
  the marshes set on fire,
  and the soldiers terrified."

³³This is what the LORD Almighty, the God of
Israel, says:

"The Daughter of Babylon is like a threshing
    floor
  at the time it is trampled;
  the time to harvest her will soon come."

NRSV

but you shall be a perpetual waste,
  says the LORD.

²⁷ Raise a standard in the land,
  blow the trumpet among the nations;
prepare the nations for war against her,
  summon against her the kingdoms,
  Ararat, Minni, and Ashkenaz;
appoint a marshal against her,
  bring up horses like bristling locusts.
²⁸ Prepare the nations for war against her,
  the kings of the Medes, with their
      governors and deputies,
  and every land under their dominion.
²⁹ The land trembles and writhes,
  for the LORD's purposes against Babylon
    stand,
to make the land of Babylon a desolation,
  without inhabitant.
³⁰ The warriors of Babylon have given up
    fighting,
  they remain in their strongholds;
their strength has failed,
  they have become women;
her buildings are set on fire,
  her bars are broken.
³¹ One runner runs to meet another,
  and one messenger to meet another,
to tell the king of Babylon
  that his city is taken from end to end:
³² the fords have been seized,
  the marshes have been burned with fire,
  and the soldiers are in panic.
³³ For thus says the LORD of hosts, the God of
    Israel:
Daughter Babylon is like a threshing floor
  at the time when it is trodden;
yet a little while
  and the time of her harvest will come.

³⁴ "King Nebuchadrezzar of Babylon has
    devoured me,
  he has crushed me;
he has made me an empty vessel,
  he has swallowed me like a monster;
he has filled his belly with my delicacies,
  he has spewed me out.

NIV

34"Nebuchadnezzar king of Babylon has
        devoured us,
    he has thrown us into confusion,
    he has made us an empty jar.
Like a serpent he has swallowed us
    and filled his stomach with our delicacies,
    and then has spewed us out.
35May the violence done to our flesh[a] be upon
        Babylon,"
    say the inhabitants of Zion.
"May our blood be on those who live in
        Babylonia,"
    says Jerusalem.

    36Therefore, this is what the LORD says:

"See, I will defend your cause
    and avenge you;
I will dry up her sea
    and make her springs dry.
37Babylon will be a heap of ruins,
    a haunt of jackals,
an object of horror and scorn,
    a place where no one lives.
38Her people all roar like young lions,
    they growl like lion cubs.
39But while they are aroused,
    I will set out a feast for them
    and make them drunk,
so that they shout with laughter—
    then sleep forever and not awake,"
                declares the LORD.
40"I will bring them down
    like lambs to the slaughter,
    like rams and goats.
41"How Sheshach[b] will be captured,
    the boast of the whole earth seized!
What a horror Babylon will be
    among the nations!
42The sea will rise over Babylon;
    its roaring waves will cover her.
43Her towns will be desolate,
    a dry and desert land,
a land where no one lives,
    through which no man travels.
44I will punish Bel in Babylon
    and make him spew out what he has swallowed.

[a]35 Or done to us and to our children   [b]41 Sheshach is a cryptogram for Babylon.

NRSV

35 May my torn flesh be avenged on Babylon,"
    the inhabitants of Zion shall say.
"May my blood be avenged on the inhabitants
    of Chaldea,"
    Jerusalem shall say.
36 Therefore thus says the LORD:
I am going to defend your cause
    and take vengeance for you.
I will dry up her sea
    and make her fountain dry;
37 and Babylon shall become a heap of ruins,
    a den of jackals,
an object of horror and of hissing,
    without inhabitant.

38 Like lions they shall roar together;
    they shall growl like lions' whelps.
39 When they are inflamed, I will set out their
        drink
    and make them drunk, until they become
        merry
and then sleep a perpetual sleep
    and never wake, says the LORD.
40 I will bring them down like lambs to the
        slaughter,
    like rams and goats.

41 How Sheshach[a] is taken,
    the pride of the whole earth seized!
How Babylon has become
    an object of horror among the nations!
42 The sea has risen over Babylon;
    she has been covered by its tumultuous
        waves.
43 Her cities have become an object of horror,
    a land of drought and a desert,
a land in which no one lives,
    and through which no mortal passes.
44 I will punish Bel in Babylon,
    and make him disgorge what he has
        swallowed.
The nations shall no longer stream to him;
    the wall of Babylon has fallen.

45 Come out of her, my people!
    Save your lives, each of you,
    from the fierce anger of the LORD!

[a]Sheshach is a cryptogram for Babel, Babylon

NIV

The nations will no longer stream to him.
And the wall of Babylon will fall.

45 "Come out of her, my people!
Run for your lives!
Run from the fierce anger of the LORD.
46 Do not lose heart or be afraid
when rumors are heard in the land;
one rumor comes this year, another the next,
rumors of violence in the land
and of ruler against ruler.
47 For the time will surely come
when I will punish the idols of Babylon;
her whole land will be disgraced
and her slain will all lie fallen within her.
48 Then heaven and earth and all that is in them
will shout for joy over Babylon,
for out of the north
destroyers will attack her,"
declares the LORD.

49 "Babylon must fall because of Israel's slain,
just as the slain in all the earth
have fallen because of Babylon.
50 You who have escaped the sword,
leave and do not linger!
Remember the LORD in a distant land,
and think on Jerusalem."

51 "We are disgraced,
for we have been insulted
and shame covers our faces,
because foreigners have entered
the holy places of the LORD's house."

52 "But days are coming," declares the LORD,
"when I will punish her idols,
and throughout her land
the wounded will groan.
53 Even if Babylon reaches the sky
and fortifies her lofty stronghold,
I will send destroyers against her,"
declares the LORD.

54 "The sound of a cry comes from Babylon,
the sound of great destruction
from the land of the Babylonians.[a]
55 The LORD will destroy Babylon;
he will silence her noisy din.

[a] 54 Or Chaldeans

NRSV

46 Do not be fainthearted or fearful
at the rumors heard in the land—
one year one rumor comes,
the next year another,
rumors of violence in the land
and of ruler against ruler.

47 Assuredly, the days are coming
when I will punish the images of Babylon;
her whole land shall be put to shame,
and all her slain shall fall in her midst.
48 Then the heavens and the earth,
and all that is in them,
shall shout for joy over Babylon;
for the destroyers shall come against them
out of the north,   says the LORD.
49 Babylon must fall for the slain of Israel,
as the slain of all the earth have fallen
because of Babylon.

50 You survivors of the sword,
go, do not linger!
Remember the LORD in a distant land,
and let Jerusalem come into your mind:
51 We are put to shame, for we have heard
insults;
dishonor has covered our face,
for aliens have come
into the holy places of the LORD's house.

52 Therefore the time is surely coming, says the
LORD,
when I will punish her idols,
and through all her land
the wounded shall groan.
53 Though Babylon should mount up to heaven,
and though she should fortify her strong
height,
from me destroyers would come upon her,
says the LORD.

54 Listen!—a cry from Babylon!
A great crashing from the land of the
Chaldeans!
55 For the LORD is laying Babylon waste,
and stilling her loud clamor.
Their waves roar like mighty waters,
the sound of their clamor resounds;

NIV

Waves ˻of enemies˼ will rage like great waters;
the roar of their voices will resound.
[56]A destroyer will come against Babylon;
her warriors will be captured,
and their bows will be broken.
For the LORD is a God of retribution;
he will repay in full.
[57]I will make her officials and wise men drunk,
her governors, officers and warriors as well;
they will sleep forever and not awake,"
declares the King, whose name is the LORD
Almighty.

[58]This is what the LORD Almighty says:

"Babylon's thick wall will be leveled
and her high gates set on fire;
the peoples exhaust themselves for nothing,
the nations' labor is only fuel for the
flames."

NRSV

[56]for a destroyer has come against her,
against Babylon;
her warriors are taken,
their bows are broken;
for the LORD is a God of recompense,
he will repay in full.
[57]I will make her officials and her sages drunk,
also her governors, her deputies, and her
warriors;
they shall sleep a perpetual sleep and never
wake,
says the King, whose name is the LORD of
hosts.

[58]Thus says the LORD of hosts:
The broad wall of Babylon
shall be leveled to the ground,
and her high gates
shall be burned with fire.
The peoples exhaust themselves for nothing,
and the nations weary themselves only for
fire.[a]

[a]Gk Syr Compare Hab 2.13: Heb *and the nations for fire, and they
are weary*

COMMENTARY

The section against Babylon stands out both by its length and by its intensity. It is made up of a series of oracles, heaping up announcements of judgment against Babylon. Standing at the end of the oracles against the nations and going on as long as it does, the prophetic word against Babylon provides a climax both to these chapters concerning the nations and to the book as a whole. Just as Babylon was there from the beginning, implicitly, in the call of Jeremiah with the Lord's announcement of disaster from the north, so also it is at the end of the book in very explicit terms. Just as Babylon has dominated the nation and the book, so also now the book announces Babylon will be dominated in the end. Just as Babylon came from the north as the Lord's judgment against Judah, so also now the Medes and the Persians shall come from the north as the Lord's judgment against Babylon. Just as the prophet called for subjection to Babylonian rule, so also now he calls for its

overthrow. Just as the Lord again and again—up to the immediately preceding verses—has called Babylon the human agent of the divine ruler, so also now the Lord announces the overthrow of that former agent on behalf of the divine rule.

This last point has been one of the most troubling issues in the interpretation of these chapters. How can the prophet, who claimed again and again that Babylonian power was the arm of the Lord in judgment against Judah and that the nation of Judah should submit to that power, now declare that Babylon and its king are enemies of the Lord, oppressors of Judah, deserving great punishment for the way in which they have treated the Lord's people? The simplest way out of that seeming contradiction is to see these chapters as the work of a later prophetic hand announcing the fall of Babylon and the restoration of Judah. Certainly, the time of restoration and return from exile is in view: (1) The oracles presuppose the destruction of the Jerusalem Temple (50:28; 51:24) and the rise of the Median Empire (51:11, 27-28); (2) as in Isaiah 40–55, Judeans now suffer in exile (50:28,33), but return is anticipated (50:4-5); (3) Babylon is still in power, but its end is on the horizon.

The book of Jeremiah, however, does not distinguish a different or later prophetic voice here. All is ascribed to Jeremiah; both the superscription (50:1) and the conclusion (51:59-64) to the oracles against Babylon make that explicit. Furthermore, the Hebrew form of the book anticipates a limited Babylonian hegemony and the Lord's punishment of Babylon and its king in 25:11-13 (cf. 27:7; 29:10).[235] Thus the book assumes that these different perspectives can be held together, that Nebuchadrezzar, the "servant" of the Lord (25:9; 27:6; 43:10), can become the object of the Lord's punishment (50:18; see the Commentary on 27:6), that submission to Babylonian power as the Lord's will does not mean that oppressive power has the last word.

> The message of the Book of Jeremiah is that Babylon was divinely destined for ultimate judgment and collapse, but it would be the hand of God that delivered the fatal blow. Meanwhile the People of God, whether in Judah or among the exiles in Babylon, were bound to await God's time. The eschatological reality would emerge from the historical process, and it would achieve a full and complete realization. Nevertheless it demanded patience, faith, and painful submission to a less than satisfactory present experience before this divine purpose achieved its end.[236]

Babylon is not an automaton, a tool in the hands of the Lord. It is a flesh-and-blood military-political power, accountable for its actions, even if those actions serve as a vehicle for the Lord's wrath against a sinful nation. That accounting is laid out in these chapters. Unlike some of the preceding oracles against other nations, the reason for the judgment against Babylon is clear and repeated. The new word in these chapters is the promise of deliverance and return for Judah and Israel as a part of the judgment against Babylon. The repetition of hope for both kingdoms, Israel and

Judah, provides part of the theological closure to the book of Jeremiah (50:4-5, 17-20, 33-34; 51:5). The *whole* of Israel is promised a return and restoration as a consequence and a feature of the judgment of Babylon.

There is much scholarly debate about the appropriate division of these chapters into oracles or sections. Different arrangements can be defended. The text "does not have a tight, logical structure characterized by a clear thematic progression." As one interpreter has put it:

> It is quite possible that the concluding prophecy of Jeremiah's book *deliberately* takes such a wide sweep and offers such a kaleidoscope image. When the topic in this prophecy turns to the great opponent of Judah, the destroyer of the city and temple of God, the oppressor of the peoples, all the stops are pulled. Past, present, and future follow each other in quickly shifting metaphors. Commands to advance and instructions to retreat tumble over each other. The entirety can best be compared to a musical composition in which the basic thematic elements reappear in continually changing combinations to emphasize, with all colour and language, the one message of the retributive and liberating vengeance of the God who punishes Babylon and restores Israel's justice.[237]

Consistent with this view of the oracle against Babylon, the commentary that follows does not treat the material in sections, as is customary. Rather, the opening section, 50:1-20, serves as an avenue by which to open and explore prominent themes and aspects of the oracle as a whole. Two interlocking themes dominate the initial oracles of this block: the fate of Babylon (50:2-3, 8-16), and the fate of Israel and Judah (50:4-7). They are brought together abrasively in 50:17-20 and then are spun out in the rest of the chapters in the following ways:

(1) The announcement of judgment against Babylon begins with proclamations and banners heralding the demise of Babylon before all the nations that have been its victims (50:2). The announcements are short and punchy in both Hebrew and English: Babylon is captured! Bel (the chief Babylonian god) is ashamed! Marduk (another name for the same god) is terrified! The following chapters simply fill in the details for those who are interested. If previous chapters have pointed to

235. The absence of these references to Babylon from the Greek translation suggests that they may be later and redactional in the Hebrew text.

236. Ronald Clements, *Jeremiah,* Interpretation (Atlanta: John Knox, 1988) 264-65.

237. H. G. L. Peels, *The Vengeance of God: The Meaning of the Root NQM and the Function of NQM-Texts in the Context of Divine Revelation in the Old Testament,* OTS 31 (Leiden: Brill, 1995) 182.

Babylonian power as the agency of destruction against the other nations, those nations now are given the good word that this power itself will be broken and destroyed. The shift of perspective between chaps. 46–49 and chaps. 50–51 is immediately evident.[238]

(2) At the beginning of this long section, an important feature of its style and theology becomes apparent. The experience of Babylonian defeat is comparable to that inflicted on the other nations by Babylon: a shaming of people (50:12) and gods (50:2). The shame of Babylon (cf. 51:47) will correspond to the shame it has inflicted on others (51:51). This is the first instance of a continuing undercurrent of reciprocity and reversal in these oracles. At some points, it is made explicit:

Do to her as she has done (50:15*b*)
Repay her according to her deeds; just as she has done, do to her. (50:29)

He is repaying her for what is due. (51:6*b*; cf. v. 24)

Babylon must fall for the slain of Israel,
as the slain of all the earth have fallen because of Babylon. (51:49)

For the Lord is a God of recompense,
he will repay in full. (51:56*b*)

The text conveys such reward by taking words from earlier in the book and reversing their meaning. An excellent example is found in the way in which 6:22-24 is quoted in 50:41-43. In the earlier text, the "people from the north" are the Babylonians, who come against "daughter Zion," whose hands fall helpless. In chap. 50, the people from the north are the Medes and the Persians, who come against "daughter Babylon," and it is "the king of Babylon" whose hands fall helpless.

In many other ways, this reversal and reciprocal judgment are present indirectly, but clearly. The cup in the Lord's hand, making the other nations drunk (51:7), will itself be made drunk by the Lord (51:39, 57). The "plunderers of my heritage" (שסה *šāsâ*, 50:11) will be "plundered" (שלל *šālal*, 50:10; בזז *bāzaz*, 50:37). "The hammer of the whole earth" (50:23) will become "the last of the nations" (50:12). The mountain that destroys the whole earth will become a burned-out mountain

(51:25). The hunter and devourer of the sheep (50:6-7, 17) will be a flock that is dragged away (50:45). The enemy who came from the north, Babylon, is now itself to be visited by an enemy from the north (50:3, 9, 41; 51:48). This latter foe from the north is described as "a company of great nations" (50:9; cf. 51:27*a*), but the Medes and the Persians are probably in view (51:11, 27*b*-28). And the nation that carried the gods of other nations into exile will find its own gods and images dismayed and punished (50:18; 51:44, 47, 52).

(3) This polemic against the gods and their images, which is as old as Elijah's encounter with the priests of Baal at Mt. Carmel (1 Kings 18) and is a recurring theme in Isaiah 40–55, is as political as it is theological. It represents a claim of power over the Babylonians that seems to contradict Israel's present circumstances but that will be vindicated in the future. The conflict between the Lord and the gods of the nations surfaces again. What is finally at stake is a claim about divine rule, about who is the power at work in the world. That point is made in various ways in this text. One is the repeated use of the title "LORD of hosts" (50:18, 25, 34; 51:5, 14, 19, 33, 57), an insistent hammering home of the claim of the God of Israel (see 50:18; 51:33) over all the hosts of heaven and earth. Another formulation of this claim occurs in 51:15-19, which repeats 10:12-16 (see the Commentary on 10:12-16 for details), setting the power of the Lord who created all the universe over against the powerless idols of the Babylonians. The oracle against Babylon reiterates the persistent biblical theme that the Lord of hosts is the only truly effective power in the world. The conflict between the Lord and the other gods, manifest here in the punishment and destruction of the Babylonian divine powers, helps Israel to reject other claims, of denying any successful challenges to the rule of the Lord of Israel (50:24). In this way, the words of these chapters about the fate of the Babylonian gods and images, like so many such biblical references, become a theodicy, a claim on behalf of the Lord against the evidence of history and politics, a claim that history and politics are, in fact, the realm of the Lord's "plan" and "purposes" and "work" of God (50:25, 45; 51:10-12), through which vindication will be achieved for both God and people (50:10; cf. 50:34).

---

238. On this shift of perspective, see Walter Brueggemann, *A Commentary on Jeremiah: Exile and Homecoming* (Grand Rapids: Eerdmans, 1998) 461-63.

(4) That vindication is signaled also in the theme of the Lord's vengeance against Babylon (50:15, 28; 51:6, 11, 36). It is surely no accident that of the eleven times the Hebrew root נקם (*nqm*) appears in the oracles against the nations to speak of divine judgment as the "vengeance" or "vindication" of the Lord, nine occurrences are in the oracle against Babylon. The notion of the vengeance of God involves two elements. When used in a judgmental sense—and it can be used positively—the vengeance of God is both a retribution, "a day of retribution" (46:10a NRSV), for past deeds by the party under judgment, and an act of vindication of the purposes and the sovereignty of the Lord. With regard to Babylon, both dimensions are critical. The retribution is explicit: "Take vengeance on her, do to her as she has done" (50:15); "vengeance for his temple" (50:28; 51:11); and "This is the time of the Lord's vengeance; he is repaying her what is due" (51:6). The vengeance of God is thus a part of the justice of God against Babylon and on behalf of Israel; it is directly associated with arguing and defending the cause of oppressed Israel (51:36; cf. 50:34). But this divine "vengeance" is also a manifestation of the Lord's rule over the nations, even over the strongest and most powerful. The vengeance of God is concerned with maintaining the honor and sovereignty of the Lord, whose abode and people have been abused (e.g., 50:28, 33; 51:24, 50-51), as well as with accomplishing the justice and the deliverance of both Judah/Zion (50:18-20, 34; 51:5-6, 10, 34-36) and the peoples of the earth (50:34; 51:48).[239] It is motivated by Babylon's haughty pride, first indicated in the picture of Babylon rejoicing and exulting, frisking about like a heifer in the field and neighing like great stallions (50:11), a depiction underscored by labeling Babylon as the "arrogant one" (50:51-52) and as "challenging" or "opposing" the Lord (50:24). But the vengeance of God is grounded as much in the Babylonian oppression of Israel/Judah and the other nations as it is in the arrogance of Babylon.[240]

(5) Along with the shame of the gods and the people, the divine judgment will reduce a once powerful and wealthy nation to a land of desola-

tion, uninhabited and uninhabitable. This outcome is signaled thematically at the very beginning: It is a land of desolation, and no one will live in it (50:3).[241] That theme, present also in the other oracles against the nations, is then hammered out in great detail. The language is piled on: "a wilderness, dry land, and a desert" (50:12b); "she shall never again be peopled, or inhabited for all generations" (50:39); the land is winnowed and emptied (51:2), "a desolation without inhabitant" (51:29, 37), a "heap of ruins, a den of jackals" (51:37), "a land in which no one lives, and through which no mortal passes" (51:43; cf. 50:40). One word, however, is used in two ways to underscore by its repetition and its double meaning the terrible plight of the land. The root שמם (*šmm*, "be desolated" or "be appalled") recurs and characterizes both the state of the devastated and desolate land (50:3, 13a; 51:26b, 29; cf. 46:19; 48:9) and the reaction of all who see the fate of Babylon and are horrified (50:13b; 51:37, 41, 43; cf. 49:13, 17, 20).[242] In some instances, both the objective state and the subjective reaction may be caught up in a single reference (e.g., 50:23; NRSV, "horror"; NIV, "desolate"; cf. 51:41). Indeed, the dual meaning may be implied in every case. The force of the recurring use of this root may be discerned best by observing the repetition of the exclamation: "How Babylon has become an object of horror among the nations!" (50:23; 51:41). This great and astonishing reversal is especially obvious in the reaction of the nations who suffered under Babylonian oppressive power. They react not in terror but in horror, not in fear but in derisive hissing (50:13b; 51:37). The tables are truly turned. The poetic justice of this fate is found in the realization that Babylon now suffers the divine judgment for which it was the instrument against Jerusalem and Judah (19:8; 25:9, 18; 29:18) and the nations.

(6) The opening verses of this long oracle against Babylon also make a twofold claim about Israel and Judah (50:2-4). First is the announcement that a suffering ("weeping," 50:4) people shall find their way back to the Lord and to Zion. This language suggests return from exile, of

239. H. G. L. Peels, *The Vengeance of God: The Meaning of the Root NQM and the Function of NQM-Texts in the Context of Divine Revelation in the Old Testament*, OTS 31 (Leiden: Brill, 1995) 187
240. Ibid.

241. On this depiction of Babylon's fate, see D. J. Reimer, *The Oracles Against Babylon in Jeremiah 50–51: A Horror Among the Nations* (San Francisco: Mellen Research University Press, 1993) 180-85.
242. Ibid., 180-82.

course, but it is couched in thoroughly theological and religious language: "seek the LORD" (cf. Deut 4:29; Amos 5:4, 6, 14), "turn the face," "an everlasting covenant." The return home means nothing if it is not a return to the Lord. These verses pick up the note that is sounded earlier in the book, envisioning beyond judgment a new and eternal covenant, written on the heart, never to be forgotten (31:31-34; see also the Commentary on 31:31-34). Second, the oracle identifies a double responsibility for the plight of "my people" (50:6-7; cf. 50:11; 51:19): Bad leadership, portrayed here in the imagery of shepherds who have led the flock astray so that they do not know where their home fold is (cf. 23:1-4; 50:44), and enemies who have assumed the guilt of the straying sheep meant they could devour the sheep with no culpability. In the quotation of the enemies, two things happen: A rationale is given for explaining the Lord's turn against Babylon in its assumption that the sin of Israel meant it could do what it pleased to the Lord's people, and their explanation provides a Yahwistic explanation for the fate of Israel in the mouths of their enemies: "They have sinned against the LORD, the true pasture, the hope of their ancestors, the LORD" (50:7*b;* cf. 51:5). That is, indeed, the problem, and deliverance from exile presupposes this proper understanding of the deeper reality of Babylonian power over Israel/Judah (cf. Isa 40:2).

The sheep imagery carries forward in 50:8 as the exiles are to be like rams leading the way out of exile; it recurs in 50:14-17 as the enemies of 50:7, identified as Assyrians and then Babylonians, are portrayed as lions preying on the sheep. The restoration of Israel is anticipated as a restoration of the flock to its home pasture. Something else happens in that restoration: The sin/guilt disappears (50:20)! If one looks for it, it is not there. It cannot be found. This is in some respects an astonishing word in the light of all that has gone before. But it is also given a clear explanation: The Lord has forgiven. Those who are left after the destruction will have their sins taken away, literally.

(7) Thematically and stylistically, the strong military language of the opening section is carried through the text as a whole. Shouts and commands ring throughout the text:

> "Take up your positions." (50:14)
> "Go up against her and attack." (50:21)
> "Come against her from every quarter . . . Kill all her bulls." (50:26-27)
> "Sharpen the arrows! Fill the quivers!" (51:11)
> "Raise a standard." (51:12, 27)
> "Prepare [lit., "sanctify"] the nations for war against her." (51:27-28)
> "Destroy her utterly. (50:26; cf. 50:21; 51:3)[243]

The text says that "the noise of battle is in the land" (50:22). It is also in the text! Its strongest form occurs in the weaponry imagery, created by the picture of the Lord's opening up "his armory" containing all "the weapons of his wrath." There are two primary weapons: the sword (50:16) and the war club or mace (51:20; the combination of 51:1 and 16*b* suggests the wind is also a weapon in the armory). Each of these weapons becomes the subject of a kind of war song, the sword in 50:33-38, where it is set to cut down everything and everybody in Babylon because of their fascination with idols and images, and the mace in 51:20-23, where the subject and object are uncertain. The war club smashes kingdoms and nations, young and old, girl and boy, farmers and their animals. This sounds more like the Babylonians as the wielder of the club rather than the recipient of its violence. The repeated verb "I smash" could be understood as past tense, referring to Babylon's activities against other nations as the agent of the Lord's wrath. In 50:23, Babylon is the "hammer" of the whole earth, but a different noun is used there for "hammer" than the word for "war club." The bottom line is that the mace is in the hands of the divine warrior; it will wreak havoc on whatever object comes under the Lord's judgment. (See Reflections at 51:59-64.)

---

243. These latter two expressions are reminiscent of the ancient call to holy war and the ban against the enemy, the total destruction of the enemy, and all its goods as a vow to the deity.

JEREMIAH 51:59-64, SEALING BABYLON'S FATE

NIV

59This is the message Jeremiah gave to the staff officer Seraiah son of Neriah, the son of Mahseiah, when he went to Babylon with Zedekiah king of Judah in the fourth year of his reign. 60Jeremiah had written on a scroll about all the disasters that would come upon Babylon—all that had been recorded concerning Babylon. 61He said to Seraiah, "When you get to Babylon, see that you read all these words aloud. 62Then say, 'O LORD, you have said you will destroy this place, so that neither man nor animal will live in it; it will be desolate forever.' 63When you finish reading this scroll, tie a stone to it and throw it into the Euphrates. 64Then say, 'So will Babylon sink to rise no more because of the disaster I will bring upon her. And her people will fall.' "

The words of Jeremiah end here.

NRSV

59The word that the prophet Jeremiah commanded Seraiah son of Neriah son of Mahseiah, when he went with King Zedekiah of Judah to Babylon, in the fourth year of his reign. Seraiah was the quartermaster. 60Jeremiah wrote in a*a* scroll all the disasters that would come on Babylon, all these words that are written concerning Babylon. 61And Jeremiah said to Seraiah: "When you come to Babylon, see that you read all these words, 62and say, 'O LORD, you yourself threatened to destroy this place so that neither human beings nor animals shall live in it, and it shall be desolate forever.' 63When you finish reading this scroll, tie a stone to it, and throw it into the middle of the Euphrates, 64and say, 'Thus shall Babylon sink, to rise no more, because of the disasters that I am bringing on her.' "*b*

Thus far are the words of Jeremiah.

*a*Or *one*   *b*Gk: Heb *on her. And they shall weary themselves*

COMMENTARY

At the end of the long oracle against Babylon, a narrative tells of Jeremiah's writing down the oracles against Babylon on a scroll and committing it to an official named Seraiah, who is to take it to Babylon and read it there before throwing the scroll into the Euphrates River, a symbolic action signifying the destruction of Babylon, which will sink from sight as permanently as does the scroll in the river.

Such action is dated to the fourth year of Zedekiah's reign, 594 BCE, the same year as Jeremiah's counseling of submission to Babylon (chaps. 27–28; see 28:1). The inclusion of this narrative at the end of the oracle against Babylon serves several purposes:

(1) It reinforces the association of the oracle with Jeremiah. However the oracle concerning Babylon may have come into being, the narrative forcefully insists on the Jeremianic voice lying behind it, even quoting the oracle at two places (cf. 51:62 with 50:3 and 51:26*b*).

(2) Presenting the oracle against Babylon as

coming from Jeremiah in 594 BCE is a way of claiming that the different perspectives on Babylon are not to be explained by assigning the oracle to another person or a later date. In the midst of the counsel to submit to Babylon, the prophet announces the ultimate doom of Babylon. This tactic places the whole Babylonian story in the plan of God, so that both exile and its end are anticipated. Babylonian dominance and the harsh reality of exile for those who resist are part of the Lord's plan, but so is the overthrow of Babylon. So the prophet can tell the people to submit to the judgment of God while also announcing the ultimate judgment of the Babylonians. Whatever critical judgments may be made or proposed about authorship and time of writing, this narrative offers an integrated perspective—authorially, temporally, and theologically.

(3) Taking the scroll to Babylon ensures that the then dominant Babylonians and the exiles living in Babylon will hear these words and know what the Lord intends for the future. These words are not

hidden from those whose judgment they announce.

(4) The text also says that the reading of the scroll is so that God will listen and be reminded: "O God, you are the one who said you would destroy this place" (v. 62*a*). The prophet has spoken often to the Lord in this book. This is the last time, and it is through a surrogate. It is a way of the prophet's calling on God to follow through on what the prophet has announced. "We are being given a picture of the scroll being waved in God's face."[244]

(5) The fate of Babylon is in contrast with that of several other nations. Not only does the oracle go on much longer in describing the terrible end of Babylon, but also these final words seem to offer

244. Walter Brueggemann, *A Commentary on Jeremiah: Exile and Homecoming* (Grand Rapids: Eerdmans, 1998) 485.

an implicit contrast to other final words that speak of a restoration of Egypt (46:26), Moab (48:47), Ammon (49:6), and Elam (49:39). Lest one think that such restoration is an eventual possibility for the Babylonian tyrant, the symbolic action at the end says no! In the course of the scriptures, both Egypt and Assyria, hated opponents of Israel, are presented as having a future in God's mercy. Babylon, however, remains entirely a continuing symbol for opposition to the work of God.

(5) Closure to the prophecy of Jeremiah and to the book is given at the end of v. 64 with "the words of Jeremiah," which are the same words with which the book opens (1:1). This is the extent of Jeremiah's words, Jeremiah's oracles. This note closing Jeremiah's prophecy alerts the reader to the character of the final chapter as an appendix, standing outside the prophecy of Jeremiah.

REFLECTIONS

1. The collection of oracles against the nations is a reminder of the geopolitical character of the reign of God. The reader may not be all that interested in Elam, Philistia, Moab, and Kedar. Then and now the primary agenda of the listeners to Jeremiah's oracles is set around what happens to the elect community of faith, those with whom the Lord has covenanted. Whether resistant or receptive to Jeremiah's often harsh oracles, we expect them to have to do with us. The prophet is not likely to be killed over words about Kedar. What happens to other nations may be of direct interest to those in the community of faith in that their fate is inextricably bound up with that of the other nations. So it is that the oracles against the other nations incorporate words of hope and deliverance for Judah.

But these oracles are not simply to show the elect a way out. The connections between the affairs of the nations and those of Judah are, except for Babylon, not all that clear. The nations are an audience for the word of the Lord in their own right. Jeremiah's call at this point is not simply a nationalistic reflex. Whatever good possibilities they may include for the community under judgment—and some good possibilities are definitely indicated—these oracles are not primarily to or for that community. The kingdom of God is universal and cosmic in scope, and the affairs of all the nations come under its sway. One of the most telling indicators of that in the scriptures is the prophetic propensity for addressing and speaking about the affairs and fate of others than Israel and the insistent claim throughout these oracles that what is going on is entirely the Lord's doing.

2. One cannot help wondering about the actual audience for these oracles. Surely Jeremiah did not wander off to Elam, Philistia, Moab, or Kedar—although we do know by now that he ended up in Egypt, and at the end of the oracle against Babylon he sets in motion a plan for the oracle against Babylon to be read in that city. Furthermore, some of the oracles have been associated with the visit of emissaries from other nations to Jerusalem to plan a revolt in 594 BCE. But it is still not possible to assume that all of these oracles were announced in the hearing of persons who were members of the nation being addressed.

To that extent, they belong to a cadre of biblical texts that seem to address a larger community that may not or cannot hear them. Thus the hymns of praise call the nations to the praise of the Lord, even though those hymns were sung in a Judean temple. Both the oracles addressed to other nations far off and the call to those same nations to join in the praise of the Lord are a testimony to the claim of the Lord of Israel to a universal rule, one that does not depend on the acquiescence of its subjects or even whether they hear the words addressed to them. The claim that is inherent in these oracles concerning other nations, oracles that are often addressed quite directly to them, is all the more radical if they were not spoken in their presence. There are indicators that God has other stories with other nations, but Israel's *own* story claims that the Lord is involved with the nations near and far, that they stand under divine judgment for their sins and may also stand under that same divine mercy that so often saved Israel.

3. One of the consistent outcomes of the experience of destruction and defeat is *shame* (46:12, 24; 48:1, 13, 20, 39; 50:2, 47). The shame may be that of the nation as a whole or of its gods. In either case, what is a painful personal and interpersonal experience is here transferred to the national level and confronts us with the reality of national shame. National disaster creates a pain that can best be understood as shame, a nation embarrassed by either its deeds or its fate. It is an exposure like nakedness, the whole people revealed in their "stripped" condition and laughed at by others. We are so accustomed to shame as a personal experience that we may not realize that there are corporate experiences also, manifest especially when in some way the community "falls," is "tripped up" or stripped down. Then everyone experiences on a quite personal level a sense of humiliation and embarrassment at being a part of this nation and this people. The opposite of ethnic pride is ethnic shame, and it is out of the terrible experience of the latter that some have learned to claim the former.

4. If the fate of the various nations depicted in these oracles is not dissimilar to that of Judah, then the promises to the nations are also commensurate with God's promises to the covenant community of Israel. Several times the oracles against the nations end up with a specific word of restoration, of new life for the defeated and exiled nation (46:26; 48:47; 49:6, 39). The eschatological word of hope ("in the latter days," 48:47), which is always understood to have universal dimensions, is not simply a general word about the future but a quite specific promise of restoration for particular peoples and nations that have also undergone divine judgment. The potential for chauvinism and nationalism, for the hubris of election, that is carried by the "good news" of the judgment and shame of our enemies is broken open by the word that they will also share the "good news" of restoration of fortunes and renewal of life. Couching this word of restoration as the actual "last word" of the oracles against Egypt (46:26), Moab (48:47), Ammon (49:6), and Elam (49:39) is a literary way of indicating the theological point that the Lord's last word is not judgment and death but hope and new life. Nor is that last word to be heard only by a select few. It is encompassing, not excluding. These snippets of hope for the other nations join with more elaborated texts, such as Isaiah 19, where Israel, "my heritage," is joined with Egypt, "my people," and Assyria, "the work of my hands," to be "a blessing in the midst of the earth" (Isa 19:24-25) to remind us that the universality of God's reign is good news for everyone, not simply for the chosen people.

5. But the word of restoration beyond judgment may not be universal. The Babylons among us may hear only silence. Indeed, Babylon confronts us with that terrible possibility of a community so under divine judgment for its sins and crimes that there is no possibility of restoration. "Babylon" joins with "Sodom and Gomorrah," another topos in these texts (49:18; 50:40; 51:43), to become biblical symbols for evil that is so great that the only outcome is judgment without amelioration. In the book of Revelation, Babylon serves as a metaphor for great evil, matched only by the greatness of God's wrath against it (Rev 16:19; 18:2-3, 10, 21-24). More specifically, it becomes a "code-word for the oppressive temporary world power that ruled over the nations."[245]

6. Often in these oracles against various nations (e.g., in the case of the destruction of the Philistines in chap. 47 or the judgment against Damascus in 49:23-27), there is no rationale for the terrible devastation. Its agency is clear. This is the Lord's doing, the Lord's day, the sword of the Lord. But the typical grounding of destruction in rationality, in accusations of misconduct of some sort, a grounding that can transform destruction into judgment, is often missing in these texts. The reader confronts head-on this terrible God who moves in wrath that cannot be softened or covered up. Its color is blood. Its outcome is death. That these oracles may not have had any concrete reality in some instances begs the theological issue that disturbs us and has helped to paint the God of the Old Testament in a single color: red.

The questions we bring to such texts may be as likely to get satisfactory answers as those Job raised. We are before a great and terrible God who is known to be for us but who cannot be domesticated and moralized into a gentle, loving force. The Bible assumes a moral ground for the divine activity even when it cannot show it. "It is an odd way *in extremis* to assert moral coherence in public reality."[246] So we are in that uncomfortable but unavoidable spot—between a rock and a hard place—unable to tell why the Lord God has done this awful deed and knowing that the work of this transcendent God is beyond our comprehension. If we are going to protest this savage and ungrounded destruction—as, indeed, we must, for we are moral creatures in God's own image—then we may also, like Job, need to repent in dust and ashes when our questioning is over rather than go home with satisfactory answers to settle into our personal and theological easy chairs.

7. There is at least one motivation that is given for the destruction of the nations in these oracles, though it is confined to the oracles against the traditional enemies of Israel/Judah: Egypt and Babylon. It is the *vengeance* or *vindication* of God (46:10; 50:15, 28; 51:6, 11, 36). The notion of vengeance may be no more acceptable to theological sensibilities than is the bloody sword. Indeed, we are inclined to equate the two, as these texts do. But the vengeance of God is a profound and widespread theme in Scripture that cannot be confined to our customary notions of brutal revenge. As the translations sometimes indicate, what is in view is *vindication* against the Lord's enemies (see 46:10 NRSV), enemies who, at some moments, are also the Lord's agents (cf. Isa 10:5-19). The destruction is not a mindless bloody act, though bloody it is. It is the work of the Lord in resistance to and in overcoming those forces at work in the world who ultimately stand against the power of God. Just as the jealousy of the Lord is at the same time the zeal of the Lord on behalf of God's people and the right, so also the vengeance of God is at the same time the vindication of God on behalf of justice and righteousness as manifest in the sovereign rule of the Lord.[247] The divine warrior who goes with sword in hand is the ruler whose kingdom and power are at stake and the righteous judge who acts on behalf of a moral order that is not always comprehensible but is discernible in those fragmentary moments when we are given a glimpse of heaven (e.g., Psalm 82). The geopolitical context in which the Old Testament always understands that rule produces a very concrete and material messiness that more spiritual conflicts may avoid. The Bible insists that this often messy world is where God does battle as much as within the human soul.

8. In some cases, there is a complexity to the judgment of God that bears noting. Against the Moabites, for example, the destruction seems to have to do with Moab's arrogance and self-

245. Ronald Clements, *Jeremiah,* Interpretation (Atlanta: John Knox, 1988) 266.

246. Brueggemann, *A Commentary on Jeremiah,* 442.

247. On the vengeance/vindication of God, see esp. H. G. L. Peels, *The Vengeance of God: The Meaning of the Root NQM and the Function of NQM-Texts in the Context of Divine Revelation in the Old Testament,* OTS 31 (Leiden: Brill, 1995), and, more briefly, the exposition of Psalm 139 in Patrick D. Miller, *Interpreting the Psalms* (Philadelphia: Fortress, 1986).

confidence, but also with its mocking and taunting reaction to the fate of Israel. But chap. 48 also sees the judgment of the Lord against Moab as bringing to an end the sacrifices and offerings on the high places to the gods of the Moabites, and elsewhere in the chapter Chemosh, the chief god of the Moabites, is seen as shamed and powerless. In much of the prophecy of the Old Testament, judgment seems to be a specific act in response to a specific sin or a particular type of sin: apostasy, injustice, pride, disobedience. These oracles suggest that the judgment of God is not always that simple, that it may be rooted in many different aspects of a people's life. The search for a single cause, a single sin to be confessed, may be on the wrong track. National pride, attitudes toward other nations, forgetting who is our Lord—all of these and perhaps many other kinds of things are the features of our life that evoke a negative divine response. At this point, the general confession of sin is an important liturgical act to be carried out with absolute seriousness, not so much because there is no good within us but because our sins are manifold and complicated but discernible to the eyes of God precisely in all their complexity.

9. One specific sin that brings judgment on more than one nation is the exalted sense of security and confidence in oneself and one's god that assumes an imperviousness to any danger or to greater forces. It is clearly a national sin. The Moabites, the Ammonites, and the Edomites are so characterized (48:7, 29-30; 49:4, 16), but the Egyptians also are quoted as planning to cover the earth and destroy its inhabitants (46:8). The arrogance and self-sufficiency of pride is not a corporate sin only, but it is certainly a besetting temptation for national entities. The oracles against the nations inevitably force a consideration of their resonance with the activities, sins, and consequences practiced and incurred by later states and nations. The dominance of national arrogance as the ground for divine judgment rings bells that can hardly be unheard. From tyrannical imperialism to mild chauvinism, contemporary nations turn love of country into national arrogance, appropriate respect for national heritage into exalted claims for moral superiority, and military preparedness into the conviction that our nation is impervious to the powers of other nations and our weapons systems and armies are so strong that we need not worry in any serious way. Whether such assumptions are accurate or well grounded is not apparently an issue in the oracles against the nations. Simply holding such views is perceived as an inappropriate national self-idolization that brings the terror of divine judgment through the destructive forces of those seemingly superior nations. Whatever form the national god may take, it will probably end up in exile under those circumstances. The national flag may have to come down from its heights to be a ground cover for those whose secure homes are gone before the wind.

10. The judgment against Babylon includes some words about the fate of Israel and Judah. One of those is the rather surprising announcement that their sin is going to disappear (50:20). The point is made in some detail. If you look for their sin, you will not find it. It is not there anymore. This is no magic act, much less a kind of erosion or attrition of responsibility. The explanation is straightforward and clear. The Lord forgives them. In these verses, therefore, we hear the good news that runs throughout the Scriptures, that the Lord's judgment is not the final word, that God can and will simply take away our sin. That is a way of saying what forgiveness is all about. It means the sin is not there anymore. The radical act of God in forgiveness is often blurred and not heard fully as the good news it is when we do not make clear that forgiveness is real, that it wipes away the sin. When the minister says to the congregation, "I declare unto you in the name of Jesus Christ, your sins are forgiven," that's it! We can let those sins go. They are not there anymore.

There are various images for this radical act of God. The notion of being cleansed (e.g., Ps 51:7), of sins being washed away, carries the same wonderful news. The "dirt" is gone. In our speech about these matters, we often talk about forgiving and forgetting or about doing one without the other. Forgiving is forgetting. In a passage echoed here, Jer 31:34, the Lord says, "I will forgive their iniquity, and I will no longer remember their sin." If the Lord forgets it, it is forgotten. If the Lord forgives, the sin is forgotten. We really do not carry that heavy baggage around anymore. Perhaps such grace is not possible between human beings. But if it is, there is a joining of the mind and the heart, a letting go of the offense and letting go of its memory. When that happens, both parties lose their heavy burden. Another word for this is *grace*.

JEREMIAH 52:1-34

THE DESTRUCTION OF JERUSALEM

NIV

52 Zedekiah was twenty-one years old when he became king, and he reigned in Jerusalem eleven years. His mother's name was Hamutal daughter of Jeremiah; she was from Libnah. ²He did evil in the eyes of the LORD, just as Jehoiakim had done. ³It was because of the LORD's anger that all this happened to Jerusalem and Judah, and in the end he thrust them from his presence.

Now Zedekiah rebelled against the king of Babylon.

4So in the ninth year of Zedekiah's reign, on the tenth day of the tenth month, Nebuchadnezzar king of Babylon marched against Jerusalem with his whole army. They camped outside the city and built siege works all around it. ⁵The city was kept under siege until the eleventh year of King Zedekiah.

6By the ninth day of the fourth month the famine in the city had become so severe that there was no food for the people to eat. ⁷Then the city wall was broken through, and the whole army fled. They left the city at night through the gate between the two walls near the king's garden, though the Babylonians*ᵃ* were surrounding the city. They fled toward the Arabah,*ᵇ* ⁸but the Babylonian*ᶜ* army pursued King Zedekiah and overtook him in the plains of Jericho. All his soldiers were separated from him and scattered, ⁹and he was captured.

He was taken to the king of Babylon at Riblah in the land of Hamath, where he pronounced sentence on him. ¹⁰There at Riblah the king of Babylon slaughtered the sons of Zedekiah before his eyes; he also killed all the officials of Judah. ¹¹Then he put out Zedekiah's eyes, bound him with bronze shackles and took him to Babylon,

ᵃ7 Or Chaldeans; also in verse 17   ᵇ7 Or the Jordan Valley   ᶜ8 Or Chaldean; also in verse 14

NRSV

52 Zedekiah was twenty-one years old when he began to reign; he reigned eleven years in Jerusalem. His mother's name was Hamutal daughter of Jeremiah of Libnah. ²He did what was evil in the sight of the LORD, just as Jehoiakim had done. ³Indeed, Jerusalem and Judah so angered the LORD that he expelled them from his presence.

Zedekiah rebelled against the king of Babylon. ⁴And in the ninth year of his reign, in the tenth month, on the tenth day of the month, King Nebuchadrezzar of Babylon came with all his army against Jerusalem, and they laid siege to it; they built siegeworks against it all around. ⁵So the city was besieged until the eleventh year of King Zedekiah. ⁶On the ninth day of the fourth month the famine became so severe in the city that there was no food for the people of the land. ⁷Then a breach was made in the city wall;*ᵃ* and all the soldiers fled and went out from the city by night by the way of the gate between the two walls, by the king's garden, though the Chaldeans were all around the city. They went in the direction of the Arabah. ⁸But the army of the Chaldeans pursued the king, and overtook Zedekiah in the plains of Jericho; and all his army was scattered, deserting him. ⁹Then they captured the king, and brought him up to the king of Babylon at Riblah in the land of Hamath, and he passed sentence on him. ¹⁰The king of Babylon killed the sons of Zedekiah before his eyes, and also killed all the officers of Judah at Riblah. ¹¹He put out the eyes of Zedekiah, and bound him in fetters, and the king of Babylon took him to Babylon, and put him in prison until the day of his death.

12In the fifth month, on the tenth day of the month—which was the nineteenth year of King Nebuchadrezzar, king of Babylon—Nebuzaradan the captain of the bodyguard who served the king of Babylon, entered Jerusalem. ¹³He burned the

ᵃHeb lacks wall

NIV

where he put him in prison till the day of his death.

12On the tenth day of the fifth month, in the nineteenth year of Nebuchadnezzar king of Babylon, Nebuzaradan commander of the imperial guard, who served the king of Babylon, came to Jerusalem. 13He set fire to the temple of the LORD, the royal palace and all the houses of Jerusalem. Every important building he burned down. 14The whole Babylonian army under the commander of the imperial guard broke down all the walls around Jerusalem. 15Nebuzaradan the commander of the guard carried into exile some of the poorest people and those who remained in the city, along with the rest of the craftsmen[a] and those who had gone over to the king of Babylon. 16But Nebuzaradan left behind the rest of the poorest people of the land to work the vineyards and fields.

17The Babylonians broke up the bronze pillars, the movable stands and the bronze Sea that were at the temple of the LORD and they carried all the bronze to Babylon. 18They also took away the pots, shovels, wick trimmers, sprinkling bowls, dishes and all the bronze articles used in the temple service. 19The commander of the imperial guard took away the basins, censers, sprinkling bowls, pots, lampstands, dishes and bowls used for drink offerings—all that were made of pure gold or silver.

20The bronze from the two pillars, the Sea and the twelve bronze bulls under it, and the movable stands, which King Solomon had made for the temple of the LORD, was more than could be weighed. 21Each of the pillars was eighteen cubits high and twelve cubits in circumference[b]; each was four fingers thick, and hollow. 22The bronze capital on top of the one pillar was five cubits[c] high and was decorated with a network and pomegranates of bronze all around. The other pillar, with its pomegranates, was similar. 23There were ninety-six pomegranates on the sides; the total number of pomegranates above the surrounding network was a hundred.

[a]15 Or populace   [b]21 That is, about 27 feet (about 8.1 meters) high and 18 feet (about 5.4 meters) in circumference   [c]22 That is, about 7 1/2 feet (about 2.3 meters)

NRSV

house of the LORD, the king's house, and all the houses of Jerusalem; every great house he burned down. 14All the army of the Chaldeans, who were with the captain of the guard, broke down all the walls around Jerusalem. 15Nebuzaradan the captain of the guard carried into exile some of the poorest of the people and the rest of the people who were left in the city and the deserters who had defected to the king of Babylon, together with the rest of the artisans. 16But Nebuzaradan the captain of the guard left some of the poorest people of the land to be vinedressers and tillers of the soil.

17The pillars of bronze that were in the house of the LORD, and the stands and the bronze sea that were in the house of the LORD, the Chaldeans broke in pieces, and carried all the bronze to Babylon. 18They took away the pots, the shovels, the snuffers, the basins, the ladles, and all the vessels of bronze used in the temple service. 19The captain of the guard took away the small bowls also, the firepans, the basins, the pots, the lampstands, the ladles, and the bowls for libation, both those of gold and those of silver. 20As for the two pillars, the one sea, the twelve bronze bulls that were under the sea, and the stands,[a] which King Solomon had made for the house of the LORD, the bronze of all these vessels was beyond weighing. 21As for the pillars, the height of the one pillar was eighteen cubits, its circumference was twelve cubits; it was hollow and its thickness was four fingers. 22Upon it was a capital of bronze; the height of the one capital was five cubits; latticework and pomegranates, all of bronze, encircled the top of the capital. And the second pillar had the same, with pomegranates. 23There were ninety-six pomegranates on the sides; all the pomegranates encircling the latticework numbered one hundred.

24The captain of the guard took the chief priest Seraiah, the second priest Zephaniah, and the three guardians of the threshold; 25and from the city he took an officer who had been in command of the soldiers, and seven men of the king's council who were found in the city; the secretary of the commander of the army who mustered the people of the land; and sixty men of the people of

[a]Cn: Heb that were under the stands

NIV

²⁴The commander of the guard took as prisoners Seraiah the chief priest, Zephaniah the priest next in rank and the three doorkeepers. ²⁵Of those still in the city, he took the officer in charge of the fighting men, and seven royal advisers. He also took the secretary who was chief officer in charge of conscripting the people of the land and sixty of his men who were found in the city. ²⁶Nebuzaradan the commander took them all and brought them to the king of Babylon at Riblah. ²⁷There at Riblah, in the land of Hamath, the king had them executed.

So Judah went into captivity, away from her land. ²⁸This is the number of the people Nebuchadnezzar carried into exile:

in the seventh year, 3,023 Jews;
²⁹in Nebuchadnezzar's eighteenth year,
832 people from Jerusalem;
³⁰in his twenty-third year,
745 Jews taken into exile by Nebuzaradan the commander of the imperial guard.
There were 4,600 people in all.

³¹In the thirty-seventh year of the exile of Jehoiachin king of Judah, in the year Evil-Merodach[a] became king of Babylon, he released Jehoiachin king of Judah and freed him from prison on the twenty-fifth day of the twelfth month. ³²He spoke kindly to him and gave him a seat of honor higher than those of the other kings who were with him in Babylon. ³³So Jehoiachin put aside his prison clothes and for the rest of his life ate regularly at the king's table. ³⁴Day by day the king of Babylon gave Jehoiachin a regular allowance as long as he lived, till the day of his death.

[a]31 Also called *Amel-Marduk*

NRSV

the land who were found inside the city. ²⁶Then Nebuzaradan the captain of the guard took them, and brought them to the king of Babylon at Riblah. ²⁷And the king of Babylon struck them down, and put them to death at Riblah in the land of Hamath. So Judah went into exile out of its land.

28This is the number of the people whom Nebuchadrezzar took into exile: in the seventh year, three thousand twenty-three Judeans; ²⁹in the eighteenth year of Nebuchadrezzar he took into exile from Jerusalem eight hundred thirty-two persons; ³⁰in the twenty-third year of Nebuchadrezzar, Nebuzaradan the captain of the guard took into exile of the Judeans seven hundred forty-five persons; all the persons were four thousand six hundred.

31In the thirty-seventh year of the exile of King Jehoiachin of Judah, in the twelfth month, on the twenty-fifth day of the month, King Evil-merodach of Babylon, in the year he began to reign, showed favor to King Jehoiachin of Judah and brought him out of prison; ³²he spoke kindly to him, and gave him a seat above the seats of the other kings who were with him in Babylon. ³³So Jehoiachin put aside his prison clothes, and every day of his life he dined regularly at the king's table. ³⁴For his allowance, a regular daily allowance was given him by the king of Babylon, as long as he lived, up to the day of his death.

COMMENTARY

This chapter functions as an appendix to the book of Jeremiah. It is a slightly modified version of 2 Kgs 24:18–25:30, recounting in summary fashion the Babylonian destruction of Jerusalem, the looting of the Temple, the execution of some of the leaders, and the exile of many Judeans. The account concludes with a report of King Jehoiachin's release from prison so that he would sit at table with the king of Babylon. The version in Jeremiah offers more detail about the items taken from the Temple, enumerating the exiles taken to Babylon during three different deportations (in 598, 587, and an otherwise unknown one in 582 BCE), whereas the version in 2 Kings includes an account of the appointment and murder of Gedaliah as well as the subsequent journey of Judeans to Egypt (see Jeremiah 40–43).

The destruction of Jerusalem, the death of Zedekiah, the taking of the temple vessels, and the exile have already been reported in the book. Why, then, has this appendix been added? No explicit reason is given. The central event around which Jeremiah's prophecies revolved was the fate of Jerusalem and its Temple, what led up to that momentous event, and ways it could have been avoided. The same is true of the narrative portions of the book, so prominent in the later chapters. This final chapter underscores the significance of that event for the book and for the community. It summarizes what had happened, though leaving the door to the future open.

The summary character of the chapter works in two ways. First, the text offers a concise theological judgment (vv. 2-3). It indicts the wickedness of the king, the city, and the whole people, moving out from the center but incorporating the community in the indictment, even identifying the king whose sins, according to the book of Jeremiah, were most numerous: Jehoiakim. Destruction and exile, which are recounted in the verses that follow, are first interpreted as the result of God's anger and judgment.

Second, and sharply different, chap. 48 includes an extended historical summary. The only time the God of Israel is mentioned in the rest of the chapter occurs in the phrase "the house of the LORD," one of the titles for the Temple in Jerusalem. The political and experiential reality of God's judgment was harsh, concrete, and personal. It is spelled out here in some detail. The starting point of this historical summary is the note that all the events resulted from Zedekiah's rebellion against the king of Babylon. The preceding chapters have forcefully made this point. Again and again, the Lord sent word to both king and people through Jeremiah to submit to the king of Babylon as punishment for their sins. The rebellion of Zedekiah was the final disobedience. The result of that rebellion is narrated in gory detail: seige; famine; flight; royal executions and maiming; the looting and burning of the Temple, the palace, and houses; and massive exile.

One of the differences between Jeremiah 52 and 2 Kings 25 is the more extended account of the looting of the temple vessels (52:17-23). The report records and helps to preserve the memory of the beauty and value of that which had been in the Temple. When Hananiah challenged Jeremiah and prophesied an end to Babylonian domination, evidence of such would include the return of the king and the return of the vessels from the Temple, some of which must have already been carried to Babylon (28:3-4). No mention is made of the ark of the covenant, but the pillars of bronze and the bronze sea in the courtyard, together with the large bulls that supported the sea, were among the items carried off. The text emphasizes their size and ornamentation. Many other valuable pieces were also taken.

No theological comment is made on these matters at the end. None is necessary. The king and the Temple were so significant that the pain and sense of hopelessness would have been self-evident. The paragraphs numbering the executed leaders (vv. 24-27) and the exiled citizens over the course of three deportations (vv. 28-30) underscore the decimation of Judah, a point emphasized more thoroughly here than in the parallel account in 2 Kings 25. The painstaking attention to how many went into exile in each deportation highlights those episodes and focuses the reader's attention on those who were led away, not on those who remained. The text calls attention to Nebuzaradan, the Babylonian official in charge, who left some of the poorest people to tend the land. But it is much more explicit about those who were taken (vv. 15, 28-30), even noting that some of the poor were taken along with "the rest of the people who were left in the city" (v. 15). The reader knows from earlier chapters about a significant number who remained in Judah. The book closes by shifting attention entirely to those in exile, indicating that is what needs to be remembered. It also sets the future there.

The final paragraph offers a modest anticipation of restoration. Its modesty can hardly be overstated, since the last word of this book is about the death of the king, who is still in exile. But the inclusion of the word about the release of the Judean king Jehoiachin from prison, and especially about his eating before the king in a place above that of other exiled kings, offers a modest encouragement about the royal line. In the context of the larger story of God's people, one may see in this event the beginnings of restoration, a coda to the story that keeps alive the hope in a ruler from the line of David.

REFLECTIONS

1. A small item in this story worthy of reflection is the note about Nebuzaradan's leaving the poor to tend the vineyards and till the land. That is a way of saying that the Babylonian Empire was not interested in simply wiping out the people and rendering the land permanently destroyed. But there is something more here. One of the things that regularly puzzles and disturbs us about the fact of corporate judgment upon a people because of their injustice toward others in the community is that it seems to do in the victims with the oppressors. That may well be the case in many instances, but it may also be true that the victim is no worse off with the judgment than before. Here, at least, some of the poor who suffered under the oppression of others in the community continued to live in the land and were given the right and opportunity to enjoy its productivity. It is a risky thing to try to find good news for victims who are caught up in the larger downfall of a people, and this story does not dwell on this matter long enough to tell us much. After all, some of the poor went into exile also. But our interest in the fate of leading citizens, kings, and temples should not lead us to miss the poor one more time. They deserve better, and sometimes they may get better in the judgment. (See also the Reflections at 37:1–39:18.)

2. The juxtaposition of the theological interpretation at the beginning (52:1-3) with the extended archival account of what actually happened sets this event as a kind of paradigm of the biblical understanding of God's activity in history. The two realities are placed side by side and are identified with each other: the anger of God that expels Judah and Jerusalem from the very presence of the Lord; and the devastating destruction of Jerusalem, the Temple, and the people. The one is a purely theological statement: "God cast them out." The other is a purely historical report of a geopolitical or military event. How these two things are to be seen together is not disclosed. They are simply placed alongside each other so that we are to hear them as one reality with a double perspective, each as real as the other. But we are given no clues as to how it is that God acted in this event. We may be reminded of the story of Joseph and his interpretation of all that happened at the end (Gen 50:20). He knows two things are true about the story: The brothers purposed evil, and God purposed that evil for good. There is no effort to say how those two things are both true. So it is here that the activity of God is the most important datum. Where that is located is spelled out in detail. But there is a mystery in the relation between the two that cannot be overcome. It is spelled out no better in the Bible than it is in our common life or in the events of later times where we search for the activity of God, believe it to be there, but cannot give a phenomenology of the divine activity any more than does Scripture.

THE BOOK OF BARUCH

INTRODUCTION, COMMENTARY, AND REFLECTIONS

BY

ANTHONY J. SALDARINI

THE BOOK OF
BARUCH

INTRODUCTION

T he book of Baruch is a five-chapter pseudepigraphic work attributed to Baruch, the highly placed Jerusalem scribe who appears in the book of Jeremiah (chaps. 32; 36; 43; 45). It is often called 1 Baruch to distinguish it from *2* and *3 Baruch,* apocalyptic narratives from the late first and second centuries CE and from *4 Baruch,* or *Paraleipomena of Jeremiah,* a narrative about the destruction of the Temple in 586 BCE. Baruch is part of a cluster of writings associated with the prophet Jeremiah and the destruction of the Temple in 586 BCE. It is extant in Greek, though parts or all of it were translated from a Hebrew original. In the Septuagint it immediately follows the book of Jeremiah and precedes Lamentations; in the Vulgate it follows Lamentations and includes the Letter of Jeremiah as a sixth chapter. Baruch is recognized as canonical by Roman Catholics and the Orthodox communities. It is not recognized as canonical by the Jewish and Protestant communities, but is classified with the apocrypha.

Many commentators have described Baruch as a very derivative, composite work, lacking in originality and unity, and "substandard" in comparison with the Hebrew Bible. Carey Moore, for example, explains that the Christian church bypassed Baruch because "the book's literary style, which at best is uneven in quality, was not sufficiently strong or memorable to compensate for the book's theological and religious weaknesses, especially in the book's lack of originality and consistency."[1] Such comments imply

1. Carey A. Moore, *Daniel, Esther and Jeremiah: The Additions,* AB 44 (Garden City, N.Y.: Doubleday, 1977) 261.

that Baruch and other Second Temple Jewish literature reflect a time of decline. They fail to appreciate the vitality and creativity of Second Temple Jewish literature, of which Baruch is an example. Like all prayers and poems of that era, Baruch uses biblical words, phrases, themes, and ideas. But Baruch and Second Temple literature are notable for their innovative uses of biblical traditions to meet new circumstances and to express intense community distress and aspirations.

STRUCTURE, UNITY, AND GENRES

Baruch may be divided into four uneven parts, the first two of which are prose and the second two, poetry: (1) narrative introduction (1:1-14); (2) prayer of confession and repentance (1:15–3:8); (3) wisdom poem of admonition and exhortation (3:9–4:4); (4) poem of consolation and encouragement (4:5–5:9). Their distinctive styles, themes, and language have led commentators to postulate multiple authors or to deny to the book any coherence or substantial unity. Although the parts of Baruch are based on biblical and Second Temple models and may have been written independently before being incorporated into the final work, the final author has linked the parts with words, themes, and traditions so that they work together to form a rhetorical and literary unity. Such composite works, which underwent extensive editing, are common in Second Temple literature (see, e.g., *1 Enoch; Testaments of the Twelve Patriarchs*) as well as in the Bible (see, e.g., Daniel and especially the versions of the book of Jeremiah to which Baruch is related). In Baruch the final author has melded the parts into a dramatic whole. After he sets the scene in the introduction, he moves from suffering and repentance for sin (1:15–3:8) to devotion, to wisdom and obedience, and to God's commands (3:9–4:4); he concludes with encouragement to persevere in suffering and with the promise of divine intervention (4:5–5:9).

LANGUAGES

Baruch is extant in a Greek version that was probably translated from a Hebrew original. Translations of Baruch into Latin, Syriac, Coptic, Ethiopic, Armenian, and Arabic have also survived. The Syriac version is especially helpful in interpreting the Greek. The majority of scholars agree that the Greek of the prayer of confession and repentance, along with the introduction (1:1–3:8), was translated from Hebrew. The Greek contains Hebraisms (e.g., 2:26, literally in Greek, "where your name has been called over it") and translation errors (e.g., 1:9, where the Greek translator chose the wrong meaning for the Hebrew מסגר [*masgēr*], which can refer either to "prisoners" or to "smiths"; see the Commentary on 1:8-9). In general, a comparison of the Greek version of Jeremiah with Bar 1:15–3:8 indicates that the same person translated both Jeremiah and Baruch from Hebrew.[2] Whether the wisdom poem and the poem of consolation and encouragement

2. Emanuel Tov, *The Septuagint Translation of Jeremiah and Baruch: A Discussion of an Early Revision of the LXX of Jeremiah 29–52 and Baruch 1:1–3:15,* HSM 8 (Missoula, Mont.: Scholars Press, 1976) 111-33.

derive from Hebrew originals is still debated, though a successful retroversion of these poems into Hebrew with extensive commentary by David Burke has tipped the balance toward a Hebrew original.[3]

DATES AND PROVENANCE

Since Baruch contains four distinct sections, many scholars assign separate dates to them and another to the final form of the book. Modern commentators generally place the final form somewhere in the Greco-Roman period, from 300 BCE to 135 CE, not in the Babylonian period assigned it by the narrative frame. Beyond that there is little consensus. All acknowledge that the book contains only the vaguest allusions to events contemporary with the author(s) and that since the book is couched in traditional language, it has a "timeless" quality. Arguments for the dates of the book and its parts depend upon the Greek translation of the book, literary relationships with other works, and the tone and atmosphere of the whole book.

1. The Greek Translation of Bar 1:1–3:8. As noted in the section on language, the prayer of confession and repentance was translated from Hebrew into Greek by the same person who translated Jeremiah. Since the grandson of Ben Sira, who translated the Wisdom of Ben Sira (Ecclesiasticus) into Greek in Egypt by 116 BCE, refers to the Law and the Prophets as a well-known and accepted collection in the Greek-speaking community of Alexandria, the Greek version of Bar 1:1–3:8 must have been completed before 116 BCE.

2. Literary Relationships. The prayer of confession and repentance (Bar 1:15–2:18) has a detailed literary relationship with the Hebrew prayer of repentance in Dan 9:4-19 (see Commentary on 1:15–3:8 for specifics). Many have interpreted Bar 1:15–2:8 as dependent on Daniel 9 and thus later than 165 BCE.[4] However the type of dependency and the dates of both works are uncertain. Even though the prayer in Baruch is much more expansive that that in Daniel, both may have independently adapted an earlier prayer that is now lost. Even if Baruch depends on Daniel 9, the prayer in Daniel 9 is probably an earlier work incorporated into the apocalyptic visions of Daniel 7–12.[5]

The poem of consolation and encouragement (Bar 4:5–5:9) contains a passage (Bar 5:5-9) that has a close literary relationship with *Psalms of Solomon* 11 (see fig. 1, 972).

3. David G. Burke, *The Poetry of Baruch: A Reconstruction and Analysis of the Original Hebrew Text of Baruch 3:9–5:9*, SBLSCS 10 (Chico, Calif.: Scholars Press, 1982). A hundred years previously J. J. Kneucker, *Das Buch Baruch. Geschichte und Kritik, Übersetzung, und Erklärung* (Leipzig: Brockhaus, 1879), also provided a retroversion with extensive comments. For arguments pro and con see R. H. Pfeiffer, *History of New Testament Times with an Introduction to the Apocrypha* (New York: Harper, 1949) 417-21, and George W. E. Nickelsburg, "The Bible Rewritten and Expanded" in *Jewish Writings of the Second Temple Period*, ed. Michael E. Stone (Philadelphia: Fortress, 1984) 144-45.

4. E.g., Odil Hannes Steck, *Das apokryphe Baruchbuch: Studien zu Rezeption und Konzentration "kanonischer" Überlieferung* (Göttingen: Vandenhoeck & Ruprecht, 1993) 88-92, 286, argues that Baruch used Daniel 9 as it appears in the context of Daniel 7–12 and like that text it stems from the Maccabean crisis in the 160s BCE.

5. John J. Collins, *Daniel*, Hermeneia (Minneapolis: Fortress, 1993) 359, notes correctly that "the prayer in Daniel 9 is a traditional piece that could have been composed at any time after the Exile."

Commentators have frequently used this relationship to date either the poem of consolation and encouragement or the whole of the book of Baruch, but uncertainties about the literary relationship and the date of *Psalms of Solomon* 11 undermine the arguments for the date of Baruch. Many commentators have argued that the author of Baruch used *Psalms of Solomon* 11 because they see Baruch as more tightly organized and literarily unified.[6] But other commentators have argued that *Psalms of Solomon* is dependent on Baruch.[7] On the other hand, the poem is so traditional in language and thought that both *Psalms of Solomon* 11 and Baruch 5 could be independent variations on a common source.

Thus arguments that the whole of Baruch or at least the last section is based on the date of the *Psalms of Solomon* (after the Roman conquest in 63 BCE, since these psalms allude to Pompey, the Roman general) rest on shaky ground. In addition, some commentators think that *Psalms of Solomon* 11 may have been an earlier poem incorporated into the collection.[8] If so, then the author of Baruch would have had access to this psalm before 63 BCE.

In summary, a hypothesis of a common source for the *Psalms of Solomon* 11 and Bar 5:5-9 is more consonant with the shared themes, forms, and expressions found in Second Temple Jewish prayers. The author of Baruch draws upon widespread and deeply felt hopes for the vindication and reconstitution of Israel as a nation under God's protection. Baruch's literary relationships with Daniel 9 and *Psalms of Solomon* 11 locate Baruch solidly within the Second Temple period but do not support a more precise date. Similarly, the thought and wording throughout Baruch depend on the biblical Law and Prophets, especially Deuteronomy, Jeremiah, and Isaiah 40–66. Thus Baruch is probably from the Hellenistic period (late 4th cent. BCE on), when the OT canon began to take shape and became communally recognized.

3. Internal Evidence. The internal atmosphere of the book and allusions to its time of composition are vague and sometimes contradictory. The introduction (1:1-14), which assumes goodwill toward the reigning monarchs for whom it requests prayers, contrasts to the final prayer of consolation and encouragement, which manifests intense anger against the oppressive nations (see 4:31-35). The chronology of the introduction understands the deportation as a recent event (1:11-12), but the wisdom poem alludes to an exile of long duration (2:4-5; 3:10-11; 4:2-3). In the introduction either the

6. Moore, *Daniel, Esther, and Jeremiah: The Additions,* 314-16, argues that the close parallels are confined to Bar 5:5-9 and that the past tenses inserted into 5:8-9 indicate that Baruch is secondary to the Psalms of Solomon. But he also argues that Bar 5:5-9 was added to the end of Baruch at a later date, so that the parallels with Psalms of Solomon cannot be used to date Baruch. Rather, Bar 4:5–5:4 could be from the early second century or even the previous two centuries BCE. Jonathan A. Goldstein, "The Apocryphal Book of Baruch," *PAAJR* 46-47 (1979-80) 191-92n. 41, argues against Moore's case for the secondary nature of Bar 5:5-9.

7. Wilhelm Pesch, "Die Abhängigkeit des 11. Salomonischen Psalms vom letzten Kapitel des Buches Baruch," *ZAW* 67 (1955) 251-63; Burke, *The Poetry of Baruch,* 30, following Pesch; Steck, *Das apokryphe Baruchbuch,* 240-42, further argues that Bar 4:5–5:9 is so integrally related to the whole of Baruch that it is an original composition and never existed as an independent poem.

8. Nickelsburg, "The Bible Rewritten and Expanded," 145n. 327.

Temple is standing (1:10) or sacrifices are being offered at the Temple site in Jerusalem, but in the prayer of repentance the Temple has been destroyed (2:26). As noted previously the content of the prayers resembles that of Second Temple literature in general and does not help with dating.

4. Conclusion. The Greek period (332–63 BCE) is the most probable setting for most of the materials in Baruch, and within that period the second century has found most favor with commentators.[9] The lack of a detailed polemic and crisis atmosphere leads Moore to place Baruch early in the second century BCE, before the Maccabean war with Antiochus IV (167–164 BCE) and the conflicts with his successors.[10] Others, such as Goldstein (followed by Steck), put it after the Maccabean war.[11] Other scholars differ and put Baruch in the Roman-Herodian period (63 BCE–70 CE) with its simultaneous accommodation to Roman rule and fierce resentment of oppression. Others associate the hope of restoration in Baruch with the aftermath of the destruction of the Temple by the Romans in 70 CE.[12] In the end, no firm and widely persuasive conclusion has been reached because the urgent prayers of Israel, the lamentation over the sufferings of exile, and the hopes for the restoration of Israel and Jerusalem are common themes in Jewish literature from the sixth century BCE to the second century CE and have a protean quality that allows them to be applied to various situations.

PLACE, AUTHORSHIP, AUDIENCE, AND PURPOSE

Baruch as a whole is oriented toward Jerusalem. The author addresses a personified Jerusalem and her inhabitants; and Jerusalem addresses the exiles, her former inhabitants. The prayers and exhortations seek the restoration of Jerusalem and her inhabitants. Exile is a temporary state, to be ended by God's intervention. Thus Baruch probably originated in Jerusalem. The author knew thoroughly the biblical and Second Temple traditions and supported worship at the Temple, the holiness of Jerusalem, the restoration of Israel, and obedience to the Torah. Baruch, the pseudonymous author chosen for the book, was a highly placed Jerusalem scribe in the time of Jeremiah. The author may also have been a teacher or an official in Jerusalem, part of a learned circle devoted to the study and promotion of the traditions of Israel. In the swirl of Hellenistic

9. See the detailed survey of numerous scholars of the past two centuries in Burke, *The Poetry of Baruch,* 26-29. Only a few recent or very influential scholars will be cited in this commentary.

10. Moore, *Daniel, Esther, and Jeremiah: The Additions,* 260.

11. Goldstein, "The Apocryphal Book of Baruch"; Steck, *Das apokryphe Baruchbuch,* 294-303; Nickelsburg, *Jewish Literature Between the Bible and the Mishnah* (Philadelphia: Fortress, 1981) 113-14, opts for either the early second century BCE or the Maccabean period. According to Goldstein, the author of Baruch was promoting peaceful coexistence with the Seleucids through cooperation with Antiochus V after the death of his father, the notorious Antiochus IV, and after the rededication of the Temple. In this scenario, the hostility toward the nations would be a response to the oppression suffered during and after the reign of Antiochus IV Epiphanes, and the goodwill toward the ruling powers in the introduction (1:11-12) would reflect the gradually emerging detente with the Seleucids.

12. Doron Mendels, "Baruch, Book of," *ABD* 1:620, prefers either post-70 or early second century BCE. Emil Schürer, Geza Vermes, Fergus Millar, and Martin Goodman, *The History of the Jewish People in the Age of Jesus Christ (175 b.c.–a.d. 135),* vol. 3.2 (Edinburgh: T. & T. Clark, 1987) 737-38, suggest that the introduction, the compilation of Baruch, and perhaps the last section (4:5–5:9) are post-70 CE.

conflicts and threats to safety, the author sought to influence the outlooks, commitments, and policies of the Jerusalem leadership and people. Political, social, cultural, and religious groups were numerous and varied during this period. The book of Baruch encouraged all to adhere to the traditional deuteronomic theology, the wisdom of Israel articulated in the Torah, the commandments as a guide for life, and the post-exilic prophetic hopes for restoration of Jerusalem and Israel. It sought to clarify and establish the political, social, and religious traditions of Israel in Jewish society and to guide Jews in their responses to oppressive imperial rule and attractive foreign culture.

THOUGHT AND THEOLOGY

Baruch draws upon the traditions of Israel as they developed from the Babylonian exile (586 BCE) through the Second Temple period. Each of the parts of Baruch has been influenced by different biblical books and traditions—for example, but not exclusively, 1:15–3:8 by Daniel 9, Jeremiah, and Deuteronomy; 3:9–4:4 by Job 28 and the wisdom tradition, and 4:5–5:9 by Isaiah 40–66. The theological emphases of each section correspond to their literary genres and purposes. The confession and prayer of repentance addresses God with the liturgically proper title "Lord" and petitions for forgiveness. The wisdom poem addresses God with the most general and universal Greek word for "God", θεός (theos), in the manner of international wisdom. Despite that, the author identifies true wisdom with the biblical law (Torah) and wise behavior with obedience to God's commandments, as do other second-century writings, such as Sirach (Ecclesiasticus) 24. The poem of consolation and encouragement promises the eventual restoration of Israel and Jerusalem and the overcoming of the nations who dominate and oppress them. Here God is frequently designated as eternal or everlasting, as befits God's comprehensive, long-term restorative role.

The particularities of Baruch can best be seen against the background of the outlooks, political stances, and religious programs of other Jewish literature and groups in the Second Temple period. Contrary to many sectarian polemical texts, such as those found at Qumran, Baruch does not distinguish between those Jews who are faithful to a certain way of keeping the law and those who are unfaithful. The author of Baruch invites all Jews to acknowledge the nation's sinfulness, to repent, to obey the commandments, and to hope for divine assistance. He desires the reunification of all exiles with the Judeans in the land, and his norms for correct attitudes and behavior are drawn from the mainstream biblical traditions without emphasis on special practices or beliefs. The arguments over laws and calendar found in the book of *Jubilees,* the *Damascus Document,* and other works are entirely absent.

Baruch does not promote any of the new beliefs and world views that appeared in apocalyptic literature. Like the Hebrew Bible (except for Daniel 12), Baruch does not look forward to life after death but expects divine intervention and restoration of Israel in this world. The nations, which have persecuted Israel, will be punished and subjugated; but no messiah will come to defeat them or lead Israel, nor is any universal judgment or wholesale destruction envisioned. Rather, the desired result of the restoration is for Israel to dwell in its land in peace. Special revelations and cosmic battles between good and evil, such as those found in Daniel, do not appear here.

The author of Baruch has produced a middle-of-the-road, traditional theology to which Israel can adhere under all circumstances. Baruch's very generality and lack of originality, for which it has often been criticized, made it attractive and available to Jews of every inclination. The book seems to have been especially useful to Jews in the Greek-speaking diaspora, since it survived in Greek.

Baruch has not been greatly or directly influential on Christian literature. It shares with Christianity a stress on confession and repentance for sin, but both derived it from the Hebrew Bible. The sin of sacrificing to demons rather than to God appears in 1 Cor 10:20 and Bar 4:7, but both may be dependent on Deut 32:17. Both Baruch and Paul attack Greco-Roman wisdom as false (Bar 3:16-28; 1 Cor 1:18-25), but no direct literary relationship can be established.

The wisdom poem in Baruch may have had a literary influence on Paul's Letter to the Romans and the Gospel of John. Paul's argument that one does not need to ascend to heaven or descend into the abyss to find righteousness (Rom 10:6-8) is based on Deut 30:12-14, a text that has also influenced Bar 3:29-30. Baruch stresses both the impossibility of humans' finding wisdom on their own and the presence of wisdom among humans as a divine gift (Bar 3:36–4:1). This interpretation and elaboration of Deuteronomy accords closely with Paul's analysis of the divine gift of righteousness brought by Jesus.

Baruch 3:29–4:4 also speaks of wisdom in a way parallel to the Gospel of John's discourse about Jesus the son of God in John 3:13-21 and 31-36. In both Baruch and John humans cannot ascend to heaven to get wisdom, but rather wisdom in Baruch and the son of the Father in John descend from heaven to humans as a divine gift. In Baruch, wisdom is associated with life, light, and salvation, as is Jesus in John. Wisdom understood as the law dwells with Israel in Baruch just as Jesus dwells with humans as the truth, the word, and the way in John. In Deuteronomy 30, Baruch, and John, God's presence on earth (commandments, wisdom, Jesus) is available to all who will accept it.[13]

13. For an analysis of the detailed relationships between John and Baruch, see Norman R. Petersen, *The Gospel of John and the Sociology of Light: Language and Characterization in the Fourth Gospel* (Valley Forge, Pa.: Trinity, 1993) 114-19.

BIBLIOGRAPHY

Commentaries:
Fitzgerald, Aloysius. "Baruch." *New Jerome Biblical Commentary.* Edited by Raymond Brown et al. Englewood Cliffs, N.J.: Prentice-Hall, 1990. A short introductory commentary providing the non-specialist reader with commentary on historical background; meanings of various words, phrases, and sentences; and basic theological interpretation.

Harrington, Daniel J. "Baruch." In *Harper's Bible Commentary.* Edited by James L. Mays. San Francisco: Harper & Row, 1988. An introductory commentary with particular focus on the meaning of the text.

Moore, Carey A. *Daniel, Esther, and Jeremiah: The Additions.* AB 44. Garden City, N.Y.: Doubleday, 1977. Provides a general introduction and moderately detailed textual notes. Sparing in interpretation. Advances the thesis that Baruch consists of five separate compositions loosely edited into one work.

Steck, Odil Hannes. *Dask apokryphe Baruchbuch: Studien zu Rezeption und Konzentration "kanonischer" Überlieferung.* Göttingen: Vandenhoeck & Ruprecht, 1993. The most highly detailed technical commentary available. Offers almost seventy pages of general discussion (including the modern theological meaning of Baruch) and almost two-hundred fifty pages of translation and detailed exegesis.

Whitehouse, O. C. "1 Baruch." In *The Apocrypha and Pseudepigrapha of the Old Testament.* Volume 1. Edited by R. H. Charles. Oxford: Clarendon, 1913. Though in many ways now substantially outdated, this volume offers a highly detailed and still relevant discussion of Baruch's textual history, language, authorship, and similar issues. Detailed textual notes accompany the author's translation, which is similar to the KJV in style.

Specialized Studies:

Nickelsburg, George W. E. "The Bible Rewritten and Expanded." In *Jewish Writings of the Second Temple Period.* Edited by Michael E. Stone. Philadelphia: Fortress, 1984. A general discussion of Baruch in light of the state of scholarly knowledge and discussion in the early nineteen eighties. Analyzes Baruch's compositional history and relationship to other texts including the books of Jeremiah and Daniel.

———. *Jewish Literature Between the Bible and the Mishnah.* Philadelphia: Fortress, 1981. A short discussion and summary of Baruch, which is treated as a unified composition.

Schürer, Emil, Geza Vermes, Fergus Millar, and Martin Goodman. *The History of the Jewish People in the Age of Jesus Christ (175 B.C.–A.D. 135).* Volume 3.2. Edinburgh: T. & T. Clark, 1987. An update of a (seriously flawed) classic early twentieth century German work. Provides a general introduction and summary of Baruch, a concise but strong discussion of composition history, Baruch's place in the canon, and its use by the early church and patristic writers. Good bibliography up through the early nineteen eighties.

OUTLINE OF BARUCH

I. Baruch 1:1-14, Narrative Introduction

    A. 1:1-9, Narrative Introduction

    B. 1:10-14, The Cover Letter

II. Baruch 1:15–3:8, Prayer of Confession and Repentance

    A. 1:15–2:10, Confession of the Judean Community

    B. 2:11–3:8, Prayer of Repentance for Mercy and Deliverance

III. Baruch 3:9–4:4, Wisdom Admonition and Exhortation

    A. 3:9-14, Rebuke and Call to Israel

    B. 3:15-31, Wisdom Hidden from Humans

    C. 3:32–4:1, God Gives Wisdom to Israel

    D. 4:2-4, Final Exhortation to Accept Wisdom

IV. Baruch 4:5–5:9, A Poem of Consolation and Encouragement

    A. 4:5-9*a*, Introductory Poem of Consolation

    B. 4:9*b*-16, Jerusalem's Lament to Neighboring Peoples

    C. 4:17-29, Jerusalem's Exhortation to Her Children

    D. 4:30–5:9, Poem of Consolation to Jerusalem

BARUCH 1:1-14

NARRATIVE INTRODUCTION

OVERVIEW

The narrative introduction to Baruch sets the scene for the prayers and exhortations that follow in the rest of the book (1:15–5:9). However, the introduction is notorious for its conflicts with the body of the book and for historical errors. These conflicts undercut the narrative coherence of the book as a whole and raise questions concerning the purposes of the author of Baruch. (Theories about the actual historical setting, author, and date of Baruch are treated in the Introduction.) For example, in the introduction (1:6-7, 10), the Babylonian exiles send money for the priests in Jerusalem to offer sacrifices; but the prayer of confession and repentance (1:15–3:8) alludes to the destruction of the Temple (2:26), and the lament in the final section implies that Zion has been devastated (4:9-35). The introduction requests that prayers be offered for the Babylonian king and his son so that the exiles may live under their protection (1:11-12). By contrast, the prayer of confession and repentance stresses the shame and suffering of exile (2:4, 13; 3:8), and the poem of consolation and encouragement (4:5–5:9) attacks the savagery of the nations and promises punishment for them (4:14-16, 25, 31-35). The introduction treats the exile as an event that began five years previously (1:2), while the wisdom poem treats it as having been lengthy (3:10-11; 4:2-3). In identifying Belshazzar as the son of Nebuchadnezzar (1:11-12), the introduction repeats an error found in Dan 5:2. Actually, Nabonidus was the father of Behshazzar, and they were coregents when defeated by Cyrus the Persian in 539 BCE. Finally, the narrative framework of Baruch fits uneasily into some biblical narratives. Baruch is placed in Babylon, contrary to Jer 43:1-6, which recounts his forced flight with Jeremiah into Egypt.

The introduction's mention of money sent for sacrifices in the Temple assumes the period between the first and second deportations of Jerusalemites to Babylon (597–586 BCE) while the Temple was still standing (1:11-12). The allusion to the Temple's destruction in 2:26 supports a narrative setting between the Babylonian destruction of Jerusalem and the Temple and the return of some exiles under Cyrus the Persian (586–538). The dates of events cited or alluded to in the introduction are muddled. The month in 1:2 is unnamed in the text, though it is usually taken to be the fifth month, Ab, which is the month in which Jerusalem was destroyed. The next date is Siwan, the third month (1:8), which puts the arrival of the collection ten months later than it was gathered in Babylon. The final "date" is the "the day of the festival and the days of the [sacred] season" (1:14), which is usually taken as a reference to the feast of Tabernacles in the seventh month, Tishri.

Each of these problems will be taken up in the commentary. Here two general comments and two conflicting hypotheses concerning the narrative chronology will provide orientation to the world of the text and to the purposes of the author(s) in creating this narrative world. The author of Baruch works with a variety of traditions found in other literature from the Second Temple period, sometimes interpreting scriptural verses in a surprising way and sometimes drawing upon alternative narratives and scenarios that were common stock in his time. He does not seek historical accuracy in the modern sense, nor does he have earlier, reliable historical sources. Furthermore, granted the complex literary and social context of Second Temple Judaism, no theory can fully explain all the narrative elements, much less discover what happened historically at the time in which the narrative is set. The goal must be to understand the book through understanding the narrative world envisioned by the author.

The chronological setting of Baruch can be understood as 597–586 BCE, between the first and second deportations, or as 586–538 BCE, between the destruction of the Temple and the return of some of the exiles. The case for 597–586 is based mainly on the request that sacrifices be offered in Jerusalem (1:10-11). The "fifth year" in 1:1 is the fifth year of King Jeconiah (593/592 BCE), who replaced his father during the first siege of Jerusalem in 598/597. The initial visions of the book of Ezekiel are dated to that same year (Ezek 1:2). According to this chronology, the exiles send offerings to the Temple, which is still standing. This situation corresponds to that of the actual audience of Baruch during the Second Temple period, when the Temple was once again standing. Many Jews lived in the diaspora and sent offerings to the Temple in Jerusalem. This hypothesis solves some problems but leaves others outstanding. The setting between the deportations does not correspond to the allusions to a long exile in later sections (a new generation in 3:4; endurance in 4:5, 21, 27, 30). The return of the Temple vessels (1:8-9) is unnecessary, since worship has presumably been carried on from 597 to 592 BCE.

The more common chronological setting for the narrative is 586–538 BCE, between the destruction of Jerusalem and the return of some exiles under Cyrus.[14] The sense of overwhelming tragedy and

14. For an extended defense of this hypothesis, see Odil Hannes Steck, *Das apokryphe Baruchbuch: Studien zu Rezeption und Konzentration "kanonischer" Überlieferung* (Göttingen: Vandenhoeck & Ruprecht, 1993).

loss, the mourning of Zion (4:5–5:9), the promise of return, the deuteronomic theology of punishment for sin all point to the Babylonian exile following the destruction of Jerusalem and the Temple in 586. The major obstacle to this interpretation is the lack of a Temple in Jerusalem to receive the collection for sacrificial offerings and to provide a setting for Joakim and the priests. In this scenario, Baruch envisions the continuation of sacrifice in Jerusalem after the exile of 586. The exiles provide the necessities for the cult, money to buy sacrificial animals, and the holy implements and vessels with which to carry out the rituals (1:6-10). The possibility of sacrifices without the Temple derives from Ezra 3:1-6, where the returned exiles set up an altar and reinstituted sacrifice at the site of the Temple. The author of Baruch merely moves this act forward to provide for greater continuity of worship and for a closer connection of the exiles to Jerusalem all during the exile. In this understanding of events, the expression "house of the Lord" (1:14) would refer to the temple area, not to the building itself, which had been destroyed.

Both hypotheses are far from certain, and neither solves all the problems of the introduction. The latter is more simple and closer to the text. Yet, on a quick reading it appears that the author still seems to presume the existence of the Temple, not just an altar. Perhaps the author left the chronology and setting vague so as to have the richest social and religious context for this teaching. The details of these problems and hypotheses will be addressed in the commentary.

BARUCH 1:1-9, NARRATIVE INTRODUCTION

NAB

1 Now these are the words of the scroll which Baruch, son of Neriah, son of Mahseiah, son of Zedekiah, son of Hasadiah, son of Hilkiah, wrote in Babylon, **2** in the fifth year [on the seventh day of the month, at the time when the Chaldeans took Jerusalem and burnt it with fire]. **3** And Baruch read the words of this

NRSV

1 These are the words of the book that Baruch son of Neriah son of Mahseiah son of Zedekiah son of Hasadiah son of Hilkiah wrote in Babylon, [2]in the fifth year, on the seventh day of the month, at the time when the Chaldeans took Jerusalem and burned it with fire.

[3]Baruch read the words of this book to

NAB

scroll for Jeconiah, son of Jehoiakim, king of Judah, to hear it, as well as all the people who came to the reading: **4** the nobles, the kings' sons, the elders, and the whole people, small and great alike—all who lived in Babylon by the river Sud.

5 They wept and fasted and prayed before the LORD, **6** and collected such funds as each could furnish. **7** These they sent to Jerusalem, to Jehoiakim, son of Hilkiah, son of Shallum, the priest, and to the priests and the whole people who were with him in Jerusalem. **8** [This was when he received the vessels of the house of the LORD that had been removed from the temple, to restore them to the land of Judah, on the tenth of Sivan. These silver vessels Zedekiah, son of Josiah, king of Judah, had had made **9** after Nebuchadnezzar, king of Babylon, carried off Jeconiah, and the princes, and the skilled workers, and the nobles, and the people of the land from Jerusalem, as captives, and brought them to Babylon.]

1, 9: *tous desmōtas* = *hammasgēr*: cf. Jer 24.1

NRSV

Jeconiah son of Jehoiakim, king of Judah, and to all the people who came to hear the book, [4]and to the nobles and the princes, and to the elders, and to all the people, small and great, all who lived in Babylon by the river Sud.

5Then they wept, and fasted, and prayed before the Lord; [6]they collected as much money as each could give, [7]and sent it to Jerusalem to the high priest[a] Jehoiakim son of Hilkiah son of Shallum, and to the priests, and to all the people who were present with him in Jerusalem. [8]At the same time, on the tenth day of Sivan, Baruch[b] took the vessels of the house of the Lord, which had been carried away from the temple, to return them to the land of Judah—the silver vessels that Zedekiah son of Josiah, king of Judah, had made, [9]after King Nebuchadnezzar of Babylon had carried away from Jerusalem Jeconiah and the princes and the prisoners and the nobles and the people of the land, and brought them to Babylon.

[a] Gk *the priest*   [b] Gk *he*

COMMENTARY

1:1. "The words of the book that Baruch . . . wrote" refers to the contents of Bar 1:15–5:9. The terms for "book" in Greek are βιβλίον (*biblion*) in 1:1, 3, 14 and βίβλος (*biblos*) in 1:3, translated by the NRSV as "book" in 1:1, 3 and as "scroll" in 1:14. These words come from βύβλος (*byblos*), meaning "papyrus," and may refer to a strip of papyrus, a papyrus roll, or a document written on papyrus or other material—for example, a letter, a legal document, or a book. In the Greek translation of Jeremiah 29:1 [Greek 36:1], the "words of the *biblos*" that Jeremiah sent to the exiles in Babylon after the first exile of 597 BCE are identified as a "letter" (ἐπιστολή *epistolē*). In Jeremiah 32:10-16 [Greek 39:10-16] the *biblion* that Baruch writes is a deed to land, and in Jeremiah 36 [Greek 43] the *biblion* is a scroll of Jeremiah's prophecies. The *biblion* of Baruch is a scroll of prayer, instruction, and exhortation.

Baruch, son of Neriah, son of Mahseiah the scribe, is well known from the book of Jeremiah (Jer 32:12), where he records Jeremiah's teachings (chap. 36) and with his brother Seriah, "chief quartermaster", (שׂר מנוחה *śar mĕnûḥâ*) is part of the governing class in Jerusalem for King Zedekiah (Jer 51:59). The three earlier links in his genealogy, Zedekiah, Hasadiah and Hilkiah, are unique to Baruch. The names "Baruch" and "Seriah" have turned up in Judean seal impressions from the seventh–sixth centuries, reading as follows: "Belonging to Berekhyahu son of Neriyahu the scribe" and "Belonging to Seiyahu son of Neriyahu."[15] Baruch was probably an official, as was his brother. Baruch is known for his association with Jeremiah—e.g., transferring land (Jeremiah 32), writing Jeremiah's prophecies (Jeremiah 36), being consoled by Jeremiah (Jer 45:1-2), being accused of conspiracy and going with Jeremiah to Egypt (Jer 43:3, 6).

15. Nahman Avigad, "Baruch the Scribe and Jerahmeel the King's Son," IEJ 28 (1978) 52-56. Two further examples in private hands are found in Robert Deutsch and Michael Heltzer, *Forty New Ancient West Semitic Inscriptions* (Tel Aviv-Jaffa: Archaeological Center Publication, 1994), and are reported in Hershel Shanks, "Fingerprints of Jeremiah's Scribe," BAR 22 (1996) 36-38. Nahman Avigad, *Hebrew Bullae from the Time of Jeremiah* (Jerusalem: Israel Exploration Society, 1986) #9 = Baruch, and #7 = Seraiah. For the office of scribe, including remarks on Baruch, see J. Andrew Dearman, "My Servants the Scribes: Composition and Context in Jeremiah 36," JBL 109 (1990) 403-21.

Although v. 1 says that Baruch wrote this book in Babylon, according to Jer 43:6, he and Jeremiah were taken forcibly to Egypt by the group that assassinated Gedaliah ben Ahikam, the Babylonian appointed governor of Judah. Biographical narratives about Jeremiah were common in post-exilic Jewish literature. Since the book of Jeremiah does not say when or where Baruch and Jeremiah died, they became literarily available for a variety of narrative tasks. For example, in the Dead Sea Scroll 4Q385b (earlier referred to as 4Q385 16 or ApocJer[c]) Jeremiah accompanies the exiles as far as the Euphrates River, instructing them how to be faithful to God in Babylon. Another fragment of this work places Jeremiah in Egypt, in agreement with the biblical account, instructing the exiles there.[16] The later rabbinic commentary *Pesikta Rabbati* 26:6 has Jeremiah accompany the exiles as far as the Euphrates to comfort them, a scenario that is consistent with the Qumran *Apocryphon of Jeremiah*. Presumably such narratives suggested roles for Baruch as well. In *2 Bar* 10:1-5, God tells Baruch to instruct Jeremiah to go to Babylon to support the captives while Baruch stays in Jerusalem and receives visions of the future, which he then communicates to the people. In *4 Baruch* (*Paraleipomena of Jeremiah*) 4:6-7 Jeremiah is taken as an exile to Babylon while Baruch mourns in Jerusalem. Sixty-six years later, Jeremiah leads the people back to Jerusalem from Babylon (chap. 8 of *4 Baruch*).[17]

Josephus provides a historical context for the movement of Jeremiah and Baruch from Egypt to Babylon, although he does not name them.[18] After retelling the story of Jeremiah and Baruch being taken forcibly to Egypt (Jeremiah 43), Josephus recounts how Nebuchadnezzar conquered Egypt in his twenty-third year, which was the fifth year after the destruction of Jerusalem. Nebuchadnezzar took the Jewish refugees (presumably including Jeremiah and Baruch) from Egypt to Babylon as captives. Analogously, Jer 52:30, a passage found in the Hebrew but not in the Greek (the present Hebrew of Jeremiah is a later version

than the Greek), speaks of a third exile in the twenty-third year of Nebuchadnezzar, five years after the destruction of Jerusalem. Later rabbinic interpretations also place Baruch in Babylon. *Seder Olam Rabbah* 26 tells the story of Nebuchadnezzar conquering Egypt in his twenty-seventh year and explicitly says that he exiled Jeremiah and Baruch to Babylon. Some rabbinic writings radically compress post-exilic chronology so that Baruch was the teacher of Ezra in exile,[19] but then the midrashic author must explain why Baruch and Ezra did not return with the exiles in 538 BCE (Baruch was too old, and Ezra stayed behind to care for him).

1:2. The dates given in Baruch do not make obvious and consistent narrative sense. The date at the beginning of this verse lacks the number of the month. The month probably was the fifth month, with the number of the month omitted through the scribal error of haplography, in which the repeated word "fifth" for both the year and the month was dropped.[20] The seventh day of the fifth month is the date of the destruction of the Temple by Nebuchadnezzar's armies in 586 BCE (see 2 Kgs 25:8). Zechariah, in the late sixth century BCE, mentions a fast in the fifth month (Zech 7:5; 8:19).[21] Thus the date here would refer to 581 BCE, the fifth year after the destruction of the Temple.

Some commentators, however, calculate the fifth year as 592 BCE, five years after the deportation of King Jehoiachin and other leaders from Jerusalem to Babylon in 597 (2 Kgs 24:12-16). Ezekiel's call as a prophet is also placed in the fifth year, on the fifth day of the fifth month (Ezek 1:2). The latter part of v. 2, with its reference to the destruction of Jerusalem, is not decisive in deciding between these two dates. "At the time when" (ἐν τῷ καιρῷ *en tō kairō*) may refer to the general period when these events happened, or it may refer to a specific anniversary date (as in 1 Macc 4:54). The presence of a high priest and priests in Jerusalem (v. 7), the request that they offer sacrifice at the altar (v. 10), and the reference to the house of the Lord (v. 14) suggest that the Temple

---

16. Devorah Dimant, "An Apocryphon of Jeremiah from Cave 4 (4Q385B-4Q385 16)," in *New Qumran Texts and Studies,* ed. George J. Brooke (Leiden: Brill, 1994) 11-30.

17. George W. E. Nickelsburg, "Narrative Traditions in the Paraleipomena of Jeremiah and 2 Baruch," *CBQ* 35 (1973) 60-68, shows how the Jeremiah and Baruch traditions interacted.

18. Josephus, *Antiquities of the Jews,* 10.9.6-7 (176-182)

19. *B. Megilla* 16b; *Song of Songs Rab.* 5.5, 1.

20. Steck, *Das apokryphe Baruchbuch,* 19. The majority of commentators accept the fifth month.

21. The commemoration of the destruction of the Temple on the ninth of Ab (*Tisha b'Ab*) is a rabbinic custom. Jer 52:12 puts the destruction on the tenth day of the month.

is still standing. On the other hand, the rest of Baruch presumes that the Temple has been destroyed (2:26; for further interpretation of these problems, see the Overview to this section and the Commentary on 1:10-14).

1:3-4. The audience for the reading of Baruch's book is consistent with related biblical materials. Jeconiah, son of Jehoiakim, whose name is found in 1 Chr 3:16-17; Jer 24:1; 27:20; 29:2; and elsewhere, is identical with Jehoiachin in 2 Kgs 24:6-12. He became king in 598 BCE during the Babylonian siege of Jerusalem, when his father, Jehoiachim, died. He surrendered the city in spring 597 and was taken to Babylon, where he died in exile. With him are "the people" (v. 3), or more inclusively "all the people, great and small" (v. 4). The leaders with Jeconiah are specified as the "sons of the kings"—that is, the members of the royal family ("princes" in the NRSV), the "powerful" (δυνατοί *dynatoi,* translated as "nobles" in the NRSV), and the elders. The description of the king and his entourage calls to mind the assembly of the leaders and people to hear the reading of the book found in the Temple during the reign of Josiah (2 Kgs 23:1-2), an assembly that included "all the people great and small." It also recalls the king's and his court's hearing (with displeasure) the reading of Jeremiah's prophecies by Baruch (Jeremiah 36). Finally, the gathering of the king and the people by a river or canal in Babylon replicates the gathering of Ezekiel and the exiles at the River Chebar (Ezek 1:1) and of the group returning with Ezra at the River Ahava (Ezra 8:15).[22]

1:5-7. The response of the people (weeping, fasting, and praying) is common in biblical and Second Temple literature (e.g., Neh 1:4; 9:1; Ezra 8:21-23; Dan 6:18; 9:3; Tob 12:8; Jdt 4:13). The collecting of money (lit., silver) for temple offerings according to each one's means corresponds to the instructions in Deut 16:16-17 on bringing

offerings during the pilgrimage festivals. The money is to be sent to the priest Joakim, son of Hilkiah, in Jerusalem (the NRSV has Jehoiakim, the Hebrew equivalent of this Greek name). The Greek has the simple title "priest," but here "priest" refers to the high priest, as it does in the case of Jehoiada, "the priest" in Jerusalem who opposes Athaliah and enthrones Joash (2 Kings 11–12). Joakim's name is a problem, however. He does not appear in the narrative of 2 Kings as a high priest before the destruction, nor is he on the list of high priests in 1 Chr 6:13-15. According to the biblical narratives, Seriah was the last high priest in the Temple; he was executed after the conquest of Jerusalem (2 Kgs 25:18; Jer 52:24). His son Jehozadak went with the exiles to Babylon (1 Chr 6:15). Thus none of the historical narratives or lists attests to a Joakim serving in Jerusalem immediately after the destruction of the Temple. The name "Joakim," however, is associated with the priesthood. Joakim, son of Jeshua, is high priest in the time of Ezra (Neh 12:10-11), and the fictional book of Judith contains a high priest named Joakim who exercises great power (Jdt 4:6, 8, 14; 15:8). The name is a credible priestly name used for a fictional narrative character. The author of Baruch understands Joakim to be the high priest in Jerusalem from 586 until the return of Jeshua, son of Jozadak (another name for Jehozadak, the high priest who went into exile), under Cyrus the Persian in 538 (Ezra 2:2; 3:2).[23] The author of Baruch probably pictured worship continuing at an altar without a temple before the return from Babylon. The biblical basis for such a scenario is provided by two incidents. After the destruction of the Temple and the murder of the governor Gedaliah, men from Shiloh, Shechem, and Samaria came to Mizpah with grain and incense offerings for the Temple, which was no longer standing (Jer 41:4-7).[24] This brief notice implies that some kind of cultic activity was going on. Similarly and more clearly, the returned exiles set up an altar on the site of the destroyed Temple and offered sacrifices (Ezra 3:1-6).

22. The river's name, the Sud, was for a long time unknown. However, an apocryphal version of Jeremiah (4Q389a earlier called 389 6 or 4QApocJer^e) refers to a river called סור (*swr,* probably pronounced *sûr*). If this is the Hebrew original of the Greek transliteration *soud,* then the mistaken versions in the Greek can be explained as a confusion of the final *resh* with a *dalet* by the translator (a common error). Thus the original Sur came out as Soud in Greek and as *sur* in Syriac, in which a different initial sibilant, the *sade,* was substituted for the original *samek.* The creation of this name may be a play on words based on the Hebrew word *swr,* which means "to turn aside or depart," as in Isa 52:11.

23. If Baruch was written after the Maccabean war against the Seleucids, then the name "Yoakim" may have been chosen for its similarity to "Yakim," which was the Hebrew name of the priest Alcimus. See Jonathan A. Goldstein, "The Apocryphal Book of Baruch," PAAJR 46-47 (1979-80) 194.

24. Steck, *Das apokryphe Baruchbuch,* 18-20, 29-31, 39.

1:8-9. These two verses do not fit smoothly into the narrative either grammatically or historically, and so some commentators label one or both as glosses. Neither Kings nor Chronicles has a story of King Zedekiah (597–586 BCE) making new implements for the Temple after the first deportation. The logic of the story derives partly from 2 Kings, which reports that Nebuchadnezzar cut in pieces and took all the golden temple vessels to Babylon in 597 BCE (2 Kgs 24:13). This would leave the Temple without equipment for sacrifice, so the author of Baruch envisions the king making new, less costly silver vessels. However, the biblical account is not consistent within itself or with Baruch. In the final conquest and destruction of Jerusalem in 586, the Babylonians took away both gold and silver implements and vessels (2 Kgs 25:14-15), not just Zedekiah's silver vessels.[25] In addition, the story of an early return of the temple vessels (v. 8) does not fit smoothly into the narrative. The Greek grammar does not clarify who brought the vessels back to Jerusalem, whether Hilkiah the priest (mentioned in v. 7) or Baruch (mentioned in v. 3). The NRSV and most commentators choose Baruch.[26] The letter sent to Jerusalem mentions the money for sacrifices, but not the temple vessels (v. 10). Nevertheless, the logic of the author of Baruch is still clear: Since Zedekiah's vessels would have been taken to Babylon in 586, the narrative must place their return between 586 and 538, when a group of exiles returned (Ezra 1–3). If Baruch understands that sacrifices were offered during this period, he must ensure that some sacred vessels and implements are returned to Jerusalem along with money to buy sacrificial animals.[27]

The list of groups carried off to Babylon in v. 9 is similar to the lists of those taken to Babylon in Jer 24:1 (officials of Judah, artisans, and smiths) and Jer 29:2 (the queen mother, the court officials, the leaders of Judah and Jerusalem, artisans, and smiths). The NRSV must be corrected in one place and the Greek in another, however. The first group is not "princes," as in the NRSV, but "leaders" or "officials" (ἄρχοντες *archontes,* which often translates the Hebrew שָׂרִים *śārîm*). The Greek of the second group is "prisoners" (δεσμῶται *desmōtai*), so translated by the NRSV, but this is a translation error from Hebrew. The Hebrew word מסגר (*masgēr*) has two meanings: "prison" (Isa 24:22) and "smith" (2 Kgs 24:14; Jer 24:1). "Smiths" is clearly the correct choice for a list of exiled productive leaders.[28] Baruch adds to this list of exiles the "people of the land." In Kgs 25:12, by contrast, the poor of the land ("poor of the people") are left to farm the land, and in Jer 24:1 the rich are also listed among the deportees. Baruch, however, consistently stresses the unity and cohesiveness of the people of Israel in exile and in the land. (See Reflections at 1:10-14.)

25. In 538 BCE Sheshbazzar brought 5,469 gold and silver vessels back to Jerusalem after Cyrus the Persian's conquest of Babylon (Ezra 1:7-11).

26. Goldstein, "The Apocryphal Book of Baruch," 179, suggests that, according to the narrative in the book of Baruch, the priest Hilkiah, grammatically the closest antecedent to 1:8, brought back the vessels from Babylon in the third month, two months before Baruch brought the money for sacrifices to Jerusalem. Goldstein attributes the imaginary return of the vessels to Jerusalem to the author of Baruch, who, during the Maccabean revolt, was motivated by an actual (according to Goldstein) offer to Antiochus V in 163 BCE to return the temple vessels as part of a peace process (Goldstein, "The Apocryphal Book of Baruch," 185). His hypothesis lacks a firm foundation.

27. The idea of an early return of temple implements may have been suggested by the prophet Hananiah's (false) prediction in 594 BCE that the sacred vessels taken in 597 would be returned in two years (Jer 28:3). But the prophecy is treated as false in the Jeremiah narrative and points to the wrong date for the Baruch narrative.

28. The Greek translators also chose the wrong meaning for Jer 24:1 and 29:2.

BARUCH 1:10-14, THE COVER LETTER

NAB

10 Their message was: "We send you funds, with which you are to procure holocausts, sin offerings, and frankincense, and to prepare cereal offerings; offer these on the altar of the LORD our God, **11** and pray for the life of Nebuchadnezzar, king of Babylon, and that of Belshazzar, his son, that their lifetimes may equal the duration of the heavens above the earth; **12** and that the LORD may give us strength, and light to our eyes, that we may live under the protective shadow of Nebuchadnezzar, king of Babylon, and that of Belshazzar, his son, and serve them long, finding favor in their sight.

13 "Pray for us also to the LORD, our God; for we have sinned against the LORD, our God, and the wrath and anger of the LORD have not yet been withdrawn from us at the present day. **14** And read out publicly this scroll which we send you, in the house of the LORD, on the feast day and during the days of assembly:

1, 10: (*poiē sate*) *manaa:* so LXX^{MSS};=*minḥâ:* cf. Jer 17, 26.
1, 14: *en'ē merais kairou=bime mo'ē d:* cf. Sir 50, 6.

NRSV

10They said: Here we send you money; so buy with the money burnt offerings and sin offerings and incense, and prepare a grain offering, and offer them on the altar of the Lord our God; ¹¹and pray for the life of King Nebuchadnezzar of Babylon, and for the life of his son Belshazzar, so that their days on earth may be like the days of heaven. ¹²The Lord will give us strength, and light to our eyes; we shall live under the protection^a of King Nebuchadnezzar of Babylon, and under the protection of his son Belshazzar, and we shall serve them many days and find favor in their sight. ¹³Pray also for us to the Lord our God, for we have sinned against the Lord our God, and to this day the anger of the Lord and his wrath have not turned away from us. ¹⁴And you shall read aloud this scroll that we are sending you, to make your confession in the house of the Lord on the days of the festivals and at appointed seasons.

^a Gk *in the shadow*

COMMENTARY

The exiles in Babylon request that a full range of sacrifices, "whole offerings" (עולה *'ôlâ*), "sin offerings" (חטאת *ḥaṭṭā't*), "incense offerings" (לבנה *lĕbônâ*), "grain offerings" (מנחה *minḥâ*), and prayers be offered for the long lives of the Babylonian kings so that they may protect the exiled Judeans. Clearly, the exiles anticipate serving these foreign conquerors and winning their favor. This promoting of a positive relationship with the ruling powers is one common response to conquest in Second Temple Jewish literature that is also found in the prayer of confession and repentance (1:15–3:8), in the stories in Daniel 1–4; 6, and in Esther. It corresponds to Jeremiah's pro-Babylonian prophecies (Jer 27:6-11) and instructions to the exiles to pray for Babylon (Jer 29:7). Ezekiel promotes the same attitude (Ezek 29:17-20). This school of thought recognized the Babylonian dominance of the Near East and the social and political dissolution of Judea. In its view, a well-intentioned king could be an aid to Judeans in the land and in exile. However, many other works, including the last part of Baruch (4:31-35), express intense resentment toward imperial oppression.

The introduction's link with the traditions in Daniel 1–6 can be seen in the erroneous identification of Nebuchadnezzar as the father of Belshazzar (v. 12), which is also found in Dan 5:2, 11, 18, and 22. In fact, Nabonidus was the father of Belshazzar, and they were the last two Babylonian kings, ruling as co-regents in 539 BCE, when Cyrus the Persian conquered Babylon and took over the empire. Nebuchadnezzar was earlier in the sixth century, but he is prominent in Jewish thought because he conquered Jerusalem.

The exiles in Babylon also ask that the Jerusalemites pray on their behalf to God, who is still angry with them (v. 13). They implicitly accept the deuteronomic theology that Jerusalem was destroyed as a punishment for its sins. The rest of the book of Baruch (1:5–5:9) consists of the exiles' prayers, exhortations, and hopes, which the Jerusalemites are to recite for them in the Temple during the festivals (v. 14). Thus vv. 13-14 are the immediate introduction for the prayer of confession and repentance (1:15–3:8) and for the instruction and exhortation that follow.

The reading of the book or scroll is to take place in the "house of the LORD," which is ordinarily understood as the Temple. Once again, the chronological setting of the narrative in relation to the Temple is unclear (see the Introduction and Overview). If the setting is post-586, as is most probable, then the "house of the LORD" had already been destroyed. "House of the LORD" would then refer to the temple area, where an altar was set up (see the Commentary on 1:7). The NRSV translation of the time of the prayer of confession, "on the days of the festivals and at appointed seasons," is not fully accurate. The Greek is more literally "in the day of the feast [ἑορτῆς *heortēs*] and on the days of the festival season [καιροῦ *kairou*]." This clause may refer to Jewish festivals in general, as in the NRSV, but more likely designates the new year festival in the fall, at the beginning of the seventh month, Tishri, and the eight-day Feast of Tabernacles, beginning on the fifteenth of Tishri.

REFLECTIONS

The Babylonian conquest of Jerusalem has destroyed the religious world of the exiled Judean community at the beginning of Baruch. Analogously the modern world has destroyed or severely stressed the traditional religious world of many Christians. A normal human reaction in both cases is to walk away sadly. The Babylonian conquerers probably expected the exiled Judeans to assimilate to Mesopotamian culture and cause them no more trouble, just as modern science and secular culture naively expected religion to disappear. However, contrary to expectations, the Judean exiles struggled to maintain their traditional ties and rectify their relationship with God, thus providing a model of fidelity for contemporary believers. Their classic response to disaster—confession of sin, prayer, repentance, instruction, exhortation, and trust in divine mercy and intervention—has been adopted by later Jewish and Christian groups. A return to the core convictions and practices of the religious tradition answers cultural breakdown and fragmentation of communal consciousness. Like the exiled Judean community, contemporary Christians must frankly and robustly admit their feelings and lack of attention to God in order to clarify their vision of God and meet the threats and challenges of a new world.

In Western culture, people view themselves as individuals in a large and often chaotic world. Only the family, or perhaps a small group of friends, stands between the person and an amazing, but often hazardous, universe. The ancient Judeans preserved a resolute sense of community that has been lost in much of the modern world. Although they were separated by hundreds of miles, the Judeans in Babylon and in Judea act as one unified community to confront their national disaster. Although they had suffered and lost their independence, their fellowship in loss overcame any potential rivalries or differences. The book of Baruch, contrary to much of Second Temple literature, lacks any disputes over practice, outlook, or interpretation of history. The political, social, and religious conflicts that motivate the plot of the books of Ezra and Nehemiah receive no notice in Baruch so that the Judeans may be one before God in repentance, salvation, and restoration. Baruch's all-embracing turn toward God provides a cogent example to the multiplicity of Christian churches all struggling with communal problems in the face of modern Western culture and the rich diversity of cultures and religions throughout the world.

The book of Baruch shares the inclination of both the biblical tradition and the modern world to see history as a coherent, intelligible whole. Baruch fills in the narrative of Israel's exile, where details are scarce, and does so in a way that brings coherence, unity, and expectation to Israel's history. To preserve Israel's integrity in the face of Babylonian exile, the author of Baruch provides for the continuity of settlement, worship, and priestly institutions and thus mitigates the tragedy of the destruction. In a similar way, contemporary Christian modes of worship, behavior, fellowship, and social engagement must undergo reinterpretation and revitalization so that God's work in the community may be felt in the world.

BARUCH 1:15–3:8

PRAYER OF CONFESSION AND REPENTANCE

OVERVIEW

The Babylonian exiles' prayer, which they send to Jerusalem and Judea (1:13-14), consists of two long sections: a communal confession (1:15–2:10) and a prayer of repentance (2:11–3:8). The first is a public admission of sin and an acknowledgment of just punishment. Unlike similar confessions, it is not addressed directly to God in the second person, but gives a more "objective," third-person description of sin that instructs Israel. The confession of sin is personalized by a hortatory use of "we," which invites Israel to acknowledge its failings. The second part is a prayer of repentance and a petition for mercy addressed directly to God in the second person. This combination of confession and petition is typical of Second Temple prayers and can be found in Ezra 9:6-15; Neh 1:5-11; 9:5-37; Daniel 9; the *Prayer of Azariah* (Dan 3:3-22 LXX); and the *Words of the Luminaries* (4Q504-506).[28] Second Temple prayers and hymns frequently contain petitions for mercy, forgiveness of sins and deliverance from divine punishment and oppression; prayers of repentance and confessions of sin (see 4Q393), acceptance of divine punishment and acknowledgment of God's justice; and reviews of Israel's disobedience and of God's fidelity to Israel.[29]

Second Temple prayers developed from a variety of biblical literary forms, especially the communal lament, which is found in about forty psalms (e.g., Psalms 44; 74; 79; 80; 83), the book of Lamentations, and the prophets (e.g., Isa 63:7-19).

The confession of sin can be found in a number of places (e.g., Psalms 51; 106; Jer 32:17-23). The classical lament contains at least three elements: (1) a description of Israel's enemy, (2) Israel's desperate situation because of the enemy, and (3) a petition to God for help or mercy.[30] Some psalms complain so bitterly about Israel's suffering that they essentially indict God for abandoning Israel. After the destruction of Jerusalem, a heightened consciousness of sin transformed reproaches against God into an acknowledgment and acceptance of just divine judgment and punishment. The prayer of petition (often introduced by the imperative "Hear" as in Bar 2:14, 16, 31; 3:2, 4) was bolstered by a prayer of repentance or confession of sin. Israel's confession of its disobedience and acceptance of prophetic threats of punishment for sin are often balanced by a recollection of God's past mercy and saving acts toward Israel and praise for God's justice and aid. These Second Temple prayers still reflect the biblical covenant form: "1) confession of breach of covenant, 2) admission of God's righteousness, 3) recollection of God's mercies, and 4) appeal for mercy for God's own sake."[31]

Second Temple prayers share many literary characteristics and traditional attitudes, but do not have one strictly stereotypical form. They reflect the diverse circumstances of post-exilic Jewish communities and the vitality and creativity of the literary and liturgical tradition as it adapted to new circumstances by shifting away from classical

---

28. John J. Collins, *Daniel: With an Introduction to Apocalyptic Literature*, FOTL 20 (Grand Rapids: Eerdmans, 1984) 92.

29. See Bilhah Nitzan, *Qumran Prayer and Religious Poetry*, STDJ 12 (Leiden: Brill, 1994) 6-7, 85, 90-109; David Flusser, "Psalms: Hymns and Prayers," in *Jewish Writings of the Second Temple Period*, ed. Michael E. Stone, CRINT 2:2 (Philadelphia: Fortress, 1984) 570-73; Stevan G. Reif, *Judaism and Hebrew Prayer: New Perspectives on Jewish Liturgical History* (Cambridge: Cambridge University Press, 1995).

30. Claus Westermann traces the evolution of the lament from the Psalms and prophets into the Second Temple period. See Westermann, "Struktur und Geschichte der Klage in Alten Testament," *ZAW* 66 (1954) 44-80, translated as Part Four of *Praise and Lament in the Psalms* (Atlanta: John Knox, 1981; German original 1977) 165-213. See also his *Lamentations: Issues and Interpretation* (Minneapolis: Fortress, 1994; German original, 1990) 94-98.

31. Collins, *Daniel,* 92.

biblical forms toward a great variety of expressions using traditional vocabulary and theology in new settings and combinations. The rich fund of hymns and prayers found in Second Temple literature, most recently in the Dead Sea Scrolls, shows that they were popular during the Second Temple period.[32]

Was the prayer in Bar 1:15–3:8 possibly used in a public context? According to the narrative in Baruch, this prayer was supposed to be recited when the Judean community made its "confession in the house of the Lord on the days of the festivals and at appointed seasons" (1:14). The survival of a large number of these prayers in narrative contexts (e.g., Ezra 9; Daniel 9) and independently among the Dead Sea Scrolls (4Q393; 4Q507-509, parallel to 1Q34 and 34 bis) suggests that this popular prayer form may have been used in penitential settings. For example, the Qumran *Community Rule* (1QS 1-2; see also the *Damascus Document* 20:28-30) seems to reflect a communal confession of sins and plea for mercy as part of a covenant renewal ceremony. The confession and prayer of repentance in Bar 1:15–3:8 derives from this Second Temple tradition of public confession and repentance. However, since Bar 1:15–3:8 serves the overall theology and purposes of Baruch so thoroughly, it probably was a literary creation for this work rather than a pre-existing public prayer.

Though some have claimed that the prayer is loosely constructed, repetitive, and verbose,[33] it is in fact carefully constructed with balanced parts and interlocking themes. The confession (1:15–2:10) begins and ends with similar laments (1:15-18; 2:6-10) and encloses a recital of Israel's disobedience and punishment. The prayer of repentance (2:11–3:8) begins and ends with petitions (2:11-18; 3:1-8) and encloses a contrast of God's threat of punishment for disobedience (2:19-26) with God's promise of mercy (2:27-35). The confessions, descriptions of punishment, petitions to God, etc., are connected to one another by a rich web of language and themes that are repeated

and developed in different contexts. The unifying language and themes make it unlikely that several earlier prayers have been combined, as some claim.[34] Attempts to divide the prayer into a confession written by Baruch for those remaining in Jerusalem (1:15–2:5) and a prayer for the exiles (2:6–3:8) contradicts the author's consistent treatment of all Israel as one.[35]

The language, literary forms, and theology of the confession and prayer are based on the Hebrew Bible, especially the prayer in Daniel 9, the Baruch material in Jeremiah 32 and 36, and the deuteronomic theology found in Jeremiah, Deuteronomy, and the deuteronomic history. Most strikingly, Bar 1:15–2:18 follows closely the prayer of confession and request for forgiveness in Dan 9:4-19; from Bar 2:19 on, the Danielic material has been exhausted. In contrast to Bar 1:15–2:18, the prayer in Dan 9:4-19 addresses God directly and more concisely, with only a brief third-person description of what God has done in the middle (Dan 9:12-14). Baruch has expanded the Danielic prayer with language and thought drawn from Jeremiah and deuteronomic theology. Baruch has also changed the focus of the prayer from the destruction of Jerusalem and the Temple to the sufferings of exile. In the end, though, the prayers in Daniel and Baruch are so similar that either one is dependent on the other or both draw on a lost source. Few argue that Daniel is dependent on Baruch, but no consensus has emerged on whether Baruch depends on Daniel or both on a common source. The question is further complicated because most agree that the prayer in Daniel 9 is an earlier literary unit that has been incorporated, perhaps with revisions, into Daniel. Thus Moore claims that both prayers could derive from the late fourth century BCE, while Steck argues that Baruch depends both on the Danielic prayer

32. The public prayers of the community were for the most part not fixed in their wording and regular prayer practices developed gradually. See Joseph Heinemann, *Prayer in the Talmud: Forms and Patterns* (Berlin: de Gruyter, 1977; Hebrew original 1964); Nitzan, *Qumran Prayer and Religious Poetry.*

33. See Carey A. Moore, *Daniel, Esther, and Jeremiah: The Additions,* AB 44 (Garden City, N.Y.: Doubleday, 1977) 292.

34. Moore, ibid., 282, 291, argues that the prayer has four parts, all of which may have been independent. Moore's position is rejected by George W. E. Nickelsburg, *Jewish Literature Between the Bible and the Mishnah* (Philadelphia: Fortress, 1981) 110 and 152n. 24, and by Emil Schürer, Geza Vermes, Fergus Millar, and Martin Goodman, *The History of the Jewish People in the Age of Jesus Christ (175 B.C.–A.D. 135),* vol. 3.2 (Edinburgh: T. & T. Clark, 1987) 734n. 351. Recently, Goldstein and Steck have argued in detail for the literary unity of 1:15–3:8 within Baruch. See Goldstein, "The Apocryphal Book of Baruch," 187; Odil Hannes Steck, *Das apokryphe Baruchbuch: Studien zu Rezeption und Konzentration "kanonischer" Überlieferung* (Göttingen: Vandenhoeck & Ruprecht, 1993) 93-95.

35. See Moore, *Daniel, Esther, and Jeremiah: The Additions,* 282, 291, for the thesis of two addressees. See Steck, *Das apokryphe Baruchbuch,* 72-75, for the unity of the addressee as Israel.

and on its literary context in Daniel 9. In the end, both prayers were probably written in the mid-second century BCE during the Maccabean period.[36]

As has been noted, the author of Bar 1:15–3:8 has drawn heavily from the language and interpretations of Israel's history as it is found in Jeremiah. For example, Jeremiah 32 has especially influenced Baruch. During the Babylonian siege of Jerusalem, God instructs Jeremiah to purchase a family field (Jer 32:6-15) as a sign that Judah's defeat will not be permanent. Jeremiah then prays to understand God's purpose, reviewing the exodus, Israel's disobedience, and the ongoing Babylonian attack on Jerusalem. God replies with a description of Jerusalem's imminent defeat and destruction (Jer 32:26-35) and with a promise of restoration and a new covenant (Jer 32:27-44). Not just the words and phrases, but also the assumptions, theology, and attitudes in Jeremiah 32 have influenced the author of Baruch.[37] Baruch also draws upon and fills in the Jeremianic narrative.

36. See Moore, *Daniel, Esther, and Jeremiah: The Additions,* 293; Steck, *Das apokryphe Baruchbuch,* 88-92, 115.
37. See Steck, *Das apokryphe Baruchbuch,* 93, for this thesis.

For example, the transition from the description of Israel's punishment to the promise of restoration (Jer 32:35-36) implies, but does not state, that Israel has repented. Baruch 1:15–3:8 expresses Israel's repentance.

Behind both Jeremiah and Baruch lies the theology, language, and outlook of Deuteronomy. The theme of Baruch may be summarized by Deut 4:30-31:

> In your distress, when all these things have happened to you in time to come, you will return to the LORD your God and heed him. Because the LORD your God is a merciful God, he will neither abandon you nor destroy you; he will not forget the covenant with your ancestors that he swore to them.

The language of the blessing and curses in Deuteronomy 28 and of the covenant in Deuteronomy 30 are especially rich as a source for Baruch. Though dozens of linguistic and theological parallels could be given, this commentary will be limited to major cross-references and concentrate on the internal coherence and integrity of Baruch.

BARUCH 1:15–2:10, CONFESSION OF THE JUDEAN COMMUNITY

NAB

15 "Justice is with the LORD, our God; and we today are flushed with shame, we men of Judah and citizens of Jerusalem, **16** that we, with our kings and rulers and priests and prophets, and with our fathers, **17** have sinned in the LORD's sight **18** and disobeyed him. We have neither heeded the voice of the LORD, our God, nor followed the precepts which the Lord set before us. **19** From the time the LORD led our fathers out of the land of Egypt until the present day, we have been disobedient to the LORD, our God, and only too ready to disregard his voice. **20** And the evils and the curse which the LORD enjoined upon Moses, his servant, at the time he led our fathers

1,17: '*ōn* = '*ăšer.*
1,20: (*tous pateras 'ēmōn*) *ek gēs Aigyptou* (*dounai*): so LXX[MSS].

NRSV

15And you shall say: The Lord our God is in the right, but there is open shame on us today, on the people of Judah, on the inhabitants of Jerusalem, 16and on our kings, our rulers, our priests, our prophets, and our ancestors, 17because we have sinned before the Lord. 18We have disobeyed him, and have not heeded the voice of the Lord our God, to walk in the statutes of the Lord that he set before us. 19From the time when the Lord brought our ancestors out of the land of Egypt until today, we have been disobedient to the Lord our God, and we have been negligent, in not heeding his voice. 20So to this day there have clung to us the calamities and the curse that the Lord declared through his servant Moses at the

NAB

forth from the land of Egypt to give us the land flowing with milk and honey, cling to us even today. **21** For we did not heed the voice of the LORD, our God, in all the words of the prophets whom he sent us, **22** but each one of us went off after the devices of our own wicked hearts, served other gods, and did evil in the sight of the LORD, our God.

2 "And the LORD fulfilled the warning he had uttered against us: against our judges, who governed Israel, against our kings and princes, and against the men of Israel and Judah. **2** He brought down upon us evils so great that there has not been done anywhere under heaven what has been done in Jerusalem, as was written in the law of Moses: **3** that one after another of us should eat the flesh of his son or of his daughter. **4** He has made us subject to all the kingdoms round about us, a reproach and a horror among all the nations round about to which the LORD has scattered us. **5** We are brought low, not raised up, because we sinned against the LORD, our God, not heeding his voice.

6 "Justice is with the LORD, our God; and we, like our fathers, are flushed with shame even today. **7** All the evils of which the LORD had warned us have come upon us; **8** and we did not plead before the LORD, or turn, each from the figments of his evil heart. **9** And the LORD kept watch over the evils, and brought them home to us; for the Lord is just in all the works he commanded us to do, **10** but we did not heed his voice, or follow the precepts of the LORD which he set before us.

2,1: (*Iouda*) *tou agagein eph' ēmas kaka megala' a* (*ouk epoiētē*): so LXX[MSS].
2.2: *epoiēsen | epoiēthē = 'āśā* (impersonal)
2,4: (*edōken*) *'ēmas . . .* (*diespeiren*) *'ēmas*: so Lat[MSS], Armen. *abaton=śammâ*: cf. Jer 29 (49), 13.
2,5: (*kai*) *egenēthēmen* (*'ypotatō*): so LXX[MSS], Lat, P.
2,7: Omit *'a* after *tauta*: so LXX[MSS]; dittog.

NRSV

time when he brought our ancestors out of the land of Egypt to give to us a land flowing with milk and honey. [21]We did not listen to the voice of the Lord our God in all the words of the prophets whom he sent to us, [22]but all of us followed the intent of our own wicked hearts by serving other gods and doing what is evil in the sight of the Lord our God.

2 So the Lord carried out the threat he spoke against us: against our judges who ruled Israel, and against our kings and our rulers and the people of Israel and Judah. [2]Under the whole heaven there has not been done the like of what he has done in Jerusalem, in accordance with the threats that were[a] written in the law of Moses. [3]Some of us ate the flesh of their sons and others the flesh of their daughters. [4]He made them subject to all the kingdoms around us, to be an object of scorn and a desolation among all the surrounding peoples, where the Lord has scattered them. [5]They were brought down and not raised up, because our nation[b] sinned against the Lord our God, in not heeding his voice.

[6]The Lord our God is in the right, but there is open shame on us and our ancestors this very day. [7]All those calamities with which the Lord threatened us have come upon us. [8]Yet we have not entreated the favor of the Lord by turning away, each of us, from the thoughts of our wicked hearts. [9]And the Lord has kept the calamities ready, and the Lord has brought them upon us, for the Lord is just in all the works that he has commanded us to do. [10]Yet we have not obeyed his voice, to walk in the statutes of the Lord that he set before us.

[a] Gk *in accordance with what is*   [b] Gk *because we*

COMMENTARY

The prayer, sent by exiles in Babylon to be read aloud during the festivals, begins with a terse, blunt, and balanced description of the present relationship of Israel to God that acknowledges Israel's fault and vindicates God:

> To our Lord God righteousness,
> but to us shame of faces
> until this day.
> (Bar 1:15a, author's trans.)

Israel's shame is neither a feeling of embarrassment nor a sense of personal guilt; it is, rather, a loss of honor of "face"—that is, proper and expected public standing. A shamed or dishonored person no longer could participate normally in social relationships or function as an integral part of the village or nation. In this case, Israel frankly admits its disordered and untenable relationship with the most important member of its social world, God. This admission, elaborated in 1:15–2:10, lays a foundation for the lengthy appeal to God in 2:11–3:8.

The shame includes all Israel throughout history: the people of Judea and the inhabitants of Jerusalem, their traditional leaders from the top down (kings, rulers, priests, and prophets), and finally their ancestors who were in the same unacceptable relationship with God as Israel is in the present (1:15-16). Baruch adopts the outlook of Jeremiah, who condemns everyone, including (false) prophets (Jer 32:32). This view is contrary to Dan 9:6, which omits the prophets. Israel's shame derives from sin, disobedience, and failure to listen to God's voice and live according to divinely given statutes (vv. 17-18; cf. Deut 9:23; Jer 9:13; Dan 9:8-10). The prayer follows the deuteronomic tradition in which Israel's failings provide the stimulus for exhortation and prophecy.

The Greek verb for "negligent" (ἐσχεδιάζομεν *eschediazomen*, 1:19), which occurs here only in the LXX, may also mean to be "hasty" or "careless," so that Israel is ironically "quick not to listen." As a result (Bar 1:20), the curses promised in Deut 28:15-68 for disobedience have "clung" to Israel (3:4; Deut 28:21, 60). (The expression "calamities and the curse" is more literally and grammatically rendered, "the evil things, namely the curse.") Although God spoke to Israel through the prophets (1:21; see also 2:20, 24), as God had through Moses (cf. the unfaithful, corrupt prophets of 1:16), Israel did not listen but instead rejected God through idolatry and evil behavior. God in turn confirmed and carried out (ἔστησεν *estēse*; וַיָּקֶם *wayyāqem*) God's word (2:1). That is, God is faithful in punishing unfaithful Israel, from the judges and kings of the Bible to the time of the author of Baruch.

This lamentable history provokes a reflection from the author on the severity and uniqueness of the punishments associated with the destruction of Jerusalem (2:2-5). The reference to cannibalism (2:3) is threatened in the Bible (Lev 26:29; Deut 28:53; Jer 19:9) and is a stock horror story of sieges.[38] The author shields himself somewhat from the horrors of the destruction and exile by referring to the exiles as "them" (2:4-5). But at the end of v. 5, the author again identifies himself and his audience (the NRSV inserts "our nation" in place of "we") as the sinners who failed to listen to God's voice. This failure to listen appears frequently as the radical rupture in the relationship of people with God (1:19, 21; 2:10, 22, 24, 29; 3:4).

The confessional prayer ends just as it began, with an acknowledgment of God's justice and Israel's shame (2:6; cf. 1:15) and a summary of Israel's punishments and refusal to repent (2:7-10; cf. 1:18-22). All the disasters suffered by Israel were threatened by God in Scripture (2:7), were kept ready or watched over by God (2:9; cf. Dan 9:14), and were actuated by God (2:9). In all this, God is just (2:6) as are all the demands God makes (2:9). The phrase "all the works which he has commanded us [to do]" (2:9) may also mean "all his actions which he has ordered against us." (See similar phrases in the prayers in Neh 9:33; Dan 9:14.) The final verse (2:10) repeats and summarizes the confession with which the prayer began: Israel has neither listened to God's voice nor done what God commanded (cf. 1:18). They have shamed God and God's honor—that is, God's status

---

38. The reference to cannibalism (2:3) has been associated by some scholars with Josephus's story of the mother who ate her child during the siege of Jerusalem in 70 CE. See Josephus *The Jewish War* 5.3.4 201-13. This story was used to date Baruch to the first century CE. But cannibalism is a stock theme that cannot be used for dating.

as Creator and Ruler requires defense. Thus God has punished Israel, and in response Israel must honor God by acknowledging God's justice and turning to God for help. This Israel does in its prayer for mercy and deliverance.

Some commentators understand 2:6-10 as the beginning of the following prayer, but this paragraph is still in first- and third-person speech,[39] in contrast to 2:11–3:8, which is in the second person; and 2:6-10 summarizes and concludes (with an inclusio) the confession begun in 1:15. Israel's full confession of its failure to listen and obey and of its sin and just punishment lead to an extended request for divine mercy and deliverance motivated by desperate need. (See Reflections at 2:11–3:8.)

39. Moore, *Daniel, Esther, and Jeremiah: The Additions*; Doron Mendels, "Baruch, Book of," *ABD* 1:620.

BARUCH 2:11–3:8, PRAYER OF REPENTANCE FOR MERCY AND DELIVERANCE

NAB

11 "And now, LORD, God of Israel, you who led your people out of the land of Egypt with your mighty hand, with signs and wonders and great might, and with your upraised arm, so that you have made for yourself a name till the present day: 12 we have sinned, been impious, and violated, O LORD, our God, all your statutes. 13 Let your anger be withdrawn from us, for we are left few in number among the nations to which you scattered us. 14 Hear, O LORD, our prayer of supplication, and deliver us for your own sake: grant us favor in the presence of our captors, 15 that the whole earth may know that you are the LORD, our God, and that Israel and his descendants bear your name. 16 O LORD, look down from your holy dwelling and take thought of us; turn, O LORD, your ear to hear us. 17 Look directly at us, and behold: it is not the dead in the nether world, whose spirits have been taken from within them, who will give glory and vindication to the LORD. 18 He whose soul is deeply grieved, who walks bowed and feeble, with failing eyes and famished soul, will declare your glory and justice, LORD!

19 "Not on the just deeds of our fathers and our kings do we base our plea for mercy in your sight, O LORD, our God. 20 You have brought your wrath and anger down upon us, as you had warned us through your servants the prophets: 21 'Thus says the LORD: Bend your shoulders to the

2,18: Omit *autou* after *psychē*: so LXX[MSS].

NRSV

11And now, O Lord God of Israel, who brought your people out of the land of Egypt with a mighty hand and with signs and wonders and with great power and outstretched arm, and made yourself a name that continues to this day, 12we have sinned, we have been ungodly, we have done wrong, O Lord our God, against all your ordinances. 13Let your anger turn away from us, for we are left, few in number, among the nations where you have scattered us. 14Hear, O Lord, our prayer and our supplication, and for your own sake deliver us, and grant us favor in the sight of those who have carried us into exile; 15so that all the earth may know that you are the Lord our God, for Israel and his descendants are called by your name.

16O Lord, look down from your holy dwelling, and consider us. Incline your ear, O Lord, and hear; 17open your eyes, O Lord, and see, for the dead who are in Hades, whose spirit has been taken from their bodies, will not ascribe glory or justice to the Lord; 18but the person who is deeply grieved, who walks bowed and feeble, with failing eyes and famished soul, will declare your glory and righteousness, O Lord.

19For it is not because of any righteous deeds of our ancestors or our kings that we bring before you our prayer for mercy, O Lord our God. 20For you have sent your anger and your wrath upon us, as you declared by your servants the prophets,

NAB

service of the king of Babylon, that you may continue in the land I gave your fathers: **22** for if you do not hear the LORD's voice so as to serve the king of Babylon,

23 I will make to cease from the cities of Judah
and from the streets of Jerusalem
The sounds of joy and the sounds of
gladness,
the voice of the bridegroom
and the voice of the bride;
And all the land shall be deserted,
without inhabitants.'

24 But we did not heed your voice, or serve the king of Babylon, and you fulfilled the threats you had made through your servants the prophets, to have the bones of our kings and the bones of our fathers brought out from their burial places. **25** And indeed, they lie exposed to the heat of day and the frost of night. They died in dire anguish, by hunger and the sword and plague. **26** And you reduced the house which bears your name to what it is today, for the wickedness of the kingdom of Israel and the kingdom of Judah.

27 "But with us, O LORD, our God, you have dealt in all your clemency and in all your great mercy. **28** This was your warning through your servant Moses, the day you ordered him to write down your law in the presence of the Israelites: **29** If you do not heed my voice, surely this great and numerous throng will dwindle away among the nations to which I will scatter them. **30** For I know they will not heed me, because they are a stiff-necked people. But in the land of their captivity they shall have a change of heart; **31** they shall know that I, the LORD, am their God. I will give them hearts, and heedful ears; **32** and they shall praise me in the land of their captivity, and shall invoke my name. **33** Then they shall turn back from their stiff-necked stubbornness, and from their evil deeds, because they shall remember the fate of their fathers who sinned against the LORD. **34** And I will bring them back to the land which with my oath I promised to their fathers, to Abraham, Isaac and Jacob; and they shall rule it. I will make them increase; they shall not then diminish. **35** And I will establish for them, as an

2,23: *kai exōthen (ierousalēm)=ûmēḥûsôt*: cf Jer 7, 34.
2,25: *kai en apostolē=ûbaddeber*: cf Jer 32(39), 36.

NRSV

saying: [21]Thus says the Lord: Bend your shoulders and serve the king of Babylon, and you will remain in the land that I gave to your ancestors. [22]But if you will not obey the voice of the Lord and will not serve the king of Babylon, [23]I will make to cease from the towns of Judah and from the region around Jerusalem the voice of mirth and the voice of gladness, the voice of the bridegroom and the voice of the bride, and the whole land will be a desolation without inhabitants.

[24]But we did not obey your voice, to serve the king of Babylon; and you have carried out your threats, which you spoke by your servants the prophets, that the bones of our kings and the bones of our ancestors would be brought out of their resting place; [25]and indeed they have been thrown out to the heat of day and the frost of night. They perished in great misery, by famine and sword and pestilence. [26]And the house that is called by your name you have made as it is today, because of the wickedness of the house of Israel and the house of Judah.

[27]Yet you have dealt with us, O Lord our God, in all your kindness and in all your great compassion, [28]as you spoke by your servant Moses on the day when you commanded him to write your law in the presence of the people of Israel, saying, [29]"If you will not obey my voice, this very great multitude will surely turn into a small number among the nations, where I will scatter them. [30]For I know that they will not obey me, for they are a stiff-necked people. But in the land of their exile they will come to themselves [31]and know that I am the Lord their God. I will give them a heart that obeys and ears that hear; [32]they will praise me in the land of their exile, and will remember my name [33]and turn from their stubbornness and their wicked deeds; for they will remember the ways of their ancestors, who sinned before the Lord. [34]I will bring them again into the land that I swore to give to their ancestors, to Abraham, Isaac, and Jacob, and they will rule over it; and I will increase them, and they will not be diminished. [35]I will make an everlasting covenant with them to be their God and they shall be my people; and I will never again remove my people Israel from the land that I have given them."

NAB

eternal covenant, that I will be their God, and they shall be my people; and I will not again remove my people Israel from the land I gave them.

3 "LORD Almighty, God of Israel, afflicted souls and dismayed spirits call to you. **2** Hear, O LORD, for you are a God of mercy; and have mercy on us, who have sinned against you: **3** for you are enthroned forever, while we are perishing forever. **4** LORD Almighty, God of Israel, hear the prayer of Israel's few, the sons of those who sinned against you; they did not heed the voice of the LORD, their God, and the evils cling to us. **5** Remember at this time not the misdeeds of our fathers, but your own hand and name: **6** for you are the LORD our God; and you, O LORD, we praise! **7** For this, you put into our hearts the fear of you: that we may call upon your name, and praise you in our captivity, when we have removed from our hearts all the wickedness of our fathers who sinned against you. **8** Behold us today in our captivity, where you scattered us, a reproach, a curse, and a requital for all the misdeeds of our fathers, who withdrew from the LORD, our God."

3,2: (*akouson, Kyrie*) '*oti theos eleēmon ei*, (*kai eleēson*): cf LXX^MSS, Lat.
3,4: *tōn tethnēkotōn Israel*= *m^etē* (not *mētē*) *yiśrā'ēl*: cf. IS 41, 14. (*tēs phōnēs*) *Kyriou* (*theou autōn*): so LXX^MSS.
3,7: ('*emōn*) *tou* (*epikaleisthai*): so LXX^MSS.

NRSV

3 O Lord Almighty, God of Israel, the soul in anguish and the wearied spirit cry out to you. [2]Hear, O Lord, and have mercy, for we have sinned before you. [3]For you are enthroned forever, and we are perishing forever. [4]O Lord Almighty, God of Israel, hear now the prayer of the people[a] of Israel, the children of those who sinned before you, who did not heed the voice of the Lord their God, so that calamities have clung to us. [5]Do not remember the iniquities of our ancestors, but in this crisis remember your power and your name. [6]For you are the Lord our God, and it is you, O Lord, whom we will praise. [7]For you have put the fear of you in our hearts so that we would call upon your name; and we will praise you in our exile, for we have put away from our hearts all the iniquity of our ancestors who sinned against you. [8]See, we are today in our exile where you have scattered us, to be reproached and cursed and punished for all the iniquities of our ancestors, who forsook the Lord our God.

[a] Gk *dead*

COMMENTARY

2:11-18. The prayer of repentance includes further confession and a plea for mercy addressed directly to God in the second person. The beginning (vv. 15-19) draws phrases and themes from the end of the prayer in Dan 9:15-19. However, Baruch's prayer for restoration focuses on the people, in contrast to Dan 9:15-19, where the restoration of the city of Jerusalem is central to the author's concerns. The introduction to the prayer of repentance (vv. 11-13) invokes the founding event of Israel's relationship with God: liberation from slavery in Egypt, followed by memories of God's benevolent power and Israel's sins and just punishments. The language and theology of this appeal stand squarely in the deuteronomic tradi-

tion (e.g., Deut 6:21-23; Jer 32:20-21; Dan 9:15). The NRSV follows the Greek in stating that Israel has done wrong *"against all your [God's] ordinances"* (v. 11), but the Hebrew of Dan 9:16 suggests that the original text may have connected that final phrase with the following sentence. If so, then Israel would be asking God to turn away from anger on the basis of God's sense of justice: "Lord our God, *by all your just actions* let your anger turn away from us." At the end of the introduction (v. 13) the author cites other reasons for the exiles' prayer: They are few in number, scattered, and under the control of other nations (see also 2:14, 23, 29-30, 32, 34-35; 3:7-8). This prayer will seek to overcome the distance between

God and the people that has been opened up by sin, exile, and loss of autonomy.

The next two petitions (vv. 14-15 and vv. 16-18) appeal to God's self-interest as a motive for listening to Israel's requests. Since Israel and its people are called by God's name (see 2 Sam 12:28 for the custom of imposing a ruler's or an owner's name upon something), and since all the world knows of God through Israel, then the nations that have captured Israel will think ill of God if the people die and cannot testify to God's glory and justice. The people's requests are modestly appropriate to their powerless position in exile. First, they desire to find favor in the sight of their captors (v. 14), a practical good sought in several other biblical texts (1:12; 1 Kgs 8:50; Ps 106:46; Ezek 8:9), and then they ask to remain alive so that they can praise God (v. 18): "The person who is deeply grieved, who walks bowed and feeble, with failing eyes and famished soul, will declare your glory and righteousness, O Lord" (Bar 2:18).

This latter request turns the tables on God by transforming a deuteronomic punishment into a petition in lieu of death. In Deut 28:62-67, Moses threatens that if Israel disobeys God, it will be left few in number and scattered among all peoples; here in v. 13 these things have happened. Deuteronomy further warns that God will give Israel "a trembling heart, failing eyes and a languishing spirit" and constant fear because their lives are threatened (Deut 28:65-67). Baruch, after pointing out that the dead cannot praise God (v. 17), cleverly accepts the promised grief, debilitation, and fear in order to avoid the threat of death (v. 18). The very limited goals of these petitions bespeak a long experience of exile and political powerlessness and contrast strikingly with many prophetic promises and apocalyptic visions of national restoration.

2:19-35. The author begins his plea for God's mercy in v. 19 by confessing again that his ancestors and their kings did not act justly and by implicitly acknowledging that he has no right to God's help. He substantiates this admission with a narrative of Judah's disobedience, which led to the destruction of Jerusalem and the disinterring of their kings and ancestors by the victorious Babylonians. Baruch's narrative draws upon the accounts and prophetic threats in Jeremiah.

The Hebrew expression used to ask for God's

mercy (lit., "throw down a plea for mercy [ἔλεος eleos] before your face," 2:19) is found with similar Greek wording only in Dan 9:18 and in Jer 36:7; 37:20; 38:26; 42:2. Israel has been punished for disobeying prophetic commands (1:21; 2:24) to submit to Babylonian rule (cf. Jeremiah 27) by a miserable death from famine, war, and disease (Bar 2:25 and often in Jeremiah and elsewhere) and also by dishonor that continues up to the present, through the disinterment of royal bones (v. 24) and the ruin and decay of the Temple (v. 26). Jeremiah had predicted that King Jehoiakim's corpse would be exposed to the elements (Jer 36:30) as punishment for his rejection and burning of the scroll of Jeremiah's prophecies. The vague expression "you have made [the Temple] as it is today" (v. 26) refers to the Temple that was destroyed in the sixth century BCE and perhaps also to the sad state of the Temple or its administration when Baruch was written.

Baruch's prayer and the poems in 3:8–4:4 and 4:5–5:9 do not end with punishment, but with God's kindness and compassion toward Israel (v. 27). The Greek word translated as "kindness" (ἐπιείκεια epieikeia) refers to fairness and clemency in applying the law in a court, and the word for "compassion" (οἰκτιρμός oiktirmos) refers to those people or situations deserving of pity because of the suffering or loss involved. God's mercy was already promised and predicted in Scripture at the time when God told Moses to write down the law (Exod 24:2; Deut 31:9; cf. Josh 8:32). The "quotation" that follows (vv. 29-35) is not word for word from the Bible, but contains phrases and clauses from Moses' teaching in Deut 4:30-31; 30:1-10; and numerous places in Jeremiah, especially chap. 32. The use of Moses and Jeremiah here is consistent with references to Moses and the prophets earlier (Bar 1:20-21; 2:2, 20). The repetition of God's promises to Israel in a traditional form implies that God has already set the process in motion and that the end result of the promises is assured. Rejection of God's commands has led to the scattering of the people among the nations and a diminution of their numbers (vv. 29-30), but in exile the people will recognize their God (vv. 30-32) and obey because they acknowledge the sins of their ancestors. In Baruch, the people have precisely recognized God and acknowledged their sin through confession and prayer. Just as rejection of God in the promised land led to its loss, so also now recognition of God in exile leads to a return to the land (vv. 34-35). The promises made to the patriarchs will be fulfilled again in the restoration of the people as inhabitants and rulers of the land. The cycle of history will be complete when God binds the people through a permanent covenant, never to exile them again (v. 35). Sin, which soured Israel's relationship with God, has been overcome through this confession of sin, repentance, and remembering of God. Now all that is required is the return to the land of Israel.

3:1-8. The final petition of the prayer returns the focus to the exigencies of present exile and recapitulates many of the themes of the preceding prayer. Commentators have often understood this final section as an independent prayer because (1) it has a different tone; (2) it addresses God as the "Almighty" (vv. 1, 4 and nowhere else in Baruch; (3) it is spoken by the children of the original exiles (v. 7), not the Judean leaders and people listed in 1:13-16 or the original exiles themselves (2:13-14); and (4) it articulates Israel's urgent need for deliverance from exile and oppression, in contrast to 2:14, which seeks only a lightening of oppression. These tensions may indicate that an earlier source was used, but vv. 1-8 now bring Israel's confession and prayer of repentance to an acute and intense conclusion, preparing for the final two poems.

God is addressed for the first time as "Lord Almighty," Κύριος Παντοκράτωρ (*Kyrios Pantokratōr*) in Greek and יהוה צבאות (*Yahweh Ṣĕbāʾôt*) in Hebrew, by "a soul in anguish and a wearied spirit" appropriate to a lengthy exile. The prayer progresses expeditiously from a plea for mercy and a confession of sin (v. 2) to a striking contrast between God, who is permanently enthroned in heaven, and Israel, which is continually perishing (v. 3). The actors, their relationships, and the problem are patent and lead to a repeated, more urgent petition for help. The second half of the prayer begins with a repetition of

the call in v. 2 for God to hear Israel (v. 4). In the Greek, Israel is characterized as "dying" or "dead" (מיתי ישראל *mêtê Yiśrāʾēl*) Israel. The Greek translator probably misread the Hebrew מתי (*mĕtê*), meaning "men" (Isa 41:14; NRSV, "people") as *mĕtê Iśrāʾēl,* "the dead of Israel." Yet the Greek makes symbolic sense in this context (מיתי ישראל *mêtê Isrāʾēl*), for "dying Israel" recalls 2:17, which reminded God that the dead cannot praise God. The exiles point out that they are the generation subsequent to those whose sins caused the destruction of Jerusalem and exile (v. 2). Although they concede that their parents did not listen to God, they call on God to hear them because the evils (the literal meaning of κακά [*kaka*], translated by the NRSV here and in 1:20 as "calamities"; cf. Deut 28:21, 60) that "clung" to their sinful parents have also clung to them.

Baruch's prediction at the end of chap. 2 that Israel would remember God and then repent is now fulfilled. Israel remembers and praises God (vv. 6-7) and calls on God, with ironic appropriateness, *not* to remember its ancestors' sins (v. 5). The petitioners protest that they have fear of God in their hearts (v. 7) and have rejected their ancestors' iniquity (v. 8; cf. v. 4), and they urgently remind God again of their social dislocation and disorder ("scattered, cursed, reproached and punished," v. 8). The Greek word for "punished" (ὄφλησις *ophlēsis*) connotes a judicial penalty or fine in a lawsuit.

In summary, Israel's prayer of confession and repentance ends with a call to God to hear (vv. 2, 4) and to see (v. 8), but without a response and closure. God's redemption of Israel will be dramatically recounted at the end of Baruch (chap. 5). In the meantime, since the people claim to fear God (v. 7), the author of Baruch continues with a wisdom poem (3:9–4:4), which, like all wisdom literature, presumes a sense of awe, reverence, and fear of God. The wisdom poem also explains more fully why Israel is suffering in exile and how it should act while waiting for God.

REFLECTIONS

Modern spirituality stresses positive attitudes and goals such as growth, fulfillment, relationships, and love. Confessing and repenting of sin, error, and failure unsettle us and clash with our positive religious sensibility. Believers in the lonely contemporary world spontaneously seek God's love and promises of salvation. Unfortunately, many of us also seek to evade pervasive evil and the onerous labor of asking for forgiveness. Americans especially turn away too quickly from the pain and shame of sin and fail to envision a bright new future and a fresh start on the road to success. Our lack of self-esteem frequently prompts evasion and denial, rather than admission of responsibility or guilt. Few people know how to begin an apology or admit gracefully that they are wrong.

The confession and prayer of repentance in Baruch guides us through the necessary stages of healing and growth from acknowledging sin to admitting helplessness, calling on God, and repenting. The author of the confession cuts the knot of repentance in the fourteen English words that were cited at the beginning:

> To our Lord God righteousness,
> but to us shame of faces
> until this day. (Bar 1:15, author's trans.)

Frankly and openly, he contrasts human shame and failure with God's integrity and honor. From this admission all else follows in Baruch, including forgiveness, the revelation of God's law, renewed fidelity, the consolation of Jerusalem, and the return of the exiles.

In contrast to Baruch, many modern corporate and political leaders speak of moral, professional, and personal failure and evil in impersonal terms. They say, "Mistakes were made." But no name, least of all that of the speaker, appears. Sins that destroy body and spirit become lapses in judgment. The exposure of misdeeds arouses not a robust admission of wrongdoing, but attacks on the media or "whistleblowers," who are labeled enemies or liars.

The author of the confession in Baruch does not hide behind evasive rhetoric. Israel has refused to listen to and obey God from the exodus to the time of Baruch. God warned Israel, but the people did what they wanted. God responded with punishment. This concise history of Israel functions like the stories told at Alcoholics Anonymous meetings or like the feelings of participants in therapy sessions. No excuses, rationalizations, or extenuating circumstances can erase or hide the cold, painful facts of lives gone wrong, nor can they mitigate the destructive consequences to self, family, friends, and society.

Rigorous honesty, no matter how great the anguish, opens the way out. Paradoxically, the painful review of sin and guilt at the beginning of the prayer in Baruch brings coherence and consolation to the lives of those who ask for forgiveness. Authentic comprehension of the cause of the exile and Babylonian oppression opens the way for a different outcome. The rehearsal of disobedience and sin contrasts ironically and painfully with an urgent appeal for mercy from the very God who has been rejected. The refusal to hear God in the past (1:17, 21; 2:5) silently reproaches the petitioners even as it motivates their call for God to hear them now in their need (2:14, 16, 31; 3:2, 4). A stark awareness of God's anger and an immediate experience of punishment permeate the prayer. Yet the petitioners' very disarray and sense of loss turn them inevitably toward a restored community. A frank admission of fault sensitizes them to the most important things they have lost and seek to regain.

From talk shows to poetry readings, everyone complains about the disarray of society, the futility of work, the corruption of politics, and the collapse of the family. We blame impersonal bureaucracies, venal governments, "other" social groups and irrational, unknown forces for our misfortunes. Disconnected from our immediate world, we inevitably misunderstand the real causes of our confusion, alienation, and anxiety. Looking for a scapegoat, we lack responsibility and so, like children, cry out in frustrated impotence.

In Baruch, confession of sin and repentance make sense of Israel's disasters. When we admit our failings, misunderstandings, weaknesses, and harmful, sinful behaviors, we begin to understand the chaos and suffering of life as a consequence of disobedience to the laws that were meant to give shape to a just society. By that very act we diminish the scope and power of disorder and confusion within ourselves and in the world around us. In Baruch, Israel mourns the lost Temple (2:26), the ignored Torah (2:28), the conquered land (2:34), and the exiled people (2:23, 35). As a result, these four—Temple, Torah, land, and people—became the pillars of Second Temple Judaism, appearing constantly in Jewish prayers, poems, and narratives, most especially in the final two poems of Baruch. Reconstruction of modern life awaits a similar, frank inventory of our sins and losses so that we may know what God has given us as a foundation for our lives.

BARUCH 3:9–4:4

WISDOM ADMONITION AND EXHORTATION

OVERVIEW

This section of poetic wisdom admonition and exhortation differs significantly in style, terminology, genre, and background from the preceding prayer of confession and repentance; yet, it fits coherently into the argument of the book of Baruch as a whole. The admonition and exhortation teach Israel what to do after its confession and repentance by exploring the origins of sin and suggesting a better way to live through wisdom. The poem attributes the problem of sin and exile to the people's abandonment of wisdom and their inability to find it on their own. It argues that the law, especially Deuteronomy, is wisdom itself. Wisdom has been given to Israel by God as a basis for a renewed life of fidelity, and it demands understanding and obedience.

The logical structure of the poem is relatively simple, though attempts to recover its poetic structure vary greatly because we do not have its Hebrew original. The sections of the wisdom poem in this commentary follow the flow of its argument rather than a hypothetical reconstruction of the poetic form. The poem begins with a rebuke of Israel for abandoning wisdom and a call to learn wisdom (3:9-14). The question of where wisdom is to be found (3:15) leads to a long section that argues that different groups of people and even the ancient giants have been unable to find wisdom (3:16-31). God, the Creator who knows wisdom and gives it to Israel in the law, solves the problem (3:32–4:1). The poem ends with an exhortation for Israel to accept wisdom (4:2-4) as the solution to Israel's sinfulness and as the key to reestablishing a proper relationship with God.

This wisdom poem was probably written originally in Hebrew,[40] though many scholars still hold that it was composed in Greek. It may have circulated independently before being modified and incorporated into Baruch. It uses language and thought found in biblical and Second Temple wisdom literature, rather than the prophetic language dominant in the other parts of Baruch. It also contains the deuteronomic terms and ideas that appear in all sections of Baruch. The wisdom poem refers to God by the generic Greek term for God, Θεός (theos), a usage that accords with the international nature of ancient wisdom literature. In contrast, the first section of Baruch (1:1–3:8) calls God "Lord," in agreement with the Hebrew Bible and the Septuagint; however, the final section (4:5–5:9), which uses God (theos) frequently, also addresses God as "Everlasting" or "Eternal." The wisdom poem does not attribute anthropomorphic actions, feelings, or thoughts to God, in contrast to other parts of Baruch (e.g., 1:13; 2:11, 13, 16-17, 20; 4:9, 25, 27).[41] Consistent with the instructional and exhortatory purposes of the wisdom poem, the author frequently addresses Israel/Jacob by name ("Israel," 3:9-10, 24, 36; 4:4; "Jacob," 3:36; 4:2).

If the wisdom poem had an independent existence before being incorporated into Baruch, it provides little evidence for its date. The introduction suggests that the exile has been long (3:10-11), but this section may be a redactional link with the preceding prayer of repentance.[42] Most have dated the poem from the second century BCE to the first century CE.[43] Some have suggested a

---

40. See David G. Burke, *The Poetry of Baruch: A Reconstruction and Analysis of the Original Hebrew Text of Baruch 3:9–5:9,* SBLSCS 10 (Chico, Calif.: Scholars Press, 1982) for a recent and thorough argument of the case.

41. Carey A. Moore, *Daniel, Esther, and Jeremiah: The Additions,* AB 44 (Garden City, N.Y.: Doubleday, 1977) 304.

42. See B. N. Wambacq, "L'unité du livre de Baruch," *Bib* 47 (1966) 574-76; George W. E. Nickelsburg, *Jewish Literature Between the Bible and the Mishnah* (Philadelphia: Fortress, 1981) 153n. 31.

43. See Burke, *The Poetry of Baruch,* 26-28, for a summary of positions.

pre–Maccabean date,[44] and others hold that no date can be determined.[45] The affinities of this poem with Sirach 24 slightly favor the second century BCE, but wisdom themes persisted over the centuries. The wisdom poem has some thematic similarities with the prayer for wisdom in the book of Wisdom (Wis 9:1-18), but the correspondences are rather vague and too imprecise to support an argument for dependency. (See Bar 3:29 and Wis 9:4 on bringing Wisdom down from heaven; Bar 4:4 and Wis 9:10 on learning what is pleasing to God from wisdom; Bar 3:36 and Wis 9:17 on God's sending wisdom to humans.) Even if a relationship could be established, the date of the book of Wisdom is very uncertain (1st cent. BCE–1st cent. CE). Finally, those who date the final section of Baruch using *Psalms of Solomon* 11 sometimes try to date the wisdom poem along with it, but the relationship of Baruch with *Psalms of Solomon* is disputed (see the next section).

Of more interest and utility for understanding Baruch is the place of the wisdom poem in Israelite and Second Temple wisdom literature. Poems about wisdom, especially personified Wisdom, have their major biblical source in Proverbs 1–9, and prayers for wisdom often stem from Solomon's prayer in 1 Kgs 3:6-9. Sirach begins with poems on wisdom (Sir 1:1-10) and fear of God (Sir 1:11–2:18) and continues with several more wisdom poems (Sir 4:11-19; 14:20–15:10; 24:1-29; 39:1-11). The book of Wisdom contains both poems to wisdom (Wis 6:12-25; 7:22–8:21; chap. 10) and prayers for wisdom (Wis 7:15-22; 9:1-18). The *Letter of Aristeas* affirms the necessity of praying as part of living the philosophical life (#256). The Dead Sea Scrolls contain an exhortation to seek wisdom (4Q185), a warning concerning the seductive evil woman as a symbol of foolishness (4Q184), and a series of blessings of the wise (4Q525). Interestingly,

wisdom and apocalyptic perspectives are joined in the Dead Sea Scrolls (e.g., 4Q415-418, Sapiential Work A). Although Baruch lacks any apocalyptic influences, its wisdom poem leads to the final section of Baruch, where God intervenes in history and returns Israel from exile (Bar 4:5–5:9).

The wisdom influences in Bar 3:9–4:4 are patent. Four Greek words concerned with wisdom appear frequently with overlapping meanings that are not consistently translated in the NRSV. The most common biblical Greek word for "wisdom," σοφία (*sophia*), occurs twice (3: 12, 23). Three other Greek words are more prominent: φρόνησις (*phronēsis*), which has the connotation of "prudence," is translated by the NRSV as "wisdom" (3:9, 14, 28), the same word used for *sophia*. The other two words are ἐπιστήμη (*epistēmē*), translated as "knowledge" (3:20, 27, 36), and σύνεσις (*synesis*), translated as "understanding" (3:14, 23 [twice], 32). All four words are in the Greek feminine gender and are referred to as "she" or "her" in other verses. "Understanding"/*synesis* (3:14) seems to be the referent in the thematic 3:15. "Knowledge"/*epistēmē* (3:20) is the referent to the series of pronouns in 3:20-22. In the next verse (3:23), "understanding"/*synesis* occurs twice in parallel, followed by *sophia* and a pronoun in parallel. After "knowledge"/*epistēmē* in 3:27, *phronēsis*/"wisdom" (3:28) becomes the referent to the pronouns in 3:29-32, a critical turning point in the poem. At the end of the poem God finds "knowledge"/*epistēmē* (3:36), which remains the referent through 3:37–4:2 and is identified with the law and the book of commandments of God. A mapping of these usages and of the poetic parallelisms in the poem suggests that the author is not distinguishing these four words from one another in any meaningful way and that he is using them all to refer to what is usually called "wisdom" in English. The close relationship of the words for "knowledge," "understanding," and "wisdom" can be seen in the cluster of terms in Prov 1:1-7.

"Way" (ὁδός *hodos*) is a dominant metaphor both in this poem and in wisdom literature. The way of wisdom, which humans cannot find and which God knows, appears in Bar 3:13, 20-21, 23, 27, 31, 36. The common poetic pair "way" and "path(s)" appears in 3:31, as it does in Pss 27:11; 77:19 and in Prov 2:8, 20; 4:11, 14; 8:20. "Way"

44. Burke, ibid., 29, suggests a pre-Maccabean date because of the emphasis on fidelity to Torah. But Odil Hannes Steck, *Das apokryphe Baruchbuch: Studien zu Rezeption und Konzentration "kanonischer" Überlieferung* (Göttingen: Vandenhoeck & Ruprecht, 1993) 161-63, suggests the Maccabean period partly for the same reason. Steck stresses the strong thematic relationships and outlooks shared among the parts of Baruch and so dates the poem to the time he suggests for the composition of the whole book, the Maccabean period. See ibid., 158-63, 285-303.

45. Moore, *Daniel, Esther, and Jeremiah: The Additions,* 305; Emil Schürer, Geza Vermes, Fergus Millar, and Martin Goodman, *The History of the Jewish People in the Age of Jesus Christ (175 B.C.–A.D. 135)* (Edinburgh: T. & T. Clark, 1987) 3:736.

can also be used in a negative sense of the way to death (Prov 2:18). Baruch draws upon specific biblical usages of this metaphor. For example, in Bar 3:13 the prophet says to Israel, "If you had walked in the way of God, you would be living in peace forever." Similarly, Prov 3:17 says of wisdom, "Her ways are ways of pleasantness, and all her paths are peace." In Job 28, on which part of this poem is modeled, mortals do not know the way to wisdom (Job 28:13; Bar 3:16-31) but God does (Job 28:23; Bar 3:36). Baruch combines the deuteronomic and wisdom traditions. Deuteronomy speaks of following the path God has commanded in order to live (5:33) and frequently admonishes Israel not to turn away from the way God has commanded (9:12, 16; 11:28; 13:5; 31:29).

The author of Baruch further enriches this deuteronomic linking of the way with God's commandments by identifying wisdom with the commandments and by having God, who knows "the whole way to knowledge" (Bar 3:36) reveal knowledge to Israel in the commandments and in the law (4:1). Deuteronomy has profoundly affected the wisdom poem, as it has the other parts of Baruch. The threat that God will exile the people from the land if they disobey the commandments, the promise that God will be merciful if the people will repent, and the praise of God's power and accomplishments (Deut 4:25-40) are especially influential, as is the warning about exile and choosing life through the commandments rather than death through disobedience (Deuteronomy 30).

The most obvious, immediate influence on Bar 3:15-37 is the wisdom poem in Job 28. Baruch 3:9–4:4 does not follow Job 28 as closely as Bar 1:15–2:18 followed Dan 9:4-19, but it draws numerous thematic units and words from Job. For example, in both texts the wisdom of the nations is viewed negatively (Job 28:1-22; Bar 3:16-31), and God's wisdom is viewed positively (Job 28:23-27; Bar 3:32-37). Both refer extensively to the parts of the cosmos, including the earth (Job 28:1-13; Bar 3:16-23) and the sea (Job 28:21; Bar 3:26-29). Sequences of thought are also reproduced (Bar 3:30, 31, 33 from Job 28:15-19, 23-24, 26).

Baruch is not simply a revision of Job 28, since it is also influenced by the phraseology and thought of some psalms (e.g., Psalms 49; 119; 147). Psalm 147 has a cluster of themes found in Baruch, such as God's control over the stars (Ps 147:4; Bar 3:34), the giving of the commandments to Israel/Jacob (Ps 147:19; Bar 3:36), and Israel's special advantage in relationship with God (Ps 147:20; Bar 4:3). Similarly, the wisdom poem in Sirach 24 shares themes with the end of this poem (3:36–4:1). In Sirach, Wisdom leaves the heavenly assembly on God's command to live in Jerusalem among God's people. Sirach narrates the story of Wisdom's descent in detail, along with her subsequent flourishing in Israel. In contrast, Baruch briefly states that God gave knowledge to Israel, and so she lived with humans on earth (3:36-37). Each poem then states in a verse that wisdom is the biblical law: "All this is the book of the covenant of the Most High God, the law that Moses commanded us" (Sir 24:23); "She is the book of the commandments of God, the law that endures forever" (Bar 4:1). Sirach and Baruch here share a tradition, but it is not clear whether one has influenced the other or whether they have drawn on a similar source.

In summary, the language, themes, and thought of Baruch share much with the wisdom tradition, but, except for Job 28 and Sirach 24, no substantial literary connection between Baruch's wisdom poem and the wisdom poems in Proverbs, Ecclesiastes, or the book of Wisdom emerges.

BARUCH 3:9-14, REBUKE AND CALL TO ISRAEL

<table>
<tr><td>

NAB

9 Hear, O Israel, the commandments of life:
  listen, and know prudence!
10 How is it, Israel,
    that you are in the land of your foes,
    grown old in a foreign land,
  Defiled with the dead,
11   accounted with those destined for the
      nether world?
12 You have forsaken the fountain of wisdom!
13   Had you walked in the way of God,
    you would have dwelt in enduring peace.
14 Learn where prudence is,
    where strength, where understanding;
  That you may know also
    where are length of days, and life,
    where light of the eyes, and peace.

</td><td>

NRSV

⁹ Hear the commandments of life, O Israel;
  give ear, and learn wisdom!
¹⁰ Why is it, O Israel, why is it that you are in
      the land of your enemies,
    that you are growing old in a foreign
      country,
    that you are defiled with the dead,
¹¹ that you are counted among those in Hades?
¹² You have forsaken the fountain of wisdom.
¹³ If you had walked in the way of God,
    you would be living in peace forever.
¹⁴ Learn where there is wisdom,
    where there is strength,
    where there is understanding,
  so that you may at the same time discern
    where there is length of days, and life,
    where there is light for the eyes, and peace.

</td></tr>
</table>

COMMENTARY

The initial exhortation for Israel to hear the commandments and wisdom combines the deuteronomic call to hear God's voice and commandments (Deut 5:1; 6:3-4; 30:12-13; 31:12-13), wisdom literature's instruction that children/students listen to their parent/teacher (Prov 1:8; 4:1; 8:32-33), and Lady Wisdom's invitation to the people to learn from her (Prov 1:20-21; 8:1-5). The identification of wisdom with the commandments is also found in Sir 24:23. The phrase "commandments of life" (3:9) comes from Ezek 33:15, but it echoes the sapiential and deuteronomic commonplace that obedience to the commandments leads to life and prosperity, and disobedience to death and disaster (Deut 4:1; Prov 4:4, 13). The parallel second half of 3:9 says, literally, "give ear in order to know prudence." The choice of the Greek word φρόνησις (phronēsis, "prudence"; translated by the more inclusive term "wisdom" in the NRSV) emphasizes practical wisdom, oriented to action, and thus corresponds to the commandments in the first half of the verse. Ben Sira has a similar expression when he turns

from describing God's revelation to all humans to God's revelation to Israel: "He bestowed knowledge upon them, and allotted to them the law of life" (Sir 17:11).

The poet next rebukes Israel with a four-part question that taunts them to explain the reality of their lengthy exile, which is like death and burial (vv. 10-11). Then he answers the questions in terms of the exhortation in v. 9: If Israel had heard the commandments of life, then they would have walked in the way of God and would be living in peace instead of exile (vv. 9*a*, 13). But Israel has abandoned the fountain of prudence (wisdom), rather than listening and learning (vv. 9*b*, 12). The final admonition (v. 14) holds out the promise of wisdom, strength, life, light, and peace in contrast to exile and death in the earlier rebuke (vv. 10-11). Wisdom as defined here powerfully and directly affects the course and quality of life. The metaphor of "light" at the end of v. 14 consistently connotes life, wisdom, and God in Baruch (vv. 14, 20, 33; 4:2 in this poem and 1:12; 5:9 in the rest of

Baruch). The hopeful message of this introductory section is worked out in the argument of the poem and will be repeated in the conclusion (4:2-4). (See Reflections at 4:2-4).

BARUCH 3:15-31, WISDOM HIDDEN FROM HUMANS

NAB	NRSV

15 Who has found the place of wisdom,
    who has entered into her treasuries?
	[15] Who has found her place?
	    And who has entered her storehouses?

16 Where are the rulers of the nations,
    they who lorded it over the wild beasts of
    the earth,
	[16] Where are the rulers of the nations,
	    and those who lorded it over the animals
	        on earth;

17   and made sport of the birds of the heavens:
    They who heaped up the silver
    and the gold in which men trust;
    of whose possessions there was no end?
	[17] those who made sport of the birds of the air,
	    and who hoarded up silver and gold
	    in which people trust,
	    and there is no end to their getting;

18 They schemed anxiously for money,
    but there is no trace of their work:
	[18] those who schemed to get silver, and were
	        anxious,
	    but there is no trace of their works?

19 They have vanished down into the nether
        world,
    and others have risen up in their stead.
	[19] They have vanished and gone down to Hades,
	    and others have arisen in their place.

20 Later generations have seen the light,
    have dwelt in the land,
    But the way to understanding they have not
        known,
	[20] Later generations have seen the light of day,
	    and have lived upon the earth;
	    but they have not learned the way to
	        knowledge,

21   they have not perceived her paths, or
    reached her;
    their offspring were far from the way to her.
	nor understood her paths,
	    nor laid hold of her.
	[21] Their descendants have strayed far from her[a]
	    way.

22 She has not been heard of in Canaan,
    nor seen in Teman.
	[22] She has not been heard of in Canaan,
	    or seen in Teman;

23 The sons of Hagar who seek knowledge on earth,
    the merchants of Midian and Teman,
    the phrasemakers seeking knowledge,
    These have not known the way to wisdom,
    nor have they her paths in mind.
	[23] the descendants of Hagar, who seek for understanding on the earth,
	    the merchants of Merran and Teman,
	    the story-tellers and the seekers for understanding,
	    have not learned the way to wisdom,
	    or given thought to her paths.

24 O Israel, how vast is the house of God,
    how broad the scope of his dominion:
	[24] O Israel, how great is the house of God,
	    how vast the territory that he possesses!

25 Vast and endless,
    high and immeasurable!
	[25] It is great and has no bounds;
	    it is high and immeasurable.

26 In it were born the giants, renowned at the first,	

3,18: Omit *'oti* before *'oi to*: so LXX^{MSS}, Lat; dittog.
3,21: (*tes'odou*) *autēs* (*porrō*): so 2 LXX^{MSS}, P.
3,23: *oute* (*'uiou Agar*) . . . *synesin epi gēs*: so LXX^{MSS}. *Madian* for *Merran*: confusion in Hebrew.
3,26: (*'oi onomastoi*) *'oi* (*ap archēs*): so LXX^{MSS}.

[a] Other ancient authorities read *their*

NAB

stalwarts, skilled in war.
27 Not these did God choose,
nor did he give them the way of
understanding;
28 They perished for lack of prudence,
perished through their folly.
29 Who has gone up to the heavens and taken
her,
or brought her down from the clouds?
30 Who has crossed the sea and found her,
bearing her away rather than choice gold?
31 None knows the way to her,
nor has any understood her paths.

NRSV

26 The giants were born there, who were famous
of old,
great in stature, expert in war.
27 God did not choose them,
or give them the way to knowledge;
28 so they perished because they had no wisdom,
they perished through their folly.

29 Who has gone up into heaven, and taken her,
and brought her down from the clouds?
30 Who has gone over the sea, and found her,
and will buy her for pure gold?
31 No one knows the way to her,
or is concerned about the path to her.

COMMENTARY

After exhorting Israel to seek wisdom, the author must help them acquire it. Unfortunately, humans have a dismal record in the search for wisdom. To the opening question: "Who has found her place?/ And who has entered her storehouses?" (v. 15), the author must answer: "No one knows the way to her,/ or is concerned about the path to her" (v. 31). In quick succession he summarizes the failures of the powerful and wealthy (vv. 16-19) along with generations of humankind, including the neighbors of Israel (vv. 20-23) and even the giants (vv. 24-28).

The author of Baruch was guided by an earlier poem about hidden wisdom in Job 28:

"But where shall wisdom be found?
And where is the place of understanding?
Mortals do not know the way to it,
and it is not found in the land of the living.
The deep says, 'It is not with me,'
and the sea says, 'It is not with me.'
It cannot be gotten for gold,
and silver cannot be weighed out as its price.
It cannot be valued in the gold of Ophir,
in precious onyx or sapphire.
Gold and glass cannot equal it,
nor can it be exchanged for jewels of fine gold."
(Job 28:12-15 NRSV)

Both Job and Baruch comment on the difficulty of finding wisdom and the ineffectiveness of ordinary human efforts to acquire it. Baruch dramatizes the search by reviewing the efforts of various classes of people who might be expected to be wise. Preeminently in a hierarchical society, the "rulers of the nations" might be expected to be as wise as they are powerful and rich, but they have died (vv. 16-19). Baruch's critique of the rulers subtly comments on several types of human failure. That they are leaders of the "nations" implicitly differentiates Israel from the nations and leaves room for God's gift of wisdom to Israel at the end of the poem, in contrast to the nations' lack of wisdom (vv. 21-23). The leaders are described as "those who lord it over the animals on earth" (v. 16), a tradition found also in Jer 27:6; Dan 2:27-28; and Jdt 11:7, where the king rules humans and animals. These leaders are subtly identified with all humanity, which was given dominion over the earth and its creatures in the creation story (Gen 1:28). The strongest criticism is reserved for the triviality and irresponsibility of the wealthy (vv. 17-18). They make sport with or tease the birds of the air (see also Job 41:5), instead of learning wisdom about God and creation from them (Job 12:7-12); they rely on their wealth for everything, rather than seeking wisdom.

The author articulates his harsh comments on the excessive, foolish reliance on wealth in a string of clauses and participles in vv. 17-18. The meaning of the second half of v. 18 is difficult. It continues the train of thought of the first half of the verse, if the Greek is translated (contrary to the NRSV) to refer to the clandestine activities used to acquire wealth: "those who schemed to get silver, and were anxious, and [καί *kai*] there is no discovering their works?" Or the Greek may communicate the common wisdom theme that there is no understanding of some things (see Job 5:9 of God; Prov 25:3 of kings), applied in this case to the activity of making or acquiring silver.[46] In the end, the result of all this effort is not wisdom, but death for humanity throughout its history (v. 19).

The chronic inability of human beings to find wisdom is expanded to include later generations and is concretized with the name of countries, peoples, and occupations (vv. 20-23). Ironically, these later generations have seen the "light" of day, but they have not gained knowledge (v. 20), which would give the light of wisdom (v. 33; 4:2). The author speaks insistently of the way to knowledge (ἐπιστήμη *epistēmē*), a metaphor that reaches a climax in v. 36, where God is the one who "found the whole way to knowledge" and gave it to Israel. Neither later generations nor the descendants of Hagar have learned the "way" (ὁδός *hodos*) to knowledge (vv. 20, 31) and wisdom (v. 23), nor have they understood (v. 20), given thought (v. 23), or been concerned about (v. 31) her "paths" (τρίβοι *triboi*). Rather, humans have "strayed far from [knowledge's] way" (v. 21).

Israel's immediate neighbors are specified as the nations that have not found wisdom. Traditional eastern Mediterranean wisdom literature, including Proverbs and Job, acknowledges the universality of human wisdom. The tradition that the nations do not have wisdom comes from the prophets (e.g., Isa 19:11-15).[47] But in Baruch, Canaan, meaning cities like Tyre (Ezek 28:12; Zech 9:2) and Teman—an Edomite city noted for its wisdom in Job 2:11 (Eliphaz the Temanite); Jer 49:7; and Obad 8-9—are charged with not having heard of wisdom (v. 22). The Arabs, who were identified as descendants of Ishmael, son of Hagar, and specifically the merchants of two Arabian

cities, Merran (Midian, south of Edom) and Tema, likewise do not have wisdom, even though they are engaged in international trade and should have gained great wisdom from many peoples. (The NRSV translates "Teman" because the Greek uses the same name, θαιμαν (*Thaiman*) for Tema in Arabia and Teman in Edom.) The traditional non-Israelite storytellers who might have passed on traditional wisdom of many peoples and the generic "seekers of understanding" (σύνεσις *synesis*) have all failed to learn the way of "wisdom" (σοφία *sophia*) (v. 23). This verdict echoes the author's diagnosis of the cause of Israel's exile as failure to walk in the way of God (v. 13).

Since wisdom has not been found on earth among humans in history, the search for wisdom moves on to the universe as a whole in primeval times (vv. 24-31). The whole universe is the house of God here (v. 24), in contrast to the Hebrew Bible, where the house of God is a temple or a building. This interpretation stems from God's knowledge of, presence in, and sovereignty over the whole of the universe, ideas that are found in the Hebrew Bible (Job 28:24; 11;7-9), in the Greek Bible (Wis 7:24; 8:1) and in Philo (*De aeternitate mundi* 112). The author of Baruch is coy about whether wisdom is actually to be found in the house of God. Consistent with the previous section, he affirms that another group, the primeval giants, lacked prudence (v. 27, φρόνησις *phronēsis,* translated by the NRSV as "wisdom") and perished (vv. 26-28). The "giants" were the progeny of angels who disobeyed God and had intercourse with human women.[48] In *1 Enoch* 7, it is noted that the angels taught their human wives certain kinds of medicine and magic, but the author of Baruch judges that this kind of "knowledge" (*epistēmē*), which heals the body, is not what is required for "life" (vv. 9, 13-14; 4:1), because the giants engaged in violent, cannibalistic behavior, which is the opposite of prudent, wise behavior. Thus, even more than human figures in primeval times, they had no grasp of wisdom.

The futile search for hidden wisdom ends just as it began, with rhetorical questions that require a negative answer (vv. 29-30, parallel to v. 15). Together they eliminate wisdom's storehouses,

46. See O. C. Whitehouse, "1 Baruch," in *The Apocrypha and Pseudepigrapha of the Old Testament,* vol. 1, ed. R. H. Charles (Oxford: Clarendon, 1913) 588-59; David G. Burke, *The Poetry of Baruch: A Reconstruction and Analysis of the Original Hebrew Text of Baruch 3:9–5:9,* SBLSCS 10 (Chico, Calif.: Scholars Press, 1982) 89, for these and other options.

47. See Gerhard von Rad, *Wisdom in Israel* (Nashville: Abingdon, 1972) 318-19.

48. A synopsis of this version of the story of primeval evil is preserved in Gen 6:1-4.

heaven, and foreign lands as viable places to find wisdom. However, biblical readers will not lose hope because they know that one need not seek God's commandments in the heavens or across the sea, since they are, in fact, present among Israel (Deut 30:12-13). And after a summary statement

of the problem, "No one knows the way to her [the antecedent is *phronēsis* in v. 28], or is concerned about the path to her" (v. 31), the author turns to the solution and source of wisdom: God. (See Reflections at 4:2-4.)

BARUCH 3:32–4:1, GOD GIVES WISDOM TO ISRAEL

NAB	NRSV
32 Yet he who knows all things knows her; he has probed her by his knowledge— He who established the earth for all time, and filled it with four-footed beasts; **33** He who dismisses the light, and it departs, calls it, and it obeys him trembling; **34** Before whom the stars at their posts shine and rejoice; **35** When he calls them, they answer, "Here we are!" shining with joy for their Maker. **36** Such is our God; no other is to be compared to him: **37** He has traced out all the way of understanding, and has given her to Jacob, his servant, to Israel, his beloved son. **38** Since then she has appeared on earth, and moved among men. **4** She is the book of the precepts of God, the law that endures forever; All who cling to her will live, but those will die who forsake her.	³² But the one who knows all things knows her, he found her by his understanding. The one who prepared the earth for all time filled it with four-footed creatures; ³³ the one who sends forth the light, and it goes; he called it, and it obeyed him, trembling; ³⁴ the stars shone in their watches, and were glad; he called them, and they said, "Here we are!" They shone with gladness for him who made them. ³⁵ This is our God; no other can be compared to him. ³⁶ He found the whole way to knowledge, and gave her to his servant Jacob and to Israel, whom he loved. ³⁷ Afterward she appeared on earth and lived with humankind. **4** She is the book of the commandments of God, the law that endures forever. All who hold her fast will live, and those who forsake her will die.

COMMENTARY

To find wisdom the author turns to "the one who knows all things" (3:32). This figure is identified with active participles and is called "our God" only in 3:35, although God has already been foreshadowed in 3:24-25, where the search moved to God's house, the universe in its entirety. Similarly, here

God "found her [φρόνησις *phronēsis,* last named in 3:28] by his understanding [σύνεσις *synesis*]" (3:32) and then created, controlled, prepared, and filled the universe (3:32*b*-34). The language used here to describe God the Creator comes from the wisdom tradition. God orders light and the stars;

they obey, as they do in Job 37:11. The stars stand guard duty (3:34), as they do in Sir 43:10. God's wisdom, creative power, and control over nature are intimately related and mutually supportive here and in wisdom literature in general.

God resolves the problem of the poem, the human search for wisdom, by giving knowledge to Israel in the form of "the book of the commandments of God and the law that endures forever" (4:1)—that is, the Torah, or Pentateuch. Baruch introduces his solution to the problem of knowledge by directly addressing his audience with an expression of praise for Israel's God, who has wisdom: "This is our God; no other can be compared. . . . / He found the whole way to knowledge" (3:36)[49] The Hebrew Bible often affirms that God is incomparable or the only God. It also says that God's wisdom is greater than that of the nations (Jer 10:6-7). The claim that God found the "whole way of knowledge" rests upon acceptance of God as the Creator who knows all. Although the "way" to wisdom has been a central metaphor in this poem (see the Commentary on 3:20), the finding of the way of knowledge is less a search and more a recognition that God and knowledge/wisdom are one and the same. In view of the identity of the law with wisdom in 4:1, the idea of the whole or entire way of knowledge may be associated with the whole or entire commandment or way God placed before Israel in Deuteronomy (תורה [tôrâ] in Deut 4:8; מצוה [miṣwâ] in Deut 5:31; 6:25; 8:1; 11:8, 22; 15:5; 19:9; 27:1).

Drawing upon the whole biblical tradition of God's choice of Jacob/Israel as the forebear of God's own people, the author affirms that God gave this essential, but hard to find, knowledge to Israel and that knowledge appeared on earth and lived among humans (vv. 36-37; vv. 37-38 NAB).[50] God's gift of knowledge to Israel and wisdom's presence on earth within Israel is common in the Second Temple wisdom tradition (Sir 24:8, 10-12; Wis 9:10). The wisdom poem in Sirach 24

narrates in detail God's order to Wisdom that she leave the divine assembly in heaven and live in Jerusalem among Israel and Wisdom's flourishing and attractiveness to the people of Israel. Baruch merely alludes to this tradition in dependence on Sirach or a common source. Baruch, however, enshrines wisdom among the people in exile and in the land, in contrast to Sirach, who stresses the land and Jerusalem as the dwelling place of wisdom (Sir 24:8-14). The most concrete and satisfactory answer to the question asked in 3:15 concerning where wisdom is to be found appears finally in 4:1: Wisdom/prudence/knowledge is (in a more literal translation than the NRSV) "the book of the commandments of God and the law enduring forever." The identification of wisdom with Torah, the law and holy book of Israel, completes the incorporation of the international wisdom of the ancient Near East into Israel's developing biblical traditions. This trend began in Deuteronomy, where Moses, exhorting Israel to obey the commandments God gave them, refers to Near Eastern wisdom: "You must observe them [the commandments] diligently, for this will show your wisdom and discernment to the peoples, who, when they hear all these statutes, will say, 'Surely this great nation is a wise and discerning people!' " (Deut 4:6 NRSV). The claim to an exclusive possession of wisdom and the identification of wisdom with the law (i.e., the Bible, especially the Pentateuch) appears at the climax of the wisdom poem in Sirach 24: "All this [the wisdom he has been teaching] is the book of the covenant of the Most High God,/the law that Moses commanded us/ as an inheritance for the congregations of Jacob" (Sir 24:23 NRSV).

The book of Wisdom (1st cent. BCE or CE) does not explicitly articulate the identification of wisdom with the Bible, but its unique combination of biblical or Greek wisdom serves to support the authenticity and superiority of Jewish wisdom in a Greek world.[51] The consequences of adhering to wisdom, commandments, and law in Baruch is articulated in the deuteronomic contrast of life versus death (Bar 4:1; Deut 30:15, 19), a connection suggested also by Sirach (Sir 17:11; 24:22). The conjunction of obedience with law and life

---

49. In the Greek version and in some translations 3:34 is divided into two verses so that 3:35-37 becomes 3:36-38.

50. Some have claimed that Bar 3:37 is a Christian interpolation because wisdom's appearing on earth and living with humankind appears dependent on the Johannine tradition that "the Word became flesh and lived among us" (John 1:14). But in view of this Jewish tradition of wisdom's presence in Israel, Bar 3:37 is thoroughly Jewish. Similarly, although wisdom is personified only in this verse of the poem, the tradition goes back to Proverbs 1–9.

51. See David Winston, *The Wisdom of Solomon,* AB 43 (Garden City, N.Y.: Doubleday, 1979) 33-63, for a comprehensive review of the biblical and Greek evidence.

takes us back to the beginning of this poem, where the author associates walking in God's way with living in peace (Bar 3:13; cf. Deut 5:33 on the whole way that God commands, which leads to life). (See Reflections at 4:2-4.)

BARUCH 4:2-4, FINAL EXHORTATION TO ACCEPT WISDOM

NAB	NRSV

2 Turn, O Jacob, and receive her:
    walk by her light toward splendor.
3 Give not your glory to another,
    your privileges to an alien race.
4 Blessed are we, O Israel;
    for what pleases God is known to us!
 	
4,4: (ta aresta) tō theō, so LXX^{MSS}.
	² Turn, O Jacob, and take her;
	    walk toward the shining of her light.
	³ Do not give your glory to another,
	    or your advantages to an alien people.
	⁴ Happy are we, O Israel,
	    for we know what is pleasing to God.

COMMENTARY

The wisdom poem ends the way it began with direct address to Israel. The author advises repentance, suggested by the verb "turn" (ἐπιστρέφω 'epistrephō) and acquisition of wisdom in contrast to the vanity of acquiring silver and gold (cf. 3:17-18). "Walking" toward the "light" of wisdom recalls the frequent metaphor of the "way" of wisdom. "Light" connotes "life" (3:14), creation (3:33), and the light of God's "glory" (5:9). This exhortation is followed by an admonition to Israel not to give up its "glory" and advantage—that is, its law and wisdom—to another nation (4:3). The metaphor "glory" prepares for Israel's and Jerusalem's participation in God's glory in the final section of Baruch (4:24, 37; 5:1-2, 4, 6-8). The idea that the law gives Israel an advantage over the nations appears both in the Hebrew Bible (Ps 147:19-20) and in the New Testament (Rom 3:1-2; 9:4-5). The poem ends with a final blessing (4:4), as does Moses' final testament to the twelve tribes (Deut 33:29). It summarizes the immediate function of wisdom in the argument of Baruch: Through wisdom, Israel knows what God wants and can please God through obedience. Thus Israel has repented (1:15–3:8), knows God's will (3:9–4:4), and is ready to return from exile in the final section (4:5–5:9).

REFLECTIONS

Knowledge as depicted in this wisdom poem both attracts and repels people influenced by contemporary Western culture. Most seek what the wisdom poem promises: an accessible knowledge that solves life's problems. However, they resist acknowledging the problem of the poem: wisdom's inaccessibility due to human limitations. Our modern confidence in human intellect presumes that all problems and dangers await solution by rational, scientific inquiry and technological innovation. Science fills the role of divine and human wisdom as the way to a good life. With the help of science, rational humans should control the physical and social world by using their wits in disciplined labor. Far from seeking a hidden wisdom, we often feel overwhelmed by the unending stream of information in print and broadcast media and on the Internet.

Despite the surfeit of information available to us and our confidence in reason and science, more and more people search for a deeper wisdom and spirituality that transcends the preoccupations of the modern world. The practical accomplishments and benefits of reason and science have drawn our attention and energy away from our inner spiritual lives and have left us afloat in a complex, partially understood universe. This alienation from self and the universe has depersonalized and fragmented what used to be called wisdom.

The wisdom poem in Baruch speaks powerfully and confidently to these paradoxes and tensions of modern life. Wisdom in Baruch is personal and universally coherent at the same time. The God who created and controls the universe knows the world and its inhabitants intimately. God gives human beings the kind of wisdom that will overcome human ignorance and limitations and allow us to understand the world in its depth and live well. Divine wisdom comes to those who accept it as a concrete, comprehensible, well-articulated, and integral revelation. In the end, wisdom is the commandments and the law—that is, the Scriptures. For Baruch's audience, the formerly futile search for wisdom reaches a simple, peaceful end in the most obvious and accessible place, Israel's publicly acknowledged and accepted biblical tradition.

Baruch's solution to the problem of wisdom brings relief and closure at a price that is too high for a world dedicated to tolerance and multicultural learning. Baruch's exclusive claim for the validity of biblical wisdom to the exclusion of all else and his harsh criticism of other nations that have not found wisdom conflict with the pluralistic openness required by our diverse, international world. The wisdom of many cultures must contribute to the search for God and an understanding of God's works.

Although Baruch's exclusive and peremptory claim for Israel's wisdom does not accord with modern attitudes, his criticism of those in Israel and the nations who might be expected to find wisdom, but have not, accords well with the modern disposition to criticize political leaders, the wealthy, and experts who have failed to give guidance to society and use their resources wisely. Within the whole of Baruch the author has argued a case for how to understand life and how to live. In this poem he points the way to true, effective wisdom, drawing upon the biblical wisdom tradition. Although his solution to the problem of wisdom requires modification to take into account the diversity of the whole world as we know it, his acknowledgment of God as the source of wisdom and his insistent search for a comprehensive, integrative knowledge of the world speaks to our deepest desires.

This wisdom poem offers a kind of knowledge that demands commitment and total involvement. Similarly, the contemporary critique of rationalism and science rejects the myth of disinterested, objective knowledge and insists that all knowing includes commitment to some goal. The choice of a scientific research project implies a purpose that seeks to solve a problem or change our way of thinking about the world or acting within the world. Involvement in humanistic, historical, literary, or artistic activities supports a sensitive, sophisticated apprehension of the world and a reflective, purposeful way of life. To put this point and the thrust of the wisdom poem into deuteronomic theological categories, knowledge demands life-and-death choices. We either acknowledge and obey God in harmony with the world or reject God with a disobedience that leads to chaos.

BARUCH 4:5–5:9

A POEM OF CONSOLATION AND ENCOURAGEMENT

OVERVIEW

V arious commentators have described the poetic final section of Baruch as a psalm, a song, a poem, a hymn, a prayer, a lament, or a promise. These literary forms have been further specified by descriptors like "consolation," "encouragement," "hope," "redemption," "prophetic," and "eschatological." The poem has been divided into as few as four and as many as eleven sections or stanzas. Most agree that the poem in 4:5-9a introduces two discourses, one by a personified Jerusalem to her neighbors (4:9b-16) and her exiled inhabitants (4:17-29), and a second to Jerusalem by the author (4:39–5:9). The second discourse contains three sections introduced by imperatives (4:30-35; 4:36–5:4; 5:5-9) or perhaps four, with 5:1-4 as a separate section. Rather than try to reconstruct the poetic stanzas of what may have been a Hebrew original, I shall divide this poetic passage into four rhetorical parts, according to their speakers and audiences. After the author briefly encourages the people of Jerusalem who are a memorial of Israel (4:5-9a), a personified Jerusalem laments her children's exile in the presence of her neighbors (4:9b-16). Jerusalem then addresses her exiled children with an exhortation encouraging them to persevere and with a consoling promise that God will save them from exile (4:17-29). Finally, the author addresses Jerusalem with a four-part poem of encouragement and consolation based on the prophetic promises that God will punish Jerusalem's enemies, reestablish the city, and bring back the inhabitants (4:30–5:9).

This poem of consolation and encouragement is not a prayer and was not part of a public liturgy,[52] because it does not directly address God as "Lord," as the prayer in 1:15–3:8 does, but refers to God as the "eternal" or "everlasting" one (αἰώνιος aiōnios) as befits God's comprehensive, long-term restorative role (4:8, 10, 14, 20, 22, 24, 35; 5:2). It contains laments, prophetic promises, predictions, and exhortations. The classic biblical lament[53] begins with an expression of sorrow directed at God, followed by a petition for deliverance. Here in Baruch, Jerusalem's lament is followed by prophetic promises of divine intervention to end the exile.[54] This response to the lament has been influenced by post-exilic salvation oracles and prayers.[55]

Although the poem of consolation and encouragement differs in genre and literary tradition from the admonitory wisdom instruction that precedes, it provides a coherent conclusion to Baruch. Baruch began with a prayer of confession and repentance for past sins (1:15–3:8), which led to a wisdom instruction acknowledging God's wisdom and encouraging obedience to God's law (3:9–4:4). The repentance and instruction of these first two sections of Baruch have prepared the audience to experience proleptically the consolation and deliverance that are promised for the future. Expressions of hope in the first section (e.g., 2:30-35) have prepared for this final poem, and expressions of sorrow in this final section (e.g., 4:9b-16) acknowledge the pain expressed at the beginning of the book.

---

52. Bilhah Nitzan, *Qumran Prayer and Religious Poetry* (Leiden: Brill, 1994) 41 and n. 27.

53. Claus Westermann, *Praise and Lament in the Psalms* (Atlanta: Knox, 1981; German original 1977) 170; *Lamentations: Issues and Interpretation* (Minneapolis: Fortress, 1994; German original 1990) 94-98.

54. Westermann, *Praise and Lament in the Psalms,* 206-7, cites Bar 4:9b-16 as an example of the late form of the lament separated from the usual petitionary prayer.

55. See the Overview to Bar 1:15–3:8 for a sketch of Second Temple prayers. See also Claus Westermann, *Prophetic Oracles of Salvation in the Old Testament* (Louisville: Westminster/John Knox, 1991; orig. German 1987).

Figure 1: Literary Parallels Between *Psalms of Solomon 11* and Baruch 5

Psalms of Solomon 11*

1 Sound in Zion the signal trumpet
   of the sanctuary;
      announce in Jerusalem the voice of
      one bringing good news,
   for God has been merciful to Israel
   in watching over them.

2 Stand on a high place, Jerusalem
     and look at your children
   from the east and the west
     assembled together by the Lord.
3 From the north they come
     in the glory of their God;
   from far distant islands
     God has assembled them.
4 He flattened high mountains
     into level ground for them;
     the hills fled at their coming.

5 The forests shaded them
     as they passed by;
   God made every fragrant tree to
     grow for them.
6 So that Israel might proceed
     under the supervision of
     the glory of their God.

7 Jerusalem, put on
     (the) clothes of your glory,
     prepare the robe of your holiness
   for God has spoken well of Israel
     forevermore.

8 May the Lord do what he has
     spoken about Israel
     and Jerusalem;
   may the Lord lift up Israel
     in the name of his glory.
9 May the mercy of the Lord
be upon Israel forevermore.

Baruch 5 *(parallels)* (NRSV)

5 Arise, O Jerusalem,
     stand upon the height;
   look toward the east,
     and see your children gathered
     from west and east

7 For God has ordered
     that every high mountain and
     the everlasting hills
     be made low
   and the valleys filled up,
     to make level ground,
     so that Israel may walk safely
     in the glory of God
8 The woods and every fragrant tree
     have shaded Israel
     at God's command.

9 For God will lead Israel with joy,
     in the light of his glory,
     with the mercy and righteousness
     that come from him.

1 Jerusalem . . . put on forever
     the beauty of the glory from God;
2a Put on the robe of the righteousness
     that comes from God
4 For God will give you evermore
     the name, "Righteous Peace,
Godly Glory."

3 for God will show your splendor
     everywhere under heaven.

*From *Psalms of Solomon,* translated by R. B. Wright, in *The Old Testament Pseudepigrapha,* edited by James H. Charlesworth. Copyright © 1983, 1985 by James H. Charlesworth. Reprinted by permission of Doubleday, a division of Random House, Inc.

This final poem is influenced in its language, imagery, rhetoric, and thought by the salvation oracles in Isaiah 40–66, by the song of Moses (Deuteronomy 32), by the prayer of the afflicted in Psalm 102, and by the book of Lamentations (next to which Baruch stood in the Septuagint). For example, the personification of Zion as a grieving mother is based on Isa 51:17-20 and Lamentations 1–2; Zion's being consoled by God appears in Isa 52:1-2. Within Second Temple literature the extra-biblical psalm from Qumran, 11QPs^a 22:1-5 (called the Apostrophe to Zion), is in the same literary stream. The type of encouragement found in Baruch 4–5 resembles that in the eschatological psalm in Sir 36:1-17 and the eschatological prayer of encouragement in Tobit 13.[56]

The end of the poem of consolation (4:30–5:9) has a close literary relationship to Psalms of Solomon 11, which may be seen most easily in a chart (see *fig.* X, 000).

Commentators have thoroughly disagreed on whether one of these poems depends on the other or both on a common source with the result that the date, social setting, and author of this poem of consolation and encouragement cannot be directly determined from its relationship to the Psalms of Solomon (see the Introduction). Baruch 4:15-16 speaks of a distant, ruthless nation that may indirectly refer to the occupying power in Israel at the time of the poem's composition. But the language of these verses is highly stereotyped (see Deut 28:49-50; Jer 5:15) and could refer equally well to Antiochus IV or others of the Seleucids in the second century BCE; it may even refer to the Romans after 63 BCE. True to its purposes, the book of Baruch leaves us free to identify Israel's suffering and consolation with any historical crisis and interpret it according to the model of divine/human interaction expounded in its poems and prayers.

---

56. See the review of prayers in David Flusser, "Psalms, Hymns and Prayers," in *Jewish Writings of the Second Temple Period,* ed. Michael Stone (Philadelphia: Fortress, 1984) 551-77, esp. 556-57.

BARUCH 4:5-9*a*, INTRODUCTORY POEM OF CONSOLATION

NAB	NRSV

5 Fear not, my people!
     Remember, Israel,
6 You were sold to the nations
     not for your destruction;
 It was because you angered God
     that you were handed over to your foes.
7 For you provoked your Maker
     with sacrifices to demons, to no-gods;
8 You forsook the Eternal God who nourished
          you,
     and you grieved Jerusalem who fostered
     you.
9 She indeed saw coming upon you
     the anger of God; and she said:
	[5] Take courage, my people,
	     who perpetuate Israel's name!
	[6] It was not for destruction
	     that you were sold to the nations,
	 but you were handed over to your enemies
	     because you angered God.
	[7] For you provoked the one who made you
	     by sacrificing to demons and not to God.
	[8] You forgot the everlasting God, who brought
	          you up,
	     and you grieved Jerusalem, who reared you.
	[9] For she saw the wrath that came upon you
	          from God,
	     and she said:

4,5: *mnēmosynon=zeker* for *z^{e}kōr.*
4,7: *paröxynate* (*gar*): so LXX^{MSS}.
4,8: (*epelathesthe*) *de . . .* (*elupēsate*) *de*: so LXX^{MSS}.

COMMENTARY

The introduction reassures Israel that they will not be completely destroyed in their punishment for angering God. The author begins with the exhortation to "take courage," advice that is repeated three more times in the two discourses that follow (vv. 21, 27, 30). The Greek word for "take courage" (θαρσεῖτε *tharseite*) probably translates the common Hebrew expression אל תירא ('al tîrā'), "Do not be afraid," which is found in narratives and prophetic oracles (e.g., Gen 15:1; Isa 10:24). The addressees function as "a memorial of Israel" (a more literal rendering of the NRSV's "who perpetuate Israel's name"). The Greek for "memorial" (μνημόσυνον *mnēmosynon*) sometimes translates the Hebrew word שֵׁם (*šēm*, "name"; Deut 32:26). Although the survivors look like the vanishing remnant of a defeated people, they are actually a significant and potent token of Israel's future. The subgroup being addressed is not yet identified, but will turn out to be the exiled inhabitants of Jerusalem. The author assuages the people's fears of total destruction in a compact chiastic sentence:

A You were sold to the nations
   B not for destruction
   B´ but because you angered God
A´ you were handed over to your enemies.
   (v. 6; see Jer 30:11)

The people have been sold (Isa 50:1) like prisoners of war and led into exile. But this is not the end. The two discourses will lead finally to the destruction of Jerusalem's enemies (v. 25) and the return of the exiles (4:36–5:9).

The people's sin is compactly summarized in the next sentence (v. 7) with a charge drawn from Deut 32:17 that they provoked God by sacrificing to demons. As a result, they forgot God, and this failure to remember the exodus and all God did for Israel (e.g., Deut 5:15; 8:2, 18; 9:7; 15:15) constitutes infidelity to the covenant. Forgetting is an ironic fault, since the author understands the survivors as a "memorial" (v. 5). In v. 8 God is characterized as "eternal" or "everlasting" for the first time in Baruch. This title, that stresses God's permanence and constancy in contrast to the people's infidelity, is used seven more times in this section of Baruch (4:10, 14, 20, 22, 24, 35; 5:2).

Jerusalem enters the narrative here, personified as a mother, and remains an actor until the end of the book. Jerusalem's children (inhabitants) have saddened her personally, and her grief is expressed in a lament that immediately follows. The author uses female imagery associated with nurture to characterize the relationships of both Jerusalem and God to the people: God "brought up" (ἐπήγαγεν *epēgagen*) the people, and Jerusalem "reared" (ἀπήγαγον *apēgagon*) them. The two Greek terms are ordinarily used of a nursemaid feeding a child and seeing to its upbringing. Baruch's rhetoric makes a personal appeal to the people based on the intimate, nurturing relationship between God and Jerusalem, God's chosen city.

The intimacy of the relationship of Jerusalem to her inhabitants leads smoothly into Jerusalem's lament that follows. When Jerusalem saw the death of her children in siege and battle and the exile of others to Babylon, she lamented her loss to her neighbors. (See Reflections at 4:30–5:9.)

BARUCH 4:9b-16, JERUSALEM'S LAMENT TO NEIGHBORING PEOPLES

NAB	NRSV
"Hear, you neighbors of Zion! God has brought great mourning upon me, **10** For I have seen the captivity that the Eternal God has brought	Listen, you neighbors of Zion, God has brought great sorrow upon me; [10] for I have seen the exile of my sons and daughters,

NAB

upon my sons and daughters.
11 With joy I fostered them;
    but with mourning and lament I let them
        go.
12 Let no one gloat over me, a widow,
        bereft of many:
    For the sins of my children I am left desolate,
        because they turned from the law of God,
13   and did not acknowledge his statutes;
    In the ways of God's commandments they did
        not walk,
        nor did they tread the disciplined paths of
            his justice.

14 "Let Zion's neighbors come,
        to take note of the captivity of my sons
            and daughters,
        brought upon them by the Eternal God.
15 He has brought against them a nation from afar,
        a nation ruthless and of alien speech,
    That has neither reverence for age
        nor tenderness for childhood;
16 They have led away this widow's cherished
        sons,
        have left me solitary, without daughters.

4,15: 'oi (ouk ēschynthēsan): so LXX^{MSS}.

NRSV

    which the Everlasting brought upon them.
11 With joy I nurtured them,
        but I sent them away with weeping and
            sorrow.
12 Let no one rejoice over me, a widow
        and bereaved of many;
    I was left desolate because of the sins of my
        children,
        because they turned away from the law of
            God.
13 They had no regard for his statutes;
        they did not walk in the ways of God's
            commandments,
        or tread the paths his righteousness showed
            them.
14 Let the neighbors of Zion come;
        remember the capture of my sons and
            daughters,
        which the Everlasting brought upon them.
15 For he brought a distant nation against them,
        a nation ruthless and of a strange language,
    which had no respect for the aged
        and no pity for a child.
16 They led away the widow's beloved sons,
        and bereaved the lonely woman of her
            daughters.

COMMENTARY

Words concerning bereavement, desolation, and helplessness in the face of aggression characterize Jerusalem's lament. The personification of Jerusalem as the speaker fits a Second Temple tendency for autobiographical expression (e.g., Nehemiah, 4 Ezra). Although Jerusalem addresses her neighboring cities and peoples, the indirect addressee is God. Four times, at the beginning and at the end, Jerusalem refers to the sorrow (v. 9), the captivity (vv. 10, 14; the NRSV translates the Greek as "exile" and "capture"), and the distant nation (v. 15) that the Everlasting "brought upon" them. Through God's agency, that ruthless nation "led away" Jerusalem's sons and daughters. The nation that led Jerusalem's children into captivity in the narrative is, of course, Babylon. The author is probably applying this historical paradigm to the Seleucid ruler of his own time.

Jerusalem contrasts the joy of nurturing her children (v. 11) and her love for them (v. 16) with her present situation. She is now a widow (vv. 12, 16; cf. Lamentations 1), a metaphor for her defeat and destruction in the war. She has been left behind (NRSV, "bereaved") by her captive children (v. 12) and is sad (vv. 9, 11), weeping (v. 9), desolate (vv. 12, 16; NRSV, "bereaved" in v. 16), and lonely for her daughters (v. 16). Tucked into the middle of this lament are the conventional reasons for the Jerusalemites' captivity: turning away from God's law and disobedience (vv. 12-13); but the impassioned condemnation of Israel's sins found in 1:15–3:8 is completely missing. The author focuses on the injustice being done to Jerusalem and her captive inhabitants by Babylon, probably as an implicit reference to imperial powers in a later period. The poem focuses sharply on the ruthlessness of a foreign nation "with no respect for the aged and no pity for a child" (v. 15; cf. Deut 28:49-50), on Jerusalem's maternal sorrow, and on God's responsibility for this painful situation. The author's estrangement from God is symbolized by Jerusalem's ironic address to her "neighbors" (vv. 9, 14). The Greek term for "neighbors" (πάροικοι *paroikoi*) usually refers to strangers living in a city or territory and has a pejorative nuance. Given the generally hostile relations between Israel and neighboring nations (Jer 12:14-17), they are the last people Jerusalem should be turning to and asking to "hear" (v. 9 NAB), to "come," and to "remember" (v. 14). Jerusalem has already admonished her neighbors not to take

malicious delight in her widowhood and abandonment (v. 12; cf. Dan 9:16). Thus in addressing the lament to her neighbors Jerusalem is implicitly criticizing God. In Jer 12:7-13, God laments over Jerusalem. In the book of Lamentations, the poet sorrows over Jerusalem, which has been destroyed, and encourages the people to return to God. Here, however, the poet talks indirectly to God through the voice of widow Jerusalem, who seeks ordinary human sympathy from her neighbors. All attention and emotion turns toward the estrangement of the people from their mother Jerusalem. The people's sins and relationship with God lie in the background. (See Reflections at 4:30–5:9.)

BARUCH 4:17-29, JERUSALEM'S EXHORTATION TO HER CHILDREN

NAB

17 What can I do to help you?
18 He who has brought this evil upon you
must himself deliver you from your enemies' hands.
19 Farewell, my children, farewell:
I am left desolate.
20 I have taken off the garment of peace,
have put on sackcloth for my prayer of supplication,
and while I live I will cry out to the Eternal God.

21 "Fear not, my children; call upon God,
who will deliver you from oppression at enemy hands.
22 I have trusted in the Eternal God for your welfare,
and joy has come to me from the Holy One
Because of the mercy that will swiftly reach you
from your eternal savior.
23 With mourning and lament I sent you forth,
but God will give you back to me
with enduring gladness and joy.

NRSV

¹⁷ But I, how can I help you?
¹⁸ For he who brought these calamities upon you
will deliver you from the hand of your enemies.
¹⁹ Go, my children, go;
for I have been left desolate.
²⁰ I have taken off the robe of peace
and put on sackcloth for my supplication;
I will cry to the Everlasting all my days.

²¹ Take courage, my children, cry to God,
and he will deliver you from the power
and hand of the enemy.
²² For I have put my hope in the Everlasting to save you,
and joy has come to me from the Holy One,
because of the mercy that will soon come to you
from your everlasting savior.ᵃ
²³ For I sent you out with sorrow and weeping,
but God will give you back to me with joy
and gladness forever.
²⁴ For as the neighbors of Zion have now seen your capture,

ᵃOr *from the Everlasting, your savior*

NAB

24 As Zion's neighbors lately saw you taken
captive,
so shall they soon see God's salvation come
to you,
with great glory and the splendor of the
Eternal God.

25 "My children, bear patiently the anger
that has come from God upon you;
Your enemies have persecuted you,
and you will soon see their destruction
and trample upon their necks.
26 My pampered children have trodden rough
roads,
carried off by their enemies like sheep in a
raid.
27 Fear not, my children; call out to God!
He who brought this upon you will remember you.
28 As your hearts have been disposed to stray
from God,
turn now ten times the more to seek him;
29 For he who has brought disaster upon you
will, in saving you, bring you back
enduring joy."

NRSV

so they soon will see your salvation by God,
which will come to you with great glory
and with the splendor of the Everlasting.
²⁵ My children, endure with patience the wrath
that has come upon you from God.
Your enemy has overtaken you,
but you will soon see their destruction
and will tread upon their necks.
²⁶ My pampered children have traveled rough
roads;
they were taken away like a flock carried
off by the enemy.

²⁷ Take courage, my children, and cry to God,
for you will be remembered by the one who
brought this upon you.
²⁸ For just as you were disposed to go astray
from God,
return with tenfold zeal to seek him.
²⁹ For the one who brought these calamities
upon you
will bring you everlasting joy with your
salvation.

COMMENTARY

Mother Jerusalem begins with a sad, rhetorical question, testifying to her helplessness: "But I, how can I help you?" (v. 17). The question is immediately resolved by a confident affirmation that the one (God) who brought the evil things (NRSV, "calamities") upon Jerusalem's children will deliver them from their enemies (v. 18). The end echoes the beginning with a similar thematic claim that the God who brought the evil things upon Jerusalem's children will bring them ever-lasting joy with salvation (v. 29). Within this inclu-sio Jerusalem encourages her children to be courageous, to endure captivity, and to pray with the hope that God will return them to Jerusalem.

Jerusalem's instructions and encouragement to her children are punctuated by four imperatives to "go" (v. 19), to "take courage" (vv. 21, 27), and to "endure" (v. 25). She begins on a somber note by telling her children to go into captivity (v. 19; the

Greek verb βαδίζετε [*badizete*] has the connota-tion of "march"). This captivity is God's will and the reality from which any change will spring. Similarly, Jerusalem accepts her present desolation (v. 19; see also vv. 12, 16), clothing herself in sack-cloth rather than a robe of peace (v. 20; cf. 5:1). The first response to this tragedy is energetic prayer. Jerusalem promises to "cry" out to God (v. 20) and recommends that her captive children "take courage" and cry out to God as well (v. 21). The instruction to "take courage" (also found in vv. 5, 27, 30) introduces a series of hopeful con-trasts between the people's present oppression and Jerusalem's confidence that God "will deliver you from the power and hand of the enemy" (v. 21; cf. vv. 18, 29). God's mercy will return Jerusalem's children and give her joy instead of sorrow (v. 23; cf. v. 11); the inhabitants of Jerusalem will experi-ence salvation and glory in place of captivity (v.

24). This salvation will be witnessed by the same neighbors of Jerusalem who witnessed the people's captivity (see v. 14).

Jerusalem's confidence that God will return her children leads to joy amid sorrow, mourning, and prayer (v. 22, in contrast to vv. 19-20). This paradoxical contrast of sorrow and joy derives from Jer 31:15-17, which begins with Rachel weeping for her children. There God instructs Rachel to stop crying, because her children will return from the land of the enemy to their own country. Baruch applies this consoling prophecy to Jerusalem (vv. 19-22) and portrays Jerusalem as responding with trust to God's oracle and communicating it to her children. In the Gospel of Matthew, Rachel's weeping for her children (Matt 2:18; see also Jer

31:15) applies immediately to the children of Bethlehem who were killed by Herod the Great. But the contexts in Jeremiah, Baruch, and Matthew concern exile, hope of return, and a new relationship with God.

The second response to the tragedy of captivity is to "endure" God's punishment patiently with hope. This instruction is supported by ironic contrasts: The tables will be turned on the people's captors (v. 25); Jerusalem's pampered children have traveled rough roads (v. 26); they went astray from God (v. 28), in contrast to being taken away like a stolen flock by their enemy (v. 26). The third response to these painful disjunctures is to take courage, cry out to God, and seek God with tenfold zeal (vv. 27-28). (See Reflections at 4:30–5:9.)

BARUCH 4:30–5:9, POEM OF CONSOLATION TO JERUSALEM

NAB	NRSV
30 Fear not, Jerusalem! He who gave you your name is your encouragement.	30 Take courage, O Jerusalem, for the one who named you will comfort you.
31 Fearful are those who harmed you, who rejoiced at your downfall;	31 Wretched will be those who mistreated you and who rejoiced at your fall.
32 Fearful are the cities where your children were enslaved, fearful the city that took your sons.	32 Wretched will be the cities that your children served as slaves; wretched will be the city that received your offspring.
33 As that city rejoiced at your collapse, and made merry at your downfall, so shall she grieve over her own desolation.	33 For just as she rejoiced at your fall and was glad for your ruin, so she will be grieved at her own desolation.
34 I will take from her the joyous throngs, and her exultation shall be turned to mourning:	34 I will take away her pride in her great population, and her insolence will be turned to grief.
35 For fire shall come upon her from the Eternal God, for a long time, and demons shall dwell in her from that time on.	35 For fire will come upon her from the Everlasting for many days, and for a long time she will be inhabited by demons.
36 Look to the east, Jerusalem! behold the joy that comes to you from God.	36 Look toward the east, O Jerusalem, and see the joy that is coming to you from God.
37 Here come your sons whom you once let go, gathered in from the east and from the west By the word of the Holy One,	37 Look, your children are coming, whom you sent away;

4,34: (*to aguariama autēs*) *estai* (*eis penthos*): so LXX^{MSS}.

NAB

rejoicing in the glory of God.

5 Jerusalem, take off your robe of mourning
and misery;
put on the splendor of glory from God
forever:

2 Wrapped in the cloak of justice from God,
bear on your head the mitre
that displays the glory of the eternal name.

3 For God will show all the earth your splendor:

4 you will be named by God forever
the peace of justice, the glory of God's worship.

5 Up, Jerusalem! stand upon the heights;
look to the east and see your children
Gathered from the east and the west
at the word of the Holy One,
rejoicing that they are remembered by God.

6 Led away on foot by their enemies they left
you:
but God will bring them back to you
borne aloft in glory as on royal thrones.

7 For God has commanded
that every lofty mountain be made low,
And that the age-old depths and gorges
be filled to level ground,
that Israel may advance secure in the glory
of God.

8 The forests and every fragrant kind of tree
have overshadowed Israel at God's command;

9 For God is leading Israel in joy
by the light of his glory,
with his mercy and justice for company.

NRSV

they are coming, gathered from east and
west,
at the word of the Holy One,
rejoicing in the glory of God.

5 Take off the garment of your sorrow and
affliction, O Jerusalem,
and put on forever the beauty of the glory
from God.

2 Put on the robe of the righteousness that comes
from God;
put on your head the diadem of the glory of
the Everlasting;

3 for God will show your splendor everywhere
under heaven.

4 For God will give you evermore the name,
"Righteous Peace, Godly Glory."

5 Arise, O Jerusalem, stand upon the height;
look toward the east,
and see your children gathered from west and
east
at the word of the Holy One,
rejoicing that God has remembered them.

6 For they went out from you on foot,
led away by their enemies;
but God will bring them back to you,
carried in glory, as on a royal throne.

7 For God has ordered that every high mountain
and the everlasting hills be made low
and the valleys filled up, to make level
ground,
so that Israel may walk safely in the glory of
God.

8 The woods and every fragrant tree
have shaded Israel at God's command.

9 For God will lead Israel with joy,
in the light of his glory,
with the mercy and righteousness that come
from him.

COMMENTARY

After complaining to her neighbors and encouraging her captive people, Jerusalem herself needs
encouragement and consolation. The author
speaks prophetically to Jerusalem in the name of
God. Thus he can speak about God (4:30) and use

the first-person pronoun in God's name (4:34).
Jerusalem is told in four imperatives to "take
courage" (4:30), to "look" (4:36), to "take off" her
garment of sorrow (5:1), and to "arise" (5:5).
These imperatives mark off four sections of the

poem. (The NRSV's imperative "Look" in 4:37 is actually an exclamation, "Behold" [ἰδού *idou*]. According to another view, the middle two imperatives together make a single stanza.) The laments, indictments, repentance, and sorrow of the previous sections of Baruch are left behind in favor of a climactic expression of confidence in divine salvation. As a final solution to the destruction of Jerusalem, her enemies will be destroyed, she will arise in glory, and her people will return.

The first command for Jerusalem to take courage introduces a double contrast of Jerusalem and the cities that oppress her. Jerusalem has been mourning, destroyed, and desolate while her oppressors enjoyed the prosperity and slaves gained from Jerusalem. Eventually, those who mistreated Jerusalem, rejoiced at her fall, were proud, or accepted exiled slaves from her population will ironically and appropriately suffer the same fate themselves; they will grieve as Jerusalem has done and will finally be punished by fire (4:31-35) while Jerusalem arises, ends her mourning, and greets her returning sons and daughters (4:36–5:9).

The author alludes to God's relationship to Jerusalem as a parent (God has named Jerusalem), which will lead to a reversal in which God comforts Jerusalem (4:30*b*). The intensity of the prophetic poet's feelings about Jerusalem's enemies is communicated by a lapse into the divine first person in 4:34:

> I [God] will take away her [Babylon's] pride in her
> great population,
> and her insolence will be turned to grief.

This author's anger and resentment against Jerusalem's enemies contrast with the introductory narrative, in which the Israelites exiled in Babylon ask those remaining in Jerusalem to pray for Nebuchadnezzar and his son so that the exiles can live peacefully under them (1:11-12). The promise of divine intervention grips the end of this book, in contrast to patience under divine punishment at the beginning. The author of Baruch is probably alluding to later enemies or authorities that are hostile to Jews or Jerusalem. Identification of the enemy depends on the date of the book, with candidates ranging from the Ptolemies, the Seleucids during the Maccabean period, or the Romans after the destruction of the Second Temple.

The next brief section of the prayer (4:36-37) begins the climax of the book and the resolution of the confessions, laments, and petitions that have occupied the author thus far. A series of contrasts brings home the transformation that takes place. Earlier Jerusalem lamented: "With joy I nurtured them,/ but I sent them away with weeping and sorrow" (4:11). Now God, through the prophet, consoles Jerusalem by resolving the problem central to Jerusalem's lament: "Look toward the east, O Jerusalem,/ and see the joy that is coming to you from God" (4:36).

Jerusalem's children went east into exile, but now she is to look east for their return. Jerusalem had told her children to go obediently into exile: "Go, my children, go; for I have been left desolate" (4:19). Now the prophet consoles Jerusalem with a rectification of the situation:

> Look, your children are coming,
> whom you sent away;
> they are coming, gathered from east and west,
> at the word of the Holy One,
> rejoicing in the glory of God. (4:37)

The expression "from east and west" seems to include Jewish exiles from everywhere, not just from Babylon (see 5:5). The return "at the word of God" fulfills a promise made in the first prayer of repentance and contrition: "I will bring them [Israel] again into the land that I swore to give to their ancestors, to Abraham, Isaac, and Jacob, and they will rule over it" (2:34). And finally, the author introduces the "glory of God" (4:37), an expression that will be repeated six more times in the nine verses of chap. 5 (vv. 1, 2, 4, 6, 7, 9).

Jerusalem is instructed to change her clothing (5:1) and arise to see and greet her children (5:5). Her actions now are in stark contrast to her response to the exile of her children. Then Jerusalem laments:

> I have taken off the robe of peace
> and put on sackcloth for my supplication;
> I will cry to the Everlasting all my days. (4:20)

Now God has heard her, and so she is told to:

> Take off the garment of your sorrow and
> affliction, O Jerusalem,
> and put on forever the beauty of the glory from
> God. (5:1)

Jerusalem's situation has completely changed through divine intervention, a transition symbolized by the metaphor of God's "glory." Glory is God's honor, reputation, power, authority, importance, and divine status, especially when it is manifested to humans either as a divine radiance or through God's intervention in human events. Here God's glory appears for the decisive and final correcting of the wrongs done to Jerusalem and Israel. Jerusalem's newly acquired beauty (5:1), her crown (5:2), and her name (5:4) all come from God's glory. She and her situation are transformed by the divine power that has manifested itself. This eschatological transformation finds precedent in apocalyptic literature and in Third Isaiah (Isa 60:1-3; 62:1-4). The solution to the situation is a radical change for Jerusalem through participation in God's glory, righteousness (5:2, 4), splendor (5:3), and peace (5:4). Jerusalem's change of clothes is more than the end of mourning. Jerusalem receives from God the symbols of sovereign power, including God's glory, a robe connoting God's justice, which is the basis for God's rule, and a crown (5:1-2). Clothed this way, Jerusalem's God-given power is seen as splendor by all (5:3). Jerusalem is given the throne names "Righteous Peace" and "Godly Glory" (5:4), which contain the elements of a legitimate rule and authenticate Jerusalem's status and authority.

Once transformed by God's glory, Jerusalem arises (5:5) to see her children return in the glory of God (5:6-7, 9). The description of their return depends on prophetic descriptions of the restoration of Israel and Jerusalem. *Psalms of Solomon* 11 is very similar to Bar 5:5-9 and is related to it in some way. (See the Overview above and the Introduction to Baruch for further discussion of this relationship.) The author of Baruch draws upon widespread and deeply felt hopes for the vindication and reconstitution of Israel as a nation under God's protection. Jerusalem is again told to look toward the east and see her children returning home rejoicing (5:5 b-d, repeating 4:36-37; cf. the similar scene in Isa 40:9-11). The children rejoice because God remembered them (5:5), just as Jerusalem told them would happen (4:27). The returnees, who come from the "west and east" as well (5:5 b; see 4:37), seem to include all of exiled Israel. The people were previously designated "a memorial of Israel" (4:5), and now they rejoice "in God's remembrance" of them (5:5) and become Israel once again (5:7, 9).

The people's final and definitive return verifies the assurance given them at the beginning of this poem:

> Take courage, my people,
> who perpetuate Israel's name!
> It was not for destruction
> that you were sold to the nations. (4:5-6)

Jerusalem's people return in a divine royal procession marked by God's glory (see 4:24 for the promise of a return in glory) and made easy and safe by God (5:6-9; see also the level road in the desert in Isa 40:3-4). Sovereign Jerusalem joyfully meets her returning people so that the laments and desolation of the earlier parts of the book are at an end. The goal of the prayers, the climax of the narrative action, and the hope of the author are summarized in 5:9:

> For God will lead Israel with joy,
> in the light of his glory,
> with the mercy and righteousness that come
> from him.

REFLECTIONS

An authentic movement from discouragement and despair to hope and confidence eludes many people caught up in their own problems or trapped in destructive social and political situations. Even the divinely warranted promise carried by the thematic 4:6, "It was not for destruction that you were sold to the nations," rings hollow today for those who contemplate the enormous, dehumanizing loss of life and destruction of communities in the Holocaust during World War II and in ethnic conflicts since then. How can the restoration of Israel correct the injustices and barbarities of history? Can the biblical tradition, with its ongoing dialogue with God and its trust in God's justice, overcome the maliciousness of human behavior?

Like the author of Baruch, we frequently mobilize biblical traditions to encourage and reshape ourselves and our society in the face of injustice, poverty, human suffering, and failure. And like

Baruch's audience, we seldom experience immediate amelioration or rectification of the painful and destructive forces that threaten our physical, personal, and spiritual lives. But when we speciously deny the reality and pernicious effects of oppression, suffering, and misery, we endanger a frank and authentic response to individual and social crises. Lady Jerusalem provides a model for dealing with disaster. She responds vigorously to the dissolution of Judean society and the uprooting of her people by mourning and lamenting all that has been lost. Her full engagement with human life in all its complexity and ambiguity lays the foundations for a vision of future restoration and provides the strength to hope and endure.

Strikingly God is not a partner in the dialogue between Jerusalem and her children. They presume God's power and activity at every turn but do not address God directly in petition or praise. Like many contemporary believers, they treat God as a background force in life and history and as a guarantor of the future, rather than as a direct actor in contemporary politics and society. Those who are troubled "take courage" because God will remember, comfort, and deliver them. God, in turn, influences Israel's future through human agency rather than by direct divine action. The oppressive empire falls, the exiles return, and Jerusalem regains sovereignty. The "glory" of God manifests itself in Jerusalem and in her people, Israel; the injustices of history are rectified by the political and social restoration of God's city and people and their vindication in the eyes of their enemies. Unlike apocalypticism, here God does not appear in glory, take the faithful away to a better place, and destroy the evil world. Rather, Jerusalem wears "the robe of righteousness that comes from God" and "the diadem of the glory of the Everlasting" (5:2) in this world. As in Rom 1:17, those who are faithful to God receive God's righteousness.

The contemporary West emphasizes the problems and destinies of individuals, both in this world and the next. The book of Baruch, true to the biblical tradition, expresses its hope in social images. Jerusalem personifies the reactions of a collective reality, God's people in disarray and need. Their disorder and suffering call forth an ingathering of all Israel and the restoration of the city and nation in harmony with God and at peace with the world. In a similar way, Revelation 21 concludes with the restoration of Jerusalem as a home for those who have been faithful to God, where they will live with God.

Two uncomfortable teachings of the final poem in Baruch remain. First, under the influence of deuteronomic theology, Baruch confidently and simply asserts that Israel has suffered defeat and is suffering exile because God is punishing them for rejecting, disobeying, and sinning against God. This theology of human adversity has the merit of protecting the sovereignty and integrity of God and giving full weight to human freedom, failure, and irresponsibility. Contemporary readers can resonate with Baruch's sharp appreciation of human fragility and corruption, but with Job we will want to question God more rigorously than deuteronomic theology allows. The horrors of human history and the ambiguities of life have relativized the overarching divine order that inspires the usual theology of sin and punishment. Baruch undercuts the theology of punishment by holding the nations that have oppressed Israel culpable for their hostility and injustice. Human evil, not divine justice, operates most directly in deadly political conflicts.

Second, Baruch's aggressive condemnation of the nations that have attacked Israel and its confident anticipation of their destruction work against the modern struggle for international understanding and peace. Israel's sinful transgressions of God's commandments lead not only to God's anger and punishment, but also to repentance, mercy, and restoration. But Baruch envisions no such complete and ongoing relationship with God for the nations. Israel alone will be restored as God's people.

Today the churches struggle with the particularity of their own traditions in relationship with the modern belief that God's people include all human beings. True to the ancient world, Baruch's vision extends only to Israel as the people of God. Thus the boundaries of Baruch's narrative and symbolic world must be extended to include all. We must complement the punishment for sin that Baruch promises to the nations with the story of God's mercy and ongoing relationship with all nations in history.

THE LETTER OF JEREMIAH

INTRODUCTION, COMMENTARY, AND REFLECTIONS

BY
ANTHONY J. SALDARINI

THE LETTER OF

JEREMIAH

INTRODUCTION

T he Epistle of Jeremiah survives in Greek as well as in many versions, such as Syriac, Arabic, Coptic, Ethiopic, and Latin. In some Greek MSS (e.g., Alexandrinus, Vaticanus) and in the Syriac Hexapla and the Arabic, the epistle is separated from Baruch by Lamentations. In later LXX and other Syriac MSS and in the old Latin, the epistle comes right after Baruch. In the Vulgate, the KJV, and Catholic Bibles, the epistle is included as chapter 6 of Baruch, which itself follows Jeremiah.

GENRE AND LITERARY STRUCTURE

The superscription of the epistle (v. 1) identifies it as a copy of a letter sent by the prophet Jeremiah to Judean prisoners who were about to be shipped to Babylon. The next six verses (vv. 2-7) directly address the exiles in a form consistent with a letter and also provide a narrative framework for the document. However, the rest of the epistle consists of satirical parodies and polemics against idols[1] and prophetic admonitions and warnings,[2] all of which have literary links with the Hebrew Bible, especially the book of Jeremiah.[3] Whether the epistle is thought of as an ancient letter depends on how flexibly

---

1. Wolfgang M. W. Roth, "For Life, He Appeals to Death (Wis 13:18): A Study of Old Testament Idol Parodies," *CBQ* 37 (1975) 21-47, esp. 40-42.

2. Irene Taatz, *Frühjüdische Briefe: Die paulinischen Briefe im Rahmen der offiziellen religiösen Briefe des Frühjudentums* (Göttingen: Vandenhoeck & Ruprecht, 1991) 57-58.

3. For the invocation of the letter form for its authoritative status, even when the genre was not sustained, see Philip S. Alexander, "Epistolary Literature," in *Jewish Writings of the Second Temple Period,* ed. Michael E. Stone (Assen/Philadelphia: Van Gorcum/Fortress, 1984) 584-85 and n. 26.

the letter genre is understood.[4] The first seven verses of the epistle parallel the letter Jeremiah sent to the Babylonian exiles (Jeremiah 29),[5] and the epistle is clearly meant to supplement the materials found in the book of Jeremiah. Although the epistle's language is very much like a tract, it also addresses the exiles in its exhortatory refrains as one would address the recipients of a letter.

After the introduction (vv. 1-7), the polemics, instructions, and exhortations may be divided into ten sections: vv. 8-16, vv. 17-23, vv. 24-29, vv. 30-40*a*, vv. 40*b*-44, vv. 45-52, vv. 53-56, vv. 57-65, vv. 66-69, and vv. 70-73. Each division concludes with a refrain, which argues that the statues of the gods are not really gods and, therefore, should not be feared: "From this it is evident that they are not gods; so do not fear them" (v. 16; similarly vv. 23, 29, 65, 69); "Why then must anyone think that they are gods, or call them gods?" (v. 40; similarly vv. 44, 51, 56, 72). Similar rhetorical questions and statements also appear within sections four (v. 30), six (vv. 47, 49, 51), and eight (vv. 59, 64). These refrains keep before the reader the main themes of the epistle, "beware of becoming at all like the foreigners or of letting fear for these gods possess you" (v. 5), and "It is you, O Lord, whom we must worship" (v. 6). The fear motif comes from Jeremiah 10, which has influenced the whole epistle: "Their idols are like scarecrows in a cucumber field,/ and they cannot speak;/ they have to be carried,/ for they cannot walk./ *Do not be afraid of them,*/ for they cannot do evil,/ nor is it in them to do good" (Jer 10:5, italics added; cf. Ep Jer 5, 70). Thus the Epistle of Jeremiah, despite its repletion, transmits a unified message within the Jeremiah tradition. The Targum on Jer 10:11 says that the Aramaic slogan in that verse was quoted from this epistle, but the Targum is a late and unreliable source for this kind of information. However, the theme of Jer 10:11, "The gods who did not make the heavens and the earth shall perish from the earth and from under the heavens" (NRSV), fits well the content and focus of the epistle.

Within this narrative and thematic framework, the epistle's polemical observations and arguments are repeated frequently, often without discernible order. This repetition has led commentators to outdo one another in criticizing it. Ball wonders how a work "so formless, so confused, so utterly destitute of the graces of style" could have been preserved in the Alexandrian canon. "We are presented with a voluble but ill-connected succession of propositions, bearing little visible relation to each other beyond general animus against idolatry."[6] Torrey agreed more briefly: "It is a formless composition, rambling and repetitious."[7] Carey Moore describes the epistle more precisely: "Apart from a not infrequent uncertainty as to the antecedents of its pronouns, the text is intelligible enough; but its images, analogies, and comparison are rarely new and never memorable.

---

4. For the broad use of the term *epistle* or *letter* to name ancient documents, see ibid., 581 and n. 13.

5. Reinhard G. Kratz, "Die Rezeption von Jeremia 10 und 29 im Pseudepigraphen Brief des Jeremia," *JSJ* 26 (1995) 19.

6. Charles J. Ball, "Epistle of Jeremy," *APOT,* 597.

7. C. C. Torrey, *The Apocryphal Literature* (New Haven: Yale University Press, 1945) 65.

After the first three or four stanzas there is no further development or progression of thought; rather, the same old observations and arguments are rehashed."[8]

Others have seen more structure to the argument. The Greek conjunction γάρ (*gar,* "for") links arguments and observations in vv. 7, 8, 17, 24, 30, 50, 53, 60, 66, and 70. (These connectives are not always translated in the NRSV.) Similarly, the connective particle δέ (*de*) appears in v. 43 and the conjunction οὖν (*oun,* "therefore") in vv. 49, 51, 56, and 64. Although the lines of argument and coherence are often unclear, a recent study has divided the argument into two parts (vv. 8-29 and 30-73), with each subdivided into three sections (vv. 8-16, 17-23, 24-29 and vv. 30-65 [with subdivisions], 66-69, 70-73.)[9] Suffice it to say that the epistle marshals abundant, related evidence against the reality of the gods, but it lacks a tightly structured argument.

In form and content the Epistle of Jeremiah is closely related to the Hebrew Bible and other Second Temple literature. The rejection of statues and images of God as well as of other gods is found in the Ten Commandments (Exod 20:3-5; Deut 5:7-9) and other biblical laws (Exod 34:17; Lev 19:4; 26:1; Deut 4:16, 23; 27:15). But the Epistle of Jeremiah addresses the danger of idolatry in exile (cf. Deut 4:27-28) more specifically by drawing upon the prophetic and cultic polemics against idols (Pss 115:3-8; 135:15-18; Isa 40:18-20; 41:6-7; 44:9-20; 46:1-8; Hab 2:18-19). These materials have been drawn into the Jeremiah tradition and organized under the influence of the polemic against idols in Jer 10:1-16 and the letter to the exiles in Jeremiah 29.[10] Presumably the author of the Epistle of Jeremiah sought to address new dangers by gathering and reinterpreting the anti-idol materials in the prophets, especially Jeremiah. The epistle was one of a number of Second Temple compositions that addressed the problem of idolatry through polemic and parody (see Wis 13:10-19; 15:7-13; Bel and the Dragon; *Jub.* 12:2-5; 20:8-9). The author, who probably wrote in Hebrew, used the Hebrew version of Jeremiah, not the Greek. The image of the scarecrow in the cucumber patch (v. 70) comes from the Hebrew of Jer 10:5, but is missing in the Greek.

In a recent study, R. G. Kratz argues that the Epistle of Jeremiah is an orderly interpretation and rewriting of Jer 10:1-16 for a new situation rather than a random borrowing of themes and motifs. Thus Jer 10:2-3*a* and Ep Jer 4–6 each introduces its respective polemics. Jeremiah 10:3*b*-5*a* (along with Jer 10:9, 14) provided the themes of the first part of the epistle (vv. 8-29), and Jer 10:5*b*-16 the themes for the second, longer and more complex part (vv. 30-73).[11] Kratz places the epistle within the chronological framework of the Jeremiah tradition, which was itself undergoing extensive editing during the Persian and Greek periods. The writer of the epistle was adapting the

8. Carey A. Moore, "Jeremiah, Additions to," *ABD* 3:704.

9. Kratz, "Die Rezeption von Jeremia 10 und 29 im Pseudepigraphen Brief des Jeremia," 2-31, with a chart on 6-7.

10. W. Roth, "For Life, He Appeals to Death (Wis 13:18)," 41, notes that all the motifs in Jer 10:1-16 appear in the Epistle of Jeremiah.

11. Kratz, "Die Rezeption von Jeremia 10 und 29 im Pseudepigraphen Brief des Jeremia," 14-15.

Jeremiah tradition to his own situation in the third century BCE, which required long-term resistance to idolatry.[12] Thus the Epistle of Jeremiah is not a pale imitation of Jeremiah; rather, it is part of a vital and developing complex of prophetic traditions that were giving guidance to Jewish communities in the Hellenistic age.

LANGUAGE, DATE AND PLACE

The Epistle of Jeremiah has survived only in Greek as part of the LXX. The earliest MS evidence for the epistle is a very fragmentary copy of vv. 43-44 in Greek.[13] However, a number of peculiarities in the Greek suggest that it was translated from a Hebrew original.[14] The clearest translation error, corrected by most English versions, is found in v. 72. The Greek reads, literally: "From the purple and marble that rot upon them [the statues of the gods] you will know that they are not gods." Since marble does not rot, the statement is incoherent. However, the Hebrew word for "marble" or "alabaster" (שש *šeš*) also means "linen," which here would refer to the statues' clothing, which does rot. Similarly, in v. 12 the Greek says literally that the statues "cannot save themselves from rust and food" (the NRSV's "rust and corrosion" comes from a Greek variant reading). The translator probably read the Hebrew letters מאכל (*m'kl*) as מַאֲכָל (*ma'kāl*), "food," rather than as מֵאֹכֵל (*me'okel*), "the devourer," that is, a moth. Thus the Hebrew original referred to rust corroding the metal overlay of the statues and moths eating away at the clothing. Elsewhere, in the middle of an argument that the statues of the gods are powerless, they are said to be "like crows between heaven and earth" (v. 55), an unusually obscure simile. However, the Hebrew consonants for the word "crows" (ערבים *'rbym*) could easily have been confused with "clouds" (עבים *'bym*) by the translator. Other suggested mistranslations are less certain but improve the text. In "for just as someone's dish is useless when it is broken" (v. 17), "someone's dish" (כלי אדם *kly 'dm*; lit., "dish of a man") in Hebrew may have resulted from a misreading of כלי אדמה (*kly 'dmh*), "ceramic/earthen disk" (lit., "dish of earth"). In general, the Greek of the epistle has many Semitic characteristics and can be easily retroverted into Hebrew, so the likelihood of a Hebrew original is generally accepted.

The epistle can be assigned no secure date. It has been most frequently placed in the Hellenistic period (332–63 BCE). The Qumran Greek MS fragment of vv. 43-44 mentioned above was copied in about 100 BCE. The epistle may be referred to in 2 Macc 2:2, which recounts that Jeremiah "instructed those who were being deported [to Babylon] not . . . to be led astray in their thoughts on seeing the gold and silver statues and their adornment" (NRSV). The cover letter of 2 Maccabees (2 Macc 1:1-9) is dated in 124 BCE, and the letter it introduces (2 Macc 1:10–2:18) is generally thought to be earlier, perhaps soon after the rededication of the Temple in 164 BCE. These two pieces of external

---

12. Ibid., 20-21, 26-29.
13. M. Baillet et al., *Les "Petites Grottes" de Qumrân: Textes,* DJD 3 (Oxford: Clarendon, 1962) 7Q2, 143.
14. The most influential case in English was made by Ball, "Epistle of Jeremy," 597-98.

evidence suggest that the Epistle of Jeremiah was composed in the second century or earlier. Some commentators have taken the reference to seven generations (v. 3) literally and calculated a period of 280 years from 597 or 586 to the late fourth century (317 and 306 BCE).[15] But chronological notices of this kind are conventional and symbolic. Jeremiah speaks of seventy years (Jer 25:12; 29:10) and three generations (Jer 27:7). Daniel reinterpreted this period into seventy weeks of years (Dan 9:2, 24-27), and it may be that the author is here engaged in a similar enterprise. If so, then such chronological notices are not accurate indicators for the document's date of composition. The content and purpose of the epistle, to delegitimate other gods so that Israel will not worship them, are so general that they may pertain to any time in the Persian and Greek periods.[16]

The narrative framework of the introduction refers to the Babylonian period and to Babylonian gods. More substantively, the types of statues, processions, dressing, feeding, and care of the gods that are alluded to and mocked in the polemics of the epistle (vv. 15-22, 29-39, 40-44, 57-58) match closely what we know of Babylonian worship.[17] But Babylonian worship continued throughout the Persian and Greek periods, and Greeks, Egyptians, Syrians, and Mesopotamians worshiped and used statues of gods in analogous and similar ways. In addition, polemics and parodies against the gods were common in Hellenistic literature.[18] Thus the author of the Hebrew original of the epistle may have been in the Babylonian[19] or Judean Jewish community. There is no sign of specifically Egyptian influence except for the mention of cats (v. 22), which were first domesticated in Egypt.

THEMES

The extensive attack on the Near Eastern gods supports the main theme and goal of the Epistle of Jeremiah: that Israel should worship only the God of the Bible (v. 6) and not fear foreign gods (v. 5). The list of polemical charges brought against the statues of the gods is long, detailed, and repetitious. In general, the author lists exhaustively the gods' lack of all the attributes and aptitudes generally expected of gods in the ancient

15. See Ball, "Epistle of Jeremy," 596; Carey A. Moore, *Daniel, Esther, and Jeremiah: The Additions,* AB 44 (Garden City, N.Y.: Doubleday, 1977) 328, 334-35.

16. Kratz, "Die Rezeption von Jeremia 10 und 29 im Pseudepigraphen Brief des Jeremia," 30, suggests that the Epistle of Jeremiah is a response to Hellenistic worship that uses the book of Jeremiah in a new way.

17. For a convenient summary of the archaeological evidence for Babylonian worship, see Philip J. King, "Jeremiah and Idolatry," in *Eretz-Israel: Archaeological, Historical and Geographical Studies,* Joseph Aviram Volume 25 (Jerusalem: Israel Exploration Society, 1996) 31*-36*. See also Roth, "For Life, He Appeals to Death (Wis 13:18)," 51, on the Babylonian evidence in the Epistle of Jeremiah. The most extensive case for the Babylonian gods as objects of polemic was made by Weigand Naumann, "Untersuchungen über den apokrynphen Jeremiahsbrief," *BZAW* 25 (1913) 3-31.

18. See the parallels cited in George W. E. Nickelsburg, "The Bible Rewritten and Expanded," in *Jewish Writings of the Second Temple Period,* ed. Michael E. Stone (Philadelphia: Fortress, 1984) 148n. 341.

19. Kratz, "Die Rezeption von Jeremia 10 und 29 im Pseudepigraphen Brief des Jeremia," 2, suggests a Hebrew or Aramaic original addressed to the Babylonian community and a third-century BCE Greek translation of the Epistle of Jeremiah.

Near East. In making this attack, the epistle contrasts the ancient intuition of divine power and presence in the statues with the perceptible inactivity of those images of the gods.[20] The author repeats constantly that the gods are made of wood overlaid with gold and silver (vv. 30, 39, 55, 57-58, 70-71) and that they, far from being creators, were made by human craftsmen (vv. 4, 8-9, 39, 45-47, 50, 57) who themselves will die (v. 46). The gods cannot care for themselves or help themselves in time of crisis (vv. 12-15, 18-21, 24, 27, 55). They cannot move, but must be carried (vv. 4, 26-27, 55, 68) and must be clothed by humans (vv. 9-11). They cannot speak, see, or touch (vv. 8, 19, 41); in short, they have no breath or life within them (vv. 25, 27).

These gods cannot do good or evil for their worshipers or for themselves (vv. 34-38, 48-49, 53, 64, 67). They do not rule the heavens (vv. 60-63), make or break kings (vv. 34, 53, 66), fight wars, enforce judgments, help their clients, or protect themselves from theft (vv. 14-15, 18, 53-55, 57-59). Their wooden cores, metal plating, and clothing deteriorate (vv. 12, 20, 72). They are served by dishonest priests who steal from them (vv. 10, 28, 33). Their cults are improper and impure (judged by biblical standards), because priests have torn clothing and shaved heads (vv. 31-32) and because impure women and prostitutes serve them (vv. 11, 29-30, 42-43). As a result, these gods bring dishonor and shame upon their worshipers (vv. 26, 39-40, 47, 72-73).

20. For the Mesopotamian gods, see A. L. Oppenheim, *Ancient Mesopotamia: Portrait of a Dead Civilization* (Chicago: University of Chicago Press, 1964) 171-227; T. Jacobsen, "The Graven Image," in *Ancient Israelite Religion: Dedicated to Frank M. Cross,* ed. P. Miller et al. (Philadelphia: Fortress, 1987) 15-32; King, "Jeremiah and Idolatry," 33*.

BIBLIOGRAPHY

Commentaries:

Ball, Charles J. "Epistle of Jeremy." in *Apocrypha and Pseudepigrapha of the Old Testament.* Edited by R. H. Charles. Oxford: Clarendon, 1913. Still significant for its detailed textual notes.

Fitzgerald, Alysius. "Baruch." *New Jerome Biblical Commentary.* Edited by Raymond Brown et al. Englewood Cliffs, N.J.: Prentice-Hall, 1990. A short introductory commentary with the Letter of Jeremiah positioned as chapter six in the commentary on Baruch.

Harrington, Daniel J. "Letter of Jeremiah." In *Harper's Bible Commentary.* Edited by James L. Mays. San Francisco: Harper & Row, 1988. A brief introductory commentary that emphasizes the meaning of the text.

Moore, Cary A. *Daniel, Esther, and Jeremiah: The Additions.* AB 44. Garden City, N.Y.: Doubleday, 1977. Provides a general introduction and moderately detailed textual notes. Sparing interpretation.

Specialized Studies:

Nickelsburg, George W. E. "The Bible Rewritten and Expanded." In *Jewish Writings of the Second Temple Period.* Edited by Michael E. Stone. Philadelphia: Fortress, 1984. A short introduction to the Letter of Jeremiah in light of the state of scholarly knowledge and discussion in the early nineteen eighties.

———. *Jewish Literature Between the Bible and the Mishnah.* Philadelphia: Fortress, 1981. Contains a short discussion and summary of the Letter of Jeremiah.

Schürer, Emil, Geza Vermes, Fergus Millar, and Martin Goodman. *The History of the Jewish People in the Age of Jesus Christ (175 B.C.–A.D. 135)*. Vol. 3.2. Edinburgh: T. & T. Clark, 1987. An update of a (seriously flawed) classic early twentieth century German work providing a summary and cursory discussion of the Letter of Jeremiah. Valuable for its discussion of the use of the book in early Christianity and patristic writers.

OUTLINE OF THE LETTER OF JEREMIAH

I. Letter of Jeremiah 6:1-7, Narrative Introduction

II. Letter of Jeremiah 6:8-16, First Instruction

III. Letter of Jeremiah 6:17-23, Second Instruction

IV. Letter of Jeremiah 6:24-29, Third Instruction

V. Letter of Jeremiah 6:30-40a, Fourth Instruction

VI. Letter of Jeremiah 6:40b-44, Fifth Instruction

VII. Letter of Jeremiah 6:45-52, Sixth Instruction

VIII. Letter of Jeremiah 6:53-56, Seventh Instruction

IX. Letter of Jeremiah 6:57-65, Eighth Instruction

X. Letter of Jeremiah 6:66-69, Ninth Instruction

XI. Letter of Jeremiah 6:70-73, Tenth Instruction

THE LETTER OF JEREMIAH 6:1-7

NARRATIVE INTRODUCTION

NAB

6 **1** A copy of the letter which Jeremiah sent to those who were being led captive to Babylon by the king of the Babylonians, to convey to them what God had commanded him:

For the sins you committed before God, you are being led captive to Babylon by Nebuchadnezzar, king of the Babylonians. **2** When you reach Babylon you will be there many years, a period seven generations long; after which I will bring you back from there in peace. **3** And now in Babylon you will see borne upon men's shoulders gods of silver and gold and wood, which cast fear upon the pagans. **4** Take care that you yourselves do not imitate their alien example and stand in fear of them, **5** when you see the crowd before them and behind worshiping them. Rather, say in your hearts, "You, O LORD, are to be worshiped!"; **6** for my angel is with you, and he is the custodian of your lives.

6,1: Omit 'ymōn: so LXX^MSS.

NRSV

6 *a* A copy of a letter that Jeremiah sent to those who were to be taken to Babylon as exiles by the king of the Babylonians, to give them the message that God had commanded him.

2 Because of the sins that you have committed before God, you will be taken to Babylon as exiles by Nebuchadnezzar, king of the Babylonians. ³ Therefore when you have come to Babylon you will remain there for many years, for a long time, up to seven generations; after that I will bring you away from there in peace. ⁴ Now in Babylon you will see gods made of silver and gold and wood, which people carry on their shoulders, and which cause the heathen to fear. ⁵ So beware of becoming at all like the foreigners or of letting fear for these gods*b* possess you ⁶when you see the multitude before and behind them worshiping them. But say in your heart, "It is you, O Lord, whom we must worship." ⁷For my angel is with you, and he is watching over your lives.

a The King James Version (like the Latin Vulgate) prints The Letter of Jeremiah as Chapter 6 of the Book of Baruch, and the chapter and verse numbers are here retained. In the Greek Septuagint, the Letter is separated from Baruch by the Book of Lamentations.
b Gk for them

COMMENTARY

As was noted in the Introduction, even though this work is called a letter, it contains admonitions, exhortations, and especially polemics against idolatry.[21] The epistle is meant to fit into the sequence of events found in the book of Jeremiah. The letter of Jeremiah to the exiles settled in Babylonia (Jeremiah 29), on which this work is modeled, is addressed to the Judeans already taken to Babylon by Nebuchadnezzar in the first exile (597 BCE; see 2 Kgs 24:10-17). This epistle precedes that letter, since it is addressed to "those who were to be taken to Babylon as exiles," before they were led away. However, it is

21. The verses here are numbered 1-73, as in the NRSV. The Greek verse numbers, followed by some translations, vary by one or two verses because the superscription (v. 1 here) is often not numbered and because verse divisions vary in several places.

also possible that the author envisioned the second exile, which followed the destruction of Jerusalem in 586 BCE. After Nebuzaradan, Nebuchadnezzar's captain of the bodyguard, took Jerusalem (2 Kgs 25:8-12; Jer 39:1-10), Nebuchadnezzar ordered Jeremiah's release from jail and offered him transport to Babylon if he wished; but Jeremiah chose to stay in Mizpah with Gedaliah, who was appointed governor (Jer 39:1–40:6). This scenario from the biblical book of Jeremiah provides a context for Jeremiah to address a letter to the exiles as they are gathered for the trip to Babylon. Similar apocryphal expansions of the Jeremiah stories can be found in the Greek and Hebrew versions of Jeremiah and in the Jeremiah Apocryphon found at Qumran (4Q385b). According to the Qumran text, Jeremiah traveled to Babylon before he was taken to Egypt (see Jeremiah 43 for his exile in Egypt).

The first statement of the epistle (v. 2) gives the deuteronomic explanation for exile: sin. The prediction that the people will remain in exile for a long time (v. 2) agrees with Jeremiah's letter (Jeremiah 29) in which he advises the exiles to settle down in Babylon and build houses, families, and gardens. Twice the book of Jeremiah predicts an exile of seventy years (Jer 25:12; 29:10) and elsewhere indirectly alludes to three generations (Jer 27:7, extant only in the Hebrew). Here the author, writing much later, extends the time of exile to seven generations in order to encompass his own time. All these round numbers, along with the further revision in Dan 9:2, 24-27 to "seventy weeks of years," only approximate the length of exile.

The topic of the Epistle of Jeremiah is a simple deuteronomic problem (v. 4): The people will be tempted to assimilate into Babylonian culture and worship their gods. They will experience the attractions of worship and ritual, including gold- and silver-plated wooden statues (common in Babylon; see Isa 40:19; Jer 10:3-4), festival processions (known from Mesopotamian reliefs and Isa 46:1), and popular reverence for these gods ("fear" means awe, respect, reverence, acceptance). The solution to this problem is to remain distinct from the Babylonians and not to fear their gods. The instruction not to fear the Babylonian gods will be repeated in five of the ten refrains that end the sections of the epistle (vv. 16, 23, 29, 65, 69). When attracted by a festival procession and the religion of the native population, Israel should affirm its commitment to God alone: "It is you, O Lord, whom we must worship" (v. 6; cf. Deut 6:4 and the commandments in Exod 20:3; Deut 5:7). In response, God will watch over faithful Israel through the agency of an angel, connoting divine presence and care (v. 7), just as God cared for them during the exodus (see Exod 14:19; 23:20, 23; 32:34, where the angel is a euphemism for God's activity; for a later understanding of angelic guardians, see Tob 5:4-5). The Greek verb for "watching over" (ἐκζητῶν *ekzetōn*) Israel's lives has an added connotation of judicial investigation and accountability for any harm done (to or by the exiles?). The rest of the epistle exhorts the exiles to reject other gods by convincing them that God alone is genuine and powerful and that other gods are inauthentic. (See Reflections at 6:70-73.)

FIRST INSTRUCTION

NAB

7 Their tongues are smoothed by woodworkers; they are covered with gold and silver—but they are a fraud, and cannot speak. **8** People bring gold, as to a maiden in love with ornament, **9** and furnish crowns for the heads of their gods. Then sometimes the priests take the silver and gold from their gods and spend it on themselves, **10** or give part of it to the harlots on the terrace. They trick them out in garments like men, these gods of silver and gold and wood; **11** but though they are wrapped in purple clothing, they are not safe from corrosion or insects. **12** They wipe their faces clean of the house dust which is thick upon them. **13** Each has a scepter, like the human ruler of a district; but none does away with those that offend against it. **14** Each has in its right hand an axe or dagger, but it cannot save itself from war or pillage. Thus it is known they are not gods; do not fear them.

6,9: (*eis 'eautous*) *katanalōsousi*: so LXX^MSS.
6,10: Omit *theous* before *chrysous*: so LXX^MSS.

NRSV

8 Their tongues are smoothed by the carpenter, and they themselves are overlaid with gold and silver; but they are false and cannot speak. [9]People[a] take gold and make crowns for the head of their gods, as they might for a girl who loves ornaments, [10]and make crowns for the heads of their gods. Sometimes the priests secretly take gold and silver from their gods and spend it on themselves, [11]or even give some of it to the prostitutes on the terrace. They deck their gods[b] out with garments like human beings—these gods of silver and gold and wood [12]that cannot save themselves from rust and corrosion. When they have been dressed in purple robes, [13]their faces are wiped because of the dust from the temple, which is thick upon them. [14]One of them holds a scepter, like a district judge, but is unable to destroy anyone who offends it. [15]Another has a dagger in its right hand, and an ax, but cannot defend itself from war and robbers. [16]From this it is evident that they are not gods; so do not fear them.

[a] Gk *They*   [b] Gk *them*

COMMENTARY

The author argues for his position (the Greek sentence begins with "For" [γάρ *gar*]) by mocking the statues of the gods and the people who attend to them. His conclusion is repeated at the beginning and the end, "they are false" (v. 8) and "they are not gods" (v. 16); and his advice, "do not fear them" (v. 16), corresponds to his theme in the opening narrative (vv. 5-6). He proves his position by describing the gods and their worshipers. The gods need to be clothed and adorned like children (vv. 9, 11), they get dirty and must be cleaned, and they deteriorate through the attacks of rust on their metal plating and moths on their clothing (v. 12; see the Introduction for this interpretation of "corrosion."). Although they bear royal, judicial, and military insignia (vv. 12, 14-15), these gods cannot execute the guilty or defend themselves. The priests steal the gods' wealth (v. 10), sometimes for prostitution (v. 11). Ritual prostitution in the gods' temples may be implied by the Greek word τέγος (*tegos*), translated as "terrace" (lit., "roof," but used in idiomatic speech for any roofed building or hall, like a temple, and also for a brothel). Herodotus reports that ritual prostitutes, the "brides of Bel," slept in the top level of Bel's great pyramid temple in Babylon.[22] In summary, the gods and their priests are inauthentic, fraudulent, deceptive, and corrupt. (See Reflections at 6:70-73.)

22. Herodotus *History* 1.181.

LETTER OF JEREMIAH 6:17-23

SECOND INSTRUCTION

NAB

15 As useless as one's broken tools **16** are their gods, set up in their houses; their eyes are full of dust from the feet of those who enter. **17** Their courtyards are walled in like those of a man brought to execution for a crime against the king; the priests reinforce their houses with gates and bars and bolts, lest they be carried off by robbers. **18** They light more lamps for them than for themselves, yet not one of these can they see. **19** They are like any beam in the house; it is said their hearts are eaten away. Though the insects out of the ground consume them and their garments, they do not feel it. **20** Their faces are blackened by the smoke of the house. **21** Bats and swallows alight on their bodies and on their heads; and cats as well as birds. **22** Know, therefore, that they are not gods, and do not fear them.

NRSV

17 For just as someone's dish is useless when it is broken, [18]so are their gods when they have been set up in the temples. Their eyes are full of the dust raised by the feet of those who enter. And just as the gates are shut on every side against anyone who has offended a king, as though under sentence of death, so the priests make their temples secure with doors and locks and bars, in order that they may not be plundered by robbers. [19] They light more lamps for them than they light for themselves, though their gods[a] can see none of them. [20]They are[b] just like a beam of the temple, but their hearts, it is said, are eaten away when crawling creatures from the earth devour them and their robes. They do not notice [21] when their faces have been blackened by the smoke of the temple. [22]Bats, swallows, and birds alight on their bodies and heads; and so do cats. [23]From this you will know that they are not gods; so do not fear them.

[a] Gk *they*   [b] Gk *It is*

COMMENTARY

The physical realities of the temple statues prompt the second series of satirical attacks. The initial thesis (v. 17), a proverbial simile that they are as useless as broken ceramic pots (cf. Jer 19:11; 22:28; Hos 8:8), is supported by the helplessness of the temple statues and leads to the concluding refrain that the gods are neither real nor to be feared (v. 23). Ironically, the worshipers who venerate the gods stir up dust, which gets in the gods' eyes (v. 18) and prevents them from seeing the light of the many lamps in the temples (v. 19; cf. Ps. 115:5); nor do they know that their faces are blackened by the smoke of those lamps (v. 21).

The comparison in the second half of v. 18 is

unclear both in Greek and in the NRSV. Probably it refers to a person who has insulted a king and is jailed in a walled (lit., fenced or fortified) courtyard (αὐλαί *aulai*) whose gates are secured as he awaits death. Jeremiah was confined in such a courtyard (Jer 32:2). The temple statues of the gods are similarly locked up like prisoners, but ironically the walls keep the robbers out, rather than keep them in. The gods cannot move (v. 4) or defend themselves (v. 15). In fact, the argument continues, living things attack the gods. Since the gods are made of wood, like the temple (cf. v. 8), insects eat their wooden "hearts" along with their robes (v. 20; cf. v. 12) and thus destroy them. Birds land on them, with the implication that they deposit feces there, and "cats" (mentioned only here in the LXX) climb on them. The beleaguered temple gods are the opposite of a real and powerful God and thus do not deserve to be feared (v. 23). (See Reflections at 6:70-73.)

THIRD INSTRUCTION

NAB

23 Despite the gold that covers them for adornment, unless someone wipes away the corrosion, they do not shine; nor did they feel anything when they were molded. **24** They are bought at any price, and there is no spirit in them. **25** Having no feet, they are carried on men's shoulders, displaying their shame to all; and those who worship them are put to confusion **26** because, if they fall to the ground, the worshipers must raise them up. They neither move of themselves if one sets them upright, nor come upright if they fall; but one puts gifts beside them as beside the dead. **27** Their priests resell their sacrifices for their own advantage. Even their wives cure parts of the meat, but do not share it with the poor and the weak; **28** the menstruous and women in childbed handle their sacrifices. Knowing from this that they are not gods, do not fear them.

6,27: *adynatō metadidoasi*; omit *mē*: so LXX^MSS.

NRSV

24 As for the gold that they wear for beauty—it^*a* will not shine unless someone wipes off the tarnish; for even when they were being cast, they did not feel it. ^25 They are bought without regard to cost, but there is no breath in them. ^26 Having no feet, they are carried on the shoulders of others, revealing to humankind their worthlessness. And those who serve them are put to shame ^27 because, if any of these gods falls^*b* to the ground, they themselves must pick it up. If anyone sets it upright, it cannot move itself; and if it is tipped over, it cannot straighten itself. Gifts are places before them just as before the dead. ^28 The priests sell the sacrifices that are offered to these gods^*c* and use the money themselves. Likewise their wives preserve some of the meat^*d* with salt, but give none to the poor or helpless. ^29 Sacrifices to them may even be touched by women in their periods or at childbirth. Since you know by these things that they are not gods, do not fear them.

^*a* Lat Syr: Gk *they*   ^*b* Gk *if they fall*   ^*c* Gk *to them*   ^*d* Gk *of them*

COMMENTARY

This instruction, beginning with the connective "for" (γάρ *gar*), continues the previous argument: The gods are so helpless that their precious gold plating (cf. v. 8) must be polished. The expression "for even when they were being cast, they did not feel it" (v. 24) makes little sense, because the statues were not cast; rather they were made from wood overlaid with gold. Probably the Greek writer mistranslated the original Hebrew, which read, "when they were polluted [חללו *ḥālĕlû*], they did not feel it," as when they produced/cast [חוללו *ḥôlĕlû*], they did not feel it. A series of sarcastic contrasts (vv. 25-27) devalue both the statues and their attendants. Although the statues are expensive to buy, they lack life (v. 25; cf. Ps 135:17; Jer 10:14), so that offering them gifts is like the traditional offering of gifts at the graves of the dead (v. 27), a practice common in the Near East but resisted by the Hebrew Bible (Deut 26:14; Ps 106:28). Because they lack locomotion, the statues must be carried (v. 26; cf. vv. 4, 68) and set up by others. This immobility dishonors their worshipers, who participate in the charade by picking up the statues if they are ignominiously dropped. The author also condemns the corrupt priests for stealing sacrifices (cf. v. 10) and their wives for preserving excess meat rather than giving it to the poor (v. 28). Finally, Babylonian rituals are judged by biblical norms: Women who are ritually impure through childbirth or menstruation (see Lev. 12:2-5; 15:19-20) touch the sacrifices (v. 29). (See Reflections at 6:70-73.)

FOURTH INSTRUCTION

NAB

29 How can they be called gods? For women bring the offerings to these gods of silver and gold and wood; **30** and in their temples the priests squat with torn tunic and with shaven hair and beard, and with their heads uncovered. **31** They shout and wail before their gods as others do at a funeral banquet. **32** The priests take some of their clothing and put it on their wives and children. **33** Whether they are treated well or ill by anyone, they cannot requite it; they can neither set up a king nor remove him. **34** Similarly, they cannot give anyone riches or coppers; if one fails to fulfill a vow to them, they cannot exact it of him. **35** They neither save a man from death, nor deliver the weak from the strong. **36** To no blind man do they restore his sight, nor do they save any man in an emergency. **37** They neither pity the widow nor benefit the orphan. **38** These gilded and silvered wooden statues are like stones from the mountains; and their worshipers will be put to shame. **39** How then can it be thought or claimed that they are gods?

6,32: ('*oi iereis*) *endyousi*: so LXX^MSS.

NRSV

30 For how can they be called gods? Women serve meals for gods of silver and gold and wood; [31]and in their temples the priests sit with their clothes torn, their heads and beards shaved, and their heads uncovered. [32]They howl and shout before their gods as some do at a funeral banquet. [33]The priests take some of the clothing of their gods*a* to clothe their wives and children. [34]Whether one does evil to them or good, they will not be able to repay it. They cannot set up a king or depose one. [35]Likewise they are not able to give either wealth or money; if one makes a vow to them and does not keep it, they will not require it. [36]They cannot save anyone from death or rescue the weak from the strong. [37]They cannot restore sight to the blind; they cannot rescue one who is in distress. [38]They cannot take pity on a widow or do good to an orphan. [39]These things that are made of wood and overlaid with gold and silver are like stones from the mountain, and those who serve them will be put to shame. [40]Why then must anyone think that they are gods, or call them gods?

a Gk *some of their clothing*

COMMENTARY

The attack on Babylonian rituals continues. Women serve in the temples (v. 30), contrary to biblical law, which does not allow women even to enter the inner precincts of the Jerusalem Temple. Priests preside with their heads uncovered, hair and beards shaved, and clothes torn, howling and shouting (vv. 31-32). Shaved heads and beards, disheveled hair, torn clothing, and even flesh wounds were normal and accepted signs of mourning in the Near East (Job 1:20; Jer 41:5; 48:37), but certain of these practices were forbidden to Israelites (e.g., "shaven temples," a rite of hair cutting, in Jer 9:26; 25:23; 49:32) and to priests serving at the Temple (Lev 10:6; 21:5, 10; Deut 14:1; Ezek 24:17; 44:17-20) because they were associated with mourning rituals for the Babylonian dying and rising god, Dumuzi or Tammuz (vv. 31-32; cf. Jer 16:5; Ezek 8:14).

The priests are again accused of stealing from the gods (v. 33; cf. vv. 10, 28) and their worshipers of shaming themselves (v. 39) because these gods lack divine attributes (vv. 34-38). These gods cannot repay good and evil, make or break kings (1–2 Samuel), guarantee a vow, make a person wealthy (2 Sam 2:7), save the weak or preserve human beings from death (Deut 32:39; Ps 49:15), give sight to a blind person, rescue someone in distress, or aid the helpless widow or orphan (Ps 146:8-9). The final comparison of gold- and silver-plated wood statues with inert stones (v. 39) is drawn from Hab 2:19. (See Reflections at 6:70-73.)

FIFTH INSTRUCTION

NAB

40 Even the Chaldeans themselves have no respect for them; for when they see a deaf mute, incapable of speech, they bring forward Bel and ask the god to make noise, as though the man could understand; **41** and they are themselves unable to reflect and abandon these gods, for they have no sense. **42** And their women, girt with cords, sit by the roads, burning chaff for incense; **43** and whenever one of them is drawn aside by some passerby who lies with her, she mocks her neighbor who has not been dignified as she has, and has not had her cord broken. **44** All that takes place around these gods is a fraud: how then can it be thought or claimed that they are gods?

6,44: *en* (*autois*) . . . *'öste* (*theous*): so LXX^MSS.

NRSV

Besides, even the Chaldeans themselves dishonor them; for when they see someone who cannot speak, they bring Bel and pray that the mute may speak, as though Bel[a] were able to understand! [41]Yet they themselves cannot perceive this and abandon them, for they have no sense. [42]And the women, with cords around them, sit along the passageways, burning bran for incense. [43]When one of them is led off by one of the passers-by and is taken to bed by him, she derides the woman next to her, because she was not as attractive as herself and her cord was not broken. [44]Whatever is done for these idols[b] is false. Why then must anyone think that they are gods, or call them gods?

[a] Gk *he*   [b] Gk *them*

COMMENTARY

The priests bring dishonor on their own gods (vv. 40-41), just as the gods shame their worshipers (v. 39), by vain efforts to cure mute people through a mute god. "Chaldeans" here probably refers to religious specialists who engaged in divination and magic. "Bel" (Isa 46:1; Jer 50:2; 51:44), more properly "Belu," is the Babylonian equivalent of "Baal," meaning "Lord," and refers to Marduk. The Greek pronominal subjects and objects in vv. 40-41 are very unclear, as is the NRSV interpretation of them. In v. 41, either the statue of Bel is brought to the mute person or the person is brought to Bel's temple. When Bel and the mute person are together, either Bel is entreated to speak or to enable the person to speak, but Bel cannot understand in either case. Verse 41 seems to mean that even this ineffective appeal to Bel does not cause the Chaledeans to perceive the impotency of Bel and abandon their gods, as the author would

expect, because the Chaldeans have no understanding. Thus they are taken in by their gods and do not recognize acts of worship and reverence as false.

Similarly women at the temples compete with one another for partners in ritual prostitution (vv. 42-43; cf. v. 11) and do not recognize their worship as false or question their gods. The cords around the women sitting in the passageways (v. 42) were probably worn around their foreheads as a sign that they were prostitutes (see v. 11 and Jer 3:2 for prostitution). Evidence for temple prostitutes in the ancient Near East and in Israel (Deut 23:17-18; 2 Kgs 15:12; 22:47; 23:7; 24:24) is plentiful, but the connection of such prostitution with fertility cults is very unclear. Sometimes prostitutes were used to support the temples. In other cases, individual women had intercourse to fulfill a vow. The burning bran (v. 42; bran is chaff, the outer covering of the wheat kernel) may have been used as an aphrodisiac. Herodotus describes the practice of a prostitute's waiting in the temple to be led away by a man for intercourse as a once-in-a-lifetime ritual practiced in Babylonian temples of Ishtar Mylitta, whom he identified with the Greek goddess Aphrodite. His interpretation of the temple women's sexual activity may not be accurate, since they could have been women fulfilling a vow.[23] Needless to say, biblical law, the prophets, and the author of the Epistle of Jeremiah (v. 44) strongly reject such fertility practices. (See Reflections at 6:70-73.)

23. Herodotus *History* 1.199.

SIXTH INSTRUCTION

NAB

45 They are produced by woodworkers and goldsmiths, and they are nothing else than what these craftsmen wish them to be. **46** Even those who produce them are not long-lived; **47** how then can what they have produced be gods? They have left frauds and opprobium to their successors. **48** For when war or disaster comes upon them, the priests deliberate among themselves where they can hide with them. **49** How then can one not know that these are no-gods, which do not save themselves either from war or from disaster? **50** They are wooden, gilded and silvered; they will later be known for frauds. To all peoples and kings it will be clear that they are not gods, but human handiwork; and that God's work is not in them.

51 Who does not know that they are not gods?

6,47: (*kataskeuasthenta*) *einai theoi*: so LXX[MSS].
6,51: (*Tini oun*) *ou (gnosteon)*: so LXX[MSS].

NRSV

45 They are made by carpenters and goldsmiths; they can be nothing but what the artisans wish them to be. [46]Those who make them will certainly not live very long themselves; [47]how then can the things that are made by them be gods? They have left only lies and reproach for those who come after. [48]For when war or calamity comes upon them, the priests consult together as to where they can hide themselves and their gods.[a] [49]How then can one fail to see that these are not gods, for they cannot save themselves from war or calamity? [50]Since they are made of wood and overlaid with gold and silver, it will afterward be known that they are false. [51]It will be manifest to all the nations and kings that they are not gods but the work of human hands, and that there is no work of God in them. [52]Who then can fail to know that they are not gods?[b]

[a] Gk *them*   [b] Meaning of Gk uncertain

COMMENTARY

The author implicitly contrasts the Babylonian gods with the biblical creator God. God created the world and lives forever, but the statues of the gods were created by artisans (Ps 115:4; Isa 40:19; Jer 10:9), who themselves soon die (v. 46). These created gods mislead and dishonor the craftsmen's descendants. The biblical God rules the world with power to destroy all opponents, in contrast to the statues of the gods, which must be hidden by their priests during war (v. 48). The public, international forum of war unmasks the gods' fraudulent claims to divinity. (See Reflections at 6:70-73.)

LETTER OF JEREMIAH 6:53-56

SEVENTH INSTRUCTION

NAB

52 They set no king over the land, nor do they give men rain. **53** They neither vindicate their own rights, nor do they recover what is unjustly taken, for they are unable; **54** they are like crows between heaven and earth. For when fire breaks out in the temple of these wooden or gilded or silvered gods, though the priests flee and are safe, they themselves are burnt up in the fire like beams. **55** They cannot resist a king, or enemy forces. **56** How then can it be admitted or thought that they are gods?

NRSV

53 For they cannot set up a king over a country or give rain to people. [54]They cannot judge their own cause or deliver one who is wronged, for they have no power; [55]they are like crows between heaven and earth. When fire breaks out in a temple of wooden gods overlaid with gold or silver, their priests will flee and escape, but the gods[a] will be burned up like timbers. [56]Besides, they can offer no resistance to king or enemy. Why then must anyone admit or think that they are gods?

[a] Gk *they*

COMMENTARY

The powerless gods of the previous instruction cannot appoint a king (cf. v. 34) or see that justice is done for themselves or others (cf. v. 14) or give rain (Deut 11:14; 28:12; Ps 147:8), as Near Eastern gods are expected to do. The statues of the gods, previously shown to be subject to dust, corrosion, and war, are now threatened with incineration in temple fires that they, unlike their priests, cannot escape. The odd simile that they are like crows between heaven and earth (v. 55) is probably based on a mistranslation of the orginal Hebrew "clouds" (see the Introduction on language). Thus the gods are powerless (v. 54), like clouds drifting in the sky. (See Reflections at 6:70-73.)

They are safe from neither thieves nor bandits, these wooden and silvered and gilded gods; **57** those who seize them strip off the gold and the silver, and go away with the clothing that was on them, and they cannot help themselves. **58** How much better to be a king displaying his valor, or a handy tool in a house, the joy of its owner, than these false gods; or the door of a house, that keeps safe those who are within, rather than these false gods; or a wooden post in a palace, rather than these false gods! **59** The sun and moon and stars are bright, and obedient in the service for which they are sent. **60** Like wise the lightning, when it flashes, is a goodly sight; and the same wind blows over all the land. **61** The clouds, too, when commanded by God to proceed across the whole world, fulfill the order; **62** and fire, sent from on high to burn up the mountains and the forests, does what has been commanded. But these false gods are not their equal, whether in beauty or in power; **63** so that it is unthinkable, and cannot be claimed, that they are gods. They can neither execute judgment, nor benefit man. **64** Know, therefore, that they are not gods, and do not fear them.

6,56: (*ou mē*) *diasōthosin:* so LXX^{MSS}.
6,58: *charēsetai* (*o kektēmenos*): so Lat.

57 Gods made of wood and overlaid with silver and gold are unable to save themselves from thieves or robbers. [58]Anyone who can will strip them of their gold and silver and of the robes they wear, and go off with this booty, and they will not be able to help themselves. [59]So it is better to be a king who shows his courage, or a household utensil that serves its owner's need, then to be these false gods; better even the door of a house that protects its contents, than these false gods; better also a wooden pillar in a palace, than these false gods.

60 For sun and moon and stars are bright, and when sent to do a service, they are obedient. [61]So also the lightning, when it flashes, is widely seen; and the wind likewise blows in every land. [62]When God commands the clouds to go over the whole world, they carry out his command. [63]And the fire sent from above to consume mountains and woods does what it is ordered. But these idols[a] are not to be compared with them in appearance or power. [64]Therefore one must not think that they are gods, nor call them gods, for they are not able either to decide a case or to do good to anyone. [65]Since you know then that they are not gods, do not fear them.

[a] Gk *these things*

COMMENTARY

This instruction contains two parts, (1) the helplessness and uselessness of statues of the gods (vv. 57-59) and (2) their inferiority to heavenly bodies, which are under God's control (vv. 60-64). Each part concludes that the gods are false (vv. 59, 64), and the whole section ends with the usual refrain not to fear them (v. 65). The charge that the gods can be robbed of their goods and stolen entirely has appeared several times pre-

viously (vv. 10, 15, 28, 33, 48). Similarly, the contrast of useful household items (a utensil, door, or column) with useless statues of the gods appeared earlier (vv. 17-18) and is common in other polemics (e.g., Wis 13:12-15; 15:7-8). The contrast between a king and a false god (v. 59) is cogent, but it does not fit the context. Perhaps the Hebrew for a "wooden staff" (מקל *maqqēl*) or a "spindle" (פלך *pelek*) has been confused with the word for "king" (מלך *melek*). If so, all four useful household items in v. 59 (staff/spindle, utensil, door, and pillar) would be made of wood.

God commands the sun, moon, stars, lightning, and wind as they travel over the whole world (vv. 60-62) and heavenly fire when it strikes the earth (v. 63). The image of the sky and storm god ruling the world and executing justice is common in the Near East and in the Hebrew Bible (e.g., Exodus 15; 19:16-19; 1 Kgs 18:44-45; Psalms 29; 135:7).

The creation story carefully subordinates powerful heavenly bodies so that they will not be worshiped (Gen 1:14-18). Here these heavenly powers are magnified in contrast to the unimpressive and powerless gods, which are dismissed as unable even to decide a case or do any good (v. 64), much less rule the cosmos. The criteria for a true God include ruling the heavens, guaranteeing justice, and protecting worshipers; the statues of the gods fail on all counts. (See Reflections at 6:70-73.)

LETTER OF JEREMIAH 6:66-69

NINTH INSTRUCTION

NAB

65 Kings they neither curse nor bless. **66** They show the nations no signs in the heavens, nor are they brilliant like the sun, nor shining like the moon. **67** The beasts which can help themselves by fleeing to shelter are better than they are. **68** Thus in no way is it clear to us that they are gods; so do not fear them.

NRSV

66 They can neither curse nor bless kings; [67]they cannot show signs in the heavens for the nations, or shine like the sun or give light like the moon. [68]The wild animals are better than they are, for they can flee to shelter and help themselves. [69]So we have no evidence whatever that they are gods; therefore do not fear them.

COMMENTARY

The Greek conjunction "for" (γάρ *gar*) connects this instruction to the previous one, and the pronominal subject of the first verb refers back to the noun "false gods" (οἱ ψευδεῖς θεοί *hoi pseudeis theoi*) in v. 59 (the noun "idols" in NRSV v. 63 is not in the Greek). Polemics continue showing that the statues of the false gods have no power over the earthly or heavenly order. The gods cannot curse or bless kings (v. 66; cf. vv. 34, 53). That they do not give light like the sun and the moon (v. 67) recalls the ironic comment that priests light lamps for them in their temples, but the gods cannot see (v. 19). The unclear observation that "they cannot show signs in the heavens for the nations" (v. 67) may refer to the use of heavenly bodies to predict the future or as signs of divine pleasure and displeasure (cf. Jer 10:2). However, the expression "signs in nations in heaven" probably springs from a confusion in the translation of the similar Hebrew words for "nations" (עמים *'amîm*) and "heaven(s)" (שמים *šāmayim*). Finally, and strikingly, these false gods are lower than heavenly bodies, human beings, and even wild animals, who can run for cover (cf. vv. 4, 26). (See Reflections at 6:70-73.)

LETTER OF JEREMIAH 6:70-73

TENTH INSTRUCTION

NAB

69 For like a scarecrow in a cucumber patch, that is no protection, are their wooden, gilded, silvered gods. **70** Just like a thornbush in a garden on which perches every kind of bird, or like a corpse hurled into darkness, are the silvered and gilded wooden gods. **71** From the rotting of the purple and the linen upon them, it can be known that they are not gods; they themselves will in the end be consumed, and be a disgrace in the land. **72** The better for the just man who has no idols: he shall be far from disgrace!

6,71: *marmarou=śēś linen. (tēs ep) autois (sēpomenes) gnōsesthe*: so LXX^MSS.

NRSV

70 Like a scarecrow in a cucumber bed, which guards nothing, so are their gods of wood, overlaid with gold and silver. [71]In the same way, their gods of wood, overlaid with gold and silver, are like a thornbush in a garden on which every bird perches; or like a corpse thrown out in the darkness. [72]From the purple and linen[a] that rot upon them you will know that they are not gods; and they will finally be consumed themselves, and be a reproach in the land. [73]Better, therefore, is someone upright who has no idols; such a person will be far above reproach.

[a] Cn: Gk *marble*, Syr *silk*

COMMENTARY

The tenth and final instruction does not provide a summary or conclusion to the letter, but reinforces previous themes with new images. The first of three similes, the scarecrow in a cucumber patch, is drawn from the Hebrew version of Jer 10:5, which stresses the muteness and immobility of a (carved?) "post" used as a scarecrow. But the author of the Epistle of Jeremiah applies this simile to a favorite theme, that the gods cannot guard themselves or prevent robbery (cf. vv. 15, 18, 57, 59). Second, the gods are compared to a thorn bush in a garden (v. 71), which is out of place and fit only to be fouled by perching birds. (Ordinarily thorn bushes were used as hedges around a garden.) Finally, and most dismally, the gods are like an unburied corpse (v. 71), abandoned under cover of darkness. In a society that respected its dead and valued proper burial, this is the ultimate dishonor and show of contempt. In Amos 8:3 a series of disasters signifying social dissolution include "dead bodies [which]

shall be many, cast out in every place." Jeremiah predicts that victims of famine and sword during war will be thrown out into the streets with no one to bury them (Jer 14:16), and Baruch makes the disinterment of the bones of kings a symbol of the destruction of Judean society (Bar 2:25). In the penultimate verse, the gods' lack of immortality, a requirement for authentic divinity, is symbolized by the rotting of their royal purple and linen clothes. In the end, the statues of the gods will be consumed—literally "devoured."

Although the epistle lacks a satisfying conclusion, the final two verses repeat and intensify the theme of dishonor. The gods are a reproach to the lands where they are present (v. 72; cf. v. 47). A reproach refers to something disgraceful or dishonorable that causes people to reject or rebuke the land and people associated with these false gods. In an honor/shame society, such an object of reproach taints the public standing of everyone and thus is a much more serious matter than in modern Western society, which emphasizes personal guilt. "Reproach" is the catchword that leads to the final verse (v. 73), which does not repeat the usual refrains that concluded the previous nine instructions. Rather, the author implicitly compares the just person who has no idols with all those mentioned in the epistle who have gods made of wood plated with gold and silver. The word "idols" (εἴδωλα *eidōla*) is used only here in the Epistle of Jeremiah, despite the NRSV's insertion of the word into its translations of vv. 44 and 63. Although the introductory narrative of the epistle aims its polemic against Babylonian gods in the time of Jeremiah, the author must have lived later when some Jews were in danger of bringing statues of the gods into their homes. Against this practice, the author holds up the wisdom ideal of the just person who retains his or her honor by avoiding any "reproach"—that is, any dishonorable or disgraceful thing or behavior. Here dishonorable behavior is owning and worshiping idols. If those addressed in the Epistle of Jeremiah follow this advice, the author's long and repetitious polemic will have achieved its goal.

REFLECTIONS

Much of the content, attitudes, and tactics in the Epistle of Jeremiah strike the modern reader as inappropriate or irrelevant. The temptation to worship gods other than the biblical God died out with the demise of polytheism in the West. The epistle's sharp rejection of other religions does not fit the pluralistic and ecumenical temper of our times. Contemporary theologies seek to understand, to learn from, and to accept as authentic other religions and their cultures. The polemics and parodies in the Epistle of Jeremiah misrepresent the views of others and so contradict our standards of rationality and fairness. Sarcastic, nihilating attacks on others' views and practices remind us of the worst in political ads and recall the destructive effects of Christian anti-Semitism throughout history, especially during the Nazi Holocaust of World War II.

For all its limitations, the Epistle of Jeremiah communicates a sharp, robust appreciation of God's vitality and power. The author defends his core theology with a determined exposition of God's reality and sovereignty in the face of massive cultural bias against monotheism in the ancient world. In the contemporary West, denial of or inattention to God has replaced polytheism as the major threat to the worship of God. Yet this change in orientation does not leave the biblical tradition silent. The epistle witnesses to a creative reinterpretation and reuse of Jeremiah and other biblical texts in order to counter the long-term threat of idolatry in the Hellenistic Empire. The Dead Sea Scrolls and other Second Temple literature witness to a similar rewriting of biblical texts to meet new challenges. Analogously, in our "Hellenistic" world two millennia later the Epistle of Jeremiah can give some guidance for a Christian response to the modern world. The polemical ripostes against false gods may be turned metaphorically against those things and obsessions that relativize or blot out God in our culture and personal lives. The critique of Babylonian cultic practices may uncover a superficial, self-serving religiosity that estranges people from one another, from their world, and ultimately from God. The promise that God will watch over the Judeans even while they are in exile may encourage confidence in a God often perceived as absent rather than present. Finally, the fundamental fidelity to God's covenant with Israel, which underlies the theology and exhortations of the epistle, continues to support Christian life today, even in a world very different from that of the Epistle of Jeremiah.

THE BOOK OF LAMENTATIONS

INTRODUCTION, COMMENTARY, AND REFLECTIONS

BY
KATHLEEN M. O'CONNOR

THE BOOK OF
LAMENTATIONS

INTRODUCTION

Lamentations is a searing book of taut, charged poetry on the subject of unspeakable suffering. The poems emerge from a deep wound, a whirlpool of pain, toward which the images, metaphors, and voices of the poetry can only point. It is, in part, the rawness of the hurt expressed in the book that has gained Lamentations a secure, if marginal, place in the liturgies of Judaism and Christianity. Its stinging cries for help, its voices begging God to see, its protests to God who hides behind a cloud—all create a space where communal and personal pain can be reexperienced, seen, and perhaps healed. Although the book of Lamentations is short, containing only five poems, it is a literary jewel and a rich resource for theological reflection and worship. Indeed, its recovery in our communal lives could lead to a greater flourishing of life amid our own wounds and the woundedness of the world.

HISTORICAL SETTING

A short collection of five poems, Lamentations is a poetic response to a national tragedy. Its poems reflect conditions following the invasion and collapse of the nation, particularly of its capital city, and of the destruction of economic and social life among the citizenry. A long-standing and firm tradition of interpretation places the book in the period following Babylonian military assaults on Judah in 597, 587, and 582 BCE.

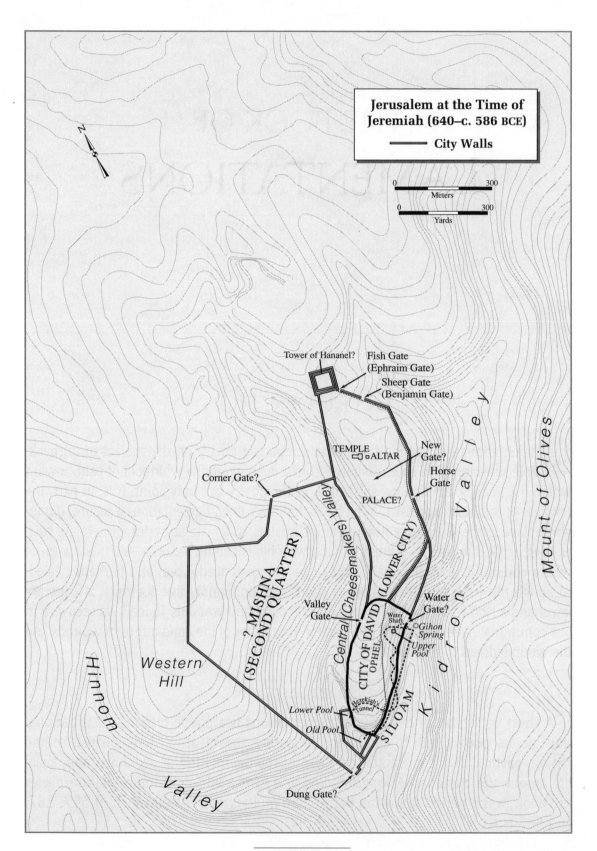

Jerusalem at the Time of Jeremiah (640–c. 586 BCE)

—— City Walls

0 300
Meters

0 300
Yards

Tower of Hananel?

Fish Gate (Ephraim Gate)

Sheep Gate (Benjamin Gate)

TEMPLE

ALTAR

New Gate?

Horse Gate

Corner Gate?

PALACE?

Central (Cheesemakers) Valley

(LOWER CITY)

? MISHNA (SECOND QUARTER)

Valley Gate

Water Gate?

CITY OF DAVID

OPHEL

Water Shaft

Gihon Spring

Upper Pool

Western Hill

Kidron Valley

Mount of Olives

Hezekiah's Tunnel

SILOAM

Lower Pool

Old Pool

Hinnom

Valley

Dung Gate?

Iain Provan, however, has disputed the traditional dating and location of the book.[1] He claims that there is insufficient evidence to tie the book firmly to this or to any other precise historical period. Not only are the poems metaphoric and the language elusive, but also the author as a poet writes with great power in ways that do not represent particular events but simply evoke them. In Provan's view, other invasions and destructions of Jerusalem could equally have produced the conditions that gave birth to this literature.

The helpful conclusion to be drawn from Provan's refreshing academic heresy is that the biblical text need not be tied to a particular historical setting to be moving and effective literature. By severing the book from precise historical connections, the interpreter quickly enables the book to serve as a metaphor that may illuminate many different situations of intense pain and suffering. Provan does not succeed, however, in dislodging Lamentations completely from the Babylonian era. Though he is correct about the paucity of evidence explicitly connecting the book to this time, he does not credit the traditional interpretations that locate the book in Palestine after the Babylonian invasion. If the invasion of Judah and Jerusalem is not the precise tragedy underlying Lamentations, then it is at least a central catastrophe in Israel's history that provides an illuminating backdrop for understanding the fury, grief, and disorientation that this book expresses.

In the aftermath of the Babylonian invasions of Jerusalem, survivors would have wondered whether they could continue to survive as a people. Leading families had been deported to Babylon; the king's palace, the Temple, and the city walls had been razed. A long siege of the city had left many dead, ill, and suffering from famine. Along with overwhelming physical and social devastation came the collapse of the community's entire theological and symbolic world. The words of the prophets and the promises to Abraham and to David had turned empty. Where was the God who promised to dwell with them in Zion, to be with the house of David forever? Where was the God who brought them to the land of promise? How had God contributed to the devastation of their world?

Whether the Babylonian invasion actually occasioned the writing and composition of this book or whether later tradition emerged from reflection on the book in the light of the nation's fall and assigned it to that time and place cannot be known for certain. But the traditional connections of Lamentations with the fall of Jerusalem and Judah to Babylon indicate the way the book served the community. The book came to be seen as an expression of grief and outrage at heart-stopping tragedy—and the tragedy that provoked its composition was massive.

AUTHORSHIP, VERSIONS, CANONICAL PLACEMENT

One of the reasons for the traditional dating of Lamentations to the Babylonian period is because tradition has also held that the prophet Jeremiah was its author. The

---

1. Iain Provan, *Lamentations,* NCB (Grand Rapids: Eerdmans, 1991) 7-19.

Hebrew or Masoretic Text (MT) does not name any author, but the later Septuagint (LXX) translation adds an interpretive opening line. After the captivity of Israel and the desolation of Jerusalem, "Jeremiah sat weeping and lamented this lamentation over Jerusalem."

Other features of the book associate it with Jeremiah. The speaker in Lam 3:52-54 portrays his captivity in terms that vaguely resemble Jeremiah's captivities in the court of the guard in Jer 37:11-21 and 38:1-13. Jeremiah's own reputation is that of the weeping prophet, and hence, the spirit of Lamentations accords with some of his gloomy prophecy.

Jeremiah is the author of Lamentations in a symbolic sense but probably not in a literal sense. Authorship in the ancient world did not follow modern customs. In order to bring books under the aura of heroes and their moral authority, writings were often ascribed to them. Despite loose thematic and metaphorical connections between Lamentations and the book of Jeremiah, numerous features of Lamentations argue against his authorship, not the least of which is the fact that many positions in Lamentations appear to contradict Jeremiah's prophecies.[2]

Just as there is inadequate data to determine Jeremiah's possible role in the production of the book, so also no clear consensus has emerged regarding how many authors were involved in composing the poems. The work of one poet or several may be gathered here. This commentary does not attempt to decide these questions but assumes a unity of material in the book's present form.

The Masoretic Text separates Lamentations from Jeremiah and places Lamentations among the Writings, though that position has varied.[3] Hebrew practice places Lamentations among the *Megillot,* or five liturgical scrolls. By contrast, the LXX, which asserts Jeremianic authorship, also places Lamentations after the prophetic books, sometimes directly following Jeremiah and sometimes with the book of Baruch intervening between them. In addition to the MT and the LXX, there is a later Aramaic version, or targum, that translates the text in a midrashic manner to highlight and expand religious aspects of the Hebrew text.[4]

LITURGICAL USE

Lamentations holds a special place in liturgical services of Judaism and Christianity. The Jewish community reads the Lamentation scroll on the ninth of Ab. That date commemorates five calamities, including the destruction of the First and Second Temples and the destruction of Jerusalem by the Romans. The liturgical atmosphere for the reading is like a public funeral, and the text may be chanted.[5]

2. Delbert Hillers, *Lamentations,* AB 7A (Garden City, N.Y.: Doubleday, 1972) xxi-xxii.
3. Ibid., xvii.
4. Etan Levine, *The Aramaic Version of Lamentations* (New York: Hermon, 1976); Shaye J. D. Cohen, "The Destruction from Scripture to Midrash," *Prooftexts* 2 (1982) 1-17.
5. Levine, *The Aramaic Version of Lamentations,* 13.

Christians use selections of Lamentations during Holy Week services in the recitation of Tenebrae and Good Friday liturgies. Christians lament the death of Jesus, their own sins, and, symbolically, their own eventual deaths. Beyond these special liturgical occasions, however, Lamentations is largely ignored in public worship, in preaching, and for meditative use. Many factors may contribute to this neglect of Lamentations, including its troubling content of relentless grief and anger and the predominance of denial in the dominant culture of North America.

STRUCTURE AND LITERARY FEATURES

Poetic beauty, dramatic power, and puzzling ambiguities converge in Lamentations. The book's artfulness gives it the capacity to draw readers into the overwhelming human struggles portrayed in the poems and to embroil readers in unanswerable questions. Alphabetical and formal structures, mixtures of voices, and the relationship of the five poems to each other contribute to the book's intense and terrible potency and raise key issues in its interpretation. These features overlap in interpretation, and decisions about form and voice contribute to the understanding of the relationships of the poems to each other.[6]

First, each of the five poems draws on the lament form and is built in some way upon the Hebrew alphabet, but within that framework are wide variations in form and structure. Second, a number of different voices or poetic speakers appear within and across the poems. Third, the relationships among the five poems are complex and strongly debated by modern interpreters, but readers must account for them in determining the book's purposes. What hangs in the balance in this decision are the purposes of the book and the status of hope in the book. Is the third, and only hopeful, poem the book's "monumental center,"[7] or is hope swallowed up by the doubt and despair of the surrounding poems?

By their very presence, these literary dilemmas prevent swift resolution and easy dismissal of the enormous sense of abandonment and injustice expressed in these poems. The book's literary puzzles, its mixtures of forms, voices, and unevenly shaped poems may give evidence of deliberate crafting, a chiseling and polishing of words, images, and poetic forms that draw readers into a maelstrom and force them to find their own way out.

Alphabetical Forms and Literary Genre. The Hebrew alphabet contributes to the structuring of the book's individual poems in two ways. First, the book's first four poems are acrostics. They are written in alphabetical order so that each verse or line begins with a sequential letter of the Hebrew alphabet. The poem in chapter 3 intensifies the

6. Alan Mintz, "The Rhetoric of Lamentations and the Representation of Catastrophe," in *Hurban: Responses to Catastrophe in Hebrew Literature,* ed. G. A. Buttrick et al. (New York: Columbia University Press, 1984) 19-48; reprinted from *Prooftexts* 2 (1982) 1-17.
7. Ibid., 33.

acrostic form by including three lines in each verse that begin with the same alphabetical letter.[8]

The second way the alphabet structures the poems concerns their length. In accordance with the twenty-two lines of the Hebrew alphabet, all five poems contain twenty-two lines or multiples thereof. The first three poems are each sixty-six lines long. The fourth poem contains only forty-four lines, and the fifth, and only non-acrostic, poem contains only twenty-two lines. While the poems gain from alphabetical structuring, the diversity of their relationships to the alphabet indicates tensions among them. Each poem stands freely on its own, but how do they relate to each other?

Chapter One	*Chapter Two*
acrostic	acrostic
22 verses of three lines each	22 verses of three lines each
(66 lines)	(66 lines)

Chapter Three
acrostic
66 verses of one line each with
three verses per letter

Chapter Four	*Chapter Five*
acrostic	not acrostic
22 verses of two lines each	22 verses of one line each
(44 lines)	(22 lines)

The acrostic form itself has been the subject of much scrutiny. What are the purposes of poetic alphabetizing? Acrostics may have been used for aesthetic purposes,[9] to show off the poet's skill, or as an aid to memory.[10] Mnemonic purposes alone, however, do not explain acrostic use, since there are many poems in the Hebrew Bible but few acrostics.[11] More evocative and symbolic purposes may better explain the use of the alphabet in Lamentations. Acrostics impose order and organization on shapeless chaos and unmanageable pain, and they imply that the suffering depicted in the poems is total. Nothing can be added to it, for suffering extends from "א to ת" (*aleph* to *taw*).

8. In chaps. 2–4 the alphabet is disturbed, reversing the usual *'ayin-pê* (ע - פ) order, but this may indicate that the alphabet itself was not yet stable. See Frank Moore Cross, "Studies in the Structure of Hebrew Verse: The Prosody of Lamentations 1:1-22," in *The Word of the Lord Shall Go Forth*, ed. Carol L. Meyers and M. O'Connor (Winona Lake, Ind.: Eisenbrauns, 1984) 148.

9. Claus Westermann, *Lamentations: Issues and Interpretation* (Minneapolis: Fortress, 1994) 99.

10. N. Gottwald, *Studies in the Book of Lamentations*, SBT (Chicago: Alec R. Allenson, 1954) 26-28.

11. Other acrostics in the Hebrew Bible include Psalms 9–10; 25; 34; 37; 111–12; 119; 145; Prov 31:10-31; and Nah 1:2-8.

Whatever the motivation for their use, however, Daniel Grossberg observes that acrostics impose unity upon various voices, images, and perspectives within the individual poems.[12] Heater observes that the acrostics divide the content of the poems with the middle letters of the Hebrew alphabet.[13]

Besides their alphabetical structures, the poems in Lamentations also draw on lament forms and funeral dirges and, in particular, on the lament over the fallen city.[14] Laments abound in the Bible and in the literature of the ancient Near East. The book of Psalms contains communal laments that speak in the plural voice of the community, and individual laments in the voice of a single person.[15] Laments are prayers of protest, complaint, and grief over a disaster, and with great passion they appeal to God for deliverance. They arise from faith in the power and willingness of God to save. They insist that the world is an open system in which divine intervention is always possible.

The lament over the city was a common literary form in the ancient Near East. Mesopotamian city laments, for example, exhibit some common features with Lamentations, including their somber mood at the destruction, themes of divine abandonment and involvement in the destruction, descriptions of calamity, massive weeping, as well as the use of poetic devices of many voices or personas, personification of the city, and marked reversals in the city's fate.[16]

Lamentations, however, significantly adapts the Mesopotamian form. It transfers the Mesopotamian treatment of the city's patron goddess to the figure of personified Jerusalem. Goddesses were heavenly patrons of their city, but they were powerless to prevent destruction caused by other gods and often wept over the city's destruction.[17] In Lamentations, Jerusalem is personified as a female, but she is merely a city, not a goddess. The many similarities between the city laments and Lamentations indicate that the biblical book emerged from a world that possessed common artistic forms for the expression of grief, rage, and protest.

Interlaced with lament forms in the book are themes typical of the funeral dirge. These include a mournful cry for the one who has died, a proclamation of death, contrast with previous circumstances of the dead person, and the reaction of bystanders.[18] When the poet or poets of Lamentations sought to give expression to the unspeakable

---

12. Daniel Grossberg, *Centripetal and Centrifugal Structures in Biblical Poetry,* SBLMS 39 (Atlanta: Scholars Press, 1989) 84-85.

13. Homer Heater, Jr., "Structure and Meaning in Lamentations," *BSac* 149 (1992) 304-15.

14. Claus Westermann, *Lamentations: Issues and Interpretation* (Minneapolis: Fortress, 1994) 1-23; F. W. Dobbs-Allsopp, *Weep, O Daughter of Zion: A Study of the City-Lament Genre in the Hebrew Bible,* BibOr 44 (Rome: Editrice Pontifico Istituto Biblico, 1993); Paul Wayne Ferris, *The Genre of Communal Lament in the Bible,* SBLDS 127 (Atlanta: Scholars Press, 1992); Norman K. Gottwald, "The Book of Lamentations Reconsidered," in *The Hebrew Bible and Its Social World and in Ours,* ed. Norman K. Gottwald, SBLSS (Atlanta: Scholars Press, 1993) 165-73.

15. See Patrick Miller, *They Cried to the Lord: The Form and Theology of Biblical Prayer* (Minneapolis: Fortress, 1994) 68-134.

16. Dobbs-Allsopp, *Weep, O Daughter of Zion,* 29-96.

17. J. J. M. Roberts, "The Motif of the Weeping God in Jeremiah and Its Background in the Lament Tradition of the Ancient Near East," *Old Testament Essays* 5 (1992) 361-74.

18. Westermann, *Lamentations,* 1-23.

pain their community endured, they drew on the repertoire of form, imagery, and metaphor available in the ancient world. From this familiar and traditional raw material, they created a complex artistic expression in the interplay of acrostic, lament, and dirge.

Voices. One of Lamentations' most effective literary devices is its use of different speakers.[19] Multiple poetic voices interweave, overlap, and contradict each other. The speakers are literary creations who offer testimony in the thick of catastrophe. Voices of a narrator, Daughter Zion, an unidentified man, and the community lament, protest, and attempt to cope with the tragedy they have survived. The book is dramatized speech.

A narrator, an omniscient third-person reporter, appears in chapters 1, 2, and 4. In the first two chapters he introduces and comments upon the circumstances and words of Daughter Zion, who appears only in the first two chapters. She is the city of Jerusalem, personified as a woman, a princess, a lover, a widow, a daughter, and above all, a mother. The principal speaker in chapter 3 is a man, a shamed and humiliated captive, entrapped and reaching for hope. The voice of the community appears briefly in chapters 3 and 4 but takes over in speech directed to God in chapter 5.

The interplay of these voices allows the book to approach the massive suffering of the destroyed city from many viewpoints. The city itself becomes a person, weeping over its pain, screaming for aid, and protesting its deplorable conditions. The defeated man in chapter 3 grasps for hope, but in chapters 4 and 5 his words are quickly replaced by dour accounts of suffering from the narrator and the community. Westermann observes that the speakers are not individuals but "are at the same time both lamenters and the lamented."[20] They signify the destroyed city and its citizens. Each voice articulates the pain of the community.

The personification of Jerusalem as Daughter Zion, or "Daughter of Zion,"[21] has an ancient tradition that receives further development in Lamentations. The ancient world commonly understood cities as female and personified them as divine wives of the resident god. Biblical representations of Daughter Zion draw on these depictions but do not understand the city as a deity. In Lamentations, the personified city is the punished wife of Yahweh, who fulfills all the prophecies against her in the books of Jeremiah, Ezekiel, and Hosea.[22]

---

19. William F. Lanahan, "The Speaking Voice in the Book of Lamentations," *JBL* 93 (1974) 41-49.

20. Westermann, *Lamentations,* 140.

21. F. W. Dobbs-Alsopp, "The Syntagma of *bat* Followed by a Geographical Name in the Hebrew Bible: A Reconsideration of Its Meaning and Grammar," *CBQ* (1995) 451-70.

22. Julie Galambush, *Jerusalem in the Book of Ezekiel: The City as Yahweh's Wife,* SBLDS 130 (Atlanta: Scholars Press, 1992) 25-59; Dobbs-Alsopp, *Weep, O Daughter of Zion,* 75-91; A. R. Pete Diamond and Kathleen M. O'Connor, "Unfaithful Passions: Coding Women, Coding Men in Jeremiah 2–3 (4:2)," *Biblical Interpretation* (1996) 288-310; Elaine Follis, "The Holy City as Daughter," in *Directions in Biblical Hebrew Poetry,* ed. Elaine Follis, JSOTSup 40 (Sheffield: JSOT, 1987) 173-84; Renita J. Weems, *Battered Love: Marriage, Sex, and Violence in the Hebrew Prophets,* OBT (Minneapolis: Fortress, 1995).

Female personification of Jerusalem and Judah in Lamentations comes with strong associations that lend themselves to poetry of woundedness and grief and shame. Daughter Zion is a woman with a past, a disastrous present, and no future. Mintz observes, "The serviceableness of Jerusalem as an abandoned fallen woman lies in the precise register of pain it articulates."[23] In contrast to the dead, whose sufferings are finished, the defiled woman who survives is a living witness to pain that knows no end.

Missing from the poetic voices in Lamentations is the voice of God. The missing voice looms over the book. The speakers refer to God, call for help, ask God to look, accuse God of hiding from them, of attacking and forgetting them—but God never responds. The speakers interpret, provide motives for, and attack the absent one, but God never steps into the sound studio. Thick, soundproof walls bar the suffering voices from the one who caused their suffering and the only one they believe can comfort them, save them, and stop the suffering. Unlike Job, who receives a divine response to his protestations, the suffering characters in this book never gain an audience. Why is God silent? No simple answer to this question emerges.

Relations Among the Poems. How the five poems with their diverse voices and viewpoints and their varied alphabetic structures fit together and interact is the major issue in the book's interpretation. Until recently, many interpreters, both Christian and Jewish, claimed that chapter 3 is the book's literary and theological center.[24] There are good reasons for such an interpretive decision. Located in the middle of the book, chapter 3 intensifies the acrostic form and expresses hope in an extended way to suggest that the triumph of hope over suffering is the book's main point.

Despite its midpoint location, however, chapter 3 is not bordered by symmetrically composed poems to clinch such an interpretive decision. The poems that precede chapter 3 do not match the poems that follow it in length or form. Instead, chapters 4 and 5 grow shorter, and the acrostic form disappears altogether in chapter 5. These formal variations create a lopsided structure of the whole, leading some interpreters to think that hope is drowned by the reality of suffering and by a silent God.

William Shea suggested that the book's asymmetrical shape imitates the rhythmic pattern found in funeral dirges in ancient Israel, called the "limping," or *qînâ*(קינה), meter.[25] This rhythmic pattern contains three long beats and two short ones. In Shea's analogy, the shortening of the poems and the disappearance of the acrostic form in the latter part of Lamentations construct an ending that drifts off, like the funeral dirge, in grief without resolution. The rhythmical pattern dies away "because it was written in remembrance of Jerusalem, the city that died away."[26]

23. Alan Mintz, "The Rhetoric of Lamentations and the Representation of Catastrophe," in *Hurban: Responses to Catastrophe in Hebrew Literature,* ed. G. A. Buttrick et al. (New York: Columbia University Press, 1984) 24.

24. Norman K. Gottwald, "The Book of Lamentations Reconsidered," in *The Hebrew Bible in Its Social World and in Ours,* SBLSS (Atlanta: Scholars Press, 1993) 165-73; Delbert Hillers, *Lamentations,* AB 7A (Garden City, N.Y.: Doubleday, 1972) XVI; Mintz, "The Rhetoric of Lamentations and the Representation of Catastrophe," 33.

25. William H. Shea, "The *qînāh* Structure of the Book of Lamentations," *Bib* 60 (1979) 103-7.

26. Ibid., 107.

Although the presence of this meter as a structuring device in the book is far from certain, since Shea transfers a meter found in single lines to five poems, his suggestion is provocative. His treatment of the book that decenters the importance of chapter 3 and its expressions of hope has found strong development in recent interpretation. Linafelt, Dobbs-Alsopp, and Provan deemphasize chapter 3 for a variety of reasons and point to the book's movement toward protest and doubt rather than faith and reconciliation.[27]

Linafelt identifies a number of interpretive biases that have led interpreters to find chapter 3 to be the book's hermeneutical key. These biases include preference for the male voice of the "strong man," Christian identification of the figure in chapter 3 with Christ, and preference for interpretation that favors human reconciliation with God through repentance.[28] But hope does not triumph in the book; it is merely one point of view, more tenuously arrived at even in chapter 3 than commentators have admitted. What the book offers instead of resolute hope, confidence, and reconciliation with God are "intersecting perspectival discourses,"[29] speeches that move across trauma, rage, hope, doubt, and tired dismay. No single speaker, no particular viewpoint silences the others. Instead, multiple speakers try to find expression for grief, "to articulate the inexpressible, and turn death into beauty."[30]

The poems try to house grief in familiar and ordered language commonly found in other biblical laments. But these poems in Lamentations use traditional lament language in ways that are gripping and concrete. Within the poems the same Hebrew roots and sounds appear, get repeated, disappear, and reappear.[31] Provan observes that the language is metaphorical, imagistic, and conventional, rather than representational.[32] The book is not trying to mimic reality but to evoke and re-create the suffering of the community. The poems are masterpieces of artistic intricacy in which the speakers hammer out their pain in rhythms and circles of sorrow. Ultimately the poems cannot build a shelter for grief and rage. Landy proposes that the poetry conveys its own inadequacy to the task by fading out in a whimper and in an effectual cry for revenge.[33]

LAMENTATIONS AND THE ARTS

A brief sampling of the artistic appropriations of Lamentations shows the potency of Lamentations in new contexts. Musicians have employed its lyrics for liturgical music

27. Tod Linafelt, "Surviving Lamentations: A Literary-Theological Study of the Afterlife of a Biblical Text" (Ph.D. diss., Emory University, 1997); F. W. Dobbs-Allsopp, *Weep, O Daughter of Zion: A Study of the City Lament Genre in the Hebrew Bible,* BibOr 44 (Rome: Editrice Pontifico Istituto Biblico, 1993) 22-24; Iain Provan, *Lamentations,* NCB (Grand Rapids: Eerdmans, 1991).

28. Linafelt, "Surviving Lamentations," 6-25.

29. Burke O'Connor Long, *Planting and Reaping Albright: Politics, Ideology and Interpreting the Bible* (University Park: Pennsylvania State University Press, 1997).

30. Francis Landy, "Lamentations," in *The Literary Guide to the Bible,* ed. Robert Alter and Frank Kermode (Cambridge, Mass.: Belknap, 1987) 329.

31. Frank Moore Cross, "Studies in the Structure of Hebrew Verse: The Prosody of Lamentations 1:1-22," in *The Word of the Lord Shall God Forth: Essays in Honor of David Noel Freedman,* ed. Carol L. Meyers and M. O'Connor, ASOR (Winona Lake, Ind.: Eisenbrauns, 1983) 129-55.

32. Provan, *Lamentations,* 13.

33. Landy, "Lamentations," 329.

and for more general compositions. In the sixteenth century, Thomas Tallis set "The Lamentations of Jeremiah" to music, and in the twentieth century Pablo Casals did likewise in "O Vos Omnes," known in English as "O Ye People." For Lent of 1956, Hungarian composer Lajos Bardos wrote a musical setting for eight verses of chapter 5 to lament national shame, entrapment, and guilt during the Soviet occupation of Hungary. Leonard Bernstein wrote a "Jeremiah" symphony that uses Lamentations, and Igor Stravinsky composed "Threni" in 1958.

Although Polish composer Henryk Gorecki's Symphony No. 3 has no direct connection with the book of Lamentations, the symphony is a haunting lament that employs lyrics of great sadness in the form of testimony from a prison wall and of a mother's lament for her disappeared child. In the exquisite sorrow of its music, this work expresses communal heartbreak at the unspeakable horrors of the twentieth century. The work's surprising popularity among classical music lovers in the United States may witness to the stored-up sorrow and unspoken anger in the general culture.

Among literary reincarnations of Lamentations two works demand attention. One is a short memoir by Naomi Seidman, "Burning the Book of Lamentations," in which Seidman yearns for the end of lamenting and for the day all Jews can burn laments forever. The other is a work of fiction by Cynthia Ozick entitled *The Shawl: A Story and Novella,* in which Daughter Zion's loss of her children is reenacted in a mother's exceedingly tragic loss of her small daughter in a concentration camp.[34]

A painting by Rembrandt, entitled *The Prophet Jeremiah Lamenting the Destruction of Jerusalem,* hangs in the Rijksmuseum in Amsterdam. For the Union Church of Pocantico Hills, New York, Marc Chagall created a small jewel of a stained-glass window of Jeremiah, whom he identified by referring to Lam 3:1-3. Fritz Eichenberg's etching of *The Lamentations of Jeremiah* pictures a man in chains, a woman clutching a baby, and a small child clinging to the captured man.[35]

THE BOOK'S TITLES

Because the Hebrew Bible names its books by their first word or words, the Hebrew title of Lamentations is ספר איכה (*Seper 'Êkâ*), literally "the book of How."[36] איכה (*'Êkâ*) is an exclamation of shock that means "how" or "alas," and should, perhaps, be pronounced with a catch in the voice or with a gasp: "How lonely lies the city upon the hill!" (Lam 1:1). Seidman suggests that behind the declarative *how* of the title lurks an interrogative "how" that questions the means and even the possibility of telling about this unspeakable catastrophe.[37] The opening exclamation of pity and astonishment hangs

34. Cynthia Ozick, *The Shawl: A Story and a Novella* (New York: Knopf, 1981). Linafelt, "Surviving Lamentations," studies the story as a "survival" of the biblical book.

35. *Fritz Eichenberg: Works of Mercy,* ed. Robert Ellsberg (Maryknoll: Orbis, 1992).

36. See Naomi Seidman, "Burning the Book of Lamentations," in *Out of the Garden: Women Writers on the Bible,* ed. Christian Buchmann and Celina Spiegel (New York: Fawcett Columbine, 1994) 282.

37. Ibid., 282.

over the entire book and reappears as the first word of chapters 2 and 4. In the literal rendering of the title, "How," as opposed to "Lamentations," which derives from the Greek translation (θρῆνοι *Thrēnoi*), Jean-Marc Droin finds a close approximation to the book's meaning. In his view, Lamentations is a quest for understanding in disaster more than simply a sorrowful lament.[38] But a lamentation, by its very nature, is also a complaint, a protest, as well as a search for meaning.

Linafelt calls Lamentations a brutal book,[39] a book that assaults us, and it surely does, even in the violence-laden climate of media, entertainment, and the streets. But the book's unmitigated violence, its expression of loneliness, abandonment, and suffering, its descriptions of death, of helplessness, of the suffering of women, children, the elderly, all have a contemporaneity to them. The poems evoke an outer world and portray an inner landscape known to many contemporary people. The book's very brutality makes it a comfort, a recognition in its metaphorical construction of the way things are for many people. The book functions as a witness to pain, a testimony of survival, and an artistic transformation of dehumanizing suffering into exquisite literature. In the process, it raises profound questions about the justice of God.

38. Jean-Marc Droin, *Le Livre des Lamentations: "Comment?" Une Traduction et un commentaire,* La Bible, porte-Parole (Geneva: Labor et Fides, 1995).
39. Linafelt, *Surviving Lamentations,* 2.

BIBLIOGRAPHY

Commentaries:
Hillers, Delbert. *Lamentations.* AB 7A. Garden City, N.Y.: Doubleday, 1972. A nontechnical commentary intended for the general audience. Includes a lengthy introduction on text-critical and translation issues, and brief discussions of interpretation and contemporary application.

Provan, Iain. *Lamentations.* NCB. Grand Rapids: Eerdmans, 1991. A brief commentary based on the RSV that emphasizes translation and text-critical issues; limited attention is given to issues of theology and interpretation.

Westermann, Claus. *Lamentations: Issues and Interpretation.* Translated by Charles Muenchow. Minneapolis: Fortress, 1994. An excellent, concise introduction to Lamentations by one of the twentieth century's leading interpreters of both the lament form and the book of Lamentations. Analyzes the ancient Near Eastern origins of laments, reviews the history of twentieth-century Lamentations research, discusses interpretive methodology, provides commentary, and explores the theological significance of Lamentations.

Specialized Studies:
Dobbs-Allsopp, F. W. *Weep, O Daughter of Zion: A Study of the City Lament Genre in the Hebrew Bible.* BibOr 44. Rome: Editrice Pontifico Istituto Biblico, 1993. An interpretation of Lamentations in the light of ancient Mesopotamian laments for the destruction of a great city.

Gottwald, Norman K. "The Book of Lamentations Reconsidered." In *The Hebrew Bible in Its Social World and Ours.* SBLSS. Atlanta: Scholars Press, 1993. Takes the measure of literary, tradition-historical, redactional, and sociological contributions to the study of Lamentations written since Gottwald's earlier work.

———. *Studies in the Book of Lamentations.* Chicago: Alec R. Allenson, 1954. A technical discussion of Lamentations' acrostic form, genre, theology, and significance as a unified response to a specific historical situation in ancient Israel.

Grossberg, Daniel. *Centripetal and Centrifugal Structures in Biblical Poetry.* SBLMS 39. Atlanta: Scholars Press, 1989. A detailed analysis of the poetic techniques found in Lamentations and two other collections of biblical poetry.

Linafelt, Tod, *Surviving Lamentations: Catastrophe, Lament, and Protest in the Afterlife of a Biblical Book.* Chicago: University of Chicago Press, 2000. A sustained interpretation of Lamentations as "literature of survival"—i.e., literature responding to the aftermath of a catastrophe. Also provides a detailed investigation of how Lamentations and its themes have "survived" in various literary forms throughout history.

OUTLINE OF LAMENTATIONS

LAMENTATIONS 1:1-22

No Comfort

Overview

Devastation, abandonment, and comfortlessness of a woman confront readers in the opening poem. That woman is Daughter Zion, the destroyed city of Jerusalem. To portray the city and its vast affliction, the first poem weaves together the voices of two poetic figures, that of a narrator (vv. 1-11) and Daughter Zion herself (vv. 11c-22). The voices divide into two overlapping poetic panels. The narrator, presumably male,[40] speaks in the first panel (vv. 1-11), except in vv. 9c and 11c, where Daughter Zion interrupts him. Daughter Zion speaks in the second panel (vv. 11c-22), except in v. 17, where the poet interrupts her.

Although the two voices overlap and echo each other, they do not address each other. He speaks to an unidentified audience about her, and she addresses God alone. Despite the absence of dia-

logue between them, the two voices offer double testimony of witness and sufferer. Together they create a geography of pain. Their discourse gives pain form and shape in a map of Daughter Zion's outer and inner worlds. The narrator tells what has happened to her; she reports how it feels to suffer as she does.

Both speakers describe Daughter Zion's condition—she has no one to comfort her—and both insist that Yahweh is the primary cause of her terrible plight. The narrator speaks in the third person as an uninvolved observer, an "objective" reporter who describes the "facts." He lets none of his own response be known and allows his plain description of her predicament to speak for itself. Daughter Zion, by contrast, speaks in the first person as the sufferer, the enunciator of pain, the victim of trauma. Her misery is immediate, personal, and intimate. Between the two voices, a totality of pain unfolds.

---

40. Barbara Bakke Kaiser, "Poet as 'Female Impersonator': The Image of Daughter Zion as Speaker in Biblical Poems of Suffering," *Journal of Religion* (1987) 164-82.

LAMENTATIONS 1:1-11b, SHE HAS NO ONE TO COMFORT HER

NIV	NRSV

1 [a]How deserted lies the city,
  once so full of people!
 How like a widow is she,
  who once was great among the nations!
 She who was queen among the provinces
  has now become a slave.
 	
 [2]Bitterly she weeps at night,
  tears are upon her cheeks.
	1 How lonely sits the city
	  that once was full of people!
	 How like a widow she has become,
	  she that was great among the nations!
	 She that was a princess among the provinces
	  has become a vassal.
	
	 [2] She weeps bitterly in the night,
	  with tears on her cheeks;
	 among all her lovers

[a]*This chapter is an acrostic poem, the verses of which begin with the successive letters of the Hebrew alphabet.*	

NIV

Among all her lovers
there is none to comfort her.
All her friends have betrayed her;
they have become her enemies.

³After affliction and harsh labor,
Judah has gone into exile.
She dwells among the nations;
she finds no resting place.
All who pursue her have overtaken her
in the midst of her distress.

⁴The roads to Zion mourn,
for no one comes to her appointed feasts.
All her gateways are desolate,
her priests groan,
her maidens grieve,
and she is in bitter anguish.

⁵Her foes have become her masters;
her enemies are at ease.
The LORD has brought her grief
because of her many sins.
Her children have gone into exile,
captive before the foe.

⁶All the splendor has departed
from the Daughter of Zion.
Her princes are like deer
that find no pasture;
in weakness they have fled
before the pursuer.

⁷In the days of her affliction and wandering
Jerusalem remembers all the treasures
that were hers in days of old.
When her people fell into enemy hands,
there was no one to help her.
Her enemies looked at her
and laughed at her destruction.

⁸Jerusalem has sinned greatly
and so has become unclean.
All who honored her despise her,
for they have seen her nakedness;
she herself groans
and turns away.

⁹Her filthiness clung to her skirts;
she did not consider her future.
Her fall was astounding;
there was none to comfort her.

NRSV

she has no one to comfort her;
all her friends have dealt treacherously
with her,
they have become her enemies.

3 Judah has gone into exile with suffering
and hard servitude;
she lives now among the nations,
and finds no resting place;
her pursuers have all overtaken her
in the midst of her distress.

4 The roads to Zion mourn,
for no one comes to the festivals;
all her gates are desolate,
her priests groan;
her young girls grieve,ᵃ
and her lot is bitter.

5 Her foes have become the masters,
her enemies prosper,
because the Lord has made her suffer
for the multitude of her transgressions;
her children have gone away,
captives before the foe.

6 From daughter Zion has departed
all her majesty.
Her princes have become like stags
that find no pasture;
they fled without strength
before the pursuer.

7 Jerusalem remembers,
in the days of her affliction and wandering,
all the precious things
that were hers in days of old.
When her people fell into the hand of the foe,
and there was no one to help her,
the foe looked on mocking
over her downfall.

8 Jerusalem sinned grievously,
so she has become a mockery;
all who honored her despise her,
for they have seen her nakedness;

ᵃ Meaning of Heb uncertain

NIV

"Look, O LORD, on my affliction,
  for the enemy has triumphed."

10The enemy laid hands
  on all her treasures;
she saw pagan nations
  enter her sanctuary—
those you had forbidden
  to enter your assembly.

11All her people groan
  as they search for bread;
they barter their treasures for food
  to keep themselves alive.

NRSV

she herself groans,
  and turns her face away.

9 Her uncleanness was in her skirts;
  she took no thought of her future;
her downfall was appalling,
  with none to comfort her.
"O Lord, look at my affliction,
  for the enemy has triumphed!"

10 Enemies have stretched out their hands
  over all her precious things;
she has even seen the nations
  invade her sanctuary,
those whom you forbade
  to enter your congregation.

11 All her people groan
  as they search for bread;
they trade their treasures for food
  to revive their strength.

COMMENTARY

1:1. To convey the external world of Jerusalem's pain, the narrator begins with an exclamation of surprise and perhaps pity. "How [איכה *'ēkâ*] lonely lies the city once so full of people!" (author's trans.). The contrast between the woman's current plight and her previous glory obsesses the speaker. It is not simply that Jerusalem is in misery, but that her fortunes have been completely overturned. Once bursting with life, the city is empty; formerly great among nations, she has become like a widow; and once a princess, she is now a vassal. That her previous life had been glorious contributes to and emphasizes the sorrow and disgrace of her current reality.

The narrator's comparison of Jerusalem to a widow underlines her aloneness and the precariousness of her future. Widows in the ancient world were not simply wives of deceased husbands, but women whose husbands' deaths left them without protection and support of extended families.[41] Widows were destitute people.

41. Paula S. Hiebert, " 'Whence Shall Help Come to Me?' the Biblical Widow," in *Gender and Difference in Ancient Israel,* ed. Peggy L. Day (Minneapolis: Fortress, 1989) 125-41.

1:2. Whether the poet feels pity or contempt for Daughter Zion is not clear, but his unremitting attention draws readers to her. Tears bring the silent and desolate figure to life. She "weeps bitterly." Perhaps simply to accommodate the Hebrew alphabet, verbs of "weeping" (בכו תבכה *bākô tibkeh*) open the verse, but the effect of the grammatical construction is to emphasize weeping as her first act in the book. The time is "night," itself symbolic of the sunlessness in which she lives. "She has no one to comfort her." She has no companion, no witness, no one who recognizes the depth of her suffering. Once friends and lovers surrounded her, but now they have betrayed her, and she is alone. Since women in the ancient world had no right to lovers, the narrator's mention of them signals that the woman may have immoral allegiances. By referring to her lovers, the narrator implies that she brought her suffering upon herself by her sinfulness.

1:3. As the narrator guides readers around the utter desolation of the city, he shifts attention briefly from the city to the nation. Judah, also personified as a woman, has gone into exile and has been overwhelmed by distress. But Judah's capital city, Daughter Zion, is the narrator's chief concern and the cause of his sad lament.

1:4-6. Grief is palpable in the city and so salient a feature of the landscape that roads, city gates, and inhabitants mourn, for Zion is in "bitter anguish" (v. 4). Her foes (צריה *ṣārêhâ*) dominate her, and most crushing of all, the same foe (צר *ṣār*) captured her children (v. 5). The narrator uses a specific noun for "children" (עולליה *'olālêhâ*), rather than the more general noun for "sons" (בנים *bānîm*), which can convey less intimate forms of relationship than mother to child (v. 5). The loss of her children will be this woman's greatest grief to which she and the narrator will continually return in this and later poems.[42] In Hebrew "enemies" (צר צריה *ṣārêhâ, ṣar*) frame the verse, and embedded between them is the poem's first mention of Yahweh, "who has made her suffer" for her sins. It is as if the foe could do nothing without divine sanction. Daughter Zion's predicament grows in horror. She faces the worst loss a mother can know, the loss of her children, and it is her fault because her sin has enraged her God against her. From the narrator's view of events, she must bear the guilt.

1:7-9. These verses expand themes of reversal of fortunes and of abandonment, for "there was no one to help her"; but they add further blame and great, nearly unspeakable, shame. Charges against her, intimated by the presence of her lovers in v. 2, become explicit. She "has sinned grievously" (v. 8). All who honored her now "despise her for they have seen her nakedness." Nakedness was cause for great shame in the ancient world, particularly

for women.[43] The narrator uses shaming of the female body as a metaphor for the city's dishonor (v. 8).

Accusations reach a low point when the narrator declares, in a reference to the menstrual functions of the female body, "Her uncleanness was on her skirts; she took not thought for her future" (v. 9). Menstrual bleeding made women ritually unclean (Lev 15:19-30). That may be the narrator's reference here, particularly since he later refers to her as a menstrual rag (נדה *niddâ*, v. 17).[44] It is unclear, however, how she could be held responsible for the natural discharges of her body. Was it her failure to care for her skirts that indicated her carelessness about the future, or does the charge against her suggest sexual license? Whatever the poem's intentions, ritual uncleanness and carelessness contribute to her fall in the narrator's interpretation of events. And "she had none to comfort her" (v. 9*b*).

Perhaps because the narrator has so fiercely accused her, or perhaps because she is in search of a comforter, Daughter Zion bursts unexpectedly into speech. She addresses Yahweh, not the narrator: "O Yahweh, see [ראה *rĕ'ēh*] my affliction" (v. 9*c*). She begs Yahweh to notice the enemies' triumph, to take into account her pain.

1:10-11b. Zion's outburst does not stop the narrator, who continues to speak coolly, removed from the struggle, like a reporter at the scene of a tragedy, standing by and explaining the trauma. He keeps noticing what she has lost—her treasures, her sanctuary, her inviolability (v. 10). He reports that the people groan and are forced to barter for food "to keep themselves alive" (v. 11). (See Reflections at 1:11*c*-22.)

---

42. Tod Linafelt, "Surviving Lamentations: A Literary-Theological Study of the Afterlife of a Biblical Text" (Ph.D. diss., Emory University, 1997) 71-125.

43. Jerome H. Neyrey, "Nudity," in *Biblical Social Values and Their Meaning: A Handbook* (Peabody, Mass.: Hendrickson, 1993) 119-25.

44. Kathleen M. O'Connor, "Lamentations," in *The Women's Bible Commentary,* ed. Carol A. Newsom and Sharon H. Ringe (Louisville: Westminster/John Knox, 1992) 178-84.

LAMENTATIONS 1:11c-22,
NO ONE TO COMFORT ME

NIV

"Look, O LORD, and consider,
for I am despised."

12"Is it nothing to you, all you who pass by?
    Look around and see.
Is any suffering like my suffering
    that was inflicted on me,
that the LORD brought on me
    in the day of his fierce anger?

13"From on high he sent fire,
    sent it down into my bones.
He spread a net for my feet
    and turned me back.
He made me desolate,
    faint all the day long.

14"My sins have been bound into a yoke[a];
    by his hands they were woven together.
They have come upon my neck
    and the Lord has sapped my strength.
He has handed me over
    to those I cannot withstand.

15"The Lord has rejected
    all the warriors in my midst;
he has summoned an army against me
    to[b] crush my young men.
In his winepress the Lord has trampled
    the Virgin Daughter of Judah.

16"This is why I weep
    and my eyes overflow with tears.
No one is near to comfort me,
    no one to restore my spirit.
My children are destitute
    because the enemy has prevailed."

17Zion stretches out her hands,
    but there is no one to comfort her.
The LORD has decreed for Jacob
    that his neighbors become his foes;
Jerusalem has become
    an unclean thing among them.

18"The LORD is righteous,

NRSV

Look, O LORD, and see
    how worthless I have become.

12 Is it nothing to you,[a] all you who pass by?
    Look and see
if there is any sorrow like my sorrow,
    which was brought upon me,
which the LORD inflicted
    on the day of his fierce anger.

13 From on high he sent fire;
    it went deep into my bones;
he spread a net for my feet;
    he turned me back;
he has left me stunned,
    faint all day long.

14 My transgressions were bound[a] into a yoke;
    by his hand they were fastened together;
they weigh on my neck,
    sapping my strength;
the Lord handed me over
    to those whom I cannot withstand.

15 The LORD has rejected
    all my warriors in the midst of me;
he proclaimed a time against me
    to crush my young men;
the Lord has trodden as in a wine press
    the virgin daughter Judah.

16 For these things I weep;
    my eyes flow with tears;
for a comforter is far from me,
    one to revive my courage;
my children are desolate,
    for the enemy has prevailed.

17 Zion stretches out her hands,
    but there is no one to comfort her;
the LORD has commanded against Jacob
    that his neighbors should become his foes;
Jerusalem has become
    a filthy thing among them.

---

[a]14 Most Hebrew manuscripts; Septuagint *He kept watch over my sins*
[b]15 Or *has set a time for me / when he will*

[a] Meaning of Heb uncertain

NIV

yet I rebelled against his command.
Listen, all you peoples;
  look upon my suffering.
My young men and maidens
  have gone into exile.

¹⁹"I called to my allies
  but they betrayed me.
My priests and my elders
  perished in the city
while they searched for food
  to keep themselves alive.

²⁰"See, O LORD, how distressed I am!
  I am in torment within,
and in my heart I am disturbed,
  for I have been most rebellious.
Outside, the sword bereaves;
  inside, there is only death.

²¹"People have heard my groaning,
  but there is no one to comfort me.
All my enemies have heard of my distress;
  they rejoice at what you have done.
May you bring the day you have announced
  so they may become like me.

²²"Let all their wickedness come before you;
  deal with them
as you have dealt with me
  because of all my sins.
My groans are many
  and my heart is faint."

NRSV

¹⁸ The LORD is in the right,
  for I have rebelled against his word;
but hear, all you peoples,
  and behold my suffering;
my young women and young men
  have gone into captivity.

¹⁹ I called to my lovers
  but they deceived me;
my priests and elders
  perished in the city
while seeking food
  to revive their strength.

²⁰ See, O LORD, how distressed I am;
  my stomach churns,
my heart is wrung within me,
  because I have been very rebellious.
In the street the sword bereaves;
  in the house it is like death.

²¹ They heard how I was groaning,
  with no one to comfort me.
All my enemies heard of my trouble;
  they are glad that you have done it.
Bring on the day you have announced,
  and let them be as I am.

²² Let all their evil doing come before you;
  and deal with them
as you have dealt with me
  because of all my transgressions;
for my groans are many
  and my heart is faint.

COMMENTARY

1:11c. At the poem's center, Daughter Zion displaces the narrator as the principal speaker (v. 11c). As soon as she speaks, her voice has an emotional intensity and urgency lacking from the narrator's speech. Nor does she look to the past and its glories as he has. Her focus is the immediacy of her pain in the present. She addresses Yahweh and intensifies her demands in what may

be a poetic shout: "Look [ראה rĕ'ēh], O Yahweh, and see [הביטה habîṭâ]" (NRSV). The first imperative repeats her demand from v. 9c, but the second verb heightens urgency. The word נבט (Nābaṭ) means "to consider," "to pay attention." She orders Yahweh to look at her and see her condition, and her reason is that she is "worthless" (זוללה zôlēlâ). In this declaration of self-loathing, she echoes the poet's view of her (זלל *zll*, v. 8*b*), like an abused woman who has lost all sense of self-esteem.

1:12. When Yahweh offers no reply and no comfort, Daughter Zion turns to address a third party, presumably the passersby, demanding with the same verbs that they "pay attention [נבט *nābaṭ*] and look [ראה *rāʾâ*]." Although the Hebrew of v. 12*a* is not entirely clear,[45] Daughter Zion uses the same verbs she used in addressing Yahweh (v. 11*c*), except in reverse order. She does not ask for relief from her suffering. She asks only for a witness, for someone who recognizes the immensity of her sorrow and its source in Yahweh's "fierce anger." Again, she echoes the poet (v. 5*b*), but she adds heat to his interpretation. Even if she has provoked divine anger, her suffering is without comparison, "Is there any sorrow like my sorrow?" (v. 12*b*). Yahweh caused it in a rage.

1:13-16. As Daughter Zion continues to address passersby, divine actions become the subject of her speech. Yahweh is "on high," outside Daughter Zion's earthly space but close enough to strike her (v. 13). Using vivid, violent verbs, she relates Yahweh's brutal treatment of her. He sent fire; he spread a net; he turned her back; he left her devastated. Divine attacks on the female body again serve as a metaphor for the destruction of the city. Like Tamar after being raped by her brother Amnon (2 Sam 13:20), Zion is desolate. But unlike Tamar, Daughter Zion believes she deserves her fate as punishment for her sins. Yahweh gathers her sins and hangs them from her neck to shame and debilitate her further. Then like a scene from a pornographic movie, he hands her over to people more powerful than she (v. 14).

In this chapter, Daughter Zion's interpretation of the national tragedy is that Yahweh is its direct cause and she the indirect one. Yahweh has rejected her warriors, crushed her young men, stamped on her as if she were grapes in a wine press (v. 15). But anger at her divine attacker fades into tears as she explains to the passersby:

This is why I weep

. . . .

No one is near to comfort me,
  no one to restore my spirit.
My children are destitute. (v. 16)

1:17. Suddenly, the narrator interrupts her just as she had interrupted him (v. 9*c*). Perhaps he is moved by her plight. He stresses again that there is no one to comfort her, and again he connects her isolation to her shame. She has become an "unclean thing" (NIV) or a "filthy thing" (NRSV). The Hebrew term used here (בדה *niddâ*) refers to a menstrual rag.[46] This woman is not only ritually unclean, but she is also repulsive and dirty.

1:18-22. As if she has not heard the poet, Daughter Zion announces to the people that Yahweh "is in the right" (צדיכ *ṣaddîq*) (v. 18). The righteous God is a just God. She also tells the people that she is to blame, but it is her inhabitants who are suffering. They, her metaphorical children, are exiled, betrayed, and scavenging for food (vv. 18-19). Frenzy quickens her speech as she turns again to the Silent One. "See [ראה *rĕʾēh*], O Lord," she screams, "how distressed I am!" (v. 20). Phrases of physical and mental pain accumulate. "I am in torment"; "my stomach churns, my heart is wrung." And she confesses, using the verb of v. 8 in emphatic form, "I have been very rebellious" (מרה *mrh*, v. 21).

Daughter Zion's feverishly described torment narrows to the same haunting refrain. Though death is inside and out (v. 20*c*), "there is no one to comfort me" (v. 21). She does not ask for comfort now but merely states her need for comfort. Instead, she asks for justice from the just judge, the God who is just. Possibly justice will comfort her. She demands that Yahweh see the evildoing of her enemies. Let it come "before you" and deal with them (1:22). Yahweh does not reply.

---

45. Delbert Hillers, *Lamentations*, AB 7A (Garden City, N.Y.: Doubleday, 1972) 10.

46. O'Connor, "Lamentations," 180.

REFLECTIONS

1. As a symbolic figure of poetry, Daughter Zion's conditions evoke experiences of contemporary suffering in countless ways. People who have known severe loss, physical and emotional abuse, or catastrophic illness may recognize themselves in her internal world of abandonment and comfortlessness. Whole peoples around the globe may see their realities mirrored in her external world of physical atrocity and social collapse. Many peoples know the devastation of war and military attack, the destruction of their cities and dwelling places and of their way of life. Many suffer abject poverty, hunger, and hopelessness and watch as their children's lives are stunted and threatened. Some live with dehumanizing rejection simply for having been born into their skin, their religion, or their social group.

Any conditions of deprivation that inhibit life and prevent full human flourishing call for—indeed, demand—lamentation.[47] Lamentation names what is wrong, what is out of order in God's world, what keeps human beings from thriving in all their creative potential. Simple acts of lament expose these conditions, name them, open them to grief and anger, and make them visible for remedy. In its complaint, anger, and grief, lamentation protests conditions that prevent human thriving, and this resistance may finally prepare the way for healing. Lamentations, therefore, needs to be a practice of the church, a continuing prayer of protest, of solidarity, and of self-expression among believers.

2. Judith Lewis Hermann writes that the typical response to atrocity or trauma is to banish it from consciousness. Certain violations of the social compact are too terrible to allow them to come to consciousness or be uttered aloud. This, she says, is "the meaning of the word unspeakable."[48] Amnesia and denial enable individuals and communities to survive and move beyond catastrophe. But when crises are past, amnesia and denial constrict hope, cut off energy, deplete life, and abort lives of praise.

The dominant culture in the United States is that of denial and amnesia that affords innumerable ways to escape and lie about pain. The culture obsesses about money and the acquisition of material things. It teaches us to hide from pain by living vicariously through celebrities or to escape into workaholism and other addictions. It encourages us to displace anger by scapegoating immigrants or to transfer pain onto others in acts of "charity" or social justice.

The book of Lamentations practices truth-telling. It refuses denial and reverses amnesia by inviting readers into pain and affliction in all their rawness. It urges us to face suffering, to speak of it, to be dangerous proclaimers of the truth that society wants to repress. Lamentations refuses to whitewash the "narrative wreckage" that occurs in Zion. Daughter Zion's expected future, her anticipated narrative of prosperity and security, has been smashed to bits. The narrator describes the "narrative wreckage" that Daughter Zion faces.[49]

Daughter Zion's own account of her tragedy is blunt, immediate, traumatic. Her version of events epitomizes what Arthur Frank calls a "chaos story."[50] A chaos story is an account of suffering with no beginning, middle, or end. It tells of destructive events from which the storyteller has no distance, no capacity for interpretation, no ability to analyze, no effective way to separate herself or himself from the calamity. Chaos stories come to speech in fragmented, repetitive ways because the storyteller's affliction is so overwhelming. Such stories represent an effort to make visible wounds that can only be hinted at, talked around.

As beginning efforts to survive insurmountable suffering, chaos stories are terribly difficult to listen to or accept because they evoke wrenching and terrifying experiences within the listener.

---

47. Rebecca Chopp, "Feminism and the Theology of Sin," *Ecumenist* (November-December 1993) 12-16.
48. Judith Lewis Hermann, *Trauma and Recovery* (New York: Basic Books, 1992).
49. Arthur Frank, *The Wounded Storyteller: Body, Illness and Ethics* (Chicago: University of Chicago Press, 1995).
50. Ibid.

It is likely, however, that the capacity to hear them is central to ministry in a community of faith. Such listening may become possible only when listeners have already embraced their own denied pain and terror.

Well-meaning efforts to push people out of chaos stories before they have sufficiently relived the emotional trauma only deny and compound the suffering. Advice like "Get over it," "Get on with it," "Look on the bright side," reinforces the dehumanization of the sufferers by refusing to accept their stammering efforts toward truth. Denial, whether in political, therapeutic, or pastoral arenas, cuts off healing, aborts true reconciliation, and replaces truth with lies. What seems to be required from the churches, both clergy and laity, in the face of suffering, therefore, is not, initially at least, answers, dogmas, or solutions. Instead what is needed is a profoundly expanded capacity to hear the pain of the afflicted.[51]

It is precisely Daughter Zion's chaos story that provides an invitation to people in what Wendy Farley calls "radical suffering," suffering that diminishes and rejects the full humanity of sufferers.[52] Pain like that of Daughter Zion can never gain full articulation because it destroys all the usual measurements of life. Like many who suffer, Daughter Zion sits in the midst of calamity and cannot go forward. Her words accumulate around the wounds. She must speak; yet her wounds are unspeakable. Thus conventional genres, traditional language, and ordinary patterns of discourse are finally inadequate.

Poetic depictions of Daughter Zion's stammerings from within the center of her pain are the first movements toward survival. The chaos story can never be surmounted, the unspeakable wound cannot be healed, until it is accepted by the sufferer in all its life-destroying power and life-bludgeoning negativity. Giving voice to chaos brings affliction into the light and creates a space where healing may be possible. This is the accomplishment of Lamentations in its mixture of voices, genres, and poetic beauty that blends pain, rage, and doubt in a burbling stew.

51. Robert J. Schreiter, *Reconciliation: Ministry and Mission in a Changing Social Order,* Boston Theological Institute Series 3 (Maryknoll, N.Y.: Orbis, 1992).
52. Wendy Farley, *Tragic Vision and Divine Compassion: A Contemporary Theodicy* (Louisville: Westminster/John Knox, 1990).

WHO WILL HEAL YOU?

OVERVIEW

Similarities between the first two chapters of Lamentations suggest that they are closely related and comment upon each other. Both chapters follow the same formal pattern. Like the poem in chap. 1, the second poem is an acrostic of twenty-two verses, each verse containing three lines of which only the first begins with the sequential alphabetical letter. Like the first poem, the second one begins with the exclamation "how" (איכה 'êkâ), and the speakers of chap. 1, the narrator and Daughter Zion, continue their discourse in chap. 2.

The book's first chapter prepares the way for the second by vividly depicting the city's destruction, its effect on Daughter Zion, and her momentous grief and shame over the loss of her children. But chap. 2 shifts attention from Daughter Zion's condition to its cause, the furious rage of Yahweh. Both the narrator and Daughter Zion accuse God unrelentingly of overseeing, catalyzing, and executing atrocities against the woman.

Chapter 2 does not split easily into two panels of speech as did chapter 1. Instead, the poet is the primary speaker with Daughter Zion's discourse limited to vv. 20-22. Strangely, both speakers frequently address Yahweh as Adonai in this chapter. Is this merely orthographic coincidence, since Adonai is the name pronounced when Yahweh is written? Does the title Adonai, meaning "lord" or "master," suggest greater respect for God than does the proper name Yahweh? Or is it a distancing as the deity comes under severe accusation?[53]

The poem divides thematically into three units: (1) God's Mighty Acts, vv. 1-10; (2) Who Will Heal You? (vv. 11-19); and (3) Look and Consider, (vv. 20-22).

---

53. William D. Reyburn, *A Handbook on Lamentations,* UBS Handbook Series (New York: United Bible Society, 1992) 9.

LAMENTATIONS 2:1-10, GOD'S MIGHTY ACTS

NIV

2 [a]How the Lord has covered the Daughter
of Zion
with the cloud of his anger[b] !
He has hurled down the splendor of Israel
from heaven to earth;
he has not remembered his footstool
in the day of his anger.

[a]This chapter is an acrostic poem, the verses of which begin with the successive letters of the Hebrew alphabet.   [b]1 Or How the Lord in his anger / has treated the Daughter of Zion with contempt

NRSV

2 How the Lord in his anger
has humiliated[a] daughter Zion!
He has thrown down from heaven to earth
the splendor of Israel;
he has not remembered his footstool
in the day of his anger.

[2] The Lord has destroyed without mercy
all the dwellings of Jacob;

[a] Meaning of Heb uncertain

NIV

²Without pity the Lord has swallowed up
  all the dwellings of Jacob;
in his wrath he has torn down
  the strongholds of the Daughter of Judah.
He has brought her kingdom and its princes
  down to the ground in dishonor.

³In fierce anger he has cut off
  every horn[a] of Israel.
He has withdrawn his right hand
  at the approach of the enemy.
He has burned in Jacob like a flaming fire
  that consumes everything around it.

⁴Like an enemy he has strung his bow;
  his right hand is ready.
Like a foe he has slain
  all who were pleasing to the eye;
he has poured out his wrath like fire
  on the tent of the Daughter of Zion.

⁵The Lord is like an enemy;
  he has swallowed up Israel.
He has swallowed up all her palaces
  and destroyed her strongholds.
He has multiplied mourning and lamentation
  for the Daughter of Judah.

⁶He has laid waste his dwelling like a garden;
  he has destroyed his place of meeting.
The Lord has made Zion forget
  her appointed feasts and her Sabbaths;
in his fierce anger he has spurned
  both king and priest.

⁷The Lord has rejected his altar
  and abandoned his sanctuary.
He has handed over to the enemy
  the walls of her palaces;
they have raised a shout in the house of
      the Lord
  as on the day of an appointed feast.

⁸The Lord determined to tear down
  the wall around the Daughter of Zion.
He stretched out a measuring line
  and did not withhold his hand from
      destroying.
He made ramparts and walls lament;
  together they wasted away.

*a3 Or / all the strength; or every king; horn here symbolizes strength.

NRSV

in his wrath he has broken down
  the strongholds of daughter Judah;
he has brought down to the ground in dishonor
  the kingdom and its rulers.

³ He has cut down in fierce anger
  all the might of Israel;
he has withdrawn his right hand from them
  in the face of the enemy;
he has burned like a flaming fire in Jacob,
  consuming all around.

⁴ He has bent his bow like an enemy,
  with his right hand set like a foe;
he has killed all in whom we took pride
  in the tent of daughter Zion;
he has poured out his fury like fire.

⁵ The Lord has become like an enemy;
  he has destroyed Israel.
He has destroyed all its palaces,
  laid in ruins its strongholds,
and multiplied in daughter Judah
  mourning and lamentation.

⁶ He has broken down his booth like a garden,
  he has destroyed his tabernacle;
the LORD has abolished in Zion
  festival and sabbath,
and in his fierce indignation has spurned
  king and priest.

⁷ The Lord has scorned his altar,
  disowned his sanctuary;
he has delivered into the hand of the enemy
  the walls of her palaces;
a clamor was raised in the house of the LORD
  as on a day of festival.

⁸ The LORD determined to lay in ruins
  the wall of daughter Zion;
he stretched the line;
  he did not withhold his hand from
      destroying;
he caused rampart and wall to lament;
  they languish together.

⁹ Her gates have sunk into the ground;

NIV

⁹Her gates have sunk into the ground;
  their bars he has broken and destroyed.
Her king and her princes are exiled among
        the nations,
  the law is no more,
and her prophets no longer find
  visions from the Lord.

¹⁰The elders of the Daughter of Zion
  sit on the ground in silence;
they have sprinkled dust on their heads
  and put on sackcloth.
The young women of Jerusalem
  have bowed their heads to the ground.

NRSV

he has ruined and broken her bars;
her king and princes are among the nations;
  guidance is no more,
and her prophets obtain
  no vision from the LORD.

¹⁰The elders of daughter Zion
  sit on the ground in silence;
they have thrown dust on their heads
  and put on sackcloth;
the young girls of Jerusalem
  have bowed their heads to the ground.

COMMENTARY

Accusations found in chap. 1 that Daughter Zion's sins caused her suffering nearly disappear in this poem. Only the narrator's attack on the prophets for failing to reprimand Zion's iniquity recalls her responsibility for her pain (v. 14). Both speakers insist, instead, that it is Yahweh's anger that fuels the furious attacks against the daughter. Yahweh is out of control in a rage that lacks proportionality to anything she might have done.

2:1-8. Words of divine anger appear in vv. 1-4 and 6 and also frame v. 1. Adonai covers Daughter Zion in a cloud of "his anger" (באפו *bĕʾapô*, 2:1*a*), and he does not remember his footstool, his resting place, "in the day of his anger" (אפו *ʾapo*, v. 1*c*). Again the narrator views the nation's suffering in the light of its past glory, but now the agent of reversal and collapse is unmistakably clear.

The narrator piles active verbs on top of one another to portray divine involvement in the city's destruction. Yahweh flings out the nation from heaven, "throwing down the glory of Israel" (v. 1*b*). "Without pity" God "swallows up," "tears down," and "brings to the ground" buildings, strongholds, the whole kingdom (v. 2). Blinding rage motivates violence, for God's anger is hot (בחרי-אף *bāḥărî-ʾap*), a singeing fire loosed upon the nation, burning it and consuming all around (v. 3).

For the narrator, God's presence is a consuming holocaust. The poem does not nuance references to fire, as for example, purgation, cleansing, or

refining, as have some of the prophets (Isa 5:24; 6:6; Jer 6:29; Amos 7:4). In Lamentations, fire is God's weapon to obliterate a world. The One whose right hand should protect the people not only withdraws protection (v. 3*b*), but also becomes "like an enemy," a warrior who attacks (vv. 4*a*, 5*a*). God's right hand strings his bow for war, kills in Daughter Zion's tent, murders in a "rage like fire" (v. 4*c*, author's trans.).[54]

To convey engulfing destruction by the divine enemy, the narrator again uses language of "swallowing" (בלע *bāla'*, v. 2*a*). God "swallowed up Israel and swallowed up her palaces" (v. 5*b*). The narrator remarks on the effects of these mighty acts of fury that "multiply mourning and lament for the daughter of Judah" (v. 5*c*). But it is the attack on Jerusalem, Yahweh's own worship-filled dwelling place, that reveals the indiscriminate reach of divine destruction (vv. 6-8). The divine warrior destroyed "his booth," "his tabernacle" (v. 6), disrupted worship, and spurned king and priest. God has lost control, turned into a mad deity whose rage destroys even the divine home.

And most appalling, this devastation was deliberate, premeditated. Adonai "determined" (חשב *ḥāšab*) to tear down the city wall (v. 8). God measured, did not turn from swallowing (בלע *bāla'*),

---

54. On the divine warrior, see Delbert Hillers, *Lamentations*, AB 7A (Garden City, N.Y.: Doubleday, 1972) 43; Patrick Miller, "God the Warrior," *Int* (1965) 39-46.

and caused the structures of the city's defense to waste away. For the speaker, divine premeditation compounds the horror of the divine attack.

2:9-10. Abruptly the narrator draws attention away from the violent mighty acts of the deity to their effects upon Daughter Zion. In swiftly passing images, vv. 9-10 create a picture of total collapse, as if the readers are watching a city sinking into the earth. The city gates are destroyed, rulers are in exile, and the Torah, the living constitution and spir-

it of the community, no longer exists. The prophets are without visions, for their connection with Yahweh is broken. And the surviving inhabitants, described by a merism, "the old and the young"— that is, everyone from the youngest to the oldest[55]— mourn and lament, stunned by the tragedy that has befallen them. (See Reflections at 2:20-22.)

55. Claus Westermann, *Lamentations: Issues and Interpretation* (Minneapolis: Fortress, 1994) 153.

LAMENTATIONS 2:11-19, WHO WILL HEAL YOU?

NIV

¹¹My eyes fail from weeping,
  I am in torment within,
my heart is poured out on the ground
  because my people are destroyed,
because children and infants faint
  in the streets of the city.

¹²They say to their mothers,
  "Where is bread and wine?"
as they faint like wounded men
  in the streets of the city,
as their lives ebb away
  in their mothers' arms.

¹³What can I say for you?
  With what can I compare you,
  O Daughter of Jerusalem?
To what can I liken you,
  that I may comfort you,
  O Virgin Daughter of Zion?
Your wound is as deep as the sea.
  Who can heal you?

¹⁴The visions of your prophets
  were false and worthless;
they did not expose your sin
  to ward off your captivity.
The oracles they gave you
  were false and misleading.

¹⁵All who pass your way
  clap their hands at you;
they scoff and shake their heads

NRSV

¹¹ My eyes are spent with weeping;
  my stomach churns;
my bile is poured out on the ground
  because of the destruction of my people,
because infants and babes faint
  in the streets of the city.

¹² They cry to their mothers,
  "Where is bread and wine?"
as they faint like the wounded
  in the streets of the city,
as their life is poured out
  on their mothers' bosom.

¹³ What can I say for you, to what compare you,
  O daughter Jerusalem?
To what can I liken you, that I may
    comfort you,
  O virgin daughter Zion?
For vast as the sea is your ruin;
  who can heal you?

¹⁴ Your prophets have seen for you
  false and deceptive visions;
they have not exposed your iniquity
  to restore your fortunes,
but have seen oracles for you
  that are false and misleading.

¹⁵ All who pass along the way
  clap their hands at you;

NIV

at the Daughter of Jerusalem:
"Is this the city that was called
   the perfection of beauty,
   the joy of the whole earth?"

16All your enemies open their mouths
   wide against you;
they scoff and gnash their teeth
   and say, "We have swallowed her up.
This is the day we have waited for;
   we have lived to see it."

17The LORD has done what he planned;
   he has fulfilled his word,
   which he decreed long ago.
He has overthrown you without pity,
   he has let the enemy gloat over you,
   he has exalted the horn[a] of your foes.

18The hearts of the people
   cry out to the Lord.
O wall of the Daughter of Zion,
   let your tears flow like a river
   day and night;
give yourself no relief,
   your eyes no rest.

19Arise, cry out in the night,
   as the watches of the night begin;
pour out your heart like water
   in the presence of the Lord.
Lift up your hands to him
   for the lives of your children,
who faint from hunger
   at the head of every street.

[a] 17 Horn here symbolizes strength.

NRSV

they hiss and wag their heads
   at daughter Jerusalem;
"Is this the city that was called
   the perfection of beauty,
   the joy of all the earth?"

16 All your enemies
   open their mouths against you;
they hiss, they gnash their teeth,
   they cry: "We have devoured her!
Ah, this is the day we longed for;
   at last we have seen it!"

17 The LORD has done what he purposed,
   he has carried out his threat;
as he ordained long ago,
   he has demolished without pity;
he has made the enemy rejoice over you,
   and exalted the might of your foes.

18 Cry aloud[a] to the Lord!
   O wall of daughter Zion!
Let tears stream down like a torrent
   day and night!
Give yourself no rest,
   your eyes no respite!

19 Arise, cry out in the night,
   at the beginning of the watches!
Pour out your heart like water
   before the presence of the Lord!
Lift your hands to him
   for the lives of your children,
who faint for hunger
   at the head of every street.

[a] Cn: Heb Their heart cried

COMMENTARY

2:11-12. It is tempting to identify the speaker in these verses as Daughter Zion, because the speech is frantically emotional and tear-laden, but the speaker's tears "for the daughter of my people" (v. 11 b) require that the voice belong to the narrator.[56]

56. See F. W. Dobbs-Allsopp, *Weep, O Daughter of Zion: A Study of the City Lament Genre in the Hebrew Bible,* BibOr 44 (Rome: Editrice Pontificio Istituto Biblico, 1993) 103; and Hillers, *Lamentations,* for a careful discussion of the importance of the children.

Both the NIV and the NRSV omit "daughter" from the translation בת־עמי (*bat-'ammî*). His emotional distance from Daughter Zion, present in chap. 1, completely disappears here. The narrator enters her world of pain and affliction. No longer is he the disaffected reporter.

Instead, the narrator is overcome with tears, his insides are in turmoil over the "breaking" (שבר

šeber) of the daughter, and the overwhelming reason for his collapse is the suffering of the children (vv. 11*c*-12). To great effect, he quotes the children as they ask their mothers for food. They are dying from hunger at their mothers' breasts. Westermann notes that it is the sight of innocent children suffering that disturbs the speaker.[57] The scene is pitiful and heart-rending because the mothers are helpless and unable to feed their little ones. But the children represent more than innocents, more than the dying offspring of a particular family; they symbolize the future of the nation dying before the eyes of the community.[58] They are the most vulnerable, and their deaths signify the death of the whole people.

It is as if the narrator required the elapse of thirty verses of poetry for the true horror of the city's destruction to reach his heart, to penetrate his distant, objective persona. Now he absorbs the horrific nature of Daughter Zion's tragedy, for her dying children have released his feelings. They have shaken him, and at last he weeps with her (v. 11).

2:13. For the first time in the book, the narrator stops speaking about Daughter Zion in the third person and addresses her directly with three unanswerable questions. "To what can I compare you?" (אעידך *'ă'îdēk*). "To what can I liken you?" Besides meaning "to compare," the Hebrew verb of the first question (עוד *'ûd*) also means "to bear witness."[59] His multileveled questions ask her how he can bear witness to her suffering. Is there something comparable to which he can appeal so that her pain will be manageable, so the mind can take hold of it and distance can be gained from it?[60]

At last, the narrator confronts her suffering in its totality, its incomparability, and in the inability of his words to bear witness to it.[61] He needs a "language of the unsayable," but such a language of direct speech that can express and encompass her suffering does not exist, for her suffering is "as vast as the sea."[62] The narrator and the poet behind him confront the limits of language. Language "breaks" on account of her "breaking" (שברך *šibrēk*).

At the same time, the narrator's language evokes the realities of her pain and potentially transforms it by witnessing to it. He sees it in its unspeakableness and incomparability. He recognizes her pain and in his speech stands by her. He addresses her with the startling title "Virgin Daughter Zion," changing her characterization from a guilty woman with many lovers (1:2) into an innocent virgin (cf. Jer 31:21). Then he asks the third unanswerable question: "Who can heal you?"

2:14-17. The next four verses eliminate all candidates for a healer. Her prophets are effete, the passersby mock her, enemies entrap her, and Yahweh planned it all (2:14-17). The prophets have proved unreliable because their visions did not warn her of her sin and thereby help her to avoid this calamity in the first place. They are liars and will not heal her. The passersby to whom she appealed for comfort in 1:12-16 hiss, shake their heads at her, and mock her with her previous glory: "Is this the city that was called/ the perfection of beauty,/ the joy of all the earth?" (v. 15). They will not heal her.

The narrator also quotes her enemies, formerly her friends and lovers (1:2). They brag about their treachery and scheming. In words that echo God's language of attack (vv. 2, 5, 8) they say, "We have swallowed her up" (בלענו *billā'nû*). They shout triumphantly that at last they "have seen" (ראינו *rā'înû*) the day of her destruction (v. 16). The rhetorical device of quoting the enemies' speech adds drama to their triumph over Daughter Zion. They have been anticipating, scheming to destroy her, and they celebrate as she mourns alone. The enemies will not heal her.

Her final court of appeal should be Yahweh, but as chap. 2 has unequivocally declared, Yahweh will not heal her. Yahweh, announces the narrator, was the planner, the originating source, the violent energy behind her destruction (v. 17). The

---

57. Westermann, *Lamentations,* 154. See also Tod Linafelt, "Surviving Lamentations: A Literary-Theological Study of the Afterlife of a Biblical Text" (Ph.D. diss., Emory University, 1997), for a careful discussion of the importance of the children.

58. A. R. Pete Diamond and Kathleen M. O'Connor, "Unfaithful Passions: Coding Women Coding Men in Jeremiah 2:1–3:25 (4:2)," *Biblical Interpretation* (1996) 288-310, study the symbolic importance of children in the family of Yahweh and wife Jerusalem/Israel.

59. The Vulgate emends to the current reading, "compare you."

60. Contra Hillers, *Lamentations,* 46.

61. Francis Landy, "Lamentations," in *The Literary Guide to the Bible,* ed. Robert Alter and Frank Kermode (Cambridge, Mass.: Belknap, 1987) 329-34.

62. Sanford Budic and Wolfgang Iser, *Languages of the Unsayable: The Play of Negativity in Literature and Literary Theory,* Irvine Studies in the Humanities (Stanford: Stanford University Press, 1987).

Hebrew wording is emphatic in assigning deliberate forethought to God: "YHWH has done what he planned [זָמַם *zāmām*], his word which he commanded from days of old" (author's trans.). It was Yahweh who incited the enemy and Yahweh who "has demolished without pity." In this verse, the narrator summarizes his interpretation of events. The city's destruction was no chance happening, nor were Zion's enemies its instigators. Yahweh planned (v. 8), determined, decided ahead of time, from days of old, to destroy Daughter Zion. God will not heal her. She is alone and totally without recourse. No one will heal her.

2:18-19. Paradoxically, the poet directs Daughter Zion to cry out to Adonai. Although the first line of v. 18 presents a translation difficulty, the poet clearly addresses Daughter Zion in these two verses.[63] Despite the hopelessness of her situation, the poet advises her to "create a scene" before Adonai: "Let your tears flow like a river, day and night" (v. 18). "Give a ringing cry in the night" (v. 19a, author's trans.). "Pour out your heart like water" in the presence of Adonai, and "lift up your hands to him." The narrator urges her to scream, carry on, act out, implore God "for the lives of your children,/ who faint from hunger/ at the head of every street" (v. 19c). Perhaps, even if God has utterly forsaken Daughter Zion, God will have pity on her children. She must not restrain her tears; she must not cease from shouting out; she must not hold back for the sake of her children that they may have a future. (See Reflections at 2:20-22.)

63. The Hebrew reads, "Their heart cried to the Lord." The NIV supplies "people." The NRSV follows BHS in correcting the text to an imperative.

LAMENTATIONS 2:20-22, LOOK AND CONSIDER

NIV

20"Look, O Lord, and consider:
  Whom have you ever treated like this?
Should women eat their offspring,
  the children they have cared for?
Should priest and prophet be killed
  in the sanctuary of the Lord?

21"Young and old lie together
  in the dust of the streets;
my young men and maidens
  have fallen by the sword.
You have slain them in the day of your anger;
  you have slaughtered them without pity.

22"As you summon to a feast day,
  so you summoned against me terrors on
      every side.
In the day of the Lord's anger
  no one escaped or survived;
those I cared for and reared,
  my enemy has destroyed."

NRSV

20 Look, O Lord, and consider!
  To whom have you done this?
Should women eat their offspring,
  the children they have borne?
Should priest and prophet be killed
  in the sanctuary of the Lord?

21 The young and the old are lying
  on the ground in the streets;
my young women and my young men
  have fallen by the sword;
in the day of your anger you have killed them,
  slaughtering without mercy.

22 You invited my enemies from all around
  as if for a day of festival;
and on the day of the anger of the Lord
  no one escaped or survived;
those whom I bore and reared
  my enemy has destroyed.

COMMENTARY

At last, Daughter Zion raises her voice, but her speech is short, as if she has energy only for a few words. Unlike the narrator, she does not interpret the cause of her plight or speak about the past. The present pain engrosses her so she describes it, not in an explanatory narrative but as a list of horrors, a chaos story. Her speech arises from the thick of trauma; it is incapable of distance, of interpretation, or of principled explanation.

She repeats her demands from chap. 1, using the same verbs to gain divine attention here as she did there (vv. 11c, 20). "Look [ראה *rĕ'ēh*], O Yahweh, and consider [הביטה *habîṭâ*]." Once again she insists that if Yahweh would only take heed, if Yahweh would only comprehend fully what she has suffered, realize how divine fury has completely overturned her world, then there might be hope. She accuses the deity of careless inattention, "Whom have you ever treated [עלל *'ālal*] like this?" (v. 20). Neither the NIV nor the NRSV captures the full force of her charges against the deity. The verb עלל (*'ālal*) conveys more aggression than does "treat" someone (NIV) or "do to" someone; rather, it suggests "affliction" and "abuse."[64] She begs Yahweh to notice that he is abusing her. But her request is not about herself; it concerns the suffering of her children, the inhabitants of her city.

What God seems not to notice are shocking atrocities to the weakest, most vulnerable. "Should women eat their offspring, the children they have cared for?" (v. 20b). That mothers would kill children in an act of cannibalism for their own survival or for the survival of other children is almost unthinkable. How can Adonai be blind to this? But the use of the word "children" (עללי *'olālê*) is parallel to Yahweh's act of abuse (עלל *'ālal*, v. 20a) and evokes divine complicity by its placement in the sentence.[65]

In an effort to persuade God to notice her suffering, she pairs the obscenities relating to the children with the murder of priests and prophets in Adonai's own sanctuary, presumably engaged in their work of worship, as if divine self-interest would compel action. Old and young, male and female, "in the day of your anger you have slaughtered them without mercy" (v. 21c). Daughter Zion's accusations against God have moved beyond charges of callous inattention to an echoing of the poet's indictments. This God is neither absent nor shortsighted, but a merciless, calculating, and angry destroyer of innocent life. This is the God who invited Daughter Zion's enemies for a festival on the day of his anger (v. 22).

64. Linafelt, "Surviving Lamentations," 117-18.

65. Ibid., 118.

REFLECTIONS

1. The most conspicuous feature of chapter 2 is its unbridled anger at God. Both speakers grow in anger, hurl accusations at God, and accuse God of pitiless attacks on the city and its people. In their interpretation of events, the deity's rage is the principal origin of the city's destruction. Both speakers abandon the belief that Daughter Zion has done herself in by her sin. It is Yahweh whose anger lies behind the catastrophe.

Many people believe that expressions of anger have no place in the prayers of the believing communities, in religious speech, or in individual efforts to live a spiritual life. Such estimates are acts of denial, instructions in lying, not biblical faith. The poems of Lamentations, and the second poem most vividly, spring from anger. They create a rhetoric of fury, a swirling language of pain, distrust, and betrayal, both divine and human. In this language what is awry and causes unspeakable suffering is the way God relates to humans, the way God has abandoned covenant mutuality and faithfulness. This causes profound rage.

The speaker's anger at God is neither blasphemous nor unfitting for prayer. Rather, it is a language of fidelity. With pounding honesty, the speakers shout toward God their experience of reality in its life-bludgeoning pain and dehumanizing terror. They hide nothing. They present God with all that is wrong with the world and their relationship, and in doing so they are eminently faithful. Their anger signifies that they have not let go of God. They scream at God that their relationship is collapsing. They keep up their side of the communication, even though they receive no response.

Lamentation is a form of prayer that may be essential to believing communities and struggling individuals because it springs from the hope that nothing about human life is inappropriate for divine attention—no chaos, no atrocity, no sinfulness cuts us off from God. Denial, refusal to make a scene, to pour out our hearts day and night until God will see cuts us off from God and from ourselves. At the root of lament, therefore, is faith that God is a God of justice who, if seeing, will act in justice and who, if attending, will restore relationship.

2. The practice of lament in public worship is a political act. Expressing anger, disclosing discontent with the world, protesting injustice to God has political ramifications. Walter Brueggemann asserts that if we cannot challenge the governance of this world, then we cannot challenge the governors of the world.[66] The churches' unwillingness or incapacity to bring radical discontent, protest, and anger before God silences and denies reality. It teaches sheepishness, lying, and cowardice. Protest of injustice and oppression is learned in prayer.

3. Daughter Zion seeks a comforter, but who or what could possibly bring her comfort? What could even temporarily soothe her wounds of abandonment, trauma, and loss that create and constrict her worlds? Her speech provides a clue. She does not ask for restoration, cessation of pain, reversal of fortune, or even for the return of her beloved children. She asks only that Yahweh see, attend to, recognize her suffering. She wants God to see her shame and worthlessness, to look carefully upon the torments of her body and her heart and the atrocities afflicting her children. She asks for a witness and that God be that witness.

The power of witnessing is that only seeing, attending to, and recognizing suffering can bring comfort and make a way for healing. Seeing and acknowledging pain validate it. Seeing helps the sufferer to know that she or he is not crazy, not an exile from the human race, but one truly overpowered by tragedy, whatever its cause. Acknowledging pain is a form of embrace.

In the book of Lamentations, God never comforts Daughter Zion, never sees her suffering. But she does have a comforter. In the second poem, the narrator himself sees her, hears her, weeps with her, and urges her to express her grief and anger. The narrator, who was previously apart from her pain, now enters into her pain. He recognizes that her suffering is enormous, more vast than the sea, beyond compare. He joins her in a kind of solidarity that accepts the truthfulness of her testimony, that offers her back her dignity, and that changes him.

The poem itself also serves as Daughter Zion's comfort and assurance. In artistic speech, it sets out in graphic vignettes the pain that has invaded every aspect of her life. This poem and the collection that the book comprises are her witness, her comfort, her assurance. The poems create a world of language that mirrors suffering back to the brokenhearted and hopeless city.

This is why communities and individuals who know great suffering find in Lamentations immense comfort, not brutal assault. Under conditions of radical pain, it is possible to find in the book a truth-telling that resonates in the readers' worlds. The poems testify to the life-thwarting and humanity-destroying character of trauma and assault. They do not whitewash its ugliness or the anger of survivors. In bearing witness, the poetry of grief and anger creates a space for healing. This poetry makes it possible for sufferers to see themselves reflected back in all their sorrowful humanity. Such witness may be the poem's principal use for the churches and for believing communities.

---

66. Walter Brueggemann, "The Costly Loss of Lament" *JSOT* 36 (1986) 57-67.

---

4. Although Daughter Zion receives no comfort from Yahweh in the book of Lamentations, Yahweh does comfort her in another biblical book. The prophetic book of Isaiah (chaps. 48–54) keeps Zion alive and provides her with a beautiful, bracing future. Her comfort comes in exquisite lyrical poetry where her conditions are reversed yet again and her family life is restored.[67] There Yahweh speaks directly to her, comforts her, promises to return her children to her.

The poems of comfort to Daughter Zion are traditionally assigned to an anonymous prophet of the exile referred to as Second Isaiah. That material may come from a later time in the exilic period when the Judean deportees in Babylon began to anticipate a return to Jerusalem. The words of consolation and comfort addressed to Daughter Zion become a vision of hope for a renewed future. But in Lamentations, there is little sign of such a turn of events. The survivors appear to be too new to their suffering even to imagine a different horizon ahead. It may be that Lamentations opens a space for renewed imagination and hope by representing the wounds, by retelling the pain. Perhaps only then can a new world open to them. It is, therefore, a danger that the Isaian passages will too soon transport contemporary biblical readers to a happy ending that shortcuts the work of grief and anger that comes to the surface in lament.

Survivors of abuse, warfare, radical suffering, assault, and tragic, life-altering loss must tell their stories over and over again. This is a way to relive trauma, to re-enter it in a space and time outside of their own space and time, and to come to terms with it and the deep emotions that accompany it.[68] Then the poems may give them the energy and hope to step ever so slowly out of their suffering story toward healing.

67. See Patricia Tull Willey, *"Remember the Former Things": The Recollection of Previous Texts in Isaiah 40–55,* SBLDS (Atlanta: Scholars Press, 1997).

68. See Judith Lewis Hermann, *Trauma and Recovery* (New York: Basic Books, 1992); Robert Schrieter, *Reconciliation: Mission and Ministry in a Changing Social Order* (Maryknoll, N.Y.: Orbis, 1992).

LAMENTATIONS 3:1-66

THE STRONG MAN'S DILEMMA

OVERVIEW

The third poem startles readers by introducing a new poetic persona into the book. The narrator and Daughter Zion are completely missing from this chapter and are replaced by an unidentified male. In its laudable effort to be gender-inclusive, the NRSV translation obscures the change in speaker by translating the opening clause, "I am the one." The genderless pronoun "one" wrongly suggests that Daughter Zion is continuing to speak from the previous chapter. But new testimony bursts out in this chapter in the voice of a strong man or soldier (גבר *geber*). The choice of the Hebrew noun *geber* and not of more generic words for "male" or "human," may bring military connotations to the speaker's voice. Although *geber* can be translated simply as "man," the word refers to a man as a defender of women, children, and other non-combatants.[69] Lanahan understands the speaker to be a soldier. Although such identification is not certain, *geber* appears also in vv. 27, 35, and 39, providing continuity in the characterization of the speaker and keeping the military connotations alive in the poem.

Whether the strong man is present in the poem or not, however, his voice is as intimate, personal, and anguished as that of Daughter Zion. He presents the testimony of another survivor of the catastrophe and offers a different viewpoint from that of either the narrator or Daughter Zion. The strong man is hopeful, reliant on theological traditions of divine mercy, and confident that Yahweh has seen his suffering. His arrival at hope, however, is through a convoluted journey, a tortured struggle, in which hope is asserted in the face of contradictory experience.

Within the literary context of the whole book, the strong man's hope is muted indeed. His hope-ful discourse creates one of the book's most vexing interpretive problems. Is the placement of the man's testimony at the book's center, in the most dense and intricate of acrostic poems, reason to find it "the monumental center of the book"[70] and the ultimate triumph of faith? Or is the voice of hope eclipsed by the trailing off of the book in the disheartened voices of the poet-narrator and the community in the final chapters? Because we do not know the significance of the book's compositional arrangement, decisions about the chapter's role must remain interpretive.

However, it is probably a false dichotomy to require a definitive interpretation of the poems' relationships to hope and to one another. Voices of hope and horror are left standing, juxtaposed with one another as a response to unspeakable tragedy. The book's open-endedness may be a deliberate rhetorical strategy to lay bare the totality of the city's devastation. Lamentations does not resolve the pain, does not absolve the deity, and does not let hope whitewash the truth of the nation's confusion and desperation. And little noticed by interpreters, these same contradictions that mark the book as a unity reside together in the words of the strong man.

Besides introducing a new speaker, chapter 3 differs from the surrounding chapters in other ways. Chapter 3 lacks the opening exclamation "how" (איכה *'êkâ*), found in 1:1; 2:1; 4:1. Further distinguishing chap. 3 from the surrounding chapters is the intensification of the acrostic form. Each of three successive lines begins with the same letter of the Hebrew alphabet in chap. 3. In addition, the poem's language repeats, overlaps, and inter-

---

69. See BDB, 149-50.

70. Alan Mintz, "The Rhetoric of Lamentations and the Representation of Catastrophe," in *Hurban: Responses to Catastrophe in Hebrew Literature*, ed. G. A. Buttrick et al. (New York: Columbia University Press, 1984) 33.

weaves across stanzas with greater density than in other poems. For example, the third stanza, or group of three alphabetic lines (vv. 7-9), uses the verb "to wall in" (גדר *gādar*) as the initial word of both v. 7 and v. 9. The noun "way" (דרך *derek*) also occurs in v. 9 and reappears as the initial word in vv. 11-12 in the fourth stanza. This linguistic interweaving within and across stanzas creates a density of language, an overlapping of sound, and a joining of horrors that express the entrapment of the speaker and contribute to the poem's literary strategies of encirclement. In exceptionally artful ways, chap. 3 circles around imagery of captivity and entrapment to enclose both the speaker and the deity within metaphorical barricades.

The poem divides into two larger sections: (1) The Strong Man's First Complaint, 3:1-42, and (2) The Strong Man's Second Complaint, vv. 43-66, each beginning with a complaint. The sections subdivide by topic, speaker, and addressee.

I. The Strong Man's First Complaint, 3:1-42
   The Enemy's Overflowing Rage, vv. 1-20
   Reasons to Expect Mercy, vv. 21-39
   Invitation to Repent, vv. 40-42
II. The Strong Man's Second Complaint, 3:43-66
   God Has Not Forgiven, vv. 43-54
   God Has Rescued—God Will Rescue, vv. 55-63
   Petition for Justice, vv. 64-66

LAMENTATIONS 3:1-42, THE STRONG MAN'S FIRST COMPLAINT

Lamentations 3:1-20, The Enemy's Overflowing Rage

NIV	NRSV
3 ^aI am the man who has seen affliction by the rod of his wrath.	**3** I am one who has seen affliction under the rod of God's^a wrath;
²He has driven me away and made me walk in darkness rather than light;	² he has driven and brought me into darkness without any light;
³indeed, he has turned his hand against me again and again, all day long.	³ against me alone he turns his hand, again and again, all day long.
⁴He has made my skin and my flesh grow old and has broken my bones.	⁴ He has made my flesh and my skin waste away, and broken my bones;
⁵He has besieged me and surrounded me with bitterness and hardship.	⁵ he has besieged and enveloped me with bitterness and tribulation;
⁶He has made me dwell in darkness like those long dead.	⁶ he has made me sit in darkness like the dead of long ago.
⁷He has walled me in so I cannot escape; he has weighed me down with chains.	⁷ He has walled me about so that I cannot escape; he has put heavy chains on me;
⁸Even when I call out or cry for help, he shuts out my prayer.	⁸ though I call and cry for help, he shuts out my prayer;
⁹He has barred my way with blocks of stone; he has made my paths crooked.	⁹ he has blocked my ways with hewn stones, he has made my paths crooked.
¹⁰Like a bear lying in wait, like a lion in hiding,	

^a *This chapter is an acrostic poem; the verses of each stanza begin with the successive letters of the Hebrew alphabet, and the verses within each stanza begin with the same letter.*

^a Heb *his*

NIV

¹¹he dragged me from the path and mangled me
and left me without help.
¹²He drew his bow
and made me the target for his arrows.

¹³He pierced my heart
with arrows from his quiver.
¹⁴I became the laughingstock of all my people;
they mock me in song all day long.
¹⁵He has filled me with bitter herbs
and sated me with gall.

¹⁶He has broken my teeth with gravel;
he has trampled me in the dust.
¹⁷I have been deprived of peace;
I have forgotten what prosperity is.
¹⁸So I say, "My splendor is gone
and all that I had hoped from the LORD."

¹⁹I remember my affliction and my wandering,
the bitterness and the gall.
²⁰I well remember them,
and my soul is downcast within me.

NRSV

¹⁰ He is a bear lying in wait for me,
a lion in hiding;
¹¹ he led me off my way and tore me to pieces;
he has made me desolate;
¹² he bent his bow and set me
as a mark for his arrow.

¹³ He shot into my vitals
the arrows of his quiver;
¹⁴ I have become the laughingstock of all
my people,
the object of their taunt-songs all day long.
¹⁵ He has filled me with bitterness,
he has sated me with wormwood.

¹⁶ He has made my teeth grind on gravel,
and made me cower in ashes;
¹⁷ my soul is bereft of peace;
I have forgotten what happiness is;
¹⁸ so I say, "Gone is my glory,
and all that I had hoped for from the LORD."

¹⁹ The thought of my affliction and my
homelessness
is wormwood and gall!
²⁰ My soul continually thinks of it
and is bowed down within me.

COMMENTARY

3:1. "I am the strong man who has seen [ראה *rāʾâh*] affliction by the rod of his overflowing rage" (author's trans.). As the poem's opening verb, the strong man's claim to have "seen" establishes a relationship with the unanswered requests of the speakers in the previous chapters for Yahweh "to see." Yahweh has not seen, but the speaker has seen his own horrors. In Hebrew, the verb "to see" also carries the nuance of "to experience." Used here with the emphatic first-person pronoun "I" (אני *ʾănî*), the verb establishes the strong man's authority to speak. Because he has experienced affliction, he has authority to speak, to give voice, to testify from inside the pain of his affliction. He uses that authority to weave together the cause of his affliction and its consequences.

The result is a portrait of an abusive relationship. The use of the first-person voice again invites readers to identify with the suffering male speaker and to experience vicariously the affliction that comes from the enemy's overflowing rage.

The NRSV prematurely identifies the abusive enemy as God.[71] For twenty verses, however, the Masoretic Text (MT) does not mention God except for a hint in v. 8. The text's silence about the enemy's identity is a powerful literary strategy. The withholding of the enemy's name avoids blasphemy by not charging God directly with the extreme cruelty described in this unit. It also

71. The NRSV translation makes sense because the preceding verse (2:22) speaks of Yahweh's anger, but the speaker is Daughter Zion. Both the MT and the LXX refer to the enemy with the pronoun "he."

invites identification of the enemy with the army that has invaded the city and destroyed the nation and suggests that divine absence caused the affliction.[72] But the withholding of the enemy's identity draws readers into the entangled relationship of torturer and victim. Only later in the poem do the full implications of the enemy's behavior become clear and, therefore, all the more appalling. Yahweh is not absent; Yahweh is the enemy (vv. 37-39).

3:2-9. Immediately the grammatical subject of the sentences shifts, however, from the speaker to the anonymous enemy: "He drove me into darkness, he turned against me, he weakened my flesh" (vv. 2-4). The enemy besieges and surrounds the strong man, places him in darkness like the dead, walls him in and binds him with a chain (vv. 5-7).

Violent and claustrophobic language energizes these verses. A brutal opponent tortures the speaker's body and holds him captive. Active verbs describe the enemy encircling the victim.[73] The enemy "builds against him," surrounds him, walls in his way. And just as the enemy "walls in" (גדר gdr) the man (v. 7) and "walls [gdr] his path with stones" (v. 9), so also the stanza (vv. 7-9)) builds a wall around his screams and "shuts out" his prayers for help, mimicking the enemy's actions (v. 8). A poetics of encirclement creates crushing metaphorical walls that silence and destroy. The speaker is trapped, captured, closed in completely. He is vulnerable, cut off, and helpless.

3:10-18. Then with his way "walled in," captive and vulnerable, an enemy assaults him as the poem adds language of attack to language of encirclement (vv. 10-13). The enemy is a lurking bear,

a hiding lion, a ravaging beast of prey who tears the speaker to pieces and leaves him desolate (v. 11). The enemy is an archer who has pierced the strong man's heart with an arrow (vv. 12-13). He has filled him with bitterness (v. 15), crushed his teeth with gravel, and made him cower in ashes (v. 16).

Language about the enemy's aggression is so abundant, multiple, drawn from so many spheres, that it nearly becomes hyperbolic in its excess, as if the narrator must draw on every possible realm of life to express the impact of the unnamed enemy upon him. Only briefly does the speaker interrupt the staccato listing of attacks to make himself again the grammatical subject and to bemoan his social shame as the laughingstock of his people (v. 14). But finally he turns from the physical and social afflictions he has experienced to speak of his inner torments. He "is rejected from peace" and has forgotten goodness (v. 17). To emphasize his present sorrows, he quotes himself and for the first time names God, but not in accusation: "So I say, 'Gone is my glory,/ and all that I had hoped for from the LORD'" (v. 18). The speaker's self-quotation articulates his vanished hope and brings the audience into his grim state of mind.

3:19-20. His mental state is anything but stable. When he remembers his affliction and hopelessness, he feels deep bitterness (v. 19). He uses the same word for "affliction" (עניי 'onyî) that he used in v. 1, encircling his own testimony in a larger poetic structure so that vv. 1-19 echo the encirclement of the speaker and the encircling created in the stanzas. The whole testimony of vv. 1-19 is framed as a "remembering" (זכר zākar), a retelling of the horrors that keeps them alive in mind and heart. This remembering makes his soul sink down upon him (v. 20). (See Reflections at 3:64-66.)

72. Pamela Jean Owens, "Personification and Suffering in Lamentations 3," *Austin Seminary Bulletin* (Spring 1990) 75-90.
73. William F. Lanahan, "The Speaking Voice in the Book of Lamentations," *JBL* 93 (1974) 46, notices the device of encirclement in the poem without specifying where.

Lamentations 3:21-39, Reasons to Expect Mercy

NIV	NRSV

[21]Yet this I call to mind
   and therefore I have hope:
	[21] But this I call to mind,
	   and therefore I have hope:

NIV

²²Because of the LORD's great love we are
    not consumed,
  for his compassions never fail.
²³They are new every morning;
  great is your faithfulness.
²⁴I say to myself, "The LORD is my portion;
  therefore I will wait for him."

²⁵The LORD is good to those whose hope is
    in him,
  to the one who seeks him;
²⁶it is good to wait quietly
  for the salvation of the LORD.
²⁷It is good for a man to bear the yoke
  while he is young.

²⁸Let him sit alone in silence,
  for the LORD has laid it on him.
²⁹Let him bury his face in the dust—
  there may yet be hope.
³⁰Let him offer his cheek to one who would
    strike him,
  and let him be filled with disgrace.

³¹For men are not cast off
  by the Lord forever.
³²Though he brings grief, he will show compassion,
  so great is his unfailing love.
³³For he does not willingly bring affliction
  or grief to the children of men.

³⁴To crush underfoot
  all prisoners in the land,
³⁵to deny a man his rights
  before the Most High,
³⁶to deprive a man of justice—
  would not the Lord see such things?

³⁷Who can speak and have it happen
  if the Lord has not decreed it?
³⁸Is it not from the mouth of the Most High
  that both calamities and good things come?
³⁹Why should any living man complain
  when punished for his sins?

NRSV

²²The steadfast love of the LORD never ceases,ᵃ
  his mercies never come to an end;
²³they are new every morning;
  great is your faithfulness.
²⁴"The LORD is my portion, says my soul,
  "therefore I will hope in him."

²⁵The LORD is good to those who wait for him,
  to the soul that seeks him.
²⁶It is good that one should wait quietly
  for the salvation of the LORD.
²⁷It is good for one to bear
  the yoke in youth,
²⁸to sit alone in silence
  when the Lord has imposed it,
²⁹to put one's mouth to the dust
  (there may yet be hope),
³⁰to give one's cheek to the smiter,
  and be filled with insults.

³¹For the Lord will not
  reject forever.
³²Although he causes grief, he will have
    compassion
  according to the abundance of his
    steadfast love;
³³for he does not willingly afflict
  or grieve anyone.

³⁴When all the prisoners of the land
  are crushed under foot,
³⁵when human rights are perverted
  in the presence of the Most High,
³⁶when one's case is subverted
  —does the Lord not see it?

³⁷Who can command and have it done,
  if the Lord has not ordained it?
³⁸Is it not from the mouth of the Most High
  that good and bad come?
³⁹Why should any who draw breath complain
  about the punishment of their sins?

ᵃ Syr Tg: Heb LORD, we are not cut off

COMMENTARY

3:21-24. In a sudden emotional reversal, the strong man remembers something else that reverses his outlook, lifts him up, gives him hope, or at least puts him in a stance of expectant waiting (v. 21). He remembers that the steadfast love and mercies of Yahweh never end: "They are new every morning!" (v. 23*a*). This arresting statement of faith seems, for the moment, to wipe away the hopelessness and suffering of the first twenty lines of the poem. Such sudden reversals in outlook are typical of the lament form and express confident faith in the face of adversity. But the strong man's lament is far more complex than suggested by the usual purposes of the lament.

For the speaker, the moral character of Yahweh radically contradicts his own experience of suffering in which the implied captor and abuser is Yahweh (vv. 1-20). The poem's sharp reversal of mood, the suddenness of the speaker's switch from despair to hope, does not require the conclusion that the poem abruptly stitches together independent literary fragments.[74] In its present form, the poem expresses the theological dilemma that faces the speaker and his community and that forms the central struggle of the chapter and of the book.

The strong man's assertions of faith and hope extend from v. 21 to v. 36, but his dilemma will not emerge with full force until vv. 37-39. What gives him hope (יחל *yāḥal*, 3:21) is Yahweh's fidelity and mercy. The חסד (*ḥesed*, "steadfast love") of Yahweh never ceases; God's mercies never come to an end; every morning "they are new" (vv. 22-23*a*). Contradicting his own words of hopelessness (v. 21), the speaker quotes himself again, declaring that Yahweh is his "portion" and, therefore, he will hope (v. 24). In its poetics of encirclement, the poem frames God's merciful fidelity with the strong man's hope (יחל *yāḥal*, vv. 21, 24). Hope encircles divine mercy, as if to support it, for it may not be able to sustain itself.

The strong man's use of self-quotations establishes a certain parity between his two conflicting experiences. Renewed hope and failed hope receive the same rhetorical attention (v. 18). The *ḥesed* (חסד) of Yahweh never ceases; God's mercies never come to an end, "therefore I will hope in him" (v. 24). In this case, hope is a decision of the speaker based on remembrance of divine mercies. For the first time in the poem, he addresses Yahweh directly to voice the confidence that underscores their mutual relationship, "Great is your faithfulness."

3:25-36. But how should the next stanzas be understood in relation to the speaker's rediscovered hope? His next words join the speaker's affirmation of divine *ḥesed* (vv. 21-24) with his experience of grief and rejection (vv. 1-21), but they do not declare unequivocal confidence in God. They suggest, instead, an internal struggle to persuade himself that his faithfulness and hope are well placed. Yahweh "is good to those who wait" (קוה *qāwāh*), he states, and "it is good that one should wait quietly" (or "hope," יחל *yāḥal*) for the "salvation of YHWH" (v. 26). It is good for the strong man (גבר *geber*) to bear the yoke. His waiting here is expectant, and it is filled with suffering. Indirectly the speaker is instructing not only himself but also his implied audience about proper behavior in suffering. Be silent, wait, bear the yoke. Accept suffering, and stop resisting.

A certain ambivalence colors this advice. The yoke is a conventional metaphor used to express burden or enslavement that here captures the predicament of the speaker.[75] He tells himself to accept the fate imposed on him as he sits alone in silence (v. 28), he abases himself (v. 29), and he accepts abuse and insult (v. 30). The chance that there still may be hope (v. 29), that right behavior may influence the deity, who "does not reject forever" (v. 31), motivates his efforts. In these declarations about the value of suffering, the strong man's dilemma becomes clear. Yahweh is the one who has imposed the yoke upon him and has rejected him. Yahweh is the one who smites (v. 30) and causes grief (v. 31). Yahweh is the abuser—but not forever, not always.[76] Divine mercy sur-

---

74. See Norman K. Gottwald, *Studies in the Book of Lamentations* (Chicago: Alec R. Allenson, 1954) 37-38; Claus Westermann, *Lamentations: Issues and Interpretation* (Minneapolis: Fortress, 1994) 67-68.

75. Patrick Skehan and Alexander DiLella, *The Wisdom of Ben Sira*, AB 30 (Garden City, N.Y.: Doubleday, 1987) 579n. 193.

76. See David Bluementhal, *Facing the Abusing God: A Theology of Protest* (Louisville: Westminster/John Knox, 1993), for a provocative and troubling theology on this point.

passes divine abuse, "according to his steadfast love" (*ḥesed,* v. 32; cf. v. 22).

Because, for the ancients, events occur by divine causation, the strong man is entangled in theological contradictions. Like Daughter Zion, he finds God at the root of his afflictions; and in God he finds the only cause for hope. His experience of suffering and his theological beliefs contradict each other so that the poem's literary strategy of encirclement finds echoes in the entangled theology of the captive.

He tries to absolve God with a richly layered claim. God does not afflict "willingly" (מלבו *millibô;* lit., "from his heart," v. 33). He uses the same word for "affliction" (ענה *'ānâ*) that he used in vv. 1-20 for affliction that came from the "rod of his overflowing anger" (v. 1). Now he claims that he knows the heart of God, that God did not want to afflict willingly, "from the heart." It is as if the suffering that the strong man has relentlessly described was somehow accidental or as if the deity were under the power of an outside force, so that these brutal attacks were against the divine will but required by some overwhelming force or principle. To the strong man it appears that God must be powerless in this matter, that the true identity of God is not abusive or wrathful but characterized by great mercy (v. 32).

Perhaps in a rhetorical effort to persuade God to act mercifully and the implied audience to behave submissively,[77] the strong man lists the deeds that God does unwillingly (vv. 34-36). Although the specific divine acts are clear, translation of these lines is difficult. The NRSV translates the stanza as a separate thought from vv. 31-33. When prisoners are crushed, when human rights are perverted, when one's case is subverted, "does the LORD not see it?" The NIV also ends the stanza with a question. But the question form is not required by the Hebrew, and the verses may be interpreted as a continuation of the thought of the previous stanza.[78] To crush prisoners of war, to turn aside the strong man, to subvert a human in his cause, Adonai does not see. If the last line is interpreted as a statement, then it provides another defense

for the deity's failure to act. God does not see; perhaps God is not to blame.

Whether the text presents a statement or a question, the poem joins the strong man with speakers in the previous two poems in his insistence that God's seeing matters. The syntactical confusions of these verses are probably best left standing, for they evoke the theological predicament of the speaker. As a captive strong man who has experienced attacks and humiliation, he cannot resolve the contradiction between his confidence in Yahweh (vv. 20-33) and the circumstances of his torture and abuse (vv. 1-20), and perhaps neither can his implied audience.

3:37-39. The speaker's struggle to make sense of his affliction continues on its erratic course. The root of his dilemma emerges in rhetorical questions addressed to the audience, as if he is inviting them to think through their bitter plight with him: "Who can speak and have it happen" besides Yahweh? No one! "Is it not from the mouth of the Most High that good and bad come?" Yes, everything comes from Yahweh! Since God controls everything, and the speaker is not willing to blame God for his troubles, he is driven back to the conclusion that humans must have provoked God by their sinfulness.

The speaker's final question affirms this conclusion and invites the audience to submit to suffering. Who can possibly complain "about the punishment of their sins?" Has the strong man taken back his own complaint, convinced himself that it was illegitimate?[79] Is he suggesting that the community is complaining inappropriately? Since complaint will reappear in the remainder of the poem, any such evaluation has no lasting significance. Instead, the speaker thinks out loud, turning over experience and tradition to arrive at a satisfactory explanation of the disaster. He seems one step removed from the affliction that he has suffered because, unlike the narrator and Daughter Zion, he has the capacity to think about causes, even as he continues to be tormented by them. To explain his painful reality, he probes tradition; but his efforts fail. (See Reflections at 3:64-66.)

---

77. Westermann, *Lamentations,* 177, calls 3:33-38 a "didactic midrash."

78. The grammatical issue is whether the infinitives in 3:34-36 depend on the ראה (*rā'āh*) of v. 36*b* or on the verbs in v. 33. See Delbert Hillers, *Lamentations,* AB 7A (Garden City, N.Y.: Doubleday, 1972) 57-58; Iain Provan, *Lamentations,* NCB (Grand Rapids: Eerdmans, 1991) 97.

79. Provan, *Lamentations,* 100.

Lamentations 3:40-42, Invitation to Repent

NIV	NRSV
[40]Let us examine our ways and test them, and let us return to the LORD. [41]Let us lift up our hearts and our hands to God in heaven, and say: [42]"We have sinned and rebelled and you have not forgiven.	[40] Let us test and examine our ways, and return to the LORD. [41] Let us lift up our hearts as well as our hands to God in heaven. [42] We have transgressed and rebelled, and you have not forgiven.

COMMENTARY

The speaker's temporary conclusion that humans cause their own suffering by their sin prepares the way for him to turn directly to the audience and try to draw them into an act of repentance.[80] He urges them to join in wholehearted worship and in general stereotypical language utters a communal confession of sin. He is convinced enough of his most recent explanation of the events to act upon it and to want to persuade others to join him.

"We have transgressed and rebelled," he states

on behalf of the community (v. 42). But how? In what way? Prophetic accusations of idolatry and social injustice surely influence the speaker's thinking that human sin caused the disaster by bringing down divine wrath. Yet the speaker is not specific. He does not make his case for their common sin; he merely assumes it. He invites a collective examination of conscience, declares their sinfulness, but he attaches to this confession a stinging accusation against Yahweh: "We have sinned and rebelled/ and you have not forgiven" (v. 42). As the speaker shifts his address from the people to Yahweh, his real anger and energy are aimed not at his community but at the deity. (See Reflections at 3:64-66)

80. Some commentators see in the first-person plural form "let us" (נחפשה *naḥpĕśâ*) evidence of redactional splicing together of more than one literary piece. Westermann, *Lamentations,* 159, thinks these verses are a late post-exilic correction to an earlier poem, but the poem makes perfect sense as it stands, whether the unity is original or secondary.

LAMENTATIONS 3:43-66, THE STRONG MAN'S SECOND COMPLAINT

Lamentations 3:43-54, God Has Not Forgiven

NIV	NRSV
[43]"You have covered yourself with anger and pursued us; you have slain without pity. [44]You have covered yourself with a cloud so that no prayer can get through. [45]You have made us scum and refuse among the nations.	[43] You have wrapped yourself with anger and pursued us, killing without pity; [44] you have wrapped yourself with a cloud so that no prayer can pass through. [45] You have made us filth and rubbish among the peoples.

NIV

46 "All our enemies have opened their mouths
    wide against us.
47We have suffered terror and pitfalls,
    ruin and destruction."
48Streams of tears flow from my eyes
    because my people are destroyed.

49My eyes will flow unceasingly,
    without relief,
50until the LORD looks down
    from heaven and sees.
51What I see brings grief to my soul
    because of all the women of my city.

52Those who were my enemies without cause
    hunted me like a bird.
53They tried to end my life in a pit
    and threw stones at me;
54the waters closed over my head,
    and I thought I was about to be cut off.

NRSV

46 All our enemies
    have opened their mouths against us;
47 panic and pitfall have come upon us,
    devastation and destruction.
48 My eyes flow with rivers of tears
    because of the destruction of my people.

49 My eyes will flow without ceasing,
    without respite,
50 until the LORD from heaven
    looks down and sees.
51 My eyes cause me grief
    at the fate of all the young women in
        my city.

52 Those who were my enemies without cause
    have hunted me like a bird;
53 they flung me alive into a pit
    and hurled stones on me;
54 water closed over my head;
    I said, "I am lost."

COMMENTARY

The speaker resumes his complaints in ways that both echo the opening complaint (vv. 1-20) and move beyond it. Both complaints see the enemy's anger as the catalyst behind the catastrophe (vv. 1, 43). Both accuse the Angry One of refusing to accept prayers (vv. 8, 44). Both describe the speaker's entrapment and capture (vv. 3, 5, 7, 9, and 53-54). Both speak of the Angry One in animal metaphors (vv. 10, 52), and in both the speaker quotes his own words (vv. 18, 24, 54). These similarities between the complaints create literary cohesion between the two sections of the poem, counterbalancing the centrifugal features that push the two complaints apart.[81]

The second complaint extends beyond the first in the breadth and directness of its charges against God. In the second complaint the speaker addresses his enemy directly, and that enemy is unmistakably Yahweh (v. 55). The speaker expands his laments beyond his own suffering to embrace the suffering of the community, expressed in first-person plural forms (vv. 43-48). And this complaint is even more bitter than the first. Its force seems virtually to cancel any power of the communal act of repentance to resolve the speaker's theological dilemma. The second complaint makes the communal confession of sin and repentance appear halfhearted and ritualistic in the face of new accusations against Yahweh.

3:43-48. The community may bear some responsibility for provoking Yahweh, states the speaker. Addressing Yahweh, the speaker also states that Yahweh has "covered yourself with anger and pursued us."[82] For these most explicit attacks, the speaker addresses God directly, "You have killed and not pitied" (v. 43, author's trans.). Advice to submit quietly to the yoke, the suggestion that no one has the right to complain, humble calls to lift up hands to God—all have disappeared from the speaker's discourse. He faces Yahweh with scathing accusations and anger that disavow his earlier confidence that God's mercies are new every morning and that God will have compassion

81. Daniel Grossberg, *Centripetal and Centrifugal Structures in Biblical Poetry*, SBLMS 39 (Atlanta: Scholars Press, 1989) 91-93.

82. Hillers, *Lamentations*, 59, reads "covered us."

"according to the abundance of his steadfast love." In this case, Yahweh is a killer (הרג *hārag*, v. 43*b*).

Yahweh's anger is out of control, and that, not human sin, is the source of the community's pain. Now further language of encirclement depicts Yahweh's deliberate distance from them. Yahweh has covered the divine self in anger, and, covered with a cloud, Yahweh is utterly impervious to prayer (v. 44). The people cannot reach God because God has built a protective, alienating barrier against them. The divine agent of their destruction, encircled in clouds, totally removed from their reach has made them "scum and refuse in the midst of the peoples" (vv. 45-46). Strange horrors have come upon the speaker and his community, fear and a snare, devastation and breaking (v. 47).

3:49-54. Then the speaker returns to first-person language (3:55, 63) not simply to revisit his personal pain but to express sorrow at the fate of his people, which will take up much of the rest of the poem. He weeps over the "breaking of the daughter of my people." His eyes flow with tears ceaselessly (v. 49) "until the LORD looks down from heaven and sees" (ראה *rā'â*, v. 50). Like the

speakers of the previous chapters, the strong man clings to the need for Yahweh to see, but Yahweh is in heaven, removed from the people's suffering. The speaker takes a stand, engages in a one-person sit-in. He will weep until Yahweh looks down, and Yahweh must look down. For the speaker, the question is not whether Yahweh will see, but when Yahweh will see.

Yet this expectant, demanding position of hope, this stubborn waiting is itself encircled in the poem by descriptions of eyes that seem to weep of their own accord, independent of human volition (vv. 49, 51). Tears drown hope. The speaker's reasons to weep extend beyond the fate of the "daughter of my people"—that is, Jerusalem—to the "daughters of my city," perhaps the female inhabitants of the city or, as Provan suggests, women of the outlying towns and satellite cities of Jerusalem.[83] The strong man again speaks of his own plight (vv. 53-54) in terms that evoke the national tragedy. The speaker personifies the suffering community. (See Reflections at 3:64-66.)

83. Provan, *Lamentations*, 83.

Lamentations 3:55-63, God Has Rescued—God Will Rescue

NIV	NRSV

[55]I called on your name, O LORD,
    from the depths of the pit.
[56]You heard my plea: "Do not close your ears
    to my cry for relief."
[57]You came near when I called you,
    and you said, "Do not fear."
 	
[58]O Lord, you took up my case;
    you redeemed my life.
[59]You have seen, O LORD, the wrong done to me.
    Uphold my cause!
[60]You have seen the depth of their vengeance,
    all their plots against me.
 	
[61]O LORD, you have heard their insults,
    all their plots against me—
[62]what my enemies whisper and mutter
    against me all day long.
[63]Look at them! Sitting or standing,
    they mock me in their songs.
	[55]I called on your name, O LORD,
	    from the depths of the pit;
	[56]you heard my plea, "Do not close your ear
	    to my cry for help, but give me relief!"
	[57]You came near when I called on you;
	    you said, "Do not fear!"
	
	[58]You have taken up my cause, O Lord,
	    you have redeemed my life.
	[59]You have seen the wrong done to me, O LORD;
	    judge my cause.
	[60]You have seen all their malice,
	    all their plots against me.
	
	[61]You have heard their taunts, O LORD,
	    all their plots against me.
	[62]The whispers and murmurs of my assailants
	    are against me all day long.
	[63]Whether they sit or rise—see,
	    I am the object of their taunt-songs.

COMMENTARY

Because the speaker uses perfect verbs that express completed action, some interpreters believe that the speaker's appeal to divine intervention recalls a different experience of suffering than depicted in vv. 1-20.[84] But temporal distinctions that separate past from present are not required to make sense of the verses. The strong man may be calling upon memories of past suffering and rescue as a means to fan hope in his present reality. Or he may simply be speaking of his immediate past (vv. 52-56), which has immediate presence for him. For the ancients, past and present were not separated by impermeable boundaries as they are for modern Westerners. The strong man's past is still a living reality, a raw open wound, even though it seems clear that the speaker is a step removed from torture and abuse because he is sufficiently composed to be able to inquire about its causes.

Again the speaker describes his circumstances in terms of encirclement and entrapment (vv. 52-54). His enemies hunted him, put him in a pit as was done to Jeremiah (Jeremiah 37–38), and closed him in with a stone. He was drowning and

cut off from life. With impressionistic images, he portrays a choking hopelessness, a situation of desperation from which escape is nearly unthinkable. And from that place, the pit of despair and death, he again addresses Yahweh directly: "I called on your name" (v. 55). It does not matter if this was an act in the past or his current plea. Even if it is memory, it functions in the poem as a cause for present expectancy, a budding hope that God has already begun to act on his behalf. Then he quotes God: "You came near when I called you,/ and you said 'Do not fear' " (v. 57). These are the only words assigned to God in the entire book, and they quote remembered divine speech, not present speech.

What the speaker claims to have found is the divine witness who has been sought throughout the first three poems. God has seen, has heard, and has taken up the speaker's case (vv. 57-63). The speaker is redeemed. In these verses of past remembrance or of current confident imagining, God serves as witness, prosecutor of the legal case, and judge between the speaker and his enemies. Yahweh has seen the wrong done to him and the malice and plots against him. And Yahweh has heard the enemies' taunts and plots, their constant scheming. Divine seeing and hearing remain the key to a different future, perhaps to any future at all. (See Reflections at 3:64-66.)

---

84. Hillers, *Lamentations*, 15, 52-53, 59. Since Westermann thinks the whole poem is a collection of pieces, he claims that the verses' tense indicates the verses' origins outside this piece. See Claus Westermann, *Lamentations: Issues and Interpretation* (Minneapolis: Fortress, 1994) 154-57. But Provan, *Lamentations*, 81-83, joins others to propose that only 3:53-54 refers to the past.

Lamentations 3:64-66, Petition for Justice

NIV

⁶⁴Pay them back what they deserve, O LORD,
    for what their hands have done.
⁶⁵Put a veil over their hearts,
    and may your curse be on them!
⁶⁶Pursue them in anger and destroy them
    from under the heavens of the LORD.

NRSV

⁶⁴ Pay them back for their deeds, O LORD,
    according to the work of their hands!
⁶⁵ Give them anguish of heart;
    your curse be on them!
⁶⁶ Pursue them in anger and destroy them
    from under the LORD's heavens.

COMMENTARY

The poem closes with a petition, typical of the lament form, for vengeance, retaliation, and justice. Pay them back, give them anguish, turn your anger against them, and destroy them. The speaker does not ask for comfort, for rescue, for restoration to old glories, or for renewed life. He asks for a balancing of terrors. The one who destroyed him, his people, and his world should be destroyed in turn. Only Yahweh can do this.

The interpretive decision to understand this chapter as the book's center has literary support in the intensification of the acrostic form, in the increased density of the poetry, and in the placement of hope at the center, as is also found in Jeremiah 30–33, located just past the midpoint of the book. But in Lamentations, even if readers determine that chap. 3 is the book's theological and literary heart, the poem's expression of hope remains muted at best. The speaker's move toward hope arises from the pit of his suffering. It represents a turning, inexplicable, unbidden, that arises without theological resolution. The status of this hope, therefore, will always be controversial.

Does the strong man's hope represent a capitulation on his part to previous ways of thinking, a submission in the form of denial of his own words that God is the torturer and abuser, the one who sends evil as well as good, that God has refused forgiveness and has hidden from their prayers? Does the speaker really believe that the community's sin is the reason for their tragedy and that God was justified in the abuse that flayed their bodies and souls? Or has the speaker arrived at some bottom point, spiritually and psychologically? Has he entered his suffering so honestly and thoughtfully that new life emerges within, as inexplicable as grace? Any answer to these questions must remain an interpretive decision. What is clear is that the speaker has not reached theological resolution.

REFLECTIONS

1. Elaine Scarry writes that God's existence seems so absolute in the Hebrew Scriptures that individuals and epochs that question the existence of a divine being appear to be no more than "a small tear in the page." Yet, she observes, at the same time, perhaps even almost simultaneously, the biblical texts describe the "incredible difficulty, the feat of imagination and agony of labor required in generating an idea of God and holding it steady in place (hour by hour, day by day) without any graphic image to assist the would-be believer."[85]

The troubled speaker in chapter 3 reflects just such difficulty as he swings back and forth between faith and doubt. Hope and despair co-inhabit his inner world. In his poem, cobbled out of confidence and despair, accusation and submission, hope is merely episodic, not enduring, not triumphant.

In times of profound suffering and disorientation, hope comes and goes. It rarely triumphs at first appearance. At such times, psychological confidence may emerge prior to theological or intellectual resolution. Trust of God and of life may return before satisfactory interpretations of tragedy and catastrophe have been created. Survival is a process—halting, reversible, yet ultimately trustworthy for those willing, at least, to look to, to wail at, to stand before the God who sees.

2. Like Job, the strong man in chapter 3 finds that his experience of pain overtakes and reduces to rubble his theological certitudes. From the depths of the pit, physical or metaphorical, it seems impossible that God's mercies "are new every morning." Divine anger at human sinfulness is the only explanation available to the strong man to explain his predicament, but he, like Job, finds suffering to be disproportionate to the engulfing pain in which he lives. His suffering and shame arise from divine fury.

85. Elaine Scarry, *The Body in Pain: The Making and Unmaking of the World* (Oxford: Oxford University Press, 1985) 198.

After a century of bloodshed, holocaust, and nuclear and ecological threat, many believers reject the notion that God is the originating source of good or evil. Many deny the existence or presence of God at all. Modern Western life creates a different climate from the ancient context in which to pray laments. Despite their therapeutic value, their capacity to mirror pain and suffering of many kinds as metaphor and symbol, their exposure of ugly, dehumanizing worlds, these poems will not create faith among the doubtful. Where faith in God is weak, these poems will not reassure.

But the strong man raises hauntingly contemporary questions about divine power. Is God the source of or able to prevent historical tragedy? Or is God in some sense limited by the world and its ways? Like his contemporaries, the strong man powerfully affirms that God is the source of "calamities and good things" (3:38 NIV). Since he believes God to be good, the strong man adopts the prophetic and deuteronomistic view that catastrophe must be the result of human sinfulness (3:39-41). Yet, he cannot convince himself of this view. The communal confession of sin is perfunctory and is followed by blame of God for failing to forgive (3:43-46).

The strong man's prayer, therefore, is a prayer of protest and resistance. Like Job, he rejects the theologies of his time, and, perhaps, also like Job, he comes to no full resolution of the problem. Yet, he does offer a glimpse of another possibility when he proposes that God "does not willingly bring affliction or grief" to anyone (3:33 NIV). The structure of his theodicy, his defense of God as the powerful source of calamity and good things, begins to crack in this verse. How could God, who can speak and have it happen (3:37), be forced to act against the divine heart? It is as if God is suddenly vulnerable, forced to act by a principle or force outside of divine control.

This slim filament of doubt concerning divine power opens the way to consider the vulnerability of God. It creates a kind of iconoclasm that separates the living One from entrenched notions of God as a relentless, chastising, warrior force. The strong man's doubt may point to a God who suffers with, who empathizes with, who is pained by the destruction of the people.

3. It would be wrong for Christian readers to assert that the strong man and Job find their answers in the New Testament—that is, not if the suffering and death of Jesus are faced in all their brutality and dehumanizing power, and in the questions of divine justice that it raises. Jesus could pray these laments in all their sense of divine abandonment and their imprecations for God to see.

LAMENTATIONS 4:1-22

THE DIMMING OF THE FUTURE

OVERVIEW

Compared to the intense fury, the cries of excruciating pain, and the rivers of tears in the first three poems, chap. 4 conveys a sense of exhaustion and remoteness, as if the strong man had brought sorrow and fury as far as they could go. The major theme of the poem is the diminishment of life, the dimming of glory, the quiet extinguishing of the future. Several of the poem's literary features work together with the theme to create what might be called a "poetics of diminishment." These include a less engaged speaker, a shortened acrostic form, and the absence of divine addressee.

A narrator, perhaps the same literary figure from chaps. 1 and 2, appears again as the poem's principal speaker. Yet this unnamed speaker never captures readers' imaginations or feelings in the same way as do the speakers in the previous poems, nor does his speech encourage readers to identify with him. This is because he speaks in the third person and uses first-person singular speech only once when he refers to "the Daughter of my people" (vv. 3*b*, 6). Although the social conditions that he describes are no less horrifying than those in the first three chapters, he seems remote from, or enervated by, the national tragedy. Neither the anger nor the hope of previous chapters is sustained here.

In accord with his initial discourse in chap. 1, the narrator's remarks are unadorned by feelings. But here his spare reporting is not supplemented by Daughter Zion's more anguished testimony, as it was in chap. 1. Not until a second communal voice, or the same voice using first-person plural forms, describes the community's own experience of the invasion (vv. 17-20) is the audience drawn directly into the poem.

Formally, the acrostic of chap. 4 diminishes in length from the book's first three acrostic poems.

Each of those poems contains sixty-six lines of poetry, with chap. 3 most intricately designed. By contrast, chap. 4 reduces the length of acrostic to a short forty-four lines and assigns successive letters of the Hebrew alphabet only to the first word of every two lines.

Perhaps of equal importance to the reduced acrostic for the artful representation of diminishment of life is the poem's omission of any speech addressed to Yahweh. Unlike all the other poems in the book, chap. 4 never speaks to, indeed barely mentions, God. The narrator mentions divine actions in scattering the religious leadership (v. 16), refers to Yahweh's anointed one (v. 20), and implies that it is God's deeds that he or the community anticipates in the future (v. 22). But the speaker abandons the dramatic efforts of the earlier poems to get Yahweh to see the devastation that has befallen the community. There are no requests of God to look or take notice. It is as if the speaker has lost hope, exhausted his energy for such an appeal. Just as the city's glory and future thematically grow dim, so also the poetic structures diminish in intensity and affective engagement.

The narrator acts like a traumatized guide to the devastated city. He focuses readers' attention on the horrifying conditions of the survivors, and his grief is buried under that weight. It is as if the emotions of the first three chapters have reached a pitch and are now spent, although nothing has changed. The poem evokes, suggests, and conveys with great clarity the sense of diminishment, dulling, and devastation that afflicts the city and its populace.

The poem divides into four thematic units: (1) The Dimming of Everything, vv. 1-10; (2) Everything Grows Dull, vv. 11-16; (3) The Retelling of the Attack, vv. 17-20; and (4) Future Reversal, vv. 21-22.

LAMENTATIONS 4:1-10, THE DIMMING OF EVERYTHING

NIV

NIV

4 [a]How the gold has lost its luster,
　　the fine gold become dull!
The sacred gems are scattered
　　at the head of every street.

[2]How the precious sons of Zion,
　　once worth their weight in gold,
are now considered as pots of clay,
　　the work of a potter's hands!

[3]Even jackals offer their breasts
　　to nurse their young,
but my people have become heartless
　　like ostriches in the desert.

[4]Because of thirst the infant's tongue
　　sticks to the roof of its mouth;
the children beg for bread,
　　but no one gives it to them.

[5]Those who once ate delicacies
　　are destitute in the streets.
Those nurtured in purple
　　now lie on ash heaps.

[6]The punishment of my people
　　is greater than that of Sodom,
which was overthrown in a moment
　　without a hand turned to help her.

[7]Their princes were brighter than snow
　　and whiter than milk,
their bodies more ruddy than rubies,
　　their appearance like sapphires.[b]

[8]But now they are blacker than soot;
　　they are not recognized in the streets.
Their skin has shriveled on their bones;
　　it has become as dry as a stick.

[9]Those killed by the sword are better off
　　than those who die of famine;
racked with hunger, they waste away
　　for lack of food from the field.

[10]With their own hands compassionate women
　　have cooked their own children,

---

[a] This chapter is an acrostic poem, the verses of which begin with the successive letters of the Hebrew alphabet.　　[b] 7 Or lapis lazuli

NRSV

4 How the gold has grown dim,
　　how the pure gold is changed!
The sacred stones lie scattered
　　at the head of every street.

[2] The precious children of Zion,
　　worth their weight in fine gold—
how they are reckoned as earthen pots,
　　the work of a potter's hands!

[3] Even the jackals offer the breast
　　and nurse their young,
but my people has become cruel,
　　like the ostriches in the wilderness.

[4] The tongue of the infant sticks
　　to the roof of its mouth for thirst;
the children beg for food,
　　but no one gives them anything.

[5] Those who feasted on delicacies
　　perish in the streets;
those who were brought up in purple
　　cling to ash heaps.

[6] For the chastisement[a] of my people has
　　been greater
　　than the punishment[b] of Sodom,
which was overthrown in a moment,
　　though no hand was laid on it.[c]

[7] Her princes were purer than snow,
　　whiter than milk;
their bodies were more ruddy than coral,
　　their hair[c] like sapphire.[d]

[8] Now their visage is blacker than soot;
　　they are not recognized in the streets.
Their skin has shriveled on their bones;
　　it has become as dry as wood.

[9] Happier were those pierced by the sword
　　than those pierced by hunger,

---

[a] Or iniquity　　[b] Or sin　　[c] Meaning of Heb uncertain　　[d] Or lapis lazuli

NIV

who became their food
when my people were destroyed.

NRSV

whose life drains away, deprived
of the produce of the field.

10 The hands of compassionate women
have boiled their own children;
they became their food
in the destruction of my people.

COMMENTARY

4:1. Chapter 4, like chaps. 1 and 2, opens with the same exclamation of shock and pity for the city. "How" (איכה 'êkâ) the gold has grown "dim" (v. 1a), "the fine gold become dull" (v. 1b). Although Hillers emends this verse because he cannot make literal sense of gold's becoming dim and dull, tampering with the Hebrew is unnecessary.[86] The golden imagery in vv. 1-2 is open and suggestive. The diminishing brightness of gold refers to the city's past glories, now ruined. The dulling of gold signifies the depletion of the city's wealth at a number of levels. Gold symbolizes the city's honor and power, its life and people, and, in particular, its children. Everything and everyone has lost its shine, its liveliness, its value. They still exist, but hardly appear to be themselves.

The sacred stones "scattered at the head of every street" are equally evocative poetic images. They may refer to temple stones or to the building stones of Zion, the holy city, now no more than rubble. Or, in a more materialistic vein, precious stones or gems and gold (v. 1b NIV) may have become so devalued in the aftermath of the invasion that people scatter them about as meaningless objects. Since the speaker turns from these diminished and scattered objects to the subject of the children, however, it may be that the "children of Zion" are the mother city's true gold, her sacred stones, her wealth, her honor, and her future. The next line suggests that this is so.

4:2. Zion's "precious children," once "worth their weight in fine gold" are now accounted as no more valuable than clay pots—dull, breakable, and unenduring. The brutal torture and devastation of the children are the speaker's overriding

concern. In the book's first two chapters, the narrator and Daughter Zion also lament the fate of the children, but chap. 4 is most graphic and blistering in its account of their suffering. And most shocking, according to the narrator, the dimming and dulling of the children's value is not the consequence of invasion by outside enemies. Rather, it results from the cruelty of their own people.

4:3-4. The narrator compares parents to wild jackals and ostriches, creatures known for carelessness regarding their young. Yet jackals and ostriches at least nurse their young. By contrast, "the daughter of my people" has become heartless (v. 3). Both the NRSV and the NIV miss the personification expressed in the Hebrew phrase "daughter of my people" (v. 3b). Mother Zion disdains her own children, whose tongues stick to the roofs of their mouths (v. 4). They are dying of hunger and thirst, and no one gives them bread. Are the people so enervated by the national catastrophe that they can no longer care for children? Is the city so devastated that there is no bread to offer the children? Whatever material conditions may lay behind the language, the picture of starving, dying children is a reversal of fortune in the extreme. The people's future dims and grows dull, for their children will not survive their hunger and thirst (v. 4).

4:5-10. Life is no longer comfortable and secure. Used to rich diets, people now perish in the streets. Accustomed to royal robes, they now "cling to ash heaps" (v. 5). Princes, purer than snow, whiter than milk, bodies more ruddy than coral, have exchanged glowing health for decaying bodies. Now their faces are blackened like soot, and their skin has shriveled up (vv. 7-8). Gone is strength, good grooming, thriving existence. Most

---

86. Hillers, *Lamentations*, 78-79.

appalling still, those who died in the siege are better off than the survivors, "whose life drains away" from hunger in the aftermath of war (v. 9).

Both the depravity and deprivation of life in the city come to expression in the charge against mothers: "With their own hands," compassionate women boiled their children and ate them in "the destruction of the daughter of my people" (v. 10). This appalling indictment of mothers for cannibalism is multileveled. The offending women are not cruel, careless, or inhumane. They are "compassionate" women (רחמניות *raḥămānîyôt*), connected to their offspring by a Hebrew wordplay on "womb" (רחם *reḥem*) to which the word for "compassion" may be connected.[87] The cannibalism of mothers is nearly unthinkable, yet it is by their hands that children become food.

The cannibalism of which the narrator accuses the women may be more symbolic than actual, although there is no way to know for certain. Lamentations may have adapted a deuteronomic curse announcing that, if Israel violates the covenant, both men and women, caring and exceedingly sensitive people, will eat the flesh of their children (Deut 28:53-57). Lamentations

alters the deuteronomic curse by accusing women alone of fulfilling it.[88] What is clear is that the "destruction [שבר *šeber*] of the daughter of my people" (lit., the "smashing" or "breaking") is also the smashing and breaking of her children. Life has drained away. What once was brilliant gold is now dross, and there is no future.

The speaker interrupts his chilling account of the dimming of life in the city with a comparative statement. The "punishment" (עון *'āwôn*) of the "daughter of my people" was more severe than what happened to Sodom (v. 6). The Hebrew noun translated "punishment" can also mean "sinfulness" or "iniquity." Sodom and its twin city Gomorrah were bywords for sinful depravity in Israel (Genesis 18–19), so the narrator's comparison of Sodom's destruction with Jerusalem's downfall implies shaming accusation of Jerusalem. Yet the comparison may go further. Sodom was destroyed in a moment, "with no hand being laid upon it"—that is, it was not invaded by human enemies. Jerusalem, by contrast, is still being destroyed in the aftermath of the siege at the hands of invaders and now from the inside at the hands of its mothers (v. 10). (See Reflections at 4:21-22.)

87. Phyllis Trible, *God and the Rhetoric of Sexuality*, OBT (Philadelphia: Fortress, 1978) 45.

88. O'Connor, "Lamentations," 181.

LAMENTATIONS 4:11-16, WHY EVERYTHING GROWS DULL

NIV

[11] The LORD has given full vent to his wrath;
  he has poured out his fierce anger.
He kindled a fire in Zion
  that consumed her foundations.

[12] The kings of the earth did not believe,
  nor did any of the world's people,
that enemies and foes could enter
  the gates of Jerusalem.

[13] But it happened because of the sins of
      her prophets
  and the iniquities of her priests,

NRSV

[11] The LORD gave full vent to his wrath;
  he poured out his hot anger,
and kindled a fire in Zion
  that consumed its foundations.

[12] The kings of the earth did not believe,
  nor did any of the inhabitants of the world,
that foe or enemy could enter
  the gates of Jerusalem.

[13] It was for the sins of her prophets
  and the iniquities of her priests,

NIV

who shed within her
  the blood of the righteous.

¹⁴Now they grope through the streets
  like men who are blind.
They are so defiled with blood
  that no one dares to touch their garments.

¹⁵"Go away! You are unclean!" men cry
      to them.
  "Away! Away! Don't touch us!"
When they flee and wander about,
  people among the nations say,
  "They can stay here no longer."

¹⁶The LORD himself has scattered them;
  he no longer watches over them.
The priests are shown no honor,
  the elders no favor.

NRSV

who shed the blood of the righteous
  in the midst of her.

¹⁴ Blindly they wandered through the streets,
    so defiled with blood
that no one was able
    to touch their garments.

¹⁵ "Away! Unclean!" people shouted at them;
    "Away! Away! Do not touch!"
So they became fugitives and wanderers;
    it was said among the nations,
    "They shall stay here no longer."

¹⁶ The LORD himself has scattered them,
    he will regard them no more;
no honor was shown to the priests,
    no favor to the elders.

COMMENTARY

4:11. Chapter 4 interprets the city's destruction in terms reminiscent of the first three chapters. All four chapters understand Yahweh as the primary agent of destruction who deliberately and actively unleashed anger upon the city. Three active verbs portray the uncontainability of Yahweh's fury. Yahweh "gave full vent" to divine wrath, poured out "fierce anger," "kindled a fire in Zion" (4:11). The heat of godly rage, overflowing and fierce, burns Jerusalem to its foundations, even though human agents actually enter the gates of Jerusalem.

4:12. When the narrator claims that no king or resident of the world could believe that such a thing could happen, what he means is that Jerusalem's destruction is simply unthinkable (4:12). The theological source of this thinking is Zion theology, articulated most beautifully by the prophet Isaiah. The theological tradition of the Davidic monarchy held that God had chosen to dwell in the Temple of Jerusalem, and that presence protected the city from invasion or destruction.[89] Hence, Lam 4:12 expresses one stream of theological tradition that was

89. Ben C. Ollenburger, *Zion, City of the Great King: A Theological Symbol of the Jerusalem Cult*, JSOTSup 41 (Sheffield: Sheffield Academic, 1987).

completely overturned by the military destruction of the city. What astonishes the narrator, the kings, and the people of the world in this poem is not only that the city is destroyed but also that the agent of that destruction is Yahweh.

4:13-16. Sharing active responsibility for the city's collapse and for unleashing divine fury, however, are the religious leaders. The sins of the prophets and the iniquities of the priests caused the invasion. They shed innocent blood in the city (v. 13). To indict the leadership, the speaker draws symbolic language from priestly traditions of ritual defilement. Contact with blood makes priests ritually unclean. These priests have not only touched blood, but they also have spilled the blood of the innocent. So wicked and defiled are they that they will contaminate anyone who comes into contact with them. To dramatize the heinous nature of the priests' offense, the narrator quotes the people's shouts, "Away!" "Unclean!" "Do not touch!" This is language that lepers were required to shout when they came near healthy people lest they spread their contagion (Lev 13:34-47). And like lepers, the religious leaders are condemned to exile. "They can no longer stay here" (v. 15*b*).

From the narrator's viewpoint, there has been a

complete upheaval of the way things should be. Priests and prophets should be leaders of worship, protectors of their own ritual purity and that of the community; but they are so perverse that they are shunned and expelled by the people. Yahweh acts toward them with equal disdain, scattering them,

no longer continuing "to look at them" (נבט *nābat,* v. 16). Once again in Lamentations, to be the object of Yahweh's gaze, of divine looking and seeing, is fundamental to human security and survival. The priests, the prophets, and the elders are cast from divine sight. (See Reflections at 4:21-22.)

LAMENTATIONS 4:17-20, THE RETELLING OF THE ATTACK

NIV

¹⁷Moreover, our eyes failed,
  looking in vain for help;
from our towers we watched
  for a nation that could not save us.

¹⁸Men stalked us at every step,
  so we could not walk in our streets.
Our end was near, our days were numbered,
  for our end had come.

¹⁹Our pursuers were swifter
  than eagles in the sky;
they chased us over the mountains
  and lay in wait for us in the desert.

²⁰The LORD's anointed, our very life breath,
  was caught in their traps.
We thought that under his shadow
  we would live among the nations.

NRSV

¹⁷Our eyes failed, ever watching
  vainly for help;
we were watching eagerly
  for a nation that could not save.

¹⁸They dogged our steps
  so that we could not walk in our streets;
our end drew near; our days were numbered;
  for our end had come.

¹⁹Our pursuers were swifter
  than the eagles in the heavens;
they chased us on the mountains,
  they lay in wait for us in the wilderness.

²⁰The LORD's anointed, the breath of our life,
  was taken in their pits—
the one of whom we said, "Under his shadow
  we shall live among the nations."

COMMENTARY

Suddenly, the speaker begins using first-person plural forms. Either the narrator speaks on behalf of the community or the community replaces him as speaker. As in chap. 3, the mixing of singular and plural voices blurs the line between individual and community, between the lamenter and the lamented. The effects of this mixture of voices are both to bring the audience into the poem and to express the totality of the disaster's impact. The collective "we" adds intensity and drama to the chilling, more distant third-person reporting of the narrator.

For the first time, the community of survivors tell their experience of the invasion. Retelling is a

way of reliving the horror. It makes the invasion present through an understated and impressionistic description that brings the audience into the thick of the attack. Retelling creates a space and a time that bring the survivors of the tragedy back into trauma. Four short verses depict their vain hope for help, their expectation of death, the terror of the attack, and the devastating loss of their symbolic anchor, the king.

Again eyes are prominent in the poetry, not the weeping eyes of the previous chapters (1:2; 2:11, 18; 3:49-51) or the unseeing eyes of Yahweh, who will not see (1:9, 11, 20; 2:20; but cf. 3:59), but the eyes of the community, worn out with the strain of looking for help. They "watched in vain . . . for a nation that could not save" (v. 17). Whether the search for help refers to an actual nation, such as Egypt, Babylon's only strong opponent, or to any external assistance is unclear. But that no nation could save them when the primary agent of destruction is Yahweh dawns upon the survivors in the wake of the invasion.

The survivors use few words to relive the siege. The enemy was inescapable; they "stalked us at every step," "chased us in the mountains,"

ambushed "us in the wilderness" (v. 19). The community knew the end was near. Their pursuers were swift as eagles, aggressive, cunning, and exhausting. And for these survivors, the final dashing of their hopes occurs in the pitiful death of the king, Yahweh's "anointed" one. He was, they thought, Yahweh's chosen king, their protection and security among the nations, "the breath [רוח *rûaḥ*] of our life" (v. 20). They were wrong, and another hope has dimmed. (See Reflections at 4:21-22.)

LAMENTATIONS 4:21-22, FUTURE REVERSAL

21Rejoice and be glad, O Daughter of Edom,
    you who live in the land of Uz.
But to you also the cup will be passed;
    you will be drunk and stripped naked.

22O Daughter of Zion, your punishment
        will end;
    he will not prolong your exile.
But, O Daughter of Edom, he will punish
        your sin
    and expose your wickedness.

21 Rejoice and be glad, O daughter Edom,
    you that live in the land of Uz;
but to you also the cup shall pass;
    you shall become drunk and strip yourself
        bare.

22 The punishment of your iniquity, O daughter
        Zion, is accomplished,
    he will keep you in exile no longer;
but your iniquity, O daughter Edom, he
        will punish,
    he will uncover your sins.

COMMENTARY

Direct address occurs for the first time in the poem, but it is not Yahweh who is addressed. In a dramatic turn, the speaker accosts the neighboring nation of Edom, personified as "Daughter of Edom," as if the capital city were standing by for conversation. A longtime enemy of Israel (see Num 20:14-21), Edom was accused of aiding the attacking Babylon and of refusing to help escapees from assaults on Jerusalem.

In this poem, the speaker interrupts the partying of Edom as it gloats over Jerusalem's destruction. Yes, rejoice and be glad, the speaker says to Edom, but your turn is certain to come. The "cup will pass to you"; Edom will become drunk and "strip yourself bare" (v. 21). More than a promise

of a future wild orgy is involved in this pronouncement. The cup coming to them is the cup of divine wrath, the cup of poison that Jeremiah prophesied would come to every nation after Israel drank of it (Jer 25:15-29). Edom will meet the same fate that Judah has suffered. Using female nudity to express the nadir of shame, the poem promises that Yahweh will punish the Daughter of Edom for her sins just as Yahweh had punished Daughter Zion.

The words condemning Edom work as solace for the survivors of the invasion of Judah. An enemy will be punished for the disaster. But the poem closes with an even stronger expression of hope for the survivors: "Daughter of Zion, your punishment will end" (v. 22*a*). As the two female figures exchange places of degradation, shame, and devastation, Zion gains a future, at least in the world of imagination. The one who gloats will be gloated over. The sins of Daughter Edom replace the sins of Daughter Zion. No sin will go unpun-

ished, and survivors begin to imagine a different world from their present one. The narrator does credit God for changing their horizons, for ultimately God punishes sin. The world, therefore, will one day be a just place.

REFLECTIONS

1. Rebecca Chopp describes sin as both depravation and deprivation. Sin as depravation refers to the usual notion of sin as depraved, evil action, wickedness in all its forms. But sin can also be understood as deprivation, those circumstances that deprive human beings of the necessary conditions for full human flourishing.[90] It is these conditions that the narrator describes in chapter 4 and the voice of the community will continue to expand in chapter 5.

Survivors of the invasion and destruction of the city can barely exist. Their conditions are subhuman. Children are starving; adults are barely recognizable from the ravages of hunger; women boil their own children for food. The people are without leadership, for religious and royal leaders have been expelled from the community. They cling to life, but human dignity and hope for full, expansive existence are overridden by deprivation and chaos. It is precisely such subhuman conditions that demand lamentation.

In Chopp's view, lamentation names as "concretely as possible the conditions that prevent human flourishing," that distort and dehumanize life.[91] Whether in literal or symbolic terms, whole peoples around the globe and near at hand subsist in similar material and spiritual conditions. Hunger, abject poverty, hopelessness, the brutality of warfare, attempted genocide, torture, abuse, catastrophic illness, and profound loss afflict countless peoples. The list of the world's suffering seems infinite.

It is for them and for all who suffer pain and the loss of human dignity that the churches can lament, call to God, demand that God see, insist that God's world become a place of justice and dignified life for all creatures. Such continual imprecation before God may energize human action for justice and work for the thriving of life among all peoples. Praying creates worlds.

2. Lamentations is a mode of prayer and a form of speech that enables people to tell the truth of their lives and to see the real lives of others in their deprivation, their pain, and their abandonment. As a practice of truth-telling, lamentations enables a type of seeing that both expresses and creates discontent. Lamentations is not only a mode of survival, but it is also a profound act of resistance and of solidarity with the afflicted.

One of the necessary tasks facing the churches is to provide believers with a repertoire of poems, forms, and artful speech of lament. Lamentations reveals the turning of wordless wounds, of pre-vocal pain into art, into beauty, into a means of survival. When disaster and tragedy strike a community, a family, or an individual, the practices of lament and the aesthetics of pain and sorrow must be in place already. Insufficient use of Lamentations in worship and preaching keeps believing people cut off from a profound spiritual and political resource. Without laments, people turn to shallow devotions and to superstitions that may offer little comfort and no mirroring, and may result in denial and repression of all kinds.

90. Rebecca Chopp, "Feminism and the Theology of Sin," *Ecumenist* (November-December 1993) 12-16.
91. Ibid., 15.

LAMENTATIONS 5:1-22

THE SURVIVORS' PRAYER

OVERVIEW

The poem in chap. 5 differs from the previous poems in a number of ways. The poem is not an acrostic, but it does continue the diminution of poetic form begun in chap. 4. As the book's shortest poem, only twenty-two lines, chap. 5 evokes the Hebrew alphabet by its length alone. The prominent poetic figures of the earlier poems, the narrator, personified Zion, and the strong man, are replaced by the voice of the many, the communal "we," although this is not the first time in the book that the community speaks. In the previous two poems the community came briefly to speech. The strong man speaks with or on behalf of the community in the confession of sin (3:40-47), and the community interrupts the narrator to describe their experience of the invasion (4:17-20). In the book's final poem, that collective voice takes over completely.

Perhaps this first-person plural speaker represents the book's imagined audience, the community of survivors who have stood by while the individual speakers among them testify to the pain of all. Now the whole community enters the colloquy, as if given courage and aroused to action by the previous speakers. They climb into the poetic frame of the book to pray for restoration in a final plea to Yahweh.

The community's speech differs from the discourse of the other speakers in its addressee. They speak to no one but Yahweh in the book's most conventional prayer of lament. They begin with a petition (v. 1), followed by a long complaint about conditions in the city (vv. 2-18). They speak with assurance that Yahweh rules forever (vv. 19-20) and close with another petition (vv. 21-22).[92] In this poetic structure, petitions frame complaint so that the complaint provides the reasons why God should act. The final petition (vv. 21-22) brings the book to a close with a request for restoration that is qualified by a disheartened and tired effort of the people to resign themselves to their reality. In relation to the previous poems, this one serves as a summation of the pain of the people, the city, the nation, and a final demand that God pay attention to them.

The poem divides into three parts: (1) Appeal to Yahweh to Look and See, v. 1; (2) What Yahweh Must See, vv. 2-18; and (3) A Qualified Plea for Restoration, vv. 19-22.

92. Claus Westermann, *Lamentations: Issues and Interpretation* (Minneapolis: Fortress, 1994) 211.

LAMENTATIONS 5:1, APPEAL TO YAHWEH TO LOOK AND SEE

NIV	NRSV
5 Remember, O LORD, what has happened to us; look, and see our disgrace.	**5** Remember, O LORD, what has befallen us; look, and see our disgrace!

COMMENTARY

The people, speaking as one voice, ask Yahweh to do two things: to "remember" (זכר *zākar*) and to "look and see" (ראה *rā'āh* and נבט *nābaṭ*). God has not remembered and has not seen. From the speakers' viewpoint, it is as if Yahweh is afflicted with attention deficit disorder. God cannot focus on "what has befallen us," cannot remember, can-

not keep it present in the divine mind long enough to act upon it. And it is as if Yahweh is blind, unable to look or unwilling to see their "disgrace." Like the previous speakers, the people insist that divine seeing would alter their reality. (See Reflections at 5:19-22.)

LAMENTATIONS 5:2-18, WHAT YAHWEH MUST SEE

NIV

²Our inheritance has been turned over to aliens,
  our homes to foreigners.
³We have become orphans and fatherless,
  our mothers like widows.
⁴We must buy the water we drink;
  our wood can be had only at a price.
⁵Those who pursue us are at our heels;
  we are weary and find no rest.
⁶We submitted to Egypt and Assyria
  to get enough bread.
⁷Our fathers sinned and are no more,
  and we bear their punishment.
⁸Slaves rule over us,
  and there is none to free us from their hands.
⁹We get our bread at the risk of our lives
  because of the sword in the desert.
¹⁰Our skin is hot as an oven,
  feverish from hunger.
¹¹Women have been ravished in Zion,
  and virgins in the towns of Judah.
¹²Princes have been hung up by their hands;
  elders are shown no respect.
¹³Young men toil at the millstones;
  boys stagger under loads of wood.
¹⁴The elders are gone from the city gate;
  the young men have stopped their music.
¹⁵Joy is gone from our hearts;
  our dancing has turned to mourning.
¹⁶The crown has fallen from our head.
  Woe to us, for we have sinned!
¹⁷Because of this our hearts are faint,
  because of these things our eyes grow dim

NRSV

²Our inheritance has been turned over
    to strangers,
  our homes to aliens.
³We have become orphans, fatherless;
  our mothers are like widows.
⁴We must pay for the water we drink;
  the wood we get must be bought.
⁵With a yoke[a] on our necks we are hard driven;
  we are weary, we are given no rest.
⁶We have made a pact with[b] Egypt and Assyria,
  to get enough bread.
⁷Our ancestors sinned; they are no more,
  and we bear their iniquities.
⁸Slaves rule over us;
  there is no one to deliver us from their hand.
⁹We get our bread at the peril of our lives,
  because of the sword in the wilderness.
¹⁰Our skin is black as an oven
  from the scorching heat of famine.
¹¹Women are raped in Zion,
  virgins in the towns of Judah.
¹²Princes are hung up by their hands;
  no respect is shown to the elders.
¹³Young men are compelled to grind,
  and boys stagger under loads of wood.
¹⁴The old men have left the city gate,
  the young men their music.
¹⁵The joy of our hearts has ceased;
  our dancing has been turned to mourning.
¹⁶The crown has fallen from our head;
  woe to us, for we have sinned!

a Symmachus: Heb lacks With a yoke   *b Heb* have given the hand to

NIV	NRSV
[18]for Mount Zion, which lies desolate, with jackals prowling over it.	[17]Because of this our hearts are sick, because of these things our eyes have grown dim: [18]because of Mount Zion, which lies desolate; jackals prowl over it.

COMMENTARY

In the long complaint that comprises the body of the poem, the people tell God what to look at. Their speech tries to draw divine attention by pointing to what God should see, should attend to, should witness. They show what has befallen them and describe their "disgrace" insistently, as if God might hear, even if God will not see. They do not recount the events of invasion as they did in 4:16-20. Instead, they describe the physical, social, emotional, and spiritual conditions of survivors in an occupied land.

5:2-3. Strangers possess their inheritance, their land, and their homes. Spiritually and emotionally they are abandoned, fully displaced "orphans" (v. 3). They are bereft of care, security, and shelter. Their mothers are widows, like Daughter Zion (1:1). Like her, they are alone; but they are also her orphans, her children, deprived of their family, which is broken and ruptured by death, fatherlessness, and widowhood.

5:4-5. Physical conditions of life are dreadful. They must pay for the produce of the land, for water and wood that belong to everyone but are now controlled by their occupiers. They are fatigued and weary from forced labor, from the yoke of slavery on their "hard driven" necks (v. 5). Occupation makes slaves of them and turns routines of daily subsistence into enormous burdens.

5:6-7. The next verse interrupts the complaint to interpret the people's plight (v. 6). They have contributed to their current condition by having made a pact with the foreign powers of Egypt and Assyria. They had given their loyalties to another, not to Yahweh. This language evokes prophetic attacks on foreign entanglements. No nation can save them; only Yahweh can. The sins of their ancestors must include these frightful alliances for which the present community must bear the punishment.

The people's portrayal of themselves as bearing the sins of their ancestors is reminiscent of the way Jeremiah portrays the survivors of the invasion of Jerusalem as children of sinful Zion. In Jeremiah's poems about the broken marriage between Yahweh and Daughter Zion (Jer 2:1–4:2), the children of the marriage appear as the survivors of the family breakup. They bear the sin of their ancestors and express repentance as they return to their father, Yahweh (Jer 3:22-25).[93]

By contrast, in this chapter of Lamentations the survivors suggest that they are being punished for the sin of the ancestors and not for their own sin. The previous generation surely sinned collectively, but for the speakers, "fatherless orphans" (v. 3), the punishment is truly excessive, for it continues into their own generation. Quietly they resist the theology of the narrator, of Daughter Zion, and of the strong man that sin explains the frightful conditions of their lives. In this poem, they express no repentance.

5:8-13. The perilous predicament of the occupation returns to the center of the people's complaint. Slaves have become their rulers. The slave rulers may refer to a puppet government or to appointees of the occupying nation, or they may signify the topsy-turvy nature of the current social order. Slaves are people unprepared and unsuitable to lead. They have displaced Judah's proper rulers, and from these new rulers the community needs to be saved.

Danger pervades the simplest circumstances of daily life. Perhaps because of military or police presence or because of general chaos in the society, the people obtain food at the "peril of their lives" (v. 9). Their appearance has changed—their skin

93. See A. R. Pete Diamond and Kathleen M. O'Connor, "Unfaithful Passions: Coding Women Coding Men in Jeremiah 2:1–3:25 (4:2)," *Biblical Interpretation* (1996).

has blackened—because of hunger that burns and destroys their bodies. Women are not safe; virgins are raped. Princes are hung by their hands, elders are disrespected, young men and boys are forced into onerous labor. Life in the occupied land threatens human survival at every turn. Is survival even possible?

5:14-18. The people turn from their impressionistic description of the horrors of their external world to its impact upon their spirits. Grief abounds, but it makes them tired and numb. Joy is gone, and mourning replaces dancing. Jeremiah's promises to turn mourning back into joy (Jer 31:13) are nowhere in sight for this community. Their joyless hearts are sick, and their eyes have "grown dim."

Tears do not flow as they did for other speakers in Lamentations. The people are beyond tears, numb from the invasion, the destruction, and their current desperate situation. Their eyes are dim because they have no hope, no future to set upon; nothing but despair stretches before them. They cannot see ahead, and the blindness of God, who will not look, will not pay attention, now spreads to the people like a contagion. Their spirits are like their beloved Mt. Zion: desolate, empty, a place where the jackals scavenge (v. 18). From this bleak world they offer a final, wavering and halfhearted plea. (See Reflections at 5:19-22.)

LAMENTATIONS 5:19-22, A QUALIFIED PLEA FOR RESTORATION

NIV	NRSV

[19]You, O LORD, reign forever;
    your throne endures from generation to
        generation.
[20]Why do you always forget us?
    Why do you forsake us so long?
[21]Restore us to yourself, O LORD, that we
        may return;
    renew our days as of old
[22]unless you have utterly rejected us
    and are angry with us beyond measure.
	[19] But you, O LORD, reign forever;
	    your throne endures to all generations.
	[20] Why have you forgotten us completely?
	    Why have you forsaken us these
	        many days?
	[21] Restore us to yourself, O LORD, that we may
	        be restored;
	    renew our days as of old—
	[22] unless you have utterly rejected us,
	    and are angry with us beyond measure.

COMMENTARY

5:19. Abruptly, in the typical style of laments, the speakers utter words of assurance in the midst of their suffering. They address directly the blind God, the One whom they are begging to remember and to see (v. 1): "You, O Yahweh," they say, "reign forever." The power of the divine ruler endures, and the divine reign still stands. A similar acclamation of faith appears in Ps 102:12-13. There the psalmist praises the divine king, "enthroned forever" with confidence that "you will rise up and have compassion on Zion."

5:20. But for the speakers in the final poem of

Lamentations, assurance of divine rule is not reassuring. Rather than continue with hopeful and flattering words of praise, they hurl their angry, unanswerable questions at the divine ruler. "Why do you keep forgetting us?" they ask. "Why have you forsaken us these many days?" The rule of God is of no benefit to them; it is no cause for praise and thanksgiving, if divine rule cannot regard them, see them, remember them.

5:21. The people conclude their prayer with a final plea for restoration. They first ask Yahweh to restore relationship with them: "Restore us to yourself." Their covenant is what has been violated by divine blindness and silence. The Hebrew verb "return" (שׁוּב *šûb*) frames the line. Literally, it reads, "return us to you that we may return" (v. 21*a*). The people recognize their powerlessness and incapacity before the divine ruler. For their relationship to resume as in the days of old, everything depends on divine willingness.

5:22. For the community, however, the resumption of divine/human relationship is in grave doubt. They ask Yahweh to renew their days, "unless you have utterly rejected us and are angry with us beyond measure." Despite the appeal for renewal, these are profoundly sad and hopeless words. The community is as desolate and abandoned at the end of the book as was their mother, Zion, at the book's beginning. They voice their fear that nothing will ever change, for it is possible that divine anger remains "beyond measure," overflowing, a potent heat that continues to reject and to destroy the people.

There is no response from God in this book. There is only the blind God, the missing voice that hovers over the entire book. Lamentations is about absence.

REFLECTIONS

1. It is remarkable that this canonical text remains so utterly empty of divine comfort, assurance, or promise of intervention. It is as if the book itself were an abandoned child, a comfortless widow, a desolate city. It may be that the book's own spirit is so bleak and frightening that the book has been nearly abandoned in worship and scholarship. Yet Lamentations is completely adequate as it stands. Why else would its composers and canonizers be content to leave it without divine response?

The experience of divine absence, blindness, and imperviousness to human suffering, expressed in countless ways by several speakers, is the book's central subject. It is God's absence from the poems, however, that creates space for the speakers to explore their momentous suffering, to move from numb silence and pre-literate groans to speech that is eloquent, beautiful, and evocative and that gives form and shape to the unspeakable. For God to speak in this book in a "happy ending" of comfort or promise would cheapen the suffering, foreshorten exploration of tragedy, and deny the depth of human experience of pain. This book offers no answers. It plunges into pain beyond words and finds words to explore realities humans prefer to deny.

By its acrostic, alphabetic forms, its voices of longing for recognition and release, its metaphors of anger and tears, Lamentations creates a house for the sorrows of the world. Whatever historical destruction produced the poetry, the book now captures in the symbolic fabric of language and forms the inner and outer worlds of survivors of oppression, abuse, genocide, and profound loss.

In a contemporary poem, theologian Delores Williams speaks of the "cataract eyes of God" that do not see the suffering on the streets of Harlem.[94] The absent deity is a major theme of modern Western literature from Holocaust testimony such as Elie Wiesel's *Night*[95] to Samuel Beckett's *Waiting for Godot*[96] and Archibald MacLeish's dramatic retelling of Job, *JB*.[97] In some of this literature, God is simply not there.

In Lamentations, God is present but hiding. The wonder of this biblical book is its daring, momentous honesty about the One who hides behind clouds, turns away prayers, and will not pay attention. Lamentations articulates a theology of absence and abandonment that is almost contemporary in its longing and emptiness. In the language of Christian mystics, it portrays "the dark night of the soul" of a whole people.

94. Delores Williams, "Songs I Meant to Sing," unpublished poem, Smythe Lectures, Columbia Theological Seminary, 1998.
95. Elie Wiesel, *Night* (New York: Hill and Wang, 1960).
96. Samuel Beckett, *Waiting for Godot* (New York: Grove, 1997).
97. Archibald MacLeish, *JB: A Play in Verse* (London: Samuel French, 1956).

2. Language of human sinfulness, guilt, and responsibility takes believers only a short distance toward resolution and comfort, and human sinfulness applies only some of the time, and contributes only to some tragedy. In Lamentations, suffering ultimately outstrips explanations of pre-exilic prophets, which rely on human responsibility. The speakers in Lamentations never abandon human sin in their interpretations; they simply displace it, reduce its importance compared to their anger and accusation of God, who is blind, who turns against them, and who finally appears to have abandoned them.

At the turn of the twenty-first century and the millennium, such a theological explanation of suffering as the result of human sinfulness no longer suffices. The Holocaust of Nazi Germany, the killing fields of Cambodia, the attempts at genocide in Rwanda—all these alone defy explanations of divine origins or simple accusations of human immorality. These experiences of human cruelty take on demonic proportions, and the suffering of the peoples "is vaster than the sea."

3. In a time when some religions and the dominant culture of the United States understand God to be the One who makes us prosper in all things, who promises us life and fortune and love and who rescues us from our enemies, the missing voice of Lamentations is subversive, iconoclastic, and cathartic. To repress this iconoclastic discourse, to deny it equal weight with other biblical testimony is to cut off correction of our syrupy notions of the deity. Easy dismissals of the missing voice, of the blind God, are not warranted, for this representation of God must stand alongside the liberating God of Exodus, the comforting God of Isaiah, and the resurrecting God of the New Testament. Nor can this text be dismissed as the misunderstanding of an earlier, less enlightened people. There can be no escape to the New Testament when we recall the cross on which Jesus faced inexplicable suffering.

Instead, Lamentations serves as brilliant, luminous iconoclasm. The missing one crushes false images, smashes sugary pictures, destroys narrow theologies. The missing voice releases God from constricting theologies, conforming churches, and dehumanizing cultures. The book is a stammering toward the unsayable, a nod to the deep pulsating silence at the heart of the universe. The book is an invitation beyond speech.

4. The eloquent Jewish thinker Elie Wiesel, survivor of Auschwitz, wrote in his book *Night* that the Holocaust brought down night upon all that he believed of God. In much of Wiesel's long public career he has brought God to court for that travesty and other travesties against humanity. After years of lamentation, grief, and anger, Wiesel has written that he would no longer speak of God in the same terms. He asks now whether the enemies at Auschwitz wanted to destroy God along with the Jews. Now he wonders, "Ought we not to think of your pain too? Watching your children suffer at the hands of your other children, haven't you also suffered?"[98] Perhaps, Wiesel arrived at this profound insight only because for years he lamented, faced, retold, railed against those horrors.

In the face of dehumanizing and radical suffering, there are no ready answers, no facile theological solutions—only partially adequate ones. But in the midst of enervating pain, overwhelming anger, and ceaseless weeping, Lamentations forms a shelter. Its poems build a sacred space where suffering is seen, acknowledged, borne witness to. And that may be comfort enough.

98. Elie Wiesel, "A Prayer for the Day of Awe," OP-ED, *New York Times,* Oct. 2, 1997, A15.

THE BOOK OF EZEKIEL

INTRODUCTION, COMMENTARY, AND REFLECTIONS

BY

KATHERYN PFISTERER DARR

THE BOOK OF
EZEKIEL

INTRODUCTION

"I n the thirtieth year, in the fourth month, on the fifth day of the month, as I was among the exiles by the river Chebar, the heavens were opened, and I saw visions of God" (Ezek 1:1). With these words, readers enter the world and work of Ezekiel, son of Buzi, a Judean priest who, along with his upper-crust compatriots, was exiled to Babylonia in 597 BCE. Ezekiel was, it seems, part of a "brain drain" by which Babylonia's King Nebuchadrezzar II attempted to subdue the troublesome vassal state of Judah. Their deportation is described in 2 Kgs 24:14-16:

> [The king of Babylon] carried away all Jerusalem, all the officials, all the warriors, ten thousand captives, all the artisans and the smiths; no one remained, except the poorest people of the land. He carried away Jehoiachin to Babylon; the king's mother, the king's wives, his officials, and the elite of the land, he took into captivity from Jerusalem to Babylon. The king of Babylon brought captive to Babylon all the men of valor, seven thousand, the artisans and the smiths, one thousand, all of them strong and fit for war. (NRSV)

From the time that Ezekiel was commissioned as Yahweh's prophet to the house of Israel in 593 BCE, until the fall of Jerusalem in 586 BCE, he engaged in the harsh task of dismantling the orthodox Yahwistic theology of his day. That theology emphasized Yahweh's promises to the Israelites—e.g., the blessings attending the covenant forged at Sinai, God's absolute commitment to the Davidic dynasty, and the inviolability of

Jerusalem, site of Yahweh's Temple. Such promises strengthened his fellow exiles' resistance to Ezekiel's relentless insistence that Yahweh had resolved utterly to destroy Judah on account of its long-lived and ongoing abominations. The end was approaching. Israel's failure to honor the obligations of its covenant with Yahweh was bringing upon its own head the full weight of the covenantal curses. Only after Nebuchadrezzar, Yahweh's weapon against Judah, destroyed Jerusalem and devastated the land of Judah did the content and tone of Ezekiel's oracles change. Israel did have a future, but that future was under God's control and was designed to ensure that the sins of the past could never be repeated. After all, Yahweh's reputation among the nations was at stake!

HISTORICAL BACKGROUND

The Decline and Defeat of Judah. What historical circumstances caused Nebuchadrezzar II to treat Judah and its capital city, Jerusalem, so harshly? In order to answer this question, we must consider certain historical events in the ancient Near East. From the ninth century BCE onward, the small kingdoms of Syro-Palestine, including Israel and Judah, struggled to survive as the armies of Assyria, Egypt, and later Babylonia marched through the Fertile Crescent—the traversable arc of land linking Egypt to the west and Mesopotamia to the east (see the maps on 557-58).

Judah was one of only a few kingdoms to survive Assyrian aggression in the eighth century. During the reigns of Tiglath-pileser III (745–727 BCE), Shalmaneser V (726–722 BCE), and Sargon II (721–705 BCE), the Assyrian Empire subjected significant areas of Syro-Palestine to destruction, depopulation, and political reorganization into Assyrian provinces. Aram-Damascus fell in 732 BCE, and Samaria, capital of the northern kingdom of Israel, followed in 722/21 BCE. Jotham, Judah's king, survived because he had refused to join with the kings of Israel and Damascus when they formed a last-ditch coalition against the Assyrians. His son and successor, Ahaz, avoided an attempt to remove him from the throne and replace him with ben Tabeel by sending an appeal for help (and a generous gift) to Tiglath-pileser (2 Kgs 16:7-9). The Assyrian king intervened, but Judah paid the price of becoming an Assyrian vassal state.

Judah did not attempt to escape Assyrian domination until the reign of Hezekiah (715/14–687/86 BCE). According to 2 Kgs 18:4-8, Hezekiah undertook three primary tasks. First, he authorized cultic reforms, removing pagan artifacts from the Temple and reinstituting Passover observance. Second, he rebelled against the king of Assyria and refused to serve (pay tribute to) him. Third, he engaged in wars with the Philistines.

In 701 BCE, Sennacherib responded to Hezekiah's initiatives with a punitive campaign against the land of "Hatti" (Syro-Palestine). After quelling centers of rebellion in Phoenicia, Palestine, and a number of cities in Judah, he besieged the city of Jerusalem (2 Kgs 18:13–19:37; Isaiah 36–37). In his annals, Sennacherib boasts of imprisoning

Hezekiah in his city "like a bird in a cage" and of exacting enormous tribute.[1] Jerusalem survived Sennacherib's campaign, but the land of Judah was severely crippled. Throughout the long reign of Hezekieh's son Manasseh (687/86–642 BCE), Judah remained an obsequious vassal of Assyria.

After Sennacherib was murdered, Esarhaddon became king of Assyria (680–669 BCE). He was followed by Ashurbanipal (668–627 BCE), whose early success in holding together the sprawling Assyrian Empire was compromised by the revolt of Pharaoh Psammetichus I, founder of the twenty-sixth Egyptian dynasty (554–610 BCE). Psammetichus both ended Assyrian domination of Egypt and planned campaigns into Syro-Palestine in order to reassert Egyptian control over the area. In Mesopotamia, Babylonia also was able to reassert its independence under Nabopolasar, the founder of the Neo-Babylonian Empire, with the help of the Medes (626 BCE).

During this period of waning Assyrian power, young Josiah (640–609 BCE) became king of Judah after his father, Amon (642–640 BCE), was assassinated in a palace intrigue. Like Hezekiah, Josiah sought to centralize worship in the Jerusalem Temple as well as to restore Judah to its earlier, broader borders. Assyria was too weak immediately to address Josiah's political ambitions and cultic reforms. Nevertheless, Josiah's attempts at reform were short-lived. Egypt and Babylonia engaged in a power struggle, and Pharaoh Necho launched a military expedition to Carchemish on the Euphrates River (609 BCE). He planned to join forces with Assuruballit, the king of Assyria, in order to prevent the Babylonians from defeating the Assyrians, lest the Babylonians gain an upper hand over Egyptian ambitions. Recognizing the negative consequences of an Egyptian/Assyrian victory for Judah, Josiah attacked Necho's forces as they passed through the Megiddo valley and was killed in battle. Necho hurried on to Carchemish, leaving the Judeans to mourn their dead king and to place his son Jehoahaz (called Shallum in 1 Chr 3:15) upon the throne.

Jehoahaz ruled for only three months. Returning from Carchemish by way of Riblah, Necho appointed another of Josiah's sons, Eliakim (whom he renamed Jehoiakim, 2 Kgs 23:35), to reign in his stead. Jehoahaz was exiled to Egypt, where he died (2 Kgs 23:31-34; 2 Chr 36:34; Jer 22:1-12; Ezek 19:1-4). Egyptian control of Syro-Palestine lasted from 609 to 605 BCE, and Jehoiakim maintained a pro-Egyptian policy throughout that period.

In 605 BCE, the scales of power tipped in favor of Babylonia. Nebuchadrezzar II met the Egyptian army at Carchemish and won a decisive victory. He also launched military expeditions into the land of Hatti and demanded tribute from its local kings. When Ashkelon—a major Philistine city—refused to surrender, its king was captured, and the city was destroyed (see Jer 36:9). Following the Babylonian victory over Philistia, another Philistine city (c. 603/602 BCE), Jehoiakim abandoned his pro-Egyptian policies and became Nebuchadrezzar's vassal.

1. J. B. Pritchard, *Ancient Near Eastern Texts Relating to the Old Testament,* 3rd ed. (Princeton: Princeton University Press, 1969) 88. This account conflicts with the biblical tradition that Sennacherib was forced to withdraw from the city when his army was decimated by "the messenger of the LORD" (see Isa 37:26-38; 2 Kgs 19:35).

Jehoiakim continued to hope for an Egyptian revival, however. In 601 BCE, Nebuchadrezzar's forces met Necho's army near the frontier of Egypt. Both sides suffered enormous casualties, and neither could claim complete victory. Nebuchadrezzar went home to reorganize his troops, and he did not return to Syro-Palestine until 598/97 BCE. Jehoiakim decided that the time was ripe for revolt. Only three years after submitting to Nebuchadrezzar, he rebelled against his overlord, no doubt with the expectation of Egyptian assistance.

Nebuchadrezzar could not immediately crush Jehoiakim's rebellion, but he deployed Babylonian troops already in the region, along with bands of Syrians, Moabites, and Ammonites, to unsettle the area until he could attend to it personally (Jer 35:11). In 597 BCE, during the seventh year of his reign, Nebuchadrezzar mounted a campaign against Judah. The Babylonian Chronicles contain the following report: "Year 7, month Kislimu: The king of Akkad moved his army into Hatti land, laid siege to the city of Judah and the king took the city on the second day of the month Addaru. He appointed in it a (new) king of his liking, took heavy booty from it and brought it into Babylon."[2]

Nebuchadrezzar's stranglehold on Jerusalem ended when Jehoiakim's successor, Jehoiachin, surrendered in March 597 BCE. He and members of the royal household were forced into exile, along with nobles, craftsmen, and smiths, as well as "the men of valor" (see 2 Kgs 24:14-16 NRSV) and Ezekiel, the priest (Ezek 1:1-3). According to 2 Kgs 24:14, only "the poorest people of the land" escaped deportation, but this is likely an exaggeration. Many people living in outlying areas probably escaped, relatively unscathed by the event. The total number of persons exiled cannot be determined, because the biblical sources disagree.

Nebuchadrezzar chose Jehoiachin's uncle Mattaniah to occupy the exiled king's throne and changed his name to Zedekiah (2 Kgs 24:17). The choice was an unfortunate one for Judah. According to the biblical witness, Zedekiah was a weak, vacillating figure who lacked the strength to make decisions in the midst of conflicting advice from pro-Babylonian and pro-Egyptian advisers. During his initial years, the king apparently fulfilled his vassal obligations to Nebuchadrezzar. In 594/93 BCE, however, a conspiracy—either in Babylonia or in Syro-Palestine itself (encouraged, perhaps, by Pharaoh Psammetichus II [593–588 BCE])—rejuvenated hopes of national freedom and the exiles' speedy return home (see Jeremiah 27–28). The rebellion apparently dissipated quickly, however; and Judean envoys, perhaps even Zedekiah himself, traveled to Babylonia to demonstrate Judah's submission to its suzerain.

2. Ibid., 564. This passage names neither the Judean king who was defeated nor the man appointed by Nebuchadrezzar to take his place. The biblical historiographers differ in their accounts of the events. According to 2 Kgs 24:6-12, Jehoiakim died and was succeeded by his son, Jehoiachin, prior to the seige against Jerusalem. However, 2 Chr 36:6-10 states that Jehoiakim was bound in fetters and exiled to Babylon at the time of the siege, and Jehoiachin followed him into exile three months and ten days afterwards. The account in 2 Kings is likely more accurate (see also Jer 22:19; 36:30).

Zedekiah did not learn his lesson. Encouraged by pro-Egyptian advisers and by offers of assistance from Egypt's new pharaoh, Hophra (588–569 BCE), as well as by the soothing words of certain prophets (see Jer 5:12; 14:13), he rebelled openly against Babylonian overlordship in 589/88 BCE. The rebellion was ill-timed, ill-planned, and doomed to failure. Nebuchadrezzar reacted almost immediately by besieging the city of Jerusalem (2 Kgs 25:1-2). The land of Judah was devastated, and many of its cities were destroyed (Jer 34:7; 44:2; Lam 2:2-5). Jerusalem itself withstood the siege until August 586 BCE (see 2 Kgs 25; Jer 21:3-7; 39; 52:4-5; Ezek 24:1-2), but it was finally taken, despite limited military assistance from Pharaoh Hophra.

Zedekiah remained in Jerusalem throughout the siege, but when the city's walls were breached, he and his military advisers attempted to flee (2 Kgs 25:4). They were captured by Babylonian forces and taken to Riblah, where Nebuchadrezzar was headquartered. After witnessing the executions of his sons, Zedekiah was blinded, fettered, and taken to Babylon.

On the ninth of Ab, Nebuzaradan, commander of the Babylonian forces, supervised the systematic destruction of Jerusalem. Its significant structures, including the royal palace, were burned, its walls were torn down; and the Temple was first looted and then torched. A number of people, including Seraiah, the chief priest; Zephaniah, the second priest; and other cultic personnel, military leaders, and "sixty men of the people of the land who were found in the city" were taken to Riblah and executed (2 Kgs 25:18-21 NRSV).

No figures concerning the number of Judeans forced into exile in the wake of Jerusalem's defeat are provided in 2 Kings 25. Verse 11 states that "Nebuzaradan the captain of the guard carried into exile the rest of the people who were left in the city and the deserters who had defected to the king of Babylon—all the rest of the population" (2 Kgs 25:11 NRSV), save for the very poorest people in the land. Jeremiah 52:28-30 states that a total of 4,600 persons were deported in three waves (3,023 in 597 BCE, 832 in 586 BCE, and 745 in 581 BCE). We do not know how many people perished during the siege and devastation of Jerusalem.

Conditions in Judah During the Exilic Period. In accord with Babylonian imperial practice, Nebuchadrezzer neither repopulated the land of Judah with exiles from other countries nor set a foreign commander over the remaining people. Instead, he appointed a Judean nobleman, Gedaliah, son of Ahikam, to a position of leadership. Settling into the Benjaminite city of Mizpah, apparently the new provincial capital, Gedaliah began to gather and reorganize the survivors. At some point, he summoned "all the leaders of the forces in the open country" (Jer 40:7 NRSV; see 2 Kgs 25:23), some of whom were apparently hiding in caves or in the Judean desert (Ezek 33:27), to return to their homes and co-exist peacefully with the Babylonian overlords in their midst. Gedaliah's invitation that these captains "gather wine and summer fruits and oil, and store them in your vessels, and live in the towns that you have taken over" (Jer 40:10 NRSV) suggests that the devastation of Judah was neither so widespread nor so thorough as the biblical accounts state.

Precisely how many and what sorts of people lived under Gedaliah's supervision is difficult to determine. The biblical witness that only a few of the "poorest people of the land" remained after the deportations of both 597 BCE (2 Kgs 24:14) and 586 BCE (2 Kgs 25:12) has already been noted, but this is probably an exaggeration. Janssen has argued that the economic status of some who remained in the land actually improved after the deportations, since they were given property (including royal estates) previously belonging to the exiles.[3]

According to Jer 40:13–41:3, Gedaliah ignored a warning from Johanan that one of Johanan's fellow captains of the forces intended to kill him. Jeremiah 40:14 suggests that the assassin, Ishmael, son of Nethaniah, was encouraged by Baalis, king of Ammon. It is possible, however, that Ishmael instigated the plan himself, for he was a descendant of David; and he may well have regarded Gedaliah's cooperation with the Babylonians as traitorous. The assassination plot succeeded. Gedaliah was killed, as were "all the Judeans who were with Gedaliah at Mizpah, and the Chaldean soldiers who happened to be there" (Jer 41:3 NRSV). The next day, Ishmael also killed eighty mourners who had traveled to Jerusalem, save for ten men who bought their lives with promises of food for Ishmael and his men. Subsequently, Ishmael captured additional people at Mizpah and attempted to enter Ammon with them. Johanan aborted their flight, however, and released Ishmael's captives. The assassin and eight accomplices escaped (Jer 41:15).

Johanan and the people went to Geruth Chimham near Bethlehem and contemplated a trip to Egypt (Jer 41:16). Their fear of Babylonian reprisal was probably well-founded, since Babylonian soldiers, as well as Judeans, had been killed during the ordeal. Over Jeremiah's vehement protests, the people decided to flee (Jer 42:7–43:7), and "all the remnant of Judah" (Jer 43:5 NRSV) migrated to Tahpanhes, an Egyptian border fortress (Jer 43:7-8). Nothing is said of surviving communities within the land of Judah, but it is reasonable to suppose that people living in outlying areas did not leave with Johanan. Some of those who fled to escape Babylonian revenge may eventually have returned.

The book of Ezekiel has nothing positive to say about the Judeans who remained in Jerusalem following the deportations of 597 and 586 BCE. To the contrary, it excoriates those who were left behind in 597 BCE, heaping accusation after accusation against them and promising punishments such as had never occurred before. To Ezekiel's mind, Yahweh's destruction of Jerusalem was fully justified, and few would survive. To be sure, Ezekiel could be extremely critical of his fellow exiles as well. But he clearly believed that Israel's future depended upon Yahweh's dealings with the diaspora living in Babylonia. Hence, his assessment of the Judeans who remained in their homeland cannot be regarded as objective.

Conditions in Babylonia During the Exilic Period. Unfortunately, Hebrew Scripture provides little information about the conditions experienced by the Judean deportees of 597 and 586 BCE. After completing the long trek to Babylonia, the king and

3. Enno Janssen, *Juda in der Exilszeit,* FRLANT 69 (Göttingen: Vandenhoeck & Ruprecht, 1956) 49-54.

members of his family were imprisoned in its capital city (2 Kgs 25:27-30 states that Jehoiachin was released from prison in the thirty-seventh year of his exile, but says nothing about the fates of his subjects). However, many, if not most, of the exiles were settled at Tel Abib in the vicinity of Nippur near the Chebar Canal, part of an intricate system of canals carrying water from the Euphrates River throughout the city and its surroundings. The "tel" (mound) in Tel Abib suggests that the Babylonians placed the deportees in an area once inhabited, but subsequently destroyed. If this is the case, then many of the exiles would have spent their time rebuilding the ruins.

In his letter to the exiles of 597 BCE (Jer 29:1-23), Jeremiah rejected any hope of a quick return home. He urged them to "build houses and live in them; plant gardens and eat what they produce. Take wives and have sons and daughters; take wives for your sons, and give your daughters in marriage, that they may bear sons and daughters; multiply there, and do not decrease" (Jer 29:5-6 NRSV). If communication flowed between Syro-Palestine and Babylonia with relative efficiency, such that Jeremiah knew of the exiles' situation, then his letter can be taken as evidence that they could obey his advice if they resolved to do so. Nevertheless, we should not suppose that all of the exiles shared similar circumstances. Military leaders likely were conscripted into the Babylonian army. Expert craftsmen undoubtedly labored on some of Nebuchadrezzar's many building projects. Imprisonment, slavery, or forced conscription was surely the fate of some exiles. It seems likely, however, that most were able to practice their trades and support their families.

If the situation at Tel Abib was reasonably benign, however, we should not presume that its inhabitants endured no suffering or distress. Renz writes of their trauma:

> Having been part of Judah's upper class, they had left behind family, social status and material possessions. They had seen people dying during the siege and must have had further losses of life on the long and arduous journey to Babylonia, where they received a humiliating "welcome," as certainly as Nebuchadnezzar made sure that he received a hero's welcome. Even with these events receding somewhat in the background, the reality was that they had exchanged their hilly homeland and the pleasant climate of Jerusalem for the flat and hot Babylonian low lands, and at least some of them were certainly not used to the hard manual labour now required of them. To this must be added, at the time before the fall of Jerusalem, the mixture of hope and fear concerning their own and Jerusalem's situation.[4]

Psalm 137 expresses the exiles' grief, frustrated nationalism, and hunger for revenge in terms that could scarcely be more extreme. Perhaps this psalm was composed not long after the people reached Babylonia. Ezekiel 37:11 attests to the sense of resignation experienced by at least some of the exiles after years in Babylonia: "Our bones are dried up, and our hope is lost; we are cut off completely." We should not suppose that all of the deportees experienced the same reactions throughout the entire exilic period. While some clung with tenacity to their distinct ethnic identity, others probably assimilated

---

4. Thomas Renz, *The Rhetorical Function of the Book of Ezekiel,* VTSup 76 (Leiden: Brill, 1999) 44-45.

into Babylonian culture rapidly. While some struggled mightily to maintain faith in Yahweh, others probably shifted their devotion to Babylonian deities.

EZEKIEL'S CRITIQUE OF THE ORTHODOX YAHWISM OF HIS DAY

Although we cannot assume that all of the exiles deported in 597 BCE subscribed to the same Yahwistic theology, it is helpful to understand prominent aspects of that theology, since doing so helps us to understand why Ezekiel's oracles were resisted by his audience prior to the fall of Jerusalem.

In his commentary, Block identifies four "pillars" of divine promise upon which the people of Judah rested their faith.[5] First, they believed that they were Yahweh's chosen people, enjoying the blessings of their covenant relationship with Yahweh forged at Sinai centuries earlier. From this belief, they derived a sense of confidence based on the power of their God to ensure their welfare and to protect them. To be sure, the Judeans knew that maintaining their covenant relationship with Yahweh brought obligations as well as benefits. Nevertheless, one can imagine that the latter were emphasized to the neglect of the former.

Second, they believed that Yahweh had granted land to Israel's ancestors and that they were inheritors of that land grant. Yahweh owned the land they inhabited, and their presence there was God's will. As their patron deity, Yahweh would fight to protect their land and to ensure that the people were not forced from it.

The third and fourth "pillars" of Israel's theology are particularly crucial for understanding the orthodox Yahwistic faith of Ezekiel's day. In both, the city of Jerusalem plays a crucial role. On the one hand, the people of Judah believed that Yahweh had entered into an eternal covenant with the descendants of David, promising that the Davidic dynasty would reign in Jerusalem in perpetuity. The people living in Jerusalem during the years leading up to the Babylonian onslaught knew well their traditions about David and about God's unconditional promise that one of his descendants would occupy Israel's throne forever. Presented as Yahweh's declaration to David through the prophet Nathan, 2 Sam 7:11b-16 is a classic statement that God established an ongoing Davidic dynasty in Israel:

> The LORD declares to you that the LORD will make you a house. When your days are fulfilled and you lie down with your ancestors, I will raise up your offspring after you, who shall come forth from your body, and I will establish his kingdom. He shall build a house for my name, and I will establish the throne of his kingdom forever. I will be a father to him, and he shall be a son to me. When he commits iniquity, I will punish him with a rod such as mortals use, with blows inflicted by human beings. But I will not take my steadfast love from him, as I took it from Saul, whom I put away from before you. Your house and your kingdom shall be made sure forever before me; your throne shall be established forever. (NRSV)

Other biblical literature declares, in exuberant poetry, the belief that Yahweh promised to ensure the continuity of the Davidic dynasty forever. Psalm 2, a royal psalm pro-

5. D. I. Block, *The Book of Ezekiel: Chapters 1–24,* NICOT (Grand Rapids: Eerdmans, 1997) 7-8.

claiming the sovereignty of Judah's king over the nations, articulates the ongoing father/adopted son relationship between Yahweh and the Davidic king:

> I will tell of the decree of the LORD:
> He said to me, "You are my son;
>   today I have begotten you.
> Ask of me, and I will make the nations your heritage,
>   and the ends of the earth your possession.
> You shall break them with a rod of iron,
>   and dash them in pieces like a potter's vessel." (Ps 2:7-9 NRSV)

These two texts, and many others, affirm Yahweh's commitment to the Davidic kings who occupied Judah's throne throughout the pre-exilic period. The king was the adopted son of Yahweh, whom God would protect against attack by any and all nations. Israel did not go so far as to deify its kings, but it asserted that the relationship between Yahweh and the Davidic king was unique. This theological tenet had implications for all of the people, not just for the royal family, for through the king, Yahweh's blessings ostensibly were mediated to the nation as a whole. The Davidic king's rule was the earthly manifestation of Yahweh's heavenly rule. The political consequences of this theology served the Davidic dynasty well; the people were expected to give their total support and loyalty to the king, for he ruled with Yahweh's sanction and blessing.

On the other hand, Jerusalem was crucial to the theology of pre-exilic Judeans because the Solomonic Temple stood within its walls. The Temple built during Solomon's reign was likely very important from the time of its completion. But the Bible testifies to its increasing significance in succeeding centuries. A little more than three hundred years after it was constructed, Judah's King Josiah initiated a reform movement that sought to close down every other Yahwistic cultic site within Judah, and even in the territory of the former northern kingdom. Josiah believed that the Solomonic Temple in Jerusalem alone was suitable for appropriate worship of Yahweh.

It follows from these beliefs that the people thought that their patron deity would not permit the city in which God's Temple stood to be destroyed. Their unswerving faith is expressed in Psalm 48:

> Great is the LORD and greatly to be praised
>   in the city of our God.
> His holy mountain, beautiful in elevation,
>   is the joy of all the earth,
> Mount Zion, in the far north,
>   the city of the great King.
> Within its citadels God
>   has shown himself a sure defense.
>
> . . . .
>
> Your name, O God, like your praise,

reaches to the ends of the earth.
Your right hand is filled with victory.
Let Mount Zion be glad,
let the towns of Judah rejoice
because of your judgments. (Ps 48:1-3, 9-11 NRSV)

Like the prophet Jeremiah, Ezekiel's contemporary who remained in Jerusalem, Ezekiel scrutinized these four tenets of the Yahwistic theology of his day and subjected them to a radical critique. True, Yahweh and Israel were covenant partners, but the people had for centuries failed to fulfill their covenant obligations. While the covenant forged at Sinai demanded Israel's undivided fidelity to God, the people of Ezekiel's day were idolatrous. Indeed, their idols had even found their way into Yahweh's own Temple (see, e.g., chap. 8). While the covenant demanded that the people observe moral and ethical laws, these laws were abrogated by each generation (see, e.g., chap. 20). While the covenant demanded that Judean society be just, its leaders were oppressors, perpetrators of violence and bloodshed (see, e.g., chap. 22). Because the rebellious house of Israel had failed to honor its covenant obligations, Yahweh would bring the covenant curses upon them, including deportation, destruction, and death.

God had, indeed, granted to Israel the land promised to its ancestors, but its failure to obey the covenant regulations meant that Israel could and would lose its right to inhabit that territory. God was either going to expel the people from their homeland (e.g., chap. 14) or cover it with their corpses (see, e.g., chap. 6).

Yahweh had determined long ago that David's descendants would rule over God's people. But Judah's kings, and especially its last monarchs, blatantly broke God's laws and ravaged their subjects like lions (chap. 19), oppressing the very people whose rights they were duty-bound to protect (chap. 22) and rebelling against the pro-Babylonian policy that Ezekiel insisted was Yahweh's will (chap. 17). Such kings would not go unpunished.

Ezekiel believed that God's glory had resided in the Temple in Jerusalem. But he insisted that Yahweh was abandoning that Temple, because the abominations committed within it had polluted the place completely. Without God's protective presence, the Temple was doomed to destruction, as was the city in which it stood—a city so corrupt that it had outsinned Sodom (see chaps. 16 and 23).

Ezekiel offered his fellow exiles no hope that their homeland might survive Babylonian aggression. To the contrary, he insisted that Yahweh was bringing about its downfall. The divine warrior was warring against "his" own people. Undergirding his pronouncements of judgment were certain presuppositions that Ezekiel steadfastly refused to abandon. These presuppositions will reappear from time to time in the pages of this commentary, but they should be stated plainly at the outset.[6]

6. The following paragraphs are based on K. P. Darr, "Ezekiel's Justifications of God: Teaching Troubling Texts," *JSOT* 55 (1992) 98-117.

First, Ezekiel asserts Yahweh's unparalleled sovereignty over history and the nations. His worldview is utterly theocentric. God is at work in the world, controlling nations and events according to God's own plan.

Second, that plan includes the destruction of Judah. Ezekiel insists that the approaching devastation is the doing, and not the undoing, of Israel's God. He spurns any notion that the Babylonian army will succeed because "The LORD does not see us; the LORD has abandoned the country" (Ezek 8:12 TNK), or that Jerusalem's demise will signal the victory of Marduk, patron deity of Babylon, over Israel's God. He ascribes historical events to Yahweh; he will not abandon Yahweh to history.

Third, Ezekiel insists that God's punishments are just. Yahweh's plan is not capricious, undertaken at the deity's whim, but the thoroughly merited response to Israel's long-lived sin. The punishment is proportionate to the crime. And because the anticipated punishment will be horrific, Israel's sins must be grievous, indeed.

In the years prior to Judah's collapse, Ezekiel ruthlessly opposes any notion that Yahweh is powerless, apathetic, or unjust. He insists that Yahweh is both in control of events and justified in the way those events are controlled. If the God who is both just and the Lord of history has determined to reduce Judean land and cities to uninhabited wasteland, and to exile or exterminate the population, then this must be because the Judeans have sinned to such a degree that no other outcome is possible without violating divine justice. Both Judah's conviction and the deity who convicts it are just.

Ezekiel's oracles of judgment are filled with passion and utterly devoid of sentimentality. The God we witness through Ezekiel's words is consumed by wrath, bent on violence, and hungry for vengeance. Little wonder that Ezekiel's readers—ancient and modern—might recoil at his portrayal of Yahweh in chaps. 4–24. In the transitional chaps. 25–32, Ezekiel directs his ire at Israel's enemies (and at one potential ally, Egypt). His oracles against foreign nations and rulers likewise are replete with images of a wrathful, violent, and vengeful God, whose preferred method of dealing with these nations is extermination in order that all be forced to acknowledge that "I am Yahweh." The assertion that God would knock Israel's foes to their knees must have been good news, indeed, for Ezekiel's late exilic readers. For moderns, however, these oracles present formidable theological obstacles.

EZEKIEL'S ORACLES OF RESTORATION

Ezekiel's words of doom are not his only words, however. Chapters 33–48 contain the preponderance of the prophet's oracles of restoration. In them, he insists that Israel will not remain in exile forever, because the people's present plight dishonors Yahweh's reputation among the nations. For the sake of Yahweh's own name, God will regather the people from the nations, return them to their homeland, and ensure that the sins of the past are never repeated. Yahweh will enter into a new covenant with the people.

Their God-given hearts and spirits will be incapable of abrogating Yahweh's statutes and ordinances; and their land will be transformed into a veritable Garden of Eden, prompting the astonishment of all who pass by (see Ezekiel 36). The people will be shepherded by a new David (see Ezekiel 34). All potential foes will be eliminated in God's final battle against Gog and his hordes (Ezekiel 38–39). And Yahweh's glory will return to a new and perfectly ordered Temple, situated at the center of a land inhabited by the reconstituted twelve tribes of Israel (Ezekiel 40–48).

THE PRIEST/PROPHET EZEKIEL

The book bearing Ezekiel's name provides readers with only a little biographical information about him. We know that his father's name was Buzi. His own name, which appears only in 1:3 and 24:24, means either "God strengthens" or "May God strengthen." He was a priest, or at least in training for the priesthood, at the time he was deported to Babylonia. We know that he had a residence in Tel Abib, for we are told that elders visited him in his house. He was married, although we do not know his wife's name. Nothing is said of their children, if any existed. We have no idea how he supported himself.

The Ezekiel we encounter in his book presents himself as an eccentric, even bizarre, figure. Little wonder that past scholars have sometimes subjected him to the psychiatrist's couch. Block acknowledges that Israel's prophets often acted and spoke in unusual ways, but he insists that Ezekiel was in a class of his own:

> The concentration of so many bizarre features in one individual is without precedent: his muteness; lying bound and naked [?]; digging holes in the walls of houses; emotional paralysis in the face of his wife's death; "spiritual" travels; images of strange creatures, of eyes, and of creeping things; hearing voices and the sounds of water; withdrawal symptoms; fascination with feces and blood; wild literary imagination, pornographic imagery; unreal if not surreal understanding of Israel's past; and the list goes on.[7]

Despite Ezekiel's apparent eccentricities, most contemporary scholars reject a psychoanalytical approach to understanding Ezekiel's personality. One exception, D. J. Halperin, believes that Ezekiel's writings betray a hatred of women and men rooted in child abuse.[8] But his speculations remain just that.

We know that Ezekiel was among the intellectual elite of his day. The book of Ezekiel reveals an author of extraordinary acumen, sophistication, and literary gifts. Ezekiel's intellect reveals itself in myriad ways: his mastery of technical vocabularies; his political expertise; his familiarity with Israel's religious traditions; and above all his creative revisions of those traditions to suit the challenges of his times. We should assume that his audience, Jerusalem's elite, was equipped to understand his words, for they shared with him a complex web of social, political, economic, military, and religious knowledge.

---

7. Block, *Ezekiel 1–24*, 10.
8. D. J. Halperin, *Seeking Ezekiel: Test and Psychology* (University Park: Penn State University Press, 1993).

EZEKIEL AND HIS AUDIENCE

Like many, though not all, contemporary scholars, I think that Ezekiel's entire "ministry" took place in Babylonia and entailed the performance of certain sign acts, and especially the oral proclamation of oracles to his exilic audience. The notion that Ezekiel was a writer, not an orator, has deep roots within the discipline. In the nineteenth century, for example, Reuss denied Ezekiel any oral ministry:

> There is not a single page in the whole book which we must suppose to have been read or proclaimed publicly. Ezekiel was not an orator; he was a writer. What he gives us are literary reflections, the product of private study and the fruit of retirement and contemplation. We should have to shut our eyes to the evidence to arrive at the view that he had ever had occasion to interfere actively in affairs, and to go out from his retreat to appear on the scene where passions are aroused and events take place.[9]

But Reuss's statement, with its tinges of Romanticism, goes too far. I do not doubt that prior to his oral performances, Ezekiel frequently committed oracles to writing. Indeed, in the case of his longest and most detailed speeches (e.g., Ezekiel 16), that seems the most likely scenario. Nevertheless, in the book, Yahweh repeatedly instructs the priest-prophet to "speak" to his compatriots, and his late exilic readers (see below) will assume that he did so.

Like Renz, I think that the book of Ezekiel derives from an oral debate with his exilic audience.[10] Ezekiel's oracles are not disinterested theological essays. They are strategic speech by which the prophet seeks to persuade his audience to perceive events (e.g., the forthcoming destruction of Jerusalem), persons (e.g., Zedekiah and his pro-Egyptian advisers), and institutions (e.g., the monarchy) in his way, rather than in some other way. The exiles, clinging to the divine promises of their faith, resisted Ezekiel's message of doom and destruction. And one can imagine that the harshness of his pronouncements of judgment further hardened the hearts of many in his audience. Nevertheless, Ezekiel refused to soften his rhetoric or to concede that alternative interpretations of events were possible. His refusal to budge testifies to the depths of his convictions, and he everywhere insists that his words are actually *God's* words, which he must proclaim in order to save his own life.

EZEKIEL AND HIS READERS

Although some scholars think that the Ezekiel scroll reached essentially its final form years, perhaps even centuries, after the prophet's lifetime, I am not persuaded to that view. It is possible, perhaps likely, that during the post-exilic period, members of

9. E. Reuss, *Ancien Testament II, Les Prophètes Littérature* II (Paris: Sandoz & Fischbacher) 10; cited and translated in W. Zimmerli, *Ezekiel 1: A Commentary on the Book of the Prophet Ezekiel, Chapters 1–24,* trans. R. E. Clements, Hermeneia (Philadelphia: Fortress, 1979) 4.

10. Renz, *The Rhetorical Function of the Book of Ezekiel,* 16.

Ezekiel's "school" further supplemented his work. But the book as a whole does not address, or even seem knowledgeable about, conditions pertaining during the post-exilic period. Like Renz, I think that the book was virtually completed by the late exilic period; and I will place my reader (see below) in that time frame. Renz astutely observes that the book does not presuppose a great chronological gulf separating Ezekiel's original audience from the book's earliest readers:

> It is remarkable that the book of Ezekiel makes little effort to distinguish the audience of the book from the prophet's original audience; rather, the former is seen in continuity with the latter. This means that even if one assumes that the book was written for a post-exilic readership (an assumption . . . I do not share), one must not overlook the fact that the book invites its readers to identify with the exilic community. It does not address directly a world beyond the world of the prophet Ezekiel, but rather invites prospective readers to enter into the world of refugees in "Tel Aviv" and their prophet. The book of Ezekiel develops its argument with the reader by narrating the story of a prophet's unfolding argument with his exilic audience. In this way the book addresses its own audience by having the audience in the book addressed by the prophet. In other words, it is a communication by being a narrative about a communication.[11]

A significant factor distinguishes Ezekiel's original audience from his earliest readership, however. The latter constituency knows what the former did not until news of Jerusalem's destruction reached Babylonia: Ezekiel was right. His predictions that Nebuchadrezzar would breach Jerusalem's walls, torch the city, slaughter many of its inhabitants, and deport others were fulfilled. As a consequence of this knowledge, Ezekiel's earliest readers are, *from the outset,* predisposed to acknowledge his status as Yahweh's authentic prophet and to read his oracles as God's own words—precisely the posture that Ezekiel's original audience resists for reasons already identified. But more is involved than the simple verification of prophetic predictions. Renz is surely correct when he states that even the reader who knows that Jerusalem was destroyed needs to understand *why* it was destroyed: "To this end the readers are put (in their imaginations) in the situation before the fall of Jerusalem. They are invited to 'judge' Jerusalem and thereby to pronounce Yahweh's judgement as just."[12] Once Jerusalem has been destroyed, and the news reaches Tel Abib, then the distance between Ezekiel's original audience and his late exilic readers diminishes. Now, both groups await the fulfillment of Ezekiel's outstanding oracles against the nations, and especially the restoration of Israel to its homeland and the restructuring of its society.

THE STRUCTURE OF THE BOOK OF EZEKIEL

Before turning to a discussion of the reading process, and of "my reader" of the book of Ezekiel, I offer the following observations about the structure of the book that are

11. Ibid.
12. Ibid., 41.

pertinent to that discussion. As noted earlier, the book of Ezekiel consists of three major sections. The first section, chaps. 1–24, consists primarily of sign acts and oracles of doom against Judah and Jerusalem. The second section, chaps. 25–32, contains most of Ezekiel's oracles against foreign nations and rulers, while the third section, chaps. 33–48, contains oracles concerning Israel's future restoration. Many of Ezekiel's oracles are dated (dates appear in 1:1-3; 3:16; 8:1; 20:1; 24:1; 26:1; 29:1, 17; 30:20; 31:1; 32:1, 17; 33:21; and 40:1), and with one understandable exception (29:17), these date notices appear in chronological order. This feature of the book contributes to the reader's sense of its coherence. This is no pastiche of oracles, but a carefully structured literary work anchored in historical events. The scroll has a beginning, a middle, and an end. Its contents can be read randomly, but it invites a sequential reading.

Moreover, four vision reports appear in the book. In 1:1–3:15, Ezekiel witnesses a vision in which "the glory of the LORD" comes to him over Babylonia in storm cloud and blazing light, and he is commissioned as Yahweh's prophet. In 8:1–11:24, Ezekiel is transported by the spirit to the Temple in Jerusalem, where he sees the abominations committed there and witnesses Yahweh's glory abandoning the city to its fate. In 37:1-14, Ezekiel is again transported by the spirit, this time to "the valley," which is filled with heaps of disconnected and thoroughly desiccated bones. Before his eyes, the bones are rejoined, bound by sinews, refleshed, covered with skin, and animated by the spirit. Finally, in chaps. 40–48, the hand of Yahweh brings Ezekiel to a "very high mountain," where he tours Yahweh's new Temple and witnesses God's glory enter it. These vision reports also tell a "story" of sorts, which unfolds chronologically. This is most obvious in the case of the second and fourth reports, which describe the departure of Yahweh's glory from the Temple and its return, respectively. The vision reports in the book also invite a sequential reading of the scroll. They can be read randomly. But a major structural component of the work is thereby obscured. One might imagine that after reading randomly in the book over a period of time, one could learn the relationship of any given pericope to another. What is lost in such a scenario, however, is the reader's experience of the *unfolding* prophetic message of Ezekiel as historical events develop. The late exilic reader whom I posit encounters Ezekiel's oracles sequentially, from beginning to end.

DISASSEMBLING AND RECONSTRUCTING THE BOOK OF EZEKIEL[13]

The history of Ezekielian scholarship shows that in biblical studies, no less than in other disciplines, our presuppositions and methodologies influence the questions we ask of texts, and those questions inevitably influence the answers we discern. Early historical investigators of Israel's prophetic corpus, for example, sought primarily to recover the

---

13. The following sections derive from my earlier research, specifically, K. P. Darr, "Ezekiel Among the Critics," *CurBS* 2 (1994) 9-24; and *Isaiah's Vision and the Family of God* (Louisville: Westminster John Knox, 1994) esp. 13-32.

prophets' "authentic" words within their original historical contexts. They wished to distinguish later supplements from these "genuine" utterances in order that the prophets' own personalities, historical circumstances, and religious beliefs might be revealed. "To borrow from a description of sculpting attributed to the great Italian artist, Michelangelo, these scholars carved into the textual block until they reached a particular prophet's 'skin' and then stopped. When their work was completed, the statue before them looked precisely like their [mental] images of Amos, or Ezekiel, or 'Deutero-Isaiah.' But littered around its base lay chunks and shards of discarded text."[14]

Some contemporary scholars, frustrated by the "dismembering" tendencies of historical-critical methods, have turned to a variety of literary-critical approaches. Such approaches can contribute fresh and important insights into biblical books. But historical-critical approaches and literary criticism are not of necessity antithetical (as advocates of each sometimes suggest). Some literary-critical approaches, including my own, rely upon historical-critical discoveries. Such reliance is necessary when examining the book of Ezekiel, for, as noted above, it presents as a carefully structured literary work anchored in historical events. In this commentary, I often set aside certain traditional agendas, such as distinguishing between "authentic" and "inauthentic" materials, and carefully tracing the composition history of the book. But I do not concomitantly devalue the myriad contributions of historical criticism to our understanding of the Ezekiel scroll.

Ezekiel Among the Critics. In 1880, Smend could confidently pen the following assessment of the Ezekiel corpus: "The whole book is . . . the logical development of a series of ideas in accordance with a well thought out, and in part quite schematic, plan. We cannot remove any part without disturbing the whole structure."[15] Smend's assessment echoed that of Ewald, who declared in 1841 that the scroll, though not composed in a single stage, nevertheless owed its final form to Ezekiel himself.[16]

This judgment was attacked, however, in the late 1800s and early 1900s. G. Hölscher's *Die Profeten* constituted one such attack.[17] Having established to his satisfaction the ecstatic character of Ezekiel's genuine prophecies, Hölscher distinguished between the prophet's own utterances and the supplements of later redactors, whose efforts threaten to obfuscate the oracles of Ezekiel, the poet:

> By freeing the poetry of Ezekiel from the dry prosaic pattern in which the redaction has
> woven his poems, the poet Ezekiel appears once again in a clear light, with his brilliant,
> imaginative and passionate rhetoric. From a religio-historical point of view also the picture
> of Ezekiel changes completely: he is no longer the stiff priestly writer and pathfinder of a

14. Darr, *Isaiah's Vision and the Family of God,* 13.

15. R. Smend, *Der Prophet Ezechiel,* KHAT (Leipzig: Hirzel, 1880) xxi; cited by W. Zimmerli, *Ezekiel 1,* 3.

16. H. Ewald, *Die Propheten des Alten Bundes erklärt.* II. *Jeremja und Hezekiel* (Göttingen: Vandenhoeck & Ruprecht) 207.

17. G. Hölscher, *Die Profeten* (Leipzig: Hinrichs, 1914); that attack was further strengthened in his *Hesekiel, der Dichter und das Buch,* BZAW 39 (Giessen: Töpelmann, 1924).

legalistic and ritualistic Judaism, for which he has been held, but a genuine prophet of Jewish antiquity, a spiritual companion of the authentic Jeremiah.[18]

Hölscher attributed only 144 of the book's 1,273 verses to Ezekiel![19]

Several years after Hölscher's commentary was published, V. Herntrich refuted the book's own claim that Ezekiel was among the exiles deported to Babylonia in 597 BCE, arguing instead that his prophetic ministry took place in Jerusalem.[20] Perhaps he was actually exiled in 587 BCE, after the city was destroyed. In any event, Ezekiel fell silent at that time. His earlier prophetic oracles were subsequently edited by a 597 BCE deportee who wished to buttress his assertion that true prophecy had traveled into exile with his own elite community. Herntrich attributed chaps. 40–48, as well as some material in prior chapters, to this editor.

Only a decade after Hölscher's commentary appeared, and beneath the cumulative weight of critical analysis, G. A. Cooke could point to an upheaval in Ezekiel studies: "In recent years the study of Ezekiel has undergone something of a revolution. . . . It is no longer possible to treat the Book as the product of a single mind and a single age."[21]

In a 1953 lecture, H. H. Rowley assessed the state of Ezekiel's studies to his own day. He rehearsed a variety of hypotheses about the book's unity, its date of composition, and Ezekiel's location(s) at the time of his prophetic career. But he also looked ahead to what he regarded as the future of Ezekiel studies. Today many, though not all, critics agree with Rowley's assessments:

> First, he noted that though the text undoubtedly contained some secondary elements, they probably were not present in large quantities. Second, he claimed that Ezekiel, a gifted poet, could not be ruled out as the author of prose passages as well, and that no compelling evidence discredited the scroll's own claims regarding the locus of his prophetic activities. Third, Rowley pointed out that the ostensible need to resort to psychological explanations of Ezekiel's behaviors and words was largely mitigated by appropriate consideration of the literary genre (for example, visions).[22]

DIACHRONIC AND SYNCHRONIC APPROACHES TO THE BOOK OF EZEKIEL

Rendtorff's observation about Isaian scholarship is true of Ezekiel studies as well: "The common starting point among scholars interested in the formation of the Book of Isaiah is the conviction, or at least the assumption, that the present shape of the book is not the result of more or less accidental or arbitrary developments but rather . . . of

18. Hölscher, *Hesekiel,* 5-6; cited in Zimmerli, *Ezekiel 1,* 5.
19. See W. Zimmerli, *Ezekiel 1,* 5. Even more extreme is J. Garscha, *Studien zum Ezechielbuch: Eine redaktionskritische Untersuchung von Ez 1–39,* Europaische Hochschulschriften 23.23 (Bern: Peter Lang, 1974). He argues that only about thirty verses of chaps. 1–39 are from the prophet himself (17:2-10; 23:2-25).
20. V. Herntrich, *Ezekielprobleme,* BZAW 61 (Giessen: Töpelmann, 1974).
21. G. A. Cooke, *A Critical and Exegetical Commentary on the Book of Ezekiel,* ICC (New York: Scribner's, 1936) 1:v.
22. K. P. Darr, "Ezekiel Among the Critics," 11-12. See also H. H. Rowley, "The Book of Ezekiel in Recent Study," *BJRL* 36 (1953–54) 149-90.

deliberate and intentional literary and theological work."[23] Like Rendtorff, I distinguish between two approaches current in contemporary Ezekiel scholarship. On the one hand, diachronic approaches attempt to reconstruct the history of a text, including its composition history. On the other hand, synchronic approaches pursue what the text, in all its complexity, means in its final form.

Diachronic Approaches and Redaction Criticism. An imposing group of scholars has applied diachronic methods to the book of Ezekiel. In the twentieth century, the most famous and influential of these was Walther Zimmerli, whose massive, two-volume commentary on the book of Ezekiel appeared first as part of the Biblischer Kommentar, Altes Testament series,[24] and later, in English translation, as part of the Hermeneia commentary series.[25] Zimmerli's approach lay between the extreme positions represented by Smend, on the one hand, and Hölscher and Herntrich, on the other. He located Ezekiel's entire ministry in Babylonia, attributed the scroll to the prophet and his "school," concluded that Ezekiel himself returned to and updated earlier oracles, and dated the book's composition largely to the exilic period.

A gifted text critic, Zimmerli both worked with the Hebrew Masoretic Text (MT) and resorted to the versions (e.g., the Greek Septuagint [LXX]) in order to produce an original text free of later accretions and scribal errors. (One can seriously question whether even an "original" text would be free of scribal errors. Text critics agree that the book of Ezekiel is difficult Hebrew. Moreover, the scroll contains many *hapax legomena*, terms found nowhere else in the Hebrew Bible. Zimmerli counted over 130 such terms in the work.)[26] He utilized methodological tools, especially form- and traditio-historical criticism, with skill and verve; and he identified forms and speeches lying behind the final shape of the text. Indeed, he went so far as to rewrite certain passages, ostensibly restoring them to their "original" forms (see, e.g., his rewrite of Ezekiel 16).[27] But he also traced the diachronic processes whereby original versions of texts attained their final forms. Willing to attribute problematic textual features to inept redactors, he nevertheless dealt seriously, though separately, with their efforts, describing a process by which "kernel elements" underwent further development.[28]

Synchronic Approaches to the Book of Ezekiel. As noted above, synchronic approaches to biblical books pursue the meaning of a text in its final form, irrespective of the process by which it attained that form. Rendtorff's defense of recent synchronic readings of Isaiah also is applicable to synchronic readings of Ezekiel:

23. R. Rendtorff, "The Book of Isaiah: A Complex Unity. Synchronic and Diachronic Reading," SBLSP 30 (1991) 9.

24. W. Zimmerli, *Ezechiel,* I, *BKAT* 13.1 (Neukirchen-Vluyn: Neukirchener Verlag, 1969); *Ezechiel,* II, *BKAT* 13.2 (Neukirchen-Vluyn: Neukirchener Verlag, 1969).

25. W. Zimmerli, *Ezekiel 1: A Commentary on the Book of the Prophet Ezekiel, Chapters 1–24,* trans. R. E. Clements, Hermeneia (Philadelphia: Fortress, 1979) and *Ezekiel 2: A Commentary on the Book of the Prophet Ezekiel, Chapters 25–48,* trans. J. D. Martin, Hermeneia (Philadelphia: Fortress, 1983).

26. Zimmerli, *Ezekiel 1,* 23.

27. Ibid., 347-48.

28. Because Zimmerli dealt with "primary" verses before moving on to secondary accretions, it it difficult to grasp the dynamic of the text *as a text.*

A changing view on the Book of Isaiah should allow, and even require, studies on topics, themes, expressions, and even ideas characteristic for the book as a whole or significant parts of it, without at the same time discussing the questions of redaction or composition. A synchronic reading, if carried out with the necessary sophistication, should have its own right.[29]

The method employed by Moshe Greenberg in the first two volumes of his three-volume commentary on Ezekiel for the Anchor Bible series bears a close familial resemblance to synchronic approaches.[30] His "holistic" interpretations of Ezekiel's oracles reflect a dissatisfaction with what he deems the anachronistic criteria of certain methodologies. He asserts, for example, that criteria commonly employed to recover the original oracles of Ezekiel "are simply *a priori,* an array of unproved (and unprovable) modern assumptions and conventions that confirm themselves through the results obtained by forcing them on the text and altering, reducing, and reordering it accordingly."[31] Unlike Zimmerli, who seeks to recover original texts by removing later accretions, Greenberg attempts to make sense of the book both textually and structurally in its received (MT) form. "His interpretations demonstrate a deep appreciation for what texts reveal about themselves when patiently probed."[32] Yet Greenberg's method should be distinguished from synchronic readings proper, because he does not intend to bracket evidence of redaction and editorial shaping. Rather, his approach reflects his judgments concerning the book's authorship and arrangement, both of which he attributes to the prophet Ezekiel:

The present Book of Ezekiel is the product of art and intelligent design. . . . A consistent trend of thought expressed in a distinctive style has emerged, giving the impression of an individual mind of powerful and passionate proclivities. . . . The persuasion grows on one as piece after piece falls into the established patterns and ideas that a coherent world of vision is emerging, contemporary with the sixth-century prophet and decisively shaped by him, if not the very words of Ezekiel himself.[33]

In a review of both commentaries, J. D. Levenson contrasts the approaches of Zimmerli and Greenberg: "Whereas Zimmerli sees the book of Ezekiel as a puzzle which the exegete must put into an intelligible order, Moshe Greenberg sees it as a subtle work of art and the exegete's task as the demonstration of its intelligibility. Where Zimmerli is a plastic surgeon, Greenberg is a midwife, carefully uncovering ever more order and symmetry in a text before which he stands in obvious reverence."[34]

29. R. Rendtorff, "The Book of Isaiah," 20.
30. Moshe Greenberg, *Ezekiel 1–20,* AB 22 (Garden City, N.Y.: Doubleday, 1983); *Ezekiel 21–37,* AB 22A (Garden City, N.Y.: Doubleday, 1997).
31. Greenberg, *Ezekiel 1–20,* 20.
32. K. P. Darr, "Ezekiel Among the Critics," 14.
33. Greenberg, *Ezekiel 1–20,* 26-27.
34. J. D. Levenson, "Ezekiel in the Perspective of Two Commentators," *Int* 38 (1984) 213.

A READER-ORIENTED APPROACH TO THE BOOK OF EZEKIEL

Many biblical scholars no longer confine their interests to recovering a prophet's original words, cleansed of later accretions. To the contrary, recent scholarship displays considerable interest in redactors as gifted literary artists and theologians in their own right. Although I value the findings of diachronic analysis, I have chosen in this commentary to focus upon a late exilic reader's construal (understanding) of the book. A reader-oriented approach differs from that of Zimmerli in many ways; notably, my reader does not bring to the text knowledge of the historical-critical methodologies developed especially in the nineteenth and twentieth centuries and of their goals. It also differs from that of Greenberg in that it focuses not only upon what is read, but also upon the reading process itself. In what follows, I am indebted to J. A. Darr, whose reader-oriented method approaches biblical books (in his case, Luke-Acts; in mine, Ezekiel) as potentially coherent literary works, rather than simply as quarries for historical data.[35]

Acknowledging the many literary methods available to critics, Darr emphasizes the importance of constructing a "text-specific" approach that is well-suited to a particular piece of literature. All too often, he observes, contemporary biblical scholars adopt literary methods developed with modern works in mind. Such anachronistic approaches inevitably prove inadequate. To paraphrase Darr, the complexities of interpreting an ancient religious text like the book of Ezekiel cannot be overlooked in our search for literary-critical methods.[36] Rather, we must construct an eclectic approach, whose features are fashioned in the light of the particular text at hand.

Three Critical Premises. Three critical premises ground Darr's method. First, he affirms that "literature functions rhetorically"—that is, "it achieves certain effects—esthetic, emotional, moral, ideological—in an audience by means of rhetorical strategies."[37] Second, he asserts that meaning arises from the "dynamic interaction of both the rhetorical strategies of the text and the interpretive strategies (a repertoire of conventions and expectations) of its reader."[38] In other words, *meaning depends not only upon what the text brings to the reader, but also upon what the reader brings to the text.* This second premise presupposes that scholars can gain access to both the text and at least some aspects of the reader's extra-textual repertoire, including: "(1) language; (2) social norms and cultural scripts; (3) classical or canonical literature; (4) literary conventions (e.g., genres, type scenes, standard plots, stock characters) and reading rules (e.g., how to categorize, rank, and process various textual data); and (5) commonly-known historical and geographical facts."[39]

35. See John A. Darr, " 'Glorified in the Presence of Kings': A Literary-Critical Study of Herod the Tetrarch in Luke-Acts" (Ph.D. diss., Vanderbilt University, Nashville, 1987), published as *Herod the Fox: Audience Criticism and Lukan Characterization,* JSNTSUP 163 (Sheffield: Sheffield Academic, 1998). He subsequently refined it in *On Character Building: The Reader and the Rhetoric of Characterization in Luke-Acts,* Literary Currents in Biblical Interpretation, ed. D. N. Fewell and D. M. Gunn (Louisville: Westminster/John Knox, 1992).

36. Darr, " 'Glorified in the Presence of Kings,' " 12-13.

37. Ibid., 15.

38. Ibid.

39. Darr, *On Character Building,* 22.

Our knowledge of this repertoire remains incomplete; and like those engaged in purely historical-critical pursuits, we can never eliminate uncertainty or the necessity for conjecture. Nevertheless, Darr insists in his third premise that a variety of text-specific factors—historical, social, linguistic, literary—remain relevant for contemporary construals of ancient texts. Some of those factors function transculturally and are easily grasped. Others are elusive. But it behooves critics to reconstruct culture-specific factors pertaining when the book of Ezekiel could be read as a coherent literary work.

With these three premises in place, Darr locates his literary method among the categories identified by M. H. Abrams:

> Abrams' analytic scheme consists of four elements: the work itself, the artist or author, the universe or nature, and the audience. While most critics blend all four of these elements in their interpretive endeavors, each "tends to derive from one of these terms his principle categories for defining, classifying and analyzing the work of art, as well as the major criteria by which he judges its value." All literary theories, by definition, pay some heed to the text; however, some approaches concentrate on it in isolation (objective theories), whereas others explain the work by relating it to something or someone else—the author (expressive theories), the audience (pragmatic theories), or aspects of the universe (mimetic theories).[40]

Darr's premises place his method on the "pragmatic" axis of Abrams's categories. Pragmatic approaches are scarcely novel; they predominated from the time of Horace through the eighteenth century. In the following two centuries, however, they were supplanted—first by expressionism (Romanticism) and then by objectivism (Formalism and the New Criticism)—primarily as a reflex against Romanticism's propensities toward "psychologistic and biographical criticism."[41]

Objective theories, by contrast, approach the text as an object "solid and material as an urn or icon."[42] "Critics read, reread, and reify the text as a complete mental 'object' whose textual features, including plot, theme, motif, character, point of view, juxtaposition, ambiguity, etc., can be analyzed and described."[43] They may, for example, read about Yahweh's abandonment of the Temple in Jerusalem (Ezekiel 11) with God's return to a new temple (Ezekiel 43) in mind. Or they may read Ezekiel's accusations against personified Jerusalem in chap. 16 with those found in chap. 23 in mind. But first-time, sequential readers encounter texts without benefit of the "big picture." Only in retrospect can they reconsider the significance of an earlier text in the light of later ones.

---

40. Darr, " 'Glorified in the Presence of Kings,' " 18, citing and discussing M. H. Abrams, *The Mirror and the Lamp: Romantic Theory and the Critical Tradition* (New York: Oxford University Press, 1953) 6.

41. Ibid., 23.

42. T. Eagleton, *Literary Theory: An Introduction* (Minneapolis: University of Minnesota Press, 1983) 47.

43. K. P. Darr, *Isaiah's Vision and the Family of God* (Louisville: Westminster John Knox, 1994) 25-26.

Like Darr, I follow critics like W. Iser and W. Booth, who focus upon "the dynamic interaction between text and reader in the temporal, conventional process of reading."[44] Admittedly, Iser's approach includes an inevitable indeterminacy: "By bringing in the reader as co-creator of the work's meaning, Iser has left himself open to . . . charges of indeterminacy and relativism. . . . Will not each individual reading of a text be different? Are some readings better than others? If so, what criteria are used to make these sorts of judgments?"[45] Daunting though these questions are, they are better faced head-on than ignored, as if readers played no role in determining a text's meaning. Hence, Darr concludes that "responsibility for maintaining a delicate balance between text and reader in the dialectical production of literary meaning lies with the critic; at this point artistry enters the interpretive enterprise":

> We envision a dialectic in which the text guides, prefigures, and attempts to persuade a reader to choose a particular path or adopt a certain world-view. At the same time, the reader is only using these textual promptings as starting points for filling in the gaps left by the text . . . and anticipating what is to come as the reading progresses. Texts have a certain determinateness, but the meanings derived from these texts are qualified by the receptivity and creativity of the individual reader in an interpretive community.[46]

Focusing upon text, reader, and the reading process does not rule out appeals to other elements in the interpretive process. As noted, Darr's eclectic method admits those social, historical, and literary contexts pertaining when more or less completed biblical books were first read. It remains pragmatic, however, because of the ways in which these "extrinsic" elements are utilized: "In essence, author and historical context are brought into the process of interpretation through the portals of text and reader, respectively."[47]

"Optical Lenses" and the Critic's Task. Critics select, order, and balance elements that shape interpretation; and their choices are not, protestations notwithstanding, utterly disinterested. To the contrary, Darr writes, "what the critic writes is no less rhetorical than the text itself, for critics actively advance one reading over alternatives":[48]

> The critic is a creative re-reader whose selections specify and limit what is to be perceived and how "best" it is to be understood by others. . . . by reconstructing a particular social-historical setting, identifying specific literary influences, and accentuating selected textual phenomena (and ignoring others), the critic attempts to persuade others to accept his or her interpretation.[49]

44. Darr, " 'Glorified in the Presence of Kings,' " 38. See also W. Iser, *The Act of Reading: A Theory of Aesthetic Response* (Baltimore: Johns Hopkins University Press, 1978); W. Iser, "The Reading Process: A Phenomenological Approach," *New Literary History* 3 (1972) 279-99; and W. C. Booth, *The Rhetoric of Fiction,* 2nd ed. (Chicago: University of Chicago Press, 1983).
45. Darr, " 'Glorified in the Presence of Kings,' " 30.
46. Ibid., 38-39.
47. Ibid., 19.
48. Ibid., 55.
49. Ibid., 56-57.

One need only to compare the commentaries by Zimmerli and Greenberg to see that competent critics can construe texts in widely divergent ways.

Darr adopts Booth's "optical lens" imagery to describe how critics negotiate various interpretive options. "Our choices of a given inquiry work like our choices of optical instruments, each camera or microscope or telescope uncovering what other instruments conceal and obscuring what other instruments bring into focus."[50] Darr's "optical instrument" requires the manipulation of four lenses: wide-angle, editorial, objective, and reading.[51] The wide-angle lens is located in the eye of the critic, and its field of vision is the broadest of the four because it includes all of the information (historical, cultural, social, literary, etc.) that critics bring to texts.

The editorial lens, Darr's second optical instrument, examines a smaller field, but at greater depth. It focuses upon a particular text; and through it, modern scholars can discern information unavailable to ancient readers—e.g., signs of multiple authorship and redactional layers.

Reading a literary work through the objective lens, critics can focus upon the entire text within the same field. As noted above, first-time sequential readers do not have access to this lens. But critics can read and reread a literary work until it becomes, in effect, a "complete mental object" whose recurring features assume their places within the larger design. "Through this lens," Darr writes, the critic "scans the entire work (in any sequence—end to beginning, beginning to end, or randomly) in an effort to compare the part to the whole."[52]

Finally, critics shape and position the reading lens. Although not always acknowledged as such, "the reader" is an interpretive construct:

> The reader is not a given (e.g., an innate property of the text), but rather, is implicitly or explicitly construed by the critic. Such a construal is inevitably based, at least in part, on the critic's own reading experience. Every audience-oriented approach is founded upon preconceived notions of (1) the nature of the reading process (in general, and with regard to the specific work in question), and (2) the identity (competence, learning, knowledge of literary and cultural codes) of the reader.[53]

Of course, critics inevitably create readers (at least to some degree) in their own image. Nevertheless, critic and reader are not simply the same. The modern critic has access to repositories of knowledge (e.g., critical methodologies) the ancient reader does not possess; and the ancient reader, native to the culture whence the book arose, has access to knowledge (historical, cultural, social, etc.) unavailable to modern scholars.

Identifying the Reader. The initial task is to construct a "text-specific" reader who possesses the knowledge necessary to interpret the book of Ezekiel competently.

---

50. Booth, *The Rhetoric of Fiction,* 405.
51. Darr, " 'Glorified in the Presence of Kings,' " 57.
52. Ibid., 60.
53. Ibid., 61.

My reader is part of the second generation of Judeans living in Babylonia. Although he does not reside in Jerusalem, he has learned from Israel's cognoscenti-in-exile about life there. Culturally literate and fully at home within his diaspora community, he knows—or at least thinks he knows—facts (historical, political, geographical, religious, ethnic) and conventions (social, cultural, literary, etc.) related to Israel and its world. Far better than those Judeans who remained in their homeland, he knows the sophisticated culture of a major Mesopotamian empire. Though this is his first reading of the Ezekiel scroll, he is familiar with other of Israel's existing religious texts. He also knows the literary "classics" of his larger culture. Finally, he enjoys the opportunity, access, expertise, and time to read and interpret the unfolding Ezekiel scroll.

As noted above, my reader reads the book of Ezekiel in order to understand why, from the perspective of this authentic prophet who proclaims God's own words, Jerusalem was destroyed, Judah collapsed, and part of the population was deported to Babylonia, where he now resides. He also reads to discover what the future of Yahweh's people, and their enemies, will be.

Aspects of the Reading Process. Iser describes the dynamic process of reading: "We look forward, we look back, we decide, we change our decisions, we form expectations, we are shocked by their nonfulfillment, we question, we muse, we accept, we reject."[54] From this quotation, Darr identifies four complementary, ongoing aspects of reading: anticipation and retrospection; consistency building; investment and identification; and defamiliarization.[55] I shall discuss each briefly.

As sequential readers progress through a text, they continually reassess earlier expectations and judgments as new insights and data emerge. "In the dialectic of reading," Darr states, "each word, sentence, or other textual unit both illuminates and is illumined by what precedes it." The further one reads, the more complex the process of anticipation and retrospection becomes.[56] This is especially true when one seeks to construe so long and complex a text as the book of Ezekiel.

Related to this first aspect is the reader's tendency toward consistency building: "By correlating discrete elements of the text . . . and adding extra-textual information when necessary, the audience [reader] is able to image patterns . . . which cover textual gaps, help to resolve tensions, and clarify ambiguities."[57] Again, consistency building is a more complex process when a lengthy and eclectic piece of prophetic literature is at issue. Nevertheless, certain textual features (e.g., chronologically arranged oracles, the Ezekielian tendency to introduce topics briefly, only to return to them at greater length later in the scroll) encourage readers to construe texts on the basis of preceding chapters and verses.

54. Iser, "The Reading Process," 293.
55. Darr, *On Character Building*, 29.
56. Darr, " 'Glorified in the Presence of Kings': A Literary-Critical Study of Herod the Tetrarch in Luke-Acts" (Ph.D. diss., Vanderbilt University, Nashville, 1987) 64.
57. Ibid., 65.

The third aspect, "investment and identification," refers to the varying distance between the reader and the text. "Consciously or unconsciously," Darr observes, "the reader oscillates between a full-scale involvement in the [world of the text] and a more detached observation of it."[58]

How are Ezekiel's late exilic readers encouraged to accept his explanation of the tragic events of Israel's past and of Yahweh's role in those events, to assume responsibility for their own actions and those of their community, to remain faithful to God, and to live in anticipation of restoration to their homeland? Here, the focus shifts from the reader to the text itself: "The *text* provides a series of stimuli which elicit and guide audience responses. In other words, it is a rhetorical framework, designed strategically to foster a sequence of mental images and cognitive acts by the reader. The text also controls point of view, a vital element in the shaping of values"[59] Moreover, text and reader share an extratext—that is, common ground that facilitates communication: "The first-time reader must bring to a text a set of expectations which provide a context for processing it. Such a meeting point between reader and text is provided by the extra-text, the repertoire of shared conventions and canonical works that exists in any literate society."[60] The literature of the ancient Near East suggests that audiences prized established literary conventions. Yet innovation also had its place. What Iser calls "defamiliarization"— setting the well-known in unfamiliar terrain—could force readers to perceive traditional elements in new ways.[61] One need only think of Ezekiel's radically innovative account of Israel's exodus and wilderness experiences in chap. 20 to recognize the rhetorical power of defamiliarization.

CONCLUSION

The book of Ezekiel enriches our canon of Scripture with its architectural majesty, sophisticated and complex theology, and literary brilliance. During a critical period in Israel's history, Ezekiel sought to teach his community about human responsibility and divine response, to convince his fellow exiles of the unparalleled power of their God, and to discern their future as the people of Yahweh. I can only respect his refusal to abandon faith in God in the midst of crippling tragedy.

The format of *The New Interpreter's Bible* commentary series affords its readers the opportunity not only to study the brilliant and complex book of Ezekiel, but also to reflect upon its significance within contemporary contexts. In so doing, readers may find parts of the book of Ezekiel difficult to swallow. In this Introduction, I have identified certain Ezekielian presuppositions and beliefs that, once recognized and understood, may ameliorate readers' discomfort somewhat. But beyond the acquisition of historical

58. Ibid.
59. John A. Darr, *On Character Building: The Reader and the Rhetoric of Characterization in Luke-Acts,* Literary Currents in Biblical Interpretation, ed. D. N. Fewell and D. M. Gunn (Louisville: Westminster/John Knox, 1992) 32.
60. Darr, " 'Glorified in the Presence of Kings,' " 67.
61. Iser, *The Act of Reading,* 69.

insight lies the responsibility to debate the issues the book of Ezekiel raises. If, in the course of such debates, readers challenge aspects of the Ezekielian tradition, they are not at odds with the priest-prophet of old. To the contrary, they are in a very real sense Ezekiel's true disciples.

BIBLIOGRAPHY

Commentaries:

Blenkinsopp, Joseph. *Ezekiel.* IBC. Louisville: John Knox, 1990. A readable commentary designed especially to assist pastors in preaching from the book of Ezekiel.

Block, Daniel I. *The Book of Ezekiel: Chapters 1–24.* NICOT. Grand Rapids: Eerdmans, 1997; and *The Book of Ezekiel: Chapters 25–48,* NICOT. Grand Rapids: Eerdmans, 1998. An exceptionally detailed and thorough commentary written by an evangelical scholar who is admirably conversant with the histories and literatures of ancient Israel and its Near Eastern neighbors.

Eichrodt, Walther. *Ezekiel.* Translated by Cosslett Quin. OTL. Philadelphia: Westminster, 1970. A sometimes helpful interpretation of Ezekiel and his book that too often dismisses material which the author judges to be later additions to Ezekiel's oracles.

Greenberg, Moshe. *Ezekiel 1–20.* AB 22. Garden City, N.Y.: Doubleday, 1983; *Ezekiel 21–37.* AB 22A. Garden City, N.Y.: Doubleday, 1997. Two excellent volumes in what will be a three-volume commentary on the book of Ezekiel. Greenberg's "holistic" approach to the text pays enormous dividends for serious students of Ezekiel. In discussing each textual segment, he moves from "Comment" (on grammatical and lexicographical issues) to "Structure and Themes."

Zimmerli, Walther. *Ezekiel 1: A Commentary on the Book of the Prophet Ezekiel, Chapters 1–24.* Translated by R. E. Clements. Hermeneia. Philadelphia: Fortress, 1979; *Ezekiel 2: A Commentary on the Book of the Prophet Ezekiel, Chapters 25–48.* Translated by J. D. Martin. Hermeneia. Philadelphia: Fortress, 1983. A massive commentary by a leading Ezekiel scholar of the twentieth century. For each pericope, Zimmerli's undertakes a five-stage analysis consisting of Text, Form, Setting, Interpretation, and Aim. He seeks especially to distinguish between Ezekiel's original oracles and subsequent expansions of them, and to recover the process by which the book attained its final form.

Books and Collections of Essays:

Darr, John A. " 'Glorified in the Presence of Kings': A Literary-Critical Study of Herod the Tetrarch in Luke-Acts" (Ph.D. diss., Vanderbilt University, Nashville, 1987). Published as *Herod the Fox: Audience Criticism and Lukan Characterization.* JSNTSUP 163. Sheffield: Sheffield Academic, 1998. Also *On Character Building: The Reader and the Rhetoric of Characterization in Luke-Acts.* Literary Currents in Biblical Interpretation. Edited by D. N. Fewell and D. M. Gunn. Louisville: Westminster/John Knox, 1992. Descriptions of the reader-oriented methodology adopted for use in this commentary.

Darr, Katheryn Pfisterer. "Ezekiel." In *The Women's Bible Commentary.* Expanded Edition with Apocrypha. Edited by Carol A. Newsom and Sharon H. Ringe. Louisville: Westminster John Knox, 1998. Brief treatments of passages within the book of Ezekiel dealing with, or of special interest for, women readers.

Davis, Ellen F. *Swallowing the Scroll: Textuality and the Dynamics of Discourse in Ezekiel's Prophecy.* Bible and Literature 21. Sheffield: Almond, 1989. An investigation of Ezekiel's oracles as literary compositions influenced by patterns of thought shaped by reading and writing.

Galambush, Julie. *Jerusalem in the Book of Ezekiel: The City as Yahweh's Wife.* SBLDS 130. Atlanta: Scholars Press, 1992. Demonstrates the rewards of patiently probing the metaphorical personification of Jerusalem as a woman whose "sexual impurity" pollutes Yahweh's temple.

Hals, Ronald M. *Ezekiel.* FOTL 19. Grand Rapids: Eerdmans, 1989. Exhaustive form-critical analyses of Ezekiel's oracles prefaced by brief discussions of textual problems and followed by discussions of a given passage's genre, setting, and intention.

Joyce, Paul. *Divine Initiative and Human Response in Ezekiel.* JSPTSup 51. Sheffield: JSOT, 1989. Insightful discussions of important issues in contemporary Ezekielian scholarship.

Klein, Ralph W. *Ezekiel: The Prophet and His Message.* Studies on Personalities of the Old Testament. Columbia: University of South Carolina Press, 1988. A succinct, straightforward, and very readable introduction to Ezekiel and his book.

Lust, J., ed. *Ezekiel and His Book: Textual and Literary Criticism and Their Interrelation.* BETL 74. Leuven: Leuven University Press, 1986. A collection of essays by an international group of scholars under three rubrics: "Textual Criticism and Its Relation with Literary Criticism"; "Literary Criticism, Its Methods and Its Relation to Other Approaches"; and "The Message of the Book and Its Relation with Other Biblical and Non-Biblical Literature."

Odell, Margaret S., and John T. Strong, eds. *The Book of Ezekiel: Theological and Anthropological Perspectives.* SBLSymS 9. Atlanta: SBL, 2000. Essays growing out of the work of the SBL seminar, "Theological Perspectives on the Book of Ezekiel." Its essays address two themes: (1) the absence of God; and (2) anthropology in the book of Ezekiel.

Renz, Thomas. *The Rhetorical Function of the Book of Ezekiel.* VTSup 76. Leiden: Brill, 1999. An insightful and persuasive identification of rhetorical strategies by which the book of Ezekiel seeks to persuade its late exilic readers to accept the prophet's explanation of why Yahweh punished the people of Judah and to anticipate the fulfillment of Ezekiel's oracles of restoration.

Stevenson, Kalinda Rose. *The Vision of Transformation: The Territorial Rhetoric of Ezekiel 40–48.* SBLDS 154. Atlanta: Scholars Press, 1996. An extremely illuminating analysis of Ezekiel's fourth and final vision report from the perspective of human geography.

OUTLINE OF THE BOOK OF EZEKIEL

I. Ezekiel 1:1–3:15, Ezekiel's Inaugural Vision and Commission

    A. 1:1-3, Superscription

    B. 1:4-28, The Appearance of Yahweh's Glory

    C. 2:1–3:15, The Commission

        2:1-2, Introduction to the Commissioning
        2:3-5, The First Commissioning Speech
        2:6-7, The Commissioning Continues
        2:8–3:3, The Act of Ordination
        3:4-9, Tough Audience, Tougher Prophet
        3:10-11, Go, Speak to the Exiles
        3:12-15, Conclusion

EZEKIEL 1:1–3:15

EZEKIEL'S INAUGURAL VISION AND COMMISSION

OVERVIEW

In Ezek 1:1–3:15, a dislocated priest sees in a vision the "glory of the LORD" coming to him through the skies over Babylonia. What brought him to the Chebar Canal that day in 593 BCE, when suddenly the heavens were opened and he perceived in storm cloud and blazing light the enthroned majesty of Israel's God? Had he, as Greenberg speculates, been cast out by an exilic community that preferred the comforting words of optimistic prophets?[62] Was he beside water because, bound as he was to foreign soil, it set the best available scene for prayer (Psalm 137)? Or was he seeking some revelation that might, in

62. Moshe Greenberg, *Ezekiel 1–20,* AB 22 (Garden City, N.Y.: Doubleday, 1983) 41.

the midst of desolate circumstances, illumine Yahweh's dealings with Israel?

Ezekiel's glimpse of God—an encounter remarkable for its wealth of detail, its reverential refusal to disclose too much, and its striking juxtapositions of tradition and innovation—literally "lays him out." A fortifying spirit sets him back on his feet, even as Yahweh, the unspecified speaker, orders him to the prophet's task, demands his unqualified obedience, warns that he must work a tough crowd, feeds him his script, armors him for a battle of wills, and then "takes off" with a roar of wings and wheels, leaving the newly commissioned prophet whose belly bulges with divine words sitting, stunned, among his fellow captives.

EZEKIEL 1:1-3, SUPERSCRIPTION

NIV

1 In the[a] thirtieth year, in the fourth month on the fifth day, while I was among the exiles by the Kebar River, the heavens were opened and I saw visions of God.

[2]On the fifth of the month—it was the fifth year of the exile of King Jehoiachin— [3]the word of the LORD came to Ezekiel the priest, the son of Buzi,[b] by the Kebar River in the land of the Babylonians.[c] There the hand of the LORD was upon him.

a1 Or ⌊my⌋   b3 Or *Ezekiel son of Buzi the priest*
c3 Or *Chaldeans*

NRSV

1 In the thirtieth year, in the fourth month, on the fifth day of the month, as I was among the exiles by the river Chebar, the heavens were opened, and I saw visions of God. [2]On the fifth day of the month (it was the fifth year of the exile of King Jehoiachin), [3]the word of the LORD came to the priest Ezekiel son of Buzi, in the land of the Chaldeans by the river Chebar; and the hand of the LORD was on him there.

COMMENTARY

Ezekiel 1:1-3 is not, strictly speaking, a superscription. By definition, superscriptions are statements prefixed to written compositions yet "standing outside the body of the work itself."[63] They provide information about the works they precede (e.g., presumed authorship, date, location, etc.), but they are not linked grammatically to what follows. Ezekiel 1:1, by contrast, is presented in the first person (by an as yet unidentified "I") and introduces the divine vision (מראות אלהים *mar'ôt 'ĕlōhîm*) and call to prophesy described in 1:4–3:15. It is, therefore, an integral part of the following autobiographical report. (The double date and precise location in 1:1-3 pertain only to Ezekiel's inaugural vision and call to prophesy, 1:1–3:15.)

The distinction between introduction and superscription notwithstanding, Ezek 1:1-3 conveys data common to the latter genre. Verse 1 begins with a date, followed by the author's location (by the Chebar Canal; see Introduction). That date, the fifth day of the fourth month (Tammuz = June-July) of the thirtieth year, immediately raises a question: The thirtieth year of what? Verse 2, probably a subsequent addition intended to shed light on this conundrum, correlates the date in v. 1 to a specific event; the thirtieth year was also the fifth year of the exile of Judah's King Jehoiachin (i.e., 593 BCE; subsequent dates in the book of Ezekiel also are based on the year of Jehoiachin's deportation, 597 BCE; see the Introduction). But the enigma persists and, not surprisingly, has provoked a variety of explanations. The Targumic tradition construed the date to mean that thirty years had passed since the discovery of a scroll in the Jerusalem Temple during King Josiah's reign (621 BCE), which had prompted religio-political reforms in Judah (according to 2 Kings 22; cf. 2 Chronicles 34).[64] But this interpretation has little to commend it, since Josiah's reform does not mark the beginning of a calendrical counting system elsewhere in the Hebrew Bible, including the book of Ezekiel.

Other ancient and modern solutions (e.g., that the thirtieth year designates the date of the scroll's completion or of a Jubilee year), are speculative as well. Hence, readers of vv. 1-2 anticipate the filling of at least three textual gaps: the significance of the thirtieth year,[65] the identity of the first-person speaker, and the content of this divine vision.

With v. 3, the autobiographical style of v. 1 shifts to third person. For this reason, among others, many critics suggest that at least v. 3*a* constitutes a later addition to v. 1 (and its partial elucidation in v. 2). An editor, wishing not to displace vv. 1-2, has here inserted further information of a type appearing in superscriptions to most other prophetic collections, and in a literary style similar to Hag 1:1 and Zech 1:1. The MT of v. 3*a* asserts that the word of Yahweh came ("was") to "Ezekiel, the son of Buzi, the priest,"[66] thereby establishing both the speaker's identity and the divine origin (authority) of what follows. It also repeats Ezekiel's location by the Chebar Canal and augments it with the phrase "in the land of the Chaldeans" (see Introduction).

In addition to identifying the first-person voice of v. 1, v. 3—with its appositional phrase, "the priest"—might be understood by readers to shed light on the mysterious "thirtieth year." According to Num 4:3, 23, 30, Levite males began their service at the tent of meeting at thirty years of age (and retired at age fifty). In the light of Ezekiel's priestly lineage, readers might reason that Ezekiel's first divine vision occurred in his thirtieth year, when he would have been ordained a priest had he remained in Jerusalem. Further into the text, they will discover that Ezekiel has witnessed "the appearance of the likeness of the glory of the LORD" (1:28). According to Lev 9:6, Yahweh's glory appeared at the climax of the consecration of Aaron (and presumably of subsequent high priests

---

63. Gene M. Tucker, "Prophetic Superscriptions and the Growth of a Canon," in *Canon and Authority,* ed. George W. Coats and Burke O. Long (Philadelphia: Fortress, 1977) 58.

64. Targums are Aramaic translations and interpretations of OT texts. They were created during the early centuries of the common era for use in synagogues as an aid to Aramaic-speaking Jews.

65. Ellen F. Davis, *Swallowing the Scroll: Textuality and the Dynamics of Discourse in Ezekiel's Prophecy,* JSOTSup 78 (Sheffield: Almond, 1989) 77-81, notes that the reference to the thirtieth year constitutes a "restricted code." Ezekiel expects his "in group" audience to know what the thirtieth year signifies without being told.

66. Both the NRSV and the NIV associate "the priest" with Ezekiel. In fact, the appositional phrase could refer to Buzi, his father. Yet the strong possibility that the son shared his father's vocation, coupled with the book's priestly caste, supports the view that Ezekiel was himself a priest. See the Introduction.

of Israel). Further still, they will learn that at the conclusion of his vision, Ezekiel rejoined the exiles at Tel-Abib and sat stunned among them "for seven days" (3:15b). Exodus 29:35 and Lev 8:33, 35; 9:1 state that the ordination of Aaron and his sons lasted seven days.[67]

The text of 1:1 does not read "in *his* thirtieth year" (or the like). For that reason, the conjecture that it originally referred to Ezekiel's age remains just that.[68] Here, I am simply suggesting that ancient readers of the scroll, conversant with regulations and details regarding the ordination and service of priests, might interpret the thirtieth year of v. 1 (and subsequent textual "clues") in the light of them.[69]

The notice that "the hand of Yahweh" was upon Ezekiel (v. 3b) will appear also in accounts of his other three great visions (8:1; 37:1; 40:1; see also 3:14, where the phrase appears at the end of a visionary account; 3:22, which introduces yet another vision of Yahweh's glory; and 33:21, where Yahweh's hand is associated with the end of Ezekiel's speechlessness). This and related phrases are found elsewhere in the Hebrew Bible:[70]

Yahweh's hand upon Elijah empowers him to run before Ahab's chariot from Carmel to Jezreel (1 Kgs 18:46). According to 2 Kgs 3:15-20, the hand of the Lord comes upon Elisha, who, assisted by trance-inducing music, utters an oracle. In Isa 8:11 and Jer 15:17, the phrase expresses the prophets' experience of being under "divine compulsion," but does not introduce a prophecy delivered in a trance.[71] On the basis of extra-biblical and biblical evidence, Roberts argues that the phrase originally referred to the "disastrous manifestation of the supernatural power," especially as evinced in illness. In its secondary meaning within Israel's prophetic narratives and literature, "the hand of Yahweh" formula was applied to the prophetic phenomenon because that phenomenon remarkably resembled symptoms of human malady conventionally designated by it.[72] The early meaning of a phrase may or may not determine its later semantic development. Does the reader, confronted by a notice of Yahweh's hand upon Ezekiel, conclude that he exhibited behavior conventionally associated with trance or seizure?[73] Or does one simply take the phrase to indicate the prophet's vivid awareness that his experience was abnormal?[74] The meaning of the text remains ambiguous. (See Reflections at 3:12-15.)

---

67. Ezekiel's last divine vision (chaps. 40–48) is dated twenty years later (40:1)—according to this interpretive scheme, Ezekiel's retirement (fiftieth) year.

68. So also W. Eichrodt, *Ezekiel,* OTL (Philadelphia: Westminster, 1970) 52.

69. Miller, by contrast, argues that the thirtieth year was from the beginning a reference to Ezekiel's age. See James E. Miler, "The Thirtieth Year of Ezekiel 1:1," *RB* 99 (1992) 499-503.

70. Zimmerli believes that the phrase is a "genuinely Israelite formulation" with origins in Israel's exodus tradition. See Walther Zimmerli, *Ezekiel 1: A Commentary on the Book of the Prophet Ezekiel, Chapters 1–24,* trans. R. E. Clements, Hermeneia (Philadelphia: Fortress, 1979) 117-18.

71. Greenberg, *Ezekiel 1–20,* 42.

72. J. J. M. Roberts, "The Hand of Yahweh," *VT* 21 (1971) 249-50.

73. For Greenberg, "susceptibility to seizure is characteristic of Ezekiel, distinguishing him from other literary prophets who never employ this expression in describing the onset of their prophecy" (Greenberg, *Ezekiel 1–20,* 42).

74. So Keith W. Carley, *The Book of the Prophet Ezekiel,* CBC (London: Cambridge University Press, 1974) 12, 25.

EZEKIEL 1:4-28, THE APPEARANCE OF YAHWEH'S GLORY

NIV	NRSV
[4]I looked, and I saw a windstorm coming out of the north—an immense cloud with flashing lightning and surrounded by brilliant light. The center of the fire looked like glowing metal, [5]and in the fire was what looked like four living creatures. In appearance their form was that of a man, [6]but each of them had four faces and four wings.	4As I looked, a stormy wind came out of the north: a great cloud with brightness around it and fire flashing forth continually, and in the middle of the fire, something like gleaming amber. [5]In the middle of it was something like four living creatures. This was their appearance: they were of human form. [6]Each had four faces, and each of

NIV

[7]Their legs were straight; their feet were like those of a calf and gleamed like burnished bronze. [8]Under their wings on their four sides they had the hands of a man. All four of them had faces and wings, [9]and their wings touched one another. Each one went straight ahead; they did not turn as they moved.

[10]Their faces looked like this: Each of the four had the face of a man, and on the right side each had the face of a lion, and on the left the face of an ox; each also had the face of an eagle. [11]Such were their faces. Their wings were spread out upward; each had two wings, one touching the wing of another creature on either side, and two wings covering its body. [12]Each one went straight ahead. Wherever the spirit would go, they would go, without turning as they went. [13]The appearance of the living creatures was like burning coals of fire or like torches. Fire moved back and forth among the creatures; it was bright, and lightning flashed out of it. [14]The creatures sped back and forth like flashes of lightning.

[15]As I looked at the living creatures, I saw a wheel on the ground beside each creature with its four faces. [16]This was the appearance and structure of the wheels: They sparkled like chrysolite, and all four looked alike. Each appeared to be made like a wheel intersecting a wheel. [17]As they moved, they would go in any one of the four directions the creatures faced; the wheels did not turn about[a] as the creatures went. [18]Their rims were high and awesome, and all four rims were full of eyes all around.

[19]When the living creatures moved, the wheels beside them moved; and when the living creatures rose from the ground, the wheels also rose. [20]Wherever the spirit would go, they would go, and the wheels would rise along with them, because the spirit of the living creatures was in the wheels. [21]When the creatures moved, they also moved; when the creatures stood still, they also stood still; and when the creatures rose from the ground, the wheels rose along with them, because the spirit of the living creatures was in the wheels.

[22]Spread out above the heads of the living

[a]17 Or aside

NRSV

them had four wings. [7]Their legs were straight, and the soles of their feet were like the sole of a calf's foot; and they sparkled like burnished bronze. [8]Under their wings on their four sides they had human hands. And the four had their faces and their wings thus: [9]their wings touched one another; each of them moved straight ahead, without turning as they moved. [10]As for the appearance of their faces: the four had the face of a human being, the face of a lion on the right side, the face of an ox on the left side, and the face of an eagle; [11]such were their faces. Their wings were spread out above; each creature had two wings, each of which touched the wing of another, while two covered their bodies. [12]Each moved straight ahead; wherever the spirit would go, they went, without turning as they went. [13]In the middle of[a] the living creatures there was something that looked like burning coals of fire, like torches moving to and fro among the living creatures; the fire was bright, and lightning issued from the fire. [14]The living creatures darted to and fro, like a flash of lightning.

[15]As I looked at the living creatures, I saw a wheel on the earth beside the living creatures, one for each of the four of them.[b] [16]As for the appearance of the wheels and their construction: their appearance was like the gleaming of beryl; and the four had the same form, their construction being something like a wheel within a wheel. [17]When they moved, they moved in any of the four directions without veering as they moved. [18]Their rims were tall and awesome, for the rims of all four were full of eyes all around. [19]When the living creatures moved, the wheels moved beside them; and when the living creatures rose from the earth, the wheels rose. [20]Wherever the spirit would go, they went, and the wheels rose along with them; for the spirit of the living creatures was in the wheels. [21]When they moved, the others moved; when they stopped, the others stopped; and when they rose from the earth, the wheels rose along with them; for the spirit of the living creatures was in the wheels.

[22]Over the heads of the living creatures there was something like a dome, shining like crystal,[c]

[a]Gk OL: Heb And the appearance of   [b]Heb of their faces   [c]Gk: Heb like the awesome crystal

creatures was what looked like an expanse, sparkling like ice, and awesome. ²³Under the expanse their wings were stretched out one toward the other, and each had two wings covering its body. ²⁴When the creatures moved, I heard the sound of their wings, like the roar of rushing waters, like the voice of the Almighty,ᵃ like the tumult of an army. When they stood still, they lowered their wings.

²⁵Then there came a voice from above the expanse over their heads as they stood with lowered wings. ²⁶Above the expanse over their heads was what looked like a throne of sapphire,ᵇ and high above on the throne was a figure like that of a man. ²⁷I saw that from what appeared to be his waist up he looked like glowing metal, as if full of fire, and that from there down he looked like fire; and brilliant light surrounded him. ²⁸Like the appearance of a rainbow in the clouds on a rainy day, so was the radiance around him.

This was the appearance of the likeness of the glory of the LORD. When I saw it, I fell facedown, and I heard the voice of one speaking.

ᵃ24 Hebrew *Shaddai*   ᵇ26 Or *lapis lazuli*

spread out above their heads. ²³Under the dome their wings were stretched out straight, one toward another; and each of the creatures had two wings covering its body. ²⁴When they moved, I heard the sound of their wings like the sound of mighty waters, like the thunder of the Almighty,ᵃ a sound of tumult like the sound of an army; when they stopped, they let down their wings. ²⁵And there came a voice from above the dome over their heads; when they stopped, they let down their wings.

26And above the dome over their heads there was something like a throne, in appearance like sapphire;ᵇ and seated above the likeness of a throne was something that seemed like a human form. ²⁷Upward from what appeared like the loins I saw something like gleaming amber, something that looked like fire enclosed all around; and downward from what looked like the loins I saw something that looked like fire, and there was a splendor all around. ²⁸Like the bow in a cloud on a rainy day, such was the appearance of the splendor all around. This was the appearance of the likeness of the glory of the LORD.

When I saw it, I fell on my face, and I heard the voice of someone speaking.

ᵃTraditional rendering of Heb *Shaddai*   ᵇOr *lapis lazuli*

COMMENTARY

The account of Ezekiel's divine vision in this unit ranks as one of the most complex and difficult passages in the entire book. At once detailed and veiled, it appears as the first of Ezekiel's attempts to describe the visible manifestation of Yahweh's "glory." Owing to its placement in chap. 1, this vision functions as the reader's entrance to the world of Ezekiel (presumed author and text). The account can be divided into five sections: (1) appearance of the storm cloud from the north, v. 4; (2) portrayal of the four living creatures, vv. 5-14; (3) description of the wheels, vv. 15-21; (4) depiction of the enthroned figure, vv. 22-27; and (5) additional details, plus statements of recognition and response, with brief reference to the divine voice, v. 28.

For many critics, the canonical description of

Ezekiel's inaugural vision emerged from a long, complex process begun by the priest himself and subsequently taken up by members of his "school" (see Introduction), who supplemented his original, briefer account and whose own expansions became the basis for even later elaborations.[75] Greenberg, by contrast, defends the original literary unity of most of 1:4-28 and attributes it to Ezekiel.[76] His "holistic" approach (see Intro-

75. See especially Zimmerli, *Ezekiel 1,* 82-89, 101-6, 118-31, who presents his own (and ostensibly Ezekiel's original) "version" of chap. 1 without later additions.

76. Greenberg, *Ezekiel 1–20,* 42-59. In Greenberg's opinion, contemporary criteria for distinguishing between the priest's own words and "inauthentic" supplements "are simply *a prioris,* an array of unproved (and unprovable) modern assumptions and conventions that confirm themselves through the results obtained by forcing them on the text and altering, reducing, and reordering it accordingly." Ibid., 20.

duction) sheds considerable light on the text, including the rationale governing the order of presentation of its various elements, yet without proving that the chapter is the product of Ezekiel almost *in toto.*

I do not wish to preclude the possibility that Ezekiel 1 is the final product of more than one hand. To the contrary, when I examine the text through the editorial lens (see Introduction), precisely those textual features that have suggested the presence of secondary expansions come into focus. Shifting to the reading lens, however, my attention turns to the ways in which ancient readers actualized the Hebrew text. I focus especially upon interpreting the scroll sequentially and in its final form. The fact that the reader moves through the text verse by verse, constructing rather than presupposing the "big picture," bears considerably upon this construal of 1:4-28, since many of its details become clearer in the light of information supplied one or more verses later. As a result, the first-time, late exilic reader's encounter with Ezekiel's apparition is even more enigmatic than critics presuming knowledge of the entire chapter, and even of the whole book, recognize.

1:4. According to this verse, Ezekiel saw a divine vision when "the heavens were opened." His account of that vision resumes in v. 4 as the priest espies—sweeping in from the northern skies—a tempestuous windstorm (רוח סערה *rûaḥ sĕʿārâ*; the fem. sing. noun *sĕʿārâ* appears, e.g., in 2 Kgs 2:1; Job 38:1; 40:6; in each case, the NRSV translates "whirlwind")—"an immense cloud with flashing lightning[77] and surrounded by brilliant light." From the midst of this fiery effulgence, he perceives something like "glowing amber" (חשמל *ḥašmal*; this word appears only here, in 1:27, and in 8:2).[78]

The notice that Ezekiel's divine apparition approaches from "the north" (הצפון *haṣṣāpôn*) is both geographically specific and fraught with multiple levels of meaning. The noun frequently designates one of the four cardinal compass points (north). Yet even this mundane meaning could be ominous, for according to a number of prophetic texts, Yahweh brings enemies (e.g., Assyria, Babylonia) against Israel and Judah from the north (see Isa 14:31; 41:25*a*; Jer 1:14-15; 4:6; 6:1, 22). Mesopotamian troops traveled northwest along the Fertile Crescent on their way to Israel and Judah.

In certain phrases (e.g., 39:2) and especially as a proper noun, however, צפון (*ṣāpôn*) could bear mythological overtones. According to Canaanite myth, Zaphon, a mountain in northern Syria, was the site of the storm god Baal-Hadad's royal palace, the place whence he issued divine proclamations, and one locus of assembly and feasting by the deities.[79] Ancient Israel both adopted and adapted mythological associations with Mt. Zaphon. Psalm 89:12, perhaps one of the earliest biblical references to Zaphon, praises Yahweh as the creator of mounts Zaphon, Amanus, Hermon, and Tabor.[80] In Isaiah 14, the king of Babylon's arrogant pretentions include ascending to heaven, sitting enthroned on the heights of Zaphon, the "mount of assembly," and making himself like the highest god (Isa 14:13-14). Instead, he is brought down to Sheol—a lesson to all who presume to challenge Yahweh's sovereignty.

Elihu's speech in Job 37:21-24 depicts God's approach from Zaphon (NRSV and NIV, "out of the north").[81] No one can gaze at the sun in a clear sky (Job 37:21); yet God's appearance is brighter still:

> From Zaphon comes golden splendor;
>   around God is awesome majesty.
>
> (Job 37:22 KJV)

This passage shares features with Ezek 1:4.[82] Yet the lexical correspondence between the two texts is not so great as to prove the literary dependence of one upon the other. More likely, both authors drew from a common well of mythic ideas.

---

77. The Hebrew phrase סערה (*sĕʿārâ*; NRSV, "fire flashing forth continually") appears elsewhere only in Exod 9:24, a description of the hailstorm that, along with other plagues, afflicted the land of Egypt. There, as here, the phrase appears within a description of a fierce lightning storm.

78. Greenberg, *Ezekiel 1–20,* 43, and others cite Akkadian *elmešû,* an unknown type of precious stone, as a possible cognate. "The word must be taken as referring to a quasi-mythical precious stone of great brilliance and with a color which one tried to imitate with dyes." *The Assyrian Dictionary* (Chicago: University of Chicago Press, 1958) 4:108a.

79. H. Avalos, "Zaphon, Mount," in *The Anchor Bible Dictionary,* 6 vols. (New York: Doubleday, 1992) 6:1040-41.

80. Mitchell Dahood, S.J., *Psalms II:51-100,* AB 17 (Garden City, N.Y.: Doubleday, 1968) 308, 314.

81. See Marvin H. Pope, *Job,* AB 15 (Garden City, N.Y.: Doubleday, 1965) 286-87.

82. See Carol A. Newsom, "The Book of Job," in *The New Interpreter's Bible,* 12 vols. (Nashville: Abingdon, 1994) 4:591-92.

Jerusalem/Zion traditions were significantly influenced by the myths and imagery of Israel's cultural neighbors. For instance, in Ps 48:1, Zion is called Yahweh's "holy mountain," while v. 2 speaks of "Mount Zion in the far north." The latter phrase cannot be a literal reference to the city's locale. Rather, it "locates" Mt. Zion within the sphere of conceptions surrounding Mt. Zaphon, as well as other mountains of Canaanite and Mesopotamian myth. Isaiah 2:2-3 (see also Mic 4:1-2) anticipates a time when "the mountain of the LORD's house/ shall be established as the highest of the mountains" (NRSV) and the locus of Yahweh's divine instructions and decrees,[83] while Isa 25:6 presages a feast for all peoples upon "this mountain," Zion.

1:5-8a. In the midst of the effulgent cloud, Ezekiel discerns something like (דמות *dĕmût*) four living creatures whose appearance (מראיהן *mar'êhen*) is something like (*dĕmût*) a human form (v. 5). (The use of such qualifiers throughout the chapter serves not only to specify but also to conceal the details of what are supranormal entities.) Each creature has four faces and four wings (v. 6). The text will return to these features. Verses 7 and 8a, however, direct attention to the creatures' legs and feet, and then to their hands. Here, obscurities abound. Has each creature two or more legs or only one, and in what sense are they "straight"? Barrick speculates that the "redactionally augmented" creatures of Ezekiel's vision were winged quadrupeds whose limbs comported with conventional ancient Near Eastern iconography, such that their forelegs, viewed frontally, appeared stationary and "straight."[84] The number of hands is also vague; we cannot determine if each of the four creatures has only one pair or if a pair is ascribed to each of the beings' four sides.[85]

1:8b-9. These verses supply additional comments about the creatures' wings and movement. According to v. 9a, the upper wings of each being are joined at the tips to those on either side. The reader imagines, therefore, that the creatures form

a square. When v. 9b adds that each "moved straight ahead, without turning as they moved"— that is, regardless of their direction of motion—it presupposes information concerning a lead (human) face not supplied until the following verse.

1:10-12. According to v. 10, each of the creatures' four faces bears a different visage: human (in front), leonine (on the right side), bovine (on the left side), and aquiline (in back). Humans are God's crowning creation; lions, bulls, and eagles take pride of place among the animals.[86] Their description, Greenberg notes, "reflects the sequence of observation. The onlooker (on any side) was confronted by a human face . . . from what could be seen on the heads of the rest of the creatures, the onlooker inferred that in back of the human face confronting him was an eagle's face."[87] Hybrid creatures are well-attested in the iconography of the ancient Near East; we have no close analogue, however, for Ezekiel's four-faced beings. Verse 11 further elaborates upon each creature's four wings. The position of the outstretched upper pair agrees with the description in v. 9a; the other (lower) pair covers its body.

In the light of v. 10, the assertion that each being moves straight ahead (v. 12; recall v. 9b) makes better sense; regardless of their direction of travel, the human countenance of one of the creatures always faces forward. Verse 12b states that they move at the direction of הרוח (*hārûaḥ*, "breath," "wind," "spirit"; the same noun, without the definite article, appeared in v. 4). Greenberg's assertion that here the noun means not "wind" but "spirit"—a reference to the animating force that directs the creatures' movements and originates "*in him who sat enthroned above them*"—also presupposes information not yet accessible to the sequential reader.[88]

1:13-14. Verse 13 speaks of something resembling burning coals or torches "moving to and fro" within the space enclosed by the four beings. In 10:2, these coals will figure in Jerusalem's conflagration. In this context, neither their appearance nor their function is clear. Verse 14 does not appear in the LXX, and commentators, including

83. See Richard J. Clifford, *The Cosmic Mountain in Canaan and the Old Testament* (Cambridge, Mass.: Harvard University Press, 1972); Jon D. Levenson, *Theology of the Program of Restoration of Ezekiel 40–48*, HSM 10 (Missoula, Mont.: Scholars Press, 1976).

84. W. Boyd Barrick, "The Straight-Legged Cherubim of Ezekiel's Inaugural Vision (Ezekiel 1:7a)," *CBQ* 44 (1982) 543-50.

85. See Moshe Greenberg, *Ezekiel 1–20*, AB 22 (Garden City, N.Y.: Doubleday, 1983) 43-44; and Zimmerli, *Ezekiel 1*, 102-3.

86. On the symbolism of these four creatures, see L. Dürr, *Ezekiels Vision von der Erscheinung Gottes (Ez. c. 1 und 10) im Lichte der vorderasiatischen Altertumskunde* (Würzburg: Richter, 1917).

87. Greenberg, *Ezekiel 1–20*, 45.

88. Ibid., 45-46, italics added.

Greenberg, agree that it is a late elaboration upon the text. At odds with the description thus far, it depicts the creatures themselves as darting to and fro.

1:15-21. These verses describe four wheels located "on the earth" (below) and beside each of the four creatures.[89] Their presence suggests that flight is not the sole means of locomotion for Ezekiel's apparition, as yet only partially sketched (the word "throne," for example, has yet to appear). Many critics, Zimmerli among them, regard this entire section as a later elaboration on the original account—an option not considered by the ancient reader.[90]

As to their appearance (v. 16*a*), the wheels gleam like chrysolite (so LXX here and in Exod 28:20; see NIV; NRSV, "beryl"); further details (v. 16*b*) are obscure. When the MT likens the wheels' construction to "the wheel in the midst of the wheel" (v. 16*b*), the translators of both the NRSV and the NIV envision intersecting wheels—that is, mechanisms capable of moving in any of four directions without turning. Possibly, however, the text describes four discrete wheels, one beneath each creature and facing in the same direction as its lead (human) face. Hence, when the creatures moved forward, Zimmerli explains, the wheels did also; and, since the leading face guided the creatures, enabling movement in all four directions, the notion of a leading, guiding wheel was introduced.[91] Greenberg suggests either a disk with a protuberance surrounding its axle that looked like an inner wheel or a wheel with concentric rims.[92] The "eyes" studding their rims ("brows") round about are best understood as nails or other (decorative?) fittings. Zimmerli's observation that these eyes signal "the all-seeing power of the Rider of the throne-chariot"[93] again presupposes information not yet available to the sequential reader, who assembles the textual pieces of Ezekiel's initial vision as one assembles pieces of a jigsaw puzzle, but without the benefit of a picture on the top of the box.

In highly repetitious language, vv. 19-21 describe the perfectly synchronized movements of the creatures and their respective wheels, despite the absence of a mechanism linking one to the other. This phenomenon is twice explained by the assertion that *hārûaḥ* ("the breath," "wind," "spirit") of the living creature(s) was in the wheels. Here as at v. 12*b*, this animating agent remains something of a mystery. Does it designate the storm blast of v. 4, such that both creatures and conveyance are swept along at the will of the wind? Or, more likely, does it derive from a previously undescribed divine source?

1:22-28. With v. 22, the reader's attention is drawn from the bottom of Ezekiel's apparition to a dazzling expanse (רקיע *rāqîa'*, "firmament"; see Gen 1:6; NRSV, "dome") over the creatures' heads. Here the text first states that the beings are supporting and transporting something. But the glimpse, though tantalizing, is restricted and brief. Again Ezekiel's focus returns to the creatures' wings. Verse 23 repeats, albeit in different language, information already provided in vv. 9 and 11. Verse 24 employs three similes to communicate the sound of their wings in motion: It is like "the sound of mighty waters" (see Ps 93:3-4);[94] like "the voice of the Almighty" (שַׁדַּי *Šadday*), an ancient divine epithet (see Exod 6:3); like the din of an army (see Isa 17:12-13). When the creatures stop moving, their wings slacken. Many critics (e.g., Zimmerli, Eichrodt) delete v. 25, in part because the reference to a voice from above the expanse strikes them as premature at this point. Greenberg counters, however, that the voice is mentioned here precisely because it only becomes audible as the clamor described in v. 24 abates.[95]

Finally, Ezekiel's (and his reader's) line of vision rises above the expanse (vv. 26-27), and he sees something like a throne, its appearance like sapphire (or lapis lazuli). Above the throne sits—what? The language of v. 26*b* (and v. 27) is imprecise: "and seated above the likeness of a throne was something that seemed like a human form." Here, Blenkinsopp observes, the reader recalls the language of humanity's creation in Gen

---

89. The phrase "on the earth," coupled with the reference to four wheels, either suggests what the text does not state explicitly—that Ezekiel's contraption (for lack of a better word at this point) has landed—or conveys general information about its mobility.

90. Zimmerli, *Ezekiel 1,* 127-30.

91. Ibid., *Ezekiel 1,* 129.

92. Greenberg, *Ezekiel 1–20,* 47.

93. Zimmerli, *Ezekiel 1,* 129.

94. Regarding the phrase "mighty waters," see Greenberg, *Ezekiel 1–20,* 48. See also H. May, "Some Cosmic Connections of *Mayim Rabbim," JBL* 74 (1955) 9-21.

95. Greenberg, *Ezekiel 1–20,* 49.

1:26-27. In that context, humanity (אדם 'ādām) is created in the likeness (דמות dĕmût) of God. In the present passage, God appears in the likeness of humanity (דמות כמראה אדם dĕmût kĕmar'ēh 'ādām).[96] Above what has the appearance of loins, the priest sees something having the appearance of glowing amber, ḥašmal (see v. 4). The following, difficult circumstantial clause, which does not appear in the LXX, apparently states that the ḥašmal-like upper portion of the figure is encased in fire. From the loins down also, the form has the appearance of fire, and the entire shape is surrounded by radiance.[97]

That radiance is likened to a rainbow (v. 28), as the phrase "in a cloud on a rainy day" makes clear. The reference evokes thoughts of the sign that, after the Noachic deluge, symbolized God's primeval covenant with the earth's living creatures never again to destroy them by flood (Gen 9:12-17). Perhaps in this context, the appearance of the multicolored radiance surrounding the enthroned figure reassures readers that Yahweh's promise to sustain creation still stands, despite the threat of chaotic times. Yet one can only wonder upon what basis W. Eichrodt claims that its appearance qualifies the meaning of Ezekiel's vision, such that "the Almighty power, whose wonders unfold before the prophet's eyes, turns toward the nations, and *no thought of Israel is involved.*"[98]

Because the reader's processing of chapter 1 has proceeded apace with Ezekiel's suspense-building account, his "moment of recognition" coincides with the text's own apex. Said differently, the reader has assembled, each in turn, the textual "pieces" of Ezekiel's divine vision. By the time one arrives at v. 26, the picture reveals with remarkable detail those elements situated beneath the expanse first identified in v. 22. When those pieces bearing the (less distinct and detailed) image of what lies above the expanse (vv. 26-27a) finally are put in place, however, the reader at last grasps the "big picture": It "was the appearance of the likeness of the glory of the LORD!" (כבוד kĕbôd yhwh).[99]

As a verb, the Hebrew root כבד (kbd) literally means "to be heavy," "weighty," "burdensome," and figuratively, "to be honored."[100] A feminine noun from the same root, כבוד (kābôd) can refer to "wealth" (e.g., Gen 31:1), "honor" (including the honor due to Yahweh), "reputation" (see Job 19:9), and "glory."[101] Biblical traditions frequently associate the visible manifestation of Yahweh's "glory" with a cloud (e.g., Exod 16:10-12; 40:34; Num 16:42) and fire (e.g., Exod 24:17; Lev 9:23; 2 Chr 7:1). Its appearance signifies sanctification and blessing in some situations (e.g., Exod 29:43; Lev 9:23; Isa 40:5), but it could also presage punishment (e.g., Exod 16:7, 10-12; Num 16:42; 20:6).

Mettinger has shown that during the pre-exilic period, kābôd denoted a divine attribute (see, e.g., Pss 24:7-10; 29:3). In later priestly traditions, however, the noun "suffered" a "semantic condensation," such that it came to designate God per se. Ezekielian references to "glory" represent a transitional stage in this development. On the one hand, "we find indications of the original usage, inasmuch as kābôd has a broad denotation in certain cases and includes both God and his chariot throne (Ezek 1:28; 3:23; 8:4; 11:23; 43:2)."[102] On the other hand, the priest "conceives of the Glory of the LORD as both speaking and acting; for example, the kābôd speaks in Ezek 9:3-7; 43:6-11; 44:4-5. Further, the word is the subject of verbs of motion; and finally, there are passages where the context requires an implicit identification of the kābôd with God."[103] Being neither a source critic nor a tradition historian, the ancient reader would have regarded both usages as extremely long-lived and their relationship as supplementary, rather than contradictory (but see Excursus, "Extra-Textual Traditions and Ezekielian Innovations," 1118-21).

96. Joseph Blenkinsopp, *Ezekiel,* IBC (Louisville: John Knox, 1990) 22.

97. נגה (nōgah) appeared also in v. 4 to describe the brightness surrounding the cloud. For a description of what Greenberg terms the "intricate quasi-balance" of this verse, see Greenberg, *Ezekiel 1–20,* 50-51. His observations notwithstanding, the presence of the circumstantial clause in v. 27a has the effect of blurring the distinction between the upper (ḥašmal-like) and lower (fiery) halves of the figure's form. See Zimmerli, *Ezekiel 1,* 131.

98. Walther Eichrodt, *Ezekiel,* trans. Cosslett Quin, OTL (Philadelphia: Westminster, 1970) 58, italics added.

99. On the basis of 1:1-28, it is not possible to determine with certainty whether Ezekiel's statement refers to the entire apparition or only to the figure enthroned upon the expanse above the creatures' heads. Tryggve N. D. Mettinger, *Dethronement of Sabaoth: Studies in the Shem and Kabod Theologies,* ConBOT 18 (Lund: CWK Gleerup, 1982) 107, supports the former view.

100. F. Brown, S. R. Driver, and C. A. Biggs, *A Hebrew and English Lexicon of the Old Testament* (Oxford: Oxford University Press, 1907; repr. Peabody, Mass.: Hendrickson, 1979) 457.

101. Ibid., 458-59.

102. Mettinger, *Dethronement of Sabaoth,* 115.

103. Ibid., 107.

Ezekiel reacts by falling on his face; according to Lev 9:23-24, the Israelites did likewise when Yahweh's glory was manifested in fire. Their examples commend such behavior to the reader, who, through the text, also has encountered the ineffable mystery of Yahweh's glory. But what are the meaning and function of the divine apparition that at last lies before the mind's eye? In addition to Ezekiel 1, the primary resource, what in the reader's extra-textual repertoire assists the attempt to make sense of Ezekiel's vision? (See Reflections at 3:12-15.)

❖   ❖   ❖   ❖

EXCURSUS: EXTRA-TEXTUAL TRADITIONS AND EZEKIELIAN INNOVATIONS

The ancient reader of Ezek 1:4-28 treads a new path, yet encounters familiar landmarks along the way. Several features have already been noted that assist the reader's interpretation of Ezekiel's inaugural vision: mythical associations with Mt. Zaphon/the north; the meaning and function of "the hand of the LORD" in other literary contexts; Yahweh's appearance to Moses in something like anthropomorphic form (Exod 33:18-23); "glory" as the visible manifestation of God's presence. Other relevant aspects of the reader's extra-textual repertoire have yet to be explored, however: knowledge of ancient Israel's ark and temple cherubim, as well as of its divine chariot and storm theophany traditions. Each of these topics has been the focus of modern investigation. Critics have labored diligently, for example, to discern why ancient Israel's ark functions one way in Zion traditions, another in the book of Deuteronomy, and yet another in priestly-pentateuchal texts. But the ancient interpreter did not wield the tools of contemporary biblical criticism. Even if he possessed dilatory knowledge of scriptural references to the ark, he undertook no tradio-historical analysis of them! To the contrary, the reader's natural tendency toward consistency building militated against such an approach (see the Introduction).

THE ARK

Critics agree that both Israel's ark and its temple cherubim traditions strongly influenced Ezekiel 1. It follows that knowledge of these traditions contributed to the reader's competent construal of the text. Biblical tradition traces the ark, a portable chest, back to Israel's post-exodus desert trek. According to the account in Exod 25:10-22, God gave Moses detailed instructions regarding its construction, including a cover consisting of a "mercy seat" flanked at each end by a golden cherub. These cherubim faced each other, their outstretched wings overshadowing the mercy seat (Exod 25:20). According to this same passage, the God-given "testimony" (העדות *hā'ēdût*) was to be placed in the ark, and the latter would function as a meeting place between Yahweh and Moses: "There I will meet with you, and from above the mercy seat, from between the two cherubim that are on the ark of the covenant, I will deliver to you all my commands for the Israelites" (Exod 25:22 NRSV). Here as elsewhere, *the ark is linked with God's presence* (see also Num 10:33, 35-36; Judg 20:26-27; 1 Sam 4:3-11). Moreover, in a number of passages, it is explicitly associated with manifestations of God's "glory" (see 1 Sam 4:19-22; Pss 24; 63:2; 78:61; 132:8).

Some years after Israel's entrance into the land, the ark was moved from Bethel to the sanctuary at Shiloh. According to 1 Samuel 4–6 (the ark narrative), Israel's elders decided to bring the object into battle against the Philistines, where it was captured (1 Sam 4:1-4 NRSV). In this context, the object is called "the ark of the covenant of the LORD of hosts, who is enthroned on the cherubim" (1 Sam 4:4). Whether this particular phrase is to be regarded as its "fullest and most ancient liturgical name"[104] or, more likely, as a retrojection of later theological concepts into

___
104. C. L. Seow, "Ark of the Covenant," *ABD* 1:387.

the premonarchical period, its presence in 1 Sam 4:4 certainly invited ancient readers to regard the cherubim-flanked ark as the throne of Yahweh, the king.[105] The same phrase appears in 2 Sam 6:2, part of the account of David's transportation of the ark to Jerusalem (2 Sam 6:1-15). During David's reign the ark was kept in a tent (2 Sam 6:17; 7:2, 5-7). With the completion of Solomon's Temple, however, it was moved into that structure's innermost sanctum, the holy of holies (דביר *děbîr*; see 1 Kgs 8:1-11), and was placed beneath the wings of the temple cherubim.

THE TEMPLE CHERUBIM

In 1 Kgs 8:1-12, "cherubim" refers not to the creatures adorning the ark's cover, but to the two gold-covered statues (each ten cubits high with a ten-cubit wingspan) that stood in the Temple's holy of holies and beneath whose inner wings the ark was placed. According to their description in 1 Kgs 6:23-28, these cherubim stood parallel to each other and faced the cella (2 Chr 3:13), the largest room in the Temple. Their wings were arranged so that "a wing of one was touching the one wall [of the *děbîr*], and a wing of the other cherub was touching the other wall; their other wings toward the center of the house were touching wing to wing" (1 Kgs 6:27-28 NRSV). Archaeologists have discovered ancient Near Eastern reliefs and sculptures of cherubim thrones upon which sit either deities or human kings. These artifacts are among the data suggesting that during Israel's monarchical period, Yahweh also was conceived of as an invisibly enthroned king whose seat was formed by the cherubims' conjoined and horizontal inner wings.[106] The ark beneath the throneseat served as Yahweh's footstool (see 1 Chr 28:2; Pss 99:5; 132:7).

THE CHARIOT THRONE AND STORM THEOPHANIES

Ezekiel's description of Yahweh's glory everywhere emphasizes mobility (via wind, wings, wheels, the spirit). Here, the divine king's chair assumes the form of a *chariot* throne. For Wevers, Ezekiel's conception of a divine chariot throne may be rooted in an anthropomorphic understanding of Yahweh as king: "The kings of Israel and Judah rode in chariots as a sign of royal dignity (I Kg. 22:35; 2 Kg. 9:27; 10:15)."[107] But neither royal appurtenances nor "enthroned on the cherubim" temple traditions can fully account for Ezekiel's divine chariot throne and its juxtaposition with stormy wind and a great cloud. We must look also to Israel's theophanic traditions, wherein "the King *enthroned* in the Temple was none other than the *coming* God . . . the cherubim, which originally basically represented a throne, came additionally to be regarded as the cloud-chariot of the coming God."[108]

The combining of Zion enthronement traditions with earlier storm theophany imagery should not, Mettinger asserts, be construed as "mere momentary enthusiasm for poetic speech":

> Rather, this idea has left unmistakable traces in later texts, and implicitly underlies both Ezekiel's description of the throne as a chariot and the Chronicler's explicit reference to the cherubim throne as a מרכבה (*merkābâ* "chariot," 1 Chr 28:18). . . . the Temple theologians seem to have counselled a *complementary*, rather than contradictory, relationship between the enthroned King [Zion Traditions] and coming God [storm theophany traditions]. These two aspects are by no means to be played off against each other. Both had origins in the cultic tradition, and, further, both were of importance for later theological reflection concerning the presence of God. The outstretched wings of the cherubim help to create an iconographic impression of "frozen motion," and thus through a brilliant paradox unify the idea of static presence implicit in the throne motif with the dymanic parousia implicit in the theophany."[109]

105. See ibid.
106. Mettinger, *Dethronement of Sabaoth*, 23; see, e.g., Pss 80:1; 99:1; Isa 6:1; 37:16 [= 2 Kgs 19:15, without "of hosts"].
107. J. W. Wevers, *Ezekiel*, NCB (London: Nelson, 1969) 47; see also Moshe Greenberg, *Ezekiel 1–20*, AB 22 (Garden City, N.Y.: Doubleday, 1983) 57.
108. Mettinger, *Dethronement of Sabaoth*, 35.
109. Ibid., 36.

EZEKIELIAN INNOVATIONS

Knowledge of these religious landmarks—ark, cherubim throne, chariot, and theophany traditions—informs the ancient reader's understanding of Ezekiel's vision. Yet this text is more than just the combination of various antecedents; it constitutes "an alchemy from which emerges someting genuinely new which nevertheless retains its links with the past."[110]

Regarding v. 28, for example, it was observed that Ezekielian references to Yahweh's "glory" sometimes designate a divine attribute and other times refer to the deity per se. It was further observed that while pre-exilic Zion traditions frequently employed the divine epithet יהוה צבאות (*yhwh ṣĕbāʾôt,* "the LORD of hosts"), priestly tradition abandoned it in favor of כבוד יהוה (*kĕbôd yhwh ,* "the glory of the LORD"). The phrase "the LORD of hosts, who is enthroned on the cherubim," with its emphasis on Yahweh's continuous presence *within* the Jerusalem Temple, never appears in Ezekiel, although enthronement imagery has certainly left its mark upon chap. 1. Rather, Yahweh's presence *comes* to Ezekiel in Babylonia, rendezvousing with him by the Chebar Canal.[111]

Ezekiel 1 is everywhere the product of decisions, conscious and unconscious. It is highly rhetorical (see Introduction), especially in the sense that it invites its readers to perceive "reality" (including divine reality) on its terms, rather than in some other way. Such invitations are extended for specific purposes—to entitle, to persuade, to disguise, to conceal;[112] of these, persuasion is most pervasive.[113]

Of what does chap. 1 seek to persuade its audience through its innovation on a foundational tenet of Zion theology? Why might Ezekiel, whose deportation coincided with the Babylonian despoiling of Yahweh's Temple and who everywhere insists that Jerusalem faced certain destruction, have chosen to portray God's presence ("glory") in Babylonia? In Ezekiel's historical context, it seems, emphasizing an inextricable link between God's presence and the Temple would have proved extremely problematic, for what would it say of Yahweh if (to put it crudely) the chosen divine residence crashed down upon God's head? Instead, Ezekiel's inaugural vision affirms Yahweh's mobility and freedom to be present when and wherever the Lord chooses. Sequential readers have only begun to explore the theological consequences of the affirmation that Israel's enthroned Lord is not "temple bound."

On a smaller scale, certain details in Ezek 1:4-28 also display the tendency both to utilize existing conventions and to introduce innovations. The descriptions of the four-winged "living creatures" in chap. 1, for example, probably reflect the influence of Mesopotamian iconography (while the creatures explicitly called "cherubim" in chaps. 10–11 will more closely resemble the Jerusalem temple cherubim).[114] We have no textual or artistic precedent for their four faces. And while the creatures attending the enthroned Lord in Isaiah 6 each had three pairs of wings (Isa 6:2), Ezekiel's have only two pairs. According to Isa 6:2, the seraphims' third pair covers their faces, perhaps to ensure appropriate reverence in Yahweh's presence. In Ezekiel 1, by contrast, a third pair may have been deemed unnecessary, since the creatures were positioned beneath, not facing, the chariot throne.[115] Nevertheless, aspects of their descriptions and their function as bearers of the enthroned "glory" invite the reader to associate, if not identify, them with the cherubim of ark, temple, and theophanic traditions. Variations in scriptural depictions of Yahweh's winged attendants would have urged readers away from a single, fixed mental picture.

A final question remains—one that surely confronted the ancient reader of Ezek 1:1-28, yet one that cannot be answered on the basis of those verses alone: For what purpose does the glory

---

110. J. Blenkinsopp, *Ezekiel,* IBC (Louisville: John Knox, 1990) 19-20.
111. Mettinger, *Dethronement of Sabaoth,* 81-82.
112. See K. P. Darr, *Isaiah's Vision and the Family of God* (Louisville: Westminster/John Knox, 1994) 24.
113. Ibid., 43.
114. See Mettinger, *Dethronement of Sabaoth,* 102.
115. Wevers, *Ezekiel,* 45.

of the Lord come to this man? Does its appearance indicate divine approval of Ezekiel, as did Moses' glimpse of the back of Yahweh's glory? Will this vision, like Isaiah 6, introduce a prophetic call narrative? Does this extraordinary theophany bode well for the captives, or ill? As Allen observes, critics who find in this appearance of Yahweh's glory an indication of divine benevolence implicitly presuppose chaps. 8–11, where Yahweh's glory is said to leave both Temple and city.[116] Though the *kābôd,* or "God's glory," has abandoned Jerusalem, it has taken up residence with the exiles in Babylonia. But the reader knows nothing of chaps. 8–11 as yet. Theophanies often had as their goal the divine warrior's defeat of Israel's enemies. But at the hands of the prophets, the genre could be turned to depict Yahweh's coming in judgment against Israel itself.[117] Which will be the case here? The purpose of Yahweh's rendezvous with Ezekiel remains uncertain.[118] But the brief reference to a voice in 1:28*b* suggests that the answer is close to hand.

116. Leslie Allen, "The Structure and Intention of Ezekiel 1," *VT* 43 (1993) 152.
117. Ibid., 153-54.
118. So also R. R. Wilson, "Prophecy in Crisis," *Int.* 38 (1984) 125.

❖   ❖   ❖   ❖

EZEKIEL 2:1–3:15, THE COMMISSION

Ezekiel 2:1-2, Introduction to the Commissioning

NIV

2 He said to me, "Son of man, stand up on your feet and I will speak to you." [2]As he spoke, the Spirit came into me and raised me to my feet, and I heard him speaking to me.

NRSV

2 He said to me: O mortal,[a] stand up on your feet, and I will speak with you. [2]And when he spoke to me, a spirit entered into me and set me on my feet; and I heard him speaking to me.

[a]Or *son of man;* Heb *ben adam* (and so throughout the book when Ezekiel is addressed)

COMMENTARY

The voice Ezekiel hears as he lies prostrate and overwhelmed addresses him directly in 2:1: "O mortal, stand up on your feet, and I will speak with you." Yet the priest cannot, it seems, rise of his own volition; a spirit (רוּח *rûaḥ*) enters him and sets him on his feet. Just as the source of the voice is not explicitly stated in 1:28*b,* so also in 2:1*a,* the verb "(and) he said" lacks an explicit subject. In these and subsequent verses, however, this voice can only belong to Yahweh; the text's omission of a specified speaker is yet another example of the reverence and reserve that characterize the account of Yahweh's advent in chapter 1 (the source of the

"spirit" likewise is not specified). Ezekiel himself will say nothing throughout his commissioning.

For the first of ninety-three times in the book (2:1), Ezekiel is called "mortal" (lit., "son of man"; each of the subsections of Ezekiel's commissioning in 2:1–3:15 has this phrase near its beginning: 2:1, 3, 6, 8; 3:4, 10; see also 3:1, 3). Yahweh will consistently use this phrase when addressing Ezekiel (his proper name does not reappear except in the third-person reference of 24:24). The epithet comports with conventional Hebrew idiom: אדם (*'ādām,* "human being") designates a class; בן (*ben-,* "son of") specifies a member of that class.

But critics attribute different nuances to the phrase. For Blenkinsopp the use of "mortal" emphasizes that Ezekiel's function as a prophet is more important than the person himself.[119] Zimmerli also plays down Ezekiel's individuality, but he discerns its purpose in the contrast between "humanity" (אדם *'ādām*) and "deity" (אל *'ēl*). Moreover, *'ādām* appears as the subject of rulings in certain legal texts (e.g., Lev 1:2; 13:2); hence Ezekiel, with his priestly background, might use that word as a matter of course.[120] Greenberg,

too, believes that designating Ezekiel as "mortal" serves to distinguish him from the divine beings he sees not only in chap. 1, but also in chaps. 8–11 and 40.[121] Eichrodt, citing Ps 8:5, asserts that the title emphasizes Ezekiel's creaturely weakness.[122] It is not possible simply to rule out one or another of these interpretations, since each has its own logic within the context of the book. In any event, the epithet is capable of bearing (and the reader of perceiving) more than one nuance, even within a single verse. (See Reflections at 3:12-15.)

119. Joseph Blenkinsopp, *Ezekiel,* IBC (Louisville: John Knox, 1990) 24.
120. W. Zimmerli, *Ezekiel 1: A Commentary on the Book of the Prophet Ezekiel, Chapters 1–24,* trans. R. E. Clements, Hermeneia (Philadelphia: Fortress, 1979) 131.

121. Moshe Greenberg, *Ezekiel 1–20,* AB 22 (Garden City, N.Y.: Doubleday, 1983) 61-62.
122. Walther Eichrodt, *Ezekiel,* trans. Cosslett Quin, OTL (Philadelphia: Westminster, 1970) 61.

Ezekiel 2:3-5, The First Commissioning Speech

[3]He said: "Son of man, I am sending you to the Israelites, to a rebellious nation that has rebelled against me; they and their fathers have been in revolt against me to this very day. [4]The people to whom I am sending you are obstinate and stubborn. Say to them, 'This is what the Sovereign LORD says.' [5]And whether they listen or fail to listen—for they are a rebellious house—they will know that a prophet has been among them.

[3]He said to me, Mortal, I am sending you to the people of Israel, to a nation[a] of rebels who have rebelled against me; they and their ancestors have transgressed against me to this very day. [4]The descendants are impudent and stubborn. I am sending you to them, and you shall say to them, "Thus says the Lord GOD." [5]Whether they hear or refuse to hear (for they are a rebellious house), they shall know that there has been a prophet among them.

[a]Syr: Heb *to nations*

COMMENTARY

"I am sending you. . . . and you shall say to them. . . . then they will know. . . ." With these words, Yahweh expresses the essential elements of Ezekiel's call. The first of these phrases, "I am sending you" (vv. 3-4), constitutes, as Zimmerli observes, the prophet's "basic authorization" (see also Isa 6:8; Jer 1:7). Indeed, the most severe form of antagonism toward a prophet is the accusation "Yahweh has not sent you" (see Ezek 13:6; Jer 28:15; 43:2).[123]

To whom is Ezekiel sent? The text minces no words: His audience consists of "the children of

Israel," the "nations of rebels"[124] who perpetuate the sins of their ancestors "to this very day" by revolting against their sovereign and violating their vassal responsibilities. These are, of course, political charges. In this context, however, Israel's sovereign is none other than God, and its covenant obligations include religious and ethical demands. Hence Greenberg uses Martin Buber's term "theopolitical."[125]

123. Zimmerli, *Ezekiel 1,* 132.

124. "To nations" (אל־גוים *'el-gôyim*), not in the LXX, is sometimes regarded as a later addition. Both the NRSV and the NIV render *gôyim* in the singular. For Greenberg, *Ezekiel 1–20,* 63, the MT makes sense.
125. Ibid., 63. See the index in M. Buber, *Moses* (London: East and West Library, 1946) s.v. "Theopolitical idea."

These "children" are "hard of face and tough of heart," that is "impudent and stubborn" (v. 4).[126] Ezekiel must proclaim to them: "thus has אֲדֹנָי יהוה [*ʾădōnāy yhwh;* lit., "(my) LORD Yahweh"] said."[127] In v. 4 this messenger formula, which is not followed by an oracle, should perhaps be construed as applicable to all of Ezekiel's forthcoming oracles.[128] Whether the "rebellious house" (a pejorative twist on the conventional epithet, "house of Israel") listens or not, "they will know that a prophet has been among them." Hence, Ezekiel's "success" does not turn on audience reaction; it depends entirely on his obedient proclamation of God's word in their presence. To judge from the

characterization of Israel throughout its generations, a positive response seems unlikely at best. Israel will "know" (recognize and acknowledge) that Ezekiel is truly Yahweh's spokesman only when his prophecies have been fulfilled. Yet the commissioning account itself speaks to God's ongoing involvement in Israel's life: "Even when little hope [exists] of averting the misfortune," Greenberg observes, "a prophet is still sent, so that afterward the people will realize that . . . God had given them warning in due time; it was no lack of consideration on his part but their own heedlessness that caused their downfall."[129] Greenberg's comment highlights divine concern for Israel, despite its perduring sin and obstinacy and their consequences. But this text also betrays concern for Yahweh's reputation. From the outset, the book of Ezekiel insists that God's punishment upon Israel is apropos to its crimes—indeed, was already thoroughly deserved centuries earlier (e.g., 2:3). The Lord is not to blame. (See Reflections at 3:12-15.)

126. The Hebrew phrases combine an exterior ("face") and an interior ("heart") figure. See Greenberg, *Ezekiel 1–20,* 64.

127. This double epithet occurs 217 times in Ezekiel, always from the prophet's mouth. See ibid, 65. See also Walther Zimmerli, *Ezekiel 2: A Commentary on the Book of the Prophet Ezekiel, Chapters 25–48,* trans. J. D. Martin, Hermeneia (Philadelphia: Fortress, 1983) 556-62; J. Lust, " 'Mon Seigneur Jahweh' dans le teste," *EThL* 44 (1968) 482-88.

128. The messenger formula appears 129 times in the book of Ezekiel, a number equalled only in Jeremiah. Its point, Wevers remarks, is plain: "Ezekiel is to speak Yahweh's words only." See Wevers, *Ezekiel,* 52.

129. Greenberg, *Ezekiel 1–20,* 75.

Ezekiel 2:6-7, The Commissioning Continues

⁶And you, son of man, do not be afraid of them or their words. Do not be afraid, though briers and thorns are all around you and you live among scorpions. Do not be afraid of what they say or terrified by them, though they are a rebellious house. ⁷You must speak my words to them, whether they listen or fail to listen, for they are rebellious.

⁶And you, O mortal, do not be afraid of them, and do not be afraid of their words, though briers and thorns surround you and you live among scorpions; do not be afraid of their words, and do not be dismayed at their looks, for they are a rebellious house. ⁷You shall speak my words to them, whether they hear or refuse to hear; for they are a rebellious house.

COMMENTARY

Verse 6 contains two pairs of negative imperatives. The first pair orders him not to fear the (obstinate, stubborn, and rebellious) exiles and not to fear their words. The second pair orders him not to fear their words and not to be dismayed because of them. (The admonition not to fear also appears, e.g., in Jeremiah's call account, Jer 1:8, 17*b.*) Between these two pairs appears a phrase that traditionally has been understood as an

acknowledgment that such fears would be well-founded.[130] Ezekiel's would-be adversaries are depicted metaphorically as thorns and briers surrounding him and as scorpions (or, perhaps, scorpion plants) upon which he must sit.[131] A quite

130. The phrase begins with כִּ (*kî*). Both the NRSV and the NIV render it concessively ("*though* briers and thorns . . ."). However, it can also be translated causally ("*because* briers and thorns . . .").

131. Stephen Garfinkel, "Of Thistles and Thorns: A New Approach to Ezekiel ii 6," *VT* 37 (1987) 430-35.

different construal of the verse is possible, however, and is suggested by two incantations in Maqlû, a Babylonian series of rituals for alleviating the effects of sorcery. Maqlû III.153-54 reads as follows:

> I am the spike of a thornbush;
> you cannot step on me!
> I am the stinger of a scorpion;
> you cannot touch me!

In these lines, the speaker describes himself as a spike and a stinger whom others approach at their peril. Obtaining this sense in Ezek 2:6 requires only that כִּי (*kî*) be translated as "because," rather than as "though." (See Reflections at 3:12-15.)

Ezekiel 2:8–3:3 The Act of Ordination

NIV

[8]But you, son of man, listen to what I say to you. Do not rebel like that rebellious house; open your mouth and eat what I give you."

[9]Then I looked, and I saw a hand stretched out to me. In it was a scroll, [10]which he unrolled before me. On both sides of it were written words of lament and mourning and woe.

3 And he said to me, "Son of man, eat what is before you, eat this scroll; then go and speak to the house of Israel." [2]So I opened my mouth, and he gave me the scroll to eat.

[3]Then he said to me, "Son of man, eat this scroll I am giving you and fill your stomach with it." So I ate it, and it tasted as sweet as honey in my mouth.

NRSV

[8]But you, mortal, hear what I say to you; do not be rebellious like that rebellious house; open your mouth and eat what I give you. [9]I looked, and a hand was stretched out to me, and a written scroll was in it. [10]He spread it before me; it had writing on the front and on the back, and written on it were words of lamentation and mourning and woe.

3 He said to me, O mortal, eat what is offered to you; eat this scroll, and go, speak to the house of Israel. [2]So I opened my mouth, and he gave me the scroll to eat. [3]He said to me, Mortal, eat this scroll that I give you and fill your stomach with it. Then I ate it; and in my mouth it was as sweet as honey.

COMMENTARY

Zimmerli aptly calls this third stage of Ezekiel's commissioning an "act of ordination." He observes, moreover, that these three stages also appear in Jeremiah's call narrative: the summons to prophesy in Ezek 2:3-5 has its counterpart in Jer 1:5(-8); the admonition not to fear (Ezek 2:6-7) appears, as noted above, in Jer 1:8, 17*b*; and the act of ordination in Jer 1:9 corresponds to the present verses.[132] Jeremiah 1:9 reads as follows:

> Then the LORD put out his hand and touched my mouth; and the LORD said to me,
> "Now I have put my words in your mouth."
> (NRSV)

Yahweh's touch bestows divine words that Jeremiah

must proclaim. Yet one does not surmise that God literally stuffs words down his throat![133] Ezekiel 2:8–3:3, by contrast, presents something both literal and astonishing: The prophet is ordered to eat "that which I am giving to you" (v. 8*b*). He sees a hand (again, lack of specificity signals reverential reserve; the hand belongs to Yahweh) extending to him a written scroll. When "he" (Yahweh) spreads out the scroll before him, Ezekiel discovers that it is inscribed front and back with lamentations, mourning, and woe. Scrolls usually bore writing on

---

132. Zimmerli, *Ezekiel 1*, 134-35.

133. The reader may well recall not only Jer 1:9, but also Isa 6:6-7 (in which a seraph touches Isaiah's mouth with a burning coal, thereby obviating his sin) and 1 Kgs 22:22 (where a member of Yahweh's divine council suggests placing a "lying spirit" in the mouths of the four hundred prophets who, against Micaiah ben Imlah, urge Ahaz and Jehoshaphat to attack Ramoth-gilead).

one side only; here, departure from normal practice signals "the distressing superabundance" of the Lord's message.[134]

The following divine address (3:1) thrice demands obedience. Twice Ezekiel is commanded to eat the scroll; then he must go, "speak to the house of Israel."[135] He immediately opens his mouth to receive the object. It does not suffice, however, simply to "chew upon" its contents; the document must fill his belly (v. 3*a*). What certainly sounds like an odious procedure is relieved in v. 3*b* by Ezekiel's claim that it tasted as sweet as honey. Readers may recall similar sentiments in Jer 15:16*a* and Ps 119:103. In these texts, however, the language is used metaphorically.

This "act of ordination" raises several interrelated issues. The first concerns the scroll's contents. Although some critics contend that the "lamentations, mourning, and woe" constitute audience *reactions* to Ezekiel's judgment oracles (so Zimmerli, Wevers, Blenkinsopp, etc.), these three words probably characterize the very words that *he must proclaim.*

So, for example, Wilson observes that "for Ezekiel, the eating of the scroll indicates that God has supplied the prophet with oracles in a fixed form that cannot be changed. All of the words which Ezekiel speaks are precisely the same words which God literally put inside the prophet."[136]

A second issue surfaces in Wilson's further comment: "There can therefore be no doubt about the prophet's authority."[137] Ancient Israel's literature, including the book of Jeremiah and subsequent passages in Ezekiel, testifies to conflict between prophets, each claiming to bear Yahweh's authentic word for tumultuous times.[138] Ezekiel emphasizes the divine origin of his words in order to separate himself from prophets who ostensibly compose and deliver oracles for self-serving reasons. Eichrodt speaks of Ezekiel's *personal* need

for reassurance that he has been entrusted with God's message.[139] But this highly rhetorical text actually seeks to reassure its *readers* that Ezekiel's words are, in fact, God's own: "The Ezekielian emphasis upon the prophet's (literal) ingestion of the divine word functions as part of his defense against charges of false, indeed, seditious prophecy."[140]

Ezekiel receives God's word as literary text. "No longer is the word of Yahweh . . . given in a personal address by God," Zimmerli observes. "It has become a book."[141] This shift cannot, of course, be explained as an increasing propensity toward writing on God's part! It has, rather, been interpreted as reflecting both Ezekiel's own literary propensities and the increasing importance of writing in his day, not only as a means of preserving earlier traditions, but also as a mode for reinterpretation and creative composition during Israel's late monarchical and exilic periods.[142]

Ellen Davis attributes to Ezekiel a "pioneering role as a writer-prophet": "Ezekiel greatly exceeded his predecessors in the degree to which he exploited the potential inherent in writing. . . . [His] was a fundamentally literate mind, i.e., his patterns of thought and expression were shaped by habits of reading and writing. . . . [through him] Israelite prophecy for the first time received its *primary* impress from the new conditions and opportunities for communication created by writing."[143] By the reader's day, of course, many of Israel's religious traditions, including some prophetic materials, had already assumed written form. Hence, neither Ezekiel's reception of a text (albeit through an unusual, indeed odious, procedure) nor the fact that his prophecies were recorded in a scroll would have struck him as remarkable. (See Reflections at 3:12-15.)

---

134. Zimmerli, *Ezekiel 1,* 135.

135. "The eating of the scroll," Greenberg observes, "is as much a test of the prophet's obedience . . . as a stocking of the prophet with a content by which to counter the defiant words of the people (cf. 3:1 with 2:7)." See Greenberg, *Ezekiel 1–20,* 73.

136. Wilson, "Prophecy in Crisis," 127. See also Greenberg, *Ezekiel 1–20,* 68; K. P. Darr, "Write or True?: A Response to Ellen Frances Davis," in *Signs and Wonders: Biblical Texts in Literary Focus,* ed. J. Cheryl Exum, SemeiaST (Atlanta: Society of Biblical Literature, 1989) 239-247.

137. Wilson, "Prophecy in Crisis," 127.

138. See James L. Crenshaw, *Prophetic Conflict,* BZAW 124 (Berlin: Walter de Gruyter, 1971).

139. Eichrodt, *Ezekiel,* 63.

140. Darr, "Write or True?" 245.

141. W. Zimmerli, *Ezekiel 1: A Commentary on the Book of the Prophet Ezekiel, Chapters 1–24,* trans. R. E. Clements, Hermeneia (Philadelphia: Fortress, 1979) 137.

142. Von Rad is but one of many critics who acknowledge that writing played a heretofore unparalleled role in creating the book of Ezekiel: "Ezekiel, more even than Jeremiah, needed to express his prophetic message in writing—in an ordered form. He makes scarcely any use of the shorter units of expression, the diatribe and the threat, which classical prophecy had employed. When he speaks, the results are as a rule literary compositions, even large-scale dissertations." See G. von Rad, *Old Testament Theology,* 2 vols., trans. D. M. G. Stalker (New York: Harper and Bros., 1965] 2:222.

143. Ellen F. Davis, *Swallowing the Scroll: Textuality and the Dynamics of Discourse in Ezekiel's Prophecy,* Bible and Literature 21 (Sheffield: Almond, 1989) 27.

Ezekiel 3:4-9, Tough Audience, Tougher Prophet

NIV

⁴He then said to me: "Son of man, go now to the house of Israel and speak my words to them. ⁵You are not being sent to a people of obscure speech and difficult language, but to the house of Israel— ⁶not to many peoples of obscure speech and difficult language, whose words you cannot understand. Surely if I had sent you to them, they would have listened to you. ⁷But the house of Israel is not willing to listen to you because they are not willing to listen to me, for the whole house of Israel is hardened and obstinate. ⁸But I will make you as unyielding and hardened as they are. ⁹I will make your forehead like the hardest stone, harder than flint. Do not be afraid of them or terrified by them, though they are a rebellious house."

NRSV

4He said to me: Mortal, go to the house of Israel and speak my very words to them. ⁵For you are not sent to a people of obscure speech and difficult language, but to the house of Israel— ⁶not to many peoples of obscure speech and difficult language, whose words you cannot understand. Surely, if I sent you to them, they would listen to you. ⁷But the house of Israel will not listen to you, for they are not willing to listen to me; because all the house of Israel have a hard forehead and a stubborn heart. ⁸See, I have made your face hard against their faces, and your forehead hard against their foreheads. ⁹Like the hardest stone, harder than flint, I have made your forehead; do not fear them or be dismayed at their looks, for they are a rebellious house.

COMMENTARY

The account of Jeremiah's "act of ordination" is followed in Jer 1:10 (see also Jer 1:17-19) by a "recapitulation" of the commissioning.[144] An analogous element appears in Ezek 3:4-9, where the "hardness" of the prophet's audience requires an even greater toughening of Ezekiel.

Again, the deity orders him to go to the house of Israel and speak Yahweh's exact words. He is not being sent to peoples whose vernacular he does not know. We can assume that within their Babylonian setting, the exiles routinely encountered diverse peoples (v. 6a) with unfamiliar languages. The reader, like Blenkinsopp, might well recall at this point the Tower of Babel myth (Gen 11:1-9), according to which a cacophony of languages led to the breakdown of both communication and community.[145] If Ezekiel were sent to one of these, Yahweh says, they would listen to him! (Does this ironic slur remind readers of the equally ironic story of Jonah, whose message [in Hebrew]—"Forty more days and Nineveh will be overturned" [Jonah 3:4b NIV]—immediately

elicits the repentance of his [Akkadian-speaking] Ninevite audience?) The house of Israel will not be willing to listen to Ezekiel because, Yahweh states, "they are not willing to listen to me" (v. 7), hard (fore)headed and stubborn of heart as they are.[146] Accusations of obstinacy run like a red thread through Israel's traditions (e.g., Exod 32:9; 33:3, 5; 34:9; Num 20:10; Deut 31:27; 9:6-13; Isa 30:9, 48:4; Jer 3:3; 5:3). Isaiah was told that his oracles would render the people even *less* receptive than before (Isa 6:9-10). Here, however, "the hardening of the people is already an established fact, corresponding to the finality of [Ezekiel's] preaching. No room is left therefore for the Isaianic concept of the hardening being brought about by the prophet's [ministry]."[147] Because their faces and foreheads (brows) are hard, Yahweh makes Ezekiel's forehead harder still—like diamond, tougher than flint. (In the threefold repetition of חזק [*ḥzq*, "to be or grow firm, strong,

---

144. Zimmerli, *Ezekiel 1,* 137.

145. Joseph Blenkinsopp, *Ezekiel,* IBC (Louisville: John Knox, 1990) 25-26.

146. Blenkinsopp, ibid., 26, may be correct when he links v. 7 to the crisis in prophecy referred to above. At a time when Israel's prophets offered diametrically opposing "divine" oracles, who could know whose words were in fact God's own? But the text nowhere considers what might be the cause of Israel's skepticism and even disillusionment.

147. Zimmerli, *Ezekiel 1,* 138.

strengthen"],[148] readers may discern a play on Ezekiel's own name [יחזקאל *yĕḥezqē'l,* "God tough-

148. *BDB,* 304.

ens"].) Thus fortified, he must neither fear them nor be intimidated by their expressions. (See Reflections at 3:12-15.)

Ezekiel 3:10-11 Go, Speak to the Exiles

NIV

[10]And he said to me, "Son of man, listen carefully and take to heart all the words I speak to you. [11]Go now to your countrymen in exile and speak to them. Say to them, 'This is what the Sovereign LORD says,' whether they listen or fail to listen."

NRSV

[10]He said to me: Mortal, all my words that I shall speak to you receive in your heart and hear with your ears; [11]then go to the exiles, to your people, and speak to them. Say to them, "Thus says the Lord GOD"; whether they hear or refuse to hear.

COMMENTARY

God's address continues in v. 10 with two commands: Ezekiel must take into his heart and hear with his ears all of Yahweh's words. The sequence "heart . . . ears" seems illogical. Greenberg labels it a *hysteron proteron* ("last first"), in which "what (chrono)logically is last in a series is placed first owing to its importance."[149] The Hebrew verb form אדבר (*'ădabbēr*), translated in the future tense ("I shall speak"), suggests (and subsequent chapters confirm) that the prophet will continue to receive God's words, in addition to those ingested in the scroll-swallowing episode. Finally, he is

149. Moshe Greenberg, *Ezekiel 1–20,* AB 22 (Garden City, N.Y.: Doubleday, 1983) 69.

ordered specifically to go to the exiles, here called "the children of your people" (v. 11*a*), and to say to them, "Thus says the LORD Yahweh," whether they listen or not. Some critics contend that the epithet in v. 11*a,* coupled with the absence of any reference to the people's rebelliousness in vv. 10-11, indicates that the exiles are less defiant than that portion of the "house of Israel" still residing in Judah.[150] Yet the reappearance of the refrain, "whether they hear or refuse to hear" (v. 11*b*), invites the reader to apply also to the captives those indictments that have suffused Ezekiel's call to prophesy. (See Reflections at 3:12-15.)

150. E.g., J. W. Wevers, *Ezekiel,* NCB (London: Nelson, 1969) 52.

Ezekiel 3:12-15, Conclusion

NIV

[12]Then the Spirit lifted me up, and I heard behind me a loud rumbling sound—May the glory of the LORD be praised in his dwelling place!— [13]the sound of the wings of the living creatures brushing against each other and the sound of the wheels beside them, a loud rumbling sound. [14]The Spirit then lifted me up and took me away, and I went in bitterness and in the anger of my spirit, with the strong hand of the LORD upon

NRSV

12Then the spirit lifted me up, and as the glory of the LORD rose[a] from its place, I heard behind me the sound of loud rumbling; [13]it was the sound of the wings of the living creatures brushing against one another, and the sound of the wheels beside them, that sounded like a loud rumbling. [14]The spirit lifted me up and bore me away; I went in bitterness in the heat of my spirit, the

[a]Cn: Heb *and blessed be the glory of the LORD*

NIV

me. [15]I came to the exiles who lived at Tel Abib near the Kebar River. And there, where they were living, I sat among them for seven days—overwhelmed.

NRSV

hand of the LORD being strong upon me. [15]I came to the exiles at Tel-abib, who lived by the river Chebar.[a] And I sat there among them, stunned, for seven days.

[a]Two Mss Syr: Heb *Chebar, and to where they lived.* Another reading is *Chebar, and I sat where they sat*

COMMENTARY

His commissioning completed, Ezekiel recounts how the spirit lifted him up (see also 8:3; 11:1, 24; 43:5) amid a loud rumbling sound. The MT of v. 12*b* reads, "Blessed be the glory of the LORD from his place!" a doxology presumably uttered either by "unspecified heavenly beings" or by the prophet himself (see Ps 135:21).[151] Its presence in this context strikes critics as awkward. Hence, they have long suggested that for ברוך (*bārûk,* "blessed") one read ברום (*bĕrûm,* "when [the glory of the LORD] arose"; see 10:4). Verse 13, then, identifies the sound's source as the wings and wheels of the living creatures bearing Yahweh's glory aloft. Ezekiel does not witness its departure; he only hears it as he is taken away by the spirit (v. 14*a;* see also 1 Kgs 18:12; Isa 40:24; 41:16). The juxtaposition of "lifted me up and bore me away" with "I went" (v. 14*b*) and "I came" (v. 15*a*) suggests, in Greenberg's words, "a passage from visionary (vss. 12-14*a*) to real experience."[152] Rejoining the exiles at Tel-abib, Ezekiel sits stunned (משמים *maśmîm,* "desolate") among them for seven days (cf. Paul's experience in Acts 9:8-9). Tel-abib literally means "a (ruin) hill of the flood"—that is, a mound

thought to have been deserted since the primeval deluge (i.e., from ancient times).

The return in these verses to images, themes, and vocabulary from Ezekiel's inaugural vision creates an envelope for Ezekiel's entire call account (1:1–3:15).[153] Many critics, Zimmerli among them, regard v. 13 as a later elaboration upon the original text.[154] In any event, references to the departure of Yahweh's glory (v. 12), the sounds of wings and wheels (v. 13), the spirit, and the hand of Yahweh (v. 14) enhance the reader's impression of the unity and coherence of those materials encountered thus far in the book.

Scholars have sometimes suggested that the connection between Ezekiel's vision (chap. 1) and his commissioning (2:1–3:15) is artificial. After all, Jeremiah's call to prophesy, which shares significant affinities with the Ezekielian report (see above), includes no comparable visionary account. Comparison with Isaiah 6 (and with a related text, 1 Kings 22), however, confirms that divine vision and prophetic commission already were linked in Israel's tradition by Ezekiel's day.[155]

151. Greenberg, *Ezekiel 1–20,* 70.
152. Ibid., 74.

153. Ibid., 70.
154. Zimmerli, *Ezekiel 1,* 139.
155. Zimmerli, ibid., 98-100, 108-10, compares and contrasts Isaiah 6 and Ezek 1:1–3:15.

REFLECTIONS

1. "Ezekiel *was* an extremist. He did go further than his peers in all his predictions. But what made him totally different, perhaps unique, is something else: In his case, vision and word merged and became one."[156]

Like many an extremist and visionary, Ezekiel has a difficult time securing a place in mainstream Christianity. With a few well-known exceptions (e.g., the valley of dry bones vision in

156. Elie Wiesel, "Ezekiel," in *Congregation: Contemporary Writers Read the Jewish Bible,* ed. David Rosenberg (New York: Harcourt Brace Jovanovich, 1987) 184.

37:1-14), his oracles seldom make their way into lectionary readings and sermons, for they are deemed too severe, too complex, and too painful to set before our congregations and Bible study groups. And Ezekiel makes us uncomfortable—a sentiment we surely share not only with his original audience in exile, but also with two and a half millennia of his interpreters, both Jewish and Christian. Among the early rabbis, for example, we find the opinion that reading the book's beginning and ending was too dangerous to be undertaken by anyone younger than thirty years of age.

If Ezekiel's oracles strike us as too much, we should recognize that his message matched his times—grim, complex, painful. In a world where holocausts happen with numbing regularity, we risk being too inured to slaughter, suffering, and mass dislocations to take in the crisis that Ezekiel not only experienced, but also felt compelled to interpret to his generation. Or perhaps we are not inured at all, but recoil from his words as if from fire and the certainty of being burned. Fire and blazing light are recurring images in the book; who can blame the reader who sometimes fears the flames? "With such visions of fire, with such memories of fire," Wiesel writes, "even prophets ought to be careful and remain silent."[157]

The brightest light emanates from above the four extraordinary creatures rushing toward Ezekiel amid a violent storm. The priest must first accustom his eyes to flashing lightning ("as if it were possible to say such a thing") before he can discern an enthroned figure encased in glowing amber and fire. What he sees, and invites his readers to see, is no less than Yahweh's visible presence—the "glory of the LORD." His audacity in recounting what he witnessed discomfited the rabbis, who pointed out that Ezekiel's commission to speak God's words did *not* include a mandate to describe what he had seen. To their minds, the very text of his inaugural vision might explode into flames if read by persons unprepared or unworthy of its words. Nobel Laureate Elie Wiesel informs us that Rabbi Yohanan ben Zakkai and his closest disciples studied Ezekiel's *merkavah* ("chariot") vision:

> And we are told that whenever they did, a heavenly fire would surround them. Was it there to shield them or to protect them or to isolate them from reality or to remind them of the fire of Sinai? Perhaps it was there to bring them closer to the fire that consumed the sanctuary in their time—and other living sanctuaries in later generations—or perhaps to teach them the dangers inherent in language, to teach them that some words have the ability to burn and burn.[158]

Ezekiel maintains silence throughout his visionary experience, including his commission to prophesy. Words go into him; they do not come out. Privy to the deliberations of the divine council, Isaiah dared to insert himself into the conversation (Isa 6:8). As a priest, Ezekiel must have been accustomed to visionary accounts, cultic appurtenances, even the transfiguring pinnacles of liturgy. Confronted by Yahweh's glory, however, his knees buckle beneath him. Is he physically unable to speak? Does God give him no chance to utter even a word? Does he maintain silence for fear that anything he says might be taken as a sign of his own rebelliousness?

God demands Ezekiel's absolute obedience. The Lord everywhere tells him what he must and must not do. Moderns dislike being told what to do, perhaps even more than Ezekiel's ancient audiences, who, after all, were forcibly accustomed to life under rulers devoid of "democratic" values and humanitarian constraints. We know nothing of Ezekiel's temperament prior to his encounter by the Chebar Canal, but what he experienced there transformed his life and set him to a task from which there was no release. Centuries later, Saul of Tarsus—a zealous persecuter of the early Christians—encounters Christ on the road to Damascus, receives his own life-transforming commission, is blinded by a light brighter than the sun, and neither eats nor drinks for three days (Acts 9:3-9; 22:6-11; 26:12-18). But the very idea that God could make such

157. Ibid.
158. Ibid., 185.

unqualified demands today is more likely to send us running than to our knees. If a vision like Ezekiel's preceded divine demands, we, too, might be dazzled and terrified enough to respond as he responded. But for how long and under what circumstances? The book of Ezekiel testifies to the prophet's continuing obedience over two decades of his life, despite isolation, discord, and audience apathy.

2. Erich von Daniken's *Chariots of the Gods? Unsolved Mysteries of the Past* quickened public interest in Ezekiel's visions with suggestions of interplanetary voyages, playing to our fascination with both science and fiction.[159] His readers might not swallow the idea of divine visions, but the notion of intelligent life "out there" has endless appeal. Ezekiel's world looked to the skies also and saw that they were filled with deities. The Babylonians studied the heavens and worshiped its inhabitants—sun, moon, and stars. Israel's poets knew the heavenly "host" both as Yahweh's army and as astral objects of worship. But the divine realm was not "out there" only. To the contrary, Ezekiel's world is radically theocentric ("God-centered"). Creation is the Lord's handiwork; empires move at the command of Israel's deity (whether they know it or not), and nations are judged by Yahweh's standards. Reality is shaped by divine speech and can be explained on no other terms. When Ezekiel does speak, he utters only God's words, because no other words make sense of his world and of Israel's experience in it.

In his day, Israel's experience must be of divine judgment. Its crimes are long-lived and intractable. God insists that this is true, even as Ezekiel is commissioned to serve as a prophet to the convicts. For years, his script of lamentations, mourning, and woe will barrage his audience, relentlessly insisting that history is yet unfolding at Yahweh's command, that all this suffering is, in fact, the form divine justice must take. "Why does the prophet insist with such fervor on Jewish weaknesses and transgressions?" Wiesel asks. "Does he enjoy shaming them? One reason may be that, knowing of the catastrophe in the making, he wants the Jewish people to have an explanation, he wants to save them from absurdity. Better that they think their plight represents punishment, rather than gratuitous cruelty. Any answer is better than no answer."[160]

The spoiled pot must be destroyed, to borrow an image from Jeremiah 18, before the potter can reshape it into a worthy vessel. Ezekiel's task will entail remolding the very foundations upon which much of Israel's theology was constructed. To do so, he must engage in the daring, daunting transformation of tradition. We see him at work already in his account of Yahweh's advent and claim upon his life. The appearance of Yahweh's glory in Babylon shatters expectations, not because the Lord is limited to Israelite soil, but because tradition has sought to make of God a permanent, protective presence there. Mere mortals (but what else is Ezekiel?), we dismiss ourselves as candidates for taking up his commission. Who dares to recast our venerable traditions? But Ezekiel, in his obedience, models the necessity of discerning God's word to his times and of fashioning his theological inheritance into a form that can both survive the collapse of old ideas and support God's new work into the future, when every divine word is fulfilled and the people acknowledge that a prophet *and* his Lord have been among them.

3. A popular adage has it that the devil is in the details. The details of Ezekiel's experience, by contrast, are filled with divine disclosures. Jewish mystics have known this for millennia. Does his visionary account indulge too much in anthropomorphic images of God? Human beings are forbidden the making of idols, but Yahweh's self-revelations can assume whatever form the deity wills, regardless of our expectations. Does his vision display a penchant for the number four (four creatures, four faces, four wings, four wheels, etc.)? Four represents totality—four compass points (Isa 11:12); four eras of world history (Daniel 2 and 7). Its prominence here teaches us that God's sovereignty is universal, spanning both space and time. Among New Testament

---

159. Erich von Daniken, *Chariots of the Gods? Unsolved Mysteries of the Past,* trans. Michael Heron (New York: Putnam, 1970).
160. Wiesel, "Ezekiel," 174-75.

writers, the author of Revelation 4 borrowed from Ezekiel 1, Isaiah 6, and other sources, adopting and adapting their images to describe his own vision of God's enthroned glory—surrounded by a rainbow, flashing forth lightning as thunder roars, and attended by four creatures: one like a lion, another like an ox, a third bearing a human face, and a fourth like an eagle. Through his eyes, details of Ezekiel's vision illuminate the very throne room of heaven. Among the ante-Nicene fathers, Irenaeus identified the Evangelists with these four creatures (Matthew with the man, Mark with the eagle, Luke with the ox, and John with the lion)[161] and discerned in their number, their faces, and their forms, the meaning of the fourfold gospel and of "the dispensation of the Son of God":

> It is not possible that the Gospels can be either more or fewer in number than they are. For, since there are four zones of the world in which we live, and four principal winds, while the Church is scattered throughout all the world, and the "pillar and ground" of the Church is the Gospel and the spirit of life; it is fitting that she should have four pillars, breathing out immortality on every side and vivifying men afresh. From which fact, it is evident that the Word, the Artificer of all, He that sitteth upon the cherubim, and contains all things, He who was manifested to men, has given us the Gospel under four aspects, but bound together by one Spirit. . . . For the cherubim, too, were four-faced, and their faces were images of the dispensation of the Son of God. For, [as the Scripture] says, "The first living creature was like a lion," symbolizing His effectual working, His leadership, and royal power; the second [living creature] was like a calf, signifying [His] sacrificial and sacerdotal order; but "the third had, as it were, the face as of a man"—an evident description of His advent as a human being; "the fourth was like a flying eagle," pointing out the gift of the Spirit hovering with His wings over the Church.[162]

4. I have stood beside the Charles River on the fourth day of the month of July and watched fireworks suffuse with dazzling light the northern sky over Boston, Massachusetts. Are contemporary readers of Ezekiel's vision too blasé, too accustomed to glittering pyrotechnics and to the "special effects" that fill our films, to stand in awe of what Ezekiel saw? Are they inured, not to suffering or by fear, but by their sophistication? The fourth century CE Rabbi Rava said, "All that Ezekiel saw, Isaiah had seen already. And yet, there is a difference between their personalities. Ezekiel could be compared to a villager who happens to come to the city where he saw the king; Isaiah is compared to a city person who is used to seeing the king frequently, even in his own palace, and therefore is not seized by such frantic desire to tell about it."[163] Perhaps moderns have outgrown their capacity to be awestruck—perhaps they are bemused, not bedazzled, by Ezekiel's vision and his stunned response to it. Who believes in visions anyway? Do we simply dismiss Ezekiel's claim to have witnessed the glory of God as the self-deluding rantings of one whose psychological state must, under his traumatic circumstances, be considered suspect? Can divine displays of power truly be seen only by those who perceive their own powerlessness?

161. Victorinus and St. Augustine followed, though each went his own way in matching author to animal.
162. *The Ante-Nicene Fathers: Translations of The Writings of the Fathers Down to A.D. 325*, ed. Alexander Roberts and James Donaldson, vol. 1: *The Apostolic Fathers—Justin Martyr—Irenaeus* (Grand Rapids: Eerdmans, 1993) 428.
163. BT *Hagigah* 13*b*. Quoted by Wiesel, "Ezekiel," 178.

EZEKIEL 3:16-27

FURTHER DEFINING EZEKIEL'S ROLE AS PROPHET

OVERVIEW

E zekiel's call narrative said virtually nothing about the content of the divine oracles he must proclaim. Ezekiel 3:16-27 does little to fill this gap, other than to reiterate that the prophet must speak Yahweh's own words. Its primary burden is further to define Ezekiel's role as God's authentic spokesperson to "the house of Israel"— more specifically, to his fellow captives at Tel-Abib.

Although most critics concede that both pericopes are linked to and elaborate upon Ezek 1:1–3:15, they insist that 3:16-21, and at least portions of vv. 22-27, are best explained as subsequent additions to their canonical context, inserted by editors late in the work's composition history for structural, thematic, and perhaps polemical reasons. Largely cobbled together from oracles appearing elsewhere in the book (e.g., chaps. 18; 24; 33), these texts must be explored and explained, they maintain, in relation to those (sequentially) later passages.

Biblical scholars have long been preoccupied with the crucial tasks of defining the boundaries of individual units, detecting secondary elements, and reconstructing a text's path to its final position within a larger work. This commentary, however, focuses especially upon how first-time, sequential readers of Ezekiel make sense of the scroll (see Introduction). The implications of this methodological approach for interpreting 3:16-27 are significant. First, the verses before us cannot be explained on the basis of subsequent texts, because the reader knows nothing of them. Rather, their meaning must be sought on their own terms and within their present contexts. As Ellen Davis observes, "a strong reading should render the text synchronically intelligible at every stage of development. That is, while a passage may have been elaborated in such a way as to enhance

or to alter its earlier meaning . . . it is assumed that the general intention and effect of these changes was to produce a meaningful text."[164]

Second, apparent efforts to smooth out inconsistencies, fill gaps, and build bridges both within and between individual units, whether ascribed to Ezekiel or to later editors, must be taken seriously for what they are: early attempts to assist the reader in understanding the text at hand. Disregarding or playing down such elements deprives the interpreter of critical clues to the meanings and functions of texts in their final form—the legacy left us by the Ezekielian tradition.

Third, boundaries separating individual units cannot be drawn absolutely. To be sure, the method here adopted must attend to formal features—e.g., opening and closing formulas—and to topical, temporal, geographical, and other shifts between pericopes. The text is not seamless. Nevertheless, the relationships between a particular passage and those preceding and following it must not be ignored. The verses before us, for example, can be meaningfully related not only to what precedes them, but also to each other and to the following verses. The text invites (consistency-seeking) readers to perceive continuity, rather than incongruity, as they make their way through it.

Ezekiel 3:16-27 continues the first-person narrative style of 1:1, 4–3:15. The prophet recounts a second divine address seven days after his initial call (3:16-21) and a third that commences with v. 22 and continues through 5:17. During both addresses, Ezekiel remains silent (save for 4:14), even as Yahweh places his life on the line and sets the boundaries within which he must work.

164. Ellen F. Davis, *Swallowing the Scroll: Textuality and the Dynamics of Discourse in Ezekiel's Prophecy,* Bible and Literature 21 (Sheffield: Almond, 1989) 26.

EZEKIEL 3:16-21, THE WATCHMAN'S RESPONSIBILITY

NIV

¹⁶At the end of seven days the word of the LORD came to me: ¹⁷"Son of man, I have made you a watchman for the house of Israel; so hear the word I speak and give them warning from me. ¹⁸When I say to a wicked man, 'You will surely die,' and you do not warn him or speak out to dissuade him from his evil ways in order to save his life, that wicked man will die for[a] his sin, and I will hold you accountable for his blood. ¹⁹But if you do warn the wicked man and he does not turn from his wickedness or from his evil ways, he will die for his sin; but you will have saved yourself.

²⁰"Again, when a righteous man turns from his righteousness and does evil, and I put a stumbling block before him, he will die. Since you did not warn him, he will die for his sin. The righteous things he did will not be remembered, and I will hold you accountable for his blood. ²¹But if you do warn the righteous man not to sin and he does not sin, he will surely live because he took warning, and you will have saved yourself."

[a]18 Or in; also in verses 19 and 20

NRSV

16At the end of seven days, the word of the LORD came to me: 17Mortal, I have made you a sentinel for the house of Israel; whenever you hear a word from my mouth, you shall give them warning from me. 18If I say to the wicked, "You shall surely die," and you give them no warning, or speak to warn the wicked from their wicked way, in order to save their life, those wicked persons shall die for their iniquity; but their blood I will require at your hand. 19But if you warn the wicked, and they do not turn from their wickedness, or from their wicked way, they shall die for their iniquity; but you will have saved your life. 20Again, if the righteous turn from their righteousness and commit iniquity, and I lay a stumbling block before them, they shall die; because you have not warned them, they shall die for their sin, and their righteous deeds that they have done shall not be remembered; but their blood I will require at your hand. 21If, however, you warn the righteous not to sin, and they do not sin, they shall surely live, because they took warning; and you will have saved your life.

COMMENTARY

Verse 16 looks in two directions: The first half looks back, temporally relating what follows to 3:15; the second half looks forward, its formula ("the word of the LORD came to me") introducing the divine speech that, in the text's final form, follows in vv. 17-21.[165] These two halves are separated in the MT by a space, most often an indication

of paragraph divisions or interruptions).[166] Moreover, the verbal sequence ויהי . . . ויהי (wayhî . . . wayhî; lit., "and it was . . . and it was"), unattested elsewhere in the book, betrays—to the minds of many critics—a later editor's somewhat clumsy touch.[167] Yet the verse, in its canonical form, does not impede comprehension. To the contrary, its transitional character abets the reader's move from 1:1–3:15 to subsequent verses.

165. This formula appears almost fifty times in the book of Ezekiel; it also is found in prophetic narratives within the Deuteronomistic History (e.g., 1 Sam 15:10; 2 Sam 7:4; 1 Kgs 13:20; 2 Kgs 20:4), in Jeremiah, in Haggai, and in Zechariah. It functions, Greenberg explains, to report "a revelation-experience by way of introducing a prophecy," but does not imply a distance between deity and prophet that must be mediated by the word. See Moshe Greenberg, *Ezekiel 1–20*, AB 22 (Garden City, N.Y.: Doubleday, 1983) 83; contra W. Zimmerli, *Ezekiel 1: A Commentary on the Book of the Prophet Ezekiel, Chapters 1–24*, trans. R. E. Clements, Hermeneia (Philadelphia: Fortress, 1979) 145.

166. See S. Talmon, "Pisqa Be'emṣa Pasuq and 11 Q Psᵃ," *Textus* 5 (1966) 11-21, cited in Greenberg, *Ezekiel 1–20*, 83.

167. According to Cooke, the original connection between 13:16a and 4:1ff. was broken with the insertion of 3:16b-21 and 3:22-27. See G. A. Cooke, *A Critical and Exegetical Commentary on the Book of Ezekiel*, ICC (New York: Scribner's, 1937) 1:44. Cf. Zimmerli, *Ezekiel 1*, 142, 144; Greenberg, *Ezekiel 1–20*, 82-83.

According to the divine word that Ezekiel heard and here relates, Yahweh uses "watchman" metaphorically to define the prophet's task to "the house of Israel." That is, the deity "speaks about one thing [Ezekiel's obligation as prophet] in terms which are seen to be suggestive of another,"[168] the watchman's duty to sound an alarm when danger threatens his community. The metaphor is not novel; it appears, for example, in Jer 6:17; Hos 9:8; and Hab 2:1 (Jer 6:17 focuses on the people's brazen response to their prophets; Ezek 3:16-21, by contrast, highlights Ezekiel's responsibility). Its usage in this context is especially apt, as we shall see, for while the watchman sounds a general alarm, his warning bears directly upon every person who hears it.

What imperils Ezekiel's audience? In Eichrodt's words, "the enemy of whom Ezekiel is to give warning is not any foreign foe but—no room is left for any doubt about it—Yahweh!"[169] When the prophet hears God's word, he must warn the exiles "against me" (NRSV and NIV, "from me"). Eichrodt notes the tension created by this situation: Yahweh's "action as judge . . . overhangs the nation and constitutes the most genuine and most menacing of dangers. Yet that same God appoints a watchman, evidently in order to give warning of himself and of the deadly danger he brings with him."[170] Following verses illustrate Ezekiel's responsibility by means of two scenarios involving "the wicked" and two others involving "the righteous." Do these cases support the view that here, Yahweh's threat "does not strike at people in general, but one wicked man among them, and the prophet is not told to deliver a general sermon to a congregation, but to address an appeal to this one threatened person among the people, in order to rescue him from the danger to which he is exposed"?[171]

Eichrodt's understanding of socioreligious dynamics within the exilic community, influenced by his interpretations of Ezekiel 18 and 33 (whence, in his view, this passage derives), con-

vinces him that these verses reflect a shift in the prophet's mode of addressing the exiles: "The individual had grown up so as to claim independence and assert his rights against the community," he explains, "and that produced a general mental attitude which either rejected or else failed to understand any message which was not couched in personal terms."[172] As a consequence, "we see Yahweh, in appointing the watchman, turning in love to his people and feeling it worth while to give a particular warning to each individual, so as to make him feel through it the mercy of the God who seeks him."[173] Eichrodt's statements are appealing. But are they relevant for this text?

Not a few critics have attributed to Ezekiel (especially after Jerusalem's destruction) a fresh emphasis upon the individual. Verses 18-21 reflect this concern, they claim, albeit "prematurely" (owing to their secondary editorial insertion near the book's beginning). Such arguments must be judged on the basis of a thorough examination of each passage at issue. In this context, it is worth recalling at the outset that Yahweh appoints Ezekiel as watchman "for the house of Israel" (v. 17), a broad epithet inclusive of its every member. He must give *them* "warning against me."

The four scenarios Yahweh sets before Ezekiel reflect the influence of biblical case (conditional or casuistic) law.[174] Typically such laws, like their ancient Near Eastern counterparts, begin with a protasis setting out the details of a case (e.g., "If someone is caught kidnaping another Israelite, enslaving or selling the Israelite," Deut 24:7*a* NRSV), followed by an apodosis spelling out its legal consequences (e.g., "then that kidnaper shall die," Deut 24:7*b* NRSV); and the subject is singular. The intent of this legal form is not to contrast the person with the community, but *to address personally every member of the larger group.* Verses 18-21 appear to function in the same way.

According to the first case (v. 18), if Yahweh pronounces the death sentence (מוֹת תָּמוּת *môt tāmût,* "you shall surely die") against any wicked person (the sentence appears in the second-person, as if addressed to the defendant in an actual court

168. Quoting J. M. Soskice's definition of metaphor, *Metaphor and Religious Language* (Oxford: Clarendon, 1985) 15. See K. P. Darr, "Figurative Language and Contemporary Theory," in *Isaiah's Vision and the Family of God* (Louisville: Westminster John Knox, 1994) 36-41.

169. Walther Eichrodt, *Ezekiel,* trans. Cosslett Quin, OTL (Philadelphia: Westminster, 1970) 443.

170. Ibid.

171. Ibid., 445.

172. Ibid., 447.

173. Ibid., 450.

174. On Ezekiel's use of legal language, see H. G. Reventlow, *Wächter über Israel. Ezechiel und seine Tradition,* BZAW 82 (Berlin: A. Topelmann, 1962).

setting, as opposed to the third-person, the usual form in law codes), but Ezekiel does not alert him to the danger, warning him from his wicked path in order to save his life; the sentence will be carried out, but Yahweh will require from the prophet's hand (an accounting for) the blood of the condemned—that is, he will suffer the death penalty as well (see 2 Sam 4:11-12). If, by contrast, the prophet warns the wicked person but he does not turn away from his wickedness, he shall die, but Ezekiel will have saved his own life.

Verse 20 takes up the case of the righteous person who turns from his or her righteousness and commits iniquity, with the result that Yahweh places a "stumbling block" (מכשול *mikšôl*) before that person. Here, Greenberg explains, *mikšôl* means " 'calamity'—not an occasion for sin but a cause of downfall and ruin"[175] (see also Isa 8:14 and Jer 6:21). Hence, the divinely placed stumbling block is the equivalent of the death sentence appearing in v. 18.[176] Felled as a consequence of inquity, the righteous person shall die; former deeds will not save him or her. And because Ezekiel failed to warn this person, Yahweh will require the blood of the righteous from his hand. But if the prophet warns the righteous and the latter heeds his warning, both parties will have saved their lives.

At first glance, the two cases in vv. 20-21 appear to parallel those in vv. 18-19. Closer inspection reveals significant differences between them, however, as Wilson has shown. First, were the form of v. 20 truly parallel to that of v. 18, it would begin, "If I say to the righteous, 'you shall surely live.' " Second, v. 20 is dependent upon vv. 18-19.[177] Third, the outcomes described in each pair of cases are not the same. In the first pair, the death sentence stands; what sets the scenarios apart is not the fate of the wicked, but that of Ezekiel. Of the second pair, v. 20 resembles v. 18 in requiring the deaths of both the lapsed righteous and the prophet. But in v. 21, both lives are spared.[178]

These instructions to Ezekiel function, in part, to demonstrate Yahweh's intention that the entire "house of Israel," both the wicked and the backsliding righteous, receive warning about the consequences of their actions. Equally clear, however, is the text's overriding concern that Ezekiel carry out his responsibility to warn them of impending danger—divinely imposed (untimely) death. To that end, the prophet's own life is placed in the balance; in cases involving the "incorrigibly" wicked, Ezekiel's singular concern must be "to acquit himself before God. Whether or not his warning is heeded matters not; as soon as he has performed his appointed task he is in the clear."[179] In one case involving the lapsed righteous (v. 21), however, the prophet's warning is efficacious: His life is saved by Ezekiel's warning. Here, Greenberg observes, the prophet's motivation extends beyond himself: "The righteous man, who . . . hears the alarm, reconsiders, and saves himself from disaster, is a character calculated to engage the sympathy of the prophet. . . . Let Ezekiel bear in mind that this, too, is part of his task."[180]

When Ezekiel utters Yahweh's death sentence, he takes up a task ascribed to other biblical prophets as well (see, e.g., Isaiah's pronouncement to Hezekiah in 2 Kgs 20:1 [= Isa 38:1]). When he adopts and adapts the form of case law, his priestly expertise becomes evident. The result of this creative combination serves his purpose well, as Greenberg explains: "Clothing the content of prophetic oracles in the form of case law is . . . a vehicle for stating principles of God's dealing with men, or, in other words, theological doctrines. . . . Ezekiel . . . made innovative use of this form for teachings which, though given for an occasion, he wished to present in the guise of general theological principles."[181]

Ezekiel's duty, then, is to sound the alarm when Yahweh pronounces the death sentence against "the house of Israel," who are guilty of long-lived, grievous sin (2:1–3:15). His life depends solely on his performance of that task; it does not hang on the people's response. Lives may be saved as a result of his warning. But Ezekiel is not told to hold that possibility before his audience. Like the preceding chapters, these verses drive home especially the obedience required of Yahweh's prophet. (See Reflections at 3:22-27.)

175. Greenberg, *Ezekiel 1–20,* 85.

176. Leviticus 19:14 forbids Israelites from placing stumbling blocks before the blind. "That God's judgment is described in terms of an act prohibited to men," Greenberg observes, "bespeaks a scandalous situation that the prophet is empowered to avert." Ibid.

177. Robert R. Wilson, "An Interpretation of Ezekiel's Dumbness," *VT* 22 (1972) 95.

178. Ibid., 95-96.

179. Greenberg, *Ezekiel 1–20,* 87.
180. Ibid., 88.
181. Ibid., 94-95.

EZEKIEL 3:22-27, LIMITATIONS ON EZEKIEL'S PROPHETIC MINISTRY

NIV

22The hand of the LORD was upon me there, and he said to me, "Get up and go out to the plain, and there I will speak to you." 23So I got up and went out to the plain. And the glory of the LORD was standing there, like the glory I had seen by the Kebar River, and I fell facedown. 24Then the Spirit came into me and raised me to my feet. He spoke to me and said: "Go, shut yourself inside your house. 25And you, son of man, they will tie with ropes; you will be bound so that you cannot go out among the people. 26I will make your tongue stick to the roof of your mouth so that you will be silent and unable to rebuke them, though they are a rebellious house. 27But when I speak to you, I will open your mouth and you shall say to them, 'This is what the Sovereign LORD says.' Whoever will listen let him listen, and whoever will refuse let him refuse; for they are a rebellious house.

NRSV

22Then the hand of the LORD was upon me there; and he said to me, Rise up, go out into the valley, and there I will speak with you. 23So I rose up and went out into the valley; and the glory of the LORD stood there, like the glory that I had seen by the river Chebar; and I fell on my face. 24The spirit entered into me, and set me on my feet; and he spoke with me and said to me: Go, shut yourself inside your house. 25As for you, mortal, cords shall be placed on you, and you shall be bound with them, so that you cannot go out among the people; 26and I will make your tongue cling to the roof of your mouth, so that you shall be speechless and unable to reprove them; for they are a rebellious house. 27But when I speak with you, I will open your mouth, and you shall say to them, "Thus says the Lord GOD"; let those who will hear, hear; and let those who refuse to hear, refuse; for they are a rebellious house.

COMMENTARY

Verses 22-24a, a brief report of yet another encounter between Ezekiel and the Lord's glory, introduce a third divine speech (3:24b–5:17). The author of this introduction has deliberately linked its theophany with Ezekiel's inaugural vision and call to prophesy (1:1–3:15); the reference to the hand of the Lord (v. 22) recalls 1:3 and 3:14; the appearance of Yahweh's glory (v. 23) is explicitly likened to its earlier manifestation by the Chebar Canal; the prophet falls on his face (v. 23; see 1:28) but is brought to his feet when the spirit enters him (v. 24; see 2:2). There are differences, of course. In chap. 1, the divine apparition swept toward Ezekiel as he stood by the Chebar Canal. Here, he is ordered "out into the valley"— Babylonia's alluvial plain—where Yahweh's glory awaits his arrival. Moreover, the text makes no attempt fully to restate details from 1:1-28. Eichrodt finds the notice of the glory's presence in v. 23 "remarkably lifeless" compared to that of Ezekiel 1; and well he should if the point were to

contrast the two texts. Such is not the purpose of v. 23, however, which stirs the reader's memories of that first, dazzling encounter and invites him to transport them to the scene on the plain. Like Zimmerli, Eichrodt attributes this reference to the glory's appearance to an editor working late in the book's composition history.[182] In their present context, however, vv. 22-24a perform their functions well—helping the reader to perceive consistency with what precedes, while introducing the next phase of Yahweh's instructions to the prophet.

Those instructions begin with Yahweh's abrupt command: "Go, shut yourself inside your house" (v. 24b; only in v. 25a do we find the formula "As for you, mortal," which, with some variations, has almost consistently introduced divine speeches and subsections of speeches to this point in the book; but see 3:22b). As the reader progresses through the work, he will discover that the text

182. Eichrodt, *Ezekiel,* 77; Zimmerli, *Ezekiel 1,* 157-58.

seldom situates Ezekiel in the public arena. When he addresses the elders of his community, for example, he does so at home (see also Elisha, 2 Kgs 6:32). At this point, however, the reader cannot specify the precise implications of Yahweh's order for Ezekiel's ability to communicate with others. The reader knows only that the prophet cannot go out among his fellow exiles.

Verse 25 places a second limitation on Ezekiel.[183] Yahweh informs him that "cords shall be placed on you, and you shall be bound with them, so that you cannot go out among the people" (NRSV; NIV, "they [the exiles] will tie [you] with ropes; you will be bound"). A great deal can depend upon whether one construes the third-person masculine plural verbs "to place" and "to bind" as actives or passives. If the former, these verbs designate the actions of others (the exiles?); if the latter, the agent who places and binds the cords is not specified (but is presumably Yahweh).

The reader cannot resolve this problem purely on grammatical grounds, since third-person plural active verbs can function as the equivalent of passives.[184] Rather, he will decide between the two options based on an understanding of vv. 24b-27 and in the light of what has been observed thus far. Yahweh's imperative in v. 24b accords well with the demands that have filled prior divine speeches. Verse 25, with its further restriction of the prophet's mobility, refers to the exiles using a third-person masculine plural suffix. If those exiles are to be regarded as the *agents* of this second limitation, however, then v. 25 constitutes a radical departure from previous texts, in which God alone has determined Ezekiel's role irrespective of his audience's response.

In v. 26, Yahweh imposes a third limitation upon the prophet: His tongue will cling to the roof of his mouth, rendering him speechless so that he cannot be an איש מוכיח (*'îš môkîaḥ*) for the exiles, because "they are a rebellious house." This verse not only bears on the reader's construal of

vv. 24b-27, but also plays an important role in shaping the understanding of Ezekiel's particular prophetic task. Hence, we must examine it closely. Crucial to its correct interpretation is the meaning of *môkîaḥ*, a Hiphil participle from the root יכח (*ykḥ*, "to decide," "adjudge," "prove") often translated "reprover" or "rebuker."[185]

In the argot of ancient Israel's pedagogical literature, the root *ykḥ* frequently denotes the activity of one who functions as a father or teacher, revealing and specifying the learner's mistakes.[186] Though his words can be harsh, their purpose is beneficial. Not surprisingly, Yahweh sometimes appears in the reprover's role (e.g., Prov 3:11-12). The wise student embraces rebuke as an opportunity for learning (Prov 25:12); the "scoffer" or "wicked" hates it (Prov 9:7-8; 13:1; 15:12), though even he may derive some benefit from the experience (Prov 19:25).

This didactic meaning of *ykḥ* appears especially to have influenced many translations and interpretations of v. 26. Greenberg, for example, maintains that in binding Ezekiel's tongue, Yahweh forbids him to assume the role of "one who reproaches wrongdoers with their wickedness and calls on them to mend their ways," adding that "the reprover" evidently fulfilled, on a communal scale, the religious injunction of Lev 19:17, and citing Prov 9:7-8. In Ezekiel's case, "reproof is checked by a moral motive: the people do not deserve it, for they are rebellious . . . ."[187] Zimmerli points to the *môkîaḥ* of Amos 5:10 and of Isa 29:20-21 as examples of those who "reprove" in the town gate, the traditional site of legal transactions.[188] Closer examination of these two texts reveals, however, that the *môkîaḥ* is not a remonstrating sage, but a participant in a juridical process.[189] In fact, the root *ykḥ* has deep and varied roots in the forensic proceedings of ancient Israel.[190] Is the meaning of *môkîaḥ* in 3:26 best illumined by its

---

183. Zimmerli, *Ezekiel 1*, 159, contends that the command in v. 24b is "quite independent" and "not related to" vv. 25-26. It is doubtful, however, that the reader of these verses would construe v. 24b in that way. Rather, vv. 24b-26 set out a series of divinely imposed limitations upon the prophet.

184. For discussion about the grammar here, see *Gesenius Hebrew Grammar*, ed. E. Kautsch and A. E. Cowley, 2nd rev. ed. (Oxford: Clarendon, 1910; repr. 1985) 144g; Cooke, *A Critical and Exegetical Commentary on the Book of Ezekiel*, 1:47; Zimmerli, *Ezekiel 1*, 160; Greenberg, *Ezekiel 1-20*, 102.

185. See *Theological Dictionary of the Old Testament*, ed. G. Johannes Botterweck and Helmer Ringgren, trans. David E. Green (Grand Rapids: Eerdmans, 1990) s.v. "יכח," where the basic meaning assigned to the root is "to set right," "to show what is right"; see also Isa 2:4; 11:3-4; Mic 4:3.

186. Ibid., 69.

187. Greenberg, *Ezekiel 1-20*, 102.

188. Zimmerli, *Ezekiel 1*, 161.

189. In both texts, the TNK translates *môkîaḥ* as "arbiter."

190. *TDOT*, 65-68.

uses in legal, rather than didactic, parlance? And does the presence of juristic elements in vv. 17-21 invite the reader to understand *môkîaḥ* on juridical, rather than sapiental, grounds?

M. B. Dick's analysis of legal metaphors in the book of Job sheds considerable light on forensic meanings of *ykḥ*, on the role of the arbiter in the ancient Near East, and on the significance of *môkîaḥ* in v. 26.[191] His thesis that Job 31:35 constitutes "a defendant's official appeal before a third party for a civil hearing at which the judge would compel the plaintiff to formalize his accusations and to present any supporting evidence" is buttressed by both extra-biblical and biblical texts. From Akkadian legal documents, for example, we learn that when a dispute arose between two parties, a trial was normally preceded by *informal* attempts at arbitration between the plaintiff and the accused. Should such efforts fail, however, either party could request a *formal* hearing before an impartial arbiter(s).[192]

One such scenario appears in Genesis 31. When Laban catches up to Jacob and ransacks his goods for "stolen" property, Jacob (the defendant) angrily confronts his father-in-law (the plaintiff), demanding material evidence of his alleged crime at a public hearing: "What is my offense? What is my sin, that you have hotly pursued me? Although you have felt about through all my goods, what have you found of all your household goods? Set it here before my kinsfolk and your kinsfolk, so that they may decide [וְיוֹכִיחוּ *wĕyôkîḥû*] between us two" (Gen 31:36b-37 NRSV). Jacob's stipulation that arbiters come from both kin groups reveals his concern that both the hearing and their ruling be fair and impartial (or at least balanced).[193] Moreover, Jacob couples his demand for a public hearing with an assertion of innocence; his behavior toward Laban has been more than exemplary in all situations (Gen 31:38-42). Similarly, when David is charged with plotting against King Saul

(1 Samuel 24), he seeks adjudication (by Yahweh) of the specious accusations against him.[194] In addition to submitting material evidence—a strip of Saul's cloak (1 Sam 24:11)—he also asserts his innocence.

In Job 9:33, Job longs for a *môkîaḥ* (NRSV, "umpire") who might ensure a fair public hearing between Yahweh and himself: "There is no umpire [or "Would that there were an umpire"] between us, who might lay his hand on us both" (NRSV). In this context also, Dick observes, "the *môkîaḥ* is the ancient Near Eastern judge. Unlike the modern magistrate who represents the state and functions with its authority, this arbiter could probably only suggest a settlement which possessed no authority unless one party swore [to forgo further litigation]."[195] Job formally requests such a hearing in chap. 31. But because his accuser (Yahweh) is also his "ultimate arbiter," Job perceives that his pleas for a neutral third party are in vain. "This incongruity," Dick writes, "reduces the legal metaphor to the absurd and thereby reveals the bankruptcy of conceiving the man-God relationship along the lines of legal justice."[196]

If, as Dick and others argue, the *môkîaḥ* is an arbiter, what might be the implications of Yahweh's decision to render Ezekiel speechless, so that he cannot assume this role for the rebellious house of Israel?

We call prophets "intermediaries" because they mediate between the divine and human spheres. Most often, biblical prophetic literature depicts one side of the coin (Israel's prophets proclaiming Yahweh's words to the people) rather than the other (Israel's prophets conveying human words to God). One result is that critics sometimes overlook the latter function of prophecy. When v. 26 states that Ezekiel cannot perform the arbiter's role, it precludes any possibility of his participation in a formal hearing in which *both* parties—Yahweh and Israel—might have their say (e.g., present witnesses and evidence). It also constrains the exiles who, like Job, might perceive that their suffering is caused by Yahweh,[197] but who cannot rely on Ezekiel's assistance in securing a fair hearing leading

191. M. B. Dick, "The Legal Metaphor in Job 31," *CBQ* 4 (1979) 37-50. However, Dick says nothing about 3:16-21 in his article.

192. See ibid., 41-42; J. G. Lautner, *Die richterliche Entscheidung und die Streitbeendigung im altbabylonischen Prozessrechte,* Leipziger rechtwissenschaftliche Studien 3 (Leipzig: Theodor Weicher, 1922).

193. When the word *môkîaḥ* designates one who presides over a trial or dispute, Wilson observes, "it seems to refer to a legal official whose task was to assure a fair hearing for both the accuser and the accused." See Wilson, "An Interpretation of Ezekiel's Dumbness," 99.

194. Dick, "The Legal Metaphor in Job 31," 44-45.
195. Ibid., 46.
196. Ibid., 50.
197. As Dick notes, ibid., 40, "the theological etiology for human suffering was not restricted to an individual's lamentation, for sin could also explain a national catastrophe (Isa 1:4-6)."

to compromise and perhaps even a dismissal of the divine charges against them (already articulated in 2:1–3:12). Why not? Because their guilt cannot be denied: "they are a rebellious house." Ezekiel is not rendered incapable of "reproving" the people because "they do not deserve it."[198] He cannot act the arbiter because Yahweh forbids it. "Now," Davis writes, "the function of the prophet is simply to make known to Israel the author of judgment and the just grounds for its execution."[199]

If Ezekiel's potential role as arbiter has been checked by divinely imposed muteness, this does not mean that he cannot speak for other reasons. Whenever Yahweh addresses him, God will open his mouth and Ezekiel will say, "Thus says Lord Yahweh," whether his audience hears or refuses to hear. "In the dialogue which Yahweh carries on with his people through the prophet, communication can now move in only one direction: from Yahweh to the people. No longer can the people argue with Yahweh through the prophet. The time for a fair trial has passed."[200]

Ezekiel's inability/ability to speak is at issue in two sequentially later passages, 24:27 and 33:22.

Modern critics have tended to analyze and interpret Ezek 3:26-27 in the light of those texts—construing v. 26 to say that Ezekiel's speechlessness is absolute and explaining v. 27 as an editorial attempt to ameliorate the problem created by the secondary placement of v. 26 in chap. 3.[201] Read on its on terms, however, v. 26 does not state that Ezekiel will be totally mute. Divinely imposed silence precludes his arbitrating between Israel and its God, but whenever Yahweh opens his mouth, he *must* proclaim God's oracles to his fellow captives (v. 27). These two parallel statements (vv. 26-27) appear problematic only when interpreted in the light of passages as yet unknown to the reader.[202] His understanding of those later texts may be influenced by his interpretation of 3:26-27; he may even be forced to rethink these earlier verses when he arrives at those later ones. At this point, however, the competent sequential reader perceives none of the problems that have plagued modern critics.

198. Greenberg, *Ezekiel 1–20*, 102.
199. Davis, *Swallowing the Scroll*, 56.
200. Wilson, "An Interpretation of Ezekiel's Dumbness," 101.

201. See ibid., 104. Cf. Davis, *Swallowing the Scroll*, 50, 52.
202. The previous passage, by contrast, may influence the reader's understanding of 3:24b-27 not only by its use of language at home in juristic settings, but also by establishing a context for Yahweh's decision not to allow Ezekiel to function as an arbiter. See Robert R. Wilson, "An Interpretation of Ezekiel's Dumbness," *VT* 22 (1972) 101, who suggests that "the legal dispute involved here [v. 26] is the one to which iii 16b-21 has already alluded. It is the dispute between the people and Yahweh. . . . In this dispute Ezekiel is forbidden to be a mediator."

REFLECTIONS

In a world where mighty empires vie for power, smaller nations are crushed in the fray, and ecological disasters threaten great and small alike, the theocentric (God-centered) people of Israel perceive Yahweh at work. And because their worldview is also ethnocentristic, they interpret Yahweh's actions, for good or for ill, especially in the light of their own. If Israel is just, righteous, and obedient, it expects to experience divine blessings. If, by contrast, the nation forgets its God, is sinful and rebellious, it should expect to endure divine judgment. In short, Israel makes causal connections between what it does and what Yahweh is doing. We call this theological equation—reward for good, punishment for evil—the "Doctrine of Retribution." Because, as the apostle Paul states, "all have sinned and fall short of the glory of God" (Rom 3:23 NRSV), this doctrine can prove an unbearable burden. If the punishment is perceived far to outweigh the crime, "theodicy"—the questioning of God's justice—almost certainly arises. (Why must blameless Job suffer so severely?) These concepts are both ancient and contemporary. They surface whenever we ask why bad things happen to good people.

Ancient Israel knows that Yahweh's judgment is no paltry thing. It affirms, nonetheless, that God's character includes a propensity toward grace. When the author of Psalm 130 cries "out of the depths" of anguish (Ps 130:1 NRSV), for example, he acknowledges that were the deity to keep account of sins, none could survive. Above all, however, he affirms that God forgives and redeems:

If you, O LORD, should mark iniquities,
  LORD, who could stand?
But there is forgiveness with you,
  so that you may be revered. (Ps 130:3-4 NRSV; see also vv. 7-8)

More than once, Hebrew Scripture asserts that "the LORD is merciful and gracious, slow to anger and abounding in steadfast love" (Ps 103:8 NRSV; see also Exod 34:6; Ps 145:8; Joel 2:13; Jonah 4:2; Nah 1:3). But in the face of relentless human sinfulness, divine justice also has its day, for God's grace does not simply obviate human accountability. When the psalmist says that "he does not deal with us according to our sins, nor repay us according to our iniquities" (Ps 103:10 NRSV), his words fly in the face of much biblical testimony that insists that though Yahweh is forbearing, divine wrath can erupt in the face of persistent rebelliousness (e.g., 2 Kgs 17:7-18). The twin themes of God's justice and grace must somehow coexist, for both are deeply rooted in tradition and in human experience.

When divine justice demands punishment, Israel's prophets sometimes intercede on the people's behalf: Yahweh shows the eighth-century BCE prophet Amos a swarm of locusts formed to devour Israel's crops. Amos intercedes: "O Lord GOD, forgive, I beg you! How can Jacob stand? He is so small!" Yahweh relents (Amos 7:1-3 NRSV). The Lord calls for fire. Amos intercedes: "O Lord GOD, cease, I beg you! How can Jacob stand? He is so small!" Yahweh relents (Amos 7:4-6 NRSV). As Amos watches, the Lord holds a plumb line to a wall. Israel is crooked, unsound. This time, God's judgment stands. Intercessory prayer and personal petition are deeply rooted in the Judeo-Christian tradition. In reciting such prayers, do believers ever seriously consider the possibility that "no" might be God's only viable response?

The book of Jeremiah dares to disclose the pathos of both deity and prophet in the face of a people seemingly bent on its own destruction. Both weep; both lament. Yahweh's pain is that of a parent whose children have turned away to their own hurt: "Return, O faithless children," God entreats, "I will heal your faithlessness" (Jer 3:22 NRSV). Both are driven to the pinnacles of rage and the craters of despair. Both lose patience, lose their tempers, lose hope that Judah will change its course, turn, and survive. At one point, Yahweh forbids Jeremiah to intercede further on Judah's behalf: "As for you, do not pray for this people, do not raise a cry or prayer on their behalf, and do not intercede with me, for I will not hear you" (Jer 7:16 NRSV). Yahweh's emotions are everywhere present in Jeremiah's prophecies. How do humans contend with the notion of a God whose pain strains the divine heart or whose anger eclipses love?

The prophet Habakkuk determines to stand at his watchpost, awaiting God's response to his complaint that Yahweh neither sees nor hears, that the Lord's own people are suffering while those more wicked than they destroy without mercy. Surely justice demands an accounting even of Yahweh's ways (Hab 1:2–2:1). But Ezekiel makes no such demand of the Lord. Who dares to follow biblical characters like Moses and Job when they contend with God?

Where in the book of Ezekiel are the prophet's cries of intercession on Israel's behalf? Where is God's pain at the prospect of Judah's demise? Where does Ezekiel call Yahweh to account for Israel's suffering at Babylonia's hand? We have read no such things thus far. God authors Ezekiel's script. Ezekiel can neither intercede nor arbitrate; both he and his tongue are tied. Israel's ultimate arbiter has already determined its guilt and pronounced sentence.

Ezekiel's prophetic ministry coincides with a deadly crisis in Israel's relationship with its God. His people have, it seems, confounded Yahweh's every attempt—grace-filled and punitive—to bring them to repentance, to change their self-destructive course, to effect reconciliation between creator and created. Now Israel must face the consequences of its obdurate propensity toward sin. It is time, to borrow words from Jeremiah's call account, "to pluck up and to pull down, to destroy and to overthrow" (Jer 1:10 NRSV). What, if anything, lies on the other side of judgment has no place here. This place is harsh, ominous, full of limitations, filled with God's no. Ezekiel must pound that no into the stubborn foreheads of the rebellious house of Israel.

EZEKIEL'S ORACLES AGAINST JUDAH AND JERUSALEM

EZEKIEL 4:1–5:17, "THIS IS A SIGN FOR THE HOUSE OF ISRAEL"

OVERVIEW

In 4:1–5:4, Yahweh commands Ezekiel to perform a series of sign acts primarily related to the fates of Jerusalem and its inhabitants. Indeed, even when the text turns to exilic conditions (e.g., 4:13), it focuses upon homeland survivors of the city's destruction in 587 BCE, not upon those Judeans (like Ezekiel) already living in Babylonia. In the following divine harangue (5:5-17), the majority of Yahweh's reproaches and threats are cast as direct address to Jerusalem (using the second-person fem. sing. pronoun "you"; see Excursus: "Cities as Females," 1221-25). Yet the prophet's audience is not the city's hapless besieged, but his fellow exiles (and late exilic readers). These verses presuppose that vital ties—familial, social, political, religious, etc.—inextricably bind the deportees of 597 BCE to Judah and events transpiring there. They also presuppose that Ezekiel's audience, no less than their counterparts in Jerusalem, must be convinced that the harsh divine judgment announced by both deeds and diatribe is imminent and unavoidable: "Their goal is not a repentance that could still change things. . . . The only repentance they seek is that which acknowledges guilt and accepts punishment."[203]

Although only one sign act requires that Ezekiel speak (4:7b), each is an "oracle"—designed by God, consigned to the prophet, and ostensibly intended for others. Medium and message are inextricable elements of such actions. In order for them to have an impact, they must reach an audience in *some* way. Critics note that Ezekiel could have performed these acts while confined to his house (3:24b). But if that were the case, then in what sense might they function as "a sign for the house of Israel" (4:3b)?

Prophetic sign acts were no Ezekielian innovation. Yet no other prophet was ordered to perform them so frequently as he. Were such acts deemed especially appropriate at critical junctures in Israel's history, when prophets felt compelled to communicate God's intentions in the most attention-grabbing of ways? Does this explain why the preponderance of Ezekiel's sign acts appears in chaps. 1–24, where horrific oracles of doom follow one upon another and hope seldom intrudes?

The sign actions performed by Israel's prophets were not miracles. They usually entailed activity within the capacity of any person (although some would certainly have elicited social sanction; one should recall Yahweh's command that Isaiah walk naked and barefoot through the streets of Jerusalem, Isa 20:2-4). Their presence discomfited the twelfth-century CE Jewish philosopher Maimonides, who contended that Ezekiel saw himself performing such actions only in visions and whose discussion in *Guide for the Perplexed* includes the following apologetic: "God forbid to assume that God would make his prophets appear an object of ridicule and sport in

---

203. Ronald M. Hals, *Ezekiel*, FOTL 19 (Grand Rapids: Eerdmans, 1989) 35.

the eyes of the ignorant, and order them to perform foolish acts."[204] In past centuries, scholars tended to explain Ezekiel's actions either as parables or as manifestations of some psychological and/or physical ailment. The former of these two interpretive turns is understandable, for several of the performances assigned to Ezekiel strain credulity: Could he actually have lain on his left side, bound with cords, for three hundred and ninety days? Klostermann's proposal that Ezekiel lay on his side for so long because he suffered from a disorder known as "periodic alalia" commands little contemporary support.[205]

Did Ezekiel actually carry out the sign acts assigned in 4:1–5:4? Many a contemporary critic insists that he did. Zimmerli opines that "a sign-action which was not actually performed but only narrated must be regarded as a late and weakened form,"[206] while Greenberg reasons that "the explicit anticipation of public reaction to such actions (e.g., Ezek 12:9) excludes taking them as

visionary."[207] Davis, by contrast, regards Ezekiel's sign act accounts as literary compositions intended by the author-prophet to enhance significantly the reader's engagement with the text. "We see in his sign-actions," she writes, "a highly conscious self-representation, a literary effort which is calculated in the best sense: one so finely coordinated and attuned to his audience's perception of reality that the imitation of an action is more persuasive than action itself."[208]

Critics should acknowledge their limitations. No one can ever know if Ezekiel actually obeyed the orders of 4:1–5:4. If he did, it is likely that only a handful of people witnessed them, and their responses were not preserved. One thing is certain, however: Millions of readers have "witnessed" Ezekiel's sign acts through Yahweh's instructions in the text. The narrative encourages the reader's *presumption* that these acts will, in fact, be executed. The reader should remember, in a related vein, how the account of Ezekiel's inaugural vision seeks, through its wealth of details, to persuade readers that Ezekiel truly saw what he claims to have seen (1:4-28).

204. Moses Maimondes, *The Guide for the Perplexed,* trans. M. Friedländer (New York: E. P. Dutton, 1947) 2.46.

205. A. Klostermann, "Ezekiel. Ein Beitrag zu besser Würdigung seiner Person und seiner Schrift," *TSK* 50 (1877) 391-439.

206. W. Zimmerli, *Ezekiel 1: A Commentary on the Book of the Prophet Ezekiel, Chapters 1–24,* trans. R. E. Clements, Hermeneia (Philadelphia: Fortress, 1979) 156.

207. Moshe Greenberg, *Ezekiel 1–20,* AB 22 (Garden City, N.Y.: Doubleday, 1983) 122.

208. Ellen F. Davis, *Swallowing the Scroll: Textuality and the Dynamics of Discourse in Ezekiel's Prophecy,* Bible and Literature 21 (Sheffield: Almond, 1989) 71.

Ezekiel 4:1-3, Enacting a Siege

NIV	NRSV
4 "Now, son of man, take a clay tablet, put it in front of you and draw the city of Jerusalem on it. ²Then lay siege to it: Erect siege works against it, build a ramp up to it, set up camps against it and put battering rams around it. ³Then take an iron pan, place it as an iron wall between you and the city and turn your face toward it. It will be under siege, and you shall besiege it. This will be a sign to the house of Israel.	4 And you, O mortal, take a brick and set it before you. On it portray a city, Jerusalem; ²and put siegeworks against it, and build a siege wall against it, and cast up a ramp against it; set camps also against it, and plant battering rams against it all around. ³Then take an iron plate and place it as an iron wall between you and the city; set your face toward it, and let it be in a state of siege, and press the siege against it. This is a sign for the house of Israel.

COMMENTARY

Still standing on the plain in the presence of Yahweh's glory, Ezekiel is ordered by God to take a sun-dried brick, a common building material, and to depict upon it a city—Jerusalem.[209] (Archaeologists have unearthed bricks and tablets inscribed with city plans and maps in the area of ancient Babylon.) This icon will serve as stage for some deadly serious "play," for he is to place it under siege, complete with siegeworks, walls, ramps, and battering rams round about. Next, he must take an iron griddle, position it between

himself and the "city," and "direct his face" (gaze with intense hostility) against it.

Although the text does not explicitly interpret these activities, their meaning seems clear: Ezekiel's siege depicts on a small scale the Babylonian army's siege against Jerusalem, while the iron griddle represents the impenetrable barrier Yahweh has placed between city and self.[210] Together, these activities will be "a sign for the house of Israel" (v. 3b). Given the divine provenance and consequent authority of the assigned act, this military game cannot be dismissed as the prophet's own machinations! (See Reflections at 5:5-17.)

209. BHS and some critics suggest that "Jerusalem" be deleted as a later addition that spoils the suspense otherwise created by leaving the city unnamed until 5:5. See Walther Eichrodt, *Ezekiel*, trans. Cosslett Quin, OTL (Philadelphia: Westminster, 1970) 83. The text presents, however, as Yahweh's private instructions to Ezekiel, who ostensibly needs fully to understand the sign act he is ordered to perform.

210. Greenberg, *Ezekiel 1–20*, 104, refers to the opinion that the barrier represents Israel's sin (see Isa 59:2).

❖   ❖   ❖   ❖

EXCURSUS: PROPHETIC SIGN ACTS

That Ezekiel is ordered to perform sign acts comes as no surprise to ancient readers familiar with the phenomenon from both pre-classical and classical prophetic traditions. The prophet Ahijah of Shiloh tears his garment into twelve pieces and hands ten to Jeroboam, son of Nebat, to indicate that God has given him ten tribes of the soon-to-be-sundered kingdom of Israel (1 Kgs 11:30-31). Hosea's marriage to Gomer and the symbolic names of their children signify Yahweh's jealousy over Israel's unfaithfulness and its consequences for the land and its inhabitants (Hosea 1–3). Jeremiah dons a yoke to portray the subservience of Judah and its neighbors to Babylon (Jeremiah 27). The prophet Hananiah breaks that yoke—a striking countersign that challenges Jeremiah's version of impending events (Jer 28:10-11).

Ezekiel's sign acts, like their counterparts in other prophetic books and narratives, have generated considerable critical debate. One aspect of that debate turns on the relationship between such actions and magic. Did the prophets and their audiences believe that sign acts had a causitive effect on the future? No, Wevers avers: "Magic attempts to effect an action by enacting such symbolically. But prophetic action was never thought to bring about that which is symbolized."[211] Eichrodt, by contrast, perceives in such performances "a remarkable resemblance to a magical act, not only in the construction, nature and method of the symbolic action but also in the belief that it will prove effective once it is accomplished."[212]

Eichrodt hurries on to add, however, that we should not term the prophetic act "magical"; its "compelling power is not based upon its mechanical performance. . . . Yahweh's consent . . . confers authority, which supplies the basis for faith in the irresistible effective might of the prophetic action."[213] Here, Eichrodt acknowledges his indebtedness to Fohrer, whose landmark study has influenced a generation of scholars.[214] Fohrer pointed to (ostensible) similarities

211. J. W. Wevers, *Ezekiel*, NCB (London: Nelson, 1969) 60.
212. Eichrodt, *Ezekiel*, 81.
213. Ibid., 81-82.
214. G. Fohrer, *Die symbolischen Handlungen der Propheten*, 2nd ed., ATANT 25 (Zurich: Zwingli, 1968).

between the prophets' sign acts, on the one hand, and magical beliefs and practices of the ancient world, on the other hand. So, for example, he linked Ezekiel's fixed gaze upon his besieged brick "city" (4:1-3) to the oriental notion of the dreaded "evil eye" (see Amos 9:4*b*). Sign acts functioned, in part, to present God's messages in striking ways. But, Fohrer insisted, prophets and audiences alike believed that such acts, like magic, could alter the future.[215] Lang summarizes Fohrer's thinking on this point:

> The symbolic act . . . influences and shapes future events simply by being performed. . . . This is magic, but magic with a difference. . . . While "real" magicians work on their own behalf and rely on mechanisms inherent in the magical manipulation itself, prophets act on behalf of the deity . . . [giving] magic an entirely new meaning. Substituting the promise and threat of magic by the promise and threat of the deity, they have transcended and indeed abolished the very notion of magic.[216]

The label "magic" applies, in Lang's view, only to those few actions that, by " 'pre-imitating' the future, or the effort required to produce it . . . [pave] the way for the historical event. In a mystical way the historical event participates in the magical game and is set in motion by the latter."[217] As examples he cites Elisha's "war magic" (2 Kgs 13:14-19) and the "drowning" of Jeremiah's papyrus scroll (Jer 51:59-64). But most prophetic sign acts belong to other categories.[218] "Teaching aids," for example, "visualize an aspect of the prophetic message or preaching." Ezekiel's military game (4:1-3) belongs to this category. A second type, "performative gestures," includes those actions that, when executed, effect some change in the status quo. Here, Lang cites Elijah's throwing of his cloak over Elisha (1 Kgs 19:19-21), an act that brings the latter into the fold of Elijah's disciples.[219] To "symbolically perceived acts" belong those instances when a prophet interprets life events in a symbolic way. Ezekiel, for example, perceives in his wife's death a parallel to Jerusalem's impending destruction (24:15-27).

Again, critics must acknowledge their limitations. We cannot ask ancient Israelites if they believed that prophetic sign acts influenced future events. We do know, however, that by attributing the commands to perform these actions to Yahweh, the author of Ezek 4:1–5:4 encourages the reader's presumption that the siege of 4:1-3, for example, will indeed be performed, not only by Ezekiel against the city plan, but also on a larger scale by God against Jerusalem itself. On the one hand, the narrative strategy of presenting these actions as divine commands imbues them with God's authority. On the other hand, it buttresses the *prophet's* authority in several ways. First, it places him in the company of past prophets who also were ordered to perform sign actions (e.g., Elijah, Amos, Hosea, Isaiah, Jeremiah). Second, it depicts Ezekiel as privy to Yahweh's exact plans for Israel's future. Third, it makes the implicit claim that God will sustain this prophet in his performance of even the most arduous tasks. Fourth, it asserts Ezekiel's prophetic authority.[220]

---

215. Many modern critics agree. See, e.g., Zimmerli *Ezekiel 1*, 156; Hals, *Ezekiel*, 33. Cf. Greenberg, *Ezekiel 1–20*, 122-23.

216. B. Lang, "Street Theater, Raising the Dead, and the Zoroastrian Connection in Ezekiel's Prophecy," in *Ezekiel and His Book: Textual and Literary Criticism and Their Interrelation*, ed. J. Lust, BETL 74 (Leuven: Leuven University Press, 1986) 303-4.

217. Ibid., 306.

218. Hence, Lang concludes, Fohrer was "on the right track, if only in a much more limited way than . . . anticipated." Ibid.

219. Lang does not explain by what power performative gestures effect such changes. Is Elijah's act performative, in part, because it is conventional?

220. Davis, *Swallowing the Scroll*, 70.

❖   ❖   ❖   ❖

Ezekiel 4:4-8, Bearing Iniquity/Punishment

NIV

[4]"Then lie on your left side and put the sin of the house of Israel upon yourself.[a] You are to bear their sin for the number of days you lie on your side. [5]I have assigned you the same number of days as the years of their sin. So for 390 days you will bear the sin of the house of Israel.

[6]"After you have finished this, lie down again, this time on your right side, and bear the sin of the house of Judah. I have assigned you 40 days, a day for each year. [7]Turn your face toward the siege of Jerusalem and with bared arm prophesy against her. [8]I will tie you up with ropes so that you cannot turn from one side to the other until you have finished the days of your siege.

[a]4 Or your side

NRSV

[4]Then lie on your left side, and place the punishment of the house of Israel upon it; you shall bear their punishment for the number of the days that you lie there. [5]For I assign to you a number of days, three hundred ninety days, equal to the number of the years of their punishment; and so you shall bear the punishment of the house of Israel. [6]When you have completed these, you shall lie down a second time, but on your right side, and bear the punishment of the house of Judah; forty days I assign you, one day for each year. [7]You shall set your face toward the siege of Jerusalem, and with your arm bared you shall prophesy against it. [8]See, I am putting cords on you so that you cannot turn from one side to the other until you have completed the days of your siege.

COMMENTARY

In 4:4-8, Yahweh commands that Ezekiel bear the "guilt" (or "punishment?") of "the house of Israel" and of "the house of Judah" by lying first on his left side (for 390 days) and then on his right (for 40 days), respectively. Above all others, Eichrodt observes, this sign act commends the view that descriptions of most such actions should not be taken literally, but "regarded as a poetical way of expressing their message in parabolic or pictorial form."[221] His comment arises from the implausibility that Ezekiel could lie "absolutely still" for so lengthy a period of time.

We miss the point of this act if we focus foremost upon its credulity, or if we attempt to explain Ezekiel's ability to execute it by resorting to diagnoses of mental and/or physical disability.[222] The ancient reader's extra-textual repertoire included countless examples of persons who, at Yahweh's command, performed feats beyond normal human ability and/or outside acceptable social behavior,

in some cases for extraordinary periods of time (the prophet Isaiah is said to have walked naked and barefoot through Jerusalem's streets for *three years,* Isa 20:3). Again, the fact that Yahweh commands this conduct of Ezekiel encourages the reader's presumption that the prophet will obey orders.

Critics identify numerous conundrums in Ezek 4:4-8; a glance at the text through the "editorial lens" (see Introduction) reveals many of them. Consider the following observations and questions: (1) Verse 4 contains no introductory formula. Do vv. 4-8 constitute a separate sign act or a continuation of the siege enactment demanded in 4:1-3? (2) Up to this point, "the house of Israel" has designated all of Israel throughout its history. Does the presence of "the house of Judah" in v. 6 require that vv. 4-5 pertain only to the northern kingdom? (3) What does it mean for Ezekiel to נשא (*nāśā',* "bear") עון (*'āwōn,* "iniquity" or "punishment"), and which of these two translations of *'awōn* is best suited to each of the verses in which the phrase appears? (4) What is the significance of the numbers of days/years in the MT? How might we explain the absence of forty days of lying on

221. Eichrodt, *Ezekiel,* 83.
222. This is *not* to deny that traditional ways of speaking about various physical anomalies may have influenced accounts of Ezekiel's immobility. See Stephen Garfinkel, "Another Model for Ezekiel's Abnormalities," *JANES* 19 (1989) 39-50.

the right side in 4:9? (5) If cords prevent Ezekiel from turning "from one side to the other" (v. 8), how could he change sides, as dictated in vv. 4 and 6?

Certain critics explain these and other features of 4:4-8 by pointing to the text's complex history of composition. Verse 4 lacks an introductory formula, they insist, because it is a later accretion; "the house of Israel" only came to designate the northern kingdom with the subsequent addition of v. 6. No single explanation for the numbers suffices, because their significance changed as the text was expanded. Does our approach, which focuses upon the way the late exilic, sequential reader construed the book of Ezekiel, justify setting these issues aside as ancillary to our task?

This text, more than any we have examined thus far, raises two questions: (1) Was the reader aware that in his era, Israel's traditions—including its religious traditions—were the object of substantial literary activity? (2) Might he have considered that editorial reworking (reinterpretation) introduced at least some of the problems identified above?[223] Unfortunately, these tantalizing questions cannot be answered with any degree of certainty. We must, therefore, frame the discussion in terms of a different question—namely, do certain features of the text, combined with the reader's tendency toward consistency building, suffice to render these verses intelligible in their final form?

That the sign act described in these verses does not begin with a usual introductory formula will probably not discomfit the sequential reader (3:24b also lacked such a formula). True, the activity prescribed differs from that of vv. 1-3. Yet references to "the siege"/"your siege" in vv. 7 and 8 respectively link it to the preceding military game. As a consequence, the reader regards Ezekiel's bearing of iniquity/punishment as an act successive and related to, rather than utterly distinct from, the siege enactment and extends the introduction in v. 1 to it also. (By the same token, the order to prepare siege rations [vv. 9-17], likewise introduced by ואתה [wĕ'attâ, "and you"] in v. 9, will be linked to previous verses not only by the theme of siege, but also by the reference to lying

on the side for 390 days, v. 9b. Hence this act also appears to follow upon and relate to the previous two, and the fuller introductory formula of v. 1 suffices for it as well.) Historical critics detect in these "bridging" verses the work of a redactor. We should rather say that such bridges, regardless of their origins, perform their task well: smoothing the transition from one sign act to the next.

In v. 4 Yahweh commands that the prophet lie on his left side and, placing the guilt or punishment of the "house of Israel" upon it, bear it for "the number of the days that you lie there." Verse 5 speaks more specifically: He must so lie for three hundred and ninety days, "equal to the number of the years." To this point, the reader naturally takes "the house of Israel" to mean what it has meant in earlier chapters—that is, all of Israel throughout its history to Ezekiel's day. Does v. 6 force him to reinterpret vv. 4-5 as referring to the northern kingdom alone? In order to answer this question, we must first consider the possible meaning(s) of the phrase nāśā' 'āwōn in these verses.

Zimmerli's analysis of the thirty-five appearances of nāśā' 'āwōn in the MT reveals that in its twenty-seven occurrences in the Priestly source of the Pentateuch (eighteen) and in the book of Ezekiel (nine), this phrase conveys one of three meanings:

(1) In the sphere of sacral law it is used in concluding formulations to establish a condition of guilt.

(2) In a weaker usage the expression can take on the meaning "to be responsible for something" (such as the sanctuary, Num 18:1).

(3) In substitutionary acts it can express the "guilt bearing" of the substitute. Thus the scapegoat bears the guilt of the people on itself into the desert (Lev 16:22).[224]

Critics agree that in vv. 4-6, the phrase falls within the third category of meaning.[225] Yet Ezekiel's bearing of 'āwōn does not function to "bear away" the people's guilt (or punishment); rather, it confronts them in a most concrete and sustained

---

223. Even Greenberg, who everywhere seeks to discern the intelligibility of the canonical text, concludes that the present position of 4:4-8 results from "editorial decision." See Greenberg, *Ezekiel 1–20*, 126.

224. Zimmerli, *Ezekiel 1*, 164.

225. In fact, many scholars suggest that this passage has influenced the famous "suffering servant" poem in Isaiah 53. See, e.g., Joseph Blenkinsopp, *Ezekiel*, IBC (Louisville: John Knox, 1990) 35-36.

way with the reality of their 'āwōn. Zimmerli's cautionary note is apropos:

> We must not be too hasty here in introducing an elaborate theory of substitution, especially since Ezek 4:4 is . . . an attempt at interpreting an event of the prophet's life in a new way, making use of this phrase drawn from the priestly vocabulary. . . . The idea is expressed that Ezekiel portrayed publicly . . . a condition of guilt. . . . by lying bound, [he] became a revealer of guilt, an accuser, as he had been previously in threatening punishment.[226]

The reference to "three hundred ninety days" in v. 5 can be construed as corresponding to the approximately three hundred and ninety years that Solomon's Temple stood (or of the existence of the monarchy), such that this phase of Ezekiel's sign act constitutes a public portrayal of the guilt that sinful Israel (now reduced to the southern kingdom) incurred over the approximately four centuries of its existence. Zimmerli reminds us, however, that in addition to denoting " 'wrongdoing,' and the guilt this incurs, 'āwōn also can designate 'the punishment consequent upon such guilt.' "[227] Do aspects of v. 6, coupled with the reader's extra-textual knowledge, suggest that in this verse, 'āwōn designates forty years of punishment that Israel's surviving element ("the house of Judah") must now endure?

Verse 6 begs thoughts of Num 14:34. Moses sends spies to search out the land of Canaan (Num 13:1-21). At the end of forty days, the spies return to the Hebrews' camp with evidence of the land's astonishing abundance (Num 13:23), but also with tales of its fearsome inhabitants (Num 13:28-29, 31-33). Dispirited, the Hebrews decide to abandon the Lord's plan for their future and return to Egypt (Num 14:1-4). Yahweh, in turn, resolves to destroy them and make for Moses "a nation greater and mightier than they" (Num 14:12 NRSV). Moses and Aaron succeed in securing the people's immediate survival. But as a consequence of their iniquity, the people must wander in the wilderness for forty years—a year of punishment for each day of the spies' reconnaissance of the land (cf. the Ezekielian text, where a day is substituted for each year).

The association of forty years (a round number likely signifying a single generation) with punishment in Num 14:34 suggests that in Ezek 4:6, too, forty years of punishment is in view.[228] We have, then, a prediction that the exile will last forty years, commencing with Jerusalem's destruction and continuing (along the lines of Num 14:34) for a single generation (cf. Jeremiah's seventy years, Jer 25:11; 29:10).[229] Critics note that three hundred and ninety plus forty yields four hundred and thirty—the same number of years that, according to Exod 12:40-42, Israel lived in Egypt prior to the exodus. Does the reader anticipate that, according to Ezekiel's scheme, Israel will embark on a new exodus at the conclusion of its exile in Babylon?[230] Subsequent passages in the book will certainly support such a view (see, e.g., Ezek 20:33-44).

Because v. 7 repeats "set your face" from v. 3 and refers to "the siege of Jerusalem," it assists readers in unifying the first and second acts in the present unit. The "bare arm" is a symbol of military strength. The text does not specify the content of Ezekiel's prophesying against the city, but context confirms that his words will be ominous, indeed. Verse 8, with its reference to Yahweh's binding of the prophet (cf. 3:25), states that Ezekiel will be unable to shift from one side (presumably the left) to the other (the right) "until you have completed the days of your siege." This verse buttresses the reader's construal of vv. 4-6. Left-lying Ezekiel will, in bearing the sins of the house of Israel, depict its long-lived iniquity. But when "the days of your siege" have passed and a new phase in Israel's history begins, he must turn to his right side and publicly portray ("bear") its punishment for those sins. (See Reflections at 5:5-17.)

---

226. Zimmerli, *Ezekiel 1*, 164-65.
227. Ibid., 167.
228. Greenberg *Ezekiel 1–20*, 118.
229. In order for this number to make sense as a prediction," Hals writes, "this material would have to have originated prior to . . . 547 B.C.E." See Hals, *Ezekiel*, 34.
230. See, e.g., Zimmerli, *Ezekiel 1*, 167.

Ezekiel 4:9-17, Siege Rations

NIV

⁹"Take wheat and barley, beans and lentils, millet and spelt; put them in a storage jar and use them to make bread for yourself. You are to eat it during the 390 days you lie on your side. ¹⁰Weigh out twenty shekels^a of food to eat each day and eat it at set times. ¹¹Also measure out a sixth of a hin^b of water and drink it at set times. ¹²Eat the food as you would a barley cake; bake it in the sight of the people, using human excrement for fuel." ¹³The LORD said, "In this way the people of Israel will eat defiled food among the nations where I will drive them."

¹⁴Then I said, "Not so, Sovereign LORD! I have never defiled myself. From my youth until now I have never eaten anything found dead or torn by wild animals. No unclean meat has ever entered my mouth."

¹⁵"Very well," he said, "I will let you bake your bread over cow manure instead of human excrement."

¹⁶He then said to me: "Son of man, I will cut off the supply of food in Jerusalem. The people will eat rationed food in anxiety and drink rationed water in despair, ¹⁷for food and water will be scarce. They will be appalled at the sight of each other and will waste away because of^c their sin.

^{a}10 That is, about 8 ounces (about 0.2 kilogram) ^{b}11 That is, about 2/3 quart (about 0.6 liter) ^{c}17 Or away in

NRSV

9And you, take wheat and barley, beans and lentils, millet and spelt; put them into one vessel, and make bread for yourself. During the number of days that you lie on your side, three hundred ninety days, you shall eat it. ¹⁰The food that you eat shall be twenty shekels a day by weight; at fixed times you shall eat it. ¹¹And you shall drink water by measure, one-sixth of a hin; at fixed times you shall drink. ¹²You shall eat it as a barley-cake, baking it in their sight on human dung. ¹³The LORD said, "Thus shall the people of Israel eat their bread, unclean, among the nations to which I will drive them." ¹⁴Then I said, "Ah Lord GOD! I have never defiled myself; from my youth up until now I have never eaten what died of itself or was torn by animals, nor has carrion flesh come into my mouth." ¹⁵Then he said to me, "See, I will let you have cow's dung instead of human dung, on which you may prepare your bread."

16Then he said to me, Mortal, I am going to break the staff of bread in Jerusalem; they shall eat bread by weight and with fearfulness; and they shall drink water by measure and in dismay. ¹⁷Lacking bread and water, they will look at one another in dismay, and waste away under their punishment.

COMMENTARY

In its present form, this sign act—like the preceding one—pertains not only to the siege of Jerusalem, but also to conditions beyond the city's destruction, when survivors will be forced to dwell "among the nations" (v. 13). Many scholars contend that the original account, Yahweh's command that Ezekiel consume scanty rations of bread and water, said nothing of exile—a topic only introduced with the subsequent addition of vv. 12-15.[231] Are we able to make satisfactory sense of the canonical text?

The prophet must take cereals and vegetables,

prepare bread (לחם *leḥem*), and eat it during the three hundred and ninety days that he lies on his side (v. 9). In our age, "multi-grain" bread is lauded for its nutritional benefits. Here, however, Ezekiel's resort to a bit of this and that signals shortages in Jerusalem, where no single foodstuff is available in sufficient amount to make a loaf.[232] Some critics, citing Deut 22:9 and Lev 19:19*b*, assert that the prophet's bread is unclean by virtue of its mixed contents. But those laws only prohibit sowing fields with more than one type of seed.

231. See, e.g., Greenberg, *Ezekiel 1–20*, 118-19.

232. The Babylonian Talmud (*Erubin* 81a) tells of a third-century CE experiment that proved that even a dog would not eat Ezekiel's bread. See Greenberg, *Ezekiel 1–20*, 106.

They say nothing about combining different grains in food. Twenty shekels is the equivalent of eight ounces of bread. The prophet must eat it at "fixed times" during each day; likewise, he must drink only one-sixth of a hin (*hin* = gallon; hence, two-thirds of a quart) of water daily (v. 11).

Verse 9*b* makes no reference to lying on the right side (cf. v. 6). The reader concludes, therefore, that the prophet must limit himself to siege rations only during the period when he is "bearing" Israel's iniquity. Jerusalem's fall will constitute the turning point from Israel's era of iniquity to its years of punishment (exile). According to v. 8, Ezekiel may switch sides only after he has completed "the days of your siege."

Verse 12*a* is obscure. Zimmerli suggests that Ezekiel's bread ("it," NRSV; "the food," NIV) must be prepared as are barley cakes—that is, baked in hot ashes.[233] This reading makes sense in the light of v. 12*b*, which demands that the fare be prepared in plain view "on human dung." If the reader relates v. 12 to siege conditions in Jerusalem, then the use of such fuel can be understood as a defiling but necessary energy source under desperate circumstances.

But what of v. 13, which abruptly shifts from limited rations to Israel's eating of "defiled food [*lehem*] among the nations"? This question, coupled with certain grammatical incongruities, leads Greenberg to conclude that preparing and eating bread (vv. 9-10) and the making of barley cakes (v. 12) are two separate activities: the former pertains to siege conditions; the latter (involving the use of human excrement) represents the defiled food that Israel will eat in exile.[234] (Is any food consumed outside the land of Israel regarded as unclean? see Hos 9:3). In Greenberg's view, vv. 6, 12-15 were once a self-contained unit which required that Ezekiel eat barley cake while lying on his right side. But his hypothetical rearrange-

ment of these verses is just that. The reader is not bewildered by the juxtaposition of siege and exile within a single sign act, for the same phenomenon occurred also in vv. 4-8 (it will recur in 5:1-4). More likely, he understands vv. 9-15 to say that just as Ezekiel's siege bread is unclean (by virtue of the defiling way in which it is baked), so also the survivors' food will be unclean (as a consequence of being eaten outside the land of Israel).

Ezekiel, who has been eating food outside the land of Israel for some years now, breaks silence for the first time in the book to protest God's command that he eat bread prepared on human dung (v. 14). Through three "protestations of innocence,"[235] he reminds God of his life-long adherence to Israel's dietary laws. He has not consumed the meat of an animal that died "of itself" (see Lev 17:15; Deut 14:21) or was mutilated (see Exod 22:31), and he has not eaten sacrifical meat left over until the third day (Lev 7:18; 19:7). Yahweh responds with a concession: Ezekiel can prepare his bread (*lehem*, not a barley cake) on cow's dung instead (v. 15).

Verses 16-17 return to the topic of shortages in Jerusalem. Yahweh's threat against the city's inhabitants draws upon traditional, metaphorical language. In Lev 26:26, for example, God's warnings to Israel include "break[ing] the staff of bread."[236] Food will be doled out "by weight," and those who eat it "shall not be satisfied" (Yet another divine threat in Isa 3:1 refers to both the staff of bread and the staff of water). Shortages and the danger that occasions them reduce the besieged to fear and dismay. (See Reflections at 5:5-17.)

233. Zimmerli, *Ezekiel 1*, 149, 170.
234. Moshe Greenberg, *Ezekiel 1–20*, AB 22 (Garden City, N.Y.: Doubleday, 1983) 118.
235. W. Zimmerli, *Ezekiel 1: A Commentary on the Book of the Prophet Ezekiel, Chapters 1–24*, trans. R. E. Clements, Hermeneia (Philadelphia: Fortress, 1979) 171.
236. "Staff of bread" may reflect actual practice. Koehler refers to the placing of loaves of bread on staffs. See L. Koehler, *Kleine Lichter; fünfzig Bibelstellen erklärt*, Zwingli-Bücherei 47 (Zürich: Livingli, 1945) 25-27.

Ezekiel 5:1-4, Symbolic Shaving

NIV

5 "Now, son of man, take a sharp sword and use it as a barber's razor to shave your head and your beard. Then take a set of scales and divide up the hair. ²When the days of your siege come to an end, burn a third of the hair with fire inside the city. Take a third and strike it with the sword all around the city. And scatter a third to the wind. For I will pursue them with drawn sword. ³But take a few strands of hair and tuck them away in the folds of your garment. ⁴Again, take a few of these and throw them into the fire and burn them up. A fire will spread from there to the whole house of Israel.

NRSV

5 And you, O mortal, take a sharp sword; use it as a barber's razor and run it over your head and your beard; then take balances for weighing, and divide the hair. ²One third of the hair you shall burn in the fire inside the city, when the days of the siege are completed; one third you shall take and strike with the sword all around the city;ᵃ and one third you shall scatter to the wind, and I will unsheathe the sword after them. ³Then you shall take from these a small number, and bind them in the skirts of your robe. ⁴From these, again, you shall take some, throw them into the fire and burn them up; from there a fire will come out against all the house of Israel.

ᵃHeb *it*

COMMENTARY

In this, the last sign act of the series, Yahweh commands Ezekiel to take a sharp blade, wield it like a razor over his head and beard, then weigh and divide the shorn hair. One-third he is to burn inside the city (an apparent reference to the inscribed brick of 4:1-3). He must strike one-third with a sword "all around it," and the last third will be scattered to the winds. Verses 3-4 further describe the fates of this third portion; for many critics, they constitute a later elaboration.[237]

The impact of this activity depends, in no small measure, on the reader's awareness of associations with shaving in Israel's world. On the one hand, shaving one's head and beard was a sign of mourning, a "self-imposed ritual dishonoring, just as the rending of garments is a form of ritualized nudity and fasting a kind of premortem dying."[238] On the other hand, shaving imposed by one party (e.g., a military conqueror) upon another was a gross insult of the sort that could incite thoughts and acts of violent revenge (see 2 Samuel 10).

The description of this act echoes Isa 7:20, a prophetic threat in which the king of Assyria is cast metaphorically as a razor wielded by the divine barber to shave the Judeans' heads, genitals, and beards. Once again (see the Commentary on 2:8–3:3), Ezekiel has taken up an earlier prophecy and transformed its figurative language into literal action. His use of "sword" (חרב *ḥereb*), rather than Isaiah's "razor" (תער *taʿar*), in v. 1 *a* drives home the military nature of the catastrophe.

Fire frequently appears in biblical metaphors for punishment (e.g., Lam 1:13). Some critics assert that in v. 2, it refers to famine (see Lam 5:10).[239] Second Kings 25:3 states that at the time of Jerusalem's destruction, the famine had become so severe that "there was no food for the people of the land" (NRSV). Because Ezekiel is told to burn his hair "when the days of the siege are completed," however, the sequential reader might construe the flames of v. 2 as the actual fires set by Nebuzaradan's forces (2 Kgs 25:9). The reader knows, after all, that the Babylonians torched the city. One interpretation should not rule out the

237. See, e.g., Zimmerli, *Ezekiel 1,* 173-74.
238. Joseph Blenkinsopp, *Ezekiel,* IBC (Louisville: John Knox, 1990) 38.

239. See Walther Eichrodt, *Ezekiel,* trans. Cosslett Quin, OTL (Philadelphia: Westminster, 1970) 87.

other, since both famine and burning buildings are apt in this context. Ezekiel's act assails the senses, for a heap of hair does not simply burn. It sparks and stinks.

The Bible does not state how many of Jerusalem's inhabitants perished in battle once the Babylonians breached its walls. Ezekiel portrays their plight by taking his sword and striking a second portion of hair all around the inscribed brick. The third portion, scattered to the winds, represents immediate survivors of the city's destruction. What chance have they of escaping, however, if Yahweh pursues them with unsheathed sword? Verse 3 holds out hope for a few, since one binds (hides) something in the end of one's robe to protect it (see 1 Sam 25:29). Yet even some of these are doomed, for Ezekiel must consign part of this portion of hair to the fire (here, judgment more generally defined) as well. Verse 4*b*, with its initial "from it" (MT; NRSV and NIV, "from there"; LXX, "And you shall say to the whole house of Israel"; it functions, on that reading, to introduce vv. 5-17), is difficult; but its sense seems to be that all of Israel's survivors face further judgment. (See Reflections at 5:5-17.)

Ezekiel 5:5-17, "This Is Jerusalem": A Diatribe Against Judah's Capital

NIV

5"This is what the Sovereign LORD says: This is Jerusalem, which I have set in the center of the nations, with countries all around her. 6Yet in her wickedness she has rebelled against my laws and decrees more than the nations and countries around her. She has rejected my laws and has not followed my decrees.

7"Therefore this is what the Sovereign LORD says: You have been more unruly than the nations around you and have not followed my decrees or kept my laws. You have not even*a* conformed to the standards of the nations around you.

8"Therefore this is what the Sovereign LORD says: I myself am against you, Jerusalem, and I will inflict punishment on you in the sight of the nations. 9Because of all your detestable idols, I will do to you what I have never done before and will never do again. 10Therefore in your midst fathers will eat their children, and children will eat their fathers. I will inflict punishment on you and will scatter all your survivors to the winds. 11Therefore as surely as I live, declares the Sovereign LORD, because you have defiled my sanctuary with all your vile images and detestable practices, I myself will withdraw my favor; I will not look on you with pity or spare you. 12A third of your people will die of the plague or perish by famine inside you; a third will fall by the sword

a7 Most Hebrew manuscripts; some Hebrew manuscripts and Syriac You have

NRSV

5Thus says the Lord GOD: This is Jerusalem; I have set her in the center of the nations, with countries all around her. 6But she has rebelled against my ordinances and my statutes, becoming more wicked than the nations and the countries all around her, rejecting my ordinances and not following my statutes. 7Therefore thus says the Lord GOD: Because you are more turbulent than the nations that are all around you, and have not followed my statutes or kept my ordinances, but have acted according to the ordinances of the nations that are all around you; 8therefore thus says the Lord GOD: I, I myself, am coming against you; I will execute judgments among you in the sight of the nations. 9And because of all your abominations, I will do to you what I have never yet done, and the like of which I will never do again. 10Surely, parents shall eat their children in your midst, and children shall eat their parents; I will execute judgments on you, and any of you who survive I will scatter to every wind. 11Therefore, as I live, says the Lord GOD, surely, because you have defiled my sanctuary with all your detestable things and with all your abominations—therefore I will cut you down;*a* my eye will not spare, and I will have no pity. 12One third of you shall die of pestilence or be consumed by famine among you; one third shall fall by the sword around you; and one third I will scatter to

a Another reading is I will withdraw

NIV

outside your walls; and a third I will scatter to the winds and pursue with drawn sword.

13"Then my anger will cease and my wrath against them will subside, and I will be avenged. And when I have spent my wrath upon them, they will know that I the LORD have spoken in my zeal.

14"I will make you a ruin and a reproach among the nations around you, in the sight of all who pass by. 15You will be a reproach and a taunt, a warning and an object of horror to the nations around you when I inflict punishment on you in anger and in wrath and with stinging rebuke. I the LORD have spoken. 16When I shoot at you with my deadly and destructive arrows of famine, I will shoot to destroy you. I will bring more and more famine upon you and cut off your supply of food. 17I will send famine and wild beasts against you, and they will leave you childless. Plague and bloodshed will sweep through you, and I will bring the sword against you. I the LORD have spoken."

NRSV

every wind and will unsheathe the sword after them.

13My anger shall spend itself, and I will vent my fury on them and satisfy myself; and they shall know that I, the LORD, have spoken in my jealousy, when I spend my fury on them. 14Moreover I will make you a desolation and an object of mocking among the nations around you, in the sight of all that pass by. 15You shall be[a] a mockery and a taunt, a warning and a horror, to the nations around you, when I execute judgments on you in anger and fury, and with furious punishments—I, the LORD, have spoken— 16when I loose against you[b] my deadly arrows of famine, arrows for destruction, which I will let loose to destroy you, and when I bring more and more famine upon you, and break your staff of bread. 17I will send famine and wild animals against you, and they will rob you of your children; pestilence and bloodshed shall pass through you; and I will bring the sword upon you. I, the LORD, have spoken.

[a]Gk Syr Vg Tg: Heb *It shall be*   [b]Heb *them*

COMMENTARY

Having ordered Ezekiel to perform certain sign acts, Yahweh launches into a ferocious diatribe, inveighing against Jerusalem and threatening its inhabitants with horrific punishments. Here, Hals writes, "God's emotions surface . . . cold objectivity is replaced with a hot-blooded proclamation of wrath rooted in sovereign jealousy."[240] Verses so filled with divine fury are difficult to read, but they are not without precedent. Leviticus 26, the final chapter of the "holiness code" (priestly legislation found in Leviticus 17–26) appears especially to have influenced this passage. In that context, God warns Israel what will happen if it abrogates their covenant. In this passage, by contrast, covenant violations have already occurred, and the threats have become announcements of imminent punishments.[241]

The introductory messenger formula, "Thus says the Lord GOD," appears three times in vv.

5-12, emphasizing that the prophet (who, from the narrative's perspective, remains on the plain in the presence of Yahweh's glory) will be but a mouthpiece for God's own words. "This is Jerusalem," Yahweh says, immediately orienting the reader to that city which, according to Israel's traditions, was uniquely the site of God's protective presence and home to the dynasty descended from David. Yahweh has given Judah's capital a central place among the nations, yet it has rebelled by rejecting its covenant obligation to obey God's ordinances and statutes. As an unfaithful covenant (treaty) partner, Jerusalem should expect to experience the fulfillment of treaty curses. Indeed, many of the ensuing threats are drawn from treaty curses appearing elsewhere in Hebrew Scripture and in other ancient Near Eastern literature.

Having spoken of what was done on Jerusalem's behalf and of its disobedience, Yahweh moves to an announcement of punishment, twice initiated by "therefore" (לכן *lākēn*), followed by the messenger formula (vv. 7-8). Because Jerusalem (i.e.,

240. Ronald M. Hals, *Ezekiel,* FOTL 19 (Grand Rapids: Eerdmans, 1989) 36.
241. See Greenberg, *Ezekiel 1–20,* 124-28.

its inhabitants) has rejected Yahweh's laws, choosing instead the practices of surrounding nations, God will personally attack the city. Note the emphatic "I, I myself am coming against you."[242] The city's punishment will be no private affair; it will be witnessed by the nations whose ways it has chosen over Yahweh's (v. 8).

Verse 9 is careful to state that God's judgment occurs "because of all your abominations." The term תועבה (tô'ēbâ "abomination") refers to ritually impure activities, including idolatrous practices, as well as to other forms of wickedness. Horrifying as Yahweh's judgment will be, it is proportionate to Jerusalem's detestable practices (see the discussion of the Doctrine of Retribution in the Reflections at 3:16-27). God asserts that these punishments have no parallel either in the past or in the future. First comes cannibalism, an appalling consequence of sin and siege, according to Lev 26:29; 2 Kgs 6:29; Jer 19:9; Lam 4:10, etc. In these and other texts, parents are threatened with having to eat their children in order to survive. Ezekiel goes a step further, proclaiming that children will eat their parents (v. 10a). Verse 10b adds that any survivors will be "scattered to every wind." These words evoke thoughts of v. 2; indeed, in subsequent verses, readers encounter commentary on several of the aforementioned sign acts.

Verse 11, initiated with an oath formula, further explains Yahweh's motivation for the threatened judgments: Jerusalem's abominations have defiled God's Temple. Pity has no place here.[243] Verse 12, a reiteration of v. 2, interprets the "fire" of that earlier verse as pestilence and famine.

In v. 13, God anticipates that the execution of these judgments will accomplish two things. On the one hand, Yahweh will enjoy, as it were, a divine catharsis. "Jealousy" (קנאה qin'â, "zeal," NIV) refers to "the resentful rage of one whose prerogatives have been usurped by, or given to,

another."[244] On the other hand, the exercise of divine anger through these punishments will bring Yahweh's unfaithful people to the inescapable recognition that only God, the sovereign Lord to whom they owe utter obedience, has brought these judgments against them.

At present, the anticipation of these accomplishments does nothing to assuage Yahweh's ostensible need further to articulate the horrors awaiting Jerusalem and its inhabitants. The city will become a desolation (i.e., both destroyed and depopulated), the object of mocking among the nations. Elsewhere in Hebrew Scripture, including the book of Ezekiel, the notion that God's people might be subjected to ridicule from other nations functions rhetorically to motivate Yahweh's intervention on their behalf for the sake of the divine reputation (see, e.g., Ezek 36:20-21). Here, God presents Israel's humiliation as part and parcel of its punishment. Not only will the nations witness and celebrate the outworking of divine wrath against this people, but also they will take warning from it, since it testifies to a deity of fearsome power.

Ezekiel's reference to Yahweh's "deadly arrows of famine" echoes Deut 32:23-24, where such arrows are identified as "wasting hunger, burning consumption, bitter pestilence" (NRSV). According to Israel's traditions, Yahweh fought as a mighty warrior against its foes. Here, however, the divine warrior turns weaponry against God's own people with devastating effect (note the repetition of "staff of bread" from 4:16). Like this text, Lev 26:22 threatens that wild animals will kill Israel's children, while Lev 26:33 speaks of Yahweh's unsheathed sword.

The Lord's speech, then, draws upon stereotypical threats present also in other literary contexts. That they are conventional, however, does not diminish their impact. Infused with repeated expressions of divine wrath and determination to bring upon Jerusalem the consequences of its sins, God's diatribe points relentlessly to horrors from which no escape is possible.

---

242. The formula "I am coming against you" elsewhere appears in a report of a duel; see 1 Sam 17:45-49.

243. See Greenberg, *Ezekiel 1–20*, 115.

244. Ibid., 115. The same noun appears in the Decalogue (Exod 20:5).

REFLECTIONS

What does the Lord require? If we put this question to the present unit—indeed, to the book of Ezekiel as a whole—one answer must surely be obedience. In 2:8, Yahweh forbade Ezekiel to be "rebellious like that rebellious house." In the present unit, the prophet recounts God's command that he portray, in a physical way, divine purposes, enduring physical, psychological, and social mortifications. Several of his sign acts (eating bread baked on human dung, shaving) threaten to ravage his self-identity:

> Cast in the role of narrator, Ezekiel speaks for God in commanding and interpreting the sign-actions as a vivid depiction of Israel's fate. But in representing his performance of them, Ezekiel shows his own profound and costly involvement in the people's suffering . . . the fact that Ezekiel is enjoined to perform acts which are unnatural for any person (24.16), abhorrent to him as an observer of the law (4.14), and even in violation of the special restrictions laid upon him as a priest (shaving his hair) reinforces the claim asserted in the repeated messenger formula: this prophecy comes from YHWH. So far is it from being Ezekiel's own invention that he is even obliged to become alienated from his own identity in order to serve as its vehicle.[245]

Modeling obedience to Yahweh's commands, the prophet functions as a foil for human rebelliousness. The text encourages the expectation that Ezekiel will carry out to the letter even the most arduous of Yahweh's sign acts. Only once does he raise his voice in protest. On that occasion, he objects on behalf of a religious injunction. And God's mind is changed (4:13-15). Ezekiel teaches Yahweh a lesson about obedience to divine law!

The eighth-century BCE prophet Micah asked what Yahweh requires and, in the words of Mays, concluded that "it is not sacrifice of something outside a person. . . . It is rather a yielding of life itself to God and his way, 'repentance' of the most radical sort. . . . What YHWH requires is not the life of some thing, but the living of the man who stands before him."[246] Jesus probed the same question on the Mount of Olives when, confronted with the prospect of his own death, he prayed, "Father, if you are willing, remove this cup from me." He models utter obedience when, in the next breath, he adds, "yet, not my will but yours be done" (Luke 22:42 NRSV).

Ezekiel's God demands obedience and, when it is not forthcoming, vows to bring upon Israel the full force of the covenant curses ostensibly first articulated at Mt. Sinai. The commentary has noted Ezekiel's indebtedness to Leviticus 26. Readers of that chapter discover that near its end, Yahweh actually speaks of hope in the face of genuine repentance:

> But if they confess their iniquity and the iniquity of their ancestors, in that they committed treachery against me and, moreover, that they continued hostile to me . . . then will I remember my covenant with Jacob; I will remember also my covenant with Isaac and also my covenant with Abraham, and I will remember the land . . . when they are in the land of their enemies, I will not spurn them, or abhor them so as to destroy them utterly and break my covenant with them; for I am the LORD their God; but I will remember in their favor the covenant with their ancestors whom I brought out of the land of Egypt in the sight of the nations, to be their God: I am the LORD. (Lev 26:40, 42, 44-45 NRSV)

This final chapter of Israel's "holiness code" (see Introduction) moves in a direction that Ezekiel does not—not yet.

Ezekiel's sign acts are much more than small-scale enactments of imminent events (though that is part of their function). His words confront readers with the magnitude of human iniquity, not only with its dreadful toll in terror, suffering, and carnage, but also with its cost to God.

---

245. Ellen F. Davis, *Swallowing the Scroll: Textuality and the Dynamics of Discourse in Ezekiel's Prophecy,* Bible and Literature 21 (Sheffield: Almond, 1989) 71.
246. James L. Mays, *Micah*, OTL (Philadelphia: Westminster, 1976) 142.

Elsewhere biblical traditions assert that grace and mercy are integral to Yahweh's character. Here, Ezekiel cuts such characteristics off at the quick. Israel must be forced fully to confront its iniquity, to acknowledge and accept that finally, partners who break promises pay for their actions.

Christians may rebel against the notion that a time comes when grace cannot abound. Surely this unit fuels the popular opinion that the God of the Old Testament is wrathful, as opposed to the loving God of the New Testament. Neither generalization holds water, of course; divine wrath and love appear in both parts of the Bible. Better to recognize that this unit forces readers to grapple with a profound biblical anthropomorphism: God, like human beings, possesses a full range of emotions. The extremes of those emotions are not love and mercy at one end of the spectrum, the *dispassionate* administration of justice on the other. The God of Ezek 4:1–5:17 can become angry, express wrath, and act out of jealousy in response to mortal sins. Here, Yahweh borders on the sadistic, reveling in the prospect of Israel's punishments. Moderns may or may not accept the portrayal of a deity who, in this sense, has been fashioned in the image of humanity. But those who take seriously their biblical heritage must wrestle with it.

Does God really behave this way? On first reflection this question may impress us with its "cut to the chase" character. In fact, however, the so-called direct approach sidesteps crucial aspects of Ezekiel's worldview that, if neglected, distort and confine the perimeters of our thinking. Here, I am reminded of advice given by John Robert Seeley, a nineteenth-century educator, to Cambridge college students: "In history," he said, "everything depends upon turning narrative into problems. . . . Break the drowsy spell of narrative; ask yourself questions; set yourself problems; you will become an investigator, you will cease to be solemn and begin to be serious."[247]

In the light of Seeley's remarks, we should rather ask: What problems did the prophet face, and what presuppositions and beliefs influenced his way of dealing with them? At least four answers come to mind. First, Ezekiel believed that Jerusalem faced certain destruction. In Judah (e.g., Jer 28:1-4), and perhaps in Babylonia as well (Jer 29:15-23), other prophets were predicting a speedy reversal of Judah's misfortunes. Despite their opposing views, however, Ezekiel insisted to his fellow exiles that he, not they, was speaking the Lord's own words.

Second, Ezekiel was convinced that the approaching catastrophe was "the doing, and not the undoing, of Israel's God."[248] Elsewhere in the book, the prophet attributes to Israel's elders the following words: "Yahweh does not see us; the LORD has abandoned the country" (8:12). But Ezekiel spurns the notion that divine apathy has become Babylon's opportunity to squelch a recalcitrant vassal state or that Jerusalem's demise will signal the Babylonian god Marduk's victory over Israel's deity. Ezekiel claims historical events for Yahweh. He will not surrender Yahweh to history.[249]

Third, Ezekiel's acts and speech reflect his bedrock belief that God's actions are not capricious, the result of some divine whim, but punishment for Israel's sins. If Yahweh has determined to destroy Judah's land, cities, and population, it must be on account of human culpability. Israel is at fault, not God. Fourth, the prophet is convinced that Yahweh is just. Because the punishment—horrific beyond words—is proportionate to the crime, Israel's abominations must be exorbitant. More than once, his fellow Judeans challenge this view, asserting that "the way of the LORD is unfair!" (18:25, 29 NRSV; see also 33:17, 20). But Ezekiel refuses to abandon his defense of divine justice.[250]

Ezekiel cannot blame events on some "demonic power" opposing Yahweh; the notion of a "devil" had not yet made its way into Israelite thought. He does not regard the catastrophes of 597 and 587 BCE as the price one pays for settling along what we moderns call the Fertile

---

247. John Robert Seeley, *The Expansion of England,* ed. J. Gross (Chicago: University of Chicago Press, 1971) 139. The following paragraphs are much influenced by the discussion in K. P. Darr, "Ezekiel's Justifications of God: Teaching Troubling Texts," *JSOT* 55 (1992) 98-117.

248. Darr, "Ezekiel's Justifications of God," 111.

249. Ibid.

250. Ibid.

Crescent, the strategic arc of traversable land joining Egypt and Mesopotamia. He rejects any notion that Yahweh is powerless or apathetic or unjust. "He insists that Yahweh is both in control of events, and justified in the way those events are controlled. Ezekiel's [acts and oracles], with their charges of human guilt, are constructed . . . to convince his audience that both their conviction, and their convictor, are just."[251]

Encountering so difficult a unit as 4:1–5:17, then, we are obliged first to understand, as best we are able, Ezekiel's own problems and perspectives. But we cannot rest there; because these verses are Scripture—God's living word—we must also explore their significance for modern-day believers. What choices have we in coming to terms with Ezekiel's message? Jonathan Smith asserts that we must learn how to "argue" about interpretations—that is, to "bring private percept into public discourse . . . learn[ing] to negotiate difference with civility."[252] "Argument exists for the purpose of clarifying choices," Smith says, and "choices are always consequential, that is to say, they require the acceptance of responsibility."[253]

Both Jews and Christians may be uncomfortable with the notion of "arguing" with Ezekiel, or with any other biblical author. Acknowledging that some aspect of a biblical text bothers them, they may conclude with resignation that what the Bible says must be true—someday, they will understand. But one crucial aspect of religious growth entails assuming responsibility for the decisions we make in interpreting the Bible.

Toward that end, Smith offers a helpful suggestion when he asserts that "*nothing must stand alone* . . . every item encountered [must have] a conversation partner, so that each may have, or be made to have, an argument with another in order that [interpreters] may negotiate difference, evaluate, compare, and make judgments."[254] The book of Job, with its stark challenges to the adequacy of retributive theology, makes an excellent conversation partner for Ezek 5:5-17. But Elie Wiesel's famous account of how he and other prisoners in a Nazi concentration camp were forced to witness the hanging of a young boy is a compelling option as well, for it points to very different understandings of Yahweh's relationship to human agony. According to Wiesel, the child weighed so little that his death was slow and agonizing. "Where is God?" one man asked. And again, "Where is God now?" And Wiesel writes, "I heard a voice within me answer him: 'Where is He? Here He is—He is hanging here on this gallows.' "[255]

Juxtaposing opposing, yet compelling, texts encourages contemporary believers to evaluate the claims of each and to make judgments—open to further learning though they be. Within my own school of theology context, it is crucial that students see me participating in such arguments, weighing options, and making choices that I can defend.[256] When, for example, students ask what I think about Ezekiel's assertions that destruction, death, and exile at the hands of the Babylonians were God's punishment upon a sinful people, I respond that in a world where holocausts happen, I dare not agree. "I must tell Ezekiel, 'No, in this, I cannot follow you.' "[257]

At a critical period in Judah's history, Ezekiel struggled with issues of human responsibility and divine response. Modern-day believers should work to understand how and why he dealt with problems as he did. We can only respect his absolute refusal to abandon faith in Yahweh in the face of so much tragedy. On reflection, we may conclude that Ezekiel's cannot be the final word. That does not mean, however, that 5:5-17 is less important than other biblical passages. Sometimes, we embrace painful texts not because we agree with their answers, but because they force us to wrestle with crucial questions.[258]

---

251. Ibid., 112.
252. Jonathan Z. Smith, " 'Narratives into Problems': The College Introductory Course and the Study of Religion," *JAAR* 56 (1988) 733.
253. Ibid.
254. Ibid., 112-13.
255. E. Wiesel, *Night,* trans. S. Rodway (New York: Farrar, Straus & Giroux, 1960) 61-62.
256. Darr, "Ezekiel's Justifications of God," 113.
257. Ibid., 114.
258. Ibid., 117.

EZEKIEL 6:1–7:27, PUNISHMENT UPON ISRAEL'S LAND AND ITS INHABITANTS

OVERVIEW

The bulk of Ezekiel 4–5, both Yahweh's commands that the prophet perform certain sign acts and the following divine tirade, focused upon Jerusalem and its inhabitants (though Ezekiel's immediate audience consisted of his fellow exiles in Babylon). In 6:1-14, he must again address home ground. Here, however, his perimeters broaden to include the entire land. Sin, it seems, is not restricted to the nation's capital. Yahweh has determined not only utterly to destroy illicit cultic sites (called במות *bāmôt,* "high places") scattered across Israel's landscape and to slaughter those who frequent them, but also to reduce all of Israel's habitations to desolate ruins (6:1-7, 11-14).

Chapters 4–5 only hinted that some of Jerusalem's residents, like the hairs remaining in the end of Ezekiel's robe (5:3), would escape with their lives. Ezekiel 6:8-10 speaks more fully of their future. In this sense also, the prophet's horizon stretches beyond that of preceding units. Those remaining in Judah will perish (6:11-14).

But the few who survive the sword (6:8) will be forced in exile finally to "know" (acknowledge and accept) Yahweh, whose sovereign power is unrivaled (6:9-10).

Like Ezekiel 6, chapter 7 begins with God's order that Ezekiel address Israel's land. The following poem proclaims that the "end" has come: The impending Day of Yahweh will bring utter annihilation. Although riddled with textual difficulties, many of which may have confounded the ancient reader as well as contemporary scholars, its overriding message is clear: The pitiless outpouring of Yahweh's wrath spells doom for every facet of Judah's social order. This "end" is not the result of divine capriciousness or simply "what happens" when a powerful empire determines to prey upon lesser kingdoms. It is, rather, the punishment of a just God who brings upon a sinful people the full measure of their own, festering abominations.

Ezekiel 6:1-14, Judgment upon Illicit Cultic Sites

NIV

6 The word of the LORD came to me: [2]"Son of man, set your face against the mountains of Israel; prophesy against them [3]and say: 'O mountains of Israel, hear the word of the Sovereign LORD. This is what the Sovereign LORD says to the mountains and hills, to the ravines and valleys: I am about to bring a sword against you, and I will destroy your high places. [4]Your altars will be demolished and your incense altars will be smashed; and I will slay your people in front of your idols. [5]I will lay the dead bodies of the Israelites in front of their idols, and I will scatter your bones around your altars. [6]Wherever you live, the towns will be laid waste and the high places demolished, so that your altars will be laid waste and devastated, your idols smashed and

NRSV

6 The word of the LORD came to me: [2]O mortal, set your face toward the mountains of Israel, and prophesy against them, [3]and say, You mountains of Israel, hear the word of the Lord GOD! Thus says the Lord GOD to the mountains and the hills, to the ravines and the valleys: I, I myself will bring a sword upon you, and I will destroy your high places. [4]Your altars shall become desolate, and your incense stands shall be broken; and I will throw down your slain in front of your idols. [5]I will lay the corpses of the people of Israel in front of their idols; and I will scatter your bones around your altars. [6]Wherever you live, your towns shall be waste and your high places ruined, so that your altars will be waste and

NIV

ruined, your incense altars broken down, and what you have made wiped out. [7]Your people will fall slain among you, and you will know that I am the LORD.

[8]" 'But I will spare some, for some of you will escape the sword when you are scattered among the lands and nations. [9]Then in the nations where they have been carried captive, those who escape will remember me—how I have been grieved by their adulterous hearts, which have turned away from me, and by their eyes, which have lusted after their idols. They will loathe themselves for the evil they have done and for all their detestable practices. [10]And they will know that I am the LORD; I did not threaten in vain to bring this calamity on them.

[11]" 'This is what the Sovereign LORD says: Strike your hands together and stamp your feet and cry out "Alas!" because of all the wicked and detestable practices of the house of Israel, for they will fall by the sword, famine and plague. [12]He that is far away will die of the plague, and he that is near will fall by the sword, and he that survives and is spared will die of famine. So will I spend my wrath upon them. [13]And they will know that I am the LORD, when their people lie slain among their idols around their altars, on every high hill and on all the mountaintops, under every spreading tree and every leafy oak—places where they offered fragrant incense to all their idols. [14]And I will stretch out my hand against them and make the land a desolate waste from the desert to Diblah[a]—wherever they live. Then they will know that I am the LORD.' "

[a]14 Most Hebrew manuscripts; a few Hebrew manuscripts *Riblah*

NRSV

ruined,[a] your idols broken and destroyed, your incense stands cut down, and your works wiped out. [7]The slain shall fall in your midst; then you shall know that I am the LORD.

[8]But I will spare some. Some of you shall escape the sword among the nations and be scattered through the countries. [9]Those of you who escape shall remember me among the nations where they are carried captive, how I was crushed by their wanton heart that turned away from me, and their wanton eyes that turned after their idols. Then they will be loathsome in their own sight for the evils that they have committed, for all their abominations. [10]And they shall know that I am the LORD; I did not threaten in vain to bring this disaster upon them.

[11]Thus says the Lord GOD: Clap your hands and stamp your foot, and say, Alas for all the vile abominations of the house of Israel! For they shall fall by the sword, by famine, and by pestilence. [12]Those far off shall die of pestilence; those nearby shall fall by the sword; and any who are left and are spared shall die of famine. Thus I will spend my fury upon them. [13]And you shall know that I am the LORD, when their slain lie among their idols around their altars, on every high hill, on all the mountain tops, under every green tree, and under every leafy oak, wherever they offered pleasing odor to all their idols. [14]I will stretch out my hand against them, and make the land desolate and waste, throughout all their settlements, from the wilderness to Riblah.[b] Then they shall know that I am the LORD.

[a]Syr Vg Tg: Heb *and be made guilty*   [b]Another reading is *Diblah*

COMMENTARY

Although the original unity of Ezekiel 6 has been questioned, Greenberg's analysis discloses the skillful manner in which the chapter, in its final form, has been structured.[259] Verses 1-14 consist of two judgment oracles (vv. 3-7 and 11-13*a*), each beginning with an expressive gesture (vv. 2, 11) and followed by an elaborating

259. Moshe Greenberg, *Ezekiel 1–20*, AB 22 (Garden City, N.Y.: Doubleday, 1983) 137-41.

"afterwave" (vv. 8-10, 13*a*-14). Both oracles and afterwaves conclude with recognition formulae ("then you [or "they"] shall know . . . "), expressing the intended effect of Yahweh's devastating punishments (see below).

6:1-7. At some later time, God again orders Ezekiel to prophesy against Israel's land. The orientation formula "set your face toward" (v. 2) appears nine times in the book; readers recall its earlier appearances in 4:3, 7. Critics, citing the Moabite king Balak's attempts to elicit a curse against the Israelites from Balaam, a Mesopotamian diviner, suggest that visual contact with the addressee was once a prerequisite for pronouncing negative prophetic oracles (Num 22:41–24:25; see esp. Num 22:41; 23:13; 24:2).[260] Such cannot be the case here, of course, for Ezekiel resides at a considerable distance from Judah. The formula (and accompanying gesture?) conveys hostility nonetheless and further intensifies the power of the prophet's message.

The phrase "mountains of Israel" also recurs in the book (seventeen times); as further elaboration in v. 3 shows, it designates Israel's entire land, not only the mountains per se. The summons, "You mountains of Israel, hear the word of the Lord GOD! Thus says the Lord GOD. . . ." echoes the proclamations of royal heralds (e.g., "Hear the word of the great king, the King of Assyria! Thus says the king . . ." 2 Kgs 18:28 NRSV).[261]

In v. 3*b* (recall 5:8), Yahweh's self-asseveration, "I, I myself" emphatically identifies the author/executor of impending punishments. Here as often, Ezekiel by-passes the Babylonians' role, insisting that the Lord will personally demolish Israel's high places and cultic appurtenances and scatter the bodies and bones of devotees among their idols (called גלולים [*gillûlîm*], likely a coarse pun on גללים [*gelālîm*, "dung pellets"]), thereby inflicting corpse defilement upon those ostensibly holy shrines.

260. See Ronald M. Hals, *Ezekiel,* FOTL 19 (Grand Rapids: Eerdmans, 1989) 39-40; W. Zimmerli, *Ezekiel 1: A Commentary on the Book of the Prophet Ezekiel, Chapters 1–24,* trans. R. E. Clements, Hermeneia (Philadelphia: Fortress, 1979) 182-83.

261. See Greenberg, *Ezekiel 1–20,* 131.

❖   ❖   ❖   ❖

EXCURSUS: ISRAEL'S "HIGH PLACES"

What do we know about Israel's high places? Of the approximately one hundred references to במות (*bāmôt,* "high places") in Hebrew Scripture, over four-fifths (including Ezekiel 6) designate a locus of cultic activity (e.g., animal and other sacrifices, the burning of incense, festival observances).[262] A traditional hypothesis holds that these *bāmôt,* Canaanite in origin, were rustic, open-air sanctuaries situated atop mountains or hills in vegetal settings (e.g., 1 Kgs 14:23: "For they also built for themselves high places, pillars, and sacred poles on every high hill and under every green tree," NRSV). Though dedicated to Yahweh, they were especially susceptible to syncretistic religious beliefs and practices, including fertility rituals (see below). According to Num 33:52 and Deut 12:2-4, God ordered the Israelites to destroy these sites upon entering the land. They flourished nonetheless until Judah's seventh-century king Josiah (640–609 BCE) launched religiopolitical reforms leading to their destruction (2 Kings 23).[263] Yet Josiah's reforms, like the ruler himself, were short-lived, and the "high places" resumed operation not long after his death. Hence Jeremiah's and Ezekiel's condemnations of them.

Against this traditional view, Whitney reminds us that *bāmôt* were "different things in different places at different times."[264] Some of these man-made constructions may have been small and rustic, but others consisted of substantial buildings and even building complexes (e.g., 2 Kgs 23:19). Most biblical references situate high places in urban, rather than rural, settings. The prophet Samuel, for example, is said to have supervised sacrifices at a high place in a city within the district of Zuph (1 Sam 9:5-27). It is noted in 2 Kgs 17:9 that the northern Israelites built high places "in all their towns"; 2 Kgs 23:8 locates them in Judean cities as well. Indeed, Ezek 6:6 associates the *bāmôt* with settlements.

An anatomical meaning of במה (*bāmâ*) refers to the back (trunk? shank?) of a human or animal

262. W. Boyd Barrick, "High Place," *ABD,* 3:197.

263. King Hezekiah of Judah (715–687/86 BCE) earns the approval of the Deuteronomistic Historians in part because "he removed the high places" (2 Kgs 18:4). His successor, Manasseh, however, is said to have rebuilt them (2 Kgs 21:3).

264. J. T. Whitney, " 'Bamoth' in the Old Testament," *TynBul* 30 (1979) 147.

(e.g., Deut 33:29). A topographical meaning suggests "heights." De Vaux notes, however, that *bāmâ* can designate the "back" of clouds or "waves" of the sea: "The idea which the word expresses . . . is something which stands out in relief from its background," he concludes, "but the idea of a mountain or hill is not contained in the word itself."[265] While some high places may have been built on elevated ground, biblical references suggest that many were not. Possibly *bāmâ* refers to architectural platforms characteristic of such sites.

High places are objects of bitter censure not only in Ezekiel 6, but also in many other biblical texts (e.g., Lev 26:30-33; 2 Kgs 17:11; 2 Chr 33:3; Ps 78:58; Hos 10:8; Amos 7:9). Indeed, Ezek 20:27-29 will identify cultic activities at these sanctuaries as paradigmatic of Israel's sinfulness upon entering Canaan. Yet certain early traditions link venerable figures (e.g., Samuel) to such shrines without a disapproving word, suggesting that the polemic against them gained momentum as Israel's history unfolded, fueled especially by the deuteronomists' attempts during Josiah's reign to centralize worship at the Temple in Jerusalem.

W. B. Barrick cautions against simply equating high places with the rural installations roundly condemned, for example, in the books of Kings: "It is commonly supposed that bamoth are the object of the frequent polemic against worship conducted in the countryside 'upon every high hill and under every green tree.' . . . But 2 Kgs 16:4 (= 2 Chr 28:4) argues against the identification: Ahaz is said to have 'slaughtered animals and burned food offerings in the bamoth *and* upon the hills and under every green tree.' "[266] Barrick's caution is apropos; such an equation may indeed run awry of historical reality. It is likely, however, that on the basis of biblical texts like 1 Kgs 14:23; 2 Kgs 17:10-11; Ezekiel 6, etc., the ancient reader presupposed that Israel's high places and these rural installations were essentially the same, bringing negative associations with one to the other.

Biased biblical accounts cannot serve as reliable sources either for the sorts of religious activities that transpired at high places, or for how those activities were understood by the folk who frequented them. On the basis of texts like Hos 4:12-14 and Jer 3:6, 13, many critics argue that fertility rituals (e.g., so-called cultic prostitution, sexual intercourse at sacred sites intended to prompt gods and goddesses also to mate, thereby ensuring the fertility of land, livestock, and humans) were integral to worship in Israel's high places. Yet the existence of cultic prostitution rests on dubious "evidence"— not only a prejudiced biblical witness, but also imaginative reconstructions of ancient Near Eastern rituals, archaeological evidence that is susceptible to more than one interpretation, and the writings of several classical "historians" whose accuracy is suspect.[267] True, Ezekiel accuses worshipers at Israel's high places of having "wanton" hearts and eyes (6:9). Reading sexual activity into such accusations, however, misconstrues this figurative use of language (see the Commentary on 16:1-63; 23:1-49).

265. R. de Vaux, *Ancient Israel: Its Life and Institutions,* trans. John McHugh (New York: McGraw-Hill, 1961) 284.
266. Barrick, "High Place," 199.
267. K. P. Darr, "Ezekiel's Justifications of God: Teaching Troubling Texts," *JSOT* 55 (1992) 105.

Ezekiel 6 nowhere asserts that Israel's doomed high places are places for fertility rituals. Yet his verbal assault against these shrines affirms in no uncertain terms that they host horrific practices. The thorough eradication of these sites will at last bring an end to long-lived arenas of Israelite apostasy. But beyond that end lies an even larger purpose: The people in whose midst the slain have fallen (v. 7) will be forced at last to an inescapable recognition: "then you shall know that I am Yahweh" (v. 7*b*).

This "recognition formula," ("then you [or "they"] shall know that I am Yahweh"), which appears some sixty times in the book of Ezekiel, often at the end of oracles or of subsections within oracles, "expresses the intended effect of the event predicted in the oracle."[268] Greenberg's succinct statement of its import bears repeating:

268. Greenberg, *Ezekiel 1–20*, 133.

The name YHWH is properly synonymous with power (to punish and to rescue), sovereignty, holiness, and authorship and control of events. Presently it is not recognized as such either in Israel, who are apostate or faithless, or among the nations, who are idolatrous. But when disaster strikes them or they experience a miraculous deliverance, the God who announced the event through the prophet will be acknowledged as possessing the attributes properly attached to his name.[269]

Destruction, death, and defilement, then, are only part of Yahweh's intentions. A larger goal demands that those who discover the carnage acknowledge the activity of their sovereign divine judge.

6:8-10. Death will not befall all who presently reside in the homeland. Some will escape, for that, too, is part of God's plan. Exiled among the nations, they will "remember" how with wanton (idolatrous) hearts and eyes they broke God's heart ("how I was brokenhearted," 6:9 TNK) and "loathe themselves" on account of all their cultic abominations. Through this painful repentance, the people will come to know Yahweh, whose threats were neither unwarranted nor unfulfilled (v. 10).

6:11-14. The oracle in vv. 11-13a commences with the messenger formula, followed by Yahweh's command that Ezekiel perform other expressive gestures: "Clap your hands and stamp your foot, and say, Alas. . . ." By these actions and exclamation, Ezekiel will publicly portray Yahweh's malevolent delight in venting fury against Israel (see Deut 28:63).

Following verses return to and heighten the chapter's original theme (God's destruction of illicit cultic sites and their devotées), thereby rounding off the unit. Although the reader recalls that some Judeans will survive Yahweh's purge (vv. 8-10), vv. 11-12 give no hint of this idea. To the contrary, these verses announce the entire population's demise. Those outside Jerusalem will perish, whether they are located far from the city (by pestilence) or in closer proximity to it (by the sword); urban survivors of Jerusalem's destruction will die of famine. Who, then, will be left to "know that I am Yahweh"? Does the recognition formula in v. 13 ("And *you* shall know," italics added) remind Ezekiel's fellow exiles (and the reader)

of Yahweh's intention that they, too, be forced both to acknowledge and to accept that their God wields unparalleled power to punish? The subsequent shift to a third-person plural pronoun ("they") in v. 14 parallels the alternation in pronouns one also finds when comparing the recognition formulae in vv. 7 and 10.

Verse 13 does not refer to "high places" per se, employing, rather, the stereotypical language of deuteronomistic-related condemnations of rural shrines. As noted above, the reader is likely simply to conflate the two on the basis of this and other texts.

Like the "bared arm" (see 4:7), the "outstretched hand" (v. 14) is an image of military power. While v. 6 threatened the ruin of Israel's towns, v. 14 speaks of the depopulation and destruction of its entire land. The MT reading, "from the desert of Diblathah," makes no sense; most critics read "from the desert to" and emend the place-name to "Riblah," a town in Hamath, Israel's traditional northern border (see 2 Kgs 14:25; Ezek 48:1; Amos 6:14). Since "wilderness" refers to the desert constituting Judah's southwestern edge, the text as emended encompasses the entire land from a southern boundary to its approximate northern limits.

For the ancient reader, Riblah was fraught with horrific associations. When the Babylonians breached Jerusalem's walls in 587 BCE, Judah's King Zedekiah attempted to flee. But Nebuchadrezzar's forces captured him and brought him to Riblah: "Then they captured the king and brought him up to the king of Babylon at Riblah, who passed sentence on him. They slaughtered the sons of Zedekiah before his eyes, then put out the eyes of Zedekiah; they bound him in fetters and took him to Babylon" (2 Kgs 25:6-7 NRSV). Zimmerli, among other critics, asserts that the reference to this tragic site was added to Ezekiel 6 sometime after the events of 587 BCE.[270] But the ancient reader might well conclude that the place-name *presaged*, rather than *recalled*, the tragedy of Zedekiah and his sons and of other of Judah's religious and civic leaders (see 2 Kgs 25:18-21). (See Reflections at 7:1-27.)

269. Ibid., 133.

270. W. Zimmerli, *Ezekiel 1: A Commentary on the Book of the Prophet Ezekiel, Chapters 1–24*, trans. R. E. Clements, Hermeneia (Philadelphia: Fortress, 1979) 190-91.

Ezekiel 7:1-27, The Day of Yahweh Draws Near

NIV

7 The word of the LORD came to me: [2]"Son of man, this is what the Sovereign LORD says to the land of Israel: The end! The end has come upon the four corners of the land. [3]The end is now upon you and I will unleash my anger against you. I will judge you according to your conduct and repay you for all your detestable practices. [4]I will not look on you with pity or spare you; I will surely repay you for your conduct and the detestable practices among you. Then you will know that I am the LORD.

[5]"This is what the Sovereign LORD says: Disaster! An unheard-of[a] disaster is coming. [6]The end has come! The end has come! It has roused itself against you. It has come! [7]Doom has come upon you—you who dwell in the land. The time has come, the day is near; there is panic, not joy, upon the mountains. [8]I am about to pour out my wrath on you and spend my anger against you; I will judge you according to your conduct and repay you for all your detestable practices. [9]I will not look on you with pity or spare you; I will repay you in accordance with your conduct and the detestable practices among you. Then you will know that it is I the LORD who strikes the blow.

[10]"The day is here! It has come! Doom has burst forth, the rod has budded, arrogance has blossomed! [11]Violence has grown into[b] a rod to punish wickedness; none of the people will be left, none of that crowd—no wealth, nothing of value. [12]The time has come, the day has arrived. Let not the buyer rejoice nor the seller grieve, for wrath is upon the whole crowd. [13]The seller will not recover the land he has sold as long as both of them live, for the vision concerning the whole crowd will not be reversed. Because of their sins, not one of them will preserve his life. [14]Though they blow the trumpet and get everything ready, no one will go into battle, for my wrath is upon the whole crowd.

[15]"Outside is the sword, inside are plague and famine; those in the country will die by the sword, and those in the city will be devoured by

[a]5 Most Hebrew manuscripts; some Hebrew manuscripts and Syriac *Disaster after*   [b]11 Or *The violent one has become*

NRSV

7 The word of the LORD came to me: [2]You, O mortal, thus says the Lord GOD to the land of Israel:

An end! The end has come
    upon the four corners of the land.
[3]Now the end is upon you,
    I will let loose my anger upon you;
I will judge you according to your ways,
    I will punish you for all your abominations.
[4]My eye will not spare you, I will have no pity.
    I will punish you for your ways,
    while your abominations are among you.
Then you shall know that I am the LORD.

    [5]Thus says the Lord GOD:
Disaster after disaster! See, it comes.
[6] An end has come, the end has come.
It has awakened against you; see, it comes!
[7]Your doom[a] has come to you,
    O inhabitant of the land.
The time has come, the day is near—
    of tumult, not of reveling on the
        mountains.
[8] Soon now I will pour out my wrath upon you;
    I will spend my anger against you.
I will judge you according to your ways,
    and punish you for all your abominations.
[9]My eye will not spare; I will have no pity.
    I will punish you according to your ways,
    while your abominations are among you.
Then you shall know that it is I the LORD who strike.

[10]See, the day! See, it comes!
    Your doom[a] has gone out.
The rod has blossomed, pride has budded.
[11] Violence has grown into a rod of
        wickedness.
None of them shall remain,
    not their abundance, not their wealth;
    no pre-eminence among them.[a]
[12]The time has come, the day draws near;
    let not the buyer rejoice, nor the seller
        mourn,
    for wrath is upon all their multitude.
[13]For the sellers shall not return to what has been

[a]Meaning of Heb uncertain

NIV

famine and plague. ¹⁶All who survive and escape will be in the mountains, moaning like doves of the valleys, each because of his sins. ¹⁷Every hand will go limp, and every knee will become as weak as water. ¹⁸They will put on sackcloth and be clothed with terror. Their faces will be covered with shame and their heads will be shaved. ¹⁹They will throw their silver into the streets, and their gold will be an unclean thing. Their silver and gold will not be able to save them in the day of the LORD's wrath. They will not satisfy their hunger or fill their stomachs with it, for it has made them stumble into sin. ²⁰They were proud of their beautiful jewelry and used it to make their detestable idols and vile images. Therefore I will turn these into an unclean thing for them. ²¹I will hand it all over as plunder to foreigners and as loot to the wicked of the earth, and they will defile it. ²²I will turn my face away from them, and they will desecrate my treasured place; robbers will enter it and desecrate it.

²³"Prepare chains, because the land is full of bloodshed and the city is full of violence. ²⁴I will bring the most wicked of the nations to take possession of their houses; I will put an end to the pride of the mighty, and their sanctuaries will be desecrated. ²⁵When terror comes, they will seek peace, but there will be none. ²⁶Calamity upon calamity will come, and rumor upon rumor. They will try to get a vision from the prophet; the teaching of the law by the priest will be lost, as will the counsel of the elders. ²⁷The king will mourn, the prince will be clothed with despair, and the hands of the people of the land will tremble. I will deal with them according to their conduct, and by their own standards I will judge them. Then they will know that I am the LORD."

NRSV

sold as long as they remain alive. For the vision concerns all their multitude; it shall not be revoked. Because of their iniquity, they cannot maintain their lives.ᵃ

¹⁴ They have blown the horn and made everything ready;
  but no one goes to battle,
  for my wrath is upon all their multitude.
¹⁵ The sword is outside, pestilence and famine
  are inside;
  those in the field die by the sword;
  those in the city—famine and pestilence
    devour them.
¹⁶ If any survivors escape,
  they shall be found on the mountains
  like doves of the valleys,
  all of them moaning over their iniquity.
¹⁷ All hands shall grow feeble,
  all knees turn to water.
¹⁸ They shall put on sackcloth,
  horror shall cover them.
  Shame shall be on all faces,
  baldness on all their heads.
¹⁹ They shall fling their silver into the streets,
  their gold shall be treated as unclean.

Their silver and gold cannot save them on the day of the wrath of the LORD. They shall not satisfy their hunger or fill their stomachs with it. For it was the stumbling block of their iniquity. ²⁰From theirᵇ beautiful ornament, in which they took pride, they made their abominable images, their detestable things; therefore I will make of it an unclean thing to them.

²¹ I will hand it over to strangers as booty,
  to the wicked of the earth as plunder;
  they shall profane it.
²² I will avert my face from them,
  so that they may profane my treasuredᶜ
    place;
  the violent shall enter it,
  they shall profane it.
²³ Make a chain!ᵃ
  For the land is full of bloody crimes;
  the city is full of violence.
²⁴ I will bring the worst of the nations
  to take possession of their houses.

ᵃMeaning of Heb uncertain   ᵇSyr Symmachus: Heb *its*   ᶜOr *secret*

NRSV

I will put an end to the arrogance of the
strong,
and their holy places shall be profaned.
25 When anguish comes, they will seek peace,
but there shall be none.
26 Disaster comes upon disaster,
rumor follows rumor;
they shall keep seeking a vision from the
prophet;
instruction shall perish from the priest,
and counsel from the elders.
27 The king shall mourn,
the prince shall be wrapped in despair,
and the hands of the people of the land
shall tremble.
According to their way I will deal with them;
according to their own judgments I will
judge them.
And they shall know that I am the LORD.

COMMENTARY

Again, Ezekiel receives from Yahweh an extended pronouncement of doom and havoc against Israel's soil (and its inhabitants). This chapter, like the preceding one, says nothing of the time or place of Yahweh's utterances or of the circumstances under which the prophet must relay them to his audience. Rather, as Ellen Davis observes, Ezekiel "casts himself in the role of first listener and model respondent to what is effectively a divine monologue."[271] Said differently, the text presents the prophet as Yahweh's immediate audience, rather than as a speaker with an audience of his own. This rhetorical strategy focuses the reader's attention squarely upon God as source and agent of the impending catastrophe. Yet Ezekiel does not recede altogether, for he is both the author of vv. 1-2*a* and Yahweh's conduit between divine oracle and designated recipients.

The chapter shares formal features with chap. 6 (e.g., introductory elements, recurrence of the recognition formula; see above). The prophet is beholden to various of Israel's literary traditions—especially the book of Amos, but also Isaiah,

Zephaniah, Jeremiah, Exodus, certain psalms, and the priestly account of the Noachic flood.[272] The reader's ability to discern such allusions depends, of course, upon the breadth and depth of his extratextual repertoire (see Introduction). The basic meaning of the text can be understood (with effort; textual problems and rare words abound) by a reader lacking such knowledge, but much of its richness will remain untapped. Hence our imaginative scholarly construction of a reader steeped in Israel's existing literary traditions.

Two principal sections are evident:[273] a two-part announcement of doom (vv. 2*b*-4 and vv. 5-9, each concluding with a recognition formula) and descriptive statements concerning the imminent unraveling of Judean society (vv. 10-27*b*, also concluding with a recognition formula, v. 27*b*).[274]

272. Note that the NIV arranges the lines of this text as if the entire chapter were composed in prose, rather than poetry. The NRSV reflects the translator's judgment that Ezekiel 7 consists mostly of poetic lines, with some prosaic elements. The distinction between Hebrew poetry and prose can be difficult to determine. Hence, some scholars prefer to speak of "elevated prose."

273. The LXX has produced a quite different version of this chapter. For a detailed discussion of differences, see Zimmerli, *Ezekiel 1*, 194-214.

274. See Moshe Greenberg, *Ezekiel 1–20*, AB 22 (Garden City, N.Y.: Doubleday, 1983) 157-58.

271. Ellen F. Davis, *Swallowing the Scroll: Textuality and the Dynamics of Discourse in Ezekiel's Prophecy*, Bible and Literature 21 (Sheffield: Almond, 1989) 136.

Blenkinsopp calls Ezekiel 7 a "sermon in verse" based largely upon Amos 5:18-20 and 8:2-3, 9-10.[275] During the reign of Jeroboam II (786–746 BCE), the prophet Amos traveled from Judah into the prosperous northern kingdom of Israel. Perceiving that the poor suffered at the hands of the rich and powerful, whose immoral and unjust practices belied their thin veneer of piety, Amos pronounced judgments and predicted national disaster. Did the Israelites long for "the day of the LORD," when Yahweh, their mighty warrior, would triumph over their foes? They would discover that on that day, Yahweh's wrath would turn against them (Amos 5:18-20; 8:9-10). The "end" (8:2-3) was at hand.

Amos 7:1–9:5 recounts the prophet's five visions of Yahweh's proposed punishments. In the fourth of these (8:1-3), the Lord shows Amos a basket of "ripened fruit" (קיץ *qayiṣ*) and asks what he sees. To Amos's response Yahweh replies, "The end [הקץ *haqqēṣ*] has come upon my people Israel" (NRSV). This vision account plays upon the aural similarity between *qayiṣ* ("ripened fruit") and *qēṣ* (the "end").[276]

7:1-4. Ezekiel takes up Amos's pronouncements concerning the "end" and the "day of Yahweh" with a vengeance. Equating the two concepts, he proclaims the impending destruction of Israel's soil in a series of short, stark lines (vv. 2-4). The phrase "the soil of Israel" (אדמת ישראל *'admat yiśrā'ēl*) appears only in the book of Ezekiel (17 times). Far more frequent is ארץ ישראל (*'ereṣ yiśrā'ēl,* "the land of Israel"). Because *'ădāmâ* and *ereṣ* share a number of meanings and can function as virtual synonyms, it is difficult to discern what the significance of Ezekiel's choice might be. In many contexts, however, *'ădāmâ* bears such nuances as "dirt," "(tilled) ground," "soil," and the like. Said differently, the meaning of *'ădāmâ* can be more "earthy" than that of *'ereṣ.* Zimmerli discerns in *'admat yiśrā'ēl* "a recollection of the splendor of the beloved land, the land 'which Yahweh thy God gives you' (Ex 20:12; cf. Dtn 4:40f and other passages)."[277] If he is correct, then Ezekiel's use of "Israel's soil" carries a special

pathos: a cherished, life-sustaining gift is about to be destroyed by the one who gave it.

Many critics insist that in the doom announcement begun in v. *2b,* the phrase "the four corners of the land" (*'ereṣ*) refers to the entire earth.[278] Analogous language in Isa 11:12, Akkadian literature, and Rev 7:1 designates all the lands. Moreover, certain other passages concerning the "day of Yahweh" envision global upheaval (e.g., Isa 2:12-16), so such must also be the case here. However the reader's primary resource for construing this text is the text itself, interpreted in the light of the book of Ezekiel to this point: v. *2b* follows immediately upon Yahweh's command that Ezekiel address *Israel's* soil; 6:14 referred explicitly to two Israelite borders, so the reader has only just been reminded of its traditional geographical limits. It seems hasty, therefore, already to conclude on the basis of 7:1-2 that Yahweh is threatening all-encompassing destruction. Only as the reader proceeds through the chapter will he discover whether its focus remains fixed on Israel per se or stretches beyond its land to speak of universal upheaval.

Verses 3-4 already leave no doubt that the end comes as a consequence of Israel's sins. In one sense, it is the inevitable outworking of the people's own ways and abominations. In another sense, its cause is Yahweh's anger in response to those sins. Both Ezekiel's exilic audience and his readers must not be allowed to resort to any other explanations (e.g., divine apathy, powerlessness, or injustice) for the horrific events inexorably bearing down upon their homeland. Here, as in chap. 6, the purpose of Yahweh's destruction is precisely that those who experience it firsthand, those who hear of it in exile, and those who encounter Yahweh's words as text be constrained to interpret the cataclysm as God's own punishment upon a people whose impurity has exceeded the limits of divine mercy (v. 4).

7:5-9. These verses share striking affinities with vv. 1-4. It is small wonder, then, that modern critics often regard them as a parallel variant of those verses, inserted into their present context by Ezekiel or a later editor, either intentionally or by

275. Joseph Blenkinsopp, *Ezekiel,* IBC (Louisville: John Knox, 1990) 44-46.

276. See Hans Walter Wolff, *Joel and Amos,* trans. W. Janzen, S. D. McBride, and C. A. Moenchors, Hermeneia (Philadelphia: Fortress, 1977) 318-20.

277. Zimmerli, *Ezekiel 1,* 203.

278. E.g., Ronald M. Hals, *Ezekiel,* FOTL 19 (Grand Rapids: Eerdmans, 1989) 44 ; Zimmerli, *Ezekiel 1,* 203; Walther Eichrodt, *Ezekiel,* trans. Cosslett Quin, OTL (Philadelphia: Westminster, 1970) 101; J. W. Wevers, *Ezekiel,* NCB (London: Nelson, 1969) 72.

mistake.[279] Focusing upon similarities between the two passages encourages this hypothesis. Yet the units are distinguished by significant differences, as well. For example, while v. 2 consistently addresses Israel's land, v. 7a speaks to the inhabitant(s) of the land. Verses 2-4 use language associated with the "day of Yahweh," but explicit reference to "the day" does not appear until v. 7b. When these and other differences also are duly considered, we may well conclude that the ancient reader both recognized the iterative (namely, emphatic) effect of the second oracle upon the first *and* attended to how variations between the two units modified or restricted or extended meaning. This literary strategy comports well with synonymous parallelism, a commonplace of Hebrew poetry in which the thought of one line is repeated, often with slight modification, in a second (or even third) line in order both to underscore and to modulate the message.

Again, Yahweh precludes the possibility that divine pity might save Judah from the punishment it deserves (v. 9). Israel's religious traditions repeatedly affirm that God is "merciful and gracious, slow to anger, and abounding in steadfast love and faithfulness . . . forgiving iniquity and transgression and sin" (Exod 34:6-7a NRSV; see also Num 14:18; Neh 9:17, 31; Ps 103:8; Jer 32:18; Jonah 4:2). But tradition also teaches that Yahweh "by no means clear[s] the guilty" (Exod 34:7b NRSV). Israel's impurity has become so great that only a thorough purge of land and people can eradicate it. The modified form of the recognition formula in v. 9b further emphasizes Yahweh's direct role in Israel's imminent destruction.

7:10-27. Preceding verses have repeatedly pressed Yahweh's authorship of Israel's demise. Readers can scarcely have missed this point, and it influences their construal of these verses. Hence we should not follow Zimmerli in unduly emphasizing the latter's "impersonal" style. True, a significant portion of these verses is couched in objective, rather than subjective, language. In the light of vv. 1-9, however, the reader is certain to regard vv. 10-27a, and not just v. 27b, as "formulated personally of Yahweh."[280] When Zimmerli claims that "everything that is to happen to men

[in vv. 10-27a] is first described as though it were unrelated to God and did not concern him,"[281] he misconstrues the text.

Verse 10 begins with yet another announcement of impending catastrophe. "Doom" (v. 10a) is as good as any translation of the obscure Hebrew צפרה (šĕpirâ; the same word appeared in v. 7). Verses 10b-11a employ floral imagery to describe "the automatic link between deed and consequence with the ripening of the blossom of injustice and violence into the flower of doom."[282] They elicit thoughts of Numbers 17, the story of the budding of Aaron's rod, confirming Yahweh's selection of Aaron as high priest over all of Israel's tribes. In Ezekiel 7, Greenberg observes, these verses function as a "grim parody of election." Greenberg also notes the ambiguity (polyvalence) of מטה (matteh, "rod," "staff") in this passage. In addition to recalling the story of Aaron's blossoming rod, the noun evokes the metaphor of a powerful, hostile kingdom as a rod wielded by Yahweh to punish Israel (Isa 19:5). But in conjunction with זדון (zādôn, "pride") and in the light of its proximity to חמס (hāmās, "violence" or "lawlessness") in v. 11a, matteh also evokes מטה (mutteh, "perversion of law").[283] The translations of v. 11b in the NRSV and the NIV are reasonable attempts to make sense of a hopelessly obscure text.

Verse 12a again emphasizes the imminence of Yahweh's day. Buyers will not rejoice over newly acquired commodities, and sellers will not mourn the loss of possessions. What matter if one increases or decreases one's estate, when the economy is certain to crash? (The same idea appears in Isa 24:2.) Verse 13 elaborates in prose: Sellers will never be able to reacquire their property. These ideas likely bore special significance in the light of Ezekiel's insistence that those currently dwelling in Judah would soon perish or be forced into exile with only the few necessities they could carry on their backs. The prophet Jeremiah's seemingly foolish purchase of familial land in Anathoth just prior to Babylonia's defeat of Judah signaled that beyond catastrophe, Israel had a future in its land (Jer 32:1-44). Ezekiel says nothing of the sort.

279. See Zimmerli's refined analysis in *Ezekiel 1*, 194-96, 201-7.
280. Ibid., 206.
281. Ibid., 213.
282. Hals, *Ezekiel*, 45.
283. Greenberg, *Ezekiel 1–20*, 149.

Verses 14-16 describe Israel's utter paralysis in the face of enemy forces. Tradition taught that on the day of Yahweh, Israel's mighty God would lead its troops in victory over all its foes. Verse 14*a* speaks of preparations for warfare, only to add that no one goes forth to battle. The Lord's own people have become the object of the divine warrior's wrath. In language somewhat akin to 5:2-4, 12; 6:11-12, the prophet proclaims that those outside Jerusalem will die by the sword, while those inside the city will succumb to the ravages of pestilence and famine. Should some Judeans survive, they will flee to the mountains. Ezekiel, like the authors of Ps 11:1; Isa 16:2; Jer 48:28, employs bird similes to describe the distress of refugees seeking shelter and safety on Israel's heights.

In the face of such horrors, the people experience uncontrollable terror. Enfeebled hands are a physiological manifestation of psychological anguish in the face of impending doom (see Isa 13:7; Jer 50:43). The NRSV translation of v. 17*b*, "all knees turn to water" (see also NIV), is misleading. The image refers to losing control of one's bladder. Concerning this and preceding lines, Greenberg aptly cites an Assyrian description of enemies fleeing: "Their hearts beat like that of a fledgling dove chased away, they passed hot urine."[284] Wearing sackcloth and shaving one's head are signs of mourning. "In the shame which lies on their faces," Zimmerli observes, "there is betrayed a humiliation which is more than the simple psychological reaction to the surrounding world. It is the specific loss of honor and all that this means in the way of righteousness, which alone makes life possible."[285]

Two ideas are interwoven in vv. 19-20: (1) the worthlessness of silver and gold when basic necessities are unavailable and (2) the use of these precious metals in making idols.[286] Verse 19*a* sets the stage for the subsequent development of both ideas—worthlessness and cultic impurity—for it speaks of flinging silver into the streets and of gold being treated like נדה (*niddâ*; this noun denotes bodily secretions, especially menstrual blood—a

source of extreme contamination; see, e.g., Lev 12:2; 15:19-24; as such, it can refer to a range of unclean things).[287] The assertion that neither silver nor gold can save the people on the day of Yahweh's wrath echoes Zeph 1:18.

Verse 19*a* develops the first of these two ideas: What good are valuable metals if famine has become so severe that food cannot be had at any price? Verse 20 develops the second: From their ("his") beautiful "ornaments" (עדיו *'edyô*), the people have fashioned idols—objects of human pride, but "abominable images," "detestable things" in Yahweh's eyes. Verse 19*b* ("For it was the stumbling block of their iniquity" [i.e., the iniquity that caused their downfall; see the Commentary on 3:20])[288] pivots between the two ideas. On the one hand, it suggests that greed has been part of the people's stumbling block of iniquity. On the other hand, it opens the way to the following accusation of idolatry. Because God's people have made images of their ornaments, Yahweh will make of them ("it") an unclean thing (again, the noun is נדה *niddâ*), handing them over to strangers and the wicked of the earth (here, the Babylonians). They will be able to enter and defile the Temple's holy of holies only because Yahweh turns away: "I will avert my face from them" (v. 22).

Verses 19-20 evoke thoughts of Israel's golden calf episode and its immediate aftermath (Exod 32:1–33:6). In response to Moses' prolonged absence from the camp, Israel's first wilderness generation demands that Aaron "make gods for us, who shall go before us" (Exod 32:1 NRSV). Aaron commands that women and children bring their gold earrings to him, and from them he fashions a calf. Atop Mt. Sinai, Yahweh informs Moses of Israel's apostasy, and Moses immediately returns to the people. Enraged at their idolatrous revelry, Moses orders the Levites to commit mass murder, then burns the calf, grinds it to powder, throws the powder into water, and forces the surviving Israelites to drink it (Exod 32:20). A subsequent plague from Yahweh takes additional lives (Exod 32:35).

284. Ibid., 152.
285. Zimmerli, *Ezekiel 1*, 208.
286. The prophet Isaiah spoke of Yahweh's day as a time when people would seek refuge among rocks and crags and cast away their silver and gold idols (Isa 2:12-22). See also Isa 30:22, where silver and gold-clad idols are rejected with disgust.

287. The conjunction of נדה (*niddâ*; lit., "menstrual blood"; figuratively, an extreme pollutant) and עדיו (*'edyô*, "[his] ornaments") is suggestive. In Ezekiel 7, Yahweh twice insists that Israel's precious metals will become *niddâ* (vv. 19-20). Ezekiel 16:7 suggests that in ancient Israel, the phrase "ornament of ornaments" (בעדי עדיים *ba'ădî 'ădāyîm*) referred to the onset of menstrual periods ("maturity").
288. See Greenberg, *Ezekiel 1–20*, 153.

Following this episode, God commands that Moses and the people depart Mt. Sinai. They will enter Canaan, accompanied by God's messenger (Exod 32:34; 33:2). But the Lord will not go with them, lest this "stiff-necked people" be consumed by divine holiness on the way (Exod 33:1-4). Learning of these harsh words, the people mourn, and no one puts on ornaments. There follows in Exod 33:5 a modified reiteration of Yahweh's command to Moses (Exod 33:1-3) with further elaboration: "So now take off your ornaments, and I will decide what to do to you" (NRSV). Exodus 33:6 reports that the Israelites did strip themselves of their ornaments from Mt. Horeb onward.[289]

The precise meaning of "ornaments" in Exod 33:4-6 is uncertain. Brueggemann is probably correct when he identifies them as "gold rings like those in 32:2-3, out of which the calf was made":

> There is no doubt a reference here to the materials used for the calf. In this post-calf situation, reconstituted Israel . . . is to unburden itself of such provocative possessions . . . Because Yahweh speaks, Israel has a post-calf possibility. But it must forego the commodities that seduce and distort . . . In v. 5, this unburdening becomes the precondition of Yahweh's next act: "I will decide what to do to you."[290]

The reader whose extratext includes Exod 32:1–33:6 (and who has only just encountered an ironic allusion to Aaron's blossoming rod in Ezek 7:10-11), recalls features of the former that link it to the book of Ezekiel, especially 7:19-20. Both Exod 33:1-6 and the prophet Ezekiel repeatedly characterize God's people as stubborn and obstinate. In each text, Israel engages in cultic abomination by turning its gold into idols. In the aftermath of the golden calf incident, Yahweh orders that the people remove their "ornaments" (ʿedyô) "from Mount Horeb onward." Ezekiel 7:20 charges the people with using (forbidden) ornaments to make abominable idols. Hence, a sin committed at the beginning of Israel's history persists to the present, when its "end" is pending.

The opening imperative of v. 23, "Make a chain!," evokes the image of manacled captives who must journey into exile on foot.[291] As Greenberg observes, the charge that Israel's land is full of bloodshed and lawlessness introduces yet another facet of the people's sin:

> Bloody crimes (mišpaṭ dāmîm) and lawlessness (ḥāmās) fill the land. Heretofore Ezekiel arraigned the people for cultic "abominations" and "loathsome things," in line with the priestly covenant threats of Lev 26. . . . Now social wrongs are added, in the idiom of the Flood story ("the earth was filled with lawlessness," Gen 6:11, 13) and earlier prophecy (e.g., Isa 1:15, "Your hands are full of bloodguilt").[292]

Verse 24 both repeats the charge of human hubris ("arrogance") and threatens the destruction of Israel's sanctuaries. (This threat stirs thoughts of Ezekiel 6, judgment against the homeland's high places.) Terror-filled, the people will seek שלום (šālôm, "peace," "wholeness," "well-being"), but to no avail (v. 25). In the face of relentless calamity, they will pursue guidance and advice from three leadership groups: prophets ("vision"), priests ("instruction"), and elders ("counsel"). But these traditional resources will fail (v. 26; cf. Jer 18:18).

Verse 27a describes the impending despair of Judah's populace. The king will mourn, the prince will be clothed with despair, and the hands of the people will tremble (see v. 17). The sequential reader does not yet know that in later chapters of the book, Ezekiel will employ נשׂיא (nāśîʾ, "chief," "prince") to designate Israel's future monarchs (e.g., chap. 46). Hence, the reader may understand it as a collective noun referring to "clan chiefs."[293]

The assertion that Yahweh's punishment is both proportionate and apropos to the people's sin (vv. 3, 8-9) is reiterated in v. 27b. The chapter concludes with the recognition formula. As a consequence of Yahweh's punishment upon them, the Judeans will at last be forced to acknowledge and accept who their Lord is—sole sovereign, author and executor of their "end."

---

289. As Childs observes, Exod 33:4-6 appears to preserve two accounts of why the ornaments are removed: spontaneously at the people's initiative (Exod 33:4) and in response to divine command. See Brevard Childs, *Exodus,* OTL (Philadelphia: Westminster, 1974) 585.

290. W. Brueggemann, "The Book of Exodus," in *The New Interpreter's Bible,* 12 vols. (Nashville: Abingdon, 1994) 1:937-38.

291. The word רתוק (*rattôq,* "chain," "bond") is a *hapax legomenon*—that is, it appears in Hebrew Scripture only once.

292. Moshe Greenberg, *Ezekiel 1–20,* AB 22 (Garden City, N.Y.: Doubleday, 1983) 162-63.

293. See ibid., 156.

We return to a question raised at the beginning of the commentary on this chapter. Does it, with its pronouncements concerning "the day of the LORD," envision worldwide destruction (v. 2)? On the basis of this analysis, we may conclude that it does not. Throughout its verses, Israel's land, its inhabitants, and the society they have constructed remain the objects of Yahweh's devastating wrath. Other peoples (e.g., "foreigners," "the wicked of the earth," the "violent," the "worst of the nations") are mentioned, but nothing is said of their concomitant demise. To the contrary, they will be the beneficiaries of what Israel has lost. Focusing first upon what the text at hand says should caution commentators against importing to Ezekiel 7 a universalism that, while apt to certain other "day of Yahweh" passages, has no place here.

REFLECTIONS

Modern readers of Ezekiel 6–7 are barraged with divine threats of death-dealing assaults and the collapse of every vestige of social stability to which people cling in the face of catastrophe. Judah's end is rushing upon it—devastating, inexorable. Soon, the people must walk "through the valley of the shadow of death" (Ps 23:4 NIV). The trek cannot be avoided, and Ezekiel allows no hope that Yahweh's presence along the way might be experienced as protective and life-sustaining. To the psalmist's confident claim, "I will fear no evil, for you are with me" (Ps 23:4 NIV), Ezekiel might well reply that Yahweh will accost fear-stricken Israel with the lethal consequences of its own evil.

A modern-day poet might paraphrase Ezekiel's message with the images and argot of the atomic age. Nuclear warheads can pulverize reality in a heartbeat. Historically, such weapons have been aimed at a nation by an outside enemy. But Ezekiel's "eve of destruction" is authored by the enemy within—the self-same deity who has gifted Israel with every blessing. Blows from a stranger are one thing; blows from a protector, provider, the object of devotion and trust and love, are quite another.

The eighth-century BCE prophet Hosea insisted that Ephraim (the northern kingdom of Israel) must be steeped in steadfast love and knowledge of God (e.g., Hos 6:6). Ezekiel's recurring use of the recognition formula ("then they shall know that I am Yahweh") within and at the end of judgment oracles reflects his conviction that Israel lacks such knowledge and finally must be forced to it. Knowledge of God cannot be had by rote memorization of religious traditions. It eludes those who think that Yahweh can be "managed" in high-handed ways or dismissed from everyday life or taken for granted, as if both human sin and divine forgiveness were cheap. If, as Israel's own cult asserts, Yahweh is the sovereign Lord of history—just, holy, wielding unrivaled power—then this people must be made to acknowledge and accept that fact, facing fully its consequences for their existence.

Here, we recognize that there are different levels of "knowing." A substance abuser, for example, may "know" for years that he or she has a serious problem, yet do nothing about it. When abuse reaches a critical stage, however, that person may come to know in a fundamentally different way the reality and implications of the disease. That kind of knowledge can lead to a radical reorientation in life—to the willingness to work at maintaining an abstinent life.

Ezekiel is not saying that the people have forgotten that Yahweh is Israel's particular deity or that they have neglected to worship God (though he excoriates the high places and their cultic trappings). His oracles presuppose that his audience is familiar with Yahwistic faith—its traditions, its theological presuppositions and beliefs, etc. No doubt many who were confronted by his oracles could have recited from memory the community's prayers or accurately described its cultic rituals, for they had participated in festivals and other religious observances for years. What is lacking, Ezekiel insists, is knowing "to the bone" who God is and what are the implications of Yahweh's role, demands, and character traits for Israel's life.

Chapters 6–7 make us uncomfortable for many reasons. First, Ezekiel nowhere suggests that acquiring such knowledge will commute Israel's sentence. To the contrary, he insists that the people will only truly learn who Yahweh is through the experience of divine judgment. Both the prophet Jeremiah and Dietrich Bonhoeffer, the German theologian imprisoned and ultimately murdered by the Nazis, were forced to will the destruction of their own nations, in order that their people might survive. Thus far, Ezekiel has said little of survival. But he believes that Israel's impurity has become so great that only a thorough purge of people and land can remove it. Christians often think of a progression of steps leading from sin to salvation: One acknowledges God's sovereignty, confesses wrongdoings, and asks the Lord for forgiveness. God pardons, and wholeness is restored. Ezekiel insists upon the first of these steps, but he says nothing of the others. If his contemporaries are making confessions and asking for forgiveness, he does not acknowledge it. Because his God forswears pity, the consequences of sin cannot be ameliorated. If a modern-day Ezekiel were to proclaim a comparable message—such as asserting that we have made material wealth our gods, insisting upon the Lord's irrevocable intention utterly to destroy our land and cities and to desolate their inhabitants—how might we defend ourselves? Which of our traditions might we invoke?

Second, these chapters make no distinction between the righteous and sinners. Nowhere is the possibility raised that persons not deserving of death might be found in Judah. Ezekiel 6–7 mentions survivors, but neither chapter suggests that they are less guilty than those who will perish. The prophet Jeremiah claimed to have searched the streets of Jerusalem for one just and truth-seeking individual on whose behalf Yahweh might pardon the city. Behind his claim lies the problem of theodicy: Can God truly be just if the innocent suffer along with the guilty? Jeremiah contended that the search was unsuccessful (Jer 5:1-3). His assertion is hard to swallow; surely there were righteous people there, as well as innocents—children, the not yet born. But unlike Jeremiah (who at least addressed the issue), Ezekiel condemns the people in Judah en masse.

Third, these chapters, like Ezek 5:5-17, draw us into scenes of savagery and degradation. "By means of vivid imagery," Blenkinsopp writes, "Ezekiel shows up the fragility and impermanence of those realia which make up the fabric of our taken-for-granted existence and contribute to our sense of personal and social identity. One has only to speak to a survivor of the Nazi concentration camps," he observes, "or watch the old newsreels with their images of unspeakable degradation, or visit Yad Va-Shem, the memorial to the Holocaust in Jerusalem, to appreciate how quickly the veneer of civilized life and humanity can be stripped away. It is this process of the dehumanizing of the defeated which Ezekiel is here describing in terms of brutal realism."[294]

Elsewhere in the scroll, Ezekiel's virulent attacks against his people evoke responses: anger, denial, and countercharges that God is unjust. No doubt these oracles did as well. To be sure, his audience probably included persons who interpreted the nation's plight as he did, because no other explanation made sense. What, after all, was worse: the despairing uncertainty of collapsing social structures or the despairing uncertainty of alienation from the God whose words at least offered an explanation for their collapse? But many others surely protested his utter lack of hope, his endless pointing of the finger of guilt, his insistence that divine wrath could exceed mercy. His words stood at odds with so many of their treasured Yahwistic traditions. How could he proclaim Judah's demise at the hands of a more wicked nation, mocking its sacred traditions of election and casting Yahweh in the role of a ruthless murderer?

It may be helpful to recall the prophet's presuppositions and beliefs, as discussed in the Reflections on 4:1–5:17. First, he is convinced that Judah's demise is imminent. Second, he attributes its collapse to Yahweh, rather than to some other deity (e.g., Marduk, a principal god in the Babylonians' pantheon). Third, he insists that the Lord is not acting capriciously: Judah's punishment is a consequence of its own sinfulness. Fourth, he steadfastly maintains that God is

---

294. Joseph Blenkinsopp, *Ezekiel*, IBC (Atlanta: John Knox, 1990) 51, 48.

just; the punishment is proportionate to the crime. Recognizing these fundamentals of the prophet's worldview helps us to understand what is at stake in his depictions of both Yahweh and Israel. The people must interpret their plight as God's justifiable punishment upon a sinful nation. Any other interpretation challenges Yahweh's sovereign and just control of history.

More must be said, however, for if we feel content or compelled uncritically to adopt Ezekiel's perspective as our own, we are only a short step away from "blaming the victims"—a powerful, prevalent, and hurtful strategy in ancient and modern times. Ezekiel's voice is but one of many in Scripture through which Israel blames itself for the bad things befalling it. This propensity takes seriously divine justice and righteousness, as well as human sin. It also is fraught with danger. A people has the right to point the finger of blame at itself. But others may take its self-accusations as license also to blame that people. And doing so "has murderous implications which murderers will in time spell out."[295]

Numerous texts in Scripture "create" God in the image of human beings. Ezekiel attributes to Yahweh a range of human thoughts, emotions, and reactions. His God, no less than his people, can erupt in rage when betrayed or ignored. Who has not wished that evil might redound upon its perpetrators? Yahweh has the power to make that wish reality. But at what price? Reconciliation is essential for wholeness. One thinks, for example, of Jesus' teaching: "If you are offering your gift at the altar and there remember that your brother has something against you, leave your gift there in front of the altar. First go and be reconciled to your brother; then come and offer your gift" (Matt 5:23-24 NIV). Ezekiel denies his people even a glimpse of reconciliation. But he denies it to God as well. Often in the Hebrew Bible, God's feelings for Israel are characterized as deeply personal and emotional. (Recall, for example, Hos 11:8-9, where God is overwhelmed by love for Ephraim and forswears the punishment it deserves.) Ezekiel does not speak overtly of the brokenness Yahweh suffers as a consequence of Israel's sins. It is evident, nonetheless, in his portrayal of a deity so consumed by anger that divine mercy is cut off. For all of Ezekiel's insistence that Yahweh's behavior is justified, he presents a deity whose unbridled rage bespeaks personal loss and pain.

The apostle Paul knows that human sin causes a breach in the relationship between creator and creation. But he proclaims that the death and resurrection of Christ—who was without sin, yet has borne the sins of all humankind—has made possible a "new creation" for anyone who is "in Christ" (2 Cor 5:17). "All this is from God," Paul continues, "who reconciled us to himself through Christ, and has given us the ministry of reconciliation; that is, in Christ God was reconciling the world to himself, not counting their trespasses against them, and entrusting the message of reconciliation to us" (2 Cor 5:18-19 NRSV). Reading Paul's words, we may think first in terms of humanity's need for reconciliation with God. But that interpretation does not exhaust his meaning. God also needs the reconciliation that is essential to wholeness. So great is God's desire for relationship with humankind that God willingly gives "God's" own son in order that the breach might be healed. In the world of ancient Israel, there could be no greater sacrifice (see, e.g., Genesis 22).

---

295. Franklin Littell, *The Crucifixion of the Jews: The Failure of Christians to Understand the Jewish Experience* (New York: Harper & Row, 1975) 2. Littell uses this phrase in a discussion of the "displacement myth"—that is, "the myth that the mission of the Jewish people was finished with the coming of Jesus Christ, that 'the old Israel' was written off with the appearance of 'the new Israel.' "

EZEKIEL 8:1–10:22, EZEKIEL'S SECOND VISION: YAHWEH'S GLORY ABANDONS JERUSALEM

OVERVIEW

The sequential reader who embarks with Ezekiel on a visionary translocation to Jerusalem (chaps. 8–11) already knows that the city and its inhabitants are doomed. Although Yahweh's plan for the Babylonian exiles remains something of a mystery, passages like 5:5-17 have stated all too clearly that the vast majority of Jerusalemites (and also their rural counterparts throughout Judah) are, in effect, living on "death row."

In this vision, Ezekiel witnesses four cultic abominations committed in the immediate vicinity of Yahweh's own Temple (chap. 8). These accounts—vivid illustrations of the depravity of Jerusalem's inhabitants, including its leaders—justify the following mass execution (chap. 9). In chap. 10, God commands an enigmatic man clothed in linen to set the city afire, even as Yahweh's glory prepares to abandon the city aboard a chariot throne borne aloft by four cherubim. Ezekiel 11 further castigates Jerusalem's leaders and takes to task those who arrogantly assume a privileged position vis-à-vis the exiles. Their sins will redound upon them; the exilic community, by contrast, will be restored and transformed by God's grace. Ezekiel's vision ends as Yahweh's glory abandons Jerusalem, and the prophet is returned by the spirit to Babylonia, there to tell his fellow exiles what he has seen.

Most modern scholars contend that this vision account is not, in its final form, simply the prophet's product. They agree that chaps. 8 and 9 were, from the outset, paired. But detailed descriptions (in chap. 10) of the cherubim who bear aloft Yahweh's glory are often regarded as later expansions of the original version. Even Greenberg concedes that the beginning of chap. 11 might once have belonged to another, parallel vision account.[296] But his analysis of these four chapters, which seeks to make sense of the canonical text as an "intentional product," succeeds in demonstrating that it has been constructed with care. Despite the occasional bump or gap, the sequential reader is able to make sense of the text as a unified narrative.

Ezekiel's vision purports to reveal both what is transpiring in Jerusalem on the fifth day of the sixth month of 592 BCE (8:1) and what will occur there some years hence (the city was not destroyed until 587 BCE). Said differently, it not only describes present conditions, but also predicts/describes future events. The reader need not be unsettled, as are some modern critics, to discover, for instance, that after the man clothed in linen and armed with fiery coals has set out to burn the city (10:7), the scene shifts to the entrance of the Temple's east gate, where twenty-five men have gathered with nary a flame in sight (chap. 11).[297] The point is not that Ezekiel witnesses events in logical, chronological order and within a single time frame (this is, after all, a vision), but that the extremity of Jerusalem's sinfulness (both cultic abominations and social wrongdoings) be shown to justify God's exodus from the city and its future demise.

296. Moshe Greenberg, "The Vision of Jerusalem in Ezekiel 8–11: A Holistic Interpretation," in *The Divine Helmsman: Studies on God's Control of Human Events, Presented to Lou H. Silberman,* ed. James L. Crenshaw and Samuel Sandmel (New York: KTAV, 1980) 158; Moshe Greenberg, *Ezekiel 1–20,* AB 22 (Garden City, N.Y.: Doubleday, 1983) 199.

297. Greenberg, e.g., states that the latter scene is misplaced: "After the general slaughter depicted in 9:6-8, how did twenty-five men come to be at the east gate of the temple?" *Ezekiel 1–20,* 192.

Ezekiel 8:1-18, Ezekiel Witnesses Cultic Abominations Near and in the Temple

NIV

8 In the sixth year, in the sixth month on the fifth day, while I was sitting in my house and the elders of Judah were sitting before me, the hand of the Sovereign LORD came upon me there. [2]I looked, and I saw a figure like that of a man.[a] From what appeared to be his waist down he was like fire, and from there up his appearance was as bright as glowing metal. [3]He stretched out what looked like a hand and took me by the hair of my head. The Spirit lifted me up between earth and heaven and in visions of God he took me to Jerusalem, to the entrance to the north gate of the inner court, where the idol that provokes to jealousy stood. [4]And there before me was the glory of the God of Israel, as in the vision I had seen in the plain.

[5]Then he said to me, "Son of man, look toward the north." So I looked, and in the entrance north of the gate of the altar I saw this idol of jealousy.

[6]And he said to me, "Son of man, do you see what they are doing—the utterly detestable things the house of Israel is doing here, things that will drive me far from my sanctuary? But you will see things that are even more detestable."

[7]Then he brought me to the entrance to the court. I looked, and I saw a hole in the wall. [8]He said to me, "Son of man, now dig into the wall." So I dug into the wall and saw a doorway there.

[9]And he said to me, "Go in and see the wicked and detestable things they are doing here." [10]So I went in and looked, and I saw portrayed all over the walls all kinds of crawling things and detestable animals and all the idols of the house of Israel. [11]In front of them stood seventy elders of the house of Israel, and Jaazaniah son of Shaphan was standing among them. Each had a censer in his hand, and a fragrant cloud of incense was rising.

[12]He said to me, "Son of man, have you seen what the elders of the house of Israel are doing in the darkness, each at the shrine of his own idol? They say, 'The LORD does not see us; the LORD has forsaken the land.'" [13]Again, he said, "You will

NRSV

8 In the sixth year, in the sixth month, on the fifth day of the month, as I sat in my house, with the elders of Judah sitting before me, the hand of the Lord GOD fell upon me there. [2]I looked, and there was a figure that looked like a human being;[a] below what appeared to be its loins it was fire, and above the loins it was like the appearance of brightness, like gleaming amber. [3]It stretched out the form of a hand, and took me by a lock of my head; and the spirit lifted me up between earth and heaven, and brought me in visions of God to Jerusalem, to the entrance of the gateway of the inner court that faces north, to the seat of the image of jealousy, which provokes to jealousy. [4]And the glory of the God of Israel was there, like the vision that I had seen in the valley.

[5]Then God[b] said to me, "O mortal, lift up your eyes now in the direction of the north." So I lifted up my eyes toward the north, and there, north of the altar gate, in the entrance, was this image of jealousy. [6]He said to me, "Mortal, do you see what they are doing, the great abominations that the house of Israel are committing here, to drive me far from my sanctuary? Yet you will see still greater abominations."

[7]And he brought me to the entrance of the court; I looked, and there was a hole in the wall. [8]Then he said to me, "Mortal, dig through the wall"; and when I dug through the wall, there was an entrance. [9]He said to me, "Go in, and see the vile abominations that they are committing here." [10]So I went in and looked; there, portrayed on the wall all around, were all kinds of creeping things, and loathsome animals, and all the idols of the house of Israel. [11]Before them stood seventy of the elders of the house of Israel, with Jaazaniah son of Shaphan standing among them. Each had his censer in his hand, and the fragrant cloud of incense was ascending. [12]Then he said to me, "Mortal, have you seen what the elders of the house of Israel are doing in the dark, each in his room of images? For they say, 'The LORD does not see us, the LORD has forsaken the land.'" [13]He

[a]2 Or *saw a fiery figure*

[a]Gk: Heb *like fire*   [b]Heb *he*

NIV

see them doing things that are even more detestable."

¹⁴Then he brought me to the entrance to the north gate of the house of the LORD, and I saw women sitting there, mourning for Tammuz. ¹⁵He said to me, "Do you see this, son of man? You will see things that are even more detestable than this."

¹⁶He then brought me into the inner court of the house of the LORD, and there at the entrance to the temple, between the portico and the altar, were about twenty-five men. With their backs toward the temple of the LORD and their faces toward the east, they were bowing down to the sun in the east.

¹⁷He said to me, "Have you seen this, son of man? Is it a trivial matter for the house of Judah to do the detestable things they are doing here? Must they also fill the land with violence and continually provoke me to anger? Look at them putting the branch to their nose! ¹⁸Therefore I will deal with them in anger; I will not look on them with pity or spare them. Although they shout in my ears, I will not listen to them."

NRSV

said also to me, "You will see still greater abominations that they are committing."

14Then he brought me to the entrance of the north gate of the house of the LORD; women were sitting there weeping for Tammuz. 15Then he said to me, "Have you seen this, O mortal? You will see still greater abominations than these."

16And he brought me into the inner court of the house of the LORD; there, at the entrance of the temple of the LORD, between the porch and the altar, were about twenty-five men, with their backs to the temple of the LORD, and their faces toward the east, prostrating themselves to the sun toward the east. 17Then he said to me, "Have you seen this, O mortal? Is it not bad enough that the house of Judah commits the abominations done here? Must they fill the land with violence, and provoke my anger still further? See, they are putting the branch to their nose! 18Therefore I will act in wrath; my eye will not spare, nor will I have pity; and though they cry in my hearing with a loud voice, I will not listen to them."

COMMENTARY

8:1-6. In v. 1 Ezekiel situates the following scene in time and place. The date is the fifth day of the sixth month (called "Ab") of the sixth year (of King Jehoiachin's exile; see 1:2)—about September 18, 592 BCE by my reckoning.[298] The location is Ezekiel's house, where the "elders of Judah" have gathered to sit before him. Ezekiel does not tell us why the elders have come. Perhaps they required priestly instruction concerning some legal or cultic dispute. Alternatively, they may have sought an oracle from Yahweh. The reader whose extra-textual repertoire includes traditions about Elisha, the ninth-century BCE northern prophet and miracle worker, will recall that he, too, is described as sitting in his house with the "elders" (2 Kgs 6:32; see also 2 Kgs 4:38; 6:1).

In the midst of this scene, "the hand of Yahweh" falls upon Ezekiel (as in Ezek 1:3; 3:14, 22; for the meaning of the phrase, see the Commentary on 1:3), and suddenly he sees a fiery figure.[299] The description of the being in v. 2 resembles in significant ways the depiction of Yahweh's enthroned glory in 1:26-27. As a consequence, the reader might assume that the prophet is again in God's presence.

According to v. 3, the figure grasps a lock of Ezekiel's hair. (In the Akkadian myth "A Vision of the Nether World," an Assyrian prince named Kummâ visits the realm of the dead in a dream; and the enthroned god Nergal [?] siezes him "by

---

298. Over a year has passed since Ezekiel first witnessed the approach of Yahweh's glory in the sky over Babylonia (about July 31, 593 BCE; see the Commentary on 1:1-2). The LXX reads, "in the fifth month." See the discussion of these chronological difficulties in Walther Eichrodt, *Ezekiel,* trans. Cosslett Quin, OTL (Philadelphia: Westminster, 1970) 121. See also Greenberg, *Ezekiel 1–20,* 166.

299. So MT; commentators (probably correctly) read אישׁ (*'îš*; "human") instead of אשׁ (*'ēš*; "fire"), following the LXX (the Hebrew text may have arisen from scribal error). The reference to "fire" is not, in itself, jarring to the reader, who in the following verse will encounter several references to fire/gleaming brightness. That the figure has an appendage like a hand (v. 3) suggests an anthropomorphic form, although the hybrid living creatures bearing Yahweh's glory also have hands (1:8).

the locks of my forehead.")[300] Yet Ezekiel is borne aloft and brought in a divine vision to Jerusalem not by God (if so this figure be), but by the "spirit"—the same force that set him back on his feet following his first vision of Yahweh's glory by the Chebar Canal (2:2). Again, the reader associates the prophet with Elisha, for the latter also claimed a type of bilocation (2 Kgs 5:26). Ezekiel is not the first of Israel's intermediaries to speak of being in one place, yet observing firsthand what transpires in another. Such links root him deeply in Israel's prophetic movement; in this case, the association both provides Ezekiel's claims with a traditional precedent and imparts to him some of the authority of his predecessors.

The prophet is set down in the Temple's outer court, just beyond the north gate leading to its inner court, and in proximity to "the image of jealousy, which provokes to jealousy"—that is, evokes Yahweh's jealous wrath (v. 3). The following brief notice of God's glory in Jerusalem (v. 4) says nothing of the apparatus and living beings described in chap. 1. The prophet simply asserts that "the glory of the God of Israel was there, like the vision that I had seen in the valley" (referring back to 3:22-23; in that context also nothing is said of the chariot per se, though Ezekiel expressly likens what he saw there to the glory witnessed by the Chebar Canal, 3:23). In his inaugural vision, Ezekiel identifies what he sees only after his gaze has risen beyond the living creatures to the human-like figure enthroned above the dome over their heads (1:28). Does "the appearance of the likeness of the glory of the LORD" refer only to that figure, or does it include the chariot throne and its conveyors? Mettinger observes that in some Ezekielian texts, "glory" (כבוד kābôd) apparently refers to both. But in others, the priest "conceives of the Glory of the Lord as both speaking and acting" as God.[301] The latter usage will predominate in chaps. 8, 9, and 11, where Yahweh speaks (to Ezekiel and others) and acts (leading the prophet from one place to another).

Though vague, the brief reference to God's glory in Jerusalem performs its function: "The narrative has to establish its presence in the temple area; whether with or without its bearers, inside the Temple or outside, are matters of no consequence and so not noted."[302] Still v. 4 likely raises questions in the reader's mind: What precisely did Ezekiel see? Whence has the glory come? Zimmerli insists that the glory "has plainly come from a distance,"[303] but the text neither supports nor refutes his view.

God orders Ezekiel to direct his eyes north toward the "image of jealousy"—apparently a statue of the goddess Asherah, "queen of heaven."[304] The cult of this Canaanite deity already was part of Israelite religion early in the history of the divided monarchy (see 1 Kgs 15:13; 18:19). According to 2 Kgs 21:7, King Manasseh of Judah placed her carved image in the Jerusalem Temple. But Josiah, the seventh-century BCE reforming monarch, is said to have removed the statue and pulverized it at the Wadi Kidron (2 Kgs 23:6). Did an Asherah idol actually stand just outside the Temple's inner court in Ezekiel's day? If so, then a new statue must have been constructed sometime after Josiah's death. It is equally possible, however, that Ezekiel's account of what he witnesses is retrospective—that is, he speaks of a defunct cultic object as if it (and its altar) were still standing. God's question, "Mortal, do you see. . .?" (v. 6) underscores the necessity that Ezekiel personally and carefully observe this first abomination.[305]

8:7-13. God then leads Ezekiel to the wall of the entrance to the north gate. In the wall, he spies a hole (חר ḥōr; here, ḥōr is better rendered "recess," analogous to the "hiding place" of 1 Sam 14:11; Job 30:6).[306] After all, if a hole already were present in the wall, why would God command the prophet to dig another one?

300. *ANET*, 110a.

301. T. N. D. Mettinger, *Dethronement of Sabaoth: Studies in the Shem and Kabod Theologies,* ConBOT (Lund: C.W.K. Gleerup, 1982) 107, 115.

302. Greenberg, *Ezekiel 1–20,* 196-97.

303. W. Zimmerli, *Ezekiel 1: A Commentary on the Book of the Prophet Ezekiel, Chapters 1–24,* trans. R. E. Clements, Hermeneia (Philadelphia: Fortress, 1979) 254.

304. The Hebrew word translated "image" is סמל (*semel*). Greenberg suggests that the statue's position in the area north of the Temple may be significant, since Mt. Zaphon was, in Ugaritic mythology, Baal's abode. Canaanite literature identifies Asherah as Baal's mother. Certain biblical and extra-biblical texts, however, suggest that at least some Israelites regarded her as Yahweh's consort. See Greenberg, *Ezekiel 1–20,* 168.

305. The phrase rendered "drive me far from my sanctuary" by both the NRSV and the NIV should be understood to mean that Asherah's devotees distance themselves from (i.e., remain outside of) Yahweh's Temple proper in order to worship at her image. See J. W. Wevers, *Ezekiel,* NCB (London: Nelson, 1969) 68.

306. See Greenberg, *Ezekiel 1–20,* 169.

Rather, an already obscure recess must itself be gouged before the prophet can reach a secret entrance (v. 8). Hals plausibly suggests that Ezekiel's excavation may be "a graphic way of portraying the hiddenness" of what is transpiring beyond that entrance.[307]

At God's order, Ezekiel enters a chamber to witness the "vile abominations that [the elders of the house of Israel] are committing here" (v. 9; note that Ezekiel's house guests are called "the elders of Judah"). The chamber walls are covered with unclean creatures—"creeping things" (רמשׂ remeś), "loathsome animals" (בהמה שׁקץ běhēmâ šeqeṣ), and "all the idols of the house of Israel." Readers who have visited ancient Egyptian burial chambers and seen walls covered with bas-relief sculptures of deities in animal forms or the famous "Ishtar Gate" of Babylon, with its inlaid lions and serpents, can imagine the sight that met his eyes. And standing before them, incense censers in hand, are seventy of Israel's elders—including Jaazaniah son of Shaphan (v. 11).[308]

To "stand before" (v. 11a) means to engage in cultic activity, in this case, to worship the deities represented on the secret chamber's walls. These elders, like Asherah's devotées, violate both the second and third commandments (Exod 20:1-6). Incense had a place within the cult of Yahweh. According to Lev 16:12-13, for example, Aaron was to bring a censer with him when, on the Day of Atonement, he entered the holy of holies. But it was used in idolatrous cultic rituals as well (see Isa 65:3; Jer 19:4, 13).

Again, Yahweh asks—"Mortal, have you seen . . . ?"[309] It is crucial that Ezekiel witness what is transpiring in secrecy and darkness. God intends, moreover, that he know what the elders are saying: "Yahweh does not see us; the LORD has forsaken the land." As Daniel Block observes, these two clauses constitute the climax of the scene, and both are ambiguous:

The comment about Yahweh not seeing may reflect despair at having lost his protective care, or the belief that Yahweh is blind to what they are doing in this dark room. In the first instance, his oblivion serves as a pretext for turning to other deities for aid in a time of crisis; in the second it offers a pretext for the elders' audacious entry into the sacred precincts, their usurpation of priestly prerogatives, and their introduction of these abominable images and practices.[310]

As for the second comment, do the elders believe that the Lord has abandoned the land because a threat from some more powerful deity has forced Yahweh to flee? Have they concluded that God has grown indifferent to the city's plight? Are theirs the actions of "people who have lost faith in the covenant God and are desperate for divine aid from any source?"[311] Whatever thoughts and doubts lurk in the elders' minds, Ezekiel and his reader know the truth: God sees; no recess is deep enough, no chamber so concealed that it escapes Yahweh's notice. And the Lord has not abandoned the land—not yet. Ezekiel's "tour" continues. For a second time, Yahweh states, "You will see still greater abominations that they are committing" (v. 13).

8:14-15. A third cultic abomination is described in vv. 14-15. Yahweh brings the prophet to the north gate of the court, where he sees women sitting on the ground, lamenting the "Tammuz." Here, it seems, is the Bible's only reference to a shepherd king (also called "Dumuzi") who, according to the Sumerian King List, ruled Bad-tibira for 36,000 years. Revered as a deity, husband of the goddess Inanna, Tammuz was apparently associated with the annual cycles of fertility (manifested in rising tree sap, the date palm and its fruit, the grain used to produce bread and beer, the quickening of the fetus, and mothers' milk) and barrenness.[312] Surviving Mesopotamian literature focuses especially upon the deity's death and descent to the underworld. In the fourth month (named "Tammuz" in his honor), when nature withered beneath the summer sun, devotées mourned his passing in poetic laments.

---

307. Ronald M. Hals, *Ezekiel*, FOTL 19 (Grand Rapids: Eerdmans, 1989) 52.

308. On the significance of "seventy elders," see the etiology (story of origin) in Num 11:16-30. If Jaazaniah's family included the Shaphan mentioned in 2 Kings 22 (a court official associated with Josiah's reform efforts), then the presence of this elder within the secret chamber signaled not only the failure of the reform, but also the ubiquity of Israelite idolatry.

309. The phrase "each in his room of images" (NRSV) suggests that each elder occupies a separate or semi-separate chamber (cf. 8:10). Better is the NIV translation: "each at the shrine of his own idol."

310. D. I. Block, *The Book of Ezekiel: Chapters 1–24*, NICOT (Grand Rapids: Eerdmans, 1997) 293.

311. Ibid., 294.

312. Thorkild Jacobsen, *Toward the Image of Tammuz and Other Essays on Mesopotamian Culture*, HSS 21 (Cambridge, Mass.: Harvard University Press, 1970) 73-74.

His cult was especially popular among women, whose grief and bereavement were expressed, perhaps at different stages in their own life cycles, as that of a sister for her deceased brother, a wife bereft of her husband, or a mother bewailing the death of her beloved son.

Block suggests that "the Tammuz" refers to a particular genre of lament, rather than to a god.[313] Because the two prior abominations (like the fourth to follow) involve Israel's veneration of a deity other than Yahweh, however, the reader likely will conclude that this one does as well. Ezekiel's vision of atrocities committed in Jerusalem occurs in the sixth month (8:1), not the fourth (Tammuz) when, in Mesopotamia, the deity's descent to the underworld was lamented. But the women's ritual he witnesses, like the other abominations, need not have transpired in Jerusalem on that precise date.

8:16-18. The fourth and worst abomination brings Ezekiel to a place of particular sanctity within the Temple's inner court, "between the porch and the altar" (vv. 16-18). According to Joel 2:17, priests positioned themselves there to weep and pray on fast days. But the twenty-five men Ezekiel sees are not called "priests," and their postures—backs to the Temple, faces toward the east, prostrate before the sun—bespeak both contempt for Yahweh and reverence of the sun god Shemesh/Shamash. Deuteronomy 4:19 and 17:2-5 expressly forbade Israel from worshiping the heavenly bodies. In 2 Kings, we read that the seventh-century BCE Judean king Manasseh built altars to the "host of heaven" in the two courts of Yahweh's Temple (2 Kgs 21:5). King Josiah was credited with disposing of horses dedicated to the sun, burning their chariots, and destroying Manasseh's altars (2 Kgs 23:11-12).

God asks Ezekiel a pair of rhetorical questions: "Have you seen this, O mortal? Is it not bad enough that the house of Judah commits the abominations done here?" But before the prophet can answer in the affirmative, Yahweh directs his attention to a greater evil. Acts of social violence (חמס *ḥāmās*; the same word describes the "violence" or "lawlessness" that provoked God to let loose the flood of Noah's day) committed by Judeans against their less powerful victims stir Yahweh to even fiercer anger. This is not the first time in Ezekiel that accusations of violence have followed charges of abominations (see chap. 7), so the reader is not thrown by their abrupt juxtaposition here. As a priest, Ezekiel knows Yahweh's abhorrence of Israel's incessant idolatry. But here he avers the Lord's greater outrage over atrocities committed by people against others. By their actions, God insists, "they are putting the branch to my nose!" (MT, "their nose," a deliberate scribal emendation). The meaning of this action is obscure; scholars have identified it as a gesture of entreaty, an obscene gesture, or a euphemistic reference to "breaking wind."[314] Whatever the phrase's literal referent, its present use is probably metaphorical: Just as a painful blow provokes outrage, so also Judah's deeds unleash divine wrath, expressed in a threefold declaration: "My eye will not spare, nor will I have pity" (see 5:11; 7:4); "I will not listen to [their outcries]" (v. 18). Note the cluster of references to the senses in these two verses; an offense against one results in God's refusal to turn two others benevolently toward the people. (See Reflections at 11:22-25.)

---

313. Block, *Ezekiel 1–24*, 294-96.

314. See Block's discussion and bibliography. Ibid., 299.

Ezekiel 9:1-11, The Wicked Are Slaughtered, Despite Ezekiel's Attempt at Intervention

NIV

9 Then I heard him call out in a loud voice, "Bring the guards of the city here, each with a weapon in his hand." ²And I saw six men coming from the direction of the upper gate,

NRSV

9 Then he cried in my hearing with a loud voice, saying, "Draw near, you executioners of the city, each with his destroying weapon in his hand." ²And six men came from the direction

NIV

which faces north, each with a deadly weapon in his hand. With them was a man clothed in linen who had a writing kit at his side. They came in and stood beside the bronze altar.

³Now the glory of the God of Israel went up from above the cherubim, where it had been, and moved to the threshold of the temple. Then the Lord called to the man clothed in linen who had the writing kit at his side ⁴and said to him, "Go throughout the city of Jerusalem and put a mark on the foreheads of those who grieve and lament over all the detestable things that are done in it."

⁵As I listened, he said to the others, "Follow him through the city and kill, without showing pity or compassion. ⁶Slaughter old men, young men and maidens, women and children, but do not touch anyone who has the mark. Begin at my sanctuary." So they began with the elders who were in front of the temple.

⁷Then he said to them, "Defile the temple and fill the courts with the slain. Go!" So they went out and began killing throughout the city. ⁸While they were killing and I was left alone, I fell face-down, crying out, "Ah, Sovereign Lord! Are you going to destroy the entire remnant of Israel in this outpouring of your wrath on Jerusalem?"

⁹He answered me, "The sin of the house of Israel and Judah is exceedingly great; the land is full of bloodshed and the city is full of injustice. They say, 'The Lord has forsaken the land; the Lord does not see.' ¹⁰So I will not look on them with pity or spare them, but I will bring down on their own heads what they have done."

¹¹Then the man in linen with the writing kit at his side brought back word, saying, "I have done as you commanded."

NRSV

of the upper gate, which faces north, each with his weapon for slaughter in his hand; among them was a man clothed in linen, with a writing case at his side. They went in and stood beside the bronze altar.

3Now the glory of the God of Israel had gone up from the cherub on which it rested to the threshold of the house. The Lord called to the man clothed in linen, who had the writing case at his side; ⁴and said to him, "Go through the city, through Jerusalem, and put a mark on the foreheads of those who sigh and groan over all the abominations that are committed in it." ⁵To the others he said in my hearing, "Pass through the city after him, and kill; your eye shall not spare, and you shall show no pity. ⁶Cut down old men, young men and young women, little children and women, but touch no one who has the mark. And begin at my sanctuary." So they began with the elders who were in front of the house. ⁷Then he said to them, "Defile the house, and fill the courts with the slain. Go!" So they went out and killed in the city. ⁸While they were killing, and I was left alone, I fell prostrate on my face and cried out, "Ah Lord God! will you destroy all who remain of Israel as you pour out your wrath upon Jerusalem?" ⁹He said to me, "The guilt of the house of Israel and Judah is exceedingly great; the land is full of bloodshed and the city full of perversity; for they say, 'The Lord has forsaken the land, and the Lord does not see.' ¹⁰As for me, my eye will not spare, nor will I have pity, but I will bring down their deeds upon their heads."

11Then the man clothed in linen, with the writing case at his side, brought back word, saying, "I have done as you commanded me."

COMMENTARY

The people's outcries will have no effect. But then Yahweh cries aloud in the prophet's hearing, and the summons ("Draw near, you executioners of the city") is immediately efficacious. Through the north gate come six men armed with clubs (or battle axes), accompanied by a linen-clothed man with a writing case at his waist (vv. 1-2). His garment is that of a priest, his equipment that of a

scribe. The band halts in the Temple's inner court, "beside the bronze altar"—that is, Solomon's altar (1 Kgs 8:64), which had been moved from its original location to the northeast corner of the temple court in order to make room for a stone altar erected by the eighth-century BCE Judean king Ahaz (2 Kgs 16:14).

Verse 3*a,* a parenthetical, explanatory clause,

informs the reader that "the glory of the God of Israel" (mentioned briefly in 8:4) "had gone up from the cherub [sing., from Akkadian *kurimbu,* a type of divine or semi-divine creature] on which it rested to the threshold of the house." Its movement was, it seems, contemporaneous with events narrated thus far. What will the reader make of this observation? If he knows the well-established tradition that God's glory resided within the Temple's holy of holies, enthroned upon Solomon's pair of gold covered cherubim, their wings outspread and the ark of the covenant resting between and beneath them (see 1 Kgs 6:23-28; 8:1-12), he likely will imagine that the glory has risen off of the cherub pair and moved outward to the Temple's threshold. (The singular "cherub" does not rule out this understanding, since it can be construed as a collective referring to the [one] pair.) Can the reader square this understanding with the larger narrative context of v. 3*a*? In preceding (and subsequent) verses, Yahweh addresses the man clothed in linen, the executioners, and Ezekiel, all of whom are located in the Temple's inner court (outside the structure proper). Hence, the reader has likely presumed that Yahweh is with them there. Can the Lord be conceived as present in two locales simultaneously? Yes. Common to ancient religions was the belief that "the deity is at once localized in its temple and 'in heaven' (or ubiquitous)."[315] Still, v. 3*a* gives pause: What can it mean that God's glory has abandoned its site within the Temple's most sacred space? Block explains: Its departure "signaled Yahweh's suspension of rule and raised the possibility of his departure from the city. The people's accusation/rationalization that Yahweh has abandoned them is about to be fulfilled, and when that happens there will be no hope. By inserting this observation here the author has intentionally correlated Yahweh's departure with the judgment of Jerusalem."[316]

Yahweh orders the man clothed in linen to go through Jerusalem, placing a "tau" (the last letter of the Hebrew alphabet, written as an "X" in the old Canaanite script) on the foreheads of all who "sigh and groan" over the abominations committed there (v. 4).[317] For the first time, the reader learns that God intends to preserve the lives of Jerusalemites who bewail its sinfulness. The narrative does not follow after the man in linen; the reader is left wondering about the search.

Jeremiah claims to have searched Jerusalem's streets for a single just and truth-seeking individual on whose behalf Yahweh might save the city (Jer 5:1-3). Ezekiel's God sets no less than a divine or semi-divine emissary to the task of marking some for survival—a clear affirmation of Yahweh's intention only to punish the culpable. In the next breath, God sets the executioners to their deadly task: "Pass through the city after him, and kill." They must model their behavior on the Lord's: "Your eye shall not spare, and you shall show no pity." Verse 5 makes clear that the presence of righteous individuals will not prevent the execution of their fellow Jerusalemites. To the contrary, *all* whose foreheads are not marked will perish, be they old or very young, male or female.[318] First to die are the elders whose worship of the sun constituted the greatest of the cultic abominations Ezekiel has witnessed (8:16-18). That the massacre commences at the Temple presents a double irony: Not only is Yahweh's own sanctuary, the city's most sacred site, first to be defiled by corpses, but also it provides no asylum for those sentenced to death.

With their departure, Ezekiel is left alone in the inner court (v. 8*a*). Yet he is not alone. Yahweh is there also, and the two engage in a coversation of sorts. Heretofore, the prophet has spoken Yahweh's script. Only in 4:14 did he take the initiative to speak on his own, protesting the Lord's command that he consume defiled meat. But now, Ezekiel takes up the traditional prophetic task of interceding with God on Israel's behalf: "Ah Lord GOD!" he cries, "will you destroy all who remain of Israel as you pour out your wrath upon Jerusalem?" Must this be the end of God's people, or is there some hope that he, like his prophetic predecessors (e.g., Moses, Num 14:13-19; Amos,

315. Moshe Greenberg, *Ezekiel 1–20,* AB 22 (Garden City, N.Y.: Doubleday, 1983) 196.

316. Block, *Ezekiel 1–24,* 306.

317. The Hebrew phrase is alliterative: *hanne'ĕnāḥîm wĕhanne'ĕnāqîm.* Block, ibid., 307, translates, "moan and groan." Readers recall the "mark of Cain" (Gen 4:15) and perhaps the Passover, when Yahweh's messenger of destruction passed by the blood-smeared doors of the Hebrews enslaved in Egypt (Exodus 12).

318. Here, Block observes, "Yahweh singles out the defenseless, the frail, and the innocent, those who seek refuge behind a city's walls in times of crisis." Ibid., 308.

Amos 7:2, 5) can change Yahweh's mind? The Lord's response is immediate, negative, and self-justifying: The guilt of *all* God's people ("the house of Israel and Judah") is very, very great. Hence, their execution is fully justified; the land is filled with bloodshed, evidence of the people's ubiquitous acts of social violence (see 8:17); Jerusalem itself is full of perversity (injustice). The people's own words testify against them (v. 9*b*); here, the order of the two clauses quoted earlier (8:12) has switched. Is this reversal intended to suggest that the elders' sentiments also are voiced (in slightly different form) by other Judeans? But Yahweh has not abandoned the land (though the glory's move-

ment from the holy of holies to the threshold [9:3*a*] presages that possibility). Yahweh *sees* Judah's sins; as a consequence, Yahweh's *eye* will not spare them, and pity has no place. Their own deeds will redound upon their heads (an echo of 7:4, 8-9, 27; 8:18; and the Lord's instructions in 9:5). If there be hope for a remnant surviving in Judah (Ezekiel's fellow exiles are a separate matter), it resides with the possibility that the linen-clothed man has identified some righteous Jerusalemites. Verse 11 affirms that he has carried out Yahweh's instructions, but says nothing of results. (See Reflections at 11:22-25.)

Ezekiel 10:1-22, Jerusalem Will Burn, and Yahweh's Glory Prepares to Abandon the City

NIV

10 I looked, and I saw the likeness of a throne of sapphire[a] above the expanse that was over the heads of the cherubim. [2]The LORD said to the man clothed in linen, "Go in among the wheels beneath the cherubim. Fill your hands with burning coals from among the cherubim and scatter them over the city." And as I watched, he went in.

[3]Now the cherubim were standing on the south side of the temple when the man went in, and a cloud filled the inner court. [4]Then the glory of the LORD rose from above the cherubim and moved to the threshold of the temple. The cloud filled the temple, and the court was full of the radiance of the glory of the LORD. [5]The sound of the wings of the cherubim could be heard as far away as the outer court, like the voice of God Almighty[b] when he speaks.

[6]When the LORD commanded the man in linen, "Take fire from among the wheels, from among the cherubim," the man went in and stood beside a wheel. [7]Then one of the cherubim reached out his hand to the fire that was among them. He took up some of it and put it into the hands of the man in linen, who took it and went out. [8](Under the wings of the cherubim could be seen what looked like the hands of a man.)

NRSV

10 Then I looked, and above the dome that was over the heads of the cherubim there appeared above them something like a sapphire,[a] in form resembling a throne. [2]He said to the man clothed in linen, "Go within the wheelwork underneath the cherubim; fill your hands with burning coals from among the cherubim, and scatter them over the city." He went in as I looked on. [3]Now the cherubim were standing on the south side of the house when the man went in; and a cloud filled the inner court. [4]Then the glory of the LORD rose up from the cherub to the threshold of the house; the house was filled with the cloud, and the court was full of the brightness of the glory of the LORD. [5]The sound of the wings of the cherubim was heard as far as the outer court, like the voice of God Almighty[b] when he speaks.

6When he commanded the man clothed in linen, "Take fire from within the wheelwork, from among the cherubim," he went in and stood beside a wheel. [7]And a cherub stretched out his hand from among the cherubim to the fire that was among the cherubim, took some of it and put it into the hands of the man clothed in linen, who took it and went out. [8]The cherubim appeared to have the form of a human hand under their wings.

*a*1 Or *lapis lazuli*   *b*5 Hebrew *El-Shaddai*

*a*Or *lapis lazuli*   *b*Traditional rendering of Heb *El Shaddai*

NIV

⁹I looked, and I saw beside the cherubim four wheels, one beside each of the cherubim; the wheels sparkled like chrysolite. ¹⁰As for their appearance, the four of them looked alike; each was like a wheel intersecting a wheel. ¹¹As they moved, they would go in any one of the four directions the cherubim faced; the wheels did not turn about[a] as the cherubim went. The cherubim went in whatever direction the head faced, without turning as they went. ¹²Their entire bodies, including their backs, their hands and their wings, were completely full of eyes, as were their four wheels. ¹³I heard the wheels being called "the whirling wheels." ¹⁴Each of the cherubim had four faces: One face was that of a cherub, the second the face of a man, the third the face of a lion, and the fourth the face of an eagle.

¹⁵Then the cherubim rose upward. These were the living creatures I had seen by the Kebar River. ¹⁶When the cherubim moved, the wheels beside them moved; and when the cherubim spread their wings to rise from the ground, the wheels did not leave their side. ¹⁷When the cherubim stood still, they also stood still; and when the cherubim rose, they rose with them, because the spirit of the living creatures was in them.

¹⁸Then the glory of the LORD departed from over the threshold of the temple and stopped above the cherubim. ¹⁹While I watched, the cherubim spread their wings and rose from the ground, and as they went, the wheels went with them. They stopped at the entrance to the east gate of the LORD's house, and the glory of the God of Israel was above them.

²⁰These were the living creatures I had seen beneath the God of Israel by the Kebar River, and I realized that they were cherubim. ²¹Each had four faces and four wings, and under their wings was what looked like the hands of a man. ²²Their faces had the same appearance as those I had seen by the Kebar River. Each one went straight ahead.

ᵃ11 Or aside

NRSV

⁹I looked, and there were four wheels beside the cherubim, one beside each cherub; and the appearance of the wheels was like gleaming beryl. ¹⁰And as for their appearance, the four looked alike, something like a wheel within a wheel. ¹¹When they moved, they moved in any of the four directions without veering as they moved; but in whatever direction the front wheel faced, the others followed without veering as they moved. ¹²Their entire body, their rims, their spokes, their wings, and the wheels—the wheels of the four of them—were full of eyes all around. ¹³As for the wheels, they were called in my hearing "the wheelwork." ¹⁴Each one had four faces: the first face was that of the cherub, the second face was that of a human being, the third that of a lion, and the fourth that of an eagle.

15The cherubim rose up. These were the living creatures that I saw by the river Chebar. ¹⁶When the cherubim moved, the wheels moved beside them; and when the cherubim lifted up their wings to rise up from the earth, the wheels at their side did not veer. ¹⁷When they stopped, the others stopped, and when they rose up, the others rose up with them; for the spirit of the living creatures was in them.

18Then the glory of the LORD went out from the threshold of the house and stopped above the cherubim. ¹⁹The cherubim lifted up their wings and rose up from the earth in my sight as they went out with the wheels beside them. They stopped at the entrance of the east gate of the house of the LORD; and the glory of the God of Israel was above them.

20These were the living creatures that I saw underneath the God of Israel by the river Chebar; and I knew that they were cherubim. ²¹Each had four faces, each four wings, and underneath their wings something like human hands. ²²As for what their faces were like, they were the same faces whose appearance I had seen by the river Chebar. Each one moved straight ahead.

COMMENTARY

Chapter 10 consists of two sections (vv. 1-8 and vv. 9-22), both beginning with the phrase "Then I looked" (וארא והנה *wā'er'eh wĕhinnēh*). Section one notes the arrival of God's cherubim throne, the glory's departure from the holy of holies, and the commissioning and equipping of the linen-clothed man who, having marked some Jerusalemites for survival, now functions as the agent of the city's destruction by fire. Section two presents interwoven descriptions of the cherubim and their wheels and signals the movement of Yahweh's glory from the Temple's threshold to its east gate. Modern critics who assert not only the essential literary unity of chaps. 8–9, but also the integrity of their juxtaposition, perceive in chap. 10 problems of a more serious sort. Zimmerli, for example, regards virtually all of 10:8-22 as secondary, the result of multiple levels of ongoing editorial expansion.[319]

Focusing upon the ancient reader's sequential construal of the received text, rather than upon its compositional history, should not be viewed as a means of avoiding or "explaining away" textual difficulties. Chapter 10 confronts readers, ancient and modern, with certain conundrums. Yet the modern critic's methods of analysis will identify problems not perceived by, and suggest complex explanations for those problems not conceivable to, ancient interpreters. Moreover, we should remember that Ezekiel's earliest readers undoubtedly took many problems in stride. Perhaps they were predisposed to anticipate less than absolute clarity and realism in vision accounts. They certainly expected both to find and to negotiate errors by all-too-human copyists. Despite the existence of computer spell-check programs, professional proofreaders, and photocopy machines, we must do the same. And like our ancient counterparts, we manage nicely unless the problems are so severe that meaning is hopelessly mangled.

The commentary proceeds, therefore, with the assumption that the sequential reader is able to make sense of Ezekiel 10 as a continuation of the vision account of chaps. 8–9. Consciously and unconsciously the reader seeks both to fill gaps encountered along the way (aided by knowledge acquired thus far in reading the book and drawn from his extra-textual repertoire) and to smooth out inconsistencies (both within this chapter and across chapter lines, esp. chap. 1)—a strategy explicitly encouraged in chap. 10. The appearance of Yahweh's (empty) chariot throne in v. 1 confronts the reader with both: Its (re)appearance at this point is abrupt, and while the verse is reminiscent of 1:22, 26, its reference to cherubim is alien to Ezekiel's inaugural vision by the Chebar Canal. What creatures are these, and what has become of the "living beings"? Again, what is the relationship between the cherubim of 10:1 and the cherub of 9:3a?

Zimmerli postulates that the original text of chap. 10 spoke only of a single cherub; references to multiple cherubs, whose appearance both resembles and differs from that of the "living beings" of chap. 1, constitute a subsequent editorial "overlay."[320] Greenberg, by contrast, asserts that the singular "cherub" (v. 4a) refers only to Solomon's pair of gold-clad statues, while "cherubim" (plural) designates the actual living conveyors of Yahweh's throne.[321] The ancient reader might well construe the text as Greenberg has done. Zimmerli's complex hypothesis would not have occurred to him and so offers no help.

If v. 1 constitutes something of a jolt, v. 2 returns the reader to a familiar figure: the man clothed in linen. But how his function has changed! In chap. 9, his mark meant survival; here, God instructs him to go in to the wheelwork (called הגלגל *haggalgal*) beneath the cherubim,[322] and having filled his hands with burning coals, to scatter them over the city. (1:13 spoke of "something that looked like burning coals of fire, like torches moving to and fro among the living creatures," but without explanation of its

---

319. W. Zimmerli, *Ezekiel 1: A Commentary on the Book of the Prophet Ezekiel, Chapters 1–24,* trans. R. E. Clements, Hermeneia (Philadelphia: Fortress, 1979) 231-32.

320. Ibid., 250.
321. Greenberg, *Ezekiel 1–20,* 196-97.
322. In MT the noun is singular. Versional evidence for the plural is strong, however, and the MT may have resulted from haplography. If the text before read "cherub," then we may assume that the wheelwork the man approaches lies between and beneath the pair of cherubs standing in the holy of holies (see 9:3a). But the plural "cherubim" appears further in the same verse, and v. 3 will explicitly locate these cherubs south of the Temple, not within it.

---

significance. Now, the reader learns of [at least one of] its function.) The man's priest-like linen attire has been discussed. The term זרק (*zāraq* "to strew," "to scatter"; often "to dash" [blood]) further underscores his priestly status, for the verb sometimes describes priestly lustrations (e.g., Lev 3:2, 8, 13).[323] Here, ironically, it depicts the process by which Jerusalem will be set ablaze.

Ezekiel looks on as the man sets to his appointed task. Parenthetically, he locates the living cherubim—the sapphire-like form of an (empty) throne above their heads, and the wheel-work beneath and between them—to the south of the "house" (temple),[324] and he observes that "the cloud" has filled the inner court. Verse 4*a*, also parenthetical, essentially reiterates the action described in 9:3*a*, which transpires within the holy of holies, beyond Ezekiel's field of vision. Yahweh's glory rises from above the cherub statues and moves to the threshold of the house (temple). With its departure (v. 4*b*), the house is filled with the cloud, while the court grows bright with the glory of the Lord. Juxtaposed to the information in v. 3*b*, this notice is perplexing. The reader is not surprised that the cloud is associated with God's glory, for such is part and parcel of Israel's cultic traditions (see Exod 16:10-12; 40:34; Num 16:42). Also not new is the notion that exiting from the holy of holies "releases," so to speak, the cloud; according to 1 Kgs 8:10-11, it filled Yahweh's Temple when the priests who first placed the ark of the covenant in that most sacred space emerged from it. Nonetheless, the two notices are not easily reconciled.

Some scholars contend that the notice of the glory's movement is original to v. 4*a;* its presence in 9:3*a* is secondary—an awkward scribal intrusion. Block, by contrast, regards v. 4*a* as "a flashback to and an expansion of 9:3." In his view also, these verses do not recount two separate events. Rather, 9:1-11 and 10:1-8 detail the same event from two different persperspectives: "The former [chapter] highlights the judgment of Jerusalem directly as an expression of divine wrath, with Yahweh's departure being a secondary theme. The latter reverses this ranking, treating the divine abandonment of the temple by Yahweh as the primary motif, and the judgment of the city as ancillary."[325]

If, as both Greenberg and Block suggest, the text distinguishes between the pair of statues (cherub) standing in the holy of holies (9:3*a;* 10:4*a*) and the "real" cherubim of 10:1-2, 5-22, then the sudden appearance of Yahweh's actual chariot throne becomes explicable: As God's glory abandons its position above the replica, the real thing arrives—its appearance signaled by the sound of the cherubim's wings (v. 5)—ready to transport the glory as needed.[326]

As the man moves in to obey Yahweh's command, one of the cherubs stretches out its hand, takes some of the fire, and gives it to him. He then sets out. As was the case with his earlier mission, the narrative does not follow him. The stage for Ezekiel's vision remains the temple precinct. Like the audience of a play, his reader assumes that significant events are transpiring off-stage.

With the notice that the cherub's hand is human in form, the text embarks on a lengthy description of the chariot's wheels and the cherubim themselves. The following verses both resemble and depart from the descriptions in chap. 1:

> Where material from ch. 1 is repeated, most of the grammatical difficulties have been smoothed out . . . much of the analogical language has disappeared. The indefinite expression "creatures" [chap. 1] . . . has been replaced by the specific "cherubim" . . . the wheels (*'ôpannîm*) are identified specifically as *galgal* (10:13), and the sheer brilliance of the first vision has been toned down. Furthermore, the description of the creatures has been rationalized (10:14; cf. 1:10), and details that seemed out of place in ch. 1 now have vital parts to play (the burning coals and the wheels).[327]

Readers, ancient and modern, certainly recognize these and other differences between the two descriptive passages—e.g., the discrepancy

---

323. See Greenberg, *Ezekiel 1–20,* 181.

324. Heretofore, Ezekiel's vision has focused on events transpiring on the north and east sides of the temple precinct. Locating the cherubim to the south of the Temple distances the vehicle of God's glory from the abominations, as well as the executions, north of the Temple.

325. D. I. Block, *The Book of Ezekiel: Chapters 1–24,* NICOT (Grand Rapids: Eerdmans, 1997) 315.

326. Moshe Greenberg, *Ezekiel 1–20,* AB 22 (Garden City, N.Y.: Doubleday, 1983) 195-97; Block, *Ezekiel 1–24,* 319-20.

327. Block, *Ezekiel 1–24,* 316-17.

between 1:18, which speaks of "eyes" (decorative studs?) covering the rims of the chariot wheels, and 10:12, which apparently envisions eyes covering not only the four wheels, but also the cherubim's entire bodies—backs, hands, and wings (NIV; cf. NRSV), and the replacement of the ox face (1:10) with the face of a cherub (10:14). Dijkstra may be correct when, having examined evidence of editorial glosses in Ezekiel 10, he concludes that "originally, the text of ch. 10 was a visionary report independent from ch. 1. It is not those elements, which makes ch. 10 differ from ch. 1, which have to be excised as later additions to the text. On the contrary, the additions are those elements which harmonize the text of ch. 10 according to ch. 1. . . . The vision of the cherubim was indeed the vision of the cherubim and not, as textual tradition grad-

ually wanted to reshape it, the vision of the [chariot throne] in ch. 1."[328] But that "textual tradition" seeks to diffuse such differences for the reader by explicitly identifying the "wheels" of Ezekiel 1 with the "wheelwork" of 10:13 and by repeatedly asserting that the "living creatures" first witnessed by the Chebar Canal, and the cherubim of this vision, are the same beings (10:15, 20, 22).

With v. 18, Yahweh's glory departs the Temple's threshold and takes its place above the cherubim. In the prophet's sight, they lift off from the earth, bearing the glory to the Temple's east gate. (See Reflections at 11:22-25.)

328. Meindert Dijkstra, "The Glosses in Ezekiel Reconsidered: Aspects of Textual Transmission in Ezekiel 10," in *Ezekiel and His Book: Textual and Literary Criticism and Their Interrelation,* ed. J. Lust, BETL 74 (Leuven: Leuven University Press, 1986) 77.

EZEKIEL 11:1-25, THE CONCLUSION OF EZEKIEL'S SECOND VISION

OVERVIEW

Ezekiel 11 both continues and concludes the prophet's visionary "visit" to Jerusalem. Scholars question the original relationship of chap. 11 to chaps. 8–10, noting, for example, that v. 1 reads like a formal introduction to a different vision, that the twenty-five men gathered at the Temple's east gate are oblivious to the city's immolation, osten-

sibly carried out in 10:6-7, and that vv. 1-21 interrupt the glory's exit from the city. Yet most specialists both attribute the bulk of chap. 11 to Ezekiel and acknowledge that numerous links between it and previous chapters invite the reader to construe all of chaps. 8–11 as a single vision account.

Ezekiel 11:1-13, Ezekiel Castigates Jerusalem's Leaders

NIV

11 Then the Spirit lifted me up and brought me to the gate of the house of the LORD that faces east. There at the entrance to the gate were twenty-five men, and I saw among them Jaazaniah son of Azzur and Pelatiah son of Benaiah, leaders of the people. ²The LORD said to me, "Son of man, these are the men who are plotting evil and giving wicked advice in this city. ³They say, 'Will it not soon be time to build

NRSV

11 The spirit lifted me up and brought me to the east gate of the house of the LORD, which faces east. There, at the entrance of the gateway, were twenty-five men; among them I saw Jaazaniah son of Azzur, and Pelatiah son of Benaiah, officials of the people. ²He said to me, "Mortal, these are the men who devise iniquity and who give wicked counsel in this city; ³they say, 'The time is not near to build houses; this city

NIV

houses?[a] This city is a cooking pot, and we are the meat.' [4]Therefore prophesy against them; prophesy, son of man."

[5]Then the Spirit of the LORD came upon me, and he told me to say: "This is what the LORD says: That is what you are saying, O house of Israel, but I know what is going through your mind. [6]You have killed many people in this city and filled its streets with the dead.

[7]"Therefore this is what the Sovereign LORD says: The bodies you have thrown there are the meat and this city is the pot, but I will drive you out of it. [8]You fear the sword, and the sword is what I will bring against you, declares the Sovereign LORD. [9]I will drive you out of the city and hand you over to foreigners and inflict punishment on you. [10]You will fall by the sword, and I will execute judgment on you at the borders of Israel. Then you will know that I am the LORD. [11]This city will not be a pot for you, nor will you be the meat in it; I will execute judgment on you at the borders of Israel. [12]And you will know that I am the LORD, for you have not followed my decrees or kept my laws but have conformed to the standards of the nations around you."

[13]Now as I was prophesying, Pelatiah son of Benaiah died. Then I fell facedown and cried out in a loud voice, "Ah, Sovereign LORD! Will you completely destroy the remnant of Israel?"

[a]3 Or *This is not the time to build houses.*

NRSV

is the pot, and we are the meat.' [4]Therefore prophesy against them; prophesy, O mortal."

[5]Then the spirit of the LORD fell upon me, and he said to me, "Say, Thus says the LORD: This is what you think, O house of Israel; I know the things that come into your mind. [6]You have killed many in this city, and have filled its streets with the slain. [7]Therefore thus says the Lord GOD: The slain whom you have placed within it are the meat, and this city is the pot; but you shall be taken out of it. [8]You have feared the sword; and I will bring the sword upon you, says the Lord GOD. [9]I will take you out of it and give you over to the hands of foreigners, and execute judgments upon you. [10]You shall fall by the sword; I will judge you at the border of Israel. And you shall know that I am the LORD. [11]This city shall not be your pot, and you shall not be the meat inside it; I will judge you at the border of Israel. [12]Then you shall know that I am the LORD, whose statutes you have not followed, and whose ordinances you have not kept, but you have acted according to the ordinances of the nations that are around you."

13Now, while I was prophesying, Pelatiah son of Benaiah died. Then I fell down on my face, cried with a loud voice, and said, "Ah Lord GOD! will you make a full end of the remnant of Israel?"

COMMENTARY

The text addresses three topics: judgment upon the city's smug civil leaders, who will suffer the lethal consequences of their own, death-dealing crimes against fellow Judeans (vv. 1-13); a rebuttal of the Jerusalemites' claim that the exiles have been written out of God's history, including words of judgment against the former and hope-filled promises for the latter (vv. 14-21); and the departure of Yahweh's glory from the city, followed by Ezekiel's return to the exiles in Babylonia (vv. 22-25).

Scholars point to similarities between Ezekiel's account of Yahweh's glory abandoning the Temple and the Neo-Babylonian *Poem of Erra,* a literary classic of the ancient Near East. Bodi compares this poem to the book of Ezekiel and, more specifically, to the present passage. In *Erra,* the gods Erra and Marduk become angry at the neglect of their cults, moral decay, the tumult of the peoples, and the threat human beings pose to the deities. Marduk abandons his shrine; in his absence, Erra, the god of destruction and chaos, destroys Babylon and forces its inhabitants into exile to serve as slaves for seventy years. After only eleven years, however, Marduk's anger abates, and he brings the people back to rebuild Babylon. Similarly, Ezekiel 8–9 describes the cultic abominations committed in Yahweh's Temple, as well as moral and social crimes; and these are presented as justifying Yahweh's abandonment of the city.[329]

The spirit transports Ezekiel (see 8:3*b*) to the east gate of God's Temple, where, according to 10:18, the glory-bearing cherubim are hovering. There, the prophet sees twenty-five city officials, "men who devise iniquity and who give wicked counsel in this city," including Jaazaniah son of Azzur (not the Jaazaniah son of Shaphan of 8:11) and Pelatiah son of Benaiah. That Ezekiel is able to name two members of the group adds a realistic note.

These verses take the form of a prophetic disputation speech, in which a popular opinion of the people is quoted and then refuted (see also 8:12; 12:22, 27; 18:2, 19, 25, 29). In this instance, Yahweh first quotes the officials and then twice commands Ezekiel to prophesy against them.

What is the meaning of the officials' ostensible statements? Although the phrase "build houses" can, in other contexts, refer metaphorically to establishing families (e.g., Deut 25:9; Ruth 4:11; Prov 24:27), it is best construed literally here. But why is this not the time to build? Are the officials boasting of their appropriation of the exiles' properties? Or are they acknowledging that all of the city's resources are best used securing Jerusalem from attack? The following two assertions are metaphorical, and their meaning also is not immediately apparent to the reader. Do they convey the officials' sense of security, that they are choice cuts of meat safely stewing within a cooking pot or preserved in a storage vessel (the city's protective walls)? Perhaps, when the prophet obeys Yahweh's double imperative to prophesy against them, the meaning of their metaphors will become clear.

According to v. 5, Yahweh's spirit falls upon Ezekiel, and he receives the script of his prophecy (elsewhere, the text speaks of Yahweh's hand falling upon the prophet; see 3:22). God knows what "the house of Israel" is thinking, and also what they have done, killing the city's inhabitants and filling its streets with the slain.[330] Therefore, the Lord God takes up the officials' metaphors and

redefines their referents. Not they, but their victims are the meat within the "pot" (city). The reader whose extra-textual repertoire includes the oracles of the eighth-century BCE prophet Micah might well recall his use of butcher imagery in an indictment of Israel's leaders:

> And I said:
> Listen, you heads of Jacob
>   and rulers of the house of Israel!
> Should you not know justice?—
>   you who hate the good and love the evil,
> who tear the skin off my people,
>   and the flesh off their bones;
> who eat the flesh of my people,
>   flay their skin off them,
> break their bones in pieces,
>   and chop them up like meat in a kettle,
>   like flesh in a caldron. (Mic 3:1-3 NRSV)

Yahweh will remove the officials from the pot/city, and they will fall by the sword they have feared and hoped to avoid within its walls. They will be handed over to foreigners, instruments of God's own judgment. Verse 10, "I will judge you at the border," may remind the reader of Riblah (recall 6:14), where Nebuchadrezzar passed sentence on King Zedekiah and other of Judah's leaders in the wake of Jerusalem's fall (2 Kgs 25:5-7, 18-21; see also Lam 1:3*b*). Here as elsewhere, the recognition formula ("and you shall know that I am Yahweh") expresses the intended effect of God's judgment upon those whose self-deluding take on reality will soon be shattered. Yahweh, not they, controls events. The city is not their pot, and they are not the meat (v. 11)—a direct refutation of the quote in v. 3. Again, the recognition formula appears, insisting that through disaster, the officials will be forced to acknowledge the absolute power, sovereignty, and control of their God, whose statutes and ordinances they have flouted in favor of the ordinances of surrounding nations.[331] In 5:6-7 also Ezekiel charged Jerusalem with rejecting God's statutes and ordinances while following the ordinances of the nations.

While Ezekiel is prophesying, Pelatiah son of Benaiah dies. We cannot know, of course, whether a man bearing this name actually perished at that

---

329. D. Bodi, *The Book of Ezekiel and the Poem of Erra,* OBO 104 (Freiburg; Universitätsverlag, 1991) 215.

330. חלל (*ḥālāl*), "slain," often designates those who have perished in battle (see, e.g., Lam 2:12). But it also refers to victims of death penalties imposed by corrupt courts.

331. See Moshe Greenberg, *Ezekiel 1–20,* AB 22 (Garden City, N.Y.: Doubleday, 1983) 133.

time. But within the world of Ezekiel's vision, the notice of his death functions to drive home with inescapable force the truth of the prophet's words. Ezekiel himself, it seems, is horrified by this event. He falls on his face and cries out, "Ah Lord God! You are making a full end of the remnant of Israel." Both the NRSV and the NIV translate his

exclamation as a question, in conformity with 9:8. But the Hebrew text contains no interrogative. Rather, the death of Pelatiah, whose name means "Yahweh rescues a remnant," forces Ezekiel to answer his own earlier query in the affirmative. (See Reflections at 11:22-25.)

Ezekiel 11:14-21, A Prophetic Disputation: Land Rights

NIV

[14]The word of the LORD came to me: [15]"Son of man, your brothers—your brothers who are your blood relatives[a] and the whole house of Israel—are those of whom the people of Jerusalem have said, 'They are[b] far away from the LORD; this land was given to us as our possession.'
[16]"Therefore say: 'This is what the Sovereign LORD says: Although I sent them far away among the nations and scattered them among the countries, yet for a little while I have been a sanctuary for them in the countries where they have gone.'
[17]"Therefore say: 'This is what the Sovereign LORD says: I will gather you from the nations and bring you back from the countries where you have been scattered, and I will give you back the land of Israel again.'
[18]"They will return to it and remove all its vile images and detestable idols. [19]I will give them an undivided heart and put a new spirit in them; I will remove from them their heart of stone and give them a heart of flesh. [20]Then they will follow my decrees and be careful to keep my laws. They will be my people, and I will be their God. [21]But as for those whose hearts are devoted to their vile images and detestable idols, I will bring down on their own heads what they have done, declares the Sovereign LORD."

[a]15 Or are in exile with you (see Septuagint and Syriac)   [b]15 Or those to whom the people of Jerusalem have said, 'Stay

NRSV

[14]Then the word of the LORD came to me: [15]Mortal, your kinsfolk, your own kin, your fellow exiles,[a] the whole house of Israel, all of them, are those of whom the inhabitants of Jerusalem have said, "They have gone far from the LORD; to us this land is given for a possession." [16]Therefore say: Thus says the Lord GOD: Though I removed them far away among the nations, and though I scattered them among the countries, yet I have been a sanctuary to them for a little while[b] in the countries where they have gone. [17]Therefore say: Thus says the Lord GOD: I will gather you from the peoples, and assemble you out of the countries where you have been scattered, and I will give you the land of Israel. [18]When they come there, they will remove from it all its detestable things and all its abominations. [19]I will give them one[c] heart, and put a new spirit within them; I will remove the heart of stone from their flesh and give them a heart of flesh, [20]so that they may follow my statutes and keep my ordinances and obey them. Then they shall be my people, and I will be their God. [21]But as for those whose heart goes after their detestable things and their abominations,[d] I will bring their deeds upon their own heads, says the Lord GOD.

[a]Gk Syr: Heb people of your kindred   [b]Or to some extent
[c]Another reading is a new   [d]Cn: Heb And to the heart of their detestable things and their abominations their heart goes

COMMENTARY

Like 11:1-13, vv. 14-21 take the form of a prophetic disputation. Again, God quotes an opinion current among Jerusalem's residents. They have reasoned that the exiles,[332] far removed from their homeland, are also removed from Yahweh, while they are the recipients of the deportees' portion of Israel's inheritance, its land gift from God. This opinion, no less than that expressed in v. 3, reflects the self-congratulatory illusions of the city's inhabitants, whose theological interpretation of reality God will confound, along with Ezekiel's own horrific conclusion that no remnant will be spared. Yahweh, who is not restricted to Israel's land but free to be wherever God wills, acknowledges that the exiles are living among the nations, scattered throughout other countries. But geographical distance does not equal divine alienation. With the image of the departure of Yahweh's glory from the Temple still fresh, the reader "hears" God affirm the Lord's presence with the exiles scattered abroad. Yahweh has become a מקדש מעט (*miqdāš měʿaṭ*) to them. Scholars debate the meaning of this phrase. Zimmerli discerns in it a reference to "the limited forms of a worship practiced far from the sanctuary,"[333] while Greenberg reasons that "since the divine presence is fully manifest only in the Jerusalem sanctuary (cf. 37:26-28), the reduced presence among the exiles is boldly figured as 'a small sanctuary.' "[334] On either interpretation, an ironic contrast is being drawn between the Jerusalemites, who would take their continuing presence in the city as a sign of divine favor and a basis for security, and the exiles, so far removed from the traditional site of divine presence, but its beneficiaries nonetheless.

Verse 17 addresses Ezekiel's exilic audience. God intends to regather them and to give them Israel's land. Back home, they will rid their land of

its detestable trappings, the abominations of its former inhabitants. To this point in the book, neither God nor Ezekiel has voiced the opinion that the deportees are undeserving victims of divine judgment upon a sinful people. That sentiment has no place here, either. The extraordinary transformation of which Yahweh now speaks is the Lord's own initiative, and not a response to genuine repentance: God will give the exiles one heart—that is, singleness of mind (the antithesis is "two hearts," inconstancy; see Ps 12:2)—and a new spirit. The metaphor "heart of stone" artfully conveys the notion of a people stubbornly bent on disobedience; its antithesis, "heart of flesh," bespeaks a people responsive to God's leading. Indeed, obedience to the Lord's statutes and ordinances will be the consequence of Yahweh's "organ transplant" and the basis of the covenant God reinstitutes with this people (note the covenant formula, "they shall be my people, and I will be their God"). Hope-filled words to the exiles give way to a reiteration of judgment against those Jerusalemites who stand accused of not following the divine statutes and ordinances (v. 13), and whose hearts are bound to their detestable things and abominations. Their deeds will redound upon their own heads, yet another echo of a pronounced theme in chaps. 7–9.

Scholars wonder that so optimistic a note should be struck amid the near-ubiquitous pessimism of Ezekiel's previous (and following) oracles. For many, these verses dilute the force of the prophet's continual efforts to convince his exilic audience (and the reader) that Judah's present troubles and future demise are, in fact, God's just and inescapable punishment upon a sinful people. Accordingly they claim vv. 17-21 for Ezekiel, but attribute their present placement to later editors who wished already to affirm that God's message to this people was also and finally a promise of reconciliation. For those living in exile, Ezekiel's words are indeed good news—if the destruction of their beloved city and its inhabitants can be called such. But for the inhabitants of Jerusalem, objects of Yahweh's wrath and the chapter's principal focus, these verses

---

332. The Hebrew, "your brothers, your brothers, your redeeming kinsmen, the whole house of Israel, all of them," may, in the first instance, refer to the prophet's own extended family. More likely, however, the text intends to underscore that the exiles constitute a community that alone can still be called the "house of Israel." Those who would exclude them not only from the nation but also from the sphere of God's concern are themselves excluded.

333. W. Zimmerli, *Ezekiel 1: A Commentary on the Book of the Prophet Ezekiel, Chapters 1–24,* trans. R. E. Clements, Hermeneia (Philadelphia: Fortress, 1979) 262.

334. Greenberg, *Ezekiel 1–20,* 190.

constitute a continuation of God's judgment against them. Articulating the exiles' far brighter prospects puts the lie to their smug and self-righteous claims to be God's sole legitimate heirs (v. 15). (See Reflections at 11:22-25.)

Ezekiel 11:22-25, Yahweh's Glory Abandons Jerusalem

NIV

²²Then the cherubim, with the wheels beside them, spread their wings, and the glory of the God of Israel was above them. ²³The glory of the LORD went up from within the city and stopped above the mountain east of it. ²⁴The Spirit lifted me up and brought me to the exiles in Babylonia*a* in the vision given by the Spirit of God.

Then the vision I had seen went up from me, ²⁵and I told the exiles everything the LORD had shown me.

a24 Or Chaldea

NRSV

²²Then the cherubim lifted up their wings, with the wheels beside them; and the glory of the God of Israel was above them. ²³And the glory of the LORD ascended from the middle of the city, and stopped on the mountain east of the city. ²⁴The spirit lifted me up and brought me in a vision by the spirit of God into Chaldea, to the exiles. Then the vision that I had seen left me. ²⁵And I told the exiles all the things that the LORD had shown me.

COMMENTARY

The cherubim bear aloft God's glory, which rises above the city, crosses the Kidron Valley, and lands on the Mount of Olives. Does God's glory stop there out of reluctance to leave the city? Greenberg quotes the interpretation of Rabbi Johanan: "For three and a half years the Presence . . . tarried on the Mount of Olives, proclaiming thrice daily, 'Return, wayward sons' (Jer 3:22). When it saw they would not repent, it flew away,

saying, 'I will go back to my [heavenly] abode till they realize their guilt; in their distress they will seek me and beg for my favor' (Hos 5:14)."[335] With its departure, the spirit returns the prophet to Babylonia and his fellow exiles. Only then does the vision end. Ezekiel tells them all the things that the Lord has shown him.

335. From *Pesikta de-Rav Kahana* 13.11. See also Greenberg, *Ezekiel 1–20*, 191.

REFLECTIONS

Ezekiel's vision of events transpiring in Jerusalem—horrific in its detail, damning in its insistence that the city and its inhabitants are doomed—serves well the prophet's purposes: claiming the past, present, and future for Yahweh; justifying God's judgment; explaining how it can be that the defeat of a nation signals the sovereignty of its God, whose wrath is righteous, whose presence cannot be contained within walls or by self-serving theologies, and whose freedom confounds every human strategy.

At the outset, we are confronted with God's jealousy (8:3), a self-professed characteristic that, already in the Ten Commandments, rules out resort to any other gods (Exod 20:3-6). Yet, at the heart of God's own city—indeed, at the very door of Yahweh's house—clusters of Jerusalemites pay homage to alien deities. Ezekiel's four examples of Israel's cultic abominations are so blatant, so extreme in their depictions of a people daring to defy God's most basic articulation of Israel's covenant obligations, that modern readers may be tempted to dismiss them as ancient caricatures of no consequence for contemporary life. What have we to do with idols? But the modern world has no shortage of "Asherahs," no limit to temptations to place faith in other gods—material wealth, the exercise of power, self-aggrandizing ideologies—and to seek security inside "pots" of our own making (11:3).

Yahweh's jealous wrath is so great, Ezekiel asserts, that it disables the deity: God's eye is blinded to the possibility of pity, God's ear deafened to the people's screams. Jealousy—irrational, reckless, self-sustaining—accounts for many a contemporary homicide, and Ezekiel's Lord is not immune to its murderous impulse. The executioners must be as ruthless as their divine commander. If the text gives with one hand the comforting affirmation that those who moan and groan over Jerusalem's abominations will be spared, it takes with the other any hope that the city's youngest and most vulnerable inhabitants will survive (9:6). Here, indeed, is a surplus of rage—rhetorical and real overkill. Our sympathies lie not with God, but with Ezekiel, who at long last attempts to intercede on the people's behalf, sinful though they be (9:8). His attempt fails, because unbounded jealousy and mercy cannot co-exist; the former will consume the latter. But we love him for trying.

The truth, of course, is that victorious armies do not distinguish between righteous and sinful victims. Defending God's justice demands, it seems, that Ezekiel envision the sparing of the former. But they, too, will perish. Such is the way of war. Contemporary believers who think that their only obligation is to live "good" lives overlook the inescapable consequences of systemic evil all around them. But individual pietism is no protective pot, and bewailing social violence is no substitute for prophetic critique.

Within the prophet's vision, God's judgment takes two forms: heated engagement and cool disentanglement. To Ezekiel's mind, Israel's sin has so polluted its environment that God must personally destroy it all; the land becomes a killing field; and the city must be burned off. Nebuchadrezzar's soldiers will turn Ezekiel's vision into brutal reality, but the prophet insists that Yahweh is the executioners' and the arsonists' actual commander-in-chief. To whom but God would Ezekiel ascribe the power to destroy the Lord's own people? Intermingled images of Yahweh's glory speak differently, insisting that the divine presence will not abide with an idolatrous, violent people. The same God who issues deadly orders silently abandons the city to its fate.

Even as Ezekiel insists that we view Jerusalem's destruction through God's eyes, he opens our ears to the people's perspectives. Twice God quotes them as saying, "Yahweh does not see us; the LORD has forsaken the land" (8:12; 9:9). Their construal of reality is utterly false, but eventually true. God sees through every human attempt to conceal idolatrous impulses and acts, hears even unspoken thoughts (11:5), but then declares, "I will not look on them with pity or spare them. Although they shout in my ears, I will not listen to them" (8:18; NIV). The beginning of Ezekiel's vision explicitly locates God's glory in Jerusalem (8:4), so readers know that Yahweh has not forsaken the land. But by vision's end, the glory of the Lord will do just that. Jerusalem's officials confidently claim security for themselves ("This city is the pot, and we are the meat," 11:3) and a privileged place in God's heart ("They have gone far from the LORD; to us this land is given for a possession," 11:15 NRSV). But in the future, they will be stripped of every self-serving assertion. Here, then, is a great irony. Ezekiel's vision is God's reality; the people's construct of reality is a delusion. The prophet invites his readers—ancient and modern—utterly to condemn the Jerusalemites for their self-serving interpretations. But we understand them. They are neither the first nor the last to bend their theologies toward their own ends. Witness the early settlers' claims that America was the new "promised land," their God-given gift. Every generation devises ways of justifying its claims of God's preferential treatment to the exclusion of others.

Yahweh's concluding, hopeful words to the exiles must be understood within the context of Ezekiel's visionary experience, which everywhere focuses upon the sins of Jerusalem's inhabitants in order to justify the impending catastrophe. Their future, precisely the opposite of the fate awaiting those residing in the homeland, puts the lie to the latter's hopes and expectations. Yet the prophet nowhere suggests that the exiles will, of their own volition, repent of their obstinacy. (How can their survival be justified, when Jerusalem's most vulnerable inhabitants will perish?) Rather, God must radically transform their character. In Ps 51:10-12, a supplicant longs for just such an alchemy:

Create in me a clean heart, O God,
  and put a new and right spirit within me.
Do not cast me away from your presence,
  and do not take your holy spirit from me.
Restore to me the joy of your salvation,
  and sustain in me a willing spirit. (NRSV)

Ezekiel's unexpected (undeserved?) salvation oracle points to a truth affirmed in both the Old and the New Testament: People cannot will themselves to righteousness. True goodness requires God's transforming power, manifest in a radical reorientation of the heart (mind) and life.

EZEKIEL 12:1–14:11, TRUE AND FALSE PROPHECY: CHALLENGES TO EZEKIEL'S MINISTRY

OVERVIEW

According to 11:25, Ezekiel told his fellow exiles what he had seen and heard during his visionary transportation to Jerusalem: the cultic abominations and social injustices perpetrated by its inhabitants; Yahweh's orders of execution and immolation; the departure of God's glory; and also (the reader assumes) the Lord's promises that the exiles would be gathered from among the nations and repatriated, their (obstinate) hearts of stone replaced with (obedient) hearts of flesh (11:17-20).

These promises must be viewed within the larger context of Ezekiel's vision (chaps. 8–11), which everywhere emphasizes the depravity of those Judeans remaining in their homeland, the better to justify God's decision to destroy them and their capital city, shattering their self-serving theologies and forcing them to a new recognition of Yahweh's power. More specifically, they must be construed in the light of the Jerusalemites' arrogant assertion: "They [the exiles] have gone far from the LORD; to us this land is given for a possession" (11:15). The reader might well suppose

that Ezekiel's original audience was offended by this interpretation of the exile and took comfort in Ezekiel's unexpected restoration oracle. Yet the bulk of his vision was not "good news" for them, because his relentless insistence that Judah was doomed threatened not only to dash their hopes of national survival, but also to diminish prospects of their imminent release and repatriation.

To judge from the oracles in Ezekiel 12–14, the exiles' hopes died hard. These chapters are not dated, and so the reader can only wonder how much time separates them from the onset of the prophet's vision in 592 BCE and from each other. But each of the oracles in this larger unit presupposes that Jerusalem has not yet fallen, and in each, Ezekiel must continue the struggle to convince his audience that the catastrophe is coming— and soon.

In chap. 12, Yahweh commands Ezekiel to perform two sign acts, both vivid portrayals of the terror and misery accompanying the city's final days (vv. 3-16, 17-20). These, in turn, are followed by two disputation speeches, each of which quotes and then refutes popular challenges to the efficacy and immediacy of prophetic doom sayings (12:12-28). Chapter 13 consists of two oracles against Israelite intermediaries—male prophets at home and in exile whose pleasing, self-generated oracles lull their audiences into a false sense of security—and against female exiles who "play the prophet" using techniques that Ezekiel regards as illicit.

Chapter 14 excoriates the exiles' resort to idolatry, returns to the topic of deceiving prophets, and then refutes any notion that even the exemplary righteousness of a few might result in deliverance for the many. For the reader, each of these units fits appropriately beneath a rubric introduced already in 2:37 and reiterated in 12:2: Israel is a "rebellious house."

Ezekiel 12:1-16, A Sign Act: Deportation and Attempts to Escape

NIV

12 The word of the LORD came to me: [2]"Son of man, you are living among a rebellious people. They have eyes to see but do not see and ears to hear but do not hear, for they are a rebellious people.

[3]"Therefore, son of man, pack your belongings for exile and in the daytime, as they watch, set out and go from where you are to another place. Perhaps they will understand, though they are a rebellious house. [4]During the daytime, while they watch, bring out your belongings packed for exile. Then in the evening, while they are watching, go out like those who go into exile. [5]While they watch, dig through the wall and take your belongings out through it. [6]Put them on your shoulder as they are watching and carry them out at dusk. Cover your face so that you cannot see the land, for I have made you a sign to the house of Israel."

[7]So I did as I was commanded. During the day I brought out my things packed for exile. Then in the evening I dug through the wall with my hands. I took my belongings out at dusk, carrying them on my shoulders while they watched.

[8]In the morning the word of the LORD came to me: [9]"Son of man, did not that rebellious house of Israel ask you, 'What are you doing?'

[10]"Say to them, 'This is what the Sovereign LORD says: This oracle concerns the prince in Jerusalem and the whole house of Israel who are there.' [11]Say to them, 'I am a sign to you.'

"As I have done, so it will be done to them. They will go into exile as captives.

[12]"The prince among them will put his things on his shoulder at dusk and leave, and a hole will

NRSV

12 The word of the LORD came to me: [2]Mortal, you are living in the midst of a rebellious house, who have eyes to see but do not see, who have ears to hear but do not hear; [3]for they are a rebellious house. Therefore, mortal, prepare for yourself an exile's baggage, and go into exile by day in their sight; you shall go like an exile from your place to another place in their sight. Perhaps they will understand, though they are a rebellious house. [4]You shall bring out your baggage by day in their sight, as baggage for exile; and you shall go out yourself at evening in their sight, as those do who go into exile. [5]Dig through the wall in their sight, and carry the baggage through it. [6]In their sight you shall lift the baggage on your shoulder, and carry it out in the dark; you shall cover your face, so that you may not see the land; for I have made you a sign for the house of Israel.

[7]I did just as I was commanded. I brought out my baggage by day, as baggage for exile, and in the evening I dug through the wall with my own hands; I brought it out in the dark, carrying it on my shoulder in their sight.

[8]In the morning the word of the LORD came to me: [9]Mortal, has not the house of Israel, the rebellious house, said to you, "What are you doing?" [10]Say to them, "Thus says the Lord GOD: This oracle concerns the prince in Jerusalem and all the house of Israel in it." [11]Say, "I am a sign for you: as I have done, so shall it be done to them; they shall go into exile, into captivity." [12]And the prince who is among them shall lift his baggage on his shoulder in the dark, and shall go out;

NIV

be dug in the wall for him to go through. He will cover his face so that he cannot see the land. [13]I will spread my net for him, and he will be caught in my snare; I will bring him to Babylonia, the land of the Chaldeans, but he will not see it, and there he will die. [14]I will scatter to the winds all those around him—his staff and all his troops—and I will pursue them with drawn sword.

[15]"They will know that I am the LORD, when I disperse them among the nations and scatter them through the countries. [16]But I will spare a few of them from the sword, famine and plague, so that in the nations where they go they may acknowledge all their detestable practices. Then they will know that I am the LORD."

NRSV

he[a] shall dig through the wall and carry it through; he shall cover his face, so that he may not see the land with his eyes. [13]I will spread my net over him, and he shall be caught in my snare; and I will bring him to Babylon, the land of the Chaldeans, yet he shall not see it; and he shall die there. [14]I will scatter to every wind all who are around him, his helpers and all his troops; and I will unsheathe the sword behind them. [15]And they shall know that I am the LORD, when I disperse them among the nations and scatter them through the countries. [16]But I will let a few of them escape from the sword, from famine and pestilence, so that they may tell of all their abominations among the nations where they go; then they shall know that I am the LORD.

[a]Gk Syr: Heb *they*

COMMENTARY

Yahweh's next address to the prophet begins with a negative assessment of the exiles in whose midst he dwells. The reader has known, virtually since the book began, of God's opinion that Israel is a rebellious house (see 2:3-7). Here, Ezekiel takes up a motif of his prophetic predecessors to describe their obstinacy: Having eyes to see, they do not see; having ears to hear, they do not hear (see, e.g., Isa 6:9-10; 43:8; Jer 5:21). "For more than a year in act and word," Greenberg observes, "Ezekiel had exhibited his message to their eyes and ears, but they had disregarded him and held fast to their hope in Jerusalem's survival and their speedy return to it."[336] Perhaps, God suggests, the performance of a new sign act in their sight (this phrase will appear seven times in vv. 3-7) will break through their rebelliousness.

In the Commentary on 4:1–5:4, it is noted that prophetic sign acts are not miracles. Rather, they entail activity within the capacity of any person. Past scholarship regarded Ezekiel's sign acts either as parables or as manifestations of psychological and/or physical ailments (see, e.g., 4:4-8). Contemporary critics, by contrast, tend to think that they actually took place. One may note Zimmerli's

remark that a "sign-action which was not actually performed but only narrated must be regarded as a late and weakened form,"[337] and Greenberg's reasoning that "the explicit anticipation of public reaction to such actions (e.g., Ezek 12:9) excludes taking them as visionary."[338]

Characteristically, the sign-act account of vv. 3-16 begins with God's command (vv. 1-6), reports Ezekiel's execution of the assignment (v. 7), and then explains its significance (vv. 8-16). The prophet must reenact a painful episode from his own past, preparing an exile's baggage—a cloth or skin containing the meager necessities of life—and then, in broad daylight and before the deportees' eyes, exiting his own house for a different (unspecified) locale (v. 3; ancient Assyrian bas-relief sculptures portray the inhabitants of Lachish carrying their bundles into exile). Verse 4 expands upon God's command. Although Ezekiel must bring out

336. Moshe Greenberg, *Ezekiel 1–20*, AB 22 (Garden City, N.Y.: Doubleday, 1983) 208.

337. W. Zimmerli, *Ezekiel 1: A Commentary on the Book of the Prophet Ezekiel, Chapters 1–24*, trans. R. E. Clements, Hermeneia (Philadelphia: Fortress, 1979) 156.

338. Greenberg, *Ezekiel 1–20*, 122. In contrast, Davis regards Ezekiel's sign act accounts as literary compositions that function to enhance the reader's engagement with the text. See Ellen F. Davis, *Swallowing the Scroll: Textuality and the Dynamics of Discourse in Ezekiel's Prophecy*, Bible and Literature 21 (Sheffield: Almond, 1989) 71. On the relationship between sign acts and magic, see Excursus: "Prophetic Sign Acts," 1143-44.

his baggage in daylight, he is not to leave until the evening. Burrowing through a mud-brick wall (as if in hopes of avoiding detection?), he must shoulder his burden and depart in darkness. Moreover, he must cover his face (as if in hopes of concealing his identity?). Elsewhere in Hebrew Scripture, a covered face can signify grief (2 Sam 15:30; Esth 6:12) or shame (Mic 3:7; Esth 7:8; Jer 14:3). In this context, however, its stated purpose is to prevent Ezekiel from seeing the ground. Does his covered head portend that those forced into exile will never see their homeland again (see Jer 22:10-12)?[339]

The prophet apparently performs in silence, leaving his fellow exiles to ponder the import of his actions. Certainly, they admit more than one interpretation. "Ezekiel had made preparations for a long journey," Eichrodt observes, "and before setting off had begun to demolish his temporary dwelling—in such circumstances, why could that not be the signal for them to knock down their improvised adobe huts and start upon the longed-for journey home?"[340] Had not Ezekiel himself declared Yahweh's promise that the exilic community would return to Judah (11:17-20)? Perhaps the time has come for that prophecy to be fulfilled!

Not until morning does God authorize Ezekiel to explain his actions (in Yahweh's own words). His immediate response to the exiles' question in v. 10 dashes any hope that his performance presages their return home. The precise meaning of v. 10*b* is elusive. Both the NRSV and the NIV translate, "This oracle [הזה המשא *hammaśśāʾ hazzeh*] concerns the prince in Jerusalem and all the [NIV, "the whole"] house of Israel." The noun משא (*maśśāʾ*) means "oracle" in many contexts (e.g., Isa 13:1; 15:1; 17:1), though Ezekiel nowhere (else?) uses it in that way. Equally plausible, however, is the suggestion of Greenberg and Block that in this context, *maśśāʾ* means "burden." So translated, "this burden" refers to Ezekiel's baggage, and it, in turn, represents Judah's "prince" (נשיא *nāśîʾ*) and his subjects, who will be carried into exile.[341] Ezekiel is, indeed, a "sign" for the exiles (see v. 6) in the sense that what he has done

(taken his baggage into exile) will be done to their king and comrades back home.

With v. 12, the exile's baggage no longer represents the prince. Rather, the text predicts that he will shoulder his own bundle in the dark and head out. The verse is essentially a repetition of Ezekiel's own actions (described in vv. 4-6), except that the MT reads "they shall dig through the wall," rather than "he shall dig." Does the plural pronoun refer to aides who assist the ruler in making his escape? Verse 13, also cast in first-person divine speech, emphasizes Yahweh's role in hunting him down: God will cast a net (רשת *rešet*) over him; he will be caught in God's snare (מצודה *mĕṣûdâ*). Moreover, the Lord will scatter his troops to the wind, with the sword pursuing them. The intended effect of their deportation is that they might know Yahweh, whose unrivalled, sovereign power controls history. Yet, God says in v. 16, a few will escape the deadly triad of sword, famine, and pestilence in order that among the nations, they may tell of all their abominations (recalling chap. 8) and come to know who Yahweh is. Verse 16 may also mean that in recounting their sins among the nations, these latest exiles will justify God's judgment upon them, in order that other peoples might recognize in Judah's demise the appropriateness of God's punishment and themselves learn something of Yahweh's character.

The "prince in Jerusalem" (v. 10) is Judah's last king, Zedekiah, though Ezekiel does not deign to speak his name or to give him that title. His fate is recorded in 2 Kgs 25:4-7:

> Then a breach was made in the city wall; the king with all the soldiers fled by night by the way of the gate between the two walls, by the king's garden, though the Chaldeans were all around the city. They went in the direction of the Arabah. But the army of the Chaldeans pursued the king, and overtook him in the plains of Jericho; all his army was scattered, deserting him. Then they captured the king and brought him up to the king of Babylon at Riblah, who passed sentence on him. They slaughtered the sons of Zedekiah before his eyes, then put out the eyes of Zedekiah; they bound him in fetters and took him to Babylon. (NRSV)

Critics contend that details about Zedekiah's flight, capture, and punishment have left their mark on

---

339. See Greenberg, *Ezekiel 1–20*, 211.

340. W. Eichrodt, *Ezekiel,* trans. Cosslett Quin, OTL (Philadelphia: Westminster, 1970) 151.

341. See Greenberg, *Ezekiel 1–20*, 212; D. I. Block, *The Book of Ezekiel: Chapters 1–24,* NICOT (Grand Rapids: Eerdmans, 1997) 372-74.

the interpretation of Ezekiel's sign act in vv. 10-15. The prophet's reference to "the prince in Jerusalem" (v. 10) evokes thoughts of that hapless monarch. The statement that the prince will be brought to Babylon, yet not see it (v. 13), may refer to Zedekiah's blindness, already inflicted at Riblah (a site mentioned in 6:14 and possibly alluded to in 11:10). Moreover, Ezekiel's prediction that the prince's troops will be scattered reminds readers of 2 Kgs 25:5 ("all his army was scattered, deserting him"). True, the two texts differ: While Ezekiel exits through an opening he has dug in a wall, Zedekiah and his army escape Jerusalem through a city gate; v. 12 speaks of the prince covering his face in order not to see the ground with his eyes (see also v. 6), rather than of his being unable to see.

It seems unlikely that the sequential reader of vv. 1-8 will immediately think of Zedekiah. With the reference to "the prince in Jerusalem" in v. 10, however, Zedekiah will surely come to mind. Subsequent textual details (as noted above) will confirm the reader's suspicion that the fate of Zedekiah (and his people) is the subject of Ezekiel's sign act. Indeed, in the light of vv. 10-15, the reader may return to and reinterpret vv. 4-8 (with their repeated references to "in the evening" and "dark"), taking earlier references to Ezekiel's covered face and to his not seeing the ground as oblique allusions to Zedekiah's blindness.[342] Rather, Ezekiel's ability to presage the monarch's fate further enhances the reader's assessment that he is truly God's authentic prophet. (See Reflections at 14:1-11.)

---

342. But the reader need not resort to Zimmerli's textual surgery. Zimmerli, *Ezekiel 1*, 265-75; see his reconstruction of the "original" text, ibid., 268.

Ezekiel 12:17-20, Quaking and Trembling

NIV

[17]The word of the LORD came to me: [18]"Son of man, tremble as you eat your food, and shudder in fear as you drink your water. [19]Say to the people of the land: 'This is what the Sovereign LORD says about those living in Jerusalem and in the land of Israel: They will eat their food in anxiety and drink their water in despair, for their land will be stripped of everything in it because of the violence of all who live there. [20]The inhabited towns will be laid waste and the land will be desolate. Then you will know that I am the LORD.' "

NRSV

[17]The word of the LORD came to me: [18]Mortal, eat your bread with quaking, and drink your water with trembling and with fearfulness; [19]and say to the people of the land, Thus says the Lord GOD concerning the inhabitants of Jerusalem in the land of Israel: They shall eat their bread with fearfulness, and drink their water in dismay, because their land shall be stripped of all it contains, on account of the violence of all those who live in it. [20]The inhabited cities shall be laid waste, and the land shall become a desolation; and you shall know that I am the LORD.

COMMENTARY

These verses share a number of formal features with vv. 1-16. Both passages begin with the announcement of Yahweh's word coming to Ezekiel (addressed as "mortal"), and in each, God commands the prophet to perform a sign act. Interpretations of these acts, cast as first-person divine speech and introduced with the messenger formula ("Thus says the Lord GOD," vv. 10, 19), follow. Moreover, both passages conclude with the recognition formula, giving to each the character of a prophetic proof saying.

Critics have suggested that these formal resemblances (as opposed to similarities of content) account for the juxtaposition of these two sign acts in chap. 12. Yet both address Ezekiel's fellow exiles concerning judgment upon those

Judeans remaining in the homeland. Because neither sign act is dated, the reader cannot determine with certainty their chronological relationship. Nevertheless, formal features and similarities in content invite readers closely to relate these two units, even as they allow each its own distinctive features and emphases.

In two parallel lines, Yahweh commands Ezekiel to eat his bread with quaking (רעש *ra'aš*) and to drink his water with trembling (רגזה *rogzâ*) and fearfulness (דאגה *dĕ'āgâ*). The reader recalls an earlier sign act involving the prophet's consumption of bread and water. But while 4:9-11 highlighted the scarcity of those mainstays within the besieged city of Jerusalem, this passage focuses upon Ezekiel's deportment as he eats and drinks. Elsewhere, *ra'aš* is associated with the quaking of the earth (see, e.g., 37:7); only here does it denote human shaking. The noun *rogzâ* appears nowhere else in Hebrew Scripture, but various forms of the root, applied to the body, can describe grief (2 Sam 19:10), rage (Hab 3:2), joyous celebration (Jer 33:9), or adrenaline-fueled agitation (of a combat horse, Job 39:24). The third noun, then, specifies the emotion associated with Ezekiel's behavior: He quakes and trembles uncontrollably from fear, and the resulting impairment of dexterity imperils even the routine activities of eating and drinking. Zimmerli, like some other critics, attributes Ezekiel's tremors to a physical and/or psychological illness.[343] But, according to v. 18, the prophet quavers at God's command.

Ezekiel's explanation of his sign act is addressed to "the people of the land." Würthwein has demonstrated that during the pre-exilic period, this phrase referred to Judah's landowning, full citizens.[344] Both Isa 5:8-10 and Mic 2:1-5 take this class to task for amassing their property at the expense of poorer landowners. (Once-)wealthy owners of estates were surely represented among the upper-crust exiles of 597 BCE. In this context, Ezekiel's use of the epithet strikes an ironic chord, since the landowners own land no longer (recall the arrogant boasts of the inhabitants of Jerusalem: "They [the exiles] have gone far from the LORD; to us this land is given for a possession," 11:15).

Although he addresses his fellow deportees, Ezekiel's physical performance anticipates the behavior of "the inhabitants of Jerusalem in the land of Israel." They, like he, shall eat with fearfulness and drink with dismay (שממון *šimmāmôn*) at the prospect of their land's being stripped (תשם *tēšam*) from them as a consequence of their violence. The root שמם (*šmm*) appears many times within the book of Ezekiel. As a verb, it can mean "to be desolated" in both senses of that English word: to be devoid of inhabitants (depopulated) and to be devastated (i.e., reduced to ruins, rendered a wasteland). In v. 19, the first of these two meanings is emphasized by the conjunction of this term with מלאה (*mĕlō'āh*, "its fullness, contents"). In the following verse, by contrast, the parallel lines "The inhabited cities shall be laid waste [תחרבנה *teḥĕrabnâ*]; and the land shall become a desolation [שממה *šĕmāmâ*]" point to the second meaning.[345] The intended effect of all this devastation is that "you [the exiles] shall know that I am Yahweh."

Hence, this sign act, like the immediately preceding one, is designed to make the exiles accept the idea that Yahweh has determined to make Judah desolate. The fact that Ezekiel has returned to this theme time and again bespeaks the deportees' adamant refusal to accept the inevitability and extent of God's judgment. From the late exilic reader's perspective, this sign act and its interpretation are yet another way by which Yahweh attempts to shatter the obstinancy of a community that has eyes but does not see, has ears but does not hear. (See Reflections at 14:1-11.)

---

343. Ibid., 277. See also Eichrodt, *Ezekiel,* 153: "Ezekiel's trembling and quaking . . . [are] at least in part a result of the severe strain on his physical energy imposed by the trances and visions granted to him."

344. See E. Würthwein, *Der 'amm ha'arez im Alten Testament,* BWANT 4 (Stuttgart: Kohlhammer, 1936) 43. Only in the aftermath of the exile did the epithet become a demeaning designation for the poorer people of the land.

345. See K. P. Darr, "Desolation and Waste," in "Breaking Through the Wilderness: References to the Desert in Exilic Prophecy" (Ph.D. diss., Vanderbilt University, 1984) 267-76.

Ezekiel 12:21-28, Two Disputation Oracles

NIV

²¹The word of the LORD came to me: ²²"Son of man, what is this proverb you have in the land of Israel: 'The days go by and every vision comes to nothing'? ²³Say to them, 'This is what the Sovereign LORD says: I am going to put an end to this proverb, and they will no longer quote it in Israel.' Say to them, 'The days are near when every vision will be fulfilled. ²⁴For there will be no more false visions or flattering divinations among the people of Israel. ²⁵But I the LORD will speak what I will, and it shall be fulfilled without delay. For in your days, you rebellious house, I will fulfill whatever I say, declares the Sovereign LORD.' "

²⁶The word of the LORD came to me: ²⁷"Son of man, the house of Israel is saying, 'The vision he sees is for many years from now, and he prophesies about the distant future.'

²⁸"Therefore say to them, 'This is what the Sovereign LORD says: None of my words will be delayed any longer; whatever I say will be fulfilled, declares the Sovereign LORD.' "

NRSV

²¹The word of the LORD came to me: ²²Mortal, what is this proverb of yours about the land of Israel, which says, "The days are prolonged, and every vision comes to nothing"? ²³Tell them therefore, "Thus says the Lord GOD: I will put an end to this proverb, and they shall use it no more as a proverb in Israel." But say to them, The days are near, and the fulfillment of every vision. ²⁴For there shall no longer be any false vision or flattering divination within the house of Israel. ²⁵But I the LORD will speak the word that I speak, and it will be fulfilled. It will no longer be delayed; but in your days, O rebellious house, I will speak the word and fulfill it, says the Lord GOD.

²⁶The word of the LORD came to me: ²⁷Mortal, the house of Israel is saying, "The vision that he sees is for many years ahead; he prophesies for distant times." ²⁸Therefore say to them, Thus says the Lord GOD: None of my words will be delayed any longer, but the word that I speak will be fulfilled, says the Lord GOD.

COMMENTARY

Like the preceding pair of sign act accounts, the two disputation speeches in these verses begin with a formulaic announcement of the advent of Yahweh's word to Ezekiel (addressed characteristically as "Mortal"). In the first, God asks Ezekiel a question, more rhetorical than real, concerning a proverb (משל *māšāl*) making the rounds back in Judah. Within the biblical literature, *māšāl* applies to a variety of literary genres: parables, proverbs, allegories, poetic odes, didactic utterances, etc. The *māšāl* quoted by Yahweh in v. 22 ("Time passes, and every vision fails")[346] fits well Fontaine's definition of the "traditional saying" as:

A statement, current among the folk, which is concise, syntactically complete, consisting of at least one topic and comment which may or may not be metaphorical, but which exhibits a logical

relationship between its terms. The referents which form the image are most likely to be drawn from the experience of common, "everyday" life, but the meaning (message) of the saying may vary from context to context, and any "truth claim' for that message must be considered "relative" rather than "absolute." The transmission of the saying, however achieved, is *always* purposeful, but specific details of contextual use may be necessary to determine the purpose in any given situation.[347]

The reader has it on God's authority that this proverb is circulating among "the folk" in Israel's land. A "concise, syntactically complete" statement, it consists of two topics and two comments:

Topic A: time	Comment A: passes
Topic B: every vision	Comment B: fails

346. See D. I. Block, *The Book of Ezekiel: Chapters 1–24,* NICOT (Grand Rapids: Eerdmans, 1997) 386.

347. C. R. Fontaine, *Traditional Sayings in the Old Testament: A Contextual Study,* Bible and Literature Series 5 (Sheffield: Almond, 1982) 64.

Each topic and corresponding comment—literal, not metaphorical—exhibits "a logical relationship between its terms," and each describes an experience common to the life experience of the ancient Israelites. The saying is purposeful, but its message must be construed within the context in which it was spoken. Were the proverb "performed" within a community lamenting the ongoing nonfulfillment of prophetic *salvation* oracles, its function might be to articulate grief, frustration, and doubt, perhaps in hopes that God might be moved to act. But if, as appears to be the case here, the proverb speaks to the ongoing failure of doom oracles to be realized, then it functions not only to express popular doubts about the efficacy of prophetic predictions, but also to justify a cynical attitude toward them.

Yahweh's immediate response to the quoted saying is a command: Ezekiel must announce in the Lord's own words (note the messenger formula) God's intention to render the people's proverb obsolete (since the imminent fulfillment of prophetic doom oracles will put the lie to its "truth claim"). Now the prophet must proclaim a proverb of Yahweh's coining, which is the antithesis of the folk's own: "The time is at hand, and the event [realization] of every vision!"[348] Concomitant with the abandonment of the people's proverb will be the cessation of every false vision and empty [deluding] divination, with the result that only Yahweh's authentic word will remain. And it will be fulfilled—not at some ill-defined time in the distant future, but within the lifetime of the present generation. Yahweh's epithet for Israel, "O rebellious house," invites the reader to interpret this unit also in the light of earlier assertions of its obstinacy (vv. 1, 3).

Over the course of its history, ancient Israel identified a number of criteria intended to assist the people in differentiating between authentic and inauthentic prophecies. To judge from its canonical literature, the fulfillment or nonfulfillment of a predictive oracle was one criterion for distinguishing between the two.[349] In Deut 18:22, for example, we read: "If a prophet speaks in the name of the Lord but the thing does not take place

or prove true, it is a word that the Lord has not spoken. The prophet has spoken it presumptuously; do not be frightened by it" (NRSV). Micaiah ben Imlah advances the same guideline in his attempts to persuade King Ahab that, contrary to the prediction of four hundred court prophets, he will die in battle at Ramoth-gilead (1 Kgs 22:28). Ezekiel himself invokes it on several occasions, for instance, "When this comes—and come it will!—then they shall know that a prophet has been among them" (33:33).

Crenshaw identifies the limitations of this criterion. Two are of particular import here. It could meaningfully pertain only to predictive prophecies, and it could only be applied in retrospect. In vv. 21-25, predictive prophecies are clearly at issue, but because they have yet to be realized, their authenticity remains in doubt, fueling skepticism and defiance. Have the people concluded, in Greenberg's words, that "as the moment when the prophecy was uttered recedes further and further into the past without the prophecy's taking effect, its power peters out and it sinks into oblivion—a dead letter no one need worry about"?[350] If so, they are wrong. Yahweh's words will be fulfilled, and in the cynics' own lifetimes.[351]

In the second disputation speech, Yahweh again quotes a proverb of Israel (a משל *māšāl*, though the noun does not reappear here): "The vision which he visions is for many days [hence], and regarding distant times he prophesies." This literal utterance is cast as two lines exhibiting synonymous parallelism and a chiastic arrangement, a pattern in which the parallels occur in reverse order, ABB´A´. It also conforms to Fontaine's definition of a traditional saying. Like its predecessor, it consists of two topics with comments:

Topic A: his vision	Comment A: is for many days [hence]
Topic B: he prophesies	Comment B: regarding distant times

Unlike the previous proverb, this one appears to have circulated among the Babylonian exiles, perhaps in response to Ezekiel's own oracles of doom concerning Jerusalem and its inhabitants. This

---

348. See Moshe Greenberg, *Ezekiel 1–20*, AB 22 (Garden City, N.Y.: Doubleday, 1983) 226.
349. James L. Crenshaw, *Prophetic Conflict: Its Effect Upon Israelite Religion*, BZAW 124 (Berlin: Walter de Gruyter, 1971) 49-52.

350. Greenberg, *Ezekiel 1–20*, 227.
351. Ibid.

proverb does not challenge the credibility of his "vision," but insists that its fulfillment lies far in the future. Perhaps the exiles cling to hope that a successful rebellion against Babylonia by its vassal states will force a delay of Jerusalem's destruction (see Jeremiah 27). Perhaps they hold out hope that Ezekiel's prophecies are conditional after all. Such a perception had its precedents:

> Oracles of doom might be deferred—not canceled—for a generation or more because of the contrition of the condemned (I Kings 21:29 [Ahab]; II Kings 22:19f. [Josiah]) or God's long-suffering.... Hezekiah's punishment was expressly postponed, to his relief, until the time of his descendants (Isa 39:6f.). It was therefore possible to defuse Ezekiel's dooms without impugning their validity (as did the proverb of the first oracle) simply by "putting them far off."[352]

352. Ibid., 231.

Indeed, Ezekiel will himself speak of Yahweh's decision to postpone punishment, especially in order to protect the divine reputation from ridicule among the nations (20:9, 14, 22).

Ezekiel was by no means the first of Israel's prophets whose oracles met with popular skepticism. Isaiah condemns those mockers who say, "Let him make haste, let him speed his work that we may see it; let the plan of the Holy One of Israel hasten to fulfillment, that we may know it!" (Isa 5:19 NRSV). Jeremiah prays for vindication against his detractors who say, "Where is the word of the LORD? Let it come!" (Jer 17:15 NRSV). Here, Yahweh insists that the divine word will be fulfilled without delay. (See Reflections at 14:1-11.)

Ezekiel 13:1-23, Oracles Condemning False Prophets

OVERVIEW

In 12:21-28, Ezekiel defended the content and the relevance of his doom prophecies in the face of popular opposition to both. Now, he denounces his professional rivals: male prophets of Israel whose self-generated oracles collude with their audiences' self-deluding desire for security (13:1-16) and female deportees who "play the prophet" and whose illegitimate methods of divination not only endanger the lives of their clients, but also undercut Ezekiel's legitimate role as "watchman" to the exiles (13:17-23). Like its predecessor, this chapter is not dated. Yet both formal features (e.g., the recurring, formulaic announcement of Ezekiel's reception of Yahweh's word; repeated resort to the recognition formula) and content (challenges to Ezekiel's ministry and message; shared vocabulary) invite the reader to interpret the material in this chapter in the light of Ezekiel's ongoing struggle to convince his audience that he is the authentic spokesman of Yahweh, whose word Israel discounts or avoids to its peril.

Working through 13:1-23, the reader will discover two similarly structured oracles, each beginning with "woe" (הוֹי hôy)—the harbinger of prophecies of doom. Both oracles consist of a "pre-amble" (vv. 2-3a, 17-18a), followed by charges against the prophets (vv. 3b-7, male; vv. 18b-19, female), and two waves of judgment pronouncements (vv. 8-9 and 10-16, on the one hand, vv. 20-21 and 22-23, on the other hand), each concluding with the recognition formula (vv. 9, 14, 21, 23).[353]

Earlier prophets also contended with rival intermediaries and their messages (see, e.g., Isa 28:7 and Mic 3:5-7). Particularly in times of crisis, the people exhibited an all-too-human tendency to seek out purveyors of reassuring words (see Isa 30:9-10). Jeremiah, Ezekiel's contemporary in Jerusalem, has constantly to contend with weal-speaking opponents. "Ah, Lord GOD!" he protests, "Here are the prophets saying to them, 'You shall not see the sword, nor shall you have famine, but I will give you true peace in this place'" (Jer 14:13 NRSV; see also Jer 6:14[8:11] and Jeremiah's less than successful confrontation with Hananiah in Jeremiah 28). In Jer 23:16, Yahweh warns Jeremiah's audience not to be deceived, for "they speak visions of their own mind" (NRSV). "What

353. See Block's chart in *Ezekiel 1–24*, 394.

has straw in common with wheat?" the Lord asks. "Is not my word like fire . . . and like a hammer that breaks a rock in pieces?" (Jer 23:28*b*-29 NRSV). In his letter to the exiles (Jeremiah 29), Jeremiah both confirms the presence of professional prophets and diviners in their midst and counsels the people not to be beguiled by their deceptive messages and methods. But Ezekiel's audience, no less than Jeremiah's own, prefers reassuring words to doom pronouncements. (See Reflections at 14:1-11.)

Ezekiel 13:1-16, Oracles Against Male Prophets

NIV

13 The word of the LORD came to me: [2]"Son of man, prophesy against the prophets of Israel who are now prophesying. Say to those who prophesy out of their own imagination: 'Hear the word of the LORD! [3]This is what the Sovereign LORD says: Woe to the foolish[a] prophets who follow their own spirit and have seen nothing! [4]Your prophets, O Israel, are like jackals among ruins. [5]You have not gone up to the breaks in the wall to repair it for the house of Israel so that it will stand firm in the battle on the day of the LORD. [6]Their visions are false and their divinations a lie. They say, "The LORD declares," when the LORD has not sent them; yet they expect their words to be fulfilled. [7]Have you not seen false visions and uttered lying divinations when you say, "The LORD declares," though I have not spoken?

[8]" 'Therefore this is what the Sovereign LORD says: Because of your false words and lying visions, I am against you, declares the Sovereign LORD. [9]My hand will be against the prophets who see false visions and utter lying divinations. They will not belong to the council of my people or be listed in the records of the house of Israel, nor will they enter the land of Israel. Then you will know that I am the Sovereign LORD.

[10]" 'Because they lead my people astray, saying, "Peace," when there is no peace, and because, when a flimsy wall is built, they cover it with whitewash, [11]therefore tell those who cover it with whitewash that it is going to fall. Rain will come in torrents, and I will send hailstones hurtling down, and violent winds will burst forth. [12]When the wall collapses, will people not ask you, "Where is the whitewash you covered it with?"

[a]3 Or *wicked*

NRSV

13 The word of the LORD came to me: [2]Mortal, prophesy against the prophets of Israel who are prophesying; say to those who prophesy out of their own imagination: "Hear the word of the LORD!" [3]Thus says the Lord GOD, Alas for the senseless prophets who follow their own spirit, and have seen nothing! [4]Your prophets have been like jackals among ruins, O Israel. [5]You have not gone up into the breaches, or repaired a wall for the house of Israel, so that it might stand in battle on the day of the LORD. [6]They have envisioned falsehood and lying divination; they say, "Says the LORD," when the LORD has not sent them, and yet they wait for the fulfillment of their word! [7]Have you not seen a false vision or uttered a lying divination, when you have said, "Says the LORD," even though I did not speak?

[8]Therefore thus says the Lord GOD: Because you have uttered falsehood and envisioned lies, I am against you, says the Lord GOD. [9]My hand will be against the prophets who see false visions and utter lying divinations; they shall not be in the council of my people, nor be enrolled in the register of the house of Israel, nor shall they enter the land of Israel; and you shall know that I am the Lord GOD. [10]Because, in truth, because they have misled my people, saying, "Peace," when there is no peace; and because, when the people build a wall, these prophets[a] smear whitewash on it. [11]Say to those who smear whitewash on it that it shall fall. There will be a deluge of rain,[b] great hailstones will fall, and a stormy wind will break out. [12]When the wall falls, will it not be said to you, "Where is the whitewash you smeared on it?" [13]Therefore thus says the Lord GOD: In my wrath I will make a stormy wind break out, and

[a]Heb *they*   [b]Heb *rain and you*

¹³" 'Therefore this is what the Sovereign LORD says: In my wrath I will unleash a violent wind, and in my anger hailstones and torrents of rain will fall with destructive fury. ¹⁴I will tear down the wall you have covered with whitewash and will level it to the ground so that its foundation will be laid bare. When it*ᵃ* falls, you will be destroyed in it; and you will know that I am the LORD. ¹⁵So I will spend my wrath against the wall and against those who covered it with whitewash. I will say to you, "The wall is gone and so are those who whitewashed it, ¹⁶those prophets of Israel who prophesied to Jerusalem and saw visions of peace for her when there was no peace, declares the Sovereign LORD." '

ᵃ*14* Or *the city*

in my anger there shall be a deluge of rain, and hailstones in wrath to destroy it. ¹⁴I will break down the wall that you have smeared with white-wash, and bring it to the ground, so that its foundation will be laid bare; when it falls, you shall perish within it; and you shall know that I am the LORD. ¹⁵Thus I will spend my wrath upon the wall, and upon those who have smeared it with whitewash; and I will say to you, The wall is no more, nor those who smeared it— ¹⁶the prophets of Israel who prophesied concerning Jerusalem and saw visions of peace for it, when there was no peace, says the Lord GOD.

COMMENTARY

Yahweh's command that Ezekiel prophesy against "the prophets of Israel who are prophesying" already articulates the most stinging indictment against them: They, like Jeremiah's rivals, "prophesy out of their own minds" (v. 2). Prophets whose oracles are their own creations have no legitimate claim to that title, and Ezekiel must herald God's charges against them. Similes and metaphors serve his purpose well. First, he asserts that Israel's prophets are like jackals among ruins. Given the range of negative associations with these scavengers, the reader cannot miss the teeth in Ezekiel's accusation: Denizens of desolate wastes (e.g., Isa 34:13), they seek out sites where even Arabs and shepherds fear to tread (Isa 13:19-22). Their howls serve as apt similes for people's most profound utterances of pain and grief (Mic 1:8). Humans who must share the domains of jackals are among the most rejected of creatures (Job 30:29), but jackals eagerly appropriate the ruins of once-inhabited cities. Indeed, by burrowing, they contribute to their progressive decay.

The image of Israel's jackal prophets aprowl, scavenging among the people and contributing to their ruin, is followed (appropriately enough) by an image of Israel as a field whose fence—built to dissuade both human and animal marauders—has fallen to pieces. Israel's prophets neither "go up"

into the gaps to provide immediate defense nor repair the fence in order that it "might stand in battle on the day of the LORD" (v. 5). Here, the field fence has become a breached city wall. According to Ps 106:23, Moses, Israel's prophet par excellence, "stood in the breach" when God threatened to destroy the Israelites for worshiping the golden calf. Not so Ezekiel's prophetic rivals. Faced with Israel's disintegration, they resort to falsehood and lying divination, proclaiming their oracles in Yahweh's name and then expecting the Lord to fulfill them!

Verse 8, with its initial "therefore," moves beyond accusation to the first of two judgment announcements. Because of these prophets' false visions and lying words, Yahweh's hand will be against them (v. 9; see Ezekiel's gesture in 4:7). "Whereas elsewhere Ezekiel uses the expression . . . 'the hand of Yahweh came' of prophetic empowerment," Block observes, now God "announces that the false prophets will finally experience [what] they have been claiming all along. However, the effects of [God's] hand on them will be quite different from anything a prophet might ordinarily expect and from what these false prophets claim."³⁵⁴ Three parallel lines

354. Ibid., 404.

proclaim God's judgment upon them: They will not be part of the community; their names will not be registered in the roll of Israel's citizens (see Ezra 2:62; Neh 7:64; Jer 22:30); and they will not return to the homeland. They will, however, be forced through these punishments to recognize the unparalleled power and sovereignty of Yahweh.

A second judgment announcement, consisting of three parts, follows in vv. 10-16. First, Ezekiel restates Yahweh's charges against the false prophets (v. 10). Here, a different (though related) metaphor appears. When the people build a weak wall assembled without benefit of mortar, their weal-speaking prophets daub it with whitewash, a thin veneer that lends to it the appearance of a more substantial structure. But when a mighty storm—driving rains, large hailstones, violent wind—strikes, the wall falls. So Yahweh's wrath, like a great storm, will level the whitewashed wall, exposing its faulty construction. Here, the wall (masc.) has become the city of Jerusalem (fem.); her foundations, like those of Samaria (Mic 1:6), will be laid bare (v. 14). Israel's false prophets will perish in the rubble. So much for proclaimers of "peace" when there is no peace. (See Reflections at 14:1-11.)

Ezekiel 13:17-23, Oracles Against Female Prophets

NIV

[17]"Now, son of man, set your face against the daughters of your people who prophesy out of their own imagination. Prophesy against them [18]and say, 'This is what the Sovereign LORD says: Woe to the women who sew magic charms on all their wrists and make veils of various lengths for their heads in order to ensnare people. Will you ensnare the lives of my people but preserve your own? [19]You have profaned me among my people for a few handfuls of barley and scraps of bread. By lying to my people, who listen to lies, you have killed those who should not have died and have spared those who should not live.

[20]" 'Therefore this is what the Sovereign LORD says: I am against your magic charms with which you ensnare people like birds and I will tear them from your arms; I will set free the people that you ensnare like birds. [21]I will tear off your veils and save my people from your hands, and they will no longer fall prey to your power. Then you will know that I am the LORD. [22]Because you disheartened the righteous with your lies, when I had brought them no grief, and because you encouraged the wicked not to turn from their evil ways and so save their lives, [23]therefore you will no longer see false visions or practice divination. I will save my people from your hands. And then you will know that I am the LORD.' "

NRSV

17As for you, mortal, set your face against the daughters of your people, who prophesy out of their own imagination; prophesy against them [18]and say, Thus says the Lord GOD: Woe to the women who sew bands on all wrists, and make veils for the heads of persons of every height, in the hunt for human lives! Will you hunt down lives among my people, and maintain your own lives? [19]You have profaned me among my people for handfuls of barley and for pieces of bread, putting to death persons who should not die and keeping alive persons who should not live, by your lies to my people, who listen to lies.

20Therefore thus says the Lord GOD: I am against your bands with which you hunt lives;[a] I will tear them from your arms, and let the lives go free, the lives that you hunt down like birds. [21]I will tear off your veils, and save my people from your hands; they shall no longer be prey in your hands; and you shall know that I am the LORD. [22]Because you have disheartened the righteous falsely, although I have not disheartened them, and you have encouraged the wicked not to turn from their wicked way and save their lives; [23]therefore you shall no longer see false visions or practice divination; I will save my people from your hand. Then you will know that I am the LORD.

[a]Gk Syr: Heb *lives for birds*

COMMENTARY

At Yahweh's command, Ezekiel must set his face (an ominous gesture; see 4:3, 7) against female exiles who are accused of playing the prophet and, like their male counterparts, of "prophesy[ing] out of their own imaginations" (v. 17). But while the male prophets of Israel abet the community's attempts to cling to optimistic illusions, these women operate at the level of the individual, thwarting Ezekiel's role as Israel's "watchman" (see the Commentary on 3:16-21). The following accusations (vv. 18b-19), their technical terms drawn from the world of sorcery and witchcraft, shroud these women in the magical practices of ancient Mesopotamian society.[355]

Heretofore, Ezekiel has said nothing about the women forced into exile by the Babylonians. The reader might suppose that having settled into their new surroundings, these women returned to the daily chores of domestic life. Such may, in fact, have been the situation of many (though not all) of Judah's female deportees, for their displacement was not preceded by a lengthy period of warfare with its concomitant decimation of the male population. Under more deadly circumstances, many of these women—strangers in a land where foreign women were viewed with suspicion—might have been forced into prostitution and other activities at the fringes of civilized life in Mesopotamia.

Within the literatures of ancient Assyria and Babylonia, we find many references to witchcraft and sorcery. But one need not look that far afield to discover that such activities played a role in popular religion. Why would a law like that found in Lev 20:6 ("If any turn to mediums and wizards, prostituting themselves to them, I will set my face against them, and will cut them off from the people," NRSV) appear if resort to such intermediaries were not a persistent temptation? The story of Saul and the Endor medium (1 Samuel 28) testifies to the presence of diviners in Israel. Especially in periods of crisis, people turned to every possible means by which to secure some sense of control over their lives. Although males participated in such practices, women especially were associated

with them. Their "arts"—both feared and sought after—promised protection from the spells enlisted by one's enemies, on one hand, while holding out the possibility of harming one's foes, on the other hand. Amulets and other charms offered some security; rituals and incantations functioned to release persons who believed themselves to be victims of witchcraft.

Ezekiel seeks thoroughly to discredit these women. He mocks their appurtenances—wrist and arm bindings or pads, veils or other head coverings—even as he ascribes to them the power to kill the innocent and preserve the lives of the guilty. Scholars dispute whether the "handfuls of barley" and "pieces of bread" referred to in v. 19 were used in rituals[356] or were payment for the women's services.[357] In either case, Ezekiel accuses these women of profaning God: "With their sorcerous invocation of the divine name," Block observes, "the women have degraded Yahweh in the public's eyes to the level of the Babylonian deities and demons, who let themselves be manipulated by divination and witchcraft."[358]

One can reasonably suspect that Ezekiel has, in effect, "demonized" these women unfairly. As Bowen makes clear, the distinction between magic, on the one hand, and religion, on the other, is a social distinction.[359] Even within a single society, persons can disagree about whether certain types of behavior belong in the first category or the second. Hence, in reading both the book of Ezekiel and the commentators on the present passage, she warns that "we should be aware that their assessment of the practices of these women as 'magic' may tell us more about [their] attitude toward these women than offering any solid information about the characteristics of female prophets." Bowen suggests, on the basis of biblical and extra-biblical evidence, that these women may have

355. See Sue Rollin, "Women and Witchcraft in Ancient Assyria," *Images of Women in Antiquity,* ed. Averil Cameron and Amélie Kuhrt (Detroit: Wayne State University Press, 1993) 34-45.

356. Moshe Greenberg, *Ezekiel 1–20,* AB 22 (Garden City, N.Y.: Doubleday, 1983) 240.

357. W. Zimmerli, *Ezekiel 1: A Commentary on the Book of the Prophet Ezekiel, Chapters 1–24,* trans. R. E. Clements, Hermeneia (Philadelphia: Fortress, 1979) 297.

358. D. I. Block, *The Book of Ezekiel: Chapters 1–24,* NICOT (Grand Rapids: Eerdmans, 1997) 416.

359. Nancy R. Bowen, "The Daughters of Your People: Female Prophets in Ezekiel 13:17-23," *JBL* 118 (1999) 420.

functioned, at least in part, as medical and religious professionals whose services were important during childbirth and other sorts of "illnesses." In any event, Ezekiel condemns them because, in continuing the practices of the past (and present), they perpetuate Israel's "old identity," which must perish in order that Ezekiel's understanding of its new, post-judgment identity become reality.[360]

As with the preceding oracle, "therefore" introduces a double wave of divine judgments against these women (vv. 20-23). First, Yahweh will strip away their magical appurtenances, releasing human "prey" from their power and forcing these women to acknowledge God. Note that here and elsewhere in the passage, God speaks of "my people,"

repeatedly asserting the divine prerogative over those whom these women are accused of manipulating for their own purposes (v. 18). Second, God will bring an end to their false visions and divinatory practices, rendering them incapable of plying their trade. The righteous ought not to be disheartened, nor the wicked protected on account of their activities. The true prophet acquits himself before God by doing precisely the opposite—arming the righteous against every stumbling block and confronting the wicked with the deadly consequences of their sin (see 3:16-21). When God saves "my people" from these "prophet players," they will be forced to know Yahweh—that is, to confess the unparalleled power of Israel's Lord. (See Reflections at 14:1-11.)

---

360. Ibid., 422-33.

Ezekiel 14:1-11, "Repent and Turn Away from Your Idols"

NIV

14 Some of the elders of Israel came to me and sat down in front of me. [2]Then the word of the LORD came to me: [3]"Son of man, these men have set up idols in their hearts and put wicked stumbling blocks before their faces. Should I let them inquire of me at all? [4]Therefore speak to them and tell them, 'This is what the Sovereign LORD says: When any Israelite sets up idols in his heart and puts a wicked stumbling block before his face and then goes to a prophet, I the LORD will answer him myself in keeping with his great idolatry. [5]I will do this to recapture the hearts of the people of Israel, who have all deserted me for their idols.'

[6]"Therefore say to the house of Israel, 'This is what the Sovereign LORD says: Repent! Turn from your idols and renounce all your detestable practices!

[7]"'When any Israelite or any alien living in Israel separates himself from me and sets up idols in his heart and puts a wicked stumbling block before his face and then goes to a prophet to inquire of me, I the LORD will answer him myself. [8]I will set my face against that man and make him an example and a byword. I will cut him off from my people. Then you will know that I am the LORD.

NRSV

14 Certain elders of Israel came to me and sat down before me. [2]And the word of the LORD came to me: [3]Mortal, these men have taken their idols into their hearts, and placed their iniquity as a stumbling block before them; shall I let myself be consulted by them? [4]Therefore speak to them, and say to them, Thus says the Lord GOD: Any of those of the house of Israel who take their idols into their hearts and place their iniquity as a stumbling block before them, and yet come to the prophet—I the LORD will answer those who come with the multitude of their idols, [5]in order that I may take hold of the hearts of the house of Israel, all of whom are estranged from me through their idols.

6Therefore say to the house of Israel, Thus says the Lord GOD: Repent and turn away from your idols; and turn away your faces from all your abominations. [7]For any of those of the house of Israel, or of the aliens who reside in Israel, who separate themselves from me, taking their idols into their hearts and placing their iniquity as a stumbling block before them, and yet come to a prophet to inquire of me by him, I the LORD will answer them myself. [8]I will set my face against them; I will make them a sign and a byword and cut them off from the midst of my people; and you shall know that I am the LORD.

NIV

⁹" 'And if the prophet is enticed to utter a prophecy, I the LORD have enticed that prophet, and I will stretch out my hand against him and destroy him from among my people Israel. ¹⁰They will bear their guilt—the prophet will be as guilty as the one who consults him. ¹¹Then the people of Israel will no longer stray from me, nor will they defile themselves anymore with all their sins. They will be my people, and I will be their God, declares the Sovereign LORD.' "

NRSV

⁹If a prophet is deceived and speaks a word, I, the LORD, have deceived that prophet, and I will stretch out my hand against him, and will destroy him from the midst of my people Israel. ¹⁰And they shall bear their punishment—the punishment of the inquirer and the punishment of the prophet shall be the same— ¹¹so that the house of Israel may no longer go astray from me, nor defile themselves any more with all their transgressions. Then they shall be my people, and I will be their God, says the Lord GOD.

COMMENTARY

Despite the unexpected appearance of a salvation oracle concerning the exiles in 11:14-21, Ezekiel's subsequent pronouncements to his immediate audience (chaps. 12–13) remain grim. He continues relentlessly to press upon them the inevitability of Judah's utter demise. He condemns their defiance of that message, and he denounces their resort to intermediaries whose oracles of well-being and illicit divinatory methods are deceiving and death-dealing. In 14:1-11 Yahweh accuses the exiles of idolatry, the most heinous of sins. They, no less than their condemned counterparts in Jerusalem, have devoted themselves to other deities (e.g., chaps. 6 and 8), contravening God's demand for exclusive loyalty. The reader recalls, among many other passages, Deut 13:4: "The LORD your God you shall follow, him alone you shall fear, his commandments you shall keep, his voice you shall obey, him you shall serve, and to him you shall hold fast" (NRSV). How dare these law-breakers seek an oracle from Yahweh, as if the God who demands absolute fidelity were oblivious or indifferent to their duplicity!

In a brief narrative introduction (v. 1), Ezekiel recounts an occasion when "certain elders of Israel" gathered to sit before him. The reader recalls a similar scenario from 8:1, though in that context the officials were called "the elders of Judah." Do these two designations refer to different groups? As the reader makes the way through the following verses, it will become evident that the broader epithet of v. 1 is particularly well-suited to its context (references to "the house of

Israel" appear in vv. 4-7, 11; see also "my people Israel," v. 9). These exilic leaders represent the whole people of Israel; what Yahweh will say to them applies also and equally to all of God's people.

Why would the elders come to Ezekiel, who constantly struggles to dash their hopes? Does his status as priest and prophet preclude bypassing him? Has some particular crisis forced them to this encounter? Verse 1 provides no explicit information regarding their circumstances and purpose, though the end of v. 3 will confirm the reader's suspicion that they have come in hopes of receiving Yahweh's answer to a particular inquiry. Verse 2, with its abrupt word-event formula ("the word of the LORD came to me"), suggests that the leaders' mission will succeed; a divine oracle is in the offing. But God's response to the prophet says nothing of the issue presently on their minds. Rather, it discloses the unspoken disposition of their hearts. In two parallel lines, Yahweh reproaches the inquirers: These men have "taken their idols [גלולים gillûlîm, "dung-idols"; see 6:4-6, 9, 13 (twice)] into their hearts" and the "stumbling block of their iniquity" (i.e., idolatry) they have "put before their faces." "Shall I let myself be consulted by them?" Yahweh asks Ezekiel—a rhetorical question that, in the light of these accusations, demands a negative response.

What is the nature of the elders' idolatry? God's reproaches in v. 3 permit no precise answer to this question. Some critics have taken Yahweh's words literally: The idols they have placed upon their hearts are amulets, the stumbling blocks actual images over which they trip.[361] As Block observes, however, at issue in this passage is "the internalization of idolatry, not its external expression . . . 'to erect on one's heart' is metaphorical language for 'to commit oneself to.' The idiom 'to place before one's face,' which portrays idolatry as an intentionally fixed 'state of mind,' is similar."[362] Have the elders secretly engaged in syncretistic religious activities? Do they long for the "good old days" in Jerusalem, when they, too, participated in the idolatrous rituals described in chap. 8? Or, as Greenberg speculates, are the "idols" in their thoughts and "before their faces" more generally "a rubric for an unregenerate state of mind" that insists that normal relations between God and the people can persist, despite the latter's obduracy and disloyalty?[363]

In the light of Yahweh's speech in v. 3, the reader likely is surprised immediately to read God's command that Ezekiel declare an oracle (introduced by the messenger formula, "Thus says the Lord GOD"). That oracle, while specific to the leaders' idolatrous mindset, is cast in the impersonal argot of casuistic law (see the Commentary on 3:16-21). This oracle repeats the reproaches of v. 3 (lodged against the officials), but recasts them as formal charges in a criminal indictment against any and all idolators of the house of Israel who consult Yahweh through an illegitimate prophet. Greenberg explains the rationale for Ezekiel's rhetoric:

> Case law was the only available literary form of discourse about particulars on an abstract, generalized level. Ezekiel, whose priestly providence familiarized him with torah literature (as his idiom shows at every turn), made innovative use of this form for teachings which, though given for an occasion, he wished to present in the guise of general theological principles.[364]

Unlike absolute or apodeictic laws, which are unconditional and employ second-person speech (e.g., "*You* shall not bow down to [idols] or worship them," Exod 20:5*a*), casuistic laws consist of a protasis (e.g., "If [or "When"] X happens"), fol-

lowed by an apodosis ("then Y will follow") and are cast in the third person (e.g., "If *anyone* among all your offspring throughout your generations comes near the sacred donations, which the people of Israel dedicate to the Lord, while *he* is in a state of uncleanness, *that person* shall be cut off from my presence: I am the LORD," Lev 22:3, NRSV, italics added). Each of these two examples belongs to the category of sacral law, for both address issues endemic to the religious/cultic sphere. Israel's priests formulated these and other laws (e.g., social, civil, moral, economic) in order that in every aspect of its life, Israel might be a holy people living in the presence of its holy God. The so-called holiness code (Leviticus 17–26), whose idioms and content Ezekiel knew well, explictly grounds its demands upon Israel in divine holiness: "The LORD spoke to Moses, saying: 'Speak to all the congregation of the people of Israel and say to them: "You shall be holy, for I the Lord your God am holy" ' " (Lev 19:1-2 NRSV).

This passage shares a number of formal features with certain casuistic, sacral laws, especially those in Leviticus 17. For example, the command "speak to X and say to them" (v. 4*a*) appears in Lev 17:2, and the formula "anyone of the house of Israel" (איש איש מבית ישראל *'îš 'îš mibbêt yiśrā'ēl*, vv. 4-7) is found in Lev 17:3, 8, 10; see also v. 13 ("And anyone of the people of Israel").[365] These and other similarities (see below) signal both to Ezekiel's immediate audience and to his reader that an attempt to inquire of Yahweh has abruptly become a legal case, and culpable members of the house of Israel are the accused! On the face of things, the elders might appear faithfully to be seeking God's guidance in a particular circumstance. Yet Yahweh reveals their duplicity, indicts them, and announces the intention to "take hold" of the Israelites' idolatrous hearts,[366] seizing what by right belongs to the Lord alone (see Exod 20:2). The self-identification formula "I [am] Yahweh," which appears not only in v. 4, but also in vv. 7 and 9, stirs thoughts of the Ten Commandments and of other laws (see, e.g., Lev 18:5; 19:12, 14, 16, 18, 29, 32, 37). Its presence here and at points

---

361. See J. Schoneveld, "Ezekiel XIV 18," *OTS* 15 (1969) 193-99.
362. Block, *Ezekiel 1–24*, 425.
363. Greenberg, *Ezekiel 1–20*, 253.
364. Ibid., 94-95.

365. The *'îš 'îš*, lit., "a man, a man") is distributive—i.e., Ezekiel conveys Yahweh's message to *each* member of the elders.
366. The verb translated "take hold" (תפש *tāpaś*) refers in other contexts to the forceful taking of a person as prisoner (1 Sam 15:8; 1 Kgs 13:4), of an animal (Ezek 19:4, 8), or of a city (Deut 20:19; Josh 8:8; Isa 36:1).

within Leviticus, Block observes, may strike the reader as somewhat awkward. The formula functions, however, to impress upon the Israelites that their laws emanate from the Lord: "Ezekiel's insertions of 'I am Yahweh' are strategically placed in each instance between the statement of the offense and the announcement of the punishment, thereby emphasizing the full force of the divine involvement in the case."[367]

In the midst of juristic language, an urgent appeal for repentance, for a "turning away" from Israel's idols and abominations (v. 6), appears for the first time in Ezekiel's scroll. Its unexpected presence casts preceding verses in a somewhat different light, for it signals that Yahweh's larger goal in confronting the house of Israel with its sin is reconciliation. Commentators have questioned whether, in proclaiming this call for repentance, Ezekiel violates the prohibition against acting as an "arbiter" between Israel and its God (see the Commentary on 3:22-27). But the initial formula, "Therefore say to the house of Israel, 'Thus says the LORD God' " pointedly presents the appeal as Yahweh's own initiative, not Ezekiel's.

Returning to the legal language of v. 4, vv. 7-8 set forth a threefold punishment of the accused, here broadened also to include "the aliens who reside in Israel" (see also Lev 17:8, 10, 12, 13; 20:2; 22:18).[368] Various forms of the first judgment, "I will set my face against them," appear ten times in Scripture (recall Ezek 7:22); and Yahweh is always the subject (see, e.g., Lev 17:10; 20:3, 5-6; Jer 44:11). The antithesis of "to set the face upon" (i.e., to look favorably upon), Ezekiel's phrase describes a hostile gesture.[369] In this context, it plays off the charge appearing in vv. 4-5 and 7: "the stumbling block of their iniquity they have *set before their faces.*"

Second, Yahweh says, "I will make them a sign [אות 'ôt] and a byword [משלים mĕšālîm]." The first of these two terms, used negatively, refers to a thing or person that serves as a warning to

observers (see, e.g., Deut 28:37, as well as Num 17:10, where Aaron's sprouted staff is kept as a warning to rebels, "so that you may make an end of their complaints against me, or else they will die"). The second, the plural (intensive) form of משל (māšāl), means in this context that the idolatrous inquirers will become widespread objects of revulsion and shock. As Polk observes, these human "bywords" should not only recognize and acknowledge their own destructive course, but also function as negative paradigms for the benefit of others.[370]

The meaning of the third punishment ("I will cut them off [הכרית hikrît, hiphil] from the midst of my people") is debated. This judicial sentence, like the first, appears in various forms elsewhere in Scripture (some 36 times in the Pentateuch; see esp. Lev 20:2-5).[371] Indeed, of the ten occurrences of the first punishment ("I will set my face against them"), six are followed by a form of hikrît (hiphil), "to cut off." Often, the idiom is expressed in the passive voice (e.g., "X shall be cut off from his people"). In those cases, the phrase does not specify who will do the "cutting off." In examples (like Ezek 14:8) where the verb is active, however, the subject is always God (e.g., Lev 20:1-6), never humans. What does this "cutting off" entail? At the least, it involves ejection from the faith community (an action ostensibly undertaken by members of that community). The condemned is cast out of God's presence, expelled from society.[372] Such is itself a form of death, since "to live is to stay in the place looked upon by the face of God (Num 6:25-26; 1 Kgs 8:29; Pss 80:4, 8, 15, 20; 104:29 and other passages)."[373] But Greenberg argues that more than banishment is at issue. The phrase connotes premature death inflicted not by human agents (e.g., by stoning), but by God.[374]

With the recognition formula in v. 8b, God's words assume the character of a prophetic proof saying. That is, knowledge of Yahweh emerges as the ultimate goal of the preceding divine speech.

367. D. I. Block, *The Book of Ezekiel: Chapters 1–24,* NICOT (Grand Rapids: Eerdmans, 1997) 424.

368. The phrase, though ill-suited to the situation of the exilic community, is retained, Greenberg claims, in order to lend the pronouncement the "aura" of venerable authority. Isaiah 56:3 ("the foreigner who has attached himself to Yahweh") reflects its adaptation to the exile. See Moshe Greenberg, *Ezekiel 1–20,* AB 22 (Garden City, N.Y.: Doubleday, 1983) 249.

369. See S. Layton, "Biblical Hebrew 'to set the face' in the Light of Akkadian and Ugaritic," *UF* 17 (1986) 169-81.

370. Timothy Polk, "Paradigms, Parables, and Měšālîm: On Reading the māšāl in Scripture," *CBQ* 45 (1983) 577.

371. Block, *Ezekiel 1–24,* 431.

372. See W. Zimmerli, *Ezekiel 1: A Commentary on the Book of the Prophet Ezekiel, Chapters 1–24,* trans. R. E. Clements, Hermeneia (Philadelphia: Fortress, 1979) 303-4; and W. Zimmerli, "Die Eigenart der prophetischen Rede des Ezechiel. Ein Beitrag zum Problem an Hand von Ez 14,1-11," *ZAW* 66 (1954) 1-26.

373. Zimmerli, *Ezekiel 1,* 304.

374. Greenberg, *Ezekiel 1–20,* 250.

Here as elsewhere, Ezekiel avers that when Yahweh acts to punish Israel's idolators, those who observe God's actions will be forced to acknowledge the Lord's sovereignty and power. "The knowledge implied by the statement of recognition," Zimmerli observes, "can only be described in connection with the actions of Yahweh that precede the recognition, prompt it, and provide it with a basis. . . . There is no room here for knowledge emerging darkly from interior human meditation, from an existential analysis of human beings and the world, or from speculation. The irreversible sequence, 'Yahweh's acts—human recognition,' is constitutive for the description of the process."[375]

Returning to the idiom of casuistic sacral law, God addresses the case of the prophet who, unlike Ezekiel, responds to the idolatrous inquirer's query (v. 9).[376] Such a prophet is deceived (the niphal of the verb פתה [pātâ] means "to be enticed, deceived"), and Yahweh is his deceiver! The notion that God intentionally deceives might be startling, but it is hardly unique to this text. One may consider, for example, Deut 13:5, where Moses is said to warn the Israelites against prophets and diviners by dreams whose omens and portents come to fruition and who urge the people to serve other gods. When this occurs, the people must not heed those prophets and diviners, but must recognize that God is testing them in order to determine if they love the Lord with all their heart and being. Such a test is real and complex, not facile, because in bringing about the intermediaries' omens and portents, Yahweh has in effect enhanced their (ostensible) authority in Israel's eyes, giving ground to their idolatrous urgings.[377] After all, if the intermediaries' omens and portents were not fulfilled, the people might more easily discount their words. In this passage, Yahweh's test is not called a deception per se. Nonetheless, it creates a false impression about the

power and status of these intermediaries (the latter are guilty of a capital offense, however; see, e.g., Deut 18:20).

Two Hebrew narratives speak of deceived and/or deceiving prophets who speak in God's name. The first, 1 Kings 13, tells the story of a "man of God" who, having faithfully carried out Yahweh's commission to declare an oracle of judgment against the altar at Bethel, is deceived (the verb is a piel form of כחש [kāḥaš], meaning "to deceive, act deceptively") by an elderly prophet of that city and, as a consequence, disobeys Yahweh's command not to eat food or drink water on the way (1 Kgs 13:9). This is certainly a troubling text. "Here," Crenshaw observes, "one sees the true prophet become false to his commission, and the 'false prophet' take up the genuine word of God and let it fall with shattering force upon the erring man of God."[378] The man of God pays for his disobedience with his life, but the lying prophet is not punished. The text does not state that the latter's deception is Yahweh's doing. His motive for lying to the man of God is nowhere stated. Still, the reader wonders how this story can be squared with the notion of divine justice.

The second narrative, 1 Kings 22, recounts a scenario wherein a member of Yahweh's divine council proposes to deceive (here, as in Ezekiel, the Hebrew verb is פתה [pātâ]) King Ahab's four hundred prophets in order that they with one voice urge King Ahab to battle the forces of Aram's king at Ramoth-gilead. In assenting to this plan, God assumes responsibility for deceiving a host of prophets who, speaking in Yahweh's name (1 Kgs 22:6), encourage Ahab to action that will cost him his life. Yet from the narrative's perspective, the court prophets have spoken in good faith, since they do not know that they have been deceived. The text says nothing of punishing these puppets in God's scheme.

Finally, we recall how Jeremiah accuses Yahweh of deceiving the people through the agency of false, peace-speaking prophets). Indeed, when his own doom oracles are not quickly fulfilled, he accuses God of deceiving him with words that might easily be placed on the lips of the condemned prophets of Ezek 14:9: "You deceived

---

375. W. Zimmerli, "Knowledge of God According to the Book of Ezekiel," in *I Am Yahweh,* trans. Douglas W. Stott (Atlanta: John Knox, 1982) 64.

376. "Woe to that prophet," Eichrodt observes, "if in such circumstances he lets himself be induced by the wish to please or by a calculated compromise to make any communication in Yahweh's name, treating his client's deadly crime as if it were a venial weakness." W. Eichrodt, *Ezekiel,* trans. Cosslett Quin, OTL (Philadelphia: Westminster, 1970) 183.

377. Given human nature, the intermediary who witnesses the fulfillment of his omens and portents may, on that basis, emerge with an enhanced self-image!

378. James L. Crenshaw, *Prophetic Conflict: Its Effect Upon Israelite Religion* BZAW 124 (Berlin: Walter de Gruyter, 1971) 48.

me [פתיתני *pittîtanî*], O Yahweh, and I was deceived [ואפת *wā'eppāt*]" (Jer 20:7).

Together, these texts remind readers that intermediaries and their messages generated complex conundrums for their societies. Ezekiel is by no means the first to speak of divine deception. And given his constant insistence upon Yahweh's unrivalled power, the reader likely is not surprised to find him asserting God's control over prophets and their utterances. Yet even more is at stake in the claim that Yahweh is the source of the prophets' deception (v. 9*a*). This statement also functions to protect both God's and Ezekiel's reputations. On the one hand, an idol-minded Israelite who thinks that he can dupe Yahweh into giving a credible response to his inquiry is deceiving himself; and any prophet who acts as his intermediary betrays, by that very action, his utter lack of credibility. As a consequence, the idolatrous inquirer has lost any chance of initiating communication with God and receiving an honest response. On the other hand, Ezekiel's status as Yahweh's authentic prophet is vindicated because he has not functioned as these exiles' conduit to God. To the contrary, Yahweh has spoken on God's own initiative and about a topic of God's own choosing.

Stretching one's arm against something also is a threatening gesture (see v. 8). The following judgment ("I will destroy him from the midst of my

people Israel") recalls the third punishment of v. 8: "I will cut them off from the midst of my people." Here, however, the substitution of "destroy" for "cut off" leaves no doubt that death at Yahweh's hand awaits the deceiving prophet. Indeed, when the following verse goes on to assert that "they shall bear their punishment,[379] the punishment of the inquirer and the punishment of the prophet *shall be the same*" (italics added; see the Commentary on 4:4-8), a reader who previously understood the "cutting off" threat of v. 8 to mean excommunication only might well revise his thinking along the lines suggested by Greenberg,[380] especially since the "like X, like Y" construction (כי . . . כי *kî . . . kî*) emphasizes exact correspondence between the two punishments (in a similar vein, see Jer 14:15-16; 27:14-15). The destruction of both guilty parties will have a purging effect upon the house of Israel: No longer will they stray from God or defile themselves with their sins. "Then," Yahweh asserts, "they shall be my people, and I will be their God" (recall 11:20). Such is the ultimate goal of Yahweh's punishments—that the covenant relationship between God and Israel be restored.

---

379. See Zimmerli's comment that in the sphere of sacral law, this phrase is used in concluding formulations to establish a condition of guilt. *Ezekiel 1,* 164.
380. Greenberg, *Ezekiel 1–20,* 250.

REFLECTIONS

Some years ago, a student in my "Israel's Prophetic Tradition" course stopped me after class. This student was very upset. A few days earlier, a well-known television evangelist had announced that God had commanded him to raise an enormous amount of money. If he failed to accomplish this goal, the evangelist claimed, God was going to "call him home." From this student's perspective, this evangelist was a revered and honorable man of God. Yet she was uncomfortable with his pronouncement and uncertain of how to respond to his claim that God was speaking to, and through, him in this way. And so she stopped me after class and said, "I've always believed that he is a genuine prophet. How can I know whether he is telling the truth or not?"

Perhaps more than my student had expected, I knew how she felt. As a little girl, I used to hurry in from church on Sunday mornings to watch this same evangelist on television. In those days, he sat on a metal folding chair at the edge of a simple platform while people seeking healing from physical ailments came forward for prayer. And so I wanted to be able to give her an answer, a litmus test that would enable her to judge his claim with certainty, thereby alleviating her doubt and discomfort. But, like the people of ancient Israel, I could not do so. I could only tell her that in raising the question, she had pointed to a direct intersection between what was going to be discussed in our classroom two days later and what people of faith have struggled with for millennia: How can we know when an authentic prophet is in our midst?

Intermediaries can arise in any society that posits both a divine and a human realm and believes that communication between those realms is possible. Israel was one such society, and the Hebrew Bible informs us that Israel had many prophets, male and female. Although Scripture likely preserves only a small sliver of Israel's prophetic traditions and oracles, the ongoing struggle to distinguish between true and false prophets and prophecies is well-represented in the canon. We know that the people of ancient Israel struggled with the problem of false prophecy, because the biblical literature tells us that they did. From our perspective, looking back with the advantage of hindsight, it may appear that Israel performed poorly in that struggle, heeding false prophets while persecuting or, worse, ignoring the true prophets. If we are wise, however, we will temper our impulse to judge, for distinguishing between true and false prophets is no easy task; and there is no guarantee that we, living in ancient times, would have fared any better.

How do we test the prophet who claims to speak the word of the Lord, yet whose word offends, surprises, terrifies, or angers us? How do we determine whose prophecies are valid when two intermediaries, each claiming to be God's spokesperson, proclaim conflicting messages? We certainly cannot dismiss out of hand those prophets whose messages we would rather not hear or read. Ezekiel's audience certainly did not want to hear his oracles about Jerusalem's destruction or his explanations for why that destruction must occur. If they could not ignore his oracles completely, then at least they could comfort themselves with the thought that they would not be fulfilled until long after their lifetimes or soothe themselves with the words of Ezekiel's competitors. But Ezekiel insists that prophets who say "peace" when there is no peace, or who attempt to conceal corruption and oppression beneath a thin veneer of civility not only speak dishonestly, but also actively contribute to the chaos.

When words are hard to hear, we are wise to listen attentively for their meaning. When, for example, prophets press upon us our responsibility for our own actions, we must resist the impulse to believe that someone or something else will save us—both as individuals and as communities.

EZEKIEL 14:12–15:8, JERUSALEM IS DOOMED! TEST CASE AND METAPHOR

OVERVIEW

Ezekiel 14:12-23 and 15:1-8 buttress the prophet's ongoing argument that Yahweh has justly doomed the sinful inhabitants of Jerusalem to destruction. Both oracles move from general observation to specific application, the transition signaled by the messenger formula ("thus says the LORD God"). Each begins with Ezekiel's claim that "the word of Yahweh came to me" and ends with the formula, "says the LORD God." And each in its own way displays his rhetorical prowess.

Readers of 14:12-23 encounter a unified oracle consisting of two unequal sections: vv. 12-20 and vv. 21-23. Ezekiel casts the first in the idiom of casuistic sacral law, four times positing the case of

a hypothetical land that "sins against me [Yahweh] by acting faithlessly" (v. 13a) and, as a consequence, endures various forms of divine punishment: famine (v. 13); ravaging beasts (v. 15); the sword (v. 17); and pestilence/bloody death (v. 19; these same punishments appear in 4:17). Each juristic scenario supports the so-called Doctrine of Retribution—human sin brings on divine punishment—and each is followed by a "subcase"[381] that presupposes and is intimately related to it: Even if Noah, Daniel, and Job, three pious venerables, were in that land, they could save only their own

381. Ronald M. Hals, *Ezekiel*, FOTL 19 (Grand Rapids: Eerdmans, 1988) 94.

lives by their righteousness. Here, it seems, is the larger point of Ezekiel's fourfold hypothetical test case: Every individual bears responsibility for his or her own survival. The second section applies both principle and punishments to Jerusalem, though with a surprising twist. This unit ends with a variant expression of the recognition formula, which justifies Yahweh's administration of justice and lends to the whole the character of a prophetic proof saying.

Ezekiel's contemporaries acknowledged his mastery of metaphor (see 20:49; 33:32). In 15:1-8, he reflects upon the vine, a popular metaphor for Israel/Judah/the Davidic dynasty. But instead of focusing upon its positive associations (e.g., fruitfulness, abundant growth, durability), he focuses on its branches—useless save as fuel for a fire. Like such branches, Jerusalem's inhabitants are fit only for flames and will be burned. Again, the recognition formula ("and you shall know that I am Yahweh") makes of Ezekiel's oracle a prophetic proof saying; holocaust in the homeland will force the exiles to acknowledge the sovereignty and justice of their God.

Ezekiel 14:12-23, Salvation by Proxy?

NIV

[12]The word of the LORD came to me: [13]"Son of man, if a country sins against me by being unfaithful and I stretch out my hand against it to cut off its food supply and send famine upon it and kill its men and their animals, [14]even if these three men—Noah, Daniel[a] and Job—were in it, they could save only themselves by their righteousness, declares the Sovereign LORD.

[15]"Or if I send wild beasts through that country and they leave it childless and it becomes desolate so that no one can pass through it because of the beasts, [16]as surely as I live, declares the Sovereign LORD, even if these three men were in it, they could not save their own sons or daughters. They alone would be saved, but the land would be desolate.

[17]"Or if I bring a sword against that country and say, 'Let the sword pass throughout the land,' and I kill its men and their animals, [18]as surely as I live, declares the Sovereign LORD, even if these three men were in it, they could not save their own sons or daughters. They alone would be saved.

[19]"Or if I send a plague into that land and pour out my wrath upon it through bloodshed, killing its men and their animals, [20]as surely as I live, declares the Sovereign LORD, even if Noah, Daniel and Job were in it, they could save neither son nor daughter. They would save only themselves by their righteousness.

[a]14 Or Danel; the Hebrew spelling may suggest a person other than the prophet Daniel; also in verse 20.

NRSV

12The word of the LORD came to me: [13]Mortal, when a land sins against me by acting faithlessly, and I stretch out my hand against it, and break its staff of bread and send famine upon it, and cut off from it human beings and animals, [14]even if Noah, Daniel,[a] and Job, these three, were in it, they would save only their own lives by their righteousness, says the Lord GOD. [15]If I send wild animals through the land to ravage it, so that it is made desolate, and no one may pass through because of the animals; [16]even if these three men were in it, as I live, says the Lord GOD, they would save neither sons nor daughters; they alone would be saved, but the land would be desolate. [17]Or if I bring a sword upon that land and say, "Let a sword pass through the land," and I cut off human beings and animals from it; [18]though these three men were in it, as I live, says the Lord GOD, they would save neither sons nor daughters, but they alone would be saved. [19]Or if I send a pestilence into that land, and pour out my wrath upon it with blood, to cut off humans and animals from it; [20]even if Noah, Daniel,[a] and Job were in it, as I live, says the Lord GOD, they would save neither son nor daughter; they would save only their own lives by their righteousness.

21For thus says the Lord GOD: How much more when I send upon Jerusalem my four deadly acts of judgment, sword, famine, wild animals, and pestilence, to cut off humans and animals

[a]Or, as otherwise read, Danel

NIV

21"For this is what the Sovereign LORD says: How much worse will it be when I send against Jerusalem my four dreadful judgments—sword and famine and wild beasts and plague—to kill its men and their animals! 22Yet there will be some survivors—sons and daughters who will be brought out of it. They will come to you, and when you see their conduct and their actions, you will be consoled regarding the disaster I have brought upon Jerusalem—every disaster I have brought upon it. 23You will be consoled when you see their conduct and their actions, for you will know that I have done nothing in it without cause, declares the Sovereign LORD."

NRSV

from it! 22Yet, survivors shall be left in it, sons and daughters who will be brought out; they will come out to you. When you see their ways and their deeds, you will be consoled for the evil that I have brought upon Jerusalem, for all that I have brought upon it. 23They shall console you, when you see their ways and their deeds; and you shall know that it was not without cause that I did all that I have done in it, says the Lord GOD.

COMMENTARY

14:12. The word event formula ("The word of the LORD came to me") signals Ezekiel's reception of a fresh message from Yahweh. Yet the formula is not immediately followed by God's command to convey the impending communiqué to his exilic audience. At the outset, God appears to address Ezekiel alone. Only the reader is privy to the speech.

14:13-20. Like 14:1-11, these verses adapt the language of casuistic sacral law (if [or when] X happens, then Y will follow; see the Commentary on 3:16-22). The protasis, explicitly stated in v. 13a and presupposed in the three subsequent scenarios, both introduces the accused ("a land," a metonym for its inhabitants) and identifies its crime ("sins against me [Yahweh] by acting faithlessly"). The initial apodosis (v. 13) pronounces God's judgment—famine and its consequences—in three clauses. The first and most general clause, "I will stretch out my hand against it," describes a punitive gesture already encountered in 6:14 and 14:9. The second, "[I will] break its staff of bread and send famine upon it," proclaims the devastating loss of life-sustaining nourishment (see the Commentary on 5:16). The third, a consequence of its predecessor, states that "[I will] cut off [הכרית *hikrît*] from it human beings and animals" (i.e., all living creatures).[382] Here and in vv.

17, 19, and 21, "to cut off" certainly means something other than excommunication from Israel's cultic community (see the Commentary on 14:1-11). As in 9:9, Yahweh's "cutting off" is lethal.

How might the reader construe v. 13? The protasis operates simultaneously on two levels: international and Israel-specific. On the one hand, it simply presumes God's sovereignty over *any* land that "sins against Yahweh by acting faithlessly." This global perspective accords well with Ezekiel's ubiquitous assertions of God's unrivalled sovereignty and power to judge not only Israel, but also other nations. "Properly speaking," Greenberg reminds us, "only those who know YHWH can be guilty of trespass against him"; here alone in all of Hebrew Scripture is this specific charge lodged against a non-Israelite subject. Yet Jer 50:14 and Ezek 16:50 also indict Gentiles in terms otherwise applied only to Israel.[383]

On the other hand, v. 13 already invites the reader to consider this "everyland" with Israel in mind, since the sins of (the inhabitants of) the hypothetical land are described in terms suggestive of Israel's own misdeeds. Not only does the accusation of sinning against *Yahweh* point in this direction (since Yahweh is Israel's patron deity), but also the charge of "acting faithlessly" (למעל-מעל *limʿāl-maʿal*), though sometimes

---

382. The phrase "man and beast" is a merismus—a figure of speech in which two species represent the totality of their genus (see also vv. 17, 19, 21). Hence, its meaning is not human beings and animals only, but everything living. See A. M. Honeyman, "Merismus in Biblical Hebrew," *JBL* 71 (1952) 11-18, esp. 11-14.

383. Moshe Greenberg, *Ezekiel 1–20*, AB 22 (Garden City, N.Y.: Doubleday, 1983) 157.

descriptive of betrayal within human relationships (e.g., Num 5:12, 27), most often designates *Israel's* sin against its God. Ideally, the reader holds together both the universality and the particularity of these and following verses. The latter does not cancel out the former, even as it suggests that by the end of Yahweh's speech, the general legal ruling will be applied to Israel itself.

As noted above, the "subcase" first introduced in v. 14 insists that even if Noah, Daniel, and Job—three legendary paragons of piety—were within Ezekiel's hypothetical land, they could save only their own lives by their righteousness. Noah, like his Mesopotamian counterparts, Utnapishtim and Atrahasis, survived a great deluge. Israel's Old Epic tradition esteems him as the only righteous person of his generation (Gen 7:1), while the priestly writers, Ezekiel's near contemporaries, call him "a righteous man, blameless in his generation" who "walked with God" (Gen 6:9 NRSV). Job, also an ancient model of righteousness, is described in the book bearing his name as "blameless and upright," a "God-fearing" man who "shuns evil" (Job 1:1, 8). He, too, survives disastrous circumstances. Neither individual is an Israelite: Noah belongs to primeval (pre-Israelite) history; Job is probably an Edomite. Yet Yahweh is the God of both Noah and Job.

The second figure of this triad, Daniel, is more elusive, though the company he keeps suggests that he, too, should be sought among exemplary figures of antiquity. In the opinion of many modern scholars, we find him in the Canaanite *Epic of Aqhat,* discovered in the 1930s among the ruins of ancient Ugarit (a city-state located near the Mediterranean coast of northern Syria and destroyed soon after 1200 BCE). This epic poem tells of King Danel, a man of meticulous virtue and devotion, favored by the gods. At its beginning, we find Danel performing an incubation rite in the hope that Baal will grant his wish for a son. Baal intercedes on his behalf to El (patriarch of the Canaanite pantheon), and Aqhat is born. Though the latter is the poem's primary character, his death and restoration its principal plot, Danel reappears at significant junctures within the story, ever the model of piety and responsibility.[384]

Some scholars doubt that Ezekiel had this ancient hero in mind, since the Danel of the *Aqhat* epic is pagan, a devotee of Baal.[385] This objection presupposes, however, that the prophet knew Danel only as he appears in this particular tale. Yet Ezek 28:3 suggests that more than a single story about Danel circulated in Ezekiel's day (see the Commentary on 28:1-10). Moreover, it is possible that Israelite appropriations of this legendary character transformed him (like Noah and Job) into a worshiper of Yahweh. Block insists that Ezekiel was referring to Daniel, the hero of the biblical book bearing his name.[386] From a purely critical perspective, this option must be ruled out. The book of Daniel was not composed until centuries after Ezekiel's scroll was completed. Though it purports to tell of a wise and pious member of the Babylonian exilic community, it actually derives from the second century BCE, when Jewish resistance to forced Hellenization under Antiochus IV Epiphanes (175–163 BCE) erupted in the Maccabean revolt. The ancient reader, working through the text of Ezekiel not long after it assumed final form, did not know the as yet unwritten book of Daniel. But first-century BCE readers who had access to that work, who could not marshal the arguments of contemporary critics against its purported date and setting and who were oblivious to, or willing to overlook, its blunders of historical detail might well have thought that Ezekiel paired Noah and Job with his exilic contemporary—also a person of exceptional virtue and piety.

With Ezekiel's assertion that three such virtuous men could save only themselves from God's punishment, the problem of theodicy—divine justice—emerges. This is so, in part, because ancient Israel's traditions do not speak with one voice about the possibility of salvation for the many based on the righteousness of a few. If readers place the present text in conversation with the story about Sodom and Gomorrah's destruction (Gen 18:16–19:29), for example, they discover both agreement and disagreement concerning God's administration of justice.

According to the Genesis narrative, when

384. See Simon B. Parker, *The Pre-Biblical Narrative Tradition,* SBLRBS 24 (Atlanta: Scholars Press, 1989) 99-144.

385. See D. I. Block, *Ezekiel 1–24,* NICOT (Grand Rapids: Eerdmans, 1997) 447-49. Block's arguments mainly follow H. H. P. Dressler, "The Identification of the Ugaritic Dnil and the Daniel of Ezekiel," *VT* 30 (1980) 174-84.

386. Block, *Ezekiel 1–24,* 446-49.

Abraham learns of Yahweh's intention to destroy Sodom, home to nephew Lot and his family, he begins to question and even to barter with God:

> Then Abraham came near and said, "Will you indeed sweep away the righteous with the wicked? Suppose there are fifty righteous within the city; will you then sweep away the place and not forgive it for the fifty righteous who are in it? Far be it from you to do such a thing, to slay the righteous with the wicked, so that the righteous fare as the wicked! Far be that from you! Shall not the Judge of all the earth do what is just?" And the LORD said, "If I find at Sodom fifty righteous in the city, I will forgive the whole place for their sake." (Gen 18:23-26 NRSV)

By the end of Abraham's negotiations with Yahweh, the Lord has agreed to spare the city for the sake of only ten righteous persons (Gen 18:32). Even this number proves too large, however. Both Sodom and Gomorrah are destroyed (Gen 19:24-25), though Lot and his family escape.[387]

Ezekiel 14:13-20, like Gen 18:23-26, affirms that the righteous do not perish with the wicked. But it rules out any possibility that God might forgive/spare a land's sinful inhabitants for the sake of its pious residents. This same perspective characterizes Ezek 9:4-6, wherein God orders the man clothed in linen to place a protective mark upon the foreheads of any Jerusalemites who moan and groan over the city's abominations, but then demands the deaths of all others, including small children.

Verse 15 announces the second of Yahweh's punishments against Ezekiel's hypothetical land: Should wild beasts bereave it of its children, leaving it depopulated and impassable, the same three righteous men (here not named) alone would be saved. "As I live," Yahweh swears, "they could save neither sons nor daughters." Deuteronomy 24:16 sets out the principle that parents will not suffer for the sins of their children, nor children for the sins of their parents: "Only for their [own] crimes may persons be put to death." Ezekiel affirms this principle, but expresses its flipside: The offspring of righteous parents cannot expect preferential treatment.

The introduction of sons and daughters in v. 16,

anticipated by the image of ravaging beasts bereaving a land of its children, invites the reader to reflect upon the offspring of Ezekiel's pious triad. Spiegel has argued that Ezekiel selected Noah, Daniel, and Job as paradigms of righteousness precisely because their children figure in their stories: Not only Noah, but also his family escaped the flood. Job begot a second set of children (Job 42:13) after his first set of offspring perished (Job 1:18-19; Spiegel contends that Job prayed his first set back to life); and, if scholars' reconstructions of the conclusion of the *Aqhat* epic are accurate, Danel and his daughter were able to bring Aqhat back from the dead. Spiegel's arguments have not persuaded most scholars, who insist that righteousness, not paternity, accounts for Ezekiel's triad. But we cannot rule out the possibility that thoughts of their offspring were astir in the ancient reader's mind.

Neither, Yahweh swears, could these three righteous venerables save their sons or daughters if God's sword passed through the land, slaying all of its living creatures (v. 17). If God sent pestilence into that land and "poured out my wrath upon it with blood" (Ezekiel regularly combines pestilence and bloody death; see 5:17; 28:23; 38:22), even Noah, Daniel, and Job could save neither son nor daughter, but themselves alone.

While slight variations distinguish these test cases, their number (four) and repetitive character underscore both the thoroughness of Yahweh's punishments and God's absolute determination that each individual suffer the consequences of his or her own sin.

The reader whose extra-textual repertoire includes Jer 15:1-3 cannot help being struck by its similarity to the present text. There, Yahweh rejects the worshiping community's public plea for mercy ("Do not spurn us, for your name's sake; do not dishonor your glorious throne; remember and do not break your covenant with us" Jer 14:21), asserting that even if Moses and Samuel were present, God would not forgive Jerusalem's sinful inhabitants (Jer 15:1). They must suffer Yahweh's four deadly punishments: pestilence, sword, famine, and captivity (Jer 15:2; devouring beasts appear in Jer 15:3). Jeremiah lifts up two important Israelite intercessors; Ezekiel's extra-Israelite triad better suits the "international" dimension of his test case. But both prophets insist that a right-

387. S. Spiegel, "Noah, Daniel, and Job, Touching on Canaanite Relics in Legends for the Jews," *Louis Ginzberg Jubilee Volume* (New York: American Academy for Jewish Research, 1945) 305-55.

eous few cannot allay God's judgment upon a sinful people.

14:21-23. With the appearance of the messenger formula in v. 21, Ezekiel turns from the case of a hypothetical everyland to address the exiles concerning the inhabitants of Jerusalem. How much more, he asserts, will Yahweh send upon Judah's capital city these same four deadly judgments! Has not Israel known that abrogation of its covenant with God would bring upon it the full force of the Lord's covenant curses—among them famine (see Lev 26:26), wild beasts (see Lev 26:22), the sword (see Lev 26:25), and plague (see Lev 26:25)? Surely no one in the city will escape.

But then, as the reader expects yet another reference to a righteous few (perhaps those Jerusalemites bearing the protective mark upon their foreheads), vv. 22-23 present a starkly different idea: Some sons and daughters *will* survive God's punishments and be brought out (not "saved") to join the exiles in Babylonia. Many a critic has suggested that these verses constitute a later "update" of Ezekiel's original oracle—an "after the fact" attempt to explain how it was that some Jerusalemites actually survived the city's destruction in 586 BCE and were subsequently deported. But the reader need not have assumed as much. Ancient Near Eastern texts and iconography acknowledge the existence of survivors who, in the aftermath of national destruction, gathered their few possessions and walked into captivity in a distant land. Ezekiel's scenario of surviving sons and daughters takes account of this reality, but ascribes to Jerusalem's survivors a positive function in God's judgment. When the exiles already in Babylonia see their evil "ways and deeds," they will understand that God's treatment of the city is fully justified. Jerusalem's destruction is not the result of divine caprice, but the only apt response to so sinful a lot. Confronted by these living, breathing embodiments of faithless Jerusalem, they will acknowledge that God has not acted without just cause. (See Reflections at 15:1-8.)

Ezekiel 15:1-8, Consigning Vine Israel to the Fire

NIV	NRSV
15 The word of the LORD came to me: [2]"Son of man, how is the wood of a vine better than that of a branch on any of the trees in the forest? [3]Is wood ever taken from it to make anything useful? Do they make pegs from it to hang things on? [4]And after it is thrown on the fire as fuel and the fire burns both ends and chars the middle, is it then useful for anything? [5]If it was not useful for anything when it was whole, how much less can it be made into something useful when the fire has burned it and it is charred?	**15** The word of the LORD came to me: [2]O mortal, how does the wood of the vine surpass all other wood— the vine branch that is among the trees of the forest? [3] Is wood taken from it to make anything? Does one take a peg from it on which to hang any object? [4] It is put in the fire for fuel; when the fire has consumed both ends of it and the middle of it is charred, is it useful for anything? [5] When it was whole it was used for nothing; how much less—when the fire has consumed it, and it is charred— can it ever be used for anything!
[6]"Therefore this is what the Sovereign LORD says: As I have given the wood of the vine among the trees of the forest as fuel for the fire, so will I treat the people living in Jerusalem. [7]I will set my face against them. Although they have come out of the fire, the fire will yet consume them. And when I set my face against them, you will know that I am the LORD. [8]I will make the land desolate because they have been unfaithful, declares the Sovereign LORD."	[6]Therefore thus says the Lord GOD: Like the wood of the vine among the trees of the forest, which I have given to the fire for fuel, so I will

NRSV

give up the inhabitants of Jerusalem. ⁷I will set my face against them; although they escape from the fire, the fire shall still consume them; and you shall know that I am the LORD, when I set my face against them. ⁸And I will make the land desolate, because they have acted faithlessly, says the Lord GOD.

COMMENTARY

Like the preceding oracle, these verses consist of two parts. The first section (vv. 1-5), introduced by the word-event formula (v. 1), contains Yahweh's didactic reflection on the vine branch. The second (vv. 6-8), begun with the messenger formula, applies that reflection to Jerusalem's inhabitants with devastating consequences. The recognition formula in v. 7b lends to the whole the character of a prophetic proof saying. Cast in the second person ("and you shall know that I am Yahweh"), the presence of this formula makes clear that Ezekiel is addressing his fellow exiles concerning the fate of their compatriots in Judah. Verse 8 rounds off the oracle in language reminiscent of 14:12-23.

The arrangement of lines (stichometry) in the NRSV translation of vv. 1-5 implies that the prophet has composed this reflection in poetry. It is true that both v. 2 and v. 3 consist of a pair of lines, each exhibiting synonymous parallelism; other "poetic" features are also present. Contemporary scholars agree, however, that these verses are elevated prose, not poetry proper.

Ezekiel's decision to focus upon the vine is not benign. While his initial reflections appear banal—general observations on a common object—his readers know well that the vine is a conventional, recurring metaphor for Israel/Judah/the Davidic dynasty. This fact, coupled with the reader's awareness that heretofore Ezekiel has never introduced a topic simply for the purpose of entertainment or "secular" education, predisposes the reader to think that the prophet's reflection on this pregnant image pertains to the house of Israel in some way. Said differently, the reader quickly suspects that Ezekiel uses a metaphor by speaking about one thing (e.g., Jerusalem and its inhabi-

tants) in terms suggestive of another (vine-stock).³⁸⁸

Viticulture was an important part of agrarian life in ancient Palestine. The fruit of the vine provided both nourishment and joy (wine). According to Num 13:23-24, the spies sent by Moses to reconnoiter the land of Canaan brought back a cluster of grapes so large that it was necessary for two men to carry it on a pole between them. The account is hyperbolic to be sure, but what better way to portray the astonishing fertility of the land God had promised to this people (see also Deut 8:7-10).

Because vine imagery appears in numerous passages within the HB, critics are able to examine such tropes (i.e., figurative language) in a variety of contexts, thereby gaining some sense of their range of stereotypical associations and functions—both positive and negative. On the one hand, the eighth-century BCE prophet Hosea likens God's delight in finding Israel to the joy of one who unexpectedly discovers grapes growing in the wilderness (Hos 9:10). Elsewhere, he describes his people as "a luxuriant vine that yields its fruit" (Hos 10:1 NRSV). The author of Psalm 80 depicts Israel as a vine that God brought out of Egypt and transplanted in choice Canaanite soil. Positive associations (e.g., fruitfulness, security, durability, and abundant growth) abound:

You brought a vine out of Egypt;
    you drove out the nations and planted it.
You cleared the ground for it;
    it took deep root and filled the land.
The mountains were covered with its shade,

388. Soskice defines metaphor as "that figure of speech whereby we speak about one thing in terms which are seen to be suggestive of another." See Janet M. Soskice, *Metaphor and Religious Language* (Oxford: Clarendon, 1985) 15.

the mighty cedars with its branches;
It sent out its branches to the sea,
    and its shoots to the river. (Ps 80:8-11 NRSV)

Here, the poet takes up the vine metaphor in order to praise God, whose care has enabled this people to thrive in a fertile environment. But he also extols Israel by inviting the worshiping community to perceive itself through the lens of a luxuriant, fruitful plant.

On the other hand, negative vine imagery casts aspersions on Israel's character. Isaiah 5:1-7, for example, details both Yahweh's diligent care for "his" vineyard and God's profound disappointment when it yields only wild (inedible) grapes. In a similar vein, Jer 2:21 expresses Yahweh's complaint against the house of Israel: "Yet I planted you as a choice vine, from the purest stock. How then did you turn degenerate and become a wild vine?" (NRSV). Elsewhere in his book, Ezekiel invites readers to perceive Judah's royal dynasty as a well-watered, fertile vine with many branches (19:10-14). With the notice that its strongest stem towers above the thick boughs of other trees (19:11), however, inappropriate human pride enters the picture. In the blink of an eye, Yahweh plucks the vine from its soil, casts it to the ground, and transplants it in the desert, where its fruit is desiccated and fire consumes it.

This last example illustrates a rhetorical strategy (defamiliarization) first employed by the prophet in the present chapter, but appearing many times in subsequent ones. That is, Ezekiel takes up an image that all would agree is appropriate to the topic at hand. But in his treatment of it, he highlights previously ignored, little-explored, and/or unanticipated associations with that image in order to make a point. No doubt his exilic audience would have conceded the aptness of positive vine imagery for an oracle concerning Jerusalem, Judah's capital and home to the Davidic dynasty. Yet Ezekiel selects negative aspects of his chosen trope, flouting the exiles' hopes.

The opening line of Ezekiel's expostulation (v. 2) invites readers to reflect on "the wood of the vine." Both the NRSV and the NIV adopt a comparative translation (NIV, "Son of Man, how is the wood of a vine better than that of a branch on any of the trees of the forest?"). But this option ill accords with the point of Ezekiel's remarks, which do not assert the superiority of vine wood over that of other trees (quite the contrary), but rather distinguish between their respective *fates.* Better, then, is this translation:

> Man, what, of all trees, becomes of
>   the vinestock,
>   the vine branch, that belongs among the trees
>   of the forest?[389]

This initial, interest-engaging query is followed by a pair of rhetorical questions that point to the uselessness of vine boughs. No, the reader would respond, wood taken from the vineyard cannot be made into something useful. No, one cannot take (make) from it so much as a peg upon which to hang a vessel.[390] Its only benefit is as fuel for the fire. And when it has been burned—both ends consumed, its middle charred—how much less can it serve any useful purpose (vv. 4-5)? Here the reader observes an Ezekielian rhetorical strategy at work. The prophet focuses on negative associations with vine branches, thereby paving the way for the judgment oracle to follow.

The application of Ezekiel's reflection commences with the messenger formula ("thus says the LORD God") preceded by כִּי (*kî,* "therefore") in v. 6. With this verse, the actual tenor of Ezekiel's metaphorical vehicle surfaces: Just as Yahweh has given up (passive) the wood of the vine as fuel for the fire, so also the Lord will give up (active) the inhabitants of Jerusalem. God will set the divine face against them (a hostile gesture; see 7:22; 14:8). Although they, like vine branches, may initially emerge from the flames with some semblance of their former shape, in the end they will be utterly reduced to ashes. Then, Ezekiel's fellow exiles will acknowledge that their sovereign God, and no other, has inflicted punishment upon the Judeans in the homeland. That land, like the hypothetical land of 14:12-20, will be rendered desolate, devoid of inhabitants, on account of their faithless action (the same charge that appeared in the apodosis of 14:13).

---

389. Greenberg, *Ezekiel 1–20,* 264-65. See also Block, *Ezekiel 1–24,* 456.

390. The verb לקח (*lāqaḥ*), "to take," appears in the passive הֻקַּח (*hăyuqqaḥ*) in v. 3*a* and in the active יִקְחוּ (*yiqḥû*) in v. 3*b*. This passive/active pattern will recur in subsequent verses.

REFLECTIONS

Ezekiel's relentless insistence that Yahweh, Israel's God and covenant partner, had determined utterly to destroy Jerusalem and virtually to wipe out Judah's population cut across many of Israel's most cherished religious beliefs. Present-day readers might be tempted to wonder that his contemporaries resisted his message so ardently. Could they not perceive that Ezekiel was the Lord's authentic spokesman in their midst and that their futures depended upon obedience and acceptance of God's will—even when it ran roughshod over their hopes and expectations? But we dare not judge the exiles too quickly. Who among us welcomes vicious frontal attacks on our most basic theological affirmations, the orthodoxy we hold dear? Who of us would wish regularly to hear an Ezekiel proclaim that the God we worship has chosen to wipe us out, divine mercy obviated by the stringent standard of justice alone? What arguments might we devise in our own defense? To what biblical traditions might we hitch our hopes? To what lengths would we go to discredit the doomsayer in our midst?

In the Reflections on 14:1-11, it is acknowledged how difficult was (and is) the task of distinguishing between the authentic utterances of true prophets and the deceiving words of false ones. On the one hand, criteria for differentiating between such intermediaries and their messages is of limited value. Some are ambiguous; others are applicable only in certain situations or in hindsight. So long as Ezekiel's doom oracles were not fulfilled, for example, the people could hold out hope that he was among the prophets Yahweh had deceived (14:9), or that divine mercy might suddenly outdistance divine wrath, or that God would eventually conclude that the Babylonians were not fit to be instruments of divine judgment against Yahweh's own covenant people, the latter's long-lived history of sin notwithstanding.

On the other hand, the fact that Israel's theological traditions did not speak with one voice concerning God's administration of justice and penchant toward mercy further complicated the exiles' dilemma. What about the prophecies of Isaiah? He, too, subjected Jerusalem and its inhabitants to scathing critiques. Yet Yahweh miraculously saved the city, wiping out the Assyrian army encamped at its very gates (Isaiah 36–37). Perhaps Jerusalem could escape the Babylonians in their day, even as it had survived the Assyrian threat in Isaiah's day. Surely, in the minds of many exiles, giving up on God's promises to sustain the Davidic dynasty, to protect Jerusalem, and to be present with this people for good, not ill, would have seemed sheer blasphemy—jumping God's ship when the waves got rough. Had not Yahweh promised that even when the Israelites walked through the darkest valley, God's rod and staff would comfort and sustain them on the way (Ps 23:4)?

In 14:12-23, Ezekiel tries a different tactic to break through the people's resistance. He broadens his horizon to speak not just of Israel, but of any land whose inhabitants prove faithless to Yahweh. His hypothetical test case must surely have surprised his audience, members of which likely were preoccupied with sorting out what contemporary circumstances meant for themselves, for their fellow Judeans in the homeland, and especially for their understanding of God's will and role during this time of national crisis. Did all nations stand beneath the judgment of Israel's deity? If so, then why were the Babylonians able to flourish, while Judah faltered? The prophet Habakkuk raised this very question:

> Your eyes are too pure to behold evil,
>   and you cannot look on wrongdoing;
> why do you look on the treacherous,
>   and are silent when the wicked swallow
>   those more righteous then they? (Hab 1:13 NRSV)

Ezekiel's fellow exiles must have raised this query as well. Was the prophet's insistence that Yahweh punished the sinful as true for other nations (whose inhabitants served other deities) as it was for Israel?

In the Commentary, it is noted that biblical traditions vary on the question of whether one's own fate is influenced by the people whose company one keeps. According to Gen 18:23-33, Abraham was able to convince God to forgive/save all the inhabitants of Sodom for the sake of only ten righteous residents. In the end, the city was destroyed, but not because Yahweh reneged on the agreement. If God would consent to Abraham's proposal on behalf of Sodom, the sinful city par excellence, why not save at least some of the inhabitants of Ezekiel's hypothetical land for the sake of three paradigms of righteousness residing there? And how much more might the Lord be willing to take account of Jerusalem's righteous, the recipients of the man in linen's protective mark (9:4), and spare that city on their behalf? Where was an intercessor like Moses in the midst of Judah's crisis? Why was the God of Abraham, and of Moses, refusing so adamantly to exercise the grace of earlier times?

In one sense, Ezekiel's insistence that there could be no salvation by proxy was a liberating word. Better to bear responsibility for one's own survival than to have one's fate ensnared in the actions of others. Ezekiel's message sat well with the teaching of Deut 24:16, "Parents shall not be put to death for their children, nor shall children be put to death for their parents; only for their own crimes may persons be put to death" (NRSV). But it contradicted no less than the Ten Commandments: "for I the LORD your God am a jealous God, punishing children for the iniquity of parents, to the third and fourth generation of those who reject me" (Exod 20:5). Elsewhere in Ezekiel, the prophet will argue against that hallowed pronouncement. His fellow exiles protested that they were suffering for the sins of their ancestors, invoking the popular proverb, "The parents have eaten sour grapes, and the children's teeth are set on edge" (Ezek 18:2 NRSV). Such fatalistic thinking could have the effect not only of demoralizing the exiles altogether, but also of providing an excuse for not taking responsibility for themselves. Ezekiel's insistence that God's justice takes each generation into account liberated the exiles from the weighty sins of their ancestors, even as it challenged every member of the community to mark well his or her own thoughts and actions.

Moderns, no less than Ezekiel's audience, may wish to "have things both ways." On the one hand, we become indignant at the notion that we might be penalized for the sins of others. Who among us, for example, would wish to be held personally responsible for the shortcomings of adult family members and friends, much less for the sins and conundrums of our societies? On the other hand, we might hope, consciously or unconsciously, that we can be shielded from the consequences of our own thoughts and actions through "holy alliances"—a "health and wealth" version of Christianity, membership in the "right" church, the daily intercessory prayers of a pious parent or other relative.

Ezekiel is convinced that his exilic audience can only accept God's "no" to Judah's survival if that "no" is shown to be deeply rooted in divine justice. They must come to acknowledge that this crisis is no indication of divine weakness or apathy, but the consequence of their own sinfulness, for which God holds each individual accountable. So negative a portrait of God's people is fearsome. Contemporary people of faith, no less than Ezekiel's audience, prefer other portraits—the pleasing images of blessing, security, and prosperity. Tell us that we are the vine—fruitful, thriving, securely planted in well-watered ground. Focus upon our strengths, but do not look closely enough to perceive our weaknesses—the terrible truth that we might also be counted useless to the ongoing task of realizing God's kingdom on earth. John's Jesus proclaims that whoever does not abide in the true vine is pruned away like a worthless branch—gathered, thrown into the fire, and burned (John 15:1-6). The gospel itself can be hard to hear.

Deep in the heart of Babylon, deep in the midst of exile, Ezekiel must have known in his own heart that the righteous often perish alongside the wicked and that lesser persons can survive, even thrive, on account of their alliances—"holy" and unholy. After all, his community of upper-crust exiles would experience Jerusalem's destruction only secondhand, while the children in Judah perished in the flames. So convinced was he that all these things must be explained as

God's own, just choices and actions that he could not speak of disaster as something God might experience *with* Yahweh's people. Even as we take responsibility for our own righteousness, we must question Ezekiel's relentless claims that divine justice leads to cut-and-dried answers.

EZEKIEL 16:1-63, JERUSALEM AS YAHWEH'S WANTON WIFE

OVERVIEW

Ezekiel knew what contemporary philosophers and literary critics now acknowledge: Metaphors convey ideas that can be stated in no other way. Tropes (figurative uses of language) are not simply embellished expressions of what might just as well be said literally; nor are they significant solely for their emotive impact. They are unique cognitive vehicles. The medium is the message, because the message is conveyed in terms having an irreducible impact upon the reader's perception of its meaning.

Ezekiel has pressed upon his exilic audience (and his readers) the impending, inevitable, and fully justified destruction of Jerusalem many times in preceding chapters. The message of chap. 16 is not new.[391] Neither is the method. In chap. 15, the prophet took up a familiar vine metaphor in order to convey to his audience, in an unanticipated way, the uselessness of Jerusalem's inhabitants. So also in the present chapter, this "master of metaphor" both adopts and adapts the female city imagery of his ancient Near Eastern world in order, in an extraordinarily sustained manner (63 verses), not only to cast Jerusalem's history in the most scandalous of terms, but also to underscore Yahweh's mercy, to justify "his" (in this context, the masculine pronoun is entirely appropriate) murderous wrath and to set out a "solution" to the problem posed by a persistently faithless female (people). The result, as we shall see, is a powerful,

painful, and deeply troubling text that demands that its modern-day readers attempt both to understand why Ezekiel spoke as he did and to consider the implications of his trope for ancient and modern times (see Reflections).

Ezekiel's oracle consists of three interrelated parts.[392] The first section (vv. 3-43) tells the story of a hapless infant left to die in an open field by her Amorite father and Hittite mother. Yahweh passes by her and saves her life. When the infant has grown to sexual maturity, Yahweh passes by her again, marries her, and lavishes upon her both tender care and the finest provisions. She becomes exceptionally beautiful, fit for royalty, renowned among the nations (vv. 13-14). Tragically, however, Jerusalem forgets her humble beginnings and the husband who rescued her from certain death. She plays the harlot, worshiping male images cast from God's silver and gold, sacrificing God's children to them, and offering her body to passers-by at every crossroad. So vulgar are her nymphomaniacal actions that even Philistine women are offended. Moreover, her harlotries also include illicit liaisons with other nations—Egypt, Assyria, Babylonia. In short, Ezekiel portrays her as acting in a manner that, he insists, fully justifies the exorbitant violence her husband now threatens to inflict upon her. He will summon her former lovers and shame her in their sight. They, in turn, will inflict multiple lethal wounds upon her body.

Section two (vv. 44-58) belittles Jerusalem via a proverb ("Like mother, like daughter"), reiterates

---

391. Davis oberves: "The whole force of the first twenty-four chapters [of Ezekiel] is to convict Israel of the extent of its sin and the righteousness of God's judgment. Although there is no possibility that the judgment will be reversed, nonetheless it is necessary that Israel be brought to recognition of its own deserving (especially through the lurid portraits of chs. 16 and 23)." Ellen F. Davis, *Swallowing the Scroll: Textuality and the Dynamics of Discourse in Ezekiel's Prophecy*, Bible and Literature 21 (Sheffield: Almond, 1989) 37.

392. See the analysis of Moshe Greenberg, *Ezekiel 1–20*, AB 22 (Garden City, N.Y.: Doubleday, 1983) 292-306. Ezekiel 16 is one of several examples of what Greenberg terms a "halving" pattern: a theme (A) is followed by a variation on that theme (B), which in turn is concluded with a section in which elements of both A and B are fused (C).

her odious pedigree, and contrasts her unfavorably with her two "sisters"—Samaria and Sodom. Here, Yahweh introduces "hope" for Jerusalem's future, yet in a way that further heaps shame upon her. So abhorrent is she that her sister cities appear righteous by comparison. They also will be restored; Sodom's revival especially will shame Judah's capital, since the former was regarded as the epitome of the wicked city prior to God's exposure of Jerusalem's own abominations.

Section three (vv. 59-63) begins with Yahweh's assertion of the justice of his dealings with his adulterous wife: "I will deal with you as you deserve" (v. 59). But then, remarkably, he promises to remember the covenant with Jerusalem established in her youth. Here, indeed, is an unexpected reconciliation, especially in the light of the murderous violence inflicted upon her in vv. 35-42. Still, Ezekiel permits his readers no glimpse of a joyous reunion. Instead, his metaphorical narrative concludes with Jerusalem shamed and silenced in the face of her husband's forgiveness.

Modern critics detect in vv. 44-58 and 59-63 subsequent additions to the original oracle (within vv. 1-43). The chapter has not grown as a consequence of the juxtaposition of originally independent oracles, Zimmerli observes, but "in a process of successive supplementation of a kernel element, the ideas of which have been developed and expanded."[393] The careful reader will detect certain shifts in thought (e.g., in vv. 44-58, Samaria and Sodom appear as Jerusalem's siblings; in vv. 59-63, their status is reduced from sisters to daughters). But these are not so significant as to frustrate his attempt to construe the oracle as a whole. And, unlike contemporary critics who question whether Ezekiel, in so vicious an oracle of indictment and punishment, would have ended on a note of reconciliation and forgiveness, the reader is open to that possibility. After all, he has encountered the phenomenon before (see 11:17-21).

393. W. Zimmerli, *Ezekiel 1: A Commentary on the Book of the Prophet Ezekiel, Chapters 1–24,* trans. R. E. Clements, Hermeneia (Philadelphia: Fortress, 1979) 334.

❖   ❖   ❖   ❖

EXCURSUS: CITIES AS FEMALES

When Israel's prophets (e.g., Hosea, Isaiah, Jeremiah, and Ezekiel) described and/or addressed cities—foreign and indigenous—as females, they were not coining novel tropes.[394] Such imagery belonged to a variegated literary convention attested not only in Israel, but also elsewhere in the ancient Near East. Biddle has identified two distinct city mythologems (mythological motifs) that influenced ancient Israel's personifications of cities as women.[395] In Mesopotamia, Akkadian and Sumerian cities were not imaged as females.[396] Yet such cities were conceived as sharing a patron/protégé relationship with their respective deities, male and female. "The most fruitful such patron relationships, in terms of the mythologem under consideration," Biddle observes, "are those between city and patron goddess, often depicted as mother of her city. Although Mesopotamian cities never fully achieve the status of goddesses, they are closely *identified* with their patroness and her fortunes."[397] In the Levant (areas bordering on the eastern coast of the Mediterranean), by contrast, cities were both *personified* as females and *deified* as goddesses.[398]

The biblical authors shunned the notion of city-as-goddess, finding it theologically problematic

394. The following discussion draws from K. P. Darr, *Isaiah's Vision and the Family of God* (Louisville: Westminster John Knox, 1994) esp. 85-135, and from K. P. Darr, "Ezekiel's Justifications of God: Teaching Troubling Texts," *JSOT* 55 (1992) 102-7.

395. M. E. Biddle, "The Figure of Lady Jerusalem: Identification, Deification and Personification of Cities in the ANE," in *The Biblical Canon in Comparative Perspective,* ed. W. W. Hallo et al., Scripture in Context 4, Ancient Near Eastern Studies and Texts 11 (Lewiston, N.Y.: Mellen, 1991) 173-94.

396. The gender of nouns meaning "city" mitigated against such personification: the Akkadian term for city (*alu*) was masculine; the Sumerian term (*URU*) was neuter.

397. Biddle, "The Figure of Lady Jerusalem," 175.

398. West Semitic languages supported the personification of cities as females, for common nouns for "city" were feminine in gender. In biblical Hebrew, e.g., עיר (*'îr*), and קריה (*qiryâ*), and קרת (*qeret*) are all feminine.

for what came to be orthodox Yahwism. Hence, they modified both Mesopotamian and West Semitic versions of the city mythologem. As in Mesopotamia, Israel's indigenious cities were conceived as having a patron deity, the (male) god Yahweh. Like their West Semitic counterparts, Israel's cities were personified as females. Within Hebrew Scripture, they appear in a variety of female roles—e.g., daughters (Isa 1:8; Lam 2:18); wives (Ezekiel 16 and 23); mothers (Isa 49:14-18); and widows (Lam 1:1).[399] These and other metaphorical depictions of cities draw upon certain (culture-specific) stereotypical associations with women (e.g., barrenness and fertility; maternal devotion, nurture, and compassion; objects of familial and conjugal love; bereavement and mourning) in order to present them not as inanimate repositories of stone and mortar, but as characters in the story of Yahweh's dealings with the world and, more specifically, with the people of Israel.[400]

Such stereotypical associations may or may not have been "true" to the lives and experiences of ancient Near Eastern females. (In our own culture, we speak of "dumb blondes" and the "terrible twos," even though hair color has nothing to do with intellect and some two-year-olds are irenic.) But they were well-established, and Israel's prophets and other poets exploited them in order to urge their audiences to particular perceptions of and attitudes toward the urban centers of their world. So, for example, referring to Zion as "daughter" might, in some contexts (e.g., Isa 1:8), predispose readers to ponder Jerusalem as a weak and vulnerable maiden. A poetic portrayal of Tyre as an aging prostitute plays off negative associations with "loose women" in order to belittle a prosperous and proud enemy stronghold (Isa 23:15-18). Personified Babylon could be said to rely on spells in order to protect her "family" (inhabitants)—a charge grounded in the ancient Near Eastern commonplace that women especially were drawn to witchcraft and sorcery (Ezek 13:17-23; Isa 47:9b).

MARRIAGE: SOCIAL INSTITUTION AND THEOLOGICAL METAPHOR

The conventional associations with females identified thus far could be applied both to foreign cities and to Israel's own urban centers (especially Samaria and Jerusalem, capitals of the northern and southern kingdoms of Israel, respectively). Within the Hebrew Bible, however, one association with women is reserved solely for indigenous cities: Only Israelite cities appear in the guise of Yahweh's wives.

In order to understand Ezekiel's adulterous wife/city imagery, we must consider it against the backdrop of marriage within the society of ancient Israel.[401] In that society, marriage was an important legal and economic transaction with crucial implications for a family's continuity, status, and day-to-day existence. But it was also, as Adler notes, an artificial bond:

> As opposed to the natural and biological ties of siblings, or parents and children, that of man and woman is artificial, created and defined by the customs of a given community. The legal codes of the Bible and Mesopotamia reflect this peculiarity of marriage with their numerous statutes regulating and defining this more frail institution.[402]

Galambush compares ancient Israelite marriage to the suzerain/vassal treaty relationship:

399. Regarding the word אלמנה ('almānâ, "widow"), see Chayim Cohen, "The Widowed City," *JANESCU* 5 (1985) 78-79, who observes: "In short, the 'widowed' city motif seems to refer to a once independent city which has become a vassal of another state."
400. For stereotypical associations with females in ancient Israel, see Darr, *Isaiah's Vision and the Family of God,* 85-123.
401. The following paragraphs are reproduced from *Isaiah's Vision and the Family of God.* Copyright © 1994 by K. P. Darr. Used by permission of Westminster John Knox Press.
402. E. J. Adler, "The Background for the Metaphor of Covenant as Marriage in the Hebrew Bible" (Ph.D. diss., University of California at Berkeley, 1989) 66-67. See also K. Grosz, "Some Aspects of the Position of Women in Nuzi," in *Women's Earliest Records from Ancient Egypt and Western Asia* (Atlanta: Scholars Press, 1989) 178.

Israelite marriage was, like vassaldom, a relationship of mutual obligation between two parties, one (the husband) superior and the other (the wife) inferior in terms of their legal status. As in a treaty agreement, the husband was required to protect the wife . . . and the wife was to obey the husband, and to refrain from sexual relationships with other men. The husband, like the suzerain, was free of any such obligation of exclusivity.[403]

Just as love is part of many an intimate marital relationship, so also "love" language appears in the Amarna letters and in certain ancient Near Eastern treaties to express the vassal's obligations to the suzerain. Vassals "loved" their suzerains by being obedient to them. Married women were expected to do no less. As many biblical texts attest, however, marriage could entail more than male provision and female faithfulness and obedience: "love" could be mutual. In the book of Isaiah, for example, emotive elements frequently are emphasized in Yahweh's speeches to Jerusalem, depicted metaphorically as his wife. Such metaphors structure the reader's perceptions of the complex and enduring relationship shared by Yahweh and Jerusalem, and sometimes threatened by the actions of *both* parties.[404]

Certain biblical authors (Ezekiel among them) sought to speak of one complex and mysterious entity (the relationship between Yahweh and Israel) in terms suggestive of another, better-known experience: the marriage relationship. The metaphor "works" because the former, like the latter, entailed a relationship between unequals. Each party incurred particular obligations toward the other (see above), but the "inferior" party (in the former, Israel; in the latter, the wife) alone was required to be obedient and faithful. Moreover, both relationships admitted complex emotions—love, jealousy, and anger.

Only Israelite cities are charged with committing adultery—cuckolding their husband (Yahweh) through illicit "intercourse" with other nations and their deities. The specter of female sexual infidelity menaced the soul of ancient Israel's patrilineal society. Said plainly, a wife's illicit affair with another man could result in a family's inheritance passing to an illegitimate heir (see Sir 23:22-23). In any event, the promiscuous daughter, wife, or levirate widow was guilty of dispensing sexual and reproductive resources not hers to control, enraging her father, husband, or father-in-law, and blemishing his family's honor. If woman is the "essential thread" joining patriarchy's social fabric, she also "indicates the seams where the fabric is subject to tears."[405]

Ancient Israel's sages cautioned their young male pupils against "out-of-bounds" females, asserting that liaisons with prostitutes and foreign women brought shame, disease, poverty, even death (Prov 2:18-19; 5:5). The married seductress was especially dangerous, since adultery enraged her cuckolded husband (Prov 6:20-35). The legal penalty for adultery was death for both parties (Lev 20:10; Deut 22:22), though biblical and extra-biblical evidence suggests that the husband had some say about the offending parties' fates. One should not simply assume that biblical laws, proverbs, narratives, and poetry depict the actual legal and social customs of ancient Israel or that those customs remained the same over time. In poetic (mostly prophetic) passages, for example:

> Figurative descriptions of penalties for female faithlessness (e.g., divorce [Hos 2:4; Jer 3:8], public stripping [whether preliminary to sexual assault, or indicative of the withdrawal of support from her husband's family, and compensation for the male's loss of honor], and mutilation) may or may not accurately reflect actual practices. What such texts do reveal, however, are both extremely negative social associations with adultery, and the intention not only to inflict physical and psychological suffering upon the woman, but also to return upon her the shame and dishonor that she has brought upon the offended man and his family (Deut 22:21).[406]

---

403. Julie Galambush, *Jerusalem in the Book of Ezekiel: The City as Yahweh's Wife*, SBLDS 130 (Atlanta: Scholars Press, 1992) 33.
404. "Three relationships demand absolute fidelity by one partner for the other," Frymer-Kensky writes, "the loyalty of vassal to suzerain, the allegiance of wife for husband, and Israel's devotion to God. Love language is used for all three." See T. Frymer-Kensky, *In the Wake of the Goddesses: Women, Culture, and the Biblical Transformation of Pagan Myth* (New York: Free Press, 1992) 146.
405. Carol Newsom, "Women and the Discourse of Patriarchal Wisdom: A Study of Proverbs 1–9," in *Gender and Difference in Ancient Israel*, ed. P. L. Day (Minneapolis: Fortress, 1989) 155.
406. K. P. Darr, *Isaiah's Vision and the Family of God* (Louisville: Westminster John Knox, 1994) 120. See also E. J. Adler, "The Background for the Metaphor of Covenant as Marriage in the Hebrew Bible" (Ph.D. diss., University of California at Berkeley, 1989) 43-57; H. McKeating, "Sanctions Against Adultery in Ancient Israelite Society, with Some Reflections on Methodology in the Study of Old Testament Ethics," *JSOT* 11 (1979) 69; and G. A. Yee, "Hosea," in *The Women's Bible Commentary*, ed. C. Newsom and S. H. Ringe (Louisville: Westminster/John Knox, 1992) 105-6.

In their descriptions of the married woman's illicit sexual activity, biblical authors often employed not only נאף (nāʾap, "to commit adultery") but also זנה (zānâ, "to commit fornication," "be a harlot").[407] Galambush terms the application of zānâ to a woman who is not, properly speaking, a prostitute a "first level" metaphorical use of that root. A "second level" metaphorical use of zānâ, derived from the first, functions in a number of biblical texts (including Ezekiel 16) to shape the reader's perception of Israelite idolatry:

> The male Israelite's worship of other gods is understood as parallel to a woman's illicit sexual activity, because in each case the offender has transferred the exclusive rights of the one in authority (at the second level, Yahweh, rather than husband or father) to a second, competing party (the other god). Unlike the first level metaphor, the second level metaphor is applied to cultic activity and *does not ordinarily entail any literal sexual activity*. The subject of the verb znh as a second level metaphor is always male or of mixed gender, since it is the Israelite male whose cultic activity (like the female's sexual activity) is legally circumscribed.[408]

Critics agree that the use of prostitution terminology in both first- and second-level metaphors is a rhetorical strategy intended to cast the offending party in the worst possible light: "The use of zānâ rather than nāʾap serves to emphasize promiscuity rather than infidelity, 'wantonness' rather than violation of marriage contract or covenant," Bird observes. "The connotations [are] of repeated, habitual, or characteristic behavior. . . . The metaphorical use of zānâ invokes two familiar and linguistically identified images of dishonor in Israelite culture, the common prostitute and the promiscuous daughter or wife."[409]

Within ancient Israel's prophetic corpus, unfaithful wife imagery first appears in Hosea 1–3. Although these chapters (attributed to the eighth-century BCE northern Israelite prophet) are notoriously difficult to interpret, the marriage metaphor clearly is integral to Hosea's message. The people of Israel, their land, and perhaps their capital city, Samaria, all appear in the guise of Yahweh's adulterous wife,[410] who, like a common prostitute, has consorted with other deities (e.g., the Canaanite god Baal):

> In 2:7 (Eng 2:5) the woman claims that her "lovers" have provided for her. The list of the woman's provisions plays on commonplaces of both the marital and the cultic domains. Within the vehicle of marriage, the provisions represent the necessities of life which the husband was obligated to provide. . . . The (personified) land has failed to understand that Yahweh was the source of this abundance and believes that Yahweh's competitors have made her fertile. Moreover, in 2:10 (Eng 2:8) Hosea . . . claims that the woman has used both her agricultural produce and silver and gold "for the baal." In response to this infidelity Yahweh will take back his gifts to the woman (2:11; Eng 2:9) and expose her publicly, his rights as the divorcing husband (2:4; Eng 2:2) of an unfaithful wife.[411]

As we shall see, Hosea's use of the metaphors of marriage and the adulterous wife have influenced Ezekiel's tirade against the city of Jerusalem in chap. 16. So, too, have the oracles in Jeremiah 2 and 3. In Jer 2:2, Yahweh commands Jeremiah to proclaim in Jerusalem's hearing both her initial, bridelike devotion to her husband and her subsequent decline into promiscuity. By Jer 2:20, the reader sees her sprawled, playing the prostitute with the baals "on every high hill and under every green tree." Similes serve further to degrade her: She is like a camel and a wild ass in heat, sniffing the wind for the scent of a potential mate (Jer 2:24). Jeremiah 3:6-11 personifies both

---

407. The legal texts of ancient Israel proscribe neither prostitution nor consorting with a prostitute. Nevertheless, biblical evidence suggests that social attitudes toward prostitutes were ambiguous at best, decidedly negative at worst. See Darr, *Isaiah's Vision and the Family of God,* 115-18, and the references cited there.

408. Julie Galambush, *Jerusalem in the Book of Ezekiel: The City as Yahweh's Wife,* SBLDS 130 (Atlanta: Scholars Press, 1992) 30-31, italics added.

409. P. Bird, " 'To Play the Harlot': An Inquiry into an Old Testament Metaphor," in *Gender and Difference in Ancient Israel,* ed. P. L. Day (Minneapolis: Fortress, 1989) 80, 89.

410. See Galambush, *Jerusalem in the Book of Ezekiel,* 44-45.

411. Ibid., 47.

Israel and Judah—not their capital cities, but the nations "themselves"—as Yahweh's adulterous wives. Although the unfaithful wife imagery of this prose passage seems especially to have influenced Ezekiel 23 (see the Commentary on 23:1-49), its reappearance testifies to the metaphor's "ancestral vitality." This phrase, coined by Wheelwright for his discussion of certain symbols, here refers to the cultural and literary life of this trope, which is adopted, adapted, and passed along from author to author, in each case bringing to new contexts the meanings and associations borne in earlier ones.[412]

Ezekiel's choice of imagery opens the door to a recasting of Jerusalem's history as the biography of an abandoned babe gone bad. Is his metaphorical narrative an allegory? Northrop Frye distinguishes between an allegory proper, in which allegorical references are "continuous throughout the narrative," and a work with "allegorical tendencies"—such that allegorical elements are "intermittent . . . picked up and dropped again at pleasure."[413] In the light of Frye's definition, I agree with J. Galambush that Ezekiel's story displays allegorical tendencies, but is not an allegory per se. While certain of its features can, with reasonable certainty, be correlated with actual events in Israel's history, the metaphorical "vehicle" is most determinative of how Ezekiel's "tenor" (Jerusalem's abominations and their consequences) makes an impact on his audience.[414]

412. Philip Wheelwright, *Metaphor and Reality* (Bloomington: Indiana University Press, 1962; 1973) 98-105.

413. N. Frye, "Allegory," in *Princeton Encyclopedia of Poetry and Poetics,* ed. A. Preminger (Princeton: Princeton University Press, 1974) 12-15; quoted in Galambush, *Jerusalem in the Book of Ezekiel,* 10-11.

414. The terms "tenor" and "vehicle" were coined by I. A. Richards. "Tenor" refers to the underlying subject of a metaphor; "vehicle" to the complete utterance conveying that subject. See I. A. Richards, *The Philosophy of Rhetoric* (Oxford: Oxford University Press, 1936) 93.

❖   ❖   ❖   ❖

Ezekiel 16:1-34, From Foundling to Queen: A Tragic Tale

Ezekiel 16:1-7, Yahweh Rescues an Infant

16 The word of the LORD came to me: [2] "Son of man, confront Jerusalem with her detestable practices [3]and say, 'This is what the Sovereign LORD says to Jerusalem: Your ancestry and birth were in the land of the Canaanites; your father was an Amorite and your mother a Hittite. [4]On the day you were born your cord was not cut, nor were you washed with water to make you clean, nor were you rubbed with salt or wrapped in cloths. [5]No one looked on you with pity or had compassion enough to do any of these things for you. Rather, you were thrown out into the open field, for on the day you were born you were despised.

[6]" 'Then I passed by and saw you kicking about in your blood, and as you lay there in your blood

16 The word of the LORD came to me: [2]Mortal, make known to Jerusalem her abominations, [3]and say, Thus says the Lord GOD to Jerusalem: Your origin and your birth were in the land of the Canaanites; your father was an Amorite, and your mother a Hittite. [4]As for your birth, on the day you were born your navel cord was not cut, nor were you washed with water to cleanse you, nor rubbed with salt, nor wrapped in cloths. [5]No eye pitied you, to do any of these things for you out of compassion for you; but you were thrown out in the open field, for you were abhorred on the day you were born.

[6]I passed by you, and saw you flailing about in your blood. As you lay in your blood, I said to you, "Live! [7]and grow up[a] like a plant of the field." You

[a]Gk Syr: Heb *Live! I made you a myriad*

NIV

I said to you, "Live!"*a* *7*I made you grow like a plant of the field. You grew up and developed and became the most beautiful of jewels.*b* Your breasts were formed and your hair grew, you who were naked and bare.

a6 A few Hebrew manuscripts, Septuagint and Syriac; most Hebrew manuscripts *"Live!" And as you lay there in your blood I said to you, "Live!"*   *b7* Or *became mature*

NRSV

grew up and became tall and arrived at full womanhood;*a* your breasts were formed, and your hair had grown; yet you were naked and bare.

*a*Cn: Heb *ornament of ornaments*

COMMENTARY

With the familiar word event formula and direct address ("The word of the LORD came to me, 'Mortal' "), Ezekiel announces Yahweh's command that he inform the accused, Jerusalem, of her abominations (תועבה *tô 'ēbâ*; various forms of its root [תעב *t'b*] will appear 11 times in this chapter). The reader recalls that many times heretofore, the prophet has charged Judah's capital and inhabitants with abominable practices—both cultic and moral (see, e.g., 5:11). In particular, the reader remembers Ezekiel's visionary tour of Jerusalem (chap. 8), where the prophet witnessed the performance of four cultic abominations within the very environs of Yahweh's Temple. Now, Ezekiel unleashes his most pernicious indictment of the city, taking up the conventional metaphor of Jerusalem as Yahweh's unfaithful wife and exploiting it in ways that, almost 2,500 years later, still shock readers.

Yahweh's first words to Jerusalem recall her dishonorable past. Born in the land of the Canaanites to non-Israelite parents,[415] she was denied basic post-natal care and abandoned to certain death in an open field (vv. 3*b*-5).[416] In exposing their infant,[417] her parents ceded all legal rights to their

child.[418] Ezekiel supplies no motivation for their lack of parental compassion (v. 5), leaving his readers to think the worst of these parents.[419]

Against all odds, the foundling is saved when Yahweh passes by and notices her flailing about in her birth blood. With the power of the spoken word God twice commands her, "In your blood, live!"[420] M. Malul identifies Yahweh's words as a formal declaration of legal adoption.[421] The scenario is reminiscent of a situation legislated in §185 of the Old Babylonian law code of King Hammurabi, which reads: "If a man has adopted an infant while still in his amniotic fluid and raised him up, that adopted child may never be reclaimed."[422]

Galambush observes that Yahweh's life-saving action has the effect of moving the infant from an excluded to a liminal, or "in-between," state. Legitimated by Yahweh's adoption, she nonetheless remains unclean "in her blood" and alone.[423] The text chronicles her growth; she flourishes (grows up) "like a sprout (צמח *ṣemaḥ*) of the field," a vegetal simile conventionally signifying an increase in population, but here descriptive of

415. "Amorite" is a general biblical designation for Canaan's indigenous population; "Hittite" refers to the people of Asia Minor who, after the fall of their empire, settled in northern Syria; they, too, are listed among the peoples of Palestine in biblical tradition. Unlike Hosea and Jeremiah, who attribute to Israel a time of bridelike devotion to Yahweh prior to "her" encounter with Canaanite culture, Ezekiel says nothing of Israel's pre-conquest period (cf. Ezekiel 20 and 23). See W. Zimmerli, *Ezekiel 1: A Commentary on the Book of the Prophet Ezekiel, Chapters 1–24,* trans. R. E. Clements, Hermeneia (Philadelphia: Fortress, 1979) 336-37.

416. This text sheds light on how newborns were tended in ancient Israel. The infant was wrapped in swaddling cloths in order to ensure that its limbs grew straight. See D. I. Block, *The Book of Ezekiel: Chapters 1–24,* NICOT (Grand Rapids: Eerdmans, 1997) 475.

417. On השליך (*hišlîk,* "expose") see M. Cogan, "A Technical Term for Exposure," *JNES* 27 (1968) 133-35.

418. See M. Malul, "Adoption of Foundlings in the Bible and Mesopotamian Documents: A Study of Some Legal Metaphors in Ezekiel 16:1-7," *JSOT* 46 (1990) 97-126.

419. Blenkinsopp observes that "unflattering allusion to ancestors is a regular feature of vituperative satire." Joseph Blenkinsopp, *Ezekiel,* IBC (Louisville: John Knox, 1990) 77. See, e.g., Gen 19:30-38.

420. Both the NRSV and the NIV omit the second command as a dittograph. Often, the plural דמים (*dāmîm*) means "bloodshed." In priestly laws (and here), however, the plural refers to bloody bodily fluids (Lev 12:4-5; 15:19; 20:18).

421. See Malul, "Adoption of Foundlings in the Bible and Mesopotamian Documents," 108-13; and Block, *Ezekiel 1–24,* 481.

422. *ANET,* 174. See also Block, *Ezekiel 1–24,* 481n. 110.

423. Galambush, *Jerusalem in the Book of Ezekiel,* 93.

physical maturation. "At full womanhood" (NRSV) is, in Hebrew, "ornament of ornaments" (i.e., the loveliest of ornaments): well-formed breasts and "sprouted" [ṣimmēaḥ] pubic hair. Ezekiel's double use of ṣāmaḥ, "to sprout," in v. 7 creates a "verbal bridge" between the images of vegetal fertility and

female puberty.[424] The text invites its readers to imagine her, nubile and stark naked. (See Reflections at 16:59-63.)

---

424. Ibid. See also Greenberg, *Ezekiel 1–20*, 276. Wevers suggests that emending "the loveliest of adornments" to read "to the (time of) menses" restores the text's original meaning. See J. W. Wevers, *Ezekiel*, NCB (London: Nelson, 1969) 121.

Ezekiel 16:8-14, God Takes a Wife

NIV

8" 'Later I passed by, and when I looked at you and saw that you were old enough for love, I spread the corner of my garment over you and covered your nakedness. I gave you my solemn oath and entered into a covenant with you, declares the Sovereign LORD, and you became mine.

9" 'I bathed*a* you with water and washed the blood from you and put ointments on you. [10]I clothed you with an embroidered dress and put leather sandals on you. I dressed you in fine linen and covered you with costly garments. [11]I adorned you with jewelry: I put bracelets on your arms and a necklace around your neck, [12]and I put a ring on your nose, earrings on your ears and a beautiful crown on your head. [13]So you were adorned with gold and silver; your clothes were of fine linen and costly fabric and embroidered cloth. Your food was fine flour, honey and olive oil. You became very beautiful and rose to be a queen. [14]And your fame spread among the nations on account of your beauty, because the splendor I had given you made your beauty perfect, declares the Sovereign LORD.

a9 Or I had bathed

NRSV

8I passed by you again and looked on you; you were at the age for love. I spread the edge of my cloak over you, and covered your nakedness: I pledged myself to you and entered into a covenant with you, says the Lord GOD, and you became mine. [9]Then I bathed you with water and washed off the blood from you, and anointed you with oil. [10]I clothed you with embroidered cloth and with sandals of fine leather; I bound you in fine linen and covered you with rich fabric.*a* [11]I adorned you with ornaments: I put bracelets on your arms, a chain on your neck, [12]a ring on your nose, earrings in your ears, and a beautiful crown upon your head. [13]You were adorned with gold and silver, while your clothing was of fine linen, rich fabric,*c* and embroidered cloth. You had choice flour and honey and oil for food. You grew exceedingly beautiful, fit to be a queen. [14]Your fame spread among the nations on account of your beauty, for it was perfect because of my splendor that I had bestowed on you, says the Lord GOD.

aMeaning of Heb uncertain

COMMENTARY

Now, Yahweh passes by her again and, seeing that she has reached the age for sexual lovemaking (דדים *dōdîm;* see also Prov 7:18; Cant 4:10; 7:10-11), spreads the edge (lit., "wing") of his cloak over her, covering her nakedness. The significance of this gesture is apparent from Ruth 3:9; it signifies "the establishment of a new relationship and the symbolic declaration of the husband to provide for the sustenance of his future wife."[425] Yahweh seals their covenant union with an oath,[426] and she becomes his spouse.

A detailed description of God's tender and extravagant care for his new bride follows in vv. 9-14. This subsection plays an important role in the chapter as a whole. How much greater will Jerusalem's guilt appear when, despite all that her husband has done for her, she turns faithless! First Yahweh washes off her blood[427] and anoints her with oil (v. 9). In the following verses readers encounter a metaphor within a metaphor as Ezekiel, who already is speaking of Jerusalem in terms suggestive of a woman, now speaks of that woman in terms suggestive of Israel's wilderness tabernacle (and, by extension, Jerusalem's Temple) and of its priests' vestments. God clothes her in רקמה (*riqmâ*), "embroidered cloth" (v. 10*a*). In Ps 45:14, this same noun (NRSV, "many-colored robes") refers to the apparel of a princess; in Judg 5:30, to elegant cloth (taken as booty). On the basis of these passages alone, the reader knows that Yahweh has spared no expense in clothing his wife. But *riqmâ* also refers to embroidered cloth used to make the curtains of the tabernacle and priestly garments (e.g., Exod 26:36; 27:16; 28:39;

35:35; 36:37; 38:18, 23; 39:29).[428] Moreover, Yahweh bedecks her with jewelry, putting bracelets upon her arms, encircling her neck with a fine chain, and placing a ring in her nose (see also Gen 24:47; Isa 3:21), earrings in her ears, and a crown upon her head (see the similar gifts mentioned in Gen 24:22, 53; Isa 61:3). He shods her feet in sandals made of the same fine leather (תחש *taḥaš*) used to cover the portable tent of meeting (v. 10*a*; e.g., Exod 25:5; 26:14; 35:7, 23; 36:19; 39:34; Num 4:25). Verse 13*a* reiterates (and so further underscores) the extravagance of Jerusalem's *haute couture* wardrobe, while v. 13*b* describes the *haute cuisine* quality of her diet: Yahweh provides bread made of סלת (*sōlet,* a fine flour), oil, and honey. *Sōlet* is identified as a component of certain sacrifices within the priestly writings (see, e.g., Ezek 46:14); Yahweh will call this mixture "my bread" in v. 19. Beneficiary of such lavish care, Jerusalem becomes extraordinarily beautiful, "fit for royalty," famous throughout the world (v. 14).

Ezekiel, who depicts Jerusalem as a royal bride, nonetheless says nothing of an (at least) initial period of "bridal devotion" to her husband (unlike his predecessors, Hosea [Hos 2:14-15] and Jeremiah [Jer 2:2]). Indeed, the reader hears nothing *about* her personal attitude until v. 15, and nowhere in the entire chapter will we hear her speak. This is no oversight. When we engage the text listening not only for words, but also for silences, we are struck by the lengths to which Ezekiel goes utterly to wipe from his oracle any positive impression of Jerusalem, save for her youthful physical beauty.[429] (See Reflections at 16:59-63.)

---

425. So P. A. Kruger, "The Hem of the Garment in Marriage: The Meaning of the Symbolic Gesture in Ruth 3:9 and Ezek 16:8," *JNSL* 12 (1984) 86.

426. Greenberg, *Ezekiel 1–20,* 278, points to the novelty of Yahweh's words in v. 8: "Nowhere [in the Hebrew Scriptures] is marriage expressly called a covenant or the husband charged with an oath. The origin of the oath image here . . . seems rather to be a fusion of the divine oath to the patriarchs to give their descendants the land of Canaan (e.g., Gen 26:3; Deut 1:8, etc.) and the solemn declaration of mutual obligation connected with the Exodus and covenant with the people (in the priestly writings and Deuteronomy)."

427. The text does not specify whether this refers to her birth blood, to the menstrual blood that signals puberty in females, or to the blood of first coitus.

428. The noun שש (*šēš*) in v. 10*a* refers to "fine linen" (NRSV), also used in constructing the tabernacle curtains and priestly vestments (Exod 26:36; 27:16; 28:39; 35:35; 36:37; 38:18; 39:29). The exact meaning of משי (*mešî*; NRSV, "rich fabric") is elusive, but the context demands that it also be luxurious fabric.

429. Elie Wiesel, "In the Bible: The Vision of Ezekiel," Andrew W. Mellon Lectures in the Humanities, Boston University, October 21, 1985.

Ezekiel 16:15-34, Jerusalem as Yahweh's Unfaithful Wife

EZEKIEL 16:15-22, CONSORTING WITH IDOLS

NIV

NIV

¹⁵" 'But you trusted in your beauty and used your fame to become a prostitute. You lavished your favors on anyone who passed by and your beauty became his.ᵃ ¹⁶You took some of your garments to make gaudy high places, where you carried on your prostitution. Such things should not happen, nor should they ever occur. ¹⁷You also took the fine jewelry I gave you, the jewelry made of my gold and silver, and you made for yourself male idols and engaged in prostitution with them. ¹⁸And you took your embroidered clothes to put on them, and you offered my oil and incense before them. ¹⁹Also the food I provided for you— the fine flour, olive oil and honey I gave you to eat—you offered as fragrant incense before them. That is what happened, declares the Sovereign LORD.

²⁰" 'And you took your sons and daughters whom you bore to me and sacrificed them as food to the idols. Was your prostitution not enough? ²¹You slaughtered my children and sacrificed themᵇ to the idols. ²²In all your detestable practices and your prostitution you did not remember the days of your youth, when you were naked and bare, kicking about in your blood.

ᵃ15 Most Hebrew manuscripts; one Hebrew manuscript (see some Septuagint manuscripts) by. Such a thing should not happen   ᵇ21 Or and made them pass through ⌊the fire⌋

NRSV

15But you trusted in your beauty, and played the whore because of your fame, and lavished your whorings on any passer-by.ᵃ ¹⁶You took some of your garments, and made for yourself colorful shrines, and on them played the whore; nothing like this has ever been or ever shall be.ᵇ ¹⁷You also took your beautiful jewels of my gold and my silver that I had given you, and made for yourself male images, and with them played the whore; ¹⁸and you took your embroidered garments to cover them, and set my oil and my incense before them. ¹⁹Also my bread that I gave you—I fed you with choice flour and oil and honey—you set it before them as a pleasing odor; and so it was, says the Lord GOD. ²⁰You took your sons and your daughters, whom you had borne to me, and these you sacrificed to them to be devoured. As if your whorings were not enough! ²¹You slaughtered my children and delivered them up as an offering to them. ²²And in all your abominations and your whorings you did not remember the days of your youth, when you were naked and bare, flailing about in your blood.

ᵃHeb adds let it be his   ᵇMeaning of Heb uncertain

COMMENTARY

Despite the "royal treatment" she has received, Jerusalem forgets her ignoble origins and the husband who has given her not just life, but abundant life. "With inconceivable blindness," Eichrodt writes, "the courtship of the divine lover is rejected for a perverse sensuality, in which all self-respect and all understanding of the holy exclusiveness of the true I-Thou relationship must necessarily go by the board. At the root of this decision is that self-assertion which, instead of accepting its privileged position as a gift from God, grabs at it as if it were a piece of

plunder it had won."⁴³⁰ Eichrodt's references to the divine lover and to his wife's "perverse sensuality" partake of Ezekiel's metaphorical vehicle. However, readers must avoid the trap of construing the following verses as *literal* descriptions of the sins of Jerusalem's inhabitants (whom she, the unfaithful wife, personifies; see Excursus: "Cities as Females," 1221-25). Again, faithless wife imagery determines the way those

430. Walther Eichrodt, *Ezekiel*, trans. Cosslett Quin, OTL (Philadelphia: Westminster, 1970) 219.

sins (in the following verses, idolatry) are depicted.[431]

Trusting in her beauty, Jerusalem "plays the prostitute," offering herself to any passer-by.[432] Ezekiel's reader remembers that Yahweh twice passed by her—once in her infancy and again after the onset of puberty—with life-saving and life-style-transforming consequences. Now, she repeatedly commits the capital offense of engaging in indiscriminate illict intercourse with others, dispensing sexual and reproductive capacities not hers to control. "It was his!" the last two words of v. 15 assert, recalling v. 8, where such capacities became Yahweh's legal property ("you became mine").

Verses 16-22 further elaborate upon the woman's "whoring" with idols. From her garments, she has constructed colorful shrines (במות bāmôt, "high places"), prostituting herself with heretofore unrivaled debauchery. This image evokes thoughts of the "loose woman"/"adulteress" whose seductive ways are described in Prov 7:16-18:

> I have decked my couch with coverings,
> colored spreads of Egyptian linen;
> I have perfumed my bed with myrrh,
> aloes, and cinnamon.
> Come, let us take our fill of love until morning;
> let us delight ourselves with love."
> (NRSV; see also Isa 57:7)

Ezekiel, however, has substituted bāmôt (cultic sites where foreign deities are worshiped; see 2 Kgs 21:3; see also the Commentary on Ezekiel 6)

for "bed" or "couch," allowing the literal referent (Judah's high places) to peek through his metaphorical description.

Moreover, Jerusalem has taken her gold and silver jewelry, Yahweh's wedding gifts, and made from them male images with which she likewise "plays the whore" (see also 7:20). Verse 17 may refer to phallic images, though, as Block observes, vv. 18-19 suggest that full male figures more likely are in view.[433] Jerusalem garbs these images in her God-given embroidered garments and sets before them oil and incense. (Again, the language of literal cultic activity intrudes, since incense plays a role in worship, both licit and illicit; see 8:11.) She offers her food, "[Yahweh's] bread," to them as a "pleasing odor."[434] Perhaps most horrific, she delivers Yahweh's sons and daughters as food sacrifices to these images (vv. 20-21). Scholars debate whether in some contexts the phrase "to make pass over by [or through] fire" refers only to the dedication of an infant to a deity. Here, however, actual child sacrifice is meant.[435] References to child sacrifice appear elsewhere in Hebrew Scripture (e.g., 2 Kgs 16:3; 21:6; 23:10; Jer 3:24; 7:31; 19:5; 32:35; see also Isa 57:9). The practice, probably borrowed from the Phoenicians, appears to have entered Israel during the eighth–seventh centuries BCE. Deuteronomy 12:31; 18:10; and Lev 18:21; 20:1-5 proscribe it. Only in Ezek 16:20-21 does the reader "see" the city as mother—and a monstrous one she is! In all these activities, Jerusalem has forgotten her own infancy when, "naked and bare" she was exposed in her birth blood (v. 22). (See Reflections at 16:59-63.)

---

431. Many critics assume that behind Ezekiel's metaphorical descriptions of Jerusalem's offenses lies the reality of "cultic prostitution." See R. A. Oden, *The Bible Without Theology: The Theological Tradition and Alternatives to It* (San Francisco: Harper & Row, 1987) 132, who suggests that cultic prostitution should be investigated as "an *accusation* rather than a *reality.*"

432. Galambush conceptualizes the "first level" metaphorical application of זנה (*znh*, "adultery") to a married woman who is not actually a prostitute but who is acting as if she were. Julie Galambush, *Jerusalem in the Book of Ezekiel: The City as Yahweh's Wife,* SBLDS 130 (Atlanta: Scholars Press, 1992) 28-29.

433. D. I. Block, *The Book of Ezekiel: Chapters 1–24,* NICOT (Grand Rapids: Eerdmans, 1997) 489.

434. "Mesopotamia and Egypt offer examples of the ritual clothing of the cult image and the daily offerings, including honey, incense and oil," Greenberg observes. He notes that Ezekiel's present "allusions to Israelite idolatrous practices are unique in the Bible." Moshe Greenberg, *Ezekiel 1–20,* AB 22 (Garden City, N.Y.: Doubleday, 1983) 280.

435. Ibid., 281.

EZEKIEL 16:23-34, CONSORTING WITH FOREIGN NATIONS

NIV

23" 'Woe! Woe to you, declares the Sovereign LORD. In addition to all your other wickedness, 24you built a mound for yourself and made a lofty shrine in every public square. 25At the head of every street you built your lofty shrines and degraded your beauty, offering your body with increasing promiscuity to anyone who passed by. 26You engaged in prostitution with the Egyptians, your lustful neighbors, and provoked me to anger with your increasing promiscuity. 27So I stretched out my hand against you and reduced your territory; I gave you over to the greed of your enemies, the daughters of the Philistines, who were shocked by your lewd conduct. 28You engaged in prostitution with the Assyrians too, because you were insatiable; and even after that, you still were not satisfied. 29Then you increased your promiscuity to include Babylonia,^{a} a land of merchants, but even with this you were not satisfied.

30" 'How weak-willed you are, declares the Sovereign LORD, when you do all these things, acting like a brazen prostitute! 31When you built your mounds at the head of every street and made your lofty shrines in every public square, you were unlike a prostitute, because you scorned payment.

32" 'You adulterous wife! You prefer strangers to your own husband! 33Every prostitute receives a fee, but you give gifts to all your lovers, bribing them to come to you from everywhere for your illicit favors. 34So in your prostitution you are the opposite of others; no one runs after you for your favors. You are the very opposite, for you give payment and none is given to you.

^{a}29 Or Chaldea

NRSV

23After all your wickedness (woe, woe to you! says the Lord GOD), 24you built yourself a platform and made yourself a lofty place in every square; 25at the head of every street you built your lofty place and prostituted your beauty, offering yourself to every passer-by, and multiplying your whoring. 26You played the whore with the Egyptians, your lustful neighbors, multiplying your whoring, to provoke me to anger. 27Therefore I stretched out my hand against you, reduced your rations, and gave you up to the will of your enemies, the daughters of the Philistines, who were ashamed of your lewd behavior. 28You played the whore with the Assyrians, because you were insatiable; you played the whore with them, and still you were not satisfied. 29You multiplied your whoring with Chaldea, the land of merchants; and even with this you were not satisfied.

30How sick is your heart, says the Lord GOD, that you did all these things, the deeds of a brazen whore; 31building your platform at the head of every street, and making your lofty place in every square! Yet you were not like a whore, because you scorned payment. 32Adulterous wife, who receives strangers instead of her husband! 33Gifts are given to all whores; but you gave your gifts to all your lovers, bribing them to come to you from all around for your whorings. 34So you were different from other women in your whorings: no one solicited you to play the whore; and you gave payment, while no payment was given to you; you were different.

COMMENTARY

Verses 23-34 continue Ezekiel's tirade against Yahweh's wicked wife. But while his metaphorical "vehicle" remains the same, his "tenor" shifts. Now he accuses Jerusalem of illicit liaisons with other nations. Unfaithful wife imagery was well-suited not only to idolatry accusations, but also to prophetic condemnations of international treaties, because both activities entailed trusting in/relying upon an entity other than Yahweh. (Moreover, treaty making often opened the door to the inferior party's worship of the superior party's deities.)

The parenthetical comment " 'woe, woe to you!' says the LORD God" (v. 23) may (unbeknownst to the ancient reader) be the product of a later glossator wishing further to rebuke the city (like the last two words of v. 15—"it was his"—it does not appear in the LXX). Verses 24-25 twice repeat, using different terms, the accusation already lodged in v. 16. Jerusalem has constructed a platform (גב *gab*), a lofty place (רמה *rāmâ*) in every square.[436] At the head of every street, she has built her *rāmâ* and prostituted her beauty, spreading her legs to every passer-by (the NRSV's "offering yourself" is a euphemistic way of rendering the graphic Hebrew phrase; see also NIV).

First, Ezekiel accuses the city of repeatedly playing "the whore with the Egyptians, your 'lustful' neighbors."[437] For centuries Israel and Judah had sought Egyptian assistance in warding off aggressive Mesopotamian powers. The prophet Isaiah condemned his people's policy:

> Alas for those who go down to Egypt for help
>   and who rely on horses,
> who trust in chariots because they are many
>   and in horsemen because they are very strong,
> but who do not look to the Holy One of Israel
>   or consult the LORD!
>
> .   .   .   .
>
> The Egyptians are human, and not God;
>   their horses are flesh, and not spirit.
> When the LORD stretches out his hand,
>   the helper will stumble, and the one helped
>   will fall,
>   and they will all perish together.
> (Isa 31:1, 3 NRSV)[438]

According to one famous eighth-century BCE incident (recorded in 2 Kings 18–19; Isaiah 36–37), Judah's King Hezekiah hoped for Egyptian aid when Jerusalem was in imminent danger of falling to Assyrian forces led by King Sennacherib. Within earshot of the city's walls, Sennacherib's Rabshakeh (commander-in-chief) shouted a demoralizing message to Hezekiah's representatives, ridiculing his ostensible trust in Egyptian assistance: "See, you are relying now on Egypt, that broken reed of a staff, which will pierce the hand of anyone who leans on it. Such is Pharaoh

king of Egypt to all who rely on him" (2 Kgs 18:21 = Isa 36:6), and ultimately in Yahweh, and emphasizing God's inability to rescue Jerusalem. In this crisis, Egypt indeed proved itself to be a "broken reed of a staff." According to biblical tradition, however, God delivered Jerusalem from Sennacherib's army when, in a single night, Yahweh's messenger slew 185,000 Assyrian soldiers.

Sennacherib's Annals give a different account of Judah's rebellion and its consequences.[439] Not only was the king able to shatter Hezekiah's anti-Assyrian coalition, with its hopes of Egyptian support, but also Hezekiah was forced to render an enormous tribute. Moreover, his kingdom was diminished, for Sennacherib turned former Judean territory over to Ashdod, Ekron, and Gaza, three Philistine cities. Ezekiel appears to have this incident in mind when, in v. 27, he refers to the reducing of Jerusalem's "rations" and to giving her up to "the daughters [cities] of the Philistines." His further comment that these females experience shame at Jerusalem's depravity (זמה *zimmâ*; see also Lev 18:17; Judg 20:6; Jer 13:27) is quite the insult, for if even wicked Philistine cities regard Jerusalem's activities as degrading, they must be horrific indeed!

Second, Ezekiel accuses Yahweh's wife of insatiable whoring with the Assyrians (see also Jer 2:18*b*, 36*b*). Already in the eighth century, the prophet Hosea excoriated the northern kingdom of Israel for courting Assyrian favor during the reign of King Menahem (c. 745–738 BCE):

> For they have gone up to Assyria,
>   a wild ass wandering alone;
>   Ephraim has bargained for lovers.
> Though they bargain with the nations,
>   I will now gather them up.
> They shall soon writhe
>   under the burden of kings and princes.
> (Hos 8:9 NRSV)[440]

Eventually, Menahem was forced to surrender the Galilee region of his kingdom and to pay a large tribute to Assyria's king. But after only a few years (721 BCE), Samaria fell to the Assyrians.

Judean dependence upon, and eventual subjection to, Assyria began when Judah's King Ahaz (735–715 BCE) sent an offer of vassaldom and a

---

436. The LXX regularly renders *gab* as "brothel." See Greenberg, *Ezekiel 1–20*, 281-82.

437. Again, both the NRSV and the NIV employ a euphemism, in this case further blunting a meaning already expressed euphemistically by Ezekiel. The MT reads "big of flesh" (גדלי בשר *gidlê bāśār*), but "flesh" refers to the penis (Gen 17:13; Lev 15:2-3, 7).

438. See also Isaiah 20; 30:1-3; 36:6, 9; Jer 2:18*a*, 36*a*.

439. See *ANET*, 287-88.

440. See also Jer 22:20-23; 30:14; Lam 1:19.

gift to Tiglath-pileser III in exchange for help at a time when the kings of northern Israel and Syria were conspiring to conquer Jerusalem and to replace him with a more compliant partner in their plan to repel Assyrian hegemony (733–32 BCE; see 2 Kgs 16:5-9; Isaiah 7–8). Throughout the following century, Judah remained an Assyrian vassal, despite occasional attempts at revolt.

Third, Ezekiel accuses Jerusalem of multiple whorings with "the land of traders," Chaldea (Babylon).[441] Hezekiah was, it seems, the first of Judah's kings to court favor with the Babylonians. According to 2 Kgs 20:12-19 (=Isa 39:1-8), he welcomed Babylonian envoys to his palace and even showed them Judah's treasure troves in an effort to find favor with their king, Merodach-baladan. During the city's final days, King Zedekiah's advisers were divided, some urging reliance on Egypt, others advising capitulation to the Babylonians—now intent upon controlling

all of western Asia. Jeremiah supported the latter policy, convinced that Babylon was Yahweh's agent of Judah's destruction.

Her Chaldean consorts also prove unable to satisfy Jerusalem's lust (v. 29). Verse 30 begins with a divine outburst: "How sick is your heart!" Working the streets, she has nonetheless spurned the harlot's hire (אתנן 'etnan) or fee. Though married to (under the control of) Yahweh, she procures strangers (זרים zārîm). Greenberg explains the significance of Ezekiel's word choice:

> "Strangers" has, as its first sense, men outside the marriage bond (cf. its use in the identical metaphor in Jer 2:25; 3:13; see feminine *zara* in Prov 2:16; 5:3, etc. and *zarim* of bastards in Hosea 5:7). It also has overtones of foreign nations (Ezek 7:21; 11:9; Lam 5:2) and foreign gods (Deut 32:16, where it [parallels] "abominations")—thus in a word it embraces the whole range of infidelities referred to in this passage.[442]

נדה (*Nēdeh*), a "gift," is given to every prostitute, yet she gives her gifts (from Yahweh) to all her lovers (v. 33). In short, she has "solicited instead of being solicited . . . paid fees instead of being paid fees" (v. 34). (See Reflections at 16:59-63.)

---

441. Literally, "the land of Canaan." "Canaan" means "trade," and "Canaanite" came to be used as a general term for a trader (see Job 40:30; Prov 31:24; Isa 23:8; Zech 14:21). Behind this phrase may lie the exiles' experience of Babylonia as a thriving trade center. See W. Zimmerli, *Ezekiel 1: A Commentary on the Book of the Prophet Ezekiel, Chapters 1–24,* trans. R. E. Clements, Hermeneia (Philadelphia: Fortress, 1979) 362; Moshe Greenberg, *Ezekiel 1–20,* AB 22 (Garden City, N.Y.: Doubleday, 1983) 282.

442. Greenberg, *Ezekiel 1–20,* 284-85.

Ezekiel 16:35-43, Jerusalem's Mutilation and Murder

35" 'Therefore, you prostitute, hear the word of the LORD! [36]This is what the Sovereign LORD says: Because you poured out your wealth[a] and exposed your nakedness in your promiscuity with your lovers, and because of all your detestable idols, and because you gave them your children's blood, [37]therefore I am going to gather all your lovers, with whom you found pleasure, those you loved as well as those you hated. I will gather them against you from all around and will strip you in front of them, and they will see all your nakedness. [38]I will sentence you to the punishment of women who commit adultery and who shed blood; I will bring upon you the blood vengeance of my wrath and jealous anger. [39]Then

[a]36 Or lust

35Therefore, O whore, hear the word of the LORD: [36]Thus says the Lord GOD, Because your lust was poured out and your nakedness uncovered in your whoring with your lovers, and because of all your abominable idols, and because of the blood of your children that you gave to them, [37]therefore, I will gather all your lovers, with whom you took pleasure, all those you loved and all those you hated; I will gather them against you from all around, and will uncover your nakedness to them, so that they may see all your nakedness. [38]I will judge you as women who commit adultery and shed blood are judged, and bring blood upon you in wrath and jealousy. [39]I will deliver you into their hands, and they shall throw down your platform and break down your lofty

NIV

I will hand you over to your lovers, and they will tear down your mounds and destroy your lofty shrines. They will strip you of your clothes and take your fine jewelry and leave you naked and bare. [40]They will bring a mob against you, who will stone you and hack you to pieces with their swords. [41]They will burn down your houses and inflict punishment on you in the sight of many women. I will put a stop to your prostitution, and you will no longer pay your lovers. [42]Then my wrath against you will subside and my jealous anger will turn away from you; I will be calm and no longer angry.

[43]" 'Because you did not remember the days of your youth but enraged me with all these things, I will surely bring down on your head what you have done, declares the Sovereign LORD. Did you not add lewdness to all your other detestable practices?

NRSV

places; they shall strip you of your clothes and take your beautiful objects and leave you naked and bare. [40]They shall bring up a mob against you, and they shall stone you and cut you to pieces with their swords. [41]They shall burn your houses and execute judgments on you in the sight of many women; I will stop you from playing the whore, and you shall also make no more payments. [42]So I will satisfy my fury on you, and my jealousy shall turn away from you; I will be calm, and will be angry no longer. [43]Because you have not remembered the days of your youth, but have enraged me with all these things; therefore, I have returned your deeds upon your head, says the Lord GOD.

Have you not committed lewdness beyond all your abominations?

COMMENTARY

With "therefore," followed by the vocative ("O whore"), and the messenger formula ("Thus says the Lord GOD"), the sentencing process begins. First Yahweh summarizes his wife's offenses: "Because your lust was poured out and your nakedness uncovered in your whoring with your lovers, and because of all your abominable idols, and because of the blood of your children that you gave to them." In rendering the initial clause as "Because your lust was poured out," the NRSV (cf. NIV) again translates euphemistically. As Greenberg and Block observe, the meaning of the second term in the difficult expression השפך נחשתך (*hiššāpēk nĕḥuštēk*, "you poured out your X") is illumined by its Akkadian cognate *nahšatu* ("abnormal female genital discharge," from Akkadian *nahāšu*, "to overflow"). Here, however, "Ezekiel has transformed a pathological expression into an erotic image," such that the term now refers to the lubricating fluid discharged by sexually aroused women.[443] With such language,

Ezekiel has pushed the vehicle of female sexual imagery to its limits.

A second "therefore" introduces the sentence per se. Yahweh will summon all his wife's "lovers"—ally and foe—and strip her naked before them. Here, the reader recalls not only that public stripping (whether preliminary to sexual assault or as a sign of the withdrawal of support from her husband's family, and compensation for its loss of honor) was ostensibly among the cuckolded husband's punishments of an adulteress wife (see Jer 13:26; Hos 2:9-10), but also that in her infancy and adolescence, Jerusalem was herself stark naked (16:7-8). Her lovers will destroy her platforms and lofty places, despoil her, and assemble a mob to stone her, stab her with swords, and burn her houses (here also, the metaphor has slipped a bit) "in the sight of many women."[444] Contrary to Israelite law, adulterous Jerusalem's consorts do not suffer the death penalty alongside

443. D. I. Block, *The Book of Ezekiel: Chapters 1–24,* NICOT (Grand Rapids: Eerdmans, 1997) 500; see also Moshe Greenberg, "NAḤṢAT (Ezek 16:36): Another Hebrew Cognate of Akk. *nahāṣu*," in *Essays on the Ancient Near East in Memory of Jacob Joel Finkelstein,* ed. M. deJong Ellis (Hamden, Conn.: Archon, 1977) 85-86.

444. This last phrase can be construed in two ways. On the one hand, "women" might refer to other (female) cities in Judah and beyond. On the other hand, it might refer to actual women, for whom witnessing Jerusalem's execution serves as an object lesson. The reader need not choose one of these interpretive options to the exclusion of the other. Ezekiel's language is brimful of multiple levels of meaning.

her. Instead, they function as Yahweh's agents in her execution.

Hals observes that to this point, Yahweh's feelings concerning his wife's betrayal are not mentioned explicitly.[445] With v. 42, however, God acknowledges his fury and jealousy. Jerusalem's mutilation and murder will have a cathartic effect upon those emotions, leaving God calm, his anger abated. Lest the reader be troubled by the extravagance of violence portrayed in previous verses, Yahweh declares that in carrying out Jerusalem's bloody execution (directly and by proxy), he has only "returned [her] deeds upon [her] head." The rhetorical question of v. 43*b* demands Jerusalem's own assent, both to her culpability and to Yahweh's justice. (See Reflections at 16:59-63.)

445. Ronald M. Hals, *Ezekiel*, FOTL 19 (Grand Rapids: Eerdmans, 1989) 107.

Ezekiel 16:44-58, Like Mother, Like Daughter(s)

NIV	NRSV
44" 'Everyone who quotes proverbs will quote this proverb about you: "Like mother, like daughter." 45You are a true daughter of your mother, who despised her husband and her children; and you are a true sister of your sisters, who despised their husbands and their children. Your mother was a Hittite and your father an Amorite. 46Your older sister was Samaria, who lived to the north of you with her daughters; and your younger sister, who lived to the south of you with her daughters, was Sodom. 47You not only walked in their ways and copied their detestable practices, but in all your ways you soon became more depraved than they. 48As surely as I live, declares the Sovereign LORD, your sister Sodom and her daughters never did what you and your daughters have done.	44See, everyone who uses proverbs will use this proverb about you, "Like mother, like daughter." 45You are the daughter of your mother, who loathed her husband and her children; and you are the sister of your sisters, who loathed their husbands and their children. Your mother was a Hittite and your father an Amorite. 46Your elder sister is Samaria, who lived with her daughters to the north of you; and your younger sister, who lived to the south of you, is Sodom with her daughters. 47You not only followed their ways, and acted according to their abominations; within a very little time you were more corrupt than they in all your ways. 48As I live, says the Lord GOD, your sister Sodom and her daughters have not done as you and your daughters have done. 49This
49" 'Now this was the sin of your sister Sodom: She and her daughters were arrogant, overfed and unconcerned; they did not help the poor and needy. 50They were haughty and did detestable things before me. Therefore I did away with them as you have seen. 51Samaria did not commit half the sins you did. You have done more detestable things than they, and have made your sisters seem righteous by all these things you have done. 52Bear your disgrace, for you have furnished some justification for your sisters. Because your sins were more vile than theirs, they appear more righteous than you. So then, be ashamed and bear your disgrace, for you have made your sisters appear righteous.	was the guilt of your sister Sodom: she and her daughters had pride, excess of food, and prosperous ease, but did not aid the poor and needy. 50They were haughty, and did abominable things before me; therefore I removed them when I saw it. 51Samaria has not committed half your sins; you have committed more abominations than they, and have made your sisters appear righteous by all the abominations that you have committed. 52Bear your disgrace, you also, for you have brought about for your sisters a more favorable judgment; because of your sins in which you acted more abominably than they, they are more in the right than you. So be ashamed, you also, and bear your disgrace, for you have made your sisters appear righteous.
53" 'However, I will restore the fortunes of Sodom and her daughters and of Samaria and her daughters, and your fortunes along with them,	53I will restore their fortunes, the fortunes of Sodom and her daughters and the fortunes of

NIV

[54] so that you may bear your disgrace and be ashamed of all you have done in giving them comfort. [55] And your sisters, Sodom with her daughters and Samaria with her daughters, will return to what they were before; and you and your daughters will return to what you were before. [56] You would not even mention your sister Sodom in the day of your pride, [57] before your wickedness was uncovered. Even so, you are now scorned by the daughters of Edom[a] and all her neighbors and the daughters of the Philistines—all those around you who despise you. [58] You will bear the consequences of your lewdness and your detestable practices, declares the LORD.

[a]*57* Many Hebrew manuscripts and Syriac; most Hebrew manuscripts, Septuagint and Vulgate *Aram*

NRSV

Samaria and her daughters, and I will restore your own fortunes along with theirs, [54] in order that you may bear your disgrace and be ashamed of all that you have done, becoming a consolation to them. [55] As for your sisters, Sodom and her daughters shall return to their former state, Samaria and her daughters shall return to their former state, and you and your daughters shall return to your former state. [56] Was not your sister Sodom a byword in your mouth in the day of your pride, [57] before your wickedness was uncovered? Now you are a mockery to the daughters of Aram[a] and all her neighbors, and to the daughters of the Philistines, those all around who despise you. [58] You must bear the penalty of your lewdness and your abominations, says the LORD.

[a]Another reading is *Edom*

COMMENTARY

The second major section of Ezekiel's oracle further belittles Jerusalem by disparaging her birth family in ways that evoke, but go far beyond, vv. 3-5. Every proverb propounder, Yahweh states, will say of her, "Like mother, like daughter" (for a definition and discussion of "proverb" or "traditional saying," see the Commentary on 12:21-25).[446] The meaning of this brief alliterative traditional saying (כאמה בתה *kĕ'immâ bittàh*), like all others, depends upon the context in which it is "performed." The same proverb, uttered by someone wishing to compliment the obedient daughter of a well-respected mother, would be positive. Here, by contrast, context (including the immediately following statement about the "mother," who loathes both her husband and her children) leaves no doubt that an insult is intended. Verse 45*b* introduces new characters in Ezekiel's oracle: Jerusalem has sisters, and the proverb, "Like mother, like daughter," applies to them as well, since they also "loathed their husbands and their children." This verse also repeats v. 3, though in

446. See also T. Polk, "Paradigms, Parables, and Měšālîm: On Reading the māšāl in Scripture," *CBQ* 45 (1983) 575; C. R. Fontaine, *Traditional Sayings in the Old Testament: A Contextual Study,* Bible and Literature Series 5 (Sheffield: Almond, 1982) 244-45; and K. P. Darr, *Isaiah's Vision and the Family of God* (Louisville: Westminster John Knox, 1994) 205-17.

this case, the Hittite mother appropriately precedes her Amorite husband.

Now, Ezekiel elaborates upon his brief reference to Jerusalem's "sister" cities. The eldest is Samaria (capital of the former northern kingdom) who, along with her "daughters" (surrounding towns) lived to her left (north, if one is facing east); the youngest is Sodom, who with her "daughters" lived to her right (south). The reader may not be struck by Ezekiel's claim that Samaria is Jerusalem's sibling, but the assertion that Sodom, a non-Israelite city renowned for its wickedness, is also her sister is both shocking and particularly degrading (see Deut 29:23; Amos 4:11; Isa 1:9, 10; 3:9; 13:19; Zeph 2:9; Jer 23:14; 49:18; 50:40; Lam 4:6). Not only has Yahweh's wife followed in the footsteps of her sisters, but also within a brief span of time, her corruption has exceeded theirs (v. 47). Yahweh's oath ("As I live") and the signatory formula ("thus says the Lord GOD") underscore God's assertion that neither Sodom nor its settlements has rivaled Jerusalem's evildoings. "This was the guilt of your sister Sodom," Yahweh declares. Within the context of chap. 16, the reader most likely expects to hear of Sodom's sexual misdeeds (see Gen 19:1-11). Instead, God accuses both her and her daughters of hubris, gluttony, and affluence, which blinded them to the sufferings of the poor and the needy (see Deut 8:12; 32:15). Haughty, they committed abominations before God. With the appearance of תועבה (tô'ēbâ), the reader may impute sexual sins to Sodom also, for the same noun refers to Jerusalem's "abominations." Jerusalem, however, grew to become Yahweh's wife. Ezekiel does not claim the same status for Sodom, a foreign city. God sees the deeds performed "before my face" and "does away with" (NIV) both city and settlements—a relatively benign description of the holocaust of tradition (Gen 19:24-26).

Samaria, herself the object of prophetic scorn and condemnations, here is said not to have committed half of Jerusalem's sins (see also Jer 3:11: "Faithless Israel has shown herself less guilty than false Judah"). Indeed, so great have been Jerusalem's abominations that her sisters appear righteous by comparison! Here, indeed, is a heinous insult, and it grows worse as Yahweh elaborates upon it. Jerusalem is further disgraced to discover that her abominations cause God to soften his treatment of her already-deceased siblings. Greenberg elaborates:

Inasmuch as Jerusalem has debased herself more than her sisters, a decision of God to forgive and restore her must in all fairness entail the same for her sisters. But since she boasted of her superiority... elevating them to her level must be humiliating to her. Furthermore, the cases of her sisters

being better than hers, their restoration will take precedence over hers ... so that hers can be said to be incidental to theirs ("among them"). Jerusalem's pride is thoroughly deflated.[447]

The notion that Jerusalem might "console" her sisters, not from a position of superiority, but because her guilt is greater than theirs, robs Yahweh's declaration that she and her daughters will be restored to their former state of much of the optimism it might otherwise evoke in the audience.[448] Once Sodom was a byword on the lips of prideful Jerusalem. Now Jerusalem becomes a mockery to the "daughters" of Aram and her neighbors,[449] as well as to the daughters of the Philistines (see v. 27) and all those who despise her. The signatory formula at the conclusion of v. 58 underscores Yahweh's judgment: "You must bear the penalty of your lewdness and your abominations!" That penalty includes deep disgrace, overwhelming guilt, and mockery. (See Reflections at 16:59-63.)

447. Greenberg, *Ezekiel 1–20*, 289-90.

448. The reader, of course, knows that Yahweh's wife (and the Jerusalemites she embodies) was indeed multilated and murdered by her former "lover." From his perspective, Ezekiel's way of talking about the city's restoration (to this point in the oracle) functions both as a grim reminder of her abominable past and as an warning that in the future she must remember that past with shame, reject her former attitudes and behaviors, and conduct herself as a faithful and obedient wife should.

449. The LXX reads "of Syria"; the Syriac reads "Edom." As Greenberg, *Ezekiel 1–20*, 290, observes, the Aramaeans do not elsewhere appear among Israel's enemies.

Ezekiel 16:59-63, Remembering, Renewal, and Shame

NIV

59" 'This is what the Sovereign LORD says: I will deal with you as you deserve, because you have despised my oath by breaking the covenant. 60Yet I will remember the covenant I made with you in the days of your youth, and I will establish an everlasting covenant with you. 61Then you will remember your ways and be ashamed when you receive your sisters, both those who are older than you and those who are younger. I will give them to you as daughters, but not on the basis of my covenant with you. 62So I will establish my covenant with you, and you will know that I am

NRSV

59Yes, thus says the Lord GOD: I will deal with you as you have done, you who have despised the oath, breaking the covenant; 60yet I will remember my covenant with you in the days of your youth, and I will establish with you an everlasting covenant. 61Then you will remember your ways, and be ashamed when I[a] take your sisters, both your elder and your younger, and give them to you as daughters, but not on account of my[b] covenant with you. 62I will establish my covenant with you, and you shall know that I am the LORD,

[a]Syr: Heb *you*   [b]Heb lacks *my*

NIV

the LORD. ⁶³Then, when I make atonement for you for all you have done, you will remember and be ashamed and never again open your mouth because of your humiliation, declares the Sovereign LORD.' "

NRSV

⁶³in order that you may remember and be confounded, and never open your mouth again because of your shame, when I forgive you all that you have done, says the Lord GOD.

COMMENTARY

In this, the final section of Ezekiel's lengthy oracle, the prophet both fuses elements from its first two parts and brings his diatribe against Yahweh's wanton wife to a bittersweet conclusion. After its initial messenger formula, v. 59 states, "I will deal[450] with you as you have done, you who have despised the oath, breaking the covenant."[451] Here, as in v. 43, the prophet attempts to blunt any charge that Yahweh's treatment of his wife is unjust, disproportionate to her crimes, by presenting her punishment as a tit-for-tat consequence of her own doings.

Verse 59*b* characterizes Jerusalem's sin with language evocative of v. 8: Yahweh swore (ואשבע *wāʾeššābaʿ*) an oath to her and entered into a covenant with her. She, by contrast, has "despised the oath, breaking the covenant." The reader, interpreting this charge within the world of Ezekiel's metaphorical narrative, construes it to mean that wanton Jerusalem has ignored, if not abandoned, her wifely obligations to Yahweh, her husband. Yet "covenant" is so theologically freighted a term within the Hebrew Bible that upon further reflection, the reader might well enrich this initial construal with a broader range of associations surrounding that concept. Greenberg maintains that underlying the oath image in v. 8 is "a fusion of the divine oath to the patriarchs . . . and the solemn declaration of mutual obligation connected with the Exodus and covenant with the people (in the priestly writings and Deuteronomy)."[452]

Fundamental to all of Jerusalem's abominations

has been her failure to *remember* (v. 43 began with the admonition, "Because you have not remembered the days of your youth, but have enraged me with all these things"). Yahweh, by contrast, states most emphatically that after her punishment, "*I* will remember my covenant with you in the days of your youth." This act of remembering motivates God to (re)establish with her an eternal covenant. For the reader, versed in other biblical passages, including Leviticus 26, the notion that God might "remember" a covenant of old and be reconciled with his partner is not new:

> But if they [the Israelites] confess their iniquity and the iniquity of their ancestors, in that they committed treachery against me and, moreover, that they continued hostile to me . . . then will I remember my covenant with Jacob; I will remember also my covenant with Isaac and also my covenant with Abraham, and I will remember the land. . . . I will not spurn them, or abhor them so as to destroy them utterly and break my covenant with them; for I am the Lord their God; but I will remember in their favor the covenant with their ancestors whom I brought out of the land of Egypt in the sight of the nations, to be their God: I am the Lord (Lev 26:40, 42, 44-45).

Finally Jerusalem will remember her ways and be ashamed when Yahweh takes her sisters, the elder (Samaria and her daughters) and the younger (Sodom and her daughters), and gives them to her as daughters, dependents upon rejuvenated Jerusalem. The final two Hebrew words of v. 61 (NRSV, "but not on account of my covenant with you"; NIV, "but not on the basis of my covenant with you") are better rendered as "though not as participants in your covenant."[453] Here, the sense seems to be that although Samaria and Sodom,

450. *Qere* and multiple manuscripts. The MT suggests "you [m.] do." See GKC 44 *i*. I take this form to be a converted perfect ("I will do [deal]"); see GKC 112 *x*.

451. See Block's explanation of the significance of "oath" (אלה *ʾālâ*). D. I. Block, *The Book of Ezekiel: Chapters 1–24,* NICOT (Grand Rapids: Eerdmans, 1997) 515.

452. Greenberg, *Ezekiel 1–20,* 278.

453. W. Zimmerli, *Ezekiel 1: A Commentary on the Book of the Prophet Ezekiel, Chapters 1–24,* trans. R. E. Clements, Hermeneia (Philadelphia: Fortress, 1979) 333.

formerly described as Jerusalem's more righteous siblings (in the light of her greater abominations), will be restored, their status will be subordinated to her own. Once sisters (independent cities), now daughters (dependent towns), they will become part of Judah's territory, but they will not partake of Jerusalem's unique covenant (marriage) relationship with Yahweh.[454]

"I will establish my covenant with you [fem. sing.]," Yahweh reiterates, "and you shall know that I am Yahweh." Here appears the recognition formula that so often concludes Ezekiel's oracles and now reveals the purpose of all God's dealings with his faithless wife: that she be forced to recognize and acknowledge her husband's sovereignty, with its full implications for how she conducts her life in covenant with him. "For Israel," Davis writes, "remembering the past and acknowledging YHWH are inseparable elements of a complex interaction. Israel is brought to recognize YHWH through the same kind of restorative acts by which it was first constituted as a nation. These stir Israel's memory and sense of shame at its own deeds, and the contrast between its deserving and what YHWH has done leads to a deeper understanding of this God before whom Israel stands for judgment and blessing."[455]

Verse 63 consists of a long result clause. When Jerusalem is able truly to recognize and acknowledge Yahweh's sovereignty, she will remember her past (i.e., Yahweh's faithfulness and her own sin-drenched biography). She will be confounded and "never open [her] mouth again because of [her] shame," when Yahweh forgives all that she has done. M. Odell has noted the theological problem raised by vv. 62-63, in which the conventional order—awareness of sin followed by forgiveness—is reversed. "Jerusalem feels shame only after God forgives and, furthermore, is commanded to feel shame because God forgives." Ezekiel's sequence should be interpreted neither as an "inferior understanding of divine grace," Odell argues, nor as a statement of "the classic paradox of the workings of divine grace in the midst of human feelings of unworthiness." In ancient Israelite society, shame often had to do with a loss of status. While that loss might be the consequence of an individual's or a group's own failing, the experience of shame could also entail assigning blame to another for what that party did or failed to do. In such cases, "the expression of shame is the opposite of what we would consider the feeling of unworthiness; rather, it is the expression of an individual's outrage that others do not acknowledge and respond to his or her claims."[456]

Odell finds this social attitude toward shame-as-blame reflected in Israel's complaint psalms. In such psalms, she observes, "the plea not to be put to shame is often combined with the psalmist's confession that he has put his trust in God (Pss. 25.2, 20; 31.2). The plea, 'I have trusted in you; let me not be put to shame,' appeals to God to honor the petitioner's dependence. If the psalmist should experience distress, sickness, or the scorn of his community, then that is because God has failed him. Even though this experience can lead to the conclusion that the individual has sinned and has deserved the abandonment, the psalmist does not initially feel shame because of something he has done. Rather, he feels shame because his relationship to God has failed."[457]

Verse 63 ascribes Jerusalem's speechlessness to shame—the view advocated by Zimmerli and others.[458] The phrase פתחון פה (pithôn peh), "an opening of the mouth," which appears only twice in the Hebrew Bible (here and in Ezek 29:21), means in post-biblical Mishnaic writings "an occasion for complaint, a pretext for accusation."[459] If that meaning pertains in this passage as well, Odell reasons, then v. 63 "prohibits rituals of complaint that are called mouth openings. The succeeding prepositional phrase, מפני כלמתך mippĕnê kĕlimmātĕk, 'on account of your humiliation,' confirms this interpretation: thus the sentence should be rendered, 'You will no longer have complaints (lit. mouth openings) that are necessitated

454. Block summarizes other interpretations of this phrase in *Ezekiel 1–24*, 518.

455. Ellen F. Davis, *Swallowing the Scroll: Textuality and the Dynamics of Discourse in Ezekiel's Prophecy*, Bible and Literature 21 (Sheffield: Almond, 1989) 115.

456. M. S. Odell, "The Inversion of Shame and Forgiveness in Ezekiel 16:59-63," *JSOT* 56 (1992) 102-5.

457. Ibid., 104-5.

458. W. Zimmerli, *Ezekiel 1: A Commentary on the Book of the Prophet Ezekiel, Chapters 1–24*, trans. R. E. Clements, Hermeneia (Philadelphia: Fortress, 1979) 353. See also Moshe Greenberg, *Ezekiel 1–20*, AB 22 (Garden City, N.Y.: Doubleday, 1983) 294, who interprets the reference to silence as the loss of Jerusalem's ability to "assert" herself.

459. Greenberg, *Ezekiel 1–20*, 121.

by your shame.' "[460] Ezekiel refers to formal complaints in which the people call Yahweh to account for their experience of shame.[461]

Ezekiel's fellow exiles attributed the shame they were experiencing to a failure on God's part. But in chap. 16, the prophet shows Jerusalem's shame to be a consequence of her own failure. She has not trusted in God, but in her own beauty, idols, and alliances with her "lovers." She has despised God's oath and, in so doing, released Yahweh from any obligation to her. Nevertheless, God remembers and reestablishes the covenant with her in perpetuity: "The command to be ashamed turns the claims and complaints of the people back on themselves and forces them to examine their role in the future of the divine-human relationship. Thus the significance of the inversion lies in its call to honesty and responsibility."[462]

---

460. Odell, "The Inversion of Shame and Forgiveness in Ezekiel 16:59-63," 106.

461. Ibid., 107.

462. Ibid., 108, 111-12.

REFLECTIONS

"What shall we do with a passage like Ezekiel 16?" I ask my seminary students. Often as not, their initial response is, "Ignore it!" Within Jewish tradition, that option was advanced by Eliezer, an early rabbinical disciple of Johanan ben Zakkai, who forbade its liturgical use. The text remained in the Jewish lectionary, but with the stipulation that it always be followed by a reading of its Targum (Aramaic translation and interpretation).[463] Zimmerli cites *b. Sanh.* 44*b*, where the "contending spirit" (Gabriel, who contends on Israel's behalf) questions God about the identity of Jerusalem's parents in 16:3*b:* "Lord of the world, if Abraham and Sarah were to come and stand before you, would you tell them this and put them to shame?"[464]

Christian lectionaries do not include excerpts from Ezekiel 16. The omission is scarcely surprising, since it does not make for pleasant pulpit reading. Ezekiel pushes the vehicle of female sexual imagery to its limits. (Ralph W. Klein is simply incorrect when he remarks that Ezekiel's metaphorical indictment of unfaithful Jerusalem "proves almost to be vulgar!"[465] It *is* vulgar.) The odds are excellent, therefore, that readers of this Reflections section have never heard a sermon based on this chapter, though some religious education materials refer to it. The proverb "Like mother, like daughter" continues in use, but the text as a whole is seldom the object of careful scrutiny and reflection. Is this state of affairs "just as well," given Ezekiel's choice of metaphors? Should the passage be placed beyond the boundaries of one's "canon within the canon"? Or is it important that those whose faith includes a deep commitment to our scriptural heritage contend with this troubling text? I commend the latter view, for Ezekiel is not the only biblical author to take up these tropes, and their implications are not limited to ancient times. Moreover, his metaphorical narrative rewards those readers who—like Jacob at the Jabbok (Gen 32:24-29)—wrestle with it, knowing that they might be hurt in the process, but demanding a blessing nonetheless.

At the outset, it behooves moderns to take seriously the original sociocultural setting of Ezekiel's marriage and adulterous wife metaphors. As we have seen, marriage was not a partnership between "equals" in the world of ancient Israel. But it was an intimate relationship, admitting mutual affection, devotion, and other joys of family life. That the biblical authors regarded this union as an apt vehicle for speaking about God's relationship with Israel bespeaks the esteem accorded not only that human institution, but also the intimate and loving union shared by Yahweh and Israel with its many blessings. Positive dimensions of marriage and other familial metaphors (e.g., parent/child) for the divine/human partnership must not be overlooked.[466]

---

463. *m. Meg.* 4.10. See also Joseph Blenkinsopp, *Ezekiel,* IBC (Louisville: John Knox, 1990) 76.

464. Zimmerli, *Ezekiel 1,* 349.

465. Ralph W. Klein, *Ezekiel: The Prophet and His Message,* Studies on Personalities of the Old Testament (Columbia: University of South Carolina Press, 1988) 83.

466. See K. P. Darr, *Isaiah's Vision and the Family of God* (Louisville: Westminster John Knox, 1994).

At the same time, Yahweh is always cast in the role of the male husband, while the people, Judah, Jerusalem, etc., play the part of the female wife. This state of affairs reflects the "asymmetry" of gender relationships in ancient Israel; the man holds the more privileged and powerful position in society, and the woman is subject to his control.[467] Ancient Israelite wives who engaged in sexual relations with anyone other than their husbands were guilty of adultery, a crime punishable by death. Males were not so constrained. When Israel's prophets depict human faithlessness by means of the adultery metaphor, the female is always the culprit, "the ultimate transgressor and the epitome of evil as an adulteress and a whore";[468] and they present "her" punishment as legitimate physical abuse by her husband. As Yee observes, the adultery metaphor "comes perilously close to sanctioning a husband's domestic violence against his wife."[469]

Deprecating female imagery runs like a red thread through a variety of biblical writings.[470] It appears not only in the books of Hosea and Ezekiel, but also in Isaiah, where Jerusalem's decline from (once) faithful city to harlot is lamented (Isa 1:21*a*). It surfaces in Jeremiah's charge that Israel's lasciviousness has been outdone by her sister Judah's unfaithful acts (Jer 3:6-10) and in his threats that Jerusalem will suffer rape and other acts of violence (Jer 13:22-26). As we have seen, it receives its fullest expression in Ezekiel 16, which pushes at the boundaries of female sexual imagery with its graphic depictions of the women's lewdness and of the violence inflicted upon them as punishment for their unfaithfulness.

I must acknowledge that I become uneasy when Ezekiel employs female sexual imagery to depict the ostensible wickedness of sixth-century BCE Judeans. This is not because I am squeamish or because it offends my "Southern sensibilities," but rather because imagery, especially biblical imagery, that details the degradation and public humiliation of women, describes female sexuality as the object of male possession and control, displays women being battered and murdered, and then suggests that such violence is a means toward *healing* a broken relationship can have perilous, even lethal repercussions. The files of police officers and social workers are filled with cases of women battered and murdered by males—not only husbands, but also fathers, brothers, and boyfriends—who regard them as personal possessions, subject to their control and legitimate objects of their wrath. One pastor tells of an abusive husband who recited "appropriate" Bible verses to his wife while he was beating her.

Ezekiel 16 is but one of countless biblical passages whose adequate interpretation requires serious interaction with both historical and literary analysis. Only as the reader takes account of marriage and adultery within the world of ancient Israel, and (equally important) of the metaphorical nature of Ezekiel's narrative, is he or she equipped to deal with the present text. In earlier Reflections sections, I have indicated the importance first of identifying Ezekiel's presuppositions, convictions, and conditions (including social and cultural influences), and second of engaging troubling texts, both by placing them in conversation with other texts (including biblical texts) and by entering into "arguments" (the civil negotiation of difference) with both medium and message (see esp. the Reflections at 4:1–5:17). Weems makes much the same point:

> Reading is not the passive, private, neutral experience that we have previously believed. To read is to be prepared in many respects to fight defensively. It is to be prepared to resist, to avoid, to maneuver around some of the counterproductive impulses within the text. In short, reading does not mean simply surrendering oneself totally to the literary strategies and imaginative worlds of narrators. It also means at the very least that one must be conscious of the ways in which symbolic speech, for example, draws us into its designs and attempts to mold our beliefs and identity.[471]

467. See G. A. Yee, "The Book of Hosea," in *The New Interpreter's Bible,* 12 vols. (Nashville: Abingdon, 1995) 7:206-7, 211.
468. Ibid., 211.
469. Ibid.
470. The following paragraphs are taken from K. P. Darr, "Ezekiel's Justifications of God: Teaching Troubling Texts," *JSOT* 55 (1992) 114-16.
471. Renita Weems, *Battered Love: Marriage, Sex, and Violence in the Hebrew Prophets,* OBT (Minneapolis: Fortress, 1995) 101.

Students sometimes remind me that negative masculine imagery also appears within biblical texts (as if two wrongs could make a right!). Indeed, as Galambush observes in her discussion of second-level metaphorical uses of prostitute imagery, men as well as women are accused of "harlotry," unfaithfulness to God. But that fact scarcely obviates the problems posed by Ezekiel's metaphorical narrative. Others point out that in Ezekiel 16, female imagery is intended to be inclusive of all Jerusalem's inhabitants, male as well as female. This is true, of course, but does not speak to Ezekiel's insistence that Jerusalem's destruction can only be understood as God's mutilation and murder of the city (and her inhabitants). Moreover, the inclusive nature of his gender-specific imagery easily collapses into a threat intended for women's ears alone.

Finally, audiences may insist that imagery is only that and so exerts little impact upon our thinking. Commentators sometimes lend silent support to this view, for they are at points so keen to discern the *meaning* of a text that they overlook its literary *medium* altogether. But one cannot extract meaning intact from its literary "vessel." We must take seriously Frye's urging that we "consider the possibility that metaphor is not an incidental ornament of biblical language, but one of its controlling modes of thought.[472]

One suspects that female sexual imagery and the violence that too often accompanies it, which emerged particularly at times of crisis in the history of Israel and Judah, reflect both a disease with female sexuality and the concomitant desire to control it. Such attitudes undoubtedly had implications for Israelite women. But we dare not suppose that the repercussions of such imagery were confined to distant times and places. Because the Bible is a classic within our culture, it influences all of us to some degree, whether we have a faith commitment to it or not.

Weems reminds us, however, that the marriage metaphor can enable persons more clearly to see how they hurt each other through abuses of power, "politics" broadly defined, and untenable expectations. "For once," she writes, "we might be able to admit, with the assistance of this metaphor, that part of our pain is the realization that, to our shame, hurting and being hurt have been always a part of what it has meant for us to live together as women and men."[473] It further challenges us to recognize and take seriously the pain we inflict upon our Lord and ourselves when we ignore, trivialize, or blatantly transgress our relationship with God. In Ezekiel 16, Yahweh is neither aloof nor apathetic, but fully engaged in the lives of the people whom Jerusalem embodies. Beset by pain and anger, God nonetheless remembers "his" covenant with Israel and vows again ever to honor it.

472. N. Frye, *The Great Code: The Bible and Literature* (New York: Harcourt Brace Jovanovich, 1982) 23.
473. Weems, *Battered Love,* 114.

EZEKIEL 17:1-24, "BECAUSE HE DESPISED THE OATH AND BROKE THE COVENANT"

OVERVIEW

At Yahweh's command, Ezekiel must propound a riddle (חוד חידה *ḥûd ḥîdâ*)[474] and proclaim a

474. On "riddle" in Israel, see J. L. Crenshaw, "Riddle," *The Interpreter's Dictionary of the Bible,* supp. vol. (Nashville: Abingdon, 1976) 740-41. The most famous OT riddle was posed by Samson to the Philistines (see Judg 14:12-18).

parable (משל משל *mĕšōl māšāl*; NRSV, "allegory") to the "house of Israel," his fellow exiles. As Greenberg observes, *ḥîdâ* and *māšāl* appear in parallelism elsewhere (Ps 49:5; 78:2; Prov 1:6), but they are not synonymous: "The essence of the *ḥîdâ* was opaqueness and mystification, while that of the *māšāl* was illumination."[475] Ezekiel's oracle challenges his audience both to search out the meaning of an ambiguous fable and to be illumined as its layers of meaning unfold.

The term "fable" is appropriate in this context, because vv. 3-10 are peopled with birds and plants, to which are ascribed human motivations (see also Judg 9:8-15; 2 Kgs 14:9). Verses 11-21 explain the fable in literal language and in a manner that may prove surprising to the late exilic reader who, like the prophet's original audience, likely toys with several interpretive options while the fable is in full swing. In vv. 22-24, Ezekiel takes up the imagery of vv. 3-10 in order to proclaim Yahweh's promise to reverse the misfortunes of the Davidic dynasty and exalt it among the nations.[476]

A glance at the NRSV and the NIV reveals a difference of opinion concerning the nature of the literature. While the former arranges the lines of vv. 3*b*-10, 22-24 as poetry, the latter does not. Greenberg defends the former view,[477] pointing to the presence of characteristic poetic features—parallelisms and repetitions, chiastic structures and assonance, and recurring patterns of stressed syllables (rhythm). If this is not poetry, then it is very elevated prose indeed.

Critics have detected evidence of a complex diachronic (historical) process leading, eventually, to the text in its final form.[478] The reader, however, will not subject the oracle to the dismembering methods employed by modern critics. The reader is not, for example, surprised that Ezekiel is able to speak accurately of events lying beyond the pre-586 BCE date presupposed by the oracle as a whole. For the prophet who is privy to God's own words, the future is as accessible as the past and the present.

475. Moshe Greenberg, *Ezekiel 1–20,* AB 22 (Garden City, N.Y.: Doubleday, 1983) 309. In chap. 17, Ezekiel's *māšāl* is no short, pithy saying (cf. 12:22; 16:44), but an extended composition. Block suggests "extended metaphor." See D. I. Block, *The Book of Ezekiel: Chapters 1–24,* NICOT (Grand Rapids: Eerdmans, 1997) 525. Psalm 49:3-4 correctly associates both terms with the world of Israel's sapiential traditions.

476. This chapter, like chaps. 13 and 16, exhibits Greenberg's "halving structure": (a) a poetic fable is followed by (b) a prose interpretation which, in turn, gives way to a coda that evokes (a). See Greenberg, *Ezekiel 1–20,* esp. 241, 317-20.

477. Ibid., 318.

478. E.g., W. Zimmerli, *Ezekiel 1: A Commentary on the Book of the Prophet Ezekiel, Chapters 1–24,* trans. R. E. Clements, Hermeneia (Philadelphia: Fortress, 1979) 359-68.

Ezekiel 17:1-10, A Fable

NIV

17 The word of the LORD came to me: [2]"Son of man, set forth an allegory and tell the house of Israel a parable. [3]Say to them, 'This is what the Sovereign LORD says: A great eagle with powerful wings, long feathers and full plumage of varied colors came to Lebanon. Taking hold of the top of a cedar, [4]he broke off its topmost shoot and carried it away to a land of merchants, where he planted it in a city of traders.

[5]" 'He took some of the seed of your land and put it in fertile soil. He planted it like a willow by abundant water, [6]and it sprouted and became a low, spreading vine. Its branches turned toward him, but its roots remained under it. So it became a vine and produced branches and put out leafy boughs.

[7]" 'But there was another great eagle with powerful wings and full plumage. The vine now

NRSV

17 The word of the LORD came to me: [2]O mortal, propound a riddle, and speak an allegory to the house of Israel. [3]Say: Thus says the Lord GOD:

A great eagle, with great wings and long pinions,
  rich in plumage of many colors,
  came to the Lebanon.
He took the top of the cedar,
[4] broke off its topmost shoot;
he carried it to a land of trade,
  set it in a city of merchants.
[5] Then he took a seed from the land,
  placed it in fertile soil;
a plant[a] by abundant waters,
  he set it like a willow twig.
[6] It sprouted and became a vine

[a]Meaning of Heb uncertain

NIV

sent out its roots toward him from the plot where it was planted and stretched out its branches to him for water. [8]It had been planted in good soil by abundant water so that it would produce branches, bear fruit and become a splendid vine.'

[9]"Say to them, 'This is what the Sovereign LORD says: Will it thrive? Will it not be uprooted and stripped of its fruit so that it withers? All its new growth will wither. It will not take a strong arm or many people to pull it up by the roots. [10]Even if it is transplanted, will it thrive? Will it not wither completely when the east wind strikes it—wither away in the plot where it grew?' "

NRSV

> spreading out, but low;
> its branches turned toward him,
> its roots remained where it stood.
> So it became a vine;
> it brought forth branches,
> put forth foliage.

[7] There was another great eagle,
> with great wings and much plumage.
> And see! This vine stretched out
> its roots toward him;
> it shot out its branches toward him,
> so that he might water it.
> From the bed where it was planted
[8] it was transplanted
> to good soil by abundant waters,
> so that it might produce branches
> and bear fruit
> and become a noble vine.
[9]Say: Thus says the Lord GOD:
> Will it prosper?
> Will he not pull up its roots,
> cause its fruit to rot[a] and wither,
> its fresh sprouting leaves to fade?
> No strong arm or mighty army will be needed
> to pull it from its roots.
[10] When it is transplanted, will it thrive?
> When the east wind strikes it,
> will it not utterly wither,
> wither on the bed where it grew?

[a]Meaning of Heb uncertain

COMMENTARY

Ezekiel announces the advent of Yahweh's word, consisting first of a command that he declare to the house of Israel a "fabulous" (of the nature of a fable) parable that is both enigmatic and didactic. More than entertainment is at stake here, as the messenger formula ("Thus says the Lord GOD") makes clear (v. 3); and so the reader prepares to engage in a mental game with serious consequences. Here, in a nutshell, is Ezekiel's fable:

A certain "great" eagle with strong wings, long pinions, and colorful plumage flies to Lebanon. There, it plucks the topmost growth of a cedar tree and carries it to "the land of Canaan." Next, it takes a seed from "the land" and plants it in fertile, well-watered ground. The seed sprouts and becomes a vine, its branches spreading low, its roots going deep into the soil beneath it, its foliage abundant (vv. 3-6). A second great eagle appears on the scene. Although this eagle is less impressive than the first, the vine stretches its roots and branches toward it in order to be watered, even though its environment more than suffices to make it both luxuriant and fruitful (vv. 7-8).

At this point, the narrative world of the fable is interrupted by yet another command to speak, the messenger formula, and a series of rhetorical queries (v. 9). Speaking for Yahweh, Ezekiel asks about the vine's prospects for survival. The first question, "Will it prosper?" invites a negative response. The following three ("Will he not pull up its roots?" Will he not cause its fruit to rot and wither?" "Will not its leaves wither?") anticipate positive responses. A parenthetical remark on the vine's vulnerability appears in v. 9*b*, but with v. 10 Yahweh's questioning continues: Will the vine thrive? (no); Will it not wither before the east wind? (yes). As Block observes, both fable and questions have the effect of aligning the audience's sympathies with the first eagle.[479] The intermixing of rhetorical questions demanding positive and negative responses keeps both the audience and the reader fully engaged in Yahweh's interrogation.

How might Ezekiel's audience (including the reader) make sense of his parable?[480] Its characters—eagles, cedar, and vine—appear within many types of biblical literature, and each bears a variety of associations.

In the ancient Near East, eagles were well-established symbols of military strength and royal splendor. On the human plane, armies were said to travel with the swiftness of an eagle (Lam 4:19; Hab 1:8). Jeremiah uses eagle imagery to depict the mighty Babylonian army as it swoops down, wings spread, against Moab (Jer 48:40; see also Jer 49:22, against Edom). Deuteronomy 28:49 warns that as a consequence of Israel's disobedience, "the LORD will bring a nation from far away, from the end of the earth, to swoop down on you like an eagle" (NRSV). In his eulogy over Saul and Jonathan, David states that the deceased (both royals and warriors) were "swifter than eagles" (2 Sam 1:23*b*). Assyria's King Esarhaddon (680–669 BCE) likens himself to an enraged eagle spreading its pinions to destroy its enemies, while Sennacherib (704–681 BCE) refers to the eagle as "the prince of birds."[481] On the divine plane, Yahweh takes up eagle imagery in order to describe how God has brought Israel from the Reed Sea to Sinai: "You have seen what I did to the Egyptians, and how I bore you on eagles' wings and brought you to myself" (Exod 19:4 NRSV; see also Deut 32:11). An eagle face takes its

place among those of the living creatures supporting Yahweh's heavenly throne (Ezek 1:10; 10:14). These passages suffice to show that eagles were associated with speed, strength, and pride; eagle imagery could, depending on its context, bear either fearsome or benevolent associations.

The presence of the definite article on the noun "eagle" (הנשר *hannešer*) indicates "incomplete determination,"[482] and so should be translated "a certain great eagle." Ezekiel has a specific entity in mind, but he does not reveal its identity. Instead, he describes its impressive appearance: Its wings are strong ("wing" [כנף *kānāp*] appears also in Ps 55:6; Isa 40:31); its pinions long (see Deut 32:11; Job 39:13; Pss 68:13; 91:4); its plumage a blaze of "brilliant colors" (רקמה [*riqmâ*] appears also in 16:10, 13 to describe the fabric whence was made Jerusalem's richly embroidered [multicolored?] clothing). Lang opines that Ezekiel has in mind Babylonian reliefs on glazed tiles and dazzling sculptures.[483] Block envisions "the iridescent glistening of golden eagle's feathers in the bright sunshine."[484] Obviously, Ezekiel intends to impress his audience with the strength and splendor of this magnificent bird.

The eagle comes to Lebanon, where it breaks off the "crown" (צמרת *ṣammeret*) of a cedar, its still tender, topmost shoot. The mountains of Lebanon in Syria were especially renowned for the cedars growing there—tall, strong, and beautiful (Cant 5:15; Isa 10:34*b*). King Solomon is said to have conscripted Israelites to work in Lebanon, securing timber used to construct Yahweh's Temple (1 Kgs 5:1-14) and also the palace/administrative complex known as "the House of the Forest of the Lebanon" (1 Kgs 7:2-12 NRSV). For these reasons, and also because of the "geo-theology" of ancient Israel, Jerusalem could be called "Lebanon." Jeremiah, for example, threatens Judah's king, addressing him as the "inhabitant of Lebanon, nested among the cedars" (Jer 22:23 NRSV; see also v. 6). Hence, Ezekiel's reference is ambiguous. Does he have in mind the actual Lebanon region or Judah's own capital?

The eagle transports its shoot to "a land of

479. See Block, *Ezekiel 1–24*, 532.
480. See Greenberg, *Ezekiel 1–20*, 321.
481. See Block, *Ezekiel 1–24*, 539.

482. GKC 126 *q-t*.
483. Bernhard Lang, *Kein Aufstand in Jerusalem: Die Politik des Propheten Ezechiel*, SBS (Stuttgart: Katholisches Bibelwerk, 1978) 41-49.
484. Block, *Ezekiel 1–24*, 527.

trade"/"a city of merchants." The phrase ארץ כנען ('ereṣ kĕna 'an) can be rendered either as "the land of Canaan" or as "the land of trade."[485] In this context, the parallel "in the city of merchants" foregrounds the latter option while suppressing the former. Recalling Ezek 16:29 (where the appositional or explanatory "Chaldea" leaves no doubt that the phrase refers to Babylonia), both audience and reader are predisposed to interpret v. 4b as another reference to Babylonia. This construal likely gives the exiles (and the reader) pause, since thoughts of Nebuchadrezzar's deportation of King Jehoiachin, his royal entourage, and the people in 597 BCE will certainly come to mind as at least one option for decoding vv. 3-4. The fact that the fable ascribes no hostile or aggressive motivation to the eagle may mitigate against such an interpretation, however, as will the following two verses, which describe the eagle's magnanimous treatment of the vine seedling.

Without benefit of the interpretive material to follow, Ezekiel's notice that the eagle took a seed (or "seedling") from "the land" is really quite ambiguous. What land does the prophet have in mind? If "Lebanon" (v. 3) actually refers to Jerusalem, Judah's own territory may be in view; if "the land of trade"/"city of merchants" is its referent, then Babylonia is intended. Indeed, with its rivers and irrigation canals, Babylonia could aptly be referred to as well-watered ground. On the other hand, Deut 8:7 describes Israel's future homeland as "a land with streams and pools of water, with springs flowing in the valleys and hills" (NIV). Verses 5-6 offer the audience little help in resolving this conundrum, though the image of a plant thriving in a well-watered environ, at home in Israel's wisdom traditions, is a common enough biblical trope.[486]

In any event, this "seed from the land" is no cedar, but a vine. Here, the prophet returns to the vine imagery of Ezekiel 15. In the commentary on that chapter, it is noted that the author of Psalm 80 depicts Israel as a vine brought by God out of Egypt and transplanted in choice soil. Verses 8-11 of that psalm are akin to the text at hand:

> You brought a vine out of Egypt;
>   you drove out the nations and planted it.
> You cleared the ground for it;
>   it took deep root and filled the land.
> The mountains were covered with its shade,
>   the mighty cedars with its branches;
> It set out its branches to the sea,
>   and its shoots to the river. (Ps 80:8-11 NRSV)

Just as the psalmist uses imagery of a thriving vine to describe God's tending of Israel and its consequent growth, so also vv. 5-6 depict the eagle's benevolent treatment of its seed. Greenberg contends that the first-time reader of Ezekiel's fable might assume that a scenario similar to that appearing in Ps 80:8-11 is unfolding here as well.[487] Yet the notice that the eagle transported the cedar top to Babylonia casts some doubt upon this interpretation. By the end of v. 6, both audience and reader can only surmise that the vine, whatever its location, is so well-tended by the eagle that it flourishes. Its height cannot rival that of the cedar (it spreads out low to the ground), and its dependency upon the eagle is noted ("its branches turned toward him"); but its continued growth and well-being appear secure.

Now, a second eagle appears on the scene. It, too, is a "magnificent specimen," though no rival of the first.[488] Moreover, this eagle—unlike the first—does nothing except be on the scene. Its presence, however, suffices to cause a reorientation of the vine. Now, the plant sends out its roots and branches in his direction and, from its already well-watered bed, seeks water from him. (Note the incredulous, attention-grabbing "And see!" of v. 7b.) Verse 7 smacks of the vine's senseless ingratitude, leaving the reader to ponder what the reaction of the first eagle might be.

Verse 8 reiterates how favorable was the environment in which the vine had been (trans)-planted by the first eagle—in a good field, beside many waters—a bed where it might have continued to grow, bearing grapes and becoming a

---

485. The same phrase appeared in Ezek 16:29. "Canaanite" became a word for a trader (Prov 31:24; Isa 23:8; Zech 14:21). See Zimmerli, *Ezekiel 1*, 362.

486. Psalm 1:3 likens the person who studies Torah diligently to "trees planted by streams of water, which yield their fruit in its season, and their leaves do not wither" (NRSV). Jeremiah likens those who "trust in Yahweh" to a well-watered tree that, despite heat and drought, remains fruitful (Jer 17:8). In Isa 44:3-4, Yahweh promises to pour "my spirit" upon the Israelites, who shall "spring up like a green tamarisk, like willows by flowing streams."

487. Moshe Greenberg, *Ezekiel 1–20*, AB 22 (Garden City, N.Y.: Doubleday, 1983) 320-21.

488. D. I. Block, *The Book of Ezekiel: Chapters 1–24*, NICOT (Grand Rapids: Eerdmans, 1997) 531.

magnificent vine.[489] With the conclusion of v. 8, Ezekiel has essentially brought his fabulous parable to its end. As noted above, however, vv. 9-10 (introduced by the imperative "say" plus the messenger formula) set out a series of questions regarding the ungrateful vine's prospects. Though the reader may yet be in the dark regarding the parable's correct interpretation, he is nonetheless able, from the information in the fable, to answer Yahweh's questions along anticipated lines. Given the vine's fickle and foolish behavior, the answer to the query, "Will it prosper?" is negative.[490] To the contrary, it will be destroyed in precisely the ways described in the following three phrases. Launched by the negative interrogative "Will it not . . . ?" these questions invite a positive reply. The final phrase of v. 9 ("No [lit., "not by"] strong

arm or mighty army [lit., "not by a multitude of peoples"] will be needed to pull it from its roots") both partakes of the fable's plant imagery ("to pull it from its roots") and interjects thoughts of human beings (humans have arms, not wings) and warfare. It therefore permits interpretation to peek through parable, though its significance remains elusive. What or who is this vine, which has so compromised its former situation (deeply rooted in a fertile environment, vv. 6, 8) that it can now be uprooted without difficulty?

"See!" Ezekiel again exhorts his audience. "It was planted, but will it thrive?" The answer can only be no. Verse 10*b* introduces a new agent of destruction, the sirocco, scorching winds blowing in from the desert. As Block explains, "the redirection of the vine's branches toward the second eagle (instead of having them spread out low on the ground) and its roots upward (instead of going deeper into the fertile and well-watered soil) had rendered the plant extremely vunerable to the wind's withering force."[491] Like Jonah's gourd (Jonah 4:7), the vine faded and died. (See Reflections at 17:22-24.)

---

489. Zimmerli suggests that v. 8 be regarded as a secondary intrusion that disturbs the otherwise smooth transition from v. 7 to v. 9. Its presence, however, does not constitute a stumbling block for the reader. See W. Zimmerli, *Ezekiel 1: A Commentary on the Book of the Prophet Ezekiel, Chapters 1–24*, trans. R. E. Clements, Hermeneia (Philadelphia: Fortress, 1979) 363.

490. תצלח (*tiṣlāḥ;* lit., "it will prosper") should be read as a question, despite the absence of interrogative ה (*ha*). See GKC 150*a* 1.

491. Block, *Ezekiel 1–24*, 532.

Ezekiel 17:11-21, Interpreting the Fable

NIV

[11]Then the word of the LORD came to me: [12]"Say to this rebellious house, 'Do you not know what these things mean?' Say to them: 'The king of Babylon went to Jerusalem and carried off her king and her nobles, bringing them back with him to Babylon. [13]Then he took a member of the royal family and made a treaty with him, putting him under oath. He also carried away the leading men of the land, [14]so that the kingdom would be brought low, unable to rise again, surviving only by keeping his treaty. [15]But the king rebelled against him by sending his envoys to Egypt to get horses and a large army. Will he succeed? Will he who does such things escape? Will he break the treaty and yet escape?

[16]" 'As surely as I live, declares the Sovereign LORD, he shall die in Babylon, in the land of the king who put him on the throne, whose oath he despised and whose treaty he broke. [17]Pharaoh

NRSV

[11]Then the word of the LORD came to me: [12]Say now to the rebellious house: Do you not know what these things mean? Tell them: The king of Babylon came to Jerusalem, took its king and its officials, and brought them back with him to Babylon. [13]He took one of the royal offspring and made a covenant with him, putting him under oath (he had taken away the chief men of the land), [14]so that the kingdom might be humble and not lift itself up, and that by keeping his covenant it might stand. [15]But he rebelled against him by sending ambassadors to Egypt, in order that they might give him horses and a large army. Will he succeed? Can one escape who does such things? Can he break the covenant and yet escape? [16]As I live, says the Lord GOD, surely in the place where the king resides who made him king, whose oath he despised, and whose covenant with him he broke—in Babylon he shall

NIV

with his mighty army and great horde will be of no help to him in war, when ramps are built and siege works erected to destroy many lives. ¹⁸He despised the oath by breaking the covenant. Because he had given his hand in pledge and yet did all these things, he shall not escape.

¹⁹" 'Therefore this is what the Sovereign LORD says: As surely as I live, I will bring down on his head my oath that he despised and my covenant that he broke. ²⁰I will spread my net for him, and he will be caught in my snare. I will bring him to Babylon and execute judgment upon him there because he was unfaithful to me. ²¹All his fleeing troops will fall by the sword, and the survivors will be scattered to the winds. Then you will know that I the LORD have spoken.

NRSV

die. ¹⁷Pharaoh with his mighty army and great company will not help him in war, when ramps are cast up and siege walls built to cut off many lives. ¹⁸Because he despised the oath and broke the covenant, because he gave his hand and yet did all these things, he shall not escape. ¹⁹Therefore thus says the Lord GOD: As I live, I will surely return upon his head my oath that he despised, and my covenant that he broke. ²⁰I will spread my net over him, and he shall be caught in my snare; I will bring him to Babylon and enter into judgment with him there for the treason he has committed against me. ²¹All the pick[a] of his troops shall fall by the sword, and the survivors shall be scattered to every wind; and you shall know that I, the LORD, have spoken.

[a]Another reading is *fugitives*

COMMENTARY

With a second notice of the advent of Yahweh's word, Ezekiel is again commanded to speak to his audience (vv. 3, 9), now called "the rebellious house" (cf. "the house of Israel" in v. 2).[492] Does the presence of this different epithet suggest that the exiles should recognize themselves in the image of the disloyal vine? Or does it point to their obdurate response to the situation both revealed and concealed in the preceding parable? "Do you not know what these things mean?" Ezekiel challenges his audience. A second imperative, "Tell them!" is immediately followed by a lengthy prose interpretation that begins with events Ezekiel's audience and readers know all too well: Babylon's king came to Jerusalem, took its king, Jehoiachin (eighteen years old and only three months on the throne) and officials, and deported them to Babylon. He then placed Mattaniah (renamed Zedekiah), Jehoiachin's uncle, upon the throne as a puppet king to do his bidding. According to v. 13, Nebuchadrezzar made a covenant with Zedekiah and brought him under an (loyalty) oath (אלה *'ālâ*)—that is, he forced upon Zedekiah certain obligations that, if violated, would render

the treaty null and void, thereby releasing Nebuchadrezzar from his treaty obligations and freeing him to punish his vassal as he saw fit. Verse 13b adds that he also took the "leading men" (lit., "rams"; see Exod 15:15) of the land in order that by these measures Judah might be humble and compliant, keep "his" (Nebuchadrezzar's) covenant, and survive (v. 14).[493]

Verse 15a corresponds to vv. 7-8 of the parable, v. 15b to v. 9 (without the final comment about the vine's vulnerability). Just as the vine sent its roots and branches to the second eagle, so also Zedekiah, despite his covenant obligations to Nebuchadrezzar, rebelled against his overlord and sent ambassadors to Egypt in hopes of securing horses and a large force. Three rhetorical questions follow: Will he succeed? (This verb, like that in vv. 9a and 10a, is from the root צלח [*ṣlḥ*].) Here, as in the parable, the anticipated response is negative, though the "no" pierces the hearts of those exiles whose hopes are pinned on the success of Zedekiah's rebellion. The late exilic reader knows

---

492. What follows is no new unit, however, but a second major section within the larger oracle. See Ronald M. Hals, *Ezekiel*, FOTL 19 (Grand Rapids: Eerdmans, 1989) 114.

493. Zimmerli, *Ezekiel 1*, 365, suggests that these "leading men" (sons of nobles) were taken by Nebuchadrezzar as temporary hostages in connection with the covenant-making process. When Zedekiah rebelled, however, these hostages lost any opportunity to return to the homeland.

that the answer was no. The two following questions must also be answered negatively. Zedekiah cannot escape the consequences of his actions. He cannot abrogate the treaty stipulations and survive. Now Yahweh swears an oath ("As I live") that Judah's last monarch will die in the place where resides the king who made Zedekiah king, whose oath Zedekiah has despised, and whose covenant he has broken (i.e., in the midst of Babylon; see 12:13; 2 Kgs 25:7; Jer 39:7; 52:11).

In Ezekiel's mind, it seems, is a series of political events that began during Zedekiah's fourth year on the throne (594/93 BCE). In that same year, Psammetichus II (594–588 BCE) became Pharaoh of Egypt. According to Jer 27:1–28:1, Zedekiah met with representatives from Edom, Moab, Ammon, Tyre, and Sidon, all of whom sought Egyptian assistance in throwing off the Babylonian yoke. Jeremiah opposed Judean complicity in the rebellion. Like Ezekiel, he preached a political policy of compliance with Babylon, for such, he believed, was Yahweh's will: "Now I have given all these lands into the hand of King Nebuchadrezzar of Babylon, my servant, and I have given him even the wild animals of the field to serve him" (Jer 27:6 NRSV). For unknown reasons, that rebellion was aborted. Jeremiah 51:59 states that Zedekiah was forced to travel to Babylon in that year. (In order to justify his actions, plead his innocence, or seek mercy from its king?) But in 589/88 BCE, Zedekiah, in close association with Egypt (now ruled by Psammetichus II's successor, Hophra [Apries]), openly rebelled against his overlord, as did Tyre and perhaps Ammon. Nebuchadrezzar's response was not long in coming. In 588 BCE his troops besieged Jerusalem.

This brings us to v. 17, a significant conundrum for many critics. In its present form, the verse reads: "Not by a great force or a numerous assembly will Pharaoh do with him in the battle, when ramps are cast up and siege walls are built to cut off many lives." At issue, it seems, is an incident referred to in Jer 37:5-11 (see also Jer 34:21). There we read that Pharaoh (Hophra) brought his forces near Jerusalem in an attempt to assist his ally. Though the Jeremiah passages indicate that Babylonia's troops withdrew for a time, the reprieve was short-lived, and the Babylonians soon resumed their siege. Hence Ezekiel's "prediction" that Egyptian aid would prove futile.

That Ezekiel, ostensibly prophesying at a time prior to this historical incident, could speak accurately of its outcome raises the altogether reasonable hypothesis that in its final form v. 17 is a prophecy "after the fact" that was inserted into vv. 11-21 only after the Egyptian disaster occurred. Greenberg proposes less serious surgery, however; only "Pharaoh" is secondary. Originally, v. 17 agreed with the statement in v. 9b that Nebuchadrezzar (the first eagle) would require no large force in order to deal in a hostile manner with Zedekiah during the siege. But when events turned out otherwise (the Babylonians were forced to expend considerable force and effort to capture Jerusalem), "Pharaoh" was inserted into v. 17, transforming an inaccurate prediction (Nebuchadrezzar will take Jerusalem easily) into an accurate one (Pharaoh's lame attempt to foil the siege will fail). This maneuver did not, of course, remove the disparity between v. 9b and reality. Greenberg suggests, however, that the glossator (perhaps Ezekiel himself) expected his readers to read v. 9 through the lens of the altered v. 17.[494]

As noted in the Overview, the ancient reader, believing Ezekiel to be Yahweh's true prophet, would not have denied him the ability to predict future events accurately. To the contrary, Ezekiel's foreknowledge of the futility of Pharaoh's efforts, as announced in v. 17, underscored the credibility of both the oracle and the messenger entrusted with its proclamation. Although the problem posed by v. 9b was not resolved completely (could Ezekiel have erred on this one point?), it is conceivable that the reader smoothed out that problem, either along the lines suggested by Greenberg or by construing the text as an expression of Nebuchadrezzar's perspective: The capture of Jerusalem required a lengthy siege, but it was, on the scale of military campaigns, a minor military problem for so great an empire as Babylon.

With v. 18, the spotlight returns to Zedekiah. Because he despised the oath and broke the

494. Greenberg, *Ezekiel 1–20,* 315. Davis proposes a different solution to the problem. In her view, when history proved v. 9b wrong, Ezekiel sought to correct his earlier prediction. By creating a "near-echo" of that text in the opening phrase of v. 17 (thereby creating a link between the two that might "at first glance" appear affirming), he drew "the earlier, mistaken prophecy into the sphere of the later interpretation [Pharaoh's failure] where its content receives a subtle reinterpretation." Ellen F. Davis, *Swallowing the Scroll: Textuality and the Dynamics of Discourse in Ezekiel's Prophecy,* Bible and Literature 21 (Sheffield: Almond, 1989) 99-102.

covenant (a reiteration of v. 16, though without the third-person masc. sing. suffixes "his" [Nebuchadrezzar's] oath . . . "his" covenant), because he "gave his hand" (see 2 Kgs 10:15; 1 Chr 29:24; 2 Chr 30:8; Ezra 10:19) and acted contrary to his commitment, he will not escape. Verse 19, with its initial "therefore" (לכן *lākēn*), followed by the messenger formula, transports Ezekiel's interpretation from the human to the divine plane.

The third-person masculine singular suffixes on "oath" and "covenant" in v. 16 clearly referred to Nebuchadrezzar. The same two words appeared without suffixes in v. 18. In v. 19, however, Yahweh speaks of "my" oath and "my" covenant. To which covenant does God refer? Turning to 2 Chr 36:13, many commentators aver that when Nebuchadrezzar made a covenant with Zedekiah and forced him to take an oath of loyalty (Ezek 17:13), Zedekiah swore that oath in the name of Yahweh, who in effect became a witness to it (presumably Nebuchadrezzar called Babylonian deities to witness it as well). Hence, when Zedekiah violated his loyalty oath and covenant with Nebuchadrezzar, he also broke covenant with Yahweh. Greenberg resists this line of reasoning, however, claiming that the chroniclers' account is based upon their understanding of this passage, and so no independent witness to the process by which Nebuchadrezzar's covenant with Zedekiah was forged.[495]

Were v. 19 the beginning of a new unit, Greenberg's thesis that it refers to God's covenant with Israel would be more compelling. The presence of "therefore," coupled with the messenger formula and Yahweh's oath, certainly directs the reader's attention to the following divine pronouncement. Nonetheless, that pronouncement is most logically read in relation to preceding verses. Greenberg dismisses too easily the possibility that Nebuchadrezzar forced Zedekiah to swear loyalty to his political treaty in Yahweh's name. This practice (commended by logic) was a commonplace in ancient Hittite treaties, and it appears in the eighth-century Aramaic Sefîre inscription, as well.[496] Tsevat suggests that the same policy was in effect in Assyrian oaths.[497] Cogan acknowledges

that evidence supporting this policy is not abundant. In some cases, Assyrian treaties refer only to Assyrian deities. He maintains, however, that Assyrian treaties distinguish between "provinces administered directly by Assyria and independent vassal states." The former were regarded as Assyrian in all aspects, and so their national deities were not accorded an official position. The latter, however, maintained a degree of independence; and so their deities were invoked.[498] In Babylonian treaties also, vassals swore by their own deities, as well as those of their suzerain.[499]

Hence, Yahweh's reference to "my oath . . . my covenant" likely refers to Nebuchadrezzar's covenant and oath with Zedekiah (v. 16). From God's perspective, this was no mere political alliance. Israel's deity had a personal stake in that treaty; breaking oaths dishonored God's name (Lev 19:12), and so Zedekiah must answer to Yahweh, and not just to Babylonia's king (and deities): "Even though his oath affirmed the servitude of the 'house of Israel' to a foreign overlord, yet it was the oath of Yahweh which demanded undivided allegiance."[500] Here, as elsewhere, Ezekiel speaks of an evil deed redounding upon the head of the perpetrator (9:10; 11:21; 16:43; 22:31; 33:4)—an affirmation of divine justice.

Verse 20*a*, like 12:13, adopts hunter imagery to describe Yahweh's capture of Zedekiah.[501] God brings the hapless king to Babylon and enters into judgment with him there: "When YHWH emerges in 17:20 as the self-declared hunter and judge of Israel's king," Davis observes, "the perspective returns to the unambiguously theocentric one characteristic of the book. The gradual shift in orientation from a political to a theological frame of reference, adumbrated in the changing use of covenant language (vv. 15-19), is completed with

495. Ibid., 322.
496. See J. A. Fitzmeyer, S.J., *The Aramaic Inscriptions of Sefîre*, Bibor 19 (Rome: Pontifical Biblical Institute, 1967) 12-13, 33-39.
497. M. Tsevat, "The Neo-Assyrian and Neo-Babylonian Vassal Oaths and the Prophet Ezekiel," *JBL* (1959) 199-204.

498. M. Cogan, *Syria, Judah and Israel in the Eighth and Seventh Centuries B.C.E.,* SBLMS 19 (Missoula: Scholars Press, 1974) 46-47.
499. Zimmerli, *Ezekiel 1*, 365. See also George E. Mendenhall, "Puppy and Lettuce in Northwest-Semitic Covenant Making," *BASOR* 133 (1954) 30n. 16; Fitzmeyer, *The Aramaic Inscriptions of Sefîre*, 60-61.
500. Zimmerli, *Ezekiel 1*, 366.
501. Block notes striking similarities between this passage and Ezek 12:1-16. Beyond their common theme and vocabulary, these two texts exhibit structural parallels: each consists of a preamble, a figurative presentation, a query concerning its meaning, a divinely authorized interpretation, a ray of hope (with motive clause), and the recognition formula. See D. I. Block, *The Book of Ezekiel: Chapters 1–24*, NICOT (Grand Rapids: Eerdmans, 1997) 522-23.

this verse."[502] Nothing is said about the substance of Yahweh's sentence, but the charge, "the treachery he has committed against me" (see also 14:13; 15:8; most often מעל [*ma'al*] refers to Israel's trespass against God) is a capital offense. The reader recalls the prediction in v. 16 that Zedekiah will die in Babylon. In the Commentary on chap. 12, it is noted that details about Zedekiah's attempted

502. Ellen F. Davis, *Swallowing the Scroll: Textuality and the Dynamics of Discourse in Ezekiel's Prophecy,* Bible and Literature 21 (Sheffield: Almond, 1989) 103.

escape from Jerusalem, his capture, and his punishment (see 2 Kgs 25:4-7) appear to have entered the interpretation of Ezekiel's sign act in vv. 10-15. In the present passage, nothing is said of Zedekiah's sentencing at Riblah, of the slaughter of his sons there, or of the gouging out of his eyes. Verse 21*a*, however, refers to the deaths of his troops (MT, "and as for all his fugitives with his troops") by the sword (see 12:14) and to the scattering of survivors "to every wind" (see 12:15; 2 Kgs 25:5). (See Reflections at 17:22-24.)

Ezekiel 17:22-24, Israel Will Be Exalted

NIV

22" 'This is what the Sovereign LORD says: I myself will take a shoot from the very top of a cedar and plant it; I will break off a tender sprig from its topmost shoots and plant it on a high and lofty mountain. 23On the mountain heights of Israel I will plant it; it will produce branches and bear fruit and become a splendid cedar. Birds of every kind will nest in it; they will find shelter in the shade of its branches. 24All the trees of the field will know that I the LORD bring down the tall tree and make the low tree grow tall. I dry up the green tree and make the dry tree flourish.

" 'I the LORD have spoken, and I will do it.' "

NRSV

22Thus says the Lord GOD:
I myself will take a sprig
  from the lofty top of a cedar;
  I will set it out.
I will break off a tender one
  from the topmost of its young twigs;
I myself will plant it
  on a high and lofty mountain.
23 On the mountain height of Israel
  I will plant it,
in order that it may produce boughs and
    bear fruit,
  and become a noble cedar.
Under it every kind of bird will live;
  in the shade of its branches will nest
  winged creatures of every kind.
24 All the trees of the field shall know
  that I am the LORD.
I bring low the high tree,
  I make high the low tree;
I dry up the green tree
  and make the dry tree flourish.
I the LORD have spoken;
  I will accomplish it.

COMMENTARY

The interpretive section of Ezekiel's oracle concludes with a variation on the recognition formula that emphasizes the power of Yahweh's word. The third section, initiated by the messenger formula,

takes up the imagery (and characteristics of poetry; e.g., parallelism and repetition) of Ezekiel's fable to extend a promise of restoration based not on the sphere of human political alliances, but on God's faithfulness to the house of David. We cannot know whether Ezekiel, in proclaiming his fable and its interpretation to his audience, included the optimistic prophecy in vv. 22-24. For readers of his book, however, these three verses constitute a rare upstroke among the otherwise overwhelmingly negative oracles of chaps. 4–24. Yahweh assumes the role allotted the first eagle, taking a sprig (רַךְ *rak*, "to be tender"; this noun is unique to Ezekiel) from atop a tall cedar and planting it on "a high and lofty mountain"—in this context, a reference to Mt. Zion (= "the mountain height of Israel")—in order that it might grow and bear fruit. Verse 22 speaks of a lofty cedar, not a lowly vine, though only the latter is fruit-bearing. "That the allegory does not tell of the restoration of the vine stock, but the exaltation of the cedar shoot," Zimmerli observes, demonstrates that "the promise of the new beginning was emphatically not seen as applying to the family of those ruling in the land after 597 BCE, but through the family of those deported in 597 BCE. Cf. Jer 24."[503]

So great will be this tree that "every bird of every wing" (see Gen 7:14) will nest in its branches (v. 23b). Ezekiel's image of the tall tree and the nourishment and protection it offers "represents a Hebrew version of a widespread ancient mythological motif known as the 'cosmic tree,'" Block explains. This tree, not to be associated with the "tree of life" in a paradisiacal garden, "is typically portrayed as a huge plant with its crown reaching into the heavens. . . . Although Ezekiel may have been introduced to the 'cosmic tree' motif in Babylon, the present passage may also have been inspired by Isa 11:1-10, which conjoins the elements of a newly sprouted messianic shoot, the mountain of Yahweh, and peaceful coexistence with wild animals."[504]

When v. 24 goes on to say that "all the trees of the field shall know that I am Yahweh," it asserts God's intention that, like Israel, every nation will come to recognize and acknowledge the power and sovereignty of Israel's patron deity. Verse 24b portrays God in the role of the "Great Reverser" (see 1 Sam 2:7; Ps 18:27; 75:7; 147:6).[505] The concluding formula, "I, Yahweh, have spoken" last appeared in v. 21. Here, it is amplified by the phrase "and I will do it" (see also 22:14; 36:36; 37:14).

503. W. Zimmerli, *Ezekiel 1: A Commentary on the Book of the Prophet Ezekiel, Chapters 1–24,* trans. R. E. Clements, Hermeneia (Philadelphia: Fortress, 1979) 368.

504. Block, *Ezekiel 1-24,* 551.
505. Ronald M. Hals, *Ezekiel,* FOTL 19 (Grand Rapids: Eerdmans, 1989) 117. See also Luke 1:51-53 and Revelation 18. See also Zimmerli, *Ezekiel 1,* 367.

REFLECTIONS

Ezekiel's interpretation of his nationalistic parable is written from a thoroughly theocentric perspective. To his mind, Judah's political misfortunes can be understood only when one recognizes that behind Babylonian imperialism stands the God of Israel, who judges Judah's kings according to their faithfulness to their *divine* suzerain. Ezekiel's constant affirmations of Yahweh's unrivaled sovereignty over history challenge ancient and modern readers alike to take with utmost seriousness the psalmist's assertion, "The earth is the LORD's and all that is in it, the world, and those who live in it" (Ps 24:1 NRSV). Yahweh is not indifferent to creation and its creatures. God wills that all our interactions—social, political, environmental, international—be governed by fidelity, wisdom, and an overarching commitment so to live that we participate in bringing about the kingdom of God on earth.

At the same time, Ezekiel's insistence that historical events are controlled by Yahweh, and so should be construed as reliable indicators of divine favor or disfavor, raises crucial problems for ancients (e.g., Job) and contemporary readers alike. Although the Doctrine of Retribution (God rewards the righteous but afflicts the wicked) continues to influence many a modern-day believer, and one still hears "It was God's will" at funerals, few of us would wish to affirm that God authors all historical events and that tragedies, be they personal, communal, national, or global, must be interpreted as God's retaliation for human sin.

In previous Reflections sections, I have pointed to the importance of understanding why

Ezekiel, among other biblical authors, presupposed and defended the correlation between divine action and Judah's downfall. He believed that Jerusalem's doom was certain; he insisted that this catastrophe was the doing, and not the undoing, of Israel's God; and he everywhere affirmed that Yahweh is just and that the punishment is proportionate to the people's crimes. Ezekiel knew no demonic power opposing Yahweh, and he did not construe Israel's political and national perils as an inevitable consequence of its dangerous geographical setting. Earnest study of the Bible requires that we both identify and reflect seriously upon Ezekiel's own perspectives, recognizing that he, no less than we, was in many ways a product of his times. Nevertheless, modern readers cannot—indeed, should not—simply adopt Ezekiel's worldview or feel compelled to assent to all aspects of his theology. Hence, I take issue with Block when, in his discussion of the theological implications of Ezekiel 17, he writes that God "governs human affairs so that the schemes of the wicked are frustrated and his own objectives are ultimately achieved."[506] I am as discomfitted by his words as by Ezekiel's insistence that every historical disaster Israel experiences must be understood as God's punishment for sin. In a world where holocausts occur, Ezekiel's correlation of historical events with Yahweh's administration of justice can be lethal.

In the end, Zedekiah's political machinations failed, and his people paid a terrible price. Within the book of Jeremiah, Zedekiah appears as a weak and indecisive ruler, caught between two camps of advisers—pro-Egyptian, and pro-Babylonian. On several occasions, he sought Jeremiah's advice, but lacked both the insight and the courage to steer a straight course. Had he remained loyal to his Babylonian overlord—to whom he swore an oath of loyalty—Jerusalem might have escaped Nebuchadrezzar's wrath. Had his attempts to rebel against his suzerain succeeded, the biblical historiographers might have penned a different portrait of Zedekiah. At critical junctures in history, leaders around the world face decisions that admit no easy answers because the issues are so very complex, advisers pull them in more than one direction, loyalties compete, and each "solution" is problematic, bearing the seeds of both success and calamity. Ezekiel takes seriously Zedekiah's oath, likely sworn in Yahweh's name as well as in the names of Babylonian deities. He does not separate political strategies from religious commitments, as if one could so compartmentalize life as to relegate Yahweh to the latter sphere, while operating in the former as if God did not exist or had no place there. Among moderns there is a tendency to bifurcate life: private/public; us/them; secular/religious. For the prophet, life is a seamless garment, God the essential thread without which the garment has no substance or form. Our ultimate loyalty belongs with God, our covenant partner; without that commitment, the garments of our lives unravel.

The text does not end with the deaths of Zedekiah and his political ambitions. Suddenly, and without explanation, Yahweh proclaims a plan by which God will personally replant the cedar's topmost sprout upon "the mountain of Israel" (Zion). There it will grow into a magnificent, fruit-bearing (!) cedar. Here, indeed, is a grace note deeply rooted in nationalistic hope. With profound trust in Yahweh's enduring commitment to Israel, Ezekiel asserts that the same God who brings the house of David to an ignoble end is, at that very moment, planning its future exaltation. Elsewhere in the book of Ezekiel, and in other biblical works as well, readers are told that Israel's elevation requires a concomitant humbling, or even the destruction, of other nations. Such passages testify to the pain, humiliation, and suffering that Israel endured at the hands of its more powerful neighbors—Egypt, Assyria, Babylonia. But the author of 17:22-24 does not hold before his readers scenes of Israel's vengeance against its foes or of celebrations for battles fought and won. His is a portrait of a peaceable kingdom where, amid the great cedar's branches, every bird nests in safety. Ezekiel 17 reminds us that the metaphors we employ to talk about the future are not inconsequential. To the contrary, they play a role in shaping that future.

To no one's surprise, 17:22-24 insists that all nations ("all the trees of the field") will acknowledge

---

506. Block, *Ezekiel 1–24,* 553-54.

Yahweh's unparalleled sovereignty and power. Indeed, the presence of the recognition formula in 17:24*a* confirms that worldwide acknowledgment of Israel's God is a primary goal of Yahweh's plan to reestablish and glorify David's line. The great reverser, who brings low the high tree and exalts the low tree, thereby demonstrates that power that transcends every human expectation.

EZEKIEL 18:1-32, "HAVE I ANY PLEASURE IN THE DEATH OF THE WICKED?"

OVERVIEW

From the time Ezekiel was commissioned to be Yahweh's spokesperson to the "house of Israel" (593 BCE) until the fall of Jerusalem in 587/86, he engaged in the difficult task of dismantling the orthodox Yahwism of his day—a faith nourished by certain theological trajectories (i.e., God's ongoing commitment to the continuity of the Davidic dynasty; the protective presence of Yahweh's glory in the Jerusalem Temple), but neglectful of others (the *conditional* nature of the covenant God had forged with Israel at Sinai). The former (Davidic/Zion theology) fueled the exiles' resistance to a crucial theme of Ezekiel's pre-587 ministry: Yahweh has decided utterly to destroy Jerusalem as a direct consequence of its long-lived and ongoing sinfulness. The latter (conditional Sinai theology) provided a means to explain God's decision: Israel's failure to honor its covenant obligations brings upon its own head the full weight of the covenant curses.

Ellen F. Davis observes that while other prophets engaged in direct exchanges with kings, priests, and rival prophets, Ezekiel's primary conversation partner is Israel's tradition. "Like a creative archivist," she writes, "he desires not only to preserve the treasures of the past but also to make them available and meaningful in the present. Even his disputation speeches [e.g., Ezekiel 18] are aimed as much at the tradition as at the people, purging it of its useless elements . . . and correcting disastrous misinterpretations."[507] So, for example, the prophet corrects "disastrous misinterpretations" of David/Zion theology (God guarantees

Jerusalem's survival) by insisting that Yahweh's destruction of the city is just, but also preserves "the treasures of the past" by portraying a future *beyond the punishment* when the Davidic dynasty will again be glorified (e.g., 17:22-24) and Jerusalem restored (e.g., 16:59-63). By the same token, Ezekiel deals creatively with aspects of conditional Sinai theology. In chapter 18, he purges that tradition of the age-old notion that God's punishment upon sinners spans generations—an idea expressed most authoritatively in Exod 20:5: "For I the Lord your God am a jealous God, punishing children for the iniquity of parents, to the third and the fourth generation of those who reject me" (NRSV; see also Deut 5:9).[508] Ezekiel thinks that the notion of transgenerational retribution (a generation suffers for the sins of its predecessors), here expressed in the form of a pithy proverb ("the parents have eaten sour grapes, and the children's teeth are blunted"), also has led to "disastrous misinterpretations" for his fellow exiles. On the one hand, they can protest the injustice of their situation—though innocent, they suffer for the sins of their forebears, for such is Yahweh's way. On the other hand, they can cling to that injustice as a means of eluding responsibility for their *own* sins.

Ezekiel constructs a logical and painstaking argument against the exiles' (mis)use of tradition, for he perceives that within his historical and social context, the notion of transgenerational punishment is death-dealing, rather than life-giving, to his compatriots. In the course of his argument,

507. Ellen F. Davis, *Swallowing the Scroll: Textuality and the Dynamics of Discourse in Ezekiel's Prophecy,* Bible and Literature 21 (Sheffield: Almond, 1989) 62.

508. I do not intend to suggest that the notion of transgenerational retribution is unique to Sinai covenant theology, but only that it is a significant feature of that theological trajectory.

Ezekiel seeks not only to free them from the burden of that notion (whether they seek such release or not!), but also to convince them of the possibility of individual and communal liberation from sin accumulated in the course of a single lifetime. Yahweh "has no pleasure in the death of anyone," he proclaims. "Turn, then, and live!"

Typically, disputation speeches begin with the quotation of a popular proverb (see v. 2), followed by a counterthesis (vv. 3-4) and a refutation in the form of a "systematic exposition of the coun-terthesis" (vv. 5-18).[509] Verses 21-32, which are not to be separated from preceding ones, pursue a different but related issue: judgment and repentance within the lifetime of a single individual/generation. At points throughout his disputation, Ezekiel (ostensibly) quotes his audience's objections to the argument, inviting readers to conclude that the text has preserved a lively debate.

509. D. I. Block, *The Book of Ezekiel: Chapters 1–24*, NICOT (Grand Rapids: Eerdmans, 1997) 555. See also Adrian Graffy, *A Prophet Confronts His People: The Disputation Speech in the Prophets*, AnBib 104 (Rome: Pontifical Biblical Institute, 1984) 58-64.

Ezekiel 18:1-20: "This Proverb Shall No Longer Be Used by You"

NIV

18 The word of the LORD came to me: [2]"What do you people mean by quoting this proverb about the land of Israel:

" 'The fathers eat sour grapes,
  and the children's teeth are set on edge'?

[3]"As surely as I live, declares the Sovereign LORD, you will no longer quote this proverb in Israel. [4]For every living soul belongs to me, the father as well as the son—both alike belong to me. The soul who sins is the one who will die.

[5]"Suppose there is a righteous man
  who does what is just and right.
[6]He does not eat at the mountain shrines
  or look to the idols of the house of Israel.
He does not defile his neighbor's wife
  or lie with a woman during her period.
[7]He does not oppress anyone,
  but returns what he took in pledge for a loan.
He does not commit robbery
  but gives his food to the hungry
  and provides clothing for the naked.
[8]He does not lend at usury
  or take excessive interest.[a]
He withholds his hand from doing wrong
  and judges fairly between man and man.
[9]He follows my decrees
  and faithfully keeps my laws.

[a]8 Or *take interest*; similarly in verses 13 and 17

NRSV

18 The word of the LORD came to me: [2]What do you mean by repeating this proverb concerning the land of Israel, "The parents have eaten sour grapes, and the children's teeth are set on edge"? [3]As I live, says the Lord GOD, this proverb shall no more be used by you in Israel. [4]Know that all lives are mine; the life of the parent as well as the life of the child is mine: it is only the person who sins that shall die.

5If a man is righteous and does what is lawful and right— [6]if he does not eat upon the mountains or lift up his eyes to the idols of the house of Israel, does not defile his neighbor's wife or approach a woman during her menstrual period, [7]does not oppress anyone, but restores to the debtor his pledge, commits no robbery, gives his bread to the hungry and covers the naked with a garment, [8]does not take advance or accrued interest, withholds his hand from iniquity, executes true justice between contending parties, [9]follows my statutes, and is careful to observe my ordinances, acting faithfully—such a one is righteous; he shall surely live, says the Lord GOD.

10If he has a son who is violent, a shedder of blood, [11]who does any of these things (though his father[a] does none of them), who eats upon the mountains, defiles his neighbor's wife, [12]oppresses the poor and needy, commits robbery, does not

[a]Heb *he*

NIV

That man is righteous;
he will surely live,
declares the Sovereign LORD.

[10]"Suppose he has a violent son, who sheds blood or does any of these other things[a] [11](though the father has done none of them):

"He eats at the mountain shrines.
He defiles his neighbor's wife.
[12]He oppresses the poor and needy.
He commits robbery.
He does not return what he took in pledge.
He looks to the idols.
He does detestable things.
[13]He lends at usury and takes excessive interest.

Will such a man live? He will not! Because he has done all these detestable things, he will surely be put to death and his blood will be on his own head.

[14]"But suppose this son has a son who sees all the sins his father commits, and though he sees them, he does not do such things:

[15]"He does not eat at the mountain shrines
or look to the idols of the house of Israel.
He does not defile his neighbor's wife.
[16]He does not oppress anyone
or require a pledge for a loan.
He does not commit robbery
but gives his food to the hungry
and provides clothing for the naked.
[17]He withholds his hand from sin[b]
and takes no usury or excessive interest.
He keeps my laws and follows my decrees.

He will not die for his father's sin; he will surely live. [18]But his father will die for his own sin, because he practiced extortion, robbed his brother and did what was wrong among his people.

[19]"Yet you ask, 'Why does the son not share the guilt of his father?' Since the son has done what is just and right and has been careful to keep all my decrees, he will surely live. [20]The soul who sins is the one who will die. The son will not share the guilt of the father, nor will the father share the guilt of the son. The righteousness of the righteous man will be credited to him, and the wickedness of the wicked will be charged against him.

[a]10 Or things to a brother   [b]17 Septuagint (see also verse 8); Hebrew from the poor

NRSV

restore the pledge, lifts up his eyes to the idols, commits abomination, [13]takes advance or accrued interest; shall he then live? He shall not. He has done all these abominable things; he shall surely die; his blood shall be upon himself.

[14]But if this man has a son who sees all the sins that his father has done, considers, and does not do likewise, [15]who does not eat upon the mountains or lift up his eyes to the idols of the house of Israel, does not defile his neighbor's wife, [16]does not wrong anyone, exacts no pledge, commits no robbery, but gives his bread to the hungry and covers the naked with a garment, [17]withholds his hand from iniquity,[a] takes no advance or accrued interest, observes my ordinances, and follows my statutes; he shall not die for his father's iniquity; he shall surely live. [18]As for his father, because he practiced extortion, robbed his brother, and did what is not good among his people, he dies for his iniquity.

[19]Yet you say, "Why should not the son suffer for the iniquity of the father?" When the son has done what is lawful and right, and has been careful to observe all my statutes, he shall surely live. [20]The person who sins shall die. A child shall not suffer for the iniquity of a parent, nor a parent suffer for the iniquity of a child; the righteousness of the righteous shall be his own, and the wickedness of the wicked shall be his own.

[a]Gk: Heb the poor

COMMENTARY

Ezekiel 18:1 begins with the prophet's formulaic announcement of the advent of Yahweh's word. Unlike other passages (e.g., 17:1-2), however, this announcement is not followed by a direct address ("O mortal") and command to prophesy. Rather, Ezekiel's God immediately challenges a popular proverb concerning (or "in") the land of Israel. In Hebrew, this proverb ("the parents have eaten sour grapes [בסר *bōser*; Isa 18:5; Job 15:33; Jer 31:29-30] and the children's teeth are blunted")[510] consists of only six words. Here, then, is a *māšāl* like those in 12:22, 27 and 16:44—a succinct saying common among the folk.[511]

The proverb itself describes an event of everyday human experience and contains no reference to God. Block makes much of its "secular" cast. To his mind, Ezekiel's problem with the proverb is not that the children are being punished for the sins of their parents, or even the question of theodicy. Rather, the saying reflects "a resignation to immutable cosmic rules of cause and effect" that implies God is either disinterested in the exiles' situation or is impotent to do anything about it.[512]

Block's comments are problematic on at least two levels. First, he fails to consider that whether the proverb is secular or religious depends not upon its words per se, but upon the context in which it is uttered. In some other context, the situation described in the proverb might reflect a secular circumstance. That *Yahweh* quotes and refutes the saying strongly suggests, however, that the people have been applying the proverbial situation to their own context as construed from a *theocentric* perspective: The people's *māšāl* encapsulates divine dealings, not secular concerns. Second, Block's reference to "immutable cosmic rules of cause and effect" strikes an anachronistic chord. True, Israel's sages (and even some of its prophets) could speak of actions and their consequences without pointing to Yahweh as the force conjoining the two. But within Israel's traditions, transgenerational retribution is at issue especially in theocentric arenas—sacral law, prophetic judgment oracles, etc. Within such arenas, Israel speaks not of "an immutable law of the universe,"[513] but of the justice or injustice of divine governance.[514]

The belief that, according to the rules of a deity's reign, the penalty for sin was suffered not only by the perpetrator, but also by his contemporary family and subsequent generations, was not Israel's alone. It surfaces in the Hittite *Instructions for Temple Officials*:

> If a slave causes his master's anger, they either kill him or they will injure him . . . or they will seize him, his wife, his children, his brother, his sister, his in-laws, his kin . . . If ever he is to die, he will not die alone; his kin will accompany him. If then . . . anyone arouses the anger of a god, does the god take revenge on him alone? Does he not take revenge on his wife, his children, his descendants, his kin, his slaves, and slave-girls, his cattle (and) sheep together with his crop, and will utterly destroy him?[515]

This belief appears also in the fourteenth-century BCE complaint by the Hittite king Muršiliš II to the storm god.[516]

Within the Hebrew Bible, the principle of transgenerational retribution is applied to Achan and his family (Josh 7:22-26). King Saul adheres to it when he orders the executions not only of Ahimelech and "all [his] father's house," but also of eighty-five priests, their kin (including children), and their cattle (1 Sam 22:16-19). The Deuteronomistic historians invoke the earlier "sins of Manasseh" (687/6–642 BCE) to explain/justify Yahweh's decision to destroy Judah in Ezekiel's day. Jeremiah beseeches God to punish both his adversaries and their families, while Job flatly asserts that God punishes the wicked/oppressors by slaying and starving their children (Job 27:13-14). The author of Lam 5:7 expresses the

---

510. The verb קהה (*qāhâ*), which describes the effect of unripe grapes on the teeth, elsewhere appears only in Eccl 10:10 (of dulled iron).

511. Cf. the paradigm in 14:7-8 and the extended, fabulous parable in 17:2-10. Jeremiah also quotes the sour grapes proverb (Jer 31:29), though in a slightly different form and toward other ends.

512. Block, *Ezekiel 1–24*, 561.

513. Ibid.

514. While Block regards Ezekiel's initial task as moving the proverb propounders from reflection on "immutable cosmic laws" to his own, "radically theocentric view of the universe," from the perspective of the text, the exiles are already construing their situation in theological terms.

515. *ANET*, 207-9.

516. *ANET*, 395.

proverb's sentiment in literal language: "Our ancestors sinned; they are no more, and we bear their iniquities."

On the other hand, Korah's sons are not killed along with their rebellious father (Num 26:11), and Judah's King Amaziah spares the children of his father's assassins (2 Kgs 14:6). In the latter text, the anonymous narrator bases Amaziah's decision on "what is written in the book of the law of Moses, where the LORD commanded, 'The parents shall not be put to death for the children, or the children be put to death for the parents; but all shall be put to death for their own sins' " (Deut 24:16). This law concerns justice in the human arena; its intent is to rule out wholesale revenge against the perpetrator's family.

The effect of v. 4 is to apply Deut 24:16 to the divine sphere.[517] Yahweh quotes the people's proverb in order immediately to refute it. Both the oath formula ("As I live") and the formula for a divine saying ("says the Lord GOD") emphasize that the Lord has construed their *māšāl* as a personal, false attack and is determined so to disprove it that it falls from use (see also 12:23). That refutation (the counterthesis) first asserts God's ownership of every living person, parent as well as child. All lives belong to Yahweh; hence, no one has the right to question the ruling that "only the person who sins shall die" (v. 4*b*). Here, Ezekiel reaffirms a fundamental premise of chap. 14: Yahweh saves Noah, Daniel, and Job on account of their righteousness, but judges their offspring according to their own behavior. At the same time, however, he confutes 9:5-6. While 9:4 asserts that aggrieved persons will be rescued on the day of Jerusalem's destruction, Yahweh's order that the executioners slay without pity little children not bearing the protective mark (9:5-6) comports with the principle of transgenerational punishment for sin.

Ezekiel buttresses the counterthesis of v. 4 by relating, in the manner of casuistic law, three hypothetical test cases: a righteous man, his sinful son, and his righteous grandson.[518] Verses 5-9 set out the first case. The protasis ("If a man is righteous and does what is lawful and right")[519] is amplified in vv. 6-9*a* by a list of ordinances in thirteen short clauses, of which eight are expressed negatively. These clauses appear in pairs, with the exception of v. 7*a*, where a threefold group appears.[520] Many of Ezekiel's ordinances echo laws found in the covenant code (Exod 20:22–23:33), Deuteronomy, and especially the holiness code (Leviticus 17–26). (Few words, by contrast, are shared by 18:6-9 and the Decalogue.)[521] Others are congruent with assertions and accusations concerning Israel in extra-legal literature. These ordinances will be examined before inquiring into the original life setting of such lists.

The meaning of v. 6*a* is somewhat obscure. The phrase "to eat on the mountains" appears nowhere in Hebrew Scripture outside the book of Ezekiel. We do, however, encounter references to sacrifices atop mountains in honor (or in the presence) of deities (see 2 Kgs 16:4; Isa 65:7; Ezek 6:13; 20:28; 34:6; Hos 4:13). Ezekiel regards such activities as illicit (idolatrous); the righteous man does not participate in them. Neither does he "lift up his eyes to" (trust in help from) the "dung pellets of the house of Israel," Ezekiel's coarse and characteristic name for idols (see 6:4-6, 9, and 13 [twice]; the exact phrase appears in 8:10). He does not defile his neighbor's wife[522] or approach (for sexual intercourse) a menstruating woman (see Lev 15:19-24; 18:19).[523]

517. See Block, *Ezekiel 1–24,* 562.

518. As noted first in the Commentary on 3:16-22, biblical "casuistic" (conditional) laws, like their ancient Near Eastern counterparts, consist of a "protasis" (the subordinate clause in a conditional sentence; e.g., "If someone is caught kidnapping another Israelite, enslaving or selling the Israelite," Deut 24:7*a*), followed by an apodosis (the clause spelling out its legal consequences; e.g., "then that kidnapper shall die," Deut 24:7*b*). Characteristically, the subject in such laws is singular. Yet the intent of this law form is not to contrast the person with his or her community, but *to address personally every member of the larger group.*

519. As Block observes, "man" is preferable to "person" in this context, because the following list deals particularly with male crimes. At the same time, however, the principles articulated here and elsewhere in the chapter apply to all persons, regardless of gender. See Block, *Ezekiel 1–24,* 569n. 67.

520. See W. Zimmerli, *Ezekiel 1: A Commentary on the Book of the Prophet Ezekiel, Chapters 1–24,* trans. R. E. Clements, Hermeneia (Philadelphia: Fortress, 1979) 379.

521. Ibid., 379. Zimmerli observes, however, that Ezekiel's list of clauses appears in an order reminiscent of the Decalogue. While the first pair of clauses (v. 6*a*) deals with ordinances concerning worship of God, the second (v. 6*d*) deals with ritual regulations.

522. The prohibitions against adultery in both the Decalogue (Exod 20:14; Deut 5:18) and the holiness code (Lev 20:10) employ the verb נאף (*nāʾap*), "to commit adultery." Ezekiel, however, uses טמה (*ṭimmēh*), "to pollute," adopting the perspective of ritual uncleanness. See also Gen 34:5; Num 5:14, 27-28; Ezek 22:11; 23:13, 17; 33:26. See Zimmerli, *Ezekiel 1,* 380.

523. Tikva Frymer-Kensky, "Pollution, Purification, and Purgation in Biblical Israel," in *The Word of the Lord Shall Go Forth: Essays in Honor of David Noel Freedman in Celebration of His Sixtieth Birthday,* ed. Carol L. Meyers and M. O'Connor (Winona Lake: Eisenbrauns, 1983) 399-414.

While v. 6 reflects priestly interest in cultic and sexual pollutions, vv. 7-8 concern social morality and ethics. The former take precedence (as in the Decalogue), but the latter are double their number.[524] Matties suggests that Ezekiel has purposefully integrated the two: "Loyalty to Yahweh (cultically and ethically) will bring the reward of 'life.'"[525] The righteous man does not oppress anyone. Once a debtor has repaid him, he returns to that debtor any property (e.g., clothes, livestock) taken to secure the loan.[526] He does not rob; the verb גזל (*gāzal*) means "to tear away, seize, take violent possession of," while גנב (*gānab*), the verb employed in Exod 20:15 ("You shall not steal"), can refer to taking by stealth.[527] He feeds the hungry and clothes the naked. Though these actions are not explicitly commanded within the priestly law, they are of a piece with injunctions to care for the poor (see Lev 19:9-10; 23:22; Deut 15:7-11; 24:19-21; see also Matt 25:35-36). Moreover, he refuses to benefit from the misfortunes of others. He does not take interest (see Exod 22:24; Lev 25:35-37; Deut 23:20). The word נשך (*nešek*; from נשך [*nāšak*, "to bite"]), reflects the debtor's perspective on interest: It is "a piece of one's own pie that the creditor bites off." The word תרבית (*tarbît*; from רבה [*rābâ*]), reflects the lender's perspective on interest: It "increases" his material assets.[528] He is just and honest in his legal affairs. He refrains (lit., "takes back his hand," 20:22; Ps 74:11; Lam 2:8) from injustice and arbitrates between contenders in legal disputes.

The summary statement of v. 9*a* declares that the righteous man faithfully obeys Yahweh's statutes and ordinances. Verse 9*b* consists of two declaratory formulas, plus the signatory formula ("says the Lord God"). The first declaratory formula is צדיק הוא (*ṣaddîq hûʾ*), "righteous is he." Within the Hebrew Bible, this formula (and minor variations of it) is typically attributed to Yahweh. Here, in Harrelson's words, Ezekiel holds "before the community and its individual members the qualities of life that Yahweh approves and insists upon within

the community that approaches him as Lord."[529] The second declaratory formula, a verdict of acquittal ("he shall surely live," vv. 9*b*, 17, 19, 21; see also vv. 22, 28), is cast as the precise opposite of the death sentence, "he shall surely die," and so departs from the customary "he shall not die" (vv. 17-18, 21). Hutton explains the social function of such formulas in ancient Israel: "Declaratory formulae manifest the societal need to designate status to the members of society, to their actions and material surroundings. . . . Declaratory formulae are those formulaic statements which are made by a person authorized to do so in a given situation which declare a certain action, person or object to be in a specified status with regard to the community as a whole."[530]

Ezekiel's list of cultic and social ordinances has no precise parallel elsewhere within the Hebrew Bible. However, legal lists similar in form and/or content do appear within a variety of biblical genres. The lists in Hos 4:2 and Jer 7:9, for example, occur in prophetic judgment oracles bearing resemblances to the Decalogue.

Scholars have traced the origins of these and other lists to a number of social settings within the life of ancient Israel.[531] Wevers proposes that Ezekiel modeled his list on recitals of apodeictic (divine or unconditional) law during covenant renewal feasts.[532] Others suggest that his series of ordinances is beholden to clan lists of virtues,[533] to confessions of integrity of conduct recited by worshipers,[534] or to temple entrance liturgies.[535] Zimmerli concludes that the positive declarations in vv. 9 and 16 derive from a cultic ceremony in which worshipers approaching the temple gate were informed of the rules of the sanctuary by a priest.[536]

524. Moshe Greenberg, *Ezekiel 1–20*, AB 22 (Garden City, N.Y.: Doubleday, 1983) 342.

525. G. H. Matties, *Ezekiel 18 and the Rhetoric of Moral Discourse*, SBLDS 126 (Atlanta: Scholars Press, 1990) 104, 105.

526. Greenberg, *Ezekiel 1–20*, 329; Block, *Ezekiel 1–24*, 572.

527. BDB, s.v. "גנב."

528. Block, *Ezekiel 1–24*, 573.

529. W. Harrelson, *The Ten Commandments and Human Rights*, OBT (Philadelphia: Fortress, 1980) 39.

530. R. R. Hutton, "Declaratory Formulae: Forms of Authoritative Pronouncement in Ancient Israel" (Ph.D. diss., Claremont Graduate School, 1983) 38.

531. See Matties, *Ezekiel 18 and the Rhetoric of Moral Discourse*, 92-111.

532. J. W. Wevers, *Ezekiel*, NCB (London: Nelson, 1969) 140. His proposal is too hypothetical to command support.

533. See E. Gerstenberger, *Wesen und Herkunft des "Apodiktischen Rechts,"* WMANT 20 (Neukirchen-Vluyn: Neukirchener, 1965) 69-70.

534. See K. Galling, "Der Beichtspiegel: Eine gattungsgeschichtliche Studie," *ZAW* 47 (1929) 125-30.

535. See H. Gunkel and J. Begrich, *Einleitung in die Psalmen*, 2nd ed. (Göttingen: Vandenhoeck & Ruprecht, 1966) 408-9.

536. Zimmerli, *Ezekiel 1*, 376. For a fuller discussion of these and other proposals, see Matties, *Ezekiel 19 and the Rhetoric of Moral Discourse*, 92-111.

Each of the proposed settings in life and functions of legal lists, such as those appearing in this chapter, remains hypothetical owing to inadequate data. M. Weinfeld argues against the existence of entrance liturgies in ancient Israel, because the biblical literature provides no explicit evidence of such a ceremony.[537] He notes, nonetheless, that Psalms 15; 24:3-6; and Isa 33:14-16 share a common structure: an initial question or questions (e.g., "O LORD, who may abide in your tent?" Ps 15:1a), an answer (a list of conditions for entrance), and a promise (statement of stability, blessing, or security). "In all these passages," Weinfeld observes, "the ideal behavior of the one who is granted admission to the holy place is described both in the positive manner and in the negative. The positive formulation is mainly of a general definitive character whereas the negative enumerates the deeds in detail."[538]

Turning to Ezek 18:5-9, Weinfeld detects a similar structure: a positively formulated casuistic introduction (v. 5), followed by a negatively formulated list of the righteous man's behavior (vv. 6-8); a summarizing positive statement (v. 9a); and a promise (v. 9b). Though Ezekiel's list says nothing of the Temple, Weinfeld concludes that both the list's language and Ezekiel's priestly background point to the conclusion that "the provenance of the list is priestly and was crystallized in temple circles."[539]

If these texts are not reflections of ancient Israelite entrance liturgies, what was their original setting in life? Here, Weinfeld points to inscriptions discovered on doorposts and lentels of certain Egyptian temples dating from the Hellenistic period.[540] Particularly significant is an inscription on the lintel of a door in the forecourt of the Edfu temple by Seshat, mistress of writing, to the god Horus:

> I have come to you . . . that I may set down in writing before you the doer of good and the doer of evil, to wit:

he who initiates wrongfully
he [who enters] when unclean
he who speaks falsehood in your house
he who knows [to discern] right from wrong
he who is pure
he who is upright and walks in righteousness . . .
he who loves your attendants exceedingly
he who receives bribes . . .
he who covets the property of your temple
he who is careful . . .
he who does not take rewards or the share of any man.
I write down good for the doer of good in your city, I reject the character of the evil doer . . . [he who does righteousness] in your house [is] enduring forever, but the sinner perishes everlastingly.[541]

This inscription bears striking similarities in content with the lists in Psalms 15; 24:3-6; Isa 33:14-16; and Ezek 18:5-9.

Weinfeld observes that most of the relevant Egyptian inscriptions instructed priests about virtue and devotion.[542] He then points to parallels between such inscriptions and Ezekiel's lists: "Most of the sins found in the Egyptian texts occur in the lists of Ezekiel: abstaining from forbidden meals, sexual aberrations, and social sins like oppressing the poor, taking bribes, stealing, etc., are all represented in Ezek. 18:5ff, 22:6ff., 33:14f."[543]

Weinfeld suggests that lists of ordinances also were inscribed on temple entrances in ancient Israel (see Deut 11:20, which suggests that the *Shema* [Deut 6:4-5] was inscribed on the doorposts of Israelite houses). To his mind, this inference is more credible than the scenario of "a priest or priests standing at the Temple door and interrogating" those seeking entrance.[544] Unfortunately, no inscriptional evidence exists to substantiate this suggestion. Nonetheless, much commends his conclusion that both Egyptian temple inscriptions and Ezekiel's lists originated among the temple priests. Whether these ordinances were proclaimed by priests before worshipers seeking entrance to the Temple or by worshipers seeking entrance before priests remains speculative.

---

537. M. Weinfeld, "Instructions for Temple Visitors in the Bible and in Ancient Egypt," in *Egyptological Studies,* ed. S. Israelit-Groll, ScrHier 28 (Jerusalem: Magnes, 1982) 231.

538. Ibid., 226-27; see also Ps 5:3-8.

539. Ibid., 228.

540. Ibid., 232. Similar injunctions appear also in the Ramesside period and so derive from Old Egyptian tradition.

541. Ibid., 232-33, quoting from H. W. Fairman, "A Scene of the Offering of Truth in the Temple of Edfu," *Mitteilungen des deutschen Archaeologischen Institut Abteilung Kaira* 16/II (1958) 86-92.

542. Weinfeld, "Instructions for Temple Visitors in the Bible and in Ancient Egypt," 235.

543. Ibid., 235-36.

544. Ibid., 238.

The ancient reader probably knew little or nothing of Egyptian temple inscriptions. However, he likely associated Ezekiel's lists of cultic and moral injunctions with the priestly/temple sphere. At the same time, he realized that the prophet's original audience was far removed from the Jerusalem Temple and its cult. Matties offers helpful observations regarding the function of Ezekiel's lists within his exilic community:

> Could it be that Ezekiel is actually modelling his list after the decalogue with its "first table" of laws relating to God, especially the first two commandments? He would thereby be calling for public recognition of the continuing validity of the covenant . . . as well as a renewal of piety expressed in a transformation of behavior befitting one who wishes to worship that God. Loyalty to Yahweh (cultically and ethically) will bring the reward of "life." Thus the legal lists enable the chapter to function as a sermon exhorting the people against all appearances to trust the sovereignty of Yahweh, to act responsibly, and to take part (in spite of judgment) in the reconstitution of the people of Israel. . . . The legal lists in Ezekiel 18 have been drawn into the unique focus of the disputation—to call forth the new reality of a peoplehood committed to its covenant Lord. It is that goal to which the final traditional convention beckons—the call to conversion.[545]

According to Ezekiel's second hypothetical case, the righteous man begets a violent son (בֶּן־פָּרִיץ *bēn-pārîṣ*), a shedder of blood (see also 16:38; 22:3, 27; 23:45; 33:24), who engages in activities not committed by his father.[546] In this second list, the prophet transforms negative ordinances into positive ones and vice versa in order to present the son as the antithesis of his father. Other differences are apparent as well: Nothing is said of intercourse with a menstruous woman; in v. 12, the oppressed are called "the poor and needy" (cf. v. 7), and a new charge is added (he "commits abomination").

---

545. G. H. Matties, *Ezekiel 18 and the Rhetoric of Moral Discourse*, SBLDS 126 (Atlanta: Scholars Press, 1990) 105.

546. Verse 10*b* MT reads, "and does a brother from one of these." LXX translates "and commits sins," an attempt to smooth over the difficulty. Block suggests that אח (*āḥ*), "brother," is the result of a partial dittograph of the following word. See D. I. Block, *The Book of Ezekiel: Chapters 1–24*, NICOT (Grand Rapids: Eerdmans, 1997) 575. The reader may well stumble at the phrase, suspect an error, yet construe the text reasonably well. The text of vv. 10*b*-11*a* also presents difficulties. אלה (*'ēlleh*), "these things" likely refers to the son's violent acts of bloodshed, while the following circumstantial clause returns to the son's righteous father.

Verse 13 contains no counterpart to the verdict, "he is righteous," in v. 9*b* (one might expect רשׁע הוא [*rāšāʿ hûʾ*, "He is wicked"]). But the death sentence, "He shall not live," is the opposite of "he shall surely live" in v. 9*b*. The following formula, "he shall surely die," appears numerous times within pentateuchal legal texts (see esp. Exod 19:12-13, where both "he shall not live" and "he shall surely die" appear).[547] A third form of the death sentence, "his blood shall be upon him," echoes Lev 20:9-27. This declaratory formula originally functioned to absolve executioners of blood guilt in capital cases. Ezekiel adapts it in service of his thesis: A wicked person is executed as a consequence of his or her own sin only.[548]

Verse 14 introduces Ezekiel's third hypothetical case: This man has a son who sees his father's sins, takes thought (see Eccl 7:14), and does not repeat them. The list describing his conduct (vv. 15-17) is both the antithesis of vv. 11-13 and a near copy of vv. 5-9, save for several changes. For example, here, as in vv. 11-13, no mention is made of intercourse with a menstruous woman (cf. v. 6); he demands no pledge from his debtors (a "step above" the policy of his righteous grandfather! cf. v. 7); the two-part statement regarding interest in v. 8 appears as a single observation; "my statutes" and "my ordinances" (v. 9) appear in reverse order in v. 17. The grandson's case does not conclude with the declaratory formula "he is righteous" (cf v. 9*b*), but the verdict of acquittal, "he shall surely live," does appear (v. 17*b*). Verse 18 harks back to the case of his sinful father: On account of his sins—extortion (see Deut 24:14-15; Mal 3:5), robbery, and "not good" deeds against his community, he shall die.

Critics observe that only with the appearance of this third case does Ezekiel create a scenario germane to the saying in v. 2: The son does not suffer for the sins of his backsliding father. But the presence of the first test case is hardly extraneous to his larger purpose. By both beginning and concluding with a list of the behaviors of righteous individuals, the prophet emphasizes their importance for the ongoing pedagogical task of building and shaping a righteous community.

---

547. Ibid., 564.
548. Ibid., 577.

The question posed in v. 19*a* constitutes the second of three quotations attributed by Ezekiel to his audience. With it, the exiles challenge, or are said to challenge, the judgment rendered in his third case: "Yet you say, 'Why should not the son suffer for the iniquity of the father?'" How can Ezekiel contradict their proverb, when they are living examples of its truth?[549] The prophet's response is fourfold. First, he reiterates (in summary fashion and in the language of casuistic law) both the son's positive behavior and his "sentence" ("he shall surely live"). Second, he repeats the judgment ("the person who sins shall die") first announced in v. 4*b*. Third, he again

renounces the point of the people's saying: "A child shall not suffer for the iniquity of a parent, nor a parent suffer for the iniquity of a child." This declaration actually moves beyond the proverb's truth claim, for it asserts that transgenerational retribution moves neither forward (from one generation to the succeeding one as in v. 2) nor backward (from the present generation to the preceding one; cf. Deut 24:16). Fourth, he casts the principle of retribution using the terms "righteous(ness)" and "wicked(ness)"; each individual/generation is judged on the basis of whether he or she belongs to one category or the other. These two terms constitute a bridge from this section to the next, where they will everywhere appear. (See Reflections at 18:21-32.)

---

549. Greenberg finds the people's question in v. 19*a* "provocative." See Moshe Greenberg, *Ezekiel 21–37*, AB 22A (Garden City, N.Y.: Doubleday, 1997) 332.

Ezekiel 18:21-32, "Why Will You Die, O House of Israel?"

NIV

21"But if a wicked man turns away from all the sins he has committed and keeps all my decrees and does what is just and right, he will surely live; he will not die. 22None of the offenses he has committed will be remembered against him. Because of the righteous things he has done, he will live. 23Do I take any pleasure in the death of the wicked? declares the Sovereign LORD. Rather, am I not pleased when they turn from their ways and live?

24"But if a righteous man turns from his righteousness and commits sin and does the same detestable things the wicked man does, will he live? None of the righteous things he has done will be remembered. Because of the unfaithfulness he is guilty of and because of the sins he has committed, he will die.

25"Yet you say, 'The way of the Lord is not just.' Hear, O house of Israel: Is my way unjust? Is it not your ways that are unjust? 26If a righteous man turns from his righteousness and commits sin, he will die for it; because of the sin he has committed he will die. 27But if a wicked man turns away from the wickedness he has committed and does what is just and right, he will save his life. 28Because he considers all the offenses he has committed and turns away from them, he will

NRSV

21But if the wicked turn away from all their sins that they have committed and keep all my statutes and do what is lawful and right, they shall surely live; they shall not die. 22None of the transgressions that they have committed shall be remembered against them; for the righteousness that they have done they shall live. 23Have I any pleasure in the death of the wicked, says the Lord GOD, and not rather that they should turn from their ways and live? 24But when the righteous turn away from their righteousness and commit iniquity and do the same abominable things that the wicked do, shall they live? None of the righteous deeds that they have done shall be remembered; for the treachery of which they are guilty and the sin they have committed, they shall die.

25Yet you say, 'The way of the Lord is unfair.' Hear now, O house of Israel: Is my way unfair? Is it not your ways that are unfair? 26When the righteous turn away from their righteousness and commit iniquity, they shall die for it; for the iniquity that they have committed they shall die. 27Again, when the wicked turn away from the wickedness they have committed and do what is lawful and right, they shall save their life. 28Because they considered and turned away from all the transgressions that they had committed, they shall

NIV

surely live; he will not die. ²⁹Yet the house of Israel says, 'The way of the Lord is not just.' Are my ways unjust, O house of Israel? Is it not your ways that are unjust?

³⁰"Therefore, O house of Israel, I will judge you, each one according to his ways, declares the Sovereign Lord. Repent! Turn away from all your offenses; then sin will not be your downfall. ³¹Rid yourselves of all the offenses you have committed, and get a new heart and a new spirit. Why will you die, O house of Israel? ³²For I take no pleasure in the death of anyone, declares the Sovereign Lord. Repent and live!

NRSV

surely live; they shall not die. ²⁹Yet the house of Israel says, 'The way of the Lord is unfair.' O house of Israel, are my ways unfair? Is it not your ways that are unfair?

30Therefore I will judge you, O house of Israel, all of you according to your ways, says the Lord God. Repent and turn from all your transgressions; otherwise iniquity will be your ruin.ᵃ ³¹Cast away from you all the transgressions that you have committed against me, and get yourselves a new heart and a new spirit! Why will you die, O house of Israel? ³²For I have no pleasure in the death of anyone, says the Lord God. Turn, then, and live.

ᵃOr *so that they shall not be a stumbling block of iniquity to you*

COMMENTARY

With v. 21 Ezekiel takes up a second issue concerning divine justice. If he has succeeded in convincing his audience that Yahweh does not act according to the principle of transgenerational retribution, then they are prepared to consider a related one: the idea of a "treasury of demerit or merit."[550] The prophet repudiates this idea via two hypothetical cases, each expressed by a protasis followed by an apodosis (verdict).

The first case legislates the fate of the wicked person (community, generation)[551] who repents of (= turns away from) past sins, obeys God's laws, and does "justice and righteousness" (משפט וצדקה *mišpāṭ ûṣĕdāqâ*).[552] Such persons "shall surely live; they shall not die" (see v. 17). The trove of sin accumulated in the course of a lifetime (treasury of demerit) does not determine destiny; only one's present disposition and behavior pertain. Past transgressions will not be "remembered."[553] The

following rhetorical question ("Have I any pleasure in the death of the wicked . . . and not rather that they should turn from [repent of] their ways and live?"), with its intervening, emphatic signatory formula ("says the Lord God") seeks a positive response from the audience/reader. That response, Block observes, is what those seeking release from the bondage of fatalism and despondency need so desperately: "a new vision of God, a God who is on the side of blessing and life, not on the side of the curse and death."[554]

Verse 24 presents the second of Ezekiel's pair of cases, that of the righteous person who turns away from righteousness and commits iniquity like the abominations of the wicked (see 3:20). "Shall he live?" the prophet asks (see v. 13), inviting a negative response that will dispatch the notion of a treasury of merit. Past righteousness will not be remembered. He also is judged on the basis of present disposition and behavior.

Again, Ezekiel's assertions provoke his audience. "The way of Yahweh is unfair" (לא יתכן *lōʾ yittākēn*), they charge—a "frontal attack" on God's administration of justice (v. 25a).[555] In the Qal verbal system, תכן (*tākan*) means "to regulate,"

550. Block, *Ezekiel 1–24,* 583.
551. In the MT, this statement is cast in masculine singular forms but addresses each individual within the community.
552. This phrase, predicated of Yahweh (e.g., Gen 18:19; Ps 99:4; Jer 9:23), defines both divine and royal standards of conduct. As God acts, so must the king. David (2 Sam 8:15) and Solomon (1 Kgs 10:9) embody this ideal, and Jeremiah demands it of present and future Davidic kings (Jer 22:3, 15-17; 23:5; 33:15). Here Ezekiel, like Amos before him (Amos 5:24; see also Gen 18:19), "democratizes" this standard: Each individual must conform to it. See Greenberg, *Ezekiel 1–20,* 343.
553. The same God who graciously "remembers" the covenant with the wanton wife Jerusalem (16:60) here graciously states that the sins of those who turn back from them will not be remembered.

554. Block, *Ezekiel 1–24,* 583.
555. See W. Zimmerli, *Ezekiel 1: A Commentary on the Book of the Prophet Ezekiel, Chapters 1–24,* trans. R. E. Clements, Hermeneia (Philadelphia: Fortress, 1979) 385.

"measure," "estimate"; in the Niphal (here and in 33:17, 20), it denotes "to be adjusted to the standard, i.e., right, equitable."[556] Negating the verb, the exiles characterize God's way as inequitable and arbitrary. Are they saying that "as long as someone suffers, God does not care whether it is the sinner or not"?[557] Have they decided that they would rather Yahweh be unjust than have to acknowedge their own injustice and responsibility?[558] Is their attack an attempt abruptly to retreat from a disputation they cannot win? Or is it a product of "cognitive dissonance" (confronted by a fresh, compelling understanding of God's administration of justice, they nonetheless experience conflict [dissonance] between this new perception and the traditional one)?[559] Whatever their motivation, Yahweh responds first by lobbing the accusation back into their laps (v. 26b), and second by reiterating the cases and verdicts of vv. 21-24 (in reverse order). The phrase "he shall save his life" (v. 27b) emphasizes personal responsibility for one's fate.

For a second time, Ezekiel's audience charges that the way of the Lord is unfair (v. 29a), and Yahweh countercharges in kind. The disputation is stuck; both parties are at a standstill. But then, God speaks again—first, to reassert the divine prerogative to judge and to reiterate the principle by which judgments are made: "'I will judge you, O house of Israel, all of you according to your ways,' says the Lord GOD" (again, we encounter Ezekiel's insistence that the punishment is entirely appropriate to the crime; see, e.g., 16:43; 17:19); and second to issue a call for repentance, lest iniquity be the exiles' downfall (vv. 30b-32; see 14:6). At this point, Block observes, Ezekiel changes his rhetorical strategy: "If he cannot convince his audience of the error of their ways through logical argumentation, perhaps a more impassioned approach will succeed."[560] Verse 31 is a call to *action*. God urges the exiles both to cast away their transgressions and to "get themselves a new heart and a new spirit." The latter is an astonishing challenge—unique to the book of Ezekiel and, within that corpus, unique to this passage. In 11:19-20, Yahweh promised to gift the exiles with "one [or "a new"] heart" and a "new spirit," in order that they might henceforth obey God's statutes and ordinances. Here alone does the prophet assert that humans themselves have the capacity to acquire these qualities.[561] "Why will you die, O house of Israel?" the Lord asks/appeals. Verse 32 reiterates the substance of v. 23. But what was there issued in the form of a question now becomes an impassioned declaration. Yahweh takes no pleasure in the death of anyone. "Turn, then, and live."

556. *BDB*, 1067a.
557. So Greenberg, *Ezekiel 1–20*, 333.
558. Paul Joyce, *Divine Initiative and Human Response in Ezekiel*, JSOTSup 51 (Sheffield: JSOT, 1989) 52.
559. See R. P. Carroll, *When Prophecy Failed: Cognitive Dissonance in the Prophetic Traditions of the Old Testament* (New York: Seabury, 1979) 86-128.

560. Block, *Ezekiel 1–24*, 587.
561. See Greenberg, *Ezekiel 1–20*, 341.

REFLECTIONS

Ezekiel 18 is a text worthy of the author in whose name the prophet speaks. A masterpiece of rational argument, it confounds every attempt to "get around" God, to hide behind a kind of fatalism that discourages responsibility by whispering, "What's the use?" A testimony to courage, it dares to contradict a long-lived understanding of how God operates in the world, because at this critical moment, that understanding threatens to conceal, rather than reveal, divine justice. A clarion call to liberation, it proclaims God's freedom both to flout human expectations and to stand squarely on the side of life, and also human freedom to turn from wickedness, to choose life, and to get about the task of personal and communal transformation. Filled with passion, it eschews sentimentality. Its lessons are yet being learned; its contemporary relevance is stunning. No less than Ezekiel's exilic audience, modern readers both resist its message and long to embrace it.

Proverbs remain alive when they encapsulate, in a succinct and memorable way, an observation whose truth claim makes sense of everyday human experience. The "sour grapes" saying, circulating in Jerusalem and also among the exiles, performed this task well. It is the case that the behavior of one generation affects, negatively as well as positively, the formation, experiences, and character of the next. The notion of transgenerational *responsibility* plays a crucial role in familial and communal life. It calls us faithfully to be instruments of God's care-taking—to take seriously the tasks of raising children, of creating a society that nurtures all its members, regardless of their material wealth or social status, of teaching moral and ethical values that provide a strong foundation for life—indeed, abundant life. The people's proverb conveys a truth we all can grasp.

Within the literary world of Ezekiel 18, however, the sour grapes saying is an attempt to make sense of a different sort of experience. Its propounders are asserting that transgenerational *retribution* is the principle by which God administers justice: Yahweh enters the stage of history in order to punish not only sinners, but also their offspring. Ezekiel has already insisted that the long history of Jerusalem and of those it embodies is chock a block with abominations (e.g., chap. 16). If the exiles' construal of the proverb's truth claim is allowed to stand, then they are bound by chains they did not forge, and appeals to Yahweh are an exercise in frustration. Their current plight is a consequence of God's way and will. They can protest, but they cannot win.

Ezekiel disputes the exiles' reading of reality, rooted in tradition though it be. Their perspective is death-dealing, and as he will assert several times in subsequent verses, God takes no delight in the death of anyone. His contemporaries are not shackled by the failings of their forebears. Rather, their fate hangs on their own righteousness or wickedness. Note that Ezekiel nowhere questions Yahweh's right to judge Israel. His God holds human beings accountable for the orientation and conduct of their lives. But he everywhere insists that Israel's judge decides each case according to its own merit or demerit.

Ezekiel further perceives that behind the people's protests of transgenerational punishment lies a reluctance to accept responsibility for their own conduct and its consequences. If God is unjust, what matter that they are idolatrous, violent, oppressive, and unjust? Their fate is sealed; it is "every man for himself."

Ezekiel's three test cases perform at least two functions. On the one hand, they systematically refute the people's understanding of how divine justice operates. On the other hand, they articulate guidelines for just and righteous living. The declaration "he is righteous" (v. 9) is not equivalent to the declaration "he/she is perfect." Neither are Ezekiel's lists of what righteous persons do, and refrain from doing, a "recipe" for successful negotiations with God: Meet these obligations (no less, no more), and you will be found innocent on the day of trial. Rather, the person or community that lives according to Yahweh's statutes and ordinances is manifesting in everyday ways that its primary orientation is toward God. This orientation pervades all aspects of human life—from the most intimate relations between husband and wife, to the most public transactions between business associates.

Dispatching the notion of transgenerational retribution both frees Ezekiel's audience (ancient and modern) from the penalty of their forebears' sins and forces them to assume responsibility for their own. No one likes to be told that aspects of his or her theology are wrong, especially when those aspects provide a means of making sense of the world and of personal experience. Little wonder that the exiles resisted the prophet's refutation of the principle (v. 19)—one they had learned at their mothers' knees! But Ezekiel will not permit them to disparage God's administration of justice, as if they knew better the form that justice should take.

A related issue remains, however, and Ezekiel tackles it head-on in 18:21-28. Just as God does not judge one generation for the sins of previous ones, so also Yahweh does not keep a "scorecard" of wickedness or righteousness accumulated in the course of a single lifetime or generation. Life is not a baseball game, in which points scored over the course of nine innings are tallied to determine the winning team. Persons are judged not on the basis of past conduct, but on the choices they make about the orientation of their lives here and now. Jesus says as much when he forgives the sinful woman who, learning of his whereabouts, comes to him, washes his feet with her tears, dries them with her hair, and anoints them with her precious ointment. Though her sins were many, Jesus sends her forth pardoned and in peace (Luke 7:36-50). The very rich ruler, by contrast, can affirm that he has kept all God's commandments from his youth. But when Jesus tells him that he must sell all of his possessions, give the money to the poor, and then follow him, he is saddened by the price of reorienting his life, even though his participation in God's kingdom it at stake (Luke 18:18-25).

Humans have a choice, but they must choose. God is not apathetic about our choices and so discloses the divine predilection for life. Ezekiel 18:30-32 summons us all to select life—a decision that begins with earnest repentance (turning away from our transgressions) and continues with the daily and active pursuit of a new heart and spirit. Paul echoes that challenge when, in his Letter to the Philippians, he enjoins them to "work out your own salvation with fear and trembling; for it is God who is at work in you, enabling you both to will and to work for his pleasure" (Phil 2:12-13 NRSV).

EZEKIEL 19:1-14, A "LAMENT" OVER THE PRINCES OF JUDAH

OVERVIEW

Yahweh abruptly commands Ezekiel to lift up a קִינה (*qînâ* "dirge") concerning the princes of Israel (v. 1). Verse 14*b,* a brief colophon, states that the intervening verses actually became a dirge recited by the people after the events they recount had occurred.[562]

Although Ezekiel is ordered to perform a dirge, the chapter appears to consist of two laments. Verses 2-9 describe the frustrated efforts of a lioness to elevate first one and then another of her cubs. Her hopes are dashed as each cub is ensnared by the nations, shackled, and carried off—the first to Egypt, the second to "the king of Babylon."[563] Verses 10-14*a,* by contrast, focus upon a mothering vine (see chaps. 15 and 17) flourishing in well-watered soil, fruitful and ramified, but in the twinkling of an eye uprooted, hurled to the ground, desiccated, defoliated, scorched by flames, transplanted to dry desert ground, and further burned by a fire originating in

its own stem. Yet the two parts of this chapter are not so disparate as the shift in imagery might suggest. Both treat Judah's Davidic dynasty, more specifically, its final, tragic years; both employ tropes (lion, vine) associated with royalty and nobility; and each begins with an enigmatic reference to "your mother" (vv. 2, 10). Moreover, lions and vines appear in Gen 49:9-11 (Jacob's blessing on Judah), suggesting that the juxtaposition of these images was no Ezekielian innovation. Such similarities cannot prove that both parts of Ezekiel 19 were composed at the same time and by the same author, of course; and specialists have advanced many a theory about their earliest forms, content, redactional supplements, dates, and authorship.[564] They do, however, encourage the ancient reader to construe vv. 1-14 as a two-part unit with a single message: The house of David is coming to an ignoble end and so offers no basis for hope of national survival.

Ezekiel's dirge both recounts past events and anticipates future ones. From the reader's perspective

---

562. A colophon (finishing touch) is an inscription at the end of a literary work or, as here, a section of that work. Some colophons include a statement of subject, the author's name, and publication information. Others consist simply of a comment by the author or editor. See also Lev 26:46; Job 31:40; Ps 72:20.

563. In a highly speculative thesis, I. Kottsieper proposes that vv. 2-9 derive from a secular song about a lioness whose cub grows to terrorize its territory until at last it is captured. See I. Kottsieper, " 'Was ist deine Mutter?' Eine Studie zu Ez 19,2-9," *ZAW* 105 (1993) 444-61.

564. K. Pohlmann, who dates all of chap. 19 after 587 BCE, finds the dirge's original kernal in vv. 2, 5*b,* 6, 7*b,* 8, 9, on the one hand, and vv. 10, 11*a,* 12*a,* 12*b,* and 14*b,* on the other hand. See K. Pohlmann, *Ezechielstudien: Zur Redaktionsgeschichte des Buches Und Zur Frage noch den altesten Texten,* BZAW (Berlin: de Gruyter, 1992) 139-59.

it, like preceding oracles, presupposes a date prior to Jerusalem's destruction (and the deportation of its final Davidic king, Zedekiah). Modern critics tend to contest that conclusion, but again, ancient readers would not have denied the prophet the ability accurately to portray the future. To the contrary, this oracle, like others, further enhances their regard for Ezekiel as Yahweh's authentic spokesperson to the exiles and, through the process of appropriation and reinterpretation, for their own late exilic times as well. Ezekiel's audience, it seems, resisted his words until history forced them to acknowledge that "a prophet has been among them" (2:5; 33:33).

Ezekiel 19:1-9, Maternal Ambitions, Bitter Outcomes

NIV

19 "Take up a lament concerning the princes of Israel ²and say:

" 'What a lioness was your mother
     among the lions!
She lay down among the young lions
     and reared her cubs.
³She brought up one of her cubs,
     and he became a strong lion.
He learned to tear the prey
     and he devoured men.
⁴The nations heard about him,
     and he was trapped in their pit.
They led him with hooks
     to the land of Egypt.

⁵" 'When she saw her hope unfulfilled,
     her expectation gone,
she took another of her cubs
     and made him a strong lion.
⁶He prowled among the lions,
     for he was now a strong lion.
He learned to tear the prey
     and he devoured men.
⁷He broke down[a] their strongholds
     and devastated their towns.
The land and all who were in it
     were terrified by his roaring.
⁸Then the nations came against him,
     those from regions round about.
They spread their net for him,
     and he was trapped in their pit.
⁹With hooks they pulled him into a cage
     and brought him to the king of Babylon.
They put him in prison,
     so his roar was heard no longer
     on the mountains of Israel.

[a]7 Targum (see Septuagint); Hebrew *He knew*

NRSV

19 As for you, raise up a lamentation for the princes of Israel, ²and say:

What a lioness was your mother
     among lions!
She lay down among young lions,
     rearing her cubs.
³She raised up one of her cubs;
     he became a young lion,
and he learned to catch prey;
     he devoured humans.
⁴The nations sounded an alarm against him;
     he was caught in their pit;
and they brought him with hooks
     to the land of Egypt.
⁵When she saw that she was thwarted,
     that her hope was lost,
she took another of her cubs
     and made him a young lion.
⁶He prowled among the lions;
     he became a young lion,
and he learned to catch prey;
     he devoured people.
⁷And he ravaged their strongholds,[a]
     and laid waste their towns;
the land was appalled, and all in it,
     at the sound of his roaring.
⁸The nations set upon him
     from the provinces all around;
they spread their net over him;
     he was caught in their pit.
⁹With hooks they put him in a cage,
     and brought him to the king of Babylon;
they brought him into custody,
so that his voice should be heard no more
     on the mountains of Israel.

[a]Heb *his widows*

COMMENTARY

Without benefit of the familiar word event formula ("the word of the LORD came to me"), v. 1 begins with "But you," followed by Yahweh's command that Ezekiel perform a dirge concerning the princes of Judah. Hebrew קינה (*qînâ*) refers to a dirge or lament sung or recited at an individual's death.[565] The most famous biblical example is David's dirge over King Saul and his son Jonathan (2 Sam 1:19-27). But Ezekiel's predecessors took up the genre also to lament the destruction of their nation and people (see, e.g., Jer 7:29; 9:10; Amos 5:1). Not all biblical laments are called *qînâ*, but of the eighteen appearances of that term, ten appear within the book of Ezekiel.

The dirges of ancient Israel tend to exhibit certain characteristic features: (1) pairs of lines with a 3:2 metrical pattern; (2) an initial exclamation of grief (either איך/איכה *'êk/'êkâ* ["How"] or *hôy* ["Alas!"]); (3) direct address to the deceased; and (4) a "then/now" scheme, in which past glories are contrasted with present anguish and loss (see, e.g., Lam 1:1).[566] The first of these features is illustrated by Amos 5:2 (accented letters represent stressed syllables):

> Fállen, no móre to ríse,
> is the vírgin Isráel! (RSV)

This 3:2 ("limping") metrical pattern appears in both parts of Ezekiel's dirge (less frequently in vv. 10-14). Because the pattern is not employed consistently throughout other examples of the genre, however, recent critics are less inclined to emend a text solely on the basis of meter.[567] The second feature, an initial cry of grief, is found in Lam 1:1; 2:1; and 4:1 (all *'êkâ*, "How"), but not in Ezekiel 19. Verses 1 and 10 address a second-person masculine singular entity ("*your* mother"), although the prophet does not identify him/them by name. We might reasonably conjecture that Ezekiel's ostensible addressee is yet among the living.

Zedekiah—his contemporary, Judah's last king, and the "vine" of chap. 17—is the most likely candidate. Finally, both parts of Ezekiel's dirge present a stark contrast between past and present, though in each case a shadow is cast over the description of past glories.

As he progresses through vv. 1-14, the ancient reader will surely ponder whether Ezekiel's "lament" is sincere or sarcastic. Unlike the prophet's original audience, he (and we) are bereft of certain clues (body language, including facial expressions, intonation, gestures, etc.) that were available to the exiles. Cooke detects in Ezekiel's words "the sigh of a patriotic heart,"[568] and it is difficult to imagine that the prophet cared not at all for Yahweh's covenant with David and his descendants (2 Samuel 7), though certainly he was disappointed by and hostile toward most of Judah's final rulers. Nevertheless, his lament is peculiar in many respects. In Ezekiel's "praise" of the princes, positive and negative comments commingle (see below). Moreover, humans appear in the guise of animals and plants. Indeed, his dirge is no less a fable than 17:2-10. Block terms the present chapter a parody: Ezekiel has adopted the form of a *qînâ*, but infused it with content alien to that genre.[569] In so doing, he creates tension between form and substance, "*qînâ* and story, song and fable," provoking hearers to ponder more deeply the poem's meaning.[570]

Verses 2b-9 consist of a two-part (vv. 2b-4, vv. 5-9), fabulous lament over two of Judah's "princes."[571] Initially, it focuses on "your mother"—"a lioness [לביא *lĕbiyyā'*] among lions [אריות *'ărāyôt*]," an exemplary example of her breed. The reader is invited to admire her,

565. That dirges were sung is suggested by 2 Chr 35:25.

566. See W. R. Garr, "The Qinah: A Study of Poetic Meter, Syntax and Sytle," *ZAW* 95 (1983) 54-75; D. R. Hillers, *Lamentations*, AB 7A (Garden City, N.Y.: Doubleday, 1982) xxx-xxxvii; D. I. Block, *The Book of Ezekiel: Chapters 1–24*, NICOT (Grand Rapids: Eerdmans, 1997) 592-93.

567. For a discussion of meter and (better) rhythm in Hebrew poetry, see D. L. Petersen and K. H. Richards, *Interpreting Hebrew Poetry*, GBS (Minneapolis: Fortress, 1992) 37-47.

568. G. A. Cooke, *A Critical and Exegetical Commentary on the Book of Ezekiel*, ICC (New York: Charles Scribner's Sons, 1937) 1:210.

569. Block, *Ezekiel 1–24*, 594. Cf. W. Zimmerli, *Ezekiel 1: A Commentary on the Book of the Prophet Ezekiel, Chapters 1–24*, trans. R. E. Clements, Hermeneia (Philadelphia: Fortress, 1979) 392. G. A. Yee defines parody as "the literary imitation of an established form or style." See G. A. Yee, "Anatomy of Biblical Parody: The Dirge Form in 2 Samuel 1 and Isaiah 14," *CBQ* 50 (1988) 565.

570. Block, *Ezekiel 1–24*, 594-95. Isaiah 14 contains a mocking "lament" against the king of Babylon.

571. The noun נשיא (*nāśî'*, "prince") sometimes refers to members of Judah's upper class. Here, however, it designates male members of the royal family. Ezekiel prefers "prince" to "king" (see, e.g., 12:10, 12)—a verbal swipe at Judah's last kings.

stretched out among young lions (כפרים *kĕpirîm*), raising her cubs (גוריה *gûreyhā*). From the litter, she selects one cub that, by virtue of her maternal attention and training, grows to become a young lion and successful hunter—a prerequisite for survival. To this point, Ezekiel has said nothing negative about the lioness or her offspring. But with the notice that the latter devours humans (v. 3*b*), positive associations (strength, nobility, etc.) recede and others (rapacity and violence) predominate (see also Ezek 22:25; Pss 7:2; 10:9, 17; 12; 22:13, 21; Prov 28:15; Isa 5:29; Zeph 3:3).

In response, the nations set out on a lion hunt, a sport of ancient kings. Verse 4 sheds light on how such beasts were captured. Hebrew שחת (*šaḥat*) refers to a pit dug in the ground and then disguised so that the animal unknowingly falls into it. An eighteenth-century BCE letter from Mari describes the success of this technique:

> A lion has devoured Ḥabdu-Ami's sheep in the fold. Now he [Ḥabdu-Ami] has dug a pit in his fold in Bit-Akkaka. While searching for the fold the lion fell into the pit, when Ḥabdu-Ami was in Dur-Iaḥdun-Lim. The lion tried to escape [the pit], but the shepherds gathered wood, with which they filled the pit and set it on fire. Thus they burned the lion in the fire. He closed his jaws. There shall be no more broken arms any more.[572]

"Hook" (חח *ḥaḥ*) refers to a piercing implement (see also 29:4; 38:4). Isaiah 37:29 (= 2 Kgs 19:28) speaks of a hook through the nose.[573]

With the notice that the nations brought their catch to Egypt (v. 4*b*), Ezekiel provides his first real clue concerning the identity of the lioness's first cub: Jehoahaz (609 BCE) alone among Judah's kings was exiled to Egypt (after only a three-month reign; see 2 Kgs 23:31-34). Does he thereby disclose that the lioness is Hamutal, daughter of Jeremiah of Libnah and Jehoahaz's mother (2 Kgs 23:31)?

The second phase of Ezekiel's fable also focuses initially on the lioness. When she realizes that her son will not return, she selects a second cub; he, too, grows to become a young lion. The prophet details his behavior more fully than that of his predecessor. He swaggers among the pride, learns to hunt successfully, and, like his brother, develops a taste for human flesh. Moreover, he "knows" (i.e., has sexual intercourse with) "his 'widows' " (v. 7*a*). Though the phrase is intelligible (see below), scholars often emend it for at least three reasons. First, it appears to abandon the leonine imagery of previous lines; humans have intercourse with widows; lions do not. Second, it seems an inappropriate parallel to the following line, "he laid waste their cities." Third, none of the ancient versions support precisely the reading in the MT.[574] Hence, both the NRSV and the NIV emend אלמנותיו (*'almĕnôtāyw*, "his widows") to ארמנותיהם (*'armĕnôtêhem*, "his strongholds").

Reading with the MT, C. Begg shows how v. 7*a* continues the lion imagery of vv. 2-6. The third-person masculine singular suffix "his" (widows) refers to the first cub (Jehoahaz). As king of his pride, this young lion ruled its females and sired all of their cubs. When he was captured, however, a new leader of the pride emerged, and he claimed (mated with) these lionesses. Hence, v. 7*a* refers to the second lion's (i.e., prince's) appropriation of his predecessor's harem (see 2 Samuel 3; 12; 13:8; 16:21-22; 1 Kgs 2:13-22).[575] I would add that "widow" is itself a complex term that sometimes referred to dependent cities (see Excursus: "Cities as Females," 1221-25). Thoughts of "widowed cities" may enter the mind of the reader who considers the first half of v. 7*a* in the light of the second half of v. 7*a* ("he has laid waste their cities"). Both the land and its inhabitants are appalled by the sound of his roaring. The nations of surrounding provinces come to Israel's "rescue," capturing him by means of net (רשת *rešet*) and pit and bringing him to "the king of Babylon" in order that his roaring no longer be heard on "the mountains of Israel."

572. Quoted by Block, *Ezekiel 1–24*, 601. See also A. K. Grayson, "Ambush and Animal Pit in Akkadian," in *Studies Presented to A. L. Oppenheim*, ed. R. D. Biggs and J. A. Brinkman (Chicago: Oriental Institute, 1964) 90-94, and "New Evidence on an Assyrian Hunting Practice," in *Essays on the Ancient Semitic World*, ed. J. W. Wevers and B. D. Redford, eds. (Toronto: University of Toronto Press, 1970) 3-5.

573. See also Ashurbanipal's account of the capture of Uate', his foe, in *ANET*, 300.

574. C. Begg, "The Reading in Ezekiel 19,7a: A Proposal," *ETL* 65 (1989) 370. Begg summarizes ancient and modern resolutions to the crux on 370-77.

575. Begg, ibid., 377-79, identifies this second cub as Jehoiakim, Jehoahaz's older half brother. See also Block, *Ezekiel 1–24*, 602.

If the first cub represents Jehoahaz, who is the second? This "riddle" has exercised interpreters for centuries;[576] and each of Jehoahaz's successors (Jehoiakim, Jehoiachin, Zedekiah) has had his champions.[577] Obviously, no simple solution is to hand, as each candidate's "dossier" includes both supporting and opposing data. Begg considers each ruler in turn and opts for Jehoiakim, Jehoahaz's immediate successor to the throne, because descriptions of his reign (609–598/7 BCE) best fit those of the second cub's rule in vv. 5-9.[578] Both 2 Kgs 24:4 and Jer 22:17 charge Jehoiakim with shedding innocent blood; the latter adds that he sought "dishonest gain" and practiced "oppression and violence" (see also Jer 26:20-23; 36). Because Jehoiakim was placed on the throne by Pharaoh Necho and not by "the people of the land" (but see Ezek 19:5), he sought to solidify his position by whatever means, including, Begg conjectures, appropriating his brother's harem (19:7a).[579]

576. See C. Begg, "The Identity of the Princes in Ezekiel 19: Some Reflections," *ETL* 65 (1989) 358-65.

577. Jehoiakim, Jehoahaz's immediate successor, was the choice of the medieval Jewish commentators Rashi and Kimchi. See M. Noth, "The Jerusalem Catastrophe of 587 BCE and Its Significance for Israel," in *Laws in the Pentateuch and Other Studies,* trans. D. R. Ap-Thomas (Philadelphia: Fortress, 1967) 260-81. Wevers and Zimmerli believe that he is Jehoiachin, who, along with Ezekiel and his fellow exiles, was deported to Babylon in 597 BCE, See J. W. Wevers, *Ezekiel,* NCB (London: Nelson, 1969) 148; W. Zimmerli, *Ezekiel 1: A Commentary on the Book of the Prophet Ezekiel, Chapters 1–24,* trans. R. E. Clements, Hermeneia (Philadelphia: Fortress, 1979) 394. Cf. G. Fohrer, *Die Hauptprobleme des Buches Ezechiel,* BZAW 72 (Berlin: Alfred Töpelmann, 1952) 197; W. Eichrodt, *Ezekiel,* OTL (Philadelphia: Westminster, 1970) 253-54; A. Laato, *Josiah and David Redivivus: The Historical Josiah and the Messianic Expectations of Exilic and Postexilic Times,* ConBOT 33 (Stockholm: Almqvuist & Wiksell, 1992) 169-71.

578. Begg, "The Identity of the Princes in Ezekiel 19," 360-61, 368. See also Block, *Ezekiel 1–24,* 605.

579. Begg, "The Identity of the Princes in Ezekiel 19," 378-79, notes that 2 Kgs 24:34b says nothing of Jehoahaz's wives' accompanying him to Egypt (cf. the wives of Jehoiachin in 2 Kgs 24:15), but this is an argument from silence.

Moreover, the statement that the nations of surrounding (Babylonian) provinces captured the second cub recalls 2 Kgs 24:1-20, where we read that Yahweh sent bands of Arameans, Moabites, and Ammonites against Judah in response to Jehoakim's attempted revolt against Nebuchadrezzar.

That Jehoahaz and Jehoiakim were not the sons of a single mother (the former's was Hamutal, the latter's Zebidah, daughter of Pedaiah of Rumah; 2 Kgs 23:36) is not a compelling argument against Begg's thesis, since it is possible, even likely, that the lioness represents Judah, Jerusalem (home of Judah's royal family and the entity Ezekiel elsewhere depicts as both female and a mother), and/or the Davidic dynasty. Nonetheless, 2 Kgs 24:1-7 nowhere states that Jehoiakim was deported to Babylon. (That datum appears in 2 Chr 36:6, but its historicity is suspect; see also Dan 1:1.) Still, 19:9 states only that the second cub was "brought to the king of Babylon." Might further information about the circumstances of Jehoiakim's death and Nebuchadrezzar's whereabouts at the time (see 2 Kgs 24:1, 7) supply a vital clue?

The identity of Ezekiel's second cub remains a formidable riddle. If, as suggested, Zedekiah is the monarch addressed in the second person ("*your* mother") in v. 3, one might conclude that both of the cubs (spoken of in the third person) are his predecessors, thereby removing his name from the roster of possible candidates. Yet these observations do not constitute conclusive arguments. Because Ezekiel does not pause to "decode" this fable (cf. 17:11-21), not only his audience, but also late exilic readers will likely continue to ponder the second cub's identity, even as they move on to vv. 10-14. (See Reflections at 19:10-14.)

Ezekiel 19:10-14, The Shocking Death of the Mothering Vine and Her Stems

NIV	NRSV

10" 'Your mother was like a vine in your vineyard[a]
    planted by the water;
	10 Your mother was like a vine in a vineyard[a]
	    transplanted by the water,
	    fruitful and full of branches

[a]10 Two Hebrew manuscripts; most Hebrew manuscripts *your blood*	[a]Cn: Heb *in your blood*

NIV

it was fruitful and full of branches
    because of abundant water.
[11]Its branches were strong,
    fit for a ruler's scepter.
It towered high
    above the thick foliage,
conspicuous for its height
    and for its many branches.
[12]But it was uprooted in fury
    and thrown to the ground.
The east wind made it shrivel,
    it was stripped of its fruit;
its strong branches withered
    and fire consumed them.
[13]Now it is planted in the desert,
    in a dry and thirsty land.
[14]Fire spread from one of its main[a] branches
    and consumed its fruit.
No strong branch is left on it
    fit for a ruler's scepter.'

This is a lament and is to be used as a lament."

[a]14 Or from under its

NRSV

    from abundant water.
[11] Its strongest stem became
    a ruler's scepter;[a]
it towered aloft
    among the thick boughs;
it stood out in its height
    with its mass of branches.
[12] But it was plucked up in fury,
    cast down to the ground;
the east wind dried it up;
    its fruit was stripped off,
its strong stem was withered;
    the fire consumed it.
[13] Now it is transplanted into the wilderness,
    into a dry and thirsty land.
[14] And fire has gone out from its stem,
    has consumed its branches and fruit,
so that there remains in it no strong stem,
    no scepter for ruling.

    This is a lamentation, and it is used as a lamentation.

[a]Heb Its strongest stems became rulers' scepters

COMMENTARY

In vv. 10-14, Ezekiel continues his fabulous lament over the princes of Judah. Here, however, he abandons lion imagery in order to take up another established symbol of royalty and nobility: the vine (17:5-8; 31:4-5, 7; see also Ps 1:3; Job 29:19; Isa 44:4; Jer 17:8). Like the vine of 17:5-8, this plant thrives in well-watered soil. Unlike it, which spread its branches low to the ground (17:6), this one "mothers" impressive branches, strong stems and rulers' scepters (v. 11a), so that it towers conspicuously among the clouds. Suddenly, it is ripped from its secure and fruitful environment in fury and subjected to "overkill":[580] hurled to the ground; desiccated by the east wind (see also 17:10); stripped of its fruit, its strong stem withered; and burned (see 15:4-5). Further, the vine is transplanted (what is left to transplant?) to the antithesis of its former soil—dry, thirsty desert

ground. There, a fire originating in its own stem utterly consumes its branches and fruit, leaving it no strong stem and ruler's scepter.

The enraged agent of the vine's destruction (v. 12a) is not identified. Is he Nebuchadrezzar? Yahweh? Israel's deity is nowhere named in this chapter, but Ezekiel everywhere points to the Lord's control of Judah's fate; the "nations," including Babylonia, are merely God's agents. Hence we can confidently assume that the reader attributes the vine's demise to Yahweh. The precise location to which the vine is transplanted also is not specified (cf. vv. 4, 9). The reader knows only that it resides in the desert—a hostile, deadly place.

The literary integrity of vv. 10-14 has been challenged, with the result that clauses, even entire verses, conflicting with a particular interpretation are regarded as secondary expansions by Ezekiel,

580. See Moshe Greenberg, *Ezekiel 1–20,* AB 22 (Garden City, N.Y.: Doubleday, 1983) 355.

members of his "school," or both.[581] In general, scholars belong to one of two camps: those who maintain that the fable once described the *destruction of a specific Judaean monarch(s),* the vine representing either an actual person or Judah/Jerusalem/the royal house, and those who maintain that references to one or more specific members of the royal family were grafted to a text that originally spoke of the *destruction of the vine* (David's dynasty). The ancient reader also must tackle interpretive conundrums, but he will not prune portions of the text in order to resolve them or trim it in conformity with the 3:2 metrical pattern.

Like v. 2, v. 10 refers to "*your* [second-person masc. sing.] mother." Here also, the identities of both mother and addressee are an enigma. If the reader has identified the first and second lion cubs as Jehoahaz and Zedekiah, respectively, he might presume that vv. 10-14 also speak of Hamutal. If, on the other hand, the reader regards the second cub as either Jehoiakim or Jehoachin, he likely suspects that the vine is no human mother but, like the lioness, represents the Davidic dynasty. The second option is the more compelling of the two, since the extensive description of "her" demise ill accords with what one might conjecture to be the treatment of a deposed queen mother. Again, Zedekiah is the most likely addressee.

While v. 2 is essentially an "A is a B" metaphor (i.e., "what a lioness was your mother"), v. 10 is a simile (i.e., "your mother was *like* a vine"). If she in fact represents the house of David, then "mother" is itself metaphorical, and the following vine imagery is more properly identified as a simile within a metaphor. The MT's "in your blood" has exercised ancient and modern commentators alike.[582] The LXX renders the phrase, "like a sprig on a pomegranate"—testimony to the translator's own struggle to make sense of a difficult text. Perhaps most credible is J. A. Bewer's regrouping of the MT's consonants to read כגפן בדים כי *kaggepen baddîm kî,* "like a vine (full of) shoots because. . . ."[583] We can do no better.[584]

Verse 11, a description of the vine's prodigious growth, presents its audience with formidable problems. The MT of v. 11*a* reads, "there were to her [the vine; גפן (*gepen*) is fem.] strong stems [masc. pl.] and [fit for] rulers' scepters [masc. pl.]."[585] In the remainder of this verse, however, *gepen* is treated as a masculine noun ("*his/its* growth went up as high as the clouds and *it/he* became conspicuous for the multitude of *its/his* shoots because of its height" (see also 31:3, 10, 14; 2 Sam 23:4).[586] Verse 12 then reverts to feminine grammatical forms for *gepen.* A number of scholars (e.g., Zimmerli) view v. 11*ab* as a secondary addition to the original text. Greenberg, by contrast, suggests that the antecedent of the third-person masculine singular pronouns (*its/his*) is one of the "strong stems" or boughs of v. 11*a.* Without v. 11*ab,* he contends, the text lacks a reason for the vine's subsequent downfall—the hubris of its towering branch. In his view, that branch is Zedekiah.[587]

Begg, by contrast, identifies the lofty bough of vv. 11*b*-12 as Jehoiachin (the topmost shoot of a cedar in 17:3-4), who is desiccated and consumed by fire when the vine is uprooted and cast to the ground (v. 12). Hence, the allusion is to "the losses suffered by both king and nation at the hands of the Babylonians (the 'east wind' of v. 12*a*) in 597 BCE"[588] Do vv. 13-14*a* also speak of Jehoiachin's downfall, or do they depict the fate of a second Davidide? In order to answer this question, Begg first points to parallels between vv. 2-9, on the one hand, and vv. 10-14, on the other hand. Because his observations are crucial to his larger argument, they are quoted here at length:

581. See, e.g., W. Zimmerli, *Ezekiel 1: A Commentary on the Book of the Prophet Ezekiel, Chapters 1–24,* trans. R. E. Clements, Hermeneia (Philadelphia: Fortress, 1979) 393, 397-98.

582. Fohrer, *Die Hauptprobleme des Buches Ezechiel,* 198; Noth, "The Jerusalem Catastrophe of 587 BCE and Its Significance for Israel," 274; Walther Eichrodt, *Ezekiel,* trans. Cosslett Quin, OTL (Philadelphia: Westminster, 1970) 250; and J. W. Wevers, *Ezekiel,* NCB (London: Nelson, 1969) 149, read "in a [the] vineyard." Zimmerli, *Ezekiel 1,* 390, following in the footsteps of Rashi and Kimchi, translates, "Your mother was equal to a vine," recognizing in "in your blood" (בדמך *bĕdāmĕkā*) a derivative of דמה *dāmâ* ("to be like," "resemble"). Greenberg reads with the MT, but concedes that the word remains an unresolved crux.

583. J. A. Bewers, "Textual and Exegetical Notes on the Book of Ezekiel," *JBL* 72 (1953) 159.

584. Were "in your blood" (בדמך *bĕdāmĕkā*) identical to "in your blood" (בדמך *bĕdāmayik*) in 16:6, one might conjecture that a glossator, equating the vine with Jerusalem, added the phrase as a clue to that identification. The former phrase, however, has the second-person masc. sing. pronominal suffix, while the suffix on the latter is second-person fem. sing.

585. The NRSV follows the LXX in rendering both plural forms as singulars; the NIV splits the difference, translating "Its branches [pl.] were strong, fit for a ruler's scepter [sing.]."

586. For this translation, see Zimmerli, *Ezekiel 1,* 390-91.

587. Greenberg, *Ezekiel 1–20,* 353, 356; see also 358.

588. C. Begg, "The Identity of the Princes in Ezekiel 19: Some Reflections," *ETL* 65 (1989) 368.

That the two segments start off with a parallel invocation of "your mother" is recognized by all. In my view, however, the parallelism between them extends still further. V. 2*b* refers in a general way to the lioness's progeny, her "whelps." Corresponding to this is MT's v. 11*a*'s plural formulations concerning the vine: "She had strong stem*s* for ruler*s*' scepters." 19,3-4 recount the rise and fall of one of the whelps cited in 2*b*. The chapter's second segment has a parallel to this in 11*b* "it towered aloft . . . it was seen in its height," and 12*b* "its strong stem was withered; the fire consumed it" (RSV) with its masculine singular forms and suffixes. In 19,5 there is a clear shift in the movement of the passage with a focussing once again on the mother lioness, followed by the account of the career of "another" of her whelps in vv. 6-9. A comparable sequence may be noted in 19,13-14 where the shift is signified by the opening *wĕ·attāh* ["but it/she"] of v. 13: the mother vine itself comes briefly into focus (v. 13), and then (another) "stem" and "scepter" are presented (v. 14). In light of this widegoing parallelism between them, I suggest that like vv. 2-9, 10-14*a* speak of two distinct princes.[589]

Begg's list of parallels in content and structure between the two parts of Ezekiel's dirge is impressive, and I am swayed by his conclusion that vv. 10-14*a* address the fates of two Davidides. His further claim that those two rulers are Jehoiachin and Zedekiah, respectively, also is compelling. These two kings also appeared as plants in chap. 17, Jehoiachin being the topmost shoot of the cedar in 17:3-4 (cf. the lofty bough of 19:11), Zedekiah the lowly vine (17:6) whose own "disastrous machinations" (= the internal fire of v. 14) will bring the Davidic vine (= line) to an end.[590] With vv. 13-14*a*, Ezekiel moves beyond past events to predict the deportation and death of Zedekiah in Babylon.

589. Ibid., 367.
590. Ibid., 368.

Begg's solution does not resolve all of the problems posed by Ezekiel's lament. The identities of the second cub and of the vine's branches will remain a hotly contested topic. However, Begg has shown that vv. 2-14*a* treat, in chronological order, each of Judah's final four rulers, a pattern also present in Jeremiah 22.

With the colophon of v. 14*b*, a comment that Ezekiel's lament actually passed into use, chapter 19 ends. Its presence returns us to the question of whether Ezekiel himself composed it as a heartfelt dirge or as a parody of that genre. Perhaps the answer is twofold. On the one hand, the prophet invites his audience genuinely to admire the lioness. Her maternal behavior is altogether appropriate. When they witness the cubs' demise through her eyes, they sympathize with her—bereft of her two offspring and of hope. Likewise, his initial description of the fruitful, many-branched vine's thriving in well-watered soil is positive. The audience is shocked when she is suddenly uprooted in fury and subjected to multiple lethal afflictions. These observations, coupled with the mournful expressions "What a lioness was your mother among lions" and "Your mother was like a vine," suggest that the prophet truly laments the mother's loss (both her *experience* of bereavement [vv. 2-9] and her own *death*).[591] The demise of the Davidic dynasty is a bitter pill to swallow. Her "offspring," however, are another matter. Each is described in negative as well as some positive terms: The first cub devours humans; the second does likewise and also devastates and depopulates its territory; the lofty branch (v. 11) is arrogant; the self-combusting branch destroys both itself and whatever remains of the mothering vine. Where the text speaks of them, Ezekiel's dirge becomes parodic, a mock-song.

591. K. P. Darr, "Ezekiel," in *The Women's Bible Commentary*, ed. C. A. Newsom and S. H. Ringe (Louisville: Westminster/John Knox, 1992) 186-87.

REFLECTIONS

In his dirge over the princes of Judah, Ezekiel both laments the death of the Davidic dynasty—an institution that for centuries symbolized Yahweh's ongoing commitment to the descendants of David and to their subjects—and indicts those rulers who proved unworthy of their birthright and whose reigns brought their nation to ruin. We, too, know the pain that comes of caring so deeply about institutions (e.g., political, religious) and persons, yet having to say no to policies and behaviors that imperil them and others. Ezekiel's heart is torn—anger and love commingle and compete within it. Who knows nothing of his experience?

In its own way, Ezekiel's highly nationalistic oracle reiterates the message of chapter 18. Persons (even kings) and communities are responsible for the choices they make and must bear the consequences of those choices. Family status, power, and pride are no license to ravage others, to lay waste what they have labored to build, to leave their lives in ruins. Ezekiel must convince his audience that the Davidides have brought on the death of Judah; its downfall is not Yahweh's "fault," as if God had capriciously walked away from the perpetual covenant extended, at the Lord's initiative, to David and his line (2 Samuel 7). And so he portrays them, in the guise of lions and vine branches, inviting his audience to pursue the riddles of their identities; to perceive their behaviors through the metaphorical lenses of familiar imagery; to be appalled, angered, and dismayed by their actions; and finally to assent to the justice of their demise.

God's name nowhere appears in Ezekiel's dirge. Did the prophet perceive that the exiles might more easily be drawn into his message if he couched it in the language of fable? Ezekiel's audience resisted his words on many occasions—indeed, dared to challenge both his arguments and his conclusions—even though he everywhere asserted that he spoke for Yahweh. We are reminded of the prophet Nathan, who, commanded by God to confront David with his sinful liaison with Bathsheba, Uriah's wife, devised a strategy by which to lure the king into condemning himself (2 Samuel 12). His parable also says nothing of Yahweh. Indeed, David judges the case of the rich man who steals a poor man's ewe as he would any other, oblivious to its personal significance until the moment when Nathan charges, "You are the man!" (2 Sam 12:7 NRSV). Ezekiel cannot confront Judah's kings face to face. But he challenges his audience to recognize their rulers in his descriptions of fauna and flora and to confess the justice of God's judgment on their selfishness, their devastating practices, and their arrogance. Unlike chapter 17, Ezekiel 19 does not end with a promise that God will resurrect the Davidic line. The dirge is permitted to stand on its own. There are times for lamenting, for grieving the loss of a person, an institution, an enterprise that has failed to live up to its high calling. Laments permit the expression of sadness and anger, of love and frustration, of grief and acceptance. Ezekiel says nothing of Yahweh, but his words disclose not only his own emotions, but also the ravaged heart of God.

EZEKIEL 20:1-44, HUMAN REBELLION AND DIVINE DETERMINATION IN ISRAEL'S HISTORY

OVERVIEW

As in chapter 16, in chapter 20 Ezekiel constructs a narrative of Israel's history intended to justify God's impending judgment. But while chap. 16 sought to destroy confidence grounded in Jerusalem's unique place within Yahwistic religion, chap. 20 reveals the folly of hope rooted in Israel's "salvation history"—its exodus from Egypt, the covenant forged at Sinai, and the gift of land. Beginning with the nation's origin in Egypt, the prophet-priest recasts its past as a story of persistent and enduring rebellion and apostasy. Turning from past to present, he accuses his exilic audience of perpetuating the sins of their ancestors. At this very moment, they think that they shall be "like the nations, like the tribes of the countries, [worshiping] wood and stone" (20:32), as if they could abort the Lord's plan for this people. But that, Ezekiel insists, can never happen. Israel's future lies in God's hands, and "no action on the exiles' part can ever interfere with God's determination to see that plan fulfilled, the rebellious purged, cultic purity enforced, and human willfulness quelled in a morass of shame and contrition."[592]

Ezekiel's historical narrative is no dry, objective presentation of the "facts" of Israel's genesis, wilderness wanderings, and life in its land. As Ellen Davis reminds us, "narratives are not direct reproductions of reality; they are works of art, created by the human mind" for very specific purposes.[593] Readers familiar with pentateuchal and other biblical accounts of these periods in Israel's history will find the prophet interspersing traditional details with new and shocking ones. On the one hand, he speaks of the people's deliverance from Egypt, of lawgiving in the wilderness, and of judgment against the exodus generation, none of whom is permitted to enter the land of Canaan. Yet he crafts these familiar themes very precisely in order that they best serve his goal, while suppressing those features detrimental to its fulfillment. Hence, we do well to read texts listening not only for words, but also for silences. On the other hand, one searches in vain for biblical evidence to support Ezekiel's claim that, already in Egypt, the Israelites rebelled against Yahweh by worshiping Egyptian deities, or that God punished them by deliberately giving them "not good," death-dealing laws—an idea that impells one flatly to declare: "This time, Ezekiel went too far!"

Chapter 20 begins with a date: the seventh year (of Jehoiachin's exile), on the tenth day of the fifth month (Ab)—that is, August 14, 591 BCE. Five years later, Jer 52:12 tells us, the Jerusalem Temple will be set ablaze by the troops of Nebuchadrezzar. At present, however, Ezekiel's compatriots continue to resist his constant refrain that Judah's downfall is Yahweh's inevitable and just punishment for the nation's long-lived, ongoing, and heinous abominations. Nurtured by centuries-old traditions of God's unique relationship with Israel, the exiles turn in shock and horror from the notion that many of their bedrock beliefs about Yahweh and themselves cannot hold, indeed, are crumbling with every passing day. Ezekiel's version of Israel's salvation history functions

to hasten the disintegration of those beliefs. But alongside its deconstructive function lies a constructive purpose. "In a catastrophe," Greenberg writes, "the need to find intelligibility is existential: unless one can find some pattern in events, disintegration and collapse must ensue."[594] Davis echoes Greenberg when she observes that Ezekiel 20 seeks to explain circumstances that, in the light of the predominant theological system, are inconceivable: "Israel's future as YHWH's people depends upon their ability to reconcile this thing which was never supposed to happen with what they know—or should have known—of their God."[595]

Despite its cohesive structure and numerous unifying elements, many critics conclude that chap. 20 was not composed all at once and by a single author. Zimmerli, for example, argues that the original oracle consisted only of vv. 5-26, 30-31*. Ezekiel based his retrospect on Israel's core of credo-like summaries of its initial experiences with Yahweh.[596] After Jerusalem's destruction in 587 BCE, he supplemented the earlier prophecy with an oracle of salvation (vv. 32-44). A later glossator clumsily added the brief account of Israel's apostasy in its land (vv. 27-29).[597] Scholars who defend the original and authorial unity of this passage find their ablest spokesperson in Greenberg, whose masterful analysis of the oracle's structure and contents demonstrates that its second part (vv. 33-44) has determined the scope of the first (vv. 1-29), while vv. 30-32 function as a bridge between the two.[598] One's understanding of the composition history of this chapter affects matters of interpretation, as we shall see. Nonetheless, I find nothing in it that would cause the ancient reader to question either its pre-587 BCE date (v. 1) or its total attribution to Ezekiel.

592. K. P. Darr, "Ezekiel's Justifications of God: Teaching Troubling Texts," *JSOT* 55 (1992) 102.

593. Ellen F. Davis, *Swallowing the Scroll: Textuality and the Dynamics of Discourse in Ezekiel's Prophecy,* Bible and Literature 21 (Sheffield: Almond, 1989) 107.

594. "Prolegomenon," in C. C. Torrey, *Pseudo-Ezekiel and the Original Prophecy and Critical Articles,* The Library of Biblical Studies (New York: Ktav, 1970) xxv-xxviii.

595. Davis, *Swallowing the Scroll,* 109.

596. W. Zimmerli, *Ezekiel 1: A Commentary on the Book of the Prophet Ezekiel, Chapters 1-24,* trans. R. E. Clements, Hermeneia (Philadelphia: Fortress, 1979) 405. On Israel's "short historical credo," see G. von Rad, "The Form-critical Problem of the Hexateuch," *The Problem of the Hexateuch and Other Essays,* trans. E. W. Trueman Dicken (New York: McGraw-Hill, 1966) 1-178.

597. Zimmerli, *Ezekiel 1,* 404-18. F. Sedlmeier regards vv. 1-26, 30-39 as original, vv. 27-29 and 39b-44 as subsequent expansions. See F. Sedlmeier, *Studien zu Komposition und Theologie von Ezechiel 20,* SBB 21 (Stuttgart: Katholisches Bibelwerk, 1991).

598. Moshe Greenberg, *Ezekiel 1-20,* AB 22 (Garden City, N.Y.: Doubleday, 1983) 376-83. See also Henry van Dyke Parunak, "Structural Studies in Ezekiel" (Ph.D. diss., Harvard University, 1978) 290-300.

Ezekiel 20:1-4, To Inquire of Yahweh

NIV

20 In the seventh year, in the fifth month on the tenth day, some of the elders of Israel came to inquire of the LORD, and they sat down in front of me.

²Then the word of the LORD came to me: ³"Son of man, speak to the elders of Israel and say to them, 'This is what the Sovereign LORD says: Have you come to inquire of me? As surely as I live, I will not let you inquire of me, declares the Sovereign LORD.'

⁴"Will you judge them? Will you judge them, son of man? Then confront them with the detestable practices of their fathers

NRSV

20 In the seventh year, in the fifth month, on the tenth day of the month, certain elders of Israel came to consult the LORD, and sat down before me. ²And the word of the LORD came to me: ³Mortal, speak to the elders of Israel, and say to them: Thus says the Lord GOD: Why are you coming? To consult me? As I live, says the Lord GOD, I will not be consulted by you. ⁴Will you judge them, mortal, will you judge them? Then let them know the abominations of their ancestors,

COMMENTARY

As in 14:1, certain of Israel's elders come to Ezekiel to "inquire [דרשׁ; *dāraš*] of the LORD" (see also 8:1). The text says nothing of their precise motivation for seeking a divine oracle, but that fact has not deterred critics from attempting to ferret it out. Taking a cue from Jer 28:1-4, A. Malamat links their visit to the prophet Hananiah's prediction (in the fifth month of Zedekiah's fourth year on the throne, August 594 BCE) that within two years, Yahweh will return from exile the temple vessels seized by Nebuchadrezzar, as well as Jehoiachin and all of the other exiles. Those two years have elapsed, and so Israel's elders wish to learn of the status of Hananiah's prophecy.[599] Others have conjectured that their visit corresponded to Psammetichus II's appearance in the Levant in 592/91. The exiles sought confirmation of their hope that the presence of Egypt's pharaoh would lessen Nebuchadrezzar's stranglehold on Palestine.[600] Block suggests that the exiles

inquired of Yahweh in order to comply with Deut 4:29: "From [among the nations] you will seek the LORD your God, and you will find him if you search [*dāraš*] after him with all your heart and soul" (NRSV).[601] If that be the case, one wonders at their optimism—and their audacity. After all, their last recorded attempt to inquire of God had been flatly refused. That situation became Yahweh's opportunity to accuse them of idolatry, to threaten with death all who harbored idols in their hearts yet inquired of God, and to end the life of any prophet who mediated between them and the divine sphere (14:1-10).

Now Yahweh conveys through Ezekiel and by oath a second, absolute refusal to submit to inquiry (v. 3). How dare they come? Instead, the prophet must arraign them with the abominations of their ancestors—rooting God's rebuff in a four-phase historical retrospective saturated with sin. (See Reflections at 20:39-44.)

599. A. Malamat, "The Twilight of Judah: In the Egyptian-Babylonian Maelstrom," *Congress Volume: Edinburgh 1974*, VTSup 28 (Leiden: Brill, 1975) 138-39.

600. K. W. Freedy and D. B. Redford, "The Dates of Ezekiel in Relation to Biblical, Babylonian and Egyptian Sources," *JAOS* 90 (1970) 480.

601. D. I. Block, *The Book of Ezekiel: Chapters 1–24*, NICOT (Grand Rapids: Eerdmans, 1997) 619.

Ezekiel 20:5-9, Israel in Egypt

NIV

[5]and say to them: 'This is what the Sovereign LORD says: On the day I chose Israel, I swore with uplifted hand to the descendants of the house of Jacob and revealed myself to them in Egypt. With uplifted hand I said to them, "I am the LORD your God." [6]On that day I swore to them that I would bring them out of Egypt into a land I had searched out for them, a land flowing with milk and honey, the most beautiful of all lands. [7]And I said to them, "Each of you, get rid of the vile images you have set your eyes on, and do not defile yourselves with the idols of Egypt. I am the LORD your God."

[8]" 'But they rebelled against me and would not listen to me; they did not get rid of the vile images they had set their eyes on, nor did they forsake the idols of Egypt. So I said I would pour out my wrath on them and spend my anger against them in Egypt. [9]But for the sake of my name I did what would keep it from being profaned in the eyes of the nations they lived among and in whose sight I had revealed myself to the Israelites by bringing them out of Egypt.

NRSV

[5]and say to them: Thus says the Lord GOD: On the day when I chose Israel, I swore to the offspring of the house of Jacob—making myself known to them in the land of Egypt—I swore to them, saying, I am the LORD your God. [6]On that day I swore to them that I would bring them out of the land of Egypt into a land that I had searched out for them, a land flowing with milk and honey, the most glorious of all lands. [7]And I said to them, Cast away the detestable things your eyes feast on, every one of you, and do not defile yourselves with the idols of Egypt; I am the LORD your God. [8]But they rebelled against me and would not listen to me; not one of them cast away the detestable things their eyes feasted on, nor did they forsake the idols of Egypt.

Then I thought I would pour out my wrath upon them and spend my anger against them in the midst of the land of Egypt. [9]But I acted for the sake of my name, that it should not be profaned in the sight of the nations among whom they lived, in whose sight I made myself known to them in bringing them out of the land of Egypt.

COMMENTARY

This first phase of Ezekiel's historical retrospective, introduced by the messenger formula ("Thus says the Lord GOD"; see also v. 3) locates Israel in Egypt. On the day when Yahweh "chose" (בחר *bāḥar*) Israel, the Lord swore an oath (lit., "I lifted my hand") to the offspring of Jacob's house. That oath, a radical act of divine self-disclosure, revealed Yahweh's name and covenantal commitment to this people ("I am *Yahweh your* God"), as well as divine determination to bring them out of Egypt and into a land that the Lord has personally "searched out" for them—a choice, indeed, paradisiacal property, "a land flowing with milk and honey" [see also Exod 3:8, 17; 33:3; Lev 20:24; Num 16:13, 14; Deut 6:3; 11:9; 26:9, 15], the most glorious of all lands" (Jer 3:19). Yet Yahweh's initiative comes with an imperative: Every one of the Israelites

must "cast away" the detestable things on which their eyes "feast," no longer defiling themselves with the "dung-idols" (Ezekiel's characteristic and coarse epithet for such images) of Egypt. This command, grounded in Yahweh's self-revelation and accompanied by God's promise directly to intervene in their history in a most benevolent manner, should not fail to commend itself to the Israelites. And yet, they straightaway *rebel* against their Lord and benefactor, refusing to listen to Yahweh and holding fast to their idolatries (vv. 8-9; rebellion is the sin of both the Egypt-born generation and their children, vv. 8, 13, 21; the charge echoes 2:3-8).

Already, the reader has reason to reflect on Ezekiel's portrayal of Israel in Egypt—his (creative) adoption of some traditions to the neglect of others, and his own, heretofore unknown, "contributions."[602] He recognizes numerous links con-joining the prophet's scenario with certain penta-teuchal (especially priestly) traditions. Exodus 6, for example, also speaks of the revelation of Yahweh's name in Egypt (Exod 6:2-3, 6-8, 28-29), of God's oath ("I lifted my hand") to bring Israel into a land (Exod 6:8), and of the Israelites' refusal to listen (Exod 6:9; there, a consequence of their "broken spirit" and "cruel slavery"). He perceives in Ezekiel's selection of *bāḥar* ("to choose") a (Deuternomic) term for election imbued with rich theological overtones of Yahweh's covenant love for Israel (e.g., Deut 7:6*b*-8) and of Israel's obliga-tion to return that love by obeying Yahweh's statutes and ordinances (see, e.g., Deut 7:9-11).[603]

But where, save for the brief reference to "the offspring of the house of Jacob" in v. 5, is memory of Yahweh's covenant oath to Israel's primogeni-tors—Abraham, Isaac, and Jacob—to give the land of Canaan to their descendants (Exod 6:8; Deut 7:8)? Does Ezekiel bypass these venerables because (in line with Exod 6:3) they knew God as El Shaddai, but not as Yahweh? Has he simply sub-sumed God's ancient promise to Abraham (Gen 17:1-8) in order to focus upon the Israelites in Egypt as recipients of that oath? Or, as Greenberg suggests, is the prophet's disregard of the ancestral traditions a rhetorical strategy by which he avoids launching Israel's history of sin with "the arche-typal pious recipients of God's blessing," thereby freeing himself more powerfully to "juxtapose God's total gracious commitment to Israel with Israel's total rejection of him from their first encounter with him as a nation . . . in Egypt"?[604]

Where is Ezekiel's acknowledgment that in Egypt, the Israelites suffered "cruel slavery" and a "broken spirit" (Exod 6:9)? For him, no circum-stances mitigate their rebellious rejection of Yahweh's revelation, promise, and imperative. Whence derives his accusation that the people already were apostate in Egypt (vv. 7-8)? As noted above, one searches in vain for pentateuchal con-firmation of this charge. Joshua 24:2 states that Israel's earliest ancestors—Terah and his sons,

Abraham and Nahor—served other gods while liv-ing "beyond the Euphrates." Its purpose is not to indict them, however, but to emphasize God's ini-tiative in calling Abraham forth to a new God, progeny, and land.[605]

Critics explain that the prophet has caricatured Israel's attitude in Egypt with his compatriots' hopes of Egyptian assistance in mind. Instead of acknowledging Yahweh's sovereignty, power, and justice in the contemporary catastrophe, casting off their own idolatrous (and syncretistic) religious practices (e.g, 14:1-11) and aligning their lives with Yahweh's will and purposes (chap. 18), the exiles cleave to the "idol" of Egyptian military assistance. Here, then, is the first of many exam-ples of Ezekiel's "reorganizing Israel's view of its past from the standpoint of the present crisis."[606]

Finally, the reader notes the absence of Moses (and Aaron) in Ezekiel's scenario. Within the pen-tateuchal traditions, these men perform "signs and wonders"—testimony to the unrivaled power and sovereignty of the Lord, who hears Israel's outcries and unleashes a series of devastating plagues in order that both they (Exod 6:7; 10:2) and the Egyptians (esp. their heart-hardened pharaoh) might "know that I am Yahweh" (Exod 7:5, 17; 8:22). But Ezekiel's Israelites in Egypt know nei-ther God's emissaries nor faith-buttressing miracles.

In response to this people's rebelliousness, Yahweh thinks to destroy them in Egypt (v. 8) but desists "for the sake of my name, that it should not be profaned in the sight of the nations among whom they lived, in whose sight I made myself known to them in bringing them out of the land of Egypt" (v. 9).[607] K. W. Carley claims that when Ezekiel speaks of Yahweh's acting "for the sake of my name," he alludes "not to divine self-interest, but to the necessity of Yahweh vindicating his character as a God of compassion and forgiveness, as well as of uncompromising wrath against the impenitent."[608] In a similar vein, Eichrodt explains that "God acts . . . in accordance with his own divine nature. . . . Having given himself to be

602. One should never presume that the Hebrew Bible includes all of Israel's traditions about any aspect of its experience. Therefore, we should always temper the claim that Ezekiel (or any other biblical author) has created a new thing by acknowledging the limitations of our resources.
603. See Greenberg, *Ezekiel 1–20,* 363.
604. Ibid., 364.

605. See Corrine Patton, " 'I Myself Gave Them Laws That Were Not Good': Ezekiel 20 and the Exodus Traditions," *JSOT* 69 (1996) 76.
606. Davis, *Swallowing the Scroll,* 110.
607. Reference to the exodus in this verse is premature, since Yahweh's decision concerns whether or not to destroy Israel "in the midst of the land of Egypt" (v. 8).
608. K. W. Carley, *Ezekiel Among the Prophets,* SBT 2 (London: SCG, 1975).

Israel's own as 'Yahweh thy God,' he never ceases from endeavours to arouse a response of love and trust."[609] Palatable though their words be, they ill-accord with the tenor of Ezekiel's narrative. Rather, the prophet asserts that the Israelites owe their survival not to Yahweh's care and compassion, but to divine self-interest, since destroying Israel would profane God's name among the nations.

Other biblical authors also speak of Israel's profaning God's name through acts of disobedience (e.g., Jer 34:16; Amos 2:7), contempt (e.g., Lev 19:12), and cultic apostasy (e.g., Lev 20:3). In the psalter (e.g., 25:11; 79:9-10) and beyond (e.g., Jer 14:7), petitioners pray that Yahweh will respond to their pleas "for your name's sake." And Ezekiel is by no means the first to cite concern for God's reputation among the nations as a motivation for not punishing this people. Within the Pentateuch, for example, Moses twice appeals to God along those lines. The first incident (like Ezek 20:7-8) involves idolatry. In Moses' absence, the Israelites have begun worshiping the "golden calf," and Yahweh is determined to consume them with burning wrath (Exod 32:1-10). But Moses marshals several arguments against that decision, including the following: "Why should the Egyptians say, 'It was with evil intent that [Yahweh] brought them out to kill them in the mountains, and to consume them from the face of the earth?' Turn from your fierce wrath; change your mind and do not bring disaster on your people" (Exod 32:12 NRSV; see also Deut 9:28). The second incident follows Israel's collapse of trust in the face of the spies' report of Canaan's fortified cities and towering inhabitants (Num 13:25-33). Again, Yahweh determines to wipe out the people, but Moses points out how the nations will (mis)construe that decision: "Then the Egyptians will hear of it, for in your might you brought up this people from among them, and they will tell the inhabitants of this land. . . . Now if you kill this people all at one time, then the nations who have heard about you will say, 'It is because the Lord was not able to bring this people into the land he swore to give them that he has slaughtered them in the wilderness' " (Num 14:13-16 NRSV; note that v. 19 ends with Moses' reminder that Yahweh has pardoned this people, "*from Egypt* even until now").[610] Psalm 106:6-8, part of a poignant post-exilic communal confession of Israel's sin, certainly enters the reader's mind as well, since it speaks of both Israel's rebellion (at the Sea of Reeds) and Yahweh's decision to save them "for his name's sake, so that he might make known his mighty power."[611] There, as in the present text, concern for the divine reputation functions as a lens through which God's historical dealings with Israel are perceived.[612] (See Reflections at 20:39-44.)

609. Walther Eichrodt, *Ezekiel,* trans. Cosslett Quin, OTL (Philadelphia: Westminster, 1970) 267.

610. Regarding the formula "in the sight of the nations," compare the discussions of Henning Graf Reventlow, "Die Volker als Jahwes Zeugen bei Ezechiel," *ZAW* 71 (1959) 33-43, and Paul Joyce, *Divine Initiative and Human Response in Ezekiel,* JSOTSup 51 (Sheffield: JSOT, 1989) 96-97.

611. This psalm, unlike Ezek 20:5-8, refers to Yahweh's "wonderful works" in Egypt, yet asserts that their forebears "did not consider" them (v. 7*a*).

612. See Greenberg, *Ezekiel 1–20,* 384. Ezekiel 20 likely predates this psalm, but it may have included a repertoire of traditions that the ancient reader brought to a first encounter with Ezekiel's scroll.

Ezekiel 20:10-17, The Egyptian Generation in the Desert

NIV	NRSV
[10]Therefore I led them out of Egypt and brought them into the desert. [11]I gave them my decrees and made known to them my laws, for the man who obeys them will live by them. [12]Also I gave them my Sabbaths as a sign between us, so they would know that I the LORD made them holy. [13]" 'Yet the people of Israel rebelled against me in the desert. They did not follow my decrees but rejected my laws—although the man who obeys	[10]So I led them out of the land of Egypt and brought them into the wilderness. [11]I gave them my statutes and showed them my ordinances, by whose observance everyone shall live. [12]Moreover I gave them my sabbaths, as a sign between me and them, so that they might know that I the LORD sanctify them. [13]But the house of Israel rebelled against me in the wilderness; they did not observe my statutes but rejected my ordinances,

NIV

them will live by them—and they utterly desecrated my Sabbaths. So I said I would pour out my wrath on them and destroy them in the desert. ¹⁴But for the sake of my name I did what would keep it from being profaned in the eyes of the nations in whose sight I had brought them out. ¹⁵Also with uplifted hand I swore to them in the desert that I would not bring them into the land I had given them—a land flowing with milk and honey, most beautiful of all lands— ¹⁶because they rejected my laws and did not follow my decrees and desecrated my Sabbaths. For their hearts were devoted to their idols. ¹⁷Yet I looked on them with pity and did not destroy them or put an end to them in the desert.

NRSV

by whose observance everyone shall live; and my sabbaths they greatly profaned.

Then I thought I would pour out my wrath upon them in the wilderness, to make an end of them. ¹⁴But I acted for the sake of my name, so that it should not be profaned in the sight of the nations, in whose sight I had brought them out. ¹⁵Moreover I swore to them in the wilderness that I would not bring them into the land that I had given them, a land flowing with milk and honey, the most glorious of all lands, ¹⁶because they rejected my ordinances and did not observe my statutes, and profaned my sabbaths; for their heart went after their idols. ¹⁷Nevertheless my eye spared them, and I did not destroy them or make an end of them in the wilderness.

COMMENTARY

In Ezekiel's truncated version of this second phase of Israel's history, Yahweh leads the Israelites out of Egypt and brings them into the desert.[613] There, God gives them "my statutes" (חקותי *ḥuqqôtay*; the noun is fem. pl.) and makes known to them "my ordinances" (משפטי *mišpāṭay*). The following phrase, "by whose observance everyone shall live," recalls Lev 18:5 (also in conjunction with Yahweh's ordinances and statutes; see also Ezek 18:9 and Deut 30:15-19). Moreover, God gives them "my sabbaths" (pl.) as a sign (אות *'ôt*) between deity and people, in order that they might know that it is Yahweh who sanctifies them. But Israel responds in the desert by forgoing the Lord's statutes; rejecting the divine, life-giving ordinances; and profaning God's sabbaths (v. 13).

For a second time, the reader reflects upon Ezekiel's portrayal of the Egypt-born Israelites. Again, the prophet has creatively adopted certain familiar traditions while suppressing others. In his reference to God's giving of statutes, ordinances, and sabbaths in the desert, the reader recognizes the comprehensive lawgiving at Mt. Sinai. (Zimmerli, Wevers, and others term vv. 11-12 a

second revelation of the law, but this risks "over-reading" v. 7—a prohibition against worshiping other gods, which, while formulated as law, is essentially a single injunction).[614] Sabbath observance is a recurring pentateuchal theme (Exod 20:8-11; 23:12; 34:21; Lev 19:3, 30; 23:3; 26:2; Deut 5:12-15; see also Isa 56:2, 4, 6). Jeremiah 17:19-27 presses upon the people of Judah its importance for the continuity of David's dynasty and Jerusalem's survival (see also Neh 13:17-18). Ezekiel will return to the topic in 22:8, 26; 23:38; and 44:24. As in the present text, Exod 31:17 speaks of sabbath observance as a "sign" (*'ôt*) between Yahweh and Israel. In Exod 20:8, the Israelites are commanded to remember the sabbath day by "sanctifying it." Ezekiel, by contrast, speaks of sabbaths as a means by which Yahweh "sanctifies" Israel.[615]

Here also, the reader misses any reference to Israel's great intercessor, Moses. He is not permitted to glimpse the Israelites gathered at Sinai and proclaiming with one voice, "Everything that the

613. With these and preceding verses, Greenberg observes, "the historical Exodus acquires something of the character of an expulsion of a people redeemed against its will." Greenberg, *Ezekiel 1–20*, 384.

614. Zimmerli, *Ezekiel 1*, 410; J. W. Wevers, *Ezekiel*, NCB (London: Nelson, 1969) 153. Verse 7, of course, is the structural parallel to vv. 11-12.

615. So D. I. Block, *The Book of Ezekiel: Chapters 1–24*, NICOT (Grand Rapids: Eerdmans, 1997) 632. He maintains that Ezekiel uses the plural, "sabbaths," in order also to include special holy days, sabbatical years, and the year of Jubilees.

LORD has spoken we will do" (Exod 19:9*a*). Where is acknowledgment of the genuine hardships of desert existence (cf. 19:13; Deut 8:15; 32:10; Isa 21:1; Jer 2:6)? Ezekiel devotes not a single word to traditions bespeaking Yahweh's gracious provision for the people's physical needs; geographical hardships have no impact upon God's treatment of Israel or upon Israel's response to God.[616] Law makes life possible; nothing is said of food or water. All such elements are stripped away as extraneous to Ezekiel's larger purpose of depicting this people as idolatrous and defiant of Yahweh's Torah.

Again, God considers pouring out deadly wrath upon these rebels, but is restrained by concern for the divine reputation among the nations (v. 14). On this occasion, however, the Egypt-born genera-

tion does not escape punishment. In a second oath (cf. vv. 5-6), Yahweh declares that they will not enter the fertile and glorious land first described in v. 6,[617] because they have rejected God's ordinances and statutes, profaned the sabbaths, and their "heart" goes after their idols (for a similar charge, see 14:3-4). In spite of their narrow escape from God's wrath in Egypt (v. 8), the Israelites persist in their idolatry! Yahweh's "eye" spares them (cf. the many passages in which Ezekiel declares that the Lord's eye will not spare/pity the people, e.g., 7:4, 9; 8:18; 9:10; see also 9:5); they are not slain on the spot. But Ezekiel says nothing more of them. Instead, he turns to the third phase of his historical retrospective—the period of the second desert generation. (See Reflections at 20:39-44.)

616. See K. P. Darr, "Breaking Through the Wilderness: References to the Desert in Exilic Prophecy" (Ph.D. diss. Vanderbilt University, 1984) 167-68, 176.

617. Here, Ezekiel is beholden to the notion of a forty-year period of wilderness wandering found in Num 14:20-23; Deut 1:19-40.

Ezekiel 20:18-26, Like Parents, Like Children

NIV

18I said to their children in the desert, "Do not follow the statutes of your fathers or keep their laws or defile yourselves with their idols. 19I am the LORD your God; follow my decrees and be careful to keep my laws. 20Keep my Sabbaths holy, that they may be a sign between us. Then you will know that I am the LORD your God."

21" 'But the children rebelled against me: They did not follow my decrees, they were not careful to keep my laws—although the man who obeys them will live by them—and they desecrated my Sabbaths. So I said I would pour out my wrath on them and spend my anger against them in the desert. 22But I withheld my hand, and for the sake of my name I did what would keep it from being profaned in the eyes of the nations in whose sight I had brought them out. 23Also with uplifted hand I swore to them in the desert that I would disperse them among the nations and scatter them through the countries, 24because they had not obeyed my laws but had rejected my decrees and desecrated my Sabbaths, and their eyes ‚lusted‚ after their fathers' idols. 25I also gave them over to

NRSV

18I said to their children in the wilderness, Do not follow the statutes of your parents, nor observe their ordinances, nor defile yourselves with their idols. 19I the LORD am your God; follow my statutes, and be careful to observe my ordinances, 20and hallow my sabbaths that they may be a sign between me and you, so that you may know that I the LORD am your God. 21But the children rebelled against me; they did not follow my statutes, and were not careful to observe my ordinances, by whose observance everyone shall live; they profaned my sabbaths.

Then I thought I would pour out my wrath upon them and spend my anger against them in the wilderness. 22But I withheld my hand, and acted for the sake of my name, so that it should not be profaned in the sight of the nations, in whose sight I had brought them out. 23Moreover I swore to them in the wilderness that I would scatter them among the nations and disperse them through the countries, 24because they had not executed my ordinances, but had rejected my statutes and profaned my sabbaths, and their eyes

NIV

statutes that were not good and laws they could not live by; [26]I let them become defiled through their gifts—the sacrifice of every firstborn[a]—that I might fill them with horror so they would know that I am the LORD.'

[a]26 Or —making every firstborn pass through the fire,

NRSV

were set on their ancestors' idols. [25]Moreover I gave them statutes that were not good and ordinances by which they could not live. [26]I defiled them through their very gifts, in their offering up all their firstborn, in order that I might horrify them, so that they might know that I am the LORD.

COMMENTARY

Phase three of Ezekiel's retrospective is patterned after the first two, but with some significant differences. It does not begin with a statement of benevolent divine actions (cf. vv. 5 and 10).[618] Instead, Yahweh's first words to this new generation of Israelites are a warning, cast as a negative imperative (v. 18): "Do not follow the statutes [חקי ḥûqqê, masc. pl.] of your parents,[619] nor observe their ordinances, nor defile yourselves with their [dung] idols" (i.e., the idols their parents were already worshiping in Egypt; see vv. 7-8). Verse 19 omits notice of the life-giving nature of Yahweh's statutes and ordinances (cf. v. 11);[620] and while the sabbaths remain a sign (אות 'ôt) between God and people—indeed, the avenue to Israel's acknowledgment of Yahweh's sovereignty and power (note the recognition formula in v. 20b; cf. v. 12)—nothing is said of God's sanctifying the people through them (cf. v. 12).

Again, Israel rebels, and Yahweh refrains from destroying it solely for the sake of the divine reputation among the nations (vv. 21-22). Verse 23 inserts a troubling element into Ezekiel's account of the second desert generation—God's oath to "scatter them among the nations and disperse them throughout the countries" (see also Ps 106:26-27).

As Greenberg observes, however, antecedents to Ezekiel's idea appear, for example, in Deut 31:16-18, 20-21, where Yahweh warns Moses that after his death, the people will worship the deities of Canaan, breaking their covenant with

God.[621] In anger, Yahweh will forsake them, leaving them easy prey and subject to "many terrible troubles." Though Israel has not yet entered its land, God already knows its inclination.

In search of a precedent for the notion that a nation might already amass enough sin to justify its future exile, scholars point to Gen 15:13-16. In that passage, God informs Abraham that his offspring will be enslaved in a land (Egypt) for four hundred years, after which Yahweh will bring them into the country of the Amorites (Canaanites). This delay in the fulfillment of God's promise to Abraham is explained in v. 16: over the next four hundred years, the Amorites will accrue enough iniquity to vindicate Yahweh's present decision to expel them from their land. By analogy, the second desert generation already has accumulated enough guilt to justify Israel's eventual dispersion among the nations. Subsequent generations will only confirm, and give additional ground for, God's judgment.

Yahweh's oath (vv. 23-24) bears directly on the circumstances of Ezekiel's fellow exiles. It functions, in one sense, to undercut popular questioning of divine justice (theodicy), for how can his community protest an exile already thoroughly justified before Israel ever entered its land? In another sense, however, its implications threaten to undermine Ezekiel's own argument (in chap. 18) that Yahweh does not punish one generation for the sins of previous ones. If in the desert, Israel's iniquity already justified God's determination to impose the punishment of exile, what chance had subsequent generations to undo the damage and/or change God's mind? In the face of this apparent contradiction, we must remember that

618. See Block, Ezekiel 1–24, 635.

619. In this context, the prophet has probably departed from the fem. pl. חקות (ḥuqqôt) in v. 11 in order clearly to distinguish Yahweh's statutes from those of their parents. Elsewhere, Ezekiel employs the masc. pl. form when referring to Yahweh's statutes (11:12; 36:27).

620. As Zimmerli, Ezekiel 1, 410, observes, it is unclear whether the formula, "I am Yahweh your God" (v. 19a) functions as a motive clause of the preceding verse or as a preamble to the commandments of vv. 19a-20 (analogous to Exod 20:2; Lev 18:2).

621. Moshe Greenberg, Ezekiel 1–20, AB 22 (Garden City, N.Y.: Doubleday, 1983) 385.

the prophet was no systematic theologian. With each oracle, he constructs an argument and utilizes those rhetorical strategies best suited to advance it. Greenberg's explanation—that for the sake of God's sovereignty in the face of Israel's collapse, the prophet must establish not only that the calamity was deserved, but also that God foreknew and predetermined it centuries earlier—rings true.[622] Nevertheless, Ezekiel's own audience will rebel against his portrayal of past and present, asserting their freedom to abandon the God whose words appear to offer no exit from judgment and hopelessness (see below).

With vv. 25-26, we arrive at ideas that have consternated commentators and pastors for centuries. First, how can (even) Ezekiel say that Yahweh gave "not good" statutes (again, the form is masc. pl., differentiating between these statutes and those given in v. 11) and death-dealing ordinances to the second wilderness generation as punishment for their sins? Second (and inextricable from the first), how can he claim that God polluted them through their gifts, by their "making to pass through" fire every Israelite woman's "first born child" (כל־פטר רחם kol-peṭer rāḥam; lit., "every first womb issue")[623] in order that the Lord might desolate them and force their acknowledgment of Yahweh's sovereignty and power?

Tackling these questions requires that we take a closer look at vv. 25-26, carefully interpreting them within their larger literary context. Consider vv. 11-12, God's *first* giving of the law: "I gave them my statutes and showed them my ordinances, by whose observance everyone shall live. Moreover I gave

them my sabbaths, as a sign between me and them, so that they might know that I the Lord sanctify them." As we have seen, the Egyptian generation rebels against Yahweh and rejects the law. In vv. 19-20, the Lord warns/commands the second desert generation not to follow the statutes or observe the ordinances of their parents, but to follow and observe God's laws, including sabbath observance, in order that they might know that "I the LORD am your God." Properly speaking, that was no *second* giving of the law, but Yahweh's *reiteration* to the second wilderness generation of the laws already given to their parents and enjoined on them as well. Verse 24, then, states the grounds for God's decision to scatter these Israelites throughout the nations: They have rebelled against Yahweh's laws by not executing the Lord's ordinances, by rejecting the statutes, by profaning the sabbaths, and by clinging to their parents' idols.

Only with vv. 25-26 can we speak of a *second* giving of the law. This lawgiving is the antithesis of the first (vv. 11-12). When we compare the two verse pairs, we note several correspondences between the initial "gift" law and the second "punishment" law (see chart below). In the first imposition of the law (v. 11), Yahweh gave Israel "my statutes" and "my ordinances," both of which were life-bestowing. In the second imposition of the law (v. 25), "my statutes" is replaced by "not good statutes," and "my ordinances" is replaced by "ordinances by which they could not live." In the first giving of the law (v. 12), "my sabbaths" are singled out as exemplary of God's positive disposition toward the people. A sign between divine and human partners, sabbath observance is intended to bring about Israel's recognition that *I the Lord* "sanctify them." In the second giving of the law,

622. Ibid., 385.
623. בכור (bĕkôr), by contrast, refers to a father's firstborn.

Verse 11	Verse 25
I gave them <u>my</u> statutes and showed them <u>my</u> ORDINANCES, by whose observance everyone shall **<u>live.</u>**	Moreover **I gave them** statutes that were not good and ORDINANCES by which they could not **<u>live.</u>**
Verse 12	Verse 26
Moreover **I gave them** <u>my</u> *sabbaths* as a sign between me and them, <u>so</u> that they might know that I the Lord ***sanctify them.***	**I defiled them** through <u>their</u> very *gifts*, in their offering up all their firstborn, in order that I might ***desolate them,*** <u>so</u> that they might know that I am the Lord.

Yahweh "defiles them"[624] rather than "gives to them," and "their very gifts"—child sacrifice—are singled out as exemplary of Yahweh's negative disposition toward the people. Observance of this law leads to God's desolating them, in order to bring about the people's recognition that *I am the Lord.*

When Ezekiel speaks of "causing to pass over [העביר *ha'ăbîr,* hiphil] every first issue of the womb [כל־פטר רחם *kol-peṭer rāḥam*]," he refers to the crematory sacrifice of children (the hiphil of *'br* is a technical term for child sacrifice; e.g., Lev 18:21; Jer 32:35; Ezek 16:21; 23:37; 2 Kgs 23:10 adds "by fire"; see also Deut 18:10; 2 Kgs 16:3; 17:17; 32:6//2 Chr 33:6; Ezek 20:31). Hence the inadequacy of such benign translations as "set apart" (NRSV) and "give over" (NIV). Shocking though his statement be, the reader knows that sacrifice of the firstborn—human and animal—has some bases in Israelite law. In Exod 22:29b Yahweh commands, "The firstborn of your sons [בכור בניך *běkôr bāneykā*] you shall give to me." Exodus 13:2 reads, "Consecrate to me every firstborn [כל־בכור *kol-běkôr*]; the first issue of every womb [כל־פטר רחם *kol-peṭer reḥem*]."[625] Scholars suggest that these two laws reflect early Israel's belief that Yahweh demanded the sacrifice of all firstborn males. This belief was later modified to permit the practice of redemption: Yahweh accepts a substitute (either an animal sacrifice or money) for firstborn humans (see Genesis 22). So, for example, Exod 13:12a says, "You shall cause to pass over [העברת *ha'ăbartā*] to Yahweh every first issue [*kol-peṭer-reḥem*]"; but v. 13b adds, "Every firstborn male [*běkôr*] among your children you shall redeem" (פדה *pādâ*; see also v. 15, Exod 34:20). Regarding the priests' portion, Yahweh says to Aaron, "Every first issue of the womb [*kol-peṭer reḥem*] of all creatures, human and animal, which is offered to Yahweh shall be yours; but the firstborn of human beings [בכור־האדם *běkôr hā'ādām*] you shall redeem [*pādâ*]" (Num 18:15). According to

Num 3:12-13, 44-51; 8:16-18, Yahweh accepts the service of the Levites as a substitute for Israel's firstborn.

Ezekiel's use of העביר (*ha'ăbîr,* "to cause to pass over," hiphil) says nothing of the redemption of Israel's offspring. The following phrase confirms that he is speaking of child sacrifice. Verse 26b (NRSV) reads, "in order that I might horrify them [אשמם *'ăšimmēm,* hiphil]." The Israelites would not be "horrified" by causing their firstborn to "pass over" if substitution were in view. Moreover, "horrified" is too benign a translation of the verb שמם (*šāmēm*) in this context. Yahweh does not seek simply to "horrify" the people (as if doing so might move them to repent).[626] The meaning, rather, is "so that I might desolate them."[627]

Ezekiel's claim that Yahweh gave the Israelites "not good" statutes and deadly ordinances must be interpreted as the antithesis of the first lawgiving in the desert (vv. 11-12). God's demand for child sacrifice functions as the opposite of sabbath observance and illustrates the depth of the people's depravity. Contrary to all reason (including a healthy impulse toward self-preservation), Israel rejects Yahweh's avenues to life, yet obeys God's directives for death. The people will assuredly be desolated as they sacrifice every firstborn child, seriously eroding their population. As the reader progresses through the remainder of this oracle, he will recognize that in Ezekiel's own day, the house of Israel continues to cleave to the Lord's death-dealing laws, as exemplified in their ongoing practice of child sacrifice (v. 31).

With v. 26, the story of Israel's second wilderness generation ends. This phase has no conclusion corresponding to v. 17 ("Nevertheless my eye spared them, and I did not destroy them or make an end of them in the wilderness"). The reader's last glimpse of Israel in the desert is of the people practicing *religiously* Yahweh's punitive laws. Rebellious Israel is obedient in all the wrong ways. (See Reflections at 20:39-44.)

---

624. Nowhere else in Hebrew Scripture does Yahweh appear as the subject of the verb טמא (*ṭimmê',* piel), "to defile." However, the notion that God deliberately misleads, and then punishes the deceived, appeared in 14:9-10. Note that while "I defiled them" in v. 26 corresponds to "I gave them" in v. 12, it also forms an antithetical pair with "I sanctify them" (also in v. 12).

625. Here, *běkôr* appears to designate every firstborn child, whether male or female.

626. G. C. Heider, "A Further Turn on Ezekiel's Baroque Twist in Ezek 20:25-26," *JBL* 107 (1988) 721.

627. So Greenberg, *Ezekiel 1–20,* 361. Block, *Ezekiel 1–24,* 634, like Heider, translates "devastate."

Ezekiel 20:27-29, Illicit Worship in the Land

27"Therefore, son of man, speak to the people of Israel and say to them, 'This is what the Sovereign LORD says: In this also your fathers blasphemed me by forsaking me: 28When I brought them into the land I had sworn to give them and they saw any high hill or any leafy tree, there they offered their sacrifices, made offerings that provoked me to anger, presented their fragrant incense and poured out their drink offerings. 29Then I said to them: What is this high place you go to?' " (It is called Bamah^a to this day.)

^a29 *Bamah* means *high place.*

27Therefore, mortal, speak to the house of Israel and say to them, Thus says the Lord GOD: In this again your ancestors blasphemed me, by dealing treacherously with me. 28For when I had brought them into the land that I swore to give them, then wherever they saw any high hill or any leafy tree, there they offered their sacrifices and presented the provocation of their offering; there they sent up their pleasing odors, and there they poured out their drink offerings. 29(I said to them, What is the high place to which you go? So it is called Bamah^a to this day.)

^aThat is *High Place*

COMMENTARY

Phase four of Ezekiel's retrospective begins with Yahweh's command that he speak (continue speaking) to the house of Israel, represented by the elders sitting before him. This portion of his address, introduced by the messenger formula ("Thus says the Lord GOD"), accuses the exiles' ancestors of blaspheming Yahweh in another way: by acting treacherously against God (v. 27*b*).[628] Though the Lord fulfilled the oath to bring Israel into the land (v. 6; cf. v. 15), once there the people carried out their repertoire of cultic abominations: sacrifices, offerings, pleasing odors (incense), and drink offerings upon every high hill and under every leafy tree (v. 28).[629] This verse presupposes that the Deuteronomic mandate for cult centralization was already in force—a historical anachronism likely shared by the reader, despite evidence to the contrary in 1–2 Samuel. Greenberg suggests that Ezekiel's constellation of thoughts derives from Deuteronomy 12, itself an attack on the religious practices of Judah's late monarchical period:[630]

You must demolish completely all the places where the nations whom you are about to dispossess served their gods, on the mountain heights, on the hills, and under every leafy tree. . . . You shall not worship the Lord your God in such ways. But you shall seek the place that the Lord your God will choose out of all your tribes as his habitation to put his name there. . . . Take care that you do not offer your burnt offerings at any place you happen to see. . . . When the Lord your God has cut off before you the nations whom you are about to enter to dispossess them. . . . take care that you are not snared into imitating them. . . . They would even burn their sons and their daughters in the fire to their gods (Deut 12:2, 4-5, 13, 29, 30, 31).

Yahweh challenges Israel's illicit resort to these places with a disdainful question: "What [מה *mâ*] is the high place [במה *bāmâ*] to which you go [באים *bā'îm*]?" Though English translation conceals the Hebrew wordplay, God's query becomes, in an (editorial) aside, an artificial etiology (explanation of origin) for "high place": *bā'* ("go") + *mâ* ("what") = *bāmâ*. The subsequent phrase, "to this day," suggests that worship at the high places remains a lively, if controversial, part of Judean religious practice in Ezekiel's day (see the Commentary on 6:1-14; see also Excursus: "Israel's 'High Places,' " 1159-60). From the author's perspective, this brief characterization of Israel's behavior in the land suffices to show that the Canaan-born generations have perpetuated the sins of their earliest ancestors. (See Reflections at 20:39-44.)

628. The verb נדף (*giddēp* "blaspheme") is elsewhere found only in Num 15:30. "Act treacherously" (מעל מעל *mā'al ma'al*) appears in Ezek 14:13; 15:8; 18:24. See Block, *Ezekiel 1–24,* 462-63.
629. For a fuller description of these activities, see ibid., 642-43.
630. Greenberg, *Ezekiel 1–20,* 385.

Ezekiel 20:30-32, Idolatry and Defiance in Exile

NIV

30"Therefore say to the house of Israel: 'This is what the Sovereign LORD says: Will you defile yourselves the way your fathers did and lust after their vile images? 31When you offer your gifts—the sacrifice of your sons in[a] the fire—you continue to defile yourselves with all your idols to this day. Am I to let you inquire of me, O house of Israel? As surely as I live, declares the Sovereign LORD, I will not let you inquire of me.

32" 'You say, "We want to be like the nations, like the peoples of the world, who serve wood and stone." But what you have in mind will never happen.

[a]31 Or —making your sons pass through

NRSV

30Therefore say to the house of Israel, Thus says the Lord GOD: Will you defile yourselves after the manner of your ancestors and go astray after their detestable things? 31When you offer your gifts and make your children pass through the fire, you defile yourselves with all your idols to this day. And shall I be consulted by you, O house of Israel? As I live, says the Lord GOD, I will not be consulted by you.

32What is in your mind shall never happen—the thought, "Let us be like the nations, like the tribes of the countries, and worship wood and stone."

COMMENTARY

Thus far, Ezekiel has grounded Yahweh's refusal to submit to the elders' inquiry in his particular portrayal of Israel's long-lived history of rebelliousness and idolatry. Has his audience dismissed this retrospective as so much negative reminiscing irrelevant to their immediate situation or, at best, of limited didactic significance? If so, the following two rhetorical questions, introduced by yet another command that Ezekiel address the house of Israel and by the messenger formula, demand that the exiles reassess their understanding of reality. They have defiled *themselves* (נטמא *niṭmā'*), and so cannot blame previous generations for their situation. Moreover, they, too, have "whored" (זנה *zānâ*) after other gods, flagrantly disregarding Yahweh's exclusive right to their fealty (see the Commentary on 16:1-63).[631] Their defiling apostasy is exemplified by their offering of their "gifts" (מתנות *mattĕnôt*), by causing their children to pass through fire (בהעביר בניכם באש *bĕha'ăbîr bĕnêkem bā'ēš*) as sacrifices to other gods. The reader cannot miss how closely v. 31 in particular echoes v. 26, with its references to defiling (in v. 26, Yahweh defiles Israel; in v. 31, the people

defile themselves), to their "gifts," and to the crematory sacrifice of children (while v. 26 did not say that Israel sacrificed its children to other deities, v. 31 explicitly levels that charge). But Ezekiel is speaking of present, and not just past, apostasy (as the phrase "to this day" makes clear). Surely Yahweh's rhetorical question ("Shall I be consulted by you, O house of Israel?") admits nothing except a negative response; and God supplies it here, as in v. 3, emphatically in an oath.

Perhaps the ancient reader knows no collaborating tradition of child immolation among the exiles in Babylon. He is familiar, however, with accounts of such sacrifices within the northern (2 Kgs 17:17) and southern (e.g., Jer 19:4) kingdoms of Israel and by certain of Judah's kings: Ahaz (2 Kgs 16:3); Manasseh (2 Kgs 21:6). According to 2 Kgs 23:10, 13, King Josiah attempted to end the practice by defiling Topheth, a site especially associated with it. Speaking in Yahweh's name, Jeremiah thrice refutes any notion that God demanded such sacrifices: "And [the people of Judah] go on building the high places of Topheth, which is in the valley of the son of Hinnom, to burn their sons and their daughters in the fire—which I did not command, nor did it come into mind" (Jer 7:31; see also Jer

---

631. On "second level" metaphorical uses of *zānâ* ("to be or act like a prostitute"), see J. Galambush, *Jerusalem in the Book of Ezekiel: The City as Yahweh's Wife,* SBLDS 130 (Atlanta: Scholars Press, 1992) 29-33.

19:5; 32:35). Jeremiah himself might be horrified at the audacity of Ezekiel's claim in v. 26!

In the Overview to this oracle, I noted that one's reconstruction of the composition history of Ezek 20:1-44 affects how certain verses are interpreted. Verse 32 is one such text. Because Zimmerli, for example, believes that Ezekiel's original oracle ended with Yahweh's refusal to be inquired of (v. 31), he rules out any possibility that the following verse sheds light on the situation described in vv. 1-31 (the elders' attempts to inquire of Yahweh and God's refusal to respond). In his view, the exiles' unspoken thought ("Let us be like the nations, like the tribes of the countries, and worship wood and stone") expresses their utter despair over Jerusalem's destruction in 587/86 BCE.[632] Ezekiel responds with consoling promises for Israel's future, proclaiming "the great joy that God remains at work, even through the darkest night of his people."[633]

Zimmerli's analysis and consequent interpretation have been challenged for several reasons. First, v. 31 lacks any conventional closing formula. Moreover, the prophet never ends his oracles with an oath formula ("As I live"). To the contrary, the oath formula appears either within the context of an assertion, followed by elaboration (vv. 16:48; 18:3; 20:3; 33:11), or to confirm a pronouncement of judgment (14:16, 18, 20; 17:19), or to mark a shift from reproach to judgment (5:11; 17:19; 33:27; 35:6, 11).[634] Second, v. 33 contains none of the formulas elsewhere used by Ezekiel to initiate oracles. On formal grounds, then, neither

we nor the ancient reader finds reason to separate v. 32 from either preceding or subsequent verses.

Third, while the purported quotation is ambiguous, it nonetheless provokes thoughts of rebellion, not despair, for it recalls 1 Sam 8:19-20. The prophet Samuel has marshaled compelling arguments against the people's demand, "Give us a king to govern us" (1 Sam 8:6). Nonetheless, they refuse to listen to him, saying "No! but we are determined to have a king over us, *so that we also may be like other nations,* and that our king may govern us and go out before us and fight our battles." In 1 Sam 8:22, Yahweh instructs Samuel to acquiesce to the Israelites' demand. But Ezekiel flatly declares that the exiles' unspoken thought of becoming "like the nations" by resorting to idols will never be realized. God will not allow human beings to abort the divine plan conceived while Israel was in Egypt.[635] "Being like the nations is not and has never been an option" for Israel, Davis writes, "for its status is uniquely bound up with YHWH's honor. And that honor will be vindicated."[636] Readers who recall 1 Samuel 19–20 will not construe v. 32 as Ezekiel's comforting words to a despairing people. This judgment is buttressed by the following verse, wherein God asserts an ironclad resolve to rule over the community of exiles.

Hence, v. 32 should not be severed from preceding verses, its quotation deemed irrelevant to the situation of the elders who have gathered before Ezekiel. But neither should it be seen as disclosing the elders' purpose in coming to inquire of Yahweh, as if they were seeking permission to institute a Yahwistic cult complete with images. Rather, it reflects their rebellious impulse to abandon the God with whom they have shared so negative a history. (See Reflections at 20:39-44.)

---

632. W. Zimmerli, *Ezekiel 1: A Commentary on the Book of the Prophet Ezekiel, Chapters 1–24,* trans. R. E. Clements, Hermeneia (Philadelphia: Fortress, 1979) 414. "Wood and stone" expresses, in a pejorative way, the objects of the people's service. Ancients did not believe that their wood and stone images were themselves deities, but used the images as an avenue to a god or goddesses's presence and power. See Deut 4:28; 28:64; Isa 44:9-20; 46:5-7.

633. Ibid., 418.

634. Ellen F. Davis, *Swallowing the Scroll: Textuality and the Dynamics of Discourse in Ezekiel's Prophecy,* Bible and Literature 21 (Sheffield: Almond, 1989) 111.

635. K. P. Darr, "Ezekiel's Justifications of God," 101.

636. Davis, *Swallowing the Scroll,* 113.

Ezekiel 20:33-38, Back to the Future: Israel's Second Exodus

NIV

³³As surely as I live, declares the Sovereign LORD, I will rule over you with a mighty hand and an outstretched arm and with outpoured wrath. ³⁴I will bring you from the nations and gather you from the countries where you have been scattered—with a mighty hand and an outstretched arm and with outpoured wrath. ³⁵I will bring you into the desert of the nations and there, face to face, I will execute judgment upon you. ³⁶As I judged your fathers in the desert of the land of Egypt, so I will judge you, declares the Sovereign LORD. ³⁷I will take note of you as you pass under my rod, and I will bring you into the bond of the covenant. ³⁸I will purge you of those who revolt and rebel against me. Although I will bring them out of the land where they are living, yet they will not enter the land of Israel. Then you will know that I am the LORD.

NRSV

³³As I live, says the Lord GOD, surely with a mighty hand and an outstretched arm, and with wrath poured out, I will be king over you. ³⁴I will bring you out from the peoples and gather you out of the countries where you are scattered, with a mighty hand and an outstretched arm, and with wrath poured out; ³⁵and I will bring you into the wilderness of the peoples, and there I will enter into judgment with you face to face. ³⁶As I entered into judgment with your ancestors in the wilderness of the land of Egypt, so I will enter into judgment with you, says the Lord GOD. ³⁷I will make you pass under the staff, and will bring you within the bond of the covenant. ³⁸I will purge out the rebels among you, and those who transgress against me; I will bring them out of the land where they reside as aliens, but they shall not enter the land of Israel. Then you shall know that I am the LORD.

COMMENTARY

Again, Yahweh swears an oath, this time to rule Israel (as king) with "a mighty hand and an outstretched arm, and with wrath poured out" (v. 33). Israel's psalmists celebrated Yahweh's kingship over Israel (see, e.g., Pss 10:16; 24:8-10; 29:10; 47:2). Moreover, Ezekiel's adoption of two phrases, "with a mighty hand" and "with an outstretched arm," spurs positive thoughts of God's deliverance of Israel from Egyptian slavery (e.g., Deut 4:34; 5:15; 7:19; 11:2; 26:8). But with the third phrase, "with wrath poured out," Yahweh's kingship takes on sinister associations, for it echoes not only vv. 8, 13, and 21, but also God's threats against Jerusalem (7:8; 9:8; 14:19; 22:22) and Jeremiah's prediction that Yahweh will join with the Babylonian forces to fight against Zedekiah "with outstretched hand and mighty arm, in anger, in fury, and in great wrath" (Jer 21:5 NRSV). Likewise, God's announcement of a second exodus ("I will bring you out from the peoples and gather you out of the countries where you are scattered," v. 34a) stirs thoughts of the first exodus, Yahweh's greatest salvific act on Israel's behalf

(see also Exod 13:3; 16:6, 32; 20:2; 33:1). But the repetition of "with wrath poured out" suggests that this exodus will be a fearsome, not a joyous, event.

Verses 35-38 confirm that interpretation. First, God will bring Israel into the "wilderness of the peoples," a counterpart to the desert inhabited by its earliest generations. Attempts to identify a precise geographical setting in Ezekiel's mind are misplaced. The phrase refers, as Block observes, to "no-man's-land, a land of wandering and death, through which many tribes and peoples pass but which none recognizes as a homeland."[637] There, away from the nations' stares, Yahweh will enter into judgment with the people face to face, even as God entered into judgment with their ancestors in the wilderness of the land of Egypt—hardly a positive prospect. Tradition taught that no one could see God and live (Exod 33:20; see also Gen 32:30). Such awesome encounters were rife with

637. D. I. Block, *The Book of Ezekiel: Chapters 1–24,* NICOT (Grand Rapids: Eerdmans, 1997) 651.

danger. It is little wonder that, according to Exod 20:18-21, the Israelites were terrified by God's presence in thunder, lightning, and smoke at Mt. Sinai, and so asked Moses to mediate between God and them, lest they die (see also Deut 5:5, 23-27). In that context, Moses told the people that they need not fear. Here, however, the purpose of the encounter is judgment, and no mediator stands between the people and their wrathful deity. When, in v. 37, Yahweh appears in the metaphorical guise of a shepherd forcing the flock to pass "under the staff," the image is not of a concerned shepherd who counts the sheep to see that none is missing (Jer 33:13), but of a process for distinguishing between those to be brought under the

bond of the covenant and those who continue to rebel against Yahweh.[638] The latter will participate in this new exodus, only to be purged from the community. Presumably they, like the Egypt-born generation, will die in the desert. Then the survivors will acknowledge that Yahweh alone is God. With these events, Yahweh's purpose is, in large part, fulfilled. The people will at last be bound by God's covenant. But the story does not end in the wilderness. God's plan extends beyond judgment to include Israel living faithfully in its homeland. (See Reflections at 20:39-44.)

638. See Lev 27:32, where every tenth animal that passes under the shepherd's staff is dedicated to God. Perhaps the ancient reader understood Ezekiel as making an ironic reference to this tradition.

Ezekiel 20:39-44, Worship on Yahweh's Holy Mountain

NIV

39" 'As for you, O house of Israel, this is what the Sovereign LORD says: Go and serve your idols, every one of you! But afterward you will surely listen to me and no longer profane my holy name with your gifts and idols. [40]For on my holy mountain, the high mountain of Israel, declares the Sovereign LORD, there in the land the entire house of Israel will serve me, and there I will accept them. There I will require your offerings and your choice gifts,[a] along with all your holy sacrifices. [41]I will accept you as fragrant incense when I bring you out from the nations and gather you from the countries where you have been scattered, and I will show myself holy among you in the sight of the nations. [42]Then you will know that I am the LORD, when I bring you into the land of Israel, the land I had sworn with uplifted hand to give to your fathers. [43]There you will remember your conduct and all the actions by which you have defiled yourselves, and you will loathe yourselves for all the evil you have done. [44]You will know that I am the LORD, when I deal with you for my name's sake and not according to your evil ways and your corrupt practices, O house of Israel, declares the Sovereign LORD.' "

a40 Or and the gifts of your firstfruits

NRSV

39As for you, O house of Israel, thus says the Lord GOD: Go serve your idols, everyone of you now and hereafter, if you will not listen to me; but my holy name you shall no more profane with your gifts and your idols. [40]For on my holy mountain, the mountain height of Israel, says the Lord GOD, there all the house of Israel, all of them, shall serve me in the land; there I will accept them, and there I will require your contributions and the choicest of your gifts, with all your sacred things. [41]As a pleasing odor I will accept you, when I bring you out from the peoples, and gather you out of the countries where you have been scattered; and I will manifest my holiness among you in the sight of the nations. [42]You shall know that I am the LORD, when I bring you into the land of Israel, the country that I swore to give to your ancestors. [43]There you shall remember your ways and all the deeds by which you have polluted yourselves; and you shall loathe yourselves for all the evils that you have committed. [44]And you shall know that I am the LORD, when I deal with you for my name's sake, not according to your evil ways, or corrupt deeds, O house of Israel, says the Lord GOD.

COMMENTARY

Verse 39 begins with bitter irony. The injunction, "As for you. . . . Go serve your idols" recalls Amos's "Come to Bethel—and transgress;/ to Gilgal—and multiply transgression" (Amos 4:4 NRSV) and Jeremiah's "By all means, keep your vows and make your libations [to the Queen of Heaven]" (Jer 44:25 NRSV). The following line is best understood as introducing an unspoken threat: "but afterward, if you will not listen to me. . . ." Presumably that threat will be realized in the desert judgment described in vv. 33-38. For now, however, the people must not continue to engage in syncretistic cultic activity (including child sacrifice) in Yahweh's holy name, for in doing so they profane that name.

With v. 40, Ezekiel again looks beyond the present to speak of Israel's future life in its land. In his historical retrospective he fixed upon Israel's (illict) worship at the high places in Canaan. In his prospect, by contrast, he focuses on the house of Israel serving Yahweh "on my holy mountain." This phrase, which appears nowhere else in the book but is common outside it (see, e.g., Ps 2:6; Isa 11:9; 56:7; 57:13; 65:11, 25; 66:20; Joel 2:1; 4:17; cf. Ezek 17:23; 28:14, 16) refers to Zion (though Ezekiel nowhere uses that epithet). "There" (שָׁם šām) appears three times in v. 40. *All* the house of Israel, *all* of them, will serve Yahweh, and God will accept them and "seek" (in the sense

of "require" [אֶדְרוֹשׁ ('edrôš) is a form of the same verb [דָּרַשׁ dāraš]), that means "to inquire" in vv. 1, 3, and 31]) their contributions, choicest gifts, and *all* their sacred things. Unlike their ancestors, who "sent up their pleasing odors" as part of unacceptable religious practices, the regathered Israelites will themselves be a "pleasing odor" to God. Yahweh's holy name will no longer be profaned. Instead, God will "manifest my holiness among you in the sight of the nations." In the past, Israel survived only on account of God's concern that the divine name not be profaned in the sight of the nations. Now Ezekiel imagines all the nations witnessing God's majesty.

Here, then, is the fulfillment of Yahweh's plan begun in Egypt and defied by every generation, including Ezekiel's own. The people will acknowledge the power and sovereignty of their Lord when they are restored to their land. In the face of that utterly unmerited gift, they will remember (see 16:61) their past, polluting deeds and loathe themselves (see 6:9; 16:61-63) for all their sins. Israel will come to recognize that Yahweh has not dealt with it according to its evil ways and corrupt deeds (cf. 16:43), but mercifully "for my name's sake." At last, the nation has become an occasion for the glorification of Yahweh's name, rather than a perpetual threat to God's reputation.

REFLECTIONS

Ezekiel 20:1-44 is one of the Bible's most troubling texts. What are we to make of an oracle that intentionally portrays a people's history in the most pejorative of terms, in order utterly to erode any sense of integrity, any basis for hope? A contemporary, analogous "history" of any ethnic group would certainly lead to charges of bigotry and well-publicized lawsuits. What, indeed, are we to think of the prophet's assertion that Yahweh deliberately gave the Israelites deadly laws, including child sacrifice? Ellen Davis correctly asserts that v. 26 "resists all attempts at domestication" and "cannot be conformed to human reason."[639] Who would wish to worship, much less trust, such a deity? How can we conceive of a God whose principal motivation in dealing with human beings is neither love nor mercy, but concern for Yahweh's own reputation?

Ezekiel's oracle reminds readers in no uncertain terms that biblical literature is neither objective nor entirely separable from specific historical situations and perspectives. Ezekiel's intentions lie at the opposite extreme of presenting a fair and balanced account of Israel's past—its pinnacles of achievement as well as its failures. Relentlessly, he pursues his goal: the defense of

639. Davis, *Swallowing the Scroll*, 114.

God's impending and horrific dealing with this people. Toward that end, he resorts to any means, sacrificing every positive appraisal of Israel as Yahweh's covenant partner and casting God in a role that confounds theological expectations and hopes. Even when he turns toward the future, Ezekiel will not allow his audience (and readers) a glimpse of joy. Beyond judgment lies further judgment—death for all who fail to live up to God's standards and overwhelming guilt and shame for those who survive the journey home.

For Ezekiel, *everything* hangs on securing Yahweh's sovereignty and control over history. If human experience—past, present, and future—cannot be explained as God's direct and just governance of historical events, then Yahweh's status is imperiled. This theological presupposition undergirds every verse of 20:1-44, and modern readers cannot hope to grasp their meaning unless they keep Ezekiel's worldview firmly in mind. At the same time, however, this text challenges us to consider whether the prophet's understanding of God is one that we also should embrace. Would we, like he, ascribe to the Lord the events of human history? Are we free to blame the victims when tragedy befalls them? At what price do we accept the image of God that Ezekiel creates in this oracle?

In a sermon titled "Job's Joke," delivered at Robinson Chapel, Boston University, December 4, 1997, theologian Robert C. Neville explored the consequences of the ages-old belief that God so rules the world that good people are rewarded, while the wicked are felled by cosmic law or direct divine intervention. This notion, which permeates much of both the Old and New Testaments, conceives of God as a "big person" who controls events according to a purpose that humans are able to comprehend. We reveal our anthropomorphic understanding of God when we attempt "to read our lives as if they were dictated by some divine purpose, asking God to guide us here or there, to reward us if we are good, to look the other way when we are not." In so doing, we attempt "to domesticate life's ambiguities by domesticating our idea of God." Like Job, however, we discover that a domesticated God cannot make sense of suffering and death, or of a "fair" reading of history, where the wicked flourish and the good too often suffer. Therein lies the problem with attempting to justify God's ways in human terms—an insoluble dilemma that puts us "in bondage to an unrealistic view of life, destroying faith and betraying religion [as] we stick to the anthropomorphic conception of God as the Big Guy in the Sky who tries to run the world like a just king and fails." In chapter 20, Ezekiel's "Big Guy in the Sky" ultimately succeeds in bringing to fulfillment the plan formulated already when Israel was in Egypt. But his portrayal of God as one who orders the deaths of innocent children, pronounces judgment, and then exacts punishment on future generations and rules with wrath horrifies and desolates us. The book of Job testifies to a God who transcends our attempts to make of the creator a character in the human drama—one whose motivations and deeds can be explained (contained) in ways that conform to the exigencies of the plot, be it comedy or tragedy.

Ezekiel 20 attempts to make sense of a people's ongoing history first by distorting its story, and then by encapsulating it within an overiding plot of God's utter determination to fulfill a divine plan, despite every human effort to derail it. And it attempts to make sense of God's way in the world by ascribing to the Lord the role of a monarch who is, at the same time, just *and* ruthless, forbearing *and* wrathful, life-giving *and* death-dealing, sovereign of history *and* incapable of controlling rebellious subjects. (In truth, some of history's human kings may have fit that profile, but God cannot be forced into it.) Both attempts fail, because each entails containing the transcendent God in theological vessels shaped by human hands.

Writing this Reflection, I am reminded of a scene in Lewis Carroll's wonderful book *Alice in Wonderland.* Sometime after falling down the rabbit hole, Alice finds herself at a tea party with the Mad Hatter, the March Hare, and a pitiful little Dormouse. Carroll creates the following conversation:

The Hatter was the first to break the silence. "What day of the month is it?" he said, turning to Alice; he had taken his watch out of his pocket, and was looking at it uneasily, shaking it every now and then, and holding it to his ear.

Alice considered a little, and then said, "the fourth."

"Two days wrong!" sighed the Hatter. "I told you butter wouldn't suit the works!" he added, looking angrily at the March Hare."

"It was the *best* butter," the March Hare meekly replied.[640]

The March Hare's defense is ludicrous precisely because it does not matter that it was the best butter; butter does not belong in watches. By the same token, it matters not that people attempt to contain God within their "best" vessels—systematic theologies, creedal statements, doctrines—because God does not belong in containers.

Is there, then, no "good news" in chapter 20? Careful reading reveals that Ezekiel himself knows that Yahweh cannot be contained by the "rules of the game." Even as he portrays Israel and God locked in scenarios of human sin and divine punishment, he proclaims the Lord's freedom not to deal with people according to the tenets of retributive justice. According to that doctrine (good for good; evil for evil), rebellious Israel should already have perished in Egypt. Ezekiel grounds its survival in God's concern for the divine reputation among the nations—a motivation that accords well with his unwillingness to relieve the grim caricature he places before his exilic audience. Yet divine self-interest cannot fully account for God's attempt—not once or twice, but thrice—to gift this obdurate people with laws leading not only to life, but to abundant life and knowledge of their God. Even Ezekiel's carefully crafted narrative vessel cannot contain God's grace.

640. Lewis Carroll, *Alice in Wonderland,* ed. Donald J. Gray (New York: W. W. Norton, 1971) 55-56.

EZEKIEL 20:45–21:32, A SWORD FOR GREAT SLAUGHTER

OVERVIEW

In four interrelated oracles (20:45–21:7; 21:8-17; 21:18-27; and 21:28-32), Ezekiel traces the military "career" of a sword unsheathed by Yahweh, sharpened and polished for battle, handed over to the king of Babylonia, and finally destroyed by the fiery breath of God. The collection is remarkable for its rhetorical intensity, dazzling imagery, and befuddling ambiguities. Impassioned prophecies are interspersed with dramatic gestures that reflect blazing wrath, bitter grief, and terror. Judah's world turns topsy-turvy; social structures collapse and, with them, many of Israel's most cherished beliefs about what it means to be the people of Yahweh.

Ezekiel's initial oracle, a veiled threat against Jerusalem, its sanctuary, and Israel's land, reiterates his insistence that God has determined utterly to destroy Judah. When he complains that so ambiguous an utterance can only fuel his reputation as a "maker of metaphors," the Lord decodes it. Suddenly God's raging and inextinguishable forest fire (20:47-48) becomes an unsheathed and insatiable sword, indiscriminately wielded against righteous and wicked alike throughout the land.

The following oracle invites its readers to look on as Yahweh's sword, sharpened for slaughter and burnished to brilliance, is handed over to an unnamed warrior. Ezekiel must cry and wail, for its victims are God's own people, including their princes. Yet he also must clap his hands in camaraderie as the sword's frenetic, everywhere-at-once movements effect an inescapable, bloody massacre. Ultimately, Yahweh is the one striking hand to hand.

In a third oracle, the prophet constructs an imaginative scenario: Nebuchadrezzar stands at the fork in a road, pondering which city (Rabbah of the Ammonites? Fortified Jerusalem?) will be his next target. Although his divinatory techniques are derided by the Judeans, Yahweh works through them to set the king of Babylonia's forces on the road to their capital. The results are a deadly siege and social mayhem.

Dare the Ammonites taunt Jerusalem concerning its downfall? They, too, shall fall beneath Nebuchadrezzar's sword. But then, and without stated motive, Yahweh commands that the sword (now Babylonia's king) return to its scabbard (homeland) for judgment and irrevocable destruction. What worse fate could there be than to pass from memory, as if one had never existed at all?

While the presence of opening and closing formulas reminds readers that the text before them is a collection of oracles and not a single composition, their juxtaposition and numerous links result in a sort of overriding "plot." Yahweh's unsheathed sword passes from God's own hand (21:5) into the hand of a warrior (21:11) whose identity is revealed in vv. 18-20. Though Nebuchadrezzar is ignorant of his role in the Lord's destruction of this people, God is giving him both Judah (v. 27) and the kingdom of Ammon (vv. 28-29). But the drama cannot end there. Yahweh's sharpened and polished "sword" is judged, melted, and handed over to master craftsmen of destruction (v. 31).

Ezekiel 20:45–21:7, Fire and Sword

NIV

[45]The word of the LORD came to me: [46]"Son of man, set your face toward the south; preach against the south and prophesy against the forest of the southland. [47]Say to the southern forest: 'Hear the word of the LORD. This is what the Sovereign LORD says: I am about to set fire to you, and it will consume all your trees, both green and dry. The blazing flame will not be quenched, and every face from south to north will be scorched by it. [48]Everyone will see that I the LORD have kindled it; it will not be quenched.' "

[49]Then I said, "Ah, Sovereign LORD! They are saying of me, 'Isn't he just telling parables?' "

21 The word of the LORD came to me: [2]"Son of man, set your face against Jerusalem and preach against the sanctuary. Prophesy against the land of Israel [3]and say to her: 'This is what the LORD says: I am against you. I will draw my sword from its scabbard and cut off from you both the righteous and the wicked. [4]Because I am going to cut off the righteous and the wicked, my sword will be unsheathed against everyone from south to north. [5]Then all people will know that I the LORD have drawn my sword from its scabbard; it will not return again.'

[6]"Therefore groan, son of man! Groan before them with broken heart and bitter grief. [7]And

NRSV

[45][a]The word of the LORD came to me: [46]Mortal, set your face toward the south, preach against the south, and prophesy against the forest land in the Negeb; [47]say to the forest of the Negeb, Hear the word of the LORD: Thus says the Lord GOD, I will kindle a fire in you, and it shall devour every green tree in you and every dry tree; the blazing flame shall not be quenched, and all faces from south to north shall be scorched by it. [48]All flesh shall see that I the LORD have kindled it; it shall not be quenched. [49]Then I said, "Ah Lord GOD! they are saying of me, 'Is he not a maker of allegories?' "

21 [b]The word of the LORD came to me: [2]Mortal, set your face toward Jerusalem and preach against the sanctuaries; prophesy against the land of Israel [3]and say to the land of Israel, Thus says the LORD: I am coming against you, and will draw my sword out of its sheath, and will cut off from you both righteous and wicked. [4]Because I will cut off from you both righteous and wicked, therefore my sword shall go out of its sheath against all flesh from south to north; [5]and all flesh shall know that I the LORD have drawn my sword out of its sheath; it shall not be sheathed again. [6]Moan therefore, mortal;

[a]Ch 21.1 in Heb   [b]Ch 21.6 in Heb

NIV	NRSV
when they ask you, 'Why are you groaning?' you shall say, 'Because of the news that is coming. Every heart will melt and every hand go limp; every spirit will become faint and every knee become as weak as water.' It is coming! It will surely take place, declares the Sovereign LORD."	moan with breaking heart and bitter grief before their eyes. [7]And when they say to you, "Why do you moan?" you shall say, "Because of the news that has come. Every heart will melt and all hands will be feeble, every spirit will faint and all knees will turn to water. See, it comes and it will be fulfilled," says the Lord GOD.

COMMENTARY

The first of Ezekiel's four oracles concerning the sword commences with the word event formula ("The word of the LORD came to me"), followed by Yahweh's customary address to Ezekiel ("Mortal") and a threefold command. First, Ezekiel is told to "set your face," a hostile and foreboding gesture, "toward Teman." The same gesture, accompanied by an oracle, has already appeared in 4:3, 7; 6:2. "Teman" can be construed either as a place-name (a northern district of Edom; see 25:13) or as "south" (ימין *yāmîn*, a related term, means "right," "right hand") When one faces east, the general orientation in Israel's ancient Near Eastern world, south lies to the right. At this early stage in the oracle, the reader has no basis for deciding between these two possibilities.

Second, Ezekiel is commanded to "speak out [הטף *haṭṭēp*; NRSV and NIV, "preach"] against Darom." The verb derives from נטף (*nāṭap*), "to drip"—here, "to cause [words] to drip [from the mouth]" (see also Deut 32:2; Job 29:22; Prov 5:3). It refers to prophetic speech also in Amos 7:16 and Mic 2:6. "Darom" may designate a locality (in Mishnaic Hebrew, a region of Judea lying north of Beersheba and south of Beth-Gubrin).[641] Elsewhere in Ezekiel, however, it means "south" (e.g., Ezek 40:24, 27, 28; 41:11; see also Job 37:17; Eccl 1:6; 11:3). With the addition of this second term, the reader may lean toward interpreting both Teman and Doran as common nouns, rather than proper names.

Third, Ezekiel is to "prophesy against the forest land in the Negeb." As a place-name, "Negeb" refers to a region lying south of Judah (see, e.g.,

Num 33:40; Josh 15:19). True to the meaning of its root (נגב *ngb*, "be dry," "parched"), this is desert land (owing to insufficient rainfall). Hence "forest land" (a translation of יער השדה *ya'ar haśśādeh*; lit., "the forest of the field") is misleading and better rendered "scrubland" (see also Isa 21:13). This amplified reference to the Negeb suggests a specific (if expansive) region, and so may lead the reader to reconsider that all three terms are functioning as proper nouns. Yet as a common noun, *negeb* also means "south" (e.g., Gen 13:14; Deut 8:4, 9; Josh 17:10; 1 Kgs 7:25; Ezek 40:2; 46:9).

Hence, all three terms (rendered as place-names in the LXX) can specify a single compass point. Their precise meanings to this point in the oracle remain ambiguous, and we can assume that competent ancient (and modern) readers might have understood them in different ways.

The oracle itself, addressed to "the forest of the Negeb,"[642] begins with a summons to hear Yahweh's declaration, followed by the messenger formula ("Thus says the Lord GOD"). Yahweh intends to kindle a fire in the territory that will consume every tree—green and dry.[643] Ezekiel often speaks metaphorically of God's judgment as fire (e.g., 5:4; 10:2; 15:4-7; 19:12, 14). Would the ancient reader, like some moderns, have been disconcerted by the image of a forest fire raging through territory that was not densely vegetated, and so suspect that the oracle's addressee is some-

641. Moshe Greenberg, *Ezekiel 21–37*, AB 22A (Garden City, N.Y.: Doubleday, 1997) 418.

642. The oracle is not, of course, addressed to this third member of the triad to the exclusion of the other two. Rather, the elaborated phrase "the forest (scrubland) of the Negeb" best fits the nature of Yahweh's judgment, a roaring (forest) fire.

643. The phrase "every green tree . . . and every dry tree" is a merism—i.e., a figure of speech in which totality is indicated by the pairing of two (often opposite) elements. So also "from south to north" (= the entire area) later in this verse.

thing other than the southern scrubland (see below)? In any event, the "blazing flame" (להבת שלהבת *lahebet šalhebet*; the phrase [lit., "flame of flame"; a juxtaposition of the common noun "flame" and an Aramaized form of the same root] expresses the superlative), inextinguishable in its intensity, will "scorch" (or "scar"; a related noun appears in Lev 13:23, 28) the face of every person in its path. "All flesh," everyone, will see what Yahweh has done. In this variation on the recognition formula (normally, "then X shall know that I am Yahweh"), "see" replaces "know," and emphasis falls on witnessing what Yahweh (and no other deity) has carried out, rather than on an inward recognition of Yahweh's identity as sovereign Lord.

In a manner uncharacteristic of the prophet, Ezekiel responds with a complaint to Yahweh consisting of "Ah!" (אהה *'ăhăh*, a cry of alarm), direct address, and an indirect quotation of the people: "They are saying of me, 'Is he not a ממשל משלים [*měmaššēl měšālîm*]?' " (A piel participle, *māšal* bears the nuance of repeated engagement in the activity.) Forms of משל *māšal* have already appeared in 12:22-23; 16:44; 17:2; and 18:2. The noun encompasses a variety of literary genres, including pithy proverbs, parables, and extended tropes. Translators suggest a variety of renderings: "teller of parables" (NIV), "riddlemonger" (TNK), "maker of allegories"(NRSV). In this context, I favor "maker of metaphors." The oracle does not fit the conventional understanding of parables (stories told to make a moral or theological point). It is not, strictly speaking, either a riddle (though all metaphors have a "riddling" quality) or an allegory. Allegories present "an abstract or spiritual concept in the guise of concrete images and events."[644] Metaphors, by contrast, are figures of speech by which we "speak about one thing in terms which are seen to be suggestive of another."[645] With this oracle, Ezekiel engages in the latter activity. In subsequent verses (21:1-6) he will disclose the underlying subject ("tenor") of his metaphorical "vehicle" (the oracular utterance), clarifying some of its terms through the substitution of "literal" equivalents, while replacing others with different metaphors.

What is the gist of the people's quote, and why does the prophet complain of it to Yahweh? Does he despair of recurring gripes from the exiles that his oracles are unintelligible?[646] Does he fear that the "richness of his repertoire" inclines his audience to appreciate him as an entertainer, but not to take his words seriously (see 33:30-33)?[647] Either view is possible, though Yahweh's immediate interpretation of the metaphorical oracle especially commends the former.

The reappearance of the word event formula, address to the prophet ("Mortal"), and threefold command signals no new oracle, but Yahweh's interpretation of the oracle that began in 20:45. Ezekiel must set his face toward *Jerusalem,* speak out against the *sanctuary,*[648] and prophesy against the *land of Israel* (see similar wording in Ps 79:1). These "decodings" of Teman, Darom, and "the scrubland of the Negeb" effectively rule them out as names of disparate locales. And while they might well startle both audience and reader, they are not too far-fetched. Both Jerusalem and its Temple lie within the southern kingdom of Israel, and "the land of Israel" likely designates Judah's (southern) territory. In retrospect—if not in prospect—the reader may detect two clues in Ezekiel's phrase יער השדה נגב (*ya'ar haśśādeh negeb,* "the forest land in the Negeb"). First, it recalls "the House of the Forest (of Lebanon)"—a designation for Jerusalem's royal palace (see 1 Kgs 7:2; 10:17, 21; Isa 22:8) and perhaps for its Temple as well (see 1 Kgs 6:9-36), since both were built of Lebanon's cedars. Jeremiah appears to have both structures in mind when he speaks of Yahweh's kindling "a fire in her [Jerusalem's] forest [*ya'ar*]" (Jer 21:14). Second (and related to the first), both שדה (*śādeh*) and *ya'ar* appear in Mic 3:12, a doom prophecy.

There, it seems, the eighth-century BCE prophet Micah has with bitter irony "reversed" the meaning of a traditional epithet for Jerusalem: "the (mountain of) the house of the forest" will be reduced to a wooded (i.e., overgrown and un-

644. Richard N. Soulen, *Handbook of Biblical Criticism,* 2nd ed. (Atlanta: John Knox, 1981) 15.

645. Janet Martin Soskice, *Metaphor and Religious Language* (Oxford: Clarendon, 1985) 15.

646. So W. Zimmerli, *Ezekiel 1: A Commentary on the Book of the Prophet Ezekiel, Chapters 1–24,* trans. R. E. Clements, Hermeneia (Philadelphia: Fortress, 1979) 424.

647. So Greenberg, *Ezekiel 21–37,* 419.

648. Ronald M. Hals, *Ezekiel,* FOTL 19 (Grand Rapids: Eerdmans, 1988) 145, and others emend "sanctuaries" to "their sanctuary"—i.e., the Jerusalem Temple. Greenberg, *Ezekiel 21–37,* 419, by contrast, points to other passages where the plural refers to that Temple (e.g., Pss 68:35; 73:17) and terms this a "plural of extension."

inhabited) wild. The reader who contemplates Ezekiel's equation of Judah's southern scrubland (*ya'ar haśśādeh negeb,*) and Jerusalem/Temple/ the land of Israel with Mic 3:12 ringing in his ears will, like Jeremiah's contemporaries (Jer 26:17-18), recall that a prophet of Yahweh predicted Jerusalem's destruction centuries earlier. And (like Ezekiel's compatriots?) the reader will discern in the prophet's proleptic language the impending fulfillment of that prediction. Further, as this chapter unfolds and Nebuchadrezzar's forces appear on the scene, the reader remembers that the armies of Israel's Mesopotamian foes, Assyria and Babylonia, routinely skirted the Arabian desert by traveling northwest along the Fertile Crescent, approaching Israel from the north and then heading south to battle (a reality reflected in the many biblical references to "the enemy from the north," e.g., Jer 1:14; 6:1).

Again, the third element of Ezekiel's triad (in this case, "the land of Israel") is singled out for direct address (though not to the exclusion of the other two). Following the messenger formula, Yahweh issues the "challenge to a duel" formula ("I am coming against you!"; see also 5:8 and 13:8).[649] Drawing sword from scabbard, the Lord will cut off "both righteous and wicked." Here the blazing fire of 20:47-48 has become God's unsheathed sword, while the expression "every green tree and every dry tree," implying totality, has been supplanted by another, "righteous and wicked": the total population. Lest we pass too facilely over the latter phrase, we need to note that Yahweh's announcement appears to contravene Ezekiel's prior assertions that God does not punish the righteous and the wicked indiscriminately (9:4-6; 14:12-20; 18:1-32). Again, we must recognize that the prophet was no systematic theologian. But if Ezekiel's pair, "righteous and wicked," brings to mind Abraham's argument with God concerning the fate of Sodom ("Far be it from you to do such a thing, to slay the righteous with the wicked, so that the righteous fare as the wicked! Far be that from you! Shall not the Judge of the earth do what is just?" Gen 18:25), it nonetheless speaks realistically of warfare. When, for example, the prophet asserts that Yahweh's "X" on the foreheads of those Jerusalemites who moan and groan over abominations committed in their city will protect them from the executioners (9:4-6), he ignores the fact that warriors draw no such distinctions (see 14:12-20).

Among Yahweh's arsenal of weapons (e.g., famine, pestilence, wild animals, fire), the sword figures most prominently in Ezekiel's scroll (5:1-2; 6:3, 8, 11-12; 11:8, 10; 12:14, 16; 14:17, 21; 16:40; 17:21). Elsewhere, it appears among the curses consequent upon Israel's abrogation of its covenant obligations (e.g., Lev 26:25, 33; Deut 28:22). Amos (9:4) and Jeremiah (47:6-7) tell of Yahweh's commanding the sword to slaughter; in Amos, and also in Jer 9:16, it pursues the people in exile. While fire and sword are equated in no other Hebrew Bible text, Ezekiel may have borrowed the idea from Babylonian literary culture. In the *Erra Epic,* a poetic account of Babylon's downfall, Isûm (a masc. form of *Isâtûm*), the agent of Babylon's destruction, is first addressed as "torch." In the following line, however, he is called "the broadsword: slaught[erer]."[650]

When the Lord's unsheathed sword has killed all flesh throughout Judah ("from south to north"), then "all flesh" (a reference to humanity, which witnesses God's raging fire in 20:48) will acknowledge that Yahweh (alone) has effected the slaughter. Just as God's blazing fire will not be extinguished (20:47-48), so also the deity will not return weapon to scabbard.

Yahweh then addresses Ezekiel, twice commanding him to "moan" (אנח *'ānaḥ*; the same verb appeared in 9:4) with "breaking heart" (NRSV and NIV)[651] and "bitter grief" in the exiles' presence. This sign act (see Excursus: "Prophetic Sign Acts," 1143-44), a dramatic performance directed by the deity, intends to evoke a question from the prophet's audience (see also 12:9; 24:19; 37:18): "Why do you moan?" God scripts the reply: God is moaning on account of "the news that is coming" (NIV). What is this news? Critics have offered several explanations,

---

649. Hals, *Ezekiel,* 146.

650. D. I. Block, *The Book of Ezekiel: Chapters 1–24,* NICOT (Grand Rapids: Eerdmans, 1997) 669, citing L. Cagni, *The Poem of Erra,* Sources from the Ancient Near East 1 (Malibu: Undena, 1977) 84. See further D. Bodi, *The Book of Ezekiel and the Poem of Erra,* OBO 104 (Göttingen: Vandenhoeck & Ruprecht, 1991) 250-54. See also the description of the "pest" deity Erra's indiscriminate slaughter in the Mesopotamian Erra Epic in *Myths from Mesopotamia: Creation, the Flood, Gilgamesh, and Others,* trans. S. Dalley (Oxford: Oxford University Press, 1989) 307.

651. The Hebrew (בשברון מתנים *běšibrôn motnayim;* lit., "with rupture of tendons") is a more devastating (and in English, less stereotypical) phrase. See Greenberg, *Ezekiel 21–37,* 420-21.

but the most compelling identifies it as a report of the massive slaughter described in the immediately preceding oracle and its interpretation.[652] The arrival of that report will bring on massive physiological and psychological expressions of anguish: enfeebled hands and loss of bladder control, such that urine wets one's knees (neither the NRSV's "all knees will turn to water" nor the NIV's "every knee become as weak as water" captures the meaning in Hebrew), on the one hand,

and melting hearts and fainting spirits, on the other hand. Hillers has demonstrated that this passage, like 17:17, 27, reflects a literary convention in ancient Israel: the reaction to bad news (see also Isa 13:7-8; 21:3-4; Jer 6:24; 49:23-24).[653] This first oracle ends with Ezekiel's assurance that the news is coming, and God's oracle will be fulfilled. The prophetic utterance formula, "says the Lord GOD," both brings it to a close and further underscores its divine origin. (See Reflections at 21:28-32.)

652. Alternatively, one might say that Ezekiel's performance presages the Judeans' reaction in the face of Nebuchadrezzar's advancing troops.

653. D. R. Hillers, "A Convention in Hebrew Literature: The Reaction to Bad News," *ZAW* 77 (1965) 86-90.

Ezekiel 21:8-17, The Sword in the Slayer's Hand

NIV

[8]The word of the LORD came to me: [9]"Son of man, prophesy and say, 'This is what the Lord says:

" 'A sword, a sword,
    sharpened and polished—
[10]sharpened for the slaughter,
    polished to flash like lightning!

" 'Shall we rejoice in the scepter of my son ⌞Judah⌟? The sword despises every such stick.

[11]" 'The sword is appointed to be polished,
    to be grasped with the hand;
it is sharpened and polished,
    made ready for the hand of the slayer.
[12]Cry out and wail, son of man,
    for it is against my people;
it is against all the princes of Israel.
They are thrown to the sword
    along with my people.
Therefore beat your breast.

[13]" 'Testing will surely come. And what if the scepter ⌞of Judah⌟, which the sword despises, does not continue? declares the Sovereign LORD.'

[14]"So then, son of man, prophesy
    and strike your hands together.
Let the sword strike twice,
    even three times.
It is a sword for slaughter—

NRSV

[8]And the word of the LORD came to me: [9]Mortal, prophesy and say: Thus says the Lord; Say:
    A sword, a sword is sharpened,
        it is also polished;
[10]it is sharpened for slaughter,
        honed to flash like lightning!
How can we make merry?
    You have despised the rod,
        and all discipline.[a]
[11]The sword[b] is given to be polished,
        to be grasped in the hand;
    it is sharpened, the sword is polished,
        to be placed in the slayer's hand.
[12]Cry and wail, O mortal,
        for it is against my people;
    it is against all Israel's princes;
        they are thrown to the sword,
        together with my people.
        Ah! Strike the thigh!
[13]For consider: What! If you despise the rod, will it not happen?[a] says the Lord GOD.
[14]And you, mortal, prophesy;
        strike hand to hand.
    Let the sword fall twice, thrice;
        it is a sword for killing.
    A sword for great slaughter—
        it surrounds them;
[15]therefore hearts melt

[a]Meaning of Heb uncertain   [b]Heb *It*

NIV

a sword for great slaughter,
closing in on them from every side.
¹⁵So that hearts may melt
and the fallen be many,
I have stationed the sword for slaughter[a]
at all their gates.
Oh! It is made to flash like lightning,
it is grasped for slaughter.
¹⁶O sword, slash to the right,
then to the left,
wherever your blade is turned.
¹⁷I too will strike my hands together,
and my wrath will subside.
I the LORD have spoken."

[a]15 Septuagint; the meaning of the Hebrew for this word is uncertain.

NRSV

and many stumble.
At all their gates I have set
the point[a] of the sword.
Ah! It is made for flashing,
it is polished[b] for slaughter.
¹⁶ Attack to the right!
Engage to the left!
—wherever your edge is directed.
¹⁷ I too will strike hand to hand,
I will satisfy my fury;
I the LORD have spoken.

[a]Meaning of Heb uncertain   [b]Tg: Heb wrapped up

COMMENTARY

Any treatment of this oracle, Ezekiel's second concerning the sword, must be regarded as tentative. Hals summarizes the problems it presents to text critics and interpreters: "Not only are two lines (vv. 10b and 13b) incomprehensible and beyond translation, but much of the rest is so corrupt that virtually every line is rendered uncertain by the conjectures necessary to make any sense of it." Hals goes on to suggest that the text has suffered in preservation on account of its extremely imaginative poetic content and form.[654] By analogy, one can easily surmise how lines from E. E. Cummings's description of an approaching thunderstorm might (even in the electronic age) suffer in transmission:

dis(appeared cleverly)world

iS Slapped:with;liGhtninG
!⁶⁵⁵

Ezekiel's two-part oracle (vv. 8-13, vv. 14-17) is introduced most emphatically by the word event formula (see also 20:45; 21:1), Yahweh's direct address to the prophet, a command ("prophesy and say"), the messenger formula ("thus says the LORD"), and the imperative "say." It ends (v. 17)

with the conclusion of divine speech formula, "I the LORD have spoken." Between the two, the prophetic utterance formula ("says the Lord GOD") at the conclusion of v. 13 signals the end of its first section, while the command "And you, mortal, prophesy" (v. 14) initiates the second.

The first section of the oracle further subdivides into vv. 9b-13, on the one hand, and vv. 14-17, on the other.[656] The former launches in an impersonal, yet impassioned way (note the double exclamation "a sword! a sword!"; cf. 2 Kgs 4:19; Jer 4:19), a poem about preparing a sword for battle and handing it to an unnamed warrior. Its staccato poetic lines, repeated references to "sharpened" (הוחדה hûḥaddâ, vv. 9b, 10a, 11b) and "polished" (מרוטה mĕrûṭâ, vv. 9b, 10a, 11ab), and recurring explosive sounds (e.g., ח ḥ; ט ṭ) have sometimes prompted scholars to imagine that these verses derive from a sword song, dance, or incantation. So, for example, Hals detects in Ezekiel's poetry the residues of magical views of weapons:

One sang or pictured only . . . the successful use of one's weapons. What made such use magic was mainly the attempt thereby to predetermine the success of tomorrow's battle or hunt.

654. Hals, *Ezekiel*, 149.
655. "XXXVIII," in E. E. Cummings, *W* (New York: Liveright, 1970).
656. See Moshe Greenberg, *Ezekiel 21–37*, AB 22A (Garden City, N.Y.: Doubleday, 1997) 439-40.

However, the personification of a sword or the description of its functioning as that which happens by itself may be further aspects of magic. There is also a natural link between powerful, efficacious words and impressive eloquence, between captivating, repetitious style and the primitive verbal power of a spell.[657]

At the least, Ezekiel's poetry demonstrates his knowledge of a specialized vocabulary pertaining to the preparation, appearance, and use of swords in warfare.

The initial verb in v. 10*a*, טבח (*ṭābaḥ*), generally refers to the slaughtering of domestic animals for food (see Gen 43:16; Exod 22:1; Deut 28:31; 1 Sam 25:11; Prov 9:2; by extension, cooks are called *ṭabbāḥ* [sing.] in 1 Sam 9:23-24 and *ṭabbāḥôt* [pl.] in 1 Sam 8:13). When its object is humans, however, the verb can describe "bloody massacres," like that envisioned here (e.g., Ps 37:14; Jer 48:15).[658] Verse 15*a* likens the burnished sword to a lightning flash. The second half of this verse is, for moderns at least, largely unintelligible; many critics simply dismiss it as a garbled secondary addition (a judgment all too easily reached when the meaning of a text eludes us). Yet it is represented in the versions. According to the NRSV translation, Ezekiel dissuades his audience from thinking that they are not the sword's intended victims. Because they have despised Yahweh's rod of discipline (like the stick brandished by parents and teachers in order to punish obdurate children), the sword is wielded against them. The NIV, by contrast, interprets the verse as an admonition not to rejoice in Judah's rod (i.e., the royal scepter [שבט *šēbeṭ*; see also 19:11] of its kings), for the sword "despises" (i.e., will destroy) every such scepter (lit., "every tree"; the phrase echoes 20:47). So much for hopes of deliverance based on God's covenantal promises to the house of David (2 Samuel 7) and on Jacob's blessing that the royal scepter would never depart (the tribe of) Judah (Gen 49:10).[659] There is every reason to believe that ancient, like modern, interpreters stumbled over this line. In the light of the reference to שבטי משלים (*šibṭê mōšĕlîm*, "royal scepters") in 19:11 (see also 19:14*a*), however, the reader

is inclined to interpret v. 10*a* as a threat against Judah's royal house. Verse 11*a* refers only to "the palm" that grasps the sword, but v. 11*b* further specifies that this hand belongs to a (unnamed) warrior.

With v. 12 Yahweh again orders Ezekiel to engage in dramatic actions (see v. 6). On the one hand, he must "cry and wail" (= shriek loudly; see also Isa 65:14*b*; Hos 7:14) because, God says, the sword's victims will be "my people," including "all the princes of Israel." (Here, the largely impersonal language of vv. 9*b*-11 has given way to God's use of personal pronouns ["*my* people"] and precise identification ["all the princes of *Israel*"].) On the other hand, he must "strike the thigh," a gesture of grief. Verse 13, like v. 10*b*, has resisted the best efforts of translators. The two texts appear to be related in some way; they share the noun "rod" (or "scepter," *šēbeṭ*), as well as the verb "despises" (מאסה *mō'eseṭ*). Again, and not surprisingly, the NRSV and the NIV go separate ways in their respective renderings. The former emphasizes that the sword wielded against God's people and their princes is the inevitable consequence of their rejection of Yahweh's (disciplining) rod. The latter speaks of a time of testing (of what or whom?)[660] when the scepter of Judah will be destroyed by the sword. By this (better) construal, v. 13, like 19:10-14, portends the end of Judah's royal house. Between v. 10*a* and this verse, the reader has encountered a specific reference to the sword's execution of "all the princes of Israel" in v. 12.

The second half of this oracle (vv. 14-17) commences with God's command that Ezekiel prophesy and "strike hand to hand." The latter directive appeared in 6:11 (accompanied by stamping of the feet). Although the significance of this gesture is not clear, its reappearance in v. 17*a* suggests that it expresses anger ("I [Yahweh] too will strike hand to hand, I will satisfy my fury").[661] The command to prophesy is not followed by a statement of what the prophet is to say (cf. v. 9). Is the clapping of hands itself the (non-verbal) communication? Or should the following line ("Let the sword fall")

657. Ronald M. Hals, *Ezekiel,* FOTL 19 (Grand Rapids: Eerdmans, 1989) 151.

658. See Block, *Ezekiel 1–24,* 676.

659. See ibid., 677-78.

660. Block suggests that the sword itself must prepare for a testing—i.e., its fulfillment of the murderous mission. Ibid., 679.

661. Cf. the conclusions of Zimmerli, *Ezekiel 1,* 434; Block, *Ezekiel 1–24,* 679; K. Friebel, "Jeremiah's and Ezekiel's Sign-Acts: Their Meaning and Function as Nonverbal Communication and Rhetoric" (Ph.D. diss., University of Wisconsin at Madison, 1989) 712-16; and Greenberg, *Ezekiel 21–37,* 424.

be placed in his mouth? In vv. 14b-16, as Block observes, two descriptions of the sword's action (vv. 14b, 16) frame statements of its consequence/function (vv. 14c-15). The sword is called to double and triple itself—that is, to strike so rapidly as to create the visual illusion of more than one weapon (v. 14b).[662] Subsequently, Yahweh commands it to slash in all directions ("Attack to the right!/ Engage to the left!"),[663] whichever way its sharpened blade ("your face") is pointed (v. 16).[664] People caught in its paths will be incapacitated by terror. Even Jerusalem's walls offer no protection,

for Yahweh has positioned the sword at every gate. Verse 15b echoes imagery and vocabulary found especially in v. 10a: the sword flashes like lightning (ברק bārāq); it is grasped for bloody massacre (טבח ṭābaḥ). If the identity of the warrior into whose hand the sword is placed remains a mystery (v. 6), there can be no doubt that ultimately, it is Yahweh's weapon—effecting divine judgment upon God's own people. The carrying out of its murderous mission will have a cathartic effect upon the deity: "I will satisfy my wrath" (הנחותי חמתי hănîḥôtî ḥămātî); the same Hebrew phrase appears in 16:42, immediately following Yahweh's description of the multiple lethal punishments (including stabbing with swords) inflicted upon Jerusalem, God's unfaithful wife. (See Reflections at 21:28-32.)

---

662. For different interpretations of "twice" and "thrice," see Greenberg, *Ezekiel 21–37*, 424.

663. I.e., "from every direction." See E. Z. Melamed, "Break-up of Stereotype Phrases as an Artistic Device in Biblical Poetry," in *Studies in the Bible*, ed. C. Rabin, ScriHier 8 (Jerusalem: Magnes, 1961) 146-47.

664. D. I. Block, *The Book of Ezekiel: Chapters 1–24*, NICOT (Grand Rapids: Eerdmans, 1997) 679-80.

Ezekiel 21:18-27, The Sword of the King of Babylon

NIV

[18]The word of the LORD came to me: [19]"Son of man, mark out two roads for the sword of the king of Babylon to take, both starting from the same country. Make a signpost where the road branches off to the city. [20]Mark out one road for the sword to come against Rabbah of the Ammonites and another against Judah and fortified Jerusalem. [21]For the king of Babylon will stop at the fork in the road, at the junction of the two roads, to seek an omen: He will cast lots with arrows, he will consult his idols, he will examine the liver. [22]Into his right hand will come the lot for Jerusalem, where he is to set up battering rams, to give the command to slaughter, to sound the battle cry, to set battering rams against the gates, to build a ramp and to erect siege works. [23]It will seem like a false omen to those who have sworn allegiance to him, but he will remind them of their guilt and take them captive.

[24]"Therefore this is what the Sovereign LORD says: 'Because you people have brought to mind your guilt by your open rebellion, revealing your sins in all that you do—because you have done this, you will be taken captive.

[25]" 'O profane and wicked prince of Israel,

NRSV

18The word of the LORD came to me: [19]Mortal, mark out two roads for the sword of the king of Babylon to come; both of them shall issue from the same land. And make a signpost, make it for a fork in the road leading to a city; [20]mark out the road for the sword to come to Rabbah of the Ammonites or to Judah and to[a] Jerusalem the fortified. [21]For the king of Babylon stands at the parting of the way, at the fork in the two roads, to use divination; he shakes the arrows, he consults the teraphim,[b] he inspects the liver. [22]Into his right hand comes the lot for Jerusalem, to set battering rams, to call out for slaughter, for raising the battle cry, to set battering rams against the gates, to cast up ramps, to build siege towers. [23]But to them it will seem like a false divination; they have sworn solemn oaths; but he brings their guilt to remembrance, bringing about their capture.

24Therefore thus says the Lord GOD: Because you have brought your guilt to remembrance, in that your transgressions are uncovered, so that in all your deeds your sins appear—because you have come to remembrance, you shall be taken in hand.[c]

[a]Gk Syr: Heb *Judah in*   [b]Or *the household gods*   [c]Or *be taken captive*

whose day has come, whose time of punishment has reached its climax, ²⁶this is what the Sovereign LORD says: Take off the turban, remove the crown. It will not be as it was: The lowly will be exalted and the exalted will be brought low. ²⁷A ruin! A ruin! I will make it a ruin! It will not be restored until he comes to whom it rightfully belongs; to him I will give it.'

²⁵ As for you, vile, wicked prince of Israel,
   you whose day has come,
   the time of final punishment,
²⁶ thus says the Lord GOD:
   Remove the turban, take off the crown;
   things shall not remain as they are.
Exalt that which is low,
   abase that which is high.
²⁷ A ruin, a ruin, a ruin—
   I will make it!
   (Such has never occurred.)
Until he comes whose right it is;
   to him I will give it.

COMMENTARY

The third of Ezekiel's cluster of oracles concerning the sword is introduced by the word event formula ("The word of Yahweh came to me"), followed by God's direct address to the prophet. It consists of three sections: a sign act (vv. 19-20), an explanation of that act (vv. 21-24), and an exhortatory address to the "vile, wicked prince of Israel" (vv. 25-27).

Yahweh instructs Ezekiel to perform yet another sign act: He must mark out two roads originating in the same land, alternative routes upon which the sword of the king of Babylon might proceed. The text does not indicate how, or on what, these "roads" are to be represented. The reader likely recalls Ezekiel's brick, upon which was drawn or incised a representation of Jerusalem (4:1). At the "mother of the way"—that is, the fork ("head") of the road (v. 21)—he must carve a signpost identifying the two directions Nebuchadrezzar's forces could take; one road leads to Rabbath of the Ammonites, the other to Judah and fortified Jerusalem. Characteristically, nothing is said of Ezekiel's actual implementation of Yahweh's command.

Critics appropriately associate this oracle with Nebuchadrezzar's campaign against the west in 589/88 BCE. When Zedekiah joined with the rulers of Tyre and Ammon in rebelling against their overlord, to whom he had sworn an oath of loyalty, the king of Babylon responded quickly, besieging Jerusalem in 588 BCE (see the

Commentary on 17:1-24). The prophet's scenario at the fork in the road is not, of course, an actual episode, but an exercise of his imagination intended to create suspense and foster fear.

Which city will be Nebuchadrezzar's target? So momentous a decision calls for divine input, and so his oracle-priest carries out certain divinatory techniques (לקסם־קסם *liqsām qāsem*, "to consult an omen").[665] The first involves the manipulation of arrows, a practice known as belomancy or rhabdomancy,[666] which consists of shaking inscribed arrows, then drawing one (from the quiver?) on the presumption that the god or gods will determine which is chosen. This technique is not attested in extant ancient Babylonian literature. The second entails consulting ("ask[ing]") the teraphim. Little is known of these objects, though from Gen 31:30 one might deduce that they were small representations of deities. This practice also is not mentioned in extant Babylonian texts. The third technique, examining the liver (hepatoscopy), by contrast, is well-known from Assyrian and Babylonian sources (but referred to explicitly nowhere else in the Hebrew Bible). Archaeologists have recovered models of livers (used as

---

665. See A. Malamat, "New Light from Mari [ARM XXVI] on Biblical Prophecy (III-IV)," in *Storia e tradizioni di Israele,* ed. D. Garrone and F. Israel (Brescia: Paideia, 1991) 188, for an instance of Nebuchadrezzar's reliance on an oracle to determine his campaign route. See also Block, *Ezekiel 1–24,* 685-86).

666. See Block, *Ezekiel 1–24,* 686, on these two terms and the procedure they designate. See also S. Iwry, "New Evidence for Belomancy in Ancient Palestine and Phoenicia," *JAOS* 81 (1961) 27-33.

teaching aids?) that have been divided into numerous sections and bear markings (significant for interpretation), as well as extensive texts regarding such markings and their import in previous divinations.

Verse 22 records the result of Nebuchadrezzar's divination: The omen appears on the liver's right side. Next stop, Jerusalem![667] The remainder of this verse describes the fate awaiting Judah's capital: battering rams set up at the gates; the terrifying sound of battle cries (see Isa 42:13; Zeph 1:14); siege towers erected. Verse 23a is difficult. "Them/they" cannot be the Babylonians, since Nebuchadrezzar's troups would have presupposed the efficacy of their divinatory techniques, and a campaign against rebellious Jerusalem was a reasonable next step. Hence, Ezekiel must be talking about his compatriots back home. They are portrayed as dismissing the Babylonian oracle-priest's techniques as false divination—an orthodox assessment (see, e.g., Deut 18:10; 2 Kgs 17:17) that buttresses their persistent (but, in Ezekiel's view, misfounded) confidence that Yahweh will protect their city against all foes. The following expression, "they have sworn solemn oaths" (NRSV), is especially elusive. Does it refer to Zedekiah's oath of loyalty to Nebuchadrezzar, sworn in Yahweh's name but abrogated when an opportunity for rebellion arose (see the Commentary on 17:11-22)? If so, the people likely are criticized for having held that oath in the same contempt accorded Nebuchadrezzar's empty divination. Alternatively (and in line with 29:16—a passage not yet encountered by the ancient, sequential reader), Ezekiel's accusation may allude to Judah's ill-conceived confidence in Egypt's promises of assistance.[668]

Verse 23b poses even greater problems. Clearly, what it describes spells disaster for the Judeans, since it will lead to capture by Nebuchadrezzar. Beyond that assertion, however, its meaning is unclear and admits several interpretations (as in the quite different translations of the NRSV and the NIV). The conundrum resides in the phrase והוא־מזכיר עון (wĕhû'-mazkîr 'āwōn; lit., "and he [it?

that?] will cause iniquity to be remembered"). To what does הוא (hû') refer? What is called to remembrance, and in whose mind? Greenberg translates hû' as "that" (i.e., Judah's [and the exiles'] belittling of Nebuchadrezzar's omens, grounded in misguided trust in Egyptian aid).[669] Pagan divination may be so much hocus-pocus, but when Yahweh is involved, "even liver-omens speak 'truth.' "[670] Israel's resistance to Yahweh's verdict (paradoxically revealed through Nebuchadrezzar's divining) brings to God's mind its long-lived history of iniquity (i.e., trusting in other gods and political alliances) and results in Jerusalem's capture by Nebuchadrezzar. One finds an analogous use of the phrase "bring X's iniquity to mind" in 1 Kgs 17:18, where Elijah's Phoenician hostess complains that his presence in her home has drawn Yahweh's careful scrutiny ("brought my iniquity to [God's] mind)," resulting in her son's death as punishment for her guilt (which might otherwise have gone unrequited?).[671] But other critics (e.g., Zimmerli, Wevers) adopt H. G. Reventlow's hypothesis that mazkîr 'āwōn is the title of a judicial official, the "public prosecutor" (see 2 Sam 8:16; 20:24; 1 Kgs 4:3).[672] Ezekiel accords that role to Nebuchadrezzar, whose divination techniques elicit from Judah a response that brings its iniquity (broadly defined) to God's mind, leading to divine judgment at the hands of Babylonia's king. Verse 24, then, constitutes an accusation-packed "motivated declaration of judgment,"[673] addressed (ostensibly) to the Jerusalemites and introduced by the messenger formula, "thus says the Lord GOD." Because the people have brought their iniquity to remembrance by disclosing their transgressions (פשע peša', "rebellions") and by bringing to light ("causing to be seen") their sins by all their misdeeds, they will be seized by force.

667. See M. Greenberg, "Nebuchadnezzar at the Parting of the Ways: Ezek. 21:26-27," in Ah, Assyria: Studies in Assyrian History and Ancient Near Eastern Historiography, ed. M. Cogan and I. Eph`al, ScrHier 33 (Jerusalem: Hebrew University Press, 1990) 270-71.
668. So Moshe Greenberg, Ezekiel 21–37, AB 22A (Garden City, N.Y.: Doubleday, 1997) 431.
669. Ibid., 431.
670. Ibid., 441, 447. In a similar vein, Zimmerli proposes that "it" refers to Nebuchadnezzar's oracular decision(s) which, though dismissed by the Judeans as a "lying oracle," nevertheless "carry within themselves the full weight of a divine decision." See W. Zimmerli, Ezekiel 1: A Commentary on the Book of the Prophet Ezekiel, Chapters 1–24, trans. R. E. Clements, Hermeneia (Philadelphia: Fortress, 1979) 445.
671. Greenberg, Ezekiel 21–37, 431-32. See also Num 5:15, 18.
672. See H. G. Reventlow, "Das Amt des Mazkir. Zur Rechtsstruktur des öuffentlichen Lebens in Israel," ThZ 15 (1959) 161-75; Zimmerli, Ezekiel 1, 445; J. W. Wevers, Ezekiel, NCB (London: Nelson, 1969) 168.
673. Zimmerli, Ezekiel 1, 445.

Suddenly, Ezekiel shifts to second-person address in a scorching rebuke of Zedekiah (vv. 25-27), here called a "defiled wicked prince of Israel."[674] His day (of death) is coming (see also 1 Sam 26:10), an announcement that alludes to the terrible "Day of Yahweh," a time when, according to certain of Israel's prophets (e.g., Amos, Isaiah, Zephaniah), God will war against the Lord's own people (see the Commentary on 7:1-27). "The time of final punishment" (קֵץ *qēṣ;* lit., "in time of punishment," "end"; see also v. 29; 35:5) suggests that the day is ripe for Zedekiah's amassed iniquity to be punished. Yahweh addresses him specifically ("thus says the Lord GOD"), demanding that he remove his turban/crown, the symbol of royal authority. The following phrase, literally, "this, not

this," is in effect a call for total social upheaval. What was low is raised up; what was high is brought low (see also 17:24; Ps 75:8). The following, thrice-repeated (signaling the superlative) noun עוה (*'awwâ*), from a root meaning "to bend, twist," is nicely translated as "topsy-turvy."[675] Yahweh is turning Judah's world upside down. Critics have discerned in v. 27*b* an ironic twist on Gen 49:10, part of Jacob's blessing of Judah: "On Ezekiel's lips Gen. 49:10 is not about tribute and subordination of the world to Judah, but about the judgment of Judah by the principal representative of that world which was to bow before Judah."[676] (See Reflections at 21:28-32.)

674. Greenberg, "wicked corpse"; חלל (*ḥālāl*) appeared also in v. 12 in the phrase "a sword for great slaughter."

675. So Block, *Ezekiel 1–24,* 683.

676. Ibid., 693. See also W. L. Moran, "Gen 49:10 and Its Use in Ez 21:32," *Bib* 39 (1958) 405-25.

Ezekiel 21:28-32, The Sword Resheathed

NIV	NRSV
28"And you, son of man, prophesy and say, 'This is what the Sovereign LORD says about the Ammonites and their insults:	28As for you, mortal, prophesy, and say, Thus says the Lord GOD concerning the Ammonites, and concerning their reproach; say:

" 'A sword, a sword,
    drawn for the slaughter,
polished to consume
    and to flash like lightning!
	A sword, a sword! Drawn for slaughter,
	    polished to consume,[a] to flash like lightning.

29Despite false visions concerning you
    and lying divinations about you,
it will be laid on the necks
    of the wicked who are to be slain,
whose day has come,
    whose time of punishment has reached its
        climax.
	29Offering false visions for you,
	    divining lies for you,
	they place you over the necks
	    of the vile, wicked ones—
	those whose day has come,
	    the time of final punishment.

30Return the sword to its scabbard.
    In the place where you were created,
in the land of your ancestry,
    I will judge you.
	30Return it to its sheath!
	In the place where you were created,
	    in the land of your origin,
	    I will judge you.

31I will pour out my wrath upon you
    and breathe out my fiery anger against you;
I will hand you over to brutal men,
    men skilled in destruction.
	31I will pour out my indignation upon you,
	    with the fire of my wrath
	    I will blow upon you.
	I will deliver you into brutish hands,
	    those skillful to destroy.

32You will be fuel for the fire,	32You shall be fuel for the fire,
	    your blood shall enter the earth;
	you shall be remembered no more,
	    for I the LORD have spoken.

	aCn: Heb *to contain*

NIV

your blood will be shed in your land,
you will be remembered no more;
for I the LORD have spoken.' "

COMMENTARY

The fourth of Ezekiel's oracles concerning the sword, begun with Yahweh's address to the prophet ("As for you, mortal") and followed by a command to prophesy and the messenger formula, brings together a host of terms and phrases appearing in previous verses. Greenberg, who charts the chapter's vocabulary, notes that of the sixty-two words appearing in vv. 28b-32, only ten are new.[677] Zimmerli attributes the oracle to a later editor,[678] but the reader would draw the opposite conclusion: Ezekiel has skillfully conjoined previous elements in order to bring his group of sword oracles to its climactic conclusion.

The prophecy is said to concern the Ammonites and their taunts. Ezekiel 25:1-7, the first of the prophet's oracles against foreign nations and rulers (25:1–32:32), condemns the Ammonites for their derisive delight at Judah's destruction. Given the reference to Rabbath Ammon in v. 20, Zimmerli explains, the editor fittingly turns to the city lying along the road not taken, depicting its destruction by the sword (Nebuchadrezzar and his forces) in terms just used to describe God's judgment upon Jerusalem and its prince.[679] Rabbah has not escaped for long! But it is difficult to see how vv. 28b-29 are related to the Ammonites. B. Lang, who attributes the oracle to Ezekiel, argues that the reference to the Ammonites is secondary; originally this ruthless judgment pronouncement was aimed at Judah.[680] Greenberg believes that the oracle can only be understood if we ignore the reference to the Ammonites altogether, for it is intentionally misleading. Ezekiel's real target is Babylonia, but because a prediction of its destruction risks reprisal, he resorts to a code name.[681]

Block, by contrast, identifies vv. 28b-29 as a quotation of the Ammonites' version of the earlier sword song (vv. 9-10) by which they taunt Israel following Nebuchadrezzar's decision not to advance against their city.

Given the explicit designation in v. 28a, the reader will most likely construe vv. 28b-29 as a description of Nebuchadrezzar's future attack against Ammon. An initial double vocative "sword, sword," is followed by a varied form of vv. 9b-10a. Nebuchadrezzar's unsheathed sword, polished and flashing like lightning, turns against Ammon. The reference to false visions and lies is obscure, but it recalls the Jerusalemites' assessment of Nebuchadrezzar's divinatory techniques. Zimmerli suggests that Ammon's own diviners have erred by issuing favorable oracles. Now the Babylonians place the sword (addressed in the second person) over the necks of the Ammonites for whom, like Judah's "vile, wicked" prince, the day of death has come.

Most critics agree that vv. 30-32 address Nebuchadrezzar. The initial imperative, "Return it to its sheath," stands in stark contrast to v. 5, where is was said that Yahweh's sword would never return to its scabbard. Now the king of Babylon (the sword) is to reenter his homeland, there to face God's judgment. The reader who is familiar with the idea that God uses foreign nations as instruments of judgment against Israel, only to turn against them when their usefulness has ended (see, e.g., Isa 31:8-9, against Assyria), will not be surprised to discover that the "sword" also will suffer Yahweh's outpoured anger. Verses 31-32, like 20:47-48, contain fire imagery. But while the earlier verses spoke of a forest fire, Ezekiel now casts Yahweh in the role of a smelter whose bellow-like blowing melts the sword with the fire of divine wrath.[682] Moreover, God will hand the weapon over to barbarians, master crafts-

677. Greenberg, *Ezekiel 21–37,* 444.

678. Zimmerli, *Ezekiel 1,* 448. See also Wevers, *Ezekiel,* 169.

679. Zimmerli, *Ezekiel 1,* 448.

680. B. Lang, *Kein Aufstand in Jerusalem: die Politik des Propheten Ezekiel,* SBB (Stuttgart: Katholisches Bibelioerk, 1981) 120-31. See also B. Lang, "A Neglected Method in Ezekiel Research: Editorial Criticism," *VT* 29 (1979) 43.

681. Greenberg, *Ezekiel 21–37,* 435.

682. See ibid., 437-38; Block, *Ezekiel 1–24,* 656.

men of destruction (an allusion to the Medes? see Isa 13:17).[683] With the reference to "your blood," the human referent (Nebuchadrezzar and his sub-

jects) intrudes. Yahweh's final threat, "you will not be remembered," bespeaks permanent annihilation. The concluding formula, "for I Yahweh have spoken," grounds the foregoing oracle in the certain fulfillment of God's word.

683. So Greenberg, *Ezekiel 21–37*, 437; Zimmerli, *Ezekiel 1*, 450.

REFLECTIONS

Even in their "glory days," the nations of Israel and Judah were little more than petty kingdoms. Situated along the traversable corridor of land linking Egypt with the "megapowers" of Mesopotamia, Assyria, and Babylonia, they were routinely trapped between the political and economic ambitions of all three. In the intervals, they fought off other peoples struggling to gain a foothold in their territories and squabbled with neighboring nations.

It is little wonder that in a world of insatiable empires, Israel envisioned its national deity as a mighty warrior whose sword was unsheathed against his foes. What faith was required to assert, often in the face of overwhelming evidence to the contrary, that Yahweh was a god of unparalleled power, whose dominion over human history was absolute! And when the northern kingdom finally succumbed to Assyria, and Jerusalem's collapse was imminent, what tenacity of faith was required of those who pointed the finger of blame at the victims, Ezekiel among them! Ezekiel stands with those prophets and historiographers who refused to ascribe national tragedy to divine apathy, capriciousness, or Yahweh's defeat at the hands of rival deities, insisting that Israel's ruin be read as God's just and proportionate punishment of a relentlessly sinful people who, as beneficiaries of Yahweh's election and laws, should have known better.

Even as modern faith communities wrestle with Ezekiel's fundamental presupposition that God directly controls human history, rewarding the righteous but punishing the wicked, it behooves them to acknowledge the courage of his convictions. "Peace, peace" is always the most popular message. In times of crisis, words of comfort can be panaceas for the soul. Ezekiel eschews peace when there is no peace and, from the readers' perspective, doles out hope in rare and compact packages. Who dares to stand beside him as he takes on his own community's deeply rooted beliefs?

The Jesus of Matthew's Gospel cautions his disciples not to think that he has come to bring peace to the earth: "I have not come to bring peace, but a sword" (Matt 10:34 NRSV). That sword severs even family ties, a foundation of social stability. But militaristic images of God and of a sword-wielding savior rest uneasily within many a contemporary faith community. If we must speak of weaponry, let it be in affirmation of Isaiah's vision, wherein people beat their swords into plowshares, and nations neither raise their swords nor study war anymore (Isa 2:4; see also Mic 4:3). Among the great hymns of the church, "Lead On, O King Eternal" proclaims the paradox that God's kingdom comes "not with swords loud clashing, nor roll of stirring drums," but with "deeds of love and mercy." "We've a Story to Tell to the Nations" speaks of a song that will "conquer evil and shatter the spear and sword." And while "The Battle Hymn of the Republic" proclaims the coming of one who "hath loosed the fateful lightning of his terrible swift sword," readers may recall that its place within certain recent hymnals was secured only after a "battle" of sorts.

Ezekiel admits no paradox that would transform Yahweh's clashing sword into an instrument of "love and mercy." The story he tells to his nation is of a God who has "loosed the fateful lightning of his terrible swift sword" against the Lord's own people.

Militaristic imagery may have its place in religious oratory, and many a person of faith has taken up the implements of war to fight for causes imbued with our most cherished religious values. But like so many of our symbols, the sword cuts both ways—an unbearable cliché within this context, but one worthy of reflection. Affirming that behind the swords of nations stands God's sword is a dangerous enterprise that should force us to our knees in prayer. Casting our lot with Ezekiel's insistence that Yahweh presses the sword against us, and also against our foes, in direct response to human sin privileges one biblical image of God to the neglect of others. It casts the Lord in the role of a big warrior whose solution to the problems posed by fallible creatures is the very violence that, elsewhere in his book, Ezekiel denounces as Israel's greatest sin against God (see the Commentary on 22:1-31 and the Reflections at 22:23-31). Dare we say that God's imagination cannot move beyond the militaristic means by which human communities have sought to assert their power, resolve their conundrums, and enslave their neighbors?

EZEKIEL 22:1-31, BLOODSHED CITY: THE DESTRUCTION OF JERUSALEM AND ITS LEADERS

OVERVIEW

Ezekiel 22 juxtaposes three judgment oracles linked by common themes and vocabulary: vv. 1-16, vv. 17-22, and vv. 23-31. The first oracle concerns the legal case of "Bloodshed City," a nefarious epithet for Jerusalem. Judah's capital, ruled by violent princes and rife with social, cultic, and sexual abominations, is polluted by the bloodshed (and consequent blood guilt) within her and is defiled by idolatry. Her inhabitants abrogate God's laws in every sphere of life. Her sentence entails the dispersion of the city's population among the nations.

In his second oracle, Ezekiel employs tropes (figurative uses of language) drawn from metallurgy to describe the worthlessness of his people and their punishment. Israel is dross, the impure residue that remains after metal has been refined. Just as the smelter gathers silver, bronze, iron, lead, and tin into a fiery furnace, so also Yahweh will gather the people into Jerusalem and subject them to the liquefying heat of God's wrath.

Finally, the prophet justifies God's punishment by pointing to the failure of Judah's leaders (princes, priests, officials, prophets, and privileged classes) to discharge their duties responsibly. If God had found even a single worthy person among those groups, the destruction would not occur. Instead, Yahweh has poured out divine indignation upon the people, consuming them with the fire of wrath.

Ezekiel 22:1-5, The Case Against Bloodshed City

NIV

22 The word of the LORD came to me: [2]"Son of man, will you judge her? Will you judge this city of bloodshed? Then confront her with all her detestable practices [3]and say: 'This is what the Sovereign LORD says: O city that brings on herself doom by shedding blood in her midst and defiles herself by making idols, [4]you have become guilty because of the blood you have shed and have become defiled by the idols you have

NRSV

22 The word of the LORD came to me: [2]You, mortal, will you judge, will you judge the bloody city? Then declare to it all its abominable deeds. [3]You shall say, Thus says the Lord GOD: A city! Shedding blood within itself; its time has come; making its idols, defiling itself. [4]You have become guilty by the blood that you have shed, and defiled by the idols that you have made; you have brought your day near, the appointed time of

NIV

made. You have brought your days to a close, and the end of your years has come. Therefore I will make you an object of scorn to the nations and a laughingstock to all the countries. ⁵Those who are near and those who are far away will mock you, O infamous city, full of turmoil.

NRSV

your years has come. Therefore I have made you a disgrace before the nations, and a mockery to all the countries. ⁵Those who are near and those who are far from you will mock you, you infamous one, full of tumult.

COMMENTARY

With the announcement of a fresh message from the Lord and a double address to the prophet ("You, mortal"), Ezekiel brings Jerusalem ("Bloodshed City"; see also 24:6, 10) to trial in the court of Yahweh, who assumes the roles of accuser, judge, and executioner. The following ריב (*rîb*; a judgment oracle whose structure and contents reflect judicial proceedings) consists of three subsections: a general indictment and anticipation of doom (vv. 1-5); a detailed indictment of Jerusalem's leaders, especially its "princes" (kings; vv. 6-12); and a pronouncement of the sentence (vv. 13-16).

The oracle begins with God's twice-repeated interrogative ("Will you arraign, will you arraign the bloody city?"), a rhetorical device (see also 20:4) conveying intense affirmation (i.e., "you *will assuredly* arraign . . ."). Nahum, Ezekiel's seventh-century BCE prophetic predecessor, applied the epithet "Bloodshed City" to Nineveh, capital of the Assyrian Empire, whose forces were responsible for the downfall of the northern kingdom of Israel in 722/21 BCE and renowned for attrocities in warfare. Nineveh was destroyed in 612 BCE; hence it cannot be the object of Ezekiel's arraignment. Nevertheless, the application of Nahum's epithet to some other, as yet unidentified entity already signals that the "defendant" in this case stands accused of the most heinous of crimes. (This usage recalls 16:46-56, where Ezekiel unfavorably compares Jerusalem with its "sister" cities, Sodom and Samaria.)

Ezekiel's arraignment of the bloody city consists of making known to "her" all her abominations (see also 16:2).⁶⁸⁵ Zimmerli defines "abomination"

as a "comprehensive term for all sins of cultic impurity."⁶⁸⁶ Heretofore, Ezekiel has applied the noun especially to idolatry and sexual misconduct (as defined in Israel's law codes). Now, as following verses demonstrate, he employs it even more broadly to include not only cultic offenses (three charges) and prohibited sexual activity (five charges), but also social malfeasances (eight charges).⁶⁸⁷

With v. 3 (introduced by the messenger formula, "Thus says the Lord GOD"), Jerusalem is summoned before the court. Although the formal announcement of charges will appear in vv. 4-5, this verse already discloses her corruptions. The locus of bloodshed (violent crimes), "her time" (i.e., the time of her doom; see 7:7, 12; Eccl 9:12; Jer 27:7) has come (the pollution resulting from bloodshed threatens Yahweh's ongoing presence with Israel in its land; see Num 35:33-34). She is defiled by the ongoing manufacture of "dung" idols (Ezekiel's characteristic and coarse term for the images of other deities). Verse 4a, with its shift to direct address (second-person fem. sing.), reiterates and expands upon v. 3. As a consequence of "her blood" (i.e., the spilled blood of her victims), she has become polluted (see Num 35:33; true to Ezekiel's epithet for Jerusalem, "Bloodshed City," this oracle reverberates with references to shedding blood, vv. 3-4, 6, 9, 12-13; the recurrence of "in her midst," vv. 7, 13, and "in you," vv. 6-7, 9-12, 16, suggests that the city is, in effect, a defiled vessel filled with blood and consequently rife with blood guilt). As a consequence of her idolatry, she has become unclean (see also Isa 30:22; Jer 2:23;

---

685. In Hebrew and other West Semitic languages, common nouns for "city" were feminine in gender. See Excursus: "Cities as Females," 1121-25. Here the personification of Jerusalem as a woman is muted (compare chaps. 16; 23), but not irrelevant. Like chap. 16, this collection of oracles focuses especially on "blood" and "defilement." Repeated references to bloodshed/guilt "in her" (vv. 6-7, 9-12, 16) and "in her midst" (vv. 7, 13) evoke thoughts of a menstrous woman whose discharge is a source of uncleanness.

686. W. Zimmerli, *Ezekiel 1: A Commentary on the Book of the Prophet Ezekiel, Chapters 1–24*, trans. R. E. Clements, Hermeneia (Philadelphia: Fortress, 1979) 190.

687. Moshe Greenberg, *Ezekiel 21–37*, AB 22A (Garden City, N.Y.: Doubleday, 1997) 467-68.

7:30; Ezek 5:11; 20:7, 8, 31). While in v. 3 she was threatened with the approach of "her time" of judgment, in v. 4 she is said to have brought near (hastened) her days of judgment, the appointed time (of punishment) for her years of sin. Therefore, Yahweh is personally giving her over as a disgrace to the nations and a mockery to all the (other) lands (v. 5; see Ps 79:4). Those who are far

away and those who are near (an expression indicating "all peoples") will mock her (see also 16:57) on account of her defiled name (reputation) and the greatness (abundance) of the tumult (מהומה *mĕhûmâ,* "lawless disorder") within her (see also 7:7).[688] (See Reflections at 22:23-31.)

688. Greenberg, *Ezekiel 21–37,* 453.

Ezekiel 22:6-12, Jerusalem's Misconduct

NIV

6" 'See how each of the princes of Israel who are in you uses his power to shed blood. 7In you they have treated father and mother with contempt; in you they have oppressed the alien and mistreated the fatherless and the widow. 8You have despised my holy things and desecrated my Sabbaths. 9In you are slanderous men bent on shedding blood; in you are those who eat at the mountain shrines and commit lewd acts. 10In you are those who dishonor their fathers' bed; in you are those who violate women during their period, when they are ceremonially unclean. 11In you one man commits a detestable offense with his neighbor's wife, another shamefully defiles his daughter-in-law, and another violates his sister, his own father's daughter. 12In you men accept bribes to shed blood; you take usury and excessive interest[a] and make unjust gain from your neighbors by extortion. And you have forgotten me, declares the Sovereign LORD.

[a]12 Or *usury and interest*

NRSV

6The princes of Israel in you, everyone according to his power, have been bent on shedding blood. 7Father and mother are treated with contempt in you; the alien residing within you suffers extortion; the orphan and the widow are wronged in you. 8You have despised my holy things, and profaned my sabbaths. 9In you are those who slander to shed blood, those in you who eat upon the mountains, who commit lewdness in your midst. 10In you they uncover their fathers' nakedness; in you they violate women in their menstrual periods. 11One commits abomination with his neighbor's wife; another lewdly defiles his daughter-in-law; another in you defiles his sister, his father's daughter. 12In you, they take bribes to shed blood; you take both advance interest and accrued interest, and make gain of your neighbors by extortion; and you have forgotten me, says the Lord GOD.

COMMENTARY

In these verses, Ezekiel presents evidence against Jerusalem and her political leaders. He begins with "the princes of Israel in you" (Ezekiel routinely refers to Judah's kings as princes) who stand accused of violent abuses of power ("shedding blood") perpetrated against the very society whose order and justice they are charged to protect (v. 6). The following list of specific, but only representative, crimes (vv. 7-12a) is aptly associated with these princes, who not only commit

them, but who also fail to prevent their subjects from following suit.[689]

First, Ezekiel submits that within the city, parents are treated with contempt (v. 7a). Injunctions concerning the proper treatment of fathers and mothers by their offspring, especially adult children, are variously expressed in the Hebrew Bible. Exodus 21:17 and Lev 20:9 state that "cursing"

689. See ibid., 454.

father and mother is a capital offense. Deuteronomy 27:16 curses anyone who treats parents contemptuously. The Decalogue commandment (Exod 20:12; see also Deut 5:16), by contrast, is cast in positive language ("Honor your father and your mother") and is accompanied by a "reward" for its fulfillment ("so that your days may be long in the land that the LORD your God is giving you").[690] Greenberg compares the sentiment in Ezekiel to a Sumerian text in whose prologue King Lipit Ishtar of Isin (early second millennium BCE) describes how he set right social wrongdoings in his city: "I made the father support his children, (and) I made the children support their father; I made the father stand by his children, (and) I made the children stand by their father."[691]

Second, Ezekiel charges that the city's aliens are exploited, her widows and orphans wronged (v. 7b). Laws concerning the treatment of these, society's most vulnerable constituencies, appear in Exod 22:21; 23:9, 12; Deut 14:29; 16:11, 14; 24:19-21; 26:12-13 (see also Jer 7:6; 22:3). Here, too, Greenberg cites a Sumerian text (from the mid-third millennium BCE) that speaks to the regulation of power vis-à-vis the powerless. A list of reforms enacted by Erukagina of Lagash includes the following item: "Urukagina made a covenant with [the god] Ningirsu that a man of power must not commit an (injustice) against an orphan or widow."[692] In this respect also, Jerusalem's monarchs have failed to carry out a royal responsibility attested throughout the ancient Near East.

Thus far, Ezekiel's "evidence" has consisted of crimes of violence (shedding blood) within the sphere of social relations. Verse 8, by contrast, speaks in a general way of Jerusalem's cultic violations. She has despised Yahweh's "holy things" (e.g., the Temple and its various appurtenances, the sacrifices offered there) and profaned God's sabbaths (20:13, 16, 21, 24; see also Lev 19:30, where Yahweh commands the Israelites to "keep my sabbaths and reverence my sanctuary"). Sabbath observance was Yahweh's gift to Israel, a sign of their covenant bond (see Exod 31:13-17;

Ezek 20:12, 20) and a weekly reminder of God's roles as creator (Exod 20:11) and deliverer (Deut 5:15). When Jerusalem profanes the Lord's sabbaths, she flagrantly denies Yahweh's particular claim upon her life.

Verse 9 juxtaposes social, cultic, and sexual misconduct. Among Jerusalem's inhabitants are "slanderers" (אנשי רכיל 'anšê rākîl; lit., "merchant men"). Within the Pentateuch, only Lev 19:16 refers to the rākîl (see also Jer 6:28; 9:3), who are associated with bloodshed, killing in order to "get rid of persons obnoxious to those in power by means of false accusations."[693] In her also, meals are eaten upon the mountains (high places?). Here, as in 18:6, we encounter an obscure phrase appearing only in the book of Ezekiel. Negative references to sacrifices atop mountains in honor (or in the presence) of deities appear, however, in 2 Kgs 16:4; Isa 65:7; and Hos 4:13 (see also Ezek 6:13). The prophet clearly regards this cultic practice (whatever its precise nature) as illicit.

Moreover, acts of lewdness (זמה zimmâ) are committed in her midst (v. 9b). In Israel's priestly law codes (including the holiness code, Lev 17:1–26:46), zimmâ refers to sexual "depravity" (e.g., Lev 18:17; 19:29; 20:14; see also Ezek 16:27, 58; 22:9, 11; 23:21, 27, 35, 44, 48). Verses 10-11 cite five examples of the immorality of Jerusalem's (male) inhabitants: (1) they engage in sexual relations with their fathers' wives. To "uncover their fathers' nakedness" means to have intercourse with a woman (wife or concubine) whose sexuality ("nakedness") is legally the property of the father—that is, one's mother or "stepmother," broadly defined (see Lev 18:7-8). In Lev 20:11, this crime is a capital offense; both parties are to be put to death. (2) They engage in sexual intercourse with women who are impure on account of their menstrual flow (see Lev 18:19; 20:18; Ezek 18:6). In contexts where sexual activity is at issue, critics often translate ענה ('innâ, "violate") as "rape." Ezekiel is asserting that these men have compounded violence with ritual uncleanness. The verb can be interpreted more broadly, however, to mean "to treat abusively, without regard to proper behavior" (see, e.g., Deut 21:14,

690. W. Harrelson, *The Ten Commandments and Human Rights,* OBT (Philadelphia: Fortress, 1980) 92-105.

691. Greenberg, *Ezekiel 21–37,* 454, citing S. N. Kramer, *The Sumerians* (Chicago: University of Chicago Press, 1963) 336-37.

692. Kramer, *The Sumerians,* 319.

693. G. A. Cooke, *A Critical and Exegetical Commentary on the Book of Ezekiel,* 2 vols., ICC (Edinburgh: T. & T. Clark, 1936) 1:241.

where rape is not at issue).[694] By either rendering, Ezekiel presents these women as unwilling participants in a proscribed union.[695] (3) The men "commit abomination" (adultery) with their neighbor's wife, an act prohibited in Exod 20:14; Lev 18:20; 20:10 (Jeremiah also charges his people with adulterous acts; see Jer 5:7; 7:9; 9:1; 23:10; 29:23). (4) They lewdly defile (engage in sexual intercourse with) daughters-in-law (see Lev 18:15, 20:12, where this capital crime also is punished by the execution of both parties). (5) Finally, they demand incestuous sexual relations of their sisters (banned in Lev 18:9, 11; 20:17).

With v. 12, Ezekiel turns from sexual misconduct to economic crimes. Israelite law prohibited the acceptance of bribes, since "greasing the palms" of officials inevitably led to injustice and oppression. Exodus 3:8, for example, demands: "You shall take no bribe, for a bribe blinds the officials, and subverts the cause of those who are in the right" (see also Deut 16:18-19). Deuteronomy 10:17 grounds the ban in the nature of Yahweh, who, possessing unparalleled power, nonetheless is fair and forswears bribes. Deuteronomy 27:25, like Ezek 22:12, associates bribery with bloodshed (see also 1 Sam 8:3; Isa 1:23; 5:23). Moreover, Jerusalem's leaders demand exhorbitant interest

rates on loans (see the Commentary on 18:8, 13, 17) and amass profits by extortion at the expense of their fellows (see Exod 18:21; Lev 19:13).

The prophet's list of the violent crimes perpetrated in Jerusalem ends with a damning summary statement: "You have forgotten me" (see also 23:35).[696] Bloodshed City, polluted by violent crimes and saturated with bloodguilt, harbors a society that is the very opposite of that which God desires for/demands of this people. Ezekiel's catalog of cultic, sexual, and economic offenses represents, but does not exhaust, the nation's transgressions. They signal the collapse of that theo-ethos by which Israel might have lived as Yahweh's faithful covenant partner. In God's laws, Hals observes, "he had laid claim to every area of his people's lives, and the expression of allegiance was to be measured not just by affirmations, but by implementation. . . . the meaning of 'I am Yahweh your God and you are my people,' was to find expression much more in how one treated others than in what sacrifices one offered. In fact, to mistreat others was to enter into the sphere of guilt and uncleanness which prevented ritual contact with God."[697]

---

694. Tikva Frymer-Kensky, "Deuteronomy," in *The Women's Bible Commentary,* ed. C. A. Newsom and S. H. Ringe (Lousville: Westminster/John Knox, 1992) 53.
695. Greenberg, *Ezekiel 21–37,* 455.

696. The antithesis of this charge, to "remember" Yahweh, is found only in 6:9, of captured refugees who survive Judah's downfall and are scattered "among the nations."
697. Ronald M. Hals, *Ezekiel,* FOTL 19 (Grand Rapids: Eerdmans, 1988) 158. See also Zimmerli, *Ezekiel 1,* 459.

Ezekiel 22:13-16, Jerusalem's Sentence

NIV

13" 'I will surely strike my hands together at the unjust gain you have made and at the blood you have shed in your midst. 14Will your courage endure or your hands be strong in the day I deal with you? I the LORD have spoken, and I will do it. 15I will disperse you among the nations and scatter you through the countries; and I will put an end to your uncleanness. 16When you have been defiled[a] in the eyes of the nations, you will know that I am the LORD.' "

a16 Or When I have allotted you your inheritance

NRSV

13See, I strike my hands together at the dishonest gain you have made, and at the blood that has been shed within you. 14Can your courage endure, or can your hands remain strong in the days when I shall deal with you? I the LORD have spoken, and I will do it. 15I will scatter you among the nations and disperse you through the countries, and I will purge your filthiness out of you. 16And I[a] shall be profaned through you in the sight of the nations; and you shall know that I am the LORD.

aGk Syr Vg: Heb you

COMMENTARY

With v. 13, Ezekiel initiates the sentencing phase of Jerusalem's case. A summons to attention ("See!") is accompanied by a sign act: The prophet claps his hands in anger (see 21:14, 17) on account of Jerusalem's illicit profiteering (v. 12) and the blood shed in her (with its consequent bloodguilt). Two rhetorical questions follow: "Can your courage [lit., "heart"] stand firm/ can your hands remain strong in the days of my (punitive) dealing with you?" (v. 14a). Firm heart and strong hands are the antithesis of "melting heart" and "feeble hands" in 21:7 (see the Commentary on 20:45–21:7). The Lord's queries admit only a negative response. Verse 14b grounds the certain fulfillment of God's judgment in Yahweh's own identity. The sentence proper, though addressed directly to Jerusalem (the pronoun "you" is second-person fem. sing. throughout vv. 15-16), nonetheless speaks first of her residents, who will be scattered among the nations, dispersed throughout the lands (a fate presaged in Lev 26:33-39 and Deut 28:64; see also Ezek 12:15; 29:12; 30:23, 26). Does the following expression of Yahweh's determination to purge the city's "filthiness" from her also refer to the removal of her population (inhabitants = filthiness)? Or does it allude to the purgation of Bloodshed City itself? The NRSV and the NIV opt for two different translations of v. 16. The former emends the text to read, "And I [Yahweh] shall be profaned"; the latter follows the Hebrew text in reading "When you [second-person fem. sing.] have been defiled." Ezekiel has, of course, expressed grave concern that Yahweh's reputation might suffer among the nations should Israel receive the punishment it deserves (see, e.g., 20:9, 14, 22). In this context, however, v. 16 should be construed as the last of a series of punishments inflicted upon Jerusalem (and her inhabitants), and not as an expression of the price God pays for afflicting her. The following recognition formula ("and you shall know that I am the LORD") expresses the goal/consequence of those penalties: Jerusalem's acknowledgment of Yahweh's unrivaled sovereignty and power.[698] (See Reflections at 22:23-31.)

698. See Moshe Greenberg, *Ezekiel 21–37*, AB 22A (Garden City, N.Y.: Doubleday, 1997) 457-58.

Ezekiel 22:17-22, Israel Is Dross, Not Silver

NIV

¹⁷Then the word of the LORD came to me: ¹⁸"Son of man, the house of Israel has become dross to me; all of them are the copper, tin, iron and lead left inside a furnace. They are but the dross of silver. ¹⁹Therefore this is what the Sovereign LORD says: 'Because you have all become dross, I will gather you into Jerusalem. ²⁰As men gather silver, copper, iron, lead and tin into a furnace to melt it with a fiery blast, so will I gather you in my anger and my wrath and put you inside the city and melt you. ²¹I will gather you and I will blow on you with my fiery wrath, and you will be melted inside her. ²²As silver is melted in a furnace, so you will be melted inside her, and you will know that I the LORD have poured out my wrath upon you.' "

NRSV

17The word of the LORD came to me: ¹⁸Mortal, the house of Israel has become dross to me; all of them, silver,ᵃ bronze, tin, iron, and lead. In the smelter they have become dross. ¹⁹Therefore thus says the Lord GOD: Because you have all become dross, I will gather you into the midst of Jerusalem. ²⁰As one gathers silver, bronze, iron, lead, and tin into a smelter, to blow the fire upon them in order to melt them; so I will gather you in my anger and in my wrath, and I will put you in and melt you. ²¹I will gather you and blow upon you with the fire of my wrath, and you shall be melted within it. ²²As silver is melted in a smelter, so you shall be melted in it; and you shall know that I the LORD have poured out my wrath upon you.

ᵃTransposed from the end of the verse; compare verse 20

COMMENTARY

The second of Ezekiel's oracles in chapter 22 commences with the word event formula (v. 17), followed by Yahweh's characteristic mode of addressing the prophet ("Mortal") and a complaint: "the house of Israel has become dross[699] to me"—all of them, bronze (נחֹשֶׁת *nĕḥōšet*), tin (בדיל *bĕdîl*), iron (ברזל *barzel*), and lead (עוֹפֶרת *'ôperet*). In the midst of a furnace (כור *kûr*), "dross of silver they have become."[700] This trope, whose vehicle derives from the sphere of metallurgy,[701] signals that Ezekiel is again about the business of making metaphors (see 20:49). Unlike most modern readers, he is familiar with the method of refining silver, and he employs it creatively in order to convey to his audience the worthless nature and impending punishment of all who, fearing Nebuchadrezzar's troops, seek protection within the walls of Judah's capital. This oracle should probably be dated to 589 BCE, near the onset of the siege of Jerusalem.

Ezekiel's metaphor reflects the two-stage process by which silver was extracted from lead ore (galena), which usually contained other metals such as copper, zinc, or tin. Derry and Williams describe the smelting process:

> Silver and lead were found together in the mineral galena (lead sulphide), which could be converted into a lead-silver alloy by roasting it to get rid of the some of the sulphur and then heating it to a higher temperature, which further reduced the sulpher content and caused the alloy to form at the bottom of the furnace. . . . The silver-lead alloy was melted in a porous clay crucible (the cupel) and a blast of air was blown upon it. The lead was thus oxidized and removed.[702]

Israel has become the worthless and impure residue that remains after the silver has been collected. In constructing his oracle, Ezekiel has, in effect, placed the end (by)product of the smelting process first.

In the following interpretation of v. 18, the people are addressed directly. Because they have all become dross, God will gather them into the midst of Jerusalem. This process is illumined by two similes also derived from metallurgy. The first appears in v. 20: "As one gathers silver, bronze, iron, lead, and tin into a smelter, to blow the fire upon them in order to melt them; so I will gather you in my anger and in my wrath, and I will put you in and melt you." The inclusion of כֶסֶף (*kesep*), "silver," in this list of metals does not collide with the trope characterizing the people in v. 18. That metaphor portrayed Israel as consisting only of dross. Ezekiel's simile, by contrast, reflects the usual reality that a variety of metals must be subjected to the heat of the furnace in order to extract silver from the galena. Just so, Yahweh will gather the entire house of Israel into Jerusalem and "melt" it with the heat of God's anger and wrath (vv. 20-21). Likewise, the second simile likens Israel's destruction in Jerusalem to that of silver melted in a smelter, but does not thereby imply that Israel is silver. Both similes refer to a *process,* rather than to the nature of the ores undergoing that process. Nonetheless, the juxtaposition of metaphor (the house of Israel has become dross) and similes ("As one gathers. . . . As silver is melted") has the apparent effect of putting the cart before the horse (to mix metaphors). Because Yahweh already knows that Israel is dross, no positive result can come of smelting it. Rather, as Greenberg observes, the smelting process becomes the lens through which Yahweh's fiery punishment of the people is perceived.[703] The goal of that process, as stated in v. 22*b,* is that the people be forced to know (acknowledge) that their punishment is, in fact, the pouring out of God's wrath upon them. Yahweh is the smelter!

Smelting imagery is found in Israel's traditions about its enslavement in Egypt. In Deut 4:20, for example, Moses is said to remind the people that they are the exclusive property of the God who

---

699. The MT reads "to backslide" (לסוּג *lĕsûg*); virtually all commentators, following the versions and Qere (לסיג *lĕsîg*), read סיג (*sîg* sing.) or לסגים (*lĕsiggîm* pl.; see vv. 18*b,* 19; Ps 119:119; Prov 25:4; 26:23; Isa 1:22).

700. The NRSV moves כסף (*kesep,* "silver") to the front of the list of metals in conformity with v. 20. The NIV (properly) follows the MT. The phrase *sigîm kesep* is problematic. See S. R. Driver, *A Treatise on the Use of Tenses in Hebrew,* 3rd ed. (Oxford: Clarendon, 1892); G. R. Driver, "Linguistic and Textual Problems: Ezekiel," *Bib* 19 (1938) 69; S. Abramsky, " 'Slag' and 'Tin' in the First Chapter of Isaiah," *ErIsr* 5 (1958) 105-1; J. W. Wevers, *Ezekiel,* NCB (London: Nelson, 1969) 175; and Greenberg, *Ezekiel 21–37,* 458.

701. See R. J. Forbes, *Studies in Ancient Technology,* 2nd ed. (Leiden: Brill, 1971–72) 8:275-76 and 9:1-305.

702. T. K. Derry and Trevor I. Williams, *A Short History of Technology* (Oxford: Oxford University Press, 1961) 116.

703. Greenberg, *Ezekiel 21–37,* 459.

---

has brought them out of the "iron-smelter" (Egypt). King Solomon includes the metaphor in his prayer of dedication of the Jerusalem Temple (1 Kgs 8:51), and it appears in Jeremiah's indictment of the covenant-breaking people of Judah (Jer 11:4). Elsewhere, Jeremiah adopts smelting imagery in an impassioned indictment of his fellow Judeans. They are bronze and iron, and although the bellows blows furiously and the lead is oxidized in the fire, the refining process fails, leaving the silver impure and unfit for use (Jer 6:27-30). Isaiah 1:22, 25 speaks more optimistically. Although Jerusalem's silver has become dross, Yahweh will refine it—a harsh process that nonetheless results in the elimination of her impurity. In a text that shares Ezekiel's concern for God's reputation, Deutero-Isaiah calls the Babylonian exile a "furnace of adversity" in which God has refined Israel (Isa 46:10). (See Reflections at 22:23-31.)

Ezekiel 22:23-31, Justifying God's Judgment

NIV

23Again the word of the LORD came to me: 24"Son of man, say to the land, 'You are a land that has had no rain or showers^a in the day of wrath.' 25There is a conspiracy of her princes^b within her like a roaring lion tearing its prey; they devour people, take treasures and precious things and make many widows within her. 26Her priests do violence to my law and profane my holy things; they do not distinguish between the holy and the common; they teach that there is no difference between the unclean and the clean; and they shut their eyes to the keeping of my Sabbaths, so that I am profaned among them. 27Her officials within her are like wolves tearing their prey; they shed blood and kill people to make unjust gain. 28Her prophets whitewash these deeds for them by false visions and lying divinations. They say, 'This is what the Sovereign LORD says'—when the LORD has not spoken. 29The people of the land practice extortion and commit robbery; they oppress the poor and needy and mistreat the alien, denying them justice.

30"I looked for a man among them who would build up the wall and stand before me in the gap on behalf of the land so I would not have to destroy it, but I found none. 31So I will pour out my wrath on them and consume them with my fiery anger, bringing down on their own heads all they have done, declares the Sovereign LORD."

a24 Septuagint; Hebrew *has not been cleansed or rained on*
b25 Septuagint; Hebrew *prophets*

NRSV

23The word of the LORD came to me: 24Mortal, say to it: You are a land that is not cleansed, not rained upon in the day of indignation. 25Its princes^a within it are like a roaring lion tearing the prey; they have devoured human lives; they have taken treasure and precious things; they have made many widows within it. 26Its priests have done violence to my teaching and have profaned my holy things; they have made no distinction between the holy and the common, neither have they taught the difference between the unclean and the clean, and they have disregarded my sabbaths, so that I am profaned among them. 27Its officials within it are like wolves tearing the prey, shedding blood, destroying lives to get dishonest gain. 28Its prophets have smeared whitewash on their behalf, seeing false visions and divining lies for them, saying, "Thus says the Lord GOD," when the LORD has not spoken. 29The people of the land have practiced extortion and committed robbery; they have oppressed the poor and needy, and have extorted from the alien without redress. 30And I sought for anyone among them who would repair the wall and stand in the breach before me on behalf of the land, so that I would not destroy it; but I found no one. 31Therefore I have poured out my indignation upon them; I have consumed them with the fire of my wrath; I have returned their conduct upon their heads, says the Lord GOD.

aGk: Heb *indignation*. 25A conspiracy of its prophets

COMMENTARY

The third of Ezekiel's triad of oracles in chapter 22, addressed to Israel's land, includes scathing denunciations of the nation's civil and religious leaders. Similar indictments appear in Mic 3:11 (rulers, priests, prophets) and Jer 5:31 (prophets, priests), but this oracle so resembles Zeph 3:3-4 that most scholars believe Ezekiel adopted his seventh-century predecessor's oracle as the basis for his own, lengthier composition to further his own purposes.

Most, but not all, critics conclude that these verses were composed after the fall of Jerusalem.[704] The presence of converted imperfect (i.e., past tense) verbs in vv. 30-31 commends that judgment, but cannot confirm it, since the so-called prophetic perfect describes events that have not yet occurred, but most certainly will in the (near) future. In any case, it is clear that Ezekiel is justifying God's judgment by pointing to the utter failure of Judah's leaders to act responsibly.[705] In describing their behavior, Ezekiel in effect offers a negative "job description" for the posts of prince, official, priest, prophet, and "people of the land."

After the customary announcement of a fresh oracle from Yahweh, followed by God's address, "Mortal," Ezekiel is commanded to speak to Israel's land. It is a land not purged, not rained upon in "the day of indignation" (יום זעם *yôm zāʿam*). Israel counted adequate rainfall among the covenant blessings bestowed by Yahweh (Lev 26:4). Drought was the consequence of failure to honor that covenant (Lev 26:19; Deut 28:23-24; see also 1 Kings 17–18; Amos 4:7). Some critics detect in v. 24 a reference to an actual drought in Israel, but that explanation fails fully to tap its meaning. Block finds here a declaration that despite the land's defilement, it has never undergone "the cleansing force [טהר *ṭihar*] of a torrential

deluge [גשם *gešem*]," a metaphor rooted in the Noachic flood account, where *gešem* designates the downpour that rid the world of human wickedness, corruption, and violence (Gen 6:5, 11).[706] If something of that sort is intended here, Ezekiel does not develop the image further. "Indignation" refers to Yahweh's intervention in judgment in Isa 10:5; Jer 15:17; Nah 1:6; and Hab 3:12 (see also Dan 8:19; 11:36, where it has become, in effect, a technical term. Zephaniah, upon whose oracle Ezekiel depends, employs it in Zeph 3:8. The day of Yahweh's indignation is "doomsday."[707]

In the Hebrew text, v. 25 criticizes "a conspiracy of its [the land's] prophets." However, the ancient reader, no less than his modern counterparts, will likely conclude that the text is in error, for its animal imagery and list of offenses, ill-suited to prophets (see v. 28), repeatedly echo the charges lodged against Judah's princes in 19:1-9. In that lament also, Ezekiel cast Judah's kings as lions, a traditional symbol of royalty and nobility, only to assert that they were ferocious maneaters. In this context, metaphor is replaced by simile, as he likens Israel's rulers to roaring lions who tear into their prey, devour humans, plunder the land of its riches, and make widows of their victims' wives. Zephaniah did not include kings in his indictment, beginning instead with high-ranking officials (שרים *śārîm*); but kings head the list in Jer 1:18.

While Zephaniah next indicts Jerusalem's judges, Ezekiel targets Israel's priests (v. 26). Within chaps. 1–39, this verse alone portrays the priesthood negatively, asserting its utter disregard of its most vital professional responsibilities. They have done violence to the torah (a striking phrase found elsewhere in Hebrew Scripture only in Zeph 3:4) and desecrated God's holy things (the sanctuary and its contents, donations, etc.; see v. 8). They have not distinguished between the holy and the common, and they have failed to teach the people the difference between the unclean and the clean (see Lev 10:10; 11:47; 20:25). Finally, they have

704. See, e.g., W. Zimmerli, *Ezekiel 1: A Commentary on the Book of the Prophet Ezekiel, Chapters 1–24*, trans. R. E. Clements, Hermeneia (Philadelphia: Fortress, 1979) 467; Ronald M. Hals, *Ezekiel*, FOTL 19 (Grand Rapids: Eerdmans, 1989) 161. Wevers, *Ezekiel*, 175-76, goes so far as to attribute the entire oracle to Ezekiel's "school." Greenberg, *Ezekiel 21–37*, 465, 470, acknowledges that the composition may reflect Jerusalem's destruction. However, Block opts for the period just prior to 586 BCE. D. I. Block, *The Book of Ezekiel: Chapters 1–24*, NICOT (Grand Rapids: Eerdmans, 1997) 722.
705. Hals, *Ezekiel*, 161, calls the oracle a "prophetic explanation of punishment."

706. Block, *Ezekiel 1–24*, 723.
707. Greenberg, *Ezekiel 21–37*, 461.

disregarded (lit., "hid their eyes from") God's sabbaths, neither observing them nor pursuing other offenders. As a consequence, Yahweh is profaned in their midst.

Zephaniah depicted Jerusalem's judges as rapacious wolves that immediately consumed their prey. Ezekiel, who says nothing of judges (שׁפטים *šōpĕṭîm*), turns next to the *śārîm*, ("nobles," "officials) with whom his predecessor began (Hos 9:15; see also Isa 1:23; 3:14). These predators, like Israel's princes, tear prey, shed blood, and destroy lives for dishonest profit (see vv. 12-13).

No less than its priests, Israel's prophets betray their calling in the most fundamental ways. Ezekiel's indictment, longer and less general than Zephaniah's, returns to accusations and imagery appearing in chap. 13. They mislead their clients by "whitewashing" the truth (in 13:10, this entails proclaiming "peace" when there is no peace). Their visions are false, their divinations lies (see 13:6), for though they prophesy in Yahweh's name, God has said nothing to them.

Finally, Ezekiel condemns the "people of the land," here a designation for a landowning social class of considerable politial, economic, and social importance (see 7:27). They, like the wicked son of 18:12, 18, have committed extortion and robbery, oppressing the poor and needy, as well as the aliens residing in Israel's land (see v. 7*b*).

Verse 30 is reminiscent of Jer 5:1-5, wherein God commands Jeremiah to scour the streets of Jerusalem for a single just and truth-seeking person on whose behalf Jerusalem might be pardoned. Jeremiah alleged that his search was in vain. Ezekiel's God claims personally to have sought someone who would "repair the wall and stand in the breach before me on behalf of the land, so that I would not destroy it." The metaphor is militaristic: If a hole (פרץ *pereṣ*) in a city wall is neither repaired nor guarded by soldiers, the enemy is sure to enter it (see also 13:5). For Ezekiel, Yahweh is that enemy. In the absence of a single worthy person, God's indigation (זעם *za'am*; see v. 24) is poured out upon the people, and they are consumed by the fire of Yahweh's wrath (see Ps 106:23). Verse 30 is at odds with the prophet's previous assertion that the righteous cannot save others, even their own children (14:12-20).

Judah's destruction is justified by Ezekiel's oft-asserted claim that God has brought down upon the people's heads the consequences of their own conduct (see 9:10; 11:21; 16:43). This oracle, like the first (v. 12), concludes with the formula, "says the Lord GOD."

REFLECTIONS

Bloodshed City, Ezekiel's epithet for Jerusalem, could justifiably be applied to many contemporary cities where violent crimes are epidemic and corruption is the name of the game. In two of his three oracles, the prophet identifies Judah's leaders as those most responsible for his people's impurity. That is not the whole story, of course, for abuses of power, deceit, and brutality exist at all levels of society. Nevertheless, leaders in every sphere—political, economic, and religious—must contend with temptations to misuse their authority, to feather their own nests at the expense of others, to place themselves above the laws of justice and morality, to "play the system," because, after all, that is the way it has always been done. The corrupting propensity of power is proverbial.

Like many an author of Hebrew Scripture, Ezekiel insists that Israel's covenant with Yahweh has direct implications for every aspect of its life. The modern distinction between "sacred" and "secular" has no place in his thinking, for God demands fidelity in every arena of experience. The eighth-century BCE prophet Amos knew well that cultic observances alone did not suffice (Amos 4:4-5), for the very folk who "religiously" brought their sacrifices, tithes, and offerings to the temples were, at the same time, profiting at the expense of the poor. "Sunday-only"

Christians, no less than the pilgrims to Bethel and Gilgal, deceive themselves if they think that they are fulfilling God's claim upon their lives. Recall Hals's comment: "The meaning of 'I am Yahweh your God and you are my people' was to find expression much more in how one treated others than in what sacrifices one offered."[708] Hence, Ezekiel does not hestitate to juxtapose cultic acts with social attrocities, public life with private relationships. Life is a seamless whole, everywhere testifying to one's most fundamental commitments.

Religious leaders do not escape the prophet's censure. They also are vulnerable to the temptations that accompany power and authority. Ezekiel knows all too well that prophets can learn to "go through the motions," yet be devoid of God's word to their times. He recognizes that the pomp and circumstance of priestly ritual can conceal self-serving appetites for prestige, profit, and laxity. Jesus shares that knowledge. In Luke 11:43-44, for example, he critizes the Pharisees, who "love to have the seat of honor in the synagogues and to be greeted with respect in the marketplaces," but who in fact are sources of social defilement. They exemplify those who put their own interests ahead of the kingdom of God.[709]

Israel's torah, too often dismissed by Christians as the antithesis of "gospel," in fact testifies to existence lived out in utter awareness that life is sacred—not only one's own life, but equally the lives of others. Faithful partnership with God is not a consequence of private piety alone. Abundant life is quite different from life surrounded by abundance. Ezekiel challenges Judah's leaders, the exiles, and his readers to embody Yahweh's holiness, justice, and love.

708. Hals, *Ezekiel,* 158.
709. Greenberg, *Ezekiel 1–24,* 728.

EZEKIEL 23:1-49, THE (TRAGIC) TALE OF TWO SISTERS

OVERVIEW

True to Ezekiel's oracles thus far, chapter 23 seeks to (more than) justify Yahweh's impending destruction of Jerusalem. Here, as in chap. 16, the prophet takes up, sustains, and elaborates upon a literary convention: the personification of cities as women (see Excursus: "Cities as Females," 1221-25). Ezekiel 16 focused especially upon Jerusalem's idolatry, depicted metaphorically as adultery. This chapter emphasizes the faithless and fickle international alliances pursued by both Samaria (capital of the northern kingdom of Israel) and Jerusalem (capital of Judah). For Ezekiel, a political isolationist, such (d)alliances constituted flagrant disloyalty to Yahweh, who alone should be the object of their trust.

In vv. 2-21, Ezekiel casts God in the role of a storyteller. What follows is no objective, historical account, but an extended metaphorical narrative about two sisters whose content frequently derives from the prophet's take on events in the "lives" of both kingdoms. Already in Egypt, Oholah (Samaria), the elder, and Oholibah (Jerusalem), the younger, engaged in sexual activity unbefitting maidens, whose sexual and reproductive capacities should have been reserved for their future husbands. In time, Yahweh marries both women, and each gives birth to sons and daughters. Neither is true to her mate, however. Oholah "plays the prostitute" with Assyria's choicest males and defiles herself with their idols. Consequently, God gives her into the hands of her "lovers," who strip her naked in public, seize her children, and slay her with the sword (vv. 5-10). Oholibah witnesses Oholah's brutal demise but draws no lesson from it. Instead, she outdoes her elder sister, lusting after not only the Assyrians, but also the Babylonians and her earliest paramours, the Egyptians (vv. 11-21). Hence, Yahweh threatens her with multiple punishments, including mutilation, public stripping, despoliation, the deportation of her children, and burning at the hands of her former lovers, God's agents of her destruction (vv. 22-35).

Verses 36-45 "resurrect" Oholah in order that she, Oholibah's cohort in harlotry, be present when an expanded list of charges is lodged against them. Verses 46-49 anticipate the punishment for these crimes. Yahweh is summoning an army to carry out the sentence. The sisters' deaths will bring an end to their lewdness in the land and serve as a warning to all "women" not to follow their example. In a manner characteristic of Ezekiel's oracles, this metaphorical narrative ends with the recognition formula, "and you shall know that I am the Lord GOD." Ultimately, Yahweh acts in order that the people of Israel might be forced to acknowledge the unparalleled power and sovereignty of their God.

Most critics contend that Ezekiel 23 is the end product of a lengthy and complex process inspired by Jeremiah's story of Faithless Israel and her sister, False Judah (Jer 3:6-13), initiated by the prophet, continued by members of his "school," and concluded by later generations of redactors/editors. Jorg Garscha, for example, limits the oracle's "authentic" core to vv. 2, 4*a*, 5-6, 9, 10*a*, 11*a*, 14*b*, 15*a*, 16, 18*b*, 22(?), and 24*b*-25*a*(?).[710] Zimmerli discerns Ezekiel's hand in only seventeen of the chapter's forty-nine verses.[711] Though their judgments are extreme and, perhaps in some cases, based on overly refined criteria for determining the earliest elements, there is little doubt that the present text took shape over some time and in "conversation" with other of Ezekiel's oracles, including chaps. 16 and 22. The prophet may have played the primary role in shaping and expanding upon the earliest version of his oracle. But it is likely that later redactors/editors also have contributed to its final, canonical form. The

ancient reader had no recourse to the presuppositions and analytical methods of contemporary critics. But he, too, knew that, especially in vv. 40-44, the text makes for tough reading.

Viewing chapter 23 through the lens of an ancient reader, we must take care not to attribute to him the responses of many modern-day audiences. Contemporary interpreters of both genders express shock and dismay at Ezekiel's underlying presupposition that both women and their sexuality are properly the property of males, that violence, even death, is justifiable punishment for female infidelity (imagined or real). They decry the prophet's resort to pornographic imagery, and sometimes subject him to psychological analysis. Setel, for example, allows that it is possible "to understand the extreme misogyny of Ezekiel as the author's response to his own experience of powerlessness and humiliation. Yet it is also important to recognize and examine the fact that he used specifically female imagery and to interpret his prophecy in *relationship* to the means he chose, not as something external to it."[712]

Setel's "diagnosis" cannot be confirmed, of course, but its insight is worth pondering. Her insistence that the meaning of Ezekiel's oracle cannot be isolated from his choice of metaphor echoes the view of many a contemporary philosopher and literary critic that tropes (figurative uses of language) should not be dismissed as merely decorative ways of expressing something that might just as well be said literally (albeit with a loss of emotive impact). As noted in the Overview to chapter 16, the metaphorical medium is the message, because that message is communicated in terms having an irreducible impact upon the reader's reception of it. This observation applies equally to ancient and modern readers.

Moshe Greenberg, whose commentary on Ezekiel is fundamentally the "historical-philological search for the primary, context-bound sense of Scripture," eschews the "judgmental" work of feminists who, in his view, fail to distinguish what the text meant to its earliest readers from

710. Jorg Garscha, *Studien zum Ezechielbuch: Eine redaktionskritische Untersuchung von 1–39,* Europäische Hochschulschriften 23 (Bern: Herbert Lang, 1974) 53-63.

711. W. Zimmerli, *Ezekiel 1: A Commentary on the Book of the Prophet Ezekiel, Chapters 1–24,* trans. R. E. Clements, Hermeneia (Philadelphia: Fortress, 1979) 480-81.

712. T. Drorah Setel, "Feminist Insights and the Question of Method," in *Feminist Perspectives on Biblical Scholarship,* ed. Adela Yarbro Collins (Chico: Scholars Press, 1985) 41.

what it means in contemporary contexts, in service to "a new female reality."[713] Although his label ("feminists") is inappropriately narrow (as if only feminists make judgments about texts) and monolithic (as if all women biblical scholars were feminists as he defines that term), Greenberg's point is not ungrounded. One can profitably bring the text into dialogue with both its ancient Near Eastern (and especially Israelite) world and twenty-first century cultures, but the first conversation is an essential prerequisite for the second; and each will differ from the other in signicant ways. The "trick" is not anachronistically to impose upon ancient readers the presuppositions and agendas of today.

It should be added, however, that Ezekiel 23 presents neither ancient nor contemporary audiences with objective "truth." The prophet's metaphors and other rhetorical techniques unabashedly attempt to shape both the message and his audience's reception of it. Moreover, one dare not simply presume that the interpretations of ancient audiences (and readers) were uniform.[714]

713. Moshe Greenberg, *Ezekiel 21–37,* AB 22A (Garden City, N.Y.: Doubleday, 1997) 494.
714. Greenberg seems to make such an assumption.

One can plausibly conjecture that female and male members of that group (who were not, by the scroll's own testimony, unwilling to argue with his perspectives) construed and judged his use of female imagery in diverse ways. The ancient woman who herself had experienced violence, including sexual violence, at the hands of her husband or of soldiers might not be so persuaded. The man who watched as his sister, wife, or daughter was stripped, raped, and then murdered might well be outraged by Ezekiel's choice of imagery. In the end, both might utterly reject any portrait of Yahweh as the perpetrator and enabler of such brutality. Dare we presume that biblical portrayals of God as "merciful, slow to anger, and abounding in steadfast love" (see, e.g., Jonah 4:2) arose and were sustainable only during periods of social tranquility? Or should we discern in such words a countervailing insistence that, in good times *and* in bad times, love for Israel is fundamental to God's character and shapes divine activity? Fortunately, the format of *The New Interpreter's Bible* provides space for both efforts—construing (as best we are able) the text's meanings in its ancient context and reflecting on its implications for contemporary communities of women and men.

Ezekiel 23:1-4, Setting the Scene

NIV	NRSV
23 The word of the LORD came to me: [2]"Son of man, there were two women, daughters of the same mother. [3]They became prostitutes in Egypt, engaging in prostitution from their youth. In that land their breasts were fondled and their virgin bosoms caressed. [4]The older was named Oholah, and her sister was Oholibah. They were mine and gave birth to sons and daughters. Oholah is Samaria, and Oholibah is Jerusalem.	23 The word of the LORD came to me: [2]Mortal, there were two women, the daughters of one mother; [3]they played the whore in Egypt; they played the whore in their youth; their breasts were caressed there, and their virgin bosoms were fondled. [4]Oholah was the name of the elder and Oholibah the name of her sister. They became mine, and they bore sons and daughters. As for their names, Oholah is Samaria, and Oholibah is Jerusalem.

COMMENTARY

Like many of Ezekiel's oracles, this one begins with the word event formula ("The word of Yahweh came to me"), followed by God's direct address to the prophet ("Mortal"). Unlike many others, however, Ezekiel is not ordered to address an audience. Instead, the Lord immediately launches into the story of two women, daughters of a single mother. Nothing more is said of this mother (does she represent the Israelites in Egypt?), and not a word is devoted to their father(s). In chapter 16, Ezekiel attached a poisonous pedigree to the hapless foundling whom Yahweh discovered lying in her birth blood in an open field. Jerusalem's father was an Amorite, her mother a Hittite (16:3, 45). Here, by contrast, his point seems simply to be that these women are (at least) maternal siblings. Hard on the heels of this brief introduction comes an accusation. In their youth, they played the prostitute in Egypt. Their breasts were squeezed, their virgin nipples fondled. Such activity does not constitute adultery, for neither woman is married as yet. In a world where maidens were expected to reserve their sexuality (and reproductive capacity) for their future husbands, however, Ezekiel's charge is clearly negative. Moreover, he intensifies its effect by his choice of terms: to "play the prostitute" is to engage in sexual activity habitually;[715] harlotry accusations ascribe to those implicated a range of culture-specific, pejorative associations with common prostitutes.[716]

Verse 4a informs readers of the two women's names: the elder ("greater") is Oholah, the other, Oholibah. Both epithets derive from אהל ('ōhel), a Hebrew noun meaning "tent." A traditional view holds that in the present context, "tent" refers to sanctuaries (see, e.g., Exod 33:7; Num 11:24; Ps 15:1; 61:5). Oholah means "her (own) tent," while Oholibah means "my tent (is) in her."[717] Oholah's name is judgmental, in that "tent"

refers to the (from a Judean perspective, illicit) sanctuaries of the northern kingdom of Israel, while Oholibah's is positive, pointing to the presence of Yahweh's (legitimate) Temple in Jerusalem, capital of Judah.[718] But there are problems with this interpretation. On the one hand, the final ה (h) of both epithets is written without a mappîq, a dot placed within the letter (ה) to indicate its function as a consonant. If these final letters were part of the third-person feminine singular suffix ("her"), we would expect both to be written with a mappîq. On the other hand, Ezekiel does not refer to sanctuaries as "tents" elsewhere in his scroll (but see 41:1). That fact alone does not constitute a compelling argument for dismissing "sanctuary" as the referent of "tent," especially for the audience (and reader) familiar with Israel's traditions about the (post exodus) desert "tent of meeting" (אהל מועד 'ōhel mô'ēd; a structure outside the Israelite camp where Moses was said to meet with Yahweh; e.g., Num 12:5, 10), the wilderness tabernacle (e.g., Exod 39:32), and the tent pitched by David to house the ark in Jerusalem (2 Sam 6:17). Zimmerli concludes that both epithets are archaic-sounding Bedouin names, evocative of Israel's pre-Egyptian, semi-nomadic origins.[719] But he concedes that the Israelites might have detected a wordplay congruent with the traditional view set out above.[720] The conundrum admits no easy answers, but we should not overlook the fact that the sisters' names are similar in sound, an audible signal of their familial tie.

While chap. 16 described in considerable detail the tender care and physical abundance bestowed by Yahweh upon "his" bride (16:9-14), here Ezekiel permits only the briefest reference to God's marriage to both women ("They became mine," v. 4; see 16:8). The notice that each bore sons and daughters confirms that these unions were consummated. Verse 4b dissipates any doubt about the sisters' identities: "Oholah is Samaria,

---

715. Phyllis Bird, " 'To Play the Harlot': An Inquiry into an Old Testament Metaphor," in *Gender and Difference in Ancient Israel,* ed. P. L. Day (Minneapolis: Fortress, 1989) 80.

716. See K. P. Darr, *Isaiah's Vision and the Family of God* (Louisville: Westminster John Knox, 1994) 115-21; E. J. Adler, "The Background for the Metaphor of Covenant as Marriage in the Hebrew Bible" (Ph.D. diss., University of California at Berkeley, 1963) 311-14.

717. See W. Eichrodt, *Ezekiel,* OTL (Philadelphia: Westminster, 1970) 322.

718. Zimmerli rejects the notion that the names reflect two different evaluations of Oholah and Oholibah, based on their respective sanctuaries, since throughout Ezekiel 23 both siblings are judged negatively; indeed, Oholibah's sins surpass her sister's. See Zimmerli, *Ezekiel 1,* 483-84.

719. Ibid., 483. See also D. I. Block, *The Book of Ezekiel: Chapters 1–24,* NICOT (Grand Rapids: Eerdmans, 1997) 735-36.

720. Zimmerli, *Ezekiel 1,* 484.

and Oholibah is Jerusalem." In the excursus "Cities as Females" (1221-25), it is noted that the personification of cities as women was not an Ezekielian innovation. Like his predecessors, Hosea, Isaiah, Nahum, and Jeremiah, the prophet employed female imagery in order to evoke and exploit certain stereotypical associations with women toward strategic ends. In this context, he recasts the histories of Samaria and Jerusalem (i.e., Israel as a whole) as biographies. The sequential reader who arrives at 23:1-49 already knowing the contents of chaps. 16 and 22 expects that Ezekiel's rhetorical strategy will function to depict the offending parties in the worst possible light; vv. 3-4 go a long way toward confirming that expectation.

Here, as in chap. 16, we must ask whether the text is, properly speaking, an allegory. Clearly, it displays allegorical tendencies—that is, elements of Ezekiel's "biographies" can be correlated with actual historical events.[721] Perhaps, if our knowledge of Israel's history and traditions were fuller, we might detect even more correspondences between narrative and reality than we are presently able to do. Nonetheless, if we search the text seeking only point-for-point correlations, as if

its primary import lay in what it says about something else, we rob Ezekiel's metaphorical oracle of much of its richness, complexity, and power to evoke a range of associations. His creation is more than an indictment of Israel's political misalliances and cultic abominations. It is an invitation to his audience (and readers) to perceive one complex, mysterious, and intimate reality (the relationship between Yahweh and this people) in terms suggestive of another (marriage) that, although no less complex, mysterious, or intimate, is nonetheless better known.

Ezekiel's scenario in vv. 2-4 is, in some respects, surreal. In chap. 16, he acknowledged Jerusalem's Canaanite origins. David did not build that city. He captured a Jebusite stronghold (see Gen 10:15-16; Judg 19:11-12; 2 Sam 5:6) and established it as the capital of Israel. Here, however, the prophet places both Samaria and Jerusalem in Egypt. This rhetorical strategy makes sense only when one realizes that the two cities actually represent all of Israel from the earliest days of its existence. Ezekiel's decision to employ personified city imagery, in conjunction with marriage and adultery metaphors, in the ensuing sweep of Israel's past, present, and (impending) future shapes the plot from the outset. (See Reflections at 23:36-49.)

721. See N. Frye, "Allegory," in *Princeton Encyclopedia of Poetry and Poetics*, ed. Alex Preminger (Princeton: Princeton University Press, 1974) 12-15.

Ezekiel 23:5-10, Oholah's Adultery and Punishment

NIV

5"Oholah engaged in prostitution while she was still mine; and she lusted after her lovers, the Assyrians—warriors [6]clothed in blue, governors and commanders, all of them handsome young men, and mounted horsemen. [7]She gave herself as a prostitute to all the elite of the Assyrians and defiled herself with all the idols of everyone she lusted after. [8]She did not give up the prostitution she began in Egypt, when during her youth men slept with her, caressed her virgin bosom and poured out their lust upon her.

9"Therefore I handed her over to her lovers, the Assyrians, for whom she lusted. [10]They stripped her naked, took away her sons and

NRSV

5Oholah played the whore while she was mine; she lusted after her lovers the Assyrians, warriors[a] [6]clothed in blue, governors and commanders, all of them handsome young men, mounted horsemen. [7]She bestowed her favors upon them, the choicest men of Assyria all of them; and she defiled herself with all the idols of everyone for whom she lusted. [8]She did not give up her whorings that she had practiced since Egypt; for in her youth men had lain with her and fondled her virgin bosom and poured out their lust upon her. [9]Therefore I delivered her into the hands of her lovers, into the hands of the

[a]Meaning of Heb uncertain

daughters and killed her with the sword. She became a byword among women, and punishment was inflicted on her.

Assyrians, for whom she lusted. [10]These uncovered her nakedness; they seized her sons and her daughters; and they killed her with the sword. Judgment was executed upon her, and she became a byword among women.

COMMENTARY

The story of Oholah's illict fornications (vv. 5-8) and eventual punishment (vv. 9-10) begins with a general accusation: She betrayed her husband, Yahweh, by "playing the harlot" (v. 5a). Ezekiel has already accused both sisters of prostituting themselves in Egypt (v. 3). Such behavior was degrading, but it did not entail adultery, since neither was married at the time. By v. 5, however, Oholah's marital status has changed. Leviticus 20:10 and Deut 22:22 state that the legal penalty for adultery is the deaths of *both* parties. We can question whether that penalty was routinely enforced. Moreover, we should not simply assume that biblical portrayals of other punishments inflicted on unfaithful wives reflect actual social practices. Nonetheless, the text reveals the negative views of adulterous women and the concomitant impulse not only to inflict upon them physical and psychological pain, but also to return upon them the shame and dishonor they have brought upon their husbands and families.[722]

As noted in the Commentary on chapter 16, certain biblical authors, including Ezekiel, employ not only נאף (nāʾap, "to commit adultery"), but also זנה (zānâ, "to commit fornication," "be a harlot") to describe the married women's illict intercourse. Phyllis Bird observes that the use of zānâ rather than nāʾap foregrounds promiscuity rather than infidelity, "wantonness" rather than abrogation of the marriage contract or covenant. "The metaphorical use of zānâ invokes two familiar . . . images of dishonor in Israelite cuture, the common prostitute and the promiscuous daughter or wife."[723]

The objects of Oholah's lusting (עגב ʿāgab; see also vv. 9, 12, 16, 20; 33:31-32; Jer 4:30) are her Assyrian "lovers": guardsmen attired in expensive

blue fabric,[724] governors, and commanders, all handsome and sitting astride horses. In chap. 16, Ezekiel praised the physical beauty and rich attire of Yahweh's young bride (16:9-14). Here, by contrast, he says nothing of Oholah's appearance, emphasizing instead the attractiveness of Assyria's military and administrative officials, all "decked out," one imagines, in their finest "dress" uniforms. Bedazzled by their beauty, Oholah gives herself (as a prostitute) to *all* of them. Moreover, she defiles herself with all their idols (lit., "dung-pellets," Ezekiel's characteristic and crass label for the images of other deities). Like the proverbial dog that returns to its vomit, Oholah reverts to the lewd behavior of her youth when, according to Ezekiel, she willingly played the prostitute with Egyptian men. The phrase אותה שכבו (ʾôtāh šākĕbû) is problematic, but its clear referent is illicit intercourse.[725] The phrase "poured out . . . lust" appeared also in 16:15 ("lavished your whorings") to describe adulterous acts initiated by Jerusalem with "any passer-by."

Oholah's punishment, introduced by לכן (lākēn, "therefore"), begins when her husband delivers her into the hands of her Assyrian "lovers" (v. 9; see v. 5). Ezekiel ignores the question of how, or why, Samaria's partners in adultery should not only escape punishment, but also serve as Yahweh's instruments of her demise. Public stripping, whether preliminary to sexual assault or a signal of the loss of support of her husband and his family, or both, appears in Hos 2:3; Jer 13:26-27; and Ezek 16:36-39; in each of these texts, the victim is not a human woman, but an entity personified as a female. Seizing her sons and daughters is an apparent reference to Assyria's harsh

---

722. Darr, *Isaiah's Vision and the Family of God,* 120.
723. Bird, " 'To Play the Harlot,' " 80, 89.

724. See Greenberg, *Ezekiel 21–37,* 475, for this translation of קרובים (gĕrôbîm, "guardsmen").
725. See ibid., 476-77.

deportation policy, or to their deaths in the course of the capital's downfall. As noted in the Commentary to 20:45–21:32, the sword figures prominently in the prophet's oracles of doom (e.g., 5:1-2; 6:3, 8, 11-12; 11:8, 10; 12:14, 16; 14:17, 21; 16:40; 17:21; 21:3-32). In 16:42, Jerusalem's brutal death had a cathartic effect upon her divine husband: "So I will satisfy my fury on you, and my jealousy shall turn away from you; I will be calm, and will be angry no longer." But while the verses are filled with expressions of (misspent) erotic passion, Ezekiel's God remains aloof, admitting no emotions and recounting both "his" wife's sins and her punishment in a detached manner. The juxtaposition of "she became a byword [lit., "a name"] among women" and "judgment was executed upon her" suggests that the former was a consequence of the latter. As word of Oholah's punishment circulates, her name comes to represent the worst fate that can befall a city, just as the name of Zimri, the king-killer, is applied by Jezebel to Jehu (2 Kgs 9:31; see 1 Kgs 16:9-10), who overthrew northern Israel's Omride dynasty.[726]

Clearly, vv. 9-10 refer to Assyria's destruction of Samaria in 722/21 BCE. Critics have sought also to identify the historical referents underlying vv. 5b-8. So, for example, Samaria's initial liaison with Assyria might refer to King Jehu's payment of tribute to Shalmaneser III in 841 BCE (in hopes of securing support for his regime?).[727] Cogan has shown that the vassal states of Assyria (i.e., allied foreign nations that paid tribute but retained their independence), were bound by loyalty oaths sworn in the names of Assyrian deities (and likely their own as well).[728] Ezekiel's charge that Oholah defiled herself with the "dung-idols" of her Assyrian "lovers" reflects that religiopolitical reality.[729] Despite such an oath, however, Israel's last king, Hoshea, conspired with the Egyptians and withheld tribute from Shalmaneser, bringing on Assyrian troops and the fall of Samaria under Sargon II (2 Kgs 17:3-4; see also Hos 7:11; 12:1). Has memory of this incident motivated Ezekiel's evocation of Egypt in v. 8?[730] Given the prophet's antipathy toward Israel's repeated resorts to Egyptian aid down to his own day, we should not be surprised to find such a reference here. Yet the intent of this verse appears, rather, to assert that Oholah's whorings with the Assyrians are but a resumption of the sexual activity practiced since her youth in Egypt. Despite her union with Yahweh, her behavior has never changed; she has simply switched human partners. (See Reflections at 23:36-49.)

726. Ibid., 477.
727. ANET, 281.

728. M. Cogan, Imperialism and Religion: Assyria, Judah and Israel in the Eighth and Seventh Centuries B.C.E., SBLMS 19 (Missoula: Scholars Press, 1974) 44-49.
729. Vassalage may also have brought with it some obligation to participate in Assyria's state cult.
730. So Julie Galambush, Jerusalem in the Book of Ezekiel: The City as Yahweh's Wife, SBLDS 130 (Atlanta: Scholars Press, 1992) 112; Moshe Greenberg, Ezekiel 21–37, AB 22A (Garden City, N.Y.: Doubleday, 1997) 476; W. Zimmerli, Ezekiel 1: A Commentary on the Book of the Prophet Ezekiel, Chapters 1–24, trans. R. E. Clements, Hermeneia (Philadelphia: Fortress, 1979) 485.

Ezekiel 23:11-35, The Indictment and Punishment of Oholibah

NIV

[11]"Her sister Oholibah saw this, yet in her lust and prostitution she was more depraved than her sister. [12]She too lusted after the Assyrians—governors and commanders, warriors in full dress, mounted horsemen, all handsome young men. [13]I saw that she too defiled herself; both of them went the same way.

[14]"But she carried her prostitution still further. She saw men portrayed on a wall, figures of

NRSV

[11]Her sister Oholibah saw this, yet she was more corrupt than she in her lusting and in her whorings, which were worse than those of her sister. [12]She lusted after the Assyrians, governors and commanders, warriors[a] clothed in full armor, mounted horsemen, all of them handsome young men. [13]And I saw that she was defiled; they both took the same way. [14]But she carried her whorings further; she saw male figures carved on the

[a]Meaning of Heb uncertain

NIV

Chaldeans[a] portrayed in red, [15]with belts around their waists and flowing turbans on their heads; all of them looked like Babylonian chariot officers, natives of Chaldea.[b] [16]As soon as she saw them, she lusted after them and sent messengers to them in Chaldea. [17]Then the Babylonians came to her, to the bed of love, and in their lust they defiled her. After she had been defiled by them, she turned away from them in disgust. [18]When she carried on her prostitution openly and exposed her nakedness, I turned away from her in disgust, just as I had turned away from her sister. [19]Yet she became more and more promiscuous as she recalled the days of her youth, when she was a prostitute in Egypt. [20]There she lusted after her lovers, whose genitals were like those of donkeys and whose emission was like that of horses. [21]So you longed for the lewdness of your youth, when in Egypt your bosom was caressed and your young breasts fondled.[c]

[22]"Therefore, Oholibah, this is what the Sovereign LORD says: I will stir up your lovers against you, those you turned away from in disgust, and I will bring them against you from every side— [23]the Babylonians and all the Chaldeans, the men of Pekod and Shoa and Koa, and all the Assyrians with them, handsome young men, all of them governors and commanders, chariot officers and men of high rank, all mounted on horses. [24]They will come against you with weapons,[d] chariots and wagons and with a throng of people; they will take up positions against you on every side with large and small shields and with helmets. I will turn you over to them for punishment, and they will punish you according to their standards. [25]I will direct my jealous anger against you, and they will deal with you in fury. They will cut off your noses and your ears, and those of you who are left will fall by the sword. They will take away your sons and daughters, and those of you who are left will be consumed by fire. [26]They will also strip you of your clothes and take your fine jewelry. [27]So I will put a stop to the lewdness and prostitution you began in Egypt. You will not look

a 14 Or Babylonians   b 15 Or Babylonia; also in verse 16
c 21 Syriac (see also verse 3); Hebrew caressed because of your young breasts   d 24 The meaning of the Hebrew for this word is uncertain.

NRSV

wall, images of the Chaldeans portrayed in vermilion, [15]with belts around their waists, with flowing turbans on their heads, all of them looking like officers—a picture of Babylonians whose native land was Chaldea. [16]When she saw them she lusted after them, and sent messengers to them in Chaldea. [17]And the Babylonians came to her into the bed of love, and they defiled her with their lust; and after she defiled herself with them, she turned from them in disgust. [18]When she carried on her whorings so openly and flaunted her nakedness, I turned in disgust from her, as I had turned from her sister. [19]Yet she increased her whorings, remembering the days of her youth, when she played the whore in the land of Egypt [20]and lusted after her paramours there, whose members were like those of donkeys, and whose emission was like that of stallions. [21]Thus you longed for the lewdness of your youth, when the Egyptians[a] fondled your bosom and caressed[b] your young breasts.

[22]Therefore, O Oholibah, thus says the Lord GOD: I will rouse against you your lovers from whom you turned in disgust, and I will bring them against you from every side: [23]the Babylonians and all the Chaldeans, Pekod and Shoa and Koa, and all the Assyrians with them, handsome young men, governors and commanders all of them, officers and warriors,[c] all of them riding on horses. [24]They shall come against you from the north[d] with chariots and wagons and a host of peoples; they shall set themselves against you on every side with buckler, shield, and helmet, and I will commit the judgment to them, and they shall judge you according to their ordinances. [25]I will direct my indignation against you, in order that they may deal with you in fury. They shall cut off your nose and your ears, and your survivors shall fall by the sword. They shall seize your sons and your daughters, and your survivors shall be devoured by fire. [26]They shall also strip you of your clothes and take away your fine jewels. [27]So I will put an end to your lewdness and your whoring brought from the land of Egypt; you shall not long for them, or remember Egypt any

a Two Mss: MT from Egypt   b Cn: Heb for the sake of
c Compare verses 6 and 12: Heb officers and called ones
e Gk: Meaning of Heb uncertain

NIV

on these things with longing or remember Egypt anymore.

28"For this is what the Sovereign LORD says: I am about to hand you over to those you hate, to those you turned away from in disgust. 29They will deal with you in hatred and take away everything you have worked for. They will leave you naked and bare, and the shame of your prostitution will be exposed. Your lewdness and promiscuity 30have brought this upon you, because you lusted after the nations and defiled yourself with their idols. 31You have gone the way of your sister; so I will put her cup into your hand.

32"This is what the Sovereign LORD says:

"You will drink your sister's cup,
    a cup large and deep;
it will bring scorn and derision,
    for it holds so much.
33You will be filled with drunkenness
        and sorrow,
    the cup of ruin and desolation,
    the cup of your sister Samaria.
34You will drink it and drain it dry;
    you will dash it to pieces
    and tear your breasts.

I have spoken, declares the Sovereign LORD.

35"Therefore this is what the Sovereign LORD says: Since you have forgotten me and thrust me behind your back, you must bear the consequences of your lewdness and prostitution."

NRSV

more. 28For thus says the Lord GOD: I will deliver you into the hands of those whom you hate, into the hands of those from whom you turned in disgust; 29and they shall deal with you in hatred, and take away all the fruit of your labor, and leave you naked and bare, and the nakedness of your whorings shall be exposed. Your lewdness and your whorings 30have brought this upon you, because you played the whore with the nations, and polluted yourself with their idols. 31You have gone the way of your sister; therefore I will give her cup into your hand. 32Thus says the Lord GOD:

You shall drink your sister's cup,
    deep and wide;
you shall be scorned and derided,
    it holds so much.
33You shall be filled with drunkenness
        and sorrow.
    A cup of horror and desolation
    is the cup of your sister Samaria;
34you shall drink it and drain it out,
    and gnaw its sherds,
    and tear out your breasts;

for I have spoken, says the Lord GOD. 35Therefore thus says the Lord GOD: Because you have forgotten me and cast me behind your back, therefore bear the consequences of your lewdness and whorings.

COMMENTARY

While Ezekiel dispatched Oholah in only six verses, he devotes twenty-five verses to Oholibah's indictment (vv. 11-21) and punishments (vv. 22-35). Obviously, the already-defunct capital of northern Israel is not his central concern. Rather, Samaria's "biography" has illustrated the enormous price Yahweh exacts for illicit unions with foreign nations and their gods. Jerusalem, whose youthful whorings in Egypt paralleled her sister's, can only be expected to follow in her path. Though she should have learned from Oholah's tragic "morality tale," she has instead outdone her "in her lusting and in her whorings" (v. 11). Like

her sibling, she is captivated by the physical beauty of Assyria's young officials and horsemen (v. 12), provoking Yahweh's observation that she also is defiled, as was Oholah (v. 13)—and so already deserves to suffer her sister's fate. Again critics seek to illumine the historical events underlying Ezekiel's accusation. Has he in mind King Ahaz's alliance with Assyria, a desperate attempt (decried by the prophet Isaiah; see Isa 7:1–8:18) to hold on to Judah's throne when Pekah of Israel and Rezin of Aram-Damascus conspired to replace him with the son of Tabeel, a "puppet" who would support their attempt to halt Assyria's advance into the region (733–32 BCE)? Tiglath-pileser willingly came to Ahaz's rescue, but at the price of Judean vassalage and a huge tribute that included silver and gold from the Temple and the royal treasury (2 Kgs 16:8). The authors of 2 Kings charge Ahaz with heinous cultic sins: offering up his son as a crematory sacrifice (2 Kgs 16:3); worshiping at the "high places" (2 Kgs 16:4). Given Ezekiel's sharp condemnations of both international political alliances and these specific cultic practices (e.g., chap. 20), it seems reasonable that he might allude to this dark period in Judah's history.

Unlike her sister, Oholibah lives long enough to add the Chaldeans to her roster of lovers. The Chaldeans were an Aramaean people originally situated along the Persian Gulf. In 625 BCE they gained control of Babylon.[731] Ezekiel's use of the term in v. 14 appears to reflect his awareness that the Chaldeans were not part of Babylonia's native population.[732] Jerusalem's whorings with her new lovers are said to have begun when she saw engravings of male Chaldean nobles in full regalia (including belts [see Isa 5:27] and flowing turbans), outlined with red paint. Ezekiel may himself have seen such engravings on the buildings and monuments of Babylon, but how, one wonders, might Oholibah have witnessed them? Greenberg suggests that the scenario is a product of the prophet's escalating rhetoric. Previously, her passion was aroused by flesh-and-blood Assyrians; now her longing is unleashed by mere pictures.[733]

Oholibah sends messengers to Chaldea (v. 16). Though the sexual metaphor is prominent (their portraits have stirred her lust), the language of sending messengers derives from the sphere of diplomacy (see 17:15, where Zedekiah rebels against Nebuchadrezzar by sending ambassadors to Egypt in hopes of securing horses and a large army). The text suggests that the Babylonian officials waste no time coming to and bedding with her, so that she is defiled. In the light of her history

of illict fornications, the reader might be surprised to read that "her soul recoiled from them" (תקע נפשה מהם *têqaʿ napšāh mēhem*, v. 17b; see also vv. 18, 28; Jer 6:8). Is her reaction illumined by that of Ammon, David's son, who desired his sister, Tamar, but having raped her, hated her with a hatred greater than the love with which he had loved her (2 Sam 13:15)? There is little doubt that behind this, Ezekiel's first acknowledgment that either sister might actually pay an emotional price for her self-derogating behavior, lies the reality of Jerusalem's vacillating foreign policies (see below). Still, the comment should not be overlooked in a chapter that elsewhere narrows the emotional range of both sisters to nymphomaniacal lust.

In the face of Oholibah's unabashed whorings, Yahweh's "soul recoils from her" (תקע נפשי מעליה *têqaʿ napšî mēʿāleyhā*) as it had from her sister (v. 18). Yet she only increases her fornications, remembering her youthful days when she played the prostitute in Egypt and yearning for her earliest paramours (lit., "concubines"). Ezekiel, whose anti-Egyptian sentiments are well-established by this point in the scroll, does not deign to speak of these lovers as "handsome young men." Their attributes consist of oversized penises ("like those of donkeys"; see also the reference to "big membered" Egyptians in 16:26) and abundant ejaculations ("like that of stallions"; see Jer 5:8). Ezekiel's comment, obviously a slur, runs afoul of contemporary American culture, where size is prized; but moderns also know that sexual organs and practices can play a role in insults, especially ethnic insults. Fokkelien van Dijk-Hemmes remarks that by depicting Oholibah's desire in terms of penis size, Ezekiel has betrayed a male obsession.[734] Verses 19-21 do not state explicitly that Oholibah resumed sexual relations with the Egyptians: She "remembers the days of her youth when she played the harlot"; she "lusts after her former paramours" (but dispatches no messengers to them; cf. v. 16); she "longs for the lewdness" of her youth. Nonetheless, most critics discern in these verses references to Jerusalem's recurring hopes of securing military assistance from Egypt.[735]

731. Walther Eichrodt, *Ezekiel*, trans. Cosslett Quin, OTL (Philadelphia: Westminster, 1970) 325.

732. Zadok suggests that בני בבל (*bĕnê bābel*), "the sons of Babylon" (v. 15), refers to the Chaldean ruling classes. See R. Zadok, "West Semitic Toponyms in Assyrian and Babylonian Sources," in *Studies in Bible and in the Ancient Near East*, ed. Y. Avishur and J. Blau (Jerusalem: Rubinstein, 1978) 178-79.

733. Greenberg, *Ezekiel 21–37*, 478. Jer 22:14, an indictment of Judah's King Jehoiakim, derogates his newly built palace with its red-painted rooms.

734. Fokkelien van Dijk-Hemmes, "The Metaphorization of Women in Prophetic Speech: An Analysis of Ezekiel xxiii," *VT* 43 (1993) 168.

735. Greenberg, *Ezekiel 21–37*, 21, suggests that in this context פקד (*pāqad*) bears the specific meaning of "turning back to something after having left it" (see Exod 4:31; Judg 15:1), citing with approval the TNK translation, "you reverted to."

Two historical referents come to mind. On the one hand, Ezekiel may be thinking of King Hezekiah's reign (715/14–687/86 BCE), in the course of which Judah attempted to escape Assyrian vassalage with the assistance of Egypt and Babylon. In that case, v. 17 may contain a veiled reference to Hezekiah's welcome of envoys sent by Babylon's Chaldean king, Marduk-apal-iddin (Merodach-baladan; 721–709, 704–703 BCE). This possibility cannot be ruled out solely on the basis of chronology. Though Ezekiel lived more than a hundred years later, he most certainly would have known of strategic events of the period, including Hezekiah's rebellion, Sennacherib's retributive campaign against Judah, and his seige of Jerusalem in 701 BCE (see 2 Kgs 18:13–19:37; Isa 36:1–37:38).

On the other hand, the prophet may have been speaking of more recent events. Judah remained Assyria's vassal in the years following Sennacherib's siege. But the Assyrian Empire was beginning to unravel. When Egypt's Pharaoh Necho (c. 610–594 BCE) sent his troops north in a last-ditch effort to salvage its remnants, Judah's King Josiah (640–609 BCE) cast his lot with the Babylonians, intercepting Necho's army at Meggido. Josiah died in the encounter (2 Kgs 23:29), and his son Jehoahaz succeeded him. The Egyptian army hurried on to battle with Babylonian forces along the Euphrates River (2 Kgs 24:7). But three months later, as Necho returned home, he deposed Jehoahaz and enthroned another of Josiah's sons, Eliakim, whom he named Jehoiakim.[736] Jehoiakim maintained a pro-Egyptian policy. But in 605 BCE, the Babylonians roundly defeated the Egyptian army at Carchemish. Sometime later, Jehoiakim was forced to submit to Nebuchadrezzar. Yet after three years, and with hopes of Egyptian assistance, he rebelled against Babylon. Nebuchadrezzar responded with a punitive campaign in 598/97 and, as we know, took Jerusalem in 597 BCE, exiling its current king, Jehoiachin, and a select segment of the population, including Ezekiel. This brings us to the reign of Zedekiah, whose betrayal of his loyalty oath with Nebuchadrezzar was the subject of chap. 17 (see the Commentary on

17:11-22 for a discussion of Zedekiah's vacillating political policies and their disastrous outcome). As Galambush observes, one need not select one of these two periods and eliminate the other from consideration.[737] Ezekiel may have both periods in mind, such that vv. 19-21 indict Jerusalem for its full sweep of "infidelities" with Egypt.

With v. 22, Ezekiel addresses Oholibah directly and announces her sentence. As a consequence of her whorings, God will rouse against her the lovers from whom she turned in disgust—the Babylonians, all the Chaldeans, as well as three Aramaean tribes: Pekod (called Puqudu in Akkadian texts; see Jer 50:12), Shoa (often identified with Sutu, the name of a nomadic tribe; see Isa 22:5), and Koa (perhaps Quti/Guti, a tribe living east of the Tigris).[738] These names are ominous, since they are similar to the Hebrew words for "punish," "cry for help," and "shriek," respectively.[739] The last two may also have been chosen for their rhyming sounds. The following reference to Assyrians probably reflects the historical reality that after the empire collapsed, its soldiers were conscripted into Babylonia's fighting forces.[740] Just as Ezekiel emphasized the good looks and attractive clothing of the sisters' sexual partners, so also here he details their approach against Jerusalem, with special attention to their military machinery and battle attire.

In Hosea 2, Yahweh threatened personally to carry out the punishment of Israel/her land. In vv. 24-27, by contrast, Yahweh commits Jerusalem's judgment to the throng of officials and military officers marshaled against her who, Ezekiel adds ominously, will judge her according to their own ordinances (v. 24). God's jealous wrath is unleased in their furious dealings with her. They will cut off her nose and ears. Facial mutilation was among the attrocities practiced in Israel's ancient Near Eastern world.[741] In the domestic sphere, Middle Assyrian law permitted the husband of an adulterous wife to cut off her nose.[742] If a male or female slave received stolen property from a man's wife,

736. Jehoahaz was taken to Egypt in chains and died there; see 2 Kgs 23:31-4; 2 Chr 36:3-4; Jer 22:10-12; Ezek 19:3-4.

737. Galambush, *Jerusalem in the Book of Ezekiel,* 114-15.
738. See Zimmerli, *Ezekiel 1,* 488; Greenberg, *Ezekiel 21–37,* 481.
739. See Eichrodt, *Ezekiel,* 328.
740. Greenberg, *Ezekiel 21–37,* 481.
741. See an excerpt from the annals of Assyria's king Ashurnasirpal in D. I. Block, *The Book of Ezekiel: Chapters 1–24,* NICOT (Grand Rapids: Eerdmans, 1997) 752-53.
742. *ANET,* 181.

both nose and ears could be cut off, while the wife lost her ears only.[743] Apparently, the Israelites did not practice this mode of punishment. Does its presence here explain Ezekiel's reference to the troops judging Israel according to their own practices? The NRSV's "your survivors" (v. 25a; see also NIV) attempts to make sense of Hebrew אחריתך ('aḥărîtēk; lit., "the after-part of you"). Greenberg suggests, however, that the form refers to "the rest of you"—what is left of Oholibah after she has been mutilated. The same form reappears in the second half of v. 25, following the notice that Oholibah's sons and daughters will be seized; in that context, "posterity" seems an apt translation, though 'aḥărîtēk might also refer to property left behind to burn in the city.[744] Moreover, her former lovers will strip her and take her jewelry (see 16:39). By these punishments, Yahweh will put an end to the lewdness and whoring she has practiced since her time in Egypt. Finally, she will forget her Egyptian paramours.

Verses 28-30 consist of a second doom pronouncement against Oholibah, introduced by the messenger formula ("For thus says the Lord GOD"). Verse 28 reiterates the thought of v. 22, but with greater intensity. Yahweh will deliver her into the hands of those she *hates,* into the hands of those from whom she turned in *disgust,* and they will deal with her with *hatred,* stealing everything she has labored for (see Deut 28:33) and publicly stripping her naked, so that her shame is exposed for all to see. Ezekiel defends this punishment as the consequence of her lewdness and whorings, because she has played the prostitute with the nations and polluted herself with their idols—a fresh charge earlier leveled against Oholah alone (v. 7).

Like v. 13, v. 31*a* explicitly states that Oholibah has followed her sister's path. Hence Yahweh will place Oholah's "cup" in her hand (v. 31*b*). This second half-verse provides a felicitous transition to the following poem about "the cup of horror and desolation." The reader is alerted that Oholah also has drunk from this cup. But Ezekiel has reserved his description of the dreadful ordeal for Oholibah, the primary focus of his extended oracle. Ezekiel's poem begins with the messenger formula (v. 32) and ends with a concluding formula ("says the Lord GOD"). The cup motif was a familiar one, appearing in Hab 2:15-16 and Jer 25:15-29 ("For thus the LORD, the God of Israel, said to me: 'Take from my hand this cup of the wine of wrath, and make all the nations to whom I send you drink it. They shall drink and stagger and go out of their minds because of the sword that I am sending among them," Jer 25:15-16; see also Jer 49:12-13; 51:7; Isa 51:1, 22). This image derives from the hospitality of the host, who fills his guests' ample drinking vessels to the brim. Here as in other contexts where the motif is used negatively, however, its contents are so intoxicating that they poison the one who is forced to quaff them.[745] Drinking from her sister's ample cup, Jerusalem will become an object of scorn and derision, drunk and filled with sorrow, utterly appalled. Verse 34 is grotesque. Having drained every drop, a deranged Oholibah will smash the cup and gnaw its sherds, in order to suck out any liquid absorbed by the clay.[746] Then, in an act of self-mutilation, she will tear out her breasts, the body parts whose role in her earliest and ongoing fornications was noted in vv. 3, 8, and 21 (all in conjunction with Egypt). Despite its initial "therefore" (*lākēn*), v. 35 is actually a concluding, summarizing threat. Because Oholibah has "forgotten" Yahweh, casting her husband behind her back (see 1 Kgs 14:9; Neh 9:26), she must bear the consequences of her grossly immoral actions. (See Reflections at 23:36-49.)

743. Ibid., 180.
744. See Zimmerli, *Ezekiel 1,* 489.

745. See W. McKane, "Poison, Trial by Ordeal, and the Cup of Wrath," *VT* 30 (1980) 487-92.
746. See Greenberg, *Ezekiel 21–37,* 484; J. W. Wevers, *Ezekiel,* NCB (London: Nelson, 1969) 185.

Ezekiel 23:36-49, Oholah and Oholibah: Together Again in Sin and Judgment

NIV

³⁶The Lord said to me: "Son of man, will you judge Oholah and Oholibah? Then confront them with their detestable practices, ³⁷for they have committed adultery and blood is on their hands. They committed adultery with their idols; they even sacrificed their children, whom they bore to me,ᵃ as food for them. ³⁸They have also done this to me: At that same time they defiled my sanctuary and desecrated my Sabbaths. ³⁹On the very day they sacrificed their children to their idols, they entered my sanctuary and desecrated it. That is what they did in my house.

⁴⁰"They even sent messengers for men who came from far away, and when they arrived you bathed yourself for them, painted your eyes and put on your jewelry. ⁴¹You sat on an elegant couch, with a table spread before it on which you had placed the incense and oil that belonged to me.

⁴²"The noise of a carefree crowd was around her; Sabeansᵇ were brought from the desert along with men from the rabble, and they put bracelets on the arms of the woman and her sister and beautiful crowns on their heads. ⁴³Then I said about the one worn out by adultery, 'Now let them use her as a prostitute, for that is all she is.' ⁴⁴And they slept with her. As men sleep with a prostitute, so they slept with those lewd women, Oholah and Oholibah. ⁴⁵But righteous men will sentence them to the punishment of women who commit adultery and shed blood, because they are adulterous and blood is on their hands.

⁴⁶"This is what the Sovereign Lord says: Bring a mob against them and give them over to terror and plunder. ⁴⁷The mob will stone them and cut them down with their swords; they will kill their sons and daughters and burn down their houses.

⁴⁸"So I will put an end to lewdness in the land, that all women may take warning and not imitate you. ⁴⁹You will suffer the penalty for your lewdness and bear the consequences of your sins of idolatry. Then you will know that I am the Sovereign Lord."

ᵃ37 Or even made the children they bore to me pass through the fire; ᵇ42 Or drunkards

NRSV

36The Lord said to me: Mortal, will you judge Oholah and Oholibah? Then declare to them their abominable deeds. ³⁷For they have committed adultery, and blood is on their hands; with their idols they have committed adultery; and they have even offered up to them for food the children whom they had borne to me. ³⁸Moreover this they have done to me: they have defiled my sanctuary on the same day and profaned my sabbaths. ³⁹For when they had slaughtered their children for their idols, on the same day they came into my sanctuary to profane it. This is what they did in my house.

40They even sent for men to come from far away, to whom a messenger was sent, and they came. For them you bathed yourself, painted your eyes, and decked yourself with ornaments; ⁴¹you sat on a stately couch, with a table spread before it on which you had placed my incense and my oil. ⁴²The sound of a raucous multitude was around her, with many of the rabble brought in drunken from the wilderness; and they put bracelets on the armsᵃ of the women, and beautiful crowns upon their heads.

43Then I said, Ah, she is worn out with adulteries, but they carry on their sexual acts with her. ⁴⁴For they have gone in to her, as one goes in to a whore. Thus they went in to Oholah and to Oholibah, wanton women. ⁴⁵But righteous judges shall declare them guilty of adultery and of bloodshed; because they are adulteresses and blood is on their hands.

46For thus says the Lord God: Bring up an assembly against them, and make them an object of terror and of plunder. ⁴⁷The assembly shall stone them and with their swords they shall cut them down; they shall kill their sons and their daughters, and burn up their houses. ⁴⁸Thus will I put an end to lewdness in the land, so that all women may take warning and not commit lewdness as you have done. ⁴⁹They shall repay you for your lewdness, and you shall bear the penalty for your sinful idolatry; and you shall know that I am the Lord God.

ᵃHeb hands

COMMENTARY

These verses challenge the best efforts of every reader and critic. The Hebrew text (esp. vv. 40-44) is, in Greenberg's opinion, incoherent, odd, and disconcerting.[747] Zimmerli accounts for its peculiarities by placing it at a considerable remove from Ezekiel, and even his school, and attributing its parts to numerous editors/redactors. Greenberg suggests the opposite view, terming the text a "preliminary expectoration" (Kierkegaard) and a rare glimpse of an Ezekielian oracle in its earliest, unpolished form, before the prophet or some other editor got his hands on it.[748] The idea is intriguing and recalls Eichrodt's comment that vv. 40-44 are "so lively and vigorous" that one is tempted to detect here a fragment of an earlier and fuller account.[749] Yet his explanation that the "rough draft" of this passage escaped editorial attention because the "blatant unreality" of presenting both sisters in a single scenario was "too flagrant an excess even for the Ezekielian editor" is hardly convincing.

A "resurrected" Oholah joins her sister as Yahweh commands Ezekiel, in a manner similar to 16:2; 20:4; and 22:2, to arraign both women, informing them of the abominations with which they are charged (the introductory formula "Yahweh said to me" is unique to the book). The scene is unreal (Samaria was destroyed over a century earlier), but no more so than Ezekiel's initial decision to place both siblings (capital cities) in Egypt. Here, it seems, is another means by which the prophet speaks of God's judgment upon the whole house of Israel.

The following accusations, which include a number of quotations and allusions from previous chapters, are more diverse than those of earlier verses, where fornication (foreign alliances) was the name of both siblings' game and idolatry ran a distant second (vv. 7, 30). First comes the ubiquitous charge of adultery, here expressed by the (technically correct) נאף (nā'ap, "to commit adultery"), rather than by זנה (zānâ, "to be or act like a prostitute"), and bloodshed (a new allegation, but one reminiscent of chap. 22). These accusations are illuminated by v. 37b. They have committed

adultery with their idols (an idea at home in chap. 16), and the blood on their hands is that of Yahweh's children, sacrificed as food for those images (see also 16:20-21). God further accuses them of "defiling" (טמא ṭimmē') "my" Temple and profaning "my" sabbaths (see 22:8; Lev 19:30). The latter allegation has appeared in earlier chapters (e.g., 20, 22). The former is explained in v. 39. Having shed the blood of their offspring, the blood-stained sisters come to Yahweh's sanctuary to "profane" (חלל ḥālal) it.[750] Note the phrases "this they have done to me" (v. 38a) and "this is what they did in my house" (v. 39a), and the intervening "my sanctuary," "my sabbaths," "my sanctuary." The sisters' sins have direct implications for God, whose holy space and times they recklessly desecrate.

Verses 40-42 depict a new scenario in the lurid career of Yahweh's wives (especially Oholibah/Jerusalem). As noted, these verses are especially problematic, but they are also intriguing. In v. 16, Oholibah sent messengers (a diplomatic envoy) to the Chaldeans. In v. 40, the sisters dispatch a messenger to unidentified men "from far way"; and straightaway they come to them. Verses 40b-41 describe the elaborate toilette by which Oholibah (the likely referent of the second- and third-person fem. sing. forms) prepares for these guests: She bathes, paints her eyes, and bedecks herself with ornaments. In 16:11-12, husband Yahweh adorned Jerusalem, his young bride, with ornaments: bracelets, a chain, a nose ring, earrings, and a beautiful crown. The reader can well imagine that these are the very items with which she now bejewels herself in preparation for the arrival of men who are not her husband. She positions herself on a "stately couch" (lit., a "seat of glory"),[751] before which stands a table spread with Yahweh's incense and oil. Ezekiel creates a scene of a high-priced courtesan awaiting her upper-crust client(s), then deflates it in the following verse. Her love feast is, it seems, a bawdy public event; her clients are "rabble," drunken habitués of the

---

747. Greenberg, *Ezekiel 21–37*, 490.
748. Ibid., 490-91.
749. Eichrodt, *Ezekiel*, 333-34.

750. Galambush, *Jerusalem in the Book of Ezekiel*, 118-19, suggests that child sacrifice, temple worship, and profanation of Yahweh's sabbath are juxtaposed because the first two occured on the third, a Yahwistic "holy day."
751. See Greenberg, *Ezekiel 21–37*, 486.

desert whose gifts (bracelets, beautiful crowns; recall 16:11-12) are nothing but harlot's hire.

The references to Oholibah's "seat of glory" and to Yahweh's incense and oil suggest that behind this raunchy vignette might lie some sort of cultic ritual. The well-spread table before Oholibah's couch is reminiscent of Mesopotamian table altars, "set with the prepared rations of the divine repast."[752] Alternatively, the referent might be a political dalliance of some sort, the occasion marked by a state dinner. Galambush proposes that these verses portray Jerusalem's reception of both Egyptian diplomats (the "men from far away") and representatives from Judah's smaller, neighboring states (the drunken desert rabble), who come to Jerusalem to plot a rebellion against Babylon. Her further suggestion that the ensuing "orgy" transpires *within* the Jerusalem Temple begs the question of the location(s) where official treaty ceremonies were held.[753] What evidence we have, textual and iconographic, points to the palace as the most likely setting for such events. If Galambush is correct, then this final fornication scene is climactic (worst of all) precisely because foreigners have entered Yahweh's Temple. But Ezekiel does not explicitly state that the scene transpires there.

Verse 43 presents considerable problems. The speaker (presumably Yahweh, who has witnessed the preceding "festivities") seems first to say that Oholibah is "worn out" by her adulteries. The verb בלה (bālâ) refers to worn out sacks, wine-skins, sandals, and clothing in Josh 9:4-5, 13. Sarah employs it to describe her old (post-menopausal) age. Ezekiel may be suggesting that Oholibah is well-past her prime (hence the necessity of a more elaborate toilette and the reality of a less-desirable clientele). One thinks, for example, of Tyre, the "forgotten" prostitute who, after seventy years, takes her harp and takes to the streets in hopes of strumming up a little business (Isa 23:15-18). More likely, she is "worn out" in a

sexual sense, the result of her endless acts of intercourse. Verse 43b, literally, "now he [or "they"] will fornicate her fornications, and she," is notoriously difficult. Zimmerli suggests that we should supply the remainder of the thought, something like "(she)'ll enjoy it!"[754] Verse 44 shifts from metaphor to simile: He (they?) has entered her as one enters a prostitute; thus they have entered Oholah and Oholibah, depraved women.

The identity of the "righteous men" who will pronounce "them" (the suffix is third-person masc.) guilty of adultery and bloodshed also is elusive. The Targum (a free translation of the Hebrew text into Aramaic) adds that these men are righteous "in comparison with them" (i.e., Oholah and Oholibah). Wevers plausibly conjectures that the men are called "righteous" because their sentence befits the women's crimes (see v. 37; 16:38).[755] The text does not compel us simply to identify these judges with the murderous assembly summoned by Yahweh for terror and plunder (here, the referent [city] intrudes). As in 16:40-41, the mob's brutality consists of stoning, hacking with swords, and burning houses (again, the referent surfaces), but Ezekiel adds that these executioners will slay their sons and daughters as well (v. 47). Thus Yahweh will bring an end to the sisters' sexual depravity (זמה zimmâ; see, e.g., Lev 18:17; 19:29; 20:14; Ezek 16:27, 58; 22:9, 11; 23:21, 27, 35, 44, 48) in the land. Verse 48b suggests that their fates can serve a didactic purpose—that is, that "all women" take warning and not engage in acts of sexual depravity. Oholibah learned nothing from Oholah's experience (v. 11), though v. 10 claims that the latter's demise became "a byword among women." Has the force of Ezekiel's imagery, by which the sins of an entire people were personified in the biographies of the two females representing Samaria and Jerusalem, collapsed into a caution intended for women's ears alone? Or does the metaphor remain intact, such that "all women" refers to other cities (see 16:27, where "the daughters of the Philistines" are Philistine cities)?[756] The notice can be interpreted along either line. In fact, the reader need not

752. M. Cogan, *Imperialism and Religion: Assyria, Judah and Israel in the Eighth and Seventh Centuries B.C.E.*, SBLMS 19 (Missoula: Scholars Press, 1974) 75. In "An Oracular Dream Concerning Ashurbanipal," e.g., the goddess Ishtar instructs her devotee to "eat food, drink wine, supply music, praise my divinity." See *ANET*, 451.

753. Galambush, *Jerusalem in the Book of Ezekiel*, 119-23. She reads v. 39b as an introduction to the following scene, rather than as the conclusion of the previous charges.

754. W. Zimmerli, *Ezekiel 1: A Commentary on the Book of the Prophet Ezekiel, Chapters 1–24*, trans. R. E. Clements, Hermeneia (Philadelphia: Fortress, 1979) 479.

755. Wevers, *Ezekiel*, 188; see also Greenberg, *Ezekiel 21–37*, 487.

756. See Eichrodt, *Ezekiel*, 333.

choose one to the exclusion of the other. The object lesson will find its "teachable moments." Verse 49*a* rounds off Yahweh's threat to the women: Their punishment is (just) repayment for their sexual depravity and idolatry. The concluding recognition formula, "and you [masc. pl.] shall know that I am Lord Yahweh," lends to the whole the tone of a prophetic proof saying. Characteristic of Ezekiel's oracles, it yokes God's punishment to the ultimate goal that Israel might acknowledge the sovereign and absolute power of its Lord.

REFLECTIONS

No less than Ezekiel 16, the present chapter both thwarts and invites serious theological reflection. Its exhaustive (and ultimately exhausting) use of sexual language and tropes (e.g., metaphors, similes) to depict political and cultic activities the prophet deplores makes it an unlikely candidate for sermons and other religious education forums. Ezekiel intends to shock his audience, and modern readers remain susceptible to the aftershocks. Why spend time on a text so filled with offensive imagery and brutality?

The Reflections to chapter 16 raise issues equally germane to the present chapter, and the reader is advised to work through them in addition to the following remarks. It behooves us, for example, to remember that ancient Near Eastern marriages were not partnerships between legal and social "equals," that wives were in principle (if not always in practice!) subject to their husbands' control, and that adultery was regarded as a capital offense, in at least some circles. Like certain of his predecessors, Ezekiel discerned in the marriage bond a suitable metaphor for describing the covenant relationship between God, the "superior" party (husband) and Israel, the subordinate party (his wife)—a union that should have been characterized by deeply mutual commitment and female faithfulness. Within the world of that metaphor, Israel's violations of its covenant obligations (here, political alliances, idolatry) become acts of sexual infidelity. Ezekiel's reference to Yahweh's (consummated) marriages to Oholah and Oholibah is restricted to a single verse (v. 4), but their union (covenant) is the basis for everything that follows. As ancient Near Eastern wives, these women were, or should have been, subject to their husband's control, their sexuality and reproductive capacities his alone.

Ezekiel never questions why Yahweh was unwilling or unable to control his wives' behavior. Ezekiel's purpose lies in a different direction—namely, to justify the destruction of both women (cities and, by extension, the whole house of Israel) by depicting their "abominations" in the worst possible terms. Block raises an important point, I think, when he observes that Ezekiel's depictions of these two women cannot and should not be construed as representative of his views of women in general.[757] As we will see in the Commentary on chapter 24, Ezekiel's own wife was "the delight of [his] eyes." Nonetheless, his resort to female imagery, especially degrading female sexual imagery, to describe human sin, coupled with his recourse to physical atrocities, even murder, as God's just means of punishing "his" wanton wives, can have deadly consequences when abusive persons determine to model their behavior after "God's own"—to become, in effect, the "righteous judges" of 23:45. The courts are filled with cases of domestic violence, of women battered and murdered by men who regard "their" women—girlfriends, wives, daughters—as personal possessions and legitimate targets of their rage. For many such men, though not all, of course, biblical passages such as Ezekiel 23 sanction both their attitudes and their actions.

The chapter raises another issue as well. Each party (both genders) in the fornications Ezekiel describes is guilty of objectifying the other. Ogling stirs lust; lust demands personal gratification. But genuine concern for the other is absent. Ezekiel's metaphors point with some profundity

757. Block, *Ezekiel 1–24*, 734.

to the price both parties pay when intimate relations (including sexual relations) are motivated solely by selfish desires: eroded self-esteem; feelings of betrayal (of oneself and by the other); loathing directed inward and outward. But the truth of his observations is reserved for neither the most private of personal relations nor the most public of political exchanges. Our world cries out for persons and communities across the social spheres whose moral actions are not motivated by greed, who do not regard the other as an object of exploitation. As children of the living God, in whose image we all are created, we deserve to be treated with respect, even as we are obligated to deal respectfully with others.

EZEKIEL 24:1-14, THE PARABLE OF THE POT

NIV

24 In the ninth year, in the tenth month on the tenth day, the word of the LORD came to me: ²"Son of man, record this date, this very date, because the king of Babylon has laid siege to Jerusalem this very day. ³Tell this rebellious house a parable and say to them: `This is what the Sovereign LORD says:

" 'Put on the cooking pot; put it on
  and pour water into it.
⁴Put into it the pieces of meat,
  all the choice pieces—the leg and the
    shoulder.
Fill it with the best of these bones;
⁵   take the pick of the flock.
Pile wood beneath it for the bones;
  bring it to a boil
  and cook the bones in it.

⁶" 'For this is what the Sovereign LORD says:

" 'Woe to the city of bloodshed,
  to the pot now encrusted,
  whose deposit will not go away!
Empty it piece by piece
  without casting lots for them.

⁷" 'For the blood she shed is in her midst:
  She poured it on the bare rock;
she did not pour it on the ground,
  where the dust would cover it.
⁸To stir up wrath and take revenge
  I put her blood on the bare rock,
  so that it would not be covered.

⁹" 'Therefore this is what the Sovereign LORD says:

NRSV

24 In the ninth year, in the tenth month, on the tenth day of the month, the word of the LORD came to me: ²Mortal, write down the name of this day, this very day. The king of Babylon has laid siege to Jerusalem this very day. ³And utter an allegory to the rebellious house and say to them, Thus says the Lord GOD:

Set on the pot, set it on,
  pour in water also;
⁴ put in it the pieces,
  all the good pieces, the thigh and
    the shoulder;
  fill it with choice bones.
⁵ Take the choicest one of the flock,
  pile the logs[a] under it;
  boil its pieces,[b]
  seethe[c] also its bones in it.

⁶Therefore thus says the Lord GOD:
Woe to the bloody city,
  the pot whose rust is in it,
  whose rust has not gone out of it!
Empty it piece by piece,
  making no choice at all.[d]
⁷ For the blood she shed is inside it;
  she placed it on a bare rock;
she did not pour it out on the ground,
  to cover it with earth.
⁸ To rouse my wrath, to take vengeance,
  I have placed the blood she shed
  on a bare rock,
  so that it may not be covered.

NIV

" 'Woe to the city of bloodshed!
  I, too, will pile the wood high.
¹⁰So heap on the wood
  and kindle the fire.
Cook the meat well,
  mixing in the spices;
  and let the bones be charred.
¹¹Then set the empty pot on the coals
  till it becomes hot and its copper glows
so its impurities may be melted
  and its deposit burned away.
¹²It has frustrated all efforts;
  its heavy deposit has not been removed,
  not even by fire.

¹³" 'Now your impurity is lewdness. Because I tried to cleanse you but you would not be cleansed from your impurity, you will not be clean again until my wrath against you has subsided.

¹⁴" 'I the LORD have spoken. The time has come for me to act. I will not hold back; I will not have pity, nor will I relent. You will be judged according to your conduct and your actions, declares the Sovereign LORD.' "

NRSV

⁹Therefore thus says the Lord GOD:
  Woe to the bloody city!
    I will even make the pile great.
¹⁰ Heap up the logs, kindle the fire;
    boil the meat well, mix in the spices,
    let the bones be burned.
¹¹ Stand it empty upon the coals,
    so that it may become hot, its copper glow,
    its filth melt in it, its rust be consumed.
¹² In vain I have wearied myself;ᵃ
    its thick rust does not depart.
    To the fire with its rust!ᵇ
¹³ Yet, when I cleansed you in your filthy
      lewdness,
    you did not become clean from your filth;
  you shall not again be cleansed
    until I have satisfied my fury upon you.
¹⁴I the LORD have spoken; the time is coming, I will act. I will not refrain, I will not spare, I will not relent. According to your ways and your doings I will judge you, says the Lord GOD.

ᵃCn: Meaning of Heb uncertain   ᵇMeaning of Heb uncertain

COMMENTARY

This section consists of introductory material (vv. 1-3a) and a complex poetic judgment oracle (vv. 3b-14). The former begins with a date notice, followed by the word event formula ("the word of the LORD came to me"), Yahweh's direct address to the prophet ("Mortal") and the order that he record the "name" of that very day, an explanation of the day's significance, and God's command that Ezekiel "propound a parable" to the "rebellious house," to which the messenger formula is prefixed. The latter is launched by a metaphorical parable (vv. 3b-5), which gives way to two dissimilar, but now interwoven, interpretations (vv. 6-12). It ends with a direct address to Jerusalem justifying Yahweh's judgment (v. 13) and an expanded closing that states most emphatically the Lord's absolute determination to destroy the city (v. 14).

Yahweh commands Ezekiel to present a parable to the "rebellious house," an epithet for Israel first introduced in 2:5. For the reader, the presence of this pejorative moniker, coupled with the almost relentlessly scathing contents of the prophet's preceding oracles and the initial reference to an infamous date in Israel's history (v. 1), signals more bad news for Ezekiel's audience. The following parable, perhaps a popular ditty sung by cooks preparing a sumptuous meal, is itself devoid of negative elements. With v. 6 (introduced by "therefore," plus the messenger formula, "thus says the Lord GOD" and "Woe to the bloody city!"), however, Ezekiel identifies the cooking pot as "Bloodshed City"—Jerusalem (see 22:2). Just as the pot is contaminated by interior filth (a notion nowhere suggested in vv. 3b-5), so also Jerusalem is contaminated by the blood shed in her (and consequent bloodguilt). Verses 7-8 develop this idea more fully, though in a manner unrelated to Ezekiel's pot metaphor.

A second introduction (v. 9a), identical to that

in v. 6*a*, commences yet another interpretation of the ditty/parable, to which it more closely corresponds. Here, Yahweh assumes the cook's role, amassing a great pile of wood, kindling the fire, and boiling (down) the aromatic stew until nothing but charred bones remain in the pot. Verses 11-12 return to the image, introduced in v. 6, of the filthy copper pot that, at God's command, is placed without contents upon coals until it glows red-hot and its filth (should be) consumed. Yet even this procedure fails to cleanse the cauldron, which is finally consigned to the fire (v. 12*b*). In vv. 13-14, Yahweh addresses Jerusalem directly: God's previous attempts to cleanse her have failed, and she will not be clean again until the Lord has expended divine fury against her. The time is coming; God's mind is made up and will not change, for the judgment is apropos to Jerusalem's ways and misdeeds.

As the preceding summary indicates, Ezekiel's oracle is so complex, and its alternating interpretations of the cooking parable so distinctive, as to suggest that a complex history of composition lies behind the text. A majority opinion regards vv. 3*b*-14 as a conflation of two originally separate oracles: on the one hand, the cooking ditty and its interpretation (vv. 3*b*-5, 9-10); on the other, the filthy pot and Yahweh's resolve to cleanse it (vv. 6-8, 11-12).[758] The conflator of these two oracles was probably Ezekiel himself or members of his "school."[759] Block champions a different view: Verses 1-14 constitute a unified "disputation speech," launched by a popular work song (or, alternatively, Ezekiel's own, *ad hoc* composition) that, like the proverb quoted in 11:3*b* ("this city is the pot, and we are the meat"), assumes theological significance. Both the proverb and the song express the Jerusalemites' sense of security and well-being, grounded in faith that their city is inviolable. Yet in each case, this master of metaphor transforms positive associations into negative ones, a characteristic rhetorical ploy at which he excels.

Ezekiel's twofold rejoinder to the ditty ("thesis") consists of a "dispute" (vv. 6-8), followed by a "counterthesis" (vv. 9-14).[760] Block's identification of elements common to vv. 1-4 and (other) disputation speeches assists our efforts to make sense of the oracle in its final form. But his claim that both rebuttals of the song, the dispute and the counterthesis, clearly answer vv. 3*b*-5 founders. Contrary to his assertion, the "dominant motifs" in the ditty/parable are not the pot and the piled-up firewood (the former becoming the focus of vv. 6-8, the latter of 9-13).[761] They are, rather, the pot and its *contents,* the meat and bones. Verse 6 follows logically upon the cooking song only in the sense that both employ pot imagery. But the overriding concern of vv. 6-8, 11-12—that is, the filth in the pot—is altogether alien to the ditty.

The ancient reader, ignorant of the modern critic's presuppositions and analytical methods, undoubtedly recognizes that within the confines of vv. 6-12, the image of the cooking pot is interpreted along two distinct, but interwoven, lines. Yet he also observes that these verses are unified by shared imagery, themes, and vocabulary. Moreover, many elements of vv. 1-14 echo previous oracles: Jerusalem under siege (v. 2; see also 4:1-3; 5:2; 7:14-15; 17:17; 21:22; 22:17-22); pot/meat imagery (vv. 3*b*-5, 6*b*, 10; see 11:1-12); the command that Ezekiel propound a parable (v. 3; see also 17:2); the "rebellious house" (v. 3; see also 2:5-6; 12:2, 3, 9, 25; 17:12) and "Bloodshed City" (vv. 6, 9; see also 22:2) epithets, as well as the references to bloodshed in Jerusalem (v. 7; see also 22:3-4), to the city's depravity (v. 13; see also 16:27, 43, 58; 22:9, 11; 23:21, 27, 29, 35, 44, 48 [twice], 49), and to Yahweh's refusal to show pity (v. 14; see also 8:18; 9:10). The clustering of these echoing elements confirms the auspicious, climactic nature of this pronouncement of judgment (already insinuated by its association with the date of the onset of Nebuchadrezzar's siege) and suggests that the twinned interpretations of the parable set out only two of the oracle's multi-layered meanings. Davis observes that by replaying earlier themes, Ezekiel invites his readers to enlarge their

758. W. Zimmerli, *Ezekiel 1: A Commentary on the Book of the Prophet Ezekiel, Chapters 1–24,* trans. R. E. Clements, Hermeneia (Philadelphia: Fortress, 1979) 503-6; J. W. Wevers, *Ezekiel,* NCB (London: Nelson, 1969) 188-92; Moshe Greenberg, *Ezekiel 21–37,* AB 22A (Garden City, N.Y.: Doubleday, 1997) 503-6; and Hans F. Fuhs, "Ez 24—überlegungen zu Tradition und Redaktion des Ezechielbuches," in *Ezekiel and His Book,* ed. J. Lust, BETL 74 (Leuven: Leuven University Press, 1986) 266-82.

759. Zimmerli, *Ezekiel 1,* 498, admits either option. Greenberg, *Ezekiel 21–37,* 506, opts for the former.

760. D. I. Block, "Ezekiel's Boiling Cauldron: A Form-Critical Solution to Ezekiel XXIV 1-14," *VT* XLI (1991) 12-37. See also D. I. Block, *The Book of Ezekiel: Chapters 1–24,* NICOT (Grand Rapids: Eerdmans, 1997) 765-98.

761. Block, "Ezekiel's Boiling Cauldron," 19-20.

understanding of his "symbol system," such that they become adept at filling textual gaps and can appreciate more fully its cumulative impact. Interpretation remains an uncertain enterprise, however.[762]

For five years, Ezekiel has relentlessly pursued his God-given commission to function as Yahweh's prophet to the exilic community. His oracles and sign acts have addressed a variety of issues, but none more pressing (or frequent) than the Lord's decision utterly to destroy Jerusalem and its inhabitants—just penalty for a long-lived and ongoing history of cultic, political, and social abominations. The record suggests that Ezekiel's version of Yahweh's word to his times was mightily resisted by members of his audience, who clung tenaciously to the traditional belief that Jerusalem—home to Yahweh's Temple and the Davidic dynasty—was the impregnable object of the Lord's protection. So long as Jerusalem stood, hope persisted that God's punishment would stop short of total annihilation.

The ancient reader, who knows that Nebuchadrezzar's siege of the city ultimately succeeded in bringing about its downfall, recognizes in the date notice of v. 1 a near knock-out punch to that hope. Dates appear rather frequently in the scroll (e.g., 1:1; 8:1; 20:1; 26:1; 29:1), but this one departs from Ezekiel's conventional style both in its wording and in its position within the sentence (in Hebrew, it follows the phrase "[and] the word of the LORD came to me"). The date (January 15, 588, by my reckoning) appears in near-identical form in 2 Kgs 25:1 (see also Jer 39:1; 52:4); critics suggest that its presence in 24:1 was effected by an early addition to the text.[763] From the reader's perspective, of course, Ezekiel's ability precisely to identify the date on which the far-off siege began is but one more confirmation of his status as Yahweh's authentic prophet. God's command that Ezekiel record the "name" of this very day further suggests to the reader that when news of the siege reaches the exiles through some other source, they will be forced to acknowledge the prophet's

veracity, as demonstrated by his early access to (divinely dispensed) information.[764]

Ezekiel's oracle begins when, in obedience to Yahweh's command, he "propounds a parable" (מְשֹׁל...מָשָׁל mĕšōl... māšāl; NRSV, "utter[s] an allegory") to the "rebellious house." In reality, of course, his audience consists only of his fellow exiles. The rhetorical audience, however, embraces all of Israel—the deportees and their compatriots in Judah, as well as late exilic readers. Pointing to the so-called well-digging song of Num 21:17-18, scholars suggest that the prophet's parable is (or is based upon) a secular ditty sung by cooks as they prepared a choice meal (analogous to "Polly Put the Kettle On").[765] The song addresses a single chef, (twice) commanding that he set the pot (הַסִּיר hassîr; here construed as a masc. sing. noun; see Jer 1:13) on its stand (v. 3b; see 2 Kgs 4:38). Having poured in an appropriate quantity of water, he must place in it (the pot, now construed as fem. ["in her"]; see 2 Kgs 4:38) the best cuts of meat—thigh and shoulder—and bones (or "limbs," as in Judg 19:29).[766] Verse 5 further specifies that these top-grade cuts derive from the choicest member of the flock—additional confirmation that this is no ordinary stew. Hebrew "pile the bones" (עֲצָמִים 'ăṣāmîm) is difficult, not only because bones are unsuitable as fuel, but also because in vv. 4b and 5b, the same noun refers to the bones or limbs placed inside the pot. Critics, taking a cue from v. 10, emend the text to הָעֵצִים (hā'ēṣîm), "pieces of wood." Though nothing is said of lighting the logs, the remainder of v. 5 commands that the pot's contents be brought to a vigorous boil (lit., "boil her boilings"; the verb רתח [rātaḥ], "to boil," elsewhere appears in Job 30:27; 41:31).

As noted above, Ezekiel's ditty is devoid of negative elements. Indeed, its language creates a scenario of excitement and anticipation. Nonetheless, the reader suspects that something ominous is afoot, not only because of the contents of vv. 1-3a, but also because Ezekiel's trope (figurative use of

762. Ellen F. Davis, *Swallowing the Scroll: Textuality and the Dynamics of Discourse in Ezekiel's Prophecy*, Bible and Literature 21 (Sheffield: Almond, 1989) 95.

763. So Zimmerli, *Ezekiel 1*, 498-99; Greenberg, *Ezekiel 21–37*, 496.

764. Greenberg proposes that in the original absence of a date in v. 1, the phrases "the name of the day" and "this very day" pointed forward. The day was named by what occurred on it: "The king of Babylon has laid siege to Jerusalem this very day." See Greenberg, *Ezekiel 21–37*, 497.

765. Block, *Ezekiel 1–24*, 770, as suggested by J. B. Taylor, *Ezekiel: An Introduction and Commentary*, TOTC (Downers Grove, Ill.: InterVarsity, 1969) 178.

766. See Greenberg, *Ezekiel 21–37*, 498.

language) immediately stirs thoughts of other stew pots. The prophet has already condemned certain of Jerusalem's officials for identifying themselves as the meat within a protective pot (11:3). In that context he insists that these men's victims are actually the flesh in the cauldron, while they will be removed from it. Micah, an eighth-century BCE Judean prophet, made use of pot/meat imagery roundly to condemn Israel's rulers, portrayed as cannibalistic cooks who prepare and then consume the flesh of their victims (Mic 3:1-3). Ezekiel's original audience, brought on board only at the point of the messenger formula at the end of v. 3a, might have conjectured (against all odds, given the tenor of the prophet's earlier utterances, including 11:1-12) that the following parable concealed some positive message;[767] but no reader of vv. 1-5 in their canonical form can reach that conclusion.

As in 15:6 and 17:19, an initial לכן (*lākēn*, "therefore") introduces the (ostensible) interpretation of the parable. It, in turn, is followed by the messenger formula and a caustic pronouncement of woe upon "Bloodshed City"—a derogatory moniker applied by Nahum, Ezekiel's seventh-century prophetic predecessor, to Nineveh, capital of the Assyrian Empire (Nah 3:1), and subsequently applied to Jerusalem by Ezekiel (22:2). Its reappearance here performs two important functions. On the one hand, it discloses the referent behind Ezekiel's pot. On the other hand, it provides ample motivation for subsequent verses by bringing to the reader's mind the full range of moral, sexual, and cultic atrocities committed within Judah's capital (see, e.g., chap. 22).

Hebrew חלאתה (*hel'ātāh*; from חלא *hālā'*, "be sick," "diseased") is a crux. The NRSV renders it as "rust" (following the LXX ἰός), an attractive option. After all, the poem has just equated the pot with the "bloody city": Just as Jerusalem is filled with blood (and rife with bloodguilt), so also the pot is marred by reddish rust. A problem arises for the reader, however, when v. 11 states more precisely that the pot is made of copper. Copper does not rust; it develops, rather, a green patina. The NIV

translates *hel'ātāh* as "encrusted" (deposit), and this rendering is better suited to later verses. Following Greenberg, I translate the term as "filth."[768] Anticipating vv. 12-13, v. 6a states that the pot's interior filth cannot be dislodged. Verse 6b is especially difficult. Is the meat the pot disgorges "piece by piece" the source of its filth—a pointed confutation of the ditty's assertion that only the best cuts fill the cauldron? Or must the cuts be discarded because they have been contaminated by the already filthy pot? In 11:9, Yahweh threatened to remove Jerusalem's smug officials (the self-identified "meat") from the cooking vessel (their city), in order that they might be judged on "the borders of Israel"—an apparent reference to Riblah (see 6:14; 2 Kgs 25:20-21). Perhaps some such thought is expressed here, as well. The following phrase, "a lot has not fallen on her," is equally puzzling. Cooke conjectures that it refers to the indiscriminate removal of Jerusalem's inhabitants following the final siege; at the time of the first deportation (in 597 BCE), by contrast, lots were cast to determine who would go into exile and who would remain in Judah.[769] More plausible is Block's suggestion that this phrase also refutes the notion that the cauldron's contents are choice cuts—that is, Yahweh's select people. The sacred lot has not fallen on them; they are not "chosen."[770]

Thus far, the interpretation of Ezekiel's parable has diverged considerably from the ditty's contents per se. Verses 7-8, an elaboration on the bloody city accusation, abandon cooking imagery altogether. Jerusalem has placed her blood (i.e., the blood she [her inhabitants] has shed) upon a bare rock. According to Lev 17:13, the blood of animals and birds killed as food was to be poured out upon the ground (see also Deut 12:16, 24; 15:23) and covered with earth (lest it provoke Yahweh's wrath; see also Gen 37:26, where Joseph's brothers contemplate killing him and concealing his blood). According to Gen 4:10, the blood of Abel cries out to Yahweh from the ground for vengeance. Isaiah 26:21 foretells a time when the earth will disclose the blood of the innocent slain. Job entreats the earth not to cover his blood, in

---

767. So Greenberg, *Ezekiel 21–37,* 505. Worthy of note is his caution against a "rush to decode" the parable, such that a retrospective recognition of the ditty's significance is presumed from the outset. Here, Greenberg is, in essence, arguing for the importance of a *sequential* construal of the text.

768. Ibid., 499.
769. G. A. Cooke, *A Critical and Exegetical Commentary on the Book of Ezekiel,* 2 vols., ICC (Edinburgh: T. & T. Clark, 1936) 1:267. See also Zimmerli, *Ezekiel 1,* 501.
770. Block, *Ezekiel 1–24,* 778.

order that it might continually cry out for vindication (Job 16:18). Jerusalem's placing of blood upon bare rock precludes any possibility of its being poured out, absorbed by the ground, and covered with earth (v. 7). But in fact, her flagrant disregard of Israelite law suits perfectly the purposes of Yahweh, who claims the action as God's own: The visible blood stirs divine wrath, inciting the Lord to take vengeance on the city (v. 8).

Verses 9-10, also introduced by an initial *lākēn*, "therefore," followed by the messenger formula and an acerbic pronouncement of woe upon "Bloodshed City" (see v. 6*a*), return to and decode Ezekiel's parable in closer conformity to its content. Verse 9*b* emphatically asserts that Yahweh has assumed the role of the cook in the ditty, piling on logs and (explicitly) kindling the fire and bringing the cauldron's contents to a furious boil until, at last, the pot has boiled dry (the MT's "and anoint the anointing pot" is unintelligible; the LXX reads "and the broth becomes little"),[771] and nothing remains but charred bones. Note the contrast between the bubbling meat and bones in v. 5*b* and the desiccated, scorched bones of v. 10*b*. The divine cook's purpose is the antithesis of the human chef's goal.

Verses 11-12 return to the theme of the filthy pot, first introduced in the difficult v. 6. The contaminated vessel, devoid of contents (v. 11*a;* recall v. 6*b*), is to be placed upon "her" coals (the referent is "pot") and heated until it glows fiery hot. The verb in v. 11*b,* נתך (*nātak*), can be translated in one of two ways. On the one hand, it can mean "to pour out" (so Block, who translates the line, "and its filthiness inside it is poured out").[772] On the other hand, it can mean "to be (s)melted," as in 22:21, where the verb appears in three different forms: "I will gather you and blow upon you with the fire of my wrath, and you shall be *melted* within it. As silver is *melted* in a smelter, so you shall be *melted* in it." In that context, Jerusalem was cast as a smelting furnace into which dross (Israel) was placed and melted (for naught). The latter of these two translation options is preferable. The Hebrew phrase ונתכה בתוכה טמאתה (*wĕnittĕkâ bĕtôkāh ṭum'ātāh*) is more properly rendered, "and her impurity will be X *in her midst*" (cf.

Block's translation, "and its filthiness *inside it* is X"). With this correction, it makes no sense to translate *nātak* as "pour out," since one would not pour the pot's impurity back into it. Moreover, the corresponding verb in the following phrase, "its filth *be consumed*" (תמם *tāmam,* "to be completed, finished"), elsewhere appears in the context of smelting imagery (Jer 6:29, reading with Qere). Hence *tāmam* best parallels *nātak* when the latter also is construed as a metallurgical term. Yahweh's command, then, is that the pot be superheated in an attempt to smelt away the impurity/filth within it.

The first two words of v. 12 (תאנים הלאת *tĕ'ûnîm hel'āt*) defy translation.[773] The NIV conjectures that the pot "has frustrated all efforts"—an apropos thought in the light of the following line, "its filth has not been removed."[774] So read, this verse (excepting its final phrase) becomes an admission that the (s)melting process has failed (see also Jer 6:29). The final phrase, "in fire her filth," has no verb. The NIV reads, "not even by fire," a rendering well-suited to its context. But the NRSV's, "To the fire with its . . ." also is possible, so long as one envisions that the pot, as well as its contamination, are consigned to the fire. If the latter cannot be eliminated by any other means (including smelting), then the entire mess must be engulfed in flames—from the reader's perspective, a presage of the burning of Jerusalem.

With v. 13, Yahweh addresses Jerusalem directly. The first two words of this verse evoke charges lodged against the city in chaps. 16, 22, and 23: Jerusalem's impurity is "depravity" (זמה *zimmâ*), a term Ezekiel uses especially for sexual depravity. The remainder of the verse, in which the verb טהר (*ṭihar,* "to cleanse") thrice appears, further expresses Yahweh's utter frustration at the failure of all attempts to purge Jerusalem of her impurity. It culminates with God's declaration to the city that it will only be clean again after Yahweh's wrath against it has been satisfied (see also 5:13; 16:42; 21:17). Divine resolve is stated most emphatically in v. 14 by means of seven verbs—three expressed positively ("I, Yahweh,

771. See Zimmerli, *Ezekiel 1,* 495; Greenberg, *Ezekiel 21–37,* 501.
772. Block, *Ezekiel 1–24,* 768, 781.

773. Zimmerli, *Ezekiel 1,* 495-96, dismissess them as a scribal error. The NRSV's "in vain I have wearied myself" adopts Ziegler's proposal. See Joseph Ziegler, *Ezechiel,* EB (Würzburg: Echter, 1963) 79. The NIV and Greenberg, *Ezekiel 21–37,* 502, translate, "It [Greenberg, "She"] has frustrated all effort(s)"—i.e., resisted all attempts at cleansing.
774. See Greenberg, *Ezekiel 21–37,* 502.

have spoken"; "It is coming"; "I will carry [it] out"); three formulated as negatives ("I will not hold back"; "I will not pity"; "I will not relent"); and a final positive construction ("I will judge you"), accompanied by Ezekiel's familiar notice that Yahweh's judgment is proportionate to the city's conduct and (wanton) ways. The oracle ends with the closing formula, "says Lord Yahweh."

REFLECTIONS

For five years, Ezekiel has pressed upon his people the unbearable, intractable, and as yet unfulfilled divine word that Jerusalem and its inhabitants are doomed to destruction and death. His prophecies threaten to eviscerate their most foundational and cherished beliefs about what it means to be the covenant people of Yahweh—singled out among the nations, lifted from slavery, sustained in the desert, and gifted with a land of God's own choosing, where a perpetual stream of Davidic kings rule and Yahweh protects both the Temple and the capital city in which it stands. Was the exiles' ongoing resistance to his message mere confirmation of God's judgment that Israel was and always had been a "rebellious house"? Or was theirs a faith so deeply rooted and stalwart that it refused to bend when the nation teetered on the brink of destruction? If the latter was true of even a few of Ezekiel's compatriots, they deserve the respect that he denies them. How might we respond if a self-proclaimed prophet in our midst persisted in flaying to the bones our most revered doctrines and relentlessly condemned the church to death?

In a world where people presupposed that deities controlled the destinies of nations, Ezekiel ascribed to Yahweh the full force of Nebuchadrezzar's army. What matter that the king of Babylon was motivated by empire-building ambitions or that he attributed his victories to Marduk's unparalleled power? When the Lord's strange work was done, Nebuchadrezzar would be judged and cut off. Such was Ezekiel's belief in Yahweh's just and unrivaled reign—a faith so deeply rooted and stalwart that it refused to bend when his nation teetered on the brink of destruction and his own people confuted his attempts to make sense of chaos. He, too, deserves the respect that his audience so often denied him. How else could he respond when his ears were filled with divine words that flayed to the bones Israel's most revered doctrines and relentlessly condemned God's people to death?

Ezekiel's parable, like those of Jesus, shows how ordinary objects and activities can become powerful vehicles for religious teachings. A copper kettle of seething stew discloses Yahweh's burning wrath against people who imagine that they are prime rib in a privileged pot. A woman works yeast into flour and discloses the mysterious, permeating power and growth of the kingdom of God (Matt 13:33; Luke 13:20). In a world enamored of spectacle, revelation is everywhere present, but often overlooked.

Jesus' parable "works," in part, because it suppresses conventional, negative associations with yeast (evil, impurity; see, e.g., Mark 8:15) and foregrounds fresh, positive ones. As noted in the Commentary, Ezekiel excelled at turning conventional traditions and metaphors on their heads in service to a bodacious take on time-worn religious beliefs. In chapters 4–24, his task was overwhelmingly deconstructive. Modern-day, no less than ancient, sequential readers of his book are exhausted by his relentless assaults, though none can deny that in his efforts to be heard, Ezekiel draws from and enriches a variegated stock of beliefs, literary genres, and metaphors. Has his audience made of Jerusalem a sacred vessel? Yahweh sees the intransigent filth within it, even as Jesus perceives that the outwardly clean cup-and-dish Pharisees are filled with greed and self-indulgence (Matt 23:25-26).

Ezekiel confounds his audience's expectations not because he affirms Yahweh's sovereign control of history, but because he insists that at this moment in Israel's history, God's power and will are manifested in the enemy troops surrounding Jerusalem, settling in for a siege. For this prophet, everything depends upon his people's acceptance that Yahweh is God, and God is just.

Modern faith communities might wish to stand with him on those two points, yet question Ezekiel's concomitant, utterly theocentric reading of history. In a world where mighty nations run roughshod over small ones, and the blood of victims falls upon village paths and urban highways, his correlation of events with Yahweh's administration of justice can be dangerous. Yet, to the extent that we take up the task of engaging in dialogue with our religious traditions, accepting his invitation to fix a fresh eye on even our most treasured beliefs, in faith that revelation is everywhere present, if often overlooked, we become Ezekiel's true disciples.

EZEKIEL 24:15-27, "I AM TAKING FROM YOU THE DELIGHT OF YOUR EYES"

OVERVIEW

Ezekiel 24:15-27 brings to a close the scroll's first major section (pronouncements of doom upon Israel/Judah, 4:1–24:27) and consists of two parts. Verses 15-24, introduced by the characteristic word event formula ("The word of the LORD came to me") and direct address to the prophet ("Mortal"), announce that Yahweh intends suddenly "to take away from you [Ezekiel] the delight of your eyes" (v. 16*a*). In the aftermath of this as yet unidentified loss, Ezekiel must forgo the customary rites of mourning (vv. 16*b*-17). Verses 18-20 describe events subsequent to Yahweh's speech: the following morning, the prophet speaks to the people (the words of vv. 16-17?); that evening, his (unnamed) wife dies. The next morning, he carries out God's stipulations. His peculiar behavior evokes a question from fellow exiles ("Will you not tell us what these things mean for us, that you are acting this way?" v. 19); and Ezekiel responds with an oracle of Yahweh (vv. 21-24). Just as God has taken away the delight of his eyes, so also the Lord will profane "my" Temple—the pride of their power, the delight of their eyes, their heart's desire; and their children will fall by the sword. Like Ezekiel, they will foreswear conventional mourning rituals. Hence, the prophet functions as a sign (מופת *môpēt*) to them: As he has done, they will do. Then the exiles will know that "I am Yahweh"—that is, they will recognize and acknowledge behind these tragic events the unparalleled power and sovereignty of their Lord (v. 24*b*).

In vv. 25-27, begun with the (subsection) intro-duction "And you" followed by another direct address ("mortal"), Yahweh informs the prophet that when news of the Temple's destruction and of the deaths of the exiles' relatives arrives (via a survivor), the restriction on his speech (described in 3:26-27) will end. These three verses, whose content differs from that of vv. 15-24, are nonetheless explicitly linked to them by topic (the fall of Jerusalem), as well as by the repetition of "the delight of their eyes" (v. 25; see vv. 16, 21), the reiteration of "sons and daughters" (v. 25; see v. 21), and a second assertion that Ezekiel will be a sign to them (v. 27*b;* see v. 24). This section also closes with the recognition formula: God's ultimate goal is that through these events, the people will come to know that "I am Yahweh."

From the ancient reader's perspective, the date set out in 24:1 (January 15, 588 BCE, by my reckoning, the day Nebuchadrezzar began his eighteen-month siege of Jerusalem) applies to vv. 15-27 as well. Modern critics, however, tend to assign them to a later date, when the city's fall was imminent. The (prose) text poses several conundrums (see below). Premier among its problems (for ancient and modern readers alike, one suspects) is Yahweh's decision suddenly to kill Ezekiel's wife in order that, through his divinely prescribed responses to her death and God's accompanying words, he might confront the exiles with the harsh and excruciating reality of analogous losses pressing in upon them. The personal lives of other prophets—Hosea, Isaiah, Jeremiah—also were penetrated by their ministries. Jeremiah, for example, is forbidden the joys of marriage and children (Jer 16:2). But Ezekiel's experience exceeds all others. That Yahweh would go to this extreme—and the text itself offers no escape from that conclusion, either by labeling the incident an allegory,[775] or by suggesting that Ezekiel perceived the theological significance of his wife's passing only in retrospect—can be construed from two angles. One might say that God could find no more apt vehicle by which to convey both the Lord's and the people's pain over unbearable losses than the death of Ezekiel's beloved spouse. And yet, as Hals fittingly observes, objections arise at precisely this point. For the God of this text, whose decision is announced to the prophet in an abrupt and almost matter-of-fact way, seems shockingly hard-hearted.[776] Could no other strategy have worked as well for the deity who, according to 18:32, has "no pleasure in the death of anyone"? It is little wonder that Hals calls this the

"ugliest of all symbolic acts."[777] Here at least, Paul Joyce remarks, one might anticipate some reference to Yahweh's fondness for Israel. But while the Lord spares no words in describing the people's strong attachment to—indeed, longing for—the Jerusalem Temple, nothing is said of God's affection for the place. Ezekiel's deity is not loving: "neither the root אהב (*ahēb,* 'love') nor the root חסד (*ḥāsad,* 'steadfast love, kindness') is ever used in Ezekiel in connexion with Yahweh."[778]

While vv. 15-24 constitute a signal, if deeply troubling, conclusion to Ezekiel's collection of doom pronouncements, vv. 25-27 point forward to the time when both he and his message will be vindicated. The release from a restriction imposed (according to the canonical text) at the outset of his ministry (3:26-11) marks a new stage in Ezekiel's prophetic career. The burden of that phase is not yet clear, but the reader knows that it is coming.

775. So E. W. Hengstenberg, *Prophecies of the Prophet Ezekiel,* trans. A. C. Murphy and J. G. Murphy (Edinburgh: T. & T. Clark, 1869) 211-12.

776. Ronald M. Hals *Ezekiel,* FOTL 19 (Grand Rapids: Eerdmans, 1988).

777. Ibid., 175.

778. Paul Joyce, *Divine Initiative and Human Response in Ezekiel,* JSOTSup 5 (Sheffield: JSOT, 1989) 100.

Ezekiel 24:15-24, Losses Too Great for Grief

NIV

[15]The word of the LORD came to me: [16]"Son of man, with one blow I am about to take away from you the delight of your eyes. Yet do not lament or weep or shed any tears. [17]Groan quietly; do not mourn for the dead. Keep your turban fastened and your sandals on your feet; do not cover the lower part of your face or eat the customary food ⌊of mourners⌋."

[18]So I spoke to the people in the morning, and in the evening my wife died. The next morning I did as I had been commanded.

[19]Then the people asked me, "Won't you tell us what these things have to do with us?"

[20]So I said to them, "The word of the LORD came to me: [21]Say to the house of Israel, 'This is what the Sovereign LORD says: I am about to desecrate my sanctuary—the stronghold in which you take pride, the delight of your eyes, the object of your affection. The sons and daughters you left

NRSV

[15]The word of the LORD came to me: [16]Mortal, with one blow I am about to take away from you the delight of your eyes; yet you shall not mourn or weep, nor shall your tears run down. [17]Sigh, but not aloud; make no mourning for the dead. Bind on your turban, and put your sandals on your feet; do not cover your upper lip or eat the bread of mourners.*a* [18]So I spoke to the people in the morning, and at evening my wife died. And on the next morning I did as I was commanded.

[19]Then the people said to me, "Will you not tell us what these things mean for us, that you are acting this way?" [20]Then I said to them: The word of the LORD came to me: [21]Say to the house of Israel, Thus says the Lord GOD: I will profane my sanctuary, the pride of your power, the delight of your eyes, and your heart's desire; and your sons and your daughters whom you left behind shall

*aVg Tg: Heb *of men*

behind will fall by the sword. ²²And you will do as I have done. You will not cover the lower part of your face or eat the customary food ˌof mournersˌ ²³You will keep your turbans on your heads and your sandals on your feet. You will not mourn or weep but will waste away because of[a] your sins and groan among yourselves. ²⁴Ezekiel will be a sign to you; you will do just as he has done. When this happens, you will know that I am the Sovereign LORD.'

ª23 Or *away in*

fall by the sword. ²²And you shall do as I have done; you shall not cover your upper lip or eat the bread of mourners.[a] ²³Your turbans shall be on your heads and your sandals on your feet; you shall not mourn or weep, but you shall pine away in your iniquities and groan to one another. ²⁴Thus Ezekiel shall be a sign to you; you shall do just as he has done. When this comes, then you shall know that I am the Lord GOD.

ªVg Tg: Heb *of men*

COMMENTARY

In the Commentary on 4:1–5:17 (see Excursus: "Prophetic Sign Acts," 1143-44), it is noted that the majority of Ezekiel's sign acts appear in chaps. 1–24, where one doom pronouncement follows another and audience resistance runs deep. Like other intermediaries (e.g., Hosea, Isaiah, Jeremiah), he performed these acts in order to convey, in a most profound way, God's messages to his audience. In past centuries, critics tended to regard Ezekiel's actions either as parables or as evidence of some psychological and/or physical ailment. Contemporary scholars continue to question whether the prophet actually carried out all of the sign acts attributed to him. But few doubt the veracity of the present report, which is rooted in an event the exiles could verify.

The sign act account of vv. 15-24 consists of four parts: (1) Yahweh commands Ezekiel to perform an act (vv. 16-17); (2) he recounts its execution (v. 18); (3) the exiles ask for an explanation (v. 19); (4) the sign act is interpreted by means of a divine oracle (ending with the recognition formula, "then you shall know that I am the Lord GOD"). This structure both echoes and innovates upon those of previous sign act accounts. Often in the book, these accounts consist solely of Yahweh's instructions, and nothing is said about their actual performance (see 4:1-3, 4-8; 12:17-20; 21:18-24). Here, by contrast, Ezekiel supplies a brief report of his behavior (see 12:7). Audience reactions appear in three other sign act accounts (12:9; 21:7; 37:18), but in each case, they are incorporated into Yahweh's words. In this passage, Ezekiel quotes his audience's question.

With the advent of Yahweh's word (v. 15), Ezekiel learns that *God* is about to perform a deadly sign act: with a single blow (במגפה *bĕmaggēpâ*), the Lord will take away from the prophet "the delight of your eyes." Elsewhere in Hebrew Scripture, *bĕmaggēpâ* refers to death by plague (Exod 9:14; Num 14:37; 25:8-9; 2 Sam 24:21, 25; Zech 14:12) or on the battlefield (1 Sam 4:17; 2 Sam 18:7). Here, it conveys the notion of sudden death, but says nothing of its proximate physical cause. The Hebrew word מחמד (*maḥmad*, "desire") is based on a root whose verb (חמד *ḥāmad*) can refer to illicit coveting (e.g., Deut 5:21) and to proper enjoyment (e.g., Gen 2:9). In Lam 2:4, Yahweh is said to have killed "all who were pleasing to the eye" (NIV). Verse 16 says nothing of Ezekiel's wife per se. We cannot determine the degree of its ambiguity, for we do not know if the prophet had children or other close relatives living with him in exile. Indeed, we would not know that he was married save for this single text. Its presence piques readers' curiosity and reminds us just how little we know about the details of Ezekiel's life. But the book as a whole, including the present passage, exhibits no interest in biographical data for its own sake.

In ten imperative clauses, Yahweh constrains Ezekiel's response to his impending loss.[779] He is

779. Feldman maintains that as a priest, Ezekiel was forbidden customary mourning rituals as commanded in Lev 10:6. See Emanuel Feldman, *Biblical and Post-Biblical Defilement and Mourning: Law as Theology* (New York: Yeshiva University Press, 1977) 103. However, if such were the norm the people would not have registered surprise at his failure to perform those rituals. Moreover, one cannot simply assume that an exiled, and so inactive, priest would have been constrained by the same laws governing priests in active service within the Temple. See Greenberg, *Ezekiel 21–37*, 509-10.

forbidden to mourn and weep (see Jer 22:18, where expressions of lament appear, and Yahweh proclaims that King Jehoiakim will not be mourned with the words "Alas, lord!" and "Alas, his majesty!"). He must not shed tears, an apparent redundancy not found in the LXX. The Hebrew phrase האנק דם מתים (hēʾānēq dōm mētîm) is difficult. Zimmerli translates "moan in deathly stiffness" (דמם dāmam, "cease to move"; see, e.g., Exod 15:16),[780] an improvement over "groan quietly" (NIV) or the like—renderings Greenberg labels oxymoronic. He suggests that dōm mētîm, "moaning for the dead" was a fixed expression; hence, "groan a moaning for the dead"—a private, isolated expression of grief.[781]

The following phrase prohibits public mourning rituals. Customarily, the bereaved removed their headgear in order that their hair might hang loose and be covered with dirt or ashes. Ezekiel must wear his turban (פאר [pĕʾēr] elsewhere designates the Zadokite priest's headpiece [44:18; see also Exod 39:28], the "hats" worn by Jerusalem's wealthy women [Isa 3:20], and the garland worn by a bridegroom [Isa 61:10]). Instead of removing his sandals to go barefoot (see 2 Sam 15:30), he must put them on. He is forbidden to cover his upper lip, a practice required of lepers in Lev 13:45 and a sign of disgrace in Mic 3:7. Zimmerli, who envisions covering of the entire head down to the upper lip, finds here a very ancient custom by which survivors sought to disguise themselves, lest the ghost of the deceased return and do them harm. The practice continued, even after its "animistic basis" receded.[782] Greenberg, by contrast, suggests that the edges of a cloth wrapped around the head were used to cover the lower portion of the face—the mustache and beard.[783] Finally, Ezekiel must not eat "the bread of men" (v. 17b; see also v. 22). Many commentators emend אנשים (ʾănāšîm), "men," to אונים (ʾônîm), "mourners," taking leḥem ʾônîm (see Hos 9:4) as a technical expression for the meal brought to the bereaved.[784] As Cooke aptly observes, however, it

is difficult to explain why a later scribe would have twice altered the (ostensibly) original and intelligible reading.[785]

According to v. 18a, Ezekiel "spoke to the people in the morning." The phrase exercises critics who tend to regard it either as a continuation of Yahweh's address to Ezekiel (originally written in the imperative: "Speak to the people in the morning")[786] or as a "clumsy addition" that anticipates the prophet's response to the people's query (v. 19) in vv. 20-24.[787] What would Ezekiel have to say at this point in the narrative, when the death has not yet occurred? But Greenberg proposes that he shares with them the (still ambiguous) substance of vv. 16-17. Yahweh employs "the delight of your eyes," rather than the more straightforward "your wife," in v. 16 in order to anchor the subsequent point that the Temple is as precious to the people as Ezekiel's loved one is to him. This point is lost on the exiles, however, unless they know of God's communiqué to the prophet.[788] Verse 18 raises questions concerning the timing of events. Several scenarios are possible. One might suppose that the prophet receives Yahweh's command on one day and speaks to the people on the morning of the next day. That evening, his wife dies, and he carries out God's orders the following morning. This option best fits the testimony of the canonical text. Alternatively, Ezekiel addresses the people on the same morning that the Lord speaks to him. His wife dies that evening, and he carries out Yahweh's instructions the next morning. But if Ezekiel talks to the people just after God has spoken to him, why include the phrase "in the morning" in v. 18a? The temporal notice implies that the prophet speaks to the people on the morning *after* he receives the Lord's announcement/ demand. A third possibility is that his wife dies on the evening of the day that Yahweh speaks to him; the following morning, he speaks to the people and carries out God's command.[789] Critics tend to favor this third reconstruction of events, but at the expense of expunging v. 18a, which is attested

780. Zimmerli, *Ezekiel 1*, 502.

781. Greenberg, *Ezekiel 21–37*, 508.

782. W. Zimmerli, *Ezekiel 1: A Commentary on the Book of the Prophet Ezekiel, Chapters 1–24*, trans. R. E. Clements, Hermeneia (Philadelphia: Fortress, 1979) 506.

783. Moshe Greenberg, *Ezekiel 21–37*, AB 22A (Garden City, N.Y.: Doubleday, 1997) 509.

784. D. I. Block, *The Book of Ezekiel: Chapters 1–24*, NICOT (Grand Rapids: Eerdmans, 1997) 790.

785. G. A. Cooke, *A Critical and Exegetical Commentary on the Book of Ezekiel*, 2 vols., ICC (Edinburgh: T. & T. Clark, 1936) 1:271.

786. Walther Eichrodt, *Ezekiel*, trans. Cosslett Quin, OTL (Philadelphia: Westminster, 1970) 345.

787. Zimmerli, *Ezekiel 1*, 503. See also J. W. Wevers, *Ezekiel*, NCB (London: Nelson, 1969) 192, who regards v. 18a as a misplaced variant on the final clause of the verse.

788. Greenberg, *Ezekiel 21–37*, 513.

789. So Block, *Ezekiel 1–24*, 790.

in all the versions.[790] The ancient reader will opt for the first scenario and, as Greenberg suggests, likely conclude that Ezekiel shares the contents of vv. 16-17 with the people prior to his wife's demise—yet another of several irregularities in this sign act account. On the morning after she dies, then, he carries out Yahweh's orders, but does not speak until the exiles have questioned him concerning his aberrant behavior (v. 19).

Their query is pointedly self-interested: "Will you not tell us what these things mean for us, that you are acting in this way?" (see also 37:18).[791] Ezekiel's account of his response, which *includes* the familiar word event formula ("the word of the LORD came to me"), followed by an imperative ("Say to the house of Israel") and the messenger formula ("Thus says the Lord GOD"), is cast in first-person divine speech. Yahweh will profane Jerusalem's sanctuary, whose significance for Israel is signaled by three appositional epithets. The first, "the pride of your power," foregrounds the people's trust that the Temple, within which God's presence dwells, is inviolable—a sentiment expressed in Mic 3:11*b* ("Surely the LORD is with us! No harm shall come upon us"). The second, "the desire of your eyes," links this oracle to Yahweh's (initially ambiguous) address to the prophet in v. 16. The Temple is "the apple of their eyes." The third, "the longing of your life" (מחמל נפשכם *maḥmal napšĕkem*), also bespeaks the people's deep care for/concern about the Temple. Ezekiel frequently employs חמל (*ḥāmal*) to describe the emotion that Yahweh foreswears in punishing Israel: "My eye will not spare and *I will have no pity* (וגם אני לא אחמול *wĕgam 'ānî lō' 'eḥmôl* see also 7:4, 9; 8:18; 9:10]." Elsewhere, the same verb expresses the compassion of Pharaoh's daughter for the infant Moses (Exod 2:6) and the concern of parents for their children (Mal 3:17). Hence, Greenberg observes, it prepares the way for the following thought, "your sons and your daughters whom you left behind shall fall by the sword."[792] Here, it seems, Yahweh strikes two blows to the heart of the exiles. They will lose not

only the Jerusalem Temple and all it represents within the orthodox theology of their day, but also their offspring. Jeremiah also speaks of a grief so widespread and shattering that customary mourning rituals are eschewed (Jer 16:6-7).

Greenberg cites, by way of analogy, a passage from the ancient Egyptian *Prophecy of Neferti* concerning the collapse of the Old Kingdom: "There is no one who weeps because of death; there is no one who spends the night fasting because of death; (but) a man's heart pursues himself alone. (Disheveled) mourning is no (longer) carried out today, for the heart is completely *separated from* it."[793]

Critics regard vv. 22-23 as a later insertion into Yahweh's oracle, begun with v. 21 and concluded with the recognition formula in v. 24*b*. This judgment rests on the observation that Ezekiel appears abruptly to be speaking for and about himself. The people will do as he has done, disregarding the conventional rituals of mourning. They too will not cover their upper lip or eat bread. (Who might bring it to them, if all are bereaved?) Their turbans will remain on their heads, their sandals upon their feet. They will neither lament nor weep, but (here, the text departs from Ezekiel's own actions in order to cast an aspersion on the people) will "waste away" (NIV; מקק *māqaq,* niphal; lit., "to decay," "rot," "fester") in their iniquities (בעונתיכם *ba'ăwōnōtêkem*) and groan aloud to one another (see Prov 5:11; in 4:17 Yahweh presaged that for lack of bread and water, the besieged inhabitants of Jerusalem "will look at one another in dismay, and waste away under their punishment/iniquity" [עון *'āwōn*]).

The following verse refers to Ezekiel by name (its first appearance since 1:3). Hence, Yahweh reemerges as the speaker, reiterating the assertion of v. 22 that the people will do as the prophet has done. (The ancient reader who construes all of vv. 21-24 as God's words is left with the altogether unanticipated idea that Ezekiel's bereavement and behavior in the human sphere point to the Lord's own in the divine sphere.) When this occurs and grief befalls them, they will be forced to acknowledge the sovereignty of their Lord. (See Reflections at 24:25-27.)

790. So Zimmerli, *Ezekiel 1,* 503. *BHS* suggests that the clause is an addition, but can point to no supporting MS evidence.

791. H. A. Brongers, "Some Remarks on the Biblical Particle *hălo'*," *OTS* 21 (1981) 187, renders "will you not" as "please," an example of the emphatic affirmative.

792. Greenberg, *Ezekiel 21–37,* 510.

793. See Greenberg, *Ezekiel 21–37,* 515.

Ezekiel 24:25-27, A Final Word, a New Phase

NIV

25"And you, son of man, on the day I take away their stronghold, their joy and glory, the delight of their eyes, their heart's desire, and their sons and daughters as well— 26on that day a fugitive will come to tell you the news. 27At that time your mouth will be opened; you will speak with him and will no longer be silent. So you will be a sign to them, and they will know that I am the LORD."

NRSV

25And you, mortal, on the day when I take from them their stronghold, their joy and glory, the delight of their eyes and their heart's affection, and also*a* their sons and their daughters, 26on that day, one who has escaped will come to you to report to you the news. 27On that day your mouth shall be opened to the one who has escaped, and you shall speak and no longer be silent. So you shall be a sign to them; and they shall know that I am the LORD.

*a*Heb lacks *and also*

COMMENTARY

In the last three verses of Ezekiel 24, Yahweh speaks directly to the prophet. Introduced by the subsection formula, "And you," and direct address ("mortal"), the passage echoes v. 21 with its epithets and reference to the exiles' offspring, underscoring yet again the magnitude of their impending losses. On the day that Yahweh executes judgment upon Jerusalem, a survivor will announce the news of its fall. The repeated "on the day"/"on that day" in vv. 25 and 26, respectively, confounds critics, who point out that a survivor could scarcely have made his way to the exiles in Babylonia on the same day that the city fell. An earlier generation of scholars alleviated this difficulty by positing that, contrary to the book's explicit testimony, Ezekiel was residing in a town not far from Jerusalem at the time of its destruction—a "solution" that creates insufferable problems.

Zimmerli, who labels all three verses an appendix, suggests that originally, v. 27 (without "to the one who has escaped") followed v. 25; hence, on the very day of Jerusalem's overthrow, Ezekiel would have been released from the restriction on his speech described in 3:26-27. Verse 26 and the reference to the survivor in v. 27, then, derive from a later editor, who wished to reconcile these verses with 33:21-22, a passage not yet encountered by the sequential reader.[794] The conundrum posed by the canonical text is real enough, but so is the (apparently overriding) concern to juxtapose the city's destruction, the news of its fall, and the opening of Ezekiel's mouth. The ancient reader most likely assumes that vv. 25-27 compress events in service to that larger agenda.[795]

The fulfillment of a predictive prophecy looms large among biblical criteria for distinguishing between true and false intermediaries (see, e.g., Deut 18:21-22). So long as Jersualem stood, Ezekiel's status was open to question, his oracles concerning its demise fair game for refutation, evasion, and rationalization. Verses 25-27 anticipate an end to that state of affairs, when both the prophet and God's word through him are vindicated, and Ezekiel's ministry enters a new phrase, unrestricted by the Lord's early ban upon his acting as arbiter between Yahweh and Israel (see the Commentary on 3:26-27).

794. Zimmerli, *Ezekiel 1,* 508.
795. Greenberg, *Ezekiel 21–37,* 514.

REFLECTIONS

From the outset of his prophetic ministry, Ezekiel has predicted the deaths of thousands of people residing in Jerusalem and throughout Judah. He has spread before his fellow exiles horrific scenes of butchery, of bodies and bones strewn across the countryside, of personified (female) cities mutilated, raped, and slashed with swords. He has portrayed Yahweh as a military commander who orders "his" band of assassins to slaughter "old men, young men and young women, little children and women" (9:6 NRSV), and as an arsonist whose forest fire scorches the faces of everyone in its paths (20:45-48). Ezekiel's God executes justice by execution; and though the prophet asserts from time to time that innocents will be saved (e.g., 9:4), he more frequently speaks of the Lord's decimation of the entire population.

Why, in a book so rife with carnage, does Yahweh's decision to slay Ezekiel's wife, whose name and biography we do not know, stand out as especially troubling? Do we pity her—exiled from her homeland, joined with a man whose harsh ministry took its toll upon them both, cut down in her prime? Do we recognize what her death represents: the ever-present possibility that we or a loved one might be gone in a heartbeat, felled by stroke, or cardiovascular failure, or a highway accident? Does the particularity of her death penetrate the emotional armor we develop as a consequence of hearing about or seeing on television the remains of masses of anonymous victims? At the National Holocaust Memorial in Washington, D.C., each visitor is given a card bearing information about a European Jew whose life was imperiled or lost during World War II, in order that he or she might experience the particularity of tragedy amid a hell too immense to take in whole. Perhaps the death of Ezekiel's wife is so poignant because we can grasp it; suddenly, a beloved person nowhere condemned for any sort of sin (cf. Pelatiah son of Benaiah in 11:13) pays the ultimate price. Yet even more than this is at stake. The text declares without equivocation or apology that Yahweh takes the prophet's wife away from him. Her blood is on God's hands. Who fails to fear the idea that the Lord could simply view this woman as expendable, could slay her in service to a sign act, and then forbid her husband even to accord her the mourning rituals that would have honored her life, acknowledged who she was—in her own right, and for others—and permitted their community to come together in grief, despair, and hope of healing? Who fails to fear a God who could so manipulate human emotions—Ezekiel's and the exiles'—yet remain cooly detached in the process?

A passage like Ezekiel 24 is susceptible to the "run around." We dodge its meaning and head instead for the New Testament, with its God of love and mercy. Alternatively, we claim that though the text says *this,* it really means *that.* Yahweh did not actually kill Ezekiel's wife. She died of natural causes or in some household accident. God then assuaged her husband's grief by giving her death meaning: Ezekiel's loss could be his people's gain if, by his behavior and their openness to instruction ("Will you not tell us what these things mean for us, that you are acting this way?"), they might at last perceive the extremity of their own impending losses, acknowledge their sins, and repent.

The problem with these "remedies," of course, is that neither honors the text, which deserves—indeed, demands—a hearing on its own terms. Ezekiel might never have anticipated that the Lord would root a sign act in the death of his wife. But he everywhere insists that Yahweh controls the full sweep of history, initiating and shaping events according to God's own purposes. In his temple vision (chaps. 8–11), Ezekiel witnesses the sudden death of Pelatiah; and the experience so shakes him that he spontaneously cries aloud, "Ah, Lord GOD! will you make a full end of the remnant of Israel?" (11:13 NRSV)—a rare emotional outburst that puts the lie to caricatures of the prophet as emotionally detached, constitutionally incapable of compassion. There is every reason to believe that he was devastated by his wife's death and that refraining from culturally entrenched, meaningful expressions of grief only exacerbated his pain. But there is no basis on which to argue that he would have denied God's right to conceive and carry out this sign act strategy. Ezekiel can be consistent.

That does not mean Ezekiel was right. Throughout preceding Reflections sections (see esp. the Reflections at 4:1–5:17), I have urged that if we are to take seriously our biblical heritage, we must work both to understand the worldviews of its authors, including their theological presuppositions, *and* to enter into dialogue with them, our discourses informed, for example, by the resources identified in John Wesley's quadrilateral: scripture, tradition, reason, and experience. We are not living in an ancient Near Eastern world, and God does not demand that we think or believe or explain (away) as if we were. An utterly theocentric interpretation of history—which lays responsibility for all events at God's feet and insists that they can be directly correlated with divine favor or punishment—may be woven into the warp and woof of ancient Near Eastern thought. But even the ancients (e.g., Job) challenged it.

Troubling texts like this one are entrées into poignant and important discussions about life and death, about how we can think and speak of God's power, justice, wrath, and love in relationship with creation and each of its creatures. They admit no easy answers, but crucial issues seldom do. Ezekiel 24:15-27 is an invitation to engage in serious talk. Anyone who has lost, or will lose, a loved one needs to participate in the conversation.

ORACLES AGAINST FOREIGN NATIONS AND RULERS

EZEKIEL 25:1-17, ORACLES AGAINST NEIGHBORING FOES

OVERVIEW

In chapter 25, Ezekiel turns from pronouncements of doom against Israel/Judah to a collection of oracles against four of Judah's neighbors/enemies: Ammon (vv. 3*b*-7); Moab (vv. 8-11); Edom (vv. 12-14); and Philistia (vv. 15-17). The order of these oracles has apparently been determined by the geographical locations of the nations addressed. From Israel's perspective, Ammon lay to the east, Moab to the southeast, Edom to the south, and Philistia to the southwest.

Israel shared a history of enmity with each of these four peoples, even as it acknowledged kinship ties with three of them (Ammon, Moab, and Edom). According to Israelite tradition, both the Moabites and the Ammonites were descendants of Lot, Abraham's nephew. Genesis 19:30-38 tells an insulting story about the origins of these two peoples, a "put down" reflective of long-lived hostility: Bereft of eligible mates, Lot's two daughters conspire to get their father drunk and have sexual intercourse with him in order to bear children. The elder daughter names the son born of that union Moab; "he is the ancestor of the Moabites to this day" (Gen 19:37 NRSV). The younger daughter names her son Ben-Ammi, "the ancestor of the Ammonites to this day" (Gen 19:38 NRSV). Israelite tradition also asserts that Esau, Jacob's twin and the first to emerge from Rebekah's womb, was the ancestor of the Edomites. According to Gen 25:22, the two babies were already in conflict in utero.

The feuds between Israel and these nations were largely rooted in territorial disputes. Ammon emerged around the beginning of the Iron Age (c.

1200 BCE). According to biblical tradition, its well-defended boundaries precluded Israelite intrusion as the conquest generation made its way through the Transjordan (Num 21:24). Moses is said to have forbidden the Israelites to harass or engage in warfare with the Ammonites, since their territory was God's gift to Lot's descendants (see Deut 2:19, 37). Yet Josh 13:25 states that "half the land of the Ammonites" (NRSV) was allocated to the tribe of Gad. During the period of the judges, Jephthah waged war with the king of Ammon over contested territory (Judges 11). At King David's command, Joab "ravaged the Ammonites, and besieged Rabbah," their capital (2 Sam 11:1 NRSV). Following Israel's division into two kingdoms, however, the Ammonites reasserted their independence. Over subsequent centuries (c. 922–742 BCE), territorial battles continued (see, e.g., 2 Chr 20:1-23; 27:5). Throughout the seventh century BCE Ammon, like Judah, was a vassal of the Assyrian Empire. But with the latter's decline, the Ammonites gained control of some Israelite territory (see Zeph 2:8-11; Jer 49:1-6). They became Nebuchadrezzar's vassals in return for military assistance against Arab aggressors and, in that capacity, participated in Babylonian-sponsored raids against Judah (2 Kgs 24:2). But representatives of Ammon were among the international envoys who, according to Jer 27:1-3, gathered in Jerusalem during Zedekiah's reign to plot rebellion against their suzerain (Jer 27:3). Ezekiel 21 envisions Nebuchadrezzar at the fork of a road, employing various divinatory techniques in order to determine his next target: Rabbah of the Ammonites or Judah and fortified Jerusalem (21:19-22). Ammon escaped Judah's fate (21:28-29) and for a time remained in open revolt against Babylonia.

Following Jerusalem's destruction in 587 BCE, Nebuchadrezzar appointed a Judean, Gedaliah, governor over Judah. His conciliatory policies stirred the patriotic zeal of Ishmael, a member of Judah's royal family who, perhaps in collaboration with Ammon's king, Baalis, assassinated Gedaliah and the troops at Mizpah (Jer 40:7–41:3). When his rebellion failed, Ishmael was forced to flee to Ammon (Jer 41:15). According to Josephus, Nebuchadrezzar campaigned against Coele-Syria, as well as Moab and Ammon, in 582/81 BCE.[796]

Moab also emerged at the beginning of the Iron Age, prior to Israel's arrival in Transjordan. Its land lay east of the Dead Sea. The northern border of Moab fluctuated with the nation's fortunes. At times it extended as far as just north of the Dead Sea. During periods of weakness, however, it moved south as much as twenty-five miles, to the Arnon River. Its southern boundary was the Zered Brook, with Edom lying to its south. Deuteronomy 2:9 prohibits Israelite intrusion into Moabite territory, also Yahweh's gift to Lot's descendants. According to Josh 13:15-23, however, Moses allotted the land lying north of the Arnon to the Transjordanian tribe of Reuben. Deuteronomy 23:3-6 betrays Israel's extreme animosity toward the Moabites (and Ammonites), excluding these peoples from Yahweh's assembly to the tenth generation, "because they did not meet you with food and water on your journey out of Egypt, and because they hired against you Balaam son of Beor, from Pethor of Mesopotamia, to curse you" (Deut 23:4-5 NRSV; see Numbers 22–25). Judges 3:12-30 attests to Israel's early territorial disputes with Moabites. According to 2 Sam 8:2 (1 Chr 18:2), David conquered them and forced them to pay tribute. In the early ninth century, however, Moab attempted to reassert its independence and to regain territory north of the Arnon River. Success was blocked by Omri, king of northern Israel,

who, according to the ninth-century BCE inscription on the Moabite Stone (discovered in 1868 CE), "humbled Moab many years."[797] Following the death of Ahab, northern Israel's king (869–850 BCE), however, Moab's king Mesha withheld tribute (2 Kgs 3:5). Ahab's son J(eh)oram, assisted by Judah's king Jehoshaphat and the king of Edom, embarked on a retributive campaign, but Moab survived, as signalled in Mesha's proud and hyperbolic claim: "I have triumphed over him and over his house, while Israel hath perished for ever!"[798] During his reign, King Uzziah (c. 783-742) subjected Moab to Judah's control.

In time, Moab also was forced to pay tribute to Assyria. Even more than Ammon, it was weakened by seventh-century Arab invasions (see Isaiah 15–16). Following the Battle of Carchemish in 605 BCE, Moab became a Babylonian vassal. According to 2 Kgs 24:2, Moabites also were among Nebuchadrezzar's agents of punishment when Jehoiakim attempted to rebel against Babylonia. They too sent envoys to Jerusalem to plot against their suzerain (Jer 27:3). After Jerusalem fell, Judean refugees fled to Moab, as well as to Ammon and Edom (Jer 40:11).

The Edomites occupied territory south of the Dead Sea, from the Zered Brook to the Gulf of Aqaba. According to Gen 36:31-39, eight kings ruled Edom before Israel established its monarchy. Saul is credited with defeating Edomite forces (1 Sam 14:47), and 2 Sam 8:13-14 records David's bloody victory over the nation. During Solomon's reign, Edom struggled to regain independence (1 Kgs 11:14-22). Although it remained Judah's vassal during the reign of King Jehoshaphat, it revolted against Jehoram, his son (2 Kgs 8:20-22), and in subsequent years remained a troublesome enemy (see 2 Kgs 14:7, 22; 16:6). Like its neighbors, Edom became an Assyrian vassal. After a century of subservience to that empire, it submitted to the yoke of Babylonia. Jeremiah 27:3 includes Edomite emissaries among those who colluded with Zedekiah to rebel against Nebuchadrezzar. According to certain biblical texts (e.g., Ps 137:7; Lam 4:21; Obad 10-14), Edom took advantage of Judah's demise, gloating over Jerusalem's destruction, looting the city,

---

796. See Josephus *Antiquities of the Jews* 10.9.7.181-82. If his account is accurate—and archaeological evidence suggests that the sedentary population of Ammon was severely diminished around this time—then Nebuchadrezzar's campaign became the Arab invaders' opportunity to seize control of the land.

797. *ANET*, 320.
798. Ibid.

refusing its refugees, and grabbing Judean territory.

Biblical tradition traces the Philistines' origins to Crete, a datum not substantiated by archaeology. Repelled by the Egyptians, these "People of the Sea" settled along the western coastal plain of Palestine, capturing the cities of Ashkelon, Ashdod, Gath, and Gaza and founding Ekron to create an alliance of five city-states (Pentapolis). The Samson saga (Judges 13–15) reflects Israel's enmity toward these competitors for land. According to 1 Sam 4:1-10, Philistine forces engaged Israel at Ebenezer, destroyed Shiloh, and captured the ark of the covenant. An Israelite victory at Mizpah brought some relief (1 Sam 7:7-14); and Saul, Israel's first king, further subdued the Philistines, assisted by his son Jonathan (1 Sam 13:2–14:23). Accounts of David's Philistine wars appear in 2 Sam 5:17-23; 21:15-22. Amos 1:6-8 excoriates the Philistines for wartime attrocities. They continued to trouble Judah during the Assyrian period. In his annals, Sennacherib, king of Assyria (704–681 BCE), claims to have given a strip of Judean territory to Mitinti, king of Ashdod, Padi, king of Ekron, and Sillibel, king of Gaza.[799] Ezekiel 16:27 alludes to this loss (see the Commentary on 16:1-63). After the Assyrian Empire crumbled, the Philistines allied themselves with Egypt and against Babylonia. In 604 BCE, however, Nebuchadrezzar attacked Ashkelon and further snuffed out Philistine hopes of independence by deporting the rulers of Gaza, Ashdod, and Ashkelon. Jeremiah 27 says nothing of Philistine participation in Zedekiah's plot to rebel against Babylonia.

Although the preceding paragraphs provide an overview of Israelite/Judean relations with the four nations condemned in Ezekiel 25, neither past territorial disputes, nor Nebuchadrezzar's enlistment of Ammonite, Moabite, and Edomite troops in punitive raids against Judah, constitutes the focus of Ezekiel's oracles against Israel's neighbors/enemies. Rather, the prophet condemns these peoples because, by disparaging and victimizing Judah in its darkest hour, they impute Yahweh's dominion. Having steadfastly attributed Judah's demise to its just and sovereign Lord, Ezekiel now proclaims the folly of peoples whose mockery demeans God's power and whose vengeance quickens the Lord's desire for revenge. Moshe Greenberg, citing biblical (e.g., Prov 24:17-18) and extra-biblical literature, observes that when one party suffers according to Yahweh's purpose, its misfortune should "put the fear of God" into others who witness it.[800] When Ammon says "Aha!" over Yahweh's profaned sanctuary, Israel's desolate land, and the deportation of its inhabitants (v. 3; see also v. 6); when Moab concludes that "The house of Judah is like all the other nations" (v. 8); when Edom takes vengeance upon the house of Judah (v. 12); and when the Philistines pursue endless hostilities (v. 15), they both insult Israel's deity and undercut Ezekiel's fundamental premise that Judah's destruction is no sign of divine impotence, but terror-inducing testimony to the God whose sovereignty, justice, and wrath extend beyond Israel's borders to include all the nations.

Not one of the nations Ezekiel "addresses" was privy to his words, of course. The import and function of his oracles against the nations lies not in what they said to Israel's foes, but in their significance for his exilic audience and for readers of his scroll. In the aftermath of Jerusalem's destruction, both Israel's election and the power of its God were thrown open to survivors' questions. How could Yahweh allow the city and its Temple to be destroyed, while age-old enemies survived, gloating over and profiting from Judah's demise? Perhaps God had not permitted the catastrophe at all, much less brought it on, but had been defeated by the superior deities of a world-class empire. When Ezekiel "quotes" the Moabites' claim that "the house of Judah is like all the other nations" (v. 8), he echoes the exiles' own frustration and fears, cited in 20:32. In proclaiming that the Lord will personally "execute judgments upon Moab" (and its neighbors), forcing that nation to acknowledge in its own undoing the doing of Israel's Lord ("then they shall know that I am Yahweh," v. 11; see also vv. 7, 14, 17), Ezekiel consoles and emboldens his fellow deportees, asserting Yahweh's unrivalled sovereignty at the moment when it most seems in doubt. The God who brings upon the Judeans' heads punishment for their sins will not brook their enemies' insults.

---

799. Ibid., 288a.

800. Moshe Greenberg, *Ezekiel 21–37,* AB 22A (Garden City, N.Y.: Doubleday, 1997) 525-26.

Ezekiel's oracles against Ammon, Moab, Edom, and Philistia form a collection within the larger collection of oracles against seven foreign nations (those just named, plus Tyre, Sidon, and Egypt) inserted between the proclamation of Jerusalem's impending destruction (24:25-27) and the arrival in Babylonia of news that "the city has fallen" (33:21; see Excursus: "Ezekiel's Oracles Against Foreign Nations and Rulers," 1355-56). Unlike some other of Ezekiel's oracles against the nations, those appearing in chap. 25 are not dated. Their contents reveal, however, that each belongs to the period after the fall of Jerusalem in 586 BCE and presupposes that event.

Ezekiel 25:1-7, Two Oracles Against Ammon

<table>
<tr><td>

NIV

25 The word of the LORD came to me: [2]"Son of man, set your face against the Ammonites and prophesy against them. [3]Say to them, 'Hear the word of the Sovereign LORD. This is what the Sovereign LORD says: Because you said "Aha!" over my sanctuary when it was desecrated and over the land of Israel when it was laid waste and over the people of Judah when they went into exile, [4]therefore I am going to give you to the people of the East as a possession. They will set up their camps and pitch their tents among you; they will eat your fruit and drink your milk. [5]I will turn Rabbah into a pasture for camels and Ammon into a resting place for sheep. Then you will know that I am the LORD. [6]For this is what the Sovereign LORD says: Because you have clapped your hands and stamped your feet, rejoicing with all the malice of your heart against the land of Israel, [7]therefore I will stretch out my hand against you and give you as plunder to the nations. I will cut you off from the nations and exterminate you from the countries. I will destroy you, and you will know that I am the LORD.' "

</td><td>

NRSV

25 The word of the LORD came to me: [2]Mortal, set your face toward the Ammonites and prophesy against them. [3]Say to the Ammonites, Hear the word of the Lord GOD: Thus says the Lord GOD, Because you said, "Aha!" over my sanctuary when it was profaned, and over the land of Israel when it was made desolate, and over the house of Judah when it went into exile; [4]therefore I am handing you over to the people of the east for a possession. They shall set their encampments among you and pitch their tents in your midst; they shall eat your fruit, and they shall drink your milk. [5]I will make Rabbah a pasture for camels and Ammon a fold for flocks. Then you shall know that I am the LORD. [6]For thus says the Lord GOD: Because you have clapped your hands and stamped your feet and rejoiced with all the malice within you against the land of Israel, [7]therefore I have stretched out my hand against you, and will hand you over as plunder to the nations. I will cut you off from the peoples and will make you perish out of the countries; I will destroy you. Then you shall know that I am the LORD.

</td></tr>
</table>

COMMENTARY

Characteristically, the chapter begins with the word event formula (v. 1), followed by Yahweh's direct address to the prophet ("mortal"). The command "set your face toward . . ." is familiar from earlier oracles and sign acts (4:3, 7; 6:2; 13:17; 20:46). The pose is hostile, and Ezekiel's performance of it parallels God's own (14:8; 15:7).

The focus of the prophet's stare is the Ammonites, and he must speak against them, his oracle prefaced by a call to attention ("Hear the word of the Lord GOD," v. 3a) and the messenger formula ("Thus says the Lord GOD," v. 3b). The oracle proper (vv. 3b-5), like the four to follow, takes the form of a three-part prophetic proof saying: an initial statement of the nation's transgression ("Because. . . .") gives way to an announcement of its punishment (introduced by לכן [lākēn, "therefore"]), followed by the recognition formula ("Then you shall know that I am Yahweh," v. 5 b). As so often in Ezekiel, the presence of this third element lends to the previous two a broader agenda. Not only is the offending nation to experience God's judgment, but also through that judgment it will be forced to recognize (acknowledge) Yahweh's powerful self-manifestation in history.[801]

Though Ezekiel is commanded to speak to the Ammonites (lit., "sons of Ammon"), vv. 3b-4 address a feminine singular entity (see the Excursus: "Cities as Females," 1221-25, for the ancient Israelite literary convention of personifying cities—foreign and domestic—and sometimes nations as women). The likely referent is Rabbah (v. 5), Ammon's capital, though it, in turn, can represent the nation as a whole. Because she said "Aha!" an exclamation of malevolent glee (see also 6:11), over God's sanctuary when it was profaned, and over the land of Israel when it was made desolate, and over the "house of Judah" when its population was forced into exile, therefore, Yahweh is handing her over to "the people of the east"—that is, nomads of the Syro-Arabian desert, as a possession.[802] Such nomads, referred to also in Judges 6–8 and Jer 49:28, were renowned for their wisdom (1 Kgs 4:30), but troublesome for their incursions into settled territory.

This text amplifies the substance of Ezekiel's threat against the Ammonites. Because they ("she") expressed malicious delight over Israel's desolate land, their land will be appropriated and plundered. The nomads (who are not specified by tribe) will establish stone-encircled encampments and pitch their tents in Ammon's midst, eating the food that the Ammonites have labored to produce and drinking the milk of their livestock. The reader recalls the covenant curse of Deut 28:33a: "A people whom you do not know shall eat up the fruit of your ground and of all your labors" (NRSV). Such was Israel's experience in the time of the judges. Ammon should expect the same

fate. The threat, "I will make Rabbah a pasture for camels and Ammon a fold for flocks," is part and parcel of a literary cliché by which the destruction of cities and their environs is described as a reduction to desert-like conditions (see, e.g., Isa 7:23-25; 17:2; 27:10; 32:14; Jer 4:26; 12:10-12; 22:6-7; Zeph 2:13-15). Have the Ammonites relished the deportation of Judah's population? Even their capital city will be stripped of its inhabitants. The concluding recognition formula reverts to masculine plural address: "Then you shall know that I am the LORD."

As noted in the Overview, Ezekiel's "proclamation" to the Ammonites is actually directed to his exilic audience. Nothing is said of Judah's restoration; and the "spoils" of God's war against Ammon go to the Arabs, not to Israel. Yet by its insistence that Ammon's ruin will be Yahweh's doing, the prophet reasserts the sovereignty of Israel's God, whose power and authority are manifested in the fates of nations that (mis)perceive Judah's catastrophe as license to express contempt not only for Yahweh's own Temple, but also for the Lord's land and people.

Ezekiel's second oracle against Ammon (vv. 6-7) is linked to the preceding one by a resumptive כי (kî), "for." Like the first, this oracle is introduced by the messenger formula and structured as a three-part prophetic proof saying consisting of a statement of Ammon's transgression (introduced by "because," v. 6); the announcement of its punishment (with initial "therefore," v. 7); and the recognition formula ("Then you shall know that I am Yahweh," v. 7b). Unlike the first, it is consistently directed to a second-person masculine singular entity, perhaps the king of Ammon (who represents his nation). His offense consists of clapping his hands, stamping his feet, and rejoicing wholeheartedly over Israel's calamity. The reader recalls that in 6:11, Yahweh commanded Ezekiel to clap his hands (see 21:14, 17; 22:13), stamp his foot, and say "Aha" at all his people's abominations, thereby embodying God's malevolent glee and satisfaction at venting wrath against a faithless people. What Yahweh can do (and command his prophet to do), however, Israel's enemies can never do with impunity.

The term מחא (māḥā', "to clap"), an Aramaized form, also appears in Isa 55:12 ("all the trees of the field shall clap their hands," NRSV) and Ps

---

801. See W. Zimmerli, "The Word of Divine Self-Manifestation (Proof-Saying): A Prophetic Genre," in *I Am Yahweh,* trans. Douglas W. Stott (Atlanta: John Knox, 1982) 99-110.

802. The phrase "hand . . . over" is at home within Israel's concept of holy war, when Yahweh battles against its enemies. In this instance, however, God does not speak of handing Ammon over to Israel, but to these foreign instruments of divine judgment. See Walther Zimmerli, *Ezekiel 2: A Commentary on the Book of the Prophet Ezekiel, Chapters 25–48,* trans. James D. Martin, Hermeneia (Philadelphia: Fortress, 1983) 13.

98:8 ("Let the floods clap their hands," NRSV). Both of these tropes (figurative uses of language) are situated within hymns of praise to God. But in this context, and conjoined with references to stamped feet and "wholehearted contempt," hand clapping expresses the dark side of joy, which erupts in the face of an enemy's adversity. When Ammon expresses its contemptuous pleasure at Israel's suffering, it belittles not only the people, but also their deity. Therefore (and in the terminology of Israel's holy war tradition; see n. 802), the Lord will stretch out "his" hand against him and give him as plunder (reading with Qere) to the nations (see also 7:21; 23:46; 26:5; 34:8, 22, 28; 36:4). Two parallel clauses further describe

Ammon's fate: Yahweh will cut him off from the peoples and cause him to perish from the lands. A final threat, "I will destroy you," rounds off the punishment section. The following recognition formula functions as it did in v. 5*b*.

If this second oracle lacks the specificity of the first (the punishments are stated in general, stereotypical phrases, without reference to "the people of the east"), it intensifies the attribution of Ammon's fall to Israel's God. Does the nation and/or its king clap his *hands* in delight at Judah's demise? With outstretched *hand,* Yahweh will give him over to the nations. One assumes that they, in turn, will delight at his destruction. (See Reflections at 25:15-17.)

Ezekiel 25:8-11, An Oracle Against Moab

COMMENTARY

Moab, whose eponymous ancestor was, according to Israelite tradition, Lot's son and Ammon's brother, is the object of Yahweh's ire in Ezekiel's third, three-part prophetic proof saying (vv. 8-11). Introduced by the messenger formula, followed by "because," it speaks about, not to, Moab. The reference to Seir (the principle mountain range of Edom; it designates that nation in Gen 32:4; 36:8-9; Num 24:18; Ezekiel 35) in v. 8 is inappropriate and defies explanation (it does not appear in the LXX). Ezekiel will not address Edom until vv. 12-14.

Moab's offense lies in its (ostensible) interpretation of Judah's demise, which Yahweh quotes:

"The house of Judah is like all the other nations." These words may ring a bell in the mind of the ancient reader. When Israel's elders asked Samuel to appoint a king for them, they expressed a desire to be "like other nations." Their request displeased the prophet-judge, and God regarded it as a rejection of their divine ruler (1 Sam 8:4-7). In Ezek 20:32, the Lord emphatically renounces the exiles' latest rebellion—their thought, "Let us be like the nations, like the tribes of the countries, and worship wood and stone." Being "like the nations" is never an option for Israel, a people singled out as Yahweh's possession: "Who is like your people, like Israel?" King David prays. "Is there another nation on earth whose God went to redeem it as a people, and to make a name for himself, doing great and awesome things for them, by driving out before his people nations and their gods?" (2 Sam 7:23 NRSV). Moab's construal of Judah's disaster impugns both Israel's unique election and its deity.

Yahweh's announcement of punishment, initiated with "therefore," is cast in military language. God is opening the flank (כָּתֵף *kātēp,* "shoulder") of Moab, exposing its territory to attack. The Hebrew phrase translated "from the cities, from its cities" is difficult. The LXX lacks "its cities," and both the NRSV and the NIV omit it. The three cities mentioned are located north of the Arnon River, in land Israel regarded as its own. According to Joshua 13, Beth-jeshimoth (Josh 13:20), Baal-meon (Josh 13:17, where it is called by its full name, "Beth-baal-meon"), and Kiriathaim (Josh 13:19) lay within the land allotted to the Transjordanian tribe of Reuben. For that reason, perhaps, Ezekiel refers to them as "the glory of the land." Baal Meon was Moab's possession c. 830 BCE; according to the Moabite Stone inscription, King Mesha "built Baal-meon, making a reservoir in it."[803] By c. 772 BCE,

803. *ANET,* 320b.

it was under Israelite control. But Jeremiah knows both it (28:23) and Kiriathaim (48:1, 23) as Moabite cities.

Despite Israel's long-lived territorial disputes with Moab, Ezekiel's oracle does not promise to give the latter's land to the Israelites. To the contrary, as in the first oracle against Ammon (v. 4), Yahweh will give Moab's land to the people of the east. Ezekiel twice refers to Ammon in the punishment section of his anti-Moab oracle. Both nations will become the nomads' possession. The phrase "Ammon shall be remembered no more among the nations" recalls 21:32, part of an Ezekielian oracle against Ammon which appears, at least in vv. 30-32, to address Nebuchadrezzar. No worse fate could befall a people than to be so thoroughly eradicated that no memory of its existence survived. Yahweh will personally execute judgments upon Moab (v. 11*a*). The concluding recognition formula bears a particular poignancy in the light of Moab's interpretation of Judah's demise. The people who thought that "the house of Judah is like all the other nations" will, through their downfall, be forced to acknowledge Yahweh's devastating role in their own history. (See Reflections at 25:15-17.)

Ezekiel 25:12-14, An Oracle Against Edom

NIV

[12]"This is what the Sovereign LORD says: 'Because Edom took revenge on the house of Judah and became very guilty by doing so, [13]therefore this is what the Sovereign LORD says: I will stretch out my hand against Edom and kill its men and their animals. I will lay it waste, and from Teman to Dedan they will fall by the sword. [14]I will take vengeance on Edom by the hand of my people Israel, and they will deal with Edom in accordance with my anger and my wrath; they will know my vengeance, declares the Sovereign LORD.' "

NRSV

[12]Thus says the Lord GOD: Because Edom acted revengefully against the house of Judah and has grievously offended in taking vengeance upon them, [13]therefore thus says the Lord GOD, I will stretch out my hand against Edom, and cut off from it humans and animals, and I will make it desolate; from Teman even to Dedan they shall fall by the sword. [14]I will lay my vengeance upon Edom by the hand of my people Israel; and they shall act in Edom according to my anger and according to my wrath; and they shall know my vengeance, says the Lord GOD.

COMMENTARY

The Hebrew Bible contains many venomous excoriations of Edom. Psalm 137, a lament over the destruction of Jerusalem, speaks of the Edomites' treachery on the day the city fell:

> Remember, O LORD, against the Edomites
> the day of Jerusalem's fall,
> how they said, "Tear it down! Tear it down!
> Down to its foundations!" (NRSV)

The same theme appears in the book of Obadiah (vv. 10-12), itself an oracle against Edom. These texts, and others, testify to Israel's memory of Edomite mockery and vengeance in the face of Judean catastrophe. Scholars debate the historicity of the biblical witness,[804] but the reader would not.

Ezekiel's oracle against Edom, also a three-part prophetic proof saying, is not addressed *to* that nation. Introduced by the messenger formula, it purports to be Yahweh's words *about* Edom. Key to the oracle are forms of נקם (*nāqam*, "to avenge," "take vengeance"), which appear three times in v. 12 and twice in v. 14.

Edom's transgression is expressed in a single emphatic verse. Because it has acted vengefully against the nation of Judah, committing an irreparable offense in taking vengeance upon them (revenge for territorial battles with Judah and other resentments), therefore Yahweh (note the repetition of the messenger formula within v. 13) will stretch out "his" hand against it (see also v. 7), slaying its population—both human and animal—and rendering it a desolation. Final vengeance is the Lord's! From Teman, an Edomite locality (see Gen 36:15, 42; Jer 49:7, 20; Obadiah 9; Amos 1:12) to Dedan, a territory probably lying beyond Edom's southern frontier (see Gen 10:7; 25:3; Ezek 38:13; Jer 48:7-8 also refers to Teman and Dedan in an anti-Edom oracle), they will fall by the sword. English translation conceals a word-play; the word for "desolation" is חרבה (*ḥorbâ*), and the similar sounding word for "sword" is חרב (*ḥereb*). Verse 14 is startling for its statement that God will exact vengeance "by the hand of my people Israel." How might Israel—defeated and desolate—act as the agent of Yahweh's wrath? If Ezekiel proclaimed these words to his fellow exiles, then they move beyond the current catastrophe to a time when God's people will be reconstituted as a powerful nation.[805] The recognition formula, a modification of the conventional form, asserts that Edom will know (experience) Yahweh's vengeance—an outcome whose certainty is reinforced by the concluding utterance formula, "says the Lord GOD." (See Reflections at 25:15-17.)

---

804. Bartlett disputes biblical charges of Edomite treachery. See J. R. Bartlett, "Edom and the Fall of Jerusalem, 587 B.C.," *PEQ* 114 (1982) 13-24; Dicou accords them greater credibility. See Bert Dicou, *Edom, Israel's Brother and Antagonist: The Role of Edom in Bibilical Prophecy and Story*, JSOTSup 169 (Sheffield: JSOT, 1994).

805. Zimmerli regards v. 14a as a secondary expansion of the original text. See Walther Zimmerli, *Ezekiel 2: A Commentary on the Book of the Prophet Ezekiel, Chapters 25–48*, trans. J. D. Martin, Hermeneia (Philadelphia: Fortress, 1983) 18.

Ezekiel 25:15-17, An Oracle Against Philistia

NIV	NRSV
15"This is what the Sovereign LORD says: 'Because the Philistines acted in vengeance and took revenge with malice in their hearts, and with ancient hostility sought to destroy Judah, 16therefore this is what the Sovereign LORD says: I am about to stretch out my hand against the Philistines, and I will cut off the Kerethites and destroy those remaining along the coast. 17I will	15Thus says the Lord GOD: Because with unending hostilities the Philistines acted in vengeance, and with malice of heart took revenge in destruction; 16therefore thus says the Lord GOD, I will stretch out my hand against the Philistines, cut off the Cherethites, and destroy the rest of the seacoast. 17I will execute great vengeance on them with wrathful punishments.

NIV

carry out great vengeance on them and punish them in my wrath. Then they will know that I am the LORD, when I take vengeance on them.' "

NRSV

Then they shall know that I am the LORD, when I lay my vengeance on them.

COMMENTARY

Ezekiel's proclamation against the Philistines says nothing of a human agent of God's destruction. Like the four preceding oracles, it is cast as a three-part prophetic proof saying, initiated by the messenger formula, with a statement of the offense (introduced by "because"), followed by an announcement of punishment ("therefore . . .") and a concluding recognition formula. In this oracle, also, נקם (nāqam, "to avenge," "take vengeance") is a key term, appearing three times in v. 15 and twice in v. 17. The Philistines, Ezekiel charges, espied in Judah's destruction a moment ripe for revenge, and so acted with heartfelt malice to settle ancient scores. As in v. 13, so also here, "therefore" is followed by a reiteration of the messenger formula just prior to the proclamation of Philistia's punishment. Again the prophet resorts to holy war language to forecast that Yahweh's hand will be stretched out against the Philistines to their destruction. "Cut off the Cherethites" is another play on similar-sounding words: והכרתי את־כרתים (wĕhikrattî 'et-kĕrētîm). "Cherethites" (Cretans) reflects Israel's belief that the Philistines came by sea from Crete (see also Zeph 2:5). Moreover, God will destroy the rest of the seacoast, Philistia's homeland (see also Jer 47:7). Vengeance breeds even greater vengeance. Verse 17a proclaims in no uncertain terms Yahweh's determination to execute wrathful (see v. 14) punishments on them. The concluding recognition formula is expanded by yet another reference to God's vengeance. When the Philistines experience it, they will "know that I am Yahweh"—that is, recognize that Israel's deity is at work in the historical experience of their own demise.

Scholars question whether, in Ezekiel's day, the Philistine nation still existed or was sufficiently strong to take advantage of Judah's misfortunate. As noted in the Overview, Nebuchadrezzar attacked Ashkelon and deported the rulers of Gaza, Ashdod, and Ashkelon in 604 BCE; and Jeremiah 27 says nothing of Philistine participation in Zedekiah's plot to rebel against Babylonia. Perhaps this final oracle, which bears such striking similarities to that against Edom, was added in order to "round out" to seven the number of nations decried in Ezekiel's oracles against the nations.

❖   ❖   ❖   ❖

EXCURSUS: EZEKIEL'S ORACLES AGAINST FOREIGN NATIONS AND RULERS

Like all other prophetic collections (excluding Hosea), the book of Ezekiel contains oracles against foreign nations (and rulers). The bulk of these oracles has been gathered into chaps. 25–32 (an anti-Ammon oracle is found in 21:33-37; another oracle against Edom appears in chap. 35). Consequently, they constitute a middle section between prophecies of judgment against Israel on the one hand (chaps. 1–24) and prophecies of restoration for Israel on the other (chaps. 33–48). An analogous tripartite arrangement appears within the Jerusalem Isaiah corpus (chaps. 13–23 are directed against foreign nations) and the LXX arrangement of Jeremiah. This pattern, Lawrence Boadt observes, should be regarded as a traditional schema: "Because the judgment against Israel invariably involves domination or devastation by her enemies, [her] restoration and salvation requires their fall from arrogant power as an incentive to revived and renewed confidence in Yahweh."[806]

Chapters 25–32 excoriate seven (a symbolic number expressing totality) nations (see Deut 7:1). In addition to pronouncements against Ammon, Moab, Edom, and Philistia, the prophet devotes seven oracles to Tyre/its king, one to Sidon (like Tyre, a Phoenician seaport), and seven to Egypt/Pharaoh. As noted above, the nations addressed in chap. 25 were Israel's nearest neighbors/adversaries. Tyre, a city situated on an island one-half mile off the eastern coast of the Mediterranean Sea, drew Ezekiel's ire not only because of its ability to escape Babylonian aggression, but also because of its pride and prosperity—the latter borne, the prophet charges, of dishonest trade policies. No explicit reason is given for the impending punishment of Sidon; the ancient reader likely assumes that its sins are the same as those of its sister city, Tyre. Finally, Egypt, Judah's treaty partner, is condemned for pride and for its recurring role in inciting nations to rebel against their Babylonian overlord—a strategy that, to Ezekiel's mind, violates Yahweh's world-embracing plan.

Critics have sought to uncover the origins of prophetic oracles against foreign nations and rulers.[807] What were their earliest settings and functions? Do they point to the presence of charismatic prophetic predecessors who, during Israel's pre-monarchical period, employed curses, omens, and judgment oracles in order to justify and encourage Israel's soldiers, and to influence the outcome of their battles? Were they at home within Israelite royal theology/ideology, proclaiming the sovereignty of Jerusalem's kings over all the nations (see, e.g., Psalm 2)? Had they a role in Israel's cultic laments and prayers for national victory? Finally, what was their relationship to international politics as represented, for example, in ancient Near Eastern treaties? These questions, each the focus of ongoing debate, are crucial; yet their immediate relevance for a discussion of Ezekiel's oracles against foreign nations and rulers is limited. By the prophet's day, such oracles were part and parcel of the prophets' repertoire. Ezekiel does not encourage Judah to take up arms; to the contrary, he champions Nebuchadrezzar's martial activity as God's own instrument against his fellow Judeans. Though he everywhere insists upon Yahweh's universal control of history, he does not do so in service to the political aspirations of the Davidic monarchy as it existed in his day. In some cases, his oracles against foreign nations and rulers constitute "good news" for his compatriots; in others, they challenge hopes that an ally, e.g., Egypt, might enable Judah to escape destruction.

Modern readers should recognize that Ezekiel's actual audience for these oracles is his fellow exiles. He does not literally address, for example, Tyre's ruler or Egypt's pharaoh. Rather, his literary creations invite compatriots to particular perceptions of Yahweh's present and future activity in the broader historical arena. Do some deportees suspect that Judah's troubles are the consequence of the weakness of its patron deity? Ezekiel proclaims that Yahweh controls not only its fate, but also the fates of all other nations. Do other peoples revel in Jerusalem's destruction? God will bring calamity upon them as well. Do prideful rulers exalt themselves, as if they were gods? The Lord will shatter their pretense and force them, through defeat and destruction, to acknowledge Yahweh's unrivalled power. These perceptions, though proclaimed in the midst of specific historical contexts, are not bound by their times. The ancient reader is encouraged, chastened, and challenged by them.

---

806. Lawrence Boadt, *Ezekiel's Oracles Against Egypt: A Literary and Philological Study of Ezekiel 29–32,* BibOr 37 (Rome: Pontifical Biblical Institute, 1980) 7.

807. For a review of studies on this theme, see David L. Petersen, "The Oracles Against the Nations: A Form-Critical Analysis," SBLSP 1 (Missoula: Scholars Press, 1975) 39-62.

❖   ❖   ❖   ❖

REFLECTIONS

Ezekiel's oracles against foreign nations, like those of other of Israel's prophets and poets, are deeply imbued with nationalistic fervor. We can understand, of course, that neighboring nations, jockeying for limited land, develop visceral and long-lived animosities. Hungry for prime real estate and revenge, each generation refuels the feud, until resolution seems well-nigh impossible. In such situations, people take up weapons *and* the pen, expressing with the latter a range of sentiments both hopeful and ugly. In a day when moderns increasingly recognize the importance of profound respect and cooperation among the nations inhabiting this tiny planet, however, biblical oracles that suggest that the solution to international conflict is the extermination of one's enemies are troubling indeed.

Ironically, Ezekiel's utterly theocentric interpretation of events, which cuts to the heart of many of Israel's most cherished traditions, here cuts the other way. The same Lord of history who brings down upon Judah's head the consequences of its manifold abominations, acts to punish other nations for their misconstrual of that tragedy. We should recognize in the prophet's affirmation that Yahweh also judges other nations a "pastoral" strategy of sorts. But can the answer to human desire for vengeance and possessions be found in the attribution to God of those same impulses?

Ancient Israel's oracles against foreign nations and rulers are ideological, but they are also profoundly theological. Like the exiles, Ezekiel's God longs for revenge against those nations whose insults and profiteering belittle both Israel and its deity. And while other prophets, Deutero- and Trito-Isaiah in particular, anticipate a future in which the world's nations are converted to Yahwism and live in harmony with—indeed, materially enrich—the Lord's people, Ezekiel shares no such vision.[808]

Precisely the opposite is true. Ezekiel's expectation of universal acknowledgment of Yahweh's sovereignty and power does not include a concomitant expectation that the nations will participate in or benefit from Israel's restoration. Ezekiel's perspective is exclusive, rather than inclusive, of lands and peoples outside the land of Israel.[809] They will come to "know" Yahweh through depopulation (e.g., 21:31-32; 25:13; 26:11; 27:27, 34; 28:23; 29:8, 11; 30:6, 11; 32:12, 15, 20, 22, 24-25), devastation (e.g., 25:5; 26:4-5, 9-10, 12, 14, 19; 29:12a; 30:12), and deportation (e.g., 29:12b; 30:23, 26). But the prophet's oracles against foreign nations and rulers emphasize the *finality* of Yahweh's punishments upon them.

What are we to make of this avenging and wrathful God whose plan for Israel's enemies is largely motivated by self-vindication? We are not surprised that Ezekiel would look to the nations through the lens of Yahweh's unparalleled power and control over history. He has consistently and adamantly read Israel's experience from that perspective, and we cannot imagine that he would ascribe to (the deities of) other nations any ability to thwart that plan. At the same time, however, we are called to struggle with (against?) Ezekiel's notion that the Lord's method of choice for dealing with offending peoples is to wipe them out, so that they are "remembered no more among the nations" (25:10). Christian readers may be tempted to "run around" the prophet's worldview, taking refuge in Paul's mission to the Gentiles. But avoiding difficult biblical texts is no answer. When a prophet—ancient or modern—proclaims, "Thus says the LORD," we are free neither to accept his or her words unreflectively nor to reject them out of hand. In a world where wars continue to be fought in God's name, we are responsible for engaging in difficult conversations and making hard choices. Even as we understand why Ezekiel spoke as he did, we must listen (an active, not a passive, activity) for God's word for our day.

808. Cf. Walther Eichrodt, *Ezekiel*, trans. Cosslett Quin, OTL (Philadelphia: Westminster, 1970) 585-86.
809. See K. P. Darr, "The Wall Around Paradise: Ezekielian Ideas About the Future," *VT* 37 (1987) 271-79.

Ezekiel's oracles against the nations present one side of complex and poignant stories. He has nothing to say about Israel's long-lived hostilities toward its kin/neighbors/enemies. He casts other nations as the "bad guys" and does not acknowledge that both parties (e.g., Israel and Ammon, Israel and Edom) likely did their share to fan the flames of hatred. The desire for possessions has ripped apart many a familial tie. The kinship connection that binds Israel to Ammon, Moab, and especially Edom, reminds us of just how virulent inter-family feuds can be. The history of Jewish and Christian relations warns us of the consequences of placing God on one side or another.

EZEKIEL 26:1–28:19, SEVEN ORACLES AGAINST (THE KING OF) TYRE

Ezekiel 26:1-21, Four Oracles Against Tyre

OVERVIEW

Chapter 26 contains four of Ezekiel's seven oracles against Tyre, a Phoenician city-state situated on an island just off the eastern coast of the Mediterranean Sea. It opens with an incomplete date notice and the word event formula (v. 1), followed by Yahweh's characteristic address to the prophet ("Mortal," v. 2a). The first oracle (vv. 2-6), like the five against Israel's neighbors/enemies in chapter 25, is cast as a three-part prophetic proof saying. The *reason* for Yahweh's future punishment of the city is expressed by means of an (ostensible) quotation of Tyre's greedy and self-satisfied reaction to Jerusalem's fall (v. 2). The *penalty,* presented in language appropriate to Tyre's location "in the midst of the sea" (v. 5), entails God's bringing against Tyre many nations, which will destroy its walls, reduce its island to a bare rock, and devastate its mainland settlements ("daughters"). The concluding recognition formula ("Then they shall know that I am the LORD") articulates the ultimate purpose of God's actions: When Tyre experiences Yahweh's punishments, she will be forced to acknowledge the unrivalled power and sovereignty of Israel's deity.

The second oracle (vv. 7-14) echoes and elaborates upon the first. Beginning with resumptive כִּי (*kî,* "for") and the messenger formula, it tells of Nebuchadrezzar's destruction of Tyre's "daughter-towns" on the mainland (v. 8a), his siege against the city itself (vv. 8b-9), the influx of troops through its breached walls (v. 10) and their slaughter of Tyre's inhabitants (v. 11), looting and further demolition (v. 12), the cessation of music (v. 13), and the reduction of the island to a bare rock (v. 14). Typical of Ezekielian oracles against foreign nations, v. 14a emphasizes the finality of Yahweh's punishment.

The third oracle, initiated with a resumptive messenger formula, speaks of the effect of Tyre's fall upon the rulers of the coastlands, her trading partners. A description of their mourning rituals (vv. 15-16) is followed by a poetic lament in vv. 17-18. Finally, vv. 19-21, initiated by a supplemental *kî* and the messenger formula (so also vv. 7-14), describe Tyre's descent to the "Pit" or netherworld. This oracle also stresses the once-and-for-all nature of God's judgment: Tyre "will never be found again" (v. 21b).

As the summary indicates, these four oracles are arranged in logical order: Yahweh's reason for punishing Tyre appears already in v. 2 (when God quotes Tyre's own words; see also 25:8) and is presupposed in the second, third, and fourth oracles. The expanded description of the city's destruction in vv. 7-14 (cf. vv. 4-6a) occasions the mournful actions and lamentation of "the princes of the sea" in vv. 15-18; and the chapter concludes with the climactic, imaginative descent of Tyre to the netherworld, where ancient people live among "primeval ruins" (vv. 19-21). Moreover, verbal links (words and phrases) and themes (e.g., descent) conjoin the prophecies. Hence, from the reader's perspective, the juxtaposed oracles are interrelated and together create a sort of narrative "plot" (analogous to that produced by the sequence of "sword" oracles in chap. 21).

These observations notwithstanding, modern critics tend to deny Ezekiel the bulk of chapter 26. Walther Zimmerli, for example, attributes only vv. 2-6 (without the expansions in vv. 5*b*-6) to the prophet. Verses 7-14 constitute a later "exposition" of the original oracle, and both vv. 15-18 and vv. 19-21 are subsequent additions. While the basic oracle was composed close to the time of Jerusalem's fall in 587 BCE, vv. 7-14 derive from the period of Nebuchadrezzar's thirteen year siege of Tyre (see below). The third and fourth oracles also reflect that period and betray the influence of 27:28-36 and 32:17-32, respectively. The chapter attained its final form prior to April 26, 571 BCE, the date on which Ezekiel issued an oracle acknowledging Nebuchadrezzar's failure to destroy Tyre and promising him Egypt as compensation (29:17-20). Hence, Zimmerli attributes vv. 7-21 to Ezekiel's "school."[810] Hals, by contrast, better explains the resemblances between vv. 2-6 and vv. 7-14, between vv. 15-18 and 27:28-36, and between vv. 19-21 and 32:17-32 on the basis of the prophet's resort to stereotypical language—customary words and phrases associated with particular and recurring themes: how cities are besieged, mourning rituals, the descent to the underworld.[811] Greenberg acknowledges that the chapter likely took shape over time, but claims it for Ezekiel who, having composed an initial, brief oracle, returned to it "again and again," augmenting the text in light of subsequent events.[812] The late exilic sequential reader, presupposing Ezekiel's ability to foresee the city's fate already in 587 BCE (v. 1), might well imagine that he uttered all four oracles on a single occasion. If the reader knows that the Babylonian assault against Tyre failed to destroy the island fortress, however, that knowledge creates a problem (nonfulfillment of a prophetic prediction) that is not "resolved" until he has read 29:17-20.

810. Walther Zimmerli, *Ezekiel 2: A Commentary on the Book of the Prophet Ezekiel, Chapters 25–48,* trans. J. D. Martin, Hermeneia (Philadelphia: Fortress, 1983) 33-40.

811. Ronald M. Hals, *Ezekiel,* FOTL 19 (Grand Rapids: Eerdmans, 1989).

812. Moshe Greenberg, *Ezekiel 21–37,* AB 22A (Garden City, N.Y.: Doubleday, 1997) 544.

❖   ❖   ❖   ❖

EXCURSUS: TYRE "IN THE HEART OF THE SEAS"

In chapter 25, each of Ezekiel's five oracles against Israel's nearest neighbors and long-lived foes is brief. Tyre and Israel/Judah were not bitter adversaries, yet Ezekiel's scroll devotes some seventy-six verses to oracles against Tyre and its king. (Other oracles against Tyre appear in Amos 1:9-10; Isa 23:1-18; Joel 3:4-8; Zech 9:2-4; Jer 25:22; 27:3; 47:4). How are we to explain his deep hostility toward the island fortress? In order to answer this question, we must learn something of Tyre's history and relations with the people of Israel, of the latter's stereotypical ideas and associations with the former, and of Ezekiel's theological presuppositions concerning God's plan for other nations.

A BRIEF HISTORY OF THE CITY-STATE

In modern times, Tyre is known by its Arab name, Ṣūr. In ancient days, however, its name was Ṣôr, "Rock"—a fitting epithet for a Phoenician city located on a rocky island approximately one-half mile off the eastern coast of the Mediterranean and approximately twenty-five miles south of Sidon. In Assyrian annals, the city is called Sur-ri. "Tyre" derives from the Greek "Tyros."

The Phoenician mainland was squeezed between the mountains to its east and the Mediterranean Sea to the west. But its shores afforded some superb harbors, from which the Phoenicians set sail and conducted a thriving maritime trade. Tyre's natural harbor, situated north of the city, was called "Sidonian" because it was aligned toward Sidon. A second harbor, called "Egyptian" because it faced toward Africa, was built by the ninth-century BCE King Ithobaal (or Ethbaal) I. The two harbors were linked by a canal traversing the city. The contemporary adage "location is everything" was true for Tyre. Surrounded by the sea, it survived both Assyrian and Babylonian attempts to destroy it. At the same time, its locale rendered this city of about 30,000 inhabitants extremely dependent upon its mainland territories and cities for drinking water, agricultural products, livestock, and timber. Without those necessities, the city could not survive for long. On more than one occasion, blockades brought Tyre to its knees.

While the four nations Ezekiel condemns in chapter 25 emerged at approximately the same time as Israel, the city-state of Tyre was much older, perhaps dating back to the nineteenth century BCE. Its "golden age," however, began with the reign of Hiram I (969–936 BCE). According to legend, the city was established on rocks coupled by the roots of a sacred olive tree. But Tyrian sources credit Hiram I with conjoining two original islands in order to enlarge the city, as well as rebuilding its Sidonian harbor, adding massive shipyards, and constructing three major temples (to Melqart, Astarte, and Baal Shamen, respectively), the royal palace, etc.[813] The temple to Melqart, guardian of the city, was especially renowned for its two great pillars. (According to the classical historian Herodotus, one was made of pure gold, the other of emerald.) Old Testament readers know of Hiram I's friendship with King David, who made use of cedars and craftsmen sent from Tyre to build his palace (2 Sam 5:11), and of the commercial treaty Hiram signed with Solomon (1 Kgs 5:1-12). In exchange for building materials and technical expertise for the construction of Yahweh's Temple, Solomon provided Tyre with wheat and fine oil. The two kings also engaged in a naval partnership. At Hiram's initiative, they built a merchant fleet at Eziongeber on the Red Sea (1 Kgs 9:26). These were the famous "ships of Tarshish" (see, e.g., Isa 2:16; 1 Kgs 10:22, 29), which set sail every three years for Ophir and returned with gold, silver, precious stones, and ivory.[814] Their alliance guaranteed Tyre access to mainland trade routes leading to Syria, Mesopotamia, and Arabia. These positive relations profited both Tyre and Israel.

The ninth-century BCE king of Tyre, Ithobaal (or Ethbaal) I (887–856 BCE), was, as noted above, responsible for the construction of the city's impressive walls and its "Egyptian" seaport. He sought to consolidate political and trade relationships with mainland neighbors, in part, through marriage alliances. His daughter, the nefarious Jezebel—a zealous devotée of Baal—was wed to Israel's King Ahab (869–850 BCE; see 1 Kgs 16:31). During the reigns of Ithobaal and his successors, Tyre extended its mainland frontiers as never before.[815]

During the ninth century BCE, the ambitious Assyrian Empire sent its armies across northern Syria, imperiling Tyrian trade in the region. In order to protect their economic interests, Phoenician cities, including Tyre, were forced to pay tribute. Tyre paid to Ashur-nasir-apal II (884–860 BCE) gold, silver, tin, linen, monkeys, and wooden and ivory chests. Shalmaneser II (859–825 BCE) exacted gold, silver, bronze, lead, purple wool, ivory, and vessels. Adad-nirari II (811–784 BCE) demanded huge quantitites of iron, ivory, and purple cloth.[816] At the same time, the expansion of Assyria's empire brought to Tyre new opportunities for trade with Mesopotamia. Not until the middle of the eighth century did Assyria's king, Tiglath-pileser III (745–727 BCE), actually wage war on Phoenicia, turning part of its territory into an Assyrian province. Tyre's king, Hiram II (739–730 BCE), joined the king of Aram-Damascus in an anti-

---

813. Maria Eugenia Aubet, *The Phoenicians and the West: Politics, Colonies and Trade,* trans. Mary Turton (Cambridge: Cambridge University Press, 1993) 27.
814. Ibid., 36.
815. Ibid., 41.
816. Ibid., 46.

Assyrian coalition and paid for his folly by losing additional mainland territory, including Arvad and Byblos. Moreover, Tiglath-pileser stationed inspectors and customs officials in Tyre's ports and demanded of its king, Mattan II (730–729 BCE), an unparalleled tribute of one hundred and fifty talents of gold. Still, the city-state was permitted to continue its flourishing trade, upon which the Assyrians also relied.

The anti-Assyrian policies of Tyre's King Luli (729–694 BCE) had grave repercussions. For five years, Shalmaneser V blockaded the island, cutting off its water supply and creating severe shortages. Not content simply to annex territory, Sargon II (721–705 BCE) embarked on a campaign of destruction and mass deportation in Phoenicia and Israel, though he too could not capture Tyre. In 701 BCE, after an unsuccessful rebellion against Sennacherib (704–681 BCE), Luli was forced to flee to Cyprus. Tyre lost most of its remaining mainland territories, including Usu and Sidon. Esarhaddon (680–669 BCE) boasted of defeating the city: "I conquered Tyre which lies in the middle of the sea; from its king Baal, who trusted in Tirhakah king of Cush, I took away all his cities and his possessions."[817] A fragmentary text makes a more modest claim, however: "In the course of my campaign I threw up earthworks against Baal king of Tyre who had put his trust in his friend Tirhakah king of Cush, had thrown off the yoke of Assur my lord and had answered me insolently; I cut off bread and water, their means of subsistence."[818] By this more subdued account, the island fortress survived, though Esarhaddon, with typical "humility," says of Baal I (680–640 BCE): "The splendor of my lordship overwhelmed him . . . and he bowed down and implored me as his lord."[819] Esarhaddon's treaty with Baal I permitted Tyre to trade with the north and the west (though not with Egypt), but placed Assyrian deputies within the city and imposed tolls upon Tyrians who entered seaports under the empire's control.[820] Among the curses leveled against Tyre should it abrogate its treaty obligations, we read the following: "May Baal Shamaim, Baal Malagêc and Baal Saphon raise an evil wind against your ships to undo their moorings and tear out their mooring pole, may a strong wave sink them in the sea and a violent tide [rise] against you."[821] Ashurbanapal's subsequent blockade of Tyre (663 BCE) further weakened the city. By about 640 BCE, all of its mainland territory had become an Assyrian province.

After the Battle of Carchemish in 605 BCE, Tyre was forced to submit to Babylonia. Jeremiah 27:3 reports that Tyrian envoys came to Jerusalem, along with other of Judah's neighbors, to plot a rebellion against their overlord during Zedekiah's reign (594/93 BCE; see Jer 27:3). Thanks to its island setting, the city escaped Jerusalem's fate. But Josephus tells us that soon afterward, Nebuchadrezzar began a thirteen year siege of the city (585–572 BCE).[822] Tyre survived, but Nebuchadrezzar deported its king, Ithobaal III. Following the reign of his successor, Baal II, who died in 564 BCE, the city was governed first by Babylonian, and later by Persian, administrative officials.[823] Alexander the Great was able finally to conquer the fortress (in 332 BCE) by building a causeway from the mainland to the island. After a seven-month siege, the city capitulated. Some thirty thousand inhabitants were sold into slavery. Over subsequent centuries, alluvial deposits made of Alexander's mole a permanent peninsula linking Tyre to the mainland.

EZEKIEL'S ENMITY TOWARD TYRE

Biblical oracles against Tyre tend to criticize the city for its pride and possibly betray a bias against commercialism (spawned, perhaps, by jealousy). Isaiah 23:7 portrays "her" as a peripatetic

817. Riekele Borger, *Die Inschriften Asarhaddons, Königs von Assyrien,* AFOB 9 (Graz: Im Selbstverlag des Herausgebers, 1956) 86. See also Zimmerli, *Ezekiel 2,* 23.

818. Borger, *Die Inschriften Asarhaddons,* 112.

819. *ANET,* 291a.

820. See "Esarhaddon's Treaty with Baal, King of Tyre," in Simo Parpola and Kazuko Watanabe, eds., *Neo-Assyrian Treaties and Loyalty Oaths,* SAA 2 (Helsinki: Helsinki University Press, 1988) 24-27.

821. Ibid., 27.

822. See Josephus *Antiquities of the Jews* 10.11.1.

823. Aubet, *The Phoenicians and the West,* 49.

woman bent on colonization and the establishment of far-flung trade routes. Isaiah 23:8 extols her glory, the better to savor Yahweh's ultimate control of this wealthy, powerful, and haughty queen. The mostly prose conclusion of Isaiah 23 predicts that Tyre will be "forgotten" for seventy years, a single lifespan. Isaiah 23:15-16 then avers that at the end of that period, the city's situation will become that of an aging harlot. In this "trollop's tune," Tyre, the "forgotten" prostitute, is encouraged to play the harp while walking the streets. Apparently Tyre is being encouraged to leave retirement and attract new customers.[824] Tyre will be visited by Yahweh and will resume "intercourse" with the nations. With the assertion that Tyre's earnings, a prostitute's pay, will be dedicated to Yahweh, the final blow falls. The unfortunate consequence is that Yahweh and Israel become Tyre's pimps.[825]

In the course of Ezekiel's seven oracles against Tyre, he too will accuse the city and its king of hubris and excessive commercialism (though his use of female imagery falls far short of Isaiah's imaginative tropes). Moreover, 26:2-6, the first of his oracles against the city, condemns Tyre for perceiving in Jerusalem's destruction an opportunity further to line its own pockets. But Zimmerli is correct, I think, when he points to a broader, theological basis for the prophet's hostility. For Ezekiel, Babylon was Yahweh's instrument of judgment against Judah. In 587 BCE not only Jerusalem, but also Egypt and Tyre, were rebelling against Nebuchadrezzar. Jerusalem fell; Egypt and Tyre did not. Their ability to withstand Babylonian assault ran counter to Ezekiel's understanding of God's plan for the nations. Hence, both Tyre and Egypt were the objects of his scorn, their fates of crucial and ongoing concern.[826] Ezekiel's latest dated words (29:18-21) concern Yahweh's decision to "give the land of Egypt to King Nebuchadrezzar of Babylon" (29:19*a*) as compensation for his inability to destroy Tyre. In fact, Nebuchadrezzar was ultimately incapable of felling either foe.

824. K. P. Darr, "Ezekiel's Justifications of God: Teaching Troubling Texts," *JSOT* 55 (1992)14. Julie Galambush, *Jerusalem in the Book of Ezekiel: The City as Yahweh's Wife,* SBLDS 130 (Atlanta: Scholars Press, 1992) 39.
825. K. P. Darr, *Isaiah's Vision and the Family of God* (Louisville: Westminster John Knox, 1994) 156-57.
826. Zimmerli, *Ezekiel 2,* 24.

❖   ❖   ❖   ❖

Ezekiel 26:1-6, Introduction

NIV

26 In the eleventh year, on the first day of the month, the word of the LORD came to me: [2]"Son of man, because Tyre has said of Jerusalem, 'Aha! The gate to the nations is broken, and its doors have swung open to me; now that she lies in ruins I will prosper,' [3]therefore this is what the Sovereign LORD says: I am against you, O Tyre, and I will bring many nations against you, like the sea casting up its waves. [4]They will destroy the walls of Tyre and pull down her towers; I will scrape away her rubble and make her a bare rock. [5]Out in the sea she will become a place to spread fishnets, for I have spoken, declares the Sovereign LORD. She will become plunder for the nations,

NRSV

26 In the eleventh year, on the first day of the month, the word of the LORD came to me: [2]Mortal, because Tyre said concerning Jerusalem, "Aha, broken is the gateway of the peoples; it has swung open to me; I shall be replenished, now that it is wasted," [3]therefore, thus says the Lord GOD: See, I am against you, O Tyre! I will hurl many nations against you, as the sea hurls its waves. [4]They shall destroy the walls of Tyre and break down its towers. I will scrape its soil from it and make it a bare rock.

NIV

⁶and her settlements on the mainland will be ravaged by the sword. Then they will know that I am the LORD.

NRSV

⁵ It shall become, in the midst of the sea,
    a place for spreading nets.
I have spoken, says the Lord GOD.
    It shall become plunder for the nations,
⁶   and its daughter-towns in the country
        shall be killed by the sword.
Then they shall know that I am the LORD.

COMMENTARY

Ezekiel's initial oracle against Tyre takes the form of a three-part prophetic proof saying consisting of (1) a statement of Tyre's offense (begun with "because"; see 25:3, 8, 12, 15); (2) an announcement of its punishment (introduced by a transitional "therefore" [לכן *lākēn*]; see 25:4, 7, 9, 13, 16), plus the messenger formula ("thus says the Lord GOD"; see 25:13, 16); and (3) a concluding recognition formula, "Then they shall know that I am the LORD" (v. 6*b;* see 25:5, 7, 11, 14 [variant form], 17). The date prefixed to the word event formula in v. 1 is incomplete. Though it specifies the year (the eleventh of Jehoiachin's exile, i.e., spring 587 to spring 586 BCE) and the day ("the first of the month"), it fails to identify the month (cf. 24:1). In v. 2, the words attributed to Tyre presuppose Jerusalem's destruction in 586 BCE. According to 33:21, however, word of the city's fall did not reach the Babylonian exiles until the tenth month of the twelfth year (January 585 BCE). Scholars have "resolved" the conundrum in various ways.[827] The ancient reader might suppose that the Tyrians, by virtue of their outstretched presence in seaports and along mainland trade routes, learned of Jerusalem's fate before word reached the exilic community, and that Ezekiel (whose awareness of far-off phenomena was established already, e.g., in chaps. 8–11) was able quickly to convey Yahweh's punitive response to their reaction.

As noted in the Overview, Ezekiel's first oracle against Tyre bears striking resemblances to the five oracles against Israel's neighboring states in chapter 25. Here, as there, Tyre's offense lies in its response to Jerusalem's calamity. Like Ammon, she has exclaimed "Aha!" an expression of malicious glee. (On the personification of cities as women, see Excursus: "Cities as Females," 1221-25). Her ostensible delight springs from the realization that the destruction of a competing trade center spells additional business and profit for herself. The phrase "the doors of the peoples" is best construed as an epithet for Jerusalem, one that acknowledges its commercial and political importance.[828] We cannot know, unfortunately, whether that moniker was actually in use in Ezekiel's day, or was coined by him. (A third option views the phrase as an *ad hoc* creation of the Tyrians.) In any event, Tyre imagines that Jerusalem's broken gateway has swung open in her direction; its commerce and influence will accrue to her.

Unlike Ammon, Tyre is not depicted as relishing the profanation of Yahweh's Temple, the desolation of Judah's territory, or the deportation of its population. Unlike Moab, she is not accused of questioning Judah's uniqueness as the elect people of Yahweh. Unlike Edom and Philistia, she is not charged with seizing the moment of Judah's destruction to exercise military vengeance against it. Tyre played no role in Israel's/Judah's fierce and ongoing territorial disputes with its nearest neighbors. Yet her crime, a "calculating and selfish mockery,"[829] lays bare Tyre's failure both to stand in awe of Yahweh's sovereign power, as evinced in judgment upon God's own people, and to recognize the appropriate implications of that judgment

---

827. See the various solutions offered in J. W. Wevers, *Ezekiel*, NCB (London: Nelson, 1969) 200; Zimmerli, *Ezekiel 2*, 33; and Greenberg, *Ezekiel 21–37*, 529.

828. On עמי (*'ammî*) as "city," "fortress," see H. J. Van Dijk, *Ezekiel's Prophecy on Tyre (Ez. 26, 1–28, 19): A New Approach*, BibOr 20 (Rome: Pontifical Biblical Institute, 1968) 4-8.

829. Walther Zimmerli, *Ezekiel 2: A Commentary on the Book of the Prophet Ezekiel, Chapters 25–48*, trans. J. D. Martin, Hermeneia (Philadelphia: Fortress, 1983) 34.

for herself and for the other nations of the world. She views Judah's demise through profiteering eyes.

Ezekiel's God will not permit such greed and self-satisfaction to go unanswered. Hence v. 3, with its initial "therefore" followed by the messenger formula, announces Yahweh's hostility (note the "challenge to a duel" formula, "I am against you"; see also 21:3) and initiates a scenario of judgment in the form of attacking enemy troops, reduction of the island to bare rock, plunder, and the destruction of her "daughter-towns," the mainland settlements so vital to Tyre's survival. The description of the approach of great nations is well-suited to Tyre's locale: Yahweh will hurl them against her "as the sea hurls it waves" (v. 3).[830] Similar imagery appears in Jer 46:7-8 (where the Egyptian army is described as "rising like the Nile, like rivers whose waters surge") and 51:42 (a threat against Babylon).

These foes will destroy Tyre's walls and break down its towers. The earliest known representation of the city, a bas-relief on the bronze gates at Balawat (mid-ninth century BCE) depicts Tyre on its island and surrounded by a wall with five towers at regular intervals.[831] The second-century CE philosopher and historian Arian reports that on its eastern side, Tyre's walls reached a height of 45 meters, approximately one hundred and forty-eight feet.[832] Yahweh, either personally or through these human agents, will scrape off its rubble, reducing the island to a bare rock (see also 26:14; 24:7-8, of Jerusalem).

Scoured of every trace of human habitation, Tyre will become "a place for spreading nets."[833] The image presents a devastating antithesis to the bustling commerce of Tyre's glory days. Ezekiel will return to this image much later in his scroll when, in an oracle of restoration concerning Israel's land, he speaks of the future transformation of the Dead Sea, such that its waters team with "a great many kinds" of fish, "like the fish of the Great Sea," the Mediterranean. In that context, the announcement that a flourishing fishing industry will result in fishermen spreading out their nets to dry them "from En-gedi to En-eglaim" (probably sites on the eastern and western shores of the Dead Sea, respectively) is good news, an example of the paradisiacal conditions Israel will enjoy when Yahweh restores it to its land. Here, it describes Tyre's destruction.

Verse 5a ends with a conclusion formula that underscores the divine origin of Ezekiel's words: "I have spoken, says the Lord GOD." Yet the oracle, in its final form, does not end at that point. Verse 5b "backtracks," as it were, to refer to the plundering of Tyre, while v. 6a speaks of the destruction of its mainland settlements. The latter is described by means of a conventional (not "dead") metaphor that casts a city's surrounding settlements as her "daughters" (see also 16:27, 46). Hence, to kill Tyre's daughters by the sword is, in one sense, to destroy those settlements. But Ezekiel's trope (figurative use of language) can also be read literally, since the devastation of towns often entailed the slaughter of their inhabitants as well. Verse 6a, in effect, gives readers two thoughts in one. Polyvalence is characteristic of poetry, and critics should not insist that one construal cancels out all others.[834]

The concluding recognition formula, which appears only here in all of Ezekiel's oracles against Tyre, proclaims the ultimate goal of Yahweh's punishment of the island fortress. The Tyrians read Jerusalem's fate through the lens of how they might profit from that catastrophe. But when they have experienced God's lethal intervention, they will (in their dying moment?) be forced to acknowledge that Yahweh's sovereign control of events extends to their own history, as well. The book of Ezekiel longs for, insists upon, that moment of recognition not only for Israel, but also for other nations. (See Reflections at 26:19-21.)

830. For a discussion of textual problems in this verse, see Moshe Greenberg, *Ezekiel 21–37*, AB 22A (Garden City, N.Y.: Doubleday, 1997) 531.

831. Aubet, *The Phoenicians and the West*, 32.

832. *History of Alexander* (= *Anabasis*) 2.21.4.

833. The Hellenistic "Prophecies of a Potter" indicates that "the city by the sea will become a place where fishermen dry [their nets]." See Zimmerli, *Ezekiel 2*, 35.

834. In arguing that the reference is *only* to "a sudden attack surprising the people who are found outside the fortified city, mostly women," Van Dijk dismisses the daughters=dependent settlements metaphor so well-established in biblical literature. See Van Dijk, *Ezekiel's Prophecy on Tyre*, 12-14.

Ezekiel 26:7-14, The Siege Against Tyre

NIV

⁷"For this is what the Sovereign LORD says: From the north I am going to bring against Tyre Nebuchadnezzar*a* king of Babylon, king of kings, with horses and chariots, with horsemen and a great army. ⁸He will ravage your settlements on the mainland with the sword; he will set up siege works against you, build a ramp up to your walls and raise his shields against you. ⁹He will direct the blows of his battering rams against your walls and demolish your towers with his weapons. ¹⁰His horses will be so many that they will cover you with dust. Your walls will tremble at the noise of the war horses, wagons and chariots when he enters your gates as men enter a city whose walls have been broken through. ¹¹The hoofs of his horses will trample all your streets; he will kill your people with the sword, and your strong pillars will fall to the ground. ¹²They will plunder your wealth and loot your merchandise; they will break down your walls and demolish your fine houses and throw your stones, timber and rubble into the sea. ¹³I will put an end to your noisy songs, and the music of your harps will be heard no more. ¹⁴I will make you a bare rock, and you will become a place to spread fishnets. You will never be rebuilt, for I the LORD have spoken, declares the Sovereign LORD.

a7 Hebrew Nebuchadrezzar, of which Nebuchadnezzar is a variant; here and often in Ezekiel and Jeremiah

NRSV

7For thus says the Lord GOD: I will bring against Tyre from the north King Nebuchadrezzar of Babylon, king of kings, together with horses, chariots, cavalry, and a great and powerful army.
⁸ Your daughter-towns in the country
    he shall put to the sword.
  He shall set up a siege wall against you,
    cast up a ramp against you,
    and raise a roof of shields against you.
⁹ He shall direct the shock of his battering rams
        against your walls
    and break down your towers with his axes.
¹⁰ His horses shall be so many
    that their dust shall cover you.
  At the noise of cavalry, wheels, and chariots
    your very walls shall shake,
  when he enters your gates
    like those entering a breached city.
¹¹ With the hoofs of his horses
    he shall trample all your streets.
  He shall put your people to the sword,
    and your strong pillars shall fall to the
        ground.
¹² They will plunder your riches
    and loot your merchandise;
  they shall break down your walls
    and destroy your fine houses.
  Your stones and timber and soil
    they shall cast into the water.
¹³ I will silence the music of your songs;
    the sound of your lyres shall be heard no
        more.
¹⁴ I will make you a bare rock;
    you shall be a place for spreading nets.
  You shall never again be rebuilt,
    for I the LORD have spoken,
    says the Lord GOD.

COMMENTARY

Following a resumptive כי (*kî*) and the messenger formula, Yahweh speaks more precisely of the agents of Tyre's destruction: Nebuchadrezzar and his troops. Verse 7 contains the scroll's first refer-

ence to the king of Babylonia by name. Ezekiel's spelling of it (cf. Nebuchadnezzar, more common in the HB) is in fact closer to the Babylonian Nabûkudur(ri)uṣur, which means "May Nabu protect the eldest son" (see 29:18-19; Jer 49:28). In previous chapters, Ezekiel has referred to this ruler as "the king of Babylon" (17:12; 19:9; 21:24, 26; 24:2), and that title appears here, as well. "King of kings" appears as the title of an Egyptian pharaoh of the Eighteenth Dynasty. In Assyrian texts, it is used with reference to Ashurnasirpal II, Esarhaddon, and Ashurbanipal; and it also appears in the literature of the Persian Empire and its successors. Within extant Neo-Babylonian texts, however, it appears only as the title of the god Marduk.[835] Hence, we cannot be certain whether "king of kings" was a royal title employed by Nebuchadrezzar (the "argument from silence" is not conclusive), or a surviving "legacy" of the Assyrian age. His approach "from the north" (the conventional direction whence Israel's/Judah's enemies arrived at the doorstep) accords with geographical reality. In order to reach Phoenicia, the Babylonian army traveled northwest along what we term the "Fertile Crescent," the traversable strip of land linking Mesopotamia to Palestine and ultimately, to Egypt (see the maps on 557-58). Nebuchadrezzar's forces are formidable, including horses, chariots, horsemen,[836] and "an assemblage of a great army."[837]

Commentators observe that in the following "account" of Nebuchadrezzar's siege of Tyre (vv. 8-14), the most detailed siege description in Hebrew Scripture, the army's activities follow logically one upon the other. First, a city's outlying settlements are destroyed (v. 8a); second, siege works are erected against its defenses (vv. 8b-9); third, troops enter the city through its breached walls (vv. 10-11a); fourth, the population is slaughtered (v. 11b); fifth, the city is pillaged (v. 12a); sixth, its buildings and walls are demolished (v. 12b).[838] They also recognize, however, that this type of siege account is ill-suited to Tyre's island setting, especially in its references to a siege wall, ramp, and battering rams. "The entire description of the siege," Gustav Jahn observes, "does not suit the island of Tyre, and seems to have been drawn according to the customary scheme of siege [of mainland cities] without regard for the situation of Tyre."[839] Only v. 12b, with its reference to casting "your stones and timber and rubble . . . into the water," and the concluding v. 14, which returns to the threats in vv. 4-5 (Tyre will become a "bare rock" and "a place for spreading nets") reflect its particular location (the NRSV translates עפר ['āpār, "dry earth," "dust"] as "soil," a possible rendering; better is the NIV's "rubble"; see Lev 14:45; 2 Sam 17:13; 1 Kgs 20:10).[840] Hence, it becomes difficult to assess the extent to which the siege description sheds light on an actual assault against Tyre. Does the reference to "your strong pillars" in v. 11, for example, refer to the two famous pillars of Melqart's temple?

The description is vivid, inviting its audience both to see and to hear the onslaught: the trampling hooves of horses raise clouds of dust, the deafening din of chariots shakes the city's walls, luxurious buildings (the palace complex?) crash to the ground. The reference to the cessation of music in v. 13 recalls Amos 5:23: "Take away from me the noise of your songs;/ I will not listen to the melody of your harps" (NRSV). However, whereas Amos refers to Yahweh's rejection of Israel's cultus, the silencing of Tyre's songs results from the decimation of its population. God's lethal punishment through the agency of Nebuchadrezzar's army is irrevocable. The city shall never be rebuilt. The oracle's closing formulas reiterate that everything which Ezekiel has proclaimed will surely occur, for his words are, in fact, God's own. (See Reflections at 26:19-21.)

835. Zimmerli, *Ezekiel 2*, 35-36.
836. Possibly "spanhorses," as argued by Sigmund Mowinckel, "Drive and/or Ride in O.T.," *VT* 12 (1962) 277-99.
837. Greenberg, *Ezekiel 21–37*, 532, reading MT "[and] an assemblage and an army," as equivalent to a construct pair. See Ezek 23:24.
838. Ibid., 542.
839. Gustav Jahn, *Das Buch Ezechiel* (Leipzig: E. Pfeiffer, 1905) 186.
840. See Greenberg, *Ezekiel 21–37*, 534, who quotes Esarhaddon's description of Sidon's destruction in 677 BCE. See also *ANET*, 291a.

Ezekiel 26:15-18, Mourning and Lamentation over Tyre

NIV

15"This is what the Sovereign LORD says to Tyre: Will not the coastlands tremble at the sound of your fall, when the wounded groan and the slaughter takes place in you? 16Then all the princes of the coast will step down from their thrones and lay aside their robes and take off their embroidered garments. Clothed with terror, they will sit on the ground, trembling every moment, appalled at you. 17Then they will take up a lament concerning you and say to you:

" 'How you are destroyed, O city of renown,
peopled by men of the sea!
You were a power on the seas,
you and your citizens;
you put your terror
on all who lived there.
18Now the coastlands tremble
on the day of your fall;
the islands in the sea
are terrified at your collapse.'

NRSV

15Thus says the Lord GOD to Tyre: Shall not the coastlands shake at the sound of your fall, when the wounded groan, when slaughter goes on within you? 16Then all the princes of the sea shall step down from their thrones; they shall remove their robes and strip off their embroidered garments. They shall clothe themselves with trembling, and shall sit on the ground; they shall tremble every moment, and be appalled at you. 17And they shall raise a lamentation over you, and say to you:

How you have vanished*a* from the seas,
O city renowned,
once mighty on the sea,
you and your inhabitants,*b*
who imposed your*c* terror
on all the mainland!*d*
18 Now the coastlands tremble
on the day of your fall;
the coastlands by the sea
are dismayed at your passing.

*a*Gk OL Aquila: Heb *have vanished, O inhabited one,*   *b*Heb *it and its inhabitants*   *c*Heb *their*   *d*Cn: Heb *its inhabitants*

COMMENTARY

Ezekiel's third oracle concerning Tyre presupposes the report of the city's demise in vv. 7-14. Cast as divine speech (note the messenger formula in v. 15*a*), it addresses Tyre directly,[841] informing her of the mournful (re)actions of "the princes of the sea" to news of her catastrophe and quoting the lament they raise over her. Ezekiel composed a lament or dirge over the last of the Davidic kings and their dynasty in chapter 19, but without providing a setting for its utterance. This imaginative scenario, by contrast, attests to the anguish of Tyre's trading partners, coastal city-states for whom the catastrophy brings grave economic consequences.

Just as Tyre's walls shook (רעש *rā'aš*) at the sound of Nebuchadrezzar's chariots entering its gates, so also the coastlands shake (*rā'aš*) at the sound of Tyre's downfall (מפלה *mappelet*; see also v. 18; 27:27; 31:13; Judg 14:8; Prov 29:16), the groaning of her wounded, and the slaughter of victims in her midst. The "princes of the sea" may in fact be kings, as the image of their descending from their thrones suggests. But the title might also designate a powerful (in some cases royal) class of "mercantile elite." There was a Council of State in Byblos that may have served as a board of commercial management, presided over by the king and the "princes of the sea" (26:16). Although our understanding of this board is limited, a treaty between Asarhadon and King Baal of Tyre demonstrates that Tyre's merchant fleet was partly owned by the king and by the ship owners and merchant princes.[842]

---

841. Van Dijk suggests that לצור (*lĕṣôr*), "to Tyre," in v. 15*a* be read as a vocative, "O Tyre." See Van Dijk, *Ezekiel's Prophecy on Tyre,* 29).

842. Aubet, *The Phoenicians and the West,* 94.

These princes do not rend their robes and embroidered (or variegated) garments. Instead, they remove them and "clothe themselves with trembling." The metaphor of attiring oneself with emotions is familiar from passages like Pss 35:26; 109:29; Isa 59:17; and Ezek 7:18, 27. Sitting upon the ground appears in Isa 3:26; 47:1; Jer 14:2; Ps 137:1; and Job 2:13.[843] The princes shall tremble repeatedly and be appalled concerning Tyre.

Their lament is composed in the *qinah* (3:2) rhythm pattern typical of biblical dirges. It begins with the doleful אֵיךְ (*'ēk*), "How," which, like the fuller form, *'êkâ*, initiates many an Israelite lament (e.g., Isa 1:21; 14:4, 12; Lam 1:1; 2:1; 4:1). The NRSV omits "O inhabited one" (נוֹשֶׁבֶת *nôšebet*) from v. 17; the form itself may be a misunderstanding of the original נִשְׁבַּת (*nišbat*), "vanished," or, following Van Dijk, "broken, shattered"

843. For an Ugaritic parallel, see *ANET,* 139a.

(see 30:18).[844] Van Dijk's translation reads, "How you have perished and are you shattered by the Sea, O city renowned."[845] The once/now pattern, frequent in laments, contrasts the city's former status—"once mighty on the seas," it and its inhabitants inspiring terror (not on account of military ambitions, but because of their "primacy in commerce")[846]—with the trembling and dismay of the coastlands on account of "the day of your fall."[847] When Tyre is destroyed, its commercial "empire" verges on collapse.[848] Ezekiel's third oracle concerning Tyre ends without benefit of closing formulae. (See Reflections at 26:19-21.)

844. Van Dijk, *Ezekiel's Prophecy on Tyre,* 33.
845. Ibid., 2, retaining "you have perished," which Zimmerli deletes as an addition necessitated by misconstrual of נִשְׁבַּת (*nišbat*) See. Zimmerli, *Ezekiel 2,* 30.
846. Greenberg, *Ezekiel 21–37,* 537-38.
847. Van Dijk, *Ezekiel's Prophecy on Tyre,* 38.
848. Contra ibid.

Ezekiel 26:19-21, Tyre's Descent to the Pit

NIV

[19]"This is what the Sovereign LORD says: When I make you a desolate city, like cities no longer inhabited, and when I bring the ocean depths over you and its vast waters cover you, [20]then I will bring you down with those who go down to the pit, to the people of long ago. I will make you dwell in the earth below, as in ancient ruins, with those who go down to the pit, and you will not return or take your place[a] in the land of the living. [21]I will bring you to a horrible end and you will be no more. You will be sought, but you will never again be found, declares the Sovereign LORD."

[a]20 Septuagint; Hebrew *return, and I will give glory*

NRSV

[19]For thus says the Lord GOD: When I make you a city laid waste, like cities that are not inhabited, when I bring up the deep over you, and the great waters cover you, [20]then I will thrust you down with those who descend into the Pit, to the people of long ago, and I will make you live in the world below, among primeval ruins, with those who go down to the Pit, so that you will not be inhabited or have a place[a] in the land of the living. [21]I will bring you to a dreadful end, and you shall be no more; though sought for, you will never be found again, says the Lord GOD.

[a]Gk: Heb *I will give beauty*

COMMENTARY

The fourth of Ezekiel's oracles against Tyre, also introduced by the messenger formula, underscores that Tyre's fate is Yahweh's doing. Here, the prophet imagines Tyre's descent to the underworld: as its towers and pillars crashed down to the ground, and the princes of the sea descended from their thrones, so Tyre makes its

final journey down to the Pit (the passage shares stereotypical ideas and phrases with the fuller description of Egypt's descent to the netherworld in 32:17-32). Yahweh addresses the city of Tyre directly. When God has reduced her to an uninhabited waste, and when the Lord has covered her—one who once ruled the seas—with the primeval deep (תהום *tĕhôm*) and the "great waters" (המים הרבים; *hammayim hărabîm*) cover her (both terms are laden with mythological overtones), then Yahweh will bring her down to the Pit, where reside those who have already died, "the people of long ago" (see Lam 3:6; Ps 143:3). In the netherworld (lit., "the lowest land"), amid ancient ruins, she will dwell with the dead. Verse 20*a* (NRSV, "so that you will not be inhabited") might rather be rendered "so that you will not sit [enthroned; i.e., "reign"] any more."[849] Verse 20*b* is difficult, as the NRSV and the NIV acknowledge. Van Dijk reads ונתתי (*wĕnātattî*), ostensibly "and I will give," as a feminine form with an archaic case-ending (see Ezek 16:18), labels the absence of a negating לא (*lō'*) before the verb, as well as the lack of a second-person feminine singular suffix on "beauty,"

"glory" as ellipses, and renders, "And that you spread no longer your glory over the land of the living."[850] The NRSV's "dreadful end" and the NIV's "horrible end" are better rendered "terror"; Tyre will cease to exist. Though sought for, she will never again be found. As noted above, Ezekiel takes pains to emphasize her utter and eternal destruction. The oracle ends with the closing formula, "says the Lord GOD."

Owing to their location, the Tyrians were able to withstand the assaults of the mighty empires Assyria and Babylonia. Like the inhabitants of "inviolable" Jerusalem, they presumed their security. But Ezekiel asserts that the same deity whose judgment is manifested in Jerusalem's destruction is bent upon their demise as well.

849. K. P. Darr, *Isaiah's Vision and the Family of God* (Louisville: Westminster John Knox, 1994) 145-47; Van Dijk, *Ezekiel's Prophecy on Tyre*, 45-46.

850. Van Dijk, *Ezekiel's Prophecy on Tyre*, 46-47. Greenberg takes "glory in the land of the living" to be an epithet for Tyre; the thought then continues into the following line, "a horror [בלהה *ballāhâ*] will I make you."

REFLECTIONS

Ezekiel's first account of Tyre's demise, cast in the form of four sequential and interrelated oracles, depicts the downfall of a thriving maritime city-state and the dismayed reactions of those who have participated in her commercial empire. Israel and Judah, no less than other nations of their world, profited from Tyrian trade; and the history of their relationships with the city was not marked by the territorial disputes and bitter acrimony apparent in Ezekiel's oracles against Ammon, Moab, Edom, and Philistia (chap. 25). Yet here, as in 25:3, 6, 8, 12, and 15, Tyre's offense lies in her inappropriate response to Jerusalem's destruction (v. 2). From her economic perspective, Jerusalem's loss is her gain; and Ezekiel explicitly grounds Yahweh's punishment in her gleeful greed. As noted in the Overview, however, his ire doubtlessly is fueled by Tyre's ability to escape Nebuchadrezzar's forces, God's instrument of judgment.

The Reflections at 25:1-17 note that ancient Israel's oracles against foreign nations and rulers are not only ideological, but also profoundly theological. Ezekiel, whose own nation had recently succumbed to the massive Babylonian military machine, was determined that his people recognize in their punishment the justice and unrivalled power of their God, whose governance of history was absolute: "He insists that Yahweh is both in control of events, and justified in the way those events are controlled. Ezekiel's [acts and oracles], with their charges of human guilt, are constructed . . . to convince his audience that both their conviction, and their convictor, are just."[851] But he was also intent upon persuading his exilic audience that Yahweh's sovereign rule was by no means confined to Judah's borders. The Lord of their history was the Lord of all history.

In the aftermath of Jerusalem's destruction, Ezekiel will begin to speak of a marvelous future awaiting the people of God. According to the scroll's canonical structure, however, he turns first to the fates of certain of Israel's neighbors. (He does not prophesy against Babylon in chaps.

851. K. P. Darr, "Ezekiel's Justifications of God: Teaching Troubling Texts," *JSOT* 55 (1992) 112.

25–32; see Excursus: "Ezekiel's Oracles Against Foreign Nations and Rulers," 1355-56.) For the prophet, Israel's restoration presupposes the elimination of those nations that have provoked Yahweh's anger. As moderns, we would be more comfortable with Ezekiel's oracles against foreign nations and rulers if, in the end, they pointed toward reconciliation and peace among all of God's peoples. But Ezekiel, for whom worldwide *acknowledgment* of Yahweh as sovereign God is a crucial concern, cannot or will not envision a "utopia" that stretches beyond Israel's borders to embrace all of creation. His perspective is simply too parochial to bring him to that place. Ezekiel's vision of the future needs to be brought into dialogue with other, more inclusive biblical expressions of worldwide *shalom*, peace (e.g., Gen 12:3; Isa 49:6; and John 3:16).

Refugees around the world know the anguish of homelands torn apart and ravaged by territorial disputes and internecine stuggles. For them, ancient Israel's experience strikes an all-too-familiar chord. For many others, however, Tyre's response to Jerusalem's downfall is closer to their own life "environment." Empire building takes many forms—economic, political, technological, scientific. Competition is fierce; we describe it with terms like "cut-throat," but also with phrases like "good business practice" and "the way the game is played." We strive, sometimes by unethical means, to "come out on top." And we may relish some glee of our own when a competitor stumbles, a rival is forced to close its doors, we "kill the opposition."

Competition is not negative per se. To the contrary, we are indebted to this impulse for much of the progress achieved in aspects of our lives too numerous to count. Tyre's response to the fall of Jerusalem reminds us, however, that our competitors also are people, families, communities, with beliefs, needs, and aspirations of their own. As folk of faith, we are called by God to respect and dignify them, to treat them as we would wish to be treated. Most of us have walked both sides of success. Failure is as painful for our opponents as it is for ourselves.

If this reflection on the present text is worth pondering, we must yet concede that Ezekiel 26 does not espouse the spirit that we may feel pulled by God to exhibit in the midst of our own successes and failures with competitors. Ezekiel proclaims that the God of Israel will exact from the Tyrians the ultimate price for their greedy delight in Jerusalem's misfortune. Again, we are confronted by an ancient prophet whose (nationalistic) worldview and (theological/ideological) presuppositions create God in the image of a vengeful deity whose preferred means of dealing with offending peoples is to exterminate them: "I will bring you to a dreadful end, and you will be no more; though sought for, you will never be found again, says the Lord GOD" (Ezek 26:21 NRSV). And so, we return to the observation offered in the Reflections to chapter 25: When prophets profess to speak God's oracles, we must engage in difficult conversations and make hard choices. Even as we struggle to understand why Ezekiel spoke as he did, we must listen actively for God's word today.

Ezekiel 27:1-36, The Sinking of Ship Tyre

OVERVIEW

Ezekiel's fifth and longest oracle against Tyre, a Phoenician city-state situated on an island just off the eastern coast of the Mediterranean Sea (see the maps on 557-58), testifies to his literary prowess, including his mastery of metaphor. In earlier oracles, he has repeatedly demonstrated his powerful acumen, his in-depth knowledge of

numerous and wide-ranging topics, including their technical vocabularies, and his familiarity with and creative use of religious traditions. Ezekiel 27 itself justifies placing the prophet among the intellectual cognoscenti of his ancient Near Eastern world. To read it is to stand in awe of its author.

According to v. 1, Yahweh is the true author of

the following lamentation over Tyre (see Excursus: "Tyre 'in the Heart of the Seas,' " 1359-62). Following the word event formula ("The word of the LORD came to me"), God addresses the prophet ("Now you, mortal") and commands him to raise a dirge over the city ("and say to Tyre . . ."). Ezekiel has composed laments before; one recalls his lamentation over Judah's last kings and the Davidic dynasty in 19:1-14, as well as the dirge ostensibly uttered over Tyre by "the princes of the sea" in 26:17-18. In the first of these two texts, as with the present passage, he employed metaphor—a lioness and her whelps, a ramified vine—in order most powerfully to convey his message concerning the doom of the Davidic dynasty and to distinguish between "then" (past glory) and "now" (dead, or as good as dead), a contrast characteristic of the genre. Hals reminds us that metaphors were frequent features of ancient dirges, especially when the entity lamented was not an ordinary individual, but a city, dynasty, or nation.[852] Such is the case here, as Ezekiel takes up (coins?) a maritime metaphor: Tyre is a ship.

The oracle consists of two major sections, each of which can be further divided into subsections. The "then" section, vv. 3-25, describes in great detail the splendid merchantman—constructed of the finest materials (vv. 5-7), manned and maintained by elite Phoenician "sailors" (vv. 8-9a), and defended by mercenaries drawn from the ends of the known world (vv. 10-11). Poetry gives way to prose in vv. 12-25a as the oracle rehearses at length Tyre's trade partners and the commodities of exchange. The list is long and imposing, a literary emporium of the world's goods, ranging from necessities, like agricultural products and livestock, to luxury items—gold and silver, precious gems, ivory, and ebony (copper is noticeably absent). Itself a treasure trove for historians (presenting "information of incalculable value about Tyre's trade and zones of economic influence, so much so that it is considered to be one of the most relevant sources of information for reconstructing the Phoenician economy in the days of the Mediterranean expansion"),[853] it impresses readers ancient and modern, with the wealth, prestige, and cosmopolitanism of this ancient city "ship." As we shall see, critics are prone to excise vv. 12-25a (and other verses sharing their vocabulary) from the original oracle, as if they played no role in—indeed, detracted from—Ezekiel's lament. The ancient reader will not entertain that idea, and the oracle suffers their absence. Each detail of the prophet's dirge amplifies the impact of the whole and invites its audience to invest in this "ship of dreams"—a symbol of exotic locales, seafaring adventure, and fabulous wealth—until, in Newsom's words: "Ezekiel simply takes the ship to sea and sinks it in a single, sudden verse" (v. 26).[854]

The "now" section of the dirge, vv. 25b-36, commences with the shipwreck (vv. 26-27) and then describes the agonized responses of various constituencies for whom Tyre's sinking spells disaster. In a deft rhetorical move, Ezekiel first portrays other mariners abandoning their fleets, standing on the shore, and mourning the loss of the great vessel and its crew, and then places a dirge on their lips (vv. 32-36), thereby creating a lament within a lament.

The mariner's dirge, the reader assumes, is heartfelt, as are the emotions—appallment, fear, sorrow—of those who hear of the catastrophe at sea. Is Ezekiel's lament also a genuine outpouring of grief? The sequential reader who arrives at this oracle fresh on the heels of chapter 26, and so knows of Tyre's greedy and self-serving response to the destruction of Jerusalem (26:2) and of Yahweh's intention utterly to eradicate it, will conclude that his lamentation is an example of derision in disguise. This is true even though the oracle itself neither accuses Tyre of sin (but see below) nor gloats explicitly over its demise (or portrays others doing so) and, save for the messenger formula in v. 3, contains not a single reference to God. Its present placement, following the four preceding oracles against the city-state, determines in a significant way the reader's construal of the sinking of ship Tyre. (See Reflections at 27:26-36.)

852. Ronald M. Hals, *Ezekiel*, FOTL 19 (Grand Rapids: Eerdmans, 1989) 192.

853. Maria Eugenia Aubet, *The Phoenicians and the West: Politics, Colonies and Trade*, trans. Mary Turton (Cambridge: Cambridge University Press, 1993) 98.

854. Carol Newsom, "A Maker of Metaphors: Ezekiel's Oracles against Tyre," in *The Place Is Too Small for Us*, ed. Robert P. Gordon (Winona Lake: Eisenbrauns, 1995) 197.

Ezekiel 27:1-11, The Construction of Ship Tyre and Its Crew

NIV

27 The word of the LORD came to me: [2]"Son of man, take up a lament concerning Tyre. [3]Say to Tyre, situated at the gateway to the sea, merchant of peoples on many coasts, `This is what the Sovereign LORD says:

" 'You say, O Tyre,
  "I am perfect in beauty."
[4]Your domain was on the high seas;
  your builders brought your beauty to
    perfection.
[5]They made all your timbers
  of pine trees from Senir[a];
they took a cedar from Lebanon
  to make a mast for you.
[6]Of oaks from Bashan
  they made your oars;
of cypress wood[b] from the coasts of Cyprus[c]
  they made your deck, inlaid with ivory.
[7]Fine embroidered linen from Egypt was your
    sail
  and served as your banner;
your awnings were of blue and purple
  from the coasts of Elishah.
[8]Men of Sidon and Arvad were your oarsmen;
  your skilled men, O Tyre, were aboard as
    your seamen.
[9]Veteran craftsmen of Gebal[d] were on board
  as shipwrights to caulk your seams.
All the ships of the sea and their sailors
  came alongside to trade for your wares.

[10]" 'Men of Persia, Lydia and Put
  served as soldiers in your army.
They hung their shields and helmets on your
    walls,
  bringing you splendor.
[11]Men of Arvad and Helech
  manned your walls on every side;
men of Gammad
  were in your towers.
They hung their shields around your walls;
  they brought your beauty to perfection.

[a]5 That is, Hermon   [b]6 Targum; the Masoretic Text has a different division of the consonants.   [c]6 Hebrew *Kittim*   [d]9 That is, Byblos

NRSV

27 The word of the LORD came to me: [2]Now you, mortal, raise a lamentation over Tyre, [3]and say to Tyre, which sits at the entrance to the sea, merchant of the peoples on many coastlands, Thus says the Lord GOD:
  O Tyre, you have said,
    "I am perfect in beauty."
[4]Your borders are in the heart of the seas;
    your builders made perfect your beauty.
[5]They made all your planks
    of fir trees from Senir;
  they took a cedar from Lebanon
    to make a mast for you.
[6]From oaks of Bashan
    they made your oars;
  they made your deck of pines[a]
    from the coasts of Cyprus,
    inlaid with ivory.
[7]Of fine embroidered linen from Egypt
    was your sail,
    serving as your ensign;
  blue and purple from the coasts of Elishah
    was your awning.
[8]The inhabitants of Sidon and Arvad
    were your rowers;
  skilled men of Zemer[b] were within you,
    they were your pilots.
[9]The elders of Gebal and its artisans were
      within you,
    caulking your seams;
  all the ships of the sea with their mariners
      were within you,
    to barter for your wares.
[10]Paras[c] and Lud and Put
    were in your army,
    your mighty warriors;
  they hung shield and helmet in you;
    they gave you splendor.
[11]Men of Arvad and Helech[d]
    were on your walls all around;
  men of Gamad were at your towers.
  They hung their quivers all around your walls;
    they made perfect your beauty.

[a]Or *boxwood*   [b]Cn Compare Gen 10.18: Heb *your skilled men, O Tyre*   [c]Or *Persia*   [d]Or *and your army*

COMMENTARY

Unlike chap. 26 (v. 1), chap. 27 is not dated; hence, the reader likely assumes that the following prophecy also was delivered at a time not far removed from Jerusalem's fall (587/86 BCE), perhaps on the same occasion as Ezekiel's previous oracles against Tyre.

Following the word event formula and Yahweh's address to the prophet, Ezekiel is ordered to raise a lamentation over the city, addressed to Tyre "herself" (see Excursus: "Cities as Females," 1221-25). Two appositional phrases further define the subject of his dirge: Tyre "sits (enthroned) at the entrances [pl.] of the sea," and is "merchant of the peoples on many coastlands." The first suggests the city's geographical location—the principal factor in its commercial success. Enthroned at a point of access to the sea, Queen Tyre with her two seaports, the Sidonian to the north and the Egyptian to the south, exemplifies the truth of the popular adage, "location is everything." The second phrase highlights the role that locale affords her. The form translated "merchant" is the feminine singular participle רכלת (*rōkelet*), from רכל (*rākal*), meaning "go about, from one to another"; hence, "trade."[855] Tyre's commercial enterprise is far-flung.

Both the NRSV and the NIV follow the Masoretic Text (MT) in translating v. 3*b*. Tyre is addressed directly and with the vocative ("O Tyre"), then quoted as having said, "I am perfect in beauty." Despite the intelligibility of the MT, however, critics have long urged that אני (*'ānî*, "I") be repointed to אני (*'ŏnî* "ship"). That change, in turn, suggests the deletion of אמרת (*'āmart*), "you said," as secondary—a consequence of misreading "ship" as "I." The emended text then reads, "O Tyre, you are a ship, perfect in beauty."[856] Zimmerli's reasoning is typical in this regard: so altered, the line both introduces Ezekiel's metaphor immediately, as is his custom (see 19:2; 28:12; 32:2), and conforms to the 3 + 2 metrical

pattern characteristic of Hebrew laments. Neither argument is decisive, however, and the reader, aware that hubris is a frequent charge in prophetic oracles against foreign nations and rulers, will discern in Tyre's boast to be "perfect in beauty," an attribute elsewhere ascribed to Jerusalem (see Lam 2:15; Ps 50:2; Ezek 16:14), a reason for her subsequent demise.[857]

If Tyre's self-appraisal smacks of hubris, it nonetheless is substantiated in following verses. Ezekiel's description of her construction and crew spares no effort in conveying a sense of the vessel's magnificence, the better to drive home the economic consequences of her sinking in v. 26. Verse 4*a,* "Your borders are in the heart of the seas," is literally (geographically) true of the island. With v. 4*b* ("your builders made perfect your beauty"), however, a reader might suspect that a metaphor is afoot. Hebrew גבול (*gĕbûl*) often means "border," "boundary," "territory."[858] As Greenberg notes, however, the noun can bear an architectural meaning—that is, the "barrier" of a building (40:12) or the "rim" of an altar (43:13, 17, 20). Moreover, builders do not construct islands (though v. 4*b* might be interpreted as referring to the beauty of the city with its walls, towers, ports, temples, and palace). "Builders" might here be construed more specifically to mean "shipwrights."[859]

If v. 4 barely hints at the ship metaphor, v. 5 makes it explicit. The shipwrights of merchantman Tyre built her "ribs" or "planks" (לחתים *luḥōtāyim*; dual ending) of fir trees from (Mt.) Senir (according to Deut 3:9, the Amorite name of Mount Hermon; but see Cant 4:8; 1 Chr 5:23). They took one of the (proverbial) cedars of Lebanon, the timber of palaces and temples, to make its mast. Its oars were made from the famous

855. *BDB,* 940a.

856. See, e.g., Walther Zimmerli, *Ezekiel 2: A Commentary on the Book of the Prophet Ezekiel, Chapters 25–48,* trans. J. D. Martin, Hermeneia (Philadelphia: Fortress, 1983) 378; J. W. Wevers, *Ezekiel,* NCB (London: Nelson, 1969) 205; Jorg Garscha, *Studien Zum Ezechielbuch: eine redaktions-Kritische Untersuchung Von 1–39,* Europaische Hochschul Schriften 23 (Bern: Herbert Lang 1974) 158n. 492.

857. As Greenberg, *Ezekiel 21–37,* 548, observes, altering the MT eliminates Tyre's arrogant appropriation of Jerusalem's epithet. Moreover, "you said" (or a variant of same) frequently introduces "blameworthy" statements in Ezekiel's oracles against nations (see 25:3, 8; 26:2; 28:2; 29:3;). Ezekiel has elsewhere employed metaphorical parables without, at the outset, identifying underlying referents (see, e.g., 17:3-10; 24:3-5). See also the discussion about meter in Hebrew laments in John Thomas Strong, "Ezekiel's Oracles Against the Nations Within the Context of His Message" (Ph.D. diss., Union Theological Seminary in Virginia, 1993) 198 n. 65.

858. *BDB,* 147b-148a.

859. Greenberg, *Ezekiel 21–37,* 549.

oaks of Bashan (see Isa 2:13; Zech 11:2). Its deck (or perhaps the passenger pavillion?) was constructed of pines (or cypresses) from the coasts of Cyprus, inlaid with ivory ("[elephant's] tooth"; see 1 Kgs 20:22; Amos 3:15).[860] The precise types of trees referred to in vv. 5-6 are uncertain, but clearly, ship Tyre is constructed of the finest woods.

Tyre's sail is made from first-class fabric, Egyptian linen (שש šēš). The word רקמה (riqmâ), a term Ezekiel elsewhere uses to refer to fine, variegated (embroidered?) fabric (16:10, 13, 18; 17:3; 26:16; 27:16, 24), suggests that the linen was dyed and/or bore a design. The term נס (nēs), translated "ensign" in the NRSV and "banner" in the NIV is, properly, a second word for "sail" (see Isa 33:23).[861] Surviving depictions of Phoenician vessels do not support the notion that they sported flags. Rather, v. 7a suggests that the sail's design or pattern functions to identify the ship.[862] Her awning (protecting a portion of the deck from the sun's rays?) is made from cloths dyed blue and purple. The "coasts of Elishah" probably refers to Cyprus.

Having described the magnificent ship itself, Ezekiel turns to its crew. Its rowers (v. 8a) are the inhabitants of Sidon and Arvad (Phoenician coastal seaports lying twenty-five miles and one hundred ten miles north of Tyre, respectively).[863] Their role reflects the subservience of these cities to Tyre. Verse 8b specifies, by contrast, that Tyre's own experts are its "rope men"—that is, navigators. The NRSV emends צור (ṣōr, "Tyre") to צמר (ṣmr, "ṣemar"; see Gen 10:18), also a Phoenician coastal city, for the sake of consistency. The NIV follows the MT; so also the reader, observing that Tyre entrusts the most important responsibility to its own. Van Dijk suggests (in connection with v. 9) that the phrase היו בך (hāyû bāk; NRSV, "were within you") be translated "boarded you," rendering היה (hāyâ) in the sense of "to appear," "to come" (NIV, "were on board").[864] Verse 9a further

specifies that the elders of "Gebal" (i.e., Byblos, a Phoenician coastal seaport lying some sixty miles north of Tyre) and her wise men boarded the vessel to serve as its carpenters (see, e.g., 2 Kgs 12:6, 8), caulking its seams.

In v. 9b, Ezekiel's "Tyre is a ship" metaphor appears to slip a bit, allowing the actual referent, the island city with its seaports, to surface ("all the ships of the sea with their mariners were within you [boarded you?] to barter for your wares"). For this reason and others (e.g., meter), Zimmerli deletes it as secondary.[865] The same phenomenon occurs in other of Ezekiel's extended metaphors (see, e.g., 16:41; 17:9; 23:47), however; and the reader is accustomed to it. Diakonoff suggests that the metaphor be viewed more broadly: "ship" Tyre refers primarily to its naval prowess, but also to its island fortress.[866]

Trading vessels were prime targets for pirates, and so it comes as no surprise that this one is protected by soldiers, mercenaries from Paras (Persia), Lud (Lydia), and Put (Libya); for the latter two, see 30:5. John Thomas Strong contends that the reference to Paras (Persia) is a telling anachronism, since it did not emerge as a bona fide world power until the mid-sixth century BCE.[867] As Greenberg observes, however, the annals of Assyrian king Adad-Nirari III (c. 811–784 BCE) refer to Parsua (Persia).[868] Moreover, its pairing with two other peoples situated at the extremities of the then-known world suggests that it is not here regarded as a major world empire. An Assyrian bas-relief depicting the flight of Tyre's King Luli (early 7th cent. BCE) shows round shields hanging from both ship railings and Tyre's city walls.[869] No such evidence suggests that helmets were hung. These forces and their armaments give (to) Tyre (the suffix is dative) splendor. With v. 11, the referent (city) again intrudes. Men of Arvad (see v. 8) and Helech (Hebrew, "your army"; but is this a reference to Cilicia?) are stationed around the walls, while Gammadians (LXX, "watchmen") guard the

860. Ibid., 549.

861. See H. J. Van Dijk, Ezekiel's Prophecy on Tyre (Ez. 26, 1–28, 19): A New Approach, BibOr 20 (Rome: Pontifical Biblical Institute, 1968) 65.

862. Greenberg, Ezekiel 21–37, 550.

863. BHS suggests that Hebrew "inhabitants of" be emended to read "princes of," on the assumption that the former provides a pale parallel to the ensuing "wise men" and "elders." See Zimmerli, Ezekiel 2, 44-45. See also Van Dijk, Ezekiel's Prophecy on Tyre, 66-69, who translates "kings."

864. Van Dijk, Ezekiel's Prophecy on Tyre, 72.

865. Zimmerli, Ezekiel 2, 54.

866. I. M. Diakonoff, "The Naval Power and Trade of Tyre," IEJ 42 (1992) 171.

867. Strong, "Ezekiel's Oracles Against the Nations Within the Context of His Message," 197.

868. See ANET, 281b. See also Greenberg, Ezekiel 21–37, 551.

869. Aubet, The Phoenicians and the West, 34. It is possible, esp. in the light of v. 11, that v. 10 refers to mercenaries within the city of Tyre.

towers.[870] Their quivers (see Jer 51:11) are hung around the walls. "They made perfect your beauty" echoes Tyre's boast in v. 3 (see also v. 4*b*), bringing to a close Ezekiel's description of ship Tyre and its crew.

Plotting on a map the locales mentioned in vv. 5-11, Liverani observes a pattern of three concentric belts. The first, and tightest, belt consists of Sidon, Arvad, Tyre (according to the MT), and

Byblos—Phoenician cities supplying the vessel's crew; the second belt consists of inland mountains (Lebanon, Senir, Bashan), Cyprus (Elishah, Kittim), and Egypt. These areas provide raw materials (timber, linen); the third and loosest belt consists of Paras, Lud, and Put; these regions supply Tyre's troops. He further observes that the areas belonging to these three belts are not included in the subsequent list of Tyre's trade partners (vv. 12-25).[871] (See Reflections at 27:26-36.)

870. The Vg renders "Gammadim," from Hebrew גמד (*gōmed,* "short cubit") as *Pygmaei* ("dwarfs"), perhaps Cimmerians. See Greenberg, *Ezekiel 21–37,* 552-53.

871. M. Liverani, "The Trade Network of Tyre According to Ezek. 27," in *Ah. Assyria . . .,* ed. M. Cogan and I. Eph`al, ScrHier 33 (Jerusalem: Magnes, 1991) 71n. 27.

Ezekiel 27:12-25, Tyre's Trading Partners and Their Commodities of Exchange

NIV

12" 'Tarshish did business with you because of your great wealth of goods; they exchanged silver, iron, tin and lead for your merchandise.

13" 'Greece, Tubal and Meshech traded with you; they exchanged slaves and articles of bronze for your wares.

14" 'Men of Beth Togarmah exchanged work horses, war horses and mules for your merchandise.

15" 'The men of Rhodes[a] traded with you, and many coastlands were your customers; they paid you with ivory tusks and ebony.

16" 'Aram[b] did business with you because of your many products; they exchanged turquoise, purple fabric, embroidered work, fine linen, coral and rubies for your merchandise.

17" 'Judah and Israel traded with you; they exchanged wheat from Minnith and confections,[c] honey, oil and balm for your wares.

18" 'Damascus, because of your many products and great wealth of goods, did business with you in wine from Helbon and wool from Zahar.

19" 'Danites and Greeks from Uzal bought your merchandise; they exchanged wrought iron, cassia and calamus for your wares.

20" 'Dedan traded in saddle blankets with you.

a15 Septuagint; Hebrew *Dedan*   *b16* Most Hebrew manuscripts; some Hebrew manuscripts and Syriac *Edom*   *c17* The meaning of the Hebrew for this word is uncertain.

NRSV

12Tarshish did business with you out of the abundance of your great wealth; silver, iron, tin, and lead they exchanged for your wares. 13Javan, Tubal, and Meshech traded with you; they exchanged human beings and vessels of bronze for your merchandise. 14Beth-togarmah exchanged for your wares horses, war horses, and mules. 15The Rhodians[a] traded with you; many coastlands were your own special markets; they brought you in payment ivory tusks and ebony. 16Edom[b] did business with you because of your abundant goods; they exchanged for your wares turquoise, purple, embroidered work, fine linen, coral, and rubies. 17Judah and the land of Israel traded with you; they exchanged for your merchandise wheat from Minnith, millet,[c] honey, oil, and balm. 18Damascus traded with you for your abundant goods—because of your great wealth of every kind—wine of Helbon, and white wool. 19Vedan and Javan from Uzal[c] entered into trade for your wares; wrought iron, cassia, and sweet cane were bartered for your merchandise. 20Dedan traded with you in saddlecloths for riding. 21Arabia and all the princes of Kedar were your favored dealers in lambs, rams, and goats; in these they did business with you. 22The merchants of Sheba and Raamah traded with you;

*a*Gk: Heb *The Dedanites*   *b*Another reading is *Aram*   *c*Meaning of Heb uncertain

NIV

21" 'Arabia and all the princes of Kedar were your customers; they did business with you in lambs, rams and goats.

22" 'The merchants of Sheba and Raamah traded with you; for your merchandise they exchanged the finest of all kinds of spices and precious stones, and gold.

23" 'Haran, Canneh and Eden and merchants of Sheba, Asshur and Kilmad traded with you. 24In your marketplace they traded with you beautiful garments, blue fabric, embroidered work and multicolored rugs with cords twisted and tightly knotted.

25" 'The ships of Tarshish serve
    as carriers for your wares.
You are filled with heavy cargo
    in the heart of the sea.

NRSV

they exchanged for your wares the best of all kinds of spices, and all precious stones, and gold. 23Haran, Canneh, Eden, the merchants of Sheba, Asshur, and Chilmad traded with you. 24These traded with you in choice garments, in clothes of blue and embroidered work, and in carpets of colored material, bound with cords and made secure; in these they traded with you.[a] 25The ships of Tarshish traveled for you in your trade.

So you were filled and heavily laden
    in the heart of the seas.

[a]Cn: Heb *in your market*

COMMENTARY

As noted in the Overview, many critics deny Ezekiel the extensive list of Tyre's trade partners and their exports. Not only is such a list ill-suited to its present (poetic) context, they aver, but it also betrays, despite some reworking, its origin as a "technical" document derived from a great government agency or commercial house.[872] Even Carol Newsom, who acknowledges that "the long, slow description of the construction of the ship and its staffing" invites the reader's deep commitment to Ezekiel's ship metaphor, omits vv. 12-25 from her analysis, although the trade list can be said to perform the same function.[873]

Other critics, while acknowledging that Ezekiel might have worked from a separate source document, or from information provided by Phoenician fellows in exile, ascribe the final form of vv. 12-25*a*, with its stylistic variations, to the prophet, who put the information to good use and for identifiable reasons. M. Liverani cites a text attributed to Gudea, Ensi of Lagash, who revels in the far-flung provenances of his city's imports.[874]

Greenberg notes the incorporation of lists in Homer's poetic catalogs. A more striking analogy appears in a Sumerian myth about Enki and Ninhursag, wherein a list identifies the trade of Dilmun, a "paradisaical port city."[875] Such examples cannot establish Ezekielian authorship of the trade list. They suggest, however, that the ancient reader would not have been puzzled by its presence here, much less found reason to attribute it to some other author. As noted in the Overview, Ezekiel's wide-ranging knowledge (a reflection, the text avers, of God's own) is well-established long before the reader arrives at chapter 27.

Several general observations about the list (which begins and ends with a reference to Tarshish; vv. 12, 25*a*) will assist those who work through it. First, one notes that the products associated with particular locales (nations, cities, etc.) are mainly typical goods of those areas. Hence, the list focuses especially upon what Tyre receives (imports) from its far-flung trade partners. As Liverani observes, this emphasis is apropros to its

872. Zimmerli, *Ezekiel 2*, 63, 70. Cf. Liverani, "The Trade Network of Tyre According to Ezek. 27," 79.

873. Newsom, "A Maker of Metaphors," 197.

874. Liverani, "The Trade Network of Tyre According to Ezek. 27," 71n. 27. See also *ANET*, 268-29.

875. For Greek vessels, see Homer *Iliad* 2.484-785; for Trojan forces, see Homer *Iliad* 2.786-877. See also Greenberg, *Ezekiel 21–37*, 566; Thorkild Jacobsen, *The Harps That Once. . . : Sumerian Poetry in Translation* (New Haven: Yale University Press, 1987) 188-89.

"celebrative" purpose: "It is not a matter of Tyre working for trade, rather of trade working for Tyre."[876]

Second, the locales specified essentially move from the western Mediterranean to eastern Mesopotamia—that is, from northwest to southeast. Separate from this pattern, however, another can be discerned if one plots these locales upon a "mental map." Again, Liverani speaks of "concentric belts," this time four in number.[877] The inner ("tightest") belt includes areas closest to Tyre (Judah, "the land of Israel," Damascus). From these locales, Tyre imports agricultural products—wheat, honey, oil, wine, and resins. A second, geographically broader belt consisting of Beth-Togarmah, Arabia and Kedar, and (again) Damascus supplies Tyre with animals and animal products— horses, mules, sheep, goats, and wool. A third, even wider belt includes Javan, Tubal and Meshech, Dedan, Edom, and Eden-Harran-Assur. These areas supply manufactured products: bronze utensils, textiles, cloth, saddlecloths, and ropes, as well as slaves. Finally, the outer belt (consisting of Tarshish, Sheba and Raamah, the Rhodians, and Edom (again) supply metals and luxury goods: silver, iron, tin, lead, gold, spices, precious stones, ebony, and ivory.[878]

Verse 3b referred to Tyre as a trader (from רכל rākal, "go about, from one to another") to many coastal nations. Ezekiel's trade list employs rākal (in various forms) and also forms of סחר (sāḥar, "go around, about, travel about in")[879] as alternating synonyms for the city's trading partners (sāḥar appears in vv. 12, 15-16, 18, 21 [twice]; rākal in vv. 13, 15, 17, 20, 22-24). Aubet suggests that these "trading partners" were, in fact, Tyre's "agents"—that is, participants in an enormous mercantile organization in which such agents, under the "direct tutelage" of Tyre, worked for her from their own native countries. So construed, Ezekiel's list refers not to nations per se,

but to Tyrian agents acting as intermediaries with those nations.[880]

The word נתן (nātan, "to give") occurs frequently (vv. 12-14, 16-17, 22), the foreign countries being its subject and their exports its direct object. Van Dijk suggests that in this context, nātan be construed in the technical sense, "to sell, to exchange."[881] Also present are שׁוב (šûb) (hiphil; hence, "to get in exchange") in v. 15 and היה (hāyâ, "to be") in 27:19.[882] Two additional recurring terms (hapax legomena in this passage—i.e., they appear only here in the HB) require comment. The first, עזבון ('izzābôn; plural only), is from עזב ('āzab, "to leave," "forsake," "loose").[883] BDB defines the term as "wares (as left in the purchaser's hand)."[884] Greenberg follows Moshe ben Sheshet, who explained the term as "the merchandise that one who trades in a land leaves ['azab] there"; hence, exports Tyre has received for re-exportation to other trading partners or agents.[885] The second, מערב (ma'ărāb), is derived variously.[886] Some scholars derive it from ערב ('ārab, "to enter"),[887] hence, "incoming goods," "import"—that is, that which Tyre receives from its trading partners or agents.[888] These two terms tend to alternate in the trade list: forms of עזבון ('izzābôn, "exports") appear in vv. 12, 14, 16, 18-19a, and 22; forms of מערב (ma'ărāb, "import") appear in vv. 13, 17, and 19b).[889]

---

876. Liverani, "The Trade Network of Tyre According to Ezek. 27," 74.

877. Ibid., 71. The following discussion is much indebted to Liverani's analysis.

878. Ibid., 73; see his text-critical discussion, 73-74.

879. BDB, 695.

880. Aubet, The Phoenicians and the West, 102. Liverani suggests that סחרתך (sōḥartēk, "your trade agent") and סחרת ידך (sĕḥōrat yādēk, "trade agent of your hand"), references to Tyre's trade agents, are here applied to regions, nations, cities, etc., in order to diminish their role to that of agents under Tyre's tutelage, the better to focus on Tyre's pivotal role in international trade. See Liverani, "The Trade Network of Tyre According to Ezek. 27," 76. Such a strategy would play nicely into Ezekiel's hands if, as seems quite likely, he intends to emphasize Tyre's former (present?) glory in order to intensify its present (actually future) demise.

881. H. J. Van Dijk, Ezekiel's Prophecy on Tyre (Ez. 26, 1–28, 19): A New Approach, BibOr 20 (Rome: Pontifical Biblical Institute, 1968) 76.

882. M. Liverani, "The Trade Network of Tyre According to Ezek. 27," in Ah, Assyria . . ., ed. M. Cogan and I. Eph'al, ScrHier 33 (Jerusalem: Magnes, 1991) 77.

883. BDB, 736b-737b.

884. Ibid, 738a.

885. Moshe Greenberg, Ezekiel 21–37, AB 22A (Garden City, N.Y.: Doubleday, 1997) 553. So also I. M. Diakonoff, "The Naval Power and Trade of Tyre," IEJ 42 (1992) 193.

886. BDB, 786b, derives it from 'ārab ("take on pledge," give in pledge," "exchange") and defines it as "articles of exchange, merchandise."

887. Liverani, "The Trade Network of Tyre According to Ezek. 27," 77.

888. See Diakonoff, "The Naval Power and Trade of Tyre," 183-84.

889. See the chart in Greenberg, Ezekiel 21–37, 565.

Tarshish (probably Tartessus, a Phoenician port in southern Spain) is cited in v. 12 as the first of Tyre's trade partners (or agents). It appears, along with Elishah (v. 7), Kittim, and Rodanim (see below), as a son of Javan (see v. 13) in Gen 10:4 (the table of nations) and 1 Chr 1:7. From it, Tyre receives silver, iron, tin, and lead. Readers recall that when God ordered the prophet Jonah to travel (east) to Nineveh, capital of Assyria, he instead boarded a ship bound for Tarshish (Jonah 1:3), the farthest western locale accessible by the Mediterranean Sea. Classical writers associate Tartessus with deposits of silver, iron, tin, and lead.[890] Jeremiah 10:9 refers to "beaten silver ...brought from Tarshish" (NRSV).

Javan, Tubal, and Meshech were Tyre's traders in slaves and bronze vessels (v. 13); that is, Tyre received these human and bronze "commodities" from them. All three are mentioned, in this same order, as descendants of Japheth in Gen 10:2; 1 Chr 1:5. Javan refers to the Ionians, Greeks of western Asia Minor. Tubal and Meshech were located in central and southeastern Asia Minor. Amos 1:9 perhaps refers to Tyrian slave trade; Joel 3:6 accuses Tyre of selling Judeans to the people of Javan.

From Beth-togarmah (eastern Asia Minor) Tyre received as trade commodities horses, war horses, and mules (v. 14). Togarmah (see also Ezek 38:6) appears in Gen 10:2 as a descendant of Gomer, the brother of Javan, Tubal, Meshech, etc. According to 1 Kgs 10:28 (2 Chr 1:16), Solomon imported horses from Kue, also in eastern Asia Minor.

Both the NRSV and the NIV emend the MT (בני דדן *běnê dědān,* "the Dedanites") to בני רדן (*běnê rōdān*, "the Rhodians"), following the LXX. The association of the site with "many coastlands" ill-suits Dedan, which appears (properly) in v. 20. Cooke retains the MT, however, pointing out the unlikelihood that ivory and ebony, products of Africa and India respectively, would have come to Tyre by way of Rhodes. Diakonoff suggests that the Rhodians received these items from Naucratis, a Greek colony in Egypt.[891] On the basis of Ps 72:10, critics have translated השיבו אשכרך (*hēšîbû ʾeškārēk*) as "rendered you tribute" (see TNK).

As Greenberg observes, however, Tyre's trading partners were not her tributaries. He therefore defines *ʾeškārēk* as " 'product to be delivered'— i.e., under agency contract."[892]

The MT's "Aram" (v. 16) appears as Edom in some manuscripts; and critics tend to emend accordingly, noting that the sequence Edom, Judah, land of Israel, Damascus (hence, vv. 16-18) runs from south to north along the King's Highway.[893] Whether the items listed (turquoise, purple, embroidered work, fine linen, coral, and rubies) were appropriate to either locale is debated. In this verse, the word for linen is בוץ (*bûṣ*), better suited to an Aramaic or Edomite trade item, as opposed to שש (*šēš*), which has an Egyptian etymology (see v. 7).[894] The precise meanings of the nouns translated "coral" and "rubies" are uncertain. The former appears also in Job 28:18; the latter in Isa 54:12.

The terminology "Judah and the land of Israel" admits several interpretations. One might, on the basis of Ezek 40:2, regard "the land of Israel" as referring to all of Israel, including Jerusalem; in 47:18, it designates the future Israel's entire territory, which is limited to the western side of the Jordan River. Alternatively, one might suppose that (at least this portion of) Ezekiel's list derives from the time of the divided kingdoms; hence, "the land of Israel" designates the (then still extant) northern kingdom. Finally, it is quite possible that the references are to the (still existing) kingdom of Judah and to the territory of the former northern kingdom (see 2 Chr 30:25; 34:7).[895]

In addition to the present passage, wheat, honey, and oil appear as products of Israel's land in Deut 8:8 and Jer 41:8. The wheat is defined more precisely as "from Minnith" (v. 17). Minnith appears in Judg 11:33 as an area lying west of Rabbah Ammon, capital of the Ammonites—that is, on the eastern side of the Jordan River. According to 2 Chr 27:5, the Ammonites paid as tribute to King Jotham of Judah (8th cent. BCE) "ten thousand cors [the exact quantity of this

890. Strabo iii.2,8f.; Diodorus v.35ff. See G. A. Cooke, *A Critical and Exegetical Commentary on the Book of Ezekiel,* 2 vols., ICC (Edinburgh: T. & T. Clark, 1936) 300-301.

891. Diakonoff, "The Naval Power and Trade of Tyre," 189-90.

892. Greenberg, *Ezekiel 21–37,* 555. See also Walther Zimmerli, *Ezekiel 2: A Commentary on the Book of the Prophet Ezekiel, Chapters 25–48,* trans. J. D. Martin, Hermeneia (Philadelphia: Fortress, 1983) 64.

893. Liverani, "The Trade Network of Tyre According to Ezek. 27," 69.

894. Greenberg, *Ezekiel 21–37,* 555.

895. Zimmerli, *Ezekiel 2,* 66-67.

large measure is uncertain] of wheat and ten thousand of barley"(NRSV). If this identification is correct, one supposes that Israelite traders served as intermediaries between Transjordanian states and Tyre.[896] The NRSV's "millet" (NIV, "confections") is פנג (pannag), another hapax. Critics have associated the noun with Akkadian pannigu and translated "(type of) cake or meal."[897] Balm ("mastic resin")[898] is associated with Transjordanian Gilead (Gen 37:25; Jer 8:22; 46:11). Again, Israelite traders may have served as conduits for these goods. Within the Joseph narrative, a caravan of Ishmaelites from Gilead transports gum, balm, and resin to Egypt (Gen 37:25; see also 43:11).[899]

Damascus participates in (and profits from) Tyrian trade by virtue of its exports—wine of Helbon, and white (undyed) wool (v. 18). The city, a capital of the Aramean (Syrian) kingdom (see, e.g., 1 Kgs 11:24; 19:15; 2 Kings 8:7, 9; 14:28; 16:10-12; Isa 7:8), was conquered by Assyria's King Tiglath-pileser III in 733/32 BCE. Here, the reference appears to be to its larger (Syrian) territory.[900]

Helbon, a town located northwest of Damascus in Anti-lebanon, appears nowhere else in Hebrew Scripture. Zimmerli cites Nebuchadrezzar's offering to Marduk of "wine from the land of . . . Hilbuni," and also the report of Strabo and Athenaeus that Persian kings consumed Halybonian wine, "of which Poseidonius says that it also grows in Damascus in Syria after the Perisians planted the vines there."[901] "White wool" presupposes צחר (ṣaḥar). Diakonoff observes that the importation of undyed wool was vital to Tyre's industry and to its trade in purple-dyed wool, since the extract (dye) of the mollusk could not be transported.[902] Other critics take ṣaḥar as a place-name ("wool of Ṣaḥar"), perhaps a wilderness area northwest of Damascus.[903]

Verse 18 ends so abruptly that critics search for its original conclusion in (an emended) v. 19a. In the MT, the latter begins with the puzzling pairing of Dan (ודן wĕdān, "[and] Dan"), a northern Israelite tribe, and Javan (ויון wĕyāwān; see v. 13), the Ionian Greeks, followed by מאוזל (mĕ'ûzzal). These three forms have long confounded critics, who suggest a variety of solutions.[904] A. R. Millard proposes minor emendations (ו [waw] becomes a י [yod] in each of the three words; mĕ'ûzzal becomes מאיזל [mĕ'îzāl, "from Izalla"]) to read, "and wine casks from Izalla," the place-name designating a city in northern Mesopotamia that was famous for its wine.[905] So construed, a third item is added to the list of Damascene trade exports to Tyre. The items listed in v. 19b, "wrought iron [or "iron ingots"], cassia, and sweet cane ["calamus"]," also derive from (are mediated through) Damascus as Tyrian imports.

Biblical tradition identifies Dedan as (1) a descendant of Raamah son of Cush (Gen 10:7; 1 Chr 1:9 or (2) a descendant of Jokshan son of Keturah, whom Abraham married some time after the death of Sarah (Gen 25:3; 1 Chr 1:32). In both contexts, Dedan and Sheba (v. 22) are brothers. The site, located at the northwest oasis of al-'Ulā, not far from Teima, was a major center of south Arabian trade during the sixth–fourth centuries BCE.[906] In that capacity it reappears (along with Sheba and "the merchants of Tarshish") in 38:13 (see also Isa 21:13). Here, Dedan trades in riding cloths.

Arabia (the north Arabian desert) was home to bedouin Arab tribes (see Jer 3:2), including Kedar, identified as a son of Ishmael in Gen 25:13. Greenberg aptly suggests that "chiefs of Kedar" (NRSV and NIV, "princes of Kedar") refers to a "federation of nomad tribes."[907] As befits nomads, these Tyrian trading partners (depicted as "trade

---

896. Ibid., 67. See also Greenberg, *Ezekiel 21–37*, 556.

897. Liverani, "The Trade Network of Tyre According to Ezek. 27," 73.

898. Zimmerli, *Ezekiel 2*, 67.

899. Greenberg, *Ezekiel 21–37*, 556.

900. On Syria's significance in ancient Near Eastern trade, see M. C. Astour, "Overland Trade Routes in Ancient Western Asia," in *Civilizations of the Ancient Near East,* 4 vols. (New York: Scribner's, 1995) 3:1414-15.

901. Zimmerli, *Ezekiel 2*, 67. The reference to Nebuchadrezzar is from VAB IV 9 Col. I, 22-28 and 19A Col. IV, 50-57; the second reference is from Strabo *Geography* 15.735; Athenaeus *Deipnosophistae* 1.28.

902. Diakonoff, "The Naval Power and Trade of Tyre," 188.

903. Zimmerli, *Ezekiel 2*, 67.

904. Zimmerli deletes ודן (wĕdān, "[and] Dan"), the first form of v. 19, as a miswritten dittography of ויון (wĕyāwān; see v. 13), the verse's second form, itself an error for ויין (wĕyayin, "and wine"). The thought begun in v. 18 concludes with בעזבוניך (bĕ'izbônayik, "as your exports"), the fourth form of v. 19. He then repoints מאוזל (mĕ'ûzzāl), the verse's third word, as מאוזל (mĕ'ûzāl, "from Usal"), which becomes the source of the products identified in v. 19b. See ibid., 49.

905. A. R. Millard, "Ezekiel xxvii 19: The Wine Trade of Damascus," *JSS* 7 (1962) 201-3. See also H. J. Van Dijk, *Ezekiel's Prophecy on Tyre (Ez. 26, 1–28, 19): A New Approach,* BibOr 20 (Rome: Pontifical Biblical Institute, 1968) 80; Diakonoff, "The Naval Power and Trade of Tyre," 188; Greenberg, *Ezekiel 21–37*, 557.

906. Diakonoff, "The Naval Power and Trade of Tyre," 190.

907. Greenberg, *Ezekiel 21–37*, 558.

agents of your hand"—that is, agents under Tyrian tutelage) export livestock: lambs, rams, and goats.[908] In an inscription regarding his campaigns against Egypt, Syria, and Palestine, Assyria's King Ashurbanipal (668–627 BCE) refers to booty seized from the Kedarites—donkeys, camels, and small cattle.[909]

Sheba and Raamah (v. 22), like Tarshish, Rhodes, and Edom, belong to Liverani's fourth (outer) belt and trade in precious metals and luxury goods: spices, precious stones, and gold.[910] Located in southern Arabia, their precise locations are uncertain. According to 1 Kgs 10:10, the queen of Sheba brought these same items to Solomon as gifts.

Verse 23 is chock-a-block with place-names; along with v. 24, it challenges commentators. Hebrew חרן (ḥārān, "road"), a commercial city on the Balikh River in northwest Mesopotamia, is familiar from Israel's ancestoral traditions. According to Gen 11:31, Terah took his son Abram and daughter-in-law Sarai, along with Lot, his grandson, and migrated from Ur of the Chaldeans to Haran. After his death there, Abram and his kin left Haran for Canaan (12:1-6; see also Gen 28:10–29:1). Canneh is unknown, though scholars have identified it as the capital of the Assyrian province of Kullani, located in Mesopotamian Aramaean territory. Eden is routinely sought in Assyrian Bit-Adini, an Aramaean state conquered by Shalmaneser III in 856 BCE and turned into an Assyrian province.[911] Diakonoff looks to Arabia, however, positing dnn, the name of a north Arabian tribal group, or Aden ('Adan), a city and natural port in south Arabia that, in the sixth century BCE, played an important role in trade.[912] The city of Assur is mentioned in its commercial capacity, and not as a major political player.[913] Zimmerli takes it in the latter sense (Assyria) and regards it as secondary. The identity of Chilmad also is uncertain. Zimmerli emends כלמד (kilmad) to read "the whole of Media." The reappearance of Sheba is suspicious.

In any event, these trade partners traffic in manufactured items—fine garments, luxury fabrics, multicolored, knotted rugs (or coverlets).

Verse 25a ends where the list began, with a reference to Tarshish. The "ships of Tarshish" should not, however, be narrowly construed as Tarshish ships per se, or as ships built for trade with Tarshish alone. Rather, the phrase designates large, seaworthy vessels, "regardless of origin or port of call."[914] The remainder of the verse returns readers to the poetry of vv. 3b-11 and describes the consequence of this great influx of goods: ship Tyre is filled and very heavy/honored/rich. Here, Greenberg observes, the primary meaning is that the vessel lies "low in the water because of its weight; paired with 'full,' it connotes 'rich(ly stocked)' as well." Zimmerli regards all of v. 25 as secondary, a "bridge" joining the list to the lamentation.[915] If such be the case, it is a finely wrought link indeed.

Scholars debate the date of Ezekiel's trade list. Aubet places it prior to the period of Assyrian domination over Judah, Israel, and Damascus, perhaps during Ithobaal's reign (887–856 BCE), when Tyrian trade in the east underwent its greatest expansion.[916] Fohrer, who believed that the list originated in Egypt (hence Egypt's absence from the list), dated it to the reign of Pharaoh Amoses III (569–525 BCE), when Egypt was heavily engaged in sea trade.[917] Liverani argues well for the period 610–590 BCE, after the collapse of the Assyrian Empire, but prior to Babylonian hegemony under Nebuchadrezzar. Like Judah under Josiah, Tyre took advantage of those years, and broadened its trade network in Arabia, Anatolia, and Media. Hence, he concludes, the "trade picture of Ezek. 27:11-23 is . . . a precise political project, limited in time to a short-term juncture . . . [and not] a generic commercial horizon, valid through all of Tyrian history."[918] Ezekiel's maritime metaphor can obscure one aspect of the list. A glance at the map proves that overland trade also is crucial to Tyre's economic enterprise. (See Reflections at 27:26-36.)

908. Greenberg, ibid., cites Ashurbanipal's list of booty from the Kedarites: "donkeys, camels, large and small cattle." See *ANET,* 299b.

909. *ANET,* 299b.

910. Liverani, "The Trade Network of Tyre According to Ezek. 27," 73.

911. See Zimmerli, *Ezekiel 2,* 68.

912. Diakonoff, "The Naval Power and Trade of Tyre," 191.

913. Liverani, "The Trade Network of Tyre According to Ezek. 27," 71.

914. Greenberg, *Ezekiel 21–37,* 561.

915. Zimmerli, *Ezekiel 2,* 69.

916. Maria Eugenia Aubet, *The Phoenicians and the West: Politics, Colonies and Trade,* trans. Mary Turton (Cambridge: Cambridge University Press, 1993) 99.

917. G. Fohrer, *Ezekiel,* HAT 13 (Tübingen: Mohr [Siebeck], 1955) 158.

918. Liverani, "The Trade Network of Tyre According to Ezek. 27," 72.

Ezekiel 27:26-36, Shipwreck, Sorrow, and Disastrous Consequences

NIV

26Your oarsmen take you
    out to the high seas.
But the east wind will break you to pieces
    in the heart of the sea.
27Your wealth, merchandise and wares,
    your mariners, seamen and shipwrights,
your merchants and all your soldiers,
    and everyone else on board
will sink into the heart of the sea
    on the day of your shipwreck.
28The shorelands will quake
    when your seamen cry out.
29All who handle the oars
    will abandon their ships;
the mariners and all the seamen
    will stand on the shore.
30They will raise their voice
    and cry bitterly over you;
they will sprinkle dust on their heads
    and roll in ashes.
31They will shave their heads because of you
    and will put on sackcloth.
They will weep over you with anguish of soul
    and with bitter mourning.
32As they wail and mourn over you,
    they will take up a lament concerning you:
"Who was ever silenced like Tyre,
    surrounded by the sea?"
33When your merchandise went out on the seas,
    you satisfied many nations;
with your great wealth and your wares
    you enriched the kings of the earth.
34Now you are shattered by the sea
    in the depths of the waters;
your wares and all your company
    have gone down with you.
35All who live in the coastlands
    are appalled at you;
their kings shudder with horror
    and their faces are distorted with fear.
36The merchants among the nations hiss at you;
    you have come to a horrible end
    and will be no more.' "

NRSV

26 Your rowers have brought you
    into the high seas.
The east wind has wrecked you
    in the heart of the seas.
27 Your riches, your wares, your merchandise,
    your mariners and your pilots,
your caulkers, your dealers in merchandise,
    and all your warriors within you,
with all the company
    that is with you,
sink into the heart of the seas
    on the day of your ruin.
28 At the sound of the cry of your pilots
    the countryside shakes,
29 and down from their ships
    come all that handle the oar.
The mariners and all the pilots of the sea
    stand on the shore
30 and wail aloud over you,
    and cry bitterly.
They throw dust on their heads
    and wallow in ashes;
31 they make themselves bald for you,
    and put on sackcloth,
and they weep over you in bitterness of soul,
    with bitter mourning.
32 In their wailing they raise a lamentation for
            you,
    and lament over you:
"Who was ever destroyed[a] like Tyre
    in the midst of the sea?
33 When your wares came from the seas,
    you satisfied many peoples;
with your abundant wealth and merchandise
    you enriched the kings of the earth.
34 Now you are wrecked by the seas,
    in the depths of the waters;
your merchandise and all your crew
    have sunk with you.
35 All the inhabitants of the coastlands
    are appalled at you;
and their kings are horribly afraid,

[a]Tg Vg: Heb *like silence*

NRSV

their faces are convulsed.
[36] The merchants among the peoples hiss at you;
 you have come to a dreadful end
 and shall be no more forever."

COMMENTARY

With v. 26*a,* the vessel's rowers are said to bring it into the high seas. Verse 26*b* states, in very succinct fashion, that the east wind breaks it "in the heart of the seas." Heretofore, Ezekiel's development of the "Tyre is a ship" trope has focused upon positive associations with its vehicle (ship)— its beauty, expert crew, and thriving trade. Suddenly, however, he foregrounds a previous suppressed, but undoubtedly apt association with ships: they sometimes sink. Psalm 48:7 speaks in simile of the east wind shattering the ships of Tarshish; and other passages testify to the sirocco's destructive capacity (e.g., Ezek 17:10; 19:12; Isa 27:8; Jer 18:17; Hos 13:15; Jonah 4:8). In these contexts, the east wind is presented not as a natural phenomenon, but as an instrument of, or way of illumining, Yahweh's judgment. Hence, the reader is predisposed to interpret v. 26 as divine punishment—another way of describing God's utter destruction of Tyre (promised in chap. 26). Tyre, whose security was largely a consequence of its setting "in the heart of the seas," meets its violent end there. Verse 27 enumerates what goes down with the ship, its vocabulary drawn not only from vv. 8*b*-10, but also from the trade list ("wealth," "exports," "imports"). If the latter be secondary, it is nonetheless clear that an effort has been made to integrate its terminology into the larger passage (see also v. 3). "On the day of your fall" echoes 26:18.

The outcries of the drowning sailors reverberate in nature. The MT reads "your open country will quake"—possible if a reference to the mainland is intended. Citing Isa 57:20 and Amos 8:8, Greenberg proposes "waves will toss."[919] Verses 29-31 movingly portray sailors disembarking from their ships and standing on the shore, wailing aloud at Tyre's sinking, weeping bitterly, and engaging in various ritual acts of mourning: throwing dust upon their heads (see Josh 7:6; Job 2:12); rolling in ashes (see Mic 1:10; Jer 6:26); cutting (or plucking out) their hair (7:18; Lev 21:5 [proscribed]; Mic 1:16; Isa 22:12; Jer 16:6); and donning sackcloth (7:18; Isa 22:12; Jer 6:26).

Verse 32 introduces the sailors' woeful lament over Tyre. Unfortunately, its first line is difficult to construe. The MT's כדמה (*kĕdumâ*), perhaps "like silence" (see NIV) or "like something destroyed" (see NRSV), fails to satisfy critics, who suggest that it be read either as נדמה (*nidmâ*), "be like, resemble" (hence, "Who was like Tyre in the midst of the sea?"),[920] or as a cognate of Akkadian *dimtu,* "tower, fortified area" (hence, "Who was like Tyre, like a tower in the midst of the sea?").[921] The latter option is possible; elsewhere the city is called "the fortified city of Tyre" (Josh 19:29 NRSV). Zechariah 9:3 asserts that "Tyre has built herself a stronghold" (NIV); and Isa 23:14 reads, "Wail, you ships of Tarshish, your fortress [Tyre] is destroyed" (NIV). So emended, the sailors' dirge begins with a description of Tyre's former glory, as befits the genre. This reading does not, however, maintain the metaphor. In v. 33, the sailors recall how Tyre's exports enriched the nations and their kings. Verse 34, then, turns to the "now" portion of the lament: The ship is lost, along with its cargo and crew.

Verses 35-36*a* describe the consternation of those for whom Tyre's demise has grave economic consequences—the inhabitants of the coastlands (see 26:15, 18; 27:3) and their kings, the traders among the nations. Zimmerli states that to hiss (or whistle) is to gloat: "Tyre's rivals rejoice over her fall."[922] He has misconstrued the line's meaning,

919. Greenberg, *Ezekiel 21–37,* 561. See also Van Dijk, "the waves shake," *Ezekiel's Prophecy on Tyre,* 84-85.

920. Zimmerli, *Ezekiel 2,* 52.
921. Van Dijk, *Ezekiel's Prophecy on Tyre,* 85-86; Greenberg, *Ezekiel 21–37,* 562.
922. Zimmerli, *Ezekiel 2,* 69.

however (see 1 Kgs 9:8; Lam 2:15). Theirs is an expression of profound grief, as the context demands. Verse 36*b*, with its reference to horror ("dreadful end") and Tyre's eternal extinction, echoes 26:21.

REFLECTIONS

With consummate artistry, Ezekiel 27 invites its readers into the world of Tyre's rich and far-flung trade network. The "lament," which the prophet introduces as Yahweh's own word to Tyre (though its actual audience is his fellow exiles) describes the magnificent vessel and its crew, celebrates its commercial success, but then describes its demise and the anguished reactions of those whose fortune sinks with the ship. As noted in the commentary, the sailors' lament in 27:32-36 is heartfelt, but Ezekiel's larger lamentation, especially when read in the light of the preceding chapter, is not.

In the Reflections on chapter 26, it is observed that the prophet's anger toward Tyre likely derived from that city's ability, by virtue of its geographical setting, to survive Nebuchadrezzar's forces, God's instrument of judgment, despite its apparent complicity in a plan to rebel against Babylon (Jer 27:3). (Many of the observations in that Reflections section are germane to the present passage, as well, and readers are urged to review it.) Ezekiel says nothing of the sort here; indeed, the only hint of Tyrian wrongdoing appears in 27:3, where she boasts, "I am perfect in beauty." The text goes on to substantiate that claim in subsequent verses, but the reader who knows that hubris is a frequent charge in prophetic oracles against foreign nations and rulers will likely detect in her utterance the proverbial pride that goes before a fall. The reader will likely detect Yahweh behind the east wind that wrecks the vessel, but the lament proper contains no explicit reference to a deity. Were it not for its introduction, and our knowledge of Ezekiel's antipathy toward Tyre, we might read Ezekiel 27 as what it purports to be—an actual lament over a city which, from the prophet's perspective, is as good as dead.

Hals points out that while the "shocking jolt" of Tyre's sinking can lead to remarks about the transitory nature of splendor and riches, as well as the folly of placing one's trust in those values, the text itself makes no such observations.[923] He is correct, but it is difficult to read Ezekiel 27 without entertaining those thoughts. Today, no less than in Ezekiel's own, the forces of nature can wipe out material resources in the twinkling of an eye. During tornado season, for example, television news reports show scene after scene of devastation wrought by wind, rain, and hail. Families, even entire communities, can in a matter of moments lose all of their possessions. Fires can leave people with only the clothes on their backs. Even when life is not lost, these are lamentable catastrophes; and they force us to reckon with the impermanence of our possessions, even as we mourn their ruin. Those same news reports also testify to the strength of the human spirit, however, when they display congregations standing and worshiping at sites where churches and synagogues stood only days before.

The story of Jesus' encounter with a rich young man whose life was a model of commandment keeping, but whose many possessions were too high a price to pay even for eternal life (Matt 19:16-22), reminds us of the importance of weighing our priorities. We marvel at his short-sighted decision ("When the young man heard [Jesus'] word, he went away grieving, for he had many possessions," Matt 19:22 NRSV), but then must ask ourselves if we are guilty of following his example. The dangers posed by wealth is a recurring New Testament theme. One thinks also of Jesus' "sermon on the mountain," when he taught, "Do not store up for yourselves treasures on earth, where moth and rust consume and where thieves break in and steal; but store up for yourselves treasures in heaven, where neither moth nor rust consumes and where thieves do not break in and steal. For where your treasure is, there your heart will be also" (Matt 6:19-21 NRSV).

---

923. Ronald M. Hals, *Ezekiel,* FOTL 19 (Grand Rapids: Eerdmans, 1989) 192.

Ezekiel's oracle against ship Tyre impressed the author of Revelation 18, who used it (including a trade list) as the model for portions of his taunt concerning the fall of Rome (called "Babylon"). In three dirges, kings (Rev 18:9-10), merchants (Rev 18:11-17a), and mariners (Rev 18:17b-20) lament the great city, destroyed by fire. "Alas, alas, the great city," the shipmasters, seafarers, sailors, and sea traders intone, "where all who had ships at sea grew rich by her wealth! For in one hour she has been laid waste" (Rev 18:19 NRSV).

Ezekiel 28:1-19, The Downfall of the King of Tyre

OVERVIEW

Ezekiel's sixth (28:1-10) and seventh (28:11-19) oracles concerning Tyre, a Phoenician city-state located on an island just off the eastern coast of the Mediterranean Sea (see the maps on 557-58), address its ruler ("prince," v. 2; "king," v. 11). Neither oracle is dated; the reader likely associates them with the incomplete date notice prefixed to the prophet's first anti-Tyre oracle (26:1), 587/86 BCE. Ittobaal III ruled Tyre from 590 to 575 BCE, but that datum sheds little light upon these passages, since neither oracle appears to disclose biographical information about a particular Tyrian king. As its leading "citizen," Tyre's ruler essentially epitomizes his realm as perceived through Ezekiel's biased eyes.

Verses 1-10 pronounce judgment upon the monarch, who by virtue of his secure geographical setting "in the heart of the seas" esteems himself a god who sits upon a divine throne (v. 2a). The ancient reader, accustomed to the role that hubris ("pride") plays in many a prophetic denunciation of foreign nations and rulers, already perceives in his self-appraisal an arrogance inviting Yahweh's judgment. Verse 2b rebuts the ruler's pretention to divinity. True, his wisdom exceeds that of the legendary Dāni'ēl (v. 3), and he has used it to amass enormous wealth through trade (vv. 4-5a). But his consequent pride will be pierced by the swords of "the most terrible of the nations" (v. 7), the Babylonians. Death distinguishes mortals from deities. Tyre's ruler will meet a violent end "in the heart of the seas"—the very setting that, he has thought, made him inviolable and assured his ongoing prosperity (v. 8b; cf. v. 2a). So much for his claim to divinity.

Verses 11-19 present, by dint of the introductory formulae in vv. 11-12a, as a separate oracle—

Yahweh's own, mocking "lament" over Tyre's king. Yet this passage is closely linked to the preceding doom pronouncement (both address Tyre's ruler and describe his ruination, and they share a number of terms). Twice before in oracles against Tyre, Ezekiel has described its destruction, but then placed lamentations on the lips of those who suffer the economic and political pangs of its fate (26:17-18; 27:32-36). Hence, the reader is predisposed to construe vv. 11-19 as a complement to vv. 1-10.

This "lament," however, is distinctive in many ways. True to its genre, it contrasts the past glory of Tyre's king with his present status—if not dead, then as good as dead. But, as Hals observes, the dirge's deep indebtedness to mythological themes and motifs distinguishes this king's demise, as does the fact that Yahweh, ostensibly the speaker throughout, structures the lament along the pattern of primeval sin and punishment.[924] While vv. 1-10 are fairly straightforward (but see below), vv. 11-19 bristle with difficulties. Critics concede that the dirge over Tyre's king is among Ezekiel's most confounding compositions, and many conclude that it has undergone significant expansion at the hands of later traditionists. So, for example, Zimmerli prunes the text, recasting it in the 3 + 2 (qînah) metrical pattern characteristic of (at least portions of) many Hebrew laments.[925]

Discussion will work from the consonantal Masoretic Text (MT), presuming that the hypo-

---

924. Ronald M. Hals, *Ezekiel*, FOTL 19 (Grand Rapids: Eerdmans, 1989) 199.

925. W. Zimmerli, *Ezekiel 2: A Commentary on the Book of the Prophet Ezekiel, Chapters 25–48*, trans. J. D. Martin, Hermeneia (Philadelphia: Fortress, 1983) 87-89.

thetical ancient reader struggled to make sense of it without (anachronistic) recourse to the analytical methods and reconstructions of modern biblical scholarship. This approach does not disavow the possibility that the earliest form of the dirge was subsequently amplified. Neither does it deny that parts of the text are obscure. Indeed, the ancient reader may have experienced some frus-

tration in attempting to understand it, although it is also possible that such a reader, familiar with a broader range of paradise myth motifs and themes than have survived in the extant literature of ancient Israel's world, stumbled less often than we. Rather, it opts to treat these verses in their final (canonical) form.

Ezekiel 28:1-10, Judgment upon the King of Tyre

NIV

28 The word of the LORD came to me: [2]"Son of man, say to the ruler of Tyre, 'This is what the Sovereign LORD says:

" 'In the pride of your heart
  you say, "I am a god;
I sit on the throne of a god
  in the heart of the seas."
But you are a man and not a god,
  though you think you are as wise as a god.
[3]Are you wiser than Daniel[a] ?
  Is no secret hidden from you?
[4]By your wisdom and understanding
  you have gained wealth for yourself
and amassed gold and silver
  in your treasuries.
[5]By your great skill in trading
  you have increased your wealth,
and because of your wealth
  your heart has grown proud.

  [6]" 'Therefore this is what the Sovereign LORD says:

" 'Because you think you are wise,
  as wise as a god,
[7]I am going to bring foreigners against you,
  the most ruthless of nations;
they will draw their swords against your
      beauty and wisdom
  and pierce your shining splendor.
[8]They will bring you down to the pit,
  and you will die a violent death
  in the heart of the seas.
[9]Will you then say, "I am a god,"

[a]3 Or *Danel*; the Hebrew spelling may suggest a person other than the prophet Daniel.

NRSV

28 The word of the LORD came to me: [2]Mortal, say to the prince of Tyre, Thus says the Lord GOD:
  Because your heart is proud
    and you have said, "I am a god;
  I sit in the seat of the gods,
    in the heart of the seas,"
  yet you are but a mortal, and no god,
    though you compare your mind
    with the mind of a god.
[3]You are indeed wiser than Daniel;[a]
    no secret is hidden from you;
[4]by your wisdom and your understanding
    you have amassed wealth for yourself,
  and have gathered gold and silver
    into your treasuries.
[5]By your great wisdom in trade
    you have increased your wealth,
  and your heart has become proud in your
      wealth.
[6]Therefore thus says the Lord GOD:
  Because you compare your mind
    with the mind of a god,
[7]therefore, I will bring strangers against you,
    the most terrible of the nations;
  they shall draw their swords against the
      beauty of your wisdom
    and defile your splendor.
[8]They shall thrust you down to the Pit,
    and you shall die a violent death
    in the heart of the seas.
[9]Will you still say, "I am a god,"
    in the presence of those who kill you,
  though you are but a mortal, and no god,

[a]Or, as otherwise read, *Danel*

NIV	NRSV

in the presence of those who kill you?
 You will be but a man, not a god,
     in the hands of those who slay you.
 ¹⁰You will die the death of the uncircumcised
     at the hands of foreigners.
 	
 I have spoken, declares the Sovereign LORD.' "
	in the hands of those who wound you?
	 ¹⁰You shall die the death of the uncircumcised
	     by the hand of foreigners;
	     for I have spoken, says the Lord GOD.

COMMENTARY

The two-part judgment oracle of Ezekiel 28:1-10 identifies the sins of Tyre's ruler (vv. 2a-5) and proclaims his impending punishment (vv. 6-10). It is introduced by the prophet's claim to have received a fresh communiqué from Yahweh (v. 1), followed by God's characteristic mode of direct address ("Mortal") and a command to speak to the "prince" (נגיד *nāgîd*) of Tyre. This noun appears only here within the book of Ezekiel; elsewhere in Hebrew Scripture, it often designates the kings of Israel and Judah (e.g., Saul, 1 Sam 9:16; David, 1 Sam 13:14; 25:30; Solomon, 1 Kgs 1:35; Jeroboam, 1 Kgs 14:7; Hezekiah, 2 Kgs 20:4; but see Dan 9:25-26). Richter has argued that early in Israel's history, *nāgîd* meant "deliverer," though later prophetic usage of the term was more general.[926] Alt defined the *nāgîd* as one appointed by Yahweh to lead the nation (e.g., 1 Sam 9:16; 10:1; 13:14; 25:30; 2 Sam 7:8; 1 Kgs 14:7; 16:7; 1 Chr 11:2; 2 Chr 6:5; Isa 55:4).[927] In the light of this usage, some critics reason that Ezekiel calls Tyre's ruler "prince" in order to aver that he too was appointed by Yahweh, and so should be beholden to Israel's God. (Is the same nuance present in Psalm 76:12, where "princes" appears in parallelism with "the kings of the earth"?) But Jer 20:1 applies the term to Pashhur, "chief officer" (NRSV) in Yahweh's Temple; and in later texts also, it refers to priestly officials, including the high priest (1 Chr 9:11; 2 Chr 31:13; 35:8; Neh 11:11; Dan 11:22).[928] This usage should be kept in mind, since in subsequent verses (especially vv. 11-19), Tyre's ruler will be cast not only as king, but also

as priest (a caricature true, it seems, to the king of Tyre's dual role as monarch and as priest of Melqart, the city's principal deity).

The messenger formula, "Thus says the Lord GOD," launches the oracle per se, which commences with "because" (יען *ya'an*) and the reason for the presaged punishment. The heart of Tyre's ruler is "high"—that is, haughty. Proverbs 16:5 threatens those with lofty hearts:

> All those who are arrogant ("high of heart") are <br> an abomination to the Lord;
     be assured, they will not go unpunished.

The reader who is familiar with this tenet of sapiential thought already glimpses the inevitable outcome of Ezekiel's oracle against the prince of Tyre. That same reader soon discovers that "heart" is a key word in this passage; it appears eight times and with several different meanings. Here and in v. 5, it is the locus of pride, while in vv. 2b and 6, it designates the seat of wisdom—that is, the "mind." Its usage in the phrase "in the heart of the seas" (vv. 2, 8; see also 27:4, 26) is overtly metaphorical, designating the midst of the sea, as opposed to the shore.[929]

In the ultimate expression of self-aggrandizement, Tyre's prince has thought "I am a god;/ I sit on a divine throne,/ in the heart of the seas." To Israelite ears, even rulers risk divine wrath in uttering such a boast. To be sure, Psalm 2 ascribes to Yahweh the following assertion about Judah's monarchs: "You are my son; today I have begotten you" (v. 7). But Israel did not deify its kings. Whether or not Tyre's kings actually claimed

---

926. W. Richter, "Die nâgîd Formel," *BZ* 9 (1965) 71-84.
927. A. Alt, "The Formation of the Israelite State in Palestine," *Essays on Old Testament History and Religion*, trans. R. A. Wilson (Oxford: Basil Blackwell, 1966) 195.
928. For additional meanings of the noun, see *BDB*, 617b-618a.

929. Moshe Greenberg, *Ezekiel 21-37*, AB 22A (Garden City, N.Y.: Doubleday, 1997) 573.

divine status is a moot point.[930] The thought that Ezekiel ascribes to the prince sets him up for destruction.

The phrase אל אני (*'ēl 'ānî*) admits two different translations. One takes *'ēl* as a common noun ("A god am I"). The other reads it as the proper name of the head deity of the Canaanite pantheon ("*El* am I"). Scholars have long debated which of these two options is appropriate to v. 2. On the one hand, those who opt for the appellative sense ("god") note that in v. 9, the prince's claim to divinity is expressed differently: אלהים אני (*'ēlōhîm 'ānî*), "A god am I." Because in that context, *'ēlōhîm* is a common noun, the *'ēl* of v. 2*a* should be understood in the same way. Moreover, Ezekiel's choice of *'ēl* may have been suggested by his subsequent, two-fold use of the succinct phrase ואתה אדם ולא־אל (*wĕ'attâ 'ādām wĕlō'-'ēl*), "but you are a human and not a god" (vv. 2*b*, 9*b*).[931] Ezekiel did not coin this phrase; it appears in Isa 31:3, "but Egypt is human and not a god" (see also Num 23:19; Isa 45:22; 46:9; Hos 11:9*b*). Finally, critics point out that Melqart—"King of the City" and patron of shipping and trade—was Tyre's principal deity, not El.[932] Hence, it is far more likely that Tyre's human king is presented in the guise of that deity than of El.

On the other hand, some scholars accept Marvin Pope's thesis that Ezek 28:1-19 is best construed in the light of El myths lodged within the Ugaritic literary corpus.[933] According to his reconstruction of those myths, the aged El was deposed by the storm god Baal, who banished him from Mt. Zaphon and forced him to dwell "at the springs of the (two) rivers, in the midst of the channels of the (two) deeps."[934] Despite El's attempts to regain his former position, he was constrained to remain an underworld deity. At one level, vv. 1-10 address Tyre's proud and presumptive

monarch, whose claim of divinity rests on his secure and economically advantageous island setting ("I sit on the divine throne, in the heart of the seas"). At a deeper level, however, they betray the influence of the El myths. Like the deposed El, who was renowned for his wisdom, Tyre's wise prince will soon be ousted and forced to dwell in the underworld. Pope goes on to argue that the account of El's past glory and subsequent fall has significantly shaped vv. 11-19 as well. Once, the head of the Canaanite pantheon dwelt on the cosmic mountain in a palace constructed of precious metals and gemstones. But he was cast down from the mount and relegated to the underworld. Tyre's king will suffer the same fate.[935]

One need not accept Pope's entire argument concerning the relationship between the El myths on the one hand, and Ezek 28:1-19, on the other, in order to posit that the self-aggrandizing quotation attributed to Tyre's prince in v. 2 stirs thoughts of El and his watery abode. Pope himself suggests that Ezekiel's use of *'ēl* in v. 2*a* is "intentionally ambiguous."[936] The prophet appears to play on the two possible meanings of *'ēl*—common noun and proper name. Poetry is, of its nature, polyvalent, and we have no firm basis on which to assert that only one or the other meaning was in his mind. The reader who is familiar with the myth of El and his dwelling place might interpret the verse in that light. The reader who is not can nonetheless make sense of the statement; by either reading, it constitutes a culpable expression of pride (see also v. 8; Isa 14:13-15).

Verse 2*b* performs two functions: It (immediately) refutes the prince's claim to divinity ("but you are a human being and not a god," v. 2*b*); and it introduces the motif of wisdom ("though you compare your mind ["heart"] with the mind ["heart"] of a god," v. 2*b*) which follows in vv. 3-5 and 7*b*. In the opinion of some scholars, both functions point to the secondary status of this half-verse. On the one hand, they observe, the immediate rebuff of the prince's claim deflates the oracle's rhetorical power.[937] On the other hand,

---

930. According to Aubet, the king of Tyre claimed divinity, equating himself with the god of the city. See Maria Eugenia Aubet, *The Phoenicians and the West: Politics, Colonies and Trade,* trans. Mary Turton (Cambridge: Cambridge University Press, 1993) 123. However, Ezekiel speaks not only of Tyre's earthly ruler, but also of Tyre's patron deity, Melqart, whom the monarch both serves (as priest) and represents.

931. See, e.g., Zimmerli, *Ezekiel 2,* 77-78; Greenberg, *Ezekiel 21–37,* 573; H. J. Van Dijk, *Ezekiel's Prophecy on Tyre (Ez. 26, 1–28, 19) A New Approach,* BibOr 20 (Rome: Pontifical Biblical Institute, 1968) 97.

932. J. W. Wevers, *Ezekiel,* NCB (London: Nelson, 1969) 214.

933. Marvin H. Pope, *El in the Ugaritic Texts,* VTSup 2 (Leiden: Brill, 1955).

934. Ibid., 61-81.

935. Ibid., 97-103.

936. Ibid., 98. See also Frank Moore Cross, *Canaanite Myth and Hebrew Epic: Essays in the History of Religion of Israel* (Cambridge, Mass.: Harvard University Press, 1973) 44.

937. John Thomas Strong, "Ezekiel's Oracles Against the Nations Within the Context of His Message" (Ph.D. diss., Union Theological Seminary in Virginia, 1993) 209.

the introduction of the wisdom motif became necessary only after vv. 3-5, 7*b* had been inserted by a later hand.[938] Originally, then, the oracle consisted of vv. 1-2*a*, 6, 7, 8-10.

For this Commentary, the overriding question is whether the received text admits a coherent reading. Nothing precludes a swift rebuttal of the prince's claim to divinity (indeed, the blasphemous nature of his statement might be thought to demand it); and the ancient Near Eastern reader, who regards wisdom as an essential attribute of worthy kings, is not surprised that Ezekiel should elaborate upon the wisdom of a ruler who compares his mind to that of the gods. Verse 3 concedes that Tyre's prince is even wiser than Daniel, the legendary king of Ugarit referred to in the story of Aqhat (see the Commentary on 14:12-20), so that no mystery is hidden from him. The late date of the book of Daniel precludes the possibly that Ezekiel refers to the biblical Daniel as he appears in that text. Yet Dan 4:9 says of him, "no mystery is too difficult for you." The ability of the exceedingly wise to decode mysteries was, it seems, an established sapiential idea (see also 1 Kgs 10:3).

According to vv. 4-5, Tyre's prince has put his wisdom to a specific purpose: the acquisition of great "wealth" (חיל *ḥayil*) through "trade" (רכל *rākal*). Tyre's wealth (הון *hôn*) is emphasized in chapter 27 (vv. 12, 18, 27, 33), where forms of *rākal* also abound (vv. 3, 13, 15, 17, 20, 22-23, 24 [twice]). As a consequence, these verses, so often dismissed as secondary, not only provide the reader with an additional, specific, and already-established reason for the prince of Tyre's arrogance (wealth borne of successful commerce), but also link this chapter to the preceding one. If, as so many critics agree, vv. 3-5 are secondary additions to the basic text, they are nonetheless apropos to their context.

Verse 6*a* consists of לכן (*lākēn*, "therefore") and a second messenger formula (see v. 2). On form-critical grounds, one expects the proclamation of punishment to follow immediately thereafter. Instead, the second half of the verse, commencing with "because" (יען *ya'an*), reiterates the indictment of v. 2*b* ("though you compare your mind [heart] with the mind of a god"), creating a some-

what awkward envelope for vv 3-5. Verse 7*a*, then, begins with a second "therefore." (The sequence "therefore . . . because . . . therefore" appears elsewhere in the book; e.g., 22:19.)

Verses 7-10 describe the prince's punishment. Yahweh will bring against him/his city "strangers [זרים *zārîm*] . . . the most terrible of nations [עריצי גוים *'ārîṣê gôyim*]." For the reader, Tyre's destroyer—Nebuchadrezzar and his troops—was already identified in 26:7. (This same phrase appears in 31:12, an oracle against Egypt's pharaoh. According to 30:10-11, his end also comes at the hand of Nebuchadrezzar "and his people with him, the most terrible of the nations.") The king of Babylon's soldiers will draw their swords "against the beauty of your wisdom/and defile your splendor" (v. 7*b*). This half-verse echoes several terms appearing in previous anti-Tyrian verses: "sword" (26:11); "beauty" (27:3-4, 11); and "wisdom" (27:8*b*, 9; 28:3-5). Hebrew "splendor," "radiance" (יפעה *yip'â*) is a *hapax legomenon,* appearing only here and in v. 17. According to Oppenheim, "the sanctity of the royal person is often said to be revealed by a supernatural and awe-inspiring radiance or aura . . . characteristic of deities and of all things divine . . . [Akkadian] *melammu,* something like 'awe-inspiring luminosity,' is [the] most frequent" term for this phenomenon.[939] Hence, to "defile" the prince's splendor is to disclose his (actual) human status.[940]

According to v. 8, the ruler's foes will thrust him down to the "Pit" (שחת *Šaḥat*). Elsewhere in the book of Ezekiel, this term refers to a pit-trap employed by the nations to capture man-eating lions—a metaphor for two of Judah's last kings (19:4, 8). Here, however, it designates the netherworld (see also Ps 16:10, where *Šaḥat* parallels "Sheol," and Ps 30:10 [= Sheol, v. 4*a* (בור *bôr,* "pit," "grave," v. 4*b*)]; *bôr* appeared in 26:20, "those who go down to the pit"). "You shall die a violent death" is, in Hebrew, "you shall die the death of the slain," hence a brutal, unnatural death (see Jer 16:4). As noted in the Overview, the prince's demise "in the heart of the seas" is ironic, since he has thought himself impervious to danger there (v. 2).

---

938. The insertion of vv. 3-5, Zimmerli argues, necessitated a secondary recapitulation of the indictment (v. 6*b*) plus "therefore" (in v. 7*a*); see *Ezekiel 2,* 75.

939. A. L. Oppenheim, *Ancient Mesopotamia,* rev. ed., completed by E. Reiner (Chicago: University of Chicago Press, 1977) 98. See also Greenberg, *Ezekiel 21–37,* 575.

940. Greenberg, *Ezekiel 21–37,* 575.

Clearly, the intended answer to the rhetorical question posed in v. 9*a* ("Will you still say, 'I am a god,' in the presence of the one who kills you?") is no. Verse 9*b* echoes v. 2*b*: "but you are a human and not a god." Both the NRSV and the NIV read מְחֹלְלֶיךָ (*mĕḥōlĕleykā,* "your slayers"; see v. 8) for the MT's מְחַלְלֶיךָ (*mĕḥalleykā,* "your polluters," "desecrators"; see v. 7).[941] The emendation is supported by the LXX and some manuscripts. But Carol Newsom discerns significance in the canonical form:

> The frustration of the reader's expectation of a form of . . . *ḥll* "to slay" . . . makes one attend to the implications of . . . the reference to pollution. Just as the prince claimed to be a god because of his divine dwelling "in the heart of the seas," so Ezekiel promises him that he will be . . . "slain in the heart of the seas." Since the presence of a corpse in a holy place profanes it and makes it unsuitable for the indwelling presence

of a deity, Ezekiel is wryly telling the pretentious king of Tyre that once he is killed there, Tyre will be defiled and no longer a suitable residence for a god.[942]

Verse 10 further demeans Tyre's prince. If, as Herodotus asserts (2.104), the Phoenicians practiced circumcision, then v. 10*a* cannot be construed simply at the literal level. From Israel's perspective, uncircumcision was a disgrace (see Gen 34:14), "uncircumcised" a term of derision (see, e.g., Judg 14:3; 15:18; 1 Sam 14:6; 17:26—all references to the Philistines). To "die the death of the uncircumcised" by the hand of strangers (see v. 7) is to perish in disgrace. (Greenberg cites, as a contemporary equivalent, to "die like a dog.")[943] The oracle ends with the closing formula, "for I have spoken, says the Lord GOD."

---

941. So, e.g., Zimmerli, *Ezekiel 2,* 75. See also Greenberg, *Ezekiel 21–37,* 575.

942. Carol Newsom, "A Maker of Metaphors: Ezekiel's Oracles against Tyre," in *The Place Is Too Small for Us,* ed. Robert P. Gordon (Winona Lake: Eisenbrauns, 1995) 199-200.

943. Greenberg, *Ezekiel 21–37,* 576.

REFLECTIONS

The Hebrew Bible frequently asserts that an unbridgeable gulf separates God from human beings. Other nations might deify their kings, but the equation of the human and the divine was considered blasphemy in Israel. Ezekiel, whose antipathy toward Tyre was, in large measure, a consequence of its ability (by virtue of its secure island setting) to withstand the Babylonians, Yahweh's current instruments of punishment, attributes this blasphemous claim to Tyre's prince, then swiftly rebuts it. True, the ruler is wise and wealthy. But neither those attributes nor his seemingly impregnable location "in the heart of the seas" will deliver him from God's judgment. Pride is one of the proverbial "seven deadly sins." As Ezekiel portrays him, Tyre's prince is puffed up by a pride so great that it causes him to forget who he is—a mortal who, like all human beings, will perish. Few of us will ever know extraordinary wealth. We can imagine, however, how mortality frustrates those whose fortunes avail them of "anything money can buy," but who must die nonetheless. Two New Testament texts cited in the Reflections to Ezekiel 27 (Matt 6:19-21 and 19:16-22) are as relevant to this passage as to the preceding chapter, for both urge against a life ruled by material wealth.

In previous reflections on Ezekiel's oracles against foreign nations, I have acknowledged disease with the prophet's perspective that Yahweh's preferred method of dealing with "problematic peoples" is extermination. Ezekiel insists that this is true, even as he insisted that the destruction of Judah, including Jerusalem, its capital, was God's just punishment for Israel's long-lived and ongoing sins. Both assertions are fundamental to the prophet's understanding of Yahweh's sovereign control over history, and as serious conversation partners with our scriptural heritage, we owe it to Ezekiel to try to understand why he argued as he did. At the same time, we are not constrained simply to accept his presuppositions as our own. When Tyre was finally conquered by Alexander the Great in 332 BCE, tens of thousands of its inhabitants were sold into slavery. Dare we think that God cared nothing for the Phoenicians whose lives ended or were uprooted during those days?

Ezekiel 28:11-19, A Lament over the King of Tyre

NIV

[11]The word of the LORD came to me: [12]"Son of man, take up a lament concerning the king of Tyre and say to him: 'This is what the Sovereign LORD says:

" 'You were the model of perfection,
full of wisdom and perfect in beauty.
[13]You were in Eden,
the garden of God;
every precious stone adorned you:
ruby, topaz and emerald,
chrysolite, onyx and jasper,
sapphire,[a] turquoise and beryl.[b]
Your settings and mountings[c] were made of
gold;
on the day you were created they were prepared.
[14]You were anointed as a guardian cherub,
for so I ordained you.
You were on the holy mount of God;
you walked among the fiery stones.
[15]You were blameless in your ways
from the day you were created
till wickedness was found in you.
[16]Through your widespread trade
you were filled with violence,
and you sinned.
So I drove you in disgrace from the mount of
God,
and I expelled you, O guardian cherub,
from among the fiery stones.
[17]Your heart became proud
on account of your beauty,
and you corrupted your wisdom
because of your splendor.
So I threw you to the earth;
I made a spectacle of you before kings.
[18]By your many sins and dishonest trade
you have desecrated your sanctuaries.
So I made a fire come out from you,
and it consumed you,
and I reduced you to ashes on the ground
in the sight of all who were watching.

[a]13 Or lapis lazuli   [b]13 The precise identification of some of these
precious stones is uncertain.   [c]13 The meaning of the Hebrew for
this phrase is uncertain.

NRSV

11Moreover the word of the LORD came to me:
[12]Mortal, raise a lamentation over the king of
Tyre, and say to him, Thus says the Lord GOD:
You were the signet of perfection,[a]
full of wisdom and perfect in beauty.
[13]You were in Eden, the garden of God;
every precious stone was your covering,
carnelian, chrysolite, and moonstone,
beryl, onyx, and jasper,
sapphire,[b] turquoise, and emerald;
and worked in gold were your settings
and your engravings.[a]
On the day that you were created
they were prepared.
[14]With an anointed cherub as guardian I placed
you;[a]
you were on the holy mountain of God;
you walked among the stones of fire.
[15]You were blameless in your ways
from the day that you were created,
until iniquity was found in you.
[16]In the abundance of your trade
you were filled with violence, and you
sinned;
so I cast you as a profane thing from the
mountain of God,
and the guardian cherub drove you out
from among the stones of fire.
[17]Your heart was proud because of your beauty;
you corrupted your wisdom for the sake of
your splendor.
I cast you to the ground;
I exposed you before kings,
to feast their eyes on you.
[18]By the multitude of your iniquities,
in the unrighteousness of your trade,
you profaned your sanctuaries.
So I brought out fire from within you;
it consumed you,
and I turned you to ashes on the earth
in the sight of all who saw you.
[19]All who know you among the peoples
are appalled at you;

[a]Meaning of Heb uncertain   [b]Or lapis lazuli

NIV

¹⁹All the nations who knew you
are appalled at you;
you have come to a horrible end
and will be no more.' "

NRSV

you have come to a dreadful end
and shall be no more forever.

COMMENTARY

As noted in the Overview, Ezekiel's lamentation over the ruler (here called "king") of Tyre challenges interpreters. Not only is the text difficult at points, but also one may be certain that its motifs and imagery exceed our knowledge of ancient Near Eastern mythology. Clearly, the prophet has borrowed material appearing also in Genesis 2–3, the story of Adam and Eve, whose disobedience led to their expulsion from the Garden of Eden. But neither that text nor other surviving accounts of primeval paradise illumines every aspect of his oracle. Hence, we cannot always discern what Ezekiel intends to say, where he has borrowed from existing ideas and images, or where he has assumed the role of creative innovator. While v. 2 identifies the oracle as a lament, and the passage characteristically contrasts the subject's past glory (vv. 12b-15) with subsequent disaster (vv. 16-19), its sin/punishment scheme sets it apart from conventional dirges.

Again, Ezekiel receives Yahweh's word, a command that he raise a dirge over, and addressed to, Tyre's king (מלך *melek*; the prophet's actual audience remains his fellow exiles). The shift from "prince," (נגיד *nāgîd*) in v. 2 to "king" (*melek*) in v. 12 should be noted; perhaps these are simply two different ways of referring to the same human ruler. But because the name of Tyre's principal deity, Melqart, means "King of the City," it is also possible that Ezekiel's lament intends to stir thoughts of both entities—the mortal king and the god he serves/represents.

The lamentation commences with the messenger formula ("Thus says the Lord GOD"). In the light of the preceding judgment oracle, Yahweh's ostensibly affirming words to the monarch are startling. Unfortunately, the first phrase is obscure, as the NRSV acknowledges. The MT may be translated, "You were a sealing of proportion" (חותם תכנית *hôtēm toknît*), but most critics agree that *hôtēm*, a participle, should be repointed as the noun חותם (*hôtām*, "seal, signet ring"). The king's seal was used to authenticate documents (1 Kgs 21:8); and the bearer of his signet ring wielded royal authority (see, e.g., Esth 3:10; 8:2). In Jer 22:24, Yahweh rejects King Jehoiachin (Coniah) as "the signet ring on my right hand"; in Hag 2:23, Yahweh promises to make Zerubbabel "like a signet ring." The sense seems to be that the king, as God's signet, is the authentic representative and administrator of Yahweh's royal power on earth. Wilson notes that *hôtām* also appears in descriptions of the vestments of Israel's high priest, which include precious stones engraved like signets with the names of Israel's tribes (Exod 28:11, 21, 36; 39:6, 14, 30)—a significant observation, since in this passage, Tyre's ruler is appropriately cast as king and priest (see below).[944] But what of תכנית (*toknît*)? Is it from the root תכן (*tākan*), "to regulate, measure, estimate"; hence, "measurement, proportion" (43:10, "pattern") and, in this phrase, a "perfect signet" or the like?[945] Or, as Wevers suggests, is its root כנה (*kānâ*), "betitle, give a name," thus "an authenticating seal"?[946] Other critics have proposed more radical emendations of the text,[947] but the conundrum persists. On the basis of the two following, positive phrases, "seal of perfection" seems a reasonable rendering. "Full of wisdom" recalls vv. 3-5, 7b, and 27:8, 9; "perfect in beauty" echoes Tyre's boast in 27:3 (see also 27:4, 11). Thus Ezekiel begins his lament by praising Tyre's king, much as he initially substantiated Tyre's claim to perfect beauty in his metaphor of the city as a magnificent trade ship (chap. 27).

944. Robert R. Wilson, "The Death of the King of Tyre: The Editorial History of Ezekiel 28," in *Love and Death in the Ancient Near East: Essays in Honor of Marvin H. Pope,* ed. John H. Marks and Robert M. Good (Guilford, Conn.: Four Quarters, 1987) 215.
945. So *BDB,* 1067b.
946. Wevers, *Ezekiel,* 216.
947. See, e.g., Van Dijk, *Ezekiel's Prophecy on Tyre,* 113-14; Greenberg, *Ezekiel 21–37,* 580.

Like Adam and Eve, the royal figure dwells in Eden, the garden of God. This datum in effect casts him in the role of primeval man in paradise (nothing is said of a mate). "Every precious stone was מְסֻכָתֶךָ [*mĕsukātekā*]" is difficult. Greenberg translates "your hedge," citing Mic 7:4; Isa 5:5; and Prov 15:19. So read, the verse speaks of a (protective) hedge made of precious stones—an image akin to Isa 54:11-12, where the wall of restored Jerusalem is built of gems. As he acknowledges, however, the obscure end of v. 13 suggests that the creature wore these adornments.[948] Hence, most critics translate *mĕsukāteka* as "your covering, garment." This comment distinguishes Tyre's king from Adam and Eve, who were naked until they sinned (Gen 2:25). According to Nonnos of Panopolis, Melqart wore garments "brightly decorated with the stars."[949] Might the reader who knows of such divine attire read v. 13 in that light? The following list of precious stones certainly stirs thoughts in Israelite minds of the breastplate worn by Israel's high priest. According to Exod 28:17-20, this breastplate contained twelve stones (one for each of Israel's tribes) set in gold in four rows of three each. The gems of the first row were carnelian, chrysolite, and emerald; the second row consisted of turquoise, sapphire (or lapis lazuli), and moonstone; the third row contained jacinth, agate, and amethyst; and the stones of the fourth row were beryl, onyx, and jasper.

Ezekiel includes nine of these stones and lists them in a different order.[950] Critics tend to regard the list as secondary, a later elaboration on the preceding reference to "every precious stone" inspired by Exod 28:17-20. The author reduced the number of stones by three and changed their order lest Tyre's ruler be thought to wear a breastplate identical to that of Israel's high priest. We have no evidence that Tyre's kings/priests wore such items. The function of v. 13, however, is to associate the Tyrian king with the priesthood. This is not to say, as Wilson argues, that the list's purpose was to identify this figure as the *Israelite* high priest.[951] That thesis not only flies in the face of the text's own claim to address the king of Tyre, but also ignores the differences between this verse and the description in Exodus 28. Rather, the intent seems to be to foreground the priestly role of Tyre's king by depicting him in ways suggestive of the priesthood to Ezekiel's Israelite audience.

M. E. Aubet explains that priestly functions were integral to the Phoenician monarchy. Hence, the king of Sidon called himself "priest of Astarte," the king of Byblos, "priest of the Lady." The Annals of Tyre refer to monarchs with priestly duties.[952] The monarch's sacred nature seems to have been more emphasized in Tyre than in other Phoenician cities. Perhaps this was because of the singular importance of Melqart, the patron god of the city, who was considered to have enormous power over the city's commercial policy, in which the king was deeply involved.[953] If her assessment is correct, then we can better understand why Ezekiel drew from familiar associations with Israel's priesthood to depict Tyre's king as a priest. We shall return to this topic below.

Both תֻּפֶּיךָ (*tuppeykā*), "your settings," and נְקָבֶיךָ (*nĕqābeykā*), "your engravings," are obscure. They may be technical terms from the world of jewelry making. Exodus 28:20b specifies that the stones of the high priest's breastplate were set in gold filigree, and something of the sort may be intended here as well. When the text goes on to say that the king/priest was so adorned since the day of his creation, it uses a form of בָּרָא (*bārā'*), "to create," a word reserved for Yahweh's creative activity (see below).

Verse 14 is perhaps the most confounding of Ezekiel's lament. Difficulties arise already with the first form, אַתְּ (*'att*), which the Massoretes pointed as a second-person feminine singular independent pronoun; hence, "you [fem. sing.] were a . . . cherub [אַתְּ *'att*]." The pronoun's gender is problematic in an address to Tyre's male king (whether human or divine), though Greenberg observes that

948. Moshe Greenberg, *Ezekiel 21–37,* AB 22A (Garden City, N.Y.: Doubleday, 1997) 581-82.

949. *Dionysiaca* 40.367-369, 408-423, 578-579. See also S. Ribichini, "Melqart," *The Dictionary of Deities and Demons in the Bible,* ed. Karel van der Toorn et al. (Leiden: Brill, 1995) 563-65.

950. The LXX lists twelve jewels, in the order found in Exod 28:17-20, inserting gold and silver between the sixth and seventh gems. Zimmerli offers a thorough discussion of the stones, some of whose identities are uncertain. See W. Zimmerli, *Ezekiel 2: A Commentary on the Book of the Prophet Ezekiel, Chapters 25–48,* trans. J. D. Martin, Hermeneia (Philadelphia: Fortress, 1983) 82-84.

951. Wilson, "The Death of the King of Tyre," 214.

952. Maria Eugenia Aubet, *The Phoenicians and the West: Politics, Colonies and Trade,* trans. Mary Turton (Cambridge: Cambridge University Press, 1993) 122-23.

953. Ibid., 124.

the same phenomenon occurs in Num 11:15 and Deut 5:24.[954] One can only wonder why the Massoretes pointed *'att* as they did, especially since the same two consonants, pointed as *'attâ,* serve as the masculine singular pronoun "you" five times in Hebrew Scripture (e.g., Ps 6:4). Did they intend that the feminine singular "you" be construed as a reference to the city itself, personified (according to literary convention) as female (see Excursus: "Cities as Females," 1221-25)? Many critics follow the LXX, however, and repoint "you" to "with" (אֵת *'et*). As a consequence, the primeval creature in Eden is not called a cherub (MT; NIV), but rather is said to be *with* a cherub (so NRSV). The LXX omits from its translation the two words following "cherub" in the MT. The first, ממשח (*mimšaḥ*), is a *hapax legomenon* and, in Zimmerli's words, "totally obscure."[955] Both the NRSV and the NIV translate "anointed" (from משח *māšaḥ,* "to smear," "anoint"); Greenberg suggests "great" (see Aramaic *mšḥ,* "measure").[956] The second, הסוכך (*hassôkēk*), perhaps derives from סכך (*sākak*), "to overshadow," "screen," "cover," hence "shielding" or "guardian." This term quickens thoughts of the two cherubs whose outspread wings overshadowed (*sākak*) the cover of the ark in the tabernacle (Exod 25:20; 37:9) and of the two ten-cubit tall cherubim that stood within the holy of holies in the Jerusalem Temple (1 Kgs 6:23-28; 8:1-12; 1 Chr 28:18).

We cannot know exactly what Ezekiel meant to say in v. 14*a.* Moreover, we cannot determine how first-time, sequential readers would have construed the text. The vowel points supplied much later by the Massoretes tell us that they *equated* Tyre's king with the cherub placed by Yahweh on "the holy mountain of God." And, Aubet tells us, the winged cherub was the emblem of Melqart, the "King of the City" represented by Tyre's human ruler.[957] The LXX points to the alternative understanding: Tyre's king shares paradise with a shielding or guardian cherub. Either reading is possible; and both surely garnered support from competent ancient interpreters. The reader who recalls Gen 3:24, where cherubim and a flaming, turning sword guard the tree of life in the aftermath of the first couple's sin, might be predisposed to construe

'et as "with," though, as Wilson observes, the cherubim of Genesis 3 did not live in the garden with the primeval pair.[958] The reader who thinks especially of the celestial cherubim represented in the Jerusalem Temple—not only those standing in the holy of holies, but also those represented on its hangings and carved on its doors and walls (e.g., 1 Kgs 6:23, 25, 27-29, 32, 35; 7:29, 36; Ezek 41:18, 20, 25; see also Exod 26:1, 31; 36:8, 35; 37:7), might discern in the equation of king and cherub a metaphor by which the prophet further foregrounds the priestly role of Tyre's king. Again, this is not to say that vv. 11-19 are actually about Israel's high priest.[959] Rather, Ezekiel has employed a familiar ritual icon in order to present Tyre's ruler in the guise of a primeval, celestial king/priest. We should add that the cherub will reappear in v. 16. In the light of that verse, the reader's interpretation of v. 14*a* might receive further confirmation or be called into question.

Like the deity he sometimes claimed to be, Tyre's ruler dwells on "the holy mountain of God." This phrase too is multifaceted. On the one hand, it evokes thoughts of Mt. Zaphon, the mount of the assembly of the gods in Canaanite mythology (see Isa 14:13). On the other hand, the reader thinks of Jerusalem's Temple Mount (called "the holy mountain" in Isa 27:13; Jer 31:23; see also Ezek 20:40). Indeed, in Ps 48:1-2, Mt. Zion, "the city of the great King," is identified with Mt. Zaphon. At the same time, "the holy mountain of God" should not be construed as a contradiction of v. 3, which places the creature in "Eden, the garden of God." In Israelite religious imagination the Temple Mount, God's holy mountain, and Eden are frequently conjoined.[960]

The phrase "stones of fire" (vv. 14, 16) is obscure, and critics have proposed a number of different explanations.[961] Pope links these stones with Baal's (also El's?) abode on Mt. Zaphon—constructed of silver, gold, lapis lazuli (and perhaps other precious stones) that were fused by a (smelting) fire within the building.[962] Zimmerli identifies the fire stones as other creatures who,

954. Greenberg, *Ezekiel 21–37,* 583.
955. Zimmerli, *Ezekiel 2,* 92.
956. Greenberg, *Ezekiel 21–37,* 583.
957. Aubet, *The Pheonicians and the West,* 124.

958. Wilson, "The Death of the King of Tyre," 215.
959. Contra ibid., 215-16.
960. See Jon D. Levenson, *Theology of the Program of Restoration of Ezekiel 40–48,* HSMS 10 (Atlanta: Scholars Press, 1976) 7-36.
961. See Zimmerli, *Ezekiel 2,* 93.
962. Marvin H. Pope, *El in the Ugaritic Texts,* VTSup 2 (Leiden: Brill, 1955) 99-102.

like the cherub, inhabit God's holy mountain.[963] Greenberg, with others, points to Akkadian *aban,* "fire stone," and suggests that the phrase points back to the hedge of precious stones referred to in v. 13*a.*[964] Wilson equates the fire stones with the coals of fire found on the temple altar and representative of Yahweh's presence (Ezek 10:2; Lev 16:12; cf. Ezek 1:13; 2 Sam 22:13; Ps 18:13, 14).[965] None of the solutions sampled here is convincing. Is the reference to fire stones an Ezekielian innovation, or has he borrowed it from ancient mythic imagery? At most, we can say that these "stones of fire" contribute to the reader's impression that Tyre's king resided in a divine domain.

Verse 15 functions as a pivot for the lament. On the one hand, v. 15*a* credits Tyre's king with having been blameless since the day he was created (ברא *bārāʾ*). Because in Hebrew Scripture, *bārāʾ* ("to create") refers only to the creative activity of Israel's deity, its presence here affirms that this primeval being (whether Tyre's human king, or the god he represents) owes his perfection, wisdom, and beauty to Yahweh. Like Adam and Eve, he was sinless because God created him so. On the other hand, v. 15*b* asserts the loss of his former, blameless status. Succinctly, it states that "wrongdoing" was found in him. The author does not elaborate on the genesis or nature of this wrongdoing by means of myth (cf. Genesis 3). Instead, v. 16*a* points to an offense rooted in Tyrian commerce, here characterized as "violence" (חמס *ḥāmās*), a noun appearing also in 7:23; 8:17; and 12:19. The phrase "you were filled with violence" evokes thoughts of the Noachic flood account, wherein Yahweh destroyed all living creatures (save for the ark's inhabitants) because "the earth was filled with violence" (Gen 6:11, 13). While chap. 27 said nothing explicitly pejorative about Tyre's trade practices, this verse invites readers to perceive Tyre's (ruthless) trade as the cause of the primeval creature's "fall" from paradise and justification for his destruction.

As in Genesis 3, the creature's sin leads to his expulsion from paradise (here, "the mountain of

God," v. 16). The Hebrew phrase "so I profaned you from . . ." implies the "cast out" supplied by the NRSV (see, e.g., Ezra 2:62). Verse 16*b* contains the second reference to a shielding cherub. MT reads, "I banished you [ואבדך *wāʾabbedkā*; see 6:3; 22:27; Jer 23:1], guardian cherub, from amidst fire stones" (see NIV), reinforcing the interpretation of readers who identified Tyre's king with the celestial being in v. 14. The LXX, however, makes the cherub the subject of the verb "to banish, destroy"—hence, "the guardian cherub banished you" (see NIV). One suspects that this translation/interpretation has been influenced by Gen 3:24: The Lord God "placed the cherubim, and a sword flaming and turning to guard the way to the tree of life." According to Gen 3:23, however, Yahweh—not the cherubim—expelled the first human couple from the Garden of Eden.

Verse 17*a* echoes previous anti-Tyre oracles: Beauty (27:3, 4, 11) has fostered a proud heart (vv. 2, 5) in Tyre's king, whose wisdom (vv. 3-5; 27:8*b*, 9) he has corrupted for the sake of his splendor (v. 7). Hence, Yahweh casts him down from the mountain of God to the ground. (The reader recalls the lament in chap. 19, where the ramified vine—a symbol of the Davidic dynasty and its last rulers—was uprooted in fury and "cast down to the ground," v. 12). Yahweh's punishment of the presumptuous monarch takes place before the eyes of his peers, the kings of other nations.

While v. 15 spoke only of "wrongdoing" and v. 16*a* of the violence and sin attending Tyrian trade, v. 18*a* adds an additional charge: "you have profaned your sanctuaries." The sense seems to be that by his moral offenses, this king/priest has polluted his dwelling place—the divine throne of v. 2, Eden/the mountain of God in this oracle. Just as the mountain of God, Eden, and the Jerusalem Temple Mount are conjoined in the religious imagination of ancient Israel, so here Tyre is associated with Eden and the mountain of God; and the corrupting practices of its king/priest result in its defilement. Verse 18*b,* then, further describes God's punishment of the monarch—destruction by fire. Hals links this fire with the flaming sword of Gen 3:24, though the latter flame constitutes a barrier between primeval paradise and fallen humanity, while that of v. 18 is an ordinary fire

963. Zimmerli, *Ezekiel 2,* 93.
964. Greenberg, *Ezekiel 21–37,* 583.
965. Robert R. Wilson, "The Death of the King of Tyre: The Editorial History of Ezekiel 28," in *Love and Death in the Ancient Near East: Essays in Honor of Marvin H. Pope,* ed. John H. Marks and Robert M. Good (Guilford, Conn.: Four Quarters, 1987) 216.

capable of destroying a city.[966] Other critics detect in the "fire from within you" the notion that judgment erupts from the very locus of evil;[967] see 19:14. Aubet points, rather, to an annual spring Tyrian festival in the month of Peritios (February-March) commemorating the resurrection of Melqart, in the course of which an image of the god was subjected to ritual cremation. The immolation revived Melqart and rendered him "immortal by virtue of fire." As Melqart's representative, Tyre's king played an active role in this festival.[968] If Aubet's description of the ritual is accurate, then Ezekiel has dealt Tyrian theology a savage thrust. Yahweh brings forth a consuming fire, which reduces the king to ashes in the sight of all. This is no step toward resurrection, however, but an ultimate and irreversible destruction. Verse 19 concludes with an echo of 26:21 and 27:36.

It seems, then, that Ezekiel has drawn upon paradise themes and imagery, combining and innovating upon traditional material in order ultimately to depict Tyre's king/priest as a primeval, semi-divine being created by Yahweh, placed in Eden/the mountain of God, and endowed with royal and priestly attributes. This "concession" to the glorious past of a haughty monarch permits the prophet not only to present Tyre/Melqart, embodied in the ruler, as the creation of Israel's sovereign God, but also to depict his demise as a fall from paradise consequent upon sin, a theme familiar to his exilic audience from Genesis 3. What Ezekiel gives with one hand ("you were a . . . cherub"), he takes away with the other ("and I turned you to ashes on the earth").

966. Ronald M. Hals, *Ezekiel,* FOTL 19 (Grand Rapids: Eerdmans, 1989) 200-201.
967. Zimmerli, *Ezekiel 2,* 94.
968. Aubet, *The Phoenicians and the West,* 128-29.

REFLECTIONS

Ancient Israel did not deny the existence of deities other than Yahweh. To the contrary, throughout much of its history, the people of biblical Israel presupposed that the gods and goddesses of its neighbors ruled those peoples in much the same way that Yahweh, its God, ruled it. The biblical authors judge Israel's resort to other deities harshly. Though they might exist, Israel owed its complete fidelity to Yahweh. Over time, many biblical authors—Ezekiel among them—insisted that Israel's God alone was the sovereign ruler of all creation, and that the day would come when the Lord's unparalleled power would be recognized by all the nations of the earth.

Tyre, by virtue of its ability to survive despite Nebuchadrezzar's long and crippling siege, cast doubt on Ezekiel's affirmation of Yahweh's absolute control of history. Hence, the prophet attacked it on many fronts: its greedy delight at the economic advantage gained by Jerusalem's destruction (26:2); its claims to perfect beauty and ongoing prosperity (chap. 27); its pride in geographical security, wisdom, and wealth (chaps. 27–28); its god, represented by an arrogant ruler/priest (chap. 28). We should assume that Ezekiel's attention to Tyre was, at least to some degree, motivated by the doubts of his fellow exiles, who struggled to understand why their nation should suffer so severely, while certain neighboring nations escaped. Was Melqart, in fact, more powerful than Yahweh?

Understanding why Ezekiel, and other Old Testament prophets, spoke as they did about Yahweh's destruction of foreign nations and rulers helps moderns better to wrestle with such troubling texts. To be sure, we can easily grasp the notion that unbridled human pride is ultimately self-destructive. Hence the popular proverb, "pride goes before a fall." But Ezekiel's insistence that the foes of the people of God are doomed to destruction by that God is as dangerous today as a nuclear weapon in the hands of religious fanatics. In a world where holocausts happen, we cannot simply acquiesce to Ezekiel's worldview, even though we admire his absolute refusal to abandon the bedrock belief that God's sovereignty over the cosmos is primarily revealed in Yahweh's control of the events of history.

EZEKIEL 28:20-26, THE DESTRUCTION OF SIDON AND THE RESTORATION OF ISRAEL

OVERVIEW

The bulk of Ezekiel's oracles against foreign nations and rulers are gathered in chaps. 25–32. To this point in that collection, the prophet has pronounced doom upon five of Israel's neighboring nations: Ammon (25:1-7); Moab (25:8-11); Edom (25:12-14); Philistia (25:15-17); and Tyre (seven oracles encompassing 26:1–28:19). Ezekiel 29:1–32:32 contains seven oracles against Egypt/Pharaoh. Ezekiel 28:20-23, an oracle against Sidon, brings the total number of nations the prophet condemns in chaps. 25–32 to seven. Critics have suggested that the doom pronouncement against Sidon, a Phoenician port city located on the Lebanese coast about twenty-five miles north of Tyre (see the maps on 557-58), was included precisely to attain that significant number. Imprecations against Sidon occur in conjunction with anti-Tyre declarations elsewhere in Israel's prophetic literature (see, e.g., Isaiah 23; Jer 25:22; Joel 3:4; Zech 9:2), so the placement of this oracle immediately after the anti-Tyre ones makes sense.

Moreover, emissaries from Sidon traveled to Jerusalem, along with those of Edom, Moab, Ammon, and Tyre, in 594/93 BCE to plot with Judah's King Zedekiah a rebellion against their Babylonian overlord. Because, from Ezekiel's perspective, the Babyonians functioned as Yahweh's agents of punishment upon Judah and its neighbors, Sidon's participation in the conspiracy was a culpable offense. The ultimate (and twice-stated) goal of Sidon's demise is that its inhabitants be forced to "know that I am Yahweh"—that is, recognize and acknowledge the unparalleled power of Israel's God as manifested in their own history (vv. 22-23).

Verse 24 looks beyond the anti-Sidon oracle, summarizing the implication for Israel of Ezekiel's doom announcements concerning its surrounding nations. With their demise, the house of Israel will no longer suffer "a pricking brier or a piercing thorn" from those neighbors who have treated it with contempt. This verse also ends with the recognition formula—behind all of Yahweh's dealings with the nations lies the intention that God's sovereignty be evinced and acknowledged throughout Israel's world to its benefit. Verses 25-26, initiated with introductory formulae, further expand upon the message of v. 24, anticipating the day when Israel will be regathered from among the nations and settled safely on its own soil. This "re-membering" will be possible because, owing to the power of Israel's God, scornful nations no longer exist.

Ezekiel 28:20-24, Introduction and an Oracle Against Sidon

NIV	NRSV
[20]The word of the LORD came to me: [21]"Son of man, set your face against Sidon; prophesy against her [22]and say: `This is what the Sovereign LORD says:	[20]The word of the LORD came to me: [21]Mortal, set your face toward Sidon, and prophesy against it, [22]and say, Thus says the Lord GOD:

" 'I am against you, O Sidon,
   and I will gain glory within you.
They will know that I am the LORD,
   when I inflict punishment on her
   and show myself holy within her.
	I am against you, O Sidon,
	   and I will gain glory in your midst.
	They shall know that I am the LORD
	   when I execute judgments in it,
	   and manifest my holiness in it;
	[23] for I will send pestilence into it,
	   and bloodshed into its streets;

NIV

NIV

²³I will send a plague upon her
    and make blood flow in her streets.
The slain will fall within her,
    with the sword against her on every side.
Then they will know that I am the LORD.

²⁴" 'No longer will the people of Israel have malicious neighbors who are painful briers and sharp thorns. Then they will know that I am the Sovereign LORD.

NRSV

and the dead shall fall in its midst,
    by the sword that is against it on every side.
And they shall know that I am the LORD.
24The house of Israel shall no longer find a pricking brier or a piercing thorn among all their neighbors who have treated them with contempt. And they shall know that I am the Lord GOD.

COMMENTARY

Ezekiel's brief oracle against Sidon contains no specific indictment. In that respect, it differs from the short oracles in chap. 25 and 26:1-6, each of which accused an Israelite neighbor of reveling in Judah's/Jerusalem's destruction. Following the word event formula ("The word of the LORD came to me") and Yahweh's characteristic direct address to the prophet ("Mortal"), Ezekiel is ordered to set his face toward Sidon and prophesy against it (the same hostile gesture appears in 6:2; 21:2; 25:2; 29:2; cf. 4:3).

The oracle proper begins with the messenger formula ("Thus says the Lord GOD"), followed by the "challenge to a duel" formula ("I am against you"; see also 26:3; cf. 21:3). Yahweh then announces the intention to "glorify myself" (NRSV and NIV, "gain glory") through what God will do in Sidon's midst (see also 39:13, 21). According to Exod 14:4a and 17b, Israel's God hardens the heart of Pharaoh in order to "gain glory for myself over Pharaoh." In both cases, Yahweh's motivation is expressed in the following recognition formula: "and the Egyptians shall know that I am the LORD" (vv. 14:4b; 18a). So also here, God's self-glorification will result in the Sidonians' acknowledgment of the unparalleled power of Israel's God. "Execute judgments" appears also in Ezek 5:10, 15; 11:9; 16:41; 25:11; 28:26; and 30:14, 19 (cf. 23:10). "Manifest my holiness," like "glorify myself," is priestly terminology. Elsewhere in Ezekiel, it appears in 20:41; 28:25; 36:23; 38:16; 39:27—in each instance, Zimmerli observes, in connection with the endorsement by witnesses "before the eyes of all nations."⁹⁶⁹ Both forms appear in Lev 10:3, immediately following

the deaths of Aaron's presumptive sons, Nadab and Abihu. Verse 23 describes, in stereotypical language, Yahweh's agents of punishment against Sidon: pestilence (see, e.g., 5:12, 17; 6:12); bloodshed (see, e.g., 5:17; 14:19; 35:6; 38:22); and sword (see, e.g., 5:12; 6:12; 14:17-18). "And the slain shall fall" echoes 6:7.

If the oracle against Sidon does not include a specific accusation (though "execute judgments" implies that God acts in response to some punishable offenses), v. 24 offers a summary of the consequence of the doom of Israel's neighboring states for the people of Yahweh: The nations that have treated Israel with contempt, described metaphorically as "a pricking brier or a piercing thorn" (for similar imagery, see Num 33:55 and Josh 23:13), will exist no longer. The term סלון (*sillôn,* "brier") appears also in 2:6 (referring to the hostility Ezekiel will experience from his fellow exiles), but nowhere in Hebrew Scripture outside the book of Ezekiel. In Lev 13:51-52; 14:44, a form of ממאיר (*mam'îr,* "pricking, piercing") functions as a priestly technical term for the diagnosis of spreading skin eruptions ("spreading leprous disease," NRSV). The term קוץ (*qôṣ,* "thorn") elsewhere appears in Gen 3:18; Isa 32:13; and Hos 10:8, while the phrase קוצי המדבר (*qôṣê hammidbār*), "thorns of the desert," describes an excruciating punishment in Judg 8:7, 16. This verse also concludes with the recognition formula. Presumably "they" are Israel's once-contemptuous neighbors. Or does the plural pronoun refer to the house of Israel? (See Reflections at 28:25-26.)

969. Zimmerli, *Ezekiel 2,* 98.

❖   ❖   ❖   ❖

EXCURSUS: THE PHOENICIAN CITY OF SIDON

The Greek historian Strabo cites Sidon (modern Saïda), a coastal city with two seaports, among the most ancient of Phoenician urban centers.[970] It appears twice, paired with Tyre, in the fourteenth-century BCE *Epic of Kirta* from Ugarit. The thirteenth-century BCE Papyrus Anastasi I, a satirical Egyptian letter, includes Sidon in a north-to-south itinerary list, following Byblos and Berytos (Beirut) but before Sarepta and Tyre. The eleventh-century BCE travel report of Wen-Amon, an Egyptian official of the temple of Amon at Karnak, refers to fifty ships harbored at Sidon—part of a trade network between Phoenicia and Egypt.[971]

Early in Phoenician history, Sidon's importance exceeded Tyre's. A Hittite incantation from the early fourteen century BCE lists Sidon before Tyre.[972] Within Hebrew Scripture, Sidon is the name for the firstborn son of Canaan (Gen 10:15; 1 Chr 1:13). Moreover, Sidon and the Sidonians frequently function as synecdoches (a less inclusive entity, the single city state and its inhabitants, representing a more inclusive entity, greater Phoenicia and its inhabitants) for Phoenicia and the Phoenicians (see Deut 3:9; Judg 3:3; 10:6, 12; 18:7; 1 Kgs 5:6; 11:1, 5, 33; 16:31; 2 Kgs 23:13). In 2 Kgs 16:31, Ethbaal (Ithobaal I, 887–856 BCE) is called "king of the Sidonians" yet, according to a citation from Menander of Ephesus, he was, in fact, the ruler of Tyre.[973]

By the close of the second millennium, however, Tyre's significance superseded that of Sidon. During the Assyrian period, and owing to its more vulnerable coastal location, Sidon suffered more than Tyre. In his third campaign, Assyria's King Sennacherib (704–681 BCE) conquered "Great Sidon" and "Little Sidon," demanding a heavy annual tribute of Tuba'lu (Ethba'al), whom he installed as ruler. His successor, Esarhaddon (680–669 BCE), boasted of razing the city and killing its rebellious king.[974] Assyria's king then founded, at a different location, a settlement named Kar-Asarhaddon, "Esarhaddon's Quay," which became the center of Assyrian administration in the area.[975] Despite this harsh treatment, Sidon recovered after the collapse of the Assyrian Empire.[976]

Little is known of Sidon's situation during the years when Egypt and Babylon contended for control of Syria and Palestine. As noted in the Overview to 28:20-26, however, its ruler sent envoys to Jerusalem in 595/94 BCE, to plan a revolt against Babylon (Jer 27:3). Along with the monarchs of Tyre, Gaza, and Ashdod, Sidon's king appears among a list of captives in Nebuchadrezzer's court.[977] During the Persian period, Sidon regained its former importance, serving as an administrative center and supplying ships for the navy of King Xerxes I. In 351 BCE, however, the Sidonians rebelled against Artaxerxes III Ochus; as a consequence, some forty thousand persons lost their lives. Unlike Tyre, Sidon simply submitted to Alexander the Great in 333 BCE.

970. Strabo, *Geography* 16.2.22.
971. *ANET,* 27a.
972 Philip C. Schmitz, "Sidon (Place)," *ABD,* 6:17-18.
973. See Josephus *Antiquities of the Jews* 8.324. See also Schmitz, "Sidon (Place)," *ABD,* 6:17.
974. *ANET,* 290b.
975. Schmitz, "Sidon (Place)," *ABD,* 6:17.
976. Zimmerli, *Ezekiel 2,* 97.
977. *ANET,* 307a.

❖   ❖   ❖   ❖

Ezekiel 28:25-26, Restoration for Israel

<table>
<tr><td>

NIV

²⁵" 'This is what the Sovereign LORD says: When I gather the people of Israel from the nations where they have been scattered, I will show myself holy among them in the sight of the nations. Then they will live in their own land, which I gave to my servant Jacob. ²⁶They will live there in safety and will build houses and plant vineyards; they will live in safety when I inflict punishment on all their neighbors who maligned them. Then they will know that I am the LORD their God.' "

</td><td>

NRSV

25Thus says the Lord GOD: When I gather the house of Israel from the peoples among whom they are scattered, and manifest my holiness in them in the sight of the nations, then they shall settle on their own soil that I gave to my servant Jacob. ²⁶They shall live in safety in it, and shall build houses and plant vineyards. They shall live in safety, when I execute judgments upon all their neighbors who have treated them with contempt. And they shall know that I am the LORD their God.

</td></tr>
</table>

COMMENTARY

These verses further elaborate upon Israel's fate once Yahweh has executed judgments (v. 26; see v. 22) against derisive, surrounding nations. Ezekiel 20:34 spoke in a threatening way of God's gathering the exiles from the countries in which they were scattered—the prelude to a second judgment "in the wilderness of the peoples." Looking beyond that judgment (20:41), the prophet again speaks—this time positively—of Yahweh gathering Israel out of the countries where it has been scattered. This second text, like the present passage, describes Israel's ingathering as a manifestation of Yahweh's holiness "in the sight of the nations" (cf. 28:22). Like 20:5, v. 25

refers to the patriarch Jacob ("the house of Jacob" in the former; "my servant Jacob" in the latter; see 37:25). Israel's future safety is twice expressed in v. 26 (see also 34:25, 27-28), which describes a peaceful agrarian existence with language reminiscent of Isa 65:21 and Jer 29:5, 28 (see also Ezek 34:25-28). The final recognition formula clearly refers to *Israel's* consequent knowledge of "the LORD their God." The very God whose unrivaled power and sovereignty Israel has been forced to acknowledge in its own destruction, and then in the extermination of its enemies, will be manifested in the impending "re-membering" of Israel on its own, secure soil.

REFLECTIONS

In the Reflections sections to other of Ezekiel's oracles against foreign nations (chaps. 25–28), I have considered the long-lived and ongoing consequences of any worldview that proclaims that Israel's God, or the deity/deities of any other peoples or nations, deals with foes through extermination. Not only does such a belief raise disturbing theological questions about the nature of gods and goddesses who might act in such a way, but also it sets before humans a divinely sanctioned model for death-dealing international "relations." The reader is invited to peruse those Reflections for further discussion of this formidable and crucial issue.

In the present section, we focus instead upon the promises for Israel's future proffered in 28:24-26. Ezekiel, who has gone to any lengths to convince his fellow exiles that Judah's demise is Yahweh's just punishment for its sin—that contemporary historical events are the doing, and not the undoing, of its God—here insists with absolute consistency upon the Lord's control of history, but looks beyond judgment to restoration. This restoration enhances Yahweh's reputation, whose holiness is manifested "in the sight of nations" and whose ability to regather this people and secure its future in the homeland puts the lie to any suspicion that Israel's demise was, in fact, the consequence of worshiping a "second-rank" God. Moreover, it is not simply a reversion to Israel's pre-punishment reality, but a qualitatively different kind of existence. Apropos to the position of these verses immediately after a series of oracles against neighboring foes, that different kind of existence is defined as "safe(ty)." Building houses and planting vineyards was (is) risky business in a world where chances are great that adversaries will either level those houses or move into them themselves, and that others will reap what one has sown. One thinks of Gideon attempting to thresh out wheat in the wine press, lest the Midianites and Amalekites destroy the harvest (Judges 6), and of Jeremiah's decision to purchase a plot of family land when the Babylonians were certain soon to confiscate all property as their own—an act of astonishing faith in God's future for Israel (Jer 32:1-15).

All of us engage in that risky business to one degree or another. For many, international relations are as perilous as they were for the ancient Israelites, for the borders of hostile nations are but a short distance from home. For most, the homeland itself is fraught with certain dangers, notably crime borne of hopelessness, substance abuse, selfishness, desperation, or rampant greed. For some, peril exists within one's own family; for example, domestic abuse, physical and mental.

We, no less than the inhabitants of Israel's ancient Near Eastern world, long for safety at home. Ezekiel's promise that Israel will one day experience that safety strikes a deep chord within us. But safety is not simply a matter of trusting in God (though that is finally foundational to *šālôm*, "peace," "wholeness") to eliminate sources of danger surrounding us and ours. What Ezekiel does not say in this particular context, but must be said when one speaks of safety, is the obligation upon all of us to act as God's instruments of justice, compassion, and responsibility.

EZEKIEL 29:1–32:32, SEVEN ORACLES AGAINST (THE PHARAOH OF) EGYPT

Ezekiel 29:1-16, Pride, Punishment, and Restoration: Three Oracles Against Egypt

OVERVIEW

Ezekiel devotes seven oracles to Egypt, the seventh and last nation condemned in chaps. 25–32 (see Excursus: "Ezekiel's Oracles Against Foreign Nations and Rulers," 1355-56). Like Tyre, also the subject of seven denunciations, Egypt elicited Ezekiel's ire in part because of its ability to withstand Babylonian imperial expansion. From the prophet's perspective, Nebuchadrezzar and his forces were Yahweh's instruments of punishment against not only Judah, but also Ammon, Moab, Edom, Philistia, Tyre, Sidon, and Egypt. Egyptian resistence, coupled with its policy of encouraging these other nations to rebel against their Babylonian overlord, defied God's plans for their present and future. In particular, Egyptian promises of military assistance tempted Judah to place its trust in an entity other than Yahweh.

Ezekiel 29:1-16 consists of introductory information plus three interrelated oracles: vv. 3-6*a*, vv. 6*b*-9*a*, and vv. 9*b*-16. The date in v. 1, "In the tenth year, in the tenth month, on the twelfth day of the month" (January 7, 587 BCE, by my reckoning), is the earliest of those prefixed to the prophet's oracles against foreign nations. Nebuchadrezzar's siege against Jerusalem ("in the ninth year," 24:1) has been underway for a year;

that city will fall approximately six months later. This date may properly pertain only to vv. 3-6*a*. Zimmerli, for example, argues that vv. 1-16 were not composed all at once, but arose as a consequence of "successive enrichments"; vv. 6*b*-9*a* presuppose Egypt's failure successfully to intercede on Judah's behalf and so should be dated after the fall of Jerusalem. Verses 9*b*-16 are much later and derive from Ezekiel's school.[978] His assessment may well be correct; nonetheless, the ancient reader will likely apply the date in v. 1 to all three oracles (29:17 specifies another, much later date).

Ezekiel's initial prophecy, a two-part proof saying initiated by the "summons to a duel" formula ("I am against you"; see also 21:3; 26:3; 28:22), addresses not only "Pharaoh, king of Egypt," but also "all Egypt" (its land and inhabitants, v. 2). Again, this master of metaphor takes up a familiar and apropos trope, depicting Pharaoh as "the great crocodile" (NRSV, "dragon"; NIV, "monster") sprawled in the midst of his Nile canals. As in 28:2, so here, a foreign ruler betrays, by way of an ostensible quotation, a pride so great as to invite Yahweh's punishment (v. 3*b*). The crocodile's sense of power and safety is destroyed in two swift strokes as God, the mighty hunter, sets hooks in its jaws, draws it—along with the fish sticking to its scales—from its Nile canals, and hurls it to certain

978. W. Zimmerli, *Ezekiel 2: A Commentary on the Book of the Prophet Ezekiel, Chapters 25–48*, trans. J. D. Martin, Hermeneia (Philadelphia: Fortress, 1983) 109, 115.

death in the desert. The ultimate goal of Yahweh's successful hunt is that all of Egypt's inhabitants might recognize and acknowledge God's unparalleled power and control of history, which extends beyond Israel to include even this great world empire.

Verses 6*b*-9*a* develop a second metaphor for Pharaoh/Egypt: "because" (יַעַן *ya'an*) it is a "staff of reed" to the house of Israel, that leans upon it to its peril, therefore Yahweh will bring the sword against Egypt, cutting off humans and animals and reducing the land to desolation and waste. Here also, God acts in order that the Egyptians be forced to acknowledge the sovereignty of Israel's God (v. 9*a*).

Verses 9*b*-16 consist, first, of further elaboration upon the wholesale devastation of Egypt's land and cities. Its territory will lie uninhabited for forty years, its population dispersed in exile (vv. 9*b*-12). Remarkably, vv. 13-16 look beyond punishment to speak of the partial restoration of Egypt—a promise nowhere else found in Ezekiel's oracles against *other* foreign nations. Though Yahweh plans to restore Egypt's fortunes, its territory will be reduced to the land of Pathros—that is, Upper, or southern, Egypt (v. 14). The "most lowly of the kingdoms," it will never again be able to tempt Israel with empty promises of aid. Verse 16*b* brings this three-oracle unit to a close with yet another recognition formula. (See Reflections at 29:17-21.)

❖ ❖ ❖ ❖

EXCURSUS: EZEKIEL'S ORACLES AGAINST PHARAOH/EGYPT

Ezekiel's seven oracles against Egypt span chaps. 29–32 (29:1-16; 29:17-21; 30:1-19; 30:20-26; 31:1-18; 32:1-16; 32:17-32). Four of the seven units are addressed to Pharaoh. Six are dated (30:1-19 is not)—testimony to the prophet's concern that God's words about Egypt be preserved, correlated with current events, and verifiable upon their fulfillment. The earliest date is prefixed to the three interrelated oracles appearing in 29:1-16 (see above). The latest, "the twenty-seventh year, in the first month, on the first day of the month" (April 26, 571 BCE), pertains to 29:17-20 and is the latest recorded date in the book. The others occur in chronological order and span approximately twenty-six months.

Ancient Israel's traditions acknowledge the venerable links conjoining it with Egypt. One recalls the adventures of Joseph, whose half-brothers conspired to remove him from their lives, but who eventually attained power in Egypt second only to Pharaoh's (Genesis 37–45). Jacob's entire family soon migrated to Egypt, settling in Goshen and prospering there until, centuries later, "a new king arose over Egypt who did not know Joseph" (Exod 1:8). This pharaoh, probably Rameses II (c. 1290–1224 BCE), is said to have enslaved the Hebrews and ordered the deaths of their male infants (Exod 1:9-22). At least one baby, Moses, survived and, according to folklore, was raised in Pharaoh's court as the adopted son of the king's own daughter (Exod 2:1-10). The story of Moses and of the Hebrew's exodus from Egypt is too well-known to require rehearsal here. According to the prophet's own, distinctive version of the people's liberation, wilderness wanderings, and life in the land of Israel (Ezekiel 20), Israel was idolatrous already in Egypt (20:7-8).

Egypt's history is far too long and complex even to summarize in this excursus. It suffices to note, first, that during the periods of Assyrian and Babylonian hegemony, Egypt practiced a policy of inciting the vassal (subservient) rulers of Syria-Palestine to resist and/or rebel against their suzerains. According to 2 Kgs 17:3-6, for example, Hoshea—the last ruler of the northern kingdom of Israel (c. 732–724 BCE), committed the grave political error of withholding tribute from his Assyrian overlord, Shalmaneser V (727–722 BCE), and sought aid from Egypt. Assyria's king quickly responded with a punitive campaign leading to the besieging of Samaria and Hoshea's capture. Approximately two years later, Samaria fell to Assyria's new king, Sargon II (721–705 BCE); the city was destroyed and its inhabitants forced into exile.

In 701 BCE, Assyria's king Sennacherib marched his troops against Syria-Palestine; during the third stage of his campaign, he targeted the Philistine city of Ekron. Its inhabitants sought help from Egypt's king, "Tirhakah king of Cush" (2 Kgs 19:9). On this occasion, Egypt's army actually came to Ekron's assistance; but its force was defeated and the city captured.[979] Sennacherib then turned toward Judah. After seizing a number of its fortified cities (2 Kgs 18:13; Isa 36:1), he sent his Rabshakeh (commander-in-chief) and a large force to Jerusalem. Within earshot of the city's inhabitants, the Rabshakeh shouted demoralizing words at the representatives of Judah's King Hezekiah, ridiculing Hezekiah's ostensible trust in Egyptian aid:

> On whom do you now rely, that you have rebelled against me? See, you are relying on Egypt, that broken reed of a staff, which will pierce the hand of anyone who leans on it. Such is Pharaoh king of Egypt to all who rely on him. (Isa 36:5-6 NRSV; 2 Kgs 19-21)

Like other prophets, Isaiah consistently condemns resort to foreign alliances (Isa 10:20; 18:1-7; 22:3; 28:11-13). Isaiah 30:1-7 and 31:13 denounce reliance upon treaties with Egypt. (See also Isaiah's sign act concerning the future captivity of Egypt and Ethiopia in Isa 20:1-6.) Nonetheless, the Assyrian military commander's claim that Hezekiah was relying on Egyptian assistance was probably accurate. According to biblical tradition, Sennacherib learned that Tirhakah and his troops had again set out to fight against him (2 Kgs 19:9; Isa 37:9), and the news may have prompted him temporarily to turn his attention to that foe. Scholars question whether Tirhakah was, in fact, king of Cush at the time; indeed, the actual events of Sennacherib's siege against Jerusalem and its aftermath remain a mystery. All the same the ancient reader, who undoubtedly knows traditions about Jerusalem's escape in 701 BCE, also knows of Isaiah's imprecations against resort to Egypt and of Tirhakah's failure to play a major role in the city's survival.

Second, it behooves us to say something of the Saite period in Egyptian history (664–525 BCE), since the momentous events of Ezekiel's lifetime occurred during the rule of that (twenty-sixth) dyntasy. Despite repeated battles between the armies of Egypt and Assyria during the first half of the seventh century BCE, these two empires eventually formed an alliance. Indeed, both Pharaoh Psammetichus (662–610) and his son, Necho II (610–593), attempted to aid the crumbling Assyrian Empire during the final decades of that century. In 609 BCE, Necho's army marched

979. See *ANET,* 287b-288a.

north toward that end, but was intercepted at the pass of Megiddo by Judah's King Josiah (640–609), who had cast his hopes for a reunited Israel with the Babylonians. Judah lost the battle, and Josiah was executed. As a consequence, Judah became Egypt's vassal (2 Kgs 23:29-30). The Judeans enthroned Jehoahaz, Josiah's son, but after only three months, Necho exiled him to Egypt (see the Commentary on 19:3-4) and appointed as king another of Josiah's sons, Eliakim (Jehoiakim, 2 Kgs 23:31-34). In 605 BCE, however, Necho's forces were soundly defeated by Nebuchadrezzar at the battle of Carchemish and pursued back to Egypt's border. Its remaining power sufficed only to prevent a Babylonian invasion in 601 BCE. In connection with Ezek 29:1-6a (see below), we note that Necho's most famous internal program was the construction of a canal linking the Nile with the Red Sea.

Necho's son, Psammetichus II (594–589), avoided direct confrontation with Babylonia, but supported the attempts of Judah and its neighboring states—Edom, Moab, Ammon, Tyre, and Sidon—to rebel against Nebuchadrezzar during the reign of Judah's King Zedekiah (see Jer 27:1–28:1; see also the Commentary on 17:1-24). That revolt did not materialize, but in 589/88 BCE, Zedekiah—again seeking assistance from Egypt (now ruled by Psammetichus II's successor, Hophra [Apries; 589–570 BCE])—openly revolted against his Babylonian overlord (Ezek 17:15). Nebuchadrezzar responded by besieging Jerusalem in 588 BCE. When Hophra's troops approached the city, Babylonian forces withdrew from Jerusalem for a time (see, e.g., Jeremiah 37). But the relief proved short-lived. Ultimately, the Egyptian army left Judah's capital to its fate. In the aftermath of a revolt led by Amasis (570 BCE), one of Hophra's generals, the pharaoh was forced to flee. He returned in 567, but died in battle against Amasis in 567 BCE.

❖   ❖   ❖   ❖

Ezekiel 29:1-6a, The Death of the Great Crocodile

NIV

29 In the tenth year, in the tenth month on the twelfth day, the word of the LORD came to me: [2]"Son of man, set your face against Pharaoh king of Egypt and prophesy against him and against all Egypt. [3]Speak to him and say: 'This is what the Sovereign LORD says:

" 'I am against you, Pharaoh king of Egypt,
    you great monster lying among your
        streams.
You say, "The Nile is mine;
    I made it for myself."
[4]But I will put hooks in your jaws
    and make the fish of your streams stick to
        your scales.
I will pull you out from among your streams,
    with all the fish sticking to your scales.
[5]I will leave you in the desert,
    you and all the fish of your streams.
You will fall on the open field

NRSV

29 In the tenth year, in the tenth month, on the twelfth day of the month, the word of the LORD came to me: [2]Mortal, set your face against Pharaoh king of Egypt, and prophesy against him and against all Egypt; [3]speak, and say,
Thus says the Lord GOD:
    I am against you,
        Pharaoh king of Egypt,
    the great dragon sprawling
        in the midst of its channels,
    saying, "My Nile is my own;
        I made it for myself."
[4]I will put hooks in your jaws,
    and make the fish of your channels stick to
        your scales.
I will draw you up from your channels,
    with all the fish of your channels
        sticking to your scales.
[5]I will fling you into the wilderness,
    you and all the fish of your channels;

NIV

and not be gathered or picked up.
I will give you as food
    to the beasts of the earth and the birds of
        the air.

⁶Then all who live in Egypt will know that I am the LORD.

NRSV

you shall fall in the open field,
    and not be gathered and buried.
To the animals of the earth and to the birds of
        the air
    I have given you as food.
⁶ Then all the inhabitants of Egypt shall know
    that I am the LORD

COMMENTARY

Following the date formula (see above), Ezekiel announces the advent of a fresh message from God. He must "set [his] face against" Pharaoh king of Egypt (the phrase, denoting a hostile gesture, is unique to Ezekiel; see 6:2; 13:17; 21:2, 7; 25:2; 28:20; 29:2; 35:2; 38:2), prophesying against him and all of Egypt (its land [fem.] and inhabitants [masc. pl.]). Here, as in Ezekiel's other oracles against Egypt, Pharaoh is not named. But Hophra (Apries) is the presumed addressee.

Speaking in Yahweh's name, Ezekiel summons Pharaoh with the "challenge to a duel" formula, "I am against you" (the same formula that appears in reference to Tyre in 26:3 and against Sidon in 28:22). He then casts Egypt's king as a menacing creature, "the great תנים [*tannîm,* "serpent," "dragon," "sea monster]."⁹⁸⁰ In some contexts, this noun designates the primeval chaos dragon defeated by Yahweh (see, e.g., Job 7:12; Ps 74:13; Isa 51:9). In Exod 7:9, 10, 12, by contrast, it refers to a snake. Here, most commentators agree, Ezekiel speaks of the Nile crocodile, though associations with the mythological *tannîm* undoubtedly cling to the word in this context, as well.⁹⁸¹ Suddenly, certain fearsome traits of Pharaoh are foregrounded: he is menacing, voracious, a predator before whom others flee. In choosing to depict Pharaoh as a crocodile, Ezekiel was not breaking new metaphorical ground. Zimmerli quotes a

hymn to Thutmose III in which Amun says of Pharaoh's foes: "I have made them see thy majesty as a crocodile, Lord of fear in the water, unapproachable."⁹⁸² Moreover, the cult of Sebek, the crocodile deity, flourished in Egypt for centuries.

The impressive creature basks in the midst of his Nile streams (plural), a reference to the river's many branches and canals. As with the king of Tyre (28:2), so here Ezekiel quotes a boast of the presumptuous ruler: "My Nile is my own; I made it for myself." Zimmerli detects in Pharaoh's words a claim to ownership based on the power of creation.⁹⁸³ However, ancient readers familiar with the enormous waterworks systems constructed by Egypt's pharaohs to regulate the inundation of the Nile as it flowed north, and perhaps with Necho's construction of a canal linking the river with the Red Sea, might interpret Pharaoh's braggadoccio in the light of that knowledge.⁹⁸⁴

With v. 4, Ezekiel, in effect, flips the crocodile metaphor over to reveal its soft underbelly. Despite its ostensible security, the creature is vulnerable. With baited hooks, Yahweh will snare the beast, drawing it out of its canals. Herodotus describes a crocodile hunt: "The hunter baits a hook with a chine of pork, and lets it float into the middle of the river; he himself stays on the bank with a young live pig, which he beats. Hearing the cries of the pig, the crocodile goes after the sound and meets the chine, which it swallows; then the hunters pull the line."⁹⁸⁵ The fish sticking to the

---

980. *BDB,* 1072b. One expects תנין (*tannîn;* see Ps 74:13; Isa 27:1; 51:9), but the same form also appears in Ezek 32:2. See Lawrence Boadt, *Ezekiel's Oracles Against Egypt: A Literary and Philogical Study of Ezekiel 29–32,* BibOr 37 (Rome: Pontifical Biblical Institute, 1980) 26-27.

981. Boadt translates "dragon," asserting that "crocodile" is too mundane a rendering in this context. At the same time, however, he acknowledges that "many of the descriptive details of the sea-monster are depicted from the *apropos* attributes of the crocodile: water-dwelling, serpent-like, dangerous and certainly not under man's control!" Ibid., 28.

982. Zimmerli, *Ezekiel 2,* 111.

983. Ibid., 111.

984. K. P. Darr, "Breaking Through the Wilderness: References to the Desert in Exilic Prophecy" (Ph.D. diss., Vanderbilt University, 1984) 228-36.

985. Herodotus 2.70 in *Herodotus,* trans. A. D. Godley, LCL (New York: Putnam, 1920–24). See also Moshe Greenberg, *Ezekiel 21–37,* AB 22A (Garden City, N.Y.: Doubleday, 1997) 602.

crocodile's scales share its fate. The image is a bit bizarre; perhaps these fish represent the Egyptians or, more specifically, Pharaoh's army. More likely, they represent neighboring nations which, like Judah, have clung to Egyptian promises of military assistance.

God then tosses the crocodile, along with its fish, into the wilderness and certain death. Its carcass will be neither collected nor gathered—synonymous terms paired also in Ezek 11:17 and Mic 4:6. Rather, its exposed corpse will be eaten by animals and birds—the "ultimate disgrace" (see also Ezek 39:17-20; Deut 28:26; Jer 34:20).[986] Such a fate would horrify Egyptian rulers, who expended enormous energy and resources on royal tombs in order to ensure their safe passage into the afterlife.

In another context, I have observed that Ezekiel's crocodile metaphor is not complex. Construing it requires little more of his audience

(and readers) than an awareness that he was not speaking nonsense (he did not actually think that Pharaoh was a crocodile). Ezekiel's fellow exiles might well have heard his oracle with consternation, if they were pinning their hopes on Egyptian assistance. "Like Ehud, who ostensibly approached Eglon to share a secret, but instead planted a sword in his stomach (Judg 3:15-22), Ezekiel's crocodile metaphor invites pro-Egyptian hearers near in order to deal a deadly thrust. Exploiting the weakness implicit in a familiar image and matching metaphor and mode of punishment with deadly perfection, the prophet depicts YHWH's utter destruction of a presumptuous monarch."[987] The fulfillment of his oracle will force all of Egypt's inhabitants (and the exiles), to acknowledge the sovereignty of Israel's God (v. 6a). (See Reflections at 29:13-16.)

986. Ibid., 603. See also D. R. Hillers, *Treaty-Curses and the Old Testament Prophets,* BibOr 16 (Rome: Pontifical Biblical Institute, 1964) 68-69.

987. See K. P. Darr, "Literary Perspectives on Prophetic Literature," in *Old Testament Interpretation: Past, Present, and Future, Essays in Honor of Gene M. Tucker,* ed. J. L. Mays et al. (Nashville: Abingdon, 1995) 139-41.

Ezekiel 29:6b-9a, Egypt Is a Fragile Reed

NIV

" 'You have been a staff of reed for the house of Israel. [7]When they grasped you with their hands, you splintered and you tore open their shoulders; when they leaned on you, you broke and their backs were wrenched.[a]

[8]" 'Therefore this is what the Sovereign LORD says: I will bring a sword against you and kill your men and their animals. [9]Egypt will become a desolate wasteland. Then they will know that I am the LORD.

a7 Syriac (see also Septuagint and Vulgate); Hebrew *and you caused their backs to stand*

NRSV

because you[a] were a staff of reed
to the house of Israel;
[7]when they grasped you with the hand, you broke,
and tore all their shoulders;
and when they leaned on you, you broke,
and made all their legs unsteady.[b]

8Therefore, thus says the Lord GOD: I will bring a sword upon you, and will cut off from you human being and animal; [9]and the land of Egypt shall be a desolation and a waste. Then they shall know that I am the LORD.

[a]Gk Syr Vg: Heb *they*   [b]Syr: Heb *stand*

COMMENTARY

The second of the prophet's three interrelated oracles against Egypt begins with a "because" clause, identifying yet another reason for the impending punishment of Pharaoh and his nation. Here also, Ezekiel takes up a conventional metaphor: Egypt is a "staff of reed" to the house of Israel. Because reeds are hollow, those foolish enough to choose them as walking sticks or crutches risk bodily injury. So Judah, by leaning on Egypt, misplaces its trust to its harm.

The reader, familiar with biblical traditions concerning Sennacherib's siege of Jerusalem during the reign of Judah's King Hezekiah (701 BCE), recalls how the Rabshakeh (commander-in-chief) of Assyria's army used the same imagery to depict the folly of hopes that Tirhakah and his Egyptian army could rescue the city (see Excursus: "Ezekiel's Oracles Against Pharaoh/Egypt," 1401-3). Ezekiel's description of the consequences of leaning on this "staff of reed" goes beyond the Rabshakeh's demoralizing message. While the Assyrian official charac-terized Egypt as "that broken reed of a staff, which will pierce the hand of anyone who leans on it" (Isa 36:6; 2 Kgs 18:21), the prophet speaks of the reed staff splitting open or dislocating the shoulder and of the collapse of the loins. He who leans on Egypt falls flat on his face!

"Therefore," plus the messenger formula, initiates the announcement of punishment, now expressed in stereotypical language (vv. 8-9). Yahweh will bring upon the land of Egypt a sword (see, e.g., 6:3; 11:8; 14:17; 33:2; Lev 26:25), which shall exterminate both humans and animals—a merismus for all living creatures (see, e.g., 14:13, 17, 19, 21; 25:13; 29:8, 11; 32:13; Exod 9:19, 22; Num 31:47; Jer 7:20; 21:6)—leaving it "a desolation and a waste," uninhabited ruins (see Lev 26:31-33). Then they (the Egyptians, at the point of death or any survivors?) will know Yahweh's unparalleled power, as manifested in their own history. (See Reflections at 29:13-16.)

Ezekiel 29:9b-12, Egypt Will Be Exiled

NIV

" 'Because you said, "The Nile is mine; I made it," [10]therefore I am against you and against your streams, and I will make the land of Egypt a ruin and a desolate waste from Migdol to Aswan, as far as the border of Cush.[a] [11]No foot of man or animal will pass through it; no one will live there for forty years. [12]I will make the land of Egypt desolate among devastated lands, and her cities will lie desolate forty years among ruined cities. And I will disperse the Egyptians among the nations and scatter them through the countries.' "

[a]10 That is, the upper Nile region

NRSV

Because you[a] said, "The Nile is mine, and I made it," [10]therefore, I am against you, and against your channels, and I will make the land of Egypt an utter waste and desolation, from Migdol to Syene, as far as the border of Ethiopia.[b] [11]No human foot shall pass through it, and no animal foot shall pass through it; it shall be uninhabited forty years. [12]I will make the land of Egypt a desolation among desolated countries; and her cities shall be a desolation forty years among cities that are laid waste. I will scatter the Egyptians among the nations, and disperse them among the countries.

[a]Gk Syr Vg: Heb *he*   [b]Or *Nubia*; Heb *Cush*

COMMENTARY

The motivation clause ("because . . .") of v. 9*b* reiterates, in slightly different form, Pharaoh's boast (in v. 3*b*). The announcement of punishment ("therefore . . .") follows immediately thereafter. Again, Yahweh utters the "challenge to a duel" formula against Pharaoh (see v. 3*a*), but also against the Nile canals. All of Egypt will be reduced to a desolate ruin. Migdol ("tower") likely refers to defensive forts situated on Egypt's northeastern frontier (Exod 14:2; Jer 44:1; 46:14).[988] Syene was its southern frontier, located slightly north of the Nile's first cataract. Hence, the phrase "from Migdol (to) Syene" specifies the nation's geo-

graphical breadth, just as "from Dan to Beersheba" (e.g., Judg 20:1; 1 Sam 3:20) designates the entire land of Israel. Cush refers to territory lying south of Egypt. Here, Ezekiel declares the period of Egypt's extreme desolation—forty years, the conventional span of a single generation. In 3:6, the prophet performed a sign act signifying Judah's forty-year punishment. Moreover, Yahweh's threat, "I will scatter the Egyptians among the nations, and disperse them among the countries," echoes Israel's fate as described in 20:23. Hence, these verses proclaim against Egypt a punishment that parallels Israel's own (v. 12). (See Reflections at 29:13-16.)

988. *ANET,* 259b.

Ezekiel 29:13-16, Egypt Will Be Restored

NIV

13" 'Yet this is what the Sovereign LORD says: At the end of forty years I will gather the Egyptians from the nations where they were scattered. [14]I will bring them back from captivity and return them to Upper Egypt,[a] the land of their ancestry. There they will be a lowly kingdom. [15]It will be the lowliest of kingdoms and will never again exalt itself above the other nations. I will make it so weak that it will never again rule over the nations. [16]Egypt will no longer be a source of confidence for the people of Israel but will be a reminder of their sin in turning to her for help. Then they will know that I am the Sovereign LORD.' "

[a]*14* Hebrew *to Pathros*

NRSV

13Further, thus says the Lord GOD: At the end of forty years I will gather the Egyptians from the peoples among whom they were scattered; [14]and I will restore the fortunes of Egypt, and bring them back to the land of Pathros, the land of their origin; and there they shall be a lowly kingdom. [15]It shall be the most lowly of the kingdoms, and never again exalt itself above the nations; and I will make them so small that they will never again rule over the nations. [16]The Egyptians[a] shall never again be the reliance of the house of Israel; they will recall their iniquity, when they turned to them for aid. Then they shall know that I am the Lord GOD.

[a]Heb *It*

COMMENTARY

In the light of Ezekiel's overt hostility toward Egypt in, for example, chaps. 17 and 23, vv. 13-16 are nothing short of astonishing. Yahweh announces the intention, at the end of forty years, to regather the Egyptians from exile, repatriate them, and revive Egypt's fortunes (for similar promises to Israel, see 11:17; 20:34, 41; 28:25).

This future restoration will not restore Egypt to its former glory. To the contrary, its territory will be reduced to Pathros (Upper, or southern, Egypt), here described as the Egyptians' original homeland. So circumscribed, Egypt will become "the most lowly of the kingdoms," never again to exalt itself above the nations (v. 15). So humbled, the

Egyptians will never again tempt the house of Israel to rely upon it, rather than upon God. The Israelites, in turn, will recall their past, iniquitous resort to Egypt and acknowledge Yahweh's sole sovereignty (v. 16).

Ezekiel, or perhaps later members of his school, was not the only biblical author to speak of a future for Egypt lying beyond punishment. Jeremiah 46:26 proclaims that Egypt will be handed over to Nebuchadrezzar, yet adds that afterward, "Egypt shall be inhabited as in the days of old." Isaiah 19:1-15 speaks of Yahweh's punishment of Egypt's gods, administrators, and other inhabitants; and vv. 16-17 portray Judah as "a terror to the Egyptians." Yet vv. 18-25 also proclaim, in a remarkable way, the Egyptians' conversion to Yahwism, the future presence of a Yahwistic altar

within the land of Egypt, a highway conjoining Egypt and Assyria, and God's blessing not only upon Israel, but also upon Egypt ("Blessed be Egypt my people") and Assyria. Should we discern in such texts the authors' awareness of Jewish diaspora settlements in Egypt (e.g., the island of Elephantine)? The text says nothing of these people. Deuteronomy 23:3 precludes the admission of Ammonites or Moabites to the Lord's assembly "even to the tenth generation," but vv. 7-8 prohibit Israel from abhoring the Edomites, their kin, and the Egyptians "because you were an alien residing in their land." Are Israel's stories of its early, intertwined history with Egypt such that certain of its traditionists cannot imagine Egypt's utter extinction but chose, rather, to envision its future firmly under Yahweh's control?

REFLECTIONS

Ezekiel's three initial oracles against Egypt, a redoubtable empire but unreliable political ally, focus first upon Pharaoh, whose pride and impunity challenge the prophet's conviction that no nation, regardless of its strength and longevity, can withstand Yahweh's plan for Israel and its ancient Near Eastern neighbors. Here as elsewhere, Ezekiel resorts to metaphor—no mere embellishment, but strategic speech—not only to organize his audience's (and readers') perception of the Egyptian king (and the country he represents) as cunning and dangerous, but also to persuade it to a new or deeper understanding of God's unparalleled power over every opponent. Ezekiel could have chosen another rhetorical strategy by which to depict Pharaoh's demise. But who can deny the vigor of his hunting vignette? The Bible teems with figurative uses of language. Our prayers, teaching, and preaching are enlivened when we not only examine and perhaps appropriate certain of its most dynamic and durable tropes, but also explore fresh imagery apropos to our own cultures and challenges.

The "Egypt is a staff of reed" metaphor also functions succinctly, and with rhetorical punch, to reveal a truth basic to the prophet's message: God alone must be the ultimate object of our faith and trust. Ezekiel insists with unrivaled severity that Yahweh's punishment of Israel (and of its culpable neighbors) can no longer be avoided. To his mind, the Babylonian aggressors are God's instruments of judgment; resort to other nations in hopes of avoiding that punishment betrays both a failure to accept the fate that Israel has earned and a fundamental refusal to acknowledge God's sovereignty as manifested in history. Ezekiel insists that trust in Yahweh offers no detour around the catastrophic events bearing down upon Judah. God's people must go through judgment, for only that path offers hope for its future. Israel must cling to God, even as Yahweh orchestrates its undoing.

These are, by anyone's reckoning, harsh words. We can easily understand why his fellow exiles and readers—ancient and modern—have resisted his interpretation of reality. While working to understand why Ezekiel spoke as he did, we have also, in previous Reflections sections, questioned the viability of a worldview that both asserts God's authorship of historical events and insists that the Lord so stages those events that righteousness is rewarded and wickedness punished. God-fearing people are not immune to tragedy, violence, and suffering. By the same token, oppressors can flourish all the days of their lives. Ezekiel's difficult message is that one does not trust in Yahweh because doing so guarantees survival and success, but because only God is worthy of, and entitled to, our ultimate faith and trust.

That, in the case of Egypt, God's preferred method of dealing with an earthly foe is *not* eternal extinction gives pause. The book of Ezekiel often looks beyond Judah's destruction to envision the restoration of Israel. But among the prophet's oracles against foreign nations, only Egypt is promised a restitution of sorts after its proscribed period of punishment. It is difficult to know whether Ezekiel himself subscribed to this view, or if it reflects the perspective of later traditionists. The question is, in any event, largely irrelevant. More important is our recognition that over the course of history—a history that has spanned millennia and is still alive—Jews and Christians have struggled to understand how they might best relate to each other, and to peoples and nations whose ways are not their ways, and whose gods are not their God. The pages of our Bibles speak to this issue often and in diverse ways. The many opinions they convey cannot be reconciled into some monolithic whole, and no one text can be singled out as what "the Bible says." So, "there are matters in the Bible which are time- and culture-conditioned, there are high points and low points, and, above all, there are developments in the way divine actions and appropriate human reaction are perceived and described. If we are not to fall back on allegory . . . these must be taken into account in our own response to the texts."[989]

The modern world is far larger than Ezekiel knew, but it is also smaller. What happens, even on the other side of the planet, can have global implications. When internecine feuds foment and larger nations prey upon smaller ones, we cannot simply presuppose that the battles will go against God's foes—that some live, and others die, according to God's plan. Even as, in faith, we commend ourselves and our world into the Lord's hands, we are commissioned to seek justice, to weigh competing claims, and to act in ways that testify to a bedrock belief that God loves this world and takes no pleasure in the death of the wicked, but longs rather that they (we) should turn from evil and live (Ezek 18:23).

989. Joseph Blenkinsopp, *Ezekiel,* IBC (Louisville: John Knox, 1990) 136.

Ezekiel 29:17-21, Yahweh Will Give Egypt to Nebuchadrezzar

NIV

[17]In the twenty-seventh year, in the first month on the first day, the word of the LORD came to me: [18]"Son of man, Nebuchadnezzar king of Babylon drove his army in a hard campaign against Tyre; every head was rubbed bare and every shoulder made raw. Yet he and his army got no reward from the campaign he led against Tyre. [19]Therefore this is what the Sovereign LORD says: I am going to give Egypt to Nebuchadnezzar king of Babylon, and he will carry off its wealth. He will loot and plunder the land as pay for his army. [20]I have given him Egypt as a reward for his efforts because he and his army did it for me, declares the Sovereign LORD.

[21]"On that day I will make a horn[a] grow for the house of Israel, and I will open your mouth among them. Then they will know that I am the LORD."

a21 Horn here symbolizes strength.

NRSV

[17]In the twenty-seventh year, in the first month, on the first day of the month, the word of the LORD came to me: [18]Mortal, King Nebuchadrezzar of Babylon made his army labor hard against Tyre; every head was made bald and every shoulder was rubbed bare; yet neither he nor his army got anything from Tyre to pay for the labor that he had expended against it. [19]Therefore thus says the Lord GOD: I will give the land of Egypt to King Nebuchadrezzar of Babylon; and he shall carry off its wealth and despoil it and plunder it; and it shall be the wages for his army. [20]I have given him the land of Egypt as his payment for which he labored, because they worked for me, says the Lord GOD.

[21]On that day I will cause a horn to sprout up for the house of Israel, and I will open your lips among them. Then they shall know that I am the LORD.

COMMENTARY

The date in v. 17, "in the twenty-seventh year [of Jehoiachin's exile], in the first month, on the first day of the month" (April 26, 571 BCE), is the latest in the entire book of Ezekiel. Twenty-two years have passed since Ezekiel first was commissioned by Yahweh to prophesy to his fellow exiles in Babylonia.

The following oracle apparently was occasioned by the failure of Nebuchadrezzar's troops successfully to pillage and destroy Tyre, a Phoenician city-state situated on an island approximately one-half mile off the eastern Mediterranean coast (see Excursus, "Tyre 'in the Heart of the Seas,' " 1359-62). In a series of seven oracles (chaps. 26–28), Ezekiel had predicted that Tyre would be utterly and forever destroyed by the Babylonians. So long as Nebuchadrezzar's thirteen-year siege of the city (c. 585–572) continued, Ezekiel's predictions remained viable. In the end, however, Nebuchadrezzar's reward fell far short of the splendid spoil Ezekiel had predicted (see, e.g., 26:7-14). True, Babylonia's ruler did not labor entirely in vain: The city capitulated, and he deported Tyre's king, Ithobaal III. Nevertheless, Nebuchadrezzar's inability to pillage and sack Tyre likely cast doubt upon Ezekiel's ability accurately to foretell the future. The present passage grants us a glimpse of how the prophet sought to accommodate his (God's) word to a new situation: Yahweh will give Nebuchadrezzar the wealth of Egypt as "wages" for his army (vv. 19-20). Verse 21 correlates Babylonia's victory over Egypt with hope for Israel (note the opening formula, "On that day . . .") and reassures the prophet that he will again be able to speak with the confidence borne of credibility. In its final form, the unit ends with the recognition formula (v. 21 *b*).

29:17-20. Ezekiel announces the advent of a fresh word from Yahweh, who characteristically addresses him as "Mortal." Verses 18-20 do not speak directly to the failure of Ezekiel's predictions concerning Tyre's destruction. Instead, the Lord points to the hard labor Nebuchadrezzar's army expended in its thirteen-year siege of the city. So strenuous was the work that the soldiers' heads and shoulders were rubbed bare.

Some critics have speculated that this description reflects the Babylonians' attempt to construct a causeway between the mainland and the island—a strategy successfully implemented by Alexander the Great in 332 BCE.[990] So enormous a project would require the troops to transport countless containers of earth on the shoulders and against their heads. But we have no evidence that Nebuchadrezzar set his troops to that task.[991] J. Katzenstein thinks it likely that the "siege" was actually a blockade from the mainland.[992] An inscription of Assyria's king Assurbanipal describes his blockade of Tyre in 663 BCE: "I threw up [earthworks] against him. [To prevent the escape] of his people, I kept a strong guard (on the watch). On sea and the dry land I seized his roads, I prevented him from going (anywhere). I let little water and food, which would keep them alive, reach their mouths."[993] This text suggests that the Babylonian troops also expended most of their energy in controlling Tyre's mainland territories, in order that no supplies reach the island from those quarters.

Because neither Nebuchadrezzar nor his soldiers have received wages (booty) from Tyre,[994] Yahweh has determined to give the land of Egypt to Babylonia's king. Its wealth will become his army's wages. The participial phrase "I am giving" recalls the "assurance of victory" formula at home in ancient Israel's "holy war" traditions (see Josh 6:2; Judg 7:9),[995] but here applied to a foreign king who functions as God's instrument. Hence, Ezekiel portrays Nebuchadrezzar's impending victory over Egypt as an exercise of divine justice—that is, redress for wages not paid for hard labor.

990. See, e.g., E. L. Allen, "Exposition on the Book of Ezekiel," in *The Interpreter's Bible*, 12 vols. (Nashville: Abingdon, 1956) 6:227-28.

991. W. Zimmerli, *Ezekiel 2: A Commentary on the Book of the Prophet Ezekiel, Chapters 25–48*, trans. J. D. Martin, Hermeneia (Philadelphia: Fortress, 1983) 119.

992. J. Katzenstein, *The History of Tyre* (Jerusalem: Schocken Institute, 1973) 331.

993. See D. D. Luckenbill, ed., *Ancient Records of Assyria and Babylonia*, 2 vols. (Chicago: University of Chicago Press, 1926–27) 2:847. See also Greenberg, *Ezekiel 21–37*, 533.

994. On booty (goods, livestock, persons) as a soldier's wages, see M. Greenberg, "Is there a Mari Parallel to the Israelite Enemy *ḥerem*?" ErIsr 24, *Avraham Malamat Volume* (Jerusalem: Israel Exploration Society, 1993), 49-53; and Greenberg, *Ezekiel 21–37*, 614.

995. In those texts, however, the phrase is cast in the perfect or past tense. In v. 20*a*, the phrase reappears, but in the past tense. See G. von Rad, *Der heilige Krieg im alten Israel*, ATANT 20 (Zürich: Zwingli, 1951) 6-9.

It does not suffice to follow Zimmerli's reasoning that Ezekiel's Tyre prophecies, once quite urgent, became "unimportant" in the course of history.[996] If such were the case, how might we explain his return to the topic some thirteen years later? Ezekiel's rhetorical strategy in this oracle cannot offset entirely his unfulfilled predictions concerning the plunder and destruction of Tyre. Instead, it blunts that issue by focusing upon another, though related one—compensating Nebuchadrezzar and his army for their lengthy and laborous campaign against the Phoenician island. At the same time, these verses speak to Ezekiel's as-yet-unrealized predictions of Egypt's demise. Since the time of Hophra's unsuccessful bid to rescue Jerusalem, Nebuchadrezzar has been preoccupied with the Tyrian blockade. Now that it has ended, he is able to turn his attention to Egypt. In fact, Nebuchadrezzar died without ever conquering that country, though a damaged tablet dating from the thirty-seventh year of his reign (568/67 BCE) speaks of a Babylonian campaign against Hophra's general and successor, Amasis.[997]

996. Zimmerli, *Ezekiel 2*, 120.
997. *ANET*, 308b.

29:21. Critics tend to regard v. 21 as a subsequent addition to vv. 17-20 (note the closing formula, "says the Lord GOD," in v. 20*b*), though the ancient reader would not construe it as such. The phrase "on that day" links the following, optimistic word concerning the house of Israel to the fulfillment of Ezekiel's prediction of Egypt's destruction. References to the raising or lifting up of a horn (a symbol of strength) appear, for example, in Pss 75:5 and 148:14 (see also Lam 2:3, where Yahweh is said to have "cut off every horn" of Israel when Jerusalem was destroyed). Only Ps 132:17, however, speaks of causing a horn to sprout—a reference to the Davidic dynasty (see also Ps 89:17, where "our horn" represents Israel's king). Has Ezekiel in mind the restoration of David's line? Unfortunately, the phrase is too brief and vague to substantiate that conclusion. Clearly, however, the announcement bodes well for Israel. Ezekiel, also, is consoled by the promise that when these events transpire, he will be given " an opening of the mouth," that is, a claim to be heard based on the vindication of his prophecy (see Jer 28:8-9). (By contrast, on account of her shame, Jerusalem will never again open her mouth, 16:63.)

REFLECTIONS

In the Commentary to Ezekiel 12, ancient Israel's problem of differentiating between authentic and inauthentic prophecies is discussed. Then, no less than now, God's people had to contend with situations where two or more persons, each claiming to be Yahweh's trustworthy spokesperson, addressed the same dilemma but in very different ways. The fulfillment or non-fulfillment of a predictive oracle was one criterion for distinguishing between true and false prophecies. In Deut 18:22, for example, we read: "If a prophet speaks in the name of the LORD but the thing does not take place or prove true, it is a word that the LORD has not spoken. The prophet has spoken it presumptuously; do not be frightened by it" (NRSV). Ezekiel himself invokes this criterion (e.g., "When this comes—and come it will!—then they shall know that a prophet has been among them," 33:33 NRSV; see also 1 Kgs 22:28).

When predictive prophecies fail to materialize, skepticism follows. Isaiah condemned those who taunted him: "Let him make haste, let him speed his work that we may see it; let the plan of the Holy One of Israel hasten to fulfillment, that we may know it!" (Isa 5:19 NRSV). Jeremiah prayed for vindication in the face of detractors who asked, "Where is the word of the LORD? Let it come!" (Jer 17:15 NRSV). Ezekiel's fellow exiles employed a proverb, "The days are prolonged, and every vision comes to nothing" (12:22 NRSV), to express their doubts about the validity of the prophet's predictions that Jerusalem would soon be destroyed. A few verses later, a second skeptical saying is attributed to the exiles: "The vision that he sees is for many years ahead; he prophesies for distant times" (12:27 NRSV). This proverb does not challenge the credibility of Ezekiel's vision, but it insists that the fulfillment of that vision lies far in the future.

Ezekiel's predictions of Tyre's utter destruction by Nebuchadrezzar were not merely unfulfilled; they were invalidated.[998] In 29:17-20 he quotes no skeptical response of the exiles to their failure. But the text itself testifies to a problem that the prophet had somehow to address. By the criterion advanced in Deut 18:22, he had failed a "test" that might have confirmed his authenticity as Yahweh's prophet. But, of course, the matter was not so cut-and-dried as that. David Noel Freedman suggests that since Ezekiel knew he was a true prophet, predictions that failed to materialize did not prove him wrong but were, rather, explained by reference to the mysteries of the Divine. A prophet could only report what had been revealed to him.[999] Whatever Ezekiel's mindset, Freedman certainly reminds us of the inadequacies of a simple fulfillment or nonfulfillment criterion for authenticating prophecies. So does the book of Jonah. His unconditional message to the city of Nineveh ("Forty days more, and Nineveh shall be overthrown!" Jonah 3:4 NRSV) was not fulfilled because, in the face of the Ninevites' repentance, God decided not to destroy them. Jonah then had to learn a hard lesson about divine freedom and mercy (Jonah 4:1-11).

We are accustomed to competing voices in practically every facet of life, including the religious sphere. God-fearing people can and do disagree on the full range of issues we face. Preachers proclaim very different messages from their pulpits. How are we to discern God's will for our lives—personal and communal? The Bible provides no fail-safe criteria upon which to discern the word of the Lord among the many words we hear. John Wesley's "quadrilateral" is a helpful tool, because in addition to Scripture, it invites us to use other resources: tradition, reason, and experience.

If the Bible is God's "living word," and not simply an artifact from the ancient world, then it must be allowed to live. Life always entails growth and change. Ezekiel permits the Tyre prophecies to stand even as they are contradicted, at least in part, by subsequent events. He proclaims a fresh message from God, informed by ongoing faith in Yahweh's sovereignty over the nations and by his own construal of how history is unfolding. His prophecies are not infallible, as if attempts to understand God's will and purpose were once-and-for-all, absolutely right or dead wrong. Ezekiel also must keep listening and thinking.

998. Greenberg, *Ezekiel 21–37,* 617.
999. See ibid.

Ezekiel 30:1-19, The Day of Egypt

OVERVIEW

Only Ezek 30:1-19, the third of the prophet's seven units against Pharaoh/Egypt, is not dated; and its three interrelated subunits (vv. 2-9, vv. 10-12, and vv. 13-19) contain no explicit references to historical events. The reader likely associates it with the date (the latest in the scroll) prefixed to the immediately preceding oracle (see 29:17)—that is, the first day of the first month of the twenty-seventh year of Jehoiachin's exile (April 26, 571 BCE). Knowing of Yahweh's decision to give Egypt and its wealth to Nebuchadrezzar and his soldiers as wages for their disappointing, thir-teen-year blockade of Tyre (29:18-20), Ezekiel further describes its demise.

Verses 2-9 take up "the day of Yahweh" motif. Originally this motif expressed Israel's expectation of a time when Yahweh, its mighty warrior God, would destroy its adversaries. But during the reign of the northern kingdom's Jeroboam II (786–746 BCE), a Judean prophet named Amos traveled north and turned traditional expectations for Yahweh's day on their heads. Despite their pretense of piety, Israel's rich and powerful were afflicting the poor and vulnerable within their society. On account of their immoral and unjust practices, Yahweh's wrath would be unleashed against them (Amos 5:18-20; 8:9-10). *They* would be God's enemies on the day of the Lord!

Amos's twist on the day of Yahweh motif was adopted by succeeding prophets (see, e.g., Isa 2:12-17; Jer 30:7; Joel 1:15; 2:1-12; Zeph 1:14-18). Ezekiel himself employs it in chap. 7 to describe the destruction of Israel's soil and its inhabitants. Here, however, he sets the motif to its original function, applying it to a foreign nation and its allies. Egypt is Yahweh's foe and so should be Israel's as well. Yet, ironically, many of God's people have placed faith in that foe. Indeed, Judean soldiers also are serving in its army! For those exiles who have supported a pro-Egyptian foreign policy, the prophet's announcement of Egypt's utter demise is not good news. Indeed, the prophecy troubles the ancient reader of Ezekiel's scroll as well, because in his day, fellow Jews are living there, for example, in Alexandria and Tehaphnehes.

Verses 10-12 reiterate that Nebuchadrezzar, king of Babylon, will be Yahweh's agent of Egypt's destruction (so also 20:19*a*). The swords of his soldiers will fill the land with corpses, and Yahweh will dry up the Nile's canals and streams, desolating "the land and everything in it" (v. 12). A concluding formula (v. 12*b*) assures the fulfillment of

this prophecy. Yahweh has spoken; the outcome is assured.

Verse 13 predicts the collapse of both "pillars" of Egyptian society—its gods and government. Important cities and regions of the nation, accompanied by familiar expressions of destruction, appear in vv. 14-18. The toponyms appear without discernible order, and several place-names and phrases are repeated. The intent, Boadt opines, is to present "a kaleidoscope of simultaneous devastation."[1000] Many a critic, however, complains that the literary quality of vv. 13-19 falls short of Ezekiel's high standards and so attribute them to his disciples or "school."[1001] Greenberg, however, argues that absent justification for equating authenticity with accuracy, aesthetic merit, and consistency, the question to be asked is whether the text reflects the prophet's style and situation.[1002] In my view, nothing precludes the ancient reader's construal of these verses as what they purport to be—a series of interrelated Ezekielian oracles concerning Yahweh's future destruction of Egypt.

1000. Lawrence Boadt, *Ezekiel's Oracles against Egypt: A Literary and Philogical Study of Ezekiel 29–32,* BibOr 37 (Rome: Pontifical Biblical Institute, 1980) 74.
1001. Zimmerli observes that the list of place-names displays "more of a show of learning than actual knowledge." See W. Zimmerli, *Ezekiel 2: A Commentary on the Book of the Prophet Ezekiel, Chapters 25–48,* trans. J. D. Martin, Hermeneia (Philadelphia: Fortress, 1983) 128.
1002. See Moshe Greenberg, *Ezekiel 21–37,* AB 22A (Garden City, N.Y.: Doubleday, 1997) 629.

Ezekiel 30:1-9 Yahweh's Day Against Egypt and Its Mercenaries

NIV

30 The word of the LORD came to me: ²"Son of man, prophesy and say: 'This is what the Sovereign LORD says:

" 'Wail and say,
"Alas for that day!"
³For the day is near,
the day of the LORD is near—
a day of clouds,
a time of doom for the nations.
⁴A sword will come against Egypt,
and anguish will come upon Cush.ᵃ

ᵃ4 That is, the upper Nile region; also in verses 5 and 9

NRSV

30 The word of the LORD came to me: ²Mortal, prophesy, and say, Thus says the Lord GOD:

Wail, "Alas for the day!"
³ For a day is near,
the day of the LORD is near;
it will be a day of clouds,
a time of doomᵃ for the nations.
⁴A sword shall come upon Egypt,
and anguish shall be in Ethiopia,ᵇ
when the slain fall in Egypt,

ᵃHeb lacks *of doom*   ᵇOr *Nubia*; Heb *Cush*

NIV

When the slain fall in Egypt,
    her wealth will be carried away
    and her foundations torn down.

5Cush and Put, Lydia and all Arabia, Libya*a* and the people of the covenant land will fall by the sword along with Egypt.
    6" 'This is what the LORD says:

" 'The allies of Egypt will fall
    and her proud strength will fail.
From Migdol to Aswan
    they will fall by the sword within her,
                    declares the Sovereign LORD.
7" 'They will be desolate
    among desolate lands,
and their cities will lie
    among ruined cities.
8Then they will know that I am the LORD,
    when I set fire to Egypt
    and all her helpers are crushed.

9" 'On that day messengers will go out from me in ships to frighten Cush out of her complacency. Anguish will take hold of them on the day of Egypt's doom, for it is sure to come.

a5 Hebrew Cub

NRSV

and its wealth is carried away,
    and its foundations are torn down.
5Ethiopia,*a* and Put, and Lud, and all Arabia, and Libya,*b* and the people of the allied land*c* shall fall with them by the sword.

6 Thus says the LORD:
Those who support Egypt shall fall,
    and its proud might shall come down;
from Migdol to Syene
    they shall fall within it by the sword,
says the Lord GOD.
7 They shall be desolated among other desolated countries,
    and their cities shall lie among cities laid waste.
8 Then they shall know that I am the LORD,
    when I have set fire to Egypt,
    and all who help it are broken.
9On that day, messengers shall go out from me in ships to terrify the unsuspecting Ethiopians;*d* and anguish shall come upon them on the day of Egypt's doom;*e* for it is coming!

*a*Or *Nubia*; Heb *Cush*   *b*Compare Gk Syr Vg: Heb *Cub*
*c*Meaning of Heb uncertain   *d*Or *Nubians*; Heb *Cush*   *e*Heb *the day of Egypt*

COMMENTARY

The first of Ezekiel's three subunits against Egypt in 30:1-19 commences with the familiar word event formula ("The word of the LORD came to me"), followed by Yahweh's conventional address to the prophet ("Mortal") and a double imperative ("prophesy and say"). The oracle per se, launched by the messenger formula ("Thus says the Lord GOD"), commands an unspecified masculine (or mixed) plural audience (ostensibly the Egyptians themselves): "Wail, 'Alas the day!' "[1003] A second phrase augments the first ("For a day is near"), and a third, climatic phrase supplies even

more information: "The day *of Yahweh* is near."[1004] Like other prophets, Ezekiel describes Yahweh's day in part by means of a natural phenomenon: it will be "a day of clouds" (cf. 34:12; Zeph 1:15; Joel 2:2), an appointed time (of doom) for the nations. Verse 3*b* suggests that here, as in some other "day of Yahweh" passages, the predicted cataclysm is universal in scope. Subsequent verses, however, will speak only of the destruction of Egypt and its allies.

Ezekiel, who favors the sword among Yahweh's arsenal of weapons, announces its coming upon Egypt. When the slain fall in Egypt,[1005]

1003. The interjection "Alas" (הה *hāh*) is a variant of אהה (*'ăhāh,* "alas," "woe"); for the latter in Ezekiel, see 4:14; 9:8; 11:13; and 21:5. Contrary to the NRSV and the NIV, the Hebrew ל (*lě*) prefixed to "the day" should not be translated as the preposition "for," but as an emphatic particle. See Boadt, *Ezekiel's Oracles Against Egypt,* 58.

1004. Boadt, ibid., 60, cites these three clauses as an example of "delayed identification." Announcements of the approach of Yahweh's day also appear in Isa 13:6; Joel 2:1; 4:14; Zeph 1:7, 14.

1005. נפל (*nāpal,* "to fall") appears frequently in Ezekiel's oracles against foreign nations; see also vv. 5, 6 (twice), 17.

its "horde" or "wealth" (המון; *hāmôn*) is taken away,[1006] and its foundations are demolished (v. 4*a*), Cush (Ethiopia) will be enveloped in anguish. The fortunes of Cush, situated south of Egypt proper, were intertwined with those of its northern neighbor (see Isa 20:3, 4, 5; 43:3; 45:4; Neh 3:9; Ps 68:32). In fact, Cush was home to the twenty-fifth dynasty of pharaohs (710–663 BCE). The Twenty-sixth, or Saite, Dynasty, however, was Egyptian; and Psammetichus II (594–588 BCE), Ezekiel's contemporary, campaigned successfully to bring his southern neighbor back under Egypt's control. The prophet does not proclaim that the terror-stricken Cushites also shall die by the sword. Rather, as Greenberg observes, their despair will reflect the enormity of Egypt's destruction.[1007] Hebrew חלחלה (*ḥalḥālâ*), "anguish," "writhing" (see also Isa 21:3; Nah 2:11), from the root חול (*ḥûl*), "whirl, dance, writhe," can refer to physical pain, especially that associated with women in childbirth, but also to "the psychological anguish and physiological reactions of persons facing impending doom, or anticipating the destruction of others."[1008]

Verse 5 specifies the origins of mercenaries in Egypt's army who also will fall. Here, some critics aver, a later hand has elaborated upon the reference to Egypt's "horde" (of troops) in v. 4*b*.[1009] Ezekiel begins with Cush, Put (Lybia), and Lud (Lydia). Readers recall that he placed soldiers from Lud and Put aboard "ship Tyre" in 27:10. In Jer 46:9, the same trio of similar-sounding names identifies mercenaries in Pharaoh Necho's army at the battle of Carchemish (605 BCE). "And all Arabia" (NRSV; NIV) is based on an unnecessary emendation of the MT, which actually reads "and all the mixed people" (וכל-הערב; *wěkol-hā'ereb*).[1010]

Hebrew כוב (*kûb*; note the assonance with the first three names in this verse) is unknown. On the basis of the LXX, some scholars emend it to לוב (*lûb*)—that is, Libyans (cf. Nah 3:9).[1011] "The people of the land of the covenant" likely refers to Judeans. Jeremiah 24:8 notes their presence in Egypt at the time of the first deportation to Babylonia in 597 BCE. Following Jerusalem's destruction and the assassination of the Babylonian-appointed governor, Gedaliah, Jeremiah urged his fellow survivors not to migrate to Egypt; but they, fearing Babylonian reprisal, forced him and Baruch to flee with them to Tahpanhes (Jer 41:1–43:7). Jeremiah 44:1 addresses Jews living in Migdol, Tahpanhes, Memphis, and the land of Pathros. The *Letter of Aristeas* 13 refers to Jewish soldiers in the army of a Psammetichus during his campaign against the Ethiopians (Cushites). Does "covenant" refer to a mutual assistance treaty forged between Egypt and Judah during the reign of Zedekiah? The LXX "clarifies" the phrase to read "the people of my covenant"—that is, the covenant between Yahweh and Israel.

Perhaps the later insertion of v. 5, which interrupts the smooth connection between vv. 4 and 6, occasioned the messenger formula in v. 6*a* (it does not appear in the LXX). Two parallel clauses follow: "the support[er]s of Egypt" (סמכי מצרים *sōměkê miṣrayim*), likely a reference to troops gleaned from allies (see Ps 37:17, 24; 54:6), shall fall, and Egypt's "proud might" (perhaps a reference to the royal scepter; hence, its government) will collapse. "From Migdol [in the north] to Syene [in the south]" is a merism signifying Egypt's entire territory, within which all will fall (see the Commentary on 29:10).

With the destruction of Egypt's allies and the downfall of its government, it will be rendered desolate among other desolate countries; and his (so MT; a reference to Pharaoh?) cities will be reckoned among other ruined cities (v. 7; see 29:12).[1012] An expanded recognition formula (v. 8) identifies the ultimate goal of Egypt's overthrow: Its people and their allies will be forced to acknowledge Yahweh's power and sovereignty when God has set Egypt afire and broken its helpers (see 1 Kgs 20:16; Isa 31:3). Here, as

---

1006. המון (*hāmôn*, "horde," "wealth," "uproar," "pomp," "pride") is, as Boadt observes, a key noun in Ezekiel's anti-Egypt oracles. Of its 66 occurrences in the HB, 45 appear in Isaiah, Jeremiah, and Ezekiel; 26 of these are in Ezekiel, 16 within chaps. 29–32. See Boadt, *Ezekiel's Oracles Against Tyre*, 64. In this context, both the NRSV and the NIV opt for "wealth"; as Block observes, however, "pride" also is appropriate, being a theme of other Ezekielian oracles against foreign nations. See D. I. Block, *The Book of Ezekiel: Chapters 25–48*, NICOT (Grand Rapids: Eerdmans, 1998) 158. But see the comments to v. 5.

1007. Greenberg, *Ezekiel 21–37*, 630.

1008. K. P. Darr, *Isaiah's Vision and the Family of God* (Louisville: Westminster John Knox, 1994) 102.

1009. See, e.g., Boadt, *Ezekiel's Oracles Against Egypt*, 64-65.

1010. In Exod 12:38, הערב (*hā'ereb*) refers to an admixture of non-Hebrews who participated in the exodus from Egypt (see, e.g., Exod 12:38). In Jer 25:20, it denotes an ethnically diverse group, possibly aligned with Egypt; and in Jer 50:37, it designates various foreign soldiers serving in the army of Babylonia.

1011. Boadt, *Ezekiel's Oracles Against Egypt*, 65.

1012. See Greenberg, *Ezekiel 21–37*, 606-7, 622-23.

elsewhere in Ezekiel's oracles against foreign nations, "knowing" lacks positive connotations. It is, rather, a "last gasp" realization by the Egyptians that Israel's deity has brought about their end.

In the following prose verse (initated, like 29:21, by the phrase "on that day"), Yahweh speaks of dispatching messengers in ships (צים [ṣîm], an Egyptian loan word) to terrify the complacent Cushites with news of "the day of Egypt," that is, the day of its doom (see the analogous "the day of Midian" in Isa 9:3). Here, the author engages in "exegesis of scripture by means of scripture,"[1013] reversing the scenario of Isa 18:2. According to that passage, ambassadors from Cush sailed down the Nile in papyrus vessels toward Judah, there to encourage its support of Ashdod's rebellion against Assyria in 714 BCE (see also Isa 14:32; 20:1-6). Here, by contrast, God sends messengers up the Nile toward distant Cush in order to crush its self-confidence. (See Reflections at 30:13-19.)

1013. Zimmerli, *Ezekiel 2,* 130.

Ezekiel 30:10-12, Nebuchadrezzar and Yahweh Will Defeat Egypt

NIV	NRSV

[10]" 'This is what the Sovereign LORD says:
 	
 " 'I will put an end to the hordes of Egypt
   by the hand of Nebuchadnezzar king of
   Babylon.
 [11]He and his army—the most ruthless of
   nations—
 will be brought in to destroy the land.
 They will draw their swords against Egypt
   and fill the land with the slain.
 [12]I will dry up the streams of the Nile
   and sell the land to evil men;
 by the hand of foreigners
   I will lay waste the land and everything
   in it.
 	
 I the LORD have spoken.
	[10]Thus says the Lord GOD:
	 I will put an end to the hordes of Egypt,
	   by the hand of King Nebuchadrezzar of
	   Babylon.
	 [11] He and his people with him, the most
	   terrible of the nations,
	   shall be brought in to destroy the land;
	 and they shall draw their swords against
	   Egypt,
	   and fill the land with the slain.
	 [12] I will dry up the channels,
	   and will sell the land into the hand of
	   evildoers;
	 I will bring desolation upon the land and
	   everything in it
	   by the hand of foreigners;
	 I the LORD have spoken.

COMMENTARY

As in 29:18-20, so here Ezekiel announces that Nebuchadrezzar, king of Babylon, will function as Yahweh's agent of Egypt's destruction. More accurately, this foreign king with his troops ("the most terrible of the nations"; see also 28:7) will be brought in to battle as God's allies. With drawn swords (another echo of 28:7; see further 5:2, 12; 12:14), they will fill the land of Egypt with the slain. Meanwhile Yahweh will dry up the Nile, upon which Egypt's existence depends (see also Isa 19:5-7; 37:25, 2 Kgs 19:34; 42:15) and hand the land over to "fierce men" (see 7:24; Ps 78:49).[1014] "Foreigners" appear in conjunction with "the most terrible of the nations" in 7:21; 28:7; 31:12; 32:12; and Isa 25:2-3. (See Reflections at 30:13-19.)

1014. Greenberg, *Ezekiel 21–37,* 624.

Ezekiel 30:13-19, Devastation Throughout Egypt

NIV

13" 'This is what the Sovereign LORD says:

" 'I will destroy the idols
  and put an end to the images in Memphis.*a*
No longer will there be a prince in Egypt,
  and I will spread fear throughout the land.
14I will lay waste Upper Egypt,*b*
  set fire to Zoan
  and inflict punishment on Thebes.*c*
15I will pour out my wrath on Pelusium,*d*
  the stronghold of Egypt,
  and cut off the hordes of Thebes.
16I will set fire to Egypt;
  Pelusium will writhe in agony.
Thebes will be taken by storm;
  Memphis will be in constant distress.
17The young men of Heliopolis*e* and Bubastis*f*
  will fall by the sword,
  and the cities themselves will go into cap-
    tivity.
18Dark will be the day at Tahpanhes
  when I break the yoke of Egypt;
  there her proud strength will come to an
    end.
She will be covered with clouds,
  and her villages will go into captivity.
19So I will inflict punishment on Egypt,
  and they will know that I am the LORD.' "

a13 Hebrew *Noph*; also in verse 16   *b14* Hebrew *waste Pathros*
c14 Hebrew *No*; also in verses 15 and 16   *d15* Hebrew *Sin*; also
in verse 16   *e17* Hebrew *Awen* (or *On*)   *f17* Hebrew *Pi Beseth*

NRSV

13Thus says the Lord GOD:
I will destroy the idols
  and put an end to the images in Memphis;
there shall no longer be a prince in the land
    of Egypt;
  so I will put fear in the land of Egypt.
14I will make Pathros a desolation,
  and will set fire to Zoan,
  and will execute acts of judgment on
    Thebes.
15I will pour my wrath upon Pelusium,
  the stronghold of Egypt,
  and cut off the hordes of Thebes.
16I will set fire to Egypt;
  Pelusium shall be in great agony;
Thebes shall be breached,
  and Memphis face adversaries by day.
17The young men of On and of Pi-beseth shall
    fall by the sword;
  and the cities themselves*a* shall go into
    captivity.
18At Tehaphnehes the day shall be dark,
  when I break there the dominion of Egypt,
  and its proud might shall come to an end;
the city*b* shall be covered by a cloud,
  and its daughter-towns shall go into captivity.
19Thus I will execute acts of judgment on
    Egypt.
  Then they shall know that I am the LORD.

*a*Heb *and they*   *b*Heb *she*

COMMENTARY

In v. 13*a,* Yahweh announces the future destruction of Egypt's idols (גלולים [*gillûlîm*], "dung pellets," Ezekiel's characteristic and coarse term for the statues of foreign deities) and the end of the images (אלילים *'ĕlîlîm*) in Memphis (נֹף *nōp*). Here, the punishment of a people extends to its gods; see Exod 12:12 ("on all the gods of Egypt I will execute judgments") and Isa 19:1.[1015] Verse 13*b* proclaims that Egypt will never again have a

native ruler (נשיא *nāśî'*, "prince"). Because *'ĕlîlîm,* "images," appears nowhere else within the book of Ezekiel (but see, e.g., Lev 19:4; 26:1), some critics emend it to אילים (*'êlîm*), "rams" (see LXX), a common metaphor for leaders.[1016] The MT makes sense, however, and the ancient reader is able to understand it without difficulty. The collapse of gods and government will put fear in the land of Egypt.

1015. Ibid., 624.

1016. See Boadt, *Ezekiel's Oracles Against Egypt,* 76.

As noted in the Overview, the place-names of vv. 13-19 are not listed in any discernable order;[1017] and the subunit is characterized by repetitions. Lists of place-names appear also in other prophetic oracles (see, e.g., Mic 1:10-15, Jer 46:14; 48:1-5, against Moab). Most of the phrases in the present passage are presented as first-person threats by Yahweh; others express in the third person the victims' experiences (e.g., "writhe in anguish" [vv. 4, 9, 16], "fall by the sword" [v. 17; see also 5:12; 6:11, 12; 7:15; 11:10; 17:21; 23:25, etc.], "go into captivity" [vv. 17, 18; see 12:11]. God will make Pathros (Upper or southern Egypt; see also 29:14) a desolation. Zoan (Greek "Tanis," an administrative center in the eastern Delta) will be set afire (vv. 14, 16; see also vv. 8 and 26); and God will execute punishments (see also 5:10, 15; 11:9; 14:21; 16:41; 25:11; 28:22, 26) against No (full name "No-Amon," i.e., "City of [the god] Amon"; Greek "Thebes" [v. 14]). Sin (Egyptian "fortress"), a strategic stronghold on Egypt's northeastern frontier traditionally identified as Pelusium, will endure the outpouring of God's wrath; (see also 7:8; 9:8; 14:19; 16:38; 20:8, 13, 21; 22:22; 36:18) and the horde of No (המון נא *hămôn nōʾ*; Greenberg suspects a play on No-Amon, see Nah 3:8)[1018] will be cut off (see also 14:13, 17, 19, 21; 21:8, 9; 25:7, 13, 16; 29:8).

Verse 16 extends the threat of fire (see v. 9) to all Egypt, then predicts that Sin also will writhe in anguish (vv. 4, 9). The walls of No (Thebes) will be breached (see 13:11; 26:10); and the enemies of Noph ("Moph" in Hos 9:6; Greek "Memphis"; the translation is uncertain, and the text is likely corrupt) will attack by day. The young men of On (און *ʾāwen*, "iniquity"; but see Gen 41:45, 50), located just north of modern Cairo and the center

of solar worship in Egypt (Greek, *Heliopolis,* i.e., "the city of the sun[-god]"), and of Pi-beset (Hebrew for the Egyptian place-name meaning "house of Bastet," the Egyptian cat/lion goddess; Greek, *Bupastis*) shall fall by the sword; the women (so LXX, but likely a reference to [the remaining inhabitants of] the two cities) will go into captivity.

Tehaphnehes (Taḥpanḥes), a frontier fortress located near the northern rim of the Suez Gulf, is the last of the subunit's place-names (v. 18). According to Jer 43:7-9, Judean refugees (including Jeremiah and Baruch) settled in Tehaphnehes following Jerusalem's destruction and the assassination of Gedaliah (see Overview); and Pharaoh maintained a palace there. Both the NRSV and the NIV translate the MT's חשׂך (*ḥāśak*), "withhold," as if it were a form of חשׁך (*ḥāšak*), "darkens" (see, e.g., 32:7-8; Isa 13:10). The latter appears in multiple manuscripts and makes sense. Reading with the MT, one must supply an object such as "light."[1019] "When I break there the bars of Egypt" (מטות מצרים *môṭôt miṣrayim*) suggests an ironic play on words. Normally, שׁבר (*šābar,* "break") plus *môṭôt* ("yoke [bars]") expresses (metaphorically) an act of liberation from servitude (34:27; Neh 1:13; Jer 28:10-13; Lev 26:13). Here, however, it refers to the breaking of Egypt's supports, or strength.[1020] Verse 18*b* returns to the cloud imagery of v. 3: Gloom will accompany Tehaphnehes' doom, and her "daughters"—that is, the inhabitants of dependent settlements (see v. 17)—will be forced into exile. The execution of all these punishments will force the Egyptians to acknowledge Yahweh's sovereign and unparalleled power as manifested in their own history.

1017 Block suggests that their random arrangement reflects the chaos Egypt will experience. See his information about the eight place names of vv. 13-19. Block, *Ezekiel 25–48,* 165-70.

1018. Greenberg, *Ezekiel 21–37,* 626.

1019. Greenberg, *Ezekiel 21–37,* 627.

1020. See ibid. Perhaps the text originally spoke of breaking the scepter(s) (מטות *maṭṭôt*) of Egypt (so LXX). That trope, Boadt observes, was a common Semitic metaphor (Isa 14:5; Jer 48:17) for the collapse of government. See Boadt, *Ezekiel's Oracles Against Egypt,* 81.

REFLECTIONS

How great is Ezekiel's faith in the power of Israel's God, that he should speak of Yahweh using one mighty empire to destroy another! In an environment where the destruction of a nation often was understood to signal the *weakness* of its deity, he proclaims the Lord's control not only of little Judah, but also of major players on the world's stage. We can only wonder that he, and other like-minded Judeans, continued to assert God's sovereignty amid the taunts of hostile neighbors (e.g., Ammonites, 25:3, 6; Moabites, 25:8; Tyrians, 26:2) and the victory shouts of the Babylonians, who attributed their triumphs to their own deities. For the prophet, even the forces of nature obey Yahweh's commands: Gloom accompanies doom; the waters of the mighty Nile dry up.

This unit, like other of Ezekiel's oracles against foreign nations, raises thorny theological problems. Moderns must wrestle with the ancient Near Eastern notion that deities deal with hostile peoples by exterminating them. That perspective threatens not only to turn God into a "big warrior on *our* side" (whoever *we* might be), but also to sanction so-called "holy wars" and their atrocities. The importance of understanding why, for instance, Israel's prophets spoke as they did about the fates of foreign nations does not carry a concomitant obligation to embrace their views.

But in a world where people tend to place their trust in what is powerful, successful, and prosperous, we do well to ponder Ezekiel's steadfast faith. Living on foreign soil and experiencing (albeit from a distance) the destruction of his modest homeland, while world empires jostle for power, he insists nonetheless that the just and mighty God of Israel, who alone is worthy of faith, yet rules history. Against all "evidence," he stands with God and summons his readers to do likewise. Even as we question aspects of the content of his faith, we marvel at its unwavering tenacity.

Ezekiel 30:20-26, The Broken Arms of Pharaoh

NIV

20In the eleventh year, in the first month on the seventh day, the word of the LORD came to me: 21'Son of man, I have broken the arm of Pharaoh king of Egypt. It has not been bound up for healing or put in a splint so as to become strong enough to hold a sword. 22Therefore this is what the Sovereign LORD says: I am against Pharaoh king of Egypt. I will break both his arms, the good arm as well as the broken one, and make the sword fall from his hand. 23I will disperse the Egyptians among the nations and scatter them through the countries. 24I will strengthen the arms of the king of Babylon and put my sword in his hand, but I will break the arms of Pharaoh, and he will groan before him like a mortally wounded man. 25I will strengthen the arms of the king of Babylon, but the arms of Pharaoh will fall limp. Then they will know that I am the LORD, when I put my sword into the hand of the king of Babylon and he brandishes it against Egypt. 26I will disperse the Egyptians among the nations and scatter them through the countries. Then they will know that I am the LORD.'

NRSV

20In the eleventh year, in the first month, on the seventh day of the month, the word of the LORD came to me: 21Mortal, I have broken the arm of Pharaoh king of Egypt; it has not been bound up for healing or wrapped with a bandage, so that it may become strong to wield the sword. 22Therefore thus says the Lord GOD: I am against Pharaoh king of Egypt, and will break his arms, both the strong arm and the one that was broken; and I will make the sword fall from his hand. 23I will scatter the Egyptians among the nations, and disperse them throughout the lands. 24I will strengthen the arms of the king of Babylon, and put my sword in his hand; but I will break the arms of Pharaoh, and he will groan before him with the groans of one mortally wounded. 25I will strengthen the arms of the king of Babylon, but the arms of Pharaoh shall fall. And they shall know that I am the LORD, when I put my sword into the hand of the king of Babylon. He shall stretch it out against the land of Egypt, 26and I will scatter the Egyptians among the nations and disperse them throughout the countries. Then they shall know that I am the LORD.

COMMENTARY

This section, the fourth of seven units against Egypt (see Excursus: "Ezekiel's Oracles Against Pharaoh/Egypt," 1401-3), begins with a date notice (the seventh day of the first month of the eleventh year of Jehoiachin's exile; April 29, 587 BCE, by my reckoning), plus the customary word event formula ("the word of the LORD came to me") and God's direct address to the prophet ("Mortal"). Three months have passed since Ezekiel delivered his initial series of oracles against Egypt (29:1-16), and Nebuchadrezzar's siege of Jerusalem has been underway for about fifteen months. The present, highly repetitive unit presupposes the failure of Pharaoh Hophra's earlier attempt to end that siege. Now, lest the exiles continue to pin their hopes for national survivial on Egyptian intervention, Yahweh announces the impending, total defeat of Pharaoh's army and the scattering of Egypt's population "throughout the lands." Here, as in 29:17-20 and 30:10-12, the king of Babylon (Nebuchadrezzar) functions as God's agent of destruction.

Key words in the oracle are "arm/arms" (זרעות/זרוע *zĕrôaʿ /zĕrōʿôt*; [6x]) and "hand" (יד *yād*; [3x]). References to both body parts can function as metaphors for strength and power (see, e.g., 20:33: "As I live, says the Lord GOD, surely with a mighty hand and an outstretched arm, and with wrath poured out, I will be king over you"). Block observes that the figure of a sword- (or club-) wielding pharaoh is common in Egyptian iconography. A scene from the reign of Amenhotep II, for example, presents the king "holding the locks of his enemy in one hand and the other hand poised to bludgeon the man. The accompanying inscription reads: 'Amenhotep . . . who smites the rulers of the foreign lands of the far north, he is a god whose arm is great.' "[1021] Among Pharaoh Hophra's royal titles was "Possessor of a Strong Arm."[1022] We do not know if Ezekiel was aware of that epithet, but readers who were perceived within the text an irony lost on others.

Within the Hebrew Bible, strong (e.g., "outstretched") arm imagery is especially prominent within Israel's exodus traditions (e.g., Exod 3:19-20,

"hand"; Exod 6:6, "arm"; Exod 13:3, 14, 16, "hand"; Exod 15:16, "arm"; Deut 3:14; 6:21; 9:26, "hand"; Deut 9:29; 26:8, "arm"); hence, the reader moves through the present text mindful of Yahweh's venerable defeat of Pharaoh and his forces. Once, Israel's deity afflicted Egypt in order to liberate the Hebrews from slavery. Now, the house of Israel keeps looking to Egypt to rescue Jerusalem/Judah from Yahweh's judgment by the hand of Nebuchadrezzar! The folly of that policy is underscored by God's threat to impose upon Egypt the same punishment Israel is experiencing— dispersal among the nations. The Lord's purpose will be served when the exiled Egyptians finally are forced to acknowledge the sovereign, unrivaled power of Israel's God.

Critics point to similarities between 30:20-26 on the one hand and 29:17-21 on the other. Each begins with a date, followed by the word event formula and God's direct address to Ezekiel. In both cases, Yahweh first informs the prophet of a recent historical event (in 29:18, Nebuchadrezzar's failure to pillage and destroy Tyre; in 30:21, Pharaoh's failure to end the Babylonian siege of Jerusalem). Neither unit contains a command that Ezekiel prophesy to the exiles. Rather, לכן (*lākēn*), "therefore," plus the messenger formula ("thus says the Lord GOD") and הנה (*hinnēh*, "see now") introduces fresh divine initiatives (in 29:19-20, Yahweh's decision to give Egypt to Nebuchadrezzar and his troops as compensation for their efforts against Tyre; in vv. 22-26, God's determination to finish off Pharaoh and his army and to exile his subjects through the agency of the king of Babylon).

In v. 21, Yahweh speaks of having already "broken the arm" of Pharaoh. In the aftermath of that military defeat, his arm has been neither bound so that it might heal, nor securely bandaged so that, once strengthened, it might grasp a sword.[1023] In other words, Pharaoh has not sufficiently recovered from his last engagement of the Babylonian army to muster another. Now, God intends to

---

1021. Block, *Ezekiel 25–48*, 175.
1022. See ibid., 175-76; Greenberg, *Ezekiel 21–37*, 634.

1023. The term חבש (*ḥābaś*, "to bind") appears also in 16:10 and 24:17; חתול (*ḥittûl*, "to be bandaged") is a *hapax legomenon* (i.e., it appears only here). However, other forms of the root (see 16:4; Job 38:9), combined with the present context, suggest "to swaddle," "to wrap firmly."

break both of the king's arms, the (remaining) strong one, and the one already broken.[1024] (Note the familiar "challenge to a duel" formula, "I am against Pharaoh king of Egypt.") Disabled, Pharaoh will be utterly unable to grasp sword in hand; and Yahweh will scatter the defenseless Egyptians throughout the lands (see also 29:12*b*)—an echo of Israel's own punishment (20:23).

The same God who cripples Pharaoh's arms will strengthen the arms of Babylon's king (Nebuchadrezzar is not named in the present passage), placing Yahweh's own sword in his hand (v. 24*a*). And Egypt's king will groan before him as the mortally wounded groan. Verse 25*a* echoes the message of the preceding verse, while v. 25*b* affirms that God's ultimate goal will be achieved: the Egyptians will be forced to acknowledge ("know") who Yahweh is—the sovereign Lord of history, including their own—when the king of Babylon wields God's own sword and stretches it across their land. Verse 26*a* repeats, almost word for word, the threat of v. 23, and it, too, concludes with the recognition formula.

1024. Freedy and Redford conjecture that Ezekiel's reference to Pharaoh's two arms derives from a two-pronged attack by the Egyptian army against Nebuchadrezzar's besieging troops. See K. S. Freedy and D. B. Redford, "The Dates in Ezekiel in Relation to Biblical, Babylonian and Egyptian Sources," *JAOS* 90 (1970) 471, 482-83. Boadt, *Ezekiel's Oracles Against Egypt,* 85, suggests that Pharaoh's broken arm refers to his already defeated land forces, while the still healthy arm represents Egypt's navy, presently engaged in supplying Tyre against the Babylonian blockade.

REFLECTIONS

Neither Ezekiel nor other of Israel's prophets shrank from the most brutal descriptions of Yahweh's punishments upon Israel and other, offending nations. The tropes (figurative uses of language) they adopt, the scenarios they spin, function to seize the attention of their audiences, to shock and terrify them, or to vent their desire for grisly revenge. In this passage, the prophet presents Yahweh as a torturer who cripples Pharaoh's arms so that he groans like one mortally wounded. The resulting image, Blenkinsopp concedes, is sadistic: "Yahweh has broken Pharaoh's arm, Pharaoh will not receive medical attention to enable him to take up arms again, and, just to make sure, Yahweh will break it again and the other one also for good measure."[1025]

The purpose of Ezekiel's violent rhetoric is not difficult to discern: on this occasion, he seeks to destroy any hope among his fellow exiles that God's impending judgment upon Judah can be avoided by means of Egyptian intervention. The Lord of history, whose punishment of the house of Israel Ezekiel proclaims to be just and proportionate to its sins, is Lord of Egypt's history as well, and of all the nations on the earth. But the prophet is concerned that Yahweh's reputation will suffer, not only among the Judeans at home and in Babylonia, but also among those peoples who witness or hear about the nation's downfall. And so, he proclaims in no uncertain terms the power of his God to command and conquer mighty empires, and to bring kingdoms to their knees in the most savage of ways.

Blenkinsopp also is troubled by the violence of Ezekiel's oracles against foreign nations and rulers: "There are matters in the Bible which are time- and culture-conditioned, there are high points and low points. . . . These must be taken into account in our response to the texts."[1026] Ezekiel's world, like our own, was filled with violence. And in his view, God was capable of violent emotions and actions. His perspective plays well where people hunger for revenge, but it creates a dangerous divine role model.

1025. Joseph Blenkinsopp, *Ezekiel,* IBC (Louisville: John Knox, 1990) 136.
1026. Ibid.

Ezekiel 31:1-18, Consider Cedar Assyria

OVERVIEW

The fifth pronouncement against Pharaoh/Egypt comprises a single unit consisting of three interrelated subunits: vv. 2b-9, vv. 10-14, and vv. 15-18 (see Excursuses: "Ezekiel's Oracles Against Foreign Nations and Rulers," 1355-56, and "Ezekiel's Oracles Against Pharaoh/Egypt," 1401-3). The first, an extended metaphor in verse, speaks of a cosmic or world tree—a conventional mythological image not confined to ancient Near Eastern literature.[1027] The second (vv. 10-14) describes the tree's destruction on account of its hubris (pride); and the third (vv. 15-18) follows it to Sheol, the underworld habitat of the dead.

The unit is framed by lines exhibiting an ABB'A' chiastic pattern. After a date notice, the familiar word event formula, and Yahweh's direct address to Ezekiel, the prophet is ordered to (A) "say to Pharaoh king of Egypt and to his hordes: (B) 'Whom are you like . . .?' " (v. 2b). The unit concludes with (B') "Whom are you like . . . ?" (v. 18a), followed by (A') "This is Pharaoh and all his horde, says the Lord GOD" (v. 18b). Remarkably, intervening verses nowhere refer to Pharaoh/Egypt. In what sense, then, does Ezekiel's arboreal metaphor pertain to the fate of the kingdom on the Nile?

The answer to this question hangs largely on a text-critical judgment. Ostensibly, the first two Hebrew words of v. 3 read, "Consider Assyria" (הנה אשור *hinnēh 'aššûr*). Both the NRSV and the NIV adopt this translation, and it is championed by a number of critics.[1028] The second of these two words (*'aššûr*), however, can also be read either as a variant of תאשור (*tĕ'aššûr*), "cypress," or as a scribal error for same; many scholars prefer one of those possibilities.[1029] By the first rendering, Pharaoh is instructed to "consider Assyria" (embodied in its king[s]) as an entity comparable to

himself/Egypt; and the following poem describes Assyria/its king metaphorically as "a cedar of Lebanon"—a majestic, towering tree which, on account of its arrogance, fell just as Egypt will fall. By the second rendering, Pharaoh is instructed to "consider a cypress" as a metaphor for himself/his nation; and Assyria and its king(s) are nowhere in sight.

True to my method (see the Introduction), I read "Assyria" with the MT and all versions. Ancient readers certainly knew from experience that scribal errors could make their way into even the most carefully copied scrolls; and it is possible that some of those readers, like their modern counterparts, opted for "cypress" instead of Assyria. The MT is intelligible, however; and the resort to Assyria/its king in an anti-Egypt prophecy would not strike the reader as far-fetched. On the one hand, Egypt and Assyria appear together in analogous roles in Hos 7:11 (as allies of Ephraim); Isa 19:23 (as future converts to Yahwism); and Zech 10:11 (as Yahweh's victims). On the other hand, the past destruction of one capital/nation could buttress belief in the demise of another. In Nah 3:8-11, for example, the impending devastation of Nineveh, Assyria's capital, is likened to that of Thebes, the capital of Upper Egypt already captured by the Assyrians under Ashurbanipal in 663 BCE. Just as Thebes was conquered, so also Nineveh will be. Moreover, the reader knows that Assyria is elsewhere associated with hubris (e.g., Isa 10:12-15) and with tree imagery (see Isa 10:18-19, 33-34).[1030]

The unit demands a second critical judgment as well. All scholars recognize that the present passage is filled with mythological elements: the world tree whose top towers among the clouds, whose branches shelter the earth's living creatures, and whose roots go down to the subterranean deep (תהום *tĕhôm*);[1031] the Garden of

---

1027. See D. I. Block, *The Book of Ezekiel: Chapters 1–24*, NICOT (Grand Rapids: Eerdmans, 1997) 187-88, and the literature cited there.

1028. See, e.g., ibid., 184-85; Moshe Greenberg, *Ezekiel 21–37*, AB 22A (Garden City, N.Y.: Doubleday, 1997) 646-47; M. Fishbane, *Biblical Interpretation in Ancient Israel* (New York: Oxford University Press, 1985) 46n. 6.

1029. E.g., W. Zimmerli, *Ezekiel 2: A Commentary on the Book of the Prophet Ezekiel, Chapters 25–48*, trans. J. D. Martin, Hermeneia (Philadelphia: Fortress, 1983) 141-42, 149; J. W. Wevers, *Ezekiel*, NCB (London: Nelson, 1969) 235; Ronald M. Hals, *Ezekiel*, FOTL 19 (Grand Rapids: Eerdmans, 1989) 218.

1030. See Greenberg, *Ezekiel 21–37*, 646.

1031. There are striking similarities between Ezek 31:7-9 and the *mēsu* tree described in the Babylonian poem of Erra: "Where is the *mēsu* tree, the flesh of the gods, the ornament of the king of the univ[erse]? That pure tree, that august youngster suited to supremacy, whose roots reach as deep down as the bottom of the underwor[ld]: a hundred double hours through the vast sea waters; whose top reached as high as the sky of [Anum]." Erra I:150-53, in *The Poem of Erra*, trans. L. Cagni, SANE 1 (Malibu: Undena, 1977) 32.

Eden/garden of God; the descent to Sheol. Some regard these elements as fundamental to the text's content and meaning. Stolz, for example, speculates that undergirding vv. 3-8(9) is an ancient, lost myth about a human's attempt to conquer Lebanon, the garden of God, in order to obtain eternal life. The mortal's efforts fail, and he is consigned to Sheol. Ezekiel supposedly combined this myth with the Garden of Eden myth, such that the tree became a symbol of arrogance; and it, like the human of the lost myth, was relegated to the underworld.[1032] For others, however, Ezekiel's world tree trope (figurative use of language) functions essentially as a political metaphor, albeit one that uses mythical elements as a basis for its profundity.[1033]

Ezekiel takes up his extended arboreal metaphor toward political ends. The unit's significance lies not in its relationship to some ancient myth (though its message is enriched by multiple mythic elements), but in its insistence that proud Pharaoh and his nation will go the way of arrogant Assyria and its king. Ezekiel's actual audience does not include Pharaoh, of course. His goal is to shatter his fellow exiles' hopes that Egypt will deliver Jerusalem from Nebuchadrezzar's death grip. There is, perhaps, no better way to undermine the exiles' confidence than to make a comparison with the other major ancient Near Eastern power to whom Egypt had been subject, a power now in ruins.[1034] A political construal of the present passage comports well with two previous Ezekielian texts in which towering tree/vine tropes represent political entities: Ezekiel 17 and 19:10-14, 22-24 (see also Isa 2:12-15).

1032. Fritz Stoltz, "Die Bäume des Gottesgartens auf dem Libanon," *ZAW* 84 (1972) 141-56.

1033. Walther Eichrodt, *Ezekiel,* trans. Cosslett Quin, OTL (Philadelphia: Westminster, 1970) 425.

1034. Greenberg, *Ezekiel 21–37,* 647.

Ezekiel 31:1-9, Comparing Egypt to Assyria, the Great Cedar

NIV	NRSV
31 In the eleventh year, in the third month on the first day, the word of the LORD came to me: ²"Son of man, say to Pharaoh king of Egypt and to his hordes:	**31** In the eleventh year, in the third month, on the first day of the month, the word of the LORD came to me: ²Mortal, say to Pharaoh king of Egypt and to his hordes:

NIV

31 In the eleventh year, in the third month on the first day, the word of the LORD came to me: ²"Son of man, say to Pharaoh king of Egypt and to his hordes:

" 'Who can be compared with you in majesty?
³Consider Assyria, once a cedar in Lebanon,
    with beautiful branches overshadowing the
        forest;
  it towered on high,
    its top above the thick foliage.
⁴The waters nourished it,
    deep springs made it grow tall;
  their streams flowed
    all around its base
  and sent their channels
    to all the trees of the field.
⁵So it towered higher
    than all the trees of the field;
  its boughs increased
    and its branches grew long,
    spreading because of abundant waters.
⁶All the birds of the air

NRSV

31 In the eleventh year, in the third month, on the first day of the month, the word of the LORD came to me: ²Mortal, say to Pharaoh king of Egypt and to his hordes:

  Whom are you like in your greatness?
³   Consider Assyria, a cedar of Lebanon,
  with fair branches and forest shade,
    and of great height,
    its top among the clouds.ᵃ
⁴The waters nourished it,
    the deep made it grow tall;
  making its rivers flowᵇ
    around the place it was planted,
  sending forth its streams
    to all the trees of the field.
⁵So it towered high
    above all the trees of the field;
  its boughs grew large
    and its branches long,
    from abundant water in its shoots.
⁶All the birds of the air
    made their nests in its boughs;

ᵃGk: Heb *thick boughs*   ᵇGk: Heb *rivers going*

NIV

nested in its boughs,
all the beasts of the field
    gave birth under its branches;
all the great nations
    lived in its shade.
⁷It was majestic in beauty,
    with its spreading boughs,
for its roots went down
    to abundant waters.
⁸The cedars in the garden of God
    could not rival it,
nor could the pine trees
    equal its boughs,
nor could the plane trees
    compare with its branches—
no tree in the garden of God
    could match its beauty.
⁹I made it beautiful
    with abundant branches,
the envy of all the trees of Eden
    in the garden of God.

NRSV

under its branches all the animals of the field
    gave birth to their young;
and in its shade
    all great nations lived.
⁷It was beautiful in its greatness,
    in the length of its branches;
for its roots went down
    to abundant water.
⁸The cedars in the garden of God could not
    rival it,
nor the fir trees equal its boughs;
the plane trees were as nothing
    compared with its branches;
no tree in the garden of God
    was like it in beauty.
⁹I made it beautiful
    with its mass of branches,
the envy of all the trees of Eden
    that were in the garden of God.

COMMENTARY

This unit, like all but one (30:1-19) of Ezekiel's six other pronouncements against Pharaoh/Egypt, begins with a date notice. The new word of Yahweh came to the prophet on the first day of the third month of the eleventh year of Jehoiachin's exile (June 21, 587 BCE, by my reckoning), almost two months after the previous oracle (30:20-26) was delivered.[1035] God commands him to address Pharaoh, Egypt's king, and his hordes (military forces).[1036] His speech begins with a query: "[To] whom are you like in your greatness?" (v. 2b).[1037]

The question is more rhetorical than real. Having posed it, Ezekiel immediately profers its answer: "Consider Assyria."[1038] The following appositional phrase, "a cedar of Lebanon," introduces the arboreal trope that will dominate the entire passage. Clearly, Ezekiel did not coin the "a cedar of Lebanon is a nation" metaphor (see, e.g., Isa 2:12-13), and the reader easily accepts the following, past-tense description of Assyria as a once-majestic tree.[1039]

Critics often observe that this description is altogether positive.[1040] Were readers to encounter vv. 3-9 in isolation from their present context, they

1035. Freedy and Redford correlate this date with the arrival in Babylonia of news that Nebuchadrezzar has thrashed the second prong of Egyptian soldiers dispatched (or led) by Pharaoh Hophra to deliver besieged Jerusalem. But their hypothesis suffers from a lack of corroborating external evidence. See K. S. Freedy and D. B. Redford, "The Dates in Ezekiel in Relation to Biblical, Babylonian and Egyptian Sources," *JAOS* 90 (1970) 472.

1036. המון (*hāmôn*), a noun admitting many meanings (e.g., "horde," "wealth," "uproar," "pomp," "pride"), occurs 16 times within Ezekiel's oracles against Egypt (chaps. 29–32). At least two meanings are relevant to this context: "horde" and "pride." The former conforms to the noun's meaning in 30:1-19; the latter becomes increasingly apt as the reader progresses through 31:1-18.

1037. G. R. Driver, "Ezekiel: Linguistic and Textual Problems," *Bib* 35 (1954) 300, translates מי (*mî*), "(to) whom," impersonally as "what." Because the question is posed to a human king, however, one anticipates the comparison of like with like—in this case, the king (and the embodiment of) Assyria.

1038. Block argues that Ezekiel presents "consider Assyria" as Pharaoh's response to his query. As Greenberg observes, however, the question deals not with Pharaoh's "self-image," but with fact. It is unlikely that Ezekiel would set up a rhetorical situation in which Pharaoh chose to compare himself/Egypt to an already-defunct empire.

1039. Because Ezekiel's cedar represents the vanquished Assyrian Empire, the past tense (perfect) Hebrew verbs are appropriate. Critics who emend "Assyria" to "cypress" and relate it directly to the still-extant Pharaoh/Egypt must construe these perfect verb forms either as examples of the "prophetic perfect" (so certain is a prophet that his or her oracle will be fulfilled that he or she speaks of future events as if they had already occurred), or as indicative of the influence of dirges upon the text.

1040. See, e.g., Block, *Ezekiel 25–48*, 185.

aver, no clue would alert them to the impending indictment and punishment of the tree in vv. 10-18 (Ezekiel may have authored vv. 3-9; alternatively, he may have adopted an already existing poem, here used for his own distinctive purposes). Their judgment is open to question. The ancient Israelite reader, steeped in the argot (conventional idiom and imagery) of arrogance, might well detect in this exaggerated description of the cedar's abundant branches, protective shade, and immense height the proverbial pride preceding a fall. Perhaps they would suspect that so fantastic a description of the cedar's "past glory" is, in the manner of a satirical lament, preliminary to an account of its equally impressive demise. Such, after all, is the pattern established, e.g., in several of Ezekiel's oracles against Tyre/its king (27:1-36; 28:1-10, 11-19).

The prophet holds nothing back in his initial praise of cedar Assyria. Having extolled its branches, shade, and extraordinary height ("its top ["crown"; see 17:3, 22] among the clouds"; see 19:11), he procedes further to elaborate upon each characteristic in reverse order.[1041] The tree grew tall on account of the abundant waters sustaining it. The terms מים (mayim), "waters" (v. 4a), and תהום (tĕhôm), "the deep" (v. 4a), also are paired in the priestly creation account ("the earth was a formless void and darkness covered the face of the deep, while a wind from God swept over the face of the waters," Gen 1:2 NRSV). Scholars have long known that behind tĕhôm lurks Tiamat, the chaos monster of the Babylonian creation epic. In Genesis 1, she has been largely demythologized: the pre-creation waters of chaos do not oppose God's creative acts. In the present passage, that process has taken a further step: the deep is devoid of associations with chaos.

The waters nourished cedar Assyria; the subterranean deep (see Gen 7:11 and 8:2) made it grow tall, sending its rivers flowing around its bed[1042] and (or "but") causing its (manmade) irrigation canals (תעלות tĕ'ālôt; see, e.g., 1 Kgs 18:32, 35, 38; 2 Kgs 18:17; Isa 7:3) to release water to "all the [other] trees of the field." Do readers detect a contrast between the cedar sustained by the mayim and tĕhôm on the one hand, and the trees of the open country watered through its artificial canals on the other?[1043] If so, v. 5a supports their view: (therefore) cedar Assyria stood higher than all the other trees of the field. Its boughs grew broad, its branches long, from the great waters (מים רבים mayim rabbîm) in its conduit.[1044]

All the birds of the air nested in its boughs; all the animals gave birth beneath its branches (poignant testimony to their instinctive awareness of the safety the tree affords). The reader recalls Ps 104:16-17, part of a hymn in praise of Yahweh as creator:

> The trees of the Lord are watered abundantly,
> the cedars of Lebanon that he planted.
> In them the birds build their nests;
> the stork has its home in the fir trees. (NRSV)

In an admonition to the Jerusalemites to engage in ritual lament over the destruction of their land, by contrast, Jeremiah describes a scene antithetical to the secure existence described in Ezek 31:6:

> Take up weeping and wailing for the mountains,
> and a lamentation for the pastures of the
> wilderness,
> because they are laid waste so that no one passes
> through,
> and the lowing of cattle is not heard;
> both the birds of the air and the animals
> have fled and are gone. (Jer 9:10 NRSV)

With "all the great nations [גוים רבים gôyim rabbîm; see also 26:3; 31:6, 37:27, 28:23, 39:27] lived in its shade," Ezekiel's metaphor appears to slip a bit, so that the actual referents (Assyria's allies and vassals) intrude—a characteristic of his extended tropes (see, e.g., the Commentary on chaps. 16 and 23). In Hebrew Scripture, shade (צל ṣēl, "shade," "shadow") often serves as a metaphor for protection—divine (e.g., Pss 17:8; 36:7; 91:1; 121:5; Isa 49:2; 51:16; Lam 4:20) and human/national (e.g., Gen 19:8; Isa 30:2-3). Frequently in the literature of the ancient Near

---

1041. Ibid., 186.

1042. Readers recall the beneficent descriptions of tĕhôm in Gen 49:25 and Deut 33:13. In the former, Jacob blesses Joseph with "blessings of heaven above/blessings of the deep that lies beneath"; in the latter, Moses blesses Joseph's land with "the choice gifts of heaven above/and of the deep that lies beneath."

1043. So Greenberg, *Ezekiel 21–37*, 637-38, and, tentatively, Lawrence Boadt, *Ezekiel's Oracles Against Egypt: A Literary and Philological Study of Ezekiel 29–32*, BibOr 37 (Rome: Pontifical Biblical Institute, 1980) 107. Greenberg detects in "all the trees of the field" a reference to "king(dom)s lesser than Assyria."

1044. The MT's בשלחו (bĕšallĕḥô), "in its sending," makes little sense. See Greenberg, *Ezekiel 21–37*, 638.

East, a king's shadow represents the security he provides his people.[1045]

Verse 7 underscores the tree's magnificent appearance, a consequence of its abundantly watered roots. References to its beauty (vv. 7, 8, 9) recall Ezekiel's repeated allusions to the beauty of Tyre/its king in 27:3*b*, 4 and 28:7, 12, 17. Verse 8 declares that even the cedar, fir, and plane trees growing in the garden of God (see Gen 2:9) cannot rival its beauty. Block observes, correctly I think, that Ezekiel's evocations of "the garden of God" (vv. 8 [twice] and 9) and "Eden" (v. 9) bear little "mythological baggage."[1046] For the prophet's

audience/reader, the trees of paradise (Genesis 2) set a standard of perfection[1047] that cedar Assyria surpassed nonetheless! This is high praise, indeed, yet no greater than his statement that the king of Tyre, "full of wisdom and perfect in beauty," once resided in "Eden, the garden of God" (28:12-13).

In v. 9, cast as first person divine speech, the author (Ezekiel from the reader's perspective; a later traditionist in the opinion of most modern critics) makes the theological point that Yahweh alone was responsible for the beauty of the cedar with its mass of branches—a beauty so great that even the (personified) trees of Eden were envious. (See Reflections at 31:15-18.)

1045. D. Hillers, *Lamentations,* AB 7A (Garden City, N.Y.: Doubleday, 1972) 92.
1046. Block, *Ezekiel 25–48,* 188.

1047. In a similar vein, Deutero-Isaiah proclaims that Yahweh will make Jerusalem's ruined environs "like Eden . . . like the garden of the LORD" (Isa 51:3-4; see also Gen 13:10; Ezek 36:35; Joel 2:3).

Ezekiel 31:10-14, The Indictment and Punishment of Cedar Assyria

NIV

10" 'Therefore this is what the Sovereign LORD says: Because it towered on high, lifting its top above the thick foliage, and because it was proud of its height, [11]I handed it over to the ruler of the nations, for him to deal with according to its wickedness. I cast it aside, [12]and the most ruthless of foreign nations cut it down and left it. Its boughs fell on the mountains and in all the valleys; its branches lay broken in all the ravines of the land. All the nations of the earth came out from under its shade and left it. [13]All the birds of the air settled on the fallen tree, and all the beasts of the field were among its branches. [14]Therefore no other trees by the waters are ever to tower proudly on high, lifting their tops above the thick foliage. No other trees so well-watered are ever to reach such a height; they are all destined for death, for the earth below, among mortal men, with those who go down to the pit.

NRSV

10Therefore thus says the Lord GOD: Because it[a] towered high and set its top among the clouds,[b] and its heart was proud of its height, [11]I gave it into the hand of the prince of the nations; he has dealt with it as its wickedness deserves. I have cast it out. [12]Foreigners from the most terrible of the nations have cut it down and left it. On the mountains and in all the valleys its branches have fallen, and its boughs lie broken in all the watercourses of the land; and all the peoples of the earth went away from its shade and left it.
[13] On its fallen trunk settle
    all the birds of the air,
  and among its boughs lodge
    all the wild animals.
[14]All this is in order that no trees by the waters may grow to lofty height or set their tops among the clouds,[b] and that no trees that drink water may reach up to them in height.
    For all of them are handed over to death,
      to the world below;
    along with all mortals,
      with those who go down to the Pit.

[a]Syr Vg: Heb *you*   [b]Gk: Heb *thick boughs*

COMMENTARY

Thus far, Ezekiel has compared Egypt/Pharaoh, objects of God's ire in chaps. 29–30, to vanquished Assyria/its king(s), described as a magnificent cedar. Here, as in other of his oracles, he has lavished praise upon his ostensible addressee. But the reader, accustomed to this rhetorical strategy and alert to the frequent equation of physical height and arrogance, suspects that Ezekiel has set up Assyria (Egypt) for disaster. That suspicion is quickly confirmed in a second subunit, a judgment oracle prefaced by "therefore" plus the messenger formula. The accusation, introduced by "because" (יען אשר *ya'an 'ăšer*) and consisting mainly of perfect (past tense) verb forms (since Assyria's fall lies in the past), echoes ideas from vv. 2*b*-9 but with a sinister twist: The cedar (MT, "you") towered high;[1048] it set its top among the clouds; and *its heart* was *proud* of its height. On account of its haughtiness, it received from Yahweh the punishment Ezekiel here rehearses: God gave it into the hand of the prince (lit., "ram" [איל *'ayil*]; see the Commentary on 30:13) of the nations; and he, in turn, dealt with it proportionate to its wickedness.[1049] The reader, knowing of Babylonia's role in the collapse of the Assyrian Empire and recalling Ezekiel's previous statements that Nebuchadrezzar is God's agent of Egypt's impending demise (29:17-20; 30:10-11, 24-25), identifies this "prince" as the king of Babylon;[1050] and that judgment is confirmed in v. 12, since both "foreigners" and "the most terrible of the nations" have consistently referred to Babylonian forces in Ezekiel's oracles against foreign nations and rulers (see 28:7,

10; 30:11-12). Lest the reader conclude that credit for the victories of Babylonia's king(s) belongs to them and their deities, v. 11 concludes with Yahweh's asseveration, "*I* have cast it/him out" (alternatively, this phrase, which some critics delete as secondary—it does not appear in the LXX—can be read as the beginning of v. 12).

Like reckless lumberjacks, the Babylonians felled cedar Assyria and left it. Its branches lay upon the mountains[1051] and in the valleys, and its broken boughs littered the land's watercourses. (The series mountains, valleys, and watercourses, along with hills, appears in 6:3; 35:8; 36:4, 6 and signifies "everywhere.") In 32:5-6, Yahweh will threaten to scatter the carcass of "dragon" Pharaoh across mountains, valleys, and watercourses. In 35:8, part of a description of Yahweh's future punishment of Mt. Seir (i.e., Edom; see 25:12-14), the corpses of those slain by the sword will fill the mountains, hills, valleys, and watercourses (see also 30:11*b*). Here, Ezekiel applies this conventional imagery to the "body parts" of a tree.

Verse 14 functions as a hinge between preceding verses on the one hand, and subsequent ones on the other. Its language continues the tree imagery and anti-hubris theme of preceding verses, but it also introduces the idea of descent to the "Pit" or underworld that will dominate vv. 15-18. Because it begins so abruptly (What is the antecedent for "in order that"? the NRSV supplies "All this" in order to smooth the transition from v. 13 to v. 14; the NIV's "therefore" is too free a rendering of למען [*lĕma'an,* "in order that," "to the end that"]), exhibits a distinctly didactic

1048. Because, in the remainder of v. 10, Yahweh addresses Assyria (Egypt) in the third person, many critics (e.g., Zimmerli, *Ezekiel 2,* 143) emend "you" to "he/it." Greenberg, *Ezekiel 21–37,* 639, admits that the shift in person is disconcerting, while Block, *Ezekiel 25–48,* 190, explains it as a reflection of Ezekiel's "tension" over the referents of his oracle. The reader, accustomed to shifts in person within Ezekiel's oracles and beyond, might not be discomfited by the sudden alteration, or he might suspect a scribal error and harmonize accordingly, or he might rationalize along the lines Block suggests.

1049. The Hebrew verbs for "to give" (נתן *nātan*) and "to deal with" (עשה *'āśâ*) are imperfects, ostensibly signifying either future or habitual/durative action. Both the NRSV and the NIV translate them as if they were perfect (past tense) forms (following the LXX). The alternation of perfect and imperfect verbs is not rare in Hebrew poetry. The same phenomenon occurred in v. 6 (where "lived" appears in the imperfect) and will reappear in v. 13.

1050. Nabopolassar ruled Babylonia at the time of Assyria's collapse. Ezekiel may have had his son and crown prince, Nebuchadrezzar, in mind, however, since he led the Babylonian army to victory against Egypt at the defining battle of Carchemish in 605 BCE.

1051. Both the NRSV and the NIV follow the MT's accents in reading "On the mountains" as the beginning of a new thought. But Hals, *Ezekiel,* 218, and Wevers, *Ezekiel,* 238, suggest that the phrase belongs with the preceding verb: "cut it down and left it on the mountains." Bereft of its protective shade, the peoples of the earth (see "all the mighty nations" in v. 6*b*) abandoned the cedar. The birds who once built their nests in its boughs perched upon its (horizontal) trunk; and the beasts who formerly gave birth beneath its branches lodged among its boughs (for strikingly similiar imagery, see Isa 18:6). In 29:5, the reader recalls, Yahweh flung Pharaoh, the great Nile crocodile, into the wilderness; and both animals and birds fed on its carcass. According to 34:4, all the birds of the air will settle on sea monster Pharaoh; and wild animals will "gorge themselves" on its cadaver. In the present passage, Ezekiel refrains from describing these creatures as woodeaters! Still, v. 13 stirs ominous associations.

quality[1052] and contains new concepts, many critics assign the verse to a later hand.[1053] As Block observes, however, readers might interpret it as a continuation of Yahweh's punitive response to the cedar's arrogance in v. 11 (vv. 12-13, a description of the actions of "third parties" [the foreigners who fell the tree, the peoples of the earth who abandon it, and the birds and animals who occupy its "remains"], constitute momentary interruptions).[1054] And while Ezekiel rarely pauses to offer general instruction in morality (here, mortality!), chap. 18 offers something of an analogy.

Other trees (nations, rulers) should draw a lesson from the destruction of cedar Assyria. No "trees of water" (i.e., other trees whose roots tap the subterranean deep?) should grow to so lofty a height, setting their crowns among the clouds. The remainder of v. 14*a* is more difficult. The MT reads, "and their leaders [or perhaps "gods"

(אליהם *'êlêhem,* "rams," "chieftains"; see v. 11)] should not stand high, all drinkers of water." The personal pronoun "their" might refer to the preceding "trees of water," hence (remaining within the metaphor) the arboreal leaders of abundantly watered trees. Alternatively, "their" could refer to the following "all drinkers of water"—a larger grouping than "trees of water," since it includes humans as well. So construed, Greenberg observes, "their leaders" looks *back* to the trees and *forward* to the human referents of v. 14*b*.[1055] A majority of critics (including the translators of the NRSV and the NIV), however, read "to/against them" (*'ălêhem;* so LXX), an emendation of "their leaders" requiring no change of MT's consonants. The thought, then, is that no trees (kings/nations) should aspire to the height (hubris) of trees like cedar Assyria, thereby setting themselves up for its fate. For, v. 14*b* continues, the fate of the proud is death. Such trees descend to the underworld along with all mortals, everyone who goes down to the Pit. (See Reflections at 31:15-18.)

1052. Petersen describes this verse as "an almost sermonic conclusion for the benefit of other 'trees.'" See David L. Petersen, "Introduction and Annotations to Ezekiel," in *The HarperCollins Study Bible,* NRSV (New York: HarperCollins, 1993) 1272.

1053. See, e.g., W. Zimmerli, *Ezekiel 2: A Commentary on the Book of the Prophet Ezekiel, Chapters 25–48,* trans. J. D. Martin, Hermeneia (Philadelphia: Fortress, 1983) 151.

1054. See Block, *Ezekiel 25–48,* 192.

1055. Greenberg, *Ezekiel 21–37,* 641.

Ezekiel 31:15-18, Cedar Assyria in Sheol

NIV	NRSV
[15]" 'This is what the Sovereign LORD says: On the day it was brought down to the grave*a* I covered the deep springs with mourning for it; I held back its streams, and its abundant waters were restrained. Because of it I clothed Lebanon with gloom, and all the trees of the field withered away. [16]I made the nations tremble at the sound of its fall when I brought it down to the grave with those who go down to the pit. Then all the trees of Eden, the choicest and best of Lebanon, all the trees that were well-watered, were consoled in the earth below. [17]Those who lived in its shade, its allies among the nations, had also gone down to the grave with it, joining those killed by the sword.	15Thus says the Lord GOD: On the day it went down to Sheol I closed the deep over it and covered it; I restrained its rivers, and its mighty waters were checked. I clothed Lebanon in gloom for it, and all the trees of the field fainted because of it. [16]I made the nations quake at the sound of its fall, when I cast it down to Sheol with those who go down to the Pit; and all the trees of Eden, the choice and best of Lebanon, all that were well watered, were consoled in the world below. [17]They also went down to Sheol with it, to those killed by the sword, along with its allies,*a* those who lived in its shade among the nations.
[18]" 'Which of the trees of Eden can be compared with you in splendor and majesty? Yet you,	18Which among the trees of Eden was like you in glory and in greatness? Now you shall be brought down with the trees of Eden to the world below; you shall lie among the uncircumcised,
a15 Hebrew *Sheol*; also in verses 16 and 17	*a*Heb *its arms*

NIV

too, will be brought down with the trees of Eden to the earth below; you will lie among the uncircumcised, with those killed by the sword.

" 'This is Pharaoh and all his hordes, declares the Sovereign LORD.' "

NRSV

with those who are killed by the sword. This is Pharaoh and all his horde, says the Lord GOD.

COMMENTARY

In vv. 10-14, Ezekiel depicted in metaphorical language the destruction of the magnificent cedar representing Assyria. Now, in a third subunit, he describes the effects of the cedar's descent to Sheol on nature, the nations, and other inhabitants (trees and humans) of the underworld. The "descent to Sheol" motif appears not only in the present passage, but also in other prophetic oracles against foreign nations and rulers (e.g., 26:19-21; 28:8, both against Tyre; 32:17-32, against Egypt's pharaoh; Isa 14:9-11, 15-20, against the king of Babylon). Within Israel's prophetic literature, it is primarily associated with (satirical) laments. Ezekiel 31 is nowhere labeled a dirge/lament. Both its structure and its contents, however, betray the influence of that genre. The Hebrew text poses some formidable problems (see below). Moreover, the placement of trees in the underworld, thought consistent with the arboreal imagery that has dominated the unit, is in Hals's words "less than impressive"—an aesthetic judgment, but one I share.[1056]

The oracle, introduced by the messenger formula ("Thus says the Lord GOD"), is cast as first person divine speech. "On the day it [cedar Assyria] went down to Sheol," Yahweh begins, but the verbs in the remainder of the phrase (to the semicolon in the NRSV and the NIV) are difficult. The former finds in האבלתי (he'ĕbaltî) a denominative verb meaning "to close [a gate]," cognate to Akkadian abullu, "gate" (Aramaic 'ibbûl).[1057] By this rendering, the Lord claims either to have shut off the waters of Tehom or to have closed them over the cedar (see 26:19, where Yahweh says of Tyre, "When I bring up the deep over you, and the great waters cover you"). The latter derives the verb from אבל ('ābal), "to mourn." By this

rendering, God claims to have caused Sheol to mourn the loss of the cedar it once nourished so abundantly (see also Lam 2:8, "he caused rampart and wall to mourn").[1058] The conundrum is intensified by the following, asyndetic (not prefixed with ו [wĕ]) verb, כסתי (kissêtî, "I covered"). The MT accents separate the two verbs. The LXX deletes "I covered." Boadt (crediting Dahood) regards the verb pair as a hendiadys (two words, connected by a conjunction, that express a single thought) and translates, "I covered with mourning garments the Tehom" (see NIV). Block's rendition ("I shut off [the water supply], and I covered it with the deep") seems somewhat oxymoronic (if the deep is shut off, how can it then cover the cedar?), but "I shut off" comports well with the following "I restrained its rivers, and its mighty waters were checked." Both the NRSV and the NIV render קדר (qādar, "be dark," "cause to mourn") idiomatically as "to clothe [Lebanon] in [or "with"] gloom"—that is, to cover it with dark mourning garments, on account of cedar Assyria (see also 32:7-8, where Yahweh's murder of Pharaoh, the great sea monster, is accompanied by covering [darkening] the heavens and its luminaries [stars, sun, moon]). On its account, as well, all the trees of the field (see vv. 4-5) languished or withered.

On the earth, God caused the nations to quake at the sound of the cedar's fall (v. 16a; see also 26:15, "Shall not the coastlands shake at the sound of your (Tyre's] fall?"). Meanwhile, the ruined tree joined others in Sheol—all the trees of Eden (who once envied the cedar, v. 9), as well as the choice and best of Lebanon. All these "drinkers of water" (so also v. 14a) were consoled to see that even cedar Assyria shared their fate.

1056. Hals, *Ezekiel,* 221.
1057. Block, *Ezekiel 25–48,* 195.

1058. Boadt cites P. Skehan's proposal that the verb is a hiphil form of 'ābal II, "to cause to dry up." See Boadt, *Ezekiel's Oracles Against Egypt,* 118-19n. 70).

Verse 17*a* explains that these other trees also went down to Sheol, to (join) those humans slain by the sword. The second half-verse, however, is perplexing. Literally, it reads "and its/his arm they dwelt in its/his shade among the nations." Like some commentators, the translators of the NRSV and the NIV detect in "its/his arm" a reference to Assyria's allies and vassals who, according to v. 6*b*, once lived in the shade (protection) of its branches, but now also are residents of Sheol.

Finally, v. 18 expands upon the question put to Pharaoh in v. 2*b:* To whom among the trees of Eden does he compare "in glory and greatness"? He, like they, will be brought down to the world below, there to lie amidst its least honorable inhabitants—the uncircumcised (see the Commentary on 28:10) and those killed by the sword in battle (see v. 17). Such is the fate of Pharaoh and his horde, a declaration underscored by the concluding formula "says the Lord GOD."

Hals opines that the adjective "tragic" is genuinely apropos to this unit because there is "an undeniable element of real sympathy here for the glory that was Egypt's."[1059] I detect nothing in Ezekiel 31 that confirms his judgment. True, those Judean exiles who persistently cling to the hope that even in these final days, Egypt might yet secure Jerusalem's survival, would think this unit a sad pill to swallow. But Ezekiel, whose anti-Egyptian attitude has surfaced time and again in his scroll, presents Egypt's future destruction as signal evidence of Yahweh's sovereign control not only of Israel, but also of all mighty nations. There is strange comfort in that affirmation. If Judah's impending collapse is but one aspect of God's worldwide judgment, then Israel may, as occasional passages have suggested along the way (e.g., 11:17-20; 17:22-24; 28:24-26), hope that in its own history, the Lord who brings low the high tree and dries up the green tree will also make high the low tree and make the dry tree flourish (17:24).

1059. Hals, *Ezekiel,* 222.

REFLECTIONS

In the book of Psalms, ancient Israel repeatedly affirms the universal sovereignty and absolute power of Yahweh, its God. Psalm 93, for example, celebrates the Lord's worldwide, majestic rule:

The LORD is king, he is robed in majesty;
  the LORD is robed, he is girded with strength.
He has established the world; it shall never be moved;
  your throne is established from of old;
  you are from everlasting. (Ps 93:1-2 NRSV)

Because as powerful theological currents affirmed, the divine king's presence and power were especially associated with Jerusalem, Judah's capital, the security of that city was thought to be assured:

Great is the LORD and greatly to be praised
  in the city of our God.
His holy mountain, beautiful in elevation,
  is the joy of all the earth,
Mount Zion, in the far north,
  the city of the great King.
Within its citadels God
  has shown himself a sure defense. (Ps 48:1-3 NRSV)

A small kingdom even at the height of its power, Israel nonetheless insisted that its Deity also determined the fates of other nations:

You have rebuked the nations, you have destroyed the wicked;
    you have blotted out their name forever and ever.
The enemies have vanished in everlasting ruins;
    their cities you have rooted out;
    the very memory of them has perished. (Ps 9:5-6 NRSV)

For centuries, Israel placed its faith upon these pillars of Yahwistic theology. In the prophet's day, however, those pillars appeared to verge on collapse. If Jerusalem were destroyed by Nebuchadrezzar and his forces, it could only be because its Deity was either too weak, or too apathetic, to save it. Or was Ezekiel correct? Was God, like Samson of old (Judg 16:29-30), grasping the pillars (of orthodox Judean theology) and, straining with all "his" might, pulling them down so that the "house of Israel" would fall on all who were in it? And if that were the case, what hope might sustain Judah, at home and in exile?

Ezekiel insists that Judah's demise, far from testifying to a weak or apathetic deity, is Yahweh's just and proportionate punishment for its myriad and long-lived sins. In his oracles against foreign nations and rulers, moreover, he repeatedly proclaims that the fate of other kingdoms, large and small, rests solely in God's hands. The Lord's judgment against Israel is not an isolated event, but part of a larger plan whose goal is that Yahweh's sovereignty be experienced and acknowledged throughout the world. Jerusalem's destruction is not Yahweh's defeat, but testimony to that plan in progress:

At the set time that I appoint
    I will judge with equity,
When the earth totters, with all its inhabitants,
    it is I who keep its pillars steady.
I say to the boastful, "Do not boast,"
    and to the wicked, "Do not lift up your horn;
do not lift up your horn on high,
    or speak with insolent neck." (Ps 75:2-5 NRSV)

Against all evidence, Ezekiel maintains a relentless belief in Yahweh's power and sovereignty over all of history. In other Reflections sections, we have considered the problems that can attend this theology: the idea that God not only is the Lord of history, but also controls history such that the good always win and the evil always lose. Such thinking almost inevitably leads to blaming the victim(s), as if they were responsible for their suffering, and idolizing success (especially power and material wealth) attained through any means; the all too frequent insistence that Yahweh's preferred method of dealing with foes (Israel's enemies) is extermination. That thinking might play well to national pride and thirst for revenge, but it can also throw a sacred canopy over human acts of brutality.

Wrestling with problematic facets of Ezekiel's theology does not mean, however, that we cannot be inspired by him relentlessly to trust in God whatever life brings:

God is our refuge and strength,
    a very present help in trouble.
Therefore we will not fear, though the earth should change,
    though the mountains shake in the heart of the sea;
though its waters roar and foam,
    though the mountains tremble with its tumult. (Ps 46:1-3 NRSV)

Ezekiel 32:1-16, "You Are Like a Dragon in the Seas"

OVERVIEW

Both Yahweh's command to Ezekiel in v. 2*a* and the colophon of v. 16 identify intervening verses as a lamentation. A careful reading, however, reveals that this sixth utterance against Egypt (see Excursus: "Ezekiel's Oracles Against Pharaoh/ Egypt," 1355-56), which is scarcely composed in the 3:2 metrical scheme characteristic of at least portions of many biblical dirges, is actually a prophetic announcement of punishment against Pharaoh and his land.[1060] Laments, whether sincere or sarcastic, usually commence with a description of the past glory of the deceased (or soon to be deceased). One thinks, to give a single example, of Ezekiel's lamentation over the king of Tyre (28:11-19), which initially credits the ruler with abundant wisdom, perfect beauty, and an address in Eden, only to chronicle his banishment from God's mountain on account of his pride and corruption. In the present passage, God's first statement to Pharaoh, "You considered yourself a lion among the nations," might be construed positively (the lion being a symbol of royalty in Egypt, as well as in Israel, Mesopotamia, etc.). But the following line immediately rebuffs Pharaoh's illusion with God's reality ("but you are like a dragon in the seas"), and the prophet's development of that mythological image in vv. 3-10 is pejorative, even gruesome. In a manner reminiscent of chap. 29, Yahweh will capture the sea creature and cast its enormous carcass into an open field. Its flesh and blood will fill the mountains, valleys, and watercourses of Egypt. Simultaneously, Yahweh will darken the sky's luminaries, and all who witness the dragon's demise will be filled with terror.

Verses 11-15 speak, in more historical terms, of the vanquishing of Egypt and its inhabitants— human and animal. Though Yahweh is the ultimate power behind the nation's demise, the king of Babylon, God's agent of punishment, will bring it to ruin. Undisturbed by inhabitants, the waters of the Nile will flow as smoothly as oil.

The unit contains a number of opening and closing formulae whose present locations puzzle interpreters and suggest that behind the final product lies a complex editorial history. Garscha traces four stages in the text's development and denies Ezekiel any part of them.[1061] Zimmerli, who detects the oracle's core in v. 2, identifies four successive expansions (vv. 3-8, vv. 9-10, vv. 11-15, plus the colophon in v. 16), but he allows the possibility that the prophet authored them.[1062] Hals doubts that the unit ever functioned as an actual dirge, v. 16 notwithstanding, and deigns it a literary unit "designed more for reading than for hearing."[1063] The ancient reader will himself, I suspect, wonder that the lament label is affixed to a composition bereft of an initial description of past glory and chockablock with oracular formulae. Nothing, however, precludes his ascription of the unit to Ezekiel. In fact, the text is so replete with vocabulary, ideas, and images from previous oracles against foreign nations and rulers that even on his initial reading, he will find much familiar here.

1060. See Ronald M. Hals, *Ezekiel,* FOTL 19 (Grand Rapids: Eerdmans, 1989) 224.

1061. Järg Garscha, *Studien zum Ezechielbuch: Eine redaktionskritische Untersuchung von 1–39,* Europäische Hochschulschriften 23 (Bern: Herbert Lang, 1974) 185-92.

1062. W. Zimmerli, *Ezekiel 2: A Commentary on the Book of the Prophet Ezekiel, Chapters 25–48,* trans. J. D. Martin, Hermeneia (Philadelphia: Fortress, 1983) 157-58.

1063. Hals, *Ezekiel,* 224.

Ezekiel 32:1-10, The Gory Demise of Dragon Pharaoh

NIV

32 In the twelfth year, in the twelfth month on the first day, the word of the LORD came to me: [2]"Son of man, take up a lament concerning Pharaoh king of Egypt and say to him:

" 'You are like a lion among the nations;
    you are like a monster in the seas
thrashing about in your streams,
    churning the water with your feet
    and muddying the streams.

[3]" 'This is what the Sovereign LORD says:

" 'With a great throng of people
    I will cast my net over you,
    and they will haul you up in my net.
[4]I will throw you on the land
    and hurl you on the open field.
I will let all the birds of the air settle on you
    and all the beasts of the earth gorge
        themselves on you.
[5]I will spread your flesh on the mountains
    and fill the valleys with your remains.
[6]I will drench the land with your flowing
        blood
    all the way to the mountains,
    and the ravines will be filled with your
        flesh.
[7]When I snuff you out, I will cover the heavens
    and darken their stars;
I will cover the sun with a cloud,
    and the moon will not give its light.
[8]All the shining lights in the heavens
    I will darken over you;
I will bring darkness over your land,
            declares the Sovereign LORD.
[9]I will trouble the hearts of many peoples
    when I bring about your destruction among
        the nations,
    among[a] lands you have not known.
[10]I will cause many peoples to be appalled at
        you,
    and their kings will shudder with horror
        because of you
when I brandish my sword before them."

[a]9 Hebrew; Septuagint *bring you into captivity among the nations, / to*

NRSV

32 In the twelfth year, in the twelfth month, on the first day of the month, the word of the LORD came to me: [2]Mortal, raise a lamentation over Pharaoh king of Egypt, and say to him:

You consider yourself a lion among the nations,
    but you are like a dragon in the seas;
you thrash about in your streams,
    trouble the water with your feet,
    and foul your[a] streams.
[3] Thus says the Lord GOD:
    In an assembly of many peoples
    I will throw my net over you;
    and I[b] will haul you up in my dragnet.
[4] I will throw you on the ground,
    on the open field I will fling you,
and will cause all the birds of the air to settle
        on you,
    and I will let the wild animals of the whole
        earth gorge themselves with you.
[5] I will strew your flesh on the mountains,
    and fill the valleys with your carcass.[c]
[6] I will drench the land with your flowing blood
        up to the mountains,
    and the watercourses will be filled with
        you.
[7] When I blot you out, I will cover the heavens,
    and make their stars dark;
I will cover the sun with a cloud,
    and the moon shall not give its light.
[8] All the shining lights of the heavens
    I will darken above you,
    and put darkness on your land,
                says the Lord GOD.
[9] I will trouble the hearts of many peoples,
    as I carry you captive[d] among the nations,
    into countries you have not known.
[10] I will make many peoples appalled at you;
    their kings shall shudder because of you.
When I brandish my sword before them,
    they shall tremble every moment
for their lives, each one of them,
    on the day of your downfall.

[a]Heb *their*   [b]Gk Vg: Heb *they*   [c]Symmachus Syr Vg: Heb *your height*   [d]Gk: Heb *bring your destruction*

COMMENTARY

The present unit commences with a date notice. The word of the Lord came to Ezekiel on the first day of the twelfth month of the twelfth year of Jehoiachin's exile (March 3, 585 BCE by my reckoning) and approximately two months after news of Jerusalem's capture reached the deportees (33:21). Almost two years have elapsed since the prophet proclaimed the preceding oracle against Egypt (31:1).[1064] Now, Yahweh commands him to "raise a lamentation over Pharaoh king of Egypt." Ezekiel's doom pronouncements against Tyre/its king were followed by dirges (see 26:17-18; 27; 28:11-19), and so the reader is not surprised that such should also be the case here.

In chap. 31, Ezekiel ostensibly asked Pharaoh to whom he compared in greatness, only to supply an immediate answer: the once mighty but now vanquished Assyria. Here, the prophet begins by observing that Egypt's king considers himself "a lion among the nations." As noted in the Overview, the lion was an established royal symbol in ancient Israel's world. Not only was it "the king of beasts," but also its hunting skills and rapacity were well-suited to convey glowing praise of rulers' victories over their enemies. So, for example, an inscription concerning Seti I proclaims, "His majesty is like an enraged lion,"[1065] and "His majesty prevailed over them like a fierce lion."[1066] The Thutmose III inscription quoted in the Commentary to chap. 29 identifies Pharaoh not only as a crocodile, but also as a lion: "I caused them to see thy majesty as a fierce lion,/ as thou makest them corpses throughout their valleys" (see also Amos 3:8; Hos 5:14; 11:10-11; 13:7,

Isa 31:4; 38:13)."[1067] Ezekiel's embittered "lament" over two of the Davidic dynasty's last kings (19:1-9; see the Commentary) depicts them as man-eating despoilers of their *own* land. That "twist" notwithstanding, the reader imagines that Pharaoh would warm to a comparison with a young lion.

Ezekiel has other ideas, however. He insists that Egypt's king is actually like a dragon (תנים *tannîm*) in the seas. In 29:3, *tannîm* functioned as a metaphor for Pharaoh, the crocodile proudly basking in his Nile canals. Yahweh, the great hunter, pierced his jaws with hooks and flung him, along with the fish clinging to his scales, into the desert and certain death. In the present simile, the reader assumes, initially at least, that the croc is back, though now situated in the seas and streams. As he makes his way through the text, however, he will discover that this *tannîm* is more bloated sea monster than sinister crocodile. Ezekiel quickly invites his audience to perceive the dragon snorting (NRSV and NIV, "thrashing") about in its rivers, stirring up the waters with its feet (see 34:18),[1068] and fouling its (MT, "their") streams. An ecological disaster, it at least appears not too disruptive of life on the land.

Verse 3 commences with the messenger formula: "Thus says the Lord GOD." Both biblical and extrabiblical literature speak of the primeval chaos dragon. Within Hebrew Scripture, Yahweh's battles with this beast are recounted, for example, in Job 26:13; Ps 74:12-14; and Isa 51:9-10 (see also Isa 27:1). Canaanite mythology describes how Baal snared Yamm ("Sea") in his net.[1069] The

1064. This date is later than that prefixed to the following oracle (32:17-32). Many Hebrew MSS, along with the LXX and the Syriac, read "in the eleventh year," and some critics follow suit. See, e.g., K. S. Freedy and D. B. Redford, "The Dates in Ezekiel in Relation to Biblical, Babylonian and Egyptian Sources," *JAOS* 90 (1970) 468n. 30.

1065. *ANET*, 263b.

1066. Ibid., 254b.

1067. Ibid., 374b. See also the self-description of Ramesses II as "the living lion . . . slayer of his enemies" in A. Dardiner, *The Kadesh Inscriptions of Ramesses II* (Oxford: Oxford University Press, 1960) no. R 2.

1068. This image also appears in Akkadian literature, where it is used both literally and as a metaphor for muddying the "political" waters. See D. I. Block, *The Book of Ezekiel: Chapters 25–48,* NICOT (Grand Rapids: Eerdmans, 1998) 200.

1069. See E. L. Greenstein, "The Snaring of the Sea in the Baal Epic," *Maarav* 3/2 (1982) 195-216.

Babylonian Creation Epic recounts Marduk's victory over Tiamat, the fearsome monster goddess whom he catches in his net, kills, and then dismembers.[1070] In this passage, also, the (fishing) net is the Lord's weapon of choice, and not the hooks of 29:4. (Readers recall that in 12:13 and 17:20, Yahweh threatens to spread a net over Zedekiah, Judah's last king, and bring him to Babylon.)[1071] The capture takes place before witnesses ("an assembly of many people"); indeed, according to the MT, they (NRSV, "I") participate in hauling the monster up in God's dragnet.[1072]

Verse 4 is especially reminiscent of the scene in 29:5. Yahweh will throw the beast upon the ground, fling it onto an open field; and the cadaver will host all the birds of the air, while the wild animals of the whole earth gorge themselves on it. The unique phrase, "the whole earth," suggests the extraordinary magnitude of the dragon's body: It is a "world beast" of cosmic proportions.[1073] This idea is further underscored in vv. 5-6. First, Yahweh declares, "I will strew your flesh on the mountains,/and fill the valleys with your carcass"; see also 35:8 and Jer 25:33.[1074] (Readers recall the branches and boughs of cedar Assyria scattered on the mountains, in the valleys, and in "all the watercourses of the land," 31:12). Moreover, God will drench the land with monster Pharaoh's flowing blood up to the mountains, and the watercourses will be filled with his body fluids. As Hals observes, neither high mountains nor deep ravines

are characteristic of the Nile River valley; the language is hyperbolic, not location specific.[1075]

The term בכבותך (bĕkabbôtĕkà), "in your snuffing out" (v. 7a) lacks a subject, but it is surely Yahweh (so NRSV and NIV). The word כבה (kābâ) refers literally to snuffing out a wick/lamp (e.g., Lev 6:5-6; 1 Sam 3:3; Prov 31:18). Figuratively it can refer to death, as in Isa 43:17: "they lie down, they cannot rise,/they are extinguished, quenched like a wick" (see also 2 Sam 14:7; 21:17). On the cosmic level, God will "cover" the heavens (see also 26:19; 31:15), make their stars dark (see 30:18), and cover the sun with a cloud; and the moon will withhold its light. Here, Ezekiel changes the conventional ordering—sun, moon, and stars—found in Gen 1:15, Jer 31:35, and Ps 136:8-9. Hence, the heavens will be bereft of shining lights; and Pharaoh's land will be shrouded in darkness. Readers recognize in this motif certain prophetic descriptions of the day of Yahweh (e.g., Amos 5:18, 20: 8:9; Isa 13:10; Joel 2:10), though that phrase does not appear in these verses. Moreover, both the imagery and the vocabulary of v. 8b quicken thoughts of the pre-exodus plague of darkness that aggrieved Egypt (Exod 10:21-22). The closing formula, "says the Lord GOD," underscores the divine origin and consequent authority of Ezekiel's words.

Verses 9-10 describe the consternation of many peoples when Yahweh brings news of the dragon's downfall among the nations and even into the most distant of lands ("countries you have not known"). God will appall these many peoples; their kings' hair will stand on end (see, similarly, 26:15-16 and esp. 27:35) when the Lord brandishes "my sword" before them. If so ignominious a fate could overtake Pharaoh, then they also are vulnerable to Yahweh's sovereign power. (See Reflections at 32:11-16.)

1070. See ANET, 67.

1071. Held discusses Akkadian and Hebrew terms for spreading a net in M. Held, "Pits and Pitfalls in Akkadian and Biblical Hebrew," JANES 5 (1973) 181-89. On capture by net as a punishment for treaty oath violations, see D. Hillers, Treaty-Curses and the Old Testament Prophets, BibOr 16 (Rome: Pontifical Biblical Institute, 1964) 69-70.

1072. Their presence, Zimmerli observes, interrupts Ezekiel's metaphor and should be attributed to a later hand. See Zimmerli, Ezekiel 2, 159. As has been noted, however, the reader knows that literal referents often intrude into the prophet's extended tropes (figurative uses of language).

1073. Zimmerli, Ezekiel 2, 160.

1074. רמותך (rămûtêkā) is difficult. Greenberg translates "your bulk," deriving the form from רום (rûm "be high") and understanding it as a reference to the towering mass of the monster's carcass. But it can also be read as "maggots," from the root רמם (rāmam, "to rot," "to decay"), in which case the word functions metonymically for the decaying flesh they consume. See Lawrence Boadt, Ezekiel's Oracles Against Egypt: A Literary and Philological Study of Ezekiel 29–32, BibOr 37 (Rome: Pontifical Biblical Institute, 1980) 137.

1075. Hals, Ezekiel, 225. Cf. the following Assyrian inscription of Tiglath-Pileser I: "Like a storm demon I piled up the corpses of their warriors on mountain ledges (and) made their blood flow into the hollows and plains of the mountains." See A. K. Grayson, Assyrian Royal Inscriptions, II, RANE (Wiesbaden: Marrassowitz, 1976) 9 (I.iii.23-27). See also D. H. Müller, Ezechiel-studien (Berlin: Reuther & Reichard, 1895) 56-58; Greenberg, Ezekiel 21–37, 657.

Ezekiel 32:11-16, The Desolation of Egypt

NIV

11" 'For this is what the Sovereign LORD says:

" 'The sword of the king of Babylon
  will come against you.
12I will cause your hordes to fall
  by the swords of mighty men—
  the most ruthless of all nations.
They will shatter the pride of Egypt,
  and all her hordes will be overthrown.
13I will destroy all her cattle
  from beside abundant waters
no longer to be stirred by the foot of man
  or muddied by the hoofs of cattle.
14Then I will let her waters settle
  and make her streams flow like oil,
                    declares the Sovereign LORD.
15When I make Egypt desolate
  and strip the land of everything in it,
when I strike down all who live there,
  then they will know that I am the LORD.'

16"This is the lament they will chant for her. The daughters of the nations will chant it; for Egypt and all her hordes they will chant it, declares the Sovereign LORD."

NRSV

11 For thus says the Lord GOD:
  The sword of the king of Babylon shall come
    against you.
12 I will cause your hordes to fall
  by the swords of mighty ones,
  all of them most terrible among the
    nations.
  They shall bring to ruin the pride of Egypt,
    and all its hordes shall perish.
13 I will destroy all its livestock
    from beside abundant waters;
  and no human foot shall trouble them any
    more,
    nor shall the hoofs of cattle trouble them.
14 Then I will make their waters clear,
    and cause their streams to run like oil,
      says the Lord GOD.
15 When I make the land of Egypt desolate
    and when the land is stripped of all that
      fills it,
  when I strike down all who live in it,
    then they shall know that I am the LORD.
16 This is a lamentation; it shall be chanted.
    The women of the nations shall chant it.
  Over Egypt and all its hordes they shall
      chant it,
  says the Lord GOD.

COMMENTARY

A second messenger formula initiates a doom prophecy against all of Egypt. "My sword" in v. 10 becomes "the sword of the king of Babylon" in v. 11. Throughout Ezekiel's oracles against Egypt, he has consistently maintained that Nebuchadrezzar, Yahweh's proximate agent of punishment, will conquer the kingdom on the Nile. Egypt's hordes will fall beneath the swords of Babylonia's warriors, here as elsewhere called "the most terrible among the nations" (28:7; 30:11; 31:12). They will devastate the pride of Egypt, and all her horde (army) will be destroyed.

But God is not content simply to strip the land of human inhabitants. Its livestock also will be wiped out. Henceforth, neither human feet nor cattle hoofs (see 29:11) will trouble its abundant Nile waters (as did Pharaoh, the sea monster; see v. 2). As a consequence, the sediment in their waters will settle, and their streams will run like oil. The motif of streams running like oil is often associated with paradise, where all is peaceful and harmonious. Here, however, the tranquil waters are a by-product of the land's desolation. Verse 14, like v. 8, ends with a formula ("says the Lord GOD"), which reenforces that Ezekiel's oracle is, in fact, Yahweh's own word and so is certain to be fulfilled.

Verse 15, with its concluding recognition formula, lends to the entire unit the quality of a proof-saying. The ultimate goal of God's devastation of Egypt is that those who have lived in it be forced to acknowledge the sovereignty and unparalleled power of Yahweh as manifested in their own history.

The colophon of v. 16 identifies the preceding oracle as a lamentation, to be chanted over Egypt and all its hordes by the women of the nations. Hebrew Scripture, as well as extrabiblical evidence, suggests that women especially functioned as professional mourners throughout the ancient Near East (see, e.g., Isa 22:12; Jer 7:26; 9:17).[1076]

1076. An eleventh-century BCE sarcophagus of Ahiram of Byblos bears a portrait of four professional female Canaanite mourners. The two on the left are beating their breasts; the arms of the two on the right are raised. See J. D. Pritchard, ed., *The Ancient Near East in Pictures Relating to the Old Testament* (Princeton: Princeton University Press, 1954) no. 459.

REFLECTIONS

Ezekiel, who nowhere deigns to utter Pharaoh's name, here proclaims yet another scathing punishment against Egypt's king. To his mind, any attempt by Judah's ally on the Nile to interfere with Yahweh's judgment against Israel is an offense against God, an example of arrogance so great as to invite divine judgment; and any attempt by Judah to place faith in its treaty partner constitutes a betrayal of the fidelity that rightfully belongs only to the Lord. Now, Jerusalem has been destroyed, and the prophet remains determined to convince his fellow exiles that Egypt, too, will meet its doom *at* the hand of Yahweh *by* the hand of Nebuchadrezzar. For those who had favored a pro-Egyptian political policy and nurtured hope that Judah's ally might mount a last-minute rescue of Jerusalem, Ezekiel's oracles against Egypt must have rankled to the bone. But there is a sort of "pastoral" dimension to the prophet's diatribes. If Israel is to have any future whatsoever, it can only come at God's bidding. By asserting Yahweh's power over Egypt *and* Babylonia, Ezekiel assures his audience (and his readers) of the Lord's sovereign power over all nations. History is unfolding according to God's plan.

As inhabitants of a world no less violent than Ezekiel's own, we know too well the brutality that armies inflict upon their enemies. Indeed, atrocities on battlefields and city streets are brought into our homes by television and computer. Ezekiel, who knows nothing of such technology, uses metaphors to create vivid and memorable *word* pictures: the slaughter of Pharaoh, the chaos dragon, and the grisly dissemination of his carcass and body fluids; a Nile flowing smooth as oil because no living creatures—human or beast—disturb its waters.

The prophet's hostility toward Egypt is evident in every verse of the present passage. And when we understand what was at stake for him—convincing his fellow exiles that Judah's destruction was no sign of divine weakness or apathy, but part of Yahweh's world-wide plan of judgment, beyond which Israel could look expectantly toward salvation—we can better see why he spoke as he did. Ezekiel obviously had no theological problem with attributing to God the qualities of a vicious warrior who inflicts upon "his" victims the most gruesome and desolating of punishments, for in his view, presumptuous nations were an affront to the Lord's unrivaled sovereignty. Such, after all, was part and parcel of his ancient Near Eastern worldview and integral to Yahwistic faith. (Consider, for example, the pre-exodus plagues inflicted upon Egypt and God's pre-conquest command that the Israelites utterly exterminate the indigenous population of Canaan.)

In my judgment, we who accord the Bible a privileged place within our faith cannot simply avoid these texts by, for example, fleeing to favorite passages within the New Testament. Oracles against foreign nations and rulers appear in virtually every prophetic collection within the canon. Their sheer number alone makes them a presence with which we must contend. Ezekiel's oracles against Egypt are fruitfully placed in conversation with, for example, Isaiah 19, and with other biblical texts which speak of God's relationships with the nations in very different ways (see, e.g., Gen 12:3; Isa 49:6; and John 3:16).

A nation brought to its knees is a prime candidate for anger, bitter agony, and the desire for revenge. We hear in Ezekiel's words the outpouring of his people's pain; and we listen for God's words in his utterances. But the two cannot simply be equated, as if our ways were God's ways. Ezekiel himself spoke of Egypt's limited revival beyond destruction (29:13-16)—an astonishing fact given his acrimony toward that nation. His oracles against the nations are a starting place for fruitful dialogue about how we, as diverse children of a single God, can work toward the coming of God's kingdom on earth, as it is in heaven.

Ezekiel 32:17-32, Send Egypt Down to Sheol

OVERVIEW

In 32:17-32, Ezekiel's seventh pronouncement against Egypt and the last of his oracles against seven foreign nations/rulers in chaps. 25–32 (see Excursuses: "Ezekiel's Oracles Against Foreign Nations and Rulers," 1355-56, and "Ezekiel's Oracles Against Pharaoh/Egypt," 1401-3), Yahweh commands the prophet to wail (in lamentation) over Egypt, thereby sending its horde (army) down to the world below to take its dishonorable place among other nations (Assyria, Elam, Meshech-Tubal, Edom, the "princes of the north," and the Sidonians [Phoenicians]). Modern critics disparage the literary quality of this unit, for it is fraught with repetitions, ill-connected verses, and grammatical conundrums (which surely frustrated ancient readers as well). At the same time, they value immensely the light it sheds on ancient Israel's understanding of the netherworld and of the conditions of its deceased inhabitants.[1077]

The unit consists of introductory material and God's fresh charge to Ezekiel (vv. 17-18), plus three subsections. Verses 19-21 demand the consignment of Pharaoh and his forces to Sheol. Egypt's kings anticipated an afterlife abounding in the same pleasures they enjoyed on earth. Hence, they arranged to be buried with all of the necessities and finery required to sustain them in royal fashion. Here, however, Ezekiel dooms Pharaoh to

the sort of dreary netherworld familiar from biblical, as well as extra-biblical, texts. Consider, for example, the following excerpt from the Mesopotamian myth, "The Descent of Ishtar to the Underworld":

To Kurnugi, land of [no return],
Ishtar daughter of Sin was [determined] to go . . .
To the dark house, dwelling of Erkalla's god,
To the house which those who enter
  cannot leave,
On the road where travelling is one-way only,
To the house where those who enter
  are deprived of light,
Where dust is their food, clay their bread.
They see no light, they dwell in darkness . . .[1078]

In this gloomy, post-mortem existence, the deceased are, in effect, "living corpses."[1079] Conscious, vocal, and able to experience emotions (e.g., shame, disgrace, consolation), they are segregated according to certain criteria—social standing on earth (e.g., royalty or subjects), the circumstances of their deaths and burials (e.g., honorable or dishonorable)—and cognizant of new arrivals. But their lives are only a shadow of former, earthly existence.

In vv. 22-30, Ezekiel elaborates on the circumstances of the ignoble dead (vv. 22-28). He

1077. See, e.g., N. J. Tromp, *Primitive Conceptions of Death and the Nether World in the Old Testament,* BibOr 21 (Rome: Pontifical Biblical Institute, 1969).

1078. "The Descent of Ishtar to the Underworld," in *Myths from Mesopotamia,* trans. Stephanie Dalley (Oxford: Oxford University Press, 1989) 155.
1079. Block, *Ezekiel 25–48,* 232.

launches his "(dis)honor role"[1080] of Sheol's inhabitants with Assyria, a choice that comes as no suprise to the sequential reader, who recalls his analogy between Assyria (the great cedar) and Egypt in chap. 31. The stock phrases used to detail her circumstances and those of her company will recur, with modifications, in subsequent descriptions of the other nations (see above) residing there. Indeed, this second section is a model of repetition with variation—a characteristic of Ezekielian rhetoric. Finally, vv. 31-32 both anticipate Pharaoh's response to these fellow inhabitants of Sheol and accuse him (and his horde) of the same charges lodged against his grave-mates.

1080. Ibid., 225.

The present passage functions not only as a climax to Ezekiel's seven pronouncements against Pharaoh/Egypt, but also (by virtue of its references to other countries) as an apt finale to the oracles against foreign nations and rulers gathered in chaps. 25–32. Consistent with the prophet's theology throughout his scroll, it presupposes Yahweh's absolute control of all peoples throughout their histories and even beyond death. Unlike the Mesopotamians, for example, who assigned the realm of the dead to underworld deities (e.g., King Nergal and Queen Ereshkigal), the prophet asserts that the Lord's sovereignty extends even to the "uttermost parts of the Pit" (v. 23). Death does not release the nations from God's powerful grip.

Ezekiel 32:17-18, Wail over the Horde of Egypt

NIV

[17]In the twelfth year, on the fifteenth day of the month, the word of the LORD came to me: [18]"Son of man, wail for the hordes of Egypt and consign to the earth below both her and the daughters of mighty nations, with those who go down to the pit.

NRSV

17In the twelfth year, in the first month,[a] on the fifteenth day of the month, the word of the LORD came to me:
[18] Mortal, wail over the hordes of Egypt,
     and send them down,
 with Egypt[b] and the daughters of majestic
         nations,
     to the world below,
     with those who go down to the Pit.

[a]Gk: Heb lacks *in the first month*   [b]Heb *it*

COMMENTARY

The unit is prefaced by an incomplete date notice. The MT specifies the twelfth year (of the exile of King Jehoiachin)[1081] and the fifteenth day of the month, but fails to identify which month. The reader probably fills this gap by resorting to the date prefixed to the preceding oracle (32:1; hence, the twelfth month). Accordingly, the passage can be dated to March 18, 585 BCE (by my reckoning), two weeks later than the utterance in 32:1-16 (the LXX, followed by the NRSV, arbitrarily opts for "the first month").

1081. Other Hebrew MSS, plus the Syriac, read "in the eleventh year."

After the characteristic word event formula ("the word of the LORD came to me"), God addresses the prophet directly ("Mortal") and commands him to wail over the horde of Egypt, a performance that will send it down to the world below.[1082] The verb "to wail," "lament" (נהה *nāhâ*) elsewhere appears in Mic 2:4 and perhaps 1 Sam 7:2. In those contexts, as here, it refers to mournful wailing. (One doubts, however, that Ezekiel's mourning is heartfelt.) Nominal forms from the

1082. המון (*hāmôn*) appears often in Ezekiel's oracles against Egypt. In some contexts, it can mean "wealth," "pomp," or "pride." Here, however, it refers to Pharaoh's military forces (see also 30:10, 15; 31:18; 32:12).

same root, including נהי (*nĕhî,* "wailing," "lamentation," "mourning song"), appear more frequently (e.g., Amos 5:16; Jer 9:9, 17, 19; 31:15; Mic 2:4). Scholars speculate, but cannot prove (owing to insufficient evidence), that *nĕhî* refers to a type of lamentation with characteristics different from those of the more familiar קינה (*qînâ*) lament (see, e.g., 19:1-14; 26:17-18; 27:1-36; 28:11-19; 32:2). The latter (whether sincere or sarcastic) is distinguished by a limping, 3 + 2 rhythmic pattern (in at least some of its lines) and by its contrast between "then" (past glory) and "now" (dead or as good as dead). The present passage exhibits neither of those features. Its focus remains fixed on the ignominious conditions awaiting Pharaoh and his forces in Sheol.

Already in v. 18, textual difficulties arise. The noun המון (*hāmôn,* "horde") is masculine singular, and so one is not surprised to read that Ezekiel is to consign "it" (the object suffix on the verb also is masc. sing.) to the Pit. But in the MT, v. 18*b* commences with the feminine singular pronoun "her" (אותה *ôtāh,* "her and the daughters of majestic nations"). To what does this feminine pronoun refer? The NRSV and the NIV rightly conclude that its referent is "Egypt." After all, both nations and their important (especially capital) cities frequently appear as feminine entities in the literatures of Israel and the ancient Near East (see

Excursus: "Cities as Females," 1221-25). Perhaps, as Greenberg suggests, Ezekiel's sudden shift to a feminine pronoun for Egypt in v. 18*b* was prompted by the immediately following phrase, "and the daughters, majestic nations."[1083] Nonetheless, a number of critics emend "her" to "you" (אתה *'attâ,* referring to Ezekiel).[1084] This small change has implications for the role of the daughter nations. If it is adopted, then they—functioning as keening female mourners (see 32:16)—join Ezekiel in wailing Egypt's descent to the underworld. According to the MT, however, Ezekiel is to send both Egypt ("her") *and* the majestic nations down to the world below. Because the MT is intelligible, the ancient reader has no reason to suspect an error. But the identity of these "women" remains something of a mystery. How can they be the nations referred to in subsequent verses when, according to the text, those nations already reside in Sheol? (See Reflections at 32:19-32.)

1083. Greenberg, *Ezekiel 21–37,* 660. Both the NRSV and the NIV render the phrase, "and the daughters of. . . ." One thinks, then, of the nations' female populations. However, the phrase is probably better understood as an appositional genitive referring not to the daughters of nations, but to the nations themselves. Hence, Jer 50:42 ("O daughter Babylon," not "O daughter of Babylon") and Isa 47:1 ("virgin daughter Babylon" and "daughter Chaldea"). See W. F. Stinespring, "No Daughter of Zion: A Study of the Appositional Genitive in Hebrew Grammar," *Enc* 26 (1965) 133-42; K. P. Darr, *Isaiah's Vision and the Family of God* (Louisville: Westminster John Knox, 1994) 128-31.
1084. See Boadt, *Ezekiel's Oracles Against Egypt,* 152-53; Block, *Ezekiel 25–48,* 217.

Ezekiel 32:19-32, Go Down!

NIV

[19]Say to them, 'Are you more favored than others? Go down and be laid among the uncircumcised.' [20]They will fall among those killed by the sword. The sword is drawn; let her be dragged off with all her hordes. [21]From within the grave[a] the mighty leaders will say of Egypt and her allies, 'They have come down and they lie with the uncircumcised, with those killed by the sword.'

[22]"Assyria is there with her whole army; she is surrounded by the graves of all her slain, all who have fallen by the sword. [23]Their graves are in the depths of the pit and her army lies around her

[a]21 Hebrew *Sheol*; also in verse 27

NRSV

[19] "Whom do you surpass in beauty?
Go down! Be laid to rest with the uncircumcised!"
[20]They shall fall among those who are killed by the sword. Egypt[a] has been handed over to the sword; carry away both it and its hordes. [21]The mighty chiefs shall speak of them, with their helpers, out of the midst of Sheol: "They have come down, they lie still, the uncircumcised, killed by the sword."

[22]Assyria is there, and all its company, their graves all around it, all of them killed, fallen by

[a]Heb *It*

NIV

grave. All who had spread terror in the land of the living are slain, fallen by the sword.

24"Elam is there, with all her hordes around her grave. All of them are slain, fallen by the sword. All who had spread terror in the land of the living went down uncircumcised to the earth below. They bear their shame with those who go down to the pit. 25A bed is made for her among the slain, with all her hordes around her grave. All of them are uncircumcised, killed by the sword. Because their terror had spread in the land of the living, they bear their shame with those who go down to the pit; they are laid among the slain.

26"Meshech and Tubal are there, with all their hordes around their graves. All of them are uncircumcised, killed by the sword because they spread their terror in the land of the living. 27Do they not lie with the other uncircumcised warriors who have fallen, who went down to the grave with their weapons of war, whose swords were placed under their heads? The punishment for their sins rested on their bones, though the terror of these warriors had stalked through the land of the living.

28"You too, O Pharaoh, will be broken and will lie among the uncircumcised, with those killed by the sword.

29"Edom is there, her kings and all her princes; despite their power, they are laid with those killed by the sword. They lie with the uncircumcised, with those who go down to the pit.

30"All the princes of the north and all the Sidonians are there; they went down with the slain in disgrace despite the terror caused by their power. They lie uncircumcised with those killed by the sword and bear their shame with those who go down to the pit.

31"Pharaoh—he and all his army—will see them and he will be consoled for all his hordes that were killed by the sword, declares the Sovereign LORD. 32Although I had him spread terror in the land of the living, Pharaoh and all his hordes will be laid among the uncircumcised, with those killed by the sword, declares the Sovereign LORD."

NRSV

the sword. 23Their graves are set in the uttermost parts of the Pit. Its company is all around its grave, all of them killed, fallen by the sword, who spread terror in the land of the living.

24Elam is there, and all its hordes around its grave; all of them killed, fallen by the sword, who went down uncircumcised into the world below, who spread terror in the land of the living. They bear their shame with those who go down to the Pit. 25They have made Elam[a] a bed among the slain with all its hordes, their graves all around it, all of them uncircumcised, killed by the sword; for terror of them was spread in the land of the living, and they bear their shame with those who go down to the Pit; they are placed among the slain.

26Meshech and Tubal are there, and all their multitude, their graves all around them, all of them uncircumcised, killed by the sword; for they spread terror in the land of the living. 27And they do not lie with the fallen warriors of long ago[b] who went down to Sheol with their weapons of war, whose swords were laid under their heads, and whose shields[c] are upon their bones; for the terror of the warriors was in the land of the living. 28So you shall be broken and lie among the uncircumcised, with those who are killed by the sword.

29Edom is there, its kings and all its princes, who for all their might are laid with those who are killed by the sword; they lie with the uncircumcised, with those who go down to the Pit.

30The princes of the north are there, all of them, and all the Sidonians, who have gone down in shame with the slain, for all the terror that they caused by their might; they lie uncircumcised with those who are killed by the sword, and bear their shame with those who go down to the Pit.

31When Pharaoh sees them, he will be consoled for all his hordes—Pharaoh and all his army, killed by the sword, says the Lord GOD. 32For he[d] spread terror in the land of the living; therefore he shall be laid to rest among the uncircumcised, with those who are slain by the sword—Pharaoh and all his multitude, says the Lord GOD.

[a]Heb it   [b]Gk Old Latin: Heb of the uncircumcised   [c]Cn: Heb iniquities   [d]Cn: Heb I

COMMENTARY

Without benefit of the messenger formula ("Thus says the Lord GOD"), Ezekiel ostensibly addresses Egypt/its horde with a rhetorical question (a familiar strategy appearing also, e.g., in 31:2): "More lovely than whom are you?" Behind this question, the reader assumes, lies Egypt's boast of being the loveliest of the nations. Here, as elsewhere, the prophet does not allow self-agrandizing claims to go unchallenged. "Go down!" he commands (the verb ירד [yārad, "to go down"] appears 20 times in chaps. 31–32). "Be laid to rest with the uncircumised."

In 28:10, Ezekiel proclaimed that Tyre's king would "die the death of the uncircumcised"; in 31:18, Pharaoh was ostensibly told that he would lie among the uncircumcised in the world below. For the ancient Israelites, uncircumcision was a disgrace (see Gen 34:14) and "uncircumcised" a term of extreme derision (see, e.g., Judg 14:3; 15:18; 1 Sam 14:6; 17:26, all referring to the Philistines).[1085] Because both the Phoenicians and the Egyptians practiced circumcision,[1086] the prophet's threats are best interpreted as metaphors for dishonorable death and burial, respectively. In this context also, Egypt is not only consigned to the underworld, but also ordered to bed itself among the ignominious dead—the least "lovely" of all conceivable surroundings!

While v. 19 was cast in second-person speech, the following verses (through v. 27) are phrased in the third person. Ezekiel informs his audience that Egypt's deceased will fall in the midst of "those slain by the sword." Eissfeldt has argued that these are not simply soldiers killed in warfare (though that meaning makes sense in this context), but more specifically criminals who were executed by the sword, either left unburied or buried without honor, and then relegated (along with the uncircumcised) to Sheol's worst quarters (see also 31:17; Isa 22:2).[1087] Verse 20b confounds commentators

and is probably corrupt, but it speaks of an appointed sword (Nebuchadrezzar's, to judge from previous passages; see 30:10-11, 24-25) and of Egypt (fem.) and her hordes (pl.) being dragged off. Verse 21 also confounds. The identity of "the mighty chiefs" (lit., "the rams of the mighty men") cannot be determined on the basis of this verse, but their apparent function is to greet Sheol's latest arrivals (see, by analogy, Isa 14:9-10). Their comment about Egypt and her helpers' ignoble place among the uncircumcised and sword-slain is likely scornful mockery.

Assyria (fem.) is the first of a triad of nations on Ezekiel's "dishonor roll" situated northeast of the Fertile Crescent. She lies, surrounded by the graves of her slain array, in the deepest recess of the Pit (see also Isa 14:15). (One recalls the tombs of nobles surrounding the royal pyramids at Giza.) Ezekiel accuses them of "spread[ing] terror" while on earth. The charge is apt. Assyria's ninth-century BCE king, Shalmaneser III, boasted about his gory treatment of a foe:

> I slew their warriors with the sword, descending upon them like [the god] Adad when he makes a rainstorm pour down. In the moat (of the town) I piled them up, I covered the wide plain with the corpses of their fighting men, I dyed the mountains with their blood like red wool. I took away from him many chariots (and) horses broken to the yoke. I erected pillars of skulls in front of his town, destroyed his (other) towns, tore down (their walls) and burnt (them) down.[1088]

Assyria's dishonorable end, then, is a consequence of its brutality while "in the land of the living." Ezekiel does not explicitly refer to the Assyrian array as "uncircumcised," though the Assyrians apparently did not practice circumcision.

The prophet Isaiah portrayed Elam, the second of Ezekiel's nations in Sheol, as a violent nation accomplished in archery and chariotry (Isa 22:6; see also 21:2); and Jeremiah condemns it to God's judgment in Jer 49:35-39. In the Table of Nations, Elam appears as Shem's firstborn son (his siblings are Ashur, Arpachshad, Lud, and Aram; Gen 10:22). The history of this nation, which lay east

---

1085. Lods has argued that in ancient Israel, the uncircumcised were denied funeral rites and burial in the family grave and were thought to reside at the lowest level of the underworld. See A. Lods, "La 'mot des incirconcis,' " *CRAI* (1943) 271-83.

1086. See J. Sasson, "Circumcision in the Ancient Near East," *JBL* 85 (1966) 473-76.

1087. Eissfeldt, "Schwerterschlagene bei Hesekiel," in *Studies in Old Testament Prophecy,* ed. H. H. Rowley (New York: Scribner's, 1950) 73-81.

1088. *ANET,* 277. See also D. I. Block, *The Book of Ezekiel: Chapters 25–48,* NICOT (Grand Rapids: Eerdmans, 1998) 225-26,

of Babylonia (in modern Iran), is obscure. We know that it was ravaged by Assyria's king Ashurbanipal during a two-year campaign (647–646 BCE) and became part of the Assyrian Empire. Little is known of Elam during the neo-Babylonian period. By the mid-sixth century, it had become part of the empire of the Medes and Persians.[1089] Its capital, Susa, regained prominence under the Persian king, Darius.

The MT devotes two, highly repetitive verses to Elam; and many commentators suggest that v. 25 is a doublet, either of v. 24 or (more likely) of v. 26 (concerning Meshech-Tubal).[1090] The reader might wonder why the description of Elam is longer than that of the other nations mentioned in this oracle: What is its special significance for Ezekiel? But he will not resort to the "solutions" proposed by modern critics.

Elam's horde surrounds her grave. Victims of the sword, they went down uncircumcised to the world below. (We do not know if the Elamites practiced circumcision; Ezekiel's statement cannot simply be accepted as fact.) They too are charged with having spread terror on earth; and as a consequence, they bear their disgrace with fellow Pit-dwellers. Verse 25 states that they (?) have made her (presumably Elam) a resting-place (משכב miškāb, "couch," "bed") in the midst of the slain, the graves of her horde surrounding her. (In the ancient Near East, corpses often were laid to rest on bedlike biers with headrests.) Again, her horde is said to be uncircumcised, pierced by the sword, a former source of terror on earth who must now bear its shame, situated among the slain.

The reference to Meshech-Tubal (v. 26) is anomalous. Elsewhere, the pair appears as two separate peoples (see Gen 10:2; Ezek 27:13 [in reverse order and as Tyre's trading partners]; 38:2, 3; 39:1; 1 Chr 1:5 [also in reverse order]); here, they are presented as if a single entity. Situated in Asia Minor, these peoples also engaged in ongoing warfare against Assyria; moreover, they suffered attacks by Cimmerian and Scythian invaders during

the eighth-seventh centuries BCE. In Ezekiel 38–39, they will reappear among Gog's invaders of Israel's land. In the present passage, however, Ezekiel depicts Meshech-Tubal also as a dangerous northern power of the past. Consigned to Sheol, it lies with the graves of its uncircumcised and slain horde all about it on account of the terror they spread on earth.

Verse 27 contrasts Meshech-Tubal's disgrace with the apparently honorable burial of an obscure fourth group. The MT reads, "But they shall not lie with *the fallen warriors of the uncircumcised*" (את־גבורים נפלים מערלים 'et-gibbôrîm nōpēlîm mē'ărēlîm). The reader might identify this fourth group with the גבורים אלי ('ēlê gibbôrîm), "chief warriors" who, according to v. 21, greet Egypt and her hordes upon their arrival in Sheol. (Greenberg equates the two and suggests that this elite group resides at a higher level than the other nations; hence, they are first to acknowledge Egypt's entrance into Sheol.)[1091] They were buried with their weapons; their swords lie beneath their heads (a practice otherwise unattested) and their shields (MT, "their iniquities") upon their bones.[1092]

Who are these fallen warriors? The LXX reads "the fallen heroes *of old*," as if the MT were מעולם (mē'ôlām) and not מערלים (mē'ărēlîm), "of the uncircumcised."[1093] Perhaps, as most critics surmise, the MT preserves a scribal error; the copyist, accustomed to the many references to the uncircumcised in this passage, inadvertently substituted mē'ărēlîm here as well. Emended in the light of the LXX, the verse stirs thoughts of the Nephilim who, according to Gen 6:1-4, were offspring of "the sons of God" and "the daughters of humans" and grew to become "the heroes that were of old, warriors of renown." Does Ezekiel have in mind these primeval, pre-flood warriors, including

1089. See Moshe Greenberg, *Ezekiel 21–37*, AB 22A (Garden City, N.Y.: Doubleday, 1997) 664.
1090. See, e.g., W. Zimmerli, *Ezekiel 2: A Commentary on the Book of the Prophet Ezekiel, Chapters 25–48*, trans. J. D. Martin, Hermeneia (Philadelphia: Fortress, 1983) 167. Boadt argues that v. 25 was misplaced in the course of transmission. Originally, it followed v. 26, and vv. 25, 27-28 spoke of Egypt. See Lawrence Boadt, *Ezekiel's Oracles Against Egypt: A Literary and Philological Study of Ezekiel 29–32*, BibOr 37 (Rome: Pontifical Biblical Institute, 1980) 158-59.

1091. Greenberg, *Ezekiel 21–37*, 665.
1092. "Their iniquities" makes a poor parallel to "their swords." Cornill first proposed reading צנותם (ṣnwtm, "their shields") for עונתם ('wntm, "their iniquities"); this solution is widely accepted and might well have occurred to the ancient reader. Boadt suggests, however, that one might read with the MT if 'wntm is derived from the root עון ('wn, "to dwell") and is translated as "housing," here "sepulchre." See Boadt, *Ezekiel's Oracles Against Egypt*, 165-66.
1093. The MT is intelligible, but it is difficult to understand why "the fallen warriors of the uncircumcised" would receive more honorable burials than, for example, the uncircumcised of Elam and Meshech-Tubal. One might, as Boadt observes, translate "fallen [physically] apart from the uncircumcised." The meaning of apartness is conveyed by the preposition מן min also, e.g., in Job 19:26; Isa 14:19; 22:3. See Boadt, *Ezekiel's Oracles Against Egypt*, 165.

Nimrod, "the first on earth to be a mighty warrior" (Gen 10:8)? Block terms recourse to this ancient tradition "shocking." How could Ezekiel present these antediluvian people as honorable residents of Sheol, when they were the epitome of wickedness, corruption, and violence in his religious tradition. They had terrorized the living. Why should these mighty ancients have special status in the netherworld?[1094] Three explanations are possible, Block concedes. First, Ezekiel's reference might draw from other Israelite traditions that, unlike Gen 6:1-4, embraced these warriors as honorable characters. One thinks, for example, of Gilgamesh, the Mesopotamian hero described as two-thirds god and one-third human.[1095] Second, Ezekiel might be borrowing extra-Israelite traditions wherein deceased rulers were regarded as divinized heroes (the "Rephaim"). Third, Ezekiel might simply have revised the Genesis tradition for rhetorical purposes. Wicked though these warriors were, they appeared noble when compared to the uncircumcised slain of Meshech-Tubal.[1096]

The identity of these fallen warriors remains a mystery, despite the efforts of ancient (the translators of the LXX) and contemporary scholars. Clearly, however, their burials are favorably compared to those of Sheol's other, dishonored inhabitants. And, in v. 28, Ezekiel—ostensibly addressing Pharaoh (Egypt) directly—informs him that he will be broken (in battle; see 30:8) and that his burial will be shameful.

Having described the post-mortem circumstances of three once-powerful Mesopotamian kingdoms, Ezekiel turns to Syro-Palestinian peoples. Edom, Israel's neighbor/adversary to the south, was roundly condemned in 25:12-14 for acting vengefully against the nation of Judah. A second oracle against Edom will appear in chap. 35. Here, the prophet anticipates its future disgrace in the Pit. Nothing is said of its "horde"; rather, its kings and all its princes (chieftains), despite their might, will lie with the dishonorably slain and uncircumcised (though the Edomites practiced circumcision). Ezekiel does not charge

Edom with spreading terror on earth (cf. vv. 23, 25-26); perhaps he did not deign to credit Israel's fraternal foe with such power.

Finally, Ezekiel turns to Judah's northern neighbors, all their princes/chiefs (נסיך [*nāsîk*] refers to leaders also in Josh 13:21; Ps 83:11; Mic 5:5),[1097] and "every Sidonian"—a phrase including not only the inhabitants of the historically prominent Phoenician city condemned in 28:20-23, but other Phoenicians as well (so also in Deut 3:9; Josh 13:4, 6; Judg 3:3; 1 Kgs 16:31). Despite their might, evinced in the terror their power engendered, they too descend deep into the Pit to take their place among the dishonorable dead. "They lie uncircumcised" conflicts with Herodotus, who claimed that both the Syrians and the Phoenicians practiced circumcision. Hence, for example, Cooke reads "with the uncircumcised."[1098] But the MT might simply be taken as a demeaning (and inaccurate) slur.

When Pharoah sees them (i.e., the dishonorable circumstances of both large and small nations), he will be consoled concerning all his horde. According to 31:16, the earth's choice trees took comfort when Assyria, the great cedar, joined them in the world below (as will Egypt). Here, however, Pharaoh takes solace in the knowledge that other kingdoms also suffer his ignominious end.[1099] Verse 31 ends with the signatory formula ("says the Lord GOD"), but in its final form the oracle has a second conclusion as well. According to the MT, v. 32a describes *Yahweh's* action in the first person: "I have caused terror of him" (so also NIV; the NRSV has "he," referring to Pharaoh [Egypt], in line with preceding references to the nations' causing terror of themselves in the land of the living). With this statement, Ezekiel ascribes to God the dread-inducing power Egypt's king has wielded on earth. Now, he and all his multitude will be laid to rest amongst Sheol's least reputable residents (v. 32b).

1094. Block, *Ezekiel 25–48*, 228.
1095. *ANET*, 73b.
1096. Block, *Ezekiel 25–48*, 228.

1097. The Akkadian cognate *nakiku*, refers to Aramaean princes/chieftains. Hence, some scholars suggest that the prophet speaks of Syrian, as well as Phoenician (see below) rulers.
1098. See Herodotus 2.104. See also G. A. Cooke, *A Critical and Exegetical Commentary on the Book of Ezekiel*, ICC (New York: Scribner's, 1937) 355.
1099. Taking comfort need not, as Boadt observes, be an "honorable" emotion. According to Gen 27:42, Esau takes comfort in his plan to kill Jacob. See Boadt, *Ezekiel's Oracles Against Egypt*, 16.

REFLECTIONS

Readers of this, Ezekiel's final oracle against Egypt and the last of the oracles against foreign nations/rulers collected in chapters 25–32, should attend not only to what the prophet says about post-mortem subsistence, but also to what he does not say. In previous oracles, he has threatened Tyre's prince (26:20; 28:8) and Egypt's pharaoh (31:15-18) with a one-way trip to the Pit. But the present passage is his longest treatment of life beyond earthly existence. Ezekiel's Sheol (neitherworld, Pit) is not "hell"—a place of eternal punishment, supervised by Satan, to which the condemned wicked are consigned. Its residents are not tortured, although the dishonorably dead and buried are aware of their status and suffer shame on account of it. In the prophet's day, the notion of a devil had not yet emerged in Hebrew thought. And though the present passage focuses upon a sampling of Sheol's most ignominious inhabitants (excepting the fallen warriors of v. 27), other biblical texts inform us that the netherworld was regarded as the final resting place of all people, the wicked *and* the righteous. One thinks, for example, of the deceased judge/prophet Samuel, whom the medium at Endor brought up out of the ground at King Saul's command (1 Sam 28:3-19). To judge from the present passage, Sheol consisted of separate levels, sections, or compartments. Ezekiel's almost exclusive focus upon its most disgraceful denizens precludes consideration of its better quarters.

As noted above, 32:17-32 functions both as the finale of Ezekiel's oracles against Egypt/Pharaoh and as the conclusion to a collection of prophecies concerning the nations. Although Yahweh commands the prophet to engage in a mourning performance, the text's tone is sarcastic, not sincere. We can assume that many who witnessed Ezekiel in action, as well as his readers, ancient and modern, knew of the extraordinary efforts of Egypt's kings to provide themselves, their families, and high-ranking officials with the goods, services, and security required for a comfortable, even abundant, afterlife—witness the pyramid complex at Giza, a wonder of the ancient world. Ezekiel's consignment of Pharaoh and his horde to the depths of the Pit eviscerates their expectations in the Judeans' eyes and places Egypt's fate in Yahweh's hands. It, like other nations—great and small—is God's property and can be disposed of as the Lord sees fit.

For all his ire against his own people, Ezekiel never threatens the house of Israel with the ignominious fate in Sheol that has befallen, or soon will overtake, other nations. Again, we observe what might be called a "pastoral" agenda undergirding his words. His fellow exiles learn, in no uncertain terms, that the power of their God extends beyond Israel to determine the destinies of all peoples from beginning to end. The collapse of Judah and Jerusalem's destruction were most easily (if most painfully) interpreted as a sign of Yahweh's weakness or apathy. But the prophet insists that this is a wrong reading of history. We are astonished by the strength and tenacity of his faith.

EZEKIEL 33:1–48:35

EZEKIEL 33:1–48:35

ORACLES CONCERNING THE RESTORATION OF ISRAEL

EZEKIEL 33:1-33, THE CITY OF JERUSALEM HAS FALLEN!

OVERVIEW

Ezekiel 33 is a complex chapter, containing various themes and literary forms. Verses 2-20, prefaced by the conventional word event formula (v. 1), consist of two major sections, vv. 2-9 and vv. 10-20. Both are cast as first-person divine speech and addressed to Ezekiel, who must convey Yahweh's words to his fellow exiles in Babylonia. The first section concerns Ezekiel's role as watchman to the house of Israel. Verses 2-6 speak literally of a lookout's responsibility and of his culpability should he fail to perform his task; vv. 7-9 speak figuratively of Ezekiel as sentinel and of his accountability should he not attempt to dissuade the wicked from his (or her) evil ways. The ancient reader is familiar with the "a prophet is a watchman" metaphor. It appeared in 3:16-21 (see the Commentary on 3:16-27) and is found in Hos 9:8, Hab 2:1, and Jer 6:17. Its use in this context is entirely apropos. Just as the watchman sounds a *general* alarm that bears directly upon *every person* who hears it, so Ezekiel issues a *general* call to repentance which seeks a response from *every member* of the exilic community.

The second section, a two-part disputation, quotes and then responds to two statements attributed to Ezekiel's audience. Verse 10 contains the deportees' first (!) recorded admission of sin and ends with a question: "How then can we *live?*" Verse 11, Yahweh's initial response, begins with an oath of denial that God takes pleasure in the death of the wicked ("As I *live.* . . ."), and issues a call for repentance. It also ends with a question: "why will you die, O house of Israel?" Verses 12-16 set forth two legal cases in the style of casuistic law (see below) and elaborate on each of them. The first case concerns the backsliding righteous person; the second, the repentant wicked. The former will not be saved by previous righteousness, but the latter, by *turning away* from sin and *doing* what is just and right, shall surely *live.*

In this disputation, Yahweh intends to challenge and console the exiles who, by their own admission (v. 10), are carrying a heavy burden of sin. The reader likely is surprised, therefore, by the content of the second quotation attributed to them (vv. 17 and 20): "The way of the Lord is not just." Yahweh counters their accusation first by reversing it ("it is their own way that is not just"; v. 17*b*), then by reiterating the principle by which divine justice operates (vv. 18-19), and finally by insisting that the exiles will be judged according to their (present) ways (v. 20*b*). It is the end of the race, not the beginning, that determines one's end.[1100] The oracle has no concluding formula.

Sequential readers recognize that this passage is built largely from preceding textual material. Not only did the watchman metaphor appear in 3:16-22 (where Yahweh further defined for Ezekiel his responsibilities as God's authentic prophet to "the house of Israel"), but also vv. 10-20 are strikingly similar to 18:1-32—also a disputation, in which Ezekiel sought first to refute the deportees' belief in transgenerational punishment (vv. 2-19) and then to debunk the notion that people store up a

---

1100. D. I. Block, *The Book of Ezekiel: Chapters 25–48,* NICOT (Grand Rapids: Eerdmans, 1998) 248.

"treasury of demerit or merit" that inexorably determines their fate (vv. 21-32; see the Commentary on 3:16-27).[1101] Nevertheless, vv. 2-9 are no slavish repetition of 3:16-21, and vv. 11-20 do not repeat 18:21-32 verbatim. The contents of the present passage have been carefully crafted to suit their context.

Ezekiel 33:21-22, a rare autobiographical notice, describes the fulfillment of Yahweh's promise in 24:26-27 that on the day a survivor arrives in Babylonia with news of Jerusalem's fall, the restriction on Ezekiel's ability to speak (ostensibly imposed some seven days after his call to the prophetic office; see 3:26-27) will be lifted. The realization of his doom prophecies vindicates God (at least from the perspective of Ezekiel's theological argument) and prophet alike, and frees the latter not only to call Israel to judgment, but also to play the arbiter's reconciling role.

Verses 23-29 contain a disputation speech that, with its closing, expanded recognition formula, is cast as a prophetic proof saying. Yahweh first informs Ezekiel of a saying circulating among those remaining in Judah following Jersalem's destruction ("Abraham was only one man, yet he got possession of the land; but we are many; the land is surely given us to possess"), then demands that the prophet accuse them of six ritual/ethical wrongdoings (unlike Abraham, these homelanders are not paragons of faithfulness and virtue), and finally condemns them to death. We can be certain that Ezekiel and his fellow exiles harbored little affection for those who were busily appropriating their property in the homeland.

Finally, vv. 30-33 record Yahweh's report to the prophet concerning the actual motivation of the throngs who are entering his house to hear God's latest communiqué. They enjoy Ezekiel's "performance" but do not take his words to heart, or put them into action, because their focus is fixed on profiteering by any means. The time will come, however, when they will be forced to know (recognize and acknowledge) the prophet's status as Yahweh's genuine intermediary.

1101. Ibid., 583.

Ezekiel 33:1-20, A Call for Repentance

Ezekiel 33:1-9, Ezekiel's Responsibility as Sentinel

NIV

33 The word of the LORD came to me: [2]"Son of man, speak to your countrymen and say to them: 'When I bring the sword against a land, and the people of the land choose one of their men and make him their watchman, [3]and he sees the sword coming against the land and blows the trumpet to warn the people, [4]then if anyone hears the trumpet but does not take warning and the sword comes and takes his life, his blood will be on his own head. [5]Since he heard the sound of the trumpet but did not take warning, his blood will be on his own head. If he had taken warning, he would have saved himself. [6]But if the watchman sees the sword coming and does not blow the trumpet to warn the people and the sword comes and takes the life of one of them, that man will be taken away because of his sin, but I will hold the watchman accountable for his blood.'

NRSV

33 The word of the LORD came to me: [2]O Mortal, speak to your people and say to them, If I bring the sword upon a land, and the people of the land take one of their number as their sentinel; [3]and if the sentinel sees the sword coming upon the land and blows the trumpet and warns the people; [4]then if any who hear the sound of the trumpet do not take warning, and the sword comes and takes them away, their blood shall be upon their own heads. [5]They heard the sound of the trumpet and did not take warning; their blood shall be upon themselves. But if they had taken warning, they would have saved their lives. [6]But if the sentinel sees the sword coming and does not blow the trumpet, so that the people are not warned, and the sword comes and takes any of them, they are taken away in their iniquity, but their blood I will require at the sentinel's hand.

NIV

7"Son of man, I have made you a watchman for the house of Israel; so hear the word I speak and give them warning from me. 8When I say to the wicked, 'O wicked man, you will surely die,' and you do not speak out to dissuade him from his ways, that wicked man will die for[a] his sin, and I will hold you accountable for his blood. 9But if you do warn the wicked man to turn from his ways and he does not do so, he will die for his sin, but you will have saved yourself.

[a]8 Or in; also in verse 9

NRSV

7So you, mortal, I have made a sentinel for the house of Israel; whenever you hear a word from my mouth, you shall give them warning from me. 8If I say to the wicked, "O wicked ones, you shall surely die," and you do not speak to warn the wicked to turn from their ways, the wicked shall die in their iniquity, but their blood I will require at your hand. 9But if you warn the wicked to turn from their ways, and they do not turn from their ways, the wicked shall die in their iniquity, but you will have saved your life.

COMMENTARY

An initial oracle, introduced by Ezekiel's formulaic announcement of a fresh divine communiqué, Yahweh's direct address to the prophet ("O Mortal"), and a command that he proclaim God's words to "your people" (see also 3:11; 33:2, 12, 17, 30), begins with two hypothetical situations cast in the style of casuistic (conditional) law.[1102] The scenarios are these: Yahweh brings a sword (war) upon a land, and its people conscript a member of their community to function as watchman. If that watchman sees the enemy approaching and warns the community by blowing the trumpet, then any who hear the trumpet blast but do not take warning, so that they are slain by the sword, bear responsibility for their deaths: "their blood shall be upon their own heads" (v. 4; see also Josh 2:19).[1103] If the sentinel does not sound a warning and the enemy slays someone, however, the victim will have perished on account of personal sin, but God will hold the watchman accountable for the death ("blood")—that is, he also will die.[1104]

With vv. 7-9, Yahweh correlates elements of these hypothetical situations with Ezekiel's own. God (not the people!) has conscripted Ezekiel as sentinel to the house of Israel. Whenever the Lord speaks to him, he must give warning from God to the exiles. If Yahweh pronounces the death sentence ("you shall surely die") against the wicked, and the prophet does not warn them to turn from their (evil) ways, they shall die in their iniquity (like those who fail to heed the watchman's trumpet blast), but Ezekiel also will have committed a capital offense. If he warns the wicked to turn from their ways and they do not, they will perish, but Ezekiel will have saved his own life. Perhaps Ezekiel composed this text with Jer 6:17 in mind:

Also I raised up sentinels for you:
"Give heed to the sound of the trumpet!"
But they said, "We will not give heed." (NRSV)

These verses are remarkably similar to portions of 3:16-21. According to both passages, Yahweh is the source both of the danger and of the warning. In each text, Ezekiel's life hangs on the faithful performance of his duty as Yahweh's spokesperson. When God issues the death penalty against the wicked, Ezekiel *must* give warning, though he is not accountable for the exiles' choices (to persist in their wickedness or to repent and change their ways). But there are differences as well. Chapter 3 consists of Yahweh's instructions to *Ezekiel*; he is not commanded to share the divine communiqué with his compatriots. In 33:2-9, by contrast, God

1102. Typically casuistic laws begin with a protasis ("If you will diligently observe this entire commandment that I am commanding you," Deut 11:22) followed by an apodosis stating the legal consequence(s) of the action described in the protasis ("then the LORD will drive out all these nations before you, and you will dispossess nations larger and mightier than yourselves," Deut 11:23).

1103. See Moshe Greenberg, *Ezekiel 21-37*, AB 22A (Garden City, N.Y.: Doubleday, 1997) 673.

1104. Note that in the first instance, the victim's failure to heed the sentinel's warning is absurd, but nothing is said of his moral character. The second, by contrast, states that the unwarned slain person is culpable, dying on account of his or her sins. While the watchman's irresponsibility is the proximate cause of death, the fatality is justified on other grounds.

explicitly orders the prophet to convey his words to them. Ezekiel's responsibility is an issue, but the larger issue—the one developed in subsequent verses—is the possibility God profers: life! The death sentence can be repealed if the wicked turn from their evil ways. (See Reflections at 33:10-20.)

Ezekiel 33:10-20, Despair and Disputation

NIV

¹⁰"Son of man, say to the house of Israel, 'This is what you are saying: "Our offenses and sins weigh us down, and we are wasting away because of[a] them. How then can we live?" ' ¹¹Say to them, 'As surely as I live, declares the Sovereign LORD, I take no pleasure in the death of the wicked, but rather that they turn from their ways and live. Turn! Turn from your evil ways! Why will you die, O house of Israel?'

¹²"Therefore, son of man, say to your countrymen, 'The righteousness of the righteous man will not save him when he disobeys, and the wickedness of the wicked man will not cause him to fall when he turns from it. The righteous man, if he sins, will not be allowed to live because of his former righteousness.' ¹³If I tell the righteous man that he will surely live, but then he trusts in his righteousness and does evil, none of the righteous things he has done will be remembered; he will die for the evil he has done. ¹⁴And if I say to the wicked man, 'You will surely die,' but he then turns away from his sin and does what is just and right— ¹⁵if he gives back what he took in pledge for a loan, returns what he has stolen, follows the decrees that give life, and does no evil, he will surely live; he will not die. ¹⁶None of the sins he has committed will be remembered against him. He has done what is just and right; he will surely live.

¹⁷"Yet your countrymen say, 'The way of the Lord is not just.' But it is their way that is not just. ¹⁸If a righteous man turns from his righteousness and does evil, he will die for it. ¹⁹And if a wicked man turns away from his wickedness and does what is just and right, he will live by doing so. ²⁰Yet, O house of Israel, you say, 'The way of the Lord is not just.' But I will judge each of you according to his own ways."

[a]10 Or away in

NRSV

10Now you, mortal, say to the house of Israel, Thus you have said: "Our transgressions and our sins weigh upon us, and we waste away because of them; how then can we live?" ¹¹Say to them, As I live, says the Lord GOD, I have no pleasure in the death of the wicked, but that the wicked turn from their ways and live; turn back, turn back from your evil ways; for why will you die, O house of Israel? ¹²And you, mortal, say to your people, The righteousness of the righteous shall not save them when they transgress; and as for the wickedness of the wicked, it shall not make them stumble when they turn from their wickedness; and the righteous shall not be able to live by their righteousness[a] when they sin. ¹³Though I say to the righteous that they shall surely live, yet if they trust in their righteousness and commit iniquity, none of their righteous deeds shall be remembered; but in the iniquity that they have committed they shall die. ¹⁴Again, though I say to the wicked, "You shall surely die," yet if they turn from their sin and do what is lawful and right— ¹⁵if the wicked restore the pledge, give back what they have taken by robbery, and walk in the statutes of life, committing no iniquity—they shall surely live, they shall not die. ¹⁶None of the sins that they have committed shall be remembered against them; they have done what is lawful and right, they shall surely live.

17Yet your people say, "The way of the Lord is not just," when it is their own way that is not just. ¹⁸When the righteous turn from their righteousness, and commit iniquity, they shall die for it.[b] ¹⁹And when the wicked turn from their wickedness, and do what is lawful and right, they shall live by it.[b] ²⁰Yet you say, "The way of the Lord is not just." O house of Israel, I will judge all of you according to your ways!

[a]Heb by it   [b]Heb them

COMMENTARY

Yahweh's direct address to the prophet continues as God orders him to speak—more precisely, to quote and then respond to a comment circulating among his fellow deportees: "Our rebellions and our sins weigh upon us, and we are wasting away because of them; how then can we live?" (v. 10). Here, for the first time, Ezekiel's audience finally acknowledges its culpability. The noun פֶּשַׁע (peša'), "rebellion, transgression," is from a root whose verb, פָּשַׁע (pāša'), means "to rebel, transgress." In the case of suzerainty treaties, the vassal, or inferior partner, is threatened with curses should he rebel against the suzerain, or superior partner. In the Hebrew Bible, the same root refers to Israel's rebellions against God (see, e.g., Isa 1:2). The noun חטאה (ḥaṭā'â), "sin," is from a root whose verb, חטא (ḥāṭā'), means "to miss a goal or way, to sin." The exiles have missed the mark, abrogated God's covenant requirements, and are feeling the burden of their wrongdoing and its consequent punishment. Indeed, they claim to be "wasting away." The verb מקק (māqaq) elsewhere refers to wounded or rotting flesh (Ps 38:5; Zech 14:12), to the physical ravages of hunger and thirst (Ezek 4:17), and to pining away or languishing in grief and exile (Ezek 24:23; Lev 26:39).

So demoralized are the deportees by their crushing sense of sin and hopelessness that they even ask, "How then shall we survive?" Though their lives are not literally at risk, their despair is so deep that living seems too formidable a task. We cannot know how the exiles expressed their feelings, because the text does not preserve intonation, gestures, etc. Was their comment uttered in anger, or with the flat voice of resignation borne of severe depression? Whatever their tone, they have come a long way since the days when they taunted Ezekiel (12:21) and reassurred themselves that his threats were irrelevant to their time (12:27).

Yahweh responds to their complaint and query with an oath, by God's own life, that the Lord takes no pleasure in the death of the wicked, but in their turning from their ways (repenting) and living! (The same statement, cast as a rhetorical question, appears in 18:23; see also 18:32.) An impassioned plea ("turn back, turn back from your evil ways") ends with a question of God's own: "for why will you die, O house of Israel?" (quoting 18:31).

For a third time, Yahweh pauses to address Ezekiel directly ("And you, mortal") and reiterates the command that he speak to his people. Verse 12 sets out the principle by which divine justice operates: One's past does not determine one's present or future. Past righteousness will not save the person who sins; past wickedness will not cause persons to stumble who turn from their wickedness. Two examples of this principle in action follow. Though God pronounces the "life sentence" ("they shall surely live") to the righteous, if they trust that their righteousness has saved them and then commit iniquity, from that very day Yahweh will not remember their previous righteous deeds; they will perish on account of their sins. But if God pronounces the death sentence against the wicked, and they respond not only by turning from their sin but also by doing what is lawful and right, from that very day Yahweh will cancel their death sentence. They will live. Verse 15 provides three examples (not an exhaustive list) of what it means to do what is "lawful and right": restoring the pledge (property—e.g., clothing, livestock—taken from a debtor to secure a loan),[1105] restoring what he has taken by robbery (the verb גזל [gāzal] means "to tear away, seize, take violent possession of", see 18:7, 12, 16), and "walking in [obeying] the statutes of life" (parallel to "[he] keeps all my statutes" in 18:21) in order not to commit iniquitous acts. Hence, the repentant wicked must not only redress past misdeeds (which the stalwart righteous do not commit), but also live, as do the righteous, in obedience to God's statutes.

Are vv. 12-16 "good news" to the exiles? One would think so. After all, they have already acknowledged their heavy burden of rebellions and sins (v. 10). Surely they would identify with, and seek to emulate, the repentant wicked who, by turning from their previous ways, are released from God's death sentence. Yahweh is offering

---

1105. According to Ezekiel 18, the righteous person who does what is lawful and right "restores to the debtor his pledge" (18:7). His violent son "does not restore the pledge" (18:12). His righteous grandson "exacts no pledge" (18:16); hence, his righteousness is even greater than that of his grandfather.

Ezekiel's compatriots both a clean slate (past iniquities are promptly forgotten) and life! Yet they are insisting that "the way of the Lord is not just." Should this quotation, repeated *verbatim* from 18:25, 29, be construed as a view expressed *prior* to God's latest communiqué to the prophet, a message which he has not yet proclaimed in their hearing? If so, then one might hope that once the exiles have heard Yahweh's words, they will readily assent to the principle of divine justice Ezekiel spells out for them. After all, they have changed since Ezekiel last lectured them on this topic (chap. 18) Now, they are willing to acknowledge their culpability ("*Our* rebellions and *our* sins weigh upon us") instead of blaming preceding generations for their sorry state. Most commentators assume, however, that the people are protesting (at least some portion of) the content of vv. 2-16. (See chap. 18 where, in the context of strikingly similar material, the exiles twice charge God with unfairness, vv. 25, 29.) Perhaps they are angered by the notion that Yahweh forgets a lifetime of righteous deeds (a "treasury of merit") at the moment when a righteous person commits iniquity. Is that divine justice? But the opposite also is true: Yahweh forgets a lifetime of rebellions and sins at the moment when a wicked person turns from evil and begins to do good. And that act testifies mightily to God's mercy.

Graffy proposes that the people's complaint be translated "YHWH's way cannot be fathomed."[1106] The exiles challenge the *modus operandi* of Yahweh's justice not only because it requires them to change, but also because it strikes them as "arbitrary" and "nonsensical."[1107] They focus not on God's mercy, but on their sense of being at the mercy of God. But Ezekiel's God will not brook their objection; instead, the Lord hurls it back at them: "it is their own way that is not just" (v. 17). Yahweh's logic is consistent. People are judged on the basis of their present orientation, and not their past performance. The exiles' "logic" is illogical if they refuse God's offer of a clean slate and life in exchange for repentance and the pursuit of a righteous path. Is Yahweh's concluding assertion ("O house of Israel, I will judge all of you according to your ways!") an "impassioned appeal,"[1108] or a round rejection of their accusation?

1106. A. Graffy, *A Prophet Confronts His People,* AnBib 104 (Rome: Pontifical Biblical Institute, 1984) 77.
1107. Block, *Ezekiel 25–48,* 252.
1108. Ibid.

REFLECTIONS

A critic once observed that the eighth-century prophet, Amos, "blew in, blew off, and blew out." Amos, a denizen of Judah, traveled to the Northern Kingdom of Israel, condemned its powerful and prosperous classes, predicted its ruin, and then, so far as we know, returned home. The same cannot be said of Ezekiel. He was part of the community he addressed and bore divinely imposed responsibility for it. Should he fail to perform his role as Israel's "watchman," he would pay for his negligence with his life. He could not force his compatriots to alter their ways, but he was forced to inform them of the consequences of change and of a refusal to change.

Pastors, professors of biblical studies, and others sometimes operate as did Amos. Invited to lead a revival for a congregation not their own, or to lecture at a continuing education event for clergy in some distant conference, they too can blow in, blow off (hopefully in some helpful way!), and blow out. Within their own back yards, however, they—like Ezekiel—must work daily and faithfully to carry out their commissions and then live with the consequences—comfortable and decidedly uncomfortable.

Nowhere do I find Ezekiel softening his message for the sake of popularity, though I suspect that he occasionally felt the tug of that temptation. At the time of his call, God told him straightaway that he would carry out his ministry in "briers and thorns" amidst "scorpions," but should not fear them, proclaiming Yahweh's words "whether they hear or refuse to hear" (3:6-7). Ezekiel has been obedient, not rebellious, in the performance of his task; and he remains so in the present passage. But now, he faces a community in despair so deep that it questions the very possibility of survival.

Yahweh meets their grief with promises of a new beginning and abundant life. Their admission of rebellion and sin is itself a turning point, and God turns toward them with the good news that they need not perish for their capital offenses but can, instead, start afresh with no "criminal record" hanging over their heads. Their prison of pain and hopelessness has an open exit through which they can walk. What convict would choose to remain behind bars? Yet they respond not with gratitude, but with protestation. "The way of the Lord is not just," they insist. What madness is this?

In the Commentary, I suggested that their complaint was rooted, at least in part, in God's principle that heretofore righteous persons who committed iniquity were at that moment sentenced to death, their past righteousness erased from Yahweh's memory, while the wicked were set scot-free upon repentance and a change of course. Can we blame them for bristling at that statement? Human beings hold dear their sense of fairness. One thinks, for example, of Jesus' parable about the landowner who hired laborers for his vineyard. When some worked far longer than others, but all received the same pay, those who put in the longest day contested the landowner's fairness. No matter that they had received the agreed upon wage. They deserved more, or at least the latecomers deserved less (Matt 20:1-16)! Surely a righteous person should be allowed an occasional iniquity, or at least, the repentant wicked should bear some onus for a life of evil acts!

Ezekiel insists upon God's right to judge persons by their behavior here and now, unfettered by the past. And so those who look back over their lives and conclude that the scales are tipped on the side of righteousness grumble about the unfairness of it all, and even the wicked are disaffected by the necessity for repentance (which entails an admission of *personal* guilt) and a radical change of lifestyle. These are perfectly human responses; but they do not suit God's sense of justice, and they cannot blunt the sheer pleasure Yahweh experiences when the wicked turn from death toward life. We can see why, in another of Jesus' parables, the obedient sibling is disgruntled when Dad throws a party to celebrate the return of his prodigal son (Luke 15:11-32). But Jesus invites us to hear God's voice in the father's joyous cry, "this son of mine was dead and is alive again; he was lost and is found!"

Like the prodigal son, the wicked of Ezekiel's community are not literally dead. But they are as good as dead, because Yahweh has pronounced the death sentence against them. Like the forgiving father, however, God rejoices when they "come to themselves" (see Luke 15:17) thanks to Ezekiel's warning, turn away from their death-dealing way, and choose the path of obedience and life.

Ezekiel 33:21-22, "The City Has Fallen!"

NIV

²¹In the twelfth year of our exile, in the tenth month on the fifth day, a man who had escaped from Jerusalem came to me and said, "The city has fallen!" ²²Now the evening before the man arrived, the hand of the LORD was upon me, and he opened my mouth before the man came to me in the morning. So my mouth was opened and I was no longer silent.

NRSV

21In the twelfth year of our exile, in the tenth month, on the fifth day of the month, someone who had escaped from Jerusalem came to me and said, "The city has fallen." ²²Now the hand of the LORD had been upon me the evening before the fugitive came; but he had opened my mouth by the time the fugitive came to me in the morning; so my mouth was opened, and I was no longer unable to speak.

COMMENTARY

So long as Jerusalem survived, Ezekiel's status as Yahweh's authentic prophet remained contestable; and his oracles about its demise could be ignored, refuted, or rationalized. Yahweh promised the prophet, however, that when the city fell, a survivor (פָּלִיט *pālîṭ*) would bring the news of its destruction to Ezekiel (24:25-26).[1109] On that day, his mouth would be opened, the restriction on his speech (described in 3:26-27) would be lifted, and he would be a "sign" (מוֹפֵת; *môpēt*) to the exiles (24:27; see also 12:6, 11; 24:24). Then they would "know that I am Yahweh" (i.e., acknowledge God's absolute power and sovereignty as manifested in their history), and Ezekiel's authenticity would be vindicated.

In the book of Ezekiel, both the oracles against foreign nations/rulers in chaps. 25–32 and the oracle just examined (33:1-20) separate the prediction in 24:25-27 from its fulfillment in 33:21-22.[1110] Critics suggest that the insertion of chaps. 25–32 (whether by Ezekiel, or by an editor) occurred at a late stage in the work's composition.[1111] Ezekiel 33:1-20 was prefixed to this snippet of autobiographical narrative in order to characterize Ezekiel's ministry during the pivotal period when God's message was shifting from judgment to restoration.[1112]

Originally, many critics contend, Ezekiel's period of muteness lasted for only a single night. It began one evening (we shall consider the date in v. 21), when the hand of the Lord came upon him;

and it ended the following morning, prior to the survivor's arrival with news of Jerusalem's fall (33:22; Ezekiel speaks of Yahweh's hand upon him in 1:3; 8:1; 37:1; and 40:1; in each of those cases, Ezekiel immediately undergoes a visionary experience, but the text does not make explicit the effect of Yahweh's hand upon the prophet. For some critics, it initiates his night of muteness; cf. 3:15. For others, its effect was to free Ezekiel from his speech restriction. The former view is more plausible). Ezekiel's disciples, or "school," noting the disparity between 24:25, 27 on the one hand, and 33:22 on the other hand (the former connects the opening of the prophet's mouth and the end of his enforced silence with the day of Jerusalem's destruction; the latter connects the opening of the prophet's mouth and the end of his enforced silence with the later arrival of the survivor), inserted 24:26 ("on that day a fugitive will come to tell you the news") in an attempt to reconcile 24:25, 27 with 33:22.[1113] In fact, their addition introduced a problem since, reading 24:25-27 in its final form, the reader is left with the untenable notion that the city's destruction and the survivor's arrival in Babylonia occurred on the same day!

Later still, so the theory goes, the muteness motif was extended back to a time just seven days after Ezekiel's call to the prophetic office (3:26-27). In Wilson's view, the disciples' aim was apologetic. Detractors might charge that Jerusalem would have survived had Ezekiel performed not only the prophetic role of proclaiming Yahweh's judgment to the house of Israel, but also the prophetic task of interceding with God on Israel's behalf (cf. Gen 18:16-33). But Ezekiel's "failure" to intercede with Yahweh was not evidence that he was negligent in his duties. He did not plead Israel's case because the Lord had expressly prohibited him from doing so.[1114]

Ezekiel 3:26 is sometimes taken to mean that Ezekiel was absolutely unable to speak at all from seven days after his call until word of Jerusalem's destruction reached him (33:22). But that inter-

1109. The noun (from the root פלט [*plṭ*], which has the basic meaning of "escape") is definite; hence, "a certain survivor." "Fugitive" is not an adequate translation of פָּלִיט (*pālîṭ*), if one thinks of fugitives only as persons who flee voluntarily (and perhaps in secret). In Ezek 6:8-10, the plural form of the noun refers to people who have been carried into captivity. Hence, the "escapee" or "fugitive" who brings news of Jerusalem's destruction might well be part of the forced deportation of Judeans in the immediate aftermath of that tragic event (see also 14:22).

1110. In Zimmerli's view, 33:21-22 originally constituted a direct sequel to 24:15-24. Ezekiel 24:25-27, a secondary addition, was composed on the basis of 33:21-22 to make this connection even more explicit. See W. Zimmerli, *Ezekiel 2: A Commentary on the Book of the Prophet Ezekiel, Chapters 25–48*, trans. J. D. Martin, Hermeneia (Philadelphia: Fortress, 1983) 191.

1111. One consequence of this insertion was that the essentially chronological arrangement of the entire scroll's contents was disturbed, since a number of the prophet's oracles against other nations/rulers post-date and presuppose Jerusalem's fall.

1112. See, e.g., Ronald M. Hals, *Ezekiel*, FOTL 19 (Grand Rapids: Eerdmans, 1989) 240. One consequence of this insertion is that the exiles' utter despair (expressed in v. 10) often is interpreted as their response to the newsbearer's arrival in Babylon (reported in 33:21-22).

1113. See, e.g., W. Zimmerli, *Ezekiel 1: A Commentary on the Book of the Prophet Ezekiel, Chapters 1–24*, trans. R. E. Clements, Hermeneia (Philadelphia: Fortress, 1979) 508-9.

1114. R. R. Wilson, "An Interpretation of Ezekiel's Dumbness," *VT* 22 (1972) 104.

pretation, as we saw in the Commentary on 3:26-27, cannot be reconciled with the scroll's repeated testimony that Ezekiel indeed uttered a large number of prophetic oracles in the interim between the temporal settings of 3:26-27 and 33:22. The ancient reader, whose approach to the text did not include the presuppositions, and methodological moves (e.g., the possibility of textual translocations) of modern biblical scholarship, had to make sense of 3:26 in other ways. I proposed in the Commentary on 3:26-27 that the reader might well understand the restriction on Ezekiel's speech as his divinely imposed *inability* to function as an איש מוכיח (*'îš môkîaḥ*), an impartial arbiter who seeks justly to facilitate a juridical settlement between the plaintiff (here, Yahweh) and the defendant (here, Israel). This does not mean, however, that Ezekiel could not talk at all. Verse 27 asserts that whenever God speaks to him, his mouth will be opened and he will say to his audience, "Thus says the Lord GOD." As Wilson observes, "communication can now move in only one direction: from Yahweh to the people. No longer can the people argue with Yahweh through the prophet. The time for a fair trial has passed."[1115]

The sequential reader of 24:27 most naturally assumes that God's promise ("On that day your mouth shall be opened . . . and you shall speak and no longer be silent") presages the prophet's release from the restriction imposed in 3:26 ("and I will make your tongue cling to the roof of your mouth, so that you shall be speechess and unable to [function as] an arbiter for them, for they are a rebellious house"). The fulfillment of that promise appears in 33:21-22, a passage preceded by the exiles' first admission of wrongdoing ("Our transgressions and our sins weigh upon us, and we waste away because of them; how then can we live?"). It remains to be seen, however, what the consequences of the opening of Ezekiel's mouth will be. Will he assume the arbiter's role? Is such a role necessary now that Jerusalem has actually fallen and Judah has collapsed? Does the plethora of restoration oracles to follow blunt the exiles' felt need for an *'îš môkîaḥ*?

The date introducing Ezekiel's brief autobiographical narrative is clear in Hebrew ("In the twelfth year of our exile, in the tenth month, on

the fifth day of the month"), but problematic on other grounds. According to 24:1, a date notice closely resembling that of 2 Kgs 25:1 (=Jer 52:4) in form and content, Nebuchadrezzar's siege of Jerusalem began on the tenth day of the tenth month (Tebet) of the ninth year of *Jehoiachin's* exile: January 15, 588 BCE. The siege lasted for some eighteen months; and the city fell on the ninth day of the fourth month (Tammuz) of the tenth year of *Zedekiah's* reign (2 Kgs 25:1; Jer 39:2; 52:6): July 18, 586 BCE. According to 2 Kgs 25:9, Nebuchadrezzar's commander, Nebuzaradan, set Jerusalem ablaze on or about the seventh day of the fifth month in the nineteenth year of his reign—August 14, 586 BCE (Jer 52:12 specifies the tenth, rather than the seventh, day)—and deported survivors including, most likely, the man who brought news of the city's fall to Ezekiel.

According to Ezek 33:21, this survivor reached Babylonia on the fifth day of Tebet in the twelfth year of Jehoiachin's exile (January 8, 585 BCE). By this reckoning, the trip from Jerusalem to the exilic community took approximately five months, a reasonable span of time in light of Ezra 7:9. But a conundrum persists. It would appear that approximately three years have passed since the onset of the eighteen-month siege (24:1). Zimmerli addresses the problem by emending MT 33:21 to read "In the eleventh year . . . " on the basis of eight manuscripts of the Lucianic recension of LXX and the Syriac.[1116] Better, I think, is the suggestion that the date in 24:1 is based not on the years of Jehoiachin's exile (as are all others in Ezekiel's scroll, including that appearing in 33:21), but on the official Jewish calendar, which counted from a king's regnal year—that is, the first full year of his reign (in this case, the date would refer to Zedekiah's ninth year). The year of *Jehoiachin's* exile was 597 BCE, but Zedekiah's first regnal year did not end until 596 BCE. Perhaps Ezekiel resorted to the official dating system because the day that the siege began was so crucial ("Mortal, write down the name of this day, this very day"; 24:2*a*). Alternatively, 24:1 may not originally have contained a date notice. A later editor, noting Yahweh's command to record the precise date when Nebuchadrezzar's siege began, supplied it

1115. Ibid., 101.

1116. W. Zimmerli, *Ezekiel 2: A Commentary on the Book of the Prophet Ezekiel, Chapters 25–48*, trans. J. D. Martin, Hermeneia (Philadelphia: Fortress, 1983) 191.

on the basis of 2 Kgs 25:1.[1117] In any event, an eagle-eyed ancient reader, recalling the distinctive form of the date notice in 24:1 vis à vis Ezekiel's others, and its similarity to 2 Kgs 25:1 (as well as to Jer 39:2 and 52:6), might well conclude that the prophet chose, in this particular case, to use the official dating system, rather than his own idiomatic one.

1117. See D. I. Block, *The Book of Ezekiel: Chapters 1–24,* NICOT (Grand Rapids: Eerdmans, 1997) 773.

REFLECTIONS

Jerusalem's destruction must have caused many Judeans to question both Yahweh's power and the feasibility of Yahwistic religion. Why continue to worship a deity who, at the crucial hour, was either unwilling or unable to protect "his" chosen people, the Davidic dynasty, the Temple? From the perspective of Ezekiel's preaching, however, Judah's collapse *vindicated* God, who had used Nebuchadrezzar's army justly to punish the house of Israel for its long-lived history of sin. Moreover, the prophet was vindicated by the city's demise. No longer could his community question his status as Yahweh's authentic prophet, for his judgment oracles had been fulfilled; the eye-witness testimony of the survivor left no doubt about that. Or could they raise questions? Jeremiah's predictions that Jerusalem would be restored were realized. But afterwards, when he condemned his fellow survivors in Egypt for their idolatry, they refused to take him seriously: "As for the word that you have spoken to us in the name of the LORD, we are not going to listen to you" (Jer 44:16 NRSV).

We should not doubt that Ezekiel himself experienced profound anguish when he heard the news. Judah was his homeland, Jerusalem his home town. So many of his people had perished. Recall that in the course of his visionary return to the Temple (8:1–11:25), as God's executioners began their slaughter of the city's population, he cried out, "Ah Lord God! will you destroy all who remain of Israel as you pour out your wrath upon Jerusalem?" (9:8 NRSV). Ezekiel was not immune to sorrow and grief. Even a society's harshest internal critics can bewail its passing—so much suffering, the loss of what might have been.

Nevertheless, v. 22 says nothing of the prophet's pain or of his fellow exiles' response to the blow. Rather, Ezekiel presents himself as in some sense liberated by the survivor's news. Yahweh has opened the prophet's mouth; the years of restricted speech have ended.

In our own day, social critics, including pastors and congregations who care deeply about their society's religious, political, and economic ills, may themselves feel constrained by the necessity of negativity, the burden of their critiques. It's no easy thing to be the bearers of bad news, to speak God's word of judgment to a world that prefers praise over reproof. If their judgments are on target and confirmed by events, they may feel that both God and they have been vindicated, though at an enormous price. But just as Ezekiel's scroll does not end with his exoneration, but looks beyond it to the task of reconstruction, so our task is not only "to pluck up and to pull down, to destroy and to overthrow," but also "to build and to plant" (Jer 1:10 NRSV).

Ezekiel 33:23-29, Judgment upon the Survivors Remaining in Judah

NIV

²³Then the word of the LORD came to me: ²⁴"Son of man, the people living in those ruins in the land of Israel are saying, 'Abraham was only one man, yet he possessed the land. But we are many; surely the land has been given to us as our possession.' ²⁵Therefore say to them, 'This is what the Sovereign LORD says: Since you eat meat with the blood still in it and look to your idols and shed blood, should you then possess the land? ²⁶You rely on your sword, you do detestable things, and each of you defiles his neighbor's wife. Should you then possess the land?'

²⁷"Say this to them: 'This is what the Sovereign LORD says: As surely as I live, those who are left in the ruins will fall by the sword, those out in the country I will give to the wild animals to be devoured, and those in strongholds and caves will die of a plague. ²⁸I will make the land a desolate waste, and her proud strength will come to an end, and the mountains of Israel will become desolate so that no one will cross them. ²⁹Then they will know that I am the LORD, when I have made the land a desolate waste because of all the detestable things they have done.'

NRSV

²³The word of the LORD came to me: ²⁴Mortal, the inhabitants of these waste places in the land of Israel keep saying, "Abraham was only one man, yet he got possession of the land; but we are many; the land is surely given us to possess." ²⁵Therefore say to them, Thus says the Lord GOD: You eat flesh with the blood, and lift up your eyes to your idols, and shed blood; shall you then possess the land? ²⁶You depend on your swords, you commit abominations, and each of you defiles his neighbor's wife; shall you then possess the land? ²⁷Say this to them, Thus says the Lord GOD: As I live, surely those who are in the waste places shall fall by the sword; and those who are in the open field I will give to the wild animals to be devoured; and those who are in strongholds and in caves shall die by pestilence. ²⁸I will make the land a desolation and a waste, and its proud might shall come to an end; and the mountains of Israel shall be so desolate that no one will pass through. ²⁹Then they shall know that I am the LORD, when I have made the land a desolation and a waste because of all their abominations that they have committed.

COMMENTARY

With the fall of Jerusalem—at least a five-month-old fact in Palestine, but fairly fresh news to the exiles of 597 BCE—Ezekiel is commanded by Yahweh to "address" those Judeans who have survived the Babylonian onslaught and remain in their homeland. 2 Kings 24:11 states that Nebuzaradan carried into exile all of Jerusalem's population, as well as those who had defected to the king of Babylon. But the following verse acknowledges that he left behind "some of the poorest people of the land" to sustain its agricultural economy. No doubt the population decreased substantially, especially in the environs of Jerusalem. But we should surmise that the inhabitants of more remote, rural areas were not dis-patched in large numbers, and that those urbanites who were able, by stealth or flight, to avoid Nebuzaradan's "net," returned (no doubt cautiously) to their devastated cities ("the inhabitants of those ruins in the land of Israel," v. 24 NIV).

Ezekiel's *actual* audience remains his exilic community—not only the first deportees, but also those who have only recently arrived (Ezekiel presupposes that the deported survivors of Judah's collapse will join his community in exile; see, e.g., 14:22-23). Both constituencies will, naturally enough, long for the latest news of events occurring in, and conditions pertaining to, Judah. Those carried off by Nebuzaradan have much to tell their seasoned fellow exiles. But further information

1456

likely arrives through a variety of venues—trade caravans, reports of Babylon's latest victory, written correspondence, etc.

According to v. 24, Yahweh informs Ezekiel of a saying circulating among those who remain in the homeland: "Abraham was only one man, yet he got possession of the land; but we are many; the land is surely given us to possess." This "thesis" is followed by disputation (vv. 25-26) and a counterthesis (vv. 27-29). Hence, the oracle can be labeled a disputation speech. At the same time, the presence of the expanded recognition formula ("Then they shall know that I am the LORD") lends to the whole the character of a prophetic proof saying consisting of motivation (vv. 24-26), pronouncement of judgment (vv. 27-28), and recognition formula (v. 29). The conjoining of these two—motivation and judgment—elsewhere appears in 11:2-12 and 37:11-14.

If the quotation actually was voiced by those remaining in Judah (and we cannot know with assurance that it was), we are left to wonder about the spirit in which it was said. Critics tend to concede that these folk were enduring hard times. So, for example, Greenberg speaks of "a miserable few clinging desperately to their heritage";[1118] and Zimmerli allows that "the people are "trying to find their feet again in a war-ravaged Judah"; their words reflect "not only a purely pragmatic re-orientation," but also "a process of reflection about the fundamentals in which Israel bases her life."[1119] "One may marvel," Zimmerli further observes, "at the will to rebuild and the strength to overcome catastrophes which find expression here."[1120] But Greenberg also speaks of "the unrepentant homelanders who arrogate to themselves the title of Abraham's heirs";[1121] and Zimmerli also opts for Ezekiel's (and Yahweh's) view: theirs is a "false sense of self-security."[1122]

The reader recalls that earlier in the scroll, Ezekiel (ostensibly) addressed those who remained in Jerusalem following the deportation of 597 BCE (11:1-25; see Commentary). There, as here, the homelanders' "theses" are quoted and refuted; and countertheses are advanced. Though the Jerusalemites construe the exiles' situation as evidence that God has rejected the latter ("They have gone far from the LORD," 11:15b) and interpret their own situation as evidence of divine favor ("to us this land is given for an inheritance"; 11:15b), the opposite is true. They are not the choice meat in the pot (Jerusalem); and the deportees will be gathered from the nations to which they have been scattered and return to reclaim their property. In light of the many similarities between chap. 11 and the present passage (note, e.g., how the pre-destruction homelanders' claim, "to us this land is given for a possession," 11:15b, is echoed in the post-fall homelanders' assertion, "the land is surely given us to possess," 33:24b) the reader is predisposed to assess negatively the contention of "the inhabitants of these waste places in the land of Israel." This predisposition is validated in subsequent verses.

Yahweh's refutation, introduced by לָכֵן (lākēn), "Therefore say to them" and the messenger formula ("Thus says the Lord GOD"), counters their claim by condemning their character. The religiosity suggested by their evocation of Abrahamic tradition is belied by their actions: (1) eating meat from which the blood has not been drained;[1123] (2) worshiping idols (lit., "dung pellets"); and (3) shedding blood (committing murder).[1124] Each of these three activities violates Israel's covenantal restrictions (on the first, see Lev 17:10-16; 19:26; note also Gen 9:4-6; 1 Sam 14:32-34; on the second, see Exod 20:1-6; on the third, see the prohibition against murder in Exod 20:13). Ezekiel has already accused his fellow Judeans of these sins (24:7; 18:6, 12, 15; 22:3, 4, 9, 12). The following rhetorical question, "shall you then possess the land?" permits only a negative response.

A second triad of accusations follows: (4) the homelanders resort to violence. The Hebrew phrase translated "you depend on your swords" (NRSV; NIV, "you rely on your sword") does not reappear in Hebrew Scripture; literally, it might be rendered either as "you stand on your sword," or

---

1118. Moshe Greenberg, *Ezekiel 21–37,* AB 22A (Garden City, N.Y.: Doubleday, 1997) 689.
1119. Zimmerli, *Ezekiel 2,* 198.
1120. Ibid., 199.
1121. Greenberg, *Ezekiel 21–37,* 690.
1122. Zimmerli, *Ezekiel 2,* 199.

1123. Lit., "upon the blood they eat," a formulation also found in Lev 19:26 ("Do not eat upon the blood"). Here, עַל ('al) has the meaning "accompanied by," "in addition to." See Block, *Ezekiel 25–48,* 257.

1124. Block, ibid., 259, labels the homelanders' recourse to Abraham "a totally secular a fortiori argument," but he seems to overstate the case. We should not expect, in this context, a fully rounded theological argument.

"you live by your sword."[1125] In either case, the substance of this fourth charge is essentially that of the third. Zimmerli suggests that it speaks to the violence in Judah after its destruction (see, e.g., 2 Kgs 25:22-26; Jeremiah 41);[1126] (5) they commit abominations. Ezekiel frequently resorts to the term תועבה (*tôʿēbâ*), "abomination," to speak of a variety of sins, including idolatry (e.g., 6:9; 8:6, 9) and sexual malfeasance (e.g., 22:11); (6) they defile their neighbors' wives through illicit acts of intercourse. Here, the reader recalls not only 18:6, 15, but also 22:11. This second triad also ends with the rhetorical question, "shall you then possess the land?"

Ezekiel does not dispute that, by God's grace, Abraham was promised that his descendants would inherit the land of Canaan. But he roundly rejects any notion that the remaining homelanders can base their hopes on a similarity between their venerable ancestor's situation and their own. Their blazen violations of covenant obligations sharply distinguish them from the patriarch, a paradigm of obedience, religious fidelity, and virtue. And so he must say to them, in Yahweh's name and by divine oath, that the God whose judgment Judah experienced at the hands of Nebuchadrezzar's troops is judging them still. Those residing among the ruins of towns and cities will fall by the sword; those residing in rural areas will be devoured by the wild animals whose number increases as a land's human population decreases; and those who have fled to the strongholds and caves (see also Judg 6:2) will die by pestilence (v. 27). Yahweh will reduce the land to utter desolation (see 6:4). Its proud might will end, and no inhabitant will remain to cross Israel's mountains. The expanded recognition formula in v. 29 identifies God's ultimate purpose for this punishment. The survivors in Judah, whose sins have continued despite the fatal blow of 586 BCE, will at last be forced, by death (!) and devastation, to recognize and acknowledge Yahweh's unrivaled sovereignty.

Critics observe that in Isa 51:1-2, the anonymous exilic prophet whom we call "Second Isaiah" also refers to Abraham (and to Sarah). Second Isaiah seeks to convince his fellow exiles in Babylonia that Yahweh, their God, possesses unlimited power and is at work in history to return them to Judah. His audience might well be experiencing disillusionment, and also trepidation at the prospect of undertaking a long journey leading to a desolate homeland that many have never seen. But the prophet insists that God will do for them what Yahweh did for Israel's ancestral father and mother:

> Listen to me, you who pursue righteousness
> and who seek the Lord:
> Look to the rock from which you were cut
> and to the quarry from which you were hewn;
> look to Abraham, your father,
> and to Sarah, who gave you birth.
> When I called him he was but one,
> and I blessed him and made him many.

Second Isaiah's use of this particular ancestoral tradition is akin to the landowners' allusion in Ezek 33:24. In each case, the speaker(s) refers to Abraham in order to buttress his community's morale and belief that, though small in number, they will be able to accomplish great things. But the two texts differ in significant ways. In Ezekiel 33, the homelanders refer to Abraham, at least in part, in order to justify their appropriation of land and goods left behind by the deportees. In Isa 51:1-2, the prophet alludes to Abraham and Sarah in order to assert that the exiles will receive Yahweh's blessing, thrive, and grow in number. Ezekiel concentrates on the homelanders' sins; Second Isaiah addresses "you who pursue righteousness and who seek the LORD." Ezekiel's God condemns the homelanders. (One wonders if both they and the claim ascribed to them are judged so harshly because Ezekiel's own audience of exiles would not take kindly to the pilfering of their property by those remaining in Judah.) Second Isaiah's God sides with those exiles who have remained faithful to Yahweh and who will accept the Lord's invitation to return to Judah. (Second Isaiah never acknowledges that Israel's land is populated by Judeans who escaped deportation. He speaks as if the land were without inhabitants and awaiting the exiles' return.) (See Reflections at 33:30-33.)

1125. The second option is favored by Greenberg, who understands עמד (*ʿāmad*) to mean "to exist," "last," "be sustained." See Greenberg, *Ezekiel 21–37*, 685.

1126. Zimmerli, *Ezekiel 2*, 199.

Ezekiel 33:30-33, They Hear Your Words But Do Not Put Them into Practice

NIV

30"As for you, son of man, your countrymen are talking together about you by the walls and at the doors of the houses, saying to each other, 'Come and hear the message that has come from the LORD.' 31My people come to you, as they usually do, and sit before you to listen to your words, but they do not put them into practice. With their mouths they express devotion, but their hearts are greedy for unjust gain. 32Indeed, to them you are nothing more than one who sings love songs with a beautiful voice and plays an instrument well, for they hear your words but do not put them into practice.

33"When all this comes true—and it surely will—athen they will know that a prophet has been among them."

NRSV

30As for you, mortal, your people who talk together about you by the walls, and at the doors of the houses, say to one another, each to a neighbor, "Come and hear what the word is that comes from the LORD." 31They come to you as people come, and they sit before you as my people, and they hear your words, but they will not obey them. For flattery is on their lips, but their heart is set on their gain. 32To them you are like a singer of love songs,a one who has a beautiful voice and plays well on an instrument; they hear what you say, but they will not do it. 33When this comes— and come it will!—then they shall know that a prophet has been among them.

aCn: Heb like a love song

COMMENTARY

Formally, vv. 30-33 constitute the second sub-unit of a larger unit prefaced (in v. 23) by the familiar word event formula ("The word of the LORD came to me"). In these verses, however, Ezekiel's attention has shifted from the words and deeds of homelanders remaining in Judah to those of his fellow exiles. Like vv. 24-29, the present passage begins with God's direct address to the prophet ("As for you, mortal. . . ."). What follows is not an oracle for Ezekiel to proclaim, but Yahweh's report of what the deportees are saying about the prophet.

Ezekiel has, it seems, become a "hot topic" of conversation. Whenever people pause in a shady spot ("by the walls, and at the doors of the houses") to chat, they encourage each other to "come and hear what the word is that comes from the LORD." Entering the prophet's house, they sit before him "as my people", just as the elders have come and sat before him (8:1; 14:1; 20:1). They listen to his words, but they do not obey them: a sorry state of affairs! The people fill Ezekiel's house, ostensibly hungering for God's word; but that word has no effect upon how they live their lives. The plural noun עגבים ('ăgābîm), "flattery" (NRSV), "devotion" (NIV), actually denotes sensuous love. The verb from the same root ("to lust") appears in Ezekiel's metaphorical account of international relations involving Samaria (Oholah) and Jerusalem (Oholibah) in 23:5, 7, 9, 12, 16, and 20. Critics suggest emending the text to כזבים (kĕzābîm), "lies, deceptive things," but the reader will attempt to make sense of the MT. The exiles crave the sensuous and have mouths full of erotic speech.[1127] But their hearts are set on their בצע (beṣa'), "gain made by violence, unjust gain, profit" (see also 22:13, 27).[1128] To them, Ezekiel is like a love song beautifully sung and accompanied by a musical instrument—excellent entertainment. They listen intently, but they do not put his words into actions.

Such, Yahweh reports, is Ezekiel's situation. But it will not remain so indefinitely. When "it" (the pronominal suffix is feminine singular) comes (when what comes? predicted events?), as it surely will, then the exiles will know that a

1127. Block, Ezekiel 25–48, 266.
1128. BDB 130b.

prophet has been among them (see 2:5). This too is a "recognition formula," though here, the people will come to know and acknowledge not who Yahweh is, but who Ezekiel is—God's authentic intermediary.

REFLECTIONS

Ezekiel 33:23-33 purports to shed light on the mindset of two different constituencies: those Judeans who have survived the onslaught of Nebuchadrezzar's troops and remain in their native land; and the deportees of 597 and 586 BCE. On the one hand, the homelanders, who have experienced horrific events and conditions, are determined to persist, indeed, to prevail, over their circumstances. On the other hand, the exiles, who have endured their own brands of trauma, are frequenting Ezekiel's house in order to hear Yahweh's latest communiqué. Their time with the prophet is entertaining but, like many a Sunday morning sermon, his message has no impact upon their lives.

It is difficult to determine the accuracy of Ezekiel's portrayals of both constituencies. He has never had anything positive to say about those who escaped deportation in 597 BCE, and so we are not surprised to see him accusing them of a sampling of sins which Israelite law regards as most grievous. His God utterly rejects the homelanders' evocation of Abrahamic tradition although, as noted in the commentary, we cannot know if they were actually saying such things and, if so, the spirit in which they spoke. We can know that the deportees, Ezekiel's actual audience, would have loathed the notion that during their exile, fellow Judeans were helping themselves to their property. The prophet, who probably had some real information about conditions pertaining in post-fall Judah, has no intention of giving those who remain in Judah a fair hearing. His rebuttal is absolute; his accusations are applied to them all. We are reminded that the text is not a disinterested, objective, nothing-but-the-facts report. It was composed for a particular audience, and its author's perspectives are everywhere apparent. Reading this passage, we listen for the word of Yahweh; but we also recognize that when God speaks through human beings, their minds and hearts are neither disengaged nor deleted. We hear God's voice, but also the voice (presuppositions, beliefs, biases) of the human author. How comforting it is to realize that dialogue with the divine does not reduce us to robots!

Ezekiel's God does not condemn his exilic audience to death for its failure to put the prophet's words into action. But they too are excoriated for their post-fall behavior. Was it actually the case that not one of those who thronged to his house took his message to heart? Ezekiel's authenticity as Yahweh's true intermediary was confirmed—at least for a time—when his predictions of Judah's collapse were realized. Surely at least some who saw and heard him were transformed by his ministry! But the text does not permit that possibility, denouncing them all for their insincerity and greed. We should assume that this cream-of-the-crop exilic community faired reasonably well in Babylonia. Some may even have flourished. No doubt they were as susceptible to the infection of avarice as are we. The prophet proclaims God's word in their midst; but both Yahweh and Ezekiel know that human hearts can harden, and minds run roughshod in pursuit of wealth. The text tells us that when "it" (?) comes to pass, then the exiles will know that a prophet has been among them. But will they? If the confirmation of Ezekiel's judgment oracles did not do the trick, what will?

EZEKIEL 34:1-31, THE LORD IS YOUR SHEPHERD; YOU SHALL NOT WANT

OVERVIEW

With Ezekiel 34, the reader arrives at the onset of what commentator Daniel Block calls "the gospel according to Ezekiel (34:1–48:35)."[1129] To be sure, optimistic prophecies have appeared in some preceding chapters (e.g., 11:14-21; 17:22-24; 28:25-26); and negative comments will surface not only in chap. 34, but also in some subsequent oracles. The present prophecy of salvation, however, marks a genuine turning point in the prophet's ministry. Henceforth, he will speak frequently of Yahweh's future rescue of Israel, of its restoration to the homeland, and of conditions that will pertain there.

Ezekiel 34 draws upon (and draws together) a rich array of Israel's religious imagery, traditions, and motifs: the metaphors, common in the ancient Near Eastern world, that a king (whether divine or human) is a shepherd, and his subjects are the flock; Day of the Lord allusions; the (new) exodus; God's everlasting covenant with David and his dynasty; blessings associated with fidelity to the covenant forged at Sinai; and the establishment of a future "covenant of peace."

A complex compositional history likely underlies Ezekiel 34. Few critics would deny the prophet vv. 1-16 (sans vv. 7-8), but the "authenticity" of vv. 17-31 has been the subject of vigorous debate.[1130] Nevertheless the text invites readers to construe it as a single unit, because its subunits (vv. 2-10; 11-16; 17-31) share shepherd/flock imagery. Such imagery is less pronounced in vv. 25-30 (it returns explicitly in

v. 31). But because those verses are read in the light of preceding ones and speak of Israel's future security in ways largely apropos to animals as well as to human beings, they fit their context well.

Following the familiar word event formula (v. 1), the chapter commences with a prophecy of punishment addressed to the past shepherds of Israel (vv. 2-10). This may seem a strange way to launch an oracle of salvation, but the reader soon discovers that the shepherds' loss will be the flock's gain. Ezekiel casts his metaphorical description of the rulers' sins of commission and omission against Yahweh's people in the form of a woe oracle (vv. 2-6; note the presence of הוי [*hôy*, "woe"] in v. 2 NIV). The announcement of their punishment appears in v. 10: God will retake control of the flock, bringing an end to the shepherds' exploitive and irresponsible tending.

The second subunit (vv. 11-16) proclaims that Yahweh, the good shepherd, will seek out the sheep scattered among the nations and return them to their homeland, there to graze in fine pasturage upon the mountains of Israel and to drink from the land's watercourses. The Lord's care for the flock is the antithesis of the former shepherds' miscare (compare vv. 4 and 16).

Verse 16 *b* functions as a pivot between previous and following verses. Yahweh will destroy the fat and strong members of the flock, whose offenses are detailed in vv. 17-21, and tend the sheep with "justice." Not only do the rams and he-goats (the flock's most powerful members) feed on the best pasturage and drink the clearest water, but also they oppress the rest of the flock by trampling the remaining pasturage beneath their feet and muddying the water with their hooves. Therefore, Yahweh will judge between the "fat sheep" and their victims, the "lean sheep" who have been scattered far and wide. The text does not dwell upon the form Yahweh's judgment or arbitration will take. Rather, v. 22 focuses upon the positive—God's rescue of the flock, which will "no longer be ravaged."

1129. D. I. Block, *The Book of Ezekiel: Chapters 25–48*, NICOT (Grand Rapids: Eerdmans, 1998) 268.

1130. G. A. Cooke, *A Critical and Exegetical Commentary on the Book of Ezekiel*, ICC (New York: Scribner's, 1937), regards vv. 17-31 as a secondary expansion of the two-part, authentic oracle in vv. 1-16. J. W. Wevers, *Ezekiel*, NCB (London: Nelson, 1969) 257, 260-64, concurs. W. Zimmerli, *Ezekiel 2: A Commentary on the Book of the Prophet Ezekiel, Chapters 25–48*, trans. J. D. Martin, Hermeneia (Philadelphia: Fortress, 1983) 212-23, attributes vv. 1-15, v. 16 (a linking verse), and vv. 17-22 to the prophet. Verses 23-24 are also to be regarded as authentic, although their placement in the present text is secondary. Verses 7-8 are later expansions, while vv. 25-30(31) come from Ezekiel's disciples. By contrast, Jon D. Levenson, *Theology of the Program of Restoration of Ezekiel 40–48*, HSM 10 (Missoula: Scholars Press, 1976) 84-91, defends the chapter's unity.

An initial conjunctive (ו *waw,* "and") links vv. 23-25 to preceding verses. Yahweh intends to raise up over the flock one shepherd, "my servant David." Here, Ezekiel speaks not of the resurrection of Israel's second king, but of the reestablishment of the Davidic dynasty. Despite his earlier, brutal denunciations of Judah's last rulers (see, e.g., chaps. 17 and 19), he anticipates the restoration of Israel's only legitimate royal line.

Promising the establishment of an uncondi-tional "covenant of peace," Ezekiel describes a future free of dangers (wild animals, oppressive and insulting nations, famine) and filled with blessings (security, seasonal rains, lush vegetation). The people will know that Yahweh is with them and that they are God's own. The chapter concludes with the reassuring words, "You are my sheep, the sheep of my pasture and I am your God, says the Lord GOD."

Ezekiel 34:1-10, Woe to the Shepherds of Israel

NIV

34 The word of the LORD came to me: [2]"Son of man, prophesy against the shepherds of Israel; prophesy and say to them: 'This is what the Sovereign LORD says: Woe to the shepherds of Israel who only take care of themselves! Should not shepherds take care of the flock? [3]You eat the curds, clothe yourselves with the wool and slaughter the choice animals, but you do not take care of the flock. [4]You have not strengthened the weak or healed the sick or bound up the injured. You have not brought back the strays or searched for the lost. You have ruled them harshly and brutally. [5]So they were scattered because there was no shepherd, and when they were scattered they became food for all the wild animals. [6]My sheep wandered over all the mountains and on every high hill. They were scattered over the whole earth, and no one searched or looked for them.

[7]" 'Therefore, you shepherds, hear the word of the LORD: [8]As surely as I live, declares the Sovereign LORD, because my flock lacks a shepherd and so has been plundered and has become food for all the wild animals, and because my shepherds did not search for my flock but cared for themselves rather than for my flock, [9]therefore, O shepherds, hear the word of the LORD: [10]This is what the Sovereign LORD says: I am against the shepherds and will hold them accountable for my flock. I will remove them from tending the flock so that the shepherds can no longer feed themselves. I will rescue my flock from their mouths, and it will no longer be food for them.

NRSV

34 The word of the LORD came to me: [2]Mortal, prophesy against the shepherds of Israel: prophesy, and say to them—to the shepherds: Thus says the Lord GOD: Ah, you shepherds of Israel who have been feeding yourselves! Should not shepherds feed the sheep? [3]You eat the fat, you clothe yourselves with the wool, you slaughter the fatlings; but you do not feed the sheep. [4]You have not strengthened the weak, you have not healed the sick, you have not bound up the injured, you have not brought back the strayed, you have not sought the lost, but with force and harshness you have ruled them. [5]So they were scattered, because there was no shepherd; and scattered, they became food for all the wild animals. [6]My sheep were scattered, they wandered over all the mountains and on every high hill; my sheep were scattered over all the face of the earth, with no one to search or seek for them.

[7]Therefore, you shepherds, hear the word of the LORD: [8]As I live, says the Lord GOD, because my sheep have become a prey, and my sheep have become food for all the wild animals, since there was no shepherd; and because my shepherds have not searched for my sheep, but the shepherds have fed themselves, and have not fed my sheep; [9]therefore, you shepherds, hear the word of the LORD: [10]Thus says the Lord GOD, I am against the shepherds; and I will demand my sheep at their hand, and put a stop to their feeding the sheep; no longer shall the shepherds feed themselves. I will rescue my sheep from their mouths, so that they may not be food for them.

COMMENTARY

Yahweh commands Ezekiel to prophesy against the shepherds of Israel. Who are these shepherds? Critics agree that the prophet employs a metaphor common throughout the ancient Near East, i.e., a king is a shepherd.[1131] The Sumerian King List, for example, says of Etana, a post-flood ruler of Kish, "Etana, a shepherd, he who ascended to heaven (and) who consolidated all countries, became king and ruled 1,560 years."[1132] In the prologue to his law code, Hammurabi, a ruler of the Old Babylonian Dynasty, identifies himself as "Hammurabi, the shepherd, called by Enlil am I."[1133] Block cites two ancient Near Eastern similes employing shepherd (= king) and flock (= subjects) imagery. The first, a Babylonian proverb, asserts that "a people without a king (is like) sheep without a shepherd." The second, from Egypt, expresses the same idea: without a king, the people are "like a flock gone astray without a shepherd."[1134] These proverbs stir thoughts of the prophet Micaiah son of Imlah's prediction concerning the death of northern Israel's King Ahab: "I saw all Israel scattered on the mountains, like sheep that have no shepherd" (1 Kgs 22:17).

It is possible that Ezekiel, like Jeremiah (see, e.g., Jer 2:8; 23:1-4), intends that "shepherds" be understood to refer more broadly to leaders in Jerusalem, and not just to the nation's kings *per se*. Block challenges that option, observing that in vv. 23-24, the problem of the former, abusive shepherds is resolved by Yahweh's future appointment of a single good shepherd, David, through whose earthly rule God will exercise divine rule of the flock.[1135] His point is strong, though not decisive. In preceding judgment oracles, Ezekiel has singled out Judah's kings for rebuke (see, e.g., Ezekiel 17, with which the present passage shares striking similarities, and Ezekiel 19). But he has also condemned Israel's elders for idolatry (8:9-13) and its princes for idolatry, gross acts of social injustice (e.g., murder, oppression), the desecration of

sabbaths, and sexual misconduct (Ezekiel 22). On balance, I conclude that in 34:1-10, the prophet focuses on Judah's last kings. But competent ancient (as well as modern) readers could construe "shepherds" more broadly.

The indictment, in the form of a woe oracle, immediately sets out a situation gone awry. Israel's shepherds tended (רעה *rā'â*) themselves, when their responsibility was to tend the sheep![1136] They ate the fat, i.e., the choicest part of an animal (a sin of commission);[1137] they clothed themselves with wool (a second sin of commission); and they slaughtered the fat sheep (a third sin of commission), but (the charge is repeated) they did not tend the sheep (a sin of omission).[1138] They made no attempt to strengthen the weak animals, heal the infirmed, bind up the injured, return those who had strayed from the flock, or seek out the lost animals (all sins of omission), but ruled over them with force and harshness (a sin of commission). "With force," Greenberg reminds us, describes the brutal oppression the Israelites endured under King Jabin of Canaan (Judg 4:3), while "harshness" characterizes the Egyptians' savage treatment of the enslaved Hebrews (Exod 1:13-14).[1139] Israel's shepherds have treated their own flock as would foreign tyrants and taskmasters! As a consequence, the sheep have been scattered and have fallen prey to wild animals (at the literal level, marauding nations). Lacking a leader, the sheep—Yahweh calls them "*my* sheep," asserting that God is their true owner—have wandered

---

1131. Soskice compellingly defines metaphor as "that figure of speech whereby we speak about one thing in terms which are seen to be suggestive of another." See Janet Martin Soskice, *Metaphor and Religious Language* (Oxford: Clarendon, 1985) 15.

1132. *ANET,* 265.

1133. Ibid., 164.

1134. Block, *Ezekiel 25–48,* 281.

1135. Ibid., 282.

1136. The NIV's "take care of" is preferable to the NRSV's "feed" here and throughout the chapter. As its verses make clear, tending the flock entails a great deal more than simply feeding it.

1137. The LXX takes חלב (*ḥlb*) to mean "milk" (*ḥālāb*) rather than "fat" (*ḥēleb*). Many critics follow suit on the grounds that otherwise the MT's first sin of commission is simply repeated in the third ("they slaughter the fat sheep"). The alternative reading results in the somewhat strange notion of "eating" milk, but that apparent difficulty is resolved by pointing to solid milk products—e.g., curds and cheese; see 1 Sam 17:18; Isa 7:22). In fact, however, the first and third of the shepherds' sins need not be construed as identical. The first refers to the eating of the fat of an animal, its richest and best parts. The third refers to the slaughter of fat sheep—i.e., the choicest (and so most prized) animals of the flock.

1138. One might question whether the first, and especially the second, "sins" of commission are actually sins at all. However, the shepherds are shown to exploit the flock for their own self-tending, without exercising the basic responsibilities of caring for the sheep.

1139. Moshe Greenberg, *Ezekiel 21–37,* AB 22A (Garden City, N.Y.: Doubleday, 1997) 697.

throughout the mountains and high places of Israel, and finally been dispersed "over all the face of the earth" with no one to search (שׁרד *dāraš*) for or seek them.

The reader is surely struck by Ezekiel's metaphorical account of how his fellow Judeans entered exile. Though he has excoriated the last rulers of the Davidic dynasty in previous oracles and depicted Judean society's most helpless members as victims of their leaders (e.g., 22:6-12), for the most part Ezekiel has condemned the entire "house of Israel"—both those Judeans remaining in the homeland and those deported to Babylon. Here, by contrast, all of God's scattered people appear as helpless victims of their rulers' neglect and abuse.

Verse 7, with its initial "therefore" (לכן *lākēn*) followed by a direct address to the shepherds and the call to attention formula ("hear the word of Yahweh"), leads readers next to expect the proclamation of punishment. Instead v. 8, with its initial oath ("As I live") and prophetic utterance ("says the Lord GOD") formulas, summarizes the situation in an incomplete sentence: Because God's flock has no shepherd and has become spoil and prey for all the ravaging beasts, and because God's shepherds have not sought out Yahweh's flock, tending rather to themselves. . . . Verse 9, then, repeats v. 7; and v. 10 sets out the punishment proper, introduced by the messenger formula, "Thus says the Lord GOD." Speaking now of the shepherds in the third person, Yahweh utters the challenge to a duel formula ("I am against the

shepherds"; the formula "I am against X," formulated either in the second person [direct address] or in the third person, has appeared in 21:3; 26:3; 28:22; 29:30; 30:22). God will demand (שׁרד *dāraš;* the same root appeared in v. 6 with the meaning "to search") "my flock" from their hand and bring an end to their irresponsible tending; and they will no longer indulge themselves at the sheep's expense. The Lord will rescue "my flock" *from their mouths,* and the sheep will no longer be food for them. Readers recall that in the story of David and Goliath, the young shepherd, defending his ability to battle the giant, said to Saul: "Your servant used to keep sheep for his father; and whenever a lion or a bear came and took a lamb from the flock, I went after it and struck it down, rescuing the lamb *from its mouth*" (1 Sam 17:34-35 NRSV, italics added). When Yahweh speaks of rescuing God's flock from the mouths of the shepherds, the latter are comparable to rapacious beasts.

Some critics have argued that the verses examined thus far were composed during the pre-exilic period, when Judah still was ruled by Davidic kings.[1140] From the perspective of the sequential reader, however, Ezekiel proclaims these verses *after* the news of the nation's collapse has reached the exiles. Hence, his indictment of Judah's kings must serve some function other than proclaiming punishment to a still-enthroned royal line. That function becomes clear as the reader progresses through the following subsection, vv. 11-16.

1140. See, e.g., W. H. Brownlee, "Ezekiel's Poetic Indictment of the Shepherds," *HTR* 51 (1958) 191-203.

REFLECTIONS

In the world of ancient Israel, sheep and other livestock were valuable possessions—sources of nourishment (meat and milk) and of wool for clothing, tents, and trade. A shepherd's life was difficult and often dangerous, for he was responsible both for providing the defenseless flock with adequate food and water and for protecting it from predators—both human (see, e.g., Ezek 25:4) and animal (1 Sam 17:34-35).

The peoples of the ancient Near East spoke of kings as shepherds and of their subjects as sheep, thereby emphasizing the responsibility of the former diligently to care for and protect the latter. In ancient Israel, kings were expected to "tend" their subjects; and God held them accountable for their treatment of the flock.

The shepherd/flock metaphor is ancient but enduring. Its significance for Christian ministry is reflected in our use of "pastor" to refer to ordained ministers. Ministers serve as shepherds obedient to God. They are not self-appointed, nor are they engaged primarily by the flock. Instead, they are called by God to divine service.

Pastoring is not, however, the sole responsibility of ordained ministers. To the contrary, authentic leadership requires "pastoral" care. Everyone who, in one way or another, in one arena or another, exercises authority and influence would do well to consider how the shepherd metaphor might impact his or her mindset and actions. Pastoring begins with the psalmist's full awareness that "the earth is the LORD's and all that is in it,/ the world, and those who live in it" (Ps 24:1 NRSV). As leaders and caretakers, we are not to use persons, things, and situations to personal advantage. Neither exploitation nor neglect is acceptable. Rather, we are to act as God's stewards, protecting and providing for those who are entrusted to our care, but belong to God. Ezekiel 34 has much to say to leaders of every ilk, be they politicians, health-care providers, supervisors, teachers, pastors, or parents.

Ezekiel 34:11-16, Yahweh, Israel's Good Shepherd

NIV

11 " 'For this is what the Sovereign LORD says: I myself will search for my sheep and look after them. 12As a shepherd looks after his scattered flock when he is with them, so will I look after my sheep. I will rescue them from all the places where they were scattered on a day of clouds and darkness. 13I will bring them out from the nations and gather them from the countries, and I will bring them into their own land. I will pasture them on the mountains of Israel, in the ravines and in all the settlements in the land. 14I will tend them in a good pasture, and the mountain heights of Israel will be their grazing land. There they will lie down in good grazing land, and there they will feed in a rich pasture on the mountains of Israel. 15I myself will tend my sheep and have them lie down, declares the Sovereign LORD. 16I will search for the lost and bring back the strays. I will bind up the injured and strengthen the weak, but the sleek and the strong I will destroy. I will shepherd the flock with justice.

NRSV

11For thus says the Lord GOD: I myself will search for my sheep, and will seek them out. 12As shepherds seek out their flocks when they are among their scattered sheep, so I will seek out my sheep. I will rescue them from all the places to which they have been scattered on a day of clouds and thick darkness. 13I will bring them out from the peoples and gather them from the countries, and will bring them into their own land; and I will feed them on the mountains of Israel, by the watercourses, and in all the inhabited parts of the land. 14I will feed them with good pasture, and the mountain heights of Israel shall be their pasture; there they shall lie down in good grazing land, and they shall feed on rich pasture on the mountains of Israel. 15I myself will be the shepherd of my sheep, and I will make them lie down, says the Lord GOD. 16I will seek the lost, and I will bring back the strayed, and I will bind up the injured, and I will strengthen the weak, but the fat and the strong I will destroy. I will feed them with justice.

COMMENTARY

In this subsection Ezekiel turns from Judah's last kings, the exploitative and irresponsible bad shepherds of the past, to Yahweh as the flock's exemplary future shepherd. As the reader makes his way through vv. 11-16, he recognizes that the preceding subsection functioned as a foil for this one. Yahweh's tending of the flock is the antithesis of the kings' former, irresponsible shepherding.

As noted in the Overview, the "a god is a shepherd" metaphor was well-established in the ancient Near East. The Babylonian deity Marduk, for example, is exalted by other deities who say, "May he shepherd all the gods like a flock."[1141] Egyptian hymns speak of the gods as herdsmen,

1141. *ANET*, 72a.

and so on. Within the Hebrew Bible, this metaphor appears most famously in Psalm 23 ("The LORD is my shepherd, I shall not want") but also in other texts (e.g., Ps 80:1a: "Give ear, O Shepherd of Israel, you who lead Joseph like a flock!" see also Mic 4:6; 7:14; Jer 23:3: "Then I myself will gather the remnant of my flock out of all the lands where I have driven them, and I will bring them back to their fold, and they shall be fruitful and multiply"; and Isa 40:11: "He will feed his flock like a shepherd; he will gather the lambs in his arms, and carry them in his bosom, and gently lead the mother sheep").

Following the messenger formula, Yahweh speaks with emphatic determination: "I myself" (v. 11b). God will not withdraw from the sheep, but will actively search them out (שׁרד *dāraś*) and examine (בקר *bāqar*) them. The piel verb from the root *bāqar* can mean "to seek" but also "to inquire" in the sense of inspecting something. In Lev 13:36, it describes a priest's inspection of a person's skin for signs of disease (yellow hair); in Lev 27:33, it refers to the examination of an animal in order to determine its fitness for sacrifice. Verse 21 is difficult, but the sense seems to be that just as a shepherd examines (*bāqar*) his scattered sheep when at last he has found them, so Yahweh will examine "my sheep" after rescuing them from all of the places to which they were scattered "on a day of cloud and deep gloom."[1142] The latter phrase stirs thoughts of the theophany at Mt. Sinai (see, e.g., Deut 4:11; Ps 97:2) and, especially, of the "Day of Yahweh" motif (see Joel 2:2; Zeph 1:15, and the Commentary to Ezekiel 7). In this context, it refers to the recent destruction of Jerusalem, which Ezekiel understands to be Yahweh's just punishment for Israel's long-lived history of sin.

In describing God's future salvific activity, Ezekiel draws from vocabulary rooted in Israel's exodus (from Egypt) and entrance (into Canaan) traditions. Yahweh will *bring* them *out* from the peoples and *gather* them from the countries, and *bring* them *into* their own land.[1143] These three verbs appeared, in the same sequence, in Ezek 20:34-35—also an account of a new exodus which, in 20:37, uses shepherd imagery ("I will make you pass under the staff"). Under the (mis)care of the bad shepherds, the flock was scattered and wandered "over all the mountains and on every high hill" (v. 6). Under the direct care of shepherd Yahweh, however, the Israelites will undertake a new exodus, even greater than the first, because God will bring them out from the lands of *multiple* peoples, gathering them from *all* the nations. More than the Judean exiles in Babylonia are in view here. Yahweh intends to retrieve all members of flock Israel including, one supposes, the descendants of those northern Israelites scattered abroad in the wake of Ephraim's defeat by the Assyrians in 721 BCE and the Judeans who fled to Egypt in the aftermath of Jerusalem's fall. The mountains of Israel are thrice mentioned (in vv. 13-14) as the ideal setting for the flock, offering excellent pasturage and ample water. Verse 15, with its initial, emphatic pronoun ("*I* will be the shepherd of my sheep") speaks of rest and security for the flock and stirs thoughts of Ps 23:2 ("He makes me lie down in green pastures").

In v. 4, the irresponsible shepherds were accused of five sins of omission. In Hebrew, one expects a verb to precede its direct object. But in v. 4 normal word order was reversed for emphasis:

A   the weak you have not strengthened,
B   the sick you have not healed,
C   the injured you have not bound up,
D   the strayed you have not brought back,
E   the lost you have not sought

Verse 16 recasts these five negative statements about the shepherds' neglect into positive statements concerning Yahweh's shepherding of the flock. Again, direct objects precede verbs for emphasis. Moreover, the order of statements in v. 4 is reversed; and the A and B statements of that verse are, in v. 16, conflated and condensed:

E′   the lost I will seek,
D′   the strayed I will bring back,
C′   the injured I will bind up,
B′   the sick
A′   I will strengthen.

1142. Hence, "dark clouds." See H. A. Brongers, "Merismus, Synekdoche und Hendiadys in der Bible-Hebräischen Sprache," *OTS* 14 (1965) 108-9.

1143. Zimmerli, *Ezekiel 2*, 216. Levenson, *Theology of the Program of Restoration of Ezekiel 40–48*, 88-90, points to other links between Ezekiel 34 and Israel's exodus traditions. Block, *Ezekiel 25–48*, 290-91, cites ancient Near Eastern texts in which a human king speaks of having gathered his people using pastoral imagery. For a biblical analogy, see Isa 44:28, where Yahweh says of Cyrus, "He is my shepherd, and he shall carry out all my purpose."

In MT, the initial statement of v. 16b reads, "but the fat and the strong *I will destroy*" (אשמיד *ʾašmîd*). In two Hebrew manuscripts, however, the verb is אשמיר (*ʾašmîr*), "*I will watch over*." The latter reading is presupposed by LXX; MT can be explained as a copyist's error, since ד (*d*) and ר (*r*) were easily confused. If one emends the Masoretic text, then the first part of v. 16b continues the series of short, positive descriptions about Yahweh's good shepherding begun in v. 16a: God's tending of the flock is not restricted to its lost and disabled members, but extends to robust and healthy animals (the opposite of "the weak" [A] in v. 4) as well. The second half of v. 16b, then, pro-

claims that God will tend the flock "with justice," the antithesis of the bad shepherds' ruling with "force and harshness." However, MT can be retained if one reads all of v. 16b as a presage of the subunit to follow, in which Yahweh promises to judge or arbitrate between strong and oppressive members of the flock and their weaker victims. The sequential reader of v. 16 does not yet know the contents of vv. 17-22, so the MT's "I will destroy" is jarring. But the tension it creates is immediately resolved in the following verses. So read, v. 16b functions as a transition between preceding verses and ensuing ones.

REFLECTIONS

As noted in the Commentary, Yahweh is rather frequently depicted in Hebrew Scripture as the good shepherd who provides for the flock's every need. Although many people reading this reflection will have had little or no direct contact with shepherds and sheep, the metaphor remains powerful. Witness the popularity of Psalm 23, which affirms that even as God's sheep walk "through the valley of the shadow of death" (NIV), they need not fear, for God is with them as protector and guide.

For many Christians, Jesus assumes the role of the good shepherd. Indeed, as O'Day observes, "the image of Jesus as the good shepherd has a perennial hold on Christian imagination and piety. Some of the most popular pictures of Jesus are those that depict him as a shepherd, leading a flock of sheep."[1144] According to John 10:11, Jesus appropriates the "good shepherd" metaphor because he, like such a shepherd, "lays down his life for the sheep."

In Israel's ancient Near Eastern world, kings were expected to "tend" their subjects justly, especially those who were most vulnerable to abuse: widows, orphans, the poor, infirmed, and displaced. Israel's past shepherds neglected such responsibilities, Ezekiel charges (v. 4). But Yahweh, Israel's divine king, shepherds the entire flock including its weakest members (v. 16). How a society and its leaders treat those who struggle against disadvantages speaks volumes about that society's true values—not the ones it professes to hold, but those revealed in policy and action. North American society provides all too stark examples of our failure to imitate the divine shepherd. Too often the elderly are neglected, the homeless are disparaged, the sick are stigmatized, and foreigners are exploited.

1144. Gail R. O'Day, "The Gospel of John," in *The New Interpreter's Bible,* 12 vols. (Nashville: Abingdon, 1995) 9:671.

Ezekiel 34:17-31, Yahweh Arbitrates, Establishes, and Initiates

Ezekiel 34:17-22, Inter-flock Conflict

NIV

17" 'As for you, my flock, this is what the Sovereign LORD says: I will judge between one sheep and another, and between rams and goats. ¹⁸Is it not enough for you to feed on the good pasture? Must you also trample the rest of your pasture with your feet? Is it not enough for you to drink clear water? Must you also muddy the rest with your feet? ¹⁹Must my flock feed on what you have trampled and drink what you have muddied with your feet?

²⁰" 'Therefore this is what the Sovereign LORD says to them: See, I myself will judge between the fat sheep and the lean sheep. ²¹Because you shove with flank and shoulder, butting all the weak sheep with your horns until you have driven them away, ²²I will save my flock, and they will no longer be plundered. I will judge between one sheep and another.

NRSV

17As for you, my flock, thus says the Lord GOD: I shall judge between sheep and sheep, between rams and goats: ¹⁸Is it not enough for you to feed on the good pasture, but you must tread down with your feet the rest of your pasture? When you drink of clear water, must you foul the rest with your feet? ¹⁹And must my sheep eat what you have trodden with your feet, and drink what you have fouled with your feet?

20Therefore, thus says the Lord GOD to them: I myself will judge between the fat sheep and the lean sheep. ²¹Because you pushed with flank and shoulder, and butted at all the weak animals with your horns until you scattered them far and wide, ²²I will save my flock, and they shall no longer be ravaged; and I will judge between sheep and sheep.

COMMENTARY

The third major subsection of Ezekiel 34, which can itself be subdivided into smaller sections based on the topics addressed, is cast in the form of a three-part prophetic proof saying. Turning now to address the flock ("As for you, my flock") Yahweh declares, following a resumptive messenger formula, the intention to judge or arbitrate between strong and weak sheep. The reasons why such arbitration is necessary are identified in a series of accusations expressed as questions (vv. 18-19). Verse 20, introduced by the transitional "therefore" (לכן *lākēn*) followed by the messenger formula, promises Yahweh's intervention on behalf of the lean sheep. Verse 21, introduced by "because" (יען *ya'an*) continues the indictment of vv. 18-19, adding the charge that the strong animals physically abuse the weak ones. In v. 22 God declares,

"I will save my flock"; as a consequence, they will no longer be ravaged. Ezekiel does not provide specifics about the consequences of Yahweh's arbitration for the flock's *oppressive* members. One certainly presumes that God's intervention will bring inter-flock conflict to an end. The strong sheep will not continue to bully the weak. Nevertheless, the reader who construes vv. 20-22 in the light of MT v. 16*b* ("but the fat and the strong I will destroy") and with 20:37-38 in mind might well assume that oppressive and violent members of the flock will be eliminated. In this particular context, has Ezekiel blunted the extermination of abusive animals in order to foreground his overriding interest, God's positive efforts on the flock's behalf?

REFLECTIONS

Ezekiel 34 speaks to the issue of what we would call responsible ecological stewardship. God's creation is not ours to exploit, as Judah's former kings exploited the flock entrusted to their care. Neither are we, like the strong, selfish members of the flock addressed in vv. 17-22, free to take more than our share of its resources, consuming at will and polluting what remains. Ezekiel's world knew the devastation of flood and earthquake, of famine and drought, of warfare and plunder. We too know of such things; perhaps we have even experienced some of them. But Ezekiel's world did not know the devastation of nuclear waste and chemical landfills, of cracked-open oil tankers and mountains of non-biodegradable trash. Today, chap. 34 speaks with a piercing relevance the prophet could not have imagined.

Ezekiel 34:23-24, Israel Tended by One Shepherd, God's Servant David

NIV	NRSV
[23]I will place over them one shepherd, my servant David, and he will tend them; he will tend them and be their shepherd. [24]I the LORD will be their God, and my servant David will be prince among them. I the LORD have spoken.	[23]I will set up over them one shepherd, my servant David, and he shall feed them: he shall feed them and be their shepherd. [24]And I, the LORD, will be their God, and my servant David shall be prince among them; I, the LORD, have spoken.

COMMENTARY

Commentators sometimes express surprise at the contents of vv. 23-24, Yahweh's promise to raise up over the sheep a single human shepherd, "my servant David" (the emphasis on a *single* shepherd likely reflects Ezekiel's expectation that in the future, Israel will consist not of two separate kingdoms, but of one united kingdom), to tend them and to be prince among them. Hals speaks, for example, of "the unanticipated promise of a Davidic shepherd."[1145] For several reasons, however, the ancient reader likely is not surprised that Ezekiel moves in this direction. First, he has read chap. 17, which—like the present passage—speaks first of the failures of Judah's last kings, second of Yahweh's punitive response to their sins, and third of God's future restoration of the Davidic dynasty. Ezekiel uses different imagery in that chapter—eagles, cedars, vines (see the Commentary on chap. 17). But the progression of thought in the two passages is essentially the

same.[1146] Second, the reader knows Jer 23:1-6(8), which likewise exhibits both shepherd/flock metaphors and the same sequence.[1147] Third, he recognizes that references to David as shepherd and as Yahweh's servant ruler fit sublimely into their context. On the one hand, tradition remembers David, the youthful shepherd, as a faithful tender of his father's flock—one who risked his own life in order to protect the animals entrusted to his care (1 Sam 17:34-35). David's actual shepherding style was the antithesis of the evil shepherds' (metaphorical) "tending." On the other hand, tradition remembers David as Israel's king par excellence, the ruler for whom God established an unconditional, everlasting covenant:

1146. Levenson identifies similarities between Ezekiel 17 on the one hand, and chap. 34 on the other. See Jon D. Levenson, *Theology of the Program of Restoration of Ezekiel 40–48*, HSM 10 (Missoula: Scholars Press, 1976) 84-101.

1147. Some scholars argue that Ezekiel knew this passage in Jeremiah and was influenced by it. But there are significant differences, as well as similarities, between the two texts. If Jer 23:1-6[8] was not a direct influence on Ezekiel 34, then it is possible that both reflect a pattern of thought present elsewhere (e.g., Jer 30:8-11; 33:12-26).

1145. Ronald M. Hals, *Ezekiel*, FOTL 19 (Grand Rapids: Eerdmans, 1989) 249.

"your house and your kingdom shall be made sure forever before me; your throne shall be established forever" (2 Sam 7:16; see also Jer 33:17, 20-21, 25-26). Critical though he be of Judah's final Davidic kings, Ezekiel still insists that its only legitimate dynasty will be reinstituted in Israel's future.

The references to David in vv. 23 and 24, then, address the dilemmas of preceding verses at multiple levels. Israel's shepherds failed to tend their flock and, in fact, exploited it in order to care for themselves. Young David, by contrast, cared for his father's flock as an obedient and faithful shepherd should. A future Davidic shepherd (here called "prince," נשׂיא *nāśîʾ*) will tend Yahweh's flock as did King David of old, God's servant ruler (the title "my servant" is, in this context, both honorific and expressive of one's obligation to obey one's master). Unlike Israel's past shepherds, who helped themselves to the best of Yahweh's flock, this Davidide will tend the sheep on behalf of their true owner. As Levenson observes. "God does not send his messiah to rule; he rules through his messiah."[1148]

At its outset, v. 24 echoes half of the traditional Sinai covenant formulation (e.g., "You are my people, and I am your God"; see, e.g., Deut 27:9; Jer 31:11; Hos 2:25). But the second half of v. 24 evokes thoughts of the Davidic covenant. Hence, the verse not only echoes both covenant traditions, but also yokes them. (See Reflections at 34:25-31.)

1148. Levenson, *Theology of the Program of Restoration of Ezekiel 40–48,* 87.

Ezekiel 34:25-31, A Covenant of Peace

NIV

25 " 'I will make a covenant of peace with themand rid the land of wild beasts so that they may live in the desert and sleep in the forests in safety. 26I will bless them and the places surrounding my hill.*a* I will send down showers in season; there will be showers of blessing. 27The trees of the field will yield their fruit and the ground will yield its crops; the people will be secure in their land. They will know that I am the LORD, when I break the bars of their yoke and rescue them from the hands of those who enslaved them. 28They will no longer be plundered by the nations, nor will wild animals devour them. They will live in safety, and no one will make them afraid. 29I will provide for them a land renowned for its crops, and they will no longer be victims of famine in the land or bear the scorn of the nations. 30Then they will know that I, the LORD their God, am with them and that they, the house of Israel, are my people, declares the Sovereign LORD. 31You my sheep, the sheep of my pasture, are people, and I am your God, declares the Sovereign LORD.' "

a26 Or I will make them and the places surrounding my hill a blessing

NRSV

25I will make with them a covenant of peace and banish wild animals from the land, so that they may live in the wild and sleep in the woods securely. 26I will make them and the region around my hill a blessing; and I will send down the showers in their season; they shall be showers of blessing. 27The trees of the field shall yield their fruit, and the earth shall yield its increase. They shall be secure on their soil; and they shall know that I am the LORD, when I break the bars of their yoke, and save them from the hands of those who enslaved them. 28They shall no more be plunder for the nations, nor shall the animals of the land devour them; they shall live in safety, and no one shall make them afraid. 29I will provide for them a splendid vegetation so that they shall no more be consumed with hunger in the land, and no longer suffer the insults of the nations. 30They shall know that I, the LORD their God, am with them, and that they, the house of Israel, are my people, says the Lord GOD. 31You are my sheep, the sheep of my pasture*a* and I am your God, says the Lord GOD.

aGk OL: Heb pasture, you are people

COMMENTARY

Yahweh's promise of a future "covenant of peace" (ברית שלום *bĕrît šālôm*) is followed by a description of its attending blessings: the eradication of dangerous beasts, such that one can rest securely throughout the land, including its least hospitable regions; lush vegetation sustained by adequate and reliable seasonal rains; and freedom from oppression and fear. Here, we find one of the fullest descriptions of Israel's understanding of *šālôm* as more than the absence of hostility or tension. "[*Shalom*] speaks of wholeness, harmony, fulfillment, humans at peace with their environment and with God."[1149]

What is this "covenant of peace" that God will make *for* (not "with") them? What is its relationship to other covenants within the book of Ezekiel and beyond? Bernard Batto argues convincingly that the "covenant of peace" motif derives from ancient Near Eastern mythology about the primeval period. When divine/human hostility ended, the deities ceased their efforts to exterminate humankind and took an oath "to maintain peace and harmony with humankind and even with the whole of creation."[1150] The oath was confirmed by a "permanent visible sign" symbolizing the perpetuity of this new era of peace. The myth appears in two variations, designated by Batto as Pattern A and Pattern B. In the former, the gods attempt to exterminate humankind by flood. The latter lacks a flood account. Rather, a goddess seeks to slay humanity with her sword.[1151] The influence of Pattern A is patent in the biblical flood accounts (J and P) found in Genesis 6–9. Pattern B may have left its imprint on the present passage, as we shall see below. According to Batto, certain of Israel's prophets (Hosea, Ezekiel, Deutero-Isaiah, Zechariah) adopted the covenant of peace motif, which had grown and developed over the centuries. But they unlatched it from the primeval period and projected it into the future (Hos 2:18-25; Isa 54:10; Zech 8:10-12, Ezekiel 37). So, for example, in the present passage and in Isa 54:9-10, the assuaging of Yahweh's anger is followed by

God's promise to establish an eternal covenant of peace with Israel.

Zimmerli, and more recently Block, identify this covenant of peace with the "eternal covenant" that Yahweh will establish with Jerusalem, "his" faithless wife, in Ezek 16:60. To be sure, that passage says nothing of a covenant of "peace." For Zimmerli, the addition of that word in this passage simply makes explicit the essence of covenant. A covenant establishes well-being, a healthy relationship between the covenant's partners. This well-being extends throughout the nation's sphere of life when Yahweh is the covenant partner who brings about peace.[1152]

It is by no means clear, however, that an ancient reader of Ezek 34:25-31 would identify its "covenant of peace" with the eternal covenant of 16:60. The latter appeared within the context of a metaphorical narrative about Jerusalem, a personified (female) city whose idolatrous cultic practices and inappropriate royal policies (e.g., forging and relying on international alliances) were presented as sexual infidelities threatening her marriage with Yahweh. To be sure, faithless Jerusalem embodies her inhabitants. But the female personification of the urban center is ubiquitous throughout chap. 16. Yahweh speaks of remembering God's covenant with *her* in the days of *her* youth (most obviously a reference back to their marriage in 16:9) and establishing with *her* an everlasting bond, i.e., one that cannot be abrogated because Yahweh determines that it will not be.

The "covenant of peace" in the present passage, by contrast, says little about God's relationship with that city. To the contrary, the blessings of this covenant focus especially upon idyllic agrarian conditions. One wonders if Zimmerli, Block, and others have associated this passage with 16:60 under the influence of Hosea 2, where both female imagery (Israel's land and its people are personified as women) and reference to a beneficent covenant (v. 18) appear. I do not deny that Ezek 34:25-30 bears some similarities to Hosea 2,

---

1149. D. I. Block, *The Book of Ezekiel: Chapters 25–48,* NICOT (Grand Rapids: Eerdmans, 1998) 303.

1150. Bernard Batto, "The Covenant of Peace: A Neglected Ancient Near Eastern Motif," *CBQ* 49 (1987) 187.

1151. Ibid., 187-88.

1152. W. Zimmerli, *Ezekiel 2: A Commentary on the Book of the Prophet Ezekiel, Chapters 25–48,* trans. J. D. Martin, Hermeneia (Philadelphia: Fortress, 1983) 220.

though there are differences as well.[1153] As Batto has shown, both texts reflect the influence of the ancient Near Eastern motif discussed above (they share, for example, the notion of lying down in safety and of abundant harvests). Nevertheless, the equation of this passage's covenant of peace with the eternal covenant of Ezek 16:60 seems strained.

More probable is the reader's conclusion that Yahweh's covenant of peace is somehow associated with the one forged at Sinai. How could he not think of that treaty, when Ezekiel's description of the blessings Israel will enjoy in the future echoes blessings associated with human fidelity to that ancient bond? The present passage evokes thoughts of the Sinaitic covenant blessings of Lev 26:1-13 and their counterpart in Deut 28:2-14. Yet this covenant of peace *cannot* adequately be explained simply as a renewing of the conditional Sinai covenant. In vv. 25-30, Ezekiel nowhere says that Yahweh's covenant of peace depends upon the people's obedience to a set of stipulations. Rather, he focuses upon Yahweh's initiative ("I will make a covenant of peace for them") and unconditional promises of safety, blessing, security, and freedom from oppression. So, while the benefits of the covenant in vv. 25-30 stir thoughts of that ancient treaty with its blessings (and curses), this covenant is presented as something new.

The first consequence of Yahweh's covenant of peace is the eradication of dangerous animals from Israel's land (cf. Hos 2:18; Isa 11:6-8). Even the desert and its opposite, the forest, will be so safe that one can live and sleep in them. The desert is home to wild and noxious creatures. Forests are especially dangerous at night, when beasts prowl in search of food (see Ps 104:20-22).

In the covenant curse of Lev 26:22, Yahweh threatens to bring ravenous beasts against Israel: "I will let loose wild animals against you, and they shall bereave you of your children and destroy your livestock; they shall make you few in number, and your roads shall be deserted." Ezekiel has previously referred to such beasts as God's instruments of punishment (5:17; 14:15, 21; 31:12-14;

33:27). Now, his promise recalls the covenant blessings of Lev 26:6: "And I will grant peace in the land, and you shall lie down and no one shall make you afraid; I will remove dangerous animals from the land, and no sword shall go through your land." There, as here, "peace" is associated with the eradication of wild beasts, though Leviticus speaks also of sword-wielding foes.

Verse 25 makes sense as an address to human beings. But the reader also can easily understand it as a promise to Yahweh's "flock." On the one hand, enemy nations are depicted as wild animals ravaging the sheep in Ezek 34:5, 8. On the other hand, eliminating fierce beasts would benefit flocks both literal and metaphorical. Indeed, the reference to residing securely in the desert and sleeping in the woods might be more appropriate to the flock metaphor.

Verse 26 is difficult because the referent for "them" in the phrase "I will make them" is unclear, the identity of "my hill" is disputed, and its relationship to v. 25 is ambiguous. In the light of the immediately preceding verse, "them" might refer to the recipients of Yahweh's covenant ("I will make with them a covenant of peace"), who can reside securely even in the land's most harrowing areas. Alternatively "them" might be understood as a reference to the desert and forests of v. 25b. This second possibility is buttressed by the fact that the following phrase ("the region around my hill") is, like desert and forests, a reference to place(s). "My hill" might well be construed by the ancient reader as a reference to Jerusalem (see Isa 10:32; 31:4). The fact that Ezekiel has not (and will not) use the name "Zion" does not rule out that possibility, since Jerusalem and its Temple are often his focus. (It is true, however, that the prophet does not elsewhere use "hill" in this way; cf. 6:3, 13; 20:28; 34:6; 35:8; 36:4, 6).

The first half of v. 26, then, likely asserts Yahweh's promise to make all of Israel's land, including its most formidable regions, into a "blessing"—that is, "an exemplar of blessedness."[1154] In v. 26b, God promises that the land

---

1153. In Hos 2:20, Yahweh initiates a new covenant, but not one between God and Israel. To the contrary, the covenant, mediated by Yahweh, is between Israel and the beasts, birds, and creeping things. The consequence of this covenant is peace and security. Ezekiel's "covenant of peace" entails the absolute elimination of animals that threaten the human population.

1154. Moshe Greenberg, *Ezekiel 21–37*, AB 22A (Garden City, N.Y.: Doubleday, 1997) 703. Zimmerli, *Ezekiel 2*, 210, and Walther Eichrodt, *Ezekiel*, trans. Cosslett Quin, OTL (Philadelphia: Westminster, 1970) 474, follow the LXX, deleting ברכה (*běrākâ*, "blessing"). They then emend the MT to read ונתתי את־הרביבים (*wěnātattî 'et-hārěbîbîm*, "And I shall send showers of dew in its season").

---

will receive its seasonal rains, "showers of blessing." As a consequence, lush vegetation will grow (v. 27 a).[1155] The trees of the field will yield their fruit, and the earth will bring forth its various crops. The people will be freed from the danger of drought, famine, starvation, and death. Secure on their soil, they will know that "I am Yahweh," when God has freed them from slavery as in the exodus of old.[1156] No longer will they be plunder for other nations or food for savage beasts. Fear will have no place in so safe an existence.

In MT, v. 29 begins as follows: "And I shall establish for them a planting of renown" (מטע לשם *maṭṭāʿ lĕšēm*). The NRSV translates "a splendid vegetation"; the NIV reads "a land renowned for its crops." The Hebrew text makes sense: so great will be the fertility of Israel's land that the people will never again experience famine or the consequent insults of other nations. LXX, however, presupposes מטע שלם (*maṭṭāʿ šālōm*), "a peaceful planting"; and commentators often emend the MT

accordingly. Batto's investigation of the "covenant of peace" motif offers some support for emending MT, for Pattern B examples of the core myth he examines include a submotif about the planting of peace in the earth. If, as Batto suggests, the text is one of several biblical references to this submotif, then it is possible that a knowledgeable reader might espy in MT a slight scribal error and read accordingly. Verses 28-29 address the Israelites literally (as people), rather than metaphorically (as the sheep of Yahweh's flock). By this point, however, the reader is accustomed to Ezekiel's tendency to permit literal referents to surface within metaphorical oracles (see, e.g., 16:41).

Verse 30 commences with the opening words of the recognition formula ("and they shall know that . . ."), followed by assurance of God's presence with the people, itself a modified version of the Sinai covenant formula (see, e.g., Lev 26:12). The closing formula, "says the Lord GOD," assures Ezekiel's audience and his reader that his words are, in fact, God's own. Verse 31, yet another variation on the Sinai covenant formula, explicitly returns to the flock metaphor. The NIV translation follows the MT (translating אדם [*ʾādām,* "human"] as "people"), while the NRSV translation follows the LXX (where a Greek equivalent of *ʾādām* does not appear). This verse, like its predecessor, ends with the formula, "says the Lord GOD."

1155. Some commentators believe that Ezekiel goes still further, describing a future fructification of the desert. But such a reading goes too far. The text promises reliable and abundant seasonal rains, but it says nothing about the desert's being transformed. Verse 25 presupposes that both the desert and the forests will remain after Yahweh institutes the covenant of peace. They simply will no longer be inhabited by voracious beasts.

1156. Both a reference to slavery and the expression "I will break the bars of your yoke" appear in Lev 26:13. Readers recall also the scenario of Jeremiah 28 (Jeremiah's confrontation with the prophet Hannaniah) and Jer 30:8.

REFLECTIONS

Ezekiel's use of the shepherd/sheep metaphor has the power to realign our understanding of what responsible leadership entails. Like all metaphors, however, it requires thoughtful critique. Ezekiel anticipates that the reversal of his people's plight will be initiated and sustained solely by God. When Yahweh, the good shepherd, reclaims the sheep, their every need will be met: the flock's fat and abusive members will no longer ravage the other sheep or the environment; the good old days of David's rule will return; the blessings of God's unconditional covenant of peace will make possible life that, if not edenic, is certainly idyllic.

Fertile soil, freedom from foe and fear—who among us does not yearn for such conditions? But if, for the prophet, the covenant of peace comes only as a result of divine volition, then what remains for humans to do? What role have we to play in setting the world right? It is one thing to acknowledge Yahweh as creator and liberator. It is quite a different thing passively to await God's creative and liberating activity. Ezekiel's metaphor affirms that ultimately, God is the source of salvation. But we are not sheep. We are, Genesis 1 insists, created in God's image and entrusted with dominion over all other living things. Ironically, exercising dominion is an act of servantship. It demands responsibility; it certainly is not a license to exploit God's "very good" creation.

EZEKIEL 35:1–36:15, GOD'S WORD TO MT. SEIR AND TO THE MOUNTAINS OF ISRAEL

OVERVIEW

Ezekiel 35:1–36:15 consists of a judgment oracle against Mt. Seir (the land of Edom) in 35:1-15, followed by an announcement of salvation to the mountains of Israel in 36:1-15. Critics agree that the juxtaposition of these two passages, whether by the prophet or by a later editor, was intentional. As in chap. 34, so also here, Ezekiel's God promises to reverse a negative situation. Edom especially has mocked Israel and set its sights on Yahweh's land. Now God vows to carry out a brutal retribution against Israel's foes. Beyond their punishment, however, lies a glorious future for Israel's mountains (land) and God's people, who "will soon come home" (36:8). Mount Seir will become a desolation and a waste, but the mountains of Israel will be tilled, sown, and fertile. Edom's mountains, hills, valleys, and watercourses will be filled with corpses, but Israel's mountains, hills, watercourses, valleys, desolate wastes, and deserted towns will no longer suffer plunder and ridicule. Mount Seir will become a "perpetual desolation"; its decimated cities will never be reinhabited. Israel's land, including its "ghost towns," will teem with human beings and animals. Despite their diametrically different futures, both nations will fulfill God's larger purpose: Each will come to recognize and acknowledge Yahweh as the unrivaled divine sovereign who controls all of history.

Ezekiel 35:1-15, An Oracle Against Mt. Seir

OVERVIEW

Ezekiel's diatribe against Mt. Seir begins with the customary word event formula ("The word of the LORD came to me"), followed by God's direct address to the prophet ("Mortal"). Ezekiel is commanded to "set his face" against Mt. Seir—a hostile gesture familiar from preceding oracles (4:3, 7; 6:2; 15:7; 20:46; 21:7; 25:2; 38:2)—and to prophesy against it. The messenger formula, "Thus says the Lord GOD," asserts that the following words are in fact divine speech.

"Seir" is an ancient epithet; it is attested already in the fourteenth-century Amarna tablets. Originally, it may have referred to the wooded slopes of mountains lying east of the Arabah, Edom's western border. In the present text, however, as well as in Gen 32:4, 36:8, and Num 24:18, Seir functions as a synonym for the entire land of Edom, which lay south of the Dead Sea and stretched from the Zered Brook (its northern boundary) almost to the Gulf of Aqabah in the south (see map, 551-58). According to Deut 2:12, 22, Seir was inhabited by Horites until the descendants of Esau displaced them and seized the land for themselves.

The sequential reader of 35:1-15 does not yet know that Ezekiel's judgment oracle against Mt. Seir will serve as a foil for the following announcement of salvation to the mountains of Israel. He does know, however, of the enduring hatred between Israel and Edom—a family feud that, according to tradition, began while Jacob and Esau were within Rebekah's womb (Gen 25:22-23). The Hebrew Bible contains a number of scathing excoriations of Edom (e.g., Amos 1:11-12; Isa 34:5-17; Jer 49:7-22; Mal 1:2-5). Several, including Obad 11-14, Ps 137:7, and Lam 4:21-22, charge Edom with gloating over Jerusalem's destruction in 586 BCE, looting, refusing and even killing Judean refugees, and/or landgrabbing.

Edom was among the small Syro-Palestinian states the prophet denounced in the aftermath of Jerusalem's fall (Ezekiel 25). In 25:12-14, Ezekiel accused Edom of taking vengeance against the house of Israel. The root נקם (*nqm*), "to avenge, take vengeance," appeared three times in 25:12 to describe Edomite action and twice in 25:14 to describe Yahweh's reaction—the extermination of its population "by the hand of my people Israel." In 35:1-15, by contrast, the key root is שׁמם (*šmm*, "to be desolate," "laid waste"; forms of it appear ten times); and Yahweh vows that with outstretched hand, God will personally quash Mt. Seir.

Close analysis suggests that chap. 35 is not a single unit, but a collection of four short oracles (vv. 3-4; 5-9; 10-13; 14-15) not unlike the brief oracles against Israel's neighbors in chap. 25. These prophecies may not have been uttered on a single occasion; and it is possible that they originally belonged with Ezekiel's other oracles against foreign nations (chaps. 25–32).

Ezekiel 35:1-4, Yahweh Will Make Mt. Seir a Desolation

NIV

35 The word of the LORD came to me: [2]"Son of man, set your face against Mount Seir; prophesy against it [3]and say: 'This is what the Sovereign LORD says: I am against you, Mount Seir, and I will stretch out my hand against you and make you a desolate waste. [4]I will turn your towns into ruins and you will be desolate. Then you will know that I am the LORD.

NRSV

35 The word of the LORD came to me: [2]Mortal, set your face against Mount Seir, and prophesy against it, [3]and say to it, Thus says the Lord GOD:

I am against you, Mount Seir;
   I stretch out my hand against you
   to make you a desolation and a waste.
[4]I lay your towns in ruins;
   you shall become a desolation,
   and you shall know that I am the LORD.

COMMENTARY

The first oracle is cast as a two-part prophetic proof saying. After instructing Ezekiel to prophesy (vv. 1-2), in part one (vv. 3-4*a*) Yahweh addresses Mt. Seir directly, issuing the threatening "challenge to a duel" formula ("I am against you," see 5:8; 13:8; 26:3; 28:22; 29:3, 10; 34:10; 38:3; and 39:1), followed by a stereotypical threat emphasizing God's power ("I will stretch out my hand against you"; see also, e.g., Ezek 6:14; 14:9; 25:7, 13). The effects of Yahweh's intervention in Edomite history follow: Seir will become "a desolation and a waste" (שממה ומשמה *šĕmāmâ*

ûmĕšammâ);[1157] its cities will be reduced to ruins, and it will become a desolation (*šĕmāmâ*). In part two (v. 4*b*) the recognition formula points to the broader purpose of this overpowering display of divine strength: Mt. Seir will be forced to acknowledge Yahweh's unrivaled power and sovereignty. (See Reflections at 35:14-15.)

1157. These are the first two occurrences of the key root שמם (*šmm*) in chap. 35. "Sometimes the completeness of an action or state is expressed by placing together two or even three substantives of the same stem and of similar sound." *GKC* 113 1. See also Moshe Greenberg, *Ezekiel 1–20,* AB 22 (Garden City, N.Y.: Doubleday, 1983) 136-37.

Ezekiel 35:5-9, Edomite Atrocities Against Israel Will Be Punished

NIV

[5]" 'Because you harbored an ancient hostility and delivered the Israelites over to the sword at the time of their calamity, the time their punish-

NRSV

[5]Because you cherished an ancient enmity, and gave over the people of Israel to the power of the sword at the time of their calamity, at the time of

ment reached its climax, ⁶therefore as surely as I live, declares the Sovereign LORD, I will give you over to bloodshed and it will pursue you. Since you did not hate bloodshed, bloodshed will pursue you. ⁷I will make Mount Seir a desolate waste and cut off from it all who come and go. ⁸I will fill your mountains with the slain; those killed by the sword will fall on your hills and in your valleys and in all your ravines. ⁹I will make you desolate forever; your towns will not be inhabited. Then you will know that I am the LORD.

their final punishment; ⁶therefore, as I live, says the Lord GOD, I will prepare you for blood, and blood shall pursue you; since you did not hate bloodshed, bloodshed shall pursue you. ⁷I will make Mount Seir a waste and a desolation; and I will cut off from it all who come and go. ⁸I will fill its mountains with the slain; on your hills and in your valleys and in all your watercourses those killed with the sword shall fall. ⁹I will make you a perpetual desolation, and your cities shall never be inhabited. Then you shall know that I am the LORD.

COMMENTARY

While vv. 3*a*-4 proclaimed God's determination to destroy Mt. Seir without providing an explicit reason for the judgment, the succeeding three-part proof saying (vv. 5-9) begins with a formal accusation (introduced by יַעַן [*ya'an,* "because"], v. 5). This, in turn, is followed by an announcement of punishment (introduced by לָכֵן [*lākēn,* "therefore"], vv. 6-9*a*) and a concluding recognition formula (v. 9*b*). Yahweh accuses Mt. Seir (the Edomites) of clinging to an ancient enmity. (The same charge was lodged against the Philistines in 25:15.) Here, readers recall not only Gen 25:23 but also Gen 27:41 where, in response to Jacob's usurpation of Esau's blessing, they learn that "Esau hated Jacob" (see also Gen 32:4-22; 33:1-16). At the time of Judah's collapse ("the time of their calamity, at the time of their final punishment"), Edom delivered the people of Israel over to the power (lit., "hand") of the sword. "Their calamity" (אֵידָם *'êdām*) appears only here in the book of Ezekiel. Greenberg points not only to its assonance with דָּם (*dām,* "blood"), the key term in the following verse, but also to its similarity to אֱדוֹם (*'ĕdôm,* "Edom"), which will appear in v. 15. "Thus," he observes, "disaster, blood, and Edom are linked by sound."[1158] I would add that both blood and the root whence derives the proper noun Edom ("to be red") are linked by color.

The announcement of punishment follows in vv. 6-9*a*. At the outset, it is intensified by the

divine oath formula ("as I live"). As noted already, "blood" is a key term in v. 6 (it appears four times). Unfortunately the verse teems with difficulties. It begins with Yahweh's announcement of an impending intervention into Edomite history. The meaning of MT (lit., "I shall make you into blood") is elusive; witness but three attempts to render it (NRSV, "I will prepare you for blood"; NIV, "I will give you over to bloodshed"; TNK, "I will doom you with blood"). Next, Yahweh states the result of that intervention: "blood will pursue you." Neither the announcement of intervention nor its result is represented in the LXX, and critics note that their presence in the MT breaks the expected connection between the beginning of the oath formula in 6*a* and its continuation in v. 6*b*.[1159] Hence, they delete them as an altered dittograph of v. 6*b*.

But v. 6*b* has its problems as well. According to MT, Yahweh's second reason for Edom's punishment (the first, cherishing an "ancient enmity," appeared in v. 5) reads as follows: "surely you hated blood." Such a rendering makes little sense in this context. Hence, BHS and many commentators emend the MT in the light of the LXX and read "you have incurred guilt with respect to blood" (cf. Ezek 22:4).[1160] The NRSV and the NIV avoid the difficulty by negating the verb, i.e., "since you did not hate bloodshed, bloodshed shall

1158. Moshe Greenberg, *Ezekiel 21–37,* AB 22A (Garden City, N.Y.: Doubleday, 1997) 713.

1159. G. A. Cooke, *A Critical and Exegetical Commentary on the Book of Ezekiel,* ICC (Edinburgh: T. & T. Clark, 1936) 2:384.

1160. See W. Zimmerli, *Ezekiel 2: A Commentary on the Book of the Prophet Ezekiel, Chapters 25–48,* trans. J. D. Martin, Hermeneia (Philadelphia: Fortress, 1983) 224.

pursue you." The problem with this solution is that in oaths (as here) לא (*lōʾ*) preceded by אם (*ʾim*) expresses not the negative, but an emphatic affirmation.[1161] G. R. Driver suggests a better solution: the problem is a consequence of scribal error, a metathesis (reversal) of שׁ (*ś*) and נ (*n*). Once the two consonants are restored to their correct order, we arrive at the elliptical reading "you bear [the guilt] of blood," a meaningful statement in this context.[1162]

Although the precise meaning of v. 6 remains elusive, the gist of the entire verse is not entirely lost: what the Edomites have done to the Israelites will be done to them. Yet even more can be said, viz., what Yahweh has done to the Israelites on account of their sins will be done to Edom on account of its offenses against Israel, its homeland, and especially its God.

Verse 7 returns to the theme (introduced in v. 3) of the utter desolation awaiting Mt. Seir.[1163] While v. 3 was cast as a direct address *to* Mt. Seir, however, vv. 7-8*a* speak *about* it; and the pronominal suffixes are third-person masculine singular. Yahweh will reduce Mt. Seir to a waste and a desolation, cutting off (exterminating) its entire population (literally, "all who go to and fro") and filling its mountains with the slain. Verse 8*b*, returning to

second-person singular direct address, elaborates: Mt. Seir's hills, valleys, and ravines (i.e., the land in its entirety) will be chock-a-block with the corpses of those killed by the sword. As a consequence, God again informs Mt. Seir, "I will make you a perpetual desolation, and your cities shall never be inhabited." Then, the Lord declares, "you [masc. pl., addressing Edom's population] shall know that I am Yahweh."

Attentive readers recognize several striking similarities between Ezek 6:1-10, a judgment oracle addressed to "the mountains of Israel," and the present passage. In both texts, Ezekiel is ordered to perform a hostile gesture ("set your face toward [or "against"]") and prophesy against mountainous terrain. Both passages refer to Yahweh's outstretched hand (6;14; 35:3), to the fallen slain (6:4, 7; 35:8), and to ruined towns (6:6; 35:4). To be sure, the two texts differ in significant ways. Chapter 6 focuses especially upon Israel's illicit cultic practices at its high places, while chap. 35 says nothing of Edomite religious practices. Nonetheless, the similarities make the point that the same God who brought judgment against Yahweh's own people will just as surely bring judgment against its ancient, cruel, and arrogant foe. The infliction of the same punishment that Israel has endured upon Edom is good news. Not only does Yahweh continue to care about Israel's land, but also God plans to wipe out the Edomites whose usurpation of that land might be an obstacle to Israel's restoration. (See Reflections at 35:14-15.)

1161. *BDB*, 50a.

1162. G. R. Driver, "Linguistic and Textual Problems: Ezekiel," *Bib* 19 (1938) 181. Cf. Greenberg, *Ezekiel 21–37*, 713.

1163. The first word of the MT's phrase, לשממה ושממה (*lĕśimmâ ûśĕmāmâ*), is not attested elsewhere and may be an error. The reader might suspect that a scribe has here bungled the phrase שממה ומשמה (*šĕmāmâ ûmĕšammâ*; see v. 3). In any event, the meaning and significance of forms derived from שׁמם (*šmm*) have already become more than clear.

Ezekiel 35:10-13, Yahweh Will Punish Mt. Seir

NIV

10" 'Because you have said, "These two nations and countries will be ours and we will take possession of them," even though I the LORD was there, [11]therefore as surely as I live, declares the Sovereign LORD, I will treat you in accordance with the anger and jealousy you showed in your hatred of them and I will make myself known among them when I judge you. [12]Then you will know that I the LORD have heard all the con-

NRSV

10Because you said, "These two nations and these two countries shall be mine, and we will take possession of them,"—although the LORD was there— [11]therefore, as I live, says the Lord GOD, I will deal with you according to the anger and envy that you showed because of your hatred against them; and I will make myself known among you,[a] when I judge you. [12]You shall know

[a]Gk: Heb *them*

NIV	NRSV
temptible things you have said against the mountains of Israel. You said, "They have been laid waste and have been given over to us to devour." ¹³You boasted against me and spoke against me without restraint, and I heard it.	that I, the LORD, have heard all the abusive speech that you uttered against the mountains of Israel, saying, "They are laid desolate, they are given us to devour." ¹³And you magnified yourselves against me with your mouth, and multiplied your words against me; I heard it.

COMMENTARY

Verses 10-13 constitute a second three-part prophetic proof saying. Like its immediate predecessor, this oracle begins with a formal accusation introduced by יַעַן (ya'an, "because," v. 10), followed by an announcement of punishment introduced by לָכֵן (lākēn, "therefore," v. 11). A variant form of the recognition formula, expanded by an ostensible quotation of the Edomites (v. 12) and additional comments about the reason for God's punishment (v. 13), bring this prophecy to a close.

Yahweh's accusation against Mt. Seir (the reason for its impending punishment) is cast as a quotation of Edom's aspiration to "possess" (יָרַשׁ yāraš) "the two nations and the two countries," presumably a reference to the territory once held by the Northern and the Southern Kingdoms of Israel (see also 25:3, 8 and 26:2 for similar quotations appearing as reasons for judgment). Modern critics suspect that Edomites would not actually have spoken in this way, since the Northern Kingdom would have been a faded memory by Ezekiel's day (it fell in 721 BCE). Rather, the prophet's personal hope for the future reunification of Judah and Ephraim into one nation is expressed here. (That expectation will be stated specifically in 37:15-28.) He hyperbolically presents Edom as aspiring to encroach upon *all* of *both* kingdoms' former territory. Its grandiose plans are an affront to Yahweh who, readers are told in an "interruptive objection" not attributed to God,[1164] was there.

Although Jerusalem was destroyed and Judah collapsed, these events—which Ezekiel consistently depicts as the "doing" and not the "undoing" of Israel's deity—should not be interpreted as evidence that Yahweh had abandoned the land, or been forced out of it, or lost ownership of it. Therefore, Yahweh vows to recompense Mt. Seir tit-for-tat for the anger and jealousy it has exhibited on account of its hatred for Israel (v. 11a). Verse 11b casts the recognition formula not as a consequence of Yahweh's intervention, but as the intervention itself ("I will make myself known"). The NIV reads with the MT "known among *them* when I judge you" (emphasis mine). According to this rendering, Yahweh will "make myself known" to the Israelites through the act of punishing Mt. Seir.[1165] The NRSV, by contrast, follows the LXX and translates "and I will make myself known among *you*" (masc. sing., italics added)—that is, Mt. Seir.

The descendants of Esau will discover, to their doom, that Yahweh has indeed heard their abusive speech against the mountains of Israel. Again, Ezekiel ostensibly quotes their very words: "They are laid desolate, they are given us to devour." Israel's land is, in their opinion, fair game and easy prey. But their endless boastings are an affront to Yahweh because derision of the land of Israel taunts its true owner.[1166] (See Reflections at 35:14-15.)

1164. Ronald M. Hals, *Ezekiel,* FOTL 19 (Grand Rapids: Eerdmans, 1989) 255.

1165. See Greenberg, *Ezekiel 21–37,* 716, who cites Ezek 39:7 as analogous.
1166. D. I. Block, *The Book of Ezekiel: Chapters 25–48,* NICOT (Grand Rapids: Eerdmans, 1998) 320.

Ezekiel 35:14-15, Rejoicing over Desolate Edom

NIV	NRSV
¹⁴This is what the Sovereign Lord says: While the whole earth rejoices, I will make you desolate. ¹⁵Because you rejoiced when the inheritance of the house of Israel became desolate, that is how I will treat you. You will be desolate, O Mount Seir, you and all of Edom. Then they will know that I am the Lord.' "	¹⁴Thus says the Lord God: As the whole earth rejoices, I will make you desolate. ¹⁵As you rejoiced over the inheritance of the house of Israel, because it was desolate, so I will deal with you; you shall be desolate, Mount Seir, and all Edom, all of it. Then they shall know that I am the Lord.

COMMENTARY

Introduced by the messenger formula, vv. 14-15 threaten Mt. Seir with a deadly reversal. Verse 14*b* is often regarded as corrupt, and it is not idiomatic Hebrew.[1167] Nevertheless, ancient readers discern its gist with little difficulty: while all the earth delights in Edom's calamity, Yahweh will make it a desolation. Verse 15*a,* which some commentators regard as an editorial attempt to clarify the meaning of v. 14*b,* renders the reversal more explicit. Just as (the inhabitants of) Mt. Seir rejoiced over the land Yahweh allotted to the house of Israel (נחלת בית־ישראל *naḥlat bêt-yiśrāʾēl*) when it was desolate, so Yahweh will render Mt. Seir—indeed, all of Edom—desolate.[1168] The concluding recognition formula again articulates Yahweh's ultimate aim—that the Edomites be forced to acknowledge God's sovereign control over their history.[1169]

1167. See Greenberg, *Ezekiel 21–37,* 716.

1168. The fem. Hebrew noun נחלה (*naḥălâ*; construct *naḥlat*) is translated "inheritance" in both the NRSV and the NIV. Forshey has shown, however, that the Hebrew root נחל (*nḥl*) refers to "the practice of giving loyal servants the utilization of land as a reward for past service—fundamentally military service is involved—and in expectation of future service." H. O. Forshey, "The Hebrew Root *NHL* and Its Semitic Cognates" (Th.D. diss., Harvard University, 1973) 233. Hence, Israel has not inherited the land as its very own possession. Yahweh has allotted the land to Israel, but God remains its true owner.

1169. The MT's "and they shall know . . ." shifts from the second-person masc. sing. suffixes of vv. 14-15*b.* The LXX translates "and you shall know." The MT makes sense, however, when one recognizes that while Mt. Seir is Ezekiel's ostensible audience, his actual audience consists of his fellow exiles.

REFLECTIONS

When too many people claim ownership of too little land, conflict is inevitable. One need not master ancient Near Eastern history to recognize the truth of this observation. We confront it routinely in newspapers and magazines, and on television, radio, and the Internet. Oftentimes, hatred and violence are linked with religious beliefs. *We* own this land because *God* gave it to *us,* and competing claimants are not only *our* enemies but also *God's* foes.

The Reflections accompanying the Commentary to Ezekiel 25 are equally apropos to Ezekiel 35. In that context, I wrote:

> We can understand . . . that neighboring nations, jockeying for limited land, develop visceral and long-lived animosities. Hungry for prime real estate and revenge, each generation refuels the feud, until resolution seems well-nigh impossible. In such situations, people take up weapons *and* the pen, expressing with the latter a range of sentiments both hopeful and ugly. In a day when moderns increasingly recognize the importance of profound respect and cooperation among the nations inhabiting this tiny planet, however, biblical oracles that suggest that the solution to international conflict is the extermination of one's enemies are troubling indeed.

Perhaps the last sentence quoted is too optimistic. In many cases, it seems, moderns are no closer to recognizing the importance of profound respect and cooperation among the nations than were the peoples of Ezekiel's day; and they are all too ready to hurl both insults and artillery at their enemies. An uncritical reading of ancient Israel's oracles against foreign nations seems to endorse such an approach, for they unabashedly affirm that Yahweh not only sanctions the butchery of Israel's foes, but also is "himself" the death-dealer. The same deity who quashed the Northern and Southern Kingdoms of Israel for their sins turns now to their neighbors with murderous rage.

What are we to make of this characterization of God as a wrathful and avenging deity whose actions are motivated largely by the desire for self-vindication, and whose modus operandi is wholesale murder and destruction? This question cannot, I believe, simply be ignored. It demands of us a willingness honestly to wrestle with these canonical texts. Also in the Reflections to Ezekiel 25, I observed that we should not be surprised that Ezekiel and other ancient Israelites depicted Yahweh as an avenging warrior whose power and control over the nations was unparalleled by any other deity. And we can commend Ezekiel for maintaining a steadfast faith in God despite the fact that reality ran roughshod over that depiction. But we should beware of texts that create God in the image of humanity, that attribute to the Lord the basest human beliefs and behaviors. In a world where battles continue to be fought in God's name, we are responsible for engaging in difficult conversations and making hard choices about those texts. Even as we understand why Ezekiel spoke as he did, we must listen (an active, not a passive, activity) for God's word in our day.

Ezekiel 36:1-15, Salvation for the Mountains of Israel

OVERVIEW

Ezekiel 36:1 lacks the word-event formula ("The word of the LORD came to me") that so regularly introduces Yahweh's disclosures to the prophet. Hence, the ancient reader likely regards it and subsequent verses as a continuation of the divine speech begun in 35:1 (36:16 is introduced by the word-event formula). Nonetheless, 36:1 obviously signals a significant transition in God's communiqué. Addressing Ezekiel directly ("Mortal"), Yahweh commands him to prophesy to "the mountains of Israel," which are summoned to "hear the word of the LORD." Obviously Ezekiel, living in Babylonia, cannot literally speak to Israel's personified homeland; his actual audience consists of his fellow exiles. But the identification of his rhetorical audience is signficant, in part, because it reminds readers of two preceding addresses. On the one hand, the reader remembers that in Ezek 6:2 also, the prophet was ordered to set his face toward the mountains of Israel and to prophesy to them. In that context, his words were of God's impending judgment. Here, by contrast, he will speak of their imminent salvation. On the other hand, the reader immediately

recalls that in 35:2, Ezekiel was told to set his face against Mt. Seir. In that context, his words referred to its utter desolation. Here, by contrast, he will speak to Israel's mountains of their revivification and repopulation. The punishment that Israel's mountains have suffered will become Edom's eternal fate, but Israel's homeland will experience fully God's beneficence.

Ezekiel's salvation oracles habitually commence with a past or present problem that Yahweh must resolve before Israel's plight is reversed (see, e.g., the Commentary on Ezekiel 34). Ezekiel 36:1-15 exhibits this resolved problem→salvation pattern; an initial section (vv. 1b-7) reassures the addressees (rhetorical and real) that surrounding nations, and especially (or paradigmatically) Edom, will suffer the consequences of their mockery, slander, and greedy appropriation of Yahweh's land; a second section (vv. 8-15) focuses upon the impending fructification of Israel's mountains, the not-too-distant return of their inhabitants from exile, and the restoration of the land's reputation. Because this pattern is present in 36:1-15, some critics suggest that, originally, 35:1-15 was not prefixed to 36:1-15. Be that as it may, in its present position chap. 35 not only introduces the offenses also cited in 36:2*b*-7, but also provides a more detailed description of the punishments (desolate land, ruined cities, border-to-border corpses) Yahweh will inflict on Edom (36:7).

Even a casual reader of Ezek 36:1-15 cannot avoid the conclusion that these verses are filled with prophetic formulae. The messenger formula ("Thus says the Lord GOD"), for example, appears in vv. 2-7, and 13. Ezekiel is four times commanded to prophesy (vv. 1, 3, 6, 8), and Israel's mountains are twice summoned to "hear the word of the LORD" (vv. 1, 4). The frequently paired יען (*ya'an*, "because . . .) followed by לכן (*lākēn*, "therefore . . .") appears in vv. 2-4, 6*b*-7, 13-14, and *lākēn* alone appears in vv. 5 and 6*a*. In addition to these repetitions of formulae and form, there are repetitions or near repetitions of stock phrases (e.g., "to the mountains and to the hills, to the watercourses and to the valleys," vv. 4*b* and 6*b*) and content (cf., e.g., v. 5, "I am speaking in my hot jealousy," and v. 6*b*, "I am speaking in my jealous wrath"). For these reasons and others, many a critic has concluded that 36:1-15 consists of a core oracle subsequently expanded by editors—either Ezekiel himself or members of his "school"—who cobbled together oracle fragments and added interpretive comments.[1170]

Other critics, such as Block, counter that blaming the editors is illogical. "Later editors would have been concerned to create a smoother and clearer text, not one that was more confused."[1171]

On first reading, Block's critique makes sense. On further reflection, however, one wonders if he has not allowed modern presuppositions to creep into his thinking. While it is true that today's editors work to produce smoother, clearer texts, we cannot simply presume that ancient editors had the same goal. It is by no means self-evident that they would have regarded repetition as a vice, rather than a virtue. Rather, they might have thought that the presence of multiple messenger formulae, of repeated commands to prophesy and summonses to attention, and of the prophetic utterance formula ("says the Lord GOD") contributed to their readers' acceptance of texts as authentic and authoritative. Moreover, such editors often exercised the freedom to integrate their interpretations and "clarifications" into earlier texts. Far from concluding that Ezekiel or his later editors bungled their job (Zimmerli) or strove for "uncluttered" texts (Block), we should judge these editors on the basis of their own criteria, as best we can discern them. Because certain later prophetic collections (e.g., Trito-Isaiah, Zechariah, Malachi) display a propensity toward repetition, the loosening of traditional forms, and so on, we should not assume that the ancient reader of Ezekiel's scroll would have deemed the present passage (and many others) choppy or clumsy. This judgment does not, of course, rule out the possibility that scribal errors entered the text in the course of its composition and transmission. Ancient readers surely knew well that all-too-human copyists could and did make mistakes; and they, like we, would have tried by various mental means to make sense of the text before them.

1170. E.g., Zimmerli, *Ezekiel 2*, 232-33.
1171. Block, *Ezekiel 25–48*, 322.

Ezekiel 36:1-7, Reassurances for the Mountains of Israel

NIV

36 "Son of man, prophesy to the mountains of Israel and say, 'O mountains of Israel, hear the word of the LORD. ²This is what the Sovereign LORD says: The enemy said of you, "Aha! The ancient heights have become our possession."' ³Therefore prophesy and say, 'This is what the Sovereign LORD says: Because they

NRSV

36 And you, mortal, prophesy to the mountains of Israel, and say: O mountains of Israel, hear the word of the LORD. ²Thus says the Lord GOD: Because the enemy said of you, "Aha!" and, "The ancient heights have become our possession," ³therefore prophesy, and say: Thus says the Lord GOD: Because they made you desolate

NIV

ravaged and hounded you from every side so that you became the possession of the rest of the nations and the object of people's malicious talk and slander, ⁴therefore, O mountains of Israel, hear the word of the Sovereign LORD: This is what the Sovereign LORD says to the mountains and hills, to the ravines and valleys, to the desolate ruins and the deserted towns that have been plundered and ridiculed by the rest of the nations around you— ⁵this is what the Sovereign LORD says: In my burning zeal I have spoken against the rest of the nations, and against all Edom, for with glee and with malice in their hearts they made my land their own possession so that they might plunder its pastureland.' ⁶Therefore prophesy concerning the land of Israel and say to the mountains and hills, to the ravines and valleys: 'This is what the Sovereign LORD says: I speak in my jealous wrath because you have suffered the scorn of the nations. ⁷Therefore this is what the Sovereign LORD says: I swear with uplifted hand that the nations around you will also suffer scorn.

NRSV

indeed, and crushed you from all sides, so that you became the possession of the rest of the nations, and you became an object of gossip and slander among the people; ⁴therefore, O mountains of Israel, hear the word of the Lord GOD: Thus says the Lord GOD to the mountains and the hills, the watercourses and the valleys, the desolate wastes and the deserted towns, which have become a source of plunder and an object of derision to the rest of the nations all around; ⁵therefore thus says the Lord GOD: I am speaking in my hot jealousy against the rest of the nations, and against all Edom, who, with wholehearted joy and utter contempt, took my land as their possession, because of its pasture, to plunder it. ⁶Therefore prophesy concerning the land of Israel, and say to the mountains and hills, to the watercourses and valleys, Thus says the Lord GOD: I am speaking in my jealous wrath, because you have suffered the insults of the nations; ⁷therefore thus says the Lord GOD: I swear that the nations that are all around you shall themselves suffer insults.

COMMENTARY

In 36:1a, Yahweh commands Ezekiel to address "the mountains of Israel," here personified and representing the homeland as a whole. Verses 1b-7 constitute the first part of that address. Their function is twofold: on the one hand, they indirectly indict "the enemy"—a general term that will be clarified in v. 3 with reference to "the rest of the nations" and "the people," and in v. 5 with reference to "the rest of the nations" and "all Edom"—for malice, mockery, plunder, and the illicit appropriation of the land Yahweh allotted to Israel. On the other hand, they reassure the addressees (ostensibly the mountains, but actually the exiles) that God knows of these indignities, is enraged by them, and will soon turn the tables on Israel's enemies. They will themselves become the objects of insults.

Verses 2-3 are structured according to the familiar "because . . . therefore, . . ." pattern. The "because" clause supplies the reasons for Yahweh's impending intervention. In this case, the reasons are cast as quotations: Israel's foe has said

"Aha!" of the mountains (an expression of malicious glee earlier placed in the mouths of the Ammonites [25:3] and Tyre [26:2] in the aftermath of Jerusalem's destruction) and also claimed Israel's "ancient heights" as their own possession (מורשׁה [môrāšâ] from the root ירשׁ [yrš]; the same root appeared in 35:10), though Yahweh is the true owner of the land.

Normally, one expects the following "therefore" clause (v. 3) to announce a pending punishment of the offenders. That expectation is thwarted, however, for several verses. Instead, Ezekiel is again commanded to prophesy to Israel's mountains, and his words once more include indirect indictments of their foes. This pronouncement also is structured according to the "because . . . therefore . . ." pattern. Because Israel's enemies have perceived in its land's calamity an opportunity to improve their own situations, making the mountains desolate (שׁמות [šammôt]) and crushing (שׁאף [šā'ōp]) them from all sides, not only claiming the land God allotted to Israel, but also engaging in vicious gossip and mockery of it, therefore. . . . Again, the expected pronouncement of punishment does not follow. Instead, after "therefore," Israel's mountains are summoned for a second time to "hear the word of the Lord GOD" (v. 4*a*). The messenger formula introduces Ezekiel's (God's) address to "the mountains and the hills, the watercourses and the valleys, the desolate wastes and the deserted towns" that have been the victim of plunder and derision by surrounding nations. (Verse 4 recalls 6:3, which introduced a devastating list of punishments. In the present passage, however, Yahweh assures them that God will act punitively—not against Israel's land, but against its enemies.)

Clearly, the compiler of this material, whether Ezekiel or a later editor, does not intend simply and immediately to proclaim punishment upon the enemies of Israel's homeland (and of Yahweh, its owner). Rather, as noted above, he wishes also to alert the addressees (ostensibly the mountains of Israel, but actually the exiles) that God knows of the indignities the land has suffered in the aftermath of its divinely authored destruction. Yahweh, not the nations, was responsible for Judah's desolation. Ezekiel never wavers on that point. But subsequent to God's just punishment of Israel, the nations have reveled in its downfall and seized its land. Their responses dishonor both the land and Yahweh.

In v. 5, also introduced by "therefore" followed by the messenger formula, Yahweh speaks "in my hot jealousy" against Israel's foes (Edom is singled out, connecting this unit with 35:1-15), who with "wholehearted joy and utter contempt" have claimed God's land as their own possession (*môrāšâ*). Yet another "therefore" introduces v. 6, and Ezekiel again is commanded to prophesy to Israel's land, "the mountains and hills, the watercourses and valleys." In these verses, Israel's God is no dispassionate arbiter of justice, but a deity who speaks in "my jealous wrath," who is on the scene, and who will not permit the nations' insults of Yahweh's land and honor to continue. Because Israel's mountains have "suffered the insults of the nations" (v. 6*b*), therefore (v. 7*a*)—at last, readers arrive at the anticipated pronouncement of punishment—God lifts the divine hand in oath that those nations will themselves suffer insults, experiencing the same desolation that Israel endured. An eye for an eye; a tooth for a tooth. (See Reflections at 36:8-15.)

Ezekiel 36:8-15, "See Now, I Am for You"

8 " 'But you, O mountains of Israel, will produce branches and fruit for my people Israel, for they will soon come home. 9I am concerned for you and will look on you with favor; you will be plowed and sown, 10and I will multiply the number of people upon you, even the whole house of Israel. The towns will be inhabited and the ruins rebuilt. 11I will increase the number of men and animals upon you, and they will be fruitful and become numerous. I will settle people on you as in the past and will make you prosper more than before. Then you will know that I am the LORD. 12I will cause people, my people Israel, to walk upon you. They will possess you, and you will be their inheritance; you will never again deprive them of their children.

8But you, O mountains of Israel, shall shoot out your branches, and yield your fruit to my people Israel; for they shall soon come home. 9See now, I am for you; I will turn to you, and you shall be tilled and sown; 10and I will multiply your population, the whole house of Israel, all of it; the towns shall be inhabited and the waste places rebuilt; 11and I will multiply human beings and animals upon you. They shall increase and be fruitful; and I will cause you to be inhabited as in your former times, and will do more good to you than ever before. Then you shall know that I am the LORD. 12I will lead people upon you—my people Israel—and they shall possess you, and you shall be their inheritance. No longer shall you bereave them of children.

NIV

13" 'This is what the Sovereign LORD says: Because people say to you, "You devour men and deprive your nation of its children," [14]therefore you will no longer devour men or make your nation childless, declares the Sovereign LORD. [15]No longer will I make you hear the taunts of the nations, and no longer will you suffer the scorn of the peoples or cause your nation to fall, declares the Sovereign LORD.' "

NRSV

13Thus says the Lord GOD: Because they say to you, "You devour people, and you bereave your nation of children," [14]therefore you shall no longer devour people and no longer bereave your nation of children, says the Lord GOD; [15]and no longer will I let you hear the insults of the nations, no longer shall you bear the disgrace of the peoples; and no longer shall you cause your nation to stumble, says the Lord GOD.

COMMENTARY

Verse 8, with its initial "But you" plus vocative address to Israel's mountains, signals a turning point in chap. 36. Heretofore, Ezekiel has addressed Israel's mountains with two apparent goals: first, to assure the addressees (rhetorical and real) that Yahweh knows of the greedy land aspirations and mockery of Israel's surrounding enemies, of which Edom is the paradigmatic example; second, to reassure those addressees that their desolation and humiliation are about to end. The true owner of Israel's homeland will ensure that these foes experience both the destruction and the consequent disparagement that Israel has endured. Now, however, Ezekiel begins to speak not of reparation, but of refructification, repopulation, and the repair of the land's reputation. The exiles, here called "my people," are returning soon;[1172] and in preparation for their arrival, Israel's mountains will become verdant, their trees bearing fruit for the returnees' nourishment. In Greenberg's words, "branches and fruit are ascribed directly to the soil that nourishes them ("*your* branches"; "*your* fruit").[1173]

Elsewhere in the book of Ezekiel—indeed, in the entire Hebrew Bible—the phrase הנני אליכם

(*hinnî ʾălêkem*) functions as the ominous "challenge to a duel" formula: "See now, I am coming against you" (or "coming to you [to attack you]"). Now the prophet turns its conventional meaning on its head. In this context, the words mean "I am coming to you [for your welfare]." The following phrase, "I will turn my face to you" echoes the covenant blessing of Lev 26:9 and is the antithesis of "hide my face from you" (see, e.g., 39:29; Isa 59:2). But while the blessings of Leviticus 26 are contingent upon Israel's obedience vis-à-vis its covenant obligations, here the blessings are promised unconditionally to the mountains of Israel. They will be tilled and sown.

The promise that the land will be cultivated leads naturally to vv. 10 and 11. While trees could bear fruit without human assistance, tiling and sowing the soil required human beings. Verse 10 states emphatically that the population of Israel's homeland will be wonderfully restored. The unequivocal "the whole house of Israel, all of it" extends God's promise not only to the population of the former southern kingdom and their offspring, but also to the descendants of the northern Israelites deported by the Assyrians in 721 BCE. What has come of Mt. Seir's boast, "These two nations and these two countries shall be mine, and we will take possession of them" (35:10)! Cities will again teem with inhabitants, and the ruined places will be rebuilt. God will multiply not only human beings but also animals upon Israel's mountains. The phrase "They shall increase and be fruitful" also stirs thoughts of Lev 26:9; and readers will think as well of God's blessing of animals in Gen 1:22 and of humans in Gen 1:28, 9:1,

1172. Scholars sometimes search for a historical event that might have precipitated Ezekiel's assertion that the exiles would soon return home. See J. W. Wevers, *Ezekiel*, NCB (London: Nelson, 1969) 270, who points to Jehoiachin's release from prison proper in 561 BCE (2 Kgs 25:27-30;). The phrase is hopeful; it is also vague—intentionally so. I incline toward Greenberg's suggestion that its presence advances a theological agenda. For him, Ezekiel's God speaks of "shortening the term of exile" in the light of "the need for YHWH to vindicate his honor." Greenberg, *Ezekiel 21–37*, 720, 724. His point is substantive, but the promise that the exiles will soon return home also buttresses their hopes. The homecoming of which Ezekiel speaks is not "for many years . . . for distant times" (12:27); it is imminent.

1173. Greenberg, *Ezekiel 21–37*, 719.

and 9:7. These ideal conditions will exceed anything Israel has ever experienced. "Then," the Lord says, identifying the larger purpose underlying the transformation of Israel's land, "you shall know that I am Yahweh."

Beyond the recognition formula of v. 11*b*, v. 12 further elaborates upon the consequences of Yahweh's intervention on behalf of Israel's mountains. God will cause human beings to walk upon them—not just any human beings, mind up, but the Lord's own people, Israel. This statement not only reverses the absolute desolation with which the mountains of Israel were threatened in Ezek 6:14, but also constitutes the antithesis of the perpetual desolation that Edom will become, with no one coming or going (35:7-9). The Israelites will (re)possess their land (MT "you")[1174] and again it shall be Israel's נחלה (*naḥălâ*), its divinely allotted possession.[1175] So much for the nations' intentions to possess the land (35:10; 36:3, 5). So much for Edom's rejoicing over Israel's loss of its *naḥălâ* (35:15)!

In MT, the final clause of v. 12 reads, "and you shall never again bereave them [of their children]" (see also 5:17; 14:15). The statement seems odd. Heretofore in the present unit, Israel's land has been depicted sympathetically—the victim of the surrounding nations' ridicule and greed. Now, however, it is presented as a murderer of children. Does the author have in mind the droughts and consequent famine that plagued the land, or actual plagues? Is he thinking about the battles that Israel fought, and lost, there? The translators of LXX render שכל (*škl*) "bereave" as a passive, rather than an active, verb; hence "and you [Israel's land] shall no more be bereaved of them," that is of its inhabitants, God's people Israel. Without benefit of the Masoretes' vowel pointing, the ancient reader may well have understood the verb as passive, as well. Such a rendering makes better sense, Greenberg affirms, because "the point is not that parents shall no longer be bereft of their children, but that the country shall never again be depopulated and thus subject to seizure by its neighbors." He translates *škl* as "to lose" and suggests that a similar metaphor occurs in 2 Kgs 2:19: "and the

water is bad and the land keeps losing her children."[1176]

If the final clause of v. 12 might, at this point in the text, be construed such that the land of Israel is cast as a victim, rather than a culprit, as bereaved, rather than the bereaver, there can be no doubt that in v. 13, the nations are quoted as uttering two decidedly pejorative accusations, introduced by "because" (יען *ya'an*), against that land. The first, "You devour people," charges that Israel's land, like the rapacious lion/kings of 19:3, 6, kills the very people it should protect. The spies sent by Moses to reconnoiter the land of Canaan spoke similarly of Israel's future homeland: "The land that we have gone through as spies is a land that devours its inhabitants" (Num 13:32). Precisely why they would have said such a thing in the story is unclear, but the accusation may well have been a stereotypical slur. Their second accusation, "you bereave your nation of children" echoes v. 12*b*; and in this context, there can be no doubt that the land's foes depict it as the perpetrator, not the victim. Remarkably in v. 14, introduced by "therefore" (לכן *lākēn*), Yahweh does not defend Israel's land against these accusations. Rather, God asserts that in the future, the charges will no longer be true! The land will not continue to devour human beings (as it presumably has been doing) and it will no longer bereave (not "be bereaved") its nation of children. The MT of v. 14 reads, "and you will not again cause your nation to stumble" (כשל *kšl*). That reading is certainly possible. In light of the two occurrences of *škl*, "to bereave," in vv. 12 and 13, however, the reader might suspect a scribal error. Yet v. 15 also contains a form of the root *kšl* (see NIV and NRSV). Would the reader suspect that the same error occurred twice? In any event, v. 15 contains three divine promises: Never again will Yahweh cause the land to hear the insults of the nations; it will never again bear the disgrace of the peoples; and it will no longer cause its nation to stumble (or, perhaps, bereave its nation of its children). Is it the case, as Zimmerli suggests, that vv. 14-15 speak to "a hidden despondency" among the exiles, who are wrestling with the question of whether a new beginning in the land can turn out any differently than did the first?[1177]

1174. At this point in v. 12, the pronouns shift from masc. pl. to sing. The MT marks them as masc. sing., but the ancient reader, without benefit of MT vowel points, would likely read them as fem. sing., the implied referent being "land" (ארץ *'ereṣ*, a fem. sing. noun).

1175. Concerning *naḥălâ*, see Forshey, "The Hebrew Root NHL and Its Semitic Cognates" 233; Block, *Ezekiel 25-48,* 321.

1176. Greenberg, *Ezekiel 21–37,* 721.

1177. W. Zimmerli, *Ezekiel 2: A Commentary on the Book of the Prophet Ezekiel, Chapters 25–48,* trans. J. D. Martin, Hermeneia (Philadelphia: Fortress, 1983) 239.

REFLECTIONS

In both this text and 35:1-15, Ezekiel's actual audience is the exilic community of which Ezekiel was a part. We can assume that that audience was pleased to hear of Edom's future demise and also to learn that Yahweh's concern for the homeland had not abated—if, in fact, they still held hope that God had not utterly abandoned them or proven incapable of rescuing them. But perhaps some, at least, sensed the tragedy of kindred nations so caught in the cancer of hatred that each experienced malicious glee at the thought of the other's catastrophic demise.

Verses 8-15 are of a different sort. Having reassured Israel's homeland that its enemies will be targets of God's "hot jealousy" and "jealous wrath," Yahweh now speaks tenderly (rare in the book of Ezekiel!) of its restoration and rehabilitated reputation, and of the impending return of "my people Israel." It is interesting to read such a text and to recognize what, for its ancient Near Eastern author, constituted an idyllic existence: a homeland fertile, cultivated, and filled with inhabitants, animal and human, all reproducing at impressive rates; ruined cities rebuilt and reinhabited; a deep knowledge and acknowledgment of the God who creates and sustains these conditions; a reputation that commands the respect of others. One wonders if Ezekiel's audience dismissed his assurances as so much hyperbole, or if they derived from them some comfort that conditions would improve during their lifetimes, and that full realization of God's promises would transpire some day.

We too can long for such an existence, yet despair that it is not possible. Many people around our world are living in exile with little chance of returning home. Crops still fail on account of drought or infestation; and unlike the inhabitants of the ancient world, we are threatened by the pesticides and other chemicals used to keep critters away. Overpopulation is a perduring problem in many parts of the planet, with consequences for us all. Cities can become hotbeds of violence and poverty. The list goes on and on.

Texts like Ezek 36:8-15 can inspire hope in us, but we—like the prophet's original audience—cannot sit back and wait for God to fulfill them. When at last the exiles returned to their homeland, they did not find the paradisiacal conditions promised them by Ezekiel, and to an even greater degree, by the anonymous prophet we call Second Isaiah (Isaiah 40–55). No, after completing the long trek home, they had to deal with endless and complex problems: cities still lying in ruins; a severely eroded population; opponents who did not welcome them back, thank you; famine; etc. By the same token we, while longing for a better world and praying, "your kingdom come, your will be done on earth as it is in heaven," must be willing to tackle our problems in intelligent, compassionate, and sustained ways.

In our attempts to address ecological problems and disasters, we do well to remember that God cares about this world. In the present passage, Yahweh addresses Israel's homeland with reassurances and promises. "See now," the Lord says, "I am for you; I will turn to you." Ezekiel was focused squarely upon Israel's homeland. But, as the psalmist declares, "the earth is the LORD's, and everything in it,/ the world, and all who live in it" (Ps 24:1 NRSV). When we waste and contaminate our natural resources, we offend God the creator.

EZEKIEL 36:16-38, FOR THE SAKE OF MY HOLY NAME

OVERVIEW

The word event formula of Ezek 36:16 signals the beginning of a new communication from Yahweh to the prophet, while the recognition formula in v. 38b ("Then they shall know that I am the LORD") marks its end. Intervening verses summarize a number of ideas that have appeared earlier in the scroll. Their theological significance is considerable. Strictly speaking, they constitute an oracle of salvation. At the same time, however, they might strike an ancient audience—and contemporary readers—as harsh, even fearsome.

Commentators generally agree that the unit consists of three sections: the first (vv. 16-32), often described as the "core" of the prophecy, can be divided further into vv. 17-21 (a divine monologue addressed to Ezekiel ["Mortal"] with no command that he proclaim it to the exiles) and vv. 22-32 (introduced by Yahweh's demand that Ezekiel deliver the following oracle to "the house of Israel").[1178] To the core have been added, whether by Ezekiel or by a later redactor(s), two appendices: vv. 33-36 and 37-38.

In the monologue, the Lord offers a brief account of the people's defiling sinfulness and identifies an extremely negative consequence of the exile, Israel's punishment: Yahweh's holy name has been profaned among the nations to which the people were scattered (vv. 17-21). The

oracle proper immediately emphasizes what God's motivation for impending actions is not ("It is not for your sake, O house of Israel, that I am about to act") and what it is ("for the sake of my holy name"). Yahweh will gather the dispersed from the nations, return them to their land, purify them, and remove their "stony" hearts, replacing them with a "heart of flesh." Moreover, God will infuse them with God's own spirit and render them utterly incapable of violating the Lord's statutes and ordinances. Nothing is said about either human contrition or the people's loss of freedom to choose between good and evil. Returned to "the land that I gave to your ancestors," the Israelites will resume their life as God's covenant people (v. 28) without fear of famine and its consequent disgrace. Verse 31 expresses a thought found previously in Ezek 20:43: back in their homeland, the people will remember their long-lived history of iniquity and loathe themselves for their sinfulness (see also 16:53-63). Verse 32 reiterates v. 22: God will not act for Israel's sake.

The first of the two appendixes, each with its own, initial messenger formula ("Thus says the Lord GOD"), speaks of the restoration of Israel's land and cities. So great will be their transformation that passers-by will place Israel's territory on par with the mythical Garden of Eden and acknowledge Yahweh's power and sovereignty. The second addresses a problem raised most recently in 36:10-11—underpopulation. God intends to make the people as numerous as the flocks of sacrificial animals gathered in Jerusalem for festivals in former times. (The analogy returns readers to the image of Israel as Yahweh's flock in Ezekiel 34.) Then, "they shall know that I am the LORD."

1178. Ezekiel 36:23b-30 does not appear in Papyrus 967, an early Greek text (late 2nd or 3rd third cent. CE) or in the Old Latin Codex Wirceburgensis (6th cent. CE). Scholars have tended in the past to regard the omission of these verses as a consequence of scribal error. See F. V. Filson, "The Omission of Ezek. 12:26-28 and 36:23b-38 in Codex 967," *JBL* 62 (1943) 27-32. Lust finds this explanation implausible and has argued instead that Papyrus 967 preserves an earlier form of the text. See Johan Lust, "Ezekiel 36–40 in the Oldest Greek Manuscript," *CBQ* 43 (1981) 517-33. His arguments are summarized and scrutinized in Moshe Greenberg, *Ezekiel 21–37,* AB 22A (Garden City, N.Y.: Doubleday, 1997) 738-40; D. I. Block, *The Book of Ezekiel: Chapters 25–48,* NICOT (Grand Rapids: Eerdmans, 1998) 337-43. True to my method, I shall follow the MT.

Ezekiel 36:16-32, Yahweh Redeems Israel for the Sake of the Divine Name

Ezekiel 36:16-21, Israel's Sins and Their Consequences for God

NIV

16The word of the LORD came to me: 17Mortal, when the house of Israel lived on their own soil, they defiled it with their ways and their deeds; their conduct in my sight was like the uncleanness of a woman in her menstrual period. 18So I poured out my wrath upon them for the blood that they had shed upon the land, and for the idols with which they had defiled it. 19I scattered them among the nations, and they were dispersed through the countries; in accordance with their conduct and their deeds I judged them. 20But when they came to the nations, wherever they came, they profaned my holy name, in that it was said of them, "These are the people of the LORD, and yet they had to go out of his land." 21But I had concern for my holy name, which the house of Israel had profaned among the nations to which they came.

NRSV

16The word of the LORD came to me: 17Mortal, when the house of Israel lived on their own soil, they defiled it with their ways and their deeds; their conduct in my sight was like the uncleanness of a woman in her menstrual period. 18So I poured out my wrath upon them for the blood that they had shed upon the land, and for the idols with which they had defiled it. 19I scattered them among the nations, and they were dispersed through the countries; in accordance with their conduct and their deeds I judged them. 20But when they came to the nations, wherever they came, they profaned my holy name, in that it was said of them, "These are the people of the LORD, and yet they had to go out of his land." 21But I had concern for my holy name, which the house of Israel had profaned among the nations to which they came.

COMMENTARY

With words ostensibly intended for Ezekiel's ears alone, Yahweh recounts how Israel, while living on its own soil, defiled (טמא ṭimmē᾽) the land by its "ways and deeds" (the same word pair appeared in 14:23; 20:43-44 with reference to idolatry and in 24:14 with reference to bloodshed; the phrase is imprecise, but the reader, recalling its previous association with these two offenses, will think especially of them). According to v. 17b, the people's conduct—the pollution of the very soil upon which they lived—was for Yahweh like menstrual impurity. Ezekiel's choice of analogy might seem strange in this context. According to the Torah (see especially Leviticus 15), a woman's menstrual flow rendered her impure for seven days; her impurity was contagious, and it could be contracted by anyone who touched her, her chair, or her bed (see Ezek 18:6; 22:10). But unlike the willful people's "ways and deeds," menstruation itself was no moral offense; and women were not expected to experience guilt or shame on account of it.[1179] Why, then, this particular trope? Looking beyond the pages of Torah, we discover that menstrual imagery could be used in a pejorative way to describe activites (violent bloodshed) and states of being so impure as to elicit utter disgust and revulsion (see, e.g., Lam 1:9; Ezra 9:11). Here, the menstrual impurity analogy functions graphically to convey a sense of Israel's defiling conduct, which has led in turn to the defilement of God's land.[1180]

1179. Deborah Klee, "Menstruation in the Hebrew Bible" (Ph.D. diss., Boston University, 1998).

1180. The defilement incurred through immoral behavior could not be purified simply by performing a ritual. It could be removed only through an act of divine cleansing, brought on by genuine repentance, sacrifice, and gratitude. See Block, *Ezekiel 25–48,* 345; Tikva Frymer-Kensky, "Pollution, Purification, and Purgation in Biblical Israel," in *The Word of the Lord Shall Go Forth,* ed. Carol L. Meyers and M. O'Connor (Winona Lake: Eisenbrauns, 1983) 401-6.

Only in 36:17-18 does Ezekiel accuse Israel of having *defiled* (from the root *ṭmʾ*) its homeland. Beyond his book, however, the topic appears in a variety of contexts. According to Num 35:33-34, unredressed bloodshed defiled the land, which was home not only to the Israelites, but also to their God: "You shall not pollute the land in which you live; for blood pollutes the land, and no expiation can be made for the land, for the blood that is shed in it, except by the blood of the one who shed it. You shall not defile the land in which you live, in which I also dwell; for I the LORD dwell among the Israelites." The land also contracted impurity through the illicit sexual activities of its inhabitants (see, e.g., Lev 18:6-28), or when the corpse of a hanged criminal was not removed from a tree until the day after his execution (Deut 21:22-23). Ezekiel believed that idolatry defiled God's sanctuary (5:11); in v. 18 (see also Jer 2:7) it appears, along with bloodshed, as a cause of the land's defilement.

Deuteronomy 18:9-12 cautions Israel not to resort to the illicit practices of Canaan's inhabitants lest it too be dispossessed. And in the book of Leviticus, the land's rejection of its population is described in language suggestive of a person who, sickened by the contents of his stomach, vomits them out.

God's response to Israel's defilement of its land is described in vv. 18-19: "I poured out my wrath upon them" (see also 7:8; 9:8; 14:19; 20:8, 13, 21, 33-34; 22:22; 30:15) on account of the blood they had shed upon the land, and because by their "dung pellets" (Ezekiel's characteristic and crude term for idols), they had defiled it. Yahweh scattered (פוץ *pûṣ*) the people among the nations, and they were dispersed (זרה *zārâ*) throughout the countries (see also 12:15; 20:23; 22:15; 29:12;

30:23, 26). Verse 19*b* insists that the penalty was proportionate to the crime.

Despite the appropriateness of God's dealings with the people, their dispersion among the nations has had an (apparently unforeseen; but see 20:9, 14, 22) negative consequence for Yahweh's *name* (שם *šēm*), i.e., for the divine reputation, among the nations. By their very presence abroad, the Israelites have profaned the Lord's holy name, for onlookers witnessing their fate exclaim, "These are the people of Yahweh, and yet they had to go out of his land!" (v. 20*b*). How and why have the relationships between God, the people, and their homeland been broken? The nations might conclude that Yahweh allowed the Judeans to be exiled because God was angry at them. Such a theological explanation is reflected, for example, in the fifth line of the Moabite Stone: Omri, "king of Israel, oppressed Moab for a long time, because Chemosh [Moab's patron deity] was angry at his land." But Ezekiel's words disclose that his (and Yahweh's) concern lies in a different direction: the nations believe that Israel's God was either *unwilling* (see the Judeans' own comments in 8:12 and 9:9) or, worse, *unable* to protect the Judeans against the assault of Marduk, Babylon's principal deity, and his forces, the troops led by Nebuchadnezzar.

The profanation of the divine name, which Ezekiel (and Yahweh) takes with the utmost seriousness, here appears as the sole motivation for God's future dealings with Israel: the divine reputation must be restored to its previous luster. Ezekiel says nothing to suggest that Yahweh is motivated by love, covenant faithfulness, or mercy for Israel.[1181] (See Reflections at 36:37-38.)

1181. Zimmerli, *Ezekiel 2*, 247-48.

Ezekiel 36:22-32, I Will Bring You into Your Own Land

NIV

22Therefore say to the house of Israel, Thus says the Lord GOD: It is not for your sake, O house of Israel, that I am about to act, but for the sake of my holy name, which you have profaned among the nations to which you came. ²³I will sanctify

NRSV

22Therefore say to the house of Israel, Thus says the Lord GOD: It is not for your sake, O house of Israel, that I am about to act, but for the sake of my holy name, which you have profaned among

NIV

my great name, which has been profaned among the nations, and which you have profaned among them; and the nations shall know that I am the LORD, says the Lord GOD, when through you I display my holiness before their eyes. [24]I will take you from the nations, and gather you from all the countries, and bring you into your own land. [25]I will sprinkle clean water upon you, and you shall be clean from all your uncleannesses, and from all your idols I will cleanse you. [26]A new heart I will give you, and a new spirit I will put within you; and I will remove from your body the heart of stone and give you a heart of flesh. [27]I will put my spirit within you, and make you follow my statutes and be careful to observe my ordinances. [28]Then you shall live in the land that I gave to your ancestors; and you shall be my people, and I will be your God. [29]I will save you from all your uncleannesses, and I will summon the grain and make it abundant and lay no famine upon you. [30]I will make the fruit of the tree and the produce of the field abundant, so that you may never again suffer the disgrace of famine among the nations. [31]Then you shall remember your evil ways, and your dealings that were not good; and you shall loathe yourselves for your iniquities and your abominable deeds. [32]It is not for your sake that I will act, says the Lord GOD; let that be known to you. Be ashamed and dismayed for your ways, O house of Israel.

NRSV

the nations to which you came. [23]I will sanctify my great name, which has been profaned among the nations, and which you have profaned among them; and the nations shall know that I am the LORD, says the Lord GOD, when through you I display my holiness before their eyes. [24]I will take you from the nations, and gather you from all the countries, and bring you into your own land. [25]I will sprinkle clean water upon you, and you shall be clean from all your uncleannesses, and from all your idols I will cleanse you. [26]A new heart I will give you, and a new spirit I will put within you; and I will remove from your body the heart of stone and give you a heart of flesh. [27]I will put my spirit within you, and make you follow my statutes and be careful to observe my ordinances. [28]Then you shall live in the land that I gave to your ancestors; and you shall be my people, and I will be your God. [29]I will save you from all your uncleannesses, and I will summon the grain and make it abundant and lay no famine upon you. [30]I will make the fruit of the tree and the produce of the field abundant, so that you may never again suffer the disgrace of famine among the nations. [31]Then you shall remember your evil ways, and your dealings that were not good; and you shall loathe yourselves for your iniquities and your abominable deeds. [32]It is not for your sake that I will act, says the Lord GOD; let that be known to you. Be ashamed and dismayed for your ways, O house of Israel.

COMMENTARY

The oracle proper, which Yahweh commands Ezekiel to proclaim to "the house of Israel," is linked to the preceding by לכן (*lākēn*), "therefore," and commences with the messenger formula, "Thus says the Lord God." What Yahweh has shared with the prophet must now be made perfectly clear to his fellow exiles: God is *not* acting for *Israel's* sake, but solely for the sake of Yahweh's *holy name,* which the people have profaned by their presence among the nations. This untenable situation will be reversed, God avers, as Yahweh sanctifies "my great name" and the nations are compelled to recognize and acknowledge the

power and sovereignty of Israel's deity, manifested before their eyes through God's dealings with Israel (v. 23).

This is not the only time that Israel has benefited from Yahweh's concern for the divine reputation. When the forty spies sent by Moses to reconnoiter the land of Canaan returned with talk of its strong inhabitants and fortified cities, the Hebrew were ready to return to Egypt. Yahweh was ready to destroy them on the spot. But Moses successfully intervened on their behalf, reminding God that the nations would misconstrue the cause of their deaths: "If you kill this people all at one time, then the nations who have heard about you will say, 'It is because the LORD was not able to bring this people into the land he swore to give them that he has slaughtered them in the wilderness'" (Num 14:15-16). Similarly, when three thousand Hebrews suffered an embarrassing defeat at the city of Ai, Joshua appealed to Yahweh: "O LORD, what can I say, now that Israel has turned their backs to their enemies! The Canaanites and all the inhabitants of the land will hear of it and surround us, and cut off our name from the earth. Then what will you do for your great name?" (Josh 7:8-9).

Striking similarities exist between the present passage and Ezekiel 20. In that lengthy oracle, Ezekiel asserts that on three occasions, only Yahweh's concern for the divine reputation among the nations dissuaded the Lord from destroying the Hebrews. Despite God's oath to bring them out of Egypt and into "a land flowing with milk and honey, the most glorious of all lands" (20:6), the people rebelled against God's command not to worship the idols of Egypt. In the wilderness, that same generation rebelled again, failing to observe God's statutes, rejecting the divine ordinances, and profaning the sabbaths. Their offspring, the second wilderness generation, followed in their parents' footsteps. On each occasion, Ezekiel claims, God thought to "pour out my wrath" upon the people to destroy them (20:8, 13*b*, 21*b*; see 36:18); but thrice Yahweh was restrained by concern for the divine name. According to 20:32, however, God swore to the obdurate Israelites in the wilderness that "I would scatter them among the nations and disperse them through the countries." Ezekiel does not, in that oracle, consider the ramifications of this action for God's reputation. But in the present passage, it is his major concern.

As in Ezek 20:41, so here, Yahweh intends that the nations witness the manifestation of God's holiness at work in Israel's history (v. 23). Verses 24-30 describe Yahweh's restorative plan. First, the Lord will *gather* the scattered Israelites from all the countries to which they have been dispersed and *bring them into* their homeland: a new exodus lies ahead! Ezekiel spoke of a new exodus in chapter 20 as well. In that context, he proclaimed that the event would be launched by an enraged deity and followed by the judging and purging of rebels in the wilderness prior to the sur-

vivors' return to their homeland. Now, Ezekiel says nothing of that fearsome desert encounter. Everything he describes is intended to *glorify* God's reputation, and to cast no further doubts about Yahweh's ability to gather, sustain, and repatriate this people. According to Ezek 36:16-38, Yahweh intends to deal with the problem of Israel's recalcitrance in a quite different way, as we shall see.

In the book of Deuteronomy, Moses is said to have warned the Israelites that if they failed to fulfill their covenant obligations, God would bring upon them a long and horrific list of curses, including exile. But he also told them that if, while they were living among the nations, they returned to the Lord and obeyed God "with all your heart and with all your soul," then Yahweh would have compassion upon them: "Even if you are exiled to the ends of the world, from there the LORD your God will gather you, and from there he will bring you back" (Deut 30:4). In this passage from Deuteronomy, the initiative lies with Israel: repenting and being obedient are choices the people are capable of making.

Ezekiel's concern for the divine reputation cannot wait for human initiative, and repentance is not a prerequisite for Yahweh's restorative acts (so also in Jer 33:6-9). Having returned the people to their land, God will both cleanse them of their past impurity and ensure their future compliance. Verse 25 addresses the problem of Israel's defiled status and land (vv. 17-18). Forms of טהר (*ṭāhēr*), "to be clean, pure," appear three times in this single verse. Yahweh will sprinkle *purifying* water upon them and *cleanse* them; as a consequence, they will be *clean* from their impurities and "dung pellets," the idols they have served. Ezekiel's language is a mixed metaphor of priestly cleansing rituals and blood sprinkling ceremonies.[1182] Rituals involving the use of water include the consecration of priests (Exod 29:4) and Levites (Num 8:7), as well as the ritual cleansing of the chief priest on the Day of Atonement (Lev 16:4, 24, 26); the ceremonial washing of clothes (in Exod 19:10, in preparation for a theophany); and the red heifer ashes ceremony, designed to cleanse persons defiled by contact with a corpse (Num 19:1-22).[1183]

1182. Ibid., 248-49; Block, *Ezekiel 25–48.*
1183. Block, *Ezekiel 25–48,* 354.

Once the people have been purified from all their iniquities, Yahweh will replace their "heart of stone"—obstinate, rebellious, unfeeling—with a "heart of flesh" and infuse them with God's own spirit. As a consequence, the Israelites will at last "follow my statutes and be careful to observe my ordinances" (v. 27*b*). This is no turn of heart on the Israelites' part but a heart transplant performed unilaterally by Yahweh to ensure the people's utter and unending obedience (here Ezekiel goes beyond both Deut 30:6 and Jer 31:31-34). Verses 26-27 closely resemble Ezek 11:19-20*a*, part of a (sequentially) earlier restoration oracle concerning those deported Judeans whose counterparts in Jerusalem were claiming the homeland as their own possession. In that context also, Yahweh promised to insure the exiles' absolute and ongoing compliance: "Thus I will cause you to follow my laws and faithfully to observe my rules" (TNK). In 18:31, by contrast, Ezekiel's God exhorts the house of Israel: "Get yourselves a new heart and a new spirit!" as if human beings were perfectly capable of doing so (see the Commentary on 18:1-32). Here, then, is a theme that Ezekiel uses in different ways, depending upon the contexts in which it appears and the strategies motivating its use.

Purified, transformed, and totally obedient, the people will be able to live "in the land that I gave to your ancestors." Moreover, Yahweh will renew the covenant with them: "you shall be my people, and I will be your God" (v. 28).

Returning to the topic of v. 25, Yahweh promises to rescue Israel from all its uncleanness. Thus far, the root ישׁע (*yrš*), "to rescue, save, deliver," has appeared in the book of Ezekiel only in 34:22 (God will save flock Israel's vulnerable sheep from its stronger, ravaging members). Here, in effect, God rescues Israel from itself, that is, from the defilement that the people have brought upon themselves. Moreover, God will "summon (קרא *qārā'*) the grain"—an unusual phrase, the reversal of Yahweh's summoning of famine in 2 Kg 8:1 and Ps 105:16—and make it abundant. Famine is a recurring concern in Ezekiel's oracles of restoration. In 34:29, Yahweh promises that Israel's soil will be so fruitful that its inhabitants will experience neither the pangs of hunger nor the insult of nations (see also 36:8). The two concerns are paired again in 36:29-30. Abundant harvests will

rule out famine and the consequent disgrace inflicted upon the famished by mocking onlookers. The reader who picks up on the importance of these two issues will likely interpret (or reinterpret) 36:13-15 in light of them. Famine takes a society's weakest members first; and a land that "devours" its starving inhabitants is culpable and therefore vulnerable to insults and disgrace.

Having articulated the various stages of Yahweh's plan for restoration, God turns to what the people's response will (and ostensibly should) be. Recalling their evil ways and not good dealings, they will "loathe themselves" for their iniquities and abominable deeds. Returning to the assertion of v. 22, Yahweh again stresses what Israel must know: God will not act for the sake of the house of Israel. The people are commanded to be ashamed (בושׁ *bôš*) and humiliated (niphal of כלם *kālam*) on account of their past misconduct.

How somber and stern is Ezekiel's "good news." When Jeremiah, by contrast, speaks of Israel's restoration, he permits a glimpse of human joy and thanksgiving, and even of divine love for Israel:

> There shall once more be heard the voice of mirth and the voice of gladness, the voice of the bridegroom and the voice of the bride, the voices of those who sing, as they bring thank offerings to the house of the LORD:
> "Give thanks to the LORD of hosts,
> for the LORD is good,
> for his steadfast love endures forever!
> (Jer 33:10-11 NRSV)

Ezekiel denies his audience, and his readers, any such glimpse. This harsh passage is reminiscent of others appearing earlier in the book. In 6:9, the prophet proclaims that those who escape Judah's destruction will, in exile, loathe themselves for their evil doings. In Ezek 16:61-63 Jerusalem, personified as Yahweh's faithless wife, remembers her abominations and is ashamed in the face of Yahweh's reconciling actions. Indeed, her shame is such as to silence her for life.

Again we note pronounced similarities between Ezekiel 20 and 36. Both Ezek 20:43-44 and 36:31-32 appear within a context where Ezekiel is deeply concerned about the profanation of the divine name among the nations. Both are prefaced with an announcement that God will regather the people and return them to their ancestral home—

not because they merit such treatment, but for the sake of God's own reputation. In each case, the people's proper responses include self-loathing. (See Reflections at 36:37-38.)

Ezekiel 36:33-36, "Like the Garden of Eden"

NIV

33" 'This is what the Sovereign LORD says: On the day I cleanse you from all your sins, I will resettle your towns, and the ruins will be rebuilt. 34The desolate land will be cultivated instead of lying desolate in the sight of all who pass through it. 35They will say, "This land that was laid waste has become like the garden of Eden; the cities that were lying in ruins, desolate and destroyed, are now fortified and inhabited." 36Then the nations around you that remain will know that I the LORD have rebuilt what was destroyed and have replanted what was desolate. I the LORD have spoken, and I will do it.'

NRSV

33Thus says the Lord GOD: On the day that I cleanse you from all your iniquities, I will cause the towns to be inhabited, and the waste places shall be rebuilt. 34The land that was desolate shall be tilled, instead of being the desolation that it was in the sight of all who passed by. 35And they will say, "This land that was desolate has become like the garden of Eden; and the waste and desolate and ruined towns are now inhabited and fortified." 36Then the nations that are left all around you shall know that I, the LORD, have rebuilt the ruined places, and replanted that which was desolate; I, the LORD, have spoken, and I will do it.

COMMENTARY

Following the messenger formula, vv. 33-36 commence with the phrase "On the day that I cleanse you from all your iniquities." "On the day" links these verses with the preceding ones; and the root of the word translated "cleanse" (טהר *ṭāhēr*) is the same one that thrice appeared in v. 25. Addressing the issue of Israel's desolate land, God promises to repopulate the towns, whose ruins will be rebuilt. Moreover, the soil will be tilled, ceasing to be the desolation that has been witnessed by "all who passed by." The present text reverses Yahweh's punishment of Judah's inhabitants as anticipated in Ezek 5:14-16. In that context, Yahweh threatened to make them "a desolation and an object of mocking among the nations . . . in the sight of all that pass by." As a consequence, they would be "a mockery and a taunt, a warning and a horror, to the nations

around you." Verse 16 spoke of Yahweh loosening "my deadly arrows of famine" against the Israelites. In the present context, by contrast, future famine has already been ruled out (36:10-12, 29-30), the desolate land will be revived, and mockery will be replaced by an awestruck observation cast as a direct quotation of the passers-by: "This land that was desolate has become like the garden of Eden; and the waste and desolate and ruined towns are now inhabited and fortified." Then the surrounding nations, whose taunts have demeaned and angered Israel's God, and whose punishment Israel awaits, will be forced to acknowledge that Yahweh has *rebuilt* the ruins, and *replanted* the desolate soil (see Jer 1:10). This outcome is certain, for "I, the LORD, have spoken, and I will do it." (See Reflections at 36:37-38.)

Ezekiel 36:37-38, Israel's Population Explosion

NIV	NRSV
37"This is what the Sovereign LORD says: Once again I will yield to the plea of the house of Israel and do this for them: I will make their people as numerous as sheep, 38as numerous as the flocks for offerings at Jerusalem during her appointed feasts. So will the ruined cities be filled with flocks of people. Then they will know that I am the LORD."	37Thus says the Lord GOD: I will also let the house of Israel ask me to do this for them: to increase their population like a flock. 38Like the flock for sacrifices,*a* like the flock at Jerusalem during her appointed festivals, so shall the ruined towns be filled with flocks of people. Then they shall know that I am the LORD. *a*Heb *flock of holy things*

COMMENTARY

Following an initial messenger formula (vv. 37-38 are linked to preceding verses by עוד זאת ['ôd zō't, "this too"]), Yahweh makes an astonishing announcement. Heretofore in the scroll, God has absolutely refused "to be inquired" of (דרש *dāraš*) by Israel's elders (14:3; 20:3, 31; see also 8:18). In the future, however, that ban will be lifted; and Yahweh will permit the house of Israel "to request" (*dāraš*) that its population be increased "like a flock." This God will do to so great an extent that the streets of the once-ruined towns will teem with human beings as numerous as the flocks of animals for sacrifice that once filled the streets of Jerusalem during festivals (see the [likely hyperbolic] accounts of the very large numbers of animals sacrificed [2 Chr 29:31-36 and 35:7-9]).

As so often in the book of Ezekiel, the oracle ends with the recognition formula, which articulates the ultimate goal of God's intervention in Israel's (and the other nations') history: the acknowledgement of who Yahweh is in all God's glory and sovereignty.

REFLECTIONS

Viewed from a theological perspective, Ezek 36:16-38 is one of the most important passages in the entire book. The priest-prophet articulates, in forceful language permeated by priestly thought, a thoroughly theocentric ("God-centered") account of: (1) Israel's defiling past and proportionate punishment; (2) the negative consequences of its punishment for Yahweh's "name" (reputation) among the nations; and (3) God's solution to that intolerable state of affairs.

Many a modern reader may find the text unsettling, if not distasteful. The analogy between Israel's defiling impurity and a woman's menstrual flow imbues the latter—a natural bodily function essential to procreation—with negative connotations. The portrait of an enraged deity pouring out wrath upon a people, ripping the survivors of Nebuchadrezzar's siege and assault from their homeland, and scattering them among their conquerors, is troubling, even terrifying. Having apparently failed to anticipate the consequence of deportation for the divine reputation, that same deity resolves to reverse the situation. The plan of restoration set out in vv. 24-38 involves regathering the people, returning them to their homeland, purifying them, fructifying their desolate territory, and rebuilding their ruined cities, such that the mocking taunts of neighboring nations are replaced by awestruck acknowledgment of what Yahweh has accomplished. All of this will be done not for the sake of the people themselves, however, but only for the glorification of their God. The statement "It is not for your sake, O house of Israel, that I am about to act" (vv. 22, 32) does not *rule out* the possibility that Yahweh cares about Israel. Indeed, Ezekiel elsewhere suggests that God cares deeply about the people (see, e.g., 18:31-32; 33:11).

But here, no such divine sentiments are permitted. The people will benefit greatly from Yahweh's restorative acts, but their response should and will be self-loathing—a state of mind that moderns know can inflict extreme psychological and physiological injury.

Even vv. 26-27, God's well-known promise to replace Israel's stony heart with a heart of flesh and to imbue it with Yahweh's own spirit, can be problematic. Some Jews and Christians will wonder how spiritual transformation is possible without prior human repentance. Would God really purge people of their sins without contrition and confession? And what becomes of human freedom to choose between good and evil if God acts unilaterally to "reprogram" human nature? These verses exhibit, on the one hand, radical despair of Israel's repentance. For Ezekiel, Israel has from its beginning and throughout its history been rebellious, disobedient, and unfaithful (see, e.g., Ezekiel 16, 20, and 23). And the sins of the past are very much present not only among those who have remained in the homeland, but also among his fellow exiles. The prophet may believe that Israel's future resides with those who were "scattered among the nations," rather than with those who remained in Judah, but he does not hold them any less culpable of the widespread and ongoing transgressions he describes. From the time of his call through succeeding decades, he has known the reality of Israel's "heart of stone." The restoration of Yahweh's reputation cannot depend upon or wait for Israel's initiative.

On the other hand, Greenberg observes, the text exhibits "a radical certainty that God's holiness (majesty, authority) would be vindicated and acknowledged by all nations, through the agency of Israel.[1184] Here, as everywhere in his book, Ezekiel insists that God ultimately is in control of history, Israel's and the nations'; and human obduracy will never derail Yahweh's plan to be acknowledged in all God's holiness, power, and glory. Because the nations know that Israel is Yahweh's people and are aware of the losses it has endured, they question and even mock Yahweh's ability to function as an ancient Near Eastern patron deity should. What sort of god or goddess permits a land and its people to be ripped apart so savagely? Is such a deity worthy of praise? Or should he or she be abandoned, so that loyalty and devotion can shift to a more "successful" patron?

For Ezekiel, the profanation of God's name creates an untenable situation which must be set right, irrespective of human merit or the lack thereof. Israel's guarantee of restoration is the indissoluble link between God's reputation and Israel's fortunes.[1185] For all that Ezekiel has insisted, especially in judgment oracles, that Yahweh's treatment of Israel has been appropriate to its behavior (most recently in 36:19), in this case, the people's status (their sinfulness, their willingness or unwillingness to repent) is simply irrelevant. Nothing must stand in the way of the sanctification of Yahweh's name.

Ezekiel insists that once Yahweh restores, purifies, and transforms Israel, the people will be capable only of obedience. Disobedience has, from Ezekiel's perspective, been Israel's core defect since its days of slavery in Egypt. What is to keep them from continuing their past practices, defiling their native soil, and incurring yet another punishment that imperils Yahweh's reputation? "So that God's name never again suffer disgrace," Greenberg observes, "Israel's restoration must be irreversible. Such it can be only if Israel be denied the ability ever again to disobey God's law. God's uninterrupted glorification entails the curtailment of human freedom."[1186]

I suspect that modern readers respond to Yahweh's "curtailment of human freedom" in a variety of ways. Indeed, individuals may find themselves with a divided mind on this topic. On the one hand, we despair (often with good reason) of the prospect that human beings will, in and of themselves, effect radical transformations. This is true not only on a grand scale (global transformation, cultural and social transformation), but also on a personal scale (transformation of the self). The idea that God might so reconfigure human beings that they would simply be incapable of misconduct (but who defines what "misconduct" is?) has a strong appeal. On the other hand,

1184. Greenberg, *Ezekiel 21–37*, 735.
1185. Ibid.
1186. Ibid.

vv. 26-27 describe a process which leaves its recipients incapable of exercising the freedom to choose between one path and another. No one lives entirely free of prohibitions and restrictions, of course. But is the cost of obedience to God too high in this case? Can one even speak of "obedience" if the obedient party is constitutionally incapable of being disobedient? Can one affirm with Michael Fox that "when one has God's spirit in him he does God's will because he *wants* to do God's will"?[1187]

At this point, one wonders about the degree to which personal and cultural presuppositions are influencing one's construal of the text. I have described this passage as "harsh," for example, but would it have struck Ezekiel's fellow exiles in that way? After all, so long as Yahweh's name and Israel's fate are conjoined, the people need not fear total extinction. Indeed, they can anticipate a marvelous restoration that does not hang upon their merit. And perhaps the loss of human freedom to choose would not be problematic for ancient readers who realize that obdurate choices could occasion unbearable punishments. Yet the importance of human choice is a recurring idea in Hebrew Scripture. One thinks of Deut 30:19-20: "I have set before you life and death, blessings and curses. Choose life so that you and your descendants may live, loving the LORD your God, obeying him, and holding fast to him." Joshua allows that the Hebrews can choose to serve deities other than Yahweh: "Now if you are unwilling to serve the LORD, choose this day whom you will serve, whether the gods your ancestors served in the region beyond the River or the gods of the Amorites in whose land you are living; but as for me and my household, we will serve the LORD" (Josh 24:15). The people's ability to *choose* to be faithful to Yahweh is crucial in that context. And, of course, choice lies at the heart of the exhortation in Ezek 18:5-21. Wrong choices have negative consequences, but one can cite many biblical texts that indicate that God values human obedience based on genuine choice.

In the Commentary, I noted that Ezekiel twice speaks of God's giving the house of Israel a new heart and a new spirit (11:19, 36:26), while elsewhere, he exhorts the house of Israel to "Cast away from you all the transgressions that you have committed against me, and get yourselves a new heart and a new spirit! Why will you die, O house of Israel?" (18:31). One can understand, I think, why the prophet speaks as he does in each context. Still, when these verses are juxtaposed, we perceive in them a kind of paradox—on the one hand, the call for human responsibility, on the other hand, the assertion that God is in complete control and effects all in terms of salvation. This tension is by no means limited to the Ezekiel scroll. To the contrary, it appears both in Paul's letters and in the Gospels. Paul, for example, feels comfortable in exhorting the Corinthian believers to "clean out the old leaven that you may be a new lump, just as you are in fact unleavened. For Christ our Passover also has been sacrificed" (1 Cor 5:7). Why, one wonders, is it necessary to "clean out the old leaven" if one is already unleavened? Or again, Paul can tell the Galatians, "if we live by the Spirit, let us also walk by the Spirit" (Gal 5:25; "live" and "walk" are essentially synonyms. The Spirit moves us, but at the same time, we must follow the Spirit). The paradox is even clearer in Phil 2:12*b*-13, where Paul tells his readers to "work out your salvation with fear and trembling, for it is God who is at work in you both to will and to work for his good pleasure." Of this striking but common Pauline paradox Günther Bornkamm observes:

Note that the action is not divided up between God and men, making the two propositions supplementary to each other. Nor is the sense: Bend all your endeavors on this, and God will add his and crown it. Nor: He has made the beginning; see to it that it comes to a successful issue. No, each proposition substantiates the other: Because God does everything, you too have everything to do. . . . The believer's actions derive from God's act, and the decisions taken by obedience from God's antecedent decision for the world in Christ. Thus the two come together in equilibrium: to live on the basis of *grace,* but also to *live* on the basis of grace."[1188]

1187. Michael Fox, "The Rhetoric of Ezekiel's Vision of the Valley of the Bones," *HUCA* 51 (1980) 15.
1188. Günther Bornkamm, *Paul* (New York: Harper and Row, 1971) 201-3.

From this perspective, faith is not simply mental assent to doctrine or truth. Rather, it is full participation in the life of God and the church. God's gracious outreach toward the believer and the believer's activity toward God coalesce. Each is integral to the other.

The evangelists also know of the paradoxical relationship between divine and human willing and acting. In Luke's presentation of the story of the ministering woman (Luke 7:36-50), for example, Jesus tells the woman that "your sins have been forgiven" (v. 48). But is this forgiveness the *consequence* of her actions (anointing Jesus' feet with tears and expensive perfume, and then kissing and wiping his feet with her hair) or the *cause* of them? The narrator provides no specific clues as to the motivation of the woman's strange actions. Gap-filling sequential readers may identify the woman as one of the sinners whom the narrative has just characterized as "having been baptized with the baptism of John," that is, as having repented (Luke 7:29).[1189] But even this only removes the issue by one step. Why have they repented? The paradox of divine and human interaction, gift and call, faith and obedience, belief and duty remains.

1189. John A. Darr, *On Character Building: The Reader and the Rhetoric of Characterization in Luke-Acts* (Louisville: Westminster/John Knox, 1992) 33-34.

EZEKIEL 37:1-14, "MORTAL, CAN THESE BONES LIVE?"

OVERVIEW

These verses, often referred to as the vision of the valley of dry bones, are arguably the most famous in all the book of Ezekiel. Their importance for Jews and Christians is indicated by the signal periods when they are read liturgically. They accompany the Torah reading, Exod 33:12–34:26, on the sabbath of Passover week.[1190] *The Revised Common Lectionary* associates it with the fifth Sunday in Lent (year A), the Easter vigil (years A, B, and C), and Pentecost (year B).

This is the third of Ezekiel's four visionary reports (the others appear in 1:1-3:15, 8:1–11:25, and 40:1–48:35). Elsewhere in the book, oracles are routinely introduced with the word event formula "the word of the LORD came to me." Here, as in the other three vision accounts, Ezekiel states that "the hand of the LORD came upon me." Transported by the spirit of the Lord to "the valley," Ezekiel is astonished to see that it is filled with a multitude of disconnected and thoroughly desiccated bones. The image is of a battlefield whose slain never received proper burial, but were left to decay (and be ravaged by birds and beasts) where they fell. Having led Ezekiel around these piles of bones, Yahweh asks him a question: "Mortal, can these bones live?" (v. 3). The prophet's response is enigmatic (see Commentary): "O Lord GOD, you know." Yahweh then orders Ezekiel to prophesy to the bones (as if they had ears to hear!). In response to the prophet's words, the bones are re-membered, bound by sinews, refleshed, covered with skin, and animated by the spirit.

The vision proper is followed in vv. 11-14 by a modified disputation speech which, the reader comes to realize, is actually a salvation oracle directed to Ezekiel's fellow deportees. The bones, Yahweh informs Ezekiel, are "the whole house of Israel." The exiles are lamenting that their bones are dried up, their hope has perished, and they are utterly cut off (v. 11). The first of these three assertions has most probably occasioned the metaphorical vision of vv. 1-10. The third suggests the quite different metaphor appearing in vv. 12-14. Yahweh instructs the prophet to inform his audience that their present situation and consequent despair will be transformed. God will open their

---

1190. A biblical text read in tandem with the Torah selection is called a Haftorah.

graves, bring them forth from those graves, and return them to their homeland. The recognition formula in v. 13 ("And you shall know that I am Yahweh") points to God's greater purpose in all this activity—that Israel should know and acknowledge who its unrivaled deity is, in all of God's power and sovereignty. Verse 14, like 36:27, affirms that the Lord will place "my spirit" within the people and they shall live, reestablished on their own soil. This verse also contains a modified recognition formula, which insists that Yahweh's words will indeed be fulfilled (see most recently 36:36*b*).

Ezekiel 37:1-10, The Dry Bones Are Re-membered

NIV	NRSV
37 The hand of the LORD was upon me, and he brought me out by the Spirit of the LORD and set me in the middle of a valley; it was full of bones. ²He led me back and forth among them, and I saw a great many bones on the floor of the valley, bones that were very dry. ³He asked me, "Son of man, can these bones live?"	**37** The hand of the LORD came upon me, and he brought me out by the spirit of the LORD and set me down in the middle of a valley; it was full of bones. ²He led me all around them; there were very many lying in the valley, and they were very dry. ³He said to me, "Mortal, can these bones live?" I answered, "O Lord GOD, you know." ⁴Then he said to me, "Prophesy to these bones, and say to them: O dry bones, hear the word of the LORD. ⁵Thus says the Lord GOD to these bones: I will cause breath*a* to enter you, and you shall live. ⁶I will lay sinews on you, and will cause flesh to come upon you, and cover you with skin, and put breath*a* in you, and you shall live; and you shall know that I am the LORD."

NIV body (continued):

I said, "O Sovereign LORD, you alone know."

⁴Then he said to me, "Prophesy to these bones and say to them, 'Dry bones, hear the word of the LORD! ⁵This is what the Sovereign LORD says to these bones: I will make breath*a* enter you, and you will come to life. ⁶I will attach tendons to you and make flesh come upon you and cover you with skin; I will put breath in you, and you will come to life. Then you will know that I am the LORD.' "

⁷So I prophesied as I was commanded. And as I was prophesying, there was a noise, a rattling sound, and the bones came together, bone to bone. ⁸I looked, and tendons and flesh appeared on them and skin covered them, but there was no breath in them.

⁹Then he said to me, "Prophesy to the breath; prophesy, son of man, and say to it, 'This is what the Sovereign LORD says: Come from the four winds, O breath, and breathe into these slain, that they may live.' " ¹⁰So I prophesied as he commanded me, and breath entered them; they came to life and stood up on their feet—a vast army.

NRSV body (continued):

7So I prophesied as I had been commanded; and as I prophesied, suddenly there was a noise, a rattling, and the bones came together, bone to its bone. ⁸I looked, and there were sinews on them, and flesh had come upon them, and skin had covered them; but there was no breath in them. ⁹Then he said to me, "Prophesy to the breath, prophesy, mortal, and say to the breath:*a* Thus says the Lord GOD: Come from the four winds, O breath,*b* and breathe upon these slain, that they may live." ¹⁰I prophesied as he commanded me, and the breath came into them, and they lived, and stood on their feet, a vast multitude.

*a*Or *spirit*   *b*Or *wind* or *spirit*

*a*5 The Hebrew for this word can also mean *wind* or *spirit* (see verses 6-14).

COMMENTARY

Ezekiel's autobiographical vision narrative begins with the statement, "The hand of Yahweh came upon me." References to Yahweh's powerful hand upon the prophet appeared in the vision reports in Ezekiel 1–3 (1:3; 3:14, 22) and 8:1–11:25 (8:1); and the phrase will reappear in 40:1, the beginning of his final vision account (40:1–48:35). The statement probably suggests that the prophet exhibited behavior associated with spirit possession, perhaps a trance-like state (see the Commentary on Ezek 1:3). Because Ezekiel's other vision narratives are dated, scholars have suspected that originally, this account also bore a date. If that was the case, however, there is no way to retrieve it.

While in God's grip, Ezekiel claims to have been transported "by the spirit of the Lord" to "the valley" and deposited there. (The phrase "the spirit of Yahweh" elsewhere appears in 11:5. In that context, it prefaces God's command that Ezekiel prophesy to the house of Israel. Here, however, it functions much as the phrase "by the spirit of God" functions in 11:24. There, too, the spirit is a means of transportation. The presence of the definite article on בקעה [biq'â, "valley," "plain"] suggests, as in 3:22, that a particular valley is in mind.) To the prophet's astonishment (הנה [hinnēh, "lo!" or "behold!"] will appear twice in v. 2 and once in vv. 5, 7-8), it is filled with bones. In order that Ezekiel get the full impact of the sight before his eyes, Yahweh leads him round about them. He is struck both by their great number and by their extreme dryness. Then, God poses a question to the prophet: "Mortal, can these bones live?" Ezekiel's response, "O Lord GOD, you know," is vague. Had we access to vocal inflection and possible gestures, we might be able to determine whether he spoke with conviction ("O Lord God, *you* know"), hesitation, or resignation ("O Lord GOD . . . you know"). In any event, he does not rule out that possibility; and readers would not expect him to do so. Throughout his scroll to this point, Ezekiel has never suggested that anything lies beyond Yahweh's power and control.

Scholars have sought the source of Ezekiel's imagery both in Mesopotamian battle accounts and in treaty curses. In his annals, Assyria's King

Sennacherib (704–681 BCE) brags "With the bodies of [the enemy's] warriors I filled the plain, like grass."[1191] If the vassals of Assyrian King Esarhaddon (680–669 BCE) were disloyal, they risked the following curse: "May Ninurta, leader of the gods, fell you with his fierce arrow, and fill the plain with your corpses, give your flesh to eagles and vultures to feed upon."[1192] The reader recalls a similar covenant curse in Deut 28:25-26. Ezekiel's vision account says nothing of marauding birds and beasts. Presumably, those creatures have long since completed their feast. His emphasis falls, rather, upon the legion of desiccated bones. According to Num 19:16, anyone in an open field who touched a human bone remained unclean for seven days. But the priest-prophet voices no such concern here (cf. Ezek 4:14). This is, after all, a visionary experience, not actual contact with human remains.

Yahweh commands Ezekiel, a spectator to this point, to prophesy to the bones, calling them to attention and demanding that they "hear the word of the LORD." Following the messenger formula ("Thus says the Lord GOD") he is to announce to them their impending revivification. The outcome, introduced by *hinnēh*, is proclaimed first: God will cause "breath" or "spirit" to enter them, and they will live. This end will be accomplished through a four-fold process. First, God will lay sinews upon them, binding bone to bone. Second, Yahweh will cause flesh to come upon them. Third, skin will cover the flesh. This sequencing of events reverses the process by which bodies decompose. Finally, God will infuse them with breath (or "spirit"). As a consequence of these procedures, the bones will live; more importantly, the Lord's larger purpose will be accomplished: the revived people will know and acknowledge who Yahweh is.

Ezekiel reports that he prophesied as commanded—to exceedingly dramatic effect. He hears a sound, a quaking or rattling. As Greenberg observes, one cannot determine whether the quaking of the earth causes the bones to stir, or if

1191. D. D. Luckenbill, *The Annals of Sennacherib*, OIP (Chicago: University of Chicago Press, 1924) 46, ll.9-10. See also Moshe Greenberg, *Ezekiel 21–37*, AB 22A (Garden City, N.Y.: Doubleday, 1997) 748.
1192. *ANET*, 538b.

the ground quakes on account of the animated bones.[1193] According to Yahweh, the first step of the vivification process entailed the laying on of sinews (v. 6). In Ezekiel's account, by contrast, the process commences as bones approach each other, bone to its appropriate bone, to constitute skeletons (v. 7). Suddenly, they are stitched together by sinews, flesh has come upon them, and they are covered with skin!

The bones have become bodies but, Ezekiel observes, the bodies are lifeless, for there is no breath (רוח *rûaḥ*) within them. Now, in an act unanticipated in vv. 5-6, Ezekiel is twice commanded to prophesy again, summoning "the breath" or "the spirit" (הרוח *hārûaḥ*). It is unclear at this point which translation of *hārûaḥ* best suits the context. The matter is further complicated when he is ordered, following the messenger formula, to evoke the *rûaḥ* from "the four winds" (מארבע רוחות *mě'arba' rûḥôt*) to "breathe" (or "blow"?) upon "these slain." "Wind" is yet another meaning of *rûaḥ,* and the four winds (the winds that blow from the four compass points— i.e., all winds) appear to be the powerful source of the *rûaḥ* Ezekiel must summon.

1193.   Greenberg, *Ezekiel 21–37,* 743.

The verb "to breathe" in v. 9 is from the root נפח (*nph*). That same verb appears in Gen 2:7 to describe how God, having formed a human body from the soil, breathed into its nostrils the breath of life. Critics point out that the creation account in Genesis 2 is educed here not just by the presence of that same verb, but especially by the fact that in both passages, the human body is formed before the breath (or spirit, or wind) enlivens it. Ezekiel's distinction between body and breath is not, Zimmerli reminds us, an expression of the dualistic understanding of human beings, which contrasts "a creaturely body which is from below" with "an immortal soul which is from above." Rather, the prophet "distinguishes between the body, which can be seen with the eyes and felt with the hands, and the life force, which animates the body, is intangible, but is no less effective and can be discerned in the breath."[1194]

Ezekiel prophesies as commanded. The breath or wind enters the corpses and they come alive. More, they stand up on their feet, "a vast army." (See Reflections at 37:11-14.)

1194. W. Zimmerli, *Ezekiel 2: A Commentary on the Book of the Prophet Ezekiel, Chapters 25–48,* trans. J. D. Martin, Hermeneia (Philadelphia: Fortress, 1983) 261.

Ezekiel 37:11-14, Disputation, Interpretation, and Salvation

[11]Then he said to me: "Son of man, these bones are the whole house of Israel. They say, 'Our bones are dried up and our hope is gone; we are cut off.' [12]Therefore prophesy and say to them: 'This is what the Sovereign LORD says: O my people, I am going to open your graves and bring you up from them; I will bring you back to the land of Israel. [13]Then you, my people, will know that I am the LORD, when I open your graves and bring you up from them. [14]I will put my Spirit in you and you will live, and I will settle you in your own land. Then you will know that I the LORD have spoken, and I have done it, declares the LORD.' "

11Then he said to me, "Mortal, these bones are the whole house of Israel. They say, `Our bones are dried up, and our hope is lost; we are cut off completely.' [12]Therefore prophesy, and say to them, Thus says the Lord GOD: I am going to open your graves, and bring you up from your graves, O my people; and I will bring you back to the land of Israel. [13]And you shall know that I am the LORD, when I open your graves, and bring you up from your graves, O my people. [14]I will put my spirit within you, and you shall live, and I will place you on your own soil; then you shall know that I, the LORD, have spoken and will act, says the LORD."

COMMENTARY

Verses 11-14 have been termed a modified disputation speech. A sentiment ostensibly shared by the exiles is quoted, and then Yahweh responds to it. In many disputation speeches, God challenges the quotation head on, as in Ezek 12:21-25, 26-28 and 18:1-32. Here, however, the Lord does not deny that the exiles' deadly despair is real. Rather Yahweh describes, in both metaphorical and literal language, what will be done to transform their lives.

Verse 11 pivots between the preceding vision account (vv. 1-10) and what follows (vv. 12-14). At its outset, Yahweh "decodes" the extraordinary events Ezekiel has just witnessed with a simple equation: "Mortal, these bones are *the whole house* of Israel" (emphasis mine). Here, as elsewhere (see, e.g., 36:10), the prophet thinks not just of the fallen kingdom of Judah, but also of Israel's northern kingdom, destroyed by the Assyrians in 721 BCE. God then calls Ezekiel's attention to a three-line lament circulating among the people:

> Our bones are dried up,
> and our hope is lost;
> we are cut off completely.

In Hebrew, each of these three lines consists of two words; and the second word of each line ends with either *-ênû* or *-ānû,* creating a mournful rhyming sound.

The despondency experienced by Ezekiel's fellow exiles in the aftermath of Judah's collapse was expressed by means of a quotation already in 33:10: "Our transgressions and our sins weigh upon us, and we waste away because of them; how then can we live?" Here, the exiles do not question whether life is possible. To the contrary, in the first line of their lament, they speak metaphorically as if they were already dead and their bodies reduced to desiccated bones. If the lament was actually abroad among the exiles, then its first line, "Our bones are dried up," expresses a sentiment that may well have inspired Ezekiel's metaphorical vision in vv. 1-10. Among ancient Israel's didactic literature, that same sentiment is expressed in the second line of a proverb: "A cheerful heart is a good medicine,/ but a down-cast spirit dries up the bones" (Prov 17:22). The author of Prov 15:30 affirms that "a cheerful look brings joy to the heart,/ and good news gives health to the bones" (NIV). Proverbs 3:7-8 instructs: "Do not be wise in your own eyes;/ fear the LORD and shun evil./ This will bring health to your body/ and nourishment to your bones" (NIV). Within the book of Psalms, "bones" appears in expressions of praise ("All my bones shall say,/ 'O LORD, who is like you?' " (32:10*a*). But they also appear in petitionary prayers. The psalmist of 31:10 laments both emotional and physical distress ("For my life is spent with sorrow, and my years with sighing;/ my strength fails because of my iniquity,/ and my bones waste away"), while the author of Ps 102:3 sighs, "For my days pass away like smoke,/ and my bones burn like a furnace."

The second line of the exiles' lament acknowledges an utter absence of hope (see also 19:5). The NRSV translates, "our hope is lost"; the NIV, "our hope is gone." Both renderings are proper. However, the root אבד (*'bd*) means not only "to vanish" but also "to perish." The former option is apropros to inanimate things like "hope," but the latter meaning should not, in this context of deadly despair, be suppressed: "our hope has perished."

The third line employs the root גזר (*gzr*). In the qal verbal system, the root means "to cut, divide." It is used literally in 2 Kgs 6:4 to describe the felling of trees. It appears within the complex and multilayered trope of Isa 9:18-21 to refer to cutting off a piece of meat for consumption. In the present text, the root appears in the niphal verbal system and means "to be cut off" or "destroyed." From what have the people been cut off? The text does not elaborate, but on the basis of the two preceding lines, we should expect the third also to deal with death in some way. Greenberg has shown that this verb can refer to one who has died and been buried. Striking examples of this usage appear in Ps 88:3-5; Isa 53:8-9; and Lam 3:54-55. Hence, the third line of the people's lament presages the figurative language of vv. 12-13, which depicts the exiles not as scattered piles of desiccated bones lying *on* the ground, but as buried corpses which Yahweh brings up from *below* the ground.[1195]

Having shown Ezekiel the vision of revived bones and informed (or reminded) him of the people's lament, Yahweh now commands him to utter a public prophecy. In the following oracle, which is introduced by the messenger formula, God speaks first of opening the people's graves and then of bringing them up from those graves. Obviously, the lamenting exiles are no more dead and interred than they are dried bones spread across the plain of the Euphrates. Here, as in vv. 1-10, the prophet wields the power of metaphor to persuade his audience, and his readers, to accept a new perception of their reality.[1196] Finally, Yahweh will bring them back to the land of Israel. The verbs translated "bring up" and "bring back" evoke thoughts of a new exodus.

The expanded recognition formula of v. 13 reiterates the metaphorical promise of national disinterment. When their graves are opened and they are brought up from them, they will know and acknowledge who Yahweh is. The vocative address, "O my people," which appeared also in v. 12, is repeated, further emphasizing that a covenantal bond yet exists between Yahweh and Israel.

Verse 14 both elaborates upon v. 13 and advances a thought expressed at the end of v. 12. At the beginning of v. 14, Yahweh promises to place God's own spirit within them, with the consequence that "you shall live." Recognizing the near parallel between "[I will] put breath [or spirit] in you, and you shall live" in v. 6*a* on the one hand, and v. 14*a* on the other, Greenberg observes that just as the restored bodies of vv. 7-8 were inanimate until the wind breathed upon them, so the corpses emerging from their graves will be "lifeless clay" until God's spirit enters them.[1197] Does the reference to "my spirit" clarify for the reader the ambiguous references to רוח (*rûaḥ*), both without and with the definite article, in preceding verses, or is it to be differentiated from them? For consistency-seeking readers, the appearance of

"my spirit" (or "my breath") may illumine the references to *rûaḥ* in vv. 5 and 6 especially. The noun with pronominal suffix appeared earlier in 36:27, where an infusion of Yahweh's spirit renders once-rebellious Israel capable only of following Yahweh's statutes and observing carefully God's ordinances. In the present passage, life—not obedience—is specified as the consequence of the infusion of Yahweh's spirit. But obedience and life are inextricably linked in Ezekiel's thought. In chap. 20, for example, we read in vv. 11 and 21 "I gave them my statutes and showed them my ordinances, by whose observance everyone shall live" (see also chap. 18).

While in v. 12, Yahweh promised to bring God's people back to their homeland, v. 14 goes a step further: God will "place" (or "settle" or "establish") the people in the land of Israel. The root נוח (*nûaḥ*) appeared also at the beginning of the oracle (v. 1) to describe Yahweh's placing of the prophet in the midst of the valley. All of this, v. 14 asserts, God will do in order that the people will know that the Lord whose words Ezekiel speaks will surely fulfill these promises.

Do Ezekiel's choices of metaphors—dried bones and bringing people up from their graves—suggest that in his day, corporeal resurrection of individuals was an established idea? Based on biblical and extra-biblical evidence, most scholars have answered this question in the negative. True, the notion was abroad in Jewish thought by the first century CE. But the first articulation of it appears in the book of Daniel (which post-dates significantly the book of Ezekiel) with reference to those who died during the persecutions of the Seleucid king Antiochus IV during the years 167–164 BCE: "Many of those who sleep in the dust of the earth shall awake, some to everlasting life, and some to shame and everlasting contempt" (Dan 12:2).[1198]

Fox suggests that at the time of Ezekiel, his audience would have regarded the notion of corporeal resurrection as "basically absurd." They, like he, would have answered the rhetorical questions of Ps 88:10-12 with the expected "no":

1195. See Greenberg, *Ezekiel 21–37*, 745-46.

1196. K. P. Darr, *Isaiah's Vision and the Family of God* (Louisville: Westminster John Knox, 1994) 42-44. Fox notes the suasive quality of rhetoric: "Rhetoric is persuasive discourse (persuasive in intent if not in accomplishment)." See Michael Fox, "The Rhetoric of Ezekiel's Vision of the Valley of the Bones," *HUCA* 51 (1980) 2.

1197. Greenberg, *Ezekiel 21–37*, 746.

1198. As Fox observes, this verse is not indebted to Ezekiel's language. But because other passages in Daniel (e.g., Dan 4:7-15; 7:9-10; 10:4-6) reveal the author(s) dependence on Ezekiel, it is possible that this passage also presupposes knowledge of the present passage. See Fox, "The Rhetoric of Ezekiel's Vision of the Valley of the Bones," 187.

Do you work wonders for the dead?
  Do the shades rise up to praise you?
Is your steadfast love declared in the grave,
  or your faithfulness in Abaddon?
Are your wonders known in the darkness,
  or your saving help in the land of
    forgetfulness?

"Ezekiel shows the dead rising," Fox avers, "but not because he believes that actual corpses will do so. Rather he depicts the extreme case of unpredictable salvation in order to enable the people to expect a salvation that though unlikely is yet less radical, the return of the nation from exile."[1199]

1199. Ibid., 186.

REFLECTIONS

Fox is correct when he asserts that the prophet has singled out seemingly impossible events in order to buttress his claims that other highly improbable, but not *as* preposterous, feats are indeed possible. If Yahweh can restore desiccated bones and buried bodies to life, then there are absolutely no limits to God's power. Ezekiel's fellow exiles do not view the vision directly, as he alleges to have done, but they "see" it through his astonished eyes.

As noted in the commentary, Ezek 37:1-14 is the third of four visionary accounts in the book. In the first, 1:1–3:15, Ezekiel begins his recounting as follows: "In the thirtieth year, in the fourth month, on the fifth day of the month, as I was among the exiles by the river Chebar, the heavens were opened, and I saw *visions of God*" (1:1, italics added). The words I have just emphasized do not appear in the present visionary report, but if they did, their presence would be apropos. Critics sometimes translate those words as "divine visions," and that is not a bad rendering of מראות אלהים (*mar'ōt 'ĕlōhîm*). But for the purposes of reflection, I should like not only to retain the translation appearing in both the NIV and the NRSV, but also to change it slightly and, in so doing, to alter its meaning. That is, I wish to consider not "visions of God," but "God's vision." What does it mean to look at our world, and at ourselves, through God's eyes?

Ezekiel's fellow deportees lament that they are (as good as) dead. Their hope has perished; and without hope, they might as well be dead. The future, if one can even speak of such, seems as barren as the past years and present experience of exile. Moreover Ezekiel himself has repeatedly insisted, in his oracles of condemnation and judgment, that their suffering is Yahweh's just punishment for a history of unrelenting rebelliousness and sin. Surely in the light of Judah's collapse, Jerusalem's destruction, the exiles' own situation, and Ezekiel's past denunciations, good news was, for many, hard to hear, well-nigh impossible to envision.

When, in a vision, Yahweh brought the prophet out to a broad valley and showed him the mounds, all around, of desiccated and dismembered bones, Ezekiel saw them through his own eyes. As noted in the Commentary, his answer to God's question—"Mortal, can these bones live?"—can be interpreted in at least two ways, either as an absolute affirmative, or as an uncertain throwing of the ball back into Yahweh's court. If the latter, then God's ensuing command, "Prophesy to these bones, and say to them: O dry bones, hear the word of the LORD,' " required of Ezekiel a leap of faith. But then, the bones began rattling, coming together to form skeletons; and suddenly, Ezekiel was no longer looking at them through his own eyes. His vision was lifted to a higher plane; now he was viewing them through God's eyes. The skeletons were clothed with flesh and skin and animated by breath, and they stood up on their feet!

In recounting his vision, Ezekiel challenges his fellow exiles and generations of his readers to view their circumstances not through their own, limited vision, but through God's eyes. Can these bones live? Of course not. But look at them through God's eyes, and watch bones rushing to their appropriate partners. Watch as ligaments bind them together, flesh blankets them, and skin seals them tightly. Watch as God's spirit, which heals hopelessness, infuses them, so that they rise up—a great army testifying to the power of Yahweh. Can corpses be brought forth from graves and become living beings again? Absurd! But look through God's eyes, and watch them come up, receive God's spirit, and return home. When we raise our vision to look beyond what our mundane eyes can see, we watch the impossible happen through God's eyes. "I can't believe my eyes," we say when we have witnessed an utterly unanticipated and/or seemingly impossible event take place. But we can believe God's eyes and, looking through them, glimpse unimagined reasons to keep on hoping, though the desert be dry and dark, and the promised land far, far away.

Ezekiel urges his audience to view their situation through the eyes of a God for whom all things are possible. And as I reflect on Ezek 37:1-14, I am reminded of "A Hard Death," a poem by Amos Wilder. The poem is too long to cite in full, but I share three lines from it:

> Accept no mitigation,
> But be instructed at the null point.
> The zero breeds new algebras.[1200]

Ezekiel's fellow exiles were at the null point, as good as dead and without hope. Facile words of reassurance could not cut through their despair. But Ezekiel invited them to view reality through God's eyes by means of a divine vision wherein the zero breeds new and unanticipated algebras.

The Judeo-Christian tradition brims with accounts of the zero breeding new algebras. Consider, for example, the crucifixion and death of Jesus. Surely, for Jesus' friends and family—those who had pinned their hopes on him—the cross must have seemed the starkest of "zeros," the hardest of deaths not only for Jesus, but also for their hopes. And yet, that instrument of scandalous, disgraceful death becomes for Christians of every age a powerful symbol of hope, of life beyond death, of salvation.

Nobel Laureate and Holocaust survivor Elie Wiesel has observed that Ezekiel's vision of the valley of dried bones bears no date because *every generation* needs to hear *in its own time* that these bones can live again.[1201] Like the exiles of old, we too can at times feel as good (rather, bad) as dead. We are null and void inside. But if we look through God's eyes, we can see broader realities, bases for hope. God can sustain us and fill our barren experiences with lively hope. Is it possible? Absolutely not, disbelievers aver. But look with God's vision and watch it happen!

1200. Amos Niven Wilder, *Grace Confounding: Poems* (Philadelphia: Fortress, 1972) 26-27.
1201. Elie Wiesel, "Ezekiel," in *Congregation: Contemporary Writers Read the Jewish Bible,* ed. David Rosenberg (San Diego: Harcourt Brace Jovanovich, 1987) 186.

EZEKIEL 37:15-28, THE RE-UNION AND RESTORATION OF THE PEOPLE OF ISRAEL

OVERVIEW

As is his custom, Ezekiel introduces 37:16-28 with the word event formula, "the word of the LORD came to me" (v. 15). This same formula reappears in 38:1, the beginning of yet another unit. In intervening verses, readers initially encounter God's command that the priest/prophet perform a sign-act—the last of his scroll and the only one

appearing among Ezekiel's salvation oracles. He must take for himself one "stick" (עֵץ 'ēṣ; on the other possible meanings of this noun, see below) on which he has either written or carved words (according to the MT) "of Judah, and the Israelites associated with it." Next, he must take a single stick on which he has either written or carved the words (again, according to the MT) "of Joseph, the stick of Ephraim, and all the house of Israel associated with it." Then, he must take the two sticks and (somehow) conjoin them so that they appear to be one stick, a single object in his hand (vv. 16-17). Performing this sign-act, Yahweh informs the prophet, will rouse the curiosity of his fellow exiles, who will ask, "Please tell us what you mean by these" (v. 18). Ezekiel must inform them that what he has done with the sticks Yahweh also will do (v. 19). Verse 19 does not provide the interpretation one expects to follow God's demand for a prophetic sign-act. Rather, the interpretation proper, introduced by v. 20, appears in vv. 21-23 (24*a*). Yahweh's plan for the people encompasses not only those who survived the collapse of Judah and their offspring, but also the descendants of those northern Israelites who, in the wake of Assyria's defeat of their kingdom in 721 BCE, were dispersed across the Assyrian Empire a century and a half earlier. Farfetched as this might sound, it was a pulsating hope at the time. Ezekiel's contemporary, Jeremiah, also predicted the return of the Northern Kingdom's diaspora (3:11-14; 30; 31).

Subsequent verses, which lack any explicit reference to the preceding sign-act material, constitute an amalgam of many important themes appearing in Ezekiel's previous salvation oracles. Emphasis falls not upon the unification of two disparate entities, but upon the eternality of God's gifts to all Israel, including the reestablishment of their covenant relationship. The unit attains its apex in the promises that Yahweh will set "my sanctuary" in the midst of the people and that God's protective presence will be over them. Verse 28 articulates, by means of a modified recognition formula, the ultimate purpose of God's actions: that the nations know (acknowledge) that Yahweh has sanctified Israel when the Lord's sanctuary is in its midst forever.

While most critics attribute the sign-act account (minus glosses) in vv. 15-19 to Ezekiel, the authorship of vv. 20-28 has been much debated. By what process did the text assume its final form? This is not a question that the ancient reader would ask. He presumes Ezekielian authorship, and there is nothing in this passage that would cause him to rethink that presumption. To the contrary, the fact that the salvation promises of vv. 21-28 echo many of Ezekiel's sequentially prior promises of weal underscores his sense that these verses are of a piece with the prophet's other oracles. Nevertheless, there is—from the perspective of many modern-day commentators—evidence to suggest that in addition to clarifying glosses interspersed here and there, the original sign-act account was subsequently expanded by vv. 20-24*a* (a contribution either of Ezekiel or of a redactor) and, at a later stage, by vv. 24*b*-28 (probably the product of another hand).[1202]

1202. E.g., W. Zimmerli, *Ezekiel 2: A Commentary on the Book of the Prophet Ezekiel, Chapters 25–48,* trans. J. D. Martin, Hermeneia (Philadelphia: Fortress, 1983).

Ezekiel 37:15-19, A Sign Act

[15]The word of the LORD came to me: [16]"Son of man, take a stick of wood and write on it, 'Belonging to Judah and the Israelites associated with him.' Then take another stick of wood, and write on it, 'Ephraim's stick, belonging to Joseph and all the house of Israel associated with him.' [17]Join them together into one stick so that they will become one in your hand.

[18]"When your countrymen ask you, 'Won't you tell us what you mean by this?' [19]say to them, 'This is what the Sovereign LORD says: I am going

[15]The word of the LORD came to me: [16]Mortal, take a stick and write on it, "For Judah, and the Israelites associated with it"; then take another stick and write on it, "For Joseph (the stick of Ephraim) and all the house of Israel associated with it"; [17]and join them together into one stick, so that they may become one in your hand. [18]And when your people say to you, "Will you not show us what you mean by these?" [19]say to them, Thus says the Lord GOD: I am about to take the stick of Joseph (which is in the hand of Ephraim) and the

NIV

to take the stick of Joseph—which is in Ephraim's hand—and of the Israelite tribes associated with him, and join it to Judah's stick, making them a single stick of wood, and they will become one in my hand.'

NRSV

tribes of Israel associated with it; and I will put the stick of Judah upon it,[a] and make them one stick, in order that they may be one in my hand.

[a]Heb I will put them upon it

COMMENTARY

Following the customary word event formula in v. 15, Ezekiel recounts his latest communiqué from Yahweh. Addressing the prophet directly ("Mortal"), God has commanded him to engage in a sign-act (for the significance of prophetic sign-acts, see the Commentary on 4:1–5:17). The description of this sign act is dominated by references to "one" (אחד 'eḥād); the word appears eight times in vv. 16-19 (once in the plural!) and one time each in vv. 22a, 22b, and 24a. He must take one עץ ('ēṣ) and write or carve upon it, "Of Judah and the Israelites associated with him" (TNK). Next, he must take another 'ēṣ and inscribe upon it, "Of Joseph—the stick of Ephraim—and all the House of Israel associated with him" (TNK). Then he must somehow conjoin the two (end to end?) so that they appear to be a single object in his hand. (The plural form of "one" suggests that the two objects Ezekiel grasps have the appearance of a single object. When Yahweh speaks of the two sticks, and kingdoms, becoming one object in the divine hand, the singular form appears [v. 19].) The bringing together of disparate objects to form a whole reminds readers of the re-membered bones in the previous oracle, Ezek 37:1-14.

Immediately, we confront a problem: How should 'ēṣ be translated? The word can have a handful of different meanings. Oftentimes, it refers to a tree (or, as a collective noun, to "trees"). Ezekiel uses it to refer to a tree(s) in, for instance, 6:13; 31:8; and 34:27. This meaning of 'ēṣ is probably not appropriate in the present context. Ezekiel is ordered literally to perform this sign act; and while it is conceivable that he could carry it out were he to uproot and use very small trees, it seems unlikely that he did so.[1203]

The term 'ēṣ can also mean "wood"—that is, a material utilized for building. Ezekiel uses it with this meaning in 26:12, where he refers to the timber of a city. It is possible that Ezekiel resorted to construction lumber, assuming that the two pieces of wood were not too large to be held together in a single hand. The noun can also be used to specify that certain objects have been fashioned from wood: idols (certainly not in this context, but see, Isa 40:2; Hos 4:12), vessels (Exod 7:19), staves, etc.[1204] Hence, we have several options.

Perhaps Ezekiel was ordered to inscribe and then join together two rods or staffs. (One thinks of Num 17:1-13 where, at Yahweh's command, Moses collects one staff from the leader of each of Israel's twelve tribes and writes or inscribes upon each of them its owner's name.) These objects would have been readily available. Although the reader of vv. 15-19 has not yet arrived at 37:24, after he has read that verse he might think shepherds' staffs an especially likely choice, given its reference to David as Israel's future shepherd (king). Against this view, commentators observe that when Ezekiel refers to staffs elsewhere, he uses more precise terms, (e.g., מטה maṭṭeh, "staff," "rod," "shaft," "branch," "tribe," 4:16; 5:16; משענת mišʿenet, "staff," 29:6; and מקל maqqēl, "rod," "staff," 39:9).[1205] Why not do so here, as well, if such objects were in his mind?

Another possibility is that Ezekiel conjoined two scepters. This option has commended itself to quite a few commentators, who observe that such objects would be apropos to Yahweh's goal of reuniting Israel's two former kingdoms. In Ezek 19:11, the prophet spoke of a vine tree's strongest branches becoming rulers' scepters. One can

1203. Barnes opts for "trees," but presumes that the sign act is metaphorical. See W. E. Barnes, "Two Trees Become One: Ezek. xxxvii 16-17," JTS 39 (1938) 391-93.

1204. BDB, 781-82.
1205. D. I. Block, The Book of Ezekiel: Chapters 25–48, NICOT (Grand Rapids: Eerdmans, 1998) 398.

question, however, how the prophet could have acquired such objects. Certainly, genuine scepters would not have been available to him. Perhaps one should suppose that Ezekiel carved or otherwise constructed two scepter-like objects. But then, one would expect Yahweh to have commanded him to "make," rather than simply "take" them (see, e.g., 12:3). Still, the reference in v. 19 to the 'ēṣ that "is in the hand of Ephraim" (a gloss?), the tribe whence came the northern kingdom's rulers, might invite the reader to take this option seriously at that point. In any event, such scepters should not be conceived as representing two dynasties, but rather two kingdoms. Ezekiel has already made it clear (in 34:23-24) that Israel's future ruler ("prince") will be a Davidide.

Another view, reflected already in the Targum (which renders 'ēṣ by Aramaic לוחא [lwḥ'] as "tablet"; the Hebrew cognate is לוח [lûaḥ]), is that Ezekiel brought together in his hand two wooden writing boards. Block has most recently championed this option. Citing, among other resources, D. J. Wiseman's article, "Assyrian Writing Boards,"[1206] he describes such objects as "flat pieces of wood, and occasionally ivory or metal, covered on the writing surface with a compound of beeswax and 25 percent orpiment, into which a message would be etched."[1207] Two or more writing boards could be linked together by leather straps or hinges.

Critics have objected to this option claiming that Ezekiel would not have had access to expensive, beeswax-covered writing boards. This challenge cannot be overcome, as Block attempts to do, by pointing to the "remarkable antiquity and breadth of distribution of writing boards." I certainly do not deny their existence in the ancient Near East and beyond, or that Ezekiel would have been familiar with them. But it is a leap to suggest on that basis that Ezekiel "may even have possessed some of his own leaves."[1208] Neither, I think, can the case be made by referring to Isa 8:1 ("take a large tablet [גליון gillāyôn]"), to Isa 30:8 ("Go now, write it before them on a tablet [לוח lûaḥ]/ and inscribe it in a scroll [ספר sēper]," or to Hab 2:2, where the prophet is commanded to record the vision he has experienced on הלחות

(halluḥôt), "tablets." To be sure, such tablets could have been made of wood; but in none of these passages is the inscribed object called 'ēṣ. Notices that other prophets sometimes recorded their prophecies in writing does not necessarily buttress an argument that Ezekiel carried out his sign-act with two wooden writing boards. When Block goes even further to argue that these tablets contained not only the brief identifications God demands in v. 16, but also the text of vv. 21-24a (inscribed on one of the tablets) and of vv. 24b-28 (inscribed on the other), he is, by his own admission, being speculative.[1209]

Another, and to my mind most likely, option is that Ezekiel simply took two sticks (or pieces of wood) of manageable size (see 1 Kgs 17:12). Sticks would have been easily to hand; and, as Block observes, Ezekiel has tended on other occasions to use common objects in his sign acts.[1210] One can well imagine his audience's curiosity (v. 18) if the prophet simply picked up sticks, as opposed to man-made wooden objects. In the end, however, we must admit that 'ēṣ is susceptible to more than one translation; perhaps the prophet purposefully chose an ambiguous term. The reader's uncertainty would not have been shared by the prophet's original audience if, in fact, he actually carried out the sign-act in the presence of his fellow exiles. Here, as with other of Ezekiel's sign-acts, however, the description of the act, the audience's anticipated response, and subsequent interpretation are all cast as divine speech; and the text nowhere reports its actual, public performance.

Although I prefer the TNK's succinct rendering of the preposition ל (lě), prefixed both to "Judah" and to "Joseph," as "of," the NIV's "belonging to" conveys the preposition's meaning in this context better than does the NRSV's "for." Ezekiel's two sticks are not, as one might think based on the NRSV rendering, intended for the (now defunct) entities addressed. Rather, they represent those entities. One is not surprised that "Judah" refers to Israel's southern kingdom, for it was the most prominent tribe of that nation (to which it lent its name) and the Davidic dynasty derived from it.

1206. *Iraq* 17 (1955) 7.
1207. Block, *Ezekiel 25–48*, 400.
1208. Ibid., 400-401.
1209. Ibid., 404.
1210. Ibid., 399.

When Ezekiel (or a later editor) adds "and the Israelites associated with it," he refers to other constituencies of that kingdom—for example, the Simeonites and sometimes the Benjaminites, etc. The tribe of Joseph, whose name sometimes refers to Israel's northern kingdom (see, e.g., Amos 5:15; Obad 18; Ps 77:15, etc.), actually consisted of two tribes ostensibly bearing the names of Joseph's two sons, the elder Manasseh (Gen 41:51) and the younger Ephraim (Gen 41:52). The Ephraimites dominated the history of the northern kingdom (its kings were all Ephraimites). Following Assyria's annexation of the nation's outlying territories (a consequence of the failure of the Syro-Ephraimite war in 734–732 BCE), its remaining heartland—the domain of Manasseh and Ephraim—was called after the dominant tribe. Hence, many critics conclude, the parenthetical reference to "the stick of *Ephraim*" is a clarifying gloss.

When the public performance of this sign-act elicits queries from Ezekiel's fellow exiles, Yahweh commands the prophet, he must respond with words prefaced by the messenger formula, "Thus says the Lord GOD." As Ezekiel has done, God promises, so Yahweh will take the stick of Joseph (here described as "in the hand of Ephraim") and of the tribes associated with it and conjoin it with the stick of Judah in the divine hand in order that they become one. Literally, v. 19*b* reads, "and I shall place them upon it, the stick of Judah," with "them" presumably refering to the "tribes of Israel" associated with the stick of Joseph. But the sign act entails joining stick to stick, not stick to tribes. Moreover, the MT suggests that the stick of Joseph is to be placed upon the stick of Judah—an unanticipated outcome. The problem is alleviated by the deletion of "them." We then read, "and I will place the stick of Judah upon it" (i.e., the stick of Joseph). (See Reflections at 37:24*b*-28.)

Ezekiel 37:20-24*a*, The Significance of the Sign Act

NIV

[20]Hold before their eyes the sticks you have written on [21]and say to them, 'This is what the Sovereign LORD says: I will take the Israelites out of the nations where they have gone. I will gather them from all around and bring them back into their own land. [22]I will make them one nation in the land, on the mountains of Israel. There will be one king over all of them and they will never again be two nations or be divided into two kingdoms. [23]They will no longer defile themselves with their idols and vile images or with any of their offenses, for I will save them from all their sinful backsliding,[a] and I will cleanse them. They will be my people, and I will be their God.

[24]" 'My servant David will be king over them, and they will all have one shepherd.' "

[a]23 Many Hebrew manuscripts (see also Septuagint); most Hebrew manuscripts *all their dwelling places where they sinned*

NRSV

[20]When the sticks on which you write are in your hand before their eyes, [21]then say to them, Thus says the Lord GOD: I will take the people of Israel from the nations among which they have gone, and will gather them from every quarter, and bring them to their own land. [22]I will make them one nation in the land, on the mountains of Israel; and one king shall be king over them all. Never again shall they be two nations, and never again shall they be divided into two kingdoms. [23]They shall never again defile themselves with their idols and their detestable things, or with any of their transgressions. I will save them from all the apostasies into which they have fallen,[a] and will cleanse them. Then they shall be my people, and I will be their God.

24My servant David shall be king over them; and they shall all have one shepherd.

[a]Another reading is *from all the settlements in which they have sinned*

COMMENTARY

This divine promise to repeat the prophet's actions suggests, but does not actually interpret, their significance. Hence, Ezekiel is further instructed that while he displays the stick in his hand for all to see, he must again proclaim to his fellow exiles a divine oracle prefaced by the messenger formula. "Look," God asserts, I will take (לקח *lāqaḥ*, as in vv. 16 [twice], 19; see also 36:24) the Israelites from the nations to which they have been dispersed, will gather them "from every quarter," and will bring them into their own land. Here, Ezekiel's language again evokes the second exodus theme so crucial to his salvation oracles (see, e.g., 34:13; 36:12, 24; 37:12) and elaborated upon, with a decidedly harsher tone, in 20:33-44 (see Commentary).

With v. 22, the significance of stick conjoining is at last spelled out. Having regathered the Israelites from the nations and returned them to their soil, Yahweh will make them "one nation" (גוי אחד *gôy 'eḥād*) in the land. The use of גוי (*gôy*), "nation," is significant here; God will not only bring the people home, but also constitute them as an established political entity, a *single* state on "the mountains of Israel" (i.e., the land as a whole), rather than as the two kingdoms that existed as a consequence of the schism occurring shortly after Solomon's death (see 1 Kgs 11:26–12:20). Never again will Israel be divided into two nations. According to 1 Kgs 11:29-39, Ahijah, the prophet of Shiloh, informed Jeroboam, future ruler of the future Northern Kingdom, that Yahweh was giving him ten of the nation's twelve tribes on account of the people's religious apostasy and disobedience under Solomon's dubious leadership. But, the Deuteronomistic Historians report, Jeroboam's decision to set up two golden calves, one in Bethel and the other in Dan, cost him God's favor. Ezekiel's oracle expresses the Judahite theo-political perspective that the creation of a nation made up of the ten tribes under Jeroboam was an illegitimate move, contrary to Yahweh's wishes.

All of this single nation will, moreover, be ruled by one king. In v. 22, nothing more is said about this monarch. But the reader, recalling 34:23-24 ("I will place over them one shepherd, my servant David, and he will tend them; he will tend them and be their shepherd. I the LORD will be their God, and my servant David will be prince among them. I the LORD have spoken," NIV), has quite definite ideas about this figure from that passage; and those ideas will be reenforced in subsequent verses. Never again will they be two nations; never again will they be divided into two kingdoms.[1211]

Verse 23 returns to subjects already encountered in 36:25, 29a. Never again will the people defile themselves with idolatry and other detestable practices, or by any of their former transgressions (from פשע *pāšaʿ*, "to rebel," "transgress"), for Yahweh will rescue (from ישע *yāšaʿ*, "to rescue," "deliver") them from all the apostasies (see the Commentary on 36:16-38) and cleanse (from טהר *tāhēr*, "to cleanse," "purify"; see the Commentary on 36:16-38) them.[1212] Then, they will again become Yahweh's people, and the Lord will be their God. The old rupture in their covenant relationship, brought on by Israel's failure faithfully to uphold its obligations, will be repaired. Verse 24a echoes 34:23-24, save that here, "my servant David" is called "king" (מלך *melek*), rather than "prince" (נשיא *nāśîʾ*), which elsewhere is Ezekiel's preferred term for Israel's rulers. For the reader, who has not yet encountered the many references to the *nāśîʾ* in chaps. 40–48, the appearance of "king" in this verse is scarcely surprising. After all, v. 22 already has spoken of the one nation having one king (*melek*) as king (*melek*) over all the people. That king will be "my servant David"—not the resurrected monarch of old, but a Davidide who, like his revered namesake, will tend and serve flock Israel according to Yahweh's will. (See Reflections at 37:24b-28.)

1211. The MT reads, "never again will it be [יהיה *yihyeh*; third-person masc. sing.] two nations." *Qere* pluralizes the verb form (יהיו *yihyû*). The error can be understood, since *yihyeh* appeared just four words earlier.

1212. The MT reads, "I will save them from all their settlements in which they have sinned." The ancient reader would have tried to make sense of this reading, but will be hampered by the fact that according to its oracular context, the exiles have already been repatriated prior to the actions described in v. 23. By simply switching the order of two consonants (reading משבתיהם [*mĕśûbōtêhem*] for the MT's מושבתיהם [*môšbōtêhem*]) one attains the meaning "from all their turnings [aways]."

Ezekiel 37:24b-28, God's Unending Blessings

NIV

They will follow my laws and be careful to keep my decrees. ²⁵They will live in the land I gave to my servant Jacob, the land where your fathers lived. They and their children and their children's children will live there forever, and David my servant will be their prince forever. ²⁶I will make a covenant of peace with them; it will be an everlasting covenant. I will establish them and increase their numbers, and I will put my sanctuary among them forever. ²⁷My dwelling place will be with them; I will be their God, and they will be my people. ²⁸Then the nations will know that I the LORD make Israel holy, when my sanctuary is among them forever.' "

NRSV

They shall follow my ordinances and be careful to observe my statutes. ²⁵They shall live in the land that I gave to my servant Jacob, in which your ancestors lived; they and their children and their children's children shall live there forever; and my servant David shall be their prince forever. ²⁶I will make a covenant of peace with them; it shall be an everlasting covenant with them; and I will bless[a] them and multiply them, and will set my sanctuary among them forevermore. ²⁷My dwelling place shall be with them; and I will be their God, and they shall be my people. ²⁸Then the nations shall know that I the LORD sanctify Israel, when my sanctuary is among them forevermore.

[a]Tg: Heb give

COMMENTARY

Verse 24b, like 36:27, stresses that the (long-rebellious) people will live in obedience to the Lord's statutes and ordinances. In this, they shall follow their shepherd of old, for David is remembered as the king who walked in God's ways, did what was right in Yahweh's eyes, and kept the divine statutes and commands (1 Kgs 11:38).

When, in v. 25, Ezekiel refers to the land to which all Israel will be returned, he identifies that territory as "the land that I gave to my servant Jacob, in which your ancestors lived." His wording is apropos to its context: Jacob was the father of the eponymous ancestors of all twelve of Israel's tribes. Ezekiel not only reaches back to past generations but also stretches forward to subsequent generations. The land given in the distant past will be the eternal homeland in the future, forever ruled by the Davidic line.[1213] In v. 26a, as in 35:25-31 (see Commentary), Ezekiel's God promises the people to make with them a "covenant of peace." True to its present context, the eternality of that covenant is emphasized (see also Lev 26:4; Isa 55:3; Jer 32:40). Moreover, God will bless them

and multiply them (see Ezek 36:11 and recall the priestly blessing in Gen 1:22. The words echo Yahweh's promise to Abraham in Gen 22:17a ["I will indeed bless you, and I will make your offspring as numerous as the stars of heaven and as the sand that is on the seashore"]).

At the text's climax, Yahweh promises to set "my sanctuary" among the people forever. ("Sanctuary" [מקדש‎ miqdāš] has appeared in 5:11; 8:6; and 9:6; it is from the root קדש‎ [qdš], meaning "to be holy.") Block understands miqdāš, with its emphasis upon divine holiness, to emphasize God's transcendence, while משכן‎ (miškān) focuses upon God's immanence. The latter was associated in Exodus with the "tent of meeting." According to Exod 33:7-11, Moses would pitch this tent some distance from camp and go there to meet with Yahweh, who descended in a pillar of cloud to the tent entrance and spoke to him "face to face, as a man speaks to his friend" (v. 11). Greenberg has offered an interesting interpretation of vv. 26-27. In his view, one should attend to the two prepositions used: on the one hand, God's sanctuary will be *in the midst of* (בתוך‎ bĕtôk) the people; on the other hand, Yahweh's "presence"

1213. Jenni suggests that the basic meaning of עולם‎ ('ôlām) is probably "most distant time." Ernst Jenni, "Time," *IDB* 4:644.

will be *over* (על *'al*) them "like a protective tent." In Ezekiel's reuse of the "antique priestly term for the desert Tabernacle," he writes, the word *miškān* now refers to "a sheltering divine presence—a mere step away from the post-biblical concept of the Shekinah."[1214]

Block offers the important observation that, while this passage does not speak of the "end times," it is eschatological literature nonetheless. Ezekiel imagines not the "end times," but "endless

time." "The prophet's vision concerns not so much the consummation, the end of history, as its climax."[1215]

The covenant formula, "I will be their God and they shall be my people," brings to a close Yahweh's promises to Israel, a list resembling Lev 16:1-13. The concluding modified recognition formula avers that the nations will know that Yahweh has sanctified Israel when they witness God's sanctuary eternally in its midst.

1214. Moshe Greenberg, *Ezekiel 21–37,* AB 22A (Garden City, N.Y.: Doubleday, 1997).

1215. Block, *Ezekiel 25–48,* 416-17.

REFLECTIONS

In 37:15-28, Ezekiel adopts a rhetorical strategy not unlike that which he employed in 37:1-14. He speaks of Israel's future in terms that must have struck his audience as absurd. Perhaps his fellow exiles could—at the extremes of their imaginations—hope that they might one day return to their homeland and become an independent nation again. But how could they possibly envision a future that included the descendants of those northern Israelites who were driven into exile by the Assyrians in 721 BCE? And how could they possibly envision a future so utopian that *nothing* would go wrong *forever?* Has Ezekiel gone too far? We balk at perfect portraits. Look at the woman in that picture. Was she really that beautiful? Did she not have a hair out of place? Was her skin actually perfectly smooth? She looks so magnificent that we suspect the artist has idealized her appearance beyond what is humanly possible. Do we harbor that same suspicion when we read Ezek 37:15-28? Ezekiel promises that every dream his audience and readers could imagine will come true. Did some shun his optimism? That Ezekiel, always speaking of things that could not possibly happen. Good old Ezekiel, trying to corral our hopes with picture-perfect possibilities. Life is not like that, Ezekiel. Reality is hard; we've known that for decades now. Why tempt us with "pie-in-the-sky" perfection?

But faith is like that. Faith summons us beyond the possible to what might be. In Ezek 37:1-14, the prophet invited his audience and readers to look through God's eyes, such that even the dead might be revived. Here, he does much the same. By means of a sign act, dictated by God, Ezekiel portrays the impossible becoming possible. The scattered tribes of Israel can be reunited. The homeland can be reclaimed. The covenant can be renewed. The nations can be overwhelmed by what Yahweh has accomplished.

We cannot know how Ezekiel's fellow exiles responded to his perfect portrait of Israel's future. The text gives no clue to their response. Surely some thought the prophet to be crazy—a madman living in an unreal reality. Others may have caught a glimpse of his reality and perceived in Ezekiel's description of the future a basis for hope. Where do we stand? We pray, "Your kingdom come, your will be done." But do we really believe in such a possibility?

For some, faith is belief in things seen. Because we believe, religion supplies us with all the answers. What the Bible says goes—if the text includes contradictions and conundrums, the fault lies with us. We simply do not perceive perfectly. But for others, faith is belief in things unseen. We, like Jacob at Jabbok (Gen 32:22-32), wrestle with our uncertainties, are wounded, and demand a blessing. We live in the expectation that the impossible is plausible, all evidence to the contrary.

EZEKIEL 38:1–39:29, THE FINAL BATTLE: YAHWEH DEFEATS GOG AND HIS HORDES

OVERVIEW

With graphic, mysterious, and sometimes grue-some language, Ezekiel 38–39 describes the battle to end all battles. The opponents will be Yahweh, the Divine Warrior of Israel, whose just (so Ezekiel) punishment of Judah has damaged Yahweh's reputation among the nations, and Gog of Magog, chief prince of Meshech and Tubal, along with the vast hordes of his allies. The battle will begin at Yahweh's initiative (38:4); the battle-ground will be "the mountains of Israel" (38:8). The conflagration will occur at some time in the distant future—long after the ingathering and resettlement of Israel's diaspora, when the people are living securely in their restored homeland. "Like a cloud covering the land" (38:9, 16), Gog and his forces will advance against Israel. This will occur, Yahweh declares, "so that the nations may know me, when through you, O Gog, I display my holiness before their eyes" (38:16*b*). As this and later verses confirm, the defeat of Gog is not Yahweh's ultimate goal, but the means by which larger goals of extreme importance within the Ezekielian corpus will be achieved.

Across the many centuries since its creation, Ezekiel 38–39 has stirred readers' imaginations, fantasies, fears, and hopes. It has been reinter-preted by generations, such that the portraits of persons, nations, and forces identified with the mysterious Gog of Magog are numerous indeed. During the centuries and millennia following the pericope's composition, J. Blenkinsopp observes: "Gog will be identified successively with Ethopians (*Sibylline Oracles* 3.319, 512), Goths, the Muslim invaders of Europe, the Mongols, Stalin, Hitler, and so on."[1216]

Over the past century, biblical scholars have raised myriad questions about the Gog of Magog material: Who or what did Gog *originally* repre-sent; who authored the text; what was its history of composition; what accounts for its present position within the Ezekiel scroll; and what is its genre?

The original identity of Gog of Magog is, to my mind, forever shrouded in mystery. Did Ezekiel (if, in fact, he authored this text, or at least some por-tion of it) have a particular individual in mind? Did he draw from legendary tales about a fearsome military figure from the past? Did Gog represent a contemporary barbarian horde threatening the Mesopotamian plain? Was he a personification of darkness (the Sumerian word for "darkness" is *gûg*), evil, and/or chaos? Writers who date the Gog materials after Ezekiel's lifetime point to such figures as Alexander the Great, or the Seleucid king Antiochus Eupator (second century BCE). Perhaps Gog of Magog was a product of Ezekiel's imagination, enhanced by references to earlier tra-ditions (including prophetic traditions) and leg-ends, and to fear-inspiring, edges-of-the-earth peoples and locales.[1217] Fortunately, discerning the significance of the Gog of Magog material within the book of Ezekiel does not hinge upon recover-ing the original identity of Yahweh's opponent.

As noted, some critics have insisted that Ezekiel played no role in creating the Gog of Magog ora-cle. So, for example, R. Ahroni assigns a late, post-exilic date to the pericope (38:1–39:24), thereby eliminating the prophet from the possible cast of authors.[1218] Others assign him only a bit-part: Walther Zimmerli reduces the original oracle to 38:1-9 (minus many glosses), 39:1-5, and 17-20. Remaining verses, then, are the elaborations and additions of more than a single member and gen-eration of Ezekiel's "school."[1219] John W. Wevers discerns the original oracle in 39:1-4, 6;[1220]

1216. Joseph Blenkinsopp, *Ezekiel,* IBC (Louisville: John Knox, 1990) 184.

1217. The *NIV Study Bible* suggests that the name "Gog of Magog" was purposely vague. See *The NIV Study Bible,* ed. Kenneth Barker (Grand Rapids: Zondervan, 1985) 1280.

1218. R. Ahroni, "The Gog Prophecy and the Book of Ezekiel," *HAR* 1 (1977) 1-27.

1219. W. Zimmerli, *Ezekiel 2: A Commentary on the Book of the Prophet Ezekiel, Chapters 25–48,* trans. J. D. Martin, Hermeneia (Philadelphia: Fortress, 1983) 296-99.

1220. J. W. Wevers, *Ezekiel,* NCB (London: Nelson, 1969) 286.

Hossfeld admits a basic oracle consisting only of 38:1-3a and 39:1b-5 (later expanded in six stages).[1221]

More recently, however, certain critics have argued that the Gog of Magog material is essentially a unified oracle authored by Ezekiel himself prior to Cyrus' liberating edict of 539 BCE.[1222] M. S. Odell reads chaps. 38–39 as a coherent unit and an integral part of the book as a whole.[1223] Block also adopts a holistic approach: true, the final pericope probably includes secondary additions, but Ezekiel himself may have been responsible for them.[1224]

When I view this passage through the lens of modern critical biblical scholarship, I detect reasons to doubt that Ezekiel alone composed it in its final, canonical form. To be sure, in many ways its literary style, contents, and vocabulary are congruent with previous chapters of the book, as we shall see. But consider, for example, that nowhere in Ezekiel's preceding oracles of salvation (chaps. 34–37) does he speak of Yahweh's final battle with Gog. Was this passage inserted at the end of these salvation oracles by a post-exilic person(s) who, realizing that the edenic conditions Ezekiel predicted in those earlier oracles had yet fully to materialize, added this final battle as a precondition for the ultimate realization of the marvelous future described in chaps. 34–37?[1225]

When I view this pericope through the lens of an ancient reader of the scroll as a whole, however, I conclude that such a reader could and would have assumed Ezekielian authorship. True, he might be startled by the sudden and unanticipated arrival of Gog and his hordes on the literary scene. But he might also reason that the prophet did not speak of the conflagration earlier because his prior task was to describe the future ingathering and resettlement of those exiles who would return to and rebuild their homeland. Only then did Ezekiel turn to subsequent events. After all, the Gog of Magog pericope states that the battle will be fought only after the ingathered Judeans have been living securely in the land of Israel for a very long time. My ancient reader knows that this final battle still has not taken place.

Finally, scholars have questioned the genre of this passage. F. Hitzig was the first to term it "apocalyptic;"[1226] and it does display features associated with later apocalyptic literature. The text does not, however, meet important criteria for apocalyptic literature identified by J. J. Collins in his well-known definition of "apocalypse." Collins defines the term as "a genre of revelatory literature with a narrative framework, in which a revelation is mediated by an otherworldly being to a human recipient, disclosing a transcendent reality which is both temporal, insofar as it envisages eschatological salvation, and spatial insofar as it involves another, supernatural world."[1227] Ezekiel 38–39 is cast as narrative, but it includes no mediating "otherworldly being" and its spatial (the mountains of Israel) and temporal (far in the future) settings are not radically discontinuous with this-worldly space and time.

Paul Hanson distinguishes between "prophetic eschatology" and "apocalyptic eschatology," the latter being largely an outgrowth of the former. He defines prophetic eschatology as "a religious perspective which focuses on the prophetic announcement to the nation of the divine plans for Israel and the world which the prophet has witnessed unfolding in the divine council and which he translates into the terms of plain history, real politics, and human instrumentality." Apocalyptic eschatology, he continues, is "a religious perspective which focuses on the disclosure (usually esoteric in nature) to the elect of the cosmic vision of Yahweh's sovereignty—especially as it relates to his acting to deliver his faithful—which disclosure the visionaries have largely ceased to translate into the terms of plain history, real politics, and human instrumentality."[1228] To my mind, the Gog of

1221. F. Hossfeld, *Untersuchungen zu Komposition und Theologie des Ezechielbuches,* FB 20 (Würzburg: Echter, 1977) 402-09.

1222. See Ralph W. Klein, *Ezekiel: The Prophet and His Message,* Studies on Personalities of the Old Testament (Columbia: University of South Carolina Press, 1988) 157-58.

1223. M. S. Odell, " 'Are You He of Whom I Spoke by My Servants the Prophets?' Ezekiel 38–39 and the Problem of History in the Neobabylonian Context" (Ph.D. diss., University of Pittsburgh, 1988).

1224. D. I. Block, *The Book of Ezekiel: Chapters 25–48,* NICOT (Grand Rapids: Eerdmans, 1998) 426-27. See also Klein, *Ezekiel,* 157-58.

1225. Hanson excludes chaps. 38–39 from his discussion of Ezekiel's relationship to apocalyptic. See Paul D. Hanson, *The Dawn of Apocalyptic* (Philadelphia: Fortress, 1975).

1226. F. Hitzig, *Der Prophet Ezechiel,* Kurzgefasstes exegetisches Handbuch Zum Alten Testament 8 (Leipzig: Weidmannïsche Buchhandlung, 1847) xiv-xv.

1227. J. J. Collins, "Towards the Morphology of a Genre," in *Apocalypse: The Morphology of a Genre,* ed. J. J. Collins, Semeia 14 (Missoula: Scholars Press, 1979) 9.

1228. Hanson, *The Dawn of Apocalyptic,* 11-12.

Magog pericope is situated not at one end of this continuum or the other, but between the two. Invoking tree imagery (as does Ezekiel in chaps. 17 and 31), we can say that the multiple roots of this passage are deeply embedded in prophetic eschatology, while its branches stretch toward the cosmic plane of apocalyptic eschatology.

The Gog of Magog material presents as an extremely complex oracle. It begins with the word event formula in 38:1 and ends with the concluding formula, "says the Lord God," in 39:29. Ezekiel 40:1 commences with a date notice and introduces a visionary account with a very different focus.

Chapters 38–39 confront readers with a striking example of the typically Ezekielian "halving" pattern identified by M. Greenberg.[1229] The oracle's two major sections consist of 38:1-23 on the one hand, and 39:1-29 on the other. The first focuses upon Yahweh's defeat of Gog and his hordes, while the second describes especially the disposition of their corpses. A comparison of 38:1-4a and 39:1-2a, the introductions to these two major sections, reveals that they are remarkably similar, though the former contains more information than the latter (see below). Each of these two sections is further divided by a fresh address to the prophet and a command that he speak (38:14; 39:17). Hence we discern four principal sub-

sections (and even smaller units) consisting of 38:2-13, 14-23; 39:1-16, 17-29. Within the first subsection, the messenger formula ("thus says the Lord God") appears in vv. 3 and 10; in the second, it appears in vv. 14 and 17. Within the third subsection, the formula is present in 39:1; and in the fourth, in vv. 17 and 25. Obviously, the creator(s) of this material is much concerned that its hearers/readers attribute these words to the divine author, with all the authority that attribution conveys.

Other formulas are present as well, particularly the recognition formula which, in a variety of forms, appears in 38:16, 23; 39:6-7, 22-23, and 28. This, Block notes, is a "denser concentration" of the formula than is found within any other oracle in the book—a statistic that sheds light not only on the passage's form (a series of proof sayings which, combined, yield "a single powerful proof oracle") but also on its intentions: the expression of "Yahweh's determination once and for all to reveal to the nations his holiness, and to his own people his covenant loyalty."[1230] A third intention should be added, viz., Yahweh's determination to restore the divine reputation among the nations by forcing them to recognize that "the house of Israel went into captivity for their iniquity, because they dealt treacherously with me" (39:23-24). Ultimately "the house of Israel," and not Yahweh, was responsible for Judah's collapse and the exiles' deportation.

1229. Moshe Greenberg, *Ezekiel 1–20*, AB 22 (Garden City, N.Y.: Doubleday, 1983) 25-26.

1230. Block, *Ezekiel 25–48*, 430-31.

Ezekiel 38:1-9, Yahweh Will Bring Gog Against Israel

NIV

38 The word of the LORD came to me: [2]"Son of man, set your face against Gog, of the land of Magog, the chief prince of[a] Meshech and Tubal; prophesy against him [3]and say: 'This is what the Sovereign LORD says: I am against you, O Gog, chief prince of[b] Meshech and Tubal. [4]I will turn you around, put hooks in your jaws and bring you out with your whole army—your horses, your horsemen fully armed, and a great horde with large and small shields, all of them brandishing their swords. [5]Persia, Cush[c] and Put will be

[a]2 Or *the prince of Rosh,*   [b]3 Or *Gog, prince of Rosh,*   [c]5 That is, the upper Nile region

NRSV

38 The word of the LORD came to me: [2]Mortal, set your face toward Gog, of the land of Magog, the chief prince of Meshech and Tubal. Prophesy against him [3]and say: Thus says the Lord GOD: I am against you, O Gog, chief prince of Meshech and Tubal; [4]I will turn you around and put hooks into your jaws, and I will lead you out with all your army, horses and horsemen, all of them clothed in full armor, a great company, all of them with shield and buckler, wielding swords. [5]Persia, Ethiopia,[a] and Put

[a]Or *Nubia;* Heb *Cush*

with them, all with shields and helmets, ⁶also Gomer with all its troops, and Beth Togarmah from the far north with all its troops—the many nations with you.

⁷" 'Get ready; be prepared, you and all the hordes gathered about you, and take command of them. ⁸After many days you will be called to arms. In future years you will invade a land that has recovered from war, whose people were gathered from many nations to the mountains of Israel, which had long been desolate. They had been brought out from the nations, and now all of them live in safety. ⁹You and all your troops and the many nations with you will go up, advancing like a storm; you will be like a cloud covering the land.

are with them, all of them with buckler and helmet; ⁶Gomer and all its troops; Beth-togarmah from the remotest parts of the north with all its troops—many peoples are with you.

7Be ready and keep ready, you and all the companies that are assembled around you, and hold yourselves in reserve for them. ⁸After many days you shall be mustered; in the latter years you shall go against a land restored from war, a land where people were gathered from many nations on the mountains of Israel, which had long lain waste; its people were brought out from the nations and now are living in safety, all of them. ⁹You shall advance, coming on like a storm; you shall be like a cloud covering the land, you and all your troops, and many peoples with you.

COMMENTARY

In typical Ezekielian style, the oracle against Gog of Magog commences with the word event formula ("The word of the LORD came to me") followed by Yahweh's direct address to the prophet ("Mortal"). Ezekiel is told to "set his face" toward the target of Yahweh's utterance (the gesture is familiar; in preceding chapters, Ezekiel has been commanded to set his face toward/against persons and entities; see 4:3, 7; 6:2; 13:17; 20:46; 21:2; 25:2; 28:21; 29:2; 35:2). God's first words to Gog, "I am against you," are familiar. This "challenge to a duel" formula has already appeared in Ezek 5:8; 13:8, 20; 21:3; 26:3; 28:22; 29:3, 10; 30:22; 34:10; 35:3. In this case, the label attached by moderns to this formula is particularly apt: In Ezek 39:3, the battle between Yahweh and Gog will be presented as a duel between the two parties.

As noted in the Overview, scholars of the past century have expended considerable energy seeking to discover the original identity of Gog of Magog. A Reubenite named Gog is very briefly mentioned in 1 Chr 5:4, but critics agree that the reference sheds no light on the mystery. *Gaga* appears in the fourteenth-century BCE Amarna tablets referring to peoples of the north,[1231] and the Ugaritic materials include reference to a deity

named *Gaga*. Among legendary figures from the past, the most likely candidate is the Lydian king Gyges (ca. 680–650 BCE), the *Gûgu* mentioned in the annals of Assyria's king Ashubanipal (668–627 BCE).[1232]

Other scholars have argued that Gog is Nebuchadrezzar, or a personification of Babylonia. Advocates of this view assert that the defeat of Judah's lethal foe is a necessary precondition for Yahweh's reenthronement in Jerusalem. Against this argument, one notes that elsewhere in the book, Nebuchadrezzer is consistently presented as Yahweh's instrument of judgment, while Babylonia is nowhere decried in Ezekiel's oracles against foreign nations. Proponents counter, however, that given Ezekiel's locale, any oracle he might utter against Nebuchadrezzar/Babylonia would of necessity be couched in mysterious language.

Writers who deny the Gog materials to Ezekiel suggest that he represents some figure who lived after Ezekiel's death. Alexander the Great is the favorite among several such candidates. B. F. Batto does not identify Gog with a particular person of any age. He describes the Gog oracle as "proto-

---

1231. See W. F. Albright, "Gog and Magog," *JBL* 43 (1924) 381-82.

1232. Gyges' exploits appear in Herodotus *Histories* 1.8-13. Since Gyges was deceased in Ezekiel's day, the reference could not literally be to him. He would, rather, serve as a cipher for a threatening and most fearsome foe.

apocalyptic" and argues that Gog symbolizes chaos.[1233]

Equally obscure is the reference to Magog, here presented as Gog's domain. In Gen 10:2 and 1 Chron 1:5, Magog appears as a descendant of Noah's son Japheth, along with Gomer, Madai, Javan, Tubal, Meshech, and Tiras. If Gog represents Gyges, then the reference might be to Lydia in western Asia Minor. But the place-name has not appeared in any extant ancient Near Eastern texts and may well be an artificial construction, created by the prefixing of Hebrew מ (*ma*), meaning "place of," to the name Gog.[1234]

Both the NIV and the NRSV render the Hebrew phrase נְשִׂיא רֹאשׁ מֶלֶךְ וְתֻבָל (*nĕśîʾ rōʾš melek wĕtubāl*) as "[the] chief prince of Meshech and Tubal."[1235] Hence, Gog is identified as the head of a regional group of rulers. There are problems with this translation, however. In the Hebrew text, "prince" is in construct with the following noun; hence, "prince of the chief (or "head") of Meshech and Tubal."[1236] Block renders the phrase "the prince, chief of Meshech and Tubal."[1237] Another approach finds in רֹאשׁ (*rōʾš*) a proper noun designating a land and/or its people.[1238] In that case, the phrase would read "the prince of Rosh, Meshech, and Tubal." I shall follow the NIV and NRSV rendering.

Meshech (Musku/Muśku) and Tubal (Tabal) are known to us from neo-Assyrian inscriptions. Peoples of Asia Minor, they engaged in ongoing warfare against Assyria. Here, they make their third appearance in the book of Ezekiel. They appeared (in reverse order and prefaced by "Javan") among Tyre's trading partners in 27:13. In 32:26-28, Meshech and Tubal (lit., "Meshech-Tubal") were describing as lying in their graves in the Pit, a dishonorable burial consequent upon their having "spread terror in the land of the

living" (v. 26). The reader recalls that charge in the present context. Why would Ezekiel focus upon these groups? Block's speculation makes sense:

> Informed citizens of Judah were probably aware of . . . peoples in the distant north [who] were shrouded in mystery. The reports of these mysterious people groups that filtered down spoke of wild peoples, brutal and barbaric. This combination of mystery and brutality made Gog and his confederates perfect symbols of the archetypical enemy.[1239]

Whatever plans Gog might have harbored for himself will be interrupted when Yahweh turns him around and puts hooks into his jaws. Readers recall that in Ezekiel 29, Yahweh threatened to put hooks through the jaws of Pharaoh, there depicted as a great crocodile lounging in his Nile canals, to draw him up from the water, and to cast him to his death in the wilderness. To be hooked in the jaws like an animal by the divine hunter is an ominous prospect indeed. Yahweh will then bring Gog out, along with his vast and extremely well-equipped army, horses, and war horses. Each warrior is protected by full armor, shield, and buckler, and each wields a sword (v. 4). The reader suspects that this detailed description of so fearsome an army plays a rhetorical role: Great indeed is the deity who can crush such legions.

In vv. 5-6, the reader learns of five additional allies of Gog. The entities referred to in v. 6 appear, as do Magog, Tubal, and Meshech, in Gen 10:2-4 (=1 Chron 1:6). Gomer is identified as the first of Japheth's sons. The descendants of Gomer should likely be identified with the Cimmerians (Akkadian *gimmiraia*). Indo-Europeans from the Ukraine, they were driven from their homeland by the Scythians. After threatening the Assyrians in the eighth century BCE, they pushed west into Asia Minor and conquered Gordion and its Phrygian king Midas (of "golden touch" fame in the well-known legend) in 676 BCE. The Cimmerians were defeated by the Assyrians in the seventh century BCE. This is the sole reference to Gomer in the book of Ezekiel. Beth-togarmah ("the house of Togarmah") likewise appears in Genesis 10, where Togarmah is identified as one of Gomer's three sons (v. 3). Neo-Assyrian texts locate the city of

1233. B. F. Batto, *Slaying the Dragon: Mythmaking in the Biblical Tradition* (Louisville: Westminster/John Knox, 1992) 157-62. For fuller discussions of candidates for the original identity of Gog, see Zimmerli, *Ezekiel 2*, 300-302; Block, *Ezekiel 25–48*, 433.

1234. Zimmerli, *Ezekiel 2*, 301.

1235. See ibid., 305.

1236. J. Galambush finds in this translation a covert clue that Gog is, in fact, Nebuchadrezzar, whose deputy was able successfully to broker peace in the Anatolian region when a dispute developed between the Lydians and the Medes over control of Meshech and Tubal. See Julie Galambush, "Ezekiel," in *The Oxford Bible Commentary* (Oxford: Oxford University Press, forthcoming).

1237. Block, *Ezekiel 25–48*, 424-25.

1238. So J. D. Price, "Rosh: An Ancient Land Known to Ezekiel," *Grace Theological Journal* 6 (1985) 67-89, who identifies Rosh with the Râshu/Rêshu appearing in neo-Assyrian annals.

1239. Block, *Ezekiel 25–48*, 436.

Til-garimmu on the eastern border of Tubal. Sennacherib's forces destroyed the city in 695 BCE. In Ezek 27:14, Beth-togarmah appeared as a trade partner of Tyre, dealing in horses and mules. Here, Ezekiel locates it in "the remotest parts of the north."

Hence, my knowledgeable reader likely would have associated four of Gog's allies with locales lying north of Israel. The same cannot be said, however, of the three allies identified in v. 5— Persia, Cush (Ethopia); and Put (Libya). For this reason, among others,[1240] many modern scholars dismiss v. 5 as a later addition. Zimmerli, for example, opines that Persia, Cush, and Put "basically have no business in the army of these wild, warrior tribes who are capable of waging their own wars."[1241] But it is by no means certain that an ancient reader would have stumbled over the verse. Nothing in the pericope thus far has suggested that Gog's hordes of allies could include *only* forces from the north.[1242] In its present position, v. 5 brings the number of Gog's allies to seven, a number symbolizing totality or completeness;[1243] and it depicts those allies as coming from both the northern and southern extremities of the known world. Together, these two factors convey to the reader that the future battle will be what we moderns call a world war.[1244]

With v. 7, Yahweh summons Gog: "Be prepared; get ready." The masculine singular imperatives address Gog, but they extend also to the hordes at his command. Despite the urgency of this summons, the battle for which God has conscripted Gog does not lie in the immediate future. "After many days"[1245] and "in future years" (NIV;

באחרית השנים [bĕ'ahărît haššānîm] appears only here in the HB), Gog will be mustered and brought to a land restored from warfare (lit. "a land restored from [the] sword"), a land whose diaspora has been brought out from many nations to the mountains of Israel (recall Ezek 20:34-42), a land long devastated but now reinhabited (see Ezek 36:33-34) whose population is living in safety (see Ezek 28:26; 34:25, 27, 28). In addition to those passages just cited in the preceding sentence, the reader recalls 36:8-12—part of an oracle addressed to the mountains of Israel in which Yahweh promises the return of their inhabitants and the rebuilding of their waste places. Together, these echoes of Ezekiel's earlier salvation oracles confirm that such conditions will already pertain before Yahweh's battle with Gog begins. The phrase "dwelling securely" (NRSV "living in safety") evokes thoughts of, e.g., Lev 26:5. There we read that if Israel follows God's statutes and keeps the divine commandments, observing them faithfully (i.e., is a responsible covenant partner with Yahweh), "your threshing shall overtake the vintage, and the vintage shall overtake the sowing; you shall eat your bread to the full, and live securely in your land." Hence, the reader concludes that prior to the time of Gog's attack, the once-ruptured covenant between Yahweh and all of Israel will be restored.

The description of Gog's advance employs two similes. First, he will come up "like a storm" (כשאה *kaššō'â*; the fem. noun שאה [*šō'â*], from the root *š'h*, refers to "devastation," "ruin," "waste"; in this context it is best translated "storm" since it appears in parallelism with the second simile, "like a cloud"; the same noun appears in Isa 20:3, where we read of "the storm that will come from afar"). Second, he will come "like a cloud" (כענן *ke'ānān*) covering the land. The prophet Jeremiah also employed storm imagery (see, e.g., Jer 4:13) to describe an advancing army. Together, these two similes convey a sense of the ferocity and vastness of Gog's troops and the "many peoples" with him (repeating the concluding phrase of v. 6). (See Reflections at 39:21-29.)

1240. Wevers, *Ezekiel*, 287, regards the verse as a secondary addition in part because, if it were original, it would read "with you," rather than "with them."

1241. Zimmerli, *Ezekiel 2*, 306.

1242. This is the case even if, as most critics agree, Ezekiel draws in v. 6 upon the "foe from the north" motif, found, for example, in Jer 1:13-14; 4:6-17; 6:1-30.

1243. The reader recalls that seven nations were denounced in chaps. 25–32. The prophet pronounces seven oracles against Tyre and its king (chaps. 26–28) and seven against Egypt and its pharaoh (chaps. 29–32). According to 37:17-32, seven nations are present with Egypt in Sheol.

1244. Odell, " 'Are You He of Whom I Spoke by My Servants the Prophets?' " 103-5, argues for the retention of v. 5.

1245. The phrase מימים רבים (*miyyāmîm rabbîm*) elsewhere appears in Josh 23:1 to designate the period between Israel's entry into Canaan and Joshua's farewell address.

Ezekiel 38:10-13, Gog Eyes Israel's Defenseless Villages

NIV

¹⁰" 'This is what the Sovereign LORD says: On that day thoughts will come into your mind and you will devise an evil scheme. ¹¹You will say, "I will invade a land of unwalled villages; I will attack a peaceful and unsuspecting people—all of them living without walls and without gates and bars. ¹²I will plunder and loot and turn my hand against the resettled ruins and the people gathered from the nations, rich in livestock and goods, living at the center of the land." ¹³Sheba and Dedan and the merchants of Tarshish and all her villages*ᵃ* will say to you, "Have you come to plunder? Have you gathered your hordes to loot, to carry off silver and gold, to take away livestock and goods and to seize much plunder?" '

ᵃ13 Or *her strong lions*

NRSV

10Thus says the Lord GOD: On that day thoughts will come into your mind, and you will devise an evil scheme. ¹¹You will say, "I will go up against the land of unwalled villages; I will fall upon the quiet people who live in safety, all of them living without walls, and having no bars or gates"; ¹²to seize spoil and carry off plunder; to assail the waste places that are now inhabited, and the people who were gathered from the nations, who are acquiring cattle and goods, who live at the center*ᵃ* of the earth. ¹³Sheba and Dedan and the merchants of Tarshish and all its young warriors*ᵇ* will say to you, "Have you come to seize spoil? Have you assembled your horde to carry off plunder, to carry away silver and gold, to take away cattle and goods, to seize a great amount of booty?"

ᵃHeb *navel*   ᵇHeb *young lions*

COMMENTARY

To this point in the oracle, Gog's future attack against the mountains of Israel has been ascribed solely to Yahweh's initiative. Israel's own God will drag him to its restored homeland. No charges have been lodged against Gog. In vv. 10-13, however, Gog and his followers are said to be motivated by greed. These verses are, in Zimmerli's opinion, a secondary expansion introduced first by the messenger formula ("Thus says the Lord God") and then by "on that day," a "loose connecting formula" which signals an expansion.[1246] Its purpose is to justify Yahweh's decision to bring Gog against the mountains of Israel and their inhabitants: the future conflagration, which will result in the demise of Gog and his allies, will be an act of divine justice, a punishment for avarice.

Although moderns might be persuaded to Zimmerli's opinion, my ancient reader can easily

1246. Zimmerli, *Ezekiel 2,* 310.

construe these verses as a logical "next step" in the action. "On that day" when Gog advances upon the land at Yahweh's initiative, he will discover that its inhabitants are living in villages without benefit of protective walls, bars, or gates (cf. Ezek 36:35). In short, Gog will survey easy prey. In his mind he will devise an "evil scheme," for the peaceful people who are dwelling securely in the center of the earth will have spoil to seize and plunder to carry off. Gog apparently is encouraged to act on his evil scheme by merchants from Sheba and Dedan and from Tarshish (each a trade partner of Tyre, see Ezekiel 27). Their rhetorical questions invite positive responses: yes, Gog has come to seize spoil. He has assembled his horde to carry off plunder, to steal away silver and gold, to take away cattle and goods, and to seize a great amount of booty. Moreover, they suggest that these merchants hope to profit from the spoils of war. (See Reflections at 39:21-29.)

Ezekiel 38:14-16, Displaying God's Holiness Before the Nations

NIV

¹⁴"Therefore, son of man, prophesy and say to Gog: 'This is what the Sovereign LORD says: In that day, when my people Israel are living in safety, will you not take notice of it? ¹⁵You will come from your place in the far north, you and many nations with you, all of them riding on horses, a great horde, a mighty army. ¹⁶You will advance against my people Israel like a cloud that covers the land. In days to come, O Gog, I will bring you against my land, so that the nations may know me when I show myself holy through you before their eyes.

NRSV

14Therefore, mortal, prophesy, and say to Gog: Thus says the Lord GOD: On that day when my people Israel are living securely, you will rouse yourself[a] ¹⁵and come from your place out of the remotest parts of the north, you and many peoples with you, all of them riding on horses, a great horde, a mighty army; ¹⁶you will come up against my people Israel, like a cloud covering the earth. In the latter days I will bring you against my land, so that the nations may know me, when through you, O Gog, I display my holiness before their eyes.

[a]Gk: Heb *will you not know?*

COMMENTARY

Verse 14 commences with לכן (*lākēn*), "therefore," which links what follows to previous verses. For a second time, Yahweh addresses the prophet ("Mortal"), commands him to prophesy to Gog, and commissions him to speak. Verses 14-16a essentially reiterate what has been stated in vv. 1-9. "On that day" when the people are living securely, Gog will take note (so the MT; the NRSV emends with the LXX) and advance from the most remote parts of the north along with his hordes. Striking, however, is the two-fold reference to "my people Israel" (vv. 14, 16), and the phrase "my land" in v. 16a. This people whom Gog plans to pillage belong to their patron deity, and the land they occupy is God's property.

Because the covenant between Yahweh and Israel has been restored, Gog's scheme is doomed to failure. Why, then, will God turn him around, hook him through his jaws, and impel him toward Israel's homeland? Verse 6b provides the first

answer to this question. "In the latter days" (literally, "at the end of days"), Yahweh will bring Gog against the land of Israel in order that the nations may know—that is, recognize and acknowledge—God's unparalleled sovereignty and power. Gog is God's instrument—the means by which the Lord's holiness will be displayed in the nations' sight.[1247] Universal recognition of Yahweh as the supreme and unrivaled deity is a major concern of the Ezekielian tradition, which wrestled with the theological consequences of Judah's collapse for Yahweh's reputation (see especially Ezekiel 36). Looking toward the future, this pericope anticipates the demonstration of Yahweh's holiness by means of the defeat of Gog, the fiercest of foes, and his hordes. (See Reflections at 39:21-29.)

1247. Three times prior to the present passage, the text speaks of Yahweh displaying God's holiness "in the sight of the nations." In each case (20:431; 28:25; 36:23), the nations will witness God's ingathering of the diaspora. In 28:22, Yahweh's holiness is manifested in the destruction of Sidon.

Ezekiel 38:17-23, Yahweh's Theophany Convulses Creation

NIV

17" 'This is what the Sovereign LORD says: Are you not the one I spoke of in former days by my servants the prophets of Israel? At that time they prophesied for years that I would bring you against them. 18This is what will happen in that day: When Gog attacks the land of Israel, my hot anger will be aroused, declares the Sovereign LORD. 19In my zeal and fiery wrath I declare that at that time there shall be a great earthquake in the land of Israel. 20The fish of the sea, the birds of the air, the beasts of the field, every creature that moves along the ground, and all the people on the face of the earth will tremble at my presence. The mountains will be overturned, the cliffs will crumble and every wall will fall to the ground. 21I will summon a sword against Gog on all my mountains, declares the Sovereign LORD. Every man's sword will be against his brother. 22I will execute judgment upon him with plague and bloodshed; I will pour down torrents of rain, hailstones and burning sulfur on him and on his troops and on the many nations with him. 23And so I will show my greatness and my holiness, and I will make myself known in the sight of many nations. Then they will know that I am the LORD.'

NRSV

17Thus says the Lord GOD: Are you he of whom I spoke in former days by my servants the prophets of Israel, who in those days prophesied for years that I would bring you against them? 18On that day, when Gog comes against the land of Israel, says the Lord GOD, my wrath shall be aroused. 19For in my jealousy and in my blazing wrath I declare: On that day there shall be a great shaking in the land of Israel; 20the fish of the sea, and the birds of the air, and the animals of the field, and all creeping things that creep on the ground, and all human beings that are on the face of the earth, shall quake at my presence, and the mountains shall be thrown down, and the cliffs shall fall, and every wall shall tumble to the ground. 21I will summon the sword against Gog[a] in[b] all my mountains, says the Lord GOD; the swords of all will be against their comrades. 22With pestilence and bloodshed I will enter into judgment with him; and I will pour down torrential rains and hailstones, fire and sulfur, upon him and his troops and the many peoples that are with him. 23So I will display my greatness and my holiness and make myself known in the eyes of many nations. Then they shall know that I am the LORD.

[a]Heb *him*   [b]Heb *to* or *for*

COMMENTARY

Verses 18-23 describe, in graphic and terrifying detail, the effects on nature of Yahweh's battle with Gog. Verse 17, which commences with the messenger formula, is unanticipated in light of preceding verses and quite different from those following it. According to the MT, Yahweh's address to Gog takes the form of a question: "Are you he of whom I spoke in former days by my servants the prophets of Israel, who in those days prophesied for years that I would bring you against them?" (NRSV; the phrase is difficult; the MT reads "in those days years"; the LXX adds the copula to "years," hence, "in those days and years"). Because Yahweh presumably would not ask such a question of Gog in order actually to secure infor-

mation, the query should be regarded as a rhetorical question. But what is its presumed answer? We shall return to that issue below. In the LXX, by contrast, there is no question. Yahweh's words to Gog are cast as an indicative sentence: "You are he of whom I spoke." The NIV retains the question but, by translating "Are you not the one," inclines its readers to a positive response: "Yes, you are the one."

Many scholars regard v. 17 as a secondary expansion of the basic text. Not only does it not fit easily into its context, they observe, but also its style and content are distinctive. Ezekiel elsewhere speaks of "the prophets of Israel" (e.g., 13:2, 16), but only here in the book do we encounter "my servants the prophets of Israel"; "my servants the prophets" is a phrase familiar from the Deuteronomistic History (2 Kgs 9:7; 17:13), deuteronomistically influenced passages in Jeremiah (7:25; 26:5; 29:19; 35:15; 44:4), and Zech 1:6. Moreover, as Zimmerli observes, the phrase seems to reflect "a stage of distanced reflection on past prophecy which one does not expect in Ezekiel."[1248] It is likely that v. 17 is a later addition; it is unlikely, however, that my reader would regard it as such. Of what prophecies would he think as he considered Ezekiel's reference to the oracles of former days? Scholars point often to Isa 14:24-25, where Yahweh swears to defeat "the Assyrian" on the mountains of Israel ("my mountains"), and Isa 14:31 (where the Assyrian army is described metaphorically as smoke coming out of the north), as well as Jeremiah's foe from the north passages in 1:13-15; 4:5-18; and 6:22. Of course, Gog is neither an Assyrian nor a Babylonian. For that reason, Block concludes that the proper answer to the rhetorical question is "no."[1249] Isaiah was not prophesying concerning Gog, and Jeremiah eventually identified his foe from the north as Nebuchadrezzar and the Babylonians. But Block's discussion, in particular, begs the question he nowhere asks: If the author intends that the answer to the rhetorical question attributed to Yahweh be "no," then why pose it at all? Without a positive response, the question has no point.

I conclude that the author of v. 17, whether Ezekiel or a later redactor, intends that Yahweh's query link Gog with the prophecies of other prophets who spoke of a foe from the north. This does not mean that the Isaian and early Jeremian oracles were regarded as "unfulfilled." Of course they were fulfilled! The Assyrians indeed wreaked havoc in Israel's neighborhood during the eighth-century BCE; and Nebuchadrezzar and his forces destroyed Jerusalem, just as Jeremiah had said they would. It means rather that when a predictive prophecy was fulfilled by an historical event, it was not then discarded as if its significance were "used up." To the contrary, it was subject to continual reinterpretation in light of changing circumstances. Israel's prophets had proclaimed that God

used the "foe from the north" as an instrument by which Yahweh punished the Israelites for a variety of sins. Ezekiel, who consistently maintained in his oracles of judgment that Yahweh was using Nebuchadrezzar in just that way, now looks forward to Yahweh's future, consummate victory over the ultimate foe from the north. God brings Gog and his forces against Israel's land, not as an instrument for its destruction, but for the occasion of Gog's destruction. Never again will God's people, living securely in their land and incapable of incurring Yahweh's wrath (36:26-27) and consequent punishment, fear such a foe.

With v. 18, the divine speech shifts from second-person direct address to Gog to third-person indirect address about Gog. Critics often observe that the following description of cosmic, earth-shattering power was composed in the style of later apocalyptic and so ascribe it to a later redactor.[1250] Such may in fact be the case. However, the ancient reader knows that precedents exist for this type of imagery in earlier prophecies; see, e.g., Jer 4:23-26, which speaks of a horrific earthquake shaking the mountains as creation teeters on the edge of returning to primordial chaos. On the day—the day that Gog comes to the land of Israel—Yahweh declares, God's wrath will be roused against him. The different terms used to describe God's passionate outburst have appeared earlier in the corpus, but here they are piled, one after the other, in a manner unparalleled within Ezekiel and possibly the entire Hebrew Scriptures.[1251]

A mighty earthquake will shake the land of Israel and all of its living creatures. The list of animals shaken by the quake occasioned by Yahweh's theophany—the fish of the sea, the birds of the air, the animals of the field, and all creeping things that creep on the ground, as well as all human beings—recalls the language of the priestly creation account in Genesis 1. So severe will that earthquake be that the mountains and their cliffs, symbols of stability, will be thrown down; and every wall constructed by human hands will crash to the ground. That Israel's human and animal populations would do more than quake under such circumstances, and that its land would suffer horrific devastation, does not deter the author,

1248. Zimmerli, *Ezekiel 2*, 312.
1249. See D. I. Block, "Gog in Prophetic Tradition: A New Look at Ezekiel XXXVIII 17," *VT* 42 (1992) 170-72; *Ezekiel 25–48*, 452-56.

1250. See, e.g., Zimmerli, *Ezekiel 2*, 312-14.
1251. Block, *Ezekiel 25–48*, 457.

who focuses solely upon the fate of Gog and his forces. Yahweh will summon the sword against Gog throughout God's mountains. Panic-stricken, Gog's hordes will turn their swords against each other (as did the Midianites in their battle with Gideon, Judg 7:22). The text preoccupies them with self-destruction, and so need say nothing about the possibility of Israel's inhabitants being slaughtered. This war is between Yahweh on the one hand, and Gog and his army on the other. The author affords the Israelites no role in the former's victory and the latter's defeat.

Among Yahweh's arsenal of weapons are pestilence and bloodshed. In 5:16-17, these afflictions, as well as the sword, appeared among the many punishments Yahweh threatened to inflict upon the sinful inhabitants of Jerusalem. Moreover, God will punish Gog and his vast forces with torrential floods and hailstones, and with fire and sulfur (recall the destruction of Sodom and Gomorrah in Gen 19:24). By these means, Yahweh engages in a great self-disclosure: God's greatness and holiness are revealed in the eyes of the many nations which witness that "battle to end all battles." As a consequence, they are forced to acknowledge Yahweh.

With the destruction of this, the ultimate "foe from the north," Yahweh reassures God's people that they need not fear that some further, future foe will swoop down upon them. Both Assyria and Babylonia were foes from the north, instruments of Yahweh's judgment upon the Northern and Southern Kingdoms respectively. But under the conditions described by Ezekiel, including new hearts and spirits that are incapable of disobedience (36:26-27), Israel will not again sin against its God. No future judgment will ever be needed. (See Reflections at 39:21-29.)

Ezekiel 39:1-8, Gog's Defeat; God's Holy Name Protected

NIV

39 "Son of man, prophesy against Gog and say: 'This is what the Sovereign LORD says: I am against you, O Gog, chief prince of[a] Meshech and Tubal. [2]I will turn you around and drag you along. I will bring you from the far north and send you against the mountains of Israel. [3]Then I will strike your bow from your left hand and make your arrows drop from your right hand. [4]On the mountains of Israel you will fall, you and all your troops and the nations with you. I will give you as food to all kinds of carrion birds and to the wild animals. [5]You will fall in the open field, for I have spoken, declares the Sovereign LORD. [6]I will send fire on Magog and on those who live in safety in the coastlands, and they will know that I am the LORD.

[7]" 'I will make known my holy name among my people Israel. I will no longer let my holy name be profaned, and the nations will know that I the LORD am the Holy One in Israel. [8]It is coming! It will surely take place, declares the Sovereign LORD. This is the day I have spoken of.

[a]1 Or Gog, prince of Rosh,

NRSV

39 And you, mortal, prophesy against Gog, and say: Thus says the Lord GOD: I am against you, O Gog, chief prince of Meshech and Tubal! [2]I will turn you around and drive you forward, and bring you up from the remotest parts of the north, and lead you against the mountains of Israel. [3]I will strike your bow from your left hand, and will make your arrows drop out of your right hand. [4]You shall fall upon the mountains of Israel, you and all your troops and the peoples that are with you; I will give you to birds of prey of every kind and to the wild animals to be devoured. [5]You shall fall in the open field; for I have spoken, says the Lord GOD. [6]I will send fire on Magog and on those who live securely in the coastlands; and they shall know that I am the LORD.

[7]My holy name I will make known among my people Israel; and I will not let my holy name be profaned any more; and the nations shall know that I am the LORD, the Holy One in Israel. [8]It has come! It has happened, says the Lord GOD. This is the day of which I have spoken.

COMMENTARY

For a third time in the Gog of Magog pericope, Yahweh addresses Ezekiel directly ("Mortal") and commands that he prophesy against Gog. Unlike 38:1, 39:1 makes no reference to Magog and does not include the command that Ezekiel set his face against God's foe. The "challenge to a duel" formula (39:1), found also in 38:3, is followed by a series of verbal clauses announcing Yahweh's deadly plans for this adversary: Israel's divine warrior will turn Gog around (v. 2; see also 38:4); drive him forward;[1252] bring him up from the remotest stretches of the north; and lead him against the mountains of Israel. Having forced Gog to the battle site, Yahweh will engage him in a duel. Verse 3 offers only the briefest description of their clash: Yahweh will knock Gog's bow from his left hand and cause his arrows to fall from his right hand. Defenseless, Gog will fall upon the mountains of Israel, along with all his troops and accompanying peoples (see 38:9). This account of Gog's demise lacks not only the vivid, earth-shattering, and cosmic imagery of 38:19-22, but also its emphasis upon Yahweh's passionate and burning wrath. However, the consistency-building reader of the Gog oracle will likely import both into the present account, construing the latter as further detail about Yahweh's actual, face-to-face encounter with this ultimate enemy.

God will then give the carcasses of Gog and his hordes to every kind of scavenging bird—vultures, eagles, ravens, etc.—and to the wild animals (literally "creatures of the field")—lions, jackals, hyenas, etc. When they have done their work, only the bones will remain, like the bones strewn across the valley in Ezekiel's vision in chap. 37. But Yahweh will not be content simply to defeat Gog and his forces and then to abandon their remains to scavengers. According to v. 6, Yahweh will send fire (shades of Sodom and Gomorrah!) on Magog, Gog's domain, and on the inhabitants of the coastlands, the shores and islands of the Mediterranean Sea. With great irony, the text describes those inhabitants as "dwelling securely." The same phrase appeared in 38:8, 11, and 14 to describe the Israelites' situation prior to Gog's unanticipated assault. Now, Yahweh will assault with fire those subjects of Gog who believe themselves to be out of harm's way.

As noted in the Overview, the destruction of Gog and his hordes is not Yahweh's ultimate goal in chaps. 38–39; rather it is the means by which larger goals of crucial importance within the book of Ezekiel will be achieved. In 38:16b, one of those goals was identified: that the nations come to know Yahweh's unparalleled sovereignty and power. Gog is Yahweh's vehicle—the means by which Yahweh will display the Lord's holiness in the sight of the nations. In 39:7, Yahweh further states the goals that will be achieved by means of the divine warrior's victory over Gog and his forces. First, God will make known God's holy name among the people of Israel. With this final battle, the Lord's own people will come to full awareness of the nature of their unrivalled patron deity. The NRSV translation follows MT in placing the direct object of the verb, "My holy name," at the very beginning of the sentence, thereby emphasizing its importance. Second, God will never again allow God's holy name to be profaned. The reader recognizes in Gog's future defeat the resolution of a problem that has plagued the prophet: the profanation of God's holy name as a consequence of the exile. According to 36:20-23, God's holy name was profaned when the nations, witnessing the exiles whom Yahweh had dispersed throughout the countries, wondered how such a thing could have happened: Had Yahweh simply abandoned them, or had Israel's God proven too weak to defend it? (In 20:39, Ezekiel's fellow exiles were accused of profaning God's holy name by engaging in illicit religious practices.) Yahweh's victory over Gog will forever end such speculations. Third, the nations will be forced to acknowledge the identity of Yahweh as "the Holy One in Israel." This epithet, which resembles the Isaian title "the Holy One of Israel" (Isa 12:6; 43:3; 55:5; 50:9, 14), affirms God's abiding presence in, and commitment to, Israel and its land.

Verse 8 emphatically asserts that the events described thus far will indeed transpire. The

---

1252. Hebrew שִׁשֵּׁאתִיךְ (šiššē'tîkā) is a hapax legomenon—i.e., a word appearing only once in the HB. BDB identifies the form as a pilpel from the root שאה (šš'), probably meaning "lead on."

phrase "Look! It is coming. It will be done" (author's trans.) echoes 21:7. In that context, what was coming was the sword of Yahweh, drawn in punishment against God's own people. Here, by stark contrast, these words assert "the inevitability of the coming salva-

tion."[1253] The day of Yahweh's defeat of Gog, about which God has spoken through Ezekiel, will be the ultimate "day of the LORD." (See Reflections at 39:21-29.)

1253. W. Zimmerli, *Ezekiel 2: A Commentary on the Book of the Prophet Ezekiel, Chapters 25–48*, trans. J. D. Martin, Hermeneia (Philadelphia: Fortress, 1983) 315.

Ezekiel 39:9-10, Disposing of Gog's Weaponry

NIV

9" 'Then those who live in the towns of Israel will go out and use the weapons for fuel and burn them up—the small and large shields, the bows and arrows, the war clubs and spears. For seven years they will use them for fuel. [10]They will not need to gather wood from the fields or cut it from the forests, because they will use the weapons for fuel. And they will plunder those who plundered them and loot those who looted them, declares the Sovereign LORD.

NRSV

9Then those who live in the towns of Israel will go out and make fires of the weapons and burn them—bucklers and shields, bows and arrows, handpikes and spears—and they will make fires of them for seven years. [10]They will not need to take wood out of the field or cut down any trees in the forests, for they will make their fires of the weapons; they will despoil those who despoiled them, and plunder those who plundered them, says the Lord GOD.

COMMENTARY

With v. 9, the scene shifts from Yahweh's deadly battle with Gog to its aftermath. The Israelites, making their first appearance in the oracle, will go forth from their cities, collect the weapons (נשק *nešeq*) of Gog and his hordes, and burn them (literally "and they will burn and kindle"). Six types of weapons are enumerated: small shields ("bucklers") and body shields; bows and arrows; javelins (NRSV, "handpikes"; NIV, "war clubs") and spears.

So numerous will these weapons be that they will fuel Israel's fires for seven years, alleviating the necessity of gathering wood from the land's fields and forests. Like the later creator of the book of Esther, the author of v. 10*b* relishes a reversal: The Israelites will despoil those who despoiled them, and plunder those who plundered them. (See Reflections at 39:21-29.)

Ezekiel 39:11-16, The Burial of Gog and His Hordes

NIV

11" 'On that day I will give Gog a burial place in Israel, in the valley of those who travel east toward[a] the Sea.[b] It will block the way of travelers, because Gog and all his hordes will be buried there. So it will be called the Valley of Hamon Gog.[c]

[a]11 Or of   [b]11 That is, the Dead Sea   [c]11 *Hamon Gog* means *hordes of Gog.*

NRSV

11On that day I will give to Gog a place for burial in Israel, the Valley of the Travelers[a] east of the sea; it shall block the path of the travelers, for there Gog and all his horde will be buried; it shall be called the Valley of Hamon-gog.[b] [12]Seven months the house of Israel shall spend burying them, in order to cleanse the land. [13]All the peo-

[a]Or *of the Abarim*   [b]That is, *the Horde of Gog*

NIV

¹²" 'For seven months the house of Israel will be burying them in order to cleanse the land. ¹³All the people of the land will bury them, and the day I am glorified will be a memorable day for them, declares the Sovereign LORD.

¹⁴" 'Men will be regularly employed to cleanse the land. Some will go throughout the land and, in addition to them, others will bury those that remain on the ground. At the end of the seven months they will begin their search. ¹⁵As they go through the land and one of them sees a human bone, he will set up a marker beside it until the gravediggers have buried it in the Valley of Hamon Gog. ¹⁶(Also a town called Hamonah*ᵃ* will be there.) And so they will cleanse the land.'

ᵃ16 Hamonah means horde.

NRSV

ple of the land shall bury them; and it will bring them honor on the day that I show my glory, says the Lord GOD. ¹⁴They will set apart men to pass through the land regularly and bury any invaders*ᵃ* who remain on the face of the land, so as to cleanse it; for seven months they shall make their search. ¹⁵As the searchers*ᵃ* pass through the land, anyone who sees a human bone shall set up a sign by it, until the buriers have buried it in the Valley of Hamon-gog.*ᵇ* ¹⁶(A city Hamonah*ᶜ* is there also.) Thus they shall cleanse the land.

ᵃHeb travelers   ᵇThat is, the Horde of Gog   ᶜThat is The Horde

COMMENTARY

Verses 11-16 describe the meticulous collection of the physical remains of Gog and his allies and the burial of those remains in Israel. The reader may initially be surprised to discover that the birds of prey and wild animals summoned by Yahweh in v. 4 have left anything behind to bury! The apparent problem recedes, however, with the reference to "human bone" in v. 15.

"On that day"—at a time in the future, perhaps on the same day that Gog attacks (38:18)—Yahweh will allocate a burial site for Gog and his hordes (v. 1). The location of that site has vexed scholars. One wonders if the author was intentionally vague on this point, or if he intended to pose a riddle for his audience to ponder, or if ancient readers would have known what we do not know, such that the site would have been immediately apparent to them. Some critics believe that גֵי הָעֹבְרִים (*gê hāʿōbĕrîm*), said to lie "east of the sea," is a variant spelling of "the Valley of the Abarim." By this reckoning, "the sea" is the Dead Sea, and the reference is to a mountainous region lying west of northern Moab.¹²⁵⁴ According to Num 33:47-48, the Israelites camped in the mountains of Abarim before setting out for the plains of Moab by the Jordan Sea at Jericho. This

identification is problematic, however, in light of the verse's assertion that Gog's burial site will be "in Israel."

A second view proposes that עברים (*ʿōbĕrîm*) be construed as a Qal masculine plural participle from the root עבר (*ʿbr*) meaning "to pass over, through, by"—hence, "the Valley of the Travelers" (so NRSV; the NIV's "those who travel east toward the Sea" is not supported by the MT). By this reckoning, "the sea" might be either the Mediterranean Sea (called simply "the sea[s]" in 25:16, 26:5, 16-18; 27:3-4, 9, 25-27, 29, 32, 34) or the Dead Sea (so NIV), and the reference would likely be to a caravan route.

A third possibility claims that *ʿōbĕrîm* refers to "those who pass on"—that is, those who have passed from this life to the next.¹²⁵⁵ Odell cites Ps 144:4 and Job 34:20 in support of this view;¹²⁵⁶ Block cites an Ugaritic text, which associates *ʿbrm* with *mlkm* ("kings") and speaks of deceased heroes.¹²⁵⁷ Odell and Block further suggest that the future, new name of the valley, "the Valley of Hamon-gog" (that is, the Valley of Gog's Horde) is

1254. So J. W. Wevers, *Ezekiel,* NCB (London: Nelson, 1969) 292.

1255. M. S. Odell, "The City of Hamonah in Ezekiel 39:11-16: The Tumultuous City of Jerusalem," *CBQ* 56 (1994) 479-89; D. I. Block, *The Book of Ezekiel: Chapters 25–48,* NICOT (Grand Rapids: Eerdmans, 1998) 468-69.

1256. Odell, "The City of Hamonah in Ezekiel 39:11-16," 485.

1257. Block, *Ezekiel 25–48,* 468, citing KTU 1.22.1.12-17.

a wordplay on the Valley of the Son of Hinnom (the valley is elsewhere called simply the Valley of Hinnom or the Valley of the Sons of Hinnom), a narrow valley lying along the western and southern sides of Jerusalem which, according to Josh 15:8 and 18:16, marked the west to east boundary between the tribal lands of Judah and Benjamin. The books of Kings (and Chronicles) and Jeremiah condemn Topheth, in the Valley of (the son of) Hinnom, for the cultic practices carried out there—practices which included the ritual immolation of infants. Kings Ahaz and Manasseh are said to have sacrificed their own sons in the Valley of Hinnom as burnt offerings to Molech (2 Chr 28:3; 33:6).

The prophet Jeremiah proclaimed that in the future, the valley would receive a new name, marking its transformation from cultic site to burial ground:

> And they [the people of Judah] go on building the high place [MT, "high places"] of Topheth, which is in the valley of the son of Hinnom, to burn their sons and their daughters in the fire—which I did not command, nor did it come into my mind. Therefore, the days are surely coming, says the Lord, when it will no more be called Topheth, or the valley of the son of Hinnom, but the valley of Slaughter: for they will bury in Topheth until there is no more room. The corpses of this people will be food for the birds of the air, and for the animals of the earth; and no one will frighten them away. (Jer 7:31-33 NRSV)

If the author of Ezek 39:11 indeed had the Valley of Hinnom in mind, and if he knew this text from Jeremiah, then it seems likely that the latter has influenced the former. All of this remains uncertain, of course, but it is tempting to conclude with Odell and Block that Ezekiel (or some later author) discerned in the Valley of the Son of Hinnom the perfect (perfectly horrible) site for the burial of Gog and his hordes. Jeremiah's statement that they will bury in Topheth "until there is no more room" would then shed light on the Ezekielian assertion that the burial site will "block the way of travelers" (v. 11).

A full seven months will be required in order for the house of Israel, all the people of the land, to bury the dead in order cultically to purify the terrain. Numbers 19:11-22 speaks of the contaminating effect of contact with a corpse and the process by which one is ritually cleansed. In v. 16, for example, we read: "Whoever in the open field touches one who has been killed by a sword, or who has died naturally, or a human bone, or a grave, shall be unclean seven days." But Ezekiel the priest says nothing about the contamination incurred by the people during their seven month stint; his focus remains fixed upon the land. In fulfilling their task, the people will bring honor upon themselves (lit., "and it will become for them a name") on the day when God reveals God's own glory. Ezekiel has previously shown great concern for God's name, or reputation. But now he is concerned for Israel's name. Scrupulously burying the enemy testifies to Israel's passion for the land's purity and the newfound security that rests in God.[1258]

Verses 14-16 elaborate upon the importance of purifying the land after the defeat of Gog. Even the scrupulous efforts of the land's population over a seven month period will not suffice to insure that no remains of Gog and his hordes are overlooked. Hence, further steps must be taken. With priestly precision, the author tells how the people will establish a standing commission of men, passers-through (the root 'br reappears here), who for seven (additional) months will traverse the land and bury any "passers-on" (i.e., the dead) they discover. Verse 15 provides greater detail about this operation. The passers-through will comb the land, and if they spot a human bone, they will place a marker beside it. A second group, called the buriers, will follow behind them and, seeing these markers, will bury the remains in the Valley of Hamon-gog.

Verse 16 is, at best, an enigma. Many critics dismiss it as a gloss whose meaning cannot be recovered.[1259] However Odell, again followed by Block, believes that the city there called "Hamonah" ("horde") is in fact Jerusalem.[1260] More specifically, it is the turbulent Jerusalem condemned by Ezekiel in 5:7-9 and 7:10-14 which, in the hands of the Judeans who remained in the homeland during the years of the Babylonian exile, yet requires purification by those returning home.

1258. Block, *Ezekiel 25–48*, 470.
1259. So Zimmerli, *Ezekiel 2*, 319; Walther Eichrodt, *Ezekiel*, trans. Cosslett Quin, OTL (Philadelphia: Westminster, 1970) 528.
1260. Odell, "The City of Hamonah in Ezekiel 39:11-16," 481-89; Block, *Ezekiel 25–48*, 471-72.

Now it is true that Ezekiel is critical of those who remained in Jerusalem (see Ezekiel 11 and 33:23-29), and he links the land's restoration with the regathered and restored diaspora. Odell's argument has the virtue of explaining a cryptic compound sentence, but it is a very complex and "studied" solution that begs the question of why, in this context, Ezekiel (or some other author) would choose to take a swipe at (those who

remained in) Jerusalem following its destruction. One notes that none of the salvation oracles in chaps. 34–37 address this issue. To the contrary, they (like the oracles of Second Isaiah) speak as if the land of Judah were devoid of inhabitants (another way of taking a swipe at those who remained in the land) until the exiles return. (See Reflections at 39:21-29.)

Ezekiel 39:17-20, A Grisly Sacrificial Feast

NIV

[17]"Son of man, this is what the Sovereign LORD says: Call out to every kind of bird and all the wild animals: 'Assemble and come together from all around to the sacrifice I am preparing for you, the great sacrifice on the mountains of Israel. There you will eat flesh and drink blood. [18]You will eat the flesh of mighty men and drink the blood of the princes of the earth as if they were rams and lambs, goats and bulls—all of them fattened animals from Bashan. [19]At the sacrifice I am preparing for you, you will eat fat till you are glutted and drink blood till you are drunk. [20]At my table you will eat your fill of horses and riders, mighty men and soldiers of every kind,' declares the Sovereign LORD.

NRSV

17As for you, mortal, thus says the Lord GOD: Speak to the birds of every kind and to all the wild animals: Assemble and come, gather from all around to the sacrificial feast that I am preparing for you, a great sacrificial feast on the mountains of Israel, and you shall eat flesh and drink blood. [18]You shall eat the flesh of the mighty, and drink the blood of the princes of the earth—of rams, of lambs, and of goats, of bulls, all of them fatlings of Bashan. [19]You shall eat fat until you are filled, and drink blood until you are drunk, at the sacrificial feast that I am preparing for you. [20]And you shall be filled at my table with horses and charioteers,[a] with warriors and all kinds of soldiers, says the Lord GOD.

[a]Heb chariots

COMMENTARY

In this subunit, Yahweh issues an invitation to scavenging birds and carnivorous beasts to be God's guests at a grisly sacrificial feast at the Lord's table on the mountains of Israel. This feast, called a זבח (zebaḥ; the qal verb from the same root [זבח; zbḥ] means "to slaughter, to slaughter for sacrifice"), refers to a ritual act in which the flesh of a sacrificed animal was consumed by those presenting that animal, save for a few choice cuts given to the priests; and the blood and fat were reserved for Yahweh. Careful readers will note that Gog and his hordes are nowhere explicitly listed on the bill of fare. Read within its context, however, the passage appears clearly to speak further of the fate of their remains.

Critics rightly warn moderns against imposing Western understandings of logic and consistency on ancient Near Eastern texts. Nonetheless, it is difficult to imagine that the ancient reader would not have experienced some surprise that, after reading of the deaths and meticulous burials of Gog and his army, he should suddenly encounter a scenario in which their flesh and blood are the makings of a great banquet. One can only surmise that Ezekiel, or some later author, chose this point in the text further to elaborate upon the notice in v. 4b that Yahweh will give the corpses of Gog and his cohorts to the birds of prey and wild animals.

As Block observes, the subunit takes the form of an official invitation. After the address to Ezekiel, the herald ("As for you, mortal"), the notice of the superior's message ("thus says the Lord God"), and the commissioning of the herald ("Speak to the birds of every kind and to all the wild animals") comes the invitation proper (vv. 17-20), followed by the "signature of the host."[1261] With three imperatives, God summons the guests, enticing them with the prospect of eating flesh and drinking blood prepared for them by Yahweh. Verse 18 further details the menu: The birds and beasts will dine on the flesh of warriors and drink the blood of the princes of the earth. The list of animals that follows might appear out of place within this context until the reader realizes that the rams, lamb, goats, and bulls—all fatlings of Bashan—are metaphorical terms for Gog's elite warriors. (Bashan, a region lying north of the Transjordan, was renowned for its fertility and for its powerful and sleek beasts; see Deut 32:14; Ps 22:13; Amos 4:1.) In v. 19, Yahweh is said to promise those

invited to the sacrificial meal at the Lord's table that they will gorge on fat until thoroughly sated and drink blood until thoroughly drunk. Verse 20 then reminds readers that the menu consists of horses and charioteers (the NRSV and the NIV correctly understand רכב [*rekeb,* "chariot(s)"] as a reference to riders in chariots), of warriors, and of soldiers of every stripe.

These verses brim with irony. The *zebaḥ* feast is all but turned on its head. Instead of worshipers bringing an animal to be sacrificed and consumed in Yahweh's presence, Yahweh brings together ravaging birds and beasts to feast upon human flesh, blood, and fat. In conventional *zebaḥ* feasts, the blood and fat are reserved for Yahweh (placed upon the altar; see Lev 3:16-17). Here, God offers these most holy portions to unclean living creatures. One might wonder that priest Ezekiel, or a later author, would set out such a scene. Anyone who has read chaps. 16 and 23, however, knows that Ezekiel does not shy away from the grotesque. (See Reflections at 39:21-29.)

1261. Block, *Ezekiel 25–48*, 473-74.

Ezekiel 39:21-29, Looking Back, Looking Forward

NIV	NRSV
[21]"I will display my glory among the nations, and all the nations will see the punishment I inflict and the hand I lay upon them. [22]From that day forward the house of Israel will know that I am the LORD their God. [23]And the nations will know that the people of Israel went into exile for their sin, because they were unfaithful to me. So I hid my face from them and handed them over to their enemies, and they all fell by the sword. [24]I dealt with them according to their uncleanness and their offenses, and I hid my face from them. [25]"Therefore this is what the Sovereign LORD says: I will now bring Jacob back from captivity[a] and will have compassion on all the people of Israel, and I will be zealous for my holy name. [26]They will forget their shame and all the unfaithfulness they showed toward me when they lived in safety in their land with no one to make them afraid. [27]When I have brought them back from the nations and have gathered them from the countries	[21]I will display my glory among the nations; and all the nations shall see my judgment that I have executed, and my hand that I have laid on them. [22]The house of Israel shall know that I am the LORD their God, from that day forward. [23]And the nations shall know that the house of Israel went into captivity for their iniquity, because they dealt treacherously with me. So I hid my face from them and gave them into the hand of their adversaries, and they all fell by the sword. [24]I dealt with them according to their uncleanness and their transgressions, and hid my face from them. [25]Therefore thus says the Lord GOD: Now I will restore the fortunes of Jacob, and have mercy on the whole house of Israel; and I will be jealous for my holy name. [26]They shall forget[a] their shame, and all the treachery they have practiced against me, when they live securely in their land with no one to make them afraid, [27]when I have
[a]25 Or *now restore the fortunes of Jacob*	[a]Another reading is *They shall bear*

of their enemies, I will show myself holy through them in the sight of many nations. [28]Then they will know that I am the LORD their God, for though I sent them into exile among the nations, I will gather them to their own land, not leaving any behind. [29]I will no longer hide my face from them, for I will pour out my Spirit on the house of Israel, declares the Sovereign LORD."

brought them back from the peoples and gathered them from their enemies' lands, and through them have displayed my holiness in the sight of many nations. [28]Then they shall know that I am the LORD their God because I sent them into exile among the nations, and then gathered them into their own land. I will leave none of them behind; [29]and I will never again hide my face from them, when I pour out my spirit upon the house of Israel, says the Lord GOD.

COMMENTARY

The Gog of Magog pericope is set in the future, when the exiles have already resettled in their homeland. Hence, vv. 21-29 look forward to events anticipated, but not yet realized. Witnessing Yahweh's defeat of Gog and his hordes, however, the nations will look back to events lying in the past and reinterpret them in a way that exonerates Yahweh's damaged reputation. Critics often regard these verses as two appendices (vv. 21-24 on the one hand, vv. 25-29 on the other) from authors other than Ezekiel. But the ancient reader, discerning in them a cornucopia of important Ezekielian themes, will attribute vv. 21-29 to the priest-prophet, despite the fact that they contain words and phrases that are rare, or previously unattested, in the book.

Hals's statement that these two appendices are "unconnected to the battle with Gog"[1262] is in fact an overstatement. Verses 21-22 are best understood within the context of the aftermath of that battle. When in v. 21 we read, "my hand that I have laid on them," the referent of *them* is best construed as Gog and his army; when in v. 22 we read that "the house of Israel shall know that I am the Lord their God, from that day forward," *that day* is best construed as the day of Yahweh's victorious battle over those same foes.

Ezekiel 39:13 spoke of the manifestation of Yahweh's glory. Verse 21 speaks of same among the nations. The glory of the Lord, first revealed to Ezekiel in a vision as he stood beside the Chebar Canal, will be displayed for all eyes to see in light of God's great victory. Both NRSV and NIV translate משפטי (*mišpāṭî*) in v. 21 b as "my judgment." Block, by contrast, argues that the correct rendering is "my justice" ("justice" is the required translation of the term in Ezek 18:8).[1263] In the present context, it seems unnecessary to pit one translation against the other. Rather, the reader may recognize that the administration of divine justice here requires judgment against Gog and his hordes who, though forced to approach Israel's homeland by Yahweh, discerned in the situation an opportunity to line their pockets. The phrase "my hand that I have laid on them" (v. 21 b) appears nowhere else in the book of Ezekiel.

Verse 22 affirms that one of the foremost objectives in the Ezekielian tradition will be fully and forever realized. Henceforth, the house of Israel will know that Yahweh is their God. The nations, too, will be instructed by God's victory over Gog. In the past, they had speculated that defeat and exile befell Yahweh's people because their patron deity was incapable of protecting them. Seeing God's triumph, however, they will realize that Israel's captivity was a consequence not of divine impotence but of human sinfulness (v. 23). In the past, the Lord explains, "I hid my face from them" and handed them over to their adversaries for slaughter by the sword. The phrase "I hid my face from them" has not previously appeared in the book of Ezekiel, but the notion that a deity's hidden face brought disastrous consequences is well attested not only in Hebrew Scripture (e.g., Ps 13:1;

1262. Ronald M. Hals, *Ezekiel,* FOTL 19 (Grand Rapids: Eerdmans, 1989) 279.

1263. Block, *Ezekiel 25–48,* 481.

27:9; 104:29; Isa 54:8; 59:2; 64:7), but also in other ancient Near Eastern texts. In "A Prayer of Lamentation to Ishtar," for example, we read:

> Accept the abasement of my countenance;
> Hear my prayers.
> Faithfully look upon me and accept my
>   supplication.
> How long, O my Lady, wilt thou be angered
>   so that thy face is turned away?
> How long, O my Lady, wilt thou be infuriated,
>   so that thy spirit is enraged?
> Turn thy neck which thou hast set against me;
> Set thy face [toward] good favor.[1264]

Verse 24, then, further asserts the justice of God's judgment upon Yahweh's own people. They got what they deserved while the Lord's face was hidden from them.

The second so-called appendix, vv. 25-29, speaks of the exiles' return to their land as an event yet lying in the future. At present, they remain in Babylonia. But the Gog of Magog material has challenged them to steadfast hope that their superpower patron deity will soon intervene in history and bring them home.

Verse 25 begins with *lākēn,* "therefore," which not only links what follows to preceding verses but also functions as a "rhetorical attention getter."[1265] Following the messenger formula, Yahweh speaks in the first person. The audience is Ezekiel's fellow exiles, but Yahweh refers to them in the third person. God will restore the fortunes of Jacob and have mercy on the whole house of Israel. The phrase "restore the fortunes" appeared earlier in 16:53 in Yahweh's address to personified Jerusalem and in 29:14, in a surprising twist on an oracle against Pharaoh. It appears frequently in the so-called Book of Consolation within the Jeremiah scroll (30:3, 18; 31:23; 33:7, 11, 26). Ezekiel has referred to the patriarch Jacob on three prior occasions (20:5; 28:25; 37:25). In this context, the epithet is applied to his descendants, the exiles. For the reader familiar with the Jacob cycle of stories in Genesis, the reference to Jacob is particularly significant since he was forced to go to Paddan-Aram in northern Mesopotamia, but eventually returned to Canaan (Genesis 27–33). The root רחם (*rḥm*) appears here for only the second time in

the book of Ezekiel. In 20:26, the phrase *kol-peṭer rāḥam* referred to every Hebrew woman's firstborn child. Here, it refers to Yahweh's compassion (NRSV "mercy") for all of God's people. Elsewhere, Ezekiel has used חמל (*ḥāmal*) "spare, have compassion," (5:11; 7:4, 9; 8:18; 9:5, 10; 16:5; 36:21) but in every case, with the exception of 36:21, it is used in a negative sense, i.e., Yahweh rules out the possibility that divine compassion might enable Israel to escape judgment. The end of v. 25 adds a second motivation for Yahweh's future, salvific actions. The Lord will act not only for Israel's sake, but also out of passionate zeal for God's holy name (see 36:22-23; 39:7).

What will be Israel's response to Yahweh's compassionate intervention in its history? The answer to this question hinges upon the first word in the MT. The form, preceded by a conjunctive ו (*wě*; "and") is נשׁו (*nāśû*), from the root נשׁא (*nś'*) meaning "to bear." However, many translations (including NRSV and NIV) render it as if it were from the root נשׁה (*nāšâ* "to forget"). The notion that the people, securely resettled in their homeland with no one to fear, would be able to forget their sinful past is appealing, but it is not Ezekielian. This verse reminds readers of Ezekiel 16, where personified Jerusalem responds to Yahweh's promise of an everlasting covenant on the other side of judgment by remembering her ways and being ashamed (v. 61). It evokes thoughts of Ezekiel 20, where the exiles, having been returned to Yahweh's holy mountain, will remember their ways and polluting deeds and loathe themselves for all their evils (v. 43). And it calls to mind Ezek 36:22-32, where the to-be-restored house of Israel is reminded that Yahweh will act not for its sake, but for the sake of Yahweh's holy name, and then is commanded to "be ashamed and dismayed for your ways" (v. 32). Within the Ezekielian tradition, memory of one's sinful past surfaces amidst the (anticipated) experience of God's salvific actions. Verse 27 further states that when Yahweh has brought the exiles back from among the peoples and gathered them from the lands of their enemies (one would expect "gathered them from their enemies' lands" to precede "bought them back from the peoples"), God's holiness will be manifest "in the sight of many nations" (see, most recently, 39:25).

1264. Ibid., 385.
1265. Block, *Ezekiel 25–48,* 485.

Verses 28-29 consist of a much elaborated recognition formula. The nations will know that Yahweh is Israel's God, who sent "his" people into exile (on account of their sinfulness; see, most recently, 39:24) but who then (re)gathered them to their homeland, leaving nary a soul behind. (The word for "gathered" is כנס [*kinnēs*], which appears in 22:21, rather than Ezekiel's customary קבץ [*qābaṣ*]. The last two statements of v. 28 do not appear in the LXX.) The reader who is familiar with Detueronomy 4 will discern in v. 28 the fulfillment of God's ancient promise that after the people are exiled, they will return to Yahweh their God and be obedient:

> In your distress, when all these things have happened to you in time to come, you will return to the Lord your God and heed him. Because the Lord your God is a merciful God, he will neither abandon you nor destroy you; he will not forget the covenant with your ancestors that he swore to them (Deut 4:30-31; see also Lev 26:44-45).

Verse 29 expresses Yahweh's commitment never again to hide the divine face from God's people (see vv. 23-24). Transforming the phrase "I will pour out my wrath" that has occurred so often in the Ezekiel scroll (7:8; 9:8; 20:8, 13, 21, 33, 34, etc.), Yahweh promises to "pour out my spirit upon the house of Israel." Block observes that in each of the five appearances of this idea in the Hebrew Bible (see Isa 32:15; 44:1-5; Joel 2:28; Zech 12:10), the outpouring of Yahweh's spirit signals "the ratification and sealing of the covenant relationship with his people."[1266] The passage ends with the citation formula, "says the Lord GOD."

1266. Ibid., 488.

REFLECTIONS

Deeply lodged in the human spirit is the longing for security, for freedom from fear. That longing intensifies when people know themselves to be vulnerable, when their fears are very real, when they are far from home. Many of Ezekiel's fellow exiles knew such longing well. To be sure, some born-in-Babylonia Judeans would have opted for security in the only home they had ever known. For such persons, Ezekiel's salvation oracles functioned as invitations to view reality differently, to perceive that the future of Yahweh's people lay not in Mesopotamia, but in the homeland promised to the descendants of Abraham and Sarah, Isaac and Rebekah, Jacob and Leah and Rachel—a land that would soon be transformed into a veritable Garden of Eden. (The later oracles of Second Isaiah [Isaiah 40–55] often employ the same rhetorical strategy; see, e.g., Isa 51:3.)

For many others, however, the longing to return to Judah and to resume a life now free of fear must have been fierce and passionate. Ezekiel's salvation oracles, including the Gog of Magog pericope, fueled their hopes that Yahweh would indeed intervene in history to bring about the conditions the priest-prophet described—if not for their sakes, then for the sake of the divine reputation which had been sullied among the nations with Judah's collapse and the exiles' forced residency in Babylonia (see, e.g., Ezek 36:22-32). The Gog of Magog pericope speaks *about* the distant future, but it speaks *to* the diaspora community about issues most crucial to it, including the desire to be reunited with Yahweh in covenant fidelity. The ancient reader, who knows that God's battle to end all battles has not yet transpired, also awaits the fulfillment of Ezekiel's oracle. So does the Christian author of Revelation 19–20, who anticipates that following a thousand years of Messianic rule, Satan will deceive "the nations at the four corners of the earth, Gog and Magog" (now two distinct entities), and bring them against "the camp of the saints" and "the beloved city" (Jerusalem) where they will be consumed by fire descending from heaven.

Modern readers, no less than their ancient counterparts, long for security. We want to believe that good will triumph over evil—said theologically, that God will intervene in human history to reward the righteous and to punish the wicked. The Gog of Magog pericope is, within the book of Ezekiel, the ultimate expression of that longing. Jacob's descendants fell beneath the deadly blows of foes from the north. The prophet Isaiah described the Assyrian army as "smoke coming from the north," and the Northern Kingdom was defeated by that army in 721 BCE. The prophet Jeremiah identified the foe from the north as Nebuchadrezzar's forces, and the Southern Kingdom was defeated by that army in 586 BCE (Jer 25:8-14). But, as indicated in the Commentary, chaps. 38–39 present Yahweh's battle with Gog and his hordes as the conclusive victory which eliminates forever the threat posed by foes from the north—indeed, according to Ezek 38:5-6, from the totality of the earth's evil and aggressive forces.

Gog of Magog is the supreme (incomparably evil) enemy. Although the attack against the land of Israel which he spearheads is initiated by Yahweh alone, the text in its canonical form dehumanizes Gog (he is hooked through the jaws like an animal). Indeed, Gog is more caricature than character. The only human personality traits ascribed to him are avarice and a concomitant desire to assail an ostensibly unprotected people (38:10-12). Nowhere does this material invite its readers to consider Gog and his hordes as fellow human beings. In fact, the very notion that one might do so seems, on the surface, patently absurd.

Yet at a time when we are forced increasingly to recognize the importance of profound respect and cooperation among the nations sharing this tiny planet, biblical oracles which suggest that the solution to a people's (any people's) problems is the extermination of its enemies are extremely problematic. Even more difficult is the idea that God would, for the sale of self-vindication, deliberately drag Gog to the battlefield and utterly exterminate him and his forces. To be sure, the text speaks also of Yahweh's compassion for, and covenant loyalty to, God's people. But to the extent that Ezekiel depicts Yahweh as a deity who resolves problems by means of massacre, he turns God into a negative role model for people with problems of their own.

EZEKIEL 40:1–48:35, EZEKIEL'S VISION OF AN ALL NEW, THOROUGHLY IMPROVED ISRAEL

OVERVIEW

In this, his fourth and final vision report, Ezekiel describes a perfectly ordered Israelite society living in a perfectly ordered homeland under the leadership of a perfectly ordered priesthood serving in a perfectly ordered Temple complex. Moshe Greenberg divides chaps. 40–48 into three major subunits plus two transitional passages. In the first subunit, 40:1–43:12, Ezekiel is transported to a high mountain, where he is given a guided tour of its Temple complex and then witnesses Yahweh's glory enter and fill the Temple. The second subunit, 44:1–46:24, sets out rules governing access to the temple complex and the activities carried out within it. The third subunit, 47:13–48:35, describes the apportionment of land among Israel's twelve tribes. The first transitional passage, 43:13-27, focuses on the altar and links the static vision of the first subunit with the activity prescribed in the second subunit. The second transitional passage, 47:1-11, follows a vivifying stream of water that issues from the Temple and grows as it flows to the east; this passage links the Temple of the first two subunits to the third.[1267]

Ambitious readers who determine to work through these chapters find themselves confronted with a morass of details and much confusion. I would venture that many an ancient reader would also have experienced bewilderment and frustration at points. This is technical language—the argot of architecture and especially of ritual practice—and it undoubtedly was best understood by priests conversant with the structures, inner workings, and rituals of cultic life.

1267. M. Greenberg, "The Design and Themes of Ezekiel's Program of Restoration," *Int.* 38 (1984) 189-90.

How can moderns lacking such information make sense of this vision and understand the theology undergirding it? Stevenson offers three keys to unlocking Ezekiel's "vision of transformation" that are apropos in the context of this Overview. First, she argues persuasively that the vision is best construed when approached from the perspective of human geography. "Human geography shows that every society is organized in space," she writes. "Changing the spatial organization of the society changes the society. Ezekiel 40–48 is a vision of a new society organized according to a new set of spatial rules. *It is a temple society with controlled access to sacred space, based on a spatial theology of holiness.*"[1268]

Second, Stevenson maintains that the genre of Ezekiel 40–48 is territorial rhetoric. Territoriality, she explains, is a technical term used within the discipline of human geography. Robert Sack defines territoriality as "the attempt by an individual or group to affect, influence, or control people, phenomena, and relationships, by delimiting and asserting control over a geographic area."[1269] According to Sack, space becomes territory when an attempt is made to control access to it by means of a boundary of some sort—a structure, or even a password.[1270] Territoriality is "place specific" and "always involves issues of power."[1271]

One way to assert territoriality, Stevenson maintains, is to describe areas, boundaries, and rules of access in a written text such as Ezekiel 40–48.[1272] Within the world of the vision, Yahweh asserts territoriality as the victorious divine king who returns from battle (chaps. 38–39) and is enthroned within his palace (Temple). But the priests also assert territoriality by controlling access to sacred space and performing the most crucial religious rituals.

Third, Sevenson emphasizes "the shape of the holy." In Ezekiel's vision, the square is of primary symbolic significance. "In the landscape of temple and land in Ezekiel," she writes, "the square is not simply an accident of design. It is rhetorically

meaningful and is intended to be the material representation of a theology of holiness . . . the command to measure the proportion in 43:10 is part of a rhetorical strategy to restructure a society according to a theology of holiness."[1273] In the course of the temple tour, Ezekiel learns through the measurements of his guide that the outer court, inner court, Temple, *binyān* ("building," "structure"), holy of holies, and altar are all square in shape. Careful readers will discover that many of the measurements provided for these and other features of the Temple complex are multiples of five—five, twenty-five, fifty, etc.

Before turning to the first subunit of Ezekiel 40–48, more should be said about the "theology of holiness" referred to several times thus far. This theology of holiness is much illumined by Jacob Milgrom's extensive analysis of Israel's priestly cultic system. Like other ancient Near Eastern theologies, this cultic system conceives of people, places, and things as holy or common, pure or impure. Milgrom insists that holiness is not, as many moderns might think, an abstract ethical quality. It is a "thing," a dynamic and contagious substance emanating from deities. Its antagonist is impurity, also a dynamic and contagious physical substance which emanates, in Israelite thought, from human beings. Because holiness and impurity are dynamic and contagious, contact with them renders persons or objects either holy or impure. (By contrast, the common and pure are stative, i.e., stating a condition or state, and non-contagious substances.)[1274]

Some moderns might view the concept of contagious holiness positively, but in the thought world of ancient Israel, illicit contact with the holy could have deadly consequences. One thinks, for example, of the hapless Uzzah, who reached out his hand to steady the ark as it was being carted to Jerusalem and died as a consequence (2 Sam 6:6-7). Or one thinks of Korah and his cohorts, Dathan and Abiram (Numbers 16), who believed that they should be able to offer incense to Yahweh and who confronted Moses and Aaron on the issue. Korah made a theological argument for his position: "All the congregation are holy, every one of them, and the Lord is among them. So why

1268. Kalinda Rose Stevenson, *The Vision of Transformation: The Territorial Rhetoric of Ezekiel 40–48,* SBLDS 154 (Atlanta: Scholars Press, 1996) xviii, italics added.
1269. Robert David Sack, *Human Territoriality: Its Theory and History,* Cambridge Studies in Historical Geography (Cambridge: Cambridge University Press, 1986) 19.
1270. Ibid., 9.
1271. Stevenson, *The Vision of Transformation,* 12.
1272. Ibid., 13.
1273. Ibid., 42.
1274. J. Milgrom, *Leviticus 1–16,* AB 3 (New York: Doubleday, 1991) 257.

1533

then do you exalt yourselves above the assembly of the Lord?" (Num 16:3). But as they stood with their censers and incense at the entrance of the tent of meeting, Yahweh threatened to destroy the entire "congregation of Israel." Moses intervened, and the congregation was permitted to distance itself from Korah, Dathan, and Abiram. But Yahweh is said to have caused the earth to "open its mouth"; and the men, together with their families and possessions, "went down alive into Sheol."

Impurity has the power to pollute a temple. This potential is exceeding dangerous because, as Ezekiel's second vision report (chaps. 8–11) makes perfectly clear, Yahweh's glory will not reside in a grossly impure temple. Ezekiel 5:11 warned of the consequences of temple defilement: "Therefore, as I live, says the Lord God, surely, because you have defiled my sanctuary with all your detestable things and with all your abominations—therefore I will cut you down; my eye will not spare, and I will have no pity." When God abandons the Temple, the land, its people, indeed, the Temple itself, are doomed to destruction at the hands of Yahweh's punitive instruments. Such, from Ezekiel's perspective, was the hard lesson of 586 BCE, when the Babylonian army broke through Jerusalem's walls, burned every large structure, including the Solomonic Temple, and either killed or exiled the majority of the city's inhabitants. The sins of the past must not be repeated. And, Stevenson writes, one corrects the sins of the past by controlling access to space in the future. The concern for measurements, which the modern reader may find bothersome and irrelevant, is con-

sistent with a "worldview in which the cultic abuses of the past were perceived as boundary violations of sacred space."[1275]

Although impurity is dangerous and unacceptable to God, temple impurity is inevitable. In his commentary on Leviticus 1–16, Milgrom notes that, from the perspective of the priestly pentateuchal authors, impurity pollutes the priestly tabernacle in three stages: (1) an individual's inadvertent misdeed or severe physical impurity pollutes the courtyard altar, which must then be purged by daubing its horns with blood from the purification sacrifice (see below). (Ezekiel diminishes this possibility by placing the altar in the inner court, an area accessible only to priests); (2) an inadvertent misdeed committed by priest or people pollutes the Temple, which must then be purged by the high priest, again by blood from the purification sacrifice; (3) "wanton unrepented sin not only pollutes the outer altar and penetrates into the shrine but it pierces the veil and enters the adytum [innermost sanctuary], housing the holy Ark and . . . the very throne of God."[1276] Purifying the Temple by means of the ongoing sacrificial system is the task of the priests.

The issues here addressed—human geography, territoriality, the shape of the holy, and the theology of holiness—enable modern readers more fully to understand Ezekiel's vision of a perfectly ordered and temple-centered Israelite society in the midst of which Yahweh's glory dwells. The devil is *not* in the details! The details make possible God's abiding presence.

1275. Stevenson, *The Vision of Transformation*, xxiv.
1276. Milgrom, *Leviticus 1–16*, 257.

Ezekiel 40:1–43:12, A Purified and Perfectly Ordered Temple

Overview

Some scholars think that the detailed measurements of structures and spaces identify chaps. 40–42 as a building plan. If such it be, however, it is not a very good one. With its almost total lack of vertical measurements and its failure to give measurements for at least some structures, it does not provide adequate information for the construction

of a Temple complex.[1277] I agree with Stevenson that the issue in these chapters is not the proper *building* of structures, but "the *creation* of spaces, and even more importantly, *keeping these spaces*

1277. See W. Zimmerli, *Ezekiel 2: A Commentary on the Book of the Prophet Ezekiel, Chapters 25–48,* trans. J. D. Martin, Hermeneia (Philadelphia: Fortress, 1983).

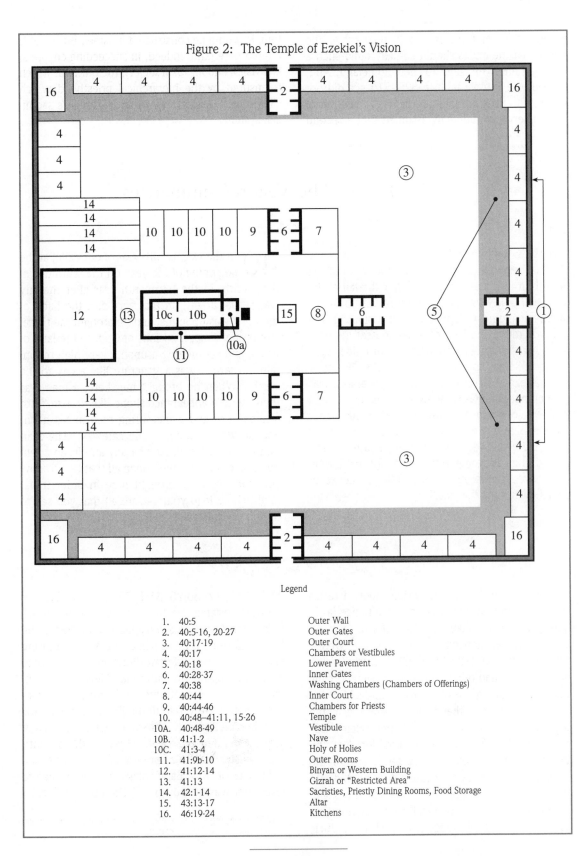

Figure 2: The Temple of Ezekiel's Vision

Legend

1.	40:5	Outer Wall
2.	40:5-16, 20-27	Outer Gates
3.	40:17-19	Outer Court
4.	40:17	Chambers or Vestibules
5.	40:18	Lower Pavement
6.	40:28-37	Inner Gates
7.	40:38	Washing Chambers (Chambers of Offerings)
8.	40:44	Inner Court
9.	40:44-46	Chambers for Priests
10.	40:48–41:11, 15-26	Temple
10A.	40:48-49	Vestibule
10B.	41:1-2	Nave
10C.	41:3-4	Holy of Holies
11.	41:9b-10	Outer Rooms
12.	41:12-14	Binyan or Western Building
13.	41:13	Gizrah or "Restricted Area"
14.	42:1-14	Sacristies, Priestly Dining Rooms, Food Storage
15.	43:13-17	Altar
16.	46:19-24	Kitchens

separate."[1278] Nothing is said in the text to the effect that the exiles should actually build such a complex after returning to their homeland. And, indeed, the Temple built in 520–515 BCE did not conform to Ezekiel's measurements. The author of this material undoubtedly assumed that a second temple would be constructed in Israel. But what is offered here (and, indeed, in succeeding chapters) is a *vision* and an *ideal* society, the purity of which is ensured by the hierarchical priesthood which carries out the perfectly ordered Temple's sacrificial system.

1278. Stevenson, *The Vision of Transformation,* 19, italics added.

Ezekiel 40:1-4, The Vision Commences

40 In the twenty-fifth year of our exile, at the beginning of the year, on the tenth of the month, in the fourteenth year after the fall of the city—on that very day the hand of the LORD was upon me and he took me there. [2]In visions of God he took me to the land of Israel and set me on a very high mountain, on whose south side were some buildings that looked like a city. [3]He took me there, and I saw a man whose appearance was like bronze; he was standing in the gateway with a linen cord and a measuring rod in his hand. [4]The man said to me, "Son of man, look with your eyes and hear with your ears and pay attention to everything I am going to show you, for that is why you have been brought here. Tell the house of Israel everything you see."

40 In the twenty-fifth year of our exile, at the beginning of the year, on the tenth day of the month, in the fourteenth year after the city was struck down, on that very day, the hand of the LORD was upon me, and he brought me there. [2]He brought me, in visions of God, to the land of Israel, and set me down upon a very high mountain, on which was a structure like a city to the south. [3]When he brought me there, a man was there, whose appearance shone like bronze, with a linen cord and a measuring reed in his hand; and he was standing in the gateway. [4]The man said to me, "Mortal, look closely and listen attentively, and set your mind upon all that I shall show you, for you were brought here in order that I might show it to you; declare all that you see to the house of Israel."

COMMENTARY

Ezekiel's fourth and final vision report, like his first, is introduced with a double date notice (as in 1:1-2). On the one hand, Ezekiel informs his readers that he experienced this vision in the twenty-fifth year of "our exile," which began in 597 BCE when Ezekiel and other Judean elites were forcibly displaced, along with King Jehoiachin, to Babylonia. On the other hand, it occurred in the fourteenth year after "the city" (Jerusalem) was destroyed. The intervening information ("at the beginning of the year, on the tenth day of the month") is problematic because it does not indicate the number of the month that marked the beginning of the New Year. (Ezekiel habitually numbers months in his date notices; see 1:1; 8:1; 20:1; 24:1; 29:1, 17; 30:20; 31:1; 32:1, 17; 33:21. The phrase translated "at the beginning of the year" [בראש השנה *bĕrōʾš haššānâ*] appears only here in the HB.) Unfortunately, the biblical data are confusing and point in two different directions. While some texts presuppose an autumnal New Year commencing in the seventh month (Tishri), others suppose a spring New Year in the first month (Nisan).

Julius Wellhausen observed that Israel's New Year, celebrated on the first day of the seventh month, gave way to a spring New Year under the influence of the Babylonians not long before Jerusalem was destroyed.[1279] The book of Ezekiel

1279. Julius Wellhausen, *Prolegomena to the History of Ancient Israel* (Gloucester, Mass.: Peter Smith, 1973) 109.

is among several exilic and post-exilic writings that refer to months not by names, but by numers; and this practice too seems to have begun under Babylonian influence. Although Ezekiel's other dates presuppose a spring New Year (as does the discussion of festivals in Ezek 45:18-25), Wellhausen believed that the date in 40:1 was based on a fall New Year. He drew a connection between the text and Leviticus 25. According to Lev 25:9, a trumpet blast on the tenth day of the seventh month of the fiftieth year marked the beginning of the year of Jubilee, when land was restored to its original owners and enslaved Hebrews were released ("And you shall hallow the fiftieth year and you shall proclaim liberty throughout the land to all its inhabitants. It shall be a jubilee for you: you shall return, every one of you, to your property and every one of you to your family," v. 10). Zimmerli agreed with Wellhausen's dating, noting that if it is correct, then the reference to "the twenty-fifth year of our exile" gains new significance, because the twenty-fifth year marks (approximately) the mid-point of the fifty year Jubilee cycle. If Ezekiel conceived of the exilic period as a jubilee cycle that would end with the exiles' release in the fiftieth year of their "enslavement" to the Babylonians, then the twenty-fifth year marked a turning point of sorts. With approximately half of their exilic experience behind them, the deportees could begin to anticipate their release.[1280]

Despite the force of Wellhausen's argument, it is more likely that Ezekiel presupposed a spring New Year. As noted above, the other dates in the book are based on that calendar. For at least twenty-five years, he and his fellow exiles had lived in a society where the New Year commenced in the spring with the month of *Nisannu* (March/April). In Babylonia, the New Year was celebrated with the *akitu* ceremony. This eleven-day festival took place with "great pomp and rejoicing" during the first eleven days of the month.[1281] Jacob Klein describes the ritual, based on a detailed description in a Seleucid-era (third century BCE) text containing instructions to the high priest (*sesgallu*) concerning cultic rituals to be performed in the Temple during the second to fifth days of the festival:

During these days, prayers and incantations are recited to Marduk, beseeching him to calm his anger and bless the king and the people for the coming year. On the fourth day, the great Babylonian mythic poem *enuma elis*, describing Marduk's victory over Tiamat (the primeval sea) and the creation of the world by him, is recited before the god. On the fifth day, after the Temple has been thoroughly purified, the king is led before Marduk. The high priest takes away from him his royal insignia, strikes him on his cheeks, pulls his ears, and makes him bow down to the ground. At this point, the king has to utter a declaration of innocence, in which he asserts that he did not neglect the worship of the god, nor did he harm the sacred city of Babylon or its protected people. Thereupon, the high priest utters a favorable oracle, assuring the king that Marduk listened to his prayer and will bless his kingship and destroy his enemies. After the high priest returns to the king his royal insignia, he again strikes his cheek, and if "his tears flow—Bel [Marduk] is appeased; if his tears do not flow—Bel is angry; an enemy will rise and bring about his downfall" (*ANET,* 334, 429-52).[1282]

Although the description of the remainder of the ritual has been lost from the Seleucid-era text, Klein has reconstructed highlights of the *akitu* on the basis of certain neo-Assyrian and neo-Babylonian royal inscriptions: Most likely on the ninth of Nisan, the king "seized" Marduk's hand and conducted him in a festive procession to the *akitu* temple outside the city. In some way, a cultic drama was enacted there on the following day that symbolized Marduk's primordial victory over Tiamat and the forces of chaos. The festival ended on the eleventh day, and all the gods returned to their cities on the twelfth day.[1283]

In addition to comparing Ezekiel's final vision with the *akitu* festival, scholars point to similarities between the book of Ezekiel and the neo-Babylonian "Poem of Erra," a literary classic in the ancient Near Eastern world. Daniel Bodi has highlighted a theme common to certain ancient Near Eastern texts including the Poem of Erra: "the absence of divinity from its shrine."[1284] This poem describes the grave consequences when the gods Erra and Marduk are angered by neglect of their rituals, moral decay, the tumult of the peoples, and

---

1280. Zimmerli, *Ezekiel 2,* 345-46.
1281. Jacob Klein, "Akitu," *ABD,* 1:138.
1282. Klein, "Akitu," 139.
1283. Ibid.
1284. Daniel Bodi, *The Book of Ezekiel and the Poem of Erra,* OBO 104 (Freiburg: Universitätsverlag, 1991) 52, 215.

the threat humans pose to the deities. Marduk abandons his shrine; and in his absence, Erra—the god of destruction and chaos—destroys Babylon and forces the Babylonians into exile, there to serve as slaves for seventy years. After only eleven years Marduk's wrath is abated, however, and he brings the exiles back to rebuild Babylon.

Bodi compares this poem with the book of Ezekiel and, more specifically, with Ezekiel's second visionary report (Ezekiel 8–11), wherein Yahweh's glory abandons Jerusalem and its Temple on account of cultic abuses and moral decay, leaving the land vulnerable to attack by the Babylonians. The departure of the deity from its shrine because of society's moral, social, cultural, and political offenses is a theme that the book of Ezekiel shares with the Erra Epic and a number of other Akkadian texts. Ezekiel 8 describes the cultic abominations found in the Jerusalem Temple, while 9:9 cites additional moral and social crimes as the reasons for God's merciless destruction of Israel's population.[1285]

Stevenson argues persuasively that together, the "absence of the divinity from his shrine" theme and the *akitu* ceremony, which enacts Marduk's return to his temple, are crucial for a reader's understanding of the structure of the book of Ezekiel, especially Ezekiel 40–48. Ezekiel's fourth visionary report narrates God's return from exile to God's shrine in order to renew divine rule and take possession of God's house. Unlike in the Babylonian *akitu* ceremony, God comes alone.[1286]

The ancient reader arrives at Ezek 40:1 with the expectation that Yahweh will return to "the mountain height of Israel" and that proper worship of God will be restored there (see, e.g., 20:40-44). He does not yet know exactly how these changes will occur, but if he is conversant with ancient literatures (like the Poem of Erra) and cultic ceremonies (like the Babylonian *akitu* festival), such knowledge will enrich his reading of Ezekiel's final visionary account, and indeed, of the book as a whole.

"On that very day," v. 1 continues, "the hand of the Lord was upon me, and he brought me there." Does "on that very day" function to emphasize the preceding date information, or does it refer to the

anniversary of Jehoiachin's deportation—a possibility suggested by the notice in 2 Chr 36:10 that "In the spring of the year, King Nebuchadrezzar sent and brought him [Jehoiachin] to Babylon"? The latter is possible,[1287] but the former seems more likely.[1288]

Ezekiel experiences "the hand of the Lord" upon him, as he did at the outset of his first (1:3), second (8:1), and third (37:1) vision reports (on the significance of this phrase, see the Commentary on 1:3). But he says nothing here of a supernatural being with the form of a man who, according to 8:2-3, stretched out his hand to seize a lock of Ezekiel's hair, or of "the spirit" lifting him up. According to 8:3, this supernatural being tranported Ezekiel in visions of God (divine visions) to Jerusalem. Ezekiel 40:1 states only that Yahweh brought the prophet *there*. The term שׁם (*šām*, "there") is an important word in Ezekiel's final vision report; but this, its first appearance in that report, is ambiguous. Where is there? The ambiguity is short-lived. In v. 2 Ezekiel states that Yahweh brought him to "the land of Israel," and more specifically, placed him upon a "very high mountain." Jon Levenson has demonstrated that recognizing the significance of the mountain of Ezekiel's vision requires readers to reflect upon several traditions. The mountain is, of course, Mt. Zion; but it also evokes associations with Eden, Mt. Sinai, and Mt. Abarim.[1289]

On the mountain's southern slope, Ezekiel sees a city-like structure (using a simile; the prophet beholds a complex resembling a city, rather than an actual city). His arrival has, it seems, been anticipated. When Yahweh's hand has brought him "there," he sees a "man" whose appearance shines like bronze. The creatures supporting the chariot throne of Yahweh's glory likewise were said to sparkle like (burnished) bronze (1:7). Clearly, the "man" standing in the gateway is no mere mortal, but a denizen of the divine sphere. His tasks are twofold: (1) he is a surveyor; with the linen cord in his hand, he will measure lengthy objects, and with the measuring reed, he will

1285. Ibid., 215.
1286. Stevenson, *The Vision of Transformation*, 53.

1287. See D. I. Block, *The Book of Ezekiel: Chapters 25–48,* NICOT (Grand Rapids: Eerdmans, 1998) 513.
1288. A more plausible scenario is that the composer of 2 Chr 36:10 knew the present passage and inserted the reference to "the spring of the year," which does not appear in 2 Kgs 24:10-12, on the basis of it.
1289. Jon D. Levenson, *Theology of the Program of Restoration of Ezekiel 40–48,* HSM 10 (Missoula: Scholars Press, 1976) 5-53.

measure shorter lengths; (2) he is a tour guide. The man instructs Ezekiel ("Mortal") to "look closely and listen attentively, and set your mind upon all that *I shall show you*," for the priest has

been brought there precisely to absorb everything that the man *shows him* in order to declare it to the house of Israel, his fellow exiles. (See Figure 2, 1535; see Reflections at 43:10-12.)

Ezekiel 40:5-16, The Exterior Wall and Its Outer East Gate

NIV

[5]I saw a wall completely surrounding the temple area. The length of the measuring rod in the man's hand was six long cubits, each of which was a cubit[a] and a handbreadth.[b] He measured the wall; it was one measuring rod thick and one rod high.

[6]Then he went to the gate facing east. He climbed its steps and measured the threshold of the gate; it was one rod deep.[c] [7]The alcoves for the guards were one rod long and one rod wide, and the projecting walls between the alcoves were five cubits thick. And the threshold of the gate next to the portico facing the temple was one rod deep.

[8]Then he measured the portico of the gateway; [9]it[d] was eight cubits deep and its jambs were two cubits thick. The portico of the gateway faced the temple.

[10]Inside the east gate were three alcoves on each side; the three had the same measurements, and the faces of the projecting walls on each side had the same measurements. [11]Then he measured the width of the entrance to the gateway; it was ten cubits and its length was thirteen cubits. [12]In front of each alcove was a wall one cubit high, and the alcoves were six cubits square. [13]Then he measured the gateway from the top of the rear wall of one alcove to the top of the opposite one; the distance was twenty-five cubits from one parapet opening to the opposite one. [14]He measured along the faces of the projecting walls all around the inside of the gateway—sixty cubits. The measurement was up to the portico[e] facing the courtyard.[f] [15]The distance from the entrance of the

NRSV

5Now there was a wall all around the outside of the temple area. The length of the measuring reed in the man's hand was six long cubits, each being a cubit and a handbreadth in length; so he measured the thickness of the wall, one reed; and the height, one reed. [6]Then he went into the gateway facing east, going up its steps, and measured the threshold of the gate, one reed deep.[a] There were [7]recesses, and each recess was one reed wide and one reed deep; and the space between the recesses, five cubits; and the threshold of the gate by the vestibule of the gate at the inner end was one reed deep. [8]Then he measured the inner vestibule of the gateway, one cubit. [9]Then he measured the vestibule of the gateway, eight cubits; and its pilasters, two cubits; and the vestibule of the gate was at the inner end. [10]There were three recesses on either side of the east gate; the three were of the same size; and the pilasters on either side were of the same size. [11]Then he measured the width of the opening of the gateway, ten cubits; and the width of the gateway, thirteen cubits. [12]There was a barrier before the recesses, one cubit on either side; and the recesses were six cubits on either side. [13]Then he measured the gate from the back[b] of the one recess to the back[b] of the other, a width of twenty-five cubits, from wall to wall.[c] [14]He measured[d] also the vestibule, twenty cubits; and the gate next to the pilaster on every side of the court.[e] [15]From the front of the gate at the entrance to the end of the inner vestibule of the gate was fifty cubits. [16]The recesses and their pilasters had windows, with shutters[e] on the inside of the gateway all around, and the vestibules also had windows on the inside all around; and on the pilasters were palm trees.

a5 The common cubit was about 1 1/2 feet (about 0.5 meter). b5 That is, about 3 inches (about 8 centimeters) c6 Septuagint; Hebrew *deep, the first threshold, one rod deep* d8,9 Many Hebrew manuscripts, Septuagint, Vulgate and Syriac; most Hebrew manuscripts *gateway facing the temple; it was one rod deep.* [9]*Then he measured the portico of the gateway; it* e14 Septuagint; Hebrew *projecting wall* f14 The meaning of the Hebrew for this verse is uncertain.

aHeb *deep, and one threshold, one reed deep* bGk: Heb *roof* cHeb *opening facing opening* dHeb *made* eMeaning of Heb uncertain

NIV

gateway to the far end of its portico was fifty cubits. ¹⁶The alcoves and the projecting walls inside the gateway were surmounted by narrow parapet openings all around, as was the portico; the openings all around faced inward. The faces of the projecting walls were decorated with palm trees.

COMMENTARY

(See Figure 2, 1535.) The first feature Ezekiel observes is an exterior wall surrounding the entire city-like structure. The tour guide measures the dimensions of this outer wall (חומה *ḥômâ,* "wall"; in 42:20, the noun also refers to this temple-enclosing wall; elsewhere in Ezekiel and the remainder of the HB, it refers to city walls): It is one reed (approx. 10.25 feet) thick and one reed tall. (Although the reader does not yet know it, this will be the sole vertical measurement in the description of the temple complex, with the exceptions of the tables in 40:42 and the wooden altar in 41:22.) One expects a wall to be higher than its thickness. What is the purpose of this massive structure? In the aftermath of the definitive defeat of Gog and his hordes (Ezekiel 38–39), the reader does not imagine that the complex needs to be defended against foreign foes. This wall serves other functions, including separating the holy and the common, defining sacred space, and limiting access to that space lest it be contaminated. According to the MT, the wall surrounds (and so encloses) a "house" (בית *bayit).* Both the NRSV and the NIV translate *bayit* as "temple area," aware that this same noun will be used throughout the text to refer to the entire Temple compound. Perhaps the ancient, sequential reader would not yet make that identification, though "house" is used frequently in Hebrew Scripture to describe Yahweh's "house"—that is, temple (e.g., 2 Sam 7:13). With the detail characteristic of Ezekiel's other vision accounts, readers are told that the measuring reed used by the man is six long cubics, each cubit (approximately 20.5 inches) consisting of seven handbreadths, as opposed to the normal cubit (approximately 17.7 inches) of six handbreadths.

Those who would enter this "house" must do

so through one of the outer wall's three, carefully controlled gateways. These gateways are not typical of ancient temple complexes, archaeologists tell us, but they resemble the gates of certain fortified cities from the Solomonic era (Hazor, Gezer, Megiddo).¹²⁹⁰ Little wonder, then, that Ezekiel likens the complex to a city, since its massive exterior wall and enormous gates resemble those of a well-fortified urban center.

Ezekiel's tour guide approaches the gateway on the east side of the wall. Gates function to control access to and from an area. In this case, Stevenson observes, the gate is massive because it is the "first line of defense against unauthorized entry."¹²⁹¹ It is apropos that the tour begin there; readers recall that when Yahweh's glory abandoned the city, it exited toward the east (10:19; 11:23). Moreover, they will soon discover that the Temple of Ezekiel's vision is oriented toward the east. The bronze-skinned man climbs an unspecified number of steps (on the basis of 40:22, 26, one can deduce that there were seven steps; the LXX provides that number here) and, setting foot upon the gate's threshold, measures its depth. The threshold, like the outer wall, is one reed deep (again, about 10.25 feet). Beyond the threshold stretches a corridor with square recesses on either side. Each recess, v. 7 *a* informs us, is one reed wide and one reed deep; and the space between them is five cubits. Verse 10 will return to these recesses, stating that there are six of them, three on each side of the corridor. The guide measures the threshold

1290. For diagrams and discussion, see Zimmerli, *Ezekiel 2,* 350-54. Archaeologists have tended to date these structures to the time of Solomon. See A. Mazar, *Archaeology of the Land of the Bible 10,000–586 B.C.E.,* ABRL (Garden City, N.Y.: Doubleday, 1990) 384-87, 465-70.
1291. Stevenson, *The Vision of Transformation,* 45.

of a vestibule lying at the gate's interior end; this threshold, like the one through which he entered the outer east gate, is one reed deep.[1292] The vestibule itself is eight cubits deep and as wide as the gate itself. Its supporting jambs are two cubits.

As noted, v. 10 provides further information about the recesses lying on both sides of the central corridor. Each is equal in size to the other five, and the jambs or pilasters on either side of the second recess on both sides of the gate are equal in size (five cubits). Nothing is said about the function of these recesses; if we compare them to similar areas in the gateways of certain cities, we can surmise that they served as guard rooms for those protecting the complex from illegitimate entry. Block observes that in "real life," such recesses often had benches running around their sides. City officials could sit on these benches as they carried out legal and administrative responsibilities (see, e.g., Job 29:7).[1293]

With v. 11, the guide returns to the front entrance of the gateway and measures its width, ten cubits. The width of the main corridor is thirteen cubits, about 22.2 feet. Going back yet again to the recesses, the reader learns of one cubit barriers or boundaries distinguishing the rooms from the main corridor. Nothing more is said of their appearance, but in 43:13, the same noun (גבול *gĕbûl*, "barrier," "boundary") refers to a one-span rim surrounding the base of the Temple's altar. According to v. 13 the guide also measures the ceiling of the structure, from the back of one recess to the back of the next, a horizontal distance of twenty-five cubits.[1294] This agrees with the earlier statement that the recesses are each six cubits deep, while the width of the gateway's corridor is thirteen cubits. Because this is an interior measurement, it is not possible to determine the exterior width of the gate. Verse 14 is so corrupt

as to be unintelligible. Ancient readers surely stumbled over it as well.[1295] Verse 15 states that the full distance of the gateway facing east, from the front of the gate to the front of the vestibule at its end, is fifty cubits. Hence, the interior gateway is a perfectly proportioned (2:1) rectangle.

Verse 16 provides further information about the gate's walls. They are, it seems, punctuated by an unspecified number of windows, or niches. Both the NRSV ("windows") and the NIV ("parapet openings") choose the former option. Zimmerli reasonably suggests that their function was to provide the means by which light might illumine the interior of the gate structure.[1296] But comparison with the Qumran *Temple Scroll* suggests that the reference may be to niches (i.e., recesses that do not penetrate the walls) which were used as storage cupboards.[1297] The verse also provides detail concerning the gateway's jambs or pilasters; they are decorated with palm fronds, as were various structures and items in Solomon's Temple (see 1 Kgs 6:29-36).

Amid the complexity of structures, measurements, and proportions, modern readers do well to remember Stevenson's point that "what is actually being measured are the spaces created by the structures, rather than the structures themselves."[1298] The structures indeed provide boundaries, but their principal functions are to define and defend those spaces. The enormity of the gate facing east (and of the other two exterior gates as well) bespeaks Ezekiel's conviction that access to the sacred temple complex must be carefully controlled. (See Reflections at 43:10-12.)

1295. Allen attempts to reconstruct how this verse attained its final, difficult formulation. See Leslie C. Allen, *Ezekiel 20–40*, WBC 29 (Dallas: Word, 1990) 522-23.

1296. W. Zimmerli, *Ezekiel 2: A Commentary on the Book of the Prophet Ezekiel, Chapters 25–48*, trans. J. D. Martin, Hermeneia (Philadelphia: Fortress, 1983) 351.

1297. See Block, *Ezekiel 25–48*, 522-23, for description and bibliography.

1298. Kalinda Rose Stevenson, *The Vision of Transformation: The Territorial Rhetoric of Ezekiel 40–48*, SBLDS 154 (Atlanta: Scholars Press, 1996) 19.

1292. Block, *Ezekiel 25–48*, 521, observes that "vestibule" (אלם *'ûlām*) denotes "a (roofed) antechamber or hall."

1293. Ibid., 521.

1294. גג (*gāg*) usually refers to the roof of a building. As Block observes, however, this is an interior measurement, so "ceiling" is more appropriate. See ibid., 521.

Ezekiel 40:17-19, The Outer Court

NIV

¹⁷Then he brought me into the outer court. There I saw some rooms and a pavement that had been constructed all around the court; there were thirty rooms along the pavement. ¹⁸It abutted the sides of the gateways and was as wide as they were long; this was the lower pavement. ¹⁹Then he measured the distance from the inside of the lower gateway to the outside of the inner court; it was a hundred cubits on the east side as well as on the north.

NRSV

17Then he brought me into the outer court; there were chambers there, and a pavement, all around the court; thirty chambers fronted on the pavement. ¹⁸The pavement ran along the side of the gates, corresponding to the length of the gates; this was the lower pavement. ¹⁹Then he measured the distance from the inner front of[a] the lower gate to the outer front of the inner court, one hundred cubits.[b]

[a]Compare Gk: Heb *from before*   [b]Heb adds *the east and the north*

COMMENTARY

(See Figure 2, 1535.) Having passed through the outer east gate, Ezekiel's guide provides him a first viewing of the Temple's outer court. The priest/prophet observes thirty chambers or porticoes (לשׁכות *lĕšākôt*), whose function(s) is not immediately defined (perhaps the author assumes, for the time being, that his ancient readers know well their function[s]; Jer 35:2-4 and Neh 13:4-14 suggest that they were used for meetings, for eating and drinking, and for storage). He also sees a pavement (רצפה *riṣpâ*), which runs parallel to the outer wall all around the outer court.[1299] Verse 18*b* describes this as the lower pavement. The chambers are situated around the perimeter of the

court, and they give on to this lower pavement, which lies between them and the area of the outer court proper. The dimensions of the chambers and of the pavement are not provided, but Stevenson assists us in imagining the relationship of gate, pavement, and outer court. The gate structures "jut into the open space." The pavement that runs along the outer wall fills in the extra space in the outer court, which is in the form of a perfect square. This pavement is both "boundary marker and buffer zone between the thirty Chambers and the area of the Outer Court."[1300] According to v. 19, the guide then measures the distance from the inner front of the outer east gate to the outer front of the inner east gate, a distance of one hundred cubits. (See Reflections at 43:10-12.)

1299. The same word is used in 2 Chr 7:3 to describe the pavement upon which the people bow their faces after seeing Yahweh's glory enter the Solomonic Temple.

1300. Stevenson, *Vision of Transformation,* 21.

Ezekiel 40:20-27, The Outer Gates

NIV

²⁰Then he measured the length and width of the gate facing north, leading into the outer court. ²¹Its alcoves—three on each side—its projecting walls and its portico had the same measurements as those of the first gateway. It was fifty cubits long and twenty-five cubits wide. ²²Its openings, its portico and its palm tree decorations had the same measurements as those of the gate facing

NRSV

20Then he measured the gate of the outer court that faced north—its depth and width. ²¹Its recesses, three on either side, and its pilasters and its vestibule were of the same size as those of the first gate; its depth was fifty cubits, and its width twenty-five cubits. ²²Its windows, its vestibule, and its palm trees were of the same size as those of the gate that faced toward the east. Seven steps

NIV

east. Seven steps led up to it, with its portico opposite them. ²³There was a gate to the inner court facing the north gate, just as there was on the east. He measured from one gate to the opposite one; it was a hundred cubits.

²⁴Then he led me to the south side and I saw a gate facing south. He measured its jambs and its portico, and they had the same measurements as the others. ²⁵The gateway and its portico had narrow openings all around, like the openings of the others. It was fifty cubits long and twenty-five cubits wide. ²⁶Seven steps led up to it, with its portico opposite them; it had palm tree decorations on the faces of the projecting walls on each side. ²⁷The inner court also had a gate facing south, and he measured from this gate to the outer gate on the south side; it was a hundred cubits.

NRSV

led up to it; and its vestibule was on the inside.ᵃ ²³Opposite the gate on the north, as on the east, was a gate to the inner court; he measured from gate to gate, one hundred cubits.

24Then he led me toward the south, and there was a gate on the south; and he measured its pilasters and its vestibule; they had the same dimensions as the others. ²⁵There were windows all around in it and in its vestibule, like the windows of the others; its depth was fifty cubits, and its width twenty-five cubits. ²⁶There were seven steps leading up to it; its vestibule was on the inside.ᵃ It had palm trees on its pilasters, one on either side. ²⁷There was a gate on the south of the inner court; and he measured from gate to gate toward the south, one hundred cubits.

ᵃGk: Heb *before them*

COMMENTARY

(See Figure 2, 1535.) Ezekiel's tour guide moves to the interior end of the outer North Gate in order to measure its length and width. The description of this gate is considerably briefer than that of the previous one because the two gates are identical. The north gate also consists of three recessed rooms along both sides of the interior corridor, as well as vestibules, jambs, windows or niches, and palm tree decorations; and the measurements of its spaces and structures are the same as those given for the outer east gate. It too is a perfect rectangle. Here, unlike in v. 6, we are told specifically that seven steps lead up to the gate's exterior entrance. In this case, also, one hundred cubits separate the inner end of the outer north gate from the outer end of the inner north gate.

Ezekiel next recounts that his tour guide brought him to the south gate of the exterior wall. This gate is identical to the other two, and its interior end also is separated from the outer end of its corresponding inner south gate by one hundred cubits. (See Reflections at 43:10-12.)

Ezekiel 40:28-37, The Inner Gates

NIV

²⁸Then he brought me into the inner court through the south gate, and he measured the south gate; it had the same measurements as the others. ²⁹Its alcoves, its projecting walls and its portico had the same measurements as the others. The gateway and its portico had openings all around. It was fifty cubits long and twenty-five cubits wide. ³⁰(The porticoes of the gateways

NRSV

28Then he brought me to the inner court by the south gate, and he measured the south gate; it was of the same dimensions as the others. ²⁹Its recesses, its pilasters, and its vestibule were of the same size as the others; and there were windows all around in it and in its vestibule; its depth was fifty cubits, and its width twenty-five cubits. ³⁰There were vestibules all around, twenty-five

NIV

around the inner court were twenty-five cubits wide and five cubits deep.) [31]Its portico faced the outer court; palm trees decorated its jambs, and eight steps led up to it.

[32]Then he brought me to the inner court on the east side, and he measured the gateway; it had the same measurements as the others. [33]Its alcoves, its projecting walls and its portico had the same measurements as the others. The gateway and its portico had openings all around. It was fifty cubits long and twenty-five cubits wide. [34]Its portico faced the outer court; palm trees decorated the jambs on either side, and eight steps led up to it.

[35]Then he brought me to the north gate and measured it. It had the same measurements as the others, [36]as did its alcoves, its projecting walls and its portico, and it had openings all around. It was fifty cubits long and twenty-five cubits wide. [37]Its portico[a] faced the outer court; palm trees decorated the jambs on either side, and eight steps led up to it.

[a]37 Septuagint (see also verses 31 and 34); Hebrew *jambs*

NRSV

cubits deep and five cubits wide. [31]Its vestibule faced the outer court, and palm trees were on its pilasters, and its stairway had eight steps.

[32]Then he brought me to the inner court on the east side, and he measured the gate; it was of the same size as the others. [33]Its recesses, its pilasters, and its vestibule were of the same dimensions as the others; and there were windows all around in it and in its vestibule; its depth was fifty cubits, and its width twenty-five cubits. [34]Its vestibule faced the outer court, and it had palm trees on its pilasters, on either side; and its stairway had eight steps.

[35]Then he brought me to the north gate, and he measured it; it had the same dimensions as the others. [36]Its recesses, its pilasters, and its vestibule were of the same size as the others;[a] and it had windows all around. Its depth was fifty cubits, and its width twenty-five cubits. [37]Its vestibule[b] faced the outer court, and it had palm trees on its pilasters, on either side; and its stairway had eight steps.

[a]One Ms: Compare verses 29 and 33: MT lacks *were of the same size as the others*   [b]Gk Vg Compare verses 26, 31, 34: Heb *pilasters*

COMMENTARY

(See Figure 2, 1535.) These verses describe three gates (south, east, and north) which lead from the outer court to the inner court. Scholars often opine that these must be the gates of an inner wall, though no such structure is mentioned. Zimmerli acknowledges the silence, but insists that one must "assume" its existence since the inner gates "only make sense as openings in a wall."[1301] But Stevenson argues that an inner wall is unnecessary. The outer and inner courts are sufficiently distinguished by a difference in elevation, since in order to enter the gates leading to the inner court, one must first ascend a flight of eight steps (v. 31). Not only are the stairways and gates sufficient to control access to the inner court, she avers, but also "without a wall, worshipers can see the rituals conducted at the Altar in the inner court, and the priests in the inner Court can see what is occuring in the Outer Court

below."[1302] The fact that one goes up to enter the inner gates reflects the ascending sacrality of the inner court.

The three inner gates are as massive as are their outer counterparts, and their measurements and proportions likewise are identical to the latter with one exception. In the case of the outer gates, the large vestibules are the last areas one traverses before entering the outer court. In the case of the inner gates, the large vestibules are the first areas one traverses as one passes through the gates to arrive at the inner court.

In the case of the inner gates, the guide begins with the gate facing south—a logical next step since he has only just left the south outer gate. Problematic in this description is v. 30, which has no counterpart in the descriptions of the other two inner gates, which speaks inappropriately of

1301. Zimmerli, *Ezekiel 2*, 355.

1302. Stevenson, *Vision of Transformation*, 44.

large vestibules (plural), and which provides dimensions for those vestibules that differ from those of the outer gates.[1303]

Verses 32-34 describe the inner east gate, whose dimensions, recesses, jambs, and vestibule are said to be identical to those of the gates described thus far. In vv. 35-37, the guide brings Ezekiel to the north inner gate and measures it as well. It too is described as identical to the gates previously measured and described.

Stevenson asserts that the emphasis on gates that the reader cannot have missed thus far in Ezekiel is evidence of "territoriality."[1304] When one reflects upon the dimensions, structures, and especially the spaces created by the massive outer and inner gates from this perspective, they cease to be "picky" and tedious details of no relevance. Rather, they convey a sense of Ezekiel's absolute insistence that Israel's Temple should forever be protected from the impurities of the past, recounted especially in chapter 8, which led to the catastrophes of 586 BCE, including the destruction of the Solomonic Temple. (See Reflections at 43:10-12.)

1303. See Block, *Ezekiel 25–48.* The verse is absent from the LXX.

1304. Stevenson, *The Vision of Transformation,* 45.

Ezekiel 40:38-43, Chambers for Sacrifices

NIV

38A room with a doorway was by the portico in each of the inner gateways, where the burnt offerings were washed. 39In the portico of the gateway were two tables on each side, on which the burnt offerings, sin offerings and guilt offerings were slaughtered. 40By the outside wall of the portico of the gateway, near the steps at the entrance to the north gateway were two tables, and on the other side of the steps were two tables. 41So there were four tables on one side of the gateway and four on the other—eight tables in all—on which the sacrifices were slaughtered. 42There were also four tables of dressed stone for the burnt offerings, each a cubit and a half long, a cubit and a half wide and a cubit high. On them were placed the utensils for slaughtering the burnt offerings and the other sacrifices. 43And double-pronged hooks, each a handbreadth long, were attached to the wall all around. The tables were for the flesh of the offerings.

NRSV

38There was a chamber with its door in the vestibule of the gate[a] where the burnt offering was to be washed. 39And in the vestibule of the gate were two tables on either side, on which the burnt offering and the sin offering and the guilt offering were to be slaughtered. 40On the outside of the vestibule[b] at the entrance of the north gate were two tables; and on the other side of the vestibule of the gate were two tables. 41Four tables were on the inside, and four tables on the outside of the side of the gate, eight tables, on which the sacrifices were to be slaughtered. 42There were also four tables of hewn stone for the burnt offering, a cubit and a half long, and one cubit and a half wide, and one cubit high, on which the instruments were to be laid with which the burnt offerings and the sacrifices were slaughtered. 43There were pegs, one handbreadth long, fastened all around the inside. And on the tables the flesh of the offering was to be laid.

[a]Cn: Heb *at the pilasters of the gates*   [b]Cn: Heb *to him who goes up*

COMMENTARY

(See Figure 2, 1535.) Ezekiel's guided tour of the temple complex, which has proceeded apace to this point, is now delayed by descriptions of areas and provisions for the preparation of offerings and, in the next section, by descriptions of priestly chambers located in the inner court beside the north and south gates, respectively (vv. 44-47). Because these passages interrupt the tour, differ in style and focus from the tour texts proper (40:1-37, 47-49, 41:1-4), and introduce topics "prematurely," Zimmerli regards them as later additions to the original text functioning, each in its own way, further to "elucidate" the "picture of the temple seen by the prophet."[1305] Block, by contrast, defends the authenticity of both, refusing to regard them as "the work of later hands."[1306]

As a modern critic versed in the methodological tools of critical biblical scholarship, I find much merit in Zimmerli's detailed arguments. At the same time, I realized that my ancient reader was not interested in determining textual seams, splitting those seams, and then examining each swatch in order to determine how it became part of the larger fabric of the text. Readers who are not trained to be seam spotters are more naturally consistency builders who attempt to make sense of the text before them in its received form (see Introduction). Indeed, Block himself displays this very tendency toward consistency building when, in arguing for the "authenticity" of vv. 38-43, he observes that "the insertion lends realism to the account. As anyone who has been led around a new site by a tour guide knows, the leader often pauses along the way to describe a particular feature with greater detail, thereby adding both understanding and interest to what could otherwise become routine."[1307]

Because vv. 35-37 have dealt with the inner gate facing north, it is likely that the gate mentioned in v. 38 is one and the same. (Actually, the word for "gate" does not appear in v. 38. Both the NIV and the NRSV emend the MT's "pilasters," "jambs," to "gate," which makes much better sense in this context. Ancient readers knew that scribes sometimes made errors, and they made mental adjustments when necessary. Because the MT form is plural, some scholars have argued that each gate has a chamber like the one described here.) Ezekiel notices a chamber, ostensibly situated beside the vestibule since we are told that its door opens onto the vestibule. Within this chamber, the burnt offering victims are washed. The burnt offering (עולה 'ôlâ from the root עלה 'lh, "to go up") was a sacrifice involving the burning of an

entire animal (bulls, sheep, goats). Persons bringing this sacrifice to the Temple were not permitted to eat any of the meat. This offering served two primary functions—to subdue divine anger, and to atone for sin.[1308]

Block speaks of washing the sacrificial animals before slaughter, but it is difficult to understand how the entrails could be washed while the animal was still alive.[1309] Leviticus 1:9 and 13, which he cites, suggest rather that the lower legs and entrails were washed after the animal had been killed and dismembered, and that its entrails and lower legs were washed prior to placing them upon the altar. First Kings 7:38 states that King Solomon made (had made) ten bronze basins, stationing five on the south side of the Temple and the other five on the north side of the Temple. According to 2 Chr 4:6, these basins held water used to rinse the burnt offerings.

In the vestibule of the gate, Ezekiel sees two tables standing on one side and two more standing on the other side. On these tables, the burnt offerings, the purification offerings (NRSV and NIV "sin offerings") and the reparation offerings (NRSV and NIV "guilt offerings") are slaughtered. The Hebrew noun חטאת (ḥaṭṭā't), "purification offering" derives from the root חטא (ḥṭ') and, more specifically, from the Piel verb meaning "to cleanse, expurgate, decontaminate."[1310] Block identifies six stages in the ritual:[1311] (1) the sacrificial victim is brought to the Temple; (2) the person offering the sacrifice lays hands on the animal; (3) the animal is killed; (4) its blood is daubed on sacred objects;[1312] (5) the remains of the animal are disposed of either by burning them, or by eating them; (6) the purification ritual is pronounced.[1313] The purpose of this offering is not the purification of its offerer; in fact, the blood is never applied to a person. Its function, rather, is to purify the sanctuary of pollution. This is an essential

---

1305. Zimmerli, *Ezekiel 2,* 365-69, esp. 368.

1306. D. I. Block, *The Book of Ezekiel: Chapters 25-48,* NICOT (Grand Rapids: Eerdmans, 1998) 531, 535.

1307. Ibid., 531.

1308. J. Milgrom, *Leviticus 1-16,* AB 3 (New York: Doubleday, 1991) 172-77.

1309. Block, *Ezekiel 25-48,* 532. Zimmerli, *Ezekiel 2,* 367, is correct in asserting that this washing takes place only after the slaughtering.

1310. Milgrom, *Leviticus 1-16,* 253, insists that translating the purification offering as "sin offering" is contextually, morphologically, and etymologically inaccurate.

1311. Block, *Ezekiel 25-48,* 532-33.

1312. Milgrom thinks that the blood of the purification ritual is "the purging element, the ritual detergent" that is confined to the sanctuary, but never applied to a person. See Milgrom, *Leviticus 1-16,* 254-55; on the purification offering, 253-64; on Ezekiel's use of the term, 281-84.

1313. Block, *Ezekiel 25-48,* 532-33.

concern because if the Temple becomes polluted, Yahweh will abandon it, as Ezekiel 8–11 has shown.

The third kind of sacrifice referred to in v. 39 is the reparation offering (אשם *'āšām*). Milgrom defines cultic usages of the root אשם (*'šm*):

> The noun *'āšām* is the restitution for desecration by either composition or sacrifice and should be rendered "reparation" and "reparation offering," respectively. The verb *'āšām* is a stative. When it is followed by the preposition *l* and a personal object it means "to incur liability to" someone for reparation; without an object, it refers to the inner experience of this liability, meaning "to feel guilt."[1314]

Two pairs of tables flank the threshold, one pair on each side, just outside the vestibule of the gate. Robert Haak has argued that כתף (*kātēp*) refers to the gate's facade, which runs perpendicular to its main corridor.[1315] Moreover, v. 41 specifies that two more pairs of tables are positioned just inside the vestibule wall, opposite those standing outside of the vestibule. On these eight tables the animals for the sacrifices are slaughtered. Verse 42 then speaks in greater detail of four tables of hewn

stone for the burnt offerings.[1316] The dimensions, including the height, of these tables, are specified: each is a cubit and a half long, a cubit and half wide (hence, square), and one cubit high. According to the MT, the instruments needed to slaughter animals for the burnt offerings and sacrifices are placed upon these tables. Are these four additional tables, or are they the same four already referred to in v. 40*b*? The answer to this question is obscure, because the text itself is obscure.[1317]

The meaning of שפתים (*šĕpattayim*) in v. 43 is uncertain. Because the noun has a dual ending, the NIV translates "double-pronged hooks." The NRSV finds here a reference to "pegs" which, like the NIV's "hooks," are a handbreadth long. Zimmerli follows the LXX in translating "storage trays," but he suspects that the reference is to a ledge running around the walls.[1318] Block opts for small niches, one handbreadth deep, in the walls, citing as support the "receptacles for the altar utensils" on the walls of the "house of the laver" referred to in the Qumran *Temple Scroll*.[1319] (See Reflections at 43:10-12.)

1314. Milgrom, *Leviticus 1–16*, 339. See his wider discussion, 319-78.

1315. Robert Haak, "The 'Shoulder' of the Temple," *VT* 33 (1983) 274-75; see also Block, *Ezekiel 25–48*, 533.

1316. Here, for the first time, mention is made of the material used to construct a temple furnishing. See Zimmerli, *Ezekiel 2*, 365.

1317. Zimmerli engages in some rearranging in order to clarify the meaning of these verses. However, he says nothing about how such dislocations might have occurred. Zimmerli would rearrange the text as follows: vv. 40-42*a*, 43*a*, 42*b*, and 43*b*. See his translation in ibid., 367-68.

1318. Zimmerli, Ezekiel 2, 367-68.

1319. Block, *Ezekiel 25–48*, 534.

Ezekiel 40:44-47, Chambers for Priests and Singers

NIV

[44]Outside the inner gate, within the inner court, were two rooms, one[a] at the side of the north gate and facing south, and another at the side of the south[b] gate and facing north. [45]He said to me, "The room facing south is for the priests who have charge of the temple, [46]and the room facing north is for the priests who have charge of the altar. These are the sons of Zadok, who are the only Levites who may draw near to the LORD to minister before him."

[47]Then he measured the court: It was square—a hundred cubits long and a hundred cubits wide. And the altar was in front of the temple.

[a]44 Septuagint; Hebrew *were rooms for singers, which were*
[b]44 Septuagint; Hebrew *east*

NRSV

[44]On the outside of the inner gateway there were chambers for the singers in the inner court, one[a] at the side of the north gate facing south, the other at the side of the east gate facing north. [45]He said to me, "This chamber that faces south is for the priests who have charge of the temple, [46]and the chamber that faces north is for the priests who have charge of the altar; these are the descendants of Zadok, who alone among the descendants of Levi may come near to the LORD to minister to him." [47]He measured the court, one hundred cubits deep, and one hundred cubits wide, a square; and the altar was in front of the temple.

[a]Heb lacks *one*

COMMENTARY

(See Figure 2, 1535.) Having described in detailed (and sometimes obscure) words the places where animals are prepared for sacrifice, vv. 38-43 give way to a notice concerning chambers for the singers in the inner court.[1320] One lies beside the north gate and faces south; the other lies beside the south (MT erroneously has "east") gate and faces north. The tour guide reappears in v. 45 ("Then he said to me . . ."), but he provides no measurement for these chambers. The chamber facing south, he explains, is for the priests who guard the Temple; and the chamber facing north is for the priests who guard the altar.[1321] Presumably, these chambers are sleeping spaces for the priests when they are "on duty." This is the first time that a differentiation between priests, if such it be, has appeared in the book of Ezekiel. It is a topic to which the text will return in 44:15-31.

In v. 47, Ezekiel informs readers that his tour guide/surveyor measures the inner court; it is one hundred cubits long (approximately 170 feet) and one hundred cubits wide, a perfect square. The altar is said to be in front of the Temple. Nothing else is said of the altar at this point, but Ezekiel will return to it in 43:13-17. (See Reflections at 43:10-12.)

1320. In translating "chambers for the singers," the NRSV follows the MT. The NIV, by contrast, follows the LXX in translating "two chambers." Only a minor emendation is involved, and the LXX is preferable. Block, *Ezekiel 25–48,* 536, argues that this text suggests a later period when the role of music in worship had been set.

1321. Milgrom has argued that the idiom שׁמרי משׁמרת (*šōmrê mišmeret*) is a military term referring to guard duty. The priests are the Temple's guards, defending it from pollution and illicit access. See J. Milgrom, *Studies in Levitical Terminology, I: The Encroacher and the Levite: The Term 'Aboda* (Berkeley: University of California Press, 1970) 8-11.

Ezekiel 40:48–41:26, The Temple Building

EZEKIEL 40:48–41:4, VESTIBULE, NAVE, AND INNER ROOM

NIV

⁴⁸He brought me to the portico of the temple and measured the jambs of the portico; they were five cubits wide on either side. The width of the entrance was fourteen cubits and its projecting walls were[a] three cubits wide on either side. ⁴⁹The portico was twenty cubits wide, and twelve[b] cubits from front to back. It was reached by a flight of stairs,[c] and there were pillars on each side of the jambs.

41 Then the man brought me to the outer sanctuary and measured the jambs; the width of the jambs was six cubits[d] on each side.[e] ²The entrance was ten cubits wide, and the projecting walls on each side of it were five cubits wide. He also measured the outer sanctuary; it was forty cubits long and twenty cubits wide.

³Then he went into the inner sanctuary and

---

a48 Septuagint; Hebrew entrance was   *b49 Septuagint; Hebrew eleven*   *c49 Hebrew; Septuagint Ten steps led up to it*   *d1 The common cubit was about 1 1/2 feet (about 0.5 meter).*   *e1 One Hebrew manuscript and Septuagint; most Hebrew manuscripts side, the width of the tent*

NRSV

48Then he brought me to the vestibule of the temple and measured the pilasters of the vestibule, five cubits on either side; and the width of the gate was fourteen cubits; and the sidewalls of the gate were three cubits[a] on either side. ⁴⁹The depth of the vestibule was twenty cubits, and the width twelve[b] cubits; ten steps led up[c] to it; and there were pillars beside the pilasters on either side.

41 Then he brought me to the nave, and measured the pilasters; on each side six cubits was the width of the pilasters.[d] ²The width of the entrance was ten cubits; and the sidewalls of the entrance were five cubits on either side. He measured the length of the nave, forty cubits, and its width, twenty cubits. ³Then he went into the inner room and measured the pilasters of the entrance, two cubits; and the width of the

---

aGk: Heb and the width of the gate was three cubits   *bGk: Heb eleven*   *cGk: Heb and by steps that went up*   *dCompare Gk: Heb tent*

NIV

measured the jambs of the entrance; each was two cubits wide. The entrance was six cubits wide, and the projecting walls on each side of it were seven cubits wide. ⁴And he measured the length of the inner sanctuary; it was twenty cubits, and its width was twenty cubits across the end of the outer sanctuary. He said to me, "This is the Most Holy Place."

NRSV

entrance, six cubits; and the sidewalls*a* of the entrance, seven cubits. ⁴He measured the depth of the room, twenty cubits, and its width, twenty cubits, beyond the nave. And he said to me, This is the most holy place.

*a*Gk: Heb *width*

COMMENTARY

(See Figure 2, 1535.) Having noted that the altar is proximate to the temple building proper, Ezekiel's guide brings him to the temple vestibule. First, he measures the jambs on either side of the entrance; they are five cubits wide. The width of the entrance to the vestibule is fourteen cubits (23.91 feet; the MT does not include the expression "and the width of the gate was fourteen cubits"; the NRSV and the NIV resort to the LXX), and its sidewalls are three cubits wide. The vestibule itself is a rectangle; its measurements are twenty cubits (34.16 feet) by twelve cubits (20.5 feet). The reader learns that ten steps lead up to the vestibule. Added to the number of other steps, the elevation from the north outer gate to the vestibule of the temple building is twenty-five steps—a significant number, as we have noted, in Ezekiel's final vision. The text refers also to two pillars or columns standing in proximity to the jambs at the entrance to the vestibule. Readers will recall the eighteen-cubit, hollow bronze columns—one named Jachin, the other Boaz—that stood at the entrance to the Solomonic Temple (see 1 Kgs 7:15-22). The exact location of Ezekiel's columns is uncertain, however, and scholars remain uncertain about their appearance, function, and symbolic significance. Are they free-standing columns, or do they provide support for the structure? Are they merely ornamental, or an architectural commonplace in temple design, as temple ruins found elsewhere in the ancient Near East suggest? Were they giant incense stands, stylized forms of sacred poles, or, since the Temple faced the east, were they pillars between which the sun was thought to rise? We cannot answer these questions with certainty.

The tour guide then brings Ezekiel to the next room on the linear axis, called the *hêkāl*.[1322] He measures the jambs flanking its entrance, which are six cubits in width (that is 20.25 feet). The entrance itself is ten cubits (17.08 feet), and its sidewalls are five cubits. The guide then measures the nave's length (forty cubits; 68.33 feet) and width (twenty cubits; 34.16 feet). It, like the outer and inner gate structures, is a perfectly proportioned rectangle. Finally, the guide enters the third room of the building. Ezekiel does not enter this room with him, but he apparently is able to observe the guide as he measures its structures and dimensions. The jambs on either side of its entrance are two cubits wide. The entrance itself is six cubits wide, and its sidewalls are seven cubits. The room itself is a perfect square measuring twenty cubits deep and twenty cubits wide. The guide then informs Ezekiel that this room is קדש הקדשים (*qōdeš haqqŏdāšîm*), "the holy of holies"—that is, the most holy space.

The careful reader notices that as one progresses from the temple building's front to its third room, the entrances decrease in size: the entrance to the vestibule is fourteen cubits wide (40:48), that of the nave is ten cubits wide, while that of the most holy room is only six cubits wide. This decreasing access corresponds to the increasing sacrality as one approaches the holy of holies. The jambs on either side of the entrance to the nave

1322. The term היכל (*hêkāl*) derives from the Sumarian ÉGAL meaning "big house." In Hebrew, it may refer either to a temple (Yahweh's palace) or to the palace of a human king. The NRSV translates the noun as "nave," the NIV as "(outer) sanctuary."

(six cubits) are wider than those flanking the vestibule (five cubits), but the jambs on either side of the entrance to the most holy space are only two cubits wide. One might expect that these would exceed the width of the nave's jambs.

Readers familiar with (descriptions of) the Solomonic Temple notice that Ezekiel's temple building resembles its predecessor in many ways. We already have observed that both structures have pillars or columns at their entrances. Both have three rooms arranged on a linear axis, and the nave and most holy room of the two structures have identical dimensions (in the account of Solomon's Temple, Ezekiel's "holy of holies" is called a דביר [debîr], "rear room"; this noun is absent from the book of Ezekiel). But there are differences as well: Ezekiel's vestibule, for example, is two cubits deeper than that of Solomon's Temple; and nothing is said of a surrounding palace complex (cf. 1 Kings 6–7).[1323] (See Reflections at 43:10-12.)

1323. See Zimmerli, *Ezekiel 2*, 359. This latter difference will be dealt with later when Ezekiel describes the role of the prince in his vision.

EZEKIEL 41:5-12, THE STRUCTURES AND SPACES SURROUNDING THE TEMPLE

NIV

[5]Then he measured the wall of the temple; it was six cubits thick, and each side room around the temple was four cubits wide. [6]The side rooms were on three levels, one above another, thirty on each level. There were ledges all around the wall of the temple to serve as supports for the side rooms, so that the supports were not inserted into the wall of the temple. [7]The side rooms all around the temple were wider at each successive level. The structure surrounding the temple was built in ascending stages, so that the rooms widened as one went upward. A stairway went up from the lowest floor to the top floor through the middle floor.

[8]I saw that the temple had a raised base all around it, forming the foundation of the side rooms. It was the length of the rod, six long cubits. [9]The outer wall of the side rooms was five cubits thick. The open area between the side rooms of the temple [10]and the ˌpriests'ˌ rooms was twenty cubits wide all around the temple. [11]There were entrances to the side rooms from the open area, one on the north and another on the south; and the base adjoining the open area was five cubits wide all around.

[12]The building facing the temple courtyard on the west side was seventy cubits wide. The wall of the building was five cubits thick all around, and its length was ninety cubits.

NRSV

[5]Then he measured the wall of the temple, six cubits thick; and the width of the side chambers, four cubits, all around the temple. [6]The side chambers were in three stories, one over another, thirty in each story. There were offsets[a] all around the wall of the temple to serve as supports for the side chambers, so that they should not be supported by the wall of the temple. [7]The passageway[b] of the side chambers widened from story to story; for the structure was supplied with a stairway all around the temple. For this reason the structure became wider from story to story. One ascended from the bottom story to the uppermost story by way of the middle one. [8]I saw also that the temple had a raised platform all around; the foundations of the side chambers measured a full reed of six long cubits. [9]The thickness of the outer wall of the side chambers was five cubits; and the free space between the side chambers of the temple [10]and the chambers of the court was a width of twenty cubits all around the temple on every side. [11]The side chambers opened onto the area left free, one door toward the north, and another door toward the south; and the width of the part that was left free was five cubits all around.

[12]The building that was facing the temple yard on the west side was seventy cubits wide; and the wall of the building was five cubits thick all around, and its depth ninety cubits.

[a]Gk Compare 1 Kings 6.6: Heb *they entered*   [b]Cn: Heb *it was surrounded*

COMMENTARY

(See Figure 2, 1535.) Ezekiel's guide next measures the wall of the temple building; it is six cubits (10.25 feet) thick, as were the outer wall surrounding the entire temple complex (40:5) and the jambs separating the temple building's vestibule from its nave (41:1). Verse 5b states that side rooms measuring four cubits in width surround the Temple. Nothing is said about the function of these rooms, but they likely were used as storage spaces in which were placed temple appurtences and revenue.[1324] Verse 6a is difficult to visualize. MT reads "side room over side room, thirty-three times" (LXX, "And the sides were twice ninety, side against side"), but one cannot imagine that a thirty-three floor structure is in view. The description of the Solomonic Temple may provide a key to unlocking the conundrum. 1 Kings 6:5-6 refers to three stories of side rooms built around the sides and back of that temple building: "He [Solomon] also built a structure against the wall of the house, running around the walls of the house, both the nave and the inner sanctuary; and he made side chambers all around. The lowest story was five cubits wide, the middle one was six cubits wide, and the third was seven cubits wide." Insets (NIV, "ledges") in the sides and back of the temple wall's terraced, exterior side serve as interior supports for the roof beams of these chambers.[1325]

Verse 7 is even more difficult to comprehend. At issue is an architectural structure that enables persons to move from the first story of side chambers up to the second and third stories. Zimmerli noted that the rabbinical use of מסבה (mĕsibbâ, "gallery") refers to a passageway which changes direction as it goes. Preceded here by the noun רחבה (rāḥābâ, "broadening"), it refers to "a staircase or ramp running round the outside of the Temple and 'broadening' it." According to b. Mid. 4.5a, Zimmerli noted, the structure "begins in the northeast corner of the temple, that is on the right as one stands in front of the temple building, leads along the north side, turns south along the rear of the temple and on the south side comes eastwards to reach the 'top story' (עליה ʿãlîyâ)." Zimmerli

recognized, however, that Ezekiel's account says nothing of this, and that Solomon's Temple had no such exterior ramp.[1326] Block dismisses the notion of a single, large exterior ramp as "physically impossible," since such a structure would block light from the side rooms. It is better, he plausibly argues, to interpret this verse in the light of the description of the Solomonic Temple in 1 Kgs 6:8 than to opt for the interpretation found in a rabbinical tractate.[1327] According to 1 Kgs 6:8, the middle story of side chambers was accessed by means of לולים (lûlîm) on the Temple's south side. The precise meaning of this architectural term is uncertain. BDB defines it as a "shaft of enclosed space, with steps or ladder."[1328] Noth envisioned trap doors,[1329] but internal spiral staircases progressing upward with ninety degree turns are more likely.[1330]

Verse 8 also presents considerable problems. It states that the temple building was surrounded by a גבה (gōbah), a noun from the root גבה (gbh) meaning "be high, exalted," which likely should be rendered as "raised platform." The temple base presumably sits upon this platform, which makes its first appearance here and has no parallel in the description of Solomon's Temple. The consistiency-building reader will likely conclude that the platform is accessed by the ten steps mentioned in 40:49. Beyond the Temple's side rooms (and exterior supporting walls; see below), this difficult text suggests, the raised platform continues for a distance of six cubits all around until the platform ends.[1331]

Verse 9a informs readers that the exterior support for the side chambers is a wall five cubits (8.54 feet) wide. With this information, one can determine the width of the Temple with its surrounding siderooms which, by virtue of their thick

---

1324. See Block, *Ezekiel 25–48,* 552, who observes that Mesopotamian temples often had storage facilities that were three or four times the size of the temple proper.

1325. For details, see Zimmerli, *Ezekiel 2,* 377.

1326. Ibid., 377.

1327. Block, *Ezekiel 25–48,* 549.

1328. *BDB,* 533.

1329. M. Noth, *I. König,* BKAT 9 (Neukirchen-Vuyn: Neukirchener, 1964) 99.

1330. So Block, *Ezekiel 25–48,* 550-51. He points out that this understanding of the לולים (lûlîm) better fits extra-biblical analogues, such as the Egyptian temples of Sahure (c. 2500 BCE) and Amun at Karnak, built by Thutmose III (c. 1479–1425 BCE). See also K. A. Kitchen, "Two Notes on the Subsidiary Rooms of Solomon's Temple," *ErIsr* 20 (1989) 108.

1331. See Zimmerli, *Ezekiel 2,* 377-78, for the many difficulties attending this text.

exterior walls, have in effect become part of the temple structure itself.[1332] The exterior walls supporting the side chambers are ten cubits (five on each side). The chambers themselves are eight cubits (four on each side), the temple walls are twelve cubits (six on each side) and the interior of the Temple is twenty cubits (85.41 feet). Added together these buildings total fifty cubits, yet another multiple of five. One can also determine the length of the Temple with its side rooms to the west. The interior of the Temple is eighty-five cubits long. Its wall is six cubits, the side rooms are four cubits, and their exterior side rooms are one hundred cubits (170.83 feet). Hence, the total dimensions are one hundred cubits by fifty cubits (both multiples of five), a perfectly proportioned rectangle.

Verses 9b-10 focus upon the open spaces lying between the exterior supporting walls of the side rooms and yet another set of chambers, the לשכות (lĕšākôt). This set of chambers, previously not mentioned, has sometimes been identified as the priestly vestries described in 42:1-9, but this is by no means certain. Zimmerli opines that nowhere else in Ezekiel's vision is anything said about these chambers. Moreover, he observes, this information is incompatible with the reference to a wall[1333] which, according to v. 11b, is the next structure in the continued movement outward. He therefore concludes that vv. 9b-10 is a secondary expansion inserted by someone of a later time who "knows of chambers on the sides of the square temple area." The priestly vestries, he adds, were located further to the west.[1334] In any event, Ezekiel's primary concern is the size of these open spaces, which are said to lie "all around the temple on every side." The spaces are twenty cubits (34.16 feet) deep (east and west), twenty cubits wide (north and south).

Verse 11a informs readers that two doors enable persons inside the side chambers to exit onto the open spaces. One of these doors is on the north side, the other is on the south. Some scholars have argued that one could enter the side chambers not only through these doors but also from inside the

Temple itself.[1335] Others contend that access to the side rooms was limited to these two external doors. The exterior doors were designed to protect the nave's sanctity.[1336] Verse 11b poses nefarious problems, as comparison of the translations of the NRSV and the NIV makes evident. The MT reads, "And the width of the space [מקום māqôm] that was left free was five cubits all around." But this statement appears to contradict v. 10, which states that the free spaces between the side rooms of the Temple and the mysterious chambers referred to in v. 10a were twenty cubits wide. Block entertains, but does not endorse, the notion that a paved area surrounding the building is in view. If that were the case, then this special area would be part of the twenty-cubits wide areas described in v. 10.[1337] Zimmerli judges MT māqôm to be "incomprehensible." Taking a cue from LXX, he argues that the original Hebrew text had גדר (gādēr, "wall") or גדרת (gĕderet, "wall," fem. sing.), not māqôm.[1338] However, he cannot explain how māqôm might have replaced gdr.

In v. 12, Ezekiel writes of yet another exterior structure, located to the west of the temple building and separated from it by a גזרה (gizrâ, "restricted area," v. 13) twenty cubits (34.16 feet) deep. This בנין (binyān), "structure, building," is imposing by virtue of its size: it is ninety cubits long (153.75 feet) and seventy cubits wide (119.58 feet); and it is surrounded by walls five cubits thick (8.54 feet). Hence, its length, including the walls, is five plus ninety plus five cubits equaling one hundred cubits; and its width is five plus seventy plus five cubits equaling eighty cubits. This structure has no counterpart in the description of Solomon's Temple complex, and nothing is said here of its function. One might assume that it too was used as storage space for ritual and other items. It is, of course, possible that Ezekiel does not spell out its use because such would have been well known to his early readers. (See Reflections at 43:10-12.)

1332. Such was not the case with the Solomonic Temple. See ibid., 379-80.

1333. In order to read "wall," Zimmerli must emend the MT.

1334. Zimmerli, *Ezekiel 2*, 378.

1335. So, T. A. Busink, *Der Tempel von Jerusalem, von Salomo bis Herodes: Eine Archäologisch-historische Studie unter Berücksichtigung des westsemitischen Tempelbaus*, 2 vols. (Leiden: Brill, 1980) 2:760.

1336. D. I. Block, *The Book of Ezekiel: Chapters 25–48*, NICOT (Grand Rapids: Eerdmans, 1998) 551-52.

1337. Ibid., 552.

1338. See W. Zimmerli, *Ezekiel 2: A Commentary on the Book of the Prophet Ezekiel, Chapters 25–48*, trans. J. D. Martin, Hermeneia (Philadelphia: Fortress, 1983) 373.

EZEKIEL 41:13-15a, THE DIMENSIONS OF THE TEMPLE COMPLEX

NIV

13Then he measured the temple; it was a hundred cubits long, and the temple courtyard and the building with its walls were also a hundred cubits long. 14The width of the temple courtyard on the east, including the front of the temple, was a hundred cubits.

15Then he measured the length of the building facing the courtyard at the rear of the temple, including its galleries on each side; it was a hundred cubits.

NRSV

13Then he measured the temple, one hundred cubits deep; and the yard and the building with its walls, one hundred cubits deep; 14also the width of the east front of the temple and the yard, one hundred cubits.

15Then he measured the depth of the building facing the yard at the west, together with its galleries[a] on either side, one hundred cubits.

aCn: Meaning of Heb uncertain

COMMENTARY

(See Figure 2, 1535.) Ezekiel recounts that his guide then measures the Temple, which is one hundred cubits (170.83 feet) long. The space including the twenty cubit restricted area behind the Temple and the eighty-cubit long *binyān* to its west, likewise measured one hundred cubits deep (v. 13). The front of the Temple and the restricted area to its east are one hundred cubits in width (v. 14). Ezekiel's guide then measures the depth of the *binyān* opposite the restricted area to the west together with its galleries;[1339] Again, the depth is one hundred cubits.[1340] (See Reflections at 43:10-12.)

1339. The term אתוקיהא (*'attwqêhā'*) is obscure. The noun reappears in v. 16 and in 42:3, 5. Some translators envision windows, ledges, or corridors. Block, *Ezekiel 25–48*, 554, acknowledges that a firm conclusion eludes us, but suggests that galleries or balconies may be in view and that balconies are also ledges and walkways.

1340. Recall that the interior width of the *binyān* is 90 cubits, and its walls are 5 cubits thick.

EZEKIEL 41:15b-26, TEMPLE FURNISHINGS AND INTERIOR ORNAMENTATION

NIV

The outer sanctuary, the inner sanctuary and the portico facing the court, 16as well as the thresholds and the narrow windows and galleries around the three of them—everything beyond and including the threshold was covered with wood. The floor, the wall up to the windows, and the windows were covered. 17In the space above the outside of the entrance to the inner sanctuary and on the walls at regular intervals all around the inner and outer sanctuary 18were carved cherubim and palm trees. Palm trees alternated with cherubim. Each cherub had two faces: 19the face of a man toward the palm tree on one side and the face of a lion toward the palm tree on the other. They were carved all around the whole temple.

NRSV

The nave of the temple and the inner room and the outer[a] vestibule 16were paneled,[b] and, all around, all three had windows with recessed[c] frames. Facing the threshold the temple was paneled with wood all around, from the floor up to the windows (now the windows were covered), 17to the space above the door, even to the inner room, and on the outside. And on all the walls all around in the inner room and the nave there was a pattern.[d] 18It was formed of cherubim and palm trees, a palm tree between cherub and cherub. Each cherub had two faces: 19a human face turned toward the palm tree on the one side, and the face of a young lion turned toward the palm

aGk: Heb *of the court*   bGk: Heb *the thresholds*   cCn Compare Gk 1 Kings 6.4: Meaning of Heb uncertain   dHeb *measures*

NIV

²⁰From the floor to the area above the entrance, cherubim and palm trees were carved on the wall of the outer sanctuary.

²¹The outer sanctuary had a rectangular door-frame, and the one at the front of the Most Holy Place was similar. ²²There was a wooden altar three cubits high and two cubits square*ᵃ*; its corners, its base*ᵇ* and its sides were of wood. The man said to me, "This is the table that is before the LORD." ²³Both the outer sanctuary and the Most Holy Place had double doors. ²⁴Each door had two leaves—two hinged leaves for each door. ²⁵And on the doors of the outer sanctuary were carved cherubim and palm trees like those carved on the walls, and there was a wooden overhang on the front of the portico. ²⁶On the sidewalls of the portico were narrow windows with palm trees carved on each side. The side rooms of the temple also had overhangs.

ᵃ22 Septuagint; Hebrew *long*   *ᵇ22* Septuagint; Hebrew *length*

NRSV

tree on the other side. They were carved on the whole temple all around; ²⁰from the floor to the area above the door, cherubim and palm trees were carved on the wall.*ᵃ*

21The doorposts of the nave were square. In front of the holy place was something resembling ²²an altar of wood, three cubits high, two cubits long, and two cubits wide;*ᵇ* its corners, its base,*ᶜ* and its walls were of wood. He said to me, "This is the table that stands before the LORD." ²³The nave and the holy place had each a double door. ²⁴The doors had two leaves apiece, two swinging leaves for each door. ²⁵On the doors of the nave were carved cherubim and palm trees, such as were carved on the walls; and there was a canopy of wood in front of the vestibule outside. ²⁶And there were recessed windows and palm trees on either side, on the sidewalls of the vestibule.*ᵈ*

*ᵃ*Cn Compare verse 25: Heb *and the wall*   *ᵇ*Gk: Heb lacks *two cubits wide*   *ᶜ*Gk: Heb *length*   *ᵈ*Cn: Heb *vestibule. And the side chambers of the temple and the canopies*

COMMENTARY

(See Figure 2, 1535.) Virtually every one of these verses poses problems of translation and interpretation. Even so fine a textual critic as Block concedes that his translation is only suggestive and open to challenge. Suddenly, and without explanation, Ezekiel has returned to the interior of the three-room (vestibule, nave, holy of holies) temple building. There is no statement to the effect that the guide has brought him there, although he is said to speak to the priest/prophet in v. 22.

Verses 15*b*-16 suggest that all three of the rooms of the Temple (MT, "vestibules"; LXX, "vestibule") were paneled with wood[1341] as were their closed niches (or, windows with recessed frames; see the Commentary on 40:16), from the floor to the top of these niches and beyond to the space above the door both on the inside and on the outside.[1342] First Kgs 6:15 reports that in Solomon's Temple, the floor was covered with cypress, and the walls up to the ceiling were covered with cedar.

Verses 17*b*-20 state that the walls of the nave and of the holy of holies, from floor to ceiling, are decorated with carvings of cherubim and palm trees. Reference to these carvings stirs thoughts of Solomon's Temple, where they also appeared in the nave and the inner sanctuary, accompanied by carvings of open flowers. Ezekiel's cherubim in chapters 1 and 10 had four faces; the cherubim here described have only two—one human, the other like that of a lion. Each cherub is flanked on both sides by a palm, such that its humanoid face is turned toward the palm tree on one side, and its leonine face is turned toward the palm tree on its other side. Verse 20 essentially reiterates the information already supplied concerning these carvings. The significance of palm and cherubim is not explained in the text. Noting that palmette trees flanked by pairs of animals is attested not only on ancient ivories, but also elsewhere, Block suggests that they are more than mere decorations. Rather, these figures reflect human aspirations for life and prosperity (represented by the palm tree) and for security (represented by the cherubim).[1343]

1341. The term הספים (*hassippîm*) is likely a scribal error of a term derived from the root ספן (*spn*), whose verb means "cover," "cover in," "panel." *BDB*, 706a.

1342. The text is difficult at this point. For an alternative interpretation, see Block, *Ezekiel 25–48*, 557-58.

1343. Ibid., 558.

Verse 21a is obscure. The NIV states that the outer sanctuary, or nave, has a "rectangular doorframe," as does the entrance to the holy of holies. The NRSV, by contrast, envisions square doorposts.[1344] Zimmerli speaks of doors and their doorposts, citing Noth, who pictured a fourfold gradition of the door casing which became narrower towards the rear.[1345] Verses 21b and 22 (note the awkward versification) describe something resembling an altar of wood. (The phraseology may remind readers of chap. 1, where similar language describes the priest-prophet's vision of Yahweh's glory and of the cherubim and chariot that transports it to Babylonia.) Critics are quick to point out that this "altar" could never be used for burnt offerings, since the table would burn right along with the offering! The author's phraseology invokes thoughts of the "table of showbread" referred to in Exod 25:23-30; Lev 24:7-9 (both of a structure within the tabernacle) and 1 Kgs 6:20-22 (of a similar structure in Solomon's Temple). This table, with its showbread, was placed before "my [Yahweh's] face" (in Exod 25:29). Ezekiel provides the dimensions for his table—it is three cubits (approx. 5.13 feet) high, two cubits (approx. 3.42 feet) long, and two cubits wide; hence, the top of the table is square in shape (cf. the dimensions of the table in Exod 25:23, which measures 2 x 1 x 1½ cubits). This description reflects the Ezekielian predisposition toward squares. Verse 22b specifies that, indeed, its corners, its base (the MT's "length" makes no sense; the LXX reads "base"; the two words are similar in Hebrew, and

the Hebrew reader likely would recognize the mistake and mentally compensate), and its walls were made of wood. The reference to the table's "corners" suggests that it, like a number of altars of the ancient Near East unearth by archaeologists, has raised corners or "horns." Ezekiel's guide informs him that "this is the table that stands before the Lord."

Zimmerli plausibly argues that the description of the altar has been secondarily inserted into its present position. When it is excised, the description moves from the doorposts (v. 21a) to the doors of the nave and holy of holies ("the holy place") in v. 23.[1346] These doors are in fact double doors. Each entrance consists of two leaves or panels, each of which swings open on its own hinge, such that when both are opened, one leaf flanks one side of the entrance, and the other leaf flanks the entrance's other side. Verse 25 informs readers that the doors of the nave are carved with the same cherubim and palm trees appearing on the walls of the nave and the holy of holies (vv. 17b-20). The reference to a "canopy of wood" (NIV, "wooden overhand"; TNK, "lattice of wood") in front of the vestibule (v. 25b) is obscure, for we do not know the precise meaning of the architectural noun עב ('āb). Part of the description of Solomon's Palace, the "house of the Forest of the Lebanon," 1 Kgs 7:6b also speaks of an 'āb in front of the front porch. Some critics envision a wooden railing that in some way limited access to the Temple's exterior vestibule.[1347] Verse 26b, which is also obscure, notes that the vestibule is decorated with covered niches or windows and palm tree carvings. In this case, nothing is said of cherubim. (See Reflections at 43:10-12.)

1344. According to 1 Kgs 6:31, Solomon's Temple had five-sided doorposts at the entrance to the dĕbîr, "hindmost chamber," "innermost room of the temple of Solomon," which is synonymous with Ezekiel's "holy of holies" and "most holy place." See BDB, 184. If we have understood this difficult text correctly, then here is another example of Ezekiel's predilection toward square shapes.

1345. Zimmerli, Ezekiel 2, 388, citing Noth, I. Könige, 127.

1346. Zimmerli, Ezekiel 2, 389.

1347. See ibid., 390.

Ezekiel 42:1-14, The Priestly Sacristies

NIV

42 Then the man led me northward into the outer court and brought me to the rooms opposite the temple courtyard and opposite the outer wall on the north side. [2]The building whose door faced north was a hundred cubits[a] long and fifty cubits wide. [3]Both in the section twenty cubits from the inner court and in the section opposite the pavement of the outer court, gallery faced gallery at the three levels. [4]In front of the rooms was an inner passageway ten cubits wide and a hundred cubits[b] long. Their doors were on the north. [5]Now the upper rooms were narrower, for the galleries took more space from them than from the rooms on the lower and middle floors of the building. [6]The rooms on the third floor had no pillars, as the courts had; so they were smaller in floor space than those on the lower and middle floors. [7]There was an outer wall parallel to the rooms and the outer court; it extended in front of the rooms for fifty cubits. [8]While the row of rooms on the side next to the outer court was fifty cubits long, the row on the side nearest the sanctuary was a hundred cubits long. [9]The lower rooms had an entrance on the east side as one enters them from the outer court.

[10]On the south side[c] along the length of the wall of the outer court, adjoining the temple courtyard and opposite the outer wall, were rooms [11]with a passageway in front of them. These were like the rooms on the north; they had the same length and width, with similar exits and dimensions. Similar to the doorways on the north [12]were the doorways of the rooms on the south. There was a doorway at the beginning of the passageway that was parallel to the corresponding wall extending eastward, by which one enters the rooms.

[13]Then he said to me, "The north and south rooms facing the temple courtyard are the priests' rooms, where the priests who approach the LORD will eat the most holy offerings. There they will put the most holy offerings—the grain offerings,

NRSV

42 Then he led me out into the outer court, toward the north, and he brought me to the chambers that were opposite the temple yard and opposite the building on the north. [2]The length of the building that was on the north side[a] was[b] one hundred cubits, and the width fifty cubits. [3]Across the twenty cubits that belonged to the inner court, and facing the pavement that belonged to the outer court, the chambers rose[c] gallery[d] by gallery[d] in three stories. [4]In front of the chambers was a passage on the inner side, ten cubits wide and one hundred cubits deep,[e] and its[f] entrances were on the north. [5]Now the upper chambers were narrower, for the galleries[g] took more away from them than from the lower and middle chambers in the building. [6]For they were in three stories, and they had no pillars like the pillars of the outer[d] court; for this reason the upper chambers were set back from the ground more than the lower and the middle ones. [7]There was a wall outside parallel to the chambers, toward the outer court, opposite the chambers, fifty cubits long. [8]For the chambers on the outer court were fifty cubits long, while those opposite the temple were one hundred cubits long. [9]At the foot of these chambers ran a passage that one entered from the east in order to enter them from the outer court. [10]The width of the passage[h] was fixed by the wall of the court.

On the south[i] also, opposite the vacant area and opposite the building, there were chambers [11]with a passage in front of them; they were similar to the chambers on the north, of the same length and width, with the same exits[k] and arrangements and doors. [12]So the entrances of the chambers to the south were entered through the entrance at the head of the corresponding passage, from the east, along the matching wall.[d]

[13]Then he said to me, "The north chambers and the south chambers opposite the vacant area are the holy chambers, where the priests who approach the LORD shall eat the most holy offerings;

[a]2 The common cubit was about 1 1/2 feet (about 0.5 meter). [b]4 Septuagint and Syriac; Hebrew and one cubit [c]10 Septuagint; Hebrew Eastward

[a]Gk: Heb door [b]Gk: Heb before the length [c]Heb lacks the chambers rose [d]Meaning of Heb uncertain [e]Gk Syr: Heb a way of one cubit [f]Heb their [g]Gk: Heb lacks outer [h]Heb lacks of the passage [i]Gk: Heb east [k]Heb and all their exits

NIV

the sin offerings and the guilt offerings—for the place is holy. [14]Once the priests enter the holy precincts, they are not to go into the outer court until they leave behind the garments in which they minister, for these are holy. They are to put on other clothes before they go near the places that are for the people."

NRSV

there they shall deposit the most holy offerings—the grain offering, the sin offering, and the guilt offering—for the place is holy. [14]When the priests enter the holy place, they shall not go out of it into the outer court without laying there the vestments in which they minister, for these are holy; they shall put on other garments before they go near to the area open to the people."

COMMENTARY

(See Figure 2, 1535.) Jonathan Z. Smith differentiates between "three zones of relative sacrality" in the Temple complex.[1348] The center "spine" runs from east to west and includes the steps leading up to the outer east gate, the east gate itself, the inner court stairs leading to the inner east gate, the inner east gate, the altar, the stairs leading up to the vestibule, the vestibule itself, the nave, the holy of holies, the restricted space to the west of the Temple, and the *binyān* ("structure," "building") lying at the westernmost end of the spine. "In both legal and ritual terms," Smith writes, "it is this axis that may be understood as the "god's house," centered on the throne room, marked off to the west by the 'restricted space,' to the north and south by the lateral 'open space' (*munnāḥ,* Ezekiel 41:9), and frontally by the funnel of entranceways and shifts in height described above."[1349]

With Ezek 42:1, Ezekiel's tour of this "god's house" ends. His guide leads him out, by way of the north inner gate, to the outer court. He approaches a building lying north of the restricted area (between the Temple proper and the *binyān*). Nothing is said of the guide taking measurements, but such measurements are provided, and so one must assume the process, and not simply its results. Verse 2 informs the reader that this building on the north side is one hundred cubits (that is, 170.83 feet) long and fifty cubits (approximately 85.42 feet) wide. The building is a perfect rectangle, and its cubit length and width are multiples of five. Numerous difficulties confront readers

of vv. 3-6, with every detail open to debate, and reconstructions purely tentative.[1350] Verse 3 is extremely confusing; it obviously attempts further to situate this building and to provide architectural details about its form, but the most that can be said is that this building is the depth of the *binyān* plus the restricted area, and it is likely a multi-chambered, three story building with doors that open to the north.

Verse 4 tells of an inner passageway running in front of the chambers' doors. The measurements for this passageway according to the MT are ten cubits wide by one cubit deep. But this, of course, cannot be correct. Both the LXX and the Syriac read "and its length was one hundred cubits." This number is plausible since the passageway would, in that case, run down the entire northern length of the building. Verses 5-6 provide additional, obscure architectural information about the sacristy building. The levels of the three-story structure appear to be terraced, that is, the middle level is set farther back than the first, and the third farther back than the second.

Verses 7-8 inform readers that a fifty cubit long wall runs parallel to the chambers on the other side of the passageway. The additional fifty cubits are provided by the wall of an adjacent chamber in the outer court. Verse 9, then, describes how the priests gain access to the building. From the outer court, they enter the passageway running east to west in front of the chamber doors. Clearly, this arrangement is intended to protect the chamber from illicit access. The people cannot enter the building's chambers from the outer court; only the

1348. To these three zones he adds a fourth, the outer court, described in Ezek 42:14 as "the place where the people are." See Jonathan Z. Smith, *To Take Place: Toward Theory in Ritual* (Chicago: University of Chicago Press, 1987) 59-60.
1349. Ibid. 60.
1350. Block, *Ezekiel 25–48,* 564.

priests can enter, and they only through this passageway. Presumably, it is protected by a guard(s). Its width ("of the passageway" does not appear in MT and must be supplied by the reader) is determined by the wall on its northern side (v. 10a). Verses 10b-12 state summarily that a corresponding structure of priestly chambers to the south (the MT's "to the east" makes no sense; the reference should be, rather, to the south [so LXX]; the reader would recognize the erroneous word and assume that south should replace it) of the restricted area and the binyān is like that just described in vv. 1-10b.

In vv. 13-14, Ezekiel's guide informs him of the functions of the sacristies, which are threefold. First, the "priests who approach the Lord" eat those portions of the "most holy offerings" allocated to them in these chambers. The offerings include the grain (or cereal) offering, which can take the form of raw flour, or of baked, toasted, or fried grain. The cereal offering must not be leavened, and is seasoned with salt. It often is mixed with oil and frankincense. this offering can be brought to the Temple by those too poor to afford an animal sacrifice. According to Lev 2:8-10, the priest takes a token portion of the grain offering and burns it on the altar, creating an aroma pleasing to Yahweh. The remainder of the grain offering is given to the priests—Aaron and his sons (Lev 2:10)—as a most sacred portion of Yahweh's food gifts.[1351] On the purification (NIV and NRSV, "sin") and reparation (NIV and NRSV, "guilt") offerings, see the commentary to Ezek 40:38-43. These most holy consumables are appropriately eaten in the priestly sacristy because, as v. 13b states, the place, like the sacrifices, is holy. Second, the priests' food is to be stored there. Third, when the priests who have entered this holy place emerge from it onto the outer court, they must leave the sacred vestments, in which they served Yahweh, there because these garments are holy. The priests must don other garments before leaving the chambers. In this context, we are not told whether this must be done in order to prevent these holy garments from unpurity (impurity is contagious) or to prevent the transmission of their (contagious) holiness to those in the outer court Ezekiel will return to this issue in 44:19. (See Reflections at 43:10-12.)

1351. Following Milgrom, *Leviticus 1–16,* 177-78.

Ezekiel 42:15-20, Final Measurements of the Temple Complex

NIV

[15]When he had finished measuring what was inside the temple area, he led me out by the east gate and measured the area all around: [16]He measured the east side with the measuring rod; it was five hundred cubits.[a] [17]He measured the north side; it was five hundred cubits[b] by the measuring rod. [18]He measured the south side; it was five hundred cubits by the measuring rod. [19]Then he turned to the west side and measured; it was five hundred cubits by the measuring rod. [20]So he measured the area on all four sides. It had a wall around it, five hundred cubits long and five hundred cubits wide, to separate the holy from the common.

[a]16 See Septuagint of verse 17; Hebrew *rods*; also in verses 18 and 19.   [b]17 Septuagint; Hebrew *rods*

NRSV

15When he had finished measuring the interior of the temple area, he led me out by the gate that faces east, and measured the temple area all around. [16]He measured the east side with the measuring reed, five hundred cubits by the measuring reed. [17]Then he turned and measured[a] the north side, five hundred cubits by the measuring reed. [18]Then he turned and measured[a] the south side, five hundred cubits by the measuring reed. [19]Then he turned to the west side and measured, five hundred cubits by the measuring reed. [20]He measured it on the four sides. It had a wall around it, five hundred cubits long and five hundred cubits wide, to make a separation between the holy and the common.

[a]Gk: Heb *measuring reed all around. He measured*

COMMENTARY

(See Figure 2, 1535.) In these verses, Ezekiel states that when his guide finished measuring the interior of the temple area, he brought Ezekiel out by the outer east gate (the same gate by which they entered the complex, 40:6) and then measured the exterior of the entire temple complex. Using the measuring reed, he determined that the east side is five hundred cubits (a total of 284.72 yards). Next he measured the north side; it too is five hundred cubits, as are the south and west sides. The temple complex is a perfect square. A massive wall surrounds it in order to separate the holy from the common or profane beyond its exterior. The wall is five hundred cubits long on each of its four sides. (See Reflections at 43:10-12.)

Ezekiel 43:1-9, Yahweh's Glory Returns to the Temple

NIV

43 Then the man brought me to the gate facing east, ²and I saw the glory of the God of Israel coming from the east. His voice was like the roar of rushing waters, and the land was radiant with his glory. ³The vision I saw was like the vision I had seen when he[a] came to destroy the city and like the visions I had seen by the Kebar River, and I fell facedown. ⁴The glory of the LORD entered the temple through the gate facing east. ⁵Then the Spirit lifted me up and brought me into the inner court, and the glory of the LORD filled the temple.

⁶While the man was standing beside me, I heard someone speaking to me from inside the temple. ⁷He said: "Son of man, this is the place of my throne and the place for the soles of my feet. This is where I will live among the Israelites forever. The house of Israel will never again defile my holy name—neither they nor their kings—by their prostitution[b] and the lifeless idols[c] of their kings at their high places. ⁸When they placed their threshold next to my threshold and their doorposts beside my doorposts, with only a wall between me and them, they defiled my holy name by their detestable practices. So I destroyed them in my anger. ⁹Now let them put away from me their prostitution and the lifeless idols of their kings, and I will live among them forever.

[a]3 Some Hebrew manuscripts and Vulgate; most Hebrew manuscripts I   [b]7 Or their spiritual adultery; also in verse 9   [c]7 Or the corpses; also in verse 9

NRSV

43 Then he brought me to the gate, the gate facing east. ²And there, the glory of the God of Israel was coming from the east; the sound was like the sound of mighty waters; and the earth shone with his glory. ³The[a] vision I saw was like the vision that I had seen when he came to destroy the city, and[b] like the vision that I had seen by the river Chebar; and I fell upon my face. ⁴As the glory of the LORD entered the temple by the gate facing east, ⁵the spirit lifted me up, and brought me into the inner court; and the glory of the LORD filled the temple.

6While the man was standing beside me, I heard someone speaking to me out of the temple. ⁷He said to me: Mortal, this is the place of my throne and the place for the soles of my feet, where I will reside among the people of Israel forever. The house of Israel shall no more defile my holy name, neither they nor their kings, by their whoring, and by the corpses of their kings at their death.[c] ⁸When they placed their threshold by my threshold and their doorposts beside my doorposts, with only a wall between me and them, they were defiling my holy name by their abominations that they committed; therefore I have consumed them in my anger. ⁹Now let them put away their idolatry and the corpses of their kings far from me, and I will reside among them forever.

[a]Gk: Heb *Like the vision*   [b]Syr: Heb *and the visions*   [c]Or *on their high places*

COMMENTARY

(See Figure 2, 1535.) With these nine verses, the description of Yahweh's pure and perfectly ordered Temple complex (chaps 40–42) reaches its climax. All is prepared for the return of God's glory. Verse 1 states that Ezekiel's guide ("he") leads the priest/prophet to the gate facing east. Ezekiel's tour of the city-like Temple complex began at this site (40:6); and according to 42:15, the guide/surveyor had already returned him to that place. But the consistency-building reader will understand that Ezekiel subsequently followed his guide as the latter measured the lengths of the four sides of the exterior wall (vv. 16-20), ending with the west side, and so must be led back to the entrance of the east gate a second time.

Suddenly, with a sound like the roar of mighty waters, the Glory of the God of Israel comes from the east; and the land is illumined by his glory. Readers recall that in Ezekiel's initial vision of Yahweh's glory, the powerful beating of the cherubims' wings was likened to three phenomena: the sound of mighty waters, the sound of Shaddai (approaching), and the din of an army (1:24). In that context also, much was made of flashing fire, an amber-like gleam, burning coals of fire, etc. Here, the brightness of Yahweh is described with less detail, but the statement that God's glory lights up the land suffices to convey a sense of its dazzling brilliance.

Ezekiel informs his audience/readers that this vision is like the vision he saw when Yahweh (the MT reads "I," but this makes no sense; most commentators emend the text, supported by six MSS and two ancient versions) came to destroy the city (Ezekiel 8–11). This statement about the Lord's involvement in the destruction represents something of a departure from what appears in Ezekiel 10–11. Although in 10:6-7, Yahweh commands the man dressed in linen to take fire from the cherubs, the immediate effect of this command upon the city is not recorded. Rather, the predominate idea is that Yahweh's glory abandons the still extant city to its fate at the hands of Babylonian soldiers. This statement serves the theological purpose of explaining how it is possible for an invading army to destroy Yahweh's own Temple. Marduk did not defeat Yahweh; God's presence no

longer resided in the city at the time of its destruction.

Ezekiel also likens this vision to what he beheld by the Chebar Canal (1:4–3:15). Now, as then (1:28b), he responds by falling upon his face (43:3b). The glory of Yahweh enters the Temple by means of the east gate. According to Ezek 10:19, Yahweh's enthroned glory hovered above the entrance to the east gate and departed the city toward the east (11:23). Here, as in 3:12, 14; 8:3; and 11:1, 24, the "spirit" transports Ezekiel to a different place—in this case, the inner court (in 2:2, the spirit raises Ezekiel to his feet so that he might be addressed by God)—and behold! Yahweh's glory fills the Temple! No human king is responsible for its construction—a startling departure from ancient Near Eastern practice as attested in the emphasis upon Solomon's role in building the First Temple for Yahweh in Jerusalem.[1352]

Ezekiel 40:6 locates "the man" (i.e., the tour guide) beside the priest-prophet when the latter hears a voice speaking to him from inside the Temple. The source of the voice is not the tour guide, but God. Yahweh addresses Ezekiel in customary fashion as "Mortal," and issues a formal announcement replete with monarchical language and imagery. "This" is the place of (King) Yahweh's (royal) throne and the place for the soles of God's feet (i.e., God's footstool). Both throne and footstool are associated with the ark of the covenant in Israel's traditions. Exodus 26:31-35 identifies the tabernacle's holy of holies with Yahweh's throne room, and the ark assumes the function of Yahweh's throne or footstool. The latter expression both refers to the object on which one rests one's feet and infers domination over one's subjects or foes (see also Ps 132:7; Lam 2:10).[1353]

Ezekiel says nothing of the ark of the covenant and never holds out hope for its return. Ark of the covenant terminology now receives new life.[1354] Critics are reminded of Jeremiah's words concerning the future absence of the ark in Jer 3:16-17: "They shall no longer say, 'The ark of the covenant

---

1352. See Kalinda Rose Stevenson, *The Vision of Transformation: The Territorial Rhetoric of Ezekiel 40–48*, SBLDS 154 (Atlanta: Scholars Press, 1996) 111-17.
1353. Block, *Ezekiel 25–48*, 581.
1354. Zimmerli, *Ezekiel 2*, 415.

of the LORD.' It shall not come to mind, or be remembered, or missed; nor shall another one be made. At that time Jerusalem shall be called the throne of the LORD, and all nations shall gather to it, to the presence of the LORD in Jerusalem." But Ezekiel's final vision has not, heretofore, mentioned a city—only a complex resembling a city. Hence, the exact referent for "this" is unclear. Does it refer to the entire Temple complex or—more specifically—to the Temple building or—even more specifically—to the holy of holies?

Yahweh's assertion of ownership and dominion is followed by a declaration of divine intention: God will reside there in the midst of the Israelite people forever. This decision rules out any possibility that the people might be permitted to perpetuate the sins of the past. Never again will the house of Israel and its kings *defile God's holy name* (a recurring Ezekielian concern; see esp. the Commentary on 37:20-24*a*) by their "whoring" (worship of other deities; alliances with foreign nations; see the Commentary on 16 and 23), or by the veneration of Israel's deceased kings (פגרי מלכיהם במותם *pigrê malkêhem bāmôtām*). The exact nature of this second, never-to-be repeated sin is unclear. In Ezek 6:5, *pĕgārîm* referred to the bodies of idolators scattered over Israel's land; and so some critics speak here of the corpses of Israel's former kings which were buried in close proximity (with only a wall between them) to the Temple. Two scoundel kings of Judah, Manasseh (2 Kgs 21:18; see also 2 Chr 33:20) and Amon (2 Kgs 21:26) are said to be buried in "the garden of Uzza," presumably in the area of the royal palace (and hence, of the Temple). But Judah's kings were most often buried in "the city of David," at some remove from the Temple. Hence, other critics think of royal steles erected to commemorate deceased kings, or of the veneration of "the deified spirits of Israel's royal ancestors, analogous to the cult of the dead at Urgarit."[1355]

A third offense, related to the second, registers Yahweh's complaint that in the past, the close proximity of Temple and palace ("they placed their threshold by my threshold and their doorposts beside my doorposts, with only a wall between me and them") defiled Yahweh's holy name on account of the abominations they committed. The Temple built by Solomon was part of a larger palace complex (see 2 Kgs 11); and the Deuteronomistic History, which credits Solomon with Temple building, registers no complaint about that arrangement. But Ezekiel bristles at the possibility that such might again be the case, and attributes their demise to Yahweh's consuming wrath. Indeed, I would argue that Ezekiel's reference to the enormous structure lying west of the Temple building (the *binyān*), as well as his emphasis upon open spaces lying to the Temple's north, south, and east sides, betrays expressly his polemic against such encroachment upon the sacred space of Israel's divine king by its former, human rulers. Verse 9 reiterates the offenses of the past and repeats the promise that in their absence, God will reside in the midst of the Israelites forever. (See Reflections at 43:10-12.)

1355. See M. H. Pope, "The Cult of the Dead at Ugarit," in *Ugarit in Retrospect: Fifty Years of Ugarit and Ugaritic,* ed. G. D. Young (Winona Lake: Eisenbrauns, 1981) 159-79.

Ezekiel 43:10-12, The Conclusion of the Temple Vision

NIV

10"Son of man, describe the temple to the people of Israel, that they may be ashamed of their sins. Let them consider the plan, 11and if they are ashamed of all they have done, make known to them the design of the temple—its arrangement, its exits and entrances—its whole design and all its regulations[a] and laws. Write these down before

[a]11 Some Hebrew manuscripts and Septuagint; most Hebrew manuscripts *regulations and its whole design*

NRSV

10As for you, mortal, describe the temple to the house of Israel, and let them measure the pattern; and let them be ashamed of their iniquities. 11When they are ashamed of all that they have done, make known to them the plan of the temple, its arrangement, its exits and its entrances, and its whole form—all its ordinances and its entire plan and all its laws; and write it down in

NIV

them so that they may be faithful to its design and follow all its regulations.

¹²"This is the law of the temple: All the surrounding area on top of the mountain will be most holy. Such is the law of the temple.

NRSV

their sight, so that they may observe and follow the entire plan and all its ordinances. ¹²This is the law of the temple: the whole territory on the top of the mountain all around shall be most holy. This is the law of the temple.

COMMENTARY

(See Figure 2, 1535.) At the beginning of Ezekiel's tour of the temple complex, his guide instructed him to look closely and listen attentively, and to focus his mind upon everything he was shown in order that he might declare it all to the house of Israel. Now, at the end of that tour, Yahweh instructs Ezekiel (again addressed as "mortal") to describe the Temple to the house of Israel, in order that the people might measure its proportion or design. The purpose of this thorough explanation is plainly stated: They will be ashamed of their (past) iniquities. One thinks especially of the abominations carried out in the First Temple as described in Ezekiel 8. This explanation might startle a reader unfamiliar with other portions of the book, but the ancient sequential reader is not surprised. Here, as elsewhere, God's restorative action elicits shame from the people for their past iniquities.[1356] True to form, Ezekiel permits no glimpse of a restored community celebrating the return of Yahweh's glory in their midst. When they are ashamed, Ezekiel must make known to them the plan of the Temple, its arrangement, its exits and entrances, and its entire form—all of its ordinances and its entire plan and all of its laws. The specificity of this statement signals its importance: Yahweh's glory will not dwell in the midst of an impure people. Ezekiel must commit all of this to writing in their sight. One presumes that having access to this written document (likely including diagrams or illustrations of some sort) will assist the people in observing and following the plan in its entirety and all of its ordinances.

The function of 43:12 is disputed. While some critics regard it as the conclusion of the temple tour section,[1357] others view it as a preamble to the second major subsection of Ezekiel 40–48, that is, 43:12–46:24.[1358] The disagreement stems, in significant measure, from the fact that its opening and closing words ("This is the law [better rendered "instruction"] of the temple") conform to a formula ("This is . . .") that can occur either at the beginning (e.g., Lev 72:11; Num 19:2) or at the end (e.g., Lev 7:31; 14:32) of priestly instructions. Perhaps the (twice stated) formula here does double duty, both bringing the descriptive section to a close and introducing the regulations sections that follow. Between the two formulas, Yahweh asserts that the entire area on the top of the mountain all around is uniquely holy. To be sure, the reader has learned that within the Temple complex there are gradations of holiness, culminating with the holy of holies in which Yahweh's glory is enthroned.[1359] But the mountaintop itself all around is the holiest area of Israel's territory.

1356. So, e.g., Zimmerli, *Ezekiel 2*, 420.

1357. So Steven Tuell, *The Law of the Temple in Ezekiel 40–48*, HSM 49 (Atlanta: Scholars Press, 1992) 45-46.

1358. I prefer to speak of gradations of holiness. To my mind, Smith's statement that "with respect to the temple mount, the land is profane; with respect to the temple, the temple mount is profane; with respect to the throne place, the temple is profane" goes too far. See Smith, *To Take Place,* 56).

1359. Block, *Ezekiel 25-48*, 589.

REFLECTIONS

I have never heard a preacher deliver a sermon on any verse of Ezek 40:1–43:12. This is certainly not to say that no one has ever done so. I do not doubt that preachers of the past and present have proclaimed the gospel ("good news") that Yahweh's dazzing glory fills the Temple in order to be present with God's people (43:1-11). But I suspect that within Christian circles, these are neglected texts. One can, having read them, understand why preachers and lay people might wish to avoid Ezekiel's final vision. After all, much of the material strikes them as tedious; and textual obscurities abound. Perhaps they reason that since Ezekiel's Temple was never built, its significance is slight. The notion that Yahweh's "glory" might permanently dwell inside a temple building seems alien to our worldview, as does a sacrificial system involving the slaughter of animals and birds. The concept of contagious holiness and impurity also is difficult to understand. Indeed, without access to ideas appearing in the Overview to this unit—human geography, territoriality, the symbolism of sacred shapes, the "theology of holiness," etc.—one has little hope of glimpsing the meaning and purpose of this rhetorical unit.

That said, I would like to suggest that the answer to these difficulties is not neglect, as if this portion of Scripture had nothing to teach us and was an unworthy conversation partner. Though there are dramatic disjunctions between the ancient priestly worldview and that held by many (though not all) moderns, there may yet be points of conjunction as well.

1. Consider the attention to detail that characterizes Ezek 40:1–43:11. Readers may care little about the width of a particular wall or court. But most can understand that when something, or someone, is genuinely precious, attention to detail becomes very important. Think about the parents who study the face and form of their newborn child, about the spouse who studies his or her mate's face while the latter lies sleeping, about the adult child who studies the beautiful, lined face of a beloved, aging parent. Imagine the art critic who suddenly is given the opportunity to study a masterpiece previously seen only in pictures. Will she give it only a passing glance, or will she study it hour after hour, attentive to its every detail? Yes, when something, or someone, is truly cherished, we want to know everything we can about it. Indeed, it is precisely my love of the Bible that compels me to learn everything about it that I can. For the authors and sympathetic readers of Ezekiel's vision, the Temple—its place, spaces, structures, and its every ritual—are of utmost significance. Ezekiel's temple vision challenges exilic and early post-exilic readers, and us as well, to believe that a community disordered, dismembered, and dislocated may yet be healed by the sovereign God of creation. Yes, we can understand Ezekiel's attention to detail.

2. Ezekiel's Temple is perfectly ordered. Perfection is rarely had in the real world, including the world of religious symbolism and ritual. No actual temple could be built on the basis of the information Ezekiel provides. We should not wonder that a post-exilic community, struggling with problems within and without, would not have undertaken so massive a building project, even if some in its midst believed that it should. But the imperfection, or implausibility of perfection, of "real world" communities, persons, and objects should not prevent us from aspiring to perfection, from "going on to perfection" in John Wesley's words.

Achieving some degree of orderliness and discipline brings not only religious, but also psychological, benefits to many people. Before beginning a project (like the writing of this commentary), I inevitably find myself cleaning my office; and I must do so on at least a somewhat regular basis. When my office is clean, orderly, and organized (if only for a day or two!), my thinking seems clearer, more orderly, and organized. The exilic and early post-exilic community experienced drought, famine, "family" feuds, and opposition from those whom they regarded as outsiders. Ezekiel's vision invites them and us to contemplate an orderly and holy existence, where present-day chaos is replaced by God's well-ordered creation (see especially Gen 1:1–2:4*a*, itself a product of priests and reflective of their worldview). Yes, we can understand Ezekiel's longing for order and discipline.

3. Several years ago, as I sat in church one Sunday morning, the pastor's young son—notorious for his behavior during worship services—ran down the main aisle toward his father, stopped, and yelled, "Daddy, this is God's house!" In that child's mind, God really did live in a house; and that house was his father's church building. As children grow and mature, they can develop more abstract notions of God's presence and perhaps reject the idea that God "lives", albeit invisibly, in a temple or church. But the notion of sacred space is not lost on most of us. The church in which we have worshiped for many years, where we married, where our children and our friends' children have been baptized, where the funeral of a beloved family member was held, is not like just any other space. It is sacred space, and we may experience God's presence in that space as we do in no other. The people of ancient Israel did not confine God to a single space; but they believed that God's presence could be experienced in a most profound way in proximity to Yahweh's Temple, where the glory of the Lord chose to dwell. Yes, we can understand Ezekiel's longing for God's presence and his emphasis upon sacred space.

4. What of the practice of slaughtering animals because their blood cleanses impurity? Such an idea is, to the minds of many, intolerable. But we should remember that our worldview is not the same as that of ancient priests. The Jewish sacrificial system underwent dramatic changes after 70 CE, when the Second Temple was destroyed and animal sacrifice ended. But throughout the years of Jesus' life, animal sacrifice was integral to religious ritual. The Jesus of the synoptic gospels says nothing negative about this type of sacrifice. In fact, he signals its importance when he teaches that even "when you are offering your gift at the altar, if you remember that your brother or sister has something against you, leave your gift there before the altar and go; first be reconciled to your brother or sister, and then come and offer your gift" (Matt 5:23-24; in Mark 1:44 and Luke 17:15 also, sacrifice is taken for granted). Certainly sacrificial motifs and imagery were woven into Christian traditions about the Last Supper, and about the death of Jesus as the ultimate fulfillment of the sacrificial cult. One thinks, for example, of Paul's statement that "our paschal lamb, Christ, has been sacrificed" (1 Cor 5:7, NRSV) and of the deutero-Pauline statement in Eph 5:2 ("and live in love, as Christ loved us and gave himself up for us, a fragrant offering and sacrifice to God," NRSV). Sacrificial motifs and imagery also appear in Christian hymnody, such as "There is a Fountain filled with Blood" and "There is Power in the Blood of the Lamb." Yes, we can understand the power of sacrifice and of its motifs and imagery.

Ezekiel's theology of holiness insists that neither God's holy presence nor the consequences of human sinfulness are to be taken lightly. This is, to my mind, an important word for contemporary Jews and Christians. A theology of holiness is a relational theology. The relationship between God and those who worship God depends upon divine mercy and human faithfulness. Ezekiel 40:1—43:11 is one vision of how that relationship can be sustained. Perhaps it is not our vision in every respect. But we are not so far removed from it that we cannot feel its power.

Ezekiel 43:13–46:24, The Torah of Ezekiel's Temple

Ezekiel 43:13-17, Regulations Concerning the Altar

NIV

13"These are the measurements of the altar in long cubits, that cubit being a cubit[a] and a handbreadth[b]: Its gutter is a cubit deep and a cubit wide, with a rim of one span[c] around the edge. And this is the height of the altar: 14From the gutter on the ground up to the lower ledge it is two cubits high and a cubit wide, and from the smaller ledge up to the larger ledge it is four cubits high and a cubit wide. 15The altar hearth is four cubits high, and four horns project upward from the hearth. 16The altar hearth is square, twelve cubits long and twelve cubits wide. 17The upper ledge also is square, fourteen cubits long and fourteen cubits wide, with a rim of half a cubit and a gutter of a cubit all around. The steps of the altar face east."

[a]13 The common cubit was about 1 1/2 feet (about 0.5 meter).
[b]13 That is, about 3 inches (about 8 centimeters)   [c]13 That is, about 9 inches (about 22 centimeters)

NRSV

13These are the dimensions of the altar by cubits (the cubit being one cubit and a handbreadth): its base shall be one cubit high,[a] and one cubit wide, with a rim of one span around its edge. This shall be the height of the altar: 14From the base on the ground to the lower ledge, two cubits, with a width of one cubit; and from the smaller ledge to the larger ledge, four cubits, with a width of one cubit; 15and the altar hearth, four cubits; and from the altar hearth projecting upward, four horns. 16The altar hearth shall be square, twelve cubits long by twelve wide. 17The ledge also shall be square, fourteen cubits long by fourteen wide, with a rim around it half a cubit wide, and its surrounding base, one cubit. Its steps shall face east.

[a]Gk: Heb lacks *high*

COMMENTARY

The importance of the altar in Ezekiel's vision can scarcely be overstated. While the holy of holies, where Yahweh's glory dwells, is the most sacred space in the Temple, the altar standing before the Temple provides the means for purifying it, thereby making it possible for Yahweh's glory to abide with the people.[1360]

Ezekiel 40:47b referred to an altar situated in front of the Temple. Now, the text returns to this object in greater detail. Verses 13-27 can be divided into two sections. On the one hand, vv. 13-17 provide the dimensions of the altar. On the other hand, vv. 18-27 legislate its purification/consecration process. A number of commentators regard both of these sections as secondary additions to the original text, in part because they

judge them not to be linked either to preceding, or to following, material.[1361] To my mind, however, my reader would immediately have understood that the sacrificial system must commence as soon as Yahweh's glory enters the Temple. Prior to that event, there is no need for the sacrificial system. Block has written that in this passage, "there is no hint of any awareness of the return of the *kabôd* ["glory"], so graphically described in the foregoing."[1362] I, by contrast, would argue that the passage presupposes Yahweh's return and, indeed, appears here precisely on account of that event.

Verse 13 begins with a formulaic announcement: "These are the dimensions of the altar." The concern for dimensions reminds readers of

1360. See Kalinda Rose Stevenson, *The Vision of Transformation: The Territorial Rhetoric of Ezekiel 40–48,* SBLDS 154 (Atlanta: Scholars Press, 1996) 40-41.

1361. So W. Zimmerli, *Ezekiel 2: A Commentary on the Book of the Prophet Ezekiel, Chapters 25–48,* trans. J. D. Martin, Hermeneia (Philadelphia: Fortress, 1983) 422.
1362. D. I. Block, *The Book of Ezekiel: Chapters 25–48,* NICOT (Grand Rapids: Eerdmans, 1998) 595.

40:5–42:20, but nothing is said here of a surveyor/guide. The dimensions are by cubits, and readers are again informed (see 40:5) that the long cubit (approximately 20.5 inches) is being used.

We must concede at the outset that the description of the altar contains architectural terms whose precise meanings elude us. Scholars can and do disagree about its shape and size. So, for example, the altar's height is disputed, as is the progress of the description. Has an editor sought to bring an originally six-cubit altar into conformity with the ten-cubit altar of Solomon's (and perhaps of the post-exilic) Temple? Does the description of the altar move from bottom to top, and then from top to bottom, or does it move only from bottom to top? These are but two of a myriad of questions confronting critics.

According to v. 13, the altar is surrounded by a sunken gutter (so NIV; NRSV, "base") one cubit deep and one cubit wide. This gutter functions as a receptacle for the blood and bits of the animals burned upon the altar. Its outer edge is protected by a curb or rim one-half cubit high (10.25 inches). This curb helps to contain the blood and gore, lest it slosh onto the inner court. Verse 13*b* signals that the altar's height is a major concern of the author. This is somewhat surprising, since the measurements provided for the temple complex seldom include height dimensions.[1363]

Verse 14 states that the distance from the bottom of the sunken gutter to the altar's lowest ledge is two cubits (approximately 41 inches), and the width of the ledge is one cubit. The distance from the lowest ledge (עזרה *'ăzārâ*)[1364] to the top of the higher ledge (this must be the sense of the Hebrew, which refers to the lowest ledge as the "lesser" ledge and to the next as the "greater" ledge, even though the greater ledge has smaller dimensions; height, not size, is at issue) is four cubits; and this ledge too is a cubit wide. Verse 15 then states that the height of the altar hearth (הראל *har'ēl*) is four cubits, with four horns projecting upward from the hearth, one at each corner. Added together, these measurements depict an altar at least ten cubits in height, depending upon the height of the horns. Archaeologists have

uncovered horned altars in the ancient Near East;[1365] and they appear in the descriptions of the Mosaic altar (Exod 29:12; Lev 4:7, 18 and elsewhere), and of the altar used by Solomon (1 Kgs 1:50-53; 2:28-29). Their function is unknown but, as Block observes, the fact that blood was smeared on them (see Lev 4:7) suggests that they bore some special significance.[1366] Persons seeking asylum in sanctuaries seized the horns of the altar hoping for divine protection (see, e.g., 1 Kgs 2:28-34).

The altar hearth itself is called both *har'el* (v. 15) and האריאל *hā'ări'êl* (v. 16). Translated literally, *'ări'êl* means "lion of El." It appears as a personal name in 2 Sam 23:20 (= 1 Chr 11:22) and Ezra 8:16. In Isa 29:1-2, 7, *'ări'êl* refers to Jerusalem, or perhaps more precisely, to the Temple's altar of burnt-offering.[1367] Block derives the word from *' arâ*, meaning "to burn," a cognate to Arabic *'ry* from which developed *'irat*, "hearth, fireplace."[1368] He concedes, however, that this rendering of the word has no parallel in the Hebrew Bible.

Equally difficult is *har'el*, "mountain of God." W. F. Albright proposed a link between *'ări'êl* and the Akkadian *arallûm*, a term which he thought could refer either to the netherworld, or to the mountain of the gods.[1369] However, this Sumerian loan word refers only to the former, not to the latter. Dijkstra suggests that *har'el* is either a "folkloristic corruption" of *'arî'el* or a "learned 'etymological' spelling."[1370] Block treats the term as a theologizing wordplay on an architectural term for the surface of the hearth.[1371]

Verse 16 provides the dimensions of the hearth; it is a perfect square measuring twelve cubits long by twelve cubits wide. Its containment wall also is a perfect square measuring fourteen by fourteen

1363. Ibid.

1364. The etymology of the architectural term *'ăzārâ* is uncertain. Here, it likely refers to a row of stones one cubit in height that served as the base of the superstructure.

1365. See, e.g., Y. Aharoni, "The Horned Altar of Beer-sheba," *BA* 37 (1974) 2-6.

1366. Block, *Ezekiel 25–48*, 601.

1367. R. E. Clements, *Isaiah 1–39*, NCB (Grand Rapids: Eerdmans, 1980) 235. R. Youngblood contends that "ariel" means "city of God," but acknowledges a play on words, such that the "city of God" is threatened with becoming an "altar-hearth." See R. Youngblood, "Ariel, 'City of God,'" in *Essays on the Occasion of the Seventieth Anniversary of The Dropsie University*, ed. A. I. Katsh and L. Nemoy (Philadelphia: Dropsie University Press, 1979) 461.

1368. Block, *Ezekiel 25–48*, 600.

1369. W. F. Albright, "The Babylonian Temple-Tower and the Altar of Burnt Offering," *JBL* 39 (1920) 137-39; and *Archaeology and the Religion of Israel*, Ayer Lectures, 5th ed. (Baltimore: Johns Hopkins University Press, 1968) 151-52.

1370. Meindert Dijkstra, "The Altar of Ezekiel: Fact or Fiction," *VT* 42 (1992) 29.

1371. Block, *Ezekiel 25–48*, 600.

cubits. The containment wall, like the bottom of the altar substructure, has a half-cubit rim surrounding a gutter one cubit deep. The description of the altar ends with the notice that it is accessed by steps on its east side. For readers familiar with the Mosaic prohibition against altar steps (Exod 20:22), this feature is startling. Because the altar faces the Temple, rather than the east, the sacrifices can truly be said to be offered in the presence of God. Block provides data which impress upon his readers the altar's massive size:

Viewed from the top, inclusive of the bottom gutter and its lip, the outer perimeter measured 20 x 20 cubits (about 34 ft.), covering an area of 1,156 square ft.; the altar proper . . . was 14 x 14 cubits (about 24 ft.), an area of 576 square ft.; and the hearth . . . was 12 x 12 cubits (about 20.5 ft.), 420 square ft.[1372]

Here, as so often in Ezekiel's vision, the immense size of the structure signals its significance. (See Reflections at 46:19-24.)

1372. Ibid., 601.

Ezekiel 43:18-27, The Consecration of the Altar

[18]Then he said to me, "Son of man, this is what the Sovereign LORD says: These will be the regulations for sacrificing burnt offerings and sprinkling blood upon the altar when it is built: [19]You are to give a young bull as a sin offering to the priests, who are Levites, of the family of Zadok, who come near to minister before me, declares the Sovereign LORD. [20]You are to take some of its blood and put it on the four horns of the altar and on the four corners of the upper ledge and all around the rim, and so purify the altar and make atonement for it. [21]You are to take the bull for the sin offering and burn it in the designated part of the temple area outside the sanctuary.

[22]"On the second day you are to offer a male goat without defect for a sin offering, and the altar is to be purified as it was purified with the bull. [23]When you have finished purifying it, you are to offer a young bull and a ram from the flock, both without defect. [24]You are to offer them before the LORD, and the priests are to sprinkle salt on them and sacrifice them as a burnt offering to the LORD.

[25]"For seven days you are to provide a male goat daily for a sin offering; you are also to provide a young bull and a ram from the flock, both without defect. [26]For seven days they are to make atonement for the altar and cleanse it; thus they will dedicate it. [27]At the end of these days, from the eighth day on, the priests are to present your burnt offerings and fellowship offerings[a] on the altar. Then I will accept you, declares the Sovereign LORD."

[a]27 Traditionally peace offerings

[18]Then he said to me: Mortal, thus says the Lord GOD: These are the ordinances for the altar: On the day when it is erected for offering burnt offerings upon it and for dashing blood against it, [19]you shall give to the levitical priests of the family of Zadok, who draw near to me to minister to me, says the Lord GOD, a bull for a sin offering. [20]And you shall take some of its blood, and put it on the four horns of the altar, and on the four corners of the ledge, and upon the rim all around; thus you shall purify it and make atonement for it. [21]You shall also take the bull of the sin offering, and it shall be burnt in the appointed place belonging to the temple, outside the sacred area.

[22]On the second day you shall offer a male goat without blemish for a sin offering; and the altar shall be purified, as it was purified with the bull. [23]When you have finished purifying it, you shall offer a bull without blemish and a ram from the flock without blemish. [24]You shall present them before the LORD, and the priests shall throw salt on them and offer them up as a burnt offering to the LORD. [25]For seven days you shall provide daily a goat for a sin offering; also a bull and a ram from the flock, without blemish, shall be provided. [26]Seven days shall they make atonement for the altar and cleanse it, and so consecrate it. [27]When these days are over, then from the eighth day onward the priests shall offer upon the altar your burnt offerings and your offerings of well-being; and I will accept you, says the Lord GOD.

COMMENTARY

As soon as the altar is erected, it must be cleansed of impurity. The text provides no clue as to who will construct it, but its consecration is mandatory and must take place before burnt offerings can be placed upon it and blood dashed against it. The sacrificial regulation itself is introduced by the formula, "These are the ordinances for the altar" (v. 18b). But this formula is preceded by Yahweh's direct address to the priest/prophet ("mortal"), followed by the prophetic messenger formula, "thus says the Lord GOD." The presence of the formula for a divine saying ("says the Lord GOD") in vv. 19 and 27 will further reenforce that these ritual regulations are presented as authoritative divine speech.

The regulations themselves are cast in conventional form. The sacro-legal heading cited above (v. 18b; see also Exod 12:43) is followed by the body of the text (vv. 19-27a), which dictates the process by which the altar is to be consecrated (see also Exod 29:36-37). This, in turn, is followed by a summary of how the consecrated altar will function in the future (v. 27b).[1373] Ritual regulations routinely open in the second person, then shift to the third person. Such is not the case here: vv. 19-21a, 22a, 23-24a, and 25a are second person singular addresses to Ezekiel; v. 21b uses the third person singular; vv. 22b, 24b, and 25b-27b employ the third person plural; in v. 27c, Yahweh speaks in the first person singular, "I." While some critics have emended the suffixes to read the third person plural throughout, it is better to assume several agents in the consecration process, including both Ezekiel and the officiating priests.[1374]

The reader is perhaps surprised to discover that Ezekiel will take part in the consecration ritual. Critics who believe that Ezekiel was denied the privilege of serving in the Jerusalem Temple because he was deported in "the [his] thirtieth year"—the age at which Levite males began their sanctuary service (see the Commentary on 1:1-3)—discern here a compensation of sorts. In any event, a comparison of this text with the altar purification ceremony in Exodus 29 strongly suggests that Ezekiel is depicted as assuming the role of Moses—is, in effect, a new Moses. According to v. 19, he must acquire a young bull of the herd for a purification offering (see the Commentary on 40:38-43 for a discussion of the purification [NIV and NRSV, "sin"] offering). This he gives to the levitical priests descended from Zadok, identified as those who "draw near to me to serve [NIV and NRSV, "minister to"] me." The singling out of priests of Zadokite descent reminds readers of 40:46, where the distinction between these priests and other levitical priests appeared for the first time in the book.

Ezekiel also must take some of the bull's blood and place it not only upon the four horns of the altar (as in Lev 16:18), but also upon the four corners of its (upper) ledge (or, perhaps, the four sides of its wall)[1375] and its rim all around (v. 20). The application of this "ritual detergent," as J. Milgrom calls the blood,[1376] will purge the altar and "atone" (כפר kippēr) for it. The idea of "atoning" for an object strikes moderns as strange, but the term must be understood correctly. The root's primary meaning is "to rub off, wipe"; in this context, it refers to the removal of impurity accruing to the altar. Only at a later, abstract stage of its development does it assume the meaning "atone, expiate."[1377] Verse 21 specifies that Ezekiel ("you") must take the bull selected for the purification offering, which will then be burned (presumably by a designated person; see Lev 16:27-28) at an appointed area outside the sanctuary (מקדש miqdāš; heretofore in Ezekiel's final vision, the Temple has been called "house").

On the second day of the consecration ritual, Ezekiel must offer, also as a purification offering, an unblemished (תמים tāmîm) male goat. When this purging ritual is completed (v. 22), he must then offer an unblemished bull and ram as whole burnt offerings. (On the whole burnt offering [עולה 'ôlâ], see the Commentary on 40:38-43; Lev 16:18-19 also describes the purification of the altar by means of the blood of two animals, a bull and a goat. In that context, however, both are

1373. Rolf Rendtorff, *Die Gesetze in der Priesterschrift,* FRLANTT 44 (Göttingen: Vandenhoeck & Ruprecht, 1954) 12; Block, *Ezekiel 25–48,* 605.

1374. So also Block, *Ezekiel 25–48,* 605.

1375. Ibid., 608.

1376. J. Milgrom, *Leviticus 1–16,* AB 3 (New York: Doubleday, 1991) 254.

1377. Ibid., 1079-84.

offered on the same day, and Aaron not only applies the blood of each to the horns of the altar, but also sprinkles the rest of the blood on the altar seven times with his finger.) Ezekiel is told to present them to Yahweh; however, v. 24*b* states that the priests both salt the meat and offer it up to God. Readers recalling the whole burnt offering legislation in Leviticus 1 realize that it says nothing about salt, though Lev 2:13 demands that grain offerings be salted. The present reference to salt reminds one of the so-called "everlasting covenant of salt" (NIV) referred to in Num 18:19 (see also 2 Chr 13:5). Salt was, of course, an important preservative in Israel's ancient Near Eastern world, and so an apt symbol for the perrmanence of the covenant relationship between Yahweh and Israel.

In contradiction to v. 22, which states that the purification ritual ends on the second day, vv. 25-26 speak of a seven-day purification process. Zimmerli, who views these verses as a secondary expansion, finds here an attempt to bring Ezekiel into line with the "P" (priestly) pentateuchal source, which legislates a seven-day altar consecration in Exod 29:37.[1378] According to v. 25, Ezekiel must prepare a goat as a purification offering, and the priests must prepare an unblemished bull and ram. At the end of seven days, the purging of the altar is completed. It has been atoned for, cleansed, and consecrated. The Hebrew idiom

underlying "consecrated," literally "to fill the hand(s)," is most often used to refer to the ordination of persons, especially priests. It may reflect the practice of giving a token payment upon assuming an office, or it may be a symbol of the office. Nowhere else in Scripture is it used of the consecration of the cultic object.[1379]

From the eighth day onward, the priests will offer upon the altar the people's (note the switch to second-person plural ["your"] address) sacrifices (v. 27). Two frequently paired types of sacrifices are mentioned in this context: the burnt offering, which is completely consumed on the altar hearth; and the well-being sacrifices (שלמם *šĕlāmîm*), which are eaten by the people. According to Lev 7:11-18, the latter category consists of thanksgiving sacrifices (תודה *tôdâ*), vow sacrifices (נדר *neder*), which were offered upon the fulfillment of a vow, and freewill offerings (נדבה *nĕdābâ*), which were offered at any time as spontaneous expressions of joy.[1380] One imagines that the Temple's outer court provided an enjoyable social environment for persons with sufficient resources to bring such offerings. Chapter 43 ends with Yahweh's promise to accept "you" (the people, and not just their sacrifices!), followed by the signatory formula. (See Reflections at 46:19-24.)

1378. Zimmerli, *Ezekiel 2*, 435.

1379. See Block, *Ezekiel 25–48*, 611.
1380. See Milgrom, *Leviticus 1–16*, 117-25.

Ezekiel 44:1-3, The Outer East Gate Is Shut

NIV

44 Then the man brought me back to the outer gate of the sanctuary, the one facing east, and it was shut. ²The LORD said to me, "This gate is to remain shut. It must not be opened; no one may enter through it. It is to remain shut because the LORD, the God of Israel, has entered through it. ³The prince himself is the only one who may sit inside the gateway to eat in the presence of the LORD. He is to enter by way of the portico of the gateway and go out the same way."

NRSV

44 Then he brought me back to the outer gate of the sanctuary, which faces east; and it was shut. ²The LORD said to me: This gate shall remain shut; it shall not be opened, and no one shall enter by it; for the LORD, the God of Israel, has entered by it; therefore it shall remain shut. ³Only the prince, because he is a prince, may sit in it to eat food before the LORD; he shall enter by way of the vestibule of the gate, and shall go out by the same way.

COMMENTARY

Verse 1 is cast in the familiar language of Ezekiel's temple tour. "He"—the referent is not stated—brings Ezekiel back to the outer east gate of the sanctuary, where his tour began (40:6-23) and through which Yahweh's glory entered the Temple (43:1-5).[1381] The prophet-priest observes that the gate is closed. It must remain closed, the Lord insists; it will not be opened. No human being (including the priests) can pass through the east gate because "Yahweh, the God of Israel," has entered through it. As a consequence, it must remain closed to humans (note the emphatic repetition of this demand). This permanently closed gate testifies to Yahweh's determination to be present with God's people forever (see 43:7, 9). The disastrous departure of Yahweh's glory, recounted in 11:22-23, will not be repeated. With v. 2, the outer east gate is a "gate" no longer. Commentators detect in these verses a polemic against pagan practices. The Babylonian *akitu* (New Year) festival (see the Commentary on 40:1) included a ritual "opening of the gate" (*pît bâbi*). This sacred gate (*babu ellu*) apparently remained closed to all human commerce throughout the year, save for the period when the god Marduk

would exit, and later return, through it.[1382] But Yahweh requires no human assistance in entering the Temple, and God's glory will never again leave the sanctuary.

Verse 3 permits access to (but not through) the gate to one person, the "prince" (נָשִׂיא *nāsîʾ*). Critics express surprise that this figure should emerge so unexpectedly and without introduction. Sequential readers, however, recall that a prince was promised in two salvation oracles (Ezek 34:23; 37:24-25), so his appearance is not totally unexpected. We shall return to this figure when the text does so (see 45:21–46:12). Here, we simply are told that the prince, by virtue of his office, is permitted to sit in the gate when consuming sacrificial meals before Yahweh. The former gate has become his royal dining room! He must enter and exit the gate's inner vestibule after accessing the outer court by means of one of the two remaining gates. He has no access to the inner court. How different is his role from that played by King Solomon in 1 Kings 6–8! Solomon oversees the building of his Temple, a royal cultic site. He offers the dedicatory prayer before the altar, blesses the assembly, and he himself offers sacrifices. Ezekiel's prince does none of these things. (See Reflections at 46:19-24.)

1381. According to the MT, Yahweh speaks to Ezekiel (v. 2), so readers may conclude that God is the guide of v. 1.

1382. See Zimmerli, *Ezekiel 2*, 440-41; Block, *Ezekiel 25–48*, 615.

Ezekiel 44:4-31, Regulations Governing Temple Service

NIV	NRSV
⁴Then the man brought me by way of the north gate to the front of the temple. I looked and saw the glory of the LORD filling the temple of the LORD, and I fell facedown. ⁵The LORD said to me, "Son of man, look carefully, listen closely and give attention to everything I tell you concerning all the regulations regarding the temple of the LORD. Give attention to the entrance of the temple and all the exits of the sanctuary. ⁶Say to the rebellious house of Israel, 'This is what the Sovereign LORD says: Enough of your detestable practices, O house of Israel! ⁷In addition to all your other detestable	⁴Then he brought me by way of the north gate to the front of the temple; and I looked, and lo! the glory of the LORD filled the temple of the LORD; and I fell upon my face. ⁵The LORD said to me: Mortal, mark well, look closely, and listen attentively to all that I shall tell you concerning all the ordinances of the temple of the LORD and all its laws; and mark well those who may be admitted to*a* the temple and all those who are to be excluded from the sanctuary. ⁶Say to the rebellious house,*b* to the house of Israel, Thus says the Lord GOD: O house of Israel, let there be an end
	*a*Cn: Heb *the entrance of* *b*Gk: Heb lacks *house*

NIV

practices, you brought foreigners uncircumcised in heart and flesh into my sanctuary, desecrating my temple while you offered me food, fat and blood, and you broke my covenant. [8]Instead of carrying out your duty in regard to my holy things, you put others in charge of my sanctuary. [9]This is what the Sovereign LORD says: No foreigner uncircumcised in heart and flesh is to enter my sanctuary, not even the foreigners who live among the Israelites.

[10]" 'The Levites who went far from me when Israel went astray and who wandered from me after their idols must bear the consequences of their sin. [11]They may serve in my sanctuary, having charge of the gates of the temple and serving in it; they may slaughter the burnt offerings and sacrifices for the people and stand before the people and serve them. [12]But because they served them in the presence of their idols and made the house of Israel fall into sin, therefore I have sworn with uplifted hand that they must bear the consequences of their sin, declares the Sovereign LORD. [13]They are not to come near to serve me as priests or come near any of my holy things or my most holy offerings; they must bear the shame of their detestable practices. [14]Yet I will put them in charge of the duties of the temple and all the work that is to be done in it.

[15]" 'But the priests, who are Levites and descendants of Zadok and who faithfully carried out the duties of my sanctuary when the Israelites went astray from me, are to come near to minister before me; they are to stand before me to offer sacrifices of fat and blood, declares the Sovereign LORD. [16]They alone are to enter my sanctuary; they alone are to come near my table to minister before me and perform my service.

[17]" 'When they enter the gates of the inner court, they are to wear linen clothes; they must not wear any woolen garment while ministering at the gates of the inner court or inside the temple. [18]They are to wear linen turbans on their heads and linen undergarments around their waists. They must not wear anything that makes them perspire. [19]When they go out into the outer court where the people are, they are to take off the clothes they have been ministering in and are to leave them in the sacred rooms, and put on

NRSV

to all your abominations [7]in admitting foreigners, uncircumcised in heart and flesh, to be in my sanctuary, profaning my temple when you offer to me my food, the fat and the blood. You[a] have broken my covenant with all your abominations. [8]And you have not kept charge of my sacred offerings; but you have appointed foreigners[b] to act for you in keeping my charge in my sanctuary.

[9]Thus says the Lord GOD: No foreigner, uncircumcised in heart and flesh, of all the foreigners who are among the people of Israel, shall enter my sanctuary. [10]But the Levites who went far from me, going astray from me after their idols when Israel went astray, shall bear their punishment. [11]They shall be ministers in my sanctuary, having oversight at the gates of the temple, and serving in the temple; they shall slaughter the burnt offering and the sacrifice for the people, and they shall attend on them and serve them. [12]Because they ministered to them before their idols and made the house of Israel stumble into iniquity, therefore I have sworn concerning them, says the Lord GOD, that they shall bear their punishment. [13]They shall not come near to me, to serve me as priest, nor come near any of my sacred offerings, the things that are most sacred; but they shall bear their shame, and the consequences of the abominations that they have committed. [14]Yet I will appoint them to keep charge of the temple, to do all its chores, all that is to be done in it.

[15]But the levitical priests, the descendants of Zadok, who kept the charge of my sanctuary when the people of Israel went astray from me, shall come near to me to minister to me; and they shall attend me to offer me the fat and the blood, says the Lord GOD. [16]It is they who shall enter my sanctuary, it is they who shall approach my table, to minister to me, and they shall keep my charge. [17]When they enter the gates of the inner court, they shall wear linen vestments; they shall have nothing of wool on them, while they minister at the gates of the inner court, and within. [18]They shall have linen turbans on their heads, and linen undergarments on their loins; they shall not bind themselves with anything that causes sweat. [19]When they go out into the outer court to the

[a]Gk Syr Vg: Heb *They*   [b]Heb lacks *foreigners*

NIV

other clothes, so that they do not consecrate the people by means of their garments.

20 " 'They must not shave their heads or let their hair grow long, but they are to keep the hair of their heads trimmed. 21No priest is to drink wine when he enters the inner court. 22They must not marry widows or divorced women; they may marry only virgins of Israelite descent or widows of priests. 23They are to teach my people the difference between the holy and the common and show them how to distinguish between the unclean and the clean.

24 " 'In any dispute, the priests are to serve as judges and decide it according to my ordinances. They are to keep my laws and my decrees for all my appointed feasts, and they are to keep my Sabbaths holy.

25 " 'A priest must not defile himself by going near a dead person; however, if the dead person was his father or mother, son or daughter, brother or unmarried sister, then he may defile himself. 26After he is cleansed, he must wait seven days. 27On the day he goes into the inner court of the sanctuary to minister in the sanctuary, he is to offer a sin offering for himself, declares the Sovereign LORD.

28 " 'I am to be the only inheritance the priests have. You are to give them no possession in Israel; I will be their possession. 29They will eat the grain offerings, the sin offerings and the guilt offerings; and everything in Israel devoted*a* to the LORD will belong to them. 30The best of all the firstfruits and of all your special gifts will belong to the priests. You are to give them the first portion of your ground meal so that a blessing may rest on your household. 31The priests must not eat anything, bird or animal, found dead or torn by wild animals.

a29 The Hebrew term refers to the irrevocable giving over of things or persons to the LORD.

NRSV

people, they shall remove the vestments in which they have been ministering, and lay them in the holy chambers; and they shall put on other garments, so that they may not communicate holiness to the people with their vestments. 20They shall not shave their heads or let their locks grow long; they shall only trim the hair of their heads. 21No priest shall drink wine when he enters the inner court. 22They shall not marry a widow, or a divorced woman, but only a virgin of the stock of the house of Israel, or a widow who is the widow of a priest. 23They shall teach my people the difference between the holy and the common, and show them how to distinguish between the unclean and the clean. 24In a controversy they shall act as judges, and they shall decide it according to my judgments. They shall keep my laws and my statutes regarding all my appointed festivals, and they shall keep my sabbaths holy. 25They shall not defile themselves by going near to a dead person; for father or mother, however, and for son or daughter, and for brother or unmarried sister they may defile themselves. 26After he has become clean, they shall count seven days for him. 27On the day that he goes into the holy place, into the inner court, to minister in the holy place, he shall offer his sin offering, says the Lord GOD.

28This shall be their inheritance: I am their inheritance; and you shall give them no holding in Israel; I am their holding. 29They shall eat the grain offering, the sin offering, and the guilt offering; and every devoted thing in Israel shall be theirs. 30The first of all the first fruits of all kinds, and every offering of all kinds from all your offerings, shall belong to the priests; you shall also give to the priests the first of your dough, in order that a blessing may rest on your house. 31The priests shall not eat of anything, whether bird or animal, that died of itself or was torn by animals.

COMMENTARY

Ezekiel's rules governing Temple service are long and complex. Reading them may well stretch the patience of modern readers almost to the breaking point. But they are crucial to the ideal cult Ezekiel envisions. No doubt, they are the product of much theological reflection. But they do not demand that participants engage in such *reflection*. Rather, they legislate *actions* both prescribed and proscribed. Throughout, Ezekiel appears in the guise of a new Moses whose Temple torah is fully authorized by Yahweh.

44:4-6a. Zimmerli observes that 44:4-5 performs double duty. On the one hand, these verses introduce the ordinances and instructions in 43:6-31. On the other hand, they also introduce the larger series of divine regulations which continues through 46:24. The verses are, in his opinion, an addition inserted by a member of Ezekiel's school who (rather clumsily) produced a pastiche of earlier verses in order to emphasize the full authority of the divine ordinances that follow.[1383] His judgment may well be correct. Nevertheless the late exilic reader attempts to make sense of the text as is, and within its literary context. In fact, vv. 4-5 function as a pivot. Until this point in the vision, Ezekiel has been called to focus attention upon everything his guide *shows* him (40:4); now, he is told to focus attention upon everything Yahweh *tells* him (44:5). Said differently, within these two verses attention turns from the *visual* revelation of Yahweh's glory filling the Temple (v. 4) to God's *aural* revelation in the form of ordinances and instructions concerning access to the Temple and its personnel (v. 5).[1384]

Because the east gate can no longer be traversed by humans, "he" (the guide/surveyor? Yahweh?) leads Ezekiel from the outer east gate to the front of the Temple by way of the north gate. Ezekiel looks and, with language echoing 43:5, sees that the Temple is suffused with the glory of Yahweh. As in 1:28 and 43:3, the priest-prophet responds by falling on his face (v. 4b). Readers might well wonder why the theophany recorded so clearly in 43:1-6 reappears here in an abridged edition. Did Ezekiel twice witness Yahweh's glory

fill the Temple? That "solution" seems implausible. More likely, this verse, coupled with vv. 5-6a, functions to authorize what follows, as Zimmerli perceived. Block finds in them a "mini-recommissioning" of Ezekiel, reminiscent of the first, which underscores both his divinely-bestowed authority and the significance of the ordinances and instructions to follow.[1385] As in the first commissioning, Ezekiel witnesses the vision of Yahweh's glory, is addressed by God as "mortal," and then is urged to hear what God will say to him. On the earlier occasion, he was ordered to consume a scroll containing words of lamentation, mourning, and woe (2:10). Here, he is to listen intently to all the ordinances of Yahweh's Temple and all its instructions, marking well those permitted entrance to the Temple, and those denied access. (The verse recalls 43:11, where Ezekiel's guide commands him to make known to the house of Israel "the plan of the temple, its arrangement, its exits and its entrances, and its whole form—all its ordinances and its entire plan and all its laws.") Verse 5 recalls 40:4: "The man said to me, 'Mortal, look closely and listen attentively, and set your mind upon all that I shall show you, for you were brought here in order that I might show it to you; declare all that you see to the house of Israel.' " But in this text, Yahweh, not the guide, is the speaker; and this too contributes to one's sense of the authority of subsequent legislation. According to v. 6a, Ezekiel will be commissioned to speak to the "rebellious [house], the house of Israel." This characterization of the Israelites also links these verses to Ezekiel's initial commissioning, when Yahweh sent him to "the people of Israel, to a nation of rebels who have rebelled against me" (2:3; see also 2:5-6, 8; 3:9, 26-27; 17:12; 24:3).

44:6b-10. The messenger formula ("Thus says the Lord GOD") signals the full authority of the following utterance, while the emphatic idiom, "Enough!" (רב־לכם *rab-lākem*; NRSV, "let there be an end to"), leads readers to expect an outbreaking of divine exasperation/wrath. With these words, Korah, Dathan, and Abiram initiated their challenge to any priestly prerogatives claimed by the Levites (Num 16:3). Using this same idiom,

1383. Zimmerli, *Ezekiel 2*, 444-45.
1384. Block, *Ezekiel 25–48*, 618-19.

1385. Ibid., 620.

Moses refuted their challenge, now cast as an attempt by the Levites to usurp the prerogatives of the Aaronide priesthood (Num 16:7). The rebels paid the ultimate price for their revolt, as did their families (Num 16:31-33). Deuteronomy 3:26 also employs this idiom when recounting God's angry response to Moses' request to enter the land beyond the Jordan River. This is strong language, and so both audience and reader take notice.

The cause of Yahweh's anger is all of the abominations of *the house of Israel*. The noun תוֹעֵבָה (*tôʿēbâ*), "abomination," appears frequently in the book of Ezekiel and refers to a variety of sins, including moral sins. Often, however, it pertains to cultic offenses; and such is the case here. In the past the Israelites permitted foreigners (בְּנֵי־נֵכָר *bĕnê-nēkar*; lit., "sons of foreignness") to perform guard duty for them in Yahweh's sanctuary (elsewhere, Ezekiel employs the plural noun זָרִים [*zarîm*] to refer to foreign nations; here, he refers not to nations, but to non-Israelites who, to his mind, are not fit to engage in cultic activity of any sort). These foreigners are described as "uncircumcised in heart and flesh." "Uncircumcised" is used literally in the second instance, figuratively in the first. On the literal level, the uncircumcised male is excluded from Yahweh's covenant community. Moreover, he is polluted, since circumcision was thought to remove impurity. Hence, the presence of uncircumcised foreigners pollutes Yahweh's Temple—a crucial concern of Ezekiel 40–48, which everywhere seeks to structure a society in which divine holiness cannot be violated. On the figurative level, the circumcised heart is open and obedient to God; the uncircumcised heart is stubborn and disobedient. So, for example, Deut 10:16 urges the Israelites to circumcise the foreskin of their hearts and be stubborn no longer; and Jer 4:4 enjoins the people of Judah to "remove the foreskin of your hearts" (NRSV), that is, to repent of their sins and submit to God's will.

The foreigners illicitly functioning as sanctuary guards polluted Yahweh's Temple in Jerusalem when God's food, that is, the fat and the blood of the sacrificial victim, were offered upon the altar. The reference to God's food suggests that these foreigners participated in ritual offerings—a flagrant violation of laws prohibiting laypersons from performing the sacred functions of the priests and Levites, lest they be killed by those guarding the sanctuary (Num 1:51; 3:10, 38-18:7). One might expect that the supervising priests especially would be blamed here. However, Ezekiel emphasizes that these are abominations of the *entire house of Israel*. As a consequence of permitting foreigners to participate in the cult, the Israelites have broken their covenant with Yahweh. The tone is grave indeed. Note, however, that nothing is said of punishing these interlopers in the future. Ezekiel apparently is not interested in pursuing punishment in this context. He is, rather, concerned to prevent any future defilement of Yahweh's sanctuary.

Scholars have questioned who these foreigners might have been. Obvious candidates are the people of Canaanite Gibeon, whom Joshua appointed to be "hewers of wood and drawers of water for the congregation and for the altar of the Lord, to continue to this day, in the place that he should choose" (Josh 9:27, NRSV). Other candidates include the Nethinim, "temple servants," identified in Ezra 2:43-54, whose names are predominantely non-Israelite, the descendants of Solomon's servants, identified in Ezra 2:55-57, and the Carites, mercenaries who served as members of the royal guard and whose duties included guarding the king's palace and the Temple (2 Kgs 11:4-8). Certainty eludes us. Interesting, however, is Zimmerli's observation that no mention is made of these foreigners in Ezekiel 8, the visionary account of Temple abominations.[1386]

Verse 9 begins with the messenger formula, again signalling the full authority of the divine regulations to follow. Any foreigner living in Israel's midst who has not become part of the covenant community may not enter the temple precinct. Rather, v. 10*a* states, the Levites [will enter] and serve in the Temple. This is the first reference to "the Levites" (the descendants of Levi, one of Jacob's 12 sons, Gen 34: 25-30; 49:5) as opposed to "the levitical priests," in the book of Ezekiel. Their responsibilities and restrictions are identified in vv. 11-14.

1386. Zimmerli, *Ezekiel 2*, 454.

❖   ❖   ❖   ❖

EXCURSUS: ARE THE LEVITES PUNISHED OR RESTORED IN EZEKIEL 44:10-14?

Before turning to vv. 11-14, we should recognize at the outset that the interpretation of Ezek 44:10-14 has played a crucial role in a major conundrum in biblical studies. At issue are answers to the following questions: what is the history of the Levites? Are they, on account of former iniquity, being demoted from full-fledged priests to secondary temple personnel? And are the temple tasks assigned to them a punishment for that iniquity? Traditionally, scholars have answered these questions affirmatively, accepting Julius Wellhausen's hypothesis that certain Levites who once functioned as priests here receive, as punishment for offenses they committed at Israel's high places (on illicit cultic activity on the "high places," see the Commentary on 6:1-7 and 20:27-31), a role subordinate to that of the Zadokite priests.[1387]

Wellhausen noted the apparent discrepancy between the priestly pentateuchal account of the subordination of the Levites on one hand, and Ezek 44:6-16 on the other. According to P, Aaron and his sons alone among the Levites were set apart to serve as priests. But Yahweh gave the Levites to Aaron and his sons as a "gift, dedicated to the Lord, to perform the service of the tent of meeting" (Num 18:6 NRSV). Their tasks included assembling and disassembling the tabernacle as Israel wandered in the wilderness, transporting the ark of the covenant, serving guard duty lest the tabernacle be profaned, and performing certain other duties of the cultic site. The Levites were *denied* access to the tabernacle's utensils, altar (Num 18:30), and holy of holies (Num 18:7). Should Aaron and his sons fail to guard these *sacra* from the Levites, they would perish right along with them. From this perspective the Levites play a role subordinate to the officiating priests, but their tasks are honorable, essential, and not a punishment in any sense.

The estimation of the Levites in Ezekiel 44 was, to Wellhausen's mind, very different from that of P. Wellhausen viewed vv. 10-14 through the lens of his understanding of Josiah's Reformation, with its destruction of the high places and centralization of worship at the Temple in Jerusalem (2 Kgs 23:1-27). In this regard, he believed that Deut 18:6-8 and 2 Kgs 23:8-9 provided important interpretive clues. The Deuteronomy passage describes circumstances ostensibly pertaining after the high places were abolished. The Levites, who had officiated at these illicit sites, were to be permitted to serve in the Jerusalem Temple should they wish to do so. 2 Kings 23:8-9 suggests, however, that the Levites were in fact rejected: "He [Josiah] brought all the priests out of the towns of Judah, and defiled the high places where the priests had made offerings. . . . The priests of the high places, however, did not come up to the altar of the Lord in Jerusalem, but ate unleavened bread among their kindred" (NRSV). As punishment for having presided over the illicit high places, the Levites were demoted from their former priestly status and reduced to inferior cultic service.

Read through the lens of Wellhausen's hypothesis, vv. 10-14 can be understood as a harsh critique of the Levites. So, for example, the NRSV translates v. 10 as follows: "But the Levites who went far from me, going astray from me after their idols when Israel went astray, shall bear their punishment." By this rendering, the *Levites* are depicted as going far away from (i.e., abandoning) Yahweh and straying after *their* idols (גלולים *gillulîm*, "dung pellets") during a period of Israelite apostasy.

Other critics, however, have countered Wellhausen's hypothesis in ways that erode much of its force. Stevenson, for example, offers a translation of v. 10 which takes seriously the syntactical relationship of its clauses:

1387. Julius Wellhausen, *Prolegomena to the History of Ancient Israel* (Gloucester, Mass.: Peter Smith, 1973) 121-51.

> Rather, the Levites who were far from me,[1388]
> when Israel went astray,
> going astray from me after their idols
> shall bear their guilt.[1389]

According to this rendering, it was the *Israelites* who went astray from Yahweh to worship *their* idols. The Levites, who had abandoned Yahweh, bear the guilt of the straying Israelites because they failed to perform their divinely-appointed tasks. The Israelites' apostasy occurred, as it were, on their watch.

The meaning of the phrase "to bear the guilt" (עון נשׂא *nāśā' 'awōn*) is uncertain in this context. According to Milgrom, when the phrase refers to guard duty of the wilderness tabernacle, it has a technical meaning. This meaning is apparent in Num 18:1: "The LORD said to Aaron: You and your sons and your ancestral house [i.e., both priests and Levites] shall bear responsibility [*nāśā' 'awōn*] for offenses connected with the sanctuary, while you and your sons alone [i.e., the priests only] shall bear responsibility for offenses connected with the priesthood" (NRSV). While the Hebrew words are the same, bearing responsibility does not carry in English the same meaning as "bear iniquity" or "bear punishment." The context of this verse is important for construing its meaning in Numbers 18. It appears, Stevenson observes, in P's response to the Korah rebellion cited above. When the earth opened beneath the feet of the rebels and their families, the Israelites fled for fear that the earth might swallow them as well. Moreover, fire from Yahweh consumed the two hundred and fifty co-rebels who had attempted to burn incense, a priestly prerogative (Num 16:32-35). God's violent response to their trespass terrified the people, who became afraid to approach the sacred place. Numbers 18:1 (and v. 23; see below) provides a "solution" to this problem. Henceforth, the priests and Levites are held responsible for all illicit access to the sacred space. The goal of this solution, was "to protect the well-being of the community because such intrusion into the holy place threatens the well-being of the whole community."[1390]

According to Num 18:23, "But the Levites shall perform the service of the tent of meeting, and they shall bear responsibility for their own offenses" (NRSV). By this construal, the referent of "their [own]" is the Levites. Milgrom rejects this interpretation, however, arguing that the correct rendering is "the Levites shall bear their [the Israelites'] guilt." In this context, Milgrom's understanding makes a great deal of sense: the Levites function as a "lightning rod to attract God's wrath upon themselves" if the Israelites violate the rules of holiness.[1391]

In the priestly pentateuchal system (Num 17:27–18:7, 23), then, the Levites bear responsibility for guarding the sanctuary, thereby preventing the people from violating rules of access and holiness. If they fail to do so, then they (the Levites) bear responsibility for the Israelites' infractions. If this technical meaning is intended in Ezekiel 44 as well, then the issue is not punishing of the Levites for past failures while serving at the cultic high places (about which nothing is said here), but the Levites' responsibility to fulfill their honorable tasks in the areas of the temple precinct to which they have access. Milgrom's argument would make perfect sense here, were it not for the references to the Levites being (or "going") far from Yahweh when the Israelites went astray after idols (v. 10), and to the Levites serving the Israelites before idols, which were a stumbling block to Israel (v. 12). These references cannot simply be ignored; they speak negatively of the Levites of the past. Hence, the phrase "they shall bear their guilt" is polyvalent. It not only carries the technical cultic meaning identified by Milgrom, but also points an accusing

---

1388. Stevenson, *The Vision of Transformation*, 73, contends that the verb רחק (*rāḥaq*) should be translated statively (i.e., expressing a condition or state) rather than as an active verb; hence, "who were," rather than "who went."

1389. Ibid., 74.

1390. Ibid., 70-71.

1391. J. Milgrom, *Studies in Levitical Terminology, I: The Encroacher and the Levite: The Term 'Aboda* (Berkeley: University of California Press, 1970) 31.

finger at the Levites.[1392] Nevertheless, I find no evidence that the temple complex responsibilities allotted them in vv. 11-14 are "punishment" for those past failures. To the contrary, these verses reinstate the Levites as privileged temple servants whose status is only one step below that of the Zadokite priests.

1392. Block assumes that the phrase must either be understood in the technical sense identified by Milgrom or in its "normal sense": "For their own failure to guard the house against encroachment, the Levites will experience Yahweh's punishment." See Block, *Ezekiel 25–48*, 629. I would argue, however, that this is not an either/or situation. The phrase can bear both meanings.

❖   ❖   ❖   ❖

44:11-14. These verses assign the Levites responsibilities in the ideal temple of Ezekiel's vision. On the one hand, the Levites serve (שׁרת *šārat*) as armed guards of the gates of the temple complex,[1393] protecting them from illicit entry and consequent pollution. On the other hand, they serve (*šrt*) the people, preparing their burnt offerings and other sacrifices.[1394] Here, Rodney Duke detects an Ezekielian innovation, for this regulation is more restrictive than those in P which permit laypersons to slaughter, flay, and wash their own sacrifices before the priests place them upon the altar (see, e.g., Lev 1:5-6, 9).[1395] In Ezekiel 44, laypersons are indeed "demoted," because they are barred from the inner court where the altar stands; and the Levites, who also are banned from the inner court, slaughter and prepare the people's sacrificial victims for them. Verse 12, with its initial "because," likewise points an accusing finger at the Levites for past failures, but its translation also is disputed. At issue once again are the referents to the third person masculine plural suffixes. Like Stevenson, I understand the verse to say that because they (the Levites) served them (the Israelites) before their (the Israelites') idols,[1396] which were a stumbling block for them (the Israelites), therefore, Yahweh lifted "his" hand upon/against them (the Levites) and they (the

Levites) bore their (the Israelites') guilt.[1397] But again, the Levites are not absolved of guilt. The phrase "they shall bear their guilt" not only carries the technical meaning identified by Milgrom, but also criticizes the Levites, because they served the Israelites before their idols.

Verse 13*a* forbids the Levites from performing priestly tasks, as does the priestly legislation in Num 18:3. They cannot approach Yahweh to serve as priests, and they are denied access to Yahweh's holy things/areas and the things that are most holy/holy of holies.[1398] But the denial of these priestly duties is no punishment inflicted upon demoted ex-priests. It simply rules out any possibility that the Levites might enter the inner court and participate in altar sacrifice.

Verse 13*b* identifies two consequences of the Levites' past actions. On the one hand, they will bear shame (כלמה *kĕlimmâ*). This concept should, as Block correctly observes, be interpreted not in the context of judgment, but in the context of restoration.[1399] Elsewhere in Ezekiel, shame and humiliation are only experienced when wrongdoers have been restored by Yahweh (see 16:53-54, 60-63; 20:39-44; 36:31-32; 39:25-26; 43:10-11). In Ezek 16:61, for example, Jerusalem—Yahweh's unfaithful wife—experiences shame when Yahweh remembers her and establishes with her an everlasting covenant (see the Commentary on Ezekiel 16). In Ezek 36:31-32, the restored house of Israel is ordered to self-loathing, shame, and dismay on account of its iniquities and abominable deeds. On the other hand, they will bear "their"

1393. The Hebrew פקדות (*pĕquddôt*) "armed guards," appeared in 9:1 to designate the armed guards (NRSV, "executioners") commissioned by Yahweh to slay those in Jerusalem who had defiled the Temple—indeed, the city as a whole.
1394. Milgrom states that the verb שׁרת (*šārat*) can have several cultic meanings: "Thus priests 'officiate' (in which case the direct object is rarely used), whereas Levites 'guard' the Tabernacle and 'assist' the laity and the priesthood (the direct object always being used.) In any case, the usual translation 'minister' . . . is inadequate." See Milgrom, *Studies in Levitical Terminology*, 67.
1395. Rodney Duke, "Punishment or Restoration? Another Look at the Levites of Ezekiel 44.6-16," *JSOT* 40 (1988) 68-69.
1396. Kalinda Rose Stevenson, *The Vision of Transformation: The Territorial Rhetoric of Ezekiel 40–48*, SBLDS 154 (Atlanta: Scholars Press, 1996) 67-68, 73-74.

1397. The phrase "to lift up the hand" with the preposition על (*'al*) appears nowhere else in the HB. Traditionally, it is understood either as a divine oath or as a jesture of judgment. But it can be construed not as a future punishment upon the Levites, but as "a negative action that has already taken place, that is, the exile." Duke, "Punishment or Restoration?" 69.
1398. See Stevenson, *The Vision of Transformation*, 75.
1399. D. I. Block, *The Book of Ezekiel: Chapters 25–48*, NICOT (Grand Rapids: Eerdmans, 1998) 632.

abominations. Again, the pronoun's referent is not absolutely clear. If the abominations in view were committed by the Levites, then the consequences of them are indeed theirs to bear. However, the most recent reference to "abominations" spoke of those committed by the house of Israel (v. 6). This suggests that the abominations are not the Levites' alone, but also include the abominations of the Israelites, who brought foreigners into Yahweh's Temple and strayed after idols. Verse 14, then, positively restates the Levites' responsibilities: they will guard the temple precinct; perform all of its chores; and supervise the activities in the outer court.

44:15-16. Having banned foreigners from the temple complex and assigned the Levites to their appropriate tasks, the text turns next to the highest level of temple personnel, the levitical priests descended from Zadok (the disjunctive ו [wĕ], prefixed to הכהנים [hakkōhănîm], signals the introduction of new subject matter), a priest in Jerusalem during David's rule (2 Sam 20:25) who supported the ascendancy of Solomon and became the first high priest of Solomon's Temple (1 Kgs 1:41-45; Ezekiel says nothing of a high priest in his Temple vision. Are all Zadokites to be considered equal in rank?). Readers have already encountered references to the Zadokites in 40:46 (where they alone among the descendants of Levi are permitted to offer sacrifices) and 43:19 (where they participate in the consecration of the altar).

In vv. 15-16, the rights and responsibilities of the Zadokite priests are presented in a style that imitates the legislation concerning the Levites in 44:10-14; v. 15 looks *back* to the Zadokites' past (exemplary) behavior, while v. 16 legislates their *future* (exemplary) roles within Ezekiel's idealized cult. In his judgment oracles, Ezekiel was capable of criticizing Israel's priests. In 22:26, he indicted them for numerous failures: "Its priests have done violence to my teaching and have profaned my holy things; they have made no distinction between the holy and the common, neither have they taught the difference between the unclean and the clean, and they have disregarded my sabbaths, so that I am profaned among them" (NRSV). In this context, however, no mention is made of these past offenses. The following regulations will demand that the Zadokites responsibly perform their obligations.

At the time when the people of Israel "went astray" from God (see v. 10), the levitical descendants of Zadok faithfully guarded Yahweh's sanctuary. They alone will draw near to serve Yahweh (The independent personal pronoun המה [hēmmâ] emphasizes that this right belongs to the Zadokites only), and they alone will present to God the fat and blood of the sacrificial victims. (The Levites cannot draw near to serve Yahweh; they stand before the people to serve them.) The Zadokites alone will enter God's sanctuary (i.e., the inner court and temple building), and only they will approach God's table (the altar) to serve God and to purify Yahweh's sanctuary (hēmmâ appears twice in v. 16).

44:17-31. Having established the supremacy of the Zadokites, the text now turns to regulations governing their behavior in all aspects of life, many of which also appear in Leviticus. As priests serving the Holy God, they must themselves be fastidious about maintaining holiness. Verses 17-19 deal with the priests' clothing. When they enter the gates of the inner court, the priests must wear linen vestments. They are not permitted woolen clothing, because such would cause them to sweat; and perspiration, like other bodily emissions, is impure. From turban to undergarments, they must be clothed in linen; and they cannot bind themselves with anything causing perspiration. Before they exit the inner court, the Zadokites must remove their linen vestments in the sacred chambers (referred to in 42:13-14) and don other garments, lest their linen garments transmit holiness to the people. Here again is expressed the belief that holiness is both contagious and dangerous (see the Commentary on 42:13-14).

Verse 20 forbids Zadokite priests from both shaving their heads and allowing their hair to grow long. Neither extreme is acceptable. Leviticus 21:5 prohibits the Aaronide priests from making bald spots on their heads, and also from shaving off the edges of their beards and gashing their flesh. Neither there, nor in this passage, is the rationale for this prohibition provided. One suspects, however, that shaving the head is forbidden because the practice was associated with death, mourning, and lamentation rituals (see Lev 19:27-28). In Ezek 7:18, for example, we read that on the Day of Yahweh, the people of Judah will don sackcloth, and shave their heads (see also Ezek 27:31, which involves sackcloth, shaving, and weeping). Leviticus 13:45 legislates that a leprous person must wear torn clothing, let the hair of his head be disheveled, cover his upper lip, and announce himself with "unclean, unclean." Perhaps the priests are forbidden to grow their hair long lest others suspect that they are unclean.

Verse 21 prohibits priests from drinking wine prior to entering the inner court. The same prohibition, more strongly worded, appears in Lev 10:9: "Drink no wine or strong drink, neither you [Aaron] nor your sons, when you enter the tent of meeting, that you may not die; it is a statute forever throughout your generations" (NRSV). This regulation may reflect a negative reaction to pagan ritual intoxication.[1400] But it may also reflect concern that the priests, if inebriated, might fail fully and perfectly to perform their duties (see Isa 28:7).

Verse 22 specifies that Zadokite priests cannot marry widows or divorcées. Only Israelite virgins (they need not be the daughters of priests) and widows of deceased priests are eligible mates. In Lev 21:7, Aaronide priests are forbidden to marry prostitutes and other "defiled" women, as well as divorcees; and in Lev 21:13-14, they are limited to virgins of their own kin. At issue, according to Lev 21:15, is the prospect that their children might be profaned among their kin.

The Zadokite priests' responsibilities are not limited to officiating in the most sacred areas of the Temple complex. They also bear obligations in the public realm. First, they are to teach Yahweh's laypeople how to distinguish between the holy and the profane, the unclean and the clean. This regulation addresses a deficiency of the pre-exilic priests (Ezek 22:26). Although the people are not permitted acess to the inner court and temple building, they are allowed into the outer court; and they are not irrelevant to the maintenance of holiness in Yahweh's land. Second, the priests must function as judges when controversies arise. Their decisions must meet the highest criteria: they must be in accord with God's own judgments. Third, they must fastidiously keep Yahweh's instruction and statues regarding appointed festivals, and keep God's sabbaths holy (cf. Ezek 22:46).

Verses 25-27 deal with priestly contact with the

dead. Contact with a corpse was thought to be defiling; here, the priests can defile themselves only for deceased blood relatives—father, mother, son, daughter, brother, or unmarried sister (so also Lev 21:1-3). Nothing is said of contact with a deceased wife, but such is ruled out in Lev 21:4: "But he shall not defile himself as a husband among his people and so profane himself" (NRSV). Verses 26-27 describe the process by which a priest defiled by corpse contact resumes his Temple functions. The text is best understood in conjunction with Numbers 19. There, we read that the defiled person is to wash in purification water containing ashes from a red heifer on both the third and the seventh days after contact with a corpse. At the end of that time, he is considered clean. Ezekiel 44:26 specifies that two weeks must pass before a priest resumes his temple responsibilities (v. 26). Upon returning to the Temple, he must immediately present a purification offering. The importance of these regulations concerning the dead is reenforced by the signatory formula "says the Lord GOD."

Verses 28-30 address the issue of the Zadokites' inheritance (נחלה naḥălâ). Yahweh is their inheritance; they shall be given no (land) holding (אחזה 'ăḥuzzâ) in Israel. Yahweh is their holding. The former Hebrew noun often is understood against the background of a familial metaphor: Yahweh is the father, and Israel is his firstborn son.[1401] But another metaphor may also be in view—that of the overlord who grants land holdings to his vassals.[1402] The second term, from the root אחז ('ḥz), "to seize, grasp," refers more broadly to a legal holding. The text recalls not only Josh 13:14 and 18:7, but also Num 18:20, where Yahweh instructs Aaron "You shall not receive as a possession [לא תנחל lōʼ tinḥāl] an allotment in their land, nor shall you have any share among them; I am your share and your possession [naḥălâ] among the Israelites" (NRSV). Because Yahweh is the priests' inheritance, they have access to both Yahweh's Temple and Yahweh's food—that is, the various sacrifices brought to the Temple. Only the whole burnt offering, which is completely consumed

1400. See *Enuma Elish* 3:134-38, in *ANET,* 66.

1401. See J. H. Wright, *God's People in God's Land: Family, Land, and Property in the Old Testament* (Grand Rapids: Eerdmans, 1990) 18-20.
1402. See D. I. Block, *The Gods of the Nations: Studies in Ancient Near National Theology,* Evangelical Theological Society Monograph Series 2 (Winona Lake: Eisenbrauns, 1988) 76-79.

upon the altar, is denied them. They may eat the cereal, purification, and reparation offerings (on these offerings, see the Commentary on 40:38-42). They also may eat every devoted thing. The Hebrew word חרם (ḥērem), "devoted thing" has two different meanings. In the context of holy war, it refers to humans, animals, cities, and objects which are devoted to Yahweh and must be utterly destroyed. In this context, however, it refers to foodstuffs which are dedicated to Yahweh and reserved for consumption by the priests. They also will eat the select grain from the first cutting of the harvest and the first gathering of grapes, olives, and every other crop, and all the gifts (תרומה

těrûmâ) of every kind, all the gifts given to God (see also Num 18:8-20). Finally, the priests shall receive from the people the first (best) of their coarse meal (see Num 15:20-21). The motivation for the people's generosity appears in v. 30b. As a consequence of their gifts, the people will receive a blessing upon their houses. The priestly preroga-tive to pronounce a blessing upon the Israelites appears in Num 6:22-27. Verse 31 forbids the priests from eating any carrion, bird or animal, that dies of natural causes or is killed by beasts. The last proscription is extended to all Israelites in Exod 22:31; Lev 22:8 applies it to the Aaronide priests. (See Reflections at 46:19-24.)

Ezekiel 45:1-9, The Holy Portion

NIV

45 " 'When you allot the land as an inheri-tance, you are to present to the LORD a portion of the land as a sacred district, 25,000 cubits long and 20,000[a] cubits wide; the entire area will be holy. [2]Of this, a section 500 cubits square is to be for the sanctuary, with 50 cubits around it for open land. [3]In the sacred district, measure off a section 25,000 cubits[b] long and 10,000 cubits[c] wide. In it will be the sanctuary, the Most Holy Place. [4]It will be the sacred portion of the land for the priests, who minister in the sanctuary and who draw near to minister before the LORD. It will be a place for their houses as well as a holy place for the sanctuary. [5]An area 25,000 cubits long and 10,000 cubits wide will belong to the Levites, who serve in the temple, as their pos-session for towns to live in.[d]

[6]" 'You are to give the city as its property an area 5,000 cubits wide and 25,000 cubits long, adjoining the sacred portion; it will belong to the whole house of Israel.

[7]" 'The prince will have the land bordering each side of the area formed by the sacred district and the property of the city. It will extend west-ward from the west side and eastward from the east side, running lengthwise from the western to

[a]1 Septuagint (see also verses 3 and 5 and 48:9); Hebrew *10,000* [b]3 That is, about 7 miles (about 12 kilometers) [c]3 That is, about 3 miles (about 5 kilometers) [d]5 Septuagint; Hebrew *temple; they will have as their possession 20 rooms*

NRSV

45 When you allot the land as an inheri-tance, you shall set aside for the LORD a portion of the land as a holy district, twenty-five thousand cubits long and twenty[a] thousand cubits wide; it shall be holy throughout its entire extent. [2]Of this, a square plot of five hundred by five hun-dred cubits shall be for the sanctuary, with fifty cubits for an open space around it. [3]In the holy district you shall measure off a section twenty-five thousand cubits long and ten thousand wide, in which shall be the sanctuary, the most holy place. [4]It shall be a holy portion of the land; it shall be for the priests, who minister in the sanctuary and approach the LORD to minister to him; and it shall be both a place for their houses and a holy place for the sanctuary. [5]Another section, twenty-five thousand cubits long and ten thousand cubits wide, shall be for the Levites who minister at the temple, as their holding for cities to live in.[b]

6Alongside the portion set apart as the holy dis-trict you shall assign as a holding for the city an area five thousand cubits wide, and twenty-five thousand cubits long; it shall belong to the whole house of Israel.

7And to the prince shall belong the land on both sides of the holy district and the holding of the city, alongside the holy district and the hold-ing of the city, on the west and on the east, cor-responding in length to one of the tribal portions,

[a]Gk: Heb *ten*   [b]Gk: Heb *as their holding, twenty chambers*

NIV

the eastern border parallel to one of the tribal portions. [8]This land will be his possession in Israel. And my princes will no longer oppress my people but will allow the house of Israel to possess the land according to their tribes.

[9]" 'This is what the Sovereign LORD says: You have gone far enough, O princes of Israel! Give up your violence and oppression and do what is just and right. Stop dispossessing my people, declares the Sovereign LORD.

NRSV

and extending from the western to the eastern boundary [8]of the land. It is to be his property in Israel. And my princes shall no longer oppress my people; but they shall let the house of Israel have the land according to their tribes.

[9]Thus says the Lord GOD: Enough, O princes of Israel! Put away violence and oppression, and do what is just and right. Cease your evictions of my people, says the Lord GOD.

COMMENTARY

Abruptly and without introduction, the text turns to a future (re)allocation of Israel's land. Unbeknownst to a first-time, sequential reader, Ezek 47:13–48:29 (especially 48:8-22) will return to the same issue and address it at greater length. Zimmerli, among other critics, believes that the author(s) of 45:1-9 knows that sequentially later material and writes under its influence. The text betrays the concern of a later age, which had difficulty reconciling the allotment of land to priests in chapter 48 in the light of 44:28 (which denied them a holding because Yahweh was their inheritance).[1403] Block cannot prove that Ezekiel himself composed the text, but he shows that its present literary setting is appropriate. Verses 1-8a are fully integrated into the torah of the Temple (44:4–46:18); indeed, they appear at the "midpoint" of this unit. Moreover, they function as a hinge between priestly concerns (44:5-31) and princely concerns (45:8b–46:18).[1404]

Verse 1 states that when the Israelites apportion (רום *rûm*) the land as an inheritance (*naḥălâ*; lit., "when you cast the land"; the phrase is an abbreviated version of the fuller, "when you cast the lot" for the land), they shall first reserve a "gift" תרומה (*tĕrûmâ*) for Yahweh—that is, a portion of land of God's own choosing.[1405] According to MT, this

holy district is twenty-five thousand cubits long (from east to west) and ten thousand cubits wide (from north to south). However, the translators of both the NRSV and the NIV, like most scholars, emend MT (also at Ezek 48:9) and read "twenty thousand cubits wide" with the LXX. Their underlying assumption is that the phrase "the holy portion" (תרומת הקדש *tĕrûmat haqqōdeš*), which appears in 45:6, 7 (twice), is synonymous with Yahweh's portion (תרומה ליהוה *tĕrûmâ laYHWH*), which appears only in v. 1. On that assumption, Yahweh's portion consists of *both* the twenty-five thousand by ten thousand cubit strip allocated for the Temple and the Zadokite priests *and also* the twenty-five thousand by ten thousand cubit holding of the Levites. Zimmerli understands the change from "twenty" to "ten" to be "a further tendentious distortion in the interests of the anti-Levitical standpoint: only the priestly land is to be described as holy." To his mind, the LXX preserves the original number.[1406] Stevenson, by contrast, rejects the assumption that the two phrases are synonymous. To her mind, MT preserves the original text, which already distinguished between Yahweh's portion—site of the temple complex, home to the priests, and holy throughout—and the holy portion, which includes *both* Yahweh's portion and the possession of the Levites.[1407]

The issue cannot be resolved with certainty. It is possible that the translators of the LXX did not understand the distinction Stevenson points to and so "corrected" MT. Verse 2 supports Stevenson's

1403. W. Zimmerli, *Ezekiel 2: A Commentary on the Book of the Prophet Ezekiel, Chapters 25–48,* trans. J. D. Martin, Hermeneia (Philadelphia: Fortress, 1983) 467. See also Ronald M. Hals, *Ezekiel,* FOTL 19 (Grand Rapids: Eerdmans, 1989) 323; J. W. Wevers, *Ezekiel,* NCB (London: Nelson, 1969) 324.

1404. Block, *Ezekiel 25–48,* 650.

1405. The noun *tĕrûmâ* appeared twice in 44:30 to refer to the people's gifts to Yahweh which the Zadokites could consume. Block, *Ezekiel 25–48,* 651, observes that Ezekiel's use of the noun to refer to real estate (here and in 48:8-10) is unique.

1406. Zimmerli, *Ezekiel 2,* 468.
1407. Stevenson, *The Vision of Transformation,* 31.

argument: within Yahweh's portion stands the sanctuary complex, measuring five hundred by five hundred cubits (so also 42:20 of the dimensions of its outer wall) and surrounded by a buffer zone of fifty cubits.[1408] But vv. 3-4 support the opposing argument, stating that within the holy district, the people must measure off a section twenty-five thousand cubits long and ten thousand cubits wide. Yahweh's sanctuary, the most holy place, will be located within this space, as will the houses of the priests who serve in the sanctuary and have access to the altar—that is, the Zadokites.

Another area with the same dimensions will be the holding (אחזה 'ăḥuzzâ) of the Levites who serve at the temple complex (v. 5). This area likely lies north of the section described in vv. 3-4. The remainder of v. 5 is difficult: the Hebrew text reads "as their holding, twenty chambers." Scholars generally follow the LXX and emend the MT on the basis of other biblical texts to read "for cities to live in." Numbers 35:2-8 grants the Levites forty-eight cities throughout the land of Israel as "cities to live in," as well as pasture lands for their animals (so also Josh 14:4; 21:41). In Ezekiel's vision, by contrast, the Levites are not scattered across Israel's land. Rather, they are gathered within the Levites' holding. I can offer no better solution than the proposed emendation; but, like Stevenson, I wonder how many cities could fit into an area the size of the Levites' allotment.[1409] Nothing is said of offerings designated for consumption by the Levites.

Verse 6 specifies that alongside (to the south of?) the holy district, the people shall set aside as the holding of the (unnamed) city an area twenty-five thousand (cubits) long from west to east (aproximately eight miles) by five thousand (cubits) wide from north to south (approximately 1.6 miles). This space will belong to the whole house of Israel. Nothing more is said of its function in this context. On the (reasonable) assumption

that "the city" is Jerusalem, readers realize that Ezekiel's Temple complex is not situated within the city (as was Solomon's Temple) but only in proximity to it. Here again, one detects Ezekiel's persistent concern that the holy Temple be protected from impurity.

Verses 7-8a return to the prince who first appeared in Ezekiel's final vision in 44:3. His holding consists of two large pieces of land lying to the east and west of the holy portion and the holding of the city (which together constitute a perfect square twenty-five thousand by twenty-five thousand cubits). Hence, the north-to-south length of each piece of land is twenty-five thousand cubits. Its other boundaries are the Mediterranean Sea to the west, and the Jordan to the east. The reference to "tribal portions" in v. 7 recalls v. 1 and presages the full discussion of tribal holdings in 48:1-29. Why the prince needs so much land will become clearer as the reader works through the remainder of Ezekiel's final vision.

In the Israelite society of Ezekiel's vision, the abuses of past princes will not be repeated (see Ezekiel 19; 21:12). In v. 8, Yahweh mandates that "my princes" shall no longer oppress "my people"; they will permit the house of Israel to occupy their tribal lands. In 1 Sam 8:14, Samuel is said to have warned the Israelites that a king would "take the best of your fields and vineyards and olive orchards and give them to his courtiers" (NRSV). The best-known biblical account of royal confiscation of a tribal holding appears in 1 Kings 21, the story of Naboth, whose vineyard King Ahab coveted. Verse 9 addresses these princes; it begins with the messenger formula ("Thus says the Lord God"), followed by the exclamatory "Enough!" an expression of wrath and exasperation (see the Commentary on 44:6). The princes are to put away violence and oppression, and to do justice (משפט mišpāt) and righteousness (צדקה ṣĕdāqâ). The imperative, "Cease your evictions of my people," is underscored by the concluding formula, "says the Lord GOD." (See Reflections at 46:19-24.)

1408. Zimmerli, Ezekiel 2, 468, regards v. 2 as a later accretion.
1409. Stevenson, The Vision of Transformation, 85.

Ezekiel 45:10-12, Standardized Weights and Measurements

NIV

¹⁰You are to use accurate scales, an accurate ephah[a] and an accurate bath.[b] ¹¹The ephah and the bath are to be the same size, the bath containing a tenth of a homer[c] and the ephah a tenth of a homer; the homer is to be the standard measure for both. ¹²The shekel[d] is to consist of twenty gerahs. Twenty shekels plus twenty-five shekels plus fifteen shekels equal one mina.[e]

[a]10 An ephah was a dry measure.   [b]10 A bath was a liquid measure.   [c]11 A homer was a dry measure.   [d]12 A shekel weighed about 2/5 ounce (about 11.5 grams).   [e]12 That is, 60 shekels; the common mina was 50 shekels.

NRSV

10You shall have honest balances, an honest ephah, and an honest bath.[a] ¹¹The ephah and the bath shall be of the same measure, the bath containing one-tenth of a homer, and the ephah one-tenth of a homer; the homer shall be the standard measure. ¹²The shekel shall be twenty gerahs. Twenty shekels, twenty-five shekels, and fifteen shekels shall make a mina for you.

[a]A Heb measure of volume

COMMENTARY

Having demanded justice and righteousness of Israel's princes, the text turns next to the subject of righteous, that is, honest (צדק ṣedeq) balances, an honest ephah (a dry measurement for grain), and an honest bath (a liquid measurement; see also Lev 19:35-36 and Deut 25:13-16). Because these verses follow on the heels of vv. 8-9, they seem especially, though by no means exclusively, to address Israel's leaders. Again, Ezekiel is concerned that past evils of Israelite society be eliminated from the ideal society he envisions. Without standardized weights and measurements, fraud flourishes in the marketplaces. So, for example, Amos 8:4-6 inveighs against corrupt purveyors who oppress the needy and poor saying: "We will make the ephah small and the shekel great, and practice deceit with false balances, buying the poor for silver and the needy for a pair of sandals, and selling the sweepings of the wheat" (vv. 5b-6,

NRSV). Micah 6:10-11 also indicts those who use scant measures, dishonest scales, and "a bag of dishonest weights" (NRSV; see also Hos 12:8; Prov 11:1).

In Ezek 45:11-14, an attempt is made to equate the size of the ephah and the bath; both are to be one-tenth of a homer, the latter being the standard measure. The word homer, which ultimately derives from "assload," refers to the weight load one donkey could bear, approximately four to six bushels.[1410] (See Reflections at 46:19-24.)

1410. For the complexities of ancient Near Eastern units of measure, see Marvin A. Powell, "Weights and Measures," *ABD* 6:897-908. Verse 12a turns to the weights used with balances. The Hebrew שקל (šeqel) refers to a stone weighing approximately 0.4 ounces (the weight of twenty of the smallest units of weight, called "gerahs"). The remainder of v. 12 in MT is difficult. It possibly calls for a mina of twenty-five plus twenty plus fifteen shekels. The normal number elsewhere in the Hebrew Bible is fifty shekels per mina. But Ezekiel's figuring may reflect the influence of the sexagesimal Babylonian system, according to which the mina consisted of sixty shekels.

Ezekiel 45:13-17, Sacrificial Obligations

NIV

¹³" 'Testing will surely come. And what if the scepter ⌊of Judah⌋, which the sword despises, does not continue? declares the Sovereign LORD.'
¹⁴"So then, son of man, prophesy
   and strike your hands together.

NRSV

13This is the offering that you shall make: one-sixth of an ephah from each homer of wheat, and one-sixth of an ephah from each homer of barley, ¹⁴and as the fixed portion of oil,[a] one-tenth of a

[a]Cn: Heb *oil, the bath the oil*

NIV

Let the sword strike twice,
    even three times.
It is a sword for slaughter—
    a sword for great slaughter,
    closing in on them from every side.
¹⁵So that hearts may melt
    and the fallen be many,
I have stationed the sword for slaughter*ᵃ*
    at all their gates.
Oh! It is made to flash like lightning,
    it is grasped for slaughter.
¹⁶O sword, slash to the right,
    then to the left,
    wherever your blade is turned.
¹⁷I too will strike my hands together,
    and my wrath will subside.
I the LORD have spoken."

ᵃ15 Septuagint; the meaning of the Hebrew for this word is uncertain.

NRSV

bath from each cor (the cor,ᵃ like the homer, contains ten baths); ¹⁵and one sheep from every flock of two hundred, from the pastures of Israel. This is the offering for grain offerings, burnt offerings, and offerings of well-being, to make atonement for them, says the Lord GOD. ¹⁶All the people of the land shall join with the prince in Israel in making this offering. ¹⁷But this shall be the obligation of the prince regarding the burnt offerings, grain offerings, and drink offerings, at the festivals, the new moons, and the sabbaths, all the appointed festivals of the house of Israel: he shall provide the sin offerings, grain offerings, the burnt offerings, and the offerings of well-being, to make atonement for the house of Israel.

ᵃVg: Heb *homer*

COMMENTARY

The information in vv. 10-12 assists readers as the text now turns to the people's gifts for the regular sacrificial offerings (תרומה *tĕrûmâ*). At issue are their grain, oil, and animal contributions. The "tax" consists of one-sixth of an ephah from each homer of wheat (1.5 percent) and one-sixth of an ephah from each homer of barley. it also includes one-tenth of a bath of olive oil from each kor (one percent). The parenthetical information at the end of v. 14 intends, one suspects, to equate the kor with the homer (as does the Vg). As it stands, however, the MT twice states that ten baths equal one homer. The sheep are taxed at one per two hundred, or 0.5 percent. These contributions are for the grain and whole burnt offerings (see the Commentary on 40:38-43), the peace offerings (see the Commentary on 43:18-27), and the libation offerings (olive oil, wine and/or water) to atone for the people.

This section also ends with the formulaic "thus says the Lord God." To it is added information about the prince's role *vis á vis* the people's contribution (vv. 16-17). The people of the land are accountable to him in fulfilling their obligations; the prince, in turn, must provide their offerings to the priests at the national cultic festivals: the new moon festivals; the sabbaths; and all the other appointed observances. He shall provide the purification offerings, the grain offerings, the burnt offerings, and the well-being offerings to make atonement for the house of Israel. These are no small tasks and responsibilities; and readers begin to understand why the prince requires significant tracts of land. (See Reflections at 48:19-24.)

Ezekiel 45:18–46:15, Regulations for National Festivals

OVERVIEW

In 45:17, Ezekiel referred to Israel's national festivals (חגים *ḥaggîm*).[1411] In this section, the priest/prophet sets out regulations governing these festivals. Even so sympathetic a critic as

---

1411. The verb חגג (*ḥgg*) means "to make pilgrimage, keep a pilgrim-feast"; the noun חג (*ḥag*) means "festival-gathering, feast, pilgrim-feast." See *BDB*, 290b).

Block concedes that the literary style is "stiff, if not monotonous."[1412] At issue, however, is the maintenance of cultic purity; and upon that, as we have seen thus far in Ezekiel's final vision, hangs Yahweh's covenant relationship with Israel.

1412. Block, *Ezekiel 25–48*, 660.

EZEKIEL 45:18-20, NEW YEAR'S PURIFICATION

NIV

[18]" 'This is what the Sovereign LORD says: In the first month on the first day you are to take a young bull without defect and purify the sanctuary. [19]The priest is to take some of the blood of the sin offering and put it on the doorposts of the temple, on the four corners of the upper ledge of the altar and on the gateposts of the inner court. [20]You are to do the same on the seventh day of the month for anyone who sins unintentionally or through ignorance; so you are to make atonement for the temple.

NRSV

[18]Thus says the Lord GOD: In the first month, on the first day of the month, you shall take a young bull without blemish, and purify the sanctuary. [19]The priest shall take some of the blood of the sin offering and put it on the doorposts of the temple, the four corners of the ledge of the altar, and the posts of the gate of the inner court. [20]You shall do the same on the seventh day of the month for anyone who has sinned through error or ignorance; so you shall make atonement for the temple.

COMMENTARY

Before turning to these regulations, vv. 18-20*a* describe an otherwise unattested ritual whose purpose is the purification of the sanctuary on the first day of the first month—that is, New Year's day (see the Commentary on 40:1).[1413] One assumes that various activities marked the beginning of the year, but Ezekiel's focus is, predictably, purging the Temple of impurity. Verse 18 states that "you" (Ezekiel?) must take a young bull without blemish (see also 43:20 where "you," ostensibly Ezekiel, participates in the purification/consecration of the altar). The priest ("he") then applies some of its blood (Milgrom's "ritual detergent")[1414] to the

---

1413. Recall that according to Exod 40:2, the wilderness tabernacle was erected on the first day of the first month. The present date may reflect Babylonian influence.
1414. J. Milgrom, *Leviticus 1–16*, AB 3 (New York: Doubleday, 1991) 254.

doorposts of the Temple, the four sides of the ledge of the altar (cf. 43:20), and an unspecified gate of the inner court.[1415] This same procedure is to be repeated on the seventh day of the month,[1416] benefiting persons who have sinned either inadvertently (see Lev 4:13; Num 15:22) or out of ignorance. (Note that nothing is said of persons who sin willfully.) Thus the Temple is purified. Zimmerli believes that Ezekiel's Torah here introduces an *annual* ritual which functions, much like the Day of Atonement in the Mosaic Torah, to cleanse both the sanctuary and the people.[1417] Block sees,

---

1415. Zimmerli, *Ezekiel 2*, 483, reasonably ventures that the east gate is intended.
1416. The LXX reads "on the seventh month on the first day of the month"—i.e., at the beginning of the year's second half.
1417. Zimmerli, *Ezekiel 2*, 482. See also Wevers, *Ezekiel*, 327-28.

rather, a one-time decontamination ritual which is at least analogous to the inaugural purification of the altar described in 43:18-27. He cites similarities between the two texts: in both, for example, Ezekiel ("you") plays a role in the ritual. But that does not, to my mind, mean that the ritual would have been limited to "the lifetime of the prophet."[1418] Given Ezekiel's extraordinary concern to ensure the ongoing purity of the Temple, one would expect an annual ritual of this sort. (See Reflections at 46:19-24.)

1418. Block, *Ezekiel 25-48,* 662, 664.

EZEKIEL 45:21-25, PASSOVER

21 " 'In the first month on the fourteenth day you are to observe the Passover, a feast lasting seven days, during which you shall eat bread made without yeast. ²²On that day the prince is to provide a bull as a sin offering for himself and for all the people of the land. ²³Every day during the seven days of the Feast he is to provide seven bulls and seven rams without defect as a burnt offering to the LORD, and a male goat for a sin offering. ²⁴He is to provide as a grain offering an ephah for each bull and an ephah for each ram, along with a hin^a of oil for each ephah.

²⁵" 'During the seven days of the Feast, which begins in the seventh month on the fifteenth day, he is to make the same provision for sin offerings, burnt offerings, grain offerings and oil.

^a24 That is, probably about 4 quarts (about 4 liters)

21 In the first month, on the fourteenth day of the month, you shall celebrate the festival of the passover, and for seven days unleavened bread shall be eaten. ²²On that day the prince shall provide for himself and all the people of the land a young bull for a sin offering. ²³And during the seven days of the festival he shall provide as a burnt offering to the LORD seven young bulls and seven rams without blemish, on each of the seven days; and a male goat daily for a sin offering. ²⁴He shall provide as a grain offering an ephah for each bull, an ephah for each ram, and a hin of oil to each ephah. ²⁵In the seventh month, on the fifteenth day of the month and for the seven days of the festival, he shall make the same provision for sin offerings, burnt offerings, and grain offerings, and for the oil.

COMMENTARY

Ezekiel turns first to the Passover (הפסח *happāsaḥ*). The story of the original Passover experience, along with instructions regarding its observance, appears in Exod 12:1-28. In order to ward off Yahweh's tenth plague against Egypt (the death of all firstborn males), each Israelite household obtained an unblemished lamb, slaughtered it on the fourteenth day of the first month, and daubed its blood on the doorposts and lintel of their houses in order to ward off Yahweh's deadly presence. That night, they ate the roasted lamb quickly, dressed in traveling clothes (v. 11). According to this account, Passover was to be celebrated privately in the home.

Ezekiel's Passover observance is a public event in which the prince plays an important role; and its purpose is purification. Verse 21 enjoins the Israelites ("you"; 2 m. pl.) to observe passover on the fourteenth day of the first month; for seven days, unleavened bread will be eaten. The prince must supply on his own behalf and on behalf of all the people of the land a young bull for a purification offering (see the Commentary on 40:38-43). Throughout the seven days of the festival he also must provide each day as burnt offerings to Yahweh seven young bulls and rams without blemish, and also a male goat (cf. Exodus 12:13; Num 28:16-25). To these he must add a grain offering (one ephah) for each bull and ram, as well as a hin of oil to every ephah. Verse 25 then speaks briefly of a seven day autumnal festival commencing on the fifteenth day of the seventh month, when the prince must provide these same offerings. (See Reflections at 46:19-24.)

EZEKIEL 46:1-15, GATE REGULATIONS, SACRIFICES, ENTERINGS, AND EXITS

NIV

46 " 'This is what the Sovereign LORD says: The gate of the inner court facing east is to be shut on the six working days, but on the Sabbath day and on the day of the New Moon it is to be opened. ²The prince is to enter from the outside through the portico of the gateway and stand by the gatepost. The priests are to sacrifice his burnt offering and his fellowship offerings.ᵃ He is to worship at the threshold of the gateway and then go out, but the gate will not be shut until evening. ³On the Sabbaths and New Moons the people of the land are to worship in the presence of the LORD at the entrance to that gateway. ⁴The burnt offering the prince brings to the LORD on the Sabbath day is to be six male lambs and a ram, all without defect. ⁵The grain offering given with the ram is to be an ephah,ᵇ and the grain offering with the lambs is to be as much as he pleases, along with a hinᶜ of oil for each ephah. ⁶On the day of the New Moon he is to offer a young bull, six lambs and a ram, all without defect. ⁷He is to provide as a grain offering one ephah with the bull, one ephah with the ram, and with the lambs as much as he wants to give, along with a hin of oil with each ephah. ⁸When the prince enters, he is to go in through the portico of the gateway, and he is to come out the same way.

⁹" 'When the people of the land come before the LORD at the appointed feasts, whoever enters by the north gate to worship is to go out the south gate; and whoever enters by the south gate is to go out the north gate. No one is to return through the gate by which he entered, but each is to go out the opposite gate. ¹⁰The prince is to be among them, going in when they go in and going out when they go out.

¹¹" 'At the festivals and the appointed feasts, the grain offering is to be an ephah with a bull, an ephah with a ram, and with the lambs as much as one pleases, along with a hin of oil for each ephah. ¹²When the prince provides a freewill offering to the LORD—whether a burnt offering or

NRSV

46 Thus says the Lord GOD: The gate of the inner court that faces east shall remain closed on the six working days; but on the sabbath day it shall be opened and on the day of the new moon it shall be opened. ²The prince shall enter by the vestibule of the gate from outside, and shall take his stand by the post of the gate. The priests shall offer his burnt offering and his offerings of well-being, and he shall bow down at the threshold of the gate. Then he shall go out, but the gate shall not be closed until evening. ³The people of the land shall bow down at the entrance of that gate before the LORD on the sabbaths and on the new moons. ⁴The burnt offering that the prince offers to the LORD on the sabbath day shall be six lambs without blemish and a ram without blemish; ⁵and the grain offering with the ram shall be an ephah, and the grain offering with the lambs shall be as much as he wishes to give, together with a hin of oil to each ephah. ⁶On the day of the new moon he shall offer a young bull without blemish, and six lambs and a ram, which shall be without blemish; ⁷as a grain offering he shall provide an ephah with the bull and an ephah with the ram, and with the lambs as much as he wishes, together with a hin of oil to each ephah. ⁸When the prince enters, he shall come in by the vestibule of the gate, and he shall go out by the same way.

9When the people of the land come before the LORD at the appointed festivals, whoever enters by the north gate to worship shall go out by the south gate; and whoever enters by the south gate shall go out by the north gate: they shall not return by way of the gate by which they entered, but shall go out straight ahead. ¹⁰When they come in, the prince shall come in with them; and when they go out, he shall go out.

11At the festivals and the appointed seasons the grain offering with a young bull shall be an ephah, and with a ram an ephah, and with the lambs as much as one wishes to give, together with a hin of oil to an ephah. ¹²When the prince provides a freewill offering, either a burnt offering

ᵃ2 Traditionally *peace offerings*; also in verse 12   ᵇ5 That is, probably about 3/5 bushel (about 22 liters)   ᶜ5 That is, probably about 4 quarts (about 4 liters)

NIV

fellowship offerings—the gate facing east is to be opened for him. He shall offer his burnt offering or his fellowship offerings as he does on the Sabbath day. Then he shall go out, and after he has gone out, the gate will be shut.

¹³ " 'Every day you are to provide a year-old lamb without defect for a burnt offering to the LORD; morning by morning you shall provide it. ¹⁴You are also to provide with it morning by morning a grain offering, consisting of a sixth of an ephah with a third of a hin of oil to moisten the flour. The presenting of this grain offering to the LORD is a lasting ordinance. ¹⁵So the lamb and the grain offering and the oil shall be provided morning by morning for a regular burnt offering.

NRSV

or offerings of well-being as a freewill offering to the LORD, the gate facing east shall be opened for him; and he shall offer his burnt offering or his offerings of well-being as he does on the sabbath day. Then he shall go out, and after he has gone out the gate shall be closed.

13He shall provide a lamb, a yearling, without blemish, for a burnt offering to the LORD daily; morning by morning he shall provide it. ¹⁴And he shall provide a grain offering with it morning by morning regularly, one-sixth of an ephah, and one-third of a hin of oil to moisten the choice flour, as a grain offering to the LORD; this is the ordinance for all time. ¹⁵Thus the lamb and the grain offering and the oil shall be provided, morning by morning, as a regular burnt offering.

COMMENTARY

46:1-3. These verses, introduced by the divine messenger formula, provide regulations concerning the cult and especially the prince's role at the time of various observances and festivals. At the outset, however, we encounter regulations related to the east inner gate. Readers recall that according to Ezek 43:1-5, Yahweh's glory enters Ezekiel's Temple through the outer east gate—the very gate by which, according to Ezek 10:18-19, Yahweh's glory exited the Solomonic Temple. In Ezek 44:1-2, the Lord informs the prophet that this gate shall remain permanently sealed; humans may not pass through it, because Yahweh has entered it. Ezekiel 44:3 states, however, that the prince, by virtue of his office, is permitted to enter the gate by way of its vestibule in the outer court, to eat sacrificial meals "before Yahweh," and then to exit by the same route. Now, the reader discovers that the inner east gate also must remain closed during the (six) working days of the week. It is to be opened only on the sabbath day and on the day of the new moon. As was the case with the outer east gate, the prince has access to this gate during these observances, and at other times as well (see below).

The prince enters the inner east gate through its vestibule in the outer court. He is to position himself by the "post" of the gate. Precisely which post

is in mind is uncertain, but it seems likely that this post lies at the other end of the gate, just before it opens onto the inner court. The prince must not enter the inner court; only the priests have access to that space. But from his position, he is able to observe as the priests offer his burnt offerings and offerings of well-being. The prince must bow down at the threshold and then exit the gate in the same manner that he entered it. On these occasions, the inner east gate remains open until evening. The people of the land—that is, members of the community who are neither priests nor prince—shall prostrate themselves at the entrance of the inner east gate on the sabbaths and new moon festivals. They can approach the gate's outer opening, but unlike the prince, they are not permitted to enter it.

46:4-5. These verses establish the sacrifices which the prince must bring to the Temple every sabbath. The burnt offering consists of six unblemished lambs and a ram without blemish, as well as a cereal offering with the ram (one ephah), as much of a cereal offering as he chooses with the lambs, and a hin of oil for each ephah. Numbers 28:9-10 also addresses the issue of Sabbath sacrifices, but the two texts are not identical. For example, the Mosaic torah in Numbers demands the offering of only two lambs; and nothing is said of a ram.

46:6-7. Ezekiel turns now to the sacrifices for the new moon festivities, a monthly observance. In Israel's ancient Near Eastern world, veneration of the moon deity was common; and it is possible that such transpired in Israel, as well. (Recall the sun worshipers of Ezek 8:6). However, orthodox Yahwism insisted that the sun, moon, and stars were God's creations (see, e.g., Gen 1:14-16), not deities; and it forbade their worship. Hosea (2:11; 5:7) and Isaiah (1:13-14) condemn the participants in new moon festivals because they are faithless to Yahweh, or because their cultic practices have no impact on their immoral behavior. But Ezekiel says nothing negative about the observance.

Because the new moon festival takes place only once per month, it is not surprising that the required sacrifices are greater than those for weekly sabbath observance. The prince shall provide a young bull without blemish, and six lambs and a ram, also without blemish. The cereal offering consists of an ephah with the bull and with the ram, as well as what he chooses for the lambs, and a hin of oil to each ephah (of flour?; see Num 28:12). Numbers 28:11-15 specifies the sacrifices required for monthly observances; and again, there are differences between its demands and those set out by Ezekiel. The Numbers legislation, for example, requires two young bulls, one ram, and seven male lambs a year old and without blemish. Moreover, it specifies the amounts of wine to accompany each animal sacrifice. Ezekiel says nothing about wine offerings. Does he suppress them for fear that inebriated worshipers might compromise the Temple's purity? Readers recall his prohibition against priests drinking wine when they enter the inner court (see also Lev 10:9).

46:8-11. Verses 8-10 return to regulations regarding exits and enterings during the festivals. Verse 8 repeats information about the prince already provided in 46:2. He must enter and exit the inner east gate in the same way; he may not enter the inner court. Verses 9-10 attend not only to the prince, but also to the "people of the land" (ordinary folk) who are permitted to enter the outer court ("come before the LORD") in order to worship God. Verse 9 states that whoever enters by way of the north outer gate must exit through the south outer gate, and vice versa. Zimmerli leaves open the possibility that behind this regulation lies some old taboo against turning around in a sacred precinct. But he rightly concludes that the regulation bears "the sober intention of preventing congestion on occasions of great crowds in the Temple and of insuring an orderly flow of the crowd through the Temple from north to south and from south to north."[1419] Verse 10 both limits the amount of time that the prince spends in the Temple and expresses his commonality with the people. When they enter the Temple, he will enter with them; when they exit, he will exit. Verse 11 repeats the information in v. 7 concerning the prince's offerings at festivals and appointed seasons.

46:12-15. The remainder of this subsection deals with the prince's freewill (v. 12) and daily offerings (vv. 13-15). Verses 13-14, unlike vv. 1-12, are cast in the second person, although the NRSV does not reflect the shift. In addition to his required offerings, the prince is free to offer spontaneous offerings of joy and well-being. On those occasions when he chooses to do so, the inner east gate will be opened for him. But after he has left the gate, it will be closed behind him. On a daily basis the prince must provide an unblemished, year-old lamb as a burnt offering, a grain offering of one-sixth an ephah, and one-third of a hin of oil to moisten the fine flour (סלת *sōlet*). The importance of this ongoing obligation is underscored by a phrase found also in the Pentateuch: this is an eternal ordinance (חקות עולם *ḥuqqôt 'ôlām*). Verse 15, which returns to the third person address of vv. 1-12, reiterates that the lamb and grain offerings, along with the oil, must be provided morning by morning as a regular burnt offering to Yahweh. Again, Ezekiel says nothing about wine offerings (cf. Num 28:7). He also is silent on the topic of evening sacrifices (cf. Num 28:8). Does he simply presuppose them? (See Reflections at 46:19-24.)

1419. Zimmerli, *Ezekiel 2*, 492.

Ezekiel 46:16-24, Additional Regulations

EZEKIEL 46:16-18, LANDHOLDING REGULATIONS

NIV

16" 'This is what the Sovereign LORD says: If the prince makes a gift from his inheritance to one of his sons, it will also belong to his descendants; it is to be their property by inheritance. 17If, however, he makes a gift from his inheritance to one of his servants, the servant may keep it until the year of freedom; then it will revert to the prince. His inheritance belongs to his sons only; it is theirs. 18The prince must not take any of the inheritance of the people, driving them off their property. He is to give his sons their inheritance out of his own property, so that none of my people will be separated from his property.' "

NRSV

16Thus says the Lord GOD: If the prince makes a gift to any of his sons out of his inheritance,[a] it shall belong to his sons, it is their holding by inheritance. 17But if he makes a gift out of his inheritance to one of his servants, it shall be his to the year of liberty; then it shall revert to the prince; only his sons may keep a gift from his inheritance. 18The prince shall not take any of the inheritance of the people, thrusting them out of their holding; he shall give his sons their inheritance out of his own holding, so that none of my people shall be dispossessed of their holding.

[a]Gk: Heb *it is his inheritance*

COMMENTARY

These verses, introduced by the messenger formula, address two issues. The first (vv. 16-17) concerns the crown lands of the prince. Readers recall that in 45:7-8, the prince was allocated two large tracts of land lying east and west of the holy portion and the holding of the city. In the light of the prince's responsibilities to provide abundant sacrificial animals and agricultural products to the priests, the reader understands that the prince must have land. Should the prince choose to make a gift of land to his sons out of his "inheritance," that land shall belong to his sons. This situation presents no problem, since the land gift remains in the prince's family. If the prince chooses to give a land grant to one of his servants, however, that servant retains the property only until the year of liberty; at that time, it reverts to the (family of the) prince.

The second issue concerns the land holdings of the people. Verse 18a prohibits the prince from confiscating any of their land holdings. The same concern was addressed in 45:8-9 (see the Commentary on 45:8-9). According to 1 Sam 8:14, Samuel warned the people who sought a king that "He will take the best of your fields and vineyards and olive orchards and give them to his courtiers" (NRSV). The story of Ahab's confiscation of Naboth's land is the most famous passage in the Hebrew Bible dealing with a king's forced confiscation of a subject's familial property. Unlike the former kings of Israel and Judah, the prince shall not alienate the people from their land holdings. His sons' inheritance must come from his own holding, so that none of Yahweh's people will be dispossessed from their land. This limitation upon the power of the prince is yet another example of Ezekiel's final vision attempting to set right the wrongs of the past. (See Reflections at 46:19-24.)

EZEKIEL 46:19-24, THE TEMPLE KITCHENS

NIV

¹⁹Then the man brought me through the entrance at the side of the gate to the sacred rooms facing north, which belonged to the priests, and showed me a place at the western end. ²⁰He said to me, "This is the place where the priests will cook the guilt offering and the sin offering and bake the grain offering, to avoid bringing them into the outer court and consecrating the people."

²¹He then brought me to the outer court and led me around to its four corners, and I saw in each corner another court. ²²In the four corners of the outer court were enclosed*a* courts, forty cubits long and thirty cubits wide; each of the courts in the four corners was the same size. ²³Around the inside of each of the four courts was a ledge of stone, with places for fire built all around under the ledge. ²⁴He said to me, "These are the kitchens where those who minister at the temple will cook the sacrifices of the people."

a22 The meaning of the Hebrew for this word is uncertain.

NRSV

19Then he brought me through the entrance, which was at the side of the gate, to the north row of the holy chambers for the priests; and there I saw a place at the extreme western end of them. ²⁰He said to me, "This is the place where the priests shall boil the guilt offering and the sin offering, and where they shall bake the grain offering, in order not to bring them out into the outer court and so communicate holiness to the people."

21Then he brought me out to the outer court, and led me past the four corners of the court; and in each corner of the court there was a court—²²in the four corners of the court were small*a* courts, forty cubits long and thirty wide; the four were of the same size. ²³On the inside, around each of the four courts*b* was a row of masonry, with hearths made at the bottom of the rows all around. ²⁴Then he said to me, "These are the kitchens where those who serve at the temple shall boil the sacrifices of the people."

aGk Syr Vg: Meaning of Heb uncertain   bHeb the four of them

COMMENTARY

Ezekiel has said much about sacrificial animals, grain offerings, and hins of oil, and also about who is permitted to consume what. According to these verses, he is shown first one (vv. 19-20), and then four other (vv. 21-24) kitchen facilities within the temple complex. These facilities serve different constituencies. The first is for the priests and is located in an area accessible only to them. The others are located in each of the four corners of the outer court and are used by the Levites to prepare sacrificial meals for the lay people.

When last the text referred to Ezekiel's tour guide, he and Ezekiel entered the inner court by way of the north gate and stood before the Temple in order to see Yahweh's glory filling it. Presumably, they have remained at that location to this point. Now, the guide leads Ezekiel back through the gate to the outer court, where they turn west (left) and enter the corridor running east

to west before the doors of the priestly sacristies lying to the north (see 42:1-4). At the rear of that corridor, Ezekiel sees a space. This, he is told, is the place where the priests boil their portions of the reparation and purification offerings, and bake their portions of the grain offerings. These portions must not be prepared in the outer court, he is told, lest their contagious holiness be transmitted to the people. The reader recalls that the priests also were required, upon leaving the inner court, to deposit their holy vestments in these sacred chambers (see the Commentary on 44:17-19). Illicit access to the holy can be deadly.

Next, the guide leads Ezekiel into the outer court and past each of its four corners. In each corner of the court, Ezekiel sees an enclosure. The NRSV, and others emend the MT's "joined" קתרות *qĕturôt* to קטנות *qĕṭannôt* and read "small," following the LXX. The problem with this emendation is that the enclosures, each measuring forty cubits long and thirty cubits wide, are scarcely small (nor should they be, given their function). Each is approximately sixty-eight by fifty-one feet.[1420] Verse 23 provides some information about the interiors of these four kitchens, but its terminology is uncertain. The word טור (*ṭûr*) usually means "row"; here, it possibly refers to a row or ledge of masonry beneath which all around are

hearths (so TNK). These kitchens, his guide informs Ezekiel, are where the temple servants (i.e., Levites) boil the people's sacrifices.

Neither descriptions of the wilderness tabernacle, nor descriptions of the Solomonic Temple, refer to kitchens. An account of Passover observance during the reign of Josiah (2 Chr 35:11-13) presupposes kitchens but says nothing of them. Ezekiel's brief descriptions of these facilities are yet another example of the vision's overriding concern to keep things in their proper place and to protect and maintain cultic purity.

1420. The TNK reads "unroofed," citing *M. Mid.* 2.5. Block commends the Aramaic rendering found in the Targum, *mqtrn,* meaning "fenced in," (*Ezekiel 25–48,* 685).

REFLECTIONS

I confess that when I read Ezek 43:13–46:24, I often feel like a stranger in an alien world. I suspect that this is true of many people—especially, perhaps, Protestant Christian readers. To be sure, I can understand, along the lines suggested in the Overview to Ezekiel 40–48, the presuppositions and thinking undergirding a theology of holiness: the absolute conviction that without God's holy presence in its midst, Israel is doomed; the insistence that ensuring Yahweh's abiding presence depends upon the maintenance of cultic purity, because a holy God will not dwell amidst an impure people. But having understood this, I still resist the idea, for example, that bodily emissions (like perspiration on priests, or menstrual blood) render persons unfit for public worship.

I can understand, along the lines suggested in the Reflections to Ezek 40:1–43:12, that the importance of maintaining purity leads to an emphasis upon detail, upon ensuring that everything is done in the right place, in the right way, and by the right persons. Organization and attention to detail can reflect the utmost importance of sacred rituals transpiring in sacred spaces; and it can bring benefits both psychological (a sense of control in chaotic times) and spiritual (the discipline of regular prayer and meditation). At the same time, however, an overplus of attention to detail, including ritual detail, can become numbing, or alienating to those excluded from participation. Finally, I become suspicious when a privileged group (e.g., the Zadokite priests) grounds its privilege in the word of God.

Perhaps I most feel like a stranger in an alien world when I read about Israel's sacrificial system. I can understand that for the author(s) of this material, the sacrificial slaughtering of animals was regarded as essential, because the blood of the victim removed impurity. However, I cannot imagine participating in such cultic rituals.

Despite the dramatic disjunctions between the world view reflected in Ezekiel 40–48 and that held by many (though not all) moderns, however, I do not want simply to shove this Scripture aside. I need to reflect more deeply on what it can teach us. And so, for example, I wish sympathetically to consider the meaning and significance of animal sacrifices in ancient Israel.

In order to do so, I must recognize the close, symbiotic relationship that existed between people and their animals in ancient Israelite society. In many a contemporary culture, animals are routinely brought to slaughterhouses, where they are regarded only as commodities to be processed, packaged, and distributed. But in ancient Israel's world, the lives of people and animals were intertwined in ways best known in modern North America, perhaps, to farmers and zookeepers. Rural Israelites and their animals lived together in houses and on compounds. Herdsmen knew each head of their cattle and, recognizing when one had strayed, exerted tremendous effort to retrieve it. Think for example, of the parable of the lost sheep so diligently sought by its shepherd (Matt 18:10-14; Luke 15:3-7). They protected their animals from rustlers, and even against ravaging beasts. Recall David's statement to King Saul: "your servant used to keep sheep for his father; and whenever a lion or a bear came, and took a lamb from the flock, I went after it and struck it down, rescuing the lamb from its mouth; and if it turned against me, I would catch it by the jaw, strike it down, and kill it" (1 Sam 17:34-35 NRSV).

Animals were crucial to the survival of the clan, because they provided milk, and wool for clothing. The economic consequences of sacrificing animals were significant, because the owner forfeited not only the animal itself, but also its reproductive capacity. In short, a sacrificed animal was a *genuine* sacrifice for those whose economic resources were limited. To offer such a gift to Yahweh was no empty ritual; rather, it expressed concretely the importance placed by the giver upon his or her relationship with God. In fact, the most important aspect of sacrifice might not have been the animal itself, but the fact that the giver was doing something unusual and in a special way in order to acknowledge the importance of his or her commitment to God. And what was true then remains true today. Being in relationship with God brings upon us responsibilities. God does demand sacrifices of us. And when we respond, we are indicating the importance of a vital covenant relationship with God for our lives.

Ezekiel insists that the animals sacrificed upon Yahweh's altar be without blemish. When the ancient Israelites sacrificed unblemished animals, they were offering their *best* to God. The temptation to do otherwise surely existed. According to the post-exilic prophet Malachi, Yahweh rejected the priests at Jerusalem's rebuilt Temple because they offered blind, lame, and sick animals upon the altar. They would never have tried to pass off such animals as taxes to the governor since such would be displeasing and he would show them no favor! Yet they brought these sacrifices to Yahweh's altar. The quality of their sacrifices betrayed their contempt for God (Mal 1:6-14). Ezekiel reminds us that what we offer to God (time, service, values lived out in concrete ways, money) must be our best, the best that we can offer.

Ezekiel 47:1–48:35, Yahweh's Land Is Made Fruitful and Is Distributed

OVERVIEW

To this point, Ezekiel's fourth and final vision account has focused primarily upon cultic matters: the temple complex and its structures; its personnel; the sacrificial system; the prince's role in providing sacrificial animals, grain, and oil; the holy contribution; and so on. Now, his vision moves beyond these matters to identify the boundaries of Israel's land, allot territory to each of the twelve tribes, provide additional information about the holy contribution, identify the city's twelve gates, and finally, to rename the city. The transitional passage facilitating this shift in focus is 47:1-12.

Ezekiel 47:1-12, Ezekiel's Transforming Stream

NIV

47 The man brought me back to the entrance of the temple, and I saw water coming out from under the threshold of the temple toward the east (for the temple faced east). The water was coming down from under the south

NRSV

47 Then he brought me back to the entrance of the temple; there, water was flowing from below the threshold of the temple toward the east (for the temple faced east); and the water was flowing down from below the south end of

NIV

side of the temple, south of the altar. ²He then brought me out through the north gate and led me around the outside to the outer gate facing east, and the water was flowing from the south side.

³As the man went eastward with a measuring line in his hand, he measured off a thousand cubits*a* and then led me through water that was ankle-deep. ⁴He measured off another thousand cubits and led me through water that was knee-deep. He measured off another thousand and led me through water that was up to the waist. ⁵He measured off another thousand, but now it was a river that I could not cross, because the water had risen and was deep enough to swim in—a river that no one could cross. ⁶He asked me, "Son of man, do you see this?"

Then he led me back to the bank of the river. ⁷When I arrived there, I saw a great number of trees on each side of the river. ⁸He said to me, "This water flows toward the eastern region and goes down into the Arabah,*b* where it enters the Sea.*c* When it empties into the Sea,*c* the water there becomes fresh. ⁹Swarms of living creatures will live wherever the river flows. There will be large numbers of fish, because this water flows there and makes the salt water fresh; so where the river flows everything will live. ¹⁰Fishermen will stand along the shore; from En Gedi to En Eglaim there will be places for spreading nets. The fish will be of many kinds—like the fish of the Great Sea.*d* ¹¹But the swamps and marshes will not become fresh; they will be left for salt. ¹²Fruit trees of all kinds will grow on both banks of the river. Their leaves will not wither, nor will their fruit fail. Every month they will bear, because the water from the sanctuary flows to them. Their fruit will serve for food and their leaves for healing."

a3 That is, about 1,500 feet (about 450 meters)   *b8* Or *the Jordan Valley*   *c8* That is, the Dead Sea   *d10* That is, the Mediterranean; also in verses 15, 19 and 20

NRSV

the threshold of the temple, south of the altar. ²Then he brought me out by way of the north gate, and led me around on the outside to the outer gate that faces toward the east;*a* and the water was coming out on the south side.

3Going on eastward with a cord in his hand, the man measured one thousand cubits, and then led me through the water; and it was ankle-deep. ⁴Again he measured one thousand, and led me through the water; and it was knee-deep. Again he measured one thousand, and led me through the water; and it was up to the waist. ⁵Again he measured one thousand, and it was a river that I could not cross, for the water had risen; it was deep enough to swim in, a river that could not be crossed. ⁶He said to me, "Mortal, have you seen this?"

Then he led me back along the bank of the river. ⁷As I came back, I saw on the bank of the river a great many trees on the one side and on the other. ⁸He said to me, "This water flows toward the eastern region and goes down into the Arabah; and when it enters the sea, the sea of stagnant waters, the water will become fresh. ⁹Wherever the river goes,*b* every living creature that swarms will live, and there will be very many fish, once these waters reach there. It will become fresh; and everything will live where the river goes. ¹⁰People will stand fishing beside the sea*c* from En-gedi to En-eglaim; it will be a place for the spreading of nets; its fish will be of a great many kinds, like the fish of the Great Sea. ¹¹But its swamps and marshes will not become fresh; they are to be left for salt. ¹²On the banks, on both sides of the river, there will grow all kinds of trees for food. Their leaves will not wither nor their fruit fail, but they will bear fresh fruit every month, because the water for them flows from the sanctuary. Their fruit will be for food, and their leaves for healing."

*a*Meaning of Heb uncertain   *b*Gk Syr Vg Tg: Heb *the two rivers go*   *c*Heb *it*

COMMENTARY

These verses describe the course of an astonishing stream that trickles forth from the foundation of the Temple and grows as it flows to the east. Led by his guide, Ezekiel follows this stream until it becomes so deep that he can no longer cross it on foot. At that point, his guide informs him of the river's further progress through the eastern region of Yahweh's land and into the Dead Sea. Its waters transform the desiccated Arabah region into a place of extraordinary vegetation, and the deadly water of the Salt Sea becomes pure and fish-filled.

Contemporary scholars agree that when Ezekiel composed his description of a sacred stream that fructifies the Arabah, he was not creating *ex nihilo*.[1421] Rather, he drew from a vast and commingling pool of mythic elements current in the ancient Near East. In the Hebrew Bible, the sacred stream motif is especially at home within two mythic complexes: (1) the myth of Zion as the cosmic mountain (see, e.g., Isa 8:6-7; 33:20-24; Joel 4:18; Zech 14:8); and (2) the paradise, or Garden of Eden, myth (e.g., Gen 2:8-14; Ezek 28:13; 31:8).[1422] Levenson has investigated the influence of these two mythic complexes upon the author(s) of Ezekiel 40–48. Regarding the first, he examines texts depicting Zion as "the navel of the world, the seat of the divine presence,[1423] capital of the divine government, and source of the redemption of nature."[1424] The belief that Zion was the inviolable mountain upon which Yahweh dwelt, and where the supranatural effects of the divine presence were manifested, is clearly attested in such "songs of Zion" as Psalms 2; 46; 48; and 76. Of these, Ps 46:4 refers explicitly to a sacred river:

> There is a river whose streams
> make glad the city of God,
> the holy habitation of the Most High. (NRSV)

Regarding the second mythic complex, Levenson examines texts in which the paradise myth has influenced the depiction of Mount Zion. According to Gen 2:10-14, a river issuing from Eden and watering the garden subsequently divides into four branches that water the world, serving as conduits of divine blessing and fertility. Levenson acknowledges that the mountain of 40:2 is the Garden of Eden only because it is identified with Mt. Zion.[1425] But he finds both in the flora and fauna of 47:1-2 and in the reference to two stands of trees in 47:7 echoes of the Eden narratives.[1426] Explicit references to the "Garden of Eden" or "Garden of God" are lacking in Ezekiel 40–48, but forms of these phrases have appeared earlier in the book. (According to 28:13, the king of Tyre dwelt in "Eden, the garden of God"; see also the "holy mountain of God" in v. 14. According to 31:8, Assyria, the great cedar, surpassed in beauty the trees in God's garden; therefore, the trees of Eden, in the garden of God, envied it. With Assyria's demise, these trees were comforted, 31:16.) Ezekiel 36:35 states that passers-by will liken Israel's restored land to the Garden of Eden.

47:1-2. Following Ezekiel's tour of the temple kitchens (46:19-24), his guide brings him back to the entrance of the Temple building. There, Ezekiel observes a tiny trickle of water bubbling forth from below its threshold. This trickle initially flows south, thereby avoiding the altar standing in front of the Temple. His guide then leads him out of the temple complex by way of the north gate (the outer east gate being permanently sealed) and around on the outside to the outer east gate. Now, Ezekiel sees the water trickling out from its south side. The Hebrew word for "trickling," מפכים (*mĕpakkîm*), is a *hapax legomenon*, that is, it appears only here in the OT. From the same root comes the noun meaning "bottle," פך (*pak*). The verb is an example of onomatopoeia—that is, it sounds like its referent ("buzz" and "crack" are

1421. Most scholars attribute at least significant portions of this text to Ezekiel. See W. Zimmerli, *Ezekiel 2: A Commentary on the Book of the Prophet Ezekiel, Chapters 25–48*, trans. J. D. Martin, Hermeneia (Philadelphia: Fortress, 1983) 547-53; Walther Eichrodt, *Ezekiel*, trans. Cosslett Quin, OTL (Philadelphia: Westminster, 1970) 580-87; J. W. Wevers, *Ezekiel*, NCB (London: Nelson, 1969) 333-36. This discussion follows K. P. Darr, "The Wall Around Paradise: Ezekielian Ideas about the Future," *VT* 37 (1987) 271-79.

1422. Clifford notes that in Ugarit literature, El dwells at "the source of the two rivers" or the "pools of the double-deep." See R. Clifford, *The Cosmic Mountain in the Old Testament*, HSM 4 (Cambridge, Mass.: Harvard University Press, 1972) 48-57.

1423. The idea that a deity dwells in a temple atop a mountain is by no means limited to Mt. Zion traditions. Clifford points to similarities between Mt. Zaphon in Ugaritic texts and Mt. Zion in the Hebrew Bible: "On both, the deity dwells in his temple from which he exercises his rule." Ibid., 131.

1424. J. D. Levenson, *Theology of the Program of Restoration of Ezekiel 40–48*, HSM 10 (Missoula: Scholars Press, 1976) 14.

1425. Ibid., 31.

1426. Ibid., 32.

but two examples of onomatopoeia in English). One hears the sound of water being poured from the narrow neck of a small bottle.

47:3-6a. With v. 3, the tour guide heads eastward with a measuring instrument in his hand. This device, called a קָו (*qāw*), is neither the linen cord nor the measuring reed of 40:3.[1427] After walking a distance of one thousand cubits, the guide measures the water. It is ankle deep. Traveling another one thousand cubits, he measures the water again. Now it is knee deep. One thousand cubits further, and the water is up to their loins. Finally, the guide progresses an additional one thousand cubits to the east and measures the water. The former "trickle" has swollen into a river that can only be traversed by swimming. The guide then asks Ezekiel, "Mortal, have you seen this?" The reader knows that the answer to this rhetorical question is a resounding "yes!" Indeed, he can imagine that Ezekiel is wide-eyed with astonishment that what began as the tiniest dribble has, without benefit of tributaries, swollen into a river! For Zimmerli, the significance of the stream's minute beginnings is best tapped by analogy to Jesus' parable of the mustard seed and leaven (Matt 13:31-33).[1428] Perhaps the most obvious explanation why the trickle remains so tiny until it has exited the temple complex is that one would not wish to have water sweeping through the courts!

47:6b-12. Returning to dry land, Ezekiel is startled to observe that both banks of the river are filled with very many trees. Zimmerli regards vv. 6*b*-7 as a later addition, designed to prepare readers for v. 12. To his mind, they create an "inelegant delay" in the flow of the narrative.[1429] It is easy to imagine, however, that Ezekiel would notice these trees immediately after arriving on shore. The guide then describes the vivifying river's further course. It traverses the land between Jerusalem and the Jordan River, flowing down through the 'arabâ.[1430] Finally, it pours into

the "sea," more specifically, what moderns call the Dead (or Salt) Sea.[1431]

In Ezekiel's vision, the Dead Sea will no longer be "virtualy devoid of life" when the river that originates in Yahweh's Temple reaches it and its waters are "healed" (*rapa'*), made fresh. In language reminiscent of Gen 1:20-21, v. 9 emphasizes that wherever the river flows,[1432] every creature that swarms will live.[1433]

Verse 10 provides further detail about the transformed Dead Sea. People will fish on its banks from En-gedi to En-eglaim. The former site (modern 'Ain Jidi) is an oasis on the western shore of the Dead Sea whose waters "emerge from a permanent spring on top of an escarpment 600 ft. above the lake."[1434] It has been excavated.[1435] The site of En-Englaim is less certain. Zimmerli, following Yadin, locates it on the southeastern shore of the Dead Sea.[1436] If this identification is correct, then the references to settlements on the Sea's eastern and western shores underscores that the entire body of water will become capable of supporting life. Learning that the Sea's shores will become "a place for the spreading of nets," the reader perceives an irony. In Ezekiel 26, the prophet twice threatened that Tyre, a prominent Phoenician city-state situated on an island off the eastern coast of the Mediterranean Sea, would be reduced to a bare rock, "a place for spreading nets." In that context, the image was a devastating reversal of Tyre's security, strength, and bustling commerce. Here, however, the same image bespeaks the marvelous transformation of the Dead Sea's stagnant and life-

---

1427. The phrase קָו מִדָּה (*qaw middâ*, "measuring line") appears in Jer 31:39.

1428. Zimmerli, *Ezekiel 2*, 516.

1429. Ibid., 512.

1430. עֲרָבָה (*'arabâ*) appears only here in the book of Ezekiel, and it refers specifically to a desiccated area within Yahweh's land. Ezekiel uses מִדְבָּר (*midbār*) when referring to the area lying beyond Israel's southwestern border (6:14)—i.e., "the desert of the land of Egypt" (20:36)—or to the "desert of the nations" (20:35; possibly a reference to the Syro-Arabian desert) or simply to any region outside cultivated land that lacks water (19:13; 29:5) and is the habitat of dangerous beasts (34:25) and "uncivilized" people (23:42).

1431. The MT reads "to the sea which have been brought out." The LXX renders the phrase "to the outlet of the water." Both Zimmerli, *Ezekiel 2*, 507, and Eichrodt, *Ezekiel*, 581, derive the meaning of MT הַמּוּצָאִים (*hammûṣā'îm*) from חמיץ (*ḥāmîṣ*), "salted" (Isa 30:24). G. R. Driver, "Linguistic and Textual Problems: Ezekiel," *Bib* 19 (1938) 186-87, derives the form from צוֹא (*ṣw'*), "to be foul," "polluted." See also Levenson, *Theology of the Program of Restoration of Ezekiel 40–48*, 22. D. I. Block, *The Book of Ezekiel: Chapters 25–48*, NICOT (Grand Rapids: Eerdmans, 1998), follows the Syriac "stagnant," as does the NRSV. See also Block's detailed discussion about the Dead Sea, ibid., 694.

1432. The MT's "two rivers" is not supported in any of the versions and makes no sense, since only one river is described in 47:1-2.

1433. Zimmerli, *Ezekiel 2*, 513, regards v. 9 as a later supplement to the text. Block, by contrast, finds significance in its fourfold כֹּל (*kol*, "each," "every") and the repetition of the phrase "wherever the stream flowed." Verse 9 emphasizes "the thoroughness of the 'healing.'"

1434. Block, *Ezekiel 25–48*, 695.

1435. See B. Mazar, T. Dothan, and I. Dunayevsky, *En-Gedi: The First and Second Seasons of Excavations, 1962–62, Atiqot* (English Series) 5 (Jerusalem: Department of Antiquities and Museums, 1966).

1436. Yigael Yadin, "Expedition D—The Cave of the Letters," *IEJ* 12 (1962) 250-51. See also Zimmerli, *Ezekiel 2*, 514-15.

less waters. But wait! Salt is an important commodity, not only as a preservative and flavor enhancer, but also within ritual practice (Ezek 43:24). Hence, Ezekiel's guide states, the Sea's shallow swamps and marshes will remain salty.

The miraculous, fertilizing effects of the river are everywhere evident, for on both of its banks stands every kind of food-producing tree (see v. 7). These trees never lose their leaves; and they bear fresh fruit monthly, not annually. Moreover, their leaves are medicinal; they are for "healing." All of this is possible because the water flows from Yahweh's sanctuary. Ezekiel's stream, originating at Yahweh's Temple on a "very high mountain" (Ezek 40:2), transforms the most diseased areas of Israel's land into a veritable Garden of Eden. This passage stands in stark contrast to preceding ones, in which the dangers of communicating holiness to the people prevented the priests from wearing their ritual garments and consuming their meals while in the outer court. (See Reflections at 48:30-35.)

❖   ❖   ❖   ❖

EXCURSUS: THE PERIMETERS OF PARADISE

Readers may wonder about the breadth of the return to paradise that Ezekiel envisions. In his commentary, Walther Eichrodt maintains that the return "is of its very nature a universal event embracing the whole world." He views the recurring formula "They shall know that I am Yahweh" as expressing "how the light of the new fellowship which God bestowed upon Israel also shines out over the Gentile world."[1437]

Peter R. Ackroyd shares Eichrodt's opinion that this passage is characterized by a universalism not unlike that found in Isaiah 40–55. Regarding the restoration of Israel's Temple and land, Ackroyd argues that "the concentration is upon the nature of God which motivates his action, and it is with a wider view, too, a prospect of the knowledge of God among the nations. This broader outlook is significant because it indicates the appropriateness of placing Ezekiel alongside Deutero-Isaiah."[1438]

I agree with both scholars to a point. It is true that within the book of Ezekiel, the restoration of Israel is a universally witnessed event that will force the nations to recognize that Yahweh is the sovereign Lord of history. But does this Ezekielian "universalism" actually express "how the light of the new fellowship which God bestowed upon Israel also shines out over the Gentile world," as Eichrodt believes? Is the return of paradise in this passage only the beginning of a transformation embracing the whole world, or does this text lead us to an altogether different judgment concerning the perimeters of paradise regained? In "The Wall Around Paradise," I have argued that "the Ezekielian expectation for universal acknowledgment of Yahweh's sovereignty and power does not include a concomitant expectation that the nations will benefit from Israel's future restoration." To the contrary, "the description of marvelous future conditions . . . is exclusive, rather than inclusive, of lands and peoples outside the land of Israel. To be sure, the author(s) of Ezek xlvii 1-12 used [e]denic imagery to describe the marvelous stream and its transforming effects. However, such imagery was employed in ways that were consonant with his own aims and expectations."[1439]

"THEN YOU WILL KNOW THAT I AM YAHWEH"

The recognition formula ("then you [or "they"] will know that I am Yahweh") plays a crucial role in Eichrodt's and Ackroyd's understanding of Ezekiel's ideas about the future. Moshe

1437. Eichrodt, *Ezekiel*, 585-86.
1438. Peter R. Ackroyd, *Exile and Restoration* (Philadelphia: Westminster, 1968) 115.
1439. Darr, "The Wall Around Paradise," 272.

Greenberg says that this formula, which appears in regular and expanded forms seventy-two times in the book of Ezekiel, "expresses the intended effect of the event predicted in the oracle."[1440]

In Ezekiel 1–24, this formula is found exclusively within oracles addressed to Israel, the vast majority of which are announcements of judgment and punishment. Repeatedly, the reader is told that through depopulation (e.g., 5:17; 9:5-6; 14:21), devastation (e.g., 5:6; 12:20; 21:27; 33:28-29) and deportation (e.g., 4:13; 6:8-10; 12:14-16; 22:15), Israel will be forced to acknowledge Yahweh's sovereign power in history. In Ezekiel 25–32, however, the formula appears in oracles against foreign nations (and rulers), who likewise will be forced to acknowledge Yahweh's unrivaled sovereignty. Accused of pride, or of gleefully taking advantage of Judah's collapse to feather their own nests (e.g., 25:3, 6, 8, 12; 26:2; 35:10, 12-13; 36:2, 20b), Israel's enemies will suffer the same punishments as Israel: Through depopulation (e.g., 21:31–22:2; 25:13; 26:11; 27:27, 34; 28:23; 29:8, 11; 30:6, 11; 32:12, 15, 20, 22, 24-25), devastation (e.g., 25:5; 26:4-5, 9-10, 12, 14, 19; 29:12a; 30:12) and deportation (e.g., 29:12b; 30:23, 26), they, too, will "know that I am Yahweh."

Israel's final fate differs from its foes', however. In Ezekiel 34–48, judgment pronouncements are replaced, for the most part, by oracles concerning its future rescue and restoration. Virtually nowhere within the book is it stated that, having suffered Yahweh's punishments, other nations also will enjoy the rescue and restoration promised to Israel. (Ezek 29:13-15, which states that Yahweh will restore the Egyptians to their homeland following forty years of exile, is hardly an exception to my point. The text emphasizes Egypt's future lowly status among the nations. So small will Egypt be that Israel will never again be tempted to look to it for aid. Nothing suggests that the future Egypt will share in Israel's paradisiacal prosperity.) To the contrary, oracles against foreign nations (and rulers) emphasize the finality of Yahweh's punishments (e.g., 26:14, 21; see also 27:36b; 28:19; 35:9a). Culpable nations will be destroyed—an outcome clearly stated in Ezek 28:24-26, where God promises to punish any nations threatening Israel's peaceful existence in its land.

Israel's enemies will come to know who Yahweh is not only when they themselves are punished, but also when they witness Israel's final destiny. Yahweh's reputation among the nations—clearly a deep concern to the author(s) of Ezekiel—will be vindicated when God's people are restored to their edenic homeland. The future restoration of Israel and its land will silence the scoffing nations (see, e.g., the nations' taunt in 36:20). Indeed, persons passing through the land will exclaim: "This land that was desolate has become like the garden of Eden; and the waste and desolate and ruined cities are now inhabited and fortified" (36:35, NRSV).

THE PERIMETERS OF FUTURE EDENIC CONDITIONS

Will the transformation effected by Ezekiel's sacred stream be confined within the carefully defined territories of Israel's homeland (see 6:14; 47:13-20; 48:1), or will the return to paradise be a universal event, as Eichrodt and Ackroyd suggest? If we concur with Eichrodt's statement that return to paradise imagery is, by its very nature, universalistic; and if we also agree that the use of such imagery confirms that the author held a universalistic perspective, then we must agree that Ezek 47:1-12 envisions what we moderns might term a "transglobal" transformation. The river flows on, creating edenic conditions world-wide, despite the fact that its progress is here traced no farther than the shores of the Dead Sea, and in spite of the striking lack of evidence elsewhere in Ezekiel's book that the nations will partake of Yahweh's future acts of rescue and restoration. We are, however, ill-advised to agree with Eichrodt, for his presupposition that return to paradise imagery necessarily includes universal transformation is arbitrary. To the con-

---

1440. Moshe Greenberg, *Ezekiel 1–20*, AB 22 (Garden City, N.Y.: Doubleday, 1983) 133.

---

trary, groups championing quite different viewpoints within Israel could and did lay claim to the same mythic motifs, using them in ways that legitimated their own expectations and goals.

In the light of this perspective, variations in the use of mythic motifs are important. We should not, for example, ignore the differences between the description of a river in Eden which waters the garden and eventually divides to water all four regions of the world, and Ezekiel's account of a sacred stream flowing only to the east, because "this conception [of a sacred stream] could take many different forms and was not confined to any single systemized shape."[1441] Rather, we must hear Ezek 47:1-12 with ears attuned not only to what we are told, but also to what we are not told. We must, as Elie Wiesel instructs us, listen for both words and silences.[1442] When we listen carefully to the text, we cannot avoid hearing the silence concerning any edenic transformation of land lying beyond Israel's territory. And we cannot avoid being struck by how precisely the regions through which the river flows are located within the boundaries of Israel's homeland.

Ezekiel's depiction of the fruitful effects of the sacred stream are exclusive, rather than inclusive, of nations and lands outside the land of Israel. The transformation of Israel's barren territory and of the Salt Sea does not presage a universal return to edenic conditions. Ezekiel was simply too parochial to envision such a scenario. Rather, it is a manifestation of blessing poured out upon Israel's land, which does not extend beyond its borders.

1441. Eichrodt, *Ezekiel*, 584.

1442. Elie Wiesel, "In the Bible: The Vision of Ezekiel," Andrew W. Mellon Lectures in the Humanities, Boston University, October 21, 1985.

❖   ❖   ❖   ❖

Ezekiel 47:13-23, The Boundaries of Israel's Homeland

NIV

13This is what the Sovereign LORD says: "These are the boundaries by which you are to divide the land for an inheritance among the twelve tribes of Israel, with two portions for Joseph. 14You are to divide it equally among them. Because I swore with uplifted hand to give it to your forefathers, this land will become your inheritance.

15"This is to be the boundary of the land:

"On the north side it will run from the Great Sea by the Hethlon road past Lebo[a] Hamath to Zedad, 16Berothah[b] and Sibraim (which lies on the border between Damascus and Hamath), as far as Hazer Hatticon, which is on the border of Hauran. 17The boundary will extend from the sea to Hazar Enan,[c] along the northern border of Damascus, with the border of Hamath to the north. This will be the north boundary.

[a]15 Or *past the entrance to*   [b]15,16 See Septuagint and Ezekiel 48:1; Hebrew *road to go into Zedad,* [16]Hamath, Berothah   [c]17 Hebrew *Enon,* a variant of *Enan*

NRSV

13Thus says the Lord GOD: These are the boundaries by which you shall divide the land for inheritance among the twelve tribes of Israel. Joseph shall have two portions. 14You shall divide it equally; I swore to give it to your ancestors, and this land shall fall to you as your inheritance.

15This shall be the boundary of the land: On the north side, from the Great Sea by way of Hethlon to Lebo-hamath, and on to Zedad,[a] 16Berothah, Sibraim (which lies between the border of Damascus and the border of Hamath), as far as Hazer-hatticon, which is on the border of Hauran. 17So the boundary shall run from the sea to Hazar-enon, which is north of the border of Damascus, with the border of Hamath to the north.[b] This shall be the north side.

18On the east side, between Hauran and Damascus; along the Jordan between Gilead and the land of Israel; to the eastern sea and as far as Tamar.[c] This shall be the east side.

[a]Gk: Heb *Lebo-zedad,* [16]Hamath   [b]Meaning of Heb uncertain   [c]Compare Syr: Heb *you shall measure*

NIV

18"On the east side the boundary will run between Hauran and Damascus, along the Jordan between Gilead and the land of Israel, to the eastern sea and as far as Tamar.[a] This will be the east boundary.
19 "On the south side it will run from Tamar as far as the waters of Meribah Kadesh, then along the Wadi ˻of Egypt˼ to the Great Sea. This will be the south boundary.
20"On the west side, the Great Sea will be the boundary to a point opposite Lebo[b] Hamath. This will be the west boundary.

21"You are to distribute this land among yourselves according to the tribes of Israel. 22You are to allot it as an inheritance for yourselves and for the aliens who have settled among you and who have children. You are to consider them as native-born Israelites; along with you they are to be allotted an inheritance among the tribes of Israel. 23In whatever tribe the alien settles, there you are to give him his inheritance," declares the Sovereign LORD.

[a]18 Septuagint and Syriac; Hebrew *Israel. You will measure to the eastern sea*   [b]20 Or *opposite the entrance to*

NRSV

19On the south side, it shall run from Tamar as far as the waters of Meribath-kadesh, from there along the Wadi of Egypt[a] to the Great Sea. This shall be the south side.
20On the west side, the Great Sea shall be the boundary to a point opposite Lebo-hamath. This shall be the west side.
21So you shall divide this land among you according to the tribes of Israel. 22You shall allot it as an inheritance for yourselves and for the aliens who reside among you and have begotten children among you. They shall be to you as citizens of Israel; with you they shall be allotted an inheritance among the tribes of Israel. 23In whatever tribe aliens reside, there you shall assign them their inheritance, says the Lord GOD.

[a]Heb lacks *of Egypt*

COMMENTARY

After exiting the temple complex to follow the course of the sacred stream, Ezekiel turns to the task of identifying the outer boundaries of Israel's homeland. According to Num 34:1-15, Moses assumed this God-given responsibility prior to the Hebrew's entrance into the land of Canaan. Once again, Ezekiel is presented as a new Moses. The subunit is introduced by the messenger formula ("Thus says the Lord GOD") and concludes with the signatory formula "says the Lord GOD"; hence, it presents as divine speech. The initial announcement, "This[1443] is the boundary" (the form is sing., not pl., as in the NRSV and the NIV), introduces a key word in what follows, for גבול (*gĕbûl,* "boundary, territory") will appear a total of nine times in vv. 15-20 alone.

1443. Emending גה (*gēh*) to זה (*zeh*), "this," with the LXX; the reader would immediately recognize and mentally correct the error.

The people must divide the land defined by Yahweh among Israel's twelve tribes. Readers recall that the subject of land allotment was broached already in 45:1; this is but one of several similarities between the present passage and 45:1-8. The notice that Joseph will have two portions seems somewhat intrusive, but it answers a question that might easily arise in the reader's mind: if the tribe of Levi, which has been allocated land within the holy contribution, is not included among the twelve tribes receiving territorial strips, how does one arrive at that number? Readers familiar with the episode recounted in Gen 48:8-22 will recall that on his deathbed, Jacob claimed Joseph's two sons, Ephraim and Manasseh, as his own.

Each tribe will receive its portion of land as a *naḥălâ.* Block insists that translating *naḥălâ* as "inheritance" is inappropriate, because the Israelites never refer to the donor, Yahweh, as a father; rather, they portray him as a suzerain. Hence, "*naḥalâ* denotes property, in this case land, specially granted by a superior to his inferiors as a reward for services rendered, or in anticipation of services yet to be performed."[1444] However, the translation appearing in both the NIV and the NRSV is not altogether inappropriate, given the reminder in v. 14*b* that Yahweh swore to give (in that case, granted) land to their ancestors. The twelve tribes receive the land God apportions to them because they are the descendants of Jacob and his sons.

The phrase, "this land shall fall to you," reflects the practice of casting lots for land. According to Num 33:54 and 34:13, this method was to be used to apportion the land among the tribes. Here, the idiom remains, but nothing more is said about casting lots. Yahweh has already determined the territory of each tribe. According to Ezek 47:14, the homeland must be allocated equitably among the tribes. In Num 33:54, by contrast, the size of land apportioned to any given tribe depends upon each tribe's population.

Following the formal announcement, "This shall be the boundary of the land," Ezekiel establishes its northern, eastern, southern, and western borders. Each boundary is introduced by לפאת (*lipʾat,* v. 15) or ופאת (*ûpeʾat,* vv. 18-20), "On the (compass point) side"; and each concludes with את פאת (*ʾēt peʾat,* vv. 17-19) or זאת פאה (*zōʾt peʾat,* vv. 17-19) or זאת פאה (*zōʾt peʾat,* v. 20), followed by the compass point.[1445]

The northern boundary receives the most detailed treatment. It stretches from the "great sea" (the Mediterranean) by way of Hethlon to Lebo-hamath, and further to Zedad, Berothah, Sibraim, and as far as Hazer-hatticon, which borders Hauran. For the purposes of this commentary, we shall not pursue every place name appearing in Ezekiel's boundary definitions. Some are known (e.g., Damascus, the Aramean kingdom lying north and northeast of Israel). But many others are uncertain (e.g., Hethlon) if not unknown (e.g., Sibraim). Indeed, the reference to Sibraim appears to have required parenthetical comment to assist ancient readers unfamiliar with the site; so also Hazer-hatticon. Lebo-hamath appears also in Num 34:8; and in other biblical texts (Num

13:21; Josh 13:5; Judg 3:3; 1 Kgs 8:65; 2 Kgs 14:25; 1 Chr 13:5; 2 Chr 7:8; Amos 6:14), it designates the northernmost point of Israel's land.

The eastern territory is defined with less detail. Ezekiel's boundary begins somewhere on the border between Mount Hauran and the territories of Damascus. It then turns southwest, edges the southern end of Damascus-controlled land, east of the Sea of Galilee, and from there to the Jordan River.[1446] The Jordan River provides the border until it reaches the Dead Sea, here called "the eastern sea." Its southern limit, according to a meaningless MT, is "you shall measure." The LXX and Syriac read "Tamar" ("date palm"), i.e, Jericho. Ezekiel's eastern boundary excludes any land lying east of the Jordan River. In Num 34:12, also, the Jordan River provides the eastern border of Israel's territory. Numbers 34:14 concedes, however, that the tribes of Reuben, Gad, and one half of Manasseh settled east of the Jordan.

Ezekiel's southern boundary begins at Tamar and procedes southwest to Meribath-kadesh (another name for Kadesh-barnea), an oasis located on the southern border of the Desert of Zin. From there, it traverses the Wadi of Egypt (not the Nile, but a wadi separating Egypt and Canaan) to the Mediterranean Sea, which serves as the land's western boundary.

This, then, is the land to be divided among the tribes of Israel. Verses 22-23 address a related issue. Among those receiving land allotments are the גרים (*gērîm*), resident aliens who live among the Israelites and are raising children in the land. Their allotments will come from the portion of land designated for the tribe in whose midst they reside. Ezekiel 14:7 spoke pejoratively of resident aliens who, like the Israelites, worshiped idols. Ezekiel 22:7, 29, however, grouped these aliens with other persons susceptible to oppression— widows, orphans, the poor—and condemned Judah's princes for exploiting them. The legislation in Lev 19:33-34 not only forbids the oppression of resident aliens, but also provides a reason why Israel should not mistreat them: "When an alien resides with you in your land, you shall not oppress the alien. The alien who resides with you shall be to you as the citizen among you; you

1444. Block, *Ezekiel 25–48,* 706.
1445. Many critics emend vv. 17-19 to read זאת (*zōʾt,* "this").

1446. Block, *Ezekiel 25–48,* 716.

shall love the alien as yourself, for you were aliens in the land of Egypt; I am the Lord your God" (NRSV). Deuteronomy 24:17-22 enjoins the Israelites to permit aliens to glean for food on their land, though nothing is said about allocating territory to them. Levenson regards Ezekiel's provision for resident aliens in 47:21-23 as "much more radical than anything else in all the legal

corpora of the Hebrew Bible," adding, "how idiotic now seems the antique canard that the priesthood was mean-spirited, exclusivistic and power-hungry!"[1447] (See Reflections at 48:30-35.)

1447. J. D. Levenson, *Theology of the Program of Restoration of Ezekiel 40–48, HSM* 10 (Missoula: Scholars Press, 1976) 123-24.

Ezekiel 48:1-29, The Tribal Allotments

NIV

48 "These are the tribes, listed by name: At the northern frontier, Dan will have one portion; it will follow the Hethlon road to Lebo[a] Hamath; Hazar Enan and the northern border of Damascus next to Hamath will be part of its border from the east side to the west side.

2"Asher will have one portion; it will border the territory of Dan from east to west.

3"Naphtali will have one portion; it will border the territory of Asher from east to west.

4"Manasseh will have one portion; it will border the territory of Naphtali from east to west.

5"Ephraim will have one portion; it will border the territory of Manasseh from east to west.

6"Reuben will have one portion; it will border the territory of Ephraim from east to west.

7"Judah will have one portion; it will border the territory of Reuben from east to west.

8"Bordering the territory of Judah from east to west will be the portion you are to present as a special gift. It will be 25,000 cubits[b] wide, and its length from east to west will equal one of the tribal portions; the sanctuary will be in the center of it.

9"The special portion you are to offer to the Lord will be 25,000 cubits long and 10,000 cubits[c] wide. 10This will be the sacred portion for the priests. It will be 25,000 cubits long on the north side, 10,000 cubits wide on the west side, 10,000 cubits wide on the east side and 25,000 cubits long on the south side. In the center of it will be the sanctuary of the Lord. 11This will be for the consecrated priests, the Zadokites, who were faithful in serving me and did not go astray

a1 Or *to the entrance to*   *b8* That is, about 7 miles (about 12 kilometers)   *c9* That is, about 3 miles (about 5 kilometers)

NRSV

48 These are the names of the tribes: Beginning at the northern border, on the Hethlon road,[a] from Lebo-hamath, as far as Hazar-enon (which is on the border of Damascus, with Hamath to the north), and[b] extending from the east side to the west,[c] Dan, one portion. 2Adjoining the territory of Dan, from the east side to the west, Asher, one portion. 3Adjoining the territory of Asher, from the east side to the west, Naphtali, one portion. 4Adjoining the territory of Naphtali, from the east side to the west, Manasseh, one portion. 5Adjoining the territory of Manasseh, from the east side to the west, Ephraim, one portion. 6Adjoining the territory of Ephraim, from the east side to the west, Reuben, one portion. 7Adjoining the territory of Reuben, from the east side to the west, Judah, one portion.

8Adjoining the territory of Judah, from the east side to the west, shall be the portion that you shall set apart, twenty-five thousand cubits in width, and in length equal to one of the tribal portions, from the east side to the west, with the sanctuary in the middle of it. 9The portion that you shall set apart for the Lord shall be twenty-five thousand cubits in length, and twenty[d] thousand in width. 10These shall be the allotments of the holy portion: the priests shall have an allotment measuring twenty-five thousand cubits on the northern side, ten thousand cubits in width on the western side, ten thousand in width on the eastern side, and twenty-five thousand in length on the southern side, with the sanctuary of the Lord in the middle of it. 11This shall be for the consecrated priests,

*a*Compare 47.15: Heb *by the side of the way*   *b*Cn: Heb *and they shall be his*   *c*Gk Compare verses 2-8: Heb *the east side the west*   *d*Compare 45.1: Heb *ten*

as the Levites did when the Israelites went astray. ¹²It will be a special gift to them from the sacred portion of the land, a most holy portion, bordering the territory of the Levites.

¹³"Alongside the territory of the priests, the Levites will have an allotment 25,000 cubits long and 10,000 cubits wide. Its total length will be 25,000 cubits and its width 10,000 cubits. ¹⁴They must not sell or exchange any of it. This is the best of the land and must not pass into other hands, because it is holy to the LORD.

¹⁵"The remaining area, 5,000 cubits wide and 25,000 cubits long, will be for the common use of the city, for houses and for pastureland. The city will be in the center of it ¹⁶and will have these measurements: the north side 4,500 cubits, the south side 4,500 cubits, the east side 4,500 cubits, and the west side 4,500 cubits. ¹⁷The pastureland for the city will be 250 cubits on the north, 250 cubits on the south, 250 cubits on the east, and 250 cubits on the west. ¹⁸What remains of the area, bordering on the sacred portion and running the length of it, will be 10,000 cubits on the east side and 10,000 cubits on the west side. Its produce will supply food for the workers of the city. ¹⁹The workers from the city who farm it will come from all the tribes of Israel. ²⁰The entire portion will be a square, 25,000 cubits on each side. As a special gift you will set aside the sacred portion, along with the property of the city.

²¹"What remains on both sides of the area formed by the sacred portion and the city property will belong to the prince. It will extend eastward from the 25,000 cubits of the sacred portion to the eastern border, and westward from the 25,000 cubits to the western border. Both these areas running the length of the tribal portions will belong to the prince, and the sacred portion with the temple sanctuary will be in the center of them. ²²So the property of the Levites and the property of the city will lie in the center of the area that belongs to the prince. The area belonging to the prince will lie between the border of Judah and the border of Benjamin.

²³"As for the rest of the tribes: Benjamin will have one portion; it will extend from the east side to the west side.

the descendants[a] of Zadok, who kept my charge, who did not go astray when the people of Israel went astray, as the Levites did. ¹²It shall belong to them as a special portion from the holy portion of the land, a most holy place, adjoining the territory of the Levites. ¹³Alongside the territory of the priests, the Levites shall have an allotment twenty-five thousand cubits in length and ten thousand in width. The whole length shall be twenty-five thousand cubits and the width twenty[b] thousand. ¹⁴They shall not sell or exchange any of it; they shall not transfer this choice portion of the land, for it is holy to the LORD.

15The remainder, five thousand cubits in width and twenty-five thousand in length, shall be for ordinary use for the city, for dwellings and for open country. In the middle of it shall be the city; ¹⁶and these shall be its dimensions: the north side four thousand five hundred cubits, the south side four thousand five hundred, the east side four thousand five hundred, and the west side four thousand five hundred. ¹⁷The city shall have open land: on the north two hundred fifty cubits, on the south two hundred fifty, on the east two hundred fifty, on the west two hundred fifty. ¹⁸The remainder of the length alongside the holy portion shall be ten thousand cubits to the east, and ten thousand to the west, and it shall be alongside the holy portion. Its produce shall be food for the workers of the city. ¹⁹The workers of the city, from all the tribes of Israel, shall cultivate it. ²⁰The whole portion that you shall set apart shall be twenty-five thousand cubits square, that is, the holy portion together with the property of the city.

21What remains on both sides of the holy portion and of the property of the city shall belong to the prince. Extending from the twenty-five thousand cubits of the holy portion to the east border, and westward from the twenty-five thousand cubits to the west border, parallel to the tribal portions, it shall belong to the prince. The holy portion with the sanctuary of the temple in the middle of it, ²²and the property of the Levites and of the city, shall be in the middle of that which belongs to the prince. The portion of the prince shall lie between the territory of Judah and the territory of Benjamin.

ᵃOne Ms Gk: Heb *of the descendants*   ᵇGk: Heb *ten*

NIV

24"Simeon will have one portion; it will border the territory of Benjamin from east to west.

25"Issachar will have one portion; it will border the territory of Simeon from east to west.

26"Zebulun will have one portion; it will border the territory of Issachar from east to west.

27"Gad will have one portion; it will border the territory of Zebulun from east to west.

28"The southern boundary of Gad will run south from Tamar to the waters of Meribah Kadesh, then along the Wadi ,of Egypt, to the Great Sea.[a]

29"This is the land you are to allot as an inheritance to the tribes of Israel, and these will be their portions," declares the Sovereign LORD.

[a]28 That is, the Mediterranean

NRSV

23As for the rest of the tribes: from the east side to the west, Benjamin, one portion. 24Adjoining the territory of Benjamin, from the east side to the west, Simeon, one portion. 25Adjoining the territory of Simeon, from the east side to the west, Issachar, one portion. 26Adjoining the territory of Issachar, from the east side to the west, Zebulun, one portion. 27Adjoining the territory of Zebulun, from the east side to the west, Gad, one portion. 28And adjoining the territory of Gad to the south, the boundary shall run from Tamar to the waters of Meribath-kadesh, from there along the Wadi of Egypt[a] to the Great Sea. 29This is the land that you shall allot as an inheritance among the tribes of Israel, and these are their portions, says the Lord GOD.

[a]Heb lacks of Egypt

COMMENTARY

These verses take up the task anticipated in 47:13-14, 21. That is, they situate the land allotted to each of Israel's twelve tribes. In vv. 1-7, seven tribes are given land grants lying north of the holy contribution, described already in 45:1-9. At that point, the list of tribal allotments is interrupted by a more detailed description of that contribution (vv. 8-22). The list then resumes, situating the five remaining tribes whose land lies south of the contribution.

48:1-7. Verse 1 commences with the introductory phase, "These are the names of the tribes" (see the similar formulas in Num 34:17, 19), followed by a second, less detailed description of the northern border of Israel's land, first identified in 47:15-17. Stretching from the eastern boundary to its western limits (the MT reads "the east side, the west"; cf. vv. 2-8), this portion is allotted to Dan (in each case, the tribal allotments end with אחד [′eḥād, "one"]). Directly south of Dan lies the tribal territory of Asher. Here and elsewhere, the western boundary is the Mediterranean Sea, but the eastern boundaries are not given. To Asher's south is Naphtali's portion, followed by the portions of Manasseh, Ephraim, Reuben, and Judah, which borders on the holy contribution.

At this point, vv. 8-22 digress from the tribal list to comment further on the sacred strip, the תרומה terûmâ or "gift" of land reserved for Yahweh. Sequential readers already know about this strip from 45:1-9 (see the Commentary on 45:1-9). Some critics believe that 48:8-22 was composed prior to 45:1-9, which was composed under its influence. However, the reader is thoroughly familiar with the Ezekielian tendency to introduce a topic, only to return to it later and in greater detail. In what follows, vv. 10-12 deal with the priests' territory, vv. 13-14 with the Levites' portion, vv. 15-20 with the city's allotment, and vv. 21-22 with the prince's land holdings.

Verse 8 introduces the topic, locating the contribution (to Yahweh) south of Judah's territory and running from east to west. Its width is twenty-five thousand cubits, and its length equal to the tribal allotments. In its midst sits the sanctuary. According to the MT, this strip will measure twenty-five thousand cubits long and ten thousand cubits wide. Most scholars, however, emend the MT and read "twenty thousand cubits wide" with the LXX. Here, as with 45:1, Zimmerli concludes that "the figure twenty thousand has been tendentiously reduced to ten thousand, since the intention has been to regard only the priestly portion as תרומה, i.e., sacred תרומה."[1448] The priests are allotted a strip of land measuring twenty-five thousand cubits on its northern side, ten thousand cubits wide on the western side, ten thousand cubits in width on its eastern side, and twenty-five thousand in length on the southern side. In its midst stands Yahweh's sanctuary.

The consecrated area will be for the priests, more specifically, for the priests descended from Zadok, who performed guard duty for Yahweh and who, unlike the Levites, did not wander away when the Israelites did. Here again is raised, in terse language, the accusation that the Levites also strayed when the Israelites went astray (after idols, according to Ezek 44:10-14; see the Excursus "Are the Levites Punished or Restored in Ezekiel 44:10-14?" 1575-77). This land, then, shall be the Zadokites' special reserve, distingushed from the remainder of the contribution as most holy and lying adjacent to the Levites' allotment. The latter consists of a comparable strip, also twenty-five thousand cubits in length and ten thousand cubits wide. The entire length will be twenty-five thousand cubits and the width ten thousand cubits (so MT; LXX reads "twenty thousand cubits"; see above). None of this, the choicest of the land, may be sold, exchanged, or transferred to others, because it is holy to Yahweh.

The remainder (הנותר hannôtar) of the contribution, a strip measuring five thousand cubits in width and twenty-five thousand in length, will be for "ordinary" use for the city. The term translated "ordinary" is חל ḥōl, meaning "profane," but its usage here is not pejorative. This is simply public space, providing the city in its midst with dwellings and pasturage. The city itself is a square measuring forty-five hundred cubits along its north side, and equal numbers on its south, east, and west sides (v. 16). It is surrounded by מגרש migrāš, a zone of open land outside all four sides of the exterior walls that stretches a distance of two hundred fifty cubits in each direction. The remainder of the land lying to the east and west of the city and its migrāš stretches ten thousand cubits in both directions. Its produce is intended for the workers of the city who, according to v. 19, are chosen from each of Israel's twelve tribes. Verse 20 then summarizes

the dimensions of the entire holy contribution, a twenty-five thousand cubits square.

The large tracts of land lying east and west of the holy contribution are the crownlands. According to 45:21-25, the prince requires land in order to provide the Temple with animal, grain, and oil offerings on his and the people's behalf. He cannot be permanently alienated from this land (46:11), and he is forbidden to enlarge it by confiscating the tribal holdings (46:18).

48:23-29. Verse 23 begins with the resumptive phrase, "As for the rest of the tribes." South of the holy contribution lies the territory allotted to Benjamin, followed by the portions of Simeon, Issachar, Zebulun, and finally, Gad. Verse 28 virtually repeats the southern boundary of Israel's land provided in 47:19. A concluding colophon (v. 29) summarizes the contents of 47:13–48:7, 23-29.

A few observations about Ezekiel's distribution list are in order. First, it presupposes that all twelve of Israel's tribes will return to the homeland—this despite the fact that the Assyrians exiled many of the inhabitants of the (ten tribe) northern kingdom and dispersed them throughout Mesopotamia following the defeat of Samaria in 721 BCE. Ezekiel expressed this same expectation by means of a sign act (the conjoining of two sticks in his hand) in 37:15-23.

Second, Ezekiel seeks tribal parity. He insists that the land be distributed equally (lit., "each man like his brother," 47:14). Despite his attempts, however, geographical reality intrudes. Block notes that while each portion is the same width, its east to west boundaries create inequities: "whereas the distance from the Mediterranean to the Jordan River at the south end of the Sea of Galilee is only 40 mi., the tip of the Dead Sea is 70 mi. from the Mediterranean. Even more problematic is the massive eastward bulge of the border north of the Sea of Galilee, where the strips could have been 100 mi. long."[1449]

Third, Ezekiel's distribution of land is hierarchical. The strips of land located farthest from the holy contribution are allotted to the tribes (Dan, Asher, Naphtali, and Gad) descended from the handmaidens of Leah (Zilpah) and Rachel (Bilhah). The eight tribes descended from Leah and Rachel (Manasseh, Ephraim, Reuben, Judah, Benjamin,

1448. Zimmerli, *Ezekiel 2,* 533-34. For a different view, see Kalinda Rose Stevenson, *The Vision of Transformation: The Territorial Rhetoric of Ezekiel 40–48,* SBLDS 154 (Atlanta: Scholars Press, 1996) 31, 89.

1449. Block, *Ezekiel 25–48,* 723.

Simeon, Issachar, and Zebulun) are closest to the contribution, with four lying to the north, and four to the south. (See Reflections at 48:30-35.)

Ezekiel 48:30-35, The Sacred City

NIV

30"These will be the exits of the city: Beginning on the north side, which is 4,500 cubits long, 31the gates of the city will be named after the tribes of Israel. The three gates on the north side will be the gate of Reuben, the gate of Judah and the gate of Levi.

32"On the east side, which is 4,500 cubits long, will be three gates: the gate of Joseph, the gate of Benjamin and the gate of Dan.

33"On the south side, which measures 4,500 cubits, will be three gates: the gate of Simeon, the gate of Issachar and the gate of Zebulun.

34"On the west side, which is 4,500 cubits long, will be three gates: the gate of Gad, the gate of Asher and the gate of Naphtali.

35"The distance all around will be 18,000 cubits.

"And the name of the city from that time on will be:

THE LORD IS THERE."

NRSV

30These shall be the exits of the city: On the north side, which is to be four thousand five hundred cubits by measure, 31three gates, the gate of Reuben, the gate of Judah, and the gate of Levi, the gates of the city being named after the tribes of Israel. 32On the east side, which is to be four thousand five hundred cubits, three gates, the gate of Joseph, the gate of Benjamin, and the gate of Dan. 33On the south side, which is to be four thousand five hundred cubits by measure, three gates, the gate of Simeon, the gate of Issachar, and the gate of Zebulun. 34On the west side, which is to be four thousand five hundred cubits, three gates,a the gate of Gad, the gate of Asher, and the gate of Naphtali. 35The circumference of the city shall be eighteen thousand cubits. And the name of the city from that time on shall be, The LORD is There.

aOne Ms Gk Syr: MT *their gates three*

COMMENTARY

Ezekiel now turns to envision Israel's future, sacred city, which he nowhere calls "Jerusalem." Verses 30-34 identify the twelve gates in the city's walls, each of which bears the name of one of the tribes. The sequence of directions—north, east, south, west—is identical to that appearing in 47:15-20, where the exterior limits of Israel's territory as a whole are established. On the north side, which measures forty-five hundred cubits, are gates named for Reuben, Judah, and Levi. On the east side, which likewise measures forty-five hundred cubits (as do the south and west sides), are the gates of Joseph, Benjamin, and Dan. When the land allocations were announced in Ezek 48:1-7, 23-27, the Joseph tribes (Manasseh and Ephraim) were each given a separate strip. Because the tribe of Levi has its own gate, how-ever, they are here subsumed under Joseph's name in order to retain the number twelve. The west side includes the gates of Gad, Asher, and Naphtali. The ancestresses apparently have affected the placement of the tribal gates, as well as the allotment of tribal strips. Hence, the three most important Leah tribes are to the north, with Judah in the middle, while the three remaining Leah tribes are to the south. Rachel's two sons, Joseph and Benjamin, are on the east side, while the two Zilpah tribes are on the west. The gates named for the two tribes descended from Bilhah, Naphtali, and Dan, are on the east and west sides of the city.

Donald Wiseman has pointed to similarities between Ezekiel's square city with its twelve gates and to Etemenanki, the Babylonian temple tower of Marduk. Its sacred precinct, also square-shaped, could be entered through twelve gates, though these were not evenly distributed on each side.[1450] We do not know if Ezekiel ever visited this temple, or even knew of its design.

Verse 35*a* provides the circumference of the city whose gates Ezekiel has named—18,000

cubits. In v. 35*b*, the hitherto unnamed urban center receives its name, יהוה שׁמה (*YHWH šammâ*, "Yahweh is there"). Scholars detect in this new name a wordplay on ירושלים (*yĕrûšālayim*). But the old city is not simply being renamed here. Rather, the name of this city proclaims that it is part of a new and perfectly ordered creation. The problems of its past are resolved, and the people of Israel can live in it with the certainty of God's presence. Yahweh is there!

1450. Donald Wiseman, *Nebuchadrezzar and Babylon,* Schweich Lectures 1983 (Oxford: Oxford University Press, 1985) 69.

REFLECTIONS

1. Ezekiel's account of a miraculous stream that issues from the Temple, fructifies the land, and transforms the Dead Sea into fresh, fish-filled water is so delightful that it brings a smile to the faces of its readers. Would that such a stream might traverse the most diseased regions of our planet, ridding the world of the poison inflicted on creation by our own gross exploitations of natural resources! But we dare not wait until Ezekiel's final vision is fulfilled to address ecological disasters. If we have so thoroughly deforested the land that it is reduced to desert-like terrain, then our responsibility is to replant and tend it. If we have transformed our lakes, rivers, and oceans into "dead seas," then our responsibility is to clean them up.

2. Ezekiel's account of the fructifying stream that issues from Yahweh's Temple reminds us that when we permit God's power to enter us, it can transform even the most barren and bruised aspects of our lives. The observation is simple, but the experience can be life transforming. For Christians, God's ability to transform us is expressed beautifully in the words of the hymn "Heal Me, Hands of Jesus," the first verse of which pleads:

Heal me, hands of Jesus, and search out all my pain;
  restore my hope, remove my fear, and bring me peace again.[1451]

3. Finally, Ezekiel's description of the transforming river can function as an exquisite metaphor for how God's blessings should flow out from our experiences of worship to transform the world in which we live. We can become conduits of God's refreshing, life-giving power. But we dare not, in this day and age, be satisfied with Ezekiel's parochialism. God's blessings are not limited to any particular community.

1451. "Heal Me, Hands of Jesus," Michael Perry, in *The United Methodist Hymnal* (Nashville: The United Methodist Publishing House, 1989) 262.

TRANSLITERATION SCHEMA

HEBREW AND ARAMAIC TRANSLITERATION

Consonants:

א	=	ʾ	ט	=	ṭ	פ or ף	=	p
ב	=	b	י	=	y	צ or ץ	=	ṣ
ג	=	g	כ or ך	=	k	ק	=	q
ד	=	d	ל	=	l	ר	=	r
ה	=	h	מ or ם	=	m	שׂ	=	ś
ו	=	w	נ or ן	=	n	שׁ	=	š
ז	=	z	ס	=	s	ת	=	t
ח	=	ḥ	ע	=	ʿ			

Masoretic Pointing:

Pure-long			Tone-long			Short			Composite *shewa*		
הָ	=	â	ָ	=	ā	ַ	=	a	ֲ	=	ă
ֵ or ֵי	=	ê	ֶ	=	ē	ֶ	=	e	ֱ or	=	ĕ
or ִי	=	î				ִ	=	i			
or וֹ	=	ô	ֹ	=	ō	ָ	=	o	ֳ	=	ŏ
or וּ	=	û				ֻ	=	u			

GREEK TRANSLITERATION

α	=	a	ι	=	i	ρ	=	r
β	=	b	κ	=	k	σ or ς	=	s
γ	=	g	λ	=	l	τ	=	t
δ	=	d	μ	=	m	υ	=	y
ε	=	e	ν	=	n	φ	=	ph
ζ	=	z	ξ	=	x	χ	=	ch
η	=	ē	ο	=	o	ψ	=	ps
θ	=	th	π	=	p	ω	=	ō

INDEX OF EXCURSUSES, MAPS, CHARTS, AND ILLUSTRATIONS

ABBREVIATIONS

BCE   Before the Common Era
CE   Common Era
c.   circa
cf.   compare
chap(s).   chapter(s)
d.   died
Dtr   Deuteronomistic historian
esp.   especially
fem.   feminine
HB   Hebrew Bible
lit.   literally
l(l).   line(s)
LXX   Septuagint
masc.   masculine
MS(S)   manuscript(s)
MT   Masoretic Text
n.(n.)   note(s)
NT   New Testament
OL   Old Latin
OT   Old Testament
par.   parallel(s)
pl(s).   plate(s)
sing.   singular
v(v).   verse(s)
Vg   Vulgate

Names of Biblical Books (with the Apocrypha)

Gen	Nah	1–4 Kgdms	John
Exod	Hab	Add Esth	Acts
Lev	Zeph	Bar	Rom
Num	Hag	Bel	1–2 Cor
Deut	Zech	1–2 Esdr	Gal
Josh	Mal	4 Ezra	Eph
Judg	Ps (Pss)	Jdt	Phil
1–2 Sam	Job	Ep Jer	Col
1–2 Kgs	Prov	1–4 Macc	1–2 Thess
Isa	Ruth	Pr Azar	1–2 Tim
Jer	Cant	Pr Man	Titus
Ezek	Eccl	Sir	Phlm
Hos	Lam	Sus	Heb
Joel	Esth	Tob	Jas
Amos	Dan	Wis	1–2 Pet
Obad	Ezra	Matt	1–3 John
Jonah	Neh	Mark	Jude
Mic	1–2 Chr	Luke	Rev

Names of Dead Sea Scrolls and Related Texts

Q	Qumran
1Q, 2Q, etc.	Numbered caves of Qumran, yielding written material; sometimes followed by abbreviation of biblical or apocryphal book
4Q385[b]	Fragmentary remains of Pseudo-Jeremiah which implies that Jeremiah went into Babylonian exile. Also known as ApocJer[c] or 4Q385 16.
4Q389[a]	Several scroll fragments now thought to contain portions of three pseudepigraphal works including Pseudo-Jeremiah. Also known as 4QApocJer[e].
4Q390	Contains a schematized history of Israel's sin and divine punishment. Also known as psMos[e].

b. Megilla	baraita Megilla
b. Mid.	Beraita Middoth
m. Mid.	midrash Middoth
p. Shekal	pesahim Shekalim

Song of Songs Rab.	Song of Songs Rabbah

AB	Anchor Bible
ABD	Anchor Bible Dictionary
ABT	Australian Biblical Review
AfOB	Archiv für Orientforschung: Beiheft
AnBib	Analecta biblica
ANET	Ancient Near Eastern Texts Relating to the Old Testament, ed. James B. Pritchard, 3d ed. Princeton: Princeton University Press, 1969.
ATANT	Abhandlungen zur Theologies des Alten und Neuen Testaments
BAR	Biblical Archaeology Review
BDB	F. Brown, S. R. Driver, and C. A. Briggs, Hebrew and English Lexicon of the Old Testament
BETL	Bibliotheca ephemeridum theologicarum lovaniensium
Bib	Biblica
BibOr	Biblica et orientalia
BKAT	Biblischer Kommentar, Altes Testament
BSac	Bibliotheca Sacra
BWANT	Beiträge zur Wissenschaft vom Alten (und Neuen) Testament
BZAW	Beihefte zur ZAW
CBQ	Catholic Biblical Quarterly
CBQMS	Catholic Biblical Quarterly Monograph Series
ConBOT	Coniectanea biblica, Old Testament
CRAI	Comptes rendus de l'Académie des inscriptions et belles-lettres
EB	Echter Bibel
Enc	Encounter
ErIsr	Eretz-Israel
ETL	Ephemerides theologicae lovanienses
FAT	Forschungen zum Alten Testament
FB	Forschung zur Bibel
FOTL	Forms of Old Testament Literature
FRLANT	Forschungen zur Religion und Literatur des Alten und Neuen Testaments
Gkc	Gesenius' Hebrew Grammar. Edited by E. Kautzsch. Translated by A. E. Cowley. 2d ed. Oxford: Oxford University Press, 1910.
HAR	Hebrew Annual Review
HAT	Handbuch zum Alten Testament
HBC	Harper Bible Commentary
HSM	Harvard Semitic Monographs
HUCA	Hebrew Union College Annual
IB	Interpreter's Bible
IBC	Interpretation: A Bible Commentary for Teaching and Preaching
ICC	International Critical Commentary
IEJ	Israel Exploration Journal
Int	Interpretation
JANESCU	Journal of the Ancient Near Eastern Society of Columbia University
JBL	Journal of Biblical Literature
JNES	Journal of Near Eastern Studies
JNSL	Journal of Northwest Semitic Languages
JSOT	Journal for the Study of the Old Testament
JSOTSup	Journal for the Study of the Old Testament–Supplement Series
KAT	Kommentar zum Alten Testament
LCL	Loeb Classical Library
NAB	New American Bible
NCB	New Century Bible
NEB	New English Bible
NIB	New Interpreter's Bible
NICOT	New International Commentary on the Old Testament
NIV	New International Version
NJB	New Jerusalem Bible
NRSV	New Revised Standard Verion
OBT	Overtures to Biblical Theology
OIP	Oriental Institute Publications
OTG	Old Testament Guides